The Production GUIDE

2003

credits & acknowledgements

Published by
Emap Information
33-39 Bowling Green Lane
London EC1R ODA

For further copies of
The Production Guide
please contact:

01858 438847
pg@subscription.co.uk

emap information

© EMAP Information 2003

ISSN 1461-2585

ISBN 1-898609-04-7

Editor
Mei Mei Rogers

Contributing Editor
Keith Drew

Senior Researcher
Caroline Adkin

Researchers Graeme Aymer,
Maria Bonet, Alberto Callero,
Sayaka Carville, Christina Fang,
Connor Gilmore, Susanna
Lindström, Kevin Linnett, Pablo
Rodera, Geraldine Sherrard

Feature Writer
Michael Burns

Research Production
David Lewis

Systems Developer
Jim Holmes

Production Manager
Karen Turner

Advertisement Manager
Charles Said

Sales Manager
Jean-Frederic Garcia

Senior Sales Executive
Samantha Turner

Sales Executives
Gianni Cerretani,
Michael Tookey

Marketing Manager
Martha Hawkins

Marketing Executive
Izzie Sadiq

Designer
Lise Meyrick

Art Director
Sarah Watson

Publishing Director
Mike Jones

Cover Image
Jacey, Debut Art

Printing in Great Britain by
Unwin Brothers Ltd
The Gresham Press
Old Woking
Surrey GU22 9LH

The Production Guide 2002
acknowledges the assistance of the
following in the compilation of this
publication:

Broadcast

Jon Baker, Publishing Director
Conor Dignam, Editor
Katy Elliott, Deputy Editor
Jonathan Rogers, Editorial Assistant
Paul Moran, Digital Production Manager
Adam Bryan, Display Advertising
Manager

Broadcastnow.co.uk

Jon Baker, Publishing Director
Luke Satchell, Online Editor
Alison Ronald, Marketing Manager

The Production Show

Simon Marett, Marketing Manager
Imogen Jones, Event Manager
Francesca Ambrosini, Conference
Producer

Screen International

Anne-Marie Flynn, Publishing Director
Leo Barraclough, Managing Editor
Louise Tutt, Features Editor

shots

Mike Jones, Publishing Director
Lyndy Stout, Editor
Martha Hawkins, Head of Marketing
Charles Said, Advertising Manager
Karen Turner, Production Manager

EMAP Information

Catherine Pusey, Managing Director

contents

Sanctuary Town House

Studio #1 SSL 4000G PLUS 72/32/4 with ULTIMATION & TOTAL RECALL. G Series mic pre-amps with E series EQ.
Acoustics by Sam Toyoshima
Monitors: GENELEC 1035a, NS10. Pro Tools HD
Studio #2 SSL 8072 G Series 72/24/8 with ULTIMATION & TOTAL RECALL. Acoustics by Sam Toyoshima
Monitors: 5.1 surround monitoring, GENELEC
1035a & 1038a, NS10. Pro Tools HD
Studio #4 SSL 4000E 72/32/4 with G series computer & Total Recall. Acoustics by Sam Toyoshima
Monitors: Genelec 1035a, NS10. Pro Tools HD
Contact: Nikki Affleck Tel: 020 8932 3200 Fax: 020 89323207 Email: townhouse@sanctuarystudios.co.uk
Sanctuary Towhouse 150 Goldhawk Road, London, W12 8HH

Sanctuary Westside Studios

Studio #1
Neve VR 60 channel console
Live area measuring 132 square metres
and two isolation booths. Monitors: Quested 4 X12 system, Yamaha NS10M, AR & Auratone
Studio #2
64 channel SSL 4064E with G series computer
The large ambient live area measuring 80 square meters. Monitors: Quested 2 X15 system, Munro
MA1 active, Yamaha NS10M, AR & Auratone
Contact: Jo Buckley Bookings Coordinator Tel: 020 7221 9494 Fax: 020 7727 0888
Email: westside@sanctuarystudios.co.uk
Westside Studios 10 Olaf Street, London W11 4BE

Sanctuary Pro Tools Room

56 Channel Mackie with Meter Bridge. Apple Macintosh G4 Dual 1.25Ghz, 1.5Gb RAM, DVD-R/CD-R.
Pro-Tools 24 Mix Plus with extra mixfarm card.
3 x 888/24 Interfaces. Various Samplers, Keyboards, Sound Modules and Outboard.
Live area with stone drum room. MTR 90 2in Tape Machine.
Experienced Pro Tools engineer included. Restaurant and bar.
Contact: Nikki Affleck Tel: 020 8932 3200 Fax: 020 89323207 Email: protools@sanctuarystudios.co.uk
Sanctuary House 45-53 Sinclair Road, London W14 0NS

Sanctuary Mobiles

Mobile Recording, Mixing - Stereo and 5.1 and Postproduction for Radio, Television Broadcast
and Comercial Release - Worldwide

Contact: Ian Dyckhoff Tel: 08700 771 071 Fax: 08700 771 068 Email: mobiles@sanctuarystudios.co.uk
Sanctuary Mobiles Bray Film Studios Water Oakley, Windsor, Berkshire SL4 5UG

Sanctuary Mastering

All current Audio Post Production processes available:
Sadie, Sonic Solutions, Cutting, Editing, High Resolution Mastering – DVDA, SACD & DSD, 5.1 Surround, Cleaning
& Restoration, Duplication, Compiling & Enhanced CD.

Contact: Lavinia Burrell and Sophie Nathan, Bookings Coordinators – Post Production
Tel: 020 8932 3200 Fax: 020 8932 3209   Email: mastering@sanctuarystudios.co.uk
Sanctuary Mastering 140 Goldhawk Rd, London W12 8HH

Sanctuary Town House Vision

Audio Postproduction Suite mixing stereo and 5.1. Dialogue, Effects Tracklaying, ADR Voice Over
and Foley for Features, Documentary, Animation, Broadcast and DVD.

Contact: Julian MacDonald – Head of THV
Tel: 020 7932 3200 Fax: 020 7932 3209 Email: thv@sanctuarystudios.co.uk
Sanctuary Town House Vision, 150 Goldhawk Road, London, W12 8HH

index : categories

AaBbCcDdEeFfGgHhIiJjKkLlMmNnOoPpQqRrSsTtUuVvWwXxYyZz

AaBbCcDdEeFfGgHhIiJjKkLlMmNnOoPpQqRrSsTtUuVvWwXxYyZz

Vv

Ww

THE PRODUCTION MANAGERS ASSOCIATION

Telephone: 020 8758 8699   E-Mail: pma@pma.org.uk

www.pma.org.uk

The PMA is a professional body of more than 180 highly skilled and experienced Production Mangers working in film, television and multimedia.

The association provides its members with a unique network of support and information via its website, regular events and bi-monthly newsletter.

FOR PRODUCERS LOOKING FOR A PRODUCTION MANAGER :

All PMA members have at least 3 years' experience and 6 credits as a Production Manager. You can view their CV's on our website and search for a suitable PM for your project by name, area of expertise, previous credits and language skills.

The **AVAILABILITY LIST** is a constantly up-dated list of available members. Click the 'AVAILABLE PMs' button on the homepage. You will see dates and contact details for the members and can link through to their CV page. Each member will negotiate their own rates of pay.

An **ANNUAL DIRECTORY OF MEMBERS**, containing contact details and credits, is available for sale through the PMA office priced @ £20.

FOR MEMBERS:

A whole host of benefits including Networking, Employment availability list, Business Support Help Line, Social Events, Sponsor events, Training Workshops, Bi-monthly Newsletter, Pension Scheme, Pact Affiliation, Co-ordinators list and the Forum. The Forum is an e-mail newsgroup where members ask each other for advice and contacts such as finding fixers in various parts of the world.

FOR CO-ORDINATORS:

Who have worked for at least two PMA members

The **CO-ORDINATORS DIRECTORY** is on a secure part of our website which can only be viewed by PMA members. Once eligibility has been confirmed, passwords enable the co-ordinators to up-date their own CV's and give their availability dates.

THE PMA IS CURRENTLY SPONSORED BY

Molinare, Picture Canning Company, Visions, Media Insurance Brokers, Film and TV Services, Dynamic International, Ricall, TSI TX, BBC Resources, Pinewood Studios, National Geographic Television, Soho Images, Home, Take 1, Coutts, Richard Howard and Co, and Anna Valley.

foreword

NOT LONG AGO, I worked on a documentary about a man called Alec Reeves. Reeves was a scientist who worked on radar defence systems during the Second World War but, rather than being a white-coated technician, he was more a crazy dreamer. At weekly meetings that he called "Sunday Soviets", Reeves and his teams would kick ideas around or, to use a phrase that wasn't around at the time, they would "brainstorm". Reeves would have the big idea, but the men in white coats would then be given the task of making them a reality. One of Reeves' big ideas which never really came to much was that just about anything could be reduced to a set of numbers or, in the modern idiom, "digitised". I'm sure there were probably people like Reeves all over the world at that time, coming up with similar ideas. Every country will claim a hero. Nonetheless, the resulting technology has changed all our lives. Now, of course, digital technology is all around us - everything from your ansafone to your radio is gradually going digital, at the same time as new inventions arise like DVDs and MP3s.

The production industry is at the forefront of those advances, both in making use of new technologies as they arise and in driving the development of further advances. It's at times like this that the Production Guide is an invaluable tool in searching for what's best for your production. It's timely, therefore, that this year's Guide puts the spotlight on digital developments. As a production manager who's supposed to keep up with just about every technical development from pre-production to the end of post-production, I'm grateful for all the help I can get.

Right now, as I'm writing this, I'm on location in Calcutta. Even here there's no VHS player in my hotel room - just a DVD. And my local contributors are asking for a CD copy of the documentary we're producing. Looks like I might have to catch up with them!

Justin Johnson
Chairman, Production Managers' Association (PMA)

**Available for all purchasers of the Production Guide
www.productionguideonline.com
is the ultimate online research tool for the UK TV,
film, video
and commercials
production industries.**

- Contains over 15,000 completely revised and updated entries – with named key personnel

- Over 250 categories allow producers and directors to find all relevant information on the best suppliers, contacts and products in the UK.

- Sophisticated online database enables quick and advanced searches, all at the touch of a button

SEARCH NOW !
Search from within a variety of different classifications, including company, person, location, credits and business type.
The online listings are constantly updated to ensure that your search results are current, all year round.
Activate your online account today by visiting:
www.productionguideonline.com.

from the editor

THE TASK OF completely revising a book as comprehensive as The Production Guide is a challenge, to say the least, especially when you consider how dynamic the UK production industry is. But, through the sheer hard work and determination of our research team, we've managed to make this edition the most comprehensive and up-to-date ever.

As a result I'm confident that you'll find The Production Guide 2003 the most indispensable resource for the industry with, just for starters, much more in-depth personnel and credits lists for the vast majority of listings - in fact this year we have over 11,000 named personnel and over 13,000 listings for companies and individuals working within the industry.

In recognition of the impact which new technology and in particular the digital revolution is having on our industry at the moment, you will also find that we've added ten new categories - amongst them High Definition, Interactive TV and Mobile Interactive Services - with four feature articles to back them up, looking specifically at what this means for producers when dealing with High Definition, Motion Control, DVD Services and Post Production.

That's in addition to the industry information and statistics which we've put together with the co-operation of the many guilds and associations involved in the film, television and commercials industry within the UK.

This year we've also managed to introduce an international flavour to The Production Guide, with a production services focus looking at some of the most popular locations for filming around the world, with three of our new categories covering international production companies, location facilities and services.

And don't forget that as the owner of a copy of the brand new Production Guide you also have access to www.productionguideonline.com which gives you entry to our vast database of companies which we are constantly adding to and updating. Contact us at theproductionguide@emap.com if you need help logging on.

Lasty, my thanks go to those people who braved my temper and worked many unsociable hours to help put together this the latest and greatest edition of The Production Guide. I hope that the result of our efforts is self evident.

Have a great year filming.

Mei Mei Rogers
Editor

The Production Guild

The Production Guild represents the largest and most experienced group of senior production personnel in the United Kingdom's film, television and visual media industry.

With over 550 individual members – Producers, Production and Assistant Accountants, Production and Location Managers, Production and Post Production Co-ordinators, Financial Administrators and Studio Executives, and many of the industry's most experienced and valued service and facility companies as Affiliates, the Production Guild is at the heart of UK feature film and television drama production.

For more information on the Guild, its services and details on how to apply for membership please contact:

Lynne Hames
Administrator
The Production Guild
Pinewood Studios
Iver Heath
Bucks SLO ONH

T: 01753 651767
F: 01753 652803
E: admin@productionguild.com
W: www.productionguild.com

Representation to government, its executives and the key film bodies

Access to professional advice and guidance across a wide range of production, fiscal and legal issues

Ongoing professional development and current production and in development information through members' seminars, weekly bulletins, quarterly newsletter and the PG website

Members' Availability Service used and trusted by incoming, UK and European feature film and television drama production

A full programme of formal and informal social and networking events

THE PRODUCTION GUILD

how to use this guide

OUR AIM remains to make the guide as lightweight and easy to use as possible. We have divided the guide into major and minor categories, with the major categories consisting of several sub-sections.

To access the information for the category in which you wish to find a contact simply refer to the contents page and turn to the corresponding page within the book. Or if you already know the company or individual name you are seeking, refer to the index in the back of the guide, which is listed alphabetically.

Each major category will begin with a table of contents that will enable you to navigate through the various sub-sections and editorial content, which is distinguished from the sub-sections by being highlighted in boldface type. You will also find overseas companies listed throughout the guide.

Example of a listing

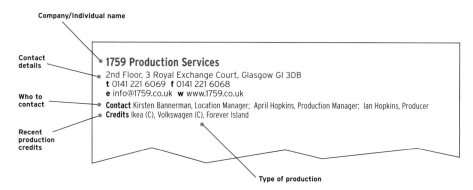

Company/Individual name

Contact details

Who to contact

Recent production credits

1759 Production Services
2nd Floor, 3 Royal Exchange Court, Glasgow GI 3DB
t 0141 221 6069 **f** 0141 221 6068
e info@1759.co.uk **w** www.1759.co.uk
Contact Kirsten Bannerman, Location Manager; April Hopkins, Production Manager; Ian Hopkins, Producer
Credits Ikea (C), Volkswagen (C), Forever Island

Type of production

Key to type of production
A	Animation
C	Commercial
D	Documentary
F	Feature Film
I	Industrial (Corporate) Film
M	Music Video
S	Short Film
T	TV Programme
W	Internet/Multimedia

Is any of our information wrong? If it is, we'd like to hear from you, as it is our aim to provide a service that is both accurate and up to date. If you find a mistake, please contact The Production Guide by e-mail on theproductionguide@emap.com.

international flight times

From London Heathrow/Gatwick to stated destination

Destination	Duration
Argentina, Buenos Aires	13hr 35min
Australia, Sydney	21hr 25min
Austria, Vienna	2hr 10min
Belgium, Brussels	1hr
Brazil, Rio de Janeiro	13hr 20min
Canada, Toronto	7hr
Chile, Santiago	17hr
Cyprus, Lamaca	4hr 25min
Czech Republic, Prague	1hr 45min
Denmark, Copenhagen	1hr 45min
Egypt, Cairo	4hr 50min
Finland, Helsinki	2hr 50min
France, Paris	1hr 5min
Germany, Frankfurt	1hr 15min
Greece, Athens	3hr 30min
Hong Kong, Victoria	11hr 45min
Hungary, Budapest	2hr 25min
India, Calcutta	9hr 45min
Ireland, Dublin	1hr 10min
Israel, Tel Aviv	4hr 40min
Italy, Rome	2hr 20min
Japan, Tokyo	11hr 30min
Kenya, Nairobi	8hr 35min
Malaysia, Kuala Lumpur	12hr 30min
Mexico, Mexico City	12hr
Netherlands, Amsterdam	1 hr
New Zealand, Auckland	26hr
Nigeria, Lagos	6hr 25min
Northern Ireland, Belfast	1 hr 10min
Norway, Oslo	2hr
Pakistan, Islamabad	7hr 45min
Philippines, Manila	15hr 5min
Poland, Warsaw	2hr 20min
Portugal, Lisbon	2hr 30min
Russia, Moscow	3hr 40min
Scotland, Edinburgh	1 hr 15min
Singapore, Singapore City	12hr 40min
South Africa, Cape Town	11hr 30min
Spain, Madrid	2hr 10min
Sweden, Stockholm	2hr 10min
Switzerland, Zurich	1hr 30min
Turkey, Istanbul	3hr 25min
USA, Washington	8hr 5min
USA, New York	7hr 35min
USA, Los Angeles	10hr 10min
USA, Chicago	8hr 30min
Venezuela, Caracas	9hr 40min
Zambia, Lusaka	10hr
Zimbabwe, Harare	9hr 50min

Local standard time is calculated by adding to or subtracting from Greenwich Mean Time

Abu Dhabi	+4	Bombay	+5.5	Chicago	-6
Adelaide	+9.5	Bonn	+1	Copenhagen	+1
Amsterdam	+1	Brisbane	+10	Damascus	+2
Anchorage	-9	Brussels	+1	Darwin	+8.5
Auckland	+12	Bucharest	+2	Detroit	-5
Baghdad	+3	Budapest	+1	Dubai	+4
Bangkok	+7	Buenos Aires	-3	Dublin	0
Beijing	+8	Cairo	+2	Gibralta	+1
Beirut	+2	Calcutta	+5.5	Helsinki	+2
Belgrade	+1	Cape Town	+2	Hong Kong	+8
Berlin	+1	Caracas	-4	Istanbul	+2

Jakarta	+7	Manila	+8	Panama	-5	Shanghai	+8	Warsaw	+1
Jerusalem	+2	Melbourne	+10	Paris	+1	Singapore	+8	Washington	-5
Karachi	+5	Mexico City	-6	Perth	+8	Stockholm	+1	Wellington	+12
Kuala Lumpur	+8	Miami	-5	Prague	+1	Sydney	+10	Winnipeg	-6
Kuwait	+3	Milan	+1	Quebec	-5	Tehran	+3.5		
Lagos	+1	Montreal	-5	Rangoon	+6.5	Tokyo	+9		
Lima	-5	Moscow	+3	Reykjavik	0	Toronto	-5		
Lisbon	0	Nairobi	+3	Rio de Janeiro	-3	Tripoli	+1		
Luxembourg	+1	New York	-5	Rome	+1	Tunis	+1		
Madras	+5.5	Oslo	+1	San Francisco	-8	Vancouver	-8		
Madrid	+1	Ottawa	-5	Santiago	-4	Vienna	+1		

international dialling codes

SHOWN OPPOSITE are the numerical
prefixes needed to dial most countries from
the UK. Dial the international access code,
00, followed by the country's code, then the
local phone number.

For example: to dial the USA from the UK,
you will need to dial 001 before the local
phone number. Most local numbers whose
area codes start with a zero will drop this
zero when the international dialling code is
added, so the telephone number 01 23 45 67
89 in Paris would be reached by dialling
00 33 123 45 67 89 from the UK.

The international operator can be contacted
on 155. International Directory Enquiries can
be contacted on 153.

Directory Enquiries for the UK, Northern
Island and the Rebuplic of Ireland can be
contacted on 192.

Aa

Afghanistan	93
Albania	355
Algeria	213
Andorra	376
Angola	244
Anguilla	1264
Antartica	672
Antiqua & Barbuda	1268
Argentina	54
Armenia	374
Aruba	297
Ascension Island	247
Australia (including Cocos Islands)	61
Austria	43
Azerbaijan	994
Azores	351

Bb

Bahamas	1242
Bahrain	973
Balearic Islands	34
Bangladesh	880
Barbados	1246
Belarus	375
Belgium	32
Belize	501
Benin	229
Bermuda	1441
Bhutan	975
Bolivia	591
Bosnia & Herzegovia	387
Botswana	267
Brazil	55
Brunei	673
Bulgaria	359
Burkina Faso	226
Burundi	257

Cc

Cambodia	855
Cameroon	237
Canada	1
Cape Verde	238
Cayman Islands	1345
Central African Republic	236
Chad	235
Chile (inlcuding Easter Island)	56
China	86
Christmas Island	61
Colombia	57

Comoros	269
Congo	242
Congo (Democratic Republic of)	243
Cote d'Ivoire	225
Cook Islands	682
Costa Rica	506
Croatia	385
Cuba	53
Cuba (Guantanamo Bay)	5399
Curaçao	599
Cyprus	357
Czech Republic	420

Dd

Denmark	45
Diego Garcia	246
Djibouti	253
Dominica	1767
Dominican Republic	1809

Ee

East Timor	670
Ecuador	593
Egypt	20
El Salvador	503
Equatorial Guinea	240
Eritrea	291
Estonia	372
Ethiopia	251

Ff

Falkland Islands	500
Faroe Islands	298
Fiji	679
Finland	358
France	33
French Guyana	594
French Polynesia	689

Gg

Gabon	241
Gambia	220
Georgia	995
Germany	49
Ghana	233
Gibraltar	350
Greece	30
Greenland	299
Grenada (including Carriacou)	1473
Guadeloupe	590

Guam	1671
Guatemala	502
Guinea	224
Guinea-Bissau	245
Guyana	592

Hh

Haiti	509
Honduras	504
Hong Kong	852
Hungary	36

Ii

Iceland	354
India	91
Indonesia	62
Inmarsat (satellite mobile)	870
Iran	98
Iraq	964
Ireland	353
Israel	972
Italy	39

Jj

Jamaica	1876
Japan	81
Jordan	962

Kk

Kazakhstan	7
Kenya	254
Kiribati	686
Korea (North)	850
Korea (South)	82
Kuwait	965
Kyrgyzstan (Kyrghyzia)	996

Ll

Laos	856
Latvia	371
Lebanon	961
Lesotho	266
Liberia	231
Libya	218
Lichtenstein	423
Lithuania	370
Luxembourg	352

Mm

Macau	853
Macedonia	389
Madagascar	261
Malawi	265
Malaysia	60
Maldives	960
Mali	223
Malta	356
Marshall Islands	692
Martinique	596
Mauritania	222
Mauritius (including Rodriguez Islands)	230
Mayotte	269
Mexico	52
Micronesia	691
Midway Island	1808
Moldova	373
Monaco	377
Mongolia	976
Monserrat	1664
Morocco	212
Mozambique	258
Myanmar (Burma)	95

Nn

Namibia	264
Nauru	674
Nepal	977
Netherlands	31
Netherlands Antilles	599
New Caledonia	687
New Zealand	64
Nicaragua	505
Niger	227
Nigeria	234
Nive	683
Norfolk Island	672
Northern Marianas	1670
Norway	47

Oo

Oman	968

Pp

Pakistan	92
Palau	680
Panama	507
Papau New Guinea	675
Paraguay	595
Peru	51
Philippines	63
Poland	48
Portugal (including Azores & Madeira)	351
Puerto Rico	1787

Qq

Qatar	974

Rr

Reunion	262
Romania	40
Russia (Federation)	7
Rwanda	250

Ss

St Helena	290
St Kitts & Nevis	1869
St Lucia	1758
St Pierre & Miquelon	508
St Vincent & the Grenadines	1784
Samoa (USA)	684
Samoa (Western)	685
San Marino	378
Sao Tomé & Principle	239
Saudi Arabia	966
Senegal	221
Serbia	381
Seychelles	248
Sierra Leone	232
Singapore	65
Slovakia	421
Slovenia	386
Solomon Islands	677
Somalia	252
South Africa	27
Spain	34
Sri Lanka	94
Sudan	249
Surinam	597
Swaziland	268
Sweden	46
Switzerland	41
Syria	963

Tt

Taiwan	886
Tajikistan	992
Tanzania	255
Thailand	66
Togo	228
Tokelau	690
Tonga	676
Trinidad & Tobago	1868
Tristan da Cunha	2897
Tunisia	216

Turkey	90
Turkmenistan	993
Turks & Caicos Islands	1649
Tuvalu	688

Uu

Uganda	256
Ukraine	380
United Arab Emirates	971
United Kingdom	44
United States of America	1
Uruguay	598
Uzbekistan	998

Vv

Vanuatu	678
Vatican City	39
Venezuela	58
Vietnam	84
Virgin Islands (UK)	1284
Virgin Islands (USA)	1340

Ww

Wake Island	808

Yy

Yemen	967
Yugoslavia	381

Zz

Zaire	243
Zambia	260
Zanzibar	255
Zimbabwe	263

conversion tables

distance

Metric > Imperial		Imperial > Metric	
1 centimetre	0.3937 inches	1 inch	2.54 centimetres
1 metre	3.281 feet	1 foot	0.3048 metres
1 metre	1.094 yards	1 yard	0.9144 metres
1 kilometre	0.6214 miles	1 mile	1.609 kilometres

area

Metric > Imperial		Imperial > Metric	
1 cubic centimetre	0.061 cubic inches	1 cubic inch	16.39 cubic centimetres
1 sq centimetre	0.1550 sq inches	1 sq inch	6.452 sq centimetres
1 sq metre	10.76 sq feet	1 sq foot	0.0929 sq metres
1 sq metre	1.196 sq yards	1 sq yard	0.8361 sq metres
1 sq kilometre	0.3861 sq miles	1 sq mile	2.591 sq kilometres
1 hectare	2.471 acres	1 acre	0.4047 hectares

volume

Metric > Imperial		Imperial > Metric	
1 litre	61.03 cubic inches	1 cubic inch	0.01639 litres
1 litre	0.22 gallons	1 gallon	4.546 litres
1 cubic metre	35.316 cubic feet	1 cubic foot	0.2832 cubic metres
1 cubic metre	1.308 cubic yards	1 cubic yard	0.7646 cubic metres
1 cubic metre	61,026 cubic inches		

mass

Metric > Imperial		Imperial > Metric	
1 gram	15.43 grains	1 grain	0.0648 grams
1 gram	0.035 ounces	1 ounce	28.35 grams
1 gram	0.0022 pounds	1 pound	453.6 grams
1 kilogram	2.205 pounds	1 pound	0.4536 kilograms
1 tonne	0.984 tons	1 ton	1,016 kilograms

temperature

Celsius > Fahrenheit
Multiply by 9/5 and add 32
Example: 100°C x 9/5 + 32 = 212°F

Fahrenheit > Celsius
Subtract 32 and multiply by 5/9
Example: (212°F - 32) x 5/9 = 100°C

DIRECTORS GUILD
OF GREAT BRITAIN

...is the only organisation that unites directors in all media
representing directors in film, television & theatre

advice on contract issues

directory of members

quarterly magazine

masterclasses, workshops
& panel discussions

rate cards

model contracts

codes of practice

directors training website :
www.directorstraining.org.uk

presence at festivals
& media fairs

a campaigning voice

DIRECTORS GUILD
OF GREAT BRITAIN
The Union for Directors in All Media
T: 020 7278 4343 F: 020 7278 4742 E: guild@dggb.co.uk or visit www.dggb.co.uk

Country	Lines/Colour	Voltage	Frequency
Aa			
Abu Dhabi	625 PAL	240V	50Hz
Afghanistan	624 PAL	220V	50Hz
Alaska	525 NTSC	240/120V	50/60Hz
Albania	625 SECAM	220V	50Hz
Algeria	625 PAL	220V	50Hz
Andorra	625 PAL	220/127V	50/60Hz
Angola	625 PAL	220V	50Hz
Antarctica	525 NTSC	240/120V	50/60Hz
Antigua/Barbuda	525 NTSC	230V	60Hz
Antilles	525 NTSC	240/120V	50/60Hz
Argentina	625 PAL N	220V	50Hz
Armenia	625 SECAM	220/127V	50Hz
Aruba	525 NTSC		
Australia	625 PAL	240V	50Hz
Austria	625 PAL	220V	50Hz
Azerbaijan	625 PAL		50Hz
Azores	625 PAL	240/220V	50Hz
Bb			
Bahamas	525 NTSC	120V	60Hz
Bahrain	625 PAL	230/110V	50/60Hz
Bangladesh	625 PAL	230V	50Hz
Barbados	525 NTSC	230/110V	50Hz
Belarus	625 SECAM	220V	50Hz
Belau	525 NTSC		
Belgium	625 PAL	220V	50Hz
Belize	525 NTSC		
Benin	625 SECAM	220V	50Hz
Bermuda	525 NTSC	208/120V	60Hz
Bolivia	525 NTSC	230/115V	50Hz
Bophuthatwana	625 PAL		
Bosnia & Herzegovina	625 PAL		50Hz
Botswana	625 PAL	220V	50Hz
Brazil	525 PAL M	220V	60Hz
British Indian Ocean Territories	525 NTSC	240/220V	50/60Hz
British Virgin Islands	525 NTSC	230V	60Hz
Brunei	625 PAL	230V	50Hz
Bulgaria	625 SECAM V	220V	50Hz
Burkina Faso	525 NTSC	220V	50Hz
Burma	525 NTSC		
Burundi	625 SECAM	220V	50Hz
Cc			
Cambodia (Kampuchea)	625 PAL	120V	50Hz
Cameroon	625 PAL	220V	50Hz
Canada	525 NTSC	240/120V	50/60Hz
Canary Islands	525 NTSC	240/220V	50/60Hz

Country	Lines/Colour	Voltage	Frequency
Central African Republic	625 SECAM	220V	50Hz
Chad	625 SECAM	220V	50Hz
Channel Islands	625 PAL	240/220V	50Hz
Chechnya	625 SECAM		50Hz
Chile	525 NTSC	220V	50Hz
China	625 PAL	220V	50Hz
China, Taiwan	525 NTSC		
Ciskei	625 PAL		
Colombia	525 NTSC	120V	60Hz
Congo	625 SECAM	220V	50Hz
Costa Rica	525 NTSC	120V	60Hz
Cote d'Ivoire	625 SECAM V	220V	50Hz
Croatia	625 SECAM		50Hz
Cuba	525 NTSC	115V	60Hz
Curaçao/Aruba	525 NTSC	240/220V	50/60Hz
Cyprus (Greek)	625 SECAM	240V	50Hz
Cyprus (Turkish)	625 PAL	240V	50Hz
Czech Republic	625 SECAM	220V	50Hz
Dd			
Denmark	625 PAL	220V	50Hz
Diego Garcia	525 NTSC		
Djibouti	625 SECAM	220V	50Hz
Dominican Republic	525 NTSC	110V	60Hz
Dubai	625 PAL	240/220V	50/60Hz
Ee			
Eire (UK)	625 PAL	220/380V	50Hz
Egypt	625 SECAM	220V	50Hz
El Salvador	525 NTSC	240/120V	60Hz
Equatorial Guinea	625 SECAM		
Estonia	625 SECAM	220V	50Hz
Ethiopia	625 PAL	240/220V	50/60Hz
Ff			
Fiji	525 NTSC	240/220V	50Hz
Finland	625 PAL	220V	50Hz
France	625 SECAM	220V	50Hz
French Polynesia	625 SECAM H	220V	50Hz
Fujairah	625 PAL	220V	50Hz
Gg			
Gabon	625 SECAM	220V	50/60Hz
Galapagos Islands	525 NTSC	240/120V	50/60Hz
Gambia	625 PAL	230V	50Hz
Georgia	625 SECAM	220/127V	50Hz
Germany	625 (new)		
	PAL/SECAM	230/133V	50Hz
Ghana	625 PAL	230V	50Hz
Gibraltar	625 PAL	240V	50Hz
Greece	625 SECAM	220V	50Hz

Country	Lines/Colour	Voltage	Frequency
Greenland	525 NTSC	240/120V	50/60Hz
Grenada	625 NTSC	230V	50Hz
Guadeloupe	625 SECAM	220V	50/60Hz
Guatemala	525 NTSC	240/120V	60Hz
Guyana	625 PAL	240/220V	50/60Hz

Hh

Country	Lines/Colour	Voltage	Frequency
Haiti	625 SECAM V	230/220V	60Hz
Hawaii	525 NTSC	240/120V	60Hz
Honduras	525 NTSC	110V	60Hz
Hong Kong	625 PAL	200V	50Hz
Hungary	625 PAL	220V	50Hz

Ii

Country	Lines/Colour	Voltage	Frequency
Iceland	625 PAL	220V	50Hz
India	625 PAL (mostly)	230V	50Hz
Indonesia	625 PAL	220/127V	50Hz
Iran	625 SECAM H	220V	50Hz
Iraq	625 SECAM H	220V	50Hz
Republic of Ireland	625 PAL	230/220V	50Hz
Israel	625 PAL	230V	50Hz
Italy	625 PAL	220V	50Hz

Jj

Country	Lines/Colour	Voltage	Frequency
Jamaica	525 NTSC	220V	50Hz
Japan	525 NTSC	100V	50/60Hz
Jordan	625 PAL	220V	50Hz

Kk

Country	Lines/Colour	Voltage	Frequency
Kazakhstan	625 SECAM		50Hz
Kenya	625 PAL	240V	50Hz
Korea (North)	625 PAL	220V	50Hz
Korea (South)	525 NTSC	100V	60Hz
Kuwait	625 PAL	240V	60Hz

Ll

Country	Lines/Colour	Voltage	Frequency
Laos	625 SECAM V	380/220V	50Hz
Laos Republic	625 PAL M	380/220V	50Hz
Latvia	625 SECAM		50Hz
Lebanon	625 SECAM V	220/110V	50Hz
Leeward Islands	525 NTSC	240/120V	50/60Hz
Leichtenstein	625 PAL/SECAM V		
Lesotho	625 PAL	220V	50Hz
Liberia	625 PAL	240/120V	60Hz
Libya	625 PAL	230/127V	50Hz
Lithuania	625 SECAM	220/127V	50Hz
Luxemburg	625 SECAM	220V	50Hz

Mm

Country	Lines/Colour	Voltage	Frequency
Macau	625 PAL	240/220V	50/60Hz
Macedonia	625 PAL	220V	50Hz
Madagascar	625 SECAM V	220/127V	50Hz
Madeira	625 PAL	240/220V	50/60Hz
Malaysia	625 PAL	240V	50Hz
Maldives	625 PAL	230V	50Hz
Mali	625 SECAM		
Malta	625 PAL	240V	50Hz
Martinique	625 SECAM V	127V	50Hz
Mauritania	625 SECAM H		
Mauritius	625 SECAM	230V	50Hz
Mayotte	625 SECAM		
Mexico	525 NTSC	220V	60Hz
Micronesia	525 NTSC	240/120V	50/60Hz
Midway Island	525 NTSC	240/120V	50/60Hz
Moldova	625 SECAM		50Hz
Monaco	625 SECAM V/PAL	220/127V	50Hz
Mongolia	625 SECAM	220V	50Hz
Montenegro	625 PAL		
Montserrat	525 NTSC	230V	60Hz
Morocco	625 SECAM V	220/127V	50Hz
Mozambique	625 PAL	220V	50Hz

Nn

Country	Lines/Colour	Voltage	Frequency
Namibia	625 PAL		
Nepal	625 PAL	220V	50Hz
Netherlands	625 PAL	220V	50Hz
Netherlands Antilles	525 NTSC	240/120V	50/60Hz
New Caledonia	625 SECAM V	240/220V	50/60Hz
New Zealand	625 PAL	230V	50Hz
Nicaragua	525 NTSC	240/120V	60Hz
Niger	625 SECAM V	220V	50Hz
Nigeria	625 PAL	230/220V	50Hz
Norway	625 PAL	230V	50Hz

Oo

Country	Lines/Colour	Voltage	Frequency
Oman	625 PAL	240V	50Hz

Pp

Country	Lines/Colour	Voltage	Frequency
Pakistan	625 PAL	230V	50Hz
Panama	525 NTSC	240/120V	60Hz
Papua New Guinea	625 PAL	240V	50Hz
Paraguay	625 PAL N	220V	50Hz
Peru	525 NTSC	225V	60Hz
Philippines	525 NTSC	220V/110V	60Hz
Poland	625 PAL	220V	50Hz
Ponape	525 NTSC	240/120V	50/60Hz
Portugal	625 PAL	220V	50Hz
Puerto Rico	525 NTSC	240/120V	60Hz

Country	Lines/Colour	Voltage	Frequency
Qq			
Qatar	625 PAL I	240V	50Hz
Rr			
Ras Al-Khaimah	625 PAL		50Hz
Reunion	625 SECAM V	240/120V	50/60Hz
Romania	625 PAL	220V	50Hz
Russia	625 SECAM	220/127V	50Hz
Rwanda	625 SECAM	220V	50Hz
Ss			
Sabah/Sarawak	625 PAL	240V	50Hz
Saipan	525 NTSC		
Samoa (Eastern)	525 NTSC	240/120V	50/60Hz
Samoa (Western)	525 NTSC	240/120V	50/60Hz
San Andreas Islands	525 NTSC		
San Marino	625 PAL	240/220V	50/60Hz
Sao Tome & Principe	625 PAL		50 Hz
Saudi Arabia	625 SECAM H	220/127V	50Hz
Saudi Arabia	625 PAL	220/127V	50Hz
Senegal	625 SECAM V	127V	50Hz
Serbia	625 SECAM		50Hz
Seychelles	625 PAL	240/220V	50/60Hz
Sharjah	625 PAL		50Hz
Sierra Leone	625 PAL	230V	50Hz
Singapore	625 PAL	230V	50Hz
Slovakia	625 PAL	220V	50Hz
Slovenia	625 PAL	220V	50Hz
Society Islands	625 SECAM H		
Somalia	625 PAL	230/220V	50Hz
South Africa	625 PAL	220V	50Hz
Spain	625 PAL	220/127V	50Hz
Sri Lanka	625 PAL	230V	50Hz
St Kitts & Nevis	525 NTSC	230V	60Hz
St Lucia	625 PAL	240V	50Hz
St Thomas	525 NTSC		60Hz
St Vincent	525 NTSC	230V	50Hz
Sudan	625 PAL	240V	50Hz
Surinam	525 NTSC	127/115V	50/60Hz
Swaziland	625 PAL	230V	50Hz
Sweden	625 PAL	220V	50Hz
Switzerland	625 PAL	220V	50Hz
Syria	625 SECAM H/PAL	220/115V	50Hz

Country	Lines/Colour	Voltage	Frequency
Tt			
Tahiti	625 SECAM H	240/220V	50/60Hz
Taiwan	525 NTSC	220/110V	60Hz
Tajikistan	625 SECAM		50Hz
Tanzania	625 PAL	400/230V	50Hz
Thailand	625 PAL	220V	50Hz
Togo	625 SECAM V	220V	50Hz
Trinidad & Tobago	525 NTSC	230/115V	60Hz
Tunisia	625 SECAM V	220V	50Hz
Turkey	625 PAL	230V	50Hz
Turkmenistan	625 SECAM		50Hz
Uu			
Uganda	625 PAL	240V	50Hz
Ukraine	625 SECAM	220/127V	50Hz
Umm Al-Quwain	625 PAL		
United Arab Emirates	625 PAL	240/220V	50Hz
United Kingdom	625 PAL	230V	50Hz
Upper Volta	625 SECAM V		
Uruguay	625 PAL N	220V	50Hz
USA	525 NTSC	240/120V	60Hz
Uzbekistan	625 SECAM	220/127V	50Hz
Vv			
Vatican	625 PAL	220V	50Hz
Venezuela	525 NTSC	240/120V	60Hz
Vietnam	525 NTSC/	220/120V	50Hz
	625 PAL & SECAM		
Virgin Islands	525 NTSC	240/120V	50/60Hz
Yy			
Yemen	625 PAL/NTSC	220V	50Hz
Yugoslavia	625 PAL	220V	50Hz
Zz			
Yemen	625 PAL/NTSC	220V	50Hz
Yugoslavia	625 PAL	220V	50Hz
Zaire	625 SECAM V	220V	50Hz
Zambia	625 PAL	220V	50Hz
Zanzibar	625 PAL	220V	50Hz
Zimbabwe	625 PAL	225V	50Hz

Many thanks to Dubbs for supplying this information.
www.dubbs.co.uk

uk : map

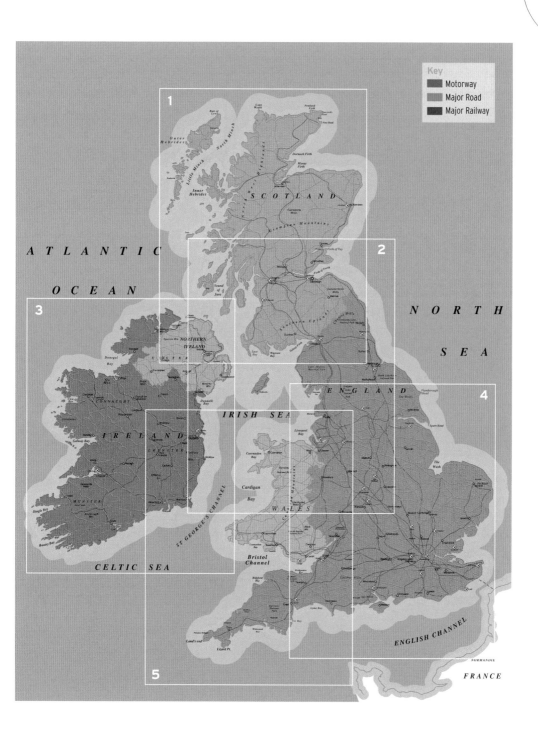

Key
- Motorway
- Major Road
- Major Railway

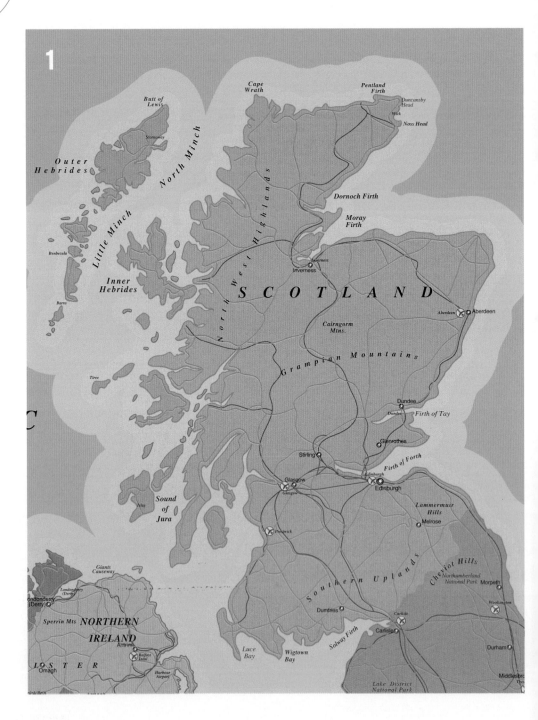

1

Cape Wrath

Pentland Firth

Butt of Lewis

Duncansby Head

Wick

Noss Head

Stornoway

Outer Hebrides

North Minch

Dornoch Firth

Moray Firth

Little Minch

North West Highlands

Inverness
Inverness

Benbecula

Inner Hebrides

S C O T L A N D

Barra

Aberdeen Aberdeen

Cairngorm Mtns.

Grampian Mountains

Tiree

Dundee
Dundee   Firth of Tay

Glenrothes

Stirling

Firth of Forth

Glasgow
Glasgow

Edinburgh
Edinburgh

Sound of Jura

Islay

Prestwick

Lammermuir Hills

Melrose

Giants Causeway

Cheviot Hills

Northumberland National Park   Morpeth

Londonderry (Derry)

Londonderry (Derry)

Sperrin Mts   NORTHERN

Antrim

Southern Uplands

Woolington

IRELAND

Belfast Intnl

Dumfries

Carlisle
Carlisle

Durham

U L S T E R
Omagh

Harbour Airport

Luce Bay

Wigtown Bay

Solway Firth

Middlesbro

Lake District National Park

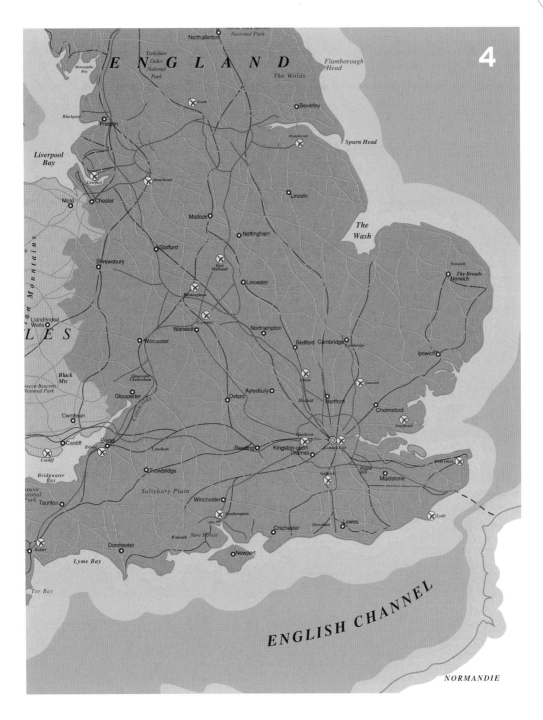

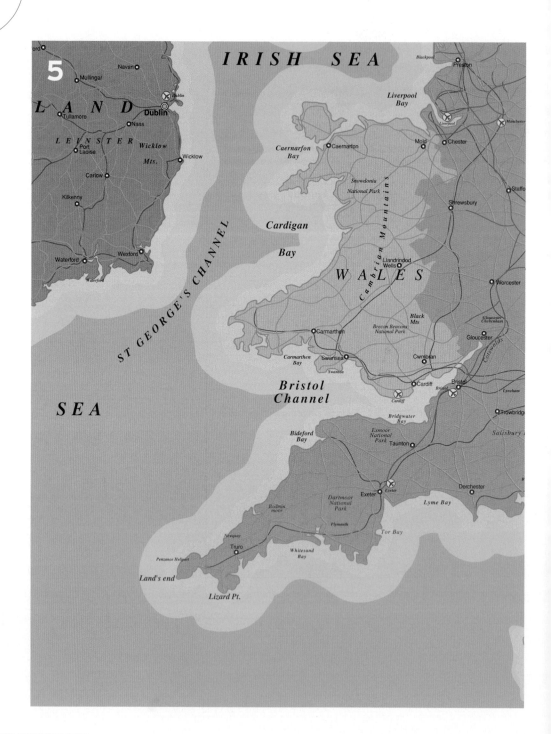

travel information

UK travel distances

Key

00	00	distance in kilometers
00	00	distance in miles

Each cell shows distance in kilometers (top) / distance in miles (bottom).

From \ To	Stanraer	Penzance	Oxford	Newcastle	Manchester	Liverpool	Hollyhead	Glasgow	Fishguard	Edinburgh	Cardiff	Cambridge	Bristol	Birmingham	Aberdeen	London
Aberdeen																864 / 537
Birmingham															688 / 430	187 / 117
Bristol														136 / 85	818 / 511	190 / 119
Cambridge													286 / 178	162 / 101	749 / 468	96 / 60
Cardiff												351 / 213	72 / 45	171 / 107	851 / 532	248 / 155
Edinburgh											629 / 393	542 / 337	597 / 373	469 / 293	203 / 127	645 / 401
Fishguard										737 / 398	181 / 113	513 / 319	193 / 120	285 / 177	843 / 524	418 / 260
Glasgow									626 / 398	72 / 45	629 / 393	562 / 349	595 / 372	466 / 291	238 / 149	644 / 400
Hollyhead								514 / 321	261 / 163	523 / 327	336 / 209	396 / 246	373 / 232	248 / 155	734 / 459	425 / 264
Liverpool							170 / 106	354 / 221	268 / 167	360 / 255	320 / 200	330 / 205	285 / 178	157 / 98	581 / 361	336 / 210
Manchester						54 / 34	200 / 125	342 / 214	304 / 189	349 / 218	301 / 188	246 / 153	267 / 167	141 / 88	566 / 354	317 / 197
Newcastle					226 / 141	272 / 170	402 / 250	240 / 150	527 / 328	174 / 109	498 / 311	365 / 228	466 / 291	317 / 198	378 / 236	441 / 276
Oxford				407 / 253	246 / 154	264 / 165	339 / 212	568 / 355	344 / 214	579 / 362	174 / 109	128 / 80	118 / 74	101 / 63	797 / 498	90 / 56
Penzance			426 / 265	768 / 477	573 / 358	592 / 370	654 / 409	901 / 563	547 / 340	907 / 567	373 / 232	592 / 368	314 / 195	445 / 278	1110 / 690	502 / 312
Stanraer		922 / 576	594 / 371	262 / 164	362 / 226	378 / 236	534 / 334	141 / 88	661 / 411	214 / 133	650 / 406	591 / 361	618 / 386	486 / 304	390 / 244	662 / 414
Strat.u.Avon	535 / 335	422 / 264	77 / 48	362 / 226	186 / 116	200 / 124	277 / 173	510 / 319	310 / 194	521 / 324	158 / 99	158 / 99	120 / 75	38 / 24	742 / 461	152 / 95

london underground

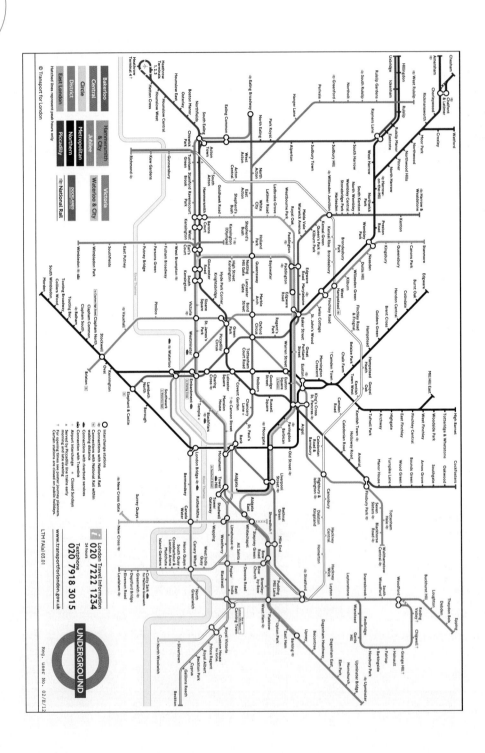

useful websites

broadcasters : terrestrial

Anglia TV	http://www.anglia.tv.co.uk
BBC	http://www.bbc.co.uk
Border TV	http://www.border-tv.com
Carlton	http://www.carlton.com
Channel 4	http://www.channel4.com
Channel 5	http://www.channel5.co.uk
Channel Television	http://www.channeltv.co.uk
Grampian	http://www.grampiantv.com
Granada TV	http://www.granadatv.co.uk
HTV West	http://www.htvwest.com
HTV Wales	http://www.htvwales.com
ITN	http://www.itn.co.uk
ITV	http://www.itv.com
LWT	http://www.lwt.co.uk
Meridian	http://www.meridian.tv.co.uk
S4C	http://www.s4c.co.uk
Scottish Television	http://www.scottishtv.co.uk
Tyne Tees Television	http://www.tynetees.tv
Ulster TV	http://www.utvlive.com
West Country Television	http://www.carlton.com/westcountry
Yorkshire Television	http://www.yorkshire-television.tv

broadcasters : satellite/cable

Arte	http://www.artefrance.fr
BBC Three	http://www.bbc.co.uk/bbcthree
BBC Four	http://www.bbc.co.uk/bbcfour
The Box	http://www.thebox.co.uk
Bravo	http://www.bravo.co.uk
British Sky Broadcasting	http://www1.sky.com
Carlton Food Network	http://www.cfn.co.uk
Cartoon Network	http://www.cartoon-network.co.uk/
Challenge TV	http://www.challengetv.co.uk
Channel TV	http://www.channeltv.co.uk
CNBC Europe	http://www.cnbceurope.com
CNN Cable News Network	http://www.cnn.com
Discovery Channel	http://www.discoveryeurope.com
Disney Channel	http://www.disneychannel.co.uk
Eurosport	http://www.eurosport.com
Fox Kids	http://www.foxkids.co.uk
Granada Sky Broadcasting	http://www.gsb.co.uk
Granada Breeze	http://www.gbreeze.co.uk
Granada Men	http://www.menandmotors.com
Granada Plus	http://www.gplus.co.uk
History Channel	http://www.thehistorychannel.co.uk
Knowledge TV	http://www.knowledgeTV.co.uk/
Landscape TV	http://www.cablenet.net/landscape
Living	http://www.livingtv.co.uk
MTV	http://www.mtv.co.uk

useful websites

broadcasters : satellite/cable: continued

National Geographic Channel	http://www.nationalgeographic.co.uk
Nickelodeon	http://www.nick.co.uk
QVC – The Shopping Channel	http://www.qvcuk.com
Sky One	http://www1.sky.com/skyone/
TCC	http://www.tcc.co.uk
Television X – The Fantasy Channel	http://www.televisionx.co.uk
Travel Channel	http://www.travelchannel.co.uk
Trouble	http://www.trouble.co.uk
VH1	http://www.vh1.co.uk

organisations & associations

Advertising Association	http://www.adassoc.org.uk
Association of National Tourist Offices	http://www.tourist-offices.org.uk
Association of Photographers	http://www.the-aop.co.uk
British Actors' Equity	http://www.equity.org.uk
British Design & Art Direction Association	http://www.dandad.org/
British Film Commission	http://www.britfilmcom.co.uk
British Film Institute Online (BPI)	http://www.bpi.co.uk
Carlton plc	http://www.carltonplc.co.uk/
Radio Advertising Bureau	http://www.rab.co.uk
Community Media Association (CMA)	http://www.commedia.org.uk
Department of Culture, Media and Sport	http://www.heritage.gov.uk/
European Broadcasting Union	http://www.ebu.ch/
Foreign & Commonwealth Office	http://www.fco.gov.uk/
Granada Sky Broadcasting	http://www.gsb.co.uk
Incorporated Society of Musicians (ISM)	http://www.ism.org
Moving Image Society/BKSTS	http://www.bksts.com
National Film Theatre	http://www.bfi.org.uk/showing/nft
National Trust	http://www.nationaltrust.org.uk/
Pearson Television	http://www.pearsontv.com/
Performing Rights Society	http://www.prs.co.uk
Producers' Alliance for Cinema & Television	http://www.pact.co.uk
Produxion.com	http://www.produxion.com
Radio Academy	http://www.radioacademy.org
Radio Authority	http://www.radioauthority.org.uk
Royal Parks of London	http://www.royalparks.gov.uk
TAC – Welsh Independent Producers	http://www.teledwyr.com
United News & Media	http://www.unm.com/
West Midlands Arts Board (Regional Arts page)	http://www.arts.org.uk

crew finders

Actors' Worldlink	http://members.aol.com/AWorldLink/index.htm
Castcall Information Services	http://www.castcall.demon.co.uk
Connections	http://www.connectionsuk.com
Creative Directory	http://www.creativedir.com
Showbiz Jobs	http://www.showbizjobs.com
Force One Entertainment	http://www.forceoneentertainment.com
Hobson's Artists	http://www.hobsons-international.com
LBS Manchester	http://www.lbs.co.uk
Lee's People	http://www.lees-people.co.uk
Mandy's Film & TV Production Directory	http://www.mandy.com/
Peters Fraser & Dunlop	http://www.pfd.co.uk
Production Access Network	http://www.prodnet.com
Rhubarb Personal Management	http://www.rhubarb.co.uk
Seifert Dench Associates	http://www.seifert-dench.co.uk
Sports Workshop Promotions	http://www.btinternet.com/~sports.promotions
Swedish Film Network	http://www.swedishfilm.net
Vincent Shaw Associates	http://home.clara.net/vincentshaw
Videography	http://www.videography.com/

studios & production facilities

Air-Edel Recording Studios Ltd	http://www.air-edel.co.uk
BBC Resources	http://www.bbcresources.co.uk
CTS Studios	http://www.cts-lansdowne.co.uk
Eastside Studios	http://www.eastsidestudios.com
Elstree Film Studios	http://www.elstreefilmtv.com
Enfys	http://www.enfys.co.uk
Fleetwood Mobiles Ltd	http://www.fleetwoodmobiles.com
Fountain Television Ltd	http://www.ftv.co.uk
Go Ahead Music	http://www.amphonic.co.uk
Grand Central Recording Studios	http://www.grand-central-studios.com
The Intrepid Aviation Company Ltd	http://www.deltaweb.co.uk/intrepid
ITN Studios	http://www.itn.co.uk
Jacobs Studios	http://www.jacobs-studios.co.uk
The London Studios	http://www.londonstudios.co.uk
Megahertz Communications Ltd	http://www.megahertz.co.uk
Metro Studios	http://www.metroimaging.co.uk
Millennium Studios	http://www.elstree-online.co.uk
Ministry of Production	http://www.skarda.net
Moles Studio	http://www.moles.co.uk
Parr Street Studios	http://www.parrstreet.co.uk
Plough Studios	http://www.ploughstudios.com
Shepperton Studios	http://www.sheppertonstudios.com
Shots Television	http://www.shots.demon.co.uk
SLV	http://www.slvision.co.uk
The Sound Company Ltd	http://www.sound.co.uk
Sound Moves	http://www.sound-moves.com
The Studio	http://www.the-studio.co.uk
The Tape Gallery	http://www.tape-gallery.co.uk
Teddington Studios	http://www.teddington.co.uk
Waterfall Studios	http://www.silver-road-studios.co.uk
Wise Buddah Ltd	http://www.wisebuddah.com

useful websites

post-production facilities

Applecart Television Facilities Ltd	http://www.applecart.co.uk
Arena Digital	http://www.arenadigital.co.uk
Asert Media Group Ltd	http://www.asert-media.co.uk
AVC Media Productions	http://www.avc-enterprises.co.uk
Avid Technology	http://www.avid.com
BBC Resources	http://www.bbcresources.co.uk
BC's Sound & Vision	http://www.beecees.demon.co.uk
Boxer Systems Ltd	http://www.boxer.co.uk
Component Ltd	http://www.component.co.uk
Computamatch	http://www.sohogroup.com
Creative Video Associates	http://www.cva.co.uk
Editz	http://www.editz.co.uk
Eidos Technologies	http://www.eidos.co.uk
Elite Television	http://www.elitetv.dircon.co.uk
The Farm	http://www.farmpost.co.uk
Fountain Television	http://www.ftv.co.uk
FrameStore	http://www.framestore.co.uk
Frontier Post	http://www.frontierpost.co.uk
Frontline TV	http://www.frontline-tv.co.uk
Gemini Audio	http://www.geminiaudio.co.uk
Headline Media	http://www.headlinemedia.co.uk
Holloway Film & Television	http://www.hollowayfilm.co.uk
Image Makers	http://www.im-digital.co.uk
Key Video Communications	http://www.keyvideo.co.uk
The London Studios	http://www.tvstudios.co.uk
Lynx Video	http://www.lynxdigital.tv
M2 Television	http://www.m2tv.com
The Machine Room	http://www.themachineroom.co.uk
Mad Editing Facilities	http://www.masterworks.com
Media Production Facilities	http://www.media-production.demon.co.uk
The Mill	http://www.mill.co.uk
The Moving Picture Company	http://www.moving-picture.co.uk
Oakslade Studios	http://www.oakslade.co.uk
Ocean Post Production	http://www.oceanpost.co.uk
One Stop Digital (OSD) Ltd	http://www.osd-uk.com
Pan Com Ltd	http://www.pancom.ie
Peak White Video	http://www.peakwhite.com
Picardy Television (Edinburgh)	http://www.picardy.co.uk
PMPP Facilities	http://www.pmpp.dircon.co.uk
Pyramid Post Production	http://www.pyramidtv.co.uk
Quadrillion	http://www.quadrillion.net
Rainbow Post Production	http://www.rainbowpost.com
Random Post Production	http://www.randompost.com
Red Post Production	http://www.red-post.co.uk
The Reel Editing Company	http://www.ad921.dial.pipex.com
Resolution	http://www.resolutionpostgroup.co

post-production facilities : continued

Salon Productions	http://www.salonrentals.com
Saunders & Gordon	http://www.sgss.co.uk
SD Post	http://www.sdpost.co.uk
Silk Sound Ltd	http://www.silk.co.uk
Simpsons Creative Communications	http://www.converge.co.uk
Soho Images	http://www.sohogroup.com
The Sound Company Ltd	http://www.sound.co.uk
Teddington Studios	http://www.teddington.co.uk/page3.html
The Television Set	http://www.arenadigital.co.uk
TVE Group	http://www.tvegroup.com
Vector Television Facilities	http://www.vectortv.co.uk
The Video Lab	http://www.videolab.net
Video London	http://www.ftech.net/~videolon
Videosonics	http://www.videosonics.com
VMI	http://www.vmi.co.uk
VPTV	http://www.vptv.com
VTR Limited Ltd	http://www.vtr.co.uk
Wheelers	http://www.wheelers.co.uk
White Lightning Group	http://www.thebridge.co.uk
Wild Tracks Audio Studios Ltd	http://www.wildtracks.co.uk
XTV Cell	http://www.xtv.co.uk

festivals and awards

may

Cannes Film Festival
14-25 May 2003
Cannes, France
www.festival-cannes.com
+ 33 1 53 59 61 00

The Production Show
20-22 May 2003
Olympia, London
www.productionshow.com
+44 20 7505 8000

Mediacast
20-22 May 2003
ExCel, London
www.mediacast.co.uk
+44 20 8910 7910

june

BANFF 2003
8-13 June 2003
Canmore, Alberta, Canada
www.banff2003.com
+1 403 678 9260

Cannes Lions 2003
15-21 June 2003
Cannes, France
www.canneslions.com
+44 20 7291 8444

july

Rushes Soho Short Film Festival
26 July-1 August 2003
Soho, London
www.sohoshorts.com
+44 20 7851 6207

august

The Edinburgh International Film Festival
13-24 August 2003
Edinburgh
www.edfilmfest.org.uk

The Guardian International Television Festival
22-24 August 2003
Edinburgh
www.geitf.co.uk
+44 20 7430 1333

september

International Broadcast Convention (IBC)
12-16 September 2003
RAI Centre, Amsterdam
www.ibc.org.uk
+44 20 7611 7500

october

MIPCOM
10-14 October 2003
Cannes, France
www.mipcom.com
+ 33 1 41 90 45 63

Digital Arts World
28-30 October 2003
Earls Court, London
www.digmedia.co.uk
+44 20 8987 0900

november

London Film Festival
5-20 November 2003
South Bank, London
www.rlff.org.uk
+44 20 7815 1322

january

The Palm Springs International Film Festival
8-19 January 2004
Palm Springs, USA
www.psfilmfest.org
+ 1 800 898 7256

The Sundance Film Festival
15-25 January 2004
Park City, USA
www.sundance.org
+ 1 801 328 3456

NATPE
19-22 January 2004
New Orleans, USA
www.natpe.org
+ 1 310 453 4440

february

Video Forum
10-12 February 2004
Wembley, London
www.videoforum.co.uk
+44 1273 836804

march

MIPTV
22-26 March 2004
Cannes, France
www.miptv.com
+33 1 41 90 45 63

Milia
24-26 March 2004
Cannes, France
www.milia.com

april

National Exhibition of Broadcasters (NAB)
17-22 April 2004
Las Vegas, USA
www.nab.org
+1 800 622 3976

2003 : calendar

january

s	m	t	w	t	f	s
			1	2	3	4
5	6	7	8	9	10	11
12	13	14	15	16	17	18
19	20	21	22	23	24	25
26	27	28	29	30	31	

february

s	m	t	w	t	f	s
						1
2	3	4	5	6	7	8
9	10	11	12	13	14	15
16	17	18	19	20	21	22
23	24	25	26	27	28	

march

s	m	t	w	t	f	s
						1
2	3	4	5	6	7	8
9	10	11	12	13	14	15
16	17	18	19	20	21	22
23	24	25	26	27	28	29
30	31					

april

s	m	t	w	t	f	s
		1	2	3	4	5
6	7	8	9	10	11	12
13	14	15	16	17	18	19
20	21	22	23	24	25	26
27	28	29	30			

may

s	m	t	w	t	f	s
				1	2	3
4	5	6	7	8	9	10
11	12	13	14	15	16	17
18	19	20	21	22	23	24
25	26	27	28	29	30	31

june

s	m	t	w	t	f	s
1	2	3	4	5	6	7
8	9	10	11	12	13	14
15	16	17	18	19	20	21
22	23	24	25	26	27	28
29	30					

july

s	m	t	w	t	f	s
		1	2	3	4	5
6	7	8	9	10	11	12
13	14	15	16	17	18	19
20	21	22	23	24	25	26
27	28	29	30	31		

august

s	m	t	w	t	f	s
					1	2
3	4	5	6	7	8	9
10	11	12	13	14	15	16
17	18	19	20	21	22	23
24	25	26	27	28	29	30
31						

september

s	m	t	w	t	f	s
	1	2	3	4	5	6
7	8	9	10	11	12	13
14	15	16	17	18	19	20
21	22	23	24	25	26	27
28	29	30				

october

s	m	t	w	t	f	s
			1	2	3	4
5	6	7	8	9	10	11
12	13	14	15	16	17	18
19	20	21	22	23	24	25
26	27	28	29	30	31	

november

s	m	t	w	t	f	s
						1
2	3	4	5	6	7	8
9	10	11	12	13	14	15
16	17	18	19	20	21	22
23	24	25	26	27	28	29
30						

december

s	m	t	w	t	f	s
	1	2	3	4	5	6
7	8	9	10	11	12	13
14	15	16	17	18	19	20
21	22	23	24	25	26	27
28	29	30	31			

2004 : calendar

january

s	m	t	w	t	f	s
				1	2	3
4	5	6	7	8	9	10
11	12	13	14	15	16	17
18	19	20	21	22	23	24
25	26	27	28	29	30	31

february

s	m	t	w	t	f	s
1	2	3	4	5	6	7
8	9	10	11	12	13	14
15	16	17	18	19	20	21
22	23	24	25	26	27	28
29						

march

s	m	t	w	t	f	s
	1	2	3	4	5	6
7	8	9	10	11	12	13
14	15	16	17	18	19	20
21	22	23	24	25	26	27
28	29	30	31			

april

s	m	t	w	t	f	s
				1	2	3
4	5	6	7	8	9	10
11	12	13	14	15	16	17
18	19	20	21	22	23	24
25	26	27	28	29	30	

may

s	m	t	w	t	f	s
						1
2	3	4	5	6	7	8
9	10	11	12	13	14	15
16	17	18	19	20	21	22
23	24	25	26	27	28	29
30	31					

june

s	m	t	w	t	f	s
		1	2	3	4	5
6	7	8	9	10	11	12
13	14	15	16	17	18	19
20	21	22	23	24	25	26
27	28	29	30			

july

s	m	t	w	t	f	s
				1	2	3
4	5	6	7	8	9	10
11	12	13	14	15	16	17
18	19	20	21	22	23	24
25	26	27	28	29	30	31

august

s	m	t	w	t	f	s
1	2	3	4	5	6	7
8	9	10	11	12	13	14
15	16	17	18	19	20	21
22	23	24	25	26	27	28
29	30	31				

september

s	m	t	w	t	f	s
			1	2	3	4
5	6	7	8	9	10	11
12	13	14	15	16	17	18
19	20	21	22	23	24	25
26	27	28	29	30		

october

s	m	t	w	t	f	s
					1	2
3	4	5	6	7	8	9
10	11	12	13	14	15	16
17	18	19	20	21	22	23
24	25	26	27	28	29	30
31						

november

s	m	t	w	t	f	s
	1	2	3	4	5	6
7	8	9	10	11	12	13
14	15	16	17	18	19	20
21	22	23	24	25	26	27
28	29	30				

december

s	m	t	w	t	f	s
			1	2	3	4
5	6	7	8	9	10	11
12	13	14	15	16	17	18
19	20	21	22	23	24	25
26	27	28	29	30	31	

2005 : calendar

january

s	m	t	w	t	f	s
						1
2	3	4	5	6	7	8
9	10	11	12	13	14	15
16	17	18	19	20	21	22
23	24	25	26	27	28	29
30	31					

february

s	m	t	w	t	f	s
		1	2	3	4	5
6	7	8	9	10	11	12
13	14	15	16	17	18	19
20	21	22	23	24	25	26
27	28					

march

s	m	t	w	t	f	s
		1	2	3	4	5
6	7	8	9	10	11	12
13	14	15	16	17	18	19
20	21	22	23	24	25	26
27	28	29	30	31		

april

s	m	t	w	t	f	s
					1	2
3	4	5	6	7	8	9
10	11	12	13	14	15	16
17	18	19	20	21	22	23
24	25	26	27	28	29	30

may

s	m	t	w	t	f	s
1	2	3	4	5	6	7
8	9	10	11	12	13	14
15	16	17	18	19	20	21
22	23	24	25	26	27	28
29	30	31				

june

s	m	t	w	t	f	s
			1	2	3	4
5	6	7	8	9	10	11
12	13	14	15	16	17	18
19	20	21	22	23	24	25
26	27	28	29	30		

july

s	m	t	w	t	f	s
					1	2
3	4	5	6	7	8	9
10	11	12	13	14	15	16
17	18	19	20	21	22	23
24	25	26	27	28	29	30
31						

august

s	m	t	w	t	f	s
	1	2	3	4	5	6
7	8	9	10	11	12	13
14	15	16	17	18	19	20
21	22	23	24	25	26	27
28	29	30	31			

september

s	m	t	w	t	f	s
				1	2	3
4	5	6	7	8	9	10
11	12	13	14	15	16	17
18	19	20	21	22	23	24
25	26	27	28	29	30	

october

s	m	t	w	t	f	s
						1
2	3	4	5	6	7	8
9	10	11	12	13	14	15
16	17	18	19	20	21	22
23	24	25	26	27	28	29
30	31					

november

s	m	t	w	t	f	s
		1	2	3	4	5
6	7	8	9	10	11	12
13	14	15	16	17	18	19
20	21	22	23	24	25	26
27	28	29	30			

december

s	m	t	w	t	f	s
				1	2	3
4	5	6	7	8	9	10
11	12	13	14	15	16	17
18	19	20	21	22	23	24
25	26	27	28	29	30	31

skillset 2002 census

2000 SAW the first ever employment census of the audio-visual industries. One of the major recommendations of the Skillset/DCMS Audio-Visual Industries Training Group (AVITG), and conducted by Skillset, it provided the first reliable estimates of employment in these vital and growing sectors, and invaluable information on the representation of women, ethnic minorities and disabled people.

The census has now become a yearly exercise and is recognised by major employers, trade associations, government departments and unions as making a hugely important contribution to mapping industry change and planning for the future.

The third census achieved its highest response to date, with a total of 844 companies responding. Complete coverage was retained in the broadcast TV and cinema exhibition sectors, with substantial increases in the response from the interactive media and facilities sectors. The response remained relatively low in commercials and decreased in the corporate production sector. The methodology used in the census is less appropriate for film production than other sectors, so these figures should be treated with some caution.

It should be noted that the snapshot methodology captures only those freelancers who were economically active on 26 June 2002, and thus may underestimate the total number of people available or seeking work as freelancers in the industry. It nevertheless indicates the level of activity within each sector on one day in employment terms.

A full report of the 2002 census is available on Skillset's website at www.skillset.org

skillset
The Sector Skills Council for the Audio Visual Industries

Total Employed and Percentages of Freelancers 2000-2002

Total Numbers					% Freelance		
	2000	2001	2002	% Change	2000	2001	2002
Animation	1,300	1,600	1,500	-8	26	54	41
Broadcast Radio	22,900	20,200	20,700	+2	18	18	35
Broadcast Television	24,100	23,200	24,900	+7	22	23	19
Cable/Satellite	6,100	5,500	4,900	-12	18	4	4
Cinema Exhibition	n/a	15,900	16,000	0	n/a	n/a	n/a
Commercials	10,600	3,200	7,200	+125	82	54	70
Corporate Production	3,600	3,700	3,200	+14	52	42	48
Facilities	13,000	9,000	8,200	-9	55	12	16
Films in Production	n/a	1,100	1,500	+44	n/a	98	98
Independent Production	11,600	13,600	13,300	-2	51	49	47
Interactive Media	20,000	42,000	46,200	+10	31	16	14
Other	2,300	2,200	3,300	+50	27	8	29
Total	116,000	141,000	151,000		35	23	23

Total Numbers of Employees and Freelancers in Each Occupational Group

Occupational Group	Employees	Freelancers	Total
Animation	1,000	1,100	2,100
Art and Design	1,800	1,700	3,500
Broadcast Engineering	2,100	100	2,200
Camera	900	1,700	2,600
Cinema Box Office	11,700	0	11,700
Cinema Cleaners	500	0	500
Cinema Management	2,700	0	2,700
Cinema Projectionist	1,100	0	1,100
Costume/Wardrobe	200	800	1,000
Interactive Media	21,800	3,100	24,900
Journalism and Sport	8,600	1,400	10,000
Library/Archive	1,200	200	1,400
Lighting	700	1,000	1,700
Make Up and Hairdressing	100	1,000	1,100
Post-Production	5,300	1,900	7,200
Producing	6,300	7,000	12,300
Production	7,200	6,200	13,400
Programme Distribution	300	0	300
Radio Broadcasting	2,200	1,900	4,100
Runners	700	600	1,300
Sound	700	600	1,300
Special Physical Effect	100	100	200
Studio Operations	1,600	600	2,200
Television Broadcasting	4,300	300	4,600
Transmission	500	0	500
Other	31,900	3,300	35,200
Total	115,500	34,600	150,100

Total employment and use of freelancers on 26 June 2002

Sector	Total	% Freelance
Animation	1,500	41
Broadcast Radio	20,700	35
Broadcast Television	24,900	19
Cable/Satellite	4,900	4
Cinema Exhibition	16,000	0
Commercials	7,200	70
Corporate Production	3,200	48
Facilities	8,200	16
Films in Production	1,500	98
Independent Production	13,300	47
Interactive Media	46,200	14
Other	3,300	29
Total	151,000	23

skillset

Skillset, the Sector Skills Council for the Audio Visual Industries, is a UK-wide strategic training body for the TV, Radio, Film, Video and Interactive Media Industries. Owned and managed by the industry itself, Skillset receives its licence to operate from government. Working with the industry and government, Skillset's principal goals are to:

> • produce informed research about skills availability and requirements
> and the current provision of training and education

Most recently Skillset produced the Developing UK Film Talent report, the most in-depth study of the UK film industry ever compiled. Which has given rise to the establishment of the Film Skills Action Group and will prepare a wide-ranging and comprehensive training strategy as part of the drive to make the UK's film workforce world leaders in their fields.

> • promote investment in skills and talent and support the provision of
> learning and skills development programmes in identified priority areas

To enhance the skills of the existing workforce, Skillset offers bursaries and course subsidises in high priority areas. A variety of courses are subsidised up to 60% off the normal price. For an up to date list of current subsidised courses visit: www.skillset.org

Skillset also directs industry funds into New Entrants Training schemes, and the SIF Network, a groundbreaking web-based service showcasing the brightest new talent available to producers looking to crew-up for production.

> • provide advice, information and guidance

skillsformedia is the industry careers service managed by Skillset and BECTU, the specialist industry trades union. skillsformedia offer informed advice and guidance and are run by working media professionals, who have been trained as careers advisors and provide honest, confidential advice tailored to the individuals needs. For more information visit: www.skillsformedia.com or call 08000 300 900

> • work actively to promote the achievement of diversity in the industry

The fourth and final round of the Skillset Millennium Awards opened in February 2003. The Awards offer individuals from ethnic minorities a grant to complete a media project beneficial to their community, up to £10,000 worth of BBC training and the support needed to get their careers off the ground.

> • develop, update, promote and implement standards and qualifications
> to inform training, education and employment practice

Skillset Standards are quality guidelines devised by industry leaders for specific job areas. Skillset is currently developing a Quality Approvals System for training partners and providers. This guide will ensure available training provision meets the changing needs of the industry.

skillset

The Sector Skills Council for the Audio Visual Industries

terrestrial channels

Anglia Television

Anglia Television Limited
Anglia House, Norwich NR1 3JG
Tel 01603 615151
Fax 01603 761245
URL www.anglia.tv.co.uk
E-mail duty office@angliatv.co.uk
Managing Director Graham Creelman
Broadcast and Regional Affairs Executive Jim Woodrow
Head Of Documentaries, Features & Education
Andrea Cornes
Controller of Programmes Neil Thompson
Head of News Guy Adams

BBC Broadcasting

Television Centre, Wood Lane,
London, W12 7RJ
Tel 020 8743 8000
Fax 020 8743 0883
URL www.bbc.co.uk/info

BBC White City

200 Wood Lane, London W12 7TS
Director-General Greg Dyke
Director of Television designate Jana Bennett
Director Radio Jenny Abramsky
Director BBC World Service Mark Byford
Director News Richard Sambrook
Director Drama, Entertainment and Children Alan Yentob
Director Nations and Regions Pat Loughrey
Director Finance, Property and Business Affairs John Smith
Director of Human Resources & Internal Communications
Stephen Dando
Director of Sport Peter Salmon
Director of Public Policy Caroline Thomson
Director of New Media Ashley Highfield
Director of Marketing & Communications Andy Duncan
Deputy Controller for Documentaries and Head of Development
David Mortimer
Chief Executive BBC Worldwide Rupert Gavin
Commercial Director, BBC Resources Ltd, BBC Technology Ltd
Roger Flynn
Commissioning Editor, Storyville Nick Fraser
Commissioning Editor, Drama Gareth Neame
Commissioning Editor, Entertainment Alan Brown
Commissioning Editor, Factual Richard Klein
Commissioning Editor, Specialist Factual Krishan Arora
Commissioning Editor, Current Affairs Peter Horrocks
Channel Controller, BBC ONE Lorraine Heggassey
Channel Controller, BBC TWO Jane Root
Channel Controller, BBC THREE Stuart Murphy
Channel Controller, BBC FOUR Roly Keating
Controller of Daytime Alison Sharman

Controller, Drama Jane Tranter
Controller, Entertainment Jane Lush
Controller, General Factual Anne Morrison
Controller, Specialist Factual Keith Scholey
Joint Director of Factual and Learning Glenwyn Benson
Joint Director of Factual and Learning Michael Stevenson
Programme Acquisition James Wills
Head of Publicity Vandra Rumney

BBC Worldwide

Woodlands
30 Wood Lane,
London, W12 0TT
Tel 020 8433 2000
URL www.bbc.co.uk/info
Director, Business Affairs Sarah Cooper
Managing Director, BBC World Patrick Cross
Chief Executive Rupert Gavin
Managing Director, Internet and Interactive Drew Kaza
Finance Director David King
Director, New Ventures and Strategy Jeremy Mayhew
Director, Human Resources Bob McCall
Director, International Television Mike Phillips
President/CEO, BBC Worldwide Americas Peter Phippen
Technology Director Gary Richards
Director, Global Marketing and Brand Development Jeff Taylor
Deputy Chief Executive and Managing Director, UK Peter Teague
Managing Director, Asia Pacific David Vine
**Managing Director, Europe, Middle East, India and
Africa** Mark Young

BBC Northern Ireland

BBC Broadcasting House,
Ormeau Road,
Belfast, BT2 8HQ
Controller Anna Carragher
Head of Entertainment, Events & Sport Mike Edgar
Head of Factual and Learning Bruce Batten
Head of Public Affairs Rosemary Kelly
Head of Marketing and Development Peter Johnston
Head of Finance Crawford McLean
Head of Drama Robert Cooper
Head of News and Current Affairs Andrew Colman
Head of Broadcasting Tim Cooke
Head of Programme Operations Stephen Beckett

terrestrial channels

BBC Scotland

BBC Scotland, Programme Information
Queen Margaret Drive
Glasgow G12 8DG
Tel 0870 100 222
Enquiries.scot@bbc.co.uk
Controller John McCormick
Commissioning Editor Ewan Angus
Head of Programmes Ken McQuarrie
Head of Network Development Colin Cameron
Head of Television Drama Barbara McKissack
Head of Entertainment Mike Bolland

BBC Wales/Cymru

BBC Wales, Broadcasting House
Llandrisant Road, Cardif CFC 2YQ
Tel 01248 370 880
Controller Menna Richards
Head of Programmes (English) Clare Hudson
Head of Programmes (Welsh) Keith Jones
Head of Public Affairs Manon Williams
Head of News and Current Affairs Aled Eirug
Head of Marketing and Communications David Jones
Head of Finance and Business Affairs Gareth Powell
Head of Personnel and Internal Communications Keith Rawlings
Head of Operations Toby Grosvenor
Commissioning Editor, Independents Nick Evans
Head of Arts Paul Islwyn Thomas
Head of Factual Adrian Davies
Head of Music David Jackson
Head of Drama Matthew Robinson
Head of Sport Nigel Walker
Head of Education Eleri Wyn Lewis
Head of Talent Maggie Russell
Legal & Business Affairs Manager Dewi Vaughan Owen
Contracts Executive, Independents Clare Jenrick
Finance Manager, Programmes Pauline Sandford
Head of Audience Research & Planning Eilir Jones
Business Development Manager Ian Grutchfield
Head of Brand Communication Phillip Moss

BBC Birmingham

Pebble Mill
Pebble Mill Road
Birmingham
B5 7QQ
Tel 0121 432 8888
Fax 0121 432 8039
Email birmingham@bbc.co.uk
Head of Programming Factual & Learning Tessa Finch
Head of Press & PR Andrew Pike
Head of Political & Community Affairs Anita Bhalla
Head of Regional & Local Programming David Holdsworth
Controller for the English Regions Andrew Griffee

BBC Bristol

BBC Broadcasting House
Whiteladies Road
Bristol
BS8 2LR
Tel 0117 973 2211
Email bristol@bbc.co.uk
Acting Head of Press & Public Relations Chris Parker
Head of Regional and Local Programming Andrew Wilson
Head of Natural History Unit Neil Nightingale
Acting Head of Documentaries & Factual Mark Hill
Head of Network Radio Production Clare McGinn

BBC Leeds

Broadcasting Centre
Woodhouse Lane
Leeds LS2 9PX
Tel 0113 224 7140
Fax 0113 224 7146
Email leeds@bbc.co.uk
Head of Region Colin Philpot
Editor Look North Jake Fowler
Editor News Gathering Kate Watkins

BBC Manchester

New Broadcasting House
PO Box 27
Oxford Road
Manchester
M60 1SJ
Tel 0161 200 2020
Fax 0161 236 1005
Email manchester@bbc.co.uk
Head of Press Rachael Wallace
Head of Entertainment Wayne Garvie
Head of Religion Alan Bookbinder
Head of Local Programme Martin Brookes

Border Television Ltd

TV Centre, Carlisle,
Cumbria, CA1 3NT
Tel 01228 525101
Fax 01228 541384
URL www.bordertv.com
Chairman Charles Allen
Managing Director Douglas Merrall
Vice Controller of Programmes Neil Robinson

Carlton UK Television

Carlton Productions (Network)
35-38 Portman Square, London W1H 6NU
Tel 020 7486 6688
URL www.itv.com/carltonlondon

Carlton Productions (Regional)
101 St Martins Lane, London WC2N 4RF
Tel 020 7240 4000

ATV Carlton Television,
35-38 Portman Square, London W1H ONU
Tel 020 7486 6688

Carlton Group
Chairman/Director of Broadcasting Michael Green
Chief Executive Clive Jones
Director of Programmes Steve Hewlett

Carlton International
Deputy Financial Director Andy Coker
Head of Business Affairs Karen Henson
Head of Rights Sylvia Thompson
Head of Operations and Financing Fiona Maxwell
Press and marketing manager Rachel Glaister
Controller of Programme Development Mark Gray

Channel Four

124 Horseferry Road,
London SW1P 2TX
Tel 020 7396 4444
Fax 020 7306 8351
Head of Business Affairs Andrew Brann
Senior Business Affairs Executive Alexandra Hobbs
Head of Entertainment & Comedy, Controller of E4 Danielle Lux
Head of Comedy Caroline Heddy
Commissioning Editor, Music Jo Wallace
Commissioning Editor, Factual Entertainment Steven D Wright
Deputy Commissioning Editor Ben Adler
Business Affairs Mark Ainsworth
Head of UK Acquisitions Bobby Allen
Commissioning Editor, Special Projects for Learning Paul Ashton
Head of Press Matt Baker

Channel 4, Nations & Regions
4th Floor, 227 West George Street,
Glasgow G2 2ND
Tel 0141 568 7100
Tel 0141 568 7103

five

Duty Office, Five
22 Long Acre
London WC2E 9IY
Tel 08457 050505
Head of Press Paul Leather
Head of Entertainment/ Deputy Head of Press Tracey O'Conner
Entertainment Publicist Nick Dear
Head of Factual and Features Publicity Louise Plank
Publicity Assistant for news, Factual & Features
Lesley Anne Saville
Children's Programmes Amy Corbett
Preview/Review Tapes Richard Webster
Head of Picture Publicity Sally Leonard
Listings Co-ordinator Natasha Mensha
Publicity Events Anita Rimmer

GMTV Ltd

The London Television Centre,
Upper Ground,
London SE1 9TT
Tel 020 7827 7000
URL www.gm.tv
Director Michael Green

Grampian Television

Duty Office, Queen's Cross
Aberdeen AB15 4XJ
Tel 01224 846 846
Fax 01224 846 800
URL www.grampiantv.co.uk
Chairman Dr Callum MacLeod

Granada plc

The London Television Centre, Upper Ground
London SE1 9LT
Tel 020 7620 1620
URL www.granadamedia.com

Granada Television
Quay Street
Manchester M60 9EA
Tel 0161 832 7211
Managing Director Brenda Smith

Granada Sky Broadcasting
Granada Breeze
Granada Men + Motors
Granada Plus
Franciscan Court, 1 Hatfields
London SE1 8DJ
Tel 020 7578 4040
URL www.gsb.co.uk
Head of Press Malcolm Packer
Listings Editor Brian Butler

HTV Wales

The Television Centre, Culverhouse Cross, Cardiff, Wales CF5 6XJ
Tel 02920 590 590
Fax 02920 597 183
URL www.htvwales.com
Head of Drama Development Peter Edwards
Head of Corporate Affairs Iona Jones
Head of Press & Public Relations Mansel Jones
Controller & Director of Programmes Elis Owen
HTV Group Managing Director Jeremy Payne
Head of HR Julie Cassley

HTV West

The Television Centre, Bath Road,
Bristol BS4 3HG
Tel 0117 972 2215
Fax 0117 972 2558
URL www.htvwest.com
HTV Group Managing Director Jeremy Payne
Director of Regional Programmes Jane McCloskey
Head of Corporate Affairs Iona Jones

Independent Television News

200 Grays Inn Road, London WC1X 8XZ
URL www.itn.co.uk
Chairman Mark Wood
Finance Director Andrew Whitaker

LWT

The London Television Centre,
Upper Ground,
London SE1 9LT
Tel 020 7620 1620
URL www.yorkshire-tv.co.uk
Managing Director Lindsay Charlton
Controller of Arts Melvyn Bragg
Controller of Entertainment Nigel Hall

Meridian Broadcasting

Television Centre,
Southampton SO14 OPZ
Tel 023 80220 2555
URL www.meridian.tv.co.uk
Managing Director Mary McAnally
Director of Sports Jim Raven

S4C (Sianel Pedwar Cymru)

Parc Ty Glas, Llanishen,
Cardif CF4 5DU
Tel 029 2074 7444
URL www.s4c.co.uk

S4C
Lon Ddewi, Caernarfon LL55 1ER
Tel 01286 674 622

S4C International team
Head of Advertising & Broadcast Sponsorship Richard Moremon
Sponsorship Sales Consultant Valerie Harmer
Production Services manager Jo Tame
Finance Director Kathrine Morris

Scottish Television

20 Renfield Street, Glasgow G2 3PR
Tel 0141 300 3000
URL www.scottishtv.com
Chief Executive, Scottish Broadcasting Andrew Flanagan
Chief Executive, TV Donald Emslie
Managing Director, Network Productions Jagdip Jagpal
Managing Director, Scottish TV Sandy Ross

Thames Television

Fremantle Media Enterprises Ltd,
1 Stephen Street, London W1T 1AL
Tel 020 7691 6000
URL www.thamestv.co.uk
Head of Press Stephanie Faber
Marketing Director Wendy Thompson
Financial Controller Ian Ayres
Financial Director Ian Osey

Tyne Tees Television

City Road, Newcastle-upon-Tyne NE1 2AL
Tel 0191 261 0181
Fax 0191 261 0181
URL www.tynetees-tv.com
Managing Director Margaret Fay
Controller of Programmes Graeme Thompson
Client Liaison Janice Casely

UTV (Ulster)

Ormeau Road, Belfast BT7 1EB
Tel 028 9032 8122
Fax 028 9032 8122
URL www.utvlike.com
Director of Television Alan Bremner
Head of News & Current Affairs Rob Morrison
Presentation & Promotions Manager Brian Owens
Senior Producer Robert Lamrock
Press & Public Relations Manager Orla McKibbin
Group Director of Engineering Bob McCourt
Group Chief Executive John McCann
Television Administration Manager Morris Goodwin

Yorkshire Television

Kirkstall Road, Leeds LS3 1JS
Tel 0113 243 8283
Fax 0113 244 5107
URL www.yorkshire-television.tv
Director of Programming John Whiston
Controller of Regional Production Clare Morrow
Head of Press & Media Relations Sally Ryle

film classification

film classification

There are seven classification categories: U, Uc and PG, which are advisory only; 12, 15 and 18, which restrict viewing by age; and R18, which is only available to adults in licensed outlets.

Occasionally, a work lies on the margin between the two categories. In making a final judgement, the BBFC takes into account the intentions of the film-maker, the expectations of the public in general and the work's audience in particular, and any special merits of the work.

Classification decisions may be stricter on video than on film. This is because of the increased possibility of underage viewing recognised in the Video Recordings Act, and of works being replayed or viewed out of context. Accordingly, a work may receive a higher age classification on video, or require heavier cuts.

Classification decisions are most strict on trailers and advertisements. This is because difficult content, which may be mediated by the context of the original work, may have a much starker effect in the brief and unprepared context of the trailer/advertisement.

Classification decisions may be less strict where they are justified by context.

Anything not permitted in these guidelines at a particular category (PG to 18) is unacceptable also at all preceding lower categories. Similarly, anything permitted at one level is acceptable at all higher levels.

production directory

the latest details for everything from advertising agencies to writers

ADVERTISING AGENCIES

1576 Advertising
25 Rutland Square, Edinburgh EH1 2BW
t 0131 473 1576 **f** 0131 473 1577
e firstname@1576.co.uk **w** www.1576.co.uk
Contact Kiri James; Katherine Reynolds

Abbott Mead Vickers BBDO Ltd
151 Marylebone Road, London NW1 5QE
t 020 7616 3500 **f** 020 7616 3600
e scott@amvbbdo.com **w** www.amvbbdo.com
Credits Guinness: Butcher, Mabbutt, Anderson (C); Wrigley's: Dog Breath (C)

The Advertising Brasserie
22 Newman Street, London W1T 3PH
t 020 7878 5600 **f** 020 7878 5656 **e** mischa@adbrasseria.co.uk
Contact Mischa Alexander, Managing Partner; Jade Puspan

Advertising Principles Ltd
Devonshire Hall, Devonshire Avenue, Street Lane, Leeds LS8 1AW
t 0113 226 2222 **f** 0113 269 6097
e talktome@adprinciples.co.uk **w** www.adprinciples.co.uk
Contact Richard Dudleston, Managing Director

AFA O'Meara Advertising
46 James's Place East, Dublin 2, Rep of Ireland
t +353 1 676 2500 **f** +353 1 676 2506 **w** www.desomeara.ie
Contact Shane Lynch, Account Director; Ruth Allen, Account Executive;
Fergal Jennings, Account Executive; Frank Neary, Account Director;
Gareth O'Gornam, Account Executive

AMV BBDO Ltd
151 Marylebone Road, London NW1 5QE
t 020 7616 3500 **f** 020 7616 3510 **w** www.amubbdo.co.uk
Contact Peter Knowland, New Business Director

ASA O'Meara
23 Fitzwilliam Place, Dublin 2, Rep of Ireland
t +353 1 676 2753 **f** +353 1 500 0660
Contact Gary Power, Media Director

Banks Hoggins O'Shea
55 Newman Street, London W1T 3EB
t 020 7947 8000 **f** 020 7947 8001 **w** www.fcb.com
Contact Brendon Payne, Head of TV

Barkers Scotland
234 West George Street, Glasgow G2 4QY
t 0141 248 5030 **f** 0141 204 0033
e pr@barkers-scot.com **w** www.barkersscotland.co.uk
Contact Nick Lang, Head of TV

Bartle Bogle Hegarty
60 Kingly Street, London W1B 5DS
t 020 7734 1677 **f** 020 7437 3666
e nicolam@bbh.co.uk **w** www.bbh.co.uk
Contact Nicola Mendelsohn, Business Development Director

Bates UK
121-141 Westbourne Terrace, London W2 6JR
t 020 7262 5077 **f** 020 7724 3834
e elizabeth_austin@batesuk.com
Contact Barry Stephenson, Head of TV

BBA Active Ltd
Unit 1, Hampstead West, 224 Iverson Road, London NW6 2HU
t 020 7625 7575 **f** 020 7625 7575
e bba@bbagenius.com **w** www.bbagenius.com
Contact Lauren Granard, Office Manager; Christian Cochrane, Art Director;
Lynne Lepard, Production Manager; Amrit Hunjan, Chief Designer; Stephen
Benjamin, Executive Creative Director

BCMB Ltd
2 Brindley Road, Old Trafford, Manchester M16 9HQ
t 0161 877 0521 **f** 0161 877 7994
e j.ingham@bcmb.co.uk **w** www.bcmb.co.uk
Contact Joanne Ingham, Head of TV

BDH TBWA
St Pauls, 781 Wilmslow Road, Didsbury Village, Manchester
M20 5RW
t 0161 908 8600 **f** 0161 908 8601
e info@bdhtbwa.co.uk **w** www.bdhtbwa.co.uk
Contact Lou Vasey, Head of TV

BMP DDB
12 Bishops Bridge Road, London W2 6AA
t 020 7258 3979 **w** www.bmpddb.com
Contact Maggie Blundell, Head of Television; Richard Morris, New Business

Bray Leino Ltd
The Old Rectory, Filleigh EX32 0RX
t 01598 760700 **f** 01598 760225
e mail@brayleino.co.uk **w** www.brayleino.co.uk
Contact Tony Atkinson, Production Manager

Camp Chipperfield Hill Murray Ltd
12-18 Grosvenor Gardens, London SW1W 0DH
t 020 7881 3200 **f** 020 7730 3977
e info@cchm.co.uk **w** www.cchm.co.uk
Contact Paul Gordon, Managing Director; Jayne Darbyshire, Client Services Director

Citigate Albert Frank
26 Finsbury Square, London EC2A 1SH
t 020 7282 8000 **f** 020 7282 8070 **w** www.citigateaf.co.uk
Contact Paul Anderson, Executive/Creative Director; Paul Anderson,
Creative Director

Cogent
Heath Farm, Hampton Lane, Meriden, Coventry CV7 7LL
t 0121 627 5040 **f** 0121 627 5038
Contact Tamzin Locise, Head of TV

Cravens Advertising Ltd
42 Leazes Park Road, Newcastle-upon-Tyne NE1 4PL
t 0191 232 6683 **f** 0191 261 2498 **e** reception@cravens.co.uk
w www.cravens.co.uk
Contact Peter Straughan, Creative Director

Creative Partnership

13 Bateman Street, London W1D 3AF
t +44 20 7439 7762 **f** +44 20 7437 1467
e info@thecreativepartnership.co.uk
w www.creativepartnership.co.uk
Contact Jim Sturgeon, Managing Director

CSA Partnership Ltd

Dragon Court, Macklin Street, Covent Gardens,
London WC2B 5LX
t 020 7316 7300 **f** 020 7316 7400
e solutions@csapartnership.co.uk **w** www.csapartnership.co.uk
Contact Ian Martin, Media Director

Culturecide Communications

2 Great Ormond Street, London WC1N 3RB
t 020 7404 7555 **t** 020 7404 7557
f 0709 226 8141 **m** 07930 809281
e schofieldmusic@stones.com **w** www.culturecide.com
Contact Frank Shofield, Creative Director
Credits www.bv.com (W); www.filedudes.com (W); www.boogie-box.com (W); www.culturecide.com (W)

Da Costa & Co Ltd

9 Gower Street, London WC1E 6HA
t 020 7916 3791 **f** 020 7916 3799 **e** info@dacosta.co.uk
Contact Nick Costa, Creative Director

Danemere Street Creative Ltd

PO Box 128, Petersfield GU32 3WJ
t 0845 080 4400 **f** 0845 080 5500 **m** 07006 303304
e enquiries@danemere-street.com **w** www.danemere-street.com
Contact Chris Powell, UK Accounts Director; Steve O'Neill, Internet and Telecoms Technical Director; Peter Powell, Director - Video Production
Credits Action Trampoline (W); Danemere Street Creative (W); Bluemondayfilms (W); 2 Tech Solutions (W)

DDFH & B

3 Christchurch Square, Dublin 8, Rep of Ireland
t +353 1 410 6666 **f** +353 1 410 6699
e firstname.surname@ddfhb.ie
Contact Derek Lawlor, Head of Production

Delaney Lund Knox Warren

25 Wellington Street, London WC2E 7DA
t 020 7836 3474 **f** 020 7240 8739 **w** www.dlkw.co.uk
Contact Greg Delaney, Chairman

Dentsu Holdings Europe Ltd

Berger House 38, Berkeley Square, London W1J 5AH
t 020 7499 9124

Dewynters

48 Leicester Square, London WC2H 7QD
t 020 7321 0488 **f** 020 7321 0104
e info@dewynters.com **w** www.dewynters.com
Contact Diane Warren, Head of TV

Doner Cardwell Hawkins

26-34 Emerald Street, London WC1N 3QA
t 020 7734 0511 **f** 020 7437 3961
e donermail@doner.co.uk **w** donercardwellhawkins.co.uk
Contact Nick Jackson, Head of Account Management

EMO Ltd

The Old Rectory, Vicarage Lane, Highworth, Swindon SN6 7AD
t 01793 767300 **f** 01793 767307 **e** ppearce@emo.uk.com
Contact Bernie Miles, Creative Director

England Agency

Marshall Mill, Marshall Street, Leeds LS11 9YJ
t 0113 234 5600 **f** 0113 234 5601 **e** info@englandagency.com
w www.englandagency.com
Contact David McIntosh, Managing Director; Tony Stanton, Chief Executive

Euro RSCG Wnek Gosper

11 Great Newport Street, London WC2H 7JA
t 020 7240 4111 **f** 020 7465 0559
e name.surname@eurorscg.co.uk **w** www.eurorscg.co.uk
Contact Sue Lee-Stern, Producer, Head of TV

Faulds Advertising

Sutherland House, 108 Dundas Street, Edinburgh EH3 5DQ
t 0131 557 6003 **f** 0131 557 2261
e rallan@faulds.co.uk **w** www.faulds.co.uk
Contact Ray Allan, Head of Television

Grey Worldwide

215-227 Great Portland Street, London W1W 5PN
t 020 7636 3399 **f** 020 7637 7473 **w** www.grey.com
Contact Dee Butler

Handley Kvester Ltd

161 Herne Hill, London SE24 9LR
t 020 7733 8947 **e** mail@handleykvester.com
Contact Mike Handley, Partner

HHCL & Partners

14-17 Market Place, Great Titchfield Street, London W1W 8AJ
t 020 7436 3333 **f** 020 7436 2677 **w** www.hhcl.com
Contact Emma Rooklidge, Head of TV

HHCL / Red Cell

Kent House, 14-17 Market place, Great Titchfield Street,
London W1W 8AJ
t 020 7436 3333 **f** 020 7436 2677 **w** www.hhcl.com
Contact Nick Howarth, Managing Director

Holly Benson Communications

Communications House, Garsington Road, Cowley, Oxford OX4 2NG
t 01865 384000 **f** 01865 749854 **w** www.hollybenson.co.uk
Contact Mike Black, Creative Director

Interfocus

Lancer Square, London W8 4ES
t 020 7376 9000 **f** 020 7376 9090
e matthew.hooper@interfocus.co.uk **w** www.interfocus.co.uk
Contact Vanessa Hogg, New Business; Paul McCarthy, New Business

J Walter Thompson Company Ltd

1 Knightsbridge Green, London SW1X 7NW
t 020 7656 7000 **f** 020 7656 7010
e firstname.surname@jwt.com
Contact Paul Fenton, Head of TV
Credits Kit Kat: Salmon (C); Smirnoff: Trainer (C); Kellogg's Special K: Security (test) (C)

JM Creative

74-78 Park Road, Whitchurch, Cardiff CF14 7BR
t 029 2052 9925 **f** 029 2052 9998
e enquiries@jmcreative.tv **w** www.jmcreative.tv
Contact Anya Lewis, Production Assistant; John Morgan, Managing Director; Tony Lakin, Creative Director; Louise Harry, Head Of Production

Lavery Rowe Advertising Ltd

69-71 Newington Causeway, London SE1 6BD
t 020 7378 1780 **f** 020 7407 4612

Leagas Delaney London

1 Alfred Place, London WC1E 7EB
t +44 20 7758 1758 **f** +44 20 7758 1750
e information@leagasdelaney.com **w** www.leagasdelaney.com
Contact Will Orr, Marketing Director
Credits Ikea (C); Virgin Mobile (C); Hyundai (C); Intercontinental Hotels (C)

Leith London
1-4 Vigo Street, London W1X 1AH
t 020 7758 1400 **f** 020 7434 3280
e intial.surname@leith.co.uk **w** www.leith.co.uk
Contact Emma Johnston, Head Of Television; John Messum, Creative Director

Leo Burnett
60 Sloane Avenue, London SW3 3XB
t 020 7591 9111 **w** www.leoburnett.com
Contact Graham Light, Head of TV

London Creative Ltd
4th Floor, 116 Great Portland Street, London W1N 5PG
t 020 7255 1616 **f** 020 7255 1617 **e** tim@londoncreative.com

Lowe & Partners
Bowater House 68-114, Knightsbridge, London SW1X 7LT
t 020 7584 5033 **f** 020 7584 9557
e simon.mcquiggan@loweworldwide.com
w ww.loweworldwide.com

Luxford Advertising Ltd
28 Great Queen Street, London WC2B 5BB
t 020 7831 3636 **f** 020 7831 1451 **e** reception@luxford.co.uk
w www.luxford.co.uk
Contact Brendan James, Managing Director

M&C Saatchi
36 Golden Square, London W1F 9EE
t 020 7543 4500 **f** 020 7543 4501 **e** judym@mcsaatchi.com
w www.mcsaatchi.com
Contact Bruce McKelvie, Head of Television

Magic Hat
7-11 Herbrand Street, London WC1N 1EX
t 020 7837 4001 **f** 020 7961 2868
e firstname.surname@europe.mccann.com
w www.mccann.co.uk
Contact Tim Clyde, Managing Director

MAP Plc
Talbert House, Manchester M16 0JJ
t 0161 907 3000 **f** 0161 907 3030
e ads@map-plc.co.uk **w** www.map-plc.co.uk
Contact Pete Johnson, Head of TV

Martin Tait Redheads Ltd
Buxton House, 1 Buxton Street, Newcastle-upon-Tyne NE1 6NJ
t 0191 232 1926 **f** 0191 232 1866 **w** www.mtra.co.uk
Contact Steve Bowen, Production Director

Masius
Warwick Building, Avonmore Road, London W14 8HQ
t 020 7751 1664 **f** 020 7348 3857 **w** www.masius.com
Contact Andrew Porter, CEO

McCann-Erickson
6 King Street, Bristol BS1 4EQ
t 0117 921 1764 **f** 0117 929 0603
e bristol_mail@europe.mccann.com
w www.mccann-erickson.co.uk

McCann-Erickson
7-11 Herbrand Street, London WC1N 1EX
t 020 7837 3737 **f** 020 7837 3773 **w** www.mccann.co.uk

MGA
11 Little College Street, London SW1P 3SH
t 020 7340 1900 **f** 020 7222 2211 **e** lbaker@mga-advertising.co.uk **w** www.mga-advertising.co.uk
Contact James McLoughlin, Board Director; Andrew Basham, Contact

Michael K Howard
Victoria House, Victoria Street, Luton LU1 2SR
t 01582 693000 **f** 01582 693297
Contact Kath Gannon, Head of Production
Credits Volkswagon (C); Choice Hotels (C)

Mitchell Patterson Grime Mitchell
137 Regent Street, London W1B 4HZ
t 020 7734 8087 **f** 020 7434 3081

Mustoe's
2-4 Bucknall Street, London WC2H 8LA
t 020 7379 9999 **f** 020 7379 8487
e damian.h@mustoes.co.uk **w** www.mustoes.co.uk
Contact Damian Horner, New Business Manager

Ogilvy
10 Cabot Square, Canary Wharf, London E14 4QB
t 020 7345 3000 **f** 020 7345 9000 **w** www.ogilvy.com
Contact Christin Clark, Head of TV

Ogilvy Primary Contact Ltd
10 Cabot Square, Canary Wharf, London E14 4GB
t 020 7468 6900 **f** 020 7468 6950

Owens DDB
38 Fitzwilliam Place, Dublin 2, Ireland
t +353 1 676 1191 **f** +353 1 676 1206
e ruth.mcguinness@owensddb.com **w** www.owensddb.com
Credits The Hearing

Partners BDDH
Cupola House, 15 Alfred Place, London WC1E 7EB
t 020 7467 9200 **f** 020 7467 9210
e enquiry@partnersbddh.co.uk **w** www.partnersbddh.co.uk
Contact Charlotte Edmunds, Head of TV; Caroline Frith, New Business Manager

Peter Kane & Company
12 Burleigh Street, London WC2E 7PX
t 020 7836 4561 **f** 020 7836 4073 **w** www.peterkane.co.uk
Contact Gary Jenner, Head of Production

Poulter Partners
Rose Wharf, East Street, Leeds LS9 8EE
t 0113 285 6500 **f** 0113 285 6501 **e**
twilson@poulterpartners.com **w** www.poulterpartners.com
Contact Sarah Emery, Head of TV

Publicis Ltd
82 Baker Street, London W1U 6AE
t 020 7935 4426 **f** 020 7487 5351 **e** judy.ross@publicis.co.uk
w www.publicis.co.uk
Contact Judy Ross, Head of TV

Radioville
143 Wardour Street, London W1F 8WA
t 020 7534 5999 **f** 020 7534 5888 **w** www.radioville.co.uk
Contact Sean Carnegie, Head of Production Coordination

Rainey Kelly Campbell Roalfe/Y&R
Greater London House, Hampstead Road, London NW1 7QP
t 020 7404 2700 **f** 020 7611 6011 **w** www.yr.com
Contact Tim Page, Deputy Head of TV; Helen Durkin, Deputy Head of TV

Riley Cardiff
Sophia House, 28 Cathedral Road, Cardiff CF11 9LJ
t 029 2066 0101 **f** 029 2066 0141 **e** neilt@riley.co.uk
w www.riley.co.uk

Roose & Partners
100 Gray's Inn Road, London WC1X 8AL
t 020 7349 6800
Contact Nikki Abraham, Marketing Director

RZed Ltd
11-12 Tottenham Mews, London W1T 4AG
t 020 7436 8747 **f** 020 7436 8748
e rzed95@rzed.com **w** www.rzed.com
Contact A Squires, New Business Manager; N Rippingale, Managing Partner; E Zographos, Managing Partner

Saatchi & Saatchi
80-84 Charlotte Street, London W1A 1AQ
t 020 7636 5060 **f** 020 7637 8489
w www.saatchi-saatchi.com
Contact James Hall, Senior Group Designer
Credits Savage Seas (D); Strange (T)

Scholz & Friends
80 Clerkenwell Road, London EC1M 5RJ
t 020 7961 4000 **f** 020 7961 4087
e friends@scholzandfriends.co.uk **w** www.s-f.com

Senior King Communications Group
14-15 Carlisle Street, London W1D 3BS
t 020 7734 5855 **f** 020 7439 1443
e agency@senior-king.co.uk **w** www.seniorkinggroup.co.uk
Contact Andrew Hall, Head of Production

Soup
Elme House, 133 Long Acre, Covent Garden, London WC2E 9DT
t 020 7420 7992
Contact Phil Capon, Creative Director

Spirit Media Scotland
24 Broughton Street, Edinburgh EH1 3RH
t 0131 478 3456 **f** 0131 478 8899 **e** morag@mediaspirit.co.uk
Contact Morag Gray; Maria Ross, Office Manager

St Luke's Communications
22 Duke's Road, London WC1H 9PN
t 020 7380 8888 **f** 020 7380 8899 **w** www.stlukes.co.uk
Contact Jochar Lesworth, Producer; Anthony Austin, Editor; Kate Male, Head of TV; Jessie Middleton, Producer; Trudy Waldron, Producer

The Target Marketing Group
Brandon House, 62 Painswick Road, Cheltenham GL50 2EU
t 01242 633100 **f** 01242 584417
e tal@targetgroup.co.uk **w** www.targetgroup.co.uk

TBWA/London
76-80 Whitfield Street, London W1T 4EZ
t 020 7573 6666 **f** 020 7573 6667
e sarah.mudge@tbwa-london.com **w** www.tbwa-london.com
Contact Diane Croll, Head of TV

Wieden + Kennedy
Elsley Court, 20-22 Great Titchfield Street, London W1W 8BE
t 020 7299 7500 **f** 020 7323 4183
Contact Rob Steiner, Head of TV; Charlie Tinson, Producer; Sarah Gough, Business Affairs Manager; Amy Smith, Managing Director; Tony Davidson, Creative Director; Kim Papworth, Creative Director

Young & Rubicam Ltd
Greater London House, Hampstead Road, London NW1 7QP
t 020 7387 9366 **f** 020 7611 6570 **w** www.rkcryr.com
Contact Tim Page, Head of TV

AGENTS

Agents Artiste

A&J Management
551 Green Lanes, Palmers Green, London N13 4DR
t 020 8882 7716 **f** 020 8882 5983 **m** 07850 281066
e ajmanagement@bigfoot.com **w** www.ajmanagement.co.uk
Contact Jackie Michael, Managing Director

Acorn Entertainments
PO Box 64, Cirencester GL7 5YD
t 01285 644622 **f** 01285 642291
e shows@huttrussell.co.uk **w** www.huttrussellorg.com
Contact Su Cooper, Personal Assistant; Dudley Russell, Managing Director

Acting Associates
71 Hartham Road, London N7 9JJ
t 020 7607 3562 **f** 020 7607 3562 **m** 07968 754 094
e fiona@actingassociates.co.uk **w** www.actingassociates.co.uk
Contact Fiona Farley, Theatrical Agent

Actors Alliance
Disney Place House, 14 Marshalsea Road, London SE1 1HL
t 020 7407 6028 **f** 020 7407 6028 **e** actors@alliance.fsnet.co.uk
Contact Max Harvey, Agent

The Actors File
63-71 Collier Street, London N1 9BE
t 020 7278 0087 **f** 020 7278 0364 **e** mail@theactorsfile.co.uk

AIM (Associated International Management)
Nederlander House, 7 Great Russell Street, London WC1B 3NH
t 020 7637 1700 **f** 020 7637 8666
e info@aim.demon.co.uk **w** www.a-i-m.net
Contact D Webster; S Gittins; L Assenheim

Air Ltd
Air House, Spennymoor DL16 7SE
t 01388 814632 **f** 01388 812445
e air@agents-uk.com **w** www.airagency.com
Contact J Wray, Director

Alander Agency
135 Marion Avenue, Stanmore HA7 4RZ
t 020 8954 7685
Contact S Deswarte, Proprietor

Allsorts The Agency
1 Cathedral Street, London SE1 9DE
t 020 7403 4834 **f** 020 7403 1656 **m** 07876 715772
e joanneallsorts@aol.com **w** www.childsplaylondon.co.uk
Contact Veronica Peacock, Head of Administration; Bob Puthill, Director; Tara Sutherland, Head of Administration; Emma Jones, Head of Entertainment
Credits Crimewatch (T); Sugababes (M); Holby City (T); British Airways (C)

Alpha Personal Management
Studio B4, Bradbury Street, London N16 8JN
t 020 7241 0077 **f** 020 7241 2410 **e** alphamanagement3@aol.com
Contact John Bleasdale, Member
Credits Band Of Brothers (T); Harry Potter And The Chamber Of Secrets (F)

Angie Bainbridge Management
3 New Cottages, The Holt, Washington RH20 4AW
t 01903 893748 **f** 01903 891320 **m** 07958 219974
e angie.bainbridge@btopenworld.com
Contact Angie Bainbridge, Managing Director

Anna Scher Theatre Management Ltd
70-72 Barnsbury Road, London N1 OES
t 020 7278 2101 **f** 020 7833 0442
e abby@astm.co.uk **w** www.astm.co.uk
Contact Abby Meckin, Agent; Andy Smith, Director

Artists Independent Network
32 Tavistock Street, London WC2E 7PB
t 020 7257 8727 **f** 020 7240 9029
e mail@artistsindependent.com **w** www.artistsindependent.com
Contact Abi Harris; Angharad Wood; Charles Finch; Vanessa Pereira

Associated International Management Inc.
John Redway Associates
Nederlandel House, 7 Great Russell Street, London WC1B 3NH
t 020 7637 1700 **f** 020 7637 8666
e info@aim.demon.co.uk **w** www.a-i-m.net
Contact Stephen Gittins, Agent; Lisa-Malie Assenheim, Agent; Derek Webster, Managing Director

Avalon Management Group Ltd
4A Exmoor Street, London W10 6BD
t 020 7598 8000 **f** 020 7598 7300
Contact Richard Allen-Turner, Director; Jon Thoday, Director
Credits The Harry Hill Show (T); Time Gentleman Please (T); The Frank Skinner Show (T)

AXM
206 Great Guildford Business Square, 30 Great Guildford Street, London SE1 OHS
t 020 7261 0400 **f** 020 7261 0408
e info@axmgt.com **w** www.axmgt.com
Contact David Charles; Alison Goldie; Jeremy Spriggs; Mufrida Hayes, Producer; Andrew Callaway

BaK Management
30 Spedan Close, Branch Hill, London NW3 7XF
t 020 7794 8980 **f** 020 7794 8980 **e** bkmanagement@aol.com
Contact Debbie Killingback

Benjamin Taylor Associates
73 Palace Road, London SW2 3LB
t 020 8671 1628 **f** 020 8671 1626
Contact Keith Taylor, Director

Big Chief Productions Ltd
Power Studio 5, 114 Power Road, Chiswick, London W4 5PY
t 020 8996 0300 **f** 020 8996 0400 **m** 07702 332030
e angie@bigchiefproductions.co.uk
w www.bigchiefproductions.co.uk
Contact Angie Fernandes, Producer

Billboard Personal Management
The Co-op Centre, 11 Mowll Street, London SW9 6BG
t 020 7735 9956 **f** 020 7793 0426
e billboardpm@easynet.co.uk **w** www.billboardpm.com

Billy Marsh Associates Ltd
174-178 North Gower Street, London NW1 2NB
t 020 7388 6858 **f** 020 7388 6848
e bmarsh@bmarsh.demon.co.uk

Bishop Burnett
47 Dean Street, London W1D 5BE
t 020 7734 9995 **f** 020 7734 9996
e bishopburnett@mcsagency.co.uk
Contact Keith Bishop, Chief Executive; Roger Burnett, Director

Boden Agency
99 East Barnet Road, Barnet EN4 8RF
t 020 8447 0909 **f** 020 8449 5212
e bodens2692@aol.com **w** www.bodenstudios.com
Contact Mo Boden, Proprietor

Brazil Productions/Yes!!! Brazil
Suite 11, Hanovia House, 28-29 Eastman Road, London W3 7YG
t 020 8743 7563 **f** 020 8743 7563
e brazil@dircon.co.uk **w** www.brazil.dircon.co.uk/gallery.html
Contact Tony Ferre, Director; N Da Cruz Braz, Assistand Director

Brian Taylor/Nina Quick Associates
50 Pembroke Road, Kensington, London W8 6NX
t 020 7602 6141 **f** 020 7602 6301
e briantaylor@nqassoc.freeserve.co.uk
Contact Brian Taylor, Director

Brunskill Management Ltd
Suite 8a, 169 Queens Gate, London SW7 5HE
t 020 7581 3388 **f** 020 7589 9460
e contact@brunskill.com **w** www.brunskill.com
Contact Aude Powell, Agent; Geoff Stanton, Agent

Bryan Drew Ltd
Mezzanine, Quadrant House, 80-82 Regent Street, London W1B 5AU
t 020 7437 2293 **f** 020 7437 0561
e bryan@bryandrewltd.com **w** www.bryandrewltd.com
Contact Mina Parmar, Assistant to Managing Director; Bryan Drew, Managing Director

Burnett Granger Associates
Prince of Wales Theatre, 31 Coventry Street, London W1D 6AS
t 020 7839 0202 **f** 020 7839 0438
e associates@burnettgranger.co.uk
Contact Lindsay Granger, Director; Barry Burnett, Director

CADS Management
209 Abbey Road, Bearwood, Birmingham B67 5NG
t 0121 420 1996 **f** 0121 434 4909 **m** 07710 028 823
e admin@cadsmanagement.co.uk **w** www.cadsmanagement.co.uk
Contact Terry Smith, Proprietor
Credits Crimewatch (T); Emmerdale (T); Anita And Me (F); Doctors (T)

Cardiff Casting
Chapter Arts Centre, Market Road, Canton, Cardiff CF5 1QE
t 029 2023 3321 **f** 029 2023 3380
e admin@cardiffcasting.co.uk **w** www.cardiffcasting.co.uk
Contact Chris Durnell, Production Director

Caroline Dawson Associates
19 Sydney Mews, London SW3 6HL
t 020 7581 8111 **f** 020 7589 4800 **e** cda@cdalondon.com
Contact Belinda Wright, Partner; Caroline Dawson, Partner

Cassie Mayer Ltd
11 Wells Mews, London W1T 3HD
t 020 7462 0040 **f** 020 7462 0041
e cassandra.mayer@cassiemayerltd.co.uk
Contact Cassie Mayer, Proprietor

Celebrity Group
12 Nottingham Place, London W1M 3FA
t 020 7224 5050 **f** 020 7224 6060
e info@celebrity.co.uk **w** www.celebrity.co.uk
Contact Ron Mowlam, Director; Geoff Gray, Business Development Coordinator
Credits Billy Connolly - Camelot (C); Martin Kemp - Abbey National (C); Leslie
Ash - Axa Sun Life (C); Ainsley Harriot - Fairy Liquid (C)

Central Agency
112 Gunnersbury Avenue, Ealing, London W5 4HB
t 020 8993 7441 **f** 020 8992 9993
e info@dorm.co.uk **w** www.thedormgroup.com

City Actors' Management Ltd
24 Rivington Street, London EC2A 3DU
t 020 7613 2636 **f** 020 7613 2656
w www.city-actors.freeserve.co.uk
Contact Mary Sheen, Agent

Claude Brooks Entertainments
1 Burlington Avenue, Slough SL1 2JY
t 01753 520717 **f** 01753 520424
Contact Claude Brooks, Proprietor

CMA (Coulter Management Agency) Personal Management
74 Victoria Crescent Road, Glasgow G12 9JN
t 0141 579 1400 **f** 0141 579 4700 **e** cmaglasgow@aol.com
Contact Anne Coulter

Lou Colson
37 Berwick Street, London W1F 8RS
t 020 7734 9633 **f** 020 7439 7569

Conway van Gelder Ltd
Third Floor, 18-21 Jermyn Street, London SW1Y 6HP
t 020 7287 0077 **f** 020 7287 1940 **e** john@conwayvg.co.uk
Contact Jeremy Conway, Director; Nicola Van Gelder, Director; Kate Plumpton,
Commercials; John Grant, Director

Abigail Coult
2 Hillary House, Boyton Close, London N8 7BB

Crawfords
6 Brook Street, London W1S 1BB
t 020 7629 6464 **f** 020 7355 1084
e info@crawfordsagency.com **w** www.crawfordsagency.com
Contact Nicholas Young, Director

Creative Artists Management Ltd (CAM)
19 Denmark Street, London WC2H 8NA
t 020 7497 0448 **f** 020 7240 7384 **e** info@cam.co.uk
Contact Michael Wiggs, Managing Director; Kevin O''Shea, Managing Director

Crouch Associates
9-15 Neal Street, London WC2H 9PW
t 020 7379 1684 **f** 020 7379 1991 **e** crouchassociates@aol.com
Contact Jeanette Scott, Agent; Andrew Lennox, PA

Dancers
1 Charlotte Street, London W1T 1RD
t 020 7636 1473 **f** 020 7636 1657 **e** info@dancersagency.co.uk
Contact Roy Clarke, Director

Dave Winslett Associates
6 Kenwood Ridge, Kenley CR8 5JW
t 020 8668 0531 **f** 020 8668 9216
e info@davewinslett.com **w** www.davewinslett.com
Contact Dave Winslett, Proprietor

David Daly Associates
586a Kings Road, London SW6 2DX
t 020 7384 1036 **f** 020 7610 9512 **e** agents@daviddaly.co.uk
Contact David Daly, Proprietor/Agent; Georgina Coombs, Agent; Rosalie
Nimmo, Agent

Dennis Lyne Agency
108 Leonard Street, London EC2A 4RH
t 020 7739 6200 **f** 020 7739 4101 **e** d.lyne@virgin.net
Contact Derick Mulvey, Agent; Dennis Lyne, Agent

Edward Wyman Agency
67 Llanon Road, Llanishen, Cardiff CF14 5AH
t 029 2075 2351 **f** 029 2075 2444
e edward@wymancasting.fsnet.co.uk
w www.wymancasting.fsnet.co.uk
Contact Edward Wyman

Eric Glass Ltd
25 Ladbroke Crescent, London W11 1PS
t 020 7229 9500 **f** 020 7229 6220 **e** eglassltd@aol.com
Contact Daniela Szmigielska, Director; Sissi Liechtenstein, Agent; Janet Glass,
Managing Director/Agent

Essanay Ltd
6 Brook Street, London W1S 1BB
t 020 7409 3526 **f** 020 7355 1084 **m** 07836 249607
e info@essanay.co.uk
Contact Nicholas Young, Director

Features
1 Charlotte Street, London W1P 1DH
t 020 7636 1473 **f** 020 7636 1657 **e** info@features.co.uk
Contact Roy Clarke, Director

Felix de Wolfe
Garden Offices, 51 Madia Vale, London W9 1SD
t 020 7289 5770 **f** 020 7289 5731 **e** felixdewolfe@aol.com

Film Rights Ltd
Mezzanine, Quadrant House, 80-82 Regent Street,
London W1B 5AU
t 020 7734 9911 **f** 020 7734 0044
e information@filmrights.ltd.uk
e information@laurencefitch.com **w** www.filmrights.ltd.uk
Contact Brendan Davis, Managing Director

Fushion
27 Old Gloucester Street, London WC1N 3XX
t 08700 111100 **f** 08700 111020
e info@fushion-uk.com **w** www.fushion-uk.com

Galloways One
15 Lexham Mews, London W8 6JW
t 020 7376 2288 **f** 020 7376 2416 **m** 07976 878535
e gallowaysone@galloways.ltd.uk
Contact Hugh Galloway, Director

Garricks
5 The Old School House, The Lanterns, Bridge Lane,
London SW11 3AD
t 020 7738 1600 **f** 020 7738 1881
e megan@garricks.net **w** www.garricks.net
Contact Megan Willis

Gary Trolan Management
30 Burrard Road, London NW6 1DB
t 020 7431 4367 **f** 020 7794 4429 **e** garytrolanmgmt@aol.com
Contact Gary Trolan, Proprietor

Gavin Barker Associates Ltd
2d Wimpole Street, London W1G 0EB
t 020 7499 4777 **f** 020 7499 3777 **e** gbarker@dircon.co.uk
Contact Gavin Barker, Managing Director

Gordon & French Associates
12-13 Poland Street, London W1F 8QB
t 020 7734 4818 **f** 020 7734 4832 **e** mail@gordonandfrench.net

Gordon Poole Agency Ltd
The Limes, Brockley BS48 3BB
t 01275 463222 **f** 01275 462252
e agents@gordonpoole.com **w** www.gordonpoole.com
Contact James Poole, Marketing Director; Gordon Poole, Managing Director

Grays Personal Management Associates Ltd
Panther House, 38 Mount Pleasant, London WC1X 0AP
t 020 7278 1054 **f** 020 7278 1091
e e-mail@graymanagement.idps.co.uk **w** www.graysman.com
Contact Mary Elliott Nelson
Credits Holby City (T); My Family (T); Casualty (T); EastEnders (T)

Hamilton Hodell
1st Floor, 24 Hanway Street, London W1T 1UH
t 020 7636 1221 **f** 020 7636 1226 **e** katie@hamiltonhodell.co.uk
Contact Lorraine Hamilton; Pauline Asper; Katie Boreham

Harris Agency Ltd
52 Forty Avenue, Wembley Park HA9 8LQ
t 020 8908 4451 **f** 020 8908 4455 **m** 07956 388716
e sharrisltd@aol.com
Contact Sharon Harris, Director
Credits Toyota (C); Hula Hoops (C); The Beach (F); Harry Potter And The Philosopher's Stone (F)

Harrispearson Managment Ltd
64-66 Millman Street, Bloomsbury, London WC1N 3EF
t 020 7430 9890
e agent@harrispearson.co.uk **w** www.harrispearson.co.uk
Contact Melanie Harris, Managing Director

Hatton McEwan
PO Box 37385, London N1 7XF
t 020 7253 4770 **f** 020 7251 9081
e info@thetalent.biz **w** www.thetalent.biz
Contact Aileen McEwan, Agent; Stephen Hatton, Managing Director; Gavin Humphries, Junior Agent

Hilda Physick Agency
78 Temple Sheen Road, London SW14 7RR
t 020 8876 0073 **f** 020 8876 5561
Contact Hilda Physick, Proprietor

Hobson's Actors
62 Chiswick High Road, London W4 1SY
t 020 8995 3628 **f** 020 8996 5350
e actors@hobsons-international.com
w www.hobsons-international.com
Contact Christina Beyer, Actors Agent; Linda Sachs, Corporate & Commercial Agent

hotdog
2 Hillary House, Boyton Close, London N8 7BB
Contact Abigail Coult, Proprietor

Ian Amos Music Management
The Studio, Seychelles House, 53 Regent Road, Brightlingsea CO7 0NN
t 01206 306222 **f** 01206 306333 **m** 07711 008989
e ian@amosmusic.com **w** www.amosmusic.com
Contact Ian Amos

International Artistes Ltd
4th Floor, Holborn Hall, 193-197 High Holborn, London WC1V 7BD
t 020 7025 0600 **f** 020 7404 9865
e firstname@intart.co.uk **w** www.intart.co.uk
Contact Laurie Mansfield, Chairman; Manely Ward, Managing Director; Bob Vorce, Managing Diretcor
Credits Jolson (T); Zipp! (T); Defending The Caveman (T); The Buddy Holly Story (T)

International Theatre & Music Ltd
Shakespeare House, Theatre Street, London SW11 5ND
t 020 7801 6316 **f** 020 7801 6317 **e** inttheatre@aol.com
Contact Piers Chater Robinson, Director

J Gurnett Personal Management Ltd
2 New Kings Road, London SW6 4SA
t 020 7736 7828 **f** 020 7736 5455
e mail@jgpm.co.uk **w** www.jgpm.co.uk
Contact Jo Gurnett, Managing Director

James Grant Management Ltd
Syon Lodge, 201 London Road, Isleworth TW7 5BH
t 020 8232 4100 **f** 020 8232 4101
e enquiries@jamesgrant.co.uk **w** www.jamesgrant.co.uk
Contact Paul Worsley, Joint Managing Director; George Ashton, Senior Artist Manager; Sue Hill

Janet Howe Agency
Studio 1, Whitebridge Estate, Whitebridge Lane, Stone ST15 8LQ
t 0161 233 0700 **f** 01785 816888
e janet@jhowecasting.fsbusiness.co.uk
Contact Janet Howe, Proprietor
Credits Forsythe Saga (T); Cold Feet (T); Linda Green (T); Doctors (T)

Janet Plater Management Ltd
D Floor Milburn House, Dean Street, Newcastle-upon-Tyne NE1 1LF
t 01912 212490 **f** 01912 212491 **e** magpie@tynebridge.demon.co.uk

Joan Gray Personal Management
29 Sunbury Court Island, Sunbury-on-Thames TW16 5PP
t 01932 783544 **f** 01932 783544
Contact Joan Gray, Proprietor

John Markham Associates
1a Oakwood Avenue, Purley CR8 1AR
t 020 8763 8941 **f** 020 8763 8942
e info@johnmarkhamassociates.co.uk
Contact David Marsden, Associate Agent; John Markham, Proprietor

The John Miles Organisation
Cadbury Camp Lane, Clapton-in-Gordano, Bristol BS20 7SB
t 01275 856770 **f** 01275 810186 **e** john@johnmiles.org.uk

Jonathan Altaras Associates
11 Garick Street, London WC2E 9AR
t 020 7836 8722 **f** 020 7836 6066
Contact Jonathan Altaras, Chairman; Annette Stone, Agent

Julian Belfrage Associates
46 Albemarle Street, London W1S 4DF
t 020 7491 4400 **f** 020 7493 5460 **e** email@julianbelfrage.co.uk
Contact Victoria Belfrage, Managing Director

Kate Feast Management
10 Primrose Hill Studios, Fitzroy Road, London NW1 8TR
t 020 7586 5502 **f** 020 7586 9817
Contact Kate Feast, Agent

Ken McReddie Ltd
91 Regent Steet, London W1B 4EL
t 020 7439 1456 **f** 020 7734 6530
Contact Ken McReddie, Proprietor

Kerry Gardner Management Ltd
7 St Georges Square, London SW1V 2HX
t 020 7828 7748 **f** 020 7828 7758 **e** kerrygardner@freeuk.com
Contact Andy Herrity, Company Director; Kerry Gardner, Proprietor; Shopie Houghton, Assistant

Leigh Management
14 St David's Drive, Edgware HA8 6JH
t 020 8952 5536 **f** 020 8951 4449 **e** leighmanagment@aol.com
Contact Nathan Leigh, Partner; Michelle Leigh, Partner

Liz Hobbs Group Ltd
65 London Road, Newark NG24 1RZ
t 08700 702702 **f** 08703 337009
e info@lizhobbsgroup.com **w** www.lizhobbsgroup.com
Contact Liz Hobbs MBE, Chief Executive Officer; Richard Kort, Associate Director (Management); Ginette Taylor, Events Manager; Rachael Lubia, Assistant Events Manager; Sylvia Millington, Office Manager

Lookalikes
26 College Crescent, London NW3 5LH
t 020 7387 9245 **f** 020 7722 8261
e susan@lookalikes.info **w** www.lookalikes.info
Contact Susan Scott, Manager

Magnet Personal Management
Unit 743, The Big Peg, 120 Vyse Street, Birmingham B18 6NF
t 0121 628 7788 **f** 0121 628 7788
e magnetagency@talk21.com **w** www.magnetactors.fsnet.co.uk

Malcolm Shedden Management
1 Charlotte Street, London W1T 1RD
t 020 7636 1473 **f** 020 7636 1657 **e** info@features.co.uk
Contact Roy Clarke, Director

Mark Summers Management
9 Hansard Mews, Kensington, London W14 8BJ
t 0870 443 5621 **f** 0870 443 5623
m 07050 227885 **m** 07957 114175
e mark@marksummers.com **w** www.marksummers.com
Contact Mark Summers, Proprietor; David Hall, Head Booker

Markham & Froggatt Ltd
4 Windmill Street, London W1T 2HZ
t 020 7636 4412 **f** 020 7637 5233
e admin@markhamfroggatt.co.uk
Contact Pippa Markham, Company Director

Marlene Zwickler & Associates
2 Belgrave Place, Edinburgh EH4 3AN
t 0131 343 3030 **f** 0131 343 3030
e marlenezwickler@mza-1.demon.co.uk
Contact Marlene Zwickler, Proprietor

McIntosh Rae Management
Thornton House, Thornton Road, London SW19 4NG
t 020 8944 6688 **f** 020 8944 6624 **e** mcinrae@talk21.com
Contact Joyce Rae, Partner; Sheila McIntosh, Partner

MCS Agency
47 Dean Street, London W1D 5BE
t 020 7734 9995 **f** 020 7734 9996
e info@mcsagency.co.uk **w** www.mcsagency.co.uk
Contact Keith Bishop, Chief Executive

Michael Summerton Management
Mimosa House, Mimosa Street, London SW6 4DS
t 020 7731 6969 **f** 020 7731 0103 **e** msminfo@btconnect.com
Contact Martin Taylor-Brown, Office Manager

Missing Link Productions Ltd
t 020 8341 7645 **m** 07989 321593 **w** www.circusperformers.com
Contact Anna Strickland, Head of Entertainment Solutions Department
Credits Rory Bremner Who Else? (T); Mark Thomas Comedy Project (T); French And Saunders Christmas Special (T); V Graham Norton (T)

MKA
11 Russell Kerr Close, London W4 3HF
t 020 8994 1619 **f** 020 8994 2992 **e** mka.agency@virgin.net
Contact Malcolm Knight, Proprietor

Morgan & Goodman
Mezzanine, Quadrant House, 80-82 Regent Street, London W1B 5RP
t 020 7437 1383 **f** 020 7494 3446 **e** mg1@btinternet.com
Contact Lyndall Goodman, Proprietor

New Faces
2nd Flloor, The Linen Hall, 162-168 Regent Street, London W1B 5TB
t 020 7439 6900 **f** 020 7287 5481
e info@newfacestalent.co.uk **w** www.newfacestalent.co.uk
Contact Val Horton, Casting Agent; Caz Butcher, Manager; Rachel Oratis, Casting Agent

Noel Gay Organisation
19 Denmark Street, London WC2H 8NA
t 020 7836 3941 **f** 020 7287 1816
e mail@noelgay.com **w** www.noelgay.com
Contact Alex Armitage, Chief Executive

Norwell Lapley Associates
Lapley Hall, Lapley ST19 9JR
t 01785 841991 **f** 01785 841992
e norwelllapley@freeuk.com **w** www.norwelllapley.co.uk
Contact Chris Davis, Director; Claire Sibley, Artiste Manager

Oriental Casting Agency Ltd
1 Wyatt Park Road, Streatham Hill, London SW2 3TN
t 020 8671 8538 **f** 020 8674 9303
e peggy.sirr@btconnect.com **w** www.orientalcasting.com
Contact Peggy Sirr, Director
Credits BT (C); Tomb Raider II (F); Out For The Kill (F); Die Another Day (F)

Pan Artists Agency
1 Hollins Grove, Sale, Manchester M33 6RE
t 0161 969 7419 **f** 0161 973 9724
e bookings@panartists.freeserve.co.uk
Contact Dorothy Hall, Proprietor

Park Management Ltd
Unit C3, 62 Beechwood Road, London E8 3DY
t 020 7923 1498 **e** park-management@hotmail.com
Contact Roz McCutcheon, Secretary; Ian Hallard, Secretary

Parrot Productions Ltd
24 Cavendish Buildings, Gilbert Street, London W1K 5HJ
t 020 7629 2998 **f** 020 7355 3510
e parrot@cerbernet.co.uk **w** www.sohoball.com
Contact Cindy Hacker, Director

Paul Bailey Agency
32 Hampton Court Crescent, East Molesey KT8 9BA
t 020 8941 2034 **f** 020 8941 6304
e paul@paulbaileyagency.com **w** www.paulbaileyagency.com
Contact Paul Bailey, Director

PBJ Management Ltd
7 Soho Street, London W1D 3DQ
t 020 7287 1112 **f** 020 7287 1191
e general@pbjmgt.co.uk **w** www.pbjmgt.co.uk
Contact Melanie Harris; Jo Beasy

PC Theatrical & Model Agency
10 Strathmore Gardens, Edgware HA8 5HJ
t 020 8381 2229 **t** 020 8357 9739 **f** 020 8933 3418
e twinagy@aol.com **w** www.twinagency.com
Contact Sandra Mooney, Director
Credits Bright Young Things (F); Holby City (T); American Girl (F); EastEnders (T)

PHA Icon Ltd
Tanzaro House, Ardwick Green North, Manchester M12 6FZ
t 0161 273 4444 **f** 0161 273 4567 **e** info@pha-agency.co.uk
w www.pha-agency.co.uk **w** www.iconactors.net
Contact Lorna McDonough, Managing Director

Physicality Ltd
265-267 Ilford Lane, Ilford IG1 2SD
t 020 8491 2800 **f** 020 8491 2801
e info@physicality.co.uk **w** www.physicality.co.uk
Contact Wayne Pritchett, Managing Director; Rachel Wedderburn, Senior Booker; Nikki Bond, Booker; Charlotte Windley, Booker
Credits Royal Warrant Holder's Jubilee Ball

PLA (Pat Lovett Associates)
39 Sandhurst Court, Acre Lane, London SW2 5TX
t 020 7733 1110 **f** 020 7733 4440 **e** pla.london@blueyonder.co.uk
Contact Dolina Logan, Associate

Price Gardner Management Ltd
85 Shorrolds Road, London SW6 7TU
t 020 7610 2111 **f** 020 7381 3288
e info@pricegardner.com **w** www.pricegardner.com
Credits Mortgage Excellence (C); TV Thoga advert (C)

Rent-A-Band
Burnside House, 10 Burns Court, Birstall WF17 9JB
t 01924 441441 **f** 01924 441441

Representation Joyce Edwards
275 Kennington Road, London SE11 6BY
t 020 7735 5736 **f** 020 7820 1845 **e** joyce.edwards@virgin.net
Contact Joyce Edwards, Proprietor

Roberta Kanal Agency
82 Constance Road, Twickenham TW2 7JA
t 020 8894 2277 **f** 020 8894 7952
Contact Roberta Kanal, Director

Roger Carey Associates
7 St Georges Square, London SW1V 2HX
t 020 7630 6301 **f** 020 7630 0029 **e** rogercarey@freeuk.com
Contact Roger Carey, Proprietor

Roxane Vacca Management
73 Beak Street, London W1F SR
t 020 7734 8085 **f** 020 7734 8086
e roxane.vacca@roxanevaccamanagement.com
Contact Roxane Vacca, Proprietor

Royce Management
34a Sinclair Road, London W14 0NH
t 020 7602 4992 **f** 020 7371 4985
Contact Ronald Chenery, Proprietor

Sandra Boyce Management
1 Kingsway House, Albion Road, London N16 0TA
t 020 7923 0606 **f** 020 7241 2313 **e** info@sandraboyce.com

Satellite Artists
34 Salisbury Street, London NW8 8QE
t 020 7402 9111 **f** 02 7723 3064 **e** satellite_artists@hotmail.com
Contact Eliot Cohen, Director

Scot Baker Agency
35 Caithness Road, London W14 0JA
t 020 7603 9988 **f** 020 7603 7698 **e** info@scot-baker.com

Scott Marshall Partners Ltd
Suite 9, 54 Poland Street, London W1F 7NJ
t 020 7432 7240 **f** 020 7432 7241 **e** fmpm@scottmarshall.co.uk
Contact Manon Palmer, Agent

Tim Scott
284 Grays Inn Road, London WC1X 8EB
t 020 7833 5733 **f** 020 7278 9175 **e** timscott@btinternet.com

Shane Collins Associates
39-41 New Oxford Street, London WC1A 1BN
t 020 7836 9377 **f** 020 7836 9388
e info@shanecollins.co.uk **w** www.shanecollins.co.uk
Contact Shane Collins, Agent

Shoot Represents
Studio 5, Church Studios, Camden Park Road, London NW1 9AY
t 020 7267 4333 **f** 020 7485 4111 **m** 07802 783 482
e adele@shootproduction.com
Contact Adele Rider, Director

South West Casting Co Ltd
(inc Robert Smith Agency)
The Courtyard, Whitchurch, Ross on Wye HR9 6DA
t 01600 891160 **t** 01600 892005 **f** 01600 891099
e agent@southwestcasting.co.uk **w** www.southwestcasting.co.uk
Contact Lynn Hazel; Trevor Hazel
Credits Teachers (T); Crimewatch (T); Casualty (T)

Stan Green Management
PO Box 4, Dartmouth TQ6 0YD
t 01803 770046 **f** 01803 770075
e sgm@clara.co.uk **w** www.stangreenmanagement.co.uk
Contact Adrian Worsley, Production Manager; Keith Floyd, Managing

Stiven Christie Management (Edinburgh)
1 Glen Street, Edinburgh EH3 9JD
t 0131 228 4040 **f** 0131 228 4645 **m** 07831 403030
e info@stivenchristie.co.uk **w** www.stivenchristie.co.uk
Contact Simon Christie, Partner; Dougie Stiven, Partner

Stiven Christie Management (London)
Richmond Buildings, 80A Dean Street, London W1V 5AD
t 020 7434 4430 **f** 020 7434 4430 **m** 07831 403030
e scm@tad.co.uk **w** www.tad.co.uk/scm
Contact Douglas Stiven, Partner

Susan Angel + Kevin Francis Ltd
First Floor, 12 D'Arblay Street, London W1F 8DU
t 020 7439 3086 **f** 020 7437 1712 **e** angelpair@freeuk.com
Contact Susan Angel, Director; Kevin Francis, Director

Talent Artists Ltd
59 Sydner Road, London N16 7UF
t 020 7923 1119 **f** 020 7923 2009 **e** talent.artists@btconnect.com
Contact Jayne Wynn Owen, Managing Director; Stephen Miles, Agent

The Talent Partnership Ltd
Riverside Studios, Crisp Road, London W6 9RL
t 020 8237 1040 **f** 020 8237 1041
e info@thetalentpartnership.co.uk
Contact Lisa Willoughby, Agent; Maddie Burdett-Coutts, Managing Director / Agent; Maggi Sangwin, Agent; Beth Sangwin, Agent; Andrew Braidford, Agent

Thomas & Benda Associates Ltd
15-16 Ivor Place, London NW1 6HS
t 020 7723 5509 **t** 020 7724 0946 **f** 020 7723 5509
Contact Ann Thomas

United Colours of London Ltd
4th Floor, 20-24 Kirby Street EC1N 8TS
t 020 7242 5542 **f** 020 7242 8125
e fbi@dircon.co.uk **w** www.fullybooked-inc.com
Contact Richard Starnowski, Director

Urban Circus Ltd
The Arts Exchange, Mill Green, Congleton CW12 1JG
t 01260 276627 **f** 01260 270777
e cg@arts-exchange.com **w** www.arts-exchange.com

Agents Children

Abacus
The Studio, 4 Bailey Road, West Cort, Dorking RH4 3QS
t 01306 877144 **f** 01306 877813 **e** admin@abacusagency.com
Contact Sue Scarrott, Proprietor; Linda Davis

Barbara Speake Theatre School & Agency
East Acton Lane, London W3 7EG
t 020 8743 1306 **f** 020 8740 6542
Contact Carole Collins-Deamer, Children's Agent
Credits Kerching (T); Emperors New Clothes (F); 2000 Acres Of Sky (T)

Bright Sparks Theatre School & Agency
16 Wellfield Road, Streatham, London SW16 2BP
t 020 8669 8995 **f** 020 8669 4020
e admin@bsparks.fsnet.co.uk **w** www.bsparks.fsnet.co.uk
Contact Gloria Berry, Principal
Credits Holby City (T); Casualty (T)

Bubblegum Model Agency
Ardreigh, Beaconsfield Road, Farnham Royal SL2 3BP
t 01753 646348 **f** 01753 669255 **m** 07768 347329
e kids@bubblegummodels.com **w** www.bubblegummodels.com
Contact Heather Morton, Proprietor

Childsplay Allsorts
1 Cathedral Street, London SE1 9DE
t 020 7403 4834 **f** 020 7403 1656
e childsplaylondon@aol.com **w** www.childsplaylondon.co.uk
Contact Mr Tuthill, Partner
Credits Woolworths (C); Johnson & Johnson (C); C.O.I (C)

Chrystel Arts Agency & Theatre School
15 Churchill Road, Edgware HA8 6NX
t 01494 773336 **f** 01494 773336 **e** chrystelarts@talk21.com
Contact Christine Minter, Principal

D&B Theatre School
Centre Studio, 470 Bromley Road, London BR1 4PN
t 020 8698 8880 **f** 020 8697 8100
e bonnie@dandbperformingarts.co.uk
Contact Donna Sullivan, Proprieter
Credits Face At The Window (T); Dr Zhivago (T); Holby City (T); A Touch Of Frost (T)

Dacia Stevens Stage School
Glenavon Lodge, Landsdowne Road, South Woodford E18 2BE
t 020 8989 0166
Contact Dacia Stevens, Proprietor

Elisabeth Smith Ltd
81 Headstone Road, Harrow HA1 1PQ
t 020 8863 2331 **f** 020 8861 1880
e models@elisabethsmith.co.uk **w** www.elisabethsmith.co.uk
Contact Elisabeth Smith, Managing Director; Charlotte Evans, Bookings

Eurokids & Adults International Casting & Model Agency
The Warehouse Studio, Glaziers Lane, Culcheth,
Warrington WA3 4AQ
t 08717 501575 **f** 01925 767563
e info@eka-agency.co.uk **w** www.eka-agency.com
Contact Annabel Ralph, Licensing Manager; Annie McElroy, TV/Film Casting; Sue Carr, Office Manager; Rebecca Keeley, TV/Film Casting; Nicola Davies, Model/Actor Admissions; Debbie Ikin, Proprietor; Karen McGreevey, Model Booker
Credits Grange Hill (T); David Beckham - Marks & Spencers (C); Coronation Street (T)

Hobson's Kids
62 Chiswick High Road, London W4 1SY
t 020 8995 3628 **f** 020 8996 5350
e kids@hobsons-international.com
w www.hobsons-international.com
Contact Gaynor Shaw, Agent

Italia Conti Academy of Theatre Arts
Italia Conti, House 23, Goswell Road, London EC1M 7AJ
t 0207 7608 7500 **f** 0207 253 1430
e sca@italiaconti36.freeserve.co.uk
Contact Gaynor Sheward, Director

Jackie Palmer Agency/JPA Management
30 Daws Hill Lane, High Wycombe HP11 1PW
t 01494 520978 **f** 01494 510479 **e** jackie.palmer@btinternet.com
Contact Marylyn Phillips, Principal

Kids London Ltd
67 Dulwich Road, London SE24 0NJ
t 020 7924 9595 **f** 020 7924 9766 **m** 07957 249 911
e kidslondon@btconnect.com **w** www.kidslondon.uk.com
Contact Sue Walker, Director
Credits PlayStation (C); Huggies (C); MacDonalds (C); Daimler Chrysler (C)

Kids Plus
54 Grove Park, London SE5 8LG
t 020 7737 3901 **f** 020 7737 3901 **m** 07759 944 215
e janekidsplus@aol.com **w** www.kidsplusuk.com
Contact Jane Green, Contact
Credits Grange Hill (T); Horizon (T); Bright Young Things (F); Boots (C)

Little Acorns
271-273 King Street, Hammersmith, London W6 9LZ
t 020 8563 0773 **f** 020 8408 3077
e acorns@dircon.co.uk **w** www.littleacorns.co.uk
Contact June Abey, Manager

Rascals Child Model Agency
13 Jubilee Parade, Snakes Lane East, Woodford Green IG8 7QG
t 020 8504 1111 **f** 020 8559 1035
e kids@rascals.abel.co.uk **w** www.rascals.co.uk
Contact Vivien Little, Director; Fiona Little, Director

Ravenscourt Management & Theatre School
Tandy House, 30-40 Dalling Road, London W6 0JB
t 020 8741 0707 **f** 020 8741 1786 **m** 07831 150200
e ravenscourt@hotmail.com **w** www.dramaschoollondon.com
Contact Robin Phillips BT, Principal; Christopher Price, Head Agent; Roe Brooks, Agent; Mark Jermin, Agent

Real Kids
4 Debenshire Gardens, Glasgow G12 0UX
t 0141 581 5889 **f** 0141 581 7385
Contact David Bell

Redroofs Theatre School & Agency
Redroofs Theatre School
t 01628 822982 **f** 01628 822461
Contact June Rose, Principal

Sylvia Young Theatre School
Rossmore Road, London NW1 6NJ
t 0207 723 0037 **f** 0207 723 1040 **e** sylviayoung@freeuk.com
w www.sylviayoungtheatreschool.co.uk
Contact Sylvia Young

Truly Scrumptious Child Model Agency
The Works, 16-24 Underwood Street, London N1 7JQ
t 020 7608 3806 **f** 020 7251 5767
Contact Sharon Obee, Director

Agents Extras

2020 Casting
2020 Hopgood Street, London W12 7JU
t 020 8746 2020 **f** 020 8735 2727
e info@2020casting.com **w** www.2020casting.com
Contact Chuck Douglas, Assistant Manager; Ben Thomas, IT Manager; Christopher Villiers, Managing Director
Credits Silent Witness (T); What A Girl Wants (F); Love Actually (F); Bloody Sunday (F)

Avenue Artistes Ltd
8 Winn Road, Southampton SO17 1EN
t 023 8055 1000 **f** 023 8090 5703

The Casting Collective
Olympic House, 317-321 Latimer Road, London W10 6RA
t 020 8962 0099 **f** 020 8962 0333
e enquiries@castingcollective.co.uk **w** www.castingcollective.co.uk
Contact Rob Martin, Director; Rosie Collins, Casting Director; Laura Sheppard, Director; Sarah Dickinson, Director
Credits Love Actually (F); Johnny English (F); First Knight: The Gauntlet Machine (F)

Clacton Top Spots
53 Rosemary Way, Jaywick, Clacton on Sea CO15 2SB
t 01255 220787 **f** 01255 220922 **m** 07785 594389
e enquiry@top-spots.u-net.com
Contact Clare Thorpe; Dee Mulcahy

The David Agency
153 Battersea Rise, London SW11 1HP
t 020 7223 7720 **f** 020 7924 2334 **m** 07831 679165
e casting@davidagency.net **w** www.davidagency.net
Contact Laila Debs, Director

Denman Casting Agency
Burgess House, Main Street, Farnsfield NG22 8EF
t 0162 388 2272 **f** 0162 388 2272
Contact Jack Denman, Proprietor

The Dolly Brook Casting Agency
PO Box 5436, Dunmow CM6 1WW
t 01371 879775 **f** 01371 875996
Contact Dolly Brook, Proprieter

Extras Unlimited
Ava House, 9 Hansford Mews, Kensington, London W14 8BJ
t 087 0443 5622 **f** 087 0443 5623 **m** 07956 254246
e info@extrasunlimited.com **e** mark@marksummers.com

FBI Ltd
4th Floor, 20-24 Kirby Street, London EC1N 8TS
t 020 7242 5542 **f** 020 7242 8125
e fbi@dircon.co.uk **w** www.fullybooked-inc.com
Contact Cherry Parker, Partner; Richard Starnowski, Partner

Fresh Agents
Albert House, 82 Queens Road, Brighton BN1 3XE
t +44 1273 711777 **f** +44 1273 711778
m 07714 672233 **m** 07714 672244
e info@freshagents.com **w** www.freshagents.com
Contact Kate Merrin, Partner; Lauren Lambe, Partner
Credits Trigger Happy TV (T); Sony Coporate (I); Butlins - Fun Police (C); Divine Inspiration - My Way (M)

G2
15 Lexham Mews, London W8 6JW
t 020 7376 2133 **f** 020 7376 2416 **m** 07831 848571
e g2@galloways.ltd.uk
Contact Maren Dallman; John Setrice, Bookings

Historical Promotions (Extras & Locations)
Butstone Business Centre, Petrockstowe, Okehampton EX20 3ET
t 01837 811243 **f** 01837 811243 **m** 07944 524657
e info@historicalpromotions.com **w** www.historicalpromotions.com
Contact Rob Butler, Managing Director
Credits Henry II (E); Hornblower (T); Royals And Riots (T); Cannibal (T)

Jaclyn 2000
52 Bessemer Road, Norwich NR4 6DQ
t 01603 622027
Contact Julian Sandiford, Proprietor
Credits Aldiss Bettys (T); Crime Watch (T)

JB Agency Online Ltd
7 Stonehill Mansions, 8 Streatham High Road, London SW16 1DD
t 020 8679 0123 **f** 020 8769 9567 **m** 07956 266344
e christian@jb-agency.com **w** www.jb-agency.com
Contact Bill Richards, Partner

Lakeside Castings (Lake District)
63 Scotland Road, Carlisle CA3 9HT
t 01228 401093 **f** 01228 401093 **m** 07850 597 689
e info@lakesidecastings.com **w** www.lakesidecastings.com
Contact Philip McKay, Director/Casting Agent
Credits Magdalene Sisters (F); Ted And Alice (T); If Only (F); 2000 Acres Of Sky (T)

Lee's People Ltd
60 Poland Street, London W1V 3DF
t 020 7734 5775 **f** 020 7734 3033 **m** 07970 527252
e lee@lees-people.co.uk **w** www.lees-people.co.uk
Contact Lee Towsey, Director

PCA Casting
3 George Street, Bath BA1 2EH
t 01225 469866 **f** 01225 469866 **m** 07884 214922
e pca@casting.fslife.co.uk
Contact Paul Cresswell, Proprietor
Credits Servants (T); BBC Digital (I); Bertie And Elizabeth (T); HTV Weather (C)

Phoenix Agency
PO Box 387, Bristol BS99 3JZ
t 0117 973 1100 **f** 0117 973 4160
e caron@phoenix-agency.demon.co.uk
Contact Caron Hughes

Ray Knight Casting Agency
21a Lambolle Place, London NW3 4PG
t 020 7722 1551 **f** 020 7722 2322
e casting@rayknight.co.uk **w** www.rayknight.co.uk
Contact Ray Knight, Managing Director

Screenlite Agency
Shepperton Film Studios, Studios Road, Shepperton TW17 0QD
t 01932 566977 **f** 01932 572507
e sreenlite@dial.pipex.com **w** www.screenliteagency.co.uk
Contact Kerry Tovey, Senior Booker; Carlie Tovey, Managing Director

Solomon Artistes Management International
30 Clarence Street, Southend on Sea SS1 1BD
t 01702 392370 **f** 01702 392385 **m** 07801 140042
e info@solomons-artistes.co.uk **w** www.soloman-artistes.co.uk
Contact Anita Houser, Agent

Agents **Hand**

Artimis Models & Promotions
PO Box 10062, Shirley, Solihull B90 4WH
t 0121 703 3168 **f** 0121 703 3168
e helen@artimis.co.uk **w** www.artimis.co.uk

Derek's Hands
153 Battersea Rise, London SW11 1HP
t 020 7924 2484 **f** 020 7924 2334 **m** 07831 679165
e casting@derekshands.com **w** www.derekshands.com
Contact Laila Debs, Director

Hired Hands
t 020 7267 9212 **f** 020 7267 1030
e models@hiredhands.freeserve.co.uk
Contact Steve Barker, Partner

Agents **Model**

'A' Class Management
PO Box 10201, Redditch B98 0AT
t 01527 453003 **e** vacancies@aclassmanagement.co.uk
w www.aclassmanagement.co.uk

Adage Models

314 The Greenhouse, The Custard Factory, Gibb Street, Birmingham B9 4AA
t 0121 693 4040 **f** 0121 693 4041
e info@adagemodels.net **w** www.adagemodels.net
Contact Tracie Bedwood, Managing Director; Kathy McDonald, Financial Director; Stuart Alexander, Model Booker

Bookings Model Agency

Studio 6, 27A Pembridge Villas, London W11 3EP
t 020 7221 2603 **f** 020 7229 4567 **e** mail@bookingsmodels.co.uk
Contact Patti Carling; Edmund Mitchell

castingontheweb.com

Russell Farm, New Road, Maulden MK45 2BG
t 01525 408179 **f** 01525 406886
e info@woburnstudios.com **w** www.castingontheweb.com
Contact Tim Liggins

IMG Models

Bentinck House, 3-8 Bolsover, London W1W 6AA
t 020 7580 5885 **f** 020 7580 5868 **e** lonmodels@imgworld.com

International Model Management (IMM)

H/21 Heathmans Road, London SW6 4TJ
t 020 7610 9111 **f** 020 7736 2221 **m** 07973 753 993
e karstenimm@aol.com
w www.internationalmodelmanagement.com
Contact Karsten Edwards, Director

NEVS Model Agency

Regal House, 198 Kings Road, London SW3 5XP
t 020 7352 4886 **f** 020 7356 6068
e getamodel@nevs.co.uk **w** www.nevs.co.uk
Contact Paul Cavalier, Director

Norrie Carr Modelling Agency

Holburn Studios, 49 Eagle Wharf Road, London N1 7ED
t 020 7253 1771 **f** 020 7253 1772
e info@norriecarr.com **w** www.norriecarr.com

Number One Model Management

408F The Big Peg, 120 Vyse Street, Birmingham B18 6NF
t 0121 233 2433 **f** 0121 233 2454
w www.numberonemodelagency.co.uk
Contact Trudi Brown, Director

Premier Model Agency

40-42 Parker Street, London WC2B 5PQ
t 020 7333 0888 **f** 020 7323 1221
e info@premiermodelmanagement.com
w www.premiermodelmanagement.com

Profile Management

London
t 0207 836 5282 **f** 0207 497 2255
e info@profile-models.com **w** www.profile-models.com
Contact C Chalvet de Recy, Director

Samantha Bond Management

10 Castelnau, London SW13 9RU
t 020 8741 0609 **f** 020 8741 4632 **m** 07703 327701
w www.samanthabond.net
Contact Mike Diamond, Contact

Sandra Reynolds Agency

62 Bell Street, London NW1 6SP
t 020 7387 5858 **f** 020 7387 5848
e tessa@sandrareynolds.co.uk **w** www.sandrareynolds.co.uk
Contact Tessa Reynolds, Proprietor; Emma Sahnerude, Head Booker

Scallywags Model Agency Ltd

1 Cranbrook Rise, Ilford IG1 3QW
t 020 8518 1133 **f** 020 8924 0262
e kids@scallywags.co.uk **w** www.scallywags.co.uk
Contact David York; Rachel York; Kim Smith; Simon Penn

Spare Parts

153 Battersea Rise, London SW11 1HP
t 020 7924 2484 **f** 020 7924 2334 **m** 07831 679165
e casting@sparepartsmodels.co.uk **w** www.sparepartsmodels.co.uk
Contact Laila Debs, Managing Director

Sports Promotions

PO Box 878, Crystal Palace Sports Centre, London SE19 2BH
t 020 8659 4561 **f** 020 8776 7772
e chris@sportspromotions.com
Contact Yvonne Adair, Booker; Chris Snode, Director
Credits Ford Transit (C); The Commonwealth Games (C); John Smiths Bitter (C)

Storm Model Agency

t 020 7368 9900 **f** 020 7376 5145
e nick@stormmodels.co.uk **w** www.stormmodels.co.uk
Contact Simon Chambers, Director

Ugly Models/Rage

Tigris House, 256 Edgware Road, London W2 1DS
t 020 7262 0515 (Rage) **t** 020 7402 5564 (Ugly)
f 020 7402 0507 **e** info@ugly.org **w** www.ugly.org

Agents **Personal**

A&B Personal Management Ltd

Paurelle House, 91 Regent Street, London W1B 4EL
t 020 7734 6047 **f** 020 7734 6318 **e** billellis@aandb.co.uk

The Actors Group Personal Management

21-31 Oldham Street, Manchester M1 1JG
t 0161 834 4466 **f** 0161 834 5588 **e** agent@tagactors.co.uk
Contact Paula Horton, Member; Deborah Bouchard

ADS

Shepperton Studios, Studios Road, Shepperton TW17 0QD
t 01932 592303 **f** 01932 592492 **e** ads@carlincrew.co.uk
Contact Sara Putt, Director

Andrew Manson Personal Management

288 Munster Road, Fulham, London SW6 6BQ
t 020 7386 9158 **f** 020 7381 8874
e amanson@aol.com **w** www.talentroom.com
Contact Andrew Manson, Proprietor

APM (Alexander Personal Management)

PO Box 834, Hemel Hempstead HP3 9ZP
t 01442 252907 **f** 01442 241099
e apm@apmassociates.net **w** www.apmassociates.net
Contact Linda French, Director

BAM Associates

41 Bloomfield Road, Bristol BS4 3QA
t 0117 971 0636 **f** 0117 971 0636 **e** bamassociates@aol.com
Contact Lee Walker; Alison Comley

Bigfish Management

55 Bendon Valley, London SW18 4LZ
t 020 8877 7111 **f** 020 8874 6623
e info@bigfishmanagement.com **w** www.bigfishmanagement.com
Contact Gregory Apprey, Agent

Bill McLean Personal Management Ltd

23B Deodar Road, Putney, London SW15 2NP
t 020 8789 8191
Contact Bill McLean, Managing Director

Brown & Simcocks

1 Bridgehouse Court, 109 Blackfriars Road, London SE1 8HW
t 020 7928 1229 **f** 020 7928 1909
e barryandcarrie@lineone.net

Contact Barry Brown, Partner; Carrie Simcocks, Partner

CA Artistes Management

153 Battersea Rise, London SW11 1HP
t 020 7223 7827 **f** 020 7924 2334
e casting@caartistes.com **w** www.caartistes.com

Contact Laila Debs, Director

Casarotto Marsh Ltd

National House, 60-66 Wardour Street, London W1V 4ND
t 020 7287 4450 **f** 020 7287 5644
e casarottomarsh@casarotto.uk.com **w** www.casarotto.uk.com

Contact Emma Trounson, Agent, TV & Short Film; Izzy Barker-Mill, Agent, Commercials; Sara Pritchard, Agent, Film

CCA Management

7 St George's Square, London SW1V 2HX
t 020 7630 6303 **f** 020 7630 7376

Contact Dulcie Houston

The Central Line

11 East Circus Street, Nottingham NG1 5AF
t 0115 941 2937 **f** 0115 950 8087 **e** mail@the-central-line.co.uk **w** www.the-central-line.co.uk

Creating Faces Agency

5 Hamilton House, 4A The Avenue, London E4 9LD
t 020 8531 8498 **f** 020 8531 9048
e info@creatingfaces.com **w** www.creatingfaces.com

Contact S Bennett, Director; N Chambers, Director

Creative Media Management

Unit 3B, Walpole Court, Ealing Studios, Ealing Green, London W5 5ED
t 020 8584 5363 **f** 020 8566 5554
e enquiries@creativemediamanagement.com

Contact Jacqui Fincham, Managing Director; Caroline Cornish-Trestrall, Agent; Owen Massey, Director; Amanda McAllister, Agent

Cruickshank Cazenove Ltd

97 Old South Lambeth Road, London SW8 1XU
t 020 7735 2933 **f** 020 7820 1081 **e** hjcruickshank@aol.com

Contact Harriet Cruickshank, Managing Director

Curtis Brown

Haymarket House, 28-29 Haymarket, London SW1Y 4SP
t 020 7396 6600 **f** 020 7396 0110 **e** cb@curtisbrown.co.uk

Contact Nick Marston, Film Agent; Ben Hall, Film Agent

The Dench Arnold Agency

24 D'Arblay Street, London W1F 8EH
t 020 7437 4551 **f** 020 7439 1355
e contact@dencharnoldagency.co.uk **w** www.dencharnold.co.uk

Dinedor Management

81 Oxford Street, London W1D 2EU
t 020 7851 3575 **f** 020 7851 3576
e info@dinedor.com **w** www.dinedor.com

Henry Foster

Roger Carey Associates, 7 St Georges Square, London SW1V 2HX
t 020 7630 6301 **f** 020 7630 0029 **e** rogercarey@freeuk.com

Gems

The Media House, 87 Glebe Street, Penarth CF64 1EF
t 029 2071 0770 **f** 029 2071 0771
e gems@gems-agency.co.uk **w** www.gems-agency.co.uk

Gilbert & Payne

Suite 73-74, Kent House, 87 Regent Street, London W1B 4EH
t 020 7734 7505 **f** 020 7494 3787 **m** 07802 640499
e ee@successtheatrical.com

Grade One TV & Film Personnel

Elstree Studios, Shenley Road, Borehamwood WD6 1JG
t 020 8324 2224 **f** 020 8324 2328 **m** 07836 778303
e gradeone.tvpersonnel@virgin.net

Contact Helen Crowe, Contact

Greasepaint Make-Up Placement Agency

143 Northfield Avenue, London W13 9QT
t 020 8840 6000 **f** 020 8840 3983
e info@greasepaint.co.uk **w** www.greasepaint.co.uk

Contact Catherine Langridge; Hannah Cruttenden

Green & Underwood

6 Brook Street, London W1S 1BB
t 020 7493 0308 **f** 020 7355 1084 **m** 07836 249 607
e info@greenandunderwood.com **w** www.greenandunderwood.com

Contact Nicholas Young, Agent

HERS

t 01884 242248 **f** 01884 251221
e hers@hersagency.co.uk **w** www.hersagency.co.uk

Contact Julia Hetherington, Proprietor

Holland-Ford's

103 Lydyett Lane, Barnton, Northwich CW8 4JT
t 01606 76960

Contact Bob Holland-Ford, Proprietor

Independent Post Company

65 Goldhawk Road, London W12 8EH
t 020 8746 2060 **f** 020 8743 2345 **e** anthony@indepost.co.uk

Contact Simon Frodsham, Managing Director; Anthony Crossby, Head Of Bookings; Caroline Duncan, General Manager

International Creative Management Ltd

Oxford House, 76 Oxford Street, London W1D 1BS
t 020 7636 6565 **f** 020 7323 0101 **w** www.icmlondon.co.uk

Contact Nick Pitt

Jeffrey & White Management

9-15 Neal Street, London WC2H 9PW
t 020 7240 7000 **f** 020 7240 0007

Contact Jeremy White, Partner

Jessica Carney Associates

Suite 90-92 Kent House, 87 Regent Street, London W1B 4EH
t 020 7434 4143 **f** 020 7434 4173 **e** info@jcarneyassociates.co.uk

Contact Jessica Carney, Director

JLM

259 Acton Lane, Chiswick, London W4 5DG
t 020 8747 8223 **f** 020 8747 8286 **e** jlm@skynow.net

Contact Nichol Urwin, Junior Agent

Jonathan Altaras Associates

13 Shorts Gardens, London WC2H 9AT
t 020 7836 8722 **f** 020 7836 6066 **e** antonia@jaa.indirect.co.uk

Contact Jonathon Altaras, Managing Director

Limelight Management

33 Newman Street, London W1T 1PY
t 020 7637 2529 **e** limelight.management@virgin.net
w www.limelightmanagement.com

Contact Fiona Lindsay, Managing Director; Linda Shanks, Director

Linda Seifert Management
91 Berwick Street, London W1F ONE
t 020 7292 7390 **f** 020 7292 7391
e contact@lindaseifert.com **w** www.lindaseifert.com
Contact Carly Peacock, Contact; Craig Smith

London Management & Representation
2-4 Noel Street, London W1V 3RB
t 020 7287 9000 **f** 020 7287 3236
Contact Fiona Williams, Contact

Magnolia Management
136 Hicks Avenue, Greenford UB6 8HB
t 020 8578 2899 **f** 020 8575 0369 **m** 07973 617 168
e jaffreymag@aol.com
Contact Jennifer Jaffrey, Proprietor

McKinney Macartney Management
The Barley Mow Centre, 10 Barley Mow Passage, London W4 4PH
t 020 8995 4747 **f** 020 8995 2414
e fkb@mmtechsrep.demon.co.uk **w** www.mckinneymacartney.com
Contact Flic McKinney, Film Technicians Agent; Kim Macartney, Film Technicians Agent

Nigel Britten Management Ltd
Riverbank House, 1 Putney Bridge Approach, Fulham, London SW6 3JD
t 020 7384 3842 **f** 020 7384 3862 **e** nbm.office@virgin.net
Contact Nigel Britten, Agent

Peters Fraser & Dunlop
Drury House, 34-43 Russell Street, London WC2B 5HA
t 020 7344 1000 **f** 020 7836 9543
e postmaster@pfd.co.uk **w** www.pfd.co.uk
Contact Alex Greig

Princestone
49 Waldeck Road, London N15 3EL
t 020 8881 8788 **f** 020 8881 2857
e princestone@madasafish.com
Contact Sarah Prince, Agent; Tim Stone, Agent

Re:Solution
90 Raglan Avenue, Waltham Cross EN8 8DD
t 020 7580 5766 **f** 01992 025506 **m** 07973 371718
e jacqui@re-solution.tv **w** www.re-solution.tv
Contact Jacqui Sesstein, Freelance Manager
Credits Where There's Muck (D); Extreme Sex (D); Bridezilla (D); Sin Cities (D)

The Research Register
47 Anson Road, London N7 0AR
t 020 7700 7573 **f** 020 7700 2627
Contact Alex Ireson, Assistant; Diana Miller, Proprietor

Richard Hatton Ltd
29 Roehampton Gate, London SW15 5JR
t 020 8876 6699 **f** 020 8876 8278
Contact Richard Hatton, Director

Roger Hancock Ltd
4 Water Lane, London NW1 8NZ
t 020 7267 4418 **f** 020 7267 0705
e hancockltd@aol.com **w** ww.rogerhancock.com
Contact Tim Hancock

Sara Putt Associates
Shepperton Studios, Studios Road, Room 923, The Old House, Shepperton TW17 0QD
t 01932 571044 **f** 01932 571109 **e** sara@saraputt.co.uk
e kate@saraputt.co.uk **w** www.saraputt.com
Contact Sara Putt, Agent

Stella Richards Management
42 Hazlebury Road, London SW6 2ND
t 020 7736 7786 **f** 020 7731 5082
Contact Stella Richards, Proprietor

Success
Suite 74, Kent House, 87 Regent Street, London W1B 4EH
t 020 7734 3356 **f** 020 7494 3787 **e** ee@successtheatrical.com

Susi Earnshaw Management
5 Brook Place, Barnet EN5 2DL
t 020 8441 5010 **f** 020 8364 9618
e enq@susiearnshaw.co.uk **w** www.susiearnshaw.co.uk

talentfile.co.uk
Red Bus Studios, 34 Salisbury Street, London NW8 8QE
t 020 7724 2243 **f** 020 7724 2871 **e** info@crimson.globalnet.co.uk

Tessa Le Bars Management
54 Birchwood Road, Petts Wood BR5 1NZ
t 01689 837084 **f** 01689 837084 **m** 07860 287255
e tessa.lebars@ntlworld.com **w** www.galtonandsimpson.com
Contact Tessa Le Bars, Manager

Clare Vidal-Hall
28 Perrers Road, London W6 0EZ
t 020 8741 7647 **f** 020 8741 9459 **e** clarevidalhall@email.com

Valedayt Management
C/o The Flat, 37 Derbyshire Lane, Hucknall, Nottingham NG15 7JX
m 07949 086470 **e** valedaytmanagement@yahoo.com
Contact Valerie Day, Director
People management, photographic artist, literary. Supporting artistes through personal transformation.

Valerie Hoskins Associates
20 Charlotte Street, London W1T 2NA
t 020 7637 4490 **f** 020 7637 4493
e vha@vhassociates.co.uk **w** www.vhassociates.co.uk
Contact Valerie Hoskins; Rebecca Watson

Vincent Shaw Associates Ltd
51 Byron Road, London E17 4SN
t 020 8509 2211 **f** 020 8509 2211
e vincentshaw@clara.net **w** www.vincentshaw.co.uk

Yardley Management
Halliford Studios, Manygate Lane, Shepperton TW17 9EG
t 01932 253325 **f** 01932 253325 **m** 07810 748710
e pete@yardleymanagement.co.uk
w www.yardleymanagement.co.uk
Contact Pete Nash, Agent

Agents Presenters

Arlington Enterprises Ltd
1-3 Charlotte Street, London W1T 1RD
t 020 7580 0702 **f** 020 7580 4994
e info@arlington-enterprises.co.uk
w www.arlingtonentreprises.co.uk
Contact Debbie Schiesser, Agent; Suzanne Goddard, Office Administrater; Lili Panagi, Agent; Hilary Murray, Agent; Anne Sweetbaum, Managing Director; Lois McBride, Agent; Suzanne Goddard, Office Administrater

Blackburn Sachs Associates
88-90 Crawford Street, London W1H 2BS
t 020 7258 6158 **f** 020 7258 6162
e presenters@blackburnsachsassociates.com
w www.blackburnsachsassociates.com
Contact Anthony Blackburn, Partner; John Sacks, Partner

Cunningham Management Ltd
London House, 271 King Street, London W6 9LZ
t 020 8233 2824 **e** info@cunningham-management.co.uk
w www.cunningham-management.co.uk
Contact Simon Fairclough, Account Manager; Chloe Cunningham, Director;
Brizee Young, Agent

Inspirational TV presenters.

David Anthony Promotions
PO Box 286, Warrington WA2 8GA
t 01925 632496 **f** 01925 416589
e dave@davewarwick.co.uk **w** www.davewarwick.co.uk
Contact David Warwick, Agent

Downes Presenters' Agency
96 Broadway, Bexleyheath DA6 7DE
t 020 8304 0541 **f** 020 8301 5591 **m** 07973 601332
e downes@presentersagency.com **w** www.presentersagency.com
Contact Wendy Downes, Agent

The Excellent Voice Company
Top Floor, 53 Goodge Street, London W1T 1TG
t 020 7636 1636 **f** 020 7636 1631 **m** 07971 680271
e info@excellentvoice.co.uk **w** www.excellentvoice.co.uk
Contact Liz Pape; Pete Gold; Ruth Underwood; Jon Briggs, Managing Director

Fletcher Associates
25 Park Way, London N20 0XN
t 020 8361 8061 **f** 020 8361 8866 **m** 07958 977 985
e fletcher.associates@lineone.net
Contact Francine Fletcher, Director

Fox Artist Management
Concorde House, 101 Shepherds Bush Road, London W6 7LP
t 020 7602 8822 **f** 020 7603 2352 **m** 07768 721 034
e fox.artist@btinternet.com
Contact Tony Fox

Jacque Evans Management Ltd
Top Floor, 14 Holmesley Road, London SE23 1PJ
t 020 8699 1202 **f** 020 8699 5192 **m** 07831 340378
e jacque@jemltd.demon.co.uk **w** www.jacqueevansltd.com
Contact Jacque Evans, Managing Director; Lesley Evans, Director

John Noel Management
10A Belmont Street, London NW1 8HH
t 020 7428 8400 **f** 020 7428 8401 **e** john@johnnoel.com

Knight Ayton Management
114 St Martin's Lane, London WC2N 4BE
t 020 7836 5333 **f** 020 7836 8333
e info@knightayton.co.uk **w** www.knightayton.co.uk
Contact Sue Knight, Partner; Sue Ayton, Partner

MPC Entertainment
MPC House, 15/16 Maple Mews, Maida Vale, London NW6 5UZ
t 020 7624 1184 **f** 020 7624 4220
e mpc@mpce.com **w** www.mpce.com
Contact Nick Canham, Artist Manager
Credits Kit Kat: Salmon (C); Guinness: Butcher, Mabbutt, Anderson (C)

Presenter Promotions
123 Corporation Road, Gillingham ME7 1RG
t 01634 851077 **f** 01634 316771 **m** 07958 582270
e info@presenterpromotions.com
w www.presenterpromotions.com
Contact Colin Cobb, Proprieter

The Roseman Organisation
51 Queen Anne Street, London W1G 9HS
t 020 7486 4500 **f** 020 7486 4600
e info@therosemanorganisation.co.uk
w www.therosemanorganisation.co.uk
Contact Jon Roseman, MD

Speak-Easy Ltd
1 Dairy Yard, High Street, Market Harborough LE16 7NL
t 01858 461961 **t** 08700 135126 **f** 01858 461994
e enquiries@speak-easy.co.uk **w** www.speak-easy.co.uk
Contact Sarah Pickering (Voice-overs); Kate Moon (Presenters)

Take Three Management
110 Gloucester Avenue, London NW1 8HX
t 020 7209 3777 **f** 020 7209 3770
e info@take3management.co.uk **w** www.take3management.co.uk
Contact Melanie Cantor, Director; Sara Cameron, Director; Vicki McIvor, Director

Unique Management Group
Beaumont House, Kensington Village, Avonmore Road,
London W14 8TS
t 020 7605 1100 **f** 020 7605 1101 **e** celebrities@uniquegroup.co.uk
Contact Joanna Carlton, Senior Agent; Sara Hersheson, Agent

VRM (Presenters)
PO Box 82, Altrincham WA15 0QD
t 01619 283222 **f** 01619 287849
e vrm@thevoicebox.co.uk **w** www.thevoicebox.co.uk
Contact Vicki Hope-Robinson, Managing Director

Agents **Sports**

APSA
Federation House, Stoneleigh Park CV8 2RF
t 024 7641 4999 **f** 024 7641 4990
e apsa@sportslife.org.uk **w** www.apsa.org.uk

Sports Locations
PO Box 878, Crystal Palace National Sports Centre,
London SE19 2BH
t 020 8659 4561 **f** 020 8776 7772 **m** 07770 994043
e enquiry@sportspromotions.co.uk
w www.sportspromotions.co.uk
Contact Yvonne Adair; Chris Snode, Director

Wizard Management
5 Clare Lawn, London SW14 8BH
t 020 8487 1173 **f** 020 8878 3821 **m** 07836 566868
e attwiz@aol.com
Contact David Ryan; Bob Louis

Agents **Voiceover**

Ad Voice
Oxford House, 76 Oxford Street, London W1D 1BS
t 020 7323 2345 **f** 020 7323 0101
Contact Susan Barritt, Director

Calypso Voices
25-26 Poland Street, London W1F 8QN
t 020 7734 6415 **f** 020 7437 0410
e calypso@calypsovoices.com **w** www.calypsovoices.com
Contact Jane Savage, Manager

Castaway
7 Garrick Street, London WC2E 9AR
t 020 7240 2345 **f** 020 7240 2772
e sheila@castaway.org.uk **w** www.castaway.org.uk
Contact Sheila Britten, Managing Director

Genuine Arab Casting
28 Otterfield Road, West Drayton UB7 8PE
t 01895 420836 **f** 01895 846599 **m** 07791 495619
e gac@genuinecasting.com **w** www.genuinecasting.com
Credits The Mummy Returns (F); The Mummy (F); The English Patient (F)

LUCCHESI

Foreign voice-overs
Translation
Casting

Sound recording
Dubbing
Subtitling

132 Cleveland Street
London W1T 6AB UK
T: +44 (0)20 7692 7700
F: +44 (0)20 7692 7711
info@vsi.tv www.vsi.tv

VSI
SUBTITLING & DUBBING
FOREIGN-LANGUAGE VERSIONS

Hobson's Voices

62 Chiswick High Road, London W4 1SY
t 020 8995 3628 **f** 020 8996 5350
e voices@hobsons-international.com
w www.hobsons-international.com
Contact Leigh Matty, Voice Agent; Sue Bonnici, Managing Director; Tania
Edwards, Voice Agent; Kate Davie, Voice Agent; Janet Ferguson-Lees, Voice Agent

INTER-COM Translations

Inter-Com Translations

Hurlingham Studios, Ranelagh Gardens, London SW6 3PA
t 020 7731 8000 **f** 020 7731 5511 **m** 07946 546531
e mail@intercom-translations.co.uk
w www.intercom-translations.co.uk
Contact Patrick Beacom, Partner; Carolina Lehrian, Partner

*Looking for a dependable professional team, with a major client list to
handle your foreign versions? All languages, all subjects. Translations,
transcriptions, time-coded scripts, subtitling, type-setting, interpreting,
voiceovers.*

Lip Service Casting Ltd

4 Kingly Street, London W1B 5PE
t 020 7734 3393 **f** 020 7734 3373 **m** 07973 298196
e jo@lipservice.co.uk **w** www.lipservice.co.uk
Contact Susan Mactavish, Managing Director

Media Ambitions Ltd

Suite 2, Ground Floor, 127 Ladbroke Grove, London W11 1PN
t 020 7229 6610 **f** 020 7229 8497 **m** 07967 726806
e elizabeth@mediaambitions.com **w** www.mediaambitions.com
Contact Elizabeth Aylo, Managing Director

Paul Daniels Voice Overs

XVO 53 Goodge Street W1T 1TG
t 020 7636 1636 **f** 020 7636 1631 **m** 07775 563225
e paul.daniels@thebollox.co.uk **w** www.thebollox.co.uk
Contact Paul Daniels, Artist; Liz Pape, Agent
Credits BBC1 (T); SKY TV (T); National Geographic (C)

Peter Dickson

Voice Shop, 304 Edgware Road, London W2 1DY
t 020 7402 3966
e studio@peterdickson.co.uk **w** www.peterdickson.co.uk
Credits Family Fortunes (T); They Think It's All Over (T); Bruce's Price Is Right
(T); Today With Mel And Des (T)

Roxane Vacca Voices

73 Beak Street, London W1F 9SR
t 020 7734 8085 **f** 020 7734 8086
e jayne.nelson@roxanevaccamanagement.com
Contact Jane Rose Nelson, Voiceover Agent

Shurwood Management

Totehill Cottage, Stedham, Midhurst GU29 0PY
t 01730 817400 **f** 01730 815846
Contact Shurley Selwood, Managing Director

Speak-Easy Ltd

1 Dairy Yard, High Street, Market Harborough LE16 7NL
t 01858 461961 **t** 08700 135126 **f** 01858 461994
e enquiries@speak-easy.co.uk **w** www.speak-easy.co.uk
Contact Sarah Pickering (Voice-overs); Kate Moon (Presenters)

Speakers Corner at Crawfords

6 Brook Street, London W1S 1BB
t 020 7629 6464 **f** 020 7355 1084 **m** 07836 249607
e vo@crawfords.tv **w** www.crawfords.tv
Contact Nicholas Young, Director

Talking Heads - The Voice Agency

88-90 Crawford Street, London W1H 2BS
t 020 7258 6161 **f** 020 7258 6162
e voices@talkingheadsvoices.com

foreignvoices.co.uk

Translations To Picture

24 Hawgood Street, London E3 3RU
t 020 7517 3550 **f** 020 7537 2839 **m** 07956 577668
e info@foreignvoices.co.uk **w** www.foreignvoices.co.uk
Contact Susan Cunningham, Production Assistant; James Bonallack, Director

*A one stop shop for timed translations, foreign voices in 25 languages —
listen to them now at www.foreignvoices.co.uk, subtitling and our in-
house Sadie suite from £60 per hour to picture.*

The Voice Box

PO Box 82, Altrincham WA15 0QD
t 01619 283222 **e** vb@thevoicebox.co.uk
Contact Vicki Hope-Robinson, Managing Director

Voice Shop

Bakerloo Chambers, 304 Edgware Road, London W2 1DY
t 020 7402 3966 **f** 020 7706 1002
e info@voice-shop.co.uk **w** www.voice-shop.co.uk
Contact Maxine Wiltshire; Susie ; Debby Sofidiya

Voice Squad

62 Blenheim Gardens, London NW2 4NT
t 020 8450 4451 **f** 020 8452 7944
e voices@voicesquad.com **w** www.voicesquad.com
Contact Neil Conrich, Director

VSI
Aradco House, 132 Cleveland Street, London W1T 6AB
t 020 7692 7700 **t** 020 7692 7702 **f** 020 7692 7711
e info@vsi.tv **w** www.vsi.tv
Contact Norman Dawood, Director; Carla Mercer, PA to Managing Director;
Virginie Verdier, Head of Subtitling; Jenny Morris, Head of Voice-Overs; Lola
Smith, Project Manager
Credits National Geographic - Africa (D); Heineken (C); What Lies Beneath (F)

Agents Writers

The Agency (London) Ltd
24 Pottery Lane, Holland Park, London W11 4LZ
t 020 7727 1346 **f** 020 7727 9037 **e** info@theagency.co.uk

Alan Brodie Representation
211 Piccadilly, London W1J 9HF
t 020 7917 2871 **f** 020 7917 2872
e info@alanbrodie.com **w** www.alanbrodie.com
Contact Alan Brodie

Alexandra Cann Representation
12 Abingdon Road, London W8 6AF
t 020 7938 4002 **f** 020 7938 4228
e enquiries@alexandracann.com

Andrew Mann Ltd
1 Old Compton Street, London W1D 5JA
t 020 7734 4751 **f** 020 7287 9264 **e** manscript@onetel.net.uk
Contact Anne Dewe, Literary Agent; Sacha Elliot, Literary Agent; Tina Betts,
Literary Agent

Blake Friedmann Literary, Film+TV Agency Ltd
122 Arlington Road, London NW1 7HP
t 020 7284 0408 **f** 020 7284 0442 **e** julian@blakefriedman.co.uk
Contact Julian Friedmann, Joint Managing Director

Francesca Bossert-Vecchi
Brie Burkeman, 14 Neville Court, Abbey Road, London NW8 9DD
t 07092 239113 **f** 07092 239111 **e** brie.burkeman@mail.com

Brie Burkeman
14 Neville Court, Abbey Road, London NW8 9DD
t 0709 223 9113 **f** 0709 223 9111 **e** brie.burkeman@mail.com

Casarotto Ramsay & Associates Ltd
National House, 60-66 Wardour Street, London W1V 4ND
t 020 7287 4450 **f** 020 7287 9128
e agents@casarotto.uk.com **w** www.casarotto.uk.com
Contact Tracey Hyde; Charlotte Kelly; Mel Kenyon; Jenne Casarotto; Jodi Shields;
Joe Phillips; Giorgio Casarotto, Managing Director

Culverhouse & James Personal Management
Shepperton Studios, Studio Road, Shepperton TW17 0QD
t 01932 592151 **f** 01932 592233
e dculverhouse@onetel.net.uk **e** jilljames4@aol.com
Contact Diane Culverhouse, Personal Manager; Jill James, Literary Agent

Darley Anderson Literary TV & Film Agency
Estelle House, 11 Eustace Road, London SW6 1JB
t 020 7385 6652 **f** 020 7386 5571
e darley.anderson@virgin.net

Futerman Rose & Associates
Heston Court Business Park, Wimbledon, London SW19 4UW
t 020 8947 0188 **f** 020 8605 2162
e guy@futermanrose.co.uk **w** www.futermanrose.co.uk
Contact Guy Rose

M Steinberg Playwrights
4th Floor, 104 Great Portland Street, London W1W 6PE
t 020 7631 1310 **f** 020 7631 1146 **e** info@steinplays.com

Macnaughton Lord 2000 Ltd
Douglas House, 19 Margvavine Gardens, London W6 8RL
t 020 7834 4646 **f** 020 7834 4949
e info@ml2000.org.uk **w** www.ml2000.org.uk

MBA Literary Agents Ltd
62 Grafton Way, London W1T 5DW
t 020 7387 2076 **f** 020 7387 2042 **e** firstname@mbalit.co.uk
Contact Diana Tyler, Managing Director; Meg Davis, Agent; Jean Kitson, Agent

Micheline Steinberg Playwrights
409 Triumph House, 187-191 Regent Street, London W1R 7WF
t 020 7287 4383 **e** steinplays@aol.com
Contact Michelline Steinberg, Managing Director

Michelle Kass Associates
36-38 Glasshouse Street, London W1B 5DL
t 020 7439 1624 **f** 020 7734 3394
Contact Michelle Kass

Real Creatives Worldwide
14 Dean Street, London W1D 3RS
t 020 7437 4188 **f** 020 7437 4221 **e** realcreate@aol.com
Contact Mark Macho

Rochelle Stevens & Company
2 Terretts Place, Upper Street, London N1 1QZ
t 020 7359 3900 **f** 020 7354 5729 **e** info@rochellestsvens.com

The Script Development Company Ltd
Fleet House, 173 Haydons Road, London SW19 8TB
t 020 8477 5438 **f** 020 8395 9988
e iqtadarhasnain@scriptdevelopment.co.uk
w www.scriptdevelopment.co.uk
Contact Iqtadar Hasnain; John Wilson

The Sharland Organisation Ltd
The Manor House, Manor Street, Raunds NN9 6JW
t 01933 626600 **f** 01933 624860 **e** tsoshar@aol.com
Contact Mike Sharland, Managing Director; Alice Sharland, Director

Sheil Land Associates Ltd
43 Doughty Street, London WC1N 2LH
t 020 7405 9351 **f** 020 7831 2127 **e** info@sheilland.co.uk
Contact John Rush

William Morris Agency (UK)
52-53 Poland Street, London W1F 7LX
t 020 7534 6800 **f** 020 7534 6900
Contact Stephanie Cabot, Managing Director

ANIMALS

A-Z Animals
The Bell House, Bell Lane, Fetcham KT22 9ND
t 01372 377111 **f** 01372 377666 **m** 07836 721288
e xl@a-zanimals.com **w** www.a-zanimals.com
Contact Gerry Cott, Managing Director
Credits Uniqlo (C); Abbey National (C); 28 Days Later (F)

A-Z Dogs
The Bell House, Bell Lane, Fetcham KT22 9ND
t 01372 377111 **f** 01372 377666 **m** 07836 721288
e xl@a-zanimals.com **w** www.a-zanimals.com
Contact Gerry Cott, Proprietor

A1 Animals
Folly Farm, Folly Lane, Bramley, Tadley RG26 5BD
t 01256 880993 **f** 01256 880653 **m** 07860 416545
e info@a1animals.freeserve.co.uk **w** www.a1animals.co.uk
Contact Elizabeth Thornton, Producer

AAA Alternative Animals
28 Greaves Road, High Wycombe HP13 7SU
t 01494 442750 **t** 01494 441385
f 01494 448710 **m** 07956 564715
e animalworld@bushinternet.com **w** www.animalworld.org.uk
Contact Carol Jones, Manager
Credits Luminal (F); Harry Enfield (T); Alice Cooper (M); Centre Parcs (C)

Actadog (SAP Dog Training)
Potterbyers, Pelton Farm, Pelton, Chester-le-Street DH2 1LX
t 0191 370 2305 **f** 0191 370 2305 **m** 07850 348761
Contact Sue Potter, Managing Director/Proprietor
Credits Black And White (C); Enemy At The Gates (F); Winalot Prime (C); Purely Belter (F)

Amazing Animals
Haythorpe Zoological Gardens Ltd, Heythrop,
Chipping Norton OX7 5TU
t 01608 683389 **f** 01608 683420
e info@amazinganimals.co.uk **w** www.amazinganimals.co.uk

Animal Acting Agency
15 Wolstenvale Close, Middleton, Manchester M24 2HP
t 0800 387755 **f** 0161 655 3700 **m** 07831 800 567
e information@animalacting.com **w** www.animalacting.com
Contact Wayne Docksey, Managing Director
Credits The Bridget Jones Diary (T); About A Boy (F); 28 Days Later (F)

Animal Actors
2 Hillingdon Avenue, Stanwell, Staines TW19 7AG
t 020 8654 0450

Animal Ambassadors
Old Forest, Hampstead Norrey's Road, Hermitage, Thatcham RG18 9SA
t 01635 200900 **f** 01635 200900 **m** 07831 558594
e kayweston@tiscali.co.uk
Contact Kay Weston

Animal Ark
29 Somerset Road, Brentford TW8 8BG
t 020 8560 3029 **f** 020 8560 5762 **m** 07957 846425
e info@animal-ark.co.uk **w** www.animal-ark.co.uk
Contact Jenny Seymour, Manager; David Manning, Proprietor
Credits Nicholas Nickleby (T); Badly Drawn Boy: Spitting in the Wind (M); BT - Broadband (C); About A Boy (F)

Animal Consultants & Trainers Association
Warwick House, 181-183 Warwick Road, London W14 8PU
t 020 7244 6999 **f** 020 7370 2823 **w** www.acta4animals.com

Animal Fair
17 Abingdon Road, London W8 6AH
t 020 7937 0011
Contact Colin Thorpe, Manager

Animal House
8 Burcott Close, Bierton, Aylesbury HP22 5DH
m 07973 155671
Contact Nigel Skeet, Proprietor

Animal Promotions
White Rocks Farm, Underriver, Sevenoaks TN15 0SL
t 01732 762913 **f** 01732 763767 **m** 07778 156513
e happyhoundsschool@yahoo.com
Contact Sue Woods, Proprietor
Credits With Nature (T); Basil Brush (T); Brilliant Creatures (T); Thompson's Directory (C)

Animal World
19 Greaves Road, High Wycombe HP13 7JU
t 01494 442750 **t** 01494 448710
f 01494 441385 **m** 07956 564 715
e animalworld@bushinternet.com **w** www.animalworld.org.uk
Contact Trevor Smith, Managing Director
Credits Twinfants (F); So Graham Norton (T); Westlife Horse (M); Esso Tigers (C)

Animals & Birds @ Parrot & Seal
Mill Farm, Hurst Green, Brightlingsea, Colchester CQ7 0EH
t 01653 668371 **t** 01206 302346
f 01653 668541 **f** 01206 304838 **m** 07774 625321
e parrotandseal@hotmail.com **w** www.parrotandseal.com
Contact Peter Bloom, Partner
Credits People vs Animals (Pilot) (T); Eureka TV (T); Mr Bean (T); Down To Earth (T)

Animals Galore
208 Smallfield Road, Horley RH6 9LS
t 01342 842400 **f** 01342 841546 **m** 07850 870 884
e info@animals-galore.co.uk **w** www.animals-galore.co.uk
Contact Cindy Newman, Managing Director

Animals O Kay
3 Queen Street, Chipperfield WD4 9BT
t 01923 291277 **f** 01923 269076 **m** 07831 305793
e kay@animalsokay.com

Animals On Blue Ltd
Montrose House, 38 Fitzjohns Avenue, London NW3 5NB
t 020 7794 3145 **f** 020 7794 5898 **m** 07798 822524
e fk@animalsonblue.com **w** www.animalsonblue.com
Contact Farokh Kherooshi, Producer/Director
Credits Mercedes (C); NesQuick (C); Johnson And Johnson (C); Samsung (C)

Aquarep
East Lodge, Heythrop, Chipping Norton OX7 5TU
t 01608 683389 **f** 01608 683420 **m** 07860 432408
e jclubb@amazinganimals.co.uk **w** www.amazinganimals.co.uk
Contact James Clubb, Director
Credits Lost in Space (F); Twelve Monkeys (F)

The Aquatic Design Centre Ltd
107-111 Great Portland Street, London W1W 6QG
t 020 7636 6388 **f** 020 7323 4305
e nick@aquaticdesign.co.uk **w** www.aquaticdesign.co.uk
Contact Nicholas Lloyd

Asoka Horse Stud
Barbrook Farm, Rock Bank, 278 Leigh Road, Worsley M28 1LH
t 0161 790 4186 **e** peggy@asokaclassicalstud.co.uk
w www.asokaclassicalstud.co.uk
Contact Margaret Litton, Managing Director

Batwatch
8 Mostyn Avenue, Lower Heswall, Wirral CH60 9LA
t 0151 342 7708
Contact Fiona Angwin, Co-Director

animals in entertainment

The HSE has produced the following guidelines for producers working with animals. In this information sheet 'must' denotes a legal obligation. Words such as 'do', 'should' etc are used to give advice on good practice.

This information was prepared by the Joint Advisory Committee for Broadcasting and Performing Arts. It gives specific advice for production activities involving animals, on stage or in a studio or on location, with or without an audience.

The work may involve putting animals in strange situations, getting them to do things for the purposes of the production, or simply recording what they do in nature.

Consideration should also be given to situations where animals may be present although they are not part of the script, eg location work in sewers.

While this information is primarily concerned with the health and safety of those who work with animals, consideration should always be given to the welfare of the animals themselves.

It should be noted that The Dangerous Wild Animals Act 1976 (enforced by the Local Authority) requires persons keeping specified animals to hold a licence, and there are many other legal requirements affecting work with animals - take expert advice.

Hazards

'Animals' include birds, reptiles, fish, insects, spiders and many other species. Two apparently similar animals can present very different hazards - venomous and non-venomous snakes for example, or domestic and feral cats.

Animals can cause injury, by bites, scratches, stings, kicking or crushing; infection or infestation from micro-organisms or parasites they carry; allergy, in some people.

Some people have phobias about particular kinds of animals - extreme fears about spiders or snakes, for example.

Many veterinary products are hazardous to human health. Hazards may also arise from hay or straw used in connection with an animal, eg. fire, soiled materials, dust, allergies.

Risk assessment

Assessments are required by: The Management of Health and Safety at Work Regulations 1992. These require a risk assessment to be carried out for all work activities. This must include the measures that are to be taken to control the significant risks that are identified.

The Control of Substances Hazardous to Health Regulations 1994 (COSHH). These require that risks of infection and allergy be assessed and adequately controlled. Veterinary products may have an Occupational Exposure Standard (OES) under these Regulations.

Unless you have expertise, the advice of a competent person may be necessary when completing the assessments. The best source of advice is likely to be the owner, handler, trainer or keeper, since that person will understand the character of the animals that are to be used. Handlers etc may, however, underestimate the risks because of their familiarity with the animals. If there is no one directly responsible for the animals, veterinary surgeons, zoos or university departments may be able to advise.

Some animals may seem to present a negligible risk - domestic cats, rabbits and guinea pigs for example. 'Tame' or 'semi-tame' animals may, however, still cause injuries - people expect them to be safe, and the animals have less fear of people.

The main points to consider in the risk assessment are:

a   What hazards does the animal present, ie. what harm could it cause?

b   What contact will there be with the animal? If there is no possibility of contact the risk of physical injury is low. There may still, however, be a health risk, eg of Leptospirosis which can be contracted from surfaces contaminated with rat urine;

c   By what routes can any micro-organisms be transmitted to humans, eg hand to mouth contact, bites, scratches, or through the air?

d   All animals (alive or dead) should be regarded as likely sources of infection or infestation. This includes those kept as pets and most laboratory animals. The most dangerous in this respect are those closest to humans in the evolutionary scale, ie other primates.

e   What influence will you have on the animal? For example, filming quietly from a hidden position is less dangerous than arranging a stunt in which the animal is required to do something it does not like;

f   How much contact will there be? Working from a distance is safer than holding an animal in your hand. Getting very close to wild or large animals may require a more detailed assessment of risks;

g   Who is exposed? A fit and healthy technician may be able to escape when children or elderly people cannot. Do any of those involved have allergies or phobias? Are any pregnant workers involved in the project?

h   What other animals may be present?

i   What could go wrong? Is it possible that the tame rat will bite the performer? If wild animals turn on you, can you defend yourself? Could the animal escape into the studio or theatre?

j   Is there an audience that could come into contact with the animal?

→→

→→→ **animals** in entertainment

Precautionary measures

In most cases expert advice will be needed about the specifics of the production but there are some basic points to consider:

Where practicable, risks should be eliminated or minimised, eg by selecting animals which present least risk, or by containing or restricting the animal.

People should always be told in advance if they are to work with animals so they have an opportunity to say if they have allergies or phobias.

Obtaining performing animals from a reputable handler should reduce the risks of the animal carrying disease.

Everyone involved should be properly briefed on risks and control measures, eg feeding arrangements or instructions not to feed, the need to avoid disturbance, and what to do in an emergency.

Animals can cause infections that threaten pregnancy. In particular, pregnant women should not enter areas in which mammals have recently given birth.

You may need to have a minimum number of people to manage an animal, but everyone else should be kept well clear.

Animals can be provoked to attack by disturbance or discomfort. Take advice about the animal's needs, provide food, water and suitable temperature. It may be necessary for the animal to be held in a quiet place until it is needed.

Keep the length of time animals are required to a minimum. Rehearse the item last and perform it first where possible. If a retake is necessary do this straight away. A tired animal may become fractious.

Material such as hay or straw used in studios or on stage is usually fireproofed or fire-retarded. However, this would be toxic for animals and arrangements may have to be made for untreated material with alternative fire precautions.

In order to minimise risk, animals should be handled no more than necessary and always with at least basic hygiene - wash afterwards, and especially before meals. Protective clothing such as gloves and overalls may be required. When bites and scratches can be expected it may be necessary to ensure that those exposed have adequate immunity to tetanus - seek advice.

Make provision for first aid. Unless they are life-threatening, bites and scratches should be encouraged to bleed, washed with clean water and dressed. The casualty should then have medical attention. Where there is the possibility of exposure at a distance from medical facilities, specific antidotes may be required for hazards such as snake bites, but this option should be considered carefully.

With thanks to HSE for supplying this information.

Blewbury Riding & Training Centre
Bessels Way, Blewbury OX11 9NH
t 01235 851016 **f** 01235 851016 **m** 07809 040914
e blewburycentre@tiscali.co.uk
Contact Jane Dexter

The British School of Falconry at Gleneagles
The Gleneagles Hotel, Auchterarder PH3 1NF
t 01764 694347 **f** 01764 664345 **w** www.gleneagles.com
Contact Emma Ford, Director

Butterfly World
Preston Park, Yarm Road, Stockton-on-Tees TS18 3RH
t 01642 791414
Contact Mrs Welsh, Manager

Cindy Morris & Company
Ty Coch Farm, Penmachno LL25 0HJ
t 01690 760248 **t** 07885 313455 **f** 01690 760248
m 07759 134329 **e** tycoch@amserve.net
Contact Cindy Morris, Director
Credits Willow (F); First Knight (F); Lesley Garret - The Singer (M); Robin Hood (F)

Classic Horsedrawn Carriages
Valley Farm, Valley LL65 3LF
t 01407 741800 **f** 01407 741800 **m** 07050 273070 **e** classiccarriages@freezone.co.uk **w** www.horsedrawn.co.uk
Contact Sue Buckingham, Manager
Credits The Proposition (F); August (F); Merlin (F)

Pauline Clift
15 Gwendale, Maidenhead SL6 6SH
t 01628 788564 **f** 01628 788564 **m** 07808 724433
e paulineclift@lineone.net

Cnoc Animal Agency
Polygon Enterprises Ltd, Cnoc Lodge, Creagan, Appin PA38 4BQ
t 0131 557 8222 **f** 0131 558 3020 **m** 0788 7482039
e d_h_montgomery@compuserve.com **w** www.animaldirector.com
Contact Janet Montgomery, Director
Credits Baxter Soup (C); Glen Grant Whiskey (C); Para Handy (T)

Cotswold Farm Park
Guiting Power, Cheltenham GL54 5UG
t 01451 850307 **f** 01451 850423 **m** 07973 326503
e info@cotswoldfarmpark.co.uk
Contact Adam Henson , Partner

Creature Feature - The Scottish Animal Agency
Gubhill Farm, Forest of Ae, Dumfries DG1 1RL
t 01387 860648 **f** 01387 860369 **m** 07770 774866
w www.creaturefeature.co.uk

PD Cundell
Roden House, Compton, Newbury RG20 6QR
t 01635 578267 **f** 01635 578267

Durham Wildlife Trust
Rainton Meadows, Chilton Moor, Houghton-le-Spring DH4 6PU
t 0191 584 3112 **f** 0191 584 3934
e durhamwt@cix.core.uk **w** www.wildlifetrust.org.uk/durham/

G&L Morton & Sons
Hasholme Carr Farm, Holme-on-Spalding-Moor, York YO43 4BD
t 01430 860393 **f** 01430 860057 **m** 07768 346 905
Contact Geoff Morton

Gill Raddings Stunt Dogs
Gill Raddings Stunt Dogs, 3 The Chestnuts, Clifton,
Deddington, Banbury OX15 0PE
t 01869 338546 **f** 01869 338546 **m** 07836 717 822
e gill@euro-stuntdogs.co.uk **w** www.euro-stuntdogs.co.uk
Contact Gill Raddings

Hayden Webb Carriages
Lambs Farm, Spencers Wood, Reading RG7 1PQ
t 0118 988 3334 **f** 0118 988 3334 **m** 07767 215404
Contact Hayden Webb, Proprietor

Heart of England Falconry
The Shakespeare Countryside Museum, Mary Arden's House,
Wilmcote, Stratford-upon-Avon CV37 9YA
t 01789 298365 **f** 01789 298365
e info@heartofenglandfalconry.co.uk
w www.heartofenglandfalconry.co.uk
Contact Stephen Wright; Richard Wall, Proprietor
Credits Lifesense - BBC Wildlife Unit (E); Cinderella (T); The Visitors (F);
Guiness (C)

James Mackie - Cavalry & Other Horses
Cownham Farm, Broadwell, Moreton-in-the-Marsh GL56 0TT
t 01451 830294 **f** 01451 832442 **m** 07860 533356

Janimals Ltd
25 Strathcona Avenue, Bookham KT23 4HW
t 013 7245 6969 **f** 013 7245 6232
Contact Liz Rutherford; Redi Neill, Director

Adrian O'Meara B.V.sc. M.R.C.V.s Veterinary Surgeon

Film
Television
Commercials

Surgery	Home	Mobile
020 8393 6049	020 8393 5428	07831 149680

North Lodge, 150 Kingston Road
Ewell Surrey KT17 2ET

For a Professional
Service on Set call... *Vetcetera*

Magri's Pets
205 Roman Road, London E2 0QY
t 020 8980 3822
Contact Andy Magri

Massey Shire & Carriage Horses
Brook Villa, Swineyard Lane, High Legh, Knutsford WA16 0SD
t 01925 753357 **m** 07836 514 970
Contact Judith Massey, Proprietor

National Birds of Prey Centre
Newent, Gloucester GL18 1JJ
t 0870 990 1992 **t** 01531 821581 **f** 01531 821389
e jpj@nbpc.demon.co.uk/katherine@nbpc.co.uk
w www.nbpc.co.uk
Contact Jemima Parry-Jones, Director; Katherine Hinton, Business Manager

Nigel Tate's Dogstars
4 Hoads Wood Gardens, Ashford TN25 4QB
t 01233 635439 **f** 07092 031929
e animals@dogstars.co.uk **w** www.dogstars.co.uk

Northumberland Wildlife Trust
The Garden House, St Nicholas Park, Jubilee Road,
Newscastle-upon-Tyne NE3 3XT
t 0191 284 6884 **f** 0191 284 6794
e mail@northwt.org.uk
w www.wildlifetrust.org.uk/northumberland
Contact Tom Andrews, Commercial Manager

Pili Palas
Fford Penmynydd, Menai Bridge LL59 5RP
t 01248 712474 **f** 01248 716518
Contact H Hughes, Partner

Prop Farm
Grange Farm, Elmton, Creswell S80 4LX
t 01909 723100 **f** 01909 721465 **m** 07836 373 322
e les@propfarm.free-online.co.uk
Contact Les Powell, Contact; Pat Ward, Managing Director
Credits At Home With The Braithwaites (T); Clocking Off (T); Where The Heart Is (T)

Raphael Falconry
35 Chichester Road, Halesworth IP19 8JL
t 01986 873928 **f** 01986 873928 **m** 07711 369805
e info@raphaelfalconry.com **w** www.raphaelfalconry.com
Contact Mike Raphael, Contact; Emma Raphael, Contact
Credits Warrior School (D); The Witchfinder General (D); Alan Partridge
Talks Back (T)

Rockwood Animals on Film
17 Lewis Terrace, Llanbradach CF83 3JZ
t 02920 885420 **m** 07973 930983
e rockwood@gxn.co.uk **w** www.rockwoodanimals.com
Contact Martin Winfield, Director; Ellen Winfield, Assistant Director
Credits Casualty (T); Teachers (T)

Rona Brown & Associates
9 King Lane Cottages, Over Wallop, Stockbridge SO20 8JF
t 01264 781804 **f** 01264 782471 **m** 07850 820086
e ronabrown@movie-animals.co.uk **w** www.movie-animals.co.uk
Contact Rona Brown
Credits Anna And The King (F); Daziel And Pascoe (T); My Hero (T);
Gorillas In The Mist (F)

Sue Clark Timbertops
Timbertops, Jackson Lane, Wentbridge WF8 3HZ
t 01977 620374 **f** 01977 621039 **m** 07718 675197
e timbertops@sue-clark.co.uk **w** www.sue-clark.co.uk
Contact Sue Clark, Proprietor
Credits Calender Girls (F); Gormenghast (S); Nice Guy Eddie (S); Mean Machine (W)

Tony Smart Special Action Horses

Parkview Stables, Maidenhead Road, Billingbear, Wokingham RG40 5RR
t 01344 424531 **f** 01344 360548 **m** 07710 604482
e tony@tonysmart.com **w** www.tonysmart.com
Contact Tony Smart
Credits Chariot Race (D); Guinness - Surfing Horses (C); Braveheart (F)

The UK Wolf Conservation Trust

The UK Wolf Centre, Butlers Farm, Beenham, Reading RG7 5NT
t 0118 971 3330 **f** 0118 971 3330
e ukwct@ukwolf.org **w** www.ukwolf.org
Contact Roger Palmer, Director

Vet On Set

Keanter, Stoke Charity Road, Kingsworthy, Winchester SO23 7LS
t 0870 243 0385 **f** 0870 243 0385 **m** 07836 217686
e pscott@zarg.co.uk
Contact Peter Scott
Credits Fierce Creatures (F); 102 Dalmatians (F); 101 Dalmatians (F)

Vetcetera

150 Kingston Road, Ewell, Epsom KT17 2ET
t 020 8716 6077 **f** 020 8393 5428 **m** 07831 149680
e omvs@yahoo.com
Contact Adrian O'Meara, Veterinary Surgeon

Welsh Bird Of Prey Centre

Manordeifi, Llechryd SA43 2PN
t 01239 682800 **m** 07771 573 950
e enquiries@welshbirdofpreycentre.co.uk
w www.welshbirdofpreycentre.co.uk
Contact Mike Wakeman, Partner

Welsh Mountain Zoo

Old Highway, Colwyn Bay LL28 5UY
t 01492 532938 **f** 01492 530498
e info@welshmountainzoo.org **w** www.welshmountainzoo.org
Contact Chris Jackson, Administration Director; Nick Jackson, Zoological Director

West Country Film Horses

St Leonard's Equitation Centre, Polson, Launceston PL15 9QR
t 01566 775543 **f** 01566 774926 **m** 07860 431225
Contact Andy Reeve

Wildfowl & Wetlands Trust

Pattinson, Washington NE38 8LE
t 0191 416 5454 **f** 0191 416 5801
e info@wwt.org.uk **w** www.washington.co.uk/wwt
Contact Chris Francis

Animatics/Animatronics

Animated Extras

12 Shepperton Studios, Studios Road, Shepperton TW17 0QD
t 01932 592347 **f** 01932 572342
e animated.extras@virgin.net **e** info@animate-extras.com
Contact Nick Williams, Partner; Daniel Parker, Partner; Pauline Fowler, Partner

BBC Special Effects

BBC Special Effects

Kendal Avenue, London W3 0RP
t 020 8993 9434 **f** 020 8993 8741 **e** special.effects@bbc.co.uk
w www.bbcresources.com/specialeffects

Crawley Creatures & Associates

Unit 22-23, Rabans Close, Aylesbury HP19 3RS
t 01296 336315 **f** 01296 339590
e jez@gibsonharris.freeserve.co.uk
w www.crawley-creatures.com
Credits Walking With Dinosaurs (A)

Animation/Computer Graphics/Motion Capture

3D Films

Plaza One, Telford Plaza, Ironmasters Way, Telford TF3 4NT
t 01952 208701 **f** 01952 208704
e enquires@3dfilms.co.uk **w** www.3dfilms.co.uk
Contact David Griffiths, Chief Executive

3D Graphics & Effects - Steven Bray

283A London Road, Greenhithe DA9 9DA
t 01322 386690 **m** 07957 976131
e stevenbray1@yahoo.co.uk **w** www.stevenbray1.com
Contact Steven Bray, Designer/Animator
Credits Visitor (T); Motion Picture House (I); Hill's (I); Walker's Crisps (I)

3D Imaging

12 Woodside Road, Simonstone, Burnley BB12 7JG
t 0870 740 9016 **f** 0870 131 5997 **m** 07879 682519
e info@3d-imaging.co.uk **w** www.3d-imaging.co.uk
Contact Geoff Hodbod, Creative Director
Credits Ribena (W)

422 South

St John's Court, Whiteladies Road, Bristol BS8 2QY
t 0117 946 7222 **f** 0117 946 7722
e debbiet@422.com **w** www.422.com
Contact Andy Davies-Coward, Chief Creative Officer; Craig Howarth, Managing Director; Debbie Taylor, Head of Business Development; Debbie Taylor, Head of Business Development; Peter Levy, Director Of Operations
Credits Plan DRTV (A); Life Of Mammals (T); A History Of Britain (T); The Blue Planet (T)

A for Animation

52 Old Market Street, Bristol BS2 0ER
t 0117 929 9005 **f** 0117 929 9004
e info@aproductions.co.uk **w** www.aproductions.co.uk

A Productions Ltd

52 Old Market Street, Bristol BS2 0ER
t +44 117 929 9005 **f** +44 117 929 9004
e info@aproductions.co.uk **w** www.aproductions.co.uk
Credits Candle Power

Aardman Animations

Gas Ferry Road, Bristol BS1 6UN
t 0117 984 8485 **f** 0117 984 8486
e 1stname.surname@aardman.com **w** www.aardman.com
Contact Liz Keynes, Executive Producer/Development & Sales; Heather Wright, Head of Production
Credits Chicken Run (A); Angry Kid (A); Rex The Runt (A); Wallace And Gromit (A)

Acme Graphics

2 Park Street, Teddington TW11 0LT
t 020 8395 5130 **f** 020 8395 5129 **e** info@acmegraphics.co.uk

Alias/Wavefront

1 Newmans Row, Lincoln's Inn, Lincoln Road, High Wycombe HP12 3RE
t 01494 441273 **f** 01494 444867
e infouk@aw.sgi.com **w** www.aliaswavefront.com
Contact Richard Love, Marketing Manager; Stephanie Meli, PR&Fvents Co-ordinator; Jane Bryan, Education, Consulting&Training; Jodie Wright, Sales Information

Ambit New Media Ltd

Horatio House, Horatio Street, Quayside, Newcastle-upon-Tyne NE1 2PE
t 0191 232 8882 **f** 0191 230 2346
e info@ambitnewmedia.com **w** www.ambitnewmedia.com

Animage Films Ltd

67 Farringdon Road, London EC1M 3JB
t 020 7831 9209 **f** 020 7831 9226
e mail@animagefilms.com **w** www.animagefilms.com
Contact Richard Burdett, Director; Ruth Beni, Director

Animation Partnership

13-14 Golden Square, London W1F 9JF
t 020 7636 3300 **f** 020 7580 9153 **m** 07785 302298
e carl@animationpartnership.co.uk
Contact David Parvin, Animation Director; Carl Gover, Executive Producer, Producer, Producer/Managing Director; Carl Gover, Managing Director/Producer
Credits Adventures Of Jackie Chan (A); Banquet - Wrigley's (A); Milltimes (A); Sharp - Strepsils (A)

Probably Europe's most well-known one-stop studio for quality 2D/3D animation.

Anthropics Technology Ltd

Unit 1, 1 Walpole Court, Ealing Studios, Ealing Green, London W5 5ED
t 020 8758 8619 **f** 020 8758 8619
e info@anthropics.com **w** www.anthropics.com
Contact Matt Minor, Production Director

Arcana Digital

Garrard House, 2-6 Homesdale Road, Bromley BR2 9LZ
t 020 8466 0655 **f** 020 8466 6610
e info@arcanadigital.com **w** www.arcanadigital.com
Contact John Fox

Architech Animation Studios

25 Baron Taylor's Street, Inverness IV1 1QG
t 01463 222201 **f** 01408 622099 **m** 07770 746416
e info@architechav.com **w** www.architechav.com
Contact Alan Macdonald, Director
Credits The Way Ahead - KCRC (Hong Kong) (A); Final Phase - KPF Sun Hung Kai (Hong Kong) (A)

Pioneering company in visualisation techniques, 3D animation and image compositing. Specialists in technical, scientific, environmental, historical and architectural projects. Full in-house production facilities including 1:1 Avid Composer editing suite.

AudioMotion Ltd

e info@audiomotion.com **w** www.audiomotion.com
Contact Mick Morris, MD; Bryan Mitchell, Operations Director
Credits Enemy At The Gate (F); UEFA Champions League (T); Gladiator (F); Rock DJ (M)

AVIDFX Ltd

12 Eric Wilkins House, Avondale Square Estate, Old Kent Road, London SE1 5ES
t +44 20 7237 7317 **f** +44 20 7237 7317 **m** 07950 285493
e avidfx@avidfx.co.uk **w** www.avidfx.co.uk
Contact Jibro Isaac, Design Manager; Willy Mutzir, Art Director

BBC Design

Broadcasting House, Whiteladies Road, Clifton BS8 2LR
t 0117 974 2175 **f** 0117 946 7741
Contact James Hall, Senior Group Designer
Credits BBC Choice: Sin Bin

BBC Post Production

BBC Post Production
(Sites across London, Bristol & Birmingham)

5550 Television Centre, Wood Lane, London W12 7RJ
t 020 8225 7702 (London) **t** 0117 9746 666 (Bristol)
t 0121 432 8621 (Birmingham)
w www.bbcresources.com/postproduction

Bermuda Shorts

1 Lower John Street, London W1F 9DT
t 020 7437 7335 **f** 020 7437 7334
e info@bermudashorts.com **w** www.bermudashorts.com
Contact Lisa Hill, Producer; Julie Pye, Managing Director; Trevor Murphy, Director; Sam Hope, Producer; Emma Cooke, Producer
Credits Death In Vegas (M); Pepsi (C); Badly Drawn Boy (M); Budweiser (C)

Bernard Heyes Design

7 Meard Street, London W1F 0EW
t 020 7287 0202 **f** 020 7434 9334 **m** 07860 369781
e bernardheyes@btconnect.com
Contact Bernard Heyes, Creative Director
Credits The Real ER (A); Coupling (A); Parkinson (A); Sahara With Michael Palin (A)

Blazkho

49-50 Eagle Wharf Road, London N1 7ED
t +44 20 7608 2939 **f** +44 20 7608 2979
e ask@blazkho.com **w** www.blazkho.com
Contact Andrew Stanning, Producer

Blue-Zoo

18 Rupert Street, London W1D 6DE
t 020 7434 4111 **e** adam@blue-zoo.co.uk **w** www.blue-zoo.co.uk
Contact Tom Box, Technical Director; Adam Shaw, Director; Oli Hyatt, Creative Director
Credits Simons Heroes (D); Curriculum English - Todd And Blod (E); Disney - Toon Disney Rebrand (T); The Story Makers - Blue Cow (A)

Box

5th Floor, 121 Princess Street, Manchester M1 7AD
t 0161 228 2399 **f** 0161 228 2399 **m** 07944 44606
e mike@the-box.co.uk **w** www.the-box.co.uk
Contact Michael Kirwin, Director; Jeremy Hogg, Creative Director
Credits The Day That Shook The World (C); Esure (C); DB Boulevard - Point Of View (M)

Brandt Animation

11 D'Arblay Street, London W1F 8DT
t 020 7734 0196 **e** finn@brandtanim.co.uk
w www.brandtanim.co.uk
Contact Finn Brandt, Creative Director
Credits BDO International (A); Opera Babes (C)

Cambridge Animation Systems

Wellington House, East Road, Cambridge CB1 1BH
t 01223 451048 **f** 01223 451145
e sales@cambridgeanimation.com
w www.cambridgeanimation.com
Contact Naomi English, Global Sales Manager

Capital Studios

Wandsworth Plain, London SW18 1ET
t 020 8877 1234 **f** 020 8877 0234
e info@capitalstudios.com **w** www.capitalstudios.com
Contact Bobbi Johnstone, Contact; Clare Phillips, Contact
Fully equipped digital broadcast studios: 3000 sq ft (60x50x19.5) and 2000 sq ft (50x50x19.5). Supported by galleries, dressing rooms, wardrobe, green room and audience facilities. Tx lines, Cafe with courtyard garden. New digital Post-Production facilities.

Carl Gover Animation

13-14 Golden Square, London W1F 9JF
t 020 7636 3300 **f** 020 7580 9153 **m** 07785 302298
e carl@animationpartnership.co.uk
Contact Carl Gover, Producer/Managing Director
Credits The Universe In A Nutshell (D)

Celaction

PO Box LB608, London W1A 9LB
t 020 7226 3649 **f** 020 7354 8868
e info@celaction.com **w** www.celaction.com
Contact Andy Blazdell
Credits Yoko! Jakamoko! Toto! (A); Big Knights (T); 2DTV (T)

Cine Wessex Ltd

Westway House, 19 St Thomas Street, Winchester SO23 9HJ
t 01962 865454 **f** 01962 842017
e nick@cinewessex.co.uk **w** www.cinewessex.co.uk
Contact Jeny Cave-Penney; Nick Frampton; Ema Branton; Ema Branton; Jeny Cave-Penney, Post Production Manager

Clockwork Digital

Studio A, 14 Lilian Road, London SW16 5HN
t 020 8679 3677 **m** 07736 383612
e richard@clockworkdigital.com **w** www.clockworkdigital.com
Contact Richard Rickitt, Managing Director
Credits Thunder Races (T); Big Dig (T); Sunken Kingdoms Of The Ice Age (D); Tweenies (T)

The Consortium of Gentlemen Ltd

27 Beethoven Street, London W10 4LG
t 020 8964 0234 **f** 020 8968 7710
e mail@cogonline.co.uk **w** www.cogonline.co.uk
Contact Julian Roberts, Producer; Mark Slater, Director; Simi Mougne, Production Manager; Mole Hill, Director
Credits PB Bear And Friends (T); Yoho Ahoy (T)

Creative TV Facilities Ltd

92 New Cavendish Street, London W1N 7FA
t 020 7224 4281 **f** 020 7935 5847
e office@creativetvfacilities.com **w** www.creativetvfacilities.com
Contact Steve Breeze, Director; Sue Francis, Director
Credits Empire (T); Time Team (T); Horizon (D); Meet The Ancestors (T)

Eye

Kirkman House, 12-14 Whitfield Street, London W1T 2RF
t 020 7436 5540 **f** 020 7436 5541
e enquiries@eye-animation.com **w** www.eye-animation.com
Contact Ian Bird, Managing Director; Amy Robson, Producer; Stephanie Cleak, Managing Director
Credits Vauxhall (C); KFC (C); Boohbah (A)

Field Of Vision

The Bryn, Stoke Prior, Leominster HR6 0LG
t 01568 760545
e mail@fieldofvision.co.uk **w** www.fieldofvision.co.uk
Contact Tim Coupland, Partner

Fotomotion

Vahljon, Green Lane, Stanmore HA7 3AB
t 020 8954 4696 **f** 020 8954 7705 **m** 07796 612883
e info@fotomotion.net **w** www.fotomotion.net
Contact Jonathan Highman; Alex Highman

Goldcrest Post Production Facilities

36-44 Brewer Street, London W1F 9LX
t 020 7437 7972 **f** 020 7437 5402 **m** 07836 204283
e mailbox@goldcrest-post.co.uk
Contact Poppy Quinn, Bookings and Customer Services Manager; Raju Raymond, General Manager

Griffilms (CYF) Ltd

Gronant, Penrallt Isaf, Caernarfon LL55 1NS
t 01286 676678 **f** 01286 676577
e mail@griffilms.com **w** www.griffilms.com
Contact Dylan Jones, Producer; Hywel Griffith, Managing Director
Credits Jack The Rubber (A); The Big Snow (A); Bibi (A); Bubz (A)

Gritt Design

9 Cornerstone, Woodbridge Road, Moseley, Birmingham B13 9EN
t 0121 258 7770 **f** 0121 258 7771
e info@gritt.com **w** www.gritt.com
Contact John Griffiths, Creative Director
Credits JB Group Ltd (A); Homeofficehomes.com (W); The Entertainer - Toy Store (A); Western Corn Ltd (A)

Halcyon Designs

25 Cortayne Road, London SW6 3QA
t 020 7736 8744 **f** 020 7736 8407
e halcyon@dial.pipex.com **w** www.halcyondesigns.com
Contact Fabrice Le Roux, Contact
Credits SAS In-Flight Video (I); Grand Designs (T); Lost Gardens (T)

Birgitta Hosea

2 Mansfield Court, Laburnum Street, London E2 8BL
t 020 7256 1307 **f** 020 7256 1307 **m** 07769 701495
e b@studiovenus.co.uk **w** www.studiovenus.co.uk
Credits 90 (S); Virus (S); Adobe (C); Nickelodeon (C)

Keyframe Computer Graphics

Unity Court, 431 Meanwood Road, Leeds LS7 2LL
t 0113 246 5913 **f** 0113 234 0038
e info@keyframe.co.uk **w** www.keyframe.co.uk
Contact Helen Simpson, Production Manager

Lane Fabian-Jones Productions Ltd

Studio 70, Shepperton Studios, Studio Road, Shepperton TW17 0QD
t 01932 592309 **e** mfj@dial.pipex.com
Credits Tango (C); Kickin & Pickin (C)

London Post

34-35 Dean Street, London W1D 4PR
t 020 7439 9080 **f** 020 7434 0714
e info@londonpost.co.uk **w** www.londonpost.co.uk
Contact Soraya Robertson, Bookings Manager; Verity Laing

Rod Lord

Old Lodge Farm, Coningsby Lane, Fifield SL6 2PF
t 01628 627032 **e** rod@rodlord.com **w** www.rodlord.com
Credits A400M The Versatile Airlifter (A)

Lynx Digital Ltd

The Barn, Court Farm, Denham Village UB9 5BG
t 01895 834433 **f** 01895 834933 **w** www.lynxdigital.tv
Contact Emma Goodall, Sales/Marketing Manager; Jeremy Pinner, General Manager; Kunle Barker, Business Development Manager

M2 Television

Ingestre Court, Ingestre Place, London W1F 0JL
t 020 7343 6543 **f** 020 7343 6555
e info@m2tv.com **w** www.m2tv.com
The Forum, 74-80 Camden Street, London, NW1 0EG
t 020 7343 6789 **f** 020 7343 6777
Contact Kabir Malik; Jennie Jones

Based in Soho and Camden, we offer a full range of video and audio post production as well as the award-winning co:de design. 5 digital online suites, 5 Editbox FX online suites, 2 Symphony online suites, Avid unity server, Clipbox video server, 14 Avid offline, 5 digital audio suites, Hal, and Illusion.

Mac Million

61 Gray's Inn Road, London WC1X 8LT
t 020 7831 5357 **f** 020 7404 6872
e info@macmillion.com **w** www.macmillion.com
Contact Mads Nybo Jorgensen, Managing Director
Credits The Ride (F); Hard Talk (T); Tonight With Trevor MacDonald (T)

Maddogs Animation

19 Deansway, Trenthady, Stoke on Trent ST4 8DD
t 01782 641292 **f** 01782 658529
e production@maddogsanimation.com
w www.maddogsanimation.com
Contact Shaun Magher, Director; Tony Jopia, Producer; Adam Cootes, Director

Magnesium Films

109 Cavendish Road, Highams Park, London E4 9NG
m 07973 389088 **e** magnesium_films@hotmail.com
Contact Paul Woodford, Head Of Animation
Credits Bad Lad Space Pirates (A); Yeast Extract (A)

Melendez Films

Julia House, 44 Newman Street, London W1T 1QD
t 020 7323 5273 **e** StevenMelendez@compuserve.com
Contact Dick Horn, Animation Director; Kaj Melendez, Technical Director (3D); Steve Melendez, Director/Producer; Javed Baig, Head of Design
Credits Babe 100 (T); Safari Joe (W); Genesis - Dance (C); Jasper (T)

MGB Facilities Ltd

Sheepscar Court, Leeds LS7 2BB
t 0113 243 6868 **f** 0113 243 8886
e contact@mgbtv.co.uk **w** www.mgbtv.co.uk

Contact Mike Gaunt, Managing Director; Elaine Wigglesworth, Facility Manager
Credits Quick Grip (I); Sport On Five (T); Hasbro (W); BUPA (C)

Minds Eye Productions Ltd

Westfalia House, Old Wolverton Road, Milton Keynes MK12 5PY
t 01908 318315 **f** 01908 316855 **m** 07764 241571
e info@minds-eye.net **w** www.minds-eye.net

Contact Martin Batten, Managing Director; Stu Middleton, Technical Director

Molinare

34 Fouberts Place, London W1F 7PX
t 020 7478 7000 **f** 020 7478 7199
e bookings@molinare.co.uk **w** www.molinare.co.uk

Contact Kate George, Facilities Manager
Credits Dorada Especial: Painting; AXN: Cornice; Walkers Dorito's: Idents; The Wind

For 30 years Molinare has been offering the best in Post Production, helping the best people make the best programmes, we have about the widest selection of facilities in one location in the industry. Based in the heart of Soho, we offer, 5 digital Online Suites, Editbox FX V8, Ursa Gold Telecine, High Definition Online, 10 Avid Offline suites and 2 Avid Online suites, 5 Audio Dubbing suites with voice over booths, Tracklay, Discreet Flint, Media Illusion, Drive in 1500 sq ft Video studio, 400 sq ft Virtual Studio, Duplication, Transmission Services, as well as the Molinare Design team for all your branding and design needs.

Oliver Murray

46 Ferme Park Road, London N4 4ED
m 07932 674657 **e** oliver.murray@lycos.com

Credits Boo For Tell-Tale Productions (I)

Nats Post Production

10 Soho Square, London W1D 3NT
t 020 7287 9900 **f** 020 7287 8636 **e** bookings@nats.ltd.uk

Contact Sara Hill, Bookings; Jo Manser; Louise Knight; Louise Thomas

One of Soho's leading facilities, Nats Post Production is fully equipped in all aspects of television post production, from offline to online, design and graphics, grade and audio dub. With over 40 suites, we strive to make sure your whole experience is as pleasant and productive as possible by offering you creative excellence, intelligent solutions and home comforts.

One

71 Dean Street, London W1D 3SF
t 020 7439 2730 **f** 020 7734 3331
e amanda.smalley@onepost.tv **w** www.onepost.tv

Contact Paul Jones, Managing Director; Will Byles, CGI; Matt Adams, Head of Production; Amanda Smalley, Sales & Marketing
Credits Kit Kat: Rap (Test) (C)

Optical Image

The Production Centre, Broome, Near Stourbridge DY9 0HA
t 01562 700404 **f** 01562 700930
e info@optical-image.com **w** www.optical-image.com

Contact David Clement, Managing Director; Jacky Clement, Company Secretary; Julie Farrington-Griffiths, Director of Resources
Credits Red Arrows - Beyond the Horizon (I); Jellabies/Jellikins (C); Butt Ugly Martians (C)

Can't find an entry?

Turn to the alphabetical Index of entries on page 705

The Production GUIDE

Turn to the alphabetical Index of entries on page 705

Passion Pictures

3 Floor, 33-34 Rathbone Place, London W1T 1JN
t 020 7323 9933 **f** 020 7323 9030
e info@passion-pictures.com **w** www.passion-pictures.com

Nick Price

10 Church Close, Church Street, Epsom KT17 4PT
t 01372 723294

PS Creative

Studio 512/513, The Greenhouse, The Custard Factory, Gibb Street, Birmingham B9 4AA
t 0121 224 8484 **f** 0121 224 8485
e mail@pscreative.co.uk **w** www.pscreative.co.uk

Contact Martin Povey, Animation Director
Credits Excalibur - Drayton Manor (C); Spectrum - S4C (T); Videodrone - Serotonin (M); Mums The Word - Carlton TV (T)

Ragavi

65 Outram Road, London E6 1JP
t 020 8552 3723 **m** 07958 739939 **e** yuthyarajah@aol.com

Red Kite Productions

89 Giles Street, Edinburgh EH6 6BZ
t 0131 554 0060 **f** 0131 553 6007
e info@redkite-animation.com **w** www.redkite-animation.com

Contact Katja Anderson, Producer; Ken Anderson, Managing Director; Rachel Bevan Baker, Creative Director; Mary Morrison, Producer
Credits Lunar Jig (A); Nightwindows (A); The Witches (A); Wilf The Witch's Dog (A)

Red Post Production

Hammersley House, 5-8 Warwick Street, London W1B 5LX
t 020 7439 1449 **f** 020 7439 1339
e production@red.co.uk **w** www.red.co.uk
Contact James Lamb, Producer; Fiona Byrne, Bookings; Stephen Luther, Managing Director; Matt White, Senior Producer; Tara Geraughty, New Business/Account Management; Tanya Johnson, Head Of Production; Annika Ahl, Bookings; Aimee Posner, Bookings
Credits Blur - Crazy Beat (M); Tennants - Bollywood (C); S Club Movie - Double Vision (F)

RJDM Animations

York Studios, Cold Ashby Road, Guilsborough, Northampton NN6 8QP
t 01604 743222 **f** 01604 743222 **m** 07808 264812
e production@rjdm.com **w** www.rjdm.com
Contact Ricky O'Donnell, Head of Animation/Director

Sega Europe Ltd

266-270 Gunnersbury Avenue, London W4 5QB
t 020 8995 3399 **f** 020 8996 4499 **w** www.sega-europe.com

SGI

1530 Arlington Business Park, Theale, Reading RG7 4SB
t 0118 925 7500 **f** 0118 925 7505 **w** www.sgi.co.uk

Skaramoosh

9-15 Neal Street, Covent Garden, London WC2H 9PW
t 020 7379 9966 **f** 020 7240 7111
e will@skara.co.uk **w** www.skara.co.uk
Contact Will Stern, Sales & Marketing Manager

Skyline Imaging Ltd

4th Floor, Oakfield House, 35 Perrymount Road, Haywards Heath RH16 3BW
t 01444 884217
e info@skylineimaging.co.uk **w** www.skylineimaging.co.uk
Contact David Mack, Creative Director; Chris Haynes
Credits The Human Body - Nerve Cells (D); The Discovery Dock (A); Away With The Fairies (F); The Chart Show Channel (T)

Slave Studios Ltd

28 Fourberts Place, London W1F 7PR
t 020 7734 5336 **f** 020 7734 5337
e info@slave-studios.co.uk **w** www.slave-studios.co.uk
Contact Andy Frain, Managing Director; Tony Krivit, Company Secretary; Chris Rais, Animation Director; Paul Beilby, Technical Director
Credits Free Jimmy (A); Tractor Tom (A); Spherics (A)

Small MEDIA

25 High Farm Meadow, Badsworth, Pontefract WF9 1PB
t 01977 608820
e richard@smallmedia.co.uk **w** www.smallmedia.co.uk
Contact Richard Burgess-Dawson

Spider Eye Ltd

Town Hall, Chapel Road, St Just, Penzance TR19 7HT
t 01736 788000 **f** 01736 788103
e post@spider-eye.com **w** www.spider-eye.com
Contact John Brooks; Ivan Richardson; Ben Weschke, Director; Morgan Francis, Director; Erica Darby, Producer

Stinkbug

28 Lucerne Road, Thornton Heath CR7 7BA
t 020 8665 1634 **m** 07952 347135
e dan@stinkbug.co.uk **w** www.stinkbug.co.uk
Contact Dan Mellor, Creative Director

Subvision

7 Zetland Road, Bristol BS6 7AG
t 0117 942 0149 **f** 0117 909 6657
e info@subvision.co.uk **w** www.subvision.co.uk
Contact Stefan Wernik, Partner; Jarema Wernik, Partner
Credits Aspects Video (C); Boots Various (C); Bassetts Moo Chews (C); Vinny (A)

Synthetic Dimensions Ltd

Silver Birches House, 72 Wergs Road, Wolverhampton WV6 8TH
t 01902 742442 **f** 01902 750578
e kate@syndime.com **w** www.syndime.com
Contact Kevin Bulmer, Director; Kate Copestake, Director
Credits Iron Maiden: The Angel And The Gambler (A); Astro Knights (A)

Telegraphics

34 Fusilier Way, Weedon NN7 4TH
t 01327 342278 **f** 01327 342432 **m** 07850 750875
e dick.laing@btinternet.com **w** www.telegraphics.co.uk
Contact Dick Laing, Designer/Director

Triffic Films Ltd

6 St Paul's Court, Stony Stratford MK11 1LJ
t 01908 261234 **f** 01908 263050
e info@triffic.co.uk **w** www.triffic.co.uk
Credits Human Remains (T); Have I Got News for You (T); 2DTV (T)

Viewpoint Digital

Pinewood Studios, Pinewood Road, Iver SL0 0NH
t 01753 650104 **f** 01753 654081
e carolcaddle@viewpoint.com **w** www.viewpoint.com
Contact Carol Caddle, Account Manager; Daphne Rowan, Managing Director

Wurmser Aids

Unit 23, Cumberland Business Park, Cumberland Avenue, London NW10 7RT
t 020 8961 4005 **f** 020 8961 3886 **e** wurmsers@btclick.com
Contact Jeremy Tidy, Director; John Tidy, Director

Graham Young

Longmeadow Thatch, Spring Lane, Cold Ash, Thatcham RG18 9PL
t 01635 861732 **m** 07990 516205 **e** gygraphics@aol.com
Credits DTS Surround Sound Experience (I); The French At War (T); Sounds Of Underground London (T); Ready Steady Cook (T)

Animation **Animators**

AAber Yowe Production

Baltasound UNST ZE2 9DS
t 01595 694383 **f** 01595 694383
e elizabeth.johnson@aaberyowe.com **w** www.aaberyowe.com
Contact Elizabeth Johnson, Producer
Credits Wise And Wonderful (A)

The Animation People

22 Churchmead Close, East Barnet EN4 8UY
t 020 8449 1601 **f** 020 8449 1601 **m** 07714 203737
e brianlarks@aol.com **w** www.animationpeople.co.uk
Contact Brian Larkin, Animation Director
Credits I'm A Celebrity...Get Me Out Of Here Promo (A); SMTV Live Promo (A); Le Crunch Crevy (A); Billy Connolly Live Greatest Hits Video (A)

Animation Post UK

24 Oakhill Road, East Putney, London SW15 2QR
t 020 8874 9602
e jeff@animationpost.co.uk **w** www.animationpost.co.uk
Contact Jeff Goldner

Animax Studios

Trace House, Clay of Allan, Fearn by Tain
t 01862 832001 **f** 01862 832002 **m** 07721 331991
e info@animaxstudios.com
Contact Claire Armstrong, Animation Director

B B C Post Production

BBC Post Production
(Sites across London, Bristol & Birmingham)
5550 Television Centre, Wood Lane, London W12 7RJ
t 020 8225 7702 (London) **t** 0117 9746 666 (Bristol)
t 0121 432 8621 (Birmingham)
w www.bbcresources.com/postproduction

Blue Sunflower Animation
50 Eagle Wharf Road, London N1 7ED
t 020 7490 2990 **f** 020 7336 7996 **w** www.bluesunflower.com

Cartwn Cymru
Ben Jenkins Court, 19A High Street Llandaf, Cardiff CF5 2DY
t 029 2057 5999 **f** 029 2057 5919
e production@cartwn-cymru.com
Contact Naomi Jones, Producer

Chromacolour International
Unit 5, Pilton Estate, Pitlake, Croydon CR0 3RA
t 020 8688 1991 **f** 020 8688 1441
e joanneh@chromacolour.co.uk **w** www.chromacolour.co.uk

The Cut-Out Animation Company
15 Avenue Road, St Albans AL1 3QG
t 01727 831061 **e** info@cut-out.co.uk **w** www.cut-out.co.uk
Contact Alan Rogers, Director; Peter Lang, Director
Credits South Pole (A); Bonny, Banana & Mo (A)

Hedgehog Animation
19 Fairfield Place, Southville, Bristol B53 1LH
m 07730 257969 **e** hedgehoganimation@hotmail.com
w members.lycos.co.uk/hedgehoganimation
Contact Fictious Egg, Freelance Flash Animator; Acme Filmworks, Renderer/Illustrator
Credits Floyd Lute (A); Animal School (A); Charmin Ultra (A); Johnny Casanova Shorts (A)

Hedley Griffin Films
Old Bank House, High Street, Laxfield, Woodbridge IP13 8DX
t 01986 798613 **f** 01986 798172
e gjc94@dial.pipex.com **w** www.hedleygriffinfilms.com
Contact Hedley Griffin, Animation Director
Credits Eyes Of Karras (A); Maths Mansion (A); Word Machine (A)

Russell Hicks
Flat 2, 8 Clarendon Road, Whalley Range, Manchester M16 8LD
t 0161 232 7238 **m** 07776 023257 **e** hicks_russell@hotmail.com
Credits Little Robots (A); The Animal Shelf (A); Bob The Builder (A); Bill And Ben (A)

Kerrupt Animation
m 07884 055836 **e** j.kerr@ic24.net
Contact James Kurr, Managing Director
Credits Jenson Jeans (A); Alan And Kath (A); MTV Shorts (A)

King Rollo Films
Dolphin Court, High Street, Honiton EX14 1HT
t 0 1404 45218 **f** 0 1404 45328 **e** admin@kingrollofilms.co.uk
Credits Paz The Penguin (A); Fimbles Animation (A); Spot (A); Maisy (A)

Russell Murch
19 Amies Street, London SW11 2JL
t 020 7228 7718 **f** 020 7228 7718 **m** 07812 506855
e rdjmurch@onetel.net.uk
Credits The Tidings (A); The Mole Sisters (A); Clifford The Big Red Dog (A); Sabrina The Teenage Witch (A)

Animation productions on all platforms - on time and on budget.

Andrew Robertson
20A Westside Common, London SW19 4UF
t 020 8947 9923 **f** 020 8947 5658 **m** 07740 320355
Credits Interbrand (C)

Rory Fellowes Animations
3 Littlesworth, Naunton, Cheltenham GL54 3AX
t 01451 850448 **f** 01451 850448 **m** 07976 784701
e rory@roryanimations.com **w** www.roryanimations.com
Credits Harry Potter And The Chamber Of Secrets (F); Hellbound: Hellraiser II (F); The Little Vampire (F)

Siriol Productions
3 Mount Stuart Square, Butetown, Cardiff CF10 5EE
t 029 2048 8400 **f** 029 2048 5962
e enquiries@siriol.co.uk **w** www.siriolproductions.com
Contact Les Orton, Animation Director; Lynne Stockford, Studio Manager; Robin Lyons, Managing Director; Andrew Offiler, Head of Development; Simon Quinn, Head of Stop Motion Production
Credits The Bobinogs (A); Hilltop Hospital (A); Fireman Sam (A); Sali Mali (A)

Skunk
87 Lancaster Road, London W11 1QQ
t 020 7908 9400 **f** 020 7908 9500
e info@skunk.tv **w** www.skunk.tv
Contact Hyun-Ho Khang, Executive Producer
Credits Peacekeeping

The Teds Agency
17 Mill Lane, Welwyn AL6 9EU
t 01438 718000 **f** 01438 718001
e production@teds.co.uk **w** www.teds.co.uk
Contact Chris Williams, Animator
Credits Filippo Berio (A); NTL (A)

Vis Television Media International Ltd
Aimex, Suite 405, Bondway Commercial Centre, London SW8 1SQ
t 0870 011 0020 **f** 0870 011 0030
e media@vismediaint.com **w** www.vismediaint.com
Contact Martin Bibby; Stuart Bristow
Credits Making Of A Millionaire (T); Culture Beat (T); Eurospice (T)

ART DEPARTMENT

Art Department
Assistants

Sarah-Jane Barnes
86A Cricklewood Broadway, London NW2 3EL
t 020 8438 9922 **f** 020 8438 9922 **e** sarah.jb@virgin.net

Emma Davis
C/o BECTU, 333-377 Clapham Road, London SW9 9BT
m 07808 401 420
e emmadesign@tiscali.co.uk **w** www.emmadavis.com
Credits Winter Solstice (T); When She Died (T); Keen Eddie (T)

Jessica Graham
ADS, Shepperton Studios, Studios Road, Shepperton TW17 0QD
t 01932 592303 **f** 01932 592492 **e** ads@carlincrew.co.uk
Credits Hot Gold (F); Let Them Eat Cake (F); Room To Rent (F); My Brother (F)

Emma Marie Jenkins
13 Tamesis Gardens, Worcester Park KT4 7JX
t 020 8337 9591 **f** 020 8286 6685 **m** 07813 205285
e jenkins_emma@hotmail.com
Credits Only Fools And Horses (T); Below (F); Jeffrey Archer - The Truth (T); Cambridge Spies (T)

Simon Linton
Gems, The Media House, 87 Glebe Street, Penarth CF64 1EF
t 029 2071 0770 **f** 029 2071 0771
e gems@gems-agency.co.uk **w** www.gems-agency.co.uk
Credits Twentieth Century Landmarks

Toby Riches
10 Alpine Grove, London E9 7SX
t 020 8986 3267 **m** 07817 415778 **e** tobyriches@yahoo.co.uk
Credits Born To Die (D); Nightmares On Wax (M); McDonald's (C); Rush Series III (T)

Mary Simcox
23 Chelsea Road, Easton, Bristol BS5 6AR
t 0117 954 0284 **m** 07773 677438 **e** mary.simcox@virgin.net
Credits Sir Gadabout (T)

Art Department
Set Dressers/Decorators

Celia Bobak
The Garden House, 11A Berkeley Place, London SW19 4NN
t 020 8947 2817 **f** 020 8947 3720 **m** 07836 236467
Credits Family Business (F); Last Orders (F)

John Bush
27 Melrose Avenue, Wimbledon Park, London SW19 8BU
t 020 8946 5372 **f** 020 8946 9640 **m** 07850 205949
Credits Topsy Turvy (F); House Of Mirth (F); Captain Corelli's Mandolin (F)

Ruth Collier
Experience Counts - Call Me Ltd, 5th Floor, 41-42 Berners Street, London W1P 3AA
t 020 7637 8112 **f** 020 7580 2582

Robyn Hamilton-Doney
Flat 8, 144-146 Westbourne Grove, London W11 2RR
t 020 7229 3988 **f** 020 7229 3988

Caroline Smith
9 Brackley Road, London W4 2HW
t 0208 747 8131 **f** 0208 747 8131 **m** 07860 483318
Credits Love Actually (F); Love In A Cold Climate (T); The Way We Live Now (T)

Tony Strong's Tapestry Services
12-16 Brunel Road, London W3 7XR
t 020 8743 7616 **f** 020 8749 9435
Contact John West

Simon RS Wakefield
36 Roxwell Road, London W12 9QF
t 020 8749 7901 **f** 020 8749 7901 **m** 07801 099917
Credits Die Another Day (F); Reign Of Fire (F); Enemy At The Gates (F); The World Is Not Enough (F)

Watts of Westminster incorporating Belinda Cootes Tapestries
Showroom, 3/14 Chelsea Harbour Design Centre, London SW10 0XE
t 020 7376 4486 **f** 020 7376 4636
e sales@wattsofwestminster.co.uk **w** www.wattsofwestminster.com
Contact Danuta Bildziuk

Ian Whittaker
Little Croft, Glebe Estate, Studland BH19 3AS
t 01929 450322 **f** 01929 450322 **m** 07802 203497
e ianwhittaker@peelstreet.u-net.com
Agent International Creative Management Ltd, Oxford House, 76 Oxford Street, London W1D 1BS
t 020 7636 6565 **f** 020 7323 0101 **w** www.icmlondon.co.uk
Credits Sense And Sensibility (F); Anna And The King (F); The Importance Of Being Earnest (F)

Art Department **Specialists**

Natalie Abadzis
13 Mereway Road, Twickenham TW2 6RF
t +44 20 8898 7145 **f** +44 20 8898 7145 **m** 07977 154422
e natalie.abadzis@blueyonder.co.uk **w** www.natalieabadzis.co.uk
Credits Sky News Promo (T); Smart on the Road (T); Blue Peter (T); Smart Programme (T)

Ann Bowen
t 01737 246171 **f** 01737 246171 **m** 07803 840 948

Art Directions
College Mansions, Winchester Avenue, London NW6 7TY
t 0207 625 5939 **f** 0207 372 1344 **e** ruthven@easynet.co.uk
Contact Ginette St Clair Ruthven, Proprietor

The Calligraphers
37 Shakespeare Street, Stratford-upon-Avon CV37 6RN
t 01789 264114 **m** 07866 347021
Contact Deborah Hammond, Partner; Denise Hagon, Partner
Credits The Hound Of The Baskervilles (T); Four Feathers (F); Monarch Of The Glen (T); Poirot (T)

Simon Clarke
7 Lochaline Street, Hammersmith, London W6 9SJ
t 020 8741 9127 **f** 0870 136 3553 **m** 07801 163108
e clarkeyboy55@btopenworld.com

Dartura
3 Station Terrace, Twyford RG10 9NE
t 0118 934 2534 **f** 0118 934 2534 **m** 07779 267055
Contact Peter Whiteman
Credits The Mummy (F); Gladiator (F); Harry Potter And The Prisoner Of Azkaban (F); Harry Potter And The Philosopher's Stone (F)

Katie Gabriel
30 The Rise, Loudwater, High Wycombe HP13 7BB
t 01494 816412 **m** 07885 484994 **e** katie@heavens-gate.demon.co.uk
Credits Die Another Day (F); Entrapment (F); The World Is Not Enough (F); Four Feathers (F)

Fred Gray
Sistine Chapel, 32 Mill Lane, Frampton Cotterell, Bristol BF36 2AA
t 01454 774499 **f** 01454 774499 **m** 07831 417479

Julieann Heskin
Stoney Side Cottage, Stoney Side, Youlgreave, Near Bakewell DE45 1WH
t 01629 636964 **m** 07890 681212 **e** julieannuk@yahoo.co.uk
Credits Commonwealth Games 2002 (T); Pepsi (C); Midland Bank (C); Two Wheels And A Baby (C)

Tony Statham Studio
100 Vauxhall Walk, London SE11 5EL
t 01843 825762 **f** 01843 825792 **m** 07973 483768
e statart@dircon.co.uk
Contact Tony Statham
Credits American Girl (F); Byron (T); The Lost Prince (T)

Timna Woollard
43C Brondesbury Villas, London NW6 6AJ
t 020 7328 6608 **f** 020 7328 6608 **m** 07710 132 602
e timna@btopenworld.com
Credits Jonny English (F); Daniel Deronda (T); Nicholas Nickleby (T)

Art Department Stylists

Trish Appleton
t 020 7706 7576 **f** 020 7706 7399 **m** 07973 909304
e trish@trishappelton.co.uk **w** www.trishappelton.co.uk

Sarah Babb
Art Department, 51 Pratt Street, London NW1 0BJ
t 020 7428 0500 **f** 020 7916 2167 **m** 07973 639785
e info@art-department.co.uk

Catherine Bates
Art Department, 51 Pratt Street, London NW1 0BJ
t 020 7428 0500 **f** 020 7916 2167 **m** 07973 639785
e info@art-department.co.uk

Natacha Du Pont de Bie
Art Department, 51 Pratt Street, London NW1 0BJ
t 020 7428 0500 **f** 020 7916 2167 **m** 07973 639785
e info@art-department.co.uk

Maria Bonet
m 07767 776046 **e** maria@wagging-tongues.freeserve.co.uk
Credits Sophie Ellis-Bextor - Take Me Home (M); Sophie Ellis-Bextor - Murder On The Dancefloor (M)

Justine Burns
Art Department, 51 Pratt Street, London NW1 0BJ
t 020 7428 0500 **f** 020 7916 2167 **m** 07973 639785
e info@art-department.co.uk

Beverley Butcher
ADS, Shepperton Studios, Shepperton Road,
Shepperton TW17 0QD
t 01932 592303 **f** 01932 592492 **e** ads@carlincrew.co.uk
Credits Daily Mail (C); Lego (C); Andrex (C); In Deep (T)

Ed Butcher Cheeky
Art Department, 51 Pratt Street, London NW1 0BJ
t 020 7428 0500 **f** 020 7916 2167 **m** 07973 639785
e info@art-department.co.uk

Clare Clarkson
Art Department, 51 Pratt Street, London NW1 0BJ
t 020 7428 0500 **f** 020 7916 2167 **m** 07973 639785
e info@art-department.co.uk

Jane Cooke
Art Department, 51 Pratt Street, London NW1 0BJ
t 020 7428 0500 **f** 020 7916 2167 **m** 07973 639785
e info@art-department.co.uk

Abigail Coult
2 Hillary House, Boyton Close, London N8 7BB

Niamh Coulter
Art Department, 51 Pratt Street, London NW1 0BJ
t 020 7428 0500 **f** 020 7916 2167 **m** 07973 639785
e info@art-department.co.uk

Belinda de Lyle-Turner
ADS, Shepperton Studios, Studios Road, Shepperton TW17 0QD
t +44 1932 592303 **f** +44 1932 592492 **e** ads@carlincrew.co.uk

Jenny Dyer
Art Department, 51 Pratt Street, London NW1 0BJ
t 020 7428 0500 **f** 020 7916 2167 **m** 07973 639785
e info@art-department.co.uk

Melanie Fisher
London W11 4NR
t 020 7371 3128 **f** 020 7371 3128 **m** 07958 327774
e melfishdes@hotmail.com

Julie-Anne Fulford
Art Department, 51 Pratt Street, London NW1 0BJ
t 020 7428 0500 **f** 020 7916 2167 **m** 07973 639785
e info@art-department.co.uk

Antonia Gibbs
Art Department, 51 Pratt Street, London NW1 0BJ
t 020 7428 0500 **f** 020 7916 2167 **m** 07973 639785
e info@art-department.co.uk

Karen Granger
Art Department, 51 Pratt Street, London NW1 0BJ
t 020 7428 0500 **f** 020 7916 2167 **m** 07973 639785
e info@art-department.co.uk

Sue Hollis
Wizzo & Co, 35 Old Compton Street, London W1D 5JX
t 020 7437 2055 **f** 020 7437 2066
e wizzo@wizzoandco.co.uk **w** www.wizzoandco.co.uk

Lucy Howe
Art Department, 51 Pratt Street, London NW1 0BJ
t 020 7428 0500 **f** 020 7916 2167 **m** 07973 639785
e info@art-department.co.uk

Jane Harris
35B Regents Park Road, London NW1 7SY
t 020 7586 2403 **f** 020 7586 2403 **m** 07976 612887
e janeharris@blueyonder.co.uk

Terry Jones
Art Department, 51 Pratt Street, London NW1 0BJ
t 020 7428 0500 **f** 020 7916 2167 **m** 07973 639785
e info@art-department.co.uk

Antonia Lake
34 Mora Road, London NW2 6TG
t 020 8208 2958 **m** 07786 517 685 **e** altitude@macunlimited.net

Cynthia Lawrence-John
Shoot Production Ltd
t 020 7267 4333 **e** shootpen@aol.com

Jenny Lawrence-Smith
20 Bryanston Mews East, London W1H 2DB
t 020 7262 5713 **m** 07989 350205 **e** jenlawrencesmith@aol.com
Credits KPMG (C); Levis (C); Mean Machine (W); Eurostar (C)

Paula Lovell
Wizzo & Co, 35 Old Compton Street, London W1D 5JX
t 020 7437 2055 **f** 020 7437 2066
e wizzo@wizzoandco.co.uk **w** www.wizzoandco.co.uk

Sarah Lovett
2 Elm Park, London SW2 2UB
t 020 8674 0335 **m** 07976 272590 **e** artdept@cwcom.net
Credits Prada (C); Stella Street (T)

Stephanie McMillan
Art Department, 51 Pratt Street, London NW1 0BJ
t 020 7428 0500 **f** 020 7916 2167 **m** 07973 639785
e info@art-department.co.uk

Marina Morris
Art Department, 51 Pratt Street, London NW1 0BJ
t 020 7428 0500 **f** 020 7916 2167 **m** 07973 639785
e info@art-department.co.uk

Sophie Newman
Art Department, 51 Pratt Street, London NW1 0BJ
t 020 7428 0500 **f** 020 7916 2167 **m** 07973 639785
e info@art-department.co.uk

Sian Penn
Art Department, 51 Pratt Street, London NW1 0BJ
t 020 7428 0500 **f** 020 7916 2167 **m** 07973 639785
e info@art-department.co.uk

Glyn Ramsbottom
93 Highlever Road, London W10 6PW
t 020 8969 4228 **f** 020 8960 3282 **m** 07973 263155
e glynis@forevermail.com

Lee Sandales
Art Department, 51 Pratt Street, London NW1 0BJ
t 020 7428 0500 **f** 020 7916 2167 **m** 07973 639785
e info@art-department.co.uk

Julie Signy
Art Department, 51 Pratt Street, London NW1 0BJ
t 020 7428 0500 **f** 020 7916 2167 **m** 07973 639785
e info@art-department.co.uk

Fanny Taylor
Art Department, 51 Pratt Street, London NW1 0BJ
t 020 7428 0500 **f** 020 7916 2167 **m** 07973 639 785
e info@art-department.co.uk

Art Directors/ Production Designers

Sylke Abinghoff
Art Department, 51 Pratt Street, London NW1 0BJ
t 020 7428 0500 **f** 020 7916 2167 **m** 07956 978003
e info@art-department.co.uk

Stephen Adams
54 Barnfield Place, London E14 9YA
t 020 7943 1721 **f** 020 7943 1722 **m** 07791 046186
e stephenadams@go.com
w www.geocities.com/stephenadams2003
Credits The Trouble With Girls (S); The I Inside (F)

Caroline Amies
Casarotto Marsh Ltd, National House, 60-66 Wardour Street, London W1V 4ND
t 020 7287 4450 **f** 020 7287 9128
e agents@casarotto.uk.com **w** www.casarotto.uk.com

Heather Armitage
34 Barons Keep, Gliddon Road, London W14 9AT
t 020 7603 8718 **e** add@heatherarmitage.com
w www.heatherarmitage.com
Credits Hammer House Of Mystery And Suspense (T); God's Outlaw (T); Blood Bath At The House Of Death (F); The Curse Of King Tutankhamoun's Tomb (T)

Anna Asp
Casarotto Marsh Ltd, National House, 60-66 Wardour Street, London W1V 4ND
t 020 7287 4450 **f** 020 7287 9128
e agents@casarotto.uk.com **w** www.casarotto.uk.com

Jille Azis
Creative Media Management, Unit 3B, Walpole Court, Ealing Studios, Ealing Green, London W5 5ED
t 020 8584 5363 **f** 020 8566 5554
e enquiries@creativemediamanagement.com
Credits Timeline (F); Around The World In 80 Days (F); Gladiator (F); Spy Game (F)

Humphrey Bangham
Gems, The Media House, 87 Glebe Street, Penarth CF64 1EF
t 029 2071 0770 **f** 029 2071 0771 **e** gems@gems-agency.co.uk
w www.gems-agency.co.uk
Credits Relic Hunter (T); Pinocchio II (A); New World Disorder (F); Arthur's Dyke (F)

Sam Barbic
Art Department, 51 Pratt Street, London NW1 0BJ
t 020 7428 0500 **f** 020 7916 2167 **m** 07973 118089
e info@art-department.co.uk

Neil 'Fairplay' Barnes
1 Hunt Road, High Wycombe HP13 7RE
t 01494 521402 **f** 01494 521402 **m** 07768 760260
e neilfairplaybarnes@hotmail.com

Ian Barratt
Art Department, 51 Pratt Street, London NW1 0BJ
t 020 7428 0500 **f** 020 7916 2167 **m** 07973 625817
e info@art-department.co.uk

Carlotta Barrow
30 Cluny Crescent, Swanage BH19 2BT
t 01929 425544 **f** 01929 425967 **m** 07850 313910
e zooks77@hotmail.com
Credits Me And Mrs Jones (T); Mrs Dalloway (F); Gentlemen's Relish (T)

Oliver Bayldon
t 020 8998 5554 **f** 020 8998 5554 **m** 07744 678977

John Beard
61 Gloucester Avenue, London NW1 7BA
t 020 7485 8320 **f** 020 7267 6729 **e** johnbeard@btconnect.com
Agent ADS, Shepperton Studios, Studios Road, Shepperton TW17 0QD
t 01932 592303 **f** 01932 592492 **e** ads@carlincrew.co.uk
Agent International Creative Management Ltd, Oxford House, 76 Oxford Street, London W1D 1BS
t 020 7636 6565 **f** 020 7323 0101 **w** www.icmlondon.co.uk
Credits The Last Temptation Of Christ (F); The Wings Of The Dove (F); Enigma (F); K-Pax (F)

Sophie Becher
McKinney Macartney Management Ltd, The Barley Mow Centre, 10 Barley Mow Passage, London W4 4PH
t 020 8995 4747 **f** 020 8995 2414
e fkb@mmtechsrep.demon.co.uk **w** www.mckinneymacartney.com

Simon D Beresford
McKinney Macartney Management Ltd, The Barley Mow Centre, 10 Barley Mow Passage, London W4 4PH
t 020 8995 4747 **f** 020 8995 2414
e fkb@mmtechsrep.demon.co.uk **w** www.mckinneymacartney.com

Amanda Bernstein
Creative Media Management, Unit 3B, Walpole Court, Ealing Studios, Ealing Green, London W5 5ED
t 020 8584 5363 **f** 020 8566 5554
Credits Star Wars: Episode I - The Phantom Menace (F); The Beach (F); Simon: An English Legionnaire (F)

Patrick Bill
96 Lilford Road, Camberwell, London SE5 9HR
t 020 7733 8619 **m** 07951 634678 **e** emth@aol.com
Credits Dambusters (T); Surrealissimo (T); The Coldest March (D); Touching The Void (F)

David Blight
Gems, The Media House, 87 Glebe Street, Penarth CF64 1EF
t 029 2071 0770 **f** 029 2071 0771
e gems@gems-agency.co.uk **w** www.gems-agency.co.uk
Credits The Medicis (T); Georgiana (T); The Great Plague (T); The Great Fire Of London (T)

Gavin Bocquet
McKinney Macartney Management Ltd, The Barley Mow Centre, 10 Barley Mow Passage, London W4 4PH
t 020 8995 4747 **f** 020 8995 2414
e fkb@mmtechsrep.demon.co.uk **w** www.mckinneymacartney.com

Sophie Boddington
Dinedor Management, 81 Oxford Street, London W10 2EU
t 020 7851 3575 **f** 020 7851 3576
e info@dinedor.com **w** www.dinedor.com
Credits Norwich Union (C); Seafrance (C); Shreddies (C); Shark Week (T)

Martin John Boddison
The Lodge, 2 York Road, Priorslee, Telford TF2 9UU
t 01952 200113 **f** 01952 210515 **m** 07885 214506
e martinboddison@supanet.com
Credits Preston Front (T); Dalziel & Pascoe II-VIII (T); Peak Practice (T); EastEnders (T)

Bollom TV & Film
Croydon Road, Beckenham BR3 4BL
t 020 8658 2299 **f** 020 8658 8672
e sales@bollom.com **w** www.bollom.com/tvandfilm
Contact Laurie Rippingale

Tom Bowyer
The Dench Arnold Agency, 24 D'Arblay Street, London W1F 8EH
t 020 7437 4551 **f** 020 7439 1355 **w** www.dencharnold.co.uk

John Bramble
Art Department, 51 Pratt Street, London NW1 0BJ
t 020 7428 0500 **f** 020 7916 2167 **m** 07973 639785
e info@art-department.co.uk

Richard Bridgland
t 514 968 4433 **m** 07860 682 973
Credits Gangster No 1 (F); The Sight (F); Resident Evil (F)

John Bristow
t 01227 458355 **f** 01227 458355 **m** 07973 830 545
e johnbristow@jbristow-design.fsnet.co.uk

Kay Brown
Gems, The Media House, 87 Glebe Street, Penarth CF64 1EF
t 029 2071 0770 **f** 029 2071 0771 **e** gems@gems-agency.co.uk
w www.gems-agency.co.uk
Credits United (T); Trinity (F); Family Affairs (T); Honour Thy Father (F)

William Bryce
112 Parc Tyn-y-Waun, Llangynwyd, Maesteg CF34 9RH
t 01656 736826 **m** 07885 379150 **e** billbryce@mac.com
Credits Casualty (T); Mind Games (T); Eldra (T); Trial And Retribution III-VI (T)

BS Design & Associates
Ibert Lodge, Ibert Road, Killearn, Glasgow G63 9PY
t 01360 550882 **f** 01360 550882 **m** 07901 554 546
e bsdesign@talk21.com
Credits Cheating Heart; Maelstrom; Tutti Frutti (C)

Martina Buckley
McKinney Macartney Management Ltd, The Barley Mow Centre, 10 Barley Mow Passage, London W4 4PH
t 020 8995 4747 **f** 020 8995 2414
e fkb@mmtechsrep.demon.co.uk **w** www.mckinneymacartney.com

Jon Bunker
t 020 7603 3762 **e** artifx@aol.com
Agent ADS, Shepperton Studios, Studios Road, Shepperton TW17 0QD
t 01932 592303 **f** 01932 592492 **e** ads@carincrew.co.uk
Credits Memory Of Water (F); Gladiators (F); Vertical Limit (F); Croupier (F)

Millie Burns
Art Department, 51 Pratt Street, London NW1 0BJ
t 020 7428 0500 **f** 020 7916 2167 **m** 07973 639785
e info@art-department.co.uk

Tony Burrough
International Creative Management Ltd, Oxford House, 76 Oxford Street, London W1D 1BS
t 020 7636 6565 **f** 020 7323 0101 **w** www.icmlondon.co.uk
Credits Richard III (F); Great Expectations (F); A Knight's Tale (F)

Tom Burton
The Dench Arnold Agency, 24 D'Arblay Street, London W1F 8EH
t 020 7437 4551 **f** 020 7439 1355
e contact@dencharnoldagency.co.uk **w** www.dencharnold.co.uk
Credits Dot The I (F)

Ed Butcher
12 Stadium Street, London SW10 0PT
t 020 7376 4816 **f** 020 7376 4816 **m** 07768 287420
e ed.butcher@virgin.net
Credits Bradford And Bingley (C); Oasis 'Little By Little' (M); Jonny Vaughan's World Cup Extra (T); Army Recruitment (C)

David Butterworth
ADS, Shepperton Studios, Studios Road, Shepperton TW17 0QD
t 01932 592303 **f** 01932 592492 **e** ads@carincrew.co.uk
Credits Take Me (T); Wyrdsister (T); Wire In The Blood (T); Cutting It (T)

Maurice Cain
International Creative Management Ltd, Oxford House, 76 Oxford Street, London W1D 1BS
t 020 7636 6565 **f** 020 7323 0101 **w** www.icmlondon.co.uk
Credits Unconditional Love (T); Frenchman's Creek (T); The Scarlet Pimpernel (T); The Infinite Worlds Of H.G. Wells (T)

Rodney Cammish
18 Lower King's Road, Kingston Upon Thames KG2 5HR
t 020 8546 5990 **m** 07956 261 780
Agent Experience Counts - Call Me Ltd, 5th Floor, 41-42 Berners Street, London W1P 3AA
t 020 7637 8112 **f** 020 7580 2582
Credits Murder In Mind (T); London's Burning (T); The Knock (T)

Roger Cann
International Creative Management Ltd, Oxford House, 76 Oxford Street, London W1D 1BS
t 020 7636 6565 **f** 020 7323 0101 **w** www.icmlondon.co.uk
Credits David Copperfield (T); My Fragile Heart (T); Tom Jones (T)

Michael Carlin
Casarotto Marsh Ltd, National House, 60-66 Wardour Street, London W1V 4ND
t 020 7287 4450 **f** 020 7287 9128
e agents@casarotto.uk.com **w** www.casarotto.uk.com

Alan Cassie
Moorthatch, Cookham Village SL6 9QQ
t 01628 523234 **f** 01628 523234
Credits The Muppets Treasure Island (F); Dr Zhivago (T); High Binders (F)

Julia Castle
29 Drayton Road, West Ealing, London W13 0LD
t 020 8997 6412 **f** 020 8998 0345 **m** 07885 836565
e julia.cc@virgin.net
Credits Hearts And Bones - Series I & II (T); To Kill A King (F); Birthday Girl (F); Inspector Lynley's Mysteries - Series I & II (T)

Ray Chan

ADS, Shepperton Studios, Studios Road, Shepperton TW17 OQD
t 01932 592303 **f** 01932 592492 **e** ads@carlincrew.co.uk
Credits Wings Of The Dove (F); Jonny English (F); Enigma (F); ThunderBirds (F)

Martin Childs

International Creative Management Ltd, Oxford House,
76 Oxford Street, London W1D 1BS
t 020 7636 6565 **f** 020 7323 0101 **w** www.icmlondon.co.uk
Credits The Madness Of King George (F); Shakespeare In Love (F); From Hell (F)

Alison Chitty

Curtis Brown Group Ltd, Haymarket House, 28-29 Haymarket,
London SW1Y 4SP
t 020 7396 6600 **f** 020 7396 0110 **e** cb@curtisbrown.co.uk

Ged Clarke

Sandford Manor, Sandford Lane, Woodlen RG8 4SY
t 01189 448090 **f** 01189 449080 **m** 07860 239 398

Clasur

3 Dorchester Avenue, Penylan, Cardiff CF23 9BQ
t 029 2049 4381 **f** 029 2049 4382 **m** 07860 297420
e gerald@clasur.tv
Contact Gerald Murphy, Production Designer
Credits Enchantment (T); FA Cup Classic (T); Late Night Poker (T)

Jim Clay

Casarotto Marsh Ltd, National House, 60-66 Wardour Street,
London W1V 4ND
t 020 7287 4450 **f** 020 7287 9128
e agents@casarotto.uk.com **w** www.casarotto.uk.com

Joel Collins

Art Department, 51 Pratt Street, London NW1 OBJ
t 020 7428 0500 **f** 020 7916 2167 **m** 07973 639785
e info@art-department.co.uk

Tom Conroy

The Dench Arnold Agency, 24 D'Arblay Street, London W1F 8EH
t 020 7437 4551 **f** 020 7439 1355
e contact@dencharnoldagency.co.uk **w** www.dencharnold.co.uk
Credits Intermission (F); Intermission; East Is East (F); Heartlands (F)

Stephen Cooper

12571 Allin Street, Los Angeles 90066, USA
t +1 310 306 1174 **f** +1 310 745 8996 **e** scoopers1275@aol.com
Credits Just Visiting (F); Alien Resurrection (F)

Sara-Jane Cornish

ADS, Shepperton Studios, Shepperton Road,
Shepperton TW17 OQD
t 01932 592303 **f** 01932 592492 **e** ads@carlincrew.co.uk
Credits David Copperfield (T); Best (F); The Luzhin Defence (F); Dust (F)

Alex Craig

10 Salamander Court, 135 York Way, London N7 9LG
t 020 7485 1404 **f** 020 7485 1471 **m** 07958 326353
e alex@alexcraig.com **w** www.alexcraig.com
Credits Hotel Babylon (T); Clive Anderson Now (T); A Question Of Sport (T); Shooting Stars (T)

Jessica Curtis

London Management & Representation, 2-4 Noel Street,
London W1F 8GB
t 020 7287 9000 **f** 020 7287 3236

Alice Cuttance

Art Department, 51 Pratt Street, London NW1 OBJ
t 020 7428 0500 **f** 020 7916 2167 **m** 07810 573125
e info@art-department.co.uk

Tim Dann

Art Department, 51 Pratt Street, London NW1 OBJ
t 020 7428 0500 **f** 020 7916 2167 **m** 07973 639785
e info@art-department.co.uk

Suzie Davies

t 01844 274156 **m** 07850 533 411
Credits Fakers (F); Tipping The Velvet (T); William And Mary (T); Othello (T)

Dennis De Groot

50 Callcott Road, London NW6 7EA
t 020 7625 4677 **f** 020 7624 4468 **m** 07831 217490 **e**
penden@globalnet.co.uk
Credits Little Britian (T); Hardware (T); Frank Skinner (T); Black Books (T)

Russell Derozario

3 Lushington Road, London NW10 5UX
t 020 8961 1066 **f** 020 8838 2229 **m** 07831 893427
e russell@purple.com
Credits Mean Machine (W)

James Dillon

t 020 7585 2284 **f** 020 7585 2289 **m** 07831 501514

Alison Dominitz

The Dench Arnold Agency, 24 D'Arblay Street, London W1F 8EH
t 020 7437 4551 **f** 020 7439 1355 **w** www.dencharnold.co.uk
Art Department, 51 Pratt Street, London NW1 OBJ
t 020 7428 0500 **f** 020 7916 2167 **m** 07973 639785
e info@art-department.co.uk

Don Grant Design

Studio 24, Ransome's Dock, 35-37 Parkgate Road, London
SW11 4NP
t 020 7350 1434 **f** 020 7350 2389 **e** dg@easynet.co.uk
Contact Don Grant, Creative Director
Credits Blackadder Back and Forth

Laurence Dorman

McKinney Macartney Management Ltd, The Barley Mow
Centre, 10 Barley Mow Passage, London W4 4PH
t 020 8995 4747 **f** 020 8995 2414
e fkb@mmtechsrep.demon.co.uk **w** www.mckinneymacartney.com

Eric Doughney

Clare Vidal Hall, 28 Perrers Road, London W6 OEZ
t 020 8741 7647 **f** 020 8741 9459 **e** clarevidalhall@email.com
w www.clarevidalhall@email.com

Amanda Duncan

t 020 7231 3815 **f** 020 7231 3815 **m** 07957 422665
e manda.duncan@virgin.net
Credits Virgin Megastore (C); Paramount Comedy Channel (C); Crimenight (T);
Stones In Their Pockets (F)

John Ebden

ADS, Shepperton Studios, Studios Road, Shepperton TW17 OQD
t 01932 592303 **f** 01932 592492 **e** ads@carlincrew.co.uk
Credits Dead Heat (F); Underworld (F); Waking Ned (F); Conspiracy Of Silence (F)

Einsteins Octopus

22 Clapton Square, London E5 8HP
t 020 8985 9850 **f** 020 8985 8221
e tony@einsteinsoctopus.co.uk **w** www.einsteinsoctopus.co.uk
Contact Tony Pletts, Managing Director

Peter Elliott

Valley Cottage, Water Lane, Albury, Guildford GU5 9BD
t 01483 203911 **m** 07966 186896 **e** despeterelliott@lineone.net
Credits EastEnders (T); Emmerdale (T); The Bill (T)

Simon Elliott

The Dench Arnold Agency, 24 D'Arblay Street, London W1F 8EH
t 020 7437 4551 **f** 020 7439 1355
e contact@dencharnoldagency.co.uk **w** www.dencharnold.co.uk
Credits I Saw You (T); Final Demand (T); Rescue Me (T)

John Ellis
Clare Vidal-Hall, 28 Perrers Road, London W6 0EZ
t 020 8741 7647 **f** 020 8741 9459
e clarevidalhall@email.com **w** www.clarevidalhall@email.com

Nick Ellis
Art Department, 51 Pratt Street, London NW1 0BJ
t 020 7428 0500 **f** 020 7916 2167 **m** 07973 639785
e info@art-department.co.uk

Philip Elton
Rookfield Hammers Lane, London NW7 4DJ
t 020 8959 2359 **f** 020 8959 2359 **m** 07710 458493
e phile333@aol.com
Credits Timeline (F); Gangster No 1 (F); Event Horizon (F); Perfect Strangers (T)

Bruce Everard
Wizzo & Co, 35 Old Compton Street, London W1D 5JX
t 020 7437 2055 **f** 020 7437 2066
e wizzo@wizzoandco.co.uk **w** www.wizzoandco.co.uk

Ricky Eyres
Casarotto Marsh Ltd, National House, 60-66 Wardour Street, London W1V 4ND
t 020 7287 4450 **f** 020 7287 9128
e agents@casarotto.uk.com **w** www.casarotto.uk.com

Tony Ferris
7 West View Road, St Albans AL3 5JX
t 01727 832209 **f** 01727 832209 **m** 07979 804130
e t_ferris@hotmail.com
Credits The Upper Hand (T); Loved By You (T); Kiss Me Kate (T); Barbara (T)

The Film Garden
104 Augustus Road, London SW19 6ER
t 020 8785 9725 **f** 020 8785 9725 **m** 07836 781498
e tim.art@filmgarden.com **w** www.filmgarden.com
Contact Tim Keates

Peter Findley
Farthings, Water Lane, Little Horkesley CO6 4DF
t 01206 273200 **f** 01206 273200 **e** interzone@btconnect.com
w www.interzone-design.co.uk
Agent ADS, Shepperton Studios, Studio Road, Shepperton TW17 0QD
t 01932 592303 **f** 01932 592492 **e** ads@carlincrew.co.uk
Credits Hope And Glory (T); Seven Wonders (T); Star Street (T); MerseyBeat (T)

Steve Fineran
International Creative Management Ltd, Oxford House, 76 Oxford Street, London W1D 1BS
t 020 7636 6565 **f** 020 7323 0101 **w** www.icmlondon.co.uk
Credits The Forsythe Saga (T); Sunday (T); Liam (F)

Ian Fisher
Clare Vidal Hall, 28 Perrers Road, London W6 0EZ
t 020 8741 7647 **f** 020 8741 9459 **e** clarevidalhall@email.com
w www.clarevidalhall.com

John Frankish
ADS, Shepperton Studios, Studios Road, Shepperton TW17 0QD
t 01932 592303 **f** 01932 592492 **e** ads@carlincrew.co.uk
Credits The Match (F)

Suzanne French
Art Department, 51 Pratt Street, London NW1 0BJ
t 020 7428 0500 **f** 020 7916 2167 **m** 07956 666192
e info@art-department.co.uk

Sarah Frere
Art Department, 51 Pratt Street, London NW1 0BJ
t 020 7428 0500 **f** 020 7916 2167 **m** 07974 395109
e info@art-department.co.uk

Julian Fullalove
Experience Counts - Call Me Ltd, 5th Floor, 41-42 Berners Street, London W1P 3AA
t 020 7637 8112 **f** 020 7580 2582

Lee Gammon
31 Richmond Road, Cardiff CF24 3AQ
m 07977 570904 **e** gammonlee@hotmail.com
Credits Vampire Craig (S); Arthur's Dyke (F); Brookside (T); Casualty (T)

Marr Gant
Art Department, 51 Pratt Street, London NW1 0BJ
t 020 7428 0500 **f** 020 7916 2167 **m** 07718 586393
e info@art-department.co.uk

Charles Garrard
International Creative Management Ltd, Oxford House, 76 Oxford Street, London W1D 1BS
t 020 7636 6565 **f** 020 7323 0101 **w** www.icmlondon.co.uk
Credits The Englishman Who Went Up A Hill But Came Down A Mountain (F); The Serpent's Kiss (F); Paranoia (F)

Norman Garwood
53 Amyand Park Road, Twickenham TW1 3HG
t 020 8891 2239 **f** 020 8891 2239 **m** 07710 475604
Credits Misery (F); Glory (F); Brazil (F); Hook (F)

Mark Geraghty
International Creative Management Ltd, Oxford House, 76 Oxford Street, London W1D 1BS
t 020 7636 6565 **f** 020 7323 0101 **w** www.icmlondon.co.uk
Credits Welcome To Sarajevo (F); The Count Of Monte Cristo (F); The Actor (F)

Annette Gillies
36 Polwarth Street, Glasgow G12 9TX
t 0141 334 3319 **f** 0141 334 3319 **m** 07831 441373
e gilliesannette@hotmail.com
Credits The Crow Road (T); Taggart (T); Monarch Of The Glen (T); 2000 Acres Of Sky - Series 3 (T)

Very experienced Production Designer for film and television drama. Over 60 hours of screen drama in the last 10 years. Languages: French & Spanish.

Max Gottlieb
International Creative Management Ltd, Oxford House, 76 Oxford Street, London W1D 1BS
t 020 7636 6565 **f** 020 7323 0101 **w** www.icmlondon.co.uk
Credits The Full Monty (F); Still Crazy (F); Lucky Break (F)

Jonathan Paul Green
23 Links Drive, Radlett WD7 8BD
t 01923 850870 **f** 07092 248719 **m** 07831 348719
e jpg@set-design.tv **w** www.set-design.tv
Credits Danepak - Rapid Rashers (C); ITV Formula 1 (T); Da Ali G Show (T); Smack The Pony (T)

Sarah Greenwood
International Creative Management Ltd, Oxford House, 76 Oxford Street, London W1D 1BS
t 020 7636 6565 **f** 020 7323 0101 **w** www.icmlondon.co.uk
Credits Nature Boy (T); Born Romantic (F); The Governess (F)

Annie Gregson
Art Department, 51 Pratt Street, London NW1 0BJ
t 020 7428 0500 **f** 020 7916 2167 **m** 07973 639785
e info@art-department.co.uk

Caroline Greville-Morris
ADS, Shepperton Studios, Studios Road, Shepperton TW17 0QD
t 01932 592303 **f** 01932 592492 **e** ads@carlincrew.co.uk
Credits Intimate Relations (T); Vigo - A Passion For Life (T); Lady Audley's Secret (T); Dr Jekyll And Mr Hyde (T)

Hayden Griffin

London Management & Representation, 2-4 Noel Street,
London W1F 8GB
t 020 7287 9000 **f** 020 7287 3236
Credits Intimacy (F)

Giovanni Guardino

11 Gainsborough Road, Felixstowe IP11 7HT
t 01394 285090 **f** 01394 285091 **m** 07802 312274
e gio@guarino.com **w** www.gio.guarino.com

Mike Gunn

12 Montague Street, Glasgow G4 9HX
t 0141 564 9789 **f** 0141 564 9790 **m** 07973 198478
e mikegunn@sol.co.uk
Credits The Book Group (T); Cambridge Spies (T); The Acid House (F);
Late Night Shopping (F)

Roger Hall

Art Department, 51 Pratt Street, London NW1 0BJ
t 020 7428 0500 **f** 020 7916 2167 **m** 07973 639785
e info@art-department.co.uk
The Dench Arnold Agency, 24 D'Arblay Street, London W1F 8EH
t 020 7437 4551 **f** 020 7439 1355
e contact@dencharnoldagency.co.uk **w** www.dencharnold.co.uk
Credits Alice In Wonderland (F); Don Quixote (T); Jason And The Argonauts (T)

Andy Hamilton

Lantern Cottage, Bashley Road, New Milton BH25 5RY
t 01425 616047
Credits Hot Wax - Ruby Wax (T); Jack Dee - Jeremy Hardy Show (T); Jasper
Carrott (T)

Peter Hampton

ADS, Shepperton Studios, Studios Road, Shepperton TW17 0QD
t 01932 592303 **f** 01932 592492 **e** ads@carlincrew.co.uk
Credits Dealers (F); Nostradamus (T); White Squall (T); Shanghai Noon (F)

Caroline Hanania

The Dench Arnold Agency, 24 D'Arblay Street, London W1F 8EH
t 020 7437 4551 **f** 020 7439 1355
e contact@dencharnoldagency.co.uk **w** www.dencharnold.co.uk
Credits Surviving Christmas (F); Serendipity (F); Anita And Me (F)

Luana Hanson

Casarotto Marsh Ltd, National House, 60-66 Wardour Street,
London W1V 4ND
t 020 7287 4450 **f** 020 7287 9128
e agents@casarotto.uk.com **w** www.casarotto.uk.com

Christopher Hardinge

15 Tintern Close, Putney, London SW15 2HF
t 0208 789 7339 **f** 0208 789 7339 **m** 07932 669279
e hardinge@freenet.co.uk

Andy Harris

41 Kelvinside Gardens, Glasgow G20 6BQ
t 0141 945 3636 **f** 0141 945 3636 **m** 07831 851295
e andy.harris1@btinternet.com
Agent International Creative Management Ltd, Oxford House,
76 Oxford Street, London W1D 1BS
t 020 7636 6565 **f** 020 7323 0101 **w** www.icmlondon.co.uk
Credits American Cousins (F); The Key (T); My Life So Far (F); The Woodlanders
(F); Gabriel And Me (F); The Escapist (F)

Rob Harris

The Dench Arnold Agency, 24 D'Arblay Street, London W1F 8EH
t 020 7437 4551 **f** 020 7439 1355
e contact@dencharnoldagency.co.uk **w** www.dencharnold.co.uk
Credits Hornblower (T); The Lost World (T); Auf Wiedersehen Pet (T)

Roger Harris

Gems, The Media House, 87 Glebe Street, Penarth CF64 1EF
t 029 2071 0770 **f** 029 2071 0771
e gems@gems-agency.co.uk **w** www.gems-agency.co.uk
Credits Grange Hill (T); Bodger And Badger (T); There's A Viking In My Bed (T);
Ghost Stories For Christmas (T)

Jayne Harvey

41 Prospect Road, Carlton, Nottingham NG4 1LX
t 0115 987 2491 **f** 0115 987 2491 **m** 07967 816921
e jayne_harvey@hotmail.com
Credits Sedgefield Park (S); Picture This; Icing on the Cake; Food Network Daily

Penny Harvey

Gems, The Media House, 87 Glebe Street, Penarth CF64 1EF
t 029 2071 0770 **f** 029 2071 0771
e gems@gems-agency.co.uk **w** www.gems-agency.co.uk
Credits The Ghost Hunter (T); Plots With A View (F); Midnight Jazz (T); Casualty (T)

Tim Harvey

International Creative Management Ltd, Oxford House,
76 Oxford Street, London W1D 1BS
t 020 7636 6565 **f** 020 7323 0101 **w** www.icmlondon.co.uk
Credits Frankenstein (T); Hamlet (F); Last Orders (F)

Alix Harwood

36 Maiden Lane, London WC2E 7LJ
t 020 7836 6889 **m** 07831 827223 **e** alixharwood@hotmail.com
Credits British Airways 'Shopping the World' (C); Mark Lewis' Peeping Tom (F);
Ho Ho Ho! (T)

Jane Harwood

Art Department, 51 Pratt Street, London NW1 0BJ
t 020 7428 0500 **f** 020 7916 2167 **m** 07957 574858
e info@art-department.co.uk

Jemima Hawkins

Art Department, 51 Pratt Street, London NW1 0BJ
t 020 7428 0500 **f** 020 7916 2167 **m** 07989 972580
e info@art-department.co.uk

Joanne Hellerman

Art Department, 51 Pratt Street, London NW1 0BJ
t 020 7428 0500 **f** 020 7916 2167 **m** 07767 484672
e info@art-department.co.uk

James Hendy

Dinedor Management, 81 Oxford Street, London W10 2EU
t 020 7851 3575 **f** 020 7851 3576 **e** info@dinedor.com
w www.dinedor.com
Credits Rolling Rock (C); Quaker Oats (C); Volvo (C); Caught In The Act (F)

Henry Harris

3 Amy Road, Oxted RH8 0PX
t 01883 715038 **m** 07774 412410 **e** henryharris@btinternet.com
Credits Withnail And I (F); East Is East (F); The Warrior (F)

Jon Henson

Casarotto Marsh Ltd, National House, 60-66 Wardour Street,
London W1V 4ND
t 020 7287 4450 **f** 020 7287 9128
e agents@casarotto.uk.com **w** www.casarotto.uk.com

Careen Hertzog

Wizzo & Co, 35 Old Compton Street, London W1D 5JX
t 020 7437 2055 **f** 020 7437 2066
e wizzo@wizzoandco.co.uk **w** www.wizzoandco.co.uk

Anna Higginson

Casarotto Marsh Ltd, National House, 60-66 Wardour Street,
London W1V 4ND
t 020 7287 4450 **f** 020 7287 9128
e agents@casarotto.uk.com **w** www.casarotto.uk.com

Bruce Hill
Vine House, 86 Tilford Road, Farnham GU9 8DS
t 01252 724359 **f** 01252 724961 **m** 07836 203 871
e bruce.hill58@aol.com **w** www.createascene.co.uk
Agent ADS, Shepperton Studios, Shepperton Road,
Shepperton TW17 0QD
t 01932 592303 **f** 01932 592492 **e** ads@carlincrew.co.uk
Credits Chelsea Flower Show (C); British Gas (C); Love Potion No 9 (F)

Rob Hinds
t 01684 541429 **f** 01684 541429 **m** 07774 150950
Credits 10th Kingdom (T); Our Friends In The North (T); My Uncle Silas (T)

David Hitchcock
24 Bridgemah Road, Teddington TW11 9AH
t 020 8943 2857 **f** 020 8943 2857 **m** 07885 284536
Credits Roger Roger - Series I and II (T); Al Murray - The Pub Landlord (T);
Lee Evans - So What Now (T); Only Fools And Horses (T)

Martin Hitchcock
ADS, Shepperton Studios, Shepperton Road, Shepperton
TW17 0QD
t 01932 592303 **f** 01932 592492 **e** ads@carlincrew.co.uk
Credits Hurricane Smith (F); 1492 (F); Cleopatra (F); The Monkey King (F)

Christopher Hobbs
International Creative Management Ltd, Oxford House,
76 Oxford Street, London W1D 1BS
t 020 7636 6565 **f** 020 7323 0101 **w** www.icmlondon.co.uk
Credits Velvet Goldmine (F); Mansfield Park (F); Gormenghast (T)

Frederick Hole
26 The Greenway, Gerrards Cross SL9 8LX
t 01753 887482 **f** 01753 887482 **m** 07801 240 072
Credits The Attack of the Clones (F); Below (F); Die Another Day (F); The World
Is Not Enough (F)

Jim Holloway
13 Spezia Road, London NW10 4QJ
t 020 8961 5308 **f** 020 8961 5308 **m** 07860 863377
e jim.holloway@ukgateway.net
Credits Life Force (T); Hetty Wainthropp Investigates (T); Phoenix Nights (T)

Marc Homes
ADS, Shepperton Studios, Shepperton Road, Shepperton
TW17 0QD
t 01932 592303 **f** 01932 592492 **e** ads@carlincrew.co.uk
Credits Fish (F); ThunderBirds (F)

Don Homfray
Old Cottage, South Creake NR21 9PR
t 01328 823514 **f** 01328 823514 **e** donhomfray@aol.com

Grenville Horner
Casarotto Marsh Ltd, National House, 60-66 Wardour Street,
London W1V 4ND
t 020 7287 4450 **f** 020 7287 9128
e agents@casarotto.uk.com **w** www.casarotto.uk.com

Duncan Howell
ADS, Shepperton Studios, Studios Road, Shepperton TW17
0QD
t 01932 592303 **f** 01932 592492 **e** ads@carlincrew.co.uk
Credits Al's Lads (F); Sunday (F); Liam (F); The Forsyte Saga (T)

Michael Howells
Casarotto Marsh Ltd, National House, 60-66 Wardour Street,
London W1V 4ND
t 020 7287 4450 **f** 020 7287 9128
e agents@casarotto.uk.com **w** www.casarotto.uk.com

Mark Hudson
5 The Spinney, Muxton, Telford TF2 8RZ
t 01952 603896 **m** 07721 625763 **e** mark.hudson@tesco.net
Credits Grease Monkeys (T); Large (F); Dalziel & Pascoe (T); Peak Practice (T)

Will Hughes-Jones
Jessica Carney Associates, Suite 90-92 Kent House,
87 Regent Street, London W1B 4EH
t 020 7434 4143 **f** 020 7434 4173 **e** info@jcarneyassociates.co.uk
Credits Storm Damage (T); In the Name of Love (T); The Inspector Lynley
Mysteries (T)

Steve Hudson
Dinedor Management, 81 Oxford Street, London W1O 2EU
t 020 7851 3575 **f** 020 7851 3576
e info@dinedor.com **w** www.dinedor.com
Credits My Vitriol (M); Way Out West (M); AOL (C); Burger King (C)

Charlotte Humpston
Folly Lodge, Folly Lane, North Wootton BA4 4ER
t 01749 890610 **f** 01749 890018 **m** 07976 370984
e c.humpston@btopenworld.com **e** flaxton@btinternet.com
w www.flaxton.btinternet.co.uk/charlotte1.htm

Mick Hurd
Art Department, 51 Pratt Street, London NW1 0BJ
t 020 7428 0500 **f** 020 7916 2167 **m** 07973 639785
e info@art-department.co.uk

Tim Hutchinson
7 Addison Grove, London W4 1EP
t 020 8994 3157 **f** 020 8987 2761 **m** 07836 245 625
e tim@hutchinson53.fsnet.co.uk
Credits Sons And Lovers (T); Margery & Gladys (T); Lucky Jim (T); Polly Anna (T)

Martyn John
International Creative Management Ltd, Oxford House,
76 Oxford Street, London W1D 1BS
t 020 7636 6565 **f** 020 7323 0101 **w** www.icmlondon.co.uk
Credits Trust (T); End Game (F); The Criminal (F); Strictly Sinatra (F)

Ashling Johnson
ADS, Shepperton Studios, Studios Road, Shepperton TW17 0QD
t 01932 592303 **f** 01932 592492 **e** ads@carlincrew.co.uk

Nigel Jones
t 01564 826025 **f** 01564 826317 **m** 07768 525 034

SJ Kaye
7 Ashbrook Road, London N19 3DF
t 020 7687 7317 **f** 020 7687 6261 **m** 07973 407849
e susannah.k@blueyonder.co.uk
Credits Baby Juice Express (F)

John-Paul Kelly
The Dench Arnold Agency, 24 D'Arblay Street, London W1F 8EH
t 020 7437 4551 **f** 020 7439 1355
e contact@dencharnoldagency.co.uk **w** www.dencharnold.co.uk
Credits Byron (T); I Capture The Castle (F); The Lost Prince (T)

Claire Kenny
International Creative Management Ltd, Oxford House,
76 Oxford Street, London W1D 1BS
t 020 7636 6565 **f** 020 7323 0101 **w** www.icmlondon.co.uk
Credits Queer As Folk (T); Messiah (T); Servants (T)

Jennifer Kernke
The Dench Arnold Agency, 24 D'Arblay Street, London W1F 8EH
t 020 7437 4551 **f** 020 7439 1355
e contact@dencharnoldagency.co.uk **w** www.dencharnold.co.uk
Credits Angels And Insects (F); Institute Benjamenta (F); Natural History (T)

Jean Kerr
ADS, Shepperton Studios, Studios Road, Shepperton TW17 0QD
t 01932 592303 **f** 01932 592492 **e** ads@carlincrew.co.uk
Credits Some Voices (F); River City (T); The Innocents (T); Whistleblower (T)

Paul Kirby
6 Woodbines Avenue, Kingston-upon-Thames KT1 2AY
t 020 8541 1991 **m** 07768 384164 **e** k2kirby@yahoo.co.uk
Credits Complicity (F); Die Another Day (F); The Four Feathers (F); Lara Croft
And The Cradle Of Life: Tomb Raider 2 (F)

George Kyriakides
ADS, Shepperton Studios, Shepperton Road,
Shepperton TW17 0QD
t 01932 593303 **f** 01932 592492 **e** ads@carlincrew.co.uk
Credits Gypsey Girl (T); Urban Gothic (T); Where The Heart Is (T); A Is For Acid (T)

Niel Lamont
Art Department, 51 Pratt Street, London NW1 0BJ
t 020 7428 0500 **f** 020 7916 2167 **m** 07973 639785
e info@art-department.co.uk

Richard Lassalle
Art Department, 51 Pratt Street, London NW1 0BJ
t 020 7428 0500 **f** 020 7916 2167 **m** 07973 639785
e info@art-department.co.uk

Mark Lavis
Art Department, 51 Pratt Street, London NW1 0BJ
t 020 7428 0500 **f** 020 7916 2167 **m** 07973 639785
e info@art-department.co.uk

Ken Ledsham
t 01753 866342 **f** 01753 794894 **m** 07778 555660

Jamie Leonard
International Creative Management Ltd, Oxford House,
76 Oxford Street, London W1D 1BS
t 020 7636 6565 **f** 020 7323 0101 **w** www.icmlondon.co.uk
Credits Tom And Viv (F); A Man Of No Importance (F); Complicity (F)

Kit Line
t 020 8994 7002 **f** 020 8994 7002 **m** 07973 631222
e kit.line@btopenworld.com
Agent ADS, Shepperton Studios, Shepperton Road,
Shepperton TW17 0QD
t 01932 592303 **f** 01932 592492 **e** ads@carlincrew.co.uk
Credits Stell Street - The Movie (F); Hanging Around (F); Expecting (F); House! (F)

Sue Lipscombe
Art Department, 51 Pratt Street, London NW1 0BJ
t 020 7428 0500 **f** 020 7916 2167 **m** 07973 639785
e info@art-department.co.uk

Nicky Lowe
Art Department, 51 Pratt Street, London NW1 0BJ
t 020 7428 0500 **f** 020 7916 2167 **m** 07949 484453
e info@art-department.co.uk

Hugo Luczyc-Wyhowski
The Dench Arnold Agency, 24 D'Arblay Street, London W1F 8EH
t 020 7437 4551 **f** 020 7439 1355
e contact@dencharnoldagency.co.uk **w** www.dencharnold.co.uk
Credits Havana Nights - Dirty Dancing II (F); Dirty Pretty Things (F); The Truth
About Charlie (F)

Bruce Macadie
CCA Management, 7 St George's Square, London SW1V 2HX
t 020 7630 6303 **f** 020 7630 7376

Alan MacDonald
International Creative Management Ltd, Oxford House,
76 Oxford Street, London W1D 1BS
t 020 7636 6565 **f** 020 7323 0101 **w** www.icmlondon.co.uk
Credits Love Is The Devil (F); Rogue Trader (F); Nora (F)

Adele Marolf
304 Walton Road, Molesey KT8 2HY
t 020 8941 5312 **f** 020 8941 5312 **m** 07850 551170
e aemarolf@aol.com
Credits The Musketeer (F); House of Eliot (T); Ivanhoe (T)

Giles Masters
Creative Media Management, Unit 3B, Walpole Court, Ealing
Studios, Ealing Green, London W5 5ED
t 020 8584 5363 **f** 020 8566 5554
e enquiries@creativemediamanagement.com
Credits Tomorrow Never Dies (F); Van Helsing (F); The Mummy (F); Shanghai
Knights (F)

Andrew McAlpine
Casarotto Marsh Ltd, National House, 60-66 Wardour Street,
London W1V 4ND
t 020 7287 4450 **f** 020 7287 9128
e agents@casarotto.uk.com **w** www.casarotto.uk.com

Amanda McArthur
Art Department, 51 Pratt Street, London NW1 0BJ
t 020 7428 0500 **f** 020 7916 2167 **m** 07973 639785
e info@art-department.co.uk

Julian McGowan
Cruickshank Cazenove Ltd, 97 Old South Lambeth Road,
London SW8 1XU
t 020 7735 2933 **f** 020 7820 1081 **e** hjcruickshank@aol.com

David McHenry
Jessica Carney Associates, Suite 90-92 Kent House, 87
Regent Street, London W1B 4EH
t 020 7434 4143 **f** 020 7434 4173 **e** info@jcarneyassociates.co.uk
Credits Shine (F); A & E (T); Love And Death On Long Island (F)

John McHugh
Experience Counts - Call Me Ltd, 5th Floor, 41-42 Berners
Street, London W1P 3AA
t 020 7637 8112 **f** 020 7580 2582

Bridget Menzies
Art Department, 51 Pratt Street, London NW1 0BJ
t 020 7428 0500 **f** 020 7916 2167 **m** 07815 047966
e info@art-department.co.uk

Catrin Meredydd
3 Sydney Road, Teddington TW11 8PQ
t 020 8255 7485 **m** 07973 862 812 **e** catmeredydd@hotmail.com
Credits White Teeth (T); Young Adam (T)

James Merifield
Creative Media Management, Unit 3B, Walpole Court, Ealing
Studios, Ealing Green, London W5 5ED
t 020 8584 5363 **f** 020 8566 5554
e enquiries@creativemediamanagement.com
Credits Revelation (F); The Life And Adventures Of Nicolas Nickleby (T);
Henry VIII (T)

Drogo Michie
Wizzo & Co, 35 Old Compton Street, London W1D 5JX
t 020 7437 2055 **f** 020 7437 2066
e wizzo@wizzoandco.co.uk **w** www.wizzoandco.co.uk

Model Box
20 Merton Industrial Park, Jubilee Way, Wimbledon, London
SW19 3WL
t 020 8254 4720 **f** 020 8254 4721
e info@modelbox.co.uk **w** www.modelbox.co.uk
Contact Bryan Raven

Andrew Mollo
Creative Media Management, Unit 3B, Walpole Court, Ealing
Studios, Ealing Green, London W5 5ED
t 020 8584 5363 **f** 020 8566 5554
e enquiries@creativemediamanagement.com
Credits Nanov (F); The Pianist (F); Pascali's Island (T); Hornblower (T)

Colin Monk

m 07785 110324

Agent Experience Counts - Call Me Ltd, 5th Floor, 41-42 Berners Street, London W1P 3AA
t 020 7637 8112 f 020 7580 2582

Credits The Knock (T); Murder In Mind (T); London's Burning (T)

Shaun Moore

Striblehills, Priest End, Thame OX9 2AE
t 01844 218072 f 01844 217558 m 07909 521754
e shaun@productiondesign.co.uk w www.productiondesign.co.uk

Deborah F Morley

23 Margate Street, Victoria Park, Bristol BS3 4SP
t 0117 971 5863 m 07831 615 338 e deborah.morley@virgin.net

Brian Morris

International Creative Management Ltd, Oxford House, 76 Oxford Street, London W1D 1BS
t 020 7636 6565 f 020 7323 0101 w www.icmlondon.co.uk

Credits Evita (F); The Insider (F); Unfaithful (F)

David Morrison

Hope Cottage, Middlehill, Egham TW20 0JG
t 01784 433521 f 01784 433521 m 07802 412587
e dave.moz@virgin.net

Credits Tales From The Tower (T); Discovery Today (T)

Peter Mullins

11 Warwick Gardens, Kensington, London W14 8PH
t 020 7603 8514 f 020 7602 0624

Agent Creative Media Management, Unit 3B, Walpole Court, Ealing Studios, Ealing Green, London W5 5ED
t 020 8584 5363 f 020 8566 5554
e enquiries@creativemediamanagement.com

Credits A Knight In Camelot (F); Back To The Secret Garden (F); The Pink Panther (F); Alfie (F); Stepping Out (F); Conspiracy - A Meeting At Wansee (F)

Paul Munford

13 Bramber Court, Sterling Place, Brentford TW8 9QP
t 020 8560 3184 m 07970 267865
e paulmunford@blueyonder.co.uk
w paulmunford.pwp.blueyonder.co.uk

Credits Titania (C); Monarch Of The Glen III (T); No Surrender (D); Bloody Sunday (F)

Andrew Munro

The Dench Arnold Agency, 24 D'Arblay Street, London W1F 8EH
t 020 7437 4551 f 020 7439 1355
e contact@dencharnoldagency.co.uk w www.dencharnold.co.uk

Credits Gormenghast (T); Mansfield Park (F); Anita And Me (F)

Julian Nagel

Art Department, 51 Pratt Street, London NW1 0BJ
t 020 7428 0500 f 020 7916 2167 m 07734 692183
e info@art-department.co.uk

Anthea Nelson

29 Urban Road, Sale M33 TTG
t 0161 969 4386 f 0161 969 4386 m 07973 952 235
e antheanelson@mac.com

Credits Snakeboy And The Sandcastle (S); One 2 One (C); Once Upon A Time In The Midlands (F)

Victoria Nelson

10 Glentham Road, Barnes, London SW13 9JB
t 020 8748 1934 f 020 8748 1934 m 07973 890303

Credits Casualty (T); As If (T); Ruth Rendell Mysteries (T); Bad Girls (T)

Tony Noble

93 Clarence Road, Tellington TW11 0BN
t 020 8977 3459 f 020 8943 1560 m 07956 414 227
e suto.noble@virgin.net

Credits Tesco (C); Homebase (C); Whoops Apocalypse (F); Don't Go Breaking My Heart (F)

Alice Normington

The Dench Arnold Agency, 24 D'Arblay Street, London W1F 8EH
t 020 7437 4551 f 020 7439 1355
e contact@dencharnoldagency.co.uk w www.dencharnold.co.uk

Credits Miranda (F); Great Expectations (T); Hilary And Jackie (F)

Alice Norris

Gems, The Media House, 87 Glebe Street, Penarth CF64 1EF
t 029 2071 0770 f 029 2071 0771
e gems@gems-agency.co.uk w www.gems-agency.co.uk

Credits Urban Ghost Story (F); The Great Indoors (T); Maestro (F); Born To Die (F)

Lee Oliver

Art Department, 51 Pratt Street, London NW1 0BJ
t 020 7428 0500 t 01923 440605 f 020 7916 2167
e info@art-department.co.uk

Nick Ormerod

London Management & Representation, 2-4 Noel Street, London W1F 8GB
t 020 7287 9000 f 020 7287 3236

Nic Pallace

45 Annett Road, Walton-on-Thames KT12 2JS
m 07831 193554 e nic@nicpallace.com w www.nicpallace.com

Credits Coupling (T); Blackadder Back And Forth (F); Love Again (F)

Bill Palmer

Martin Farm, Whiddon Down, Okehampton EX20 2QL
t 01647 231465 f 01647 231465 m 07970 527150
e bill_palmer@lineone.net w www.billpalmer.co.uk

Credits Titmus Regained (T); Agatha Christie Hour (T); Under the Hammer (T); Down To Earth (T)

Gina Parr

t 020 7272 1192 f 020 7272 1192 m 07976 750846
e gina.parr@virgin.net w www.ginaparr.com

Credits Mercury Music Prize 2002 (T); The Royal Variety Performance 2002 (T); The Brit Awards 1999 (T)

Cath Pater

Art Department, 51 Pratt Street, London NW1 0BJ
t 020 7428 0500 f 020 7916 2167 m 07973 639785
e info@art-department.co.uk

Phil Williams Design Partnership

72 Kimberley Road, Penylan, Cardiff CF23 5DN
t 029 2049 3665 f 029 2049 0658 m 07774 613451
e philwilliamsdesign@talk21.com

Contact Phil Williams, TV & Film Production Designer/Art Director

Michael Pickwoad

3 Warnborough Road, Oxford OX2 6HZ
t 07865 511106 m 07973 664015

Credits Death In Holy Orders (T); Hans Christian Andersen (T); LD50 (F)

Joe Plume

Art Department, 51 Pratt Street, London NW1 0BJ
t 020 7428 0500 f 020 7916 2167 m 07903 324134
e info@art-department.co.uk

John Plush

Badge Court Cottage, Cooksey Green, Droitwich WR9 0NJ
t 01299 851208 f 01299 851208 m 07977 460058
e john@theplushes.com

Harriet Porter

ADS, Shepperton Studios, Studios Road, Shepperton TW17 0QD
t +44 1932 592303 f +44 1932 592492
e ads@carlincrew.co.uk

Credits Worthingtons (C); Harry Potter Spell Book (C); Debenhams (C); Organics (C)

Clement Price-Thomas

16 Windsor Court, The Pavement, London SW4 0JF
m 07979 804080 **e** clemwork@yahoo.co.uk
Agent ADS, Shepperton Studios, Shepperton Road,
Shepperton TW17 0QD
t 01932 592303 **f** 01932 592492 **e** ads@carlincrew.co.uk
Credits L'Oreal (C); Fiat (C); Heineken (C); The Innocent Sleep (F)

Gary Pritchard

ADS, Shepperton Studios, Studios Road, Shepperton TW17 0QD
t 01932 592303 **f** 01932 592492 **e** ads@carlincrew.co.uk
Credits After Celia (F); Roughnecks (T); Casualty (T); The Bill (T)

Andrew Purcell

ADS, Shepperton Studios, Shepperton Road, Shepperton
TW17 0QD
t 01932 592303 **f** 01932 592492 **e** ads@carlincrew.co.uk
Credits Forgive And Forget (T); Teachers (T); Without Motive (T);
Waking The Dead III (T)

Tom Pye

Cruickshank Cazenove Ltd, 97 Old South Lambeth Road,
London SW8 1XU
t 020 7735 2933 **f** 020 7820 1081 **e** hjcruickshank@aol.com
Credits Christie Malry's Own Double Entry (F); Helen West (T); Twelfth Night (T)

Kave Quinn

Casarotto Marsh Ltd, National House, 60-66 Wardour Street,
London W1V 4ND
t 020 7287 4450 **f** 020 7287 9128
e agents@casarotto.uk.com **w** www.casarotto.uk.com

Ian Reade-Hill

ADS, Shepperton Studios, Studios Road, Shepperton TW17 0QD
t 01932 592303 **f** 01932 592492 **e** ads@carlincrew.co.uk
Credits Hostile Water (F); The Rotten Trolls (T); Red Dwarf (T); Croupier (F)

David Reekie

21 St Andrew's Square, London W11 1RH
t 020 7221 6562 **m** 07855 214829 **e** david.reekie@dk.com
Credits Intimate With A Stranger (F); The Trial Of Lee Harvey Oswald (T);
The Miracle (S); The Bill (T)

Lawrence Van Reiss

Bankview Studios, 29 Bank Road, Crumpsall, Manchester M8 4QE
t 01617 957931 **f** 01617 957931 **m** 07768 998166
e canineursa@tinyworld.co.uk **w** www.lawrencevanreiss.com
Credits Cook in the Castle (T); Madly Yours (F); Amy Foster (F)

Sally Reynolds

10 Hampden Road, Muswell Hill, London N10 2HL
t 020 8883 1520 **f** 020 8883 1520 **m** 07889 056657
e reynoldssj@dialstart.net
Credits The Cruise (T); Bad Girls (T); The Sins (T); Swallow (T)

Lucy Richardson

3 Breer Street, London SW6 3HE
t 020 7384 1327 **m** 07770 886766 **e** lucy.richardson@virgin.net
Credits Ella Enchanted (F); Chocolat (F); Spider (F); Mystic Masseur (F)

Hauke Richter

Dinedor Management, 81 Oxford Street, London W1O 2EU
t 020 7851 3575 **f** 020 7851 3576
e info@dinedor.com **w** www.dinedor.com
Credits Conspiracy (F); Mad Dogs (F); Independent (C); Volkswagen Golf (C)

Phil Roberson

4 Brecon Road, London W6 8PU
t 020 7385 6911 **m** 07973 223726 **e** philroberson@btinternet.com
Credits The Biographer (F); Warriors (T); Impact (T); Nice Guy Eddie (T)

Robert Innes Hopkins

Cruickshank Cazenove Ltd, 97 Old South Lambeth Road,
London SW8 1XU
t 020 7735 2933 **f** 020 7820 1081 **e** hjcruickshank@aol.com

Rachel Robertson

Gems, The Media House, 87 Glebe Street, Penarth CF64 1EF
t 029 2071 0770 **f** 029 2071 0771 **e** gems@gems-agency.co.uk
w www.gems-agency.co.uk
Credits Napisane Na Ciele (F); Ed Stone Is Dead (T); Grandad's Magic Lantern
(T); Boxed (F)

Roger Harris Production Design

2 Burnaby Crescent, Chiswick, London W4 3LH
t 020 8747 8545 **f** 020 8747 8545 **m** 07885 723433
e rogerharris@dsl.pipex.com
Contact Roger Harris, Proprietor
Credits Inmarsat (I); Tyndale Bible (D); Viking In My Bed (T); Christmas Ghost
Stories (T)

Scott Rogers

Art Department, 51 Pratt Street, London NW1 0BJ
t 020 7428 0500 **f** 020 7916 2167 **m** 07968 970208
e info@art-department.co.uk

Chris Roope

International Creative Management Ltd, Oxford House,
76 Oxford Street, London W1D 1BS
t 020 7636 6565 **f** 020 7323 0101 **w** www.icmlondon.co.uk
Credits Princess Of Thieves (T); Keen Eddie (T); Thunderpants (F)

Paul Rowan

3 Spring Road, Hale WA14 2UQ
t 01619 712840 **m** 07885 332 869
e user@paulrowan.softnet.co.uk
Credits The Grand (T); Murder On The Orient Express (T); Wuthering Heights (T)

Marcus Rowland

Art Department, 51 Pratt Street, London NW1 0BJ
t 020 7428 0500 **f** 020 7916 2167 **m** 07973 639785
e info@art-department.co.uk

Christine Ruscoe

45 Hatherley Road, Winchester SO22 6RR
t 01962 851321 **f** 01962 851321 **m** 07850 099589
e saberuscoe@waitrose.com
Contact Christine Ruscoe, Designer
Credits Art Attack (T); Ruth Rendell Mysteries (T)

Ian Russell

76 Mallard Place, Twickenham TW1 4SR
t 020 8395 9141 **m** 07802 259959 **e** i_russell@hotmail.com
Credits The Treasure Seekers (T); EastEnders (T); The Bill (T); The Canterville
Ghost (T)

Nina Russell-Cowan

Art Department, 51 Pratt Street, London NW1 0BJ
t 020 7428 0500 **f** 020 7916 2167 **m** 07870 646691
e info@art-department.co.uk

Crispian Sallis

Creative Media Management, Unit 3B, Walpole Court, Ealing
Studios, Ealing Green, London W5 5ED
t 020 8584 5363 **f** 020 8566 5554
e enquiries@creativemediamanagement.com
Credits Gladiatress (F); My Little Eye (F); Once Upon A Time In The Midlands
(F); Hannibal (F)

Andrew Sanders

International Creative Management Ltd, Oxford House,
76 Oxford Street, London W1D 1BS
t 020 7636 6565 **f** 020 7323 0101 **w** www.icmlondon.co.uk
Credits Wings Of The Dove (F); The Golden Bowl (F); Spider (F)

Andrew Sanders
Art Department, 51 Pratt Street, London NW1 0BJ
t 020 7428 0500 f 020 7916 2167 m 07973 639785
e info@art-department.co.uk

Tom Sayer
Flat 2, 8 Gladstone Place, Edinburgh EH6 7LY
t 0131 554 2909 f 0131 554 2909 m 07768 655377
e tom@tomsayer.demon.co.uk
Credits Skegerrak (F); Witchcreze (F); Cry For Bobo (S); Last Great Wilderness (F)

Ben Scott
The Dench Arnold Agency, 24 D'Arblay Street, London W1F 8EH
t 020 7437 4551 f 020 7439 1355
e contact@dencharnoldagency.co.uk w www.dencharnold.co.uk
Credits Sword Of Hornor (F); Armadillo (T); Boudica (T)

Carolyn Scott
Gems, The Media House, 87 Glebe Street, Penarth CF64 1EF
t 029 2071 0770 f 029 2071 0771
e gems@gems-agency.co.uk w www.gems-agency.co.uk
Credits Nightbreed (F); A Castle Christmas (F); Princess In Love (F)

Gerry Scott
t 01753 662936 f 01753 662936 m 07770 872256
Credits Wives And Daughters (T); Pride And Prejudice (T); Love In A Cold Climate (T); Messiah II (T)

James 'Sid' Scott
25 Paget Street, Grangetown, Cardiff CF11 7LB
t 029 2021 4881 f 029 2021 4869 m 07785 795421
e scott-callaghan.artpro@ntlworld.com w www.sidart.co.uk
Credits The Snowman (A); The Jogger (S); Cave OF Secrets (T); Lucky Bag (T)

Stephen Scott
20 Southern Road, London N2 9LE
t 020 8883 7750 f 020 8883 7750 m 07776 257118
Credits Hellboy (F); Tomorrow Never Dies (F); Highlander IV (F); Die Another Day (F)

Chris Seagers
18 Trafalgar Road, Twickenham TW2 5EJ
t 020 8894 4822 f 020 8985 936 m 07831 787762
Agent International Creative Management Ltd, Oxford House, 76 Oxford Street, London W1D 1BS
t 020 7636 6565 f 020 7323 0101 w www.icmlondon.co.uk
Credits Saving Private Ryan (F); Spy Game (F); Johnny English (F); Captain Corelli's Mandolin (F); Spy Game (F)

Richard Selway
Art Department, 51 Pratt Street, London NW1 0BJ
t 020 7428 0500 f 020 7916 2167 m 07870 646691
e info@art-department.co.uk

Nadine Sender
Art Department, 51 Pratt Street, London NW1 0BJ
t 020 7428 0500 f 020 7916 2167 m 07714 102405
e info@art-department.co.uk

Julia Sherborne
Art Department, 51 Pratt Street, London NW1 0BJ
t 020 7428 0500 f 020 7916 2167 m 07973 639785
e info@art-department.co.uk

Georgina Shorter
Art Department, 51 Pratt Street, London NW1 0DJ
t 020 7428 0500 f 020 7916 2167 m 07899 724509
e info@art-department.co.uk

Lester Smith
Experience Counts - Call Me Ltd, 5th Floor, 41-42 Berners Street, London W1P 3AA
t 020 7637 8112 f 020 7580 2582

Nick Somerville
f 020 8840 0375 m 07850 556716 e nick.somerville@virgin.net
Agent Jessica Carney Associates, Suite 90-92 Kent House, 87 Regent Street, London W1B 4EH
t 020 7434 4143 f 020 7434 4173 e info@jcarneyassociates.co.uk
Credits The Gift (T); The Dark Room (T); The Bombmaker (T)

Isolde Sommerfeld
Flat G, 37 Southwark Bridge Road, London SE1 9HH
t 020 7357 0317 f 020 7357 6164 m 07973 693161
e isolde@sommerfeldt.fsnet.co.uk
Credits Vodaphone (C); The Jury (T); My Brother Tom (F)

Alan Spalding
20 Boileau Road, Ealing, London W5 3AH
t 020 8997 6400 m 07850 315350 e spaldingdesign@aol.com
Credits The Great Ship (D); Zzapp And The Wordmaster (T); The Mirror Cracked From Side To Side (T); The Chronicles Of Narnia (T)

Chris Stephenson
CCA Management, 7 St George's Square, London SW1V 2HX
t 020 7630 6303 f 020 7630 7376

Mark Stevenson
International Creative Management Ltd, Oxford House, 76 Oxford Street, London W1D 1BS
t 020 7636 6565 f 020 7323 0101 w www.icmlondon.co.uk
Credits Beautiful Thing (F); In A Land Of Plenty (T); Murphy's Law (T)

Eve Stewart
International Creative Management Ltd, Oxford House, 76 Oxford Street, London W1D 1BS
t 020 7636 6565 f 020 7323 0101 w www.icmlondon.co.uk
Credits Topsy-Turvy (F); All Or Nothing (F); Nicholas Nickleby (F)

Jamie Stimpson
Art Department, 51 Pratt Street, London NW1 0BJ
t 020 7428 0500 f 020 7916 2167 m 07903 990498
e info@art-department.co.uk

Graeme Story
Experience Counts - Call Me Ltd, 5th Floor, 41-42 Berners Street, London W1P 3AA
t 020 7637 8112 f 020 7580 2582

Tony Stringer
Art Department, 51 Pratt Street, London NW1 0BJ
t 020 7428 0500 f 020 7916 2167 m 07973 639785
e info@art-department.co.uk

Madeleine Swinglehurst
Dinedor Management, 81 Oxford Street, London W10 2EU
t 020 7851 3575 f 020 7851 3576
e info@dinedor.com w www.dinedor.com
Credits B&Q (C); Baby Father (T); Big Brother 2 (T)

Brian Sykes
Dinedor Management, 81 Oxford Street, London W10 2EU
t 020 7851 3575 f 020 7851 3576
e info@dinedor.com w www.dinedor.com
Credits Sunny Delight (C); Heat Magazine (C); A Line In The Sand (T); Silent Witness (T)

Nigel Talamo
Dinedor Management, 81 Oxford Street, London W10 2EU
t 020 7851 3575 f 020 7851 3576
e info@dinedor.com w www.dinedor.com
Credits Sting (M); Kylie Minogue (M); Adidas (C); Cravendale Milk (C)

Robin Tarsnane
20 Manor View, Finchley, London N3 2SS
t 020 8349 1449 f 020 8343 4136 m 07802 713772
e 25frames@lineone.net
Credits Into The Blue (T); Kavanagh QC (T); Shooters (F); Inspector Morse (T)

Don Taylor

International Creative Management Ltd, Oxford House,
76 Oxford Street, London W1D 1BS
t 020 7636 6565 **f** 020 7323 0101 **w** www.icmlondon.co.uk
Credits Little Voice (F); House Of Mirth (F); Dr Sleep (F)

Jeff Tessler

109 Hemingford Road, London N1 1BY
t 020 7609 1097 **f** 020 7697 9727 **m** 07860 415603
e jitessler@aol.com
Agent International Creative Management Ltd, Oxford House,
76 Oxford Street, London W1D 1BS
t 020 7636 6565 **f** 020 7323 0101 **w** www.icmlondon.co.uk
Credits Wire In The Blood II (T); Queer As Folk II (T); Touching Evil (T); Serious
And Organised (T); Is Harry On The Boat (T)

Malcolm Thornton

International Creative Management Ltd, Oxford House,
76 Oxford Street, London W1D 1BS
t 020 7636 6565 **f** 020 7323 0101 **w** www.icmlondon.co.uk
Credits Our Mutual Friend (T); Othello (T); Tipping The Velvet (T)

Anne Tilby

The Dench Arnold Agency, 24 D'Arblay Street, London W1F 8EH
t 020 7437 4551 **e**
contact@dencharnoldagency.co.uk **w** www.dencharnold.co.uk
Credits Mozart In Turkey (D); Brazen Hussies (T); Alice Through The Looking
Glass (T)

Anne Tilby

Art Department, 51 Pratt Street, London NW1 0BJ
t 020 7428 0500 **f** 020 7916 2167 **m** 07973 639785
e info@art-department.co.uk

Tim Farmer Design

Glanrafon, Llanbedrog, Pwllheli LL53 7NU
t 01758 740297 **f** 01758 740297 **m** 07976 275748
e timfarmeroz@hotmail.com
Credits Buried (T); Cold Feet (T)

Jane Tomblin

Flat 1, Oak Lodge, 6 Oak Lodge Drive, West Wickham BR4 0RQ
t 020 8777 5266 **f** 020 8777 5266 **m** 07885 183924
e thelabelqueen@hotmail.com
Agent Dinedor Management, 81 Oxford Street, London W10 2EU
t 020 7851 3575 **f** 020 7851 3576
e info@dinedor.com **w** www.dinedor.com
Credits Long Time Dead (F); True Blue (F); The Sculptress (T); Peak Practice (T)

Chris Townsend

Creative Media Management, Unit 3B, Walpole Court, Ealing
Studios, Ealing Green, London W5 5ED
t 020 8584 5363 **f** 020 8566 5554
e enquiries@creativemediamanagement.com
Credits Rehab (T); Face (T); Waking The Dead II & III (T); The Darkest Light (F)

Ben van Os

International Creative Management Ltd, Oxford House,
76 Oxford Street, London W1D 1BS
t 020 7636 6565 **f** 020 7323 0101 **w** www.icmlondon.co.uk
Credits Orlando (F); It's All About Love (F); The Girl With The Pearl Earring (F)

Voytek

23b Woodland Road, Isleworth TW7 6NR
t 020 8847 2250 **f** 020 8847 2250
Credits Worst of All (T); Dandelion Dead (T); Black Rainbow (F)

Leigh Walker

The Old School House, High Street, Chipping Camden GL55 6AG
t 01386 841155 **f** 01386 841155 **m** 07774 190020
e leigh.walker1@btinternet.com
Credits Gentleman's Relish (T); Othello (T); Tipping The Velvet (T); I Capture
The Castle (F)

Stuart Walker

Casarotto Marsh Ltd, National House, 60-66 Wardour Street,
London W1V 4ND
t 020 7287 4450 **f** 020 7287 9128
e agents@casarotto.uk.com **w** www.casarotto.uk.com

Leslie Wallace

27 Falcon Heights, Mountainside, Newtownards BT23 4GF
t 028 9182 0089 **f** 028 9182 0080 **m** 07885 229823
e lesliewallacedesign@ntlbusiness.com

Peter Walpole

Art Department, 51 Pratt Street, London NW1 0BJ
t 020 7428 0500 **f** 020 7916 2167 **m** 07973 639785
e info@art-department.co.uk

Frank Walsh

35 New Barn Lane, Seer Green, Beaconsfield HP9 2QZ
t 01494 875921 **m** 07760 176160
e frank.s.walsh@lineone.net **w** www.frankwalsh.co.uk
Credits Lara Croft And The Cradle Of Life: Tomb Raider 2 (F); Buffalo Soldiers
(F); Fungus The Bogeyman (T); Cleopatra (T)

Niki Wateridge

3 Carver Close, Church Path, Chiswick, London W4 9BP
t 020 8994 6499 **m** 07939 463610 **m** 07900 287450
e ndever2000@yahoo.com
Credits Blackwater (T); The Waiting Time (T); Kavanagh QC Special (T); The
Hidden City (T)

Simon Waters

Creative Media Management, Unit 3B, Walpole Court, Ealing
Studios, Ealing Green, London W5 5ED
t 020 8584 5363 **f** 020 8566 5554
e enquiries@creativemediamanagement.com
Credits Chaos And Cadavers (T); The Squeeze (T); Randall And Hopkirk
Deceased, Series II (T)

Ian Watson

Gems, The Media House, 87 Glebe Street, Penarth CF64 1EF
t 029 2071 0770 **f** 029 2071 0771
e gems@gems-agency.co.uk **w** www.gems-agency.co.uk
Credits Jinnah (F); Sunset Heights (F); The Honey Trap (F); Three Blind Mice (F)

Ken Wheatley

Experience Counts - Call Me Ltd, 5th Floor, 41-42 Berners
Street, London W1P 3AA
t 020 7637 8112 **f** 020 7580 2582

Susan Whitaker

t 020 8896 9557 **m** 07831 186182 **w** www.film-design.co.uk
Credits Incognito (F); Entrapment (F); Sleepy Hollow (F)

Lynne Whiteread

The Dench Arnold Agency, 24 D'Arblay Street, London W1F 8EH
t 020 7437 4551 **f** 020 7439 1355
e contact@dencharnoldagency.co.uk **w** www.dencharnold.co.uk
Credits The Lowest Heat (T); Second Generation (T); Stella Does Tricks (F)

Fleur Whitlock

135 Perryfield Way, Ham, Richmond TW10 7SN
t 020 8948 0016 **m** 07831 415780
e fleur_whitlock@yahoo.co.uk
Credits Dot The I (F); Love And Death On Long Island (F); The Bill (T); A&E (T)

Sarah Whittle

Art Department, 51 Pratt Street, London NW1 0BJ
t 020 7428 0500 **f** 020 7916 2167 **m** 07870 674740
e info@art-department.co.uk

Jamie Williams

Art Department, 51 Pratt Street, London NW1 0BJ
t 020 7428 0500 **f** 020 7916 2167 **m** 07974 302420
e info@art-department.co.uk

Donal Woods

International Creative Management Ltd, Oxford House,
76 Oxford Street, London W1D 1BS
t 020 7636 6565 **f** 020 7323 0101 **w** www.icmlondon.co.uk
Credits All The King's Men (T); Take A Girl Like You (T); State Of Play (F)

Marcus Wookey

Dinedor Management, 81 Oxford Street, London W10 2EU
t 020 7851 3575 **f** 020 7851 3576 **e** info@dinedor.com
w www.dinedor.com
Credits Sony (C); Tango (C); Vigo (F); Sexy Beast (F)

Jackie Yau

Art Department, 51 Pratt Street, London NW1 0BJ
t 020 7428 0500 **f** 020 7916 2167 **m** 07799 411617
e info@art-department.co.uk

Art Directors **Assistant**

Eileen Aldous

11 Gainsborough Road, Felixstowe IP11 7HT
t 01394 285090 **f** 01394 285091 **m** 07889 437319
e eileen.aldous@btopenworld.com

Steve Bream

16 Park Crescent, Elstree, Borehamwood WD6 3PU
t 020 8953 9684 **m** 07811 345048
e stevebream519@hotmail.com
Credits The World Is Not Enough (F); Around The World In 80 Days (2003) (F);
Beyond Boarders (F); Reign Of Fire (F)

Richard Bullock

Art Department, 51 Pratt Street, London NW1 0BJ
t 020 7428 0500 **f** 020 7916 2167 **m** 07973 639785
e info@art-department.co.uk

Peter Dorme

25 Malthouse Square, Beaconsfield HP9 2LD
t 01494 670806 **m** 07889 214 717
Credits Harry Potter And The Chamber Of Secrets (F); Harry Potter And The
Philosopher's Stone (F); Enemy At The Gates (F)

Catherine Evenden

130A Graham Road, Hackney, London E8 1BS
t 020 7923 4985 **f** 020 7241 2289 **m** 07767 810005
e kate_evenden@hotmail.com
Credits U Get Me (T); Helen West (T); The Basil Brush Show (T)

Jon Houlding

m 07979 654745 **e** jonathan@houlding.co.uk
Credits Love Actually (F); The Good Thief (F); Band Of Brothers (T); Reign Of Fire (F)

Peter James

11 Radnor Road, Weybridge KT13 8JU
t 01932 821401 **f** 01932 821402 **m** 07973 188541
Credits The Lion In Winter (T); Vodaphone (C); Band Of Brothers (T); Jack And
The Beanstalk (T)

Jason Knox-Johnson

Art Department, 51 Pratt Street, London NW1 0BJ
t 020 7428 0500 **f** 020 7916 2167 **m** 07973 639785
e info@art-department.co.uk

Annelies Lovell

102 Arodene Road, London SW2 2BH
t 020 8671 3662 **m** 07710 305268
Credits The Bill (T)

Stephen Morahan

5 Piercefield, Calcot, Reading RG31 7AS
t 0118 962 4691 **m** 07944 606112
e steve@filmdesign.co.uk **w** www.filmdesign.co.uk
Credits Die Another Day (F); Lara Croft And The Cradle Of Life: Tomb Raider II
(F); Harry Potter And The Philosopher's Stone (F)

David Morrison

Art Department, 51 Pratt Street, London NW1 0BJ
t 020 7428 0500 **f** 020 7916 2167 **m** 07973 639785
e info@art-department.co.uk

Tom O'Donnell

Art Department, 51 Pratt Street, London NW1 0BJ
t 020 7428 0500 **f** 020 7916 2167 **m** 07973 639785
e info@art-department.co.uk

Mark Scruton

Art Department, 51 Pratt Street, London NW1 0BJ
t 020 7428 0500 **f** 020 7916 2167 **m** 07973 639785
e info@art-department.co.uk

Gary Tomkins

22 London Road, Aston Clinton, Aylesbury HP22 5HQ
t 01296 632024 **m** 07778 325430
Credits Harry Potter And The Chamber Of Secrets (F); Sleepy Hollow (F); The
Mummy Returns (F); Harry Potter And The Philosopher's Stone (F)

Yvonne Toner

Cross Dunn Llangarron, Ross-on-Wye HR9 6NL
t 01989 770131 **f** 01989 770131 **m** 07970 898933
e yvonnejtoner@btinternet.com
Credits Jacob's Ladder (T); Life And Debt (T); Teletubbies (T); Alone (F)

Teresa Weston

t 020 8789 6208 **m** 07785 948293 **e** teresaweston@hotmail.com

David A Wood

September House, Millbrook, Chertsey Road,
Shepperton TW17 9LA
t 01932 243242 **f** 01932 243242 **m** 07798 524316
Contact David Wood
Credits League Of Extraordinary Gentlemen (F); Resident Evil (F); Dr Zhivago (T)

Verity Woolf

ADS, Shepperton Studios, Studios Road, Shepperton TW17 0QD
t 01932 592303 **f** 01932 592492 **e** ads@carlincrew.co.uk
Credits Martini (F); Five (M); Sugar Babes (M); Robot Wars (T)

ASSOCIATIONS

Advertising Association

Abford House, 15 Wilton Road, London SW1V 1NJ
t 020 7828 4831 **f** 020 7931 0376
e ic@adassoc.org.uk **w** www.adassoc.org.uk

Advertising Film & Videotape Producers Association (AFVPA)

26 Noel Street, London W1V 3RD
t 020 7434 2651 **f** 020 7434 9002
e info@a-p-a.net **w** www.a-p-a.net
Contact Stephen Davies

Advertising Standards Authority

2 Torrington Place, London WC1E 7HW
t 020 7580 5555 **f** 020 7631 3051
e enquiries@asa.org.uk **w** www.asa.org.uk
Contact Debra Huntley, Communications Department

The Agents' Association

54 Keyes House, Dolphin Square, London SW1V 3NA
t 020 7834 0515 **f** 020 7821 0261
e association@agents-uk.com **w** www.agents-uk.com
Contact Carol Richards, Administrator

American Society of Composers, Authors & Publishers (ASCAP)

8 Cork Street, London W1X 1PB
t 020 7439 0909 **f** 020 7434 0073
e info@ascap.com **w** www.ascap.com
Contact Roger Greenaway

AND Association

10 Back Church Lane, London E1 1LX
t 020 7481 9053 **f** 020 7481 3044
e jenni@and.org.uk **w** www.and.org.uk
Contact Ismail Saray, Co-Editor; Jenni Boswell-Jones, Editing Manager
Credits Children's World-London (W)

Animal Filming & Training Commission

9 King Lane Cottages, Over Wallop, Stockbridge SO20 8JF
t 01264 781804 **m** 07850 820086
e info@aftc.org.co.uk **w** www.movie-animals.couk
Contact Rona Brown
Credits My Hero (T); Daziel And Pascoe (T)

Association of Model Agents (AMA)

122 Brompton Road, London SW3 1JE
t 020 7584 6466 **f** 020 7581 2113 **e** amalondon@btinternet.com

Association of Motion Picture Sound

28 Knox Street, London W1H 1FS
t 020 7723 6727 **f** 020 7723 6727
e admin@amps.net **w** www.amps.net
Contact Brian Hickin, Admin Secretary

Association of Photographers (AOP)

81 Leonard Street, London EC2A 4QS
t 020 7739 6669 **f** 020 7739 8707
e general@aophoto.co.uk **w** www.the-aop.org

Association of Professional Recording Services (APRS)

PO Box 22, Totnes TQ9 7YZ
t 01803 868600 **f** 01803 868444
e info@aprs.co.uk **w** www.aprs.co.uk

Brief Encounters International Short Film Festival

Watershed Media Centre, 1 Cannon's Road, Harbourside, Bristol BS1 5TX
t 0117 927 5102 **f** 0117 930 9967
e info@brief-encounters.org.uk **w** www.brief-encounters.org.uk
Contact Eimear Carolan, Festival Director; Claire Causton, Development Officer; Lucy Jefferies, Festival Administrator; Abigail Youngman, Festival Director; Alice Bennett-Leyh, Marketing & Development Assistant

Bristol Interactive Cluster

The Production House, 147A St Michaels Hill, Bristol BS2 8DB
t 0117 904 0234 **f** 0117 9040235
e team@cluster.org.uk **w** www.cluster.org.uk

British Acadamy of Film & Television Arts Scotland

249 West George Street, Glasgow G2 4QE
t 0141 302 1770 **f** 0141 302 1771
e info@baftascotland.co.uk **w** www.baftascotland.co.uk
Contact Alison Forsyth, Director

British Academy of Composers & Songwriters

British Music House, 26 Berners Street, London W1T 3LR
t 020 7636 2929 **f** 020 7636 2212
e info@britishacademy.com **w** www.britishacademy.com
Contact Fergal Kilroy, Head of Membership

British Academy of Film & Television Arts (BAFTA) Wales/Cymru

Chapter Arts Centre, Market Road, Canton, Cardiff CF5 1QE
t 029 2022 3898 **f** 029 2066 4189
e post@bafta-cymru.org.uk **w** www.bafta-cymru.org.uk
Contact Sarah Howells, Manager; Geraint Evans, Director

The British Academy of Film & Television Arts (BAFTA)

195 Piccadilly, London W1J 9LN
t 020 7734 0022 **f** 020 7734 1792
e reception@bafta.org **w** www.bafta.org
Contact Amy Minyard, Events & Membership Officer

The British Association of Choreographers

c/o Dance UK, Battersea Arts Centre, Lavender Hill, London SW11 5TF
t 020 7228 4990
e danceuk@easynet.co.uk **w** www.danceuk.org

British Association of Communicators in Business

Suite A, 1st Floor, The Auriga Building, Davy Avenue, Knowlhill, Milton Keynes MK5 8ND
t 0870 121 7606 **f** 0870 121 7601
e enquiries@cib.uk.com **w** www.cib.uk
Contact Brenda Scott, Administrator

British Council

Films Department, 10 Spring Gardens, London SW1A 2BN
t 020 7389 3065 **f** 020 7389 3041
e ftvd@britishcouncil.org **w** www.britfilms.com
Contact Julian Pye, Contact

British Design & Art Direction

9 Graphite Square, Vauxhall, London SE11 5EE
t 020 7840 1111 **f** 020 7840 0840
e info@dandad.co.uk **w** www.dandad.co.uk
Contact Louise Fowler, Awards Director

British Film Commission (BFC)

10 Little Portland Street, London W1W 7JG
t 020 7861 7860 **f** 020 7861 7864
e info@bfc.co.uk **w** www.bfc.co.uk
Contact Alison Sawkill, Head of Information

British Institute of Professional Photography (BIPP)

Fox Talbot House, 2 Amwell End, Ware SG12 9HN
t 01920 464011 **f** 01920 487056
e bippware@aol.com **w** www.bipp.com
Contact Alex Mair, Executive Secretary

British Interactive Media Association (BIMA)

Briarlea House, Southend Road, Billericay CM11 2PR
t 01277 658107 **f** 0870 051 7842
e enquiries@bima.co.uk **w** www.bima.org.uk
Contact Janice Cable, Principal Administrator; Liz Citron, Marketing Director

British Phonographic Industry (BPI)

Riverside Building, County Hall, Westminster Bridge Road, London SE1 7JA
t 020 7803 1300 **f** 020 7803 1310
e general@bpi.co.uk **w** www.bpi.co.uk
Contact Kaylee Coxall

British Society of Cinematographers

PO Box 2587, Gerrards Cross SL9 7WZ
t 01753 888052 **f** 01753 891486
e Britcinematograpters@compuserve.com **w** www.Bscine.com

British Television Advertising Awards

37 Berwick Street, London W1F 8RS
t 020 7734 6962 **f** 020 7437 0748
e info@btaa.co.uk **w** www.btaa.co.uk
Contact Peter Bigg

British Video Association

167 Great Portland Street, London W1W 5PE
t 020 7436 0041 **f** 020 7436 0043
e general@bva.org.uk **w** www.bva.org.uk

Broadcast Advertising Clearance Centre (BACC)
200 Grays Inn Road, London WC1X 8HF
t 020 7843 8232 **f** 020 7923 5484
e steph_hughes@bacc.gov.uk **w** www.bacc.org.uk
Contact Stephanie Hughes, PA To Director

Broadcasting Entertainment Cinematograph & Theatre Union (BECTU)
373-377 Clapham Road, London SW9 9BT
t 020 7346 0900 **f** 020 7346 0901
e janice@stagescreenandradio.org.uk **w** www.bectu.org.uk

Broadcasting Standards Commission
7 The Sanctuary, London SW1P 3JS
t 020 7808 1000 **f** 020 7233 0397
e bsc@bsc.org.uk **w** www.bsc.org.uk

Celtic Film & Television Festival
249 West George Street, Glasgow G2 4QE
t 0141 302 1737 **f** 0141 302 1738
e mail@celticfilm.co.uk **w** www.celticfilm.co.uk
Contact Frances Hendron, Chief Executive

The Chartered Institute of Journalists
2 Dock Offices, Surrey Quays Road, London SE16 2XU
t 020 7252 1187 **f** 020 7232 2302
e memberservices@ioj.co.uk **w** www.ioj.co.uk
Contact Dominic Cooper, Deputy General Secretary

Chief Engineers of Facilities Forum
Hillside, Merryhill Road, Bushey, Watford WD23 1DR
t 020 8950 4426 **f** 020 8421 8085
Contact Chris Hillier, Chairman; Roger Cumner, Secretary; Brian Stephens, Treasurer

Cine Guilds of Great Britain
72 Pembroke Road, London W8 6NX
t 020 7602 8319 **f** 020 7602 8319 **m** 07974 966665
e cineguildsgb@btinternet.com
Contact Sally Fisher, Secretary

Cinema & Television Benevolent Fund (CTBF)
22 Golden Square, London W1F 9AD
t 020 7437 6567 **f** 020 7437 7186
e charity@ctbf.co.uk **w** www.ctbf.co.uk
Contact Sandra Bradley, Head of Events & Marketing; Mark Roberts, Head of Welfare

Cinema Exhibitors Association (CEA)
22 Golden Square, London W1F 9JW
t 020 7734 9551 **f** 020 7734 6147 **e** cea@cinemauk.ftech.co.uk
Contact John Wilkinson, Chief Executive

Commercial Radio Companies Association
The Radio Centre, 77 Shaftesbury Avenue, London W1D 5DU
t 020 7306 2603 **f** 020 7470 0062
e info@crca.co.uk **w** www.crca.co.uk

Commonwealth Broadcasting Association
17 Fleet Street, London EC4Y 1AA
t 020 7583 5550 **f** 020 7583 5549
e cba@cba.org.uk **w** www.cba.org.uk
Contact Elizabeth Smith, Secretary General

Community Media Association (CMA)
15 Paternoster Row, Sheffield S1 2BX
t 0114 279 5219 **f** 0114 279 8976
e cma@commedia.org.uk **w** www.commedia.org.uk
Contact Beth Barker, Marketing Assistant; Keeley Scott, Administrator

Directors & Producers Rights Society
Victoria Chambers, 16-18 Strutton Ground, London SW1P 2HP
t 020 7227 4757 **f** 020 7227 4755 **e** info@dprs.org
Contact Suzan Dormer, Chief Executive

The Directors Guild of Great Britain
Acorn House, 314-320 Gray's Inn Road, London WC1X 8DP
t 020 7278 4343 **f** 020 7278 4742
e guild@dggb.co.uk **w** www.dggb.co.uk
Contact Jim Whiteford, General Manager; Maria Balermpa, Training & Events Manager; Jane Grater, Administrative Director; Malcolm Moore, Chief Executive; Pat Trueman, Chief Executive

Equity
Guild House, Upper St Martin's Lane, London WC2H 9EG
t 020 7379 6000 **f** 020 7379 7001
e info@equity.org.uk **w** www.equity.org.uk
Contact Martin Brown, Campaigns, Press and PR Offices; Helen Buckley-Hoffman, Film/TV/Radio Help Desk

Federation of Entertainment Unions
1 Highfield, Twyford, Winchester SO21 1QR
t 01962 713134 **f** 01962 713134 **m** 07889 289249
e harris@interalpha.co.uk
Contact Steve Harris, Secretary

The Film Council
10 Little Portland Street, London W1W 7JG
t 020 7861 7861 **f** 020 7861 7862
e info@filmcouncil.org.uk **w** www.filmcouncil.org.uk
Contact John Woodward, Chief Executive Officer; Paul Trijbits, Head of New Cinema Fund; Jenny Borgars, Head of Development Fund; Helen Bagnall, Head of Training Fund; Robert Jones, Head of Premier Fund
Credits The Magdalene Sisters (F); Ted and Sylvia (F); Bloody Sunday (F); Gosford Park (F)

The Film Council is the strategic body for film in the UK and uses lottery money and government grant funding to generate cultural and economic benefits. The organisation provides funding for film development, production, training, regional development, and distribution and exhibition.

Film Distributors' Association (FDA)
22 Golden Square, London W1R 3PA
t 020 7437 4384 **f** 020 7734 0912 **w** www.launchingfilms.com
Contact Mark Batey, Chief Executive

The Grierson Award
6 Washingley Road, Folksworth, Peterborough PE7 3SY
t 01733 245841 **f** 01733 240020
e awards@multimediaventures.com **w** www.griersontrust.org
Contact Jane Callaghan, Awards Co-ordinator
Credits The Grierson Awards 2002 (T)

Guide Dogs for the Blind Association
Hillfields, Burghfield Common, Reading RG7 3YG
t 0118 983 5555 **f** 0118 983 1302 **m** 07771 778 365
e pat.farr@gdba.org.uk **w** www.guidedogs.org.uk
Contact Mr Pat Farr, Media Development Manager

The Guild of British Film Editors
72 Pembroke Road, London W8 6NX
t 020 7602 8319 **f** 020 7602 8319
e secretarygbfe@btopenworld.com
Contact Brian Sinclair, Chairman; Sally Fisher, Secretary; John Glover, Vice Chairman; Sally Fisher, Secretary; Alfred Cox, Honorary Secretary

The Guild of International Songwriters & Composers
Sovereign House, 12 Trewartha Road, Praa Sands, Penzance TR20 9ST
t 01736 762826 **f** 01736 763328 **e** songmag@aol.com
w www.songwriters-guild.co.uk
Contact Carole Jones, General Secretary

Guild of Television Cameramen
1 Churchhill Road, Whitchurch, Tavistock PL19 9BU
t 01822 614405 **e** administration@gtc.org.uk
w www.gtc.org.uk

Guild of Vision Mixers
e guild@visionmixers.tv w www.visionmixers.tv
Contact Peter Turl, Chairman

Incorporated Society of British Advertisers (ISBA)
44 Hertford Street, London W1J 7AE
t 020 7499 7502 f 020 7629 5355
e info@isba.org.uk w www.isba.org.uk
Contact Malcolm Earnshaw, Director

Incorporated Society of Musicians (ISM)
10 Stratford Place, London W1C 1AA
t 020 7629 4413 f 020 7408 1538
e membership@ism.org w www.ism.org
Contact Neil Hoyle, Chief Executive

Institute of Broadcast Sound
27 Old Gloucester Street, London WC1N 3XX
t 01483 575450 f 01483 300735
e membership@ibs.org.uk w www.ibs.org.uk
Contact Malcolm Johnson, Secretariat

International Artist Managers' Association
23 Garrick Street, Covent Graden, London WC2E 9BN
t 020 7379 7336 f 020 7379 7336
e info@iamaworld.com w www.iamaworld.com

International Association of Broadcasting Manufacturers (IABM)
PO Box 2264, Reading RG31 6WA
t 0118 941 8620 f 0118 941 8630
e info@theiabm.org w www.theiabm.org
Contact Elaine Bukiej, Secretariat

International Visual Communication Association (IVCA)
19 Pepper Street, Glengall Bridge, Docklands, London E14 9RP
t 020 7512 0571 f 020 7512 0591
e info@ivca.org w www.ivca.org

The MCPS-PRS Alliance
29-33 Berners Street, London W1T 3AB
t 020 7580 5544 f 020 7306 4455
e press@mcps-prs-alliance.co.uk w www.mcps-prs-alliance.co.uk
Contact Adrian Crookes, Media Relations Manager; Andy Rock, Broadcasting Director

Musicians Union (MU)
60-62 Clapham Road, London SW9 0JJ
t 020 7582 5566 f 020 7582 9805
e hel@musiciansunion.org.uk w www.musiciansunion.org.uk
Contact Howard Evans, Sesion Organiser

National Union of Journalists (NUJ)
308-312 Grays Inn Road, London WC1X 8DP
t 020 7278 7916 f 020 7837 8143
e acorn.house@nuj.org.uk w www.nuj.org.uk
Contact Paul McLaughlin, National Broadcasting Organiser

New Producers Alliance
9 Bourlet Close, London W1W 7BP
t 020 7580 2480 f 020 7580 2484
e queries@npa.org.uk w www.newproducer.co.uk
Contact Yalda Armian, Publications & Information Manager; Kevin Dolan, Events Manager; David Castro, CEO

pact.

PACT
45 Mortimer Street, London W1W 8HJ
t 020 7331 6040 f 020 7331 6700 m 07711 706529
e enquiries@pact.co.uk w www.pact.co.uk
Contact Sarah Walker, Director of Communications & Marketing; John McVay, Chief Executive

PACT is the UK trade association that represents the commercial interests of independent feature film, television, animation and interactive media companies. PACT has 1,000 members, making it the largest representative group of screen-based content producers in the UK and the largest trade association in the film, television and interactive media sectors.

PACT in Scotland
249 West George Street, Glasgow G2 4QE
t 0141 222 4880 f 0141 222 4881
e jenny@pact.co.uk w www.pact.co.uk

Phonographic Performance Ltd (PPL)
1 Upper James Street, London W1R 3HG
t 020 7534 1000 f 020 7534 1111
e pete.rogers@ppluk.com w www.ppluk.com
Contact Pete Rogers, Head of Broadcasting

THE PRODUCTION GUILD

The Production Guild of Great Britain
Pinewood Studios, Pinewood Road, Iver Heath SL0 0NH
t 01753 651767 f 01753 652803
e admin@productionguild.com w www.productionguild.com
Contact David Chief Executive Officer, david@productionguild.com; Lynne Administrator, lynne@productionguild.com

Production Managers Association
Ealing Studios, Ealing Green, London W5 5EP
t 020 8758 8699 f 020 8758 8647
e pma@pma.org.uk w www.pma.org.uk
Contact Caroline Fleming, Administrator

Radio Academy
5 Market Place, London W1W 8AE
t 020 7255 2010 f 020 7255 2029
e info@radioacademy.org w www.radioacademy.org
Contact John Bradford, Director

The Radio Authority
Holbrook House, 14 Great Queen Street, Holborn, London WC2B 5DG
t 020 7430 2724 f 020 7405 7062
e info@radioauthority.org.uk w www.radioauthority.org.uk

Radiocommunications Agency
Wyndham House, 189 Marsh Wall, London E14 9SX
t 020 7211 0211 f 020 7211 0507
e library@rq.gsi.gov.uk w www.radio.gov.uk

Royal Television Society
Holborn Hall, 100 Grays Inn Road, London WC1X 8AL
t 020 7430 1000 f 020 7430 0924
e info@rts.org.uk w www.rts.org.uk
Contact Tom Gutteridge, Managing Director; Katie Morris, Office Manager; Deborah Halls, Membership Manager

Society for Screen-Based Learning
9 Bridge Street, Tadcaster LS24 9AW
t 01937 530520 f 01937 530520
e josie.key@learningonscreen.u-net.com
w www.learningonscreen.org.uk
Contact Josie Key, Administrator

TAC - Welsh Independant Producers
Crichton House, 11-12 Mountstuart Square, Cardiff CF10 6EE
t 02920 463322 **f** 02920 463344
e caerdydd@teledwyr.com **w** www.teledwyr.com
Contact Dafydd Hughes, Chief Executive

Video Standards Council (VSC)
Kinetic Business Centre, Theobald Street,
Borehamwood WD6 4PJ
t 020 8387 4020 **f** 020 8387 4004
e vsc@videostandards.org.uk **w** www.videostandards.org.uk
Contact Laurie Hall, Secretary General

Voice of The Listener & Viewer (VLV)
101 Kings Drive, Gravesend DA12 5BQ
t 01474 352835 **f** 01474 351112
e vlv@btinternet.com **w** www.vlv.org.uk

Women In Film & Television
6 Langley Street, London WC2H 9JA
t 020 7240 4875 **f** 020 7379 1625
e info@wftv.org.uk **w** www.wftv.org.uk
Contact Emily Compton, Administrator; Jane Cussons, Executive Director

The Writers' Guild of Great Britain
15 Britannia Street, London WC1X 9JN
t 020 7833 0777
e admin@writersguild.org.uk **w** www.writersguild.org.uk
Contact Bernie Corbett, General Secretary; Christine Paris, Assistant General
Secretary; Carmen Tabares, Membership Manager; Anne Hogben, Assistant
General Secretary

Audience Provision

Applause Store Productions Ltd
Elstree Film & Television Studios, Shenley Road,
Borehamwood WD6 1JG
t 020 8324 2700 **t** 0845 644 5678 (ticket hotline - local rate)
f 020 8953 9093 **m** 07767 685115
e mathew@applausestore.com **w** www.applausestore.com
Contact Mathew Firsht, Managing Director
Credits Ready Steady Cook (T); Your Face Or Mine (T); Top Gear (T); The Brit
Awards 2003 (T)

*Applause Store — UK's Leading Free Television & Radio Audience Ticket
Unit. We offer an audience package unlike any other in the UK,
specifically designed to find the right audience for each production. Our
team of full-time Audience Researchers are seriously committed to the
supply of targeted or general audience nationwide, and pride ourselves
on our ability to consistently hit studio capacity for every production. For
more information/competitive quote, please give us a call.*

BBC Audience Services
BBC Television Centre, Wood Lane, PO Box 3000, Room 309,
London W12 7RJ
t 020 8576 1227 **f** 020 8576 8802 **e** tv.ticket.unit@bbc.co.uk
Contact Arwin Tugwell, Manager

Live Art Development Agency
Truman's Brewery, 91 Brick Lane, London E1 6QN
t 020 7247 3339 **f** 020 7247 1149
e info@liveartlondon.demon.co.uk
w www.liveartlondon.demon.co.uk
Contact Lois Keidan; Daniel Brine

RNIB
PO Box 173, Peterborough PE2 6WS
t 08457 669999 **f** 020 7388 2034
e cservices@rnib.org.uk **w** www.rnib.org.uk

Auto-prompting Services

anthony jordan
ipromptu·tv

Anthony Jordan www.ipromptu.tv
13 Child's Place, Earls Court, London SW5 9RX
t 020 7373 6767 **f** 020 7373 7748
Credits So Graham Norton (T); Ali G (T); Lenny Henry In Pieces (T)
*Supplier of Prompting systems for studio, OBs and lightweight systems
for cranes, steadicam and hand-held cameras.*

Autocue Midlands
Unit 7, Shaw Lane Industrial Estate, Bromsgrove B60 4DT
t 01527 878782 **m** 07711 665898
e pete@autocuemidlands.co.uk **w** www.autocue.co.uk
Contact Peter Larter, Manager

Autocue North
Unit 1, Kingfisher Court, Northwich CW9 7TT
t 01606 47076 **f** 01606 443320 **m** 07836 663011
e autocuenorth@autocue.fsbusiness.co.uk
Contact James Cooper, General Manager

Autoscript Ltd
Unit 8A, Poplar Business Park, 10 Prestons Road,
London E14 9RL
t 020 7538 1427 **f** 020 7515 9529
e hire@bdlautoscript.com **w** www.bdlautoscript.com
Contact Christopher Lambert, Managing Director; Juliette Epsom, Contact
Manager, Rental

Cuebox
1 Balmoral Crescent, Farnham GU9 0DN
t 01252 690046 **f** 01252 690047 **m** 07774 712712
e info@cuebox.com **w** www.cuebox.com
Contact Ros Ince, Proprietor
Credits Geri Yoga (I); Tecnogames (T); Animals Do The Funniest Things (T);
Robot Wars (T)

EDS Portaprompt
Lane End Road, Sands, High Wycombe HP12 4JQ
t 01494 450414 **f** 01494 437591 **e** sales@portaprompt.co.uk
w www.portaprompt.co.uk

Anthony Jordan
Carlin Crew Ltd, Shepperton Studios, Studios Road,
Shepperton TW17 0QD
t 01932 568268 **f** 01932 571109
e carlin@netcomuk.co.uk **w** www.carlincrew.com

(vertical sidebar) associations • audience provision • auto-prompting services

Perfect Prompting
c/o Carlin & Company, Shepperton Studios,
Shepperton TW17 0QP
t 020 7373 6767 **m** 07850 704 066 **w** www.ipromptu.tv
Contact Anthony Jordon, Proprietor
Credits Harry Potter And The Chamber Of Secrets (F); Lara Croft Tomb Raider
II - The Cradle Of Life (F); V Graham Norton (T); Johnny Vaughan Tonight (T)

Portaco
3 Penrallt, Menai Bridge LL59 5LP
t 01248 713611 **f** 01248 713611 **e** g.ellen@btinternet.com
Contact Gillian Ellen, Prompting, Continuity

ScotPrompt
194 Lanark Road West, Edinburgh EH14 5NX
t 0131 449 2384 **f** 0131 449 7654 **e** martinbone@cwcom.net
Contact Norma Bone, Managing Director

SuzieCue

SuzieCue Autocue & Teleprompting Hire
45 Windmill Road, London W4 1RN
t 020 8994 0121 **f** 020 8994 0059 **m** 07740 097965
e hire@suziecue.co.uk **w** www.suziecue.co.uk
Contact Keith Shaw

Telescript Prompting Ltd
The Barn, Handpost Farmhouse, Maiden Green RG42 6LD
t 01344 890470 **f** 01344 890655 **m** 07802 276511
e sales@telescript.co.uk **w** www.telescript.co.uk
Contact Avril Voller, Managing Director

AVIATION

Aviation
Aerial Cameramen

Aerial Shots
4 The Sycamores, Radlett WD7 7LJ
t 01923 854944 **e** jbeament@hotmail.com
Contact Jonathan Beament, Cameraman
Credits The Matrix III (F); The Matrix II (F)

BBC Outside Broadcasts

BBC Outside Broadcasts
Kendal Avenue, London W3 0RP
t 020 8993 9333 **f** 020 8993 4510
e ob@bbc.co.uk **w** www.bbcresources.com/ob

Chris Bonass
Rush Green Airfield, London Road, Langley, Hitchin SG4 7PQ
t 01438 726969 **f** 01438 726969 **m** 07850 971491
e flightonfilm@beeb.net
Credits Easyjet TV Clip (T); Monday Night Football (T); Cricket World Cup 2003 (T)

Adam Dale
Flying Pictures, Stonefield Park, Chilbolton SO20 6BL
t 01264 861100 **f** 01264 861163
e filmservices@flying pictures.com **w** www.flyingpictures.com
Credits If Only (F); Bridget Jones's Diary (F); 28 Days Later (F)

Flying Pictures Ltd
Stonefield Park, Chilbolton SO20 6BL
t 01264 861100 **f** 01264 860033
e filmservices@flyingpictures.com **w** www.aerialfilmservices.com
Credits Ella Enchanted (F); Jonny English (F); Bridget Jones' Diary (F);
28 Days Later (F)

Colin Hazelwood
79 Nightingale Road, Hampton TW12 3HZ
t 020 8941 2318 **m** 07711 263318 **e** hazelwood@beeb.net
Credits Horizon (D); Queen's Golden Jubilee 2002 (T); Commonwealth Games
Manchester 2002 (T); Olympic Games Sydney 2000 (T)

HoverCam Ltd
The White House, Drakes View, Staddon Heights,
Plymouth PL9 9SP
t 01752 482711 **f** 01752 482744 **m** 07831 225440
e info@hovercam.com **w** www.hovercam.com
Contact Phil George
Credits BMW (C); Down To Earth (F); The Bee (F)

L&M Dickinson
Fudge Cottage, Dalditch Lane, Budleigh Salterton EX9 7AH
t 01395 446242 **m** 07711 787737
e leo@adventurearchive.com **w** www.adventurearchive.com
Contact Andrew Smart; Mandy Dickinson; Leo Dickinson
Over 20 years of freefall skydiving filming. 16mm and video.

John Marzano
Flying Pictures Ltd, Stonefield Park, Chilbolton SO20 6BL
t 01264 861100 **f** 01264 861163
e filmservices@flyingpictures.com **w** www.flyingpictures.com
Credits Spy Game (F); The World Is Not Enough (F); Blackhawk Down (F)

ParaMedia
16 The Grove, Aldershot GU11 1NL
t 01252 312540 **f** 01252 651938 **m** 07941 845385
e ian@paramedia.co.uk
Contact Ian Barraclough
Credits Gravity Powered Adventure (I); A Rough Guide To Careers (T); You Bet!
(T); One In A Million (T)

Simon Werry Flying Cameras Ltd
Southview Trehunist, Quethiock, Liskeard PL14 3SD
t 01579 344087 **f** 01579 342883 **m** 07971 020 088
e simonwerry@aol.com **w** www.flyingcameras.co.uk
Contact Simon Werry, Managing Director
Credits Thunderbirds (F); The Mummy Returns (F); Harry Potter And The
Philosopher's Stone (F); Harry Potter And The Chamber Of Secrets (T)

Veritair Helicopters Ltd
Cardiff Heliport, Foreshore Road, East Moors, Cardiff CF10 4LZ
t 029 2046 5880 **f** 029 2048 7506 **e** julian.verity@talk21.com
Contact Julian Verity, Managing Director

Aviation
Aerial Cameramounts

Aerial Camera Systems
Douglas Drive, Godalming GU7 1JX
t 01483 426767 **f** 01483 413900
e info@aerialcamerasystems.com
w www.aerialcamerasystems.com
Contact Richard Henney, Operations; Matthew Allwork, Group CEO; Matt Coyde, Marketing Manager; Martin Philp, General Manager; Sam Philp, Operations; David Rashleigh, Operations

Arena Aviation
Hanger 7, Redhill Aerodrome, Redhill RH1 5JY
t 01737 822011 **f** 01737 821145 **e** info@arena-aviation.com
w www.arena-aviation.com
Contact Richard Barlow; Richard Yeowart; Richard Snow; Mark Barry-Jackson, Chief Pilot
Credits Spooks (T); Sky High (T); Great Britons (T); Invasions (T)

BBC Outside Broadcasts

BBC Outside Broadcasts
Kendal Avenue, London W3 0RP
t 020 8993 9333 **f** 020 8993 4510
e ob@bbc.co.uk **w** www.bbcresources.com/ob

Flight Logistics
Unit 12, Garrick Centre, Hendon, London NW9 6AQ
t 020 8201 5200 **f** 020 8201 5147 **m** 07831 627878
e operations@flight-logistics.co.uk **w** www.flight-logistics.com
Contact Tim Desbois, Flight Coordinator; Anne Kennedy, Administration; Dave McKay
Credits Mindhunters (F); Clockwork Mice (F); The Gathering (F); XXX (F)

Aviation Aircraft

Air World Limited
Llanwnda, Caernarfon LL54 5TP
t 01286 830800 **f** 01286 830280 **w** www.caeairparc.com

Ballooning Network
73 Winterstoke Road, Bristol BS3 2NP
t 0117 947 1050 **f** 0117 963 9555
e flights@balnet.co.uk **w** www.balnet.co.uk

Bianchi Aviation Film Services Ltd
Wycombe Airpark, Booker, Nr Marlowe SL7 3DP
t 01494 449810 **f** 01494 461236 **m** 07836 318053
e info@bianchiaviation.com
Contact Tony Bianchi, Managing Director; Pia Kemp, Senior Administrator
Credits The Mummy (F); The Blue Max (F); These Magnificent Men and Their Flying Machines (F)

Business Air Centre
BAC House, 112 Clerkenwell Road, London EC1M 5TW
t 020 7456 7123 **f** 020 7456 7130
e charter@bac-london.com **w** www.businessaircentre.co.uk

Cormack Aircraft Services Ltd
Cumbernauld Airport, Duncan McIntosh Road, Cumbernauld, Glasgow G68 0HH
t 01236 457777 **f** 01236 738322
Contact George Cormack, Managing Director

The Fighter Collection
The Imperial War Museum, Duxford Airfield, Cambridge CB2 4QR
t 01223 834973 **f** 01223 836956
e larks@fighter-collection.com **w** www.fighter-collection.com
Contact Jane Larcombe, Manager
Credits BBC Knowledge (D); Dark Blue World (F); 28 Days Later (F)

Fineminster Europe
Worth Corner, Pound Hill, Crawley RH10 7SL
t 01293 885888 **f** 01293 883238
e charter@fineminster.com **w** www.fineminster.com
Contact Graham Plunkett, Managing Director; Joanna Bundy, Director; Sam Wood, Sales Executive

Flight Management (Charter) Ltd
West End Farm, Blackford, Wedmore BS28 4PA
t 0870 770 5575 **f** 0870 770 5576 **m** 07947 254201
e charters@flightmanagement.co.uk
w www.flightmanagement.co.uk

Flying Flicks
15 Marlborough Road, London W4 4EU
t 020 8995 1884 **f** 020 8995 5648 **m** 07966 165169
e flicks@eagletv.co.uk **w** www.eagletv.co.uk

Historic Aircraft Collection
PO Box 39, Rye TN31 6ZT
t 01580 830215 **f** 01580 830875
e hac@aerovintage.co.uk **w** www.historicaircraftcollection.ltd.uk

Hunt & Palmer International
The Tower, Goff's Park Road, Crawley RH11 8XX
t 01293 558000 **f** 01293 558099
e aircharter@huntpalmer.com **w** www.huntpalmer.com
Contact Terry Ellacott, UK Sales Manager

International Air Charter Plc
Unit 16/17 Southampton House, London Heathrow Airport, Hounslow TW6 3BZ
t 020 8897 8979 **f** 020 8897 8969
e sales@aircraftcharter.com **w** www.aircraftcharter.com

International Jet Services
International Jet Centre, 67-69 St John's Road, Isleworth TW7 6NL
t 020 8380 4468 **f** 020 8569 8746 **e** frauke@ijsltd.co.uk

Laurelgrove Productions
Unit 6A, The Old Forge, Dovecot Workshops, Barnsley Park Est, Cirencester GL7 5EG
t 01285 740123 **m** 07860 817280 **e** laurelgrove@compuserve.com
Contact Stephen Makin, Managing Director
Credits Born To Fly (I); Battle Of Britain Airshow (T); Flying Legends, Duxford (T); Royal International Air Tattoo (T)

London Executive Aviation
London City Airport, London E16 2PX
t 020 7474 3344 **f** 020 7474 5566
e info@flylea.com **w** www.flylea.com
Contact George Galanopoulos, Managing Director; Amanda Petchey, Operations Director; Patrick Margetson-Rushmore, Chief Executive; Karl Ratcliffe, Chief Pilot

The Old Flying Machine Company
Imperial War Museum, Duxford Airfield, Cambridge CB2 4QR
t 01223 836705 **f** 01223 834117
e info@ofmc.co.uk **w** www.ofmc.co.uk
Contact Laura Wetton, Operations Manager; Nigel Lamb; Sarah Hanna
Credits Battle Of Britain (F); Memphis Belle (F); Saving Private Ryan (F)

Prop Shop Ltd
Duxford Airfield, Duxford CB2 4QR
t 01223 835313 **f** 01223 837290 **e** anna@arc-duxford.co.uk
Contact John Romain, Managing Director; Anna McDowell, Company Secretary

The Shuttleworth Collection
Old Warden Park, Biggleswade SG18 9EA
t 01767 626207 **f** 01767 626229
e enquiries@shuttleworth.org **w** www.shuttleworth.org
Contact Tony Podmore, Administration

Spotlight Balloons
Rookery Cottage Gills Lane, Rooksbridge BS26 2TU
t 01934 750315 **f** 01934 750394
e peter.bird@spotlight-group.com
Contact Peter Bird; Louise Briggs; Stuart Mann
Credits Channel 4 'Mark Thomas' (T); BBC 'Ballooning' (T)

Aviation **Airports**

Aberdeen Airport
Dyce, Aberdeen AB21 7DU
t 01224 722331 **f** 01224 725724 **w** www.baa.com
Contact Lesley Bale, Managing Director; Bertram Smith, Managing Director

Airfield Systems & Components Ltd
Avcom House 11, St Leonards Road, Amersham HP6 6DT
t 01494 727703 **f** 01494 728007

Airfields-UK
Abbey House, Wellington Way, Weybridge KT13 0TT
t 01932 248221 **t** 08700 779988 **f** 08700 779989
e info@airfields-uk.com **w** www.airfields-uk.com

Airways Aero Associations Ltd
Wycombe Air Park, Booker, Marlowe SL7 3DP
t 01494 529261 **f** 01494 461237
e info@bafc.co.uk **w** www.bafc.co.uk

Avionic Services Plc
53 Portland Road, Kingston-upon-Thames KT1 2SH
t 020 8974 5225 **f** 020 8974 5023
w www.avionicservices.co.uk

Badminton Airfield
Badminton GL9 1DD
t 01454 218333 **f** 01454 218333
Contact Howard Richardson
Credits Pearl Harbour (F)

Bagby Airfield
Bagby, Thirsk YO7 2PH
t 01845 597385 **f** 01845 597747
e bagbyair@aol.com **w** www.bagbyairfield.freeserve.co.uk

Belfast International Airport
Belfast BT29 4AB
t 028 9442 2888 **f** 028 9448 4849
e info@bial.co.uk **w** www.bial.co.uk

Bickerton's Aerodromes
Denham Aerodrome, Tilehouse Lane, Denham, Uxbridge UB9 5DE
t 01895 832060 **f** 01895 831161
e manager@elgd.com **w** www.egld.com

Biggin Hill Airport Ltd
Biggin Hill, Westerham TN16 3BN
t 01959 578500 **f** 01959 540406
e enquiries@bigginhillairport.com **w** www.bigginhillairport.com
Credits Murphy's Law (T); The Fourth Angel (F)

Birmingham International Airport Ltd
Airport Way, Birmingham B26 3QJ
t 0121 767 5511 **f** 0121 782 8802 **w** www.bhx.co.uk

Blackpool Airport Ltd
Squires Gate Lane, Blackpool FY4 2QS
t 01253 343434 **f** 01253 405009
e admin@blackpoolairport.com **w** www.blackpoolairport.com

Bristol International Airport
Bristol BS48 3DY
t 0870 121 2747

British Airways Plc
Benbecula Airport, Balivanich, Isle of Benbecula HS7 5LA
t 01870 602310

Caernarfon Airpark Ltd
Dinas Dinlle, Caernarfon LL54 5TP
t 01286 830800

Cardiff International Airport
CF67 3BD
t 01446 711111 **f** 01446 711675 **w** www.cial.co.uk

City of Derry Airport
Airfield Road, Eglinton, Londonderry BT47 3PZ
t 028 7181 0784 **f** 028 7181 1426 **e** www.derry.net/airport

Cumbernauld Airport Ltd
Duncan McIntosh Road, Cumbernauld, Glasgow G68 0HH
t 01236 722100 **f** 01236 781 646

Dundee Airport
Riverside Drive, Dundee DD2 1UH
t 01382 643242 **f** 01382 641263
e david.johnston@dundeecity.gov.uk

Edinburgh Airport Ltd
Thornhosue Road, Edinburgh EH12 9DN
t 0131 333 1000 **f** 0131 335 3181 **w** www.baa.com

Elstree Aerodrome
Elstree, Borehamwood WD6 3AR
t 020 8953 7480

Exeter & Devon Airport Ltd
Exeter Airport, Exeter EX5 2BD
t 01392 367433 **f** 01392 364593
e exeterair@eclipse.co.uk **w** www.exeter-airport.co.uk
Contact Sandra Roberts, PR Manager; Stephen Ayres, PR Manager; Sue Crossland, Business Development Manager

Exeter International Airport
Exeter EX5 2BD
t 01392 367433 **f** 01392 364593
e marketing@exeter-airport.co.uk **w** www.exeter-airport.co.uk

Fairoaks Airport Ltd
Fairoaks Airport, Chobham, Woking GU24 8HU
t 01276 857700 **f** 01276 856330
e janet.hoare@alanmann.co.uk **w** www.alanmann.co.uk
Contact Diane Bennett, Airport Administrator

Gamston Aviation
Gamston Airport, Retford DN22 0QL
t 01777 838593

Glasgow Airport International Ltd
Paisley, Glasgow PA3 2ST
t 0141 887 1111 **w** www.baa.com

Haverfordwest Airport
Fishguard Road, Haverfordwest SA62 4BN
t 01437 765283 **e** hwest.airport@pembrokeshire.gov.uk

Heathrow Airport Ltd
234 Bath Road, Heathrow Airport UB3 5AP
t 08700 000123 **w** www.baa.com

Highlands & Islands Airports Ltd
Islay Airport, Glenegedale, Isle of Islay PA42 7AS
t 01496 302361 **f** 01496 302096
Contact Andrew Lindsay, Station Manager

Highlands & Islands Airports Ltd
Machrihanish, Campbeltown Airport PA28 6NU
t 01586 553797 **f** 01586 552620 **e** campadmin@hial.co.uk

Humberside Airport
Grimsby Road, Kirmington, Ulceby DN39 6YH
t 01652 688456 **e** enquiries@humbairport.co.uk
w www.humberside-airport.co.uk

Isle of Wight Airport Ltd
Scotchells Brook Lane, Sandown PO36 0JP
t 01983 405125 **f** 01983 405125

Kemble Air Services
Kemble Airfield, Kemble, Cirencester GL7 6BA
t 01285 771076 **w** www.kemble.com

Leeds Bradford International Airport
Leeds LS19 7TU
t 0113 250 9696 **f** 0113 250 5426
e general@lbia.co.uk **w** www.lbia.co.uk

Liverpool John Lennon Airport
South Terminal, Liverpool L24 1YD
t 0151 288 4000 **w** www.liverpoolairport.com
Contact Mark Povall, Commercial and Marketing Manager; Peter Tormey, Operations Director; Neil Pakey, Managing Director

London City Airport Ltd
Royal Docks, London E16 2PB
t 020 7646 0088 **f** 020 7474 5747
e info@londoncityairport.com **w** www.londoncityairport.com

London Luton Airport
Navigation House, Airport Way, Luton LU2 9LY
t 01582 405100 **e** info@london-luton.com
w www.london-luton.com

London Southend Airport Company Ltd
London Southend Airport, Southend-on-Sea SS2 6YF
t 01702 608100 **f** 01702 608110
e enquiries@southendairport.net **w** www.southendairport.net
Contact Diane Hollander, Airport Marketing

London Stansted Airport Ltd
Enterprise House, Bassingbourne Road, Stansted Airport CM24 1QW
t 08700 000303 **f** 01279 662066
e info@baa.com **w** www.baa.com
Contact R Barrisan, Communications Manager

Manchester Airport Plc
t 0161 489 3000

National Air Traffic Services Ltd
Windyhead Radio Station, New Aberdour, Fraserburgh AB43 6JH
t 01346 561255 **w** www.nats.co.uk

Newcastle International Airport
Newcastle Airport, Woolsington, Newcastle-upon-Tyne NE13 8BZ
t 01912 860966 **f** 01912 716080
e suemac@newcastleairport.com **w** www.newcastleairport.com

Oaksey Park Airfield
Oaksey, Malmesbury SN16 9SD
t 01666 577130

Perranporth Airfield
Higher Trevellas, St Agnes TR5 0XS
t 01872 552266 **f** 01872 552261 **w** www.perranporthairfield.co.uk

Redhill Aerodrome
Redhill RH1 5YP
t 01737 823377 **f** 01737 823640
e atc@redhillaerodrome.com **w** www.redhillaerodrome.com
Contact Keith Woodward, Airfield Manager
Credits Mitutoyo (C); Honda (C)

Swansea Airport
Fairwood Common, Swansea SA2 7JU
t 01792 204063 **f** 01792 297 923
e enquiries@swanseaairport.com **w** www.swanseaairport.com

Tatenhill Airfield
Newborough Road, Needwood, Burton-on-Trent DE13 9PD
t 01283 575283 **f** 01283 575650
e mail@tatenhill.com **w** www.tatenhill.com
Contact Paula Tolley, Office Manager

Teesside International Airport Ltd
Darlington DL2 1LU
t 01325 332811 **f** 01325 332810 **m** 07710 659632
e johnwaiting@teessideairport.com **w** www.teessideairport.com
Contact John Waiting, Business Services Manager
Credits Jimmy Nail (T); Byker Grove (T)

Truro Airfield
Tregavethan Chacewater, Truro TR4 8PW
t 01872 560488
Contact Graham Barral, Airfield Manager

Willowair Executive Flight Centre
Southend Airport, Southend-on-Sea SS2 6YF
t 01702 531555 **f** 01702 542 070 **e** sales@willowair.co.uk

Wolverhampton Airport
Stourbridge DY7 5DY
t 01384 221350 **f** 01384 221328
e info@wolverhamptonairport.com
w www.wolverhamptonairport.com

Aviation Helicopters

Aeromega Helicopters
Hangar 1, Stapleford Aerodrome, Stapleford Tawney RM4 1SJ
t 01708 688361 **f** 01708 688584
e James@aeromega.demon.co.uk **w** www.aeromega.com
Contact James White, Operations Manager
Credits Holby City (T); Brookside (T); Johnny English (F); Die Another Day (F)

Alan Mann Helicopters Ltd
Fairoaks Airport, Chobham, Woking GU24 8HX
t 01276 857471 **f** 01276 857037
e operations@alanmann.co.uk **w** www.alanmann.co.uk
Contact Barry Hodgkinson, Operations Manager

Arena Aviation
Hanger 7, Redhill Aerodrome, Redhill RH1 5JY
t 01737 822011 **f** 01737 821145
e info@arena-aviation.com **w** www.arena-aviation.com
Contact Richard Barlow; Richard Yeowart; Richard Snow; Mark Barry-Jackson, Chief Pilot
Credits Spooks (T); Sky High (T); Great Britons (T); Invasions (T)

Biggin Hill Helicopters
Building 159, Biggin Hill Airport, Biggin Hill TN16 3BN
t 01959 540803 **f** 01959 571176
e sales@bhh.co.uk **w** www.bhh.co.uk

Cabair Helicopters
Elstree Aerodrome, Borehamwood WD6 3AW
t 020 8236 2400 **f** 020 8905 1527
e helicopters@cabair.com **w** www.cabair.com
Contact Marion Melbourn, Operations Manager; Rod Wood, Chief Helicopter Pilot

Castle Air
Trebrown, Liskeard PL14 3PX
t 01503 240543 **f** 01503 240747
e ops@castleair.co.uk **w** www.castleair.co.uk
Contact Michael Malric-Smith, Filming Pilot; Keith Thompson, Filming Pilot; Kevin Grey, Filming Pilot; Peter Thompson, Aerial Cameraman
Credits Treasure Hunt (T); Time Flyers (T); Flying Gardener (T)

Eagle Helicopters
Newcastle City Heliport, Railway Street, Newcastle-upon-Tyne NE4 7AD
t 0191 256 8000 **f** 0191 256 8008
e Martin @newcastleheliport.freeserve.co.uk
w www.eaglehelicopters.co.uk
Contact Martin Burgin, Managing Director

using helicopters for filming

The only reason that any production uses a helicopter is because the shot or sequence is important, so simply the most important aspect is who you select to supply you.

There are many companies that claim to be "specialised film flyers", and indeed there are some very good local operators. Many may well be telling the truth in claiming that they film several times a week, but only a few understand the difference between hand held shots for the local news and the co-ordination and skill levels required for feature film quality work.

There are a number of companies, cameramen and pilots who truly specialise in aerial work, and using them will normally save time and money and produce better results.

In making your selection, only the genuine "specialist" companies will be able to provide a list of credits, references and/or a company showreel for recently completed work.

Getting a quote

Provide as much detail as possible i.e. are there any special requirements, night flying or over water flights etc. More than any other area of filming, tiny requirement changes can produce huge cost variations.

Choice of helicopters

Single or twin engined? As camera platforms single engined helicopters are a reasonable cost, but on filming flights they may not work at night, in cloud, extensively over water, or over built-up areas such as London (except on specified routes or directly over the Thames). For these areas and conditions a twin engined machine is required.

Both single and twin engined helicopters come in different sizes, all the interiors are small with very limited baggage space.

Mounts and equipment

The hire cost of better camera mounts is often offset by the efficiency they bring to a shoot, reducing helicopter flying hours and enabling work to take place in windier conditions.

The various mounts available fall into 3 categories:

a   Fixed and tilting nose mounts.

b   Sophisticated balanced side mounts,
     i.e. Tyler Middle and Major Mounts with
     Gyro Assist, Continental and the Kestrel.

c   High tech gyro stabilised camera sphere,
     i.e. Film and Video Wescam, Video
     Ultramedia. Film and Video Stab C

Allow for the cost of a technician and at least two hours for fitting and one for removal of the mount. When fitted the mount becomes part of the helicopter; it must be 'signed off' by a licensed helicopter engineer.

Ideally it is best to consider the aerial team as a separate unit and not plan to share camera equipment.

Insurance

All helicopters are required by law to carry Third Party Liability Insurance (but not Hull insurance at all!). The production company can be named as additionally assured under this policy.

Be very careful of a grey area in helicopter insurance, "the excess". Many companies fully insure, less the first 7.5 % of any claim. On a helicopter valued at £750,000 this represents a £56,250 uninsured risk working on your shoot! Check this out each time.

Helicopter work is considered a hazardous risk and hired camera equipment must be specially covered. Talk to the hire company.

Costs and minimum times

As a broad guide, single engined helicopters are £480-750 per flying hour, twins £780 £1400, and very large helicopters £1500-£3500 per flying hour.

You only pay for the time rotors are running, but the helicopter operators normally require 2-3 hours usage per day minimum.

Specialist film pilots often charge a separate daily rate.

Fuel bowser

Sending the helicopter to the nearest airfield to re-fuel often doesn't make economic sense, e.g. 15 minutes each way, and a landing fee could cost £450 each time, plus you lose the helicopter for an hour.

Location permissions

Get the location manager to talk to the helicopter supply company before he goes recce'ing. For instance, a wide area around London requires CAA clearance for a non-standard flight. Even when a 'special flight' number has been issued, its use is at the discretion of the Heathrow controller on the day.

Landing within congested areas of cities requires special permission. Helicopters can land on any suitable site in the UK subject to airspace and safety considerations. You must have written permission of the owners before arriving.

Ensure you inform the local police and relevant local residents; check on local livestock. Sheep and cows are obvious but don't forget racehorses in stables and battery hens, (who panic and don't lay eggs for a couple of days!).   →→→

Flight Works (Wycombe) Ltd
Wycombe Air Park, Near Marlow SL7 3DR
t 01494 451111 **f** 01494 769989
e info@flightworks.co.uk **w** www.flightworks.co.uk
Contact Paul Curtis, Operations Coordinator

Christopher Forrest
McAlpine Aviation Services, Swallowfield Way, Hayes UB3 1SP
t 020 8848 9647 **f** 020 8569 3230
e info@mcalpine-aviation.co.uk

Heli-charter Ltd
The Helicopter Centre, The Hangar, Manston CT12 5DE
t 01843 822555 **f** 01843 822444 **e** helicharter@hotmail.com
Contact Gary Slater, Managing Director

HoverCam Ltd
The White House, Drakes View, Staddon Heights, Plymouth PL9 9SP
t 01752 482711 **f** 01752 482744 **m** 07831 225440
e info@hovercam.com **w** www.hovercam.com
Contact Phil George
Credits BMW (C); Down To Earth (F); The Bee (F)

Kevin Grey
Castle Air, Trebrown, Liskeard, Liskeard PL14 3PX
t 01503 240543 **f** 01503 240747 **e** ops@castleair.co.uk
w www.castleair.co.uk
Credits Grafters (T); Other Peoples Children (T); Dinatopia (T)

Lloyd Ross Aviation
16 Beresford Court, Park Road, East Twickenham TW1 2PU
f 020 8891 6851 **m** 07736 444245
e duncan@lloydrossaviation.com **w** www.lloydrossaviation.com
Contact Duncan Prentice, Director/Film Pilot
Credits Air America (F); Kavanagh QC (T); Cliffhanger (F); Lancia/Opel (C)

Independent consultancy/aerial co-ordination ensures best helicopter operators, optimum prices.

Lomas Helicopters
Lake Heliport, Abbotsham, Bideford EX39 5BQ
t 01237 421054 **f** 01237 424060 **m** 07836 616 171
e lomashelos@aol.com **w** www.lomashelicopters.co.uk
Contact Emma Cocks, Operations Manager
Credits Down To Earth Programme (T); Zurich Insurance (C)

Michael Malric-Smith
Castle Air, Trebrown, Liskeard PL14 3PX
t 01503 240543 **f** 01503 240747
e ops@castleair.co.uk **w** www.castleair.co.uk
Contact Michael Smith

PDG Helicopters
The Heliport, Dalcross, Inverness IV2 7XB
t 0870 607 9000 **f** 01667 462376
e enquiries@pdg-helicopters.co.uk **w** www.pdg-helicopters.co.uk
Contact Darroch Harkness, Filming Specialist

PLM Dollar Helicopters (Glasgow)
Cumbernauld Airport, Cumbernauld, Glasgow G68 0HH
t 0870 607 9000 **f** 01236 457550
e sales@pdg-helicopters.co.uk **w** www.pdg-helicopters.co.uk
Contact Darroch Harkness, Sales

Polo Aviation Ltd
Urchinwood Manor, Congresbury, Bristol BS49 5AP
t 01934 877000 **f** 01934 834683 **m** 07765 401418
e poloaviation@aol.com **w** www.poloaviation.com
Contact Peter Hall, Managing Director; Robin Tutcher, Flight Operations

PremiAir Aviation Services Ltd
Denham Airport, Hangar Road, Uxbridge UB9 5DF
t 01895 830950 **f** 01895 830950
e j.mayhew@premiair-aviation.com **w** www.premiair-aviation.com
Contact Christopher Forrest, General Manager; James McAlpine, Chairman
Credits Sky News (T); BBC News (T); Dalziel And Pascoe (T)

Roger Savage Gyroplanes Ltd
Croft House, Berrier, Penrith CA11 0XD
t 01768 483859 **f** 01768 483693
e gyroplanes@rogersavage.co.uk **w** www.rogersavage.co.uk
Contact Roger Savage, Managing Director

Starspeed Ltd
Cherry Orchard, Weild Road, Medstead, Alton GU34 5LY
t 07000 778277 **f** 01420 562904 **m** 07966 280 150
e david.voy@virgin.net **w** www.starspeed.co.uk
Contact David Voy

Keith Thompson
Castle Air, Trebrown, Liskeard PL14 3PX
t 01503 240543 **f** 01503 240747 **m** 07967 381 922
e ops@castleair.co.uk **w** www.castleair.co.uk

Helicopters positioning
Helicopters are not fast (120-180mph) and are speed restricted, with doors off, as low as 70mph. On average they have a 300-400 mile range so allow plenty of time for positioning trips.

Minimum heights
Minimum heights vary. As standard you may not fly closer than 500' to people, vehicles and buildings. However you may not fly over a built-up area lower than 1500' or over large crowds lower than 3000'. Special dispensations can be available.

Thanks to Tim Desbois   www.flight-logistics.com

CAMERA

camera : contents

Camera **Assistants Video**

Ahmet Bekir
The Firm Booking Company Ltd, 31 Oval Road, Camden,
London NW1 7EA
t 020 7248 9090 f 020 7248 9089 e kirsty@thefirm.co.uk

Jim Bishop
Stella's Diary, 9 Hormead Road, London W9 3NG
t 020 8735 2776 t 020 8969 1855 f 020 8964 2157
m 07831 354970 m 07836 594622
e stella'sdiary@btinternet.com

Gordon Buchanan
The Firm Booking Company Ltd, 31 Oval Road, Camden,
London NW1 7EA
t 020 7248 9090 f 020 7248 9089 e kirsty@thefirm.co.uk

Alan Buckley
Stella's Diary, 9 Hormead Road, London W9 3NG
t 020 8969 1855 f 020 8964 2157 m 07775 631 562
e stella'sdiary@btinternet.com

Rupert Burton
TOVS Ltd, The Linen Hall, 162-168 Regent Street, London W1B 5TB
t 020 7287 6110 f 020 7287 5481
e info@tovs.co.uk w www.tovs.co.uk

Andy Clifford
Stella's Diary, 9 Hormead Road, London W9 3NG
t 020 8969 1855 f 020 8964 2157 m 07968 629648
e stella'sdiary@btinternet.com

Matt Conway
Flat3, 195 Ravenslea Road, Balham, London SW12 8RT
t 020 8355 7333 t 020 8908 6262 f 020 8355 7333
m 07801 341413 e mattconway100@hotmail.com
Credits Faking It (D); Restoration (D); Blackwater (T); Rush Series III (T)

Joe Cooper
Grade One TV & Film Personnel, Elstree Studios, Shenley
Road, Borehamwood WD6 1JG
t 020 8324 2224 f 020 8324 2328
e gradeone.tvpersonnel@virgin.net

Richard Cornelius
32 Kimble Road, London SW19 2AS
t 020 8286 3245 f 0208 946 8772 m 07775 893722
e djdomain@blueyonder.co.uk
Credits The Pilot Show (T); Snack A Jacks (E); Bollywood Queen (F);
Drexyle (M)

Russell Day
Grade One TV & Film Personnel, Elstree Studios, Shenley
Road, Borehamwood WD6 1JG
t 020 8324 2224 f 020 8324 2328
e gradeone.tvpersonnel@virgin.net

Mauro Dellapina
The Firm Booking Company Ltd, 31 Oval Road, Camden,
London NW1 7EA
t 020 7248 9090 f 020 7248 9089 e kirsty@thefirm.co.uk

John Dibley
The Firm Booking Company Ltd, 31 Oval Road, Camden,
London NW1 7EA
t 020 7248 9090 f 020 7248 9089 e kirsty@thefirm.co.uk

Chris Dodds
Callbox Communications Limited, 66 Shepperton Studios,
Studios Road, Shepperton TW17 0QD
t 01932 592572 f 01932 569655 m 07710 572572
e callboxdiary@btinternet.com w www.callboxdiary.co.uk

Paul Dugdale
The Firm Booking Company Ltd, 31 Oval Road, Camden,
London NW1 7EA
t 020 7248 9090 f 020 7248 9089 e kirsty@thefirm.co.uk

Jason Edwards
The Firm Booking Company Ltd, 31 Oval Road, Camden,
London NW1 7EA
t 020 7248 9090 f 020 7248 9089 e kirsty@thefirm.co.uk

James Foster
Callbox Communications Limited, 66 Shepperton Studios,
Studios Road, Shepperton TW17 0QD
t 01932 592572 f 01932 569655 m 07710 572572
e callboxdiary@btinternet.com w www.callboxdiary.co.uk

Steve Fuller
Grade One TV & Film Personnel, Elstree Studios, Shenley
Road, Borehamwood WD6 1JG
t 020 8324 2224 f 020 8324 2328
e gradeone.tvpersonnel@virgin.net

Stafford Gillott
The Firm Booking Company Ltd, 31 Oval Road, Camden,
London NW1 7EA
t 020 7428 9090 f 020 7428 9089 e kirtsy@thefirm.co.uk

Martin Gooch
Grade One TV & Film Personnel, Elstree Studios, Shenley
Road, Borehamwood WD6 1JG
t 020 8324 2224 f 020 8324 2328
e gradeone.tvpersonnel@virgin.net

Nick Helm
TOVS Ltd, The Linen Hall, 162-168 Regent Street, London
W1B 5TB
t 020 7287 6110 f 020 7287 5481 e info@tovs.co.uk
w www.tovs.co.uk

Leon Henry
The Firm Booking Company Ltd, 31 Oval Road, Camden,
London NW1 7EA
t 020 7248 9090 **f** 020 7248 9089 **e** kirsty@thefirm.co.uk

Ben Howells
Grade One TV & Film Personnel, Elstree Studios, Shenley
Road, Borehamwood WD6 1JG
t 020 8324 2224 **f** 020 8324 2328
e gradeone.tvpersonnel@virgin.net

Karl Hui
Callbox Communications Limited, 66 Shepperton Studios,
Studios Road, Shepperton TW17 0QD
t 01932 592572 **f** 01932 569655 **m** 07710 572572
e callboxdiary@btinternet.com **w** www.callboxdiary.co.uk

Matthew Clarke Irons
Grade One TV & Film Personnel, Elstree Studios, Shenley
Road, Borehamwood WD6 1JG
t 020 8324 2224 **f** 020 8324 2328
e gradeone.tvpersonnel@virgin.net

Jim Jolliffe
Callbox Communications Limited, 66 Shepperton Studios,
Studios Road, Shepperton TW17 0QD
t 01932 592572 **f** 01932 569655
e callboxdiary@btinternet.com **w** www.callboxdiary.co.uk

Keep It Simple Productions
34-36 Overnhill Road, Bristol BS16 5DP
t 0117 904 1208 **t** 0117 956 7757 **m** 07803 040380
e purgaus@hotmail.com
Contact Matthew Purgaus, Camera/Editor; Katie Jennings, Director; Danielle
Somerfield, Producer; Dean Ferris, Director
Credits Spiked (D); Yam (S); Ten Thousand Bastards (S); Powys Renewable
Energy Video (I)

Katie Lawes
The Firm Booking Company Ltd, 31 Oval Road, Camden,
London NW1 7EA
t 020 7248 9090 **f** 020 7248 9089 **e** kirsty@thefirm.co.uk

Oli Ledwith
Stella's Diary, 9 Hormead Road, London W9 3NG
t 020 8969 1855 **t** 020 8769 3919 **f** 020 8964 2157
m 07973 725137 **e** stella'sdiary@btinternet.com

Chris Lopez
The Linen Hall, 162-168 Regent Street, London W1B 5TB
t 020 7287 6110 **f** 020 7287 5481 **e** info@tovs.co.uk
w www.tovs.co.uk

Gareth Lowdnes
Callbox Communications Limited, 66 Shepperton Studios,
Studios Road, Shepperton TW17 0QD
t 01932 592572 **f** 01932 569655 **m** 07710 572572
e callboxdiary@btinternet.com **w** www.callboxdiary.co.uk

Caroline Luguet
117 Asylum Road, London SE15 2LB
t 020 7277 8154 **f** 020 7277 8154 **m** 07956 509018
e carolineluguet@mac.com
Credits Women Entrepreneur (I); Morgan Cars (D); London - Pet Shop Boys (M);
Thunder - At The Marquee (M)

Dave Maxwell
Grade One TV & Film Personnel, Elstree Studios, Shenley
Road, Borehamwood WD6 1JG
t 020 8324 2224 **f** 020 8324 2328
e gradeone.tvpersonnel@virgin.net

Richard Merritt
Callbox Communications Limited, 66 Shepperton Studios,
Studios Road, Shepperton TW17 0QD
t 01932 592572 **f** 01932 569655 **m** 07710 572572
e callboxdiary@btinternet.com **w** www.callboxdiary.co.uk

Lewis Mutongwizo
The Firm Booking Company Ltd, 31 Oval Road, Camden,
London NW1 7EA
t 020 7248 9090 **f** 0207248 9089 **e** kirsty@thefirm.co.uk

Joseph Oliver
The Firm Booking Company Ltd, 31 Oval Road, Camden,
London NW1 7EA
t 020 7248 9090 **f** 020 7248 9089 **e** kirsty@thefirm.co.uk

Simon Oliver
Callbox Communications Limited, 66 Shepperton Studios,
Studios Road, Shepperton TW17 0QD
t 01932 592572 **f** 01932 569655 **m** 07710 572572
e callboxdiary@btinternet.com **w** www.callboxdiary.co.uk

Tom Parr
The Firm Booking Company Ltd, 31 Oval Road, Camden,
London NW1 7EA
t 020 7248 9090 **f** 020 7248 9089 **e** kirsty@thefirm.co.uk

Ray Forsythe
23 Greystoke Drive, Ruislip HA4 7YL
t 01895 677316 **f** 01895 677316 **m** 0771 352 2742
e raforsythe@ndirect.co.uk

Earl Rhodes
Grade One TV & Film Personnel, Elstree Studios, Shenley
Road, Borehamwood WD6 1JG
t 020 8324 2224 **f** 020 8324 2328
e gradeone.tvpersonnel@virgin.net

Chris Rusby
4 Crossfield, Holywell Green, Halifax HX4 9ES
m 07967 595989 **e** chrisrusby@hotmail.com
Credits Brookside (T); Grange Hill (T); Hollyoaks (T)

Ben Shayler
Grade One TV & Film Personnel, Elstree Studios, Shenley
Road, Borehamwood WD6 1JG
t 020 8324 2224 **f** 020 8324 2328
e gradeone.tvpersonnel@virgin.net

Jodi Smart
e jodimarcelle@hotmail.com
Agent Grade One TV & Film Personnel, Elstree Studios,
Shenley Road, Borehamwood WD6 1JG
t 020 8324 2224 **f** 020 8324 2328
e gradeone.tvpersonnel@virgin.net

Tim Stephenson
Grade One TV & Film Personnel, Elstree Studios, Shenley
Road, Borehamwood WD6 1JG
t 020 8324 2224 **f** 020 8324 2328
e gradeone.tvpersonnel@virgin.net

Simon Surtees
Stella's Diary, 9 Hormead Road, London W9 3NG
t 020 8847 3363 **t** 020 8969 1855 **f** 020 8964 2157
m 07974 392995 **e** stella'sdiary@btinternet.com

Nadia Thomas
The Firm Booking Company Ltd, 31 Oval Road, Camden,
London NW1 7EA
t 020 7428 9090 **f** 020 7428 9089 **e** kirsty@thefirm.co.uk

Peter Wheeler
The Firm Booking Company Ltd, 31 Oval Road, Camden,
London NW1 7EA
t 020 7248 9090 **f** 020 7248 9089 **e** kirsty@thefirm.co.uk

Andrew Wiggins
Callbox Communications Limited, 66 Shepperton Studios,
Studios Road, Shepperton TW17 0QD
t 01932 592572 **f** 01932 569655
e callboxdiary@btinternet.com **w** www.callboxdiary.co.uk

Leanne Wilkins
The Firm Booking Company Ltd, 31 Oval Road, Camden, London NW1 7EA
t 020 7248 9090 **f** 020 7248 9089 **e** kirsty@thefirm.co.uk

Simon Williams
The Firm Booking Company Ltd, 31 Oval Road, Camden, London NW1 7EA
t 020 7428 9090 **f** 020 7428 9089 **e** kirsty@thefirm.co.uk

Mari Yamamura
Gems, The Media House, 87 Glebe Street, Penarth CF64 1EF
t 029 2071 0770 **f** 029 2071 0771 **e** gems@gems-agency.co.uk
w www.gems-agency.co.uk
Credits As If (T); Relic Hunter (T); Screen Gems (F)

Camera **Clapper Loaders**

Richard Ackland
t 07970 425356 **f** 07970 809812

Ben Appleton
Gems, The Media House, 87 Glebe Street, Penarth CF64 1EF
t 029 2071 0770 **f** 029 2071 0771 **e** gems@gems-agency.co.uk
w www.gems-agency.co.uk
Credits The Worst Witch (T); Revenger's Tragedy (T); Cutting It (T)

Marc Atherford
Annie's Answering Service, Pinewood Studios, Pinewood Road, Iver Heath SL0 0NH
t 01753 651303 **f** 01753 651848
e info@annies.co.uk **w** www.annies.co.uk

Genevieve Atlas
Silverwood, Marsh Lane, Bolton Percy, York YO23 7BA
t 01904 744385 **m** 07803 529119 **e** gennyatlas@hotmail.com
Credits Brookside (T); Hollyoaks (T); Stan The Man (T); Helen West (T)

Aggie Balogh
Suz Cruz, Halliford Studios, Manygate Lane, Shepperton TW17 9EG
t 01932 252577 **f** 01932 253323 **m** 07956 485593
e zoe@suzcruz.co.uk **w** www.suzcruz.co.uk

John Barbour
GAS (Guild Answering Service), C/o Panavision UK, Metropolitan Centre, Bristol Road, Greenford UB6 8GD
t 020 8813 1999 **f** 020 8813 2111
e admin@gbct.org **w** www.gbct.org

Peter Bateson
Wizzo & Co, 35 Old Compton Street, London W1D 5JX
t 020 7437 2055 **f** 020 7437 2066
e wizzo@wizzoandco.co.uk **w** www.wizzoandco.co.uk

Peter Bathurst
Callbox Communications Limited, 66 Shepperton Studios, Studios Road, Shepperton TW17 0QD
t 01932 592572 **f** 01932 569655 **m** 07710 572572
e callboxdiary@btinternet.com **w** www.callboxdiary.co.uk

Ben Battersby
Callbox Communications Limited, 66 Shepperton Studios, Studios Road, Shepperton TW17 0QD
t 01932 592572 **f** 01932 569655 **m** 07710 572572
e callboxdiary@btinternet.com **w** www.callboxdiary.co.uk

Edward Bishop
Suz Cruz, Halliford Studios, Manygate Lane, Shepperton TW17 9EG
t 01932 252577 **f** 01932 253323 **m** 07956 485593
e zoe@suzcruz.co.uk **w** www.suzcruz.co.uk

Harry Bowers
13 Wingfield Street, London SE15 4LN
t 020 7639 0487 **f** 07970 715341 **m** 07976 237 476
e harryb1@orange.net
Credits Brassed Off (F); House Of Mirth (F); Thunderpants (F)

Catherine Brown
Suz Cruz, Halliford Studios, Manygate Lane, Shepperton TW17 9EG
t 01932 252577 **f** 01932 253323 **m** 07956 485593
e zoe@suzcruz.co.uk **w** www.suzcruz.co.uk

Warren Buckingham
Suz Cruz, Halliford Studios, Manygate Lane, Shepperton TW17 9EG
t 01932 252577 **f** 01932 253323 **m** 07956 485593
e zoe@suzcruz.co.uk **w** www.suzcruz.co.uk

Dale Buckton
67a Kingswood Road, London SW2 4JN
f 07092 355844 **m** 07980 655 236
e pinsharp@dalebuckton.co.uk **w** www.dalebuckton.co.uk
Credits Salvation Army 'Link' (I); Conchie (S); Family Affairs (T)

James Burgess
Annie's Answering Service, Pinewood Studios, Pinewood Road, Iver Heath SL0 0NH
t 01753 651303 **f** 01753 651848
e info@annies.co.uk **w** www.annies.co.uk

Peter Byrne
Stella's Diary, 9 Hormead Road, London W9 3NG
t 020 7351 3203 **t** 020 8969 1855 **f** 020 8964 2157
m 07967 162133 **e** stella'sdiary@btinternet.com

Tony Byrne
Suz Cruz, Halliford Studios, Manygate Lane, Shepperton TW17 9EG
t 01932 252577 **f** 01932 253323 **m** 07956 485593
e zoe@suzcruz.co.uk **w** www.suzcruz.co.uk

Richard Carroll
Annie's Answering Service, Pinewood Studios, Pinewood Road, Iver Heath SL0 0NH
t 01753 651303 **f** 01753 651848
e info@annies.co.uk **w** www.annies.co.uk

Jenny John Chuan
10 Brentford Close, Yeading, Hayes UB4 9QG
t 020 8845 2269 **f** 020 8845 2269 **m** 07973 830066
e jjohnchuan@aol.com
Agent Suz Cruz, Halliford Studios, Manygate Lane, Shepperton TW17 9EG
t 01932 252577 **f** 01932 253323 **m** 07956 485593
e zoe@suzcruz.co.uk **w** www.suzcruz.co.uk

Shaun Cobley
Annie's Answering Service, Pinewood Studios, Pinewood Road, Iver Heath SL0 0NH
t 01753 651303 **f** 01753 651848
e info@annies.co.uk **w** www.annies.co.uk

Chris Connatty
Suz Cruz, Halliford Studios, Manygate Lane, Shepperton TW17 9EG
t 01932 252577 **f** 01932 253323 **m** 07956 485593
e zoe@suzcruz.co.uk **w** www.suzcruz.co.uk

Lee Connelly
28 Nellgrove Road, Hillingdon UB10 0SX
t 020 8581 1497 **f** 020 8581 1497 **m** 07721 009049

Bob Cooke
Suz Cruz, Halliford Studios, Manygate Lane, Shepperton TW17 9EG
t 01932 252577 **f** 01932 253323 **m** 07956 485593
e zoe@suzcruz.co.uk **w** www.suzcruz.co.uk

Jason Coop
Annie's Answering Service, Pinewood Studios, Pinewood Road,
Iver Heath SLO 0NH
t 01753 651303 **f** 01753 651848
e info@annies.co.uk **w** www.annies.co.uk

Richard Copeman
EXEC, 6 Travis Court, Farnham Royal SL2 3SB
t 01753 646677 **f** 01753 646770
e sue@execmanagement.co.uk **w** www.execmanagement.co.uk

Liz Courtney
GAS (Guild Answering Service), C/o Panavision UK,
Metropolitan Centre, Bristol Road, Greenford UB6 8GD
t 020 8813 1999 **f** 020 8813 2111
e admin@gbct.org **w** www.gbct.org

Chris Dale
Annie's Answering Service, Pinewood Studios, Pinewood Road,
Iver Heath SLO 0NH
t 01753 651303 **f** 01753 651848
e info@annies.co.uk **w** www.annies.co.uk

Mark Dempsey
8 Sunnybank Avenue, Horsforth, Leeds LS18 4LZ
t 0113 258 1927 **m** 07930 371314
e mark@clapperloader.co.uk **w** www.mddempsey.fsnet.co.uk
Credits Strange (T); Real Men (T); A Touch of Frost - Series IX (T); Cutting It -
Series I (T)

Milly Donaghy
Annie's Answering Service, Pinewood Studios, Pinewood Road,
Iver Heath SLO 0NH
t 01753 651303 **f** 01753 651848
e info@annies.co.uk **w** www.annies.co.uk

Toby Eedy
GAS (Guild Answering Service), C/o Panavision UK,
Metropolitan Centre, Bristol Road, Greenford UB6 8GD
t 020 8813 1999 **f** 020 8813 2111
e admin@gbct.org **w** www.gbct.org

Rosalyn Ellis
Annie's Answering Service, Pinewood Studios, Pinewood Road,
Iver Heath SLO 0NH
t 01753 651303 **f** 01753 651848
e info@annies.co.uk **w** www.annies.co.uk

Charlie England
Suz Cruz, Halliford Studios, Manygate Lane, Shepperton TW17 9EG
t 01932 252577 **f** 01932 253323 **m** 07956 485593
e zoe@suzcruz.co.uk **w** www.suzcruz.co.uk

Guy Frost
Callbox Communications Ltd, PO Box 66, Shepperton Studios,
Shepperton Lane TW17 0QD
t 01932 592572 **f** 01932 569655 **m** 07710 572572
e callboxdiary@btinternet.com **w** www.callboxdiary.co.uk

Jeremy Fuzco
Suz Cruz, Halliford Studios, Manygate Lane, Shepperton TW17 9EG
t 01932 252577 **f** 01932 253323 **m** 07956 485593
e zoe@suzcruz.co.uk **w** www.suzcruz.co.uk

Dominic Gaughan
Callbox Communications Limited, 66 Shepperton Studios,
Studios Road, Shepperton TW17 0QD
t 01932 592572 **f** 01932 569655 **m** 07710 572572
e callboxdiary@btinternet.com **w** www.callboxdiary.co.uk

Sam Goldie
Wizzo & Co, 35 Old Compton Street, London W1D 5JX
t 020 7437 2055 **f** 020 7437 2066
e wizzo@wizzoandco.co.uk **w** www.wizzoandco.co.uk

Chris Greenwood
329A Abbeydale Road, Sheffield S7 1FS
t 0114 255 3637 **m** 07939 130887 **e** magic.hour@virgin.net
Credits Cutting It Series II (T); League Of Gentlemen Series III (T); 24 Hour
Party People (F)

Camille Griffin
Annie's Answering Service, Pinewood Studios, Pinewood Road,
Iver Heath SLO 0NH
t 01753 651303 **f** 01753 651848
e info@annies.co.uk **w** www.annies.co.uk

Kash Halford
Callbox Communications Limited, 66 Shepperton Studios,
Studios Road, Shepperton TW17 0QD
t 01932 592572 **f** 01932 569655 **m** 07710 572572
e callboxdiary@btinternet.com **w** www.callboxdiary.co.uk

Alan Hall
Annie's Answering Service, Pinewood Studios, Pinewood Road,
Iver Heath SLO 0NH
t 01753 651303 **f** 01753 651848
e info@annies.co.uk **w** www.annies.co.uk

Rab Harling
Flat 5, 16 Grand Avenue, Muswell Hill, London N10 3BB
t 020 8352 5285 **m** 07956 434510 **e** rabs@mailcity.com
w www.kodacat.com
Agent GAS (Guild Answering Service), C/o Panavision UK,
Metropolitan Centre, Bristol Road, Greenford UB6 8GD
t 020 8813 1999 **f** 020 8813 2111
e admin@gbct.org **w** www.gbct.org
Credits LD50 (F); Al's Lads (F); Circus (F)

Star Hart
Suz Cruz, Halliford Studios, Manygate Lane, Shepperton TW17 9EG
t 01932 252577 **f** 01932 253323 **m** 07956 485593
e zoe@suzcruz.co.uk **w** www.suzcruz.co.uk

Elizabeth Hoar
Callbox Communications Limited, 66 Shepperton Studios,
Studios Road, Shepperton TW17 0QD
t 01932 592572 **f** 01932 569655 **m** 07710 572572
e callboxdiary@btinternet.com **w** www.callboxdiary.co.uk

Bradley Hogan
Annie's Answering Service, Pinewood Studios, Pinewood Road,
Iver Heath SLO 0NH
t 01753 651303 **f** 01753 651848
e info@annies.co.uk **w** www.annies.co.uk

Dan Holland
Annie's Answering Service, Pinewood Studios, Pinewood Road,
Iver Heath SLO 0NH
t 01753 651303 **f** 01753 651848
e info@annies.co.uk **w** www.annies.co.uk

Robin Horn
Suz Cruz, Halliford Studios, Manygate Lane, Shepperton TW17 9EG
t 01932 252577 **f** 01932 253323 **m** 07956 485593
e zoe@suzcruz.co.uk **w** www.suzcruz.co.uk

Phil Humphries
134 Haven Green Court, Ealing, London W5 2UX
t 020 8997 6703 **m** 07801 336007
e philjhumphries@yahoo.com **w** www.philhumphries.co.uk
Credits Starstreet (C); Revelation (C)

Gabriel Hyman
Watford
m 07980 747133
e gabriel@doutbfulsound.co.uk **w** www.doubtfulsound.co.uk

Jani Jance
11G Rowley Way, Abbey Road, London NW8 0SF
t 020 7328 8647 **f** 020 7328 8647 **m** 07958 550259
Credits Bodily Harm (T); Odours Of Chrisanthemums (S); Calender Girls (F);
Ted And Sylvia (F)

Ed Jones
EXEC, 6 Travis Court, Farnham Royal SL2 3SB
t 01753 646677 **f** 01753 646770
e sue@execmanagement.co.uk **w** www.execmanagement.co.uk

Russell Kennedy
EXEC, 6 Travis Court, Farnham Royal SL2 3SB
t 01753 646677 **f** 01753 646770
e sue@execmanagement.co.uk **w** www.execmanagement.co.uk

Raymond Knutsen
Edinburgh/London
m 07808 837667 **e** oxgangs@hotmail.com
Credits South Bank Show (T); Rockface (T); Arabia Insurance - Shark (C); IRS -
Tire Change (C)

James Layton
Warren House, Waddlane, Snape IP17 1RB
m 07787 500474
Credits Second Nature (T); Blackball (F)

Danny Lee
GAS (Guild Answering Service), C/o Panavision UK,
Metropolitan Centre, Bristol Road, Greenford UB6 8GD
t 020 8813 1999 **f** 020 8813 2111
e admin@gbct.org **w** www.gbct.org

Edward Lindsley
Suz Cruz, Halliford Studios, Manygate Lane, Shepperton TW17 9EG
t 01932 252577 **f** 01932 253323 **m** 07956 485593
e zoe@suzcruz.co.uk **w** www.suzcruz.co.uk

Sally Low
Suz Cruz, Halliford Studios, Manygate Lane, Shepperton TW17 9EG
t 01932 252577 **f** 01932 253323 **m** 07956 485593
e zoe@suzcruz.co.uk **w** www.suzcruz.co.uk

Chaz Lyon
Annie's Answering Service, Pinewood Studios, Pinewood Road,
Iver Heath SL0 0NH
t 01753 651303 **f** 01753 651848
e info@annies.co.uk **w** www.annies.co.uk

Rachel Macgregor
Suz Cruz, Halliford Studios, Manygate Lane, Shepperton TW17 9EG
t 01932 252577 **f** 01932 253323 **m** 07956 485593
e zoe@suzcruz.co.uk **w** www.suzcruz.co.uk

Alysia Maciejowska
57 Haliburton Road, St Margarets, Twickenham TW1 1PD
m 07967 011251 **e** hotlysh@hotmail.com
Credits The Key (T); Les Liasions Dangereuses (F); Straight Out (D); Taggart (T)

David Mackie
Annie's Answering Service, Pinewood Studios, Pinewood Road,
Iver Heath SL0 0NH
t 01753 651303 **f** 01753 651848
e info@annies.co.uk **w** www.annies.co.uk

Neil McKay
25 Courtney Close, Wollaton, Nottingham NG8 2BS
t 07774 226155 **e** n_a_mckay@hotmail.com
Credits Function At The Junction (T); Peak Practice (T); Picking Up The Pieces
(T); Just Like My Dad (T)

Chris Meadows
t 01424 216255 **m** 07711 806 361
Credits Midsomer Murders V (T)

Spencer Murray
21 Burchley Avenue, Borehamwood WD6 2JG
t 020 8207 2644 **t** 020 8813 1999
Agent GAS (Guild Answering Service), C/o Panavision UK,
Metropolitan Centre, Bristol Road, Greenford UB6 8GD
t 020 8813 1999 **f** 020 8813 2111
e admin@gbct.org **w** www.gbct.org
Credits Die Another Day (F); 102 Dalmatians (F); Chocolat (F); Harry Potter And
The Philosopher's Stone (F)

Gabi Norland
473A Green Lanes, London N4 1AJ
t 020 8341 1165 **m** 07974 147106 **e** supershapsister@hotmail.com

Chin Okoronkwo
Suz Cruz, Halliford Studios, Manygate Lane, Shepperton TW17 9EG
t 01932 252577 **f** 01932 253323 **m** 07956 485593
e zoe@suzcruz.co.uk **w** www.suzcruz.co.uk

Robert Palmer
Annie's Answering Service, Pinewood Studios, Pinewood Road,
Iver Heath SL0 0NH
t 01753 651303 **f** 01753 651848
e info@annies.co.uk **w** www.annies.co.uk

Ben Perry
EXEC, 6 Travis Court, Farnham Royal SL2 3SB
t 01753 646677 **f** 01753 646770
e sue@execmanagement.co.uk **w** www.execmanagement.co.uk

Derrick Peters
Annie's Answering Service, Pinewood Studios, Pinewood Road,
Iver Heath SL0 0NH
t 01753 651303 **f** 01753 651848
e info@annies.co.uk **w** www.annies.co.uk

Danny Preston
Callbox Communications Limited, 66 Shepperton Studios,
Studios Road, Shepperton TW17 0QD
t 01932 592572 **f** 01932 569655 **m** 07710 572572
e callboxdiary@btinternet.com **w** www.callboxdiary.co.uk

Ben Pritchard
Suz Cruz, Halliford Studios, Manygate Lane, Shepperton TW17 9EG
t 01932 252577 **f** 01932 253323 **m** 07956 485593
e zoe@suzcruz.co.uk **w** www.suzcruz.co.uk

Miles Proudfoot
t 07976 732762 **f** 020 8977 0338
Agent EXEC, 6 Travis Court, Farnham Royal SL2 3SB
t 01753 646677 **f** 01753 646770
e sue@execmanagement.co.uk **w** www.execmanagement.co.uk
Credits Bright Young Things (F); American Girl (F); Hidalgo (F)

Damon Randall
Annie's Answering Service, Pinewood Studios, Pinewood Road,
Iver Heath SL0 0NH
t 01753 651303 **f** 01753 651848
e info@annies.co.uk **w** www.annies.co.uk

Sam Renton
EXEC, 6 Travis Court, Farnham Royal SL2 3SB
t 01753 646677 **f** 01753 646770
e sue@execmanagement.co.uk **w** www.execmanagement.co.uk

Niki Robertson
Suz Cruz, Halliford Studios, Manygate Lane, Shepperton TW17 9EG
t 01932 252577 **f** 01932 253323 **m** 07956 485593
e zoe@suzcruz.co.uk **w** www.suzcruz.co.uk

Susi Rowell
Suz Cruz, Halliford Studios, Manygate Lane, Shepperton TW17 9EG
t 01932 252577 **f** 01932 253323 **m** 07956 485593
e zoe@suzcruz.co.uk **w** www.suzcruz.co.uk

Duncan Scott
Gems, The Media House, 87 Glebe Street, Penarth CF64 1EF
t 029 2071 0770 **f** 029 2071 0771 **e** gems@gems-agency.co.uk
w www.gems-agency.co.uk
Credits The Grimleys (T); London's Burning Series XIV (T); Murder In Mind (T)

James Scott
Annie's Answering Service, Pinewood Studios, Pinewood Road,
Iver Heath SL0 0NH
t 01753 651303 **f** 01753 651848
e info@annies.co.uk **w** www.annies.co.uk

Nigel Seal
GAS (Guild Answering Service), C/o Panavision UK,
Metropolitan Centre, Bristol Road, Greenford UB6 8GD
t 020 8813 1999 **f** 020 8813 2111
e admin@gbct.org **w** www.gbct.org

Sky Sharrock
EXEC, 6 Travis Court, Farnham Royal SL2 3SB
t 01753 646677 **f** 01753 646770
e sue@execmanagement.co.uk **w** www.execmanagement.co.uk

Matt Shaw
Suz Cruz, Halliford Studios, Manygate Lane, Shepperton TW17 9EG
t 01932 252577 **f** 01932 253323 **m** 07956 485593
e zoe@suzcruz.co.uk **w** www.suzcruz.co.uk

Penny Shipton
London
m 07958 738817 **e** penny_shipton@hotmail.com
Credits McDonalds (C); Sparkling Cyanide (T); William And Mary (T);
Dead Gorgeous (T)

Basil Smith
EXEC, 6 Travis Court, Farnham Royal SL2 3SB
t 01753 646677 **f** 01753 646770
e sue@execmanagement.co.uk **w** www.execmanagement.co.uk

Debbie Smith
8 Romola Road, Herne Hill, London SE24 9AZ
t 020 8355 0817 **f** 020 8355 0817 **m** 07710 385 481
e simon.scarboro@virgin.net
Credits Every Woman Knows a Secret (S); Relative Values (F); North Square (T)

Nigel Southall
GAS (Guild Answering Service), C/o Panavision UK,
Metropolitan Centre, Bristol Road, Greenford UB6 8GD
t 020 8813 1999 **f** 020 8813 2111
e admin@gbct.org **w** www.gbct.org

Simon Surtees
39A Vera Road, Lion's Wharf, London SW6 6QP
m 07974 392995 **e** simonsurtees@hotmail.com

Joylon Thompson
Callbox Communications Limited, 66 Shepperton Studios,
Shepperton TW17 0QD
t 01932 592572 **f** 01932 569655 **m** 07710 572572
e callboxdiary@btinternet.com **w** www.callboxdiary.co.uk

Daniel Trapp
Suz Cruz, Halliford Studios, Manygate Lane, Shepperton TW17 9EG
t 01932 252577 **f** 01932 253323 **m** 07956 485593
e zoe@suzcruz.co.uk **w** www.suzcruz.co.uk

Elizabeth Trott
224D Walm Lane, London NW2 3BS
t 020 8248 3868 **m** 07887 646009
e liz.trott@connectfree.co.uk
Credits The Family Business (F); Rehab (T); Keen Eddie (T); Daniel Deronda (T)

Jason Walker
Wizzo & Co, 35 Old Compton Street, London W1D 5JX
t 020 7437 2055 **f** 020 7437 2066
e wizzo@wizzoandco.co.uk **w** www.wizzoandco.co.uk

Brian Warner
GAS (Guild Answering Service), C/o Panavision UK,
Metropolitan Centre, Bristol Road, Greenford UB6 8GD
t 020 8813 1999 **f** 020 8813 2111
e admin@gbct.org **w** www.gbct.org

Fran Weston
Wizzo & Co, 35 Old Compton Street, London W1D 5JX
t 020 7437 2055 **f** 020 7437 2066
e wizzo@wizzoandco.co.uk **w** www.wizzoandco.co.uk

Paul Wheeldon
Annie's Answering Service, Pinewood Studios, Pinewood Road,
Iver Heath SL0 0NH
t 01753 651303 **f** 01753 651848
e info@annies.co.uk **w** www.annies.co.uk

Glyn Williams
Callbox Communications Limited, 66 Shepperton Studios,
Studios Road, Shepperton TW17 0QD
t 01932 592572 **f** 01932 569655 **m** 07710 572572
e callboxdiary@btinternet.com **w** www.callboxdiary.co.uk

Scott Williams
Suz Cruz, Halliford Studios, Manygate Lane, Shepperton TW17 9EG
t 01932 252577 **f** 01932 253323 **m** 07956 485593
e zoe@suzcruz.co.uk **w** www.suzcruz.co.uk

Sophie Wilson
Suz Cruz, Halliford Studios, Manygate Lane, Shepperton TW17 9EG
t 01932 252577 **f** 01932 253323 **m** 07956 485593
e zoe@suzcruz.co.uk **w** www.suzcruz.co.uk

Charlie Woodburn
Callbox Communications Limited, 66 Shepperton Studios,
Studios Road, Shepperton TW17 0QD
t 01932 592572 **f** 01932 569655 **m** 07710 572572
e callboxdiary@btinternet.com **w** www.callboxdiary.co.uk

Sarah Woodward
22 Maypole Gardens, Cawood, Selby YO8 3TG
t 01757 268919 **m** 07810 207449 **e** columbo96@hotmail.com
Credits The Second Coming (T); Bupa - Clocks (C); Flesh And Blood (T); At
Home With The Braithwaites (T)

Joe Wright
Callbox Communications Limited, 66 Shepperton Studios,
Studios Road, Shepperton TW17 0QD
t 01932 592572 **f** 01932 569655 **m** 07710 572572
e callboxdiary@btinternet.com **w** www.callboxdiary.co.uk

Iain Young
Suz Cruz, Halliford Studios, Manygate Lane, Shepperton TW17 9EG
t 01932 252577 **f** 01932 253323 **m** 07956 485593
e zoe@suzcruz.co.uk **w** www.suzcruz.co.uk

Camera **Crew Hire**

195 Television
Arjang, Main Road, Lacey Green, Princes Risborough HP27 0QU
t 01844 344178 **f** 01844 274724 **m** 07860 864 608
e 195tv@ukgateway.net
Contact John Poynter, Lighting Cameraman

The 400 Company
Unit B3, The Workshops, 2A Askew Crescent, Shepherds Bush,
London W12 9DP
t 020 8746 1400 **e** info@the400.co.uk **w** www.the400.co.uk
Contact Mark Sloper, Director, Director; Paul Giordani, Business Development
Manager; Jo Haynes, Production Manager; Barry Woods, Facilities Manager

A1 Camera Crews (Scotland)
193 Silvertonhill Avenue, Hamilton ML3 7PG
t 01698 427893 **f** 01698 427893 **m** 07836 574 966
e ian193@connectfree.co.uk
Contact Ian Boddie, Managing Director

Actioncam
49 Woodfield Lane, Ashtead KT21 2BT
t 01372 278919 **f** 01372 279983 **m** 07831 492 024
e actioncam@btinternet.com **w** www.actioncamtv.com
Contact Glenn Wilkinson, Director/lighting cameraman
Credits Outdoor Quest (T); Tour De France 2002 (T); The Mole (T)

And Action Ltd
5 Windsor Close, St Ives, Ringwood BH24 2LJ
t 01425 472377 **f** 01425 473779 **m** 07860 257744
e richard@cameracrew.org.uk **w** www.cameracrew.org.uk
Contact Richard Edwards, Director; Denise Ryan, Stunt Co-ordinator
Credits O'Shea's Big Adventure (T)

Steve Beer
44 Archery Steps, St George's Fields, London W2 2YF
t 020 7723 2049 **m** 07860 511628 **e** stevebeer@talk21.com
w http://stevebeer_film.tripod.com
Credits Fish For Brains (S); Like Me (S); Murder-In-Law (F)

Big Yellow Feet Production Company Ltd
Borrows Lea Farm, Hook Lane, Shere GU5 9QQ
t 01483 209500 **f** 01483 209500 **m** 07941 318280
e bigyellowfeet@hotmail.com **w** www.bigyellowfeet.com
Contact Simon Sharp, Technical Director; Byron Vaisey, Crewing Manager; Greg Mandry, Managing Director
Credits Bradford City Of Culture 2008 (I); The Politics Show (T)

Bigfoot Media
79 Carshalton Park Road, Carshalton SM5 3SJ
t 020 8647 1485 **m** 07771 592963
e info@bigfoot-media.co.uk **w** www.bigfoot-media.co.uk
Contact Mark Thompson, Partner

Blue Fin Television Ltd
34 Fitzwilliam Road, London SW4 0DN
t 020 7622 0870 **f** 020 7720 7875 **m** 07973 502349
e antleake@bluefin-tv.demon.co.uk **w** www.bluefintv.com
Contact Anthony Leake, Head of Cameras; Diane Porter, Bookings
Credits The Fugitives (T); Vandals (D); Escape From Experiment Island (T); The South Bank Show (T)

Blue Planet Television Ltd
Unit 9, Regis Road, London NW5 3EW
t 020 7267 4537 **f** 020 7428 0252 **e** info@blueplanet.tv.com
w www.blueplanet-tv.com
Contact Dominic Kipling, Facilties Manager

BROADCAST TELEVISION
facilities

Broadcast Television Facilities
Acuba House, Lymm Road, Little Bollington, Altrincham WA14 4SY
t 0161 9269808 **f** 0161 9299000 **m** 07974 151617
e info@broadcast-tv.co.uk **w** www.broadcast-tv.co.uk
Contact Robert Foster, Managing Director; Erin Mactague, Bookings Co-ordinator
Credits Brookside (T); Inside The Mind Of Roy Keane (T); Tonight With Trevor MacDonald (T); Cuba: The Other Side Of Armageddon (T)

Cine Wessex Ltd
13 Winnall Valley Road, Winchester SO23 0LD
t 01962 844900 **f** 01962 840004
e joe@cinewessex.co.uk **w** www.cinewessex.co.uk
Contact Kelly Dyer; Joe Conlan

Peter Coldwell
Karma, Glasgow Road, Hardgate, Clydebank G81 5QX
t 01389 878236 **f** 01389 878236 **m** 07831 221512
e cameras@ntlworld.com

Creation Company Films Ltd
Unit 1, The Sandycombe Centre, 1 Sandycombe Road, Kew TW9 2EP
t 020 8332 0888 **f** 020 8332 1123
e production@creationcompany.tv **w** www.creationcompany.tv
Contact Louise Glen, Production Manager; Steve Montgomery, Managing Director; Scott Drummond, Director; J Warburton, Lighting Cameraman
Credits The John Thaw Story (T); Being Victoria Beckham (T)

Creative Camera Partnership
Slades Farm, Bushcombe Lane, Cleeve Hill, Cheltenham GL52 3PN
t 01242 676003 **f** 01242 676003 **m** 07860 598323
Contact Rickie Gauld, Director of Photography
Credits Horizon (D); Discovery - Tornadoes (T); The Parent Trap (F)

Crew Digital
14A Pavilion Terrace, Wood Lane, London W12 0HT
t 020 8354 3298 **f** 020 8354 3298 **m** 07801 731942
e matt@crewdigital.com **w** www.crewdigital.com
Contact Matt Sumner, Business Manager/Lighting Cameraman
Credits Trainers (M); Great Speeches (D); Cisco Systems Live Webcasting (W); Mac World Corporate Awards (I)
DVCam Format Producers. Enhance the production value of your project without compromising the budget... unbeatable camera packages for low-budget producers.

Crewed Up Ltd
Room 321, c/o Granada TV, Quay Street, Manchester M60 9EA
t 0161 827 2971 **f** 0161 827 2972 **m** 07802 283459
e crews@crewedup.co.uk **w** www.crewedup.co.uk
Contact Mike Turnbull, Director; Jessica Leech, Crew Manager
Credits Everyman (T); Stars In Their Eyes (T); Tonight With Trevor McDonald (T)

Crews@Magpie
31-32 Cheapside, Birmingham B5 6AY
t 0121 622 5884 **f** 0121 666 6077 **m** 07836 585518
e crews@magpiefilms.co.uk **w** www.magpiefilms.co.uk
Contact Sabrina Millward, Schedules Director

Cumbria Films Ltd
The Limes, Plains Road, Wetheral, Carlisle CA4 8LE
t 01228 560778 **f** 01228 562084 **m** 07850 702853
e gren@cumbriafilms.co.uk **w** www.cumbriafilms.co.uk
Credits Countryfile (T); BBC Sport (T); Blue Peter (T); Walking With Beasts (T)

Dales Broadcast Ltd
Nettle Hill, Brinklow Road, Ansty, Coventry CV7 9JL
t 024 7662 1763 **f** 024 7660 2732 **m** 07803 584925
e sales@dales-ltd.com **w** www.dales-ltd.com
Contact Kate Boden, Marketing Director; Julian Boden, Managing Director
Credits Tickle, Patch And Friends (T); Young Choirs 2001 (T); Network Q Rally (T); Horseracing for Racetech, ATR And Channel 4 (T)

Debrouillard Ltd
74 Ashland Road, Sheffield S7 1RJ
t 0114 220 0667 **f** 0114 220 0668 **m** 07831 531416
e jonathan@debrouillard.tv **w** www.debrouillard.tv
Contact Jonathan Young, Director/Senior Cameraman
Credits The Money Programme (T); Macintyre Investigates (D); Louis Theroux Meets (D)

Decent Exposure TV Ltd
The Gardens, Watchet Lane, Little Kingshill HP16 0DR
t 01494 862667 **f** 01494 864583
e office@decentexposure.tv **w** www.decentexposure.tv
Contact Michelle O''Donoghue, Company Secretary; Carmen Radmore, Production Co-ordinator

The Digital Garage Company Ltd

13 Devonshire Mews, Chiswick, London W4 2HA
t 07000 785821 **f** 07000 785822 **m** 07788 145577
e mail@digitalgarage.co.uk **w** www.digitalgarage.co.uk
Contact Janie Willsmore, Crew Manager; Oliver Hickey, Facilities Manager
Credits Castle (D); Faking It - Drag Queen (T); Leonardo (T); Six Wives Of Henry VIII (T)

Electra Film & Television Ltd

Wharf House, Brentwaters Business Park, The Ham, Brentford TW8 8HQ
t 020 8232 8899 **f** 020 8232 8877
e mail@electra-tv.com **w** www.electra-tv.com

The Electronic Camera Company

5 Portland Square, London E1W 2QR
t 020 7734 5021 **f** 020 7480 6253
e johntarby@elecamco.demon.co.uk **w** www.elecamco.demon.co.uk
Contact John Tarby, Director of Photography

Extra Veg
(Extra Vegetables Television Crews Scotland)

Glenlockhart House, 6 The Steils, Edinburgh EH10 5XD
t 0131 446 0444 **f** 0131 446 0333 **m** 07887 571770
e cindy@extraveg.com **w** www.extraveg.com
Contact Paul Gavin, DOP & Lighting Cameraman; Cindy Thomson, Production Manager
Credits Good Driver (D); Jack Daniels (C); Candy Bar Kid (S)

EZ Film Services

243 Alcester Road South, Kings Heath, Birmingham B14 6DT
t 0121 441 2834 **f** 0121 441 2834 **m** 07941 010698
Contact Rob Southam, Camera Operator
Credits Clocking Off (T); Dazeil And Pascoe (T); Where The Heart Is (T); Hope And Glory (T)

First Sight Communications Ltd

10 Novello Croft, Old Farm Park, Milton Keynes MK7 8QT
t 07050 276484 **f** 07050 133389
e crewhire@firstsightcomms.co.uk
Contact Andy Smith, Lighting Cameraman
Credits 21st Century Medicine; Breakfast With Frost; Car Wars

Fuel Film & TV Ltd

30 Kingsfield Road, Oxhey, Watford WD19 4PS
t 01923 233956 **f** 01923 224289 **m** 07774 183366
e debbie@fuelfilm.com **w** www.fuelfilm.com
Contact Debbie Delle-Valle, Manager

Broadcast Camera Kits

Crew Diary Service

24/7 Support

www.digitalgarage.co.uk   07000 785821

Garton Film & Video

Tranby Croft, Tranby Lane, Anlaby, Hull HU10 7EF
t 01482 651317 **f** 01482 651317 **m** 07721 007100
e info@gartonmedia.fsnet.co.uk
Contact Howard Garton, Proprietor/Cameraman
Credits BBC Newsnight (T)

Glenn Wilkinson

49 Woodfield Lane, Ashtead KT21 2BT
t 01372 278919 **f** 01372 279983 **m** 07831 492024
e actioncam@btinternet.com
Credits Surpirise Chefs (T); Tour De France (T); The Mole (T)

Goldmoor Television Ltd

30 Granby Court, Bletchley, Milton Keynes MK1 1NE
t 01908 370516 **f** 01908 643119 **e** crewhire@goldmoor.co.uk
w www.goldmoor.co.uk
Credits Steerbuild (I); The Queen's Concerts (T); TOTP Awards (T)

Chris Hall

1 The Gatehouse, Gatehouse Drive, Wirksworth DE4 4DL
t 01629 824818 **f** 01629 824818 **m** 07836 652937
e chrishall48@hotmail.com
Credits Room 801 - Britain's Secret UFO Hunters (D); Blood Ties (D); What The Butler Saw - The Paul Burrell Story (D)

Hammerhead Television Facilities Ltd

Unit 22, Waters Edge Business Park, Modwen Road, Manchester M5 3EZ
t 0161 872 6200 **f** 0161 872 6300
e manchester@hammerheadtv.com **w** www.hammerheadtv.com
Contact Darren Carrig, Facilities Manager; Matt Turnbull

Hammerhead Television Facilities Ltd

9 Merchiston Mews, Edinburgh EH10 4PE
t 0131 229 5000 **f** 0131 429 4211
e scotland@hammerheadtv.com **w** www.hammerheadtv.com
Contact Chris Orvis, Production Sound Mixer; Gail Glenwright, Facilities Manager

Hammerhead Television Facilities Ltd

42 Webbs Road, London SW11 6SF
t 020 7924 3977 **f** 020 7924 2154
e london@hammerheadtv.com **w** www.hammerheadtv.com
Contact Will Wilkinson, Facilities Manager; Dan Jarmany, Facilities Manager

Heavy Pencil

41 Shakespeare Road, Hanwell, London W7 1LT
t 020 8579 3008 **f** 020 8579 3009 **m** 07776 184481
e sb@heavypencil.net **w** www.heavypencil.net
Contact Mike Howell, Rentals Manager; Simon Bishop, Director; Martyn Rissen, Cameraman; Paul Bulley, Cameraman
Credits Sunday Times Rugby Special (C); Junkyard Wars Flight Special (T); Making The Band (T)

Hoi Polloi Film & Video

PO Box 5052, Newcastle-upon-Tyne NE99 1LR
t 0191 233 0050 **f** 0191 233 0052 **m** 07974 925477
e info@filmcrew.co.uk **w** www.filmcrew.co.uk
Contact Andy Greenwood, Lighting Cameraman; Chris Sutcliffe, Lighting Cameraman; Chris Watson, Sound Recordist; Paul Gunn, Sound Recordist
Credits Trouble At The Top (T); Life Of Mammals (T); After They Were Famous (T); Great Railway Journeys (T)

Logan Baird Camera Crews

Crafthole, Torpoint, Plymouth PL11 3DD
t 01503 230739 **f** 01503 230739 **m** 07860 426540
e logan.baird@virgin.net
Contact Logan Baird, Cameraman

John Lubran

19 Mill View Close, Howey, Llandrindod Wells LD1 5RA
t 01597 860575 **f** 01597 860655 **m** 07721 429181
e john@lubran.demon.co.uk **w** www.movingvision.co.uk
Credits Centre For Alternative Technology (I); Kingdom Of The Asante (D); Driven (T); Deadline 2000 (T)

M&K Jones

15 Star Lane, Lymm WA13 9LE
t 01925 753893 **f** 01925 751455 **m** 07768 766032
e fisticufffilms@aol.com
Contact Martin David Jones, Camerman; Karen Jones, Sound Recordist

Mac Film & Video Services

37 The Chase, Penns Park, Sutton Coldfield B76 1JS
t 0121 384 2093 **f** 0121 350 7500 **m** 07831 890802
e robinmcdonald@blueyonder.co.uk
Contact Robin McDonald, DOP/Lighting Cameraman

Mighty Fine Production Facilities

28 Willows Avenue, Morden SM4 5SG
t 020 8286 2867 **f** 020 8286 2826 **m** 07050 054482
e mightyfine@blueyonder.co.uk
Contact Mark Jackson

Millbank Studios

4 Millbank, Westminster, London SW1P 3JA
t 020 7233 2020 **f** 020 7233 3158
e facilities@millbank-studios.co.uk **w** www.millbank-studios.co.uk
Contact Richard Rose, Managing Director; Pippa Walker, Head of Operations;
Nick Hattingh, Technical Operations Manager; Nicola Goulding,
Head of Production

Never Never Films

57 Rowan Close, Ealing, London W5 4AL
t 020 8567 1568 **f** 020 8567 1568 **m** 07802 883943
e ianftyoung@eurcom.net

NewsCrews Ltd

The Gables, The Green, Pulham Market IP21 4SY
t 01379 608071 **f** 01379 608071 **m** 07860 223943
e news@newscrews.co.uk **w** www.newscrews.co.uk
Contact Lesley Venables

Northland Broadcast

3 Demesne Gardens, Derry BT48 9NA
t 028 7137 2432 **m** 07831 315 830
e enquiries@northlandbroadcast.com
w www.northlandbroadcast.com
Contact Vinny Cunningham, Partner/Lighting Cameraman
Credits Newsround (T); Xchange (T); Blue Peter (T)

Orchid Video & Crewing

11 Sommerville Road, St Andrews, Bristol BS7 9AD
t 0117 924 5687 **f** 0117 924 7323 **m** 07831 236300
e orchidvideo@blueyonder.co.uk
Contact Naomi Knott, Managing Director
Credits Wildlife On One (T); Big Cat Diary (T); Driven (T);
Anglia TV National History (T)

Out of the Blue

Red Willows, Urgashay, Yeovil BA22 8HH
m 07831 598537 **e** mike@outoftheblue.eu.com
w www.outoftheblue.eu.com
Contact Mike Barnott, Lighting Cameraman
Credits Amadeus (I); Cross Country (T); Crime Squad (T)

Roger Pearce

Bramble Cottage, 6 Hunstrete, Nr Pensford, Bristol BS39 4NT
t 01761 490611 **f** 01761 490611 **m** 07831 110883
e get.shortie@dial.pipex.com
Credits Around The World In 80 Days (2003) (F); Entrapment (F); The World Is
Not Enough (F); The Mask of Zorro (F)

Picture Canning Company

55 Bendon Valley, London SW18 4LZ
t 020 8874 9277 **f** 020 8874 6623
e info@picturecanning.co.uk **w** www.picturecanning.co.uk
Contact Leslie Zunz, Managing Director; Paul Taylor, General Manager;
Phil Wade, Managing Director
Credits Escape To The Country (D); Watchdog (T); Is Harry On The Boat (T);
Holiday (D)

Picture It

50 Church Road, London NW10 9PY
t 020 8961 6644 **f** 020 8961 2969
e rosemary@picit.net **w** www.picit.net
Contact Trevor Hunt, Managing Director; Rosemary Element,
Sales & Marketing; Chris Sellers, Studio Manager
Experienced broadcast in-house crew, location and studio base.

Pollen Productions

10 Bromley Avenue, Urmston, Manchester M41 6HZ
t 0161 613 8031 **f** 0161 613 8031 **m** 07899 9154940
e tom.jeffs4@ntlworld.com **w** www.soundman.tv
Contact Tom Jeffs

Prima Vista

Unit A1, The Workshops, Askew Crescent, London W12 9DP
t +44 20 8743 7597 **f** +44 20 8740 5859
e andy@primavista.co.uk **w** www.primavista.co.uk
Contact Ross Fall, Lighting Cameraman; Andy Fairgrieve, Lighting Cameraman
Credits Ballot Box - Sunday Record (C); Pizza Hut - The Edge Relaunch (I);
Biography - Donatella Versace (D); Page To Screen - Road To Perdition (D)

Prime Television International

Latimer Road, London W10 6RQ
t 020 8969 6122 **f** 020 8969 6144
e info@primetv.com **w** www.primetv.com
Contact Chris Earls, Hire Manager; Mark Jackson, Operations Manager

Procam Television Ltd

Unit 28, Southbank Business Centre, Ponton Road, London
SW8 5BL
t 020 7622 9888 **f** 020 7498 1580
e info@procamtv.com **w** www.procamtv.com
Contact John Brennan, Operations Manager; Cal Barton, Director
Credits Tonight With Trevor McDonald (T); Tigerfly (I); Urban Media (T); The
Farmer Wants A Wife (T)

PTO Crews Ltd

10 Lambs Business Park, Tilburston Road, South Godstone
RH9 8LJ
t 01342 893399 **f** 01342 892925
e booking@ptocrews.com **w** www.ptocrews.com
Contact Claire Hill, Accounts; Stephen Shadrake, Bookings; Sallie Anne Lent,
Facilities Manager; Carol Scott, New Business Manager
Credits Daz (C); Panorama (T); Songs Of Praise (T)

camera : crew hire

camera : crew hire

Quadrillion Video Productions
The Old Barn, Kings Lane, Cookham Dean, Maidenhead SL6 9AY
t 01628 487522 **f** 01628 487523
e enq@quadrillion.net **w** www.quadrillion.net
Contact Roland Armstrong, Managing Director

Redapple Television Facilities
214 Epsom Road, Guildford GU1 2RA
t 01483 455044 **f** 01483 455022 **m** 07802 246076
e redappletv@msn.com
Contact Nigel Reynolds
Credits Blind Date (T); Through The Keyhole (T); Antiques Roadshow (T)

Redwood Television
The Milk Room, Barnham Court Farm, Barnham PO22 0BP
t 01243 554009 **f** 07967 075521 **m** 07831 604338
e chris@redwoodtv.co.uk
Contact Chris Evans, Lighting Cameraman

Rob Dean Productions
Brookfield House, 64 Lower Village Road, Sunninghill, Ascot SL5 7AS
t 01344 624234 **e** www.rdptv@aol.com
Contact Rob Dean

Sean Savage
t 01491 834521 **f** 01491 834521 **m** 07973 195144
e oldbakehouse@virgin.net
Credits The Parole Officer (F); Dirty Pretty Things (F); Elizabeth (F)

Shooting Partners Ltd
9 Mount Mews, High Street, Hampton TW12 2SH
t 020 8941 1000 **f** 020 8941 0077 **e** mail@shooting-partners.co.uk **w** www.shooting-partners.co.uk
Contact Jenny Bigrave, Production Coordinator; Mark Holdway, Displays & Projection; Phil White, Managing Director; Chris Dingley, Technical Director; Darrin Dart, Facilities Manager; Matthew Tomkinson, Head of Resources
Credits Brainteaser (T); Wish You Were Here...? (T); Laureus World Sports Awards (T); Spy TV (T)

Smashing Glass Television
19 Alderwood, Warraton, Washington NE38 9BS
t 0191 415 5855 **f** 0191 415 5825 **m** 07802 815555
e sglass1003@aol.com
Contact Simon Glass, Lighting Cameraman
Credits Against All Odds (D); Get A New Life (D)

Take One Video
116 Richmond Park Road, Kingston-upon-Thames KT2 6AJ
t 020 8549 0652 **m** 07711 623621
Contact Geoff Lewis, Production Manager
Credits Sarah (T); The Politician's Wife (T); BBC News (T)

Television News
9 Chesterton Mill, French's Road, Cambridge CB4 3NP
t 01223 366220 **f** 01223 361508 **e** dave@masons-news.co.uk
Contact Melvyn Sibson, Partner

Torque Media
The Old Post Office, Main Street, Rockingham LE16 8TG
t 01536 771768 **f** 01536 772220
e admin@torquemedia.com **w** www.torquemedia.com
Contact David Harmon

Track Two Ltd
17 Fallowfield, Ancells Farm, Fleet GU51 2UU
t 01252 812022 **f** 01252 810486 **m** 07768 830838
e crews@track2.co.uk **w** www.track2.co.uk
Contact Caroline Troy, Assignments Manager

Transmission (TX) Ltd
Unit 2A, Shepperton Studios, Studios Road, Shepperton TW17 0QD
t 020 8547 0208 **f** 01932 572571 **m** 07769 688813
e info@ttx.co.uk **w** www.ttx.co.uk

Contact Steve Lloyd, General Manager; Melanie Parkin, Bookings Contact; Peter Hughes, Bookings Contact; Malcom Bubb, Bookings Contact
Credits The Hoobs (T); Doctors (T); Teletubbies (T)

TX supply a comprehensive range of Digi Beta, Hi Def & DVCAM Shooting Facilities. Units available with either an Assistant or a Full Crew plus Transport Multi Camera Packages. Portable Triax/CCU Production Units, Timelapse Facilities, Cable Free Systems, Minicams, Microwave Links, Jimmy Jibs, Lightweight Track & Dollies, Lighting & Sound — see website.

Ultracam Production Facilities
Unit 17, Kings Park, Kings Langley WD4 8ST
t 01923 270380 **f** 01923 270386 **m** 07885 951 201
e ultracam@btconnect.com **w** www.ultracam..co.uk
Contact Jim O'Donnell, Lighting Cameraman

Vector Broadcast Camera Crews
19 Belchamps Road, Wickford SS11 8LJ
t 01268 733908 **m** 07860 444634
e info@vectorbroadcastnews.co.uk
w www.vectorbroadcastnews.co.uk
Contact Steve Verdon, Director
Credits Xray (I); Week In Week Out (D); Discovery Health - Cosmetic Surgery (D)

Video Europe
The London Broadcast Centre, 11-13 Point Pleasant, London SW18 1NN
t 020 8433 8000 **f** +4 20 8433 8001
e crewing@videoeurope.co.uk **w** www.videoeurope.co.uk

VMI Crews

Unit 1, Granville Industrial Estate, 146-148 Granville Road, London NW2 2LD
t 020 8922 9488 **f** 020 8922 9489
e vmi@vmi.co.uk **w** www.vmi.co.uk
Contact Tony Lewis, Crew Co-ordinator
Credits Tonight With Trevor McDonald (T); Green and Pleasant Land (T); Crime Squad (T)

Widescreen

The Garth, Barnet Lane, Elstree WD6 3HJ
t 020 8953 5190 **f** 020 8236 0553
e info@widescreen.uk.com **w** www.widescreen.uk.com
Contact Shirley Taylor, Manager
Credits Creative Services (C); Stake Out (T); Diggit (T)

Camera
Equipment Hire Film

Aaton @ Ice Film

Bridge Wharf, 156 Caledonian Road, London N1 9UU
t 020 7278 0908 **f** 020 7278 4552
e sales@icefilm.com **w** www.aaton.co.uk
Contact Patrick Ralston, Bookings Manager

Acorn Film & Video Ltd

13 Fitzwilliam Street, Belfast BT9 6AW
t 028 9024 0977 **f** 028 9022 2309
e info@acorntv.com **w** www.acorntv.com
Contact Roger Fitzpatrick, Manager; Sarah Reid

ARRI MEDIA

3 Highbridge, Oxford Road, Uxbridge UB8 1LX
t 01895 457100 **f** 01895 457101
e info@arrimedia.com **w** www.arrimedia.com
Contact Bill Lovell, Video Manager; Russell Allen, Head of TV Drama; Philip Cooper, General Manager; Judith Petty, Group Marketing Manager; Eugene McDonagh, Grip Manager
Credits Johnny English (F); Spooks (T); The Way We Live Now (T); Neverland (F)

Axis Films

47 Shepperton Studios, Studios Road, Shepperton TW17 0QD
t 01932 592244 **f** 01932 592246
e info@axisfilms.co.uk **w** www.axisfilms.co.uk
Contact Paul Carter, Managing Director
Credits Murder In Mind (T); Taggart (T); Walkng With Beasts (T)

Axis Films - Glasgow

64-68 Brand Street, Glasgow G51 1DW
t 0141 427 9944 **f** 0141 427 1199 **m** 07971 494902
e glasgow@axisfilms.co.uk **w** www.axisfilms.co.uk
Contact Mark Thomas, Rental Manager; Eileen Byrne, Client Contact; Tim Critchell, Grip Technician; Bram Jeevons, Managing Director
Credits Clarissa And The Countryman (T); Blind Flight (F); Taggart (T)

Bow Visions

94 Fairfoot Road, London E3 4EH
t 020 7515 5102 **m** 07959 672385
Contact Begonia Tamarit, Director; William Raban, Director

Broadcast Television Facilities

Acuba House, Lymm Road, Little Bollington, Altrincham WA14 4SY
t 0161 9269808 **f** 0161 9299000 **m** 07974 151617
e info@broadcast-tv.co.uk **w** www.broadcast-tv.co.uk
Contact Robert Foster, Managing Director; Erin Mactague, Bookings Co-ordinator
Credits Brookside (T); Inside The Mind Of Roy Keane (T); Tonight With Trevor MacDonald (T); Cuba: The Other Side Of Armageddon (T)

Complete Media Services Ltd

Caledonia Cottage, Caledonia, Blaydon-on-Tyne NE21 6AX
t 0191 414 4466 **f** 0191 414 4499 **m** 07970 191606
e jon@completemedia.org **w** www.completemedia.org
Contact Nicole Kavanagh; Jon Stubbs
Credits Football Association (C); Castrol Oil (C); What My Heart Wants To Say (M); I Dld It (C)

Daniels Film

3A Runnymeade Road, Canvey Island SS8 0EF
Contact Eddie Daniels

Green Door Films

38 Glenham Road, Thame OX9 3WD
t 01844 217148 **f** 01844 217148 **m** 07831 396266
e hi-speed@greendoorfilms.co.uk **w** www.greendoorfilms.co.uk
Contact John Hadfield, Proprietor
Specialists in high-speed film and video cameras.

Hammerhead Television Facilities Ltd

42 Webbs Road, London SW11 6SF
t 020 7924 3977 **f** 020 7924 2154
e london@hammerheadtv.com **w** www.hammerheadtv.com
Contact Will Wilkinson, Facilities Manager; Dan Jarmany, Facilities Manager

Hammerhead Television Facilities Ltd

Unit 22, Waters Edge Business Park, Modwen Road, Manchester M5 3EZ
t 0161 872 6200 **f** 0161 872 6300
e manchester@hammerheadtv.com **w** www.hammerheadtv.com
Contact Darren Carrig, Facilities Manager; Matt Turnbull

Hammerhead Television Facilities Ltd

9 Merchiston Mews, Edinburgh EH10 4PE
t 0131 229 5000 **f** 0131 429 4211
e scotland@hammerheadtv.com **w** www.hammerheadtv.com
Contact Chris Orvis, Production Sound Mixer; Gail Glenwright, Facilities Manager

Ice Film Equipment

Bridge Wharf, 156 Caledonian Road, London N1 9UU
t 020 7278 0908 **f** 020 7278 4552 **m** 07764 536000
m 07802 257185 **e** sales@icefilm.com **w** www.icefilm.com
Contact Marie MacDonald, Manager; Peter Bryant, Managing Director; Phil White, Rental Manager
Credits William And Mary (T); Fat Friends (T); Waking The Dead II & III (T); The Lost Prince (T)

Joe Dunton & Company

Elstree Film Studio, Shenley Road, Borehamwood WD6 1JG
t 020 8324 2311
e info@joedunton.com **w** www.joedunton.com
Contact Joe Dunton, Proprietor
Credits Unfaithful (F); Dawsons Creek (T); Beyond Borders (F); The Life Of David Gale (F)

Movietech Camera Rentals Ltd

7 Northfield Estate, Beresford Avenue, Wembley MA0 1NW
t 020 8903 7311 **f** 020 8903 6713
e info@movietech.co.uk **w** www.movietech.co.uk
Contact John Venables, Director

ONE 8 SIX Ltd

12 Garrick Centre, Irving Way, London NW9 6AQ
t 020 8203 8155 **f** 020 8457 2445
e info@one8six.com **w** www.one8six.com
Contact Marie Nicolas, Manager; Craig Game, Client Contact

OpTex UK

20-26 Victoria Road, New Barnet, London EN4 9PF
t 020 8441 2199 **f** 020 8449 3646
e info@optexint.com **w** www.optexint.com
Contact Edward Catton-Orr, Sales; Mike Robinson, Rentals

Panavision London

The Metropolitan Centre, Bristol Road, Greenford UB6 8GD
t 020 8839 7333 **f** 020 8839 7300
e enquiries@panavision.co.uk **w** www.panavision.co.uk
Contact Mark Nicholls, Bookings Manager

Panavision Shepperton
Shepperton Studios, Studios Road, Shepperton TW17 0QD
t 01932 592440 **f** 01932 592450 **w** www.panavision.co.uk
Contact Allan Smith

Pirate
St Leonard's Road, London NW10 6ST
t 020 8930 5000 **f** 020 8930 5001
e help@pirate.co.uk **w** www.pirate.co.uk
Contact Michael Ganss, Managing Director

South London Filter Ltd
3 Richborne Terrace, London SW8 1AS
t 020 7735 1900 **f** 020 7820 1718
e info@camerafilters.co.uk **w** www.camerafilters.co.uk
Contact Carey Duffy, Managing Director

VFG Hire Ltd
8 Beresford Avenue, Wembley HA0 1LA
t 020 8795 7000 **f** 020 8795 3366
e enquiries@vfg.co.uk **w** www.vfg.co.uk
Contact Chris Youlton, Client Contact; Marc Irwin, Marketing Manager; Ann Marie Woodhall, Rental Desk Manager; George Martin, Client Contact Lighting; Graham Hawkins, Head of Cameras; Del Jones, Client Contact; Claire Wiles, Client Contact; Jeremy Sassen, Client Contact
Credits Silent Witness (T); Waking The Dead (T); Midsomer Murders (T); Judge John Deeds (T)

Pinewood: 01753 631 133. Belfast: 028 9057 2525. Cardiff: 02920 561 900. Dublin: 00 353 (0) 1286 3811. Isle of Man: 01624 862559. Scotland: 0141 948 0101. Manchester: 0161 848 7744.

Camera
Equipment Hire Rostrum

Animated Opticals Ltd
10 D'Arblay Street, London W1F 8DS
t 020 7494 0464 **f** 020 7287 3548
e phil@animops.co.uk **w** www.animops.co.uk
Contact Phil Campbell

B B C Post Production

BBC Post Production
(Sites across London, Bristol & Birmingham)
5550 Television Centre, Wood Lane, London W12 7RJ
t 020 8225 7702 (London) **t** 0117 9746 666 (Bristol)
t 0121 432 8621 (Birmingham)
w www.bbcresources.com/postproduction

Frameline
33-34 Rathbone Place, London W1T 1JN
t 020 7636 1303 **f** 020 7436 8878
Contact Nick Comley; Chris Shelley; Nick Summers
Video to Digi/Beta SP. Film to 35mm/16mm. Titles.

Ken Morse Ltd
Unit B5 The Workshops, Askew Crescent, London W12 9DP
t 020 8749 0245 **f** 020 8749 0309
Contact Ken Morse, Managing Director

King Camera Services
73A Beak Street, London W1F 9SR
t 020 7439 7445 **f** 020 7439 7166 **m** 07714 654765
e chris@kingcamera.co.uk **w** www.kingcamera.co.uk
Contact Christopher King, Managing Director; Adele King, Accounts; Tim Barter, Senior Digital Artist
Credits South Bank Show (T); Lost Highway (T); Great Britons (T)

Neilson Hordell
Ashford Business Complex, Feltham Road, Ashford TW15 1YQ
t 01784 423670 **f** 01784 423672 **m** 07083 675353
e sales@nehor.ndirect.co.uk **w** www.nehor.ndirect.co.uk
Contact Nigel Holden, Manager

Peter Jones Rostrums Ltd
County House, 33-34 Rathbone Place, London W1T 1JN
t 020 7637 7628 **f** 020 7637 7658 **m** 07885 282968
e pjrostrums@btinternet.com
Contact Peter Jones, Managing Director

Camera
Equipment Hire Video

The 400 Company
Unit B3, The Workshops, 2A Askew Crescent, Shepherds Bush, London W12 9DP
t 020 8746 1400 **e** info@the400.co.uk **w** www.the400.co.uk
Contact Mark Sloper, Director, Director; Paul Giordani, Business Development Manager; Jo Haynes, Production Manager; Barry Woods, Facilities Manager

AFL Television Facilities Ltd
181A Verulam Road, St Albans AL3 4DR
t 01727 844117 **f** 01727 847649 **m** 07802 682424
e facilities@afltv.com **w** www.afltv.com
Contact Chris Blake, Director; Graham Howe, Lighting Camerman; Dave Chapman, Director; Jenny Lane, Facilities Manager; Athos Gabriel, Sound
Credits Cheer For Charlie (T); Time Team (T); Holiday (T)
Broadcast video shooting facilities with state-of-the-art equipment and top technicians plus the best service and backup. We supply Digital Single Camera Units and 2/3/4/5 Camera OB units.

Aimimage Camera Company
Unit 5, St Pancras Commercial Centre, London NW1 0BY
t 020 7482 4340 **f** 020 7267 3972 **m** 07976 160990
e cameras@aimimage.com **w** www.aimimage.com
Contact Atif Ghani, Production; Mark Puffett, Hire; Michael White, Hire
Credits Tableau Of Love (T); Terra Circa; Rainbow (M); The White Darkness (D)

AT Productions
6 Curley Hill Road, Lightwater GU18 5YG
t 01276 472179 **f** 01276 451112 **e** mailbox@atproductions.co.uk
w www.atproductions.co.uk
Contact Chris Rule, Production Manager

Bow Tie Television
Unit 20, Bourne Industrial Park, Bourne Road, Crayford DA1 4BZ
t 01322 524500 **f** 01322 527777
e john@bowtietv.com **w** www.bowtietv.com
Contact John Knopp, Managing Director
Credits Endemol - King Of Sport (T); NHK Enterprises Europe Ltd - Red Demon (T)

broadcast SERVICES

broadcast video equipment
hire and facilities

For a copy of our latest

hire guide

**containing hire rates and
useful technical information**

please telephone

01932 570001

www.broadcast-services.co.uk
The Coach House, Ruxbury Road, Chertsey, SURREY, KT16 9EP
Tel: (01932) 570001 Fax: (01932) 570443

Broadcast Services

The Coach House, Ruxbury Road, Chertsey KT16 9EP
t 01932 570001 **f** 01932 570443
e hire@broadcast-services.co.uk **w** www.broadcast-services.co.uk
Contact David Scrutton, Director; Peter Scrutton, Director; Darren Moss, Hire Manager

Broadcast Television Facilities

Acuba House, Lymm Road, Little Bollington, Altrincham WA14 4SY
t 0161 9269808 **f** 0161 9299000 **m** 07974 151617
e info@broadcast-tv.co.uk **w** www.broadcast-tv.co.uk
Contact Robert Foster, Managing Director; Erin Mactague, Bookings Co-ordinator
Credits Brookside (T); Inside The Mind Of Roy Keane (T); Tonight With Trevor MacDonald (T); Cuba: The Other Side Of Armageddon (T)

The Camera Store Ltd

Teddington Studios, Broom Road, Teddington TW11 9NT
t 020 8781 2797 **f** 020 8781 2759 **m** 07774 264939
e hire@thecamerastore.ltd.uk **w** www.thecamerastore.ltd.uk
Contact David Fader; Tim Highmoor; Rob Sargent

The Camera Store is a television equipment hire company specialising in camera pedestals and pan and tilt heads. Established in 1996 by three TV cameramen, The Camera Store offers a professional, reliable and friendly service. Based at Teddington Studios, The Camera Store can deliver anywhere in the UK.

Charter Broadcast Ltd

Unit 4, Elstree Distribution Park, Elstree Way, Borehamwood WD6 1RU
t 020 8905 1213 **f** 020 8905 1424 **m** 07836 521 987
e charter@charter.co.uk
Contact Helen Frost, Bookings Coordinator

Equipment hire company, offering a comprehensive range of broadcast video, audio, graphics and RF facilities for dry hire. In addition, Charter Broadcast offers Mobile Production Units and Flyaway Systems worldwide. Please contact us for further information or visit our website.

Cine Wessex Ltd

13 Winnall Valley Road, Winchester SO23 0LD
t 01962 844900 **f** 01962 840004
e joe@cinewessex.co.uk **w** www.cinewessex.co.uk
Contact Kelly Dyer; Joe Conlan

Cineflex Productions

Frogs Hole Barn, Sissinghurst Road, Biddenden TN27 8EY
t 01580 291845 **f** 01580 291845 **m** 07774 141910
Contact George Pellett, Partner; Penny Pellett, Partner

The Cruet Company

11 Ferrier Street, London SW18 1SN
t 020 8874 2121 **f** 020 8874 9850
e hire@cruet.com **w** www.cruet.com
Contact Sam Schwind, Bookings Co-ordinator; Bill Morrey, Director, Managing Director; Don Knee, Operations Manager; Emma Dow, Head of Bookings
Credits Changing Rooms (T); George Harrison Tribute Concert (M); The Villa (T)

Dales Broadcast Ltd

Nettle Hill, Brinklow Road, Ansty, Coventry CV7 9JL
t 024 7662 1763 **f** 024 7660 2732 **m** 07803 584925
e sales@dales-ltd.com **w** www.dales-ltd.com
Contact Kate Boden, Marketing Director; Julian Boden, Managing Director
Credits Tickle, Patch And Friends (T); Young Choirs 2001 (T); Network Q Rally (T); Horseracing for Racetech, ATR And Channel 4 (T)

The Digital Garage Company Ltd

13 Devonshire Mews, Chiswick, London W4 2HA
t 07000 785821 **f** 07000 785822 **m** 07788 145577
e mail@digitalgarage.co.uk **w** www.digitalgarage.co.uk
Contact Janie Willsmore, Crew Manager; Oliver Hickey, Facilities Manager
Credits Castle (D); Faking It - Drag Queen (T); Leonardo (T); Six Wives Of Henry VIII (T)

Extreme Facilities

15-17 Este Road, London SW11 2TL
t 020 7801 9111
e andrew@extremefacilities.com **w** www.extremefacilities.com
Contact Andrew Schaale

Fine Point Broadcast

Furze Hill, Kingswood KT20 6EZ
t 0800 970 2020 **f** 0800 970 2030
e hire@finepoint.co.uk **w** www.finepoint.co.uk
Contact Roger Wedlake, Chief Engineer; Colin Smith, Hire Co-ordinator; Linda Pressley, Hire Co-ordinator; Sam Barley, Hire Co-ordinator

Giltbrook Studios

10 Giltway, Giltbrook, Nottingham NG16 2GN
t 0115 938 4040 **f** 0115 938 4020 **w** www.giltbrookstudios.co.uk
Contact Cleo Lacey, Production Assistant; George Camm, Facilties Manager

The Hire Company (UK) Ltd

The Picture House, 4 Lower Park Row, Bristol BS1 5BJ
t 0117 927 7473 **f** 0117 923 0862 **m** 07860 341141
e mail@thehireco.co.uk **w** www.thehireco.co.uk
Contact Andy Bennett, Hire Manager

HOTCAM

t 020 8742 1888 **e** info@hotcam.co.uk **w** www.hotcam.co.uk

Impact Rental

170 Windmill Road West, Sunbury on Thames, London GW16 7HB
t 01932 733705 **f** 01932 733715
e hiredesk@impact-europe.com **w** www.impact-europe.com
Contact Richard Pope, Head of Hire & Staging; Fran Marsh, Head of Hire and Staging

Lighthouse Films

The Lighthouse, Guy's Head PE12 9QJ
t 01406 351522 **m** 07850 054590
e simon@lighthouse-films.co.uk **w** www.lighthouse-films.co.uk
Contact Simon Normanton, Managing Director

Suppliers of location crews and camera equipment

Maintaining quality

Tel: 020 8742 1888
Email: trevorhotz@hotcam.co.uk
Web: www.hotcam.co.uk

HOTCAM™
VIDEO FACILITIES

Metro Broadcast

5-7 Great Chapel Street, London W1F 8FF
t 020 7434 7700 **f** 020 7434 7701
e info@metrobroadcast.com **w** www.metrobroadcast.com
Contact Elaine Jaxon, Duplications Manager; Nayle Kemal, Digital Media Manager; Paul Beale, Business Development; Barry Noakes, Facilities Manager; Steve Cairns, Broadcast Services Manager; Mark Cox, Director
We offer the latest broadcast equipment (including high definition) covering production, post production and outside broadcast.

MGB Facilities Ltd

Sheepscar Court, Leeds LS7 2BB
t 0113 243 6868 **f** 0113 243 8886
e contact@mgbtv.co.uk **w** www.mgbtv.co.uk
Contact Mike Gaunt, Managing Director; Elaine Wigglesworth, Facility Manager
Credits Quick Grip (I); Sport On Five (T); Hasbro (W); BUPA (C)

Mutiny Hire

London
t 020 7207 0816 **m** 07808 724439 **e** mutinyhire@ntlworld.com
Contact George Butler, Director

New Day Pictures

84 Lambton Road, West Wimbledon, London SW20 0LP
t 020 8947 7177 **f** 020 8947 5559 **m** 07786 070239
e bradday@newdaypictures.com **w** www.newdaypictures.com
Contact Dave Knight, Hire; Eddie Taylor, Crews; Brad Day, Director; Claire Day, Production
Credits Nuggets (T); The Man Who Invented Linear B (T); Great British Architects (T)
Experienced DV-Cam crews, editing facilities, training, production. Helpful, knowledgeable staff.

OpTex UK

20-26 Victoria Road, New Barnet, London EN4 9PF
t 020 8441 2199 **f** 020 8449 3646
e info@optexint.com **w** www.optexint.com
Contact Edward Catton-Orr, Sales; Mike Robinson, Rentals
OpTex rents a wide range of production equipment including camera formats from DV to Hi-Def 24P plus miniature and covert cameras, on-camera & portable lighting, Satchler tripods, audio equipment and remote camera systems.

Picture Canning Company

55 Bendon Valley, London SW18 4LZ
t 020 8874 9277 **f** 020 8874 6623
e info@picturecanning.co.uk **w** www.picturecanning.co.uk
Contact Leslie Zunz, Managing Director; Paul Taylor, General Manager; Phil Wade, Managing Director
Credits Escape To The Country (D); Watchdog (T); Is Harry On The Boat (T); Holiday (D)

Picture It

50 Church Road, London NW10 9PY
t 020 8961 6644 **f** 020 8961 2969
e rosemary@picit.net **w** www.picit.net
Contact Trevor Hunt, Managing Director; Rosemary Element, Sales & Marketing; Chris Sellers, Studio Manager
Comprehensive range including Digibeta, DVCam, BetaSP and multi-camera portable production units.

Prima Vista

Unit A1, The Workshops, Askew Crescent, London W12 9DP
t +44 20 8743 7597 **f** +44 20 8740 5859
e andy@primavista.co.uk **w** www.primavista.co.uk
Contact Ross Fall, Lighting Cameraman; Andy Fairgrieve, Lighting Cameraman
Credits Ballot Box - Sunday Record (C); Pizza Hut - The Edge Relaunch (I); Biography - Donatella Versace (D); Page To Screen - Road To Perdition (D)

Procam Television Ltd

Unit 28, Southbank Business Centre, Ponton Road, London SW8 5BL
t 020 7622 9888 **f** 020 7498 1580
e info@procamtv.com **w** www.procamtv.com
Contact John Brennan, Operations Manager; Cal Barton, Director
Credits Tonight With Trevor McDonald (T); Tigerfly (I); Urban Media (T); The Farmer Wants A Wife (T)

Saville Audio Visual

Unit 8, Stadium Close, Cardiff CF11 7TS
t 029 2022 9411 **f** 029 2022 9412 **w** www.saville-av.com
Contact Ben Voiscy, Hire Manager

Shift 4 Ltd

18-24 Queensland Road, London N7 7AH
t 020 7609 7040 **f** 020 7609 7050
e info@shift-4.com **w** www.shift-4.com
Contact Ruth Robson, Hire Manager; Neil Burn, Managing Director; Phil Barnard, Operations Manager

Shooting|Partners

Shooting Partners Ltd

9 Mount Mews, High Street, Hampton TW12 2SH
t 020 8941 1000 **f** 020 8941 0077
e mail@shooting-partners.co.uk **w** www.shooting-partners.co.uk
Contact Jenny Bigrave, Production Coordinator; Mark Holdway, Displays & Projection; Phil White, Managing Director; Chris Dingley, Technical Director; Darrin Dart, Facilities Manager; Matthew Tomkinson, Head of Resources
Credits Brainteaser (T); Wish You Were Here...? (T); Laureus World Sports Awards (T); Spy TV (T)
Established in 1989 by a team of experienced technical and production staff, the company has grown from a small production and hiring service to a top quality facilities hire and project management operation. Shooting Partners are able to satisfy any production or display need for broadcast television, theatrical or corporate market from DV to HD.

Star Street Video Ltd

92 Star Street, London W2 1QF
t 020 7402 1330 **f** 020 7706 1084
e info@star-street-video.com **w** www.star-street-video.com
Contact Mike Harris, Director; David Holmes, Director; Alex D'Antonio, Operations Manager

Techstores.TV
15A Selly Oak Industrial Estate, Elliot Road, Birmingham B29 6LR
t 0121 415 5224 **f** 0121 41
e info@techstores.tv **w** www.techstores.tv
Contact Simon Edwards, Hire Manager
Credits KFC Conference 2003 (I)

Transmission (TX) Ltd
Unit 2A, Shepperton Studios, Studios Road, Shepperton TW17 0QD
t 020 8547 0208 **f** 01932 572571 **m** 07769 688813
e info@ttx.co.uk **w** www.ttx.co.uk
Contact Steve Lloyd, General Manager; Melanie Parkin, Bookings Contact; Peter Hughes, Bookings Contact; Malcom Bubb, Bookings Contact
Credits The Hoobs (T); Doctors (T); Teletubbies (T)

TX supply a comprehensive range of Video Camera & Camcorder equipment for hire including Digi Beta, Hi Def, DVCAM Camera Systems, Multi Camera Packages, Palmcorders, Portable Triax/CCU Production Units, Time-lapse Facilities, Cable Free Systems, Minicams, Microwave Links, Zoom & Prime Lens Kits, Matte Box & Filters, Jimmy Jibs, Lightweight Track & Dollies, Steadicams — see website.

VFG Hire Ltd
8 Beresford Avenue, Wembley HA0 1LA
t 020 8795 7000 **f** 020 8795 3366
e enquiries@vfg.co.uk **w** www.vfg.co.uk
Contact Chris Youlton, Client Contact; Marc Irwin, Marketing Manager; Ann Marie Woodhall, Rental Desk Manager; George Martin, Client Contact Lighting; Graham Hawkins, Head of Cameras; Del Jones, Client Contact; Claire Wiles, Client Contact; Jeremy Sassen, Client Contact
Credits Silent Witness (T); Waking The Dead (T); Midsomer Murders (T); Judge John Deeds (T)

Pinewood: 01753 631 133. Belfast: 028 9057 2525. Cardiff: 02920 561 900. Dublin: 00 353 (0) 1286 3811. Isle of Man: 01624 862559. Scotland: 0141 948 0101. Manchester: 0161 848 7744.

Video Europe
The London Broadcast Centre, 11-13 Point Pleasant, London SW18 1NN
t 020 8433 8000 **f** 020 8433 8001
e hire@videoeurope.co.uk **w** www.videoeurope.co.uk

Vinten Broadcast
Western Way, Bury St Edmunds IP33 3TB
t 01284 752121 **f** 01284 757914
e contact@vinten.com **w** www.vinten.com
Contact John Banham, Hire Manager

Camera **Equipment Hire Visual Effects**

Computerised Time Lapse Cinematography
27 Birstall Road, London N15 5EN
t 020 8802 8791 **f** 020 8211 8286 **m** 07966 139709
e maxim@time-lapse.co.uk **w** www.time-lapse.co.uk
Contact Maxim Ford, Proprietor

MC² Motion Control Ltd
t 020 7419 4129 **f** 020 7794 0567
e info@motioncontrol-uk.com **w** www.motioncontrol-uk.com
Contact Linda Krisman; Dennis Henry, Operator

Pirate Motion Control
St Leonards Road, London NW10 6ST
t 020 8930 5000 **f** 020 8930 5001
e help@pirate.co.uk **w** www.pirate.co.uk
Contact Michael Ganz, Managing Director

Time-Slice Films Ltd
Unit 22, Brassmill Enterprise Centre, Brassmill Lane, Bath BA1 3JN
t 01225 420988 **f** 01225 480734 **m** 07802 292084
e info@timeslicefilms.com **w** www.timeslicefilms.com
Contact Tim MacMillan, Director; Charlotte Leslie, PA
Credits Del Monte (C); Fields Of Gold (T); Ferment (A); Weird Nature (T)

Camera **Equipment Sales & Spares**

Animation & Motion Control Ltd
Chess Spring House, Pednor Bottom, Chesham HP5 2ST
t 01494 793484 **f** 01494 793485 **m** 07836 598928
e peter.brewster@dial.pipex.com **w** www.motioncontrol4u.co.uk
Contact Peter Brewster, Managing Director
Credits Die Another Day (F); The World Is Not Enough (F); The Body (F); Jack And The Beanstalk: The Real Story (F)

Canon (UK) Ltd
Woodhatch, Reigate RH2 8BF
t 01737 220000 **f** 01737 220022 **w** www.canon.co.uk

Connectronics Cable & Connection
PO Box 22618, London N4 1WW
t 020 8800 3555 **f** 07000 283461
e sales@connectronics.co.uk **w** www.connectronics.co.uk
Contact Matt Boland, General Manager

Egripment
Unit 12A, Shepperton Business Park, Govett Avenue, Shepperton TW17 8AB
t 01932 246245 **f** 01932 246248
e egripment@egripment.co.uk **w** www.egripment.com

Future Film Developments
64 Oxford Road, New Denham, Uxbridge UB9 4DN
t 01895 813730 **f** 01895 813701 **m** 07770 876552
e sales@ffd.co.uk **w** www.ffd.co.uk
Contact William Blackham, Sales

Ice Film Equipment
Bridge Wharf, 156 Caledonian Road, London N1 9UU
t 020 7278 0908 **f** 020 7278 4552 **m** 07764 536000
m 07802 257185 **e** sales@icefilm.com **w** www.icefilm.com
Contact Marie MacDonald, Manager; Peter Bryant, Managing Director; Phil White, Rental Manager
Credits William And Mary (T); Fat Friends (T); Waking The Dead II & III (T); The Lost Prince (T)

JVC Professional
Ullswater House, Kendal Avenue, London W3 0XA
t 020 8896 6000 **f** 020 8896 6060
e marketing@jvcpro.co.uk **w** www.jvcpro.co.uk
Contact D Cameron, Sales Director; Katinka Allender, Public Relations Manager; J Carpenter, Director of Marketing Services

Leica Camera Ltd
Davy Avenue, Knowlhill MK5 8LB
t 01908 256400 **t** 01908 666663 **f** 01908 671316
e info@leica-camera.co.uk **w** www.leica-camera.com
Contact Peter Melder, Sales Manager; Nobby Clark, Photographic Consultant

Libra Professional Broadcast Ltd
Chester House, 91-95 Alcester Road, Studley B80 7NJ
t 01527 853305 **f** 01527 852086
e info@libraprobroadcst.co.uk **w** www.libraprobroadcast.co.uk
Contact Whitehouse, Managing Director

Mark Roberts Motion Control Ltd
Unit 4, Birches Industrial Estate, Imberhorne Lane, East Grinstead RH19 1XZ
t 01342 334700 **f** 01342 334701
e info@mrmoco.com **w** www.mrmoco.com
Contact Assaff Rawner, Managing Director; Sophie Roberts, Marketing; Graham Gvenigault, Sales Manager

MPS Photographic
17 Carliol Square, Newcastle-upon-Tyne NE1 6UQ
t 0191 232 3558 **f** 0191 261 0990
e mps@mps-photographic.co.uk **w** www.mps-photographic.co.uk
Contact Jill Roe

OpTex UK
20-26 Victoria Road, New Barnet, London EN4 9PF
t 020 8441 2199 **f** 020 8449 3646
e info@optexint.com **w** www.optexint.com
Contact Edward Catton-Orr, Sales; Mike Robinson, Rentals

PAG
565 Kingston Road, Raynes Park, London SW20 8SA
t 020 8543 3131 **f** 020 8540 4797
e sales@paguk.com **w** www.paguk.com
Contact Nigel Gardiner, Sales Director; Ian Davies, Sales Co-ordinator; Gina O'Connor, Sales Administrator/ Manager; Steve Emmett, Publicity Manager

Pulnix Europe
Pulnix House, Aviary Court,, Wade Road, Basingstoke RG24 8PE
t 01256 475555 **f** 01256 466268
e sales@pulnix.co.uk **w** www.pulnix.co.uk
Contact B Honwood, General Sales Manager

Richardson Electronics (Europe)
Inspring House, Searby Road, Lincoln LN2 4DT
t 01522 542631 **f** 01522 545453 **w** www.rell.com
Contact Martin Evans, Managing Director

Ronford Baker Engineering Company Ltd
Oxhey Lane, Watford WD1 5RJ
t 020 8428 5941 **f** 020 8428 4743
e ronfordbaker@compuserve.com **e** www.ronfordbaker.co.uk
Contact Jeff Lawrence, Director

Supafrost Filters
25 Harwood Close, Tewin AL6 0LF
t 01438 717686 **f** 01438 717686
e mervwils@supafrost.freeserve.co.uk
Contact Mervyn Wilson, Managing Director

Van Diemen Ltd
Bridge House, Branksome Park Road, Camberley GU15 2AQ
t 01276 61222 **f** 01276 61549 **m** 07860 360851
e vandiemen@aol.com **w** www.vandiemen.tv
Contact Peter Bailey, General Manager; Christopher Smith

VDC Trading Ltd
VDC House, 4 Brandon Road, London N7 9AA
t 020 7700 2777 **f** 020 7700 3888
e sales@vdctrading.com **w** www.vdctrading.com
Contact Dugald Guthrie, Technical Director; Niall Holden, Managing Director

Video Europe
8 Golden Square, London W1F 9HY
t 020 7439 2277 **f** 020 7439 4113
e sales@videoeurope.co.uk **w** www.videoeurope.co.uk

Vinten

Vinten Broadcast
Western Way, Bury St Edmunds IP33 3TB
t 01284 752121 **f** 01284 757914
e contact@vinten.com **w** www.vinten.com
Contact John Banham, Hire Manager

Camera Focus Pullers

Kirsti Abernethy
Wizzo & Co, 35 Old Compton Street, London W1D 5JX
t 020 7437 2055 **f** 020 7437 2066
e wizzo@wizzoandco.co.uk **w** www.wizzoandco.co.uk

Mik Allen
EXEC, 6 Travis Court, Farnham Royal SL2 3SB
t 01753 646677 **f** 01753 646770
e sue@execmanagement.co.uk **w** www.execmanagement.co.uk

David Atkinson
GAS (Guild Answering Service), C/o Panavision UK,
Metropolitan Centre, Bristol Road, Greenford UB6 8GD
t 020 8813 1999 **f** 020 8813 2111
e admin@gbct.org **w** www.gbct.org

John Attwell
Suz Cruz, Halliford Studios, Manygate Lane, Shepperton TW17 9EG
t 01932 252577 **f** 01932 253323 **m** 07956 485593
e zoe@suzcruz.co.uk **w** www.suzcruz.co.uk

Matthew Ball
2A Duntshill Road, London SW18 4QL
t 020 8874 9724 **m** 07957 156954
Agent Linkline, 6 Thirlmere Gardens, Wembley HA9 8RE
t 020 8908 6262 **f** 020 8904 5179
e mail@linklinecrew.com **w** www.linklinecrew.com

Karelle Barkshire
106A Forest Road, Hackney, London E8 3BH
m 07957 450541
Agent Linkline, 6 Thirlmere Gardens, Wembley HA9 8RE
t 020 8908 6262 **f** 020 8904 5179
e mail@linklinecrew.com **w** www.linklinecrew.com

Sam Barnes
Wizzo & Co, 35 Old Compton Street, London W1D 5JX
t 020 7437 2055 **f** 020 7437 2066
e wizzo@wizzoandco.co.uk **w** www.wizzoandco.co.uk

Stuart Barrell
EXEC, 6 Travis Court, Farnham Royal SL2 3SB
t 01753 646677 **f** 01753 646770
e sue@execmanagement.co.uk **w** www.execmanagement.co.uk

Mark 'Barzie' Barrs
Callbox Communications Limited, PO Box 66, Shepperton
Studios, Shepperton Lane TW17 0QD
t 01932 592572 **f** 01932 569655 **m** 07710 572572
e callboxdiary@btinternet.com **w** www.callboxdiary.co.uk

Terry J Bartlett
79 Heol-y-Coed, Rhiwbina, Cardiff CF14 6HR
t 029 2061 6414 **f** 029 2061 6414 **m** 07831 709778
Credits Worthington (C); Unimate Force (T); Tipping The Velvet (T)

Pete Batten
Brook Cottage, Bassett Road, Letcombe Regis, Wantage Oxon,
Wantage OX12 9LJ
t 01235 764194 **m** 07768 432646 **e** petebatten@aol.com
Credits The Hours (F); Fakers (F); The Hole (F); Tomb Raider (F)

Tim Battersby
EXEC, 6 Travis Court, Farnham Royal SL2 3SB
t 01753 646677 **f** 01753 646770
e sue@execmanagement.co.uk **w** www.execmanagement.co.uk

David Bell
5 Troutbeck Close, Hawkshaw, Bury BL8 4LJ
t 01204 884539 **m** 07946 813168
Credits Danielle Cable - Eye Witness (T); Forty (T); The 2nd Coming (T);
Bob and Rose (T)

Jason Berman
Suz Cruz, Halliford Studios, Manygate Lane, Shepperton TW17 9EG
t 01932 252577 **f** 01932 253323 **m** 07956 485593
e zoe@suzcruz.co.uk **w** www.suzcruz.co.uk

Richard P Bevan
5 Primulas Close, South Anston, Sheffield S25 5JD
t 01909 578006 **f** 01709 548845 **m** 07774 453965
e rpbbevan@hotmail.com
Credits Aston Martin (C); Cutting It Series II (T); Shadow Of The Vampire (F)

Robert Binnall
EXEC, 6 Travis Court, Farnham Royal SL2 3SB
t 01753 646677 **f** 01753 646770
e sue@execmanagement.co.uk **w** www.execmanagement.co.uk

Joe Blackwell
Suz Cruz, Halliford Studios, Manygate Lane, Shepperton TW17 9EG
t 01932 252577 **f** 01932 253323 **m** 07956 485593
e zoe@suzcruz.co.uk **w** www.suzcruz.co.uk

Keith Blake
GAS (Guild Answering Service), C/o Panavision UK,
Metropolitan Centre, Bristol Road, Greenford UB6 8GD
t 020 8813 1999 **f** 020 8813 2111
e admin@gbct.org **w** www.gbct.org

Paddy Blake
Gems, The Media House, 87 Glebe Street, Penarth CF64 1EF
t 029 2071 0770 **f** 029 2071 0771 **e** gems@gems-agency.co.uk
w www.gems-agency.co.uk
Credits Jimmy Fizz (T); The Vice (T); Gypsy Girl (T); The Gentelman Thief (T)

Craig Bloor
EXEC, 6 Travis Court, Farnham Royal SL2 3SB
t 01753 646677 **f** 01753 646770
e sue@execmanagement.co.uk **w** www.execmanagement.co.uk

Ashley Bond
Suz Cruz, Halliford Studios, Manygate Lane, Shepperton TW17 9EG
t 01932 252577 **f** 01932 253323 **m** 07956 485593
e zoe@suzcruz.co.uk **w** www.suzcruz.co.uk

Neil Bradshaw
EXEC, 6 Travis Court, Farnham Royal SL2 3SB
t 01753 646677 **f** 01753 646770
e sue@execmanagement.co.uk **w** www.execmanagement.co.uk

Jessie Brough
EXEC, 6 Travis Court, Farnham Royal SL2 3SB
t 01753 646677 **f** 01753 646770
e sue@execmanagement.co.uk **w** www.execmanagement.co.uk

Lewis Buchan
Wizzo & Co, 35 Old Compton Street, London W1D 5JX
t 020 7437 2055 **f** 020 7437 2066
e wizzo@wizzoandco.co.uk **w** www.wizzoandco.co.uk

Steve Burgess
EXEC, 6 Travis Court, Farnham Royal SL2 3SB
t 01753 646677 **f** 01753 646770
e sue@execmanagement.co.uk **w** www.execmanagement.co.uk

Steven Cassidy
Suz Cruz, Halliford Studios, Manygate Lane, Shepperton TW17 9EG
t 01932 252577 **f** 01932 253323 **m** 07956 485593
e zoe@suzcruz.co.uk **w** www.suzcruz.co.uk

Paul Cave
GAS (Guild Answering Service), C/o Panavision UK,
Metropolitan Centre, Bristol Road, Greenford UB6 8GD
t 020 8813 1999 **f** 020 8813 2111
e admin@gbct.org **w** www.gbct.org

Ben Chads
Suz Cruz, Halliford Studios, Manygate Lane, Shepperton TW17 9EG
t 01932 252577 **f** 01932 253323 **m** 07956 485593
e zoe@suzcruz.co.uk **w** www.suzcruz.co.uk

Ian Chisholm
Flat 2, 42 Thrale Road, London SW16 1NX
t 020 8769 7120 **m** 07971 555885
Agent Linkline, 6 Thirlmere Gardens, Wembley HA9 8RE
t 020 8908 6262 **f** 020 8904 5179
e mail@linklinecrew.com **w** www.linklinecrew.com

Will Churchill
189 Mayall Road, London SE24 0PS
t 020 7346 8980 **m** 07775 531515
Agent Linkline, 6 Thirlmere Gardens, Wembley HA9 8RE
t 020 8908 6262 **f** 020 8904 5179
e mail@linklinecrew.com **w** www.linklinecrew.com

Matt Conway
Linkline, 6 Thirlmere Gardens, Wembley HA9 8RE
t 020 8908 6262 **f** 020 8904 5179 **e** mail@linklinecrew.com
w www.linklinecrew.com

Ewan Crispin
69 Cypress Avenue, Whitton, Twickenham TW2 7JY
t 020 8241 7858 **m** 07957 319810
Agent Linkline, 6 Thirlmere Gardens, Wembley HA9 8RE
t 020 8908 6262 **f** 020 8904 5179 **e** mail@linklinecrew.com
w www.linklinecrew.com

Nicko Cummins
Callbox Communications Limited, PO Box 66, Shepperton
Studios, Shepperton Lane TW17 0QD
t 01932 592572 **f** 01932 569655 **m** 07710 572572
e callboxdiary@btinternet.com **w** www.callboxdiary.co.uk

David Cozens
31 River Walk, Walton-on-Thames KT12 2DS
t 0193 222 9414 **f** 0193 223 4808 **m** 07711 638 115
e david.cozens@virgin.net
Contact David Cozens
Credits Band Of Brothers (T); About A Boy (F)

Ted Deason
10 Trelawney Grove, Weybridge KT13 8SS
t 01932 853739 **f** 01932 851316 **m** 07850 537363
Agent GAS (Guild Answering Service), C/o Panavision UK,
Metropolitan Centre, Bristol Road, Greenford UB6 8GD
t 020 8813 1999 **f** 020 8813 2111
e admin@gbct.org **w** www.gbct.org

Robert Dibble
10 Collingwood Avenue, London N10 3ED
t 020 8883 8487 **f** 020 8883 8487 **m** 07803 131823
e robertdibbleca@hotmail.com
Agent Annie's Answering Service, Pinewood Studios,
Pinewood Road, Iver Heath SL0 0NH
t 01753 651303 **f** 01753 651848
e info@annies.co.uk **w** www.annies.co.uk
Credits Memory of Water (F); Dot The I (F); Second Nature (F); Cheeky (F)

Marcus Domleo
Suz Cruz, Halliford Studios, Manygate Lane, Shepperton TW17 9EG
t 01932 252577 **f** 01932 253323 **m** 07956 485593
e zoe@suzcruz.co.uk **w** www.suzcruz.co.uk

Richie Donnelly
Wizzo & Co, 35 Old Compton Street, London W1D 5JX
t 020 7437 2055 **f** 020 7437 2066
e wizzo@wizzoandco.co.uk **w** www.wizzoandco.co.uk

Hamish Doyne-Ditmas
Suz Cruz, Halliford Studios, Manygate Lane, Shepperton TW17 9EG
t 01932 252577 **f** 01932 253323 **m** 07956 485593
e zoe@suzcruz.co.uk **w** www.suzcruz.co.uk

Greg Duffield
316 Rangefield Road, Bromley BR1 4QY
t 020 8461 3959 **m** 07968 038934
Agent Linkline, 6 Thirlmere Gardens, Wembley HA9 8RE
t 020 8908 6262 **f** 020 8904 5179 **e** mail@linklinecrew.com
w www.linklinecrew.com

Martyn Dunham
Warren Barn, Bedford Street, Ampthill MK45 2EX
t 01525 406603 **m** 07778 632217
Agent Linkline, 6 Thirlmere Gardens, Wembley HA9 8RE
t 020 8908 6262 **f** 020 8904 5179
e mail@linklinecrew.com **w** www.linklinecrew.com

Marc Ehrenbold GBCT
t 020 8352 1125 **f** 020 8352 1125 **m** 07956 275504
e marcam@zoom.co.uk

Jason Ellis
Suz Cruz, Halliford Studios, Manygate Lane, Shepperton TW17 9EG
t 01932 252577 **f** 01932 253323 **m** 07956 485593
e zoe@suzcruz.co.uk **w** www.suzcruz.co.uk

Miles Evans
Callbox Communications Ltd, PO Box 66, Shepperton Studios,
Shepperton Lane TW17 0QD
t 01932 592572 **f** 01932 569655 **m** 07710 572572
e callboxdiary@btinternet.com **w** www.callboxdiary.co.uk

John Ferguson
EXEC, 6 Travis Court, Farnham Royal SL2 3SB
t 01753 646677 **f** 01753 646770
e sue@execmanagement.co.uk **w** www.execmanagement.co.uk

John Fletcher
GAS (Guild Answering Service), C/o Panavision UK,
Metropolitan Centre, Bristol Road, Greenford UB6 8GD
t 020 8813 1999 **f** 020 8813 2111
e admin@gbct.org **w** www.gbct.org

Adam Forrester
GAS (Guild Answering Service), C/o Panavision UK, Metropolitan Centre, Bristol Road, Greenford UB6 8GD
t 020 8813 1999 **f** 020 8813 2111
e admin@gbct.org **w** www.gbct.org

John Foster
EXEC, 6 Travis Court, Farnham Royal SL2 3SB
t 01753 646677 **f** 01753 646770
e sue@execmanagement.co.uk **w** www.execmanagement.co.uk

Karen Fraser
Linkline, 6 Thirlmere Gardens, Wembley HA9 8RE
t 020 8908 6262 **f** 020 8904 5179
e mail@linklinecrew.com **w** www.linklinecrew.com

Karen Fraser
83 Totteridge Avenue, High Wycombe HP13 6XG
m 07989 404418

John Gamble
GAS (Guild Answering Service), C/o Panavision UK, Metropolitan Centre, Bristol Road, Greenford UB6 8GD
t 020 8813 1999 **f** 020 8813 2111
e admin@gbct.org **w** www.gbct.org

Sarah Gardiner
Annie's Answering Service, Pinewood Studios, Pinewood Road, Iver Heath SL0 0NH
t 01753 651303 **f** 01753 651848
e info@annies.co.uk **w** www.annies.co.uk

Theo Garland
Suz Cruz, Halliford Studios, Manygate Lane, Shepperton TW17 9EG
t 01932 252577 **f** 01932 253323 **m** 07956 485593
e zoe@suzcruz.co.uk **w** www.suzcruz.co.uk

Leigh Gold
05 Hood House, Dolphin Square, London SW1V 3NQ
t 020 7828 8387 **f** 020 7798 8530 **m** 07801 287453
e leighgold@hotmail.com

Merritt Gold
Suz Cruz, Halliford Studios, Manygate Lane, Shepperton TW17 9EG
t 01932 252577 **f** 01932 253323 **m** 07956 485593
e zoe@suzcruz.co.uk **w** www.suzcruz.co.uk

Michael Green
Apple Tree Cottage, Denton OX44 9JG
t 01865 872820 **f** 01865 873982 **m** 07770 592968
e mgreen9016@aol.com
Credits I'll Be There (F); Savior (F); A Christmas Carol (F); Below (F)

Mike Green
Annie's Answering Service, Pinewood Studios, Pinewood Road, Iver Heath SL0 0NH
t 01753 651303 **f** 01753 651848
e info@annies.co.uk **w** www.annies.co.uk

Kenny Groom
Annie's Answering Service, Pinewood Studios, Pinewood Road, Iver Heath SL0 0NH
t 01753 651303 **f** 01753 651848
e info@annies.co.uk **w** www.annies.co.uk

Richard Hadley
Callbox Communications Limited, PO Box 66, Shepperton Studios, Shepperton Lane TW17 0QD
t 01932 592572 **f** 01932 569655 **m** 07710 572572
e callboxdiary@btinternet.com **w** www.callboxdiary.co.uk

Oli Hallowes
1 Earlsfield Cottage, Stonards Brow, Shamley Green GU5 0UY
t 01483 892711 **m** 07779 293555
Agent Linkline, 6 Thirlmere Gardens, Wembley HA9 8RE
t 020 8908 6262 **f** 020 8904 5179
e mail@linklinecrew.com **w** www.linklinecrew.com

Tom Harding
Suz Cruz, Halliford Studios, Manygate Lane, Shepperton TW17 9EG
t 01932 252577 **f** 01932 253323 **m** 07956 485593
e zoe@suzcruz.co.uk **w** www.suzcruz.co.uk

Guy Hazel
Suz Cruz, Halliford Studios, Manygate Lane, Shepperton TW17 9EG
t 01932 252577 **f** 01932 253323 **m** 07956 485593
e zoe@suzcruz.co.uk **w** www.suzcruz.co.uk

Simon Heck
EXEC, 6 Travis Court, Farnham Royal SL2 3SB
t 01753 646677 **f** 01753 646770
e sue@execmanagement.co.uk **w** www.execmanagement.co.uk

David Hedges
75 Kipling Drive, South Wimbledon, London SW19 1TL
t 020 8543 8192 **f** 020 8543 8192 **m** 07710 271708
Credits Foyle's War (T); Outside The Rules (T); The Jury (T); Last Orders (F)

Jo Hidderley
Gems, The Media House, 87 Glebe Street, Penarth CF64 1EF
t 029 2071 0770 **f** 029 2071 0771
e gems@gems-agency.co.uk **w** www.gems-agency.co.uk
Credits Urban Gothic - Series I (T); Harry And The Wrinklies (T); Night And Day (T); Wild Justice (F)

Jamie Hogarth
17 Bargiery Road, London SE6 2LJ
t 020 8698 6634 **m** 07899 923177
Agent Linkline, 6 Thirlmere Gardens, Wembley HA9 8RE
t 020 8908 6262 **f** 020 8904 5179
e mail@linklinecrew.com **w** www.linklinecrew.com

Rupert Hornstein
Wizzo & Co, 35 Old Compton Street, London W1D 5JX
t 020 7437 2055 **f** 020 7437 2066
e wizzo@wizzoandco.co.uk **w** www.wizzoandco.co.uk

Leon Hoser
46 Moorland Road, Brixton, London SW9 8UB
t 020 7274 6185 **m** 07970 026140
Agent Linkline, 6 Thirlmere Gardens, Wembley HA9 8RE
t 020 8908 6262 **f** 020 8904 5179
e mail@linklinecrew.com **w** www.linklinecrew.com

Alex Howe
84 Brandon Street, London SE17 1ND
t 020 7703 0466 **f** 020 7703 0466 **m** 07885 305804
e alexhowe01@aol.com

William Humphris
Carlin Crew Ltd, Shepperton Studios, Studios Road, Shepperton TW17 0QD
t 01932 568268 **f** 01932 571109
e carlin@netcomuk.co.uk **w** www.carlincrew.com

Mark Isaac
26 Morlais Street, Cardiff CF23 5HQ
t 029 2049 2066 **m** 07976 411671 **e** markisaac@ntlworld.com
Credits Plots With A View (F); The I Inside (F); Messiah II (T); Hearts Of Gold (T)

Cedric James
Fairway End, The Fairway, Weybridge KT13 0RZ
t 01932 342878 **e** cedricandjean@aol.com
Credits First Knight (F); Gulliver's Travels (T); Event Horizon (F)

John Jordan
GAS (Guild Answering Service), C/o Panavision UK,
Metropolitan Centre, Bristol Road, Greenford UB6 8GD
t 020 8813 1999 **f** 020 8813 2111
e admin@gbct.org **w** www.gbct.org

Malcolm Keys
9 Southsea Street, Openshaw, Manchester M11 1BJ
t 0161 231 7496 **f** 0161 231 7496 **m** 07979 903643
e keypics@yahoo.com
Credits Interloper (S); The Forsyte Saga (T); Hollyoaks (T); La Republique
Atomique (D)

Owen Knott
4 Collard Way, Liss, Petersfield GU33 7RY
t 01730 894323 **m** 07747 011998
Agent Linkline, 6 Thirlmere Gardens, Wembley HA9 8RE
t 020 8908 6262 **f** 020 8904 5179
e mail@linklinecrew.com **w** www.linklinecrew.com

Mary Kyte
1 Wren Drive, West Drayton UB7 7NW
t 01895 443835 **f** 01895 850486 **m** 07973 341429
e kytem@aol.com
Agent Annie's Answering Service, Pinewood Studios,
Pinewood Road, Iver Heath SL0 0NH
t 01753 651303 **f** 01753 651848
e info@annies.co.uk **w** www.annies.co.uk
Credits Twelfth Night (T); Spooks I & II (F); Harry Potter And The Philosopher's
Stone (F)

Brad Larner
GAS (Guild Answering Service), C/o Panavision UK,
Metropolitan Centre, Bristol Road, Greenford UB6 8GD
t 020 8813 1999 **f** 020 8813 2111
e admin@gbct.org **w** www.gbct.org

Nic Lawson
Carlin Crew Ltd, Shepperton Studios, Studios Road,
Shepperton TW17 0QD
t 01932 568268 **f** 01932 571109
e carlin@netcomuk.co.uk **w** www.carlincrew.com

Oli Ledwith
72 Valley Road, London SW16 2XN
t 020 8769 3919 **m** 07973 725137 **e** oliled@sef1.freeserve.co.uk
Credits Samsung (C); Radio One (C); Mad Dogs (F); Bollywood Queen (F)

Oliver Loncraine
EXEC, 6 Travis Court, Farnham Royal SL2 3SB
t 01753 646677 **f** 01753 646770
e sue@execmanagement.co.uk **w** www.execmanagement.co.uk

Lorraine Luke
PO Box 2904, London W11 1JZ
m 07973 262 593
Credits Night And Day (T); Barclays Plc (W); Promoted To Glory (T); NatWest (C)

Craig Loveridge
Flat 2, 7 Parklands, Surbiton KT5 8EA
t 020 8390 4540 **m** 07808 829332
Agent Linkline, 6 Thirlmere Gardens, Wembley HA9 8RE
t 020 8908 6262 **f** 020 8904 5179
e mail@linklinecrew.com **w** www.linklinecrew.com

Paul MacKay
Suz Cruz, Halliford Studios, Manygate Lane, Shepperton TW17 9EG
t 01932 252577 **f** 01932 253323 **m** 07956 485593
e zoe@suzcruz.co.uk **w** www.suzcruz.co.uk

Clive Mackey
GAS (Guild Answering Service), C/o Panavision UK,
Metropolitan Centre, Bristol Road, Greenford UB6 8GD
t 020 8813 1999 **f** 020 8813 2111
e admin@gbct.org **w** www.gbct.org

Nathan Mann
Carlin Crew Ltd, Shepperton Studios, Studios Road,
Shepperton TW17 0QD
t 01932 568268 **f** 01932 571109
e carlin@netcomuk.co.uk **w** www.carlincrew.com

Rod Marley
GAS (Guild Answering Service), C/o Panavision UK,
Metropolitan Centre, Bristol Road, Greenford UB6 8GD
t 020 8813 1999 **f** 020 8813 2111
e admin@gbct.org **w** www.gbct.org

Sarah McCulloch
15A Cambray Road, London SW12 0XD
t 020 8675 5198 **m** 07799 413463
Agent Linkline, 6 Thirlmere Gardens, Wembley HA9 8RE
t 020 8908 6262 **f** 020 8904 5179
e mail@linklinecrew.com **w** www.linklinecrew.com

Rebecca McDonald
124 Bois Moor Road, Chesham HP5 1SS
t 01494 776297 **m** 07973 842208
Agent Linkline, 6 Thirlmere Gardens, Wembley HA9 8RE
t 020 8908 6262 **f** 020 8904 5179
e mail@linklinecrew.com **w** www.linklinecrew.com

Nadia McLeod
11A Royal Parade, Western Avenue, London W5 1ET
t 020 8997 4406 **f** 020 8997 4406 **m** 07885 310280
e nadiamcleod@onetell.net.uk

Kirsten McMahon
Suz Cruz, Halliford Studios, Manygate Lane, Shepperton TW17 9EG
t 01932 252577 **f** 01932 253323 **m** 07956 485593
e zoe@suzcruz.co.uk **w** www.suzcruz.co.uk

Toby Miles
56 Copthorne Avenue, Bromley Common BR2 8NN
m 07775 578182
Agent Linkline, 6 Thirlmere Gardens, Wembley HA9 8RE
t 020 8908 6262 **f** 020 8904 5179
e mail@linklinecrew.com **w** www.linklinecrew.com

Simon Mills
2 White Hermitage, Church Road, Old Windsor SL4 2JX
t 01753 857887 **f** 01753 857887 **m** 07778 301123
e britannic1@aol.com
Agent GAS (Guild Answering Service), C/o Panavision UK,
Metropolitan Centre, Bristol Road, Greenford UB6 8GD
t 020 8813 1999 **f** 020 8813 2111
e admin@gbct.org **w** www.gbct.org
Credits Merlin (F); Possession (F); The 10th Kingdom (T); The Four Feathers (F)

Mark Milsome
Callbox Communications Limited, 66 Shepperton Studios,
Studios Road, Shepperton TW17 0QD
t 01932 592572 **f** 01932 569655
e callboxdiary@btinternet.com **w** www.callboxdiary.co.uk

Jon Mitchell
Suz Cruz, Halliford Studios, Manygate Lane, Shepperton TW17 9EG
t 01932 252577 **f** 01932 253323 **m** 07956 485593
e zoe@suzcruz.co.uk **w** www.suzcruz.co.uk

Katie Mogg
3 Richards Close, Ash Vale GU12 5EQ
t 01252 315184 **m** 07976 947036
Agent Linkline, 6 Thirlmere Gardens, Wembley HA9 8RE
t 020 8908 6262 **f** 020 8904 5179
e mail@linklinecrew.com **w** www.linklinecrew.com

Rory Moles
EXEC, 6 Travis Court, Farnham Royal SL2 3SB
t 01753 646677 **f** 01753 646770
e sue@execmanagement.co.uk **w** www.execmanagement.co.uk

Ray Moore
GAS (Guild Answering Service), C/o Panavision UK,
Metropolitan Centre, Bristol Road, Greenford UB6 8GD
t 020 8813 1999 **f** 020 8813 2111
e admin@gbct.org **w** www.gbct.org

Ros Naylor
Suz Cruz, Halliford Studios, Manygate Lane, Shepperton TW17 9EG
t 01932 252577 **f** 01932 253323 **m** 07956 485593
e zoe@suzcruz.co.uk **w** www.suzcruz.co.uk

Zac Nicholson
Suz Cruz, Halliford Studios, Manygate Lane, Shepperton TW17 9EG
t 01932 252577 **f** 01932 253323 **m** 07956 485593
e zoe@suzcruz.co.uk **w** www.suzcruz.co.uk

Gabi Norland
Suz Cruz, Halliford Studios, Manygate Lane, Shepperton TW17 9EG
t 01932 252577 **f** 01932 253323 **m** 07956 485593
e zoe@suzcruz.co.uk **w** www.suzcruz.co.uk

Graham Norton
Callbox Communications Limited, 66 Shepperton Studios,
Studios Road, Shepperton TW17 0QD
t 01932 592572 **f** 01932 569655
e callboxdiary@btinternet.com **w** www.callboxdiary.co.uk

Eamonn O'Keeffe
Annie's Answering Service, Pinewood Studios, Pinewood Road,
Iver Heath SL0 0NH
t 01753 651303 **f** 01753 651848
e info@annies.co.uk **w** www.annies.co.uk

Vicci Orton
76 Glamorgan Street, Canton, Cardiff CF5 1QT
t 029 2033 1371 **f** 029 2066 6322 **m** 07767 445231
e vicciorton@hotmail.com
Credits Nuts & Bolts (T); Fondue, Rhyw A Deinosors (T); Belonging (T)

Sam Osborne
Suz Cruz, Halliford Studios, Manygate Lane, Shepperton TW17 9EG
t 01932 252577 **f** 01932 253323 **m** 07956 485593
e zoe@suzcruz.co.uk **w** www.suzcruz.co.uk

Luke Palmer
t 01932 252577 **f** 020 7586 1560 **m** 07973 637 011
Agent Suz Cruz, Halliford Studios, Manygate Lane,
Shepperton TW17 9EG
t 01932 252577 **f** 01932 253323 **m** 07956 485593
e zoe@suzcruz.co.uk **w** www.suzcruz.co.uk

Mark Patten
EXEC, 6 Travis Court, Farnham Royal SL2 3SB
t 01753 646677 **f** 01753 646770
e sue@execmanagement.co.uk **w** www.execmanagement.co.uk

John Patterson
EXEC, 6 Travis Court, Farnham Royal SL2 3SB
t 01753 646677 **f** 01753 646770
e sue@execmanagement.co.uk **w** www.execmanagement.co.uk

Robert Patterson
Suz Cruz, Halliford Studios, Manygate Lane, Shepperton TW17 9EG
t 01932 252577 **f** 01932 253323 **m** 07956 485593
e zoe@suzcruz.co.uk **w** www.suzcruz.co.uk

Terry Pearce
Gems, The Media House, 87 Glebe Street, Penarth CF64 1EF
t 029 2071 0770 **f** 029 2071 0771
e gems@gems-agency.co.uk **w** www.gems-agency.co.uk
Credits Peak Practice (T); Clocking Off (T); Monarch Of The Glen (T); Dalziel And Pascoe (T)

Nick Penn
EXEC, 6 Travis Court, Farnham Royal SL2 3SB
t 01753 646677 **f** 01753 646770
e sue@execmanagement.co.uk **w** www.execmanagement.co.uk

Justin Pentecost
Suz Cruz, Halliford Studios, Manygate Lane, Shepperton TW17 9EG
t 01932 252577 **f** 01932 253323 **m** 07956 485593
e zoe@suzcruz.co.uk **w** www.suzcruz.co.uk

Tim Potter
8B Gellatly Road, London SE14 5TT
t 020 7639 3263 **f** 020 7639 3263 **e** tim@timpotter.co.uk
Credits Sparkhouse (T); Lucky Jim (T); Bait (T)

Oleg Poupko
Suz Cruz, Halliford Studios, Manygate Lane, Shepperton TW17 9EG
t 01932 252577 **f** 01932 253323 **m** 07956 485593
e zoe@suzcruz.co.uk **w** www.suzcruz.co.uk

Matt Poynter
Carlin Crew Ltd, Shepperton Studios, Studios Road,
Shepperton TW17 0QD
t 01932 568268 **f** 01932 571109
e carlin@netcomuk.co.uk **w** www.carlincrew.com

Rupert Prince
Suz Cruz, Halliford Studios, Manygate Lane, Shepperton TW17 9EG
t 01932 252577 **f** 01932 253323 **m** 07956 485593
e zoe@suzcruz.co.uk **w** www.suzcruz.co.uk

Julian Pugh-Cook
Suz Cruz, Halliford Studios, Manygate Lane, Shepperton TW17 9EG
t 01932 252577 **f** 01932 253323 **m** 07956 485593
e zoe@suzcruz.co.uk **w** www.suzcruz.co.uk

Ralph Ramsden
GAS (Guild Answering Service), C/o Panavision UK,
Metropolitan Centre, Bristol Road, Greenford UB6 8GD
t 020 8813 1999 **f** 020 8813 2111
e admin@gbct.org **w** www.gbct.org

Steve Rees
8 Celandine Road, St Fagans, Cardiff CF5 4QR
t 029 2025 3463 **f** 029 2025 3463 **m** 07850 257292
e stevendavidrees@hotmail.com
Credits Restoration (T); The Story Of Tracy Beaker: Series II (T); The Falklands Play (T); Eldra (T)

Alex Reid
Annie's Answering Service, Pinewood Studios, Pinewood Road,
Iver Heath SL0 0NH
t 01753 651303 **f** 01753 651848
e info@annies.co.uk **w** www.annies.co.uk

Iwan Prys Reynolds
21A Lyne Court, Church Lane, Kingsbury, London NW9 8LE
t 020 8205 9710 **f** 020 8205 9710 **m** 07966 383 205
e iwanprys@hotmail.com
Credits Love Honour And Obey (F); South West Nine (F); Shoreditch (F)

Jonathan Richmond
EXEC, 6 Travis Court, Farnham Royal SL2 3SB
t 01753 646677 **f** 01753 646770
e sue@execmanagement.co.uk **w** www.execmanagement.co.uk

Chris Robertson
2 Welwyn Hall Gardens, Welwyn AL6 9LF
t 01438 717968 **m** 07966 253397
Agent Linkline, 6 Thirlmere Gardens, Wembley HA9 8RE
t 020 8908 6262 **f** 020 8904 5179
e mail@linklinecrew.com **w** www.linklinecrew.com

Matt Roche
221 Sooters Hill Road, London SE3 8UL
t 020 8858 9158 **m** 07768 925246
Agent Linkline, 6 Thirlmere Gardens, Wembley HA9 8RE
t 020 8908 6262 **f** 020 8904 5179
e mail@linklinecrew.com **w** www.linklinecrew.com

Sarah Rollason
Suz Cruz, Halliford Studios, Manygate Lane, Shepperton TW17 9EG
t 01932 252577 **f** 01932 253323 **m** 07956 485593
e zoe@suzcruz.co.uk **w** www.suzcruz.co.uk

Kaye Rudin
44 Heaton Road, Mitcham CR4 2BU
t 020 8648 0759 **m** 07887 886931
Agent Linkline, 6 Thirlmere Gardens, Wembley HA9 8RE
t 020 8908 6262 **f** 020 8904 5179
e mail@linklinecrew.com **w** www.linklinecrew.com

Derk Russell
Suz Cruz, Halliford Studios, Manygate Lane, Shepperton TW17 9EG
t 01932 252577 **f** 01932 253323 **m** 07956 485593
e zoe@suzcruz.co.uk **w** www.suzcruz.co.uk

Ed Rutherford
Annie's Answering Service, Pinewood Studios, Pinewood Road, Iver Heath SL0 0NH
t 01753 651303 **f** 01753 651848
e info@annies.co.uk **w** www.annies.co.uk

Steve Sadler
Annie's Answering Service, Pinewood Studios, Pinewood Road, Iver Heath SL0 0NH
t 01753 651303 **f** 01753 651848
e info@annies.co.uk **w** www.annies.co.uk

Steve Scammell
Annie's Answering Service, Pinewood Studios, Pinewood Road, Iver Heath SL0 0NH
t 01753 651303 **f** 01753 651848
e info@annies.co.uk **w** www.annies.co.uk

Duncan Scott
35 West Point, Avondale Square, London SE1 5NY
t 020 7231 3808 **m** 07958 306299
e duncan.scott@onmail.co.uk
Credits Truth (T); A is for Acid (T); Murder In Mind (T)

Gordon Segrove
Annie's Answering Service, Pinewood Studios, Pinewood Road, Iver Heath SL0 0NH
t 01753 651303 **f** 01753 651848
e info@annies.co.uk **w** www.annies.co.uk

Lucy Seymour
Suz Cruz, Halliford Studios, Manygate Lane, Shepperton TW17 9EG
t 01932 252577 **f** 01932 253323 **m** 07956 485593
e zoe@suzcruz.co.uk **w** www.suzcruz.co.uk

Robert Shacklady
Carlin Crew Ltd, Shepperton Studios, Studios Road, Shepperton TW17 0QD
t 01932 568268 **f** 01932 571109
e carlin@netcomuk.co.uk **w** www.carlincrew.com

Danny Shelmerdine
EXEC, 6 Travis Court, Farnham Royal SL2 3SB
t 01753 646677 **f** 01753 646770
e sue@execmanagement.co.uk **w** www.execmanagement.co.uk

Martin Shepherd
Lyncott, Yarnscombe, Barnstaple EX31 3LP
t 01769 560245 **f** 01769 560245 **m** 07976 799691
e martin@sheph.demon.co.uk **w** www.sheph.demon.co.uk
Agent Wizzo & Co, 35 Old Compton Street, London W1D 5JX
t 020 7437 2055 **f** 020 7437 2066
e wizzo@wizzoandco.co.uk **w** www.wizzoandco.co.uk
Credits The Hole (T); McCready And Daughter (T); Me Without You (F)

Mark Silk
Callbox Communications Limited, 66 Shepperton Studios, Studios Road, Shepperton TW17 0QD
t 01932 592572 **f** 01932 569655
e callboxdiary@btinternet.com **w** www.callboxdiary.co.uk

Patrick Smith
182-184 Dawes Road, Fulham, London SW6 7HS
t 020 7385 8644 **m** 07855 401276
Agent Linkline, 6 Thirlmere Gardens, Wembley HA9 8RE
t 020 8908 6262 **f** 020 8904 5179
e mail@linklinecrew.com **w** www.linklinecrew.com

Andy Symon
69 Union Road, London SW4 6JF
t 020 7207 4546 **m** 07973 392171
Agent Linkline, 6 Thirlmere Gardens, Wembley HA9 8RE
t 020 8908 6262 **f** 020 8904 5179
e mail@linklinecrew.com **w** www.linklinecrew.com

Olly Tellett
Carlin Crew Ltd, Shepperton Studios, Studios Road, Shepperton TW17 0QD
t 01932 568268 **f** 01932 571109
e carlin@netcomuk.co.uk **w** www.carlincrew.com

Chyna Thomson
17 Pangbourne Avenue, London W10 6DJ
t 020 8964 1104 **f** 020 8964 1274 **m** 07931 518449
e chynat@yahoo.com
Agent Annie's Answering Service, Pinewood Studios, Pinewood Road, Iver Heath SL0 0NH
t 01753 651303 **f** 01753 651848
e info@annies.co.uk **w** www.annies.co.uk
Credits The Calcium Kid (F); Hamlet (C); The Importance of Being Earnest (F)

Simon Tindall
Flat 2, 349 Clapham Road, London SW9 9BT
t 020 7326 0667 **f** 0870 135 0493 **m** 07775 658992
e simon_tindall@hotmail.com
Agent Linkline, 6 Thirlmere Gardens, Wembley HA9 8RE
t 020 8908 6262 **f** 020 8904 5179
e mail@linklinecrew.com **w** www.linklinecrew.com
Credits Surviving Extremes - Ice (D); 28 Days Later (F); History of Britain (D); Savage Planet (D)

Jonathan Tyson
62A Sudbourne Road, Brixton, London SW2 5AH
t 020 7274 0256 **m** 07947 816189
Agent Linkline, 6 Thirlmere Gardens, Wembley HA9 8RE
t 020 8908 6262 **f** 020 8904 5179
e mail@linklinecrew.com **w** www.linklinecrew.com

Axel Ulrich
GAS (Guild Answering Service), C/o Panavision UK, Metropolitan Centre, Bristol Road, Greenford UB6 8GD
t 020 8813 1999 **f** 020 8813 2111
e admin@gbct.org **w** www.gbct.org

Rosa Verge
Gems, The Media House, 87 Glebe Street, Penarth CF64 1EF
t 029 2071 0770 **f** 029 2071 0771
e gems@gems-agency.co.uk **w** www.gems-agency.co.uk
Credits Casualty (T)

Jeff Vine
Wizzo & Co, 35 Old Compton Street, London W1D 5JX
t 020 7437 2055 **f** 020 7437 2066
e wizzo@wizzoandco.co.uk **w** www.wizzoandco.co.uk

Steve Watson
Suz Cruz, Halliford Studios, Manygate Lane, Shepperton TW17 9EG
t 01932 252577 **f** 01932 253323 **m** 07956 485593
e zoe@suzcruz.co.uk **w** www.suzcruz.co.uk

John Watters

Suz Cruz, Halliford Studios, Manygate Lane, Shepperton TW17 9EG
t 01932 252577 **f** 01932 253323 **m** 07956 485593
e zoe@suzcruz.co.uk **w** www.suzcruz.co.uk

Colleen Webley

Gems, The Media House, 87 Glebe Street, Penarth CF64 1EF
t 029 2071 0770 **f** 029 2071 0771
e gems@gems-agency.co.uk **w** www.gems-agency.co.uk
Credits Footballers Wives (T); Hester (F); The Rendez Vous (F); Bad Girls (T)

Ingrid Weel

Flat 1, 1 Bridge Court, Chertsey KP16 8LX
m 07958 377 764
e ingridweel@yahoo.com **w** www.ingiontheweb.co.uk
Agent Annie's Answering Service, Pinewood Studios,
Pinewood Road, Iver Heath SL0 0NH
t 01753 651303 **f** 01753 651848
e info@annies.co.uk **w** www.annies.co.uk
Credits Holby City IV (T); Philips Expanium (C); Yorkshire Tourist Board (I)

Matt Wesson

Suz Cruz, Halliford Studios, Manygate Lane, Shepperton TW17 9EG
t 01932 252577 **f** 01932 253323 **m** 07956 485593
e zoe@suzcruz.co.uk **w** www.suzcruz.co.uk

Leon Willis

Flat 6, Charlotte Court, 68b The Old Kent Road, London SE1 4NU
t 020 7701 1665 **m** 07811 380763 **w** leon.willis@btinternet.com

Will Willis

Callbox Communications Limited, 66 Shepperton Studios,
Studios Road, Shepperton TW17 0QD
t 01932 592572 **f** 01932 569655 **m** 07710 572572
e callboxdiary@btinternet.com **w** www.callboxdiary.co.uk

Gavin Wilson

GAS (Guild Answering Service), C/o Panavision UK,
Metropolitan Centre, Bristol Road, Greenford UB6 8GD
t 020 8813 1999 **f** 020 8813 2111
e admin@gbct.org **w** www.gbct.org

Jason Wingrove

Annie's Answering Service, Pinewood Studios, Pinewood Road,
Iver Heath SL0 0NH
t 01753 651303 **f** 01753 651848
e info@annies.co.uk **w** www.annies.co.uk

David Wyatt

Suz Cruz, Halliford Studios, Manygate Lane, Shepperton TW17 9EG
t 01932 252577 **f** 01932 253323 **m** 07956 485593
e zoe@suzcruz.co.uk **w** www.suzcruz.co.uk

Douglas Young

3 Oakwood Grange, 26 Oatlands Chase, Weybridge KT13 9RY
t 01932 841804 **m** 07966 246515
Agent Linkline, 6 Thirlmere Gardens, Wembley HA9 8RE
t 020 8908 6262 **f** 020 8904 5179
e mail@linklinecrew.com **w** www.linklinecrew.com

Camera Operators

Jim Alloway

199 Ember Lane, East Molesey KT8 0BU
t 020 8398 3889 **m** 07956 443348
Credits The Dark Room (T); Seeing Red (T); Scarlet Pimpernell (T); Forsythe Saga (T)

Andrew Emslie Consultancy Ltd

Beaver Cottage North, Alderbrook Road, Winterfold,
Cranleigh GU6 8QX
t 01483 277527 **m** 07720 293822 **e** andrew_emslie@hotmail.com
Contact Andrew Emslie MBA, Director/Consultant/Cameraman
Credits Corps Business Video Productions (E); Cheltenham College (I)
*I work closely in partnership with clients to deliver
precisely what they require.*

Ray Andrew

262 Court Road, London SE9 4TY
t 020 8857 1351 **f** 020 8857 1351 **m** 07747 115532
e ray.andrew@virgin.net

Shane Appleton

TOVS Ltd, The Linen Hall, 162-168 Regent Street, London W1B 5TB
t 020 7287 6110 **f** 020 7287 5481
e info@tovs.co.uk **w** www.tovs.co.uk

Roger Backhouse

TOVS Ltd, The Linen Hall, 162-168 Regent Street, London W1B 5TB
t 020 7287 6110 **f** 020 7287 5481
e info@tovs.co.uk **w** www.tovs.co.uk

Ian 'Bunny' Baldwin

TOVS Ltd, The Linen Hall, 162-168 Regent Street, London W1B 5TB
t 020 7287 6110 **f** 020 7287 5481
e info@tovs.co.uk **w** www.tovs.co.uk

Julian Barber

Laureldene, Beechmount Road, Basset SO16 3JD
t 023 8076 6696 **f** 023 8057 7772 **m** 07770 593282
e jbarber001@aol.com
Credits Always And Everyone (T); Jonathan Creek (T); Dalziel And Pascoe (T)

Roddy Barron

Callbox Communications Ltd, Box 66, Shepperton Studios,
Shepperton Lane, Shepperton TW17 0QD
t 01932 592572 **f** 01932 569655 **m** 07710 572 572
e callboxdiary@btinternet.com **w** www.callboxdiary.co.uk

Roderick Barron

Lucknow Towers, Polesdon Lane, Ripley, Woking GU23 6DX
t 01483 224371 **f** 01483 224371 **m** 07774 655555
e recbarron@hotmail.com
Credits The Mummy (F); The Mummy Returns (F); Watership Down (A)

Klemens Becker

International Creative Management Ltd, Oxford House, 76
Oxford Street, London W1D 1BS
t 020 7636 6565 **f** 020 7323 0101 **w** www.icmlondon.co.uk
Credits The Devil's Throat (F); Hannibal (F); Spy Game (F)

Gary Beckerman

TOVS Ltd, The Linen Hall, 162-168 Regent Street, London W1B 5TB
t 020 7287 6110 **f** 020 7287 5481
e info@tovs.co.uk **w** www.tovs.co.uk

NJ Beeks-Sanders

12 Lansdowne Circus, Leamington Spa CV32 4SW
t 01926 335375 **f** 01926 335375 **m** 07980 988161
e ssutton@dircon.co.uk
Credits Cambridge Spies (T); Thunderpants (F); I Capture The Castle (F)

Brian Benjamin

TOVS Ltd, The Linen Hall, 162-168 Regent Street, London W1B 5TB
t 020 7287 6110 **f** 020 7287 5481
e info@tovs.co.uk **w** www.tovs.co.uk

Mitch Bligh

20 Marlborough Road, Archway, London N19 4NB
t 020 7272 3822 **m** 07968 774737
e mitch.bligh@ntlworld.com
Agent TOVS Ltd, The Linen Hall, 162-168 Regent Street,
London W1B 5TB
t 020 7287 6110 **f** 020 7287 5481
e info@tovs.co.uk **w** www.tovs.co.uk
Credits Disney (T); Big Brother (T); Fame Academy (T); Richard And Judy (T)

Simon Bray

Carlin Crew Ltd, Shepperton Studios, Studios Road,
Shepperton TW17 0QD
t 01932 568268 **f** 01932 571109
e carlin@netcomuk.co.uk **w** www.carlincrew.com

Jenny Budd
Top Floor Flat, 85 Hampton Park, Redland, Bristol BS6 6LQ
t 0117 974 2617 **m** 07850 860882 **e** jennybudd@talk21.com
Credits Kerching (T); Holby City (T); Judge John Deeds (T); Casualty (T)

Cosmo Campbell
Wizzo & Co, 35 Old Compton Street, London W1D 5JX
t 020 7437 2055 **f** 020 7437 2066
e wizzo@wizzoandco.co.uk **w** www.wizzoandco.co.uk

Capital Crewing
Downline Southill Road, Chislehurst BR7 5EE
t 020 8467 9842 **f** 020 8467 9872 **m** 07885 720111
e graeme@capitalcrewing.tv **w** www.capitalcrewing.tv
Contact Graeme Robertson, Camerman; Mark Bourdeaux, Camerman
Credits European Tour Weekly (T); On The Ball (T); Sky Sports (T)

Peter Carrier
29 Thornbury Avenue, Osterley, Isleworth TW7 4NF
t 07748 902559 **m** 07748 902 559
e pete@carrier-media.co.uk **w** www.carrier-media.co.uk

Peter Cavaciuti
99 Southwood Lane, London N6 5TB
t 020 8340 4555 **f** 020 8340 4555 **m** 07973 639709
Credits Neverland (F); Cat In The Hat (F); The Hunted (F); Harry Potter And The Philosopher's Stone (F)

Dave Cave
7 Monk Court, Peterlee SR8 1JL
t 0191 587 2600 **f** 0191 587 2600 **m** 07973 413013
e dave@davecave.co.uk

Paul Cave
37 Furze Common Road, Thakeham RH20 3EG
t 01798 812919 **f** 01798 812919 **m** 07850 314379
e paulalltrain@lineone.net

Tim Chester
TOVS Ltd, The Linen Hall, 162-168 Regent Street, London W1B 5TB
t 020 7287 6110 **f** 020 7287 5481
e info@tovs.co.uk **w** www.tovs.co.uk

John Clarke
TOVS Ltd, The Linen Hall, 162-168 Regent Street, London W1B 5TB
t 020 7287 6110 **f** 020 7287 5481
e info@tovs.co.uk **w** www.tovs.co.uk

Roberto Contreras
GAS (Guild Answering Service), C/o Panavision UK, Metropolitan Centre, Bristol Road, Greenford UB6 8GD
t 020 8813 1999 **f** 020 8813 2111
e admin@gbct.org **w** www.gbct.org

Trevor Coop
GAS (Guild Answering Service), C/o Panavision UK, Metropolitan Centre, Bristol Road, Greenford UB6 8GD
t 020 8813 1999 **f** 020 8813 2111
e admin@gbct.org **w** www.gbct.org

Duncan Cross
TOVS Ltd, The Linen Hall, 162-168 Regent Street, London W1B 5TB
t 020 7287 6110 **f** 020 7287 5481
e info@tovs.co.uk **w** www.tovs.co.uk

Kevan Debonnaire
TOVS Ltd, The Linen Hall, 162-168 Regent Street, London W1B 5TB
t 020 7287 6110 **f** 020 7287 5481
e info@tovs.co.uk **w** www.tovs.co.uk

Alan Denniston
3 Airyligg Drive, Eaglesham, Glasgow G76 OLJ
t 01355 303729 **m** 07971 515883
e alan@denniston.freeserve.co.uk
Credits BBC Sport (T); ITV Sport (T); Sky Sports (T)

Graeme Dunn
14 Dunsmore Avenue, Rugby CV22 5HD
t 07973 412014 **f** 07970 097686 **e** graeme.dunn@orange.net
Agent Suz Cruz, Halliford Studios, Manygate Lane, Shepperton TW17 9EG
t 01932 252577 **f** 01932 253323 **m** 07956 485593
e zoe@suzcruz.co.uk **w** www.suzcruz.co.uk
Credits Kinder Surprise (C); Baci Chocolates Italy (C); Nescafe Cold Blend (C)

Simon Edwards
10B Snowshill Drive, Bishop's Cleeve, Cheltenham GL52 8SY
t 07831 622154 **f** 07779 353408 **e** simonedwards@aol.com
Credits Guiness In The Garden (T); Wimbledon Breakfast (T); The Queen's Jubilee (T)

Equilibrium Productions
136 Lancaster Road, Barnet, London EN4 8AL
t 020 8441 7421 **m** 07968 124431
e video@eqproductions.com **w** www.eqproductions.com
Contact Michael Dodds, Proprietor
Available with or without various Sony DSR Professional DVCAM Cameras.

Simon Finney
GAS (Guild Answering Service), C/o Panavision UK, Metropolitan Centre, Bristol Road, Greenford UB6 8GD
t 020 8813 1999 **f** 020 8813 2111 **e** admin@gbct.org **w** www.gbct.org

Bruna Fionda
m 07973 667148 **e** brunafionda@hotmail.com

Martin Foley
77 Eastwood Road, Bramley, Guilford GU5 0DX
t 01483 893697 **f** 01483 893697 **m** 07778 126947
e martinjfoley@hotmail.com
Credits Love In A Cold Climate (T); Auf Wiedersehen Pet (T); Daniel Deronda (T); The Water Giant (F)

Roy Ford
GAS (Guild Answering Service), C/o Panavision UK, Metropolitan Centre, Bristol Road, Greenford UB6 8GD
t 020 8813 1999 **f** 020 8813 2111
e admin@gbct.org **w** www.gbct.org

Lewis Foster
Gems, The Media House, 87 Glebe Street, Penarth CF64 1EF
t 029 2071 0770 **f** 029 2071 0771
e gems@gems-agency.co.uk **w** www.gems-agency.co.uk
Credits Close And True (T); Al's Lads (F); Gypsy Woman (F); Glasgow Kiss (T)

Mike Fox
GAS (Guild Answering Service), Panavision, Metropolitan Centre, Bristol Road, Greenford UB6 8GD
t 020 8813 1999 **f** 020 8813 2111
e admin@gbct.org **w** www.gbct.org

Ben Frewin
Suz Cruz, Halliford Studios, Manygate Lane, Shepperton TW17 9EG
t 01932 252577 **f** 01932 253323 **m** 07956 485593
e zoe@suzcruz.co.uk **w** www.suzcruz.co.uk

Ken Garraway
GAS (Guild Answering Service), C/o Panavision UK, Metropolitan Centre, Bristol Road, Greenford UB6 8GD
t 020 8813 1999 **f** 020 8813 2111
e admin@gbct.org **w** www.gbct.org

Jeremy Gee
210 Worple Road, London SW20 8RH
t 020 8947 9261 **f** 020 8947 9261 **m** 07850 387510
Agent Bookends, 83 Maynard Drive, St Albans AL1 2JX
t 01727 841177 **e** bookgold@bookends.fsbusiness.co.uk

Keith Gibson
TOVS Ltd, The Linen Hall, 162-168 Regent Street, London W1B 5TB
t 020 7287 6110 **f** 020 7287 5481
e info@tovs.co.uk **w** www.tovs.co.uk

Adam Gillham
Carlin Crew Ltd, Shepperton Studios, Studios Road,
Shepperton TW17 0QD
t 01932 568268 **f** 01932 571109
e carlin@netcomuk.co.uk **w** www.carlincrew.com

Matthew Gladstone
44 Frieth Road, Marlow SL7 2QU
t 01628 478950 **m** 07973 673187
e matt@tvcameraman.fsnet.co.uk **w** www.tvcameraman.fsnet.co.uk

Mark Gottleib
GAS (Guild Answering Service), C/o Panavision UK,
Metropolitan Centre, Bristol Road, Greenford UB6 8GD
t 020 8813 1999 **f** 020 8813 2111
e admin@gbct.org **w** www.gbct.org

Geoff Greenslade
TOVS Ltd, The Linen Hall, 162-168 Regent Street, London W1B 5TB
t 020 7287 6110 **f** 020 7287 5481
e info@tovs.co.uk **w** www.tovs.co.uk

Paul Grice
2 Malvern Road, Liverpool L6 6BW
t 01512 631523 **m** 07802 800667 **e** p_grice@madasafish.com
Credits The Premiership (T); The Commonwealth Games (T);
Aintree Grand National (T)

Steven Hall
Brook House, Thornham Magna, Eye IP23 8HB
t 01379 678576 **f** 01379 678576 **m** 07836 335604
e hall.associates@netcom.co.uk
Agent Wizzo & Co, 35 Old Compton Street, London W1D 5JX
t 020 7437 2055 **f** 020 7437 2066
e wizzo@wizzoandco.co.uk **w** www.wizzoandco.co.uk
Credits Playing The Field (T); Gladiator (F); If Only (F); Young Adam (F)

Jamie Harcourt
Carlin Crew Ltd, Shepperton Studios, Studios Road,
Shepperton TW17 0QD
t 01932 568268 **f** 01932 571109
e carlin@netcomuk.co.uk **w** www.carlincrew.com

Alex Helfferich
TOVS Ltd, The Linen Hall, 162-168 Regent Street, London W1B 5TB
t 020 7287 6110 **f** 020 7287 5481
e info@tovs.co.uk **w** www.tovs.co.uk

Ian Hembury
TOVS Ltd, The Linen Hall, 162-168 Regent Street, London W1B 5TB
t 020 7287 6110 **f** 020 7287 5481
e info@tovs.co.uk **w** www.tovs.co.uk

Jeremy Hiles
Carlin Crew Ltd, Shepperton Studios, Studios Road,
Shepperton TW17 0QD
t 01932 568268 **f** 01932 571109
e carlin@netcomuk.co.uk **w** www.carlincrew.com

Paul Hope
TOVS Ltd, The Linen Hall, 162-168 Regent Street, London W1B 5TB
t 020 7287 6110 **f** 020 7287 5481
e info@tovs.co.uk **w** www.tovs.co.uk

Stuart Howell
Carlin Crew Ltd, Shepperton Studios, Studios Road,
Shepperton TW17 0QD
t 01932 568268 **f** 01932 571109
e carlin@netcomuk.co.uk **w** www.carlincrew.com

Gareth Hughes
Carlin Crew Ltd, Shepperton Studios, Studios Road,
Shepperton TW17 0QD
t 01932 568268 **f** 01932 571109
e carlin@netcomuk.co.uk **w** www.carlincrew.com

Martin Hume
GAS (Guild Answering Service), C/o Panavision UK,
Metropolitan Centre, Bristol Road, Greenford UB6 8GD
t 020 8813 1999 **e** admin@gbct.org **w** www.gbct.org

Clive Jackson
Carlin Crew Ltd, Shepperton Studios, Studios Road,
Shepperton TW17 0QD
t 01932 568268 **f** 01932 571109
e carlin@netcomuk.co.uk **w** www.carlincrew.com

Tony Jackson
EXEC, 6 Travis Court, Farnham Royal SL2 3SB
t 01753 646677 **f** 01753 646770
e sue@execmanagement.co.uk **w** www.execmanagement.co.uk

Tony Jackson
GAS (Guild Answering Service), C/o Panavision UK,
Metropolitan Centre, Bristol Road, Greenford UB6 8GD
t 020 8813 1999 **f** 020 8813 2111
e admin@gbct.org **w** www.gbct.org

Steve Jellyman
TOVS Ltd, The Linen Hall, 162-168 Regent Street, London W1B 5TB
t 020 7287 6110 **f** 020 7287 5481
e info@tovs.co.uk **w** www.tovs.co.uk

Paul Kateley
177D Northcote Road, London SW11 6QF
t 020 7801 0344 **m** 07985 272772 **e** paulkatuk@yahoo.com

Martin Kellett
t 07050 184378 **e** cameraman_martin@hotmail.com
Credits British Superbikes; Premiership Football (T); BBC Newsnight (T)

Ian Keown
TOVS Ltd, The Linen Hall, 162-168 Regent Street, London W1B 5TB
t 020 7287 6110 **f** 020 7287 5481
e info@tovs.co.uk **w** www.tovs.co.uk

Nigel Kirton
EXEC, 6 Travis Court, Farnham Royal SL2 3SB
t 01753 646677 **f** 01753 646770
e sue@execmanagement.co.uk **w** www.execmanagement.co.uk

Marek Kowalek
Suz Cruz, Halliford Studios, Manygate Lane, Shepperton TW17 9EG
t 01932 252577 **f** 01932 253323 **m** 07956 485593
e zoe@suzcruz.co.uk **w** www.suzcruz.co.uk

Phillip Lofthouse
TOVS Ltd, The Linen Hall, 162-168 Regent Street, London W1B 5TB
t 020 7287 6110 **f** 020 7287 5481
e info@tovs.co.uk **w** www.tovs.co.uk

Nick Lowin
GAS (Guild Answering Service), C/o Panavision UK,
Metropolitan Centre, Bristol Road, Greenford UB6 8GD
t 020 8813 1999 **f** 020 8813 2111
e admin@gbct.org **w** www.gbct.org

Ray Marlow
Suz Cruz, Halliford Studios, Manygate Lane, Shepperton TW17 9EG
t 01932 252577 **f** 01932 253323 **m** 07956 485593
e zoe@suzcruz.co.uk **w** www.suzcruz.co.uk

Eric Marquis
Suz Cruz, Halliford Studios, Manygate Lane, Shepperton TW17 9EG
t 01932 252577 **f** 01932 253323 **m** 07956 485593
e zoe@suzcruz.co.uk **w** www.suzcruz.co.uk

John Maskall
GAS (Guild Answering Service), C/o Panavision UK,
Metropolitan Centre, Bristol Road, Greenford UB6 8GD
t 020 8813 1999 **f** 020 8813 2111
e admin@gbct.org **w** www.gbct.org

Jeremy Mason
Folly Cottage, Abbotts Ann, Andover SP11 7BH
f 01264 712135 **m** 07976 267259
e jeremysmason@hotmail.com
Credits Live With Chris Moyles (T); Sky Sports Rugby Union (T); The Weakest Link (T); MTV Europe Music Awards 2002 (T)

Dave Matthews
TOVS Ltd, The Linen Hall, 162-168 Regent Street, London W1B 5TB
t 020 7287 6110 **f** 020 7287 5481
e info@tovs.co.uk **w** www.tovs.co.uk

Mark McCafferty
TOVS Ltd, The Linen Hall, 162-168 Regent Street, London W1B 5TB
t 020 7287 6110 **f** 020 7287 5481
e info@tovs.co.uk **w** www.tovs.co.uk

Andrew McDonnell
23 Oxford Road, Guiseley, Leeds LS20 9AS
t 01943 872887 **f** 01943 872887 **m** 07973 278085
e aj.mcdonnell@ntlworld.com
Credits Taggart (T); Born And Bred (T); Rebus (T); Queer As Folk (T)

Duncan McLaren
TOVS Ltd, The Linen Hall, 162-168 Regent Street, London W1B 5TB
t 020 7287 6110 **f** 020 7287 5481
e info@tovs.co.uk **w** www.tovs.co.uk

Ossie McLean
Gems, The Media House, 87 Glebe Street, Penarth CF64 1EF
t 029 2071 0770 **f** 029 2071 0771
e gems@gems-agency.co.uk **w** www.gems-agency.co.uk
Credits The Cry (T); Taggart (T); Now You See Her (T); The Cappuccino Years (T)

Patrick McLoughlin
TOVS Ltd, The Linen Hall, 162-168 Regent Street, London W1B 5TB
t 020 7287 6110 **f** 020 7287 5481
e info@tovs.co.uk **w** www.tovs.co.uk

Mark McQuoid
Carlin Crew Ltd, Shepperton Studios, Studios Road,
Shepperton TW17 0QD
t 01932 568268 **f** 01932 571109
e carlin@netcomuk.co.uk **w** www.carlincrew.com

Peter Meakin
164 Studland Road, Hanwell, London W7 3QZ
m 07801 866405 **e** petermeakin@aol.com
Credits Sahara With Michael Palin (D)

Mike Metcalfe
Suz Cruz, Halliford Studios, Manygate Lane, Shepperton TW17 9EG
t 01932 252577 **f** 01932 253323 **m** 07956 485593
e zoe@suzcruz.co.uk **w** www.suzcruz.co.uk

Mike Miller
C/o SMG TV Productions, 116 New Oxford Street, London WC1A 1HH
Credits The Forsyte Saga (T); Goodbye Mr Chips (T); Nicholas Nickleby (T); Below (F)

Nic Milner
Princestone, 49 Waldeck Road, London N15 3EL
t 020 8881 8788 **f** 020 8881 8772
Agent GAS (Guild Answering Service), C/o Panavision UK,
Metropolitan Centre, Bristol Road, Greenford UB6 8GD
t 020 8813 1999 **f** 020 8813 2111
e admin@gbct.org **w** www.gbct.org
Credits Hamlet (C); Loves Labours Lost (F); Equilibrium (F); Bridget Jones' Diary (F)

Mark Moriarty
EXEC, 6 Travis Court, Farnham Royal SL2 3SB
t 01753 646677 **f** 01753 646770
e sue@execmanagement.co.uk **w** www.execmanagement.co.uk

Sam Morrison
TOVS Ltd, The Linen Hall, 162-168 Regent Street, London W1B 5TB
t 020 7287 6110 **f** 020 7287 5481
e info@tovs.co.uk **w** www.tovs.co.uk

George Morse
59 Dorset Road, London W5 4HX
t 020 8567 3556 **m** 07860 236472
e call@georgemorse.fsnet.co.uk
Credits The Bill (T)

Julian Morson
Carlin Crew Ltd, Shepperton Studios, Studios Road,
Shepperton TW17 0QD
t 01932 568268 **f** 01932 571109
e carlin@netcomuk.co.uk **w** www.carlincrew.com

James Moss
Carlin Crew Ltd, Shepperton Studios, Studios Road,
Shepperton TW17 0QD
t 01932 568268 **f** 01932 571109
e carlin@netcomuk.co.uk **w** www.carlincrew.com
Credits Shrink (S); Casualty (T); Rockface (T)

Louis Mulvey
Suz Cruz, Halliford Studios, Manygate Lane, Shepperton TW17 9EG
t 01932 252577 **f** 01932 253323 **m** 07956 485593
e zoe@suzcruz.co.uk **w** www.suzcruz.co.uk

Ian Munday
TOVS Ltd, The Linen Hall, 162-168 Regent Street, London W1B 5TB
t 020 7287 6110 **f** 020 7287 5481
e info@tovs.co.uk **w** www.tovs.co.uk

Sian-Elin Palfrey
Gems, The Media House, 87 Glebe Street, Penarth CF64 1EF
t 029 2071 0770 **f** 029 2071 0771
e gems@gems-agency.co.uk **w** www.gems-agency.co.uk
Credits Mindblowin (T); Titanic (F); Nuts And Bolts (T)

John Palmer
Annie's Answering Service, Pinewood Studios, Pinewood Road,
Iver Heath SL0 0NH
t 01753 651303 **f** 01753 651848
e info@annies.co.uk **w** www.annies.co.uk

Mike Parker
Stella's Diary, 9 Hormead Road, London W9 3NG
t 01362 683668 **t** 020 8969 1855 **f** 020 8964 2157
m 077468 667361 **m** 07836 594622
w stella'sdiary@btinternet.com

Tom Parr
21 Longleat House, Lillington Gardens, Vauxhall Bridge Road,
Pimlico, London SW1V 2TG
t 020 7428 9090 **m** 07970 871645 **e** parrcam@aol.com
Credits Brit Awards 2003 (T); The Kumars At No 42 (T); Richard And Judy (T); Big Brother (T)

Mike Paterson
TOVS Ltd, The Linen Hall, 162-168 Regent Street, London W1B 5TB
t 020 7287 6110 **f** 020 7287 5481
e info@tovs.co.uk **w** www.tovs.co.uk

Philip Duffy Video Services
8 West Lea Garth, Leeds LS17 5DA
t 01132 696870 **f** 01132 287033 **m** 07775 528706
e info@uvr.co.uk **e** philip.duffy.video@ntlworld.com
w www.uvr.co.uk

Chris Plevin
The Homestead, Brays Lane, Hyde Heath, Amersham HP6 5RU
t 01494 783393 **f** 07976 650176 **m** 07973 208942
e cplevin@cix.co.uk
Credits Dr Zhivago (T); Brassed Off (F); Little Voice (F); Band Of Brothers (T)

Rupert Power
EXEC, 6 Travis Court, Farnham Royal SL2 3SB
t 01753 646677 **f** 01753 646770
e sue@execmanagement.co.uk **w** www.execmanagement.co.uk

Roger Prior
TOVS Ltd, The Linen Hall, 162-168 Regent Street, London W1B 5TB
t 020 7287 6110 **f** 020 7287 5481
e info@tovs.co.uk **w** www.tovs.co.uk

Michael Proudfoot
International Creative Management Ltd, Oxford House, 76 Oxford Street, London W1D 1BS
t 020 7636 6565 **f** 020 7323 0101 **w** www.icmlondon.co.uk
Credits The Wings Of The Dove (F); Unfaithful (F); The Life Of David Gale (F)

Mike Proudfoot
GAS (Guild Answering Service), C/o Panavision UK, Metropolitan Centre, Bristol Road, Greenford UB6 8GD
t 020 8813 1999 **f** 020 8813 2111
e admin@gbct.org **w** www.gbct.org

Kate Robinson
Carlin Crew Ltd, Shepperton Studios, Studios Road, Shepperton TW17 0QD
t 01932 568268 **f** 01932 571109
e carlin@netcomuk.co.uk **w** www.carlincrew.com

Ian Rolfe
London NW2 3AU
m 07719 816710 **e** ian_rolfe@hotmail.com
Credits Club Reps (T); BBC News (T); Disney Channel (T); Diggin It (T)

Steve Rouse
TOVS Ltd, The Linen Hall, 162-168 Regent Street, London W1B 5TB
t 020 7287 6110 **f** 020 7287 5481
e info@tovs.co.uk **w** www.tovs.co.uk

Ruach Ministries
122 Brixton Hill, London SW2 1RS
t 020 8678 6888x27 **f** 020 8674 0345
e bishopjaf@lineone.net **w** www.ruach-ministries.co.uk
Contact Catherine Minott, Administrator; Israel Immanuel, Editor; Malcolm Moore, Editor; Rev. John Francis, Director

Kevin Rudge
Gems, The Media House, 87 Glebe Street, Penarth CF64 1EF
t 029 2071 0770 **f** 029 2071 0771
e gems@gems-agency.co.uk **w** www.gems-agency.co.uk
Credits A Mind To Kill (T); First Sex (T); The Falklands Play (T); Anazapta (F)

Nick Schlesinger
32 Fernhurst Road, Fulham, London SW6 7JW
t 020 7384 9199 **f** 020 7384 9199 **m** 07967 593 603
e nickschlesinger@hotmail.com

Owen Scurfield
Stella's Diary, 9 Hormead Road, London W9 3NG
t 020 8674 7611 **t** 020 8969 1855 **f** 020 8964 2157
m 07973 199006 **m** 07836 594622
e stella'sdiary@btinternet.com

Philip Sindall
11 Queens Gardens, Ealing, London W5 1SE
t 020 8998 7703 **t** 020 8998 7703
e philip.sindall@btinternet.com
Agent Carlin Crew Ltd, Shepperton Studios, Studios Road, Shepperton TW17 0QD
t 01932 568268 **f** 01932 571109
e carlin@netcomuk.co.uk **w** www.carlincrew.com
Credits Sense And Sensibility (F); Elizabeth (F); Shakespeare In Love (F); The Hours (F)

Mark Smeaton
17 Prince Court, Hampton Street, Tetbury GL8 8TP
t 01666 502823 **f** 01666 502823 **m** 07973 801646
e mark@jsmeaton.freeserve.co.uk
Credits Baby Father Series 2 (T); Heartbeat (T); Casualty (T); The Bill (T)

Richard Smith
1 Crickley Cottages, Crickley Hill, Witcombe, Cheltenham GL3 4UQ
t 01452 862214 **f** 01452 862214 **m** 07976 689227
e richsmith@madasafish.com

Gary Spratling
Bookends, 83 Maynard Drive, St Albans AL1 2JX
t 01727 841177 **e** bookgold@bookends.fsbusiness.co.uk

Stefan Stankowski
Callbox Communications Ltd, PO Box 66, Shepperton Studios, Shepperton Lane TW17 0QD
t 01932 592572 **f** 01932 569655 **m** 07710 572572
e callboxdiary@btinternet.com **w** www.callboxdiary.co.uk

Andrew Stephen
6 Dale Lee, Westhoughton, Bolton BL5 3YE
t 01942 811371 **f** 01942 811371 **m** 07762 872553
e andrew.stephen@btinternet.com
Credits Where The Heart Is (T); Linda Green (T); Down To Earth (T)

Martin Stephens
Carlin Crew Ltd, Shepperton Studios, Studios Road, Shepperton TW17 0QD
t 01932 568268 **f** 01932 571109
e carlin@netcomuk.co.uk **w** www.carlincrew.com

Tony Strachan
GAS (Guild Answering Service), C/o Panavision UK, Metropolitan Centre, Bristol Road, Greenford UB6 8GD
t 020 8813 1999 **f** 020 8813 2111
e admin@gbct.org **w** www.gbct.org

Nick Swettenham
TOVS Ltd, The Linen Hall, 162-168 Regent Street, London W1B 5TB
t 020 7287 6110 **f** 020 7287 5481
e info@tovs.co.uk **w** www.tovs.co.uk

Jonathan Sykes
61 Oxford Road South, Chiswick, London W4 3DD
t 020 8400 7724 **f** 020 8400 7724 **m** 07850 065 916
e jonsky@blueyonder.co.uk
Credits State Of Play (T); The Lost Prince (T); Star Wars Episode II - The Attack Of The Clones (F)

Chris Tanner
EXEC, 6 Travis Court, Farnham Royal SL2 3SB
t 01753 646677 **f** 01753 646770
e sue@execmanagement.co.uk **w** www.execmanagement.co.uk

Christian Tester
TOVS Ltd, The Linen Hall, 162-168 Regent Street, London W1B 5TB
t 020 7287 6110 **f** 020 7287 5481
e info@tovs.co.uk **w** www.tovs.co.uk

Time Line
32 College Road, Bromsgrove B60 2NF
t 01527 579192 **f** 01527 575210 **m** 07973 159880
e peter.rance@virgin.net
Contact Peter Rance, Partner

Mark Treays
GAS (Guild Answering Service), C/o Panavision UK, Metropolitan Centre, Bristol Road, Greenford UB6 8GD
t 020 8813 1999 **f** 020 8813 2111
e admin@gbct.org **w** www.gbct.org

Malcolm Vinson (BSC)
Gems, The Media House, 87 Glebe Street, Penarth CF64 1EF
t 029 2071 0770 **f** 029 2071 0771
e gems@gems-agency.co.uk **w** www.gems-agency.co.uk
Credits Close And True (T); Harry And The Wrinklies (T); Hollyoaks (T); Urban Gothic - Series I (T)

Geraint Warrington
Suz Cruz, Halliford Studios, Manygate Lane, Shepperton TW17 9EG
t 01932 252577 **f** 01932 253323 **m** 07956 485593
e zoe@suzcruz.co.uk **w** www.suzcruz.co.uk

Jon Webb
Suz Cruz, Halliford Studios, Manygate Lane, Shepperton TW17 9EG
t 01932 252577 **f** 01932 253323 **m** 07956 485593
e zoe@suzcruz.co.uk **w** www.suzcruz.co.uk

Nick Wheeler
Suz Cruz, Halliford Studios, Manygate Lane, Shepperton TW17 9EG
t 01932 252577 **f** 01932 253323 **m** 07956 485593
e zoe@suzcruz.co.uk **w** www.suzcruz.co.uk

Tim Wigley
67 Warnham Court Road, Carshalton Beeches SM5 3ND
t 020 8643 6879 **m** 07939 151 698
e tim_wigley@yahoo.co.uk **w** www.wigleyweb.com

Peter Wignall
179 Leighton Road, Kentish Town, London NW5 2AR
m 07710 061127
Agent Carlin Crew Ltd, Shepperton Studios, Studios Road, Shepperton TW17 0QD
t 01932 568268 **f** 01932 571109
e carlin@netcomuk.co.uk **w** www.carlincrew.com
Credits Suzie Gold (T); Bend It Like Beckham (F); Snatch (F); Lock Stock And Two Smoking Barrels (F)

Andrew Wilson
9 Bridgewater Close, Penkridge ST19 5HU
t 01785 716 086 **f** 07970 080 542 **m** 07970 818293
e crashwilson@btopenworld.com
Credits Immigrants In Ireland (T); Working Mens Clubs (T); Privatization Of NHS Nurses - (T)

Bruce Wilson
92 Main Street, Scholes, Leeds LS15 4DR
t 0113 260 7574 **f** 07970 082580 **m** 07973 185748
e bruce@bwcam.com **w** www.bwcam.com
Credits Grange Hill (T); Heartbeat (T); Holby City (T); Casualty (T)

James Woods
16 Missenden Gardens, Burnham SL1 6LB
t 01628 559381 **m** 07776 233415 **e** jwoods2240@aol.com
Credits Goodyear Airship - South America (T); World Cup - Korea/Japan 2002 (T); Manchester Airport (I); Olympic Games - Sidney 2000 (I)

David Worley
Ramin, High Road, Eastcote, Pinner HA5 2EY
t 020 8429 3835 **f** 020 8429 3835 **m** 07956 263 442
e dwfilmser.camera@virgin.net
Agent Annie's Answering Service, Pinewood Studios, Pinewood Road, Iver Heath SL0 ONH
t 01753 651303 **f** 01753 651848
e info@annies.co.uk **w** www.annies.co.uk
Credits Shanghai Knights (F); The Mummy Returns (F); Reign Of Fire (F)

Jason Wrenn
EXEC, 6 Travis Court, Farnham Royal SL2 3SB
t 01753 646677 **f** 01753 646770
e sue@execmanagement.co.uk **w** www.execmanagement.co.uk

Camera Steadicam

Paul Alexander
37 Pampisford Road, Purley CR8 2NG
t 020 8660 7060 **f** 020 8660 7060 **m** 07774 131 656
Credits Dog Soldiers

Bars & Tones
4 Pymms Brook Drive, Barnet EN4 9RU
m 07973 505732
Contact Allan Barrett, Director

David Carey
Gems, The Media House, 87 Glebe Street, Penarth CF64 1EF
t 029 2071 0770 **f** 029 2071 0771
e gems@gems-agency.co.uk **w** www.gems-agency.co.uk
Credits Blue Dove (T); Micawber (T); Arthur's Dyke (F); The Rocket Post (F)

Tony Day
m 07970 057677 **e** rocksteadi@hotmail.com
Credits The Cazalet Chronical; Vision Express (C); Crust (F); The Cazalet Chronical (T)

Paul Edwards
Suz Cruz, Halliford Studios, Manygate Lane, Shepperton TW17 9EG
t 01932 252577 **f** 01932 253323 **m** 07956 485593
e zoe@suzcruz.co.uk **w** www.suzcruz.co.uk

Global Village Productions
71 Gloucester Road, Barnet EN5 1LZ
t 020 8441 3784 **f** 020 8441 3784 **e** globalvil1@aol.com
Contact Allan Barrett, Director

Alan Glover
Gems, The Media House, 87 Glebe Street, Penarth CF64 1EF
t 029 2071 0770 **f** 029 2071 0771
e gems@gems-agency.co.uk **w** www.gems-agency.co.uk
Credits Liverpool One (T); City Central (T); Hollyoaks (T); Brookside (T)

Dogan Halil
68 Banbury Road, Stratford-upon-Avon CV37 7HY
t 01789 262274 **f** 01789 262274 **m** 07973 549739
e steadidogan@hotmail.com
Credits Footballer's Wives (T); Bad Girls (T); Dinotopia (T); The Importance Of Being Ernest (F)

John Hembrough
Gems, The Media House, 87 Glebe Street, Penarth CF64 1EF
t 029 2071 0770 **f** 029 2071 0771
e gems@gems-agency.co.uk **w** www.gems-agency.co.uk
Credits Twenty-Four Hours In London (T); Wedding Tackle (F)

Infocus Television
145 Carr Lane, Dronfield, Woodhouse, Dronfield S18 8XF
t 01142 890173 **f** 01142 890830 **m** 07976 951849
e ian@infocustv.co.uk **w** www.infocustv.co.uk
Contact Ian Brown, Director; Rob Brown, Director
Credits British And World Superbikes (T); Premiership Football (T); Sculpture In Art (E); Carrier At War (D)

Dominic Jackson
Suz Cruz, Halliford Studios, Manygate Lane, Shepperton TW17 9EG
t 01932 252577 **f** 01932 253323 **m** 07956 485593
e zoe@suzcruz.co.uk **w** www.suzcruz.co.uk

Joemac Ltd
23 Kirkstall Gardens, London SW2 4HR
m 07973 226532 **e** joe@joesjibs.co.uk **w** www.joesjibs.co.uk
Contact Lesley White, PA; Joe Mcnally, Director
Credits Mo'Fire Crew (M); Tomorrow's World (T); Tonight With Trevor MacDonald (T); Bollywood Queen (F)

John Hembrough
40 Littleburn Road, London SW4 6DN
t 020 7652 2091 **f** 020 7622 4034 **m** 07973 149352
e john@hembrough.co.uk **w** www.hembrough.co.uk
Contact John Hembrough, Proprieter
Credits Waking The Dead (T); Murphy's Law (T); Phoenix Blue (F);
Ali G In Da House (F)

Fiachra Judge
The Barn, Brickwall Farm, Stisted CM77 8DB
t 01376 552922 **f** 01376 553109 **m** 07976 299 816
e fi@steadicam.demon.co.uk **w** www.gosteadi.com
Credits Wannabe (M); Martha Meet Frank, Daniel and Laurence (F);
Highbinders (F)

Alun Knott
m 07887 994406
Credits Everyman (T); I'm A Celebrity, Get Me Out Of Here (T); Wish You Were
Here...? (T); Popstars - Germany & Switzerland (T)

Vince McGahon
Suz Cruz, Halliford Studios, Manygate Lane, Shepperton TW17 9EG
t 01932 252577 **f** 01932 253323 **m** 07956 485593
e zoe@suzcruz.co.uk **w** www.suzcruz.co.uk

MK-V Modular Systems Ltd
Unit 2B, Whitehall Street, Stockport SK5 7LW
t 0161 480 3007 **f** 0161 480 3887 **m** 07768 147499
e info@mk-v.com **w** www.mk-v.com
Contact Howard Smith, Managing Director; Sue Cooper, Manager

Pete Murray
Suz Cruz, Halliford Studios, Manygate Lane, Shepperton TW17 9EG
t 01932 252577 **f** 01932 253323 **m** 07956 485593
e zoe@suzcruz.co.uk **w** www.suzcruz.co.uk

Nick Ludlow Camera & Steadicam Services
C/O Prime TV International, Latimer Road, London W10 6RQ
t 020 8969 6122 **f** 020 8969 6144 **e** nick@ludlow.co.uk

Matt Norman
29B Downs Park West, Westbury Park, Bristol BS6 7QH
t 0117 962 1057 **f** 0117 962 1057 **m** 07976 247652
e jumna@blueyonder.co.uk
Credits Slam (S); The Roman Empire (T); Brat - Sob Story (M); Running Hot (F)

Optical Support Ltd
Optical Support, 203 Belgravia Workshops, 157-163
Marlborough Rd, London N19 4NF
t 020 7281 0999 **f** 020 7561 0115 **m** 07702 606 509
e info@opticalsupport.co.uk **w** www.opticalsupport.co.uk

Poke In The Eye Films
29B Downs Park West, Westbury Park, Bristol BS6 7QH
t 0117 962 1057 **f** 0117 962 1057 **m** 07976 247652
e jumna@blueyonder.co.uk
Contact Matt Norman, Contact
Credits The Roman Empire (D); Brat - Sob Story (M)

Rupert Power
7 Coulter Road, London W6 0BJ
t 020 8563 9109 **f** 01753 646677 **f** 020 8563 9109
m 07768 698250 **e** rm.power@virgin.net
Credits Judge John Deed (T); The Vice (T); The Mummy Returns (F);
Dot The I (F)

Alistair Rae
Suz Cruz, Halliford Studios, Manygate Lane, Shepperton TW17 9EG
t 01932 252577 **f** 01932 253323 **m** 07956 485593
e zoe@suzcruz.co.uk **w** www.suzcruz.co.uk

Rock Steadi Pictures
145 Middlehill Road, Colehill, Wimborne BH21 2HJ
t 01202 840162 **f** 01202 840162 **m** 07831 106556
e rocksteadi@lds.co.uk

John Taylor
Suz Cruz, Halliford Studios, Manygate Lane, Shepperton TW17 9EG
t 01932 252577 **f** 01932 253323 **m** 07956 485593
e zoe@suzcruz.co.uk **w** www.suzcruz.co.uk

Roger 'Rock' Tooley
Suz Cruz, Halliford Studios, Manygate Lane, Shepperton TW17 9EG
t 01932 252577 **f** 01932 253323 **m** 07956 485593
e zoe@suzcruz.co.uk **w** www.suzcruz.co.uk

Alf Tramontin
t 01565 722094 **f** 01565 722188 **m** 07831 383 052
e alf@tramontin.tv

Gerry Vasbenter
Wizzo & Co, 35 Old Compton Street, London W1D 5JX
t 020 7437 2055 **f** 020 7437 2066
e wizzo@wizzoandco.co.uk **w** www.wizzoandco.co.uk

Camera Technicians

Dave Curtis
Pathways, 28 Smithy Lane, Lowerkingswood KT20 6TX
t 01737 832840 **f** 01737 832840

Laurence Edwards
96 Clarkes Avenue, Worcester Park KT4 8QB
t 020 8213 5240 **m** 07968 185 611
e laurence_edwards@hotmail.com
Credits Sleepy Hollow (F)

Guild of British Camera Technicians
C/o Panavision, Bristol Road, Metropolitan Centre, Greenford
UB6 8GD
t 020 8813 1999 **f** 020 8813 2111
e admin@gbct.org **w** www.gbct.org
Contact Wendy Fitzgerald, Editor; Harvey Harrison BSC, Chairman;
Simon Mills, Secretary

Raspberry Sound Services
9 Burghley Road, London NW5 1UG
t 020 7267 3170 **f** 020 7284 4250 **m** 07956 277880
e sharrock@raspberry-ss.com
Contact Ivan Sharrock, Production Sound Mixer
Credits Cold Mountain (F); The Talented Mr Ripley (F); U-571 (F); Gangs of New
York (F)

Peter Tyler
Peter Tyler GBCT
t 01628 525147 **f** 01628 529385 **m** 07850 929063
Credits Match of the Day (T); Lost In Space (F); Bismark and Hood (T)

Cameramen Documentary

Miah Abdulaleem
84 Warren Road, Leyton, London E10 5QA
t 020 8558 1570 **f** 020 8452 2789 **m** 07956 572454
e miahabdulaleem@hotmail.com

Acam Video Facilities
4 Finchfield Road, Finchfield, Wolverhampton WV3 9LS
t 01902 656538 **f** 01902 428840 **m** 07831 620919
e john@acamvideo.com
Contact John Czerepaninec, Proprietor
Credits Newsnight (T); Heroes And Villains (T); Tomorrow's World (D);
Panorama (T)

Richard Adam
Walton-on-Thames, London
t 01932 232047 **f** 01932 232047 **m** 07802 227 447
e richfilms@which.net

Roger Edwards
Lighting Cameraman

Broadcast & Corporate

tel	01752 830428
mobile	07778 321122
fax	07970 112894
email	roger@tanybryn.co.uk

Colin Angell
35 Redgrave Place, Marlow SL7 1J2
t 01628 475270 **m** 07802 419495 **e** colin.angell@virgin.net
Credits Equinox - Hunt For The Deathstar (D); Building The Impossible (T);
Child Brides (D); New Model Army (D)

Aspect Ratio TV
17 Savery Drive, Surbiton KT6 5RO
t 020 8398 7005 **m** 07831 411918 **m** 07775 522660
e artv@aspectratio.tv
Contact Charles Pitt, Director of Photography; Karen Bishop,
Director/Producer
Credits QED: Secret Life Of The Family (D); Buried Alive (D); Atlantis (D);
Ultimate Guide: Mummies (D)

Simon Atkins
London
t 020 8374 3509 **f** 020 8374 3509 **m** 07710 440421
e mail@simonatkins.com **w** www.simonatkins.com
Credits Revenge Of The Lost Tribe (D); The Real Macaw (D); Is Anyone Listening
(E); Murder In The Amazon (D)

David Baillie
Windy Hall, Alston CA9 3NJ
t 01434 381067 **m** 07802 406334
e dave@wildcatfilms.biz **w** www.wildcatfilms.biz
Credits Arena (D); Timewatch (D); Beyond The Fatal Shore (D); Horizon (D)

Steph Baldini
Stella's Diary, 9 Hormead Road, London W9 3NG
t 020 8969 1855 **f** 020 8964 2157 **m** 07958 350886
e stella'sdiary@btinternet.com

Bob Batchelor Ltd
Flat 2/1, 12 Langside Place, Glasgow G41 3DL
t 0141 632 0958 **f** 0141 632 0958 **m** 07831 358730
e batchel@dircon.co.uk

Blue Fin Television Ltd
34 Fitzwilliam Road, London SW4 ODN
t 020 7622 0870 **f** 020 7720 7875 **m** 07973 502349
e antleake@bluefin-tv.demon.co.uk **w** www.bluefintv.com
Contact Anthony Leake, Head of Cameras; Diane Porter, Bookings
Credits The Fugitives (T); Vandals (D); Escape From Experiment Island (T); The
South Bank Show (T)

Steve Bowles
73 Pointout Road, Southampton SO16 7DL
t 023 8039 1199 **f** 023 8039 1199 **m** 07808 725022
e stevebowles@btopenworld.com
Credits The Langsdorff Expedition (D); True Stories From The Morgue (T); The
Guernica Generation (D); Flying Into The Future (D)

Mike Charlton
Stella's Diary, 9 Hormead Road, London
t 020 8891 6382 **t** 020 8969 1855 **f** 020 8964 2157
m 077468 877480 **m** 07836 594622
e stella'sdiary@btinternet.com

Cheeky Monkey Films Ltd
Yarnbury Lodge, Yarnbury, Grassington BD23 5EQ
t 01756 753660 **f** 01756 753660 **m** 07802 478639
e paul@cheekymonkeyfilms.com
w www.cheekymonkeyfilms.com
Contact Katy Metcalfe, DV Camera Operator/Director; Paul Edwards, Lighting
Cameraman
Credits Around The World In 80 Raves (D); Wildlife Police (D); Relocation,
Relocation (D); Location, Location, Location (D)

Andy Clifford
Stella's Diary, 9 Hormead Road, London W9 3NG
t 020 8969 1855 **f** 020 8964 2157 **m** 07968 629648
e stella'sdiary@btinternet.com

Adam Clitheroe
12 Valetta Grove, London E13 OJR
t 020 7538 4699 **f** 020 7538 4699 **m** 07949 792 050
e aclitheroe@hotmail.com
Credits Interbrand Worldwide (I); Speedway (T); The Investigators (T)

Malcom Edmonds
75 Kew Green, Richmond TW9 3AH
t 020 8948 8757 **m** 07974 921030
e mx@pobox.com **w** www.catch25.com
Credits Cruel World (D); India's Hotlist (D); The Men From The Agency (D); From
Merton To Enfield (D)

JF Edwards
1 Littlewood Cottages, School Road, Drayton NR8 6EP
t +44 1603 **f** 01603 860984 **m** 07966 172909
e jf-edwards@hotmail.com

Roger Edwards
Tan-y-Bryn, Fore Street, Holbeton, Plymouth PL8 1NA
t 01752 830 428 **f** 0 7970 112894 **m** 07778 321122
e roger@tanybryn.co.uk
Credits Countryfile (T); Weight Matters (T); Crafted (T); Garden Highs (T)

Eyecon Productions Ltd
20 Micklethwaite Road, London SW6 1QD
t 07788 656267 **f** 020 7381 8887
e eyeconaust@hotmail.com
Contact Scott Barnett, Director Of Photography/Lighting Cameraman
Credits Brain Attack (D); Supermax Prisons-Inside (D); Ocean Rescue (D);
The Astronaut (D)

Nigel Fairburn
Stella's Diary, 9 Hormead Road, London W9 3NG
t 020 8677 1348 **t** 020 8969 1855 **f** 020 8964 2157
m 07970 801210 **m** 07836 594622
e stella'sdiary@btinternet.com

Robert Foster
Acuba House, Lymm Road, Little Bollington, Altrincham WA14 4SY
t 0161 926 9808 **f** 0161 929 9000 **m** 07974 151617
e robert@broadcast-tv.co.uk **w** www.broadcast-tv.co.uk
*Award-winning Cameraman. Creative, experienced and friendly crew.
Northwest based, shooting anywhere — UK or Overseas. All Latest Digital
Formats. Equipment Hire and support crew resources.*

Ian French
5 Hartford Road, Davenham, Northwich CW9 8JA
t 0 1606 45748 **f** 0 1606 45748 **m** 07966 432094
e ian@tvfilmcrew.co.uk **w** www.tvfilmcrew.co.uk
Credits Most Haunted Series I (T); Holiday Airline (T); Pet Rescue (T); Tonight
With Trevor MacDonald (T)

Richard Ganniclifft
Garden Flat, 117 Pembroke Road, Clifton, Bristol BS8 3EU
t 0117 330 9597 **f** 0117 330 9601 **m** 07836 297221
e rganniclifft@hotmail.com

Peter George
The Chantry, Burrows Lane, Gomshall GU5 9QE
t 07000 883456 **f** 01483 203566 **m** 07768 156670
e tvfilm@btinternet.com
Credits Bruce Forsyth On Bruce Forsyth (D); Real Crimes (D); Panorama (T)

Richard Gibb
Flat 1, 234 Acton Lane, London W4 5DL
t 020 8995 1792 **f** 020 8995 1792 **m** 07778 198106
e richard@rgibb.demon.co.uk
Credits Correspondent-Thirsting For War (D); Ape Man (D); Time Team (T)

Global Village Productions
71 Gloucester Road, Barnet EN5 1LZ
t 020 8441 3784 **f** 020 8441 3784 **e** globalvil1@aol.com
Contact Allan Barrett, Director

Andrew J Hartley
50 St Richard's Road, Otley LS21 2AZ
t 01943 464512 **f** 01943 464512 **m** 07831 878075

Steve Haskett
38 Melbourne Avenue, Ealing W13 9BT
t 020 8579 3558 **m** 07970 868116
e stevehaskett100@yahoo.co.uk
Credits Endurance In The Antarctic (D); South Bank Show (D); Arthur - King Of The Britons (D); Son Of God (D)

Graham Hatherley
Grooms Flat, Wolfeton House, Dorchester DT2 9QN
t 01305 259295 **f** 01305 259295 **m** 07775 783156
e graham@hatherley.fsbusiness.co.uk
Credits Living Britain (D); Voyage Of The Nautilus (D); Inside Out - Chalkfigures (D)

Paul Hennessy
11 Alder Road, London SW14 8ER
t 020 8876 6104 **f** 020 8876 6104 **m** 07836 528195

Jeremy Irving
2 Barricane, Woking GU21 1RB
t 01483 856202 **f** 01483 856203 **m** 07973 194810
e mail@jeremyirving.tv **w** www.jeremyirving.tv
Credits The Money Programme (T); 4x4 (D); Vets In Practice (D)

Sean Keane
Stella's Diary, 9 Hormead Road, London W9 3NG
t 020 8969 1855 **t** 01277 231487 **f** 020 8964 2157
m 07836 594622 **m** 07941 575604
e stella'sdiary@btinternet.com

Pat Kingston
Fairview, Toadsmoor Road, Brimscombe, Stroud GL5 2UG
t 01453 886884 **f** 01453 886884 **m** 07976 767 681
e pat@toadsmoortv.co.uk
Credits BBC News (T); Carlton TV News (T)

Charles Kinross
53 Heythorp Street, Heythorp, London SW18 5BS
t 020 8877 1570 **m** 07973 428 510
e charliekinross@fliptopfilms.com
Credits Rodney P 'The Killing' (M); Dispatches (D); Cutting Edge

Martin Lightening
10 Lynwood Grove, Sale, Manchester M33 2AN
t 0161 969 2346 **e** martin@thecameraman.co.uk
Credits Football Stories (D); A Class Act (D); Bitter Inheritance (D); Back to the Floor (D)

Eric Marquis
4H Castlebar Park, Ealing, London W5 1BX
t 020 8566 9531 **f** 020 8566 9532
w www.ukscreen.com/crew/emarquis

Paul Martin
42 Horseshoe Crescent, Hollybrook Park, Bordon GU35 0DP
t 01420 473870 **f** 01420 473870 **m** 07721 523 390
e media.attention@tiscali.co.uk

Chris Morphet
72 Victoria Road, Kilburn, London NW6 6QA
t 020 7624 3479 **f** 020 7625 7035 **m** 07771 537294
e blue-c@dircon.co.uk
Credits Jubilee Day (D); And The Winner Is (D); Missing (D); Near Miss (D)

MS Productions
112 Westcott Crescent, Hanwell, London W7 1PB
t 020 8578 7040 **f** 0870 034 6569 **m** 07973 746562
e mike@msproductions.co.uk **w** www.msproductions.co.uk
Contact Mike Shelton
Credits Abbey Vision (I); London Electricity (I); Record Breakers (T); Omnibus - Gospel Music (D)

Clive North
Minery Cottage, Tor Hole Bottom, Chewton Mendip, Radstock BA3 4LS
t 01761 241538 **m** 07831 879594
e clivenorth@btinternet.com **w** www.ukscreen.com/crew/clivenorth
Credits National Geographic - Rocket Men Of Mission 105 (D); Battle Plan - El Alamein (D)

Mark Oulson-Jenkins
Stella's Diary, 9 Hormead Road, London W9 3NG
t 01628 675669 **t** 020 8969 1855 **f** 020 8964 2157
m 07973 157995 **m** 07836 594622
e stella'sdiary@btinternet.com

George Pellett (Cineflex Productions)
Frogs Hole Barn, Sissinghurst Raod, Biddenden TN27 8EY
t 01580 291845 **f** 01580 291845 **m** 07774 141910
Credits Vauxhall Vectra Launch 2002 (I); Margate Meltdown (D); Doodle Bug Summer (D)

Toby Ralph
London
m 07939 561923 **e** toblo@freeuk.com
Credits Cash In The Attic (D); Fame Academy (T); The Money Programme (T); Pop Idol (T)

Red Earth Productions
36-38 Decima Street, London SE1 4QQ
t 020 7407 4477 **f** 020 7407 4477 **m** 07956 308453
e adam@redearthproductions.com
w www.redearthproductions.com
Contact Adam Docker
10 years experience, music videos, travel, sport, socio-historical doco's, excellent photographic imagery.

Kelvin Richard
103 Tregenna Avenue, South Harrow HA2 8QR
t 020 8864 4394 **m** 07802 463 154
e kelvin.r@tanty.demon.co.uk
Credits Raising Tennis Aces; Michael Watson Story; Legends

Colin Rogal
16 Marksbury Avenue, Richmond TW9 4JF
t 020 8878 6582 **f** 020 8878 6847 **m** 07831 232426
e colin@rogal.org **w** www.rogal.org
Credits Edward & Mary (D); Private Life Of A Masterpiece (D); The Fall of Milosevic (D)

John Samuels
14 Edgebury, Woolavington, Bridgwater TA7 8ES
t 01278 684136 **f** 01278 684136 **m** 07974 354660
e john@johnsamuels.co.uk **w** www.johnsamuels.co.uk
Credits Really Wild Show (T); Point West/Lobby (T); Testament (D); A Little Bit Of Heaven (D)

John Sennett
18 Pyrton Lane, Watlington OX49 5LX
t 01491 612367 **f** 01491 612367 **m** 07973 616180

Mike Shelton
112 Westcott Crescent, London W7 1PB
t 020 8578 7040 **f** 08700 346569 **m** 07973 746562
e mike@msproductions.co.uk **w** www.msproductions.co.uk
Credits Holiday (T); Wild About the Garden (T); Omnibus - Gospel Music (D)

Andy Shillabeer
t 01752 771946 **m** 07767 233286
e acsfilms@aol.com **w** www.acsfilms.com
Credits Africa (D); River Wolves- Giant Otters of Peru (D); The Shape of Life (D)

Alasdair Smith
25 Whitehall Road, Aberdeen AB25 2PP
m 07836 225 192
e info@video-cameraman.com **w** www.video-cameraman.com
Credits Battle of Britain; Grime Files; Beechgrove Garden

Mark Alistair Smith
87 Queens Drive, Mossley Hill, Liverpool L18 2DU
t 0151 733 5892 **m** 07050 117149
e psccameraman@hotmail.com
Credits Manchester Commonwealth Games (T); What's the Story (T); Cutting Edge 'Brian's Story' (T); Frontline NHS (T)

Robin Smith
Flat 2, 51 Fernbank Road, Redland, Bristol BS6 6PX
t 0117 942 7729 **m** 07970 283 720
e robinsmith1000@ukonline.co.uk
Credits Industrial Revelations (D); Clarissa And The Countryman (T); Raptures Of The Deep (D); Batchelor (D)

Charles Stewart
Hill View, Hinders Lane, Huntley GL19 3EZ
t 01452 830500 **m** 07802 967369
e charlescstewart@aol.com
Credits Watching The Detectives (D); Ethopia (D); Town Hall (D)

David Swan
2 Queensdale Place, London W11 4SQ
t 020 7602 4883 **f** 020 7603 2764 **m** 07768 362476
e swan@base.enterprise-plc.com
Credits Curse Of Tutankhamen (D); Secret History - Natural Born Americans (D); Yasser Arafat (D); Natural Wonders Of The World (D)

Phil Taylor
Stella's Diary, 9 Hormead Road, London W9 3NG
t 020 8969 1855 **f** 020 8964 2157 **m** 07976 655990
e stella'sdiary@btinternet.com

Triangle Images
Pond Cottage, The Triangle, Upper Basildon RG8 8LU
t 01491 671392 **f** 01491 671392 **m** 07767 658678
e iansken@aol.com
Contact Ian Kennedy
Credits Gambling (D); Topacco Wars (D)

Video One Ltd
18 Battersea Square, London SW11 3RA
t 07050 696242 **f** 07050 696243 **m** 07785 330616
e claudio@vonplanta.net **w** www.vonplanta.net
Contact Claudio von Planta
Credits A Place In France (D); Karzan's Brothers - Escape from Iraq (D); Saddam's Secret Time-Bomb (D)

Ian Watts
18 Streatham Common South, Rylstone, London SW16 3BU
t 020 8333 6555 **f** 020 8333 6555 **m** 07956 262808
e ianwattcam@aol.com
Credits First Edition (D); Surviving Extremes - Ice (D); Panorama (T); Faking It (D)

Wide-Angle
Swan Mill, 10A Swan Street, West Malling ME19 6LP
t 01732 220500 **f** 01732 220500 **m** 07836 340686
e djb@wildangel.co.uk
Contact David Brazier, Director
Credits Living With Depression (T); Mongolia Today (D); Here Comes The Bogeyman (D); Madam And Company (D)

Cameramen **General Video**

Lincoln Abraham
The Firm Booking Company Ltd, 31 Oval Road, Camden, London NW1 7EA
t 020 7248 9090 **f** 020 7248 9089 **e** kirsty@thefirm.co.uk

Chris Adams
23 Albion Hill, Exmouth EX8 1JS
t 01395 224647 **f** 01395 224647 **m** 07971 253 028
e mcvideo@eclipse.co.uk **w** www.mcvideoproductions.co.uk
Credits Seeking Somerset (T); Carlton West Country News (T)

David Allen
17 York Road, Weybridge KT13 9DY
t 01932 852596 **f** 01932 701352 **m** 07836 355 287
e dwallan@ntlworld.com

Ivor Allison
Connections, The Meadlands, Oakleigh Road, Hatch End, Pinner HA5 4HB
t 020 8420 1444 **f** 020 8428 5836 **m** 07831 305518
e mail@connectionsuk.com **w** www.connectionsuk.com

Alun Hughes Productions
Tan yr Allt, Fachwen, Llanberis LL55 3HD
t 01286 871977 **f** 01286 871977 **w** www.fachwen.org/alhughes
Contact Alun Hughes, Climbing/mountaineering cameraman
Credits Haf Ganol Gaeaf (T); BYD PWS (T)

Bill Ashworth
The Firm Booking Company Ltd, 31 Oval Road, Camden, London NW1 7EA
t 020 7248 9090 **f** 020 7248 9089 **e** kirsty@thefirm.co.uk

Barnes Lion
37 South Worple Way, London SW14 8PB
t 020 8876 6694 **m** 07976 659 333

Mark Barrett
The Firm Booking Company Ltd, 31 Oval Road, Camden, London NW1 7EA
t 020 7248 9090 **f** 0207248 9089 **e** kirsty@thefirm.co.uk

Mark Baynes
Connections, The Meadlands, Oakleigh Road, Hatch End, Pinner HA5 4HB
t 020 8420 1444 **f** 020 8428 5836 **m** 07831 305518
e mail@connectionsuk.com **w** www.connectionsuk.com

John Beck
Connections, The Meadlands, Oakleigh Road, Hatch End, Pinner HA5 4HB
t 020 8420 1444 **f** 020 8428 5836 **m** 07831 305518
e mail@connectionsuk.com **w** www.connectionsuk.com

Blue Fin Television Ltd

34 Fitzwilliam Road, London SW4 0DN
t 020 7622 0870 **f** 020 7720 7875 **m** 07973 502349
e antleake@bluefin-tv.demon.co.uk **w** www.bluefintv.com
Contact Anthony Leake, Head of Cameras; Diane Porter, Bookings
Credits The Fugitives (T); Vandals (D); Escape From Experiment Island (T); The South Bank Show (T)

Stuart Brown

Myrtle Cottage, 76 Hare Lane, Claygate KT10 0QU
t 01372 464357 **m** 07710 110011 **e** stu@stubrown.co.uk

Robert Brownhill

1 Henleaze Gardens, Bristol BS9 4HH
t 01179 620680 **f** 01179 401292 **m** 07831 688788
e singularity@onetel.net.uk
Credits Question Time; PGA European Tour Golf; La Boheme

Charlie Bryan

The Firm Booking Company Ltd, 31 Oval Road, Camden, London NW1 7EA
t 020 7428 9090 **f** 020 7428 9089 **e** kirsty@thefirm.co.uk

Jon Bunch

Experience Counts - Call Me Ltd, 5th Floor, 41-42 Berners Street, London W1P 3AA
t 020 7637 8112 **f** 020 7580 2582

Andrew Calvert

18 Hawthorne Avenue, Eastcote, Ruislip HA4 8SS
t 020 8866 3937 **f** 020 8866 3937 **m** 07973 129 074
e acdop@hotmail.com
Credits Anti Smoking Promotions (C); Honey Punks (M); Unconditional Love (F); Scrapheap Challenge (T)

Tim Capp

73 Wells House Road, London NW10 6ED
t 079 7672 2498 **m** 07976 722 498 **e** capp@tinyonline.co.uk

Jamie Carroll

Grade One TV & Film Personnel, Elstree Studios, Shenley Road, Borehamwood WD6 1JG
t 020 8324 2224 **f** 020 8324 2328
e gradeone.tvpersonnel@virgin.net

Matt Cashman

The Firm Booking Company Ltd, 31 Oval Road, Camden, London NW1 7EA
t 020 7428 9090 **f** 020 7428 9089 **e** kirsty@thefirm.co.uk

Nick Cazaly

Grade One TV & Film Personnel, Elstree Studios, Shenley Road, Borehamwood WD6 1JG
t 020 8324 2224 **f** 020 8324 2328
e gradeone.tvpersonnel@virgin.net

Jim Cox

4 Belfield Road, Epsom KT19 9SY
m 07956 371475
e jim@videovillage.net **w** www.videovillage.net

Crewcut

25 Swallow Road, Larkfield, Aylesford ME20 6LE
t 01732 842746 **f** 01732 875746 **m** 07831 311414
e trevor.hawkins@which.net
Contact Trevor Hawkins, Lighting cameraman
Credits Home Alone (T); Time Team (T)

Mark Cruickshank

The Firm Booking Company Ltd, 31 Oval Road, Camden, London NW1 7EA
t 020 7248 9090 **f** 020 7248 9089 **e** kirsty@thefirm.co.uk

Christopher W Davies

74 Tangmere Drive, Radyr Way, Llandaf, Cardiff CF5 2PQ
t 029 2057 6242 **f** 029 2057 6242 **m** 07774 269563
e daviescw@aol.com **w** http://hometown.aol.com/daviescw
Credits Funeral Of Diana, Princess Of Wales (T); Pobol Y Cwm (T); Rugby (T); Nelson Mandela's 70th Birthday Tribute Concert (T)

Also USA based 'Green Card' holder. Tel/Fax: +1 608 2778237. Mobile: +1 608 308 9738. Experienced in Studios, OB's, PSC, ENG/EFP.

Ian Dicker

3 Duckamere, Bramford, Ipswich IP8 4AH
t 01473 749774 **f** 08701 362186 **m** 07879 812 691
e iandicker@beeb.net

Graham Dougall

Connections, The Meadlands, Oakleigh Road, Hatch End, Pinner HA5 4HB
t 020 8420 1444 **f** 020 8428 5836 **m** 07831 305518
e mail@connectionsuk.com **w** www.connectionsuk.com

Phil Dow

Flat 3, 45 Reighton Road, London E5 8SQ
t 020 8806 3530 **m** 07966 443904 **e** porcee@hotmail.com

Martin Doyle

Connections, The Meadlands, Oakleigh Road, Hatch End, Pinner HA5 4HB
t 020 8420 1444 **f** 020 8428 5836 **m** 07831 305518
e mail@connectionsuk.com **w** www.connectionsuk.com

Vince Doyle

Grade One TV & Film Personnel, Elstree Studios, Shenley Road, Borehamwood WD6 1JG
t 020 8324 2224 **f** 020 8324 2328
e gradeone.tvpersonnel@virgin.net

Mike Dugdale

The Firm Booking Company Ltd, 31 Oval Road, Camden, London NW1 7EA
t 020 7248 9090 **f** 020 7248 9089 **e** kirsty@thefirm.co.uk

David Erswell

m 07990 972334 **e** d.oaf@usa.net

Dave Evans

The Firm Booking Company Ltd, 31 Oval Road, Camden, London NW1 7EA
t 020 7248 9090 **f** 020 7248 9089 **e** kirsty@thefirm.co.uk

David Fader

The Firm Booking Company Ltd, 31 Oval Road, Camden, London NW1 7EA
t 020 7248 9090 **f** 020 7248 9089 **e** kirsty@thefirm.co.uk

Sue Farrants

t 01531 890712

Jonathan Flanagan

24 Cavendish House, Chertsey Road, Twickenham TW1 1JD
t 020 8891 0674 **f** 020 8607 9073 **m** 07879 816 293
e flanagan.eng@btinternet.com

Matt Ford

Connections, The Meadlands, Oakleigh Road, Hatch End, Pinner HA5 4HB
t 020 8420 1444 **f** 020 8428 5836 **m** 07831 305518
e mail@connectionsuk.com **w** www.connectionsuk.com

Allan T Forsyth

8 The Watermill, Bracondale Millgate, Norwich NR1 2EB
t 01603 760802 **f** 01603 760802 **m** 07799 033465
Credits FIFA World Cup 2002 (C)

Robert Foster

Acuba House, Lymm Road, Little Bollington, Altrincham WA14 4SY
t 0161 926 9808 **f** 0161 929 9000 **m** 07974 151617
e robert@broadcast-tv.co.uk **w** www.broadcast-tv.co.uk

James French

3 Alexander Avenue, Droitwich Spa WR9 8NH
t 01905 796910 **f** 07977 002042 **m** 07855 743845
e jkfrench@mac.com
Credits Channel 4 Horse Racing (T); Brum (T); Commonwealth Games (T); EastEnders (T)

Mervyn Gagen

Connections, The Meadlands, Oakleigh Road, Hatch End, Pinner HA5 4HB
t 020 8420 1444 **f** 020 8428 5836 **m** 07831 305518
e mail@connectionsuk.com **w** www.connectionsuk.com

Lisha Gilbert

The Firm Booking Company Ltd, 31 Oval Road, Camden, London NW1 7EA
t 020 7428 9090 **f** 020 7428 9089 **e** kirsty@thefirm.co.uk

Paul Granville

Shadow Hall, The Green, Ubbeston, Halesworth IP19 0HA
t 01986 798489 **m** 07850 319861
e yhx62@dial.pipex.com **w** www.nozey.tv
Credits Football (T); Robbie Fulks Live (M); The Borderline (I); Salma's Day (S)

Alan Haddow

The Firm Booking Company Ltd, 31 Oval Road, Camden, London NW1 7EA
t 020 7248 9090 **f** 020 7248 9089 **e** kirsty@thefirm.co.uk

Jonathon Henderson

The Firm Booking Company Ltd, 31 Oval Road, Camden, London NW1 7EA
t 020 7248 9090 **f** 020 7248 9089 **e** kirsty@thefirm.co.uk

David Hicks

Connections, The Meadlands, Oakleigh Road, Hatch End, Pinner HA5 4HB
t 020 8420 1444 **f** 020 8428 5836 **m** 07831 305518
e mail@connectionsuk.com **w** www.connectionsuk.com

Tim Highmoor

The Firm Booking Company Ltd, 31 Oval Road, Camden, London NW1 7EA
t 020 7428 9090 **f** 020 7428 9089 **e** kirsty@thefirm.co.uk

Nat Hill

The Firm Booking Company Ltd, 31 Oval Road, Camden, London NW1 7EA
t 020 7248 9090 **f** 020 7248 9089 **e** kirsty@thefirm.co.uk

Adrian Homeshaw

The Firm Booking Company Ltd, 31 Oval Road, Camden, London NW1 7EA
t 020 7248 9090 **f** 020 7248 9089 **e** kirsty@thefirm.co.uk

Matt Ingham

The Firm Booking Company Ltd, 31 Oval Road, Camden, London NW1 7EA
t 020 7248 9090 **f** 020 7248 9089 **e** kirsty@thefirm.co.uk

Paul Jarvis

The Firm Booking Company Ltd, 31 Oval Road, Camden, London NW1 7EA
t 020 7248 9090 **f** 020 7248 9089 **e** kirsty@thefirm.co.uk

Flemming Jetmar

Connections, The Meadlands, Oakleigh Road, Hatch End, Pinner HA5 4HB
t 020 8420 1444 **f** 020 8428 5836 **m** 07831 305518
e mail@connectionsuk.com **w** www.connectionsuk.com

John Nettleship Video

Mooredge Cottage, Leeds Road, Pool in Wharfedale, Otley LS21 3BR
t 0113 284 3515 **f** 0113 284 3515 **m** 07850 293 180
e nettleship@jnv-tv.co.uk **w** www.jnv-tv.co.uk
Contact J Nettleship, Freelance Cameraman
Credits OB: British/World Superbikes (T); Pet Rescue (T); Cook Report (T)

Tony Keene

The Firm Booking Company Ltd, 31 Oval Road, Camden, London NW1 7EA
t 020 7428 9090 **f** 020 7428 9089 **e** kirsty@thefirm.co.uk

Shelley Kingston

The Firm Booking Company Ltd, 31 Oval Road, Camden, London NW1 7EA
t 020 7428 9090 **f** 020 7428 9089 **e** kirsty@thefirm.co.uk

Marek Kowalek

Connections, The Meadlands, Oakleigh Road, Hatch End, Pinner HA5 4HB
t 020 8420 1444 **f** 020 8428 5836 **m** 07831 305518
e mail@connectionsuk.com **w** www.connectionsuk.com

Steve Leach

Malthill Cottage, 25 Hillside Street, Hythe CT21 5EJ
t 01303 237227 **f** 01303 237228 **m** 07860 665355
e steve@steveleach.co.uk
Agent Grade One TV & Film Personnel, Elstree Studios, Shenley Road, Borehamwood WD6 1JG
t 020 8324 2224 **f** 020 8324 2328
e gradeone.tvpersonnel@virgin.net

Leonard Lee

Trevianni Cottage, Jamaica Place, Gosport PO12 1LS
t 023 9235 6769 **m** 07710 152636
e leonard@betacamsp.co.uk **e** leonard@hollywoodmagic.co.uk
w www.betaccmsp.co.uk
Credits Proctor And Gamble: Lacoste Launch (I); Oracle: The Power To Empower Yourself (I); Juggling Work And Care (I); Nikon UK: Training For Life (I)

Littleshed TV

58 Rothsmans Avenue, Great Baddow, Chelmsford CM2 9UF
t 01245 476798 **e** peter@littleshed.co.uk **w** www.littleshed.co.uk
Contact Peter Rawlings

Joss Lowe

Experience Counts - Call Me Ltd, 5th Floor, 41-42 Berners Street, London W1P 3AA
t 020 7637 8112 **f** 020 7580 2582

Brian Marden-Jones

Connections, The Meadlands, Oakleigh Road, Hatch End, Pinner HA5 4HB
t 020 8420 1444 **f** 020 8428 5836 **m** 07831 305518
e mail@connectionsuk.com **w** www.connectionsuk.com

Rob Marsh

43 Chevin Avenue, Leicester LE3 6PX
t 0116 287 0489 **f** 0116 299 6304 **m** 07774 735538
e r_marsh@btinternet.com
Credits Boots Chemists - Christmas Campaign Video (I); BBC Good Food Show - Celebrity Theatre (T); Virgin Trains - Regional Operator's Video (I)

Jeremy Mason

The Firm Booking Company Ltd, 31 Oval Road, Camden, London NW1 7EA
t 020 7248 9090 **f** 020 7248 9089 **e** kirsty@thefirm.co.uk

Bahram Manocheri

22A Dealtry Road, London SW15 6NL
t 020 8785 9240 **f** 020 8785 9240 **m** 07762 079696
Credits Boxed (F)

Neil McLintock

The Firm Booking Company Ltd, 31 Oval Road, Camden, London NW1 7EA
t 020 7248 9090 **f** 020 7248 9089 **e** kirsty@thefirm.co.uk

Patti Musicaro

Experience Counts - Call Me Ltd, 5th Floor, 41-42 Berners Street, London W1P 3AA
t 020 7637 8112 **f** 020 7580 2582

Tim Normington
The Firm Booking Company Ltd, 31 Oval Road, Camden,
London NW1 7EA
t 020 7428 9090 f 020 7428 9089 e kirsty@thefirm.co.uk

Saria Ofogba
Connections, The Meadlands, Oakleigh Road, Hatch End,
Pinner HA5 4HB
t 020 8420 1444 f 020 8428 5836 m 07831 305518
e mail@connectionsuk.com w www.connectionsuk.com

David Owen
AP Digital, The Works Business Centre Ltd, 5 Union St,
Ardwick, Manchester M12 4JD
t 0161 613 1988 f 0161 747 8235
e dave@apdigital.co.uk w www.apdigital.co.uk
Credits Match Of The Day (T); Rugby Special

Phil Palmer
The Firm Booking Company Ltd, 31 Oval Road, Camden,
London NW1 7EA
t 020 7248 9090 f 020 7248 9089 e kirsty@thefirm.co.uk

Terry Pearce
19 Queen Anne's Close, Twickenham TW2 5NN
t 020 8977 7400 m 07831 634863 e tp.wigwam@talk21.com

Neil Peggs
136 Newton Street, Macclesfield SK11 6RN
t 01625 422410 m 07836 368698 e peggsy@totalise.co.uk
Credits BBC, ITV, Channel 4, Sky (T)

Derek Pennell
The Firm Booking Company Ltd, 31 Oval Road, Camden,
London NW1 7EA
t 020 7248 9090 f 020 7248 9089 e kirsty@thefirm.co.uk

Perfect Pictures TV (PPTV)
The Stables, 31 Colonnade, London WC1N 1JA
t 020 7841 0290 f 020 7713 6320 m 07766 093469
e mail@perfectpictures.tv w www.perfectpictures.tv
Contact Tim Andrew Wilmott, Operations Manager

Nicholas Phelpsl
Connections, The Meadlands, Oakleigh Road, Hatch End,
Pinner HA5 4HB
t 020 8420 1444 f 020 8428 5836 m 07831 305518
e mail@connectionsuk.com w www.connectionsuk.com

Phil Piotrowsky
The Firm Booking Company Ltd, 31 Oval Road, Camden,
London NW1 7EA
t 020 7248 9090 f 020 7248 9089 e kirsty@thefirm.co.uk

Ken Platten
Connections, The Meadlands, Oakleigh Road, Hatch End,
Pinner HA5 4HB
t 020 8420 1444 f 020 8428 5836 m 07831 305518
e mail@connectionsuk.com w www.connectionsuk.com

Martyn Porter
The Firm Booking Company Ltd, 31 Oval Road, Camden,
London NW1 7EA
t 020 7248 9090 f 020 7248 9089 e kirsty@thefirm.co.uk

Peter W Powell
Highbank, 26 Chapel Street, Petersfield GU32 3DZ
t 01730 264868 m 07791 445939 e peterpowell@beeb.net
Credits BBC TV News (T); Kurdestan - Newsnight (T); Iran TV Eye -The Ayotollah
Returns (T); Fisheries Of Zambia - Progress And Prosperity (D)
*Multiskilled Video Producer, Director, Cameraman. 42 Years - 58
Countries - Anywhere.*

Proximity Manchester
St Medans, 33 Gibwood Road, Northenden, Manchester M22 4BR
t 0161 998 3402 m 07929 248323 e benny@van-den-burg.co.uk
w www.stuartpeters.co.uk/bindex.htm
Contact Benny Van Den Burg, Managing Director

James Ramsay
The Firm Booking Company Ltd, 31 Oval Road, Camden,
London NW1 7EA
t 020 7248 9090 f 020 7248 9089 e kirsty@thefirm.co.uk

Graham Reed
Connections, The Meadlands, Oakleigh Road, Hatch End,
Pinner HA5 4HB
t 020 8420 1444 f 020 8428 5836 m 07831 305518
e mail@connectionsuk.com w www.connectionsuk.com

Hayley Reid
The Firm Booking Company Ltd, 31 Oval Road, Camden,
London NW1 7EA
t 020 7428 9090 f 020 7428 9089 e kirsty@thefirm.co.uk

Andy Reik
10 Malcom House, 405 Kilburn High Road, London NW6 7QF
t 020 7328 5107 f 07970 058161 e andyreik@aol.com

Richard Faulkner
Holly Bank, Hollington, Ashbourne DE6 3GA
t 01335 360531 f 01335 360531 m 07973 616343

Rick Child Film & TV
Ebenezar Cottage, Mill End, Damerham, Nr Fordingridge SP6 3HU
t 01725 518598 f 01725 518598 m 07802 270055
e rajchild@supanet.com

Arthur Ross
The Firm Booking Company Ltd, 31 Oval Road, Camden,
London NW1 7EA
t 020 7428 9090 f 020 7428 9089 e kirsty@thefirm.co.uk

Keith Salmon
11 Rickard Close, Knowle, Solihull B93 9RD
t 01564 776747 m 07989 202 756 e k.salmon@tesco.net
Credits Boboh (T); Boys From The Blackstuff (T); Waking The Dead (F)

Rob Sargent
The Firm Booking Company Ltd, 31 Oval Road, Camden,
London NW1 7EA
t 020 7248 9090 f 020 7248 9089 e kirsty@thefirm.co.uk

Martin Schlote
The Firm Booking Company Ltd, 31 Oval Road, Camden,
London NW1 7EA
t 020 7248 9090 f 020 7248 9089 e kirsty@thefirm.co.uk

David Scott
Bracken Hill House, Hillside, Holloway, Matlock DE4 5AX
t 01629 534512 f 01629 534512 m 07831 632 669
e daves@onetel.net.uk

Adam Sculthorp
73 Midhurst Road, Liphook GU30 7UP
m 07966 483736 e scullyshoots@hotmail.com
Credits Sky Sports Rugby Union (T); FIA World Rally (T); Top Of The Pops Plus
(T); The Hoobs (T)

Andy Shaw
Grade One TV & Film Personnel, Elstree Studios, Shenley
Road, Borehamwood WD6 1JG
t 020 8324 2224 f 020 8324 2328
e gradeone.tvpersonnel@virgin.net

Prav Shetty
The Firm Booking Company Ltd, 31 Oval Road, Camden,
London NW1 7EA
t 020 7248 9090 f 020 7248 9089 e kirsty@thefirm.co.uk

Shoot First
15 Wilbury Grove, Hove BN3 3JQ
t 01273 772990 **f** 01273 774990 **m** 07860 863302
e nic@shootfirst.co.uk **w** www.shootfirst.co.uk
Contact Nic Small, Cameraman

James Simpson
Holly House, Bridgewater Road, Weybridge KT13 0EE
m 07956 994910

James Sloss
High Pines, The Avenue, Fleet GU51 4DC
t 01252 628159 **f** 01252 811809 **m** 07970 694 673
e jsloss@eurobell.co.uk

David Smith
Grade One TV & Film Personnel, Elstree Studios, Shenley
Road, Borehamwood WD6 1JG
t 020 8324 2224 **f** 020 8324 2328
e gradeone.tvpersonnel@virgin.net

Ian R Stanyon
35 Newton Road, New Denham, Uxbridge UB9 4BE
t 01895 859019 **f** 01895 851254 **m** 07767 324275
e ianstan@blueyonder.co.uk

T Pearce
19 Queen Anne's Close, Twickenham TW2 5NN
t 020 8977 7400 **m** 07831 634863 **e** tp-wigwam@talk21.com

Phil Taylor
Flat 38, Elphinstone Court, Barrow Road, London SW16 5NG
t 020 8769 4729 **m** 07976 655990 **e** philtails@yahoo.com
Credits Black And Decker (T); Women Talk Sex (T); Bremner, Bird And Fortune
(T); Would Like To Meet ... (T)

Ross Thomas
Grade One TV & Film Personnel, Elstree Studios, Shenley
Road, Borehamwood WD6 1JG
t 020 8324 2224 **f** 020 8324 2328
e gradeone.tvpersonnel@virgin.net

Verve Video Productions
3 Compton Lodge, Green Lanes, Winchmore Hill, London N21 3RU
t 020 8360 2153 **m** 07887 722728 **e** info@vervevideo.co.uk
Contact John Bennett, Proprietor

Video Services UK
105 Station Road, Sutton-In-Ashfield NG17 5GB
t 01623 557284
e andrew.halfpenny@ntlworld.com **w** www.videoservicesuk.org.uk
Contact Andrew Halfpenny, Partner; Don Halfpenny, Partner; Janet Halfpenny,
Partner

Christopher Ware
65 Trinity Street, Barry CF62 7EX
t 01446 732816 **m** 07802 865999 **e** crware@ntlworld.com
Credits Y Byd Ar Bedwar (T); Wales This Week (T)

Jonathan Watts
Gems, The Media House, 87 Glebe Street, Penarth CF64 1EF
t 029 2071 0770 **f** 029 2071 0771 **e** gems@gems-agency.co.uk
w www.gems-agency.co.uk

Kevin White
Grade One TV & Film Personnel, Elstree Studios, Shenley
Road, Borehamwood WD6 1JG
t 020 8324 2224 **f** 020 8324 2328
e gradeone.tvpersonnel@virgin.net

Yonder Films
Yonder Thatch, Easton Cross, Chagford TQ13 8DG
m 07796 331760 **e** talldunk@fsmail.net
Contact Duncan Coventry, Cameraman
Credits Flog It! (T); See Hear (T); BT (C); WestCountry Tales (T)

Cameramen **Lighting**

Bill Abbott
20 Cross Meadow, Chesham HP5 2RU
t 01494 784883 **m** 07860 300525
Agent Linkline, 6 Thirlmere Gardens, Wembley HA9 8RE
t 020 8908 6262 **f** 020 8904 5179
e mail@linklinecrew.com **w** www.linklinecrew.com

John Adderley
46 Wilton Crescent, London SW19 3QS
t 020 8542 4847 **f** 020 8241 8729 **m** 07973 730 042
e john@adderley.net **w** http://www.adderley.net/

Ali Asad
Carlin Crew Ltd, Shepperton Studios, Studios Road,
Shepperton TW17 0QD
t 01932 568268 **f** 01932 571109
e carlin@netcomuk.co.uk **w** www.carlincrew.com

Tom Astbury
8 Holding, Lower Auchinlay, Dunblane FK15 9NA
t 01786 825441 **f** 01786 825441 **m** 07802 816753
e mail@auchinlay.freeserve.co.uk

Luke Atkinson
124 Richmond Park Road, Kingston-upon-Thames KT2 6AT
t 07710 409470
Credits Dream Team (T); Mile High (T); Ant And Dec's Saturday Night Takeaway
(T); Popstars (T)

Dan Balcam
134 Cromer Road, Norwich NR6 6XN
t 01603 466335 **f** 01603 466335 **m** 07941 698754
e dan@dreamweavers.freeserve.co.uk
w www.geocities.com/dan_dreamweavers

Ian Barnes
St Mabyn, Bodmin PL30 3BJ
t 01208 841402 **m** 07836 228937
e ian@ianbarnes.co.uk **w** www.ianbarnes.co.uk
Credits Tomorrow Never Dies (F); Country File (T); Small Town's Gardens (T)

Michael Barnes
3 Birklands Park, London Road, St Albans AL1 1TS
t 01727 848395 **m** 07860 544417 **e** michael@immages.co.uk
Credits Anna Anne - Ride Ride Ride (M); Prudential (I); Hyatt Hotels
International (I)

Nick Barnett
Linkline, 6 Thirlmere Gardens, Wembley HA9 8RE
t 020 8908 6262 **f** 020 8904 5179
e mail@linklinecrew.com **w** www.linklinecrew.com

Nick Barnett
47 Rodenhurst Road, London SW4 8AE
t 020 8877 9789 **m** 07836 541934

Alan Barrett
Grade One TV & Film Personnel, Elstree Studios, Shenley
Road, Borehamwood WD6 1JG
t 020 8324 2224 **f** 020 8324 2328
e gradeone.tvpersonnel@virgin.net

Alan Beal
Grade One TV & Film Personnel, Elstree Studios, Shenley
Road, Borehamwood WD6 1JG
t 020 8324 2224 **f** 020 8324 2328
e gradeone.tvpersonnel@virgin.net

Karl Beattie
Grade One TV & Film Personnel, Elstree Studios, Shenley
Road, Borehamwood WD6 1JG
t 020 8324 2224 **f** 020 8324 2328
e gradeone.tvpersonnel@virgin.net

Andrew J Begg
1F3, 15 Lochrin Terrace, Edinburgh EH3 9QL
m 07977 005280 **e** andrew@vydor.com **w** www.vydor.com

Rob Bennett
Grade One TV & Film Personnel, Elstree Studios, Shenley Road, Borehamwood WD6 1JG
t 020 8324 2224 **f** 020 8324 2328
e gradeone.tvpersonnel@virgin.net

Kevin Bettle
72 Tennyson Road, London NW6 7SB
m 07958 695363 **e** kevinbettle@btinternet.com

Philipp Blaubach
Callbox Communications Limited, Box 66 Shepperton Studios, Shepperton TW17 0QD
t 01932 572572 **f** 01932 569655 **e** callboxdiary@btinternet.com

Blue Fin Television Ltd
34 Fitzwilliam Road, London SW4 0DN
t 020 7622 0870 **f** 020 7720 7875 **m** 07973 502349
e antleake@bluefin-tv.demon.co.uk **w** www.bluefintv.com
Contact Anthony Leake, Head of Cameras; Diane Porter, Bookings
Credits The Fugitives (T); Vandals (D); Escape From Experiment Island (T); The South Bank Show (T)

Blue Marlin Pictures
7 Thorndyke Court, Pinner HA5 4JG
t 020 8428 2007 **f** 020 8428 2007 **m** 07831 211706
Contact Ken Garraway, Cameraman/Lighting Operator

Mark Bond
Stella's Diary, 9 Hormead Road, London W9 3NG
t 020 8374 3132 **t** 020 8969 1855 **f** 020 8964 2157
m 07973 325392 **m** 07836 594622
e stella'sdiary@btinternet.com
Credits Hot Wax (T); Pilgrimage (D); Gods In The Sky (D); Equinox, Orgasmatron (D)

Nick Bond
Grade One TV & Film Personnel, Elstree Studios, Shenley Road, Borehamwood WD6 1JG
t 020 8324 2224 **f** 020 8324 2328
e gradeone.tvpersonnel@virgin.net

Jon Bowden
Grade One TV & Film Personnel, Elstree Studios, Shenley Road, Borehamwood WD6 1JG
t 020 8324 2224 **f** 020 8324 2328
e gradeone.tvpersonnel@virgin.net

Steve Bowers
Experience Counts - Call Me Ltd, 5th Floor, 41-42 Berners Street, London W1P 3AA
t 020 7637 8112 **f** 020 7580 2582

Keith Bradshaw
Grade One TV & Film Personnel, Elstree Studios, Shenley Road, Borehamwood WD6 1JG
t 020 8324 2224 **f** 020 8324 2328
e gradeone.tvpersonnel@virgin.net

Stephen J Brand GBCT, BECTU
20 Teal Close, Bradley Stoke, Bristol BS32 0EL
m 07976 731725
Credits Space Invaders (S); Making - It (T); Alien Nation (D); Everything Must Go (T)

Stephen Brind
t 01444 454945 **m** 07973 506 068 **e** sbrind@orange.net
Credits Rosie & Jim (T)

Phil Britton
3949 Veselich Avenue, Los Angeles 90039, USA
t 913 1130 **f** 913 1130
e phil@philbritton.com **w** www.philbritton.com
Credits Pilot Season (D); Junkyard Wars (T); The Really Wild Show (T)

Max Browne
217 North Hill, Highgate, London N6 4EH
t 020 8340 3036 **m** 07966 436973

Max Browne
Linkline, 6 Thirlmere Gardens, Wembley HA9 8RE
t 020 8908 6262 **f** 020 8904 5179
e mail@linklinecrew.com **w** www.linklinecrew.com

Bruce Heideman Enterprises
185 Old Birmingham Road, Marlbrook, Bromsgrove B60 1DQ
t 0121 445 2741 **f** 0121 445 2741 **m** 07813 218589
e bhemedia@hotmail.com **w** www.bhemedia.co.uk
Contact Bruce Heideman, Managing Director
Credits 5th World Productions (I)

Tom Bryan
38A Coleraine Road, Blackheath, London SE3 7PE
t 020 8378 7086 **e** thomasgbryan@hotmail.com
Credits Agony (T); London Today/London Tonight (T); Health & Spirituality Series (T)

Paul Caddis
Stonefish Films, 22 Normanby Road, London NW10 1BX
f 020 8452 4487 **m** 07710 385183 **e** stonefish.films@virgin.net

Michael Caine
1 Launcelot Court, Duston, Northampton NN5 6LA
t 01604 591330 **t** 0700 062 2633
Agent Linkline, 6 Thirlmere Gardens, Wembley HA9 8RE
t 020 8908 6262 **f** 020 8904 5179 **e** mail@linklinecrew.com
w www.linklinecrew.com

Andy Calvert
18 Hawthorne Avenue, Eastcote, Ruislip HA4 8SS
t 020 8866 3937 **m** 07973 129074
Agent Linkline, 6 Thirlmere Gardens, Wembley HA9 8RE
t 020 8908 6262 **f** 020 8904 5179 **e** mail@linklinecrew.com
w www.linklinecrew.com

Douglas Campbell
Finglen House, Campsie Glen, Glasgow G66 7AZ
t 01360 310279 **f** 01360 310279 **m** 07831 235191
e douglas6@supernet.com
Credits Sorley McLean (D); Raploch Stories (T); Ferry Up The Amazon (D)

Nic Cartwright
43 Whitelaw Road, Chorlton, Manchester M21 9HG
t 0161 881 8836 **f** 0161 881 8836 **m** 07778 046378
e niccars@ntlworld.com,
Credits Watchdog (T); Panorama (T); Gardener's World (D); This Is Your Life (T)

David Chilton
3 Oakden Street, Kennington, London SE11 4UQ
t 020 7582 4067 **e** dchiltern@netcomuk.co.uk

Richard Clutterbuck
29 Ashville Road, Bristol BS3 2AP
t 07074 781917 **f** 0117 904 0507 **m** 07778 599084

Terrance Cole
49 Oakwood Avenue, Borehamwood WD6 1SS
t 020 8953 7444 **f** 020 8207 1432

Chris Coles
Grade One TV & Film Personnel, Elstree Studios, Shenley Road, Borehamwood WD6 1JG
t 020 8324 2224 **f** 020 8324 2328
e gradeone.tvpersonnel@virgin.net

Mike Coles
13 Lincoln Road, East Finchley, London N2 9DJ
t 020 8444 7909 **f** 020 8365 3062 **m** 07968 158379
e mikecoles@dial.pipex.com
Credits The Ultimate Guide To Pyramids (D); The Day The World Took Off (D); The Elegant Universe (D); The Curse Of The Methusala Tree (D)

Communique Productions

Cranbourne House, Mill Road, Little Melton, Northwich NR9 3NT
t 01603 812747 **f** 01603 811954 **m** 07885 841 913
e philip@communique.uk.com
w www.communiqueproductions.freeserve.co.uk
Contact Philip Burne
Credits Hero to Zero (T); Brookside (T); Heartbeat (T)

James Daniels

Tumblewood, Radyr Court Road, Cardiff CF5 2QF
t 029 2055 2414 **f** 029 2055 2414 **m** 07831 337694
e dragonfly258@hotmail.com
Credits Diversity (I); Bloody Towers (D); Real Rooms (T); Horizon (D)

Jamie Daniels

Tumblewood, Radyr Court Road, Llandaff, Cardiff CF5 2QF
t 029 2055 2414 **f** 029 2055 2414 **m** 07831 337 694
e dragonfly258@hotmail.com
Credits You're The Boss; Dispatches; Bloody Towers (D)

Dave Davies

4 The Litten, Kingsclere, Newbury RG20 5NH
t 01635 299244 **f** 01635 299244 **m** 07831 809346

Allen Della-Valle

Callbox Communications Ltd, PO Box 66, Shepperton Studios, Shepperton Lane, Shepperton TW17 0QD
t 01932 592572 **f** 01932 569655 **m** 07710 572572
e callboxdiary@btinternet.com **w** www.callboxdiary.co.uk

Peter Ditch

Flat 5, 2 Brunswick Square, Hove BN3 1EG
t 01273 777122 **m** 07957 871759
Agent Linkline, 6 Thirlmere Gardens, Wembley HA9 8RE
t 020 8908 6262 **f** 020 8904 5179
e mail@linklinecrew.com **w** www.linklinecrew.com

Anne Dodsworth

m 07768 682536
e anne@lightingcamera.com **w** www.lightingcamera.com
Credits The Bill (T); The Ring (S); Temptation Island (T); Timewatch (D)

Brian Drysdale

6 Richhill Park, Belfast BT5 6HG
t 028 9065 3223 **f** 028 9065 3223 **m** 07860 477728
e 113133.1601@compuserve.com
Contact Brian Drysdale, Cameraman
Credits The Terms (S); Road To Dumcree (D); Rebel Hearts (T); Castle Court (C)

Nigel Dupont

19 Salford Road, London SW2 4BJ
t 020 8674 1221 **m** 07973 136715
Agent Linkline, 6 Thirlmere Gardens, Wembley HA9 8RE
t 020 8908 6262 **f** 020 8904 5179
e mail@linklinecrew.com **w** www.linklinecrew.com

Philip Eastabrook

Botany House, Wheeler End, High Wycombe HP14 3ND
t 01494 883039 **f** 01494 881923 **m** 07770 482652
e phil@quadrillion.tv
Credits This Is The Met Office (I); De Beers Industrial Diamonds (Element 6) (I); The Nanny State (T); Justice (T)

15 years of lighting camera experience. Resourceful, multi-skilled, own kit (if required). Beta/DVCAM including Laptop Editor and Espace.

Damien Eggs

9 Oakdene Road, Brocham RH3 7JU
t 01737 841675 **m** 07785 276674
Agent Linkline, 6 Thirlmere Gardens, Wembley HA9 8RE
t 020 8908 6262 **f** 020 8904 5179
e mail@linklinecrew.com **w** www.linklinecrew.com

Kit Elliott

77 Firtree Lane, Bristol BS5 8BJ
t 0117 935 2592 **f** 07971 131580 **m** 07710 406615
e kit@kelliott.demon.co.uk

Eric Samuel Productions - ESP

38 West Avenue, Pinner, London HA5 5BY
t 020 8868 8653 **f** 020 8868 8670 **m** 07860 636527
e believeinesp@btinternet.com
Believe in 'ESP' - a versatile asset to any production.

Derek Firmin

32 Ridge Avenue, Harpenden AL5 3LT
t 01582 713734 **m** 07711 672 862
e delboy@firmin57.freeserve.co.uk
Credits Hollywood Science; Rough Science; Romans in Britain

Ben Foster

Stella's Diary, 9 Hormead Road, London W9 3NG
t 020 8969 1855 **t** 020 8674 7611 **f** 020 8964 2157
m 07973 199006 **e** owen.scurfield@hotmail.com
e stella'sdiary@btinternet.com

Robert Foster

Acuba House, Lymm Road, Little Bollington, Altrincham WA14 4SY
t 0161 926 9808 **f** 0161 929 9000 **m** 07974 151617
e robert@broadcast-tv.co.uk **w** www.broadcast-tv.co.uk
Award-winning Cameraman. Creative, experienced and friendly crew. Northwest based, shooting anywhere — UK or Overseas. All Latest Digital Formats. Equipment Hire and support crew resources.

Colin Fox

4 Marksbury Avenue, Richmond TW9 4JF
t 020 8876 7853 **m** 07860 341088
Agent Linkline, 6 Thirlmere Gardens, Wembley HA9 8RE
t 020 8908 6262 **f** 020 8904 5179
e mail@linklinecrew.com **w** www.linklinecrew.com

Conall Freeley

The Cottage, Franche Court Road, Earlsfield, London SW17 1LB
t 020 8946 3268 **f** 020 8947 6073 **m** 07831 442714
Contact Conall Freeley
Credits River Cottage Forever (T); Femtochemistry (T); Murder in Paradise (T)

Paul Freeman

Grade One TV & Film Personnel, Elstree Studios, Shenley Road, Borehamwood WD6 1JG
t 020 8324 2224 **f** 020 8324 2328
e gradeone.tvpersonnel@virgin.net

Tony Freeman

Grade One TV & Film Personnel, Elstree Studios, Shenley Road, Borehamwood WD6 1JG
t 020 8324 2224 **f** 020 8324 2328
e gradeone.tvpersonnel@virgin.net

Kevin French

The Firm Booking Company Ltd, 31 Oval Road, Camden, London NW1 7EA
t 020 7428 9090 **f** 020 7428 9089 **e** kirsty@thefirm.co.uk

Front Element Camera Services

2 Barricane, Woking GU21 7RB
t 01483 856202 **f** 01483 856203 **m** 07973 194810
e mail@jeremyirving.tv **w** www.jeremyirving.tv
Credits Pulling Power (D); 4x4 (D); Money Program (D); Vets In Practice (D)

Matthew Gammage

52 Churchfields Drive, Bovey Tracey TQ13 9QU
t 01626 835805 **m** 07374 235921
Agent Linkline, 6 Thirlmere Gardens, Wembley HA9 8RE
t 020 8908 6262 **f** 020 8904 5179
e mail@linklinecrew.com **w** www.linklinecrew.com

Richard Gammons

17 Pages Hill, London N10 1PX
t 020 8444 0435 **f** 020 8374 2961 **m** 07770 852280
e rg7@blueyonder.co.uk
Credits Camp X-Ray (D); James Bond - The Making Of A Movie (D); We Are The Treasury (D)

Rickie Gauld
Bushcombe Lane, Cleeve Hill, Chotenham GL52 3PN
t 01242 676003 **m** 07860 598323
Credits Live Telly From The Stock Exchange (T); Discovery - Tornadoes (T); Reuegers Comedies (T)

Mike George
Callbox Communications Ltd, PO Box 66, Shepperton Studios, Shepperton Lane, Shepperton TW17 0DQ
t 01932 592572 **f** 01932 569655 **m** 07710 572572
e callboxdiary@btinternet.com **w** www.callboxdiary.com

Martyn Gibson
Little Mount, Riding Lane, Hildenborough TN11 9LR
t 01732 832382 **m** 07831 553063
Agent Linkline, 6 Thirlmere Gardens, Wembley HA9 8RE
t 020 8908 6262 **f** 020 8904 5179
e mail@linklinecrew.com **w** www.linklinecrew.com

Global Village Productions
71 Gloucester Road, Barnet EN5 1LZ
t 020 8441 3784 **f** 020 8441 3784 **e** globalvil1@aol.com
Contact Allan Barrett, Director

John Goodyer
7 Grosvenor Gardens, Sheen, London SW14 8BY
t 020 8876 1854 **f** 020 8876 1854 **m** 07973 733421
e johngoodyer@beeb.net **w** http://johngoodyer.members.beeb.net

Adam Gordon
Grade One TV & Film Personnel, Elstree Studios, Shenley Road, Borehamwood WD6 1JG
t 020 8324 2224 **f** 020 8324 2328
e gradeone.tvpersonnel@virgin.net

Jonathan Gout
Grade One TV & Film Personnel, Elstree Studios, Shenley Road, Borehamwood WD6 1JG
t 020 8324 2224 **f** 020 8324 2328
e gradeone.tvpersonnel@virgin.net

Adam Graig
54 Midmoor Road, London SW12 0EN
t 020 8772 1015 **m** 07710 420801 **e** adamcraig@compuserve.com
Credits This Morning (T); Pet Rescue (T); Escape To The Country (D); The Salon (T)

Jaimie Gramston
Flat 1, 42 Manse Road, London N16 7QD
t 020 7503 4665 **m** 07976 684842
Agent Linkline, 6 Thirlmere Gardens, Wembley HA9 8RE
t 020 8908 6262 **f** 020 8904 5179
e mail@linklinecrew.com **w** www.linklinecrew.com

Douglas Gray
Basement Flat, 20A Cologne Road, Battersea, London SW11 2AJ
t 020 7223 1621 **m** 07770 936976 **e** douglas_gray@hotmail.com
Credits Flengdang (S); SSGA (I); Witness To History (D); Webwise For Business (D)

Gordon Gronbach
Stella's Diary, 9 Hormead Road, London W9 3NG
t 020 8200 1018 **t** 020 8969 1855 **f** 020 8964 2157
m 07850 055628 **m** 07836 594622
e stella'sdiary@btinternet.com
Credits The Real A&E (D); Prudential (C); House Invaders (T); British Telecom (C)

Derek Gruszeckyj
162 Cubbington Road, Lillington, Leamington Spa CV32 7AH
t 01926 773485 **f** 01926 773486 **m** 07976 255136
e derek@derekg.co.uk **w** www.derekg.co.uk
Contact Derek Gruszeckyj, Lighting Cameraman
Credits Diana's Rock, The Paul Burrel Story (D); Bill Wyman's 'Blues Odyssey'; Antiques Roadshow (T); Rosie and Jim (T)

Julian Harries
Grade One TV & Film Personnel, Elstree Studios, Shenley Road, Borehamwood WD6 1JG
t 020 8324 2224 **f** 020 8324 2328
e gradeone.tvpersonnel@virgin.net

Paul Harris
Grade One TV & Film Personnel, Elstree Studios, Shenley Road, Borehamwood WD6 1JG
t 020 8324 2224 **f** 020 8324 2328
e gradeone.tvpersonnel@virgin.net

Jonathan Harrison
11 Corney Reach Way, Chiswick, London W4 2TY
t 020 8987 8810 **m** 07860 825950
Agent Linkline, 6 Thirlmere Gardens, Wembley HA9 8RE
t 020 8908 6262 **f** 020 8904 5179
e mail@linklinecrew.com **w** www.linklinecrew.com

Mike Harrison
Blaen Y Garnant, Gwaun Cae Gurwen SA18 1DU
t 01269 822103 **f** 01269 822103 **m** 07767 690296
e miketheccamerauk@hotmail.com
Credits To Hell With Hollywood (T); History Of Welsh (T); The Swagman (T); Scorpion King (T)

Douglas Hartington
Carlin Crew Ltd, Shepperton Studios, Studios Road, Shepperton TW17 0QD
t 01932 568268 **f** 01932 571109
e carlin@netcomuk.co.uk **w** www.carlincrew.com

Chris Hartley
7 Hillman Close, Uxbridge UB8 1QA
t 01895 258085 **m** 07850 690040
e chris@chrishartley.com **w** www.chrishartley.com
Credits Great Britains - Brunel (D); Walking With Cavemen (D); Teachers (T); The Human Body - Nerve Cells (D)

Pete Hayns
Bristol
f 07970 480982 **m** 07977 538511
e pete@hayns.com **w** www.petehayns.com
Credits Auschwitz: The Business Of Death (D); Heroes Of World War II (D); Flooded Britain (D)

David Hilton
166 Addiscombe Road, Croydon CR0 7LA
t 020 8656 1067 **f** 020 8656 1067 **e** dehilton@yahoo.co.uk
Credits I Need Your Love (M); Coors Lite (C); This Land Is My Land (D); Hard Men (F)

Ian Hilton
Experience Counts - Call Me Ltd, 5th Floor, 41-42 Berners Street, London W1P 3AA
t 020 7637 8112 **f** 020 7580 2582

Tim Hirst
92 Tunstall Road, Biddulph, Stoke-on-Trent ST8 6HH
t 01782 523225 **f** 01782 523225 **m** 07831 440564
e timvidcam@tbps.co.uk
Credits Michelin UK (I); Facelift Diaries (T); Royal Doulton (C); Sky News (T)
Experienced cameraman with kit including SP, SX and DigiBeta.

Maxwell Hodgetts
7 Long Ley, Cheddington, Nr Leighton Buzzard LU7 0SU
t 01296 660550 **f** 01296 668517 **m** 07768 861924
e max@max-cam.co.uk **w** www.max-cam.co.uk
Credits Bargain Hunt (T)

Alan Holey
Grade One TV & Film Personnel, Elstree Studios, Shenley Road, Borehamwood WD6 1JG
t 020 8324 2224 **f** 020 8324 2328
e gradeone.tvpersonnel@virgin.net

Nic Holman
32A Glenwood Road, Catford, London SE6 4NF
t 020 8960 6359 **m** 07967 485017
Agent Linkline, 6 Thirlmere Gardens, Wembley HA9 8RE
t 020 8908 6262 **f** 020 8904 5179
e mail@linklinecrew.com **w** www.linklinecrew.com

Richard Hookings
2 Powdrill Cottages, Loperwood Lane, Old Calmore,
Southampton SO40 2RL
t 02380 866123 **m** 07976 399959
e info@thecameraman.tv **w** www.thecameraman.tv
Credits The Year of the Artist (D); Hollywood - How It Was; Scrapped (D);
Musiceye.com (M)

John Howarth
1 The Beechams, Mursley MK17 0RX
t 01296 720409 **f** 01296 720409 **m** 07973 465017
e john.howarth@uk.com
Credits Ride The Wild Surf (T); Body Hits (T); Walking With Beasts (T); Walking
With Dinosaurs (T)

Keith Hunter
Grade One TV & Film Personnel, Elstree Studios, Shenley
Road, Borehamwood WD6 1JG
t 020 8324 2224 **f** 020 8324 2328
e gradeone.tvpersonnel@virgin.net

In Camera
Overdale, The Spinney, off Cragwood Drive, Rawdon, Leeds
LS19 6LH
t 0113 250 3173 **f** 0113 250 3173 **m** 07831 611979
e swd@incamera.tv **w** www.incamera.tv; www.atvcrew.com
Contact Stuart Dunbar

Mark Insoll
t 01483 533703 **f** 01483 533442 **m** 07774 705476
e markinsoll@aol.com
Credits The Trial Of Matthew Welkes - Bodmin Museum (E); Net Lectures -
Series For Optometrists (W); Club Zebra - Series For Homechoice (T); Six
European Enterprise Stories - Unilever (I)

Will Jacob
12 Melgund Road, Highbury, London N5
t 020 7700 7605 **m** 07973 292661
Agent Linkline, 6 Thirlmere Gardens, Wembley HA9 8RE
t 020 8908 6262 **f** 020 8904 5179
e mail@linklinecrew.com **w** www.linklinecrew.com

Paul Jaruis
11 Station Road, Shepperton TW17 8AU
t 01932 269960 **m** 07973 405293 **e** pjaruis@ntlworld.com

Jeffcam
34 A Back Lane, Ham, Richmond TW10 7LF
t 020 8255 7392 **m** 07900 033 280
e jeffcam@blueyonder.co.uk **w** www.homeofficebizz.co.uk
Credits Sky Sports - Football And Motorsport (T); BBC News 24 (T); Mr Right (T)

Mark Jerome
Grade One TV & Film Personnel, Elstree Studios, Shenley
Road, Borehamwood WD6 1JG
t 020 8324 2224 **f** 020 8324 2328
e gradeone.tvpersonnel@virgin.net

Peter Johnson
Grade One TV & Film Personnel, Elstree Studios, Shenley
Road, Borehamwood WD6 1JG
t 020 8324 2224 **f** 020 8324 2328
e gradeone.tvpersonnel@virgin.net

Jon Lane Associates
Garden Flat 43, Gloucester Avenue, London NW1 7BA
t 020 7419 7200 **m** 07973 733363 **e** jon@jon-lane.com

Sean Keane
62 Ardleigh Court, Hutton Road, Shenfield CM15 8NA
t 020 8969 1855 **f** 01277 230632 **m** 07941 575604
e ke@necamera.com

Adrian Kelly
Grade One TV & Film Personnel, Elstree Studios, Shenley
Road, Borehamwood WD6 1JG
t 020 8324 2224 **f** 020 8324 2328
e gradeone.tvpersonnel@virgin.net

Gerard Kelly
66 Wentworth Road, High Barnet, London EN5 4NV
t 020 8441 3640 **f** 020 8441 3640 **m** 07850 487631
e kellycam@kellyj62.fsnet.co.uk
Credits Greg Dyke At London Business School (W); Orquestra Do Algarve (M);
Trocadero Bands London (M); BBC National And Regional News (T)

Sam Key
104 Strathville Road, London SW18 4RE
t 020 8874 8260 **m** 07976 352681 **e** samkey1@aol.com
Agent Linkline, 6 Thirlmere Gardens, Wembley HA9 8RE
t 020 8908 6262 **f** 020 8904 5179
e mail@linklinecrew.com **w** www.linklinecrew.com

Daryl Kibblewhite
'The Old Police House', Church Hill, Bishops Tachbrook,
Leamington Spa CV33 9RJ
t 01926 881578 **f** 01926 881578 **m** 07778 679 264
e darylkib@lineone.net
Credits UKOOL (T); The Game Of Their Lives (D); Grandstand - Football Focus (T)

Lamplight
30 Horton View, Banbury OX16 9HP
t 01295 275708 **m** 07932 166193
e mark@lamplight-uk.com **w** www.digibeta.tv
Contact Mark Howe, Lighting Cameraman

Walter Lassally
The Abbey, Eye IP23 7NJ
t 01379 870263 **f** 01379 870263
Credits Tom Jones (F); Zorba The Greek (F)

Ann Latimer
76 Greenwood Road, London E8 1NE
t 020 7254 1177 **m** 07951 815111 **e** annl@aglatimer.fsnet.co.uk
Credits Dialogues (E); The Shoelace Adventure (T); The Ten Estates (I); The Lyric (E)

Anthony Leake
34 Fitzwilliam Road, London SW4 0DN
t 020 7622 0870 **f** 020 7720 7875 **m** 07973 502349
e antleake@bluefin-tv.demon.co.uk **w** www.bluefintv.com
Credits Vandals (D); The South Bank Show (T); The Fugitives (T); Escape From
Experiment Island (T)

Casper Leaver
Flat 3, 176 Bedford Hill, Balham, London SW12 9HL
t 020 8673 6089 **m** 07973 281555
Agent Linkline, 6 Thirlmere Gardens, Wembley HA9 8RE
t 020 8908 6262 **f** 020 8904 5179
e mail@linklinecrew.com **w** www.linklinecrew.com

Piers Leigh
Callbox Communications Ltd, PO Box 66, Shepperton Studios,
Shepperton Lane TW17 0QD
t 01932 592572 **f** 01932 569655 **m** 07710 572572
e callboxdiary@btinternet.com **w** www.callboxdiary.co.uk

Andy Leonard
12 Milner Road, Horfield, Bristol BS7 9PQ
t 0117 924 3523 **f** 0117 924 3523 **m** 07973 321 708
e crews@andycamfilms.co.uk
Credits 999 (D); Skies Of Ice (T); My Favourite Hymns (T); The Bill (T)

Alvin Leong
Gems, The Media House, 87 Glebe Street, Penarth CF64 1EF
t 029 2071 0770 **f** 029 2071 0771
e gems@gems-agency.co.uk **w** www.gems-agency.co.uk
Credits London Bridge (T); Dream Team (T); Offending Angels (S);
Sunburn II (T)

Jim Littlehales
Grade One TV & Film Personnel, Elstree Studios, Shenley
Road, Borehamwood WD6 1JG
t 020 8324 2224 **f** 020 8324 2328
e gradeone.tvpersonnel@virgin.net

Guy Littlemore
Linkline, 6 Thirlmere Gardens, Wembley HA9 8RE
t 020 8908 6262 **f** 020 8904 5179
e mail@linklinecrew.com **w** www.linklinecrew.com

Don Lord
Karibu, London Road, Brighton BN1 8PU
t 01273 558888 **f** 01273 558888 **m** 07774 450469

Peter Loring
11 Bedford Close, Chenies, Rickmansworth WD3 6EJ
t 01923 283407 **f** 01923 283407 **m** 07850 690058
e peter@peterloring.com **w** www.peterloring.com
Credits Hitting Home (D); Food Police (D); Megamaths (E);
One Foot In The Grave (T)

Stuart Luck
32 Craven Gardens, Wimbledon, London SW19 8LV
t 020 8540 4072 **m** 07831 193010
Agent Linkline, 6 Thirlmere Gardens, Wembley HA9 8RE
t 020 8908 6262 **f** 020 8904 5179
e mail@linklinecrew.com **w** www.linklinecrew.com

Andy Macdonald
Grade One TV & Film Personnel, Elstree Studios, Shenley
Road, Borehamwood WD6 1JG
t 020 8324 2224 **f** 020 8324 2328
e gradeone.tvpersonnel@virgin.net

Simon Makin
2 Bosden Hall Road, Hazel Grove, Stockport SK7 4JJ
t 0161 456 5420 **m** 07974 191932
e simon_makin@yahoo.co.uk **w** www.simonmakin.com
Credits Gus Home Shopping (I); JD Sports (C); Wakestock (T); ASL 2002 (T)

Henry Marcuzzi
59 Norfolk Avenue, Sanderstead, South Croydon CR2 8BT
t 020 8657 5520 **t** 01403 751551 **f** 020 8657 4374
m 07753 675656 **e** marcuzzi.dawson@talk21.com
Credits The Edge (I); Play For Today (T); Doctors (T)

Simon Margetts
78 Albany Road, West Green, Crawley RH11 7BZ
t 01293 447 859 **f** 01293 421 886 **m** 07971 518143
e simonmargetts@yourshowreel.com
Credits Construction Site (T); Resident Evil (Effects DP) (E)

Mike Marmion
99A Busheyhill Road, Camberwell, London SE5 8QQ
t 020 7703 1595 **m** 07860 444343
Agent Linkline, 6 Thirlmere Gardens, Wembley HA9 8RE
t 020 8908 6262 **f** 020 8904 5179
e mail@linklinecrew.com **w** www.linklinecrew.com

Lee Marriott
Grade One TV & Film Personnel, Elstree Studios, Shenley
Road, Borehamwood WD6 1JG
t 020 8324 2224 **f** 020 8324 2328
e gradeone.tvpersonnel@virgin.net

Matthew Marschner
34 Gaynesford Road, Forest Hill, London SE23 2UQ
t 020 8699 7224 **m** 07831 625612
Agent Linkline, 6 Thirlmere Gardens, Wembley HA9 8RE
t 020 8908 6262 **f** 020 8904 5179
e mail@linklinecrew.com **w** www.linklinecrew.com

Alan Marsden
Town End Farm, Gamblesby, Penrith CA10 1HY
t 01768 881137 **m** 07831 358361 **e** felledger@freeserve.co.uk

Andy Martin
23 Spencer Gate, St Albans AL1 4AD
t 01727 843036 **f** 01727 863638 **m** 07850 303143
e andy@andymartin.tv **w** www.andymartin.tv
Credits Wish You Were Here (T); Derail (D); Hobby Of Death (F);
Cloud Cuckoo Land (F)

David Matthews
Experience Counts - Call Me Ltd, 5th Floor, 41-42 Berners
Street, London W1P 3AA
t 020 7637 8112 **f** 020 7580 2582

Mark Mayling
Pond Cottage, Beamond End, Amersham HP7 0QT
t 01494 712255 **m** 07831 724628
Agent Linkline, 6 Thirlmere Gardens, Wembley HA9 8RE
t 020 8908 6262 **f** 020 8904 5179
e mail@linklinecrew.com **w** www.linklinecrew.com

Duncan McCallum
21 Oswald Court, Grange, Edinburgh EN9 2HY
m 07768 202147
Credits To the Ends of the Earth - The Abyss (T); The Face & The Edge (T)

David McCormick
789A Wandsworth Road, Clapham, London SW8 3JQ
t 020 7627 4467 **m** 07801 336440
Agent Linkline, 6 Thirlmere Gardens, Wembley HA9 8RE
t 020 8908 6262 **f** 020 8904 5179
e mail@linklinecrew.com **w** www.linklinecrew.com

Roger McDonald
Callbox Communications Ltd, PO Box 66, Shepperton Studios,
Shepperton Lane, Shepperton TW17 0DQ
t 01932 592572 **f** 01932 569655 **m** 07710 572572
e callboxdiary@btinternet.com **w** www.callboxdiary.com

Martin McGlone
Callbox Communications Limited, PO Box 66, Shepperton
Studios, Shepperton Lane, Shepperton TW17 0QD
t 01932 572572 **f** 01932 569655
e callboxdiary@btinternet.com **w** www.callboxdiary.co.uk

MD Camera Services
21 Claygate Road, London W13 9XG
t 020 8567 4482 **f** 020 8840 2138 **m** 07831 101654
e martin.doyle@virgin.net
Contact Martin Doyle, Proprietor

Dave Meadows
East Highlands, Three Gates Lane, Haslemere GU27 2ET
t 01428 644942 **m** 07973 167022
Agent Linkline, 6 Thirlmere Gardens, Wembley HA9 8RE
t 020 8908 6262 **f** 020 8904 5179
e mail@linklinecrew.com **w** www.linklinecrew.com

Alex Melman
Carlin Crew Ltd, Shepperton Studios, Studios Road,
Shepperton TW17 0QD
t 01932 568268 **f** 01932 571109
e carlin@netcomuk.co.uk **w** www.carlincrew.com

Peter Milic
Grade One TV & Film Personnel, Elstree Studios, Shenley Road, Borehamwood WD6 1JG
t 020 8324 2224 **f** 020 8324 2328
e gradeone.tvpersonnel@virgin.net

David Miller
Stella's Diary, 9 Hormead Road, London W9 3NG
t 020 7326 4074 **t** 020 8969 1855 **f** 020 8964 2157
m 07710 406750 **m** 07836 594622
e stella'sdiary@btinternet.com

Dan Mindel
Callbox Communications Ltd, Box 66, Shepperton Studios, Shepperton Lane, Shepperton TW17 0QD
t 01932 592572 **f** 01932 569655 **m** 07710 572572
e callboxdiary@btinternet.com **w** www.callboxdiary.co.uk

Angus Mitchell
86 Marlborough Park Central, Belfast BT9 6HP
t 028 9096 4086 **m** 07711 340479 **e** gucam@ntlworld.com

Sam Montague
23 Lavers Road, London N16 0DU
t 020 7249 7718 **m** 07973 269693
Agent Linkline, 6 Thirlmere Gardens, Wembley HA9 8RE
t 020 8908 6262 **f** 020 8904 5179
e mail@linklinecrew.com **w** www.linklinecrew.com

Mark Moreve
6 Hawkesley Close, Strawberry Hill, Twikenham TW1 4TR
t 020 8891 6881 **f** 020 8891 6881 **m** 07976 327130
e mmoreve@globalnet.co.uk
Credits Scrapheap Challenge (T); Slinky Malinky (M); World Travel Market Hands" (I); Monty Don's Don Roaming (T)"

Garry Morrison
75 Clouston Street, Glasgow G20 8QW
t 0141 946 3332 **f** 0141 946 3332 **m** 07831 503444
e garry@garrymo.co.uk

Steve Moss
67 King Edwards Grove, Teddington TW11 9LZ
m 07889 075484 **e** mail@stevemoss.tv **w** www.stevemoss.tv
Credits Dreamspaces (T); Tony And Georgio (T); Crimewatch UK (T); The Plantsman (T)

Andrew Muggleton
2 St Johns Buildings, Canterbury Crescent, London SW9 7QH
t 020 7737 6952 **m** 07802 722120
Agent Linkline, 6 Thirlmere Gardens, Wembley HA9 8RE
t 020 8908 6262 **f** 020 8904 5179
e mail@linklinecrew.com **w** www.linklinecrew.com

William Mullen
Gems, The Media House, 87 Glebe Street, Penarth CF64 1EF
t 029 2071 0770 **f** 029 2071 0771
e gems@gems-agency.co.uk **w** www.gems-agency.co.uk

Paul Mungeam
33B Heathfield Road, London SW18 2PH
m 07710 908482 **e** paulmungeam@hotmail.com
Credits BBC Correspondent (T); Streetmate; Pop Idol (T); Lonely Planet Guides/Treks

Ian Nelson
8 Halleys Walk, Addlestone KT15 2DH
t 01932 842524 **f** 07974 080695 **m** 07976 200809
e iannelson@bigfoot.com **w** www.iannelson.com
Credits Make my Day (T); Teletubbies (T); Blue Peter (T)

David Niblock
Carlin Crew Ltd, Shepperton Studios, Studios Road, Shepperton TW17 0QD
t 01932 568268 **f** 01932 571109
e carlin@netcomuk.co.uk **w** www.carlincrew.com

Barbara Nicholls
t 020 8348 5792 **f** 020 8348 5792 **m** 07798 525 977
e barbie.blisscam@virgin.net
Credits India Calling (D); Public Enemy #1: Superstar on Trial (D); I Love The 80s, 90s (D); Great Excavations: World Archaeological Series (T)

Ostrowski Film & TV Services
The Old Chapel, Capheaton NE19 2AQ
t 01830 530064 **f** 01830 530064 **m** 07860 763143
e janusz.ostrowski@btconnect.com
Contact Janusz Ostrowski

Bruce Parker
Strawberry Cottage, 17 Giggs Hill Road, Thames Ditton KT7 0BT
t 020 8398 9330 **f** 020 8873 7536 **m** 07774 805 460
e bruce.parker@virgin.net

Paul Robinson
Stella's Diary, 9 Hormead Road, London W9 3NG
t 020 8969 1855 **t** 020 8682 4416 **f** 020 8964 2157
m 07836 594622 **m** 07973 255815
e stella'sdiary@btinternet.com

Chris Payne
1 Newbolt Close, Paulerspury NN12 7NH
t 01327 811294 **f** 01327 811753 **m** 07711 239557
e eco1pro@aol.com
Agent Grade One TV & Film Personnel, Elstree Studios, Shenley Road, Borehamwood WD6 1JG
t 020 8324 2224 **f** 020 8324 2328
e gradeone.tvpersonnel@virgin.net
Credits The Royal Bank Of Scotland (C); Prince's Trust (S); Time Team - Behind the Scenes (D); Island Gems (D)

Kevin Pearcy
7 Stapleton Close, Bristol BS16 1AX
t 0117 965 1694 **m** 07973 173384
Agent Linkline, 6 Thirlmere Gardens, Wembley HA9 8RE
t 020 8908 6262 **f** 020 8904 5179
e mail@linklinecrew.com **w** www.linklinecrew.com

Perspective Video
t 020 8995 0251 **m** 07860 435480
e nick@perspective-video.com **w** www.perspective-video.com
Contact Nick Whittfeld, Cameraman
Credits Horizon - The Great Balloon Race (D); This Morning (T)

Ben Philpott
Carlin Crew Ltd, Shepperton Studios, Studios Road, Shepperton TW17 0QD
t 01932 568268 **f** 01932 571109
e carlin@netcomuk.co.uk **w** www.carlincrew.com

Mark Pigden
8 Wycombe Place, London SW18 2LT
t 020 8874 5810 **f** 020 8874 5810
m 07885 620760 **e** mark.pigden@talk21.com

Gerry Pinches
11 Miller Street, Summerseat BL9 5PX
t 01706 281426 **t** +33 2 9624 2559
f +33 2 9624 2577 **m** 07801 142049
Credits Secret Underworld (T); Air Plane Ski (T); Into Africa (T); A Cry from the Grave (T)

Joe Piotrowski
Grade One TV & Film Personnel, Elstree Studios, Shenley Road, Borehamwood WD6 1JG
t 020 8324 2224 **f** 020 8324 2328
e gradeone.tvpersonnel@virgin.net

Tim Piper
2 Alexandra Street, Blanford Forum DT11 7EY
t 01258 454985 **f** 01258 211786
e tim@reddragonpictures.freeserve.co.uk

Geoff Plumb
Experience Counts - Call Me Ltd, 5th Floor, 41-42 Berners Street, London W1P 3AA
t 020 7637 8112 **f** 020 7580 2582

Brady Pollard
Grade One TV & Film Personnel, Elstree Studios, Shenley Road, Borehamwood WD6 1JG
t 020 8324 2224 **f** 020 8324 2328
e gradeone.tvpersonnel@virgin.net

Charles Ponniah
192 Trevelyan Road, London SW17 9LW
t 020 8767 5518 **m** 07973 219182
Agent Linkline, 6 Thirlmere Gardens, Wembley HA9 8RE
t 020 8908 6262 **f** 020 8904 5179
e mail@linklinecrew.com **w** www.linklinecrew.com

Christopher Preston
Gems, The Media House, 87 Glebe Street, Penarth CF64 1EF
t 029 2071 0770 **f** 029 2071 0771
e gems@gems-agency.co.uk **w** www.gems-agency.co.uk
Credits The Southbank Show (T); Brookside (T); Black Soles (S); Beginners Luck (F)

Tom Pridham
67 Trentham Street, London SW18 5AP
t 020 8871 2962 **m** 07778 298708
Agent Linkline, 6 Thirlmere Gardens, Wembley HA9 8RE
t 020 8908 6262 **f** 020 8904 5179
e mail@linklinecrew.com **w** www.linklinecrew.com

Lee Pulbrook
Flat D, 54 Harwood Road, London SW6 4PY
t 020 7384 1229 **m** 07831 838534
Agent Linkline, 6 Thirlmere Gardens, Wembley HA9 8RE
t 020 8908 6262 **f** 020 8904 5179
e mail@linklinecrew.com **w** www.linklinecrew.com

Paul Quinn
m 07850 920327 **e** paul.quinn@bskyb.com

Mark Raeburn
Brighton
m 07947 742 561 **e** markraeburn@callnetuk.com
Credits My Daughter's Face (S); The Onion Bar (C); Home (S); Daddy's Girl (T)

Wayne Ratcliffe
Grade One TV & Film Personnel, Elstree Studios, Shenley Road, Borehamwood WD6 1JG
t 020 8324 2224 **f** 020 8324 2328
e gradeone.tvpersonnel@virgin.net

Mark Regan
Apartment 5, 1 Goat Wharf, Brentford TW8 0AS
t 020 8580 5644 **m** 07973 776009
Agent Linkline, 6 Thirlmere Gardens, Wembley HA9 8RE
t 020 8908 6262 **f** 020 8904 5179
e mail@linklinecrew.com **w** www.linklinecrew.com

Robin Riseley
Hill Cottage, Spring Lane, Watlington OX49 5QN
Agent Linkline, 6 Thirlmere Gardens, Wembley HA9 8RE
t 020 8908 6262 **f** 020 8904 5179
e mail@linklinecrew.com **w** www.linklinecrew.com
Credits Bill Oddie Goes Wild (T); Secret Lives Of The Pharaohs (T); Flying Gardener (T)

Chris Roach
West Dene, 5 Knull Road, Fleet GU51 4PR
m 07703 347 661 **e** chrisroach811@hotmail.com
w www.chrisroach.com
Credits Family Affairs (T); Night And Day (T); Hollyoaks (T); Brookside (T)

Nigel Roake
m 07932 644197 **e** nigel@nroake.freeserve.co.uk
Credits The Dawlish Donkey (D); The Growth Of The University Of Sunderland (D); NVH (I)

Mark Robinson
Fieldhurst, 86 Liberty Lane, Addlestone KT15 1NH
t 01932 845494 **m** 07973 559898
Agent Linkline, 6 Thirlmere Gardens, Wembley HA9 8RE
t 020 8908 6262 **f** 020 8904 5179
e mail@linklinecrew.com **w** www.linklinecrew.com

Steve Robson
Carlin Crew Ltd, Shepperton Studios, Studios Road, Shepperton TW17 0QD
t 01932 568268 **f** 01932 571109
e carlin@netcomuk.co.uk **w** www.carlincrew.com

Patrick Rowe
18 Reigate Road, Leatherhead KT22 8RA
t 01372 374887 **m** 07860 233948 **e** mail@patrickrowe.com
Agent Linkline, 6 Thirlmere Gardens, Wembley HA9 8RE
t 020 8908 6262 **f** 020 8904 5179
e mail@linklinecrew.com **w** www.linklinecrew.com

Titus Rowlandson
22A Maxted Road, London SE15 4LF
t 020 7639 1818 **m** 07779 799476 **e** titus_r100@yahoo.co.uk
Credits Pulp (M); BBC3 Idents (T); Change Makers (D); Tracing Ché (D)

John Ryan
45 Forster Road, Beckenham DR3 4LH
t 020 8402 5947 **m** 07774 851085
Agent Linkline, 6 Thirlmere Gardens, Wembley HA9 8RE
t 020 8908 6262 **f** 020 8904 5179
e mail@linklinecrew.com **w** www.linklinecrew.com

Bruce A Sabin
Astwood Court Barn, Astwood Lane, Stoke Prior B60 4BB
t 01527 821741 **f** 01527 821041 **m** 07831 305457
e brucesabin@aol.com
Credits Garden Invaders (T); House Invaders (T); ATP Tennis Masters (T); At The Races (T)

Nic Sadler
Callbox Communications Ltd, Box 66, Shepperton Studios, Shepperton Lane, Shepperton TW17 0QD
t 01932 592572 **f** 01932 569655 **m** 07710 572572
e callboxdiary@btinternet.com **w** www.callboxdiary.co.uk

Paul Sadourian
1 Peary Place, London E2 0QW
t 020 8880 6352 **f** 020 8880 6352 **m** 07973 629 441
e paul@virgin.net
Credits Nike (C); Married / Unmarried (F); Subway Cops (F); Nailing Vienna (F)

Trevor Salmon
Grade One TV & Film Personnel, Elstree Studios, Shenley Road, Borehamwood WD6 1JG
t 020 8324 2224 **f** 020 8324 2328
e gradeone.tvpersonnel@virgin.net

Eric Samuel
Bookends, 83 Maynard Drive, St Albans AL1 2JX
t 01727 841177 **e** bookgold@bookends.fsbusiness.co.uk

Jason Shepherd
Grade One TV & Film Personnel, Elstree Studios, Shenley Road, Borehamwood WD6 1JG
t 020 8324 2224 **f** 020 8324 2328
e gradeone.tvpersonnel@virgin.net

David W. Smith
Lower Ardentallan House, Lerags, Oban PA34 4SF
t 01631 562070 **m** 07710 516010 **e** cameraman@btinternet.com
Credits Neighbours From Hell (D); Starry Night (F); Horizon - Exodus (D);
Trouble At The Top (D)

Ian Bruce Smith
34A Ryelands Street, Hereford HR4 0LB
t 01432 340729 **m** 07973 432697 **e** info@brucecam.tv
Credits David Gray Live DVD (M); ATP World Tennis Tour (T); Sydney Olympic
Games (T); Breakfast With Frost (T)

Mike Spragg
13 Perryn Road, London W3 7LR
t 020 8742 9819 **m** 07973 422567
Agent Linkline, 6 Thirlmere Gardens, Wembley HA9 8RE
t 020 8908 6262 **f** 020 8904 5179
e mail@linklinecrew.com **w** www.linklinecrew.com

Paul Stephens
2 Old Corn Mews, Fern Road, Farncombe GU7 3ER
m 07778 033373
Agent Linkline, 6 Thirlmere Gardens, Wembley HA9 8RE
t 020 8908 6262 **f** 020 8904 5179
e mail@linklinecrew.com **w** www.linklinecrew.com

Richard Stevenson
t 020 8994 3200 **f** 07989 382150 **m** 07973 632631
w www.richardstevenson.co.uk

Nicholas Struthers
Turnstone Cottage, Main Road, East Boldre SO42 7WU
t 01590 626728 **f** 01590 626422 **m** 07860 390932

Orlando Stuart
9 Colville Houses, London W11 1JB
t 020 7460 5134 **m** 07860 661557
Agent Linkline, 6 Thirlmere Gardens, Wembley HA9 8RE
t 020 8908 6262 **f** 020 8904 5179
e mail@linklinecrew.com **w** www.linklinecrew.com

Robin Sunderland
Burton-on-Trent
m 07860 183903
e robin@robinsunderland.tv **w** www.robinsunderland.tv
Credits A Life Of Grime (T); Countryfile (T); Gardeners' World (T); Top Gear (T)

John Sushams
Stone House, 10 Portsmouth Avenue, Thames Ditton KT7 0RT
t 020 8339 0406 **m** 07949 100099
Agent Linkline, 6 Thirlmere Gardens, Wembley HA9 8RE
t 020 8908 6262 **f** 020 8904 5179
e mail@linklinecrew.com **w** www.linklinecrew.com

SVP
94 Blackford Avenue, Edinburgh EH9 3ES
t 0131 668 2433 **f** 0131 668 2277 **m** 07831 252515
e dave-svp@dircon.co.uk
Contact David Flett, Sole Proprietor
Credits Psychopaths; The Occult; Planet Patio

Derik Tan
Callbox Communications Ltd, Box 66, Shepperton Studios,
Shepperton Lane, Shepperton TW17 0QD
t 01932 592572 **f** 01932 569655 **m** 07710 572572
e callboxdiary@btinternet.com **w** www.callboxdiary.co.uk

John Templeton
90 Mintern Close, London N13 5SY
t 020 8882 2400 **f** 07980 670572 **m** 07768 165989
e john@johntempleton.org

Clive Thom
Flat 2, 33B Chalk Hill, Bushey WD19 4BL
t 01923 352047 **m** 07929 735091
e smilepleaseuk@yahoo.co.uk

Steve Tickner MBKS
Carlin Crew Ltd, Shepperton Studios, Studios Road,
Shepperton TW17 0QD
t 01932 568268 **f** 01932 571109
e carlin@netcomuk.co.uk **w** www.carlincrew.com

Tri-Cam
5 Jesmond Grove, Bridge Of Don, Aberdeen AB22 8UZ
t 01224 705250 **m** 07836 355751 **e** george.tricam@virgin.net
Contact George Leslie, Proprieter / Lighting Cameraman
Credits Songs Of Praise (T); Countryfile (T); Beechgrove Garden (T)

Ben Turley
180 Canbury Park Road, Kingston KT2 6LE
m 07973 390358
Agent Linkline, 6 Thirlmere Gardens, Wembley HA9 8RE
t 020 8908 6262 **f** 020 8904 5179
e mail@linklinecrew.com **w** www.linklinecrew.com

Patrick Turley
Crowds, Hamm Court, Weybridge KT13 8YG
m 07850 836995 **e** pturley@ukgateway.net
Credits Who Killed The Pagent Queen? (D); Admiral Insurance (C); George Bush
Profile (D); Eyes Wide Shut (F)

Andy Watt
Grade One TV & Film Personnel, Elstree Studios, Shenley
Road, Borehamwood WD6 1JG
t 020 8324 2224 **f** 020 8324 2328
e gradeone.tvpersonnel@virgin.net

Jim Watters
4 Brook Street, Twyford RG10 9NX
t 01189 342797 **f** 01189 342797 **m** 07702 433847
e jimwatters@macunlimited.net **w** www.ukscreen.com/crew/jimbob
Credits Treasures Of The Americas (D); NME - Bringing Rock Home (M); Cleo's
World (D); Only Food For Forces (D)

Ian Watts
Linkline, 6 Thirlmere Gardens, Wembley HA9 8RE
t 020 8908 6262 **f** 020 8904 5179
e mail@linklinecrew.com **w** www.linklinecrew.com

Keith Watts
Grade One TV & Film Personnel, Elstree Studios, Shenley
Road, Borehamwood WD6 1JG
t 020 8324 2224 **f** 020 8324 2328
e gradeone.tvpersonnel@virgin.net

Geoffrey Wharton
Callbox Communications Ltd, Box 66, Shepperton Studios,
Shepperton Lane, Shepperton TW17 0QD
t 01932 592572 **f** 01932 569655 **m** 07710 572572
e callboxdiary@btinternet.com **w** www.callboxdiary.co.uk

Grahame Wickings
72 Lordswood Road, Harborne, Birmingham B17 9BY
t 01214 278884 **f** 01214 282526 **m** 07860 477474
e grahamewickings@supanet.com
Credits Bad Girls (D); Would Like To Meet (D); Drivers Perspective (S);
Instrument Of War (D)

Glenn Wilkinson
Grade One TV & Film Personnel, Elstree Studios, Shenley
Road, Borehamwood WD6 1JG
t 020 8324 2224 **f** 020 8324 2328
e gradeone.tvpersonnel@virgin.net

Toby Wilkinson
19 Cowper Road, Bromley BR2 9RT
t 020 8289 6030 **m** 07771 714969
Agent Linkline, 6 Thirlmere Gardens, Wembley HA9 8RE
t 020 8908 6262 **f** 020 8904 5179
e mail@linklinecrew.com **w** www.linklinecrew.com

Marco Windham
Top Flat, 104 Landor Road, London SW9 9NX
t 020 7737 5954 **f** 020 7737 5954 **m** 07768 330 027
e marcowindham@onetel.net.uk
Credits Weak At Denise (F)

Woodward Film & Sound
24/26 Hulne Avenue, Tynemouth NE30 2SC
t 01912 570501 **f** 01912 570501 **e** woodwardfilming@hotmail.com
Contact Eric Woodward, Cameraman

Xube
The Garden Cottage, Park Corner, Nettlebed,
Henley-upon-Thames RG9 6DR
m 07836 363686 **e** mail@nettlebed.net
Contact Michael Haynes
Credits Life Etc (D); Lotus Cars (C); Life Before Birth (D)

Chris Yacoubian
19 Hummer Road, Egham TW20 9BW
t 01784 439271 **f** 01784 439271 **m** 07977 565143
e chrisyacoubian@bigfoot.com
Credits Pet Rescue (T); Smile (T); Boohbah (T); The Quick Trick Show (T)

Cars Chauffeur Driven

AA Chauffeur Drive
PO Box 3366, Wokingham RG40 1ZG
t 01189 775896 **f** 01189 770880 **m** 07770 901020
e info@vipdrive.co.uk **w** www.vipdrive.co.uk

Black & White Cars
208-212 Amyand Park Road, St Margarets, Twickenham
TW1 3HY
t 020 8891 4424 **f** 020 8891 0643
e operations@blackandwhitecars.com
w www.blackandwhite.com
Contact Malcolm Holland, Operations Manager

Braemar Location Vehicles
76 Dukes Wood Drive, Gerrards Cross SL9 7LF
t 01753 884000 **f** 01753 885284
Contact Michael Sherrocks, Managing Director

Rolls Royces, ancient and modern Bentleys, Mercedes, Jaguars, Daimlers plus 52 other cars. Huge choice. You want it we've got it.

Carey Worldwide Chauffeured Services
11-15 Headfort Place, London SW1X 7DE
t 020 7235 0234 **f** 020 7823 1278
e resuk@careyuk.com **w** www.ecarey.com
Contact Beth Sampson, Regional Vice President Sales, Europe

Chauffeur Link
The Coach House (BSH), Sydney Road, Bath BA2 6JF
t 01225 446936 **f** 01225 483640 **m** 07712 767000
e select@chauffeurlink.co.uk **w** www.chauffeurlink.co.uk
Contact Kirsten Stewart, Personal Assistant

CWB Chauffeuring
49 Tandridge Drive, Crofton Lane, Orpington BR6 8BY
t 01689 870783 **f** 01689 878061 **m** 07971 082594
Contact C Wells-Beeney, Proprietor

Falcon Chauffeur Drive
Eton Walk, 2 Upton Park, Slough SL1 2DP
t 01753 554477 **f** 01753 553535
e falconcd@usa.net **w** www.falconlimos.co.uk
Contact Andy Panue, Proprietor

Focus International
The Garage Workshop, 7/8 St Stephens Mews, Bayswater,
London W2 5QZ
t 020 7221 3055 **t** 020 7229 5713
f 020 7229 7967 **m** 07831 539953
e jonnyformby@aol.com **w** www.focustransport.com
Contact Sophia Wood, Director; Jonny Formby, Director; Eddie Wilcox,
Executive Director
Credits Birthday Girl (F); East Of Harlem (F); George And The Dragon (F);
Resident Evil (F)

Gleneagles Chauffeur Drive Service
Gleneagles Garage, 155 Victoria Road, Wargrave, Reading
RG10 8AH
t 0118 940 3228 **f** 0118 940 4321
e glenlimos@aol.com **w** www.gleneaglescds.co.uk
Contact David Lowe, Director

Greyhound Private Hire
t 01628 773224 **f** 01628 778947
Contact George Vinton

Heritage Carriages
8 Wells Drive, Kingsbury, London NW9 8DD
t 020 8200 0033 **f** 020 8905 9944 **m** 07831 145300
Contact G Wingrove-Harris, Proprietor

In-Style Chauffeur Hire
23 Arnside Gardens, Wembley HA9 8TJ
t 020 8904 5356 **f** 020 8930 0142
e instylecars@hotmail.com
Contact Tony Blanchett, Director; Angie Blanchett, Director

International Executive Chauffeur Driven Cars Ltd
3A Princes Parade, Golders Green, London NW11 9PS
t 020 8455 1117 **f** 020 8455 5374
e bookings@internationalexecutive.co.uk
w www.internationalexecutive.co.uk
Contact Jeff Blenford, Managing Director

LA Stretch Limo's
115 Beehive Lane, Gants Hill, Ilford IG1 3RW
t 020 8554 9292 **f** 020 8554 9393
e lalimos@aol.com **w** www.lastretchlimos.co.uk
Contact Carl Westwood, Manager

Multi-Media Transport Ltd
Brentford Station House, Boston Manor Road, Brentford TW8 8DT
t 020 8560 2111 **f** 020 8560 2123
Contact Steve Edwards, Director

Network Chauffeur Drive
The Manor House, Rafern Road, Birmingham B11 2BE
t 0870 242 2442 **f** 0870 242 2443
e info@networktransportgroup.co.uk
w www.networktransportgroup.co.uk
Contact Tracy Kimberley, Director

Radlett Radio Cars Ltd
40 Watling Street, Radlett WD7 7NN
t 01923 469800 **f** 01923 469804
w www.members.aol.com/radiocars/
Contact Terry Armstrong; Vincent Sampson, Managing Director

CASTING

Casting Agents

Ann Fielden
5 Rectory Lane, London SW17 9PZ
t 020 8767 3939 **f** 020 8672 4803 **m** 07796 173111
e ann@fieldena.freeserve.co.uk
Contact Ann Fielden, Proprieter
Credits Beech On The Run (T); Green Eyed Monster (T); Without Motive (T)

Bettws Shires
Berry Farm, Llanvihangel, Crucorney, Abergavenny NP7 8EF
t 01873 890413 **f** 01873 890413 **m** 07977 055689
Contact Barbara Morgan

Castnet Ltd
99 Windmill Lane, Bushey Heath WD23 1NE
t 020 8420 4209 **f** 020 8386 6563
e admin@castingnetwork.co.uk **w** www.castingnetwork.co.uk
Contact P Somerston, Casting; D Richman, Managing Director; A Sharron, Casting
Credits Ascend (D); Kid In The Corner (T); The Man Who Cried (F);
Band Of Brothers (T)
Over 1000 trained, professional British Actors - search online FREE!

Edward Wyman Agency
67 Llanon Road, Llanishen, Cardiff CF14 5AH
t 029 2075 2351 **f** 029 2075 2444
e edward@wymancasting.fsnet.co.uk
w www.wymancasting.fsnet.co.uk
Contact Edward Wyman, Casting Director; Judith Gay, Casting Director; Judith Gay, Casting Director
Credits Week In Week Out (D); Crimewatch (D); Belonging (T); Arachnid (T)

Laine Management
Laine House, 131 Victoria Road, Hope, Salford M6 8LF
t 0161 789 7775 **f** 0161 787 7572
e elaine@lainemanagement.co.uk **w** www.lainemanagement.co.uk
Contact Elaine Greeley

Livewires Partnership
Livewires Casting Agency, PO Box 23199, Edinburgh EH7 5XB
t 0131 557 2647 **f** 0131 557 9788 **m** 07730 399 722
e livewiresscotland@gevir.co.uk
Contact Fran Holmes; Pam Wardell

Media Modelling & Casting Agency
First Floor, 18 Castle Street, Dover CT16 2PP
t 01304 204715 **t** 01304 204739 **f** 01304 204739
m 07812 245512 **e** info@mediamc.co.uk **w** www.mediamc.co.uk
Contact Frances Metcalfe, Founder Partner; Anita Thompson, Partner

Northern Professionals Casting Company
21 Cresswell Avenue, North Shields, Tyne and Wear NE29 9BQ
t 0191 257 8635 **f** 0191 296 3243
e bill.gerard@northpro83.freeserve.co.uk
w www.northernprofessionalscastingco.com
Contact Bill Gerard, Proprietor

Paul De Freitas Casting
6 Brook Street, Mayfair, London W1S 1BB
t 020 7434 4233 **f** 020 7355 1084 **m** 07836 559 585
e pauldefreitascasting@lineone.net
Contact Paul de Freitas, Managing Director
Credits Soapstars (T); What Larry Says (S); Sizzle and Stirr (C)

PLA Scotland (Pat Lovett Associates)
5 Union Street, Edinburgh EH1 3LT
t 0131 478 7878 **f** 0131 478 7070
e info@pla.uk.com **w** www.pla.uk.com
Contact Pat Lovett; Dolina Logan

Power Promotions
PO Box 61, Liverpool L13 0EF
t 0151 230 0070 **f** 0151 230 0070 **m** 07850 779466
e tom@powerpromotions.co.uk **w** www.powerpromotions.co.uk
Contact Tom Staunton, Director
Credits Goldeneye (T); The Beat Goes On (T); RAC (C); Brookside (T)

PVA Management Ltd
Hallow Park, Worcester WR2 6PG
t 01905 640663 **f** 01905 641842 **e** post@pva.co.uk
Contact Paul Vaughan, Managing Director

Real People Casting & Research
t 0207 610 1966 **f** 0207 610 1994 **m** 07976 958 173
e jolo@beeb.net
Contact Johanna Lowe, Director

Rinky Dink Ltd
38 Langham Street, London W1W 7AR
t 020 7255 2563 **f** 020 7323 9526
e info@rinky-dink.co.uk **w** www.rinky-dink.co.uk
Contact Kerrie , Casting Director; Raz , New Business Director

Screensearch Extras Directory
Suite 401 Langham House, 302 Regent Street, London W1B 3HH
t 0870 441341 **w** www.screensearch.co.uk
Contact Ian Turner, Managing Director
Credits Snatch (F); Casualty (T); Mean Machine (W)

Script Breakdown Services
Suite 1, 16 Sidmouth Road, London NW2 5JX
t 020 8459 2781 **f** 020 8459 7442
e casting@sbsltd.demon.co.uk
Contact Lydia Martin, Managing Director

The Searchers
70 Sylvia Court, Cavendish Street, London N1 7PG
t 07958 922829 **f** 020 8964 4800 **m** 07801 151751
e wayne.searchers@virgin.net
Contact Wayne Waterson, Director; Ian Sheppard, Director
Credits Apple Macintosh (C); Cisco Systems (C); Coca-Cola (C); Nike (C)

Tinseltown Online
44-46 St Johns Street, London EC1M 4DF
t 020 7689 4000 **f** 020 7689 0458
e info@tinseltownonline.com **w** www.tinseltownonline.com

Casting Directors

Amanda Stewart Casting
Apartment 1, 35 Fortess Rd, London NW5 1AD
t 020 7485 7973 **f** 020 7482 5699
e amanda@ascasting.demon.co.uk
Contact Amanda Stewart, Proprietor

Sarah Bird
PO Box 32658, London W14 0XA
t 020 7371 3248 **f** 020 7602 8601
Credits Madam Bovary (T); Two Men Went To War (F); The Gathering (F)

Wendy Brazington
2 Old School Buildings, Archdale Road, London SE22 9HP
t 020 8299 9660 **f** 020 8299 9661 **m** 07775 638170
e wendy@castingoffice.demon.co.uk
Credits Code 46 (F); Bright Young Things (F); Heartlands (F);
24 Hour Party People (F)

Bunny Fildes Casting
56-60 Wigmore Street, London W1U 2RZ
t 020 7935 1254 **f** 020 7298 1871
Contact Bunny Fildes, Casting Director

Candid Casting
111-113 Great Titchfield Street, London W1W 6RY
t 020 7636 6644 **f** 020 7636 5522 **m** 07973 231853
e mail@candidcasting.co.uk
Contact Janine Snape, Assistant to Amanda Tabak; Amanda Tabak,
Casting Director
Credits Is Harry On The Boat? (F); The Low Down (F)

The Casting Company (UK)
112-114 Wardour Street, London W1F 0TS
t 020 7734 4954 **f** 020 7434 2346 **e** casting@michguish.com
Contact Gaby Kester, Associate; Michelle Guish, Casting Directors
Credits Bridget Jones' Diary (F); Shakespeare In Love (F); Death In Holy Orders
(T); Cold Mountain (F)

Casting Unlimited
9 Hansard Mews, London W14 8BJ
t 0870 443 5621 **f** 0870 443 5622 **m** 07956 254246
e mark@castingdirector.co.uk
Contact Mark Summers, Casting Director

Alison Chard
23 Groveside Court, 4 Lombard Road, Battersea, London SW11 3RQ
t 020 7223 9125 **f** 020 7223 9125 **m** 07808 855421
e alisonchard@castingdirector.freeserve.co.uk
Credits Dr Willoughby (T); Think Murder (T); Real Women (T); The Bill (T)

Charkham Casting
Suite 5.1, Moray House, 23-31 Great Titchfield Street,
London W1W 7PA
t 020 7436 4842 **f** 020 7436 4943 **m** 07956 456 630
e charkhamcasting@btconnect.com
Contact Gary Ford, Assistant Casting Director; Beth Charkham, Casting
Director/Proprietor
Credits Portrait of a Lady (F); Silent Witness (T); Men Behaving Badly (T)

The Crocodile Casting Company
9 Ashley Close, Hendon, London NW4 1PH
t 020 8203 7009 **f** 020 8203 7711 **m** 07774 468223
e croccast@aol.com **w** www.crocodilecasting.com
Contact Tracie Saban, Partner; Claire Gibbs, Partner
Credits Kellogg (C); Iceland (C); Powerade (C)

Crowley Poole Casting
11 Goodwins Court, London WC2N 4LL
t 020 7379 5965 **f** 020 7379 5971
Contact Suzanne Crowley, Casting Director; Gilly Poole, Casting Director
Credits Nicholas Nickleby (T); A Knight's Tale (F); Conspiracy: The Meeting at
Wannsee (F)

Debbie Shepherd Casting
Suite 16, 63 St Martins Lane, London WC2H 4JS
t 020 7240 0400 **f** 020 7240 4640
e general@debbieshepherdcasting.com
Contact Debbie Shepherd, Proprietor

Di Carling Casting
1st Floor, 49 Frith Street, London W1D 4SG
t 020 7287 6446 **f** 020 7287 6844 **m** 07748 655006
Contact Di Carling, Casting Director

Doreen Jones Casting
PO Box 22478, London W6 0WJ
t 020 8746 3782 **f** 020 8748 8533 **m** 07885 464479
Contact Doreen Jones, Casting Director; Liz Vincent Fernie,
Assistant Casting Director
Credits Shipman (T); Messiah II (T); The Vice (T); Prime Suspect VI (T)

Celestia Fox
5 Clapham Common, Northside, London SW4 0QW
t 020 7720 6143 **f** 020 7720 2734

Gail Stevens Casting
54a Clerkenwell Road, London EC1M 5PS
t 020 7253 6532 **f** 020 7253 6574
Contact Maureen Duff, Casting Director; Gail Stevens, Casting Director

Get Real Casting
13 Dents Road, London SW11 6JA
t 020 7223 5313 **f** 020 7223 5316 **m** 07778 768 195
e grcasting@aol.com **w** www.getrealcasting.com
Contact Sally Millson, Casting Director

Marcia Gresham
3 Langthorne Street, London SW6 6JT
t 020 7381 2876 **f** 020 7381 4496 **e** greshamcast@aol.com
Credits The Debt (T); The Project (T); The Inspector Linley Mysteries (T);
Warriors (T)

Grosvenor Casting
27 Rowena Crescent, London SW11 2PT
t 020 7738 0449 **f** 020 7652 6256
e angela.grosvenor@virgin.net
Contact Angela Grosvenor, Casting Director

Polly Hootkins CDG
Po Box 25191, London SW1V 2WN
t 020 7233 8724 **f** 020 7828 5051

Hubbard Casting
19 Charlotte Street, London W1T 1RL
t 020 7636 9991 **f** 020 7636 7117
e email@hubbardcasting.com
Contact Amy McClean, Casting Director; John Hubbard, Casting Director;
Dan Hubbard, Casting Director; Ros Hubbard, Casting Director

Irene East Casting
Casting Directors' Guild, BECTU, Equity, 40 Brookwood
Avenue, Barnes, London SW13 0LR
t 020 8876 5686 **f** 020 8876 5686 **m** 07967 280811
e irneast@aol.com
Credits Three In One (S); Murder In Paris; Jealousy (F); Picasso's Women

Jane Frisby Casting
51 Ridge Road, London N8 9LJ
t 020 8341 4747 **f** 020 8348 9122 **e** jane.frisby@tiscali.co.uk
Contact Jane Frisby, Casting Director

Jayne Collins Casting Ltd
38 Commercial Street, London E1 6LP
t 020 7422 0014 **f** 020 7422 0015 **m** 07956 578258
e info@jaynecollinscasting.com **w** www.jaynecollinscasting.com
Contact Jayne Collins, Managing Director
Credits Gareth Gates & Will Young (M); Kylie Minogue (M); PlayStation (C); Audi (C)

Jeremy Zimmermann Casting
26/27 Oxendon Street, London SW1Y 4EL
t 020 7925 0707 **f** 020 7925 0708
e casting@jzimmermann.com
Contact Jeremy Zimmermann, Casting Director; Andrea Clark, Associate
Credits Dog Soldiers (F); Hellboy (F); Victoria And Albert (T); Blade II (F)

Priscilla John
26A Bradmore Park Road, London W6 0DT
t 020 8741 4212 **f** 020 8741 4005
Credits Van Helsing (F); Johnny English (F); Shanghai Knights (F); About A Boy (F)

Doreen Jones
Paul Stevens @ ICM, 20 Redmore Road, London W6 0HZ
t 020 8746 3782 **f** 020 8748 8533 **m** 07885 464479

Kompani Lande
Tavastgatan 16, Stockholm 118 24, Sweden
t +468 720 5006 **f** +468 720 5075
e tusse@kompanilande.com **w** www.kompanilande.com
Contact Tusse Lande, Casting Director; Pernilla Ericsson, Casting Director

Irene Lamb
Flat 4, Avenue House, 97 Walton Street, London SW3 2HP
t 020 7589 6452 **f** 020 7584 3080

Lauren Goldwyn Casting
14 Dean Street, London W1D 3RF
t 020 7437 4417 **f** 020 7437 4221 **e** realcreate@aol.com
Contact Mark Macho, Chief Operating Officer

Lee Dennison Associates
Fushion, 27 Old Gloucester Street, London WC1N 3XX
t 08700 111100 **f** 08700 111020
e leedennison@fushion-uk.com
Credits Going To The Dogs (F); Birthday Boy (F); E-Mail (S);
Goodbye Sheila Ferguson (T)

Lesley Grayburn Casting
74 Leigh Gardens, London NW10 5HP
t 020 8969 6112 **f** 020 8969 2846
Contact Lesley Grayburn, Proprietor

Susanna Lindstrom
SBFC, Unit 8, Sandhurst House, Wolsey Street, London E1 3BD

Lisa Makin
Kerry Gardner Management, 7 St Georges Square, London
SW15 2HX
t 020 7828 7748 **f** 020 7828 7758
e kerrygardner@freeuk.com
Contact Kerry Gardner, Proprietor

Malcom Bullivant Casting
9 Montrose Villas, London W6 9TT
t 020 8748 4146 **f** 020 8748 1793
Contact Malcom Bullivant, Casting Director

Marilyn Johnson Casting
11 Goodwins Court, London WC2N 4LL
t 020 7497 5552 **f** 020 7497 5530
e marilynjohnson@lineone.net

Mary Selway Casting
Twickenham Studios, The Barons, St Margarets, Twickenham
TW1 2AW
t 020 8607 8888 **f** 020 8607 8701
Contact Mary Selway, Casting Director

Maureen Bewick Casting
104A Dartmouth Road, London NW2 4HB
t 020 8450 1604
Contact Maureen Bewick, Casting Director

Christine McMurrich
16 Spring Vale Avenue, Brentford TW8 9QH
t 020 8568 0137 **f** 020 8568 0137 **m** 07734 206190
Credits Sex Chips And Rock 'N' Roll (T); The Commander (T); Trial And
Retribution (T)

Joyce Nettles
16 Cressida Road, London N19 3JW
t 020 7263 0830 **f** 020 7263 9404

Nina Gold Casting
10 Kempe Road, London NW6 6SJ
t 020 8960 6099 **f** 020 8968 6777 **e** nina@ninagold.co.uk
Contact Nina Gold, Proprietor

Pat O'Connell
Kerry Gardner Management, 7 St Georges Square, London
SW1V 2HX
t 020 7828 7748 **f** 020 7828 7758 **e** kerrygardner@freeuk.com

Sue Odell
t 020 7267 5839 **f** 020 7284 1562 **m** 07831 811506
e sue@sueodell.com **w** www.sueodell.com
Credits Pit Bull (T)

Pearce Woolgar Casting
6 Langley Street, London WC2H 9JA
t 020 7240 0316 **f** 020 7379 8250
w www.pearcewoolgar.com
Contact Francesca Woolgar, Casting Director

Penny Barbour Casting
Rosemary Cottage, Fontridge Lane, Etchingham TN19 7DD
t 01580 819306
Contact Penny Barbour, Proprietor

Simone Reynolds
60 Hebdon Road, London SW17 7NN
t 020 8672 5443 **f** 020 8767 0280
Credits Priestley Shorts (T); Quicksand (F); The Vicar Of Dibley (T); The Bill (T)

Laura Scott
56 Rowena Crescent, London SW11 2PT
t 020 7978 6336 **f** 020 7924 1907 **e** lscott@dircon.co.uk

Michelle Smith
220 Church Lane, Woodford, Stockport SK7 1PQ
t 0161 439 6825 **f** 0161 439 0622 **m** 07860 951568
e michelle.smith18@btopenworld.com

Suzanne Smith
33 Fitzroy Street, London W1T 6DU
t 020 7436 9255 **f** 020 7436 9690 **m** 07966 236846
e zan@dircon.co.uk
Credits Black Hawk Down (F); Spider (F); Stig Of The Dump (T);
Band Of Brothers (T)

Susie Parriss Casting
53 Braemer Avenue, London SW19 8AY
t 020 8944 9552 **f** 020 8944 9553
e susie-parriss@lineone.net
Contact Susie Parriss, Proprietor
Credits Secrets & Lies (F); Where the Heart Is (T); Hornblower (T)

Suzy Korel Casting
20 Blenheim Road, London NW8 0LX
t 020 7624 6435 **f** 020 7372 3964 **m** 07973 506793
e suzy@korel.org
Contact Suzy Korel, Casting Director

Sarah Trevis
Twickenham Studios, The Barons, St Margarets, Twickenham
TW1 2AW
t 020 8607 8888 **f** 020 8607 8766
Credits Shallow Grave (F); Sweet November (F); Regeneration (F);
To Kill A King (F)

Toby Whale
80 Shakespeare Road, London W3 6SN
t 020 8993 2821 **f** 020 8993 8096 **m** 07778 992978
e toby@whalecasting.com **w** www.whalecasting.com
Credits East Is East (F); Hearts and Bones (T); Men Only (T)

Van Ost & Millington Casting
PO Box 115, Petersfield GU31 5BB
t 020 7436 9838 **f** 020 7436 9858 **m** 07831 619793
e vom@tcp.co.uk
Contact Valerie Van Ost, Partner; Andrew Millington, Partner

Casting **Facilities**

The Broadcasting Company
Unit 7, Canalot Studios, 222 Kensal Road, London W10 5BN
t 020 8969 3020 **m** 07977 570899
e broadcasting@btclick.com
Contact Sophie North, Casting

Casting Studios International Ltd
First Floor, North Wing, Ramillies House, 1-2 Ramillies Street,
London W1F 7LN
t 020 7287 0900 **f** 020 7437 2080
e info@castingstudios.com **w** www.castingstudios.com
Contact Colin Sweeny, Chairman

The Casting Suite
10 Warwick Street, London W1R 5RA
t 020 7434 2331 **f** 020 7494 0803
e info@thecastingsuite.com **w** www.thecastingsuite.com
Contact Sadis Jenour, Manager; Russell Taylor, Manager

Face to Face
50 Frith Street, London W1D 4SQ
t 020 7734 6556 **f** 020 7734 6656 **e** facetofacestudios@aol.com
Contact Becky

Kitsch Kasting Ltd
1-6 Falconburg Court, London W1V 5FG
t 020 7734 2734 **f** 020 7734 2262
e mugshotsdm@aol.com **w** www.mugshots.co.uk
Contact David Morris, Studio Manager

The London Casting Studio
5 Vigo Street, London W1S 3HB
t 020 7287 2882 **f** 020 7287 3992
e patte@londoncastingstudio.com
w www.londoncastingstudio.com
Contact Patte Griffith

Mobile Video
3 Netherhall Gardens, London NW3 5RN
t 020 7794 3825 **m** 07778 931544
e j.macinnes@btinternet.com
Contact John MacInnes, Proprietor
Credits The Others (F); Ned Kelly (F); The Pianist (F); Harry Potter (F)

Mugshots Casting Studio
20 Greek Street, London W1D 4DU
t 020 7437 9245 **f** 020 7437 0308
e mugshotsstudio@aol.com
Contact Amanda Ashed , Agent; Heather March , Agent; Becky Kidd, Studio Manager

Picture It
50 Church Road, London NW10 9PY
t 020 8961 6644 **f** 020 8961 2969
e rosemary@picit.net **w** www.picit.net
Contact Trevor Hunt, Managing Director; Rosemary Element, Sales & Marketing; Chris Sellers, Studio Manager
Flexible packages white infinity cove, fully equipped with dressing rooms.

QD Casting Studio
45 Poland Street, London W1F 7NA
t 020 7437 2823 **f** 020 7437 2830 **e** alicia.w@gotd.co.uk
Contact Alicia Winter, General Manager

Steve Norris Productions
215 Chessington Road, Ewell KT19 9XE
t 020 8394 0616 **m** 07711 669503
e norris@tall-chimneys.fsnet.co.uk
Contact Steve Norris, Proprietor

Take Five Casting Studio
25 Ganton Street, London W1S 9BP
t 020 7287 2120 **f** 020 7287 3035
e info@takefivestudio.co.uk **w** www.takefivestudio.co.uk
Contact James Clenhehan, Managing Director

Casting **Information**

Castcall Information Services
106 Wilsden Avenue, Luton LU1 5HR
t 01582 45613 **f** 01582 480736 **m** 07768 795 960
e admin@castcall.co.uk **w** www.castcall.co.uk
Contact Ron O'Brien, Proprietor

Castnet Ltd
99 Windmill Lane, Bushey Heath WD23 1NE
t 020 8420 4209 **f** 020 8386 6563
e admin@castingnetwork.co.uk **w** www.castingnetwork.co.uk
Contact P Somerston, Casting; D Richman, Managing Director;
A Sharron, Casting
Credits Ascend (D); Kid In The Corner (T); The Man Who Cried (F); Band Of Brothers (T)
Over 1000 trained, professional British Actors - search online FREE!

The Presenters Club
123 Corporation Road, Gillingham ME7 1RG
t 01634 851077 **f** 01634 316771 **m** 07958 582270
e club@presenterpromotions.com
w www.presenterpromotions.com
Contact Colin Cobb, Proprietor

Production & Casting Report (PCR)
PO Box 11, London N1 7JZ
t 020 7566 8282 **f** 020 7566 8284 **w** www.pcrnewsletter.com
Contact Bobbi Dunn, Editor

THE CASTING INFORMATION SERVICE

Script Breakdown Services
Suite 1, 16 Sidmouth Road, London NW2 5JX
t 020 8459 2781 **f** 020 8459 7442
e casting@sbsltd.demon.co.uk
Contact Lydia Martin, Managing Director
SBS Ltd is a unique service in the UK which circulates casting requirements for TV, Film and Theatre producers, directors and casting personnel throughout Great Britain. (The information is not circulated to individual artists). This speedy and efficient service reduces the cost and time for those involved in casting.

Shaun Esden
Holly House, Rectory Avenue, Wollaton Village, Nottingham NG8 2AL
t 0115 928 4105 **f** 0115 942 2483 **m** 07768 910007
e shaun@television-presenter.com
w www.television-presenter.com
Credits Carlton Food Network (T); Great Escapes (D); Wish You Were Here...? (T)

UK Theatre Network
Po Box 3009, Glasgow G60 5ET
t 08707 606033 **f** 08707 606033
e info@uktheatre.net **w** www.uktheatre.net
Contact Douglas McFarlane, Director

Video Casting Directory

1 Triangle House, 2 Broomhill Road, London SW18 4HX
t 020 8874 3314 **f** 020 8874 8590 **e** simon@fightingfilms.com
Contact Simon Hicks, Managing Director
Credits Leon The Pig Farmer (F); The Stone Forest Experience: China (W)

Catering

AV Catering

Flat 2, 14 Victoria Street, Slough SL1 1PR
t 01753 575685 **f** 01753 574878 **m** 07836 636252
Contact Vince Jordan, Partner
Credits ThunderBirds (F); Love Actually (F); Johnny English (F); The Hours (F)

Big Apple Catering

351 Leatherhead Road, Chessington KT9 2NQ
t 01372 727552 **f** 01372 727552 **m** 07774 259414
e ellpet@aol.com
Contact Peter Elliot, Proprietor
Credits KFC (C); Carphone Warehouse (C); Cadbury's All Star (C); Diet Coke (C)

Blas Ar Fwyd

25 Heol yr Orsaf, Llanrwst LL26 0BT
t 01492 640215 **f** 01492 642215 **m** 07860 658383
e deiniol@freeserve.uk
Contact Deiniol Ap Dafydd, Proprieter/Manager
Credits Noson Lawen (T); Granada (F); Dadidilde (T); Maserati (C)

Blends Catering Service

16 High Street, Caterham CR3 5UA
t 01883 345900 **f** 01883 345911 **m** 07703 291351
e st@blends.org **w** www.blends.org
Contact Steve Thornton, Proprietor

Bon Appetit

2 Convent Road, Ashford, Ashford TW15 2EW
t 01784 256368 **f** 01784 256368 **m** 07831 852874
Contact Steven Barnett, Proprietor

Busters Catering

Harmondsworth Hall, Summerhouse Lane, West Drayton UB7 0BG
m 07710 305 960
e peter@busterscatering.com **w** www.busterscatering.com

Bwyd Barça

39 New Street, Caernarfon LL55 2PU
t 01286 676359 **t** 01286 673835
Contact Martin Rigby, Proprietor
Credits Am Dani (T); Eldra (T); Rownd A Rownd (T); Timewatch (T)

Carry On Cooking

7 Palgrave House, Sultan Street, London SE5 0XS
t 07976 264299 **e** maggie@hartdyke.com
Contact Maggie Magee, Proprietor

The Catering Company

Callbox Communications Limited, 66 Shepperton Studios, Studios Road, Shepperton TW17 0QD
t 01932 592572 **f** 01932 569655 **m** 07710 572572
e callboxdiary@btinternet.com **w** www.callboxdiary.co.uk

Chevalier Catering Company Ltd

Studio 5, Garnett Close, Watford WD24 7GN
t 01923 211703 **f** 01923 211704 **m** 07767 674111
e catering@chevalier.co.uk **w** www.chevalier.co.uk
Contact Bonnie May, Operations Manager

Chevalier Event Design

Studio 4/5, Garnett Close, Watford WD24 7GN
t 01923 211703 **t** 020 8950 8998 **f** 01923 211704
e catering@chevalier.co.uk **w** www.chevalier.co.uk
Contact Bonnie May, Operations Manager; Tony Laurenson, Managing Director; Liz Madden, Sales Manager

Clarkson Catering

45 Colvin Gardens, Ilford IG6 2LH
t 01769 560686 **f** 01769 560686 **m** 07850 727 026
e clarksoncatering@supanet.com
Contact Amanda Clarkson, Proprietor
Credits Dirty Pretty Things (F); Onegin (F); Redcap (T); The Vice (T)

Clemence Caterers

Castle Street, Conwy LL32 8AY
t 01492 593248 **f** 01492 593253
Contact James Pritchard, Director

Coleman Caterers

140 Ridgeway Dr, Bromley BR1 5BX
t 020 8857 8308 **f** 020 8857 8308 **m** 07802 426749
Contact Sue Coleman, Proprieter; Brian Coleman, Proprieter

The Cooking Crew

Wizzo & Co, 35 Old Compton Street, London W1D 5JX
t 020 7437 2055 **f** 020 7437 2066
e wizzo@wizzoandco.co.uk **w** www.wizzoandco.co.uk

Crew to Crew

Callbox Communications Limited, 66 Shepperton Studios, Studios Road, Shepperton TW17 0QD
t 01932 592572 **f** 01932 569655 **m** 07710 572572
e callboxdiary@btinternet.com **w** www.callboxdiary.co.uk

Crown Society

113 Bishopsgate, London EC2N 3BA
t 020 7236 2149 **f** 020 7329 2511
e society@crowngroup.co.uk **w** www.crowngroup.co.uk
Contact Colin Sayers, Director of Customer Services

Eat To The Beat

Studio 5, Garnett Close, Watford WD24 7GN
t 01923 211702 **f** 01923 211704 **m** 07767 674117
e catering@eattothebeat.com **w** www.eattothebeat.com
Contact Tony Laurenson, Managing Director

Eat Your Hearts Out

The Basement Flat, 108A Elgin Avenue, London W9 2HD
t 020 7289 9446 **f** 020 7266 3160
e eyho@dial.pipex.com
Contact Kim Davenport, Managing Director

Fat B'Stards Catering

22 Graces Road, London SE5 8PA
t 020 7703 2726 **f** 020 7703 2726 **m** 07973 311918
e adam@hartdyke.com
Contact Adam Dyke, Director
Credits McCains Vibes (F); Best Air Guiter Album...Ever 2 (C); The Fugitives (T); Sacred Trust - One True Voice (M)

Food Goodness Sake

Callbox Communications Limited, 66 Shepperton Studios, Studios Road, Shepperton TW17 0QD
t 01932 592572 **f** 01932 569655 **m** 07710 572572
e callboxdiary@btinternet.com **w** www.callboxdiary.co.uk

Food On The Move

Callbox Communications Limited, 66 Shepperton Studios, Studios Road, Shepperton TW17 0QD
t 01932 592572 **f** 01932 569655 **m** 07710 572572
e callboxdiary@btinternet.com **w** www.callboxdiary.co.uk

Gong

Y Bwthyn Caeathro, Caernarfon LL55 2SS
t 01286 673835 **f** 01286 671657
Contact Gwenllian Daniel, Proprietor

The Good Eating Corporation Ltd
2 Chiltern Road, Newbury Park, Ilford 1G2 7JR
t 020 8590 8902 **e** tsupercook@aol.com
Contact Terry Jones, Director; Caroline Jones, Director

Goodlookin' Cooking Corporate
54 Hillbury Avenue, Harrow HA3 8EW
t 020 8907 6066
Contact Vivian Myrant-Wilson, Proprietor

Grillo's
8 Field Rise, Horninglow, Burton-upon-Trent DE13 0NR
t 01283 845124 **f** 01283 845124 **m** 07956 522 847
e grillo@supanet.com
Contact Adrian Grillo, Manager/Managing Director
Credits Sweet Medicine (T); Margery And Gladys (T); Mersey Beat III & IV (T)

GT Catering & Facilities
Unit 1, Howley Park Close, Morely, Leeds LS27 0BW
t 0113 253 7773 **f** 0113 252 6773 **m** 07787 127207
e paul@gtcaterers.com
Contact Paul Garth, Operations Director; Sharon McGuire, Office Administrator
Credits Heartbeat (T); Grange Hill (T); Hollyoaks (T); Emmerdale (T)

J&J Preparations
Unit 5, Midas Industrial Park, Longbridge Way, Uxbridge UB8 2YT
t 01895 232627 **f** 01895 257033 **m** 07774 864310
e jnj.int@virgin.net **w** www.jji.co.uk
Contact John Lane, Director; Kim Kelly, Secretary
Credits Bend It Like Beckham (F); EastEnders (T); The Inspector Linley Mysteries (T); Harry Potter And The Chamber Of Secrets (F)

John Timson Catering
83 Highfield Way, Rickmansworth WD3 2PN
t 01923 779819 **f** 01923 775108 **m** 07860 627 781
e john@john-timson-catering.co.uk
w www.john-timson-catering.co.uk
Contact John Timson, Managing Director

Lets Do Lunch
Wizzo & Co, 35 Old Compton Street, London W1D 5JX
t 020 7437 2055 **f** 020 7437 2066
e wizzo@wizzoandco.co.uk **w** www.wizzoandco.co.uk

Location Café
5 Firs Close, Iver Heath SL0 0QY
t 01753 651491 **f** 01753 651455 **m** 07774 459056
e andy@locationcafe.com **w** www.locationcafe.com
Contact Andy Aldridge, Proprietor
Credits Blackball (F); Ali G: The Movie (F); Othello (F); Tipping The Velvet (T)

Mange on the Move Ltd
Unit 19, City North, Fonthill Road, London N4 3HF
t 020 7263 5000 **f** 020 7263 2233
e info@mange.co.uk **w** www.mange.co.uk
Contact Anthony Issroff

The Mobile Mouthful
The Old Garden, Cambridge Park, Twickenham TW1 2JW
t 020 8994 8888 **f** 020 8892 2104 **m** 07802 229099
e mobilemouth@hotmail.com
Contact Sammy Mead, Partner; Duncan Manning, Partner

Moodies
Unit A, Station Road Industrial Estate, Liphook GU30 7DR
t 01428 644310 **f** 01428 661620
e moodies@btinternet.com **w** www.moodies.co.uk
Contact Jenine Moodie, Managing Director

Pamela Price Caterer
33 Iveley Road, London SW4 0EN
t 020 7622 6818 **f** 020 7622 6818 **m** 07956 673295
e pamela.price@lineone.net

Partycooks
38 Cardiff Road, Pwllheli LL53 5NT
t 01758 612140 **f** 01758 612285
Contact Ann Williams

The Pie Man Catering Company
Ventura House, 176-188 Acre Lane, London SW2 5UL
t 020 7737 7799 **f** 020 7738 7045 **e** info@the-pie-man.com
Contact Amy Evans-Tipping, Catering Events Manager

Reel Food
141 Eastwoodmains Road, Clarkston, Glasgow G76 7HB
t 0141 638 5262 **f** 0141 638 5590 **m** 07810 258950
m 07950 151703 **e** spaghettiB@aol.com
Contact Guy Cowan, Proprietor
Credits State Of Play (T); Messiah II (T); The One And Only (F); Bridget Jones' Diary (F)

Reel to Reel
Callbox Communications Limited, Box 66 Shepperton Studios, Shepperton TW17 0QD
t 01932 592572 **f** 01932 569655 **e** callboxdiary@btinternet.com

Saucery
Watchcott, Nordan, Leominster HR6 0AJ
t 01568 614221 **f** 01568 610256 **m** 07836 389160
Contact Alison Taylor, Proprietor

Set Meals
Unit 7, The Tower Workshops, Riley Road, London SE1 3DG
t 020 7237 0014 **f** 020 7231 8477
e setmeals@aol.com **w** www.setmeals.co.uk
Contact Phillip Small, Location Caterers; Neil Jones

Jane Southern
14-16 Bagleys Lane, London SW6 2AR
t 020 7731 2684 **m** 07970 319872

St Clements Catering
Unit 25, Argyle Way, Ely Distribution Centre, Cardiff CF5 5NJ
t 029 2059 8121 **f** 029 2059 2846 **m** 07836 605600
e stclements@fsbusiness.net
Contact Danny Yong, Director

Take Five
t 01442 259560 **f** 01442 250560 **m** 07850 723860
Contact Dick Conisbee, Managing Director

THEM
Wizzo & Co, 35 Old Compton Street, London W1D 5JX
t 020 7437 2055 **f** 020 7437 2066
e wizzo@wizzoandco.co.uk **w** www.wizzoandco.co.uk

Tony Bowlie
Tony Bowlie Location Catering, 88 Glyn Rhosyn East, Pentwyn, Cardiff CF23 7DT
t 029 2073 3499 **f** 029 2073 3499 **m** 07887 837458
e tonybowlie@aol.com
Contact Anthony Hill, Proprieter
Credits Belongings (T); Bertie And Elizabeth (T); Plot with a View (F)

VIP Location Catering
505 GT Great Western Road, Glasgow G12 8HN
t 0141 638 1920 **m** 07860 759975

children in entertainment

All performances for children of compulsory school age and under must be licensed under s.37(2) of the Children and Young Person's Act 1963. Licenses should be obtained from the Local Education Authority (LEA) where the child's parent lives.

Acts and recent developments

New regulations to implement the EC Directive in the protection of young people at work came into effect on 4 August 1998. The licensing requirements have been extended to include children involved in paid modelling and sporting activities.

The relevant legislation is contained in : The Children and Young Persons Act 1933 and 1963 and The Children (Performances) Regulations 1968

Below is a step by step guide to the licensing procedure which needs to be considered before any decision can be made regarding the need to licence or grant exemptions. It is re-printed with kind permission of Norman Rouse from his guide 'A Guide to Children's Licensing' - which is available from Bristol City Council.

Guide to licensing

Is the applicant below the minimum school leaving age?
* Children & Young Persons Act 963, s37 (1)
* Education Act 996, s8
* Statutory Instrument 1997 No 1970 - School Leaving Date Order

Does applicant reside in the Local Authority area?
* Children & Young Persons Act 1963, s37 (1)

Is there are charge made for admission or otherwise?
* Is it within licensed premises?
* Is it a broadcast performance?
* Is it intended for filming?
* Children & Young Persons Act 1963, s37 (2)

Is exemption possible?
* No payment to the child and not taken part in performances in the previous 6 months on more than 3 days, or
* No payment to the child for performance/activity and given under arrangements made by school, or
* No payment to the child and performance is made by a body approved by the Secretary of State or LEA (ie the Scouts Gang Show is an exemption granted by the Secretary of State).
* Children & Young Persons Act 1963 s 37 (3)
NB: Certain restrictions also apply with exemptions, see part V1 of 1968 regulations.

Is the applicant fit to take part in performance/activity?
* Children & Young Persons Act 1963, s37 (4)
* Children Regulation 1968, Regulations 8

Education, where necessary consult the headteacher (if school time affected)
* Children & Young Persons Act 1963, a37(4)
* Child Regulation 1968, Regulation 10
* Education, Pupil regulations 1995, Regulation 8,2 (b)   →→→

CHILDREN

Children Chaperones

Crêchendo Events Ltd
1 Grange Mills, Weir Road, London SW12 ONE
t 020 8772 8140 **f** 020 8772 8141
e eventsweb@crechendo.com **w** www.crechendo.com
Credits Jimmy Neutron (Movie Premier) (F); Ice Age (Movie Premier) (F); Harry Potter (Movie Premier) (F)

Jelly Kelly
Callbox Communications Limited, 66 Shepperton Studios, Studios Road, Shepperton TW17 OQD
t 01932 592572 **f** 01932 569655 **m** 07710 572572
e callboxdiary@btinternet.com **w** www.callboxdiary.co.uk

Teresa Moreno
47 North Lane, Teddington TW11 OHU
t 020 8943 1653
Credits The Mother (F); EastEnders (T); The Bill (T); The Worst Witch (T)

Sue Summerskill
58 Victoria Road, London N22 7XF
t 0208 826 0516 **f** 020 8883 0331 **m** 07976 937021
Credits 24/Seven (T); Cheeky (F); The Hoobs (F)

Karen Swan
m 07951 215183
Credits Charcoal Vision (T); Casualties (T); Holby City (T); Teachers (T)

Children Tutors

John Constable
t 020 8590 6516 **f** 020 8590 6516 **m** 07957 686817
e cjohnconstable@aol.com
Credits Teachers Series III (T); Wonderous Oblivion (F); Tom and Thomas (F)

Steve Fletcher
56 Lakeside Road, London N13 4PR
t 020 8882 4117 **f** 020 8372 3064
e arrowsmithlondon@hotmail.com
Credits About A Boy (F); The Gathering (F); White Teeth (T); The World Is Not Enough (F)

Julie Ingham Graham
27 Old Broadway, Withington, Manchester M20 3DH
t 0161 445 1754 **f** 0161 4451754 **m** 07721 048 718

Muriel McKeown
17 Engelfield Road, Islington, London N1 4LJ
t 020 7241 5340 **m** 07816 379 588
e murielmck@hotmail.com

Victoria Theakston
t 01285 653915 **f** 01285 642398 **m** 07967 815 286
Credits Hope And Glory (T); The Whistle Blower (T); Harry Potter And The Prisoner Of Azkaban (F); Harry Potter And The Philosopher's Stone (F)

Is it a safe activity?
- Children & Young Persons Act 1933, s23 - as amended by The Children (Protection at Work) Regulations 2000.
- Management of Health and Safety at Work Regulations 1992
- The Health & Safety (Young Persons) Regulations 1997

Are the application form and supporting documents satisfactorily completed?
- Children & Young Persons Act 1963, s37 (1)

See table below

Paid or Unpaid Work	Type of Work	Absence from School?	Length of Performance	Medical Required?	Licence Required?
Paid (see note 1)	TV or Filming	Yes (see note 3)	Any period of time	Yes - unless one provided within previous 6 months	Yes (see note 5)
Paid (see note 1)	TV or Filming	No	Any period of time	Yes - unless one provided within previous 6 months	Yes (see note 5)
Paid (see note 1)	Theatre, Sport or Modelling	Yes (see note 3)	Any period of time	No (see note 4)	Yes (see note 5)
Paid (see note 1)	Theatre, Sport or Modelling	No	Any period of time	No (see note 4)	Yes (see note 5)
UnPaid (see note 2)	TV or Filming	Yes (see note 3)	Any period of time	Yes - unless one provided within previous 6 months	Yes (see note 5)
UnPaid (see note 2)		No	Any period of time up to and including 4 days (and not performed within previous 6 months)	No	No
UnPaid (see note 2)	Theatre, Sport or Modelling	Yes (see note 3)	Any period of time up to and including 4 days (and not performed within previous 6 months)	No (see note 4)	Yes (see note 5)
UnPaid	Theatre, Sport or Modelling	No	Any period of time up to and including 4 days (and not performed within previous 6 months)	No (see note 4)	No
UnPaid (see note 2)	TV or Filming	Yes (see note 3)	5 days or more	Yes - unless one provided within previous 6 months	Yes (see note 5)
UnPaid (see note 2)	TV or Filming	No	5 days or more	Possibly (see note 4)	Yes (see note 5)
UnPaid (see note 2)	Theatre, Sport or Modelling	Yes (see note 3)	5 days or more	Possibly (see note 4)	Yes (see note 5)
UnPaid	Theatre, Sport or Modelling	No	5 days or more	Possibly (see note 4)	Yes (see note 5)

1 **Paid performances.** Payment to the child in respect of the child in respect of the child's taking part in the performance whether to him/her of to any other person.

2 **Unpaid Performance** "...no payment in respect of the child's taking part in the performance is made, whether to him/her or to any other person except for defraying expenses means that there is no question of any payment or consideration to procure the services of any child taking part in the performance:... A Guide to the Children (Performances) Regulations 1968.

3 **Absence from School** "...leave of absence may not be given to enable a pupil to undertake employment except in accordance with the licence. The Act and regulations contain no provision under which absence from school may be authorised for an unlicensed performance..." - A guide To the Children (Performances) Regulations 1968. Also see The Education (Pupil Restriction) Regulations 1995, Regulation 8(2)(b).

4 **Medical Certificates** are required with applications for children wishing to take part in licensed performances in any television or film work, regardless of any number of days or half days under the conditions of the licence. For broadcast performances, such as radio productions, a child can perform on up to and including 6 days in a six-month period without need for a medical.

5 **When a licence is required** a child shall not take part in a performance or activity except under the authority of a licence. Backdated licences should not be issued, they undermine the licensing process which is, after all, a safeguard for the children.

When licenses are requested at short notice, Local Authorities will invariably try to accommodate requests. However, there must be enough time to deal with the application detail beforehand. Productions should be mindful that the LEA can insist upon 21 days notice - The Children (Performances) Regulations 1968, Regulation 1 (3).

When sending details from one LEA to another - "the licensing authority must send to those authorities copies of the application form and the licence, together with any information they think should be brought to the notice of the other authorities" Children (Performance) Regulations 1968, Regulation 4.

*For further information please contact the relevant LEA.

Choreographers

Kevan Allen
14 Chertsey Road, Leytonstone, London E11 4DG
t 020 8558 7081 **f** 020 8558 7081 **m** 07889 772210
e awesomekj@aol.com
Credits Black Betty - Tom Jones (M); So Graham Norton (T); Sony Playstation (C); Popstars (T)

Micha Bergese
Tommy Tucker Agency, Suite 66, 235 Earls Court Road, London SW5 9FE
t 020 7370 3911 **f** 020 7370 4784 **e** tttommytucker@aol.com

Karen Bruce
Clare Vidal Hall, 28 Perrers Road, London W6 0EZ
t 020 8741 7647 **f** 020 8741 9459
e clarevidalhall@email.com

Pat Garrett
2 Edward Road, St Leonards-on-Sea TN37 6ES
t 020 7287 9000 **m** 07702 270895
e ptgrrtt@aol.com **w** www.kickme.to/patgarrett.com
Credits Monarch Of The Glenn (T); Muppet Treasure Island (F); Little Shop Of Horrors (F); League Of Gentlemen Christmas Special 2000 (T)

Nicky Hinkley
Tommy Tucker Agency, Suite 66, 235 Earls Court Road, London SW5 9FE
t 020 7370 3911 **f** 020 7370 4784 **e** tttommytucker@aol.com

Scarlett Mackmin
Clare Vidal Hall, 28 Perrers Road, London W6 0EZ
t 020 8741 7647 **f** 044 2087 419459
e clarevidalhall@email.com

Wayne McGregor
Cruickshank Cazenove Ltd, 97 Old South Lambeth Road, London SW8 1XU
t 020 7735 2933 **f** 020 7820 1081 **e** hjcruickshank@aol.com
Credits Symbiont - The Dancer's Body (S); Chrysalis (S); Nemesis (S)

Anthoula Papadakis
London Management c/o R. Daniels, Noel House, 2-4 Noel Sreet, London W1V 3RB
t 020 7287 9000 **e** rdaniels@lonman.co.uk
Credits Andrea Chenier SVT (T); Our Friends In The North (T)

Arlene Phillips
9 Perceval Ave., London NW3 4PY
t 020 7794 0715 **f** 020 7794 3647 **m** 07788 755567
e aphgi@yahoo.com
Contact Martin Taylor-Brown, Office Manager
Credits The Royal Variety Show (T); Monty Python's Meaning of Life (F); Commonwealth Games Ceremonies 2002 (T); We Will Rock You

Pineapple Agency
Montgomery House, 159-161 Balls Pond Road, London N1 4BG
t 020 7241 6601 **f** 020 7241 3006
e pineapple.agency@btopenworld.com
w www.pineapple-agency.com
Credits Sure Deodorant (C); French Connection (C); The Way We Live Now (T); My Family (T)

Simon Shelton
Tommy Tucker Agency, Suite 66, 235 Earls Court Road, London SW5 9FE
t 020 7370 3911 **f** 020 7370 4784 **e** tttommytucker@aol.com

Sophie's People
26 Reporton Road, London SW6 7JR
t 787 6446 **f** 787 6447
e sophies.people@btinternet.com **w** www.sophiespeople.com
Contact Sophie Pyecroft, Agent & Live Action Co-ordinator

Tommy Tucker Agency
Suite 66, 235 Earls Court Road, London SW5 9FE
t 020 7370 3911 **f** 020 7370 4784 **e** tttommytucker@aol.com

Bruno Tonioli
86A Sutherland Avenue, London W9 2QR
t 020 7289 1398 **m** 07765 232604
e bruno.tonioli@uksafeway.net
Credits The Gathering Storm (F); American Girl (F); Ella Enchanted (F); Little Voice (F)

UK Choreographers Directory
Dance UK, Battersea Arts Center, Lavender Hill, London SW11 5TN
t 020 7228 4990 **f** 020 7223 0074
e adrienn@danceuk.org **w** www.danceuk.org
Contact Adrienn Szabo, Programme Manager

Sue Weston
St John's Court, Isleworth TW7 6PA
t 020 8560 9347 **m** 07900 362060 **e** sue.weston@virgin.net
Credits Peter Pan (T); Forsyte Saga (T); Feast Of July (F); Ted And Alice (T)

Colourists

Mike Kinsella
Experience Counts - Call Me Ltd, 5th Floor, 41-42 Berners Street, London W1P 3AA
t 020 7637 8112 **f** 020 7580 2582

Luke Rainey
Broomfield House, Lapford, Devon EX17 6LX
t 01363 83101 **f** 01363 83848 **m** 07714 092251
e luke.rainey@talk21.com
Credits Malena (F); Stella Street (F); The Tenth Kingdom (T); Band Of Brothers (T)

COMPUTERS

Computers **Companies**

Albion Computers (PLC)
53-55 Mortimer Street, London W1W 8HR
t 020 7323 0220 **f** 020 7550 7551
e info@albion.co.uk **w** www.albion.co.uk

Chalfont Computer Centre
28 Market Place, Chalfont St Peter, Gerrards Cross SL9 9DU
t 01753 886400 **f** 01753 892077 **e** info@itsjustit.co.uk
Contact John Puttergill, Managing Director

Computer Support Ltd
2 The Polygon, Clifton, Bristol BS8 4PW
t 0117 929 7656 **f** 0117 929 7668
e support@ithelp.co.uk **w** www.ithelp.co.uk

Computers Unlimited
The Technology Park, Colindeep Lane, London NW9 6BX
t 020 8358 5857 **f** 020 8200 3788
e general@unlimited.com
e sales@unlimited.com **w** www.unlimited.com
Contact James Sanson, Managing Director

Enterprise Solutions Group
Enterprise House, C62, Barwell Business Park, Leatherhead
Road, Chessington KT9 2NY
t 020 8879 5800 **f** 020 8879 5801
e sales@esg3.com **w** www.esg3.com

Freehand Ltd
The Courtyard, Eastwood Road, Bramley, Guildford GU5 0DL
t 01483 894000
e jamescw@freehand.co.uk **w** www.freehand.co.uk
Contact Gary Chalk, Sales Manager; Phil Darkin, Sales Director; James Walton,
DVE/DCC Solutions Account Manager

IBM United Kingdom Ltd
PO Box 118, Normandy House, Alencon Link, Basingstoke
RG21 7NZ
t 01256 343000 **f** 08705 426329
e uk_crc@uk.ibm.com **w** www.ibm.com

Northern Computers (UK) Ltd
Charles Avenue, Burgess Hill RH15 9UF
t 01444 251180 **f** 01444 871074
e sales@northern-computers.co.uk
w www.northern-computers.co.uk
Contact Leon Rose, Sales Manager

Pixelution
29 Bridge Street, Hitchin SG5 2DF
t 01462 433558 **f** 01462 435949
e info@pixelution.co.uk **w** www.pixelution.co.uk
Contact Giles Parker, Managing Director; Piers Godden, Software Specialist;
Cliff Ray, Sales Director

Reality Computing
Home Farm, Shere Road, Albury, Guildford GU5 9BL
t 01483 202051 **f** 01483 203078
e sales@realitycomputing.com **w** www.reality-comp.co.uk
Contact Paul Brown, Managing Director

Sun Microsystems
Bagshot Manor, Green Lane, Bagshot GU19 5NL
t 01276 451440 **f** 01276 451287 **w** www.sun.com
Contact Martin Lambert, Marketing Director

Transmedia Dynamics Ltd
Tower House, High Street, Aylesbury HP20 1SQ
t 01296 745080 **f** 01296 745055
e info@tmd.tv **w** www.tmd.tv
Contact Tony Taylor, Chairman; Justin Elkerton, Managing Director; Carlton
Smith, Technical Director; Jon Maynard, Director

Xyratex
Langstone Technology Park, Langstone Road, Havant PO9 1SA
t 023 9249 6000 **f** 023 9249 6001 **w** www.xyratex.com

Computers **Consultants**

Artefactory Ltd
50 Crowborough Road, Furzedown, London SW17 9QQ
t 020 8682 1212 **m** 07711 161497 **e** data@artefactory.com
Contact Dickon Thompson, Computor

Astel UK Ltd
23 The Metro Centre, Britannia Way, London NW10 7PA
t 020 8453 0400 **f** 020 8453 0442
e jeff@astel-uk.com **w** www.astel-uk.com
Contact Jeff Taylor, Manager

Atos KPMG Consulting
1-2 Dorset Rise, London EC4Y 8EN
t 020 7311 3015 **f** 020 7694 8422 **m** 07711 473201
e kevin.yuen@atoskpmgconsulting.co.uk
Contact Kevin Yuen, Principal Consultant

Bitsoft Ltd
193 Hempstead Road, Watford WD17 3HG
t 01923 237575 **f** 01923 237616 **m** 07710 247787
e ira@bitsoft.demon.co.uk **w** www.bitsoft.co.uk
Contact Ira Coleman, Managing Director
Credits Felicia's Journey (F); The Hole (T); Rouge Traper (F); Lighthouse (S)

Jonny Bradley
London
e pgmail@nospaces.net **w** www.nospaces.net
Credits Asterley Clarke Ltd (W); Dalsouple Direct Ltd (W); Automatic Television
(W); The Agreement (W)

Computing Suppliers Federation
PO Box 7418, Great Dunmow CM6 3WF
t 08700 606901 **f** 08700 606902
e info@csf.org.uk **w** www.csf.org.uk

Image Cellar
36 London Road, Cirencester GL7 1AG
t 07813 313183
e tom@image-cellar.co.uk **w** www.image-cellar.co.uk

KAI Computer Services Ltd
245 Gray's Inn Road, London WC1X 8QY
t 020 7713 6060 **f** 020 7713 5566 **m** 07710 478976 **e**
info@kaiuk.com **w** www.kaiuk.com
Contact John Chong, Director; Niall McMahon, Applications Manager
*London TV/Film/Media focused IT applications consultancy,
support and outsource services.*

MRG Systems
Willow Court, Beeches Green, Stroud GL5 4BJ
t 01453 751871 **f** 01453 753125
e sales@mrgsystems.co.uk **w** www.mrgsystems.co.uk
Contact Bryan Corbin, Director

Multimedia UK
91-95a Alcester Road, Studley B80 7NJ
t 01527 852777 **f** 01527 852086
e multi@libraprobroadcast.co.uk
Contact Andrew Whitehouse, Tech Sales

Nu Media Research

5 Charlotte Mews, London W1P 1LP
t 020 7255 2700 **f** 020 7255 2702
e neil@nmr.com **w** www.nmr.com
Contact Craig Whitfield, Technical Operations Manager; Neil Anderson, Business Manager

Computers **Scheduling, Accountancy, Software**

Axium (UK) Ltd

Shepperton Studios, Studios Road, Shepperton TW17 0QD
t 01932 592445 **f** 01932 592228
e kevina@axium.com **w** www.axium.com
Contact David Kerney, Director of Operations
Credits Gosford Park (F); Spy Game (F); Calendar Girls (F); 102 Dalmatians (F)

Clarendon Computer Services Ltd

24 Sandy Lane, Teddington TW11 0DR
t 020 8977 9190 **f** 020 8977 5887 **m** 07774 259 717
e suemcnab@filmtrack.co.uk **w** www.filmtrack.co.uk
Contact Sue McNab, Director; Anita Cox, Marketing Consultant

KAI Computer Services Ltd

245 Gray's Inn Road, London WC1X 8QY
t 020 7713 6060 **f** 020 7713 5566 **m** 07710 478976
e info@kaiuk.co.uk **w** www.kaiuk.co.uk
Contact John Chong, Director; Niall McMahon, Applications Manager
Production Cost/Management software integrated with Microsoft, Sage and other financials.

Pilat Media Ltd

19th Floor, Wembley Point, 1 Harrow Road, Wembley HA9 6DE
t 020 8782 0700 **f** 020 8782 0701
e info@pilatmedia.com **w** www.pilatmedia.com
Contact Jules Elliott-Sysum, Vice President of Global Sales & Marketing

Sargent Disc Ltd

Pinewood Studios, Pinewood Road, Iver Heath SL0 0NH
t 01753 630300 **f** 01753 655881 **w** www.sargent-disc.com
Contact John Sargent, Managing Director; Scott Hardy, IT Manager; Marija Sargent, Payroll Manager; Jimmy Baldwin, Software Sales
Credits Band Of Brothers (T); Gathering Storm (T); Harry Potter I, II & III (F); Tombraider II (F)

ScheduALL by VizuALL Inc

Princess House, 50 East Castle Street, London W1W 8EA
t 020 7436 6655 **f** 020 7436 3555
e eurosales@ScheduALL.com **w** www.scheduall.co.uk
Contact Ron Carey, Account Manager

Virage Europe Ltd

Royal Albert House, Sheet Street, Windsor SLY 1BE
t 01753 705 035 **f** 01753 705 036
e info@virage.com **w** www.virage.com
Contact Janet Davis, Marketing Director; Dan Ambrosi, Marketing Director

Xytech

Gainborough House, 81 Oxford Street, London W1D 2EU
t 020 7903 5170 **f** 020 7903 5169
w www.xytechsystems.com
Contact Simon Hadfield, UK Account Manager

CONSTRUCTION

Construction
Companies (Sets)

Aden Hynes Sculpture Studios

3 Hornsby Square, Southfield Industrial Park, Laindon, Basildon SS15 6SD
t 01268 418837 **f** 01268 414118 **w** www.sculpturestudios.co.uk
Contact Aden Hynes, Proprietor

Andy Knight Ltd

2-6 Occupation Road, London SE17 3BE
t 020 7252 5252 **f** 020 7252 5111
e info@andyknight.co.uk **w** www.andyknight.co.uk
Contact Andy Knight, Managing Director

Aztec Design Group Ltd

PO Box 600, Harpenden AL5 1WE
t 01582 763676 **f** 01582 767766
e studio@aztecdesign.co.uk **w** www.aztecdesign.co.uk
Contact Adam Hodgson, Designer/Director; Jeremy Howell, Managing Director
Credits Cannes/Amsterdam Expos

Bi-Lines Scenery Ltd

2A Eagle Road, North Moons Moat Industrial Estate, Redditch B98 9HF
t 0 1527 63584 **f** 0 1527 66084 **m** 07976 426378

BJ's

Bray Film Studios, Down Place, Water Oakley, Windsor SL4 5UG
t 01628 622111 **f** 01628 770381 **m** 07774 174872
Contact Louise DeHaan, Secretary

BNW Enterprises Ltd

Unit 11, Verulam Industrial Estate, 224 London Road, St Albarns AL1 1JB
t 01727 868 866 **f** 01727 863 355 **m** 07802 931062
e bnw@dial.pipex.com
Contact Paul Warwick, Managing Director

Brian Eatough Film Set Construction

Unit 27, Mountheath Industrial Estate, Ardent Way, Prestwich, Manchester M25 9WB
t 0161 773 9059 **f** 0161 773 9189
e eatoughbrian.filmset@zoom.co.uk
Contact Brian Eatough, Director

Brilliant Stages

Unit 2, Hillgate, Hitchin SG4 0RY
t 01462 455366 **f** 01462 436219
e info@bstages.com **w** www.brilliantstages.com
Contact Mitch Clark, Managing Director; Tony Bowern, General Manager
Credits We Will Rock You - The Dominion Theatre; Rolling Stones Licks Tour

British Harlequin Plc

Festival House, Chapman Way, Tunbridge Wells TN2 3EF
t 01892 514888 **f** 01892 514222
e anita.wheeler@harlequinfloors.co.uk
w www.harlequinfloors.com
Contact Monica Arnott, Marketing Manager

Camouflage

Totom House, Stanley Gardens, Acton, London W3 7SZ
t 020 8742 9292 **f** 020 8749 7347 **m** 07958 513161
w www.totom.co.uk
Contact Ray Churchouse, General Manager

Creator Constructions Ltd
Unit 1, Willow Business Centre, 17 Willow Lane, Mitcham CR4 4NX
t 020 8687 3800 **f** 020 8687 3810 **m** 07979 658876
e giles@creator.uk.com **w** www.creator.uk.com
Contact Sian Lyn-Jones, New Business Manager

Davison & Woods
Unit28 The Business and Innovation Centre, Sunderland
Enterprise Park, Sunderland SR5 2TA
t 0191 516 6317 **f** 0191 516 6318 **e** davison&woods@bicne.co.uk
Contact Les Davison, Partner

DRS Construction
Art Department, 51 Pratt Street, London NW1 0BJ
t 020 7428 0500 **f** 020 7916 2167 **m** 07973 639785
e info@art-department.co.uk

Estdale Ltd
Unit G, Deseronto Wharf, St Marys Road, Langley SL3 7EW
t 01753 548422 **f** 01753 580149
Contact Ian Ivey, Managing Director
Credits Survivor (T); Dog Eat Dog (T); Alistair McGowan's Biggest Impressions (T)

Fabry Trading Ltd
Units 9-11, Silver Road, White City Industrial Park, Shepherds
Bush, London W12 7SG
t 020 8740 7776 **f** 020 8749 8782 **m** 07850 826962
e fabry@btinternet.com
Contact David Gray, Managing Director
Credits The Great Ship (T); Jonathan Creek (T); Only Fools And Horses (T)

Get Set Scenery
Unit 3A, John Withey Properties, Bedwas Road, Caerphilly
CF83 3GF
t 029 2088 8990 **f** 029 2088 5994
e corporatedisplays@freenet.co.uk **w** www.getsetscenery.co.uk
Contact Peter Gillard, Director/Paint; Tony Wilkes, Director/Construction; Kevin
Richmond, Director/Construction
Credits Bryn Terfel (T); Mike Doyle (T); Choir Of The Year (T); Late Night Poker (T)

Hardial Ltd
HDS Studios, Springfield Road, Hayes UB4 0LE
t 020 8573 4000 **f** 020 8561 1754
e info@hdsstudios.com **w** www.hdsstudios.com
Contact Pom Bhabra, Director

J&B Scenery
Unit 1, East Court, The Griffon Centre, Vale Of Leven Industrial
Estate, Dumbarton G82 3PD
t 01389 721221 **f** 01389 721221 **m** 07850 115376
Contact Ben Barry, Foreman/Carpenter; James Baxter, Construction Manager

JKL Scenic Ltd
Hoyland House, Scotch Park Trading Estate, Pickering Street,
Leeds LS12 2PY
t 0113 231 1200 **f** 0113 279 9700 **m** 07767 217082
e jklscenicltd@btinternet.com
Contact Kevin Waite, Construction Manager

John Frost Scenery Ltd
15 Maswell Park Road, Hounslow TW3 2DL
t 020 8898 0190 **f** 020 8755 3838 **m** 07860 451626
e frost_@btclick.com
Contact Mike Parker, Managing Director
Credits The National Television Awards (T); Ant 'N' Dec's Saturday Night
Takeaway (T); Stars In Their Eyes (T); Who Wants To Be A Millionaire? (T)

Keep For Series
Unit 16, Mitre Bridge Industrial Estate, Mitre Way, London W10 6AU
t 020 8962 0300 **f** 020 8960 7373
e kfsltd@kfsltd.fsnet.co.uk **w** www.keepforseries.com
Contact Les White, Managing Director; Joe Sheehan, Managing Director
Credits Blue Peter (T); Single (T); Footballers Wives (T); Judge John Deed (T)

The Ladder Company Ltd
40 Montagu Square, London W1H 2LL
e peterverard@aol.com
Contact Peter Verard, Director
Credits Princess Bride (F); Brazil (F); Enigma (F); Hartland (F)

Lewis Set Construction Ltd
26 Sunbeam Road, London NW10 6JL
t 020 8838 6211 **f** 020 8838 0734 **m** 07860 805150
e lewisset@aol.com
Contact Simon Lewis, Construction Manager

Maltbury
11 Hollingbury Terrace, Brighton BN1 7JE
t 0845 130 8881 **f** 0845 130 8881
e info@maltbury.com **w** www.maltbury.com
Contact Philip Sparkes, Managing Director

O&A Associates
198 Drakefell Road, Brockley, London SE4 2DS
t 020 7635 9155 **f** 020 7277 5120
e hannah@oasets.demon.co.uk
Contact Hannah Hunter

Parker Butler
Hibernia House, 99-101 High Street, Holywood BT18 9AG
t 028 9042 6047 **f** 028 9042 1082
e design@parkerbutler.co.uk **w** www.parkerbutler.co.uk
Contact Louise Kelly, Sales and Marketing Executive

Perry Scenic Ltd
Units D&E, 100 Dudley Rd East, Old Bury B69 3EB
t 0121 552 9696 **f** 0121 552 9697 **e** info@perryscenic.com
e jonathan@perryscenic.com **w** www.perryscenic.com
Contact Jonathan Perry, Director; David Perry, Proprietor

PF Burridge & Sons
Unit 8/9, Wesley Way, Benton Square Industrial Estate,
Newcastle upon Tyne NE12 9TA
t 0191 266 5332 **f** 0191 266 9250
e main@pfburridge.co.uk **w** www.pfburridge.co.uk
Contact David Burridge, Managing Director

Pine Film Construction Ltd
Pinewood Studios, Pinewood Road, Iver Heath SL0 0NH
t 01753 651 700 **t** 01753 654 157 **f** 01753 654 165
e john@pinefilms.f9.co.uk **w** www.pinefilms.f9.co.uk
Contact John Maher

The Production Design Company
Wallnut Tree Cottage, Ockham Lane, Ockham, Woking
GU23 6NR
t 01483 211033 **f** 01483 211352 **e** jdomhill@pdco.co.uk
Contact Jane Domhill, Managing Director

Propshop
1A Carlyon Road, Wembley HA0 1HP
t 0870 900 4311 **f** 0870 900 4311 **m** 07971 000001
e chris@the-propshop.co.uk **w** www.the-propshop.co.uk
Contact Christopher Dann, Managing Director; Rick Locker, Director

Sanctuary Set Construction
8 Olaf Street, London W11 4BE
t 020 7221 9041 **f** 020 7221 9399
e setconstruction@sanctuarystudios.co.uk
w www.sanctuarystudios.co.uk
Contact Iain Hill, Construction Manager
*Servicing any size of build for stage, screen or exhibition. Constructing
in house or on location as required anywhere in the world.*

Scott Fleary Ltd
Units 1&2, Southside Industrial Estate, Havelock Terrace,
London SW8 4AS
t 020 7978 1787 **f** 020 7622 0322 **m** 07771 596689
e ken@scottflearyltd.com
Contact Ken Fleary, Director; Matthew Scott, Director
Credits Duchess Of Malfi (T); Peter Pan At The Royal Festival Hall (E); Celebrity
Big Brother (T); Who Wants To Be A Millionaire? (T)

Set 1
The Studio, Pean Hill CT5 3BD
t 01227 763653 **f** 01227 452791 **m** 07785 547995
e set1@orange.net
Contact Bill Collom, Manager
Credits Sunset and Vine (T); Channel 4 News (T); Channel 5 News (T);
Open Golf (T)

Set 2
Westminster Industrial Estate, 216c Siemens Road, Woolwich,
London SE18 5TT
t 020 8855 2080 **f** 020 8855 1090 **m** 07831 431741
e set2jones@aol.com
Contact Peter Jones, Proprietor

Set 2 (Setting The Standards) Ltd
Riverside Drive, Cleckheaton BD19 4DH
t 01274 865888 **f** 01274 855522
e info@set-2.co.uk **w** www.set-2.co.uk
Contact Paul Murgatroyd, Managing Director; Chris Murgatroyd,
Managing Director

Set The Scene Ltd
Home Field House, Burcott, Wing, Leighton Buzzard LU7 0KW
t 01296 682344 **f** 01296 682197 **m** 07970 753142
e shargreaves@btinternet.com
Contact Stephen Hargreaves, Construction Manager

Stage One Creative Services Ltd
Briar Rhydding House, Otley Road, Shipley BD17 7JP
t 01274 531738 **f** 01274 599000
e sales@socs.co.uk **w** www.socs.co.uk
Contact Mark Johnson, Account Director; Simon Wood, Director,
Sales Director

Stephen Hayward Film & TV Constructions
Estate Yard, High Canons, Borehamwood WD6 5PL
t 020 8953 1745 **f** 020 8953 9044 **m** 07768 965857
e set-up@talk21.com **e** stephen@setbuild.tv **w** www.setbuild.tv
Contact Stephen Hayward, Construction Manager

TC Lenman
14 Lower Tail, Watford WD19 5DD
t 020 8428 9687 **f** 020 8428 9687 **m** 07850 221274
e tlenman@yahoo.co.uk

WM Display Studio Ltd
Unit C, Enterprise West, Craigmont Street, Glasgow G20 9BT
t 0141 945 5666 **f** 0141 945 5511 **e** billminnis@wnstudio.co.uk
Contact Bill Minnis, Managing Director
Credits Snoddy (T); 50/50 (T); Chilling the Fact (T)

Construction
Crew, Carpenters

Graham John Blinco
46 Stonecraft Avenue, Iver SL0 9QG
t 01753 654443
Credits Possession (F); First Knight (F); The World Is Not Enough (F)

Stephen Eels
7 Greenacre Mount, Tilehurst, Reading RG30 4UD
t 0118 941 9410 **m** 07880 976084
e steveshelly@btopenworld.com
Credits Lara Croft: Tomb Raider (F); Die Another Day (F); The World Is Not
Enough (F)

Chris Harding
19 Goat Street, St Davids SA62 6RF
t 01437 720898 **e** hardinggang@tiscali.com

Derek Honeybun
72 Old Castle Road, Weymouth DT4 8QE
t 01305 789428 **m** 07732 176502
Credits Goodnight Mr Tom (T); Pride And Prejudice (T); Topsy Turvy (F);
Brassed Off (F)

Set & Strike Ltd
55 Vernon Drive, Stanmore HA7 2BW
t 020 8861 3900 **f** 020 8861 3900 **m** 07802 932370
Contact Samuel Winterman, Director, Studio and Location
Credits The National Lottery (T); Generation Game (T); Weekend Watchdog (T)

Showforce
Unit 001a, Stratford Workshops, Burford Road, London E15 2SP
t 020 8519 5252 **f** 020 8519 9006 **m** 07770 276 301
e info@showforce.com **w** www.showforce.com

Construction **Managers**

Alex Henebury Construction
Studio 131, Great Western Studios, Great Western Road,
London W9 3NG
t 020 8374 8658 **f** 020 8374 8658 **m** 07768 892682
e alexhenebury@hotmail.com

Nick Bloom
PO Box 27006, Fortis Green, London N2 9WY
t 020 8365 3806 **f** 0709 238 2213 **m** 07768 354010
e nickbloom@compuserve.com
Credits Never Never (T); The Swap (T); Lenny Blue (T)

Dave Channon
12 French Street, Sunbury-on-Thames TW16 5JJ
t 01932 787197 **f** 01932 787697 **m** 07860 748182
Credits Auf Wiedersehn Pet (T); Brittanic (F); The Lost World (T); Hornblower (T)

Dave Creed Construction
Yew Tree Cottage, Ferry Lane, Laleham TW18 1SP
t 01784 469278 **f** 01784 469278 **m** 07764 190 914
e dave@dcreed.fsnet.co.uk
Credits Trust (T); Waking The Dead (F); LD50 (F); Wild West (T)

Frame By Frame Construction Ltd
29 Drayton Road, West Ealing, London W13 0LD
t 020 8997 6412 **f** 020 8998 0345 **m** 07860 929761
Credits Goodbye Mr Chips (T); Dirty Pretty Things (F); Bridget Jones' Diary (F);
The Hours (F)

Russell Fulton
Unit C11, Dundonald Enterprise Park, Enterprise Drive,
Cararowreagh Road, Belfast BT16 1QT
t 028 9055 7557 **f** 028 9055 7558 **m** 07885 737095
e russellfulton@fsmall.net
Contact Russell Fulton

Len Furey
t 01736 787356 **m** 07989 972017

Jonathan Dickson Construction

Unit D3, Cooper House Depot, London SW6 2AD
t 020 7371 8384 **f** 020 7371 8384 **m** 07956 351500
e jd@jonathandicksonconstrucion.co.uk
w www.jonathandicksonconstrucion.co.uk
Contact Jonathan Dickson , Construction Manager
Credits The Bunker

AJ King

29 Old Street, Haughley, Stowmarket IP14 3NT
t 01449 674126 **f** 01449 674126 **m** 07785 511705
e ajkingfilmsets@aol.com

John Maher

ADS, Shepperton Studios, Studios Road, Shepperton TW17 0QD
t 01932 592303 **f** 01932 592492 **e** ads@carlincrew.co.uk
Credits Birthday Girl (F); Unconditional Love (F); Eyes Wide Shut (F); Spy Game (F)

James McNeil

149 Ashford Road, Iver Heath SL0 0QE
t 01753 654175 **m** 07801 150470 **e**
james.mcneil1@btinternet.com
Credits Under the Hammer (T); Virtual Sexuality (F)

Barry Moll

56 Claremont Road, Ealing, London W13 0DG
t 020 8998 8595 **f** 020 8998 8595 **m** 07710 444759
Credits Last Orders (F); Daniel Deronda (T); Topsy Turvy (F);
The Way We Live Now (T)

John Thorpe

3 Bank Parade, Otley LS21 3DY
t 01943 456040 **f** 01943 456040 **m** 07860 394586
e jotleyjohn@aol.com
Credits Tipping The Velvet (T); Great Expectations (T); Our Mutual Friend (T);
The Forsyte Saga (T)

Kevin Waite

t 0113 231 1200 **f** 0113 231 1200 **m** 07767 217082
e jklscenicltd@btinternet.com
Credits League Of Gentlemen (T); The Office (T)

Augustus (Gus) Wookey

4 Forge Cottages, Caerleon, Newport NP18 3NX
m 07775 691889
e guswookey@guswookey.freeserve.co.uk
w www.guswookey.freeserve.co.uk
Credits Serious And Organised (T); The I Inside (F); Stig Of The Dump (T);
Thunderpants (F)

Continuity Script Supervisors

Arnna Alexander

Gems, The Media House, 87 Glebe Street, Penarth CF64 1EF
t 029 2071 0770 **f** 029 2071 0771
e gems@gems-agency.co.uk **w** www.gems-agency.co.uk
Credits Strange (T); Dream Team (T); Mile High (T); The Haunting (F)

Angela Allen

t 020 7286 5743 **f** 020 7289 0790 **m** 07721 412598
e angelablomfield@aol.com
Agent EXEC, 6 Travis Court, Farnham Royal SL2 3SB
t 01753 646677 **f** 01753 646770
e sue@execmanagement.co.uk **w** www.execmanagement.co.uk
Credits Tea With Moussellini (F); Callas Forever (F); Ronin (F)

Hazel Allinson

Gems, The Media House, 87 Glebe Street, Penarth CF64 1EF
t 029 2071 0770 **f** 029 2071 0771
e gems@gems-agency.co.uk **w** www.gems-agency.co.uk
Credits Grown Ups (T); Thin Blue Line (T); Kiss Me Kate (T); The Bill (T)

Hazel Allinson

Experience Counts - Call Me Ltd, 5th Floor, 41-42 Berners
Street, London W1P 3AA
t 020 7637 8112 **f** 020 7580 2582

Linda Baker

52 Menelik Road, West Hampstead, London NW2 3RH
t 020 7431 7010 **f** 020 7431 7011 **m** 07958 358 247
e Linda1baker@hotmail.com
Agent EXEC, 6 Travis Court, Farnham Royal SL2 3SB
t 01753 646677 **f** 01753 646770
e sue@execmanagement.co.uk **w** www.execmanagement.co.uk
Credits Hearts and Bones (T); Shooters (F); My Brother Tom (F)

Suzanne Baron

136 Sinclair Road, Olympia, London WI4 0NL
m 07973 749230 **e** suzannebaron@lycos.co.uk
Credits BBC Comic Relief Red Nose Night (T); Johnny Vaughan Tonight (T);
UGetMe (T); I'm Alan Partridge 2003 (T)

Libbie Barr

84 Aylmer Road, Stamford Brook, London W12 9LQ
t 020 8749 2099 **f** 020 8749 2099 **m** 07778 844694
w www.hitlist.co.uk/continuity/libbiebarr
Agent Callbox Communications Limited, 66 Shepperton
Studios, Studios Road, Shepperton TW17 0QD
t 01932 592572 **f** 01932 569655 **m** 07710 572572
e callboxdiary@btinternet.com **w** www.callboxdiary.co.uk
Contact Cathy Lord, Producer; David Barron, Producer; Paula Weinstein, Producer;
Barnaby Thompson, Producer; Sarah Curtis, Producer; Mark Cooper, Producer
Credits Notting Hill (F); Chocolat (F); Charlotte Gray (F)

Jo Beckett

Gems, The Media House, 87 Glebe Street, Penarth CF64 1EF
t 029 2071 0770 **f** 029 2071 0771
e gems@gems-agency.co.uk **w** www.gems-agency.co.uk
Credits Paradise (T); The Brontes (T); The One And Only (F); Wondrous Oblivion (F)

Alice Bell

72 Gap Road, Wimbledon, London SW19 8JF
t 020 8946 1087 **m** 07956 000770 **e** alicejbell@hotmail.com
Agent The Production Switchboard, North Down, Down Lane,
Compton GU3 1DN
t 01483 812011 **f** 01483 812027
e aly@productionswitch.freeserve.co.uk
Credits The Hoobs (T); Nescafe - Therapy (C); Neil's Party (F)

Jane Berry

The Production Switchboard, North Down, Down Lane,
Compton GU3 1DN
t 01483 812011 **f** 01483 812027
e aly@productionswitch.freeserve.co.uk
Credits Tosspot (F); Bridget Jones Diary; Spy Game (F)

Sue Binding

Gems, The Media House, 87 Glebe Street, Penarth CF64 1EF
t 029 2071 0770 **f** 029 2071 0771
e gems@gems-agency.co.uk **w** www.gems-agency.co.uk
Credits Doctors (T); Where The Heart Is (T)

Jenny Bowman

48 Cotton Road, Potters Bar EN6 5JG
t 01707 662705 **f** 01707 662705 **m** 07950 254371
Credits The Falklands Play (T); Crossroads (T); EastEnders (T); The Bill (T)

Francine Brown

19 Staunton Road, Kingston KT2 5TJ
t 020 8549 2499 **f** 020 8549 2499 **m** 07790 401343

Mary Bugg

Callbox Communications Limited, 66 Shepperton Studios,
Studios Road, Shepperton TW17 0QD
t 01932 592572 **f** 01932 569655 **m** 07710 572572
e callboxdiary@btinternet.com **w** www.callboxdiary.co.uk

Anwen Bull
Flat 6 124, Sinclair Road, London W14 0NL
t 020 7348 3773 **f** 020 7348 3773 **m** 07768 305314
e anwen_uk@yahoo.com
Agent Gems, The Media House, 87 Glebe Street, Penarth CF64 1EF
t 029 2071 0770 **f** 029 2071 0771
e gems@gems-agency.co.uk **w** www.gems-agency.co.uk
Credits Addicted To The Stars (F); Born And Bred (T); Helen Of Peckham (F); Midsomer Murders IV & V (T)

Daphne Carr
m 07799 526 929 **e** daphne.carr@scriptsupervisor.fsnet.co.uk
Credits Night & Day; Stone Scissors Paper; Headless

Karen Carter
Gems, The Media House, 87 Glebe Street, Penarth CF64 1EF
t 029 2071 0770 **f** 029 2071 0771
e gems@gems-agency.co.uk **w** www.gems-agency.co.uk
Credits The Missing Postman (T); The Bill (T); The Wilsons (T); Family Affairs (T)

Irene Chawko
Flat J25, Du Cane Court, Balham High Road, London SW17 7JU
t 020 8675 8707 **f** 020 8675 8890 **m** 07860 277502
e ichawko@aol.com
Agent Gems, The Media House, 87 Glebe Street, Penarth CF64 1EF
t 029 2071 0770 **f** 029 2071 0771
e gems@gems-agency.co.uk **w** www.gems-agency.co.uk
Credits The Mayor Of Casterbridge (T); Take A Girl Like You (T); Teachers (T); Judge John Deeds (T)

Nicky Cooney
Experience Counts - Call Me Ltd, 5th Floor, 41-42 Berners Street, London W1P 3AA
t 020 7637 8112 **f** 020 7580 2582

Lesley Cross
Cornerside, 16 Clarendon Road, Alderbury, Salisbury SP5 3AT
t 01722 710719 **f** 01722 710719 **m** 07798 678781
Agent Gems, The Media House, 87 Glebe Street, Penarth CF64 1EF
t 029 2071 0770 **f** 029 2071 0771
e gems@gems-agency.co.uk **w** www.gems-agency.co.uk
Credits The Widow Maker (F); Tom And Viv (F); Jinnah (F); Milk (F)

San Davey
Callbox Communications Limited, 66 Shepperton Studios, Studios Road, Shepperton TW17 0QD
t 01932 592572 **f** 01932 569655 **m** 07710 572572
e callboxdiary@btinternet.com **w** www.callboxdiary.co.uk

Diana Dill
13 Chiswick Staithe, Hartington Road, Chiswick, London W4 3TP
t 020 8995 9049 **m** 07970 895269
Agent EXEC, 6 Travis Court, Farnham Royal SL2 3SB
t 01753 646677 **f** 01753 646770
e sue@execmanagement.co.uk **w** www.execmanagement.co.uk
Credits The Good Thief (F); Imagining Argentina (F); The End Of The Affair (F); The Affair Of The Necklace (F)

Sam Donovan
t 020 8789 9804 **f** 020 8789 9804 **m** 07850 429139
e samdonovan@samdonovan.freeserve.co.uk
Credits Virtual Sexuality (F); Footballers Wives (F); Nil By Mouth (F)

Cathy Doubleday
t 01273 324604 **f** 01273 324604 **m** 07973 193009
e cathydday@aol.com
Credits Spooks (T); Iris (F); Neverland (F); Ted And Sylvia (F)

Kirsty Edgar
Experience Counts - Call Me Ltd, 5th Floor, 41-42 Berners Street, London W1P 3AA
t 020 7637 8112 **f** 020 7580 2582

Lucy Enfield
17 Bonnington Grove, Edinburgh EH6 4BL
t 0131 467 3231 **f** 0131 467 3098 **m** 07623 708026
e lucy_enfield@hotmail.com
Credits Skagerrak (F); Late Night Shopping (F); Gas Attack (T); Taggart (T)

Ceri Evans-Cooper
Bookends Ltd, 83 Maynard Drive, St Albans AL1 2JX
t 01727 841177 **e** bookgold@bookends.fsbusiness.co.uk

Penny Eyles
28 Corsica Street, London N5 1JY
t 020 7226 4611 **m** 07885 617782
Agent The Production Switchboard, North Down, Down Lane, Compton GU3 1DN
t 01483 812011 **f** 01483 812027
e aly@productionswitch.freeserve.co.uk
Credits The Man Who Cried (F); Waking Ned (F); Dirty Pretty Things (F); Gosford Park (F)

Lorely Farley
Carlin Crew Ltd, Shepperton Studios, Studios Road, Shepperton TW17 0QD
t 01932 568268 **f** 01932 571109
e carlin@netcomuk.co.uk **w** www.carlincrew.com

Kay Fenton
EXEC, 6 Travis Court, Farnham Royal SL2 3SB
t 01753 646677 **f** 01753 646770
e sue@execmanagement.co.uk **w** www.execmanagement.co.uk

Sue Field
EXEC, 6 Travis Court, Farnham Royal SL2 3SB
t 01753 646677 **f** 01753 646770
e sue@execmanagement.co.uk **w** www.execmanagement.co.uk

Liz Finch
Experience Counts - Call Me Ltd, 5th Floor, 41-42 Berners Street, London W1P 3AA
t 020 7637 8112 **f** 020 7580 2582

Dionne Fletcher
Gems, The Media House, 87 Glebe Street, Penarth CF64 1EF
t 029 2071 0770 **f** 029 2071 0771
e gems@gems-agency.co.uk **w** www.gems-agency.co.uk
Credits Ed Stone Is Dead (T); Search (T); The Last Of The Summer Wine (T); Crossroads (T)

Jill Forbes
34 Jameson Drive, Corbridge NE45 5EX
t 01434 632428 **f** 01434 632428 **m** 07770 895877
e jillforbes@connectfree.co.uk
Credits Coronation Street (T); Byker Grove (T); 2000 Acres Of Sky (T); Where The Heart Is (T)

Dorothy Friend
Gems, The Media House, 87 Glebe Street, Penarth CF64 1EF
t 029 2071 0770 **f** 029 2071 0771 **e** gems@gems-agency.co.uk
w www.gems-agency.co.uk
Credits A&E (T); Twenty Four Seven (T); Cold Feet (T); Coronation Street (T)

Ann Gallivan
70 Whitestile Road, Brentford TW8 9NL
t 020 8569 9463 **m** 07850 141192 **e** annie.galli@virgin.net
Credits The Garden Of Herbs (T); The Bill (T); Othello (T); Margery And Gladys (T)

Carol Gardner
Gems, The Media House, 87 Glebe Street, Penarth CF64 1EF
t 029 2071 0770 **f** 029 2071 0771
e gems@gems-agency.co.uk **w** www.gems-agency.co.uk
Credits Ultimate Force (T); The Bill (T); The Hour Of The Pig (F); Cold Comfort Farm (F)

Sarah Garner
51 Wellington Road, Ealing, London W5 4UJ
t 020 8567 0262 **f** 020 8567 0262 **m** 07770 500543
e garners@freenet.co.uk
Credits Keen Eddie (T); Johnson English (F); The Gathering (F); Band Of Brothers (T)

Linda Gibson
Gems, The Media House, 87 Glebe Street, Penarth CF64 1EF
t 029 2071 0770 **f** 029 2071 0771
e gems@gems-agency.co.uk **w** www.gems-agency.co.uk
Credits Hornblower (T); Unconfidential Love (T); Cinderella (F); An Angel For May (F)

Laura Goulding
Callbox Communications Limited, 66 Shepperton Studios,
Studios Road, Shepperton TW17 0QD
t 01932 592572 **f** 01932 569655 **m** 07710 572572
e callboxdiary@btinternet.com **w** www.callboxdiary.co.uk

Lindsay Grant
m 07711 298283 **e** lindz.i@virgin.net
Credits Sons And Lovers (T); State Of Mind (T); Cambridge Spies (T); Outside
The Rules (T)

Laura Gwynne
Gems, The Media House, 87 Glebe Street, Penarth CF64 1EF
t 029 2071 0770 **f** 029 2071 0771
e gems@gems-agency.co.uk **w** www.gems-agency.co.uk
Credits Playing The Field (T); Bridget Jone's Diary (F); Large (F); Octane (F)

Mary Haddow
Gems, The Media House, 87 Glebe Street, Penarth CF64 1EF
t 029 2071 0770 **f** 029 2071 0771
e gems@gems-agency.co.uk **w** www.gems-agency.co.uk
Credits My Uncle Silas (T); Mean Machine (W); Swept Away (F); Blueberry (F)

Katie Harlow
Gems, The Media House, 87 Glebe Street, Penarth CF64 1EF
t 029 2071 0770 **f** 029 2071 0771
e gems@gems-agency.co.uk **w** www.gems-agency.co.uk
Credits Night And Day (T); In His World (F); Queen Of Swords (F); Dark Realm (F)

Sarah Hayward
The Homestead, Brays Lane, Hyde Heath, Amersham HP6 5RU
t 01494 783393 **f** 07968 085191 **m** 07973 640 133
e sarah_hayward@btinternet.com
Credits The Last Detective (T); Tabloid TV; 3 Guesses

Peter Hodgson
EXEC, 6 Travis Court, Farnham Royal SL2 3SB
t 01753 646677 **f** 01753 646770
e sue@execmanagement.co.uk **w** www.execmanagement.co.uk

Caroline Holder
Gems, The Media House, 87 Glebe Street, Penarth CF64 1EF
t 029 2071 0770 **f** 029 2071 0771
e gems@gems-agency.co.uk **w** www.gems-agency.co.uk
Credits The Bill (T); Where The Heart Is (T); Grange Hill (T); Peak Practice (T)

Jane Houston
Gems, The Media House, 87 Glebe Street, Penarth CF64 1EF
t 029 2071 0770 **f** 029 2071 0771
e gems@gems-agency.co.uk **w** www.gems-agency.co.uk
Credits Sweet Revenge (F); Trust (T); The Parole Officer (F); State Of Play (F)

Nichol Hoye
Gems, The Media House, 87 Glebe Street, Penarth CF64 1EF
t 029 2071 0770 **f** 029 2071 0771
e gems@gems-agency.co.uk **w** www.gems-agency.co.uk
Credits Bad Girls (T); Murder Rooms (T); Dalziel And Pascoe (T); In Deep (T)

Kathy Hughes
Agent EXEC, 6 Travis Court, Farnham Royal SL2 3SB
t 01753 646677 **f** 01753 646770
e sue@execmanagement.co.uk
w www.execmanagement.co.uk
Agent Callbox Communications Limited, 66 Shepperton
Studios, Studios Road, Shepperton TW17 0QD
t 01932 592572 **f** 01932 569655 **m** 07710 572572
e callboxdiary@btinternet.com **w** www.callboxdiary.co.uk
Agent Gems, The Media House, 87 Glebe Street,
Penarth CF64 1EF
t 029 2071 0770 **f** 029 2071 0771
e gems@gems-agency.co.uk **w** www.gems-agency.co.uk
Credits Always And Everyone (T); The Insiders (T); Jimmy Spud (F);
Anazapta (F)

Pam Humphreys
'Aquarius', Canal Bank, Abercanaid CF48 1HX
t 01443 690202 **f** 01443 691872 **m** 07885 261204
e pam@prodmed.fsnet.co.uk
Agent Gems, The Media House, 87 Glebe Street,
Penarth CF64 1EF
t 029 2071 0770 **f** 029 2071 0771
e gems@gems-agency.co.uk **w** www.gems-agency.co.uk
Credits Peak Practice (T); Candle In The Dark (F); Rancid Aluminium (F); The
Testimony Of Taliesin Jones (F)

Jane Jackson
Agent EXEC, 6 Travis Court, Farnham Royal SL2 3SB
t 01753 646677 **f** 01753 646770
e sue@execmanagement.co.uk **w** www.execmanagement.co.uk
Agent Gems, The Media House, 87 Glebe Street, Penarth
CF64 1EF
t 029 2071 0770 **f** 029 2071 0771
e gems@gems-agency.co.uk **w** www.gems-agency.co.uk
Credits Roy Dance Is Dead (T); It's A Girl Thing (T); Thick, Twisted And Harry
(F); Mr In Between (F)

Emma John
The Production Switchboard, North Down, Down Lane,
Compton GU3 1DN
t 01483 812011 **f** 01483 812027
e aly@productionswitch.co.uk
Credits 20 Things To Do Before You're 30 (C); The Book Group Series II (T);
Teachers Series II (T)

Karen Jones
The Production Switchboard, North Down, Down Lane,
Compton GU3 1DN
t 01483 812011 **f** 01483 812027
e aly@productionswitch.freeserve.co.uk
Credits Lenny Blue (T); Messiah II (T); Daniel Deronda (T)

Rowena Ladbury
Callbox Communications Limited, 66 Shepperton Studios,
Studios Road, Shepperton TW17 0QD
t 01932 592572 **f** 01932 569655 **m** 07710 572572
e callboxdiary@btinternet.com **w** www.callboxdiary.co.uk

Amanda Lean
Gems, The Media House, 87 Glebe Street, Penarth CF64 1EF
t 029 2071 0770 **f** 029 2071 0771
e gems@gems-agency.co.uk **w** www.gems-agency.co.uk
Credits Ghosthunters (T); Hidden City (T); Sam's Circus (F); Crust (F)

Layla Lee-Curtis
Callbox Communications Limited, 66 Shepperton Studios,
Studios Road, Shepperton TW17 0QD
t 01932 592572 **f** 01932 569655 **m** 07710 572572
e callboxdiary@btinternet.com **w** www.callboxdiary.co.uk

Cheryl Leigh
t 020 8998 4368 f 020 8998 4368 m 07831 772423
Agent EXEC, 6 Travis Court, Farnham Royal SL2 3SB
t 01753 646677 f 01753 646770
e sue@execmanagement.co.uk w www.execmanagement.co.uk
Credits Batman (F); Felicia's Journey (F); Buffalo Soldiers (F)

Susanna Lenton
Gems, The Media House, 87 Glebe Street, Penarth CF64 1EF
t 029 2071 0770 f 029 2071 0771
e gems@gems-agency.co.uk w www.gems-agency.co.uk
Credits Land And Freedom (F); Sweet Sixteen (F); A Certain Age (F); The Rocket Post (F)

Maggie Lewty
21 Alexandra Road, Kew, Richmond TW9 2BT
t 020 8940 3777 f 020 8940 3777 m 07710 160097
e mlewty@freenet.co.uk
Credits Pearl Harbor (F); Dalziel And Pascoe (T); The Scarlet Pimpernel (T); Trial And Retribution V (T)

Harri Logan
The Production Switchboard, North Down, Down Lane, Compton GU3 1DN
t 01483 812011 f 01483 812027
e aly@productionswitch.freeserve.co.uk
Credits The Chase (F); Nine Dead Gay Guys (F); Number 1 Longing - Number 2 Regret (F)

Steve Lunnon
Suz Cruz, Halliford Studios, Manygate Lane, Shepperton TW17 9EG
t 01932 252577 f 01932 253323 m 07956 485593
e zoe@suzcruz.co.uk w www.suzcruz.co.uk

Sue Mahoney
Agent Experience Counts - Call Me Ltd, 5th Floor, 41-42 Berners Street, London W1P 3AA
t 020 7637 8112 f 020 7580 2582
Agent Annie's Answering Service, Pinewood Studios, Pinewood Road, Iver Heath SL0 0NH
t 01753 651303 f 01753 651848
e info@annies.co.uk w www.annies.co.uk
Agent Gems, The Media House, 87 Glebe Street, Penarth CF64 1EF
t 029 2071 0770 f 029 2071 0771
e gems@gems-agency.co.uk w www.gems-agency.co.uk
Credits They Think It's All Over (T); Night And Day (T); EastEnders (T); The Bill (T)

Tess Malone
EXEC, 6 Travis Court, Farnham Royal SL2 3SB
t 01753 646677 f 01753 646770
e sue@execmanagement.co.uk w www.execmanagement.co.uk

Emily Marston
Gems, The Media House, 87 Glebe Street, Penarth CF64 1EF
t 029 2071 0770 f 029 2071 0771
e gems@gems-agency.co.uk w www.gems-agency.co.uk
Credits The Queen's Nose (T); Twinfants (F); Early Morning Blues And Greens (S); Devil's Gate (F)

Billie L Mayer
Experience Counts - Call Me Ltd, 5th Floor, 41-42 Berners Street, London W1P 3AA
t 020 7637 8112 f 020 7580 2582

Alex Middleton
EXEC, 6 Travis Court, Farnham Royal SL2 3SB
t 01753 646677 f 01753 646770
e sue@execmanagement.co.uk w www.execmanagement.co.uk

Alex Moat
Gems, The Media House, 87 Glebe Street, Penarth CF64 1EF
t 029 2071 0770 f 029 2071 0771
e gems@gems-agency.co.uk w www.gems-agency.co.uk
Credits Playing The Field (T); Throw Away The Key (T); Teachers (T); EastEnders (T)

Helen Moran
51 Heys Road, Prestwich, Manchester M25 1JZ
t 0161 798 8839 f 0161 798 8839 m 07768 477205
e phmoran@msn.com
Credits Moll Flanders (T); Blue Zone (F); Blue Murder (T); Cold Feet

Zoe Morgan
EXEC, 6 Travis Court, Farnham Royal SL2 3SB
t 01753 646677 f 01753 646770
e sue@execmanagement.co.uk w www.execmanagement.co.uk

Helene Oosthuizen
EXEC, 6 Travis Court, Farnham Royal SL2 3SB
t 01753 646677 f 01753 646770
e sue@execmanagement.co.uk w www.execmanagement.co.uk

Caroline Sutton Osbourne
Gems, The Media House, 87 Glebe Street, Penarth CF64 1EF
t 029 2071 0770 f 029 2071 0771
e gems@gems-agency.co.uk w www.gems-agency.co.uk
Credits Romeo And Juliet (T); The Bill (T); Night And Day (T); Project Shadowchaser (F)

Sylvia Parker
m 07930 757109 e sparker27@talk21.com
Agent Gems, The Media House, 87 Glebe Street, Penarth CF64 1EF
t 029 2071 0770 f 029 2071 0771
e gems@gems-agency.co.uk w www.gems-agency.co.uk
Credits Helen Of Peckham (F); Rockface (T); Down To Earth (T); The Whistle Blower (T)

Paul Daniels Production & Voice Talent
23 Gosfield Street, London W1P 7HB
t 07775 563225 e info@thebollox.co.uk w www.thebollox.co.uk

Shan Prosser
Gems, The Media House, 87 Glebe Street, Penarth CF64 1EF
t 029 2071 0770 f 029 2071 0771
e gems@gems-agency.co.uk w www.gems-agency.co.uk
Credits My Uncle Silas (T); McCready And Daughter (T); Hans Christian Andersen (T); Emma Brodie (T)

Pat Rambaut
The Haven, Culross, Fife KY12 8HN
t 01383 880499 f 01383 882644 m 07768 235855
e pat@rambaut.freeserve.co.uk
Agent EXEC, 6 Travis Court, Farnham Royal SL2 3SB
t 01753 646677 f 01753 646770
e sue@execmanagement.co.uk w www.execmanagement.co.uk
Credits I'll Be There (F); Bridget Jone's Diary (F); The Magdalene Sisters (F); The Warrior (F)

Wendy J Rollason
21 Greenfields, Hixon ST18 0NF
t 01889 271009 f 01889 271584 m 07768 706723
Credits Brookside (T); Floyd's India (T); Coronation Street (T)

Vivianne Royal
Gems, The Media House, 87 Glebe Street, Penarth CF64 1EF
t 029 2071 0770 f 029 2071 0771
e gems@gems-agency.co.uk w www.gems-agency.co.uk
Credits Me And Mrs Jones (T); Solitaire For Two (F); Such A Long Journey (F); Gypsy Woman (F)

Marinella Setti
Gems, The Media House, 87 Glebe Street, Penarth CF64 1EF
t 029 2071 0770 f 029 2071 0771
e gems@gems-agency.co.uk w www.gems-agency.co.uk
Credits Come Together (T); Come Together; Pandamonium (T); The Hole (F)

Sian Prosser
Flat 2, Lambsdowne House, St Julian Street, Tenby SA70 7BA
t 01834 845662 **f** 01834 844551 **m** 07802 419870
e sianprosser@yahoo.com
Credits Hearts Of Gold (T); Foyle's War (T); Second Generation (T); Hans Christian Andersen (F)

Jane Simon
Callbox Communications Limited, 66 Shepperton Studios, Studios Road, Shepperton TW17 0QD
t 01932 592572 **f** 01932 569655 **m** 07710 572572
e callboxdiary@btinternet.com **w** www.callboxdiary.co.uk

Danuta Skarszewska
Gems, The Media House, 87 Glebe Street, Penarth CF64 1EF
t 029 2071 0770 **f** 029 2071 0771
e gems@gems-agency.co.uk **w** www.gems-agency.co.uk
Credits Where The Heart Is (T); Deadly Obsession (F); Shadow Of The Vampire (F); Attila The Hun (F)

Jayne Spooner
88 Ravenscourt Road, Hammersmith, London W6 0UG
t 020 8741 1871 **f** 020 8741 1871 **m** 07785 791200
e ravenscourt@ukonline.co.uk
Agent Gems, The Media House, 87 Glebe Street, Penarth CF64 1EF
t 029 2071 0770 **f** 029 2071 0771
e gems@gems-agency.co.uk **w** www.gems-agency.co.uk
Credits The Vice (T); Close And True (T); Walking The Dead (T); Truely, Madly, Deeply (F) The Project (T); Spooks (T); Warriors (T); The Heart Of Me (F)

Maggie Stevens
32 Fowlers Walk, Ealing, London W5 1BG
t 020 8997 8591 **f** 020 8997 8591 **m** 07970 503163
e maggiestevens@beeb.net
Credits Nature Boy (T); The Way We Live Now (T); Paradise Heights (T)

Heather Storr
The Production Switchboard, North Down, Down Lane, Compton GU3 1DN
t 01483 812011 **f** 01483 812027
e aly@productionswitch.freeserve.co.uk
Credits Miranda (F); All Or Nothing (F); Cold Mountain (F)

Diane Taylor
Callbox Communications Limited, 66 Shepperton Studios, Studios Road, Shepperton TW17 0QD
t 01932 592572 **f** 01932 569655 **m** 07710 572572
e callboxdiary@btinternet.com **w** www.callboxdiary.co.uk

Heather Taylor
Gems, The Media House, 87 Glebe Street, Penarth CF64 1EF
t 029 2071 0770 **f** 029 2071 0771
e gems@gems-agency.co.uk **w** www.gems-agency.co.uk
Credits Casualty (T); Night And Day (T); Monsignor Renard (S); In A Land Of Plenty (S)

Emma Thomas
Gems, The Media House, 87 Glebe Street, Penarth CF64 1EF
t 029 2071 0770 **f** 029 2071 0771
e gems@gems-agency.co.uk **w** www.gems-agency.co.uk
Credits Jack And The Beanstalk (F); My Hero (T); Teachers (T); The War Bride (F)

Alison Thorne
5 Wilmington Avenue, Chiswick, London W4 3HA
t 020 8994 6286 **f** 020 8994 6286 **m** 07860 876834
e aligeorge52@msn.com
Agent Annie's Answering Service, Pinewood Studios, Pinewood Road, Iver Heath SL0 0NH
t 01753 651303 **f** 01753 651848
e info@annies.co.uk **w** www.annies.co.uk

Elizabeth Tremblay
Gems, The Media House, 87 Glebe Street, Penarth CF64 1EF
t 029 2071 0770 **f** 029 2071 0771
e gems@gems-agency.co.uk **w** www.gems-agency.co.uk
Credits Hysteria - Def Lepard Story (M); After Amy (T); Swindle (F); Fear Of The Dark (F)

Lisa Vick
22 Charter Road, Slough SL1 5JE
t 01628 666896 **f** 01628 666896 **m** 07778 917630
e lisa.vick@virgin.net
Agent EXEC, 6 Travis Court, Farnham Royal SL2 3SB
t 01753 646677 **f** 01753 646770
e sue@execmanagement.co.uk **w** www.execmanagement.co.uk
Credits Love Actually (F); Birthday Girl (F); Entrapment (F)

Louise Wade
EXEC, 6 Travis Court, Farnham Royal SL2 3SB
t 01753 646677 **f** 01753 646770
e sue@execmanagement.co.uk **w** www.execmanagement.co.uk

Liz West
Annie's Answering Service, Pinewood Studios, Pinewood Road, Iver Heath SL0 0NH
t 01753 651303 **f** 01753 651848
e info@annies.co.uk **w** www.annies.co.uk

Angela Noakes Wharton
37 Magdalen Road, London SW18 3ND
t 020 8870 3533 **f** 020 8870 3533 **m** 07973 550006
e whartonar@aol.com
Credits Last Orders (F); Keen Eddie (T); Enigma (F); The Hours (F)

Helen Williams
89 Fairleigh Road, Pontcanna, Cardiff CF11 9JW
t 029 2022 7903 **m** 07901 695647 **e** helwils@totalise.co.uk

Beverley Winston
28 St Crispins Close, London NW3 2QF
t 020 7431 1565 **m** 07974 925860
e beverleywinston@aol.com
Credits A Knight's Tale (F); The Importance Of Being Earnest (F); What The Girl Wants (F); I'll Sleep When I'm Dead (F)

Pu San Wong
8 Tollgate Drive, Waterside View, Hayes UB4 0NP
t 020 8797 2673 **f** 020 8797 2673 **m** 07050 677628
e pusanwong@hotmail.com
Agent Gems, The Media House, 87 Glebe Street, Penarth CF64 1EF
t 029 2071 0770 **f** 029 2071 0771 **e** gems@gems-agency.co.uk
w www.gems-agency.co.uk
Credits Al's Lads (F); Braun Silk - Epil 100% (C); William And Mary (T); Teachers Series II (T)

Anna Worley
EXEC, 6 Travis Court, Farnham Royal SL2 3SB
t 01753 646677 **f** 01753 646770
e sue@execmanagement.co.uk **w** www.execmanagement.co.uk

Annie Wotton
EXEC, 6 Travis Court, Farnham Royal SL2 3SB
t 01753 646677 **f** 01753 646770
e sue@execmanagement.co.uk **w** www.execmanagement.co.uk

Copyright Clearance Services

United Kingdom Copyright Bureau
110 Trafalgar Road, Portslade BN41 1GS
t 01273 277333 **f** 01273 705451
e info@copyrightbureau.co.uk **w** www.copyrightbureau.co.uk

COSTUME

Costume Designers

Rebecca Allen
m 07850 830912 e rc.allen@virgin.net
Credits All About Me (T); Perfect World (T); The Grimleys (T)

Claire Anderson
The Dench Arnold Agency, 24 D'Arblay Street, London W1F 8EH
t 020 7437 4551 f 020 7439 1355
e contact@dencharnoldagency.co.uk w www.dencharnold.co.uk
Credits Rescue Me (T); State Of Play (F); Human Traffic (F)

Joey Attawia
Casarotto Marsh Ltd, National House, 60-66 Wardour Street,
London W1V 4ND
t 020 7287 4450 f 020 7287 9128
e agents@casarotto.uk.com w www.casarotto.uk.com

Anne Barfield
Gems, The Media House, 87 Glebe Street, Penarth CF64 1EF
t 029 2071 0770 f 029 2071 0771
e gems@gems-agency.co.uk w www.gems-agency.co.uk
Credits All Creatures Great And Small (T); Coronation Street (T); The Bill (T);
Holby City (T)

Yves Barre
25 Lynton Avenue, Ealing, London W13 0EA
t 020 8997 6995 f 020 8997 6995 m 07976 926 070
e yves.barre@btinternet.com
Contact Yves Barre, Costume Designer
Credits Deadly Summer (T); Ted And Alice (T); The League of Gentlemen (T)

Michelle Barrett
24A Wightman Road, London N4 1RU
t 020 8341 7688 m 07860 116547
e michelleb@styless.co.uk w www.styless.co.uk
Agent Gems, The Media House, 87 Glebe Street, Penarth
CF64 1EF
t 029 2071 0770 f 029 2071 0771
e gems@gems-agency.co.uk w www.gems-agency.co.uk
Credits BT (C); Oh Marbella (F); Blue Peter (E); Captain Eager And The Mark Of
Voth (F)

Trisha Biggar
Peters Fraser & Dunlop, Drury House, 34-43 Russell Street,
London WC2B 5HA
t 020 7344 1000 f 020 7836 9543
e postmaster@pfd.co.uk w www.pfd.co.uk

Angela Billows
Wizzo & Co, 35 Old Compton Street, London W1D 5JX
t 020 7437 2055 f 020 7437 2066
e wizzo@wizzoandco.co.uk w www.wizzoandco.co.uk

John Bloomfield
Creative Media Management, Unit 3B, Walpole Court, Ealing
Studios, Ealing Green, London W5 5ED
t 020 8584 5363 f 020 8566 5554
e enquiries@creativemediamanagement.com
Credits The Chronicles Of Riddick (F); To Kill A King (F); Open Range (F); The
Mummy Returns (F)

Carolyn Boult
Art Department, 51 Pratt Street, London NW1 0BJ
t 020 7428 0500 f 020 7916 2167 m 07970 089592
e info@art-department.co.uk

Consolata Boyle
International Creative Management Ltd, Oxford House, 76
Oxford Street, London W1D 1BS
t 020 7636 6565 f 020 7323 0101 w www.icmlondon.co.uk
Credits The Winslow Boy (F); Angela's Ashes (F); The Actor (F)

Georgia Boyle
Art Department, 51 Pratt Street, London NW1 0BJ
t 020 7428 0500 f 020 7916 2167 m 07973 639785
e info@art-department.co.uk

Dennis Brack
Gems, The Media House, 87 Glebe Street, Penarth CF64 1EF
t 029 2071 0770 f 029 2071 0771
e gems@gems-agency.co.uk w www.gems-agency.co.uk
Credits EastEnders (T); The Knock II (F); The Bill (T); The Full Monty (F)

Howard Burden
McKinney Macartney Management Ltd, The Barley Mow
Centre, 10 Barley Mow Passage, London W4 4PH
t 020 8995 4747 f 020 8995 2414
e fkb@mmtechsrep.demon.co.uk w www.mckinneymacartney.com

Vin Burnham
The Dench Arnold Agency, 24 D'Arblay Street, London W1F 8EH
t 020 7437 4551 f 020 7439 1355
e contact@dencharnoldagency.co.uk w www.dencharnold.co.uk
Credits The Chronicles Of Narnia (T); The Fifth Element (F); Lost In Space (F)

Susannah Buxton
12 Wiseton Road, London SW17 7EE
e peterwestby@yahoo.com
Agent International Creative Management Ltd, Oxford House,
76 Oxford Street, London W1D 1BS
t 020 7636 6565 f 020 7323 0101 w www.icmlondon.co.uk
Credits Tipping The Velvet (T); Shooting The Past (T); Anita And Me (F)

Alexandra Byrne
International Creative Management Ltd, Oxford House,
76 Oxford Street, London W1D 1BS
t 020 7636 6565 f 020 7323 0101 w www.icmlondon.co.uk
Credits Hamlet (F); Elizabeth (F); Captain Corelli's Mandolin (F)

Kate Carin
The Dench Arnold Agency, 24 D'Arblay Street, London W1F 8EH
t 020 7437 4551 f 020 7439 1355
e contact@dencharnoldagency.co.uk w www.dencharnold.co.uk
Credits The 51st State (F); Hideous Kinky (F); Spice World (F)

Brian Castle
Field House, 12 Manor Court, Shadwell Village, Leeds LS17 8JE
t 01132 733855 f 01132 733855 m 07768 688353
e bacastle@btopenworld.com

Alexandra Caulfield
Creative Media Management, Unit 3B, Walpole Court, Ealing
Studios, Ealing Green, London W5 5ED
t 020 8584 5363 f 020 8566 5554
e enquiries@creativemediamanagement.com
Credits Al's Lads (F); Liam (F); The Parole Officer (F)

costume : clothing sizes

men

suits/overcoats

British	36	38	40	42	44	46	48	50
American	36	38	40	42	44	46	48	50
Continental	46	48	50/52	54	56	58/60	62	64

shirts (collar sizes)

British	14	14 ½	15	15 ½	16	16 ½	17	17 ½
American	14	14 ½	15	15 ½	16	16 ½	17	17 ½
Continental	35	36/37	38	39/40	41	42/43	44	45

shoes

British	7	7 ½	8	8 ½	9	9 ½	10	10 ½
American	7 ½	8	8 ½	9	9 ½	10	10 ½	11
Continental	41		42		43		44	

women

dresses/suits

British	8	10	12	14	16	18	20	22
American		8	10	12	14	16	18	20
Continental		40	42	44	46	48	50	52

stockings

British	7	7 ½	8	8 ½	9	9 ½	10	10 ½
American	7	7 ½	8	8 ½	9	9 ½	10	10 ½
Continental	0		1		2		3	

shoes

British	4	4 ½	5	5 ½	6	6 ½	7	7 ½
American	5 ½	6	6 ½	7	7 ½	8	8 ½	8½
Continental	36 ½	37	37 ½	38 ½	39	39½	40	40½

Moira Chapman
Callbox Communications Limited, 66 Shepperton Studios,
Studios Road, Shepperton TW17 0QD
t 01932 592572 f 01932 569655 m 07710 572572
e callboxdiary@btinternet.com w www.callboxdiary.co.uk

Fiona Chilcott
m 07973 366743 e fichill@hotmail.com
Credits Ed Stone is Dead (T); The Bunker (F); Human Remains (T)

Deirdre Clancy
Creative Media Management, Unit 3B, Walpole Court, Ealing
Studios, Ealing Green, London W5 5ED
t 020 8584 5363 f 020 8566 5554
e enquiries@creativemediamanagement.com
Credits The Biographer (F); The Clandestine Marriage (F)

Michele Clapton
The Dench Arnold Agency, 24 D'Arblay Street, London W1F 8EH
t 020 7437 4551 f 020 7439 1355
e contact@dencharnoldagency.co.uk w www.dencharnold.co.uk
Credits Miranda (F); The Nine Lives Of Tomas Katz (F); Simon Magus (F)

Stephanie Collie
Casarotto Marsh Ltd, National House, 60-66 Wardour Street,
London W1V 4ND
t 020 7287 4450 f 020 7287 9128
e agents@casarotto.uk.com w www.casarotto.uk.com

Dinah Collin
The Dench Arnold Agency, 24 D'Arblay Street, London W1F 8EH
t 020 7437 4551 f 020 7439 1355
e contact@dencharnoldagency.co.uk w www.dencharnold.co.uk
Credits The Intended (F); Bloody Sunday (F); Gladiatress (F)

Abigail Coult
2 Hillary House, Boyton Close, London N8 7BB

Philip Crichton
Gems, The Media House, 87 Glebe Street, Penarth CF64 1EF
t 029 2071 0770 f 029 2071 0771
e gems@gems-agency.co.uk w www.gems-agency.co.uk
Credits The Bill (T); Mile High (T); Dragonworld (F); Club Le Monde (F)

Annie Curtis Jones
158 Essex Road, London N1 8LY
t 020 7226 5857 f 020 7226 5857 m 07774 626366
e anniecurtisjones@freedomland.co.uk
Credits Paradise Omeros (S); Vagabondia (S); Single Voices (T)

Elvis Davis
Gems, The Media House, 87 Glebe Street, Penarth CF64 1EF
t 029 2071 0770 f 029 2071 0771
e gems@gems-agency.co.uk w www.gems-agency.co.uk
Credits Redemption Road (F); Angel For May (F)

Julian Day
Gems, The Media House, 87 Glebe Street, Penarth CF64 1EF
t 029 2071 0770 f 029 2071 0771
e gems@gems-agency.co.uk w www.gems-agency.co.uk
Credits Me And Mrs Jones (T); Burn It (T); Entering Blue Zone (F); Helen Of
Peckham (F)

Fiona Dealey
Wizzo & Co, 35 Old Compton Street, London W1D 5JX
t 020 7437 2055 f 020 7437 2066
e wizzo@wizzoandco.co.uk w www.wizzoandco.co.uk

Odile Dicks-Mireaux
Casarotto Marsh Ltd, National House, 60-66 Wardour Street,
London W1V 4ND
t 020 7287 4450 f 020 7287 9128
e agents@casarotto.uk.com w www.casarotto.uk.com

Maggie Donnelly
37 Church Road, New Town, Belfast BT8 7AL
t 028 9064 7221 f 028 9064 7221 m 07801 708904
Credits Straight To Video (F); Table Twelve (T); Bally Kiss Angel (T); No Tears (T)

Pam Downe
The Dench Arnold Agency, 24 D'Arblay Street, London W1F 8EH
t 020 7437 4551 f 020 7439 1355
e contact@dencharnoldagency.co.uk w www.dencharnold.co.uk
Credits Forty Something (T); My Uncle Silas (T)

Christian Le Drezen
The Dench Arnold Agency, 24 D'Arblay Street, London W1F 8EH
t 020 7437 4551 f 020 7439 1355 w www.dencharnold.co.uk

Kate Duffy
m 07803 505127 e kateduffyw@msn.com

Nadia Dunn-Hill
Flat 1, 18 Cornwall Gardens, London SW7 4AW
t 020 7937 3176 **f** 020 7937 7156 **m** 07802 441825
Agent Wizzo & Co, 35 Old Compton Street, London W1D 5JX
t 020 7437 2055 **f** 020 7437 2066
e wizzo@wizzoandco.co.uk **w** www.wizzoandco.co.uk

Joanna Eatwell
Casarotto Marsh Ltd, National House, 60-66 Wardour Street,
London W1V 4ND
t 020 7287 4450 **f** 020 7287 9128
e agents@casarotto.uk.com **w** www.casarotto.uk.com

Nigel Egerton & Anja Mai
8 Okeover Manor, Clapham Common Northside, London SW4 ORH
t 020 7622 4185 **f** 020 7622 4185 **m** 07770 694 319
e name.1@virgin.net
Credits Inferno; Secret Society; Endgame

Nic Ede
Peters Fraser & Dunlop, Drury House, 34-43 Russell Street,
London WC2B 5HA
t 020 7344 1000 **f** 020 7836 9543
e postmaster@pfd.co.uk **w** www.pfd.co.uk

Ffion Elinor
Peters Fraser & Dunlop, Drury House, 34-43 Russell Street,
London WC2B 5HA
t 020 7344 1000 **f** 020 7836 9543
e postmaster@pfd.co.uk **w** www.pfd.co.uk

Dany Everett
Dinedor Management, 81 Oxford Street, London W10 2EU
t 020 7851 3575 **f** 020 7851 3576
e info@dinedor.com **w** www.dinedor.com
Credits August (F); A Dance To The Music Of Time (T); Talking Heads (T); Jack
And Sarah (F)

Kim Foster
37 Levendale Road, Forest Hill, London SE23 2TP
t 020 8699 6322 **f** 020 8699 6322 **w** www.kimfoster.co.uk
Credits UGetMe (T); Diggit (T); Smart Programme (T); The Bill (T)
Multiskilled costume designer with additional expertise in make-up design.

Jane Fox
Callbox Communications Limited, 66 Shepperton Studios,
Studios Road, Shepperton TW17 OQD
t 01932 592572 **f** 01932 569655 **m** 07110 572572
e callboxdiary@btinternet.com **w** www.callboxdiary.co.uk

Robin Fraser Paye
Creative Media Management, Unit 3B, Walpole Court, Ealing
Studios, Ealing Green, London W5 5ED
t 020 8584 5363 **f** 020 8566 5554
e enquiries@creativemediamanagement.com
Credits Love Again (T); Sharpe (T); A Room For Romeo Brass (F); Once Upon A
Time In The Midlands (F)

Andrea Galer
International Creative Management Ltd, Oxford House, 76
Oxford Street, London W1D 1BS
t 020 7636 6565 **f** 020 7323 0101 **w** www.icmlondon.co.uk
Credits The Way We Live Now (T); Take A Girl Like You (T); Mansfield Park (F)

Phoebe de Gaye
The Dench Arnold Agency, 24 D'Arblay Street, London W1F 8EH
t 020 7437 4551 **f** 020 7439 1355
e contact@dencharnoldagency.co.uk **w** www.dencharnold.co.uk
Credits Forsythe Saga (T); Killing Me Softly (F); Birthday Girl (F)

Tudor George
5 Wilmington Avenue, Chiswick, London W4 3HA
t 020 8994 6286 **f** 020 8994 6286 **m** 07702 909851
e tudorg50@hotmail.com
Agent ADS, Shepperton Studios, Shepperton Road,
Shepperton TW17 OQD
t 01932 592303 **f** 01932 592492 **e** ads@carlincrew.co.uk
Credits Where The Heart Is (T); A Mind To Murder (T); Cracker (T); Silent Witness (T)

Jayne Gregory
114 The Avenue, London NW6 7NN
t 020 8459 4859 **f** 020 8451 7135 **m** 07973 197321
e jayne@theavenue.ukf.net
Agent Dinedor Management, 81 Oxford Street, London W10 2EU
t 020 7851 3575 **f** 020 7851 3576
e info@dinedor.com **w** www.dinedor.com
Credits The Falklands Play (T); Rose And Maloney (T); Attachments Series I, II
(T); Lock Stock (T)

Kim Grossman
t 020 7428 0500
Agent Art Department, 51 Pratt Street, London NW1 OBJ
t 020 7428 0500 **f** 020 7916 2167 **m** 07973 639785
e info@art-department.co.uk
Credits Pizza Express (C); WH Smith (C); Putting Down the King (F)

Annie Hardinge
The Dench Arnold Agency, 24 D'Arblay Street, London W1F 8EH
t 020 7437 4551 **f** 020 7439 1355
e contact@dencharnoldagency.co.uk **w** www.dencharnold.co.uk
Credits Spaced (T); Black Books (T); Ali G In Da House (F)

Suzannah Harman
The Dench Arnold Agency, 24 D'Arblay Street, London W1F 8EH
t 020 7437 4551 **f** 020 7439 1355
e contact@dencharnoldagency.co.uk **w** www.dencharnold.co.uk
Credits Honour Thy Father (F); Married/Unmarried (F); Baby Juice Express (F)

Caroline Harris
International Creative Management Ltd, Oxford House,
76 Oxford Street, London W1D 1BS
t 020 7636 6565 **f** 020 7323 0101 **w** www.icmlondon.co.uk
Credits Still Crazy (F); A Knight's Tale (F); An Ideal Husband (F)

Evangeline Harrison
3 Walham Grove, London SW6 1QP
t 020 7385 9839 **f** 020 7385 9839
Credits I'll Sleep When I'm Dead (F)

Lyn Harvey
Brierwood Tite Hill, Englefield Green, Egham TW20 ONJ
t 01784 433349 **f** 01784 438141 **m** 07836 567924
e lyn.harvey@btinternet.com
Contact Lyn Harvey, Head of Costume
Credits Family Affairs (T); The Bill (T); Kiss Me Kate (T)

Shuna Harwood
Casarotto Marsh Ltd, National House, 60-66 Wardour Street,
London W1V 4ND
t 020 7287 4450 **f** 020 7287 9128
e agents@casarotto.uk.com **w** www.casarotto.uk.com

Verity Hawkes
Peters Fraser & Dunlop, Drury House, 34-43 Russell Street,
London WC2B 5HA
t 020 7344 1000 **f** 020 7836 9543
e postmaster@pfd.co.uk **w** www.pfd.co.uk

Kate Hawley
Clare Vidal Hall, 28 Perrers Road, London W6 OEZ
t 020 8741 7647 **f** 020 8741 9459
e clarevidalhall@email.com **w** www.clarevidalhall@email.com

Lindy Hemming
Peters Fraser & Dunlop, Drury House, 34-43 Russell Street, London WC2B 5HA
t 020 7344 1000 **f** 020 7836 9543
e postmaster@pfd.co.uk **w** www.pfd.co.uk

Chas Hines
4E Peabody Buildings, Southwark Street, London SE1 0TG
m 07980 266373 **e** chines@czlpd.co.uk
Credits Renford Rejects (T); Preaching to the Perverted (F);
Renford Rejects I, III, IV (T)

Andrew Holden
Art Department, 51 Pratt Street, London NW1 0BJ
t 020 7428 0500 **f** 020 7916 2167 **m** 07973 639785
e info@art-department.co.uk

Charlotte Holdich
International Creative Management Ltd, Oxford House,
76 Oxford Street, London W1D 1BS
t 020 7636 6565 **f** 020 7323 0101 **w** www.icmlondon.co.uk
Credits New Tricks (T); Agatha Christie's Poirot (T); The Young Indiana Jones Chronicles (T)

Ralph Holes
International Creative Management Ltd, Oxford House,
76 Oxford Street, London W1D 1BS
t 020 7636 6565 **f** 020 7323 0101 **w** www.icmlondon.co.uk
Credits Trust (T); Messiah (T); Bend It Like Beckham (F)

Ray Holman
12 Tensing Close, Llanishen, Cardiff CF14 5AW
t 029 2075 0258 **f** 029 2075 0258 **m** 07831 091428
e rayholman12@aol.com **w** www.costume-designer.co.uk
Credits Born And Bred (T); This is Personal: The Hunt of the Yorkshire Ripper (T); Peak Practice (T); Heart of the Valley (T)

Ray Holman
Peters Fraser & Dunlop, Drury House, 34-43 Russell Street, London WC2B 5HA
t 020 7344 1000 **f** 020 7836 9543
e postmaster@pfd.co.uk **w** www.pfd.co.uk

Mary Husband
The Costume Design Centre, PO Box 5877, Nottingham NG15 9GG
t 01623 491158 **f** 07811 918395 **m** 07811 918395

Joanna Johnston
International Creative Management Ltd, Oxford House,
76 Oxford Street, London W1D 1BS
t 020 7636 6565 **f** 020 7323 0101 **w** www.icmlondon.co.uk
Credits Saving Private Ryan (F); The Sixth Sense (F); About A Boy (F)

James Keast
The Dench Arnold Agency, 24 D'Arblay Street, London W1F 8EH
t 020 7437 4551 **f** 020 7439 1355
e contact@dencharnoldagency.co.uk **w** www.dencharnold.co.uk
Credits The Keys (T); Keys; The Hound Of The Baskervilles (T); Warriors (T)

Barbara Kidd
Peters Fraser & Dunlop, Drury House, 34-43 Russell Street, London WC2B 5HA
t 020 7344 1000 **f** 020 7836 9543
e postmaster@pfd.co.uk **w** www.pfd.co.uk

Franca Knight
Gems, The Media House, 87 Glebe Street, Penarth CF64 1EF
t 029 2071 0770 **f** 029 2071 0771
e gems@gems-agency.co.uk **w** www.gems-agency.co.uk
Credits It's Good To Talk (F); Horizon Special (T); The Wings Of Angels (T); Casualty (T)

John Krausa
The Dench Arnold Agency, 24 D'Arblay Street, London W1F 8EH
t 020 7437 4551 **f** 020 7439 1355
e contact@dencharnoldagency.co.uk **w** www.dencharnold.co.uk
Credits Stretford Wives (T); Revelations (T); Clocking Off (T)

Vee Layton
Experience Counts - Call Me Ltd, 5th Floor, 41-42 Berners Street, London W1P 3AA
t 020 7637 8112 **f** 020 7580 2582

Marie-Jeanne Lecca
Peters Fraser & Dunlop, Drury House, 34-43 Russell Street, London WC2B 5HA
t 020 7344 1000 **f** 020 7836 9543
e postmaster@pfd.co.uk **w** www.pfd.co.uk

Mark Lewis
Wizzo & Co, 35 Old Compton Street, London W1D 5JX
t 020 7437 2055 **f** 020 7437 2066
e wizzo@wizzoandco.co.uk **w** www.wizzoandco.co.uk

Maria Liljefors
31 Greenhill Park, London NW10 9AN
t 020 8838 1448 **f** 020 8961 0752 **m** 07802 155593
e mia.liljefors@btinternet.com
Credits Dr Zhivago (T); Sir Gadabout Series I & II (T); Pirates (T)

Nadya Lubrani
Callbox Communications Limited, 66 Shepperton Studios, Studios Road, Shepperton TW17 0QD
t 01932 592572 **f** 01932 569655 **m** 07710 572572
e callboxdiary@btinternet.com **w** www.callboxdiary.co.uk

Justine Luxton
International Creative Management Ltd, Oxford House,
76 Oxford Street, London W1D 1BS
t 020 7636 6565 **f** 020 7323 0101 **w** www.icmlondon.co.uk
Credits The Commander (T); Auf Wiedersehen, Pet (T); Out Of Control (T)

Ashley Martin-Davis
Cruickshank Cazenove Ltd, 97 Old South Lambeth Road, London SW8 1XU
t 020 7735 2933 **f** 020 7820 1081 **e** hjcruickshank@aol.com

Chris Marlowe
79c Askew Crescent, London W12 9DW
t 020 8749 7633 **f** 020 8749 7633 **m** 07973 877719
e cvm0104@yahoo.com
Agent Clare Vidal-Hall, 28 Perrers Road, London W6 0EZ
t 020 8741 7647 **f** 020 8741 9459
e clarevidalhall@email.com **w** www.clarevidalhall.com
Credits Professionals (T); Gimme Gimme Gimme (T); Big Kids (T)

Veronica McAuliffe
Flat 7, Exeter Mansions, 106 Shaftesbury Avenue, London W1D 5EQ
t 020 7437 5488 **f** 020 7437 5488 **m** 07831 248398
e veronica@costume-design.fsbusiness.co.uk
Credits Danone (C); Tina Modotti (D); Midnight Breaks (F); Samsung (C)

Katy McPhee
Art Department, 51 Pratt Street, London NW1 0BJ
t 020 7428 0500 **f** 020 7916 2167 **m** 07973 639785
e info@art-department.co.uk

Stewart Meachem
McKinney Macartney Management Ltd, The Barley Mow Centre, 10 Barley Mow Passage, London W4 4PH
t 020 8995 4747 **f** 020 8995 2414
e fkb@mmtechsrep.demon.co.uk **w** www.mckinneymacartney.com

Val Metheringham
CCA Management, 7 St George's Square, London SW1V 2HX
t 020 7630 6303 **f** 020 7630 7376

Eimer Ní Mhaoldomhnaigh
Peters Fraser & Dunlop, Drury House, 34-43 Russell Street, London WC2B 5HA
t 020 7344 1000 **f** 020 7836 9543
e postmaster@pfd.co.uk **w** www.pfd.co.uk

Jacqueline Mills
Gems, The Media House, 87 Glebe Street, Penarth CF64 1EF
t 029 2071 0770 **f** 029 2071 0771
e gems@gems-agency.co.uk **w** www.gems-agency.co.uk
Credits Search (T); Dream Team (T); Shadow Run (F); Devil's Gate (F)

Aideen Morgan
The Dench Arnold Agency, 24 D'Arblay Street, London W1F 8EH
t 020 7437 4551 **f** 020 7439 1355
e contact@dencharnoldagency.co.uk **w** www.dencharnold.co.uk
Credits Sweet Revenge (F); Daddy's Girls (T); Danielle Cable - Eye Witness (T)

Catherine Morgan-Jones
4A Princess Road, London NW1 8JJ
t 020 7722 2541 **m** 07973 619896

Diana Moseley
Peters Fraser & Dunlop, Drury House, 34-43 Russell Street,
London WC2B 5HA
t 020 7344 1000 **f** 020 7836 9543
e postmaster@pfd.co.uk **w** www.pfd.co.uk

Simon Moseley
McKinney Macartney Management Ltd, The Barley Mow
Centre, 10 Barley Mow Passage, London W4 4PH
t 020 8995 4747 **f** 020 8995 2414
e fkb@mmtechsrep.demon.co.uk **w** www.mckinneymacartney.com

Ita Murray
4 Brecon Road, London W6 8PU
t 020 7385 6911 **m** 07966 235691
Credits As If (T); Dreamteam (T); Is Harry On The Boat (T); Burnside (T)

Sheena Napier
International Creative Management Ltd, Oxford House,
76 Oxford Street, London W1D 1BS
t 020 7636 6565 **f** 020 7323 0101 **w** www.icmlondon.co.uk
Credits Backbeat (F); The Heart Of Me (F); Ravenous (F)

Anushia Nieradzik
Casarotto Marsh Ltd, National House, 60-66 Wardour Street,
London W1V 4ND
t 020 7287 4450 **f** 020 7287 9128
e agents@casarotto.uk.com **w** www.casarotto.uk.com

Inez Nordell
Gems, The Media House, 87 Glebe Street, Penarth CF64 1EF
t 029 2071 0770 **f** 029 2071 0771
e gems@gems-agency.co.uk **w** www.gems-agency.co.uk
Credits Daylight Robbery (T); Clocking Off (T); Bob And Rosie (T); Anytime Now (T)

Michael O'Connor
The Dench Arnold Agency, 24 D'Arblay Street, London W1F 8EH
t 020 7437 4551 **f** 020 7439 1355
e contact@dencharnoldagency.co.uk **w** www.dencharnold.co.uk
Credits Harry Potter And The Chamber Of Secrets (F); The Mystic Masseur (F)

Louise Page
Creative Media Management, Unit 3B, Walpole Court, Ealing
Studios, Ealing Green, London W5 5ED
t 020 8584 5363 **f** 020 8566 5554
e enquiries@creativemediamanagement.com
Credits The Young Indiana Jones Chronicles (T); The Strangerers (T); Rockface (T); Beautiful People (F)

Judy Pepperdine
Creative Media Management, Unit 3B, Walpole Court, Ealing
Studios, Ealing Green, London W5 5ED
t 020 8584 5363 **f** 020 8566 5554
e enquiries@creativemediamanagement.com
Credits The Broker's Man (T); Two Thousand Acres Of Sky (T); For Love Or Money (T)

Emma Porteous
International Creative Management Ltd, Oxford House,
76 Oxford Street, London W1D 1BS
t 020 7636 6565 **f** 020 7323 0101 **w** www.icmlondon.co.uk
Credits 1984 (F); Aliens (F); Judge Dredd (F)

Anthony Powell
c/o Andrew Glynne, 6th Floor, Empire House, 175 Piccadilly,
London W1J 9TB
t 020 7486 3166 **f** 020 7486 2164
e solicitors@glynnes.co.uk **e** www.glynnes.co.uk

Sandy Powell
Peters Fraser & Dunlop, Drury House, 34-43 Russell Street,
London WC2B 5HA
t 020 7344 1000 **f** 020 7836 9543
e postmaster@pfd.co.uk **w** www.pfd.co.uk

Mary Jane Reyner
International Creative Management Ltd, Oxford House,
76 Oxford Street, London W1D 1BS
t 020 7636 6565 **f** 020 7323 0101 **w** www.icmlondon.co.uk
Credits The Debt (T); Gabriel And Me (F); The War Zone (F)

Alyson Ritchie
Experience Counts - Call Me Ltd, 5th Floor, 41-42 Berners
Street, London W1P 3AA
t 020 7637 8112 **f** 020 7580 2582

Amy Roberts
McKinney Macartney Management Ltd, The Barley Mow
Centre, 10 Barley Mow Passage, London W4 4PH
t 020 8995 4747 **f** 020 8995 2414
e fkb@mmtechsrep.demon.co.uk **w** www.mckinneymacartney.com

Jane Robinson
International Creative Management Ltd, Oxford House,
76 Oxford Street, London W1D 1BS
t 020 7636 6565 **f** 020 7323 0101 **w** www.icmlondon.co.uk
Credits Memphis Belle (F); Ordinary Decent Criminal (F); The Virginian (F)

Delphine Roche-Gordon
Peters Fraser & Dunlop, Drury House, 34-43 Russell Street,
London WC2B 5HA
t 020 7344 1000 **f** 020 7836 9543
e postmaster@pfd.co.uk **w** www.pfd.co.uk

Anne Rudd
t 01225 744367 **f** 01225 744367 **m** 07970 279523
e annerudd@cwcom.net

Vicki Russell
Wizzo & Co, 35 Old Compton Street, London W1D 5JX
t 020 7437 2055 **f** 020 7437 2066
e wizzo@wizzoandco.co.uk **w** www.wizzoandco.co.uk

Reg Samuel
McKinney Macartney Management Ltd, The Barley Mow
Centre, 10 Barley Mow Passage, London W4 4PH
t 020 8995 4747 **f** 020 8995 2414
e fkb@mmtechsrep.demon.co.uk **w** www.mckinneymacartney.com

Astrid Schulz
38 Maude House, Ropley Street, London E2 7RY
t 020 7613 0339 **f** 020 7613 0339 **m** 07947 155611
e astridschulz@hotmail.com
Agent Art Department, 51 Pratt Street, London NW1 0BJ
t 020 7428 0500 **f** 020 7916 2167 **m** 07973 639785
e info@art-department.co.uk
Credits Peaches - Stranglers (M); Frankenphone - One 2 One (I); The Serpent (T); Flyfishing (F)

Sammy Sheldon
Peters Fraser & Dunlop, Drury House, 34-43 Russell Street,
London WC2B 5HA
t 020 7344 1000 **f** 020 7836 9543
e postmaster@pfd.co.uk **w** www.pfd.co.uk

Anna Sheppard
International Creative Management Ltd, Oxford House,
76 Oxford Street, London W1D 1BS
t 020 7636 6565 **f** 020 7323 0101 **w** icmlondon.co.uk
Credits Schindler's List (F); Band Of Brothers (T); The Pianist (F)

Anne Sinclair
The Dench Arnold Agency, 24 D'Arblay Street, London W1F 8EH
t 020 7437 4551 **f** 020 7439 1355
e contact@dencharnoldagency.co.uk **w** www.dencharnold.co.uk
Credits Active Defence (T); Children Of The New Forest (F); The Hidden City (T)

Louise Stjernsward
The Dench Arnold Agency, 24 D'Arblay Street, London W1F 8EH
t 020 7437 4551 **f** 020 7439 1355
e contact@dencharnoldagency.co.uk **w** www.dencharnold.co.uk
Credits The Dreamers (F); The Warrior (F); Sexy Beast (F)

Annie Symons
Peters Fraser & Dunlop, Drury House, 34-43 Russell Street,
London WC2B 5HA
t 020 7344 1000 **f** 020 7836 9543
e postmaster@pfd.co.uk **w** www.pfd.co.uk

Jennie Tate
Clare Vidal Hall, 28 Perrers Road, London W6 0EZ
t 020 8741 7647 **f** 020 8741 9459
e clarevidalhall@email.com **w** www.clarevidalhall@email.com
Credits Peak Practice (T); Happy Birthday Shakespeare (T); Night And Day (T);
The Queen's Nose (T)

Jill Taylor
Peters Fraser & Dunlop, Drury House, 34-43 Russell Street,
London WC2B 5HA
t 020 7344 1000 **f** 020 7836 9543
e postmaster@pfd.co.uk **w** www.pfd.co.uk

Jany Temime
McKinney Macartney Management Ltd, The Barley Mow
Centre, 10 Barley Mow Passage, London W4 4PH
t 020 8995 4747 **f** 020 8995 2414
e fkb@mmtechsrep.demon.co.uk **w** www.mckinneymacartney.com

Frances Tempest
16 College Terrace, Brighton BN2 0EE
t 01273 680750 **f** 01273 680750 **m** 07850 710999
Credits The Calendar Girl (F); New Year's Day (F); The Cazalets (T); Bertie and
Elizabeth (F)

Dawn Thomas-Mondo
Gems, The Media House, 87 Glebe Street, Penarth CF64 1EF
t 029 2071 0770 **f** 029 2071 0771
e gems@gems-agency.co.uk **w** www.gems-agency.co.uk
Credits History Of Piracy (F); Paved With Gold I,II,III&IV (T); In The Company Of
Strangers (F); Tulse Luper Suitcase (F)

Jilly Thornley
Gems, The Media House, 87 Glebe Street, Penarth CF64 1EF
t 029 2071 0770 **f** 029 2071 0771
e gems@gems-agency.co.uk **w** www.gems-agency.co.uk
Credits Child Of Love (F); Realms Of Gold (T); Chameleon (F); The Theory Of
Flight (F)

Claire Todd
Mandy Coakley Represents, 18 Mandeville Courtyard, Warriner
Gardens, London SW11 4NB
t 020 7720 6234 **f** 020 7720 0199
e mc@mandycoakley.co.uk **w** www.mandycoakley.co.uk

Jeremy Turner
Creative Media Management, Unit 3B, Walpole Court, Ealing
Studios, Ealing Green, London W5 5ED
t 020 8584 5363 **f** 020 8566 5554
e enquiries@creativemediamanagement.com
Credits Coliseum (T); Dalziel And Pascoe (T); Martin Chuzzlewit (T); The
Scarlet Pimpernel (T)

Kirstie Jo Turner
Callbox Communications Limited, 66 Shepperton Studios,
Studios Road, Shepperton TW17 0QD
t 01932 592572 **f** 01932 569655 **m** 07710 572572
e callboxdiary@btinternet.com **w** www.callboxdiary.co.uk

Sally Turner
t 01844 218878 **f** 01844 214655 **m** 07802 412643

Jackie Vernon
Flat 4, 61 Carleton Road, London N7 0ET
t 020 7609 1075 **f** 020 7609 1075 **m** 07860 899 111
Agent CCA Management, 7 St George's Square, London SW1V 2HX
t 020 7630 6303 **f** 020 7630 7376
Credits Gladiatrix (D); Meet The Magoons (T); 1940's House (D)

Elizabeth Waller
Peters Fraser & Dunlop, Drury House, 34-43 Russell Street,
London WC2B 5HA
t 020 7344 1000 **f** 020 7836 9543
e postmaster@pfd.co.uk **w** www.pfd.co.uk

Charlotte Walter
The Dench Arnold Agency, 24 D'Arblay Street, London W1F 8EH
t 020 7437 4551 **f** 020 7439 1355
e contact@dencharnoldagency.co.uk **w** www.dencharnold.co.uk
Credits I Capture The Castle (F); Murder Rooms (T); Cambridge Spies (T)

Anthony Ward
Cruickshank Cazenove Ltd, 97 Old South Lambeth Road,
London SW8 1XU
t 020 7735 2933 **f** 020 7820 1081 **e** hjcruickshank@aol.com
Credits A Midsummer Night's Dream (F)

Natalie Ward
Peters Fraser & Dunlop, Drury House, 34-43 Russell Street,
London WC2B 5HA
t 020 7344 1000 **f** 020 7836 9543
e postmaster@pfd.co.uk **w** www.pfd.co.uk

Hazel Webb-Crozier
CCA Management, 7 St George's Square, London SW1V 2HX
t 020 7630 6303 **f** 020 7630 7376

Lizzy Wilson
48 Forburg Road, Stoke Newington, London N16 6HS
t 020 7502 1033 **m** 07976 388751
e lizzyfwilson@hotmail.com
Credits Dream Team (T); Not To The Euro Campaign (C); Lenny Henry In Pieces
I & II (T)

Lucinda Wright
International Creative Management Ltd, Oxford House,
76 Oxford Street, London W1D 1BS
t 020 7636 6565 **f** 020 7323 0101 **w** www.icmlondon.co.uk
Credits The Jury (T); Deathwatch (F); Henry VIII (T)

Allison Wyldeck
Gems, The Media House, 87 Glebe Street, Penarth CF64 1EF
t 029 2071 0770 **f** 029 2071 0771
e gems@gems-agency.co.uk **w** www.gems-agency.co.uk
Credits Attachments (T); Secrets And Lies (F); Birthday Girl (F); A Lonely War (F)

Susan Yelland
Creative Media Management, Unit 3B, Walpole Court, Ealing
Studios, Ealing Green, London W5 5ED
t 020 8584 5363 **f** 020 8566 5554
e enquiries@creativemediamanagement.com
Credits Always And Everyone (T); Without Motive (T); A Line In The Sand (T);
Monsignor Renard (S)

Costume
Designers Assistant

Jill Blundell
Gems, The Media House, 87 Glebe Street, Penarth CF64 1EF
t 029 2071 0770 **f** 029 2071 0771 **e** gems@gems-agency.co.uk
w www.gems-agency.co.uk
Credits City Central (T); The Clandestine Marriage (F); Wives And Daughters (T)

Sallyann Dicksee
29 Yerbury Road, Tufnell Park, London N19 4RN
t 020 7263 3946 **m** 07768 367515
e sallyann@dickseedesign.fsnet.co.uk
Credits Jack And The Beanstalk (T); Johnny English (F)

Lezli Everitt
26 Natal Road, London N11 2HX
m 07961 427670 **e** lezli.everitt@talk21.com
Credits Poirot (T); Spaced II (T); Baby Father (T)

Rosie Grant
11 Jack Walker Court, Panmure Close, Highbury, London N5 1SG
f 020 7288 0604 **m** 07973 710843
Credits Dead Gorgeous (T); State Of Mind (T); The Foresight Saga (T); The Swap (T)

Kate Halfpenny
Wizzo & Co, 35 Old Compton Street, London W1D 5JX
t 020 7437 2055 **f** 020 7437 2066
e wizzo@wizzoandco.co.uk **w** www.wizzoandco.co.uk

Aimi Hopkins
1 Penrallt Villas, Groeslon, Caernarfon LL54 7UF
t 01286 831661 **m** 07899 848 049 **e** aimi@aimihopkins.co.uk
Credits Porc Peis Bach (T); The Heather Mountain (F)

Bet Huws
59 Henwalsa, Caernarfon LL55 2LB
t 01286 676283 **f** 01286 676283 **m** 07774 125 165
e bethuws@yahoo.co.uk
Credits Welsh Tourist Board; Brynfest @ the Vaynol

Kevin Jones
32 Austen Walk, West Bromwich B71 1RD
t 0121 588 6801 **f** 0121 588 6801 **m** 07775 623738
m 07751 467186 **e** kevin.jones0@amserve.net
e kevinjones58@vizzavi.net
Credits Party At The Palace (T); Royal Variety 2001/2002 (T)

Mary Judge
Flat 4, 69 Hillfield Park, Muswell Hill, London N10 3QU
t 020 8444 5285 **f** 020 8444 5285 **m** 07768 511131
Credits Mersey Beat (T); Tipping The Velvet (T); Hidden City (T); Playing The Field (T)

Charlotte Kay
Callbox Communications Limited, 66 Shepperton Studios,
Studios Road, Shepperton TW17 0QD
t 01932 592572 **f** 01932 569655 **m** 07710 572572
e callboxdiary@btinternet.com **w** www.callboxdiary.co.uk

Anita Lad
31 Hartington Road, London W13 8QL
t 020 8840 5173 **f** 020 8840 5173 **m** 07966 295371
Credits This Year's Love (F); The Knock (T); EastEnders (T); The Bill (T)

Susie Lewis
35 Ty-Wern Road, Rhiwbina, Cardiff CF14 6AB
t 029 2061 2751 **m** 07780 708 761
Credits Y Graith; Belonging; The Bench (T)

Charlotte Morris
t 020 7602 0043 **m** 07771 734380
e charlie@tricks.fsnet.co.uk
Credits Boudica (F); Take a Girl Like You (T); The Way we Live Now (T)

Katrina Perkins
Gems, The Media House, 87 Glebe Street, Penarth CF64 1EF
t 029 2071 0770 **f** 029 2071 0771 **e** gems@gems-agency.co.uk
w www.gems-agency.co.uk
Credits Relic Hunter (T); Alone (F); Anazapta (F); Plots With A View (F)

Phillip Rainforth
Balaclava, 3 Nuns Walk, Hyde, Winchester SO23 7EE
t 01962 856676 **m** 07050 104598
e philthebear@madasafish.com

Barbara Rutter
t 01795 890979 **m** 07050 046 469
Credits Bright Young Things (F); Event Horizon (F); 1492 (F); Horatio Hornblower (T)

Lucy Sampson
m 07976 364 062 **e** lc.sampson@btopenworld.com
Credits The Royal (T); A Good Thief (T); Fat Friends II (T)

Anne Marie Woods
m 07810 437 352 **e** woodsannemarie@hotmail.com

Jane Wrigley
t 020 7402 3192 **m** 07711 142780

Paul Yeowell
524 High Road, Leyton, London E10 6RL
t 020 8539 8382 **m** 07976 844 178 **e** paulyeowell@aol.com
Credits Unconditional Love (F); EastEnders (T); Dr Sleep (F); Nicholas Nickelby (T)

Costume Hire

The 1920s-1970s Crazy Clothes Connection
134 Lancaster Road, Ladbroke Grove, London W11 1QU
t 020 7221 3989 **f** 020 7221 3989 **w** www.crazyclothes.co.uk
Contact Esther Falconer, Contact; Derrick Falconer, Proprietor

20th Century Frox Costume Hire
614 Fulham Road, Fulham, London SW6 5RP
t 020 7731 3242 **w** www.20centuryfrox.co.uk
Contact L J Eyre, Partner; S G Marques, Partner

Academy Costumes Ltd
50 Rushworth Street, London SE1 0RB
t 020 7620 0771 **f** 020 7928 6287
e andrew2001@mac.com **w** www.academycostumes.com

Allan Scott Costumes
Offley Works, Unit F, Prima Road, London SW9 0NA
t 020 7793 1197
Contact Allan Scott, Proprietor

Angels The Costumiers
1 Garrick Road, London NW9 6AA
t 020 8202 2244 **f** 020 8202 1820 **e** angels@angels.uk.com
Contact Jonathan Lipman, Production Director

The Antique Clothing Shop
282 Portobello Road, London W10 6BY
t 020 8993 4162
Contact Sandy Stagg, Proprieter, Manager, Buyer & Seller

Arms & Archery
The Coach House, London Road, Ware SG12 9QU
t 01920 460335 **f** 01920 461044
e terry@armsandarchery.co.uk **w** www.armsandarchery.co.uk
Contact Terry Goulden, Contact

Bath Theatircal Costume Hire

Unit 8, Wallbridge Mill Industrial Estate, Frome BA11 5JX
t 01373 472786 **f** 01225 832846 **e** info@baththeatrical.co.uk
Contact Dinah Auton, Proprietor

BBC Costume + Wigs

BBC Costume & Wigs

Victoria Road, London W3 6UL
t 020 8576 1761 **f** 020 8993 7040 **e** costume@bbc.co.uk
e wigs@bbc.co.uk **w** www.bbcresources.com/costumewig

Birmingham Costume Hire

Suite 209, Jubilee Trade Centre, 130 Pershore Street,
Birmingham B5 6ND
t 0121 622 3158 **f** 0121 622 2758
e info@birminghamcostumehire.co.uk
Contact Lynn Smith, Proprietor

Bristol Costume Services Ltd

Units 4/5, Whitby Road, St Philips, Bristol BS4 3QF
t 0117 300 9233 **f** 0117 300 9244
e bcsbristol@aol.com **w** www.bristolcostumeservices.com
Contact Catriona Tyson, Managing Director

The Business

Unit F36, The Acton Business Centre, School Road, London
NW10 6DT
t 020 8963 0668 **f** 020 8838 0867
e bronwen@costume-rental.com
Contact Bronwen Nolan, Proprietor

Butterfield 8

Rose Cottage, Preston, Newton Abbot TQ12 3PP
t 01626 366437 **f** 01626 366437
e enquiries@c2ovintagefashion.co.uk
w www.c2ovintagefashion.co.uk
Contact Mark Butterfield, Managing Director; Cleo Butterfield, Managing Director

Carlo Manzi Rentals

31-33 Liddell Road, London NW6 2EW
t 020 7625 6391 **f** 020 7625 5386
Contact Carlo Manzi, Proprietor

Contemporary Wardrobe

The Horse Hospital, Colonnade, Bloomsbury, London WC1N 1HX
t 020 7713 7370 **f** 020 7713 7269
e popculture@thehorsehospital.com
Contact Roger Burton, Proprieter

Cosprop

26-28 Rochester Place, London NW1 9JR
t 020 7485 6731 **f** 020 7485 5942
e enquiries@cosprop.com **w** www.cosprop.com
Contact Bernie Chapman, Manager
Credits Sleepy Hollow (F); Forsyte Saga (T); Daniel Deronda (T); Gosford Park (F)

Costello & Sons

284-294 Ley Street, Ilford IG1 4BS
t 020 8478 2780 **f** 020 8553 3336 **w** www.costello.co.uk
Contact Mark Costello, Proprietor

The Costume Department

Building B, Sugar House Yard, Sugar House Lane, London E15 2QS
t 020 8221 0648 **f** 020 8221 0623
e info@thecostumedepartment.com
Contact M Reyner, Company Director; V Illing, Costume Assistant; J Wright, Costume Assistant
Credits Honest (F); Gabriel And Me (F); My Kingdom (F); The Debt (T)

Costume Studio Ltd

159-169 Balls Pond Road, Islington, London N1 4BG
t 020 7275 9614 **f** 020 7837 6576
e costume.studio@easynet.co.uk **w** www.costumestudio.co.uk
Contact Richard Dudley, Director

Dance Depot

Unit B7, Hortonwood 10, Telford TF1 7YA
t 01952 676002 **f** 0845 606 0216
Contact Simon Grigg, Managing Director

Escapade

150 Camden High Street, London NW1 0NE
t 020 7485 7384 **f** 020 7485 0950
e escapade@dircon.co.uk **w** www.escapade.co.uk/esc

Flame Torbay Costume Hire

Old Victorian Police Station, 31-35 Market Street, Torquay TQ1 3AW
t 01803 211930 **f** 01803 293554
e flametorbay@hotmail.com **w** www.flametorbay.co.uk
Contact Lionel Digby, Managing Director
Credits Children of the New Forest (T); Battle of the Atlantic (T); Land Girls (F)

Funn Stockings

PO Box 102, Steyning BN44 3DS
t 0870 784 0814 **f** 01903 892841
e funnorders@mailcity.com **w** www.funnorders.com
Contact Karen Coleman, Head of Marketing; Graham Huntley, Technical Manager
Credits Harry Potter (F); The Hours (F); Titanic (F)

Harveys of Hove

110 Trafalgar Road, Portslade BN41 1GS
t 01273 430323 **f** 01273 708699
e harveys.costume@ntlworld.com **w** www.harveysofhove.co.uk
Contact Wayne de Strete, Managing Director

Laurel Herman

18A Lambolle Place, London NW3 4PG
t 020 7586 7925 **f** 020 7586 7926
e info@pospres.co.uk **w** www.pospres.co.uk

Hirearchy Classic & Contemporary Costume

45-47 Palmerston Road, Boscombe, Bournemouth BH1 4HW
t 01202 394465 **e** hirearchy1@aol.com **w** www.hirearchy.co.uk
Contact Paul Tarrant, Managing Director

Laurence Corner Theatricals

62-64 Hampstead Road, London NW1 2NU
t 020 7813 1010 **f** 020 7813 1413 **w** www.laurencecorner.com
Contact Kim Jamilly, Director, Director
Vast selection of military outfits. Huge stock of headwear. Catalogue on request.

Losner Formals

232 Stamford Hill, London N16 6TT
t 020 8800 9281 **f** 020 8809 6540
e losnersbridalwear@aol.com **w** www.losners.co.uk
Contact Lawrence Sorner, Managing Director

Meculo Costumes

Myfyrian Uchaf, Gaerwen LL60 6NW
t 01248 421945
e georgescarbrough@hotmail.com **e** zoe@meculo.com
Contact Helen Scarbrough, Costume Designer/Manufacturer

Merola

195 Fulham Road, South Kensington, London SW3 6JL
t 020 7351 9338 **f** 020 7795 1414
e info@merola.co.uk **w** www.merola.co.uk
Contact Maria Ward, Proprietor

Midland Costume

Theatre Court, Derrington Avenue, Crewe CW2 7JB
t 01270 251288 **f** 01270 251289
e midlandcostume@btconnect.com

Modern Age Vintage Clothing

65 Chalk Farm Road, London NW6 7YD
t 020 7482 3787 **f** 020 8452 5321 **m** 07719 005456
e vintage-clothing@modern-age.co.uk
w www.modern-age.co.uk
Contact Basil Anastasi, Manager
Credits Light My Fire - Will Young (M); Chevrolet (C); Cadillac (C)

Movietone Frocks

Linton House, Lower Ground Floor, 39-51 Highgate Road,
London NW5 1RS
t 020 7482 1066 **f** 020 8452 5321 **m** 07702 958995
e movietone.frocks@btinternet.com
w www.movietonefrocks.co.uk
Contact Julia Dollimore, Proprietor

One Night Stand

8 Chelsea Manor Studios, Flood Street, London SW3 5SR
t 020 7352 4848 **f** 020 7376 8866 **m** 07973 540364
e joanna@onenightstand.co.uk **w** www.onenightstand.co.uk

Royal National Theatre Costume & Furniture Hire

Chichester House, 1-3 Brixton Rd, London SW9 6DE
t 020 7735 4774(Costumes) **t** 020 7820 1358(Props)
f 020 7582 8233(Costumes) **f** 020 7820 3512(Props)
e costumehire@nationaltheatre.org.uk
w www.nationaltheatre.org.uk

Sabre Sales

85-87 Castle Road, Southsea, Portsmouth PO5 3AY
t 023 9283 3394 **f** 023 9283 7394 **m** 07850 260148
e roy.smith5@virgin.net **w** www.millweb.net/go/sabre
Contact Nick Hall, Proprietor; Richard Ingram, Manager
Credits Inside Deep (T); Die Another Day (F); Four Feathers (F)

Script To Screen

Unit J7, Colchester Industrial Estate, Colchester Avenue,
Cardiff CF23 9AP
t 029 2045 4222 **f** 029 2045 4400
e lindsay@scripttoscreencostumes.co.uk
w www.scripttoscreen.co.uk
Contact Lindsay Wood, Partner; Chrissie Pegg, Costume Designer

Squirrel Films Distribution Ltd

Grices Wharf, 119 Rotherhithe Street, London SE16 4NF
t 020 7231 2209 **f** 020 7231 2119
e ostockman@sandsfilms.co.uk **w** www.sandsfilms.co.uk
Contact Olivier Stockman, Managing Director; Christine Goodwin, Director

Struts

12 Dixon Street, Carlisle CA3 8XA
t 01228 818317 **t** 01228 547996
e info@struts.co.uk **w** www.struts.co.uk
Contact Jane Robles-Peragon, Director; Michael Ayre, Director

Studio Four Costumes

4 Warple Mews, Warple Way, London W3 0RF
t 020 8749 6569 **f** 020 8749 6569
Contact Linda Burtenshaw, Proprietor

Swans Flight Productions Ltd

Swansnest, 2 Windmill Road, Hampton Hill TW12 1RH
t 020 8941 1595 **f** 020 8783 1366 **m** 07860 169278
e swansflight@aol.com **w** www.swansflight.com
Contact T Denton de Gray, Proprietor

Costume Makers

BBC Costume + Wigs

BBC Costume & Wigs

Victoria Road, London W3 6UL
t 020 8576 1761 **f** 020 8993 7040 **e** costume@bbc.co.uk
e wigs@bbc.co.uk **w** www.bbcresources.com/costumewig

Dana Bolton

t 020 8347 9880 **m** 7786 **e** danabolton2@hotmail.com

Alison Callaghan

25 Paget Street, Grangetown, Cardiff CF11 7LB
t 029 2021 4881 **f** 029 2021 4869 **m** 07711 867351
e scott-callaghan.artpro@ntlworld.com
Credits Jacob's Ladder (F); Pobl Y Cwm (T); The Bench (T)

Costume World Ltd

2-3 Red Park Place, Milton Abbas DT11 0BD
t 01258 881162 **f** 01258 880912 **m** 07967 107955
e office@costume-world.co.uk **w** www.costumeworld.co.uk
Contact Cheryl Price, Production; Michael Dyson, Secretary; Carly Griffith, Creative

Davies & Son (London) Ltd

38 Saville Row, London W1S 3QE
t 020 7434 3016
Contact Alan Bennett, Managing Director
Credits Pop Idol (T); Cavanaugh QC (T)

Embroidery Techniques

118-120 Great Titchfield Street, London W1P 7AJ
t 01848 600246 **f** 01848 600301
e alan@embtech.co.uk **w** www.embtech.co.uk
Contact Alan Fischelis, Managing Director

English Arms & Armour

Mellanowerth House, Back Lane, Angarrack, Hayle TR27 5JE
t 07136 753444 **f** 07136 753444 **m** 07713 114142
Contact Terry English, Metal Costume Fabricator & Designer

FB-FX Ltd

Unit 1, Dockwells Estate, Central Way, Feltham TW14 0RD
t 020 8751 5321 **f** 020 8890 2928
e info@fbfx.co.uk **w** www.fbfx.co.uk
Contact Grant Pearmain, Director
Credits Judge Dredd (F); Star Wars Episode I & II (F); Lost In Space (F); Gladiator (F)

From The Neck Up

84 Hampden Road, Harrow Weald HA3 5PR
t 020 8427 7429 **f** 020 8427 7429
e inness.family@btinternet.com
Contact Denise Innes, Milliner
Credits The Brits (T)

Stephan Harrington

Pembroke Cottage, Hindon Road, East Knoyle SP3 6AA
t 01747 830743 **f** 01747 830743 **m** 07702 884208
Contact Stephan Harrington, Proprietor
Credits Harry Potter (F); First Knight (F); The Gauntlet Machine (F)

Hightower Crafts (LRP)

Clwt Melyn, Pen Lon, Newborough LL61 6RS
t 01248 440500 **f** 01248 440233
e paul@hightowercrafts.com **w** www.hightowercrafts.com
Contact Paul Curtis, Director

Karen Spurgin Textile Design

39 Sundorne Road, London SE7 7PR
t 020 8355 4729 **f** 020 8858 9789
e karen.spurgin@cwcom.net **w** www.spurgin.co.uk
Contact Karen Spurgin, Contact

Kevin Darby Costumes
Unit 10, Douglas Buildings, Royal Stuart Lane, Cardiff CF10 5EL
t 029 2045 1646 **f** 029 2045 1628
e gren@dercon.co.uk **w** www.kevinderbycostumes.com
Contact Kevin Darby, Proprietor
Credits Plots With a View (F)

MBA Costumes
Goodyear House, 52-56 Osnaburgh Street, London NW1 3ND
t 020 7388 4994 **f** 020 7383 2038 **e** nhowarduk@aol.com
Contact Noel Howard, Managing Director

Mike & Rosi Compton
11 Woodstock Road, Croydon CRO 1JS
t 020 8680 4364 **f** 020 8681 3126 **m** 07770 810234
m 07900 258646 **e** mikeandrosicompton@btopenworld.com
Contact Rosi Compton, Partner; Mike Compton, Partner
We specialise in the unusual: where costume and props coincide.

Mike Coltman Costume Construction
21A Silchester Rd, London W10 6SF
t 020 8968 9136 **f** 020 8968 9136
w www.costumeconstruction.co.uk

Nicola Killeen Textiles (Dyeing & Printing)
Unit A 42-43, 50-56 Wharf Road, London N1 7SF
t 020 7250 1188 **f** 020 7250 1164
e nicola@nktextiles.com **w** www.nktextiles.com
Contact Nicola Killeen, Director

Original Knitwear (including Fake Fur)
Waterside, 99 Rotherhithe Street, London SE16 4NF
t 020 7231 9020 **f** 020 7231 9051
Contact Gina Pinnick, Proprietor

Patricia Smith Costumes
86 Parkstone Road, Hastings TN34 2NU
t 01424 442763
Contact Patricia Smith, Proprietor

Portico Leisure
Theme House, Park Hall Road, Charnock Richard, Chorley PR7 5LP
t 01257 453758 **f** 01257 453108 **m** 07744 499681
e info@theme1.com
Contact Richard Timson
Credits Die Another Day (F); Stalingrad (F); Captain Correlli's Mandolin (F);
Band Of Brothers (T)

Pullons PM Productions
St George's Studio, Wood End Lane, Fillongley CV7 8DF
t 01676 541390 **f** 01676 541390 **m** 07732 275180
w www.pm-productions.co.uk
Contact June Pullon, Proprietor
Credits Kitkat (C); www.elephant.com (C); Mr Blobby Generation Game
Costumes; Generation Game (T)

Rose-Davies Costume Builders
Daffodil Studios, Brick Hill Lane, Harvest Hill CV5 9BU
t 02676 405040 **t** 02676 404646
e info@promotioncostumes.com
w www.promotioncostumes.com
Contact Mandy Davies, Partner

Samuel Hogarth & Sons
10 Stratton Street, Mayfair, London W1X 5FD
t 020 7544 6863 **f** 020 7544 6870
e sales@samuelhogarth.co.uk
Contact Darrel Kent-Morris, Partner
Credits Shanghai Knights (F)

Linda May Sanderson
116 Mortlake Road, Kew, Richmond TW9 4AR
t 020 8876 3728 **f** 020 8876 3728 **m** 07939 610249

Margarethe Schmoll
40 Joseph Trotter Close, Skinner Street, London EC1R 1UB
t 020 7278 1680 **m** 07740 229979 **e** mschmoll99@aol.com
Credits Shanghai Knights (F); To Kill A King (F); Harry Potter And The Prisoner
Of Azkaban (F); Band Of Brothers (T)

Sheila Hallatt Costumes
4 Comely Bank Place, Edinburgh EH4 1DU
t 0131 332 1978 **t** 01330 833653 **f** 01330 833653
e shallatt@supanet.com **w** www.shallattcostumes.co.uk
Credits Farscape (T); Mopatop's Shop (T); Honey Monster (C); The Hoobs (T)

Barbara Shulman
The Garden Flat, 52c Warrington Crescent, Maida Vale,
London W9 1EP
t 020 7286 7142 **f** 020 7286 7142
e barbarashulman@hotmail.com

Stylemode Ltd
Unit 15, 24 Sugar House Lane, Stratford, London E15 2QS
m 07831 872076
Contact Paul Skipper, Director; Jac Bhakar, Director; Suheb Uddin, Director

Costume Stylists

Marianne Agertoft
3 De Beauvoir Square, London N1 4LG
t 020 7249 0119 **f** 020 7249 0119 **m** 07976 909 891
Credits Villa des Roses (F); Bride Of Ice (F)

Chris Baker
Mandy Coakley Represents, 18 Mandeville Courtyard, Warriner
Gardens, London SW11 4NB
t 020 7720 6234 **f** 020 7720 0199
e mc@mandycoakley.co.uk **w** www.mandycoakley.co.uk

Karen N Binns
Mandy Coakley Represents, 18 Mandeville Courtyard, Warriner
Gardens, London SW11 4NB
t 020 7720 6234 **f** 020 7720 0199
e mc@mandycoakley.co.uk **w** www.mandycoakley.co.uk

Helen Carey
50 Glengarry Road, London SE22 8QD
t 020 8299 1559 **f** 020 8693 5209 **m** 07860 796866
e helen.carey@pipemedia.co.uk **w** www.helencarey-stylist.com

Bo Chapman
Mandy Coakley Represents, 18 Mandeville Courtyard, Warriner
Gardens, London SW11 4NB
t 020 7720 6234 **f** 020 7720 0199
e mc@mandycoakley.co.uk **w** www.mandycoakley.co.uk

Jane Dundas
ADS, Shepperton Studios, Studios Road, Shepperton TW17 0QD
t 01932 592303 **f** 01932 592492 **e** ads@carlincrew.com
Credits Fairy (C); Shreddies (C); Sainsbury's (C); McDonalds (C)

Glenis Foster
Mandy Coakley Represents, 18 Mandeville Courtyard, Warriner
Gardens, London SW11 4NB
t 020 7720 6234 **f** 020 7720 0199
e mc@mandycoakley.co.uk **w** www.mandycoakley.co.uk

Anna Haig
8 Royal Oak Court, Pitfield Street, London N1 6EL
t 020 7729 7181 **f** 020 7729 7181 **m** 07980 552232
e anna@annahaig.co.uk
Credits Sony Playstation (C); BBC London (C); Suzuki (C)

Catherine Hanicotte
Ethos Represents, 23 Albert Square, London SW8 1BS
t 020 7735 7006 **f** 020 7735 7009
e ethosrepresents@btinternet.com

Becky John
The Chestnut, 91 Liddle Lane, London N8 8NX
t 020 8341 2368 **f** 020 8340 8936 **m** 07778 518305
e beckyjohn15@hotmail.com

Jenny Lawrence-Jones
ADS, Shepperton Studios, Shepperton Road, Shepperton
TW17 0QD
t 01932 592303 **f** 01932 592492 **e** ads@carlincrew.co.uk
Credits Levis (C); Eurostar (C); Pedigree Chum (C); Mean Machine (F)

Debbie Moles
ADS, Shepperton Studios, Shepperton Road, Shepperton
TW17 0QD
t 01932 592303 **f** 01932 592492 **e** ads@carlincrew.co.uk
Credits High Stakes (F); Perfect World (F); Fields Of Gold (F)

Suzi Pride
32 Loveridge Road, London NW6 2DT
t 020 7372 5203 **m** 07973 117751 **e** suzipride@talk21.com
Credits A Little Worm (S)

Heidi Taylor
Mandy Coakley Represents, 18 Mandeville Courtyard, Warriner
Gardens, London SW11 4NB
t 020 7720 6234 **f** 020 7720 0199
e mc@mandycoakley.co.uk **w** www.mandycoakley.co.uk

Courier Services

A-Z Couriers Ltd
Texryte House, Balmes Road, London N1 3JH
t 020 7254 2000 **f** 020 7241 3093 **w** www.a-z.co.uk
Contact Paul Fisher, Branch Manager

Air Courier International Ltd
Unit 0469, Colndale Road, Colnbrook SL3 0HQ
t 01753 561300 **f** 01753 561301
e car@aircourieruk.com **w** www.aircourier.com
Contact Darren Winter, Director

Associated Air Services Ltd
Units 4-6 Feltham Business Complex, Browells Lane, Feltham
TW13 7EQ
t 020 8844 0805 **f** 020 8844 0878
e info@aasuk.co.uk **w** www.aasuk.co.uk
Contact Lee Russell, Sales Director

Cars & Bikes
19 Enterprise Way, London NW10 6UG
t 020 8962 2222 **f** 020 8962 2299 **m** 07973 333555
e mail@carsandbikes.biz **w** www.carsandbikes.biz
Contact David Potts, Manager

Chain Gang
River Reach, Gartons Way, Battersea, London SW11 3SX
t 020 7978 4044 **f** 020 7978 4055
Contact Brian Taylor, Business Development Manager

Churchill Express
Churchill House, 43 Colville Road, London W3 8BL
t 020 8993 2211 **f** 020 8993 7769
e enquiries@churchillexpress.co.uk
Contact Damian Milson, Director

City Sprint
Lower Ground, 58 - 62 Scrutton Street, London EC2A 4PH
t 08707 335 4837 **f** 020 7880 1088
e info@citysprint.co.uk **w** www.citysprint.co.uk
Contact Emma Johns, Customer Services Manager

The Courier Group
21a Brownlow Mews, London WC1N 2LA
t 020 7831 0000 **f** 020 7404 6045 **e** mach1@aol.com
Contact Kevin Lockhead, Office Manager

Creative Couriers Ltd
75 Berwick Street, London W1F 8TG
t 020 7437 2724 **f** 020 7440 1900
Contact Tim Webb, Operations Director; Lisa Byrne, Managing Director

CYC Logistics & Distribution
Milcote House, Milcote Street, London SE1 0RX
t 020 7928 2251 **f** 020 7928 2246
e lisa@cyclogistics.com **w** www.cyclogistics.com
Contact Lisa Reynolds, Sales Manager; Dean Ali, Operations Manager

Cyclone Car & Courier Company Ltd
Cyclone House, 27-29 Whitfield Street, London W1T 2SE
t 020 7436 0902 **f** 020 7307 9818
e info@cyclone-couriers.com **w** www.cyclone-couriers.com
Contact Laurie Telfer, Sales & Marketing Director

DHL International (UK) Ltd
178-188 Great Southwest Road, Hounslow TW4 6JS
t 020 8818 8000 **f** 020 8818 8018 **w** www.dhl.co.uk
Contact Kate Hanson, Media Manager; Karren Piesley, Public Relations
Executive; John Hicks, Corporate Affairs Executive

Ecosse World Express
Unit 11, Airlink Industrial Estate, Inchinnan Road, Glasgow
Airport PA3 2RS
t 0141 887 1221 **f** 0141 887 1331
e enquiries@ecosseworldexpress.co.uk
w www.ecosseworldexpress.co.uk
Contact George Wilson, Director

Esprit Europe
Esprit House, 1 Lower Road, Waterloo Station, London SE1 8SJ
t 020 7902 3516 **f** 020 7902 3710
e julie.smith@eurostar.co.uk **w** www.espriteurope.co.uk
Contact Julie Smith, Sales & Marketing Manager

Fleet Street Flyer
21 Brownlow Mews, John''s Mews, London WC1N 2NA
t 020 7242 1233 **f** 020 7404 6045
Contact J Thompson, Manager

Hare in the Gate Couriers Ltd
21 Foley Street, London W1W 6DR
t 020 7323 3237 **f** 020 7323 2739 **e** thehare@btinternet.com
Contact R West, Director; C West, Managing Director
Credits Band Of Brothers (T); Murder In Mind III (T); Dirty Pretty Things (F);
The Hours (F)
Expert Rushes collection/delivery. Offices W1 and Pinewood Studios.

Marken Time Critical Express
Unit 2, Metro Centre, St Johns Road, Isleworth TW7 6NJ
t 020 8388 8555 **f** 020 8388 8666 **w** www.marken.com

Media Freight Services Ltd
Media House, Springfield Road, Hayes UB4 0DD
t 020 8573 9999 **f** 020 8573 9592
e services@mediafreight.co.uk **w** www.mediafreight.co.uk
Contact John Joce, Director

Midnite Express International Couriers Ltd
Unit 16, Saxon Way, Wert Drayton UB7 0LW
t 020 8607 5530 **f** 020 8607 5531
e midniteexpress@mnx.com
Contact Julie Hughes, Director

Moves Ltd
Moves House, 141 Acton Lane, London NW10 7PB
t 08700 104410 **f** 020 8267 6003
e enquiries@moves.co.uk **w** www.moves.co.uk

Night Flight International
Unit N103-104, Westminster Business Square, 1-45 Durham Streeet, London SE11 5JH
t 020 7820 1111 **f** 020 7793 1202
e katie@nightflightinternational.co.uk
w www.nightfligthinternational.co.uk
Contact Mark Entwistle, Managing Director

Point to Point
Unit 2, Bustace Studios, Conlan Street, London W10 5AT
t 020 8960 2222 **f** 020 8960 0956
e kevin@point-to-point.co.uk
Contact Kevin Gray, Manager

Precision Cargo Services Ltd
Pinewood Stuios, Pinewood Road, Iver SL0 0NH
t 01753 650551 **f** 01753 650601
e info@precisioncargo.co.uk **w** www.precisioncargo.co.uk
Contact Les Taylor, Director; Wendy Williams, Sales Manager; Gary Green, Director; Dave Powell, Director; Paul Bauldwin, General Manager

Priority Express (Couriers) Ltd
The Media Centre, Culverhouse Cross, Cardiff CF5 6XJ
t 029 2059 0464 **f** 029 2059 0313
e support@priorityexpress.co.uk **w** www.priorityexpress.co.uk
Contact Paul Havill, Joint Managing Director

Seaborne Express Couriers
Unit 13, Saxon Way Trading Estate, Moor Lane, Harmondsworth UB7 0LW
t 020 8322 1700 **f** 020 8322 1701
w www.seaborne-express.com
Contact Daniel Flitterman, CEO

Skynet Worldwide Express
Unit D, Stockley Close, West Drayton UB7 9BL
t 01895 466466 **f** 01895 466215
e skylondon@skynetworldwide.com **w** www.skynetworldwide.com
Contact Suzanne Darnington, Sales Manager; Tim Frost, Sales Manager

Specialist Air Express
Hornblowers House, Galley-Mead Road, Colnbrook SL3 0EN
t 01753 687763 **f** 01753 687764 **m** 07976 158135
e jonathan@specialistair.co.uk **e** info@specialistair.co.uk
w www.specialistair.co.uk
Contact Jonathan Fiddy, Director

Sprint International
Unit 3, The Mercury Centre, Central Way, Feltham TW14 0RN
t 020 8751 1111 **f** 020 8890 9090
e open@sprintexpress.co.uk **w** www.sprintexpress.co.uk
Contact S Tudgay, General Manager

TNT UK Ltd
Unit 6, Spitfire Trading Estate, Spitfire Way, Hounslow TW5 9NW
t 020 8561 2345 **f** 020 8848 3285 **w** www.tnt.co.uk

Total Market Support Ltd
Unit 9, Spaceway, North Feltham Trading Estate, Feltham TW14 0TH
t 020 8751 7232 **t** 020 8751 7233 **f** 020 8751 7222
e karen@totalmarkets.co.uk
Contact Karen Parker, Managing Director; Graham Seeley, Director
Credits Film Rushes (F)

Warwick
Central House, 142 Central Street, London EC1V 8AR
t 020 7250 1883 **f** 020 7549 5100
e sales@warwickgroup.co.uk **w** www.warwickgroup.co.uk
Contact Mary Thorn, Managing Director

Worlds End Couriers
Unit 6B, Farm Lane Trading Estate, 101 Farm Lane, London SW6 1QJ
t 020 7731 0454 **f** 020 7385 4468 **m** 07956 398 742
w www.wecouriers.co.uk
Contact Dave Norman, Sales Manager

Cranes, Cherrypickers

Ainscough Crane Hire Ltd
Bradley Hall, Bradley Lane, Standish, Wigan WN6 0XQ
t 01257 473423 **f** 01257 473286
e general@ainscough.co.uk **w** www.aincough.co.uk

Brogan Access Ltd
Nethan St, Motherwell ML1 3TF
t 01698 265132 **f** 01698 262547
Contact Alastair Brogan, Director

EPL Access
Unit 2, Tyne Road, Sandy SG19 1SA
t 01767 688160 **f** 01767 688161
e info@eplaccess.co.uk **w** www.eplaccess.co.uk
Contact Danny Cooper, Business Development Manager

Facelift Aerial Platforms
London Road, Hickstead, Haywards Heath RH17 5LZ
t 01444 881188 **f** 01444 881199
e hiredesk@facelift-access.co.uk **w** www.facelift-access.co.uk

Louma UK
43 Parkside, Mill Hill, London NW7 2LN
t 020 8959 3082 **f** 020 8906 3217 **m** 07831 805624
e info@louma.co.uk
Contact Lynne Samuelson, Company Secretary
Credits Die Another Day (F); Harry Potter And The Chamber Of Secrets (F); Charlotte Gray (F); Harry Potter And The Philosopher's Stone (F)

Loxam Access (Alfreton)
Unit 7, Garnham Close, Cotes Park Industrial Estate, Alfreton DE55 4QG
t 01773 835511 **f** 01773 522840
Contact Wendy Robinson, Secretary to the Managing Director; Agnes Rippault, Secretary to the Managing Director

Loxam Access (Birmingham)
14 Leopold Street, Highgate, Birmingham B12 0UP
t 0121 440 6688 **f** 0121 440 6699
e birmingham@ptp-access.com **w** www.ptp-access.com
Contact Wendy Robinson, Secretary to the Managing Director; Alan Bishop, Manager

Loxam Access (Bristol)
Victoria Road, Avonmouth, Bristol BS11 9DB
t 0117 982 8111 **f** 0117 938 2820 **m** 07831 538282
Contact Wendy Robinson, Secretary to the Managing Director; John Mather

Loxam Access (Dublin)
Unit 1A, Cookstown Industrial Estate, Tallaght, Dublin 24, Rep of Ireland
t +353 1452 0103 **f** +353 1462 1863
Contact Paul Collins, Manager; Wendy Robinson, Secretary to the Managing Director

Loxam Access (East London)
Maybells Industrial Estate, Ripple Road, Barking IG11 7NY
t 020 8595 7614 **f** 020 8595 9007 **w** www.ptp-access.com
Contact Wendy Robinson, Secretary to the Managing Director

Loxam Access (Edinburgh)
Unit 18, Tartraven Place, East Mains Industrial Estate, Broxburn EH52 5LT
t 01506 859220 **t** 0800 626220
f 01506 859221 **m** 07831 538284
e edinburgh@p+p-access.com **w** www.loxom.tv
Contact Leigh Colville, Branch Manager; Margaret Cole, Hire Consultant
Credits Rebus (T); Trans World (T); BSkyB (T); CBF Media (T)

Loxam Access (Glasgow)
45 Methil Street, Glasgow G14 0AG
t 0141 959 1299 **f** 0141 950 1439
Contact Wendy Robinson, Secretary to the Managing Director

Loxam Access (Limerick)

Units 1 & 2, Park Road, Rhebogue, Limerick, Rep of Ireland
t +353 61 317 700 **f** +353 61 317 710
Contact Wendy Robinson, Secretary to Managing Director; Niamh Graham, Manager

Loxam Access (Liverpool)

Haydock Lane, Haydock, Liverpool WA11 9UH
t 01942 722395 **f** 01942 722425
Contact Wendy Robinson, Secretary to the Managing Director

Loxam Access (Middlesborough)

Macklin Avenue, Cowpen Industrial Estate, Billingham TS23 4BY
t 01642 563417 **f** 01642 562468
e teeside@ptp-access.com **w** www.ptp-access.com
Contact Wendy Robinson, Secretary to the Managing Director

Loxam Access (Plymouth)

Mill Close, Lee Mill Industrial Estate, Ivybridge, Plymouth PL21 9GL
t 01752 690365 **f** 01752 690968 **e** plymouth@p+p-access.com

Loxam Access (Pontefract)

Bondgate Industrial Estate, Pontefract WF8 2JJ
t 01977 600122 **f** 01977 600009
Contact Wendy Robinson, Secretary to the Managing Director

Loxam Access (Portsmouth)

Crompton Way, Segensworth Industrial Estate, Fareham PO15 5SP
t 01489 575762 **f** 01489 582414

Loxam Access (Scunthorpe)

Atkinsons Way, Foxhill Industrial Estate, Scunthorpe DN15 8JQ
t 01724 749000 **f** 01724 749001
Contact Wendy Robinson, Secretary to the Managing Director

Loxam Access (West London)

731-761 Harrow Road, Kensal Green, London NW10 5NY
t 020 8964 1077 **f** 020 8960 7934
Contact Wendy Robinson, Secretary to the Managing Director

Marshall Branson

Chain Bridge Road, Blaydon-on-Tyne NE21 5SX
t 0191 414 2041 **f** 0191 414 9312
Contact Gordon Morrison, Director

Nationwide Access Ltd

1 Midland Court, Central Park, Lutterworth LE17 4PN
t 01455 206719 **f** 01455 550974
e marketing@nationwideaccess.co.uk
w www.nationwideaccess.co.uk
Contact Karen Moulds, Marketing Executive

Nationwide Skylift

1 Midland Court, Central Park, Lutterworth LE17 4PN
t 02476 408600 **f** 02476 407314
e connect@nationwideaccess.co.uk
w www.nationwideaccess.co.uk
Contact Gary Brady, Key Account Manager
Credits Iris (F); Harry Potter And The Philosopher's Stone (F)

Technovision UK Ltd

Unit 4, St Margarets Business Centre, Drummond Place,
Twickenham TW1 1JN
t 020 8891 5961 **f** 020 8744 1154 **e** info@technovision-uk.com
Contact Janet Da Cruz, Company Secretary
Credits Blue Featuring Elton John - Sorry Seems To Be... (M); Harry Potter And The
Philosopher's Stone (F); Who Wants To Be A Millionaire? (T); Pop Stars: The Rivals (T)

The Universal Aerial Platforms Service Ltd

Drury Way, Brent Park, London NW10 OJH
t 020 8830 3333 **f** 020 8830 4444
e access@universal-platforms.co.uk
w www.universal-platforms.co.uk
Contact David Howse, Manager

DESIGN FACILITIES

Design Facilities
Drapes

Acre Jean Drape Hire

Unit 7, The Kimber Centre, 54 Kimber Road, London SW18 4PP
t 020 8877 3211 **f** 020 8877 3213
e enquires@acrejean.com **w** www.acrejean.com
Contact Ross Maxwell, Managing Director; Gary Cooper-Burrows, Hire
Manager; Colin Hannah, Installations Director; Gary Holder, General Manager

Black Velvet Hire

Shepperton Drape Shop, Shepperton Studio Centre, Studios
Road, Shepperton TW17 OQD
t 01932 560175 **f** 01932 560175 **m** 07831 198127
Contact Cleo Nethersole, Partner; Gary Handley, Partner
Credits Sleepy Hollow (F); Titanic (F); The Mummy Returns (F); Harry Potter
And The Philosopher's Stone (F)

Blackout Ltd

280 Western Road, London SW19 2QA
t 020 8687 8400 **f** 020 8687 8500
e info@blackout-ltd.com **w** www.blackout-ltd.com
Contact Kevin Monks, Project Manager; Lucy Stevens, Hire and Sales Adviser;
Tony Lambert, Technical Manager; Chris Brain, Installations Director

Elstree Drape Hire & Services

Elstree Studios, Shenley Road, Borehamwood WD6 1JG
t 020 8324 2666 **f** 020 8324 2694 **m** 07956 372662
Contact Karl Wilson, Proprieter; Barry Wilson, Proprieter

Ken Creasy Ltd

34 Queens Row, London SE17 2PX
t 020 7277 1645 **f** 020 7277 1701
Contact Peter Everett, Managing Director

S&H Technical Support Group

Unit A, The Old Laundry, Chambercombe Road, Ilfracombe
EX34 9PH
t 01271 866832 **f** 01271 865423
e shtsg@aol.com **w** www.starcloth.co.uk
Contact Jo Newton, Office Manager; Nigel Smith, Partner; Dave Baxter,
Sales & Marketing Director; Terry Murtha, Partner

Design Facilities
Portrait Painters

Bollom T.V. & Film

Croydon Road, Beckenham, Kent BR3 4BL
t 020 8658 2299 **f** 020 8658 8672
e sales@bollom.com **w** www.bollom.com/tvandfilm

Sally Dray
Victoria Lodge, Victoria Close, Weybridge KT13 9QJ
t 01932 842538 **f** 01932 842538
Credits The Lost Prince (T); Hound of the Baskervilles (T); Harry Potter And
The Prisoner Of Azkaban (F); Harry Potter And The Philosopher's Stone (F)

Design Facilities
Scenic Artists

Chris Bradley
Art Department, 51 Pratt Street, London NW1 0BJ
t 020 7428 0500 **f** 020 7916 2167 **m** 07973 639785
e info@art-department.co.uk

CI Banks
68 Chatsworth Gardens, Acton, London W3 9LW
t 020 8992 0206 **f** 020 8992 0206
Contact Carolynne Banks, Scenic Artist

Stuart Clarke
8 Arlington Avenue, Leamington Spa CV32 5UA
t 01926 332844 **m** 07831 567 228
Credits Van Helsing (F); Trainspotting (F); The World Is Not Enough (F);
The Four Feathers (F)

Sally Fletcher
Wealthly Lodge, Towpath, Shepperton TW17 9LL
t 01932 227679 **m** 07778 370571 **e** sallyps@onetel.net.uk

James Gemmill
1 Church Street, Beckley OX3 9UT
t 01865 351324 **f** 01865 358525 **m** 07889 508888
e james.gemmill@talk21.com
Credits Tombraider II (F); The Mummy Returns (F); The Mummy (F); Star Wars:
Episode I - The Phantom Menace (F)

Jonathan Holbrook
24 Archfield Road, Cotham, Bristol BS6 6BE
t 01179 248467 **m** 07768 323735 **e** zoella5@aol.com
Credits Four Feathers (F); Plots with a View (F); Doctor Sleep (F)

Nick Holmes
Art Department, 51 Pratt Street, London NW1 0BJ
t 020 7428 0500 **f** 020 7916 2167 **m** 07973 639785
e info@art-department.co.uk

Eddie Howe
2 Woburn, Clivedon Court, Ealing, London W13 8DS
t 020 8998 0858 **f** 020 8998 0858 **m** 07976 747146
Experienced in TV film, commercials, adverts and mural work.

Magnus Irvin
11 Lancaster Road, London N4 4PJ
t 020 7263 3846 **f** 020 7254 0601 **e** magno@obe.abelgratis.com
Credits MTV Music Awards; Ruby Wax Live; Michael Jackson World Tour

Roy Monk
Wilton End Cottage, Radlett Lane, Shenley WD7 9AJ
t 01923 856338 **f** 01923 856338 **m** 07860 285594
Credits Love Actually (F); Band Of Brothers (T)

Rob Smiley
91 Costock Avenue, Sherwood, Nottingham NG5 3AX
t 0115 859 8931 **m** 07968 167854 **e** fracture_maze@ntlworld.com
Credits Star Wars - Episode I: The Phantom Menace (F); A Room for Romeo
Brass (F); Once Upon A Time In The Midlands (F)

Howard Weaver
25 Green Lane, Chesham Bois HP6 5LN
t 01494 722721 **e** h@howard-weaver.demon.co.uk
Credits Gosford Park (F); Neverland (F); Daniel Deronda (T); Iris (F)

Design Facilities
Signwriters

Almik Signs Ltd
10 Wendell Road, London W12 9RT
t 020 8743 1090 **f** 020 8749 5774
e 3d@almik-signs.co.uk **w** www.eclipse.co.uk/almik-signs

Bill Hodgins
Winters Tale Farm Studio, Old Blackmoor Hill, Steeple Claydon
MK18 2EZ
t 01296 730215 **f** 01296 730140 **m** 07831 766268
e bill@billhodgins-signartist.co.uk
w www.billhodgins-signartist.co.uk
Credits EuroDisney Theme Park; Weetabix (C); Pearl Harbour (F); Baby Father (T)

Spa Display Ltd
North Street Industrial Estate, Droitwich Spa WR9 8JB
t 01905 775428 **f** 01905 795417
Contact Paul Caffull, Director

Mike Stevenson
Studio 100, Shepperton Studios, Studios Road, Shepperton
TW17 0QD
t 01932 592892 **f** 01932 592294 **m** 07710 069723
e whorocket@hotmail.com

Diary Services

Annie's Answering Service
Pinewood Studios, Pinewood Road, Iver Heath SL0 0NH
t 01753 651303 **f** 01753 651848
e info@annies.co.uk **w** www.annies.co.uk

Art Department
51 Pratt Street, London NW1 0BJ
t 020 7428 0500 **f** 020 7916 2167 **m** 07973 639 785
e info@art-department.co.uk
Contact Deborah Randall-Cutler, Director

Bookends
83 Maynard Drive, St Albans AL1 2JX
t 01727 841177 **e** bookgold@bookends.fsbusiness.co.uk
Contact Marge Gold, Assistant; Sharon Gold, Company Director

Callbox Communications Ltd
PO Box 66, Shepperton Studios, Shepperton TW17 0QD
t 01932 592572 **f** 01932 569655 **m** 07710 572572
e callboxdiary@btinternet.com **w** www.callboxdiary.co.uk
Contact Patsy Brinkworth; Claire Lewis; Julia Morris

Carlin Crew Ltd
Shepperton Studios, Studios Road, Shepperton TW17 0QD
t 01932 568268 **f** 01932 571109
e carlin@netcomuk.co.uk **w** www.carlincrew.com
Contact Julia Franklin, Contact

Connections
The Meadlands, Oakleigh Road, Hatch End, Pinner HA5 4HB
t 020 8420 1444 **f** 020 8428 5836 **m** 07831 305518
e mail@connectionsuk.com **w** www.connectionsuk.com
Contact Martin Roberts; Barbara Roberts
Personal diary service for film and video technicians.

Crew 2
The London Broadcast Centre, 11-13 Point Pleasant,
London SW18 1NN
t 020 8433 8185 **f** 020 8433 8001
e steve@crew2.com **w** www.crew2.com

Diary
111 The School House, Pages Walk, London SE1 4HG
t 020 7394 9911 **f** 020 7232 2355
Contact Irene Angadi, Proprietor

The Digital Garage Company Ltd
13 Devonshire Mews, Chiswick, London W4 2HA
t 07000 785821 **f** 07000 785822 **m** 07788 145577
e mail@digitalgarage.co.uk **w** www.digitalgarage.co.uk
Contact Janie Willsmore, Crew Manager; Oliver Hickey, Facilities Manager
Credits Castle (D); Faking It - Drag Queen (T); Leonardo (T);
Six Wives Of Henry VIII (T)

Edit-Base
70A Waldegrave Road, Teddington TW11 8NY
t 020 8614 6937 **e** alison@edit-base.co.uk
Contact Alison Wren, Director

Ethos Represents
22 Albert Square, London SW8 1BS
t 020 7735 7006 **f** 020 7735 7009
e ethosrepresents@btinternet.com
Contact Susan Robertson; Melissa Baker

Exec
6 Travis Court, Farnham Royal SL2 3SB
t 01753 646677 **f** 01753 646770
e sue@execmanagement.co.uk **w** www.execmanagement.co.uk
Contact Sue Jones; Pam Riley

Experience Counts - Call Me Ltd
5th Floor, 41-42 Berners Street, London W1P 3AA
t 020 7637 8112 **f** 020 7580 2582
Contact Erika Klausner, Director

The Firm Booking Company Ltd
31 Oval Road, Camden, London NW1 7EA
t 020 7428 9090 **f** 020 7428 9089 **m** 07976 244979
e kirsty@thefirm.co.uk
Contact Kirsty Howe

GAS (Guild Answering Service)
C/o Panavision, Bristol Road, Metropolitan Centre,
Greenford UB6 8GD
t 020 8813 1999 **f** 020 8813 2111
e admin@gbct.org **w** www.gbct.org
Contact Louise Tregidgo

Linkline
6 Thirlmere Gardens, Wembley HA9 8RE
t 020 8908 6262 **f** 020 8904 5179 **e** mail@linklinecrew.com
w www.linklinecrew.com
Contact Nick Hunter, Director; Gerry Kliman, Director

The Production Switchboard Ltd
Northdown, Down Lane, Compton GU3 1DN
t 01483 812011 **f** 01483 812027
e aly@productionswitch.freeserve.co.uk
Contact Aly Burge, Managing Director

Stella's Diary
9 Hormead Road, London W9 3NG
t 020 8969 1855 **f** 020 8964 2157 **m** 07836 594622
e stella'sdiary@btinternet.com
Contact Stella Rooke

Suz Cruz
Halliford Studios, Manygate Lane, Shepperton TW17 9EG
t 01932 252577 **f** 01932 253323 **m** 07956 485593
e zoe@suzcruz.co.uk **w** www.suzcruz.co.uk
Contact Zoe Matthews, Manager

Tech II VT & Vision Engineers
135 Glenwood Gardens, Gants Hill, Ilford IG2 6XX
t 020 8924 5190 **e** sue@tech-2.net **w** www.tech-2.net
Contact Sue Herbert, Partner; Mike Herbert, Partner

TOVS Ltd
The Linen Hall, 162-168 Regent Street, London W1B 5TB
t 020 7287 6110 **f** 020 7287 5481
e info@tovs.co.uk **w** www.tovs.co.uk
Contact Irene Hanley; Val Horton, Casting Agent

Unit Call
m 07785 390254

Warpaint
16B Witherington Road, London N5 1PP
t 020 7700 5777 **f** 020 7609 4903 **e** jo_warpaint@virgin.net
Contact Joesphine Pierre, Director

Wizzo & Co
35 Old Compton Street, London W1D 5JX
t 020 7437 2055 **f** 020 7437 2066
e wizzo@wizzoandco.co.uk **w** www.wizzoandco.co.uk
Contact Cathy Henderson; Wizzo ; Collette Lillis

DIRECTORS OF PHOTOGRAPHY

Directors of Photography

Barry Ackroyd
Casarotto Marsh Ltd, National House, 60-66 Wardour Street,
London W1V 4ND
t 020 7287 4450 **f** 020 7287 9128
e agents@casarotto.uk.com **w** www.casarotto.uk.com
Credits Very Annie Mary (F); Beautiful People (F); Dust (F)

Film footage times

Shooting/playback length

Format	8mm		Super 8		16mm			35mm		All formats		
	(80 frames/ft)		(72 frames/ft)		(40 frames/ft)			(16 frames/ft)		Frames		
fps	18	24	18	24	18	24	25	24	25	18	24	25
1 sec	2.7in	3.6in	3in	4in	5.5in	7in	71.5in	18in	18.75in	18	24	25
1 min	13.5ft	18ft	15ft	20ft	27ft	36ft	37.5ft	90ft	93.75ft	1080	1440	1500
10 min	135ft	180ft	150ft	200ft	270ft	360ft	375ft	900ft	937.5ft			

Running time

Format	8mm		Super 8		16mm			35mm	
fps	18	24	18	24	18	24	25fps	24fps	25fps
100ft	7'24	5'33	6'40	5'	3'42	2'46	2'40	1'6	64"
400ft				20'	14'48	11'	10'40	4'26	4'16
1000ft						27'40	26'40	11'6	10'40
1600ft			106'	80'	59'16	44'27	n/a		n/a

Remi Adefarasin
Casarotto Marsh Ltd, National House, 60-66 Wardour Street,
London W1V 4ND
t 020 7287 4450 **f** 020 7287 9128
e agents@casarotto.uk.com **w** www.casarotto.uk.com

Martin Ahlgren
Dinedor Management, 81 Oxford Street, London W1O 2EU
t 020 7851 3575 **f** 020 7851 3576
e info@dinedor.com **w** www.dinedor.com
Credits China Airlines (C); Virgin Mobile (C); Faith Yang (M); Groove Armada (M)

Koutaiba Al-Janabi
35 Launceston Road, Perivale UB6 7GX
t 020 8998 6920 **f** 020 8998 8577 **m** 07956 831060
e koutaiba@hotmail.com
Credits Travels In Dictionaryland (D); Jiyan-Life (F); The English Sheikh & The Yemen Gentleman (D); Double Agent (S)

Robert Alazraki AFC
Peters Fraser & Dunlop, Drury House, 34-43 Russell Street,
London WC2B 5HA
t 020 7344 1000 **f** 020 7836 9543
e postmaster@pfd.co.uk **w** www.pfd.co.uk

Federico Alfonzo
Suz Cruz, Halliford Studios, Manygate Lane, Shepperton TW17 9EG
t 01932 252577 **f** 01932 253323 **m** 07956 485593
e zoe@suzcruz.co.uk **w** www.suzcruz.co.uk

Alan Almond
International Creative Management Ltd, Oxford House,
76 Oxford Street, London W1D 1BS
t 020 7636 6565 **f** 020 7323 0101 **w** www.icmlondon.co.uk
Credits My Son The Fanatic (F); Gabriel And Me (F); Forsyte Saga (T)

Dave Amphlett
Suz Cruz, Halliford Studios, Manygate Lane, Shepperton TW17 9EG
t 01932 252577 **f** 01932 253323 **m** 07956 485593
e zoe@suzcruz.co.uk **w** www.suzcruz.co.uk

Simon Archer
Creative Media Management, Unit 3B, Walpole Court, Ealing
Studios, Ealing Green, London W5 5ED
t 020 8584 5363 **f** 020 8566 5554
e enquiries@creativemediamanagement.com
Credits Stiff Upper Lips (F); The Bachelor (F); Another Life (F)

Howard Atherton BSC
EXEC, 6 Travis Court, Farnham Royal SL2 3SB
t 01753 646677 **f** 01753 646770
e sue@execmanagement.co.uk **w** www.execmanagement.co.uk

Stephen Atkinson
3 Lancaster Avenue, Hadley Wood, London EN4 0EP
t 020 8440 7227 **f** 020 8440 7337 **m** 07836 736772
e stephenjatkinson@aol.com **w** www.stephenatkinson.com
Credits How To Breed Gibbons (S); Cutting Edge/40 Minutes (D); Pretty Poly (C); Audi 80 (C)

Dewald Aukema
Creative Media Management, Unit 3B, Walpole Court, Ealing
Studios, Ealing Green, London W5 5ED
t 020 8584 5363 **f** 020 8566 5554
e enquiries@creativemediamanagement.com
Credits Witchcraze (F); My Kingdom (F); Lucia (F)

Andrei Austin
EXEC, 6 Travis Court, Farnham Royal SL2 3SB
t 01753 646677 **f** 01753 646770
e sue@execmanagement.co.uk **w** www.execmanagement.co.uk

Chas Bain
EXEC, 6 Travis Court, Farnham Royal SL2 3SB
t 01753 646677 **f** 01753 646770
e sue@execmanagement.co.uk **w** www.execmanagement.co.uk

Howard Baker
13 Oxford Road, Teddington TW11 0QA
t 020 8977 6538 **f** 020 8977 6538 **m** 07860 882093
e hmbaker55@hotmail.com
Agent Jessica Carney Associates, Suite 90-92 Kent House, 87 Regent Street, London W1B 4EH
t 020 7434 4143 **f** 020 7434 4173 **e** info@jcarneyassociates.co.uk
Credits Trial And Retribution VI (T); In Deep (T); Monsignor Renard (T); Dalziel & Pascoe (T)

Derek Banks
59 Alphington Avenue, Frimley, Camberly GU16 8LY
m 07774 126392 **e** clapperboard@ntlworld.com
Credits Strangeways Revisited (T)

Allan Barrett
EXEC, 6 Travis Court, Farnham Royal SL2 3SB
t 01753 646677 **f** 01753 646770
e sue@execmanagement.co.uk **w** www.execmanagement.co.uk

Dominic Bartels
Wizzo & Co, 35 Old Compton Street, London W1D 5JX
t 020 7437 2055 **f** 020 7437 2066
e wizzo@wizzoandco.co.uk **w** www.wizzoandco.co.uk

Jeff Baynes
27 Willes Road, London NW5 3DT
m 07956 221313 **e** jeffbaynesuk@yahoo.co.uk
Credits Art Crime (T); The Anatomists (T); The Scandalous Success Of Salvador Dali (T); The Gunpowder Plot (T)

Jonathan Beech
EXEC, 6 Travis Court, Farnham Royal SL2 3SB
t 01753 646677 **f** 01753 646770
e sue@execmanagement.co.uk **w** www.execmanagement.co.uk

David Bennett
Yardley Management, Halliford Studios, Manygate Lane, Shepperton TW17 9EG
t 01932 253325 **t** 020 8998 9418 **f** 01932 253323
e pete@yardleymanagement.com **e** davebennett.jd@virgin.net
w www.yardleymanagement.com

Gabriel Beristain BSC
Peters Fraser & Dunlop, Drury House, 34-43 Russell Street, London WC2B 5HA
t 020 7344 1000 **f** 020 7836 9543
e postmaster@pfd.co.uk **w** www.pfd.co.uk

Mirko Beutler
46-48 Broadway Market, London E8 4QJ
t 020 7241 9807 **f** 020 7241 9807 **m** 07775 651923
e mirkobeutler@hotmail.com
Credits Easy TV (I); Benefit Fraud (C); Racing Post (S); A Place To Stay (F)

Marcus Birsel
Suz Cruz, Halliford Studios, Manygate Lane, Shepperton TW17 9EG
t 01932 252577 **f** 01932 253323 **m** 07956 485593
e zoe@suzcruz.co.uk **w** www.suzcruz.co.uk

Peter Biziou
Wizzo & Co, 35 Old Compton Street, London W1D 5JX
t 020 7437 2055 **f** 020 7437 2066
e wizzo@wizzoandco.co.uk **w** www.wizzoandco.co.uk

Stephen Blackman
40 Green Street, London W1K 7FP
t 020 7355 4060 **f** 020 7355 4090 **m** 07831 717717
e mail@stephenblackman.com **w** www.stephenblackman.com
Credits Trigger Happy; Strictly Sinatra; The Cement Garden

Jonathan Bloom
The Dench Arnold Agency, 24 D'Arblay Street, London W1F 8EH
t 020 7437 4551 **f** 020 7439 1355
e contact@dencharnoldagency.co.uk **w** www.den255.co.uk
Credits The Inspector Lynley Mysteries (T); Silent Witness (T); Speak Like A Child (F)

Sean Bobbitt
Casarotto Marsh Ltd, National House, 60-66 Wardour Street, London W1V 4ND
t 020 7287 4450 **f** 020 7287 9128
e agents@casarotto.uk.com **w** www.casarotto.uk.com

Balazs Bolygo
Big Fish Management, 55 Bendon Valley, London SW18 4LZ
t 020 8877 7111 **f** 020 8874 6623
e info@bigfishmanagement.com **w** www.bigfishmanagement.com

Paul Bond
51 Half Moon Lane, London SE24 9JX
t 020 7737 3807 **m** 07980 926945

Roger Bonnici
148 Garlands Road, Redhill RH1 6NZ
t 01737 767948 **f** 01737 767948 **m** 07976 529619
e rog@rbonnici.fsnet.co.uk **w** www.rogerbonnici.co.uk
Agent Jessica Carney Associates, Suite 90-92 Kent House, 87 Regent Street, London W1B 4EH
t 020 7434 4143 **f** 020 7434 4173 **e** info@jcarneyassociates.co.uk
Credits The Poet (F); Sunset Heights (F); Boston Kickout (F); Harry on the Boat (F)

Niels Boon
Wizzo & Co, 35 Old Compton Street, London W1D 5JX
t 020 7437 2055 **f** 020 7437 2066
e wizzo@wizzoandco.co.uk **w** www.wizzoandco.co.uk

John de Borman
McKinney Macartney Management Ltd, The Barley Mow Centre, 10 Barley Mow Passage, London W4 4PH
t 020 8995 4747 **f** 020 8995 2414
e fkb@mmtechsrep.demon.co.uk **w** www.mckinneymacartney.com

Geoff Boyle FBKSTS
Bigfish Management, 55 Bendon Valley, London SW18 4LZ
t 020 8877 7111 **f** 020 8874 6623
e info@bigfishmanagement.com **w** www.bigfishmanagement.com

Henry Braham
Casarotto Marsh Ltd, National House, 60-66 Wardour Street, London W1V 4ND
t 020 7287 4450 **f** 020 7287 9128
e agents@casarotto.uk.com **w** www.casarotto.uk.com

Martyn Bray
Yardley Management, Hlliford Studios, Manygate lane, Shepperton TW17 9EG
t 01932 253325 **t** 020 8758 1232 **f** 01932 253323
m 07860 493 538 **e** pete@yardleymanagement.co.uk
e mray.light@virgin.net **w** wwww.yardleymanagement.com

Ronnie Bridger
8 Ladies Mile Road, Patcham, Brighton BN1 8QF
t 01273 507617 **e** ronniebridger@aol.com

Ken Brinsley BSC
Greenhill Farmhouse, The Street, Otham Maidstone ME15 8RR
t 01622 862228 **f** 01622 861183 **m** 07747 630078
Credits Monarch Of The Glen (T)

Damian Bromley
34 Dudley Gardens, Ealing, London W13 9LT
t 020 8840 4142 **f** 020 8840 4142 **m** 07710 161000
e mail@damianbromley.com **w** www.damianbromley.com
Agent Bigfish Management, 55 Bendon Valley, London SW18 4LZ
t 020 8877 7111 **f** 020 8874 6623
e info@bigfishmanagement.com **w** www.bigfishmanagement.com
Credits N-Trance 'Forever' (M); The Hidden City (T); Re-Inventing Eddie (F); Going Off Big Time (F)

Daniel Bronks
Suz Cruz, Halliford Studios, Manygate Lane, Shepperton TW17 9EG
t 01932 252577 **f** 01932 253323 **m** 07956 485593
e zoe@suzcruz.co.uk **w** www.suzcruz.co.uk

Film stocks

Super 8 Colour (Sound & Silent)

	Stock #	ASA	Sound	Silent
Kodak	KMA 594	40	X	
Kodak	ELA 594	160	X	
Kodak	KMA 464	40		X
Kodak	ELA 464	160		X
Kodak	EG 464	160		X

Super 8 Black & White

	Stock #	ASA	Sound	Silent
Kodak	PXR464	120		X
Kodak	TXR 494	250		X

35mm Colour Negative

	Stock #	Speed	100 Foot	200 Foot
Kodak	5277	320T	$70	NA
Kodak	5279	500T	$70	NA
Kodak	5245	50D	$60	NA
Kodak	5297	250D	NA	$120
Kodak	5248	100T	$60	NA
Kodak	5293	200T	$60	NA
Kodak	5247	125D	$60	NA
Kodak	5298	500T	NA	NA
Fuji	8532	F-125T	NA	NA
Fuji	8552	F-250T	NA	NA
Fuji	8572	F-500T	NA	NA
Fuji	8582	F-400T	NA	NA
Fuji	8522	F-64D	NA	NA
Fuji	8562	F-250D	NA	NA

35mm Black & White Negative

	Stock #	Speed 1	100 Foot	200 Foot
Kodak	5231	64T/80D	NA	NA
Kodak	5222	200T/250D	NA	NA

16mm Colour

	Stock #	Type	Speed
Kodak	7239	Neg	160D
Kodak	7240	Neg	125T
Kodak EXR	7245	Neg	50D/12D
Kodak Vision	7246	Neg	250T/64D
Kodak EXR	7248	Neg	100T/64D
Kodak	7250	Neg	400T
Kodak	7251	Neg	400D
Kodak Vision	7274	Neg	200T/125D
Kodak Vision	7277	Neg	320T/200D
Kodak Vision	7279	Neg	500T/300D
Kodak Vision	7289	Neg	800T/500D
Kodak	7293	Neg	200T
Kodak	7297	Neg	250D
Fuji	F-64D	Neg	64D
Fuji	F-125	Neg	125T
Fuji	F-250	Neg	250T
Fuji	F-250D	Neg	250D
Fuji	F-500	Neg	500T

16mm Black & White

	Stock #	Type	Speed
Kodak	7222	Neg	200T/250D
Kodak	7231	Neg	64T/80D
Kodak	7276	Positive	40T/50D
Kodak	7278	Positive	160T/200D

Steve Brook-Smith
GAS (Guild Answering Service), C/o Panavision UK, Metropolitan Centre, Bristol Road, Greenford UB6 8GD
t 020 8813 1999 f 020 8813 2111
e admin@gbct.org w www.gbct.org

Trevor Brooker
EXEC, 6 Travis Court, Farnham Royal SL2 3SB
t 01753 646677 f 01753 646770
e sue@execmanagement.co.uk w www.execmanagement.co.uk

Bill Broomfield
Grove Farm, Beckley, Oxford OX3 9YS
t 01865 351670 f 08701 638280 m 07973 134219
e post@billbroomfield.com w www.billbroomfield.com
Credits Dalziel & Pascoe (T); Teachers Series II (T); People Like Us (T)

Tony Brown
EXEC, 6 Travis Court, Farnham Royal SL2 3SB
t 01753 646677 f 01753 646770
e sue@execmanagement.co.uk w www.execmanagement.co.uk

Robin Browne BSC
Bigfish Management, 55 Bendon Valley, London SW18 4LZ
t 020 8877 7111 f 020 8874 6623
e info@bigfishmanagement.com w www.bigfishmanagement.com

Nicolaj Bruel
Yardley Management, Halliford Studios, Manygate Lane, Shepperton TW17 9EG
t 01932 253325 t 839 1250 f 01932 253323
e pete@yardleymanagement.com
w www.yardleymanagement.com

Eigil Bryld

International Creative Management Ltd, Oxford House,
76 Oxford Street, London W1D 1BS
t 020 7636 6565 **f** 020 7323 0101 **w** www.icmlondon.co.uk
Credits Wisconsin Death Trip (D); Crime And Punishment (T); To Kill A King (F)

Mike Bulley

EXEC, 6 Travis Court, Farnham Royal SL2 3SB
t 01753 646677 **f** 01753 646770
e sue@execmanagement.co.uk **w** www.execmanagement.co.uk

Riki Butland

5 Southlands Avenue, Horley RH6 8BS
t 01293 782371 **m** 07976 366949
e riki@cinematographer.dop.com
w www.cinematographer-dop.com
Agent Bigfish Management, 55 Bendon Valley, London SW18 4LZ
t 020 8877 7111 **f** 020 8874 6623
e info@bigfishmanagement.com **w** www.bigfishmanagement.com
Credits Middleton's Changeling (F); Redemption Road (F)

Ben Butler

Wizzo & Co, 35 Old Compton Street, London W1D 5JX
t 020 7437 2055 **f** 020 7437 2066
e wizzo@wizzoandco.co.uk **w** www.wizzoandco.co.uk

Fredrik Callinggard

Yardley Management, Halliford Studios, Manygate Lane,
Shepperton TW17 9EG
t 01932 253325 **t** 020 7460 2900 **f** 253353
m 07900 606269 **e** pete@yardleymanagement.co.uk
e f.callinggard@shadowboxerfilm.com

Mark Carey

t 01932 592572 **e** mark@lightingcamera.co.uk
Credits Life For Daniel (T); Saying It For The Girls (D); Sports Personality (C);
National Poetry Day (C)

Olivier Cariou

Yardley Management, Halliford Studios, Shepperton TW17 9EG
t 01932 253325 **t** 020 8968 4300 **f** 01932 253323
m 07775 713843 **e** pete@yardleymanagement.co.uk
e olivier.cariou@btinternet.com **w** www.yardleymanagement.co.uk

Dion M Casey

Dinedor Management, 81 Oxford Street, London W10 2EU
t 020 7851 3575 **f** 020 7851 3576
e info@dinedor.com **w** www.dinedor.com
Credits Long Time Dead (F); Lara Croft: Tomb Raider (F); The Verve (M);
Coldplay (M)

Peter Chapman

Bigfish Management, 55 Bendon Valley, London SW18 4LZ
t 020 8877 7111 **f** 020 8874 6623
e info@bigfishmanagement.com **w** www.bigfishmanagement.com

Simon Chaudoir

Peters Fraser & Dunlop, Drury House, 34-43 Russell Street,
London WC2B 5HA
t 020 7344 1000 **f** 020 7836 9543
e postmaster@pfd.co.uk **w** www.pfd.co.uk

Oliver Cheesman

13 St John's Road, Pollokshields, Glasgow GL41 5QP
t 0141 423 4571 **f** 0141 423 4571 **m** 07710 098 776
e oliver.catchlight@virgin.net
Credits The Practicality Of Magnolia (T); That Old One (S); Taggart - Blood
Money (T); Taggart - Fade To Black (T)

Steve Chivers

Yardley Management, Halliford Studios, Manygate Lane,
Shepperton TW17 9EG
t 01932 253325 **f** 01932 253323
e pete@yardleymanagement.com **e** splosh@msn.com
w www.yardleymanagement.com

Dominic Clemence

Jessica Carney Associates, Suite 90-92 Kent House,
87 Regent Street, London W1B 4EH
t 020 7434 4143 **f** 020 7434 4173
e info@jcarneyassociates.co.uk
Credits The Dark Room (T); Tough Love (T); The Cry (T)

Clouds Hill Imaging Ltd

Clouds Hill Farm, Little Offley, Hitchin SG5 3BZ
t 01462 769346 **f** 01462 769347
e david@cloudshillimaging.co.uk **w** www.cloudshillimaging.co.uk
Contact David Spears, Managing Director
Credits Kill Or Cure (D); How To Build A Human (T); The Human Body - Nerve
Cells (T); Neanderthals (T)

Ray Coates

Suz Cruz, Halliford Studios, Manygate Lane, Shepperton TW17 9EG
t 01932 252577 **f** 01932 253323 **m** 07956 485593
e zoe@suzcruz.co.uk **w** www.suzcruz.co.uk

Daniel Cohen

Peters Fraser & Dunlop, Drury House, 34-43 Russell Street,
London WC2B 5HA
t 020 7344 1000 **f** 020 7836 9543
e postmaster@pfd.co.uk **w** www.pfd.co.uk

Tony Coldwell

Jessica Carney Associates, Suite 90-92 Kent House,
87 Regent Street, London W1B 4EH
t 020 7434 4143 **f** 020 7434 4173 **e** info@jcarneyassociates.co.uk
Credits Falling Apart (T); Blue Murder (T); Macbeth (T)

Andy Collins

CCA Management, 7 St George's Square, London SW1V 2HX
t 020 7630 6303 **f** 020 7630 7376

Eddie Collins

56 Burkes Road, Beaconsfield HP9 1EE
t 01494 681243 **f** 01494 681243 **m** 07767 765687
Credits Shadowlands (F); Tomorrow Never Dies (F); Braveheart (F)

Mike Connor

EXEC, 6 Travis Court, Farnham Royal SL2 3SB
t 01753 646677 **f** 01753 646770
e sue@execmanagement.co.uk **w** www.execmanagement.co.uk

Simon Coull

Wizzo & Co, 35 Old Compton Street, London W1D 5JX
t 020 7437 2055 **f** 020 7437 2066
e wizzo@wizzoandco.co.uk **w** www.wizzoandco.co.uk

Mick Coulter BSC

McKinney Macartney Management Ltd, The Barley Mow
Centre, 10 Barley Mow Passage, London W4 4PH
t 020 8995 4747 **f** 020 8995 2414
e fkb@mmtechsrep.demon.co.uk **w** www.mckinneymacartney.com

Julian Court

Casarotto Marsh Ltd, National House, 60-66 Wardour Street,
London W1V 4ND
t 020 7287 4450 **f** 020 7287 9128
e agents@casarotto.uk.com **w** www.casarotto.uk.com

Vincent Cox

Unital Films, 20 Crawford Place, London W1H 5NG
t 020 7724 5720 **f** 020 7724 5720
e vincent@unitalfilms.com **w** www.unitalfilms.com
Credits The Meeksville Ghost (F); Dazzle (F); Beserkers (F); Hooded Angels (F)

Richard Craske

Gems, The Media House, 87 Glebe Street, Penarth CF64 1EF
t 029 2071 0770 **f** 029 2071 0771
e gems@gems-agency.co.uk **w** www.gems-agency.co.uk
Credits The Phoenix And The Magic Carpet (T); In The Name Of The Father (F);
The Hope (F)

2003/2004 Phases of the Moon

2003 Phases of the Moon: Universal Time

New Moon d h m	First Quarter d h m	Full Moon d h m	Last Quarter d h m
Jan 2 20 23	Jan 10 13 15	Jan 18 10 48	Jan 25 8 33
Feb 1 10 48	Feb 9 11 11	Feb 16 23 51	Feb 23 16 46
Mar 3 2 35	Mar 11 7 15	Mar 18 10 35	Mar 25 1 51
Apr 1 19 19	Apr 9 23 40	Apr 16 19 36	Apr 23 12 18
May 1 12 15	May 9 11 53	May 16 3 36	May 23 0 31
May 31 4 20	June 7 20 28	June 14 11 16	June 21 14 45
June 29 18 39	July 7 2 32	July 13 19 21	July 21 7 1
July 29 6 53	Aug 5 7 28	Aug 12 4 48	Aug 20 0 48
Aug 27 17 26	Sep 3 12 34	Sep 10 16 36	Sep 18 19 3
Sep 26 3 9	Oct 2 19 9	Oct 10 7 27	Oct 18 12 31
Oct 25 12 50	Nov 1 4 25	Nov 9 1 13	Nov 17 4 15
Nov 23 22 59	Nov 30 17 16	Dec 8 20 37	Dec 16 17 42
Dec 23 9 43	Dec 30 10 3		

2004 Phases of the Moon: Universal Time

New Moon d h m	First Quarter d h m	Full Moon d h m	Last Quarter d h m
		Jan 7 15 40	Jan 15 04 46
Jan 21 21 05	Jan 29 06 03	Feb 6 08 47	Feb 13 13 39
Feb. 20 09 18	Feb 28 03 24	Mar 6 23 14	Mar 13 21 01
Mar 20 22 41	Mar 29 00 48	Apr 5 12 03	Apr 12 04 46
Apr 19 14 21	Apr 27 18 32	May 4 21 33	May 11 12 04
May 19 05 52	May 27 08 57	June 3 05 19	June 9 21 02
June 17 21 27	June 25 20 08	July 2 12 09	July 9 08 33
July 17 12 24	July 25 04 37	July 31 19 05	Aug 7 23 01
Aug 16 02 24	Aug 23 11 12	Aug 30 03 22	Sept 6 16 10
Sept 14 15 29	Sept 21 16 53	Sept 28 14 09	Oct 6 11 12
Oct 14 03 48	Oct 20 22 59	Oct 28 04 07	Nov 5 05 53
Nov 12 14 27	Nov 19 05 50	Nov 26 20 07	Dec 5 00 53
Dec 12 01 29	Dec 18 16 40	Dec 26 15 06	

These times are in Universal Time (GMT), except between 0100 on Mar.28 and 0100 on Oct.31 when the times are in BST (1 hour in advance of GMT). Reproduced, with permission, from data supplied by HM Nautical Almanac Office. © Council for the Central Laboratory of the Research Councils.

Denis Crossan BSC
McKinney Macartney Management Ltd, The Barley Mow Centre, 10 Barley Mow Passage, London W4 4PH
t 020 8995 4747 f 020 8995 2414
e fkb@mmtechsrep.demon.co.uk w www.mckinneymacartney.com

Neve Cunningham
Peters Fraser & Dunlop, Drury House, 34-43 Russell Street, London WC2B 5HA
t 020 7344 1000 f 020 7836 9543
e postmaster@pfd.co.uk w www.pfd.co.uk

Oliver Curtis BSC
97 South Hill Park, London NW3 2SP
t 020 7433 3391 f 020 7433 3391 m 0770 840975
e oliver.curtis@virgin.net
Agent International Creative Management Ltd, Oxford House, 76 Oxford Street, London W1D 1BS
t 020 7636 6565 f 020 7323 0101 w www.icmlondon.co.uk
Credits Love And Death On Long Island (F); Vanity Fair (T); Owning Mahoney (F)

John Daly BSC
International Creative Management Ltd, Oxford House, 76 Oxford Street, London W1D 1BS
t 020 7636 6565 f 020 7323 0101 w www.icmlondon.co.uk
Credits Our Friends In The North (T); Far From The Madding Crowd (T); The Parole Officer (F)

Shane Daly
London
t 020 7585 1811 **m** 07973 445428
e s.daly@orange.net **w** www.shanedaly.net
Credits Librarians' Dream (S); Revelation (F)

Nick Dance
53 Malthouse Drive, Chiswick, London W4 2NR
t 020 8987 0249 **f** 020 8987 2249 **m** 07860 283 274
Credits Children of the New Forest; Bad Girls (T); Footballers Wives I&II (T)

Ben Davis
McKinney Macartney Management Ltd, The Barley Mow
Centre, 10 Barley Mow Passage, London W4 4PH
t 020 8995 4747 **f** 020 8995 2414
e fkb@mmtechsrep.demon.co.uk **w** www.mckinneymacartney.com

Roger A Deakins (ASC, BSC)
International Creative Management Ltd, Oxford House,
76 Oxford Street, London W1D 1BS
t 020 7636 6565 **f** 020 7323 0101 **w** www.icmlondon.co.uk
Credits Fargo (F); The Man Who Wasn't There (F); A Beautiful Mind (F)

Seamus Deasy
International Creative Management Ltd, Oxford House,
76 Oxford Street, London W1D 1BS
t 020 7636 6565 **f** 020 7323 0101 **w** www.icmlondon.co.uk
Credits The General (F); Everlasting Piece (F); Seventh Stream (T)

Benoit Delhomme
Casarotto Marsh Ltd, National House, 60-66 Wardour Street,
London W1V 4ND
t 020 7287 4450 **f** 020 7287 9128
e agents@casarotto.uk.com **w** www.casarotto.uk.com

Allen Della-Valle
30 Kingsfield Road, Oxhey WD19 4PS
t 01923 233956 **f** 01923 224289 **m** 07774 183366
e allen@fuelfilm.com

Uinkar 'Bobby' Dhillon
EXEC, 6 Travis Court, Farnham Royal SL2 3SB
t 01753 646677 **f** 01753 646770
e sue@execmanagement.co.uk **w** www.execmanagement.co.uk

Anthony Dod-Mantle
International Creative Management Ltd, Oxford House,
76 Oxford Street, London W1D 1BS
t 020 7636 6565 **f** 020 7323 0101 **w** www.icmlondon.co.uk
Credits Dogville (F); It's All About Love (F); 28 Days Later (F)

Steve Downer
The Gatehouse, High Street, Ratley, Banbury OX15 6DT
t 01295 670836 **f** 01295 670836 **m** 07785 228397
e downerfilm@aol.com
Agent Dinedor Management, 81 Oxford Street, London W1O 2EU
t 020 7851 3575 **f** 020 7851 3576
e info@dinedor.com **w** www.dinedor.com
Credits Denali - Alaska's Last Wilderness (D); Dragons Alive (D); Animal Camera
(D); Wildlife Special - Serpents (D)

Jon Driscoll
Creative Media Management, Unit 3B, Walpole Court, Ealing
Studios, Ealing Green, London W5 5ED
t 020 8584 5363 **f** 020 8566 5554
e enquiries@creativemediamanagement.com
Credits Midnight's Children (W); Mona (S); Dim Sum (S); Last Rumba In
Rochdale (S)

Andrew Dunn BSC
Peters Fraser & Dunlop, Drury House, 34-43 Russell Street,
London WC2B 5HA
t 020 7344 1000 **f** 020 7836 9543
e postmaster@pfd.co.uk **w** www.pfd.co.uk

Joe Dunton BSC
Annie's Answering Service, Pinewood Studios, Pinewood Road,
Iver Heath SL0 0NH
t 01753 651303 **f** 01753 651848
e info@annies.co.uk **w** www.annies.co.uk

Roger Eaton
33 Lime Grove, London W12 8EE
f 08701 272165 **m** 07831 606310
e roger_eaton@compuserve.com
Credits The Dinosaur Hunters (T); Where We Came From (T); Cold Fish (F); Lava (F)

Michael Elphick
2 Rushmead, Ham, Richmond TW10 7NW
t 020 8332 6958 **f** 020 8332 6741 **m** 07850 9982962
e michael@elphickacs.fsnet.co.uk
Agent Big Fish Management, 55 Bendon Valley, London SW18 4LZ
t 020 8877 7111 **f** 020 8874 6623
e info@bigfishmanagement.com **w** www.bigfishmanagement.com
Credits Nescafe - Classic (C); Naked Yoga (D); Kingdom Holdings - Global (C);
What's My Name (D)

Fred Fabre
145 Bermondsey Street, London SE1 3UW
t 020 7378 0336 **m** 07710 521038 **e** fredericfabre@aol.com
Credits Live Forever (F); Queen Victoria (T); Battle Of The Atlantic (T); Dickens (T)

Mary Farbrother
10 Galton Street, London W10 4QN
t 020 8969 0247 **f** 07802 753123 **m** 07802 753 123
e mary.farbrother@virgin.net
Agent Wizzo & Co, 35 Old Compton Street, London W1D 5JX
t 020 7437 2055 **f** 020 7437 2066
e wizzo@wizzoandco.co.uk **w** www.wizzoandco.co.uk
Credits The Darkest Light (F)

Fat Herdsman Films Ltd
7 Blake House, 82 Charlwood Street, Pimlico, London SW1V 4PE
t 020 7821 1510 **f** 020 7821 1510 **m** 07973 315733
e fhfilms@hotmail.com **w** www.fhfilms.co.uk
Contact Mark Hamilton, Director / DOP
Credits Fred Dibnah's Industrial Age (T); The Cure (M); Adidas - The Road To
Australia (C); Capital Punishment (F)

Jon Felix
London
t 020 7352 5535 **m** 07802 486005
e jon@jonfelix.com **w** www.jonfelix.com
Credits Fishy (S); One Night Stand (S); Breath Of Life (S)

John Fenner BSC
Creative Media Management, Unit 3B, Walpole Court, Ealing
Studios, Ealing Green, London W5 5ED
t 020 8584 5363 **f** 020 8566 5554
e enquiries@creativemediamanagement.com
Credits The Borrowers (F); Muppet Treasure Island (F); Jack And The
Beanstalk: The Real Story (F)

Lynn Ferguson
Peters Fraser & Dunlop, Drury House, 34-43 Russell Street,
London WC2B 5HA
t 020 7344 1000 **f** 020 7836 9543
e postmaster@pfd.co.uk **w** www.pfd.co.uk

Gavin Finney BSC
McKinney Macartney Management Ltd, The Barley Mow
Centre, 10 Barley Mow Passage, London W4 4PH
t 020 8995 4747 **f** 020 8995 2414
e fkb@mmtechsrep.demon.co.uk **w** www.mckinneymacartney.com

Gerry Fisher BSC
Pebble Cottage, River Bank, Hurstfield Road, West Molesey
KT8 1QX
t 020 8979 5498 **f** 020 8979 5498
Credits Furia (F); K (F); Highlander (F); The Go-Between (F)

Terry Flaxton

Folly Lodge, Folly Lane, North Wootton BA4 4ER
t 01749 890610 **f** 01749 980018 **m** 07976 370984
e flaxton@btinternet.com **w** www.flaxton.btinternet.co.uk
Credits The Glastonbury Movie (F); Living in Hope (F)

Gerry Floyd

Agent The Dench Arnold Agency, 24 D'Arblay Street,
London W1F 8EH
t 020 7437 4551 **f** 020 7439 1355
e contact@dencharnoldagency.co.uk **w** www.dencharnold.co.uk
Agent Yardley Management, Halliford Studios, Manygate Lane,
Shepperton TW17 9EG
t 01932 253325 **t** 01769 520434 **f** 01932 253323
e pete@yardleymanagement.com **e** flogerry@ecglobalnet.co.uk
w www.yardleymanagement.com
Credits Brazen Hussies (T); Tomorrow La Scala (F)

Cinders Forshaw

International Creative Management Ltd, Oxford House,
76 Oxford Street, London W1D 1BS
t 020 7636 6565 **f** 020 7323 0101 **w** www.icmlondon.co.uk
Credits Perfect Strangers (T); Anita And Me (F); Tipping The Velvet (T)

Graham Fowler

63A Alderton Hill, Loughton IG10 3JD
f 087 051 2912 **m** 07768 551532
e grahamfowler@tradingfaces.co.uk **w** www.grahamfowler.co.uk
Credits Porsche Cayenne (I); Qatar Airlines (I); SW9 (F)

Freddie Francis BSC

McKinney Macartney Management Ltd, The Barley Mow
Centre, 10 Barley Mow Passage, London W4 4PH
t 020 8995 4747 **f** 020 8995 2414
e fkb@mmtechsrep.demon.co.uk **w** www.mckinneymacartney.com

Martin Fuhrer

International Creative Management Ltd, Oxford House,
76 Oxford Street, London W1D 1BS
t 020 7636 6565 **f** 020 7323 0101 **w** www.icmlondon.co.uk
Credits Wilde (F); The Gathering (F); Sweeny Todd (F)

Simon Fulford

EXEC, 6 Travis Court, Farnham Royal SL2 3SB
t 01753 646677 **f** 01753 646770
e sue@execmanagement.co.uk **w** www.execmanagement.co.uk

Brendan Galvin

Peters Fraser & Dunlop, Drury House, 34-43 Russell Street,
London WC2B 5HA
t 020 7344 1000 **f** 020 7836 9543
e postmaster@pfd.co.uk **w** www.pfd.co.uk

Lucy Gannon

Peters Fraser & Dunlop, Drury House, 34-43 Russell Street,
London WC2B 5HA
t 020 7344 1000 **f** 020 7836 9543
e postmaster@pfd.co.uk **w** www.pfd.co.uk

Michael Garfath BSC

Little Westwood, Bucks Hill, Chipperfield WD4 9AR
t 01923 269606 **f** 01923 269606 **m** 07802 853203
e mgarfath@yahoo.com
Credits I'll Sleep When I'm Dead (F); Nuns On The Run (F); A Prayer For The
Dying (F); Croupier (F)

Sam Garwood

Dinedor Management, 81 Oxford Street, London W10 2EU
t 020 7851 3575 **f** 020 7851 3576
e info@dinedor.com **w** www.dinedor.com
Credits Hot Dog (S); The Dummy (S); Cheeky (F); Plunket & Macleane (F)

Sunrise/Sunset, London
May 2003-April 2004

Date	Sunrise	Sunset
1/5/02	5.33 am	8.23 pm
8/5/02	5.21 am	8.34 pm
15/5/02	5.10 am	8.45 pm
22/5/02	5.00 am	8.55 pm
29/5/02	4.52 am	9.04 pm
5/6/02	4.47 am	9.12 pm
12/6/02	4.44 am	9.17 pm
19/6/02	4.43 am	9.21 pm
26/6/02	4.45 am	9.22 pm
3/7/02	4.49 am	9.20 pm
10/7/02	4.55 am	9.16 pm
17/7/02	5.03 am	9.10 pm
24/7/02	5.12 am	9.01 pm
31/7/02	5.22 am	8.51 pm
7/8/02	5.33 am	8.39 pm
14/8/02	5.43 am	8.26 pm
21/8/02	5.55 am	8.12 pm
28/8/02	6.06 am	7.57 pm
4/9/02	6.17 am	7.41 pm
11/9/02	6.28 am	7.25 pm
18/9/02	6.39 am	7.09 pm
25/9/02	6.51 am	6.53 pm
2/10/02	7.02 am	6.37 pm
9/10/02	7.14 am	6.21 pm
16/10/02	7.25 am	6.06 pm
23/10/02	7.37 am	5.52 pm
30/10/02	6.50 am	4.38 pm
6/11/02	7.02 am	4.26 pm
13/11/02	7.14 am	4.15 pm
20/11/02	7.26 am	4.05 pm
27/11/02	7.37 am	3.58 pm
4/12/02	7.47 am	3.54 pm
11/12/02	7.56 am	3.52 pm
18/12/02	8.02 am	3.52 pm
25/12/02	8.05 am	3.56 pm
1/1/03	8.06 am	4.02 pm
8/1/03	8.04 am	4.10 pm
15/1/03	8.00 am	4.20 pm
22/1/03	7.53 am	4.31 pm
29/1/03	7.44 am	4.43 pm
5/2/03	7.33 am	4.56 pm
12/2/03	7.21 am	5.09 pm
19/2/03	7.08 am	5.22 pm
26/2/03	6.54 am	5.34 pm
4/3/03	6.39 am	5.46 pm
11/3/03	6.23 am	5.59 pm
18/3/03	6.07 am	6.11 pm
25/3/03	5.51 am	6.22 pm
1/4/03	6.35 am	7.34 pm
8/4/03	6.20 am	7.46 pm
15/4/03	6.04 am	7.58 pm
22/4/03	5.50 am	8.09 pm
29/4/03	5.36 am	8.21 pm

* With thanks to Steffen Thorsen, http://www.timeanddate.com/

Paul Gavin

Glenlockhart House, 6 The Steils, Edinburgh EH10 5XD
t 0131 446 0444 **f** 0131 446 0333 **m** 07885 258383
e paul@extraveg.com **w** www.extraveg.com
Credits Love Alone (S); Dream Chasers (D); Candy Bar Kid (S)

Frank Gell

McKinney Macartney Management Ltd, The Barley Mow
Centre, 10 Barley Mow Passage, London W4 4PH
t 020 8995 4747 **f** 020 8995 2414
e fkb@mmtechsrep.demon.co.uk **w** www.mckinneymacartney.com

Sue Gibson BSC

McKinney Macartney Management Ltd, The Barley Mow
Centre, 10 Barley Mow Passage, London W4 4PH
t 020 8995 4747 **f** 020 8995 2414
e fkb@mmtechsrep.demon.co.uk **w** www.mckinneymacartney.com

Clive Gill

139 Brixton Hill Court, London SW2 1QZ
t 020 7326 0569 **f** 020 7274 7365 **m** 07860 459565
e clive@clivegill.co.uk **w** www.clivegill.co.uk

Global Village Productions

71 Gloucester Road, Barnet EN5 1LZ
t 020 8441 3784 **f** 020 8441 3784 **e** globalvil1@aol.com
Contact Allan Barrett, Director

Geoff Glover

1 Otways Close, Potters Bar EN6 1TE
t 01707 657240 **f** 01707 850067 **m** 07770 365566
e ggeoffcam@aol.com **w** www.hitlist.co.uk/camgeoffglover
Credits Space Truckers (F); Falling For A Dancer (T); Rag Nymph (T)

Keith Goddard BSC

EXEC, 6 Travis Court, Farnham Royal SL2 3SB
t 01753 646677 **f** 01753 646770
e sue@execmanagement.co.uk **w** www.execmanagement.co.uk

Paul Godfrey BSC

Agent Gems, The Media House, 87 Glebe Street,
Penarth CF64 1EF
t 029 2071 0770 **f** 029 2071 0771
e gems@gems-agency.co.uk **w** www.gems-agency.co.uk
Agent Dinedor Management, 81 Oxford Street, London W10 2EU
t 020 7851 3575 **f** 020 7851 3576
e info@dinedor.com **w** www.dinedor.com
Credits Goodbye Charlie Bright (F); Lighthouse Hill (F); The Forsyte Saga (T);
A&E (T); Grandad's Magic Lantern (T); Always And Everyone (T)

Merritt Gold

35 Private Road, Enfield, London EN1 2EH
t 020 8363 2030 **f** 08701 328036 **m** 07973 908472
e merritt1@tinyworld.co.uk

Rob Goldie

86 Underhill Road, East Dulwich, London SE22 0QU
t 020 8299 2547 **f** 020 8637 0537 **m** 07831 423143
e robgoldie1@aol.com **w** www.robgoldie.tv
Credits The 1940's House (D); Horizon - The England Patient (D); Bad Girls IV
(T); The Tournament (D)

Nick Gordon Smith

117 Underhill Road, London G13 1PP
t 020 8693 3789 **f** 020 8693 9814 **m** 07714 719430
e nrgsmith@btinternet.com
Credits Gallivant (F); This Filthy Earth (F); One For The Road (F)

Matt Gray

Casarotto Marsh Ltd, National House, 60-66 Wardour Street,
London W1V 4ND
t 020 7287 4450 **f** 020 7287 9128
e agents@casarotto.uk.com **w** www.casarotto.uk.com

Richard Greatrex BSC

McKinney Macartney Management Ltd, The Barley Mow
Centre, 10 Barley Mow Passage, London W4 4PH
t 020 8995 4747 **f** 020 8995 2414
e fkb@mmtechsrep.demon.co.uk **w** www.mckinneymacartney.com

Francis de Groote

Grange Farm House, South Newington, Banbury OX15 4JW
t 01295 721518 **f** 01295 721518 **m** 07931 913219
e francis.degroote@talk21.com
Credits Border Cafe (T); Human Remains (T); Cruise Of The Gods (T)

Dominique Grosz

Yardley Management, Halliford Studios, Manygate Lane,
Shepperton TW17 9EG
t 01932 253325 **t** 020 8740 4301 **f** 01932 253323
e pete@yardleymanagement.com **e** domgrosz@ntlworld.com
w www.yardleymanagement.com

Jess Hall

International Creative Management Ltd, Oxford House,
76 Oxford Street, London W1D 1BS
t 020 7636 6565 **f** 020 7323 0101 **w** www.icmlondon.co.uk
Credits The Cicerones (S); Stander (F)

Doug Hallows

Jessica Carney Associates, Suite 90-92 Kent House,
87 Regent Street, London W1B 4EH
t 020 7434 4143 **f** 020 7434 4173 **e** info@jcarneyassociates.co.uk
Credits Midsomer Murders (T); Dalziel And Pascoe (T); Arthur's Dyke (F)

Peter Hannah

Wizzo & Co, 35 Old Compton Street, London W1D 5JX
t 020 7437 2055 **f** 020 7437 2066
e wizzo@wizzoandco.co.uk **w** www.wizzoandco.co.uk

Peter Hannan

The Dench Arnold Agency, 24 D'Arblay Street, London W1F 8EH
t 020 7437 4551 **f** 020 7439 1355
e contact@dencharnoldagency.co.uk **w** www.dencharnold.co.uk
Credits Withnail And I (F); Longitude (T); The Gathering Storm (F)

Stephanie Hardt

Dinedor Management, 81 Oxford Street, London W10 2EU
t 020 7851 3575 **f** 020 7851 3576
e info@dinedor.com **w** www.dinedor.com
Credits Flextech (C); American Embassy (T); As If (T)

Robert Hardy

Wizzo & Co, 35 Old Compton Street, London W1D 5JX
t 020 7437 2055 **f** 020 7437 2066
e wizzo@wizzoandco.co.uk **w** www.wizzoandco.co.uk

Geoff Harrison

141 Binscombe, Godalming GU7 3QL
t 01483 421604 **f** 01483 426769 **m** 07973 392913
e geoffharrisonltd@aol.com

Douglas Hartington

t 0700 032 1007 **f** 0700 032 1008 **m** 07860 339937
e info@doughartington.com **w** www.doughartington.com
Credits David Starkey's William And Mary (D); The Spartans (D); Andy Warhol -
The Complete Picture (D); This Is Modern Art (D)

Harvey Harrison Ltd

17 Newton Road, Wimbledon, London SW19 3PJ
t 020 8540 2590 **f** 020 8287 3540 **m** 07836 616080
e sally4hhfilms@compuserve.com
Credits The Mummy Returns (F); Equilibrium (F); Shanghai Knights (F); Lara
Croft And The Cradle Of Life: Tomb Raider 2 (F)

Peter Harvey

Bigfish Management, 55 Bendon Valley, London SW18 4LZ
t 020 8877 7111 **f** 020 8874 6623
e info@bigfishmanagement.com **w** www.bigfishmanagement.com

Simon Hawken
Wizzo & Co, 35 Old Compton Street, London W1D 5JX
t 020 7437 2055 **f** 020 7437 2066
e wizzo@wizzoandco.co.uk **w** www.wizzoandco.co.uk

Martin Hawkins
1 Frith Cottages, Partingdale Lane, Mill Hill, London NW7 1NT
t 020 8346 8106 **f** 020 8349 3123 **m** 07831 252585
e marthawk@aol.com
Credits The Sketch Show (T); Coupling (T); Alistair McGowan's Big Impression (T); Holby City (T)

James Henry
Suz Cruz, Halliford Studios, Manygate Lane, Shepperton TW17 9EG
t 01932 252577 **f** 01932 253323 **m** 07956 485593
e zoe@suzcruz.co.uk **w** www.suzcruz.co.uk

Will Henshaw
Suz Cruz, Halliford Studios, Manygate Lane, Shepperton TW17 9EG
t 01932 252577 **f** 01932 253323 **m** 07956 485593
e zoe@suzcruz.co.uk **w** www.suzcruz.co.uk

Brian Herlihy
EXEC, 6 Travis Court, Farnham Royal SL2 3SB
t 01753 646677 **f** 01753 646770
e sue@execmanagement.co.uk **w** www.execmanagement.co.uk

Andrew Hibbert
5 Alkrington Hall Road South, Manchester M24 1NJ
t 0161 643 3724 **m** 07966 271540
e andyhibbert@andyhibbert.com **w** www.andyhibbert.com
Credits Wilmot (T); Holby City (T); Hollyoaks (T); Phoenix Nights (T)

Daf Hobson BSC
C/o Sara Putt Associates, Shepperton Studios, Shepperton TW17 0QD
t 01932 571044 **f** 01932 571109
Credits Sword of Honour (T); Swallow (T); Othello (T)

Andy Horner
Suz Cruz, Halliford Studios, Manygate Lane, Shepperton TW17 9EG
t 01932 252577 **f** 01932 253323 **m** 07956 485593
e zoe@suzcruz.co.uk **w** www.suzcruz.co.uk

Tania Hoser
4 Mayton Cottages, Heel Lane, Broadoak, Canterbury CT2 0QL
t 01227 710302 **f** 01227 710302 **m** 07977 212404
e taniah2000@hotmail.com

Ian Howes
Bigfish Management, 55 Bendon Valley, London SW18 4LZ
t 020 8877 7111 **f** 020 8874 6623
e info@bigfishmanagement.com **w** www.bigfishmanagement.com

Angus Hudson
Wizzo & Co, 35 Old Compton Street, London W1D 5JX
t 020 7437 2055 **f** 020 7437 2066
e wizzo@wizzoandco.co.uk **w** www.wizzoandco.co.uk

Richard Wyn Huws
Llywel, 1 Hen Lon, Penygroes, Caernarfon LL54 6RG
t 01286 880806 **f** 01286 880806 **m** 07831 578516
e richardwyn1@aol.com
Credits Y Twr (T); Tallen Called (T); The Secret Room (T)

John Ignatius
International Creative Management Ltd, Oxford House, 76 Oxford Street, London W1D 1BS
t 020 7636 6565 **f** 020 7323 0101 **w** www.icmlondon.co.uk
Credits Randall & Hopkirk (Deceased) (T); Two Men Went To War (F); The Water Giant (F)

Jakob Ihre
The Dench Arnold Agency, 24 D'Arblay Street, London W1F 8EH
t 020 7437 4551 **f** 020 7439 1355
e contact@dencharnoldagency.co.uk **w** www.dencharnold.co.uk
Credits Dust (F); The Virgin Of Liverpool (F)

Tony Imi BSC
48 Chestnut Avenue, Esher KT10 8JF
t 020 8224 0603 **m** 07703 536405 **e** tony.imi@ntlworld.com
Agent Dinedor Management, 81 Oxford Street, London W10 2EU
t 020 7851 3575 **f** 020 7851 3576
e info@dinedor.com **w** www.dinedor.com
Credits Scarlett (T); Sunshine Boys (T); Firebirds (F); Rancid Aluminium (F)

Tom Ingle
McKinney Macartney Management Ltd, The Barley Mow Centre, 10 Barley Mow Passage, London W4 4PH
t 020 8995 4747 **f** 020 8995 2414
e fkb@mmtechsrep.demon.co.uk **w** www.mckinneymacartney.com

Baz Irvine
Wizzo & Co, 35 Old Compton Street, London W1D 5JX
t 020 7437 2055 **f** 020 7437 2066
e wizzo@wizzoandco.co.uk **w** www.wizzoandco.co.uk

Igor Jadue-Lillo
The Dench Arnold Agency, 24 D'Arblay Street, London W1F 8EH
t 020 7437 4551 **f** 020 7439 1355
e contact@dencharnoldagency.co.uk **w** www.dencharnold.co.uk
Credits Disco Pigs (F)

Graham Jaggers
84 Langham Road, Teddington TW11 9HJ
t 020 8977 5787 **f** 020 8977 5787 **m** 07831 629314
e graham@jaggers.co.uk
Credits Secret History (D); The Bill (T); Holby City (T); Casualty (T)

Peter James
Wizzo & Co, 35 Old Compton Street, London W1D 5JX
t 020 7437 2055 **f** 020 7437 2066
e wizzo@wizzoandco.co.uk **w** www.wizzoandco.co.uk

John Golding Associates BSC
15 Ashchurch Terrace, London W12 9SL
t 020 8749 3854 **f** 020 8740 9563 **m** 07767 444512
e johnegolding@yahoo.co.uk

John Lamborn TV Film Services
3 Mount Pleasant Cottages, Broadford Road, Shalford GU4 8DP
t 01483 306067 **f** 01483 306067 **m** 07836 625831
e john@johnlamborn.co.uk **w** www.johnlamborn.co.uk
Contact Doug Smith, Associate
Credits Uli Jon Roth (S); Billy Fiske Story (S); Colours Of Infinity (D)

Laurence V Jones
Yardley Management, Halliford Studios, Manygate Lane, Shepperton TW17 9EG
t 01932 253325 **t** 01398 361455 **f** 01932 253323
e pete@yardleymanagement.com **e** lvjones@eclipse.co.uk
w www.yardleymanagement.com

David Katznelson
Casarotto Marsh Ltd, National House, 60-66 Wardour Street, London W1V 4ND
t 020 7287 4450 **f** 020 7287 9128
e agents@casarotto.uk.com **w** www.casarotto.uk.com

John Keedwell
55 Gosforth Lane, Watford WD19 7AY
t 020 8421 3672 **f** 01923 448571 **m** 07831 209232
e john@echelonfilms.co.uk
Credits Pitch People (F); OK Magazine (C); Sunday Express (C); Private Girls (C)

Steve Keith-Roach
EXEC, 6 Travis Court, Farnham Royal SL2 3SB
t 01753 646677 **f** 01753 646770
e sue@execmanagement.co.uk **w** www.execmanagement.co.uk

Nina Kellgren BSC
McKinney Macartney Management Ltd, The Barley Mow
Centre, 10 Barley Mow Passage, London W4 4PH
t 020 8995 4747 **f** 020 8995 2414
e fkb@mmtechsrep.demon.co.uk **w** www.mckinneymacartney.com

John Kenway BSC
International Creative Management Ltd, Oxford House, 76
Oxford Street, London W1D 1BS
t 020 7636 6565 **f** 020 7323 0101 **w** www.icmlondon.co.uk
Credits My Life As A Fairy Tale (T); Ready When You Are, Mr McGill (T); Auf
Wiedersehen, Pet (T)

Martin Kenzie
International Creative Management Ltd, Oxford House,
76 Oxford Street, London W1D 1BS
t 020 7636 6565 **f** 020 7323 0101 **w** www.icmlondon.co.uk
Credits Angels At My Bedside (S); Dinotopia (F); Keen Eddie (F)

Darius Khondji
International Creative Management Ltd, Oxford House,
76 Oxford Street, London W1D 1BS
t 020 7636 6565 **f** 020 7323 0101 **w** www.icmlondon.co.uk
Credits Seven (F); Evita (F); Panic Room (F)

Paul Kirsop
m 07889 777759

Nic Knowland
The Dench Arnold Agency, 24 D'Arblay Street, London W1F 8EH
t 020 7437 4551 **f** 020 7439 1355
e contact@dencharnoldagency.co.uk **w** www.dencharnold.co.uk
Credits Jesus Christ Superstar (F); Al's Lads (F); Simon Magus (F)

Lajos Koltai
McKinney Macartney Management Ltd, The Barley Mow
Centre, 10 Barley Mow Passage, London W4 4PH
t 020 8995 4747 **f** 020 8995 2414
e fkb@mmtechsrep.demon.co.uk **w** www.mckinneymacartney.com

Simon Kossoff
38 Carbery Avenue, London W3 9AL
t 020 8992 0610 **f** 020 8992 9494 **m** 07702 542121
e simonkossof@aol.com
Agent The Dench Arnold Agency, 24 D'Arblay Street,
London W1F 8EH
020 7437 4551 **f** 020 7439 1355 **w** www.dencharnold.co.uk
Credits Dead Gorgeous (T); Sinners (T); Trial and Retribution IV & V (T)

Michael Kubicki
The Cottage, Foxmead, Maddox Lane, Little Bookham KT23 3BS
t 01372 458184 **f** 01372 458184 **m** 07718 225112
e michaelkubicki@amserve.com

Alwin Kuchler
Peters Fraser & Dunlop, Drury House, 34-43 Russell Street,
London WC2B 5HA
t 020 7344 1000 **f** 020 7836 9543
e postmaster@pfd.co.uk **w** www.pfd.co.uk

Brett Lamb-Shine
47C St Philip Street, London SW8 3SR
t 020 7622 8175 **f** 020 7622 8175 **m** 07876 688899
e bls@freeuk.com

Daniel Landin
28 Bramshill Gardens, London NW5 1JH
f 020 7281 5105 **m** 07796 950002 **e** dl@ndin.co.uk
Agent Suz Cruz, Halliford Studios, Manygate Lane,
Shepperton TW17 9EG
t 01932 252577 **f** 01932 253323 **m** 07956 485593
e zoe@suzcruz.co.uk **w** www.suzcruz.co.uk

Norman Langley BSC
118 Dulwich Village, London SE21 7AQ
t 020 8299 4438 **f** 020 8299 3795 **m** 07812 063224
e nly@cbsnews.com

Vernon Layton BSC
Warren House, Waddlane, Snape IP17 1RB
t 01728 688488 **m** 07879 625336 **e** layton@freebie.net
Agent McKinney Macartney Management Ltd, The Barley Mow
Centre, 10 Barley Mow Passage, London W4 4PH
t 020 8995 4747 **f** 020 8995 2414
e fkb@mmtechsrep.demon.co.uk **w** www.mckinneymacartney.com
Credits Second Nature (T); Blackball (F); The Young Americans (F); I Still Know
What You Did Last Summer (F)

Piers Leigh
21a Macfarlane Road, London W12 7JY
t 020 8742 9170 **f** 020 8742 9170 **m** 07956 443674
e pleigh@dircon.co.uk

Ryszard Lenczewski (PSC)
International Creative Management Ltd, Oxford House,
76 Oxford Street, London W1D 1BS
t 020 7636 6565 **f** 020 7323 0101 **w** www.icmlondon.co.uk
Credits Tabloid (F); Intermission (F); The Last Resort (F)

Mike Lloyd
Dinedor Management, 81 Oxford Street, London W10 2EU
t 020 7851 3575 **f** 020 7851 3576
e info@dinedor.com **w** www.dinedor.com
Credits Max Factor (C); Pantene (C); Dove (C)

Mike Lloyd
EXEC, 6 Travis Court, Farnham Royal SL2 3SB
t 01753 646677 **f** 01753 646770
e sue@execmanagement.co.uk **w** www.execmanagement.co.uk

Scott Lloyd-Davies
CCA Management, 7 St George's Square, London SW1V 2HX
t 020 7630 6303 **f** 020 7630 7376

Bryan Loftus BSC
Dinedor Management, 81 Oxford Street, London W10 2EU
t 020 7851 3575 **f** 020 7851 3576
e info@dinedor.com **w** www.dinedor.com
Credits The Cure (M); Madonna (M); The Assam Garden (F); In The Company Of
Wolves (F)

David Luther
London
t 020 7287 4450 **m** 07930 408253

John Lynch
McKinney Macartney Management Ltd, The Barley Mow
Centre, 10 Barley Mow Passage, London W4 4PH
t 020 8995 4747 **f** 020 8995 2414
e fkb@mmtechsrep.demon.co.uk **w** www.mckinneymacartney.com

David MacDonald
Yardley Management, Halliford Studios, Manygate Lane,
Shepperton TW17 9EG
t 01932 253325 **t** 172831 **f** 01932 253323
e pete@yardleymanagement.com **e** davidmac@skynet.be
w www.yardleymanagement.com

Stewart MacKay
7 Tutton Hill, Colerne, Chippenham SN14 8DN
t 01249 712302 **f** 01249 701987 **m** 07974 315806
e stewart_mackay@btinternet.com
Credits Room 36 (F); The Hard Approach (T); Rough Justice (D); Waiting For A Killer (T)

Simon Maggs
Peters Fraser & Dunlop, Drury House, 34-43 Russell Street, London WC2B 5HA
t 020 7344 1000 **f** 020 7836 9543
e postmaster@pfd.co.uk **w** www.pfd.co.uk

Brendan Maguire
Yardley Management, Halliford Studios, Manygate Lane, Shepperton TW17 9EG
t 01932 253325 **t** 987290 **f** 01932 253323
e pete@yardleymanagement.com **e** maguireb@iol.ie
w www.yardleymanagement.com

Rex Maidment
Casarotto Marsh Ltd, National House, 60-66 Wardour Street, London W1V 4ND
t 020 7287 4450 **f** 020 7287 9128
e agents@casarotto.uk.com **w** www.casarotto.uk.com

Bily Malone
McKinney Macartney Management Ltd, The Barley Mow Centre, 10 Barley Mow Passage, London W4 4PH
t 020 8995 4747 **f** 020 8995 2414
e fkb@mmtechsrep.demon.co.uk **w** www.mckinneymacartney.com

Hong Manley
McKinney Macartney Management Ltd, The Barley Mow Centre, 10 Barley Mow Passage, London W4 4PH
t 020 8995 4747 **f** 020 8995 2414
e fkb@mmtechsrep.demon.co.uk **w** www.mckinneymacartney.com

Ed Mash
Wizzo & Co, 35 Old Compton Street, London W1D 5JX
t 020 7437 2055 **f** 020 7437 2066
e wizzo@wizzoandco.co.uk **w** www.wizzoandco.co.uk

David Matches
Suz Cruz, Halliford Studios, Manygate Lane, Shepperton TW17 9EG
t 01932 252577 **f** 01932 253323 **m** 07956 485593
e zoe@suzcruz.co.uk **w** www.suzcruz.co.uk

Brian McDairmant
Jesmond House, Wetheral Pasture, Carlisle CA4 8HR
t 01228 560663 **f** 01228 562299
e brainmcdairmant@hotmail.com

Tom McDougal
The Dench Arnold Agency, 24 D'Arblay Street, London W1F 8EH
t 020 7437 4551 **f** 020 7439 1355
e contact@dencharnoldagency.co.uk **w** www.dencharnold.co.uk
Credits The Inspector Lynley Mysteries (T); Cold Feet - Series III (T); The Politician's Wife (T)

Seamus McGarvey
Casarotto Marsh Ltd, National House, 60-66 Wardour Street, London W1V 4ND
t 020 7287 4450 **f** 020 7287 9128
e agents@casarotto.uk.com **w** www.casarotto.uk.com

Walter McGill
CCA Management, 7 St George's Square, London SW1V 2HX
t 020 7630 6303 **f** 020 7630 7376

John McGlashan BSC
21 Hollingbourne Gardens, Ealing, London W13 8EN
t 020 8997 9449 **f** 020 8997 9449 **m** 07931 540232
Credits Blue Dove (T); Where There's Smoke (T); Silent Witness (T)

Phil Meheux BSC
McKinney Macartney Management Ltd, The Barley Mow Centre, 10 Barley Mow Passage, London W4 4PH
t 020 8995 4747 **f** 020 8995 2414
e fkb@mmtechsrep.demon.co.uk **w** www.mckinneymacartney.com

Nemone Mercer
International Creative Management Ltd, Oxford House, 76 Oxford Street, London W1D 1BS
t 020 7636 6565 **f** 020 7323 0101 **w** www.icmlondon.co.uk

Chris Merry
t 020 8299 4686 **m** 07703 599 012
e chris@chrismerry.com **w** www.chrismerry.com
Credits Journey To The Edge Of Space (D); The Science Of Secrecy (D); The Survival of Saddam (D); The Real Stephen Hawking (D)

Alastair Meux
Yardley Management, Halliford Studios, Manygate Lane, Shepperton TW17 9EG
t 01932 253325 **t** 020 7928 4810 **f** 01932 253323
e pete@yardleymanagement.com **e** topdop@btinternet.com
w www.yardleymanagement.com

Chris Middleton
Old Village Shop, The Green, Culworth, Banbury OX17 2BB
t 01295 760125 **f** 01295 760125 **m** 07808 491562
e cmiddleton@pulse-uk.biz
Credits E=MC^2 (F); Beg (F)

Peter Middleton BSC
Peters Fraser & Dunlop, Drury House, 34-43 Russell Street, London WC2B 5HA
t 020 7344 1000 **f** 020 7836 9543
e postmaster@pfd.co.uk **w** www.pfd.co.uk

Sebastian Milaszewski
McKinney Macartney Management Ltd, The Barley Mow Centre, 10 Barley Mow Passage, London W4 4PH
t 020 8995 4747 **f** 020 8995 2414
e fkb@mmtechsrep.demon.co.uk **w** www.mckinneymacartney.com

Tony Miller
The Dench Arnold Agency, 24 D'Arblay Street, London W1F 8EH
t 020 7437 4551 **f** 020 7439 1355
e contact@dencharnoldagency.co.uk **w** www.dencharnold.co.uk
Credits The American (F); Murphy's Law (T); The Honey Trap (F)

Alec Mills BSC
Creative Media Management, Unit 3B, Walpole Court, Ealing Studios, Ealing Green, London W5 5ED
t 020 8584 5363 **f** 020 8566 5554
e enquiries@creativemediamanagement.com
Credits Christopher Columbus - The Discovery (F); Pointmen (F); Licence To Kill (F)

Zubin Mistry
EXEC, 6 Travis Court, Farnham Royal SL2 3SB
t 01753 646677 **f** 01753 646770
e sue@execmanagement.co.uk **w** www.execmanagement.co.uk

Max Modray
EXEC, 6 Travis Court, Farnham Royal SL2 3SB
t 01753 646677 **f** 01753 646770
e sue@execmanagement.co.uk **w** www.execmanagement.co.uk

Peter Morgan
Bigfish Management, 55 Bendon Valley, London SW18 4LZ
t 020 8877 7111 **f** 020 8874 6623
e info@bigfishmanagement.com **w** www.bigfishmanagement.com

Nic Morris BSC
5 Sutherland Gardens, London SW14 8DB
t 020 8392 9762 **m** 07860 515154 **e** mail@nicmorris.com
Credits Without You (T); Firelight (F); Long Time Dead (F); Before You Go (F)

Richard Mott
Suz Cruz, Halliford Studios, Manygate Lane, Shepperton TW17 9EG
t 01932 252577 **f** 01932 253323 **m** 07956 485593
e zoe@suzcruz.co.uk **w** www.suzcruz.co.uk

Wayne Mottershead
Hampstead, London NW3 6EX
t 020 794 3116 **f** 020 794 3116 **m** 07973 323127
e waynemottershead@aol.com
Credits The Bill (T); Holby City (T)

Colin Munn
Creative Media Management, Unit 3B, Walpole Court, Ealing
Studios, Ealing Green, London W5 5ED
t 020 8584 5363 **f** 020 8566 5554
e enquiries@creativemediamanagement.com
Credits Peak Practice (T); Never Say Never Mind (F); Rockface (T)

AJ Murray
m 07973 983 907 **e** ajmurray@iname.com
Credits Direct Holidays (C); CNN - European Footprint Launch (C); Scot Rail (C);
Adidas (C)

Mike Muschamp
CCA Management, 7 St George's Square, London SW1V 2HX
t 020 7630 6303 **f** 020 7630 7376

Giles Nuttgens
International Creative Management Ltd, Oxford House,
76 Oxford Street, London W1D 1BS
t 020 7636 6565 **f** 020 7323 0101 **w** www.icmlondon.co.uk
Credits The Deep End (F); Swim Fan (F); Young Adam (F)

Mattias Nyberg
5 Harborough Road, London SW16 2XP
t 020 8677 0291 **m** 07970 718896 **e** ma_nyberg@hotmail.com
Credits The Real Eve (D); Green Party - Waterbaby (C)

Chris O'Dell BSC
Pierce House, Skeaghanore West, Ballydehob, Rep of Ireland
t +353 28 37296 **m** 07710 057957 **e** cod@iol.ie
Agent Peters Fraser & Dunlop, Drury House, 34-43 Russell
Street, London WC2B 5HA
t 020 7344 1000 **f** 020 7836 9543
e postmaster@pfd.co.uk **w** www.pfd.co.uk
Credits Margery And Gladys (T); Pollyanna (T); Hornblower II & III (T)

Eugene O'Connor
Yardley Management, Halliford Studios, Manygate Lane,
Shepperon TW17 9EG
t 01932 253325 **t** 020 8998 1361 **f** 01932 253323
e pete@yardleymanagement.com **e** euge@eoc.demon.co.uk
w www.yardleymanagement.com

David Odd
Casarotto Marsh Ltd, National House, 60-66 Wardour Street,
London W1V 4ND
t 020 7287 4450 **f** 020 7287 9128
e agents@casarotto.uk.com **w** www.casarotto.uk.com

Ray Orton
Penrhos, Llanbister LD1 6UL
t 01597 840297 **f** 01597 840297 **m** 07836 542 848
e rayorton@hotmail.com
Credits Laura Ashley (D); Hedd Wyn (F); Belonging (T); Casualty (T)

Roman Osin
International Creative Management Ltd, Oxford House,
76 Oxford Street, London W1D 1BS
t 020 7636 6565 **f** 020 7323 0101 **w** www.icmlondon.co.uk
Credits Under The Stars (F); The Warrior (F); I Am David (F)

Karl Oskarsson
Wizzo & Co, 35 Old Compton Street, London W1D 5JX
t 020 7437 2055 **f** 020 7437 2066
e wizzo@wizzoandco.co.uk **w** www.wizzoandco.co.uk

Gyula Pados
The Dench Arnold Agency, 24 D'Arblay Street, London W1F 8EH
t 020 7437 4551 **f** 020 7439 1355
e contact@dencharnoldagency.co.uk **w** www.dencharnold.co.uk
Credits The Heart Of Me (F); Hotel Splendide (F)

Tim Palmer
Casarotto Marsh Ltd, National House, 60-66 Wardour Street,
London W1V 4ND
t 020 7287 4450 **f** 020 7287 9128
e agents@casarotto.uk.com **w** www.casarotto.uk.com

John Pardue
McKinney Macartney Management Ltd, The Barley Mow
Centre, 10 Barley Mow Passage, London W4 4PH
t 020 8995 4747 **f** 020 8995 2414
e fkb@mmtechsrep.demon.co.uk **w** www.mckinneymacartney.com

Steve Parker
Annie's Answering Service, Pinewood Studios, Pinewood Road,
Iver Heath SL0 0NH
t 01753 651303 **f** 01753 651848
e info@annies.co.uk **w** www.annies.co.uk

Austin Parkinson
Rosemary Croft, Rosemary Lane, Alford, Cranleigh GU6 8EU
t 01403 752225 **f** 01403 753856 **m** 07802 777 392
Credits Invesco Continental Europe (I); Rolls Royce Asian Corporate (C); Toys R
Us (C); Ace Air (Spain-Italy-Portugal) (C)

Vicky Parnall
Suz Cruz, Halliford Studios, Manygate Lane, Shepperton TW17 9EG
t 01932 252577 **f** 01932 253323 **m** 07956 485593
e zoe@suzcruz.co.uk **w** www.suzcruz.co.uk

Mark Partridge
McKinney Macartney Management Ltd, The Barley Mow
Centre, 10 Barley Mow Passage, London W4 4PH
t 020 8995 4747 **f** 020 8995 2414
e fkb@mmtechsrep.demon.co.uk **w** www.mckinneymacartney.com

Robert Payton
Wizzo Vision, 35 Old Compton Street, London W1V 5PL
t 020 7439 4657 **f** 020 7437 2066 **m** 07970 284535
e rob@paytontv.com **w** www.paytontv.com
Credits Andrex (C); Sainsburys (C); Youngs (C); McDonalds (C)

Ian Perry (FRPS, FBIPP)
266 Esplanade, Maylandsea CM3 6AL
t 01621 741810 **f** 01621 744450 **m** 07860 232854
e perry266@aol.com
Credits The Hunt For Red November (T); Two Weddings And The Rouble (T)

Jan Pester
t 0141 334 8887 **f** 0141 576 9670 **m** 07831 875608
e janpester@ntlworld.com
Agent Bigfish Management, 55 Bendon Valley, London SW18 4LZ
t 020 8877 7111 **f** 020 8874 6623
e info@bigfishmanagement.com **w** www.bigfishmanagement.com
Credits Yo! Diary (T); The Devil's Tattoo (F); The Little Vampire (Second Unit) (S)

Tony Pierce-Roberts BSC
McKinney Macartney Management Ltd, The Barley Mow
Centre, 10 Barley Mow Passage, London W4 4PH
t 020 8995 4747 **f** 020 8995 2414
e fkb@mmtechsrep.demon.co.uk **w** www.mckinneymacartney.com

Den Pollitt
EXEC, 6 Travis Court, Farnham Royal SL2 3SB
t 01753 646677 **f** 01753 646770
e sue@execmanagement.co.uk **w** www.execmanagement.co.uk

Jake Polonsky

85 Plimsoll Road, London N4 2EE
t 020 7359 4293 **e** jake@jpolonsky.com
Agent McKinney Macartney Management Ltd, The Barley Mow
Centre, 10 Barley Mow Passage, London W4 4PH
t 020 8995 4747 **f** 020 8995 2414
e fkb@mmtechsrep.demon.co.uk **w** www.mckinneymacartney.com
Credits Groove Armada (M); Nicorette (C); BBC Talent (C); An Ideal Husband (F)

Dick Pope BSC

International Creative Management Ltd, Oxford House,
76 Oxford Street, London W1D 1BS
t 020 7636 6565 **f** 020 7323 0101 **w** www.icmlondon.co.uk
Credits Topsy-Turvy (F); All Or Nothing (F); Nicholas Nickleby (F)

Simon Poulter

Yardley Management, Halliford Studios, Manygate Lane,
Shepperon TW17 9EG
t 01932 253325 **t** 020 7602 8005 **f** 01932 253323
e pete@yardleymanagement.com **e** simon@bigrig.uk.com
w www.yardleymanagement.com

Declan Quinn

Peters Fraser & Dunlop, Drury House, 34-43 Russell Street,
London WC2B 5HA
t 020 7344 1000 **f** 020 7836 9543
e postmaster@pfd.co.uk **w** www.pfd.co.uk

Pascal Rabaud

International Creative Management Ltd, Oxford House,
76 Oxford Street, London W1D 1BS
t 020 7636 6565 **f** 020 7323 0101 **w** www.icmlondon.co.uk
Credits The Horseman On The Roof (F); End Of Violence (F); Addicted To Stars (F)

Tat Radcliffe

Peters Fraser & Dunlop, Drury House, 34-43 Russell Street,
London WC2B 5HA
t 020 7344 1000 **f** 020 7836 9543
e postmaster@pfd.co.uk **w** www.pfd.co.uk

Mike Radford

Inglefell, Heath Ride, Finchampstead, Wokingham RG40 3QN
t 01189 328368 **f** 01189 735624 **m** 07050 127009
e 114030.665@compuserve.com
Credits TV To Go (T); I'm Alan Partridge (T); Posh Nosh (T); Dead Ringers (T)

Jeremy Read

34 Stodart Road, London SE20 8ET
t 020 8289 9780 **m** 07836 594832 **e** jeremyread@lineone.net

John Record

Bigfish Management, 55 Bendon Valley, London SW18 4LZ
t 020 8877 7111 **f** 020 8874 6623 **m** 08750 690033
e johnrecord@cinematography.net
w www.bigfishmanagement.com
Credits Ballykissangel (T); French And Saunders (T); Jeopardy (T); Down To Earth (T)

John Rhodes

Creative Media Management, Unit 3B, Walpole Court, Ealing
Studios, Ealing Green, London W5 5ED
t 020 8584 5363 **f** 020 8566 5554
e enquiries@creativemediamanagement.com
Credits 16 Years (T); Only Fools And Horses (T); Rockface (T)

Kelvin Richard

Suz Cruz, Halliford Studios, Manygate Lane, Shepperton TW17 9EG
t 01932 252577 **f** 01932 253323 **m** 07956 485593
e zoe@suzcruz.co.uk **w** www.suzcruz.co.uk

Simon Richards

42 Croftdown Road, London NW5 1EN
t 020 7284 4273 **f** 020 7284 4888 **m** 07774 842 771
e rascal1@onetel.net.uk
Agent Peters Fraser & Dunlop, Drury House, 34-43 Russell
Street, London WC2B 5HA
t 020 7344 1000 **f** 020 7836 9543
e postmaster@pfd.co.uk **w** www.pfd.co.uk

George Richmond

EXEC, 6 Travis Court, Farnham Royal SL2 3SB
t 01753 646677 **f** 01753 646770
e sue@execmanagement.co.uk **w** www.execmanagement.co.uk

Jan Richter-Friis

Wizzo & Co, 35 Old Compton Street, London W1D 5JX
t 020 7437 2055 **f** 020 7437 2066
e wizzo@wizzoandco.co.uk **w** www.wizzoandco.co.uk

Philip Robertson

Creative Media Management, Unit 3B, Walpole Court, Ealing
Studios, Ealing Green, London W5 5ED
t 020 8584 5363 **f** 020 8566 5554
e enquiries@creativemediamanagement.com
Credits Beyond The Ocean (F); Resurrecting Bill (F); Babyfather (T)

Paul Robinson

34A Louisville Road, London SW17 8RW
t 020 8682 4416 **m** 07973 255815
e paulrobinson.cameraman@virgin.net
Credits Sacred Sites (T); Diana Ross (D); Black And Decker (C); Cadbury Mye (C)

Adam Rogers

Yardley Management, Halliford Studios, Manygate Lane,
Shepperon TW17 9EG
t 01932 253325 **t** 01252 821058 **f** 01932 253323
e pete@yardleymanagement.com **e** air@dircon.co.uk
w www.yardleymanagement.com

Geoff Rogers

SBFC, Unit 8, Sandhurst House, Wolsey Street, London E1 3BD

Ashley Rowe BSC

International Creative Management Ltd, Oxford House,
76 Oxford Street, London W1D 1BS
t 020 7636 6565 **f** 020 7323 0101 **w** www.icmlondon.co.uk
Credits The Governess (F); Ali G In da house (F); Calendar Girls (F)

Simon Rowles

11 Kenley Road, St Margarets, Twickenham TW1 1JT
t 020 8891 5765 **f** 020 8891 5765 **m** 07702 364023
e s.rowles@virgin.net
Agent Suz Cruz, Halliford Studios, Manygate Lane,
Shepperton TW17 9EG
t 01932 252577 **f** 01932 253323 **m** 07956 485593
e zoe@suzcruz.co.uk **w** www.suzcruz.co.uk
Credits Jesus In The Himalayas (D); The Dream Team (T); Comedy About Us (C);
Lloyds (C)

Manuel Ruiz

Yardley Management, Halliford Studios, Manygate Lane,
Shepperon TW17 9EG
t 01932 253325 **t** 190270 **f** 01932 253323
e pete@yardleymanagement.com **e** ma_nel@hotmail.com
w www.yardleymanagement.com

Richard Rutkowski

Yardley Management, Halliford Studios, Manygate Lane,
Shepperon TW17 9EG
t 01932 253325 **t** 732 9331 **f** 01932 253323
e pete@yardleymanagement.com **e** cnoevil@rcn.com
w www.yardleymanagement.com

Robbie Ryan

Suz Cruz, Halliford Studios, Manygate Lane, Shepperton TW17 9EG
t 01932 252577 **f** 01932 253323 **m** 07956 485593
e zoe@suzcruz.co.uk **w** www.suzcruz.co.uk

directors of photography

Alex P Ryle
1 Shorelands Road, Barnstaple EX31 3AA
t 01271 375545 **f** 01271 375545 **m** 07971 572037
e alex@alexryle.com **w** www.alexryle.com
Credits Alice (M); The Chosen And The Damned (F); Gunner (F)

Paul Sadourian
Creative Media Management, Unit 3B, Walpole Court, Ealing
Studios, Ealing Green, London W5 5ED
t 020 8584 5363 **f** 020 8566 5554
e enquiries@creativemediamanagement.com
Credits Making Vienna (T); Married Unmarried (T)

Ian Samels
2 Hindhead, Wanborough Drive, Roehampton SW15 4AN
t 020 8788 4115 **m** 07961 813480 **e** iansamels@hotmail.com
Credits In, Son - Time Lapse (I); MC TY (M); Big Brovaz (M); Execution Squodd (M)

Paul Sarossy CSC BSC
Peters Fraser & Dunlop, Drury House, 34-43 Russell Street,
London WC2B 5HA
t 020 7344 1000 **f** 020 7836 9543
e postmaster@pfd.co.uk **w** www.pfd.co.uk

Nick Sawyer
Wizzo & Co, 35 Old Compton Street, London W1D 5JX
t 020 7437 2055 **f** 020 7437 2066
e wizzo@wizzoandco.co.uk **w** www.wizzoandco.co.uk

Jane Scanlan
Flat 1, 297 Green Lanes, London N4 2ES
t 020 8880 1697 **m** 07956 430 362 **e** jlscanny@hotmail.com

Luke Scott
Suz Cruz, Halliford Studios, Manygate Lane, Shepperton TW17 9EG
t 01932 252577 **f** 01932 253323 **m** 07956 485593
e zoe@suzcruz.co.uk **w** www.suzcruz.co.uk

Chris Seager BSC
6 Elmwood Gardens, Hanwell, London W7 3HA
t 020 8840 3564 **f** 020 8248 0408 **m** 07801 353502
e c.seager@ntlworld.com
Agent McKinney Macartney Management Ltd, The Barley Mow
Centre, 10 Barley Mow Passage, London W4 4PH
t 020 8995 4747 **f** 020 8995 2414
e fkb@mmtechsrep.demon.co.uk **w** www.mckinneymacartney.com
Credits State Of Play (T); Ashes And Sand (F); Lenny Blue (T); The Way We Live
Now (T)

Ben Seresin
International Creative Management Ltd, Oxford House,
76 Oxford Street, London W1D 1BS
t 020 7636 6565 **f** 020 7323 0101 **w** www.icmlondon.co.uk
Credits Best Laid Plans (F); Lara Croft: Tomb Raider (F); Terminator 3: Rise Of
The Machines (F)

Jean Paul Seresin
International Creative Management Ltd, Oxford House,
76 Oxford Street, London W1D 1BS
t 020 7636 6565 **f** 020 7323 0101 **w** www.icmlondon.co.uk

Eduardo Serra AFC
Peters Fraser & Dunlop, Drury House, 34-43 Russell Street,
London WC2B 5HA
t 020 7344 1000 **f** 020 7836 9543
e postmaster@pfd.co.uk **w** www.pfd.co.uk

Gary Shaw
Wizzo & Co, 35 Old Compton Street, London W1D 5JX
t 020 7437 2055 **f** 020 7437 2066 **m** 07836 600714
e gshawdop@btinternet.com
Credits Cobra Beer - Indian Ingenuity (C); Nurofen - Kids (C); Ford Focus - No (C)

Antony Shearn
78 Elsham Road, West Kensington, London W14 8HH
t 020 7371 2327 **f** 020 7371 2327 **m** 07973 261396
e antonyshearn@aol.com **w** www.bigtonemegaproductions.com
Credits Izzy (M); Tenacious (I); Lullabelle (S); Signal To Noise (F)

Jason Shepherd
CCA Management, 7 St George's Square, London SW1V 2HX
t 020 7630 6303 **f** 020 7630 7376

David Shillingford
Wizzo & Co, 35 Old Compton Street, London W1D 5JX
t 020 7437 2055 **f** 020 7437 2066
e wizzo@wizzoandco.co.uk **w** www.wizzoandco.co.uk

Yang Shu
International Creative Management Ltd, Oxford House,
76 Oxford Street, London W1D 1BS
t 020 7636 6565 **f** 020 7323 0101 **w** www.icmlondon.co.uk
Credits Restless (F); Killing Me Softly (F); Dr. Sleep (F)

John Simmons
159 Goldhawk Road, London W12 8EN
t 020 8740 4183 **f** 020 8740 4183 **m** 07976 423130
e johnsimmons01@aol.com
Credits Big Bad World (T); The Stretch (T); Murder In Mind (T)

Kenneth Simpson
The Dench Arnold Agency, 24 D'Arblay Street, London W1F 8EH
t 020 7437 4551 **f** 020 7439 1355
e contact@dencharnoldagency.co.uk **w** www.dencharnold.co.uk
Credits Home (S); Home; Home; Girls In Love (T)

Peter Sinclair
The Dench Arnold Agency, 24 D'Arblay Street, London W1F 8EH
t 020 7437 4551 **f** 020 7439 1355
e contact@dencharnoldagency.co.uk **w** www.dencharnold.co.uk
Credits Murder Rooms (T); In Deep (T); Donovan Quick (T)

Howard Smith
GAS (Guild Answering Service), C/o Panavision UK,
Metropolitan Centre, Bristol Road, Greenford UB6 8GD
t 020 8813 1999 **f** 020 8813 2111
e admin@gbct.org **w** www.gbct.org

Mark Smythe
62A St Michaels Street, London W2 1QR
t 020 7723 5765 **f** 020 7723 5765 **m** 07710 348997

Steffen Led Sorensen
CCA Management, 7 St George's Square, London SW1V 2HX
t 020 7630 6303 **f** 020 7630 7376

Mike Southon BSC
Creative Media Management, Unit 3B, Walpole Court, Ealing
Studios, Ealing Green, London W5 5ED
t 020 8584 5363 **f** 020 8566 5554
e enquiries@creativemediamanagement.com
Credits Snow White - A Tale Of Terror (F); Replicant (F)

Andrew Speller
AGS Film Services, East Lealands, Box Village, Stroud GL6 9HR
t 01453 832064 **f** 01453 832064 **m** 07966 379764
e ags@macunlimited.net
Agent CCA Management, 7 St George's Square, London SW1V 2HX
t 020 7630 6303 **f** 020 7630 7376
Credits BT Openworld (C); Jordans Muesli Bars (C); Aids Awareness (C);
Medicinema (C)

Mike Spragg
Jessica Carney Associates, Suite 90-92 Kent House,
87 Regent Street, London W1B 4EH
t 020 7434 4143 **f** 020 7434 4173 **e** info@jcarneyassociates.co.uk
Credits Waking The Dead (T); The Knock (T); London's Burning XIII (T)

Oliver Stapleton BSC

International Creative Management Ltd, Oxford House,
76 Oxford Street, London W1D 1BS
t 020 7636 6565 **f** 020 7323 0101 **w** www.icmlondon.co.uk
Credits The Cider House Rules (F); Pay It Forward (F); The Shipping News (F)

Kate Stark

Suz Cruz, Halliford Studios, Manygate Lane, Shepperton TW17 9EG
t 01932 252577 **f** 01932 253323 **m** 07956 485593
e zoe@suzcruz.co.uk **w** www.suzcruz.co.uk

Simon Starling

Dinedor Management, 81 Oxford Street, London W10 2EU
t 020 7851 3575 **f** 020 7851 3576
e info@dinedor.com **w** www.dinedor.com
Credits BT (C); Kellog's (C); McDonald's (C); Club Le Monde (F)

Richard Stewart

Yardley Management, Halliford Studios, Manygate Lane,
Shepperton TW17 9EG
t 01932 253325 **t** 01326 231208 **f** 01932 253323
e pete@yardleymanagement.com **e** rsdop@hotmail.com
w www.yardleymanagement.com

Witold Stok BSC

McKinney Macartney Management Ltd, The Barley Mow
Centre, 10 Barley Mow Passage, London W4 4PH
t 020 8995 4747 **f** 020 8995 2414
e fkb@mmtechsrep.demon.co.uk **w** www.mckinneymacartney.com

Nigel Stone BSC

42 Barkus Way, Stokenchurch, High Wycombe HP14 3RE
t 01494 485392 **m** 07957 187885 **e** nigel.stone2@virgin.net
Credits Harry Potter And The Philospher's Stone (F); Harry Potter And The
Chamber Of Secrets (F); Entrapment (F); Band Of Brothers (T)

Ivan Strasburg

The Dench Arnold Agency, 24 D'Arblay Street, London W1F 8EH
t 020 7437 4551 **f** 020 7439 1355
e contact@dencharnoldagency.co.uk **w** www.dencharnold.co.uk
Credits The Murder Of Stephen Lawrence (T); Bloody Sunday (F); Live From
Baghdad (F)

Lukas Strebel

Peters Fraser & Dunlop, Drury House, 34-43 Russell Street,
London WC2B 5HA
t 020 7344 1000 **f** 020 7836 9543
e postmaster@pfd.co.uk **w** www.pfd.co.uk

Gavin Struthers

m 07956 133301 **e** mail@gavinstruthers.co.uk
Credits Dream Team (T); Fly Fishing (F); Baby Juice Express (F)

Adam Suschitzky

London Management & Representation, 2-4 Noel Street,
London W1F 8GB
t 020 7287 9000 **f** 020 7287 3436

Peter Suschitzky BSC

Peters Fraser & Dunlop, Drury House, 34-43 Russell Street,
London WC2B 5HA
t 020 7344 1000 **f** 020 7836 9543
e postmaster@pfd.co.uk **w** www.pfd.co.uk

Katie Swain

McKinney Macartney Management Ltd, The Barley Mow
Centre, 10 Barley Mow Passage, London W4 4PH
t 020 8995 4747 **f** 020 8995 2414
e fkb@mmtechsrep.demon.co.uk **w** www.mckinneymacartney.com

Fraser Taggart

Annie's Answering Service, Pinewood Studios, Pinewood Road,
Iver Heath SL0 0NH
t 01753 651303 **f** 01753 651848
e info@annies.co.uk **w** www.annies.co.uk

Peter Talbot

EXEC, 6 Travis Court, Farnham Royal SL2 3SB
t 01753 646677 **f** 01753 646770
e sue@execmanagement.co.uk **w** www.execmanagement.co.uk

Fred Tammes BSC

McKinney Macartney Management Ltd, The Barley Mow
Centre, 10 Barley Mow Passage, London W4 4PH
t 020 8995 4747 **f** 020 8995 2414
e fkb@mmtechsrep.demon.co.uk **w** www.mckinneymacartney.com

David Tattersall BSC

McKinney Macartney Management Ltd, The Barley Mow
Centre, 10 Barley Mow Passage, London W4 4PH
t 020 8995 4747 **f** 020 8995 2414
e fkb@mmtechsrep.demon.co.uk **w** www.mckinneymacartney.com

Peter Taylor

EXEC, 6 Travis Court, Farnham Royal SL2 3SB
t 01753 646677 **f** 01753 646770
e sue@execmanagement.co.uk **w** www.execmanagement.co.uk

Duncan Telford

Creative Media Management, Unit 3B, Walpole Court, Ealing
Studios, Ealing Green, London W5 5ED
t 020 8584 5363 **f** 020 8566 5554
e enquiries@creativemediamanagement.com
Credits Denial (S); Fishing (S); The Ultimate Cocktail (S)

Richard Terry

Suz Cruz, Halliford Studios, Manygate Lane, Shepperton TW17 9EG
t 01932 252577 **f** 01932 253323 **m** 07956 485593
e zoe@suzcruz.co.uk **w** www.suzcruz.co.uk

Martin Testar

50 Wandsworth Common Westside, Wandsworth, London
SW18 2EE
t 020 8874 4040 **m** 07798 524040
Agent Call Polly, 24 Dalby Road, London SW18 1AW
t 020 8871 2727

Yoshi Tezuka

Unit 203, Welsbach House, 3-9 Broomhill Road, London SW18 4JQ
t 020 8871 5127 **f** 020 8871 5128 **m** 07968 984727
e yoshi@chimerafilm.co.uk **w** www.chimerafilms.co.uk

Mike Thomson

Jessica Carney Associates, Suite 90-92 Kent House,
87 Regent Street, London W1B 4EH
t 020 7434 4143 **f** 020 7434 4173 **e** info@jcarneyassociates.co.uk
Credits Junk (T); The Coral Island (T); Urban Gothic (T)

Mike Thomson

Little Pippins, Spring Lane, Great Herwood MK17 0QN
m 07941 071759 **e** mikethomson@yahoo.com
Credits Junk (T); The Coral Island (T); Urban Gothic - Series I (T)

Thornton Film Service

24 Marina Approach, Yeading, Hayes UB4 9TB
t 020 8845 8755 **f** 07974 350075 **m** 07976 725493
e ptfilms@blueyonder.co.uk
Contact Susan Thornton, Accounts Manager; Peter Thornton,
Director of Photography
Credits Code Name Corgi (A); Fairy King Of AR (F); A Mind To Kill (T); Alone (F)

Clive Tickner BSC

McKinney Macartney Management Ltd, The Barley Mow
Centre, 10 Barley Mow Passage, London W4 4PH
t 020 8995 4747 **f** 020 8995 2414
e fkb@mmtechsrep.demon.co.uk **w** www.mckinneymacartney.com

Steve Tickner MBKS

88 Kenilworth Avenue, Harrow HA2 8SA
t 020 8423 2337 **f** 020 8723 4272 **m** 07836 765668
e stevetickner@mac.com

Darran Tiernan
Yardley Management, Halliford Studios, Manygate Lane,
Shepperton TW17 9EG
t 01932 253325 **f** 01932 253323 **m** 07957 646004
e pete@yardleymanagement.com **e** darrantiernan@yahoo.co.uk
w www.yardleymanagement.com

John Toll (ASC)
International Creative Management Ltd, Oxford House,
76 Oxford Street, London W1D 1BS
t 020 7636 6565 **f** 020 7323 0101 **w** www.icmlondon.co.uk
Credits Legends Of The Fall (F); Almost Famous (F); Vanilla Sky (F)

Jo Eken Torp
Dinedor Management, 81 Oxford Street, London W10 2EU
t 020 7851 3575 **f** 020 7851 3576
e info@dinedor.com **w** www.dinedor.com
Credits Kavanagh QC (T); Queer as Folk (T); One of the Hollywood Ten (T)

Jan Tovey
Princestone, 49 Waldeck Road, London N15 3EL
t 020 8881 8788 **f** 020 8881 2857
e princestone@madasafish.com
Credits King Girl (T); Norman Ormal (T); Blackwater (T)

Alan M Trow BSC
Agent Gems, The Media House, 87 Glebe Street, Penarth
CF64 1EF
t 029 2071 0770 **f** 029 2071 0771
e gems@gems-agency.co.uk **w** www.gems-agency.co.uk
Agent Dinedor Management, 81 Oxford Street, London W10 2EU
t 020 7851 3575 **f** 020 7851 3576
e info@dinedor.com **w** www.dinedor.com
Credits Ruth Rendall's Harm Done (T); Monolith (F); Dragonworld (F); The Punk (F)

Brian Tufano BSC
McKinney Macartney Management Ltd, The Barley Mow
Centre, 10 Barley Mow Passage, London W4 4PH
t 020 8995 4747 **f** 020 8995 2414
e fkb@mmtechsrep.demon.co.uk **w** www.mckinneymacartney.com

Brett Turnbull
Suz Cruz, Halliford Studios, Manygate Lane, Shepperton TW17 9EG
t 01932 252577 **f** 01932 253323 **m** 07956 485593
e zoe@suzcruz.co.uk **w** www.suzcruz.co.uk

Garry Turnbull
Dinedor Management, 81 Oxford Street, London W10 2EU
t 020 7851 3575 **f** 020 7851 3576
e info@dinedor.com **w** www.dinedor.com
Credits Reverb (F); Dress To Kill (F); Scottish Power (C); Toyota (C)

Sean Van Hales
Creative Media Management, Unit 3B, Walpole Court, Ealing
Studios, Ealing Green, London W5 5ED
t 020 8584 5363 **f** 020 8566 5554
e enquiries@creativemediamanagement.com
Credits Avenging Angels (T); The Vice (T); Cold Feet (T); Rockface (I)

Robin Vidgeon
Lammas Lodge, 16A Mayfield Road, Weybridge KT13 8XD
t 01932 848948 **f** 01932 848948 **m** 07860 764907
e robinvidgeon@onetel.net
Credits A Is For Acid (T); Rock Face (T); Cazalets (T)

Ernest Vincze BSC
25 Marville Road, London SW6 7BB
t 020 7385 3413 **f** 020 7381 4209 **m** 07711 664773
e el.vincze@virgin.net **e** tk6@mmtechsrep.demon.co.uk
Agent McKinney Macartney Management Ltd, The Barley Mow
Centre, 10 Barley Mow Passage, London W4 4PH
t 020 8995 4747 **f** 020 8995 2414
e fkb@mmtechsrep.demon.co.uk **w** www.mckinneymacartney.com
Credits Shooting The Past (T); Macbeth (F); Mystic Masseur (F)

John Walker
CCA Management, 7 St George's Square, London SW1V 2HX
t 020 7630 6303 **f** 020 7630 7376

Nigel Walters
29 Boscombe Road, Shepherds Bush, London W12 9HT
t 020 8740 6732 **f** 020 8354 0609 **m** 07774 115988
e waltatbush@aol.com **w** www.seifert-dench.co.uk
Agent The Dench Arnold Agency, 24 D'Arblay Street, London
W1F 8EH
t 020 7437 4551 **f** 020 7439 1355 **w** www.dencharnold.co.uk

John Ward
5 Dulwich Wood Park, London SE19 1XQ
t 0208 761 5431 **f** 0208 761 3545 **m** 07768 451 239
e johnward@jwfilms.demon.co.uk
Agent EXEC, 6 Travis Court, Farnham Royal SL2 3SB
t 01753 646677 **f** 01753 646770
e sue@execmanagement.co.uk **w** www.execmanagement.co.uk
Credits Dance With an Angel (T); Love Honour and Obey (F); The Final Cut (T)

Mark Waters
International Creative Management Ltd, Oxford House,
76 Oxford Street, London W1D 1BS
t 020 7636 6565 **f** 020 7323 0101 **w** www.icmlondon.co.uk
Credits Babyfather (T); Buried (T); Judge John Deed (T)

Karl Watkins
Suz Cruz, Halliford Studios, Manygate Lane, Shepperton TW17 9EG
t 01932 252577 **f** 01932 253323 **m** 07956 485593
e zoe@suzcruz.co.uk **w** www.suzcruz.co.uk

Colin Watkinson
Wizzo & Co, 35 Old Compton Street, London W1D 5JX
t 020 7437 2055 **f** 020 7437 2066
e wizzo@wizzoandco.co.uk **w** www.wizzoandco.co.uk

James Welland
Casarotto Marsh Ltd, National House, 60-66 Wardour Street,
London W1V 4ND
t 020 7287 4450 **f** 020 7287 9128
e agents@casarotto.uk.com **w** www.casarotto.uk.com

Jason West
Yardley Management, Halliford Studios, Manygate Lane,
Shepperton TW17 9EG
t 01932 253325 **t** 609395 **f** 01932 253323
e pete@yardleymanagement.com **e** daisy-films@t-online.de
w www.yardleymanagement.com

Jeremy Westgate
Suz Cruz, Halliford Studios, Manygate Lane, Shepperton TW17 9EG
t 01932 252577 **f** 01932 253323 **m** 07956 485593
e zoe@suzcruz.co.uk **w** www.suzcruz.co.uk

Paul Wheeler
45 St Leonards Road, East Sheen, London SW14 7LY
t 020 8878 7193 **m** 07836 593740 **e** cinewheeler@aol.com
Agent Creative Media Management, Unit 3B, Walpole Court,
Ealing Studios, Ealing Green, London W5 5ED
t 020 8584 5363 **f** 020 8566 5554
e enquiries@creativemediamanagement.com
Credits The Merchant Of Venice (T); Oklahoma! (T); Cor Blimey! (F)

David Whitson
Bigfish Management, 55 Bendon Valley, London SW18 4LZ
t 020 8877 7111 **f** 020 8874 6623
e info@bigfishmanagement.com **w** www.bigfishmanagement.com

Mark Wiggins
4 Cottage Close, Sharp's Lane, Ruislip HA4 7JE
t 01895 638785 **f** 01895 638785 **m** 07702 196876
e scare@dircon.co.uk
Credits Scare! (S); The Basketball Killer (S); Superstitious Minds (S)

Adrian Wild
Wizzo & Co, 35 Old Compton Street, London W1D 5JX
t 020 7437 2055 **f** 020 7437 2066
e wizzo@wizzoandco.co.uk **w** www.wizzoandco.co.uk

Ed Wild
Suz Cruz, Halliford Studios, Manygate Lane, Shepperton TW17 9EG
t 01932 252577 **f** 01932 253323 **m** 07956 485593
e zoe@suzcruz.co.uk **w** www.suzcruz.co.uk

Jo Willems
Suz Cruz, Halliford Studios, Manygate Lane, Shepperton TW17 9EG
t 01932 252577 **f** 01932 253323 **m** 07956 485593
e zoe@suzcruz.co.uk **w** www.suzcruz.co.uk

Nigel Willoughby
Agent Annie's Answering Service, Pinewood Studios,
Pinewood Road, Iver Heath SL0 0NH
t 01753 651303 **f** 01753 651848
e info@annies.co.uk **w** www.annies.co.uk
Agent International Creative Management Ltd, Oxford House,
76 Oxford Street, London W1D 1BS
t 020 7636 6565 **f** 020 7323 0101 **w** www.icmlondon.co.uk
Credits The Escapist (F); The Magdalene Sisters (F); The Key (T)

Paul Wilson BSC FBKS
15 The Meadows, Flackwell Heath HP10 9LX
t 01628 523514 **f** 01628 523513 **m** 07973 327526
e paulro@onetel.net.uk
Credits Tomorrow Never Dies (F); Goldeneye (F); The World Is Not Enough (F);
Die Another Day (F)

Ian Wilson BSC
McKinney Macartney Management Ltd, The Barley Mow
Centre, 10 Barley Mow Passage, London W4 4PH
t 020 8995 4747 **f** 020 8995 2414
e fkb@mmtechsrep.demon.co.uk **w** www.mckinneymacartney.com

Romain Winding
International Creative Management Ltd, Oxford House,
76 Oxford Street, London W1D 1BS
t 020 7636 6565 **f** 020 7323 0101 **w** www.icmlondon.co.uk
Credits The Revengers Comedies (F); The Misadventures Of Margaret (F); Tosca (F)

Gary Young
Dinedor Management, 81 Oxford Street, London W10 2EU
t 020 7851 3575 **f** 020 7851 3576
e info@dinedor.com **w** www.dinedor.com
Credits US3 (M); Marissa (M); ntl (C); JD Sports (C)

Zivko Zalar
31 Somerset Road, London W4 5DW
t 020 8994 0958 **f** 020 8932 4459 **m** 07762 110182
e zzalar@cs.com

Haris Zambarloukos
Peters Fraser & Dunlop, Drury House, 34-43 Russell Street,
London WC2B 5HA
t 020 7344 1000 **f** 020 7836 9543
e postmaster@pfd.co.uk **w** www.pfd.co.uk

DIRECTORS

Directors **1st Assistant**

Nael Abbas
36 Burdon Park, Sunnside, Newcastle-upon-Tyne NE16 5HA
t 0191 496 0813 **m** 07885 203033 **e** naelabbas@supanet.com
Credits Byker Grove (T); Rebus 'Dead Souls' (T); Lexx IV (T)

Tony Aherne
Gems, The Media House, 87 Glebe Street, Penarth CF64 1EF
t 029 2071 0770 **f** 029 2071 0771
e gems@gems-agency.co.uk **w** www.gems-agency.co.uk
Credits On Home Ground (T); The Secret (F); Happiness (T); Afraid Not Afraid (F)

Claire Alderton
16B Yerbury Road, London N19 4RL
t 07812 596878 **e** claire1st@blueyonder.co.uk
Agent Callbox Communications Limited, 66 Shepperton
Studios, Shepperton TW17 0QD
t 01932 592572 **f** 01932 569655 **m** 07710 572572
e callboxdiary@btinternet.com **w** www.callboxdiary.co.uk
Credits Trailer's Guilt (T); Blur UK Tour (M); Ocean's Eleven (C)

Jay Arthur
Suz Cruz, Halliford Studios, Manygate Lane, Shepperton TW17 9EG
t 01932 252577 **f** 01932 253323 **m** 07956 485593
e zoe@suzcruz.co.uk **w** www.suzcruz.co.uk

Jane Ashmore
Gems, The Media House, 87 Glebe Street, Penarth CF64 1EF
t 029 2071 0770 **f** 029 2071 0771
e gems@gems-agency.co.uk **w** www.gems-agency.co.uk
Credits Brum (T); Family Affairs (T); Hollyoaks (T); The Ring And The Steal (F)

Clare Awdry
EXEC, 6 Travis Court, Farnham Royal SL2 3SB
t 01753 646677 **f** 01753 646770
e sue@execmanagement.co.uk **w** www.execmanagement.co.uk

Andrew Bainbridge
Wizzo & Co, 35 Old Compton Street, London W1D 5JX
t 020 7437 2055 **f** 020 7437 2066
e wizzo@wizzoandco.co.uk **w** www.wizzoandco.co.uk

Ken Baker
ADS, Shepperton Studios, Studios Road, Shepperton TW17 0QD
t 01932 592303 **f** 01932 592492 **e** ads@carlincrew.co.uk
Credits Wings And A Prayer (F); Princess Bride (F); Labrynth (F); Willow (F)

Peter Bennett
23 Manor Farm Avenue, Shepperton TW17 9AD
t 01932 886714 **m** 07715 034537
e p-bennet-jnr@darcon.co.uk
Credits Sparkling Cyanide (T); Bice in Deep (T); The Mummy Returns (F);
The Mummy (F)

Jonathan Benson
Creative Media Management, Unit 3B, Walpole Court, Ealing
Studios, Ealing Green, London W5 5ED
t 020 8584 5363 **f** 020 8566 5554
e enquiries@creativemediamanagement.com
Credits Little Voice (F); I Dreamed Of Africa (F); Hope (F)

Rohan Berry
6B Park View, Church Grove, Hampton Wick KT1 4AL
t 020 8943 3910 **f** 020 8943 3910 **m** 07973 303360
e rohanberry@hotmail.com
Credits Carpet Right (C); Evening Standard (C); Rolo (C); South Kensington (F)

Grietje Besteman
Gems, The Media House, 87 Glebe Street, Penarth CF64 1EF
t 029 2071 0770 **f** 029 2071 0771
e gems@gems-agency.co.uk **w** www.gems-agency.co.uk
Credits An Urban Ghost Story (F); The Honey Trap (F); Mr In Between (F);
Brookside (T)

William Booker
EXEC, 6 Travis Court, Farnham Royal SL2 3SB
t 01753 646677 **f** 01753 646770
e sue@execmanagement.co.uk **w** www.execmanagement.co.uk

Bill Brennan
The Old Rectory, Rosary Road, Norwich NR1 1TA
t 01603 664727 **m** 07880 553365
Agent Gems, The Media House, 87 Glebe Street, Penarth
CF64 1EF
t 029 2071 0770 **f** 029 2071 0771
e gems@gems-agency.co.uk **w** www.gems-agency.co.uk
Credits The Cry (T); Foyles War I & II (T); The Swap (T); My Uncle Silas I (T)

Alex Bridcut
Gems, The Media House, 87 Glebe Street, Penarth CF64 1EF
t 029 2071 0770 **f** 029 2071 0771
e gems@gems-agency.co.uk **w** www.gems-agency.co.uk
Credits London's Burning (T); As Time Goes By (T); Inspector Lynley: Series II
(T); Clockwork Mice (F)

Dean Byfield
Gems, The Media House, 87 Glebe Street, Penarth CF64 1EF
t 029 2071 0770 **f** 029 2071 0771
e gems@gems-agency.co.uk **w** www.gems-agency.co.uk
Credits Attachments (T); Park Stories (S); Randall And Hopkirk Deceased (T);
The Bill (T)

Ian Cameron
Callbox Communications Limited, 66 Shepperton Studios,
Studios Road, Shepperton TW17 0QD
t 01932 592572 **f** 01932 569655 **m** 07710 572572
e callboxdiary@btinternet.com **w** www.callboxdiary.co.uk

Jude Campbell
Callbox Communications Limited, 66 Shepperton Studios,
Studios Road, Shepperton TW17 0QD
t 01932 592572 **f** 01932 569655 **m** 07710 572572
e callboxdiary@btinternet.com **w** www.callboxdiary.co.uk

Paddy Carpenter
Bookends, 83 Maynard Drive, St Albans AL1 2JX
t 01727 841177 **e** bookgold@bookends.fsbusiness.co.uk

Ed Chalkley
EXEC, 6 Travis Court, Farnham Royal SL2 3SB
t 01753 646677 **f** 01753 646770
e sue@execmanagement.co.uk **w** www.execmanagement.co.uk

Bill Challoner
Gems, The Media House, 87 Glebe Street, Penarth CF64 1EF
t 029 2071 0770 **f** 029 2071 0771 **e** gems@gems-agency.co.uk
w www.gems-agency.co.uk
Credits The Bill (T)

Marcus Collier
Gems, The Media House, 87 Glebe Street, Penarth CF64 1EF
t 029 2071 0770 **f** 029 2071 0771
e gems@gems-agency.co.uk **w** www.gems-agency.co.uk
Credits Road Movies (T); Moving On (T); Brookside (T); Hollyoaks (T)

Rozmer T Courtnay
208, 1-200 North Service Road West, Oakville L6M 2Y1, Canada
t 334 8570
e rtc_films@hotmail.com **w** http://www.rtc-films.20m.com
Credits Tuff Luk Klub (F); Gum Ball (S); Vince (S); Lorrain Pritters - He's The One (M)

Paul Dale
Gems, The Media House, 87 Glebe Street, Penarth CF64 1EF
t 029 2071 0770 **f** 029 2071 0771
e gems@gems-agency.co.uk **w** www.gems-agency.co.uk
Credits Attachments (T); Walking With Cavemen (D); Footballer's Wives (T);
Bad Girls (T)

Chris Dando
Gems, The Media House, 87 Glebe Street, Penarth CF64 1EF
t 029 2071 0770 **f** 029 2071 0771 **e** gems@gems-agency.co.uk
w www.gems-agency.co.uk
Credits Rockface (T); Silent Witness (T); Murder On The Orient Express (F);
Footballers' Wives (T)

Mark Dean
Callbox Communications Limited, 66 Shepperton Studios,
Studios Road, Shepperton TW17 0QD
t 01932 592572 **f** 01932 569655 **m** 07710 572572
e callboxdiary@btinternet.com **w** www.callboxdiary.co.uk

Melanie Dicks
EXEC, 6 Travis Court, Farnham Royal SL2 3SB
t 01753 646677 **f** 01753 646770
e sue@execmanagement.co.uk **w** www.execmanagement.co.uk

John Dodds
14 Manor Garden, Richmond TW9 1XX
t 020 8940 6670 **t** 020 7419 2323 **m** 07801 441010
Agent Bookends, 83 Maynard Drive, St Albans AL1 2JX
t 01727 841177 **e** bookgold@bookends.fsbusiness.co.uk
Credits Murder Room - Kingdom Of Bones (T); A Good Thief (T); Nice Guy Eddie
(T); Waking The Dead (T)

David Downing
Gems, The Media House, 87 Glebe Street, Penarth CF64 1EF
t 029 2071 0770 **f** 029 2071 0771 **e** gems@gems-agency.co.uk
w www.gems-agency.co.uk
Credits Peak Practice (T); The Bill (T); The Heart Surgeon (T)

Jonathan Eckersley
14 Thirlstane Street, Aigburth, Liverpool L17 9PD
t 0151 283 9073 **f** 0151 283 8077 **m** 07931 352513
e jonathaneckersley@hotmail.com
Credits Bad Girls (T); Merseybeat (T); Me And Mrs Jones (T); A&E Series IV (T)

Mark Egerton
Callbox Communications Limited, 66 Shepperton Studios,
Studios Road, Shepperton TW17 0QD
t 01932 592572 **f** 01932 569655 **m** 07710 572572
e callboxdiary@btinternet.com **w** www.callboxdiary.co.uk

Paul Elkins
Gems, The Media House, 87 Glebe Street, Penarth CF64 1EF
t 029 2071 0770 **f** 029 2071 0771
e gems@gems-agency.co.uk **w** www.gems-agency.co.uk
Credits A Is For Acid (T); Brookside (T); Heartbeat (T); Emmerdale (T)

british academy of film and television arts:
membership and events

BAFTA allows unrivalled opportunities to network with people working at all levels of the film, television and interactive industries. Membership is open to anyone with three years professional experience in the film, television or interactive industries (or any combination of these).

Benefits of membership include:

The British Academy Awards
Members can purchase substantially discounted tickets to all BAFTA awards ceremonies. These are:
Film
Television
Television Craft
Children's Film and Television
Interactive

Club facilities
BAFTAs headquarters are available for BAFTA members to use for meetings, drinks, meals and snacks. Its facilities, including one of the best equipped cinemas in London, are available to hire to members.

BAFTA events
BAFTA Members are given access to BAFTA events at no charge.
The Academy events programme showcases the best in the creative industries as well as providing a forum for debating current and controversial issues. Recent events include Spike Lee in conversation with Bonnie Greer, a Tribute to Sir John Mills, Shortcuts to Screen, and In the Frame: The Art of Product Placement.
Members can also attend social functions and events at BAFTA in Scotland, Wales, and in the North of England, as well as in Hollywood and in New York.

For more information on events at BAFTA please contact:
Amy Minyard, Events and Membership Officer, BAFTA
Tel: 020 7292 5800

Film Screenings
Almost all major feature films are screened for BAFTA members at 195 Piccadilly, usually before release. The Academy organises question and answer sessions with the stars and creators of these films on several occasions throughout the year. This year the Academy has played host to Harrison Ford, Liam Neeson, Ken Loach, Robert Altman, Tom Hanks, Director Kathryn Bigelow, Writer Paul Laverty, Spike Lee, John Malkovich, Javier Bardem, and Stephen Frears among others.

Television programmes
Many new television programmes are also now screening in advance of transmission at BAFTA, followed by a Q & A with the cast and/or crew.

Voting
Members are entitled to participate in the voting process for the annual Film, Television, Children's Film and Television and the Television Craft Awards.

Other benefits
The Academy is currently developing a far-reaching programme to bring members discounts on travel including airline flights and car hire, hotels, restaurants, health clubs, bookshops, art galleries and museums, etc.

For more information on Academy Membership, please contact:
Toby Coke, Events and Membership Assistant, BAFTA
Tel: 020 7292 5808
Email: membership@bafta.org

Cultural Diversity
As a member of the Cultural Diversity Network, BAFTA is committed to playing a front-line role in raising awareness of our multi-cultural society.

BRITISH ACADEMY OF FILM AND TELEVISION ARTS

Peter F Errington
11 Vincent Row, Hampton-Hill TW12 1RB
t 020 8979 0572 **f** 020 8979 0572 **m** 07050 030112
e avidx@screaming.net
Credits Children Of The New Forest (F); Family Affairs (T); Nine Dead Gay Guys (F); The Bill (T)

Ian Ferguson
Quartier Le Dragon, Avenue Frederic-Henri Manhes, Draguignan 83300, France
t 9468 1263 **f** 9468 1263 **e** ifrgsn@aol.com
Credits The Bill (T); Taggart (T); London's Burning (T); Jonathan Creek (T)

Micky Finch
Callbox Communications Limited, 66 Shepperton Studios, Studios Road, Shepperton TW17 0QD
t 01932 592572 **f** 01932 569655 **m** 07710 572572
e callboxdiary@btinternet.com **w** www.callboxdiary.co.uk

Grant Freeman
Wizzo & Co, 35 Old Compton Street, London W1D 5JX
t 020 7437 2055 **f** 020 7437 2066
e wizzo@wizzoandco.co.uk **w** www.wizzoandco.co.uk

Peter Freeman

EXEC, 6 Travis Court, Farnham Royal SL2 3SB
t 01753 646677 **f** 01753 646770
e sue@execmanagement.co.uk **w** www.execmanagement.co.uk

Rawdon de Fresnes

EXEC, 6 Travis Court, Farnham Royal SL2 3SB
t 01753 646677 **f** 01753 646770
e sue@execmanagement.co.uk **w** www.execmanagement.co.uk

Dominic Fysh

29 Vaughan Road, Thames Ditton KT7 0UF
t 020 8398 8798 **m** 07831 137146 **e** dfysh@aol.com
Credits Mindhunters (F); Second Nature (T); The Hole (F); Auf Wiedersehen Pet (T)

Gerry Gavigan

Bookends, 83 Maynard Drive, St Albans AL1 2JX
t 01727 841177 **e** bookgold@bookends.fsbusiness.co.uk

Marcia Gay

Creative Media Management, Unit 3B, Walpole Court, Ealing Studios, Ealing Green, London W5 5ED
t 020 8584 5363 **f** 020 8566 5554
e enquiries@creativemediamanagement.com
Credits The World Of Tomorrow (F); The Point Men (F); Silent Cry (F); Harry Potter And The Philosopher's Stone (F)

Ben Gill

Callbox Communications Limited, 66 Shepperton Studios, Studios Road, Shepperton TW17 0QD
t 01932 572572 **f** 01932 569655 **m** 07710 572572
e callboxdiary@btinternet.com **w** www.callboxdiary.co.uk

Trevor Gittings

Gems, The Media House, 87 Glebe Street, Penarth CF64 1EF
t 029 2071 0770 **f** 029 2071 0771
e gems@gems-agency.co.uk **w** www.gems-agency.co.uk
Credits Rockface (T); Byker Grove (T); Break Out (F); Liam (F)

Sean Glynn

Callbox Communications Limited, 66 Shepperton Studios, Studios Road, Shepperton TW17 0QD
t 01932 572572 **f** 01932 569655 **m** 07710 572572
e callboxdiary@btinternet.com **w** www.callboxdiary.co.uk

Daniel Goldstein

EXEC, 6 Travis Court, Farnham Royal SL2 3SB
t 01753 646677 **f** 01753 646770
e sue@execmanagement.co.uk **w** www.execmanagement.co.uk

Tommy Gormley

International Creative Management Ltd, Oxford House, 76 Oxford Street, London W1D 1BS
t 020 7636 6565 **f** 020 7323 0101 **w** www.icmlondon.co.uk
Credits Elizabeth (F); The Tailor Of Panama (F); The Four Feathers (F)

Richard Graysmark

EXEC, 6 Travis Court, Farnham Royal SL2 3SB
t 01753 646677 **f** 01753 646770
e sue@execmanagement.co.uk **w** www.execmanagement.co.uk

Griffin

Suz Cruz, Halliford Studios, Manygate Lane, Shepperton TW17 9EG
t 01932 252577 **f** 01932 253323 **m** 07956 485593
e zoe@suzcruz.co.uk **w** www.suzcruz.co.uk

Mark Griffiths

EXEC, 6 Travis Court, Farnham Royal SL2 3SB
t 01753 646677 **f** 01753 646770
e sue@execmanagement.co.uk **w** www.execmanagement.co.uk

Neil Grigson

Wizzo & Co, 35 Old Compton Street, London W1D 5JX
t 020 7437 2055 **f** 020 7437 2066
e wizzo@wizzoandco.co.uk **w** www.wizzoandco.co.uk

Lucas Harding

Suz Cruz, Halliford Studios, Manygate Lane, Shepperton TW17 9EG
t 01932 252577 **f** 01932 253323 **m** 07956 485593
e zoe@suzcruz.co.uk **w** www.suzcruz.co.uk

Cordelia Hardy

The Production Switchboard, North Down, Down Lane, Compton GU3 1DN
t 01483 812011 **f** 01483 812027
e aly@productionswitch.freeserve.co.uk
Credits Bright Young Things (F); A Rather English Marriage (T); BUPA (C)

Brian Harris

EXEC, 6 Travis Court, Farnham Royal SL2 3SB
t 01753 646677 **f** 01753 646770
e sue@execmanagement.co.uk **w** www.execmanagement.co.uk

Sam Harris

Creative Media Management, Unit 3B, Walpole Court, Ealing Studios, Ealing Green, London W5 5ED
t 020 8584 5363 **f** 020 8566 5554
e enquiries@creativemediamanagement.com
Credits Touch Of Frost (T); The War Bride (F); Dog Soldiers (F)

Mark Hassell

17 Landseer Close, Merton Abbey, London SW19 2UT
t 020 8286 7793 **f** 020 8286 7793 **m** 07970 426688
e assitantdirector@email.com
w www.hitlist.co.uk/production/assistantdirector
Agent Callbox Communications Limited, 66 Shepperton Studios, Studios Road, Shepperton TW17 0QD
t 01932 572572 **f** 01932 569655 **m** 07710 572572
e callboxdiary@btinternet.com **w** www.callboxdiary.co.uk
Credits Cloudbuster (S); Suede (M); Anxiety (F); Cancer Research (C)

Michael Hayes

Wizzo & Co, 35 Old Compton Street, London W1D 5JX
t 020 7437 2055 **f** 020 7437 2066
e wizzo@wizzoandco.co.uk **w** www.wizzoandco.co.uk

Julian Hearne

EXEC, 6 Travis Court, Farnham Royal SL2 3SB
t 01753 646677 **f** 01753 646770
e sue@execmanagement.co.uk **w** www.execmanagement.co.uk

Ben Hughes

EXEC, 6 Travis Court, Farnham Royal SL2 3SB
t 01753 646677 **f** 01753 646770
e sue@execmanagement.co.uk **w** www.execmanagement.co.uk

Monica Heath

Gems, The Media House, 87 Glebe Street, Penarth CF64 1EF
t 029 2071 0770 **f** 029 2071 0771
e gems@gems-agency.co.uk **w** www.gems-agency.co.uk
Credits Back Home (T); Rock Face (T); 2,000 Acres Of Sky (T); Monarch Of The Glen (T)

Dee Hellier

The Production Switchboard, North Down, Down Lane, Compton GU3 1DN
t 01483 812011 **f** 01483 812027
e aly@productionswitch.freeserve.co.uk
Credits Rebus Series III & IV (T); As If (T); Night & Day (T)

Richard Hewitt

International Creative Management Ltd, Oxford House, 76 Oxford Street, London W1D 1BS
t 020 7636 6565 **f** 020 7323 0101 **w** www.icmlondon.co.uk
Credits An Ideal Husband (F); The Importance Of Being Earnest (F); Cold Mountain (F)

Simon Hinkly

Creative Media Management, Unit 3B, Walpole Court, Ealing Studios, Ealing Green, London W5 5ED
t 020 8584 5363 **f** 020 8566 5554
e enquiries@creativemediamanagement.com
Credits Birthday Girl (F); Impact (F)

Ben Hughes
27 Gubyon Avenue, Herne Hill, London SE24 0DU
t 020 7274 3685 **f** 020 7978 8586 **m** 07710 115135
e ben.hughes@apisfilms.co.uk
Credits My Brother Tom (F); Ashes And Sand (F); Twelfth Night (T); Suzie Gold (F)

Bruce Jackson
Callbox Communications Limited, 66 Shepperton Studios,
Studios Road, Shepperton TW17 0QD
t 01932 592572 **f** 01932 569655 **m** 07710 572572
e callboxdiary@btinternet.com **w** www.callboxdiary.co.uk

Ian Jenkins
63 Garfield Road, Wimbledon, London SW19 8RZ
t 020 8542 9604 **m** 07973 143479 **e** iwjenkins@aol.com
Agent Gems, The Media House, 87 Glebe Street,
Penarth CF64 1EF
t 029 2071 0770 **f** 029 2071 0771
e gems@gems-agency.co.uk **w** www.gems-agency.co.uk
Credits Attachments (T); Big Train (T); Holby City (T); The Bill (T)

Bernie Jones
Wizzo & Co, 35 Old Compton Street, London W1D 5JX
t 020 7437 2055 **f** 020 7437 2066
e wizzo@wizzoandco.co.uk **w** www.wizzoandco.co.uk

Chris Kelly
Suz Cruz, Halliford Studios, Manygate Lane, Shepperton TW17 9EG
t 01932 252577 **f** 01932 253323 **m** 07956 485593
e zoe@suzcruz.co.uk **w** www.suzcruz.co.uk

Gil Kenny
Wizzo & Co, 35 Old Compton Street, London W1D 5JX
t 020 7437 2055 **f** 020 7437 2066
e wizzo@wizzoandco.co.uk **w** www.wizzoandco.co.uk

Bill Kirk
Creative Media Management, Unit 3B, Walpole Court, Ealing
Studios, Ealing Green, London W5 5ED
t 020 8584 5363 **f** 020 8566 5554
e enquiries@creativemediamanagement.com
Credits Murder Rooms (T); The Commander (T)

Barry Langley
31 Westwood Road, London SW13 0LA
t 020 8878 2479

David Lawley-Wakelin
Callbox Communications Limited, 66 Shepperton Studios,
Studios Road, Shepperton TW17 0QD
t 01932 592572 **f** 01932 569655 **m** 07710 572572
e callboxdiary@btinternet.com **w** www.callboxdiary.co.uk

Nick Laws
Callbox Communications Limited, 66 Shepperton Studios,
Studios Road, Shepperton TW17 0QD
t 01932 592572 **f** 01932 569655 **m** 07710 572572
e callboxdiary@btinternet.com **w** www.callboxdiary.co.uk

Philip A. Lewis
6 Marcia Rice Court, High Street, Abbots Bromley, Rugeley
WS15 3BL
t 0 9664 87492 **e** philip@philiplewis.co.uk **w** www.philiplewis.co.uk
Credits Doctors (T); Stig (T); Coronation Street (T); EastEnders (T)

Steve Lincoln
6 Newlands Manor, Everton, Lymington SO41 0JH
t 01590 643263 **f** 01590 642830 **m** 07980 584711
Agent The Production Switchboard, North Down, Down Lane,
Compton GU3 1DN
t 01483 812011 **f** 01483 812027
e aly@productionswitch.freeserve.co.uk
Credits Posh Nosh (T); 15 Storeys High (T); Beg; Gimme Six

Richard Lingard
3 Brookside Cottages, Brook Street, Moreton Pinkney NN11 3SL
t 01295 760878 **f** 01295 760878 **m** 07831 386914
e lingard@easynet.co.uk
Credits Being Victoria (T); Abbey National (I); Trust (T); Strange (T)

David MacDonald
Gems, The Media House, 87 Glebe Street, Penarth CF64 1EF
t 029 2071 0770 **f** 029 2071 0771
e gems@gems-agency.co.uk **w** www.gems-agency.co.uk
Credits Monarch Of The Glen (T); Murder In Mind (T); Where The Heart Is (T);
Brothers In Trouble (F)

Joanna Macdonnell
Gems, The Media House, 87 Glebe Street, Penarth CF64 1EF
t 029 2071 0770 **f** 029 2071 0771
e gems@gems-agency.co.uk **w** www.gems-agency.co.uk
Credits Crazy Jonathans (T); Crash Bang Wallop (T); Holby City (T)

Joanna MacDonnell
9 Elm Park Road, South Norwood, London SE25 6UA
t 020 8771 5444 **f** 020 8771 5444 **m** 07774 237072
e jo@macdonnell.info
Credits Holby City (T)
Single and multi camera, movie magic scheduling, fluent German.

David Mack
Gems, The Media House, 87 Glebe Street, Penarth CF64 1EF
t 029 2071 0770 **f** 029 2071 0771
e gems@gems-agency.co.uk **w** www.gems-agency.co.uk
Credits Night And Day (T); Attachments (T); Blackball (F); Bridget Jones' Diary (F)

Norman Miles
Silver Birches, Widmoor, Wooburn Common, High Wycombe
HP10 0JG
t 01628 522377 **f** 01628 522377 **m** 07768 454743
e namronselim@hotmail.com
Credits Crossroads (T); The Magic Seed; Smack The Pony (T); The Bill (T)

Suzy Mills
Shandon, Fulmer Common Road, Iver SL0 0NP
t 07071 203095 **f** 01753 662219 **e** zm@suzymills.co.uk

Dave Moor
Suz Cruz, Halliford Studios, Manygate Lane, Shepperton TW17 9EG
t 01932 252577 **f** 01932 253323 **m** 07956 485593
e zoe@suzcruz.co.uk **w** www.suzcruz.co.uk

James Murphy
266 Kew Road, Richmond TW9 3EE
t 020 8940 4959 **f** 020 8940 4958 **m** 07970 818 652
e zelenkoff@hotmail.com
Credits The Last Which (T); Mad Dogs (F); Paradise Grove (F)

Justin Murphy
m 07970 077460 **e** justinmurphy@btopenworld.com
Credits Making a Killing (F); Weak At Denise (F)

Terry Needham
EXEC, 6 Travis Court, Farnham Royal SL2 3SB
t 01753 646677 **f** 01753 646770
e sue@execmanagement.co.uk **w** www.execmanagement.co.uk

Radford Neville
Gems, The Media House, 87 Glebe Street, Penarth CF64 1EF
t 029 2071 0770 **f** 029 2071 0771
e gems@gems-agency.co.uk **w** www.gems-agency.co.uk
Credits Hornblower (T); Wire In The Blood (T); Martin Amis Project (F);
Peak Practice (T)

Chris Newman
EXEC, 6 Travis Court, Farnham Royal SL2 3SB
t 01753 646677 **f** 01753 646770
e sue@execmanagement.co.uk **w** www.execmanagement.co.uk

Martin O'Malley
Callbox Communications Limited, 66 Shepperton Studios,
Studios Road, Shepperton TW17 0QD
t 01932 592572 **f** 01932 569655 **m** 07710 572572
e callboxdiary@btinternet.com **w** www.callboxdiary.co.uk

Jez Oakley
Callbox Communications Limited, 66 Shepperton Studios,
Studios Road, Shepperton TW17 0QD
t 01932 592572 **f** 01932 569655 **m** 07710 572572
e callboxdiary@btinternet.com **w** www.callboxdiary.co.uk

Jon Older
t 0117 985 1511 **f** 0117 985 1511 **m** 07710 987685
e jonolder@talk21.com
Credits The Stratosphere Girl (T); Blue Dove (T); Paradise Heights (T);
Starhunter (T)

Nick Page
m 07973 339 541

Mick Pantaleo
Gems, The Media House, 87 Glebe Street, Penarth CF64 1EF
t 029 2071 0770 **f** 029 2071 0771
e gems@gems-agency.co.uk **w** www.gems-agency.co.uk
Credits Relic Hunter (T); I Saw You (T); Metrosexuality (T); Tom And Thomas (F)

Bill Payn
Suz Cruz, Halliford Studios, Manygate Lane, Shepperton TW17 9EG
t 01932 252577 **f** 01932 253323 **m** 07956 485593
e zoe@suzcruz.co.uk **w** www.suzcruz.co.uk

Eugenio Perez
Gems, The Media House, 87 Glebe Street, Penarth CF64 1EF
t 029 2071 0770 **f** 029 2071 0771
e gems@gems-agency.co.uk **w** www.gems-agency.co.uk
Credits Dream Team (F); Double Take (F)

Kieron Phipps
EXEC, 6 Travis Court, Farnham Royal SL2 3SB
t 01753 646677 **f** 01753 646770
e sue@execmanagement.co.uk **w** www.execmanagement.co.uk

Marcus Prince
Gems, The Media House, 87 Glebe Street, Penarth CF64 1EF
t 029 2071 0770 **f** 029 2071 0771
e gems@gems-agency.co.uk **w** www.gems-agency.co.uk
Credits Love In The Twenty-First Century (D); Casualty (T); Born And Bred (T);
EastEnders (T)

Matthew Purves
97 Studley Grange Road, London W7 2LU
t 020 8567 2923 **f** 020 8567 2923 **m** 07976 728752
e matty@mpurves.demon.co.uk
Agent Gems, The Media House, 87 Glebe Street, Penarth
CF64 1EF
t 029 2071 0770 **f** 029 2071 0771
e gems@gems-agency.co.uk **w** www.gems-agency.co.uk
Credits The Bill (T); Casualty (T); Care (T); Rehab (T)

Aidan Quinn
t 020 7625 9867 **m** 07957 361 818
e aidanquinn@onetel.net.uk
Agent Wizzo & Co, 35 Old Compton Street, London W1D 5JX
t 020 7437 2055 **f** 020 7437 2066
e wizzo@wizzoandco.co.uk **w** www.wizzoandco.co.uk

Stuart Renfrew
EXEC, 6 Travis Court, Farnham Royal SL2 3SB
t 01753 646677 **f** 01753 646770
e sue@execmanagement.co.uk **w** www.execmanagement.co.uk

Francesco Reidy
EXEC, 6 Travis Court, Farnham Royal SL2 3SB
t 01753 646677 **f** 01753 646770
e sue@execmanagement.co.uk **w** www.execmanagement.co.uk

Julian Richards
Callbox Communications Limited, 66 Shepperton Studios,
Studios Road, Shepperton TW17 0QD
t 01932 592572 **f** 01932 569655 **m** 07710 572572
e callboxdiary@btinternet.com **w** www.callboxdiary.co.uk

Carrie Rodd
Gems, The Media House, 87 Glebe Street, Penarth CF64 1EF
t 029 2071 0770 **f** 029 2071 0771
e gems@gems-agency.co.uk **w** www.gems-agency.co.uk
Credits Thrilling Chillers (T); Bring Me The Head Of Mavis Davies (F); Office
Gossip (T); Flight (F)

Deborah Saban
International Creative Management Ltd, Oxford House,
76 Oxford Street, London W1D 1BS
t 020 7636 6565 **f** 020 7323 0101 **w** www.icmlondon.co.uk
Credits Shakespeare In Love (F); Captain Corelli's Mandolin (F); The Good Thief (F)

Martin Serene
Suz Cruz, Halliford Studios, Manygate Lane, Shepperton TW17 9EG
t 01932 252577 **f** 01932 253323 **m** 07956 485593
e zoe@suzcruz.co.uk **w** www.suzcruz.co.uk

Ken Shane
97 Kings Ave, London SW4 8EL
t 020 8678 6652 **f** 020 8678 6652 **m** 07831 580 482
e kshane1961@aol.com

James Sharpe
The Production Switchboard, North Down, Down Lane,
Compton GU3 1DN
t 01483 812011 **f** 01483 812027
e aly@productionswitch.freeserve.co.uk
Credits Muraspec - Wall Coverings (C); Ryze - In My Life (M); Funk Foolin' (M)

Suzanna Shaw
Gems, The Media House, 87 Glebe Street, Penarth CF64 1EF
t 029 2071 0770 **f** 029 2071 0771
e gems@gems-agency.co.uk **w** www.gems-agency.co.uk
Credits Maria's Child (T); The Brontes (T); Brothers (F); Dead In The Water (F)

James Sherwood
Wizzo & Co, 35 Old Compton Street, London W1D 5JX
t 020 7437 2055 **f** 020 7437 2066
e wizzo@wizzoandco.co.uk **w** www.wizzoandco.co.uk

Adam Somner
EXEC, 6 Travis Court, Farnham Royal SL2 3SB
t 01753 646677 **f** 01753 646770
e sue@execmanagement.co.uk **w** www.execmanagement.co.uk

Martin Sosa
EXEC, 6 Travis Court, Farnham Royal SL2 3SB
t 01753 646677 **f** 01753 646770
e sue@execmanagement.co.uk **w** www.execmanagement.co.uk

Peter Stenning
2 Bullsfield, The Green, Newick BN8 4LA
t 01825 724225 **f** 01825 723354 **m** 07768 843 538
Credits Moi Cesar (F); Fidel! (F); Ali G Inda House (F); Bertie and Elizabeth (T)

Roy P Stevens
EXEC, 6 Travis Court, Farnham Royal SL2 3SB
t 01753 646677 **f** 01753 646770
e sue@execmanagement.co.uk **w** www.execmanagement.co.uk

Gareth Tandy
EXEC, 6 Travis Court, Farnham Royal SL2 3SB
t 01753 646677 **f** 01753 646770
e sue@execmanagement.co.uk **w** www.execmanagement.co.uk

Mechael Taylor
McKinney Macartney Management Ltd, The Barley Mow
Centre, 10 Barley Mow Passage, London W4 4PH
t 020 8995 4747 **f** 020 8995 2414
e fkb@mmtechsrep.demon.co.uk **w** www.mckinneymacartney.com

Henry Tomlinson
Bookends, 83 Maynard Drive, St Albans AL1 2JX
t 01727 841177 **e** bookgold@bookends.fsbusiness.co.uk

Guy Travers
Creative Media Management, Unit 3B, Walpole Court, Ealing
Studios, Ealing Green, London W5 5ED
t 020 8584 5363 **f** 020 8566 5554
e enquiries@creativemediamanagement.com
Credits Stander (F); House Of Mirth (F); Conspiracy - The Meeting at Wansee
(F); A Knight's Tale (F)

Lee Trevor
EXEC, 6 Travis Court, Farnham Royal SL2 3SB
t 01753 646677 **f** 01753 646770
e sue@execmanagement.co.uk **w** www.execmanagement.co.uk

David Tringham
40 Langthorne Street, Fulham, London SW6 6JY
t 020 7385 4975

Joe Tumelty (JTTVF)
12 East Drive, Edgbaston, Birmingham B5 7RX
t 0121 472 3402 **m** 07710 160715 **e** joetumelty@aol.com
Credits RTE Productions; Sport - Outside Broadcast (T); BBC News & Current
Affairs (T); Crossroads (T)

Andrew Tutte
The Production Switchboard, North Down, Down Lane,
Compton GU3 1DN
t 01483 812011 **f** 01483 812027
e aly@productionswitch.freeserve.co.uk
Credits Labour Party (C); Stereo MC's (M); Saatchi & Saatchi (C)

Gerard Wall
Callbox Communications Limited, 66 Shepperton Studios,
Studios Road, Shepperton TW17 0QD
t 01932 592572 **f** 01932 569655 **m** 07710 572572
e callboxdiary@btinternet.com **w** www.callboxdiary.co.uk

Barry Wasserman
EXEC, 6 Travis Court, Farnham Royal SL2 3SB
t 01753 646677 **f** 01753 646770
e sue@execmanagement.co.uk **w** www.execmanagement.co.uk

Charlie Watson
7 Garfield Road, London SW11 5PL
t 020 7228 8370 **f** 020 7228 8370 **m** 07973 793411
e charlie.watson1@btinternet.com
Agent Creative Media Management, Unit 3B, Walpole Court,
Ealing Studios, Ealing Green, London W5 5ED
t 020 8584 5363 **f** 020 8566 5554
e enquiries@creativemediamanagement.com
Credits A Sound Of Thunder (F); The Musketeer (F); Fear Dot Com (F)

Julia Waye
EXEC, 6 Travis Court, Farnham Royal SL2 3SB
t 01753 646677 **f** 01753 646770
e sue@execmanagement.co.uk **w** www.execmanagement.co.uk

Gary White
22 Almington Street, London N4 3BG
t 020 7272 5667 **f** 020 7272 5667 **m** 07836 538002
e garywhite@onetel.net.uk
Agent ADS, Shepperton Studios, Shepperton Road,
Shepperton TW17 0QD
t 01932 592303 **f** 01932 592492 **e** ads@carlincrew.co.uk
Credits Governor II (T); Feast of July (F); Crocodile Shoes II (T); Fatherland (F)

Mat Whitley
Wizzo & Co, 35 Old Compton Street, London W1D 5JX
t 020 7437 2055 **f** 020 7437 2066
e wizzo@wizzoandco.co.uk **w** www.wizzoandco.co.uk

Gerry Wigzell
Gems, The Media House, 87 Glebe Street, Penarth CF64 1EF
t 029 2071 0770 **f** 029 2071 0771
e gems@gems-agency.co.uk **w** www.gems-agency.co.uk
Credits Little Big Man (T); Men Only (T); Tracy Beaker (T); The Bill (T)

Celia-Jane Willett
Gems, The Media House, 87 Glebe Street, Penarth CF64 1EF
t 029 2071 0770 **f** 029 2071 0771
e gems@gems-agency.co.uk **w** www.gems-agency.co.uk
Credits Belonging (T); Clocking Off (T); Score (T); Ghosthunters (T)

Marc Wilson
Callbox Communications Limited, 66 Shepperton Studios,
Studios Road, Shepperton TW17 0QD
t 01932 592572 **f** 01932 569655 **m** 07710 572572
e callboxdiary@btinternet.com **w** www.callboxdiary.co.uk

Stephen Woolfenden
Carlin Crew Ltd, Shepperton Studios, Studios Road,
Shepperton TW17 0QD
t 01932 568268 **f** 01932 571109
e carlin@netcomuk.co.uk **w** www.carlincrew.com

Directors 2nd Assistant

Bart Bailey
EXEC, 6 Travis Court, Farnham Royal SL2 3SB
t 01753 646677 **f** 01753 646770
e sue@execmanagement.co.uk **w** www.execmanagement.co.uk

Mark Bond
Gems, The Media House, 87 Glebe Street, Penarth CF64 1EF
t 029 2071 0770 **f** 029 2071 0771
e gems@gems-agency.co.uk **w** www.gems-agency.co.uk
Credits Family Affairs (T); Crossroads (T); Casualty (T)

Shea Bradley
Flat 10, Block C, Peabody Trust Estate, Wild Street, London
WC2B 4AF
t 020 7836 2617 **m** 07887 920147
Agent The Production Switchboard, North Down, Down Lane,
Compton GU3 1DN
t 01483 812011 **f** 01483 812027
e aly@productionswitch.freeserve.co.uk
Credits Wrigleys (C); DFS (C); British Gas (C)

Emmet Cahill
The Production Switchboard, North Down, Down Lane,
Compton GU3 1DN
t 01483 812011 **f** 01483 812027
e aly@productionswitch.freeserve.co.uk
Credits Three Non Blondes (T); The Day Britain Stopped (D); Peugeot (C)

Caspar Campbell
Callbox Communications Limited, 66 Shepperton Studios,
Studios Road, Shepperton TW17 0QD
t 01932 592572 **f** 01932 569655 **m** 07710 572572
e callboxdiary@btinternet.com **w** www.callboxdiary.co.uk

Matthew Carver
The Production Switchboard, North Down, Down Lane,
Compton GU3 1DN
t 01483 812011 **f** 01483 812027
e aly@productionswitch.freeserve.co.uk
Credits The Inspector Linley Mysteries (T); Luminal (F); Promoted To Glory (T)

Paul Cathie
Suz Cruz, Halliford Studios, Manygate Lane, Shepperton TW17 9EG
t 01932 252577 **f** 01932 253323 **m** 07956 485593
e zoe@suzcruz.co.uk **w** www.suzcruz.co.uk

Brigitte Chandless
Callbox Communications Limited, 66 Shepperton Studios,
Studios Road, Shepperton TW17 0QD
t 01932 592572 **f** 01932 569655 **m** 07710 572572
e callboxdiary@btinternet.com **w** www.callboxdiary.co.uk

Adam Coop
EXEC, 6 Travis Court, Farnham Royal SL2 3SB
t 01753 646677 **f** 01753 646770
e sue@execmanagement.co.uk **w** www.execmanagement.co.uk

Andy Cornforth
Gems, The Media House, 87 Glebe Street, Penarth CF64 1EF
t 029 2071 0770 **f** 029 2071 0771
e gems@gems-agency.co.uk **w** www.gems-agency.co.uk
Credits Brookside (T); Care (T); Hollyoaks (T)

Jane Denholm
Experience Counts - Call Me Ltd, 5th Floor, 41-42 Berners
Street, London W1P 3AA
t 020 7637 8112 **f** 020 7580 2582

Sara Desmond
37 Hubert Grove, Clapham, London SW9 9PA
t 020 7978 8664 **m** 07973 412691
e sara.desmond@virgin.net
Credits 28 Days Later (F); Gosford Park (F); Band Of Brothers (T)

Geoff Dibben
EXEC, 6 Travis Court, Farnham Royal SL2 3SB
t 01753 646677 **f** 01753 646770
e sue@execmanagement.co.uk **w** www.execmanagement.co.uk

William Dutton
Gems, The Media House, 87 Glebe Street, Penarth CF64 1EF
t 029 2071 0770 **f** 029 2071 0771
e gems@gems-agency.co.uk **w** www.gems-agency.co.uk
Credits The Arnando Ianucci Show (T); Sarajevo (F); Foyles War I & II (T); Liam (F)

Al Edirisinghe
Callbox Communications Limited, 66 Shepperton Studios,
Studios Road, Shepperton TW17 0QD
t 01932 592572 **f** 01932 569655 **m** 07710 572572
e callboxdiary@btinternet.com **w** www.callboxdiary.co.uk

Carlos Fidel
Callbox Communications Ltd, 66 Shepperton Studios, Studios
Road, Shepperton TW17 0QD
t 01932 592572 **f** 01932 569655 **m** 07710 572572
e callboxdiary@btinternet.com **w** www.callboxdiary.co.uk

Richard Goodwin
EXEC, 6 Travis Court, Farnham Royal SL2 3SB
t 01753 646677 **f** 01753 646770
e sue@execmanagement.co.uk **w** www.execmanagement.co.uk

Sallie Hard
Callbox Communications Limited, 66 Shepperton Studios,
Studios Road, Shepperton TW17 0QD
t 01932 592572 **f** 01932 569655 **m** 07710 572572
e callboxdiary@btinternet.com **w** www.callboxdiary.co.uk

Philip Hartley
25 Hurst Lane, East Molesey KT8 9EA
t 020 8873 7690 **m** 07831 178866 **e** philhartley@lineone.net

Ben Howarth
EXEC, 6 Travis Court, Farnham Royal SL2 3SB
t 01753 646677 **f** 01753 646770
e sue@execmanagement.co.uk **w** www.execmanagement.co.uk

Matt Huntley
Top Flat, 5 Guernsey Grove, London SE24 9DF
t 020 8488 2105 **m** 07967 192227
e aly@productionswitch.freeserve.co.uk
Agent The Production Switchboard, North Down, Down Lane,
Compton GU3 1DN
t 01483 812011 **f** 01483 812027
e aly@productionswitch.freeserve.co.uk
Credits Barclay Card (C); Max Factor (C); Sainsbury's (C)

Mark Inglis
EXEC, 6 Travis Court, Farnham Royal SL2 3SB
t 01753 646677 **f** 01753 646770
e sue@execmanagement.co.uk **w** www.execmanagement.co.uk

Diane Kasperowicz
Gems, The Media House, 87 Glebe Street, Penarth CF64 1EF
t 029 2071 0770 **f** 029 2071 0771
e gems@gems-agency.co.uk **w** www.gems-agency.co.uk
Credits The Royal Family (T); Bob Martin II (T); Paradise Heights (T); Doctors (T)

Trevor Kaye
60 Richmond Gardens, Harrow HA3 6AJ
t 020 8954 2763 **f** 020 8933 4519 **m** 07703 258595
e trevorkaye@compuserve.com

Mark Layton
EXEC, 6 Travis Court, Farnham Royal SL2 3SB
t 01753 646677 **f** 01753 646770
e sue@execmanagement.co.uk **w** www.execmanagement.co.uk

Richard Lynn
Gems, The Media House, 87 Glebe Street, Penarth CF64 1EF
t 029 2071 0770 **f** 029 2071 0771
e gems@gems-agency.co.uk **w** www.gems-agency.co.uk
Credits Family Affairs (T); Casualty (T)

Finn MacGrath
8 Paramount Apartments, 42 Putney Hill, London SW15 6AQ
t 020 8789 3479 **f** 020 7937 3938 **m** 07778 933782
e finn@johnfinn.freeserve.co.uk
Credits Neverland (F); Bridget Jones's Diary (F); Iris (F); Billy Elliot (F)

Argyle Mallett
Callbox Communications Ltd, 66 Shepperton Studios, Studios
Road, Shepperton TW17 0QD
t 01932 592572 **f** 01932 569655 **m** 07710 572572
e callboxdiary@btinternet.com **w** www.callboxdiary.co.uk

Stephen Money
Callbox Communications Limited, 66 Shepperton Studios,
Studios Road, Shepperton TW17 0QD
t 01932 592572 **f** 01932 569655 **m** 07710 572572
e callboxdiary@btinternet.com **w** www.callboxdiary.co.uk

Carla de Nicola
Wizzo & Co, 35 Old Compton Street, London W1D 5JX
t 020 7437 2055 **f** 020 7437 2066
e wizzo@wizzoandco.co.uk **w** www.wizzoandco.co.uk

Alexander Oakley
37 Hubert Grove, Clapham, London SW9 9PA
t 020 7978 8664 **f** 020 7733 6709 **m** 07976 242982
e aloakley@yahoo.co.uk
Credits The Four Feathers (F); 28 Days Later (F); Love Actually (F)

Tony Payne
Callbox Communications Limited, 66 Shepperton Studios,
Studios Road, Shepperton TW17 0QD
t 01932 592572 **f** 01932 569655 **m** 07710 572572
e callboxdiary@btinternet.com **w** www.callboxdiary.co.uk

Louis Pazos
144 Brantley Road, Witton, Birmingham B6 7DP
t 0121 240 2771 **f** 0121 240 2771 **m** 07799 323825
e lpazos@hotmail.com
Credits Multimedia Expo (I); The Perfect Host - Langkawi Malaysia (I); Trapeze -
Bank Bumi Commerce (C); Big Time - Vidal Sassoon (C)

Sam Powell
6 Glamorgan Road, Hampton Hill, Kingston-upon-Thames KT1 4HP
t 020 8979 8599 **f** 020 8977 9441 **m** 07976 306421
Agent The Production Switchboard, North Down, Down Lane,
Compton GU3 1DN
t 01483 812011 **f** 01483 812027
e aly@productionswitch.freeserve.co.uk
Credits Sarah Connor (M); Blue Featuring Elton John - Sorry Seems To Be...
(M); Gareth Gates (M)

Danny Pruett
Gems, The Media House, 87 Glebe Street, Penarth CF64 1EF
t 029 2071 0770 **f** 029 2071 0771
e gems@gems-agency.co.uk **w** www.gems-agency.co.uk
Credits Frightmares (T)

Alex Rendell
Callbox Communications Ltd, 66 Shepperton Studios, Studios
Road, Shepperton TW17 0QD
t 01932 592572 **f** 01932 569655 **m** 07710 572572
e callboxdiary@btinternet.com **w** www.callboxdiary.co.uk

Nathan Richards
Gems, The Media House, 87 Glebe Street, Penarth CF64 1EF
t 029 2071 0770 **f** 029 2071 0771
e gems@gems-agency.co.uk **w** www.gems-agency.co.uk
Credits Sausalito (F); Haiku Tunnel (F); Nash Bridges (T); Woman on Top (F)

Sian Robinson
Yr Uncorn, Pengelli Wyn, Ffordd Bethel, Caernarfon LL55 1EA
t 01286 673584 **m** 07702 341930 **e** sianrobinson@yahoo.co.uk

Tom Rye
14 Glynswood, Chalfont St Peter, Gerrads Cross SL9 0DP
t 01753 885075 **f** 01753 885075 **m** 07734 648705
e tom_rye@hotmail.com
Credits Spellits (T); Dream Team (T)

Niveen Saleh
Callbox Communications Ltd, 66 Shepperton Studios, Studios
Road, Shepperton TW17 0QD
t 01932 592572 **f** 01932 569655 **m** 07710 572572
e callboxdiary@btinternet.com **w** www.callboxdiary.co.uk

Nickie Sault
EXEC, 6 Travis Court, Farnham Royal SL2 3SB
t 01753 646677 **f** 01753 646770
e sue@execmanagement.co.uk **w** www.execmanagement.co.uk

Mark Sinton
Callbox Communications Limited, 66 Shepperton Studios,
Studios Road, Shepperton TW17 0QD
t 01932 592572 **f** 01932 569655 **m** 07710 572572
e callboxdiary@btinternet.com **w** www.callboxdiary.co.uk

Roger Skuse
Gems, The Media House, 87 Glebe Street, Penarth CF64 1EF
t 029 2071 0770 **f** 029 2071 0771
e gems@gems-agency.co.uk **w** www.gems-agency.co.uk
Credits Silent Witness (T); Crossroads (T); The Bill (T); Casualty (T)

Charly Smith
Wizzo & Co, 35 Old Compton Street, London W1D 5JX
t 020 7437 2055 **f** 020 7437 2066
e wizzo@wizzoandco.co.uk **w** www.wizzoandco.co.uk

Alex Streeter
Callbox Communications Limited, 66 Shepperton Studios,
Studios Road, Shepperton TW17 0QD
t 01932 592572 **f** 01932 569655 **m** 07710 572572
e callboxdiary@btinternet.com **w** www.callboxdiary.co.uk

Daren Thomas
17 Hargrave Road, Maidenhead SL6 6JR
t 01628 783539 **m** 07971 016361
e daren.thomas@ntworld.com
Agent The Production Switchboard, Northdown, Down Lane,
Compton GU3 1DN
t 01483 812011 **f** 01483 812027
e aly@productionswitch.freeserve.co.uk
Credits The Crooked Man (T); British Gas - Warmer Homes (C); EastEnders (T)

Davide Tozzi
The Production Switchboard, North Down, Down Lane,
Compton GU3 1DN
t 01483 812011 **f** 01483 812027
e aly@productionswitch.freeserve.co.uk
Credits General Electric (C); Terry's Chocolate Orange (C); IBM (C)

Patti Walker-Booth
Agent Experience Counts - Call Me Ltd, 5th Floor,
41-42 Berners Street, London W1P 3AA
t 020 7637 8112 **f** 020 7580 2582
Agent Gems, The Media House, 87 Glebe Street,
Penarth CF64 1EF
t 029 2071 0770 **f** 029 2071 0771
e gems@gems-agency.co.uk **w** www.gems-agency.co.uk
Credits Story Of Tracy Beaker (T); Men Only (T); The Troll (F); Julie And The
Cadillacs (F)

Anthony Whiteway
The Garden Flat, 22 kidbrooke Park Road, Blackheath, London
SE3 0LW
m 07980 586787 **e** twhiteway@hotmail.com
Credits Come Back Around - Feeder (M); Burst Pipe - British Telecom (C);
Hungryman (C); Yellow Pages (C)

Josh Wilkins
Callbox Communications Limited, 66 Shepperton Studios,
Studios Road, Shepperton TW17 0QD
t 01932 592572 **f** 01932 569655 **m** 07710 572572
e callboxdiary@btinternet.com **w** www.callboxdiary.co.uk

Rob Willden
EXEC, 6 Travis Court, Farnham Royal SL2 3SB
t 01753 646677 **f** 01753 646770
e sue@execmanagement.co.uk **w** www.execmanagement.co.uk

Directors 3rd Assistant

Miranda Bowen
Wizzo & Co, 35 Old Compton Street, London W1D 5JX
t 020 7437 2055 **f** 020 7437 2066
e wizzo@wizzoandco.co.uk **w** www.wizzoandco.co.uk

Andrew Cameron
Wizzo & Co, 35 Old Compton Street, London W1D 5JX
t 020 7437 2055 **f** 020 7437 2066
e wizzo@wizzoandco.co.uk **w** www.wizzoandco.co.uk

Adam Coop
The Mollies, Nash Lee, Wendover HP22 6BG
t 01296 625414 **f** 01296 696323 **m** 07958 474079
e adam@angelicfilms.co.uk **w** www.angelicfilms.co.uk
Credits Dinotopia (T); Tomorrow La Scala (F); Jonathan Creek IV (T); Garth
Marengui's The Told (T)

Matt Cusworth
186 Balden Road, Harborne, Birmingham B32 2EU
t 0121 682 2664 **f** 0121 682 2664 **m** 07905 302799
e cussy@hotmail.com
Credits Popcorn (T); Judge John Deeds (T); Doctors (T); Forsythe Saga (T)

Albion Gray
Wizzo & Co, 35 Old Compton Street, London W1D 5JX
t 020 7437 2055 **f** 020 7437 2066
e wizzo@wizzoandco.co.uk **w** www.wizzoandco.co.uk

Anya Gripari
EXEC, 6 Travis Court, Farnham Royal SL2 3SB
t 01753 646677 **f** 01753 646770
e sue@execmanagement.co.uk **w** www.execmanagement.co.uk

Ellena Faith Harris
7 Vale Mill Lane, Crossroads With Lees, Haworth, Keighley BD22 OEF
t 01535 642750 **m** 07808 860564 **e** ellena_8@hotmail.com
Credits The Glass (T); Rockface (I); Only Fools And Horses (T)

James Harvey
The Production Switchboard, North Down, Down Lane, Compton GU3 1DN
t 01483 812011 **f** 01483 812027
e aly@productionswitch.freeserve.co.uk
Credits Asda (C); Edwin Collins (M); The Doves (M)

Christopher Hughes
EXEC, 6 Travis Court, Farnham Royal SL2 3SB
t 01753 646677 **f** 01753 646770
e sue@execmanagement.co.uk **w** www.execmanagement.co.uk

Robert Hunter
Bank House, 1 Churton Street, London SW1V 2JX
t 020 7976 5160 **m** 07816 346266
Agent The Production Switchboard, North Down, Down Lane, Compton GU3 1DN
t 01483 812011 **f** 01483 812027
e aly@productionswitch.freeserve.co.uk
Credits If Only (F); Murder Rooms II (T); Ultimate Force (T)

Alex Kirby
EXEC, 6 Travis Court, Farnham Royal SL2 3SB
t 01753 646677 **f** 01753 646770
e sue@execmanagement.co.uk **w** www.execmanagement.co.uk

Graham Linton
Gems, The Media House, 87 Glebe Street, Penarth CF64 1EF
t 029 2071 0770 **f** 029 2071 0771
e gems@gems-agency.co.uk **w** www.gems-agency.co.uk
Credits Auf Wiedersehen Pet (T); Is Harry On The Boat (T)

Eliot Mathews
The Production Switchboard, North Down, Down Lane, Compton GU3 1DN
t 01483 812011 **f** 01483 812027
e aly@productionswitch.freeserve.co.uk
Credits Hornblower (F); Helen Of Troy (T); Johnny English (F)

Simon Maxwell
Wizzo & Co, 35 Old Compton Street, London W1D 5JX
t 020 7437 2055 **f** 020 7437 2066
e wizzo@wizzoandco.co.uk **w** www.wizzoandco.co.uk

Jamie McKay-Haynes
115A Turnpike Lane, London N8 OOU
t 020 8342 9316 **m** 07887 563564 **e** jamiemch@mail.com
Credits Midsomer Murders (T); Possession (F); Foyle's War (T); 2000 Acres Of Sky - Series 3 (T)

James Mellor
85 Becontree Avenue, Dagenham RM8 2UJ
t 020 8597 1411 **m** 07887 994790 **e** jam22tv@tiscali.co.uk
Credits London's Burning Series XIV (T); Last Of The Summer Wire (T); Dots Story - EastEnders Bubble (T)

Steven Sander
Wizzo & Co, 35 Old Compton Street, London W1D 5JX
t 020 7437 2055 **f** 020 7437 2066
e wizzo@wizzoandco.co.uk **w** www.wizzoandco.co.uk

Lynne Tremain
Gems, The Media House, 87 Glebe Street, Penarth CF64 1EF
t 029 2071 0770 **f** 029 2071 0771
e gems@gems-agency.co.uk **w** www.gems-agency.co.uk
Credits Grange Hill (T); Family Affairs (T); The Bill (T); Holby City (T)

Directors
Commercials & Promos

Michael Anderson
Glebe House, Brookhouse Road, Framfield TN22 5NH
t 01825 890253 **f** 01825 890253 **m** 07768 356073
e michaelanderson@dialstart.net
Credits Towering Vision (S); Echoes (F); Gulag (F)

Jeff Boult
Victoria House, Wards Cross, Hurst RGo oDS
t 0118 934 1932 **m** 07768 114 556 **e** jeff@jeffboult.co.uk
Credits ASPIRA (I); 24 Hours (C); Welcome To Compass Group (C)

Sarah Bowen
m 07949 251680 **e** sarahbowen@madasafish.com
Credits Daze (S); Jarcrew (M); Shotgun Slideshow (T); One Click (I)

Champagne Film & Television Productions
Grosvenor House, 19 Westham Road, Weymouth DT4 8NU
t 01305 750100 **f** 01305 750102 **m** 07836 600 112
e info@filmaker.co.uk **w** www.filmaker.co.uk
Contact Rob Goodwin, Producer/Director

Allen Coulter
Hungryman UK, 19 Grafton Mews, London W1T 5JB
t 020 7380 8280 **f** 020 7380 8299
e mail@hungryman.com **w** www.hungryman.com

Michael Cuesta
Hungryman UK, 19 Grafton Mews, London W1T 5JB
t 020 7380 8280 **f** 020 7380 8299
e mail@hungryman.com **w** www.hungryman.com

Richard Dale
Garden Films, 34 Lexington Street, London W1F OLH
t 020 7439 4080 **f** 020 7439 4083
e garden@gardenfilms.com
Credits Teachers (T); Walking With Cavemen (D); The Human Body (D)

Darling Films
12 Cambridge Square, London W2 2QE
t 020 7402 3111 **f** 020 7402 7876 **e** darlingfilms@btinternet.com

Michel Gemmell
88 Albert Road, Caversham, Reading RG4 7PL
t 0118 947 5600 **f** 0118 947 5600 **m** 07860 393945
e michel.gemmell@mg-films.co.uk **w** www.mg-films.co.uk
Credits Maxivision (C); Burton (I)

Hammer & Tongs
C/o Holbourn Studios, 49-50 Eagle Wharf Road, London N1 7ED
t 020 7684 0011 **e** post@tongs.net **w** www.tongsville.com
Contact Nick Goldsmith, Producer; Garth Jennings, Director
Credits Badly Drawn Boy: Spitting in the Wind (M); Polish Plums (Experimental Film)

Owen Harris
Hungryman UK, 19 Grafton Mews, London W1T 5JB
t 020 7380 8280 **f** 020 7380 8299
e oharris@hunrgyman.com **w** www.hungryman.com

Jay Jeffrey Jones
Thornbank, 193 Victoria Road, Dartmouth TQ6 9EQ
t 01752 664262 **e** jjones@clearcommunications.co.uk

KSA Film & Video
63 Dean Street, London W1D 4QG
t +44 20 7287 4001 **f** +44 20 7287 4002
e info@ksa-film.co.uk **w** www.ksa-film.co.uk
Contact Jo Manser; David Kellehar; Adele Longden; John Snelgrove

David Levin
Hungry Man UK, 19 Grafton Mews, London W1T 5JB
t 020 7380 8280 **f** 020 7380 8299 **w** www.hungryman.com

Jason Martin
Garden Films, 34 Lexington Street, London W1F 0LH
t 020 7439 4080 **f** 020 7439 4083 **e** garden@gardenfilms.com

Kevin McKiernan
Garden Films, 34 Lexington Street, London W1F 0LH
t 020 7439 4080 **f** 020 7439 4083
e garden@gardenfilms.com
Credits Ericsson (C); Ford (C); Sky (I); Lost Dances Of Egon Schiele (T)

Bennett Miller
Hungry Man UK, 19 Grafton Mews, London W1T 5JB
t 020 7380 8280 **f** 020 7380 8299 **w** www.hungryman.com

Open Gate
15 Marmora Road, East Dulwich, London SE22 0RX
t 020 8299 3203 **m** 07946 352646 **e** opengateml@hotmail.com
Contact Mike Lithgow, Director
Credits Mario Andretti (C); Happit (C); Ice Hockey (C); Spaghetti Speed Cop (C)

Daniel Outram
Production Switchboard, North Down, Down Lane, Compton
GU3 1DN
m 07932 618017
e danieloutram@hotmail.com **w** www.maverickmedia.co.uk
Credits Jesus Bumps (W); Racing Post (S); Rough Trade – How Does It Go? (C)

Brian Percival
Big Fish Management, 55 Bendon Valley, London SW18 4LZ
t 020 8877 7111 **f** 020 8874 6623
e info@bigfishmamagement.com **w** www.bigfishmanagement.com

Hank Perlman
Hungryman UK, 19 Grafton Mews, London W1T 5JB
t 020 7380 8280 **f** 020 7380 8299 **e** mail@hungryman.com
w www.hungryman.com

Marcos Siega
Hungryman UK, 19 Grafton Mews, London W1T 5JB
t 020 7380 8280 **f** 020 7380 8299
e mail@hungryman.com **w** www.hungryman.com

Martin Smith
C/o Independents Management, 10-12 Ettrick Grove, Edinburgh
EH10 5AW
m 07971 230571
e martins_film@yahoo.com **w** www.bentrovato.co.uk
Credits The Black Death (F); 50 Stories - Thirteen:13 (M); Cold Winter - Malcolm
Middleton (M); Stand Up - Smoke (M)

Philip Taylor
17 Westbourne Avenue, London W3 6JL
t 020 8896 0805 **f** 020 8354 0329 **m** 07968 625 634
e philip@taylors.tv **w** www.taylors.tv
Credits Community Forum (I); Department Of Education And Skills - The Big
Idea (I); Harper Collins – The Company of Strangers (C); Shell Renewables -
2002 Into 2003 (I)

taylors.tv
17 Westbourne Avenue, London W3 6JL
t 020 8896 1247 **f** 020 8896 1247 **m** 07968 625634
e info@taylors.tv **w** www.taylors.tv
Contact Ian Puddick, Communications Director; David Taylor, Producer; Philip
Taylor, Creative Director; Lalita Taylor, Producer
Credits Acton Community Forum - Community Forum (I); Shell Renewables -
2002 Into 2003 (I); The Company of Strangers (C); Stephen King's Black House (C)

Peter Thwaites
McKinney Macartney Management Ltd, The Barley Mow
Centre, 10 Barley Mow Passage, London W4 4PH
t 020 8995 4747 **f** 020 8995 2414
e fkb@mmtechsrep.demon.co.uk **w** www.mckinneymacartney.com

Tony Vanden-Ende
The Corner House, Cidermill Lane, Leysbourne, Chipping
Campden GL55 6HL
t 01386 841453 **t** +44 20 **m** 07831 453372
e tonyvandenende@hotmail.com

Videofone Productions
49 Wellington Road, Hampton Hill TW12 1JY
t 020 8977 9112 **f** 020 8943 1147
Contact Sandy Fone, Producer; Simon Fone, Director/Scriptwriter

Scott Vincent
Hungryman UK, 19 Grafton Mews, London W1T 5JB
t 020 7380 8280 **f** 020 7380 8299
e mail@hungryman.com **w** www.hungryman.com

Leia Vogelle
9A Inglebert Street, London EC1R 1XR
t 020 7689 5567 **m** 07960 121234
e leia@leiavogelle.com **w** www.leiavogelle.com
Credits Just The Ticket (C); Jonny Lolly (S); Mary And Her Invisible Date (A);
The Bench (S)

Peter Webber
Garden Films, 34 Lexington Street, London W1F 0LH
t 020 7439 4080 **f** 020 7439 4083 **e** garden@gardenfilms.com
Credits Girl With A Pearl Earring (F); The Stretford Wives (T); Underground (T);
Men Only (T)

Eric Will
22 Clevedon Mansions, Lissenden Gardens, London NW5 1TU
m 07771 788715 **w** www.eric-will.com
Credits LG Flatron (C); Flonase (C); Hyundai (C); Coca Cola (C)

The Workshop Presents
4 Watchfield Court, Sutton Court Road, Chiswick, London W4 4NB
t 020 8747 1363 **e** craiggriffith@fsmail.net
w www.cooltubetheatre.co.uk; www.whatsyourreflection.com
Credits Through The Looking Glass (F); Musicman (C); Radio (C); Gamebox (M)

Directors Film & TV

Keith Ackrill
5 Greenfield Cottages, Scarfield Hill, Alvechurch, Birmingham
B48 7SF
t 0121 445 3563 **f** 0121 445 3563 **m** 07887 698074

Marcus Adams
Peters Fraser & Dunlop, Drury House, 34-43 Russell Street,
London WC2B 5HA
t 020 7344 1000 **f** 020 7836 9543
e postmaster@pfd.co.uk **w** www.pfd.co.uk

Carine Adler
Casarotto Ramsay & Associates Ltd, National House,
60-66 Wardour Street, London W1V 4ND
t 020 7287 4450 **f** 020 7287 9128
e agents@casarotto.uk.com **w** www.casarotto.uk.com

Joe Ahearne
Peters Fraser & Dunlop, Drury House, 34-43 Russell Street,
London WC2B 5HA
t 020 7344 1000 **f** 020 7836 9543
e postmaster@pfd.co.uk **w** www.pfd.co.uk

Jonas Akerlund
Peters Fraser & Dunlop, Drury House, 34-43 Russell Street,
London WC2B 5HA
t 020 7344 1000 **f** 020 7836 9543
e postmaster@pfd.co.uk **w** www.pfd.co.uk

Tim Albery
Cruickshank Cazenove Ltd, 97 Old South Lambeth Road,
London SW8 1XU
t 020 7735 2933 **f** 020 7820 1081 **e** hjcruickshank@aol.com
Credits Siegfried (T); Peter Grimes (T)

Yousaf Ali Khan
Peters Fraser & Dunlop, Drury House, 34-43 Russell Street,
London WC2B 5HA
t 020 7344 1000 **f** 020 7836 9543 **e** postmaster@pfd.co.uk
w www.pfd.co.uk

James Allen
5 Napier Close, Puncknowle, Dorchester DT2 9BQ
t 01308 897755 **f** 01308 897755 **m** 07884 430364

Jon Amiel
t 020 8964 8811 **f** 020 8964 8966
Credits Entrapment (F)

Gordon Anderson
Cruickshank Cazenove Ltd, 97 Old South Lambeth Road,
London SW8 1XU
t 020 7735 2933 **f** 020 7820 1081 **e** hjcruickshank@aol.com
Credits Channel 4 Sitcom Festival (T)

Paul Annett
Peters Fraser & Dunlop, Drury House, 34-43 Russell Street,
London WC2B 5HA
t 020 7344 1000 **f** 020 7836 9543
e postmaster@pfd.co.uk **w** www.pfd.co.uk

Appletree House Productions
26 Dower Park, Windsor SL4 4BQ
t 01753 865736 **m** 07967 990727
Contact John Reardon
Credits Having It Off (T); London's Burning (T); Heartbeat (T); Moving On (T)

Moira Armstrong
10 Ceylon Road, London W14 0PY
f 020 7371 4547 **e** marmst5111@aol.com
Credits Hereafter (T); Tipping The Velvet (T)

Laura Ashton
Peters Fraser & Dunlop, Drury House, 34-43 Russell Street,
London WC2B 5HA
t 020 7344 1000 **f** 020 7836 9543
e postmaster@pfd.co.uk **w** www.pfd.co.uk

Tom Atkinson
1 Trinity Court, Main Road, Colden Common, Winchester SO21 1TJ
t 01962 714359 **e** tom@dtkinsons77.fsnet.co.uk
Credits 100% (T); Television Scrabble (T); Heroes Of Comedy (T); Des O'Connor
At 40 (T)

Michael Attree
14 Oriental Place, Brighton BN1 2LJ
t 01273 885986 **m** 07855 062033
e michaelattree@yahoo.com **w** www.handlebarclub.org.uk
Credits Omnipotence Of A Wet Shave (S); Sex Talk (D); Double Life Of The
English Gentleman (T); The Divine Comedy (D)

David Attwood
International Creative Management Ltd, Oxford House,
76 Oxford Street, London W1D 1BS
t 020 7636 6565 **f** 020 7323 0101 **w** www.icmlondon.co.uk

Shona Auerbach
The Dench Arnold Agency, 24 D'Arblay Street, London W1F 8EH
t 020 7437 4551 **f** 020 7439 1355
e contact@denchanoldagency.co.uk **w** www.dencharnold.co.uk
Credits Seven (F); Seven; Natural History (T)

Michael Austin
Peters Fraser & Dunlop, Drury House, 34-43 Russell Street,
London WC2B 5HA
t 020 7344 1000 **f** 020 7836 9543
e postmaster@pfd.co.uk **w** www.pfd.co.uk

Samina Baig
Peters Fraser & Dunlop, Drury House, 34-43 Russell Street,
London WC2B 5HA
t 020 7344 1000 **f** 020 7836 9543
e postmaster@pfd.co.uk **w** www.pfd.co.uk

Lucy Bailey
Casarotto Ramsay & Associates Ltd, National House,
60-66 Wardour Street, London W1V 4ND
t 020 7287 4450 **f** 020 7287 9128
e agents@casarotto.uk.com **w** www.casarotto.uk.com

Robert Bailey
Curtis Brown, Haymarket House, 28-29 Haymarket, London
SW1Y 4SP
t 020 7396 6600 **f** 020 7396 0110 **e** cb@curtisbrown.co.uk
Credits Casualty (T); The Bill (T); Redcap (T)

Graham Baker
Peters Fraser & Dunlop, Drury House, 34-43 Russell Street,
London WC2B 5HA
t 020 7344 1000 **f** 020 7836 9543
e postmaster@pfd.co.uk **w** www.pfd.co.uk

Justin Baldwin
151 Strand, London WC2R 1HL
t 020 7836 2762 **f** 020 7836 2784

Rob Bangura
The Dench Arnold Agency, 24 D'Arblay Street, London W1F 8EH
t 020 7437 4551 **f** 020 7439 1355
e contact@dencharnoldagency.co.uk **w** www.dencharnold.co.uk

Mike Barker
Peters Fraser & Dunlop, Drury House, 34-43 Russell Street,
London WC2B 5HA
t 020 7344 1000 **f** 020 7836 9543
e postmaster@pfd.co.uk **w** www.pfd.co.uk

John Barlow
Carpenters Cottage, Preshaw Estate, Upham SO32 1SU
t 01962 771971 **f** 01962 771971 **m** 07887 687 081
e johnbarlow66@hotmail.com

Clio Barnard
Curtis Brown, Haymarket House, 28-29 Haymarket, London
SW1Y 4SP
t 020 7396 6600 **f** 020 7396 0110 **e** cb@curtisbrown.co.uk
Credits Random Acts of Intimacy (S); Messiah II (T)

Ian Barnes
Peters Fraser & Dunlop, Drury House, 34-43 Russell Street,
London WC2B 5HA
t 020 7344 1000 **f** 020 7836 9543
e postmaster@pfd.co.uk **w** www.pfd.co.uk

David Barrie

23 Hazelmere Road, London NW6 7HA
t 020 7372 7105 **m** 07775 945302
e david@lusttv.com **w** www.lusttv.co.uk
Credits In Excess: The Death Of Michael Hutchence (D); When Steptoe Met Son (D); Lost Wounds: Secrets Of The Sands (D); Blood Under The Carpet (D)

David Bartlett

20 Kenley Road, St Margaret's, London TW1 1JU
t 020 8891 2066 **m** 07767 250519
e david.bartlett@virgin.net **w** www.kewhavenpictures.com
Credits House Of Horrors (T); Happy Birthday Shakespeare (T); Nightmare Families (D); The Goodbye Plane (S)

Michael J Bassett

Linda Seifert Management, 91 Berwick Street, London
W1F ONE
t 020 7292 7390 **f** 020 7292 7391
e contact@lindaseifert.com **w** www.lindaseifert.com

Colin Bateman

Curtis Brown, Haymarket House, 28-29 Haymarket, London
SW1Y 4SP
t 020 7396 6600 **f** 020 7396 0110 **e** cb@curtisbrown.co.uk
Credits The Baby Snatchers (F); Chapter and Verse (T); Murphy's Law (T)

Otto Bathurst

Peters Fraser & Dunlop, Drury House, 34-43 Russell Street,
London WC2B 5HA
t 020 7344 1000 **f** 020 7836 9543
e postmaster@pfd.co.uk **w** www.pfd.co.uk

Roy Battersby

Peters Fraser & Dunlop, Drury House, 34-43 Russell Street,
London WC2B 5HA
t 020 7344 1000 **f** 020 7836 9543
e postmaster@pfd.co.uk **w** www.pfd.co.uk

Brian Becker

2 Somerville Drive, Sutton Coldfield B73 6JB
t 0121 355 4099 **f** 0121 355 5549 **m** 07836 205050
e info@brianbecker.co.uk **w** www.brianbecker.co.uk
Credits Mole Manor (T); Porsche- The Legend (I); Sightsavers (C)

Alan JW Bell

Linda Seifert Management, 91 Berwick Street, London W1F ONE
t 020 7292 7390 **f** 020 7292 7391
e contact@lindaseifert.com **w** www.lindaseifert.com

Michael Bell

12 Springwood Road, Oakwood, Leeds LS8 2QA
t 0113 265 1221 **m** 07812 069962
e mikebell_uk_2000@yahoo.com

Charles Leigh Bennett

75 Shaw Road, Newbury RG14 1HH
t 01635 44621 **f** 01635 44621 **m** 07050 207659
e charles.leighbennett@btinternet.com
Credits The Killer Behind The Wheel (I); In Safe Hands (I); The Brendan Voyage (T); How We Used To Live (T)

Edward Bennett

Linda Seifert Management, 91 Berwick Street, London W1F ONE
t 020 7292 7390 **f** 020 7292 7391
e contact@lindaseifert.com **w** www.lindaseifert.com

Rodney Bennett

London Management & Representation, 2-4 Noel Street,
London W1F 8GB
t 020 7287 9000 **f** 020 7287 3236

Chris Bernard

The Dench Arnold Agency, 24 D'Arblay Street, London W1F 8EH
t 020 7437 4551 **f** 020 7439 1355
e contact@dencharnoldagency.co.uk **w** www.dencharnold.co.uk

Indra Bhose

C/o Rochelle Stevens & Company, 2 Terretts Place, London N1 1QZ
t 020 7359 3900
e ibhose@hotmail.com **w** www.bhose.btinternet.co.uk
Credits Holby City (T); Bombay Blue (T); The Grand (T); Down To Earth (T)

Bigshot Films Ltd

46 Upper Mall, London W6 9TA
t 020 8748 1626 **m** 07768 700420 **e** bigshot@dircon.co.uk
Contact Jonathan Gershfield, Director
Credits Big Train (T); Dead Ringers (T); Wild West (T)

Olly Blackburn

Peters Fraser & Dunlop, Drury House, 34-43 Russell Street,
London WC2B 5HA
t 020 7344 1000 **f** 020 7836 9543
e postmaster@pfd.co.uk **w** www.pfd.co.uk

Bob Blagden

Widmoor Lodge, Widmoor, Woodburn Common HP10 0JG
t 01628 526312 **f** 01628 526312 **e** readblagden@btinternet.com
Agent Peters Fraser & Dunlop, Drury House, 34-43 Russell
Street, London WC2B 5HA
t 020 7344 1000 **f** 020 7836 9543
e postmaster@pfd.co.uk **w** www.pfd.co.uk
Credits Hope I Die Before I Get Old (T); Ashes And Sand (F); Long Haul (S)

Emma Bodger

Peters Fraser & Dunlop, Drury House, 34-43 Russell Street,
London WC2B 5HA
t 020 7344 1000 **f** 020 7836 9543
e postmaster@pfd.co.uk **w** www.pfd.co.uk

Darrol Blake

Peters Fraser & Dunlop, Drury House, 34-43 Russell Street,
London WC2B 5HA
t 020 7344 1000 **f** 020 7836 9543
e postmaster@pfd.co.uk **w** www.pfd.co.uk

Keith Boak

International Creative Management Ltd, Oxford House,
76 Oxford Street, London W1D 1BS
t 020 7636 6565 **f** 020 7323 0101 **w** www.icmlondon.co.uk

Sylvie Boden

Linda Seifert Management, 91 Berwick Street, London W1F ONE
t 020 7292 7390 **f** 020 7292 7391
e contact@lindaseifert.com **w** www.lindaseifert.com

Emma Bodger

Curtis Brown, Haymarket House, 28-29 Haymarket, London
SW1Y 4SP
t 020 7396 6600 **f** 020 7396 0110 **e** cb@curtisbrown.co.uk
Credits Hollyoaks (T); Brookside (T); Night And Day (T)

Jane Bokova

London Management & Representation, 2-4 Noel Street,
London W1F 8GB
t 020 7287 9000 **f** 020 7287 3236

Christine Booth

78 Yeldham Road, Hammersmith, London W6 8JG
t 020 8748 2733 **f** 020 8748 2733 **m** 07931 366275
e christin@dircon.co.uk
Credits Trevor Bayliss: A Very British Inventor (D); Garden Therapy (D); A Fighting Chance (D); Signs From the Heart (D)

Michael Boyd

Pauline Asper Management, Jacobs Cottage, Reservoir Lane,
Sedlescombe TN33 0PJ
t 01424 870412 **f** 01424 870412 **e** pauline.asper@virgin.net

Marcus Boyle

The Dench Arnold Agency, 24 D'Arblay Street, London W1F 8EH
t 020 7437 4551 **f** 020 7439 1355
e contact@dencharnoldagency.co.uk **w** www.dencharnold.co.uk

Harry Bradbeer
Peters Fraser & Dunlop, Drury House, 34-43 Russell Street,
London WC2B 5HA
t 020 7344 1000 **f** 020 7836 9543
e postmaster@pfd.co.uk **w** www.pfd.co.uk

Ray Brady
8 Cottons Garden, London E2 8DN
t 020 7673 5882
Credits Love Life (F); Kiss Kiss Bang Bang (F); Boy Meets Girl (F)

John Breen
Curtis Brown, Haymarket House, 28-29 Haymarket, London
SW1Y 4SP
t 020 7396 6600 **f** 020 7396 0110 **e** cb@curtisbrown.co.uk
Credits Alone it Stands (F)

David Bridel
Peters Fraser & Dunlop, Drury House, 34-43 Russell Street,
London WC2B 5HA
t 020 7344 1000 **f** 020 7836 9543
e postmaster@pfd.co.uk **w** www.pfd.co.uk

Alan Bridges
London Management & Representation, 2-4 Noel Street,
London W1F 8GB
t 020 7287 9000 **f** 020 7287 3236

Bill Britten
Linda Seifert Management, 91 Berwick Street, London
W1F ONE
t 020 7292 7390 **f** 020 7292 7391
e contact@lindaseifert.com **w** www.lindaseifert.com

Tony Britten
The Old Reading Room, The Street, Brinton, Melton Constable
NR24 2QF
t 01263 862263 **m** 07831 243942 **e** tonybritten@hotmail.com
Credits Boheme (T)

William Brookfield
Peters Fraser & Dunlop, Drury House, 34-43 Russell Street,
London WC2B 5HA
t 020 7344 1000 **f** 020 7836 9543
e postmaster@pfd.co.uk **w** www.pfd.co.uk

Pip Broughton
Peters Fraser & Dunlop, Drury House, 34-43 Russell Street,
London WC2B 5HA
t 020 7344 1000 **f** 020 7836 9543
e postmaster@pfd.co.uk **w** www.pfd.co.uk

Mark Brozel
International Creative Management Ltd, Oxford House,
76 Oxford Street, London W1D 1BS
t 020 7636 6565 **f** 020 7323 0101 **w** www.icmlondon.co.uk

John Bruce
CCA Management, 7 St George's Square, London SW1V 2HX
t 020 7630 6303 **f** 020 7630 7376

Richard Bryan
Newlands Farm, Kerdiston, Reepham NR10 4RX
t 01603 873043 **f** 01603 873046 **m** 07831 661663
e rbryan1000@aol.com
Credits Gerry and the Treatmakers; Junior Masterchef; Masterchef

Paul Bryers
Peters Fraser & Dunlop, Drury House, 34-43 Russell Street,
London WC2B 5HA
t 020 7344 1000 **f** 020 7836 9543
e postmaster@pfd.co.uk **w** www.pfd.co.uk

Frank Budgen
International Creative Management Ltd, Oxford House,
76 Oxford Street, London W1D 1BS
t 020 7636 6565 **f** 020 7323 0101 **w** www.icmlondon.co.uk

Rudolf Buitendach
Top Flat, 191 Archway Road, London N6 5BN
t 020 8347 6811 **f** 020 8347 6811 **m** 07712 044429
e rudolfb@mac.com
Credits Mary (M); Wavy Gravy (M); Suck (S); Expiry Date (S)

Jonathan Bullen
C/o John Noel Management, 10a Belmont Road, London NW1 8HH
t 020 7428 8400 **m** 07973 334 228
e jonathan_bullen@hotmail.com
Credits National Lottery (T); Who Wants To Be A Millionaire? (T); Pop Idol (T)

Rodney Butcher
91 Ashleigh Road, Mortlake, London SW14 8PY
f 020 8876 0647 **m** 07780 675666
e rodneybutcher@btopenworld.com
Credits Pas De Trois (S); Jaguar (C); British Telecom (C); Medicinema (C)

Stephen Butcher
21 Tullaghbrow, Tullaghgarley, Ballymena BT42 2LY
t 028 2563 9479 **f** 028 2563 9479 **m** 07798 528797
e stephen@tullaghbrow.freeserve.co.uk
Credits Ros Na Run (T); Fair City (T); EastEnders (T); Coronation Street (T)

Rena Butterwick
25 Queens Terrace, Isleworth TW7 7DB
t 020 8560 2430 **f** 020 8560 2430
e rena.butterwick@virgin.net

Jez Butterworth
Curtis Brown, Haymarket House, 28-29 Haymarket, London
SW1Y 4SP
t 020 7396 6600 **f** 020 7396 0110 **e** cb@curtisbrown.co.uk
Credits Christmas (T); Birthday Girl (F)

Sue Butterworth
The Dench Arnold Agency, 24 D'Arblay Street, London W1F 8EH
t 020 7437 4551 **f** 020 7439 1355
e contact@dencharnoldagency.co.uk **w** www.dencharnold.co.uk

Tom Butterworth
Curtis Brown, Haymarket House, 28-29 Haymarket, London
SW1Y 4SP
t 020 7396 6600 **f** 020 7396 0110 **e** cb@curtisbrown.co.uk
Credits Hippie Hippie Shake (F)

Nick Bye
London Management & Representation, 2-4 Noel Street,
London W1F 8GB
t 020 7287 9000 **f** 020 7287 3236

Simon Callow
Cruickshank Cazenove Ltd, 97 Old South Lambeth Road,
London SW8 1XU
t 020 7735 2933 **f** 020 7820 1081 **e** hjcruickshank@aol.com
Credits The Ballad Of The Sad Cafe (F)

Tom Cairns
Cruickshank Cazenove Ltd, 97 Old South Lambeth Road,
London SW8 1XU
t 020 7735 2933 **f** 020 7820 1081 **e** hjcruickshank@aol.com
Credits Big Day (S); Amongst Women (T); Trouble In Tahiti (T)

Anya Camilleri
2 Hillside, Highgate Road, London NW5 1QT
t 020 7482 1667 f 020 7482 1668
e anya@sleekpanther.fsnet.co.uk
Agent The Dench Arnold Agency, 24 D'Arblay Street, London W1F 8EH
t 020 7437 4551 f 020 7439 1355
e contact@dencharnoldagency.co.uk w www.dencharnold.co.uk
Credits 2GBS (T); Liverpool 1 (T); Moving On (T); Perfect (T)

Jonny Campbell
Agent Peters Fraser & Dunlop, Drury House, 34-43 Russell Street, London WC2B 5HA
t 020 7344 1000 f 020 7836 9543
e postmaster@pfd.co.uk w www.pfd.co.uk
Agent Pauline Asper Management, 1st Floor, 24 Hanway Street, London W1T 1UH
t 020 7636 1221 f 020 7636 1226 e info@hamiltonasper.co.uk

Corin Campbell Hill
176 Regents Park Road, London NW1 8XP
m 07710 251290 e corina@talk21.com
Credits Criminal (T)

Jo Cantello
Flat 2, 48 Tremadoco Road, London SW4 7LL
m 07818 067 951 e jo_cantello@hotmail.com

Peter Capaldi
Pauline Asper Management, Jacobs Cottage, Reservoir Lane, Sedlescombe TN33 0PJ
t 01424 870412 f 01424 870412 e pauline.asper@virgin.net

Annette Carducci
t 020 8964 8811 f 020 8964 8966

James Carew
10 Wesley Square, Lancaster Road, London W11 1TP
t 020 7221 1645 f 020 7221 1645 m 07939 159286
e nobeastsofierce@freenet.co.uk

Paul Carney
Jessica Carney Associates, Suite 90-92 Kent House, 87 Regent Street, London W1B 4EH
t 020 7434 4143 f 020 7434 4173
e info@jcarneyassociates.co.uk
Credits Dream Team (T); Baby Father (T); Hollyoaks (T)

Peter Cattaneo
International Creative Management Ltd, Oxford House, 76 Oxford Street, London W1D 1BS
t 020 7636 6565 f 020 7323 0101 w www.icmlondon.co.uk

James Cellan Jones
London Management & Representation, 2-4 Noel Street, London W1F 8GB
t 020 7287 9000 f 020 7287 3236

Celtic Broadcasting Ltd (London Office)
3 Church Close, Cuffley EN6 4LS
t 01707 875873 f 01707 888128 e garry.grant@ntlworld.com
Contact Garry Grant, Managing Director
Credits The Other Loch Ness Monster (T); Mario Bava: Master Of The Macabre (T); EBR (T)

Gurinder Chadha
International Creative Management Ltd, Oxford House, 76 Oxford Street, London W1D 1BS
t 020 7636 6565 f 020 7323 0101 w www.icmlondon.co.uk

Ross Chadler
Experience Counts - Call Me Ltd, 5th Floor, 41-42 Berners Street, London W1P 3AA
t 020 7637 8112 f 020 7580 2582

Hazel Chandler
33 Kirkstall Road, London SW2 4HD
t 020 8678 6028 m 07989 414007
e hazel.chandler@btinternet.com
Credits Lumpy Custard's Last Stand (D); Not Forgotten (D); Miracles (D); Comrade (T)

Peter Chelsom
The Dench Arnold Agency, 24 D'Arblay Street, London W1F 8EH
t 020 7437 4551 f 020 7439 1355
e contact@dencharnoldagency.co.uk w www.dencharnold.co.uk

Robert Chetwyn
Casarotto Ramsay & Associates Ltd, National House, 60-66 Wardour Street, London W1V 4ND
t 020 7287 4450 f 020 7287 9128
e agents@casarotto.uk.com w www.casarotto.uk.com

Phil Chilvers
t 020 8878 8033 m 07970 697 775
e phchilvers@aol.com e phil.chilvers@virgin.net
Credits Night Fever (T); Crimewatch UK (T); Top Of The Pops (T)

Chocolate Films Ltd
e info@chocolatefilms.com
Contact Rachel Wang, Director; Mark Currie, Director

Emma Clark
Stonefish Films, 22 Normanby Road, London NW10 1BX
f 020 8452 4487 m 07710 385183 e stonefish.films@virgin.net

Richard Clark
International Creative Management Ltd, Oxford House, 76 Oxford Street, London W1D 1BS
t 020 7636 6565 f 020 7323 0101 w www.icmlondon.co.uk

Sue Clayton
Peters Fraser & Dunlop, Drury House, 34-43 Russell Street, London WC2B 5HA
t 020 7344 1000 f 020 7836 9543
e postmaster@pfd.co.uk w www.pfd.co.uk

Tom Clegg
Peters Fraser & Dunlop, Drury House, 34-43 Russell Street, London WC2B 5HA
t 020 7344 1000 f 020 7836 9543
e postmaster@pfd.co.uk w www.pfd.co.uk

Martyn Coates
155 Waldegrave Road, Teddington TW11 8LU
t 020 8287 2998 m 07831 667757 e martyncoates@mac.com
Credits Art Attack International (T); This Morning (T); Trisha (T); The Big Match (T)

Mike Cocker
Peters Fraser & Dunlop, Drury House, 34-43 Russell Street, London WC2B 5HA
t 020 7344 1000 f 020 7836 9543
e postmaster@pfd.co.uk w www.pfd.co.uk

Barney Cokeliss
Peters Fraser & Dunlop, Drury House, 34-43 Russell Street, London WC2B 5HA
t 020 7344 1000 f 020 7836 9543
e postmaster@pfd.co.uk w www.pfd.co.uk

Aletta Collins
Cruickshank Cazenove Ltd, 97 Old South Lambeth Road, London SW8 1XU
t 020 7735 2933 f 020 7820 1081 e hjcruickshank@aol.com
Credits The Girl In The Red Dress (S)

Tim Conrad
t 020 8960 7645 m 07860 809946 e timconrad2@aol.com
Credits A Different Ball Game (D); The Scariest Places On Earth (D); Watercolour Challenge (T); The Mystic Knights Of Tyr Na Nog (T)

John Crome
Creative Media Management, Unit 3B, Walpole Court, Ealing Studios, Ealing Green, London W5 5ED
t 020 8584 5363 **f** 020 8566 5554
e enquiries@creativemediamanagement.com
Credits Black Beauty (T); Prospects (T); Lovejoy (T)

David Crossman
Experience Counts - Call Me Ltd, 5th Floor, 41-42 Berners Street, London W1P 3AA
t 020 7637 8112 **f** 020 7580 2582

DAA
Dalswinton, London Road, Chesterford CB10 1NY
t 01799 531200 **f** 01799 531221 **m** 07768 821096
e daa@btinternet.com
Contact David Anderson, Director
Credits Ascential Software (I); Royal Garden Hotel (I); Prudential Assurance (I)

Daniel Wilson
40 Rosemont Road, Richmond TW10 6QL
m 07971 075108 **e** dan@wilsond.fslite.co.uk
Credits EastEnders (T); The Mole (T); Emmerdale (T)

Pepe Danquart
The Dench Arnold Agency, 24 D'Arblay Street, London W1F 8EH
t 020 7437 4551 **f** 020 7439 1355
e contact@dencharnoldagency.co.uk **w** www.dencharnold.co.uk

Rachel Das
Peters Fraser & Dunlop, Drury House, 34-43 Russell Street, London WC2B 5HA
t 020 7344 1000 **f** 020 7836 9543
e postmaster@pfd.co.uk **w** www.pfd.co.uk

Howard Davies
Peters Fraser & Dunlop, Drury House, 34-43 Russell Street, London WC2B 5HA
t 020 7344 1000 **f** 020 7836 9543
e postmaster@pfd.co.uk **w** www.pfd.co.uk

Michael Davies
Abbey Lodge, Hollybush Lane, Stoke Bishop, Bristol B59 1BH
t 0117 968 4382 **f** 0117 968 4389
Credits The Red Baron (D); The Real Amy Johnson (D); Officers And Gentlemen (D); The War Behind The Wire (D)

Terence Daw
31 Samuel Manor, Chelmer Village, Chelmsford CN2 6PU
t 01245 493350 **e** td@audiencefilms.co.uk
Agent CCA Management, 7 St George's Square, London SW1V 2HX
t 020 7630 6303 **f** 020 7630 7376
Credits Solea (F); Thief Takers (T); Emmerdale Revenge Video (T); Heartbeat (T)

Jamil Dehlavi
Peters Fraser & Dunlop, Drury House, 34-43 Russell Street, London WC2B 5HA
t 020 7344 1000 **f** 020 7836 9543
e postmaster@pfd.co.uk **w** www.pfd.co.uk

Gary Dell
The Willow, 138 Cock Lane, High Wycombe HP13 7EA
t 01494 817136 **f** 01494 817620 **m** 07768 848526
e gary.dell@virgin.net
Credits Horse Racing (T); London Mayor And Assembly Coverage (T); Friday Night Live (T); 2001 General Election (T)

Savina Dellicour
London Management & Representation, 2-4 Noel Street, London W1F 8GB
t 020 7287 9000 **f** 020 7287 3236
Credits Hollyoaks (T)

Peter Demetris
2 De Morgan Road, London SW6 2RP
t 020 7384 2181 **m** 07831 196346 **e** subs@peterdltd.com
Credits On Air (T); The Jack Docherty Show (T); Can Jam (T); RI:SE (T)

Kate Dennis
Peters Fraser & Dunlop, Drury House, 34-43 Russell Street, London WC2B 5HA
t 020 7344 1000 **f** 020 7836 9543
e postmaster@pfd.co.uk **w** www.pfd.co.uk

Martin Dennis
International Creative Management Ltd, Oxford House, 76 Oxford Street, London W1D 1BS
t 020 7636 6565 **f** 020 7323 0101 **w** www.icmlondon.co.uk

Barry Devlin
Peters Fraser & Dunlop, Drury House, 34-43 Russell Street, London WC2B 5HA
t 020 7344 1000 **f** 020 7836 9543
e postmaster@pfd.co.uk **w** www.pfd.co.uk

Tania Diez
International Creative Management Ltd, Oxford House, 76 Oxford Street, London W1D 1BS
t 020 7636 6565 **f** 020 7323 0101 **w** www.icmlondon.co.uk

Jasmin Dizdar
Casarotto Ramsay & Associates Ltd, National House, 60-66 Wardour Street, London W1V 4ND
t 020 7287 4450 **f** 020 7287 9128
e agents@casarotto.uk.com **w** www.casarotto.uk.com

Alan Dossor
Peters Fraser & Dunlop, Drury House, 34-43 Russell Street, London WC2B 5HA
t 020 7344 1000 **f** 020 7836 9543
e postmaster@pfd.co.uk **w** www.pfd.co.uk

Tony Dow
International Creative Management Ltd, Oxford House, 76 Oxford Street, London W1D 1BS
t 020 7636 6565 **f** 020 7323 0101 **w** www.icmlondon.co.uk

Tim Dowd
International Creative Management Ltd, Oxford House, 76 Oxford Street, London W1D 1BS
t 020 7636 6565 **f** 020 7323 0101 **w** www.icmlondon.co.uk

Duchy Parade Films Ltd
20 Glebe Road, Harrogate HG2 0LZ
t 01423 526835 **f** 01423 526835 **m** 07799 765481
e duchyfilms@aol.com **w** www.duchyparadefilms.co.uk
Contact Peter Kershaw, Producer/Director
Credits Strange Meeting (T); That's Entertainment (T); Just Another Day (T); Wilfred (S)

Alicia Duffy
Peters Fraser & Dunlop, Drury House, 34-43 Russell Street, London WC2B 5HA
t 020 7344 1000 **f** 020 7836 9543
e postmaster@pfd.co.uk **w** www.pfd.co.uk

Ben Duncan
5 Ravensbury Terrace, Wandsworth, London SW18 4RL
t 020 8879 3087 **e** benduncan@tesco.net
Credits Britains Worst... (T); Around With Ellen McArthur (T); Holiday (T)

Jeremy Dyson
Peters Fraser & Dunlop, Drury House, 34-43 Russell Street, London WC2B 5HA
t 020 7344 1000 **f** 020 7836 9543
e postmaster@pfd.co.uk **w** www.pfd.co.uk

Robert Eagle
15 Marlborough Road, London W4 4EU
t 020 8995 1884 **f** 020 8995 5648
e robert@eagletv.co.uk **w** www.eagletv.co.uk

Christiana Ebohon
4 Howell Walk, London SE1 6TL
t 020 7701 5265 **f** 020 7701 5265 **m** 07939 026469
e christiana_ebohon@hotmail.com
Credits Dogma TV: Alister Meek Gets A Result (T); Hollyoaks (T); Doctors (T); EastEnders (T)

David Innes Edwards
Peters Fraser & Dunlop, Drury House, 34-43 Russell Street, London WC2B 5HA
t 020 7344 1000 **f** 020 7836 9543
e postmaster@pfd.co.uk **w** www.pfd.co.uk

Billie Eltringham
Curtis Brown, Haymarket House, 28-29 Haymarket, London SW1Y 4SP
t 020 7396 6600 **f** 020 7396 0110 **e** cb@curtisbrown.co.uk
Credits Closee Encounter (T); The Darkest Light (T); This is not a Love Song (F)

Zak Emerson
International Creative Management Ltd, Oxford House, 76 Oxford Street, London W1D 1BS
t 020 7636 6565 **f** 020 7323 0101 **w** www.icmlondon.co.uk

David Evans
Casarotto Ramsay & Associates Ltd, National House, 60-66 Wardour Street, London W1V 4ND
t 020 7287 4450 **f** 020 7287 9128
e agents@casarotto.uk.com **w** www.casarotto.uk.com

Susan Everett
18 Moorgate Drive, Kippax, Leeds LS25 7QT
t 0113 286 5001 **f** 0113 286 5001 **m** 07946 519824
e susan.everett@ukgateway.net
Credits White Rabbits (S); Moose (S); Puss Puss (S)

Peter Eyre
5 Castle Road, Camberley GU15 2DS
t 0 1276 24961 **m** 07754 277088
e post@petereyre.co.uk **w** www.petereyre.co.uk
Credits Trivial Pursuit (T); Mad About Pets (T); Dimbleby (T); Art Attack (T)

Ferdinand Fairfax
Peters Fraser & Dunlop, Drury House, 34-43 Russell Street, London WC2B 5HA
t 020 7344 1000 **f** 020 7836 9543
e postmaster@pfd.co.uk **w** www.pfd.co.uk

Julian Farino
International Creative Management Ltd, Oxford House, 76 Oxford Street, London W1D 1BS
t 020 7636 6565 **f** 020 7323 0101 **w** www.icmlondon.co.uk

Brian Farnham
Casarotto Ramsay & Associates Ltd, National House, 60-66 Wardour Street, London W1V 4ND
t 020 7287 4450 **f** 020 7287 9128
e agents@casarotto.uk.com **w** www.casarotto.uk.com

David Fielding
Cruickshank Cazenove Ltd, 97 Old South Lambeth Road, London SW8 1XU
t 020 7735 2933 **f** 020 7820 1081 **e** hjcruickshank@aol.com

Martha Fiennes
International Creative Management Ltd, Oxford House, 76 Oxford Street, London W1D 1BS
t 020 7636 6565 **f** 020 7323 0101 **w** www.icmlondon.co.uk

Vic Finch
82 Florence Road, London SW19 8TJ
t 020 8296 8983 **f** 020 8296 8983 **m** 07801 432953
e vyk82@yahoo.co.uk

Mike Figgis
Cruickshank Cazenove Ltd, 97 Old South Lambeth Road, London SW8 1XU
t 020 7735 2933 **f** 020 7820 1081 **e** hjcruickshank@aol.com
Credits Cold Creek Manor (F); Timecode 2000 (F); Hotel (F)

Tony Fisher
Peters Fraser & Dunlop, Drury House, 34-43 Russell Street, London WC2B 5HA
t 020 7344 1000 **f** 020 7836 9543
e postmaster@pfd.co.uk **w** www.pfd.co.uk

Sheree Folkson
Casarotto Ramsay & Associates Ltd, National House, 60-66 Wardour Street, London W1V 4ND
t 020 7287 4450 **f** 020 7287 9128
e agents@casarotto.uk.com **w** www.casarotto.uk.com

Viv Fongenie
Peters Fraser & Dunlop, Drury House, 34-43 Russell Street, London WC2B 5HA
t 020 7344 1000 **f** 020 7836 9543
e postmaster@pfd.co.uk **w** www.pfd.co.uk

Footloose Films
17 Langland Gardens, London NW3 6QE
t 020 7435 1330 **f** 020 7284 0442 **m** 07790 720040
e charlie@harris.u-net.com
Contact Charles Harris
Credits Link (C); Sex, Drugs And Dinner (D); On The Eight Ball (S); Paradise Grove (F)

Bill Forsyth
Peters Fraser & Dunlop, Drury House, 34-43 Russell Street, London WC2B 5HA
t 020 7344 1000 **f** 020 7836 9543
e postmaster@pfd.co.uk **w** www.pfd.co.uk

Giles Foster
Peters Fraser & Dunlop, Drury House, 34-43 Russell Street, London WC2B 5HA
t 020 7344 1000 **f** 020 7836 9543
e postmaster@pfd.co.uk **w** www.pfd.co.uk
Credits Talking Heads (T); Silas Marner (T); Hotel Du Lac (T); Bertie And Elizabeth (T)

Ian Foster
EXEC, 6 Travis Court, Farnham Royal SL2 3SB
t 01753 646677 **f** 01753 646770
e sue@execmanagement.co.uk **w** www.execmanagement.co.uk

Suzanne Foster
210 Broomwood Road, Battersea, London SW11 6JY
t 020 7228 2010 **f** 020 7228 2226 **m** 07941 227464
e sfoster569@aol.com
Credits the Streakers (T); Lad's Army (T); Hard Bastards (T); Tonight With Trevor McDonald (T)

Chris Fox
Experience Counts - Call Me Ltd, 5th Floor, 41-42 Berners Street, London W1P 3AA
t 020 7637 8112 **f** 020 7580 2582

Rebecca Frayn
Peters Fraser & Dunlop, Drury House, 34-43 Russell Street, London WC2B 5HA
t 020 7344 1000 **f** 020 7836 9543
e postmaster@pfd.co.uk **w** www.pfd.co.uk

Stephen Frears

Casarotto Ramsay & Associates Ltd, National House,
60-66 Wardour Street, London W1V 4ND
t 020 7287 4450 **f** 020 7287 9128
e agents@casarotto.uk.com **w** www.casarotto.uk.com

Free Spirits Film Productions

Flat 3, 130 Muswell Hill Road, London N10 3JD
t 020 8444 2668 **m** 07817 317856
e jmees30272@aol.com **w** www.free-spirits-film.co.uk
Contact Jaap Mees, Director, Director
Credits The Primrose Place (S); Off The Beaten Track (D); Rainbow Days (D);
Deeply Estranged (S)

Free Spirits' motto is: Films with quality, passion and integrity.

Martyn Friend

Peters Fraser & Dunlop, Drury House, 34-43 Russell Street,
London WC2B 5HA
t 020 7344 1000 **f** 020 7836 9543
e postmaster@pfd.co.uk **w** www.pfd.co.uk

Morag Fullarton

Peters Fraser & Dunlop, Drury House, 34-43 Russell Street,
London WC2B 5HA
t 020 7344 1000 **f** 020 7836 9543
e postmaster@pfd.co.uk **w** www.pfd.co.uk

Mike Furness

30 Woodland Drive, St Albans AL4 0EU
t 01727 830827 **f** 01727 830827 **m** 07973 403363
e m.furness@ntlworld.com
Credits Fujitsu Siemens Servers - McCann Erickson (T); What's The Big Idea (T);
Techno Games 2003 (T); Popstar's The Rivals (T)

Rick Gardner

t 01895 633280 **f** 01895 624625 **m** 07831 113939
e rickg@tesco.net

David Garfath

Casarotto Ramsay & Associates Ltd, National House,
60-66 Wardour Street, London W1V 4ND
t 020 7287 4450 **f** 020 7287 9128
e agents@casarotto.uk.com **w** www.casarotto.uk.com

Charles Garland

London Management & Representation, 2-4 Noel Street,
London W1F 8GB
t 020 7287 9000 **f** 020 7287 3236

Sarah Garrod

8 Coleraine Road, Blackheath, London SE3 7PQ
t 020 8305 0751 **m** 07885 782371 **e** sarah@sarahgarrod.co.uk

Roger Gartland

Peters Fraser & Dunlop, Drury House, 34-43 Russell Street,
London WC2B 5HA
t 020 7344 1000 **f** 020 7836 9543
e postmaster@pfd.co.uk **w** www.pfd.co.uk

Rebecca Gatward

Peters Fraser & Dunlop, Drury House, 34-43 Russell Street,
London WC2B 5HA
t 020 7344 1000 **f** 020 7836 9543
e postmaster@pfd.co.uk **w** www.pfd.co.uk

Sarah Gavron

Casarotto Ramsay & Associates Ltd, National House,
60-66 Wardour Street, London W1V 4ND
t 020 7287 4450 **f** 020 7287 9128
e agents@casarotto.uk.com **w** www.casarotto.uk.com

Carlo Gebler

Derryhillagh Schoolhouse, Enniskillen BT74 4LP
t 028 6632 4588 **e** cgebler.email@virgin.net
Credits A Little Local Difficulty (D); Student Life (D); Plain Tales From Northern
Ireland (D); Put To The Test (D)

Lorna Dean Gibbs

The Laurels, Church Street, Gawcott, Buckingham MK18 4HY
t 01280 812459 **f** 01280 823184 **m** 07774 212125
e lgibbs@newsroomink.com
Credits Commonwealth Games (T); LBC News (T); Wimbledon 2002 (T); Premier
League Football (T)

Dan Gifford

International Creative Management Ltd, Oxford House,
76 Oxford Street, London W1D 1BS
t 020 7636 6565 **f** 020 7323 0101 **w** www.icmlondon.co.uk

Brian Gilbert

Peters Fraser & Dunlop, Drury House, 34-43 Russell Street,
London WC2B 5HA
t 020 7344 1000 **f** 020 7836 9543
e postmaster@pfd.co.uk **w** www.pfd.co.uk

Jonathan Gili

28 Ifield Road, London SW10 9AA
t 020 7351 1407 **f** 020 7351 3541 **e** jonathan.gili@virgin.net
Credits The Oklahoma Outlaw (D); Tales Of The Eiffel Tower (D); The Empire
State Story (D); Queen Elizabeth, The Queen Mother (D)

Jim Gillespie

Peters Fraser & Dunlop, Drury House, 34-43 Russell Street,
London WC2B 5HA
t 020 7344 1000 **f** 020 7836 9543
e postmaster@pfd.co.uk **w** www.pfd.co.uk

Terry Gilliam

Casarotto Ramsay & Associates Ltd, National House,
60-66 Wardour Street, London W1V 4ND
t 020 7287 4450 **f** 020 7287 9128
e agents@casarotto.uk.com **w** www.casarotto.uk.com

François Girard

Casarotto Ramsay & Associates Ltd, National House,
60-66 Wardour Street, London W1V 4ND
t 020 7287 4450 **f** 020 7287 9128
e agents@casarotto.uk.com **w** www.casarotto.uk.com

Kenny Glenaan

Peters Fraser & Dunlop, Drury House, 34-43 Russell Street,
London WC2B 5HA
t 020 7344 1000 **f** 020 7836 9543
e postmaster@pfd.co.uk **w** www.pfd.co.uk

Clara Glynn

Peters Fraser & Dunlop, Drury House, 34-43 Russell Street,
London WC2B 5HA
t 020 7344 1000 **f** 020 7836 9543
e postmaster@pfd.co.uk **w** www.pfd.co.uk

Andy Goddard

Peters Fraser & Dunlop, Drury House, 34-43 Russell Street,
London WC2B 5HA
t 020 7344 1000 **f** 020 7836 9543
e postmaster@pfd.co.uk **w** www.pfd.co.uk

Jack Gold

Peters Fraser & Dunlop, Drury House, 34-43 Russell Street,
London WC2B 5HA
t 020 7344 1000 **f** 020 7836 9543
e postmaster@pfd.co.uk **w** www.pfd.co.uk

Roger Goldby

Casarotto Ramsay & Associates Ltd, National House,
60-66 Wardour Street, London W1V 4ND
t 020 7287 4450 **f** 020 7287 9128
e agents@casarotto.uk.com **w** www.casarotto.uk.com

Robert Golden

The Dench Arnold Agency, 24 D'Arblay Street, London W1F 8EH
t 020 7437 4551 **f** 020 7439 1355
e contact@dencharnoldagency.co.uk **w** www.dencharnold.co.uk

Henrique Goldman
The Dench Arnold Agency, 24 D'Arblay Street, London W1F 8EH
t 020 7437 4551 **f** 020 7439 1355
e contact@dencharnoldagency.co.uk **w** www.dencharnold.co.uk

Mick Gordon
Peters Fraser & Dunlop, Drury House, 34-43 Russell Street,
London WC2B 5HA
t 020 7344 1000 **f** 020 7836 9543
e postmaster@pfd.co.uk **w** www.pfd.co.uk

John Gorrie
Kerry Gardner Management, 7 St Georges Square, London
SW1V 2HX
t 020 7828 7748 **f** 020 7828 7758 **e** kerrygardner@freeuk.com

Brian Grant
Peters Fraser & Dunlop, Drury House, 34-43 Russell Street,
London WC2B 5HA
t 020 7344 1000 **f** 020 7836 9543
e postmaster@pfd.co.uk **w** www.pfd.co.uk

Brian Grant
75 Overhill, Southwick, Brighton BN42 4WH
m 07932 052424 **e** zhora@lineone.net
Credits Clocking Off (T); Gladiatress (F); Complex Of Fear (T); As If I-III (T)

Steve Green
Peters Fraser & Dunlop, Drury House, 34-43 Russell Street,
London WC2B 5HA
t 020 7344 1000 **f** 020 7836 9543
e postmaster@pfd.co.uk **w** www.pfd.co.uk

John Greening
8 Wain Close, Alcester B49 6LA
t 01789 765275 **f** 01789 765942 **m** 07970 648818
e greeningfam@wainclose.freeserve.co.uk
Credits Speed (T); Doctors Series III (T); Doctors Series II (T); EastEnders (T)

Cavan Greenwood
53 Elgar Avenue KT5 9JH
t 020 8241 3543 **f** 020 8241 3558 **m** 07866 750269
e cavang@blueyonder.co.uk
Credits Hollyoaks (T); Emmerdale (T)

Dewi Gregory
38A Brailsford Road, London SW2 2TE
t 020 8488 2877 **f** 07976 870252 **m** 07970 696266
e dwgrgry@aol.com
Credits Just Write (T); Risky Business (T); The Night Before The Morning After
(T); Torri Bol (T)

Chris Griffin
Alan Brodie Representation, 211 Piccadilly, London W1J 9HF
t 020 7917 2871 **f** 020 7917 2872
e info@alanbrodie.com **w** www.alanbrodie.com

Alan Grint
44 Greeway lane, Hackney, Matlock DE4 2QA
t 01629 733976 **f** 01629 735825 **m** 07885 404 831
e analtring2@hotmail.com
Credits Brookside (T); Catherine Cookson (T); Chancer (T); Peak Practice (T)

Nick Grosso
Casarotto Ramsay & Associates Ltd, National House,
60-66 Wardour Street, London W1V 4ND
t 020 7287 4450 **f** 020 7287 9128
e agents@casarotto.uk.com **w** www.casarotto.uk.com

Piers Haggard
Casarotto Ramsay & Associates Ltd, National House,
60-66 Wardour Street, London W1V 4ND
t 020 7287 4450 **f** 020 7287 9128
e agents@casarotto.uk.com **w** www.casarotto.uk.com

Ian Hamilton
11 New England Street, St Albans AL3 4QG
t 01727 834873 **f** 01727 834873 **m** 07831 639870
e ianrham@aol.com
Credits Baffa TV Awards (T); Laureus World Sports Awards (T); I'm A Celebrity
Get Me Out Of Here! (T); Party In The Park (2001) (T)

Trevor Hampton
16 Chapel Lane, Letty Green, Hertford SG14 2PA
t 01707 261285 **f** 01707 276234 **m** 07976 955330
e trevor.hampton@ntlworld.com
Credits Ragtime (T); Proms (T); Fidelio (T); Trisha (T)

Mike Hand-Bowman
45 Vernon Road, East Sheen, London SW14 8NU
t 020 8876 0579 **f** 020 8876 0579 **m** 07710 319 348
e handbow@compuserve.com

Ken Hannam
The Dench Arnold Agency, 24 D'Arblay Street, London W1F 8EH
t 020 7437 4551 **f** 020 7439 1355
e contact@dencharnoldagency.co.uk **w** www.dencharnold.co.uk

Sarah Harding
Peters Fraser & Dunlop, Drury House, 34-43 Russell Street,
London WC2B 5HA
t 020 7344 1000 **f** 020 7836 9543
e postmaster@pfd.co.uk **w** www.pfd.co.uk

Geoff Harris
26 Gothic Road, Twickenham TW2 5EH
t 020 8241 8974 **e** geoffharris@lunch.icom43.net
Credits EastEnders (T); The Knock (T); The Bill (T); London's Burning (T)

Nigel P Harris
6 Douglas Avenue, Hodge Hill, Birmingham B36 8EN
t 0121 783 6568 **m** 07941 199411 **e** nigel@the-film.biz
Credits Rosie & Jim (T); Brum (T); The Saturday Show Extra (T); 50/50 (T)

Paul Harrison
Flat 4, 14 Riverdale Road, East Twickenham TW1 2BS
t 020 8744 3912 **m** 07779 409257
Credits A Touch Of Frost (T); Grafters (T); Ballykissangel (T); Blue Dog (T)

Caroline Hawkins
13 Becketts Place, Lower Teddington Road, Hampton Wick KT1 4EQ
t 020 8977 6432 **m** 07831 802511 **e** ca.hawkins@ntlworld.com

David Hayman
International Creative Management Ltd, Oxford House,
76 Oxford Street, London W1D 1BS
t 020 7636 6565 **f** 020 7323 0101 **w** www.icmlondon.co.uk

Robert Heath
The Dench Arnold Agency, 24 D'Arblay Street, London W1F 8EH
t 020 7437 4551 **f** 020 7439 1355
e contact@dencharnoldagency.co.uk **w** www.dencharnold.co.uk

Elliot Hegarty
Peters Fraser & Dunlop, Drury House, 34-43 Russell Street,
London WC2B 5HA
t 020 7344 1000 **f** 020 7836 9543
e postmaster@pfd.co.uk **w** www.pfd.co.uk

Sarah Hellings
London Management & Representation, 2-4 Noel Street,
London W1F 8GB
t 020 7287 9000 **f** 020 7287 3236
Credits Taggart (T); Lucy Sullivan Is Getting Married (T); Midsomer Murders (T)

John Henderson
Linda Seifert Management, 91 Berwick Street, London W1F ONE
t 020 7292 7390 **f** 020 7292 7391
e contact@lindaseifert.com **w** www.lindaseifert.com

Julian Henriques
Alan Brodie Representation, 211 Piccadilly, London W1J 9HF
t 020 7917 2871 **f** 020 7917 2872
e info@alanbrodie.com **w** www.alanbrodie.com

Mark Herman
Peters Fraser & Dunlop, Drury House, 34-43 Russell Street,
London WC2B 5HA
t 020 7344 1000 **f** 020 7836 9543
e postmaster@pfd.co.uk **w** www.pfd.co.uk

Peter Hewitt
Casarotto Ramsay & Associates Ltd, National House,
60-66 Wardour Street, London W1V 4ND
t 020 7287 4450 **f** 020 7287 9128
e agents@casarotto.uk.com **w** www.casarotto.uk.com

Danny Hiller
Peter McFarlane, 3 Percy Street, London W1
t 020 7636 7750

Steve Hilliker
London Management & Representation, 2-4 Noel Street,
London W1F 8GB
t 020 7287 9000 **f** 020 7287 3236
Credits South Of The Border (T); The Darkening (F)

Michael Hines
The Dench Arnold Agency, 24 D'Arblay Street, London W1F 8EH
t 020 7437 4551 **f** 020 7439 1355
e contact@dencharnoldagency.co.uk **w** www.dencharnold.co.uk

PJ Hogan
Casarotto Ramsay & Associates Ltd, National House,
60-66 Wardour Street, London W1V 4ND
t 020 7287 4450 **f** 020 7287 9128
e agents@casarotto.uk.com **w** www.casarotto.uk.com

Pat Holden
Peters Fraser & Dunlop, Drury House, 34-43 Russell Street,
London WC2B 5HA
t 020 7344 1000 **f** 020 7836 9543
e postmaster@pfd.co.uk **w** www.pfd.co.uk

Simon Holder
16 Chancery Mews, Tooting Bec, London SW17 7TD
t 020 8767 8062 **f** 020 8767 8062 **m** 07850 884595
e simonholder@totalise.co.uk

Paul Holmes
London Management & Representation, 2-4 Noel Street,
London W1F 8GB
t 020 7287 9000 **f** 020 7287 3236
Credits Live And Kicking (T); Fame Academy (T)

Richard Holthouse
McKinney Macartney Management Ltd, The Barley Mow
Centre, 10 Barley Mow Passage, London W4 4PH
t 020 8995 4747 **f** 020 8995 2414
e fkb@mmtechsrep.demon.co.uk
w www.mckinneymacartney.com

Martyn Hone
84 Bartlholmew Road, London NW5 2AS
t 020 7267 1287 **e** martynhone@hotmail.com
Credits Mad About Machines (D); Sheriff Street Kids (D); The Matchmaker (F);
Omnibus - The Billy Elliot Boy (D)

Joel Hopkins
Peters Fraser & Dunlop, Drury House, 34-43 Russell Street,
London WC2B 5HA
t 020 7344 1000 **f** 020 7836 9543
e postmaster@pfd.co.uk **w** www.pfd.co.uk

Simon Horton
9 Yelverton Close, Walsall WS3 3XE
t 01922 712467 **m** 07703 164174 **e** simhort@hotmail.com
Credits E, Claudius (I); Car Sharks (T); Embarrassing Illnesses (D); Home From
Home (D)

Bob Hoskins
Casarotto Ramsay & Associates Ltd, National House,
60-66 Wardour Street, London W1V 4ND
t 020 7287 4450 **f** 020 7287 9128
e agents@casarotto.uk.com **w** www.casarotto.uk.com

Howard Hall
6 Foster Road, Abingdon OX14 1YN
t 01235 533981 **f** 01235 533981 **m** 07860 775438
e howardhall@filmdirector.freeserve.co.uk
w www.filmdirector.freeserve.co.uk
Contact Howard Hall, Director
Credits Law & Order (T); I Know What You Cleaned Last Night (C)

Menhaj Huda
International Creative Management Ltd, Oxford House,
76 Oxford Street, London W1D 1BS
t 020 7636 6565 **f** 020 7323 0101 **w** www.icmlondon.co.uk

Enda Hughes
Casarotto Ramsay & Associates Ltd, National House,
60-66 Wardour Street, London W1V 4ND
t 020 7287 4450 **f** 020 7287 9128
e agents@casarotto.uk.com **w** www.casarotto.uk.com

Andy Humphreys
25 Springwell Road, Streatham, London SW16 2QU
t 020 8769 3436 **f** 020 8769 3436 **m** 07734 680983
e andyghumphreys@aol.com **w** www.directorcam.co.uk
Credits Battle For Docklands (I); Ferry Up The Amazon (D); The Biggest Wheel
In The World (D)

Tom Hunsinger
Casarotto Ramsay & Associates Ltd, National House,
60-66 Wardour Street, London W1V 4ND
t 020 7287 4450 **f** 020 7287 9128
e agents@casarotto.uk.com **w** www.casarotto.uk.com

Catherine Hunter
17 Durham Road, East Finchley, London N2 9DP
m 07880 704 430 **e** minceyourwords@hotmail.com
Credits World Rally Championships (D); History of Wimbledon; Nobel Prizes 2001

Neil Hunter
Casarotto Ramsay & Associates Ltd, National House,
60-66 Wardour Street, London W1V 4ND
t 020 7287 4450 **f** 020 7287 9128
e agents@casarotto.uk.com **w** www.casarotto.uk.com

Nick Hurran
International Creative Management Ltd, Oxford House,
76 Oxford Street, London W1D 1BS
t 020 7636 6565 **f** 020 7323 0101 **w** www.icmlondon.co.uk

Nicholas Hytner
Peters Fraser & Dunlop, Drury House, 34-43 Russell Street,
London WC2B 5HA
t 020 7344 1000 **f** 020 7836 9543
e postmaster@pfd.co.uk **w** www.pfd.co.uk

Dalia Ibelhauptaite
Cruickshank Cazenove Ltd, 97 Old South Lambeth Road,
London SW8 1XU
t 020 7735 2933 **f** 020 7820 1081 **e** hjcruickshank@aol.com
Credits Feeling Good (S); Let The Good Times Roll (S)

Scott Imren
18 Ruskin Road, Hove BN3 5HA
t 01273 733672 **m** 07958 706047
e scott@parsleyproductions.co.uk
w www.parsleyproductions.co.uk
Credits ITV & Channel 4 News (T); Nickelodeon Live Links (T); Formula One Grand Prix (T)

Andy Isaac
26 Heber Road, London NW2 6AA
t 020 7792 4321 **t** 020 7243 9840 **f** 020 7792 9802
m 07714 203374 **e** andy@gjpro.com

James Ivory
Peters Fraser & Dunlop, Drury House, 34-43 Russell Street,
London WC2B 5HA
t 020 7344 1000 **f** 020 7836 9543
e postmaster@pfd.co.uk **w** www.pfd.co.uk

David Jackson
Peters Fraser & Dunlop, Drury House, 34-43 Russell Street,
London WC2B 5HA
t 020 7344 1000 **f** 020 7836 9543
e postmaster@pfd.co.uk **w** www.pfd.co.uk

Pedr James
C/o Judy Daish Associates, 2 St Charles Place, London W10 6EG
t 020 8964 8811 **f** 020 8964 8966
e sara@judydaish.demon.co.uk
Credits Nicetown; Martin Chuzzlewit; Our Friends in the North

Vadim Jean
Peters Fraser & Dunlop, Drury House, 34-43 Russell Street,
London WC2B 5HA
t 020 7344 1000 **f** 020 7836 9543
e postmaster@pfd.co.uk **w** www.pfd.co.uk

Jenny Jones
6 Sydney Row, Spike Island, Bristol BS1 6UU
t 0117 925 3574 **m** 07836 538873
e shark@thesea.co.uk **w** www.thesea.co.uk
Credits Shark Encounters (T); The Road to Certain Death (T)

John Lawrence Enterprises
3 Callcott Road, London NW6 7EB
t 07808 228067 **f** 020 8933 8414 **e** jlawrence@hotmail.com
Contact John Lawrence, Producer
Credits Streetstream (D)

Johnforrest.tv
PO Box 207, Sale M33 2WW
t 0161 973 4536 **f** 0161 976 2917

Sandy Johnson
Linda Seifert Management, 91 Berwick Street, London W1F ONE
t 020 7292 7390 **f** 020 7292 7391
e contact@lindaseifert.com **w** www.lindaseifert.com

Genevieve Jolliffe
Casarotto Ramsay & Associates Ltd, National House,
60-66 Wardour Street, London W1V 4ND
t 020 7287 4450 **f** 020 7287 9128
e agents@casarotto.uk.com **w** www.casarotto.uk.com

Martin Jones
Peters Fraser & Dunlop, Drury House, 34-43 Russell Street,
London WC2B 5HA
t 020 7344 1000 **f** 020 7836 9543
e postmaster@pfd.co.uk **w** www.pfd.co.uk

Simon Cellan Jones
International Creative Management Ltd, Oxford House,
76 Oxford Street, London W1D 1BS
t 020 7636 6565 **f** 020 7323 0101 **w** www.icmlondon.co.uk

Terry Jones
Casarotto Ramsay & Associates Ltd, National House,
60-66 Wardour Street, London W1V 4ND
t 020 7287 4450 **f** 020 7287 9128
e agents@casarotto.uk.com **w** www.casarotto.uk.com

Neil Jordan
Casarotto Ramsay & Associates Ltd, National House,
60-65 Wardour Street, London W1V 4ND
t 020 7287 4450 **f** 020 7287 9128
e agents@casarotto.uk.com **w** www.casarotto.uk.com

Mathias Julin
19A Downside Crescent, London NW3 2AN
m 07768 880808 **e** mathiasjulin@mac.com
Credits Ace Of Base (M); Nintendo (C); Family Affairs (T); Hollyoaks (T)

Laura Jury
7 Speedwell Close, Brixham TQ5 9NJ
m 07855 090589 **e** warrior_of_bushido@yahoo.co.uk
w www.angelfire.com/movies/movieproduction
Credits White Bread (S); An Introduction To Aikido (E); The Cry Of The Worm (S); The Zen Scrolls (F)

Mika Kallwass
The Dench Arnold Agency, 24 D'Arblay Street, London W1F 8EH
t 020 7437 4551 **f** 020 7439 1355
e contact@denrancholdagency.co.uk **w** www.dencharnold.co.uk

Asif Kapadia
International Creative Management Ltd, Oxford House,
76 Oxford Street, London W1D 1BS
t 020 7636 6565 **f** 020 7323 0101 **w** www.icmlondon.co.uk

Lukasz Karwowski
Peters Fraser & Dunlop, Drury House, 34-43 Russell Street,
London WC2B 5HA
t 020 7344 1000 **f** 020 7836 9543
e postmaster@pfd.co.uk **w** www.pfd.co.uk

JJ Keith
54 St Quintin Avenue, London W10 6PA
t 020 8968 9859 **f** 020 8968 9859 **m** 07973 146911
e jj.keith@ntlworld.com
Agent Peters Fraser & Dunlop, Drury House, 34-43 Russell
Street, London WC2B 5HA
t 020 7344 1000 **f** 020 7836 9543
e postmaster@pfd.co.uk **w** www.pfd.co.uk
Credits Ho Ho Ho! (T); Holiday Romance (S); Sainsbury's (C); The Bill (T)

Peter M Kershaw
C/o Duchy Parade Films Ltd, 20 Glebe Road, Harrogate HG2 0LZ
t 01423 526835 **f** 01423 526835 **m** 07799 765 481
e duchyfilms@aol.com **w** www.duchyparadefilms.co.uk
Credits That's Entertainment; No More Cry-The Corrs in Concert; Wilfred (S)

David Kester
Peters Fraser & Dunlop, Drury House, 34-43 Russell Street,
London WC2B 5HA
t 020 7344 1000 **f** 020 7836 9543
e postmaster@pfd.co.uk **w** www.pfd.co.uk

Clare Kilner
Casarotto Ramsay & Associates Ltd, National House,
60-66 Wardour Street, London W1V 4ND
t 020 7287 4450 **f** 020 7287 9128
e agents@casarotto.uk.com **w** www.casarotto.uk.com
Credits Janice Beard 45wpm (F)

Huen Swee Kim
176 The Spinney, Bar Hill CB3 8TP
t 01954 200527 **e** sweekim.huen@ntlworld.com
Credits Chinatown In Transition (T); When The Bough Breaks (T)

Brian Kirk
International Creative Management Ltd, Oxford House,
76 Oxford Street, London W1D 1BS
t 020 7636 6565 **f** 020 7323 0101 **w** www.icmlondon.co.uk

Gareth Knowles
Renshaw House, Renshaw Wood Lane, Coldsall Wood,
Wolverhampton WV8 1QU
m 07760 352921
Credits High On Daughter's London Palladium (T); Parliamentary Coverage -
Palace Of Westminster (T); The FLow Comedy (S); Home Shopping Europe (T)

Ian Knox
Peters Fraser & Dunlop, Drury House, 34-43 Russell Street,
London WC2B 5HA
t 020 7344 1000 **f** 020 7836 9543
e postmaster@pfd.co.uk **w** www.pfd.co.uk

Peter Kosminsky
Peters Fraser & Dunlop, Drury House, 34-43 Russell Street,
London WC2B 5HA
t 020 7344 1000 **f** 020 7836 9543
e postmaster@pfd.co.uk **w** www.pfd.co.uk

Antal Kovacs
27 Morrab Road, Penzance TR18 4EZ
t 01736 350019 **e** antal@west-coastproductions.fsnet.co.uk
Credits The Samaritan Kind (S); Hwerow Hweg (F); Bitter Sweet (F)

Suri B Krishnamma
Peters Fraser & Dunlop, Drury House, 34-43 Russell Street,
London WC2B 5HA
t 020 7344 1000 **f** 020 7836 9543
e postmaster@pfd.co.uk **w** www.pfd.co.uk

Tinge Krishnan
Peters Fraser & Dunlop, Drury House, 34-43 Russell Street,
London WC2B 5HA
t 020 7344 1000 **f** 020 7836 9543
e postmaster@pfd.co.uk **w** www.pfd.co.uk

Andy Lambert
London Management & Representation, 2-4 Noel Street,
London W1F 8GB
t 020 7287 9000 **f** 020 7287 3236

Christine Langan
Peters Fraser & Dunlop, Drury House, 34-43 Russell Street,
London WC2B 5HA
t 020 7344 1000 **f** 020 7836 9543
e postmaster@pfd.co.uk **w** www.pfd.co.uk

Philippa Langdale
The Lighthouse, York Rise, London NW5 1ST
m 07976 257091 **e** philippalangdale@orange.net
Agent Peters Fraser & Dunlop, Drury House, 34-43 Russell
Street, London WC2B 5HA
t 020 7344 1000 **f** 020 7836 9543
e postmaster@pfd.co.uk **w** www.pfd.co.uk
Credits Lloyd And Hill (T); The Vice (T); North Square (T); Trust (T)

Simon Langton
Newnham Hill Farmhouse, Newnham Hill, Henley-on-Thames
RG9 5TL
t 01491 642158 **f** 01491 642158 **m** 07770 596827
e langton3@hotmail.com
Credits Mother Love (F); Pride And Prejudice (T); The Scarlet Pimpernel (F)

Patrick Lau
Peters Fraser & Dunlop, Drury House, 34-43 Russell Street,
London WC2B 5HA
t 020 7344 1000 **f** 020 7836 9543
e postmaster@pfd.co.uk **w** www.pfd.co.uk

David Lawless
55A The Broadway, London
t 020 8374 6278 **m** 07879 474767
e info@brazenfilms.demon.co.uk
Credits Can't Help - Pulszar (M); Only One - Lima (M); If Silence Should End (S);
Kingdom Of The Asante (D)

Ringan Ledwidge
Peters Fraser & Dunlop, Drury House, 34-43 Russell Street,
London WC2B 5HA
t 020 7344 1000 **f** 020 7836 9543
e postmaster@pfd.co.uk **w** www.pfd.co.uk

Riitta Leena-Lynn
The Dench Arnold Agency, 24 D'Arblay Street, London W1F 8EH
t 020 7437 4551 **f** 020 7439 1355
e contact@dencharnoldagency.co.uk **w** www.dencharnold.co.uk

Mike Leigh
Peters Fraser & Dunlop, Drury House, 34-43 Russell Street,
London WC2B 5HA
t 020 7344 1000 **f** 020 7836 9543
e postmaster@pfd.co.uk **w** www.pfd.co.uk

David Leland
Casarotto Ramsay & Associates Ltd, National House,
60-66 Wardour Street, London W1V 4ND
t 020 7287 4450 **f** 020 7287 9128
e agents@casarotto.uk.com **w** www.casarotto.uk.com

Chris Lethbridge
72 Cranbrook Road, London W4 2LH
m 07973 224021 **e** chris@digitalscripts.com
Credits How To Build A Human (T); The Sci-Fi Files (T); Under the Knife (T)

Damien Lewis
42 Lockhurst Street, London E5 0AP
t 020 8533 6196 **f** 020 7682 1371 **m** 07770 844270
e mediac21@aol.com
Credits Life On The Line; Investigating Asia (T); War Hospital (T)

Ian Lewis
34 Burnt Hill Road, Lower Bourne, Farnham GU10 3LZ
t 01252 710313 **f** 01252 725855
e ian@farnfilm.com **w** www.ianlewis.biz
Credits Open University German (E); Rooted (T); The Chef's Apprentice (T);
Takeaway (T)

Jonathan Lewis
Peters Fraser & Dunlop, Drury House, 34-43 Russell Street,
London WC2B 5HA
t 020 7344 1000 **f** 020 7836 9543
e postmaster@pfd.co.uk **w** www.pfd.co.uk

Graham Linehan
Peters Fraser & Dunlop, Drury House, 34-43 Russell Street,
London WC2B 5HA
t 020 7344 1000 **f** 020 7836 9543
e postmaster@pfd.co.uk **w** www.pfd.co.uk

Matt Lipsey
International Creative Management Ltd, Oxford House,
76 Oxford Street, London W1D 1BS
t 020 7636 6565 **f** 020 7323 0101 **w** www.icmlondon.co.uk

Jim Loach
The Dench Arnold Agency, 24 D'Arblay Street, London W1F 8EH
t 020 7437 4551 **f** 020 7439 1355
e contact@dencharnoldagency.co.uk **w** www.dencharnold.co.uk

Richard Loncraine
Casarotto Ramsay & Associates Ltd, National House,
60-66 Wardour Street, London W1V 4ND
t 020 7287 4450 **f** 020 7287 9128
e agents@casarotto.uk.com **w** www.casarotto.uk.com
Credits Wide-Eyed and Legless (F); Richard III (F)

London Film Lab
1, 14 Ovington Square, London SW3 1LN
t 020 7823 9085 **f** 0870 124 2253
e londonfilmlab@hotmail.com **w** www.reelplay.com/streamfilms
Contact Alex Azabal, Producer; Elena Lario, Film Maker
Credits Nigel The Plonker (S); My Baby (S); Piece Of Cake (F); Oliver's Crimes (F)

Ian Lorimer
2 Westwood Road, London SW13 0LA
t 020 8876 8140 **f** 020 8876 8140 **m** 07836 363066
e ian.lorimer@blueyonder.com
Credits Ruby Wax (T); It's Only TV But I Like It (T); They Think It's All Over (T)

Gary Love
International Creative Management Ltd, Oxford House,
76 Oxford Street, London W1D 1BS
t 020 7636 6565 **f** 020 7323 0101 **w** www.icmlondon.co.uk

Nick Love
International Creative Management Ltd, Oxford House,
76 Oxford Street, London W1D 1BS
t 020 7636 6565 **f** 020 7323 0101 **w** www.icmlondon.co.uk

Jeremy Lovering
Peters Fraser & Dunlop, Drury House, 34-43 Russell Street,
London WC2B 5HA
t 020 7344 1000 **f** 020 7836 9543
e postmaster@pfd.co.uk **w** www.pfd.co.uk

Declan Lowney
International Creative Management Ltd, Oxford House,
76 Oxford Street, London W1D 1BS
t 020 7636 6565 **f** 020 7323 0101 **w** www.icmlondon.co.uk

Tim Lucas
Flat 20, 93 Elm Park Gardens, London SW10 9QW
t 020 7352 7452 **f** 020 7352 7452
e lucas_timothy_ford@hotmail.com

Avie Luthra
Peters Fraser & Dunlop, Drury House, 34-43 Russell Street,
London WC2B 5HA
t 020 7344 1000 **f** 020 7836 9543
e postmaster@pfd.co.uk **w** www.pfd.co.uk

Jonathan Lynn
Peters Fraser & Dunlop, Drury House, 34-43 Russell Street,
London WC2B 5HA
t 020 7344 1000 **f** 020 7836 9543
e postmaster@pfd.co.uk **w** www.pfd.co.uk

Syd Macartney
McKinney Macartney Management Ltd, The Barley Mow
Centre, 10 Barley Mow Passage, London W4 4PH
t 020 8995 4747 **f** 020 8995 2414
e fkb@mmtechsrep.demon.co.uk **w** www.mckinneymacartney.com

Bruce MacDonald
Peters Fraser & Dunlop, Drury House, 34-43 Russell Street,
London WC2B 5HA
t 020 7344 1000 **f** 020 7836 9543
e postmaster@pfd.co.uk **w** www.pfd.co.uk

Dominic MacDonald
The Dench Arnold Agency, 24 D'Arblay Street, London W1F 8EH
t 020 7437 4551 **f** 020 7439 1355
e contact@denpcharnoldagency.co.uk **w** www.dencharnold.co.uk

Fraser MacDonald
Casarotto Ramsay & Associates Ltd, National House,
60-66 Wardour Street, London W1V 4ND
t 020 7287 4450 **f** 020 7287 9128
e agents@casarotto.uk.com **w** www.casarotto.uk.com

James MacDonald
Cruickshank Cazenove Ltd, 97 Old South Lambeth Road,
London SW8 1XU
t 020 7735 2933 **f** 020 7820 1081 **e** hjcruickshank@aol.com

Kevin MacDonald
Peters Fraser & Dunlop, Drury House, 34-43 Russell Street,
London WC2B 5HA
t 020 7344 1000 **f** 020 7836 9543
e postmaster@pfd.co.uk **w** www.pfd.co.uk

Toby MacDonald
Casarotto Ramsay & Associates Ltd, National House,
60-66 Wardour Street, London W1V 4ND
t 020 7287 4450 **f** 020 7287 9128
e agents@casarotto.uk.com **w** www.casarotto.uk.com

John Mackenzie
Peters Fraser & Dunlop, Drury House, 34-43 Russell Street,
London WC2B 5HA
t 020 7344 1000 **f** 020 7836 9543
e postmaster@pfd.co.uk **w** www.pfd.co.uk

Keith Mackenzie
10 Legh Road, Prestbury SK10 4HX
t 01625 828493 **f** 01625 829460 **m** 07770 865888
e keith_kmp@hotmail.com
Credits British Touring Cars Championships (T); Commonwealth Games (T);
Cricket (T); Formula One Motor Racing (T)

Anna Mackmin
Pauline Asper Management, Jacobs Cottage, Reservoir Lane,
Sedlescombe TN33 0PJ
t 01424 870412 **f** 01424 +44 1424 **e** pauline.asper@virgin.net

Alan G Macmillan
C/o Peter MacFarlane, MacFarlane Chard Associates, 3 Percy
Streeet, London W1T 1DE
t 020 7636 7750 **f** 020 7636 7751 **w** www.macfarlane-chard.co.uk
Credits Jeopardy (T); Taggart (T); Ballykissangel (T); Nice Guy Eddie (T)

John Madden
Casarotto Ramsay & Associates Ltd, National House, 60-66
Wardour Street, London W1V 4ND
t 020 7287 4450 **f** 020 7287 9128
e agents@casarotto.uk.com **w** www.casarotto.uk.com

Lorne Magory
Honeysuckle Cottage, Whitmoor Vale Road, Hindhead GU26 6JA
t 01428 607697 **f** 01428 606112 **m** 07958 509531
e lornemagory@yahoo.com
Credits Emmerdale (T); Press Gang (T); Press Gang; Tomorrow People (T)

Raza Mallal
10 Park View, Swillington, Leeds LS26 84J
t 0113 239 2648 **f** 0113 287 0303
e raza@filmmakers.co.uk **w** www.filmmakers.co.uk

Martin Malone
Stonefish Films, 22 Normanby Road, London NW10 1BX
f 020 8452 4487 **m** 07710 385183 **e** stonefish.films@virgin.net

Paul Marcus
The Dench Arnold Agency, 24 D'Arblay Street, London W1F 8EH
t 020 7437 4551 **f** 020 7439 1355
e contact@dencharnoldagency.co.uk **w** www.dencharnold.co.uk

Andrew Margetson
Peters Fraser & Dunlop, Drury House, 34-43 Russell Street,
London WC2B 5HA
t 020 7344 1000 **f** 020 7836 9543
e postmaster@pfd.co.uk **w** www.pfd.co.uk

Pip Marks
t 020 8780 9591 f 020 8780 9591 m 07771 628 712
e thecultsltd@yahoo.co.uk
Credits A Summer's Day (S); The Hare (S)

Pati Marr
f 020 8746 3376 m 07973 510330 e patimarr@aol.com

Neil Marshall
London Management & Representation, 2-4 Noel Street,
London W1F 8GB
t 020 7287 9000 f 020 7287 3236
Credits Dog Soldiers (F)

Philip Martin
Peters Fraser & Dunlop, Drury House, 34-43 Russell Street,
London WC2B 5HA
t 020 7344 1000 f 020 7836 9543
e postmaster@pfd.co.uk w www.pfd.co.uk

Simon Massey
Peters Fraser & Dunlop, Drury House, 34-43 Russell Street,
London WC2B 5HA
t 020 7344 1000 f 020 7836 9543
e postmaster@pfd.co.uk w www.pfd.co.uk

Juliet May
International Creative Management Ltd, Oxford House,
76 Oxford Street, London W1D 1BS
t 020 7636 6565 f 020 7323 0101 w www.icmlondon.co.uk

John Maybury
Casarotto Ramsay & Associates Ltd, National House, 60-66
Wardour Street, London W1V 4ND
t 020 7287 4450 f 020 7287 9128
e agents@casarotto.uk.com w www.casarotto.uk.com

Andrew McCarthy
98 Goodrich Road, London SE22 0ER
t 020 8299 4327

Conor McDermattroe
Peters Fraser & Dunlop, Drury House, 34-43 Russell Street,
London WC2B 5HA
t 020 7344 1000 f 020 7836 9543
e postmaster@pfd.co.uk w www.pfd.co.uk

Charles McDougall
Peters Fraser & Dunlop, Drury House, 34-43 Russell Street,
London WC2B 5HA
t 020 7344 1000 f 020 7836 9543
e postmaster@pfd.co.uk w www.pfd.co.uk

Elizabeth McIntyre
37 Northolme Road, Highbury, London N5 2UU
t 020 7359 7785 m 07703 568201
e e.mcintyre@btinternet.com
Credits The Lost Children Of Berlin (D); Dangerous Love (D)

Iain McLean
The Dench Arnold Agency, 24 D'Arblay Street, London W1F 8EH
t 020 7437 4551 f 020 7439 1355
e contact@dencharnoldagency.co.uk w www.dencharnold.co.uk

Mary McMurray
43 Shirland Road, London W9 2JD
t 020 7289 6667 m 07767 261632
e marymcmurray@chelmac.clara.co.uk

Nancy Meckler
Casarotto Ramsay & Associates Ltd, National House,
60-66 Wardour Street, London W1V 4ND
t 020 7287 4450 f 020 7287 9128
e agents@casarotto.uk.com w www.casarotto.uk.com

Media Production
19 Shirley Road, Nottingham NG3 5DA
t 01159 606243 m 07985 087647
e molpress@madasafish.com w www.mediaproduction.demon.co.uk
Contact Michael Pressman, Director; Michael Pressman, Director
Credits Greenpeace UK (I)

Leslie Megahey
Peters Fraser & Dunlop, Drury House, 34-43 Russell Street,
London WC2B 5HA
t 020 7344 1000 f 020 7836 9543 e postmaster@pfd.co.uk
w www.pfd.co.uk

Christopher Menaul
Peters Fraser & Dunlop, Drury House, 34-43 Russell Street,
London WC2B 5HA
t 020 7344 1000 f 020 7836 9543 e postmaster@pfd.co.uk
w www.pfd.co.uk

Chris Menges
Casarotto Ramsay & Associates Ltd, National House,
60-66 Wardour Street, London W1V 4ND
t 020 7287 4450 f 020 7287 9128
e agents@casarotto.uk.com w www.casarotto.uk.com

Nigel Mercer
Fieldside, Northend Road, Fenny Compton, Southam CU47 2YY
t 01295 770230 m 07836 351070 e mercern@tinyonline.co.uk
Credits The Vanessa Show (T); Changing Rooms (T); Better Homes (T);
Celebrity Sleepover (T)

Chloe Mercier
Flat 12, 82 Westbourne Park Villas, London W2 5EB
t 020 7229 0725 m 07946 413210
e chloe@chloemercier.com w www.chloemercier.com
Credits Lost In Buddha's World (D); The Lepidopteran (S); The Race Around The
World (T); Embryonic Dreams (S)

Nick Metcalfe
67 Clavering Road, London E12 5EY
t 020 8925 6361 f 020 8925 6361 m 07775 644935
e nick.metcalfe1@ntlworld.com
Credits Mysteries In The Landscape (D); Accident Blackspot (D); The People
Detective (D); Time Team (T)

Gavin Millar
Peters Fraser & Dunlop, Drury House, 34-43 Russell Street,
London WC2B 5HA
t 020 7344 1000 f 020 7836 9543
e postmaster@pfd.co.uk w www.pfd.co.uk

Sam Miller
Casarotto Ramsay & Associates Ltd, National House, 60-66
Wardour Street, London W1V 4ND
t 020 7287 4450 f 020 7287 9128
e agents@casarotto.uk.com w www.casarotto.uk.com

Minds Eye Films Ltd
Shepperton Studios, Studios Road, Shepperton TW17 0QD
t 020 8995 7437 f 020 8995 5196 m 07887 563518
e info@mindseyefilms.com e johnny@mindseyefilms.com
w www.mindseyefilms.com
Contact Johnny Kevorkian, Director-Producer; Neil Murphy, Producer
Credits Seizures (S); The Wake (S)

Viral Mistry
London
e viralmistry@yahoo.com w www.ukscreen.com/crew/viral
Credits Lonely Angel; Psychic Love; Haunted Heart

Tony Mitchell
Curtis Brown, Haymarket House, 28-29 Haymarket, London
SW1Y 4SP
t 020 7396 6600 f 020 7396 0110 e cb@curtisbrown.co.uk
Credits Neanderthal (T); Ancient Egyptians (F)

Dominique Moloney
Peters Fraser & Dunlop, Drury House, 34-43 Russell Street, London WC2B 5HA
t 020 7344 1000 **f** 020 7836 9543
e postmaster@pfd.co.uk **w** www.pfd.co.uk

Kevin Molony
The Dench Arnold Agency, 24 D'Arblay Street, London W1F 8EH
t 020 7437 4551 **f** 020 7439 1355
e contact@dencharnoldagency.co.uk **w** www.dencharnold.co.uk

Justin Molotnikov
Pauline Asper Management, Jacobs Cottage, Reservoir Lane, Sedlescombe TN33 0PJ
t 01424 870412 **f** 01424 870412 **e** pauline.asper@virgin.net

David Moore
Peters Fraser & Dunlop, Drury House, 34-43 Russell Street, London WC2B 5HA
t 020 7344 1000 **f** 020 7836 9543
e postmaster@pfd.co.uk **w** www.pfd.co.uk

Andy Morahan
Linda Seifert Management, 91 Berwick Street, London W1F ONE
t 020 7292 7390 **f** 020 7292 7391
e contact@lindaseifert.com **w** www.lindaseifert.com

Christopher Morahan
Highcombe Farmhouse, The Devil's Punchbowl, Portsmouth Road, Thursley, Godalming GU6 6NS
t 01428 607031 **f** 01428 607989 **m** 07860 580434
e chrismorahan@solutions-inc.co.uk
Credits Paper Mask (F); The Jewel In The Crown (T); Clockwise (F); After Pilkington (T)

Andrew Morgan
Peters Fraser & Dunlop, Drury House, 34-43 Russell Street, London WC2B 5HA
t 020 7344 1000 **f** 020 7836 9543
e postmaster@pfd.co.uk **w** www.pfd.co.uk

Ben Morris
Peters Fraser & Dunlop, Drury House, 34-43 Russell Street, London WC2B 5HA
t 020 7344 1000 **f** 020 7836 9543
e postmaster@pfd.co.uk **w** www.pfd.co.uk

Betsan Morris Evans
Pauline Asper Management, Jacobs Cottage, Reservoir Lane, Sedlescombe TN33 0PJ
t 01424 870412 **f** 01424 870412 **e** pauline.asper@virgin.net

Ewan Morrison
Peters Fraser & Dunlop, Drury House, 34-43 Russell Street, London WC2B 5HA
t 020 7344 1000 **f** 020 7836 9543
e postmaster@pfd.co.uk **w** www.pfd.co.uk

Paul Morrison
APT Films, 255A, Brecknock Road, London N19 5AA
t 020 7284 1695 **f** 020 7482 1587 **e** paul@aptfilms.com
Credits Wondrovs Oblivion (F); Solomon & Gaenor (F)

David Morrissey
International Creative Management Ltd, Oxford House, 76 Oxford Street, London W1D 1BS
t 020 7636 6565 **f** 020 7323 0101 **w** www.icmlondon.co.uk

Malcolm Mowbray
Peters Fraser & Dunlop, Drury House, 34-43 Russell Street, London WC2B 5HA
t 020 7344 1000 **f** 020 7836 9543
e postmaster@pfd.co.uk **w** www.pfd.co.uk

Mozaic The Full Picture Limited
74 Rahere House, Central Street, London EC1V 8DQ
m 07855 414666 **e** sundos@zoom.co.uk
Contact Sundos Al-Qais, Director

Peter Mullan
Pauline Asper Management, Jacobs Cottage, Reservoir Lane, Sedlescombe TN33 0PJ
t 01424 870412 **f** 01424 870412 **e** pauline.asper@virgin.net

Peter Mumford
Cruickshank Cazenove Ltd, 97 Old South Lambeth Road, London SW8 1XU
t 020 7735 2933 **f** 020 7820 1081 **e** hjcruickshank@aol.com
Credits Forty-Eight Preludes And Fugues (T); Swan Lake (T); Nutcracker Sweeties (T)

Marc Munden
Casarotto Ramsay & Associates Ltd, National House, 60-66 Wardour Street, London W1V 4ND
t 020 7287 4450 **f** 020 7287 9128
e agents@casarotto.uk.com **w** www.casarotto.uk.com

Julian Murphy
Peters Fraser & Dunlop, Drury House, 34-43 Russell Street, London WC2B 5HA
t 020 7344 1000 **f** 020 7836 9543
e postmaster@pfd.co.uk **w** www.pfd.co.uk

Howard Myers
25 Rythe Road, Claygate KT10 9DG
m 07050 104432 **e** howardmyers@tiscali.co.uk
Credits Travel Bug; Timebusters (T); Disney Channel Kids Awards (T); Diggit (T)

Mark Mylod
Casarotto Ramsay & Associates Ltd, National House, 60-66 Wardour Street, London W1V 4ND
t 020 7287 4450 **f** 020 7287 9128
e agents@casarotto.uk.com **w** www.casarotto.uk.com

Anna Negri
Casarotto Ramsay & Associates Ltd, National House, 60-66 Wardour Street, London W1V 4ND
t 020 7287 4450 **f** 020 7287 9128
e agents@casarotto.uk.com **w** www.casarotto.uk.com

New Forest Pictures
43 Lumley Road, Cheam SM3 8NP
t 020 8641 0170 **f** 020 8296 8337 **m** 07974 168670
e nick.sherard@newforestpictures.com
w www.newforestpictures.com
Contact Natascia Phillips, Production Manager; Geoff Searle, Director; Nicholas Sherard, Director
Credits World Record Bungee Jump - Dubai (T); Folly Hill (T); Don't Look Back! (F)

Peter J Nicholson
London Management & Representation, 2-4 Noel Street, London W1F 8GB
t 020 7287 9000 **f** 020 7287 3036

Ted Nicolaou
Gems, The Media House, 87 Glebe Street, Penarth CF64 1EF
t 029 2071 0770 **f** 029 2071 0771
e gems@gems-agency.co.uk **w** www.gems-agency.co.uk
Credits In The Shadow Of The Cobra (F); Dragonworld (F); Bloodstorm (F); Subspecies (F)

Alec Nisbett
115 King Henry's Road, London NW3 3RB
t 020 7624 0584 **t** 020 7483 4728 **e** alecnisbett@beeb.net
w www.alecnisbett.co.uk
Credits Wonders Of Weather (T); Raging Planet: Tidalwave (T); Storm Force: El Niño Of The Century/Tornado (T); Horizon (T)

Omid Nooshin
The Dench Arnold Agency, 24 D'Arblay Street, London W1F 8EH
t 020 7437 4551 **f** 020 7439 1355
e contact@dencharnoldagency.co.uk **w** www.dencharnold.co.uk

Declan O'Dwyer
Peters Fraser & Dunlop, Drury House, 34-43 Russell Street,
London WC2B 5HA
t 020 7344 1000 **f** 020 7836 9543
e postmaster@pfd.co.uk **w** www.pfd.co.uk

Billy O'Brien
Peters Fraser & Dunlop, Drury House, 34-43 Russell Street,
London WC2B 5HA
t 020 7344 1000 **f** 020 7836 9543
e postmaster@pfd.co.uk **w** www.pfd.co.uk

Joe O'Byrne
Peters Fraser & Dunlop, Drury House, 34-43 Russell Street,
London WC2B 5HA
t 020 7344 1000 **f** 020 7836 9543
e postmaster@pfd.co.uk **w** www.pfd.co.uk

Damien O'Donnell
Casarotto Ramsay & Associates Ltd, National House, 60-66
Wardour Street, London W1V 4ND
t 020 7287 4450 **f** 020 7287 9128
e agents@casarotto.uk.com **w** www.casarotto.uk.com

Shane O'Sullivan
Peters Fraser & Dunlop, Drury House, 34-43 Russell Street,
London WC2B 5HA
t 020 7344 1000 **f** 020 7836 9543
e postmaster@pfd.co.uk **w** www.pfd.co.uk

Thaddeus O'Sullivan
Peters Fraser & Dunlop, Drury House, 34-43 Russell Street,
London WC2B 5HA
t 020 7344 1000 **f** 020 7836 9543
e postmaster@pfd.co.uk **w** www.pfd.co.uk

Paul Olding
42 Pitfold Road, Lee, London SE12 9HX
m 07970 155 303
e paul@bongoreef.co.uk **w** www.bongoreef.co.uk
Credits Harry Enfield's Big Arts (T); Holiday (D); Tomorrow's World (T); Animal Hospital (T)

Optimum Productions
32 Thames Eyot, Cross Deep, Twickenham TW1 4QL
t 020 8892 1403 **f** 020 8892 6014 **m** 07980 983 613
w www.optiprod.co.uk
Contact Yvonne Hewett, Producer/Director/Writer

Deborah Paige
Peters Fraser & Dunlop, Drury House, 34-43 Russell Street,
London WC2B 5HA
t 020 7344 1000 **f** 020 7836 9543
e postmaster@pfd.co.uk **w** www.pfd.co.uk

John A Parry
22 Trefoil Road, London SW18 2EQ
t 020 8874 5084 **m** 07860 564484
Credits Ramp (I); Digger And The Gang (T); Student Choice (D)

Palio Pictures Ltd
96 Brondesbury Road, London NW6 6RX
t 020 7625 6362 **f** 020 7625 6362 **m** 07703 182 478
e brunosorrentino@yahoo.com
Contact Gianfranco Norelli, Director; Bruno Sorrentino, Director/Cameraman
Credits Secrets Of A Saudi State (T); Unreported: Islam And America Through The Eyes Of Imran Khan (T); Dispatches: A Saudi Slave (T); Correspondent: City Of Dreams (T)

Panvideo
6 Woodland Park, Girton, Cambridge CB3 0QB
t 01223 276263 **f** 01223 276136 **m** 07885 379436
e panvideo@supernet.com
Contact Keith Carpenter, Director/Secretary; Mike Collins, Director

Rupert Parker
151 Wilberforce Road, London N4 2SX
t 020 7226 4490 **e** rupert@rupertparker.co.uk
w www.rupertparker.co.uk
Credits Fossil Hunters (T); Scrapheap Mega Challenge - Reach For The Skies (T); Scrapheap Challenge (T); Junkyard Wars (T)

Phatibha Parmar
Peters Fraser & Dunlop, Drury House, 34-43 Russell Street,
London WC2B 5HA
t 020 7344 1000 **f** 020 7836 9543
e postmaster@pfd.co.uk **w** www.pfd.co.uk

Murilo Pasta
48 Carmichael Court, Grove Road, Barnes, London SW13 0HA
m 07970 256870
Agent Jessica Carney Associates, Suite 90-92 Kent House, 87
Regent Street, London W1B 4EH
t 020 7434 4143 **f** 020 7434 4173 **e** info@jcarneyassociates.co.uk
Credits Brookside (T); Grange Hill (T); Hollyoaks (T)

Willi Patterson
Linda Seifert Management, 91 Berwick Street, London W1F ONE
t 020 7292 7390 **f** 020 7292 7391
e contact@lindaseifert.com **w** www.lindaseifert.com

Tom Paulin
Peters Fraser & Dunlop, Drury House, 34-43 Russell Street,
London WC2B 5HA
t 020 7344 1000 **f** 020 7836 9543
e postmaster@pfd.co.uk **w** www.pfd.co.uk

Pawel Pawlikowski
Peters Fraser & Dunlop, Drury House, 34-43 Russell Street,
London WC2B 5HA
t 020 7344 1000 **f** 020 7836 9543
e postmaster@pfd.co.uk **w** www.pfd.co.uk

Jamie Payne
Creative Media Management, Unit 3B, Walpole Court, Ealing
Studios, Ealing Green, London W5 5ED
t 020 8584 5363 **f** 020 8566 5554
e enquiries@creativemediamanagement.com
Credits Suspicion (T); At Home With The Braithwaites (T); The Dance Of Shiva (T)

Ashley Pearce
Peters Fraser & Dunlop, Drury House, 34-43 Russell Street,
London WC2B 5HA
t 020 7344 1000 **f** 020 7836 9543
e postmaster@pfd.co.uk **w** www.pfd.co.uk

Mark Peploe
Peters Fraser & Dunlop, Drury House, 34-43 Russell Street,
London WC2B 5HA
t 020 7344 1000 **f** 020 7836 9543
e postmaster@pfd.co.uk **w** www.pfd.co.uk

Joy Perino
Peters Fraser & Dunlop, Drury House, 34-43 Russell Street,
London WC2B 5HA
t 020 7344 1000 **f** 020 7836 9543
e postmaster@pfd.co.uk **w** www.pfd.co.uk

PHD Productions
8 Eldon Road, London W8 5PU
t 020 7937 5301 **f** 020 7380 0405 **m** 07951 025 386
e aidan-williams@hotmail.com **w** www.phdproductions.com
Contact Thomas Veness, Director; Aidan Williams, Producer
Credits Mugged (F); Shades of Time (F)

Nic Phillips
Linda Seifert Management, 91 Berwick Street, London W1F 0NE
t 020 7292 7390 **f** 020 7292 7391
e contact@lindaseifert.com **w** www.lindaseifert.com
Credits 40 Something (T); Barbara (T); Casualty (T)

Andy Picheta
Gems, The Media House, 87 Glebe Street, Penarth CF64 1EF
t 029 2071 0770 **f** 029 2071 0771
e gems@gems-agency.co.uk **w** www.gems-agency.co.uk
Credits Go Go Joseph (D); The Carer (T)

Steven Pimlott
Cruickshank Cazenove Ltd, 97 Old South Lambeth Road,
London SW8 1XU
t 020 7735 2933 **f** 020 7820 1081 **e** hjcruickshank@aol.com
Credits Joseph And The Amazing Technicolor Dream Coat (F)

Richard Platt
The Dench Arnold Agency, 24 D'Arblay Street, London W1F 8EH
t 020 7437 4551 **f** 020 7439 1355
e contact@dencharnoldagency.co.uk **w** www.dencharnold.co.uk

Polkadotsonraindrops
25C Josephine Avenue, London SW2 2JX
t 020 8674 4638 **m** 07957 588283
e polkadotsonraindrops@beeb.net
Contact Mark Aitken, Director
Credits La Ultima Viva (S); Ways Of....(courses) (E); Same Same But Different (F)

Tom Poole
The Dench Arnold Agency, 24 D'Arblay Street, London W1F 8EH
t 020 7437 4551 **f** 020 7439 1355
e contact@dencharnoldagency.co.uk **w** www.dencharnold.co.uk

Angela Pope
Casarotto Ramsay & Associates Ltd, National House,
60-66 Wardour Street, London W1V 4ND
t 020 7287 4450 **f** 020 7287 9128
e agents@casarotto.uk.com **w** www.casarotto.uk.com

Tim Pope
International Creative Management Ltd, Oxford House,
76 Oxford Street, London W1D 1BS
t 020 7636 6565 **f** 020 7323 0101 **w** www.icmlondon.co.uk

Edward Porembny
Peters Fraser & Dunlop, Drury House, 34-43 Russell Street,
London WC2B 5HA
t 020 7344 1000 **f** 020 7836 9543
e postmaster@pfd.co.uk **w** www.pfd.co.uk

Geoff Posner
London Management & Representation, 2-4 Noel Street,
London W1F 8GB
t 020 7287 9000 **f** 020 7287 3236
Credits The Brit Awards (T); Dinnerladies (T); Hearts And Bones (T); Queen's
Golden Jubilee Rock And Pop Concert (T)

Gerry Poulson
Maureen Moore, London Managment, Colne Cottage, The
Quay, Wivenhoe CO7 9TA
t 01206 825224 **m** 07802 410906 **e** jezpoulson@hotmail.com
Credits Heartbeat (T); The Knock (T); Murder In Mind (T)

Jane Powell
London Management, Noel House, 2-4 Noel Street, London
W1F 8GB
t 020 7287 9000 **m** 07973 511968 **e** fgw@lonman.co.uk
Credits Mersey Beat (T); Doctors (T); Holby City (T); Judge John Deeds (T)

Tristram Powell
Casarotto Ramsay & Associates Ltd, National House,
60-66 Wardour Street, London W1V 4ND
t 020 7287 4450 **f** 020 7287 9128
e agents@casarotto.uk.com **w** www.casarotto.uk.com

Udayan Prasad
Casarotto Ramsay & Associates Ltd, National House,
60-66 Wardour Street, London W1V 4ND
t 020 7287 4450 **f** 020 7287 9128
e agents@casarotto.uk.com **w** www.casarotto.uk.com

Elaine Proctor
Peters Fraser & Dunlop, Drury House, 34-43 Russell Street,
London WC2B 5HA
t 020 7344 1000 **f** 020 7836 9543
e postmaster@pfd.co.uk **w** www.pfd.co.uk

Nicholas Prosser
26B Melrose Road, Wandsworth, London SW18 1NE
t 020 8871 0458 **m** 07778 865 628
e nicholasprosser@iolfree.ie
Credits The Bill (T); Thief Takers (T); House of Eliot (T)

AJ Quinn
Peters Fraser & Dunlop, Drury House, 34-43 Russell Street,
London WC2B 5HA
t 020 7344 1000 **f** 020 7836 9543
e postmaster@pfd.co.uk **w** www.pfd.co.uk

Nina Raine
Peters Fraser & Dunlop, Drury House, 34-43 Russell Street,
London WC2B 5HA
t 020 7344 1000 **f** 020 7836 9543
e postmaster@pfd.co.uk **w** www.pfd.co.uk

Alvin Rakoff
1 The Orchard, Chiswick, London W4 1JZ
t 020 8994 1264 **f** 020 8742 0507 **m** 07808 401999
e berry@alvinrakoff.com **w** www.alvinrakoff.com
Credits The Adventures Of Don Quixote (T); A Voyage Round My Father (F); A
Dance To The Music Of Time (T); Too Marvelous For Words (M)

Lynne Ramsay
Casarotto Ramsay & Associates Ltd, National House,
60-66 Wardour Street, London W1V 4ND
t 020 7287 4450 **f** 020 7287 9128
e agents@casarotto.uk.com **w** www.casarotto.uk.com

Ben Rea
15 The Knolls, Epsom KT17 3ND
t 01737 350358 **f** 01737 350358 **e** benrea@ukonline.co.uk
Credits 2000 Today (T); Grange Hill (T); Lovejoy

John Reardon
London Management & Representation, 2-4 Noel Street,
London W1F 8GB
t 020 7287 9000 **f** 020 7287 3236
Credits Heartbeat (T); London's Burning Series XIV (T); Hollyoaks - Moving On (T)

Crispin Reece
Casarotto Ramsay & Associates Ltd, National House,
60-66 Wardour Street, London W1V 4ND
t 020 7287 4450 **f** 020 7287 9128
e agents@casarotto.uk.com **w** www.casarotto.uk.com

Gareth Rees
e cargo@dircon.co.uk
Credits The Beggar' Opera (S); Road Wars (D); Driven To Protest (D); What
Happens When We Are Killing People (W)

Barbara Rennie
Peters Fraser & Dunlop, Drury House, 34-43 Russell Street,
London WC2B 5HA
t 020 7344 1000 **f** 020 7836 9543
e postmaster@pfd.co.uk **w** www.pfd.co.uk

Ann Richardson
62 Fairlawn Grave, London W4 5EH
t 020 8994 5964 **f** 020 8995 0969 **e** ann@onlychild-icom43.net

Kerry Richardson

Peters Fraser & Dunlop, Drury House, 34-43 Russell Street,
London WC2B 5HA
t 020 7344 1000 **f** 020 7836 9543
e postmaster@pfd.co.uk **w** www.pfd.co.uk

Matthew Richardson

Cruickshank Cazenove Ltd, 97 Old South Lambeth Road,
London SW8 1XU
t 020 7735 2933 **f** 020 7820 1081 **e** hjcruickshank@aol.com
Credits The Marriage Of Figaro (T)

Ian Rickson

Curtis Brown, Haymarket House, 28-29 Haymarket, London
SW1Y 4SP
t 020 7396 6600 **f** 020 7396 0110 **e** cb@curtisbrown.co.uk

Alrick Riley

Curtis Brown, Haymarket House, 28-29 Haymarket, London
SW1Y 4SP
t 020 7396 6600 **f** 020 7396 0110 **e** cb@curtisbrown.co.uk
Credits The Cops (T); Always & Everyone (T); William And Mary (T)

Sid Roberson

Linda Seifert Management, 91 Berwick Street, London W1F ONE
t 020 7292 7390 **f** 020 7292 7391
e contact@lindaseifert.com **w** www.lindaseifert.com

Amanda Roberts

Peters Fraser & Dunlop, Drury House, 34-43 Russell Street,
London WC2B 5HA
t 020 7344 1000 **f** 020 7836 9543
e postmaster@pfd.co.uk **w** www.pfd.co.uk

Jill Robertson

London Management & Representation, 2-4 Noel Street,
London W1F 8GB
t 020 7287 9000 **f** 020 7287 3236
Credits Hollyoaks (T); Brookside (T)

Geoff Rogers

SBFC, Unit 8, Sandhurst House, Wolsey Street, London E1 3BD

Christoph Rohl

Casarotto Ramsay & Associates Ltd, National House,
60-66 Wardour Street, London W1V 4ND
t 020 7287 4450 **f** 020 7287 9128
e agents@casarotto.uk.com **w** www.casarotto.uk.com

Tim Rolt

London Management & Representation, 2-4 Noel Street,
London W1F 8GB
t 020 7287 9000 **f** 020 7287 3236

Mark Roper

Gems, The Media House, 87 Glebe Street, Penarth CF64 1EF
t 029 2071 0770 **f** 029 2071 0771
e gems@gems-agency.co.uk **w** www.gems-agency.co.uk
Credits Peak Practice (T); Relic Hunter (T); High Adventure (F); Sea Wolf (F)

Bernard Rose

Casarotto Ramsay & Associates Ltd, National House,
60-66 Wardour Street, London W1V 4ND
t 020 7287 4450 **f** 020 7287 9128
e agents@casarotto.uk.com **w** www.casarotto.uk.com

Colin Rothbart

Flat 77, 25 Gresse Street, London W1T 1QP
t 020 7681 7421 **m** 07958 601415
e colin@rothbart.co.uk **w** www.rothbart.co.uk
Credits Britain's Most Embarrassing Parents (T); The Chelsea Set (T); Richard
And Judy (T)

Dom Rotheroe

Peters Fraser & Dunlop, Drury House, 34-43 Russell Street,
London WC2B 5HA
t 020 7344 1000 **f** 020 7836 9543
e postmaster@pfd.co.uk **w** www.pfd.co.uk

Paul Rowbotham

International Creative Management Ltd, Oxford House,
76 Oxford Street, London W1D 1BS
t 020 7636 6565 **f** 020 7323 0101 **w** www.icmlondon.co.uk

Chris Rushton

1 Matthew Terrace, Dinas Powys CF64 4LL
t 029 2051 2514 **f** 029 2051 2514 **m** 07971 529851
e chris@c-rushton.freserve.co.uk **w** www.productionbase.co.uk
Credits Aberfan 25 Years of Experience (D); The Munchausen File (D); Cert 18 (D)

Gwennan Sage

The Dench Arnold Agency, 24 D'Arblay Street, London W1F 8EH
t 020 7437 4551 **f** 020 7439 1355
e contact@dencharnoldagency.co.uk **w** www.dencharnold.co.uk

Dominic Santana

Peters Fraser & Dunlop, Drury House, 34-43 Russell Street,
London WC2B 5HA
t 020 7344 1000 **f** 020 7836 9543
e postmaster@pfd.co.uk **w** www.pfd.co.uk

Peter Sasdy

London Management & Representation, 2-4 Noel Street,
London W1F 8GB
t 020 7287 9000 **f** 020 7287 3236

Philip Saville

Casarotto Ramsay & Associates Ltd, National House,
60-66 Wardour Street, London W1V 4ND
t 020 7287 4450 **f** 020 7287 9128
e agents@casarotto.uk.com **w** www.casarotto.uk.com

Caroline Sax

The Dench Arnold Agency, 24 D'Arblay Street, London W1F 8EH
t 020 7437 4551 **f** 020 7439 1355
e contact@dencharnoldagency.co.uk **w** www.dencharnold.co.uk

Thorsten Schmidt

Linda Seifert Management, 91 Berwick Street, London W1F ONE
t 020 7292 7390 **f** 020 7292 7391
e contact@lindaseifert.com **w** www.lindaseifert.com

Frank Schofield

2 Great Ormond Street, London WC1N 3RB
t 020 7404 7555 **t** 020 7404 7557 **f** 07092 268141 **m** 07930
809281 **e** frank/schofield@usa.net **w** www.bv.com
Credits Unluck For Some (S); Insurance Man (S); Hedgehog (S); 24 Pounds To
Tulse Hill (S)

Stefan Schwartz

International Creative Management Ltd, Oxford House,
76 Oxford Street, London W1D 1BS
t 020 7636 6565 **f** 020 7323 0101 **w** www.icmlondon.co.uk

Paul Seed

Peters Fraser & Dunlop, Drury House, 34-43 Russell Street,
London WC2B 5HA
t 020 7344 1000 **f** 020 7836 9543
e postmaster@pfd.co.uk **w** www.pfd.co.uk

Ian Sellar

Peters Fraser & Dunlop, Drury House, 34-43 Russell Street,
London WC2B 5HA
t 020 7344 1000 **f** 020 7836 9543
e postmaster@pfd.co.uk **w** www.pfd.co.uk

Jon Sen
Peters Fraser & Dunlop, Drury House, 34-43 Russell Street,
London WC2B 5HA
t 020 7344 1000 **f** 020 7836 9543
e postmaster@pfd.co.uk **w** www.pfd.co.uk

Eva Sereny
The Dench Arnold Agency, 24 D'Arblay Street, London W1F 8EH
t 020 7437 4551 **f** 020 7439 1355
e contact@dencharnoldagency.co.uk **w** www.dencharnold.co.uk

Seton Production
12 The Arundel Wing, Tortington Manor, Arundel BN18 0FG
t 01903 883720 **m** 07770 236938
Contact Paul Gawith, Director
Credits Teletubbies Everywhere (T); One In Three (D); BBC Commonwealth
Games (T); Carlton Debate (T)

Tristram Shapeero
Casarotto Ramsay & Associates Ltd, National House,
60-66 Wardour Street, London W1V 4ND
t 020 7287 4450 **f** 020 7287 9128
e agents@casarotto.uk.com **w** www.casarotto.uk.com

Adrian Shergold
Peters Fraser & Dunlop, Drury House, 34-43 Russell Street,
London WC2B 5HA
t 020 7344 1000 **f** 020 7836 9543
e postmaster@pfd.co.uk **w** www.pfd.co.uk

Jo Shoop
Peters Fraser & Dunlop, Drury House, 34-43 Russell Street,
London WC2B 5HA
t 020 7344 1000 **f** 020 7836 9543
e postmaster@pfd.co.uk **w** www.pfd.co.uk

Simon Shore
Peters Fraser & Dunlop, Drury House, 34-43 Russell Street,
London WC2B 5HA
t 020 7344 1000 **f** 020 7836 9543
e postmaster@pfd.co.uk **w** www.pfd.co.uk

Jeremy Silberston
Pigeons Green, St Mary's Platt, Sevenoaks TN15 8NL
t 01732 882462 **f** 01732 884993 **m** 07973 272055
e jeremy@silberston.freeserve.co.uk
Agent London Management & Representation, 2-4 Noel
Street, London W1F 8GB
t 020 7287 9000 **f** 020 7287 3236
Credits House Of Elliot (T); Where the Heart Is (T); Midsomer Murders (T);
Foyles War I & II (T)

Simon Hammond TV
Manor Cottage, Court Lane, Offenham, Evesham WR11 8RP
t 0 1386 47013 **e** info@simonhammond.co.uk
w www.simonhammond.co.uk
Contact Simon Hammond, Director; Sheila Hammond, Director
Credits Jesus For Today (W); Music Live! (T); White Sings Robeson (T); Songs Of
Praise (T)

Brian Simmons
8 Necton Road, Wheathampstead, St Alban's AL4 8AU
t 01582 834528 **m** 07930 304 607
e brian.simmons1@ntlworld.com
Credits Arts (T); Energize (T); The Disney Club (T)

Roger Singleton-Turner
15 Sleegill, Richmond DL10 4RH
t 01748 822863 **f** 01748 822149 **m** 07866 252439
e roger@singletonturner-fsnet.co.uk
Credits Grange Hill (T); The Demon Headmaster (T); Welcome To Orty-Fou (T);
The Ark (T)

*Director/Producer, award winning drama, live action, puppets,
animation, teaching.*

David Skynner
Peters Fraser & Dunlop, Drury House, 34-43 Russell Street,
London WC2B 5HA
t 020 7344 1000 **f** 020 7836 9543
e postmaster@pfd.co.uk **w** www.pfd.co.uk

George Sluizer
Casarotto Ramsay & Associates Ltd, National House,
60-66 Wardour Street, London W1V 4ND
t 020 7287 4450 **f** 020 7287 9128
e agents@casarotto.uk.com **w** www.casarotto.uk.com

Chris Smith
Peters Fraser & Dunlop, Drury House, 34-43 Russell Street,
London WC2B 5HA
t 020 7344 1000 **f** 020 7836 9543
e postmaster@pfd.co.uk **w** www.pfd.co.uk

Frank Smith
Peters Fraser & Dunlop, Drury House, 34-43 Russell Street,
London WC2B 5HA
t 020 7344 1000 **f** 020 7836 9543
e postmaster@pfd.co.uk **w** www.pfd.co.uk

Peter Smith
Peters Fraser & Dunlop, Drury House, 34-43 Russell Street,
London WC2B 5HA
t 020 7344 1000 **f** 020 7836 9543
e postmaster@pfd.co.uk **w** www.pfd.co.uk

Steve Smith
3-4 Overton Cottages, East Kennett, Marlborough SN8 4EZ
t 01672 861464 **f** 07971 434711 **m** 07973 512676
e mail@steve-smith.tv **w** www.steve-smith.tv
Credits Da Ali G Show (T); Big Brother (T); So Graham Norton (T)

Tony Smith
Peters Fraser & Dunlop, Drury House, 34-43 Russell Street,
London WC2B 5HA
t 020 7344 1000 **f** 020 7836 9543
e postmaster@pfd.co.uk **w** www.pfd.co.uk

Mary Soan
EXEC, 6 Travis Court, Farnham Royal SL2 3SB
t 01753 646677 **f** 01753 646770
e sue@execmanagement.co.uk **w** www.execmanagement.co.uk

Iain Softley
Casarotto Ramsay & Associates Ltd, National House,
60-66 Wardour Street, London W1V 4ND
t 020 7287 4450 **f** 020 7287 9128
e agents@casarotto.uk.com **w** www.casarotto.uk.com

SomaFilms Ltd
26 Godfrey Avenue, Twickenham TW2 7PF
t 07971 277923 **f** 07970 632786
e somafilms@enterprise.net **w** www.somafilms.com
Contact Arun Kumar, Writer/Director/Producer
Credits Venus (F); Looters (S); The Search For Kurtz (D)

Tim van Someren
2 Mulberry Close, Hampstead, London NW3 5UP
t 07767 700909 **f** 020 7435 5679 **e** tim@vansomeren.co.uk
Credits Puff Daddy Live In Concert In Cape Town (T); Fear Factor (T); Cilla's
Moment of Truth (T); MTV Asia Music Awards (T)

Barnaby Southcombe
London Management & Representation, 2-4 Noel Street,
London W1F 8GB
t 020 7287 9000 **f** 020 7287 3236
Credits Night And Day (T); As If (T)

Spacexploration Ltd
21 Chesham Street, Brighton BN2 1NA
m 07973 151432
e chester@spacexploration.com **w** www.spacexploration.com
Contact Chester Dent

Richard Spence
Peters Fraser & Dunlop, Drury House, 34-43 Russell Street, London WC2B 5HA
t 020 7344 1000 **f** 020 7836 9543
e postmaster@pfd.co.uk **w** www.pfd.co.uk

Simon Spencer
The Dench Arnold Agency, 24 D'Arblay Street, London W1F 8EH
t 020 7437 4551 **f** 020 7439 1355
e contact@dencharnoldagency.co.uk **w** www.dencharnold.co.uk

Bob Spiers
International Creative Management Ltd, Oxford House, 76 Oxford Street, London W1D 1BS
t 020 7636 6565 **f** 020 7323 0101 **w** www.icmlondon.co.uk

Ian Spink
Cruickshank Cazenove Ltd, 97 Old South Lambeth Road, London SW8 1XU
t 020 7735 2933 **f** 020 7820 1081 **e** hjcruickshank@aol.com
Credits Heaven Ablaze In His Breast (T); Fugue (S)

Max Stafford-Clark
Peters Fraser & Dunlop, Drury House, 34-43 Russell Street, London WC2B 5HA
t 020 7344 1000 **f** 020 7836 9543
e postmaster@pfd.co.uk **w** www.pfd.co.uk

Richard Standeven
The Dench Arnold Agency, 24 D'Arblay Street, London W1F 8EH
t 020 7437 4551 **f** 020 7439 1355
e contact@dencharnoldagency.co.uk **w** www.dencharnold.co.uk

Nick Stevens
The Dench Arnold Agency, 24 D'Arblay Street, London W1F 8EH
t 020 7437 4551 **f** 020 7439 1355
e contact@dencharnoldagency.co.uk **w** www.dencharnold.co.uk

Whit Stillman
International Creative Management Ltd, Oxford House, 76 Oxford Street, London W1D 1BS
t 020 7636 6565 **f** 020 7323 0101 **w** www.icmlondon.co.uk

Karen Stowe
London Management & Representation, 2-4 Noel Street, London W1F 8GB
t 020 7287 9000 **f** 020 7287 3236
Credits EastEnders (T); Grange Hill (T); 24/Seven (T)

Toni Strasburg
Flat 3, 38 Canfield Gardens, London NW6 3LA
t 020 7328 2536 **f** 020 7372 6649 **m** 07713 471817
e tonistraz@aol.com
Credits Paying The Price (D); Phelophepa (D); Bread And Water (D); Chain Of Hope (D)

Paul Street
International Creative Management Ltd, Oxford House, 76 Oxford Street, London W1D 1BS
t 020 7636 6565 **f** 020 7323 0101 **w** www.icmlondon.co.uk

John Stroud
The Dench Arnold Agency, 24 D'Arblay Street, London W1F 8EH
t 020 7437 4551 **f** 020 7439 1355
e contact@dencharnoldagency.co.uk **w** www.dencharnold.co.uk

Charles Sturridge
Peters Fraser & Dunlop, Drury House, 34-43 Russell Street, London WC2B 5HA
t 020 7344 1000 **f** 020 7836 9543
e postmaster@pfd.co.uk **w** www.pfd.co.uk

Donald Sturrock
Peters Fraser & Dunlop, Drury House, 34-43 Russell Street, London WC2B 5HA
t 020 7344 1000 **f** 020 7836 9543
e postmaster@pfd.co.uk **w** www.pfd.co.uk

Eric Styles
Peters Fraser & Dunlop, Drury House, 34-43 Russell Street, London WC2B 5HA
t 020 7344 1000 **f** 020 7836 9543
e postmaster@pfd.co.uk **w** www.pfd.co.uk

Tim Sullivan
Peters Fraser & Dunlop, Drury House, 34-43 Russell Street, London WC2B 5HA
t 020 7344 1000 **f** 020 7836 9543
e postmaster@pfd.co.uk **w** www.pfd.co.uk

Sun Chariot Film & TV Productions
61 Tattenham Crescent, Epsom KT18 5NX
t 01737 357460 **f** 01737 357460
Contact Joan Lewiston, Company Director
Credits Shergar (F)

Jeremy Swan
Kerry Gardner Management, 7 St Georges Square, London SW1V 2HX
t 020 7828 7748 **f** 020 7828 7758 **e** kerrygardner@freeuk.com

Piotr Szkopiak
1 Abbotswood Road, London SW16 1AJ
t 020 8769 2192 **f** 020 8677 4274 **m** 07949 151295
e pszkopiak@sniffout.com **w** www.solofilms.co.uk
Credits Let Sleeping Dogs Lie (S); Small Time Obsession (F)

Rachel Talalay
Casarotto Ramsay & Associates Ltd, National House, 60-66 Wardour Street, London W1V 4ND
t 020 7287 4450 **f** 020 7287 9128
e agents@casarotto.uk.com **w** www.casarotto.uk.com

Tangent Loop Productions
t 020 7732 7001 **m** 07939 275649 **e** tangent.loop@virgin.net
Contact Roberta Thompson, Director
Credits Poison Arrows (F); Into Swans (S); The Rubber Ball (D); Soul Train (S)

Julien Temple
Casarotto Ramsay & Associates Ltd, National House, 60-66 Wardour Street, London W1V 4ND
t 020 7287 4450 **f** 020 7287 9128
e agents@casarotto.uk.com **w** www.casarotto.uk.com

Graham Theakston
Peters Fraser & Dunlop, Drury House, 34-43 Russell Street, London WC2B 5HA
t 020 7344 1000 **f** 020 7836 9543
e postmaster@pfd.co.uk **w** www.pfd.co.uk

Colin Thomas
62 York Road, Bristol BS6 5QF
t 0117 909 2862 **m** 07974 927811
e colinthomas.hazelgower@blueyonder.co.uk
Credits Death Of A Sociologist (T); Rebels & Red Coats (T)

Delyth Thomas
C/o Judy Daish Associates, 2 St Charles Place, London W10 6EG
t 02920 222185 **m** 07968 591411
Credits The Story Of Tracy Beaker: Series II (T); Hope And Glory (T); A&E (T); Without Motive (T)

May Miles Thomas
Peters Fraser & Dunlop, Drury House, 34-43 Russell Street, London WC2B 5HA
t 020 7344 1000 **f** 020 7836 9543
e postmaster@pfd.co.uk **w** www.pfd.co.uk

Neil Thomson
Peters Fraser & Dunlop, Drury House, 34-43 Russell Street,
London WC2B 5HA
t 020 7344 1000 **f** 020 7836 9543
e postmaster@pfd.co.uk **w** www.pfd.co.uk
Credits Dalziel And Pascoe (T); Residents (T); Teachers (T); Wire In The Blood (T)

John Tiffany
Casarotto Ramsay & Associates Ltd, National House,
60-66 Wardour Street, London W1V 4ND
t 020 7287 4450 **f** 020 7287 9128
e agents@casarotto.uk.com **w** www.casarotto.uk.com

Philip Traill
Peters Fraser & Dunlop, Drury House, 34-43 Russell Street,
London WC2B 5HA
t 020 7344 1000 **f** 020 7836 9543
e postmaster@pfd.co.uk **w** www.pfd.co.uk

Jane Treays
Creative Media Management, Unit 3B, Walpole Court,
Ealing Studios, Ealing Green, London W5 5ED
t 020 8584 5363 **f** 020 8566 5554
e enquiries@creativemediamanagement.com
Credits Public Enemy - Mother And Son (D); What Sort Of Gentleman Are You
After? (T)

Joachim Trier
Casarotto Ramsay & Associates Ltd, National House,
60-66 Wardour Street, London W1V 4ND
t 020 7287 4450 **f** 020 7287 9128
e agents@casarotto.uk.com **w** www.casarotto.uk.com

Joe Tucker
Peters Fraser & Dunlop, Drury House, 34-43 Russell Street,
London WC2B 5HA
t 020 7344 1000 **f** 020 7836 9543
e postmaster@pfd.co.uk **w** www.pfd.co.uk

Roger Tucker
The Dench Arnold Agency, 24 D'Arblay Street, London W1F 8EH
t 020 7437 4551 **f** 020 7439 1355
e contact@dencharnoldagency.co.uk **w** www.dencharnold.co.uk

Sue Tully
International Creative Management Ltd, Oxford House,
76 Oxford Street, London W1D 1BS
t 020 7636 6565 **f** 020 7323 0101 **w** www.icmlondon.co.uk

Paul Unwin
Peters Fraser & Dunlop, Drury House, 34-43 Russell Street,
London WC2B 5HA
t 020 7344 1000 **f** 020 7836 9543
e postmaster@pfd.co.uk **w** www.pfd.co.uk

Willem Van De Sande Bakhuyzen
Peters Fraser & Dunlop, Drury House, 34-43 Russell Street,
London WC2B 5HA
t 020 7344 1000 **f** 020 7836 9543
e postmaster@pfd.co.uk **w** www.pfd.co.uk

Tom Vaughan
Peters Fraser & Dunlop, Drury House, 34-43 Russell Street,
London WC2B 5HA
t 020 7344 1000 **f** 020 7836 9543
e postmaster@pfd.co.uk **w** www.pfd.co.uk

Olivier Venturini
Peters Fraser & Dunlop, Drury House, 34-43 Russell Street,
London WC2B 5HA
t 020 7344 1000 **f** 020 7836 9543
e postmaster@pfd.co.uk **w** www.pfd.co.uk

Malcolm Walker
t 01256 704031 **f** 01256 704279 **m** 07774 227 622
e mtwalker@easynet.co.uk
Credits Another Life (F); Streetlife (T); Doctors (T)

Nicholas Walters
373 Harrow Road, Maida Hill, London W9 3NA
t 020 8968 4365 **m** 07803 404422
e enquiry@nicholaswalters.co.uk **w** www.nicholaswalters.co.uk
Credits Attitude (S); Tie Rack (C); Sugar Daddy (C); The Bill (T)

Matthew Warchus
Pauline Asper Management, Jacobs Cottage, Reservoir Lane,
Sedlescombe TN33 0PJ
t 01424 870412 **f** 01424 870412 **e** pauline.asper@virgin.net

Merlin Ward
118 Clonmore Street, London SW18 5HB
t 020 8637 0955 **f** 020 8516 5948 **m** 07870 487132
e merlin@creativewizard.com
Credits Out Of Bounds - Aka Dead In The Water (F)

Norman J Warren
216 Boston Road, London W7 2AD
t 020 8579 3674 **f** 020 8579 3674 **m** 07957 487167
e terror@tesco.net
Credits Talking With The Stars (D); Christopher Lee - A Life In Films (D); Terror
(F); Inseminoid (F)

Keith Washington
Oxford House, 76 Oxford Street, London W1D 1BS
t 020 7636 6565 **f** 020 7323 0101 **w** www.icmlondon.co.uk
Credits London's Burning (T); The Knock (T); My Wonderful Life (T);
Jonathan Creek (T)

John Walsh
Walsh Bros, 4 The Heights, London SE7 8JH
t 020 8854 5557 **f** 020 8854 5557 **m** 07879 816426
e walshbros@lycosmail.com
Credits Headhunting The Homeless (T); Trex II (T); Trex (T); Monarch (F)

Emma Wass
The Dench Arnold Agency, 24 D'Arblay Street, London W1F 8EH
t 020 7437 4551 **f** 020 7439 1355
e contact@dencharnoldagency.co.uk **w** www.dencharnold.co.uk

Luke Watson
The Dench Arnold Agency, 24 D'Arblay Street, London W1F 8EH
t 020 7437 4551 **f** 020 7439 1355
e contact@dencharnoldagency.co.uk **w** www.dencharnold.co.uk
Credits The Architect (T); The Fear (T); Brookside (T)

Paul Watson
32 Leitrim Avenue, Shoebury SS3 9HD
t 01702 296528 **f** 01702 296528 **m** 07774 202671
e paulofilm@aol.com

Jeremy Webb
The Dench Arnold Agency, 24 D'Arblay Street, London W1F 8EH
t 020 7437 4551 **f** 020 7439 1355
e contact@dencharnoldagency.co.uk **w** www.dencharnold.co.uk
Credits Casualty (T); Ultimate Force II (T)

Peter Webber
Peters Fraser & Dunlop, Drury House, 34-43 Russell Street,
London WC2B 5HA
t 020 7344 1000 **f** 020 7836 9543
e postmaster@pfd.co.uk **w** www.pfd.co.uk

Paul Weiland
Casarotto Ramsay & Associates Ltd, National House,
60-66 Wardour Street, London W1V 4ND
t 020 7287 4450 **f** 020 7287 9128
e agents@casarotto.uk.com **w** www.casarotto.uk.com
Credits Zero 7: Distractions

Simon Welsford
London Management & Representation, 2-4 Noel Street,
London W1F 8GB
t 020 7287 9000 **f** 020 7287 3236

Derek Wheeler

23 Raeburn Avenue, Dartford DA1 3BQ
t 01322 270194 **f** 01322 294746 **m** 07774 943586
e visability@lineone.net
Credits Treasure Hunt (T); I'd Do Anything (T); An Audience With Brian Conley (T); Robot Wars Extreme Warriors (T)

Paul Wheeler

Experience Counts - Call Me Ltd, 5th Floor, 41-42 Berners Street, London W1P 3AA
t 020 7637 8112 **f** 020 7580 2582

Camilla Whitby

Crofts House, Kirdford RH14 0JH
t 01403 820299 **m** 07860 405582
e info@cwfilms.com **w** www.camillawhitby.i12.com
Credits Safe Skiing (I); Defence In Depth (I); A Summer In Provence (D); For The Love Of Liddy (D)

Tim Whitby

Casarotto Ramsay & Associates Ltd, National House, 60-66 Wardour Street, London W1V 4ND
t 020 7287 4450 **f** 020 7287 9128
e agents@casarotto.uk.com **w** www.casarotto.uk.com

Leonard White

Highlands, 40 Hill Crest Road, Newhaven BN9 9EG
t 01273 514473 **f** 01273 514473 **e** leoguy.white@virgin.net

Marcus White

Pauline Asper Management, Jacobs Cottage, Reservoir Lane, Sedlescombe TN33 0PJ
t 01424 870412 **f** 01424 870412 **e** pauline.asper@virgin.net

Susanna White

Peters Fraser & Dunlop, Drury House, 34-43 Russell Street, London WC2B 5HA
t 020 7344 1000 **f** 020 7836 9543
e postmaster@pfd.co.uk **w** www.pfd.co.uk

Joshua Whitehead

e joshuaheed@yahoo.co.uk
Contact Joshua Whitehead, Director
Credits Unthinkable (D); $100 Taxi Ride (D); The Slot (D); Strip School (D)

Stephen Whittaker

Curtis Brown, Haymarket House, 28-29 Haymarket, London SW1Y 4SP
t 020 7396 6600 **f** 020 7396 0110 **e** cb@curtisbrown.co.uk
Credits Grafters II (T); Forsythe Saga (T); Rocket Post (F)

Daniel Wiles

10 Lonsdale Road, London W4 1ND
t 020 8995 9454 **e** daniel.wiles@granadamedia.com
Credits Crime Monthly (D); Dimbleby (D); Smash (D); The South Bank Show (T)

Martin Williams

14 St Catherine's Close, London SW17 7UA
m 079 7015 8413 **e** martin.williams@dial.pipex.com
Credits Hidden City Of London (D); Volcanic Vacations: Eruption Zone (D); Volcanic Vacations: Lava Junkies (D)

Toni Williamson

m 07768 517926 **e** toniwill@dircon.co.uk
Credits Girls Behaving Badly (T); Tenants From Hell (T); Airport (T)

Andy Wilson

Casarotto Ramsay & Associates Ltd, National House, 60-66 Wardour Street, London W1V 4ND
t 020 7287 4450 **f** 020 7287 9128
e agents@casarotto.uk.com **w** www.casarotto.uk.com

Terry Winsor

Peters Fraser & Dunlop, Drury House, 34-43 Russell Street, London WC2B 5HA
t 020 7344 1000 **f** 020 7836 9543
e postmaster@pfd.co.uk **w** www.pfd.co.uk

Claire Winyard

Casarotto Ramsay & Associates Ltd, National House, 60-66 Wardour Street, London W1V 4ND
t 020 7287 4450 **f** 020 7287 9128
e agents@casarotto.uk.com **w** www.casarotto.uk.com

Herbert Wise

13 Despard Road, London N19 5NP
t 020 7272 5047 **f** 020 7281 3767 **m** 07887 735067
e herbertwise@zoom.co.uk
Agent CCA Management, 7 St George's Square, London SW1V 2HX
t 020 7630 6303 **f** 020 7630 7376
Credits Skokie (F); I Claudius (T); Breaking The Code (T); 10th Kingdom (T)

Tony Wise

3 Corunna Drive, Horsham RH13 5HG
t 01403 274540 **f** 01403 274540 **m** 07802 740568
e tony@wisefilm.fsnet.co.uk
Credits DFID-PSA 2003 (I); Swalec Doorstep Challenge (C); Renault (I); Nissan Primera (I)

Nick Wood

Linda Seifert Management, 91 Berwick Street, London W1F 0NE
t 020 7292 7390 **f** 020 7292 7391
e contact@lindaseifert.com **w** www.lindaseifert.com

Peter Wood

Peters Fraser & Dunlop, Drury House, 34-43 Russell Street, London WC2B 5HA
t 020 7344 1000 **f** 020 7836 9543
e postmaster@pfd.co.uk **w** www.pfd.co.uk

Jeremy Wooding

The Dench Arnold Agency, 24 D'Arblay Street, London W1F 8EH
t 020 7437 4551 **f** 020 7439 1355
e contact@dencharnoldagency.co.uk **w** www.dencharnold.co.uk

Hans Fabian Wullenweber

Curtis Brown, Haymarket House, 28-29 Haymarket, London SW1Y 4SP
t 020 7396 6600 **f** 020 7396 0110 **e** cb@curtisbrown.co.uk
Credits Udenfor (S); Klatretosen (F)

Ian Wyatt

N403, BBC Elstree Centre, Clarendon Road, Borehamwood WD6 1JF
t 020 8287 8055 **t** 020 8228 7136 **f** 020 8228 8168
m 07802 212483 **e** ian.wyatt@bbc.co.uk
Credits The Pier (T); Tough Customers (T); The Law Machine (T); Signals (T)

Rupert Wyatt

Peters Fraser & Dunlop, Drury House, 34-43 Russell Street, London WC2B 5HA
t 020 7344 1000 **f** 020 7836 9543
e postmaster@pfd.co.uk **w** www.pfd.co.uk

David Yates

Curtis Brown, Haymarket House, 28-29 Haymarket, London SW1Y 4SP
t 020 7396 6600 **f** 020 7396 0110 **e** cb@curtisbrown.co.uk
Credits The Titchborne Claimant (F); Sins (T); The Way we Live Now (T)

Kfir Yefet

Casarotto Ramsay & Associates Ltd, National House, 60-66 Wardour Street, London W1V 4ND
t 020 7287 4450 **f** 020 7287 9128
e agents@casarotto.uk.com **w** www.casarotto.uk.com

Emily Young

Michelle Kass Associates, 36-38 Glasshouse Street, London W1B 5DL
t 020 7439 1624 **f** 020 7734 3394

Robert Young

28 Kew Green, Kew TW9 3BH
t 020 8948 2310 **f** 020 8948 7094 **m** 07976 705785
e rwyoung@blueyonder.co.uk
Credits GBH (T); Splitting Heirs (F); Fierce Creatures (F); Captain Jack (F)

Eleanor Yule

Peters Fraser & Dunlop, Drury House, 34-43 Russell Street, London WC2B 5HA
t 020 7344 1000 **f** 020 7836 9543
e postmaster@pfd.co.uk **w** www.pfd.co.uk

Paul Yule

46 Brookfield, London N6 6AT
t 020 7923 1998 **e** paul@paulyule.com
Credits Elgar's Tenth Muse (T); Battle For The Holocaust (D); The House Of War (D); Mugabe's Secret Famine (D)

Andrew Zikking

11 The Granary, 51 Queen Charlotte Street, Bristol BS1 3HQ
m 07799 265 863
e andrew.zikking@virgin.net
w www.andrewzikking.pwp.blueyonder.co.uk/frontpage.html
Credits Uganda (D); Take Time With Twiggy (T); Making It (T)

Display Equipment

Anna Valley Displays

9 Mounts Mews, High Street, Hampton TW12 2SH
t 020 8941 4500 **f** 020 8941 0077
e mail@annavalley.co.uk **w** www.annavalley.co.uk
Contact Mark Holdway, Displays Manager; Karen Mellor, Sales Co-ordinator; Matthew Tomkinson, Head of Resources
Credits My Family (T); The Politics Show (T); Catchphrase (T); This Is Your Life (T)

Anna Valley Displays has been providing large screen display services which includes plasmas, projectors, screens to the television industry for hire, sale, installation and consultation since 1986. We have wide experience in all types of video and data projection including HD and 3D projection.

Barco Control Rooms

50 Suttons Park Avenue, Reading RG6 1AZ
t 0118 966 4611 **f** 0118 926 7716
e sales.uk.bps@barco.com **w** www.barco.com
Contact Shane O'Reilly, Market Development Manager; Simon Turtle, Business Development Manager; Stephen Wair, Market Development Manager

DISTRUBTION & SALES

Distribution & Sales Film

Abbey Films

35 Upper Abbey Street, Dublin 1, Rep of Ireland
t +353 1804 4500 **f** +353 1872 3687
e abbeyfilms@eircom.net
Contact Leo Ward; Siobhan Flynn, Marketing and PR
Credits Austin Powers In Goldmember (F); About Schmidt (F); Gangs of New York (F); Lord Of The Rings - Two Towers (F)

Apollo Film Distributors

14 Ensbury Park Road, Bournemouth BH9 2SJ
t 01202 520962 **f** 01202 539986 **m** 07850 726728
Contact Mike Chivers, Director

Arrow Film Distributors

18 Watford Road, Radlett WD7 8LE
t 01923 858306 **f** 01923 859673
e neil@arrowfilms.co.uk **w** www.arrowfilms.co.uk
Contact Neil Agran; Alex Agran
Credits Mrs Caldicot's Cabbage War (F); Rififi (F); Girl Of Your Dreams (F); Insomnia (F)

Artificial Eye Film Company

14 King Street, London WC2E 8HR
t 020 7240 5353 **f** 020 7240 5242
e info@artificial-eye.com **w** www.artificial-eye.com
Contact Pamela Engel, Managing Director

BFI Video Publishing

21 Stephen Street, London W1T 1LN
t 020 7957 8957 **f** 020 7957 8968
e video.films@bfi.org.uk **w** www.bfi.org.uk

Blue Dolphin Film & Video

40 Langham Street, London W1W 7AS
t 020 7255 2494 **f** 020 7580 7670
e info@bluedolphinfilms.com **w** www.bluedolphinfilms.com
Contact Bernie Watters, Sales Director; Stephanie Walton, Public Relations Officer
Credits Time Of Favor (F); Fogbound (F)

BMG Video International

Bedford House, 69-79 Fulham High Street, London SW6 3JW
t 020 7384 7919 **f** 020 7384 8010
e robin.wilson@bmg.co.uk **w** www.click2music.co.uk
Contact Robin Wilson, Head of Music Programming

Buena Vista International

3 Queen Caroline Street, London W6 9PE
t 020 8222 1000 **f** 020 8222 2795 **w** www.disney.co.uk
Contact Charlotte Tudor, Publicity Director; Daniel Battsek, Managing Director; Robert Mitchell, Marketing Director
Credits Toy Story (F); Mrs Brown (F); The English Patient (F)

East West Creative Associates

Meares House, 194-196 Finchley Road, London NW3 6BX
t 0207 435 5118 **f** 0207 435 8334 **m** 07940 544560
e ebeginin@aol.com
Contact Eugene Beginin, Director General

Euro View Management Services Ltd

PO Box 80, Wetherby LS23 7EQ
t 01937 541010 **f** 01937 541083
e enquiries@euroview.co.uk **w** www.euroview.co.uk

Extreme International Ltd

The Coach House, Ashford Lodge, Halstead CO9 2RR
t 01787 479000 **f** 01787 479111
e group@extreme.com **w** www.extremeinternational.com
Contact Alistair Gosling, Managaing Director; Ben Barrett, Director International Sales

Fabulous Films

26 Loftus Road, London W12 7EN
t 020 8743 4377 **f** 020 8743 4342
e info@fabulousfilms.co.uk **w** www.fabulousfilms.co.uk
Contact Robert Starks, Proprietor

Feature Film Company

19 Heddon Street, London W1B 4BG
t 020 7851 6500 **f** 020 7851 6500
Contact Mick Southworth, Managing Director

Filmbank Distributors Ltd

Warner House, 98 Theobalds Road, London WC1X 8WB
t 020 7984 5910 **f** 020 7984 5951
e s.bryan@filmbank.demon.co.uk **w** www.filmbank.co.uk
Contact David Glennon, Bookings Coordinator

The Fremantle Corporation Ltd

Unit 2, Water Lane, Kentish Town Road, London NW1 8NZ
t 020 7284 6500 **f** 020 7209 2294
e the@fremantlecorp.couk **w** www.fremantlecorp.com
Contact Veronique Heim, Managing Director

Home Entertainment Corporation Plc

19-24 Manasty Road, Orton Southgate, Peterborough PE2 6UP
t 01733 231231 **f** 01733 238966 **i** 01733 230076
e mail@mosaic-entertainment.co.uk **w** www.hecplc.com
Contact I Muspratt, Chairman; S Barker, Development Director; J Spencer (Ms), Director of Programme Purchasing

Imperial Entertainment UK Ltd

15 Main Drive, East Lane Business Park, East Lane, Wembley HA9 7FF
t 020 8385 4455 **f** 020 8908 6785
e (name)@imperialent.co.uk
Contact RP Shah, Managing Director

Metro Tartan & Tartan Video

Atlantic House, 5 WardourStreet, London W1D 6PB
t 020 7494 1400 **f** 020 7439 1922
e info@metro-tartan.co.uk **w** www.tartanvideo.com
Contact Laura de Casto, Managing Director

Mosaic Entertainment

19-24 Manasty Road, Orton Southgate, Peterborough PE2 6UP
t 01733 363010 **f** 01733 363011
e mail@mosaic-entertainment.co.uk **w** www.mosaicmovies.co.uk
Contact Julia Spencer, Programme Purchasing; Lynda Faulkner, Programme purchasing

New Line Cinema

Turner House, 16 Great Marlborough Street, London W1F 7HS
t 020 7693 0977 **f** 020 7693 0978
e paul.saunter@turner.com **w** www.newline.com
Contact Paul Saunter

Odyssey Video

Unit 1, Dundee Way, Mollison Avenue, Enfield EN3 7SX
t 020 8804 8100 **e** amunsey@prismleisure.com
Contact Jam Elliott, General Manager; Adrian Munsey, Managing Director

Paramount Pictures

UIP House, 45 Beadon Road, Hammersmith, London W6 0EG
t 020 8741 9041 **f** 020 8741 9402 **w** www.paramount.com
Contact Michael O'Sullivan, Vice-President international; Leslie Pound, Senior Vice President International Marketing

Polar Graphics Ltd

Joel Street Farm, Joel Street, Pinner HA5 2PD
t 020 8868 2479 **f** 020 8866 8207
e info@polar-graphics.com **w** www.polar-graphics.com
Contact Peter Rowsell, Managing Director; Gary Davis, Technical Director; Holly Rowsell, Sales

Revolver Entertainment

Apex Court, Woodger Road, London W12 8NX
t 020 8222 6677 **f** 0 8222 6688
e info@revolvergroup.com **w** www.revolvergroup.com
Contact Justin Marciano, Managing Director; Natascia Phillips, Product Manager; Jezz Vernon, Marketing Director
Credits CKY2K (T); Snoop Dogg's Doggystyle (M); MTV Yoga (T); Darrins Dance Grooves (M)

Screen Edge

St Anne's House, 329 Clifton Drive South, Lytham St Anne's FY8 1LP
t 01253 712453 **f** 01253 712362
e king@outlaw23.com **w** www.screenedge.com
Contact Richard King, Label Manager

Stewart Film Distributors

The Dial House, Westmill, Buntingford SG9 9LG
t 01763 271260 **f** 01763 271473
Contact Hugh Marsh, Proprietor

Twentieth Century Fox

Twentieth Century House, 31-32 Soho Square, London W1V 3AP
t 020 7437 7766 **f** 020 7439 1806
Contact Steven Cornish, Senior Vice Presindent & Managing Director

Twentieth Century Fox Home Entertainment

Twentieth Century House, 31-32 Soho Square, London W1V 6AP
t 020 7753 8686 **f** 020 7434 2170 **w** www.fox.co.uk
Contact Gary Ferguson, VP of European Home Entertainment

United International Pictures (UIP) International

UIP House, 45 Beadon Road, London W6 0EG
t 020 8563 4130 **f** 020 8748 8990 **w** www.uip.com
Contact Paul Oneile, Chairman & CEO

United International Pictures (UIP) UK

12 Golden Square, London W1A 2JL
t 020 7534 5200 **f** 020 7534 5201
e chris_hedges@uip.com **w** www.uip.com
Contact Chris Hedges, Managing Director

Warner Bros

Warner House, 98 Theobald's Road, London WC1X 8WB
t 020 7984 5000 **f** 020 7984 5001 **w** www.warnerbros.com
Contact Shelly Groves, Director of European Technical Operations

2002 : uk box office statistics

Total UK cinema sites 692

Total UK cinema screens 3,172

(Courtesy of Dodona Research)

Total UK admissions 2002 176m (highest since 1972, up 13% on 2001)

Total box office £812.2 (up 14% on 2001)

Top 30 films in 2002

1	Harry Potter And The Chamber Of Secrets (UK-US) Warner Bros	£48,145,492 *
2	Monsters Inc (US) BVI	£37,687,829
3	Star Wars: Episode II - Attack Of The Clones (US) 20th Fox	£37,427,990
4	Die Another Day (UK-US) 20th Fox	£31,392,839 *
5	Spider-Man (US) Col TriStar	£28,729,833
6	Ocean's Eleven (US) Warner Bros	£26,361,443
7	The Lord Of The Rings: The Two Towers (NZ-US) Entertainment	£26,154,322 *
8	Austin Powers In Goldmember (US) Entertainment	£23,428,992
9	Men In Black II (US) Col TriStar	£22,164,244
10	Scooby-Doo (US) Warner Bros	£21,552,784
11	Minority Report (US) 20th Fox	£20,622,910
12	About A Boy (UK-US) UIP	£16,923,207
13	Signs (US) BVI	£16,186,153
14	Ice Age (US) 20th Fox	£14,970,631
15	My Big Fat Greek Wedding (US) Entertainment	£13,569,577
16	Lilo & Stitch (US) BVI	£13,013,345 *
17	Gosford Park (UK-US) Entertainment	£12,259,248
18	Bend It Like Beckham (UK) Helkon SK	£11,551,538
19	XXX (US) Col TriStar	£11,507,947 *
20	Stuart Little 2 (US) Col TriStar	£11,117,362
21	Ali G IndaHouse (UK-US) UIP	£10,296,604
22	Red Dragon (US) UIP	£9,593,489 *
23	Vanilla Sky (US) UIP	£9,523,575
24	Blade II (US) Entertainment	£9,118,147
25	Panic Room (US) Col TriStar	£8,307,312
26	A Beautiful Mind (US) UIP	£8,033,608
27	The Bourne Identity (US) UIP	£7,848,011
28	The Santa Clause 2 (US) BVI	£6,935,612 *
29	Road To Perdition (US) 20th Fox	£6,682,991 *
30	The Guru (UK-US) UIP	£6,497,236

* Still on release at end of year

→ →

Distribution & Sales **TV**

3DD Entertainment
190 Camden High Street, London NW1 8QP
t 020 7428 1800 **f** 020 7428 1818
e sales@3dd-entertainment.co.uk **w** www.3dd-entertainment.co.uk

Credits American Film Theatre (I); Close-Up With David Beckham (D);
The Robbie Williams Show (T); Cher - The Farewell Concert (T)

4Learning
Channel Four Television Corporation, 124 Horseferry Road,
London SW1P 2TX
t 020 7396 4444 **f** 020 7306 5599
w www.channel4.com/learning

ABC Content Sales
(Australian Broadcasting Corporation)
54 Portland Place, London W1B 1DY
t 020 7079 3201 **f** 020 7079 3251
e anne@abclondon.org **w** www.abccontentsales.com.au

Contact Anne McGrath, Sales Manager, Europe; Malcom Bood, Managing
Director; Alexandra Law, Sales Co-ordinator, Europe

→→→ 2002 : uk box office statistics

Top 15 locals

1	Harry Potter And The Chamber Of Secrets (UK-US) Warner Bros	£53,667,056
2	Die Another Day (UK-US) 20th Fox	£35,982,997
3	About A Boy (UK-US) UIP	£16,923,207
4	Gosford Park (UK-US) Entertainment	£12,259,248
5	Bend It Like Beckham (UK-Ger) Helkon SK	£11,551,538
6	Ali G IndaHouse (UK-US) UIP	£10,296,604
7	The Guru (UK-US) UIP	£6,497,236
8	28 Days later (UK-US) 20th Fox	£6,243,656
9	Iris (UK-US) BVI	£4,025,785
10	The Importance Of Being Earnest (UK-US) BVI	£3,412,587
11	Resident Evil (UK-Ger-US) Pathe	£2,760,469
12	My Little Eye (UK-Fr-US) Momentum Pictures	£2,693,396
13	Dog Soldiers (UK) Pathe	£2,050,308
14	Thunderpants (UK) Pathe	£1,940,085
15	Anita And Me (UK) Icon	£1,847,420

Arbiter Group Plc
Wilberforce Road, London NW9 6AX
t 020 8202 1199 f 020 8202 7076
e sales@arbitergroup.com w www.arbitergroup.com

BBC Worldwide
BBC Television Centre, Wood Lane, London W12 OTT
t 020 8433 2000 f 020 8749 8732 w www.bbcworldwide.com
Contact Alison Homewood, Director of Sales

Beckmann International
Meadow Court, West Street, Ramsey IM8 1AE
t 01624 816585 f 01624 816589
e videos@beckmanndirect.co.uk w www.beckmanndirect.com

Beyond Distribution Pty Ltd
22 Newman Street, London W1T 1PH
t 020 7636 9611 f 020 7636 9622
e yvonne_body@beyond.com.au w www.beyond.com.au

Boudicca Films International Sales & Distribution
t 020 7613 5882 f 020 7613 5882
e boudiccafilms@hotmail.com w www.boudiccafilms.com
Contact Deva Brady, Administrator
Credits Day of Silence (F); Kiss Kiss Bang Bang (F); Love Life (F); Boy Meets Girl (F)

Brian Hambletong TV Associates
16 Heathfield Terrace, Chiswick, London W4 4JE
t 020 8742 3212 f 020 8742 0780 e bryan@bhta.demon.co.uk
Contact Bryan Hambleton, Proprieter

Brian Jackson Films Ltd
39-41 Hanover Steps, Saint Georges Fields, Albion Street,
London W2 2YG
t 020 7402 7543 f 020 7262 5736 m 07802 216337
e brianjfilm@aol.com
Contact Brian Jackson, CEO

British Home Entertainment
5 Broadwater Road, Walton-on-Thames KT12 5DB
t 01932 228832 f 01932 247759 m 07711 848267
e cw@bhe.demon.co.uk w www.britishhomeentertainment.com

Bromley Television International
11 The Terrace, Barnes, London SW13 ONP
t 020 8876 4671 f 020 8878 3858 e bromleytv@aol.com
Contact David Bromley, Managing Director

Capricorn Programmes Ltd
Hithercroft Court, Wallingford OX10 9BT
t 01491 838888 f 01491 833333 e sales@capricornprogs.co.uk
Contact Catherine Cornick, Head of Sales; Sarah Fussell, Office Manager

Channel 4 Video
124 Horseferry Road, London SW1P 2TX
t 020 7396 4444 w www.channel4.com
Contact Catherine Crawford, Video & Merchandising Manager

CJ Productions
Newflat, Maxwelton, Upway, Redway, Porlock, Minehead TA24 8QE
t 01643 862948 f 01643 863400 m 07973 194726
e cjproductions@btconnect.com
Contact Clive Woods, Manager
Credits Reconections (M); Moor Jazz (M)

Columbia TriStar Home Video
25 Golden Square, London W1F 9LU
t 020 7533 1200 f 020 7533 1169 w www.spe.sony.com
Contact Marek Antoniak, Managing Director

Cositar International Television Ltd
78 York Street, London W1H 1DP
t 020 7625 6200
Contact Ray Byrne, Manager Business Affairs; Steve Goddard, Executive Producer

Creative Media Marketing Ltd
40 Bowling Green Lane, London EC1R ONE
t 020 7226 8551 f 020 7226 9528
Contact Gerry Easter, Managing Director

Curzon Video
110 Saint Martins Lane, London WC2N 4AD
t 020 7304 7922 f 020 7867 1131
e david.parkhill@act-arts.co.uk
Contact Daid Parkhill, Managing Director

David Finch Distribution Ltd
PO Box 264, Walton-on-Thames KT12 3YR
t 01932 882733 **f** 01932 882108 **e** sales@david-finch.com
Contact David Finch, Chief Executive

The David Lamping Company
32 Lexington Street, London W1F 0LQ
t 020 7255 8757 **f** 020 7580 3468 **m** 07836 322302
e dlamping@tdlcent.com
Contact David Lamping, Chief Executive
Credits The Slurb (Das Sams) (D); Raising Tennis Aces - The Williams' Story (D)

DCI
57 Lynton Avenue, Ealing, London W13 0EA
t 020 8998 3749 **f** 020 8566 8962 **m** 07831 614482
e davcomin@aol.com
Contact Peter Davies, Director

Derek Hill Consultancy
8 Cavendish Road, London SW12 0DG
t 020 8675 2901 **f** 020 8675 2901 **e** derek.hill@care4free.net
Contact Derek Hill, Proprietor

Digi-Box.co.uk Ltd
4 Allied Business Centre, Coldharbour Lane, Harpenden AL5 4UT
t 01582 466100 **f** 01582 768489 **m** 07803 273322
e jon@digi-box.co.uk **w** www.digi-box.co.uk
Contact Nilesh Mandalia, Business Development Executive; Nick Battle, Sales Executive; Jonathan Phillips, Managing Director

Dorling Kindersley Ltd
The Penguin Group (UK), 80 Strand, London WC2R 0RL
t 020 7010 3000 **f** 020 7010 6060 **w** www.dk.com

Eaton Films
10 Holbein Mews, Lower Sloane Street, London SW1W 8NN
t 020 7823 6173 **f** 020 7823 6017 **e** eaton.films@talk21.com
Contact Judith Bland, Director

Eros International Ltd
Unit 26, Park Royal, Metro Centre, Britannia Way, Coronation Road, London NW10 7PR
t 020 8963 8700 **f** 020 8963 0154
e eros@erosintl.co.uk **w** www.erosentertainment.com
Contact Kishore Lulla, Managing Director

Essential TV
Pinewood Studios, Pinewood Road, Iver SL0 0NH
t 01753 652494 **f** 01753 652451
e info@essential-television.com **w** www.essential-television.com
Contact David Blake, Chairman; Richard Walman, Managing Director; Julian Phelan, Producer
Credits Undead Egypt (D); The Chief Who Talks With God (D); The Path To Manhood (T); Russia's Modern Mummies (D)

European Communication Management
9b Ladbroke Grove, Holland Park, London W11 3BD
t 020 7727 5752 **f** 020 7727 6803 **e** elavelle@ecm-group.co.uk
Contact Liz Lavelle, Office Manager

Extreme International
131-151 Great Titchfield Street, London W1W 5BB
t 020 7244 1000 **f** 020 7244 0101
e sales@extremeinternational.com
w www.extremeinternational.com
Contact Jamie Li, Sales Manager; Alistair Gosling, MD/CEO; Ben Barrett, Director of Sales; Ebby Simsek, Sales Executive
Credits Game Park (D); The Right Stuff (T); When Nature Calls (D); Adventure Challenge (D)
Specialists in sports, travel, adventure and youth lifestyle programming.

Flextech Television
160 Great Portland Street, London W1W 5QA
t 020 7299 5000 **f** 020 7299 6000 **w** www.flextech.co.uk

Fremantle International Distribution
1 Stephen Street, London W1T 1AL
t 020 7691 6000 **f** 020 7691 6060
e fidsales@fremantlemedia.com **w** www.fremantlemedia.com
Contact David Ellender, Managing Director; Tony Stern, Commercial Director & Head Of Co-Productions; Rebecca Lucas, Marketing Manager
Credits The Bill (T); Think Murder (T); Oliver's Twist - Series I And II (T); Jamie's Kitchen (T)

Frontniche
Frontniche House, 14 Merrick Road, Grantham NG31 8NL
t 01476 565518 **m** 07971 601 631
e sales@frontniche.com **w** www.frontniche.com
Contact Stephen Bone, Proprieter

Global Video
96 Caledonia Street, Glasgow G5 0XJ
t 0141 420 2000 **f** 0141 420 2005
e postoffice@global-video.co.uk **w** www.global-video.co.uk
Contact Mac Rasul, Managing Director

Granada International
48 Leicester Square, London WC2H 7FB
t 020 7491 1441 **f** 020 7493 7677
e gi-marketing@granadamedia.com
w www.granadamedia.com/international
Contact Tim Mutimer, Vice President, Sales and Genre; Michelle Asik, International Marketing; Nadine Nohr, Managing Director; Clare Vincent, Vice President, Marketing; Caroline Torrance, Head of International Drama; Toby Melling, Vice President, Sales; George Sakkalli, Vice President, Sales
Credits Egypt (D); Prime Suspect (T); Engie Benjy (A)

Hearst Entertainment
136 Sloane Street, London SW1X 9AY
t 020 7565 6666 **f** 020 7565 6675
e hearst@hearstent.co.uk **w** www.hearstent.com
Contact Michael Doury, Vice President of International Sales

High Point Films & Television Ltd
25 Elizabeth Mews, London NW3 4UH
t 020 7586 3686 **f** 020 7586 3117
e sales@highpointfilms.co.uk **w** www.highpointfilms.co.uk
Contact Ronald de Neef, Principal; Piers Nightingale, Development Executive; Julie Murphy-Delaney, Director of Sales; Carey Fitzgerald, Principal
Credits The Bunker (F); Ken Russell's The Fall of the House of Usher (F); Murder Rooms (T)

HIT Entertainment PLC
5th Floor, Maple House, 149 Tottenham Court Road, London W1T 7NF
t 020 7554 2500 **f** 020 7388 9321
e consumer@hitentertainment.com **w** www.hitentertainment.com
Contact Charlie Caminada, Director of Sales
Credits Barney The Dinosaur (T); Bob The Builder (T); Angelina Ballerina (T); Thomas The Tank Engine (T)

Hypex Electroniques Ltd
19 Osram Road, East Lane Business Park, Wembley HA9 7NG
t 020 8908 3111 **f** 020 8908 3110
e sales@hypex.co.uk **w** www.hypex.co.uk
Contact Shiv Sood, Director

IAP
6a Penzance Place, London W11 4PA
t 020 7727 7158 **f** 020 7727 7158 **e** nick.doff@iapinteractive.com
Contact Nick Doff

Indigo Film & TV
116 Great Portland Street, London W1W 6PJ
t 020 7612 1701 **f** 020 7612 1705
e info@indigofilm.com **w** www.indigofilm.com
Contact Paul Shields, Chairman; David Lawley, Head of Film; Nada Cirjanic, Head of Factual; Emma Collin, Head of Vids

Inflight Studios
15 Stukeley Street, London WC2B 5LT
t 020 7400 0700 **f** 020 7400 0707
e info@inflightproductions.com **w** www.inflightproductions.com
Contact Lee Mantel, Technical Director

Journeyman Pictures Ltd
75A Walton Road, East Molesey KT8 0DP
t 020 8941 9994 **f** 020 8941 9899
e info@journeyman.tv **w** www.journeyman.tv
Contact Sam Goss, Head Of Library Sales; Kathryn Bonnici, Office Administrator;
Mark Stucke, Managing Director; Sam Bailey, Marketing & Development
Credits Kurds After The Gulf War (D); Are They Training Terrorists? (D);
Executive Outcomes (D)

Kingfisher Television Productions
Carlton Studios, Lenton Lane, Nottingham NG7 2NA
t 0115 964 5262 **f** 0115 964 5263

Medusa Communications & Marketing
Regal Chambers, 51 Bancroft, Hitchin SG5 1LL
t 01462 421818 **f** 01462 420393
Contact David Hodgins, Chairman; Stephen Rivers, Director

Minotaur International
160 Great Portland Street, London W1W 5QA
t 020 7299 5000 **f** 020 7299 5777 **e** general@minotaur.co.uk
Contact Debbie Deas, Acquisitions Executive; Sarah Tong, Vice President

NBD TV Ltd
Units 2 Royalty Studios, 105 Lancaster Road, London W11 1QF
t 020 7243 3646 **f** 020 7243 3656 **e** distribution@nbdtv.com
w www.nbdtv.com
Contact Nicky Williams, Managing Director

Nelvana Enterprises (UK)
22 Kingley Court, London W1R 5LE
t 020 7287 2770 **f** 020 7287 2740 **w** www.nelvana.com
Contact Tom Van Waveren

Octagon CSI
177-187 Arthur Road, London SW19 8AE
t 020 8944 4188 **f** 020 8944 4189
e octagoncsi@octagon.com **w** www.csi-ltd.com
Contact Marty Ehrlich; Mark Wilkin, Head of TV Production

Orbit Media
7-11 Kensington High Street, London W8 5NP
t 020 7287 4264 **f** 020 7287 0984
e enquiries@orbitmedia.co.uk **w** www.orbitmedia.co.uk
Contact Jordan Reynolds, Director

Paramount Television Ltd
49 Charles Street, London W1J 5EW
t 020 7318 6400 **f** 020 7491 2086 **w** www.paramount.com
Contact Stephen Tague, Vice President - European Sales

Park Entertainment
4th Floor, 50-51 Conduit Street, London W1S 2YT
t 020 7434 4176 **f** 020 7434 4179
e sales@parkentertainment.com **w** www.parkentertainment.com
Contact Jim Howell, Managing Director

Pearson Broadband
80 Strand, London WC2R 0RL
t 020 7010 2900 **f** 020 7010 6643
e info@pearsonbroadband.com **w** www.pearsonbroadband.com
Contact Simon Jollands, Director - Television; Laura Jones, Communications
Coordinator; Robin Gay, Communications & Marketing Manager; Eric Jones,
Executive Vice President; Natasha Hussein, Internationl Sales Manager; Brenda
Wooding, International Sales Manager; Anne Magnol, Head of Sales
Credits Spot (A); Eyewitness Series (D); Backyard Science (E);
The Way Things Work (A)

Ray Stiles Enterprises
Northumberland House, 230 High Street, Bromley BR1 1PQ
t 020 8466 0606 **f** 020 8313 9682

S4C Masnachol/Commercial
50 Lambourne Cresent, Llanishen, Cardiff CF14 5GG
t 029 2074 1440 **f** 029 2075 4444 **w** www.s4ci.com
Contact Huw Potter, Client Services Manager; Wyn Innes, Managing Director

Safir Films Ltd
49 Littleton Road, Harrow HA1 3SY
t 020 8423 0763 **f** 020 8423 7963 **e** lsafir@attglobal.net
Contact Lawrence Safir, Managing Director

Southern Star Circle
45-49 Mortimer Street, London W1W 8HX
t 020 7636 9421 **f** 020 7436 7426
e sales@sstar.uk.com **w** www.southernstargroup.com
Credits Blue Healers (T); Home And Away (T); Water Rats (T)

Sullivan Entertainment Europe Ltd
Suites 30-32, 63-65 Camden High Street, London NW1 7JL
t 020 7383 5192 **f** 020 7383 0627
e mthomas@sullivan-ent.co.uk **w** www.sullivan-ent.com
Contact Muriel Thomas, Vice President
Credits Road To Avonlea (T); Anne: The Animated Series (A); Piano Man's
Daughter (F); Anne Of Green Gables (T)

Suman Film (India Vision)
Rosebery House, Tottenham Lane, Crouch End, London N8 9BT
t 020 8348 2247 **f** 020 8348 5133 **e** films@suman.co.uk
Contact Vijay Gupta, Director

Sussex Publications
Microworld House, 4 Foscote Mews, London W9 2HH
t 020 7266 2202 **f** 020 7266 2314
e microworld@ndirect.co.uk **w** www.microworld.ndirect.co.uk
Contact Stephen Albert, Director

The Television Corporation International Division
43 Whitfield Street, London W1T 4HA
t 020 7258 6834 **f** 020 7691 8003
e international@tvcorp.co.uk
w www.televisioncorporation.co.uk/international
Contact Mark Rowland, Managing Director; Julie Quirke, Manager; Neil
Osborne, Sales Director - Advertiser Funded Programmes; Anna Fuge, Sales
Director - Formats
Credits Robot Wars (T); World's Worst Driver (T); Toyota World Of Wildlife (T);
Gillette World Sport (T)

*The Television Corporation's international division sells programming to
more than 250 broadcasters worldwide. We distribute hugely successful
sports and entertainment formats from Sunset+Vine and Mentorn and
are the UK's leading independent distributor of advertiser-funded
programming worldwide. We also represent formats from third parties
including Ludus and Shine.*

Telstar Video Entertainment
Prospect Studios, Barnes High Street, Barnes, London SW13 9LE
t 020 8878 7888 **f** 020 8878 7888 **w** www.telstar.co.uk
Contact Gareth Watson, Managing Director

Turner Broadcasting System Europe Ltd
Turner House, 16 Great Marlborough Street, London W1F 7HS
t 020 7693 1235 **f** 020 7693 1224
e helen.williams@turner.com **w** www.TCMonline.co.uk
Contact Helen Williams, Production Manager

TVF International
375 City Road, London EC1U 1NB
t 020 7837 7778 **f** 020 7278 8833
e pippa.lambert@tvf.co.uk **w** www.tvfinternational.com
Contact Robert Norton, Managing Director TVF International; Joanna Langton,
Head of TVF International
Credits Uncovering Skin (D); Mystery Of The Shroud (D); Motherland:
A Genetic Journey (D)

Universal TV International

527 Mandeville Place, London W1U 3AR
t 020 7535 3500 **f** 020 7535 3537
Contact Janet Goldsmith, Managing Director

VVL

1 Sussex Place, London W6 9XS
t 020 8910 5000 **f** 020 8910 5404
e helen.parker@unistudios.com
Contact Helen Parker, Joint Managing Director

Walt Disney Company Ltd

3 Queen Caroline Street, Hammersmith, London W6 9PE
t 020 8222 1000 **f** 020 8222 1122
w www.disneychannel.co.uk
Contact David Hulbert, President Walt Disney Television

Warner Home Video

Warner House, 98 Theobalds Road, London WC1X 8WB
t 020 7984 6400 **f** 020 7984 6400
w www.warnerbros.com

Wienerworld

Unit B2, Livingstone Court, 55-63 Peel Road, Wealdstone HA3 7QT
t 020 8427 2777 **f** 020 8427 0660
e wworld@wienerworld.com **w** www.wienerworld.com
Contact Anthony Broza, Managing Director

Draughtsmen

Alice Biddle

11 Radnor Road, Weybridge KT13 8JU
t 01932 821401 **m** 07961 325606
Credits The Trojan War (F); Die Another Day (F); Sleepy Hollow (F); Band Of Brothers (T)

Patricia Johnson

8 Fitzrobert Place, Egham TW20 9JS
t 01784 431970 **m** 07747 180951 **e** patricia_j@hotmail.com
Credits Quills (F); The Importance Of Being Earnest (F); Harry Potter And The Philosopher's Stone (F); The Mummy Returns (F)

Drivers, Unit

AJ's Passenger Transport Services

Cobwebs, St Johns Road, Sandhurst GU47 9AD
t 01252 877855 **f** 01252 877855 **m** 07860 710835
e alan.shadow@virgin.net
Contact Alan Smith, Proprietor

Barry Stevenson's Film Unit Car Service

74 Bradmore Green, Brookmans Park, Hatfield AL9 7QT
t 01707 652868 **f** 01707 652868 **m** 07774 237201
e barry@luxcar.freeserve.co.uk **w** www.luxcar.freeserve.co.uk
Credits Band Of Brothers (T); PD James' Inspector Dalgliesh (T); 28 Days Later (F); Judge John Deeds (T)

Hamish Bell

Art Department, 51 Pratt Street, London NW1 0BJ
t 020 7428 0500 **f** 020 7916 2167 **m** 07973 639785
e info@art-department.co.uk

Terry Bleasdale

12a Fairfield Close, Hayton Roby, Liverpool L36 4NR
t 0151 489 2153 **m** 07740 708836

Alex Denholm

Art Department, 51 Pratt Street, London NW1 0BJ
t 020 7428 0500 **f** 020 7916 2167 **m** 07973 639785
e info@art-department.co.uk

Phil El-Kadhi

Art Department, 51 Pratt Street, London NW1 0BJ
t 020 7428 0500 **f** 020 7916 2167 **m** 07973 639785
e info@art-department.co.uk

Film Unit Drivers Guild

136 The Crossways, Heston TW5 0JR
t 020 8569 5001 **f** 020 8569 6001 **m** 07860 700 421
e letstalk@fudg.uk.com **w** www.fudg.uk.com

Carlos Graham

Gems, The Media House, 87 Glebe Street, Penarth CF64 1EF
t 029 2071 0770 **f** 029 2071 0771
e gems@gems-agency.co.uk **w** www.gems-agency.co.uk
Credits Station Jim (T); Family Affairs (T); Metrosexuality (T); The Gift (F)

Michael Grover

The Wilkes, 16 Love lane, Morden, London SM4 6LH
t 020 8715 5832 **m** 07860 341391 **e** mr.carservices@virgin.net

David Lloyd

20 Redman House, Lant Street, London SE1 1JU
t 020 7403 4541 **f** 020 7403 5085 **m** 07850 761 969
Contact David Lloyd
Credits Roger Roger (T); Manchild (T); Serious And Organised (T)

John Noel

27 Old Gloucester Street, London WC1N 3XX
t 08708 300688 **f** 08708 303681
e johnnoel@1stpositionvehicles.co.uk
w www.1stpositionvehicles.co.uk
Credits Rescue Me (T); Sony Playstation: Medal of Honor (C); Two Men Went to War (F)

John Orsler

Art Department, 51 Pratt Street, London NW1 0BJ
t 020 7428 0500 **f** 020 7916 2167 **m** 07973 639785
e info@art-department.co.uk

Paolo di Paolo

Art Department, 51 Pratt Street, London NW1 0BJ
t 020 7428 0500 **f** 020 7916 2167 **m** 07973 639785
e info@art-department.co.uk

Mark HT Richards

t 01932 242359 **m** 07768 730887
Credits Lord Of The Rings (F); Bridget Jones' Diary (F); Lucky Break (F); Mike Bassett: England Manager (F)

Mike Richards

Art Department, 51 Pratt Street, London NW1 0BJ
t 020 7428 0500 **f** 020 7916 2167 **m** 07973 639785
e info@art-department.co.uk

Roadsmith.tv

47 Dalmain Road, Forest Hill, London SE23 1AR
f 020 8291 1963 **m** 07956 109213
e roadsmithtv@aol.com **w** www.roadsmith.tv
Contact Lennie Mortlock, Partner
Credits Wondrous Oblivion (F); Alister McGowan's Big Impression (T); Band Of Brothers (T); Harry Potter And The Chamber Of Secrets (F)

Nigel Thorpe

Art Department, 51 Pratt Street, London NW1 0BJ
t 020 7428 0500 **f** 020 7916 2167 **m** 07973 639785
e info@art-department.co.uk

DVD Services

24-7 DVD

1 Ravenscourt Park, Hammersmith, London W6 0TZ
t 020 8248 3949 **f** 020 8248 3976
e mail@24-7dvd.co.uk **w** www.24-7dvd.co.uk
Contact Symon Rove, Managing Director

Animal Tracks

6 Curley Hill Road, Lightwater GU18 5YG
t 01276 472179 **f** 01276 451112
e mailbox@atproductions.co.uk **w** www.atproductions.co.uk
Contact Nick Hemming, Director

Auteur TV

5a Clissold Road, Stoke Newington, London N16 9EX
t 020 7254 0471 **m** 07808 829650
e stream@auteur.tv **w** www.auteur.tv
Contact Digby Rumsey, Director
Credits The Pledge (F); Future Film (W); Killer Elephants (T); The Boulevard Project (W)

BBC Technology DVD Unit

BBC TV Centre, Wood Lane, London W12 7RJ
t 020 8576 7122 **e** dvd.authoring@bbc.co.uk
Contact Brendan Barbour, Business Development Manager; Julian Tow, Group Manager
Credits Aim Higher (E); Life In The Freezer - Attenborough (T); Walking With Beasts (Interactive) (I); 'Allo 'Allo (T)

Ian Grant Beushaw

84 Exmouth Road, Ruislip HA4 0UG
t 020 8845 0005 **f** 020 8845 0005 **m** 07956 229 998
e ian@boggie.fslife.co.uk

Big Blue World

98D Goldhurst Terrace, South Hamstead, London NW6 3HS
t 020 7691 2094 **m** 07764 588675
e mailbox@bigblueworld.com **w** www.bigblueworld.com
Contact Ian Greaves, Director

Bluecrest

Bluecrest International Ltd

272 Field End Road, Ruislip HA4 9NA
t 020 8582 0230 **f** 020 8582 0232
e sales@bluecrest.com **w** www.bluecrest.com
Contact Suzie Wrennall, Business Development Manager; Hannah Eiman, Business Development Executive; Denish McLeish, Production Manager; Greg Kyriacou, Managing Director; Marcelo Bustomanle, Business Development Executive; Sarah Eden, Business Development Executive; Glenn Ward, Sales and Marketing Manager

Caseys Film & Video Ltd

316-318 Latimer Road, London W10 6QN
t 020 8960 0123 **f** 020 8969 3714
e tony@caseys.co.uk **w** www.caseys.co.uk
Contact Tony Weeks, General Manager; Sue McHugh, Bookings

Comprehensive DVD production, design, encoding and authoring facilities for film distribution, commercial and corporate clients. MPEG-2 encoding for video on demand, MPEG-1 encoding for CD-R. Free demonstration available on request.

CDA Data Business Ltd

2 Benjamin Street, London EC1M 5QL
t 020 7250 3003 **f** 020 7250 3002
e sales@cdadb.co.uk **w** www.cdadb.co.uk
Contact Ian Mackay, Sales Manager

Classic Pictures Entertainment Ltd

Shepperton Services, Studios Road, Shepperton TW17 0QD
t 01932 572016 **f** 01932 572046
e lynclassicpics@aol.com **w** www.classicpictures.co.uk
Credits Classical Chillout (M); Classical Chillout (M); Naked Ibiza (M); JJ Cale (M)

Construct Image

60 Gathurst Road, London E8 3EL
t 020 7254 1436
e info@constructimage.co.uk **w** www.constructimage.co.uk
Contact Roger Schindler, Producer

De Breanski

The Media Centre, Culverhouse Cross, Cardiff CF5 6XJ
t 029 2067 9479 **f** 029 2059 0230 **m** 07970 601919
e davidgriffiths@debreanshi.co.uk **e** info@debreanshi.co.uk
w www.debreanski.co.uk
Contact David Griffiths, Manager Editor

Deluxe Digital Studios

7-11 Lexington Street, London W1F 9AF
t 020 7437 4402 **f** 020 7437 4403
e dvd.london@deluxe-digital-studios.com
w www.deluxe-digital-studios.com
Contact Gaye Sykes, DVD Producer; Jonahttan Cheesmur, Senior DVD Producer; Gerald Hinton, Technical Project Manager; Simon Valley, General Manager
Credits We Were Soldiers (T); History Of Britain (T); Red Dwarf - The Movie (T); Memento (F)

Designlab Systems Ltd

9 D'Arblay Street, London W1F 8DR
t 020 7437 5621 **f** 020 7734 1582 **m** 07785 313105
e designlab@btclick.com **w** www.designlab.co.uk
Contact Matt Stephens, Technical Manager; Barney Stoppard, Production Operator; Sarah Nugent, Production Operator; Mike Willis, Design Manager; Jim Morrison, Production Manager; Hilary Lambert, Managing Director

DGP

Portland House, 12-13 Greek Street, Soho, London W1D 4DL
t 020 7734 4501 **f** 020 7734 7034
e mail@dgpsoho.co.uk **w** www.dgpsoho.co.uk
Contact Mark Gardner, Managing Director; Rowan Bray, General Manager; Julian Day, Managing Director; Moira Brophy, Bookings Manager; Peter Hill, Sales
Credits World Chart Express (T); Gorillaz (W); Austin Powers In Goldmember (F); Murder In Mind (T)

DGP is an industry leading full service DVD facility based in Central London. A member of the GMDX affiliation programme, DGP is the only facility in the UK licensed to use Toshiba equipment and brings Hollywood studio technology, experience and creativity to all its clients, be they large or small.

The Digital Group Ltd

10 Stucley Place, Camden Town, London NW1 8NS
t 020 7284 2400 **f** 020 7284 2404
e auriol@digital-group.co.uk **w** www.digital-group.co.uk
Contact Peter Woolliscroft, Managing Director; Auriol Walker, Sales Manager

Fully comprehensive service offering Soho style facilities at competitive prices.

Digiverse Ltd

The Chequers, 28 Whitehorse Street, Baldock SG7 6QQ
t 01462 639816 **f** 01462 895777
e contact@digiverse.co.uk **w** www.digiverse.co.uk

Downstream Ltd

Willowbank House, 44 Marsh Lane, Nantwich CW5 5LH
t 01270 625125 **f** 01270 629424 **m** 07976 215152
e sales@downstream.ltd.uk
Contact Edward Leetham, Managing Director

Economical Video-to-DVD encoding. DVD mastering and duplication. Video, audio and data CD production. Audio recording and digital editing.

authoring for the future

In the topsy-turvy world of new technology, one thing at least is clear. Once people are used to high quality, they will be unsatisfied returning to a lower grade of experience. This is patently the case with the market for DVD services. From director's showreels to multi-disc movie presentations, the DVD revolution has arrived and it's growing at an incredible pace.

"Fast Internet connections at work have encouraged people to install Broadband, but the DVD market has been the complete reverse," says Anthony McCaffery, head of Rocket, the new media arm of Rushes. "The market is expanding quickly, as more players are used at home, and people in this industry expect that high-quality picture and sound in their work environment, especially as they are the ones creating the content."

"Whereas previously clients have been happy enough to review their work from a VHS or UMAT, they now crave a better way to view and approve their work back at the office, at home, or, in many cases, the final presentation for their client," continues McCaffrey. "DVD has provided them the tools to do that in a format which for many is also their domestic one of choice."

According to McCaffery, the popularity of DVD has created a renaissance in the art of providing showreels when pitching for work for many directors. "They now have the ability to create a full package with selected work and customised menus," he explains. "Presentation of their work no longer has to be in a linear format. The viewer is empowered to review the work in a way that suits them, which is also to the benefit of the director."

The quality of the MPEG-2 compression used for encoding DVD-video is far superior to VHS or CD, allowing material to be shown at the broadcast levels it was intended for. Audio too, can be presented in multi-channel formats like Dolby Digital and DTS, or high-resolution stereo audio at 24 bit, 96 kHz. In addition, enhanced DVD formats enable interactivity with Web material, DVD is ideal for archiving hours of broadcast video and the whole thing can be completely linked into on-screen menus for total viewer control.

By far the most obvious form of DVD service is that which caters to the domestic video market. Home video makes more revenue than theatrical release, so all film makers are making sure they address the needs of the DVD community by supplying more and better Value Added Material (VAM). There is also greater emphasis placed on interactive options.

"The DVD format has enabled rights owners to exploit their catalogue for a second time", says Dave Pollard of Squashpost. "The difference is that this time, at least with feature films, the home experience can come closer in quality terms to the theatrical experience. Television companies have been slower to exploit DVD and tend not to alter the programme's technical format in terms of aspect or audio dynamic. They also seem less enthusiastic about using some of the extra functionality that DVD can provide over VHS or a broadcast."

Pollard still sees the current market as buoyant, but thinks this is likely to change. "The back catalogue is disappearing," he says. "I would expect some weeding out of weaker firms during the next twelve months. Technically, there are now low-cost services that can provide cost effective and workable solutions for the type of projects that used to have to go to a specialist facility. In the feature film market, quality and experience are still the premier business drivers."

As Pollard says, repurposing TV and film material for DVD has certainly been an active market since its early days. DGP, a fully-servicing facility house offering production and post production services as well as new media, has been in the DVD business since 1999. Since then this company too, has seen more suppliers entering the market and finds competition, particularly price cutting, is fierce. "There are only a handful of major players, ourselves included, who are equipped to handle A-list titles," says Julian Day, MD of DGP. "All the major players have preferred supplier relationships with major studios to ensure volume. The current market is tough and will only get tougher. Some small companies without firm relationships with major content creators will go under. Price cutting by new entrants will damage the market for everybody."

The equipment used by these studios varies, but Toshiba, Sony and Sonic Solutions are all big vendors in this marker. Some of Sonic's products, such as DVD Producer, support the new OpenDVD specification, which provides a standard means of interchanging DVD discs that can be opened and re-edited across different applications without reference to any original source materials. Meanwhile, Sonic's patented eDVD (enhanced DVD) is the first of its extensions to the DVD format. DVD Creator is one of the Sonic products that supports this technology that integrates Web connectivity using menu buttons or from timelines within movies, and is able to drive DVD playback via the Web.

DGP uses Sonic products but turns to Toshiba for compression and authoring equipment. "This is the best equipment available and is unique to us in the UK," says Julian Day. Squashpost's setup includes networked PCs and Macs as well as hardware audio and video encoders. "We've given a great deal of attention to asset protection and both RAID networks are protected," says Dave Pollard. "Graphics for both moving and static menus are created on Apple Power Mac G4 computers using Photoshop, Combustion, After Effects, Lightwave and Final Cut Pro. For DVD, we use the Sony hardware encoder and Dolby audio encoders coupled to reference decoders. The authoring tool of choice is Spruce Maestro, although we do have Sonic Scenarist and Sonic Creator." Pollard notes that the equipment at the top end has not changed that much recently, a view shared by DGP's Julian Day, but claims that storage has got cheaper and faster, so impacting favourably on his business.

In conclusion, it seems that in this market, no two jobs are the same. "There are no typical projects, but we tend to get involved across most aspects of →→

→→→ authoring for the future

production," says Dave Pollard. "Specifically, we offer a high level of graphics expertise. This is crucial, as an attractive and logical GUI is vital to the overall success of the product. We compress both video and audio streams, and author the disc on the most appropriate of our three different systems. We perform QC checks here using both external and internal operators. The only services we do not supply in-house are sub-titling and replication. Both of these we regularly manage on behalf of customers."

"A general rule of thumb is that the earlier we are involved in the production the better," says Julian Day. "On larger, complex titles this is essential, as we can advise on how to generate assets during the pre-production process. We work closely with the client to design the disc, and encode the video and audio assets to the highest quality. We put great emphasis on client handling, with producers who are technically skilled to liase with all third-party vendors and make sure the clients wishes are met."

According to Rocket's McCaffrey, most work in the showreel end of the market, however, is at a moment's notice and this is reflected in the fast turnaround that his facility can provide. "Larger projects are often brought to us at the concept stage and we are able to advise what is possible, how the work can be presented and how we can enhance the ideas that are brought to us," he explains. "It's not rigid, we can adapt as ideas come forward during the authoring process."

Contacts: Sonic Solutions www.sonic.com
DGP, www.dgpsoho.co.uk
Squashpost, www.squashpost.co.uk/
Rocket, www.rushes.co.uk

Writer: Michael Burns

"All the major players have preferred supplier relationships with major studios to ensure volume," says DGP's Julian Day. DGP produced the menu for the 24 DVD

Sonic Solutions' DVD Creator integrates web connectivity and is able to drive DVD playback via the web.

DSM Video Ltd
Martland House, Kilbuck Lane, Haydock, St Helens WA11 9XJ
t 01942 272730 **f** 01942 272723
e card@dsm-tech.com **w** www.cdcar.org
Contact David Martland, Managing Director

Dubbs
25-26 Poland Street, London W1F 8QN
t 020 7629 0055 **f** 020 7287 8796
e sales@dubbs.co.uk **w** www.dubbs.co.uk
Contact David Wilson, Sales Manager; Seb Tyack, Digital Media Producer; Martin Rogers, Sales Manager; Lauren McCready, Business Development; Bill Gamble, Customer Services Director
Digital media facility specialising in video encoding and DVD authoring. Contact Seb Tyack.

DVD R Direct
Oakslade Studios, Station Road, Hatton CV35 7LH
t 01926 844002 **e** sales@dvdrdirect.co.uk
Contact Jack Stragnell, DVD Authorer
Credits Cadburys (W); BP Corporate DVD (W)

DVDi
t 020 7692 7700 **f** 020 7692 4120
e info@dvd-i.com **w** www.dvd-i.com
Contact Ivan Palmer; Gaelle Mechine
Credits Two Men Went To War (F)

Eagle Vision Productions
Eagle House, 22 Armoury Way, London SW18 1EZ
t 020 8870 5670 **f** 020 8874 2333
e sales@eagle-rock.com **w** www.eaglevision-int.com
Credits Classic Albums (T); Janet Jackson - Live In Hawaii (M); Marilyn Manson - Gods, Guns And Government (M); Bee Gees - One Night Only (M)

Evolutions Television Ltd
5 Berners Street, London W1T 3LF
t 020 7580 3333 **f** 020 7637 1942
e info@evolutionstelevision.com
w www.evolutionstelevision.com
Evolutions New Media department provides creative solutions for all your DVD requirements. We have a full range of DVD services and produce both simple and complex DVD-Videos of the highest quality. DVD duplication services are also available. We also offer a full range of post production, video duplication and multimedia services.

Flare
Ingestre Court, Ingestre Place, London W1F 0JL
t 020 7343 6543 **f** 020 7343 6555
e kabirm@flare-dvd.com **w** www.flare-dvd.com
Contact Kabir Malik; John Edwards; Ish Stein, Business Development
Based at M2, Flare offers a full range of DVD services: Scenarist DVD authoring and web enhancement, Digital Vision Mpeg2 video encoding, Dolby Digital audio compression and 5.1 surround mixing. Menu prod. using Photoshop, Hal, Editbox FX and Media Illusion.

creative:**brainfood**

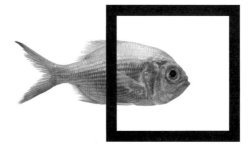

**shots online, DVD and
VHS provide you with
over 90 minutes of pure
creativity every issue.
Featuring the hottest
commercials from across
the globe, shots is your
invaluable advertising tool.**

■ **the latest mind-blowing TV
commercials**

■ **astonishing work from the most
talented new directors**

■ **ground-breaking music videos**

■ **enlightening country focus features**

■ **full credit information for every
spot featured**

■ **over 70 spots every issue**

**Increase your levels of creativity,
win your pitches and stay on top
of global advertising with shots.**

Freehand Graphics

The Courtyard, Eastwood Road, Bramley, Guildford GU5 0DL
t 01483 894000 **f** 01483 894900
e info@freehand.co.uk **w** www.freehand.co.uk
Contact Rebecca Hatrick, Animation & Computer Graphics; Matthew Wright, Production Director
Credits Grofe Grand Canyon (M); Pandemonium (M); Yes - Symphonic Live (M); Simply Red (M)

Hattrick Studios

PO Box 8, Whetstone LE8 6WX
t 0116 223 4119
e sales@hattrickstudios.co.uk **w** www.hattrickstudios.co.uk
Contact Neil Smith, Director
Credits Allround Associates (D); Automobile Association (E)

Humphries Video Services Ltd

Unit 2, The Willow Business Centre, 17 Willow Lane, Mitcham CR4 4NX
t 020 8648 6111 **t** 020 7636 3636 **f** 020 8648 5261
e sales@hvs.bdx.co.uk **w** www.hvs.co.uk
Contact David Brown, Sales and Marketing Director; Jago Michell, Business Development; Emma Lincoln, Production Co-ordinator; Mike Hudson, Production Director

Video cassette duplication and standard conversion centre. From most formats to any cassette format in any world standard. Broadcast and corporate. CD and DVD authoring/replication.

Jano Videos

97 Conway Crescent, Perivale, Greenford UB6 8JB
t 020 8997 8361 **f** 020 8537 9888 **m** 07956 339 028
e t.jeyaratnam@ntlworld.co.uk

Loadplan

Jubilee House, Townsend Lane, Kingsbury, London NW9 8TZ
t 020 8200 7733 **f** 020 8205 2615
e enquiries@loadplan.co.uk **w** www.loadplan.co.uk
Contact Nick Williams, Managing Director
Credits Jameson Whiskey (C)

London Post

34-35 Dean Street, London W1D 4PR
t 020 7439 9080 **f** 020 7434 0714
e info@londonpost.co.uk **w** www.londonpost.co.uk
Contact Soraya Robertson, Bookings Manager; Verity Laing

Meedja Ltd

10 Barley Mow Passage, London W4 4PH
t 020 8747 2055 **f** 020 8747 2049 **m** 07855 491208
e info@meedja.co.uk **w** www.meedja.co.uk
Contact Sarah Bradley, Director
Credits Feeder - Come Back Around (W); Panasonic Tau (W); Brit Awards 2003 (W); Our Friends In The North (W)

Mega-D Ltd

Europa Studios, Tadley RG26 5SU
t 01256 693135 **f** 01256 693136 **m** 07799 116266
e office@mega-d.com **w** www.mega-d.com
Contact Chris McKeeman, Managing Director

Metcom Media Ltd

10 Stocley Place, London NW1 8NS
t 020 7284 2400 **f** 020 7284 2404
Contact Mark Slingo, Sales Director; Nigel Karan, Sales Manager
Credits Pacific Institute (E); Land Rover (C); Amores Perros (F); Manga Entertainment (F)

Metro Broadcast

5-7 Great Chapel Street, London W1F 8FF
t 020 7434 7700 **f** 020 7434 7701
e info@metrobroadcast.com **w** www.metrobroadcast.com
Contact Paul Beale, Business Development; Mark Cox, Director; Nayle Kemal, Digital Media Manager

From production through to replication, our team of experienced graphic designers and DVD authors offer a comprehensive range of DVD services.

Metropolis DVD

70 Chiswick High Road, London W4 1SY
t 020 8742 1111 **f** 020 8742 2626
e dvd@metropolis-group.co.uk **w** www.metropolis-group.co.uk
Contact Sam Stubbings, Senior Producer; Anthony Owen, DVD Operations Manager

Multi Media Replication Ltd

Unit 4, Balksbury Estate, Andover SP11 7LW
t 01264 336330 **f** 01264 336694
e info@replication.com **w** www.replication.com
Contact Philip Hall, Managing Director; Karen Ireson, Software Manufacturing Sales Manager; Neil Waspe, Authoring & Encoding Manager

Music on Earth Productions

42 Barnfield Road, Ealing, London W5 1QT
t 020 8998 5675 **f** 020 8248 7404 **w** www.musiconearth.co.uk
Contact Judy Caine, Producer; Paul Balmer, Director

Original Image

68-70 Wardour Street, London W1F 0TB
t 020 7494 0777 **f** 020 7494 0309
e info@originalimage.co.uk **w** www.originalimage.co.uk
Contact David Holloway, Managing Director
Credits Hoop Dreams (F); Cold Comfort Farm (F); Gang Related (F)

the pavement

The Pavement

120-124 Curtain Road, London EC2A 3SQ
t 020 7426 5190 **f** 020 7426 5155
e info@the-pavement.com **w** www.the-pavement.com
Contact Kristen O'Sullivan

Award-winning DVD production and design for music, film/TV, and corporate clients. Experience working with directors, artists and management creating innovative titles. MPEG2, 5.1 DD and DTS encoding, DVD-Audio, DVD-R burning, etc.

Peak White Facilities

1 Latimer Road, Teddington TW11 8QA
t 08707 405625 **f** 020 8977 8357 **w** www.peakwhite.tv
Contact Richard Bonfield, Manager; Andrea Anderson, Marketing Director

Peak White offer a range of post production services for broadcast and corporate clients. DVD authoring with full graphic menus & submenus, chapter points, multiple languages, picture gallery etc. Linear and nonlinear online edit suites with DV Cam & Digital Betacam sources. Standards conversion and tape duplication.

PerfectPlay

4 Sydenham Avenue, London SE26 6UH
t 020 8778 5164 **t** 020 8776 8911
f 020 8776 8910 **m** 07939 242022
e sales@perfectplay.co.uk **w** www.perfectplay.co.uk
Contact Simon Gall, Business Development Director

Pink Pigeon Post Production

74 Berwick Street, London W1F 8TQ
t 020 7439 3266 **f** 020 7439 3277
e info@pinkpigeon.net **w** www.pinkpigeon.net
Contact Simon Boyd, Director; William Timbers, Director
Credits Chrome Dreams (W); Mark Summers Management (W); The British Council (W)

Production
Design
DVD Authoring
Web DVD
Video Encoding
Dolby Digital & DTS Encoding

Award Winning DVD production

the pavement
Tel: +44 (0)20 7426 5190
info@the-pavement.com
www.the-pavement.com

Printout Video Publishing
102 Dean Street, London W1D 3TQ
t 020 7494 0164 **f** 020 7437 7764
e info@printout.co.uk **w** www.printout.co.uk
Contact Carl Fuss, Managing Director

Quadrant Visual Solutions (Nottingham)
Unit 11, Castle Park, Queens Drive, Nottingham NG2 1AH
t 0115 840 2288 **f** 0115 840 2290 **w** www.quadrantsolutions.com
Contact Colin Dobbyne, Managing Director

Richmond Studios Ltd
83-84 George Street, Richmond TW9 1HE
t 020 8332 1690 **f** 020 8332 1691 **m** 07836 731918
e charlotte@richmondstudios.com **w** www.richmondstudios.com
Contact Charlotte Danaher, General Manager; Toby Alington, Director,
Managing Director; Robert Grieves, Designer; Miles Tudor, DVD/IT Technician;
Jonathan Potts, Video Editor; Andrea Hein, Project Manager
Credits DUP DVD (W); Ramones DVD (W); Cirque De Soleil - Alegria DVD (W);
Brit Awards (T)

*A one-stop solution for Audio, Video, DVD and Web in the centre of
Richmond, Surrey. 5.1 Dubbing, AVID and Sonic Solutions DVD suites
form part of our integrated facilities. The Brit Awards, Tina Turner, De
Beers, Cirque De Soleil, Warner Music and Universal form part of our
impressive credits.*

Sanctuary Post
53 Frith Street, London W1D 4SN
t 020 7734 4480
e post@sanctuarystudios.co.uk **w** www.sanctuarystudios.co.uk
Contact Jason Elliott, Sales and Marketing Manager

*Flame, DS editing, compositing and grading, on-line and off-line Avid
editing, Audio, graphics, CD-Rom and DVD design/authoring and
duplication services.*

Satellite Broadcast Facilities
18-20 Commercial Way, Park Royal, London NW10 7XF
t 0870 777 7888 **f** 0870 777 7800
e info@sat-facilities.co.uk **w** www.sat-facilities.co.uk
Contact Oliver Shawo, Sales & Marketing Manager; Aasha Patel, Accounts Manager

Screne Productions
126 Norwood Road, London SE24 9AF
t 020 8671 7071 **f** 020 8674 2258 **w** www.screne.org

See No Evil
6 Lillie Yard, West Brompton, London SW6 1UB
t 020 7385 8244 **f** 020 7385 0700
e info@seenoevil.net **w** www.seenoevil.net
Contact Ian Greaves, Director; Sharon Rose, Director; Steve Parr, Director

Short Run Digital Media
Leeward Farm, Heart Hall Lane, Kings Langley, Watford WD4 8JJ
t 01923 261269 **f** 01923 261267 **e** cds@tangerine.demon.co.uk
Contact Simon Hughes, Partner

Smashing Entertainment Ltd
t 01865 437682 **f** 01865 437683
e info@smashingentertainment.net
w www.smashingentertainment.net
Contact Clint Harley, Technical; Winston Smith, Sales

Sonic Solutions Europe
22 Warwick Street, Soho, London W1B 5NF
t 020 7437 1100 **f** 020 7437 1151
e info@europe.sonic.com **w** www.sonic.com
Contact Richard Linecar, Director Professional Sales, Europe

*Sonic is the leading manufacturer of DVD authoring solutions for
Windows and Macintosh. Products including Sonic DVD Creator, Sonic
Scenarist and DVD Producer are the most widely-used systems for
professional DVD publishing. Installed worldwide at major studios, post-
production facilities and corporate marketing departments, Sonic is the
DVD solution every business needs.*

Sonopress UK Ltd
Wednesbury, One Business Park, Black Country, New Road,
Wednesbury WS10 7NY
t 0121 502 7800 **f** 0121 502 7811
e sales@sonopress.co.uk **w** www.sonopress.co.uk
Contact Rob Taylor, Business Development Manager

Squash DVD Ltd
12-13 Richmond Buildings, Soho, London W1D 3HG
t 020 7292 0222 **f** 020 7292 0223
e info@squashpost.co.uk **w** www.squashpost.co.uk
Contact Christine Peacock; David Pollard; Jason Elliott
Credits Mean Machine (W); K-19 (W); Star Trek - The Next Generation (W);
The Godfather Trilogy (W)

*Squash is a DVD and digital media facility offering all forms of video
and audio encoding, interactive authoring, graphics, menu design, full
technical evaluation and QC. With a client base that includes major
Hollywood studios, distributors, advertising and communications
companies, we are able to offer you an exciting and creative alternative
for your DVD, MPEG or general digital media requirements.*

Stream Digital Media
61 Charlotte Street, London W1T 4PF
t 020 7208 1567 **f** 020 7208 1555
e info@streamdm.co.uk **w** www.streamdm.co.uk
Contact Gareth Bourne, Business Development; Paul Kind, Head of Stream;
Guy Goodger, New Business Development
Credits ALI DVD (W); The Crow Special Edition DVD (W); CSI : Crime Scene
Investigations Series 1 DVD (W); The Office - The Complete First Series DVD (W)

taylors.tv
17 Westbourne Avenue, London W3 6JL
t 020 8896 1247 **f** 020 8896 1247 **m** 07968 625634
e info@taylors.tv **w** www.taylors.tv
Contact Ian Puddick, Communications Director; David Taylor, Producer; Philip Taylor, Creative Director; Lalita Taylor, Producer
Credits Acton Community Forum - Community Forum (I); Shell Renewables - 2002 Into 2003 (I); The Company of Strangers (C); Stephen King's Black House (C)

TC Video Plond Street Ltd
1A Poland Street, London W1V 3DG
t 020 7851 9180 **f** 020 7287 5323
e info@tcvideosoho.co.uk **w** www.tcvideosoho.co.uk
Contact Mark Slingo, Sales Director; Mark Slingo, Sales Director; Clive Seer, Operations Director
Credits VideoTel (I); VideoArts (I); Westminster Council (I); Lost In La Mancha (F)

Two Plus One Ltd
1-2 Lower St James Street, London W1F 9EG
t 020 7287 2221 **f** 020 7437 4161
e sales@twoplusone.co.uk **w** www.twoplusone.co.uk
Contact Martin Rogers, Sales and Business Development; Lyndsey McPherson, Office Manager; Joy Hancock, Managing Director; Natasha Linski, Sales & Business Development

Avid DS/HD editing suite, Avid Symphony Universal, Avid Media and Film Composers, Broadcast Dubbing, Dolby Digital Encoding and Decoding, DVD Authoring and Encoding incorporating: Sonic DVD Creator and Scenarist Systems, 2D Graphics. Based in relaxed and spacious surroundings with natural light.

Warner Music Manufacturing
77 Oxford Street, London W1D 2ES
t 020 7659 2530 **f** 020 7659 2100 **m** 07813 118676
e sam.menezes@warnermusic.com **w** www.wmme.co.uk
Contact Sam Menezes, UK Sales & Marketing Manager

Wubneh Mekonnen
93 Stebbing House, Queensdale Crescent, London W11 4TF
t 020 7603 7029 **m** 07946 888440
e w.mekonnen@btopenworld.com

EDITING

editing : contents

Editing
Equipment Hire Film

MILLBANK STUDIOS

Millbank Studios
4 Millbank, Westminster, London SW1P 3JA
t 020 7233 2020 **f** 020 7233 3158
e facilities@millbank-studios.co.uk **w** www.millbank-studios.co.uk
Contact Richard Rose, Managing Director; Pippa Walker, Head of Operations; Nick Hattingh, Technical Operations Manager; Nicola Goulding, Head of Production

Philip Rigby & Sons Ltd
32 Whyteleafe Road, Caterham CR3 5EF
t 01883 332513 **f** 01883 332514
e philiprigbysonsltd@btinternet.com
Contact Philip Rigby, Proprietor

Editing
Equipment Hire Sound

Twickenham SoundStation Ltd
116 St Margarets Road, St Margarets, Twickenham TW1 2AA
t 020 8607 8760 **f** 020 8607 8965 **m** 07768 825 013
e mail@soundstation.demon.co.uk **w** www.editstation.com
Contact Chris Munro, Director; Angus Munro, Sound Enginneer; Andrew Walker, Facility Manager; Gerry Humphreys, Director; Matt Lovell

Editing
Equipment Hire Video

Addictive Editing
Building 14, Shepperton Studios, Studios Road, Shepperton TW17 0QD
t 01932 592124 **f** 01932 592134
e mail@addictive-editing.co.uk **w** www.addictive-editing.co.uk
Contact P Stapley, Proprieter; P Harris, Operations Manager
Credits Thomas The Tank Engine (T); Kavanagh QC (T); Inspector Morse (T); Red Dwarf (T)

Advance Productions Ltd
24 Park Royal Metro Centre, Britannia Way, London NW10 7PA
t 020 8838 6188 **f** 020 8838 0228 **m** 07768 874731
e info@advancedbroadcast.tv **w** www.advancedbroadcast.tv
Contact Soussan Imani, Marketing Director

Avatar Post Production Ltd
21 Abercromby Place, Edinburgh EH3 6QE
t 0131 476 7711 **f** 0131 476 7712 **m** 07956 966946
e info@avatarpp.tv **w** www.avatarpp.tv
Contact Simon Hill, Sales and Marketing/ Managing Director; Nick Wright, Senior Editor/ Managing Director
Credits The Royal Bank Of Scotland (C); The Dummy (S); Tales Of The Bow (D); The Truth About Sex And The City (D)

Broadcast Hire Centre (BHC)
81 Radcliffe New Road, Whitefield, Manchester M45 7QZ
t 0161 766 8012 **f** 0161 766 9375 **m** 07831 105856
e info@broadcasthirecentre.com
Contact Eric Langhorn, Partner

Datavision Ltd
Russell Farm, New Road, Maulden MK45 2BG
t 01525 406886 **f** 01525 840066
e info@datavision.co.uk **w** www.datavision.co.uk
Contact Mark Theobald; Tim Liggins

Harrison Avid Hire
2 Bridgemere Close, Radcliffe, Manchester M26 4FS
t 0161 723 5852 **f** 0161 724 7481 **m** 07802 982745
e clive@avidhire.co.uk **w** www.avidhire.co.uk
Contact Clive Harrison, Proprietor

Hyperactive
5 The Royston Centre, Lynchford Lane, Ash Vale GU12 5PQ
t 01252 519191 **f** 01252 513939
e hire@hyperactivebroadcast.com
w www.hyperactivebroadcast.com
Contact Lawrie Read, Deputy Managing Director; David Reeves, Managing Director
Avids, Lightworks, and Steenbeck for dry hire. Avid On-line, Film Composers, Media Composers, G4 or NT and Unity MediaNet systems at highly competitive rates. Digital and Analogue VTR's and all film accessories available.

Interbroadcast
22 Newman Street, London W1T 1PH
t 020 7580 5524 **f** 020 7637 1011
e interbroadcast@tvsetgroup.co.uk
Contact Mark Phillips; Terry Bettles

London Editing Machines Ltd
Unit 7, Waterside Trading Centre, Trumpers Way, London W7 2QD
t 020 8574 0010 **f** 020 8571 2730
e info@lemdigital.co.uk **w** www.lemdigital.co.uk
Contact Sarah Bhathena, Bookings & Marketing Manager; Peter Watson, Director; Patrick Wilbraham, Support Technician; Mike Pearce, Technical Manager
Credits Imagining Argentina (F); Mona Lisa Smile (F); The Calcium Kid (F); Gladiatress (F)

McMILLAN

McMillan
22 Soho Square, London W1D 4NS
t 020 7070 7200 **f** 020 7070 7201
e mcmillan@mcmillan.co.uk **w** www.mcmillan.co.uk
Contact Fazal Shah, Hires Manager; Kay Gilmour, Director
As Premier Resellers, McMillan are a leading broadcast equipment supplier, with confidence in their high level of service and offer special hire rates to new clients.

Picture It
50 Church Road, London NW10 9PY
t 020 8961 6644 **f** 020 8961 2969
e rosemary@picit.net **w** www.picit.net
Contact Trevor Hunt, Managing Director; Rosemary Element, Sales & Marketing; Chris Sellers, Studio Manager
Avid on-line and offline, studio and location.

Video Europe
8 Golden Square, London W1F 9HY
t 020 7494 1818 **f** 020 7494 1717
e sohohire@videoeurope.co.uk **w** www.videoeurope.co.uk

Editors Assistants

Amy Adams
Edit-Base, 70A Waldegrave Road, Teddington TW11 8NY
t 020 8614 6937 **e** alison@edit-base.co.uk

Kevin Ahern
Edit-Base, 70A Waldegrave Road, Teddington TW11 8NY
t 020 8614 6937 **e** alison@edit-base.co.uk

Marcus Alexander
Edit-Base, 70A Waldegrave Road, Teddington TW11 8NY
t 020 8614 6937 **e** alison@edit-base.co.uk

Audrey Aquilina
Edit-Base, 70A Waldegrave Road, Teddington TW11 8NY
t 020 8614 6937 **e** alison@edit-base.co.uk

David Atkinson
Edit-Base, 70A Waldegrave Road, Teddington TW11 8NY
t 020 8614 6937 **e** alison@edit-base.co.uk

Nick Baldock
Edit-Base, 70A Waldegrave Road, Teddington TW11 8NY
t 020 8614 6937 **e** alison@edit-base.co.uk

Rosalyn Ball
Edit-Base, 70A Waldegrave Road, Teddington TW11 8NY
t 020 8614 6937 **e** alison@edit-base.co.uk

Victoria Bate
Edit-Base, 70A Waldegrave Road, Teddington TW11 8NY
t 020 8614 6937 **e** alison@edit-base.co.uk

Oliver Batkin
Edit-Base, 70A Waldegrave Road, Teddington TW11 8NY
t 020 8614 6937 **e** alison@edit-base.co.uk

Alexander Baxter
Edit-Base, 70A Waldegrave Road, Teddington TW11 8NY
t 020 8614 6937 **e** alison@edit-base.co.uk

Nina Bradley
Edit-Base, 70A Waldegrave Road, Teddington TW11 8NY
t 020 8614 6937 **e** alison@edit-base.co.uk

Sarah Brewerton
Edit-Base, 70A Waldegrave Road, Teddington TW11 8NY
t 020 8614 6937 **e** alison@edit-base.co.uk

Hermione Byrt
Edit-Base, 70A Waldegrave Road, Teddington TW11 8NY
t 020 8614 6937 **e** alison@edit-base.co.uk

Ben Campbell
Edit-Base, 70A Waldegrave Road, Teddington TW11 8NY
t 020 8614 6937 **e** alison@edit-base.co.uk

Billy Campbell
11 Merredene Street, Brixton, London SW2 2AQ
t 020 8671 5600
Credits Lord Of The Rings (F)

William Campbell
Edit-Base, 70A Waldegrave Road, Teddington TW11 8NY
t 020 8614 6937 e alison@edit-base.co.uk

Paul Clegg
Edit-Base, 70A Waldegrave Road, Teddington TW11 8NY
t 020 8614 6937 e alison@edit-base.co.uk

Lisa Clifford-Owen
Edit-Base, 70A Waldegrave Road, Teddington TW11 8NY
t 020 8614 6937 e alison@edit-base.co.uk

Jason Costelloe
Edit-Base, 70A Waldegrave Road, Teddington TW11 8NY
t 020 8614 6937 e alison@edit-base.co.uk

Ruth Coulson
Edit-Base, 70A Waldegrave Road, Teddington TW11 8NY
t 020 8614 6937 e alison@edit-base.co.uk

Jo Dale
Edit-Base, 70A Waldegrave Road, Teddington TW11 8NY
t 020 8614 6937 e alison@edit-base.co.uk

Hattie Dalton
Edit-Base, 70A Waldegrave Road, Teddington TW11 8NY
t 020 8614 6937 e alison@edit-base.co.uk

Peter Dansie
Edit-Base, 70A Waldegrave Road, Teddington TW11 8NY
t 020 8614 6937 e alison@edit-base.co.uk

Ian Differ
Edit-Base, 70A Waldegrave Road, Teddington TW11 8NY
t 020 8614 6937 e alison@edit-base.co.uk

Anya Dillon
Edit-Base, 70A Waldegrave Road, Teddington TW11 8NY
t 020 8614 6937 e alison@edit-base.co.uk

Claire Dodgson
Edit-Base, 70A Waldegrave Road, Teddington TW11 8NY
t 020 8614 6937 e alison@edit-base.co.uk

Patrick Doherty
134 Carfin Road, Newarthill, Motherwell ML1 5JX
t 01698 733075 m 07951 862239
Credits River City (T); The Book Group II (T); New Tricks (T); A Line In The Sand (T)

Carlos Domeque
Edit-Base, 70A Waldegrave Road, Teddington TW11 8NY
t 020 8614 6937 e alison@edit-base.co.uk

Guy Ducker
t 020 8846 9234 f 020 8846 9234 m 07956 859750
Agent Edit-Base, 70A Waldegrave Road, Teddington TW11 8NY
t 020 8614 6937 e alison@edit-base.co.uk
Credits Warrior (F); Thunderpants (F); Calender Girls (F)

Sally-Anne Duffy
Edit-Base, 70A Waldegrave Road, Teddington TW11 8NY
t 020 8614 6937 e alison@edit-base.co.uk

Rus Ekkel
Edit-Base, 70A Waldegrave Road, Teddington TW11 8NY
t 020 8614 6937 e alison@edit-base.co.uk

Paul Elman
Edit-Base, 70A Waldegrave Road, Teddington TW11 8NY
t 020 8614 6937 e alison@edit-base.co.uk

Richard Elson
Edit-Base, 70A Waldegrave Road, Teddington TW11 8NY
t 020 8614 6937 e alison@edit-base.co.uk

Iain Erskine
Edit-Base, 70A Waldegrave Road, Teddington TW11 8NY
t 020 8614 6937 e alison@edit-base.co.uk

Laura Evans
Edit-Base, 70A Waldegrave Road, Teddington TW11 8NY
t 020 8614 6937 e alison@edit-base.co.uk

Tom Ewing
Edit-Base, 70A Waldegrave Road, Teddington TW11 8NY
t 020 8614 6937 e alison@edit-base.co.uk

Julie Foster
Edit-Base, 70A Waldegrave Road, Teddington TW11 8NY
t 020 8614 6937 e alison@edit-base.co.uk

Sharon Fuller
Edit-Base, 70A Waldegrave Road, Teddington TW11 8NY
t 020 8614 6937 e alison@edit-base.co.uk

Emma Gaffney
Edit-Base, 70A Waldegrave Road, Teddington TW11 8NY
t 020 8614 6937 e alison@edit-base.co.uk

Joanna Garrard
Edit-Base, 70A Waldegrave Road, Teddington TW11 8NY
t 020 8614 6937 e alison@edit-base.co.uk

Kim Gaster
Edit-Base, 70A Waldegrave Road, Teddington TW11 8NY
t 020 8614 6937 e alison@edit-base.co.uk

Julius Gladwell
Edit-Base, 70A Waldegrave Road, Teddington TW11 8NY
t 020 8614 6937 e alison@edit-base.co.uk

Lalit Goyal
Edit-Base, 70A Waldegrave Road, Teddington TW11 8NY
t 020 8614 6937 e alison@edit-base.co.uk

Emily Grant
Edit-Base, 70A Waldegrave Road, Teddington TW11 8NY
t 020 8614 6937 e alison@edit-base.co.uk

Adam Green
Edit-Base, 70A Waldegrave Road, Teddington TW11 8NY
t 020 8614 6937 e alison@edit-base.co.uk

Oliver Griffin
Edit-Base, 70A Waldegrave Road, Teddington TW11 8NY
t 020 8614 6937 e alison@edit-base.co.uk

Rupert Hall
Edit-Base, 70A Waldegrave Road, Teddington TW11 8NY
t 020 8614 6937 e alison@edit-base.co.uk

James Hampton
Edit-Base, 70A Waldegrave Road, Teddington TW11 8NY
t 020 8614 6937 e alison@edit-base.co.uk

Louisa Harding
Edit-Base, 70A Waldegrave Road, Teddington TW11 8NY
t 020 8614 6937 e alison@edit-base.co.uk

PJ Harling
Edit-Base, 70A Waldegrave Road, Teddington TW11 8NY
t 020 8614 6937 e alison@edit-base.co.uk

John Harris
Edit-Base, 70A Waldegrave Road, Teddington TW11 8NY
t 020 8614 6937 e alison@edit-base.co.uk

Tom Harrison-Read
Edit-Base, 70A Waldegrave Road, Teddington TW11 8NY
t 020 8614 6937 e alison@edit-base.co.uk

Kate Higham
Edit-Base, 70A Waldegrave Road, Teddington TW11 8NY
t 020 8614 6937 e alison@edit-base.co.uk

Samantha Holgate
Edit-Base, 70A Waldegrave Road, Teddington TW11 8NY
t 020 8614 6937 e alison@edit-base.co.uk

Kevin Holt
Edit-Base, 70A Waldegrave Road, Teddington TW11 8NY
t 020 8614 6937 e alison@edit-base.co.uk

Jim Howe
Edit-Base, 70A Waldegrave Road, Teddington TW11 8NY
t 020 8614 6937 e alison@edit-base.co.uk

Luke Hudson
Edit-Base, 70A Waldegrave Road, Teddington TW11 8NY
t 020 8614 6937 e alison@edit-base.co.uk

Al Hunter
2 Allison Court, 52 Allison Street, Glasgow G42 8NL
t 0141 424 0683 f 0141 424 0683 m 07752 154 551
e alhunter@ireland.com
Credits Cruel Summer (T); This Scotland: The Big Man (T); Talsi (T)

Paul Hyman
Edit-Base, 70A Waldegrave Road, Teddington TW11 8NY
t 020 8614 6937 e alison@edit-base.co.uk

Andrew Jadavji
Edit-Base, 70A Waldegrave Road, Teddington TW11 8NY
t 020 8614 6937 e alison@edit-base.co.uk

Tamsin Jeffrey
Edit-Base, 70A Waldegrave Road, Teddington TW11 8NY
t 020 8614 6937 e alison@edit-base.co.uk

Katya Jezzard
Edit-Base, 70A Waldegrave Road, Teddington TW11 8NY
t 020 8614 6937 e alison@edit-base.co.uk

Lionel Johnson
Edit-Base, 70A Waldegrave Road, Teddington TW11 8NY
t 020 8614 6937 e alison@edit-base.co.uk

Daryl Jordan
Edit-Base, 70A Waldegrave Road, Teddington TW11 8NY
t 020 8614 6937 e alison@edit-base.co.uk

Tom Kemplen
Edit-Base, 70A Waldegrave Road, Teddington TW11 8NY
t 020 8614 6937 e alison@edit-base.co.uk

Tom Kinnersley
Edit-Base, 70A Waldegrave Road, Teddington TW11 8NY
t 020 8614 6937 e alison@edit-base.co.uk

Tomomi Kitamura
Edit-Base, 70A Waldegrave Road, Teddington TW11 8NY
t 020 8614 6937 e alison@edit-base.co.uk

Ray Lau
Edit-Base, 70A Waldegrave Road, Teddington TW11 8NY
t 020 8614 6937 e alison@edit-base.co.uk

Veronique Lorin
Edit-Base, 70A Waldegrave Road, Teddington TW11 8NY
t 020 8614 6937 e alison@edit-base.co.uk

Miloslav Madacky
123 Sinclair Road, London W14 0NP
t 020 7751 1679
e memyself@btinternet.com w htttp://mmi.port5.com
Credits Out Of Bosnia (D); Venus (M); Drum Massacre (M); One Love (M)

Stefania Marangoni
Edit-Base, 70A Waldegrave Road, Teddington TW11 8NY
t 020 8614 6937 e alison@edit-base.co.uk

Keith Mason
Edit-Base, 70A Waldegrave Road, Teddington TW11 8NY
t 020 8614 6937 e alison@edit-base.co.uk

Bahader Mattu
Edit-Base, 70A Waldegrave Road, Teddington TW11 8NY
t 020 8614 6937 e alison@edit-base.co.uk

Julian May
Flat 6, 16 Chepstow Crescent, London W11 3EB
m 07050 221 887 e jumay50@hotmail.com
Agent Edit-Base, 70A Waldegrave Road, Teddington TW11 8NY
t 020 8614 6937 e alison@edit-base.co.uk
Credits The War Zone; White Teeth (T); Once Upon A Time In The Midlands (F)

Steve Mercer
Edit-Base, 70A Waldegrave Road, Teddington TW11 8NY
t 020 8614 6937 e alison@edit-base.co.uk

Ulrike Meunch
Edit-Base, 70A Waldegrave Road, Teddington TW11 8NY
t 020 8614 6937 e alison@edit-base.co.uk

Yan B Miles
Edit-Base, 70A Waldegrave Road, Teddington TW11 8NY
t 020 8614 6937 e alison@edit-base.co.uk

Lea Morement
Edit-Base, 70A Waldegrave Road, Teddington TW11 8NY
t 020 8614 6937 e alison@edit-base.co.uk

Gez Morris
Edit-Base, 70A Waldegrave Road, Teddington TW11 8NY
t 020 8614 6937 e alison@edit-base.co.uk

Karoline Moser
Edit-Base, 70A Waldegrave Road, Teddington TW11 8NY
t 020 8614 6937 e alison@edit-base.co.uk

Mark Neale
Edit-Base, 70A Waldegrave Road, Teddington TW11 8NY
t 020 8614 6937 e alison@edit-base.co.uk

Michael Nollet
Edit-Base, 70A Waldegrave Road, Teddington TW11 8NY
t 020 8614 6937 e alison@edit-base.co.uk

John Nuth
Edit-Base, 70A Waldegrave Road, Teddington TW11 8NY
t 020 8614 6937 e alison@edit-base.co.uk

Steve Pang
Edit-Base, 70A Waldegrave Road, Teddington TW11 8NY
t 020 8614 6937 e alison@edit-base.co.uk

John Pape
Edit-Base, 70A Waldegrave Road, Teddington TW11 8NY
t 020 8614 6937 e alison@edit-base.co.uk

Helen Paszyn
63 Essex Park, London N3 1ND
m 07941 352873 e helenka71@yahoo.com
Credits Pandaemonium (F); 40 (T); Doctor Sleep (F)

Tasim Persuad
Edit-Base, 70A Waldegrave Road, Teddington TW11 8NY
t 020 8614 6937 e alison@edit-base.co.uk

Ross Porter-Ward
Edit-Base, 70A Waldegrave Road, Teddington TW11 8NY
t 020 8614 6937 e alison@edit-base.co.uk

Tania Ama Reddin
Edit-Base, 70A Waldegrave Road, Teddington TW11 8NY
t 020 8614 6937 e alison@edit-base.co.uk

Matt Reed
Edit-Base, 70A Waldegrave Road, Teddington TW11 8NY
t 020 8614 6937 e alison@edit-base.co.uk

Mick Reilly
Edit-Base, 70A Waldegrave Road, Teddington TW11 8NY
t 020 8614 6937 e alison@edit-base.co.uk

Ben Renton
Edit-Base, 70A Waldegrave Road, Teddington TW11 8NY
t 020 8614 6937 e alison@edit-base.co.uk

Tina Richardson
Edit-Base, 70A Waldegrave Road, Teddington TW11 8NY
t 020 8614 6937 e alison@edit-base.co.uk

Daniel Roberts
Edit-Base, 70A Waldegrave Road, Teddington TW11 8NY
t 020 8614 6937 e alison@edit-base.co.uk

Mark Sale
Edit-Base, 70A Waldegrave Road, Teddington TW11 8NY
t 020 8614 6937 e alison@edit-base.co.uk

Charlotte Serpell
Edit-Base, 70A Waldegrave Road, Teddington TW11 8NY
t 020 8614 6937 e alison@edit-base.co.uk

Anil Sharma
Edit-Base, 70A Waldegrave Road, Teddington TW11 8NY
t 020 8614 6937 e alison@edit-base.co.uk

Tess Shepherd-Smith
Edit-Base, 70A Waldegrave Road, Teddington TW11 8NY
t 020 8614 6937 e alison@edit-base.co.uk

Lucy Smith
Edit-Base, 70A Waldegrave Road, Teddington TW11 8NY
t 020 8614 6937 e alison@edit-base.co.uk

Simone Spinazze
Edit-Base, 70A Waldegrave Road, Teddington TW11 8NY
t 020 8614 6937 e alison@edit-base.co.uk

Victoria Stevens
Edit-Base, 70A Waldegrave Road, Teddington TW11 8NY
t 020 8614 6937 e alison@edit-base.co.uk

Paul Swinburne
Edit-Base, 70A Waldegrave Road, Teddington TW11 8NY
t 020 8614 6937 e alison@edit-base.co.uk

Daniel Turner
Edit-Base, 70A Waldegrave Road, Teddington TW11 8NY
t 020 8614 6937 e alison@edit-base.co.uk

Andrew Walton
Edit-Base, 70A Waldegrave Road, Teddington TW11 8NY
t 020 8614 6937 e alison@edit-base.co.uk

Martin Weeks
Edit-Base, 70A Waldegrave Road, Teddington TW11 8NY
t 020 8614 6937 e alison@edit-base.co.uk

Claus Wehlisch
Edit-Base, 70A Waldegrave Road, Teddington TW11 8NY
t 020 8614 6937 e alison@edit-base.co.uk

Bridgette Williams
Edit-Base, 70A Waldegrave Road, Teddington TW11 8NY
t 020 8614 6937 e alison@edit-base.co.uk

Rab Wilson
Edit-Base, 70A Waldegrave Road, Teddington TW11 8NY
t 020 8614 6937 e alison@edit-base.co.uk

James Winnifrith
Edit-Base, 70A Waldegrave Road, Teddington TW11 8NY
t 020 8614 6937 e alison@edit-base.co.uk

Llyr Wynn-Jones
Edit-Base, 70A Waldegrave Road, Teddington TW11 8NY
t 020 8614 6937 e alison@edit-base.co.uk

Adam Yates
Edit-Base, 70A Waldegrave Road, Teddington TW11 8NY
t 020 8614 6937 e alison@edit-base.co.uk

Rebecca Yolland
Edit-Base, 70A Waldegrave Road, Teddington TW11 8NY
t 020 8614 6937 e alison@edit-base.co.uk

Editors Film

Melanie Adams
The Dench Arnold Agency, 24 D'Arblay Street, London W1F 8EH
t 020 7437 4551 f 020 7439 1355
e contact@dencharnoldagency.co.uk w www.dencharnold.co.uk
Credits Big Meg Little Meg (T); Vicious Circle (T); Boston Kickout (F)

Rob Alexander
m 07970 797 734 e robalexander@hotmail.com
Credits Extreme Terrain (T); Sister Wendy's American Collection (T); Fact or Fiction - Braveheart (T)

Romesh Aluwihare
19 Hall Farm Road, London W10 6ON
m 07905 056081 e romesh_aluwihare@hotmail.com
Agent Jessica Carney Associates, Suite 90-92 Kent House, 87 Regent Street, London W1B 4EH
t 020 7434 4143 f 020 7434 4173
e info@jcarneyassociates.co.uk
Credits As If III (T); Is Harry On The Boat? (T); The Bill (T)

Nick Ames
Martyr Television, 149-151 Regent Street, London W1B 4JD
t 020 7479 7830 f 0 7287 6855
e nick@martyrtv.co.uk w www.martyrtv.co.uk
Credits Spy TV (T); Black Books (T); Judge John Deeds (T); Have I Got News For You? (T)

Nick Arthurs
International Creative Management Ltd, Oxford House, 76 Oxford Street, London W1D 1BS
t 020 7636 6565 f 020 7323 0101 w www.icmlondon.co.uk
Credits The Debt (T); Lock, Stock And Two Smoking Barrels - The Series (T); Cutting It (T); Othello (T)

Mick Audsley
Casarotto Marsh Ltd, National House, 60-66 Wardour Street, London W1V 4ND
t 020 7287 4450 f 020 7287 9128
e agents@casarotto.uk.com w www.casarotto.uk.com

Clive Barrett
CCA Management, 7 St George's Square, London SW1V 2HX
t 020 7630 6303 f 020 7630 7376

Sean Barton
McKinney Macartney Management Ltd, The Barley Mow
Centre, 10 Barley Mow Passage, London W4 4PH
t 020 8995 4747 **f** 020 8995 2414
e fkb@mmtechsrep.demon.co.uk **w** www.mckinneymacartney.com

Michael J Bateman
Edit-Base, 70A Waldegrave Road, Teddington TW11 8NY
t 020 8614 6937 **e** alison@edit-base.co.uk

Guy Bensley
McKinney Macartney Management Ltd, The Barley Mow
Centre, 10 Barley Mow Passage, London W4 4PH
t 020 8995 4747 **f** 020 8995 2414
e fkb@mmtechsrep.demon.co.uk **w** www.mckinneymacartney.com

Peter Beston
Creative Media Management, Unit 3B, Walpole Court, Ealing
Studios, Ealing Green, London W5 5ED
t 020 8584 5363 **f** 020 8566 5554
e enquiries@creativemediamanagement.com
Credits Once Upon A Time In The Midlands (F); Bugs! (F); The Dance Of Shiva
(T); Don't Go Breaking My Heart (F)

Caroline Biggerstaff
The Dench Arnold Agency, 24 D'Arblay Street, London W1F 8EH
t 020 7437 4551 **f** 020 7439 1355
e contact@dencharnold.co.uk **w** www.dencharnold.co.uk
Credits Five Seconds To Spare (F); L'appartement (F); Nine And A Half Weeks (F)

David Blackmore
Casarotto Marsh Ltd, National House, 60-66 Wardour Street,
London W1V 4ND
t 020 7287 4450 **f** 020 7287 9128
e agents@casarotto.uk.com **w** www.casarotto.uk.com

John Bloom
International Creative Management Ltd, Oxford House,
76 Oxford Street, London W1D 1BS
t 020 7636 6565 **f** 020 7323 0101 **w** www.icmlondon.co.uk
Credits Gandhi (F); Damage (F); Wit (T)

Victoria Boydell
Casarotto Marsh Ltd, National House, 60-66 Wardour Street,
London W1V 4ND
t 020 7287 4450 **f** 020 7287 9128
e agents@casarotto.uk.com **w** www.casarotto.uk.com

Martin Brinkler
The Dench Arnold Agency, 24 D'Arblay Street, London W1F 8EH
t 020 7437 4551 **f** 020 7439 1355
e contact@dencharnoldagency.co.uk **w** www.dencharnold.co
Credits Last Run (F); The Honeymooners (F); Married/Unmarried (F)

Kate Buckland
t 020 8571 6952 **f** 020 8571 6952 **m** 07710 768642
e kate.filmeditor@talk21.com
Agent CCA Management, 7 St George's Square, London SW1V 2HX
t 020 7630 6303 **f** 020 7630 7376
Credits Thomas The Tank Engine (T); Panic (S); Cleopatra (T); Hidden City (T)

Julian Caidan
7 Fenwick Grove, London SE15 4HT
t 020 7639 5791 **f** 020 7639 5791 **m** 07976 946072
e jcaidan@aol.com
Credits Jimi Hendrix - Band of Gipsies; Classic Albums; South Bank Show (T)

David Campling (ACE)
Edit-Base, 70A Waldegrave Road, Teddington TW11 8NY
t 020 8614 6937 **e** alison@edit-base.co.uk

Leo Carlyon
m 07860 479962 **e** leocarlyon@hotmail.com
Credits Modern Times (D); Friends For Dinner (T); Made For Each Other (T);
Gods In The Sky (D)

Nigel Cattle
Martyr Television, 149-151 Regent Street, London W1B 4JD
t 020 7479 7830 **f** 020 7287 6855
e nigel@martyrtv.co.uk **w** www.martyrtv.co.uk
Credits London's Burning Series XIV (T); The Vice (T); Undercover Heart (T);
Inspector Lynley: Series II (T)

Celtic Broadcasting Ltd
Flowerdale House, 14 Lochalsh Road, Inverness IV3 8HS
t 01463 234000 **f** 01463 231800 **m** 07860 663566
e morag.grant@virgin.net
Contact Morag Grant, Director/Editor
Credits Mario Bava: Master of the Macabre (T); EBR (T);
The Other Loch Ness Monster (T)

Pia Di Ciaula
International Creative Management Ltd, Oxford House,
76 Oxford Street, London W1D 1BS
t 020 7636 6565 **f** 020 7323 0101 **w** www.icmlondon.co.uk
Credits Hideous Kinky (F); The Last Of The Blonde Bombshells (T); Pure (F)

Anthony Combes
International Creative Management Ltd, Oxford House,
76 Oxford Street, London W1D 1BS
t 020 7636 6565 **f** 020 7323 0101 **w** www.icmlondon.co.uk
Credits Silent Witness (T); A Respectable Trade (T); Babyfather (T)

Jon Costelloe
Jessica Carney Associates, Suite 90-92 Kent House,
87 Regent Street, London W1B 4EH
t 020 7434 4143 **f** 020 7434 4173
e info@jcarneyassociates.co.uk
Credits Messiah II (T); The Fall (F); North Square (T)

Belinda Cottrell
Jessica Carney Associates, Suite 90-92 Kent House,
87 Regent Street, London W1B 4EH
t 020 7434 4143 **f** 020 7434 4173
e info@jcarneyassociates.co.uk
Credits Dalziel & Pascoe (T); Manchild (T); Last Seduction II (F)

Peter Coulson
13 Kingslawn Close, Putney, London SW15 6QT
t 020 8788 5292 **f** 020 8788 5292
Agent CCA Management, 7 St George's Square, London SW1V 2HX
t 020 7630 6303 **f** 020 7630 7376
Credits Gulliver's Travels (T); Longitude (T); Dirty Pretty Things (F)

Abigail Coult
2 Hillary House, Boyton Close, London N8 7BB

Peter Cox
t 020 8541 3137 **e** peter100@blueyonder.co.uk
Credits Soviet Echoes (D); Africa's Child (D)

Catherine Creed
25 Straightsmouth, Greenwich, London SE10 9LB
t 020 8853 2156 **f** 07798 670865
e catherine@creedo.demon.co.uk
Agent London Management & Representation, 2-4 Noel
Street, London W1V 3RB
t 020 7287 9000 **f** 020 7287 3236
Credits Bertie And Elizabeth (T); Rogue Trader (F); I Could Read The Sky (F);
Mapmaker (F)

Eddie Daniels
3A Runnymeade Road, Canvey Island SS8 0EF

David Naden Associates
159 Wardour Street, London W1F 8WH
t 020 7734 0535 **f** 020 7437 6175
Contact Shelagh Brady
Credits Frank Auerbach (T)

THE PRODUCTION GUIDE ·253

Paul Davies
Pullastone, Kingsthorne, Hereford HR2 8AQ
t 01981 540450 **f** 01981 540101 **m** 07919 051868
e durdledavies@compuserve.com

Peter Davies
CCA Management, 7 St George's Square, London SW1V 2HX
t 020 7630 6303 **f** 020 7630 7376

Mark Day
International Creative Management Ltd, Oxford House,
76 Oxford Street, London W1D 1BS
t 020 7636 6565 **f** 020 7323 0101 **w** www.icmlondon.co.uk
Credits Cold Comfort Farm (F); The Way We Live Now (T); Anna Karenina (T)

Bob Dearberg
7 Sunnyside Road, Clevedon BS 21 7TE
t 01275 876129 **m** 07773 412824
Credits Urban Gothic - Series I (T); Junk (T); Rockface (T)

Bob Dearberg
Jessica Carney Associates, Suite 90-92 Kent House,
87 Regent Street, London W1B 4EH
t 020 7434 4143 **f** 020 7434 4173
e info@jcarneyassociates.co.uk
Credits Inspector Morse (T); Urban Gothic - Series I (T); Junk (T)

Paul Dosaj
14 Daleham Gardens, London NW3 5DA
t 020 7794 0176 **f** +4 20 7794 0176 **m** 07905 260130
e pdosaj@globalnet.co.uk
Credits Rough Ride (D); Living On The Edge (D); Danger! UXB (D); Kelly And Her Sisters (D)

John Dunstan
14 Tennyson Road, Harpenden AL5 4BB
t 01582 765796 **m** 07941 046329 **e** johndunstan@ukonline.com
Contact Tony Dow, Producer/Director
Credits Even Further Abroad (D); Holby City (T); Bob Martin (T); Roger Roger (T)

Clare Douglas
McKinney Macartney Management Ltd, The Barley Mow
Centre, 10 Barley Mow Passage, London W4 4PH
t 020 8995 4747 **f** 020 8995 2414
e fkb@mmtechsrep.demon.co.uk **w** www.mckinneymacartney.com

Paul Endacott
Creative Media Management, Unit 3B, Walpole Court, Ealing
Studios, Ealing Green, London W5 5ED
t 020 8584 5363 **f** 020 8566 5554
e enquiries@creativemediamanagement.com
Credits Forty Something (T); The Lynley Mysteries (T); Buried (T); As The Beast Sleeps (T)

Kate Evans
International Creative Management Ltd, Oxford House, `
76 Oxford Street, London W1D 1BS
t 020 7636 6565 **f** 020 7323 0101 **w** www.icmlondon.co.uk
Credits Persuasion (F); Men Only (T); Girl With A Pearl Earring (F)

Jaime Estrada
Edit-Base, 70A Waldegrave Road, Teddington TW11 8NY
t 020 8614 6937 **e** alison@edit-base.co.uk

Ian Farr
International Creative Management Ltd, Oxford House,
76 Oxford Street, London W1D 1BS
t 020 7636 6565 **f** 020 7323 0101 **w** www.icmlondon.co.uk
Credits Foyle's War (T); The Cry (T); Tough Love (T)

Neil Farrell
International Creative Management Ltd, Oxford House,
76 Oxford Street, London W1D 1BS
t 020 7636 6565 **f** 020 7323 0101 **w** www.icmlondon.co.uk
Credits Hamlet; Loves Labours Lost (F); Mindhunters (F)

Claire Ferguson
Edit-Base, 70A Waldegrave Road, Teddington TW11 8NY
t 020 8614 6937 **e** alison@edit-base.co.uk

Les Filby
62 Merivale Road, Harrow HA1 4BH
t 020 8422 1932 **m** 07970 757967 **e** lemeri@aol.com
Credits Open University (T); The Tower of London (T); Time Team (T)

The Firm
21 Carnaby Street, London W1F 7DA
t 020 7437 4535 **f** 020 7734 6176 **e** edit@thefirmeditors.tv
Contact Marc Langley, Editor

Ardan Fisher
International Creative Management Ltd, Oxford House,
76 Oxford Street, London W1D 1BS
t 020 7636 6565 **f** 020 7323 0101 **w** www.icmlondon.co.uk
Credits Edge Of Darkness (T); The Sleeper (T); The Long Run (F)

Michael T Flynn
18 Hawkeridge, Westbury BA13 4LA
e mike@theflyn.fsnet.co.uk **w** www.clearcutpictures.com
Credits A Country Estate (D); Love In The Twenty-First Century (D); Charge Of The Light Brigade (D); Africa Unmasked (D)

Brad Fuller
The Dench Arnold Agency, 24 D'Arblay Street, London W1F 8EH
t 020 7437 4551 **f** 020 7439 1355
e contact@dencharnoldagency.co.uk **w** www.dencharnold.co.uk
Credits In The Spirit (F); A Brief History Of Time (F); Nil By Mouth (F)

Helen Garrard
14 Lansdown Place, Clifton, Bristol BS8 3AF
t 0117 974 1045
Credits A Close Shave (F); The Wrong Trousers (F)

Paul Garrick
24 Endsleigh Road, Ealing, London W13 0RE
m 07971 009821
Agent Jessica Carney Associates, Suite 90-92 Kent House,
87 Regent Street, London W1B 4EH
t 020 7434 4143 **f** 020 7434 4173
e info@jcarneyassociates.co.uk
Credits Jeffrey Archer - The Truth (T); The Last Detective (T); William And Mary (T)

Nic Gaster
The Dench Arnold Agency, 24 D'Arblay Street, London W1F 8EH
t 020 7437 4551 **f** 020 7439 1355
e contact@dencharnoldagency.co.uk **w** www.dencharnold.co.uk
Credits The Mother (F); Dust (F)

Jeremy Gibbs
Edit-Base, 70A Waldegrave Road, Teddington TW11 8NY
t 020 8614 6937 **e** alison@edit-base.co.uk

David Gibson
Creative Media Management, Unit 3B, Walpole Court, Ealing
Studios, Ealing Green, London W5 5ED
t 020 8584 5363 **f** 020 8566 5554
e enquiries@creativemediamanagement.com
Credits Hope And Glory (T); The Elevat (T); Buried (T)

Chris Gill
m 07973 297113 **e** editgill@aol.com
Agent Jessica Carney Associates, Suite 90-92 Kent House,
87 Regent Street, London W1B 4EH
t 020 7434 4143 **f** 020 7434 4173 **e** info@jcarneyassociates.co.uk
Credits Strumpet (T); Crime And Punishment (T); 28 Days Later (F)

Ivor Gleek
5 Clifford Court, Tanfield Avenue, London NW2 7RY
t 020 8450 1584 **f** 020 8450 1584 **m** 07973 228258
e ivor@25fps.co.uk

Matthew Glen
Edit-Base, 70A Waldegrave Road, Teddington TW11 8NY
t 020 8614 6937 **e** alison@edit-base.co.uk

John Gow
Jessica Carney Associates, Suite 90-92 Kent House,
87 Regent Street, London W1B 4EH
t 020 7434 4143 **f** 020 7434 4173 **e** info@jcarneyassociates.co.uk
Credits 2000 Acres Of Sky - Series 3 (T); Gregory's Girl (T); Rescue Me (T)

Robin Graham-Scott
3 Poplar Avenue, Windlesham GU20 6PL
t 01276 452890 **f** 01276 452890 **m** 07831 817363

Tracy S Granger
CCA Management, 7 St George's Square, London SW1V 2HX
t 020 7630 6303 **f** 020 7630 7376

Colin Green
Casarotto Marsh Ltd, National House, 60-66 Wardour Street,
London W1V 4ND
t 020 7287 4450 **f** 020 7287 9128
e agents@casarotto.uk.com **w** www.casarotto.uk.com

Crispin Green
66 Burford Street, Hoddesdon EN11 8JN
m 07714 041809 **e** greencrispin@hotmail.com
Agent Jessica Carney Associates, Suite 90-92 Kent House,
87 Regent Street, London W1B 4EH
t 020 7434 4143 **f** 020 7434 4173 **e** info@jcarneyassociates.co.uk
Credits Holby City (T); Urban Gothic (T); In Deep (T)

Paul Green
Jessica Carney Associates, Suite 90-92 Kent House,
87 Regent Street, London W1B 4EH
t 020 7434 4143 **f** 020 7434 4173
info@jcarneyassociates.co.uk
Credits Richard III (F); The Asylum (F); The Lighthouse (F)

Jon Gregory
42 The Avenue, West Ealing, London W13 8LR
t 020 8998 8639 **f** 020 8998 8639
Agent International Creative Management Ltd, Oxford House,
76 Oxford Street, London W1D 1BS
t 020 7636 6565 **f** 020 7323 0101 **w** www.icmlondon.co.uk
Credits Pushing Tin (F); Ned Kelly (F); If Only (F); Donnie Brasco (F)

Paul Griffiths-Davies
30 Queens Road, Hazel Grove, Stockport SK7 4HX
t 01614 566169 **m** 07931 564 321 **e** hipgd@aol.com
Agent Jessica Carney Associates, Suite 90-92 Kent House,
87 Regent Street, London W1B 4EH
t 020 7434 4143 **f** 020 7434 4173
e info@jcarneyassociates.co.uk
Credits The Queen's Nose (T); A & E (T); Holby City (T)

John Grover
1 Lime Tree Close, Great Kingshill, High Wycombe HP15 6EX
t 01494 713421 **f** 01494 713421 **m** 07710 496779
e badingham@aol.com
Credits Monsignor Renard (T); Hairy Tale (F); Licence To Kill (F); Fat Friends (T)

Saadi Haeri
19 Northway Road, London SE5 9AN
t 020 7326 4493 **m** 07976 754508 **e** saadi@talk21.com
Credits Thirsting For War (D); The Dispossessed (D); Dead In The Water (D);
Diana's Top 10 (D)

Eddie Hamilton
42 Kinsley Court, 81-87 St Pauls Avenue, London NW2 5TU
m 07958 739 816 **e** eddiehamilton@email.com
w www.eddiehamilton.co.uk
Credits Mr In-Between (F); Mean Machine (F); Love, Sex, Drugs & Money (F)

Reg Harkema
Edit-Base, 70A Waldegrave Road, Teddington TW11 8NY
t 020 8614 6937 **e** alison@edit-base.co.uk

Jon Harris
International Creative Management Ltd, Oxford House,
76 Oxford Street, London W1D 1BS
t 020 7636 6565 **f** 020 7323 0101 **w** www.icmlondon.co.uk
Credits Snatch (F); Ripley's Game (F); Dot The I (F)

Martin Hay
Experience Counts - Call Me Ltd, 5th Floor, 41-42 Berners
Street, London W1P 3AA
t 020 7637 8112 **f** 020 7580 2582

Les Healey
The Dench Arnold Agency, 24 D'Arblay Street, London W1F 8EH
t 020 7437 4551 **f** 020 7439 1355
e contact@dencharnoldagency.co.uk **w** www.dencharnold.co.uk
Credits Unconditional Love (F); Croupier (F); The Passion Of Darkly Noon (F)

Kristina Hetherington
The Dench Arnold Agency, 24 D'Arblay Street, London W1F 8EH
t 020 7437 4551 **f** 020 7439 1355
e contact@dencharnoldagency.co.uk **w** www.dencharnold.co.uk
Credits Blind Flight (F); Gas Attack (T); Liam (F)

Crispin Holland
5 Mercers Road, Tufnell Park, London N19 4PH
t 020 7272 9055 **m** 07711 069 100
e crispin.holland@btinternet.com
Credits Shipwrecked (T); Secret Suburbia (D); Desert Island Discs 60th
Birthday Celebration (T); DNA - The Promise (D)

Rodney Holland
McKinney Macartney Management Ltd, The Barley Mow
Centre, 10 Barley Mow Passage, London W4 4PH
t 020 8995 4747 **f** 020 8995 2414
e fkb@mmtechsrep.demon.co.uk **w** www.mckinneymacartney.com

Peter Hollywod
53 Park Road, Hampton Hill, Hampton TW12 1HX
t 020 8979 3373 **f** 020 8941 7190 **m** 07973 121026
e editor@peterhollywood.com
Agent Edit-Base, 70A Waldegrave Road, Teddington TW11 8NY
t 020 8614 6937 **e** alison@edit-base.co.uk
Credits The Adventures of Baron Munchausen (F); The Neverending Story
II:The Next Chapter (F); Maybe Baby (F)

Mike Houghton
6 Windwill Road, Brentford TW8 0PW
t 020 8568 6498 **e** mikehoughton@beeb.net
Credits One Foot In The Grave (T); Hetty Wainthropp Investigates (T); Storm
Alert (D); Who Killed Caroline Dickinson? (D)

Niven Howie
McKinney Macartney Management Ltd, The Barley Mow
Centre, 10 Barley Mow Passage, London W4 4PH
t 020 8995 4747 **f** 020 8995 2414
e fkb@mmtechsrep.demon.co.uk **w** www.mckinneymacartney.com

Romuald Hryniewicz
6 Star Villas, Ponthir, Newport NP18 1PF
t 01633 420081 **f** 01633 420081 **m** 07900 123657
e thepoox@yahoo.com
Credits Grangehill 2003 (T); Nuts And Bolts (T); Hollyoaks (T)

Paul Hudson
Experience Counts - Call Me Ltd, 5th Floor, 41-42 Berners
Street, London W1P 3AA
t 020 7637 8112 **f** 020 7580 2582

Andrew Hulme
International Creative Management Ltd, Oxford House,
76 Oxford Street, London W1D 1BS
t 020 7636 6565 **f** 020 7323 0101 **w** www.icmlondon.co.uk
Credits Gangster Number One (F); Wicker Park (T); White Teeth (T)

Martin Hunter
The Dench Arnold Agency, 24 D'Arblay Street, London W1F 8EH
t 020 7437 4551 **f** 020 7439 1355
e contact@dencharnoldagency.co.uk **w** www.dencharnold.co.uk
Credits Event Horizon (F); Kalifornia (F); Full Metal Jacket (F)

David J Jacobs
5 Almeric Road, Battersea, London SW11 1HL
t 020 7924 1435 **m** 07884 435936 **e** djalizard@aol.com

Alan Jones
The Glebe House, Church Road, Weobley HR4 8SD
t 01544 318901 **m** 07770 612845 **e** alan@youngunter.org
Agent Jessica Carney Associates, Suite 90-92 Kent House,
87 Regent Street, London W1B 4EH
t 020 7434 4143 **f** 020 7434 4173 **e** info@jcarneyassociates.co.uk
Credits Silent Witness - Kith And Kill (T); The Mill On The Floss (F); Two
Thousand Acres of Sky (T)

Mads Nybo Jorgensen
Mac Million, 61 Gray's Inn Road, London WC1X 8LT
t 020 7831 5357 **f** 020 7404 6872 **m** 0777 6185959
e mads@macmillion.com **w** www.macmillion.com

John Jympson
McKinney Macartney Management Ltd, The Barley Mow
Centre, 10 Barley Mow Passage, London W4 4PH
t 020 8995 4747 **f** 020 8995 2414
e fkb@mmtechsrep.demon.co.uk **w** www.mckinneymacartney.com

Andy Kemp
66 Buchanan Gardens, London NW10 5AE
t 020 8969 1478 **e** andykemp@beeb.net
Credits Loyalist (T); Organ Farm (T); Death of Yugoslavia (T)

Philip Kloss
41 Woodstock Avenue, West Ealing, London W13 9UQ
m 07775 891892 **e** philipkloss@compuserve.com
Agent Jessica Carney Associates, Suite 90-92 Kent House,
87 Regent Street, London W1B 4EH
t 020 7434 4143 **f** 020 7434 4173 **e** info@jcarneyassociates.co.uk
Credits David Copperfield (T); Man And Boy (T); Daniel Deronda (T)

Paul Knight
McKinney Macartney Management Ltd, The Barley Mow
Centre, 10 Barley Mow Passage, London W4 4PH
t 020 8995 4747 **f** 020 8995 2414
e fkb@mmtechsrep.demon.co.uk **w** www.mckinneymacartney.com

Kerry Kohler
Edit-Base, 70A Waldegrave Road, Teddington TW11 8NY
t 020 8614 6937 **e** alison@edit-base.co.uk

Jason Krasucki
Creative Media Management, Unit 3B, Walpole Court, Ealing
Studios, Ealing Green, London W5 5ED
t 020 8584 5363 **f** 020 8566 5554
e enquiries@creativemediamanagement.com
Credits Love Again (T); Trance (T); Teachers (T); Manchild (T)

Justin Krish
2 Granville Road, London N4 4EL
t 020 8340 1661 **m** 07974 916530 **e** filmeditor@blueyonder.co.uk
Agent The Dench Arnold Agency, 24 D'Arblay Street, London
W1F 8EH
t 020 7437 4551 **f** 020 7439 1355 **w** www.dencharnold.co.uk

Peter Krook
25 Silver Crescent, London W4 5SF
t 020 8747 3122 **f** 020 8580 1654

Credits Playing The Field (T); Bramwell (T); Inspector Morse (T)

Sylvie Landra
The Dench Arnold Agency, 24 D'Arblay Street, London W1F 8EH
t 020 7437 4551 **f** 020 7439 1355
e contact@dencharnoldagency.co.uk **w** www.dencharnold.co.uk
Credits The Fifth Element (F); Leon (F); Jet Lag (F); A Sound Of Thunder (F)

Tony Lawson
19 The Vineyard, , Richmond RW10 6AQ
t 020 8940 7184
Credits The Butcher Boy (F); The End Of The Affair (F); The Good Thief (F)

Jerry Leon
Jessica Carney Associates, Suite 90-92 Kent House,
87 Regent Street, London W1B 4EH
t 020 7434 4143 **f** 020 7434 4173 **e** info@jcarneyassociates.co.uk
Credits Turn Of The Screw (T); Rebel Heart (T); The Whistleblower (T)

Ewa J Lind
t 020 7278 2106 **e** ewa.j.lind@virgin.net
Credits Kid In The Corner (T); September (F); Under The Skin (F); The Warrior (F)

Fiona MacDonald
69 Broughton Street, Edinburgh EH1 3RJ
t 01315 568876 **f** 07712 624525 **m** 07712 649525
Credits Flying Scots (T); Castaway (F); Pasty Faces (F)

John MacDonnell
International Creative Management Ltd, Oxford House,
76 Oxford Street, London W1D 1BS
t 020 7636 6565 **f** 020 7323 0101 **w** www.icmlondon.co.uk
Credits The Slab Boys (T); Tutti Frutti (T); Jonathan Creek (T)

Alex Mackie
McKinney Macartney Management Ltd, The Barley Mow
Centre, 10 Barley Mow Passage, London W4 4PH
t 020 8995 4747 **f** 020 8995 2414
e fkb@mmtechsrep.demon.co.uk **w** www.mckinneymacartney.com

Tim Marchant
27 Fulbrooke Road, Newnham, Cambridge CB3 9EE
t 01223 362956 **m** 07803 609397 **e** timm.13@virgin.net
Credits Safe House (T); Monarch Of The Glen II-III (T); Holby City IV-V (T);
Keen Eddie (T)

David Martin
McKinney Macartney Management Ltd, The Barley Mow
Centre, 10 Barley Mow Passage, London W4 4PH
t 020 8995 4747 **f** 020 8995 2414
e fkb@mmtechsrep.demon.co.uk **w** www.mckinneymacartney.com

Adam Masters
39 Winterdown Road, Esher KT10 8LP
t 01372 467322 **m** 07759 203195 **e** adamnast@globalnet.co.uk
Agent Edit-Base, 70A Waldegrave Road, Teddington TW11 8NY
t 020 8614 6937 **e** alison@edit-base.co.uk
Credits Lucy Sullivan Is Getting Married (T); Night And Day (T)

Laurie McDowell
Edit-Base, 70A Waldegrave Road, Teddington TW11 8NY
t 020 8614 6937 **e** alison@edit-base.co.uk

MGP
6 D'Arblay Street, London W1V 3FD
m 07802 447494

Michael Johns Associates
A1 Stylecroft Road, Chalfont St. Giles, Bucks HP8 4HZ
t 01494 872463 **f** 01494 872463 **m** 07801 657062
e michaeleditor@btinternet.com
Contact Michael Johns, Partner - Editor; Suzanne Goddard, Office
Administrater; Suzanne Goddard, Office Administrater
Credits Double X (F); Feast At Midnight (F)

Hugo Middleton
Jessica Carney Associates, Suite 90-92 Kent House,
87, London W1B 4EH
t 020 7434 4143 **f** 020 7434 4173 **e** info@jcarneyassociates.co.uk
Credits Sharpe (T); Night And Day (T); The Bill (T)

Greg Miller
Jessica Carney Associates, Suite 90-92 Kent House,
87 Regent Street, London W1B 4EH
t 020 7434 4143 **f** 020 7434 4173 **e** info@jcarneyassociates.co.uk
Credits The Vice - Walking On Water (T); Danziel & Pascoe (T); Metroland (F)

Beverley Mills
McKinney Macartney Management Ltd, The Barley Mow
Centre, 10 Barley Mow Passage, London W4 4PH
t 020 8995 4747 **f** 020 8995 2414
e fkb@mmtechsrep.demon.co.uk **w** www.mckinneymacartney.com

Richard Milward
20 Kendall Road, Isleworth TW7 6RA
t 020 8568 3554 **m** 07798 625944
e rich_jo_milward@hotmail.com
Agent CCA Management, 7 St George's Square,
London SW1V 2HX
t 020 7630 6303 **f** 020 7630 7376
Credits Twelfth Night (T); Mojo (F); Murder In Mind (T); The Bunker (F)

Minno Film Editors
28 Lexington Street, London W1F OLF
t +44 20 7439 2097 **f** +44 20 7287 2434
e info@minno.co.uk **w** www.minno.co.uk
Contact Andy Welsh

Colin Monie
The Dench Arnold Agency, 24 D'Arblay Street, London W1F 8EH
t 020 7437 4551 **f** 020 7439 1355
e contact@dencharnoldagency.co.uk **w** www.dencharnold.co.uk
Credits The Magdalene Sisters (F); Orphans (F); Young Adam (F)

Patrick Moore
The Dench Arnold Agency, 24 D'Arblay Street, London W1F 8EH
t 020 7437 4551 **f** 020 7439 1355
e contact@dencharnoldagency.co.uk **w** www.dencharnold.co.uk
Credits The Plan Man (T); Goodbye Charlie Bright (F); Human Traffic (F)

Dennis Morrison
PO Box 28314, London SE20 7WT
t 07092 366864 **f** 07092 366864 **m** 07788 441494
e dennis@dtbprod.com **w** www.dtbprod.com
Credits Headwork Surf UK (T); Bopumentary - Bop @ Midem Cannes (D);
Breakdance Special (M); Red (S)

Clive Muller
Edit-Base, 70A Waldegrave Road, Teddington TW11 8NY
t 020 8614 6937 **e** alison@edit-base.co.uk

Andrew Nelson
Dewes Green Farm, Berden, Bishop's Stortford CM23 1AR
t 01279 777784 **m** 07866 222699
e andrewnelson@berden.org.uk
Agent Jessica Carney Associates, Suite 90-92 Kent House,
87 Regent Street, London W1B 4EH
t 020 7434 4143 **f** 020 7434 4173 **e** info@jcarneyassociates.co.uk
Credits Mortimer's Law (T); London's Burning (T); Peak Practice (T)

Angus Newton
Popes Hole House, Well, Hook RG29 1TL
t 01256 862323 **f** 01256 862323 **m** 07785 745324
Agent International Creative Management Ltd, Oxford House,
76 Oxford Street, London W1D 1BS
t 020 7636 6565 **f** 020 7323 0101 **w** www.icmlondon.co.uk
Credits Ella And The Mothers (T); Complicity (F); The Crow Road (T); Scandal (T)

Nicholas Wayman Harris Ltd
81 Berwick Street, London W1F 8TQ
t 020 7734 2744

Pat O'Grady
6 Windmill Road, Brentford TW8 OPW
t 020 8568 6498 **e** poggy@tiseali.co.uk
Credits Grand Designs (T); Beloved Country - The She Chief (D);
Everyman - An Ordinary Marriage (D); Diving With The Force (D)

Jackie Ophir
11 Daniells, Welwyn Garden City AL7 1QY
t 01707 320527 **m** 07966 198698
Agent Edit-Base, 70A Waldegrave Road, Teddington TW11 8NY
t 020 8614 6937 **e** alison@edit-base.co.uk
Credits The Making Of Blake's 7 (D); Sooty (T); At Home With The Braithwaites
(T); A.K.A

William Oswald
Dol-y-Coed, Heol Pant-y-Gored, Creigian, Cardiff CF15 9NF
t 07071 237237 **m** 07796 441596 **e** willoswaldfilm@hotmail.com
Credits The Bench Series I & II (T); Otherworld (F); Do Not Go Gentle (F);
The Miracle Maker (A)

Oral Ottey
International Creative Management Ltd, Oxford House,
76 Oxford Street, London W1D 1BS
t 020 7636 6565 **f** 020 7323 0101 **w** www.icmlondon.co.uk
Credits Twin Town (F); Plunkett And Macleane (F); Band Of Brothers (T)

Russell Oxenden
Flat 12, 28 Carlton Road, Sidcup DA14 6TU
t 020 8302 0108 **f** 020 8302 0108 **m** 07956 349572
e russcut@talk21.com
Credits BT Ethnic (C); Shredded Wheat (C); Fairy (C); McDonalds (C)

Folasade Oyeleye
CCA Management, 7 St George's Square, London SW1V 2HX
t 020 7630 6303 **f** 020 7630 7376

Andrew Page
49 Priory Way, North Harrow HA2 6DQ
t 020 8863 1827 **e** andypage3@ukonline.co.uk
Credits A Strike Out Of Time (T); Real Lives (D); Cold War (D); In Britian Series (D)

Keith Palmer
Jessica Carney Associates, Suite 90-92 Kent House,
87 Regent Street, London W1B 4EH
t 020 7434 4143 **f** 020 7434 4173 **e** info@jcarneyassociates.co.uk
Credits Kavanagh QC (T); Sharpe (T); Hornblower (F)

Kant Pan
Edit-Base, 70A Waldegrave Road, Teddington TW11 8NY
t 020 8614 6937 **e** alison@edit-base.co.uk

Frances Parker
Casarotto Marsh Ltd, National House, 60-66 Wardour Street,
London W1V 4ND
t 020 7287 4450 **f** 020 7287 9128
e agents@casarotto.uk.com **w** www.casarotto.uk.com

Michael Parker
McKinney Macartney Management Ltd, The Barley Mow
Centre, 10 Barley Mow Passage, London W4 4PH
t 020 8995 4747 **f** 020 8995 2414
e fkb@mmtechsrep.demon.co.uk **w** www.mckinneymacartney.com
Credits East Is East (F); The House of Mirth (F); Thunderpants (F)

Michael Parkinson
CCA Management, 7 St George's Square, London SW1V 2HX
t 020 7630 6303 **f** 020 7630 7376

Barry Peters
Avoca, 12 Kingsway, Gerrards Cross SL9 8NR
t 01753 883369
Agent Jessica Carney Associates, Suite 90-92 Kent House,
87 Regent Street, London W1B 4EH
t 020 7434 4143 **f** 020 7434 4173 **e**
info@jcarneyassociates.co.uk
Credits The Seventh Scroll (T); Married 2 Malcolm (F); In the Beginning (F)

Alex Pikal
38 West Way, Harpenden AL5 4RD
t 01582 462885 **f** 01582 462875 **m** 07973 825549
e alex.pikal@ntlworld.com

Pixelsplice
London
m 07941 909552
e mdeignan@pixelsplice.co.uk **w** www.pixelsplice.co.uk
Credits Sophie Ellis Bextor - Watch My Lips (M); The Arts Show - If (D);
Dispatches - Seven Days In Hell (D)

Post Modern Ltd
100 Queens Road, Buckhurst Hill IG9 5BS
t 020 8281 7141 **f** 020 8281 7141 **m** 07889 914953
e colin@post-modern.co.uk
Contact Colin Green, Editor

David Pygram
22 Chamberlain Way, Pinner HA5 2AY
t 020 8866 9174 **e** d.pygram@btinternet.com
Credits Abroad In Britain With Jonathan Meades (T); Clive James: Postcard
From Bombay (T); Horizon (D)

Adam Recht
C/o Jessica Carney Associates, Suite 90-92 Kent House,
87 Regent Street, London W1B 4EH
t 020 7434 4143 **e** adam@adamrecht.com
Credits London's Burning (T); Holby City (T); Starhunter (T); Night And Day (T)

David Rees
Creative Media Management, Unit 3B, Walpole Court,
Ealing Studios, Ealing Green, London W5 5ED
t 020 8584 5363 **f** 020 8566 5554
e enquiries@creativemediamanagement.com
Credits Dead Gorgeous (T); Carrie's War (T); Pollyanna (T); Murder Rooms (T)

Michael Reichwein
International Creative Management Ltd, Oxford House,
76 Oxford Street, London W1D 1BS
t 020 7636 6565 **f** 020 7323 0101 **w** www.icmlondon.co.uk
Credits Antonia's Line (F); Mrs Dalloway (F); The Luzhin Defence (F)

John Richards
International Creative Management Ltd, Oxford House,
76 Oxford Street, London W1D 1BS
t 020 7636 6565 **f** 020 7323 0101 **w** www.icmlondon.co.uk
Credits Virtual Sexuality (F); Plots With A View (F); Band Of Brothers (T)

Julian Rodd
67 Constantine Road, Hampstead, London NW3 2LP
t 020 7485 2737 **m** 07779 965775
e j.rodd@macunlimited.net
Credits Partners In Action (F); Mumbo Jumbo (F); Revelation (F)

Liz Roe
Edit-Base, 70A Waldegrave Road, Teddington TW11 8NY
t 020 8614 6937 **e** alison@edit-base.co.uk

Xavier Russell
Jessica Carney Associates, Suite 90-92 Kent House,
87 Regent Street, London W1B 4EH
t 020 7434 4143 **f** 020 7434 4173
e info@jcarneyassociates.co.uk
Credits Red Cap (T); Teachers (T); Attachments (T)

Robin Sales
McKinney Macartney Management Ltd, The Barley Mow
Centre, 10 Barley Mow Passage, London W4 4PH
t 020 8995 4747 **f** 020 8995 2414
e fkb@mmtechsrep.demon.co.uk **w** www.mckinneymacartney.com

Gary Scott
5/1 Blackfriars Street, Edinburgh EH1 1NB
t 0131 557 4570 **m** 07976 640994 **e** g_knoll@madasafish.com
Credits Queen Elizabeth's Magician (D); Night Swimmer (S); Teenage Japanese
Killers (D); Rice Paper Stars (S)

John Scott
Casarotto Marsh Ltd, National House, 60-66 Wardour Street,
London W1V 4ND
t 020 7287 4450 **f** 020 7287 9128
e agents@casarotto.uk.com **w** www.casarotto.uk.com

Ian Seymour
Agent CCA Management, 7 St Georges Square,
London SW1V 2HX
t 020 7630 6303 **f** 020 7630 7376
e ccamanagement@btclick.com
Agent Edit-Base, 70A Waldegrave Road, Teddington TW11 8NY
t 020 8614 6937 **e** alison@edit-base.co.uk
Credits Buffalo Soldiers (F); Ned Kelly (F); Relative Values (F)

Roy Sharman
International Creative Management Ltd, Oxford House,
76 Oxford Street, London W1D 1BS
t 020 7636 6565 **f** 020 7323 0101 **w** www.icmlondon.co.uk
Credits Madam Bovary (T); The Lakes (T); I Capture The Castle (F)

Anuree De Silva
Edit-Base, 70A Waldegrave Road, Teddington TW11 8NY
t 020 8614 6937 **e** alison@edit-base.co.uk

Claire Simpson
International Creative Management Ltd, Oxford House,
76 Oxford Street, London W1D 1BS
t 020 7636 6565 **f** 020 7323 0101 **w** www.icmlondon.co.uk
Credits The Fan (F); Town And Country (F); Possession (F)

John Smith
International Creative Management Ltd, Oxford House,
76 Oxford Street, London W1D 1BS
t 020 7636 6565 **f** 020 7323 0101 **w** www.icmlondon.co.uk
Credits Sliding Doors (F); Under Suspicion (F); Proof Of Life (F)

John Victor Smith
Pen Lodge, Kingston Hill, Kingston-upon-thames KT2 7JP
t 020 8546 2390
Credits Spacetruckers (F); All The Little Animals (F); The Testimony
Of Taliesin Jones (F)

Paul Martin Smith
McKinney Macartney Management Ltd, The Barley Mow
Centre, 10 Barley Mow Passage, London W4 4PH
t 020 8995 4747 **f** 020 8995 2414
e fkb@mmtechsrep.demon.co.uk **w** www.mckinneymacartney.com

Philip Sneider
Experience Counts - Call Me Ltd, 5th Floor, 41-42 Berners Street, London W1P 3AA
t 020 7637 8112 **f** 020 7580 2582

Anne Sopel
Casarotto Marsh Ltd, National House, 60-66 Wardour Street, London W1V 4ND
t 020 7287 4450 **f** 020 7287 9128
e agents@casarotto.uk.com **w** www.casarotto.uk.com

Peter Spendeley
Experience Counts - Call Me Ltd, 5th Floor, 41-42 Berners Street, London W1P 3AA
t 020 7637 8112 **f** 020 7580 2582

Paul Steiner
4 Ashington Court, Westwood Hill, London SE26 6BN
t 020 8776 8269 **m** 07880 746447
e paulsteiner50@hotmail.com
Credits Tomorrow's World (T); EastEnders Revealed (T); Property Ladder (T); Time Team (T)

Steve Stevenson
31 Parkside Crescent, London N7 7JG
m 07050 384545 **e** steve.tvtv@virgin.net
Credits Secret History - The War The Nazis Won (T); Secrets Of The Dead - The Coldest March (T); D-Day: The Untold Story (D)

Mathew Stonehouse
m 07973 134840
e mathew@stonehouse.co.uk **w** www.stonehouse.co.uk
Credits High Speed (F); Joy-Rider (F); The Only Hotel (F)

Alan Strachan
Creative Media Management, Unit 3B, Walpole Court, Ealing Studios, Ealing Green, London W5 5ED
t 020 8584 5363 **f** 020 8566 5554
e enquiries@creativemediamanagement.com
Credits The War Bride (F); Withnail And I (F); Waking Ned (F); Saving Grace (F)

Sue Moles Editing Ltd
1 Marlborough Court, London W1F 7EE
t 020 7494 3383
e tomharcourtsmith@aol.com **w** www.suemoles.com
Contact Catherine Hendrie, Editor; Sam Mitchell, Editor; Tom Smith, Post Production Producer; Sue Moles, Managing Director
Credits McDonalds (C); Kelloggs (C); Coca Cola (C); Woolworths (C)

Ian Sutherland
International Creative Management Ltd, Oxford House, 76 Oxford Street, London W1D 1BS
t 020 7636 6565 **f** 020 7323 0101 **w** www.icmlondon.co.uk
Credits The Commander (T); Trial & Retribution IV, V, VII (T); Mind Games (T)

Scott Thomas
International Creative Management Ltd, Oxford House, 76 Oxford Street, London W1D 1BS
t 020 7636 6565 **f** 020 7323 0101 **w** www.icmlondon.co.uk
Credits I Dreamed Of Africa (F); The Lawless Heart (F); Sinners (T)

Paul Tothill
Casarotto Marsh Ltd, National House, 60-66 Wardour Street, London W1V 4ND
t 020 7287 4450 **f** 020 7287 9128
e agents@casarotto.uk.com **w** www.casarotto.uk.com

Jamie Trevill
The Dench Arnold Agency, 24 D'Arblay Street, London W1F 8EH
t 020 7437 4551 **f** 020 7439 1355
e contact@dencharnoldagency.co.uk **w** www.dencharnold.co.uk
Credits The Tichborne Claiment (F); Conspiracy Of Silence (F); Another Life (F)

Derek Trigg
Edit-Base, 70A Waldegrave Road, Teddington TW11 8NY
t 020 8614 6937 **e** alison@edit-base.co.uk

Martin Vale
Experience Counts - Call Me Ltd, 5th Floor, 41-42 Berners Street, London W1P 3AA
t 020 7637 8112 **f** 020 7580 2582

Tim Waddell
Edit-Base, 70A Waldegrave Road, Teddington TW11 8NY
t 020 8614 6937 **e** alison@edit-base.co.uk

Graham Walker
International Creative Management Ltd, Oxford House, 76 Oxford Street, London W1D 1BS
t 020 7636 6565 **f** 020 7323 0101 **w** www.icmlondon.co.uk
Credits Strange (T); When The Sky Falls (F); The Vice (T)

Joe Walker
Casarotto Marsh Ltd, National House, 60-66 Wardour Street, London W1V 4ND
t 020 7287 4450 **f** 020 7287 9128
e agents@casarotto.uk.com **w** www.casarotto.uk.com

Martin Walsh
International Creative Management Ltd, Oxford House, 76 Oxford Street, London W1D 1BS
t 020 7636 6565 **f** 020 7323 0101 **w** www.icmlondon.co.uk
Credits Bridget Jones's Diary (F); Iris (F); Chicago (F)

Frank Webb
Edit-Base, 70A Waldegrave Road, Teddington TW11 8NY
t 020 8614 6937 **e** alison@edit-base.co.uk

Tim Wellburn
Edit-Base, 70A Waldegrave Road, Teddington TW11 8NY
t 020 8614 6937 **e** alison@edit-base.co.uk

David Wendl-Berry
Experience Counts - Call Me Ltd, 5th Floor, 41-42 Berners Street, London W1P 3AA
t 020 7637 8112 **f** 020 7580 2582

Cliff West
No 4 Chapel Road, London W13 9AE
t 020 8810 1584 **e** cliff.west@talk21.com
Credits Las Bas (S); The Burger And The King (T); Gallivant (F); This Filthy Earth (F)

John Wilson
200 Elsenham Street, London SW18 5NR
t 020 8870 6049 **f** 020 8488 7877 **m** 07976 177119
e jtcwilson@ntlworld.com **w** www.johnwilsoneditor.com
Credits The Cook, The Thief, His Wife And Her Lover (F); Cheeky (F); Billy Elliot (F); Before You Go (F)

Roger Wilson
15 The Greenway, Gerrards Cross SL9 8LX
m 07831 115105
Agent Jessica Carney Associates, Suite 90-92 Kent House, 87 Regent Street, London W1B 4EH
t 020 7434 4143 **f** 020 7434 4173 **e** info@jcarneyassociates.co.uk
Credits Rockface (T); Inspector Morse (T); 2000 Acres Of Sky - Series 3 (T)

Chris Wimble
International Creative Management Ltd, Oxford House, 76 Oxford Street, London W1D 1BS
t 020 7636 6565 **f** 020 7323 0101 **w** www.icmlondon.co.uk
Credits Grace (T); Agatha Christie's Poirot (T); Firelight (F)

Justine Wright
16A Orde Hall Street, London WC1N 3JW
t 020 7831 3628 **m** 07775 783590 **e** jandalan@clara.co.uk
Credits The Game Of Their Lives (D); Being Mick (D); Late Night Shopping (F);
One Day In September (F)

Keith Wright
m 07778 004467 **e** keithjwright@hotmail.com
Credits Apple Opera (D); Where's Bingo Betty? (S); Stagnate (S); Corbin West (F)

Sue Wyatt
Casarotto Marsh Ltd, National House, 60-66 Wardour Street,
London W1V 4ND
t 020 7287 4450 **f** 020 7287 9128
e agents@casarotto.uk.com **w** www.casarotto.uk.com

Editors **Sound Assistants**

Foluso Aribigbola
Edit-Base, 70A Waldegrave Road, Teddington TW11 8NY
t 020 8614 6937 **e** alison@edit-base.co.uk

Steven Browell
Edit-Base, 70A Waldegrave Road, Teddington TW11 8NY
t 020 8614 6937 **e** alison@edit-base.co.uk

Simon Chase
Edit-Base, 70A Waldegrave Road, Teddington TW11 8NY
t 020 8614 6937 **e** alison@edit-base.co.uk

Oliver Cohen
Edit-Base, 70A Waldegrave Road, Teddington TW11 8NY
t 020 8614 6937 **e** alison@edit-base.co.uk

Sophie Cornet
Edit-Base, 70A Waldegrave Road, Teddington TW11 8NY
t 020 8614 6937 **e** alison@edit-base.co.uk

Richard Fordham
Edit-Base, 70A Waldegrave Road, Teddington TW11 8NY
t 020 8614 6937 **e** alison@edit-base.co.uk

Gagik Gharagheuzian
Edit-Base, 70A Waldegrave Road, Teddington TW11 8NY
t 020 8614 6937 **e** alison@edit-base.co.uk

Alex Joseph
Edit-Base, 70A Waldegrave Road, Teddington TW11 8NY
t 020 8614 6937 **e** alison@edit-base.co.uk

Adam Laschinger
Edit-Base, 70A Waldegrave Road, Teddington TW11 8NY
t 020 8614 6937 **e** alison@edit-base.co.uk

Ian Macbeth
Edit-Base, 70A Waldegrave Road, Teddington TW11 8NY
t 020 8614 6937 **e** alison@edit-base.co.uk

Alastair Sirkett
Edit-Base, 70A Waldegrave Road, Teddington TW11 8NY
t 020 8614 6937 **e** alison@edit-base.co.uk

Jack Whittaker
Edit-Base, 70A Waldegrave Road, Teddington TW11 8NY
t 020 8614 6937 **e** alison@edit-base.co.uk

Simon Winter
Edit-Base, 70A Waldegrave Road, Teddington TW11 8NY
t 020 8614 6937 **e** alison@edit-base.co.uk

Editors
Sound Dubbing/Mixers

Ross Adams
Holcombe Cottge, Hedsor Bourne End, Bourne End SL8 5ES
t 01628 529965 **f** 01628 529606 **m** 07771 571 172
e ross.adams@virgin.net
Agent Edit-Base, 70A Waldegrave Road, Teddington TW11 8NY
t 020 8614 6937 **e** alison@edit-base.co.uk
Credits Twin Town (F); Best Laid Plans (F); Band Of Brothers (T)

AMS Neve Plc
Billington Road, Burnley BB11 5UB
t 01282 417281 **f** 01282 417282
e enquiry@ams-neve.com **w** www.ams-neve.com
Contact Greg Cluskey, Director of Commercial Operations; Joanne Darlington,
Public Relations; David Sim, Head of Sales

Soren Andersen
London
t 020 7388 9609 **m** 07950 260078
e info@twoears.co.uk **w** www.twoears.co.uk
Credits TV3 Channel Sound Design; Viasat Broadcasting Digital (C)

Brigitte Arnold
t 020 8451 3979 **e** brigitte.arnold@btinternet.com
Agent Edit-Base, 70A Waldegrave Road, Teddington TW11 8NY
t 020 8614 6937 **e** alison@edit-base.co.uk

Alexander Cambell Askew
3 Herons Close, Kirdford, Near Billingshurst RH14 0NF
t 01403 820144 **f** 01403 820144 **m** 07831 843 811
e soundhiker@zoom.co.uk **e** soundhiker@macdream.net
Credits The Emmy Awards (T); Ever After; Band Of Brothers (T)

Campbell Askew
Edit-Base, 70A Waldegrave Road, Teddington TW11 8NY
t 020 8614 6937 **e** alison@edit-base.co.uk

Simon Branthwaite
London
t 020 8381 4283 **m** 07786 368614
e simonbranthwaite@aol.com
Credits Black Stallion Energy Drink (C); Doc Martin Shoes (C); 2001 New
Zealand Music Awards (T)

Cardiff TV Company
26-28 Dalcross Street, Roath, Cardiff CF24 4SD
t 029 2045 0950 **f** 029 2045 1151 **e** jcrossctv@aol.com
Contact John Cross, Managing Director

Colin Chapman
10 Wendover Road, Well End, Bourne End SL8 5NT
t 01628 527641 **f** 01628 527641 **m** 07860 253405
e bigsoundpost@aol.com
Agent Edit-Base, 70A Waldegrave Road, Teddington TW11 8NY
t 020 8614 6937 **e** alison@edit-base.co.uk
Credits Gladiatress (F); State Of Mind (T); Waking The Dead (T);
Song For A Rassy Boy (F)

Jonathan Cronin
Edit-Base, 70A Waldegrave Road, Teddington TW11 8NY
t 020 8614 6937 **e** alison@edit-base.co.uk

John Crumpton
109 Carrington Lane, Sale M33 5NJ
t 0161 282 6363 **m** 07976 981517
e john1crumpton@aol.com **w** www.kbsrecords.com
Credits Clocking Off IV (T); The Second Coming (T)

Paul Davies
Edit-Base, 70A Waldegrave Road, Teddington TW11 8NY
t 020 8614 6937 **e** alison@edit-base.co.uk

David Evans
Edit-Base, 70A Waldegrave Road, Teddington TW11 8NY
t 020 8614 6937 **e** alison@edit-base.co.uk

Martin Evans
Edit-Base, 70A Waldegrave Road, Teddington TW11 8NY
t 020 8614 6937 **e** alison@edit-base.co.uk

Michael Feinberg
Edit-Base, 70A Waldegrave Road, Teddington TW11 8NY
t 020 8614 6937 **e** alison@edit-base.co.uk

Richard Fettes
Tyndrum Farm, Holmbury St Mary RH5 6NB
t 01306 621410 **f** 01306 621004 **m** 07885 113906
Agent Edit-Base, 70A Waldegrave Road, Teddington TW11 8NY
t 020 8614 6937 **e** alison@edit-base.co.uk
Credits Mean Machine (F); Tea With Mussolini (F); Trainspotting (F); Muppet Treasure Island (F)

Conrad Fletcher
London
t 020 7388 9609 **m** 07950 260078
e info@twoears.co.uk **w** www.twoears.co.uk
Credits EastEnders (T); Scrapheap Challenge (T); Falklands Bound (T); The Weakest Link (T)

Michael O Flynn
Connections, The Meadlands, Oakleigh Road, Hatch End, Pinner HA5 4HB
t 020 8420 1444 **f** 020 8428 5836 **m** 07831 305518
e mail@connectionsuk.com **w** www.connectionsuk.com

Joe Gallagher
Edit-Base, 70A Waldegrave Road, Teddington TW11 8NY
t 020 8614 6937 **e** alison@edit-base.co.uk

Carl Gardiner
63 Green Lane, London W7 2PA
t 020 8567 6340 **m** 07932 783420 **e** carly.g@btopenworld.com
Credits Homefront (D); Like It Is (F); Attachments (T); London's Burning (T)

Rodney Glenn
25 Grosvenor Road, Twickenham TW1 4AD
t 020 8892 6966 **e** rodney.glenn@virgin.net
Credits Monty Python's Meaning Of Life (F); Brazil (F); Hope Springs (F); Little Voice (F)

Mick Glossop
Edit-Base, 70A Waldegrave Road, Teddington TW11 8NY
t 020 8614 6937 **e** alison@edit-base.co.uk

Rory Griffin
Edit-Base, 70A Waldegrave Road, Teddington TW11 8NY
t 020 8614 6937 **e** alison@edit-base.co.uk

Danny Hambrook
t 020 8692 2578 **f** 020 8692 2578 **m** 07050 049853
e dannyhsound@hotmail.com

Tim Hands
Edit-Base, 70A Waldegrave Road, Teddington TW11 8NY
t 020 8614 6937 **e** alison@edit-base.co.uk

Patrick Hanley
Experience Counts - Call Me Ltd, 5th Floor, 41-42 Berners Street, London W1P 3AA
t 020 7637 8112 **f** 020 7580 2582

Toby Harris
Edit-Base, 70A Waldegrave Road, Teddington TW11 8NY
t 020 8614 6937 **e** alison@edit-base.co.uk

Stefan Henrix
Edit-Base, 70A Waldegrave Road, Teddington TW11 8NY
t 020 8614 6937 **e** alison@edit-base.co.uk

Leon Horrocks
Edit-Base, 70A Waldegrave Road, Teddington TW11 8NY
t 020 8614 6937 **e** alison@edit-base.co.uk

Howard Halsall
30 Darell Road, Richmond, London TW9 4LG
t 020 8876 0892 **m** 07946 385390
Contact Colin Miller, Supervising Sound Editor; Mark Auguste, Supervising Sound Editor; Campbell Askew, Supervising Sound Editor; Nigel Mills, Supervising Sound Editor
Credits Band Of Brothers (T); Gosford Park (F); The Four Feathers (F); The Kelly Gang (F)

IADA Ltd
Ewlin, Keillour, Methven, Perth PH1 3RA
t 01738 840816 **f** 01738 840816 **m** 07785 933679
e gr1b@aol.com **w** www.iada.uk.com
Credits Moulin Rouge (F); The Magdalene Sisters (F); Chicken Run (F)

Joe Illing
Edit-Base, 70A Waldegrave Road, Teddington TW11 8NY
t 020 8614 6937 **e** alison@edit-base.co.uk

Cliff Jones
4 Grafton Mews, London W1T 5JE
t 020 7387 3230 **f** 020 7387 0718 **m** 07710 745059
e cliff@soundmonsters.com
Credits Lads Army (T); History Of DNA (D); Visions Of Space (D); Pyramid (D)

Eddy Joseph
Edit-Base, 70A Waldegrave Road, Teddington TW11 8NY
t 020 8614 6937 **e** alison@edit-base.co.uk

Christian Koefoed
London
t 020 7388 9609 **m** 07950 260078
e info@twoears.co.uk **w** www.twoears.co.uk
Credits Fresh Out Of Tears (T); Toni's War (D)

Johannes Konecny
Edit-Base, 70A Waldegrave Road, Teddington TW11 8NY
t 020 8614 6937 **e** alison@edit-base.co.uk

Simon Lang
Experience Counts - Call Me Ltd, 5th Floor, 41-42 Berners Street, London W1P 3AA
t 020 7637 8112 **f** 020 7580 2582

Peter Lennard
Edit-Base, 70A Waldegrave Road, Teddington TW11 8NY
t 020 8614 6937 **e** alison@edit-base.co.uk

Christopher Lloyd
Edit-Base, 70A Waldegrave Road, Teddington TW11 8NY
t 020 8614 6937 **e** alison@edit-base.co.uk

Derek Lomas
Edit-Base, 70A Waldegrave Road, Teddington TW11 8NY
t 020 8614 6937 **e** alison@edit-base.co.uk

Nick Lowe
Edit-Base, 70A Waldegrave Road, Teddington TW11 8NY
t 020 8614 6937 **e** alison@edit-base.co.uk

Andy Ludbrook
Woodruff Grange, Elm Park, Shotley Bridge, Consett DH8 6SE
t 01207 503959 **m** 07867 920496 **e** andy@cmsi.freeserve.co.uk
Credits Jools Holland's Piano (T); The Last Horseman (D); Millenium Movies (T); The Secrets Of The Art Factory (D)

Karl Mainzer
4 Grafton Mews, London W1T 5JE
t 020 7387 3230 **f** 020 7387 0718 **e** karl@soundmonsters.com
Credits Visions Of Space (D); Embassy Siege (D); Eminem's Mum (D); Our Sam (D)

Gerard McCann
14 Highview Road, Ealing, London W13 0HB
t 020 8566 8767
Credits To Kill A King (F); Love's Labour's Lost (F); The Beach (F); Possession (F)

Scott McEwing
TOVS Ltd, The Linen Hall, 162-168 Regent Street, London W1B 5TB
t 020 7287 6110 **f** 020 7287 5481
e info@tovs.co.uk **w** www.tovs.co.uk

Dennis McTaggart
Edit-Base, 70A Waldegrave Road, Teddington TW11 8NY
t 020 8614 6937 **e** alison@edit-base.co.uk

Paul Nickson
London
t 020 7388 9609 **m** 07950 260078
e info@twoears.co.uk **w** www.twoears.co.uk
Credits Top Of The Pops (T); MTV Music Awards 2002, Barcelona (T); Party In The Park 2001; Jazz On 3

Alan Paley
Edit-Base, 70A Waldegrave Road, Teddington TW11 8NY
t 020 8614 6937 **e** alison@edit-base.co.uk

Paul Davies Sound Design
62 Tottenham Court Road, London W1T 2ER
t 020 7323 3629 **f** 020 7580 5560 **m** 07773 776994
e info@pdsounddesign.com **w** www.pdsounddesign.com
Credits White Teeth (T); Morvern Callar (F); 40 (T)

Sandra Portman
Edit-Base, 70A Waldegrave Road, Teddington TW11 8NY
t 020 8614 6937 **e** alison@edit-base.co.uk

Simon Price (GBFE)
t 020 8870 5830 **f** 020 8870 5830 **m** 07976 826725
e simonpri@lineone.net
Credits Only Fools & Horses (T); The Musketeer (F); Saving Grace (F); Chicken Run (F)

Michael Redfern
Edit-Base, 70A Waldegrave Road, Teddington TW11 8NY
t 020 8614 6937 **e** alison@edit-base.co.uk

Colin Ritchie
Edit-Base, 70A Waldegrave Road, Teddington TW11 8NY
t 020 8614 6937 **e** alison@edit-base.co.uk

Vaughan Roberts
Connections, The Meadlands, Oakleigh Road, Hatch End, Pinner HA5 4HB
t 020 8420 1444 **f** 020 8428 5836 **m** 07831 305518
e mail@connectionsuk.com **w** www.connectionsuk.com

Sandra Roth
Edit-Base, 70A Waldegrave Road, Teddington TW11 8NY
t 020 8614 6937 **e** alison@edit-base.co.uk

John Rutherford
27 Woodland Crescent, Sedgley Park, Prestwich, Manchester M25 9WQ
t 0161 773 2659 **m** 07947 001421 **e** john-rutherford@supanet.com
Credits Prime Suspect (T); Cracker (T); The Second Coming (T); Clocking Off (T)

Ian Sands
t 1932 222704 **m** 07860 753717 **w** www.iansands.co.uk

Sound for Picture
27 Meredith Close, Pinner HA5 4RP
t 020 8421 6882 **f** 020 8421 6882 **m** 07747 626 654
e info@soundforpicture.co.uk **w** www.soundforpicture.co.uk
Contact James Berkeley, Proprietor
Credits Funny Running Into You Like This (F); Fire Power (F); Fire Fall (F)

Morten Steingrim
London
t 020 7388 9609 **m** 07950 260078
e info@twoears.co.uk **w** www.twoears.co.uk
Credits The Refuge (T)

Steven Stockford
101 Cambrian Drive, Rhos-on-Sea LL28 4SY
m 07970 794978 **e** steven@stockforwales.freeserve.co.uk
Credits Hollyoaks (T); Brookside (T); Mr Men (A); Grange Hill (T)

Richard Todman
Edit-Base, 70A Waldegrave Road, Teddington TW11 8NY
t 020 8614 6937 **e** alison@edit-base.co.uk

Twoears ltd
London
t 020 7388 9609 **m** 07950 260078
e info@twoears.co.uk **w** www.twoears.co.uk
Contact Soren Andersen, Managing Director; Melissa Brown, Bookings Manager
Agency for freelance sound engineers plus fully equipped sound studio.

Karen Warnock
Edit-Base, 70A Waldegrave Road, Teddington TW11 8NY
t 020 8614 6937 **e** alison@edit-base.co.uk

Editors Video

AD Films
10 Ducketts Mead, Roydon CM19 5EG
t 01279 793380 **f** 01279 793380 **m** 07970 255571
e andrewdenny@adfilms.freeserve.co.uk
Contact Andrew Denny, Producer/Editor
Credits Sex On TV (D); Eddie Ervine - The Inside Track (D); Cold War (D); Welcome to Australia (D)

Martin Addison
TOVS Ltd, The Linen Hall, 162-168 Regent Street, London W1B 5TB
t 020 7287 6110 **f** 020 7287 5481
e info@tovs.co.uk **w** www.tovs.co.uk

Mike Akester
Re:Solution, 90 Raglan Avenue, Waltham Cross EN8 8DD
t 020 7580 5766 **f** 01992 025506
e onthecase@totalise.co.uk **w** www.re-solution.tv
Credits Tiger Aspect (T); The South Bank Show (T); Rebuilding The Past (D); When God Goes To War (D)

Marcus Alcock
The Independent Post Company, 65 Goldhawk Road, London W12 8EH
t 020 8746 2060 **f** 020 8743 2345
e anthony@indepost.co.uk

Richard Alderson
Newcastle-upon-Tyne
t 0191 226 1558 **m** 07970 218596
e rich@rich-ideas.com **w** www.rich-ideas.com
Credits Fare Cop Club (S); Byker Grove (T); Sky Box Office (T); Sky Sports News (T)

Benet Allan
Connections, The Meadlands, Oakleigh Road, Hatch End,
Pinner HA5 4HB
t 020 8420 1444 **f** 020 8428 5836 **m** 07831 305518
e mail@connectionsuk.com **w** www.connectionsuk.com

Mohamm Andaloussi
Connections, The Meadlands, Oakleigh Road, Hatch End,
Pinner HA5 4HB
t 020 8420 1444 **f** 020 8428 5836 **m** 07831 305518
e mail@connectionsuk.com **w** www.connectionsuk.com

Simon Ardizzone
Re:Solution, 90 Raglan Avenue, Waltham Cross EN8 8DD
t 020 7580 5766 **f** 01992 025506
e onthecase@totalise.co.uk **w** www.re-solution.tv
Credits Arctic Aviators (D); Kumbh Mela (D); Top Ten Jerusalem (D); Riddles Of
The Dead (D)

Trevor Aylward
TOVS Ltd, The Linen Hall, 162-168 Regent Street, London W1B 5TB
t 020 7287 6110 **f** 020 7287 5481
e info@tovs.co.uk **w** www.tovs.co.uk

Dragomir Bajalica
Connections, The Meadlands, Oakleigh Road, Hatch End,
Pinner HA5 4HB
t 020 8420 1444 **f** 020 8428 5836 **m** 07831 305518
e mail@connectionsuk.com **w** www.connectionsuk.com

Paula Baker
The Independent Post Company, 65 Goldhawk Road, London
W12 8EH
t 020 8746 2060 **f** 020 8743 2345 **e** anthony@indepost.co.uk

Paul Trevor Bale
Edit-Base, 70A Waldegrave Road, Teddington TW11 8NY
t 020 8614 6937 **e** alison@edit-base.co.uk

Jonathan Banks
Connections, The Meadlands, Oakleigh Road, Hatch End,
Pinner HA5 4HB
t 020 8420 1444 **f** 020 8428 5836 **m** 07831 305518
e mail@connectionsuk.com **w** www.connectionsuk.com

Peter Barton
Chequers, Wilton Road, Wylye, Warminster BA12 0RF
t 01985 248303 **f** 01985 248303 **m** 07710 004632
e petebar@lineone.net
Credits Force 10 Rescue (T); How Do They Do That? (T); Animal Ark (T);
Millennium Cops (T)

Adrian Beard
TOVS Ltd, The Linen Hall, 162-168 Regent Street, London W1B 5TB
t 020 7287 6110 **f** 020 7287 5481
e info@tovs.co.uk **w** www.tovs.co.uk

Gidon Benari
TOVS Ltd, The Linen Hall, 162-168 Regent Street, London W1B 5TB
t 020 7287 6110 **f** 020 7287 5481
e info@tovs.co.uk **w** www.tovs.co.uk

Iain Bermingham
Edit-Base, 70A Waldegrave Road, Teddington TW11 8NY
t 020 8614 6937 **e** alison@edit-base.co.uk

Paul Berry
Edit-Base, 70A Waldegrave Road, Teddington TW11 8NY
t 020 8614 6937 **e** alison@edit-base.co.uk

Robert Blake
TOVS Ltd, The Linen Hall, 162-168 Regent Street, London W1B 5TB
t 020 7287 6110 **f** 020 7287 5481
e info@tovs.co.uk **w** www.tovs.co.uk

Bob Blatchford
9 Foxes Dale, Blackheath, London SE3 9BD
t 020 8852 7841 **m** 07779 918909
e bob_blatchford@hotmail.com

Adam Bokey
The Independent Post Company, 65 Goldhawk Road, London
W12 8EH
t 020 8746 2060 **f** 020 8743 2345 **e** anthony@indepost.co.uk

Paul Bolton
TOVS Ltd, The Linen Hall, 162-168 Regent Street, London W1B 5TB
t 020 7287 6110 **f** 020 7287 5481
e info@tovs.co.uk **w** www.tovs.co.uk

Adam Boome
Re:Solution, 90 Raglan Avenue, Waltham Cross EN8 8DD
t 020 7580 5766 **f** 01992 025506
e onthecase@totalise.co.uk **w** www.re-solution.tv
Credits The Concorde Disaster (D); Sin Cities (D); The Long Kiss Goodnight (F);
City Of Angels (F)

Peter Booth
Connections, The Meadlands, Oakleigh Road, Hatch End,
Pinner HA5 4HB
t 020 8420 1444 **f** 020 8428 5836 **m** 07831 305518
e mail@connectionsuk.com **w** www.connectionsuk.com

Jamie Boulton
Edit-Base, 70A Waldegrave Road, Teddington TW11 8NY
t 020 8614 6937 **e** alison@edit-base.co.uk

Phil Box
TOVS Ltd, The Linen Hall, 162-168 Regent Street, London W1B 5TB
t 020 7287 6110 **f** 020 7287 5481
e info@tovs.co.uk **w** www.tovs.co.uk

Jason Boxall
The Independent Post Company, 65 Goldhawk Road, London
W12 8EH
t 020 8746 2060 **f** 020 8743 2345 **e** anthony@indepost.co.uk

Kieron Brennan
Connections, The Meadlands, Oakleigh Road, Hatch End,
Pinner HA5 4HB
t 020 8420 1444 **f** 020 8428 5836 **m** 07831 305518
e mail@connectionsuk.com **w** www.connectionsuk.com

Jeremy Brettingham
Glebe Farmhouse, Wells Road, North Creake, Nr Fakenham
NR21 9LG
t 01328 730430 **f** 01328 730444 **m** 07818 041556
e jb@eastnortheast.co.uk
Credits Circle Line (S); Trisha Extra (T)

Bonnie Rae Brickman
5 Kirkstall Avenue, London N17 6PH
t 020 8808 9688 **e** slevart@msn.com
Credits Julie Andrews - Opening Night On Broadway (T); Pavarotti In The Park (T)

Tim Bridges
The Independent Post Company, 65 Goldhawk Road, London
W12 8EH
t 020 8746 2060 **f** 020 8743 2345 **e** anthony@indepost.co.uk

Sven Brooks
Connections, The Meadlands, Oakleigh Road, Hatch End,
Pinner HA5 4HB
t 020 8420 1444 **f** 020 8428 5836 **m** 07831 305518
e mail@connectionsuk.com **w** www.connectionsuk.com

Lee Buers
The Independent Post Company, 65 Goldhawk Road, London
W12 8EH
t 020 8746 2060 **f** 020 8743 2345 **e** anthony@indepost.co.uk

Burn Edit Ltd

12 Harrowlands Park, Dorking RH4 2RA
t 01306 743896 **m** 07776 140041 **e** burneditltd@talk21.com
Contact Alistair Burns, Video Editor
Credits Showbiz Info (T); Holidays From Hell (T); Cyberart (T)
Since 1986. Current clients - BBC.

Alistair Burns

Connections, The Meadlands, Oakleigh Road, Hatch End,
Pinner HA5 4HB
t 020 8420 1444 **f** 020 8428 5836 **m** 07831 305518
e mail@connectionsuk.com **w** www.connectionsuk.com

Brian Campbell

The Independent Post Company, 65 Goldhawk Road, London
W12 8EH
t 020 8746 2060 **f** 020 8743 2345 **e** anthony@indepost.co.uk

Canatra Ltd

27 Pine Walk, Carshalton SM5 4ES
t 020 8401 6840 **m** 07768 156661 **e** bazza76@blueyonder.co.uk
Contact Birgit Stevens, Secretary; Barry Stevens
12 years on Avid, makes me a very useful person.

Toby Carr

TOVS Ltd, The Linen Hall, 162-168 Regent Street, London W1B 5TB
t 020 7287 6110 **f** 020 7287 5481
e info@tovs.co.uk **w** www.tovs.co.uk

Charles White Productions

120 Witherford Way, Selly Oak, Birmingham B29 4AW
t 0121 472 2251 **m** 07788 414 260
e cjrwhite@hotmail.com **w** www.cut2strength.com

Chipstead Film Productions

12 Clarendon Cross, Holland Park, London W11 4AP
t 020 7229 8631 **f** 020 7221 4214 **e** c-j-davies@softhome.net
Contact Charles Davies, Proprietor
Credits The Greatest Show On Earth (T); Bugs World (T); The Great Plague (T)

Peter Christy

Connections, The Meadlands, Oakleigh Road, Hatch End,
Pinner HA5 4HB
t 020 8420 1444 **f** 020 8428 5836 **m** 07831 305518
e mail@connectionsuk.com **w** www.connectionsuk.com

Timothy Clack

TOVS Ltd, The Linen Hall, 162-168 Regent Street, London W1B 5TB
t 020 7287 6110 **f** 020 7287 5481
e info@tovs.co.uk **w** www.tovs.co.uk

Jeremy Clark

TOVS Ltd, The Linen Hall, 162-168 Regent Street, London W1B 5TB
t 020 7287 6110 **f** 020 7287 5481
e info@tovs.co.uk **w** www.tovs.co.uk

Miles Clennell

The Independent Post Company, 65 Goldhawk Road, London
W12 8EH
t 020 8746 2060 **f** 020 8743 2345 **e** anthony@indepost.co.uk

Tony Collins

Edit-Base, 70A Waldegrave Road, Teddington TW11 8NY
t 020 8614 6937 **e** alison@edit-base.co.uk

Richard Colton

The Independent Post Company, 65 Goldhawk Road, London
W12 8EH
t 020 8746 2060 **f** 020 8743 2345 **e** anthony@indepost.co.uk

Richard Colton

Edit-Base, 70A Waldegrave Road, Teddington TW11 8NY
t 020 8614 6937 **e** alison@edit-base.co.uk

Alex Cooke

Edit-Base, 70A Waldegrave Road, Teddington TW11 8NY
t 020 8614 6937 **e** alison@edit-base.co.uk

Danny Cooke

Edit-Base, 70A Waldegrave Road, Teddington TW11 8NY
t 020 8614 6937 **e** alison@edit-base.co.uk

James Cooper

TOVS Ltd, The Linen Hall, 162-168 Regent Street, London W1B 5TB
t 020 7287 6110 **f** 020 7287 5481
e info@tovs.co.uk **w** www.tovs.co.uk

Craig Cotterill

The Independent Post Company, 65 Goldhawk Road, London
W12 8EH
t 020 8746 2060 **f** 020 8743 2345 **e** anthony@indepost.co.uk

Joanna Crickmay

Edit-Base, 70A Waldegrave Road, Teddington TW11 8NY
t 020 8614 6937 **e** alison@edit-base.co.uk

Charlotte Crofts

4 Clifton View, Totterdown, Bristol B5 34SB
t 0117 971 4428 **t** 07973 444659 **e** charlotte.crofts@virgin.net

Paul Crosby

TOVS Ltd, The Linen Hall, 162-168 Regent Street, London W1B 5TB
t 020 7287 6110 **f** 020 7287 5481
e info@tovs.co.uk **w** www.tovs.co.uk

Michael Crozier

TOVS Ltd, The Linen Hall, 162-168 Regent Street, London W1B 5TB
t 020 7287 6110 **f** 020 7287 5481
e info@tovs.co.uk **w** www.tovs.co.uk

John Cryer

TOVS Ltd, The Linen Hall, 162-168 Regent Street, London W1B 5TB
t 020 7287 6110 **f** 020 7287 5481
e info@tovs.co.uk **w** www.tovs.co.uk

Mike Curd

The Independent Post Company, 65 Goldhawk Road, London
W12 8EH
t 020 8746 2060 **f** 020 8743 2345 **e** anthony@indepost.co.uk

Hal Dace

Connections, The Meadlands, Oakleigh Road, Hatch End,
Pinner HA5 4HB
t 020 8420 1444 **f** 020 8428 5836 **m** 07831 305518
e mail@connectionsuk.com **w** www.connectionsuk.com

Roger Dacier

TOVS Ltd, The Linen Hall, 162-168 Regent Street, London W1B 5TB
t 020 7287 6110 **f** 020 7287 5481
e info@tovs.co.uk **w** www.tovs.co.uk

Orly Danon

11 Strathmore Road, London SW19 8DB
m 07762 549726 **e** orlydanon@hotmail.com
Credits Flight Fantastic (D); War In The Falklands (D); Who Killed Suzie
Lamplugh (D); Thalidomide - Life At Forty (D)

Sean Davison

The Independent Post Company, 65 Goldhawk Road, London
W12 8EH
t 020 8746 2060 **f** 020 8743 2345 **e** anthony@indepost.co.uk

Paul Dawe

The Independent Post Company, 65 Goldhawk Road, London
W12 8EH
t 020 8746 2060 **f** 020 8743 2345 **e** anthony@indepost.co.uk

Brad Day
Connections, The Meadlands, Oakleigh Road, Hatch End,
Pinner HA5 4HB
t 020 8420 1444 **f** 020 8428 5836 **m** 07831 305518
e mail@connectionsuk.com **w** www.connectionsuk.com

Charlie Dean
2 Iris Cottages, Four Ashes Road, Cryers Hill, High Wycombe
HP15 6LG
t 01494 718364 **m** 07712 670404 **e** charliedean.tv@virgin.net

Patrick Denny
The Independent Post Company, 65 Goldhawk Road, London
W12 8EH
t 020 8746 2060 **f** 020 8743 2345 **e** anthony@indepost.co.uk

Kathryn DiGiacinto-Morris
Edit-Base, 70A Waldegrave Road, Teddington TW11 8NY
t 020 8614 6937 **e** alison@edit-base.co.uk

Michael Dixon
The Independent Post Company, 65 Goldhawk Road, London
W12 8EH
t 020 8746 2060 **f** 020 8743 2345 **e** anthony@indepost.co.uk

Rupert Dodds
Connections, The Meadlands, Oakleigh Road, Hatch End,
Pinner HA5 4HB
t 020 8420 1444 **f** 020 8428 5836 **m** 07831 305518
e mail@connectionsuk.com **w** www.connectionsuk.com

Ryan Driscoll
Re:Solution, 90 Raglan Avenue, Waltham Cross EN8 8DD
t 020 7580 5766 **f** 01992 025506
e onthecase@totalise.co.uk **w** www.re-solution.tv
Credits Wild Thing (D); Roses Are Red (S); The Real Full Monty (D); When
Dinosaurs Ruled (D)

Alexander Dunlop
Edit-Base, 70A Waldegrave Road, Teddington TW11 8NY
t 020 8614 6937 **e** alison@edit-base.co.uk

Mike Dutton
Connections, The Meadlands, Oakleigh Road, Hatch End,
Pinner HA5 4HB
t 020 8420 1444 **f** 020 8428 5836 **m** 07831 305518
e mail@connectionsuk.com **w** www.connectionsuk.com

Elizabeth Dyson
88 Cavendish Mansions, Clerkenwell Road, London EC1R 5DH
t 020 7837 8749 **m** 07810 377030 **e** lizzydyson@hotmail.com
Agent Edit-Base, 70A Waldegrave Road, Teddington TW11 8NY
t 020 8614 6937 **e** alison@edit-base.co.uk
Credits Christmas Unwrapped (T); French And Saunders Christmas Special
2002 (T); Spirit Of Diana (T)

James Edmonds
Edit-Base, 70A Waldegrave Road, Teddington TW11 8NY
t 020 8614 6937 **e** alison@edit-base.co.uk

Andrew Evans
TOVS Ltd, The Linen Hall, 162-168 Regent Street, London W1B 5TB
t 020 7287 6110 **f** 020 7287 5481
e info@tovs.co.uk **w** www.tovs.co.uk

Simon Evans
The Independent Post Company, 65 Goldhawk Road, London
W12 8EH
t 020 8746 2060 **f** 020 8743 2345 **e** anthony@indepost.co.uk

Mark Everson
TOVS Ltd, The Linen Hall, 162-168 Regent Street, London W1B 5TB
t 020 7287 6110 **f** 020 7287 5481
e info@tovs.co.uk **w** www.tovs.co.uk

John Fairhall
Connections, The Meadlands, Oakleigh Road, Hatch End,
Pinner HA5 4HB
t 020 8420 1444 **f** 020 8428 5836 **m** 07831 305518
e mail@connectionsuk.com **w** www.connectionsuk.com

Charlie Fawcett
The Independent Post Company, 65 Goldhawk Road, London
W12 8EH
t 020 8746 2060 **f** 020 8743 2345 **e** anthony@indepost.co.uk

Tamra Ferguson
Edit-Base, 70A Waldegrave Road, Teddington TW11 8NY
t 020 8614 6937 **e** alison@edit-base.co.uk

Freddy Fiesco
Connections, The Meadlands, Oakleigh Road, Hatch End,
Pinner HA5 4HB
t 020 8420 1444 **f** 020 8428 5836 **m** 07831 305518
e mail@connectionsuk.com **w** www.connectionsuk.com

Freddy C Fiesco
Re:Solution, 90 Raglan Avenue, Waltham Cross EN8 8DD
t 020 7580 5766 **f** 01992 025506
e onthecase@totalise.co.uk **w** www.re-solution.tv
Credits The Day That Changed The World (D); World Rally Championships (D);
The Royal Bank Of Scotland (C); World Football (T)

Nick Follows
The Independent Post Company, 65 Goldhawk Road, London
W12 8EH
t 020 8746 2060 **f** 020 8743 2345 **e** anthony@indepost.co.uk

Allan Ford
TOVS Ltd, The Linen Hall, 162-168 Regent Street, London W1B 5TB
t 020 7287 6110 **f** 020 7287 5481
e info@tovs.co.uk **w** www.tovs.co.uk

Dave Foster
Connections, The Meadlands, Oakleigh Road, Hatch End,
Pinner HA5 4HB
t 020 8420 1444 **f** 020 8428 5836 **m** 07831 305518
e mail@connectionsuk.com **w** www.connectionsuk.com

Ralph Foster
Edit-Base, 70A Waldegrave Road, Teddington TW11 8NY
t 020 8614 6937 **e** alison@edit-base.co.uk

Peter Frost
TOVS Ltd, The Linen Hall, 162-168 Regent Street, London W1B 5TB
t 020 7287 6110 **f** 020 7287 5481
e info@tovs.co.uk **w** www.tovs.co.uk

Mike Gamson
TOVS Ltd, The Linen Hall, 162-168 Regent Street, London W1B 5TB
t 020 7287 6110 **f** 020 7287 5481
e info@tovs.co.uk **w** www.tovs.co.uk

Richard Gandy
Connections, The Meadlands, Oakleigh Road, Hatch End,
Pinner HA5 4HB
t 020 8420 1444 **f** 020 8428 5836 **m** 07831 305518
e mail@connectionsuk.com **w** www.connectionsuk.com

Victor Garcia
827 Finchley Road, London NW11 8AJ
t 020 8455 4272 **m** 07980 860862 **e** victor01@nildram.co.uk

Kevin Gardam
TOVS Ltd, The Linen Hall, 162-168 Regent Street, London W1B 5TB
t 020 7287 6110 **f** 020 7287 5481
e info@tovs.co.uk **w** www.tovs.co.uk

Karamjit Gill
Edit-Base, 70A Waldegrave Road, Teddington TW11 8NY
t 020 8614 6937 **e** alison@edit-base.co.uk

Dan Goldthorp
The Independent Post Company, 65 Goldhawk Road, London W12 8EH
t 020 8746 2060 **f** 020 8743 2345 **e** anthony@indepost.co.uk

Stephen Goodall
TOVS Ltd, The Linen Hall, 162-168 Regent Street, London W1B 5TB
t 020 7287 6110 **f** 020 7287 5481
e info@tovs.co.uk **w** www.tovs.co.uk

Giles Goodman
Connections, The Meadlands, Oakleigh Road, Hatch End, Pinner HA5 4HB
t 020 8420 1444 **f** 020 8428 5836 **m** 07831 305518
e mail@connectionsuk.com **w** www.connectionsuk.com

Nigel Gourley
TOVS Ltd, The Linen Hall, 162-168 Regent Street, London W1B 5TB
t 020 7287 6110 **f** 020 7287 5481
e info@tovs.co.uk **w** www.tovs.co.uk

Mark Graham
Edit-Base, 70A Waldegrave Road, Teddington TW11 8NY
t 020 8614 6937 **e** alison@edit-base.co.uk

Peter Grain
Connections, The Meadlands, Oakleigh Road, Hatch End, Pinner HA5 4HB
t 020 8420 1444 **f** 020 8428 5836 **m** 07831 305518
e mail@connectionsuk.com **w** www.connectionsuk.com

Andy Greening
The Independent Post Company, 65 Goldhawk Road, London W12 8EH
t 020 8746 2060 **f** 020 8743 2345 **e** anthony@indepost.co.uk

Roger Guertin
The Independent Post Company, 65 Goldhawk Road, London W12 8EH
t 020 8746 2060 **f** 020 8743 2345 **e** anthony@indepost.co.uk

Luis Gutierrez
TOVS Ltd, The Linen Hall, 162-168 Regent Street, London W1B 5TB
t 020 7287 6110 **f** 020 7287 5481
e info@tovs.co.uk **w** www.tovs.co.uk

Wink Hackman
TOVS Ltd, The Linen Hall, 162-168 Regent Street, London W1B 5TB
t 020 7287 6110 **f** 020 7287 5481
e info@tovs.co.uk **w** www.tovs.co.uk

Saadi Haeri
The Independent Post Company, 65 Goldhawk Road, London W12 8EH
t 020 8746 2060 **f** 020 8743 2345 **e** anthony@indepost.co.uk

Saadi Haeri
Connections, The Meadlands, Oakleigh Road, Hatch End, Pinner HA5 4HB
t 020 8420 1444 **f** 020 8428 5836 **m** 07831 305518
e mail@connectionsuk.com **w** www.connectionsuk.com

Fiona Haigh
Connections, The Meadlands, Oakleigh Road, Hatch End, Pinner HA5 4HB
t 020 8420 1444 **f** 020 8428 5836 **m** 07831 305518
e mail@connectionsuk.com **w** www.connectionsuk.com

M Hale
TOVS Ltd, The Linen Hall, 162-168 Regent Street, London W1B 5TB
t 020 7287 6110 **f** 020 7287 5481
e info@tovs.co.uk **w** www.tovs.co.uk

Christopher Hall
TOVS Ltd, The Linen Hall, 162-168 Regent Street, London W1B 5TB
t 020 7287 6110 **f** 020 7287 5481
e info@tovs.co.uk **w** www.tovs.co.uk

Clare Hall
Connections, The Meadlands, Oakleigh Road, Hatch End, Pinner HA5 4HB
t 020 8420 1444 **f** 020 8428 5836 **m** 07831 305518
e mail@connectionsuk.com **w** www.connectionsuk.com

Eddie Hampton
Edit-Base, 70A Waldegrave Road, Teddington TW11 8NY
t 020 8614 6937 **e** alison@edit-base.co.uk

Kevin Hanna
The Independent Post Company, 65 Goldhawk Road, London W12 8EH
t 020 8746 2060 **f** 020 8743 2345 **e** anthony@indepost.co.uk

Craig Harbour
The Independent Post Company, 65 Goldhawk Road, London W12 8EH
t 020 8746 2060 **f** 020 8743 2345 **e** anthony@indepost.co.uk

Craig Harbour
Edit-Base, 70A Waldegrave Road, Teddington TW11 8NY
t 020 8614 6937 **e** alison@edit-base.co.uk

James Hart
The Independent Post Company, 65 Goldhawk Road, London W12 8EH
t 020 8746 2060 **f** 020 8743 2345 **e** anthony@indepost.co.uk

Adam Harvey
50 Frankswood Avenue, West Drayton UB7 8QS
t 01895 422014 **m** 07798 606184
e adam@pirate73.freeserve.co.uk
Credits Dinotopia (T); Formula One World Championship End Of Year Review 2000 (T); Jack & The Beanstalk -The Real Story (T); Thomas Cook TV (T)

Noel Hayes
Connections, The Meadlands, Oakleigh Road, Hatch End, Pinner HA5 4HB
t 020 8420 1444 **f** 020 8428 5836 **m** 07831 305518
e mail@connectionsuk.com **w** www.connectionsuk.com

Catherine Hendrie
1 Marlborough Court, London W1F 7EE
t 020 7494 3383 **f** 020 7287 1952
e suemoles@aol.com **w** www.suemoles.com

Richard Herring
Connections, The Meadlands, Oakleigh Road, Hatch End, Pinner HA5 4HB
t 020 8420 1444 **f** 020 8428 5836 **m** 07831 305518
e mail@connectionsuk.com **w** www.connectionsuk.com

Howard Heywood
66 Burnham Road, Tadley RG26 4QW
t 01189 815982 **m** 07850 236738
e howardheywood@hotmail.com

Dick Histed
Connections, The Meadlands, Oakleigh Road, Hatch End, Pinner HA5 4HB
t 020 8420 1444 **f** 020 8428 5836 **m** 07831 305518
e mail@connectionsuk.com **w** www.connectionsuk.com

Rick Hodgson
Connections, The Meadlands, Oakleigh Road, Hatch End, Pinner HA5 4HB
t 020 8420 1444 **f** 020 8428 5836 **m** 07831 305518
e mail@connectionsuk.com **w** www.connectionsuk.com

Christopher Hogan
Connections, The Meadlands, Oakleigh Road, Hatch End, Pinner HA5 4HB
t 020 8420 1444 **f** 020 8428 5836 **m** 07831 305518
e mail@connectionsuk.com **w** www.connectionsuk.com

Wayland Holford
Connections, The Meadlands, Oakleigh Road, Hatch End,
Pinner HA5 4HB
t 020 8420 1444 **f** 020 8428 5836 **m** 07831 305518
e mail@connectionsuk.com **w** www.connectionsuk.com

Graeme Holmes
Re:Solution, 90 Raglan Avenue, Waltham Cross EN8 8DD
t 020 7580 5766 **f** 01992 025506
e onthecase@totalise.co.uk **w** www.re-solution.tv
Credits Aussie Invasion (D); Man Overboard (D); Vodafone (C);
Passport To Mallorca (D)

Nigel Honey
Edit-Base, 70A Waldegrave Road, Teddington TW11 8NY
t 020 8614 6937 **e** alison@edit-base.co.uk

Nigel G Honey
32 Lucilla Avenue, Kingsworth TN23 3P5
m 07703 272681 **e** nhoney@lineone.net
Credits World Of Pain (T); Learning Today (E); Fastrax (E); Horizon (D)

Schuman Hoque
Edit-Base, 70A Waldegrave Road, Teddington TW11 8NY
t 020 8614 6937 **e** alison@edit-base.co.uk

Ruth Horner
Connections, The Meadlands, Oakleigh Road, Hatch End,
Pinner HA5 4HB
t 020 8420 1444 **f** 020 8428 5836 **m** 07831 305518
e mail@connectionsuk.com **w** www.connectionsuk.com

Gordon Howe
218 Oswald Road, Chorlton, Manchester M21 9GW
t 0161 881 1988 **m** 07710 434589 **e** gordonhowe@mac.com
Credits Trouble Up North (D); Three Lions (D); Z-Cars - After They Were Famous
(D); Dispatches - Wasted (D)

Andrew Hutchings
Connections, The Meadlands, Oakleigh Road, Hatch End,
Pinner HA5 4HB
t 020 8420 1444 **f** 020 8428 5836 **m** 07831 305518
e mail@connectionsuk.com **w** www.connectionsuk.com

James Iles
7 Windsor Close, Rustington, Brighton BN16 3TJ
t 01903 771432 **f** 01903 773873 **m** 07979 540955
e jamesiles82@aol.com
Credits St Peter's Church (D); A Love Supreme - Spike Wells (D); The N Gauge
Society 35th Anniversary Exhibition (I)

Marco Jackson
55a The Broadway, Crouch End, London N8 8OT
t 020 8374 6278 **m** 07968 032257 **e** marcojackson@hotmail.com
Credits Bossa: The New Wave (T); Dinner For Five (T); Secret Glory (F); Children
Of The Revolution (T)

Richard Jackson
Experience Counts - Call Me Ltd, 5th Floor, 41-42 Berners
Street, London W1P 3AA
t 020 7637 8112 **f** 020 7580 2582

Miles Johnson
TOVS Ltd, The Linen Hall, 162-168 Regent Street, London W1B 5TB
t 020 7287 6110 **f** 020 7287 5481
e info@tovs.co.uk **w** www.tovs.co.uk

Toby Jones
TOVS Ltd, The Linen Hall, 162-168 Regent Street, London W1B 5TB
t 020 7287 6110 **f** 020 7287 5481
e info@tovs.co.uk **w** www.tovs.co.uk

Mads Jorgensen
Connections, The Meadlands, Oakleigh Road, Hatch End,
Pinner HA5 4HB
t 020 8420 1444 **f** 020 8428 5836 **m** 07831 305518
e mail@connectionsuk.com **w** www.connectionsuk.com

Mads Nybo Jorgensen
Mac Million, 61 Gray's Inn Road, London WC1X 8LT
t 020 7831 5357 **f** 020 7404 6872 **m** 0777 6185959
e mads@macmillion.com **w** www.macmillion.com

Donna Joyce
Connections, The Meadlands, Oakleigh Road, Hatch End,
Pinner HA5 4HB
t 020 8420 1444 **f** 020 8428 5836 **m** 07831 305518
e mail@connectionsuk.com **w** www.connectionsuk.com

Mikhaël Junod
Re:Solution, 90 Raglan Avenue, Waltham Cross EN8 8DD
t 020 7580 5766 **f** 01992 025506
e onthecase@totalise.co.uk **w** www.re-solution.tv
Credits Hollywood Vice (D); Labatts Ice (C); The Big Cats (D); Rolling Rock (C)

Nick Kershaw
33 Landsdowne Crescent, Glasgow G20 6NH
t 0141 334 0951 **f** 0141 334 0951 **m** 07850 993157
e nick@groovyeditor.tv **w** www.groovyeditor.tv
Credits Diet Another Day (T); Football Stories: Real Footballer's Wives (T); My
Worst Week (T)

Knew Productions
The Place in the Park Studios, Bellevue Road, Wrexham LL13 7NH
t 01978 358522 **f** 01978 358522
e studio@knewmedia.co.uk **w** www.knewmedia.o.uk
Contact Richard Knew, Company Director
Credits Come Dancing (S); Labrats (F); Refresh (T)

Adam Knight
51 Croham Road, South Croydon CR2 7HD
t 020 8686 1188 **f** 020 8686 5928 **e** cbennettv@aol.com
Credits Rada, Behind The Scenes (D); Cheeky's Angels (T); Strictly Soho (D)

Kevin Lane
The Independent Post Company, 65 Goldhawk Road, London
W12 8EH
t 020 8746 2060 **f** 020 8743 2345 **e** anthony@indepost.co.uk

Jayesh Lathia
108 Brudenell Road, Tooting Bec, London SW17 8DE
t 020 8672 7624 **m** 07790 757 118
e jayeshjethalal@jlathia.fsbusiness.co.uk
Credits Flava; Public Eminem #1; Blunt ATTP Wised Up

Bruce Law
Edit-Base, 70A Waldegrave Road, Teddington TW11 8NY
t 020 8614 6937 **e** alison@edit-base.co.uk

Darren Leathley
The Independent Post Company, 65 Goldhawk Road, London
W12 8EH
t 020 8746 2060 **f** 020 8743 2345 **e** anthony@indepost.co.uk

Nicholas Lee
Connections, The Meadlands, Oakleigh Road, Hatch End,
Pinner HA5 4HB
t 020 8420 1444 **f** 020 8428 5836 **m** 07831 305518
e mail@connectionsuk.com **w** www.connectionsuk.com

Richard Legg
Connections, The Meadlands, Oakleigh Road, Hatch End,
Pinner HA5 4HB
t 020 8420 1444 **f** 020 8428 5836 **m** 07831 305518
e mail@connectionsuk.com **w** www.connectionsuk.com

Hugh Lewis
Edit-Base, 70A Waldegrave Road, Teddington TW11 8NY
t 020 8614 6937 **e** alison@edit-base.co.uk

Simon Lewis
Edit-Base, 70A Waldegrave Road, Teddington TW11 8NY
t 020 8614 6937 **e** alison@edit-base.co.uk

License To Shoot
35A Myrtle Avenue, Ruislip HA4 8SA
t 020 8868 9286 **m** 07929 260614
e kenburns@carryoons.com **w** www.carryoons.com
Contact Ken Burns, Director/Avid Editor
Credits Porn Patrol (D); What's A Carry On? (D); Mudbuster (T); The Carryoons (A)

Andy Loftus
Edit-Base, 70A Waldegrave Road, Teddington TW11 8NY
t 020 8614 6937 **e** alison@edit-base.co.uk

Simon Lowe
The Independent Post Company, 65 Goldhawk Road,
London W12 8EH
t 020 8746 2060 **f** 020 8743 2345 **e** anthony@indepost.co.uk

Jim Lownie
Edit-Base, 70A Waldegrave Road, Teddington TW11 8NY
t 020 8614 6937 **e** alison@edit-base.co.uk

Dominique Lutier
Connections, The Meadlands, Oakleigh Road, Hatch End,
Pinner HA5 4HB
t 020 8420 1444 **f** 020 8428 5836 **m** 07831 305518
e mail@connectionsuk.com **w** www.connectionsuk.com

Dominique Lutier
Re:Solution, 90 Raglan Avenue, Waltham Cross EN8 8DD
t 020 7580 5766 **f** 01992 025506
e onthecase@totalise.co.uk **w** www.re-solution.tv
Credits The Write Way (E); Suck Henry (M); The Divine David Show (T); If The
Walls Could Speak (D)

M.Y Films
373 Defoe Road, Ipswich IP1 6RZ
m 07740 651337 **e** martin.yew@btinternet.com
Contact Martin Yew, Proprietor/Managing Director; Carl Best, Head of Music
Production; Ian Dance, Head of Graphic Design; Gavin Woods, Head of
Animation; Dave Thompson, Camera Operator
Credits Vandal Youth (S); Abacus Skateboarding Apparel (C); Playing For
Success At Ipswich Town FC (I); Still Life (D)

Benjamin Macoy
Re:Solution, 90 Raglan Avenue, Waltham Cross EN8 8DD
t 020 7580 5766 **f** 01992 025506
e onthecase@totalise.co.uk **w** www.re-solution.tv
Credits Jo Guest In Jamaica (T); 4Play (T); Transworld Sports (T); Admiral
Insurance (C)

Susan Manning
TOVS Ltd, The Linen Hall, 162-168 Regent Street, London W1B 5TB
t 020 7287 6110 **f** 020 7287 5481
e info@tovs.co.uk **w** www.tovs.co.uk

Stephania Marangoni
t 020 8889 3285 **f** 020 8889 8554 **m** 07930 431143
e stephania@backroom2000.free-online.co.uk

Tim Marchant
Edit-Base, 70A Waldegrave Road, Teddington TW11 8NY
t 020 8614 6937 **e** alison@edit-base.co.uk

Stephen Matthews
m 07976 212795 **e** stephen.matthews@cheekyfilms.co.uk
Credits The 11 O'Clock Show (T); Brass Eye Special (T); Big Train (T)

Elliot McCaffrey
The Independent Post Company, 65 Goldhawk Road, London
W12 8EH
t 020 8746 2060 **f** 020 8743 2345 **e** anthony@indepost.co.uk

Rod McLean
TOVS Ltd, The Linen Hall, 162-168 Regent Street, London W1B 5TB
t 020 7287 6110 **f** 020 7287 5481
e info@tovs.co.uk **w** www.tovs.co.uk

Denis Mcwilliams
Connections, The Meadlands, Oakleigh Road, Hatch End,
Pinner HA5 4HB
t 020 8420 1444 **f** 020 8428 5836 **m** 07831 305518
e mail@connectionsuk.com **w** www.connectionsuk.com

Mikey P Ltd
6 Greenhow Park, Burley-in-Wharfedale, Ilkley LS29 7LZ
t 07771 745605 **e** mikeypees@hotmail.com
Credits Toddler Times (E); Sounds Of The Sixties (M); School (D)

Gary Miller
TOVS Ltd, The Linen Hall, 162-168 Regent Street, London W1B 5TB
t 020 7287 6110 **f** 020 7287 5481
e info@tovs.co.uk **w** www.tovs.co.uk

James Milner-Smyth
Connections, The Meadlands, Oakleigh Road, Hatch End,
Pinner HA5 4HB
t 020 8420 1444 **f** 020 8428 5836 **m** 07831 305518
e mail@connectionsuk.com **w** www.connectionsuk.com

Iain Mitchell
TOVS Ltd, The Linen Hall, 162-168 Regent Street, London W1B 5TB
t 020 7287 6110 **f** 020 7287 5481
e info@tovs.co.uk **w** www.tovs.co.uk

Sam Mitchell
1 Marlborough Court, London W1F 7EE
t 020 7494 3383 **f** 020 7287 1952
e suemoles@aol.com **w** www.suemoles.com

Sue Moles
1 Marlborough Court, London W1F 7EE
t 020 7494 3383 **f** 020 7287 1952
e suemoles@aol.com **w** www.suemoles.com

Chris Moore
TOVS Ltd, The Linen Hall, 162-168 Regent Street, London W1B 5TB
t 020 7287 6110 **f** 020 7287 5481
e info@tovs.co.uk **w** www.tovs.co.uk

John Moratiel
Re:Solution, 90 Raglan Avenue, Waltham Cross EN8 8DD
t 020 7580 5766 **f** 01992 025506
e onthecase@totalise.co.uk **w** www.re-solution.tv
Credits Mad & Angry Inventors (D); The Money Programme (T); Classic Aircraft
(D); Counterblast (D)

Sebastian Morrison
TOVS Ltd, The Linen Hall, 162-168 Regent Street, London W1B 5TB
t 020 7287 6110 **f** 020 7287 5481
e info@tovs.co.uk **w** www.tovs.co.uk

Phil Moss
TOVS Ltd, The Linen Hall, 162-168 Regent Street, London W1B 5TB
t 020 7287 6110 **f** 020 7287 5481
e info@tovs.co.uk **w** www.tovs.co.uk

Colin Moxon
Agent The Independent Post Company, 65 Goldhawk Road, London W12 8EH
t 020 8746 2060 **f** 020 8743 2345 **e** anthony@indepost.co.uk
Agent Re:Solution, 90 Raglan Avenue, Waltham Cross EN8 8DD
t 020 7580 5766 **f** 01992 025506
e onthecase@totalise.co.uk **w** www.re-solution.tv
Credits Surviving Extremes - Ice (D); Girls Nite Out (S); Citroen Saxo (C); The Ruby Wax Show (T)

Susan Muir
Connections, The Meadlands, Oakleigh Road, Hatch End, Pinner HA5 4HB
t 020 8420 1444 **f** 020 8428 5836 **m** 07831 305518
e mail@connectionsuk.com **w** www.connectionsuk.com

Clive Muller
The Independent Post Company, 65 Goldhawk Road, London W12 8EH
t 020 8746 2060 **f** 020 8743 2345 **e** anthony@indepost.co.uk

Christian Murray-Smith
The Independent Post Company, 65 Goldhawk Road, London W12 8EH
t 020 8746 2060 **f** 020 8743 2345 **e** anthony@indepost.co.uk

Mostafa Nagy
Connections, The Meadlands, Oakleigh Road, Hatch End, Pinner HA5 4HB
t 020 8420 1444 **f** 020 8428 5836 **m** 07831 305518
e mail@connectionsuk.com **w** www.connectionsuk.com

Colin Napthine
15 Aldersmead Road, Beckenham BR3 1NA
t 020 8402 7695 **f** 020 8402 7695 **m** 07941 892911
e colin.napthine1@ntlworld.com
Credits Hostage (T); Omnibus - Iris Murdoch (T); Reputations - Richard Burton (T); Living with Cancer (T)

Steve Nayler
TOVS Ltd, The Linen Hall, 162-168 Regent Street, London W1B 5TB
t 020 7287 6110 **f** 020 7287 5481
e info@tovs.co.uk **w** www.tovs.co.uk

Alan Nesbitt
7E Medina Villas, Hove BN3 2RJ
t 01273 770422 **m** 07796 953656
e alan@nesbitt.co.uk **w** www.nesbitt.co.uk/alan
Credits Clash Of The Titans (T); Artclub (T); Gardens of the Millennium (T); Great Artists (T)

Kim Nikolajsen
The Independent Post Company, 65 Goldhawk Road, London W12 8EH
t 020 8746 2060 **f** 020 8743 2345 **e** anthony@indepost.co.uk

Lee Nixon
Edit-Base, 70A Waldegrave Road, Teddington TW11 8NY
t 020 8614 6937 **e** alison@edit-base.co.uk

Anaelechi Nnadi
14B Hugh Street, London SW1V 1RP
t 020 7976 6428 **m** 07946 760692 **e** acnnadi@yahoo.co.uk
Credits Alison Cork's Countdown To Christmas (T); Get The Look (T)

Ben Nugent
Edit-Base, 70A Waldegrave Road, Teddington TW11 8NY
t 020 8614 6937 **e** alison@edit-base.co.uk

Dermot O'Brien
The Independent Post Company, 65 Goldhawk Road, London W12 8EH
t 020 8746 2060 **f** 020 8743 2345 **e** anthony@indepost.co.uk

Pat O'Grady
Edit-Base, 70A Waldegrave Road, Teddington TW11 8NY
t 020 8614 6937 **e** alison@edit-base.co.uk

Duncan O'Neill
The Independent Post Company, 65 Goldhawk Road, London W12 8EH
t 020 8746 2060 **f** 020 8743 2345 **e** anthony@indepost.co.uk

Damian O'Neil
The Independent Post Company, 65 Goldhawk Road, London W12 8EH
t 020 8746 2060 **f** 020 8743 2345 **e** anthony@indepost.co.uk

Oakfilms
5 Orchard Cottages, Wick Lane, Canerton, Bath BA2 0PQ
t 01761 470585 **f** 01761 470585 **m** 07976 661054
Contact Derek Kilkenny-Blake, Proprietor
Credits Arkive (W); At-Bristol (E); Living Europe Series (T)

Bryan Oates
C/o London Management, 2-4 Noel Street, London W1F 8GB
m 07747 611130
Credits The Sea Change (F); Waking The Dead (T); Foyle's War (T); Song For A Raggy Boy (F)

Lenaart van Oldenborgh
26 Oxford Road, London N4 3EY
m 07768 610016 **e** lenny@desk.nl
Credits Cannibals & Crampons (International Version) (D); Ian Hamilton: A Writing Life (D); A Tribute To The Likely Lads (T); The Making Of Swept Away (D)

Caroline Orme
Edit-Base, 70A Waldegrave Road, Teddington TW11 8NY
t 020 8614 6937 **e** alison@edit-base.co.uk

James Orton
293 Cowbridge Road East, Canton, Cardiff CF5 1JB
t 029 2090 3344 **f** 029 2066 6322 **m** 077 4738 0427
e me@jorton.com **w** www.jorton.com
Credits Y Ty (T); Wales This Week (T); River Patrol (D)

Barry Osment
The Independent Post Company, 65 Goldhawk Road, London W12 8EH
t 020 8746 2060 **f** 020 8743 2345 **e** anthony@indepost.co.uk

Folasade Oyeleye
f 020 8671 4347 **m** 07985 438879
Credits The Life and Songs of Kirsty MacColl (D); Just Like My Dad (S); Family Affairs (T)

Keith Palmer
The Coach House, Common Water Lane, Broadwindsor, Beaminster DT8 3QR
t 01308 867640 **m** 07816 499146
Credits Sharpe (T); Oklahoma (T); Hornblower (T); Wide In The Blood (T)

Steve Parry
Edit-Base, 70A Waldegrave Road, Teddington TW11 8NY
t 020 8614 6937 **e** alison@edit-base.co.uk

Neil Patience
TOVS Ltd, The Linen Hall, 162-168 Regent Street, London W1B 5TB
t 020 7287 6110 **f** 020 7287 5481
e info@tovs.co.uk **w** www.tovs.co.uk

Mike Pavett
The Independent Post Company, 65 Goldhawk Road, London W12 8EH
t 020 8746 2060 **f** 020 8743 2345 **e** anthony@indepost.co.uk

Mykola Pawluk
The Independent Post Company, 65 Goldhawk Road, London W12 8EH
t 020 8746 2060 **f** 020 8743 2345 **e** anthony@indepost.co.uk

Michael Pearce
The Independent Post Company, 65 Goldhawk Road, London W12 8EH
t 020 8746 2060 **f** 020 8743 2345 **e** anthony@indepost.co.uk

Polymorph Productions
22 Kirton Grove, Wolverhampton WV6 8RX
m 07773 375876 **e** fubar@orange.net
Contact Stuart Coburn
Credits League Football (T); The Sleeper (M); Wheels On The Bus (T); Party In The Park (2001) (T)

Stephen Prince
Agent Edit-Base, 70A Waldegrave Road, Teddington TW11 8NY
t 020 8614 6937 **e** alison@edit-base.co.uk
Agent Connections, The Meadlands, Oakleigh Road, Hatch End, Pinner HA5 4HB
t 020 8420 1444 **f** 020 8428 5836 **m** 07831 305518
e mail@connectionsuk.com **w** www.connectionsuk.com

Kavi Pujara
Connections, The Meadlands, Oakleigh Road, Hatch End, Pinner HA5 4HB
t 020 8420 1444 **f** 020 8428 5836 **m** 07831 305518
e mail@connectionsuk.com **w** www.connectionsuk.com

Lauren Pushkin
73 Worcester Crescent, Wooford Green IG8 OLT
f 020 8504 8704 **m** 07976 894 034 **e** laufaith@aol.com
Credits CNN (C); Evolver (C); Endzone (D); Gamer.tv (D)

David Rabin
Re:Solution, 90 Raglan Avenue, Waltham Cross EN8 8DD
t 020 7580 5766 **f** 01992 025506
e onthecase@totalise.co.uk **w** www.re-solution.tv
Credits House In The Country (T); Animal Park (T); Francis Poulenc: A Human Voice (D); Chelsea Flower Show 2002 (T)

Red Bug Productions Ltd
The Old School House, East Worldham, Alton GN34 3AT
t 01420 590420 **f** 01420 590426
e patrick@redbug.demon.co.uk **w** www.redbug.tv
Contact Patrick Redmond, Director; Nicky Hersh, Director

The Reel Editing Company
The Reel Editing Company, 65 Goldhawk Road, London W12 8EH
t 020 8743 5100 **f** 020 8743 2345 **e** penny@indepost.co.uk
Contact Penny Cassar, Facilities Manager
Credits Horizon (T)

Michiel Reichwein
International Creative Management Ltd, Oxford House, 76 Oxford Street, London W1D 3BS
t 020 7636 6565 **f** 020 7323 0101
e Firstname_Lastname@icmlondon.co.uk
w www.icmlondon.co.uk
Credits Antonia's Line (F); Woman of the North (F); The Luzhin Defence (F)

Andy Rendell
The Independent Post Company, 65 Goldhawk Road, London W12 8EH
t 020 8746 2060 **f** 020 8743 2345 **e** anthony@indepost.co.uk

Pablo Renedo
Edit-Base, 70A Waldegrave Road, Teddington TW11 8NY
t 020 8614 6937 **e** alison@edit-base.co.uk

Steve Renow
Connections, The Meadlands, Oakleigh Road, Hatch End, Pinner HA5 4HB
t 020 8420 1444 **f** 020 8428 5836 **m** 07831 305518
e mail@connectionsuk.com **w** www.connectionsuk.com

Darryl Rose
White Gables, Wayside Avenue, Bushey Heath WD23 4SH
t 020 8950 5666 **m** 07970 624424
e darryl@darrylrose.com **w** www.darrylrose.com
Credits Big Brother (T); Sky Premier Football (T); Fame Academy (T); The Brits (T)

Adrienne Ross
The Independent Post Company, 65 Goldhawk Road, London W12 8EH
t 020 8746 2060 **f** 020 8743 2345 **e** anthony@indepost.co.uk

Nicholas Roulstone
Experience Counts - Call Me Ltd, 5th Floor, 41-42 Berners Street, London W1P 3AA
t 020 7637 8112 **f** 020 7580 2582

Maggie Sackett
Connections, The Meadlands, Oakleigh Road, Hatch End, Pinner HA5 4HB
t 020 8420 1444 **f** 020 8428 5836 **m** 07831 305518
e mail@connectionsuk.com **w** www.connectionsuk.com

Simmi Sahni
Connections, The Meadlands, Oakleigh Road, Hatch End, Pinner HA5 4HB
t 020 8420 1444 **f** 020 8428 5836 **m** 07831 305518
e mail@connectionsuk.com **w** www.connectionsuk.com

Brian Sanderson
Connections, The Meadlands, Oakleigh Road, Hatch End, Pinner HA5 4HB
t 020 8420 1444 **f** 020 8428 5836 **m** 07831 305518
e mail@connectionsuk.com **w** www.connectionsuk.com

Dan Schwalm
Edit-Base, 70A Waldegrave Road, Teddington TW11 8NY
t 020 8614 6937 **e** alison@edit-base.co.uk

Assaf Scialom
Edit-Base, 70A Waldegrave Road, Teddington TW11 8NY
t 020 8614 6937 **e** alison@edit-base.co.uk

Jonathan Seal
TOVS Ltd, The Linen Hall, 162-168 Regent Street, London W1B 5TB
t 020 7287 6110 **f** 020 7287 5481
e info@tovs.co.uk **w** www.tovs.co.uk

Sam Seal
TOVS Ltd, The Linen Hall, 162-168 Regent Street, London W1B 5TB
t 020 7287 6110 **f** 020 7287 5481
e info@tovs.co.uk **w** www.tovs.co.uk

Reuben Seaton
Connections, The Meadlands, Oakleigh Road, Hatch End, Pinner HA5 4HB
t 020 8420 1444 **f** 020 8428 5836 **m** 07831 305518
e mail@connectionsuk.com **w** www.connectionsuk.com

Alan Selby
m 07092 270607 **e** alselby@orange.net

Adam Sharman
Edit-Base, 70A Waldegrave Road, Teddington TW11 8NY
t 020 8614 6937 **e** alison@edit-base.co.uk

Samantha Shepherd
Edit-Base, 70A Waldegrave Road, Teddington TW11 8NY
t 020 8614 6937 **e** alison@edit-base.co.uk

Nicholas Sherard
Edit-Base, 70A Waldegrave Road, Teddington TW11 8NY
t 020 8614 6937 **e** alison@edit-base.co.uk

Roger Shufflebottom
6 Balfour Street, Hertford SG14 3AX
t 01992 504124 **f** 01920 421672 **m** 07973 543660
e roger.shuff@cableol.co.uk
Credits Flying Squad (T); The Heat is On (T); The Lost Vikings (T)

Dave Simpson
Experience Counts - Call Me Ltd, 5th Floor, 41-42 Berners Street, London W1P 3AA
t 020 7637 8112 **f** 020 7580 2582

Slack Alice Films
6 Dron House, Adelina Grove, London E1 3AA
m 07973 265613 **e** edit@slackalicefilms.co.uk
Contact Alexander Snelling, Editor
Credits Patsy Palmer's Ibiza Workout (C); What Not To Wear Celebrity Special (T); How (Not) To Make A Short Film (S)

Final Cut Pro specialist. All Film/TV formats.

Michael Smith
12 Newenden Close, Maidstone ME14 5RU
t 01622 678723 **m** 07860 389742
Credits Pollyanna (T); Sons & Lovers (T); Margery And Gladys (T); Sparkling Cyanide (T)

Richard Snape
TOVS Ltd, The Linen Hall, 162-168 Regent Street, London W1B 5TB
t 020 7287 6110 **f** 020 7287 5481
e info@tovs.co.uk **w** www.tovs.co.uk

Sacha Sofil
Connections, The Meadlands, Oakleigh Road, Hatch End, Pinner HA5 4HB
t 020 8420 1444 **f** 020 8428 5836 **m** 07831 305518
e mail@connectionsuk.com **w** www.connectionsuk.com

David Southam
Connections, The Meadlands, Oakleigh Road, Hatch End, Pinner HA5 4HB
t 020 8420 1444 **f** 020 8428 5836 **m** 07831 305518
e mail@connectionsuk.com **w** www.connectionsuk.com

Kimaathi Spence
Connections, The Meadlands, Oakleigh Road, Hatch End, Pinner HA5 4HB
t 020 8420 1444 **f** 020 8428 5836 **m** 07831 305518
e mail@connectionsuk.com **w** www.connectionsuk.com

Janet Spiller
The Independent Post Company, 65 Goldhawk Road, London W12 8EH
t 020 8746 2060 **f** 020 8743 2345 **e** anthony@indepost.co.uk

Peter Spink
TOVS Ltd, The Linen Hall, 162-168 Regent Street, London W1B 5TB
t 020 7287 6110 **f** 020 7287 5481
e info@tovs.co.uk **w** www.tovs.co.uk

Ben Stark
TOVS Ltd, The Linen Hall, 162-168 Regent Street, London W1B 5TB
t 020 7287 6110 **f** 020 7287 5481
e info@tovs.co.uk **w** www.tovs.co.uk

Jonathan Steer
Connections, The Meadlands, Oakleigh Road, Hatch End, Pinner HA5 4HB
t 020 8420 1444 **f** 020 8428 5836 **m** 07831 305518
e mail@connectionsuk.com **w** www.connectionsuk.com

Chris Stott
The Independent Production Company, 65 Goldhawk Road, London W12 8EH
t 020 8746 2060 **f** 020 8743 2345 **e** anthony@indepost.co.uk

Julian Sykes
Edit-Base, 70A Waldegrave Road, Teddington TW11 8NY
t 020 8614 6937 **e** alison@edit-base.co.uk

Tall Order Post Production
Croft Cottage, Orchard Road, Burpham, Guildford GU4 7JH
t 01483 504429 **f** 01483 504429 **e** wink@ntlworld.com
Contact Wink Hackman, Editor

Tara Teeling-Charles
The Independent Post Company, 65 Goldhawk Road, London W12 8EH
t 020 8746 2060 **f** 020 8743 2345 **e** anthony@indepost.co.uk

Will Teversham
The Independent Post Company, 65 Goldhawk Road, London W12 8EH
t 020 8746 2060 **f** 020 8743 2345 **e** anthony@indepost.co.uk

Sandra Theron
Connections, The Meadlands, Oakleigh Road, Hatch End, Pinner HA5 4HB
t 020 8420 1444 **f** 020 8428 5836 **m** 07831 305518
e mail@connectionsuk.com **w** www.connectionsuk.com

James Thomas
The Independent Post Company, 65 Goldhawk Road, London W12 8EH
t 020 8746 2060 **f** 020 8743 2345 **e** anthony@indepost.co.uk

Alison Thompson
TOVS Ltd, The Linen Hall, 162-168 Regent Street, London W1B 5TB
t 020 7287 6110 **f** 020 7287 5481
e info@tovs.co.uk **w** www.tovs.co.uk

Duncan Thomsen
Edit-Base, 70A Waldegrave Road, Teddington TW11 8NY
t 020 8614 6937 **e** alison@edit-base.co.uk

John Thurley
Connections, The Meadlands, Oakleigh Road, Hatch End, Pinner HA5 4HB
t 020 8420 1444 **f** 020 8428 5836 **m** 07831 305518
e mail@connectionsuk.com **w** www.connectionsuk.com

Daren Tiley
Edit-Base, 70A Waldegrave Road, Teddington TW11 8NY
t 020 8614 6937 **e** alison@edit-base.co.uk

Peter Tottle
TOVS Ltd, The Linen Hall, 162-168 Regent Street, London W1B 5TB
t 020 7287 6110 **f** 020 7287 5481
e info@tovs.co.uk **w** www.tovs.co.uk

Training Matters
Unit 8B, Sparrow Hall Business Park, Edlesborough LU7 6ES
t 01525 229756 **m** 07940 562137
e mark@trainingmatters.uk.com **w** www.trainingmatters.uk.com
Contact Mark Ballantyne, Media Producer
Credits Marshall Of Cambridge (E); DAF (I); Renault (I)

Camilla Tress
25 Stowe Road, London W12 8BQ
t 020 8743 8898 **m** 07958 510416 **e** camilla.t@virgin.net
Credits Royal Treasures (D); Zarmina: Lifting The Veil (D); Kannibal (F); Sex On TV (D)

Henry Trotter
Edit-Base, 70A Waldegrave Road, Teddington TW11 8NY
t 020 8614 6937 **e** alison@edit-base.co.uk

Renoir Tuahene
Re:Solution, 90 Raglan Avenue, Waltham Cross EN8 8DD
t 020 7580 5766 **f** 01992 025506
e onthecase@totalise.co.uk **w** www.re-solution.tv
Credits Levi's (C); Concorde-The Comeback (D); Around The World In 80 Raves (D); From Here To Modernity (D)

Michelle Turkington
TOVS Ltd, The Linen Hall, 162-168 Regent Street, London W1B 5TB
t 020 7287 6110 **f** 020 7287 5481
e info@tovs.co.uk **w** www.tovs.co.uk

TV House Productions
45a Whitemore Road, Guildford GU1 1QU
t 01483 574545 **e** info@tvhouse.co.uk **w** www.tvhouse.co.uk
Contact Robert Golding, Director

Tom Ullmann
TOVS Ltd, The Linen Hall, 162-168 Regent Street, London W1B 5TB
t 020 7287 6110 **f** 020 7287 5481
e info@tovs.co.uk **w** www.tovs.co.uk

Stephen Wade
Edit-Base, 70A Waldegrave Road, Teddington TW11 8NY
t 020 8614 6937 **e** alison@edit-base.co.uk

Chris Wadsworth
The Independent Post Company, 65 Goldhawk Road, London W12 8EH
t 020 8746 2060 **f** 020 8743 2345 **e** anthony@indepost.co.uk

Johnny Wagener
Edit-Base, 70A Waldegrave Road, Teddington TW11 8NY
t 020 8614 6937 **e** alison@edit-base.co.uk

Steve Warmington
172 Compstall Road, Marple Bridge, Stockport SK6 5HA
t 07973 298417 **e** stevewarmington@beeb.net
w stevewarmington.members.beeb.net
Credits One Big Sunday (T); Top Of The Pops Awards (T); Fame, Set And Match - Band Aid (D); Commonwealth Games Highlights (T)

Nick Watson
Connections, The Meadlands, Oakleigh Road, Hatch End, Pinner HA5 4HB
t 020 8420 1444 **f** 020 8428 5836 **m** 07831 305518
e mail@connectionsuk.com **w** www.connectionsuk.com

Charlie Watts
18 Bernary Avenue, Cosham, Portsmouth PO6 2JP
m 07989 108631 **e** info@charliewatts.net **w** www.charliewatts.net
Credits Art School (T); Brown (T); The Year of the Artist (T)

Ray Weedon
37 Ringmore Rise, London SE23 3DE
t 020 8699 6224 **m** 07956 563263
Credits Airline (D); Housesitters (D); Wreck Detectives (D); Uncovered (D)

Ben Weissbort
26 Vickery Court, Mitchell Street, London EC1V 3QL
t 020 7251 2893 **m** 07961 106350
e benweissbort@blueyonder.co.uk
Agent The Independent Post Company, 65 Goldhawk Road, London W12 8EH
t 020 8746 2060 **f** 020 8743 2345 **e** anthony@indepost.co.uk

West Digital Ltd
65 Goldhawk Road, London W12 8EH
t 020 8743 5100 **f** 020 8743 2345
e edit@westdigital.co.uk **w** www.westdigital.co.uk
Contact Peter Zacaroli, Senior Editor; Catherine Preece, Assistant Editor

David R Whelton
100 Millet Road, Greenford UB6 9SJ
t 020 8578 6270 **m** 07808 120726
Credits Heart Of The Country (T); Carlton Country (T)

Peter Wiggins
Connections, The Meadlands, Oakleigh Road, Hatch End, Pinner HA5 4HB
t 020 8420 1444 **f** 020 8428 5836 **m** 07831 305518
e mail@connectionsuk.com **w** www.connectionsuk.com

Tony Wilkins
Connections, The Meadlands, Oakleigh Road, Hatch End, Pinner HA5 4HB
t 020 8420 1444 **f** 020 8428 5836 **m** 07831 305518
e mail@connectionsuk.com **w** www.connectionsuk.com

Hugh Williams
The Independent Post Company, 65 Goldhawk Road, London W12 8EH
t 020 8746 2060 **f** 020 8743 2345 **e** anthony@indepost.co.uk

Derek Wilson
m 07977 997473 **e** wilsonderek1@aol.com
Credits Music for the Millenium (T); Ally McBeal (T)

Sam Wilson
Edit-Base, 70A Waldegrave Road, Teddington TW11 8NY
t 020 8614 6937 **e** alison@edit-base.co.uk

Bob Woodward
The Independent Post Company, 65 Goldhawk Road, London W12 8EH
t 020 8746 2060 **f** 020 8743 2345 **e** anthony@indepost.co.uk

Matthew Spears Wysall
Connections, The Meadlands, Oakleigh Road, Hatch End, Pinner HA5 4HB
t 020 8420 1444 **f** 020 8428 5836 **m** 07831 305518
e mail@connectionsuk.com **w** www.connectionsuk.com

Amanda Young
m 07778 334867 **e** amandayoung@aol.com
Agent Re:Solution, 90 Raglan Avenue, Waltham Cross EN8 8DD
t 020 7580 5766 **f** 01992 025506 **e** onthecase@totalise.co.uk **w** www.re-solution.tv
Credits Peak Practice (T); Jungle Orphans (T); Industrial Revelations (D); Relocation, Relocation (T)

Education Film Schools/ Higher Education

The Art Institute at Bournemouth
Wallisdown, Poole BH15 2HH
t 01202 363269 **f** 01202 538204
Contact Rik Stratton, Course Director

Birkbeck College
Faculty of Continuing Education, 26 Russell Square, London WC1B 5DQ
t 020 7631 6639 **e** m.wood@bbk.ac.uk **w** www.bbk.ac.uk
Contact Mary Wood, Course leader

BKSTS - Moving Image Society
5 Walpole Court, Ealing Studios, Ealing Green, London W5 5ED
t 020 8584 5220 **f** 020 8584 5230 **e** info@bksts.demon.co.uk **w** www.bksts.com
Contact John Graham, Executive Director

Bournemouth Media School
Bournemouth University, Talbot Campus, Fern Barrow, Poole BH12 5BB
t 01202 524111 **t** 01202 702736
e mediaschool@bournemouth.ac.uk
w www.media.bournemouth.ac.uk
Contact Sandie Rose

Bridgwater College

Bath Road, Bridgwater TA6 4PZ
t 01278 455464 **f** 01278 444363 **e** inbox@bridgwater.ac.uk
w www.bridgwater.ac.uk
Contact Bryn Younds, Media & Animation Studies; Steve Bennison, Film & Media Studies

Brighton College of Technology

Dept of Media and Performance, Pelham Street, Brighton BN1 4FA
t 01273 667788 **f** 01273 667748
e events@bricoltech.ac.uk **w** www.bricoltech.ac.uk
Contact Paul Eustice, Director of Media

Brighton Film School

13 Tudor Close, Dean Court Road, Rottingdean BN2 7DF
t 01273 302166 **f** 01273 302163 **m** 07739 329748
e info@brightonfilmschool.org.uk
w www.brightonfilmschool.org.uk
Contact Franz von Habsburg, Director/Senior Lecturer; Meryl von Habsburg, Director of Admissions
Locations Crew, Stock, Equipment, Grip Consumables, Avid, Steenbeck, Production Office.

Brooklands College

Heath Road, Weybridge KT13 8TT
t 01932 797700 **f** 01932 797800
e central@brooklands.ac.uk **w** www.brooklands.ac.uk

Cambridge University Moving Image Studio

1 Benet Place, Lensfield Road, Cambridge CB1 7TS
t 01223 762549 **f** 01223 330571 **e** ptc20@cam.ac.uk
Contact Gaenor Moore, Administrator; Peter Cook, Studio Manager

Cardonald College

690 Mosspark Drive, Glasgow G52 3AY
t 0141 272 3322 **f** 0141 272 3444
e info_centre@cardonald.ac.uk **w** www.cardonald.ac.uk
Contact David Johnstone, Studio Manager; Adam McIlwaine, Course Leader

Chippenham College

Media & Music Department, Cocklebury Road, Chippenham SN15 3QD
t 01249 464644 **f** 01249 465326
Contact Michael Graves, Head of Media & Music

Clydebank College

Kilbowie Road, Clydebank G81 2AA
t 0141 952 7771 **f** 0141 951 1574 **w** www.clydebank.ac.uk
Contact Bob McEwan, Course Leader; Susan Steell, Tutor

Coatbridge College

Kildonan Street, Coatbridge ML5 3LS
t 01236 422316 **f** 01236 440266 **w** www.coatbridgecollege.ac.uk
Contact Josephine Peter, Senior Lecturer

Colchester Institute

Sheepen Road, Colchester CO3 3LL
t 01206 518000 **f** 01206 763041
e info@colch-inst.ac.uk **w** www.colchester.ac.uk

Coleg Harlech

Harlech LL46 2PU
t 01766 780363 **f** 01766 780169 **w** www.harlech.co.uk
Contact Trevor Andrews, Tutor

Cre8 Studios

Town Hall Studios, Regent Circus, Swindon SN1 1QF
t 01793 463210 **f** 01793 463223 **e** info@cre8studios.org.uk
Contact Vanessa Wells, Facilities Co-ordinator

Darlington College of Technology

Cleveland Avenue, Darlington DL3 7BB
t 01325 503270 **f** 01325 503275
e enquire@darlington.ac.uk **w** www.darlington.ac.uk
Contact S Campbell, Head of School of Journalism, Media, Art & Design

De Montfort University

The Gateway, Leicester LE1 9BH
t 0116 255 1551 **f** 0116 257 7353
e enquiry@dmu.ac.uk **w** www.dmu.ac.uk

Dewsbury College

Batley School of Art and Design, Wheelwright Art, Birkdale Road, Dewsbury WF13 4HQ
t 01924 451649 **f** 01924 469491
e sharman@dewsbury.ac.uk **w** www.dewsbury.ac.uk
Contact S Harman, Co-ordinator

Edinburgh College of Art

Lauriston Place, Edinburgh EH3 9DF
t 0131 221 6125 **f** 0131 221 6001
e c.parkinson@eca.ac.uk **w** www.eca.ac.uk
Contact Donald Holwill, Head of Animation; Robert Dodds, Head of Visual Communication; Noe Mendelle, Head of Film and TV

Edinburgh Video Training Company

Unit 22, John Cotton Centre, 10 Sunnyside, Edinburgh EH7 5RA
t 0131 652 1206 **f** 0131 652 9833 **e** evtc@evtc.fsnet.co.uk
Contact Rona Hunter, Course Leader

Falkirk College of Further & Higher Education

Grangemouth Road, Falkirk FK2 9AD
t 01324 403020 **f** 01324 403222
e info@falkirkcollege.ac.uk **w** www.falkirkcollege.ac.uk
Contact Sheila McKee, Course Co-ordinator

Fife College of Further & Higher Education

St Brycedale Avenue, Kirkcaldy KY1 1EX
t 01592 268591 **f** 01592 640225
e enquiries@fife.ac.uk **w** www.fife.ac.uk
Contact Rhonda Stephen, Team Leader

Glenrothes College

The Radio & TV Studios, Stenton, Glenrothes KY6 2RA
t 01592 568099 **f** 01592 568182 **e** tanderson@glenrothes.ac.uk
Contact Terry Anderson

Hackney Community College

Shoreditch Campus, Falkirk Street, London N1 6HQ
t 020 7613 9060 **f** 020 7613 9003
e enquiries@comm-coll-hackney.ac.uk
w www.comm-coll-hackney.ac.uk
Contact Alex Josephy

Halton College

Kingsway, Widnes WA8 7QQ
t 0151 257 2800 **f** 0151 420 2408
e studentservices@haltoncollege.ac.uk
w www.haltoncollege.ac.uk

Hammersmith & West London College

Gliddon Road, Barons Court, London W14 9BL
t 0800 980 2175 **f** 020 8563 8247
e cic@hwlc.ac.uk **w** www.hwlc.ac.uk
Contact Sue Dickinson, Information Services Manager

Harrogate College

Hornbeam Park, Harrogate HG2 8QT
t 01423 879466 **f** 01423 879829
e oncourse@lmu.ac.uk **w** www.harrogate.ac.uk
Contact Peter Scarth, Head of Department; Anne Pearson

Highbury College, Portsmouth

Dovercourt Road, Cosham, Portsmouth PO6 2SA
t 023 9231 3202 **f** 023 9237 8382 **e** kara.sadler@highbury.ac.uk
Contact Kara Sadler, Course Manager

International Film School Wales

PO Box 179, Caerleon Campus, Newport NP18 3YG
t 01633 432677 **f** 01633 432885
e post.ifsw@newport.ac.uk **w** www.ifsw.newport.ac.uk
Contact Clive Myer, Director; Gethin While; Humphrey Trevelyan, Head of IFSW; Beryl Llywelyn-Jones, Research & Development Officer

Kent Institute of Art & Design

Maidstone Campus, Oakwood Park, Maidstone ME16 8AG
t 01622 757286 **f** 01622 621100
e kiadmarketing@kiad.ac.uk **w** www.kiad.ac.uk
Contact Sophia Phoca, Subject Leader

Kilmarnock College of Further Education

Holehouse Road, Kilmarnock KA3 7AT
t 01563 523501 **f** 01563 538182 **w** www.kilmarnock.ac.uk
Contact Nancy Macpherson, Head of Media and Communications; Gianna Devin

Kingston University

Knights Park Campus, Kingston University School of 3D Design, Kingston-upon-Thames KT1 2QJ
t 020 8547 2000 **f** 020 8547 7365
e r.joyce@kingston.ac.uk **w** www.kingston.ac.uk
Contact Rosaleen Joyce, Course Co-ordinator

Kingsway College

Kentish Town Centre, 87 Holmes Road, London NW5 3AX
t 020 7556 8000 **f** 020 7428 2910
Contact Claire Grey, Course Leader

Lancaster University

Bailrigg, Lancaster LA1 4YL
t 01524 594193 **f** 01524 594273
e r.rushton@lancaster.ac.uk **w** www.lancs.ac.uk/depts/cmc
Contact Greg Myers, Course leader; Richard Rushton, Lecturer

Learndirect Helpline

3rd Floor, Arnhem House, Waterloo Way, Leicester LE1 6LR
t 0116 201 8509 **e** jennifer.fernandes@bss.org
Contact Jennifer Fernandes, Helpline Co-ordinatoe; Lynn Watson, Helpline Co-ordinator; Rob Philips, Helpline Co-ordinator

Leeds Metropolitan University

2 Queen Sqaure, Leeds LS2 8AF
t 0113 283 2600 ext 3860 **f** 0113 283 1901
e s.morton@lmu.ac.uk
Contact Alby James, Course Leader; Denise York, Course Leader

Liverpool John Moores University

Dean Walters Building, Cathedral Chambers, St James Road L1 7BR
t 0151 231 5047 **f** 0151 231 5049
e t.spargo@livjm.ac.uk **w** www.livjm.ac.uk
Contact Tamsin Spargo, Head of Department

London Film Academy

The Old Church, 52A Walhan Grove, London SW6 1QR
t 020 7386 7711 **f** 020 7381 6116
e info@londonfilmacademy.com **e** www.londonfilmacademy.com
Contact Lou Spain, Head Of Studies; Anna MacDonald, Media Director; Daisy Gili, Managing Director

The London Film School

24 Shelton Street, Covent Garden, London WC2H 9UB
t 020 7836 9642 **t** 020 7240 0168 **f** 020 7497 3718
e film.school@lfs.org.uk **w** www.lfs.org.uk
Contact Chrissy Bright, Librarian/Festival Co-ordinator; Ben Gibson, Director; Shirley Streete-Bharath, Head of Resources; Alan Bernstein, Head of Studies

The Manchester Metropolitan University

School of Theatre, Mabel Tylecote Building, Cavendish Street, Manchester M15 6BG
t 0161 247 1305 **f** 0161 247 6875 **e** k.daly@mmu.ac.uk
Contact Niamh Dowling, Head of School
Credits Solstis: 'Lecture' (test)

Middlesex University

School of Arts, Design and Performing Arts, Centre for Electronic Arts, Cat Hill, Barnet EN4 8HT
t 020 8202 9255 **t** 020 8411 5000 **w** www.middlesex.ac.uk
Contact Martin Pitts, Dean of School

Moonstone International

67 George Street, Edinburgh EH2 2JG
t 0131 220 2080 **f** 0131 220 2081
e info@moonshore.org.uk **w** www.moonshore.org.uk
Contact Tara Halloran, Managing Director; Karen Currie, Marketing & Information Executive; Jean Ormieres, Artictic Director; Tamara Strijthem, Programme Administrator

Napier University (Marchmont Road Campus) Dept of Photography, Film & TV

61 Marchmont Road, Edinburgh EH9 1HU
t 0131 455 5201 **e** h.davies@napier.ac.uk
Contact Huw Davis, Head of Department (Photography, Film, TV)

National Film & Television School

Beaconsfield Studios, Station Road, Beaconsfield HP9 1LG
t 01494 671234 **f** 01494 674042
e admin@nftsfilm-tv.ac.uk **w** www.nftsfilm-tv.ac.uk
Contact Susan Morgan, Deputy to the Director; S Bayly, Head of School; Richard Jenkins, Studio Manager; Deanne Edwards, Director; Marjorie Hardwick, Registry Organiser

The Northern Media School

The Workstation, 15 Paternoster Row, Sheffield S1 2BX
t 0114 225 4648 **f** 0114 225 4606
e s.wragg@shu.ac.uk **w** www.shu.ac.uk/schools/cs/nms/
Contact Suzanne Wragg, Course Administrator

North East Worcestershire College

Peakman Street, Redditch B98 8DW
t 0152 757 2870 **f** 0152 757 2870
e zblockmedia@aol.com **w** www.ne-worcs.ac.uk
Contact Mark Masters, Head of Media

North Warwickshire & Hinkley College

Hinckley Road, Numeaton CV11 6BH
t 024 7624 3000 **f** 024 7632 9056
e the.college@nwarks-hinckley.ac.uk **w** www.nwhc.ac.uk
Contact Ian Wynd

Oxford College of Further Education

City Centre Campus, Oxpens Road, Oxford OX1 1SA
t 01865 245871 **f** 01865 248871
e enquiries@oxfe.ac.uk **w** www.oxfe.ac.uk/oxfe
Contact Fiona Morey, Media Department

Oxford Film & Video Makers

The Old Boxing Club, 54 Catherine Street, Oxford OX4 3AH
t 01865 792731 **e** office@ofvm.org **w** www.ofvm.org
Contact Geron Swann, Development Officer
Credits Must Try Harder - Child Brain Injury Trust (D); Live Fast Die Young - Compassion In World Farming (D); Matsuri (D); Ups Of Downs (D)

Perth College

Goodlyburn East, Crieff Road, Perth PH1 2NX
t 01738 877000
e pieter.deuling@perth.uhi.ac.uk **w** www.perth.ac.uk
Contact David Smith, Lecturer; Pieter Deuling, Course Tutor

Plymouth College of Art & Design

School of Photography, Film and TV, Tavistock Place, Plymouth PL4 8AT
t 01752 203400 **f** 01752 203444
e mdevalk@pcad.ac.uk **w** www.pcad.ac.uk
Contact David Hotchkiss, Head of School of Photography, Film & TV; Mark de Valk, Course Leader

Raindance Film Festival/ British Independent Film Awards

81 Berwick Street, London W1F 8TW
t 020 7287 3833 **f** 020 7439 2243
e info@raindance.co.uk **w** www.raindance.co.uk

Contact Suzanne Ballantyne, Senior Programmer; Dominic Thackray, Head of Design; Tessa Collinson, British Independent Film Awards; Johanna von Fischer, Press Office and Training; Elliot Grove, Director; John Tobin, Producer

Raindance is unique, combining film training with the UK's largest independent film festival. Our courses are taught by working industry professionals.

Ravensbourne College of Design & Communication

Walden Road, Chislehurst BR7 5SN
t 020 8289 4900 **f** 020 8325 8320
e info@rave.ac.uk **w** www.rave.ac.uk

Contact Pauline Taylor, Work Placement Administrator

Redbridge College of Further Education

Little Heath, Chadwell Heath, Romford RM6 4XT
t 020 8548 7400 **f** 020 8599 8224
e lfoster@redbridge-college.ac.uk **w** www.redbridge-college.ac.uk

Contact Angela Rangecroft, Programme Area Leader; Linda Foster, Head of Creative Studies

SAE Institute London

United House, North Road, London N7 9DP
t 020 7609 2653 **f** 020 7609 6944
e saelondon@sae.edu **w** www.saeuk.com

Contact Matthias Postel, Manager; Christian De Haas, Manager

Salisbury College

Division of Art & Professional Communications, Southampton Road, Salisbury SP1 2LW
t 01722 344344
e enquiries@salisbury.ac.uk **w** www.salisbury.ac.uk

Sandwell College

Lakeside Studios, Crocketts Lane, Smethwick B66 3BU
t 0121 556 6000 **f** 0121 253 6322
e gwhitehouse@sandcis.demon.co.uk **w** www.sandwell.ac.uk

Contact Geoff Whitehouse, Head of School of Engineering

Sheffield Hallam University

City Campus, Howard Street, Sheffield S1 1WB
t 0114 225 5555 **e** liasion@shu.ac.uk **w** www.shu.ac.uk

South Thames College

Faculty of Creative and Technological Studies, Wandsworth High Street, London SW18 2PP
t 020 8918 7000 **w** www.south-thames.ac.uk

Contact Sandra Plummer, Head of Learning Programme for Media

Stevenson College

Faculty of Creative Arts, Bankhead Avenue, Edinburgh EH11 4DE
t 0131 535 4600 **f** 0131 535 4666
e mcampbell@stevenson.ac.uk **w** www.stevenson.ac.uk

Surrey Institute of Art & Design

Falkner Road, Farnham GU9 7DS
t 01252 722441 **f** 01252 892616
e pnelson@surrart.ac.uk **w** www.surrart.ac.uk

Contact Paul Nelson, Programme Leader for Fine Art

Sutton Coldfield College

Lichfield Road, Sutton Coldfield B74 2NW
t 0121 355 5671 **f** 0121 355 0799 **e** cedwards@sutcol.ac.uk

Contact Clive Edwards, Managing Director

Trinity & All Saints' College

Brownberrie Lane, Horsforth, Leeds LS18 5HD
t 0113 283 7100 **f** 0113 283 7200
e a.clifford@tasc.ac.uk **w** www.tasc.ac.uk

Contact Andrew Clifford, Head of Media Services

University of Bristol, Department of Drama: Theatre, Film, Television

Cantocks Close, Woodland Road, Bristol BS8 1UP
t 0117 928 7838 **f** 0117 928 8251
e ftv-drama@bristol.ac.uk **w** www.bris.ac.uk/depts/drama/

Contact Deborah Gibbs, Course Manager, Film and Television Production

University of East London

East Building, 4-6 University Way, London E16 2RD
t 020 8223 2740 **f** 020 8223 2898
e d.e.butler@uel.ac.uk **w** www.uel.ac.uk

Contact David Butler, Course Leader

University of Greenwich

School of Humanities, The Old Royal Naval School, London SE10 9LF
t 020 8331 8000 **f** 020 8331 8805
e courseinfo@gre.ac.uk **e** a.dawson@gre.ac.uk **w** www.gre.ac.uk

Contact Andrew Dawson, Programme Leader For Film Studies

University of Lincolnshire & Humberside

School of Art & Design, Queens Gardens, Hull HU1 3DQ
t 01482 462196 **f** 01482 462101
e padell@humber.ac.uk **w** www.uhl.ac.uk

Contact Peter Atkinson-Dell, Course Leader TV and Film Design

University of Northumbria at Newcastle

School of Arts and Social Sciences, Squires Building, Sandyford Road, Newcastle upon Tyne NE1 8ST
t 0191 227 4413 **f** 0191 227 4559
e vashti.hutton@unn.ac.uk **w** www.northumbria.ac.uk

Contact Irene Spreaggon, Senior Administrator

University of Stirling

Department of Film & Media Studies, Stirling FK9 4LA
t 01786 467520 **f** 01786 466855
e g.m.doyle@stir.ac.uk **w** www.fms.stir.ac.uk

Contact Gillian Doyle, Head of Department

University of The West of England, Bristol

Faculty of Art, Media And Design, Kennel Lodge Road, Bristol BS3 2JT
t 0117 344 4716 **f** 0117 344 4745
e amd.enquiries@uwe.ac.uk **w** www.uwe.ac.uk/amd

Contact Malcolm Brammar, Award Leader: Sound Production; Judith Aston, Award Leader: Digital Media; Alastair Oldham, Award Leader: Time-Based Media; Barbara Hawkins, Head of Communications Media

University of Wales

Centre for Advanced Development of Creative Industry, College Road, Bangor LL57 2DG
t 01248 351151 **f** 01248 382102
e elsa@bangor.ac.uk **w** www.bangor.ac.uk

Contact Graeme Harper, Director of Center for Advanced Development of Creative Industry
Credits Storytelling On DVD (E); Beyond The Moon (E)

University of Wales College, Newport

Caerleon Campus, PO Box 101, Newport NP18 3YG
t 01633 432432 **f** 01633 432850
e uic@newport.ac.uk **w** www.newport.ac.uk

Contact Prof James Lusty, Principal & Chief Executive

University of Westminster

Watford Road, Northwick Park, Harrow HA1 3TP
t 020 7911 5903 **f** 020 7911 5955
e harrow-admissions@wmin.ac.uk **w** www.wmin.ac.uk

Contact Brian Winston, Centre for Communications and Information; Michael Holland, Marketing Officer

Wiltshire College Chippenham

Cocklebury Road, Chippenham SN15 3QD
t 01249 465261 **f** 01249 464644 **f** 01249 465326
e michaelgraves@wiltscoll.ac.uk **w** www.wiltscoll.ac.uk

Contact Michael Graves, Head of Media

Education Industry Training

Actual Media Training Ltd
Cross Cottage, Caerwent, Caldicot NP26 5AZ
t 01494 714623 **f** 01494 714623 **m** 07788 933494
e actualmedia1@aol.com **w** www.actualmediatraining.co.uk
Contact Jeremy Gould, Director; Sian Lattimer, Manager

The Arvon Foundation
Sheepwash EX21 5NS
t 01409 231338 **f** 01409 231144
e t-barton@avonfoundation.org **w** www.avonfoundation.org
Contact Ian Marchant

Avril Rowlands Film & Television Training
Laxford House, Poplar Piece, Inkberrow WR7 4ID
t 01386 792051 **f** 01386 792051 **m** 07957 428548
e avriltrain@hotmail.com
Contact Avril Rowlands, Contact

BBC Training & Development
Wood Norton, Room A30, Evesham WR11 4YB
t 0870 122 0216 **f** 0870 122 0145
e training@bbc.co.uk **w** www.bbctraining.co.uk
Contact Nigel Woodcock, Business Development Manager

British Kinematograph Sound & Television Society
Ealing Studios, Ealing Green, London W5 5EP
t 020 8584 5220 **f** 020 8584 5230
e sales@bksts.com **w** www.bksts.com

Cyfle
Crichton House, 11-12 Mount Stuart Square, Cardiff Bay,
Cardiff CF10 5EE
t 029 2046 5533 **f** 029 2046 3344
e post@cyfle.co.uk **w** http://www.cyfle.co.uk/
Contact Sion Hughes, Chief Executive

The Delamar Academy of Make-Up
52A Walham Grove, Fulham, London SW6 1QR
t 020 7381 0213 **f** 020 7381 0213
e info@themake-upcentre.co.uk **w** www.themake-upcentre.co.uk
Contact David Shawyer, Proprieter

The First Film Foundation
9 Bourlet Close, London W1W 7BP
t 020 7580 2111 **f** 020 7580 2116
e info@firstfilm.demon.co.uk **w** www.firstfilm.co.uk
Contact Jonathan Rawlinson, Director

FT2 - Film & Television Freelance Training
4th Floor, Warwick House, 9 Warwick Street, London W1B 5LY
t 020 7734 5141 **f** 020 7287 9899
e info@ft2.org.uk **w** www.ft2.org.uk
Contact Sharon Goode, Director

Hall Place Studios
Leeds Metropolitan University, 3 Queens Square, Leeds LS2 8AF
t 0113 283 1906 **f** 0113 283 1713 **e** info@hallplacestudios.com
w www.hallplacestudios.com
Contact Maria Spadafora, Administrater

Hawksmere Plc
12-18 Grosvenor Gardens, London SW1W 0DH
t 020 7824 8257 **f** 020 7730 4293
e bookings@hawksmere.co.uk **w** www.hawksmere.co.uk
Contact Michael Bentley, Producer

John Lisney Associates
220 Vale Road, Tonbridge TN9 1SP
t 01732 373030 **f** 01732 373031
e info@lisneyassociates.com **e** www.lisneyassociates.com
Contact Patricia Leeds, Course Administrator

MaST International
Hermitage House, Bath Road, Taplow, Maidenhead SL6 0AR
t 01628 784062 **f** 01628 773061
e trainingsolutions@mast.co.uk **w** www.mast.co.uk

Media Interviews
26 Lansdown Heights, Bath BA1 5AE
t 01225 338 922 **f** 01225 338 924
e hugo@mediainterviews.co.uk **w** www.mediainterviews.co.uk
Contact Hugo Brooke, Proprietor

Media Know-How Ltd
New House, Bell Lane, Thame OX9 3AL
t 01844 214821 **f** 01844 214285
e mark@mediaknow-how.com **w** www.mediaknow-how.com
Contact Mark Patterson, Managing Director

Medialex Ltd
Greyhound House, 23-24 George Street, Richmond TW9 1HY
t 020 8973 2186 **f** 020 8973 2009
e info@medialex-uk.com **w** www.medialex-uk.com
Contact Pam Bernhard

National Short Course Training Programme (NSCTP)
Beaconsfield Studios, Station Road, Beaconsfield HP9 1LG
t 01494 677903 **f** 01494 678708
e info@nfts-scu.org.uk **w** www.nfts-scu.org.uk
Contact Susan Morgan, Deputy to the Director; Deanne Edwards, Director

Panico
PO Box 496, London WC1A 2WZ
t 020 7485 3533
e panico@panicofilms.com **w** www.panicofilms.com

Safesets
15 Priest End, Thame OX9 2AE
t 01844 218072 **f** 01844 217558 **m** 07909 521754
e shaun@productiondesign.co.uk **w** www.productiondesign.co.uk

Screen Yorkshire
40 Hanover Sqaure, Leeds LS3 1BQ
t 01132 944410 **f** 01132 944989 **e** info@screenyorkshire.co.uk
Contact Jo Spreckly, Chief Executive; Marsha Stankler, Administrator; Sally Joynson, Industry Training Manager; Nicola Bowen, Training Officer; Simon Moxon, Training Officer

Skillset
Prospect House, 80-110 New Oxford Street, London WC1A 1HB
t 020 7520 5757 **f** 020 7520 5758
e info@skillset.org **w** www.skillset.org

Television & Radio Techniques
The Studio, 4 Leeds Road, Sheffield S9 3TY
t 0114 242 4383 **f** 0114 242 4341 **m** 07976 328060
e info@t-r-t.co.uk **w** www.greatbritain.co.uk/trt
Contact Gary Bartram, Technical Director

TVR Television Roehampton
Television Centre, Digby Stuart, Roehampton Lane, London SW15 5PH
t 020 8392 3590 **f** 020 8392 3592 **m** 07930 300797
e tvr@roehampton.ac.uk
Contact Peter Merton, Production Manager
Credits Music & Early Years (E); Latin American Dance Syllabus (E); South Asian Dance Syllabus (E); IFWLA Women's Lacrosse World WP 2001 (C)

Warpaint School of Make-Up
7 Hadleigh Close, Merton Park, London SW20 9AW
t 020 8543 1996 **f** 020 8542 8286 **m** 07831 829230
e warpaint.school@virgin.net
Contact Teresa Kelly, Proprietor

ENGINEERS

Engineers Sound

Acoustic Engineering Services (UK)
PO Box 322, West Byfleet KT14 6YN
t 01932 352733 **f** 01932 355265 **e** aefuk@compuserve.com
Contact Alex Puttock, Director; Mark Stagg

DAT Productions Ltd
Phoenix Sound, Engineers Way, Wembley, London HA9 OET
t 020 8450 5665 **f** 020 8208 1979
e jo@datproductions.co.uk **w** www.datproductions.co.uk
Contact Cathy Ferrett, Facilities Manager; Jo Harrison, Marketing Manager
Credits White Squall (F); Keep The Aspidistra Flying (F); Brazil (F); The Last Emperor (F)

Nigel Holmes
Experience Counts - Call Me Ltd, 5th Floor, 41-42 Berners Street, London W1P 3AA
t 020 7637 8112 **f** 020 7580 2582

Tim Kerr
14 Fisher Close, Walton On Thames KT12 5PN
m 07973 543621
Credits Brain Teaser (T); My Family (T); The Sketch Show (T); Alastair McGowan's Big Impression (T)

Kevin Wood Sound Services
32 Down Road, Teddington TW11 9HA
t 020 8977 2735 **m** 07850 615311
e kevin@tvsound.co.uk **w** www.tvsound.co.uk
Contact Kevin Wood, Sound Engineer
Credits Family Affairs (T); Rumpole of the Bailey (T); Six Appeal (T); Trouble at Breakfast (T)

Gerry O'Riordan
59 Camborne Avenue, Ealing, London W13 9QZ
t 020 8566 3794 **f** 020 8932 3465
e gerryor@aol.com **w** www.snakeranch.co.uk
Credits Story of Tracy Beaker (T); The King's Beard (A); Un Chant D'Amour (S); My Kingdom (F)

Stratford Acoustics
24 Proctor Street, Birmingham B7 4EE
t 0121 333 7711 **f** 0121 333 7799
e admin@cloudone.net **w** www.cloudone.net
Contact Paul Langdon, Hire Manager

Studio File
13 Perrymead, Prestwich, Manchester M25 2QJ
t 0161 773 2664 **f** 0161 773 8290 **m** 07973 480760
e mike@osd-uk.com
Contact Mike Thornton, Director

Helen Thompson
Experience Counts - Call Me Ltd, 5th Floor, 41-42 Berners Street, London W1P 3AA
t 020 7637 8112 **f** 020 7580 2582

Engineers Video

Bristol Broadcast Engineering
4 St Pauls Road, Clifton, Bristol BS8 1LT
t 0117 907 7500 **f** 0117 907 7400 **m** 07879 422896
e alan@broadcasteng.co.uk **w** www.broadcasteng.co.uk
Contact Denise Thorne, Administrator; Derek Carr, Managing Director; Alan Griffiths, Managing Director

Ivan Burgess
24 Penwerris Avenue, Isleworth TW7 4QX
t 020 8570 4238 **m** 07966 176194
e ivan@ivanburgess.co.uk **w** www.ivanburgess.co.uk

Roger Cater
t 0117 977 5380 **m** 07774 107161 **e** production@4rog.com

Carl Dolan
TOVS Ltd, The Linen Hall, 162-168 Regent Street, London W1B 5TB
t 020 7287 6110 **f** 020 7287 5481
e info@tovs.co.uk **w** www.tovs.co.uk

GAS Electronic Systems
72 Chatham Road, London SW11 6HG
t 020 7223 1125 **f** 020 7924 4072 **m** 07860 730303
e enquiry@gasele.co.uk **w** www.gaselec.co.uk

John Stobbart
3 Bromsgrove Road, Halesowen B63 3JQ
m 07770 442851 **e** johnstobb@aol.com

Engineers Vision

Tim Allen
Grade One TV & Film Personnel, Elstree Studios, Shenley Road, Borehamwood WD6 1JG
t 020 8324 2224 **f** 020 8324 2328
e gradeone.tvpersonnel@virgin.net

Graham Barter
Grade One TV & Film Personnel, Elstree Studios, Shenley Road, Borehamwood WD6 1JG
t 020 8324 2224 **f** 020 8324 2328
e gradeone.tvpersonnel@virgin.net

Steve Bartlett
TOVS Ltd, The Linen Hall, 162-168 Regent Street, London W1B 5TB
t 020 7287 6110 **f** 020 7287 5481
e info@tovs.co.uk **w** www.tovs.co.uk

David Barton
Connections, The Meadlands, Oakleigh Road, Hatch End, Pinner HA5 4HB
t 020 8420 1444 **f** 020 8428 5836 **m** 07831 305518
e mail@connectionsuk.com **w** www.connectionsuk.com

Lotti Brunsdon
Connections, The Meadlands, Oakleigh Road, Hatch End, Pinner HA5 4HB
t 020 8420 1444 **f** 020 8428 5836 **m** 07831 305518
e mail@connectionsuk.com **w** www.connectionsuk.com

Mathew Buckley
TOVS Ltd, The Linen Hall, 162-168 Regent Street, London W1B 5TB
t 020 7287 6110 **f** 020 7287 5481
e info@tovs.co.uk **w** www.tovs.co.uk

Richard Carroll
Relko Gardens, London SM1 4TJ
m 07973 507860 **e** rich@richandkate.freeserve.co.uk
Credits The Brit Awards (T); MTV Studios; Fame Academy (T); T4 (T)

Philip Christie

Connections, The Meadlands, Oakleigh Road, Hatch End, Pinner HA5 4HB
t 020 8420 1444 **f** 020 8428 5836 **m** 07831 305518
e mail@connectionsuk.com **w** www.connectionsuk.com

Roger Conway

Connections, The Meadlands, Oakleigh Road, Hatch End, Pinner HA5 4HB
t 020 8420 1444 **f** 020 8428 5836 **m** 07831 305518
e mail@connectionsuk.com **w** www.connectionsuk.com

Mike Davies

TOVS Ltd, The Linen Hall, 162-168 Regent Street, London W1B 5TB
t 020 7287 6110 **f** 020 7287 5481
e info@tovs.co.uk **w** www.tovs.co.uk

George Fegan

TOVS Ltd, 162-168 Regent Street, London W1B 5TB
t 020 7287 6110 **f** 020 7287 5481
e info@tovs.co.uk **w** www.tovs.co.uk

Peter R Foster

176 Brodick Drive, Bolton BL2 6UE
t 01204 383695 **f** 01204 383695 **m** 07973 253464
Credits Channel 4 Horse Racing (T); BBC Commonwealth Games (T); BBC Open Golf (T); Sky Premier Football (T)

Peter Gardiner

Grade One TV & Film Personnel, Elstree Studios, Shenley Road, Borehamwood WD6 1JG
t 020 8324 2224 **f** 020 8324 2328
e gradeone.tvpersonnel@virgin.net

Keith Goodwin

Experience Counts - Call Me Ltd, 5th Floor, 41-42 Berners Street, London W1P 3AA
t 020 7637 8112 **f** 020 7580 2582

Maurice Gourd

50 Kimberley Road, Croydon CR0 2PU
t 020 8689 9181 **f** 020 8689 9181 **m** 0788 9819296
e maurice.gourd@virgin.net
Credits Rainbow (T); QVC - The Shopping Channel (T); This Week (T)
Technical Director and Studio Lighting. With fixed rigs.

Mike Hartung

Grade One TV & Film Personnel, Elstree Studios, Shenley Road, Borehamwood WD6 1JG
t 020 8324 2224 **f** 020 8324 2328
e gradeone.tvpersonnel@virgin.net

David Harvey

Experience Counts - Call Me Ltd, 5th Floor, 41-42 Berners Street, London W1P 3AA
t 020 7637 8112 **f** 020 7580 2582

David L Harvey

12 Whitton Drive, Greenford UB6 0QZ
t 020 8902 0147 **f** 020 8902 0147
Credits The Saturday Show (T); Coupling (T); Graham Norton (T); My Family (T)

Peter Harvey

TOVS Ltd, The Linen Hall, 162-168 Regent Street, London W1B 5TB
t 020 7287 6110 **f** 020 7287 5481
e info@tovs.co.uk **w** www.tovs.co.uk

Phil Hayward

TOVS Ltd, The Linen Hall, 162-168 Regent Street, London W1B 5TB
t 020 7287 6110 **f** 020 7287 5481
e info@tovs.co.uk **w** www.tovs.co.uk

Chris Hossent

TOVS Ltd, The Linen Hall, 162-168 Regent Street, London W1B 5TB
t 020 7287 6110 **f** 020 7287 5481
e info@tovs.co.uk **w** www.tovs.co.uk

John Hughes

Experience Counts - Call Me Ltd, 5th Floor, 41-42 Berners Street, London W1P 3AA
t 020 7637 8112 **f** 020 7580 2582

Richard Johnson

532 Kedleston Road, Derby DE22 2NG
m 07802 882375 **e** rich.johnson@bigfoot.com

Brian King

Agent Grade One TV & Film Personnel, Elstree Studios, Shenley Road, Borehamwood WD6 1JG
t 020 8324 2224 **f** 020 8324 2328
e gradeone.tvpersonnel@virgin.net
Agent Connections, The Meadlands, Oakleigh Road, Hatch End, Pinner HA5 4HB
t 020 8420 1444 **f** 020 8428 5836 **m** 07831 305518
e mail@connectionsuk.com **w** www.connectionsuk.com

Mike Leaback

TOVS Ltd, The Linen Hall, 162-168 Regent Street, London W1B 5TB
t 020 7287 6110 **f** 020 7287 5481
e info@tovs.co.uk **w** www.tovs.co.uk

Bryan Lockey

Experience Counts - Call Me Ltd, 5th Floor, 41-42 Berners Street, London W1P 3AA
t 020 7637 8112 **f** 020 7580 2582

Lex MacDonald

23 Albert Drive, Bearsden, Glasgow G61 2PG
t 0141 942 6359 **m** 07889 125 649 **e** lexmacd@lineone.net

Sean Mack

12 Paxton Road, Chiswick, London W4 2QX
t 020 8994 9158 **m** 07788 872844
e sean@mack9976.freeserve.co.uk

Michael McGaw

South Woodford, London E18 1AD
m 07808 068198 **e** mike@mcgawf9.co.uk
Credits RI:SE (T); Live With Chris Moyles (T); Wimbledon (T); The Big Breakfast (T)

Malcom McGregor

39 Pine Ridge, Newbury RG14 2NQ
t 01635 45124 **f** 01635 46034 **m** 07973 613 761
e malcom@videomatters.com **w** www.videomatters.com

Ian Nisbet

TOVS Ltd, The Linen Hall, 162-168 Regent Street, London W1B 5TB
t 020 7287 6110 **f** 020 7287 5481
e info@tovs.co.uk **w** www.tovs.co.uk

Peppertree Broadcast Ltd

London
m 07973 755169
e mike@peppertree-broadcast.co.uk
w www.peppertree-broadcast.co.uk
Contact Mike Hall, Managing Director
Credits EBU Salt Lake Olympics 2002 (T); Commonwealth Wealth Games 2002 (T); World Cup 2002 (T)

Mark Poor

Connections, The Meadlands, Oakleigh Road, Hatch End, Pinner HA5 4HB
t 020 8420 1444 **f** 020 8428 5836 **m** 07831 305518
e mail@connectionsuk.com **w** www.connectionsuk.com

Ed Pru

Connections, The Meadlands, Oakleigh Road, Hatch End, Pinner HA5 4HB
t 020 8420 1444 **f** 020 8428 5836 **m** 07831 305518
e mail@connectionsuk.com **w** www.connectionsuk.com

Richard Pullen
Grade One TV & Film Personnel, Elstree Studios, Shenley
Road, Borehamwood WD6 1JG
t 020 8324 2224 **f** 020 8324 2328
e gradeone.tvpersonnel@virgin.net

Alison Roberts
Grade One TV & Film Personnel, Elstree Studios, Shenley
Road, Borehamwood WD6 1JG
t 020 8324 2224 **f** 020 8324 2328
e gradeone.tvpersonnel@virgin.net

Alan James Rogers
69 Moor Lane, Wilmslow SK9 6BQ
t 01625 537620 **m** 07956 235 371 **e** alanrogers@bctalk.net
Credits Coronation Street (T); You've Been Framed (T); Holby City (T); Stars In
Their Eyes (T)

Mick Rogerson
Experience Counts - Call Me Ltd, 5th Floor, 41-42 Berners
Street, London W1P 3AA
t 020 7637 8112 **f** 020 7580 2582

John Stemp
m 07768 363133
e johnstemp@compuserve.com **w** www.vision-engineer.com
Credits Paul Weller In Hyde Park (T); Kilroy (T); At The Races (T); My Family (T)

Martin Swain
50 Chaldon Common Road, Caterham CR3 5DD
t 01833 348400 **m** 07740 355127 **e** swain.martin@virgin.net
Credits Open Golf Championship (T); Richard And Judy (T); Wimbledon (T); Last
Night At The Proms (T)

Alan Taylor
Grade One TV & Film Personnel, Elstree Studios, Shenley
Road, Borehamwood WD6 1JG
t 020 8324 2224 **f** 020 8324 2328
e gradeone.tvpersonnel@virgin.net

Paul Telco
TOVS Ltd, The Linen Hall, 162-168 Regent Street, London W1B 5TB
t 020 7287 6110 **f** 020 7287 5481
e info@tovs.co.uk **w** www.tovs.co.uk

Mike Thorne
Experience Counts - Call Me Ltd, 5th Floor, 41-42 Berners
Street, London W1P 3AA
t 020 7637 8112 **f** 020 7580 2582

Daunton Todd
TOVS Ltd, The Linen Hall, 162-168 Regent Street, London W1B 5TB
t 020 7287 6110 **f** 020 7287 5481
e info@tovs.co.uk **w** www.tovs.co.uk

Video Matters
39 Pine Ridge, Newbury RG14 2NQ
t 01645 45124 **f** 01635 46034 **m** 07973 613761
e malcolm@videomatters.com **w** www.videomatters.com

Bruce Wallis
TOVS Ltd, The Linen Hall, 162-168 Regent Street, London W1B 5TB
t 020 7287 6110 **f** 020 7287 5481
e info@tovs.co.uk **w** www.tovs.co.uk

Iain Welsh
5 Kernthorpe Road, Kings Heath, Birmingham B14 6RA
t 0121 444 6080 **f** 0121 444 6080 **m** 07092 127919
e iain.welsh@ntlworld.com

Pete Williams
TOVS Ltd, The Linen Hall, 162-168 Regent Street, London W1B 5TB
t 020 7287 6110 **f** 020 7287 5481
e info@tovs.co.uk **w** www.tovs.co.uk

Stephen Williams
TOVS Ltd, The Linen Hall, 162-168 Regent Street, London W1B 5TB
t 020 7287 6110 **f** 020 7287 5481
e info@tovs.co.uk **w** www.tovs.co.uk

EQUIPMENT

Equipment Installation

AV Kit Ltd
63 Ewer Street, London SE1 0NR
t 020 7401 3033 **f** 020 7401 3000
e enquiries@wiremech.com **w** www.avkit.com
Contact Bob Jones; Steve Muir

Boxer Scotland
Unit 1, Millennium Court, Burns Street, Glasgow G4 9SA
t 0141 564 2710 **f** 0141 564 2719
e caroline.thomson@boxer.co.uk **w** www.boxer.co.uk
Contact Caroline Thompson, Office Manager; John Dormer, Projects Manager;
Gary Welsh, Projects Manager; Stuart Currie, Managing Director

dB Broadcast Ltd
Kestrel House, Sedgeway Business Park, Witchford, Ely CB6 2HY
t 01353 661117 **f** 01353 665617
e sales@dbbroadcast.co.uk **w** www.dbbroadcast.co.uk
Contact Tom Swan, Sales And Marketing Director

Downhall Broadcast Solutions
1 Laburnum Way, Rayleigh SS6 9GN
t 01268 786588 **f** 07092 185244 **m** 07946 587554
e sales@downhallbroadcastsolutions
w www.downhallbroadcastsolutions.co.uk
Contact Mark Hooper, Broadcast Systems Engineer

John Naulls Broadcast Systems
13 First Avenue, Acton, London W3 7JP
t 020 8749 7915 **f** 020 8749 7247 **m** 07973 560472
e john@naulls.com **w** www.naulls.com
Contact John Naulls, Proprietor

Mar-Com
Europe House, 170 Windmill Road West, Sunbury-On-Thames
TW16 7HB
t 01932 733 700 **f** 01932 733 710 **w** www.mar-com.co.uk
Contact Mary Higgins, Administrator

Marcom Systems
1 Heathlands, Heath Gardens, Twickenham TW1 4BP
t 020 8891 5061 **f** 020 8892 9028
e mhiggins@mar-com.co.uk **w** www.mar-com.co.uk
Contact Mary Higgins, Contact

Mott MacDonald

Power & Communications Division, Victory House, Trafalgar Place, Brighton BN1 4FY
t 01273 365000 **f** 01273 365100 **w** www.mottmac.com
Contact Tom Allen, Director of Communications

MPI Ltd

International House, Tamworth Road, Hertford SG13 7DQ
t 01992 501111 **f** 01992 535570 **m** 07885 488254
e stuartg@mpi.ltd.uk **w** www.mpi.ltd.uk
Contact Colin Simpson, Broadcast Project Manager; Stuart Garwood, Director; Colin Green, Director; Simon Henser, Sales Consultant

Photon Beard Ltd

Unit K3, Cherry Court Way, Stanbridge Road, Leighton Buzzard LU7 4UH
t 01525 850911 **f** 01525 850922
e info@photonbeard.com **w** www.photonbeard.com
Contact Peter Daffarn, Sales Director; Mike Perry, Dealer Manager; Alan Gooch, Sales and Marketing Director

Picture Canning Company

55 Bendon Valley, London SW18 4LZ
t 020 8874 9277 **f** 020 8874 6623
e info@picturecanning.co.uk **w** www.picturecanning.co.uk
Contact Leslie Zunz, Managing Director; Paul Taylor, General Manager; Phil Wade, Managing Director
Credits Escape To The Country (D); Watchdog (T); Is Harry On The Boat (T); Holiday (D)

Tesla Systems Installation Ltd

Unit 4 Brewery Mews, St Johns Road, Isleworth TW7 6PH
t 020 8568 9007 **f** 020 8568 7656 **m** 07956 552577
e bill@teslasystems.co.uk
Contact Tony Farrington, Installation Manager; WG Briggs, Director, Managing Director
Broadcast installation specialist and outside broadcast cabling and repair work.

Test Valley Communications

79 Pond Close, Overton, Basingstoke RG25 3LZ
t 01256 771318 **f** 01256 771318 **m** 07831 370882
e systems@pvcbroadcast.com **w** www.pvcbroadcast.com
Contact PV Charman, Proprietor / Director

Wire: Broadcast Ltd

22C Fairhazel Gardens, London NW6 3SJ
m 07711 788949 **m** 07976 155998
e jonathan@wirebroadcast.co.uk **w** www.wirebroadcast.co.uk
Contact Robin Howell, Director; Jonathan Rackowe, Director
Credits JVC Studio Installation (T); BBH Transfer And Duplication System (T); MTV VT Area (T); MTV Transmission System (T)

Yellow Technology Ltd

1 The Maltings, Station Road, Newport CB11 3RN
t 01799 542105 **f** 01799 542106
e contact@yellowtechnology.co.uk
w www.yellowtechnology.co.uk
Contact Pete Eaglesfield, Commercial Manager

Equipment
Maintenance/Service

Oakleigh Cases Ltd - Flight Cases

10 The Summit Centre, Summit Road, Potters Bar EN6 3 QW
t 01707 655011 **f** 01707 646447
e info@oakleighcases.com **w** www.oakleighcases.com
Contact Liz Puxley, Accounts & Administration; Richard Puxley, Managing Director; Martin Cockton, General Manager; Andy Stroud, Account Manager

OpTex UK

20-26 Victoria Road, New Barnet, London EN4 9PF
t 020 8441 2199 **f** 020 8449 3646
e info@optexint.com **w** www.optexint.com
Contact Edward Catton-Orr, Sales; Mike Robinson, Rentals

Equipment
Manufacture, Broadcast

A&C Ltd UK

83 Headstone Road, Harrow HA1 1PQ
t 020 8427 5168 **f** 020 8861 2469
e info@powerpod.co.uk **w** www.powerpod.co.uk
Contact Dave Sherwin, Proprietor

Abakus Scientific Ltd

Grange Farm, Bourne Road, Carlby, Stamford PE9 4LU
t 01778 590117 **w** www.abakus-scientific.com
Contact Kenneth Pollitt

Abit Ltd

Unit 103, Belgravia Workshops, 159 Marlborough Road, London N19 4NF
t 020 7281 3815 **f** 020 7561 9622
e dseaborn@abit.co.uk **w** www.abit.co.uk
Contact David Seaborn, Director; Paul Baker, Head of Marketing

Accom Europe Ltd

PO Box 265, Teddington TW11 9PQ
t 020 8977 0198 **f** 020 8977 7935 **m** 07957 657911
e rob@accom.com **w** www.accom.com
Contact Rob Arnold, Eame Sales Manager

ADC Software Systems

Spencer House, 23 Sheen Road, Richmond TW9 1BN
t 020 8332 7400 **f** 020 8332 7403 **w** www.adc.com
Contact Mary Anne Trotman

Advent Communications

Preston Hill House, Nashleigh Hill, Chesham HP5 3HE
t 01494 774400 **f** 01494 791127
e sales@advent-comm.co.uk **w** www.advent-comm.co.uk

Alan Dick & Co Ltd

The Barlands, London Road, Cheltenham GL52 6UT
t 01242 518500 **f** 01242 510191
e sales@uk.alandickgroup.com **w** www.alandick.com

Alice Soundtech

Unit 34D, Hobbs Industrial Estate, Newchapel, Lingfield RH7 6HN
t 01342 833500 **f** 01342 833350
e sales@alice.co.uk **w** www.alice.co.uk
Contact Harry Bentley, Production Manager; Paul Miller, Sales Manager; Garry Thompson, General Manager

Alusett

Units F&G, Wykeham Industrial Estate, Moorside Road, Winchester SO23 7RX
t 01962 842424 **f** 01962 842425
e sales@alusett.co.uk **w** www.alusett.co.uk

Ampex Great Britain Ltd

Ampex House, Beechwood, Chineham Business Pk, Chineham, Basingstoke RG24 8WA
t 01256 814410 **f** 01256 814474
e sales@ampexgb.co.uk **w** www.ampexdata.com

ARRI GB Ltd

2 Highbridge, Oxford Road, Uxbridge UB8 1LX
t 01895 457000 **f** 01895 457001
e sales@arri-gb.com **w** www.arri.com
Contact Judith Petty, Group Marketing Manager

Aston Broadcast Systems Ltd

123-127 Deepcut Bridge Road, Deepcut, Camberley GU16 6SD
t 01252 836221 **f** 01252 837923
e sales@aston.tv **w** www.aston.tv
Contact Phil Moore, General Sales Manager; Peter Radford, Managing Director; Peter Mundan, Sales Director; Gary Pass, UK Sales Manager; Alsion Pavitt, Marketing

ATC - Loudspeaker Technology
Gypsy Lane, Aston Down, Stroud GL6 8HR
t 01285 760561 **f** 01285 760683
e info@atc.gb.net **w** www.atc.gb.net

Audio Developments Ltd
Hall Lane, Walsall Wood, Walsall WS9 9AU
t 01543 375351 **f** 01543 361051 **e** sales@audio.co.uk
Contact Roger Tromans, Technical Director; Antony Levesley, Sales Director

Audio Processing Technology Ltd
Edgewater Road, Belfast BT3 9JQ
t 028 9037 1110 **f** 028 9037 1137
e jmcclintock@aptx.com **w** www.aptx.com
Contact Jonny McClintock

Audionics
Petre Drive, Sheffield S4 7PZ
t 0114 242 2333 **f** 0114 243 3913
e info@audionics.co.uk **w** www.audionics.co.uk
Contact Phil Myers, Director; Phil Davies, Director

Audix Broadcast
Station Road, Wenden, Saffron Walden CB11 4LG
t 01799 542220 **f** 01799 541248
e sales@audixbroadcast.co.uk **w** www.audixbroadcast.co.uk
Contact Ian Jennings, Managing Director

Avitel
Berewyk Hall Court, White Colne, Colchester CO6 2QB
t 01787 220049 **f** 01787 220260
e jules@avitel.tv **w** www.avitel.tv
Contact Jules Swain, Sales Administrator//Sales Manager

BAL Broadcast Ltd
Unit 3, Buckingham Close, Nuneaton CV10 7JW
t 024 7637 5827 **f** 024 7664 2375 **e** sales@bal.co.uk
Contact Debbie Walton, Office Manager

BES Electronics Ltd
The Maltings, Charlton Road, Shepton Mallet BA4 5QE
t 01749 345005 **f** 01749 346230
e sales@beselectronics.com **w** www.beselectronics.com

Black Box
1 Greenwich Quay, Clarence Road, London SE8 3EY
t 020 8692 6992 **f** 020 8692 6957
e ra@aaa-design.com
w www.aaa-design.com/black_box/index.htm
Contact Paul Smith, Designer

Bradley Engineering
The Workshop, 2 Lovehill Cottages, Billet Lane, Iver SL3 6DQ
t 01753 654732 **f** 01753 630249
e bradders@bradders.freeserve.co.uk **w** www.bradeng.com
Contact David Bradley, Proprietor

Broadcast Developments Ltd (BDL)
Unit 8A, Poplar Business Park, 10 Prestons Road, London E14 9RL
t 020 7538 1427 **f** 020 7515 9529
e sales@bdlautoscript.com **w** www.bdlautoscript.com
Contact Christopher Lambert, Managing Director

Broadcast Technology Ltd
Sopwith Park, Royce Close, West Portway Industrial Estate, Andover SP10 3TS
t 01264 332633 **f** 01264 334509
e info@btl.uk.com **w** www.btl.uk.com

Bryant Broadcast & Data Communications
70B Stafford Road, Croydon CRO 4NE
t 020 8404 4050 **f** 020 8404 4080
e sales@bryant-broadcast.co.uk **w** www.bryant-broadcast.co.uk
Contact Graham Tottue, Sales; Ross Scott, Partner; Simon Quill, Technical; Gary Wright, Metalwork

C-MAC Microcircuits Ltd
South Denes, Great Yarmouth NR30 3PX
t 01493 743100 **f** 01493 858536 **w** www.cmac.com

Calrec Audio Ltd
Nutclough Mill, Hebden Bridge, Halifax HX7 8EZ
t 01422 842159 **f** 01422 845244
e enquiries@calrec.com **w** www.calrec.com
Contact Richard Lumb, Sales Co-ordinator; Dave Letson, UK & Europe Sales Manager; Henry Goodman, Asia Sales Manager; Jim Wilmer, US Sales Manager; John Gluck, Sales & Marketing Director

Canford Audio Plc
Crowther Road, Washington NE38 0BW
t 0191 418 1000 **f** 0191 418 1001
e info@canford.co.uk **w** www.canford.co.uk
Contact Barry Revels, Sales & Marketing Manager; Chas Kennedy, Technical Director; Phil Buckle, CEO; Iain Elliott, Director

CED Ceta Electronic Design
40 The Ridgeway, London N11 3LJ
t 020 8368 8110 **f** 020 8368 9417 **m** 07836 595 794
e sales@ced-ceta.co.uk **w** www.ced-ceta.co.uk
Contact Jim Kotak, Sales Director

Celco
Midas House, Willow Way, London SE26 4QP
t 020 8699 6788 **f** 020 8699 5056
e sales@celco.co.uk **w** www.celco.co.uk
Contact Rod Bartholomeusz, Director

Christie Digital Systems
ViewPoint, 200 Ashville Way, Wokingham RG41 2PL
t 0118 977 8000 **f** 0118 977 8100 **w** www.christiedigital.com

Cintel International Ltd
Watton Road, Ware SG12 0AE
t 01920 463939 **f** 01920 463221
e sales@cintel.co.uk **w** www.cintel.co.uk
Contact Adam Welsh, Managing Director; Simon Carter, Sales Director

The Claude Lyons Group
Brook Road, Waltham Cross EN8 7LR
t 01992 768888 **f** 01992 788000
e info@claudelyons.co.uk **w** www.claudelyons.co.uk
Contact Ian Reeves, Contact

Clyde Broadcast Products Ltd
15 North Avenue, Clydebank Business Park, Clydebank G81 2QP
t 0141 952 7950 **f** 0141 941 1224
e mail@clydebroadcast.com **w** www.clydebroadcast.com

Courtyard Electronics
Unit 13, Riverside Park, Farnham GU9 7UG
t 01252 712030 **f** 01252 722060
e info@courtyard.co.uk **w** www.courtyard.co.uk
Contact Steve Cranny, Sales Director

Crystal Sound Ltd
Meadow View, Wramplingham, Wymondham NR18 ORU
t 01603 757628 **f** 01603 759339 **m** 07789 416226
e sales@crystal-sound.co.uk **w** www.crystal-sound.co.uk
Contact David Smith, Director

Crystal Vision Ltd
Lion Technology Park, Station Road East, Whittlesford, Cambridge CB2 4NL
t 01223 497049 **f** 01223 497059
e sales@crystalvision.tv **w** www.crystalvision.tv
Contact Bill Trevelyan, International Sales Manager; Philip Scofield, Managing Director; Ray Davis, UK Sales Manager; Stewart McGhie, Technical Sales Manager

Cynergy Broadcast Ltd
Unit 1&2 Pelham Court, London Road, Marlborough SN8 2AG
t 01672 511477 **f** 01672 511474 **m** 07740 928 441
e info@cynergy.co.uk **w** www.cynergy.co.uk
Contact Ian Cunliffe, Sales Director

Digi Consoles
The School House, 4 Dorking Road, Epsom KT18 7LX
t 01372 845600 **f** 01372 845656
e sales@soundtracs.com **w** www.digiconsoles.com
Contact Todd Wells, Managing Director; James Gordon, Digital Sales Manager; Robert Doyle, Managing Director

Digital Audio Research Ltd
Harman International Industries Ltd, Cranbourne House, Cranbourne Road, Potters Bar EN6 3JN
t 01707 665000 **f** 01707 660742
e mail@dar.com **w** www.dar.uk.com
Contact Michael Parker, Managing Director

DK-Audio (UK) Ltd
t 0870 241 4118 **f** 0870 241 4119
e apa@dk-audio.com **w** www.dk-audio.com

Dolby Laboratories
Interface, Wootton Bassett SN4 8QJ
t 01793 842100 **f** 01793 842101
e info@dolby.co.uk **w** www.dolby.com

Drake Electronics Ltd
26-28 Hydeway, Welwyn Garden City AL7 3UQ
t 01727 871200 **t** 01707 371266 **m** 07802 504321
e broadcast@drake-uk.com **w** www.drake-uk.com
Contact Maurice De Jonghe, Sales Manager; Karlie Miles, Business Development Manager; Stephen Rodway, Business Development Manager

DTL Broadcast Ltd
Johnson's Estate, Silverdale Road, Hayes UB3 3BA
t 020 8813 5200 **f** 020 8813 5022
e info@dtl-broadcast.com **w** www.dtl-broadcast.com

Dubois Ltd
Arkwright Road, Corby NN17 5AE
t 01536 263653 **f** 01536 2744899
e sales@dubois.co.uk **w** www.amaray.com
Contact William Millen, Contact

E2V Technologies
106 Waterhouse Lane, Chelmsford CM1 2QU
t 01245 493493 **f** 01245 492492
e enquiries@e2vtechnologies.com **w** www.e2vtechnologies.com
Contact Barton Burmond, Publicity Manager; Ann Marsh, Publicity Manager

Edifis
The Old Bakery, Hyde End Lane, Brimpton, Reading RG7 4RH
t 0118 971 2279 **f** 0118 971 2239 **m** 07968 191473
e richard@edifis.com **w** www.edifis.com
Contact Richard Lilley, Sales Director

Electronic Visuals
25 Boundary Way, Woking GU21 5DH
t 01483 771663 **f** 01483 750358 **m** 07710 056860
e info@electronic-visuals.com **w** www.electronic-visuals.com
Contact Stuart Fordham, Sales & Marketing Director

Euphonix
2 Gayton Road, Harrow HA1 2XU
t 020 8901 7510 **f** 020 8901 7511 **m** 07968 470994
e rusty@euphonix.com **w** www.euphonix.com
Contact Jon Stansfield, Digital Product Specialist; Miles Roberts, Managing Director; Rusty Waite, VP International Sales; Jenny Langridge, Aministration Manager; John Gallen, UK Sales Manager; Ken Lancashire, Technical Manager

Flash Television Control Systems
12 Saint Kildas Road, Brentwood CM15 9EX
t 01277 218519 **f** 01277 261117
e sales@flashtcs.com **w** www.flashtcs.com
Contact Graham Roberts, Sales Manager

For A UK Ltd
Unit C71, Barwell Business Park, Leatherhead Road, Chessington KT9 2NY
t 020 8391 7979 **f** 020 8391 7978
e info@for-a.co.uk **w** www.for-a.co.uk
Contact Morecraft, Sales and Marketing Manager; M Tsuchiyama, Sales & Marketing Manager

Formula Sound
Ashton Road, Bredbury, Stockport SK6 2SR
t 01614 945650 **f** 01614 945651
e info@formula-sound.com **w** www.formula-sound.com
Contact Sandra Cockell, Sales Director

Gee Broadcast Systems Ltd
Unit 9, Grafton Way, Basingstoke RG22 6HY
t 01256 810123 **f** 01256 810061
e sales@geebroadcast.co.uk **w** www.geebroadcast.co.uk

Gigawave
Gigawave Technical Centre, Earls Colne Business Park, Colchester CO6 2NS
t 01787 223300 **f** 01787 222002
e sales@gigawave.co.uk **w** www.gigawave.co.uk
Contact Garis James, Sales Manager

Grass Valley
Thomson House, 348 Edinburgh Avenue, Slough SL1 4TU
t 01753 518200 **f** 01753 518400 **m** 07887 544677
e sales@thmulti.co.uk **w** www.thomsongrassvalley.com
Contact Richard Hartley, Marketing Director; Neils Thomas, Sales Director; Paul Wright, Service Director; David Phillips, Managing Director

Greenway
62 Wheelers Green Way, Thatcham RG19 4YF
t 01635 876500 **f** 01635 873453
e sales@greenway.co.uk **w** www.greenway.co.uk
Contact Richard Crosoer, Director

Hamlet Video International Ltd
Orchard House, Amersham Road, Chesham HP5 1NE
t 01494 793763 **f** 01494 791283
e sales@hamlet.co.uk **w** www.hamlet.co.uk
Contact Steve Nunney, Managing Director; Anna Louise Bird, Sales Manager; Steve Rutherford, Sales

Harris Broadcast
Kingfisher Way, Hinchingbrooke Business Park, Huntingdon PE29 6HB
t 01480 420200 **f** 01480 420300
e firstname.surname@harris.com **w** www.harris.com
Contact John Coubrough, Operations Director

Hawk-Woods

32 Brinkley Road, Worcester Park KT4 8JF
t 020 8335 3755 **f** 020 8330 5659
e clive@hawkwoods.com **w** www.hawkwoods.com
Contact Clive Hawkins, Director

Hitachi Denshi (UK)

The Garrick Centre, Irving Way, Hendon, London NW9 6AQ
t 020 8202 4311 **f** 020 8202 2451
e sales@hitachi-denshi-uk.com **w** www.hitachi-denshi-uk.com
Contact Richard Henwood, Sales Manager; Alex Svenson, Imaging Process
Sales Manager

Ian P Kinloch & Company Ltd

14 Commercial Road, Reading RG2 0QJ
t 0118 933 6500 **f** 0118 933 6501
e sales@ipk-broadcast.co.uk **w** www.ipk-broadcast.co.uk
Contact Ian Kinloch, Managing Director; Stephen Ellis, Sales Director

IFR Ltd

Longacres House, Six Hills Way, Stevenage SG1 2AN
t 01438 742200 **f** 01438 727601
e info@aeroflex.com **w** www.aeroflex.com

Ikegami Electronics UK

Unit E1, Brooklands Close, Sunbury-on-Thames TW16 7EB
t 01932 769700 **f** 01932 769710 **m** 07980 917451
e sales@ikegami.co.uk **w** www.ikegami.co.uk

Instant Pop-up Shelters Ltd

Units 1-3 Gowt Bank, Wrangle, Boston PE22 9BZ
t 0845 130 4242 **f** 08700 115353
e sales@instantshelters.co.uk **w** www.instantshelters.co.uk
Credits World Is Not Enough (F); Captain Corelli's Mandolin (F); Harry Potter
And The Philosopher's Stone (F); Band Of Brothers (T)

Integrated Broadcast Information Systems

Dunley Hill Court, Ranmore, Dorking RH5 6SX
t 01483 280208 **f** 01483 280244
e andrew.winter@ibistv.co.uk **w** www.ibistv.com
Contact Andrew Winter, Director of Marketing; Penny Westlake, Business Development

IPK Broadcast Systems

14 Commercial Road, Reading RG2 0QJ
t 0118 933 6500 **f** 0118 933 6501
e sales@ipk-broadcast.co.uk **w** www.ipk-broadcast.co.uk
Contact Ian Kinloch, Managing Director

Isotrack

21A Hankinson Road, Bournemouth BH9 1HJ
t 01202 247000 **f** 01202 247001 **e** proguide@isotrack.com
Contact Jonathan Finney, Proprietor

James Thomas Engineering

Navigation Complex, Navigation Road, Diglis Trading Estate
WR5 3DE
t 01905 363 600 **f** 01905 363 601
e info@jamesthomas.co.uk **w** www.jthomaseng.com
Contact Mervyn Thomas, General Manager

Kef Audio (UK)

Eccleston Road, Tovil, Maidstone ME15 6QP
t 01622 672261 **f** 01622 750653
e enquiries@kef.com **w** www.kef.com
Contact Steven Halsall, Marketing Director

Kezvale

Unit 5, Johnson's Estate, Silverdale Road, Hayes UB3 3BA
t 020 8569 2731 **f** 020 8569 2790 **m** 07976 249148
Contact M Aslam, Managing Director

Langley Design

e info@langley-design.com **w** www.langley-design.com

Leitch Europe Ltd

Holland Park House, Oldbury, Bracknell RG12 8TQ
t 01344 446000 **f** 01344 446100
e sales.europe@leitch.com **w** www.leitch.com
Contact Nigel Booth, Director of Business Development; Barry Todd, Managing
Director; Dave Dougall, Director of Sales and Marketing; Tom Gittins, Regional
Sales Manager, UK; Kelvin Bolah, Market Manager, Post Production

Lemo UK

12 North Street, Worthing BN11 1DU
t 01903 234543 **f** 01903 206231
e lemouk@lemo.com **w** www.lemo.ch
Contact Gillian James, Contact

Lund Halsey Console Systems Ltd

Gatehouse Close, Aylesbury HP19 8DE
t 01296 489964 **f** 01296 392284
e kudos@lundhalsey.com **w** www.lundhalsey.com
Contact Chris Lund, Director

Lynden Micros Ltd

Unit 48, New Forest Enterprise Centre, Totton SO40 9LA
t 02380 663200 **f** 02380 864659
e sales@lynden.co.uk **w** www.lynden.co.uk
Contact John Futter, Director

Matrox VIT Ltd

Sefton Park, Stoke Poges SL2 4JS
t 01753 665500 **f** 01753 665599
e video.info.uk@matrox.com **w** www.matrox.com/video

Media 100

Unit 11, Bracknell Beeches, Old Bracknell Lane, Bracknell RG12 7BW
t 01344 412812 **f** 01344 424936
e eurosales@media100.com **w** www.media100.co.uk
Contact Carole Ford, Internal Sales Manager; Rob Pickering, Director, Europe;
Stuart Winterbottom, Commercial Director, Europe; Pete Shaw, Marketing Director,
Europe; Paul Saint, Channel Sales Manager; Shelli Winterton, Finance Manager

Melford Electronics Ltd

Unit 14, Blenheim Road, Cressex Business Park, High Wycombe
HP12 3RS
t 01494 638069 **f** 01494 463358 **m** 07798 501358
e info@melford-elec.co.uk **w** www.melford-elec.co.uk
Contact Richard George, Managing Director; Curtis Bigg, Sales Director

MI Broadcast

Lincoln House, The Paddocks, 347 Cherry Hinton Road,
Cambridge CB1 8DH
t 01223 411625 **f** 01223 410007
e sales@tac4.com **w** www.tac4.com
Contact Robert Mackman, Broadcast Sales

Michael Stevens & Partners Ltd

Invicta Works, Elliott Road, Bromley BR2 9NT
t 020 8460 7299 **f** 020 8460 0499
e sales@michael-stevens.com **w** www.michael-stevens.com
Contact Deborah Lehmani, Export Sales Manager; Simon Adamson, Sales Manager

Microvideo Ltd

Old Farm Offices, Copley Hill Farm, Cambridge Road,
Babraham CB2 4AF
t 01223 834119 **f** 01223 834471 **m** 07776 144710
e sales@microvideo.co.uk **w** www.microvideo.co.uk
Contact Mike Dawson, Sales; Ric Brunwin, Managing Director

Miranda Technologies Ltd

Henderson House, Hithercroft Road, Wallingford OX10 9DG
t 01491 820000 **f** 01491 820001
e sales@miranda.com **w** www.miranda.com
Contact Nick Pywell, UK Sales Director

Murraypro Electronics
8 Glamorgan Road, Hampton Wick KT1 4HP
t 020 8943 1920 **e** sales@murraypro.com
Contact Tony Drummond-Murray, Proprietor

MW Video Systems Ltd
64 North Street, Fritwell OX27 7QR
t 01869 345222 **f** 01869 346002
e sales@mw-video.com **w** www.mw-video.com
Contact Brian Speck, Managing Director

Panasonic Broadcast Europe Ltd
West Forrest Gate, Wellington Road, Wokingham RG40 2AQ
t 01189 029222 **f** 01189 029348
e info@panasonic-pbe.co.uk **w** www.panasonic-broadcast.com

Pandora International Ltd
The Old Rectory, Springhead Road, Northfleet DA11 8HN
t 01474 561000 **f** 01474 566935
e sales@pandora-int.com **w** www.pogle.pandora-int.com
Contact Aine Marsland

Pebble Beach Systems Ltd
Robert Denholm House, Bletchingley Road, Nutfield RH1 4HW
t 01737 821522 **f** 01737 822202
e sales@pebble.tv **w** www.pebble.tv
Contact Peter Hajittofi, Managing Director; Ian Cockett, Technical Director; Julian Hepworth, Software Development Director

Penny & Giles Controls Ltd
Units 35-36, Nine Mile Point Industrial Estate, Cwmfelinfach, Newport NP11 7HZ
t 01495 202080 **f** 01495 202006
e studio.sales@pgcontrols.com **w** www.pgcontrols.com
Contact Andrew Clarke, Product Manager

Pharos Communications Ltd
44 West Street, Reading RG1 1TZ
t 0118 950 2323 **f** 0118 950 2525
e sales@pharos-comms.com **w** www.pharos-comms.com
Contact Roger Heath, Director

Photon Beard Ltd
Unit K3, Cherry Court Way, Stanbridge Road, Leighton Buzzard LU7 4UH
t 01525 850911 **f** 01525 850922
e info@photonbeard.com **w** www.photonbeard.com
Contact Peter Daffarn, Sales Director; Mike Perry, Dealer Manager; Alan Gooch, Sales and Marketing Director

Our service to image makers does not end with lighting manufacture, we also design and install studio lighting rigs for all types of studios and applications worldwide. Our list of successful projects includes work for state broadcasters and global corporations both in the UK and abroad. Ask for detailed catalogue.

Pixel Power Ltd
College Business Park, Coldhams Lane, Cambridge CB1 3HD
t 01223 721000 **f** 01223 721111
e enquiries@pixelpower.com **w** www.pixelpower.com
Contact Ollie Hough, Creative Specialist; Nicholas Ashley, Area Sales Manager; James Gilbert, Director, Commercial Director; Richard Jones, Area Sales Manager; Justin Moat, Area Sales Manager

PMD Magnetics
Magnetics House, Avenue Farm Industrial Estate, Stratford-upon-Avon CV37 0HR
t 01789 268579 **f** 01789 414450 **e** sales@pmdmagnetics.co.uk
Contact Veronica Finch, Sales Director

Prospect Electronics Ltd
Canterbury House, Waterside Court, Medway City Estate, Rochester ME2 4NZ
t 01634 717273 **f** 01634 716900
e sales@prospect-electronics.com
w www.prospect-electronics.com
Contact Malcolm Rankin, Managing Director

Proximity Europe
Bankshill House, Bankshill DG11 2QA
t 01576 710628 **f** 01576 710628 **m** 07855 429772
e eamesales@proximitygroup.com **w** www.proximitygroup.com
Contact Luke Tristram, Group CEO; Andy Ioannou, Managing Director

Quantel Ltd
Turnpike Road, Newbury RG14 2NX
t 01635 48222 **f** 01635 815815
e quantel@quantel.com **w** www.quantel.com
Contact Jim Totman, Sales Manager; Russell Barlow, Sales Manager; Nigel Richards, Sales Manager; Martin Mulligan, Sales Director; Roger Thornton, Corporate Relations; Vince Eade, Sales Manager

Quartz Electronics Ltd
59 Suttons Business Park, Reading RG6 1AZ
t 0118 935 0200 **f** 0118 935 0202
e sales@quartzuk.com **w** www.quartzuk.com
Contact Simon Reed, Technical Director; June Lovelock, Sales Support; Michael Hall, Sales and Marketing Manager

R&R Broadcast Systems
110-121 Belgrave Road, Portswood, Southampton SO17 3AN
t 01489 581580 **f** 01489 572716
e sales@rrbroadcast.com **w** www.rrbroadcast.com
Contact Rod Turner, Managing Director; Marvin Lane; Rob Clarke

Radamec Broadcast Systems
t 561181 **e** info@radamecbroadcast.co.uk **w** www.radamec.co.uk
Contact Mike Wolfe, Managing Director

Raycom
Technology House, 16 Tything Road, Arden Forest Industrial Estate, Alcester B49 6EP
t 01789 400600 **f** 01789 400630
e chris@raycom.co.uk **w** www.raycom.co.uk
Contact Ray Withers, Managing Director; Chris Pemberton, General Manager

Rohde & Schwarz UK Ltd
Ancells Business Park, Fleet GU51 2UZ
t 01252 818818 **f** 01252 818819
e sales@rohdeschwarz.com **w** www.rohde-schwarz.com
Contact Ian David, Production Specialist; John Surtees

RTI UK
6 Swan Wharf, Waterloo Road, Uxbridge UB8 2RA
t 07000 478485 **f** 01895 274692
e inbox@rtiuk.co.uk **w** www.rtico.com
Contact Mark McMullon, Senior Operations Manager

Shep Associates Ltd
Long Barn, North End, Meldrith, Royston SG8 6NT
t 01763 261686 **f** 01763 262154
e dgs02@globalnet.co.uk **w** www.shep.co.uk
Contact Derek Stoddart, Managing Director

Shootview Ltd
87 Cadbury Road, Sunbury-on-Thames TW16 7LS
t 01932 782823 **f** 01932 772824
e sales@shootview.com **w** www.shootview.com

Sifam
Woodland Road, Torquay TQ2 7AY
t 01803 407700 **f** 01803 407699
e info@sifam.com **w** www.sifam.com
Contact Nigel Vaughan, Managing Director; Katie Waller

Snell & Wilcox Ltd
6 Old Lodge Place, St Margarets, Twickenham TW1 1RQ
t 020 8917 4300 **f** 020 8607 9466
e info@snellwilcox.com **w** www.snellwilcox.com

Sony Broadcast & Professional Europe
Jays Close, Viables, Basingstoke RG22 4SB
t 01256 355011 **f** 01256 474585 **w** www.pro.sony-europe.com
Contact Ian Collis, Head of Broadcast Business

Sony United Kingdom Ltd
The Heights, Brooklands, Weybridge KT13 0XW
t 01932 816000 **f** 01932 817000 **w** www.sony.co.uk
Contact Pam Dhariwal, Customer Relations Manager

Soundcraft Electronics
Cranborne House, Cranborne Road, Potters Bar EN6 3JN
t 01707 665000 **f** 01707 660742
e info@soundcraft.com **w** www.soundcraft.com

SysMedia Ltd
Gatwick House, Peeks Brook Lane, Horley RH6 9ST
t 01293 814200 **f** 01293 814300
e sales@sysmedia.com **w** www.sysmedia.com
Contact Amanda Spicer, Sales and Marketing Administrator; Jonathan Swift, Major Accounts Executive
Credits SkyText (W)

Teletest Ltd
4 Shelley Road, Bournemouth BH1 4HY
t 01202 646100 **f** 01202 646101
e sales@teletest.co.uk **w** www.teletest.co.uk
Contact Nick Rose, Managing Director

Telford Technical Research Ltd
84 Bridge Road, Chertsey KT16 8LA
t 01932 564063 **f** 01932 885182
e sales@ttr.co.uk **w** www.ttr.co.uk
Contact Terry Sargeant, Managing Director

A **● THOMSON** BRAND

Thomson Broadcast Ltd
Thomson House, 348 Edinburgh Avenue, Slough SL1 4TU
t 01753 518200 **f** 01753 518400
e sales@thmulti.co.uk **w** www.thomsongrassvalley.com
Contact Mel Noonan, Sales Manager; David Phillips, Managing Director; Niels Thomas, Sales Director; Paul Wright, Service Director

Thurlby Thandar Instruments (TTI)
Glebe Road, Huntingdon PE29 7DR
t 01480 412451 **f** 01480 450409
e sales@tti-test.com **w** www.tti-test.com
Contact Mark Edwards, Sales Manager

TL Audio
2 Iceni Court, Icknield Way, Letchworth SG6 1TN
t 01462 492090 **f** 01462 492097
e info@tlaudio.co.uk **w** www.tlaudio.co.uk

Trilogy Broadcast
26 Focus Way, Andover SP10 5NY
t 01264 384000 **f** 01264 334806 **w** www.trilogy-broadcast.co.uk
Contact Barry Spencer, Sales Manager

Vortex Communications
75 The Grove, Ealing, London W5 5LL
t 020 8579 2743 **f** 020 8840 0018
e info@vtx.co.uk **w** www.vtx.co.uk
Contact Ian Prowse, Sales

Weircliffe International
Weircliffe Park, St Andrews Road, Exwick, Exeter EX4 2AG
t 01392 272132 **f** 01392 413511
e sales@weircliffe.co.uk **w** www.weircliffe.co.uk
Contact Jane Natolie, Marketing Manager

Equipment Manufacture Broadcast Compliance

Harding**FPA**
broadcast flash & pattern analyser

Cambridge Research Systems
80 Riverside Estate, Sir Thomas Longley Road, Rochester ME2 4BH
t 01634 720707 **f** 01634 720719
e enquiries@hardingfpa.co.uk **w** www.hardingfpa.co.uk
Contact Tony Carpenter
Flash and Pattern Analyser ensures ITC Compliance. Diagnostic Tool highlights accurate, creative fixes.

Dwight Cavendish Systems Ltd
The Icon, Lytton Way, Stevenage SG1 1AH
t 01438 364601 **f** 01438 311190
e admin@dwightcav.com **w** www.dwightcav.com
Contact Mazen Abdin, Managing Director

Equipment Second Hand

TNP Broadcast
Watford, Hertfordshire
t 01923 712712 **f** 01923 712777 **m** 07973 729423
e sales@tnpbroadcast.co.uk **w** www.tnpbroadcast.co.uk
Contact Tim Constable, Sales Executive; Garry Martin, Sales Executive; Howard Rose, Managing Director; Matt Robins, Sales Executive

Equipment Training

Farnborough College of Technology
Boundary Road, Farnborough GU14 6SB
t 01252 407270 **f** 01252 407271 **m** 07812 205225
e f.marden@farn-ct.ac.uk **w** www.farn-ct.ac.uk
Contact Alan Harding, Head of School; Fred Marden

Grimsby College
Nun's Corner, Laceby Road, Grimsby DN34 5BQ
t 01472 311222 **e** nicil@grimsby.ac.uk
Contact Lia Nici, Media Training Manager
Credits Skillset NVQ Training Courses (E)

Hatchet Music
176 Dereham Road, Norwich NR2 3AJ
t 01603 621882 **e** mark@hatchetmusic.co.uk
Contact Mark Narayn

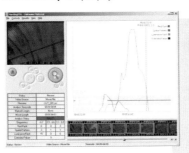
Picture Canning Company
55 Bendon Valley, London SW18 4LZ
t 020 8874 9277 **f** 020 8874 6623
e info@picturecanning.co.uk **w** www.picturecanning.co.uk
Contact Leslie Zunz, Managing Director; Paul Taylor, General Manager; Phil Wade, Managing Director
Credits Escape To The Country (D); Watchdog (T); Is Harry On The Boat (T); Holiday (D)

Signals Media Arts
Victoria Chambers, St Runwald Street, Colchester CO1 1HF
t 01206 560255 **f** 01206 369086
e admin@signals.org.uk **w** www.signals.org.uk
Contact Anita Bell, Director; Anita Bell, Acting Director
Credits Lorries & Towns Don't Mix (D); Miss Roberts (D)

Martin Uren
42 Carden Avenue, Brighton BN1 8NA
t 01273 501113 **m** 07850 994821 **e** martin.uren@ntlworld.com

VectorCommand Ltd
New Lane, Havant PO9 2LY
t 02392 449100 **f** 02392 449149
e info@vectorcommand.com **w** www.vectorcommand.com
Contact Mike Griffin, Technical Director

West Herts Media Centre
South Way, Leavesden WD25 7LZ
t 01923 681602 **f** 01923 681602
e mediacentre@westherts.ac.uk
w www.mediacentre.westherts.ac.uk
Contact Keri Jordan, Media Training Co-ordinator; Jan Spencer, Media Centre Manager; Drew Hart Shea, Technical Operations Co-ordinator; Richard Yeoman Clark, Technical Operations Co-ordinator

Film & Video Stock

Adlais
PO Box 21, Cardigan SA43 3YE
t 01239 622921 **f** 01239 622922 **m** 07768 568665
Contact Rhodri Dafis, Director

APR Video Tapes
Lea House, Frobisher Way, Taunton TA2 6BB
t 01823 251831 **f** 01823 324060
e info@aprvideo.co.uk **w** www.aprvideo.co.uk
Contact Andy Reed, Sales

Archive Film Agency
21 Lidgett Park Avenue, Leeds LS8 1EU
t 0113 266 2454 **t** 0113 268 4782 **f** 0113 266 2454
e archivefilmagency@mail.com
Contact Agnese Geoghegan, Managing Director

Carousel
Unit S-One, Inchbrook Trading Estate, Woodchester, Stroud GL5 5EY
t 0800 731 6964 **f** 01453 835508
e sales@carousel.uk.com **w** www.carousel.uk.com
Contact Rawdon Cowley, Managing Director

CCK Video Services Ltd
3 Gilbert Street, London W1Y 1RB
t 020 7495 7005 **t** 020 7409 1808
e sales@cckvideo.co.uk **w** www.cckvideo.co.uk
Contact Frank Casali; Carlo Rosso

Creative Video Associates
CVA House, 2 Cooper Road, Thornbury, Bristol BS35 3UP
t 01454 410255 **f** 01454 281868
e sales@cva.co.uk **w** www.cva.co.uk
Contact Shelly Bees, Sales Coordinator
Video tape recycling service and tape sales at competitive prices.

Emtec Magnetics UK Ltd
40 The Green, South Bar, Banbury OX16 9AE
t 01295 227800 **f** 01295 252540 **m** 07990 546903
e ian.armstrong@emtec-group.com
w www.emtec-group.com; www.mtc-open.net
Contact Kris Jessiman, Broadcast; Ian Armstrong, Applications Engineer Manager; Alan Morton

The Film Game
70 Wardour Street, London W1F 0TB
t 020 7494 9922 **f** 020 7494 9944
e mike.doyle@filmgame.co.uk **w** www.filmgame.co.uk
Contact Peter Hopkins, Managing Director
Credits Down To Earth (T); Fakers (F); If Only (F); Spooks (T)

Film Stock Centre Blanx
70 Wardour Street, London W1F 0TB
t 020 7494 2244 **f** 020 7287 2040 **m** 07831 701407
e sales@fscblanx.co.uk
Contact Pete Hopkins, Manager

First 4 Media
128 Kingston Road, Leatherhead KT22 7PU
t 0845 330 4500 **f** 0800 181347
e sales@first4media.com **w** www.first4media.com
Contact Louise Sibley, Marketing

Fuji Photo Film (UK) Ltd
Fujifilm House, 125 Finchley Road, London NW3 6HY
t 020 7586 5900 **f** 020 7722 4259
e mmorrow@fuji.co.uk **w** www.fujifilm.co.uk/motion
Contact Michelle Green; Millie Morrow, Marketing Administrator

Ilford Imaging (UK) Ltd
Town Lane, Mobberley, Knutsford WA16 7JL
t 01565 684000 **e** uk.sales@ilford.com **w** www.ilford.com
Contact Chris Taylor, Sales Executive

Jack Roe (LS) Ltd
Popular House, Peterstow, Ross-on-Wye HR9 6JR
t 01989 567474 **f** 01989 762206
e sandie@jack-roe.co.uk **w** www.jack-roe.co.uk
Contact Jonathan Worthing, Service Manager; Sandie Caffelle, Head of Sales

Kodak Ltd
PO Box 66, Station Road, Hemel Hempstead HP1 1JU
t 01442 845945 **f** 01442 844458 **w** www.kodak.com/go/motion
Contact Nicky Silver, Sales and Marketing Secretary

Massey AV
117-119 Chiswick High Road, Chiswick, London W4 2ED
t 020 8994 1317 **f** 020 8742 1456
Contact Vic Field, Shop Manager

Maxell Europe Ltd
3A High Street, Rickmansworth WD3 1HR
t 01923 494400 **f** 01923 494410
e sales@maxell.eu.com **w** www.maxell.eu.com
Contact Alex Buchanan, Uk Broadcast Sales Manager; Andy Houghton, European Engineering &Technical Support Manager; Mick Martin, European Sales and Marketing Manager

On-Air Systems Ltd
The Media Centre, 131-151 Great Titchfield Street, London W1W 5BB
t 020 7663 3663 **f** 020 7663 3664
w www.on-air-systems.com

Pak Box Stores Ltd
Unit 19, Oliver Business Park, Oliver Road, Park Royal, London NW10 7JB
t 020 8965 8111 **f** 020 8965 8222 **w** www.pakbox.co.uk
Contact David Cooper, Manager

PF Audio Visual
7 Dunrobin Court, Clydebank Business Park, Glasgow G81 2QP
t 0141 951 1811 **f** 0141 951 1587
e sales@pfav.co.uk **w** www.pfav.co.uk

Sound & Video Services (uk) Ltd
Shentonfield Road, Sharston Industrial Estate, Manchester M22 4RW
t 0161 491 6660 **f** 0161 491 6669
e sales@svsmedia.com **w** www.svsmedia.com
Contact Mike Glasspole, Managing Director; John Cooper, Sales Director

Tibet Foundation
1 St James' Market, London SW1Y 4SB
t 020 7930 6001 **f** 0 7930 6002
e enquiries@tibet-foundation.org **w** www.tibet-foundation.org
Contact Karma Hardy, Director
Credits Modern Tibetan Language (E); The Dalai Lama (S); Tibetan Performing Arts (T); Tibet 1959-1999 (D)

Topham Film & Engineering
316-318 Latimer Road, London W10 6QN
t 020 8960 0123 **f** 020 8969 3714
e caseysv@aol.com **w** www.caseys.co.uk
Contact John Casey, Managing Director

Transco Group T/A First4Media
First4Media House, 128 Kingston Road, Leatherhead KT22 7PU
t 01372 825000 **t** 0845 330 4500 **f** 01372 825050
f 0 8001 81347 **w** www.first4media.com
Contact Ruth Walkerhill, Sales Supervisor

Twinglobe
228-230 Uxbridge Rd, London W12 7JD
t 020 8743 5528 **f** 020 8742 9525 **e** twinglobe@aol.com
Contact M Thakerar, Director; D Thakerar, Director

Film & Video Stock Recycling

Creative Video Associates
CVA House, 2 Cooper Road, Thornbury, Bristol BS35 3UP
t 01454 410255 **f** 01454 281868
e sales@cva.co.uk **w** www.cva.co.uk
Contact Shelly Bees, Sales Coordinator
Video tape recycling service and tape sales at competitive prices.

FILM COMMISSIONS

Bath Film Office
Trimbridge House, Trim Street, Bath BA1 2DP
t 01225 477711 **f** 01225 477279 **m** 07770 962878
e bath_filmoffice@bathnes.gov.uk **w** www.visitbath.co.uk
Contact Maggie Ainley, Film Commissioner

Edinburgh Film Focus
63 George Street, Edinburgh EH2 2JG
t 0131 622 7337 **f** 0131 622 7338
e info@edinfilm.com **w** www.edinfilm.com
Contact Lucy Quinton, Marketing; Ros Davis, Production Liaison Manager;
Heather MacIntyre, Information Manager

The Film Council
10 Little Portland Street, London W1W 7JG
t 020 7861 7861 **f** 020 7861 7862
e info@filmcouncil.org.uk **w** www.filmcouncil.org.uk
Contact John Woodward, Chief Executive Officer; Paul Trijbits, Head of New
Cinema Fund; Jenny Borgars, Head of Development Fund; Helen Bagnall, Head
of Training Fund; Robert Jones, Head of Premier Fund
Credits The Magdalene Sisters (F); Ted And Sylvia (F); Bloody Sunday (F);
Gosford Park (F)

Guernsey Film Commision
Raymond Falla House, PO Box 459, Longue Rue, St Martins,
Guernsey GY1 6AF
t 01481 234567 **f** 01481 235015
e tony@guernseyfilms.com **w** www.guernseyfilms.com
Contact Tony Brassell; Emma Allen

IFB (Irish Film Board)
Rockfort House, St Augustine Street, Galway, Rep of Ireland
t 561398 **f** 561405 **e** louise@filmboard.ie **w** www.filmboard.ie
Contact Rod Stoneman, Chief Executive
Credits Song For A Raggy Boy (F); The Actors (F); Bloody Sunday (F); The
Magdalene Sisters (F)

Isle of Man Film Commission
First Floor, Hamilton House, Peel Road, Douglas IM1 5EP
t 01624 687173 **f** 01624 687171
e filmcomm@dti.gov.im **w** www.gov.im/dti/iomfilm
Contact Kim Fletcher, Film Officer; Hilary Dugdale, Projects Manager; Nick
Cain, Contracts Manager

London Borough of Havering
Town Hall, Main Road, Romford RM1 3BD
t 01708 432255
Contact Loraine Rossati, Film Liaison Officer

London Film Commission
20 Euston Centre, Regent's Place, London NW1 3JH
t 020 7387 8787 **f** 020 7387 8788
e lfc@london-film.co.uk **w** www.london-film.co.uk
Contact Sue Hayes, Film Commissioner; Daniela Kirchner, Head of Strategy
& Information; Julia Willis, Production Co-ordinator; Harvey Edgington, Head of
Borough Liaison; Rachel Whitburn, Borough Liaison Officer

North West Vision
BBC North, Room 2102, New Broadcasting House, Oxford
Road, Manchester M60 1SJ
t 0161 244 4560 **f** 0161 244 4559
e manchester@ftcnorthwest.co.uk **e** andys@northwestvision.co.uk
w www.northwestvision.co.uk
Contact Belinda Peach, Media Development Manager; Andrew Swarbrick

North Wales Film Commission
Mentec, Deiniol Road, Bangor LL57 2UP
t 01248 353769 **f** 01248 352497 **m** 07766 421576
e film@gwynedd.gov.uk **w** www.filmnorthwales.com
Contact Sioned Eleri Jones, Web/Office Manager; Arwyn Williams, Information
Manager; Carwyn Edwards, Film Commissioner; Hugh Jones, Commissioner
Credits Kasam Se (F); Dinotopia (T); Lara Croft And The Cradle Of Life: Tomb
Raider 2 (F); Happy Now (F)

North West Vision
109 Mount Pleasant, Liverpool L3 5TF
t 0151 708 8099 **f** 0151 708 9859 **m** 07976 629 934
e julieb@ftcnorthwest.co.uk **w** www.ftcnorthwest.co.uk
Contact Alice Morrison, Chief Executive

Northern Ireland Film Commission
3rd Floor, Alfred House, 21 Alfred Street, Belfast BT2 8ED
t 028 9023 2444 **f** 028 9023 9918
e info@nifc.co.uk **w** www.nifc.co.uk
Contact Joanne Holland; Nial Fulton; Andrew Reid, Head of Locations

Scottish Highlands & Islands Film Commission
Inverness Castle, Inverness IV2 3EG
t 01463 710637 **f** 01463 710848
e trish@scotfilm.org **w** www.scotfilm.org
Contact Jenny Yeomans, Film Liaison Officer
Credits Rock Face (T); Harry Potter And The Chamber Of Secrets (F); Monarch
Of The Glen (T)

Wales Screen Commission
Comisiwn Sgrîn Cymru

A ONE-STOP SHOP FOR LOCATIONS IN WALES

FREEFONE | **0800 849 8848**

www.walesscreencommission.co.uk

Screen East

South Way, Leavesden WD25 7LZ
t 01923 495051 **f** 01923 333007
e locations@screeneast.co.uk **w** www.screeneast.co.uk
Contact Haley Morgan, Film Liaison Officer; Katy Bishop, Film Liaison Officer; Samantha Perahia, Office & Information Manager; Chris Holt, Head Of Locations

Screen West Midlands

31-41 Bromley Street, Birmingham B9 4AN
t 0121 766 1470 **f** 0121 766 1480
e info@screenwm.co.uk **w** www.screenwm.co.uk
Contact Sue Richardson, Marketing Officer

Screen Yorkshire

40 Hanover Square, Leeds LS3 1BQ
t 0113 294 4410 **f** 0113 294 4989
Contact Emma Waite, Crew & Facilities Co-ordinator; Kaye Elliott, Production Liaison Manager; Jo Spreckley, CEO
Credits The Full Monty (F); The Hounds Of The Baskerville (T); Nicholas Nickleby (F); Calendar Girls (F)

South Wales Film Commission

The Media Centre, Culverhouse Cross, Cardiff CF5 6XJ
t 029 2059 0240 **f** 029 2059 0511
e southwalesfilm@compuserve.com
Contact Yvonne Cheal, Commissioner; Liam Hunt; David Lepla-Lewis

South West Scotland Screen Commission

Gracefield Arts Centre, 28 Edinburgh Road, Dumfries DG1 1JQ
t 01387 263666 **f** 01387 263666 **m** 07702 663297
e screencom@dumgal.gov.uk **w** www.sw-scotland-screen.com
Contact Claire Paterson, Locations Assistant; Belle Doyle, Film Officer
Credits Big Screen Britain (T); Horizon (T); 2000 Acres Of Sky (T); Magdalene Sisters (F)

South West Screen

St Bartholomews Court, Lewins Mead, Bristol BS1 5BT
t 0117 925 9977 **f** 0117 952 9988
e info@swscreen.co.uk **w** www.swscreen.co.uk
Contact Caroline Norbury, Chief Executive

Tower Hamlets Film Office

Brady Centre, 192 Hanbury Street, London E1 5HU
t 020 7364 7920 **f** 020 7364 7901 **m** 07958 304649
e filmsoffice@dial.pipex.com **w** www.towerhamlets.gov.uk
Contact Sarah Wren, Film Development Manager

Wales Screen Commission (Mid Wales Office)

Unit 6G, The Science Park, Cefn Llan, Aberystwyth SY23 3AH
t 01970 617995 **f** 01970 617942
e mathew@walesscreencommission.co.uk
e carys@walesscreencommission.co.uk
w www.walesscreencommission.co.uk
Contact Mathew Parry, Film Liaison Officer; Carys Hedd, Information Manager

Wales Screen Commission (National Enquiries)

t 0800 849 8848 **e** enquiries@walesscreencommission.co.uk
w www.walesscreencommission.co.uk

Wales Screen Commission (North Wales Office)

Mentec, Ffordd Deiniol, Bangor LL57 7UP
t 01248 353769 **f** 01248 352497
e film@gwynedd.gov.uk **w** www.walesscreencommission.co.uk
Contact Carwyn Edwards; Sioned Jones

Wales Screen Commission (South East Office)

C/o Sgrin, 10 Mount Stuart Square, Cardiff CF10 5EE
t 029 2043 5385 **f** 029 2043 5380
e penny@walesscreencommission.co.uk
e alison@walesscreencommission.co.uk
w www.walesscreencommission.co.uk
Contact Penny Skuse, Information Manager; Allison Dowzell, Film Liaison Manager

Wales Screen Commission (South West Office)

Media Technium, Gelli Aur SA38 8LR
t 01558 668573 **t** 01558 668308 **f** 01558 669003
e katherine@walesscreencommission.co.uk
e illtud@walesscreencommission.co.uk
w www.walesscreencommission.co.uk
Contact Illtud Llyr ap Dunsford, Information Manager; Katherine Thomas, Film Liaison Officer

Film Processing

Bucks Laboratories

714 Banbury Avenue, Slough SL1 4LR
t 01753 501500 **e** mail@bucks.co.uk **w** www.bucks.co.uk
Contact Dave Pitwell, Sales Director; Harry Rushton, Customer Services Director

Colour Film Services Ltd

10 Wadsworth Road, Perivale UB6 7JX
t 020 8998 2731 **f** 020 8997 8738
e johnward@colourfilmservices.co.uk
w www.colourfilmservices.co.uk
Contact Len Brown, Sales Executive; Steve Kyte, Post Production Contact; Jane Capp, Facilities Manager; Terry McCallum, Laboratory Manager; D Ward, Group Sales Manager
Credits Boy David (D); Lost in La Mancha (F); Only Fools And Horses (T)

Deluxe London

North Orbital Road, Denham, Uxbridge UB9 5HQ
t 01895 832323 **f** 01895 832446
e firstname_lastname@bydeluxe.com **w** www.bydeluxe.com
Contact Terry Lansbury, Director of Sales

Film Lab North

Croydon House, Croydon Street, Leeds LS11 9RT
t 0113 243 4842 **f** 0113 243 4323 **m** 07720 352049
e hnd@filmlabnorth.co.uk **w** www.filmlabnorth.co.uk
Contact Howard Dawson, Operations Manager; Peter Wright, General Manager
Credits Blue Planet (T); Where the Heart Is (T); Cutting It Series II (T); The Forsyte Saga (T)

Filmlab Group

Unit 1, CR Bates Industrial Estate, Wycombe Road, Stokenchurch HP14 3PD
t 01494 485271 **f** 01494 483079 **m** 07836 738853
e sue@filmlab.co.uk (for sales enquiries)
e chris@filmlab.co.uk (for all other enquiries)
w www.filmlab.co.uk
Contact Chris Brazier, Managing Director; Sue Cairns, Sales Executive

A wide range of post production equipment including Colourmaster motion picture film analysers, the Excalibur film/video post production management system, computerised laboratory systems via printernet and INPS and film processors.

UK FILM | COUNCIL

The **UK Film Council** is the strategic body for the development of film in the UK investing public money in film development, production, training, distribution and exhibition. The UK Film Council also co-funds a number of other organisations including the UK MEDIA Desk and the British Film Institute.

The UK Film Council established the **Regional Investment Fund for England** to channel public money for film to the English regions through a network of regional agencies. The Fund aims to promote and support local film industry and culture within each of the English regions by investing in the growth and expansion of production, exhibition, archives, education and training throughout the UK.

Information about the UK Film Council is available on its website www.filmcouncil.org.uk, or by applying directly to:

UK Film Council
10 Little Portland Street
London W1W 7JG
Tel: + 44 (0) 20 7861 7861
Fax: + 44 (0) 20 7861 7862

Regional Screen Agency contacts

Em-Media
Chief Executive: Ken Hay
35-37 St Mary's Gate
Nottingham NG1 1PU
Tel: 0115 934 9090
Fax: 0115 950 0988
Email: info@em-media.org.uk

Northern Film & Media
Chief Executive: Tom Harvey
Central Square
Forth Street
Newcastle-Upon-Tyne NE1 3PJ
Tel: 0191 269 9200
Fax: 0191 269 9213
Email: firstname@northernmedia.org

North West Vision
Chief Executive Alice Morrison
c/o FTC North West
109 Mount Pleasant
Liverpool L3 5TF
Tel: 0151 708 9858
Fax: 0151 708 9859
Email: firstnameinitialofsurname@northwestvision.co.uk

Screen East
Chief Executive: Laurie Hayward
Anglia House
Norwich NR1 3JG
Tel: 0845 601 5670
Fax: 01603 767191
Email: firstname@screeneast.co.uk

Screen South
Chief Executive: Gina Fegan
Folkestone Enterprise
Shearway Road
Folkestone
Kent CT19 4RH
Tel: 01303 298 222
Fax: 01303 298 227
Email: firstname.surname@screensouth.org

Screen West Midlands
31/41 Bromley Street
Birmingham B9 4AN
Tel: 0121 766 1470
Fax: 0121 766 1480
Email: info@screenwm.co.uk

Screen Yorkshire
Chief Executive: Jo Spreckley
40 Hanover Square
Leeds LS3 1BQ
Tel: 0113 294 4410
Fax: 0113 294 4989
Email: firstname@screenyorkshire.co.uk

South West Screen
Chief Executive: Caroline Norbury
St Bartholomew's
18 Christmas Street
Lewins Mead
Bristol BS1 5BT
Tel: 0117 952 9977
Fax: 0117 952 9988
Email: firstname.surname@swscreen.co.uk

Film London
For further details contact
info@filmcouncil.org.uk
or www.filmcouncil.org.uk

Henderson's Film Laboratories Ltd

18-20 Saint Dunstan's Road, South Norwood, London SE25 6EU
t 020 8653 2255 **f** 020 8653 9773
e bill@hendersonsfilmlab.com **w** www.hendersonsfilmlab.com
Contact Bill Millington, Contact

Soho Images

8-14 Meard Street, London W1F 0EQ
t 020 7437 0831 **f** 020 7734 9471
e emma.devonshire@sohoimages.com **w** www.sohoimages.com
Contact John Sears, Production Director; Len Thornton, Student and Short Film
Consultant; Paul Collard, Managing Director; Gordon Clampitt, Commercials
Director; Chris Bannister, Broadcast Sales; Nigel Horn, Features Manager; Dave
Kelly, Broadcast Manager
Credits The Magdalene Sisters (F); Bloody Sunday (F)

*Soho Images offers a complete camera to screen package for
Commercials, Features and Broadcast. We specialise in a range of film
and digital video post production services. Our Laboratory offers full
processing of 16mm and 35mm film, 24 hour rushes, PAL and NTSC
telecine transfers, 8/16/35mm gates, wet-gate option, sound-synching,
cinema bulk release prints, archive restoration and computerised
negative cutting. In conjunction with our sister companies we also
provide: film and video transfer and mastering (Standard Def or Hi-Def
formats), linear and non-linear editing (625/525/1080i), standards and
aspect ratio conversions, 2D and 3D graphics, titles and subtitling,
digital sound studios, dubbing facilities and complete DVD production.*

Technicolor Ltd

Bath Road, West Drayton UB7 0DB
t 020 8759 5432 **f** 020 8759 6270 **w** www.technicolour.com
Contact Mike Howell; Chris Gacon, Sales Controller
Credits Lord Of The Rings - Two Towers (F); Harry Potter And The Chamber Of
Secrets (F)

Todd-AO Creative Services

13 Hawley Crescent, London NW1 8NP
t 020 7284 7900 **f** 020 7284 1018
e schedules@ascent-media.co.uk **w** www.ascent-media.co.uk
Contact Matt Bowman, Head of Production; Sam Webb, Head of Post
Production; Dick Knapman, Technical Manager; Sam Lucas, In House Producer

Film Sales Agents

Gavin Film

65-66 Dean Street, London W1D 4PL
t 020 8432 2327 **f** 020 7437 3903 **m** 07753 741693
e billgavin@hotmail.com **w** www.billgavin.com
Contact Bill Gavin, Head of Sales
Credits The Hot Spot (F); The Last Tattoo (F); What Becomes Of The Broken
Hearted (F); Whale Rider (F)

Renaissance Films

34/35 Berwick Street, London W1F 8RP
t 020 7287 5190 **f** 020 7287 5191
e info@renaissance-films.com **w** www.renaissance-films.com
Contact Angus Finney, Managing Director; Sophie Janson, Head of
Development and Acquisitions
Credits The Safety Of Objects (F); The Mother (F)

Smart Egg Pictures

11/12 Barnard Mews, Barnard Road, London SW11 1QU
t 020 7350 4554 **f** 020 7924 5650 **e** sepsvs@aol.com
Contact Tom Sjoberg, Director, Acquisitions and Sales; Judy Phang, Marketing
and Servicing
Credits Dinosaurs (F); The Coca-Cola Kid (F); Montenegro (F); Martians!! Aka
Spaced Invaders (F)

Vine International Pictures

VIP House, Greenacres, New Road Hill, Downe,
Orpington BR6 7JA
t 01689 854123 **f** 01689 850990
e info@vine-international.co.uk **w** www.vine-international.co.uk
Contact Barry Gill, Managing Director; Sarah Goodwin, Sales & Marketing
Executive; Philip Setterfield, ID Film & Television/Head of Technical Services;
Marie Vine, Chief Executive Officer

Winchester Entertainment PLC

19 Heddon Street, London W1B 4BG
t 020 7851 6500 **f** 020 7851 6505
e mail@winchesterent.co.uk **w** www.winchesterent.com
Contact Andrew Brown, Vice President, Sales & Marketing; Billy Hurman,
Senior Vice President Sales & Marketing
Credits Christmas Carol -The Movie (F); Last Orders (F); Heartbreakers (F)

FINANCE

Finance Accountants

Accounteasy

175-177 Temple Chambers, Temple Avenue, London EC4Y 0DB
w www.accounteasy.co.uk
Contact David Grey
One of the easiest introductions to bookkeeping. Video training.

AGN Shipleys Chartered Accountants

10 Orange Street, London WC2H 7DQ
t 020 7312 0000 **f** 020 7312 0022
e robertsk@agnshipleys.com
Contact Ken Roberts, Partner; Steve Joberns, Partner

Baker Tilly

2 Bloomsbury Street, London WC1B 3ST
t 020 7413 5100 **f** 020 7413 5101
e media@bakertilly.co.uk **w** www.bakertilly.co.uk
Contact Mike Hearne, Partner; Keith Wilson, Partner; Christine Corner, Partner
and Head of Media Group; Tony Pierre, Partner

Beechams Chartered Accountants

3 Bedford Row, London WC1R 4BU
t 020 7242 5624 **f** 020 7405 6287
e info@beechams.com **w** www.beechams.com

Bissell & Brown

1 Legge Street, Birmingham B4 7EU
t 0121 359 7981 **f** 0121 359 1301 **e** post@bissell-brown.com
Contact B Matthews, Partner

Clayman & Co
189 Bickenhall Mansions, Bickenhall Street, London W1V 6BX
t 020 7935 0847 **f** 020 7224 2216 **e** info@claymans.co.uk
Contact M Kabel, Partner

Collard, Benzie & Hoys
2 High Street, Kingston-upon-Thames KT1 1EY
t 020 8247 4480 **f** 020 8247 4481
e mail@collardpartners.com **w** www.collardpartners.com
Contact Walter Benzie, Partner

David Grey & Co Ltd
175-177 Temple Chambers, Temple Avenue, London EC4Y 0DB
t 020 7353 3563 **f** 020 7353 3564 **e** info@davidgrey.co.uk
Contact David Grey, Director

David Hurwich & Co
8 Parkview Court, 8 Roehampton Vale, London SW15 3RY
t 020 8780 2589 **f** 020 8780 2589
e tax-accountancy@davidhurwich.co.uk **w** www.davidhurwich.co.uk
Contact David Hurwich, Chartered Tax Adviser

Deloitte & Touche
180 Strand, London WC2R 1BL
t 020 7438 3000 **f** 020 7831 1133
e ghamiltondeeley@deloitte.co.uk **w** www.deloitte.com
Contact James Bates, Senior Manager; Charles Bradbrook, Partner; Steven Andeson, Manager; Gavin Hamilton-Deeley, Partner

Elman Wall
1 Bickenhall Mansions, Bickenhall Street, London W1U 6BP
t 020 7486 6006 **f** 020 7486 6007
e jonw@elmanwall.co.uk **w** www.elmanwall.co.uk
Contact Jonathan Wall, Senior Partner

Entertainment Accounting International
26A Winders Road, Battersea, London SW11 3HB
t 020 7978 4488 **f** 020 7978 4492 **e** contact@eai.uk.com
Contact Julie Eyre; Mike Donovan

Ernst & Young
Becket House, 1 Lambeth Palace Road, London SE1 7EU
t 020 7951 2000 **f** 020 7951 1345 **w** www.ey.com/uk

Britt Gardiner
180 Lancaster Road, Notting Hill, London W11 1QU
t 020 7792 0767 **f** 020 7792 0767 **e** gardinercorrie@aol.com

Grant Thornton
Grant Thornton House, Melton Street, London NW1 2EP
t 020 7383 5100 **w** www.grant-thornton.co.uk
Contact Andrew Heffernan, Senior Manager; Sanjiv Sangar, Partner - Tax; Terry Back, Partner

Harold Everett Wreford
32 Wigmore Street, London W1U 2RP
t 020 7535 5900 **f** 020 7535 5901 **e** misaacs@hew.co.uk
Contact Michael Isaacs, Partner

Ivan Sopher & Company
5 Elstree Gate, Elstree Way, Borehamwood WD6 1JD
t 020 8207 0602 **f** 020 8207 6758
e accountants@ivansopher.co.uk **w** www.ivansopher.co.uk
Contact Ivan Sopher

KPMG
8 Salisbury Square, London EC4Y 8BB
t 020 7311 1000 **f** 020 7311 3311 **w** www.kpmg.co.uk

Lindford & Company
1 Duchess Street, London W1W 6AN
t 020 7637 2244 **f** 020 7637 2999
Contact T Lindford, Proprietor

Lubbock Fine
Russel Bedford House, 250 City Road, City Forum, London EC1V 2QQ
t 020 7490 7766 **f** 020 7490 5102
e geoffgoodyear@lubbockfine.co.uk **w** www.lubbockfine.co.uk
Contact Geoff Goodyear, Contact

Lucraft Hodgson & Dawes
2-4 Ash Lane, Rustington BN16 3BZ
t 01903 772244 **f** 01903 771071
Contact GM Butterworth, Partner; PJ Everest, Partner

MacCorkindale Alonso & Holton
4th Floor, 1-2 Langham Place, London W1B 3DD
t 020 7636 1888 **f** 020 7636 2888 **m** 07721 527975
e london@mahibm.com **w** www.mahibm.com

Mondas Information Technology Ltd
169 High Street, Rickmansworth WD3 1AY
t 01923 897333 **f** 01923 897323
e sales@mondas.com **w** www.mondas.com
Contact Bernard Snowe, Sales Director

Nyman Libson Paul (Chartered Accountants)
Regina House, 124 Finchley Road, London NW3 5JS
t 020 7433 2400 **f** 020 7433 2401
e mail@nymanlibsonpaul.co.uk **w** www.nymanlibsonpaul.co.uk

Pannell Kerr Forster
Pannell House, 6/7 Littfield Place, Clifton, Bristol BS8 3LX
t 0117 973 6841 **f** 0117 974 1238 **e** bristol@uk.pkf.com
Contact Peter Tegg, Senior Partner

PricewaterhouseCoopers LLP
1 Embankment Place, London WC2N 6RH
t 020 7804 9584 **f** 020 7822 4652
e philippa.m.machin@uk.pwcglobal.com **w** www.pwcglobal.com
Contact Peter Winkler, Chairman Of The Media Group; Robert Boyle, European Leader, Entertainment & Media Practice; Philippa Machin, Marketing Manager, Entertainment & Media

Saffery Champness
1 St Stephens Court, Bournemouth BH2 6LA
t 01202 294281 **f** 01202 290759 **w** www.saffery.com

Saffery Champness
Courtyard House, Oakfield Grove, Clifton BS8 2AE
t 0117 915 1617 **f** 0117 915 1618 **w** www.saffery.com

Saffery Champness
Sovereign House, 6 Windsor Court, Clarence Drive, Harrogate HG1 2PE
t 01423 568012 **f** 01423 501798 **w** www.saffery.com

Saffery Champness
Kintail House, Beechwood Park, Inverness IV2 3BW
t 01463 246300 **f** 01463 246301 **w** www.saffery.com

Saffery Champness
The Warrant House, High Street, Altrincham WA14 1PZ
t 0161 926 4900 **f** 0161 926 4915 **w** www.saffery.com

Saffery Champness
Stuart House, City Road, Peterborough PE1 1QF
t 01733 353300 **f** 01733 353301 **w** www.saffery.com

Saffery Champness
PO Box 141, La Tonelle House, Les Banques, St Sampson, Guernsey GY1 3HS
t 01481 721374 **f** 01481 722046 **w** www.safferyguernsey.com

Saffery Champness
Lion House, Red Lion Street, London WC1R 4GB
t 020 7841 4000 **f** 020 7841 4100
e info@saffery.com **w** www.saffery.com
Contact Lorenzo Mosca, Partner; Jason Lane, Chartered Accountant

Shariff & Company
19 Carlton Avenue, London N14 4TY
t 020 8360 7784 **f** 020 8360 7794
e enquiries@shariff-co.com **w** www.shariff-co.com
Contact Karim Shariff, Partner

Silver Levene
37 Warren Street, London W1T 6AD
t 020 7383 3200 **f** 020 7383 4168
e tony.silver@silverlevene.co.uk **w** www.silverlevene.co.uk
Contact David Martin; Tony Silver

Sloane & Company
36-38 Westbourne Grove, Newton Road, London W2 5SH
t 020 7221 3292 **f** 020 7229 4810
e david@sloane.co.uk **w** www.sloane.co.uk
Contact Annabel Fried, Office Manager; David Sloane, Partner

Linda Taylor
5 Crabtree Close, Bushey WD23 3BJ
t 020 8386 5825 **f** 020 8386 5825 **m** 07776 191 851
Credits Harry Potter And The Prisoner Of Azkaban (F); Soldier Soldier (T); Harry Potter And The Chamber Of Secrets (F); Harry Potter And The Philosopher's Stone (F)

Tenon Media
66 Chiltern Street, London W1U 4JT
t 020 7535 1400 **f** 020 7535 1401 **e** john.graydon@tenongrap.com
Contact John Graydon, Business Services Director - Film Unit

Naomi Thomas
6 Wessex Close, Thames Ditton KT7 OEJ
t 020 8398 5443 **e** naomijthomas@hotmail.com

Fran Triefus
14 Burnham Road, Hughden Valley HP14 4NY
t 01494 565895 **f** 01494 565895 **m** 07813 311643
e frantriefus@aol.com

Westbury Schotness
145-157 St John Street, London EC1V 4PY
t 020 7253 7272 **f** 020 7253 0814
e info@westbury.co.uk **w** www.westbury.co.uk
Contact Sam Clarke, Partner

Willott Kingston Smith
Quadrant House, 80-82 Regent Street, London W1B 5RP
t 020 7304 4646 **f** 020 7304 4647 **m** 07786 440536
e jmills@kingstonsmith.co.uk **w** www.kingstonsmith.co.uk
Contact John Mills, Senior Manager

Wilson & Company (Accountants) Ltd
Chiltern Chambers, St Peters Avenue, Caversham, Reading RG4 7DH
t 0118 946 4020 **f** 0118 946 4880
e wilson@wilsonco.demon.co.uk **w** www.wilson-accountants.com
Contact Andrew Wilson, Chartered Accountant

Finance
Completion Guarantors

Matheson Ormsby Prentice
30 Herbert Street, Dublin 2, Rep of Ireland
t +353 1 619 9000 **f** +353 1 619 9010 **e** mop@mop.ie
Contact Donal Roche, Managing Partner

Finance Development

Benfield Imperial Entertainment Finance Ltd
55 Bishopsgate, London EC2N 3BD
t 020 7578 7000 **f** 020 7578 7001 **w** www.benfieldgroup.com
Contact Hugo Raymond; Ed Atkinson

The Children's Film & Television Foundation
Elstree Studios, Shenley Road, Borehamwood WD6 1JG
t 020 8953 0844 **f** 020 8207 0860
e annahome@cftf.onyxnet.co.uk

East England Arts
Eden House, 48-49 Bateman Street, Cambridge CB2 1LR
t 01223 454400 **f** 0870 242 1271
e east@artscouncil.org.uk **w** www.artscouncil.org.uk
Contact Martin Ayres, Film Education and Screen Development

East Midlands Arts Board
St Nicholas Court, 25-27 Castlegate, Nottingham NG1 7AR
t 01159 897520 **f** 01159 950 2467 **w** www.arts.org.uk

European Media Development Agency (EMDA)
e emda@emda.org **w** www.emda.org
Contact David Kavanagh, Head of Office

Film Finances Ltd
14-15 Conduit Street, London W1S 2XJ
t 020 7629 6557 **f** 020 7491 7530 **w** www.filmfinances.com
Contact Graham Easton, Managing Director

Intermedia London
Unit 12, Enterprise House, 59-65 Upper Ground, London SE1 9PQ
t 020 7593 1630 **f** 020 7593 1639
e info@intermediafilm.co.uk **w** www.intermediafilm.co.uk
Contact Philip Rose, V.P. International Marketing; Gareth James, VP of UK Operations
Credits Iris (F); Hilary And Jackie (F); Sliding Doors (F)

London Production Fund
114 Whitfield Street, London W1T 5EF
t 020 7383 7755 **f** 020 7383 7745
e lfvda@demon.co.uk **w** www.lfvda.demon.co.uk
Contact Gill Henderson, Chief Executive
Credits Long Road to Mazatlan; Mavis and the Mermaid; Intolerance

MEDIA Antenna Scotland
2nd Floor, 249 West George Street, Glasgow G2 4QE
t 0141 302 1776 **t** 0141 302 1777 **f** 0141 302 1778
e scotland@mediadesk.co.uk **w** www.mediadesk.co.uk
Contact Donna Hamilton, Officer; Emma Valentine, Co-ordinator

Mediavision UK Ltd
8 Westwood Road, London SW13 OLA
m 07767 830179 **e** rlack@dircon.co.uk
Contact Russell Lack, Managing Director

Saturn Entertainment Developments Ltd
Harewood Lodge, Chapel Street, Belgrave Square, London SW1X
t 020 7235 6034 **m** 07855 755450
e info@saturn-entertainment.com
w www.saturn-entertainment.com

Sgrin Cymru Wales
10 Mount Stuart Square, Cardiff CF10 5EE
t 029 2033 3300 **f** 029 2033 3320
e sgrin@sgrin.co.uk **w** www.sgrin.co.uk

Contact Berwyn Rowlands, Chief Executive; Judith Higginbottom, Head of Production; Linda Harpwood, Company Manager/New Media; Luned Meredith, Head of Marketing; Gwion Owain, Media Antenna Wales; Dr Geraint Stanley Jones, Chair; Rhian Iolo, Exhibition Manager; Gaynor Messer Price, New Talent/Short Film Manager; Elain Dafydd, Education Manager; Hannah Raybould, Marketing Manager (UK); Sam Canham, Finance Manager; Mike Wallwork, Co-ordinator Wales Screen Commission; Anneli Jones, Lottery Manager; Gwion ap Rhisiart, Marketing Manager (International)

UK Media Desk
66-68 Margaret Street, London W1W 8SR
t 020 7323 9733 **f** 020 7323 9747
e england@mediadesk.co.uk **w** www.mediadesk.co.uk

Contact Agnieszka Moody, Director; Rachel Caddick, Assistant

Financial Services General

APT Finance
22 Reading Road, Henley on Thames RG9 1AG
t 01491 848848 **f** 01491 412372
e info@apt-finance.com **w** www.apt-finance.com

Contact Alan Archondakis, Accounts Manager; David Leno, Accounts Manager

Audio Visual Asset Management
Little Orchard House, Bears Den, Kingswood KT20 6PL
t 01737 830084 **f** 01737 830063 **m** 07831 820300
e info@avam.co.uk **w** www.avam.co.uk

Contact Duncan Rushmer, Managing Director

Bank of Scotland
Purley Business Centre, Beech House, 840 Brighton Road, Purley CR8 2BH
t 020 8668 7574 **f** 020 8763 8110 **m** 07970 566078
e robert-palmer@bankofscotland.co.uk
w www.bankofscotland.co.uk/business

Contact Yvonne Miller, Asset Finance Manager; Kerrie Peters, Media Specialist; Robert Palmer, Associate Director; Doug Balcan, Media Specialist; Darren Collett, Media Specialist

Banque Internationale a Luxembourg
Shackleton House, Hay's Galleria, 4 Battle Bridge Lane, London SE1 2GZ
t 020 7556 3000 **f** 020 7556 3055 **w** www.dexia-bil.com

Contact Gillian Duffield; Edwige Rolin, Media Department

Barclay's Bank Plc
PO Box 4WA, 27 Soho Square, London W1D 3QR
t 7455 5774

Contact M Birkenshaw, Media Banking Manager; M French, Media Banking Manager; PA Stone, Media Banking Assistant; S Pettican, Media Banking Assistant; H Costin, Media Banking Assistant

Berg Kaprow Lewis
35 Ballards Lane, London N3 1XW
t 020 8922 9222 **f** 020 8922 9223
e post@bergkaprowlewis.co.uk **w** www.bergkaprowlewis.co.uk

Contact Lesley Alexander, Partner

Chartwell Financial Ltd
5 Egerton Crescent, Withington, Manchester M20 4PN
t 0161 445 8002 **f** 0161 445 9921
e waj@chartwellfinancial.fsnet.co.uk

Contact Tony Jones, Director

Circus
1 Hardwick Street, London EC1R 4RB
t 020 7837 4466 **f** 020 7837 8828
e mail@big-top.com **w** www.big-top.com

Clockwork Capital
14 Livonia Street, London W1F 8AG
t 020 7287 3132 **f** 020 7734 6253
e sales@clockworkcapital.com **w** www.clockworkcapital.com

Compact Collections Ltd
Greenland Place, 115-123 Bayham Street, Camden, London NW1 0AG
t 020 7446 7420 **f** 020 7446 7424
e compact@palan.com **w** www.compactcollections.com

Contact Kathryn Fladgate, Copyright & Internet Co-ordinator; John O'Sullivan, General Manager; Ged Shimokwa Kelly, IT Manager

Coutts & Co
440 Strand, London WC2R 0QS
t 020 7753 1000 **w** www.coutts.com

De Lage Landen Leasing Ltd
Rushmoor Court, Croxley Business Park, Hatters Lane, Watford WD18 8EZ
t 01923 810089 **f** 01923 810011
e p.morton@delagelanden.com **w** www.delagelanden.com

Contact Peter Morton

Deloitte & Touche Consulting Group
Stonecutter Court, Stonecutter Street, London EC4A 4TR
t 020 7936 3000 **f** 020 7583 1198 **w** www.deloitte.co.uk

Contact Steve Almond

Dexia Banque Internationale a Luxembourg
Shackleton House, Hay's Galleria, 4 Battlebridge Lane, London SE1 2GZ
t 020 7556 3000 **f** 020 7556 3055
e gillian.duffield@dexia-bil.com **w** www.dexia-bil.com

Contact Gillian Duffield, Senior Manager For Media

Fineline Media Finance Ltd
Heron House, Richmond Upon Thames TW9 1EL
t 020 8334 2100 **f** 020 8334 2101
e peter.savage@fineline-finance.co.uk
e gareth.wilding@fineline-finance.co.uk
w www.finelinemediafinance.co.uk

Contact Peter Savage, Managing Director; Gareth Wilding

Medialease
30 Daventry Road, Norton, Daventry NN11 5ND
t 0800 783 5692 **f** 01327 706898 **m** 07770 372727
e info@medialease.com **w** www.medialease.com

Contact Paul Robson, Director; Carmen Evans, Administrator

Medialex Ltd
Greyhound House, 23-24 George Street, Richmond TW9 1HY
t 020 8973 2186 **f** 020 8973 2009
e info@medialex-uk.com **w** www.medialex-uk.com

Contact Pam Bernhard

NFTC
4th Floor London, 66-68 Margaret Street, London W1W 8SR
t 020 7580 6799 **f** 020 7636 6711
e info@nftc.co.uk **w** www.nftc.co.uk

Contact Alun Tyers, Director

The Royal Bank of Scotland
3rd Floor, 65 Piccadilly, London W1A 2PP
t 020 7290 4637 **f** 020 7290 4692
e karl.dye@rbs.co.uk **w** www.rbs.co.uk

Contact Lee Beasley, Business Development - Film, Television & Media Team; Karl Dye, Manager - Film, Television & Media Team; Julian Kilsby, Manager - Film, Television & Media Team; Cheryl Smith, Business Manager

Screen Partners
46 Crispin Street, London E1 6HQ
t 020 7247 3444 **f** 020 7247 9684
e information@screenpartners.com

Contact Kent Walwin, Managing Director

SME Eurofinance plc
Lombard Business Park, 8 Lombard Road, London SW19 3TZ
t 020 8544 1744 **f** 020 8545 7262 **m** 07775 852184
e gmoorcraft@smeeurofinance.com
w www.smeeurofinance.com

Contact John Dickinson, Director; Graham Moorcraft, Director

Floor Managers

Toby Baker
TOVS Ltd, The Linen Hall, 162-168 Regent Street, London W1B 5TB
t 020 7287 6110 **f** 020 7287 5481
e info@tovs.co.uk **w** www.tovs.co.uk

Ian Brown
Grade One TV & Film Personnel, Elstree Studios, Shenley Road, Borehamwood WD6 1JG
t 020 8324 2224 **f** 020 8324 2328
e gradeone.tvpersonnel@virgin.net

Alan Conley
Experience Counts - Call Me Ltd, 5th Floor, 41-42 Berners Street, London W1T 3NB
t 020 7637 8112 **f** 020 7580 2582

Jo Curtis
TOVS Ltd, The Linen Hall, 162-168 Regent Street, London W1B 5TB
t 020 7287 6110 **f** 020 7287 5481
e info@tovs.co.uk **w** www.tovs.co.uk

Phil Davies
TOVS Ltd, The Linen Hall, 162-168 Regent Street, London W1B 5TB
t 020 7287 6110 **f** 020 7287 5481
e info@tovs.co.uk **w** www.tovs.co.uk

Leigh Dawkins
m 07774 424727 **e** leighmail@tinyonline.co.uk
Credits Sky Sports (T); Mr Right (T)

Simone Dawson
TOVS Ltd, The Linen Hall, 162-168 Regent Street, London W1B 5TB
t 020 7287 6110 **f** 020 7287 5481
e info@tovs.co.uk **w** www.tovs.co.uk

Marco De Giorgi
29 Smitham Downs Road, Purley CR8 4NG
f 020 8660 4807 **m** 07802 254319
e marcodg@blueyonder.co.uk
Credits CITV White Knuckle Tour (T); World's Strongest Man 2002 (T); Housecall (T); Question Time (T)

Roger Dempster
The Firm Booking Company Ltd, 31 Oval Road, Camden, London NW1 7EΛ
t 020 7248 9090 **f** 020 7248 9089 **e** kirsty@thefirm.co.uk

Wayne Eagles
9 Cavendish Street, Peterborough PE1 5EG
t 01733 768486 **m** 07876 233999 **e** wayneeagles@hotmail.com
Credits Simply TV (T); Cisco TV Live (W); Cisco TV Live (C); Good Food Live (T)

David Gold
22 Grangeway Gardens, Redbridge IG4 5HN
t 020 8551 4580 **f** 020 8551 4580 **m** 07774 860799
e davidgold@beeb.net
Credits Commonwealth Games (T); Breakfast With Frost (T); Great Britons (T); Top Gear (T)

Michael Grenville
TOVS Ltd, The Linen Hall, 162-168 Regent Street, London W1B 5TB
t 020 7287 6110 **f** 020 7287 5481
e info@tovs.co.uk **w** www.tovs.co.uk

Geraldine Hanley
23 Kensington Court, 20 Kensington Road, Dowanhill, Glasgow G12 9NX
t 0141 339 7871 **f** 0141 339 7871 **m** 07759 398 013
m 07734 110156 **e** geraldine@horaceboris.fsnet.co.uk
Credits Elaine (T); Sky Premier Football (T); CCG (T)

Simon Hooper
43 Wiltshire Lane, Pinner HA5 2LY
m 07889 246821 **e** simonfilm@hotmail.com
Credits Big Brothers Little Brother (T); Pub Ammo (T); MTV Video Clash Live (T); International Art Attack (T)

Andy Kelk
t 01732 740677 **f** 01732 456466 **m** 07836 738368
e andykelk@hotmail.com
Credits Royal Variety (T); Gladiators (T); Popstars - Germany & Switzerland (T); Survivor (T)

Stan Kingsbury
TOVS Ltd, The Linen Hall, 162-168 Regent Street, London W1B 5TB
t 020 7287 6110 **f** 020 7287 5481
e info@tovs.co.uk **w** www.tovs.co.uk

Micheal Mollan
Experience Counts - Call Me Ltd, 5th Floor, 41-42 Berners Street, London W1T 3NB
t 020 7637 8112 **f** 020 7580 2582

Mike Morgan
Grade One TV & Film Personnel, Elstree Studios, Shenley Road, Borehamwood WD6 1JG
t 020 8324 2224 **f** 020 8324 2328
e gradeone.tvpersonnel@virgin.net

Nigel Payn
Experience Counts - Call Me Ltd, 5th Floor, 41-42 Berners Street, London W1P 3AA
t 020 7637 8112 **f** 020 7580 2582

Alec Potter
TOVS Ltd, The Linen Hall, 162-168 Regent Street, London W1B 5TB
t 020 7287 6110 **f** 020 7287 5481
e info@tovs.co.uk **w** www.tovs.co.uk

Lisa Ramsey
Experience Counts - Call Me Ltd, 5th Floor, 41-42 Berners Street, London W1P 3AA
t 020 7637 8112 **f** 020 7580 2582

Janice Shorten
t 01422 845628 **e** janiceshorten@hotmail.com

Donna Tait
TOVS Ltd, The Linen Hall, 162-168 Regent Street, London W1B 5TB
t 020 7287 6110 **f** 020 7287 5481
e info@tovs.co.uk **w** www.tovs.co.uk

Patrick Vance
Experience Counts - Call Me Ltd, 5th Floor, 41-42 Berners
Street, London W1P 3AA
t 020 7637 8112 **f** 020 7580 2582

Simon Wallace
Experience Counts - Call Me Ltd, 5th Floor, 41-42 Berners
Street, London W1P 3AA
t 020 7637 8112 **f** 020 7580 2582

Ritchie Wilkinson
TOVS Ltd, The Linen Hall, 162-168 Regent Street, London W1B 5TB
t 020 7287 6110 **f** 020 7287 5481
e info@tovs.co.uk **w** www.tovs.co.uk

Floor Managers
Assistant/Stage Managers

Sylvia Carter
27 Harvard Court, Honeydawn Road, London NW6 1HL
t 020 7435 1848 **f** 020 7435 3166 **m** 07973 320372

Keren Eliot
52 Houston Road, London SE23 2RN
t 020 8291 5510 **m** 07970 190578

First Positions Ltd
19 Fermor Road, London SE23 2HW
t 020 8225 8702 **f** 020 8576 0537 **m** 07811 123787
e janelfleury@aol.com **w** www.firstpositions.co.uk
Contact Jane Fleury, Managing Director
Credits Saturday Show (T); Absolutely Fabulous (T); Alistair McGowan Big
Impression (T); The Office (T)

Foreign Filming **Freight**

Rock-It Cargo Ltd
Delta Way, Egham TW20 8RX
t 01784 431301 **f** 01784 471052 **m** 07768 998642
e info@rock-it.co.uk **w** www.rock-itcargo.com
Contact Sonia Webb-Heath, Sales; Mark Cahill, Sales and Marketing Manager
*The world's leading freight and logistic specialist for film & TV, live
event, and entertainment production. Door to door, venue to venue
transportation, customs and documentation services via air, sea or
road. Global 24 hour support from the most experienced personnel and
network in the business.*

Government Agencies

**Department of Culture, Media & Sport
(Media Division)**
2-4 Cockspur Street, London SW1Y 5DH
t 020 7211 6432 **f** 020 7211 6417 **w** www.culture.gov.uk
Contact Alan Sutherland, Planning & Stewardship; Jon Zeff,
Policy & Innovation Delivery Unit

The Department of Trade & Industry (DTI)
1 Victoria Street, London SW1H 0ET
t 020 7215 5000 **f** 020 7222 0612
e dti.enquiries@dti.gsi.gov.uk **w** www.dti.gov.uk

Filton College
Media Department, Filton College, Filton Avenue, Filton, Bristol
BS34 7AT
t 0117 909 2272 **t** 0117 909 2331 **f** 0117 931 2233
e m.hughes@filton-college.ac.uk **w** www.filton.ac.uk
Contact Sam Wild, Lecturer; Michelle Hughes, Lecturer

Gaelic Broadcasting Committee (CCG)
4 Harbour View, Cromwell St Quay, Stornoway, Isle of Lewis
HS1 2DF
t 01851 705550 **f** 01851 706432
e admin@ccg.org.uk **w** www.ccg.org.uk

London Arts Board
2 Pear Tree Court, London EC1R 0DS
t 020 7608 6100 **t** 020 7608 4101
e info@lonab.co.uk **w** www.arts.org.uk/londonarts

London Film & Video Development Agency
114 Whitfield Street, London W1T 5EF
t 020 7383 7755 **f** 020 7383 7745
e lfvda@lfvda.demon.co.uk **w** www.lfvda.demon.co.uk
Contact Gill Henderson, Chief Executive Officer; Honnie Tang,
Information & Marketing; Maggie Ellis, Production Executive

OFTEL (Office for Telecommunication)
50 Ludgate Hill, London EC4M 7JJ
t 020 7634 8700 **f** 020 7634 8845
e infocent@oftel.gov.uk **w** www.oftel.gov.uk
Contact Jo Hamilton, Press Officer

Scottish Screen
249 West George Street, Glasgow G2 4QE
t 0141 302 1700 **f** 0141 302 1711
e info@scottishscreen.com **w** www.scottishscreen.com
Contact Claire Chapman, Head of Production; Carole Sheridan, Development
Executive; Alison Butchart, Head of Training; Steve McIntyre, Chief Executive
Credits Young Adam (F); The Magdalene Sisters (F); Morvern Callar (F);
Sweet Sixteen (F)

GRAPHICS
Graphics **Companies**

And Design
104 Felsham Road, London SW15 1DQ
t 020 8780 9806 **f** 020 8780 9804 **m** 07973 818536
e simon@and-design.com **w** www.and-design.com
Contact Gavin Reay, Director; Simon Heap, Director
Credits Haagan Dazs- 1993; Award Winning Product Design BBC

Atom Pictures
2 Weybourne Street, London SW18 4HQ
t 020 8879 3966 **f** 020 8879 0030
e atompictures@btinternet.com
Contact Bill Wilson, Designer Director; Sally Blackburn, Commercial Producer

Aurora Creative Design
14 Crown Close, Rowley Regis B65 9LF
t 0121 532 3536
Contact Paul Cobb, Proprietor

AVS Graphics and Media Ltd
19 Riverside Industrial Park, Dogflood Way, Farnham GU9 7UG
t 01252 727 266 **f** 01252 714 664
e sales.worldwide@asvgmedia.com **w** www.asvgmedia.com
Contact Chris Dixon, Sales Manager; Gavin Hunter, Sales

BBC Scotland Resources Operations

Room G51, Broadcasting House, Queen Margaret Drive, Glasgow G12 8DG
t 0141 338 2343 **f** 0141 338 2335
e resops.scotland@bbc.co.uk **w** www.bbc.co.uk/scotland/resources
Contact Natalie Adams, Facilities Co-ordinator; Alex Gaffney, Sales & Marketing Manager; Susie Miller, Marketing Assistant; Donagh Campbell, Facilities Assistant
Credits 50/50 (T); UKOOL (T); T In The Park (T); Hollywood Greats (T)

Bernard Heyes Design

7 Meard Street, London W1F 0EW
t 020 7287 0202 **f** 020 7434 9334 **m** 07860 369781
e bernardheyes@btconnect.com
Contact Bernard Heyes, Creative Director
Credits The Real ER (A); Coupling (A); Parkinson (A); Sahara With Michael Palin (A)

Blitz Graphics

100 Centennial Avenue, Elstree Way, Borehamwood WD6 3SA
t 0870 162 1200 **f** 0870 162 1222
e carol@blitzgraphics.com **w** www.blitzgraphics.com
Contact Carol Gibbs, Director; Carol Copley, Director; Les Coles, Director

Brainstorm 3D Graphics

11 Lewknor Close, Lewknor OX49 5UJ
t +44 1844 354303 **m** 07740 197922 **e** russell@fuseweb.co.uk
Contact Russell Leak, Director

Bruce Dunlop & Associates

1-6 Falconberg Court, London W1D 3AB
t 020 7440 1070 **f** 020 7440 1077
e info@brucedunlop.com **w** www.brucedunlop.com
Contact Honor Bartlett, Managing Director; Bruce Dunlop, Chief Executive Officer; Martin Poole, Sales & Marketing Director
Credits Paramount Comedy Rebrand (C); ITV1 Rebrand (C); Ford World Rally: Version 2 (C); Ford/Uefa Sponsorship Credits (C)

Burrell Durrant Hifle Design & Direction Ltd

71 South Parade, Oakfield Road, Clifton, Bristol BS8 2BB
t 0117 973 7575 **f** 0117 923 7823
e pic@bdh.net **w** www.bdh.net
Contact Rob Hifle, Senior Designer; Pic Haywood, Production Manager; John Durrant, Senior Designer; Steve Burrell, Senior Designer
Credits And Me (T); Smash Hits Poll Winners Party (T); Great Britons (T); Dinosaur Hunters (T)

Capital FX

2nd Floor, 20 Dering Street, London W1F 1AJ
t 020 7493 9998 **f** 020 7493 9997
e ian@capital-fx.co.uk **w** www.capital-fx.co.uk
Contact David Smith, Producer; Ian Buckton, Director; Tim Baxter, Film Scanning & Recording; Simon Dowling, Head of Production; Jim Davey, Director of Digital Services
Denham Media Park, North Orbital Road, Denham UB9 5HG
t 01895 831931 **f** 01895 835338
e rick.corne@capital-fx.co.uk **w** www.capital-fx.co.uk
Contact Chester Eyre, Director of Operations; Fred Chandler, Consultant; Rick Corne

Graphic design for Film & TV, digital compositing, digital to film recording, video to film transfer, laser subtitling and video rostrum.

co:de

co:de

Ingestre Court, Ingestre Place, London W1F 0JL
t 020 7343 6449 **f** 020 7343 6555
e bryony@codedesign.co.uk **w** www.codedesign.co.uk
Contact Bryony Evans
Located at M2 Soho, co:de Design & Direction is an award-winning design team recognised for channel branding, titles sequences, commercials and corporate design. Editbox FX, Hal, Illusion and audio facilities in-house.

Communicate

Brookwood House, 84 Brookwood Road, London SW18 5NS
t 020 8949 3929 **f** 020 8288 4288
e gareth@communicateworldwide.com
w www.communicateworldwide.com
Contact Gareth Mullaney, Producer

Component Graphics

1 Newman Passage, London W1T 1EF
t 020 7631 4400 **f** 020 7580 2890
e mike@component.co.uk **w** www.component.co.uk
Contact Mike Kenny, Director

Creative Pictures

38 The Drive, High Barnet, London EN5 4JQ
t 020 8440 8023 **m** 07976 952 703
e paul@creativepictures.co.uk
Contact Paul Fraser, Producer

Definition Design Ltd

21-23 Crosby Row, London
t 020 7357 6878 **f** 020 7357 6878
e neill@planetdef.co.uk **w** www.planetdef.co.uk
Contact Neil Furmston, Creative Director

G2 Video Systems

5 Mead Lane, Farnham GU9 7DY
t 01252 737151 **f** 01252 737147
e sales@g2systems.co.uk **w** www.g2systems.co.uk
Contact Marian Hollidge, Sales & Marketing; Greg Hollidge, Managing Director

General Lighting & Power

Basement Studio, 70-72 Old Street, London EC1V 4AN
t 020 7490 7975 **f** 020 7490 7955
e glp@thegeneral.co.uk **w** www.thegeneral.co.uk
Contact Jonny Halifax, Head of Production; Nic Clear, Head of Production; Ezra Holland, Head of Post Production; Danny Vaia, Head of Development

Goldcrest Post Production Facilities

36-44 Brewer Street, London W1F 9LX
t 020 7437 7972 **f** 020 7437 5402 **m** 07836 204283
e mailbox@goldcrest-post.co.uk
Contact Poppy Quinn, Bookings and Customer Services Manager; Raju Raymond, General Manager

Jump Design & Direction

Lins House, 38 Rosebery Avenue, London EC1R 4RN
t 020 7713 6316 **f** 020 7713 6322 **m** 07956 188105
e info@jumpdesign.co.uk **w** www.jumpdesign.co.uk
Contact Karon Hall, Production Manager
Credits The Luvvies (T); Real Story (T); I'm A Celebrity Get Me Out Of Here! (T)

Kemistry

Brook Green Studios, 186 Shepherds Bush Road, London W6 7NL
t 020 7371 3300 **f** 020 7603 9519
e info@kemistry.co.uk **w** www.kemisrty.co.uk
Contact Graham McCallum, Creative Director; Richard Churchill, Managing Director
Credits Monarch Of The Glen (T); Entrapment (F); Discovery (T); Film Four (T)

London Post

34-35 Dean Street, London W1D 4PR
t 020 7439 9080 **f** 020 7434 0714
e info@londonpost.co.uk **w** www.londonpost.co.uk
Contact Soraya Robertson, Bookings Manager; Verity Laing

Lost In Space

2nd Floor, 6 Ramillies Street, London W1F 7TY
t +44 20 7534 8048 **f** +44 20 7434 9289
e info@lostinspace.com **w** www.lostinspace.com
Contact Christian Hogue, Creative Director
Credits I See U In 3D (T); Disney Kids Awards 2002 (T); Orange: Business Turns to Orange (C); Autechie: Granz Graf (M)

Molinare

34 Fouberts Place, London W1F 7PX
t 020 7478 7000 **f** 020 7478 7199
e bookings@molinare.co.uk **w** www.molinare.co.uk
Contact Kate George, Facilities Manager
Credits Dorada Especial: Painting; AXN: Cornice; Walkers Dorito's: Idents; The Wind

For 30 years Molinare has been offering the best in Post Production, helping the best people make the best programmes, we have about the widest selection of facilities in one location in the industry. Based in the heart of Soho, we offer, 5 digital Online Suites, Editbox FX V8, Ursa Gold Telecine, High Definition Online, 10 Avid Offline suites and 2 Avid Online suites, 5 Audio Dubbing suites with voice over booths, Tracklay, Discreet Flint, Media Illusion, Drive in 1500 sq ft Video studio, 400 sq ft Virtual Studio, Duplication, Transmission Services, as well as the Molinare Design team for all your branding and design needs.

MotionFX Ltd

Units B4-B6, Askew Crescent Workshops, London W12 9DP
t 020 8740 4560 **f** 020 8749 0309
e johnoquigley@motionfx.co.uk **w** www.motionfx.co.uk
Contact John O'Quigley

Nats Post Production

10 Soho Square, London W1D 3NT
t 020 7287 9900 **f** 020 7287 8636 **e** bookings@nats.ltd.uk
Contact Sara Hill, Bookings; Jo Manser; Louise Knight; Louise Thomas

One of Soho's leading facilities, Nats Post Production is fully equipped in all aspects of television post production, from offline to online, design and graphics, grade and audio dub. With over 40 suites, we strive to make sure your whole experience is as pleasant and productive as possible by offering you creative excellence, intelligent solutions and home comforts.

Sanctuary Post

53 Frith Street, London W1D 4SN
t 020 7734 4480
e post@sanctuarystudios.co.uk **w** www.sanctuarystudios.co.uk
Contact Jason Elliott, Sales and Marketing Manager

Flame, DS editing, compositing and grading, on-line and off-line Avid editing, Audio, graphics, CD-Rom and DVD design / authoring and duplication services.

Schwarz Garcia

25 Harley Street, London
t 020 8203 4862 **f** 020 8202 4938 **m** 07788 666661
e matt@schwarzgarcia.com **w** www.schwarzgarcia.com
Contact Matt Garcia, Creative Director; Darren Schwarz, Technical Director
Credits Dontforgetyourcard.com (A); MTV Presentation (W)

Spaceward Graphics

Denmark House, 3B High Stret, Willingham CB4 5ES
t 01638 731795 **f** 01638 731795
e sales@satoripaint.com **w** www.satoripaint.com
Contact M Lister, Sales & Marketing Director

Superchrome Ltd

Superchrome House, 22 St Pancras Way, London NW1 0QG
t 020 7391 0862 **f** 020 7387 8609
e alan.leo@superchrome.co.uk **w** www.superchrome.co.uk
Contact David Dawson, Manager; Alan Leo

Unity Pictures

7A Newburgh Street, London W1F 7RH
t 020 7734 2888 **f** 020 7734 2999
e admin@unitypictures.co.uk **w** www.unitypictures.co.uk
Contact Chia Tucker, Production Manager; David Chiverton, Producer; Alon Ziv, Director; Hylton Tannenbaum, Director; Hilary Davis, Producer
Credits Art Crimes (T); Spitfire (C); Time Magazine (C); Spy TV (T)

XTV

71 Dean Street, London W1D 3SF
t 020 7208 1500 **f** 020 7208 1510 **w** www.xtv.co.uk
Contact Hannah Mitchel, Head of Production
Credits Snooker (T); Pepsi Chart Show (T); International Cricket (T); At The Races (T)

Graphics Designers

BBC Post Production

BBC Post Production
(Sites across London, Bristol & Birmingham)

5550 Television Centre, Wood Lane, London W12 7RJ
t 020 8225 7702 (London) **t** 0117 9746 666 (Bristol)
t 0121 432 8621 (Birmingham)
w www.bbcresources.com/postproduction

Angus Biles

TOVS Ltd, The Linen Hall, 162-168 Regent Street, London W1B 5TB
t 020 7287 6110 **f** 020 7287 5481
e info@tovs.co.uk **w** www.tovs.co.uk

Glen Bonner

TOVS Ltd, The Linen Hall, 162-168 Regent Street, London W1B 5TB
t 020 7287 6110 **f** 020 7287 5481
e info@tovs.co.uk **w** www.tovs.co.uk

co:de

co:de

Ingestre Court, Ingestre Place, London W1F 0JL
t 020 7343 6400 **f** 020 7343 6555
e bryony@codedesign.co.uk **w** www.codedesign.co.uk
Contact Bryony Evans

Located at M2 Soho, co:de Design & Direction is an award-winning design team recognised for channel branding, titles sequences, commercials and corporate design, Editbox FX, Hal, Illusion and audio facilities in-house.

Sue Cooper

TOVS Ltd, The Linen Hall, 162-168 Regent Street, London W1B 5TB
t 020 7287 6110 **f** 020 7287 5481
e info@tovs.co.uk **w** www.tovs.co.uk

Louise Corcoran

Art Department, 51 Pratt Street, London NW1 0BJ
t 020 7428 0500 **f** 020 7916 2167 **m** 07957 240665
e info@art-department.co.uk

Custom Marketing Resources

Prospect House, Hunton Road, Marden TN12 9SL
t 01622 820841 **f** 01622 820851 **m** 07802 820841
e cmr@prospect-house.demon.co.uk
Contact Alan Reading, Proprietor

E-Digital

No 1, 20 Hampden Gurney Street, London W1H 5AX
t 020 7723 9393 **f** 020 7724 3813
e jim@edigital.freeuk.com
Contact Jim Banting, CEO

Fox Displays Ltd

58 Lawrence Road, London N15 4EX
t 020 8800 2202 **f** 020 8802 7327
e sales@foxdisplays.com

The Hallmark Partnership Design Consultants

22A Arlington Way, Sadler's Wells, London EC1R 1UY
t 020 7837 3044 **f** 020 7837 7044
e info@hallmark-design.co.uk **w** www.hallmark-design.co.uk
Contact Alexandra Overton-Wood, Business Development Manager; Gary Stevens, Business Development Manager

Al Horton

Experience Counts - Call Me Ltd, 5th Floor, 41-42 Berners Street, London W1P 3AA
t 020 7637 8112 **f** 020 7580 2582

Ink Spot Design

5A Chelsea Wharf, Lots Road, London SW10 0QF
t 020 7351 2606 **f** 020 7352 3446

Alex Lemonis

Art Department, 51 Pratt Street, London NW1 0BJ
t 020 7428 0500 **f** 020 7916 2167 **m** 07941 019049
e info@art-department.co.uk

Liquid TV

1-2 Portland Mews, Soho, London W1F 8JE
t 020 7437 2623 **f** 020 7437 2618
e info@liquid.co.uk **w** www.liquid.co.uk
Contact Asra Alikhan, Managing Director; Craig Purkis, Sales Manager
Credits A Place In The Sun (T); Pop Idol (T); Extreme Sports Channel (T); Discovery Networks Europe - Diginet Channels (T)

David Martin

TOVS Ltd, The Linen Hall, 162-168 Regent Street, London W1B 5TB
t 020 7287 6110 **f** 020 7287 5481
info@tovs.co.uk **w** www.tovs.co.uk

molinare
a television corporation company

Molinare

34 Fouberts Place, London W1F 7PX
t 020 7478 7000 **f** 020 7478 7199
e bookings@molinare.co.uk **w** www.molinare.co.uk
Contact Kate George, Facilities Manager
Credits Dorada Especial: Painting; AXN: Cornice; Walkers Dorito's: Idents; The Wind

For 30 years Molinare has been offering the best in Post Production, helping the best people make the best programmes, we have about the widest selection of facilities in one location in the industry. Based in the heart of Soho, we offer, 5 digital Online Suites, Editbox FX V8, Ursa Gold Telecine, High Definition Online, 10 Avid Offline suites and 2 Avid Online suites, 5 Audio Dubbing suites with voice over booths, Tracklay, Discreet Flint, Media Illusion, Drive in 1500 sq ft Video studio, 400 sq ft Virtual Studio, Duplication, Transmission Services, as well as the Molinare Design team for all your branding and design needs.

Mook

Tuscany Wharf, 4A Orsman Road, London N1 5QJ
t 020 7749 2525 **f** 020 7749 2526 **m** 07947 840668
e adrian@mook.co.uk **w** www.mook.co.uk
Contact Adrian Wilcox, Business Development Manager; Tom Evans, Creative Director; Tom Adams, Director of Client Services; Jess Goodall, Creative Director; Paul Green, Production Director
Credits VH-1 (T); BBCi (W); Puma Shudoh Boot Launch (W); MTV European Music Awards (W)

Mark Mordue

TOVS Ltd, The Linen Hall, 162-168 Regent Street, London W1B 5TB
t 020 7287 6110 **f** 020 7287 5481
e info@tovs.co.uk **w** www.tovs.co.uk

One

71 Dean Street, London W1D 3SF
t 020 7439 2730 **f** 020 7734 3331
e amanda.smalley@onepost.tv **w** www.onepost.tv
Contact Paul Jones, Managing Director; Will Byles, CGI; Matt Adams, Head of Production; Amanda Smalley, Sales & Marketing
Credits Kit Kat: Rap (Test) (C)

Phunx Design

21 Oswin Street, Elephant & Castle, London SE11 4TF
t 020 7735 1192 **m** 07866 951225 **e** phunxgirl@hotmail.com
Contact Amanda Whittington
Credits The BBC DV Solutions Department - White City (T); Mass Club - Brixton (M); Hypnologgin (M); 9 Concrete Danced (S)

Matthew Ralph

TOVS Ltd, The Linen Hall, 162-168 Regent Street, London W1B 5TB
t 020 7287 6110 **f** 020 7287 5481
e info@tovs.co.uk **w** www.tovs.co.uk

Donna Richards

TOVS Ltd, The Linen Hall, 162-168 Regent Street, London W1B 5TB
t 020 7287 6110 **f** 020 7287 5481
e info@tovs.co.uk **w** www.tovs.co.uk

Benjamin Riley

8B Austin Street, Bethnal Green, London E2 7NB
f 020 7739 3238 **m** 07712 547412 **e** bcriley@bigfoot.com

Karen Round

TOVS Ltd, The Linen Hall, 162-168 Regent Street, London W1B 5TB
t 020 7287 6110 **f** 020 7287 5481
e info@tovs.co.uk **w** www.tovs.co.uk

Springboard Creative Solutions

Springboard Creative Solutions, 4 Holywell Road, London EC2A 4JF
t 020 7772 5000 **f** 020 7772 5020
e richardhall@springboarduk.com **w** www.springboarduk.com
Contact Andrea Tobin, Managing Director

John Tribe

Experience Counts - Call Me Ltd, 5th Floor, 41-42 Berners Street, London W1P 3AA
t 020 7637 8112 **f** 020 7580 2582

TSI

TSI Post Production

TSI Video, 10 Grape Street, London WC2H 8DY
t 020 7379 3435 **f** 020 7379 4589 **e** bookings@tsi.co.uk

Contact Simon Peach, Managing Director; Andy Wright, Producer; Simon Kanjee, Managing Director; Nathalie Roull; Shula Fitzgerald, Head of Sales; Alan Cronin, Facility Manager; Julia Gonsalves, Head of Bookings
Credits Robbie Williams In Concert (T); This Morning (T); Sir Robert Winston - The Human Instinct (T); They Think It's All Over (T)

The TSI Group includes:- TSI Post Production, TSI Transmission and TSI Design, a leading design and branding agency. The group offers high definition post production for feature films and television, digital post production for television titles, commercials and music promos.

The latest addition to the ever-expanding TSI Group is the introduction of 3D Studio Max 5 producing complex CGIs.

All in all a total and complete facility, oozing with bright, friendly, professional staff... an award winning team!"

Useful Companies

N&P Complex, Pinewood Studios, Pinewood Road, Iver Heath, Iver SL0 0NH
t 0700 087 3385 **f** 0700 087 3386
e c+v@useful.co.uk **w** www.useful.co.uk

Credits Blade 2 (F); Spy Game (F); XXX (F)

GRIPS

grips : contents

Equipment Hire	303
Services	304
Camera Car Driver	304
Key	304

Grip Equipment Hire

Camera Tracking Company

Innovation House, Douglas Drive, Godalming GU7 1JX
t 01483 426767 **f** 01483 413900
e info@aerialcamerasystems.com
w www.aerialcamerasystems.com

Contact Matthew Allwork; Malcolm Rogers, Director; Sam Heaphy, Director

The Grip Firm

24 Oxford Road, Teddington TW11 0PZ
t 020 8977 5005 **f** 020 8977 9388 **m** 07836 751080

Contact Jimmy Mullins, Hire Manager

Grip Unit

Pendeen, Copthorne Close, Croxley Green WD3 4AJ
t 01923 775785 **f** 01923 775785 **m** 07973 624185
e grip.unit@virgin.net **w** www.gripunit.co.uk

Contact Kay Read, Rental Manager; Les Dash, Camera Grip; Barry Read, Camera Grip
Credits Holby City (T); Casualty (T); Love, Honour and Obey (F)

Griplet Ltd

Willow Farm, Field Lane, Blofield Heath, Norwich NR13 4RP
t 020 8330 3331 **t** 01603 717522 **f** 01603 717661
m 07768 085711 **e** sales@griplet.co.uk **w** www.griplet.co.uk

Contact Davina Young
Credits Wild West (T); B&Q (C); The League Of Gentlemen (T); Elizabeth (F)

Gripology Ltd

65 Eastwick Drive, Bookham KT23 3PU
t 01372 452107 **m** 07798 676435
e gripology1@aol.com **w** www.gripology.co.uk

Contact Mark Ellis
Credits Willow (F); Mission To Mars (F); The Rainbow (F); Full Metal Jacket (F)

Ray Hall

20C The Elms, Warfield Park, Bracknell RG42 3RP
t 01344 891197 **f** 01344 891197 **m** 07710 488594

Off Trax

Wharf House, Brentwaters Business Park, The Ham, Brentford TW8 8HQ
t 020 8232 8822 **f** 020 8232 8877
e mail@offtrax.co.uk **w** www.offtrax.co.uk

Contact Crispin Kyle, Facilities Manager

ONE 8 SIX Ltd

12 Garrick Centre, Irving Way, London NW9 6AQ
t 020 8203 8155 **f** 020 8457 2445
e info@one8six.com **w** www.one8six.com

Contact Marie Nicolas, Manager; Craig Game, Client Contact

OpTex UK

20-26 Victoria Road, New Barnet, London EN4 9PF
t 020 8441 2199 **f** 020 8449 3646
e info@optexint.com **w** www.optexint.com

Contact Edward Catton-Orr, Sales; Mike Robinson, Rentals

Panavision Grips London

The Metropolitan Centre, Bristol Road, Greenford UB6 8GD
t 020 8839 7333 **f** 020 8578 1536 **m** 07710 313 102
e mark.furssedonn@panavision.co.uk **w** www.panavision.co.uk

Contact Tony Kent, Hire Desk Manager

Take 2 Film Services Ltd

Unit 6, West Point Trading Estate, Alliance Rd, Acton, London W3 0RA
t 020 8992 2224 **f** 020 8992 2204
e rentals@take2films.co.uk **w** www.take2films.co.uk

Contact Vince Wild, Rental Desk Manager; Glyn Edridge, Managing Director

Transmission (TX) Ltd

Unit 2A, Shepperton Studios, Studios Road, Shepperton TW17 0QD
t 020 8547 0208 **f** 01932 572571 **m** 07769 688813
e info@ttx.co.uk **w** www.ttx.co.uk

Contact Steve Lloyd, General Manager; Melanie Parkin, Bookings Contact; Peter Hughes, Bookings Contact; Malcom Bubb, Bookings Contact
Credits The Hoobs (T); Doctors (T); Teletubbies (T)

TX supply a range of light-weight grip equipment for hire including Jimmy Jibs, CamCat, Jinx Jib, Mini Jib, Micro Jib, Keywest Dolly, Focus Dolly, Tracking Systems, Hotheads, Mini cam systems, Car Rigs, Steadicam — see website.

VFG Hire Ltd

8 Beresford Avenue, Wembley HA0 1LA
t 020 8795 7000 **f** 020 8795 3366
e enquiries@vfg.co.uk **w** www.vfg.co.uk
Contact Chris Youlton, Client Contact; Marc Irwin, Marketing Manager; Ann Marie Woodhall, Rental Desk Manager; George Martin, Client Contact Lighting; Graham Hawkins, Head of Cameras; Del Jones, Client Contact; Claire Wiles, Client Contact; Jeremy Sassen, Client Contact
Credits Silent Witness (T); Waking The Dead (T); Midsomer Murders (T); Judge John Deeds (T)

Pinewood: 01753 631 133. Belfast: 028 9057 2525. Cardiff: 02920 561 900. Dublin: 00 353 (0) 1286 3811. Isle of Man: 01624 862559. Scotland: 0141 948 0101. Manchester: 0161 848 7744.

Grip Services

Gripworx Ltd

73 Silver Street, Newport Pagnell, Milton Keynes MK16 0EQ
t 01908 616634 **f** 01908 616634 **m** 07966 232362
e tony@gripworx.co.uk
Contact Tony Fabian
For all Grip requirements including GF14 crane with steadicam platform.

AJ Kennedy

67 Seaforth Road, Stornoway, Isle of Lewis HS1 2QS
t 01851 703333 **f** 01851 703322 **m** 07761 829133
e admin@islesfm.org.uk
Credits Miulaidh (T); Mo Bhalach (T); An Roghainn (T)

John Phillips

7 Park Place, Ealing, London W5 5NQ
t 020 8579 7135 **f** 020 8579 7135 **m** 0973 727630
e greaves.phillips@btinternet.com
Credits Bay College (T); Black Books (T); Spaced (T); The Bench (T)

Peter Scorah

20 New Road, Crich DE4 5BX
t 01773 857096 **f** 01773 857096 **m** 07973 147496
e p.scorah@care4free.net
Credits Baited Breath (T); The Full Monty (F); Parting Shots (F); Night And Day (T)

SSE Ltd

19 Sutton Crescent, Barnet EN5 2SW
t 020 8449 8950 **f** 020 8449 1542 **m** 07904 316105
e gripgear@aol.com **w** www.ssegripgear.co.uk
Contact Alan Saul, Director; Joyce Saul, Director

Tim Normington Ltd

54 Aslett Street, London SW18 2BH
t 020 8877 9122 **t** 07971 622615 **m** 07973 878757
e tim@normington.com **w** www.timnormington.com
Contact Julia Herbert, Production Manager; Tim Normington, Proprietor
Credits Survivor (T); The Queen's Concerts (T); Top Of The Pops Awards (T); The Royal Variety Performance (T)

Trew Grip

61 Granton Road, Birmingham B14 6HG
t 0121 443 4230 **f** 0121 443 4230 **m** 07973 786055
Contact Ian Strachan, Line Producer; Hilary Benson, Assistant Producer; Mike Treen, Line Producer
Credits Down To Earth (T); Serious And Organised (T); Second Sight (T); Midsomer Murders (T)

Grips Camera Car Driver

Ken Ashley-Johnson

Wizzo & Co, 35 Old Compton Street, London W1D 5JX
t 020 7437 2055 **f** 020 7437 2066
e wizzo@wizzoandco.co.uk **w** www.wizzoandco.co.uk

Daniel Essex

Wizzo & Co, 35 Old Compton Street, London W1D 5JX
t 020 7437 2055 **f** 020 7437 2066
e wizzo@wizzoandco.co.uk **w** www.wizzoandco.co.uk

David Summerfield

57 Little Searles, Pitsea, Basildon SS13 1NE
t 01268 583591 **f** 01268 583591 **m** 07979 462808
e dave@gripcam.freeserve.co.uk
Credits Love Me Or Leave Me Alone (S); Blackball (F); Plain Jane (T)

Simon Ward

Wizzo & Co, 35 Old Compton Street, London W1D 5JX
t 020 7437 2055 **f** 020 7437 2066
e wizzo@wizzoandco.co.uk **w** www.wizzoandco.co.uk

Grips Key

A&G Camera Grip Services

9 Park Avenue, Craig-y-Don, Llandudno LL30 1EZ
t 01492 876344 **f** 01492 873166 **e** algrips@hotmail.com
Contact Allan Hughes

David Appleby

Bookends, 83 Maynard Drive, St Albans AL1 2JX
t 01727 841177 **e** bookgold@bookends.fsbusiness.co.uk

John Arnold

EXEC, 6 Travis Court, Farnham Royal SL2 3SB
t 01753 646677 **f** 01753 646770
e sue@execmanagement.co.uk **w** www.execmanagement.co.uk

Phil Aylward

Annie's Answering Service, Pinewood Studios, Pinewood Road, Iver Heath SL0 0NH
t 01753 651303 **f** 01753 651848
e info@annies.co.uk **w** www.annies.co.uk

Rob Barlow

12A Perrymead Street, London SW6 3SP
m 07957 370619 **e** rob@k2-grips.co.uk
Agent Suz Cruz, Halliford Studios, Manygate Lane, Shepperton TW17 9EG
t 01932 252577 **f** 01932 253323 **m** 07956 485593
e zoe@suzcruz.co.uk **w** www.suzcruz.co.uk
Credits Arctic Challenge (D); Victoria Beckham (C); Truth (T)

Malcolm Beale

Agent Annie's Answering Service, Pinewood Studios, Pinewood Road, Iver Heath SL0 0NH
t 01753 651303 **f** 01753 651848
e info@annies.co.uk **w** www.annies.co.uk
Agent Gems, The Media House, 87 Glebe Street, Penarth CF64 1EF
t 029 2071 0770 **f** 029 2071 0771
e gems@gems-agency.co.uk **w** www.gems-agency.co.uk

Jason Bergh

Bookends, 83 Maynard Drive, St Albans AL1 2JX
t 01727 841177 **e** bookgold@bookends.fsbusiness.co.uk

Mark Binnall

EXEC, 6 Travis Court, Farnham Royal SL2 3SB
t 01753 646677 **f** 01753 646770
e sue@execmanagement.co.uk **w** www.execmanagement.co.uk

Jim Boorer

GAS (Guild Answering Service), C/o Panavision UK, Metropolitan Centre, Bristol Road, Greenford UB6 8GD
t 020 8813 1999 **f** 020 8813 2111
e admin@gbct.org **w** www.gbct.org

John Breedon

Suz Cruz, Halliford Studios, Manygate Lane, Shepperton TW17 9EG
t 01932 252577 **f** 01932 253323 **m** 07956 485593
e zoe@suzcruz.co.uk **w** www.suzcruz.co.uk

Paul Brinkworth

Callbox Communications Limited, 66 Shepperton Studios, Studios Road, Shepperton TW17 0QD
t 01932 592572 **f** 01932 569655 **m** 07710 572572
e callboxdiary@btinternet.com **w** www.callboxdiary.co.uk

Richard Broome

Callbox Communications Limited, 66 Shepperton Studios, Studios Road, Shepperton TW17 0QD
t 01932 592572 **f** 01932 569655 **m** 07710 572572
e callboxdiary@btinternet.com **w** www.callboxdiary.co.uk

Colin Brown

The Firm Booking Company Ltd, 31 Oval Road, Camden, London NW1 7EA
t 020 7428 9090 **f** 020 7428 9089 **e** kirsty@thefirm.co.uk

Ian Buckley

GAS (Guild Answering Service), C/o Panavision UK, Metropolitan Centre, Bristol Road, Greenford UB6 8GD
t 020 8813 1999 **f** 020 8813 2111
e admin@gbct.org **w** www.gbct.org

David Cadwallader

EXEC, 6 Travis Court, Farnham Royal SL2 3SB
t 01753 646677 **f** 01753 646770
e sue@execmanagement.co.uk **w** www.execmanagement.co.uk

Barry Calvert

Suz Cruz, Halliford Studios, Manygate Lane, Shepperton TW17 9EG
t 01932 252577 **f** 01932 253323 **m** 07956 485593
e zoe@suzcruz.co.uk **w** www.suzcruz.co.uk

James Coulter

106 Hamilton Road, Rutherghen, Glasgow G73 3DS
t 0141 647 1892 **f** 0141 647 1892 **m** 07771 775992
e jamescoultergrip@msn.com

Dave Cross

Suz Cruz, Halliford Studios, Manygate Lane, Shepperton TW17 9EG
t 01932 252577 **f** 01932 253323 **m** 07956 485593
e zoe@suzcruz.co.uk **w** www.suzcruz.co.uk

Jim Crowther

17 Kingsley Avenue, Sutton SM1 3RE
t 020 8061 6075 **f** 020 8661 6075 **m** 07973 491 641
e jimgrip@hotmail.com
Credits Mrs Caldicotts Cabbage War; Gladiator (F); Sirens

Dash Grip Unit

11 Plough Close, Lewsey Farm, Luton LU4 0SS
t 01582 662197 **f** 01582 656615 **m** 07774 234452
e les.dash@virgin.net
Credits Born And Bred (T); Alistair McGowan's Big Impression (T); Baby Father (T); Holby City (T)

Les Dash

11 Plough Close, Luton LU4 0SS
t 01582 662197 **f** 01582 656615 **m** 07774 234452
e les.dash@virgin.net
Credits EastEnders (T); Red Cap (T); Alister McGowan's Big Impression (T); Holby City (T)

Richard Davies

Callbox Communications Limited, 66 Shepperton Studios, Studios Road, Shepperton TW17 0QD
t 01932 592572 **f** 01932 569655 **m** 07710 572572
e callboxdiary@btinternet.com **w** www.callboxdiary.co.uk

Dennis Dillon

7 Braintree Road, South Ruislip HA4 0EJ
t 020 8845 7373 **f** 020 8845 7373 **m** 07802 636514
e denthegrip@msn.com

Russell Diamond

120 High Street, Stotfold, Hitchin SG5 4LH
t 01462 730946 **f** 01462 734007 **m** 07802 484668
e grumpygrip@aol.com **w** www.grumpygrip.co.uk
Agent Carlin Crew Ltd, Shepperton Studios, Studios Road, Shepperton TW17 0QD
t 01932 568268 **f** 01932 571109
e carlin@netcomuk.co.uk **w** www.carlincrew.com
Credits Jonathon Creek (T); Without Motive (T); NCS (T); Last Orders (F)

Bob Dixon

37 East Street, Tynemouth NE30 4EB
t 01912 587882 **m** 07973 310401
Credits Kathrine Cookson - The Secret (T); Emmerdale (T); Badger (T); Sharp (T)

Johnny Donne

Suz Cruz, Halliford Studios, Manygate Lane, Shepperton TW17 9EG
t 01932 252577 **f** 01932 253323 **m** 07956 485593
e zoe@suzcruz.co.uk **w** www.suzcruz.co.uk

Dave Draper

GAS (Guild Answering Service), C/o Panavision UK, Metropolitan Centre, Bristol Road, Greenford UB6 8GD
t 020 8813 1999 **f** 020 8813 2111
e admin@gbct.org **w** www.gbct.org

Harry Eckford

Annie's Answering Service, Pinewood Studios, Pinewood Road, Iver Heath SL0 0NH
t 01753 651303 **f** 01753 651848
e info@annies.co.uk **w** www.annies.co.uk

Andy Edridge

Carlin Crew Ltd, Shepperton Studios, Studios Road, Shepperton TW17 0QD
t 01932 568268 **f** 01932 571109
e carlin@netcomuk.co.uk **w** www.carlincrew.com

Mark Ellis

EXEC, 6 Travis Court, Farnham Royal SL2 3SB
t 01753 646677 **f** 01753 646770
e sue@execmanagement.co.uk **w** www.execmanagement.co.uk

John Flemming

67 Willow Crescent West, Willow Bank, New Dewham UB9 4AU
t 01895 236839 **f** 01895 253261 **m** 07850 576971
e chiefgrips@aol.com
Agent Annie's Answering Service, Pinewood Studios, Pinewood Road, Iver Heath SL0 0NH
t 01753 651303 **f** 01753 651848
e info@annies.co.uk **w** www.annies.co.uk
Credits The Mummy Returns (F); Reign Of Fire (F); Spy Game (F); The World Is Not Enough (F)

Kevin Fraser

EXEC, 6 Travis Court, Farnham Royal SL2 3SB
t 01753 646677 **f** 01753 646770
e sue@execmanagement.co.uk **w** www.execmanagement.co.uk

Bob Freeman

Carlin Crew Ltd, Shepperton Studios, Studios Road, Shepperton TW17 0QD
t 01932 568268 **f** 01932 571109
e carlin@netcomuk.co.uk **w** www.carlincrew.com

Chris Frost
Annie's Answering Service, Pinewood Studios, Pinewood Road, Iver Heath SL0 0NH
t 01753 651303 **f** 01753 651848
e info@annies.co.uk **w** www.annies.co.uk

Dan Garlick
Annie's Answering Service, Pinewood Studios, Pinewood Road, Iver Heath SL0 0NH
t 01753 651303 **f** 01753 651848
e info@annies.co.uk **w** www.annies.co.uk

Patrick Garrett
Callbox Communications Limited, 66 Shepperton Studios, Studios Road, Shepperton TW17 0QD
t 01932 592572 **f** 01932 569655 **m** 07710 572572
e callboxdiary@btinternet.com **w** www.callboxdiary.co.uk

Bill Geddes
GAS (Guild Answering Service), C/o Panavision UK, Metropolitan Centre, Bristol Road, Greenford UB6 8GD
t 020 8813 1999 **f** 020 8813 2111
e admin@gbct.org **w** www.gbct.org

Colin Ginger
Suz Cruz, Halliford Studios, Manygate Lane, Shepperton TW17 9EG
t 01932 252577 **f** 01932 253323 **m** 07956 485593
e zoe@suzcruz.co.uk **w** www.suzcruz.co.uk

Stuart Godfrey
106 Noak Hill Road, Billericay CM12 9UH
t 01277 656759 **f** 01277 656777 **m** 07831 558992
e stugrip@aol.com **w** http://members.aol.com/stugrip
Agent Annie's Answering Service, Pinewood Studios, Pinewood Road, Iver Heath SL0 0NH
t 01753 651303 **f** 01753 651848
e info@annies.co.uk **w** www.annies.co.uk
Credits Guest House Paradiso (F); Kevin And Perry Go Large (F)

Ray Hall
EXEC, 6 Travis Court, Farnham Royal SL2 3SB
t 01753 646677 **f** 01753 646770
e sue@execmanagement.co.uk **w** www.execmanagement.co.uk

Ricky Hall
Bramcote, Dedworth Road, Oakley Green, Windsor SL4 4WT
t 01753 831219 **f** 01753 831219 **m** 07802 353850
Agent EXEC, 6 Travis Court, Farnham Royal SL2 3SB
t 01753 646677 **f** 01753 646770
e sue@execmanagement.co.uk **w** www.execmanagement.co.uk
Credits Rock Face II (T); Peak Practice (T); Die Another Day (F); The World Is Not Enough (F)

Vic Hammond
10 Grove Close, Ickenham UB10 8QN
t 01895 237861 **f** 01895 237861 **m** 07956 232757
Credits Harry Potter And The Chamber Of Secrets (F); Lara Croft: Tomb Raider (F); Sleepy Hollow (F)

Paul Hatchman
EXEC, 6 Travis Court, Farnham Royal SL2 3SB
t 01753 646677 **f** 01753 646770
e sue@execmanagement.co.uk **w** www.execmanagement.co.uk

Tony Haughey
Suz Cruz, Halliford Studios, Manygate Lane, Shepperton TW17 9EG
t 01932 252577 **f** 01932 253323 **m** 07956 485593
e zoe@suzcruz.co.uk **w** www.suzcruz.co.uk

Andy Hickman
36B Foyle Road, Blackheath, London SE3 7RH
t 020 8853 3858 **f** 020 8853 3858 **m** 07659 110610
Credits Gimme 6 (T); Bounce (C); Comedy Chillers (T); The 51st State (F)

Kevin Higgins
GAS (Guild Answering Service), C/o Panavision UK, Metropolitan Centre, Bristol Road, Greenford UB6 8GD
t 020 8813 1999 **f** 020 8813 2111
e admin@gbct.org **w** www.gbct.org

Dave Holliday
GAS (Guild Answering Service), C/o Panavision UK, Metropolitan Centre, Bristol Road, Greenford UB6 8GD
t 020 8813 1999 **f** 020 8813 2111
e admin@gbct.org **w** www.gbct.org

Andy Hopkins
GAS (Guild Answering Service), C/o Panavision UK, Metropolitan Centre, Bristol Road, Greenford UB6 8GD
t 020 8813 1999 **f** 020 8813 2111
e admin@gbct.org **w** www.gbct.org

Peter Hopkins
58 Whitley Close, Stanwell, Staines TW19 7EZ
t 01784 243327 **t** 020 8813 2111 **f** 020 8813 2111
f 020 8813 1999 **m** 07976 423548
Credits Tale of Two Cities; Prince And The Pauper; Bounty

Mike House
Callbox Communications Limited, 66 Shepperton Studios, Studios Road, Shepperton TW17 0QD
t 01932 592572 **f** 01932 569655 **m** 07710 572572
e callboxdiary@btinternet.com **w** www.callboxdiary.co.uk

Bob Howland
Suz Cruz, Halliford Studios, Manygate Lane, Shepperton TW17 9EG
t 01932 252577 **f** 01932 253323 **m** 07956 485593
e zoe@suzcruz.co.uk **w** www.suzcruz.co.uk

Malcolm Huse
Callbox Communications Limited, 66 Shepperton Studios, Studios Road, Shepperton TW17 0QD
t 01932 592572 **f** 01932 569655 **m** 07710 572572
e callboxdiary@btinternet.com **w** www.callboxdiary.co.uk

Gary Hutchings
Windward, Terrace Raod North, Binfield RG42 5JG
t 01344 457324 **f** 01344 457324 **m** 07976 736757
Agent GAS (Guild Answering Service), C/o Panavision UK, Metropolitan Centre, Bristol Road, Greenford UB6 8GD
t 020 8813 1999 **f** 020 8813 2111
e admin@gbct.org **w** www.gbct.org
Credits Enigma (F); Lara Croft: Tomb Raider (F); The Hours (F)

Gary Hymns
t 01895 632043 **f** 01895 632043 **m** 07976 833 989
e g.hymns@tinyworld.co.uk
Credits Johnny English (F); The Parole Officer (F); Dirty Pretty Things (F)

JR Grip & Transport Services
10 Cross Deep Gardens, Twickenham TW1 4QU
t 020 8892 3736 **f** 020 8404 8310 **m** 07710 0735517

Phil Kenyon
Suz Cruz, Halliford Studios, Manygate Lane, Shepperton TW17 9EG
t 01932 252577 **f** 01932 253323 **m** 07956 485593
e zoe@suzcruz.co.uk **w** www.suzcruz.co.uk

Bill Van Der Kris
Carlin Crew Ltd, Shepperton Studios, Studios Road, Shepperton TW17 0QD
t 01932 568268 **f** 01932 571109
e carlin@netcomuk.co.uk **w** www.carlincrew.com

Matt Lopez-Dias
t 020 8559 8756 **m** 07810 288 954 **e** email@mattlopezdias.com
Credits Dave Matthews (M); Corndoll (S); Fallen Angels (F)

Ian Maghie
Hut 2, 31 Alexander Road, Manchester M16 8SF
m 07831 244428
Credits Foyle's War (T); Henry VIII (T)

Colin Manning
Annie's Answering Service, Pinewood Studios, Pinewood Road, Iver Heath SL0 0NH
t 01753 651303 **f** 01753 651848
e info@annies.co.uk **w** www.annies.co.uk

Keith Manning
t 01895 445753 **m** 07885 348877
e keithmanning@tesco.net **w** www.ukscreen.com/crew/keithmanni
Agent Annie's Answering Service, Pinewood Studios, Pinewood Road, Iver Heath SL0 0NH
t 01753 651303 **f** 01753 651848
e info@annies.co.uk **w** www.annies.co.uk
Credits Lenor (C); 102 Dalmatians (F); Hornblower (T); Iris (F)

Dave Maund
GAS (Guild Answering Service), C/o Panavision UK, Metropolitan Centre, Bristol Road, Greenford UB6 8GD
t 020 8813 1999 **f** 020 8813 2111
e admin@gbct.org **w** www.gbct.org

Adrian McCarthy
Suz Cruz, Halliford Studios, Manygate Lane, Shepperton TW17 9EG
t 01932 252577 **f** 01932 253323 **m** 07956 485593
e zoe@suzcruz.co.uk **w** www.suzcruz.co.uk

Adrian Simon McCarthy
10 Second Cross Road, Twickenham TW2 5RF
t 020 8894 6025 **m** 07973 256299
e asmccarthy@btopenworld.com
Credits The Good Thief (F); Dirty Pretty Things (F); Gladiator (F); Trainspotting (F)

Jamie Monks
Suz Cruz, Halliford Studios, Manygate Lane, Shepperton TW17 9EG
t 01932 252577 **f** 01932 253323 **m** 07956 485593
e zoe@suzcruz.co.uk **w** www.suzcruz.co.uk

Steve Morgan
Carlin Crew Ltd, Shepperton Studios, Studios Road, Shepperton TW17 0QD
t 01932 568268 **f** 01932 571109
e carlin@netcomuk.co.uk **w** www.carlincrew.com

Jem Morton
Drusden East, Heusden Way, Gerrards Cross SL9 7BD
t 01753 885624 **f** 01753 886255 **m** 07980 222492
e jemmorton@hotmail.com
Agent Suz Cruz, Halliford Studios, Manygate Lane, Shepperton TW17 9EG
t 01932 252577 **f** 01932 253323 **m** 07956 485593
e zoe@suzcruz.co.uk **w** www.suzcruz.co.uk
Credits Once Upon A Time In The Midlands (F)

Jimmy Mullins
Callbox Communications Limited, 66 Shepperton Studios, Studios Road, Shepperton TW17 0QD
t 01932 592572 **f** 01932 569655 **m** 07710 572572
e callboxdiary@btinternet.com **w** www.callboxdiary.co.uk

Peter Muncey
Carlin Crew Ltd, Shepperton Studios, Studios Road, Shepperton TW17 0QD
t 01932 568268 **f** 01932 571109
e carlin@netcomuk.co.uk **w** www.carlincrew.com

Ronan Murphy
Suz Cruz, Halliford Studios, Manygate Lane, Shepperton TW17 9EG
t 01932 252577 **f** 01932 253323 **m** 07956 485593
e zoe@suzcruz.co.uk **w** www.suzcruz.co.uk

Phil Murray
EXEC, 6 Travis Court, Farnham Royal SL2 3SB
t 01753 646677 **f** 01753 646770
e sue@execmanagement.co.uk **w** www.execmanagement.co.uk

Ron Nicholls
Suz Cruz, Halliford Studios, Manygate Lane, Shepperton TW17 9EG
t 01932 252577 **f** 01932 253323 **m** 07956 485593
e zoe@suzcruz.co.uk **w** www.suzcruz.co.uk

Rupert Lloyd Parry
Callbox Communications Limited, 66 Shepperton Studios, dios Road, Shepperton TW17 0QD
t 01932 592572 **f** 01932 569655 **m** 07710 572572
e callboxdiary@btinternet.com **w** www.callboxdiary.co.uk

Mickie Patten
Suz Cruz, Halliford Studios, Manygate Lane, Shepperton TW17 9EG
t 01932 252577 **f** 01932 253323 **m** 07956 485593
e zoe@suzcruz.co.uk **w** www.suzcruz.co.uk

Nick Pearson
EXEC, 6 Travis Court, Farnham Royal SL2 3SB
t 01753 646677 **f** 01753 646770
e sue@execmanagement.co.uk **w** www.execmanagement.co.uk

Toby Plaskitt
High Glade House, Warren Row, Reading
t 01628 826744 **f** 01628 820168 **m** 07884 232591
e plaskitt@tinyworld.co.uk
Credits Much Ado About Nothing (F); The Hole (F); Harry Potter And The Philospher's Stone (F)

Gary Pocock
EXEC, 6 Travis Court, Farnham Royal SL2 3SB
t 01753 646677 **f** 01753 646770
e sue@execmanagement.co.uk **w** www.execmanagement.co.uk

Tim Proctor
GAS (Guild Answering Service), C/o Panavision UK, Metropolitan Centre, Bristol Road, Greenford UB6 8GD
t 020 8813 1999 **f** 020 8813 2111
e admin@gbct.org **w** www.gbct.org

Darren Quinn
Annie's Answering Service, Pinewood Studios, Pinewood Road, Iver Heath SL0 0NH
t 01753 651303 **f** 01753 651848
e info@annies.co.uk **w** www.annies.co.uk

Alan Rank
GAS (Guild Answering Service), C/o Panavision UK, Metropolitan Centre, Bristol Road, Greenford UB6 8GD
t 020 8813 1999 **f** 020 8813 2111
e admin@gbct.org **w** www.gbct.org

David Rist
7 Stane Street, Baldock SG7 6TS
t 01462 491293 **f** 01462 491293 **m** 07885 427 638
e rist.family@virgin.net
Agent EXEC, 6 Travis Court, Farnham Royal SL2 3SB
t 01753 646677 **f** 01753 646770
e sue@execmanagement.co.uk **w** www.execmanagement.co.uk
Credits All About Adam; Band Of Brothers (T); Spy Game (F)

John Robinson
Carlin Crew Ltd, Shepperton Studios, Studios Road, Shepperton TW17 0QD
t 01932 568268 **f** 01932 571109
e carlin@netcomuk.co.uk **w** www.carlincrew.com

Geoff Rogers
SBFC, Unit 8, Sandhurst House, Wolsey Street, London E1 3BD

Nobby Roker
Suz Cruz, Halliford Studios, Manygate Lane, Shepperton TW17 9EG
t 01932 252577 **f** 01932 253323 **m** 07956 485593
e zoe@suzcruz.co.uk **w** www.suzcruz.co.uk

Gary Romaine
Carlin Crew Ltd, Shepperton Studios, Studios Road,
Shepperton TW17 0QD
t 01932 568268 **f** 01932 571109
e carlin@netcomuk.co.uk **w** www.carlincrew.com

Wayne Rowe
GAS (Guild Answering Service), C/o Panavision UK,
Metropolitan Centre, Bristol Road, Greenford UB6 8GD
t 020 8813 1999 **f** 020 8813 2111
e admin@gbct.org **w** www.gbct.org

Tony Rowland
Annie's Answering Service, Pinewood Studios, Pinewood Road,
Iver Heath SL0 0NH
t 01753 651303 **f** 01753 651848
e info@annies.co.uk **w** www.annies.co.uk

Derek Russell
EXEC, 6 Travis Court, Farnham Royal SL2 3SB
t 01753 646677 **f** 01753 646770
e sue@execmanagement.co.uk **w** www.execmanagement.co.uk

Tony Sankey
Carlin Crew Ltd, Shepperton Studios, Studios Road,
Shepperton TW17 0QD
t 01932 568268 **f** 01932 571109
e carlin@netcomuk.co.uk **w** www.carlincrew.com

Jess Saunders
Suz Cruz, Halliford Studios, Manygate Lane, Shepperton TW17 9EG
t 01932 252577 **f** 01932 253323 **m** 07956 485593
e zoe@suzcruz.co.uk **w** www.suzcruz.co.uk

Malcolm Sheehan
Callbox Communications Limited, 66 Shepperton Studios,
Studios Road, Shepperton TW17 0QD
t 01932 592572 **f** 01932 569655 **m** 07710 572572
e callboxdiary@btinternet.com **w** www.callboxdiary.co.uk

Gary Smith
EXEC, 6 Travis Court, Farnham Royal SL2 3SB
t 01753 646677 **f** 01753 646770
e sue@execmanagement.co.uk **w** www.execmanagement.co.uk

Malcolm Smith
GAS (Guild Answering Service), C/o Panavision UK,
Metropolitan Centre, Bristol Road, Greenford UB6 8GD
t 020 8813 1999 **f** 020 8813 2111
e admin@gbct.org **w** www.gbct.org

Robin Stone
62 Meadow Road, Quinton, Birmingham B32 1BA
t 0121 422 4142 **f** 0121 422 5575 **m** 07973 363566
e oscarsnest@aol.com
Agent Carlin Crew Ltd, Shepperton Studios, Studios Road,
Shepperton TW17 0QD
t 01932 568268 **f** 01932 571109
e carlin@netcomuk.co.uk **w** www.carlincrew.com
Credits Charlotte Gray (F); The Forsyte Saga (T); Saving Grace (F);
Band Of Brothers (T)

Colin Strachan
Callbox Communications Limited, 66 Shepperton Studios,
Studios Road, Shepperton TW17 0QD
t 01932 572572 **f** 01932 592572 **m** 07710 572572
e callboxdiary@btinternet.com **w** +44 7710 572572

Derek Strachan
Carlin Crew Ltd, Shepperton Studios, Studios Road,
Shepperton TW17 0QD
t 01932 568268 **f** 01932 571109
e carlin@netcomuk.co.uk **w** www.carlincrew.com

David Stratful
Carlin Crew Ltd, Shepperton Studios, Studios Road,
Shepperton TW17 0QD
t 01932 568268 **f** 01932 571109
e carlin@netcomuk.co.uk **w** www.carlincrew.com

Alex Tate
Suz Cruz, Halliford Studios, Manygate Lane, Shepperton TW17 9EG
t 01932 252577 **f** 01932 253323 **m** 07956 485593
e zoe@suzcruz.co.uk **w** www.suzcruz.co.uk

Dean Taylor
23 Gordon Road, Stratford, London E15 2DD
t 020 8539 5477 **m** 07957 208 687
e winstyles@hotmail.com
Credits Sir Gadabout Series I & II (T); Urban Chill; Three Men in a Restaurant

Kirk Thornton
Callbox Communications Limited, 66 Shepperton Studios,
Studios Road, Shepperton TW17 0QD
t 01932 592572 **f** 01932 569655 **m** 07710 572572
e callboxdiary@btinternet.com **w** www.callboxdiary.co.uk

Tony Turner
GAS (Guild Answering Service), C/o Panavision UK,
Metropolitan Centre, Bristol Road, Greenford UB6 8GD
t 020 8813 1999 **f** 020 8813 2111
e admin@gbct.org **w** www.gbct.org

Jimmy Waters
EXEC, 6 Travis Court, Farnham Royal SL2 3SB
t 01753 646677 **f** 01753 646770
e sue@execmanagement.co.uk **w** www.execmanagement.co.uk

Steve Weightman
Suz Cruz, Halliford Studios, Manygate Lane, Shepperton TW17 9EG
t 01932 252577 **f** 01932 253323 **m** 07956 485593
e zoe@suzcruz.co.uk **w** www.suzcruz.co.uk

Terry Williams
Callbox Communications Limited, 66 Shepperton Studios,
Studios Road, Shepperton TW17 0QD
t 01932 592572 **f** 01932 569655 **m** 07710 572572
e callboxdiary@btinternet.com **w** www.callboxdiary.co.uk

Rick Woollard
Carlin Crew Ltd, Shepperton Studios, Studios Road,
Shepperton TW17 0QD
t 01932 568268 **f** 01932 571109
e carlin@netcomuk.co.uk **w** www.carlincrew.com

Andy Young
Griplet Ltd, Willow Farm, Field Lane, Blofield Heath, Norwich
NR13 4RP
t 01603 717522 **f** 01603 717661 **m** 07836 263 582
e sales@griplet.co.uk **w** www.griplet.co.uk
Credits Lenny Henry In Pieces I & II (T); Elizabeth (F); The League of
Gentlemen (T)

Lucho Zuidema
Suz Cruz, Halliford Studios, Manygate Lane, Shepperton TW17 9EG
t 01932 252577 **f** 01932 253323 **m** 07956 485593
e zoe@suzcruz.co.uk **w** www.suzcruz.co.uk

Hairdressers

Jeni Dodson
Joy Goodman Agency, 3 Lonsdale Rd, London NW6 6RA
t 020 7328 3338 **e** joygoodman@aol.com

Darren Evans
Mandy Coakley Represents, 18 Mandeville Courtyard, Warriner
Gardens, London SW11 4NB
t 020 7720 6234 **f** 020 7720 0199
e mc@mandycoakley.co.uk **w** www.mandycoakley.co.uk

Eithné Fennell
32 Middlegreen Road, Langley, Slough SL3 7BW
t 01753 539482 **f** 01753 774822 **m** 07710 597040
Credits Princess Bride (F); Mission Impossible (F); Harry Potter And The
Philosopher's Stone (F); Harry Potter And The Prisoner Of Azkaban (F)

Joy Goodman
3 Lonsdale Road, London NW6 6RA
t 020 7328 3338 **f** 020 7328 3337 **w** www.joygoodman.com

Sherman Hawthorne
Mandy Coakley Represents, 18 Mandeville Courtyard, Warriner
Gardens, London SW11 4NB
t 020 7720 6234 **f** 020 7720 0199
e mc@mandycoakley.co.uk **w** www.mandycoakley.co.uk

Gerry Jones
5 Foliot Street, East Acton, London W12 0BQ
t 020 8740 6746 **f** 020 8740 6746 **m** 07885 297 970
Credits The Patriot (F); The Mummy Returns (F); Behind Enemy Lines (F)

Lisa Laudat
Mandy Coakley Represents, 18 Mandeville Courtyard, Warriner
Gardens, London SW11 4NB
t 020 7720 6234 **f** 020 7720 0199
e mc@mandycoakley.co.uk **w** www.mandycoakley.co.uk

Bernadine Long
Mandy Coakley Represents, 18 Mandeville Courtyard, Warriner
Gardens, London SW11 4NB
t 020 7720 6234 **f** 020 7720 0199
e mc@mandycoakley.co.uk **w** www.mandycoakley.co.uk

Paula Mann
12 Macklin Street, London WC2B 5SZ
t 020 7274 2746 **f** 020 7274 2746 **m** 07979 600464
Contact Joy Goodman, Agent; Nigel Barnes, Agent

Karen Mason
Mandy Coakley Represents, 18 Mandeville Courtyard, Warriner
Gardens, London SW11 4NB
t 020 7720 6234 **f** 020 7720 0199
e mc@mandycoakley.co.uk **w** www.mandycoakley.co.uk

Nat Cargius Hair & Beauty
Maverick Daffodil, 9 Chester Road, Gresford, Wrexham LL12 8DB
t 01978 855800 **m** 07967 321595
e natcut@totalise.co.uk **w** www.maverickdaffodil.com
Contact Nat Cargius, Proprietor

Helen Pham
Mandy Coakley Represents, 18 Mandeville Courtyard, Warriner
Gardens, London SW11 4NB
t 020 7720 6234 **f** 020 7720 0199
e mc@mandycoakley.co.uk **w** www.mandycoakley.co.uk

Suzanne Stokes-Munton
1A Myddelton Square, London EC1R 1XL
t 0207 837 3666 **f** 0207 837 3794 **m** 07785 246061
e sstokesmunton@hotmail.com
Credits Iron-Jawed Angels (T); Talk To Her (F); Dinotopia (T)

Antonio Surace
Mandy Coakley Represents, 18 Mandeville Courtyard, Warriner
Gardens, London SW11 4NB
t 020 7720 6234 **f** 020 7720 0199
e mc@mandycoakley.co.uk **w** www.mandycoakley.co.uk

Barbara Taylor
f 01457 869431 **m** 07836 748359
Credits Band Of Brothers (T); The Beach (F); Sense And Sensibility (F)

Mary Vango
Mandy Coakley Represents, 18 Mandeville Courtyard, Warriner
Gardens, London SW11 4NB
t 020 7720 6234 **f** 020 7720 0199
e mc@mandycoakley.co.uk **w** www.mandycoakley.co.uk

HEALTH & SAFETY
Health & Safety Advisors

Centurion Risk Assessment Services Ltd
PO Box 1740, Andover SP11 7PE
t 01264 355255 **f** 01264 355322
e main@centurion-riskservices.co.uk
w www.centurion-riskservices.co.uk
Contact Paul Rees, Director; Carole Rees, Administrator/Office Manager

H&S Advisory Service
Woodside, 19 Downwood Close, Fordingbridge SP6 1EA
t 01425 656246
Contact Brian Shemmings, Advisor

Ingrid Siebert Associates
1 Kettering Close, Calcot, Reading RG31 7DF
t 07000 464743
e isiebert@health-and-safety.co.uk **w** www.health-and-safety.co.uk
Contact Ingrid Siebert, Consultant
Credits Combat Cars (T); Beauty And The Beast(Theatrical); Pearl Harbor (F);
Star Wars: Episode I - The Phantom Menace (F)

Hilary Mahoney
3F Portman Mansions, Chiltern Street, London W1U 5AN
t 020 7224 3780 **m** 07973 139676

Michael Nevitt
t 01795 470443 **f** 01795 473030 **m** 07885 677030
e michael.nevitt@virgin.net

On-Set Safety
5 Glenside, Hythe SO45 5BA
t 02380 844751 **m** 07802 447327
e onsetsafety@aol.com **w** www.on-safety.com
Contact Dave Sutcliffe

Production Safety Services
White Gables, Cramer Gutter, Oreton DY14 0UA
t 01746 718080 **f** 01746 718080 **m** 07774 940 675
e dkt@prodsafe.demon.co.uk
Contact David King-Taylor, Main Contact

The Safety Business
49 Tottenham Court Road, London W1T 2EG
t 020 7637 5047 **f** 020 7637 3635
e info@safetybusiness.co.uk **w** www.safetybusiness.co.uk

Safety In Motion
6 Grayfriars, Ware SG12 0XW
t 01920 424812 **m** 07798 812661 **e** smckee3808@aol.com
e shaun@safetyinmotion.co.uk **w** www.safetyinmotion.co.uk
Credits The Fifth Element (F); Fame Academy (T); Jesus Christ Superstar (F);
Quills (F)

Health & Safety
Equipment Hire

The Safety Store
72 Chevening Road, London NW6 6DE
t 020 7122 2277 **f** 020 8960 2236
Credits First Knight: The Gauntlet Machine (F)

SRC UK
Patch Park Farm, Ongar Road, Abridge RM4 1AA
t 08702 404383 **f** 01708 688405
e jim@srcuk.co.uk **w** www.srcuk.com
Contact J Gaffney, Partner; JF Slater, Partner

Health & Safety
Fire Services

David Deane Associates Ltd (DDA Fire)
Pinewood Studios, Pinewood Road, Iver Heath SL0 ONH
t 01753 656181 **f** 01753 632820 **m** 07714 980323
e info@eurosafety.co.uk **w** www.ddafire.com
Contact Lynne Compton; David Deane, Director
Credits ThunderBirds (F); Lara Croft And The Cradle Of Life: Tomb Raider 2 (F);
Harry Potter And The Prisoner Of Azkaban (F); Harry Potter And The
Philosopher's Stone (F)

Midland Fire Protection Services
Paragon Park, 256 Foles-Hlll Road, Coventry CB6 5AY
t 024 7668 5252 **f** 024 7663 7575 **m** 07836 651408
e midlandfireuk@aol.com
Contact Robin Crane, Operations Director
Credits Orange (C); Heartburn Hotel (T); Dalziel & Pascoe (T)

The Pudding Lane Fire Company
5 Upper Austin Lodge Road, Eynsford, Dartford DA4 OHU
t 01322 863414 **f** 01322 863414 **m** 07970 166600
e fire@puddinglane.com **w** www.puddinglane.com
Contact Shaun McKeever, Director of Health & Safety; Roger Kendall,
Operations Director

SEC Fire Protection Ltd
Shepperton Studios, Studios Road, Shepperton TW17 0QD
t 01932 592147 **f** 01932 592402
Contact Peter Edwards, Managing Director

High Definition

Baraka Post Production
11 Greek Street, London W1D 4DJ
t 020 7734 2227 **e** bookings@baraka.co.uk **w** www.baraka.co.uk

Bow Tie Television
Unit 20, Bourne Industrial Park, Bourne Road, Crayford DA1 4BZ
t 01322 524500 **f** 01322 527777
e john@bowtietv.com **w** www.bowtietv.com
Contact John Knopp, Managing Director
Credits Endemol - King Of Sport (T); NHK Enterprises
Europe Ltd - Red Demon (T)

Faraday Technology Ltd
Croft Road Industrial Estate, Newcastle-under-Lyme ST5 0QZ
t 01782 661501 **f** 01782 630101 **m** 07769 908005
e jane@faradaytech.co.uk **w** www.faradaytech.co.uk
Contact Jane Holt, Marketing Contact

Metro Broadcast
5-7 Great Chapel Street, London W1F 8FF
t 020 7434 7700 **f** 020 7434 7701
e info@metrobroadcast.com **w** www.metrobroadcast.com
Contact Paul Beale, Business Development; Barry Noakes, Facilities Manager;
Mark Cox, Director
*Leading specialists in high definition offering HDCAM equipment
(including cameras, lenses and VTRs) crewing, duplications and
online non-linear editing.*

The Mill
40-41 Great Marlborough Street, London W1F 7JQ
t 020 7287 4041 **f** 020 7287 8393
e info@mill.co.uk **w** www.mill.co.uk
Contact Emma Shield
Credits Absolut Vodka - Mullet (C); BT Broadband - Burts Pipe (C);
Guiness - Lava (C); Levi's - Stampede (C)

Molinare
34 Fouberts Place, London W1F 7PX
t 020 7478 7000 **f** 020 7478 7199
e peterw@molinare.co.uk **w** www.molinare.co.uk
Contact Kate George, Facilities Manager
Credits Dorada Especial: Painting; AXN: Cornice; Walkers Dorito's: Idents;
The Wind

Rushes Postproduction Ltd
66 Old Compton Street, London W1D 4UH
t 020 7437 8676 **f** 07851 3002 /2519
e info@rushes.co.uk **w** www.rushes.co.uk
Contact Paul Jones, Facilities Director; Bill McNamara, Head of Visual
Effects; Sonia Ralton, Head of Production; Mike Uden, Creative Director;
Joce Capper, Managing Director; Rebecca Swegman, Head of Bookings;
Jo Morgan, Facility Manager

Screen Scene Ltd
41 Upper Mount Street, Dublin 2, Ireland
t +353 1 661 1501 **f** +353 1 661 0491
e info@screenscene.ie **w** www.screenscene.ie
Contact Jim Duggan; Alison Tully; Sinead Bagnall
Credits Acme Lager

high definition
the saviour of postproduction?

Possibly the most interesting development in the production industry also causes the most confusion. High (or Hi) Definition, or HD as it's also known, is big in the US and about to get bigger still, but elsewhere in the world, notably the UK, a strong domestic market for HD productions has yet to materialise. That is not to say that the expertise and facilities to produce high-definition work are not present in the UK. Quite the contrary, hotbeds of HD knowledge, such as St Anne's Post and Rushes, both in Soho, are pushing the format. Nor is there a lack of HD postproduction work here.

"The HD market is increasing all the time and we are working to provide our clients with all the information they need about HD and the benefits, cost savings and increased quality it offers," says Joce Capper, MD of Rushes. "There is still confusion about tape formats and whether jobs should be shot on film or HD. The industry is working together to try and dispel the myths surrounding HD, but Rushes works with HD as a tape format and in that respect it is no different to any other."

"The people with expertise in HD here are as good as anywhere else," says Bruce Everett, MD of St Anne's Post. "The great advantage with the US market is that there is much more work, more facilities and thus more people who know the format. We tend to have, in some sense, more sophisticated processes, partly because the budgets here are smaller. We have had to be innovative in the way that we deal with things, and the techniques that we've learnt over the years in Standard Definition have stood us in very good stead with HD."

However, with Digibeta and other Standard Definition formats still prevalent in European broadcast, most of the acquisition work with this format is still situated across the Atlantic. "There is much more demand now for high-definition in US television," says Tom Fletcher, vice-president of Fletcher Chicago. "There were four shows shot in HD in the 2001-02 season and twenty shows in this format last year. This season there will be fifty high-definition shows in the prime time on various networks."

The reason for this is pooling costs. Traditionally, the US has shot its programmes on film, whereas European productions have been using Digibeta much more readily. Now the US is moving straight from film to 24p. "Depending on who you talk to they're making savings of ten to twenty percent," says Fletcher. But this depends on the type of shows that are being made. Fletcher says there's a big cost saving with the likes of situation comedies, where four cameras are rolling all the time, but less so with scripted dramas that eat up less footage. "The commercial industry is moving towards it, the corporate television market is moving towards it,

all for different reasons," says Fletcher.

Fletcher's company hires acquisition equipment out of bases in five US states and has invested heavily in HD. "We have nine Sony CineAlta HDW-F900's with Zeiss lens, Fujinon cineStyle lenses," he says. "We've really gone after the high-end production crowd who would normally shoot on film, giving them all the accessories. A good piece of glass like a Zeiss lens is very important to them."

With an eye on the next burgeoning market Fletcher has just bought fifteen Panasonic variable frame rate HD cameras for use with sports programming. "Sports production has really started to pick up. This month, the NBA (National Basketball Association) launched its own station and ESPN has gone high-definition and will launch its channel at the end of the month," he explains. "The consumer is really going to notice high-definition programming because of these sports channels."

Fletcher thinks that broadcasters will have to do more to alert the audience to the benefits of high-definition, and sees the sports channels at the forefront of this awareness drive. Although HBO offers HD programming, he claims this will not drive the public to buy high-definition television sets.

"When you want to watch Saving Private Ryan, you just pop in a DVD on your high-definition player. You have 5:1 audio and the same aspect ratio as the cinema. The picture looks great, so there's not a big drive to go and buy a high-definition set. But with live sports it's a different story."

So it appears to be the sports channels like ESPN that will drive the US HD market. Another important point Fletcher makes, though, is that as ESPN is a satellite or cable service, it will get the cable companies to carry the higher bandwidth programming and so blaze a trail for the rest of the industry.

Creatives in the UK post industry have conflicting views about the format, though. "HD is a bit of a love-hate relationship," says Gavin Wellsman, flame operator at The Mill. "I love the look and definition that you get from HD, but hate the fact that simple effects take so long to create because of the processing time. Working in Pal, you are quite spoilt and can really experiment with shots. Working on HD, however, you really have to be sure that after a 20-minute process, what you are doing will work. It also seems to be a bit stop and start - I think a lot of directors would like to work with it more but avoid it because of lack of time and money."

"From a facilities perspective, HD is actually a bit of fresh air," counters Bruce Everett. "It's raised the stakes in expertise and gives facilities much more future in postproduction. It's not going to gravitate to the desktop, and the infrastructure and expertise required to make HD work lies with the video →→

→→→ HD - the saviour of postproduction

facilities. We don't have a delivery requirement in the UK for transmission in HD like there is in the US, so it's very much the influence of American money on co-productions that is driving the HD needs that we do have." In other words, according to Everett, if a producer is going to invest £800,000 to a million pounds per programme hour on a series, they're going to need to realise as much as they can of that back in the form of sales. "The overhead of HD is therefore relatively small in comparison to them not

making a sale, " he says. "By not having an HD version of their programme companies will find it's much more difficult to sell to the US."

Contacts   Fletcher Chicago, www.fletch.com
St Anne's Post, www.saintannespost.co.uk
Rushes, www.rushes.co.uk
The Mill, www.mill.co.uk

Writer   Michael Burns

St Anne's

20 St Anne's Court, London W1F OBH
t 020 7155 1500 **f** 020 7155 1501
e bruce.everett@saintannespost.co.uk
w www.saintannespost.co.uk

Contact Lucy Fuller, Bookings; Bruce Everett, Managing Director; Johnny Whitehead, Technical Operations; Portia Napier, Post Production Contacts; Becky Start, Sales; Dean Watkins, Sales
Credits State Of Mind (T); Mindhunters (F); Model Behaviour (T); Two Thousand Acres Of Sky (T)

TSI Post Production

TSI Video, 10 Grape Street, London WC2H 8DY
t 020 7379 3435 **f** 020 7379 4589 **e** bookings@tsi.co.uk

Contact Simon Peach, Managing Director; Andy Wright, Producer; Simon Kanjee, Managing Director; Nathalie Roull; Shula Fitzgerald, Head of Sales; Alan Cronin, Facility Manager; Julia Gonsalves, Head of Bookings
Credits Robbie Williams In Concert (T); This Morning (T); Sir Robert Winston - The Human Instinct (T); They Think It's All Over (T)

Home Economists

Eliza Baird
t 020 7608 3434 **f** 01884 251221
e hers@hersagency.co.uk **w** www.hersagency.co.uk

Jennie Berresford
t 020 7608 3434 **f** 01884 251221
e hers@hersagency.co.uk **w** www.hersagency.co.uk

Kit Chan
t 020 7608 3434 **f** 01884 251221
e hers@hersagency.co.uk **w** www.hersagency.co.uk

Lynne Clayton
Abbey Oaks, Farm House, Burstall Lane, Sproughton, Ipswich IP8 3DH
t 01473 747388 **f** 01473 747388 **m** 07774 113989
e lynneclayton@lineone.net
Credits Bernard Matthews Pizza (C); Bisto Gravy (C); Magnum Ice Cream (C)

Colin Capon Reel Foods
16 Sandore Road, Seaford BN25 3PR
t 01323 892429 **f** 01323 897347 **m** 07718 863603
e chef@colin-capon.fsworld.co.uk

Clare Ferguson
t 020 7608 3434 **f** 01884 251221
e hers@hersagency.co.uk **w** www.hersagency.co.uk

Christine Greaves
t 020 7608 3434 **f** 01884 251221
e hers@hersagency.co.uk **w** www.hersagency.co.uk

Beth Heald
t 020 7608 3434 **f** 01884 251221
e hers@hersagency.co.uk **w** www.hersagency.co.uk

HERS
t 01884 242248 **f** 01884 251221
e hers@hersagency.co.uk **w** www.hersagency.co.uk
Contact Julia Hetherington, Proprietor

Mary Luther
t 020 7608 3434 **f** 01884 251221
e hers@hersagency.co.uk **w** www.hersagency.co.uk

Joy Machell
t 020 7608 3434 **f** 01884 251221
e hers@hersagency.co.uk **w** www.hersagency.co.uk

Caroline Marson
t 020 7608 3434 **f** 01884 251221
e hers@hersagency.co.uk **w** www.hersagency.co.uk

Heather McInerny
Highway House, Church Lane, Ewshot, Farnham GU10 5BD
t 01252 850174 **f** 01252 850174 **m** 07860 327 329
Contact Heather McInerney

Lucy Miller
t 020 7608 3434 **f** 01884 251221
e hers@hersagency.co.uk **w** www.hersagency.co.uk

Elaine Ngan
2a Clifton Road, Wimbledon, London SW19 4QT
t 020 8947 2899 **f** 020 8944 8311 **m** 07831 888 654
e elainengan@aol.com

Jennie Reekie
Harraton Court Stables, Chapel Street, Exming, New Market CD8 7HA
t 01638 577952 **f** 01638 577952 **m** 07850 966169
e jennie@harratonstables.freeserve.co.uk

Pete Smith
81 Cornwall Gardens, London SW7 4AZ
t 020 7938 4807 **f** 020 7938 4807 **m** 07860 450 876
e peterdavid@81london.freeserve.co.uk

Camera Operator finds new angle

The ONLY show you need to visit in 2004

As the UK's largest production and broadcast exhibition, The Production Show is the most important industry event of the year. Whatever your speciality or area of interest, you need to be there to see all the latest innovations, technology, services, seminars plus free workshops.

The Production Show, 18-20 May 2004:

- Showcasing all the latest from NAB
- FREE Production and Craft workshops
- Essential seminars and masterclasses
- FREE career and training advice

It's the year's best networking opportunity and it's loaded with ways for you to learn, discover, do business and see what's hot.

To receive information about the 2004 show, log on to

www.productionshow.com

and leave your details.

THE
PRODUCTION
SHOW

18-20 MAY 2004

where **creativity**
meets **technology**

National Hall, Olympia, London

Nicole Szabason
t 020 7608 3434 f 01884 251221
e hers@hersagency.co.uk w www.hersagency.co.uk

Dagmar Vesely
t 020 7608 3434 f 01884 251221
e hers@hersagency.co.uk w www.hersagency.co.uk

Sunil Vijayakar
t 020 7608 3434 f 01884 251221
e hers@hersagency.co.uk w www.hersagency.co.uk

Hotel Booking Services

Abbey Court Hotel
20 Pembridge Gardens, Notting Hill, London W2 4DU
t 020 7221 7518 f 020 7792 3201 m 07957 588625
e info@abbeycourthotel.co.uk w www.abbeycourthotel.co.uk
Contact Abdel, Front Office Manager; Julian Hart, General Manager

Access Conference Connections
Highlawns, 53a Tamworth Road, Lichfield WS14 9HG
t 01543 411488 f 01543 411455
e sales@access-hotels.co.uk w www.access-hotels.co.uk
Contact Patricia Barnes, Director

Browns Hotel
Albermarle Street, Mayfair, London W1S 4BP
t 020 7493 6020 f 020 7493 9381
e brownshotel@brownshotel.com w www.brownshotel.com

Burnham Beeches Hotel
Grove Road, Burnham SL1 8DP
t 01628 429955 f 01628 603994 w www.regalhotels.co.uk
Contact Wendy Procter, General Manager

Cannizaro House Hotel & Restaurant
West Side, Wimbledon Common, London SW19 4UE
t 0870 333 9124 f 0870 333 9224
e cannizaro.house@thistle.co.uk w www.thistlehotels.com
Contact John Traynor, Revenue Manager

The Carlton Tower
Cadogan Place, London SW1X 9PY
t 020 7235 1234 f 020 7235 9129
e audra.taylor@carltontower.com w www.carltontower.com
Contact Audra Taylor, Marketing Executive; Rachel Evans, Marketing Manager; Liesbeth Van Geest, Reservation Manager

The Cavendish St James
81 Jermyn Street, St James's, London SW1Y 6JF
t 020 7930 2111 f 020 7839 2125 w www.devereonline.co.uk
Contact John Banks, Reservations Manager

Charlotte Street Hotel
15 Charlotte Street, London W1T 1RJ
t 020 7806 2000 f 020 7806 2002
e reservations@charlottestreethotel.co.uk
w www.charlottestreethotel.com
Contact Susannah Hall, Sales Manager; Flo Guillin, Front of House Manager

Chesterfield Hotel
35 Charles Street, Mayfair, London W1J 5ER
t 020 7491 2622 f 020 7491 4793
w www.redcarnationhotels.com
Contact Christoff Jordi, Duty & Guest Relations Manager

Claridge's
Brook Street, Mayfair, London W1A 2JQ
t 020 7629 8860 f 020 7499 2210
e info@claridges.co.uk w www.the-savoy-group.com/claridges
Contact Robert Buckolt

The Cliveden Town House
26 Cadogan Gardens, London SW3 2RP
t 020 7730 6466 f 020 7720 0236
e reservations@clivedentownhouse.co.uk
w www.clivedentownhouse.co.uk
Contact Paula Hawes, Business Development Manager

Connaught Hotel
16 Carlos Place, Mayfair, London W1K 2AL
t 020 7499 7070 f 020 7495 3262
e info@the-connaught.co.uk w www.savoy-group.co.uk

Copthorne Hotel Effingham Park Hotel
West Park Road, Copthorne RH10 3EU
t 01342 714994 f 01342 716039
e sales@effingham@mill-cop.com w www.millenniumhotels.com
Contact Nicola Hails, Events Supervisor

Copthorne Tara Hotel
Scarsdale Place, Kensington, London W8 5SR
t 020 7937 7211 f 020 7937 7100
e tara.res@mill-cop.com w www.millenniumhotels.com

Covent Garden Hotel
10 Monmouth Street, London WC2H 9HB
t 020 7806 1000 f 020 7806 1100
e covent@firmdale.com w www.firmdalehotels.com
Contact Susannah Hall, Sales Manager; Charmaine Gair, Reservations Manager

The Crowne Plaza London St James
45-51 Buckingham Gate, London SW1E 6AF
t 020 7834 6655 f 020 7630 7587
e reservations@cplonsj.co.uk w www.crowneplaza.com
Contact Alkesh Majevadia, Reservations Manager; Susanne Reus, Reservations Manager

Cumberland Hotel
Great Cumberland Place, London W1A 4RF
t 020 7262 1234 f 020 7724 4621 w www.lemeridien.com
Contact Louise Parsons, Reservations Manager

The Dorchester
Park Lane, London W1A 2HJ
t 020 7629 8888 f 020 7409 0114
e reservations@dorchesterhotel.com
w www.dorchesterhotel.com
Contact Natalie Kramer-Bawben, Director Of Sales

Dorset Square Hotel
39 Dorset Square, Marylebone, London NW1 6QN
t 020 7723 7874 e info@dorsetsquare.co.uk
w www.dorsetsquare.co.uk
Contact Janelle Baker, Reservations Supervisor; Rav Pinnel, Front Office Manager

Dukes Hotel
35 St James Place, London SW1A 1NY
t 020 7491 4840 f 020 7493 1264
e dukeshotel@csi.com w www.dukeshotel.co.uk

Eleven Cadogan Gardens
11 Cadogan Gardens, Sloane Square, London SW3 2RJ
t 020 7730 7000 f 020 7730 5217
e reservations@number-eleven.co.uk w www.number-eleven.co.uk

The Elstree Inn
148 Shenley Road, Borehamwood WD6 1EQ
t 020 8953 3175 f 020 8207 5500
e reservation@elstreeinn.demon.co.uk
w www.elstreeinn.demon.co.uk
Contact Ann Molyneux, General Manager

Executive Status Hotel Reservations Specialists
14A Kenworthy Lane, Manchester M22 4EJ
t 0161 613 9300 f 0161 613 9310
e enquiries@execstatus.com w www.execstatus.com

Flemings Mayfair Hotel
Halfmoon Street, Mayfair, London W1Y 7RA
t 020 7499 2964 **f** 020 7499 1817
e reservations@flemings-mayfair.co.uk
w www.flemings-mayfair.co.uk
Contact Jill Skidmore, Reservations Manager

Gloucester Hotel
4-18 Harrington Gardens, London SW7 4LH
t 020 7373 6030 **f** 020 7373 0409
e gloucester@mill-cop.com **w** www.millenniumhotels.com
Contact Joelle O'Neale, Reservations Manager

Go Native Ltd
26 Westbourne Grove, London W2 5RH
t 020 7221 2028 **f** 020 7221 2028
e katy@gonative.co.uk **w** www.gonative.co.uk
Contact Katy Thomas, Senior Account Manager

Gore Hotel
189 Queens Gate, London SW7 5EX
t 020 7584 6601 **f** 020 7589 8127
e reservations@gorehotel.co.uk **w** www.gorehotel.com
Contact Colin Exton, General Manager; Charnel Bunyan, Reservations Manager; Jana Zscherneck, Reservations Co-ordinator

The Goring
Beeston Place, Grosvenor Gardens, London SW1W 0JW
t 020 7396 9000 **f** 020 7834 4393
e reception@goringhotel.co.uk **w** www.goringhotel.co.uk
Contact William Cowpe, Managing Director

Grafton Hotel
130 Tottenham Court Road, London W1P 9HP
t 020 7388 4131 **f** 020 7753 0334
Contact Nesar Siddiqui, Head of Reception

Grosvenor Hotel
86 Park Lane, London W1K 7TN
t 020 7499 7248 **f** 020 7399 8111
e parklane@livebusiness.co.uk **w** www.livebusiness.co.uk
Contact Duncan Newton, Manager

Halkin Hotel
5 Halkin Street, Belgravia, London SW1X 7DJ
t 020 7333 1000 **f** 020 7333 1100
e res@halkin.co.uk **w** www.halkin.co.uk
Contact Malene Bertelson, Sales Manager

The Hampshire Hotel
31-36 Leicester Square, London WC2H 7LH
t 020 7839 9399 **f** 020 7930 8122
w www.radissonedwardian.com
Contact Colin Yap, Reservations Manager

Hilton National Hotel
Empire Way, Wembley HA9 8DS
t 020 8902 8839 **f** 020 8900 2201
Contact Andrew Stone, Reservations Manager

Holiday Inn Gatwick
Povey Cross Road, Horley RH6 0BA
t 0870 400 9030 **f** 01293 825091
Contact Orla Hines, General Manager

Hotel Booking Service Ltd
4 New Burlington Place, London W1S 2HS
t 020 7437 5052 **f** 020 7734 2124
e rooms@hotelbookingservice.com
Contact Elizabeth Smith, Reservations Manager; Ann Crooks, New Reservations Manager

Hotel Inter-Continental London
1 Hamilton Place, Hyde Park Corner, London W1J 7QY
t 020 7409 3131 **f** 020 7493 3476 **e** london@interconti.com
Contact Sharon Kilmartin, Acting General Manager; Peter Beckwith, General Manager

Hotel Number Sixteen
16 Sumner Place, South Kensington, London SW7 3EG
t 020 7589 5232 **f** 020 7584 8615
e sixteen@firmdale.com **w** www.numbersixteenhotel.co.uk
Contact Susannah Hall, Sales Manager; Andrea Ellenberger, Reservations Manager; Jean Branham

Howard Hotel
Temple Place, London WC2R 2PR
t 020 7836 3555 **f** 020 7379 4547
e reservations.london@swissotel
e emailas.london@swissotel.com **w** www.london-swissotel.com
Contact Fiona Tomase, Reservation Manager

InterContinental - The Churchill - London
30 Portman Square, London W1A 4ZX
t 020 7486 5800 **f** 020 7486 1255
e churchill@interconti.com **w** www.interconti.com
Contact Vanessa Morley, Sales Administrator

Jurys Doyles Clifton Ford Hotel
47 Welbeck Street, London W1G 8DN
t 020 7486 6600 **f** 020 7486 7492

Kensington Hilton Hotel
179-199 Holland Park Avenue, London W11 4UL
t 020 7603 3355 **f** 020 7602 9397
e sales_kensington@hilton.com **w** www.hilton.com
Contact Monika Beverus, Reservations Manager; Sarah Glanville, Reservations Manager

Knightsbridge Hotel
10 Beaufort Gardens, London SW3 1PT
t 020 7584 6300 **f** 020 7584 6355
e reservations@knightsbridgehotel.co.uk
w www.firmdalehotels.co.uk
Contact Susannah Hall, Sales Manager; Lisa Woodman, Assistant to General Manager

Lanesborough Hotel
Hyde Park Corner, London SW1X 7TA
t 020 7259 5599 **f** 020 7259 5606
e reservations@lanesborough.co.uk **w** www.lanesborough.com
Contact Jacqueline Davies, Reservations Manager

The Langham Hilton
1 Portland Place, Regent Street, London W1B 1JA
t 020 7636 1000 **f** 020 7323 2340 **w** www.hilton.com
Contact Jayne Hewitt, Public Relations Manager

Le Meridien
Bath Road, West Drayton UB7 0DU
t 020 8759 6611 **f** 020 8759 3421
w www.lemeridien-hotels.com
Contact Catriona Ryan, Reservations Manager

Le Meridien Russell
Russell Square, London WC1B 5BE
t 020 7837 6470 **f** 020 7837 2857
e reservations.russell@principalhotels.co.uk
w www.lemeridien.com

London Gatwick Airport Hilton
South Terminal, Gatwick Airport RH6 0LL
t 01293 518080 **f** 01293 528980
e hilton@gatwickairport.freeserve.com **w** www.hilton.com
Contact Christopher Rawstrom, General Manager

The London Hilton
22 Park Lane, London W1Y 4BE
t 020 7493 8000 **f** 020 7208 4142
e sale_park_lane@hilton.com **w** www.hilton.com
Contact Fabio Gallo, Business Development Director

London Mariott Hotel Grosvenor Square
Grosvenor Square, London W1K 6JP
t 020 7493 1232 **f** 020 7491 3201
e businesscentre@londonmarriot.co.uk **w** www.mariott.com
Contact Johnathon Alvin, Director of Sales and Marketing

London Outpost of the Carnegie Club
69 Cadogan Gardens, London SW3 2RB
t 020 7589 7333 **f** 020 7581 4958
e info@londonoutpost.co.uk **w** www.londonoutpost.co.uk
Contact Caroline Nolan, General Manager

Lowndes Hotel
21 Lowndes Street, London SW1X 9ES
t 020 7823 1234 **f** 020 7235 1154
e contact@lowndeshotel.com **w** www.lowndeshotel.com
Contact Micheal Morrell, Reservations Manager; Simon Venison, General Manager

Mandarin Oriental Hyde Park
66 Knightsbridge, London SW1X 7LA
t 020 7235 2000 **f** 020 7235 2001
e reserve-molon@mohg.com **w** www.mandarinoriental.com
Contact Daniela Labi, Assistant Director of Sales; Paula McColgan, Director of Sales; Spencer Yeo, Director of Sales

The Manor of Groves Hotel
High Wych, Sawbridgeworth CM21 0LA
t 01279 600777 **f** 01279 600374
e brook@brookhotels.demon.co.uk **w** www.brookhotels.co.uk

Marlborough Hotel
9-14 Bloomsbury Street, London WC1B 3QD
t 020 7636 5601 **f** 020 7636 0532
e resmarl@radisson.com **w** www.radissonedwardian.com
Contact Sherry Thompson, Front of House Manager

Mayfair Intercontinental London
Stratton Street, London W1A 2AN
t 020 7629 7777 **f** 020 7629 1459
e mayfair@interconti.com **w** www.london-mayfair.interconti.com

The Meridian London Gatwick
North Terminal, Gatwick Airport RH6 0PH
t 0870 400 8494 **f** 01293 555037
w www.lemeridian-hotels.com
Contact Danny Betteridge, Reservations Manager

Monkey Island Hotel
Bray-on-Thames, Maidenhead SL6 2EE
t 01628 623400 **f** 01628 784732 **w** www.monkeyisland.co.uk
Contact Carolyn Hendey, Events Manager

Park Lane Hotel
Piccadilly, London W1J 7BX
t 020 7499 6321 **f** 020 7499 1965
e central.reservations.london@sheraton.com
w www.sheraton.com/parklane
Contact Flavio Rizzetto, Events and Reservations Manager

The Pelham Hotel
15 Cromwell Place, South Kensington, London SW7 2LA
t 020 7589 8288 **f** 020 7584 8444
e pelham@firmdale.com **w** www.firmdalehotels.com
Contact Susannah Hall, Sales Manager; Lisa Berlyn, Reservations Manager; S Girvan, General Manager

The Pheasant Hotel
Coast Road, Kelling, Near Holt NR25 7EG
t 01263 588382 **f** 01263 588101
w www.pheasanthotelnorfolk.co.uk
Contact D Peters, Managing Director

Portobello Hotel
22 Stanley Garden, London W11 2NG
t 020 7727 2777 **f** 020 7792 9641
info@portobello-hotel.co.uk
Contact Hanna Turner, Manager

Radisson Edwardian Hotel
140 Bath Road, Hayes UB3 5AW
t 020 8759 6311 **f** 020 8759 4559 **w** www.radisson.co.uk
Contact Aleace Montgomery, Reservations Manager

Radisson Mountbatten Hotel
Seven Dials, 20 Monmouth Street, Covent Garden, London WC2H 9HD
t 020 7836 4300 **f** 020 7240 3540
e resmoun@radisson.com **w** www.radisson.com

Radisson Pastoria Hotel
326 St Martins Street, Leicester Square, London WC2H 7HL
t 020 7930 8641 **f** 020 7451 0191 **w** www.radisson .com
Contact Shahdad Jahambani, Reservations Manager

Radisson Sas Portman
22 Portman Square, London W1H 7BG
t 020 7208 6000 **f** 020 7208 6001
e portman@lonza.sih.dk **w** www.radisson.com
Contact Elizabeth Kloepfer, Reservations Manager; Eiligh Macpherson, Revenue Manager

Ramada Jarvis
150 Bayswater Road, Hyde Park, London W2 4RT
t 020 7229 1212 **f** 020 7229 2623
e sales.hydepark@ramadajarvis.co.uk
Contact Rebbeca Pooley, Reservations Manager

Regents Park Mariott Hotel
128 King Henrys Road, London NW3 3ST
t 020 7722 7711 **f** 020 7586 5822
w www.mariotthotels.com/lonrp
Contact Nikki Bagnal, Group Coordinator

The Ritz Hotel
Piccadilly, London W1J 9BR
t 020 7493 8181 **f** 020 7493 2687
e enquire@theritzhotel.co.uk **w** www.theritzlondon.com
Contact Lynda Carson, Reservations Manager

Royal Westminster Thistle Hotel
49 Buckingham Palace Road, London SW1W 0QT
t 020 7834 1302
e westminster@thistle.co.uk **w** www.thistlehotels.com/westminster
Contact Mary Pozzi, Operations Manager

Selfridge Hotel
Orchard Street, London W1H 6JS
t 020 7408 2080 **f** 020 7204 6789 **w** www.thistlehotels.com
Contact Patricia Ribiero, Assistant Revenue Manager

Shepperton Moat House
Felix Lane, Shepperton TW17 8NP
t 01932 899988 **f** 01932 245231
Contact Andrew Blythe, General Manager

Sheraton Heathrow Hotel
Colnbrook Bypass, West Drayton UB7 0HJ
t 020 8759 2424 **f** 020 8759 2091
e res293.heathrow@sheraton.com **w** www.sheraton.com/heathrow
Contact Sarah Bamford, Reservations Manager; Kelly Ford, Reservation Manager

Sheraton Skyline Hotel
Bath Road (A4), Hayes UB3 5BP
t 020 8759 2535 **f** 020 8750 9150 **w** www.sheraton.com/skyline
Contact George Anastasakos, Reservation Manager

The Ship Hotel
Russell Road, Shepperton TW17 9HX
t 01932 227320 **f** 01932 226668
Contact Gaenor Maytham, Head Receptionist

The Sloane Square Moat House
Sloane Square, London SW1W 8EG
t 020 7896 9988 **f** 020 7824 8381 **w** www.moathousehotels.com
Contact Paul Badowi, Customer Sales Manager

St Ermins Hotel
Caxtons Street, London SW1H 0QW
t 020 7222 7888 **f** 020 7222 6914
Contact Andrea Betton, Reservations Department

Stafford Hotel
St James's Place, London SW1A 1NJ
t 020 7493 0111 **f** 020 7493 7121
e info@thestaffordhotel.co.uk **w** www.thestaffordhotel.co.uk
Contact Louise Freeman, Front of House Manager; Isabella O'Donnell, Client Liason

Thistle London Heathrow
Bath Road, Longford, West Drayton UB7 0EQ
t 0870 333 9108 **f** 0870 333 9208
e londonheathrow@thistle.co.uk
w www.thistlehotels.com/londonheathrow
Contact Liz Slater, Reservations Manager

Thistle Trafalgar Square
Whitcomb Street, Trafalgar Square, London WC2H 7HG
t 0870 333 9119 **f** 0870 333 9219
e trafalgar.square@thistle.co.uk
w www.thistlehotels.com/trafalgarsquare

The Thistle Tower Hotel
St Catherines Way, London E1 9LD
t 020 7481 2575 **f** 020 7481 3799
e tower.businesscentre@thistle.co.uk **w** www.thistlehotels.com
Contact Ronald Kingston, Operations Manager

Toby Carvery & Innkeeper's Lodge
Studio Way, Borehamwood WD6 5JY
t 020 8905 1455 **f** 020 8236 9822
w www.innkeeperslodge.com
Contact Guy Birch, Manager; Lisa Birch, Manager

Vanderbilt Hotel
68-86 Cromwell Road, London SW7 5BT
t 020 7761 9000 **f** 020 7761 9001 **w** www.radison.com
Contact Vivam Abbey, Reservations Manager

Warren Lodge Hotel
Church Square, Shepperton-on-Thames TW17 9JZ
t 01932 242972 **f** 01932 253883 **e** info@warrenlodgehotel.co.uk
Contact Simon Thorneloe, Manager; Brian Shanahan, Area Manager

The Washington Hotel
Curzon Street, Mayfair, London W1J 5HE
t 020 7499 7000 **f** 020 7495 6172
w www.washingtonmayfair.co.uk

The Whipper In Hotel
Market Place, Oakham LE15 6DT
t 01572 756971 **f** 01572 757759
e whipperinhotel@brook-hotels.co.uk
w www.brook-hotels.co.uk
Contact Mairead Flynn, General Manager

Insurance Companies

Allan Chapman & James Insurance Brokers Ltd
7 Phoenix Square, Wyncolls Road, Severalls Business Park,
Colchester CO4 9PB
t 01206 500000 **f** 01206 752216
e insurance@acjltd.co.uk **w** www.acjltd.co.uk
Contact Louise Miller, Senior New Business Executive; Chris Willard,
New Business Executive

Aon Ltd
Pinewood Studios, Pinewood Road, Iver SL0 0NH
t 01753 658238 **f** 01753 653152
e liz.yuille@ars.aon.co.uk **w** www.aon.com
Contact Liz Yuille, Associate Director - Development

Charles Milnes & Co
79-80 Margaret Street, London W1W 8TA
t 020 7636 3661 **f** 020 7636 5980
Contact Charles Milnes, Managing Director

Columbus Direct Travel Insurance
17 Devonshire Square, London EC2M 4SQ
t 020 7375 0011 **f** 020 7375 0022
e sales@columbusdirect.com **w** www.columbusdirect.com
Contact Simon Victor

First Act Insurance
Simpson House, 2-6 Cherry Orchard Road, Croydon CR9 5BB
t 020 8686 5050 **f** 020 8686 5559
e mail@firstact.co.uk **w** www.firstact.co.uk
Contact Kevin Harding

Helm Group (UK) Plc
Concord House, The Centre, Feltham TW13 4BF
t 020 8844 2020 **f** 020 8844 0053
e tim@helmgroup.co.uk **w** www.helmgroup.co.uk
Contact Tim Edwards

Media & Entertainment Insurance Services
Fox House, 135 High Street, Bromley BR1 1JF
t 020 8460 4484 **t** 020 8460 4498 **f** 020 8460 6064
m 07977 409520 **e** pdc-media@netway.co.uk

Near North Entertainment Ltd
Studio 88, Shepperton Studios, Studios Road, Shepperton
TW17 0QD
t 01932 562611 **f** 01932 592524 **w** www.nnng.com
Contact Derek Townshend

Performance
Greystoke House, 80-86 Westow Street, London SE19 3AQ
t 08453 450815 **f** 08453 450816 **w** www.hpc-performance.co.uk
Contact Chris Solomon, Account Executive; Paul Smith, Business Executive;
Colin McKenna, Business Development Manager

Robertson Taylor
33 Harbour Exchange Square, London E14 9GG
t 020 7510 1234 **f** 020 7510 1134
e enquiries@rtib.net **w** www.robertson-taylor.co.uk

THB Media
20-22 Curtain Road, London EC2A 3NF
t 020 7392 1700 **f** 020 7392 1701
e mailmedia@thbgroup.com **w** www.thbmedia.com
Contact Edel Ryan, Client Services Manager

Insurance Loss Adjusters

Ashworth Mairs Group
Stratton Court, Thursby Road, Croft Business Park,
Bromborough, Wirral CH62 3PW
t 0151 343 1777 **f** 0151 343 1776
e enq@ashmg.co.uk **w** www.ashworthmairsgroup.com

Claim Specialists International Ltd
Suites 118-120, Smug Oak Business Centre, Lye Lane, Bricket
Wood AL2 3UG
t 01923 682255 **f** 01923 682256 **m** 07855 763381
e m.jones@csiclaims.co.uk
Contact Linda Wylde, Senior Adjuster; Howard Diamant, Managing Director;
Marion Jones, Director, Film & TV

Marsh UK Ltd
Tower Place, London EC3R 5BU
t 020 7357 5958 **f** 020 7929 2705 **m** 07780 670860
e terry.allen@marsh.com **w** www.marsh.com
Contact Terry Allen, Client Executive; Susan Haddow, Client Executive

Internet Services

Aardvark Media Ltd
10 Cloisters House, Cloisters Business Centre, Battersea Park
Road, London SW8 4BG
t 020 7582 7711 **f** 020 7622 4223
e info@aardvarkmedia.co.uk **w** www.aardvarkmedia.co.uk
Contact Christopher Johns, Director

Agency.com
16 Connaught Place, London W2 2ES
t 020 7964 8200 **f** 020 7964 8300
e info.london@agency.com **w** www.agency.com
Contact Craig Patton, Business Development Director

Alchemy Digital
Forresters House, 29-33 Shirley Road, Southampton SO15 3EW
t 023 8021 3400 **f** 023 8021 3401
e info@alchemydigital.com **w** www.alchemydigital.com
Contact Adrian Tennant, Creative Director

Alt Productions
33 St Giles Gate, Scawsby, Doncaster DN5 8PG
t 01302 564392 **m** 07931 741572
e steve@alt-productions.co.uk **w** www.alt-productions.co.uk

Arawak Interactive Marketing Ltd
120 Regents Street, London W1B 5RY
t 020 7734 1650 **f** 020 7734 1649
e info@arawak.co.uk **w** www.arawak.co.uk
Contact Nick Corston, Director

Arc Interactive London
Warwick Building, Kensington Village, Avonmore Road, London
W14 8HQ
t 020 7751 1663
e info@arcmarketing.com **w** www.arcmarketing.com
Contact Peter Hollins, Managing Director

The Aspect Group
Clerkenwell House, 67 Clerkenwell Road, London EC1r 5BL
t 020 7504 6900 **f** 020 7504 6901
e info@aspectgroup.co.uk **w** www.aspectgroup.co.uk
Contact Jon Russell, Commercial Director

Bates Interactive
121-141 Westbourne Terrace, Paddington, London W2 6JR
t 020 7724 7228 **f** 020 7724 3075
e chrissie_white@batesuk.com **w** www.bates-interactive.co.uk
Contact Chrissie White, Managing Director

Big Oxford Computer Company Ltd
Lincoln House, Pony Road, Oxford OX4 2RD
t 01865 717770 **f** 01865 773456
e info@bocc.co.uk **w** www.bocc.co.uk

Billco (a BMP DDB Company)
12 Bishops Bridge Road, London W2 6AA
t 020 7258 4521 **f** 020 7258 4520
e info@billco.com **w** www.billco.com
Contact Alison Parker, Managing Director

Bluewave Ltd
Mimet House, 5A Praed Street, London W2 1NJ
t 020 7706 3500 **f** 020 7262 5053
e bluewave@bluewave.co.uk **w** www.bluewave.com
Contact Mahmood Cheema, Financial Controller

Brand New Media Ltd
The Media Centre, Nepshaw Lane South, Morley, Leeds LS27 7JQ
t 0113 238 2404 **f** 0113 238 2405
e info@bnm.co.uk **w** www.bnm.co.uk
Contact Dominic O'Neill, Contact

Cable & Wireless
26 Red Lion Square, London WC1R 4HQ
t 020 7528 2000 **f** 020 8244 1599 **w** www.cwcom.com
Contact David Thain

CentraServe Ltd
Stanstead House, Shire Hill, Saffron Walden CB11 3AQ
t 01799 523882 **f** 01799 523335
e info@centraserve.com **w** www.centraserve.com
Contact Seb Clark, Project Manager

CGI Online Ltd
PO Box 292, Douglas IM99 2PT
t 01624 662264 **f** 01624 611925
e mail@cgiol.com **w** www.cgiol.com
Contact Brian Courtie, Managing Director

Clarity Communications Ltd
6 Silver Court, Bancroft, Hitchin SG5 1GB
t 01462 631287
e vicky.bradford@ntlworld.com **w** www.claritycommunication.co.uk
Contact Andy Bradford, Consultant; Victoria Bradford, Director

CMA Internet
2HQ House, Primary Court, Torr Hill, Yealmpton, Plymouth
PL8 2HQ
t 01752 881333 **f** 01752 882101 **i** 01752 882109
e info@cmanet.net **w** www.cmanet.net
Contact Amanda Leadbetter; Andy Staples, Director

Create X Design
PO Box 10219, London NW4 2WF
t 0870 870 8870 **e** info-uk@createx.com **w** www.createx.com

CST Group Ltd
Communications Centre, Lower Ground Floor, 94 Lewes Road,
Brighton BN2 3QA
t 01273 621393 **f** 01273 621390
e info@cst-group.com **w** www.cst-group.com

DNA Consulting
2-7 Brewery Square, Butlers Wharf, London SE1 2LF
t 020 7357 0573 **f** 020 7357 0574
e paula.barker@dna.co.uk **w** www.dna.co.uk
Contact Russell Jarman-Price, Chairman; Chris Perry, Managing Director; Neil
Miller, Managing Director; Steve Thompson, Creative Director
Credits www.cheltglos.co.uk (W); www.mfi.co.uk (W); www.worldvision.org.uk
(W); The Pension Service (W)

Domino Systems
The Innovation Centre, Kingston Bagpuize OX13 5AP
t 01865 821821 **f** 01865 821881
e web@domino.com **w** www.domino.com

EDL Publishing Ltd
Alexander House, Forehill, Ely CB7 4AF
t 01353 665577 **f** 01353 662489 **w** www.e-contracting.co.uk

Epic Group Plc
52 Old Steine, Brighton BN1 1NH
t 01273 728686 **f** 01273 821567
e marketing@epic.co.uk **w** www.epic.co.uk
Contact John Helmer, Marketing Manager
Credits HERO ltd 'Hero' (W); Coca-Cola Enterprises Ltd 'Welcome to the Web'
(W); Royal Bank of Scotland 'Branch Manager' (W)

Foresight Europe Ltd
Boumount House, Kensington Village, Avonmore Road,
London W14 8TS
t 020 7348 1000 **f** 020 7348 1111 **m** 07771 702 165
e tim.osler@foresight.co.uk **w** www.foresight.co.uk
Contact Lorri Whitehead, Office Manager; Charlotte Ward, Reception; Tim
Osler, New Business Development Director
Credits Early Learning Centre (W); Christian Dior (W); Gucci (W); Asprey (W)

Glide
20 The Pall Mall Deposit, 124-128 Barlby Road, London W10 6BL
t 020 7565 9007 **f** 020 7565 9008
e contact@glidetechnologies.com **w** www.glidetechnologies.com
Contact Samantha Deeks, Account Manager

Global Initiative Ltd
Clarendon House, 52 Cornmarket Street, Oxford OX1 3HJ
t 01865 304005 **f** 01865 304042
e mail@virtualgi.com **w** www.virtualgi.com
Contact Chris Sinclair, Managing Director/Creative Director; Gareth Nixon,
Technical Director
Credits www.christiehq.com (W); www.clarendon-enterprise.co.uk (W);
www.chch.ox.ac.uk/ball2002/ (W); www.streetfurnishings.co.uk (W)

GlobeCast
200 Gray's Inn Road, London WC1X 8XZ
t 020 7430 4400 **f** 020 7430 4321
e gary.champion@globecast.com
e steve.fairbrother@globecast.com **w** www.globecast.com
Contact Steve Fairbrother, Head of IP Services, Europe; William Pitt, Account
Manager; Gary Champion, Head of News and BTV, Europe

*GlobeCast - a France Telecom subsidiary - is the global leader in satellite
transmission services for professional broadcast, enterprise multimedia
and Internet content delivery. Operating 15 teleport earth stations
throughout Europe, America, Asia, Australia, the Middle East and Africa,
GlobeCast offers the complete range of satellite broadcast solutions,
including TV channel distribution, secure satellite Internet delivery,
webcasting, satellite newsgathering, direct-to-home distribution, sports
programming backhaul, studio production, special events mobile
production and audio distribution.*

GMJ
115A Cleveland Street, London W1T 5PN 6BU
t 020 7636 7112 **f** 020 7636 7110
e info@gmj.net **w** www.gmj.net
Contact Didier Madle-Jones, Marketing Director

Good Technology Ltd
332B Ladbroke Grove, London W10 5AH
t 020 7565 0022 **f** 020 7565 0020
e info@goodtech.co.uk **w** www.goodtech.co.uk
Contact Richard Davies, Managing Director

Graphico New Media Ltd
Goldwell House, Old Bath Road, Newbury RG14 1JH
t 01635 522810 **f** 01635 580621
e info@graphico.co.uk **w** www.graphico.co.uk
Contact Mark Bennett, Managing Director; Graham Darracott, Sales and
Marketing Director; Alex Weller, Creative Director
Credits www.westlife.com (W); www.pepsi-football.co.uk (W);
www.thenewbmw7series.co.uk (W); www.bbcworld.com (W)

Green Cathedral Plc
The Old Granary, Westwick, Cambridge CB4 5AR
t 01223 266700 **f** 01223 266701
e rjh@greencathedral.com **w** www.greencathedral.com
Contact Roland Henry, Head of Sales

Grey Interactive UK
Wells Point, 79 Wells Street, London W1V 3JR
t 020 7453 8320 **f** 020 7453 8339
e dick.bloomfield@greyinteractive.co.uk
w www.greyinteractive.co.uk
Contact Dick Bloomfield, Business Development Director

Headland Multimedia
11 Edison Village, Highfields Science Park, Nottingham NG7 2RF
t 0115 955 1155 **f** 0115 955 1156
e info@headland.co.uk **w** www.headland.co.uk
Contact Ken Heptonstall, Director

Host
9 Dallinger Road, Lee Green, London SE12 0TJ
t 020 8851 8974 **m** 07973 141520
e rob9@host.uk.net **w** www.host.uk.net
Contact Rob Clifford, Creative Director; Linda Clifford, Web Design
Credits www.howdle.com (W); www.thisisluck.com (W); www.arts-
technology.org (W); www.dryice-clothing.com (W)

Hyperlink Plc
8 Upper Street Martins Lane, London WC2H 9DL
t 020 7240 8121 **f** 020 7240 8121 **e** info@hyperlink.com
Contact Matteo Berlucchi, Head of Marketing

KMP Internet Solutions
Regent House, Heaton Lane, Stockport SK4 1BS
t 0161 476 6590 **f** 0161 476 0370
e info@kmpinternet.com **w** www.kmpinternet.com
Contact Bill Daring, Chairman

Leonardo
60 Sloane Avenue, London SW3 3XB
t 020 7591 9111 **f** 020 7591 9992
e info@leonardocompany.com **w** www.leonardocompany.com

Liquid Light Digital Ltd
Brighton Media Centre, 68 Middle Street, Brighton BN1 1AL
t 01273 739709 **f** 01273 739629
e info@liquidlight.co.uk **w** www.liquidlight.co.uk
Contact Robert Day, Sales Director

Motion Pixels Ltd
Milk Studios, The Old Dairy, 13B Hewer Street, London W10 6DU
t 020 8962 6238 **f** 020 8968 8004
e mail@motionpixels.com **w** www.motionpixels.co.uk
Contact Mark Mitchinson, Marketing Director; Sarah Mouncey , Head of
Marketing; Paul Baillie, Creative Director

Netdecisions
Elsinore House 3rd Floor, 77 Fulham Palace Road,
Hammersmith, London W6 8JA
t 020 8222 9400 **f** 020 8222 9401
e business_development@netdecisions.co.uk
w www.netdecisions.co.uk

NetInfo

Berkshire House, Queen Street, Maidenhead SL6 1NF
t 01628 687800 **f** 01628 687801
e info@netinfo.co.uk **w** www.netinfo.co.uk
Contact Shamus Kelly, Chief Executive Officer; Chelsi Harradine, Marketing; Gareth Walters, Accounts; Graeme Hendry, New Business; Jonathon Bradshaw, New Business
Credits www.yellgroup.co.uk (W); www.wella.co.uk (W); www.skymedia.co.uk (W); www.freeview.co.uk (W)

NetXtra Ltd

The Old Foundry, Hall Street, Long Melford, Sudbury CO10 9JG
t 01787 319393 **f** 01787 319394
e info@netxtra.net **w** www.netxtra.net
Contact Robert Schrimpff, Managing Director

NoHo Digital Ltd

10 Cabot Square, London E14 4GB
t 020 7345 3504 **f** 002 7345 3888 **w** www.ogilvy.co.uk
Contact Louise Ainsworth, Managing Director

O.I.T Ltd

7600 The Quorum, Oxford Business Park, Oxford OX4 2JZ
t 01865 785000 **f** 01865 785100 **e** oit@oit.co.uk
Contact Jannette Woodhouse, UK Sales Manager

Oyster Partners Ltd

1 Naoroji Street, London WC1X OJD
t 020 7446 7500 **f** 020 7446 7555
e cecilia.thirlway@oyster.com **w** www.oyster.com
Contact Cecilia Thirlway, Communications Manager

Perfect World Programs Ltd

1 Decima Studios, Decima Street, London SE1 4QR
t 020 7407 8992
e enq@perfect-world.co.uk **w** www.perfect-world.co.uk
Contact Denise Proctor, Managing Director
Credits www.davenportlyons.com (W); www.urbanation.net (W); Ronan Keating (W)

Pilot Interactive

Devonshire Hall, Devonshire Avenue, Street Lane, Leeds LS8 1AW
t 0113 228 2359
e davidc@pilotinteractive.co.uk **w** www.pilotinteractive.co.uk
Contact David Crawford, Client Services Director

port80 the internet consultancy

t 0870 050 8080
e enquire@port80.com **w** www.port80.co.uk

Pres.co

Beaumont House, Avonmore Road, Kensington Village, London W14 8TS
t 020 7348 1000
e philip.hunt@wheel.co.uk **w** www.pres.co.uk
Contact Paul Brooks, Creative Director

Realise Ltd

Quay House, 142 Commercial Street, Edinburgh EH6 6LB
t 0131 476 6000 **f** 0131 476 6061
e info@realise.com **w** www.realise.com
Contact Denise Lyall, Marketing Manager

Scotland On Line

Gateway East, Technology Park, Dundee DD2 1SW
t 01382 429000 **f** 01382 429001
e sales@scotlandonline.co.uk **w** www.scotlandonline.co.uk
Contact Gemma Thomson, Sales Administrator
Credits Scottish Widows (W); Dundee.com portal (W); Standard Life (W)

Scotweb Marketing Ltd

13a Albert Terrace, Edinburgh EH10 5EA
t 0131 477 8884 **f** 0701 745 6226
e info@scotweb.co.uk **w** www.scotweb.co.uk

Sequence

Media Centre, Bridge Street, Cardiff CF1 2EE
t 029 2025 2555 **f** 029 2025 2444
e chris.haresign@sequence.co.uk **w** www.sequence.co.uk
Contact Allie Symonds, Marketing Manager; Chris Haresign

state51

Rhoda Street, London E2 7EF
t 020 7729 4343 **f** 020 7729 8494
e intouch@state51.co.uk **w** www.state51.co.uk

Subnet Ltd

Glenfield Park, Lomeshaye Business Village, Nelson BB9 7DR
t 01282 616000 **f** 01282 708091
e subinfo@subnet.co.uk **e** jon@subnet.co.uk **w** www.subnet.co.uk
Contact Adrain Lord, Managing Director

TAG Interactive

29 Clerkenwell Road, London EC1M 5TA
t 020 7251 4571 **f** 020 7253 5355
e rarmstrong@tagmedia.co.uk **w** www.tagmedia.co.uk
Contact Holly Lawler, Marketing Manager; Bridget Cowan, Marketing Manager

Tamar

10 Barley Mow Passage, London W4 4PH
t 020 8995 7878 **f** 020 8995 7636
e info@tamar.com **w** www.tamar.com
Contact Neil McCarthy, Commercial Director
Credits endsleigh.co.uk (W); lpf.org.uk (W); viewgate.com (W); bravissimo.com (W)

Video Peg Web Video

55 Goldieslie Road, Sutton Coldfield, Birmingham B73 5PG
m 07956 337577 **e** info@videopeg.com **w** www.videopeg.com
Contact Andy Hayes, Partner

Virtual Internet Ltd

t 020 7854 6600 **e** info@vi.net **w** www.vi.net

Vision Interactive Ltd

16-18 Whiteladies Road, Clifton, Bristol BS9 4JF
t 0117 980 9400 **f** 0117 980 9401
e info@owta.net **w** www.owta.net
Contact Kevin Haynes, Director

Wam! Net

7 Warwick Court, London WC1R 5DJ
t 08000 937880
e uksales@wamnet.co.uk **w** www.wamnet.com
Contact Lee Myall, European Sales Director

Wickedweb Ltd

7A Enterprise Way, Edenbridge TN8 6HF
t 01732 861010 **f** 01732 863747
e newbizz@wickedweb.co.uk **w** www.wickedweb.co.uk
Contact Magnus Hakansson, Business Development Manager; Mark Meade, New Business Director
Credits ECM International (W); Friends Provident (W); Hill & Knowlton UK (W)

Wide Media Ltd

PO Box 33052, London W9 2XE
e contact@widemedia.com **w** www.widemedia.com

Zebrahosts Ltd

65 Westgate Road, Newcastle-upon-Tyne NE1 1SG
t 0191 261 7555 **f** 0191 261 4452
e info@zebrahosts.co.uk **w** www.zebrahosts.co.uk

Zynet Ltd

Rockeagle House, Pynes Hil, Exeter EX2 5AZ
t 01392 209500 **f** 01392 421762
e sales@zynet.net **w** www.zynet.net

Zyweb Ltd
Minerva House, Pynes Hill, Exeter EX2 5AZ
t 01392 209500 **f** 01392 421762
e sales@zyweb.com **w** www.zyweb.com
Contact Nova Fisher, Chairman; Steve Congrave, Managing Director

IT Services

Atos Origin UK Ltd
323 The Science Park, Milton Road, Cambridge CB4 4WG
t 01223 423355 **f** 01223 420724 **w** www.atosorigin.com
Contact Martin Moore, Facilities Manager

OCSL
East House, Newpound Common, Wisborough Green,
Billingshurst RH14 0AZ
t 01403 700959 **f** 01403 700969 **m** 07778 677 846
e info@ocsl.co.uk **w** www.ocsl.co.uk
Contact Jane Ayres, Marketing Director; Anthony May, Head of Media &
Broadcast; Tim Thrower, Managing Director; Steve Wilson, Sales Director; Neil
Thrower, Technical Director

Tiger Computer Services Ltd
387 London Road, Isleworth TW7 5XF
m 07973 185 795
e liam.westley@tigernews.co.uk **w** www.tigernews.co.uk
Credits Sky News Active Interactive; Sky News 1997&2001 General Election;
www.gmtv.co.uk

Legal Services

Baker & McKenzie Solicitors
100 New Bridge Street, London EC4V 6JA
t 020 7919 1000 **f** 020 7919 1438
e ecc@bakernet.com **w** www.bakermckenzie.com
Contact Jacqueline Dutko, Director European Coordination Centre

Berwin Leighton Paisner Solicitors
Adelaide House, London Bridge, London EC4R 9HA
t 020 7760 1000 **f** 020 7760 1111
e david.newton@berwinleightonpaisner.com **w** www.blplaw.com
Contact David Newton; Peter Stone, Partner; Adam Rose, Partner

Brian Norris Media Solutions
Greenpark, Illand, Launceston PL15 7LS
t 01566 782217 **f** 01566 782127
e rights@btopenworld.com **w** www.bnorris.btinternet.com
Contact Brian Norris, Proprietor

Brown Cooper Monier-Williams
71 Lincoln's Inn Fields, London WC2A 3JF
e clientcare@bcmw.com
Contact Nigel Urwin, Partner

Campbell Hooper Solicitors
35 Old Queen Street, London SW1H 9JD
t 020 7222 9070 **f** 020 7222 5591
e ch@campbellhooper.co.uk **w** www.campbellhooper.co.uk

Robert Carter
8 West Street, Covent Garden, London WC2H 9NG
t 020 7836 2785 **f** 020 7836 2786 **e** robert.carter@ukonline.co.uk
Credits Trinity (F)

Chilton Media Law
Legal & Busines Consultancy, 8 West Street, London WC2H 9NG
t 020 7836 2764 **f** 020 7836 2765
e chilton@medialaw.demon.co.uk
Contact Melorie Chilton

Clifford Chance
200 Aldersgate Street, London EC1A 4JJ
t 020 7600 5555 **f** 020 7600 5555 **w** www.cliffordchance.com

Clintons
55 Drury Lane, London WC2B 5RZ
t 020 7379 6080 **f** 020 7240 9310

CMS Cameron McKenna
Mitre House, 160 Aldersgate Street, London EC1A 4DD
t 020 7367 3000 **f** 020 7367 2000
e info@cmck.com **w** www.law-now.com
Contact Paul Beattie, Contact

D J Freeman
43 Fetter Lane, London EC4A 1JU
t 020 7583 4055 **f** 020 7353 7377
e media@djfreeman.co.uk **w** www.djfreeman.co.uk

Davenport Lyons
1 Old Burlington Street, London W1S 3NL
t 020 7468 2600 **f** 020 7437 8216
e helpdesk@davenportlyons.com **w** www.davenportlyons.com
Contact Leon Morgan, Partner; Richard Moxon, Partner

David Wineman Solicitors
Craven House, 121 Kingsway, London WC2B 6NX
t 020 7400 7800 **f** 020 7400 7890
e law@davidwineman.co.uk **w** www.davidwineman.co.uk

Denton Wilde Sapte
5 Chancery Lane, Cliffords Inn, London EC4A 1BU
t 020 7242 1212 **f** 020 7404 0087 **e** info@dentonwildesapte.com
Contact Steven Blundell, Marketing Director; Maddie Grindel, Marketing Director

DLA
3 Noble Street, London EC2V 7EE
t 020 7796 6069 **f** 020 7796 6113
e ruth.daniels@dla.com **w** www.dla.com
Contact Lisa Bindahnee, Solicitor; Paul Pattinson, Partner; Paul Daniels,
Solicitor; Martin Soames, Partner

Drew & Company
36-40 Glasshouse Street, London W1R 5RM
t 020 7287 7587 **f** 020 7287 7588
Contact Andrew Curtis, Principal
Credits Large (F); The Bunker (F); Bugs! (F); Lost In La Mancha (F)

Edge Manning & Company
31 Leeson Street Lower, Dublin 2, Rep of Ireland
t 662 5233 **f** 676 3609 **e** law@edgemanning.com
Contact Barry Manning, Managing Partner

Eversheds London
Senator House, 85 Queen Victoria Street, London EC4V 4JL
t 020 7919 4500 **f** 020 7919 4919
e patrickisherwood@eversheds.co.uk **w** www.eversheds.com
Contact Patrick Isherwood, Partner

Field Fisher Waterhouse
35 Vine Street, London EC3N 2AA
t 020 7861 4000 **f** 020 7488 0084
e jab@ffwlaw.com **w** www.ffwlaw.com
Contact Ellen Fleming, Partner

Finers Stephens Innocent
179 Great Portland Street, London W1W 5LS
t 020 7323 4000 **f** 020 7580 7069
e marketing@fsilaw.co.uk **w** www.fsilaw.com

Gersten & Nixon
National House, 60-66 Wardour Street, London W1F 0TA
t 020 7439 3961 **f** 020 7734 2479
e dg@gernix.co.uk **w** www.germix.co.uk
Contact Greg Wolton, Partner; Dominic Green, Solicitor

Goodman Derrick
90 Fetter Lane, London EC4A 1PT
t 020 7404 0606 **f** 020 7831 6407
e pswaffer@goodmanderrick.co.uk
Contact P Swaffer, Partner

Gordon Dadds
80 Brook Street, London W1K 5DD
t 020 74936151 **f** 020 7491 1065 **w** www.gordondadds.com

Greenwoods Solicitors
Monkstone House, City Road, Peterborough PE1 1JE
t 01733 887700 **f** 01733 887701
e mail@greenwoods.co.uk **w** www.greenwoods.co.uk
Contact Shelagh Smith, Managing Partner

Gudeon & Hodkinson
19-20 Grosvenor Street, London W1K 4QH
t 020 7493 1595 **f** 020 7493 7915
e info@usvisalaw.co.uk **w** www.usvisalaw.co.uk
Contact Edward Gudeon

Hammond
7 Devonshire Square, Cutlers Gardens, London EC2M 4YH
t 0870 839 0000 **f** 0870 839 1001
e paul.woolf@hammonds.com **w** www.hammonds.com

Harbottle & Lewis
Hanover House, 14 Hanover Square, London W1S 1HP
t 020 7667 5000 **f** 020 7607 5100
e medwyn.jones@horbottle.com **w** www.harbottle.com
Contact Robert Storer, Partner; Abigail Payne, Partner; Medwyn Jones, Partner

Harrison Curtis
8 Jockey's Fields, London WC1R 4BF
t 020 7611 1720 **f** 020 7611 1721
e mail@harrisoncurtis.co.uk **w** www.harrisoncurtis.co.uk
Contact Harrison Curtis; Tim Curtis, Solicitors

Hill Dickinson
Pearl Assurance House, Derby Square, Liverpool L2 9XL
t 0151 236 5400 **f** 0151 236 2175
e law@hilldicks.com **w** www.hilldickinson.com
Contact Christopher Manors, Public Relations Manager; Karen Park, Public Relations Manager

Catriona J Hoolahan
18A Bina Gardens, London SW5 0LA
t 020 7565 2394 **f** 020 7565 2394 **e** choolahan1@aol.com
Credits Boo! (A); Rat's Tales (T); Patrick Kielty Almost Live (T); Tweenies (T)

Howard Kennedy
11 Cavendish Square, London W1A 2AW
t 020 7636 1616 **f** 020 7491 2899 **i** 0 DX4 2748
e enquiries@howardkennedy.com **w** www.howardkennedy.com
Contact Leighton Lloyd, Partner, Media and Entertainment Department; Brian Eagles, Partner, Head of Media and Entertainment; Haken Kousetta, Partner, Media and Entertainment Department

JA Hughes
Centenary House, King Square, Barry CF62 8HB
t 01446 411000 **f** 01446 411010
e solicitors@jahughes.com **w** www.jahughes.com
Contact Duncan Kennedy, Partner

Angela Jackson
1 Lonsdale Square, London N1 1EN
t 020 7609 5615 **f** 020 7609 8684
e angelajackson@compuserve.com
Credits A Christmas Carol - The Movie (F); Last Orders (F)

Kidd Rapinet
14-15 Craven Street, London WC2N 5AD
t 020 7925 0303
Contact David Semmens, Partner

Lee & Thompson
Green Garden House, 15/22 St Christophers Place, London W1U 1NL
t 020 7935 4665 **f** 020 7563 4949
e mail@leeandthompson.com **w** www.leeandthompson.com
Contact Reno Antoniades, Partner; Richard Lever, Solicitor
Credits Linda Green (T); Bob and Rose (T); Bend It Like Beckham (T)

Leonard Lowy & Co, Solicitors
500 Chiswick High Road, London W4 5RG
t 020 8877 9260 **f** 020 8877 1337 **m** 07970 919813
e leonard@leonardlowy.co.uk **w** www.leonardlowy.co.uk

Lipkin Gorman
61 Grosvenor Street, London W1K 3JE
t 020 7493 4010 **f** 020 7409 1734
Contact Seymour Gorman, Partner

Marriott Harrison
12 Great James Street, London WC1N 3DR
t 020 7209 2000 **f** 020 7209 2001
e richard.hinchliffe@marriottharrison.co.uk
w www.marriottharrison.co.uk

LEGAL AND BUSINESS NETWORK

Medialex Ltd
Greyhound House, 23-24 George Street, Richmond TW9 1HY
t 020 8973 2186 **f** 020 8973 2009
e info@medialex-uk.com **w** www.medialex-uk.com
Contact Pam Bernhard

Nicholson Graham & Jones
110 Cannon Street, London EC4N 6AR
t 020 7648 9000 **f** 020 7648 9001
e annemarie.pryor@ngj.co.uk **w** www.ngj.co.uk
Contact Annemarie Pryor, Marketing Manager

Olswang
90 High Holborn, London WC1V 6XX
t 020 7067 3000 **f** 020 7208 8800
e olsmail@olswang.co.uk **w** www.olswang.co.uk
Contact John Routledge, Office Manager

Penningtons
Bucklersbury House, 83 Cannon Street, London EC4 N8PE
t 020 7457 3000 **f** 020 7457 3240
e info@penningtons.co.uk **w** www.penningtons.co.uk
Contact Lou Tolaini, Office Manager

Pinsent Curtis Biddle
Dashwood House, 69 Old Broad Street, London EC2M 1NR
t 020 7418 7000
e susan.biddle@pinsents.com **w** www.pinsents.com
Contact Susan Biddle, Partner; Charles Park, Partner; David Hooper, Partner

RG Pugh & Company
54 Charles Street, Cardiff CF10 2SD
t 029 2066 7689 **f** 029 2030 3709
e richardpughlaw@onetel.net.uk
Contact Richard Pugh, Head of Media Law

Richards Butler
Beaufort House, 15 St Botolph Street, London EC3A 7EE
t 020 7247 6555 **f** 020 7247 5091
e law@richardsbutler.com **w** www.richardsbutler.com
Contact Michael Maxtone Smith, Partner; Richard Philipps, Partner; Barry Smith, Partner

Sara Curran

5 Blake Mews, Kew TW9 3QA
t 020 8948 1691 **f** 020 8948 4326 **e** sc@filmit.b12

Contact Sara Curran, Principal
Credits Forty Days And Forty Nights (F); Ali G In Da House (F); The Guru (F);
About A Boy (F)

Schillings

Royalty House, 72-74 Dean Street, London W1D 3TL
t 020 7453 2500 **f** 020 7453 2600 **m** 07711 068696
e legal@schillings.co.uk **w** www.schillings.co.uk

Contact Amber Melville-Brown, Marketing Partner; Peter Goodman, Partner;
Martin Cruddace, Partner; Shelley Vincent, Office Manager; Keith Schilling,
Senior Partner; Simon Smith, Managing Partner

The Simkins Partnership

45-51 Whitfield Street, London W1T 4HB
t 020 7907 3000 **f** 020 7907 3111
e info@simkins.com **w** www.simkins.com

SJ Berwin & Co

222 Grays Inn Road, London WC1X 8XF
t 020 7533 2222 **f** 020 7533 2000 **e** info@sjberwin.com

Contact Nigel Palmer, Partner

Tarlo Lyons Solicitors

Watchmaker Court, 33 St John''s Lane, London EC1M 4DB
t 020 7405 2000 **f** 020 7814 9421
e info@tarlolyons.com **w** www.tarlolyons.com

Teacher Stern Selby

37-41 Bedford Row, London WC1R 4JH
t 020 7242 3191 **f** 020 7405 2964
e g.shear@tsslaw.co.uk **w** www.tsslaw.com

Contact Graham Shear, Partner

Tods Murray WS

66 Queen Street, Edinburgh EH2 4NE
t 0131 226 4771 **f** 0131 300 2202
e richard.findlay@todsmurray.com **w** www.todsmurray.com

Contact Richard Findlay, Media & Entertainment Law Partner; Lynn Bearmont,
Partner; Andy Harris, Assistant; David Smith, Assistant
Credits Tinsel Town (D); World War One (D); Bait (F); Gladiator (F)

Toy & Patents Development

84A Telephone Place, London SW6 1TH
t 020 7385 2848 **f** 020 7385 2848

Contact Gordon Tait, Director; Jay Blacke, Production Designer

Wayne Lewis & Associates

Waterfall Studios, 2 Silver Road, Wood Lane, London W12 7SF
t 020 8746 2000 **f** 020 8749 4222
e lawyer@waynelewis.co.uk **w** www.waynelewis.co.uk

Wiggin & Co

95 The Promenade, Cheltenham GL50 1WG
t 01242 224114 **f** 01242 224223
e law@wiggin.co.uk **w** www.wiggin.co.uk

Contact Caroline Kean, Partner

Withers

16 Old Bailey Road, London EC4M 7EG
t 020 7597 6000 **f** 020 7597 6543
e anthony.indaimoi@withers.co.uk **w** www.withers.co.uk

Contact Anthony Indaimo, Media group; Tracy Bricknall, Secretary

LIBRARIES

Libraries **Film**

AdventureArchive

Fudge Cottage, Dalditch Lane, Budleigh Salterton EX9 7AH
t 01395 446242 **m** 07711 787737
e info@adventurearchive.com
w www.adventurearchive.com

Contact Leo Dickinson; Mandy Dickinson

Archive Film

17 Conway Street, London W1P 6EE
t +44 20 7312 0300 **f** +44 20 7391 9111
e london.motion@gettyimages.com
w www.gettyimages.com

Contact Chris Blakestone

BBC

Commercial Unit, Room LG29 CB, Bush House, PO Box 76,
The Strand, London WC2B 4PH
t 020 7557 2452 **f** 020 7557 2728
w www.bbcresearchcentral.com

Credits BBC One: Rush Hour

BBC Worldwide Library Sales

Room A3057, Woodlands, 80 Wood Lane, London W12 0TT
t 020 8433 2861 **t** 020 8433 2862 **f** 020 8433 2939
e ukls@bbclibrarysales.com **w** www.bbclibrarysales.com

Contact Jeremy Cantwell, Manager for Business & Sales Development; Paul
Maidment, Sales & Marketing Director
Credits The A-Z Of Monarchy (T); Kit Kat (C); Blue Planet (T); Harry Potter And
The Prisoner Of Azkaban (F)

Black Diamond Films Ltd
Bedford Chambers, The Piazza, Covent Garden, London WC2E 8HA
t 020 7240 4071 **f** 020 7836 6339
e jim@blackdiamond.co.uk **w** www.blackdiamond.co.uk
Contact Guy Chambers, Managing Director

British Defence Film Library
Chalfont Grove, Narcot Lane, Chalfont St Peter, Gerrard's
Cross SL9 8TN
t 01494 878278 **f** 01494 878007
e robert.dungate@ssvc.com **w** www.ssvc.com
Contact Robert Dungate, Library Manager

British Movietonews Ltd
Denham Media Park, North Orbital Road, Denham UB9 5HQ
t 01895 833071 **f** 01895 834893
e library@mtone.co.uk **w** www.movietone.com
Contact Barbara Heavens, Senior Librarian; Barry Florin

British Pathe Plc
New Pathe House, 57 Jamestown Road, London NW1 7DB
t 020 7424 3636 **f** 020 7424 3637
e info@britishpathe.com **w** www.britishpathe.com
Contact Larry McKinna; Paul Gost; Paul Gost; David Haynes

Bruce Coleman Collection
16 Chiltern Business Village, Arundel Road, Uxbridge UB8 2SN
t 01895 467990 **f** 01895 467959
e library@brucecoleman.co.uk **w** www.brucecoleman.co.uk

Bulletin International
121-141 Westbourne Terrace, London W2 6JR
t 020 7479 0490 **f** 020 7479 0450
e info@bulletin-intl.com **w** www.bulletin.co.uk
Contact Rabia Bapu, Librarian

Castrol Video & Film Library (Motor Sport)
Wakefield House, Pipers Way, Swindon SN3 4SB
t 01793 452585 **f** 01793 453476 **e** skellev@castrol.com
Contact Vanna Skelley, Archivist

Chain Production Ltd
2 Clanricarde Gardens, London W2 4NA
t 020 7229 4277 **f** 020 7229 0861 **w** www.chainproduction.com

The Channel 4 Clip Library
124 Horseferry Road, London SW1P 2TX
t 020 7306 8490 **f** 020 7306 8362
e stanford@channel4.co.uk **w** www.channel4.com

Christian Aid
35 Lower Marsh, London SE1 7RL
t 020 7523 2440 **f** 020 7523 2441
e rprime@christian-aid.org **w** www.christian-aid.org.uk
Contact Robin Prime, Video Archivist

*Worldwide footage: environmental, development, habitat, people,
conflict, globalisation, trade.*

Clips & Footage
2nd Floor, 80A Dean Street, London W1D 3SN
t 020 7287 7287 **f** 020 7439 4886 **e** clipsetc@easynet.co.uk
Contact Alison Mercer, Proprietor

COI Footage File
2 The Quadrant, 135 Salusbury Road, London NW6 6RJ
t 020 7624 3388 **f** 020 7624 3377
e research@film-images.com **w** www.film-images.com
Contact Tony Dykes, Senior Researcher

Computerised Time Lapse Cinematography
27 Birstall Road, London N15 5EN
t 020 8802 8791 f 020 8211 8286
e maxim@time-lapse.co.uk w www.time-lapse.co.uk

Contemporary Films
24 Southwood Lawn Road, Highgate, London N6 5SF
t 020 8340 5715 f 020 8348 1238
e inquiries@contemporaryfilms.com
w www.contemporaryfilms.com
Contact Eric Liknaitzky

Daniels Film
3A Runnymeade Road, Canvey Island SS8 0EF
Contact Eddie Daniels

Digital Vision Motion
India House, 45 Curlew Street, London SE1 2ND
t 020 7378 5555 f 020 7378 5533
e info@digitalvisiononline.com
w www.digitalvisiononline.co.uk/motion
Contact Annabel Macadam, Motion Project Manager

Domaine
8 Whitepost Hill, Redhill RH1 6AL
t 01737 766100 f 01737 766588
e dpltv@aol.com w www.domaineproductions.com
Contact Jenny Duff, Managing Director
Credits Voyage (I)

East Anglian Film Archive
University of East Anglia, Norwich NR4 7TJ
t 01603 592664 f 01603 593475
e eafa@uea.ac.uk w www.uea.ac.uk/eafa/
Contact David Cleveland, Director

Education Distribution Services
Education House, Castle Road, Sittingbourne ME10 3RL
t 01795 427614 f 01795 437988 m 07710 362432
e b_wiles@edist.co.uk
Contact Barry Wiles, Director

Educational & Television Films
247A Upper Street, Highbury Corner, London N1 1RU
t +44 20 7226 2298 f +44 20 7226 8016
e zoe@etvltd.demon.co.uk w www.etvltd.demon.co.uk
Contact Zoe Moore, Film Librarian

Film Images (London) Ltd
2 The Quadrant, 135 Salusbury Road, London NW6 6RJ
t 020 7624 3388 f 020 7624 3377
e research@film-images.com w www.film-images.com
Contact Tony Dykes, Senior Researcher; James Kearney, Researcher; Ginny
Harrold, Acquisitions Manager; Angela Saward, Research & Marketing Manager

Film Institute of Ireland
Irish Film Centre, 6 Eustace Street, Dublin 2, Rep of Ireland
t 679 5744 f 677 8755 e info@ifc.ie w www.fii.ie
Contact Grainne Humphreys , Assistant Director//Head of Education

Focal International Ltd
Pentax House, South Hill Avenue, South Harrow HA2 0DU
t 020 8423 5853 f 020 8933 4826
e info@focalint.org w www.focalint.org
Contact Anne Johnson, Commercial Manager

Footage Farm Ltd
22 Newman Street, London W1T 1PH
t 020 7631 3773 f 020 7631 3774
e info@footagefarm.co.uk w www.footagefarm.co.uk
Contact Lin McConnell, Sales Executive

British Pathe plc **New Pathe House**
57 Jamestown Road London NW1 7DB
Tel 020 7424 3636 Fax 020 7485 3606

http://www.britishpathe.commerce...

Fremantle Archive Sales
1 Stephen Street, London W1T 1AL
t 020 7691 6733 **f** 020 7691 6080
e archive@fremantlemedia.com **w** www.fremantlemedia.com

German Film & Video Library
Education Distribution Service, Education House, Drywall
Estate, Castle Road, Sittingbourne ME10 3RL
t 01795 427614 **f** 01795 437988 **e** barry@edist.co.uk
Contact Barry Wiles, Proprietor

Graeme Peacock
56 Ashdale Crescent, Chapel House Estate, Newcastle-upon-
Tyne NE5 1AU
t 0191 267 7258 **f** 0191 267 7258
e info@graeme-peacok.com **w** www.graeme-peacok.com

Granada Visual

Granada Visual
48 Leicester Square, London WC2H 7FB
t 020 7633 2700 **f** 020 7633 2701
e granada.visual@granadamedia.com
w www.granadamedia.com/visual
Contact Bryn Downing, New Business Manager; Catherine Aleppo, Sales
Executive; Francesca Doria, Sales Executive; Victoria Thomas, Sales Executive;
Rob Molloy, Sales Executive; Mark Leaver

*Granada Visual represents 100,000+ hours of footage from the libraries of
all Granada Media companies. An amazing and diverse collection covering
every genre: arts, entertainment, factual, music, wildlife and stockshots.*

Greenpark Images
Illand, Launceston PL15 7LS
t 01566 782107 **f** 01566 782127
e info@clips.net **w** www.clips.net
Contact Leonore Morphet, Director

Greenpark Productions Ltd
Greenpark, Illand, Launceston PL15 7LS
t 01566 782178 **f** 01556 782127 **m** 07968 260778
e archives@clips.net **w** www.clips.net

Huntley Film Archives
191 Wardour Street, London W1F 8ZE
t 020 7287 8000 **f** 020 7287 8001
e films@huntleyarchives.com **w** www.huntleyarchives.com
Contact Amanda Huntley, Archivist

Images of War Ltd
31A Regents Park Road, London NW1 7TL
e derek@dircon.co.uk **w** www.warfootage.com

Imperial War Museum Film & Video Archive
Lambeth Road, London SE1 6HZ
t 020 7416 5291 **t** 020 7416 5292 **f** 020 7416 5299
e film@iwm.org.uk **w** www.iwm.org.uk
Contact Jane Fish; Paul Sargeant

*Our archive holds some 120 million feet of film and 6,500 hours of
videotape. This constantly growing collection ranges in time almost from
the birth of cinema to the present and offers detailed coverage of the
military, political, and social history of the 20th century.*

Index Stock Shots
3rd Floor, Highgate Business Centre, 33 Greenwood Place,
London NW5 1LD
t 020 7482 1953 **f** 020 7482 1967
e info@indexstockshots.com **w** www.indexstockshots.com
Contact Philip Hinds, Manager

ITN Archive
200 Gray's Inn Road, London WC1X 8XZ
t 020 7430 4480 **f** 020 7430 4453
e sales@itnarchive.com **w** www.itnarchive.com
Contact Linda Reeve, Sales Manager

London's Transport Museum
The Piazza, London WC2E 7BB
t 020 7379 6344 **f** 020 7565 7254
e resourcec@ltmuseum.co.uk **w** www.ltmuseum.co.uk
Contact Simon Murphy, Curator, Film and Video

Maverick Enterprises
31 Dobree Avenue, London NW10 2AD
t 020 8459 3858 **f** 020 8459 3895 **e** ghizela@totalise.co.uk
Contact Ghizela Rowe, Managing Director
Credits I Love The Seventies (T); The South Bank Show (T); Eurotrash (T);
Buffalo Bill (D)

Moving Image Communications
61 Great Titchfield Street, London W1W 7PP
t 020 7580 3300 **f** 020 7580 2242
e mail@milibrary.com **w** www.milibrary.com
Contact Michael Maloney, Director; Nathalie Banaigs, Acquisitions & Marketing;
Michael Maloney, Director

NATIONAL GEOGRAPHIC

National Geographic Film & Television Library
33 Ovington Square, Knightsbridge, London SW3 1LJ
t 020 7581 7175 **f** 020 7225 2315
e imorris@ngs.org **w** www.ngtlibrary.com
Contact Ian Morris, Sales Director

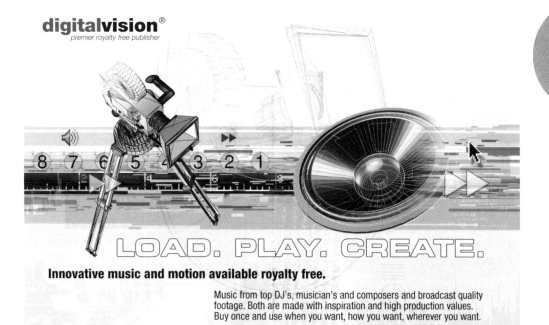
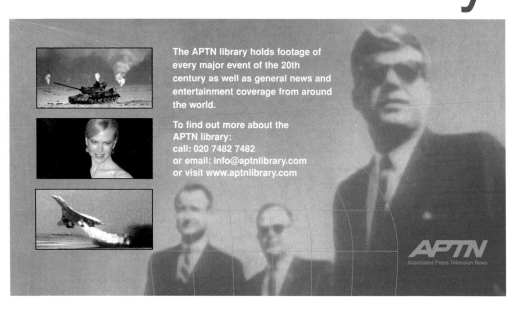

herstory

The establishment of the Welfare State and improved health provision post war directly benefited women's lot. Aguably, the advancement of women in society and their increased employment opportunities are the great success stories of the Twentieth Century.

The COI Footage File collection, a library of official films, is an invaluable resource for footage of social, economic and cultural change from 1945 onwards. Such gems as 'Light Repetitive Work' 1952 (showing the feminisation of the workforce) and 'Teenage Girl' 1961 (a mother muses on the myriad of careers choices in front of her daughter) richly illustrate these changing times.

The Sixties marked a sea-change in Britain's social fabric as well as making London into the vibrant epicentre of social and cultural change. The transformation from home-maker to liberated woman at work, rest and play is no where more evident than in 'Mr English at Home' 1940 and 'Mini Skirts Make Money' 1968.

A full on-line catalogue is available **www.film-images.com.**

Film Images was established in 1989 as a comprehensive film and video resource for organisations requiring clips and stock shots for all kinds of productions.

T: +44 (0) 20 7624 3388
F: +44 (0) 20 7624 3377
E: RESEARCH@FILM-IMAGES.COM

National Motor Museum

Film & Video Department, Beulieu, Hampshire SO42 7ZN
t 01590 614664 **f** 01590 612655 **m** 07818 454522
e stephen.vokins@beaulieu.co.uk **w** www.beaulieu.co.uk

The National Screen & Sound Archive of Wales

The National Library of Wales, Aberystwyth SY23 3BU
t 01970 632828 **f** 01970 632882 **e** agssc@llgc.org.uk
e sgrinasain@llgc.org.uk **w** www.screenandsound.llgc.org.uk
Contact Elen Jones, Administrative Assistant; Mari Stevens, Access Officer;
Dafydd Pritchard, Assistand Curator; Iestyn Hughes, Head

North West Film Archive

Minshull House, 47-49 Chorlton Street, Manchester M1 3EU
t 0161 247 3097 **f** 0161 247 3098
e n.w.filmarchive@mmu.ac.uk **w** www.nwfa.mmu.ac.uk
Contact Joanne Abley, Collections Assistant; Nick Gladden, Acquisition &
Cataloguing Assistant

The Olympic Television Archive Bureau

C/o TWI, McCormack House, Burlington Lane, London W4 2TH
t 020 8233 5353 **f** 020 8233 5354 **e** webmaster@otab.com
Contact Philippa Moore, Sales Manager

Overseas Film & Television Centre

2 The Quadrant, 135 Salusbury Road, London NW6 6RJ
t 020 7624 3388 **f** 020 7624 3377
e research@film-images.com **w** www.film-images.com
Contact Tony Muscat; James Kearney, Researcher

Reid & Casement Research

Bedford Chambers, The Piazza, Covent Garden, London WC2E 8HA
t 020 7240 4550 **f** 020 7379 0061
e research@reidandcasement.co.uk **w** www.reidandcasement.co.uk
Contact Nicola Corbett, Researcher; Joanne Mirzoeff, Researcher; Maria
O'Donnell, Researcher; Rachel McClelland, Researcher
Credits Virginmoney.com (C); Voices From The Mountains (D); After Eight (C)

Ronald Grant Archive

The Masters House, The Old Workhouse, 2 Dugard Way, Off
Renfrew Road, London SE11 4TH
t 020 7840 2200 **f** 020 7840 2299
e martin@cinemamuseum.org.uk
Contact Martin Humphries, Manager
Credits Scene By Scene (T); Legends (T); Film 2002 (T)

Royal Air Force Museum Film Archive

Grahame Park Way, Hendon, London NW9 5LL
t 020 8205 2266 **f** 020 8200 1751
e info@rafmuseum.com **w** www.rafmuseum.com
Contact Ian Thirsk, Film Archivist

RSPB Film Collection

Newsplayer Ltd, Portland House, 4 Great Portland Street,
London W1W 8QJ
t 020 7927 6699 **f** 020 7927 6698
e greg@newsplayer.com **w** www.rspb.org.uk/films
Contact Greg Owen

*The RSPB Film Collection consists of over 100 hours of film, featuring
over 100 different species of birds. RSPB material has been used in
'Gladiator', 'Father Ted', 'Miss Marple', and TV commercials in the UK
and abroad. Film Collection users can search, view, edit, order, and
licence the material, all online.*

The Scottish Screen Archive -
Scotland's Moving Image Collection

1 Bowmont Gardens, Glasgow G12 9LR
t 0141 337 7400 **f** 0141 337 7413
e archive@scottishscreen.com **w** www.scottishscreen.com
Contact kevin Cowle

THE NATIONAL SCREEN AND SOUND ARCHIVE OF WALES

ARCHIF GENEDLAETHOL SGRIN A SAIN CYMRU

screenandsound.llgc.org.uk | sgrinasain.llgc.org.uk

Llyfrgell Genedlaethol Cymru
National Library of Wales
Aberystwyth
SY23 3BU
agssc@llgc.org.uk

01970 632828
01970 615709

Shell Film & Video Unit
REF/51, Shell Centre, York Road, London SE1 7NA
t 020 7934 3318 **f** 020 7934 4090 **e** jane.poynor@shell.com
Contact Jane Poynor, Producer

The South West Film & Television Archive
Mike, Royal William Yard, Stonehouse, Plymouth PL1 3RP
t 01752 202650 **f** 01752 205025 **e** enquiries@tswsta.co.uk

Three S Films
12 Regent Square, Penzance TR18 4BG
t 01736 367912 **f** 01736 350957
e info@threesfilms.com **w** www.threesfilms.com
Contact Ian Jenkin, Video Editor; John Adams, Director

Undercurrents Productions
16b Cherwell Street, Oxford OX4 1BG
t 01865 203661 **m** 07973 298359
e underc@gn.apc.org **w** www.undercurrents.org
Contact Paul O'Connor, Director

Viewtech Educational Media
7-8 Falcons Gate, North Avon Business Centre, Dean Road,
Yate, Bristol BS37 5NH
t 01454 858055 **f** 01454 858056
e info@viewtech.co.uk **w** www.viewtech.co.uk
Contact Simon Littlechild, Director

Wellcome Trust Medical Film & Audio Collections
The Wellcome Trust, 210 Euston Road, London NW1 2BE
t 020 7611 8596 **t** 020 7611 8597 **f** 020 7611 8765
e mfac@wellcome.ac.uk
w http://catalogue.wellcome.ac.uk/search~S3
Contact Marie Williams, Contact; Michael Clark, Contact

Libraries **Music**

Active Music Library
e activemusiclibrary@yahoo.co.uk
Contact Mike Tayler, MD

ADN Creation Music Library
Sovereign House, 12 Trewartha Road, Praa Sands, Penzance
TR20 9ST
t 01736 762826 **f** 01736 763328 **m** 07721 449477
e panamus@aol.com **w** www.panamamusic.co.uk
Contact Roderick Jones, Managing Director

Amphonic Music Ltd
Kerchesters, Waterhouse Lane, Kingswood KT20 6HT
t 01737 832837 **f** 01737 833812
e mail@amphonic.co.uk **w** www.amphonic.com
Contact Ian Dale, Managing Director

Arcadia Production Music (UK)
Greenlands, Payhembury EX14 3HY
t 01404 841601 **f** 01404 841687
e admin@arcadiamusic.tv **w** www.arcadiamusic.tv

ARTL & SRTL Production Music Libraries
Record House, Record Road, Emsworth PO10 7NS
t 01243 379834 **f** 01243 430639
e info@srtl.co.uk **w** www.srtl.co.uk

Atlantic Seven Music Library
52 Lancaster Road, London N4 4PR
t 020 7263 4435 **f** 020 7436 9233
e musiclibrary@atlanticseven.com **w** www.atlanticseven.com
Contact Patrick Shart, Proprietor; Steve Jeffries, Proprietor

Audio-Visual-Media Music Library
Sovereign House, 12 Trewartha Road, Praa Sands, Penzance
TR20 9ST
t 01736 762826 **f** 01736 763328 **m** 07721 449477
e panamus@aol.com **w** www.panamamusic.co.uk
Contact Roderick Jones, Managing Director

BMG Production Music
Bedford House, 69-79 Fulham High Street, London SW6 3JW
t 020 7384 8188 **f** 020 7384 2744 **m** 07958 651379
e juliette.richards@bmg.co.uk **w** www.bmgprodmusic.com
Contact Bonamy Gauvain, Marketing; Juliette Richards, Head of Sales and
Marketing; Juliette Richards, Head of Sales and Marketing
Credits Tom McRae: A Day Like Today; Skinny: Sweet Thing

Boom! Music
16 Blackwood Close, West Byfleet KT14 6PP
t 01932 336212 **e** info@music4media.tv **w** www.music4media.tv
Contact Phil Binding, Managing Director
Credits HTV West News (T); Home On Their Own (T); Channel 5 News (T)

The British Music Information Centre
10 Stratford Place, London W1C 1BA
t 020 7499 8567 **f** 020 7499 4795
e info@bmic.co.uk **w** www.bmic.co.uk
Contact Matthew Greenall, Director; Dan Goren, Information Manager; Imogen
Mitchell, Production & Services Manager

Bruton Music
Zomba Production Music, 10-11 St Martin's Court, London
WC2N 4AJ
t 0800 0345 245 **t** 020 7497 4800 **f** 020 7497 4801
e promotions@zpm.co.uk **w** www.zpm.co.uk
Contact Tracy Bryer, Head of Promotions; Andrew Stannard, Music Consultant;
Julia Dean, Music Consultant

KPM·KOSINUS·MUSICHOUSE·MEGA-TRAX·SELECTEDSOUND·NFL·AVMUSIC

KPM|UK

TWELVE LIBRARIES: ONE CALL

VIDEOHELPER·X-RAYDOG·CASTLE CINEMUSIC·KPM CLASSICAL·DIGIFFECTS

t: 020 7412 9111
e: kpm@kpm.co.uk
w: www.playkpm.com

Caribbean Music Library
Sovereign House, 12 Trewartha Road, Praa Sands, Penzance TR20 9ST
t 01736 762826 f 01736 763328 m 07721 449477
e panamus@aol.com w www.panamamusic.co.uk
Contact Roderick Jones, Managing Director

Carlin Production Music
Iron Bridge House, 3 Bridge Approach, London NW1 8BD
t 020 7734 3251 f 020 7439 2391 m 07785 362174
e cpm@carlinmusic.co.uk w www.carlinmusic.co.uk
Contact Paul Kinane, Production Director

Cavendish Music Library
295 Regent Street, London W1B 2JH
t 020 7291 7222 f 020 7436 5675
e booseymedia@boosey.com w www.cavendishmusic.com
Contact Ann Dawson, Media Manager; Michael Shaw, Marketing Manager; Natasha Baldwin, Producer

Chappell Recorded Music Library
Zomba Production Music, 10-11 St Martin's Court, London WC2N 4AJ
t 0800 0345 245 t 020 7497 4800 f 020 7497 4801
e promotions@zpm.co.uk w www.zpm.co.uk
Contact Andrew Stannard, Music Consultant; Julia Dean, Music Consultant

Chris Worth Productions
27 Stainesway, Louth LN11 0DE
t 01507 601546 f 01507 601546
e info@chrisworthproductions.com
w www.chrisworthproductions.com
Contact Chris Worth, Managing Director
All tracks can be previewed and downloaded. Composition services available.

Connect
Zomba Production Music, 10-11 St Martin's Court, London WC2N 4AJ
t 0800 0345 245 t 020 7497 4800 f 020 7497 4801
e promotions@zpm.co.uk w www.zpm.co.uk
Contact Andrew Stannard, Music Consultant; Julia Dean, Music Consultant

Corelia Music Library
Sovereign House, 12 Trewartha Road, Praa Sands, Penzance TR20 9ST
t 01736 762826 f 01736 763328 m 07721 449477
e panamus@aol.com w www.panamamusic.co.uk
Contact Roderick Jones, Managing Director

Digital Vision Music
India House, 45 Curlew Street, London SE1 2ND
t 020 7378 5555 f 020 7378 5533
e info@digitalvisiononline.com
w www.digitalvisiononline.co.uk/music

Eventide Music Library
Sovereign House, 12 Trewartha Road, Praa Sands, Penzance TR20 9ST
t 01736 762826 f 01736 763328 m 07721 449477
e panamus@aol.com w www.panamamusic.co.uk
Contact Roderick Jones, Managing Director

Firemix
The Mill, 31 The Sadlers, Chichester PO18 0PR
t 07000 347364 f 07000 347332
e mail@firemix.com w www.firemix.com
Contact Karen Jacobs

FirstCom
Zomba Production Music, 10-11 St Martin's Court, London WC2N 4AJ
t 08000 0345 245 t 020 7497 4800 f 020 7497 4801
e promotions@zpm.co.uk w www.zpm.co.uk
Contact Andrew Stannard, Music Consultant; Julia Dean, Music Consultant

Focus Music Library
4 Pilgrims Lane, London NW3 1SL
t 020 7435 8266 f 020 7435 1505 m 07836 232367
e info@focusmusic.com w www.focusmusic.com
Contact Paul Greedus, Managing Director; Dean Mahoney, Manager

Galerie
Zomba Production Music, 10-11 St Martin's Court, London WC2N 4AJ
t 08450 345245 t 020 7497 4800
e promotions@zpm.co.uk w www.zpm.co.uk
Contact Andrew Stannard, Music Consultant; Julia Dean, Music Consultant

Gung Ho Music Library Ltd
54 Crewys Road, London NW2 2AD
t 020 8905 5955 f 020 8905 5155 e info@gunghomusic.co.uk
Contact Michelle Mullan, Managing Director

Heraldic Production Music Library
Sovereign House, 12 Trewartha Road, Praa Sands, Penzance TR20 9ST
t 01736 762826 f 01736 763328 m 07721 449477
e panamus@aol.com w www.panamamusic.co.uk
Contact Roderick Jones, Managing Director

John Fiddy Music
Unit 3, Moorgate Business Centre, South Green, Dereham NR19 1PT
t 01362 697922 f 01362 697923
e info@johnfiddymusic.co.uk w www.johnfiddymusic.co.uk
Contact John Fiddy

Justement Music Library
C/o Studio G, Cedar Tree House, Farthingsone NN12 8EZ
t 01327 360820 f 01327 360821
e library@studiog.co.uk w www.studiog.co.uk
Contact John Gale, Production Music Manager

JW Media Music Ltd
4 Whitfield Street, London W1T 2RD
t 020 7681 8900 f 020 7681 8911
e salesinfo@jwmediamusic.co.uk w www.jwmediamusic.com
Contact George Barker, Managing Director; Carl Dobbins, SFX Sales; Jenny Thornton, Music Consultant

KPM Music

127 Charing Cross Road, London WC2H 0QY
t 020 7412 9111 **f** 020 7413 0061
e kpm@kpm.co.uk **w** www.playkpm.com
Contact Tim Hardy

KPM's high quality music can now be searched, auditioned and downloaded in broadcast quality from the PLAY Music Finder system (www.playkpm.com). PLAY enables you to cross-search on eight different music libraries. This service is free of charge to all our clients.

Mediatacks Music Library

93 Columbia Way, Blackburn BB2 7EA
t 01254 691197 **m** 07951 758105
e info@mediatracks.co.uk **w** www.mediatracks.co.uk
Contact Steve Johnson, Proprietor

Melody First Production Music Library

Sovereign House, 12 Trewartha Road, Praa Sands, Penzance TR20 9ST
t 01736 762826 **f** 01736 763328 **m** 07721 449477
e panamus@aol.com **w** www.panamamusic.co.uk
Contact Roderick Jones, Managing Director

The Music Factor

The Music Factor Ltd

15 Stanhope Road, London N6 5NE
t 020 8802 5984 **f** 020 8809 7436
e themusicfactor@paulrodriguezmus.demon.co.uk
Contact Paul Rodriguez, Managing Director; Amy Coats, Copyright Manager

Recent work: BBC TV, Channel 4, Channel 5, Discovery. Facilities: music production, music publishing, music library, copyright clearance.

Music Mall

1 Upper James Street, London W1F 9DE
t 020 7534 1444 **e** info@musicmall.co.uk **w** www.musicmall.co.uk

Contact Andi Baron, Production Manager; Suzanne Willems, Production Co-ordinator; Holly Woodford, Sales and Marketing Manager; Amy Ashworth, Salea And Marketing Assistant
Credits Karaoke Party 2003 (T); Top 100 Singles Of All Time (T); Pop Stars: The Rivals (T); Fame Academy (T)

Musik' Image Music Library

Sovereign House, 12 Trewartha Road, Praa Sands, Penzance TR20 9ST
t 01736 762826 **f** 01736 763328 **m** 07721 449477
e panamus@aol.com **w** www.panamamusic.co.uk
Contact Roderick Jones, Managing Director

OGM Production Music

Kerchesters, Waterhouse Lane, Kingswood KT20 6HT
t 01737 832837 **f** 01737 833812
e post@soundstage.co.uk **w** www.amphonic.com
Contact Ian Dale, Managing Director

Panama Music Library

Sovereign House, 12 Trewartha Road, Praa Sands, Penzance TR20 9ST
t 01736 762826 **f** 01736 763328 **m** 07721 449477
e panamus@aol.com **w** www.panamamusic.co.uk
Contact Roderick Jones, Managing Director

Parry Music Library

Studio G Ltd, Cedar Tree House, Farthingstone NN12 8EZ
t 01327 360820 **f** 01327 360821
e library@studiog.co.uk **w** www.studiog.co.uk
Contact Jon Cumming, Production Music Manager

Piano Bar Music Library
Sovereign House, 12 Trewartha Road, Praa Sands, Penzance TR20 9ST
t 01736 762826 **f** 01736 763328 **m** 07721 449477
e panamus@aol.com **w** www.panamamusic.co.uk
Contact Roderick Jones, Managing Director

Powerhouse Music Library
C/o Studio G Ltd, Cedar Tree House, Farthingstone NN12 8EZ
t 01327 360820 **f** 01327 360821
e library@studiog.co.uk **w** www.studiog.co.uk
Contact John Gale, Director

Primrose Music Ltd
1 Leitrim House, 36 Worple Road, London SW19 4EQ
t 020 8946 7808 **f** 020 8946 3392
e jestersong@msn.com **w** www.primrosemusic.com
Contact Roland Rogers, Director; Brenda Wills, Cable & Satellite Manager

Promo Sonor International (GB)
Sovereign House, 12 Trewartha Road, Praa Sands, Penzance TR20 9ST
t 01736 762826 **f** 01736 763328 **m** 07721 449477
e panamus@aol.com **w** www.panamamusic.co.uk
Contact Roderick Jones, Managing Director

PSI Music Library
Sovereign House, 12 Trewartha Road, Praa Sands, Penzance TR20 9ST
t 01736 762826 **f** 01736 763328 **m** 07721 449477
e panamus@aol.com **w** www.panamamusic.co.uk
Contact Roderick Jones, Managing Director

Sound Stage Production Music
Kerchesters, Waterhouse Lane, Kingswood KT20 6HT
t 01737 832837 **f** 01737 833812
e mail@amphonic.co.uk **w** www.amphonic.com
Contact Ian Dale, Managing Director

Standard Music Ltd
Onward House, 11 Uxbridge Street, London W8 7TQ
t 020 7221 4275 **f** 020 7229 6893
e standard@bucksmusicgroup.co.uk **w** www.bucksmusicgroup.com
Contact Cliff Simms, Library Manager; Karl Selfe, Library Manager; Amanda Cockerton, Marketing Manager

Studio G Ltd
Cedar Tree House, Farthingstone, Towcester NN12 8EZ
t 01327 360820 **f** 01327 360821
e library@studiog.co.uk **w** www.studiog.co.uk
Contact John Gale, Director

Unity Production Music Library
Magnolia House, 335 Springfield Road, Chelmsford CM2 6AN
t 01245 603472 **f** 01245 603472 **m** 07949 200748
e unitymusic@blueyonder.co.uk
Contact Neil Watson, Partner

West One Music
8 Berwick Street, London W1F 0PH
t 020 7292 0000 **f** 020 7292 0010
e info@westonemusic.com **w** www.west-one-music.com
Contact Michael Shaw, General Manager; Naima Lambert, Promotions; Ciaran McNeaney, Promotions
Credits Two Men Went To War (F)

Libraries Reference

British Film Institute (BFI) Production
21 Stephen Street, London W1P 2LN
t 020 7255 1444 **f** 020 7436 2338
e library@bfi.org.uk **w** www.bfi.org.uk/library
Contact Ray Templeton, Head of Library and Education; Christopher Dupin, Annuals Librarian

British Film Institute National Library
21 Stephen Street, London W1T 1LN
t 020 7255 1444 **f** 020 7436 2338
e library@bfi.org.uk **w** www.bfi.org.uk
Contact Ray Templeton, Head of Library & Education

British Library Sound Archive
96 Euston Road, London NW1 2DB
t 020 7412 7421 **f** 020 7412 7441
e sound-archive@bl.uk **w** www.bl.uk/nsa
Contact Richard Fairman, Service Development Officer

The British Library–Business Information Service
96 Euston Road, London NW1 2DB
t 020 7412 7454 **f** 020 7412 7453
e business-information@bl.uk **w** www.bl.uk/bis
Contact Tony Corsini, Telephone Service Manager

Gwynedd Archives & Museums Service
County Offices, Victoria Dock, Caernarfon LL55 1SH
t 01286 679095 **f** 01286 679637
e archive@gwynedd.gov.uk **w** www.gwynedd.gov.uk
Contact Anne Rhydderch, Principal Archivist and Heritage Officer

National Library of Wales
Aberystwyth SY23 3BU
t 01970 632800 **f** 01970 615709
e holi@llgc.org.uk **w** www.llgc.org.uk
Contact Lestyn Hughes, Video; Sion Jobbins, Locations

National Motor Museum Film & Video Dept
Beaulieu, Montagu Ventures Ltd, John Montagu Building, Beaulieu, Brockenhurst SO42 7ZN
t 01590 612345 **f** 01590 612624 **m** 07818 454522
e filmandvideo@beaulieu.co.uk **w** www.beaulieu.co.uk
Contact Stephen Vokins

Libraries Sound FX

BBC Natural History Sound Library
Broadcasting House, Whiteladies Road, Bristol BS8 2LR
t 0117 974 2415 **f** 0117 970 6124 **e** nhu.soundenquiries@bbc.co.uk

Sound Effects Library Ltd
Tape Gallery House, 28 Lexington Street, London W1F 0LF
t 020 7439 3325 **f** 020 7734 0631
e info@sound-effects-library.com **w** www.sound-effects-library.com
Contact Lloyd Billing, Managing Director

Libraries Stills

Ace Photo Agency
Satellite House, 2 Salisbury Road, Wimbledon, London SW19 4EZ
t 020 8944 9944 **f** 020 8944 9940 **m** 07710 408 500
e info@acestock.com **w** www.acestock.com
Contact John Panton, Chairman

Anthony Blake Photo Library
20 Blades Court, Deodar Road, Putney, London SW15 2NU
t 020 8877 1123 **f** 020 8877 9787
e info@abpl.co.uk **w** www.abpl.co.uk
Contact Anna Weller, Library Manager; Graham Everitt, Client Manager

Aquarius Library
PO Box 5, Hastings TN34 1HR
t 01424 721196 **f** 01424 717704
e aquarius.lib@clara.net **w** www.aquariuscollection.com
Contact Gilbert Gibson, Managing Director; David Corkill, Head of Stills Library
Credits After They Were Famous (T); Grease (F)

Ardea Wildlife Pets Environment
35 Brodrick Road, London SW17 7DX
t 020 8672 2067 **f** 020 8672 8787
e ardea@ardea.co.uk **w** www.ardea.co.uk
Contact Sophie Napier, Company Director

Art Directors & TRIP Photo Library
57 Burden Lane, Cheam SM2 7BY
t 020 8642 3593 **f** 020 8395 7230
e images@artdirectors.co.uk **w** www.artdirectors.co.uk
Contact Bob Turner

Aspect Picture Library
40 Rostrevor Road, London SW6 5AD
t 020 7736 1998 **f** 020 7731 7362 **e** aspect.ldn@btinternet.com
Contact Derek Bayes, Director

Australia Pictures
28 Sheen Common Drive, Richmond TW10 5BN
t 020 7602 1989 **f** 020 7602 1989 **e** equilibriumfilms@hotmail.com

Aviation Photographs International
15 Downs View Road, Swindon SN3 1NS
t 01793 497179 **f** 01793 434030 **m** 07879 861110
Contact Jeremy Flack, Director

Aviation Picture Library
116 The Avenue, St Stephens, West Ealing, London W13 8JX
t 020 8566 7712 **f** 020 8566 7714 **m** 07860 670073
e avpix@aol.com **w** www.aviationpictures.com
Contact Chris Savill, Manager; Austin Brown, Proprietor

BBC
Commercial Unit, Room LG29 CB, Bush House, PO Box 76,
The Strand, London WC2B 4PH
t 020 7557 2452 **f** 020 7557 2728
w www.bbcresearchcentral.com
Credits BBC One: Rush Hour

The Bridgeman Art Library
17-19 Garway Road, London W2 4PH
t 020 7727 4065 **f** 020 7792 8509
e jenny.page@bridgeman.co.uk **w** www.bridgeman.co.uk
Contact Jenny Page, Picture Research Manager
The world's leading source of fine art images.

Christie's Images
1 Langley Lane, London SW8 1TJ
t 020 7582 1282 **f** 020 7582 5632
e imageslondon@christies.com **w** www.christiesimages.com
Contact Mark Lynch, Sales & Development

Collections
13 Woodberry Crescent, London N10 1PJ
t 020 8883 0083 **f** 020 8883 9215
e collections@btinternet.com
w www.collectionspicturelibrary.com

The Flight Collection @ Quadrant
Quadrant House, The Quadrant, Sutton SM2 5AS
t 020 8652 8888 **f** 020 8652 8933
e qpl@rbi.co.uk **w** www.theflightcollection.com

Fotomas Index UK
12 Pickhurst Rise, West Wickham BR4 0AL
t 020 8776 2772 **f** 020 8776 2236
Contact Freeman , Director

Garden Picture Library
Unit 12 Ransomes Dock, 35 Parkgate Road, London SW11 4NP
t 020 7228 4332 **f** 020 7924 3267
e info@gardenpicture.com **w** www.gardenpicture.com
Contact Iben Lund, New Business Development
Inspirational images of gardens, flowers and gardening lifestyle.

Getty Images
101 Bayham Street, London NW1 0AG
t 020 7267 8988 **t** 0800 376 7977
e sales@gettyimages.co.uk **w** www.gettyimages.com

Hulton Archive
Unique House, 21-31 Woodfield Road, London W9 2BA
t 020 7579 5730 **f** 020 7266 2414 **m** 07775 811298
w www.hultonarchive.com
Contact Jane Stevenson, Publishing Team Manager

Illustrated London News Picture Library
20 Upper Ground, London SE1 9PF
t 020 7805 5585 **e** iln.pictures@ilng.co.uk **w** www.ilng.co.uk
Contact Richard Pitkin, Marketing Manager; Elaine Hood, Manager

The Image Bank
17 Conway Street, London W1T 6EE
t 020 7312 0300 **f** 020 7428 5100
e theimagebank.uk@getty-images.com **w** www.imagebank.co.uk

Image Diggers
618B Finchley Road, London NW11 7RR
t 020 8455 4564 **f** 020 8455 4564
e ziph@macunlimited.net **w** http://imagediggers.netfirms.com
Contact Robert Lambolle, Chief Editor; Neil Hornick, Director
Credits Fulmes Television (T); Channel 4 Sitcom Festival (T); BSO - Rotterdam
BV (C); Whales Of August (F)

Image State Ltd
Ramilles House, 122 Ramillies Street, London W1F 7LN
t 020 7482 0478 **f** 020 7287 3933
e info@imagestate.co.uk **w** www.imagestate.co.uk
Contact Ben Smith, Sales Manager UK; Harry Mole, Sales Manager UK

James Davis Travel Photography
65 Brighton Road, Shoreham BN43 6RE
t 01273 440113 **f** 01273 440116
e library@eyeubiquitous.com **w** www.eyeubiquitous.com
Contact Stephen Rafferty, Library Manager

London Aerial Photo Library
PO Box 25, Ashwellthorpe NR16 1HL
t 01508 488320 **f** 01508 488282
e aerialphotos@btinternet.com **w** www.londonaerial.co.uk
Contact Nigel Stockwell

London Features International Ltd
3 Boscobel Street, London NW8 8PS
t 020 7723 4204 **f** 020 7723 9201 **m** 07802 225 520
e sales@lfi.co.uk **w** www.lfi.co.uk
Contact David Swanborough, Picture Editor

Merseyside Photo Library
Suite 6, Egerton House, Tower Road, Birkenhead, Wirral CH41 1FN
t 0151 650 6975 **f** 0151 650 6976 **e** ron@merseyside.demon.co.uk

The National Gallery Picture Library
St Vincent House, 30 Orange Street, London WC2H 7HH
t 020 7747 5994 **f** 020 7747 5999
e picture.library@nationalgallery.co.uk
w www.nationalgallery.co.uk
Contact Rebecca Snookes, Senior Account Executive; Belinda Ross, Picture
Manager; Margaret Daly, Account Executive

Picturebank Photo Library Ltd

Parman House, 30-36 Fife Road, Kingston-upon-Thames KT1 1SY
t 020 8547 2344 **f** 020 8974 5252
e info@picturebank.co.uk **w** www.picturebank.co.uk
Contact Martin Bagge, Director

Redferns Music Picture Library

7 Bramley Road, London W10 6SZ
t 020 7792 9914 **f** 020 7792 0921
e info@redferns.com **w** www.musicpictures.com
Contact Dede Millar, Partner

Rex Features

18 Vine Hill, London EC1R 5DZ
t 020 7278 7294 **f** 020 7837 4812
e rex@rexfeatures.com **w** www.rexfeatures.com
Contact Glen Marks, Library Manager

Robert Harding Picture Library

58-59 Great Marlborough Street, London W1F 7JY
t 020 7478 4000 **f** 020 7631 1070
e info@robertharding.com **w** www.robertharding.com
Contact Fraser Hall, Image Services Manager

Science Photo Library

327-329 Harrow Road, London W9 3RB
t 020 7432 1100 **f** 020 7286 8668
e info@sciencephoto-com **w** www.sciencephoto.com
Contact Justin Hobson, Research Manager

Simmons Aerofilms Ltd

Gate Studios, Station Road, Borehamwood WD6 1EJ
t 020 8207 0666 **f** 020 8207 5433
e library@aerofilms.com **w** www.aerofilms.com
Contact Michael Willis, Librarian
Credits EastEnders (T); News Night (T)

Skyscan Photolibrary

Oak House, Toddington, Cheltenham GL54 5BY
t 01242 621357 **f** 01242 621343 **m** 07831 410205
e info@skyscan.co.uk **w** www.skyscan.co.uk
Contact Brenda Marks, Library Manager

Still Moving Picture Company

8 Saxe Coburg Place, Edinburgh EH3 5BR
t 0131 332 1123 **f** 0131 332 9123
e info@stillmovingpictures.com **w** www.stillmovingpictures.com

StockShot Adventure Sports Picture Library

2B St Vincent Street, Edinburgh EH3 6SH
t 0131 557 6688 **f** 0131 566 8282 **m** 07071 201440
e info@stockshot.co.uk **w** www.stockshot.co.uk
Contact Bridget Clyde, Contact

Sue Cunningham Photographic

56 Chatham Road, Kingston-upon-Thames KT1 3AA
t 020 8541 3024 **f** 020 8541 5388
e pictures@scphotographic.com **w** www.scphotographic.com
Contact Sue Cunningham, Technical Director

Travel Pictures

3B Uplands Close, East Sheen, London SW14 7AS
t 020 8878 2226 **f** 020 8392 2920 **m** 07890 922071
e info@travelpictures.co.uk **w** www.travelpictures.co.uk

TRH Pictures

Bradleys Close, 74-77 White Lion Street, London N1 9PF
t 020 7520 7647 **f** 020 7520 7606
e trh@trhpictures.co.uk **w** www.trhpictures.co.uk

Libraries Video

Action Time (London)

35-38 Portman Square, London W1H 6NV
t 020 7486 6688 **f** 020 7612 7524
e info@actiontime.co.uk **w** www.action-time.com
Contact Tasmin Roberts, Marketing Co-ordinator; Joanne Boardman, PA to MD
& Director of Intl Sales; Elaine Michel, Clips Licensing Manager
Credits Britain's Sexiest (T); You're History (T); All Together Now (T); The Club (T)

The CCTV Archive

14 Ardilaun Road, London N5 2QR
t 01795 534448 **m** 07850 926637
e info@cctvarchive.com **w** www.cctvarchive.com

Environmental Investigation Agency

62-63 Upper Street, London N1 0NY
t 020 7354 7960 **f** 020 7354 7961
e communications@eia-international.org
w www.eia-international.org
Contact Paul Redman, Visuals Administrator; Ashley Misplon,
Communications Administrator

Film Images (London) Ltd

2 The Quadrant, 135 Salusbury Road, London NW6 6RJ
t 020 7624 3388 **f** 020 7624 3377
e research@film-images.com **w** www.film-images.com
Contact Tony Dykes, Senior Researcher; James Kearney, Researcher; Ginny
Harrold, Acquisitions Manager; Angela Saward, Research & Marketing Manager

GMTV Library Sales

The London Television Centre, Upper Ground, London SE1 9TT
t 020 7827 7363 **t** 020 7827 7366 **f** 020 7827 7043
e librarysales@gmtv.co.uk **w** www.gm.tv
Contact Sadie Willsher; Sandra Bamborough, Library Sales Manager

GNG Facilities Ltd

5 Sarum Green, Weybridge KT13 9RX
t 01932 247295 **f** 01932 247295 **e** graham.dawson@viasat.co.uk
Contact Graham Dawson, Manager

Image Bank Film

17 Conway Street, London W1T 6EE
t 020 7544 2642
e ian.morris@getty-images.com
w creative.gettyimages.com/source/tibfilm/
Contact Ian Morris, Sales Director Film; Reese Joanne, Sales Manager

Imagine Graphics Ltd

14 Alban Park, Hatfield Road, St Albans AL4 0JJ
t 01727 844744 **f** 01727 811660
e sales@imaginegraphics.co.uk **w** www.imaginegraphics.co.uk
Contact Ian Dunn, Sales
*The Artbeats royalty-free stock footage digital video library. Over 150 themes
and titles including: nature, transport, CG, timelapse, business and aerials.*

Meridian News Library

C/o Meridian, Fourth Floor, 48 Leicester Square, London
WC2H 7LY
t 020 7389 8750 **f** 020 7389 8752
e paul.johnson.meridian@granadamedia.com
Contact Paul Johnson, Senior Librarian

OSF (Stock Footage)

Lower Road, Long Hanborough OX29 8LL
t 019 9388 1881 **f** 019 9388 2808
e enquiries@osf.uk.com **w** www.osf.uk.com
Contact Jane Mulleneux, Head of Collection & Marketing; Sandra Berry,
Sales & Business Development; Vicky Turner, Sales Executive & New Business

Scene Change

284-302 Waterloo Road, London SE1 8RQ
t 020 7787 5055 **f** 020 7771 2901 **m** 07775 944289
e nigels@scene-change.com **w** www.scene-change.com

Contact Nigel Saduer, Technical Director; Diane Grant, Managing Director; Wyatt Enever, Director; Kitty Wong, Graphic Designer

Sky News Library Sales

BSkyB Ltd, Grant Way, Isleworth TW7 5QD
t 020 7705 3132 **f** 020 7705 3201
e libsales@bskyb.com **w** www.sky.com/skynewslibsales

Contact Susannah Owen, Library Sales; Paulina Porkka, Library Sales; Susannah Fritz, Library Sales; Ben White, Library Sales

Sound & Vision Management Ltd

88 Berkeley Court, Baker Street, London NW1 5ND
t 020 7402 9111 **f** 020 7723 3064
e eliot@soundandvisionmanagement.com
w www.soundandvisionmanagement.com

Contact Peter Sullivan, General Manager

Strathclyde Fire Brigade

Brigade Headquarters, Bothwell Road, Hamilton ML3 0EA
t 01698 300999 **f** 01698 459571 **e** vahian@aol.com

Contact Frank Kelly, Senior AV Engineer

Transport Research Laboratory (TRL)

Old Wokingham Road, Crowthorne RG45 6AU
t 01344 770769 **t** 01344 773131 **f** 01344 770356
e enquiries@trl.co.uk **w** www.trl.co.uk

Contact Geoff Helliwell, Video Services Manager; Frank Pond, Photographic Manager

TWI Archive

McCormack House, Burlington Lane, London W4 2TH
t 020 8233 5500 **f** 020 8233 6476
e twiarchive@imgworld.com **w** www.twiarchive.com

Contact Togo Keynes, IVP Head of Archive Worldwide
Credits ESPN Classic Sports (T); T Mobile (C); Amelie (F)

United Television News

Meridian TV Centre, Northam, Southampton SO14 0PZ
t 02380 712357 **f** 02380 712311
m 07801 522925 **i** +44 2380 337055
e shelley.hunt@granadamedia.com **w** www.inewsxchange.net/utn

Contact Shelley Hunt, Managing Editor; Julie Ovenden, Administration Assistant

UTN Meridian News Library

C/o Meridian, Fourth Floor, 48 Leicester Square, London WC2H 7LY
t 020 7389 8750 **f** 020 7389 8752
e paul.johnson.meridian@granadamedia.com

Contact Paul Johnson, Senior Librarian
Credits I Want That House (T)

Winsted Ltd

Units 7-8 Lovett Road, Hampton Lovett Industrial Estate, Droitwich WR9 0QG
t 01905 770276 **f** 01905 779791 **m** 07831 597734
e info@winsted.co.uk **w** www.winsted.com

Contact Phil Flash, Sales Manager

World Images

8 Fitzroy Square, London W1T 5HN
t 020 7388 8555 **f** 020 7387 8444
e world.images@world-television.com
w www.world-television.com/worldimages/

Contact Richard Clarke, Archivist, Sales; Minna Viro, Archivist, Sales; Julie Gambling, Archive Manager; Dominique O'Regan, Archivist

LIGHTING

Lighting **Directors**

Duncan Brown

40 Rutherwyke Close, Ewell, Epsom KT17 2NB
t 020 8393 2042

Philip Burne

Cranbourne House, Mill Road, Little Melton, Norwich NR9 3NT
t 01603 812747 **f** 01603 811954 **m** 07885 841913
e philip@communique.uk.com
w www.communiqueproductions.freeserve.co.uk

Credits The Post Office (C); Abbey National (C); Hollyoaks (T); Heartbeat (T)

Dave Bushell

6 Broadway Close, Fladbury, Pershore WR10 2QQ
f 01386 860922 **m** 07866 572395
e dave@leadinglights.tv **w** ww.leadinglights.tv

Credits Vanity Fair (T); Housecall (T); Mega Mela Awards 2002 (T); British Fashion Awards 2000/1 (T)

Dennis Butcher

Leacroft House, 37 Leacroft, Staines TW18 4PB
t 01784 457900 **f** 01784 440240 **m** 07860 662733
e denbutch@aol.com

James Campbell

m 07973 828 436
e jascamp@btinternet.com **w** www.tvlights.co.uk

Credits Crimewatch UK (T); Stand Up Show (T); Later With Jools Holland (T)

Vincent Carroll

35 Crookham Road, Fulham, London SW6 4EG
t 020 7731 4274 **m** 07974 169 345 **e** vcarroll@btinternet.com

Credits No Win No Fee Series I-II (T)

Dave Davey

231 Hampton Road, Twickenham TW2 5NG
t 020 8977 2018 **f** 020 8977 2018 **m** 07050 161779
e davedaveyld@hotmail.com

Andrew Dixon

Experience Counts - Call Me Ltd, 5th Floor, 41-42 Berners Street, London W1P 3AA
t 020 7637 8112 **f** 020 7580 2582

Andrew Dixon

39 Castlebar Park, Ealing, London W5 1DA
t 020 8998 9514 **f** 020 8998 9514 **m** 07885 731865
e adixon@iee.org **w** www.adlight.co.uk

Credits Greek Royal Weddings (T); Resurrection (T); Politics Week (T); Talk Show (T)

Mike Le Fevre
36 More Close, St Pauls Court, London W14 9BN
m 07956 305662
Contact Mike Le Fevre, Lighting Director
Credits BBC Sports Personality Of The Year (T); 2000 Today (T); Newsnight Review (T); World Cup 2002 (T)

David Finn
CCA Management, 7 St George's Square, London SW1V 2HX
t 020 7630 6303 **f** 020 7630 7376

Stuart Gain
Experience Counts - Call Me Ltd, 5th Floor, 41-42 Berners Street, London W1P 3AA
t 020 7637 8112 **f** 020 7580 2582

John James
Experience Counts - Call Me Ltd, 5th Floor, 41-42 Berners Street, London W1P 3AA
t 020 7637 8112 **f** 020 7580 2582

Andrew Leonard
Lighting Design Associates, 13 Castlepark Road, Sandycove, Rep of Ireland
t +353 1 280 5368 **f** +353 1 280 5386
e leonardlighting@esatclear.ie **w** www.lightingdesign.ie

Lighting Design Associates
13 Castlepark Road, Dalkey, Rep of Ireland
t +353 1 280 5386 **f** +353 1 280 5386
e leonardlighting@esatclear.ie **w** www.lightingdesign.ie
Contact Andrew Leonard
Credits Daniel O'Donnell Live In Belfast (T); Ronan Tynan's The Impossible Dream (T)

Michael Lingard
56 Roxeth Hill, Harrow-on-the-Hill HA2 0JW
t 020 8864 5067 **f** 020 8422 2839 **m** 07973 264130
Credits TV Scrabble (T); The Basil Brush Show (T); Play Your Cards Right (T); Big Brother (T)

Michael Lingard (MLP)
56 Roxeth Hill, Harrow HA2 0LW
t 020 8864 5067 **f** 020 8422 2839 **m** 07973 264130
e michaellingard@aol.com
Credits Play Your Cards Right (T); The Price Is Right (T); The Salon (T); Big Brother Series I,II,III (T)

Rod Litherland
2B Otteridge Road, Maidstone ME14 4JP
t 01622 735627 **m** 07778 341487 **e** LDRod@aol.com

Brian Pearce
Experience Counts - Call Me Ltd, 5th Floor, 41-42 Berners Street, London W1P 3AA
t 020 7637 8112 **f** 020 7580 2582

John Scarrott
12 Troon Close, Holmes Chapel CW4 7HS
t 01477 532231 **m** 07885 870919
e john-scarrott@supanet.com **w** www.john-scarrott.co.uk
Credits Hollyoaks (T); Brookside (T); Coronation Street (T); My Parents Are Aliens (T)

Seeing is Believing
New House, Mewith Lane, Bentham LA2 7AW
t 01524 261010 **f** 07785 599006
e design@s1b.com **w** www.seeingisbelieving.com
Contact Iain Henshaw, Managing Director

Dave Smith
1 Althorpe Street, Leamington Spa CV31 1NQ
t 01926 745366 **f** 01926 745344 **m** 07831 236000
e dave@thecolonel.uk.com **w** www.thecolonel.uk.com
Credits Cirque Du Soleil- Dralion, Alegria, Varekai (T); Miss World (T); The Brit Awards 2003 (T); Amnesty 'We Know Where You Live - Live' (T)

SNP Productions Ltd
Woodside, St Mary's Garth, Buxted, Uckfield TN22 4LY
t 07958 390034 **f** 07930 429635 **m** 07958 390034
e snp@snp-productions.co.uk **w** www.snp-productions.co.uk
Contact Simon Pugsley, Managing Director

Lighting **Electricians**

Andrew Harris
37 Hyde Green, Beaconsfield HP9 2EP
t 01494 680434 **m** 07973 745583
e andrew@harris800.freeserve.co.uk
Credits Sky Sports (T); Pop Stars Extra (T); Blue Peter (T); Big Brother (T)

Carolina Schmidtholstein
6 Austin House, Brixton Hill, London SW2 1QP
t 020 7733 8908 **m** 07788 784918 **e** caros@gmx.net
Credits Love In A Cold Climate (T); Girl On A Cycle (S); ER Campaign (C)

Travelling Light (Birmingham) Ltd
Unit 34, Boulton Industrial Centre, Icknield Street, Hockley, Birmingham B18 5AU
t 0121 523 3297 **f** 0121 551 2360 **m** 07802 418788

Lighting **Equipment/ Generator Hire**

AB Lighting
117E Shepperton Studios, Studios Road, Shepperton TW17 0QD
t 01932 592030 **t** 01932 593144
f 01932 593152 **m** 07966 484366
Contact A Berry, Managing Director

AB Lighting
Unit 117E, Shepperton Studios, Studio Road, Shepperton, London TW17 0QD
t 01932 592030 **f** 01932 593152 **m** 07966 484366
Contact Kevin Gallagher, Studio Manager/; Allan Berry, Managing Director
Credits Andrex (C); MFI (C); Pepperami (C); Asda (C)

AFL Television Facilities Ltd
181A Verulam Road, St Albans AL3 4DR
t 01727 844117 **f** 01727 847649 **m** 07802 682424
e facilities@afltv.com **w** www.afltv.com
Contact Chris Blake, Director; Chris Blake, Director; Graham Howe, Lighting Cameraman; Dave Chapman, Director; Jenny Lane, Facilities Manager; Athos Gabriel; Athos Gabriel, Sound; Chris Blake, Director
Credits Cheer For Charlie (T); Time Team (T); Holiday (T)

Broadcast video shooting facilities with state-of-the-art equipment and top technicians plus the best service and backup. We supply Digital Single Camera Units and 2/3/4/5 Camera OB units.

AFM Lighting Ltd
Waxlow Road, London NW10 7NU
t 020 8233 7000 **f** 020 8233 7001
e info@afmlighting.com **w** www.afmlighting.com
Contact Ian Suerborn, Marketing Director

AFM Lighting Ltd
Shepperton Studios, Studios Road, Shepperton TW17 0QD
t 01932 593000 **f** 01932 593001 **e** info@afmlighting.com

Alexander Lawrie
William Street, North East Lane, Edinburgh EH3 7NF
t 0131 663 2624

Arri Lighting Rental

Unit 4, Excelsior Trading Estate, Western Avenue, Cardiff CF4 3AX
t 029 2061 6160 **f** 029 2069 2383 **m** 07712 929741
e sales@arrirental.com **w** www.arri.com
Contact Steve Guy, Manager
Credits Treflan (T); Hearts Of Gold (T); The I Inside (F)

Arri Lighting Rental Ltd

4 Highbridge, Oxford Road, Uxbridge UB8 1LX
t 01895 457200 **f** 01895 457201 **e** smoran@arrirental.com
Contact Jimmy Reeves, Branch Manager; Tommy Moran, Managing Director;
Mike Ohara, General Manager; Sinead Moran, Senior Client Contact
Credits Hidalgo (F); 28 Days Later (F); Dirty Pretty Things (F); Cold Mountain (F)

Black Light

18 West Harbour Road, Edinburgh EH5 1PN
t 0131 551 2337 **f** 0131 551 6827 **m** 07775 776 819
e enquiries@black-light.com **w** www.black-light.com
Contact Gavin Stewart, Managing Director

Calumet

93-103 Drummond Street, London NW1 2HJ
t 020 7383 5127 **f** 020 7383 0841
e rental@calumetphoto.co.uk **w** www.calumetphoto.co.uk
Contact Brendan Thompson , Hire Manager

Cardiff M Light & Sound

Units 2, The Highwayman, Castle View, Bridgend CF31 1NJ
t 01656 648170 **f** 01656 648412 **e** neil@cardiffm.co.uk
Contact Phillip Evans, Managing Director

Concert Lights (UK) Ltd

Undershore Works, Brookside Road, Crompton Way, Bolton
BL2 2SE
t 01204 391343 **f** 01204 363238
e clightuk@aol.com **w** www.concertlights.com
Contact Paul Tilbury, General Manager; Chris Sinnott, Hire Manager

CVP Broadcast Rental

Priory Mill, Castle Road, Studley B80 7AA
t 01527 854222 **f** 01527 857666
e sales@creativevideo.co.uk **w** www.creativevideo.co.uk
Contact Phil Baxter, Partner

D-Tek

t 07000 347267 **e** sales@d-tek.co.uk **w** www.d-tek.co.uk
Contact John Dean, Managing Director

DDH Film & TV Lighting

351 Watford Way, Hendon, London NW4 4TE
t 020 8203 0046 **f** 020 8203 0049 **m** 07768 645845
Contact Dave Dehaan, Company Director

Direct Lighting

North London Freight Depot, York Way, London N1 0UZ
t 07000 272727 **f** 07000 262626 **m** 07970 129194
e mail@directlighting.co.uk **w** www.directlighting.co.uk
Contact Steve Knight, Managing Director; Chris Fairchild, Lighting Rental Manager

Elstree Light & Power

Millennium Studios, Elstree Way, Borehamwood WD6 1SF
t 020 8236 1300 **f** 020 8236 1333 **e** elp@elp.tv **w** www.elp.tv
Contact Tony Slee, Hire Manager; John Singer

Essential Lighting Group Ltd

Unit E, Imber Court Trading Estate, Orchard Lane, East Molsey
KT8 0BY
t 020 8335 6000 **f** 020 8398 7205
e mail@elguk.com **w** www.essential-lighting.co.uk
Contact Roger Deane, Director

Evolution Technology

1A Abbey Trading Point, Canning Road, London E15 3NW
t 08709 011130 **f** 08709 011140 **m** 07957 362560
e sean@evolutiongroupuk.com **w** www.evolutiongroupuk.com
Contact Sean Woodhead, Business Development Manager

Can't find an entry?

Turn to the alphabetical Index of entries on page 705

The Production GUIDE

Film Lighting Facilities (Republic of Ireland)

Rep of Ireland
t 1295 2479 **f** +353 295 2498 **e** info@flf.ie **w** www.flf.ie
Contact Gerry Birminghame; Eddie O''Keeffe

Futurist Projects Ltd

136 Thornes Lane, Wakefield WF2 7RE
t 01924 298900 **f** 01924 298700 **m** 07711 037 135
e sales@futuristprojects.com **w** www.futuristprojects.com
Contact Ken Byers, Sales Manager

GE Energy Rentals Ltd (Show Power)

Unit 7, Io Centre, Moorend Farm Avenue, Avonmouth, Bristol
BS11 0QL
t 0117 923 5950 **f** 0117 923 5951
e charles.crowsley@ps.ge.com **w** www.geenergyrentals.com
Contact Charles Crowsley, Project Manager

Genesis Television Ltd

46 Broadwick Street, London W1V 1FF
t 020 7734 8100 **f** 020 7734 8200
e hire@genesishire.com **w** www.genesishire.com
Contact Tim Banks, Director; Leon Powell, Hire Manager

Genetech Ltd

5 Mallory Lane, Stamford PE9 2FW
t 01780 767797 **f** 01780 767798 **m** 07747 807474
e dick@genetechltd.co.uk **w** www.genetechltd.co.uk
Contact Dick Beechey, Sales Director; Bill Logan, Director
Credits Ryder Cup Golf (T); Queen Mother's Funeral (T); F.A. Cup Final (T);
London Marathon (T)

Gofer Ltd

Woodbridge Road, Framlingham, Woodbridge IP13 9LL
t 01728 621300 **f** 01728 621301 **m** 07850 730318
e admin@gofer.co.uk **w** www.gofer.co.uk
Contact Garry Wiseman, Senior Project Manager; David Miller, Managing
Director; Eric Sedge, Project Manager

Gradav Hire & Sales Ltd

Unit C6 & C9, Hastingwood Trading Estate, Harbet Road,
Edmonton, London N18 3HU
t 020 8803 7400 **f** 020 8803 5060
e gradav@btinternet.com **w** www.gradav.co.uk
Contact Graham Threader, MD

Halo

Unit 1, Angela Davis Industrial Estate, Somerleyton Road,
London SW9 8TZ
t 020 7733 7055 **f** 020 7738 3183 **m** 07956 111515
e info@halo.co.uk **w** www.halo.co.uk
Contact Yann Guenancia, Managing Director

Hawthorn Theatrical Ltd

Crown Business Park, Old Dalby, Melton Mowbray LE14 3NQ
t 01664 821111 **f** 01664 821119
e hth@hawthorntheatrical.co.uk **w** www.hawthorntheatrical.co.uk
Contact Martin Hawthorn, Managing Director; John McAlowan, Operations Manager;
Simon Wood, Production Solutions; Richard Macrow, Hire and Sales Manager

John Hanlon Ltd

4-6 Minerva Road, Park Royal, London NW10 6HJ
t 020 8965 3335 **f** 020 8963 1250

JPL Services

15 High Street, Rampton, Cambridge CB4 8QE
t 01954 250851 **f** 01954 250543 **m** 07860 417176
Contact Jane Martin, Contact/Senior Electrician; Chris Kelk

Kave Theatre Services

15 Western Road, Hurspierpoint, Hassocks BN6 9SU
t 01273 835880 **f** 01273 834141
e enquires@kave.co.uk **w** www.kave.co.uk
Contact David Abbott, Director

Lancelyn Theatre Supplies

Electric Ave, Ferry Hinksey Road, Oxford OX2 0BY
t 01865 722468 **f** 01865 728791
e sales@lancelyn.co.uk **w** www.lancelyn.co.uk
Contact David Wilkins, Sales Manager

Lee Lighting

Wycombe Road, Wembley HA0 1QD
t 020 8900 2900 **f** 020 8902 5500
e info@lee.co.uk **w** www.lee.co.uk
Contact Martin Maund, Director; Tony Lucas, Managing Director

Lee Lighting (Bristol) Ltd

Unit 4, Avon Riverside Estate, Victoria Road, Avon Mouth,
Bristol BS11 9DD
t 0117 982 7364 **f** 0117 923 5745 **m** 07710 134559
e bristol@lee.co.uk **w** www.lee.co.uk
Contact Rod Powers

Lee Lighting (Edinburgh) Ltd

West Shore Business Centre, 7 Long Craig Rigg, Granton,
Edinburgh EH5 1QT
t 0131 552 6880 **f** 0131 552 4155 **m** 07889 793 484
e scotland@lee.co.uk **w** www.lee.co.uk

Lee Lighting (Glasgow) Ltd

110 Lance Field Street, Glasgow G3 8JD
t 0141 221 5175 **f** 0141 248 2751 **m** 07889 793484
e scotland@lee.co.uk **w** www.lee.co.uk
Contact George Thomson; Mark Ritchie

Lee Lighting (Manchester) Ltd

Manchester Road, Kearsley, Bolton BL4 8RL
t 01204 794000 **f** 01204 571877 **m** 07803 263607
e leenorth@lee.co.uk **w** www.lee.co.uk
Contact John Lawton, Sales Manager

LightTrack

89 Middlesex Street, Glasgow G41 1EE
t 0141 429 1178 **f** 0141 429 1179 **m** 07801 704596
e steve@lighttrack.co.uk
Contact Steve Arthur, Proprietor; Fiona Pollid, Manager
Credits Man Dancing (F); Balamory (T)

Lite Alternative

Unit 4, Shadsworth Business Park, Duttons Way,
Blackburn BB1 2QR
t 01254 279654 **f** 01254 278539 **m** 07973 193446
e anyone@lite-alternative.com **w** www.lite-alternative.com
Contact Jon Greaves, Hire Department

LSD/Fourth Phase (Birmingham)

201 Coventry Road, Birmingham B10 0RA
t 0121 7666 400 **f** 0121 7666 150
e uksales@lsdicon.com **w** www.lsdicon.com
Contact David Keighley, Managing Director

Neg Earth Lights

Light House, Western Road, Park Royal, London NW10 7LT
t 020 8963 0327 **f** 020 8963 0039
e enquiries@negearth.co.uk **w** www.negearth.co.uk
Contact Dave Ridgway, Managing Director

Nitelites

Unit 3E, Howdon Green Industrial Estate, Norman Terrace,
Wallsend NE28 6SX
t 0191 295 0009 **f** 0191 295 0009 **m** 07785 535632
e nitelites@onyxnet.co.uk
Contact Gordon Reay, Partner

Northern Light

Assembly Street, Leith, Edinburgh EH6 7RG
t 0131 553 2383 **f** 0131 553 3296
e enquiries@northernlight.co.uk **w** www.northernlight.co.uk
Contact Scott Walker

OpTex UK

20-26 Victoria Road, New Barnet, London EN4 9PF
t 020 8441 2199 **f** 020 8449 3646
e info@optexint.com **w** www.optexint.com
Contact Edward Catton-Orr, Sales; Mike Robinson, Rentals

Pearce Hire

Unit 27, Second Drove Industrial Estate, Fengate,
Peterborough PE1 5XA
t 01733 554950 **f** 01733 892807 **m** 07850 363543
e shaun@pearcehire.co.uk **w** www.pearcehire.co.uk
Contact Shaun Pearce, Proprietor; Stuart Battam, Electrical Manager; John
Huson, Lighting Manager

PG Stage Electrical Ltd

Northstage, Broadway, Salford M50 2UW
t 0161 869 0470 **f** 0161 869 0478 **m** 07713 214540
w www.playlight.co.uk
Contact Paul Holt; Daniel McMullan, Hire Manager

Picture It

50 Church Road, London NW10 9PY
t 020 8961 6644 **f** 020 8961 2969
e rosemary@picit.net **w** www.picit.net
Contact Trevor Hunt, Managing Director; Rosemary Element,
Sales & Marketing; Chris Sellers, Studio Manager
Full studio and location lighting hire.

Point & Source Productions
(Light Sound & Staging) Ltd

Unit 1, 37 Station Road, Belmont SM2 6DF
t 020 8661 7200 **f** 08701 696736
e hires@pslx.co.uk **w** www.pslx.co.uk
Contact Stephen Capel, Business Development Manager; Ben Marshall,
Director; Robert Meredith, Director; Kevin Ward, Hire Manager; Beverley
Marshall, Accounts

Powerent/Longville
Unit 50, Sandwich Industrial Estate, Sandwich CT13 9LY
t 01304 620062 **f** 01304 620072 **m** 07836 513122
e sales@powerent.com **w** www.powerent.com
Contact Shaun Farnes, Depot Manager

PRG Lighting Group
Ground Floor, 76 Dyne Road, London NW6 7DS
t 020 7604 2250 **f** 020 7604 2260
e ydonnelly@fourthphase.com **w** www.prg.com
Contact Hugh Frazer-Mann, Sales Director

Pro-Vision
96 Kirkstall Road, Leeds LS3 1HJ
t 0113 222 7870 **f** 0113 242 5283 **e** provision@granadamedia.com
Contact Steve May, Lighting & Generator Hire; Keith Spark, Lighting Hire Manager
Credits Heartbeat (T); Emmerdale (T); The Royal (T); Where The Heart Is (T)

Pure Productions
Unit F4, Chaucer Business Park, Kemsing, Seven Oaks TN15 6PL
t 01732 764800 **f** 01732 764801 **m** 07831 174 816
e jeremy@puregroup.com **w** www.puregroup.com
Contact Jeremy Millins, Managing Director

Sanctuary Photographic
32-36 Telford Way, London W3 7XS
t 020 8749 9171 **f** 020 8749 9683
e photographic@sanctuarystudios.co.uk
w www.sanctuarystudios.co.uk
Contact Barbara Freshwater, Studio Coordinator

Comprises five large ground floor studios and first floor food studio. Camera & lighting hire, consumables, digital photography, production services and film sales all available on site.

SPS Lighting
Manormead, Risborough Road, Terrick, Nr Wendover HP17 0UB
t 01296 614799 **f** 01296 614798
e steve@spslighting.co.uk **w** www.spslighting.co.uk
Contact Steve Smith

Stage Control Ltd
20 Station Parade, Whitchurch Lane, Edgware HA8 6RW
t 020 8952 8982 **f** 020 8951 4178

Stage Electrics
Kirkwood Road, Kings Hedges, Cambridge CB4 2PH
t 01223 423010 **f** 01223 425010
e cambridge@stage-electrics.co.uk **w** www.stage-electrics.co.uk
Contact Brian Cleary, Business Manager; Alex Keighley, Hire Manager

Stage North
The Chimes, Low Green, Woodham Village DL5 4TR
t 01325 314946 **f** 01325 311261 **m** 07860 674173
e stagenorth@btconnect.com
Contact Andy Stonely, Partner

Steve Hayward Lighting (SHL)
The Coach House, 171A Tettenhall Road, Wolverhampton WV6 0BZ
t 01902 424150 **f** 01902 424150 **m** 07860 300151
e srhayward@hotmail.com **w** www.picit.net
Contact Steve Hayward, Proprietor; Melvin Hayward, Proprietor; Patricia Hayward, Proprietor
Credits Fame Academy (T); Graham V Norton (T); The Mummys Curse (D); Space City (C)

Strathmore Film Lighting
49 Earlston Road, Stow TD1 2RL
t 01578 730398 **f** 01578 730614 **m** 07831 213594
Contact Andy Stewart, Proprietor

Technical Equipment Hire & Sales (TECH)
Unit 4, Frontier Works, 33 Queen Street, Tottenham, London N17 8JA
t 020 8493 0526 **f** 020 8493 0528 **m** 07860 679616
e office@techequip.co.uk **w** www.techequip.co.uk
Contact Lincoln Parkhouse, Proprietor; Richard Chapman

Trafalgar Lighting
9 Northway, Claverings Industrial Estate, London N9 0AD
t 020 8887 0082 **f** 020 8887 0072
e hire@trafalgarlighting.co.uk **w** www.trafalgarlighting.co.uk

Ultralight Film & Television
Unit 17, Kings Park, Kings Langley WD4 8ST
t 01923 270380 **f** 01923 270386 **m** 07885 951 200
e funkygibbon@btinternet.com
Contact Mark Gibbon, Lighting Gaffer/Rental Manager

VFG Hire Ltd
Pinewood Studios, Pinewood Road, Iver Heath SL0 0NH
t 01753 631133 **f** 01753 630485
e enquiries@vfg.co.uk **w** www.vfg.co.uk
Contact Bill Summers, Head of Lighting; Phil Wickens, Client Contact; Dick Reed, Client Contact; Tanaya Phillips, Client Contact; Jan Wilson, Client Contact
Credits Waking The Dead (T); Midsomer Murders (T); Silent Witness (T); Holby City (T)

VFG Hire Ltd
8 Beresford Avenue, Wembley HA0 1LA
t 020 8795 7000 **f** 020 8795 3366
e enquiries@vfg.co.uk **w** www.vfg.co.uk
Contact Chris Youlton, Client Contact; Marc Irwin, Marketing Manager; Ann Marie Woodhall, Rental Desk Manager; George Martin, Client Contact Lighting; Graham Hawkins, Head of Cameras; Del Jones, Client Contact; Claire Wiles, Client Contact; Jeremy Sassen, Client Contact
Credits Silent Witness (T); Waking The Dead (T); Midsomer Murders (T); Judge John Deeds (T)

Pinewood: 01753 631 133. Belfast: 028 9057 2525. Cardiff: 02920 561 900. Dublin: 00 353 (0) 1286 3811. Isle of Man: 01624 862559. Scotland: 0141 948 0101. Manchester: 0161 848 7744.

Web Lighting Ltd
Ravenscraig Road, Little Hulton, Manchester M38 9PU
t 01204 862966 **f** 01204 862977
e info@web-lighting.co.uk **w** www.web-lighting.co.uk
Contact Paul Sykes, Rental Manager; Ken Sykes; Bob Horsefield, Contact
Credits Revenger's Tragedy (T); Burn It (T); Down To Earth (T)

Lighting Equipment Sales & Spares

Anytronics
Units 5&6, Hillside Industrial Estate, London Road, Horndean PO8 0BL
t 023 9259 9410 **f** 023 9259 8723
e sales@anytronics.com **w** www.anytronics.com
Contact Bob Hall, Managing Director

BDC Music & Lights Ltd
BDC House, 40 London Road, Gloucester GL1 3NU
t 01452 521233 **f** 01452 311201 **e** barry@bdcmusic.demon.co.uk
Contact Barry Brown, Managing Director

Cinebuild Europe Ltd
Studio House, 34 Rita Road, Vauxhall, London SW8 1JU
t 020 7582 8750 **f** 020 7793 0467
e cinebuild@btclick.com **w** www.cinebuild.co.uk
Contact Tony Neale, Director; Patrick Neale, Director
Credits Ford (C); General Motors (C); Range Rover (C)

Cirro Lite (Europe) Ltd
3 Barretts Green Road, London NW10 7AE
t 020 8955 6700 **f** 020 8961 9343
e d.morphy@cirrolite.com **w** www.cirrolite.com
Contact Mike Saunders, Sales; John Coppen, Managing Director; David Morphy, Technical Director

David Lawrence Lighting
Unit 3, 22 Pakenham Street, London WC1X OLB
t 020 7833 8480 **f** 020 7833 8490
e dmlawrence13@tiscali.co.uk **w** www.studiolighting.co.uk
Contact David Lawrence

DeSisti Lighting (UK) Ltd
15 Old Market Street, Thetford IP24 2EQ
t 01842 752909 **f** 01842 753746
e desisti@globalnet.co.uk **w** www.desisti.co.uk
Contact Bill Smillie, Managing Director; Jon Reay-Young, Director

GE Lighting Ltd
Conquest House, 42-44 Wood Street, Kingston KT1 1UZ
t 020 8626 8600 **f** 020 8626 8501
e michaelhall@drakauk.com **w** www.gelighting.com

James Electrical
Castle Studios, Olmar Street, London SE1 5AY
t 020 7237 5332 **f** 020 7231 5030 **m** 07850 716814
Contact Steven James, Partner

LCA - Lights, Camera, Action Ltd
Unit 20, Fairway Drive, Greenford UB6 8PW
t 020 8575 8220 **f** 020 8575 8219
e sales@lcauk.com **w** www.lcauk.com
Contact Nick Shapley, Managing Director; Graham Kerr, Sales Director; Dave Short, Sales; Martin Carnell, Sales; Vicci Mann, Sales/Marketing

Light Support Ltd
Weir Bank, Bray-on-Thames, Maidenhead SL6 2ED
t 0118 939 3955 **f** 0118 950 5964
e sales@lightsupport.co.uk **w** www.lightsupport.co.uk
Contact Colin Morton, Managing Director

Lightfactor Sales
11 Fairway Drive, Fairway Trading Estate, Greenford UB6 8PW
t 020 8575 5566 **f** 020 8575 8678
e info@lightfactor.co.uk **w** www.lightfactor.co.uk
Contact Mick Hannaford

LightProcessor
Unit 11, Fairway Drive, Greenford UB6 8PW
t 020 8575 2288 **f** 020 8575 8678
e info@lightprocessor.co.uk **w** www.lightprocessor.co.uk
Contact Paul Fowler, Director of Sales

Northern Stage Services Ltd
Trent Industrial Estate, Duchess Street, Shaw, Oldham OL2 7UT
t 01706 849469 **f** 01706 840138
e info@northern-stage.co.uk **w** www.northern-stage.co.uk

OPTI
38 Cromwell Road, Luton LU3 1DN
t 01582 411413 **f** 01582 400613
e optiuk@optikinetics.com **w** www.optikinetics.com
Contact Glen Brown, Regional Sales Manager

Philips Lighting
The Philips Centre, 420-430 London Road, Croydon CR9 3QR
t 020 8665 6655 **f** 020 8684 0136
Contact Callum Petrie, Human Resource Manager

Photon Beard Ltd
Unit K3, Cherry Court Way, Stanbridge Road, Leighton Buzzard LU7 4UH
t 01525 850911 **f** 01525 850922
e info@photonbeard.com **w** www.photonbeard.com
Contact Peter Daffarn, Sales Director; Mike Perry, Dealer Manager; Alan Gooch, Sales and Marketing Director

Our service to image makers does not end with lighting manufacture, we also design and install studio lighting rigs for all types of studios and applications worldwide. Our list of successful projects includes work for state broadcasters and global corporations both in the UK and abroad. Ask for detailed catalogue.

Primarc Lamps & Lighting
121 Loverock Road, Reading RG30 1DZ
t 01189 596777 **f** 01189 505964
e sales@primarc.co.uk **w** www.primarc.co.uk
Contact John Edwards, Sales Director; Ian Major, Director

Pulsar Light of Cambridge Ltd
3 Coldhams Business Park, Norman Way, Cambridge CB1 3LH
t 01223 403500 **f** 01223 403501
e sales@pulsarlight.com **w** www.pulsarlight.com
Contact Sabrina Marenghi, Deputy Marketing Manager; Andy Graves, Head of Sales and Marketing

Roscolab Ltd
Kangley Bridge Road, Sydenham, London SE26 5AQ
t 020 8659 2300 **f** 020 8659 3153
e marketing@roscolab.co.uk **w** www.rosco.com
Contact Duncan Smith, Head of Marketing, Europe

Strand Lighting
Unit 3, Hammersmith Studios, Yeldham Road, London W6 8JF
t 020 8735 9790 **f** 020 8735 9799
e sales@stranduk.com **w** www.strandlighting.com
Contact Ivan Myles, Sales Director; Chris Waldron, Managing Director

Supermick Group Ltd
76 Stoneleigh Street, London W11 4DV
t 020 7221 2322 **f** 020 7727 8693 **m** 07770 755769
Contact Peter Clarke, Managing Director

Ten Out of Ten Productions
14 Forest Hill Business Centre, London SE23 3JF
t 020 8291 6885 **f** 020 8699 8968
e sales@10outof10.co.uk **w** www.10outof10.co.uk
Contact Paul Need, Director

VLPS Lighting Services Ltd
20-22 Fairway Drive, Greenford UB6 8PW
t 020 8575 6666 **f** 020 8575 0424
e info@vlps.co.uk **w** www.vlps.co.uk
Contact Peter Marshall, Account Director; Samantha Dean, Marketing Manager; Edward Pagett, General Manager; Simon Roose, European Sales Manager

Westgate Developments
Derby House, 11 Rosebery Road, Langley Vale, Epsom KT18 6AF
t 01372 800404 **f** 01372 800407 **e** westgate.power@virgin.net
Contact Mitch Hewitt, Proprietor

Lighting **Gaffers**

Brian Beaumont
62 Gloucester Avenue, London NW1 8JD
t 0117 924 6827 **f** 0117 924 6827 **m** 07710 297789
e blinklight@hotmail.com
Credits Band Of Brothers (T); Nicolas Nickleby (T); Sweet Revenge (T)

Phil Brookes
t 01204 591400 **f** 07970 083096 **m** 07778 309884
e philb@fltx.fsnet.co.uk
Credits My Kingdom (F); The Parole Officer (F); Johnny English (F)

Gary Chaisty
t 01784 439286 **m** 07973 832760 **e** gary@gchaisty.fsnet.co.uk

Larry Deacon
m 07710 230580
Credits Green Eyed Monster (T); World of Pub (T)

John Dimond
76 Exeter Road, Welling DA16 3LA
t 020 8854 8007 **f** 020 8854 8007 **m** 07774 455361
e zomuk2k@ukgateway.co.uk
Credits Halifax (C); Ernst & Young (C); Intel Pentium III (C); Whirlpool (C)

Wick Finch
White Hayes, Caldbec Hill, Battle CN33 0JS
t 01424 773181 **f** 01424 773181 **m** 07711 367832

Mark Gibbon
111 Heath Road, Beaconsfield HP9 1DJ
t 01923 270380 **f** 01923 270386 **m** 07885 951200
e ultracam@btconnect.com
Credits Single (T)

Hale Hall Lighting Associates Ltd
3 Fordson Road, Devizes SN10 3UD
t 01380 720926 **f** 01380 720926 **m** 07774 156519
e trevor@hale-hall.freeserve.co.uk
Contact Trevor Hale, Director; Richard Hall, Company Secretary

David Hedley
58 Linden Avenue, London NW10 5RG
t 020 8968 6293 **m** 07958 409506
e dhedley2000@yahoo.co.uk
Credits Promoted To Glory (T); Harold The Amazing (F); Foyle's War (T); The Jury (T)

Herbie Donnelly TV Lighting
39 Douglas Road, Sutton Coldfield, Birmingham B7Z 1NG
t 0121 354 8875 **m** 07855 350233 **e** herbiedonn@aol.com

John Higgins
124 Cromwell Road, South Kensington, London SW7 4ET
t 020 7370 1185 **f** 020 7370 1034 **m** 07836 552840
e 2biggles@msn.com
Credits Proof Of Life (F); Harry Potter And The Sorcerer's Stone (F); To Kill A King (F); The Hours (F)

Graham Hopkins
Fontygary Park, Rhoose, Barry CF62 3ZT
t 01446 710003 **m** 07836 546503

Bob Horsefield
t 01204 862966 **f** 01204 862977 **m** 07976 949329
e info@web-lighting.co.uk **w** www.web-lighting.co.uk
Credits Leeds Story (T); Baby Father (T); Down To Earth (T)

Cephas Howard
16 Summersbury Drive, Shalford, Guildford GU4 8JQ
t 01483 454939 **m** 07976 248278
e cephashoward@compuserve.com

Brian Jones
t 0161 652 4163 **f** 0161 652 4163
Credits Without Motive (F); The Last Detective (F); Wire In The Blood (T)

Ashley Kennedy
Ninewells, Austin Wood Lane, Gerrards Cross SL9 9DA
t 01753 889167 **f** 01753 889167 **m** 07973 221881
Credits The Daily Mail (C); Head & Shoulders (C); Pantene (C)

Steve Kitchen
59 East Cote Road, Ruislip HA4 8BG
t 01895 631502 **f** 01895 631502 **m** 07850 217594
e stevekitchen@btinternet.com
Credits Cry Freedom (F); Hideous Kinky (F); Aliens (F)

The Lamp Store Ltd
54 Newcome Road, Shenley, Radlett WD7 9EJ
t 01923 852635 **f** 01923 852735 **m** 07973 909 589
e nick.collier@btinternet.com
Contact Nick Collier, Lighting Director
Credits Smack the Pony (T); Survivor (T); Pop Idol (T)

Lites Film & TV Lighting
204 Thameside, Laleham, Staines TW18 2JN
t 01784 461017 **f** 01784 491617 **m** 07860 718457
Contact Terry Hunt, Proprietor

Andy Long
52 Riversley Road, Gloucester GL2 0QT
t 01452 281179 **f** 01452 381179 **m** 07973 742379
Credits Young Adam (F); What Every Girl Wants (F); Blackball (F); Morvern Callar (F)

Terry Moore
7 Starfield Avenue, Little Borough, Rochdale OL15 0NG
t 01706 377988 **f** 01706 377988 **m** 07979 745209
e tfmoore@waitrose.com
Credits At Home With The Braithwaites (T); Picking Up The Pieces (T); Wothering Heights (T); Holding On (T)

Ashley Palin
1 Ashley Walk, Mill Hill, London NW7 1DU
t 020 8346 6006 **f** 020 8346 6006 **m** 07973 347818
e palin@talk21.com
Credits Lara Croft And The Cradle Of Life: Tomb Raider 2 (F)

Larry Prinz
40 Church Walk, Thames Ditton KT7 0NW
t 020 8339 0051 **f** 020 8339 0025 **m** 07958 670765
e lpgaffer@aol.com
Credits Birthday Girl (F); Spider (F); Ali G In Da House (F); Goodbye Mr Chips (T)

Norman Smith
15 Court Road, Ickenham UB10 8TS
t 01895 635420 **f** 01895 635420 **m** 07850 532585
e smithnj@atlas.co.uk
Credits Long Time Dead (F); Dot The I (F); Belon (F)

Gavin Walters
15 Pathfinder Way, Warboys, Huntingdon PE28 2RD
t 01487 823849 **f** 01487 823849 **m** 07885 260940

Jon White
123 Balcareres Avenue, Kelvindale, Glasgow G12 0QW
t 01415 816898 **f** 01415 816898 **m** 07949 698736
e white.mccredie@ntlworld.com
Credits Wives And Daughters (T); Blind Flight (F); Taggart (T)

Micky Wilson
65 Berkeley Court, Outlands Drive, Weybridge KT13 9HY
t 01932 229745 **f** 01932 229745 **m** 07850 805392
e mickywilson@aol.com
Credits Enemy Mine (F); Sleepy Hollow (F); Longitude (T); Dinotopia (T)

LOCATION

location : contents

Location **Contacts UK**

33 Portland Place

33 Portland Place, London W1B 1QE
t 020 7636 0900 **f** 020 7495 8332 **m** 07785 718159
e edward@33portlandplace.com **w** www.33portlandplace.com
Contact Judith Dennes, House Manager

Charlestown Harbour

St Austell PL25 3NJ
t 01726 70241 **f** 01726 61839
e info@square-sail.com **w** www.square-sail.com

Clearwell Caves - Ancient Iron Mines

Clearwell, Coleford, Royal Forest of Dean GL16 8JR
t 01594 832535 **f** 01594 833362
e jw@clearwellcaves.com **w** www.clearwellcaves.com
Contact Jonathan Wright, Director; Ray Wright, Director
Credits Meet The Ancestors (T); The Jensen Code (T); The Changes (T); The Pirate Prince (T)

Corporation of London

Film Office, PO Box 270, Guildhall, London EC2P 2EJ
t 020 7332 3202 **f** 020 7332 3182 **m** 07711 277099
e joanna.burnaby-atkins@corpoflondon.gov.uk
w www.cityoflondon.gov.uk/film
Contact Joanna Burnaby-Atkins, Film Officer; Linzi Baltrunas, Assistant Film Officer

Covent Garden Market

The Management Office, 41 The Market, London WC2E 8RF
t 020 7836 9136 **f** 020 7240 5770
e info@coventgardenmarket.com **w** www.coventgardenmarket.com
Contact Sue McAinsh, Centre Manager; Jackie Nembhard

Crystal Palace National Sports Centre Leisure Connection Ltd

Jubliee Stand, Ledrington Road, London SE19 2BB
t 020 8778 0131 **f** 020 8676 8754
e crystal.palace@leisureconnection.co.uk
w www.crystalpalacensc.co.uk
Contact Eve Morris, Bookings Manager; Clare Tellam, Events Manager

Dart Valley Railway PLC

Queens Park Station, Torbay Road, Paignton TQ4 6AF
t 01803 555872 **f** 01803 664313
e pdsr@talk21.com **w** www.paignton-steamrailway.co.uk
Contact Sereny Houghton, Marketing Officer
Credits The French Lieutenant's Woman (F)

Docklands Light Railway

Castor Lane, Poplar, London E14 0DS
t 020 7363 9510 **f** 020 7363 9532 **m** 07718 195 958
e msavery@dlr.co.uk **w** www.dlr.co.uk
Contact Marie Savery, Filming Liaison; Bobbie Graham, Customer Services Manager
Credits Code 46 (F); 28 Days Later (F); Serious And Organised (T); ER (T)

English Heritage

Sarah Eastel Locations, 13 Abbey Churchyard, Bath BA1 1LY
t 01225 460022 **f** 01225 460696
e info@film-locations.co.uk **w** www.film-locations.co.uk
Contact Sarah Eastel; Vicki O'Connor, Head of Productions; Lisa Beattie, Productions Coordinator
Credits Cold Play - Yellow (M); A Lonely War (F); Harry Potter And The Philosopher's Stone (F)

English Nature

Sarah Eastel Locations, 13 Abbey Churchyard, Bath BA1 1LY
t 01225 460022 **f** 01225 460696
e info@film-locations.co.uk **w** www.film-locations.co.uk
Contact Sarah Eastel, Contact

The Enterprise Development Unit - West Somerset Council

Williton, Taunton TA4 4QA
t 01984 635360 **f** 01984 635325
e ajfowler@westsomerset.gov.uk
Contact Andrew Fowler, Economic Regeneration Officer
Credits Down To Earth (T)

Epping Ongar Railway Ltd

Station House, High Street, Ongar CM5 9BN
t 01277 366616
Contact Maureen Foley, Secretary

The Film Office

The Old Town Hall, Patriot Square, Bethnal Green, London E2 9NP
t 020 8980 8771/3 **f** 020 8981 2272
e info@thefilmoffice.fsnet.co.uk **w** www.filmoffice.co.uk
Contact Jon Hardy, Principal Film Officer/Hounslow Contact; Emma Plimmer, Islington/Hackney Contact; Chris May, Lewisham/Lambeth Contact; William Goss, Tower Hamlets Contact; Natalie Silver, Lewisham/Lambeth Contact; Michael Myrie, Islington Contact; Ben O'Farrell, Tower Hamlets Contact

g u e r n s e y f i l m s **. c o m**
For stunning locations talk to the Guernsey Film Commission

films shot in the uk 2002

Film	Country of Origin	Film	Country of Origin
American Cousins	UK	Lighthouse Hill	UK
American Girl	USA	Love Actually	UK
Ashes And Sand	UK	Mandancin	UK
Black Ball	UK	Mojhse Dosti Karoge	INDIA
The Bone Hunter	UK	The Mother	UK
Bright Young Things	UK	Neverland	USA
The Bum's Rush	UK	Nicholas Nickleby	UK/USA
Calcium Kid	UK	Neil's Party	UK
Calendar Girls	USA	Nine Lives	UK
Chaos And Cadavers	UK/SWITZ	One For The Road	UK
Cheeky	UK	Pardesi Re aka O Migrant!	INDIA
Cloud Cuckoo Land	UK	The Prodigal	UK
Day Of The Sirens	UK	Pure aka A Bad Way	UK
Devil's Gate	UK	Sixteen Years Of Alcohol	UK
Die Another Day	USA	Skagerrak	UK/DEN/SWE
Dot The I	UK/SPAIN	Solid Air	UK
Entering Blue Zone	UK	Stella Street: The Movie	UK
Fakers	UK	Suzie Gold	UK
Finding Fortune	UK	Swimming Pool	UK/FRA
Gladiatress	UK	Team One	UK
Great Ceili War	UK	Ted And Sylvia aka	
Helen Of Peckham	UK/FRA	The Beekeeper's Daughter	UK
The I Inside	USA	Tulse Luper Suitcases	UK/SPAIN/ITALY/HUN
If Only	USA	Three Blind Mice	UK/GER
I'll Be There aka Family Business	USA	To Kill A King aka Cromwell And Fairfax	UK/FRA
I'll Sleep When I'm Dead	USA	Ullaththai Killathey	INDIA
Johnny English	UK	The Virgin Of Liverpool	UK
Lara Croft And The Cradle Of Life	USA	The Water Giant	UK/USA/GER
The Last Horror Show	UK	Wilbur Wants To Kill Himself	UK/DEN
Luminal	UK/ITALY	Wondrous Oblivion	UK
LD50	UK	Young Adam	UK

Guernsey Film Commision
Raymond Falla House, PO Box 459, Longue Rue, St Martins, Guernsey GY1 6AF
t 01481 234567 **f** 01481 235015
e tony@guernseyfilms.com **w** www.guernseyfilms.com
Contact Tony Brassell; Emma Allen

Help! Unlimited
Shepperton Studios, Studios Road, Shepperton TW17 0QD
t 01932 572631 **f** 01932 569527 **e** vicki@londonend.co.uk
Contact Vicki Manning, Proprieter
Credits Hidalgo (F); Anna and the King (F); Affair of the Necklace (F); Timeline (F)

Highclere Castle
Newbury RG20 9RN
t 01635 253210 **f** 01635 255315
e theoffice@highclerecastle.co.uk **w** www.highclerecastle.co.uk
Contact WJ Moulton, Event Co-ordinator; JG Lessware, Event Co-ordinator; K Heard, Event Co-ordinator; CP Miller, General Manager; Adrian Wiley, Castle Manager

Historic Scotland Events Unit
Longmore House, Salisbury Place, Edinburgh EH9 1SH
t 0131 668 8926 **f** 0131 668 8888
e sarah.booth@scotland.gsi.gov.uk
w www.historic-scotland.gov.uk/filming/

Liverpool Film Office
Pioneer Buildings, 65-67 Dale Street, Liverpool L2 2NS
t 0151 291 9191 **f** 0151 291 9199 **m** 07711 163 878
e lfo@liverpool.gov.uk **w** www.filmliverpool.com
Contact Lynn Saunders, Film Office Manager

Loch Ness Marketing
The Village Green, Drumnadrocht, Loch Ness, Inverness IV63 6TX
t 01456 450575 **f** 01456 450045 **m** 07974 485986
e willie@nessie.sol.co.uk **w** www.lochness.scotland.net
Contact Jane Fraser, Director; Willie Cameron, Director

London Borough of Newham
Communications Unit, Newham Council, Town Hall, East Ham, London E6 2RP
t 020 8430 3888 **f** 020 8430 3777 **w** www.newham.gov.uk
Contact Ian Tompkins, Head of Communications

location : shooting in London

Borough Film Offices, based in the individual local authorities of London, are on hand to answer enquiries from the production industry and assist with all reasonable requests associated with filming in London. There are 33 local authorities in London and the London Film Commission liases between them.

Each Borough Film Office holds detailed information on local authority charges and clearances needed for filming in its own area. When planning to film, location managers will be asked to complete an Application Form, which will enable the Borough Film Office to determine quickly the particular needs of each production.

It is recognised that most production companies act in a responsible and professional manner. However, all producers are asked to take their surroundings into consideration and not obstruct others from carrying out their business, or cause a disturbance or safety hazard

The Borough Film Offices have a duty of care towards residents and businesses and will exercise control if a particular production is causing an unreasonable nuisance or noise. The local authority has the right to terminate any parking provision or other service provided by the Borough Film Office.

Any filming undertaken is the responsibility of the producer. Adequate notice (not less than one week) must be given to the Borough Film Officer when making any arrangements.

the congestion charge

From 17 February 2003, drivers in central London face paying a £5 daily congestion charge. The charge applies from 7.00am to 6.30pm, Monday to Friday, excluding public Holidays. It does not apply at weekends.

The boundary of the charging zone is the 'Inner Ring Road' linking the area from Euston Road in the north to Elephant and Castle in the south, and from Commercial Street in the east to Park Lane in the west. Drivers can pay the congestion charge either in advance or on the day of travel before, during or after their journey. An additional £5 surcharge will apply if the charge is paid from 10.00pm until midnight on the day of travel. Payment can be made up to 90 days in advance and for up to a year at a time online, by telephone, by SMS text message, by post, and at selected shops, petrol stations and car parks.

There are some exemptions and discounts to the charge, but if drivers are due to pay and don't, a Penalty Charge Notice of £80 will be issued.
For more details see www.cclondon.com

cabling

a   All cables must be made safe when they are laid and not at some later time.

b   Cables must be laid in the gutter along the highway or in the junction between a wall and the footway.

c   Cables on steps must be taped down to avoid the risk of tripping.

d   Wherever possible cables should be flown at a minimum 17ft (5.2m) above a public carriageway and 8ft 6in (2.6m) above footways. The Borough Film Office will, wherever possible, seek to make generator parking available, which avoids the need to cable across the highway.

e   If there is a need to lay cabling across a footway there may be times when it will be sufficient to lay cables at right angles under a taped rubber mat. This mat should be:
(i) a minimum of 1m wide and
(ii) visible to the public by proper lighting, cones or high-visibility hazard tape.

Rubber matting should be regarded as essential safety equipment and carried as a matter of course.

On quieter roads it may be permissible to lay cables using proper cable ramps. If so, then appropriate signage must be used and clearance given by the Borough Film Office.

It is essential to gain clearance from the Borough Film Office before any cables are attached to street furniture.

catering and removal of litter

Some local authorities do not permit any catering upon the street and it is essential to check first with the Borough Film Office and consider off-street arrangements. It is the producer's responsibility to ensure that all litter is removed before the end of each day's filming.

charges

Local authorities do not charge for filming in the street, however, some may charge for their time spent assisting filming. The following services may also incur charges at cost:

a   provision of vehicles to wet down the street

b   refuse collection

c   removal of street furniture

d   removal of unit signs that have not been removed by the production company

e   suspension of parking meters and any other parking provisions

Any damage caused by a production company to the carriageway, footway or street furniture will be charged for.   →→

Shooting in America?

Take this test:

1. Which bridge is thought to be an attractive site for people to view in the San Francisco Bay area?

A.

(Golden Gate Bridge)

B.

(Alan Moskowitz's)

2. Where do elderly middle class Americans lose a lifetime of hard-earned money?

A.

(Wall Street)

B.

(Las Vegas)

3. When searching for prehistoric dinosaurs, which location will ultimately prove most densely populated?

A.

(Ogden, Utah)

B.

(Washington D.C.)

not sure? call us.

directors film company

Executive Producer: richard coll

ph 3120.665.89.65 fax 3120.694.99.96
duivendrechtsekade 83
1096 aj amsterdam

ph 212.627.4999 fax 212.627.4999
1123 broadway, suite 1107
new york city 10010

providing worldwide film production services

◆BEE'S PICTURES◆

FOR ALL YOUR PRODUCTION NEEDS

SPAIN   ARGENTINA   CUBA   MOROCCO

children

The employment of child actors is governed by licensing regulations made in 1933, 1963, 1968 and amended in 1988.

Producers must make adequate provision for the education and health needs of all children employed when filming.

A child is a young person of less than 15 years old or still subject to full time education.

Any filming involving the employment of children (whether paid or unpaid) must be cleared through the local authority's Education Welfare service.

coning

Cones have no legal force to secure parking and their use must be agreed with the Borough Film Office.

consultation

Successful filming relies upon the local residents and businesses receiving at least one week's notice. The Borough Film Office may be able to provide contact details needed for consultation.

Letters should be sent to local residents and businesses outlining fully the intended filming and should include:

a   Date, time and exact location of filming

b   Date of letter

c   Location Manager and the Borough Film Officer's contact numbers

d   Number of crew or production personnel expected on location

e   Clear details of any stunts or dressing planned

f   Clear details of lighting plans

g   Clear details of parking proposals.

Some Borough Film Offices can supply a model letter.

The production company is strongly advised to follow the advice of the Borough Film Office concerning residents and local businesses.

cranes, camera cranes and aerial platforms

When planning to use cherrypickers or cranes on the public highway, the Borough Film Office must be informed and clearance given. The location manager or crane hire company must also discuss the exact positioning of such equipment with the Film Officer and the conditions of any permission granted should be adhered to at all times.

At night or in conditions of poor visibility, warning lights should be placed around the cherrypicker or crane. Rigging or de-rigging must be carried out at times that will not cause an unreasonable noise or nuisance.

health and safety and risk assessment

Full consideration of Health & Safety issues for all employees must be taken and proven by the producer. The producer must appoint a competent person to act as the Health & Safety representative (with a minimum of NVQ Level 3) and a full risk assessment of the location must be carried out in accordance with the Health & Safety at Work Act (1974) and the Management of Health & Safety at Work regulations (1992).

Types of Risk Assessment that may be required for filming activities include stunts, the use of flammable or toxic materials, construction work, working at heights and the use of cranes and cherry pickers. This is in addition to a comprehensive risk assessment of the location.

The Health & Safety representative appointed must be on location at all times to co-ordinate and monitor the Health & Safety systems and any control any measures put in place as a result of the risk assessment

high-visibility clothing

Crew members and production personnel working on the highway must wear high-visibility clothing to standard EN471. This is an essential safety requirement under the New Roads and Streetworks Act and it is an offence not to comply.

Failure to wear appropriate high-visibility clothing invalidates any insurance provision for the entire shoot.

indemnity and insurance

The production company will be expected to indemnify the local authority, its officers and employees against any claims or proceedings arising directly from any injury to persons or damage to property as a result of the activities of the production company or its agents. All production companies filming in the streets must carry public liability insurance.

lighting, lighting towers, scaffolding and generators

The construction and positioning of lighting towers and scaffolding must be discussed with the Borough Film Office at least one week in advance of the shoot. Any scaffolding constructed must be certified by the Borough Film Office.

When placing lighting stands on the carriageway or the footway, the Borough Film Office must be informed and clearance given. The following considerations should be taken to prevent any risk to the public or production company employees:

a   All lights above ground level and lighting stands are properly secured

b   Lighting stands placed on a footway must be attended at all times

c   Lights do not dazzle motorists   →→

◁ Lights are not shone directly towards residential properties at any time without specific permission.

Any generator used should comply with the specific requirements of the Environmental Protection Act (1990) and be positioned as far away as possible from all residential properties. The Borough Film Office can advise on the correct positioning.

night filming (20:00–08:00)

Night shoots in residential areas are naturally sensitive and it is essential to consider and consult with local residents and businesses in the planning process. (Refer to Section 6.0)

Any activity, including filming, is subject to the Environmental Protection Act (1990) regarding noise and nuisance. A legitimate complaint about noise or nuisance from a resident to the local authority can result in the termination of the shoot and the confiscation of equipment.

Therefore, it is advisable to shoot all scenes requiring noise above conversational level before 22.00hrs. Walkie-talkies should be turned down to a minimum and earpieces used.

There may be cases when equipment or heavy vehicles that cannot be removed silently at the end of filming must be left 'in situ' and attended by overnight security. This must be cleared by the Borough Film Office one week before filming.

Only essential vehicles will be allowed close to the location. Personal vehicles should be parked away from the location to minimise noise at the end of filming.

noise and nuisance

Keep noise to a minimum when setting up early in the morning. Generators should not be switched on until after 08.00 hours unless they are silent and approved by the Borough Film Office.

Local authorities have the right to take action under the Environmental Protection Act (1990) as a result of any unreasonable noise and nuisance caused by filming.(refer to section 12.2)

parking

Location managers should discuss all parking plans with the Borough Film Office at least one week in advance of filming, in particular, the on-street requirement for technical vehicles, other on-street equipment and bays to be reserved or kept empty for 'continuity'.

It is inadvisable to enter into binding contracts or assume that a location is viable until parking requirements have been agreed with the Borough Film Office.

Location Managers are responsible for the adherence to parking or vehicular movement agreements made with the Borough Film Office.

Resident's bays are rarely suspended and Disabled bays (whether for a designated person or for disabled drivers in general) will not be suspended where an alternative exists and only in very special circumstances where one does not.

Film vehicles will not be allowed to park in such a way that the passage of pedestrians or vehicular traffic is blocked or impeded or that emergency access is restricted or denied. Prior agreement must be secured from the Borough Film Office to block a footway for filming.

notification and the role of police officers on location

It is a legal requirement for the production company to inform the police of all details of filming on the street or in a public place. This includes any staging of crimes, accidents or use of firearms and special effects. The Borough Film Office can advise on contact details. Any arrangements regarding the Police in the City of London must be made through the Borough Film Office.

There will be times when it is prudent to have police officers in attendance while filming on location. Occasionally the Borough Film Office or Police will specify that filming may not proceed unless Police officers are in attendance.

If police officers are required to be in attendance on location then their role is to maintain the peace and to uphold the law. The production company must cover any costs of providing this service but Police officers are not employees of the production company.

prop or mock emergency services

The Borough Film Office and emergency service in question must be informed if there are actors to be dressed in a specific uniform (police, ambulance or fire brigade).

Uniforms and any vehicles resembling the emergency services must be covered whenever possible and in particular between takes. Any markings on vehicles must be taped over when not being used for filming or being driven on a carriageway.

Sirens should not be used at any time on location and flashing lights must be switched off when not in shot and covered when not in use.

road markings and signs

The temporary painting-out or disguising of road markings, yellow lines or other road signs requires the specific approval of the Borough Film Office and notification of the Police.

sound playback

The filming of artists to sound play-back can only be undertaken with the prior agreement from the Borough Film Office, at any time.

→→

→location : shooting in London

furniture and street lighting

The removal of street furniture, including signs, and the adjustment of street lighting is normally carried out by the local authority and charged to the production company. All arrangements for this work must be made through the Borough Film Office.

Minor work by the production company may be permissible with prior permission from the Borough Film Office but any damage or reinstatement costs would have to be met by the production company.

stunts, special effects and pyrotechnics

All stunts, special effects (including weather effects and wet downs) and pyrotechnics must be under the direct control of a named qualified stunt co-ordinator or special effects operative and comply with the Environmental Protection Act (1990).

Any plans must be discussed with the Borough Film Office at least one week in advance of the shoot. The production company is strongly advised to follow the direction of the Borough Film Office concerning the feasibility of stunts.

No firearms or replica/mock firearms should be used without consultation and consent where appropriate of the Police and the Borough Film Office on each occasion. The production company involved must ensure the safe custody of such weapons at all times.

track

All matters relating to tracking must be discussed with the Borough Film Office at least one week in advance of filming. Any obstructions or alternative footways planned must be cleared by the Borough Film Office. Tracking boards may be required in certain circumstances. The production company should ensure that pedestrians and in particular wheelchair users aren't impeded by filming.

wetdowns

Wetdowns may only be carried out with the approval of the Borough Film Office after a proper evaluation of the forthcoming weather conditions and with the proper signage as required.

notes

The descriptions highway, carriageway and footway used in this document are in conjunction with The Highways Act (1986)

The description Production refers to every type of filming. In particular, feature films, television productions, commercials, pop-promos, corporate and stills.

This document is intended as a guide to the requirements of filming on the streets and other public places in Greater London.. It is not exhaustive and film makers, location managers and production companies are advised to check with individual local authorities as to local charges, policies and practices. The London Film Commission and the Borough Film Offices will accept no liability for loss, financial or otherwise, alleged to have incurred as a result of these guidelines.

Reproduced with kind permission of the London Film Commission. www.london-film.co.uk

---

London Borough of Sutton
Civic Offices, St Nicholas Way, Sutton SM1 1EA
t 020 8770 5000 f 020 8770 5404
e suttonpr@sutton.gov.uk w www.sutton.gov.uk
Contact Joanna Simons, Chief Executive; Ian Marratt, Executive Head Of Communications

Longleat House & Safari Park
The Estate Office, Longleat, Warminster BA12 7NW
t 01985 844400 f 01985 844885
e filming@longleat.co.uk w www.longleat.co.uk
Contact Florence Wallace, Public Relations Officer

National Trust
36 Queen Anne's Gate, London SW1H 9AS
t 0870 609 5380 f 020 7222 5097
e enquires@nationaltrust.org.uk w www.nationaltrust.org.uk
Contact Philippa Lennox-Boyd, Media Liaison Officer

National Trust, Wessex & South East Regions
Sarah Eastel Locations, 13 Abbey Churchyard, Bath BA1 1LY
t 01225 460022 f 01225 460696
e info@film-locations.co.uk w www.film-locations.co.uk
Contact Vicki O'Connor, Head of Productions; Lisa Beattie, Production Assistant; Sarah Eastel, Proprietor
Credits Coldplay - Yellow (M); A Lonely War (F); Harry Potter And The Philosopher's Stone (F)

Paignton/Dartmouth Steam Railway
Queens Park Station, Torbay Road, Paignton TQ4 6AF
t 01803 555872 f 01803 664313
e pdsr@talk21.com w www.paignton-steamrailway.co.uk
Contact Sereny Houghton, Marketing Officer

Peel Airports (Finningley) Ltd
Hayfield Lane, Doncaster DN9 3XA
t 01302 773146 e rkuhnel@peelholdings.co.uk
e rkuhnel@peel.co.uk w www.doncasterfinningleyairport.co.uk
Contact Roger Kuhnel, Property Manager
Credits Naked In The Jungle (T); Secret Society (F); Jungle Run (T); Westlife (M)

Powderham Castle
Estate Office, Powderham Castle, Exeter EX6 8JQ
t 01626 890243 f 01626 890729 m 07889 103716
e castle@powderham.co.uk w www.powderham.co.uk
Contact Tim Faulkner, General Manager

Royal Society of Arts (RSA)
Sarah Eastel Locations, 13 Abbey Churchyard, Bath BA1 1LY
t 01225 460022 f 01225 460696
e info@film-locations.co.uk w www.film-locations.co.uk
Contact Sarah Eastel, Contact

Scottish Screen (Locations)
249 West George Street, Glasgow G2 4QE
t 0141 302 1724 **t** 0141 302 1723
f 0141 302 1778 **m** 07802 252172
e kevin.cowle@scottishscreen.com
w www.scottishscreenlocations.com
Contact Louise Harris; Kevin Cowle

Tayscreen
DCA, 152 Nethergate, Dundee DD1 4DY
t 01382 432321 **f** 01382 432252 **m** 07951 380403
e info@tayscreen.com **w** www.tayscreen.com
Contact Julie Craik, Commissioner
Credits Liaisons Dangereuses (F); Young Adam (F)

Test Valley Borough Council (Film Liaison Team)
Leisure Services, Beech Hurst, Weyhill Road, Andover SP10 3AJ
t 01264 368844 **f** 01264 368899
e leisure@testvalley.gov.uk **w** www.testvalley.gov.uk
Contact Kirsty Ball, Assistant Arts Officer; Michael Johnson, Arts Officer

The Welsh Development Agency
Ladywell House, Park Street, Newtown SY16 1JB
t 08457 775577 **f** 01686 627889
e enquires@wda.co.uk **w** www.wda.co.uk
Contact David Jones, Marketing Manager

West Country Production Resources
14 Victoria Grove, Bridport DT6 3AA
t 01308 420672 **f** 01308 420672 **m** 07970 981 704
e angela@dashwoodprods.freeserve.co.uk **w** www.dashwood.tv
Contact Angela Howard-Bent, Proprietor
Credits FFP Media - Rosamunde Pilcher (F); The Scarlet Tunic (F)

West London Film Office
8C Walpole Court, Ealing Studios, Ealing Green, London W5 5ED
t 020 8584 5226 **f** 020 8584 5306 **m** 07956 321862
e info@westlondonfilmoffice.co.uk
w www.westlondonfilmoffice.co.uk
Contact Lata Mulchandani, Officer; Ewan Willmott, Assistant; Mike Liddall, Manager

The Windermere Steamboat Centre
Rayrigg Road, Windermere LA23 1BN
t 01539 445565 **f** 01539 448769
e steamboat@ecosse.net **w** www.steamboat.co.uk
Contact Mike Boow, Administrator; Dave Addison, Manager
Credits North West Tonight (T); Fred Dibnah's Industrial Age (T)

Location **Facilities**

@T.I.M.E Productions Istanbul
Meydan Sokak, 6/10 Akatlar, Istanbul 80630, Turkey
t +90 212 352 3991 **f** +90 212 352 3971
e mine@timeproductions.com **e** timeprod@superonline.com
w www.timeproductions.com
Contact Mine Kalpakcioglu, Executive Producer
Credits Swiss Telecom (C); Nokia (C); Badoit - Cinderella Mineral Water (C); Agents Secrets (F)

24-6 Studio Tenerife
PO Box 49, 38611 Tenerife, Tenerife, Canary Islands, Spain
t +34 92 239 2246 **f** +34 92 239 2517
e info@24-6.com **w** www.24-6.com
Contact Norbert Schilling; Aydin Riza

The A Team Film & TV Agency
100 Fairmead Crescent, Edgware HA8 8YP
t 020 8958 8617 **f** 020 8958 8617 **m** 07831 451458
e ateamjoegibson@aol.com
Contact Joe Gibson, Company Director

A1 Mobile Ltd
New Farm, Hoveringham Lane, Horveringham, Nottingham NG14 7JX
t 01636 830111 **f** 01636 830222 **m** 07973 413584
e sales@a1mobile.co.uk **w** www.a1mobile.co.uk
Contact Richard Cave, Proprietor; Susan Filep, Senior Administrative Officer
Credits Peak Practice (T)

Aardvark Production Transport
109 Clarence Road, Grays RM17 6RD
t 01375 380349 **f** 01375 380349 **m** 07802 751954
m 07714 234048 **e** celestebirch@genie.co.uk
Contact Doug Birch; Celeste Birch

Ahh Thats Better Honeywagons
14 Sussex Road, Uxbridge UB10 8PH
t 01895 639034 **m** 07778 744292
Contact Drek Crawford, Proprietor; Melonie Walmsley, Logistics Controller
Credits Lock Stock (T); In Deep III (T); Nicholas Nickleby (T); Bad Girls (T)

American Motor Coach
Suite 16, 5 Pinner Green, Pinner HA5 2AF
t 020 8357 6756 **f** 07973 149765 **m** 07973 394708
e dvdgribler@aol.com
Contact David Gribler, Proprietor
Credits Charles Sheen (F); Big Brother (T); V 1999-James Brown (T); V 2001-Kylie Minogue (T)

Andy Dixon Facilities
3 Squire Drive, Brynmenyn Industrial Estate, Bridgend CF32 9TX
t 01656 725560 **t** 01656 725191
f 01656 725194 **m** 07768 436768
e sian@andydixonfacilities.co.uk **w** www.andydixonfacilities.co.uk
Contact Andy Dixon, Partner; Steve Haines, Transport Manager; Sian Dixon, Partner
Credits Heartlands (F); The Very Annie Mary (F); Bright Young Things (F); Down To Earth (T)

Andy Loos Ltd
Brickbarnes Farm, Evesham Road, Spetchley WR7 4QR
t 01905 345821 **f** 01905 345849
e info@andyloos.co.uk **w** www.andyloos.co.uk
Contact Tony Ray, Managing Director

A N G L I A
Television Limited

Anglia Studios
Anglia House, Norwich NR1 3JG
t 01603 615151 **f** 01603 752504
e angliastudios@granadamedia.com **w** www.angliastudios.com
Contact Dan Haddon, Location Services; Dave Wyatt, Head of Post Production; Jacky Lane, Head of Resources; Ian Osborne, Head of Studios; Beverly Bulcock, Head of Resources

Great kit, great people and the Norwich nightlife is brilliant.

ASAP Production Support Marakech
Rue Majoub El Rmiza 1, Marrakech 40000, Morocco
t +212 44 446502 **f** +212 44 446524
e info@asapps.it **w** www.asapps.it
Contact Ines Stephan

ASAP Production Support Milan
Via Gran San Bernardo 13, Milan 20154, Italy
t +39 02 3360 8783 **f** +39 02 3361 7967
e info@asapps.it **w** www.asapps.it
Contact Ines Stephan

At Your Convenience Mobile Toilets
14 Sussex Road, Ickenham Village UB10 8PH
t 01895 639034 **f** 01895 639034 **m** 07778 744292
Contact Derek Crawford, Proprietor
Credits EastEnders (T); Footballers Wives I&II (T); Band Of Brothers (T); Only Fools And Horses (T)

B&B Event Hire
Lyon Road, Hersham Industrial Estate, Hersham KT12 3PS
t 01932 253253 **f** 01932 254976 **m** 07836 507173
Contact Judith Tuck, Proprietor

BAA Gatwick Airport
Gatwick Airport RH6 0NP
t 01293 505000 **f** 01293 503794 **w** www.baa.com

Bardot Film Facilities
Shepperton Studios, Shepperton TW17 0QD
t 01932 592631 **f** 01932 569527 **e** admin@bardotfilm.com
Contact Vicki Manning, Producer; Nigel Wooll, Producer

Barking Mad Facilities
Fair View House, Church Road, Allithwaite LA11 7RF
t 08000 749237 **f** 01539 536610 **m** 07767 828 866
e enquiries@barking-mad-facilities.com
w www.barking-mad-facilities.com
Contact Tim Gorrill, Partner; Robin Gorrill, Partner; James Gorrill, Office Manager
Credits Soapstars (T); Emmerdale (T); Coronation Street (T)

The Beach Studios
Unit 1, The Sawmills, Duntshill Road, Wandsworth, London SW18 4QL
t 020 8875 0075 **f** 020 8870 5577
e office@beachstudios.freeserve.co.uk
w www.beachstudios.freeserve.co.uk

Blackbushe Airport Ltd
Terminal Building, Blackbushe Airport, Camberley GU17 9LQ
t 01252 879449 **f** 01252 874444
e blackbusheairport@bca-group.com
w www.blackbusheairport.co.uk

Bluebell Railway
Sheffield Park Station, Uckfield TN22 3QL
t 01825 720800 **f** 01825 720804
e info@bluebell-railway.co.uk **w** www.bluebell-railway.co.uk
Contact Carolyn Gray, Marketing Manager
Credits Wind In The Willows (F); Ken Russell's Mahler (F); Station Jim (T); The Railway Children (T)

Brighton Film Facilities
13 Tudor Close, Dean Court Road, Rottingdean BN2 7DF
t 01273 302166 **f** 01273 302163 **m** 07739 329748
e brightonfacilities@btopenworld.com
Contact Franz von Habsburg
Locations Crew, Stock, Equipment, Grip Consumables, Avid, Steenbeck, Production Office.

Bristol Television Film Services Ltd (BTFS)
Unit 12, Londonderry Farm, Keynsham Road, Willsbridge, Bristol BS30 6EL
t 0117 932 2046 **f** 0117 932 3335 **m** 07976 368915
e brian@btf-services.co.uk **w** www.btf-services.co.uk
Contact Brian Baker, Managing Director
Credits Silent Witness (T); Where the Heart Is (T); Murder In Mind (T); Footballers' Wives (T)

Owen Brown
Station Road, Castle Donington DE74 2NL
t 01332 850000 **f** 01332 850005 **w** www.owen-brown.co.uk

C Walton Ltd
Bruntingthorpe Airfield & Proving Ground, Bruntingthorpe, Lutterworth LE17 5QS
t 0116 247 8040 **f** 0116 247 8031 **m** 07718 158 506
e c.waltonltd@bruntingthorpe.com
Contact David Walton, Director
Credits Pulling Power (D); Driven (T); Top Gear (T)

Cabervans
Gourock PA19 1BA
t 08456 444775 **f** 01475 638775 **m** 07860 413 434
e cabervans@lineone.net **w** www.cabervans.com
Contact Patricia McKenzie, Partner; Colin McKenzie, Proprietor
Credits Harry Potter And The Chamber Of Secrets (F); Jonathan Creek (T); Harry Potter And The Philosopher's Stone (F); Monarch Of The Glen (T)

Chesham Executive Centre Ltd
Chesham House, Suite 500, 150 Regent Street, London W1B 5SJ
t 020 7432 0500 **f** 020 7432 0516
e service@chesham.co.uk **w** www.chesham.co.uk

Classic Loos
Linnets, Ogdens, Fordingbridge SP6 2PY
t 01425 650700 **f** 01425 650634
e admin@classicloos.com **w** www.classicloos.com
Contact Andrew Hay, Director

Coliseum Cinema
Wheat Street, Brecon LD3 7DG
t 01874 622504 **f** 01874 622502 **m** 07703 323235
e email@breconcoliseumcinema.freeserve.co.uk
w www.coliseumbrecon.co.uk
Contact Irene Davies, Proprietor; Peter Davies, Proprietor

Complete Events
Events House, Red Shute Hill, Hermitage, Newbury RG18 9QL
t 01635 202466 **f** 01635 202467 **m** 07973 553239
e info@completeevents.co.uk **w** www.completeevents.co.uk
Contact Mark Hutchison, Company Director

Daly Location Transport
Culverden, Crimp Hill, Old Windsor SL4 2RA
t 01753 866267 **m** 07836 537796
Contact Tom Daly, Proprietor

Devon Marquee Company Ltd
Fairview, Murchington, Chagford TQ13 8HJ
t 01647 433530 **f** 01647 433530 **m** 07976 534 927
e george@devonmarquee.co.uk **w** www.devonmarquee.co.uk
Contact Fiona Lyon-Smith, Director; George Lyon-Smith, Director

Directors Film Company of Amsterdam BV
Duivendrechtsekade 83, Amsterdam 1096 AJ, Netherlands
t +31 20 665 8965 **f** +31 20 694 9996 **e** dfc@euronet.nl
Contact Richard Coll; Piet-Hein Luykx

Directors Film Company of New York
1123 Broadway, Suite 1107, New York 10010, USA
t +1 212 627 4999 **f** +1 212 627 4499 **e** dfcnyc@aol.com
Contact Richard Coll

Elmwood Hotel for Dogs
The Lee, Great Missenden HP16 9NQ
t 01494 837420
Contact John Burton, Proprietor

Epsom Downs Racecourse
Epsom Downs KT18 5LQ
t 01372 7247 0047 **f** 01372 748253
e epsom.events@rht.net **w** www.epsomderby.co.uk
Contact Emma Neve, Sales Manager; Anita Satterley, Conference Co-ordinator; Charli North, Conference Co-ordinator
Credits Bright Young Things (F); Groove Armada - At The River (M); Maybe Baby (F); Goldeneye (F)

Film 4x4 WD Ltd
Great Barn Studios, Cippenham Lane, Slough SL1 5AU
t 01494 837134 **f** 01494 837091 **e** film4x4@aol.com
Contact Matthew Strange , Director
Credits The Mummy Returns (F); Gosford Park (F); Die Another Day (F)

Film It Sp Zoo
ul Wita Stwosza 17A, Warsaw 02 661, Poland
t +48 22 848 7811 **t** +48 22 848 3779
f +48 22 843 0607
e office@filmit.com.pl **w** www.filmit.pl
Contact Dominika Grzegdala; Mira Klajnberg

Filma-Cass
Kocamansur Sokak 115/1, Sisli, Istanbul 80260, Turkey
t +90 212 233 6018 **f** +90 212 231 0227
e filmacass@filmacass.com.tr **w** www.filmacass.com.tr
Contact Ömer Vargi; Tamer Basaran; Bahadir Arliel; Elfin Yuksekteppe; Oguz Peri

Filmflow Ltd
Adrian Avenue, London NW2 1LX
t 020 8438 9919 **f** 020 8438 9929 **m** 07831 831964
Contact Karen Hayter, Director; Alan Hayter, Managing Director

Filming Reel Production Ltd
Bahia Azul No 16, Estepona, Malaga 29680, Spain
t +34 952 798129 **f** +34 952 795838 **m** 07949 949534 (UK)
e maxine@reelproduction.co.uk **w** www.reelproduction.co.uk
Contact Maxine Parker, Producer; Leoni Cotgrove, Producer
Credits Schick Intuition/J Walter Thompson (C); Sherine, The Video (M); Love And Basketball (F); Sexy Beast (F)

Filmscope
Filmscope House, 1 Church Row, Fulmer SL3 6HW
t 01753 662528 **f** 01753 663858 **m** 07831 204223
e filmscope@aol.com **w** www.filmscope.uk.com
Contact Eleanor Bushnell, Director; Chopper Catchpole, Director

Flehner Films
Castillo 1366, Buenos Aires C 1414 AXD, Argentina
t +54 11 4771 0400 **f** +54 11 4771 6003
e rmazzeo@flehner.com.ar **w** www.flehnerfilms.com
Contact Rammero Mazzeo; Sergio Gullco
Credits Axe: 'Araña'; Renault Megane: 'Campo Traviesa'; Pajarito; Museum

The Fridge
1 Town Hall Parade, Brixton Hill, London SW2 1RJ
t 020 7326 5100 **f** 020 7274 2879
e info@fridge.co.uk **w** www.fridge.co.uk
Contact Cliffe Cooper, Production Manager; Nathalie Gomez De Vera, Marketing/PR/Press; Cliffe Cooper, Production Manager; Gary Baker, General Manager

Full Circle Partnership
Dennis Farm Studios, Dennis Farm, St Columb TR9 6DY
t 01637 881200 **f** 01637 881203 **m** 07836 317327
e fullcircle@clara.net
Contact Diana Chambers, Partner; David Chambers, Partner

Full Moon Films
22 Rue Davy, Paris 75017, France
t +33 1 4263 4648 **f** +33 1 4229 5759
e info@fullmoon-films.com **w** www.fullmoon-films.com
Contact Philippe Dugay

Full Moon Films
Via Tiburtina 521, Rome 159, Italy
t +39 06 4353 5088
f +39 06 438 0328
e info@fullmoon-films.com
w www.fullmoon-films.com
Contact Philippe Dugay

G&H Film & Television Services
182A Church Road, Holywood BT18 9RN
t 028 9039 7808 **f** 028 9042 7921 **m** 07880 711152
e info@ghfilm.freeserve.co.uk **w** www.ghfilms.co.uk
Contact Alan Crozier; David McDowell; Mark Huffam, Director; Robert Gyle, Director

The Grovefield Hotel
Taplow Common Road, Burnham SL1 8LP
t 01628 603131 **f** 01628 668078
e sales.grovefield@csmm.co.uk **w** www.grovefieldhotel.com
Contact Clare Logue, General Manager

Holiday Inn London Heathrow
M4 Junction 4, Sipson Road, West Drayton UB7 0JU
t 0870 400 8595 **f** 020 8897 8659
e fiona.mackenzie-andrew@6c.com
Contact Simon Stamper, General Manager; Fiona McKenzie-Andrews, PA to the General Manager

The Ironbridge Gorge Museums
Coachroad, Coalbrookdale, Ironbridge, Telford TF8 7DQ
t 01952 433522 **f** 01952 435999
e marketing@ironbridge.org.uk **w** www.ironbridge.org.uk
Contact Paul Gossage, Head of Marketing
Credits The Making Of The Ironbridge (D)

Jilly Green Catering
High Houses, Snittlegarth, Ireby, Carlisle CA7 1HE
t 01697 371549 **e** jillgreen1@hotmail.com
Contact Jill Green, Manager

John Anderson Hire
Smallford Works, Smallford Lane, St Albans AL4 0SA
t 01727 822485 **f** 01727 822886
e sales@superloo.co.uk **w** www.superloo.co.uk
Contact Richard Crawley, Assistant Sales Manager; Jerry Hart, Sales Director

Kempton Park Racecourse
Staines Road East, Sunbury on Thames TW16 5AQ
t 01932 782292 **f** 01932 782044
e nikki.clark@rht.net **w** www.kempton.co.uk
Contact Nikki Clark, Conference & Banqueting Co-ordinator

Knowsley Hall
Prescot L34 4AG
t 0151 4894827 **f** 0151 4805580
e events@knowsley.com **w** www.knowsley.com
Contact Diane Lofthouse, Director of Sales & Marketing; Stephen Cooper, Director of Events; Lesley Forshaw, Company Secretary

LICHTENBERG
production & mediaservice

Lichtenberg & Partners
Ludwig-Thoma Strasse 13, Oberschleissheim, Munich 85764, Germany
t +49 89 315 1366 **f** +49 89 315 1367
e manon.lichtenberg@netsurf.de **w** www.manonlichtenberg.com
Contact Manon Lichtenberg

Livingston Dining Services
Bracken Cottage, Linkside East, Hinderhead GU26 6NY
t 01428 604654 **f** 01428 609601 **m** 07836 227598
e livingstonbuses@aol.com

Location China
16 Sydner Road, London N16 7UG
t 020 7254 4395 **m** 07905 007478 **e** xatiyah@aol.com
Contact Xiaosong Atiyah
Credits The Pilt Down Turkey (D); The Strange Case Of Peking Men (D); Millennium (D); Fight School (D)

Location Facilities Ltd
Delta Way, Thorpe Industrial Estates, Thorpe TW20 8RX
t 01784 436444 **f** 01784 430117 **m** 07836 227271
w www.locationfacilities.com
Contact Mike Henley, Director; Ray Redrupp, Director

London Borough of Richmond-upon-Thames
1st Floor, Civic Centre, 44 York Street, Twickenham TW1 3BZ
t 020 8891 7160 **f** 020 8891 7718 **m** 07956 391 075
e s.lewis@richmond.gov.uk **w** www.richmond.gov.uk
Contact Sue Lewis, Filming Officer

M&B Marquees
Hawk Lane, Battlesbridge, Near Wickford SS11 7RL
t 01268 562622 **f** 01268 574228
e sales@mb-marquees.com **w** www.mb-marquees.com

M&R Production Service Srl
Via Legnano 26, Milan 20121, Italy
t +39 02 2900 6867 **f** +39 02 2900 6884
e info@mrproduction.com **w** www.mrproduction.com
Contact Michele Virgilio; Annalis Labat; Mariella Grandi

M&R Production Service Srl
Via G Nicotera 29, Rome 195, Italy
t +39 06 361 1497 **f** +39 06 361 0353
e info@mrproduction.com **w** www.mrproduction.com
Contact Annalis Labat

Mar-Key Marquees
427C, Aviation Park West, Bournemouth International Airport, Christchurch BH23 6NW
t 01202 577111 **t** 07000 627539 **f** 07000 780850
e sales@mar-key.com **w** www.mar-key.com
Contact Dave Farringdon, Director, Director; Marc , General Manager; David Tabb, Sales
Credits Gladiator (F); Saving Private Ryan (F); Braveheart (F)

Mayflower Marquees
Unit 6, Penn Street Works, Penn Street, Nr Amersham HP7 0PU
t 01494 712131 **f** 01494 713337
e ezupshelters.aol.com **w** ww.ez-up.co.uk
Contact Michael Read, Managing Director

Movie Makers
40 Crockford Park Road, Addlestone KT15 2LX
t 08700 100903 **f** 01932 844022 **m** 07785 556 772
e sales@moviemakersfacilities.com
w www.moviemakersfacilities.com
Contact Tommy Traylen, Director
Credits Analyze That (F); Shanghai Nights (F); London's Burning (T); Gosford Park (F)

Movie Makers Facilities
40 Crockford Park Road, Addlestone, Chertsey KT16 2LX
t 08700 100903 **f** 01932 844022 **m** 07785 556772
e tommytraylen@moviemakersfacilities.com
w www.moviemakersfacilities.com
Contact Tommy Traylen, Director
Credits Analyze That (F); Truth (T); Gosford Park (F); Eye Spy (F)

Namib Film
PO Box 2209, Swakopmund, Namibia
t +264 64 463371 **f** +264 64 461993
e info@namibfilms.co.za **w** www.namibfilms.co.za
Contact Guy Nockels

National Maritime Museum

Romney Road, Greenwich, London SE10 9NF
t 020 8312 6727 **t** 020 8312 8522 **f** 020 8312 6533
e filmsandfilming@nmm.ac.uk **w** www.nmm.ac.uk
Contact Lucy Hillary, Filming and Film Archive Officer; Amanda Mayne, Visual Media Manager; Annette McAllister, VM Assistant
Credits BBC Trailer - Launch Of BBC4 (C); Footballer's Wives (T); The Monarchy, The Next 50 Years (T)

Nene Valley Railway

Wansford Station, Stibbington, Peterborough PE8 6LR
t 01780 784444 **f** 01780 784440
e nurorg@aol.com **w** www.nur.org.uk
Contact Michael Warrington, General Manager

On Set Location Services Ltd

Clear Farm, South End, Bassingbourn, Royston SG8 5NL
t 01763 244886 **f** 01763 244663 **m** 07831 225544
e on.set@virgin.net
Contact Nigel Howard, Proprietor

Orlando Film

Via Cernaia 5, Milan 20121, Italy
t +39 22 901 3375 **f** +39 22 901 3407
e orlando@iol.it **w** www.orlandofilm.it
Contact Matteo Lando; Ivan Opezzi

palm**fiction**.com
production and location services in spain

Palmfiction

Plaza de la Puerta Pintada 6, Palma de Mallorca 7002, Spain
t +34 971 711444 **f** +34 971 711445
e mail@palmfiction.com **w** www.palmfiction.com
Contact Alex Gegenfurtner; David Krause

Penhow Castle

Penhow, Newport NP6 3AD
t 01633 400800 **f** 01633 400990 **m** 07970 400800
e info@penhowcastle.com **w** www.penhowcastle.com
Contact Stephen Weeks, Proprietor

Peter Ker Associates

16A Southam Street, London W10 5PH
t 020 8964 4448 **f** 020 8964 5559
e pka@pka-ministry.com **w** www.pka-ministry.com
Contact Peter Ker, Managing Director
Credits Applied Materials (C); Land Rover (C); Guinness (C); Coca Cola (W)

Place Invaders

18 Aberdour Road, Goodmayes IG3 9SB
t 020 8590 0355 **f** 020 8503 8201 **m** 07836 730295
e placeinvaders@aol.com
Contact Bill Hemmings, Director

Prepare & Repair Locations Ltd

136 Sydney Road, Muswell Hill, London N10 2RN
t 020 8883 9775 **f** 020 8883 9775 **m** 07785 776810
e austing@globalnet.co.uk
Contact Geoff Austin, Managing Director
Credits William And Mary (T); Redcap (T); Murder In Mind (T); Without Motive II (T)

PTT Films - Production Team of Turkey

Asmalimescit Minare Sok 23, Beyoglu, Istanbul 80050, Turkey
t +90 212 293 8473 **f** +90 212 293 8475
e sebnem@pttfilms.com **w** www.pttfilms.com
Contact R Sebnem Kitis

Roger Royce Ltd

Unit 1A, Impress House, Mansell Road, London W3 7QH
t 020 8743 5544 **f** 020 8749 7365
Contact Roger Royce, Proprietor

Sandown Park Racecourse, Exhibition, Conference Centre

Sandown Park, Portsmouth Road, Esher KT10 9AJ
t 01372 461249 **t** 01372 467540 **f** 01372 461334
e judith.day@rht.net **w** www.sandown.co.uk
Contact Judith Day, Sales & Marketing Manager
Credits Love Actually (F); Shirley Valentine (F)

Set Service

Via Guido Banti 34, Rome 191, Italy
t +39 06 333 2235 **t** +39 06 332 23315 **f** +39 06 332 23322
e info@setservice.it **w** www.setservice.it
Contact Massimo Di Matteo, Operations Manager; Clarissa Rosa, Company/Managing Director; Pietro Pesce, Scout/Photographer; Bruno Rosa, President
Credits Toyota Lexus (C); Spot Fiat Stilo (C); Incantesimo IV, V VI (T); L'Ora Di Religione (F)

Severn Valley Railway

The Railway Station, Bewdley DY12 1BG
t 01299 403816 **f** 01299 400839
e svrholdingsplc@btconnect.com **w** www.svr.co.uk
Contact John Leach, General Manager; Dewi Jones, Traffic manager

Sewell Films

Rua Goitacazes 112, Glória, Rio de Janeiro 22211-190, Brazil
t +55 21 205 3128 **f** +55 21 205 0477
e sewellfilms@alternex.com.br **w** www.sewellfilms.com
Contact Brian Sewell

Showwork & Co

Via Watt 5, Milan 20143, Italy
t +39 02 837 3526 **f** +39 02 835 8246
e showwork@showwork.com **w** www.showwork.com
Contact Sergio Lardera; Michele Colombo

Skyfilm Studio

Hüvösvölgyi út 35, Budapest 1026, Hungary
t +36 1 275 3066 **f** +36 1 275 3069
e skyfilm@skyfilm.hu **w** www.skyfilm.hu
Contact Andrea Orban, Casting Director; Monika Nagy, Location Manager;
Lidia Kecskemethy, Producer
Credits A Kind Of America (F); Nestlé (C); Panasonic (C); Amstel (C)

Studio Francesco Rapa

Via Dei Missionari 11, Naples 80125, Italy
t +39 081 593 5500 **f** +39 081 593 4440
e info@studiorapa.it **w** www.studiorapa.it
Contact Ivano Rapa

SUR Event Hire

Watlington Road, Cowley OX4 6SR
t 01865 747025 **f** 01865 774562
e duncan@surhire.com **w** www.mcavoygroup.com
Contact Duncan Archer, Event and Sales Manager

*SUR hire a large range of equipment to the film and event industry.
Toilets - Showers - Offices - Changing Rooms - Sleeping Accommodation -
Ticket Offices - Hospitality Units - Storage Containers etc. We have a
very modern fleet and have our own fleet of crane off load delivery
vehicles. If you've used the rest, now try the best.""*

Tetraktys Films Ltd

Apartment 201, 95 Kerynia Avenue, Aglanjia, Nicosia, Cyprus
t +357 22 337433 **f** +357 22 339286
e tetraktys@cytanet.com.cy **w** www.tetraktysmedia.com
Contact Stavros Papageorghiou, Managing Director
Credits Organic Med/Leonardo (W); Oil On Fire (F); George Seferis (D);
Perseas (A)

Thames Valley Tool Hire Ltd

193-194 High Street, Egham TW20 9ED
t 01784 433984 **f** 01784 472876
e tvth@dial.pipex.com **w** www.tvtoolhire.co.uk
Contact Stephen Storey, Managing Director; Jason Southam, Egham
Branch Manager

Theme Tech Ltd

Unit 3, Cold Harbour Industrial Estate, 129-131 Cold Harbour
Lane, London SE5 9NY
t 020 7274 1018 **f** 020 7978 9632
e info@themetech.co.uk **w** www.themetech.co.uk
Contact John Morris, Managing Director

TRAC Ltd

TRAC, Morrison House, 3A Monument Way West, Woking GU21 5EN
t 01483 768485 **f** 01483 767928
e sales@tracltd.co.uk **w** www.tracltd.co.uk
Contact Nick Russell, Director; David McLeod; Clive Brooks
Credits Queen's Jubilee Concerts At Buckingham Palace (T); Midsomer
Murders (T)

The Vibe Bar

91 Brick Lane, The Old Truman Brewery, London
t 020 7247 3479 **f** 020 7426 0641
e info@vibe-bar.co.uk **w** www.vibe-bar.co.uk
Contact Martin , General Manager; Emma , General Enquiries; Adelle Stripe,
Event Manager

Visions (Digital Outside Broadcasting) Ltd

t 020 7478 7289 **f** 020 7478 7107
e vickib@visions-ob.co.uk **w** www.visions-ob.com
Contact Vicki Betihavas, Director of Sales & Marketing

Wembley London Ltd

Elvin House, Stadium Way, Wembley, London HA9 0DW
t 020 8902 8833
e benj@wembley.co.uk
w www.whatsonwembley.com/wembley.co.uk/venues

*With 70 years of event experience, the team at Wembley can offer a
truly consultative service from start to finish. You benefit from advice
and planning skills covering everything from technical requirements
and catering through to on-the-day logistics, with a comprehensive
exhibition package for all organisers.*

Wheal's Far-Go Location Vehicles

Unit 5, 13-15 Sunbeam Road, London NW10 6JP
t 020 7727 3828 **f** 020 8965 0699
e wfg@whealsfargo.com **w** www.whealsfargo.com

Witney UK

London Road, Fairford GL7 4DS
t 01285 713370 **f** 01285 712257 **w** www.witneyuk.com
Contact Norman Amberson, Sales Manager
Credits First Knight (F); Chocolat (F); Shakespeare in Love (F)

Wrap & Roll Facilities

The Lodge, Woodcock Hill Estate, Harefield Road WD3 1PQ
t 01923 897156 **f** 01923 897156 **m** 07973 833 476
e karen@wraproll.uk.com **w** www.wrapandroll.uk.com
Contact Jim Carn, Contact; Karen Carn, Contact

Location
Facilities International

(h) Films Srl
Via Varese 12, Milan 20121, Italy
t +39 02 620051
f +39 02 6200 5215
e info@hfilms.net
w www.hfilms.net

@T.I.M.E Productions Istanbul
Meydan Sokak, 6/10 Akatlar, Istanbul 80630, Turkey
t +90 212 352 3991 **f** +90 212 352 3971
e mine@timeproductions.com **e** timeprod@superonline.com
w www.timeproductions.com
Contact Mine Kalpakcioglu, Executive Producer
Credits Swiss Telecom (C); Nokia (C); Badoit - Cinderella Mineral Water (C); Agents Secrets (F)

24-6 Studio Tenerife
PO Box 49, San Isidro, Tenerife 38611, Spain
t +34 922 392246 **f** +34 922 392246
e info@24-6.com **w** www.24-6.com
Contact Norbert Schilling

A Company
Rodeo 4, Local 40, Cerrado de Calderon, Malaga 29018, Spain
t +34 95 229 0011
f +34 95 229 8846
e seaquist@terra.es
w www.seaquistacompany.com
Contact Robert Seaquist

A Filmar Produções Lda
Rua de São Mamede (Ao Caldas), No 9 C/D, Lisbon 1100-532, Portugal
t +351 21 882 1030 **f** +351 21 886 7100
e a.filmar@ip.pt **w** www.afilmar.pt
Contact Carlos Reis, Executive Producer; Diamantino Ferreira, Director; Joana Lisboa, Producer; Julia de la Ros, Director; Hector Martinez, Director

A VideoCiencia
Rua Carlos Machado 152, Rio De Janeiro 22775-042, Brazil
t +55 21 2421 1200 **f** +55 21 2421 1711
e vc@videociencia.com.br **w** www.videociencia.com.br
Contact Sergio Brandao, Director/Executive Producer

Albiñana Films
Calle Vilana 12, Barcelona 8022, Spain
t +34 93 418 6615 **f** +34 93 212 2284
e international@albinana.com **w** www.albinana.com
Contact Juan Torres, Executive Producer

Allucinazione
Via G P da Palestrina 61A, Rome 193, Italy
t +39 06 322 6982 **f** +39 06 361 0581
e info@allucinazione.net **w** www.allucinazione.net
Contact Ricardo Magno, Managing Director; Claudia Di Mascolo, Producer

Altana Films
Girardot 1378, Buenos Aires C 1427 AKD, Argentina
t +54 11 4554 3940 **f** +54 11 4552 2547
e info@altana.com.ar **w** www.altana.com.ar
Contact Enrique Bacher

Applebox Asia

No 15, Jalan 2, Pandan Indah Industrial Park, Kuala Lumpur
55100, Malaysia
t +60 3 4294 6018 **f** +60 3 4294 6019
e khoo@appleboxasia.com **w** www.appleboxasia.com
Contact Khoo Peng Tein, Executive Producer

Artcore Productions

Nieuwendammerkade 28A12, Amsterdam 1022 AB,
Netherlands
t +31 20 531 8282 **f** +31 20 531 8280
e stef@artcore.nl **w** www.artcore.nl
Contact Monique van Beckhoven, Production Manager; Marco Both, Executive
Producer/Managing Director; Stefany Rietkerk, Executive Producer/Managing
Director; Danielle Lucassen, Production Manager
Credits NH Hotels (C); KPN (C); VW (C); Ben: Symphonies (C)

ASAP Production Support Marakech

Rue Majoub El Rmiza 1, Marrakech 40000, Morocco
t +212 44 446502 **f** +212 44 446524
e info@asapps.it **w** www.asapps.it
Contact Ines Stephan

ASAP Production Support Milan

Via Gran San Bernardo 13, Milan 20154, Italy
t +39 02 3360 8783 **f** +39 02 3361 7967
e info@asapps.it **w** www.asapps.it
Contact Ines Stephan

Banana Films

Urbanización Palma Mallorca, San Rafael Escazu, Apartado
12583-1000, San José, Costa Rica
t +506 289 3050 **f** +506 289 3049
e maria@bananafilms.com **w** www.bananafilms.com
Contact Maria Jordan

Banana Split Polska

UL JS Bacha Street 28, Warsaw 02-743, Poland
t +48 22 843 3556 **f** +48 22 843 9458
e banana@banana.pl **w** www.banana.pl
Contact Jerzy Hamkalo, Producer; Ewa Jacuta, Manager/Producer; Magda
Przezdziak, Production Manager
Credits You Decide (T); Chopin (F); Lech Beer (C)

Bee's Pictures

Calle Cordoba 10B, Fuengirola, Malaga 29640, Spain
t +34 902 118531 **t** +34 902 2667073
f +34 902 118532 **f** +34 902 2664636
e beespics@beespics.com **w** www.beespics.com
Contact Belinda Lewin, Producer; Ivo Van Vollenhoven, Producer; Iohamil
Navarro, Producer (Cuba); Simon Burge, Executive Producer

STUDIO
FRANCESCO
RAPA SRL

Production Services and Casting
in Naples, Amalfi Coast

Via dei Missionari, 11 - 80125 Napoli (Italy)
+39.081.5935500 pbx +39.081.5934440 fax

www.studiorapa.it
info@studiorapa.it

international location facilities

Searching for that special place to film? Over the next few pages, we take a look at four countries making that extra effort to attract the international producer.

CZECH REPUBLIC

"Before the revolution a lot of the economy was 20-30 years behind, but not TV. We had the same technology in Czech TV as London or Frankfurt, so the technical level was high."

Jan Petrov, Ace.

"In studios and post production houses we have better machines, better operators and friendlier services than ever."

Tomas Masin, director

"Directors and producers are satisfied they can come here for the shoot. We're in the process of persuading them to stay the extra three days and finish the project."

Bob Rickerd, Flying Colours Film Company

"Cheap facilities – that's part of the local industry's success."

Matthew Stillman, Stillking

"People grew and learned through interaction, working with the best directors in the world. We have to embrace and aggregate all the influence and talent around."

Matthew Stillman, Stillking

"On most jobs, you encounter many skilful people who are able to find solutions and come up with ideas for a minimum amount of money."

Tomas Masin, director

Unusual requests

● Create a world within Prague that included: middle eastern alleyways; an Eastern European political riot complete with Molotov cocktail throwing; a military coup in Guatemala involving truckloads of guerrillas; Laurel and Hardy look-alikes; vagrants living in an industrial estate; a football stadium. *Stillking Films* ● Reproduce an entire desert on a soundstage, complete with extensive dunes and exotic places of interest. *Prague Studios* ● Provision of everything necessary to produce a music video where the Prodigy plays to an audience of cows being milked by scantily clad maidens who feed the milk to a frenzied crowd below. *Stillking Films*

Directors recently shooting in the Czech Republic

● Rob Cohen
● David Dobkin
● Tom Carty
● Chris Palmer
● Bruce Hunt
● Traktor
● Rupert Sanders
● Laurent Heynemann
● Christian Duguay
● Jacques Fansten
● Guillermo del Toro
● David Jaffe
● Alexander Lauf

→→

SOFT PILLOW
P R O D U C T I O N S

Michalska 3, Prague
Czech Republic, Europe
tel.: +420 224 212 900
fax: +420 224 212 872

http://softpillow.tv   full service production company

Directors

Casting

Production

Location scout

Postproduction

www.armadafilms.cz

Na Zderaze 15 | 120 00 | Prague 2 | Czech Republic
Mobile: +420603472247 | Tel: +4202 21904444
Fax: +420 2 21904300 | email: info@armadafilms.cz

→→international location facilities

ITALY

"Italy is more than a typical historical location, it has amazing deserts and in some cases better beaches than the Caribbean. People go straight for the predictable: Rome, Tuscany, Venice, while great places like Naples are just ignored. The South of Italy has not been pushed enough."

Michele Anzalone, Some of Us

"Post production has been built up, is expanding and is relatively cheap."

Corrine Burns Bruno, Sunflower

"The Palace of Justice in Rome was one of the trickiest locations to get in Rome. Authorisation had never been given until this job we have just completed, and even then we had to shoot on a Sunday when all the courts of appeals were closed. The carabinieri on guard were accommodating though, and even lent us the black tie we needed for our driver... "

Ella Elliott, FilmMaster

"If you don't have the money some of the extras are brilliant in Italy and you don't have to pay buy-outs."

Corrine Burns Bruno, Sunflower

"For an Adidas shoot we had to recreate an enormous traffic jam in this Roman piazza. Thank God there wasn't a fire, because it would have been near impossible for fireman to get in... but it is amazing what you can get away with in Rome that wouldn't be allowed anywhere else."

Ella Elliott, FilmMaster

"Cinecitta Digital is the cutting edge of new technologies."

Ute Leonhardt Russell, Panorama Films

Directors recently shooting in italy
- Ji Duck Yeup ● Erick Ifergan
- Terry Gilliam ● Jonathan Glazer
- Frédéric Planchon ● David Kellogg

Unusual requests
● "Mount Etna during the eruptions: 35 people running around madly at 900 feet, with temperatures from a chilly minus 10 at the peak to 30ºC in the areas surrounded by magma." *Some of Us*

→→

ABOUT US | PRODUCTIONS | DIRECTORS | LOCATIONS | MAKING OF | CONTACT US

ITALY

A.S.A.P. Production
Via Gran San Bernardo, 13
20154 Milano
tel: 0039 02 33608783 / 34938308
fax: 0039 02 33617967
email: info@asapps.it

MOROCCO

A.S.A.P. Marrakech
Rue Majoub El Rimiza, 1
40000 Marrakech
ph: 00212.44.446502
fax: 00212.44.446524
email: info@asapps.it

www.asapps.it

→→→international location facilities

SOUTH AFRICA

"It is no secret that South Africa has diverse scenic locations, brilliant crew and cosmopolitan talent, nor that Johannesburg has the best winter climate in the world. But Jo'burg also has a plethora of urban landscapes that can be turned into replicas of a Jamaican town or European city streets. Our architecture ranges from the Edwardian through '60s and '70s decor to the very modern. Within minutes of the city there are vast sites that double as deserts, beaches and moonscapes."

Ange Ramsay, Velocity Afrika

"We have world-class facilities and operators and you never have a problem booking time, due to the unfounded belief that back home is better. There are occasions, when the production takes place over a long enough period, that we can edit during the course of the shoot, sometimes with an 'imported' editor."

Shane Bunce, Reeleyes Film Company

Unusual requests

● Like every location: "Can you do something about this weather?" ● To build a tent to cover the length of a street because it was raining *Velocity Afrika*
● At one in the morning, a demand from an agency producer that the stinkwood dresser in her five-star hotel room be changed as it was making "her underwear smell funny". Stinkwood is not only extremely rare and valuable, it also has no odour. *One Step Beyond* ● For a hooker - and it had nothing to do with a casting. That's service for you. *Reeleyes Film Company* ● "On Noordhoek Beach, the day before the actual shoot, the London-based director requested that we arrange to clear all the kelp in the water on 20km of beach and then STOP the waves" *Missing In Action Films*

Unusual locations and shoots

● Filming a lion who urinated on the DOP who stank of cat's piss for days *Freshwater Films*
● A sewage farm for a pork sausage spot *McKenzie Rudolphe* ● A beautifully appointed sitting room, entirely underwater *One Step Beyond* ● An African American transvestite skating on pink ice for an ice cream spot *McKenzie Rudolphe Film Services*
● Having to quietly kidnap a group of street people as the cast for a night shoot for a homeless support group. Fed, watered, and directed, they were released again at first light *One Step Beyond*

Directors recently shooting in South Africa

● M Grasso
● Tarsem
● Andy Morahan
● Vaughan Arnell
● Steve Reeves
● Jerry Dugan
● Antoine De Caunes
● Frank Van Passel
● Graham Rose

→→

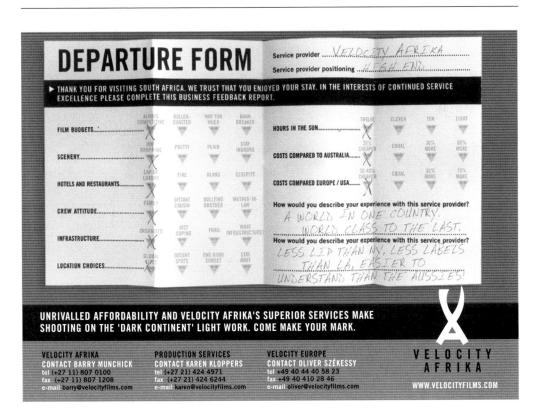

→→international location facilities

SPAIN

"There's a snobbery against the Costa Del Sol, the perception being high-rise buildings, time-share hell, new-money glitz and Sexy Beast-style gangsters – for an imaginative, creative industry it's amazing how insular the advertising community can be. We have every type of architecture and can match almost every South African location within a far smaller radius. Plus our kids casting books look like a meeting of the United Nations."

Jenni Wardle, Mundo Studios

"For casting, Barcelona draws a lot of models, plus it's a cosmopolitan city so there are lots of foreigners. Great actors are concentrated in Madrid where the theatre and features communities are based."

Santiago Morali, Director's Gallery

Unusual locations and requests

● The crater of a volcano *Quasar* ● An entire 13th century village in the desert in Almeria *On The Spot* ● A Madrid tube station that had been abandoned for 30 years *Team Works* ● A cavern with stalactites in an underground lake ● A DOP's dream *Palma Pictures* ● Asking that somebody get rid of the clouds in Bilbao, a city renowned for its foggy climate *Directors Gallery* ● Requesting an elephant for seven the next morning at 11pm *On the Spot*

Telling tales

"We were on a nightshoot in a historic bullfight square, when the director of photography decided the light from a big clock was interfering in his photography. Suddenly, the light went off and the clock stopped. The crew all broke into applause, until

the mayor of the village stormed the square with two policeman, shouting. We calmed them down, and the mayor then explained that the clock was a symbol of the village, and had been ticking since 1890. It was only at the wrap dinner that a local runner got drunk and confessed that he'd done it because he hated his village and it was his best chance for revenge."

Cayetano Chimeno, On The Spot

Directors recently shooting in Spain and Mallorca

● Matt Kirkby
● Jon Greenhalgh
● Dom & Nic
● Tarsem
● Blue Source
● Michael Kabelnikoff
● Lenny Dorfman
● Jason Smith
● Acne
● Hughes Brothers
● Vikki Blanche
● Peter Cattaneo

everything **you need:**

palm**fiction**.com

production and location services in spain

passeig de la rambla, 15   +34.971.711444 | tel   mail@palm**fiction**.com
07003 palma de mallorca   +34.971.711445 | fax   www.palm**fiction**.com
balearic islands | spain

bluesky@africaonline.co.ke
www.blueskyafrica.com
t +254 2 561841
+254 2 571851
f +254 2 574164

BLUESKY®
films

Discover...

the real Africa
in Kenya

zanzibar
tanzania
uganda
ethiopia

production coordination commercials features tv & stills

Blue Sky Croatia

Kamenarski Brijeg, Borovina 14, Zagreb 10000, Croatia
t +385 1 457 5082 **f** +385 1 457 5072
e mario@blueskycroatia.com **e** blueskycroatia@hotmail.com
Contact Sabrina Allaria, Producer; Mario Zvan, Executive Producer
Credits Kenya - White Terror (D); Dario's Sunchyme (M); Reebok (C); Lara Croft
And The Cradle Of Life: Tomb Raider 2 (F)

Blue Sky Films

PO Box 25711, 00603 Lavington, Nairobi, Kenya
t +254 2 561841 **t** +254 2 577387 **f** +254 2 574164
e bluesky@africaonline.co.ke **w** www.blueskyafrica.com
Contact Sabrina Allaria, Executive Producer, Producer; Mario Zvan, Executive
Producer; Jim Shamoon, Managing Director
Credits Kenya - White Terror (D); Dario's Sunchyme (M); Reebok (C); Lara Croft
And The Cradle Of Life: Tomb Raider 2 (F)

British American Studio Enterprises (BASE)

Rua Tavares Bastos 414/66, Rio de Janeiro RJ 22221-030, Brazil
t +55 21 2558 5547 **f** +55 21 3235 4073
e nadkarni@alternex.com.br **w** www.basebrazil.tripod.com

Bus

Calle Vicente Jimeno 11, Madrid 28035, Spain
t +34 91 376 8170 **f** +34 91 386 6193
e info@bus-pro.com **w** www.bus-pro.com
Contact Marta Delgado, Producer; Pablo Nolla, Managing Director; Pilu Pilosio,
Executive Producer; Joel Marsden, International Producer
Credits Coca Cola (C); Pepsi (C); TriNa (C); Smart (C)

Cape Direct

7 Kloofnek Road, Gardens, Cape Town 8001, South Africa
t +27 21 424 4495 **f** +27 21 424 4496
e production@capedirect.com **w** www.capedirect.com
Contact Gavin Armstrong; Dianne Bramhill
Credits Powergen (C); Lipton (C); Dell Computers (C); Peugeot (C)

Directors Film Company of Amsterdam BV

Duivendrechtsekade 83, Amsterdam 1096 AJ, Netherlands
t +31 20 665 8965 **f** +31 20 694 9996 **e** dfc@euronet.nl
Contact Richard Coll; Piet-Hein Luykx

DO Productions

PO Box 1515, Fourways, Johannesburg 2055, South Africa
t +27 11 463 1247 **t** +27 11 463 1248 **f** +27 11 706 8026
e do@doproductions.co.za **w** www.doproductions.com
Contact Marlow de Mardt; Brigid Olen
Credits A Species Odyssey (D); St George's (T); Flight Of The Phoenix (F)

Drunken Angel Entertainment

32/2 Eucharistic Congress Road, Mosta MST 09, Malta
t +356 21 418960 **f** +356 21 663116
e info@drunkenangel.net **w** www.drunkenangel.net
Contact Dennis Mahoney

Dune Films

28 Rue Tarik Bnouziad, Apartment 3, Guéliz, Marrakech, Morocco
t +212 4 443 1092 **f** +212 4 4431007
e dunefilms@iam.net.ma **w** www.cybernet.net.ma
Contact Jimmy Abounouom; Sana El Kilali; Karim Abouobayd

Easy Hell Productions

Warsaw, Poland
t +48 501 595000 **e** easyhell@easyhell.com.pl
w www.easyhell.com.pl
Contact Tomek Hryniszyn, Producer; Magda Wolosz, Managing Director
Credits Smile (E); Sprite - Passion (C); Steam Engine Depot (D); Migraine (C)

Errecerre International Productions

Passatge Torras I Bages 2, Sarria, Barcelona 8017, Spain
t +34 93 254 1200 **f** +34 93 254 0510
e rcr@errecerre.com **w** www.errecerre.com
Contact Toni Moreno; Sara Ferrer
Credits Opel Zafira (C); Premiere World (C); ö3 (C); Samsung (C)

brazil > argentina > usa > chile >

**full production &
production services
without borders**

for quotes contact
karin stuckenshmidt
kar@filmplanet.com
www.filmplanet.com

filmplanet group

The Family @ Madrid

Part of The Family Italy, Javier Ferrero 18,
Madrid 28002, Spain
t +34 915 106820 **f** +34 915 106822
e gold93@airtel.net

Contact Paloma Gardoqui; Jesus Perez Solero
Credits Toyota - Heat (C); Jeep - New Cherokee (C); Blu - 4Spots (C);
Wella - Soft Colour - Let Yourself Fall (C)

The Family

The Family

Via Ariosto 6, Milan 20145, Italy
t +39 02 4851 9711 **f** +39 02 4810 0567
e info@thefamilyfilm.it **w** www.thefamilyfilm.it

Contact Lorenzo Cefis, Executive Producer; Federico Luiselli,
Production Manager
Credits Laundry - Nintendo Game Boy Advanced (C); Wildness - Chrysler
Jeep (C); If - BMW (C)

Film It Sp Zoo

ul Wita Stwosza 17A, Warsaw
02 661, Poland
t +48 22 848 7811 **t** +48 22 848 3779
f +48 22 843 0607
e office@filmit.com.pl
w www.filmit.pl

Contact Dominika Grzegdala; Mira Klajnberg

Film Master Service

Via Morocco 18, Rome 144, Italy
t +39 06 545661 **f** +39 06 591 8865
e service.roma@filmmaster.com **w** www.filmmaster.com

Contact Janine de Wit; Ella Elliott
Credits RAI Institutional Campaign: Traffic Controllers

FILM PLANET
Full Production & Production Services Without Borders

Film Planet

Rua Fidêncio Ramos 195, 14 Andar, Sao Paulo
04551-010, Brazil
t +55 11 3049 8777 **f** +55 11 3049 8770
e hello@filmplanet.com **w** www.filmplanet.com

Contact Mércia Lima; Carlos Grübber; Karin Stuckenschmidt
Credits Barbie; Barbie

Film Positive Productions

Visegrádi u 9, Budapest 1132, Hungary
t +36 1 238 0200 **f** +36 1 238 0322
e info@filmpositive.hu **w** www.filmpositive.hu

Contact Gyorgyi Falvai
Credits Nescafe (C); Bonaqua (C); Connex - MobiFon (C); Hewlett Packard Omnibook (C)

Filma-Cass

Kocamansur Sokak 115/1, Sisli, Istanbul 80260, Turkey
t +90 212 233 6018 **f** +90 212 231 0227
e filmacass@filmacass.com.tr **w** www.filmacass.com.tr

Contact Ömer Vargi; Tamer Basaran; Bahadir Arliel; Elfin Yuksekteppe; Oguz Peri

FILM AND PHOTO PRODUCTION
SERVICE COMPANY

Filming Reel Production Ltd
Bahia Azul No 16, Estepona, Malaga 29680, Spain
t +34 952 798129 **f** +34 952 795838 **m** 07949 949534 (UK)
e maxine@reelproduction.co.uk **w** www.reelproduction.co.uk
Contact Maxine Parker, Producer; Leoni Cotgrove, Producer
Credits Schick Intuition/J Walter Thompson (C); Sherine, The Video (M); Love And Basketball (F); Sexy Beast (F)

Filmworks
PO Box 5157, Cape Town 8000, South Africa
t +27 21 461 0441 **f** +27 21 461 0572
e info@filmworks.co.za **w** www.filmworks.com
Contact Carole Prentice
Credits Cheerios (C); Saakis Rouvas (M); Amway (I); Skai (C)

Filmworks
The Production Village, PO Box 37415, Dubai, United Arab Emirates
t +39 011 347 4909 **f** +39 011 347 4590
e info@filmwks.com **w** www.filmwks.com
Contact July Tracey

FLEHNERFILMS
OTHER VISION. OTHER EXPERIENCE.

Flehner Films
Castillo 1366, Buenos Aires C 1414 AXD, Argentina
t +54 11 4771 0400 **f** +54 11 4771 6003
e rmazzeo@flehner.com.ar **w** www.flehnerfilms.com
Contact Rammero Mazzeo; Sergio Gullco
Credits Axe: 'Araña'; Renault Megane: 'Campo Traviesa'; Pajarito; Museum

Fresh Eye Film Productions
PO Box 1518, Pinegowrie, Johannesburg 2123, South Africa
t +27 11 789 3163 **f** +27 11 886 4551
e michele@fresheye.co.za **w** www.fresheye.co.za
Contact Michele Ferguson

Fresh Water Films
5 Wandel Street Gardens, Cape Town 8001, South Africa
t +27 21 461 4232 **f** +27 21461 4262
e producer@freshwatercape.co.za **w** www.freshwaterfilms.co.za
Contact Gaye Leong
Credits Thromboses (C); Infostrada (C); Maes Lager (C); Brantano (C)

Frieze Films
20 Rosebank Road, Rosebank, Johannesburg 2196, South Africa
t +27 11 788 4201 **f** +27 11 880 0268
e films@iafrica.com **w** www.friezefilms.com
Contact Neil Roberts
Credits Mobis (C); Dietorelle (C); Mild Seven (C); Galaxy Chocolates (C)

Full Moon Films
22 Rue Davy, Paris 75017, France
t +33 1 4263 4648 **f** +33 1 4229 5759
e info@fullmoon-films.com **w** www.fullmoon-films.com
Contact Philippe Dugay

Full Moon Films
Via Tiburtina 521, Rome 159, Italy
t +39 06 4353 5088
f +39 06 438 0328
e info@fullmoon-films.com
w www.fullmoon-films.com
Contact Philippe Dugay

ARGENTINA
made in
by altana films
© 2002 - 2003

MJZ - USA · MJZ - UK · Aoi Advertising - Japan · A Band Apart
Elma Garcia · Rocky Morton · Tamotsu Fujii · Wayne Isham
JWT NY · BBH UK · Nippon Design Centre · Ornelas & Assoc.
EPT · Perfetti · Muji · Budweiser

Contact:
Enrique Bacher
Julieta García
info@altana.com.ar
(5411) 4554-3940

Gatehouse Service
Unit 7, Somerset Place, 59 Somerset Road, Green Point, Cape Town 8005, South Africa
t +27 21 421 0060 f +27 21 421 0064
e bev@gatehouse.co.za w www.gatehouseservice.co.za
Contact Bev Green
Credits Volvo: ER Idents (C); Timotei - Bushes (C); Lea Jeans (C); Fanta (C)

Giant Films
Top Floor, Radio House, 92 Loop Street, Cape Town 8001, South Africa
t +27 21 422 1321 f +27 21 422 1431
e production@giantfilms.co.za w www.giantfilms.co.za
Contact Cindy Gabriel

Green Olive Films
24 Gregoriou Xenopoulou Street, Nicosia 1061, Cyprus
t +357 2276 8813 f +357 2276 8824
e athena@greenolivefilms.com w www.greenolivefilms.com
Contact Stelios Manganis; Athena Loizidou; Barbara Papa; Marinos Charalambous
Credits Tolu (M); Swiss Aid (C); Everything Wet (C); Tramboline (C)

Green Olive Films
27 Kiprou Street, Halandri, Athens 15233, Greece
t +30 210 689 7241 f +30 210 689 7243
e admin@greenolivefilms.com w www.greenolivefilms.com
Contact Stelios Manganis; Athena Loizidou; Barbara Papa
Credits Tolu (M); Swiss Aid (C); Everything Wet (C); Tramboline (C)

Ground Control AS
Gronnegata 10, Oslo 350, Norway
e mail@groundcontrol.no w www.groundcontrol.no
Contact Eirik Ohna

Groundglass
2 Nicol Street, Gardens, Cape Town 8001, South Africa
t +27 21 422 2591 f +27 21 422 2596
e groundglass@mweb.co.za w www.groundglass.com
Contact Janette de Villiers; Terry Vallet

Group Films
Margenat 73, Barcelona 8017, Spain
t +34 93 418 3302 f +34 93 212 6504
e barcelona@groupfilms.com
w www.groupfilms.com
Contact Nuria Gimpera, Executive Producer; Barbara Muschietti, Head of Services; Anna Bonet, Research & Development

I'm Film Ltd
Hajógyári Sziget 132, Budapest 1033, Hungary
t +36 1 250 0009 f +36 1 250 1473
e imfilm@imfilm.hu w www.imfilm.hu
Contact Ivan Mark
Credits KPN (C); Praxis (C); McDonalds (C); Dresner Bank (C)

THE ITALIAN JOB
Directors Bureau

The Italian Job
Via De'Castilla 24, Milan 20124, Italy
t +39 02 688 4567 f +39 02 606680
Contact Alessio Zazzera

ITI Film Studio
Ul Wiertnicza 166, Warsaw 02-952, Poland
t +48 22 453 3600 f +48 22 453 3603
e office@itifs.com w www.itifs.com
Contact Stan Dziedzic, Executive Producer
Credits Vizir: Moths

Kaktus-Production
98 Derb Sidi Bouloukat, Riad Zitoun Kdim, Marrakech 40 000, Morocco
t +212 44 442200 t +212 44 387567 f +212 44 444424
f +212 44 387605 e info@kaktus-production.com
e ahmedoudra@hotmail.com w www.kaktus-production.com
Contact Nicole Arbousset, Directors Assistant; Ahmed Oudra

Key Line Film
Avenue Sleeckx 28/32, Brussels 1030, Belgium
t +32 2 245 6450 f +32 2 245 6740
e christine@keylinefilm.be w www.keylinefilm.be
Contact Christine Mathieu, Producer
Credits Dexia Axion: Heaven Can Wait

kraftwerk
PRODUCTIONS

Kraftwerk Productions
Riddersvoldsgt 10, Oslo 258, Norway
t +47 2212 8720 f +47 2212 8721
e kraftwerk@kraftwerk.no w www.kraftwerk.no
Contact Knut Jensen; Guri Neby Hilland; Nils Kittilsen, Producer/Line Producer
Credits Stratos-Nidar: The Kid

Le Spot Productions
22A Papanikoli Street, Athens 152 32, Greece
t +30 210 817 8000 f +30 210 817 8008
e lespot@europe.mccann.com w www.lespot.gr
Contact Dimitris Alexopoulos; Elena Giamma
Credits Albacarta (C); Globul (C)

mr production service

www.mrproduction.com
info@mrproduction.com

Via Legnano, 26 · 20121 Milan · Italy
tel. +39 02 2900 6867 · fax 02 2900 6884

contact: Michele Virgilio,
Annalis Labat, Mariella Grandi

Via G. Nicotera, 29 · 00195 Rome · Italy
tel. +39 06 3611 497 · fax +39 06 3610 353

LICHTENBERG
production & mediaservice

Lichtenberg & Partners
Ludwig-Thoma Strasse 13, Oberschleissheim, Munich 85764, Germany
t +49 89 315 1366 f +49 89 315 1367
e manon.lichtenberg@netsurf.de w www.manonlichtenberg.com
Contact Manon Lichtenberg

M&R Production Service Srl
Via Legnano 26, Milan 20121, Italy
t +39 02 2900 6867 f +39 02 2900 6884
e info@mrproduction.com w www.mrproduction.com
Contact Michele Virgilio; Annalis Labat; Mariella Grandi

M&R Production Service Srl
Via G Nicotera 29, Rome 195, Italy
t +39 06 361 1497 f +39 06 361 0353
e info@mrproduction.com w www.mrproduction.com
Contact Annalis Labat

Mallorca Locations
Bahia De Palma, Apt 520, Illetas 32, Calvia, Mallorca 10782, Spain
t +34 68 624 8230 e neilpamevans@yahoo.com
Contact Neil Evans
Credits Perfect Partner (T); Prickly Heat (T); Beach Fever (T)

Mango Production
Via Vico 42, Milan 20143, Italy
t +39 02 8969 1960 f +39 02 481 7265
e email@mac.com e mangov@mac.com
Contact Vittorio Mango

Maximum Films Africa (Pty) Ltd
81 St Johns Street Gardens, Cape Town 8008, South Africa
t +27 21 461 3903 f +27 21 461 3925
e pendra@maximumfilms.com w www.maximumfilms.com
Contact Claire Dissel; Pendra Dissel, Managing Director
Credits Bubbaloo (C); Acuvue (C); Twingo (C)

McKenzie Rudolphe Film Services
47 Bloem Street, Bo-Kaap, Cape Town 8001, South Africa
t +27 21 423 1512 f +27 21 423 1516
e mcrud@iafrica.com w www.mcrud.com
Contact Ken McKenzie; Lisa Grobler; Roy Rudolphe
Credits Orangina (C); Royal Mail (C); Toyota Prado - Untamed (C); Travis (M)

Milk & Honey Films
Josefska 6, Prague 11800, Czech Republic
t +420 2 5570 7070 f +420 2 5570 7055
e info@milkandhoneyfilms.cz w www.milkandhoneyfilms.com
Contact Michaela Linhartova, Head of Production

Moonlighting Commercials
PO Box 4725, Cape Town 8000, South Africa
t +27 21 462 5300 f +27 21 462 5304
e info@moonlighting.co.za w www.moonlighting.co.za
Contact Philip Key
Credits Munkholm (C); Coors (C); Airwalk (C); Carlsberg (C)

Movie Makers International

Longacre Farm (PO Box 26914), Main Road, Hout Bay 7872, South Africa
t +27 21 790 6606 **f** +27 21 790 3664
e mmi@cis.co.za **w** www.moviemakersinternational.co.za
Contact Michael MacCarthy; Juli Lotter
Credits Cash 20000 (C); HSBC (C); Cet Alergin (C); Volksbank (C)

Movie Ventures

Alexander Boersstraat 50, Amsterdam 1071 KZ, Netherlands
t +31 20 672 0291 **f** +31 20 673 8042
e info@movieventures.nl **w** www.movieventures.nl
Contact Willem van den Brandt, Executive Producer

Mundo Studios

Centra Cadiz N340, Km 165.5, Cancelada, Estepona, Malaga 29688, Spain
t +34 952 889310 **f** +34 952 889340
e info@mundostudios.com **w** www.mundostudios.com
Contact Laura Anderson; Joanna Dogmoch
Credits Seat - Cupra (C); Moony - I'll Be Lovin' You (M); Las Ketchup - Asereje (M); TVC Airmiles (C)

Namib Film

PO Box 2209, Swakopmund, Namibia
t +264 64 463371 **f** +264 64 461993
e info@namibfilms.co.za **w** www.namibfilms.co.za
Contact Guy Nockels

NEUE SENTIMENTAL FILM

Neue Sentimental Milan

Via Novi 4, Milan 20144, Italy
t +39 02 581 5331 **f** +39 02 8942 3028 **e** milano@nsf.it
Contact Francesca Chiappetta, Executive Producer - Advertising & Music Video Awards

Ocean Films

Rua Joào Paulo 213, Florianopolis, Santa Catarina 88032-300, Brazil
t +55 48 334 8893 **t** +55 48 9960 6944
f +55 48 334 8823
e oceanfilms@oceanfilms.com.br **w** www.oceanfilms.com.br
Contact Joao Roni; Cristian Marini

One Step Beyond

PO Box 50884, V&A Waterfront, Cape Town 8002, South Africa
t +27 21 439 3352 **f** +27 21 439 8551
e info@onestepbeyond.co.za **w** www.onestepbeyond.co.za
Contact Anton Rollino; Lydia Mason; Tracey Rollino
Credits B&Q (C); Nurofen (C); Ambre Solaire (C); Skippy (C)

Orla Productions

31 Route de la Badine, Antibes 6600, France
t +33 4 9333 1185 **f** +33 4 9374 6512
e orlafrance@wanadoo.fr **w** www.orlafrance.bizland.com
Contact Francis Missana
Credits Mercedes (C); Fendi (C); BRV (C)

OrlandoFilm

Orlando Film
Via Cernaia 5, Milan 20121, Italy
t +39 02 901 3375 **f** +39 02 901 3407
e orlando@iol.it **w** www.orlandofilm.it
Contact Matteo Lando; Ivan Opezzi

Page International Services
Costa do Castelo 60, 2 Esq, Lisbon 1100-179, Portugal
t +351 21 882 1714 **f** +351 21 882 1714
e nickpage@pagelocation.com **w** www.pagelocation.com
Contact Tona Page; Nick Page

Palma Pictures The Mediterranean Production Centre
Calle Siurells 187-188, Marratxi, Mallorca 7141, Spain
t +34 971 226232 **f** +34 971 226282
e mailbox@palmapictures.es **w** www.palmapictures.es
Contact Debbie Gill
Credits Lipton Tchae; Holden Barina (C); Stefanel - Boom Boom Circus (C); Sky Blue (C)

palmfiction.com
production and location services in spain

Palmfiction
Plaza de la Puerta Pintada 6, Palma de Mallorca 7002, Spain
t +34 971 711444 **f** +34 971 711445
e mail@palmfiction.com **w** www.palmfiction.com
Contact Alex Gegenfurtner; David Krause

Partnership*pictures*

Partnership Pictures
Barrandov Film Studios, Krizeneckeho Namesti 322, Prague 5 152 53, Czech Republic
t +420 2 6707 2117 **f** +420 2 5181 4757
e office@partnershippictures.com **w** www.partnershippictures.com
Contact Petr Keller, Managing Director; Lucien Tyssendier, Executive Producer; Duncan Robson, Director, Director
Credits Hellboy (F)

PelucaFilms

Peluca Films
Congreso 3545, Capital Federal, Buenos Aires 1430, Argentina
t +54 11 4545 6200 **f** +54 11 4545 6200
e producciones@pelucafilms.com.ar
Contact Pompi Huarte, Producer; Jorge Di Benedetto, Producer; Ale Di Michele, Producer; Fabio Cimmarusti, Producer; Andrea Dibaja
Credits Philips Batteries: Cemetery (C); mundocelular.com: 'Bill'

PIONEER PRODUCTIONS

Pioneer Productions
Hajógyári Sziget 130/1, Budapest 1033, Hungary
t +36 1 457 1050 **f** +36 1 388 8950
e main@pioneer.hu **w** www.pioneer.hu
Contact Jennifer Webster, Managing Director; Dorka Klim, Producer; Juci Darvas, Producer
Credits Dior Addict (C); Nike Puddles/Stream (C); Levi's Odyssey (C); Mini: Drunkard

PIRAMIDE

Piramide
Calle Diputación 37, Local 2A, Barcelona 8015, Spain
t +34 93 327 8500 **f** +34 93 327 8501
e info@piramideproductions.com
w www.piramideproductions.com
Contact Xavier Sorolla, Executive Producer, Executive Producer; Olaf de Boer
Credits Dakar (C); Fussball (C); Sunny Side Of Life (C); Audi Quattro: Quattro

PlanetB
Bosanska 28, Zagreb 10000, Croatia
t +385 1 377 6655 **f** +385 1 390 9121 **e** mario@planetb.hr
Contact Andrej Korovljev

PTT Films - Production Team of Turkey
Asmalimescit Minare Sok 23, Beyoglu, Istanbul 80050, Turkey
t +90 212 293 8473 **f** +90 212 293 8475
e sebnem@pttfilms.com **w** www.pttfilms.com
Contact R Sebnem Kitis

Quasar Films
Calle Emilio Rubin 11, Madrid 28033, Spain
t +34 913 882466 **f** +34 913 003199
e quasarfilms@quasarfilms.com **w** www.quasarfilms.com
Contact Gema Navas
Credits B&Q - Quarry (C); B&Q - Furnace (C)

Reeleyes Film Company
1A Camden Street, Tamboerskloof, Cape Town, South Africa
t +27 21 426 2234 **f** +27 21 426 2299
e info@reeleyesfilm.com **w** www.reeleyesfilm.com
Contact Teri-Lin Robertson; Shane Brunce
Credits VW Golf 4 (C); 4 Strings - Take Me Away (M); Monsieur N (F); Garnier (C)

Rotor Productions
Kremencova 8, Prague 1 115 24, Czech Republic
t +420 2 2493 4220 **f** +420 2 2493 0843
e rotor@rotor.tv **w** www.rotor.tv
Contact Daniel Heyna-Vetrovsky
Credits Dan Curwin - Uncut (M); TPS (C); Mercedes CLK (C)

NO
HEADACHE

PTT of **T**
PRODUCTION TEAM OF TURKEY

PTT Films

Asmalı Mescit, Minare sok. no.23 80050 Beyoğlu, İstanbul-Turkey
t: +90 212 2938473   **f:** +90 212 2938475   **contact:** sebnem@pttfilms.com, balim@pttfilms.com

www.pttfilms.com

WWW.ANANADIGITAL.COM

Salento Locations

Viale Leopardi 78, Lecce 73100, Italy
t +39 832 398046
e info@salentolocation.it **w** www.salentolocation.it
Contact Francesca Grimaldi
Credits BRWD Brothers - Barilla (C)

Sardiniaproductions

Via Angioy 34, Cagliari 9124, Italy
t +39 070 6402462 **f** +39 070 673879
e info@sardiniaproductions.com **w** www.sardiniaproductions.com
Contact Michael Mueller, Managing Director; Bertram Schaenker, Office Manager; Machiel van der Does, Marketing/New Business

Set Service

Via Guido Banti 34, Rome 191, Italy
t +39 06 3332235 **t** +39 06 33223315 **f** +39 06 33223322
e info@setservice.it **w** www.setservice.it
Contact Massimo Di Matteo, Operations Manager; Clarissa Rosa, Company/Managing Director; Pietro Pesce, Scout/Photographer; Bruno Rosa, President
Credits Toyota Lexus (C); Spot Fiat Stilo (C); Incantesimo IV, V VI (T); L'Ora Di Religione (F)

1,500 LOCATIONS ON THE WEB - www.setservice.it

Not just the first image database in Rome, but the whole of Italy. It allows you to view a range of locations that are available for TV shooting, commercials, photographic shooting services or documentaries. The most complete and up-to-date source of information in Italy.

Sewell Films

Rua Goitacazes 112, Glória, Rio de Janeiro 22211-190, Brazil
t +55 21 205 3128 **f** +55 21 205 0477
e sewellfilms@alternex.com.br **w** www.sewellfilms.com
Contact Brian Sewell

The Shooting Gallery

Victoria Junction, Studio G8, Gate 1, Prestwich Street, Green Point, Cape Town 8001, South Africa
t +27 21 421 0999 **f** +27 21 421 3585
e info@theshootinggallery.co.za **w** www.theshootinggallery.co.za
Contact John Smith, Managing Director; Claire Richards, Executive Producer/Managing Director; Claudia Hall, Producer, Head of Production; Claudia Hall, Head of Production
Credits Spiderman (F); Ikea (C); Nintendo (C); Olympus (C)

Showwork & Co

Via Watt 5, Milan 20143, Italy
t +39 02 837 3526 **f** +39 02 835 8246
e showwork@showwork.com **w** www.showwork.com
Contact Sergio Lardera; Michele Colombo

Sirena Film

Rasinovo Nabrezi 6, Prague 2 120 00, Czech Republic
t +420 2 2491 8833 **f** +420 22491 9969
e info@sirenafilm.com **w** www.sirenafilm.com

Contact Artemio Benki; Kristina Hejdukova
Credits Yellow Pages (C); Canal+ (C); Oriflame (C); Paradise Found (F)

Skyfilm Studio

Hüvösvölgyi út 35, Budapest 1026, Hungary
t +36 1 275 3066 **f** +36 1 275 3069
e skyfilm@skyfilm.hu **w** www.skyfilm.hu

Contact Andrea Orban, Casting Director; Monika Nagy, Location Manager; Lidia
Kecskemethy, Producer
Credits A Kind Of America (F); Nestlé (C); Panasonic (C); Amstel (C)

SouthWest Productions

Rua Eng Antonio Maria de Avelar, 9A, Lisbon 1300-222, Portugal
t +351 21 3619470 **f** +351 21 3641669
e mail@southwest-productions.com
w www.southwest-productions.com

Contact Staffan Tranaeus, Producer
Credits E-klasse - Mercedes (I); Boiler - Limp Bizkit (M); The Portrait - Nordea Bank (C)

Stillking Films

Krizeneckeho nam 322, Prague 5 152 53, Czech Republic
t +420 267 073741 **f** +420 267 073742
e michal@stillking.com **w** www.stillking.com

Contact James Ricketts, Marketing Director; Michal Skop, Head of Production;
Pavla Burgetova, Executive Producer; Matthew Stillman, Managing Director;
David Minkowski, Head of Film
Credits The Prodigy (M); Sony Playstation (C); Van Helsing (F); The Prodigy:
Baby's Got a Temper

Strawberry Films

Bimbó út 141/B, Budapest 1026, Hungary
t +36 1 200 4040 **f** +36 1 200 6060 **m** +36 309 427589
e strawberry@strawberryfilms.hu **w** www.strawberryfilms.hu

Contact Melinda Szepesi, Producer, Producer; Katalin Krammer, Executive
Producer, Executive Producer

STUDIO
FRANCESCO
RAPA SRL

Studio Francesco Rapa

Via Dei Missionari 11, Naples 80125, Italy
t +39 081 593 5500 **f** +39 081 593 4440
e info@studiorapa.it **w** www.studiorapa.it
Contact Ivano Rapa

Tangerina Azul Internacional

Praça de Goa 2, Lisbon 1400, Portugal
t +351 21 303 1600 **f** +351 21 303 1609
e production@tangerinazul.com **w** www.tangerinazul.com
Contact Margarida Adónis, Executive Producer
Credits Audi - One Step Ahead (C); Orange (C); Mercedes - SBC (C);
Vodafone (C)

Tanit Productions

50 Rue Saint Didier, Paris 75116, France
t +33 1 4727 1731 **f** +33 1 4755 1356
e jp@tanit-prod.com **w** www.tanit-prod.com
Contact Jean-Patrick Costantini
Credits Toyota Avensis (C)

Team Works Production Services

Calle Laurín 53, Madrid 28043, Spain
t +34 11 722 9150 **f** +34 11 300 4458
e service@teamworkspain.com **w** www.teamworkspain.com
Contact Victor Minguez
Credits MBK Scooters (C); GSM Advance (C); Ford Fusion Image Film (I);
Oviesse (C)

Tetraktys Films Ltd

Apartment 201, 95 Kerynia Avenue, Aglanjia, Nicosia, Cyprus
t +357 22 337433 **f** +357 22 339286
e tetraktys@cytanet.com.cy **w** www.tetraktysmedia.com
Contact Stavros Papageorghiou, Managing Director
Credits Organic Med/Leonardo (W); Oil On Fire (F); George Seferis (D); Perseas (A)

UFO Pictures

Nad Spádem 17/202, Praha 4 140 00, Czech Republic
t +420 2 6121 3968 **f** +420 2 6121 4015
e info@ufopictures.tv **w** www.ufopictures.tv
Contact David Rauch, Executive Producer; Monika Splíchalová, Producer;
Jeffrey Brown, Producer/International Representative
Credits The Myth - Nick Cave And The Bad Seeds (D); Nissan (C); The Pied Piper
(F); Sprandi (C)

VELOCITY AFRIKA

Velocity Afrika Production Services

30 Keerom Street, Cape Town 8001, South Africa
t +21 21 424 4971 **f** +21 21 424 6244
e karen@velocityfilms.com **e** barry@velocityfilms.com
w www.velocityfilms.com
Contact Jenny Leslie, Executive Producer; Barry Munchick, Managing Director;
Nicola Valentine, Executive Producer; Karen Kloppers, Head of Production

Voodoo Productions
Calle Alegre de Dalt 55, 2C, Barcelona 8024, Spain
t +34 93 285 0229 **f** +34 93 210 5866
e contact@voodooproductions.net **w** www.voodooproductions.net
Contact Txell Sabartés; Albert Brasó

Widescope Productions
Finca la Caridad s/n, Marbella, Malaga 29600, Spain
t +34 952 860866 **f** +34 952 772237
e info@widescopeproductions.com
w www.widescopeproductions.com

Zak Productions
Avenue Mohamed V, Residence Badr 3e Etage, Marrakech, Morocco
t +212 44 439947 **f** +212 44 439945 **e** zakprods@iam.net.ma
Contact Zak Alaoui; Khadija Koulla

Location Finding Companies UK

Alba Connections
Eilean Donan, Castle Cottage, Dornie IV40 8DX
t 01599 55374 **m** 07730 122118
e albaconnections@talk21.com **w** www.albaconnections.co.uk
Contact Gordon McIntyre, Proprietor
Credits Kandukkondain (F); Lochcarron Of Scotland (I); IBM (C); Mammoth Hunters (D)

Amazing Space
74 Clerkenwell Road, London EC1M 5QA
t 020 7251 6661 **f** 020 7251 6808
e info@amazingspace.co.uk **w** www.amazingspace.co.uk
Contact Thomas Howard, Location Manager; Olivia Badnell, Librarian; Daryl Kaye, Location Co-ordinator; Tiffany Parrish, Managing Director
Credits Mr. Right (T); Fame Academy (T); Bridget Jones's Diary (F); Die Another Day (F)

Arctic Experience
29 Nork Way, Banstead SM7 1PB
t +44 1737 218010 **f** +44 1737 214245
e marketing@discover-the-world.co.uk
w www.arctic-experience.co.uk
Contact Joanne Bower, Marketing Consultant

Conwy Butterfly Jungle
Bodlondeb Park, Bangor Road, Conwy LL32 8DU
t 01492 593149 **f** 01492 593149
e info@conwybutterfly.co.uk **w** www.conwy-butterfly.co.uk
Contact Geoff Sharrock, Proprietor
Credits Mick and Geoff (T); Cool Cube (T)

E-Media-C
95-96 New Bond Street, London W1S 1DB
t 020 7518 1340 **f** 020 7518 1341
e info@emediac.net **w** www.emediac.net
Contact Paul Booth, CEO; Jo Davies, Marketing Manager

EM Media
35-37 St Mary's Gate, Nottingham NG1 1PU
t 0115 934 9090 **f** 0115 950 0988 **m** 07764 372298
e info@em-media.org.uk **w** www.em-media.org.uk
Contact Phil Nodding, Screen Commissioner - East Midlands; Emily Lappin, Location & Facilities Co-ordinator

The land of ice and fire is a spectacular place to film. With a diverse range of locations and it's proximity to the UK, it is definitely worth investigating... The UK's top Iceland tour operator now offers location advice and travel arrangements to the film/TV industry.

Arctic Experience 01737 218810

www.arctic-experience.co.uk

English Landscapes
Frilsham Nursery, Yattendon, Thatcham RG18 0XX
t 01635 200410 **f** 01635 202050
w www.thelandscapegroup.co.uk
Contact Simon Stephens, Managing Director

Film Location Associates
College Mansions, Winchester Avenue, London NW6 7TY
t 020 7625 5939 **f** 020 7372 1344 **m** 07971 546057
e filmlocations@hungryfish.com

Greenwich Film Unit
3rd Floor, Peggy Middleton House, 50 Woolwich New Road, London SE18 6HQ
t 020 8921 5873 **t** 020 8921 6048
f 020 8921 6283 **m** 07903 498681
e nicola.hogan@greenwich.gov.uk
e rachel.wegh@greenwich.gov.uk
Contact Nicola Hogan, Film Officer; Rachel Wegh, Film Unit Manager; Suzanne Hutchinson, Filming Officer
Credits Ted And Sylvia (F); All Or Nothing (F); About A Boy (F); Dirty Pretty Things (F)

jj locations
10 Harris Lane, Shenley, Radlett WD7 9EB
t 01923 853932 **f** 01923 853932 **m** 07831 239777
e info@jjlocations.co.uk **w** www.jjlocations.co.uk
Contact Johnny Jones, Location Manager

Lake District Locations
Gable Cottage, Eaglesfield, Cockermouth CA13 0SD
t 01900 823927 **f** 01900 823927 **m** 07779 956777
e e_wise@msn.com

Lavish Locations
Chiswick Town Hall, Heathfield Terrace, London W4 4JN
t 020 8742 2992 **f** 020 8742 2836
e info@lavishlocations.com **w** www.lavishlocations.com
Contact Kate Webber, Managing Director; Anna Darby, Managing Director
Credits Love Actually (F); About A Boy (F); Possession (F); Bridget Jones' Diary (F)

The Location Partnership
82 Berwick Street, London W1F 8TP
t 020 7734 0456 **f** 020 7734 5411
e info@locationpartnership.net **w** www.locationpartnership.com
Contact Sebastian Keep, Director, Location Manager; Phil Haselden, Director, Location Manager

Location Production
40 Formosa Street, London W9 2JP
t 020 7289 0304 **f** 020 7289 0139 **m** 07957 434387
e aza@locationproduction.com **w** www.locationproduction.com
Contact Charlie Somers, Location Manager; Ian Ellis, Location Manager; Wayne Moser, Location Manager; Graham Aza, Senior Location Manager; Jason Wheeler, Location Manager
Credits Sainsburys (C); Nectar (C); Ford (C); BT (C)

Location Works Ltd
42 Old Compton Street, London W1V 6LR
t 020 7494 0888 **f** 020 7287 2855
e info@locationworks.com **w** www.locationworks.com
Contact Kell Gatherer, Director; Harvey Hillyer, Director

Locationinc Ltd
Unit 2, Cooper House, 2 Michael Road, London SW6 2AD
t 020 7384 4554 **f** 020 7384 1177 **m** 07785 557161
e mail@locationinc.co.uk **e** www.locationinc.co.uk
Contact Edward Sharp, Director Of Company

North By North East
11 High Street, Gilling West, Richmond DL10 5JB
t 01748 826571 **f** 01748 829541 **m** 07785 343023
e locne@aol.com **w** www.northbynortheast.co.uk
Contact Andrew Bainbridge, Location/Production Manager
Credits Trainspotting (F); Nicholas Nickleby (T); Miranda (F);
Auf Wiedersehen, Pet (T)

Northern Film & Media
Central Square, Forth Street, Newcastle-upon-Tyne NE1 3PJ
t 0191 269 9212 **f** 0191 269 9213
e locations@northernmedia.org **w** www.northernmedia.org
Contact Paul Mingard, Commissioner; Gayle Mason, Assistant Commissioner;
Dave Watson, Production Liaison; Lynn Kirton, Administration
Credits Take Me (T); Auf Wiedersehen Pet (T); Billy Elliot (F); Harry Potter And
The Philosopher's Stone (F)

OIC Locations
66 Charlotte Street, London W1T 4QE
t 020 7419 1949 **f** 020 7419 1950 **m** 07966 399661
e info@oic.co.uk **w** www.locations.tv
Contact Annabel Francois, Library Manager; Tony Hood, Director; Henry
Camilleri, Director
Credits Adidas - Footballers (C); Sugababes (M); Wild About Harry (F);
Freeserve - Blink Productions (C)

Raymond Fisher Locations
Highfields, 27 Holt House Lane, Kings Lynn PE32 1EL
t 01553 630471 **f** 01553 630777 **m** 07768 163071
Contact Raymond Fisher, Proprietor
Credits Radiohead (M); Allo Allo (T); Panic Mechanics (T)

Roland Caine Associates
74 Swaby Road, London SW18 3QZ
t 020 8947 7597 **f** 020 8946 2987 **m** 07836 293493
e roland@locsource.com **w** www.rolandcaineassocs.com
Contact Lee Shale, Location Manager; Roland Caine, Proprietor; Simon Watson,
Location Manager
Credits Mercedes S-Type (C); Vodafone (C); Mrs Brown (F); Lady Audley's Secret (F)

Ruralocations
Pitt Farm, Frensham, Farnham GU10 3EG
t 01252 792614 **f** 01252 792614 **m** 07887 687 170
e katy.poulsom@which.net
Contact Mark Poulson, Sole Proprietor
Credits Born & Bred (T); Die Another Day (F); Gladiator (F)

Sally Mackie Locations
Cownham Farm, Broadwell, Moreton-in-the-Marsh GL56 0TT
t 01451 830294 **f** 01451 832442 **m** 07860 533355
e info@lokations.fsnet.co.uk **w** www.sallymackie-locations.com
Contact Sally Mackie, Partner
Credits Elle Fashion Brochure (C); BT Annual Report (C); Texas Instruments (C)

Sarah Eastel Locations
13 Abbey Churchyard, Bath BA1 1LY
t 01225 460022 **f** 01225 460696
e info@film-locations.co.uk **w** www.film-locations.co.uk
Contact Sarah Eastel, Contact

Strutt & Parker Film Location Agency
13 Hill Street, Berkeley Square, London W1J 5LQ
t 020 7629 7282 **f** 020 7629 0387 **m** 07802 979421
e marketing@struttandparker.com **w** www.struttandparker.com
Contact Katrina Fletcher

Wales Screen Commission (National Office)
Unit 6G, The Science Park, Cefn Llan, Aberystwyth SY23 3AH
t 0800 849 8848
e enquiry@walesscreencommission.co.uk
w www.walesscreencommission.co.uk
Contact Rachel Whitfield, Assistant to National Co-ordinator; Mike Wallwork,
National Co-ordinator

West Cornwall Film Office
Penwith District Council, St Clare, Penzance TR18 3QW
t 01736 362341 **f** 01736 336595 **e** tourism@penwith.gov.uk
Contact Sue Clarke, Tourism and Marketing Manager; Mike Foxley, Marketing &
Promotion Officer

West Country Locations
Crosslands House, Ash Thomas, Tiverton EX16 4NU
t 01884 820888 **f** 01884 821328 **m** 07774 428309
e wcl@eclipse.co.uk **w** www.wcl.eclipse.co.uk/
Contact Roger Elliott, Director; Annie Elliott, Director

Location Managers

Idris Ahmed
Gems, The Media House, 87 Glebe Street, Penarth CF64 1EF
t 029 2071 0770 **f** 029 2071 0771
e gems@gems-agency.co.uk **w** www.gems-agency.co.uk
Credits Kiss Me Kate (T); Barbara (T); Crossroads (T); Babymother (F)

Rufus Andrews
Rose Cottage, Taynton, Burford OX18 4UH
t 01993 822434 **m** 07836 222968
Credits The Rainbow (F); In A Land Of Plenty (T); Soldier Soldier (T); Dalziel
And Pascoe (T)

Dominic Barlow
Gems, The Media House, 87 Glebe Street, Penarth CF64 1EF
t 029 2071 0770 **f** 029 2071 0771
e gems@gems-agency.co.uk **w** www.gems-agency.co.uk
Credits Dead Gorgeous (T); Ashes And Sand (F); Marjorie And Gladys (F); Last
Of The Summer Wine (T)

Brian Bilgorri
Gems, The Media House, 87 Glebe Street, Penarth CF64 1EF
t 029 2071 0770 **f** 029 2071 0771
e gems@gems-agency.co.uk **w** www.gems-agency.co.uk
Credits Trial And Retribution IV (T); The Bill (T); Canterville Ghost (F);
Doomsday Gun (F)

Ian Booth
2 Hallam, Ogbourne St George, Marlborough SN8 1SG
t 01672 841596 **f** 01672 841515 **m** 07973 225095
e ian@questlocations.co.uk **w** www.thelocationdirectory.co.uk

Rhidian Bridge
PO Box 31529, London W11 4JF
t 07050 029423 **m** 07768 636936 **e** rhidian@bigfoot.com

David Broder
80 Harlescott Road, London SE15 3BZ
t 020 7277 8604 **f** 020 7277 8604 **m** 07976 397466
e broder@btopenworld.com **w** www.davidbroder.co.uk
Credits Enigma (F); Lara Croft Tomb Raider II - The Cradle Of Life (F); Star Wars Episode II - The Attack Of The Clones (F); Spider (F)

Peter Chadwick
Gems, The Media House, 87 Glebe Street, Penarth CF64 1EF
t 029 2071 0770 **f** 029 2071 0771
e gems@gems-agency.co.uk **w** www.gems-agency.co.uk
Credits Lee Evans Sitcom (T); Only Fools And Horses (T); The Bill (T); Peak Practice (T)

Rob Champion
Overend Cottage, Stinchcombe, Dursley GL11 6AR
t 01453 543876 **f** 01453 543876 **m** 07939 042361
e rob@locationmanagers.co.uk **w** www.locationmanagers.co.uk
Credits Adventure Inc (T); Casualty (T)

Clovisfilms - Locations in France
Paris, France
t +33 546 059835 **w** info@clovisfilms.com
Contact Claude Gresset, Location Director

Paul Davies
1 Ivy Street, Victoria Park, Cardiff CF5 1ER
m 07850 242266
Credits Moth (T); Lucky Bag (T); Belonging (T)

Peter Elford
34 Pyrton Lane, Watlington OX49 5LX
t 01491 612016 **f** 01491 612016 **m** 07402 422069
e p_elford@lineone.net
Credits Chaos And Cadavers (F); The Murder Of Roger Ackroyd (F); Dinotopia (T); Menace (T)

Annie Elliott
Crosslands House, Ash Thomas, Tiverton EX16 4NU
t 01884 820888 **f** 01884 821328 **m** 07774 428310
e elliott@eclipse.co.uk

Roger Elliott
Crosslands House, Ash Thomas, Tiverton EX16 4NU
t 01884 820888 **f** 01884 821328 **m** 07774 428309
e elliott@eclipse.co.uk

Mark Gladwin
Gems, The Media House, 87 Glebe Street, Penarth CF64 1EF
t 029 2071 0770 **f** 029 2071 0771
e gems@gems-agency.co.uk **w** www.gems-agency.co.uk
Credits The League Of Gentlemen - Xmas Special (T)

Richard Godfrey
34 Avondale Road, Palmers Green, London N13 4DU
t 020 8886 7342 **f** 07970 099048 **m** 07973 549137
e technical.office@virgin.net
Credits The Bombmaker (F); Murder In Mind (T); Without Motive (T); The Bill (T)

Mick Graham
27 Old Broadway, Withington, Manchester M20 3DH
t 0161 445 1754 **f** 0161 445 1754 **e** gmickloc@aol.com
Credits Wuthering Heights (T); The Forsyte Saga (T); Where The Heart Is (T); Playing The Field (T)

George Griffiths
The Production Switchboard, North Down, Down Lane, Compton GU3 1DN
t 01483 812011 **f** 01483 812027
e aly@productionswitch.freeserve.co.uk
Credits Hornblower (T); The Inspector Lynley Mysteries (T); Behind Closed Doors (T)

Derek Harrington
m 07831 308648 **e** derek@locations.demon.co.uk
Credits The Calling (F); In Deep (T); Judge John Deeds (T)

Tanya Harris
36D, Manor Road N16 5BG
m 07961 173742

Ken Holt
t 01789 204303 **m** 07778 956 778 **e** kenholt@zoom.co.uk
Credits Brumm (T); Judge John Deeds (T)

Alex van Ingen
Roland Caine Associates, 74 Swaby Road, London SW18 3QZ
t 020 8947 7597 **f** 020 8946 2987
e roland@locsource.com **w** www.rolandcaineassocs.com

Ali James
Roland Caine Associates, 74 Swaby Road, London SW18 3QZ
t 020 8947 7597 **f** 020 8946 2987 **e** roland@locsource.com
w www.rolandcaineassocs.com

Patrick Karam
97 Adelaide Grove, London W12 0JX
t 020 8742 9771 **m** 07850 972068 **e** patkaram@hotmail.com
Credits I'll Sleep When I'm Dead (F); Last Orders (F)

Sebastian Keep
73 Carlisle Mansions, Carlisle Place, London SW1P 1HZ
t 020 7834 5048 **f** 020 7233 5603 **m** 07850 045209
e batzkeep@dircon.co.uk

David Lardner
Gems, The Media House, 87 Glebe Street, Penarth CF64 1EF
t 029 2071 0770 **f** 029 2071 0771
e gems@gems-agency.co.uk **w** www.gems-agency.co.uk
Credits Hollyoaks (T); Lava (F); AKA (F); Birthday Girl (F)

Harriet Lawrence
57 Sawley Road, London W12 0LQ
t 020 8248 2586 **f** 020 8248 2586 **m** 07802 885354
e thekeylocation@aol.com
Credits Henry VIII (T); Trial & Retribution (T); Jonathon Creek (T); The Hole (F)

Gabrielle Lindemann
Gems, The Media House, 87 Glebe Street, Penarth CF64 1EF
t 029 2071 0770 **f** 029 2071 0771
e gems@gems-agency.co.uk **w** www.gems-agency.co.uk
Credits One Foot In The Grave (T); Casualty (T); The Lee Evans Show (T); Jonathan Creek (T)

Doug MacDonald
Gems, The Media House, 87 Glebe Street, Penarth CF64 1EF
t 029 2071 0770 **f** 029 2071 0771
e gems@gems-agency.co.uk **w** www.gems-agency.co.uk
Credits The Detective (T); Rides (T); Bugs (F); The Bill (T)

Chris Martin
Gems, The Media House, 87 Glebe Street, Penarth CF64 1EF
t 029 2071 0770 **f** 029 2071 0771
e gems@gems-agency.co.uk **w** www.gems-agency.co.uk
Credits Walking The Dead (T); Chains (T); 2000 Acres Of Sky (T); EastEnders (T)

Casper Mill
t 020 7652 5462 **m** 07774 407823 **e** caspermill@aol.com

Richard Moat
Gems, The Media House, 87 Glebe Street, Penarth CF64 1EF, UK
t 029 2071 0770 **f** 029 2071 0771 **e** gems@gems-agency.co.uk
w www.gems-agency.co.uk
Credits Frontiers (T); The Cambridge Spies (T); Silent Witness (T); A Breed Of Heroes (T)

Mark Mostyn
The Old Mill, Uplyme, Lyme Regis DT7 3UA
t 01297 443611 **f** 01297 443611 **m** 07850 654174
e maric.mostyr@virgin.net
Credits Morality Play (F); Nicholas Nickleby (F)

Navigator Locations
29 Parkhill Road, Belsize Park, London NW3 2YH
t 020 7813 3129 **f** 020 7813 3129 **m** 07956 613801
e navigator@hotmail.com
Contact Nick Wood, Location Manager; John Lockwood, Location Manager
Credits Royal Mail (C); Ford (C); Smirnoff (C); Rimmell (C)

Gavin Northover
Roland Caine Associates, 74 Swaby Road, London SW18 3QZ
t 020 8947 7597 **f** 020 8946 2987 **e** roland@locsource.com
w www.rolandcaineassocs.com

Ben O'Farrell
The Production Switchboard, North Down, Down Lane,
Compton GU3 1DN
t 01483 812011 **f** 01483 812027
e aly@productionswitch.freeserve.co.uk
Credits On One (S); Roadside Bloom (S); Memiton (M)

Alex Quennell
37 Foley Street, London W1W 7TN
t 020 7637 7885 **f** 020 7637 7886 **m** 07831 247 979
e alex@saltfilm.com **w** www.saltfilm.com
Credits VW (C); Lost Ships Vietnam (D); Audi (C); Audi
World-wide experience, fluent French, on-line Library at saltfilm.com

Sue Quinn
2 Avenue Mansions, Sisters Avenue, London SW11 5FL
t 020 7223 9927 **f** 020 7223 9927 **m** 07860 150627
e squinny@compuserve.com
Credits Gosford Park (F); Elizabeth (F); Dirty Pretty Things (F); Notting Hill (F)

Kevin Ramsay
Gems, The Media House, 87 Glebe Street, Penarth CF64 1EF
t 029 2071 0770 **f** 029 2071 0771
e gems@gems-agency.co.uk **w** www.gems-agency.co.uk
Credits Comic Acts (F); Body Story (T); Storm Damage (T); The Bill (T)

Mick Ratman GLM
76A Albert Street, London NW1 7NR
t 020 7380 1128 **f** 020 7916 7698 **m** 07836 208277
e mickthefish@fsmail.net
Credits Oxide And Neutrino (M); Sky TV (C); Welcome To Sarajevo (F)

Mick Ratman
Bookends Ltd, 83 Maynard Drive, St Albans AL1 2JX
t 01727 841177 **e** bookgold@bookends.fsbusiness.co.uk

Garance Rawinsky
13 Denison Hall, Hanover Square, Leeds LS3 1BQ
t 0113 244 9906 **m** 07771 893459
Credits Goodnight Sweetheart (T); The Bill (T); Omnibus On Air Promo - Talent
(C); Beech Is Back (T)

Barry Read
Experience Counts - Call Me Ltd, 5th Floor, 41-42 Berners
Street, London W1P 3AA
t 020 7637 8112 **f** 020 7580 2582

Ben Rimmer
42 Shakespeare Road, London W3 6SJ
t 020 8992 0377 **f** 020 8896 9344 **m** 07836 363638
e ben.rimmer@virgin.net
Credits Nicholas Nickleby (F); Lucky Break (F); Spy Games (F)

Scott Sidey
1 Cranborne Road, Hatfield AL10 8AW
t 01707 266641 **f** 01707 266641 **m** 07831 525630
e scott-sidey@msn.com
Contact Scott Sidey, Location Manager
Credits Baileys (C); Nine Lives (F); Sainsbury's (C)

Simon McNair Scott
The Old Rectory, Lesnewth, Boscastle PL35 0HR
t 01840 261730 **m** 07860 450376 **e** locscott@aol.com

Lee Shale
Roland Caine Associates, 74 Swaby Road, London SW18 3QZ
t 020 8947 7597 **f** 020 8946 2987
e roland@locsource.com **w** www.rolandcaineassocs.com

Jeremy Stern
337C Liverpool Road, Islington, London N1 1NH
f 020 7609 1596 **m** 07941 930203 **e** jeremy.stern@virgin.net
Agent Roland Caine Associates, 74 Swaby Road,
London SW18 3QZ
t 020 8947 7597 **f** 020 8946 2987
e roland@locsource.com **w** www.rolandcaineassocs.com
Credits Spontex (T); Rehab (T); Dead Ringers (T)

Paddy Stewart
Roland Caine Associates, 74 Swaby Road, London SW18 3QZ
t 020 8947 7597 **f** 020 8946 2987 **e** roland@locsource.com
w www.rolandcaineassocs.com

Patrick Stuart
Gems, The Media House, 87 Glebe Street, Penarth CF64 1EF
t 029 2071 0770 **f** 029 2071 0771
e gems@gems-agency.co.uk **w** www.gems-agency.co.uk
Credits Rage (T); Tales Of Uplift And Moral Improvement (T); Redemption Road (F)

Clive Trott
Roland Caine Associates, 74 Swaby Road, London SW18 3QZ
t 020 8947 7597 **f** 020 8946 2987
e roland@locsource.com **w** www.rolandcaineassocs.com

Peter Tullo
75 Magdalen Road, London SW18 3NE
t 020 8874 8533 **f** 020 8874 8533 **m** 07831 296 904
e peter@tullo.fsnet.co.uk

Bill Twiston-Davies
Roland Caine Associates, 74 Swaby Road, London SW18 3QZ
t 020 8947 7597 **f** 020 8946 2987
e roland@locsource.com **w** www.rolandcaineassocs.com

Nicholas Wade
Gems, The Media House, 87 Glebe Street, Penarth CF64 1EF
t 029 2071 0770 **f** 029 2071 0771
e gems@gems-agency.co.uk **w** www.gems-agency.co.uk
Credits The Quiet Policeman (T); Attachments (T); The Bill (T); Murphy's Law (T)

Simon Watson
Roland Caine Associates, 74 Swaby Road, London SW18 3QZ
t 020 8947 7597 **f** 020 8946 2987
e roland@locsource.com **w** www.rolandcaineassocs.com

Mathew Wortman
Roland Caine Associates, 74 Swaby Road, London SW18 3QZ
t 020 8947 7597 **f** 020 8946 2987
e roland@locsource.com **w** www.rolandcaineassocs.com

Location
Managers Assistants

Joanna Sheehan
Gems, The Media House, 87 Glebe Street, Penarth CF64 1EF
t 029 2071 0770 **f** 029 2071 0771
e gems@gems-agency.co.uk **w** www.gems-agency.co.uk
Credits The Bill (T); In The Red (T); Pet Rescue Roadshow (T); The 11 O'Clock Show (T)

MAKE-UP

make-up : contents

Make-Up Artists

Louise Abusenna
43 Lancaster Avenue, Guildford GU1 3JR
t 01483 457739 **m** 07887 851800 **e** lousalsa1@aol.com

Sallie Adams
Agent Creative Media Management, Unit 3B, Walpole Court, Ealing Studios, Ealing Green, London W5 5ED
t 020 8584 5363 **f** 020 8566 5554
e enquiries@creativemediamanagement.com
Agent Gems, The Media House, 87 Glebe Street, Penarth CF64 1EF
t 029 2071 0770 **f** 029 2071 0771
e gems@gems-agency.co.uk **w** www.gems-agency.co.uk
Agent Experience Counts - Call Me Ltd, 5th Floor, 41-42 Berners Street, London W1P 3AA
t 020 7637 8112 **f** 020 7580 2582
Agent Wizzo & Co, 35 Old Compton Street, London W1D 5JX
t 020 7437 2055 **f** 020 7437 2066
e wizzo@wizzoandco.co.uk **w** www.wizzoandco.co.uk
Credits Star Wars: Episode I - The Phantom Menace (F); The Forsyte Saga (T); The Falklands Play (T)

Sarita Allison
EXEC, 6 Travis Court, Farnham Royal SL2 3SB
t 01753 646677 **f** 01753 646770
e sue@execmanagement.co.uk **w** www.execmanagement.co.uk

Christine Allsopp
5 The Cottages, High Street, Lewknor OX49 5TW
f 01844 350184 **m** 07973 406067
e christineallsopp@aol.com **w** www.christineallsopp.com
Agent Gems, The Media House, 87 Glebe Street, Penarth CF64 1EF
t 029 2071 0770 **f** 029 2071 0771
e gems@gems-agency.co.uk **w** www.gems-agency.co.uk
Credits Supergrass - Rush Hour Soul (M); In Deep III (T); Full Metal Jacket (F); Spider (F)

Sharon Anniss
6 Lynton Close, Isleworth TW7 7ET
t 020 8744 0804 **f** 020 8744 0804 **m** 07711 314310
e sanniss@btopenworld.com
Credits Comfort Refresh (C); Green (S); Down To Earth (T); The Inspector Lynley Mysteries (T)

Jane Atkinson
50 Blackthorn Road, Attleborough NR17 1YJ
t 01953 456046 **f** 01953 456046 **m** 07860 103347
e jmamakeup@aol.com
Credits Tales Of The Unexpected (T); Kirsty's Home Videos (T); PJ James (T); London Bridge (T)

Gloria Barber
Agent EXEC, 6 Travis Court, Farnham Royal SL2 3SB
t 01753 646677 **f** 01753 646770
e sue@execmanagement.co.uk **w** www.execmanagement.co.uk
Agent Experience Counts - Call Me Ltd, 5th Floor, 41-42 Berners Street, London W1P 3AA
t 020 7637 8112 **f** 020 7580 2582

Judith Barkas
7 Richborough Road, Cricklewood, London NW2 3LU
t 020 8450 7157 **f** 020 8450 7157 **m** 07973 261637
e j.barkas@blueyonder.co.uk
Credits The Real Thomas Becket (T); The Plot To Kill Hitler (T); Blowing It (S); Smack The Pony (T)

Amanda Barker
Suz Cruz, Halliford Studios, Manygate Lane, Shepperton TW17 9EG
t 01932 252577 **f** 01932 253323 **m** 07956 485593
e zoe@suzcruz.co.uk **w** www.suzcruz.co.uk

Benita Barrell
58 Westbury Road, Southend-on-Sea SS2 4DP
t 01702 309811 **m** 007802 422153

Sue Beavis
Melville House, Newdigate Road, Beare Green RH5 4QD
t 01306 711134 **f** 01306 711107 **e** performance@freenet.co.uk
Contact Sue Beavis

Penny Bell
12 Oast House Close, Wraysbury, Staines TW19 5BX
t 01784 483168 **f** 01784 483168 **m** 07850 902384

Sarah Berry
145 Hydethorpe Road, Balham, London SW12 0JF
t 020 8673 5058 **f** 020 8675 4446 **m** 07767 264474
e sarah@make-up-artist.com **w** www.make-up-artist.com
Credits The Mummy (F); Blade 2 (F)

Chrissie Beveridge
EXEC, 6 Travis Court, Farnham Royal SL2 3SB
t 01753 646677 **f** 01753 646770
e sue@execmanagement.co.uk **w** www.execmanagement.co.uk

Allen Bills
Rose Cottage, Cleeve Road, Downend, Bristol BS16 6AD
t 0117 9551 700 **f** 0117 9560 805 **m** 07767 793034
e dauphine@lineone.co.uk

Madeleine Bills
Rose Cottage, Cleeve Road, Downend, Bristol BS16 6AD
t 0117 9551 700 **f** 0117 9560 805 **m** 07767 793034
e dauphine@lineone.co.uk

Barry Bish
t 020 7608 3434 **f** 018 8425 1221
e hers@hersagency.co.uk **w** www.hersagency.co.uk

Christine Blundell
International Creative Management Ltd, Oxford House, 76 Oxford Street, London W1D 1BS
t 020 7636 6565 **f** 020 7323 0101 **w** www.icmlondon.co.uk
Credits The Full Monty (F); Topsy-Turvy (F); Neverland (F)

Claire Bonser
16 Seymour Road, Southfields, London SW18 5JA
t 020 8877 9514 **m** 07931 728965

Jane Bradley
Mandy Coakley Represents, 18 Mandeville Courtyard, Warriner Gardens, London SW11 4NB
t 020 7720 6234 **f** 020 7720 0199
e mc@mandycoakley.co.uk **w** www.mandycoakley.co.uk

Sally-Anne Bragg
10 Arundel Road, Camberley GU15 1DL
t 0 1276 26852 **e** sabragg@talk21.com

Veronica Brebner
Peters Fraser & Dunlop, Drury House, 34-43 Russell Street, London WC2B 5HA
t 020 7344 1000 **f** 020 7836 9543
e postmaster@pfd.co.uk **w** www.pfd.co.uk

Fay De Bremaeker
131 Beauchamp Road, West Molesey KT8 2PJ
t 020 8979 0883 **f** 020 8979 0883 **m** 07973 361751
e faydebee@aol.com
Credits Second Nature (F); The Rocket Post (F); Spooks (T)

Karen Sherriff Brown
Willow End Fagnall Lane, Winchmore Hill, Amersham HP7 0PG
t 01494 433232 **f** 01494 433232 **m** 07802 712586
e ge.brown@ntlworld.com
Credits Below (F); 40 (T); Calendar Girls (F)

Karen Bryan-Dawson
EXEC, 6 Travis Court, Farnham Royal SL2 3SB
t 01753 646677 **f** 01753 646770
e sue@execmanagement.co.uk **w** www.execmanagement.co.uk

Ann Buchanan
International Creative Management Ltd, Oxford House, 76 Oxford Street, London W1D 1BS
t 020 7636 6565 **f** 020 7323 0101 **w** www.icmlondon.co.uk
Credits Four Weddings And A Funeral (F); Killing Me Softly (F); Shadow Of The Vampire (F)

Evelyn Burns
84A Stranmillis Road, Belfast BT9 5AD
e evelyn@susanrainey.com

Linda Burns
Dinedor Management, 81 Oxford Street, London W10 2EU
t 020 7851 3575 **f** 020 7851 3576
e info@dinedor.com **w** www.dinedor.com
Credits Sex Talk (T); Moviewatch (T); Audi (C); Archers (C)

Lou Burton
Gems, The Media House, 87 Glebe Street, Penarth CF64 1EF
t 029 2071 0770 **f** 029 2071 0771
e gems@gems-agency.co.uk **w** www.gems-agency.co.uk
Credits Mile High (T); Angel For May (F); Devils Gate (F); Charlie (F)

Lois Burwell
International Creative Management Ltd, Oxford House, 76 Oxford Street, London W1D 1BS
t 020 7636 6565 **f** 020 7323 0101 **w** www.icmlondon.co.uk
Credits Saving Private Ryan (F); Almost Famous (F); Catch Me If You Can (F)

Tricia Cameron
94 Hallowell Road, Northwood HA6 1DU
t +44 1923 **f** 01923 842607 **m** 07860 831454
e tricia.cameron@btinternet.com
Agent EXEC, 6 Travis Court, Farnham Royal SL2 3SB
t 01753 646677 **f** 01753 646770
e sue@execmanagement.co.uk **w** www.execmanagement.co.uk
Credits Brassed Off (F); 102 Dalmatians (F); The Mummy Returns (F); Shanghai Knights (F)

Elaine Carew
Wizzo & Co, 35 Old Compton Street, London W1D 5JX
t 020 7437 2055 **f** 020 7437 2066
e wizzo@wizzoandco.co.uk **w** www.wizzoandco.co.uk

Dawn Carl
38 Southern Drive, Loughton IG9 5BD
m 07956 340146

Angela Carradus
6 Hawthorn Gardens, Briery Meadows, Kendal LA9 6FG
t 01539 736332 **m** 07976 908897 **e** angela@artyfaces.com
Credits Ashford Entertainment (I); MVC (C); Cheeky's Angels (T)

Anna Castiello
t 0208 693 5385 **f** 0208 693 5385 **m** 07973 753143

Centre Stage Make-Up / Hair Training Studio
Brownings Farm, Blackboys, Uckfield TN22 5HG
t 01825 890080 **m** 07803 179292
Contact J Neame, Principal

My make-up and hair courses take students to a professional level. This means they are already working on productions before they finish their course. It is run more like an apprentice situation and the course takes one and a half years (part-time) to complete. All my students become successful make-up and hair artists. A prospectus can be sent and finance arranged.

Kirstin Chalmers
4 Florence Road, Stroud Green, London N4 4BU
t 020 7263 1766 **f** 020 7263 1766 **m** 07767 893786
e kirstinchalmers@cakes.demon.co.uk
Credits My Kingdom (F); Last Minute (F); Blackball (F)

Shirley Channing-Williams
137 Avenue Road, Acton, London W3 8QJ
t 020 8993 7861 **f** 020 8993 7961 **m** 07773 217 082

Diane Chenery-Wickins
Callbox Communications Limited, 66 Shepperton Studios, Studios Road, Shepperton TW17 0QD
t 01932 592572 **f** 01932 569655 **m** 07710 572572
e callboxdiary@btinternet.com **w** www.callboxdiary.co.uk

Sarah-Lee Coleman
Mandy Coakley Represents, 18 Mandeville Courtyard, Warriner Gardens, London SW11 4NB
t 020 7720 6234 **f** 020 7720 0199
e mc@mandycoakley.co.uk **w** www.mandycoakley.co.uk

Hajera Coovadia
Interactive Casting Universal, 386 The Water Gardens, Norfolk Crescent, London W2 2DL
t 020 7402 3006 **f** 020 7402 3006 **m** 07779 095924
e hajera@btconnect.com
Credits Indian Film (F); Bollywood Awards (T); Handle With Care (T); Such A Long Journey (F)

Louise Constad
Mandy Coakley Represents, 18 Mandeville Courtyard, Warriner Gardens, London SW11 4NB
t 020 7720 6234 **f** 020 7720 0199
e mc@mandycoakley.co.uk **w** www.mandycoakley.co.uk

Mary Cooper
Grove Barrs, South Road, Horsall GU21 4JN
t 01473 766244 **m** 07860 841494

Carol Cooper
CCA Management, 7 St George's Square, London SW1V 2HX
t 020 7630 6303 **f** 020 7630 7376

Yvonne Coppard
25 Coronation Rise, Great Waldingfield, Sudbury CO10 0XT
t 01787 372570

Pauline Cox
Mill Reach, Molember Road, East Molesey KT8 9NH
t 020 8398 8389 **f** 020 8873 8862 **m** 07976 988658
BBC-trained designer, make-up hairdressing prosthetics, French and German speaking (enough to get by).

Daphne Croker-Saunders
40 Archfield Road, Cotham, Bristol BS6 6BE
t 0117 9422 398 **f** 0117 9244 966 **m** 07808 466158

Julia Cruttenden
15 Waldemar Road, Ealing, London W13 9PZ
t 020 8398 8389 **f** 020 8398 8389 **m** 07973 636778

Konnie Daniel
Gems, The Media House, 87 Glebe Street, Penarth CF64 1EF
t 029 2071 0770 **f** 029 2071 0771
e gems@gems-agency.co.uk **w** www.gems-agency.co.uk
Credits Tales From Pleasure Beach (T); Diary Of A Somebody (F); The Mother (F); The Strastosphere Girl (F)

Julie Dartnell
10 Suffolk Combe, Warfield, Bracknell RG42 3TW
t 01344 444983 **f** 01344 444983 **m** 07801 354960

Suzie Davies
Flat 8, 55 Woodland Gardens, Muswell Hill, London N10 3UE
t 020 8442 1661 **m** 07956 120698

Penny Delemar-Shawyer
24 Imperial Square, Fulham, London SW6 2AE
t 020 7736 1893

Linda Devetta
1 Acacia Road, St John's Wood, London NW8 6AD
t 020 7722 4662 **f** 020 7586 0546 **m** 07785 251420
e lindanw8@aol.com
Credits The World Is Not Enough (F); Heartbreakers (F); And Now...Ladies & Gentlemen! (F)

Sarah Dickinson
40 Elder Road, London SE27 9ND
t 020 8670 5117 **m** 07973 866692

Sophie Dingwall
Callbox Communications Limited, 66 Shepperton Studios, Studios Road, Shepperton TW17 0QD
t 01932 592572 **f** 01932 569655 **m** 07710 572572
e callboxdiary@btinternet.com **w** www.callboxdiary.co.uk

Carolyn Dolby
87 Studdridge Street, London SW6 3TD
t 020 7384 3926 **m** 07939 289646

Samantha Dolding
24 Kenton Gardens, St Albans AL1 1JS
t 01727 850473 **m** 07932 941435 **e** samantha@dolding44.freeserve.co.uk

Lisa Dredge
2F Dalgarno Way, London W10 5HG
t 020 8968 7320 **m** 07885 305174
e lisadredge@btopenworld.com
Agent Stella's Diary, 9 Hormead Road, London W9 3NG
t 020 8969 1855 **f** 020 8964 2157 **m** 07885 305174
e stella'sdiary@btinternet.com
Credits Ikea (C); Comet (C); Volvo (C); Lufthansa (C)

Kathy Ducker
Moorside, 11 Cockey Moor Road, Starling, Bury BL8 2HD
t 0161 764 8429 **f** 0161 764 5080 **m** 07885 258950
e kathy@pducker.fsnet.co.uk
Credits At Home With The Braithwaites (T); Blood Strangers; Cutting It Series II (T)

Anne Edwards
33 Westbury Road, New Malden KT3 5AX
t 020 8942 2131 **m** 07801 884914

Bean Ellis
Wizzo & Co, 35 Old Compton Street, London W1D 5JX
t 020 7437 2055 **f** 020 7437 2066
e wizzo@wizzoandco.co.uk **w** www.wizzoandco.co.uk

Paul Engelen
Hawkins Barn, Stovold Hill, Cranleigh GU6 8LE
t 01483 274677 **f** 01483 274677 **m** 08850 867337

Mark English
Flat 23, 30 Grafton Way, London WC1E 6DX
t 020 7388 5903 **f** 020 7388 5903 **m** 07973 739152
e pixie001english@hotmail.com
Credits Goodbye Mr Chips (T)

Sandra Exelby
68 Sarsfield Road, Perivale UB6 7AG
t 020 8998 7494 **m** 07721 623728 **e** sandraxlb@nasmah.org.uk
Credits Highlander (F); Supply And Demand (T); Back to The Secret Garden (T); Feris Bela Gawd (Egypt) (T)

Lica Fensome
Mandy Coakley Represents, 18 Mandeville Courtyard, Warriner Gardens, London SW11 4NB
t 020 7720 6234 **f** 020 7720 0199
e mc.mandycoakley.co.uk **w** www.mandycoakley.co.uk

Emma Ferguson
Flat 9, Princes Gate, Brompton Way, Handforth, Wilmslow SK9 3NB
t 01625 530562 **m** 07768 506901
Credits Buried (T); The Parole Officer (F); Playing The Field (T); Cutting It - Series I (T)

Robert Frampton
Mandy Coakley Represents, 18 Mandeville Courtyard, Warriner Gardens, London SW11 4NB
t 020 7720 6234 **f** 020 7720 0199
e mc@mandycoakley.co.uk **w** www.mandycoakley.co.uk

Caroline Frazer
Flat 3, 9 Eton Avenue, London NW3 3EL
t 020 7794 4240 **f** 020 7794 4240 **m** 07970 888263
e frazercaroline@hotmail.com
Credits Life Laundry (T); Eurostar (C); Have I Got News For You (T); The Reckoning (F)
10 years experience, including fashion shows and celebrity photographic stills.

Magdelen Gaffney
24 Powis Terrace, London W11 0QA
t 020 7221 8289

Lisa George
m 07989 434597
e lisa.george100@virgin.net **w** www.lisageorge.co.uk
Credits Bad Girls (T); The Virgin Of Liverpool (F); Carpet Right (C)

Tracey Gifford
93 Gipsy Hill, London SE19 1QL
m 07968 016919

Renata Gilbert
58 Mead Way, Bushey WD23 2DP
t 01923 218 411 **f** 01923 218 411 **m** 07973 744823
e renatagilbert@btinternet.com **e** renata@nuttynut.com
Credits The Importance Of Being Earnest (F); Band Of Brothers (T)

Nikki Gooley
International Creative Management Ltd, Oxford House, 76 Oxford Street, London W1D 1BS
t 020 7636 6565 **f** 020 7323 0101 **w** www.icmlondon.co.uk

Grant Mason Make-Up Effects
Scottish Mask & Puppet Theatre Centre, 8-10 Balcarres Avenue, Kelvindale, Glasgow G12 0QF
t 0141 357 3757 **f** 0141 357 4484 **e** mason_grant@hotmail.com
Contact Grant Mason

Amanda Green
Dinedor Management, 81 Oxford Street, London W10 2EU
t 020 7851 3575 **f** 020 7851 3576
e info@dinedor.com **w** www.dinedor.com
Credits Daily Mail (C); Dove (C); Watercolours Challenge (T); Crimewatch (T)

Shelley Greenham
1 Linnet Close, Bushey WD23 1AX
t 020 8950 1645 **f** 020 8950 4344 **m** 07802 447403
e shelley.greenham@tesco.net
Credits Baby Father (T); My Family (T)

Belinda Green-Smith
1 Totham Lodge, Richmond Road, London SW20 0PF
t 020 8947 0273 **f** 020 8947 0273 **m** 07764 483770
e belindawainscoat@skynow.net
Credits Tomorrow La Scala (T); We Are Family (S); The Engagement (F)

Pamela Haddock
22 Cotham Road South, Cotham, Bristol B56 5TZ
t 0117 924 9917 **m** 07771 548181
Agent Gems, The Media House, 87 Glebe Street, Penarth CF64 1EF
t 029 2071 0770 **f** 029 2071 0771
e gems@gems-agency.co.uk **w** www.gems-agency.co.uk
Credits Nicholas Nickleby (T); Anazapta (F); Plots With A View (F)

Felicity Hague
17 Beacon Hill, Ovingdean, Brighton BN2 7BN
t 01273 390276 **m** 07941 279875 **e** flickhague@talk21.com

Gill Hall
On Oaks, Oakley Green Road, Oakley Green, Windsor SL4 4PZ
t 01773 859225 **m** 07970 793203

Gabrielle Hamilton
2 St Anne's Green, Headingley, Leeds LS4 2SD
t 0113 275 4871 **f** 0113 275 4871 **m** 07768 238824
e lady@gabrielle-hamilton.com
Credits Goodnight Sweetheart (T); Days Like These (T); My Family (T)

Fae Hammond
Vernons, Penton Newsey, Andover SP11 0RQ
t 01264 771397 **f** 01264 771397 **m** 07711 675466
e faehammond@cs.com
Credits Swept Away (F); Buffalo Soldiers (F); Nights Tale (T)

Maureen Hannaford-Naisbett
13 Oxford Road, Teddington TW11 0QA
t 020 8977 6358

Jan Harrison-Shell
2 Railwayside, Barnes, London SW13 0PN
t 020 8878 9048

Sam Haselhurst
21 Grand Court West, Grand Drive, Leigh-on-Sea SS9 1BQ
t 01702 714828 **m** 07980 064877

Nigel Herbert
Callbox Communications Limited, 66 Shepperton Studios, Studios Road, Shepperton TW17 0QD
t 01932 592572 **f** 01932 569655 **m** 07710 572572
e callboxdiary@btinternet.com **w** www.callboxdiary.co.uk

Maureen Hetherington
50 Woodland Terrace, Charlton, London SE7 8EN
t 020 8317 8084 **f** 020 8317 8084 **m** 07774 952251
Credits Good Night Mr. Tom (T); Romeo & Juliet (T); Morse (T); Dead Gorgeous (T)

Pauline Heys
46 Wycombe Road, Prestwood, Great Missenden HP16 0PQ
t 01494 862246 **f** 01494 868411 **m** 07787 543 600
e paulineheys@aol.com
Credits Samurai (F); Saving Private Ryan (F); Daniel Deronda (T); Captain Corelli's Mandolin (F)

Mary Hillman
23 Cambridge Park Court, Cambridge Park, East Twickenham TW1 2JN
t 020 8892 8752 **f** 020 8892 8752 **m** 07710 412961
e mary.hillman@1name.com

Brigitte Hopkins
22A St Augustines Drive, Broxbourne EH10 7NA
t 01992 448241 **f** 01992 448241 **m** 07979 426568

Jo Houtmeyers
37 Pinewood Park, New Haw KT15 3BS
m 07932 848094 **e** jo@visages.co.uk **w** www.visages.co.uk
Credits The Killing Time (D); Hollyoaks (T); Family Affairs (T)

Stella Hunter
99 Fulmers Hill, Chesham HP5 1LS
t 01494 783559

Hybrid Enterprises Ltd
Units 26-27 Armley Workshops, Pickering Street, Leeds LS12 2QG
t 0113 217 1300 **t** 01277 654862
f 0113 217 1300 **m** 07870 600 273
e studio@hybridfx.com **w** www.hybridfx.com
Contact Mike Stringer, Technical Director; Mike Bates, Production Director; Ryk Fortuna, Lead Sculptor/Technician
Credits The National Geographic (D); The Royal (T); Ant 'N' Dec's Saturday Night Takeaway (T); The Two Towers (F)

Yasmin Iqbal
Strucksbarg 49, Hamburg 21077, Germany
m 07776 250632 **e** yasminiq99@yahoo.com
Credits Dog Race (C); Darklands (F); Hidden City (T); Murder In Mind (T)

Lynne Jackett
Gems, The Media House, 87 Glebe Street, Penarth CF64 1EF
t 029 2071 0770 **f** 029 2071 0771
e gems@gems-agency.co.uk **w** www.gems-agency.co.uk
Credits Brookside (T); Planet Mirth (T); Cleopatra (T); Runaway (F)

Colin Jamison
Tremartyn, Hammersley Lane, Penn HP10 8HB
t 01494 813293

Suzanne Jansen
Creative Media Management, Unit 3B, Walpole Court, Ealing Studios, Ealing Green, London W5 5ED
t 020 8584 5363 **f** 020 8566 5554
e enquiries@creativemediamanagement.com
Credits Le Garçon Avec Les Yeux Gris (F); Two Brothers (F); The War Bride (F)

Sallie Jaye
117 Wymering Mansions, Wymering Street, Maida Vale, London W9 2NF
t 020 7266 4635 **f** 020 7266 4635 **m** 07974 402063
e s@jaye.demon.co.uk
Credits Ella Enchanted (F); Jonny English (F); Gosford Park (F); 28 Days Later (F)

Vannessa Johnson
12 Eunice Grove, Chesham HP5 1RL
m 07976 251727 **e** evanessaajohnson@hotmail.com
Credits The Crooked Man (T); Without Motive (T); My Dad Is The Prime Minister (T); Ultimate Force (T)

Meinir Jones-Lewis
Creative Media Management, Unit 3B, Walpole Court, Ealing Studios, Ealing Green, London W5 5ED
t 020 8584 5363 **f** 020 8566 5554
e enquiries@creativemediamanagement.com
Credits Insiders (F); Servants (T); Rancid Aluminium (F)

Gina Kane
C/o Blunt Agency
t 020 8960 2041

Sandra Karuza
38 Francis Road, London E10 6PP
m 07867 774177

Stephanie Kaye
1 Westbrook Avenue, Hampton TW12 2RE
t 020 8941 4938

Teressa Kelly
Hadleigh Close, Merton park, London SW20 9AW
t 020 8543 1996

Julie Kendrick
3 Rosslyn Road, Whitwick LE67 5PU
t 01530 834701 **m** 07977 042962

Marianne Kerr
Experience Counts - Call Me Ltd, 5th Floor, 41-42 Berners Street, London W1P 3AA
t 020 7637 8112 **f** 020 7580 2582

Jan Keys
Callbox Communications Limited, 66 Shepperton Studios, Studios Road, Shepperton TW17 0QD
t 01932 592572 **f** 01932 569655 **m** 07710 572572
e callboxdiary@btinternet.com **w** www.callboxdiary.co.uk

Mel Kinsman
Stella's Diary, 9 Hormead Road, London W9 3NG
t 020 8969 1855 **f** 020 8964 2157 **m** 07785 990178
e stella'sdiary@btinternet.com

Mel Kinsman
17 Chepstow Crescent, London W11 3EA
t 020 7221 7021 **m** 07785 990178
Credits Oil of Olay - Touch (C)

Kathy Kneller
Gems, The Media House, 87 Glebe Street, Penarth CF64 1EF
t 029 2071 0770 **f** 029 2071 0771
e gems@gems-agency.co.uk **w** www.gems-agency.co.uk
Credits Hidden City (T); Doctors (T); The Bill (T); Murphy's Law (T)

Cor Kwakernaak
t 020 7608 3434 **f** 018 8425 1221
e hers@hersagency.co.uk **w** www.hersagency.co.uk

Melissa Lackersteen
17 Glencoe Road, Weybridge KT13 8JY
t 01932 828117 **f** 01932 828117 **m** 07774 235681
e lackersteen@aol.com
Credits Lara Croft: Tomb Raider (F); Helen Of Troy (T); Cold Mountain (F); Die Another Day (F)

Mary Ellen Lamb
Flat 2, 3 Market Yard Mews, London SE1 3TJ
t 020 7403 1249 **m** 07718 862239 **e** melamb@ukonline.co.uk
Credits Fly Fishing

Lesley Lamont-Fisher
Creative Media Management, Unit 3B, Walpole Court, Ealing Studios, Ealing Green, London W5 5ED
t 020 8584 5363 **f** 020 8566 5554
e enquiries@creativemediamanagement.com
Credits Veru (F); Stella Street (F); The Warrior (F)

Leanne Lauri
64 Walton Street, Shadlands, Glasgow G41 3LS
m 07905 013447
e leannelauri2000@yahoo.co.uk
w www.geocities.com/leannelauri
Credits Wheel Of Fortune (T); Brookside (T); The Duel (S); In The Dark (F)

Amanda Lennox
East Kirkton, Auchterarder PH3 1DY
t 01764 662549 **m** 07762 850025

Denise Lilley
Mandy Coakley Represents, 18 Mandeville Courtyard, Warriner Gardens, London SW11 4NB
t 020 7720 6234 **f** 020 7720 0199
e mc@mandycoakley.co.uk **w** www.mandycoakley.co.uk

Tony Lilley
Gems, The Media House, 87 Glebe Street, Penarth CF64 1EF
t 029 2071 0770 **f** 029 2071 0771
e gems@gems-agency.co.uk **w** www.gems-agency.co.uk
Credits Young Adam (F); Human Traffic (F); An Ideal Husband (F); Is Harry On The Boat (T)

Katy Limmer
Wizzo & Co, 35 Old Compton Street, London W1D 5JX
t 020 7437 2055 **f** 020 7437 2066
e wizzo@wizzoandco.co.uk **w** www.wizzoandco.co.uk

Susanna Lindstrom
SBFC, Unit 8, Sandhurst House, Wolsey Street, London E1 3BD

Tanya Lodge
Callbox Communications Limited, 66 Shepperton Studios, Studios Road, Shepperton TW17 0QD
t 01932 592572 **f** 01932 569655 **m** 07710 572572
e callboxdiary@btinternet.com **w** www.callboxdiary.co.uk

Jane Logan
74 Dorien Road, Raynes Park, London SW20 8EJ
t 020 8542 4388 **f** 020 8542 4388 **m** 07958 313444
e janey.logan@virgin.net

Charlotte Lowes
Mandy Coakley Represents, 18 Mandeville Courtyard, Warriner Gardens, London SW11 4NB
t 020 7720 6234 **f** 020 7720 0199
e mc@mandycoakley.co.uk **w** www.mandycoakley.co.uk

Corrine Lucy-Howlett
43 Belgrave Close, Walton-on-Thames KT12 5PH
t 01932 223140 **m** 07756 808115

Ashley Mae-Palmer
Callbox Communications Limited, 66 Shepperton Studios, tudios Road, Shepperton TW17 0QD
t 01932 592572 **f** 01932 569655 **m** 07710 572572
e callboxdiary@btinternet.com **w** www.callboxdiary.co.uk

Make-Up Artists Provisions Ltd
6 Goldhawk Mews, Shepherds Bush, London W12 7EA
t 020 8740 0802

Antonia Malyon
23 Bembridge Close, Great Sankey, Warrington WA5 3RH
t 01925 724915 **m** 07860 733972
Credits Journey (S); Crossroads (T); The World of Lee Evans (T); Brothers and Sisters (T)

Eva Marieges-Moore
6 Richmond Avenue, Wimledon Chase, London SW20 8LA
t 020 8286 7181

Sharon Martin
Creative Media Management, Unit 3B, Walpole Court, Ealing Studios, Ealing Green, London W5 5ED
t 020 8584 5363 **f** 020 8566 5554
e enquiries@creativemediamanagement.com
Credits White Teeth (T); Red Cap (T); Final Demand (T)

Robert McCann
International Creative Management Ltd, Oxford House, 76 Oxford Street, London W1D 1BS
t 020 7636 6565 **f** 020 7323 0101 **w** www.icmlondon.co.uk
Credits The Others (F); Panic Room (F); Cold Mountain (F)

Maureen McGill
38 Somerton Avenue, Richmond TW9 4QP
t 020 8876 2241 **f** 020 8876 2241 **m** 07850 484419
e maureen.m.mcgill@btinternet.com

Ian McIntosh
Dinedor Management, 81 Oxford Street, London W10 2EU
t 020 7851 3575 **f** 020 7851 3576
e info@dinedor.com **w** www.dinedor.com
Credits Braun (C); L'Oreal Fructis (C); CD:UK (T); Top Of The Pops (T)

Deborah McKinlay
40 Lingwood Close, Bassett, Southampton SO16 7GJ
t 023 8076 0841 **m** 07768 796118

Pam Meager
9 Westfield Road, Acton, London W3 0AP
t 020 8993 0026

Kym Menzies
Mandy Coakley Represents, 18 Mandeville Courtyard, Warriner Gardens, London SW11 4NB
t 020 7720 6234 **f** 020 7720 0199
e mc@mandycoakley.co.uk **w** www.mandycoakley.co.uk

Sarah Monzani
EXEC, 6 Travis Court, Farnham Royal SL2 3SB
t 01753 646677 **f** 01753 646770
e sue@execmanagement.co.uk **w** www.execmanagement.co.uk

Lisa Moore
Mandy Coakley Represents, 18 Mandeville Courtyard, Warriner Gardens, London SW11 4NB
t 020 7720 6234 **f** 020 7720 0199
e mc@mandycoakley.co.uk **w** www.mandycoakley.co.uk

Linda A Morton
Gems, The Media House, 87 Glebe Street, Penarth CF64 1EF
t 029 2071 0770 **f** 029 2071 0771
e gems@gems-agency.co.uk **w** www.gems-agency.co.uk
Credits The Queen's Nose (T); Nightswimming (T); Miss Monday (T); Criminals (F)

Elisabeth Moss
63 Duke Road, Chiswick, London W4 2BN
t 020 8994 7401

Deborah Murphy
7A Lindley Road, Walton-on-Thames KT12 3EZ
t 01932 232369 **f** 01932 232369 **m** 07966 396447
e desmakeup@aol.com

David Myers
Peters Fraser & Dunlop, Drury House, 34-43 Russell Street, London WC2B 5HA
t 020 7344 1000 **f** 020 7836 9543
e postmaster@pfd.co.uk **w** www.pfd.co.uk

Nila Maria Myin
165A Moselle Avenue, London N22 6EY
f 020 8881 9354 **m** 07774 842778
e beyondtheline@hotmail.com
Contact John Sweeney, Producer/Director
Credits The Devils Music (F); Those Without Shadows (F)

Judy Neame
Centre Stage Make-Up Studio, Browning Farm Craft Centre, Blackboys, Uckfield TN22 5HG
t 01825 890080 **f** 01435 812165 **m** 07803 179292

Fran Needham
6 Oaklands Road, East Sheen, London SW14 8NJ
t 020 8876 4552 **f** 020 8876 4552 **m** 07778 165277
Credits Dead Gorgeous (T); Jonathan Creek (T); Great Expectations (T); All The King's Men (T)

Jan Nethercot
47 River Park, Marlborough SN8 1NH
t 01672 514019 **f** 01672 514019 **e** jan.nethercot@virgin.net

Dorka Nieradzik
Gems, The Media House, 87 Glebe Street, Penarth CF64 1EF
t 029 2071 0770 **f** 029 2071 0771
e gems@gems-agency.co.uk **w** www.gems-agency.co.uk
Credits Foyle's War (T); Circle Of Friends (F); Wild Flowers (F); I'll Sleep When I'm Dead (F)

Nosh
Callbox Communications Limited, 66 Shepperton Studios, Studios Road, Shepperton TW17 0QD
t 01932 572572 **f** 01932 592572 **m** 07710 572572
e callboxdiary@btinternet.com **w** www.callboxdiary.co.uk

Pru Oliver
Suz Cruz, Halliford Studios, Manygate Lane, Shepperton TW17 9EG
t 01932 252577 **f** 01932 253323 **m** 07956 485593
e zoe@suzcruz.co.uk **w** www.suzcruz.co.uk

Suzi Owen
18A Chandos Avenue, Ealing, London W5 4ER
t 020 8568 0810 **m** 07973 669686 **e** suzi@net-west.co.uk

Lindsay Painter
3 Springbok Farm, Alfold, Cranleigh GU6 8HT
t 01403 753985 **f** 01403 753340 **m** 07980 553574
e painterlindsay@hotmail.com
Agent Callbox Communications Limited, 66 Shepperton Studios, tudios Road, Shepperton TW17 0QD
t 01932 592572 **f** 01932 569655 **m** 07710 572572
e callboxdiary@btinternet.com **w** www.callboxdiary.co.uk

Daniel Parker
EXEC, 6 Travis Court, Farnham Royal SL2 3SB
t 01753 646677 **f** 01753 646770
e sue@execmanagement.co.uk **w** www.execmanagement.co.uk

Susan Parkinson
22 Radnor Gardens, Twickenham TW1 4NA
t 020 8891 0982 **m** 07976 248152 **e** parkisusan@aol.com

Camilla Pascucci
19 Pelham House, Mornington Avenue, London W14 8SP
t 020 7602 1878 **f** 020 7602 1878 **m** 07973 615148

Dennie Pasion
Wizzo & Co, 35 Old Compton Street, London W1D 5JX
t 020 7437 2055 **f** 020 7437 2066
e wizzo@wizzoandco.co.uk **w** www.wizzoandco.co.uk

Neil Patrick
1 Kent Street, Plaistow, London E13 8RL
t 020 8586 0215 **f** 020 8586 0215 **m** 07773 883091
e n.patrick@tesco.net

Pebbles
59 Stanley Road, East Sheen, London SW14 7EB
t 020 8878 6525 **f** 020 8876 8207 **m** 07774 697272
e mike@eccentricprods.co.uk
Credits Once Upon A Time In The Midlands (F); A Room For Romeo Brass (F); A Knight's Tale (F); Snatch (F)

Anita Perrett
Experience Counts - Call Me Ltd, 5th Floor, 41-42 Berners Street, London W1P 3AA
t 020 7637 8112 **f** 020 7580 2582

Daniel Phillips
Peters Fraser & Dunlop, Drury House, 34-43 Russell Street, London WC2B 5HA
t 020 7344 1000 **f** 020 7836 9543
e postmaster@pfd.co.uk **w** www.pfd.co.uk

Kymberley Piers Harlow
13 Anstey Road, Bear Cross, Bournemouth UB11 9HQ
t 01202 576371 **m** 07899 980161 **e** kymbersuk@yahoo.com
Credits Amoy Stir Fry (C); Sunset Heights (F); Hidden City (T); Dead In The Water (F)

Lisa Pickering
104 Elgin Avenue, Ashford TW15 1QG
t 01784 248535 **f** 01784 248535 **m** 07831 201851
Credits Elizabeth I (F); Man And Boy (T); Polyanna (T); Memory of Water (F)

Charlotte Pingriff
1 Kent Road, Plaistow, London E13 8RL
t 020 8586 0810 **m** 07773 981614 **e** charliepig@hotmail.com

Vivien Placks
Neva Villa, Summer Grove, Elstree WD6 3HH
t 020 8207 5502 **f** 020 8953 3819 **m** 07831 745884

Beverley Pond-Jones
Wizzo & Co, 35 Old Compton Street, London W1D 5JX
t 020 7437 2055 **f** 020 7437 2066
e wizzo@wizzoandco.co.uk **w** www.wizzoandco.co.uk

Gilly Popham
34 Claygate Road, Ealing, London W13 9XG
t 020 8579 0368 **m** 07961 428188 **e** hi@gillypopham.com

Premier Hair Make-Up & Styling
First Floor, 7-8 St Stephen's Mews, London W2 5QZ
t 020 7221 2333 **f** 020 7221 2444
e hms@premier-agency.com **w** www.premier-agency.com
Contact Marie Green; Lindsay Cruickshank, Director

Tina Prescott
Flat 7, Ahktar House, 131-135 Oxford Road, Manchester M1 7DY
t 0161 272 7422 **m** 07718 246490 **e** makeupartist43@aol.com

Paula Price
68 Severn Grove, Pontcanna, Cardiff CF11 9EP
t 029 2023 5099 **m** 07774 909310
Credits The Young Indiana Jones Chronicles (T); Band Of Brothers (T); The Importance of Being Earnest (F)

Rachels Make Up
32 New End Square, Hampstead, London NW3 1LS
f 020 7435 3669 **m** 07958 230919
e rachelsmakeup32@hotmail.com

Alison Rainey
Gems, The Media House, 87 Glebe Street, Penarth CF64 1EF
t 029 2071 0770 **f** 029 2071 0771
e gems@gems-agency.co.uk **w** www.gems-agency.co.uk
Credits Coming Down (F); Clancy's Kitchen (T); The Virgin Of Liverpool (F)

Pearl Rashbass
240 Caledonian Road, London N1 0NG
t 020 7278 2724

Claire Anne Ray
Mandy Coakley Represents, 18 Mandeville Courtyard, Warriner Gardens, London SW11 4NB
t 020 7720 6234 **f** 020 7720 0199
e mc@mandycoakley.co.uk **w** www.mandycoakley.co.uk

Redd
Callbox Communications Limited, 66 Shepperton Studios, Studios Road, Shepperton TW17 0QD
t 01932 592572 **f** 01932 569655 **m** 07710 572572
e callboxdiary@btinternet.com **w** www.callboxdiary.co.uk

Jeanette Redmond
15A Basement Flat, Raynam Road, Hammersmith, London W6 0HY
t 020 8741 7365 **m** 07946 226639 **e** j.redmond1@lcf.linst.ac.uk

Catrin Richards
589 Upper Richmond Road West, Richmond TW10 5DU
t 020 8287 8937 **m** 07850 683738
e catrinrichards@hotmail.com
Credits The Bill (T); A&E II (T)

Sian Richards
Creative Media Management, Unit 3B, Walpole Court, Ealing Studios, Ealing Green, London W5 5ED
t 020 8584 5363 **f** 020 8566 5554
e enquiries@creativemediamanagement.com
Credits Live From Baghdad (F); Silent Witness (T); Standing Room Only (F)

Dani Richardson
t 020 8840 8235 **m** 07802 535895
e dani@ukmakeupartist.com **w** www.ukmakeupartist.com

Steff Roeg
Wizzo & Co, 35 Old Compton Street, London W1D 5JX
t 020 7437 2055 **f** 020 7437 2066
e wizzo@wizzoandco.co.uk **w** www.wizzoandco.co.uk

Morag Ross
6 The Gables, Clapham Old Town, London SW4 0JX
t 020 7720 2497 **f** 020 7627 8415 **m** 07768 891129
e moragski@compuserve.com
Credits The Gift (F); Bandits (F); Charlotte Gray (F)

Kate Rudlin
58 Abbey Road, Chertsey KT16 8NG
t 01932 561105

Avril Russell
Meadow Cottage, Sibleys Green, Thaxted CM6 2MU
t 01371 830803 **m** 07808 801242

Julia Russell
50F Inveresk Road, Musselborough EH21 7BQ
t 0131 665 8816 **m** 07803 725152 **e** julesrussell@aol.com

RoseAnn Samuel
McKinney Macartney Management Ltd, The Barley Mow Centre, 10 Barley Mow Passage, London W4 4PH
t 020 8995 4747 **f** 020 8995 2414
e fkb@mmtechsrep.demon.co.uk
w www.mckinneymacartney.com

Catherine Scoble
Callbox Communications Limited, 66 Shepperton Studios, Studios Road, Shepperton TW17 0QD
t 01932 592572 **f** 01932 569655 **m** 07710 572572
e callboxdiary@btinternet.com **w** www.callboxdiary.co.uk

Emma Scott
Gems, The Media House, 87 Glebe Street, Penarth CF64 1EF
t 029 2071 0770 **f** 029 2071 0771
e gems@gems-agency.co.uk **w** www.gems-agency.co.uk
Credits Stig Of The Dump (T); 2000 Acres Of Sky (T); The Bee Stung Wasp (S); The Wedding Tackle (F)

Laura Jane Sessions
21 Stark Close, Diss IP22 4BY
t 01379 641092 **f** 020 7703 6873 **m** 07740 777910
e laurajanez@aol.com
Credits One Fine Day (S); Ink Me (M); Play (T)

Jan Sewell
EXEC, 6 Travis Court, Farnham Royal SL2 3SB
t 01753 646677 **f** 01753 646770
e sue@execmanagement.co.uk **w** www.execmanagement.co.uk

Angela Seyfang
12 Sydney Road, Teddington TW11 8PQ
t 020 8977 0703 **m** 07714 032050

Marella Shearer
t 020 7608 3434 **f** 018 8425 1221
e hers@hersagency.co.uk **w** www.hersagency.co.uk
Agent The Dench Arnold Agency, 24 D'Arblay Street, London
W1F 8EH
t 020 7437 4551 **f** 020 7439 1355 **w** www.dencharnold.co.uk

Shepperton Wig Company
114 Sheepwalk, Shepperton TW17 0AN
t 01932 237183 **f** 01932 254556
Contact Linda Cooley

Aaron Sherman
17 Tomswood Road, Chigwell IG7 5QP
t 020 8559 1942 **f** 020 8559 1943

Maralyn Sherman
17 Tomswood Road, Chigwell IG7 5QP
t 020 8559 1942 **f** 020 8559 1943 **m** 07713 989295

Jenny Shircore
McKinney Macartney Management Ltd, The Barley Mow
Centre, 10 Barley Mow Passage, London W4 4PH
t 020 8995 4747 **f** 020 8995 2414
e fkb@mmtechsrep.demon.co.uk **w** www.mckinneymacartney.com

Alison Smith
6 Woodside, Roffey, Horsham RH13 5UF
t 014903 264321 **m** 07860 527305

Claire Smith
27 Drayton Gardens, West Ealing, London W13 0LG
t 020 8998 6482 **m** 07961 160767

Rita Smith
27 Drayton Gardens, West Ealing, London W13 0LG
t 020 8998 6482 **m** 07778 280092

Penny Smith
Peters Fraser & Dunlop, Drury House, 34-43 Russell Street,
London WC2B 5HA
t 020 7344 1000 **f** 020 7836 9543
e postmaster@pfd.co.uk **w** www.pfd.co.uk

Barbara Southcott
Peters Fraser & Dunlop, Drury House, 34-43 Russell Street,
London WC2B 5HA
t 020 7344 1000 **f** 020 7836 9543
e postmaster@pfd.co.uk **w** www.pfd.co.uk

Jean Speak
26 Princedale Road, London W11 4NJ
t 020 7221 5942 **f** 020 7727 6095 **e** mojean@talk21.com
Credits William & Mary (T); Lorna Doone (T); Bait (T)

Helen Speyer
5 The Anglers, 57-61 High Street, Kingston-upon-Thames KT1 1NB
t 020 8541 3444 **f** 020 8541 3444 **m** 07973 910186
e helen.speyer1@orange.net

Anne Spiers
The Dench Arnold Agency, 24 D'Arblay Street, London W1F 8EH
t 020 7437 4551 **f** 020 7439 1355 **w** www.dencharnold.co.uk

Hilary Steinberg
6 Bartlett Cottages, St Albans Road, Barnet EN5 4LL
t 020 8441 0411

Sarah Stevens
Flat D, 11 Durham Terrace, London W1T 5PB
t 07967 392277 **e** sarah120477@hotmail.com

Mike Stringer
Hybrid Enterprises Ltd, Units 26-27 Armley Workshops,
Pickering Street, Leeds LS12 2QG
t 0113 217 1300 **t** 01277 654862
f 0113 217 1300 **m** 07870 600273
e studio@hybridfx.com **w** www.hybridfx.com
Credits Ant 'N' Dec's Saturday Night Takeaway (T); The National Geographic
(D); The Royal (T); The Two Towers (F)

Jane Summers
Bucks Green Cottage, Bucks Green, Bedingfield-Eye IP23 7LL
t 01728 628234 **m** 07836 729800

Elizabeth Tagg
McKinney Macartney Management Ltd, The Barley Mow
Centre, 10 Barley Mow Passage, London W4 4PH
t 020 8995 4747 **f** 020 8995 2414
e fkb@mmtechsrep.demon.co.uk **w** www.mckinneymacartney.com

Teresa Fairminer & Associates
94 Park Road, London W4 3HL
t 020 8747 4993
e tfassoc@dircow.co.uk **w** www.teresafairminer.com
Contact T Fairminer, Director
Credits Max Factor (C); Astor Cosmetics (C); Pantene (C); Olay (C)

Gillian Thomas
75 Hilliard Road, Northwood HA6 1SJ
t 01923 841001 **f** 01923 841001 **m** 07850 933955
e philbunker@hotmail.com
Credits Waking The Dead (T); Iris (F); Judge John Deeds (T)

Moira Thomson
Flat 2, Connaught Court, 14C Orford Road, Walthamstow,
London E17 9NS
t 020 8923 0190 **f** 020 8923 0190 **m** 07971 890672

Toko
t 020 7608 3434 **f** 018 8425 1221
e hers@hersagency.co.uk **w** www.hersagency.co.uk

Karen Z M Turner
Flat 4, 23 Ladbroke Crescent, London W11 1PS
t 020 7221 3206 **t** 01300 341081 **f** 020 7221 3109
m 07785 286232 **e** karenzmturner@aol.com
Agent Gems, The Media House, 87 Glebe Street,
Penarth CF64 1EF
t 029 2071 0770 **f** 029 2071 0771
e gems@gems-agency.co.uk **w** www.gems-agency.co.uk
Credits Lorna Doone (T); Servants (T); Galileo's Daughter (T); Beech On The Run (T)

Siân Turner
67 Gordon Road, West Bridgford, Nottingham NG2 5LQ
t 01159 142842 **m** 07831 855020
Credits Holby City (T); The Commander (T); Trial And Retribution IV (T); Anita
And Me (F)

Magi Vaughan
Gems, The Media House, 87 Glebe Street, Penarth CF64 1EF
t 029 2071 0770 **f** 029 2071 0771
e gems@gems-agency.co.uk **w** www.gems-agency.co.uk
Credits Jacob's Ladder (F); Adventures Inc (T); The Heather Mountain (F);
Downtime (F)

Alex Volpe
62 Carlyle Road, London W5 4BL
t 020 8568 3529 **f** 020 8568 3529

Christine Walmesley-Cotham
10 Pleydell Avenue, London W6 0XX
e cwc101@hotmail.com
Credits Peterloo (T); Waking The Dead (T); Manchild (T); Take A Girl Like You (T)

Serena Warwick
43 Vicarage Way, Colnbrook, Slough SL3 0RA
t 01753 591622 **m** 07956 008438

Geoffrey Waterman
25 Meredith Close, Hatch End, Pinner HA5 4RP
t 020 8421 1015

Norma Webb
7 Tylagarw Terrace, Pontyclun CF72 9HA
t 01443 222524 **f** 01443 222524 **m** 07802 403542
e norma.santner@virgin.net
Credits Tomorrow Never Dies (F); Gosford Park (F); Shanghai Knights (F);
Chocolat (F)

Christina Webster
36 Studios Road, Shepperton TW17 0QW
t 01932 569445 **f** 01932 701285 **m** 07771 708523
e christypink@chrissiewebster.co.uk
w www.chrissiewebster.co.uk
Credits Hetty Wainthroppe (T); Being April (T); The Face At The Window (T);
Holby City (T)

Sheelagh Wells
20A New Road, Brentford TW8 0NX
t 020 8847 6270 **m** 07979 504393

Bridget West
42 Kensington Place, London W8 7PR
t 020 7727 4280 **f** 020 7727 5047 **m** 07802 774008

Lisa Westcott
Cobbler's Cottage, Shoe Lane, East Hagbourne OX11 9LW
t 01235 512154 **f** 01235 512154 **m** 07774 869901
Credits Our Mutual Friend (T); Madness of King George (F); Wives & Daughters
(F); Shakespeare in Love (F)

Su Westwood
Gems, The Media House, 87 Glebe Street, Penarth CF64 1EF
t 029 2071 0770 **f** 029 2071 0771
e gems@gems-agency.co.uk **w** www.gems-agency.co.uk
Credits Foyles War (T); Jeffrey Archer Story (T); The I Inside (F); Susie Gold (F)

Xanthia White
75A Brondesbury Villas, Garden Flat, London NW6 6AG
t 020 7624 8258 **f** 020 7372 7876 **m** 07767 401181
e xanthia@makeup1.sflife.co.uk
Credits Waking The Dead (T); Absolutely Fabulous IV (T); Being April (T);
League Of Gentlemen Series III (T)

Vanessa White
40 Church Walk, Thames Ditton KT7 0NW
t 020 8339 0051 **f** 020 8339 0025 **m** 07802 768919
e nessiwhite@aol.com
Credits Jonathan Creek (T); The League of Gentlemen (T); Dr Terrible's House
of Horrible (T)

Eve Wignall
London
m 07885 819804
Credits Gladiatress (F); Hornblower (T); Dr Zhivago (T)

Kezia de Winne
Gems, The Media House, 87 Glebe Street, Penarth CF64 1EF
t 029 2071 0770 **f** 029 2071 0771
e gems@gems-agency.co.uk **w** www.gems-agency.co.uk
Credits Dwarfs (T); The Englishman Who Went Up A Hill But Came Down A
Mountain (F); Silas Marner (T); An Englishman Abroad (T)

Felicity Wright
London
t 020 7485 1954 **f** 020 7485 1954 **m** 07710 199216
e felicity@wrightf.freeserve.co.uk
Credits Waking The Dead Series III (T); The End Of The Affair (F); Shiner (F);
Hornblower Series III (T)

Lizzie Yianni Georgiou
47 Lancaster Avenue, Hadley Wood, Barnet EN4 0ER
t 020 8441 8707 **f** 020 8441 8707 **m** 07973 118148

Make-Up Assistants

Basia
Callbox Communications Ltd, 66 Shepperton Studios, Studios
Road, Shepperton TW17 0QD
t 01932 592572 **f** 01932 569655 **m** 07710 572572
e callboxdiary@btinternet.com **w** www.callboxdiary.co.uk

Kay Bilk
11 Tower Hill, Chipperfield WD4 9LT
m 07973 382848
Credits The Real Jane Austen (D); Waking The Dead (T); Calendar Girls (F)

Moray Binfield
19 Davis Close, Rothwell NN14 6TY
t 01536 507722 **m** 07986 945967
e moray.binfield3@ntlworld.com **w** www.bigbishop.com
Credits Closing Time (S); Roots Of Conflict (E); The Murder Of Thomas Beckett (E)

Georgina Dakeyne
m 07929 636819 **e** georgiedak@hotmail.com
Credits You're In My Seat (S); Cursed And Blessed (T)

Louise Dartford
344 Southborough Lane, Bromley BR2 8AA
t 020 8467 4482 **m** 07711 691488 **e** loudartford11@hotmail.com

Anwen Davies
10 Glanogwr Road, Bridgend CF31 3PF
t 01656 652545 **f** 01656 652545 **m** 07990 597 777
e anwendavies@supanet.com
Credits Up 'n' Under Film Llunion Lliw (F); Rampage (T); Belonging (T)

Annabel Hill
Gems, The Media House, 87 Glebe Street, Penarth CF64 1EF
t 029 2071 0770 **f** 029 2071 0771
e gems@gems-agency.co.uk **w** www.gems-agency.co.uk
Credits Doubledown (F); Dirty Pretty Things (F); The Girl With The Pearl Earing
(F); Holby City (T)

Lorraine Hill
Gems, The Media House, 87 Glebe Street, Penarth CF64 1EF
t 029 2071 0770 **f** 029 2071 0771
e gems@gems-agency.co.uk **w** www.gems-agency.co.uk
Credits TLC (T); Lenny Henry In Pieces (T); Dungeons And Dragons (F);
Revenge Of The Swedish Bikini Girls (F)

Gabbie Pall
e gabbiepall@hotmail.com

Vale
Wizzo & Co, 35 Old Compton Street, London W1D 5JX
t 020 7437 2055 **f** 020 7437 2066
e wizzo@wizzoandco.co.uk **w** www.wizzoandco.co.uk

Make-Up Prosthetics

Animated Extras
12 Shepperton Studios, Studios Road, Shepperton TW17 0QD
t 01932 592347 **f** 01932 572342
e animated.extras@virgin.net **e** info@animate-extras.com
Contact Nick Williams, Partner; Daniel Parker, Partner; Pauline Fowler, Partner

Arkane Effects

PO Box 140, Greenford UB6 9AL
t 020 8575 7550 **f** 020 8578 7880 **m** 07801 142401
e karl@arkanefx.com **w** www.arkanefx.com

Contact Deborah Hyde; Karl Derrick
Credits Gladiator (F); Harry Potter And The Prisoner Of Azkaban (F); Harry Potter And The Sorcerer's Stone (F)

Carter White FX

Shepperton Studios, Studios Road, Shepperton TW17 0QD
t 01932 562611 **f** 01932 568989 **m** 07973 193669
e carwhite@globalnet.co.uk **w** www.carterwhitefx.co.uk

Stuart Conran

61 Hyde Way, Wickford SS12 9BJ
t 01268 768130 **f** 01268 768130 **m** 07889 234459
e stucon@ukonline.co.uk

Credits Strange (T); The Hours (F); Saving Private Ryan (F); From Hell (F)

Jill Conway

21 Brancepeth Gardens, Buckhurst Hill IG9 5JL
t 020 8504 8555 **m** 07970 840 058 **e** jillconway@hotmail.com

Credits Casualty (T); Long Time Dead (F)

Coulier Creatures

Unit 2E, Building B, Wembley Commercial Centre, East Lane, North Wembley HA9 7UU
t 07973 115018 **f** 020 8908 2765
e mcoulier@dircon.co.uk **w** www.couliercreatures.com

Credits Star Wars: Episode I- The Phantom Menace (F); Harry Potter And The Philosopher's Stone (F); Stig of the Dump (T)

Creature Effects

Unit 2, 549 Eskdale Road, Uxbridge UB8 2RT
t 01895 251107 **f** 01895 251102 **m** 07771 757814
e creatfx@dircon.co.uk **w** www.creature-effects.com

Contact Alan Hedgcock, Partner; Cliff Wallace, Partner
Credits Aphex Twin - Come To Daddy (M); Black Hawk Down (F); 28 Days Later (F); Hairy Tale (F)

Fangs FX Ltd

2B Kenton Gardens, Kenton HA3 8DE
t 020 8907 4477 **f** 020 8907 4477 **m** 07831 858460
e info@fangsfx.com **w** www.fangsfx.com

Contact Chris Lyons, Director
Credits The Mummy Returns (F); Lenny Henry In Pieces I & II (T); Harry Potter And The Prisoner Of Azkaban (F); Harry Potter And The Philosopher's Stone (F)

Siobhan Harper Ryan

e siobhanharperryan@hotmail.com

Credits Tales Of Uplift And Moral Improvement (T); Leonardo's Dream Machines (T); Let's Write A Story (T); The Real Eve - Discovery Channel (T)

Hybrid Enterprises Ltd

Units 26-27 Armley Workshops, Pickering Street, Leeds LS12 2QG
t 0113 217 1300 **t** 01277 654862
f 0113 217 1300 **m** 07870 600 273
e studio@hybridfx.com **w** www.hybridfx.com

Contact Mike Stringer, Technical Director; Mike Bates, Production Director; Ryk Fortuna, Lead Sculptor/Technician
Credits The National Geographic (D); The Royal (T); Ant 'N' Dec's Saturday Night Takeaway (T); The Two Towers (F)

Groundbreaking close-up prosthetics using Hybrid's specialised silicone-designed to look, feel and move like natural skin. Also dental effects, creatures, design, bodies, key props, models, costume and materials technology.

Sinkka Ikaheima

Bere Court, Pangbourne RG8 8HT
t 0118 984 2393 **f** 0118 984 5190

Millenium FX Ltd

t 01494 775576 **f** 01494 775526 **m** 07768 848850
e nrgorton@aol.com

Contact Neill Gorton
Credits The League Of Extraordinary Gentlemen (F); The Actors (F); French And Saunders (T); Lara Croft And The Cradle Of Life: Tomb Raider II (F)

Nick Dudman/Pigs Might Fly

The Butchers Arms, The Old Shambles, Kendal LA9 4TA
t 01539 735105 **f** 01539 734674

Contact Sue Dudman, Partner; Nick Dudman, Partner
Credits Harry Potter And The Prisoner Of Azkaban (F); The Mummy Returns (F); Harry Potter And The Philosopher's Stone (F)

Mark Phillips

6 Ruscombe Close, Tunbridge Wells TN4 0SG
t 01892 619212 **m** 07767 606327
e mark@phillipsab.freeserve.co.uk

Credits Holby City (T)

Poland Dental Studio

1 Devonshire Place, London W1N 1PA
t 020 7935 6919 **f** 020 7486 3952

Geoff Portass MFX

Hill House, Heath Road, Hickling NR12 0YH
t 01692 598393 **f** 01692 598393 **m** 07050 155339
e mfx@btinternet.com **w** www.mfx.clara.co.uk

Credits Children Of Dune (T); Scratchy And Co (T); Hellraiser (F); Gladiator (F)

Janine Schneider

Wizzo & Co, 35 Old Compton Street, London W1D 5JX
t 020 7437 2055 **f** 020 7437 2066
e wizzo@wizzoandco.co.uk **w** www.wizzoandco.co.uk

Sherman Laboratories

t 020 8559 1942 **f** 020 8559 1943
e shermanfoams@btinternet.com

Contact Aaron Sherman, Director

Christopher Tucker

Bere Court, Pangbourne RG8 8HT
t 0118 984 2393 **f** 0118 984 5190

Victoria Voller

70 Boileau Road, Ealing, London W5 3AJ
t 020 8997 0197 **f** 020 8810 9997 **m** 07850 670999

Make-Up Suppliers

Cosmetics à la Carte

102 Avro House, Havelock Terrace, London SW8 4AS
t 020 7622 2318 **f** 020 7622 2318
e cosmetics@cosmeticsalacarte.com
w www.cosmeticsalacarte.com
Contact Christina Stewart, Managing Director

Charles H Fox

22 Tavistock Street, London WC2E 7PY
t 020 7240 3111 **f** 020 7379 3410
e sales@charlesfox.co.uk **w** www.charlesfox.co.uk

The Makeup Centre
52A Walham Grove, London SW6 1QR
t 020 7381 0213 **f** 020 7381 0213
e info@themake-upcentre.co.uk **w** www.themake-upcentre.co.uk
Contact David Shawyer, Managing Director

Mandy Coakley Represents
18 Mandeville Courtyard, Warriner Gardens, London SW11 4NB
t 020 7720 6234 **f** 020 7720 0199
e mandycoakley@aol.com **w** www.mandycoakley.com
Contact Lucy Roch, Booker; Jerry King, Director; Corinne Martin, Booker;
Mandy Coakley, Managing Director

MAP (Make-up Artist Provisions) Ltd
6 Goldhawk Mews, Shepherds Bush, London W12 8PA
t 020 8740 0808 **f** 020 8740 0802
e shop@makeup-provisions.com **w** www.makeup-provisions.com
Contact Niki Gallacher, Manager
Credits Harry Potter And The Philosopher's Stone (F)

Screenface
24 Powis Terrace, Notting Hill, London W11 1JH
t 020 7221 8289 **f** 020 7792 9357 **w** www.screenface.com
Contact John Danvers, Director
Credits Die Another Day (F); Harry Potter And The Prisoner Of Azkaban (F);
Harry Potter And The Chamber Of Secrets (F); Harry Potter And The
Philosopher's Stone (F)

MARKETING

Marketing Publicists

Bergmans
North House, 17 North Street East, Newcastle-upon-Tyne NE1 8DF
t 0191 232 1332 **f** 0191 232 8727 **m** 07947 114820
e bergmans@north-house.com **w** www.bergmans.co.uk
Contact Robin Ashby, Managing Partner

Big Blue Star Creative Marketing
Dunedin House, Harrow Yard, Akeman Street, Tring HP23 6AA
t 01442 826240 **f** 01442 823076 **m** 07702 252519
e admin@bigbluestar.co.uk **w** www.bigbluestar.co.uk
Contact Paul Goodwin, Managing Director

Big Life Pictures
67-69 Charlton Street, London NW1 1HY
t 020 7554 2100 **f** 020 7554 2154
e biglife@biglife.co.uk **w** www.biglife.co.uk
Contact Michelle Hudson, Fianance Director

The Braben Company
18B Pindock Mews, London W9 2PY
t 020 7289 1616 **f** 020 7289 1166
e firstname@braben.co.uk **w** www.braben.co.uk
Contact Matt Bourn, Managing Director; Sarah Braben, Chief Executive; Vicky
Hurley, Director

Bubble & Squeak Communications
Suite 325, Princess House, 50-60 Eastcastle Street, London
W1W 8EA
t 020 7636 0781 **f** 020 7636 0262
e sadie@bubblesqueak.co.uk **w** www.bubblesqueak.com
Contact Natalie Besbrode, Account Manager; Sadie Paris, Managing Director

C2U-Communications Consultancy Unlimited
PO Box 24382, London SW17 7FP
t 020 8673 0058 **f** 020 8673 0700 **m** 07770 541206
e ian@c2u.co.uk
Contact Ian Freeman, Partner

CJP Public Relations Ltd
Park House, 8 Grove Ash, Mount Farm, Milton Keynes MK1 1BZ
t 01908 275271 **f** 01908 275272
e info@cjppr.co.uk **w** www.cjppr.co.uk
Contact Theo Chalmens, Managing Director; Carolyn Jardine, Managing Director
Credits Gregory's Two Girls (F); Oklahoma! (F)

Susan d'Arcy
73 The Ridings, East Preston, Little Hampton BN16 2TW
t 01903 782994 **f** 01903 782994 **m** 07802 514407
e darcyfilm@aol.com
Credits Lara Croft And The Cradle Of Life: Tomb Raider 2 (F); The End Of The
Affair (F); The Tailor Of Panama (F)

Deborah Goodman Publicity
25 Glenmere Avenue, London NW7 2LT
t 020 8959 9980 **f** 020 8959 7875 **m** 07958 611218
e publicity@dgpr.co.uk
Contact Deborah Goodman
Credits Trance (F); The Bill (T); Badgirls (T); Footballers' Wives (T)

Dimes & Sillitoe Ltd
Clarendon House, 147 London Road, Kingston-upon-Thames
KT2 6NH
t 020 8481 1003 **f** 020 8546 8686
e info@dimes-sillitoe.com **w** www.dimes-sillitoe.com
Contact Nick Dimes, Managing Director; Sue Sillitoe, Editorial Director;
Leander Browning, Account Manager; PR Liason Manager

Francesca Smith Publicity
Church Barn, Harberton, Totnes TQ9 7SQ
t 01803 868652 **f** 01803 868444 **m** 07977 270526
e francescasmith2@compuserve.com
Contact Francesca Smith, Managing Director

Franklin Morrow Communications
55 Queen Anne Street, London W1G 9JR
t 020 7935 9368 **f** 0207935 9367
e janet@franklinmorrow.com
Contact Janet Morrow, Partner; Jill Franklin, Partner

GCI UK
30-34 Newbridge Street, London EC4V 6BJ
t 020 7072 4000 **f** 020 7072 4010 **w** www.gciuk.com
Contact Adrian Wheeler, CEO

Greg Day PR
153 Portnall Road, London W9 3BN
t 020 8960 3814 **f** 020 8960 2194 **m** 07889 861646
e greg@gregdaypr.co.uk **w** www.gregdaypr.co.uk
Contact Greg Day, Managing Director

Home Service
13 Holmesdale Road, Teddington TW11 9LJ
t 020 8255 5546 **f** 020 8943 4949 **m** 07860 228 754
e louis@yabuk.com
Contact Louis Austin, Proprietor

Joanna Kissin Public Relations
7 Erskine Hill, London NW11 6HA
t 020 8455 8532 **f** 020 8455 3136 **e** statkin@dircon.co.uk

Kirwin Media
10 Tower Court, London WC2H 9NU
t 020 7240 9224 **f** 020 7240 0979 **e** office@kirwinmedia.co.uk
Contact Lynne Kirwin; Chris Millard; Ryan Petersen

Link Us Publicity Consultants
17 Maple Close, Sandbach CW11 4JL
t 01270 750208 **f** 01270 750208 **m** 07976 266468
e mail@link-us.co.uk
Contact Rex Garratt, PR Consultant

McDonald & Rutter
34 Bloomsbury Street, London WC1B 3QJ
t 020 7637 2600 **f** 020 7637 3690
e info@mcdonaldrutter.com
Contact Jonathan Rutter, Partner; Charles McDonald, Partner
Credits Sylvia Plath Project (F); Bright Young Things (F); The Hours (F)

Merlin Digital Media
The Wharf, Schooner Way, Cardiff Bay, Cardiff CF10 4EU
t 029 2030 4050 **f** 029 2030 4051
e general@merlin-digital.co.uk **w** www.merlin-digital.co.uk
Contact Paul Cleverly, Director New Media; Catherine Tudor, Production Manager

Michael Peyton Associates
40 North End Road, London SW6 1LU
t 020 7610 2526 **f** 020 7637 1620 **m** 07961 187512
e flemingconnolly@hotmail.com
Contact Michael Peyton, Managing Director

Neil Reading PR
2-3 Golden Square, London W1F 9HR
t 020 7287 7711 **f** 020 7287 3184
e info@neilreadingpr.com
Contact Neil Reading, Chairman

Penelope James Public Relations
Wootton House, Wootton Lane, Wootton, Canterbury CT4 6RP
t 01303 844555 **f** 01303 844567 **e** pjpr@dial.pipex.com
Contact Penelope James, Managing Director

Premier PR
91 Berwick Street, London W1F ONE
t 020 7494 3478 **f** 020 7734 2024 **e** judy@prempr.co.uk
Contact Judy Mark, Office Manager
Credits Road To Perdition (F); Dirty Pretty Things (F); Catch Me If You Can (F); A Beautiful Mind (F)

Prince PR
11 Upper Camden Place, Bath BA1 5HX
t 01225 789200 **f** 01225 789300

QBO Bell Pottinger (Public Relations)
5th Floor, Holborn Gate, 26 Southampton Buildings, London WC2A 1BP
t 020 7861 2424 **f** 020 7861 2425
e tmorris@qbo-bellpottinger.co.uk **w** www.qbo-bellpottinger.co.uk

Roberts Laurence
7 Church Street, Empingham, Rutland LE15 8PN
t 01780 460777 **m** 07788 426847
e stephen@roblau.fsbusiness.co.uk
Contact Steve Roberts, Managing Director

Sue Hyman Associates Ltd
Suite 1, Waldorf Chambers, 11 Aldwych, London WC2B 4DA
t 020 7379 8420 **f** 020 7379 4944 **m** 07976 514 449
e sue.hyman@btinternet.com
Contact Sue Hyman, Managing Director

Tamesis PR
73 Wimpole Street, London W1G 8AZ
t 020 7908 3200 **f** 020 7908 3201
anthonyd@tamesis-pr.demon.co.uk
Contact Anthony Danaher, Senior Partner

tpr media consultants
3 Muswell Hill Road, London N6 5FJ
t 020 8347 7020 **f** 020 8347 6808 **m** 07974 428858
e enquiries@tpr-media.com **w** www.tpr-media.com
Contact Sophie Toumazis, Director

Warren Cowan/Phil Symes Associates
83 Charlotte Street, London W1T 4PR
t 020 7323 1200 **f** 020 7323 1070
e philsymes.cs@virgin.net
Contact Phil Symes, Managing Director
Credits Lucky Break (F); The Safety of Objects (F); Asoka (F)

WHD Publicity
PO Box 3035, Westminster, London SW1P 3BH
t 020 7799 3100 **f** 020 7976 0922
e news@whdpr.com **w** www.whdpr.com
Contact Willy Daly, Managing Director

Marketing Services

100 Percent Direct Marketing
124 Great Portland Street, London W1W 6PP
t 020 7631 3351 **f** 020 7436 9233
e a100percent@btinternet.com
Contact Michael Howe, Agency Head

232 Marketing
5 Tadcaster Court, Clarence Street, Richmond TW9 2SA
t 020 8948 8746 **m** 07710 043269
e nick232@ukonline.co.uk
Contact Nick Roberts, Product & Marketing Consultant

Allied Marketing Support Ltd
16 Longwater Lane, Finchampstead RG40 4NR
t 0118 973 2288 **f** 0118 973 1066
e info@alliedmarketing.co.uk **w** www.alliedmarketing.co.uk
Contact Hazel Cotton, Accounts Manager

Alpha Recording & Marketing
Units 1&2, Forest Industrial Park, Forest Road, Hainault IG6 3HL
t 020 8500 1981 **f** 020 8501 1319 **e** armco@globalnet.co.uk
Contact Jan Fonseca, Managing Director

Arnold Interactive
14 Welbeck Street, London W1G 9XU
t 020 7908 2700 **f** 020 7908 2701
e hello@arnoldinteractive.com **w** www.arnoldinteractive.com
Contact Ken Frakes, Managing Director; Angela Oliver; Bruce Winfield, Chief Executive Officer; Simon O'Regan, Chief Operations Officer
Credits British Sky Broadcasting Group (W); Warner Village Cinemas (W); Toyota Plc (W); Barclays Plc (W)

BCG/Creative Fx
10 Bocking End, Braintree CM7 9AA
t 01376 323461
e bcgfx@ntlworld.com **w** www.dspace.dial.pipex.com/bcgfx
Contact B Godden, Design Director

Brookes & Vernons Communications Ltd
Heath House, Cheadle Road, Uttoxeter ST14 7BY
t 01889 561000 **f** 01889 563258
e communications@brooksvernons.co.uk
w www.brooksvernons.co.uk
Contact Rob Sethna, Creative Director; Paula Davis

Concept Productions Ltd
5 Albyn Terrace, Aberdeen AB10 1YP
t 01224 625040 **f** 01224 625041
e sales@conceptproductions.co.uk
w www.conceptsolutions.co.uk

The Copyright Promotions Licensing Group plc
6th Floor, 3 Shortlands, London W6 8PP
t 020 8563 6400 **e** davidc@copyrightpromotions.co.uk
Contact David Cardwell, Chief Executive

DB Marketing Consultancy Services
81 Queens Drive, Putnoe, Bedford MK41 9BP
t 01234 268748 **f** 01234 268748 **m** 07973 843179

Deep Blue
Clerkenwell House, 67 Clerkenwell Road, London EC1R 5BE
t 020 7405 9999 **f** 0870 243 0987
e info@deepblue-i.com **w** www.deepblue-i.com
Contact Tim MacPherson, Director; Caroline Watson, Director

Denmead Marketing (Europe) Ltd
11 Russell Gardens Mews, London W14 8EU
t 020 7371 2040 **f** 020 7371 2028 **e** pr@denmeaduk.com
Contact Caroline Stott

Digital Arts World
Lamb House, Church Street, Chiswick, London W4 2PD
t 020 8987 0941 **f** 020 8987 0949
e strainor@adranstar.com **w** www.digitalartsworld.co.uk
Contact Helen Simms, Marketing Manager; Jason Moss, Sales Manager; Sophie Trainor, Festival Manager

The Digital Video Show
114 Whitchurch Road, Cardiff CF14 3LY
t 029 2066 6007 **f** 029 2066 6008 **m** 07796 262000
e info@genesis-media.co.uk **w** www.thedigitalvideoshow.co.uk
Contact Alan Torjussen, Chief Executive

Donald Smith Promotions Ltd
8 Parkfield, Menston, Ilkley LS29 6LP
t 01943 871010 **f** 01943 870322
e info@donaldsmithproductions.co.uk
Contact Alan Smith, Managing Director

Feref Ltd
14-17 Wells Mews, London W1A 1ET
t 020 7580 6546 **f** 020 7631 3156
e info@feref.com **w** www.feref.com
Contact Marie Twist, Office Manager; Chris Kinsella, Office Manager

File FX
11 Shepperton House, 83-93 Shepperton Road, London N1 3DF
t 020 7226 6646 **f** 020 7226 9810
e sales@filefx.co.uk **w** www.filefx.co.uk
Contact Richard Sutcliffe, Partner

Fisher Productions
118 Garratt Lane, London SW18 4DJ
t 020 8871 1978 **f** 020 8871 1988 **m** 07860 147801
e enquirys@fisherproductions.co.uk
w www.fisherproductions.co.uk
Contact Victoria Swift, Head of Production; Dominic Watson, Hire Manager; Philippa Bowers, Head Of Production

Globo International (London)
The Interchange, Oval Road, 2nd Floor, London NW1 7DE
t 020 7284 3590 **f** 020 7753 0089
e globo.london@tvglobo.com.br **w** www.iedeglobo.com.br
Contact Jerusah Salgado, Manager

Knekt
7 D'Arbly Street, London W1F 8DW
t 020 7434 2598
Contact Orlando Kimber, Director

Leicester Promotions Ltd
7-9 Every Street, Town Hall Square, Leicester LE1 6AG
t 0116 225 4000 **f** 0116 225 4050
e pr@leicesterpromotions.org.uk **w** www.discoverleicester.com
Contact Liz Stenning, PR Executive; Janine Williams, PR Executive

Manor Marketing
12A Manor Place, Speen, Newbury RG14 1RB
t 0 1635 44991 **f** 0 1635 34466 **m** 07748 636171
e jennie@manormarketing.tv **w** www.manormarketing.tv
Contact Jennie Evans, Managing Director; Joss Armitage, Account Manager

Marketing Projects
Projects House, Skips Lane, Christleton CH3 7BE
t 01244 330000 **f** 01244 330101
e info@marketingprojects.co.uk **w** www.marketingprojects.co.uk
Contact Jane Harrad-Roberts

The Media Show
114 Whitchurch Road, Cardiff CF14 3LY
t 029 2066 6007 **f** 029 2066 6008 **m** 07796 262000
e info@genesis-media.co.uk **w** www.themediashow.co.uk
Contact Alan Torjussen, Chief Executive

MediaXchange
10-11 Moor Street, London W1D 5NF
t 020 7734 2310 **f** 020 7287 0096
e info@mediaxchange.com **w** www.mediaxchange.com
Contact Stefan Trockle, Programme Manager; Katrina Wood, CEO

National Research Group
Martin House, 26-30 Old Church Street, London SW3 5BY
t 020 7351 4370 **f** 020 7351 9344
Contact Michael Edison, President of European Operations; Ray Ydoyaga, President Of European Operations

Porter Frith
26 Danbury Street, London N1 8JU
t 020 7359 3734 **f** 020 7226 5897
e porterfrith@hotmail.com
Contact Sue Porter, Joint Managing Director

Richardson Carpenter
Cliddesden, Basingstoke RG25 2JB
t 01256 353700 **f** 01256 358100
e tcarpenter@rca.co.uk **w** www.rca.co.uk
Contact Tony Carpenter, Managing Director

Shed 9
2 Kingsley Road, London E7 9PP
t 020 8472 3531 **f** 020 8472 3531 **m** 07957 643705
e info@shed9.com **w** www.shed9.com
Contact Malin Fabbri, Creative Director; Gary Fabbri, Director
Credits Do It...Now (S); Sisyphos (S); Alternative Photography (W); eMarketing (W)

Sky Bridge
Wimbledon Bridge House, 1 Hartfield Road, London SW19 3RU
t 020 8254 1500 **f** 020 8254 1544
e info@skybridgegroup.com **w** www.skybridgegroup.com

MEDICAL

Medical Crew Hire

British Nursing Association
The Colonnades, Beaconsfield House, Hatfield AL10 8YD
t 01707 263544 **e** info@bna.co.uk **w** www.bna.co.uk

medical information malaria vaccinations

Malaria vaccinations are required in the following countries

Aa
Afghanistan
Angola
Argentina
Armenia
Azerbaijan

Bb
Bangladesh
Belize
Benin
Bhutan
Bolivia
Botswana
Brazil
Burkina Faso
Burundi

Cc
Cambodia
Cameroon
Central African Republic
Chad
China
Colombia

Comoros
Congo
Democratic Republic of the Congo
Costa Rica
Cote d'Ivoire

Dd
Djibouti
Dominican Republic

Ee
East Timor
Ecuador
Egypt
El Salvador
Equatorial Guinea
Eritrea
Ethiopia

Ff
French Guyana

Gg
Gabon
Gambia
Georgia
Ghana
Guatemala
Guinea-Bissau
Guyana

Hh
Haiti
Honduras

Ii
India
Indonesia
Republic of Iran
Iraq

Kk
Kenya

Ll
Lao
Liberia

Mm
Madagascar
Malawi
Malaysia
Mali
Mauritania
Mauritius
Mexico
Morocco
Mozambique
Myanmar

Nn
Namibia
Nepal
Nicaragua
Niger
Nigeria

Oo
Oman

Pp
Pakistan
Panama
Papua New Guinea
Paraguay
Peru
Philippines

Rr
Rwanda

Ss
St Vincent and the Grenadines
Sao Tome and Princepe
Saudi Arabia
Senegal
Sierra Leone
Solomon Islands
Somalia
South Africa
Sri Lanka
Sudan
Surinam
Syria

Tt
Tajikistan
Tanzania
Thailand
Togo
Turkey
Turkmenistan

Uu
Uganda
United Arab Emirates

Vv
Vanuatu
Venezuela
Vietnam

Yy
Yemen

Zz
Zambia
Zimbabwe

Doctors Direct PLC
SOS House, 73-77 Britannia Road, London SW6 2JR
t 020 7751 9701 **f** 020 7610 6732
e mail@doctorsdirect.co.uk **w** www.doctorsdirect.co.uk
Contact Martin Borland

Karen Fayerty
39 Fisher Close, Enfield EN3 6WQ
t 01992 700768 **f** 01992 700320 **m** 07973 407341
e kazza.67@virgin.net

Grosvenor Nursing Agency
1st Floor Suite, Holloway Unit, Ashford Hospital, London Road, Ashford TW15 3AA
t 01784 884948 **f** 01784 884947
e info@grosvenor-nursing.com **w** www.grosvenor-nursing.com

Millstream Nursing
23 Verwood Road, North Harrow HA2 6LD
t 020 8420 1753 **f** 020 8428 9803 **m** 07860 568223
e mnurseterri@aol.com
Contact Terri Sheed, Proprietor; Lindsey Wilkinson, Nurse Manager

Paramedic Services Ltd
25 Beach Green, Shoreham-by-Sea BN3 5YG
t 01273 888899 **f** 01273 455095 **m** 07973 197887
Contact Tracy Briant, Director

South Hams Nursing Agency
Metropolitan House, The Millfields, Stonehouse, Plymouth PL1 3JB
t 01752 604555 **f** 01752 260353
e southwestnursing@eclipse.co.uk **w** www.swnursing.co.uk
Contact Barna Lewis, Director; Vivien Napper, Director

Medical **Kit**

IPS Ltd
Bridgewater Road, Broadheath, Altrincham WA14 1NA
t 0161 928 3672 **f** 0161 928 4147 **w** www.ips-healthcare.co.uk
Contact Paul Masters, Managing Director

Porter Nash Medical
120 Wigmore Street, London W1U 3LS
t 020 7486 1434 **f** 020 7224 2309
e infol@porternash.co.uk **w** www.porternash.co.uk
Contact Michael Avedissiam, General Manager

SAFA Ltd
59 Hill Street, Liverpool L8 5SB
t 0151 708 0397 **f** 0151 708 7211
e info@safa.co.uk **w** www.safa.co.uk
Contact Irene Symes, Operations Director

Wigmore Medical Ltd
23 Wigmore St, London W1U 1PL
t 020 7491 0150 **f** 020 7491 2782
e pharmacy@wigmoremedical.co.uk
Contact Peter Eghiayan, Managing Director; David Hicks, Director; Bedo Eghiayan, Chief Executive Officer; David Hicks, Managing Director

medical information yellow fever vaccinations

Yellow fever vaccinations are required in the following countries

Aa
Afghanistan
Algeria
American Samoa
Angola
Anguilla
Aruba
Australia

Bb
Bangladesh
Belize
Benin
Bhutan
Bolivia
Brazil
Brunei
Burkina Faso
Burundi

Cc
Cambodia
Cameroon
Cape Verde
Central African Republic
Chad
China

Christmas Island
Colombia
Comoros
Congo
Cote d'Ivoire

Dd
Djibouti

Ee
Ecuador
Egypt
El Salvador
Equatorial Guinea
Eritrea
Ethiopia

Ff
Fiji
French Guyana
French Polynesia

Gg
Gabon
Gambia
Ghana
Greece
Grenada
Guadeloupe
Guatemala
Guinea-Bissau
Guyana

Hh
Haiti
Honduras

Ii
India
Indonesia
Iraq

Jj
Jamaica
Jordan

Kk
Kazakhstan
Kenya
Kiribati

Ll
Laos
Lebanon
Lesotho
Liberia

Mm
Madagascar
Malawi
Malaysia
Maldives
Mauritania
Mauritius
Mozambique
Myanmar

Nn
Nauru
Nepal
Netherlands Antilles
New Caledonia
Nicaragua
Niger
Nigeria

Oo
Oman

Pp
Pakistan
Palau
Panama
Papua New Guinea
Paraguay
Peru
Philippines
Pitcairn

Rr
Reunion
Rwanda

Ss
St Helena
St Kitts & Nevis
St Lucia
St Vincent and the Grenadines
Samoa
Sao Tome and Principe
Saudi Arabia
Senegal
Seychelles
Sierra Leone
Singapore
Solomon Islands

Somalia
South Africa
Sri Lanka
Sudan
Surinam
Swaziland
Syria

Tt
Tanzania
Thailand
Togo
Tonga
Trinidad and Tobago
Turks & Caicos

Uu
Uganda

Vv
Venezuela
Vietnam

Yy
Yemen

Zz
Zambia
Zimbabwe

Medical Services

Ambulance & Medical Services
55 Cranmore Drive, Smithton, Inverness IV2 7FL
t 07050 323880 t 01463 798194
f 01463 798229 m 07866 615317
e rescuecontrol@medic3.Freeserve.co.uk
w www.rescuecontrol.co.uk
Contact Andrew Walker, Operations Manager
Credits Orange (C); Rock Face (T)

PA Barr
11 Bluehouse Lane, Oxted RH8 OAA
t 01883 713913 f 01883 713913 m 07976 759514
e patbarr@saqnet.co.uk
Credits Love Actually (F); Gosford Park (F); Possession (F); Jason And The Argonauts (F)

CLM Medical Transport Service
1 Harvest Road, Feltham TW13 7JH
t 020 8893 2020 f 020 8893 2020
e info@clmmed.com w www.clmmed.co.uk
Contact Cameron May

Doctor Doalot Unit Doctors
8 Cedar Road, East Moseley KT8 9HP
t 0208 873 3046 f 0208 873 0984
e info@doctordoalot.co.uk w www.doctordoalot.co.uk
Contact Alex Bobak, Contact

Dr John Gayner
6 Sloane Square, London SW1W 8EE
t 020 7730 3700 f 020 7730 6500 m 07785 700 700

Joseph Saber Chartered Physiotherapist
t 01962 851321 f 01962 851321

Location Medical Services
PO Box 307, Staines TW18 3WA
t 07000 633427 f 0870 750 9897
e mail@locationmedical.com w www.locationmedical.com

The London Therapeutic Massage Company
Flat 5, 28 Bryanston Street, Marble Arch, London W1H 7AE
f 020 7868 8635 m 07932 006033 e jrtaggart28@hotmail.com
Contact Jean Taggart, On-Set Massage Therapist

Medicar European Private Medical Transport
The Grange, Plumpton House, Hinxhill, Ashford TN25 5NT
t 01233 660999 f 01233 610721
e medicar@ambulanceservices.co.uk
w www.medicareuropean.co.uk
Contact Lynn Snoad, Partner; Chris Jones, Partner

Physical Therapy Clinic
1 Victoria Road, Hale, Altrincham WA15 9AF
t 0161 941 5922 f 0161 929 5402
Contact Susan Filson, Physiotherapist

Studio Clinic of Osteopathy & Acupuncture
Studio Road, Shepperton TW17 0QD
t 01932 562611 **f** 01932 246104 **m** 07976 753250
Contact Jane Wheeler

MODEL MAKING

Model Making
Model Makers

2D:3D Ltd
263 Abbeydale Road, Park Royal, London HA0 1TW
t 020 8998 3199 **f** 020 8998 7767
e rob@2d3d.co.uk **w** www.2d3d.co.uk
Contact Rob Edkins, Managing Director

3D Studios
71 Lambeth Walk, London SE11 6DX
t 020 7735 7932 **f** 020 7820 1562
Contact Terry Kemble, Proprietor; Paul Baker, Proprietor

Albatross
Unit 2, Beckett''s Wharf, Lower Teddington Road, Hampton
Wick, Kingston-upon-Thames KT1 4ER
t 020 8943 4720 **f** 020 8977 0854
e enquiries@albatrossmodels.co.uk
w www.albatrossmodels.co.uk
Contact Sean Miles, Design; Alan Mount, Managing Director
Credits Polaroid (C); Legoland (C); Blank Pathers - Gucci (C); The Steamship
Endurance (T)

Animal Instincts
30 Hollow Lane, Shinfield, Reading RG2 9BT
t 0118 988 3660
Contact Paul Draper, Director

Applied Arts
22-27 The Oval, London E2 9DT
t 020 7739 3155 **f** 020 7739 3166
Contact Bob Saunders, Proprietor

Asylum
20 Thornsett Road, London SW18 4EF
t 020 8871 2988 **f** 020 8874 8186
e info@asylumsfx.com **w** www.asylumsfx.com
Contact Kate McConnell, Director; Mark Curtis, Director; Mark Mason, Director;
Mark Ward, Director; Bob Hinks, Managing Director

Atom Ltd (Industrial Model Makers)
High Street, Sunningdale, Ascot SL5 0NG
t 01344 620001 **f** 01344 628028
e info@atomltd.com **w** www.atomltd.com
Contact Nick Mines, Director

Bad Dog Design 3D Productions
Fir Tree Cottage, Fishpool Hill, Brentry, Bristol BS10 6SW
t 0117 959 2011 **f** 0117 959 1245
e baddog@dircon.co.uk **w** www.baddogdesign.co.uk
Contact Ginny Mann, Partner

Andy Baker
11 Dunelm Street, London E1 0QQ
t 020 7790 7941 **m** 07770 390980
Credits Thunderbirds (F); Labyrinth (F); Below (F); Harry Potter And The
Philosopher's Stone (F)

Jolyon Bambridge
108 Vandyke, Bracknell RG12 8UT
t 01344 453575 **f** 01344 644408 **m** 07973 113412
e jolyonbambridge@hotmail.com
w www.flyingcamerasystems.co.uk
Credits The World Is Not Enough (F); Star Wars: Episode I - The Phantom Menace (F)

Bandit Studio
Unit 4E, Lays Farm Trading Estate, Keynsham, Bristol BS31 2SE
t 0117 951 3922 **f** 0117 951 3922 **m** 07967 120169
e info@banditstudio.com **w** www.banditstudio.com
Contact Simon Peeke, Managing Director
Credits Sky (C); Chicken Run (F); Nestea (A)

Barrow Model Makers
St Vincents School House, Greenside Street, Manchester M11 2EX
t 0161 231 2272 **f** 161 **m** 07879 410404
e barrow.models@virgin.net
Contact Stephen Dee, Partner

BBC Special Effects

BBC Special Effects
Kendal Avenue, London W3 0RP
t 020 8993 9434 **f** 020 8993 8741
e special.effects@bbc.co.uk
w www.bbcresources.com/specialeffects

Chris Lovell Studio
2 Garden Cottages, Monkshatch, Compton GU3 1DL
t 01483 810633 **f** 01483 810633 **m** 07714 096529
e chrislovell.studio@virgin.net **w** www.chrislovellstudio.co.uk
Contact Chris Lovell, Director

Cinemation
Cooleen, Church Lane, Thames Ditton KT7 0NL
t 020 8398 7307 **f** 0845 757 6333 **e** turneread@talk21.com
Contact John Read, Partner

Clive Armitage Model Making
45 Gould Road, Twickenham TW2 6RN
t 020 8894 4794 **f** 020 8894 4794 **m** 07808 346616
e cliveart2003@yahoo.co.uk
Contact Clive Armitage, Proprietor
Credits Liberty's (C); ESSO (C); British Airways (C)

Cod Steaks
Unit 18 Albion Dockside Estate, Hanover Place, Bristol BS1 6UT
t 0117 929 2729 **f** 0117 929 0885 **e** mail@codsteaks.com
Contact Susannah Lipscombe, Director, Managing Director; Lucy Wells-Fraser,
Project Manager; Lucy Fox, Project Manager
Credits Tennants Beer (C); Tennants Beer (C); Wallace And Gromit (A)

Cole Models
13 Hague Street, London E2 6HN
t 020 7729 6686 **f** 020 7739 3282 **m** 07860 382901
Contact Peter Cole, Proprietor

Complete Fabrication Ltd
Unit B108, Faircharm Studios, 8-12 Creekside, London SE8 3DX
t 020 8694 9666 **f** 020 8694 9669
e mail@completefabrication.com
w www.completefabrication.com
Contact Nicholas Corker, Manager; Toni Donati, Manager; Josephine Picket-
Baker, Manager
Credits Wok+ (C); Shreddies (C); M&M's (C); Kinder Buena (C)

CP Ceramics
150 Columbia Road, London E2 7RG
t 020 7366 9570 **f** 020 7366 9715
Contact David Richardson, Potter

Creative Glassfibre Models
266 Ralph Road, Shirley, Solihull B90 3LF
t 0121 744 9226 **f** 0121 744 9226 **m** 07778 285997

David Jones Fragile Ice & Water
Depot Road, Hounslow TW3 1SN
t 020 8572 6666 **f** 020 8577 1713
e djfm@talk21.com **w** www.fragileice.com
Contact David Jones, Proprietor

Effigy Models
Studio No 76, Shepperton Studios, Studios Road, Shepperton TW17 0QD
t 01932 241690 **f** 01932 225806 **m** 07860 844165
e sales@effigy.com **w** www.effigyuk.com
Contact Damon Wood, Contact

Emilyn Hill Design
Fieldhurst, 86 Liberty Lane, Addlestone KT15 1NH
t 01932 845494 **f** 01932 701637 **m** 07967 683799
e enzel@dircon.co.uk
Contact Emilyn Hill

Chris Fitzpatrick
Flat 5, 2 Chicksand Street, London E1 5LD
t 020 7375 1333 **m** 07949 687 641 **e** christofitz@hotmail.com
Credits Xena Warrior Princess (T); Hercules

Freeborns
2 Cobham Way, East Horsley KT24 5BH
t 01483 282986 **f** 01483 283535
e kit@freeborns.co.uk **w** www.freeborns.co.uk
Contact Kit Freeborn, Proprietor

Hands Up Puppets
C/o Peter Charlesworth & Association, 68 Old Brompton Road, South Kensington, London SW7 3LD
t 020 7581 2478
e handsuppuppets@btinternet.com **w** www.handsuppuppets.com

hb.source Ltd
77-85 Newington Causeway, London SE1 6BD
t 020 7939 9035 **f** 020 79390500
e clare@hbsource.co.uk **w** www.hbsource.co.uk
Contact Steve Blyth, Partner; Brianna Perkins, Business Manager; Clare Spencer, Business Manager

Guy Hodgkinson
Au Cachan-32550-Lasseran, France
t +33 0 562 058682 **e** hodgkinson@wanadoo.fr
Contact Guy Hodgkinson, Proprieter

Hybrid Enterprises Ltd
Units 26-27 Armley Workshops, Pickering Street, Leeds LS12 2QG
t 0113 217 1300 **t** 01277 654862
f 0113 217 1300 **m** 07870 600273
e studio@hybridfx.com **w** www.hybridfx.com
Contact Mike Stringer, Technical Director; Mike Bates, Production Director; Ryk Fortuna, Lead Sculptor/Technician
Credits The National Geographic (D); The Royal (T); Ant 'N' Dec's Saturday Night Takeaway (T); The Two Towers (F)

Jeff Cliff Models
9 Bath Buildings, Montpelier, Bristol BS6 5PT
t 0117 944 5721 **e** jeff.cliff@virgin.net
Contact Jeff Cliff, Model Maker

John Wright Modelmaking Ltd
Workshop 1, Centrespace, 6 Leonard Lane, Bristol BS1 1EA
t 0117 927 2854 **f** 0117 927 2606
e mail@jwmm.co.uk **w** www.jwmm.co.uk
Contact John Wright, Proprietor

Judah Ltd
35 Inkerman Road, London NW5 3BT
t 020 7284 1101 **f** 020 7267 0661 **m** 07831 464360
e gerry@judah.co.uk **w** www.judah.co.uk
Contact Gerry Judah

Machine Shop Special Effects Ltd
180 Acton Lane, Park Royal, London NW10 7NH
t 020 8961 5888 **f** 020 8961 5885 **m** 07973 752524
e info@machineshop.co.uk **w** www.machineshop.co.uk
Contact Paul Mann, Managing Director; Leo Todeschini, Supervisor

Mallard Models & Effects
High Gardens, Garway Hill, London HR2 8RT
t 020 8540 4430 **f** 01981 240790 **m** 07836 375248
e themodelworkshop@aol.com
Contact Mark Russell, Partner

Mattes & Miniatures
Bray Studios, Water Oakley, Windsor SL4 5UG
t 01628 506626 **f** 01628 506702 **m** 07951 724992
e mattes.miniatures@ukonline.co.uk
w www.mattesand miniatures.com
Contact Leigh Took, Partner; Ben Hall, Partner
Credits Radiohead (M); Thespian X (S); Lost In Space (F); Band Of Brothers (T)

Sarah Mayfield
29 Loder Road, Brighton BN1 6PL
m 07092 023189
e sarah@sculptress.net **w** www.sculptress.net
Credits Lara Croft: Tomb Raider (F); Die Another Day (F); The World Is Not Enough (F); The Reckoning (F)

Metro Models
2 Occupation Road, London SE17 3BE
t 020 7703 7100 **f** 020 7252 5111
e info@metromodels.co.uk **w** www.metromodels.co.uk

Model Solutions
42 Queensland Road, Islington, London N7 7AH
t 020 7700 4253 **f** 020 7700 4254
e info@modelsolutions.co.uk **w** www.modelsolutions.co.uk
Contact John Robertson, Proprietor

Neon Effects
Unit 5, Havelock Terrace, Battersea, London SW8 4AS
t 020 7498 1998 **f** 020 7498 0871
e neonfx@aol.com **w** www.neoneffect.network.net
Contact Janie Deeks-Ireland, Company Secretary

Northern Natural History
Greenhill, Brora, Sutherland KW9 6LU
t 01408 621500
e taxidermy@nnh.co.uk **w** www.nnh.co.uk/taxidermy
Contact Richard Paylor, Proprietor

Ozturk & Robotica Modelmakers
17-19 Park Terrace Lane, Glasgow G3 6BQ
t 0141 353 2261 **f** 0141 353 2614
e info@robotica.co.uk **w** www.robotica.co.uk
Contact Cemal Ozturk, Director

Parallax Models
Llwynfedwen Libanus, Brecon LD3 8NN
t 01874 638994 **f** 01874 638993 **m** 07770 328003
e mail@parallaxmodels.com
Contact Steve Coleman, Partner

John Payne
8 Stonegallows, Taunton TA1 5JN
t 01823 282347 **m** 07798 862847
Credits Harry Potter (F); K19 The Widow Maker (F); Avengers (F); Lost In Space (F)

Pennicott Payne Ltd
10-16 Gwynne Road, Battersea, London SW11 3UW
t 020 7228 6127 **f** 020 7223 3332
e info@ppl.uk.net **w** www.ppl.uk.net
Contact David Payne, Director; John Pennicott, Director

Peter Evans - Military, Models & Miniatures
38A Horsell Road, London N5 1XP
t 020 7700 7036 **f** 020 7700 4624 **e** figsculpt@aol.com
Credits Stadstoys (W); War Against Napoleon (D); The Anatomists (D); Fire Rider (S)
Military uniform research, dioramas, historical battle scenes,
individual models, war games.

Piper Modelmakers
27-25 Bevenden Street, London N1 6BH
t 020 7250 0530 **f** 020 7251 0134
e info@pipers.co.uk **w** www.pipers.co.uk
Contact Barry McKeogh, Chief Executive

Puppetspresent com
C/o Peter Charlesworth & Association, 68 Old Brompton Road,
South Kensington, London SW7 3LD
t 020 7581 2478
e puppetspresent@btinternet.com **w** www.puppetspresent.com

Richard Thomas
69 Stanhope Road, Cippenham, Burnham SL1 6JR
t 01628 669049 **m** 07776 131245
e richard@thomas0068.fsnet.co.uk
Credits Enemy At The Gates (F); Harry Potter And The Philosopher's Stone (F);
Star Wars:Episode I-The Phantom Menace (F); Die Another Day (F)

Richard Threadgill Associates
28A Grafton Square, London SW4 0DB
t 020 7207 1710 **f** 020 7207 1710
e richard@richardthreadgillassociates.co.uk
Contact Richard Threadgill, Senior Partner

RS Models
Unit 1F, Old Jamaica Business Estate, Old Jamaica Road,
London SE16 4AW
t 020 7232 2349
Contact Robin Sanders, Proprietor

The Science Museum
Exhibition Road, London SW7 2DD
t 020 7942 4373 **f** 020 7942 4383
e s.sheffield@nmsi.ac.uk **w** www.sciencemuseum.org.uk
Contact Stephen Foulger, Content/Development Manager;
Stephen Sheffield, Researcher

Sculpture & Constructional Design
Colney Park House, 100 Harper Lane, Radlett WD7 9HG
t 01727 822845 **f** 01727 823087 **m** 07831 305338
e Howarthcolneyprk@aol.com
Contact Derek Howarth, Proprietor
Credits The Count of Monte Cristo (F); All Indiana Jones (F); All Star Wars (F)

Side Effects
Unit 4, Camberwell Trading Estate, 117 Denmark Road, London
SE5 9LB
t 020 7738 5199 **f** 020 7738 5198 **e** sfx@lineone.net
Contact Patrick Vigne, Partner

Simon Cooley
Hetley Road Studios,, 62 Hetley Road, Shepherds Bush,
London W12 8BB
t 01635 200703 **m** 07950 252749 **e** gibsoncooley@supanet.com

Sirius Model Making
Lower Westfield House, Broad Lane, Leeds LS13 3HA
t 0113 255 7502 **f** 0113 255 7502 **m** 07802 152007
e sales@siriusmodelmaking.com **w** www.siriusmodelmaking.com
Contact Martin Watson, Model Maker; Iain Potts, Proprietor

Snowdonia Taxidermy Studios
School Bank Road, Llanrwst LL26 0HU
t 01492 640664 **f** 01492 641643
e sts.northwales@virgin.net **e** sales@taxidermy.com
w www.taxidermystore.com
Contact Dorothy Reid, Director
Credits Harry Potter And The Philosopher's Stone (F); Heartbeat (T); Monarch
Of The Glen (T)

Steve Wilsher Creative Effects Ltd
30 Church Road, Teddington TW11 8PB
t 020 8943 1066 **f** 020 8943 1065
e swcfx@btinternet.com **w** www.swcfx.com
Contact Steve Wilsher, Director

Stuart Murdoch Models & Effects
31A Lancaster Grove, Belsize Park, London NW3 4EX
t 020 7794 6153 **f** 020 7433 1719 **m** 07785 996622
Contact Stuart Murdoch, Proprietor
Credits Wonderland (F); House Of Mirth (F); Billy Elliott (F)

Tim Weare & Partners
The Old Courthouse, 46-48 London Road, Hurst Green TN19 7KP
t 01580 860808 **f** 01580 860068 **e** tim@wearemodels.co.uk
Contact Tim Weare, Partner

Triffic Models
Riversmeet Stables House, Sherington Road, Newport Pagnell
MK16 8NL
t 01908 211098 **f** 01908 211098 **m** 07970 028561
e pmilne@macunlimited.net
Contact Patrick Milne, Managing Director

Model Making **Supplies**

Amber Composites Ltd
94 Station Road, Langley Mill, Nottingham NG16 4BP
t 01773 530899 **f** 01773 768687
e sales@ambercomposites.co.uk **w** www.ambercomposites.co.uk
Contact Stuart Crosskill, Managing Director; Stuart Crosskill, Managing Director;
Paul Moore, Field Sales Supervisor; Steve Edwards, Senior Sales Engineer

Aquaspersions Ltd
Beacon Hill Road, Halifax HX3 6AQ
t 01422 386200 **f** 01422 386239
e info@aquaspersions.co.uk **w** www.aquaspersions.co.uk

Brent Plastics
Unit D, Cobbold Estate, Cobbold Road, London NW10 9BP
t 020 8451 0100 **f** 020 8459 3226
e sales@brentplastics.co.uk **w** www.brentplastics.co.uk
Contact P Young, Managing Director

Speciality Waxes
62 Holmethorpe Avenue, Holmethorpe Industrial Estate,
Redhill RH1 2NL
t 01737 761242 **t** 01737 761812 **f** 01737 761472
e sales@british-wax.com **w** www.british-wax.com
Contact Stephen Case-Green, Technical Director; Stuart Pooley, Manager

Woolton Wire
4 Longworth Way, Woolton Park, Liverpool L25 6JJ
t 0151 428 5097
Contact Vic Jones, Proprietor

motion control - on the move

Motion control, or 'moco' in production shorthand, is usually taken to mean mechanisms (such as film or video cameras) which have their position driven by motors and controlled by a computer. These mechanisms are known as motion control rigs, used typically for doing multiple passes over the same scene, for use in later postproduction work. There are several types of these mechanical marvels, from 'portable' systems to huge rigs, and the technology that drives them is constantly being updated.

Assaff Rawner, managing director of Mark Roberts Motion Control, says the 35-year history of his company has seen many changes. "Rostrums were the main motion control systems at the time," recalls Rawner of the early days. "These are quickly disappearing and larger systems are what most people want, like Milos and Cyclops. Computer graphics have also dramatically changed the industry."

Changed for the worse it seems, in Rawner's opinion. "Currently, the market is not doing as well as a few years ago," he says. "Moco is used mainly for commercials, but the budgets for these have dropped dramatically in the last two years, so motion control is used less and quality has dropped."

Rawner's company MRMC manufactures the rigs that are used in productions - models such as Cyclops, Milo and Juno. "We supply moco for any project, but generally our customers deal with the production company," he says. "Our systems have been used for many commercials and music videos. In terms of films, they include Matrix 2, the Tomb Raider films, Die Another Day, Terminator 3, Moulin Rouge and the two Harry Potter films among others."

CG is now closely used with motion control since all moves can be pre-visualised in 3D and then simply exported to the moco system. "This has greatly increased the flexibility of moco," says Rawner. "On the other hand, tracking software is being used in places where traditionally motion control would have been used. While tracking has given some benefits, in many cases we find the results can be worse compared to moco."

Software applications, such as boujou from 2d3 and Realviz's MatchMover, use sophisticated algorithms to analyse 2D footage and then extrapolate the camera's position in 3D space. The results can be impressive. "Boujou is so good that in most cases you don't need motion control for 3D," says Trevor Young, senior compositor at Hypnosis VFX. Built in trackers in some of the big CG animation packages use similar methods to drive virtual cameras.

"If used properly, motion control and CG can work very well together and should complement each other," counters Rob Delicata, ex-head of Mill Motion Control and now running his own company The VFX co. "We can see this in the movie Black Hawk Down,

MatchMover Professional, the automatic tracking software from REALVIZ, was used on 20th Century Fox's latest super hero action film, 'Daredevil' to complete an array of visual effects shots. Pixel Magic, a division of OCS/Freeze Frame created a seamless mix of CG and real-life elements with the software.

MRMC Cyclops in situ at the Inmotion studio in Germany. Cyclops is a purely studio based system that also has a hydraulic system to enable it to relocate itself and the track within its own or an adjacent studio.

Motion Control

Animation & Motion Control Ltd

Chess Spring House, Pednor Bottom, Chesham HP5 2ST
t 01494 793484 **f** 01494 793485 **m** 07836 598928
e peter.brewster@dial.pipex.com **w** www.motioncontrol4u.co.uk
Contact Peter Brewster, Managing Director
Credits Die Another Day (F); The World Is Not Enough (F); The Body (F); Jack And The Beanstalk: The Real Story (F)

Cinesite Europe Ltd

9 Carlisle Street, London W1D 3BP
t 020 7973 4000 **f** 020 7973 4040
e filmfx@cinesite.co.uk **w** www.cinesite.com
Contact Courtney Vanderslice, Head of Production
Credits Band Of Brothers (T); Harry Potter And The Philosopher's Stone (F)

Hypnosis VFX

Unit 1, Archer Street Studios, 10-11 Archer Street, London W1D 7AZ
t 020 7734 7676 **f** 020 7734 8260
e info@hypnosisvfx.com **w** www.hypnosisvfx.com

MC² Motion Control Ltd

t 020 7419 4129 **f** 020 7794 0567
e info@motioncontrol-uk.com **w** www.motioncontrol-uk.com
Contact Linda Krisman; Dennis Henry, Operator

where models, motion control and CG were combined seamlessly for the helicopter crash scenes. Also, the data interaction between CG and motion control has enabled pre-visualisation of some scenes that would otherwise be impossible, or would have taken far too long and cost too much to shoot. It comes down to knowing what you want and knowing how best to utilise the technology."

Delicata, who lists among his many credits moco work on Harry Potter And The Chamber Of Secrets and Black Hawk Down, says one of the problems he faces is that people are now very 2D and 3D aware, but sometimes do not approach a project with camera effects in mind. "A lot of advice on how to shoot VFX work comes from the post industry and we feel sometimes that advice is biased towards post houses and not necessarily towards how best to shoot the job. Some clients would rather fix things in post then shoot things properly, which is a false economy and sometimes leads to work being substandard. Certain clients will also avoid moco at all costs because of its reputation in taking too much time. Even on the big VFX movies everybody is always looking at the bottom line - i.e. how much does a shot cost - instead of how should we shoot this VFX shot to make it the best we can? There are too many compromises."

"We have tried hard to turn this perception around in the way that we work and the service that we offer to our clients. Some directors will always be post driven whilst others will try to achieve as much as they can in-camera, it just depends on the person and their career path in the industry. Unfortunately, the trend does seem to be towards post. The current commercial vogue seems to be more about commercials with a documentary feel and lots of dialogue as opposed to big VFX work, but this will turn around at some point in the future."

"There is not as much commercials work around," continues Delicata, who says this is more to do with the state of the industry than the effects of software, due to the fact that places like The Czech Republic and South Africa are attracting more British clients. "The agencies and production companies need to realise that if this continues for too much longer there will not be a British industry left," he says.

It's not all gloom and doom, though. "Idents, corporate productions and small ad campaigns still rely heavily on moco work," admits Delicata. "3D tracking has also had an impact on our business and has taken some work away, but motion control still has its place in the industry."

"Motion control is an invaluable tool in many different types of filming and effects, from animation to live action," concludes Assaff Rawner. "It is considered by many to be the unsung hero of special effects and postproduction; many shots are only possible because of motion control. Even the simplest shots are generally enhanced and easier to create with motion control. However good CG gets, as long as real actors and scenes are used, motion control is here to stay."

Contacts   Mark Roberts Motion Control (MRMC), www.mrmoco.com
The Mill, www.mill.co.uk
Hypnosis vfx, www.hypnosisvfx.com
RealViz, www.realviz.com
The VFX co, www.blackislandstudios.co.uk
2d3, www.2d3.com

Writer   Michael Burns

Platige Image's Milo shooting an animated scene for Proszek in Poland. Milo is a large portable moco system, designed to go from location to location, and extremely quick to build and take apart.

Brains & Picture's Milo shooting an Audi commercial in Austria. The long arm for the MRMC Milo option allows for a similar or greater reach than the Cyclops, but with lessened rigidity.

The Mill

40-41 Great Marlborough Street, London W1F 7JQ
t 020 7287 4041 **f** 020 7287 8393
e info@mill.co.uk **w** www.mill.co.uk
Contact Emma Shield
Credits Absolut Vodka - Mullet (C); BT Broadband - Burts Pipe (C); Guiness - Lava (C); Levi's - Stampede (C)

Mark Roberts Motion Control Ltd

Unit 4, Birches Industrial Estate, Imberhorne Lane, East Grinstead RH19 1XZ
t 01342 334700 **f** 01342 334701
e info@mrmoco.com **w** www.mrmoco.com
Contact Assaff Rawner, Managing Director; Sophie Roberts, Marketing; Graham Gvenigault, Sales Manager

Pirate Motion Control

St Leonards Road, London NW10 6ST
t 020 8930 5000 **f** 020 8930 5001
e help@pirate.co.uk **w** www.pirate.co.uk
Contact Michael Ganz, Managing Director

MultiMedia Services

Abbey Road Interactive
Abbey Road Studios, 3 Abbey Road, St Johns Wood, London NW8 9AY
t 020 7266 7282 **f** 020 7266 7321
e interactive@abbeyroad.com **w** www.abbeyroad.com
Contact Trish McGregor, Studio Manager; Samantha Harvey, Creative Director

Actimedia
Shelton Lodge, Shelton, Shrewsbury SY3 8BH
t 01743 355725 **f** 01743 231022 **m** 07977 889141
e info@activeye.co.uk **w** www.activeye.co.uk

Advanced Video Technologies Ltd
28 Redpost Hill, London SE24 9JQ
t 020 7501 9666 **f** 020 7501 9345
e amati@avt.it **w** www.avt.it
Contact Pietro Amati, Director

Alpha EC
100 New Kings Road, London SW6 4LX
t 0870 2011601 **e** info@alphaec.co.uk **w** www.alphaec.co.uk
Contact Ralph Brazier, Managing Director

Automatic Television Ltd
35 Bedfordbury, Covent Garden, London WC2N 4DU
t 020 7240 2073 **f** 020 7379 5210
e info@autotv.co.uk **w** www.autotv.co.uk

Big Time Pictures
Hillside Studios, Merry Hill Road, Bushey WD23 1DR
t 020 8950 7919 **f** 020 8950 1437
e info@bigtimepictures.co.uk **w** www.bigtimepictures.co.uk
Contact Tony Allen, Partner
Credits A Night Out With The Girls (D); Learning Futures (W); Fault Lines (D); Cloud Cuckoo Land (D)

Broadsystem
The Elephant House, Hawley Crescent, London NW1 8NP
t 020 7284 5000 **f** 020 7284 5200
e media@broadsystem.com **w** www.broadsystem.com
Contact Samantha Hall, Media Sales Director

John Broomhall
m 07768 181600
e john@johnbroomhall.co.uk **w** www.johnbroomhall.co.uk
Credits Grand Prix IV (W); Superman (W)

casetv.com Ltd
204 Mare Street Studios, 203-213 Mare Street, London E8 3QE
t 020 8534 5344 **f** 020 8986 8214
e case@casetv.com **w** www.casetv.com
Contact Patricia Williams, Joint Managing Director; Susan Francis, Joint Managing Director

Cinecosse
4 North Meadows, Oldmeldrum, Inverurie AB51 0GQ
t 01651 873311 **f** 01651 873300
e admin@cinecosse.co.uk **w** www.cinecosse.co.uk
Contact Marie Smith, Production Secretary; Graeme Mowat, Executive Producer

Cinécosse
North Meadows, Oldmeldrum, Inverurie AB51 0GQ
t 01651 873311 **f** 01651 873300
e admin@cinecosse.co.uk **w** www.cinecosse.co.uk
Contact Graeme Mowat, Executive Producer

Contact Group Ltd
Oakridge, Weston Road, Stafford ST16 3RS
t 01785 610966 **f** 01785 610955
e dick@contactgroup.co.uk **w** www.contactgroup.co.uk
Contact Richard Fisher, Managing Director

Contemplate
Flat 8, Durham House, 124 Old Christchurch Road, Bournemouth BH1 1NF
m 07764 500812
e info@contemplate.org.uk **w** www.contemplate.org.uk
Contact Joe Lanman, Founder/Graphic Design; Steve Bottomore, Producer
Credits The Basement (A)

The Data Business (London Office)
2 Benjamin Street, London EC1M 5QL
t 020 7251 8700 **f** 020 7253 5386
e datalondon@databiz.com **w** www.databiz.com
Contact Richard Lamb, Manager

The Data Business Ltd (Glasgow Office)
3 Lynedoch Place, Glasgow G3 6AB
t 0141 354 0050 **f** 0141 354 0055
e datascot@databiz.com **e** www.databiz.com
Contact Geraldine McDowall, Manager

The Data Business Ltd
Bankside, Kidlington OX5 1JE
t 01865 852144 **f** 01865 842223 **i** 01865 378565
e sales@databiz.com **w** www.databiz.com
Contact Geraldine McDowall, Manager - Scotland; Kildare Borrowes, Managing Director; Linda Whyte, Marketing Manager; Richard Lamb, Manager - London; Franky Marulanda, National Sales Manager

Digital Oasis
PO Box 6, Chichester PO20 7RL
t 01243 513000 **f** 01243 513355
e cd@digital-oasis.co.uk **w** www.digital-oasis.co.uk
Contact David Breen, Managing Director

Direct Image Productions Ltd
Beckside, Lindale, Grange over Sands LA11 6NA
t 01539 538817 **f** 01539 535794
e chris@directimageprod.demon.co.uk **w** www.directimageprod.demon.co.uk
Contact Chris Ware, Managing Director

Eclipse Communications
32 Phoenix International Estate, Charles Street, West Bromwich B70 0AY
t 0121 557 9521 **f** 0121 520 8924
e eclipse@eclipsecomm.com **w** www.eclipsecomm.com
Contact Peter Dallow, Chief Executive

Enlightenment Productions
1 Briars Lane, Lathom, Ormskirk L40 5TG
t 01704 896655 **f** 01704 895455
e mail@trainingmultimedia.co.uk
w www.trainingmultimedia.co.uk
Contact Adrian Tayler, Director

Eon Visual Media Ltd
Thomas Street, Hull HU9 1EH
t 01482 339650 **f** 01482 339701
e tevison@eon-media.com **w** www.eon-media.com
Contact Kim Evison, Sales and Marketing Manager
Credits Comet (W); ICI (W); Smith And Nephew (I); Burger King (W)

Espresso Productions Ltd
Riverside Studios, Crisp Road, Hammersmith, London W6 9RL
t 020 8237 1200 **f** 020 8237 1201
e info@espresso.co.uk **w** www.espresso.co.uk
Contact Tony Bowden, Managing Director

Evolutions Television Ltd
5 Berners Street, London W1T 3LF
t 020 7580 3333 **f** 020 7637 1942
e info@evolutionstelevision.com **w** www.evolutionstelevision.com
Evolutions New Media Department offers the latest technology and produces a wide range of CD-Roms from simple MPEG conversions to full authoring of complex interactive discs. Services include MPEG1 / MPEG2 / MP3 /AVI / RealVideo / QuickTime and WAV encoding, Duplication and Design. We also offer a full range of post production, video duplication and DVD services.

Forbidden Technologies
2-4 St George's, London SW19 4DP
t 020 8879 7245 **f** 020 8946 4871
e eem@forbidden.co.uk **w** www.forbidden.co.uk
Contact Greg Hirst, Business Development Director; Liz Mackenzie, Sales Manager; Stephen Streater, Chief Executive Officer; Wendy Turner, Office Manager

The Glass Page Ltd
15 De Montfort Street, Leicester LE1 7GE
e rebecca@glass-page.co.uk **w** www.glass-page.co.uk

Grey Interactive
79 Wells Street, London W1T 3QN
t 020 7453 8320 **f** 020 7453 7934
e alan.mccullogh@greyinteractive.co.uk
w www.greyinteractive.co.uk
Contact Alan McCullogh

Groovy Gecko
First Floor, 126 Long Acre, London WC2E 9PE
t 020 7240 0900 **f** 020 7240 9699
e info@groovygecko.com **w** www.groovygecko.com
Contact Eddie Robins, Technical Director

Harding FPA
80 Riverside Estate, Sir Thomas Longley Road, Rochester ME2 4BH
t 01634 720707 **f** 01604 720719
e enquiries@HardingFPA.co.uk **w** www.hardingfpa.co.uk
Contact Tony Carpenter

HB Source
77-85 Newington Causeway, London SE1 6BD
t 020 7234 0214 **f** 020 7939 0500
e clare@hbsource.co.uk **w** www.hbsource.co.uk
Credits Guitar

The Hub Communications Group Ltd
The Power House, 1 Linkfield Road, Iselworth TW7 6QG
t 020 8560 9222 **f** 020 8560 9333
e enquiry@thehub.co.uk **w** www.thehub.co.uk
Contact Amelia Hoseason, Project Executive; Sergio Falletti, Client Services Director

Inquit Films
44 Grove Hill, London E18 2JG
t 020 8252 7778 **f** 020 8532 9564
e films@inquit.co.uk **w** www.inquit.co.uk
Contact Nick Hayes, Producer

Internet Pro Video Ltd
Mount Pleasant House, 2 Mount Pleasant, Cambridge CB3 0RN
t 01223 477000 **f** 01223 506282
e sales@ipv.com **w** www.ipv.com
Contact Samuel Poupinet, Sales Manager

ITV Interactive
Oakslade Studios, Station Road, Hatton CV35 7LH
t 01926 844002 **e** sarah@oakslade.com **w** www.itvi.co.uk
Contact Sarah Vaughan, Marketing Manager
Credits Chomerics (W); BSSA (W); Worcester County Council (W); Weston Park (W)

Lighthouse Visual Communications Ltd
Sequel House, The Hart, Farnham GU9 7HW
t 01252 726302 **f** 01252 820359
e info@lvc.co.uk **w** www.lvc.co.uk
Contact Kelly Williams, Production Manager; Steve Penticost
Credits Max Factor (C); Newham Council E-Government Video (I); Highlights TV (T)

Mater
Units 4-5 Mill Lane, Cotterstock, Oundle, Peterborough PE8 5HH
t 01832 226221 **e** julie.buck@mater.co.uk **w** www.mater.co.uk
Contact Julie Buck, Managing Director

Metro New Media
35 Kingsland Road, London E2 8AA
t 020 7729 9992 **f** 020 7739 7742
e training@metronewmedia.co.uk **w** www.metronewmedia.com
Contact Claire Shovelton, Marketing & Communications Manager; Zoe Hind, Training Manager; Jag Manku, Training Co-ordinator

Mondo Ltd
PO Box 33829, London N8 9XB
t 020 8292 1064 **e** info@mondo.co.uk **w** www.mondo.co.uk

Monitor Media Ltd
120 South Street, Dorking RH4 2EU
t 01306 743838 **f** 01306 743737
e enquiries@monitormedia.co.uk **w** www.monitormedia.co.uk
Contact Robert Simmons, Managing Director; Paul Trickey
Credits Ericsson (W); Hasbro (W); Toshiba (W); Coca Cola (W)

MousePower Productions Ltd
Corsham Media Park, Westwells Road, Corsham SN13 9GB
t 01225 817600 **f** 01225 817601
e enquiries@mousepowerproductions.com
w www.mousepowerproductions.com
Contact Tracey Curtis, Head of Production; Stef Brammar, Managing Director; Tracey Harrison, Senior Producer
Credits Mayflower Centre Touch Screens (W); Oxfam Citizenship (W); BBC Web Wise (E)

MP Media Services
35 Heigham Road, London E6 2JL
t 020 8471 4760 **e** mpmediaservices@yahoo.co.uk
Contact Manji Patel-Vekaria, Managing Director

MSA Focus International
St Hilary Court, Copthorne Way, Colvohouse Cross, Cardiff CF5 6ES
t 029 2017 1760 **f** 029 2059 9733 **w** www.msafocus.com
Contact Martin Long, Projects Director

Oomf! Ltd
Unit F, 32, 40 Martell Road, West Dulwich, London SE21 8EN
t 020 8761 6636 **e** info@oomf.co.uk **w** www.oomf.co.uk
Contact Simon Dunstan, Managing Director

Orlando Digital Media Ltd
Up The Steps, Little Tew, Chipping Norton OX7 4JB
t 01608 683218 **f** 01608 683364
e info@orlandodigital.co.uk **w** www.orlandodigital.co.uk
Contact Mike Tomlinson, Director
Credits Fusion Research - EFDA Jet (I); Slices Of Life Exhibition (W); Thames Pilot (W)

Oxwood Media Ltd
Lowick House, Lincombe Lane, Oxford OX1 5DZ
t 01865 321665 f 01865 321668
e james.walsh@oxwood.com w www.oxwood.com
Contact James Walsh, Marketing Operations Officer; Howard Sears, Commercial Director

Photo-Stock Library International
14 Neville Avenue, Anchorsholme, Blackpool FY5 3BG
t 01253 864598 f 01253 864598 m 07850 988875
e enquiries@photo-stock.co.uk w www.photo-stock.co.uk
Contact Wayne Paulo, Proprietor

Pioneer Electronic (Europe)
Pioneer House, Hollybush Hill, Stoke Poges, Slough SL2 4QP
t 01753 789877 f 01753 789880
e info@pgb.pioneer.co.uk w www.pioneer-eur.com
Contact Mark Grotefeld, Marketing Manager

Pornograffiti.tv Ltd
Studio 106B, London E8 1NE
t 020 7275 0318
e bob@pornograffiti.tv w www.pornograffiti.tv
Contact Bob , Managing Director
Credits The Berlin Wall Wrap (W); The Radio Advertising Bureau (I); The Reduced Shakespeare Company (C); Bond Does Swan Lake (S)

Press Red Ltd
21 Denbigh Street, London SW1V 2HF
t 08700 136136 e info@pressred.tv w www.pressred.tv
Contact Chris Moreton, CEO; David Hughes, Sales & Marketing Director

Primal Pictures Ltd
159-163 Great Portland Street, London W1W 5PA
t 020 7637 1010 f 020 7636 7776
e email@primalpictures.com w www.primalpictures.com
Contact Catriona Kerr, International Sales Manager

Prisma Holographics Ltd
The Old Mill, Shillington Road, Gravenhurst NK45 4JE
t 01462 711171 f 01462 713258
e mail@lgfx.co.uk w www.lgfx.co.uk
Contact Mark Brown, Director; Richard Hawkins, Sales

Purple Wellies
Manor Farm, Farleigh Road, Cliddesden RG25 2JB
t 01256 392932 f 01256 353700
e claire.taylor@purplewellies.com
Contact Claire Taylor

Radimus Co UK
20 Heath Rise, Kersfield Road, London SW15 3HF
t 020 8789 2524 f 020 8789 2880 m 07711 049227
e mail@radimus.co.uk w www.radimus.co.uk
Contact Raad El-Alawi, Creative Director
Credits The Bouncers Game (W); The Bouncers (A); Those Damn Mexicans (A)

RCS (Radio Computing Services)
167-169 Great Portland Street, London W1W 5PF
t 020 7636 9636 f 020 7636 7766
e info@rcsuk.com w www.rcsuk.com
Contact Carl Landsbert, Sales Manager; Sebastian Holmes, Managing Director

The Red Green & Blue Company Ltd
29 Perryn Road, London W3 7LS
t 020 7490 1788 f 020 8746 0616 f 020 7251 0588
e info@rgbco.com w www.rgbco.com
Contact Echo Ward, Producer/Company Manager; Max Whitby, Director; Cathy Collis, Director
Credits The Elements Collection (E); Gosney In.... - Natural History Series (D); DNA Multiplatform Project (W); Mindreading: Interactive Guide to Emotions (W)

Red Lion Multimedia
1-5 Poland Street, London W1V 3DG
t 020 7734 5364
e mkilcooley@aol.com w www.redlionmultimedia.com
Contact Michael Kilcooley, Managing Director

Sanctuary Post
53 Frith Street, London W1D 4SN
t 020 7734 4480
e post@sanctuarystudios.co.uk w www.sanctuarystudios.co.uk
Contact Jason Elliott, Sales and Marketing Manager
Flame, DS editing, compositing and grading, on-line and off-line Avid editing, Audio, graphics, CD-Rom and DVD design / authoring and duplication services.

Sass Panayi & Partners Ltd
The Hay Barn, Mere Hall Park, Warrington Road, Mere, Knutsford WA16 0PY
t 01565 832832 f 01565 832833
e info@sasspanayi.com w www.sasspanayi.com

sound-motive
5 Wrotham Road, London NW1 0RE
t 020 7482 3459 f 07971 112387
e sound-motive@blueyonder.co.uk
Credits Insiders Guide (E); Culture Jockey (I); Fab:DVD (W); New From CBeebies (T)

SPR Productions
BBIC, Innovation Way, Barnsley S75 1JL
t 01226 204401 f 01226 215454
e spr@yol.co.uk e steve@yol.co.uk w www.sprdigital.co.uk
Contact Steve Rhodes, Managing Director

Squash DVD Ltd
12-13 Richmond Buildings, Soho, London W1D 3HG
t 020 7292 0222 f 020 7292 0223
e info@squashpost.co.uk w www.squashpost.co.uk
Contact Christine Peacock; David Pollard
Credits Mean Machine (W); K-19 (W); Star Trek - The Next Generation (W); The Godfather Trilogy (W)

Sync Facilities
Bank House, Wharfebank Business Centre, Ilkley Road, Otley LS21 3JP
t 01943 461461 f 01943 463388
Contact Pauline Naylor

TC Video
Wembley Commercial Centre, East Lane, Wembley HA9 7UU
t 020 8904 6271 f 020 8904 0172
e info@tcvideo.co.uk w www.tcvideo.co.uk
Contact Lissandra Xavier, Marketing Executive; Sandra Rumble, Managing Director; Clive Rumble, Managing Director

Techex
Techex House, Vanwall Road, Maidenhead SL6 4UA
t 01628 777800 f 01628 778022
e sales@techex-group.com w www.techex-group.com
Contact Nigel Sweet, Sales

Televirtual Ltd
Thorpe house, 79 Thorpe Road, Norwich NR1 1UA
t 01603 767493 f 01603 764946 m 07885 433507
e gen@televirtual.com w www.televirtual.com
Contact Tim Child, Chairman; Mark Wells, Director of Research & Development

Twentieth Century Video Ltd
Wembley Commercial Centre, East Lane, Wembley HA9 7UU
t 020 8904 6271 f 020 8904 0172 e marketing@tcvideo.co.uk
Contact Sandra Rumble, Managing Director; Lissandra Xavier, Marketing Manager

TwoFourTV.com Ltd

Boydell House, Old Newnham, Plymouth PL7 5BH
t 01752 334700 **f** 01752 340013
e enq@twofourtv.com **w** www.twofourtv.com
Contact Mark Hawkings, Chief Operating Officer

The UK Office Ltd

2 Vimy Court, Vimy Road, Leighton Buzzard LU7 1FG
t 01525 382050 **f** 01525 382060
e tuko@theukoffice.co.uk **w** www.theukoffice.com
Contact Jamie Gray, Sales Manager; Ian Kidd, General Manager; Charlie Day, Managing Director

University Of Birmingham
Multimedia & Video Production

Edgbaston, Birmingham B15 2TT
t 0121 414 6502 **f** 0121 414 6999
e a.trevis-smith@bham.ac.uk **w** www.is.bham.ac.uk/mvpt
Contact Robert Jacobs, Manager; Andrew Trevis-Smith, Facilities Manager

VBase

Llys y Fedwen, Parc Menai, Bangor LL57 4BF
t 01248 671101 **f** 01248 671102
e sales@vbase.com **w** www.vbase.com
Contact Joe Stoner

Video Arts Ltd

6-7 St Cross Street, London EC1N 8UA
t 020 7400 4800 **f** 020 7400 4900
e info@videoarts.co.uk **w** www.videoarts.co.uk

Viscom (Aberdeen) Ltd

430 Clifton Road, Aberdeen AB24 4EJ
t 01224 663500 **t** 0845 345 1987
f 01224 663520 **m** 07974 572506
e bruce@viscom-aberdeen.ltd.uk **w** www.viscom-aberdeen.ltd.uk
Contact Julie Vickers, Company Secretary; Bruce Milne, General Manager; Lisa Siwek, Multimedia Co-ordinator; Treena Giles, Senior Administrator; Murray Duguid, Multimedia Author; Elliot Hornell, Technical Operator
Credits Gulf Helicopters - Passenger Safety Briefings (I); The Robert Gordon University - Energy University (I); Grampian Business Award For Enterprise 2002 (I)

Wakefield College

Media Dept, Thornes Park, Wakefield WF2 8QZ
t 01924 789846 **f** 01924 789821 **m** 07904 789821
e m.briggs@wakcoll.ac.uk **w** www.wakcoll.ac.uk
Contact Malcom Briggs

Watershed

1 Canons Road, Harbourside, Bristol BS1 5TX
t 0117 927 6444 **f** 0117 921 3958
e info@watershed.co.uk **w** www.watershed.co.uk
Contact Dick Penny, Director; Jill Stokes, Head Of Finance; Louise Gardner, Head Of Communications
Credits www.electricdecember.org (W); www.dshed.net (W)

Westworld Interactive

Cameo House, 11 Bear Street, London WC2H 7AS
t 020 7930 6996 **f** 020 7839 1900 **e** mail@westworld.co.uk
Contact Angus Robertson

Worth Media

15-17 Middle Street, Brighton BN1 1AL
t 01273 201152 **f** 01273 710004
e info@worthmedia.net **w** www.worthmedia.net
Contact Guy Pickford, Production Director; Tris Benedict Taylor, Business Development Manager; Jonathan Martin, Communications Manager
Credits www.talkingteaching.co.uk (W); www.doc2doctor.com (W); www.nhsplus.nhs.co.uk (W)

Zendor

Bridgewater House, 58-60 Whitworth Street, Manchester M1 6LT
t 0161 237 4900 **f** 0161 237 4909
e curious@zendor.com **w** www.zendor.com
Contact Jeff Stokoe, Sales Manager

MUSIC

Music Composers

ADSR Records Ltd

35 Constantine Road, Colchester CO3 3DU
t 01206 368700 **f** 01206 368707 **m** 07946 259474
e phil@adsrrecords.com **w** www.adsrrecords.com
Contact Phil Wyard, Managing Director
Credits Extreme Sports (T); Danger Zone (C)

Advert Music Ltd

35 Durand Gardens, London SW9 0PS
t 020 7793 7426 **f** 020 7735 8965
e info@advertmusic.com **w** www.advertmusic.com
Credits "Moses, Multimania" Television and Cinema Advertisements (FCB Paris) (F)

Air-Edel Associates Ltd

18 Rodmarton Street, London W1U 8BJ
t 020 7486 6466 **f** 020 7224 0344
e air-edel@air-edel.co.uk **w** www.air-edel.co.uk
Contact Maggie Rodford, Managing Director; Beckie Bentham

Airforce Music

Media House, Hollingworth Court, Ashford Road, Maidstone ME14 5PP
t 0700 070 1111 **f** 0700 070 2222 **m** 07976 326222
e office@airforce.co.uk **w** www.airforce.co.uk
Contact Alan Bell, Managing Director; John Calvert, Managing Director

Jack Arnold

23 Croftdown Road, London NW5 1EL
t 020 7485 6227 **m** 07815 873619
e innerbeats@btopenworld.com

John Altman

Soundtrack Music Associates, 2 Kimberley Road, London NW6 7SG
t 020 7328 8211 **f** 020 7328 1444 **e** info@soundtrackcwm.co.uk

Andrew Music

Ivony, Cumnor Hill, Oxford OX2 9JA
t 01865 865654
e andrew@andrewmusic.co.uk **w** www.andrewmusic.co.uk
Contact Andrew Claxton, Director; Joan Gardner, Manager
Credits Drug-Raped (D); Polygamy (D); The Forbidden Journey (D); Health Education Authority - Immunisation (C)

Philip Appleby

Ian Amos Music Management, The Studio, Seychelles House, 53 Regent Road, Brightlingsea CO7 0NN
t 01206 306222 **f** 01206 306333 **m** 07711 008989
e ian@amosmusic.com **w** www.amosmusic.com
Credits Nothing Personal (F); Daisy-Head Mayzie (A); The Story Of Tracy Beaker (T); King's Beard (A)

Marc Aramian

Edit-Base, 70A Waldegrave Road, Teddington TW11 8NY
t 020 8614 6937 **e** alison@edit-base.co.uk

Artfield Music

5 Grosvenor Square, London W1K 4AF
t 020 7499 9941
e bb@artfieldmusic.com **w** www.artfieldmusic.com
Contact B B Cooper, Managing Director; B S Cooper, Director

Axis Music Productions

6 Linley Court, Rouse Gardens, London SE21 8AQ
t 020 8670 6710 **f** 07932 033182 **m** 07885 848188
e axis@axismusic.co.uk **w** www.axismusic.co.uk
Contact Rachael Covey, Senior Agent
Credits Freedom Fighters (F); Rocky And The Dodos (A); The Last Few (D); Nike (C)

Mark Ayres

t 020 8529 4736 **e** pg@markayres.co.uk **w** www.markayres.co.uk
Credits The Mobile (D); The Innocent Sleep (F); Doctor Who (T)

Christopher Barnett

21 Sandhurst Road, Kingsbury, London NW9 9LP
t 020 8931 0738 **m** 07974 843529 **f** 07976 647146
e chris.barnett4@virgin.net
Credits The Interview (S); The Bad Seed (S); NN (S)

Daemion Barry

Soundtrack Music Associates, 2 Kimberley Road, London NW6 7SG
t 020 7328 8211 **f** 020 7328 1444 **e** info@soundtrackcwm.co.uk

John Barry

Peters Fraser & Dunlop, Drury House, 34-43 Russell Street, London WC2B 5HA
t 020 7344 1000 **f** 020 7836 9543
e postmaster@pfd.co.uk **w** www.pfd.co.uk

Sir Richard Rodney Bennett

Ian Amos Music Management, The Studio, Seychelles House, 53 Regent Road, Brightlingsea CO7 0NN
t 01206 306222 **f** 01206 306333 **m** 07711 008989
e ian@amosmusic.com **w** www.amosmusic.com
Credits Far From The Madding Crowd (F); Swann (F); Four Weddings And A Funeral (F); Gormenghast (T)

Steve Beresford

London W10 5UN
t 020 8960 3130 **f** 020 8960 5183 **m** 07961 176459
e s.beresford@amserve.net
Credits Avril Brise (F); Pentimento (F); Bollywood Queen (F)

Nick Bicât

London Management & Representation, 2-4 Noel Street, London W1F 8GB
t 020 7287 9000 **f** 020 7287 3236
Contact Marc Berlin, Agent
Credits Stella Does Tricks (F); Micawber (T); Fields Of Gold (T); NCS Manhunt (T)

Howard Blake

Ian Amos Music Management, The Studio, Seychelles House, 53 Regent Road, Brightlingsea CO7 0NN
t 01206 306222 **f** 01206 306333 **m** 07711 008989
e ian@amosmusic.com **w** www.amosmusic.com
Credits My Life So Far (F); A Month In The Country (F); The Snowman (A)

Mathias Börgmann

19 Sandringham Road, London NW2 5EP
t 020 8933 8898 **f** 020 8933 8898
e mattborgmann@dsl.pipex.com
Credits Ether Et Terre (W); Tassilo (S); St Petersburg (D); Tristan And Ysolde Trailor (A)
Colourful and unusual atmospheres, strong music fittings to finished cuts.

Corin Buckeridge

Alan Brodie Representation, 211 Piccadilly, London W1J 9HF
t 020 7917 2871 **f** 020 7917 2872
e info@alanbrodie.com **w** www.alanbrodie.com

Niall Byrne

Ian Amos Music Management, The Studio, Seychelles House, 53 Regent Road, Brightlingsea CO7 0NN
t 01206 306222 **f** 01206 306333 **m** 07711 008989
e ian@amosmusic.com **w** www.amosmusic.com
Credits Flesh And Blood (T); Country (F); On Home Ground (T); Amongst Women (T)

Jason Carr

Alan Brodie Representation, 211 Piccadilly, London W1J 9HF
t 020 7917 2871 **f** 020 7917 2872
e info@alanbrodie.com **w** www.alanbrodie.com

Paul Carr

Peters Fraser & Dunlop, Drury House, 34-43 Russell Street, London WC2B 5HA
t 020 7344 1000 **f** 020 7836 9543
e postmaster@pfd.co.uk **w** www.pfd.co.uk

Cliff Adams Management Ltd

445 Russell Court, Woburn Place, London WC1H 0NJ
t 020 7837 6240 **f** 020 7833 4043
Contact Stella Walters, Contact

Cornucopia Music

29 North End Road, Golders Green, London NW11 7RJ
t 020 8455 4707 **e** ian@piprecords.fsnet.co.uk
Contact Ian Cameron, Managing Director; Judy Williams, Company Secretary

Cut To The Beat Limited

76 Waldegrave Road, Brighton BN1 6GG
t 01273 **m** 07931 544488
e info@cuttothebeat.com **w** www.cuttothebeat.com
Credits ICC Cricket World (T); Drug Nation (D); O'Neill - 50 Year Celebration (C); How To Blow A Billion (T)

Stephen Daltry

8 Tavistock Avenue, Walthamstow, London E17 6HR
t 020 8531 5362 **f** 020 8531 5362 **m** 07815 746167
e stephen.daltry@ntlworld.com **w** www.whiteknightpictures.com
Credits The Hunt (D); Smugglers (T); The Real Catherine Cookson (T)

Dash Dash Dot

57A Blacketts Wood Drive, Chorleywood WD3 5PY
m 07958 379189
e dashdash.dot@virgin.net **w** www.dashdashdot.net
Contact Adam Czekalowski
Credits Nine Tenths (F); Ramsleff (S); Love Life (F)

Shaun Davey

Ian Amos Music Management, The Studio, Seychelles House, 53 Regent Road, Brightlingsea CO7 0NN
t 01206 306222 **f** 01206 306333 **m** 07711 008989
e ian@amosmusic.com **w** www.amosmusic.com
Credits Ballykissangel (T); The Tailor Of Panama (F); Waking Ned (F); The Abduction Club (F)

Elliot Davis

Soundtrack Music Associates, 2 Kimberley Road, London NW6 7SG
t 020 7328 8211 **f** 020 7328 1444 **e** info@soundtrackcwm.co.uk

guild of international songwriters and composers

The Guild of International Songwriters and Composers (GISC) is an international organisation based in England in the United Kingdom. Guild members are songwriters, composers, lyricists, poets, performing songwriters, musicians, publishers, studio owners, independent record company/phonographic rights owners, music industry personnel, etc, from many countries throughout the world.

The Guild has published Songwriting and Composing magazine since 1986, which is issued free to Guild members. The Guild of International Songwriters and Composers offers advice, guidance, protection, information, encouragement and services to Guild members with regard to helping members try to achieve their aims, ambitions, progression and advancement in respect to the many different aspects of the music industry.

Free information, advice and services, such as the Guild's Copyright Service - Song and Instrumental Assessment Service - Collaboration Service – Advice, Consultancy, Information and Contact Service – Contract Vetting and Advice – Legal Contact Service and more are available to Guild members throughout their membership on music industry related matters.

The Guild's aim is to assist and help its members to gain knowledge of the music industry and to help maintain the rights of Guild members – new, amateur, semi-professional and professional songwriters, composers, lyricists, poets, performing songwriters, musicians, home/semi-pro/professional studio owners, independent record company/phonographic rights owners, music industry personnel, etc, working within the music industry, especially with the marketing and placement of Guild members' songs, instrumental themes, performances and copyright material, thus trying to assist Guild members to achieve commercial success and financial reward. Members of The Guild of International Songwriters and Composers have access to the Guild's affiliated publishing company, which is a member of The Mechanical Copyright Protection Society (MCPS) (London, England) and The Performing Right Society (PRS) (London, England). Publishing can be given to those Guild members who are contemplating their own record release, to those Guild members who are having their works broadcast on radio and television, and to those Guild members whose songs/instrumental themes are deemed to be suitable for the publishing company's various catalogues. All songs sent by Guild members to the Guild's Assessment Department are automatically heard by an A&R executive. Any songwriter member whose songs are considered to be suitable and commercially viable for the publishing company's requirements will be contacted with regard to the publishing of their works.

Panama Music Limited is the umbrella parent company of the publishing and recording trademarks and catalogues of Panama Music (Library), Scamp Music Publishing, First Time Music (Publishing) UK, Promo Sonor International (GB), Musik'Image Music Library (GB), ADN Creation Music Library (GB), PSI Music Library (GB), Caribbean Music Library (GB), Eventide Music Library, Piano Bar Music Library, Heraldic Production Music Library, Melody First Production Music Library, Audio-Visual Media Music Library, Panama Productions, First Time Records, Mohock Records, Rainy Day Records, Pure Gold Records, Heraldic Vintage Records, Heraldic Jester Records, Media UK Distribution, and has a policy to source new songs and instrumental themes for its publishing catalogues and new artistes for development from the membership of The Guild of International Songwriters and Composers. As the Guild has a large membership, Panama Music Limited primarily considers material from songwriters, composers and artistes who are members of The Guild of International Songwriters and Composers. Priority is given to all Guild members in respect to publishing and recording, this keeps everything in-house and allows decisions to be made quickly in respect to signings, if suitable for the company's catalogues. Panama Music is pleased to have the opportunity to listen to Guild members' songs, instrumental themes and/or performances through their membership of The Guild of International Songwriters and Composers, whose services to songwriters, composers, lyricists, artistes and those working and seeking to work in the music industry in general are invaluable.

For more information please visit our website at http://www.songwriters-guild.co.uk

A free songwriters newsmag/info pack is available direct from The Guild of International Songwriters and Composers, Sovereign House, 12 Trewartha Road, Praa Sands, Penzance, Cornwall TR20 9ST, England, tel: (+44) 01736 762826; fax: (+44) 01736 763328, email: songmag@aol.com

GUILD OF INTERNATIONAL SONGWRITERS & COMPOSERS

Sovereign House, 12 Trewartha Road, Praa Sands, Penzance, Cornwall TR20 9ST **Tel: 01736 762826** Fax: 01736 763328 Email:songmag@aol.com Website: songwriters-guild.co.uk Membership Sec: Carole A Jones. *International songwriters' organisation representing songwriters, composers, lyricists, artistes, musicians, publishers etc. Music industry consultants. Publishers of Songwriting and Composing magazine*

Deepwater Blue
65 Jeddo Road, London W12 9ED
t 020 8740 7727
e guy@deepwaterblue.net w www.deepwaterblue.net
Contact Guy Michelmore, Composer; George Kallis, Production Manager
Credits The Killing Zone; Cousins; Fly Fishing

Delicious Digital Ltd
Voysey House, Barley Mow Passage, Chiswick, London W4 4GB
t 020 8987 6181 f 020 8987 6182
e info@deliciousdigital.com w www.deliciousdigital.com
Contact Ian Taylor; Ollie Raphael
Credits BBC 6Music (W)

Andrew Dickson
Peters Fraser & Dunlop, Drury House, 34-43 Russell Street,
London WC2B 5HA
t 020 7344 1000 f 020 7836 9543
e postmaster@pfd.co.uk w www.pfd.co.uk

David Dundas
Ian Amos Music Management, The Studio, Seychelles House,
53 Regent Road, Brightlingsea CO7 0NN
t 01206 306222 f 01206 306333 m 07711 008989
e ian@amosmusic.com w www.amosmusic.com
Credits Freddie As FR07 (A); How To Get Ahead In Advertising (F); Withnail And I (F)

Matt Dunkley
Soundtrack Music Associates, 2 Kimberley Road, London NW6 7SG
t 020 7328 8211 f 020 7328 1444 e info@soundtrackcwm.co.uk

Dyer & Bradbury
40 Embassy Court, Regent Drive, Ruislip HA4 7ED
t 07789 436908 m 07816 855727
e dbmusic_enquiries@yahoo.co.uk
Contact Stuart Dyer, Composer; Jeremy Bradbury, Composer
Credits BBC1 Blue Peter (T); ABA Design (W); BBC Interactive (T);
www.dorec.com (W)

Steven Edis
Clare Vidal Hall, 28 Perrers Road, London W6 0EZ
t 020 8741 7647 f 020 8741 9459 e clarevidalhall@email.com

Elizabeth Shepherd Agency
29 Eversley Cres, London N21 1EL
t 020 8364 0598 f 020 8364 1624
e elizabeth@esagency.freeserve.co.uk
Contact Elizabeth Shepherd, Director
Credits Nicholas Nickleby (F); The Human Stain (F); Bruton - 'Horror Classics'
(C); Hart's War (F)

Elms Studios
10 Empress Avenue, Wanstead, London E12 5ES
t 020 8518 8629 f 020 8532 9333 m 07956 275554
e phillawrence@elmsstudios.com
Contact Rachael Covey, Agents & PR; Jim Walker, Personal Assistant; Sam
Jarrow, Engineer; Sarah Denton, Reception; Phil Lawrence, Director/Composer
Credits The Sword Of Shanarah (A); Wrigleys (C); The Times (C); Nike - Run
London (C)

CDr company reel. All digital. 20 years in professional composition.

Ernie Wood Music & Pictures
The Fairfield Studio, 15 East Parade, Harrogate HG1 5LF
t 01423 566573 f 01423 545122 m 07711 866859
e erniewood.music@virgin.net
Contact Ernie Wood, Director/Producer
Credits 911 - A Firefighter's Story (T); Builders From Hell (T); Eye Of The Storm
(T); Brambly Hedge (T)

Adam F
Soundtrack Music Associates, 2 Kimberley Road, London NW6 7SG
t 020 7328 8211 f 020 7328 1444 e info@soundtrackcwm.co.uk

Magnus Fiennes
Soundtrack Music Associates, 2 Kimberley Road, London NW6 7SG
t 020 7328 8211 f 020 7328 1444 e info@soundtrackcwm.co.uk

Michael Gibbs
Peters Fraser & Dunlop, Drury House, 34-43 Russell Street,
London WC2B 5HA
t 020 7344 1000 f 020 7836 9543
e postmaster@pfd.co.uk w www.pfd.co.uk

George Martin Music
t 020 7794 0660 f 020 7916 2784
e info@georgemartinmusic.com w www.georgemartinmusic.com

Goldfrapp
Soundtrack Music Associates, 2 Kimberley Road, London NW6 7SG
t 020 7328 8211 f 020 7328 1444 e info@soundtrackcwm.co.uk

Jonathan Goldstein
54B Church Road, Barnes, London SW13 0DQ
t 020 8563 8589 m 07973 621190 e jgmusic@globalnet.co.uk
Credits Frankfurt Motorshow (I); Cartoon - NSPCC (C); Monster.com (C)

Roger Greenaway
t 020 7486 6466 f 020 7224 0344

John E Hardy
Ael y Garth, 3 Ironbridge Road, Tongwynlais, Cardiff CF15 7NJ
m 07710 237629
e mail@johnhardymusic.com w www.johnhardymusic.com
Credits Hidden Gardens (T); Stalin (D); Rancid Aluminium (F); A Mind To Kill (T)

John Harle
Ian Amos Music Management, The Studio, Seychelles House,
53 Regent Road, Brightlingsea CO7 0NN
t 01206 306222 f 01206 306333 m 07711 008989
e ian@amosmusic.com w www.amosmusic.com
Credits Al's Lads (F); The Ship (D); Silent Witness (T); A History Of Britain (D)

Richard Hartley
Peters Fraser & Dunlop, Drury House, 34-43 Russell Street,
London WC2B 5HA
t 020 7344 1000 f 020 7836 9543
e postmaster@pfd.co.uk w www.pfd.co.uk

Richard Harvey
Ian Amos Music Management, The Studio, Seychelles House,
53 Regent Road, Brightlingsea CO7 0NN
t 01206 306222 f 01206 306333 m 07711 008989
e ian@amosmusic.com w www.amosmusic.com
Credits GBH (T); Jane Eyre (T); Animal Farm (T)

Patrick Hawes
Alan Brodie Representation, 211 Piccadilly, London W1J 9HF
t 020 7917 2871 f 020 7917 2872
e info@alanbrodie.com w www.alanbrodie.com

Nigel Hess
C/o Music Musicians & Management, 17 Elmwood Avenue,
Harrow HA3 8AJ
t 020 8907 2455 f 020 8907 4246
e nigel@myramusic.co.uk w www.myramusic.co.uk
Credits Maigret (T); Dangerfield (T); Wycliffe (T); Hetty Wainthropp Investigates (T)

Timothy Higgs
Peters Fraser & Dunlop, Drury House, 34-43 Russell Street,
London WC2B 5HA
t 020 7344 1000 f 020 7836 9543
e postmaster@pfd.co.uk w www.pfd.co.uk

Stephen Hoper
6A Casselden Road, London NW10 8QR
f 07092 047284 m 07946 533237
e info@shmdesign.co.uk w www.shmdesign.co.uk
Contact Stephen Hoper, Freelance
Credits Scooterworld (W); XL5 (W); OV05 (W); The Dark Hunter (F)

music : media licensing

MCPS Media Licensing is your main point of contact for all music clearance advice concerning a range of audio visual and creative use. The general guide includes the basics of music copyright, the different music types available and how to obtain music licences.

the basics of music copyright

When proposing to use music in any type of audio-visual production it is helpful to have a basic understanding of music copyright.

Copyright is the right granted by law to the creators of original literary, dramatic, artistic and musical works to ensure that copyright owners are rewarded for the exploitation of their works.

Copyright applies to music in three main areas:

A Musical work The copyright in a musical work, including any lyrics, belongs to the songwriter or composer who wrote the work. It is often assigned to, or exclusively licensed or administered by a music publisher. The copyright period varies but in most cases it will expire seventy years after the year of the death of the composer or last surviving co-writer.

A Sound recording The copyright in a sound recording belongs to the person who made the recording. This is usually deemed to be the record company, which holds a contract with the artist performing on the recording, or the artist itself. This copyright expires fifty years after the year in which the recording was first exploited.

A Performance The rights to an artist's performance belong to that performer or to a party they may have sold or assigned this right to. This right applies to all types of performance including a performance in a studio for recording purposes. Rights in most artists' performances on record are dealt with by the record company who own that recording, but there are circumstances when a performers' rights must be addressed separately.

As soon as an original piece of music is written or recorded, copyright protection begins. Among other things, this means that the writer (or his/her publisher if they have one) has the right to determine who can make recordings, or copy previously made recordings, of his/her work, and under what terms.

restricted acts

The Copyright Design and Patents Act (1988) gives the owners of these copyrights the exclusive right to carry out the following "restricted acts" with their property.

a   To copy the work – i.e. to make CDs, cassettes, vinyl, audio-visual synchronisations, musical chips etc.

b   To issue copies of the work to the public – i.e. to distribute or sell CDs, videos, musical toys etc.

c   To perform, show or play the work in public – i.e. playing recorded music in public, live performances, DJs, background music, the exhibition of films or corporate videos containing music etc.

d   To broadcast the work or include in a cable programme service – i.e. to transmit copyright music on radio and television.

e   To adapt the work or do any of the above in relation to an adaptation – i.e. to rearrange the music, to translate the lyrics etc.

f   To rent or lend sound carriers to the public.

Any person who does, or authorises another to do, any of these acts without consent from the copyright owner infringes copyright. Copyright owners are rewarded by collecting income, for example by licensing others to carry out "restricted acts". If anybody wishes to carry out any of the restricted acts, they have to seek permission from the copyright owner.

Producers of audio-visual material generally need to license the right to copy and issue copies only. The rights to 'broadcast' or 'perform in public' are almost always obtained from PRS or the relevant performing right society by broadcasters, exhibitors and the owners of venues.

collecting societies (MCPS)

Licensing music in general would be an extremely complicated procedure if the music user had to find out who and where the owner is, and then negotiate permission to use the music and obtain the necessary mechanical licence on an individual work-by-work basis.

However, most music copyright holders have grouped together and formed collective organisations which can license their music and collect and distribute the subsequent royalties. By choosing MCPS in this way, copyright owners have ensured that music users can get most of the mechanical licences they need from one single source.

planning to use music

When planning to use music in any of your creative projects, you are not automatically entitled to a licence and therefore must ensure all the required clearances have been obtained BEFORE you make any recordings or use your production in any way. Inadvertently using music without the necessary licence could also expose your clients to any possible claims arising from copyright infringement.

Thankfully, obtaining a licence is easy. MCPS has a specialist team of Music Licensing Consultants who provide a user-friendly service to guide producers through the process of clearing music.

This includes offering support on the licensing of publishing and some sound recording rights for the extensive range of music available for creative →→

Robert Howes
Alan Brodie Representation, 211 Piccadilly, London W1J 9HF
t 020 7917 2871 **f** 020 7917 2872
e info@alanbrodie.com **w** www.alanbrodie.com

David Hughes
Soundtrack Music Associates, 2 Kimberley Road, London NW6 7SG
t 020 7328 8211 **f** 020 7328 1444 **e** info@soundtrackcwm.co.uk

Nina Humphreys
Soundtrack Music Associates, 2 Kimberley Road, London NW6 7SG
t 020 7328 8211 **f** 020 7328 1444 **e** info@soundtrackcwm.co.uk

Roger Jackson
Ian Amos Music Management, The Studio, Seychelles House,
53 Regent Road, Brightlingsea CO7 0NN
t 01206 306222 **f** 01206 306333 **m** 07711 008989
e ian@amosmusic.com **w** www.amosmusic.com
Credits Lucy Sullivan Is Getting Married (T); Lenny Blue (T); Yoko! Jakamoko!
Toto! (A)

Adrian Johnston
Peters Fraser & Dunlop, Drury House, 34-43 Russell Street,
London WC2B 5HA
t 020 7344 1000 **f** 020 7836 9543
e postmaster@pfd.co.uk **w** www.pfd.co.uk

Roderick Jones
Sovereign House, 12 Trewartha Road, Praa Sands, Penzance
TR20 9ST
t 01736 762826 **f** 01736 763328 **m** 07721 449477
e songmag@aol.com **w** www.songwriters-guild.co.uk

Seanine Joyce
39 Great Queen Street, Covent Garden, London WC2B 5AA
t 020 7404 5104 **m** 07957 386445 **e** seanine.joyce@virgin.net
Credits Private's Progress (T); Dreamweavers (A); Fat (S); Omar: Tale Of The
Glass Splinter (S)

JPB Music Productions
4 Barns Close, Kingsteignton, Newton Abbot TQ12 3SS
t 01626 334143 **m** 07808 173741
e jpbmusic@msn.com **w** www.jpbmusic.co.uk
Contact Jason Busuttil, Composer/Music Producer; K. Michael Dixon, Creative
Manager; Tracey Dainton, Secretary

Garry Judd
C/o The Artful Corporation Ltd, Room 3, Chequers House,
Watton Road, Ware SG12 0AA
t 01920 487823 **f** 01920 487823 **m** 07870 884671
e info@artcorp.co.uk **w** www.artcorp.co.uk
Credits Fight School (T); All About Me (T); Confessions Of... (D)

Stephen Keeling
Peters Fraser & Dunlop, Drury House, 34-43 Russell Street,
London WC2B 5HA
t 020 7344 1000 **f** 020 7836 9543
e postmaster@pfd.co.uk **w** www.pfd.co.uk

Glenn Keiles
37 First Avenue, Acton, London W3 7JP
t 020 8248 1661 **f** 020 8248 7748
e glenn.keiles@virgin.net **w** www.glennkeiles.com
Credits Treasure Island II (A); Millenium (D); Simone Valentine (T); Savage
Planet (D)

Sayan Kent
Alan Brodie Representation, 211 Piccadilly, London W1J 9HF
t 020 7917 2871 **f** 020 7917 2872
e info@alanbrodie.com **w** www.alanbrodie.com

Chris Kimber
2 Peaks Hill, Purley CR8 3JE
t 020 8763 8237 **m** 07940 573118
e email@cantatemusic.co.uk **w** www.cantatemusic.co.uk
Credits Mind, Body, Spirit (M)

Martin Kiszko
Studios at the Coach House, The Coach House, 7A Richmond
Hill Avenue, Clifton, Bristol BS8 1BG
t 0117 973 8437 **f** 0117 973 8437 **e** wild.idea@virgin.net

Lambros Music
Elmina House, Old Dashwood Hill, Studley Green HP14 3XD
t 01494 483524
e lambrosmusic@supanet.com **w** www.lambrosmusic.co.uk
Contact Simon Lambros, Composer
Credits Wyvern Mystery (T); Mr Thompson's Carnation (S); The Late Twentieth
(F); Full Throttle (T)

Garratt Lee
Soundtrack Music Associates, 2 Kimberley Road, London NW6 7SG
t 020 7328 8211 **f** 020 7328 1444 **e** info@soundtrackcwm.co.uk

Paul Lewis
9 Westbourne Street, Hove BN3 5PE
t 01273 204064 **f** 01273 204064
Credits The Dark Angel (T); Bernard's Watch (T); Woof! (T)

Linden Studio
High Bankhill Farmhouse, Kirkoswald, Penrith CA10 1EZ
t 01768 870353 **f** 01768 870353 **m** 07711 898765
e guy@lindenstudio.co.uk **w** www.lindenstudio.co.uk
Contact Guy Forrester, Partner; Maire Morgan, Partner
Credits Wedded Bliss (T); Homes (T); Rural Lives (T)

Hal Lindes
Soundtrack Music Associates, 2 Kimberley Road, London NW6 7SG
t 020 7328 8211 **f** 020 7328 1444 **e** info@soundtrackcwm.co.uk

Rick Lloyd
21 Victoria Chambers, Luke Street, Shoreditch, London EC2A 4EE
t 020 7739 2134 **m** 07956 373172 **e** ricklloyd@btopenworld.com
Credits This Land (C); Porterhouse Blue (F)

Brian Lock
Ian Amos Music Management, The Studio, Seychelles House,
53 Regent Road, Brightlingsea CO7 0NN
t 01206 306222 **f** 01206 306333 **m** 07711 008989
e ian@amosmusic.com **w** www.amosmusic.com
Credits The Land Girls (F); The Gambler (F); The Portrait Of A Marriage (F)

Dario Marianelli
Ian Amos Music Management, The Studio, Seychelles House,
53 Regent Road, Brightlingsea CO7 0NN
t 01206 306222 **f** 01206 306333 **m** 07711 008989
e ian@amosmusic.com **w** www.amosmusic.com
Credits I Went Down (F); In This World (F); I Capture The Castle (F); The Warrior (F)

Mark Thomas Music
Cottons Lane Studio, Cottons Lane, Keinton Mandeville,
Somerton TA11 6DX
t 01458 224432 **t** 020 7565 2665
f 01458 224432 **m** 07990 585095
e marktmusic@aol.com **w** www.markthomas.co.uk
Contact Mark Thomas, Composer; Cool Music Ltd , Agent; Darrell Kok, Agent;
Sally Wilson, Agent

Mcasso Music Production
9 Carnaby Street, London W1F 9PE
t 020 7734 3664 **f** 020 7439 2375
e music@mcasso.com **w** www.mcasso.com
Contact Dan Hancock, Producer

Malcolm McKee
Alan Brodie Representation, 211 Piccadilly, London W1J 9HF
t 020 7917 2871 **f** 020 7917 2872
e info@alanbrodie.com **w** www.alanbrodie.com

use. Not just the commercially well-known, but also the broad range of production music offered by over 80 professional production music libraries throughout the UK.

production music and its advantages

Production music (or library music) is music specifically written for inclusion in audio and audio visual productions, such as advertisements, broadcast programmes, film and video productions. It is available on compact disc and online, for convenient, high quality and cost-effective synchronisation or dubbing into such productions. Some advantages of using production music are:

a   It is composed specifically for use with audio visual productions and is available in a variety of moods and lengths to meet the needs of any creative production.

b   There are no pre-clearance formalities involved in its use.

c   Licences issued by MCPS cover the right to reproduce the musical work, sound recording and artist performance – all the rights normally required by a production company.

d   Information on the range and type of production music can be obtained directly from the libraries – their experienced staff offer an intimate knowledge of the music available.

e   Libraries will provide copies of recordings for use in any particular production.

f   It is licensed according to the rates published in the MCPS rate card – enabling you to budget accurately.

g   Obtaining a licence is a simple process involving only a minimum of administrative involvement by the user to ensure the required licence is issued and the correct fees are paid.

Reproduced with kind permission from MCPS.
For more information please visit : www.mcps-prs-alliance.co.uk

---

Media Music
39 Norfolk Farm Road, Pyrford, Woking GU22 8LF
t 01483 766477 **m** 07957 952 277
e grahamj@media-music.co.uk
Contact Graham Jarvis, Composer
Credits Oscar Charlie (T); My Family (T); Only Fools And Horses (T)

Mermaid Music
30 Littleton Street, London SW18 3SY
t 020 8946 5046 **m** 07966 274992
e studio@mermaidmusic.co.uk **w** www.mermaidmusic.co.uk
Contact Carl Pittam, Composer / Producer
Credits Powergen (C); Help The Aged (C); Style File (T); Flora Pro Activ (C)

Michael Nyman Ltd
83 Pulborough Road, London SW18 5UL
t 020 8870 8961 **f** 020 8875 9377
e m.n.ltd@dial.pipex.com **w** www.michaelnyman.com
Contact Franziska Linke, PA; Elizabeth Lloyd, Manager

Deborah Mollison
Peters Fraser & Dunlop, Drury House, 34-43 Russell Street, London WC2B 5HA
t 020 7344 1000 **f** 020 7836 9543
e postmaster@pfd.co.uk **w** www.pfd.co.uk

Mike Moran
Soundtrack Music Associates, 2 Kimberley Road, London NW6 7SG
t 020 7328 8211 **f** 020 7328 1444 **e** info@soundtrackcwm.co.uk

Andrea Morriconne
Soundtrack Music Associates, 2 Kimberley Road, London NW6 7SG
t 020 7328 8211 **f** 020 7328 1444 **e** info@soundtrackcwm.co.uk

Mr Miller & Mr Porter
22 Bavant Road, Brighton BN1 6RD
t 01273 503003 **f** 01273 503003 **m** 07970 920303
e mrmiller@pavilion.co.uk **w** www.mrporter.co.uk
Contact Ian Porter; Peter Miller
Credits Eureka TV (T); The Quick Trick Show (T); Art Attack (T)

Daniel Mudford
London Management & Representation, 2-4 Noel Street, London W1F 8GB
t 020 7287 9000 **f** 020 7287 3236
Credits Aliens (D); Rum (T); Dicing With Debt (T); The Gene Machine (T)

Music For Film & TV Ltd
52 Eden Road, Walthamstow Village, London E17 9JT
t 020 8509 3786 **m** 07941 411550
e oliver@musicforfilm.tv **w** www.musicforfilm.tv
Contact Oliver Vessey, Director
Credits BBC Prime Idents (A); Killer Pink (S); Honda (C); Reflections Of Ground Zero (D)

Music For Films
34 Batchelor Street, London N1 0EG
t 020 7278 4288 **e** rgoldmff@aol.com
Contact Rob Gold, Director
Credits East is East (F); Bloody Sunday (F); Footballer's Wives (T); Dr. Jekyll & Mr. Hyde (F)

Music To Picture Company
12 Belsize Lane, Hampstead, London NW3 5AB
t 07000 784928 **t** 020 7794 6834 **m** 07836 262457
e pg@musictopicture.com **w** www.musictopicture.com
Contact Michael Omer, Managing Director; Polly Marshall, Production Associate
Credits Prince & The Pauper (T); Playhouse Disney (A); It's Good To Talk (F); Royal Deaths & Diseases (T)

Jennie Muskett
Peters Fraser & Dunlop, Drury House, 34-43 Russell Street, London WC2B 5HA
t 020 7344 1000 **f** 020 7836 9543
e postmaster@pfd.co.uk **w** www.pfd.co.uk

Nainita Desai & Malcolm Laws
81 George Lane, London SE13 6HN
t 020 8690 1384 **t** 020 7652 6789 **f** 020 8690 1384
m 07930 541928 **e** mn.music@virgin.net
Contact Nainita Desai, Musical Director; Malcolm Laws, Musical Director
Credits Fosters Lager (C); Benny Hill's Millions (D); Real Crimes (D); The Natural World (T)

Paul Neville

Greenfield Productions, 9 Greenfield Road, Eastbourne BN21 1JJ
t 01323 640067 **f** 087 0164 5124 **m** 07050 313180
e info@greenfieldmusic.com

Nigel Beaham-Powell & Bella Russell

7 The Paragon, Clifton, Bristol BS8 4LA
t 0117 973 1619 **f** 0117 973 0377 **e** nigel@ddmp.demon.co.uk
w www.ddmp.demon.co.uk
Contact Nigel Beaham-Powell

Notepad Music Productions

PO Box 3486, Wimborne BH11 9PJ
t 01202 570971
e info@notepadmusic.com **w** www.notepadmusic.com
Contact Liz Radford, Partner; Gavin Courtie, Partner
Credits Meet The Ancestors (T); Past Finders (T); Bumper To Bumper (T); Big Bike, Little Bike (T)

Julian Nott

222 Kensal Road, London W10 5BN
t 020 7734 5583 **f** 020 7964 2341
e julian@peninsula-films.demon.co.uk **w** www.juliannott.co.uk
Credits Christmas Carol - The Movie (F); New Year's Day (F); Wallace and Gromit (A)

Michael Palmer

219 Noel Road, London W3 0JL
t 020 8683 9775 **m** 07957 222733
e mike@mikepalmermusic.com
Credits Seriously Weird (T); Devils Gate (F); Audi (I); Audi

Alan Parker

Soundtrack Music Associates, 2 Kimberley Road, London NW6 7SG
t 020 7328 8211 **f** 020 7328 1444 **e** info@soundtrackcwm.co.uk

Jean-Claude Petit

Soundtrack Music Associates, 2 Kimberley Road, London NW6 7SG
t 020 7328 8211 **f** 020 7328 1444 **e** info@soundtrackcwm.co.uk

Phil Sawyer Music Ltd

10 Eton Road, London NW3 4SS
t 020 7586 5146 **t** 020 7586 1339
f 020 7916 7432 **m** 07956 902846
Contact Brigitte Fauny-Sawyer, Director; Phil Sawyer, Director, Director
Credits One And Only Launch (I); Lexus Wind God (C); Music Behind the Scenes (D); Harold The Contortionist Pig (S)

Andrew Phillips

Peters Fraser & Dunlop, Drury House, 34-43 Russell Street, London WC2B 5HA
t 020 7344 1000 **f** 020 7836 9543
e postmaster@pfd.co.uk **w** www.pfd.co.uk

Philip Pope

London Management & Representation, 2-4 Noel Street, London W1F 8GB
t 020 7287 9000 **f** 020 7287 3236
Credits The Fast Show (T); Swiss Toni (T); Happiness (T); Kevin And Perry Go Large (F)

Rachel Portman

International Creative Management Ltd, Oxford House, 76 Oxford Street, London W1D 1BS
t 020 7636 6565 **f** 020 7323 0101 **w** www.icmlondon.co.uk
Credits Chocolat (F); Emma (F); Nicholas Nickleby (F)

Graham Preskett

57 Grove Park Road, London W4 3RU
t 020 8747 3917 **f** 020 8747 3917 **m** 07976 354 507
e graham@preskett.com **w** www.preskett.com
Contact Graham Preskett, Composer

Paul Pritchard

12 St Leonards Road, Thames Ditton KT7 0RJ
t 020 8224 8018 **t** 020 8224 1075
f 020 8224 8018 **m** 07801 650640
e pritchmus@aol.com **e** pritchmus@fairadsl.co.uk
Credits Queen And Country (D); Power House (T); The Future Is Wild (A); Oliver Twist (T)

Red Hot Music Ltd

5th Floor, 150 Regent Street, London W1B 5SJ
t 020 7439 1505 **f** 0870 029 9802
e fastresults@redhotmusic.com **w** www.redhotmusic.com
Contact James Drew, Head of Production; John Hammersley, Managing Director

Resin

PO Box 33333, London NW11 8WA
t 07968 397957 **f** 07989 013848
e info@resinrecords.com **w** www.resinrecords.com
Contact Don Mei, Director
Credits Tik Tak (C); Aesthete (S); CVV (C); Ana - Portrait In Days (S)

Rumble Music

4 Firth Gardens, London SW6 6QA
t 020 7384 3834 **m** 07866 510592
e info@rumblemusic.co.uk **w** www.rumblemusic.com
Contact Richard Clarke
Credits Without Prejudice (T); Ant 'N' Dec's Saturday Night Takeaway (T); The National Lottery (T); I'm A Celebrity, Get Me Out Of Here (T)

Mark Russell

Soundtrack Music Associates, 2 Kimberley Road, London NW6 7SG
t 020 7328 8211 **f** 020 7328 1444 **e** info@soundtrackcwm.co.uk

Peter Salem

Peters Fraser & Dunlop, Drury House, 34-43 Russell Street, London WC2B 5HA
t 020 7344 1000 **f** 020 7836 9543
e postmaster@pfd.co.uk **w** www.pfd.co.uk

Kevin Sargent

Unit 2, Epirus Mansions, Epirus Road, London SW6 7UJ
t 020 7385 6685 **f** 020 7385 9997
w www.kevinsargent.co.uk
Credits Peugeot (C); Adidas (C); Eurostar (C); Crush (F)

Matthew Scott

Peters Fraser & Dunlop, Drury House, 34-43 Russell Street, London WC2B 5HA
t 020 7344 1000 **f** 020 7836 9543
e postmaster@pfd.co.uk **w** www.pfd.co.uk

Ilona Sekacz

Ian Amos Music Management, The Studio, Seychelles House, 53 Regent Road, Brightlingsea CO7 0NN
t 01206 306222 **f** 01206 306333 **m** 07711 008989
e ian@amosmusic.com **w** www.amosmusic.com
Credits Solomon And Gaenor (F); Mrs Dalloway (F); Antonia's Line (F); Bertie And Elizabeth (T)

Shriek

39 Margaret Street, London W1G 0JQ
t 020 7499 7778 **f** 020 7499 7654 **m** 07958 958162
e info@shriek-music.com **w** www.shriek-music.com
Contact Tim Rabjohns, Producer

Simon May Partnership Ltd

Helstonleigh, 17 South Hill, Guildford GU1 3SY
t 01483 304104 **f** 01483 301555
e simonmay.partnership@virgin.net
Contact Simon May, Head of Production & Composition
Credits Howard's Way (T); Pet Rescue (T); Castaway (F); Baby Father (T)

David Snell
29 Eversley Crescent, London N21 1EL
t 020 8364 0598 **f** 020 8364 1624 **e** davidsnell@bigfoot.com
Contact Elizabeth Shepherd, Agent
Credits Victorian Mysteries (M); Nicholas Nickleby (T); The Human Stain (F)

Sonic
8 Berkley Grove, London NW1 8XY
t 020 7722 9494 **e** reception@sonic.uk.com **w** www.sonic.uk.com
Contact P Jap, Partner; Adrienne Aiken, Partner

Soundtrack Music Associates
2 Kimberley Road, London NW6 7SG
t 020 7328 8211 **f** 020 7328 1444 **e** info@soundtrackcwm.co.uk
Contact Carolynne Wyper, Managing Director; Jeremy Finbow, Agent;
Olav Wyper, CEO
Credits Murder (T); Moulin Rouge (F); The Quiet American (F); Roman
Spring Of Mrs Stone (F)

Peter Spencer
Beech House, Watermill Lane, Icklesham, Winchelsea TN36 4AP
t 01424 813121 **f** 01424 814981 **m** 07767 896807
e peter@peterspencer.net
Credits Private Investigations (T); Mem Shaib Rita (F); Eye Of The Storm (T);
Peggy Su (F)

Stephen W Parsons & Francis Haines
99 The Avenue, London N10 2QG
t 020 8883 8625 **f** 020 8883 5079

Stanislas Syrewicz
Peters Fraser & Dunlop, Drury House, 34-43 Russell Street,
London WC2B 5HA
t 020 7344 1000 **f** 020 7836 9543
e postmaster@pfd.co.uk **w** www.pfd.co.uk

Tony Gibber Productions
116-120 Seven Sisters Road, London N7 6AE
t 020 7424 9876 **f** 020 8883 2732 **m** 07956 225891
e tony@music4ads.co.uk
Contact Tony Gibber, Composer

Ceiri Torjussen
114 Whitchurch Road, Cardiff CF14 3LY
t 029 2066 6007 **f** 029 2066 6008
e ceiri@ceiri.com **w** www.ceiri.com
Credits Dangerous Life Of Alter Boys (F); Dracula 2001 (F); Blade II (F); Scary
Movie II (F)

Colin Towns
31 Fordwich Road, Fordwich CT2 0BW
t 01227 712750 **f** 01227 712021 **e** mask@enterprise.net

Sarah Travis
Clare Vidal-Hall, 28 Perrers Road, London W6 0EZ
t 020 8741 7647 **f** 020 8741 9459
e clarevidalhall@email.com **w** www.clarevidalhall.com

Stephen Warbeck
Peters Fraser & Dunlop, Drury House, 34-43 Russell Street,
London WC2B 5HA
t 020 7344 1000 **f** 020 7836 9543
e postmaster@pfd.co.uk **w** www.pfd.co.uk

Chris Wells
Ian Amos Music Management, The Studio, Seychelles House,
53 Regent Road, Brightlingsea CO7 0NN
t 01206 306222 **f** 01206 305333 **m** 07711 008989
e ian@amosmusic.com **w** www.amosmusic.com

West Yorkshire Television
1 Daisy Lea Lane, Lindley, Huddersfield HD3 3JA
t 01484 307333
e gary@westyorkshiretv.co.uk **w** www.westyorkshiretv.co.uk
Contact Gary Smith, Director

George Wilkins
t 020 7978 9294 **m** 07905 155660
e georgewilkins@musiccomposer.fsnet.co.uk
Credits BT Chairman's Conference (I); Blue Sky Holidays (C); Kicking And
Screaming (I); Child At Our Time (T)

Debbie Wiseman
Peters Fraser & Dunlop, Drury House, 34-43 Russell Street,
London WC2B 5HA
t 020 7344 1000 **f** 020 7836 9543
e postmaster@pfd.co.uk **w** www.pfd.co.uk

Mike Woolmans
18 The Chestnuts, 70 Cleanthus Road, London SE18 3DL
t 020 8319 0696 **f** 020 8319 0696 **m** 07958 907324
e woolmans@aol.com
Credits Mike Baldwin And Me (D); Incredible Stories (D); Soapstar Lives (T);
Tonight With Trevor MacDonald (T)

Word Of Mouth Music
387 Westhorne Avenue, London SE12 9AB
t 020 8852 0163 **f** 020 8852 0163 **m** 07956 661810
e david@wordofmouthmusic.co.uk
Contact David McLeod, Music Composer

Music Consultants

Activebrief
5 Sussex Mews, Tunbridge Wells TN2 5QJ
t 01892 616042 **e** info@activebrief.com **w** www.activebrief.com
Contact Ian Sims, Director; Liz Devine, Director; Phil Begnett, Music Supervisor
Credits Rising Sun (M); Express Newspapers (C); Principles Of Lust (F)

Robin Bell
41 St Winifreds Road, Teddington TW11 9JS
t 020 8255 4125 **m** 07775 914642
e robinmbell@blueyonder.co.uk

BooseyMedia
295 Regent Street, London W1B 2JH
t 020 7291 7222 **f** 020 7436 5676
e booseymedia@boosey.com **w** www.booseymedia.com
Contact Natasha Baldwin, Producer; Andy Fernandes, Sales Executive; Michael
Shaw, Marketing Manager

*BooseyMedia encompasses the production of music for radio, film, new
media and television. BooseyMedia provides a total music service
including publishing, administration, music supervision, bespoke,
production music library & archive recordings.*

Bucks Music Group
Onward House, 11 Uxbridge Street, London W8 7TQ
t 020 7221 4275 **f** 020 7229 6893
e info@bucksmusicgroup.co.uk **w** www.bucksmusicgroup.com
Contact Simon Platz, Managing Director; Ronen Guha, ATR Manager

Michael Connell
57 Tantallon Road, London SW12 8DF
t 020 8673 5458 **f** 020 8675 5518 **e** terpsich@netcomuk.co.uk
Credits Heat (F); K-Pax (F); End of the Affair (F)

Cool Music Ltd
62A Warwick Gardens, Kensington, London W14 8PP
t 020 7565 2665 **f** 020 7603 8431
e enquiries@coolmusicltd.com **w** www.coolmusicltd.com
Contact Darrell Kok

John Gale
Cedar Tree House, Farthingstone, Towcester, Great Brington NN12 8EZ
t 01327 360820 **f** 01327 360821
e john.gale@studiog.co.uk **w** www.studiog.co.uk

Jonathan Robinson Associates
Monomark House, 27 Old Gloucester Street, London WC1N 3XX
t 07020 921450 **f** 07020 921452 **m** 07710 042958
e info@jra-music.co.uk **w** www.jra-music.co.uk
Contact Jonathan Robinson, Director
Credits Honda Accord (C); Largo (S); Search (T)

Liz Gallacher Music Supervision
23 Brickwood Road, Croydon CR0 6UL
t 020 8680 7784 **f** 020 8681 3000 **e** liz@lizg.com
Contact Gill Disley, Licensing; Liz Gallacher, Music Supervisor
Credits Calender Girls (F); Bend It Like Beckham (F); 24 Hr Party People (F); Resident Evil (F)

Media UK
Sovereign House, 12 Trewartha Road, Praa Sands, Penzance TR20 9ST
t 01736 762826 **f** 01736 763328 **m** 07721 449477
e panamus@aol.com **w** www.panamamusic.co.uk
Contact Roderick Jones, Managing Director

The Music Factor Ltd
15 Stanhope Road, London N6 5NE
t 020 8802 5984 **f** 020 8809 7436
e themusicfactor@paulrodriguezmus.demon.co.uk
Contact Paul Rodriguez, Managing Director; Amy Coats, Copyright Manager
Recent work: BBC TV, Channel 4, Channel 5, Discovery. Facilities: music production, music publishing, music library, copyright clearance.

Music Matters International Ltd
Crest House, 102-104 Church Road, Teddington TW11 8PY
t 020 8979 4580 **f** 020 8979 4590 **m** 07798 650526
e rozcolls@music-matters.co.uk
Contact Roz Colls, Director/Consultant
Credits Wish You Were Here...? (T); Judge John Deed (T); Pop Idol (T)

Paul Barrett Rock 'n' Roll Enterprises
16 Grove Place, Penarth CF6 4ND
t 029 2070 4279 **f** 029 2070 9989
e barrettrocknroll@amserve.com

Torchlight Music Ltd
34 Wycombe Gardens, London NW11 8AL
t 020 8731 9858 **f** 020 8731 9858 **e** torchlight@talk21.com
Contact Tony Orchudesch, Director
Credits The War Bride (F); Intelligent Finance (C); MFI (C); All About Me (T)

Voicebox International
Lower Flat, 69 Acre Lane, London SW2 5TN
t 020 7733 8669 **f** 020 7274 1807 **m** 07774 988377
e mail@robertbicknell.co.uk **w** www.robertbicknell.co.uk
Contact Robert Bicknell
Credits The Matchmaker (F); Give Your Mate A Break (T); Popstars - Germany & Switzerland (T); Faking It - Drag Queen (T)
Singing teacher and singing coach (pop & theatre). Many TV, record, film and theatre credits. In front and behind the camera. Have worked in Germany, Switzerland, Holland, Greece and Ireland.

Graham Walker
Creative Media Management, Unit 3B, Walpole Court, Ealing Studios, Ealing Green, London W5 5ED
t 020 8584 5363 **f** 020 8566 5554
e enquiries@creativemediamanagement.com
Credits Sleepy Hollow (F); Possession (F); The Talented Mr Ripley (F)

Music Fixers

Buick Production Ltd
283 Westbourne Park Road, London W11 1EE
t 020 7727 2322 **e** hilary@buickproduction.co.uk
Contact Hilary Skewes, Director
Credits Crust (F); Ali G (T); I Capture The Castle (F)

Tonia Davall
Can Davall, Casefabre 66130, France
t 845797 **f** 845801 **e** tonia.davall@tiscali.fr
Credits Galindez (F); Gladiator (F); If Only (F); Spirit (F)

Music Production

44 Time Productions Ltd
Takoma, Barnetts Wood Lane, Bighton, Alresford SO24 9SF
t 01962 772087 **f** 01962 773010 **m** 07740 404688
e sales@44time.com **w** www.44time.com
Contact Chris Williams, Sales Manager
Credits The 1999 FA Cup Final (T); The Festival Of Trees (T); CNN

Associated Music International Ltd
34 Salisbury Street, London NW8 8QE
t 020 7402 9111 **f** 020 7723 3064
e eliot@amimedia.co.uk **w** www.amimedia.co.uk
Contact Eliot Cohen, Managing Director

Audio Network Plc
School Farm Studios, School Farm, Little Maplestead, Halstead CO9 2SN
t 01787 477277 **f** 01787 477609
e office@audiolicense.net **w** www.audiolicense.net
Contact Ruth Jones, Account Manager; Robert Hurst, Commercial Director; Andrew Sunnucks; Juliette Squair, Business Development Manager
Credits Sugar And Spice (T); Dream Team (T); Secrets Of The Royal Kitchen (T); Mindhunters (F)

B Natural Recordings
8 West Park, 39-43 Eaton Rise, London W5 2HH
t 020 8998 7394 **f** 020 8998 7394 **m** 07775 830232
e lou.bnatural@lineone.net
Contact Lou Tate, Director

Blaze Music Ltd
2nd Floor, Hammer House, 117 Wardour Street, London W1F 0UN
t 020 7434 4313 **f** 020 7434 1511 **m** 07802 844388
e claire@blazemusic.co.uk **w** www.blazemusic.co.uk
Contact Claire Baughan, Producer

Candle
44 Southern Row, London W10 5AN
t 020 8960 0111 **f** 020 8968 7008 **m** 07860 912192
e tony@candle.org.uk **w** www.candle.org.uk
Contact Ian Ritchie, Composer; Tony Satchell, Managing Director; Charlie Spencer, Executive Producer; Phil Thurston, Composer; John Thomas, Composer
Credits Samaritans (W); Nissan (I); Powergen (C); Johnson & Johnson (C)

Carlin Production Music
Iron Bridge House, 3 Bridge Approach, London NW1 8BD
t 020 7734 3251 **f** 020 7439 2391 **m** 07785 362174
e cpm@carlinmusic.co.uk **w** www.carlinmusic.co.uk
Contact Paul Kinane, Production Director

Clifton Bank Studios
29 Jersey Way, Barwell, Leicester LE9 8HR
t 0145 584 5211 **m** 07980 089085 **e** radiomandave@aol.com
Contact David Kitto, Senior Partner

DAT Productions Ltd

Phoenix Sound, Engineers Way,
Wembley, London HA9 0ET
t 020 8450 5665 **f** 020 8208 1979
e jo@datproductions.co.uk
w www.datproductions.co.uk
Contact Cathy Ferrett, Facilities Manager;
Jo Harrison, Marketing Manager
Credits White Squall (F); Keep The Aspidistra Flying
(F); Brazil (F); The Last Emperor (F)

De Wolfe Music

Salop House, 11-20 Capper Street, London WC1E 6JA
t 020 7631 3600 **f** 020 7631 3700 **e** info@dewolfemusic.co.uk
Contact Alan Howe; Steve Rosie; Frank Barretta; Warren De Wolfe,
Producer/Consultant
Credits Infamous Murders (T); Mercedes Benz (C); Histories Raiders (T);
Family Affairs (T)

Direct2 Music Management

PO Box 38200, London NW3 5XL
t 020 7431 1609 **m** 07939 028466
e david@direct2management.co.uk
w www.direct2management.co.uk
Contact David Otzen, Chief Operating Officer; Jo Giles, General Secretary;
Robin Brattel, Director

Elizabeth Schrek Productions

Le Mailho, Cizos 65230, France
t +33 562 398289 **e** filmusic@woodworks-france.com
Contact Liz Schrek

Extreme Music

Greenland Place, 115-123 Bayham Street, London NW1 0AG
t 020 7485 0111 **f** 020 7482 4871
e info@extrememusic.com **w** www.extrememusic.com
Contact Sam Bruce, Marketing Minx; Helen O'Honlon, International Girl of
Mystery; Rosheen Scott, Client Crusader; Alison Peters, Eurostar; Olly Khoury,
Tune Raider

Factory Sound

Toftrees, Church Road, Woldingham CR3 7JX
t 01883 652386 **f** 01883 652457 **e** mackay@dircon.co.uk
Contact Brenda Mackay, Secretary
Credits Sir Les Patterson (T); House That Jack Built (T); Dame Edna Everage
(C); As Time Goes By (T)

Felt Music

82 Hertford Road, London N2 9BU
t 020 8444 4770 **f** 020 8444 4770 **e** stephen@feltmusic.com
Contact Stephen Spiro, Joint Managing Director; Richard Norris, Joint
Managing Director
Credits Ford (C); HSBC (I); Volkswagon (C); Hamilton Mattress (A)

Glass Tone Productions Ltd

1 Beech Close, Chiddingford GU8 4SB
m 07973 730161 **e** info@glasstone.co.uk **w** www.glasstone.co.uk
Contact Greg Brooker, Managing Director

James Hardway

e james@jameshardway.com **w** www.jameshardway.com

Hazard Chase Ltd

Norman House, Cambridge Place, Cambridge CB2 1NS
t 01223 312400 **f** 01223 460827
e info@hazardchase.co.uk **w** www.hazardchase.co.uk

Hippocampus Ltd

Unit 2, 22 Pakenham Street, London WC1X 0LB
t 020 7692 5170
e mail@hippocampus.uk.com **w** www.hippocampus.uk.com
Contact Daniel Thornton, Creative Director; Luvain Maximen, Producer
Credits Red Devil - Repent (C); Bluesure - Number (C); Lexus - Womb (C);
Remote Madness (T)

Holyrood Recording & Film Productions Ltd

86 Causewayside, Edinburgh EH9 1PY
t 0131 668 3366 **f** 0131 662 4463
e neil@holyroodproductions.com
w www.holyroodproductions.com

Hum

31 Oval Road, London NW1 7EA
t 020 7482 2345 **f** 020 7482 6242
e firstname@hum.co.uk **w** www.hum.co.uk
Contact Nick Payne, Producer; Don Simmons, Producer

I Like It Productions

41 Thornby Road, London E5 9QL
t 020 8923 8373 **e** ilikeit000@hotmail.com
Contact D White, Producer/Department Head/Consultant; C Harriott,
Producer/Music Fixer

Instamusic Ltd

48A Arthur Road, Wokingham RG41 2SY
t 0118 978 2408 **f** 0118 978 2408 **e** peter.fallowell@btinternet.com
Contact Peter Fallowell, Managing Director; Debbie Mills, Secretary; Julie
Fallowell, Secretary

Jeff Wayne Music Group Ltd

Oliver House, 8/9 Ivor Place, London NW1 6BY
t 020 7724 2471 **f** 020 7724 6245
e info@jeffwaynemusic.com **w** www.jeffwaynemusic.com

Joe & Co (Music) Ltd

59 Dean Street, London W1D 6AN
t 020 7439 1272 **f** 020 7437 5504
e justine@joeandco.com **w** www.joeandco.com
Contact Justine Campbell, Office Manager

John Bell Orchestrations

132 Brondesbury Villas, London NW6 6AE
t 020 7328 0060 **f** 020 7372 3860
m 07968 339003 **e** jbell.music@virgin.net

Kick Production Ltd

5D Greek Street, London W1D 4EQ
t 020 7287 3757 **f** 020 7437 0125 **e** name@kickproductions.co.uk
Contact Ian Nicholls, Partner
Credits Maisy (A); Sitting Ducks (A); Inside Las Vegas (D)

Kosinus

127 Charing Cross Road, London WC2H 0QY
t 020 7412 9111 **f** 020 7413 0061
e kpm@kpm.co.uk **w** www.playkpm.com

KPM Music

127 Charing Cross Road, London WC2H 0QY
t 020 7412 9111 **f** 020 7413 0061
e kpm@kpm.co.uk **w** www.playkpm.com
Contact Tim Hardy

*KPM's high quality music can now be searched, auditioned and
downloaded in broadcast quality from the PLAY Music Finder system
(www.playkpm.com). PLAY enables you to cross-search on eight different
music libraries. This service is free of charge to all our clients.*

Loriana Music

30A Tudor Drive, Gidea Park RM2 5LH
t 01708 750185 **f** 01708 750185 **m** 07751 450362
e info@lorianamusic.com
Contact Jean-Louis Fargier, Proprieter
Credits The World's Strongest Man (T)

Megatrax

127 Charing Cross Road, London WC2H 0QY
t 020 7412 9111 **f** 020 7413 0061
e kpm@kpm.co.uk **w** www.playkpm.com

Music By Design
Top Floor, Film House, 142 Wardour Street, London W1F 8ZU
t 020 7434 3244 f 020 7434 1064
e angela@musicbydesign.co.uk w www.musicbydesign.co.uk
Contact Steve Charles, Producer; Angela Allen, Producer

The Music Gallery Ltd
28 Lexington Street, London W1R 3HR
t 020 7287 3138 f 020 7734 0631
e marie@music-gallery.co.uk w www.tape-gallery.co.uk

Music House
143 Charing Cross Road, London WC2H 0EH
t 020 7434 9678 f 020 7434 1470
e enquiries@musichouse.co.uk w www.playmusichouse.com
Contact Rosheen Scott, Marketing Assistant

Music Sculptors
32-34 Rathbone Place, London W1T 1JQ
t 020 7636 1001 f 020 7636 1506 m 07866 385349
e info@themusicsculptors.com w www.themusicsculptors.com
Contact Michelle Spoonley, Production Manager

Nativelogic Ltd
t 08451 232833 e info@nativelogic.com w www.nativelogic.com
Contact Peter Duggal, Director

North Star Music
PO Box 868, Cambridge CB1 6SJ
t 01787 278 256 f 01787 2279 069 m 07801 701013
e nsminfo@aol.com w www.northstarmusic.co.uk
Contact Grahame MacLean, Proprietor

Old Man Jobsons Music Depot
15 Cotham Vale, Cotham, Bristol BS6 6HS
t 01179 466644 f 01179 466999 m 07973 776951
e omjmusic@netcomuk.co.uk
Contact James Barrett, Head of Production

Privileged Man Productions
PO Box 130, Stanmore HA7 4XX
t 020 8420 7532
e productions@kandystand.com w www.kandystand.com

Radiant Music
38A Elm Bank Mansions, The Terrace, London SW13 0NS
t 020 8878 9762 f 020 8878 9762 m 07957 213913
e dashiellr2@aol.com
Contact Dashiell Rae, Film Music Editor
Credits Changing Lanes (F); The Hours (F); Band Of Brothers (T); Gladiator (F)

Resonant Matrix
10 Unity Wharf, Mill Street, London SE1 2BH
t 020 7252 2661 f 08700 512594
e resonantmatrix@movingshadow.com
w www.resonantmatrix.com
Contact Rob Platford, Managing Director; Scott Garrod, Business Manager

Rhythmshop Productions Ltd
e rpl@rhythmshop.com w www.rhythmshop.com
Contact Chris Marshall, Managing Director
Credits Reputations (T); The Secret Life Of Nackers (T)

Rod Thompson Music
73 Bromfelde Road, London SW4 6PP
t 020 7720 0866 f 020 7720 0866 m 07768 288023
Contact Rod Thompson, Managing Director

Ronnie Bond Music
Churchwood Studios, 1 Woodchurch Road, London NW6 3PL
t 020 7372 2229 f 020 7372 3339 m 07932 694 117
e rbm@easynet.co.uk
Contact Ronnie Bond, Director

SBS Records
PO Box 37, Blackwood, Gwent NP12 2YQ
t 01495 201116 f 01495 201190
e glenn@sbsrecords.co.uk w www.sbsrecords.co.uk
Contact Glenn Powell, Managing Director
Credits Manic Street Preachers (C); Hot Property (T)

Selected Sound
127 Charing Cross Road, London WC2H 0QY
t 020 7412 9111 f 020 7413 0061
e kpm@kpm.co.uk w www.playkpm.com

Shake Up Music Ltd
Ickenham Manor, Ickenham, Uxbridge UB10 8QT
t 01895 672994 f 01895 633264 e mail@shakeupmusic.co.uk
Contact Joanna Tizard, Director; Rupert Gregson-Williams, Director

Simon Benson
Rosemead, South Hill Avenue, Harrow-on-the-Hill HA1 3PA
t 020 8423 1351 f 020 8423 1531 m 07973 818 586
e mon@annie-b.co.uk
Contact Simon Benson, Managing Director

Starfish
1st Floor, Block 2, 6 Erskine Road, London NW3 3AJ
t 020 7483 4344 f 020 7722 6605

TV Music Ltd
35 Durand Gardens, London SW9 0PS
t 020 7793 7426 f 020 7735 8965
e info@tvmusic.net w www.tvmusic.net
Contact Alasdair Strange, Managing Director
Credits Tele (D); Nightride (S); Moses, Multimania (C); Hands Up! (T)

Versatile Audio Services
5 Aberdeen Terrace, St James NN5 7AD
t 01604 588618 f 01604 588618 e versatile@ntlworld.com
Contact Neil Sheperd, Composer

VideoHelper
127 Charing Cross Road, London WC2H 0QY
t 020 7412 9111 f 020 7413 0061
e kpm@kpm.co.uk w www.playkpm.com

Water Music Production
First Floor, Block 2, 6 Erskine Road, London NW3 3AJ
t 020 7722 3478 f 020 7722 6605 e splash@watermusic.co.uk
Contact Tessa Lawlor, Producer

Water Music Productions Ltd
1st Floor, Block 2, 6 Erskine Road, London NW3 3AJ
t 020 7722 3478 f 020 7722 6605 e splash@watermusic.co.uk
Contact Tessa Lawlor, Executive Producer, Producer; Chris Davies, Producer, Office Manager
Credits Renewable Option - Powergen (C); Bad Barnet - Brylcream (C); Fishing - Landrover (C); Ice - Orange (C)

West One Music
8 Berwick Street, London W1F 0PH
t 020 7292 0000 f 020 7292 0010
e info@westonemusic.com w www.west-one-music.com
Contact Michael Shaw, General Manager; Naima Lambert, Promotions; Ciaran McNeaney, Promotions
Credits Two Men Went To War (F)

X-Ray Dog
127 Charing Cross Road, London WC2H 0QY
t 020 7412 9111 f 020 7413 0061
e kpm@kpm.co.uk w www.playkpm.com

Yamaha Kemble Music UK
Sherbourne Drive, Tilbrook, Milton Keynes MK7 8BL
t 01908 366700 f 01908 368872
e richard.metcalfe@yamaha-music.co.uk
w www.yamaha-music.co.uk
Contact Richard Metcalfe, Marketing Manager

Zomba Production Music

10-11 St Martin's Court, London WC2N 4AJ
t 0800 034 5245 **f** 020 7497 4801
e promotions@zpm.co.uk **w** www.zpm.co.uk
Contact Tracy Bryer, Head of Promotions; Angela Clague, Promotions Executive; Andrew Stannard, Music Consultant; Andrew Stannard, Music Consultant; Simon James, Director

Music **Publishing**

Ad-Chorel Music Ltd

86 Causewayside, Edinburgh EH9 1PY
t 0131 668 3366 **f** 0131 662 4463
e rel@relrecords.co.uk **w** www.relrecords.co.uk

Air-Edel Copyrights Ltd

18 Rodmarton Street, London W1U 8BJ
t 020 7486 6466 **f** 020 7224 0344
e air-edel@air-edel.co.uk **w** www.air-edel.co.uk
Contact Alexandra Manniln, Manager; Maggie Rodford, Managing Director

BMG Music Publishing

Bedford House, 69-79 Fulham High Street, London SW6 3JW
t 020 7384 7600 **f** 020 7384 8167 **w** www.bmgmusicsearch.com
Contact Dave Bartram, Advertising/Games Manager; Mary Ann Slim, Film/TV Manager
Credits Coca Cola - 3-Legged Striker (C); O2 Telecommunications - Launch (C); The Guru (F); Johnny English (F)

Boosey & Hawkes Music Publishing

295 Regent Street, London W1B 2JH
t 020 7580 2060 **f** 020 7291 7109
e booseymedia@boosey.com **w** www.boosey.com
Contact Natasha Baldwin, Marketing Manager; Michael Shaw, Marketing Manager

Boosey & Hawkes Music Publishers is one of the largest Classical publishers in the world. It's extensive catalogue of 20th Century music includes the works of Rachmaninoff, Stravinsky, Copland, John Adams, Steve Reich and Henryk Gorecki.

Chantelle Music

3A Ashfield Parade, Southgate, London N14 5EH
t 020 8886 6236 **f** 020 8886 6236 **w** www.chantellemusic.co.uk
Contact Riss Chantelle, Director

Chrysalis Music

The Chrysalis Building, Bramley Road, London W10 6SP
t 020 7221 2213 **f** 020 7465 6253
Contact Karina Masters, Film Manager

Classical Series (KPM)

127 Charing Cross Road, London WC2H 0EA
t 020 7412 9111 **f** 020 7413 0061
e kpm@kpm.co.uk **w** www.playkpm.co.uk
Contact Elaine van Der Schoot, Creative Manager

Edition UK Ltd

19 Woburn Place, London WC1H 0LU
t 020 8348 1038 **f** 020 8348 1038
e editionuk@btinternet.com **w** www.editionuk.co.uk
Contact David Watts, Manager

EMI Music Publishing

127 Charing Cross Road, London WC2H 0QY
t 020 7434 2131 **f** 020 7287 1041
e jchannon@emimusicpub.com **w** www.emimusicpub.co.uk
Contact Jonathan Channon, Director

Faber Music Ltd

3 Queen Square, London WC1N 3AU
e richard.paine@fabermusic.co.uk **w** www.fabermusic.co.uk
Contact Richard Paine, Director
Credits The Life Of Mammals (T); Trial And Retribution (T); Shadow Of The Vampire (T)

First Time Music (Publishing) UK

Sovereign House, 12 Trewartha Road, Praa Sands, Penzance TR20 9ST
t 01736 762826 **f** 01736 763328 **m** 07721 449477
e panamus@aol.com **w** www.panamamusic.co.uk
Contact Roderick Jones, Managing Director

Hit & Run Music Publishing Ltd

11 Denmark Street, London WC2H 8TD
t 020 7240 2408 **f** 020 7240 1818
e vanessa@hit-and-run.com
Contact Vanessa Grogan, Film and Advertising Manager

The Music Factor

The Music Factor Ltd

15 Stanhope Road, London N6 5NE
t 020 8802 5984 **f** 020 8809 7436
e themusicfactor@paulrodriguezmus.demon.co.uk
Contact Paul Rodriguez, Managing Director; Amy Coats, Copyright Manager
Recent work: BBC TV, Channel 4, Channel 5, Discovery. Facilities: music production, music publishing, music library, copyright clearance.

Orestes Music Publishing Ltd

PO Box 10653, London W5 4HB
t 020 8993 7441 **f** 020 8992 9993
e info@dorm.co.uk **w** www.thedormgroup.com

Paul Rodriguez Music Ltd

61 Queens Drive, London N4 2BG
t 020 8802 5984 **f** 020 8809 7436
e paul@paulrodriguezmus.demon.co.uk
Contact Paul Rodriguez, Director

Satellite Music Ltd

34 Salisbury Street, London NW8 8QE
t 020 7402 9111 **f** 020 7723 3064
e satellite_artists@hotmail.com **w** www.amimedia.co.uk
Contact Eliot Cohen, Managing Director

Scamp Music

Sovereign House, 12 Trewartha Road, Praa Sands, Penzance TR20 9ST
t 01736 762826 **f** 01736 763328 **m** 07721 449477
e panamus@aol.com **w** www.panamamusic.co.uk
Contact Roderick Jones, Managing Director

Songwriting Composing & Musical Productions

Sovereign House, 12 Trewartha Road, Praa Sands, Penzance TR20 9ST
t 01736 762826 **f** 01736 763328 **m** 07721 449477
e songmag@aol.com **w** www.songwriters-guild.co.uk
Contact Roderick Jones, Managing Director

World Circuit Ltd

1st Floor, Storeditch Stables, 138 Kingsland Road, London E2 8DY
t 020 7749 3222 **f** 020 7749 3232
e post@worldcircuit.co.uk **w** www.worldcircuit.co.uk
Contact Lucy Sutton, Press & Promotions; Matt Robins, Marketing Manager; Nick Gold, Managing Director; Wendy Sellars, General Manager; Jackie Harrison, Production Manager; Jo Bull, Licensing & Publishing Manager

Music
Recording Companies

Abbas Records
26 Whitehall Gardens, London W3 9RD
t 020 8992 4183 **f** 020 8354 0919 **m** 07050 114183
e simoneadon@compuserve.com
Ex-Decca engineers providing unrivalled recording experience.

ARK 21/Pagan Records
1 Water Lane, London NW1 8NZ
t 020 7267 1101 **f** 020 7267 7466
e ark21recsords@aol.com
w www.ark21.com; www.paganrecords.com
Contact Mark Haddon; Richard Breeden; Racheal Hands

First Time Records
Sovereign House, 12 Trewartha Road, Praa Sands, Penzance
TR20 9ST
t 01736 762826 **f** 01736 763328 **m** 07721 449477
e panamus@aol.com **w** www.panamamusic.co.uk
Contact Roderick Jones, Managing Director

Go Beat
Fulham Palace, Bishops Park, Bishops Avenue, London SW6 6EA
t 020 7800 4400 **f** 020 7800 4401
Contact Verdy Unger-Hamilton, Managing Director

Heraldic Jester Records
Sovereign House, 12 Trewartha Road, Praa Sands, Penzance
TR20 9ST
t 01736 762826 **f** 01736 763328
e panamus@aol.com **w** www.panamamusic.co.uk
Contact Roderick Jones, Managing Director

Heraldic Vintage Disc
Sovereign House, 12 Trewartha Road, Praa Sands, Penzance
TR20 9ST
t 01736 762826 **f** 01736 763328 **m** 07721 449477
e panamus@aol.com **w** www.panamamusic.co.uk
Contact Roderick Jones, Managing Directors

Little Piece of Jamaica Records
55 Finsbury Park Road, London N4 2JY
t 020 7359 0788 **f** 020 7226 2168
m 07973 630729 **e** paulhuepoj@yahoo.co.uk
Contact Paul Hue, Managing Director

Mohock Records
Sovereign House, 12 Trewartha Road, Praa Sands, Penzance
TR20 9ST
t 01736 762826 **f** 01736 763328
e panamus@aol.com **w** www.panamamusic.co.uk
Contact Roderick Jones, Managing Director

Natural Grooves
3 Tannsfeld Road, Sydenham, London SE26 5DQ
t 020 8488 3677 **f** 020 8473 6539 **m** 07957 251252
w www.naturalgrooves.com
Contact Jonathan Sharif, Managing Director

PVA Music
Hallow Park, Hallow, Worcester WR2 6PG
t 01905 640663 **f** 01905 641842 **e** steve@pva.co.uk
Contact Stephen Pink, Manager

REL Records Ltd
86 Causewayside, Edinburgh EH9 1PY
t 0131 668 3366 **f** 0131 662 4463
e rel@relrecords.co.uk **w** www.relrecords.co.uk

Select Music & Video Distribution Ltd
3 Wells Place, Redhill RH1 3SL
t 01737 645600 x306 **t** 01635 871338
f 01737 644065 **m** 07850 170459
e gbartholomew@selectmusic.co.uk **w** www.naxos.com
Contact Graham Bartholomew, Licensing Manager

Snapper Music PLC
3 The Coda Centre, 189 Munster Road, London SW6 6AW
t 020 7610 0330 **f** 020 7610 0355
e info@snappermusic.co.uk **w** www.snappermusic.com
Contact Brian Leafe, Music & Video Clip Licencing

Virgin Records
553 Harrow Road, London W10 4RH
t 020 8964 6000 **f** 020 8968 6533 **w** www.virgin.co.uk
Credits Junior Jack: Thrill Me; Mutiny: The Virus

ZTT Records
The Blue Buildings, 42-46 St Lukes Mews, London W11 1DG
t 020 7221 5101 **f** 020 7221 3374
e info@ztt.com **w** www.ztt.com
Contact Jill Sinclair, Managing Director

Music Recording Studios

Abbey Road Studios
Abbey Road Studios, 3 Abbey Road, St Johns Wood, London
NW8 9AY
t 020 7266 7000 **f** 020 7266 7250
e bookings@abbeyroad.com **w** www.abbeyroad.com
Contact Lucy Launder, Post Production Manager; Colette Barber, Studio
Operations Manager

Air Studios
Lyndhurst Hall, Lyndhurst Road, Hampstead, London NW3 5NG
t 020 7794 0660 **f** 020 7794 8518
e sally@airstudios.com **w** www.airstudios.com
Contact Sally Drury, Post Production Co-Ordinator
Credits Cutting It (T); Born And Bred (T); The Jury (T); Jeffrey Archer - The Truth (T)

Angel Recording Studios
311 Upper Street, London N1 2TU
t 020 7354 2525 **f** 020 7226 9624
e angel@angelstudios.co.uk **w** www.angelstudios.co.uk

Britannia Row Studios
3 Bridge Studios, 318-326 Wandsworth Bridge Road, Fulham,
London SW6 2TZ
t 020 7371 5872 **f** 020 7371 8641
e mark@britanniarowstudios.co.uk
w www.britanniarowstudios.co.uk
Contact Mark Cox, Studio Manager; Kate Koumi, Managing Director

Clock House Recording Studio
The Clock House, Keele ST5 5BG
t 01782 583301 **f** 01782 583301
e mua00@mus.keele.ac.uk
w www.keele.ac.uk/depts/mu/index.htm
Contact Cliff Bradbury, Studio Manager

Abigail Coult
2 Hillary House, Boyton Close, London N8 7BB

CTS Studios Ltd
Suite 1A, Lansdowne House, Lansdowne Road, London W11 3LP
t 020 7467 0099 **f** 020 7467 0098
e cts-lansdowne@cts-lansdowne.co.uk **w** www.cts-lansdowne.co.uk
Contact Mike Brown, Senior Mastering Engineer; Adrian Kerridge, Managing Director

Face Musical Productions

211 Wingrove Road, Newcastle-upon-Tyne NE4 9DB
t 0191 273 4443
e info@davemaugham.co.uk **w** www.davemaughan.co.uk
Contact Dave Maughan, Composer/Producer/sound designer
Credits Little Black Numbers; Kathryn Williams; Morris Quinlan

Fleetwood Mobiles Ltd

Bray Film Studios, Water Oakley, Windsor SL4 5UG
t 0870 077 1071 **f** 0870 077 1068
e sales@fleetwoodmobiles.com **w** www.fleetwoodmobiles.com
Contact Ian Dyckhoff

hotdog

2 Hillary House, Boyton Close, London N8 7BB
Contact Abigail Coult, Proprietor

Keylink Studios

Roughwood Drive, Kirkby L33 8XF
t 0151 549 2499 **f** 0151 549 0745
e keylink@keylinkstudios.org.uk **w** www.keylinkstudios.org.uk
Contact Peter Nelson, Production Manager

Konk Studios

84-86 Tottenham Lane, London N8 7EE
t 020 8340 7873 **f** 020 8348 3952 **e** linda@konkstudio.com
Contact Sarah Lockwood, Studio Manager

Lansdowne Recording Studios Ltd

Lansdowne House, Lansdowne Road, London W11 3LP
t 020 7727 0041 **f** 020 7792 8904
e info@cts-lansdowne.co.uk **w** www.cts-lansdowne.co.uk
Contact Chris Dibble, Studio Director; Vicki Pyrkos, Studio Bookings; Claire Peck, Client Coordinator

Matrix

91 Peterborough Road, London SW6 3BW
t 020 7580 9956 **t** 020 7384 6400 **f** 020 7371 8613
e matrixrecording@connectfree.co.uk
Contact Nigel Frieda, Managing Director

Mayfair Recording Studios Ltd

11a Sharpeshall Street, London NW1 8YN
t 020 7586 7746 **f** 020 7586 9721
e bookings@mayfair-studios.co.uk **w** www.mayfairstudios.com
Contact Don Mills, Manager; John Hudson, Managing Director

Metro Radio Creative Services

Radio House, Swalwell, Newcastle-upon-Tyne NE99 1BB
t 0191 420 0971 **f** 0191 421 0409
e creative@metroandmagic.com **w** www.metroradio.co.uk
Contact Mark Gregory, Creative Director; Sharon Dennis, Studio Manager

Metropolis Group

The Powerhouse, 70 Chiswick High Road, London W4 1SY
t 020 8742 1111 **f** 020 8742 3777
e hello@metropolis-group.co.uk **w** www.metropolis-group.co.uk
Contact Alison Hussey, Studio Manager

Moles Recording Studio

14 George Street, Bath BA1 2EN
t 01225 404445 **f** 01225 404447
e info@moles.co.uk **w** www.molesstudio.co.uk
Contact Jan Brown, Studio Manager

Olympic Studios

117 Church Road, London SW13 9HL
t 020 8286 8600 **f** 020 8286 8625
e info@olympicstudios.co.uk **w** www.olympicstudios.co.uk
Contact Siobhan Paine, Studio Manager
Credits Keith Flint (M); Massive Attack (M); Madonna (M)

Parr Street Studios

33-45 Parr Street, Liverpool L1 4JN
t 0151 707 1050 **f** 0151 707 1813
e info@parrstreet.co.uk **w** www.parrstreet.co.uk
Contact Paul Lewis, Bookings Manager

The Pro Tools Room

Sanctuary House, 45-53 Sinclair Road, London W14 0NS
t 020 8932 3200 **f** 020 8932 3207
e protools@sanctuarystudios.co.uk
w www.sanctuarystudios.co.uk
Contact Nikki Affleck, Studio Manager

Fully equipped Pro Tools recording studio in West London with in-house catering and licensed bar.

Radio Six Productions

PO Box 600, Glasgow G41 4SH
t 0141 427 0531 **f** 0141 427 0531
e karin@radiosix.com **w** www.radiosix.com
Contact Karin Spalter, Contact

RAK Recording Studios

42-48 Charlbert Street, London NW8 7BU
t 020 7586 2012 **f** 020 7722 5823
e trisha@rakstudios.co.uk **w** www.rakstudios.co.uk

Recording Architecture

1 Greenwich Quay, Clarence Road, London SE10 9HZ
t 020 8692 6992 **f** 020 8692 6957
e ra@aaa-design.com **w** www.aaa-design.com
Contact Roger D''Arcy, Managing Director

Red Bus TV & Recording Studios

Studio House, 34 Salisbury Street, London NW8 8QE
t 020 7402 9111 **f** 020 7723 3064 **w** www.amimedia.co.uk
Contact Eliot Cohen, Managing Director

Roundhouse Recordings Studios

91-94 Saffron Hill, Farringdon, London EC1N 8PT
t 020 7404 3333 **f** 020 7404 2947
e roundhouse@stardiamond.com
w www.stardiamond.com/roundhouse
Contact Maddy Clarke, Studio Manager; Roger McLenahan, Technical Manager; Lisa Gunther, Studio Manager

Sanctuary Town House Studios

150 Goldhawk Road, London W12 8HH
t 020 8932 3200 **f** 020 8932 3207
e townhouse@sanctuarystudios.co.uk
w www.sanctuarystudios.co.uk
Contact Nikki Affleck, Studio Manager

Excellent recording facility in West London. Studio 1: SSL4000G+ 72/32/2 with Ultimation & Total Recall. G Series mic pre-amps with E Series EQ. Studio 2: SSL 8072 G Series 72/24/8 with Ultimation & Total Recall. 5.1 Surround Monitoring. Studio 4: SSL 4000E 72/32/4 with G Series computer & Total Recall. All Monitors are Genelec 1035a & NS10. Acoustics by Sam Toyoshima. Pro Tools HD. Games Room. On-site catering and accommodation.

Sanctuary Westside Studios

10 Olaf Street, London W11 4BE
t 020 7221 9494 **f** 020 7727 0008
e westside@sanctuarystudios.co.uk **w** www.sanctuarystudios.co.uk
Contact Jo Buckley, Bookings Coordinator

Studio 1: The mixing desk is a Neve VR 60 channel console and the live area measures 132 square metres plus two sizeable isolation booths. The studio comes with a private lounge including satellite TV and hi-fi. Studio 2: The control room houses a 64 channel SSL Console with a large ambient live area measuring 80 square meters. Both studios include a Bosendorfer 7'9 grand piano."

Sarm Studios (East) Ltd

9-13 Osborn Street, London E1 6TD
t 020 7247 1311 **f** 020 7426 0009
e henri@spz.com **w** www.sarmstudios.com
Contact Graham Carpenter, Studio Manager; Henriette Cox, Studio Manager

Sarm Studios (West)
8-10 Basing Street, London W11 1ET
t 020 7229 1229 **f** 020 7221 9247
e henri@spz.com **w** www.sarmstudios.com
Contact Henriette Cox, Studio Manager; Graham Carpenter, Studio Manager

Sarner Sound Studios
16 Southsea Road, Kingston-upon-Thames KT1 2EH
t 020 8481 0600 **f** 020 8547 3038
e info@sarner.com **w** www.sarner.com
Contact Ross Magri, Bookings & Technical Director

Snake Ranch Studios
90 Lots Road, London SW10 0QD
t 020 7351 7888 **f** 020 7352 5194
e gerry@snakeranch.co.uk **w** www.snakeranch.co.uk
Contact Gerry O'Riordan, Studio Manager; Paul Richardson, Engineer; Phil Harmer, Engineer
Credits The Incredible Mrs Ritchie (F); Midsomer Murders (T); My Kingdom (F); Cold Feet (T)

Sound Stage Ltd
Kerchesters, Waterhouse Lane, Kingswood KT20 6HT
t 01737 832837 **f** 01737 833812
e ian@soundstage.co.uk **w** www.amphonic.com
Contact Ian Dale, Managing Director

Studio Remotes Ltd
2 Home Field, Caldecotte, Milton Keynes MK7 8HH
t 01908 367335 **f** 01908 367335
e info@studio-remotes.com **w** www.studio-remotes.com
Contact John Orme, Technical Manager

Village Productions
4 Midas Business Centre, Wantz Road, Dagenham RM10 8PS
t 020 8984 0322
Contact Tony Atkins, Director

Music Recording Studios Mobile

P H Music
48 Mourfield, Edgworth, Bolton BL7 0DA
t 01204 853310 **f** 01204 853445 **m** 07799 621954
e peter@phmusic.co.uk **w** www.phmusic.co.uk
Contact Peter Harrison, Managing Director

Realsound Location Recording
45 Scotland Road, Nottingham NG5 1JU
t 0115 978 7745 **f** 0115 978 7745 **m** 07973 279652
e john@realsound.fsnet.co.uk **w** www.realsound-uk.com
Contact John Moon, Proprietor

Sanctuary Mobiles
Bray Film Studios, Water Oakley, Windsor SL4 5UG
t 08700 771071 **f** 08700 771068
e mobiles@sanctuarystudios.co.uk **w** www.sanctuarystudios.co.uk
Contact Ian Dyckhoff, General Manager

Mobile Recording, Mixing — Stereo and 5.1 and Postproduction for Radio and Television Broadcast or Commercial Release worldwide

Music Musical Equipment Hire

Advanced Sounds
259 Queensway, West Wickham BR4 9DX
t 020 8462 6261 **f** 020 8462 8621 **m** 07860 310618
e advancedsoundsltd@btinternet.com
w www.advancedsounds.co.uk

The Hammond Hire Company
Islington, London
t 020 7288 0037
e mail@hammondhire.com **w** www.hammondhire.com

Mike U'Dell/Drumhire
Unit 14, Triangle Business Centre, Enterprise Way, Salter Street, London NW10 6UG
t 020 8960 0221 **f** 020 8960 0222
e mike@drumhire.com **w** www.drumhire.com

Sensible Music Hire, Sales & PA
Rebond House, 98-124 Brewery Road, London N7 9PG
t 020 7700 6655 **f** 020 7609 9478
e rental@sensible-music.co.uk **w** www.sensiblemusic.com
Contact Billy Allen, Rental Desk; Paul Kershaw, Rental Desk; Andrew Fagan, Hire Desk; Matt Russell, Hire Desk; Gavin Ellis, Rental Desk; Pat Tate, General Manager

Swans Music
Belan Moss Lane, Mobberly WA16 7BS
m 07710 341394
e hire@swannsmusic.co.uk **w** www.swansmusic.co.uk
Contact Bill Swan; David Swan

OFFICE

Office Equipment Hire

Altodigital South East Ltd
34 Pit Lake, West Croydon CR0 3RA
t 020 8688 8301 **f** 020 8688 0533
e enquiries@altodigital.com **w** www.altodigital.com
Contact Mike Stewart, Group Accountant; Jeremy Tarrant, Group Accountant

Aztec Communications Ltd
St George's House, 195-203 Waterloo Road, London SE1 8UK
t 0870 746 3000 **f** 0870 746 3001
e info@aztecuk.net **w** www.aztecuk.net/rentals
Contact Mark Parker, Sales Manager

Complete Office Systems Ltd
13 Highams Business Park, Blackhorse Lane, London E17 6SH
t 020 8527 4000 **f** 020 8527 2222
e enquiries@cosgroup.com **w** www.cosgroup.com

Hamilton Rentals
Hamilton House, North Circular Road, London NW10 7UB
t 020 8961 4300 **f** 020 8961 8385
e info@hamilton.co.uk **w** www.hamilton.co.uk
Contact Mark Watson, Sales Manager

Knightsbridge Office Services Ltd
229 Acton Lane, London W4 5DD
t 020 8995 3232 **f** 020 8995 2144 **m** 07703 937850
e enquiries@kos-hire.co.uk **w** www.kos-hire.co.uk
Contact Patrick Hayward, Director
Credits Hope & Glory II & III (T); Birthday Girl (F); Harry Potter And The Philosopher's Stone (F)

Performance Systems Ltd
8 Park Crescent, Elstree WD6 3PU
t 0845 130 0747 **f** 020 8905 1463 **m** 07860 791277
e copiers@d-cctv.co.uk
Contact Marc Green, Contact; Phil Breindel, Contact

TCE Associates Ltd
26 Midway, Walton-on-Thames KT12 3HZ
t 01932 248794 **f** 01932 228820 **m** 07860 828643
w www.tceassociates.co.uk
Contact Trevor Edwards, Managing Director
Credits The Jury (T); Harry Potter And The Philosopher's Stone (F); 102 Dalmatians (F)

Transcribe Thames Group
Phoenix House, 244 Croydon Lane, Beckenham BR3 4DA
t 020 8658 4544 **f** 020 8658 4775
e info@thamesgroup.com **w** www.thamesgroup.com
Contact Rampling, Managing Director

Office Photocopying & Printing

BPS Printers
Holtspur Top Lane, Beaconsfield HP9 1DN
t 01494 678823 **f** 01494 674457
e production@bps-printers.co.uk **w** www.bps-printers.co.uk
Contact Tom Griffiths, Managing Director; Dominic George, Production Manager

The Color Company
130 Wardour Street, London W1F 8ZN
t 020 7434 0824 **f** 020 7434 0833 **w** www.wardour@color.co.uk
Contact David Summers, Manager; Julie Summers, Manager

First Colour
15 Newman Street, London W1T 1PA
t 020 7636 2571 **f** 020 7436 4831
e westend@firstcolor.com **w** www.firstcolor.com

Kall-Kwik
21 Kingly Street, London W1B 5QA
t 020 7434 2471 **f** 020 7494 0260
e kallkwik@regent-street.demon.co.uk **e** www.kallkwik.com
Contact John Griffith, General Manager

National Screen Service
2 Wedgwood Mews, 12 Greek Street, London W1V 6VH
t 020 7437 4113 **f** 020 7287 0328
Contact Dominic Mills, Technical Support

North Film Forms - Robert North & Sons
18 Rudolph Road, Bushey WD23 3DY
t 0 5003 60300 **f** 0 5003 60123 **w** www.filmforms.co.uk
Contact Barbara Watkins, Manager

Pontaprint
52 Brewer Street, London W1R 3HN
t 020 7434 1505 **f** 020 7494 2423
e pontaprint.soho@btinternet.com
Contact Adrian Selby

printed matters ltd

Printed Matters
217 Northfield Avenue, West Ealing W13 9QU
t 020 8579 8388 **f** 020 8840 8833 **m** 07836 325586
e 1st@s4kmedia.tv
Contact Simon Bell; Tommy Wan

TSM Copiers Ltd
44B Walton Business Centre, Terrace Road, Walton-on-Thames KT12 2SA
t 08700 003050 **f** 01932 267776 **m** 07860 823050
e info@tsmcopiers.co.uk **w** www.tsmcopiers.co.uk
Contact Sean McGovern, Service Manager

Office Production Base

Coborn House Business Centre
3 Coborn Road, London E3 2DA
t 020 7267 2008 **f** 020 7267 4744 **m** 07973 176424
e susie@aaselfstorage.com **e** info@aaselfstorage.com
w www.aaselfstorage.com
Contact Suzy Adler, Manager/Director

Nauticalia Ltd
The Ferry Point, Ferry Lane, Shepperton-On-Thames TW17 9LQ
t 01932 244396 **f** 01932 241679
e sales@nauticalia.com **w** www.nauticalia.com
Contact John Hales, Sales

Office Stationers

Acton Stationers & Printers Ltd
8 Central Parade, Gunnersby Lane, London W3 8HL
t 020 8993 1555 **f** 020 8993 9763
Contact John French

Office Telephones & Faxes

DMC Business Machines Plc
59 Imperial Way, Croydon CR0 4RR
t 020 8688 4243 **f** 020 8667 0328 **w** www.dmcplc.co.uk
Contact Mr Nicholson, Managing Director

Virtual Office Services
211 Piccadilly, London W1J 9HF
t 020 7917 9917 **f** 020 7439 0262
e info@virtual-office.co.uk **w** www.voffice.co.uk
Contact Emma Kelly, Sales Manager; Lori Martin, Operations Manager; Cheryl McCormack

OUTSIDE BROADCAST

Outside Broadcast Satellite Services

BBC Outside Broadcasts

BBC Outside Broadcasts
Kendal Avenue, London W3 0RP
t 020 8993 9333 **f** 020 8993 4510
e ob@bbc.co.uk **w** www.bbcresources.com/ob

BeaconSeek Ltd
Hithermailes, 212 Mancroft Road, Aley Green, Luton LU1 4DR
t 01582 842717 **f** 01582 849013 **m** 07003 930 930
e jonathan.higgins@beaconseek.com **w** www.beaconseek.com
Contact Jonathan Higgins, Director; Ann Higgins, Director

BT Broadcast Services
BT Tower, 60 Cleveland Street, London W1P 6EA
t 0800 671848 **f** 0800 679880
e marketing@vbs.bt.co.uk **w** www.broadcast.bt.com

Com Dev Europe
Triangle Business Park, Stoke Mandaville, Alesbury HP22 5SX
t 01296 616400 **f** 01296 616500 **w** www.comdev.co.uk
Contact Peter Loweth, European Sales Manager; Rob Goldsmith, Business Development Director

Continental Microwave Ltd
1 Crawley Green Road, Luton LU1 3LB
t 01582 424233 **f** 01582 455273
e sales@continental-microwave.co.uk
w www.continental-microwave.co.uk
Contact Ian Aizlewood, Chairman

Downlink Communications Ltd
Unit 1, Avebury Court, Mark Road, Hemel Hempstead HP2 7TA
t 01442 240671 **f** 01442 240672
e downlink@downlink.co.uk **w** www.downlink.co.uk
Contact Michael Miller, Managing Director

For the corporate and broadcast client, we offer events by satellite throughout the world. Uplinks, downlinks, space segment, video-conferencing links.

Geoff Petts & Associates Satellite Express
1 The Gardens, Great Hyde Hall, Sawbridgeworth CM21 9JA
t 01279 726804 **f** 01279 722368 **m** 07802 921401
e gpetts@aol.com
Contact Geoff Petts

GlobeCast
200 Gray's Inn Road, London WC1X 8XZ
t 020 7430 4400 **f** 020 7430 4321
e gary.champion@globecast.com
e steve.fairbrother@globecast.com **w** www.globecast.com
Contact Steve Fairbrother, Head of IP Services, Europe; William Pitt, Account Manager; Gary Champion, Head of News and BTV, Europe

GlobeCast - a France Telecom subsidiary - is the global leader in satellite transmission services for professional broadcast, enterprise multimedia and Internet content delivery. Operating 15 teleport earth stations throughout Europe, America, Asia, Australia, the Middle East and Africa, GlobeCast offers the complete range of satellite broadcast solutions, including TV channel distribution, secure satellite Internet delivery, webcasting, satellite newsgathering, direct-to-home distribution, sports programming backhaul, studio production, special events mobile production and audio distribution.

ntl (Oxford)
Comtel Court, Shelley Close, Headington, Oxford OX3 8HB
t 01865 450450 **f** 01865 450535 **w** www.ntl.com
Contact Alistair Davidson, Chief Executive

ntl:broadcast

ntl : Broadcast
Crawley Court, Winchester SO21 2QA
t 01962 822400 **f** 01962 822553
e satellite-info@ntl.com **w** www.ntlbroadcast.com

Observe
Unit 19 Corrig Road, Sandyford Industrial Estate, Dublin 18
t +353 1 216 0090 **f** +353 1 216 0091
e info@observe.ie **w** www.observe.ie
Contact Alan Burns; Suzanne Colwell

PTV Prime Ltd
PO Box 34123, London NW10 7GW
t 8961 4911 **t** 8961 4914
e trevor@ptvltd.com **w** www.ptvltd.com
Contact Trevor Rogers, Managing Director

Sat-Comm Ltd
95 Hampstead Avenue, Mildenhall IP28 7AS
t 01638 515000 **f** 01638 515055
e sales@sat-comm.com **w** www.sat-comm.com
Contact Tim Williams, Managing Director

Sat-Tech Communications
24 Grecian Crescent, London SE19 9HH
t 020 8670 0089 **f** 020 8670 0136
e garywilson@sat-tech.co.uk **w** www.sat-tech.co.uk
Contact Gary Wilson, Director

Satellite Media Services
Lawford Heath Teleport, Lawford Heath Lane, Rugby CV23 9EU
t 01788 523000 **f** 01788 523001
e info@sms-internet.net **w** www.sms.co.uk
Contact Maggie Corke, Director of Sales and Marketing

SISLink

SIS Link
Satellite House, 17 Corsham Street, London N1 6DR
t 020 7696 9888 **f** 020 7608 0834
e sales@sislink.co.uk **w** www.sislink.co.uk
Contact Mark Kingston, Managing Director; Francis Lovell, Sales Manager; Helen Jeffrey, Sales Executive
Credits ITN News (T); Scottish Premiership Football (T); Orange Baftas 2003 (T); The Brit Awards (T)

SNG Broadcast Services Ltd
The London Broadcast Centre, 11-13 Point Pleasant, London SW18 1NN
t 020 8433 8080 **f** 020 8433 8081
e sales@sng.co.uk **w** www.sng.co.uk
Contact Jackie Hattingh, Production Manager; Neil Neusten, Business Development Manager

Solo Satellite
The Penthouse, 181 Northgate, Almondbury, Huddersfield HD5 8US
t 01484 424181 **f** 01484 549613 **m** 07836 333763
e info@solosat.com **w** www.solosat.com
Contact Keith Marshall

Stryder
Falcon Croft, Water Street, Somerton, Bicester OX25 6NE
t 01869 345699 **f** 01869 346699 **m** 07831 171556
e steve.ryder@stryder.tv **w** www.stryder.tv
Contact Clare Ryder, Proprietor; Steve Ryder, Proprietor
Credits BBC Newsnight (T); Sky News (T); ITV News (T)

Outside Broadcast Units

A Smith Great Bentley
Centre Park, Clacton Road, Frating, Colchester CO7 7DL
t 01206 250380 **f** 01206 250509
e ian@asgb.co.uk **w** www.asgb.co.uk
Contact Ian Smith, Managing Director

Advision TV
The Old Post House, The Street, Northbourne, Deal CT14 0LF
t 01304 366218 **f** 01304 366218 **m** 07957 625183
e enquiries@advisiontv.co.uk **w** www.advisiontv.co.uk
Contact Andy Wall; Matthew Titterton
Credits Daihatsu UK (I); Breaking The Sound Barrier With John Suchet (D); Who Wants To Be A Sillionaire? (T); Mica Paris - Live In Concert (M)

AFL Television Facilities Ltd
181A Verulam Road, St Albans AL3 4DR
t 01727 844117 **f** 01727 847649 **m** 07802 682424
e facilities@afltv.com **w** www.afltv.com
Contact Chris Blake, Director; Chris Blake, Director; Graham Howe, Lighting Camerman; Dave Chapman, Director; Jenny Lane, Facilities Manager; Athos Gabriel; Athos Gabriel, Sound; Chris Blake, Director
Credits Cheer For Charlie (T); Time Team (T); Holiday (T)

Broadcast video shooting facilities with state-of-the-art equipment and top technicians plus the best service and backup. We supply Digital Single Camera Units and 2/3/4/5 Camera OB units.

AK Speciality Vehicles UK Ltd
Unit 17, Nelson Way, Camberley GU15 3DH
t 01276 64490 **f** 01276 63350
e david.moore@aksv.co.uk **w** www.aksv.com
Contact Rob Miller, General Manager

Arena Television
Hanger 7, Redhill Aerodrome, Redhill RH1 5JY
t 01737 822011 **f** 01737 821145
e info@arena-tv.com **w** www.arena-tv.com
Contact James Bonnar, Head of Outside Broadcast; Richard Snow; Geoff Davies
Credits Iraq Day (T); Cracking Crime (T); Cracking Crime; My Favourite Hymns (T)

Barcud
Cibyn, Caernarfon LL55 2BD
t 01286 684300 **f** 01286 671679
e barcud@barcud-derwen.co.uk **w** www.barcud-derwen.co.uk
Contact Tudor Roberts

BBC Outside Broadcasts

BBC Outside Broadcasts
Kendal Avenue, London W3 0RP
t 020 8993 9333 **f** 020 8993 4510
e ob@bbc.co.uk **w** www.bbcresources.com/ob

BBC Scotland Resources Operations
Room G51, Broadcasting House, Queen Margaret Drive,
Glasgow G12 8DG
t 0141 338 2343 **f** 0141 338 2335
e resops.scotland@bbc.co.uk
w www.bbc.co.uk/scotland/resources
Contact Natalie Adams, Facilities Co-ordinator; Alex Gaffney, Sales &
Marketing Manager; Susie Miller, Marketing Assistant; Donagh Campbell,
Facilities Assistant
Credits Six Nations Rugby (T); Songs Of Praise (T); Mechanoids (T); Scottish
Premiership Football (T)

BORIS Television Ltd
Bridge House, Branksome Park Road, Camberley GU15 2AQ
t 01276 61222 **f** 01276 61549 **m** 07713 878652
Contact Christopher Smith, Managing Director

Bow Tie Television
Unit 20, Bourne Industrial Park, Bourne Road,
Crayford DA1 4BZ
t 01322 524500 **f** 01322 527777
e john@bowtietv.com **w** www.bowtietv.com
Contact John Knopp, Managing Director
Credits Endemol - King Of Sport (T); NHK Enterprises Europe Ltd - Red Demon (T)

CARLTON 021

Carlton 021
Units 11-13, Gravelly Industrial Park, Gravelly Hill, Birmingham
B24 8HZ
t 0121 327 2021 **f** 0121 327 7021
e 021info@carltontv.co.uk **w** www.carlton021.net
Contact Rob Hollier, Directer of Operations; Ed Everest, Managing Director
Credits National TV Awards (T); The Premiership (T); Choir Of The Year (T);
UEFA Champions League (T)

CBF Media Ltd
6 Springwell Court, Holbeck Lane, Leeds LS12 1AL
t 0113 242 5460 **f** 0113 255 9094
e info@cbfmedia.tv **w** www.cbfmedia.tv
Contact Cherry Salt, Facilites Manager; Mike Bryden, Managing Director;
Graham King, Managing Director

Charter Broadcast Ltd
Unit 4, Elstree Distribution Park, Elstree Way, Borehamwood
WD6 1RU
t 020 8905 1213 **f** 020 8905 1424 **m** 07836 521987
e charter@charter.co.uk
Contact Helen Frost, Bookings Coordinator

*Equipment hire company, offering a comprehensive range of broadcast
video, audio, graphics and RF facilities for dry hire. In addition, Charter
Broadcast offers Mobile Production Units and Flyaway Systems worldwide. Please contact us for further information or visit our website.*

OUTSIDE BROADCAST

Creative Technology Outside Broadcast Ltd
10 Silverglade Business Park, Chessington KT9 2QL
t 01372 747401 **f** 01372 747402
e info@ctob.co.uk **w** www.ctob.co.uk
Contact Adam Berger, Managing Director; Alexandra Stephen, Facilities Manager
Credits Coldplay At The MEN (T); Saturday Fight Night (T); Who Wants To Be A Millionaire (T)

100% fully Digital 16:9 OB fleet. Flexible and affordable solutions for all programme strands with the people who have the pedigree and know-how. You concentrate on what you do best and we'll do the same - and the result will be a credit to us both.

CT Digital Ltd
Unit 15A, Selly Oak Industrial Estate, Elliott Road, Birmingham B29 6LR
t 0121 415 5224 **f** 0121 415 5214
e info@ctdigital.tv **w** www.ctdigital.tv

CTV Outside Broadcasts
Unit 4, Matrix Park, 900 Coronation Road, Park Royal, London NW10 7PH
t 020 8453 8989 **f** 020 8838 1803 **w** www.ctvob.co.uk
Contact Yvonne Berry, Head of Production

Dales Broadcast Ltd
Nettle Hill, Brinklow Road, Ansty, Coventry CV7 9JL
t 024 7662 1763 **f** 024 7660 2732 **m** 07803 584925
e sales@dales-ltd.com **w** www.dales-ltd.com
Contact Kate Boden, Marketing Director; Julian Boden, Managing Director
Credits Tickle, Patch And Friends (T); Young Choirs 2001 (T); Network Q Rally (T); Horseracing for Racetech, ATR And Channel 4 (T)

Comprehensive OB facilities from PSC crews to our latest digital widescreen vehicles featuring up to 8 Sony cameras and 6VTRs. Edit suites offer digital, component and Avid online/offline.

E TO E Ltd
Unit 7, Swinnow Court, Stanningley Road, Leeds LS13 4ER
t 0113 257 8632 **f** 0113 255 2457
e info@etoe.co.uk **w** www.etoe.co.uk

Enfys Ltd
Unit 31, Portmanmoor Road, East Moors, Cardiff CF24 5HB
t 029 2049 9988 **f** 029 2049 5667
e mail@enfys.co.uk **w** www.enfys.co.uk
Contact Jean Roberts, Company Secretary; Sarah Jane Pain, Bookings; Martyn Roberts, Outside Broadcasts

ESP Facilities Ltd
49 Cambridge Road South, London W4 3DA
t 020 8994 1060 **f** 020 87474609
Contact Derek Oliver

Euroscope.TV
Unit B, Jubilee Close, London NW9 8TR
t 020 8205 7767 **f** 020 8205 6349 **m** 07768 876991
e info@euroscope.tv **w** www.euroscope.tv
Contact Stephen Bailey, Director; Susan Ensign, Director

ntl:broadcast

ntl : Broadcast
Crawley Court, Winchester SO21 2QA
t 01962 822400 **f** 01962 822553
e satellite-info@ntl.com **w** www.ntlbroadcast.com

On Air Media Ltd
Lammas House, 23 Clovelly Road, Ealing, London W5 5HF
t 020 8354 2294 **f** 020 8354 4288 **m** 07768 004086
e info@on-air.co.uk **w** www.on-air.co.uk
Contact Sean McHugh, Managing Director

OpTex UK
20-26 Victoria Road, New Barnet, London EN4 9PF
t 020 8441 2199 **f** 020 8449 3646
e info@optexint.com **w** www.optexint.com
Contact Edward Catton-Orr, Sales; Mike Robinson, Rentals

Partridge Electronics
54-56 Fleet Road, Benfleet SS7 5JN
t 01268 793256 **f** 01268 565759
e benfleet@partridgeelectronics.co.uk
w www.patridgeelectronics.co.uk

Picture Canning Company

55 Bendon Valley, London SW18 4LZ
t 020 8874 9277 **f** 020 8874 6623
e info@picturecanning.co.uk **w** www.picturecanning.co.uk
Contact Leslie Zunz, Managing Director; Paul Taylor, General Manager; Phil Wade, Managing Director
Credits Escape To The Country (D); Watchdog (T); Is Harry On The Boat (T); Holiday (D)

Piranha Graphics

Studio 310, Mill Studios, Crane Mead, Ware SG12 9PY
t 01920 444240 **m** 07836 202329 **e** davidc@piranhasys.co.uk
Contact David Crawley, Director
Credits ITV Sport Basketball (T); MTV Video Clash Live (T)

Pyramid TV Ltd

36 Cardiff Road, Llandaff, Cardiff CF5 2DR
t 029 2057 6888 **f** 029 2057 5777
e info@pyramidtv.co.uk **w** www.pyramidtv.co.uk
Contact Glenwen Jones, Facilities Manager

Roll to Record

Unit 6, Brook Industrial Estate, Bullsbrook Road, Hayes UB4 0JZ
t 020 8813 5622 **f** 020 8813 5620
e roll2rec@aol.com **w** www.roll2record.co.uk
Contact Peris Edwards

Scanners Television Outside Broadcasts Ltd

3 Chrysalis Way, Langley Bridge, Eastwood, Nottingham NG16 3RY
t 01773 718111 **f** 01773 716004
e info@scannerstv.com **w** www.scannerstv.com
Contact Mick Bass, Managing Director
Credits Born Sloppy (T); BBC Grandstand Horse Racing (T); Worthington Cup Football (T); Nationwide League Football (T)

Shots Television

Gravel Hill, Chalfont St Peter, Gerrards Cross SL9 9QP
t 01753 892020 **f** 01753 890612 **m** 07973 631023
e info@shotstv.co.uk **w** www.shotstv.co.uk
Contact Nick Badham, Sales; Chris Butler, Managing Director

SHOTStwo digital 8 camera scanner, SHOTSone digital 3 camera scanner and Edit/Slo-Mo vehicle. Both vehicles can provide 2 cameras, 8 audio sources, comms and CCU control via single 6mm fibre-optic cable. Ikegami HL59W digital widescreen cameras. See web for full specifications and details of de-rig PPS units and PSC.

South Midlands Communications Ltd

SM House, School House, Chandlers Ford Industrial Estate, Eastleigh SO53 4BY
t 023 8024 6200 **f** 023 8024 6206
e sales@smc-comms.com **w** www.smc-comms.com
Contact Mike Bennett, Sales Manager, Antennas & Masts; Bill Simons, Sales Manager, Radio Systems

Springfield Video Ltd

5 Kensington Road, Nottingham NG10 5PD
t 0115 939 0910 **f** 0115 939 0910 **m** 07973 410281
e roy@springfieldvideo.co.uk **w** www.springfieldvideo.co.uk
Contact Roy Bastiman

Telegenic

4 The Merlin Centre, Lancaster Road, High Wycombe HP12 3QL
t 01494 557400 **f** 01494 557410
e info@telegenic.co.uk **w** www.telegenic.co.uk
Contact Rhiannon Evans, Office Manager

Televideo Ltd

The Riverside, Furnival Road, Sheffield S4 7YA
t 0114 249 1500 **f** 0114 249 1505 **m** 07802 434749
e info@televideo.co.uk **w** www.televideo.co.uk
Contact Graham King, Director
Credits Premier League Football; British & World Superbikes

Television Mobiles

Bartlemy, Fernoy, Rep of Ireland
t +353 253 6236 **f** +353 253 6601
e helen@television-mobiles.com **w** www.television-mobiles.com
Contact Bart Arnold, Managing Director; Helen Arnold, Company Secretary

Transmission (TX) Ltd

Unit 2A, Shepperton Studios, Studios Road, Shepperton TW17 0QD
t 020 8547 0208 **f** 01932 572571
m 07769 688813
e info@ttx.co.uk **w** www.ttx.co.uk
Contact Steve Lloyd, General Manager; Melanie Parkin, Bookings Contact; Peter Hughes, Bookings Contact; Malcom Bubb, Bookings Contact
Credits The Hoobs (T); Doctors (T); Teletubbies (T)

TX supply a range of specialist Mobile & Cable-Free Camera Systems. Special Facilities include Microwave Links, Studio De-Rigs, Production Scanners, Car Rigs, Digi Beta, Hi Def & DVCAM Multi Camera & Camcorder Systems, Special Installations & Consultancy, Portable Triax/CCU Production Units, Time-lapse Facilities, Minicams, Microwave Links, Jimmy Jibs, Track & Dollies & Lighting.

Recent Credits:

BBC Television TUC live on BBC2 1999-2002

RTL Holland Wimbledon Tennis Championships
2001, 2002

TV2 Denmark
ARD Germany

Racetech ATR Horse Racing 1997-2003

● Digital Outside Broadcast
Facilities
● Trucks
● De-rigs
● PPU
● Edit System

ABC (USA) Good Morning America live from
Kuwait, Feb 2003

MTV Media Facilities for European Music
Awards, Barcelona 2002, Tony Blair Iraq Debate
March 2003

TTL are Alan Green, Nigel Cubbage and Mark Llewellyn. For the
complete solution to your outside broadcast needs, call us now on 01737-767655.

TTL Video Ltd
38 Holmethorpe Avenue, Redhill RH1 2NL
t 01737 767655 f 01737 767665
e ob@ttlvideo.com w www.ttlvideo.com
Contact Alan Green; Mark Llewellyn; Nigel Cubbage

Equipment and expertise in all areas of outside broadcast engineering.

VE Projects
The London Broadcast Centre, 11-13 Point Pleasant, London
SW18 1NN
t 020 8433 8050 f 020 8433 8051
e rlamotte@veprojects.com w www.veprojects.com

Contact Wesley Burton, Project Coordinator; Richard La Motte, Managing Director
Credits The Commonwealth Games (C); Wimbledon Tennis (T); British Open
Golf (T); The ICC Cricket Trophy (T)

Visions (Digital Outside Broadcasting) Ltd
t 020 7478 7289 f 020 7478 7107
e vickib@visions-ob.co.uk w www.visions-ob.com
Contact Vicki Betihavas,
Director of Sales & Marketing

Wired For Sound
Lee Valley Technopark, Ashley Road, London N17 9LN
t 020 8880 4840 f 020 8880 4830
e info@wiredforsound,co.uk w www.wiredforsound.co.uk

Performance Enhancement
Acting Coaches

Jenny McCracken
2 Stamford Court, Goldhawk Road, London W6 0XB
t 020 8748 7638 **m** 07979 744859
e jeremymccracken@hotmail.com

Queen Margaret's University College
36 Clerwood Terrace, Edinburgh EH12 8TY
t 0131 317 3400 **w** www.qmced.ac.uk
Contact Maggie Kinloch, Head of Drama

Performance Enhancement
Physical Training

Dave Baptiste's One on One/Jump
m 07973 600440 **e** davidb17@orange.net

Martin Weaver Health Consultancy
t 020 8580 9712 **f** 020 8580 9712 **m** 07931 387551
e health@martinweaver.co.uk **w** www.martinweaver.co.uk

Kate Armstrong Pilates Specialist
m 07946 576568 **e** katzfit@talk21.com

Startrac UK
Unit 4, The Gateway Centre, Coronation Road, Cressex
Business Park, High Wycombe HP12 3SU
t 01494 688260 **f** 01494 688269
e sales@startrac.co.uk **w** www.startrac.com
Contact Gary Knill, Managing Director

Performance Enhancement
Voice Coaches

Eileen Benskin
t 020 8455 9750 **f** 020 8455 9750 **m** 07785 791715
e ebenskin@aol.com

Barbara Berkery
International Creative Management Ltd, Oxford House,
76 Oxford Street, London W1D 1BS
t 020 7636 6565 **f** 020 7323 0101 **w** www.icmlondon.co.uk
Credits Shakespeare In Love (F); Bridget Jones's Diary (F); Nicholas Nickleby (F)

Sandra Butterworth
Joyce Edwards, 275 Kennington Road SE11 6BY
t 020 7735 5736 **f** 020 7820 1845 **e** joyce.edwards@virgin.net

Tim Charington
t 020 7735 5736 **f** 020 7820 1845 **e** joyce.edwards@virgin.net

Mel Churcher
London
f 020 7701 4593 **m** 07778 773019 **e** melchurcher@hotmail.com
Credits Tomb Raider (F); 102 Dalmations (F); The Hole (F); The Fifth Element (F)

Penny Dyer
C/o Joyce Edwards Representation, 275 Kennington Road,
London SE11 6BY
t 020 7735 5736 **f** 020 7820 1845 **e** Joyce.Edwards@Virgin.net

Gerry Grennell
International Creative Management Ltd, Oxford House,
76 Oxford Street, London W1D 1BS
t 020 7636 6565 **f** 020 7323 0101 **w** www.icmlondon.co.uk
Credits Ronin (F); From Hell (F); Ned Kelly (F)

Jessica Higgs
t 020 7735 5736 **f** 020 7820 1845 **e** joyce.edwards@virgin.net

Charmian Hoare
t 020 7735 5736 **f** 020 7820 1845 **e** joyce.edwards@virgin.net

Barbara Houseman
t 020 7735 5736 **f** 020 7820 1845 **e** joyce.edwards@virgin.net

OLM
74b The Limes Avenue, London N11 1RH
t 020 8361 0548 **f** 020 8482 1466 **m** 07960 495737
Contact Lesia Melnyk
Credits Keen Eddy (F); That 70's Show (F); Amy Foster

Elizabeth Pursey
Representation Joyce Edwards, 275 Kennington Road, London
SE11 6BY
t 020 7735 5736 **f** 020 7820 1845 **e** joyce.edwards@virgin.net

Bernard Shaw
Horton Manor, Canterbury CT4 7LG
t 01227 730843 **f** 01227 730843 **e**
bernard@bernardshaw.co.uk **w** www.bernardshaw.co.uk
The specialist director, producer, and coach for studio recorded voices.

Joan Washington
International Creative Management Ltd, Oxford House,
76 Oxford Street, London W1D 1BS
t 020 7636 6565 **f** 020 7323 0101 **w** www.icmlondon.co.uk
Credits Plunkett And Macleane (F); Captain Corelli's Mandolin (F); Charlotte Gray (F)

Julia Wilson-Dickson
t 020 7735 5736 **f** 020 7820 1845 **e** joyce.edwards@virgin.net

Neville Wortman
48 Chiswick Staithe, London W4 3TP
t 020 8994 8886 **m** 07976 805976 **e** nevillewortman@beeb.net

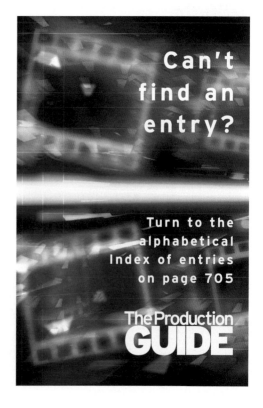

POST PRODUCTION

post production : contents

Post Production Facilities
Film Cutting Rooms

Derek Williams Film Editors Ltd
15 Bateman Street, London W1D 3AQ
t 020 7439 1091 f 020 7437 8902
e info@williamsediting.com w www.williamsediting.com
Contact Derek Williams, Facilities Manager

Goldcrest Post Production Facilities
36-44 Brewer Street, London W1F 9LX
t 020 7437 7972 f 020 7437 5402 m 07836 204283
e mailbox@goldcrest-post.co.uk
Contact Poppy Quinn, Bookings and Customer Services Manager; Raju Raymond, General Manager

Post Production Facilities
Film Neg. Cutting

Computamatch
Hammer House, 117 Wardour Street, London W1F 0UN
t 020 7287 1316 f 020 7287 0793
e kevinl@sohogroup.com w www.sohogroup.com
Contact Kevin Lynch, Commercials Manager

PNC
3 Carlisle Street, London W1D 3DH
t 020 7437 2605 t 020 7437 2025 f 020 7437 7036
e negcutting@hotmail.com w www.negcut.com
Contact Gary Campbell, Manager; Steve Ashton

Professional Negative Cutting Ltd
Heathrow Business Centre, Technicolor Laboratories, Bath Road, West Drayton UB7 0DB
t 020 8754 7584 f 020 8754 7585
e steve@negcut.com w www.negcut.com
Credits Mindhunters (F); Actors (F); The Parole Officer (F); Gosford Park (F)

Professional Negative Cutting Ltd (Commercials)
3 Carlisle Street, London W1V 5RH
t 020 7437 2025 f 020 7437 7036
e stevey@negcut.com w www.negcutting.com
Contact Nicola Franklin, Contact; Steve Ashton
Credits Orange (I); Ford Focus (C); British Airways (C); UBS (C)

Post Production Facilities
Film Storage

Bonded Services International Ltd
Unit 6, Armstrong Way, Windmill Lane, Southhall UB2 4SD
t 020 8571 5511 f 020 8571 9125
Contact Jim Walden, Customer Services; Steve Yalden, Manager

Film Management Company
Unit 8 Spaceway, North Feltham Trading Estate, Feltham TW14 0TH
t 020 8890 8780 t 020 8751 7200 f 020 8751 7222
m 07710 124786 e group@intl-vist-svcs.co.uk
Contact Colin Woods, Managing Director

Hayes Information Management
Quadrant House, 15-16 Stockwell Green, London SW9 9JJ
t 020 7526 3000 f 020 7526 3030
e howardr@stk.hayes-him.co.uk w www.hayes-him.co.uk
Contact Martin Balaam, Financial Director

Photobition Bonded Services
Unit 2, Aerodrome Way, Cranford Lane, Heston TW5 9QB
t 020 8897 7973 f 020 8759 6722 w www.ftsbonded.com
Contact Kim Cowley, Head of Business Development

Post Production Facilities
General

124 Facilities
124 Horseferry Road, London SW1P 2TX
t 020 7306 8040 f 020 7306 8041
e 124facilities@channel4.co.uk w www.124.co.uk
Contact Richard Evans, Post Production Co-ordinator; Anne-Marie Phelan, Facilities Sales Manager

303 Ltd
11 D'Arblay Street, London W1F 8DT
t 020 7437 3030 f 020 7494 0956
e info@303i.com w www.303i.com
Contact Winston Cuthbert, Manager

post production:
moving the posts

The post production industry has seen huge changes in recent times. Slammed by the worldwide recession in advertising, the facilities that traditionally depended on the cash cow of commercials have had to look for pastures new. Some have gone into film production, dabbled with new technology or amalgamated with peers to form larger multifaceted companies. Others have ceased to exist completely.

The irony is that the technology now available to facilities enables faster and more diverse work to be created than ever before. According to Patrick Jocelyn, director EMEA at Discreet, falling budgets in TV, film and broadcast has caused a need for postproduction companies to handle projects more cost-efficiently than ever. "More and more post houses are looking towards multi-resolution, multi-bit depth technology solutions and workflow pipelines," says Jocelyn. "We recognise that the industry is going through tough times, and we don't expect to see a dramatic upswing for some time. Discreet's view is that it must continue to deliver flexible software that helps customers face changing dynamics in the business, and yet remain creative and cutting edge at the same time."

Jocelyn finds that one of the chief demands from his customers is that that want to be able to do a wider range of jobs with their software. "That's why you'll find Flame 8 offers multi-resolution, multi-bit depth capability," he says. "Features such as improved timeline editing functions enable digital artists to easily do the various versions of a TV commercial as well as the main compositing. Smoke and Fire now provide more powerful effects tools to enable editors to produce a wider range of effects-based content in long form work."

In other markets, especially non-linear editing, Apple and Avid are slogging it out on the desktop. Both Apple's Final Cut Pro and Avid's Xpress DV are winning converts among both new users and old industry hands who are looking for a streamlined and often mobile, but still powerful, editing system. The Mill's director of 2D, David Smith, takes the Xpress DV system on location shoots where, with a direct feed from the camera on every take, he is able to create rough effects compositions to show the director and crew whether FX shots will work on a take-by-take basis. The new portable NLEs that offer real-time colour correction and previsualisation of effects, plus a compatibility with traditional systems, are set to start a revolution from the ground up.

So much for the products, but what about the facilities themselves? "The advertising industry has been through a tough year," says Gavin Wellsman, one of the compositors at the Mill who uses Discreet's Flame, Inferno and Combustion systems. "Things seem really busy so far this year, although I know that a full recovery is not forecast until 2004. Companies really have to be competitive to get the big jobs in now."

Pepper's MD Patrick Holzen has a view of a different side of the market. "With an economic downturn and the looming war, people want to be entertained more than ever, so long form work is on the increase," he says. "However, the budgets are shrinking which is placing greater pressure on rates." It certainly doesn't seem like a lean year for Pepper, pumping out long form postproduction for drama, documentaries and feature films such as Dr. Zhivago, Tipping the Velvet, Spooks, In this World, Gathering Storm and The Way We Live Now.

Rushes too, has an optimistic view. "The market today is far more competitive and challenging," says Joce Capper, MD. "Processes have been streamlined, meaning that the time an effect takes to achieve has reduced. Smaller budgets mean that we are constantly looking for cost-effective solutions to meet the creative needs and demands of our clients. The market will continue to evolve, as it always has, to keep up with new technologies."

So how has new technology in this field impacted on the way directors, producers and other traditional roles approach a project? From the post house's viewpoint, it seems the constantly evolving technology has enabled them to develop closer working relationships with clients. Rushes, which has pioneered many pieces of kit in its long history, including Harry and Flame, has seen just this sort of thing happen. Its operators find themselves simplifying post techniques without sacrificing the quality of effects and images. "There is now far more dialogue between the effects artists and the creative teams, and we offer a range of services from initial meetings and pre-production planning to shoot attendance," says Capper.

Pepper too, is changing the way it does business. Typical of many facilities, its telecine setup (C-Reality) has seen no real change but it has taken on board some of Avid's HD DS systems for editing. "These can effectively do the special effects that were once dependent on Inferno, Flame or Henry, making it more cost effective for the clients," says Patick Holzen, who adds, however: "as the technology is relatively new, rates are higher and the time required is longer, so clients are approaching technology like HD with caution and care and are more open to advice and guidance."

Meanwhile, Rushes, like many others, has seen a huge impact in the growth of 3D work it does. "It has been very exciting watching 3D develop from being an unattended client area to seeing clients completely involved, giving their input and creating completely new effects," says Joce Capper. "It's opened up new markets for Rushes, bringing long form work into the building and allowing us to diversify. It's a rapidly expanding area of the business."

The Mill's flame operators are also finding 3D is affecting their work. "I think the current market is about to pick up again and with new advances in

→→

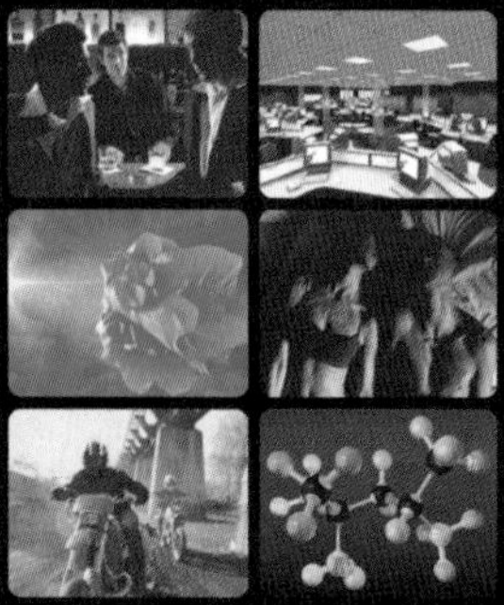

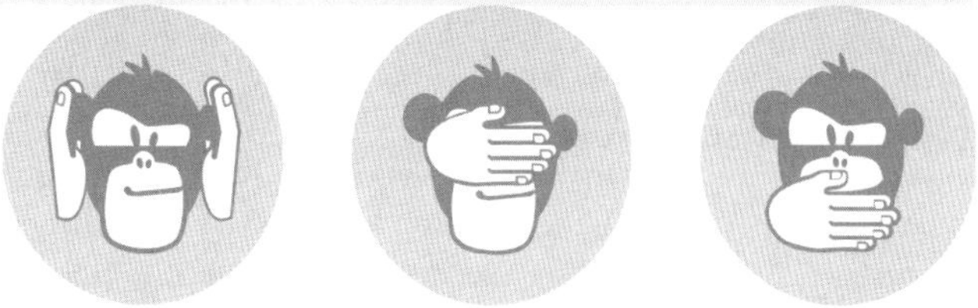

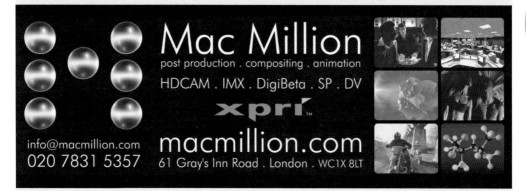

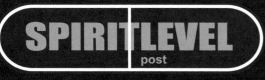

→→→ moving the posts

compositing systems and 3D I think we'll see a lot more complex and realistic effects," says flame operator Paul Marangos. "3D has changed so much in ten years. From the Bosch FGS 4000 machine that created the Dire Straits "Money For Nothing" video with really blocky flat textures, to now, where we have realistic fur in the new Levis spot with the mice (Levi's: Swap), CG is more and more a part of every aspect of our work as visual effects artists."

Other companies to benefit from 3D work include Soho 601, whose acquisition of Aardman star Will Byles led to the founding of a major new 3D department sitting atop a building filled with traditional post systems. Already turning out a series of high quality CG-animated spots, Byles has his sights set on a full-length animated feature.

Other companies have also strayed into previously untried areas of the business to fund their own development and stave off recession. Glassworks is one such company, whose combination of 3D and new art departments is responsible for some stunning new commercials. "We're establishing our art department, so there will be full-on service right from the front to the end," says Hector Macleod, Glassworks MD. "So what happens, and it's kind of ironic, is that people who

used to be our clients, are now actually turning into our competitors - specifically animation companies." Meanwhile, Glassworks' research arm is showing results, with interactive BBC Four idents, some super timeslice work on a string of spots for HP and a Formula One racing simulator for Orange. As for the industry as a whole, Macleod feels that the technology is getting cheaper; the skill base is much greater than ever it was before, the hardware is getting much faster and more affordable and as a result the whole postproduction infrastructure is much simpler.

It's clear, then, that the postproduction industry has seen changes that some would call seismic, and it's probably not over yet. The signs are there though, at least in the UK, that the aftershocks will not be all bad.

Contacts   Rushes, www.rushes.co.uk
Pepper, 020 7836 1188
The Mill, www.mill.co.uk
Soho601 www.soho601.com
Glassworks, www.glassworks.co.uk
Discreet, www.discreet.com
Avid, www.avid.com

Writer   Michael Burns

Sony PlayStation -
The Getaway, by Rushes

Virgin Mobile - The Autograph
Hunter, by Rushes

422 Manchester

4th Floor, South Central, 11 Peter Street, Manchester M2 5QR
t 0161 839 6080 **f** 0161 839 6081 **i** 0161 834 2437
e manchester@422.com **w** www.422manchester.com
Contact Martin Dixon, Managing Director; Damien Lynch, Facilities Director; Richard Wallwork, Production Director
Credits Rubba Dubbers (T); Lemsip Max Strength Direct (C); Most Haunted (T); A Question Of Sport (T)

Air Studios

Lyndhurst Hall, Lyndhurst Road, Hampstead, London NW3 5NG
t 020 7794 0660 **f** 020 7794 8518
e pip@airstudios.com **w** www.airstudios.com
Contact Sally Drury, Post Production Coordinator; Pip Norton, Dubbing Engineer
Credits Playing The Field (T); Man & Boy (F); The Jury (T)

Andrew Sumner Associates

Suite 401, Barclay House, 35 Whitworth Street West, Manchester M1 5MG
t 0161 228 0330 **f** 0161 228 0770
Contact Brian Hardman, General Manager; Janet Sumner, Bookings

Anglia Studios

Anglia House, Norwich NR1 3JG
t 01603 615151 **f** 01603 752504
e angliastudios@granadamedia.com
w www.angliastudios.com
Contact Dan Haddon, Location Services; Dave Wyatt, Head of Post Production; Jacky Lane, Head of Resources; Ian Osborne, Head of Studios; Beverly Bulcock, Head of Resources
Great kit, great people and the Norwich nightlife is brilliant.

Aquarium

122 Wardour Street, London W1F 0TX
t 020 7734 1611 **f** 020 7494 1962
e info@aquariumstudios.co.uk **w** www.aquariumstudios.co.uk
Contact Ben Baird, Dubbing Mixer; Pam Thompson, Facilities Manager; Simon Fitzpatrick, Dubbing Mixer
Credits Easy Money (D); Witchcraze (F); Murder (T); Murder

Aquila TV Ltd

94 Broad Street, Birmingham B15 1AU
t 0121 693 1881 **f** 0121 693 1880
e enquiries@aquilatv.co.uk **w** www.aquilatv.co.uk
Contact Nat Higginbottom, Facilities Manager
Credits Wrong Car Right Car (T); Network East Late (T); Big Strong Boys (T); Countryfile (T)

Arena Digital

74 Newman Street, London W1T 3EL
t 020 7436 4360 **f** 020 7436 3989
e info@arenadigital.co.uk **w** www.arenadigital.co.uk
Contact Rowan Bray, Facilities Manager; Calvin Cunningham

AVP Productions Ltd

Visual House 2, Wilmington Grove, Leeds LS7 2BQ
t 0113 383 8287 **f** 0113 383 8292

Baraka Post Production

11 Greek Street, London W1D 4DJ
t 020 7734 2227 **e** bookings@baraka.co.uk **w** www.baraka.co.uk

BBC Post Production

BBC Post Production
(Sites across London, Bristol & Birmingham)
5550 Television Centre, Wood Lane, London W12 7RJ
t 020 8225 7702 (London) **t** 0117 9746 666 (Bristol)
t 0121 432 8621 (Birmingham)
w www.bbcresources.com/postproduction

BBC Scotland Resources Operations
Room G51, Broadcasting House, Queen Margaret Drive,
Glasgow G12 8DG
t 0141 338 2343 **f** 0141 338 2335
e resops.scotland@bbc.co.uk
w www.bbc.co.uk/scotland/resources
Contact Natalie Adams, Facilities Co-ordinator; Alex Gaffney, Sales & Marketing
Manager; Susie Miller, Marketing Assistant; Donagh Campbell, Facilities Assistant
Credits The Saturday Show (T); Hollywood Greats (T); Clarissa And The
Countryman (T); Balamory (T)

Blue Post Production Ltd
58 Old Compton Street, London W1D 4UF
t 020 7437 2626 **f** 020 7439 2477
e info@bluepp.co.uk **w** www.bluepp.co.uk
Contact Amanda ; Ashley ; Alison ; Clea ; Dee ; Toby ;
Samantha Greenwood, Facilities Director

*blue - a complete serial digital facility comprising of: Spirit, master
grade, avid offline/online, flame, editbox FX, online edit & sound
studio. Broadcast, commercial & music promos catered for!!*

CFS
26 Berwick Street, London W1F 8RG
t 020 7734 4543 **f** 020 7734 6600
e cfsinsoho@colourfilmservices.co.uk
w www.colourfilmservices.co.uk
Contact Steve Dann, Facility Manager

Complete Communications Corporation
39 Long Acre, London WC2E 9LG
t 020 7845 6900 **f** 020 7845 6980
e tvhits@cellardoor.co.uk **w** www.cellardoor.co.uk

CrowTV Ltd
12 Wendell Road, London W12 9RT
t 020 8749 6071 **f** 020 8740 0795
e paul@crowtv.com **w** www.crowtv.com

Contact Mark Manning, Technical Director; Paul Kingsley, Managing Director;
Tatiana Cook, Facility Manager; Kisia Gentle, Assistant Facility Manager
Credits Adventures Of English (D); Diet Trails (D); Homefront (D); Airport (D)

Definitely Red
Unit 321/322, The Greenhouse, Gibb Street, Birmingham B94AA
t 0121 224 7740 **f** 0121 224 7741
e melanie@definitelyred.com **w** www.definitelyred.co.uk
Contact Melanie Lee, Managing Director
Credits NCDL (A); Cricket Highlights - BBC Technology (T); BBC Technology -
Cricket Highlights (T); Royal Bank Of Scotland (A)

Digital Audio Technology Ltd
Phoenix Sound, Engineers Way, Wembley, London HA9 OET
t 020 8450 5665 **f** 020 8208 1979
e jo@digitalaudiotech.com **w** www.digitalaudiotech.com
Contact Cathy Ferrett, Facilities Manager; Jo Harrison, Marketing Manager
Credits Braveheart (F); Ally McBeal (T); X-Files (T); The Full Monty (F)

 **Diverse**

Diverse Post
6 Gorleston Street, London W14 8XS
t 020 7603 4567 **f** 020 7603 2148 **w** www.diverse.tv
Contact Fay Searl; Louise Townsend, Head of Post Production
Credits Slave Nation (T); Battle Center (D); Underworld (F)

*Diverse Post offers a complete range of facilities that includes:
Smoke, Digital online, Protools audio suite, subtitling, Avid offline
and rushes transfer.*

Documentary Video Associates
7 Campbell Court, Tadley RG26 5EG
t 01256 882032 **f** 01256 882024
e barrieg@dva.co.uk **w** www.dvafacilities.co.uk

DT Productions
Unit 1, Primrose Hill Workshops, Oppidans Road,
London NW3 3AG
t 020 7916 6780 **e** diamondtime@diamondtime.co.uk
Credits Jukebox Programming, Retail Store Programming

DVA Ltd
8 Campbell Court, Bramley, Basingstoke RG26 5EG
t 01256 882032 **f** 01256 882024
e barrieg@dva.co.uk **w** www.dvafacilities.co.uk
Contact Steve Longman, Facilities Manager; Alice Meacham, Director;
Amanda Thomas, Bookings; Barrie Gibson, Managing Director; Mark Breakwell,
Head of Graphics; Steve Whettam, Head of Editing

*Editing, Audio, Graphics, Animation, Music, Duplication, DVD, Crews,
Effects, Multimedia.*

EDITHIRE Post Production Services
Soho, London W1
t 020 7529 9900 **f** 020 7434 2028
e info@edit-hire.com **w** www.edit-hire.com
Contact Janie Dahn

 evolutions

Evolutions Television Ltd
5 Berners Street, London W1T 3LF
t 020 7580 3333 **f** 020 7637 1942
e info@evolutionstelevision.com
w www.evolutionstelevision.com

*Evolutions is one of London's leading independent post production
houses offering all services from offline to online editing, graphics,
audio, new media and duplication. We provide unique creative
solutions by combining the best technology available with some of the
greatest talent in the industry. We also provide a full video duplication
and new media service.*

Exeter Phoenix
Bradninch Place, Gandy Street, Exeter EX4 3LS
t 01392 667066 **f** 01392 667599
e media@exeterphoenix.org.uk **w** www.exeterphoenix.org.uk
Contact Jonas Hawkins, Media Manager

Exposure Post Production Ltd
37-38 Newman Street, London W1P IQA
t 020 7436 1200
Contact Susan Jones
Credits Sony (C); Orange (C); Life Doctor (T); Life Laundry (T)

The Farm Digital Post Production Dublin
27 Upper Mount Street, Dublin 2, Ireland
t +353 1 676 8812 f +353 1 676 8816
e info@thefarm.ie w www.thefarm.ie
Contact Therese Caldwell, Marketing & PR Manager
Credits Health Squad (T); U2 1989 - 2000 (W); The Last (S); Bloom (F)

The Farm Group (Home)
13 Soho Square, London W1D 3QF
t 020 7437 6677 f 020 7437 4466
e info@farmpost.co.uk w www.farmpost.co.uk
Contact David Klafkowski; Nicky Sargent, Managing Director; Vikki Dunn, Managing Director; Klaf, Director; Sarah Tindall, Facility Manager - Farm; Ian Dodd, Director; Jannine Martin, General Manager - Home

Finishing Post Television Facilities Ltd
10 Giltway, Giltbrook, Nottingham NG16 2GN
t 0115 945 8800 f 0115 945 8801
e info@finishing-post.co.uk w www.finishing-post.co.uk
Contact Rod Heath, Managing Director; Jason Sarson, Director; Paul Stowe, Director; John Russell, Chairman

First Facilities
6 Studland Street, Hammersmith, London W6 0JS
t 020 8741 9088 f 020 8748 5670
e firstfacilities@jacaranda.co.uk
Contact Andy Thompson

Fusion Post Production
16 D'Arblay Street, London W1F 8EA
t 020 7758 0500 f 020 7758 0501
e edit@fusionpost.co.uk w www.fusionpost.co.uk
Contact Adam Wolff, Managing Director; Ant Hayward, Facilities Director

Golden Square Post Production
11 Golden Square, London W1F 9JB
t 020 7300 3555 f 020 7494 3288
e info@golden-square.co.uk w www.golden-square.co.uk
Contact Beth Vander, Producer; Ewan Macleod, Executive Producer; Lee Pavey, Producer; Sally Cooper, Producer

The Groucho Club
45 Dean Street, London W1D 4QB
t 020 7439 4685 e privatereceptions@grouchoclub.co.uk
Contact Helen Elk, Events Marketing Manager; Bella Parker, Events Manager

Hackenbacker Audio Post Production
10 Bateman Street, London W1D 4AQ
t 020 7734 1324
e hackenbacker@btconnect.com w www.hackenbacker.com
Contact Julian Slater, Managing Director; Nigel Heath, Managing Director; Faye Stevens, Studio Manager
Credits Spooks (T); Leaving Las Vegas (F); Hilary And Jackie (F); Mike Bassett: England Manager (F)

Harris Grant Associates
16 Trinity Churchyard, Guildford GU1 3RR
t 01483 885678 f 01483 885677
e info@harrisgrant.com w www.harrisgrant.com
Contact Neil Grant, Managing Director

Image Makers Digital Facilities
62 Dean Street, London W1D 4QF
t 020 7734 9193 f 020 7434 2786
e jason@im-digital.co.uk w www.im-digital.co.uk
Contact Alex Goodes, General Manager; Dave Austin, Audio Manager; Jason Kosbab, Director

In-House Post-Production Ltd
Building 14, Shepperton Studios, Studios Road, Shepperton
t 01932 592455 f 01932 592455
e contact@ihpp.co.uk w www.ihpp.co.uk
Contact M Stretton, Managing Director
Credits Tiny Planets (A); Red Dwarf VII (A); Tolkein (D); Hasbro (C)

International Media Production
Unit 34, 7-15 Pink Lane, Newcastle-upon-Tyne NE1 5DW
t 0191 245 1000 f 0191 245 1000 m 07801 482815
e improductions@aol.com w www.improductions.co.uk
Credits L'Enfant Peu (I); Grainger Town Poetry Films (S); The Impact Project (I)

Jae Ltd
4 Bowmont Gardens, Glasgow G12 9LR
t 0141 334 3334 f 0141 338 6662
e j@editing.co.uk w www.editing.co.uk
Credits The Boy David Story; Panorama - 'Kids on Pills' (T); Horizon - 'Twin Towers' (T)

JCA TV Facilities
Monarch House, Victoria Road, London W3 6UR
t 020 8357 5400 f 020 8357 5450
e bookings@jcatv.co.uk w www.jcatv.co.uk
Contact Perry Foran, Sales Manager; Debbie Healy, General Manager

The Joint
1st Floor, 3 Wedgewood Mews, 12-13 Greek Street, London W1D 4BD
t 020 7734 1674 f 020 7734 1391
Contact Sarah Mackay, General Manager

Kingston inmedia
PO Box 2287, Gerrards Cross SL9 8BF
t 0845 123 8787 f 01494 876006
e inmedia@kcom.com w www.kingstoninmedia.com
Contact Vicki Redstone, Marketing & Sales Co-ordinator; Lucy Green, Marketing
Credits Fat Academy (T); Blues Clues (T); Beachcomber Bay (T)

LIP S Y N C post

Lipsync Post
Screen House, 123 Wardour Street, London W1F 0UW
t 020 7534 9123 f 020 7534 9124
e admin@lipsyncpost.co.uk w www.lipsyncpost.co.uk
Contact Laura Wilson, Facilities Supervisor; Kevin Phelan, Head of Post Production; Peter Hampden, Managing Director; Jon Diamond, Managing Director
Credits S Club - Seeing Double (F); How Weird Are You? (T); The Last Detective (T); Silent Witness (T)

ADR TV/DVD mixing, Avid-DS, Graphics, HD Editing, film recording, duplication.

The London Studios Ltd
Upper Ground, London SE1 9LT
t 020 7261 3181 f 020 7737 8840
e post@londonstudios.co.uk
w www.londonstudios.co.uk
Contact Julie Sangan, Head of Post Production Sales

*Avid Offlines/Avid Symphony all on Avid Unity.
Avid Express. 7 digital Widescreen Linear suites.
6 Audio suites with Logic desks, audiofile
& voice over booths. 2 & 3D graphic areas.
2 Quantel Clipbox servers with access to
studios and Linear edit suites.*

M2 Television
Ingestre Court, Ingestre Place, London W1F 0JL
t 020 7343 6543 f 020 7343 6555
e info@m2tv.com w www.m2tv.com
The Forum, 74-80 Camden Street, London, NW1 0EG
t 020 7343 6789 t 020 7343 6777

Contact Kabir Malik; Jennie Jones

*Based in Soho and Camden, we offer a full range of video and audio
post production as well as the award-winning code design. 5 digital
online suites, 5 Editbox FX online suites, 2 Symphony online suites, Avid
unity server, Clipbox video server, 14 Avid offline, 5 digital audio suites,
Hal, and Illusion.*

Mac Million
61 Gray's Inn Road, London WC1X 8LT
t 020 7831 5357 f 020 7404 6872
e info@macmillion.com w www.macmillion.com
Contact Mads Nybo Jorgensen, Managing Director
Credits The Ride (F); Hard Talk (T); Tonight With Trevor MacDonald (T)

The Machine Room
54-58 Wardour Street, London W1D 4JQ
t 020 7734 3433 f 020 7287 3773
e info@themachineroom.co.uk w www.themachineroom.co.uk
Contact Simon Briggs, Director of Production; Wendy Field, Facilities Director;
David Clarke, Director of Client Services; Liz Clarke, Head of Sales & Marketing;
Darryl Huxley, Technical Manager; Danny Whybrow, Managing Director
Credits Morvern Callar (F); Bob The Builder Live! (A); In Deep III (T); Bad Girls V (T)

Martyr Television
Heddon House, 149-151 Regent Street, London W1B 4JD
t 020 7479 7830 f 020 7287 6855
e edit@martyrtv.co.uk w www.martyrtv.co.uk
Contact Steve Eveleigh, Director; Nick Ames, Director; Sarah Maryan,
Faculties Co-Ordinator
Credits MTV Asia: Idents (C); Bad Girls Series I-IV (T); Paradise Heights (T); Buried (T)

MGB Facilities Ltd
Sheepscar Court, Leeds LS7 2BB
t 0113 243 6868 f 0113 243 8886
e contact@mgbtv.co.uk w www.mgbtv.co.uk
Contact Mike Gaunt, Managing Director; Elaine Wigglesworth, Facility Manager
Credits Quick Grip (I); Sport On Five (T); Hasbro (W); BUPA (C)

The Mill
40-41 Great Marlborough Street, London W1F 7JQ
t 020 7287 4041 f 020 7287 8393
e info@mill.co.uk w www.mill.co.uk
Contact Emma Shield
Credits Absolut Vodka - Mullet (C); BT Broadband - Burts Pipe (C); Guiness -
Lava (C); Levi's - Stampede (C)

a television corporation company

Molinare
34 Fouberts Place, London W1F 7PX
t 020 7478 7000 f 020 7478 7199
e bookings@molinare.co.uk w www.molinare.co.uk
Contact Kate George, Facilities Manager
Credits Dorada Especial: Painting; AXN: Cornice; Walkers Dorito's: Idents; The Wind

*For 30 years Molinare has been offering the best in Post Production,
helping the best people make the best programmes, we have about the
widest selection of facilities in one location in the industry. Based in the
heart of Soho, we offer, 5 digital Online Suites, Editbox FX V8, Ursa Gold
Telecine, High Definition Online, 10 Avid Offline suites and 2 Avid Online
suites, 5 Audio Dubbing suites with voice over booths, Tracklay, Discreet
Flint, Media Illusion, Drive in 1500 sq ft Video studio, 400 sq ft Virtual
Studio, Duplication, Transmission Services, as well as the Molinare
Design team for all your branding and design needs.*

On-Line Post Production
375 City Road, London EC1V 1NB
t 020 7837 3333 f 020 7833 2185
e info@onlinepp.co.uk w www.onlinepp.co.uk
Contact Toby Daniels, Managing Director

One
71 Dean Street, London W1D 3SF
t 020 7439 2730 f 020 7734 3331
e amanda.smalley@onepost.tv w www.onepost.tv
Contact Paul Jones, Managing Director; Will Byles, CGI; Matt Adams, Head of
Production; Amanda Smalley, Sales & Marketing
Credits Kit Kat: Rap (Test) (C)

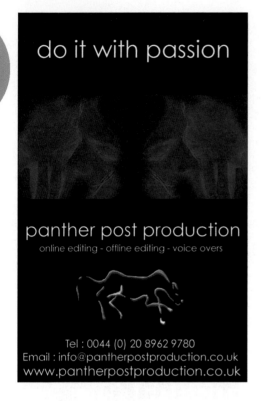

Optical Image

The Production Centre, Broome, Near Stourbridge DY9 0HA
t 01562 700404 **f** 01562 700930
e info@optical-image.com **w** www.optical-image.com
Contact David Clement, Managing Director; Jacky Clement, Company Secretary; Julie Farrington-Griffiths, Director of Resources
Credits Red Arrows - Beyond the Horizon (I); Jellabies/Jellikins (C); Butt Ugly Martians (C)

P3 Post

40-42 Lexington Street, London W1F 0LN
t 020 7287 3006 **f** 020 7439 3110
e edit@p3post.co.uk **w** www.p3post.co.uk
Contact Martin Price, Facilities Director
Credits Dave Gorman's Important Astology Experiment (T); Derrin Brown Mind Control (T); Orange Baftas 2003 (T); MTV Europe Music Awards 2002 (T)

Panther Post Production

Suite 27, Shaftsbury Centre, 85 Barlby Road, London W10 6BN
t 020 8962 9780 **f** 020 8962 9781 **m** 07973 381283
e craig@pantherpostproduction.co.uk
w www.pantherpostproduction.co.uk
Contact Craig Golding, Facilities Manager

Peach Facilities Ltd

3 Slingsby Place, Long Acre, London WC2E 9AB
t 020 7632 4240 **f** 020 7632 4250
e info@peachfacilities.co.uk **w** www.peachfacilities.co.uk
Contact Russell Parrett; Tim Whitehead; Karen Davies

Pepper

3 Slingsby Place, Long Acre, Covent Garden, London WC2E 9AB
t 020 7836 1188 **f** 020 7497 9305
e mailus@pepperpost.tv **w** www.pepperpost.tv
Contact Stephanie Goodwin; Helen Phelps; Jill Jones; Lisa Sweet
Credits Down To Earth (T); Spooks (T); Dr Zhivago (T); The Lost Prince (T)

pink pigeon

Pink Pigeon Post Production

74 Berwick Street, London W1F 8TQ
t 020 7439 3266 **f** 020 7439 3277
e info@pinkpigeon.net **w** www.pinkpigeon.net
Contact Simon Boyd, Director; William Timbers, Director
Credits Chrome Dreams (W); Mark Summers Management (W); The British Council (W)

Planet Television UK & Ireland

Planet House, 1 Canbury Park Road, Kingston-upon-Thames KT2 6JX
t 020 8974 6050 **f** 020 8974 6052
e planettv@iol.ie **w** www.planet-television.co.uk
Contact Roy Saverton, Facilities Manager; Patrick Kirby, Managing Director; Riaz Sheikh, Administration Manager; Eve Kirby, Bookings Manager
Credits Hyatt Hotels And Resorts (W); Compass Group (E); Burker King Training Series DVD (E); Lonely Lives (T)

Quadrillion

e roly@quadrillion.tv

The Quarry Ltd

Lewis Carroll House, 26-28 Brewer Street, London W1F 0SP
t 020 7437 4961 **f** 020 7437 1491
e info@the-quarry.co.uk **w** www.the-quarry.co.uk

Rainbow Post Production

16 Ingestre Place, London W1F 0JJ
t 020 7434 4566 **f** 020 7439 4565 **w** www.rainbowpost.com
Contact Nick Rogers, Dubbing Mixer; Louise , Bookings; Lyndsay , Bookings

*Based in the heart of Soho, Rainbow offers Avid Symphony and
MC9000XL online suites, two digital audio mixing suites, Avid and
Lightworks offline suites and digitising, unattended conforms,
duplication, and FTP services.*

Random Post Production

Artist's Court, Manette Street, London W1D 4AP
t 020 7434 3444 **f** 020 7434 3451
e edit@randompost.com **w** www.randompost.com
Contact Dan Weinberg; Sallyann Gray
Credits Computer Hackers (F); Harry At 18 (T); Young Musician of the Year (T)

Rapid Pictures Ltd

21-25 Goldhawk Road, London W12 8QQ
t 020 8743 8053 **e** info@rapidpictures.co.uk
Contact Jim Nichols, Managing Director

Remvision Ltd

388 City Road, Islington, London EC1V 2QA
t 020 7713 1141 **f** 020 7713 1161
e production@remvision.co.uk **w** www.remvision.co.uk
Contact Darren King

Resolution City

341-345 Old Street, London EC1V 9LL
t 020 7749 9300 **f** 020 7729 8814
e bookings@resolution.tv **w** www.resolution.tv
Contact Karen Wells, Bookings; Jacqui Rutherford, Facilities Manager

Resolution Soho

26 D'Arblay Street, London W1F 8EL
t 020 7437 1336 **e** bookings@resolution.tv **w** www.resolution.tv
Contact Christine Troughton, Bookings; Louisa Styler, Facility Co-ordinator

Revolution Post

11 Utopia Village, 7 Chalcot Road, Primrose Hill, London NW1 8LH
t 020 7586 1271 **f** 020 7586 4488
e pete@revolutionpost.tv **w** www.revolutionpost.com
Contact Torin Brown, Proprietor; Mark Woodroofe, Managing Director; Peter
Brown, Proprietor
Credits Roadies (D); Mile High (T)

Rushes Postproduction Ltd

66 Old Compton Street, London W1D 4UH
t 020 7437 8676 **f** 07851 3002 /2519
e info@rushes.co.uk **w** www.rushes.co.uk
Contact Paul Jones, Facilities Director; Bill McNamara, Head of Visual Effects; Sonia
Ralton, Head of Production; Mike Uden, Creative Director; Joce Capper, Managing
Director; Rebecca Swegman, Head of Bookings; Jo Morgan, Facility Manager

Screen Scene Ltd

41 Upper Mount Street, Dublin 2, Ireland
t +353 1 661 1501 **f** +353 1 661 0491
e info@screenscene.ie **w** www.screenscene.ie
Contact Jim Duggan; Alison Tully; Sinead Bagnall
Credits Acme Lager

*A full service post-production and outside broadcast facility. From OB
to DVD editing, Flame, XSi 3D satellite uplink facilities, telecine, sound
editing and mixing. DVD authoring and compression. 20 camera OB.
A full service in high definition and standard resolution serving
national and international markets.*

pepper

The world's only facility with **two HD Avid|DS's**
and the world's first **C-Reality S16 Wetgate**

'DR ZHIVAGO' Granada Television

'SPOOKS' BBC1

nominated for
BEST POST PRODUCTION HOUSE
BROADCAST AWARDS 2003

CREDITS

24 HOUR PARTY PEOPLE
HORNBLOWER
IN THIS WORLD
JEFFREY ARCHER: THE TRUTH
LESLEY GARRETT
MIDSOMER MURDERS
RED, WHITE AND THE BLUES
SAHARA WITH MICHAEL PALIN
THE LOST PRINCE
TIPPING THE VELVET

CONTACTS

HELEN PHELPS   JILL JONES   LISA SWEET

pepper

slingsby place   long acre   london   wc2e 9ab
+44 [0]20 7836 1188   +44 [0]20 7497 9305
mailus@pepperpost.tv   www.pepperpost.tv

Silverglade Associates Ltd

11A Enterprise House, 59 - 65 Upper Ground, London SE1 9PQ
t 020 7827 9510 **e** info@silverglade.com
w www.silverglade.com

Contact Doug Robinson, Director; Beverley Phillips, Facilities Manager; Julia Frater, Director; Charles Frater, Director
Credits Tylers Ultimate Cooking (T); Australia Uncovered (T); Gagging For It (T); Fight School (T)

The Sound House Post Production Ltd

10th Floor Astley House, Quay Street, Manchester M3 4AE
t 0161 832 7299 **f** 0161 832 7266
m 07970 920323 **i** 0161 832 4469
e suekeane@thesoundhouse.tv **w** www.thesoundhouse.tv

Contact Susan Keane, Facility Manager; Michael Stewart, Managing Director; John Wood, Dubbing Mixer
Credits Lemsip (C); King Arthur (D); Bob The Builder (A); Lord Of The Rings - Two Towers (F)

High-end audio post production and symphony online editing, city centre based with Tracklay, Foley, ADR, surround sound including 5:1, music composition and duplication.

Spiritlevel Post

43 Rivington Street, London EC2A 3QX
t 020 7729 8578 **f** 020 7729 8331
e mail@spiritlevelpost.co.uk **w** www.spiritlevelpost.co.uk

Contact Elio España, Senior Editor; Tom O'Dell, Facilities Manager
Credits Laban (I); Asylum (F); Manchild - Live In Cardiff (M); National Geographic - Hot Salsa (D)

St Anne's

20 St Anne's Court, London W1F 0BH
t 020 7155 1500 **f** 020 7155 1501
e bruce.everett@saintannespost.co.uk
w www.saintannespost.co.uk

Contact Lucy Fuller, Bookings; Bruce Everett, Managing Director; Johnny Whitehead, Technical Operations; Portia Napier, Post Production Contacts; Becky Start, Sales; Dean Watkins, Sales
Credits State Of Mind (T); Mindhunters (F); Model Behaviour (T); Two Thousand Acres Of Sky (T)

High definition and standard Def Telecine. Television and feature film sound tracks. Cutting rooms, offline, online. Linear and non-linear HD and SD.

The Station Ltd

5 D'Arblay Street, London W1F 8DE
t 020 7292 9595 **f** 020 7292 9596
e info@the-station.com **w** www.the-station.com
Contact Jenny Field, Contact
Credits Kellogg's Special K: Security (test) (C)

Swordfish Editing Ltd

7 Poland Street, London W1F 8PU
t 020 7734 2428

TSI Post Production

TSI Video, 10 Grape Street, London WC2H 8DY
t 020 7379 3435 **f** 020 7379 4589 **e** bookings@tsi.co.uk

Contact Simon Peach, Managing Director; Andy Wright, Producer; Simon Kanjee, Managing Director; Nathalie Roull; Shula Fitzgerald, Head of Sales; Alan Cronin, Facility Manager; Julia Gonsalves, Head of Bookings
Credits Robbie Williams In Concert (T); This Morning (T); Sir Robert Winston - The Human Instinct (T); They Think It's All Over (T)

The TSI Group includes:- TSI Post Production, TSI Transmission and TSI Design, a leading design and branding agency. The group offers high definition post production for feature films and television, digital post production for television titles, commercials and music promos.

The latest addition to the ever-expanding TSI Group is the introduction of 3D Studio Max 5 producing complex CGIs.

All in all a total and complete facility, oozing with bright, friendly, professional staff... an award winning team!"

Two Plus One Ltd

1-2 Lower St James Street, London W1F 9EG
t 020 7287 2221 **f** 020 7437 4161
e sales@twoplusone.co.uk
w www.twoplusone.co.uk
Contact Martin Rogers, Sales and Business Development; Lyndsey McPherson, Office Manager; Joy Hancock, Managing Director; Natasha Linski, Sales & Business Development

Avid DS/HD editing suite, Avid Symphony Universal, Avid Media and Film Composers, Broadcast Dubbing, Dolby Digital Encoding and Decoding, DVD Authoring and Encoding incorporating: Sonic DVD Creator and Scenarist Systems, 2D Graphics. Based in relaxed and spacious surroundings with natural light.

Vivid

Unit 311F, The Big Peg, 120 Vyse Street, Birmingham B18 6ND
t 0121 233 4061 **f** 0121 212 1784
e info@vivid.org.uk **w** www.vivid.org.uk

Contact Marian Hall, Facilities Manager; Paula Dower, Administration Manager; Kaye Winwood, Projects Manager; Paula Green, Administrator; Yasmeen Baig Clifford, Director, Director; Matthew Higginbottom, Production Facilitator

VPTV

Oddfellows Hall, London Road, Chipping Norton OX7 5AR
t 01608 641592 **f** 01608 641969
e info@vptv.com **w** www.vptv.com

Contact Alison Biddle, Facilities Manager; Paul Aitken, Managing Director
Credits Currys No Worries Update (I); Discover A Cleaner Tay (E); Orange - Future Home (E); I Love Mummy (T)

Complete production and post-production facilities under one roof. Broadcast Shooting - Editing (Quantel Editbox, Avids) - Large Studio - Audio Recording and Mastering - Graphics - Web Design - DVD Authoring - CDRom Production.

W6 Studio
359 Lillie Road, Fulham, London SW6 7PA
t 020 7385 2272 **f** 020 7381 5252 **m** 07836 357629
e ka2@w6studio.freeserve.co.uk **w** www.w6studio.co.uk

Waterfall Studios
2 Silver Road, Woodlane, London W12 7SG
t 020 8746 2000 **f** 020 8746 0180
e info@waterfall-studios.com **w** www.waterfall-studios.com
Contact Samantha Leese, Facilities Manager

Willcox & Willcox
12 Moor Street, London W1D 5NG
t 020 7734 9297
e willcox@dircon.co.uk **w** www.willcoxwillcox.co.uk
Credits Volkswagen Passat: Disturbance

York Student Television (ystv)
Goodricke College, University of York, Heslington, York YO10 5DD
t 01904 431431 **e** ystv@york.ac.uk **w** http://ystv.york.ac.uk

Yorkshire Tyne-Tees Television
The Television Centre, Kirkstall Road, Leeds LS3 1JS
t 0113 222 7653 **f** 0113 222 8282 **w** www.yorkshiretv.com
Contact Jim Richardson, Head of Sales and Planning
Credits Emmerdale (T); At Home With The Braithwaites (T); Where The Heart Is (T); Heartbeat (T)

Post Production Facilities
Sound ADR/Foley

Alligator Studios (previously Crocodile Studios)
7 Goodge Place, London W1T 4SG
t 020 7636 4840 **f** 020 7580 0560
e info@alligatorstudios.com **w** www.alligatorstudios.com
Contact Louise Crouch, Production Manager

Bramptons
28 Church Lane, Weston Turville, Aylesbury HP22 5SJ
t 01296 689066 **f** 01296 689067 **e** chris@musicoflife.com
Contact Chris France, Partner
Credits The Key (T); Messiah II (T); Tipping The Velvet (T); Redcaps (T)

China Blue Audio Post Production
3 Wedgwood Mews, Greek Street, Soho, London W1D 4BD
t 020 7437 5999 **f** 020 7437 5665
e info@chinablue.co.uk **w** www.chinablue.co.uk
Contact Emily Cobb , Studio Manager; David Hamilton-Smith, Managing Director
Credits Recovered (T); Freestyle (T); Heroes Of World War II (D)

De Lane Lea Ltd
75 Dean Street, London W1D 3PU
t 020 7432 3800 **f** 020 7432 3838
e info@delanelea.com **w** www.delanelea.com
Contact Katrina Rochowski, Office Manager; Anna Billington, Bookings; Yazz Rajeeball, Bookings; Peter Joly, Managing Director; Mica McGrath, Bookings
Credits Billy Elliot (F); Ned Kelly (F); Dirty Pretty Things (F); The Lost Prince (T)
The Most Competitive and Versatile Audio Post House in London.

Lunchtime Productions
117 Wise Lane, Mill Hill, London NW7 2BD
t 020 8959 3545 **f** 020 8959 3545 **m** 07973 635668
e lunchpro@dircon.co.uk
Contact Ted Kempner, Director

M2 Television
Ingestre Court, Ingestre Place, London W1F 0JL
t 020 7343 6543 **f** 020 7343 6555
e info@m2tv.com **w** www.m2tv.com
The Forum, 74-80 Camden Street, London, NW1 0EG
t 020 7343 6789 **f** 020 7343 6777
Contact Kabir Malik; Jennie Jones
Based in Soho and Camden, we offer a full range of video and audio post production as well as the award-winning co:de design. 5 digital online suites, 5 Editbox FX online suites, 2 Symphony online suites, Avid unity server, Clipbox video server, 14 Avid offline, 5 digital audio suites, Hal, and Illusion.

Samuel Moffett
21 Abbotsford Road, Redland, Bristol BS6 6EZ
m 07977 099002 **e** sam@funkphenomenon.co.uk
Credits Khad San Road Bangkok - Gateway to the East (T); Boo (T); The Land Ironclads (T)

molinare
a television corporation company

Molinare
34 Fouberts Place, London W1F 7PX
t 020 7478 7000 **f** 020 7478 7199
e bookings@molinare.co.uk **w** www.molinare.co.uk
Contact Kate George, Facilities Manager
Credits Dorada Especial: Painting; AXN: Cornice; Walkers Dorito's: Idents; The Wind
For 30 years Molinare has been offering the best in Post Production, helping the best people make the best programmes, we have about the widest selection of facilities in one location in the industry. Based in the heart of Soho, we offer, 5 digital Online Suites, Editbox FX V8, Ursa Gold Telecine, High Definition Online, 10 Avid Offline suites and 2 Avid Online suites, 5 Audio Dubbing suites with voice over booths, Tracklay, Discreet Flint, Media Illusion, Drive in 1500 sq ft Video studio, 400 sq ft Virtual Studio, Duplication, Transmission Services, as well as the Molinare Design team for all your branding and design needs.

Mosaic Studio
Portland Street, Sheffield S6 3DN
t 0114 249 5342 **t** 0114 266 6145
f 0114 266 6145 **m** 07956 654366
e info@mosaicstudio.co.uk **w** www.mosaicstudio.co.uk
Contact Brian Gray, Partner/Engineer; Helen Gray, Partner/Composer
Credits Connexions (I); NCS Manhunt (T); Baby Blues (F)

Movietrack Ltd
1 Lexington Street, London W1F 9AH
t 020 7734 4770 **f** 020 7734 4990
e tim@movietrack.freeserve.co.uk
Contact Tim Lewiston, Director
Credits Merlin (F); Among Joints (F); Shiner (F); The Boys From County Clare (F)

Outsource Media Ltd
Talisman House, 13 North Park Road, Harrogate HG3 1NH
t 01423 508500 **i** 01423 873706
e production@omuk.com **w** www.omuk.com
Credits Conflict: Desert Storm (T); Timesplitters 2 (F); Half Past Dead (T)

Sanctuary Town House Vision (THV)
150 Goldhawk Road, London W12 8HH
t 020 7932 3200 **f** 020 7932 3209
e thv@sanctuarystudios.co.uk **w** www.sanctuarystudios.co.uk
Contact Julian MacDonald, Head of Vision; D Ward, Group Sales Manager
*Audio Postproduction Suite mixing stereo and 5.1, dialogue, effects
tracklaying, ADR Voice Over and Foley for features, documentary,
animation, broadcast and DVD.*

Ten Pin Alley Ltd
Enterprise House, 19-21 Brunswick Road, Gloucester GL1 1HG
t 01452 330075 **f** 01452 382320
e tpa@tenpinalley.co.uk **w** www.tenpinalley.co.uk
Contact Keith Littler, Director; Tony Church, Business Affairs; Allison Williams,
Managing Director; Mike Cross, Technical Director; Karina Stanford-Smith, Head
of Sales
Credits Barney (A); Pond Life (A); S Club 7 Go Live (T); Clifford The Big Red Dog (A)

Universal Sound
Old Farm Lane, London Road East, Amersham HP7 9DH
t 01494 723400 **f** 01494 723500 **m** 07973 518561
e foley@justplay.co.uk **w** www.justplay.co.uk
Contact Phil Barrett, Director

Zoo Studios
145 Wardour Street, London W1F 8WB
t 020 7734 2000 **f** 020 7734 2200
e mail@zoostudios.co.uk **w** www.soho-studios.co.uk
Contact Danielle Jones, Booking Manager; Graham Ebbs, Managing Director

Post Production Facilities
Sound Dubbing

2nd Sense Broadcast Ltd
Millennium Studios, Elstree Way, Borehamwood WD6 1SF
e info@2ndsense.co.uk **w** www.2ndsense.co.uk
Credits Whistle Test (T); Boo! (A); EastEnders (T); Chuckle Vision (T)

Alligator Studios (previously Crocodile Studios)
7 Goodge Place, London W1T 4SG
t 020 7636 4840 **f** 020 7580 0560
e info@alligatorstudios.com **w** www.alligatorstudios.com
Contact Louise Crouch, Production Manager

Anvil Post Production
Denham Media Park, North Orbital Road, Denham, Uxbridge
UB9 5HL
t 01895 833522 **f** 01895 835006
e mike.anscombe@thompson.net **w** www.anvilpost.com
Contact Mike Anscombe, Studio Manager; Roger Beck, Managing Director

Arena Digital
74 Newman Street, London W1T 3EL
t 020 7436 4360 **f** 020 7436 3989
e info@arenadigital.co.uk **w** www.arenadigital.co.uk
Contact Rowan Bray, Facilities Manager; Calvin Cunningham

The Audio Suite
The Custard Factory, Gibb Street, Birmingham B9 4AA
t 0121 224 8234 **f** 0121 224 8235 **i** 0121 224 8236
e info@theaudiosuite.com **w** www.theaudiosuite.com
Contact Neil Hillman, Managing Director

Babel Media Ltd
Finsbury Business Centre, 40 Bowling Green Lane, London
EC1R ONE
t 020 7415 7029 **f** 020 7418 7001 **m** 07789 752602
e studio@babelmedia.com **w** www.babelmedia.com
Contact Lindsay Bywood, Business Development Manager

BBC Post Production

BBC Post Production
(Sites across London, Bristol & Birmingham)
5550 Television Centre, Wood Lane, London W12 7RJ
t 020 8225 7702 (London) **t** 0117 9746 666 (Bristol)
t 0121 432 8621 (Birmingham)
w www.bbcresources.com/postproduction

BC's Sound & Vision
71 Tudor Way, Bridgewater TA6 6UE
t 01278 455562 **f** 01278 446471 **m** 07860 888205
e brian@beecees.demon.co.uk **w** www.beecees.demon.co.uk
Contact Brian Comer, Director

Bell Voice Recordings
32B Fouberts Place, London W1V 1HF
t 020 7437 1034 **f** 020 7434 0870
e steve@bellvoice.com **w** www.bellvoice.com
Contact Steve Hall, Managing Director
Credits Seeboard Gas (C); Liberty Pads (C); John Charcol (C)

Big Ears Post
2 Pontcanna Place, Pontcanna, Cardiff CF11 9JY
t 029 2022 9588 **f** 029 2022 9588 **m** 07879 405199
e eira.banks@virgin.net
Contact Ian 'Spike' Banks, Sound Editor; Eira Banks, Assistant Editor
Credits The Meeksville Ghost (F); Up 'N' Under (F); Alone (F); Otherworld (F)

The Bridge Facilities Company
55-57 Great Marlborough Street, London W1F 7JX
t 020 7434 9861 **f** 020 7494 4658
e bookings@thebridge.co.uk **w** www.thebridge.co.uk
Contact Tom McComvile, Facility Manager
Credits Tetley (C); The Little Robots (A); The Lampies (A)

The Bridge
55 Great Marlborough Street, London W1F 7JX
t 020 7434 9861 **f** 020 7494 4658
e bookings@thebridge.co.uk **w** www.thebridge.co.uk
Contact Jane Babb, Bookings Manager

Capital Studios
Wandsworth Plain, London SW18 1ET
t 020 8877 1234 **f** 020 8877 0234
e info@capitalstudios.com **w** www.capitalstudios.com
Contact Bobbi Johnstone, Contact; Clare Phillips, Contact
*Fully equipped digital broadcast studios: 3000 sq ft (60x50x19.5) and
2000 sq ft (50x50x19.5). Supported by galleries, dressing rooms,
wardrobe, green room and audience facilities. Tx lines, Cafe with
courtyard garden. New digital Post-Production facilities.*

DB Post Productions
1-8 Batemans Building, Soho Square, London W1V 5TW
t 020 7434 0097 **f** 020 7287 9143
e general@dbpost.com **w** www.dbpost.com
Contact Amanda Heatley, Bookings Manager; Janie Dahn; Kevin Brazier, Director
Credits Stretfordwives (T); Teachers (T); Shackelton (T)

DE LANE LEA

De Lane Lea Ltd
75 Dean Street, London W1D 3PU
t 020 7432 3800 **f** 020 7432 3838
e info@delanelea.com **w** www.delanelea.com
Contact Katrina Rochowski, Office Manager; Anna Billington, Bookings; Yazz
Rajeeball, Bookings; Peter Joly, Managing Director; Mica McGrath, Bookings
Credits Billy Elliot (F); Ned Kelly (F); Dirty Pretty Things (F); The Lost Prince (T)
The Most Competitive and Versatile Audio Post House in London.

The Digital Audio Company

3 Carleton Business Park, Carleton New Road, Skipton BD23 2AA
t 01756 797100 **f** 01756 797101
e info@the-digital-audio.co.uk **w** www.the-digital-audio.co.uk
Credits In Deep I, II & III (T); Wire In The Blood (T); A Touch Of Frost (T); Linda Green (T)

Digital Audio Technology Ltd

Phoenix Sound, Engineers Way, Wembley, London HA9 0ET
t 020 8450 5665 **f** 020 8208 1979
e jo@digitalaudiotech.com **w** www.digitalaudiotech.com
Contact Cathy Ferrett, Facilities Manager; Jo Harrison, Marketing Manager
Credits Braveheart (F); Ally McBeal (T); X-Files (T); The Full Monty (F)

Evolutions Television Ltd

5 Berners Street, London W1T 3LF
t 020 7580 3333 **f** 020 7637 1942
e info@evolutionstelevision.com **w** www.evolutionstelevision.com

Evolutions currently offer two Pro-Tools Dubbing suites. Autoconforming can be carried out from any of the VTR formats supported at Evolutions or audio can be taken from any OMFI compatible system. Both suites have direct access to voice-over booths and 1000s of sound effects and music cds. We also offer a full range of post production, video duplication and new media services.

Fitzrovia Post Ltd

33 Gresse Street, London W1T 1QU
t 020 7209 3474 **f** 020 7209 3484
e info@fitzroviapost.com **w** www.fitzroviapost.com

Frame Film & Television Post Production

26 St Annes Court, London W1F 0BL
t 020 7734 8617 **f** 020 7287 0509 **m** 07771 605094
e frame@aol.com
Contact Stan White, Proprietor

Future Film Group

25 Noel Street, London W1F 8GX
t 020 7434 6655 **f** 020 7434 6644
e cook@futurefilmgroup.com **w** www.futurefilmgroup.com
Contact Peter Hodges, Director; Steve Cook, Post Production Supervisor; Peter Maxwell, Feature Film Mixer; Ellie Walker, Studio Bookings; Ted Swanscott, ADR & Foley mixer; Richard Lewis, TV Sound Mixer
Credits The I Inside (F); To Kill A King (F); About A Boy (F); 28 Days Later (F)

Gemini Audio

Hammer House, 117 Wardour Street, London W1F 0UN
t 020 7734 8962 **f** 020 7439 3122
e info@geminiaudio.co.uk
w www.geminiaudio.co.uk
Contact Patrick Simpson, Studio Manager
Credits Time Team Special (T); Hero - Bobby Moore (D); Ground Force (T); BBC Correspondent (T)

Goldcrest Post Production Facilities

36-44 Brewer Street, London W1F 9LX
t 020 7437 7972 **f** 020 7437 5402 **m** 07836 204283
e mailbox@goldcrest-post.co.uk
Contact Poppy Quinn, Bookings and Customer Services Manager; Raju Raymond, General Manager

Sound and vision post: two dubbing theatres, one ADR Foley Theatre, voiceovers, Foley and FX, tracklaying, Avid/Lightworks and film cutting standards conversion. Also production offices and apartments.

Hillside

Merry Hill Road, Bushey WD23 1DR
t 020 8950 7919 **f** 020 8421 8085
e enquiries@hillside-studios.co.uk **w** www.hillside-studios.co.uk
Contact David Hillier, Head of Facilities

Avid Symphony, Media Composer XL and Digibeta Suite. Dubbing to picture with Soundtracs DS3 and Audiofile. Extensive effects/music library.

David Humphries

Whitehall Farmhouse, White Horse Lane, Wingmore, Canterbury CT4 6LR
t 01227 831297 **f** 01227 831297 **m** 07957 228645
e david_humphries@hotmail.com
Credits Daziel And Pascoe (T); Longitude (T); Paradise Heights (T); Dirty Pretty Things (F)

Inspired Sands

Cardiff Bay Business Centre, Lewis Road, Ocean Park, Cardiff CF24 5EJ
t 029 2048 4298 **f** 029 2045 1200
e info@inspired-sands.co.uk **w** www.inspired-sands.co.uk
Contact John Davies, Manager

Interact Sound Ltd

160 Barlby Road, London W10 6BS
t 020 8960 3115 **f** 020 8964 3022
e info@interact-sound.co.uk **w** www.interact-sound.co.uk
Contact Tony Martin, Studio Manager; Aad Wirtz, Director; Sandie Wirtz, Director
Credits Promoted To Glory (T); The Debt (T); Biggie And Tupac (F); 24 Hour Party People (F)

The London Studios Ltd

Upper Ground, London SE1 9LT
t 020 7261 3181 **f** 020 7737 8840
e post@londonstudios.co.uk **w** www.londonstudios.co.uk
Contact Julie Sangan, Head of Post Production Sales

Avid Offlines/Avid Symphony all on Avid Unity. Avid Express. 7 digital Widescreen Linear suites. 6 Audio suites with Logic desks, audiofile & voice over booths. 2 & 3D graphic areas. 2 Quantel Clipbox servers with access to studios and Linear edit suites.

M2 Television

Ingestre Court, Ingestre Place, London W1F 0JL
t 020 7343 6543 f 020 7343 6555
e info@m2tv.com w www.m2tv.com
The Forum, 74-80 Camden Street, London, NW1 0EG
t 020 7343 6789 f 020 7343 6777

Contact Kabir Malik; Jennie Jones

Based in Soho and Camden, we offer a full range of video and audio post production as well as the award-winning co:de design. 5 digital online suites, 5 Editbox FX online suites, 2 Symphony online suites, Avid unity server, Clipbox video server, 14 Avid offline, 5 digital audio suites, Hal, and Illusion.

Marmalade Studios

143 Wardour Street, London W1F 8WA
t 020 7534 5885 f 020 7534 5884
e post@marmaladestudios.co.uk w www.marmaladestudios.co.uk

Contact Philla Marshall, Bookings & Sales; Renee Dulieu, Bookings & Sales
Credits Telemagination - Metal Headz (T); Lion TV - Bricks & Mortar (D); Discovery Channel (C); Discovery Channel: 'Nature's Call'

Martyr Sound

6 Berners Mews, London W1P 3DG
t 020 7637 2828 f 020 7637 8222
e mix@martyrsound.co.uk w www.martyrsound.co.uk

Contact Keith Marriner, Director; Danny Finn, Operations Manager; Steve Eveleigh, Director
Credits Buried (T); Bad Girls Series I-IV (T); London's Burning Series XIV (T); Judge John Deeds (T)

Molinare

34 Fouberts Place, London W1F 7PX
t 020 7478 7000 f 020 7478 7199
e bookings@molinare.co.uk w www.molinare.co.uk

Contact Kate George, Facilities Manager
Credits Dorada Especial: Painting; AXN: Cornice; Walkers Dorito's: Idents; The Wind

For 30 years Molinare has been offering the best in Post Production, helping the best people make the best programmes, we have about the widest selection of facilities in one location in the industry. Based in the heart of Soho, we offer, 5 digital Online Suites, Editbox FX V8, Ursa Gold Telecine, High Definition Online, 10 Avid Offline suites and 2 Avid Online suites, 5 Audio Dubbing suites with voice over booths, Tracklay, Discreet Flint, Media Illusion, Drive in 1500 sq ft Video studio, 400 sq ft Virtual Studio, Duplication, Transmission Services, as well as the Molinare Design team for all your branding and design needs.

The Music Factor Ltd

15 Stanhope Road, London N6 5NE
t 020 8802 5984 f 020 8809 7436
e themusicfactor@paulrodriguezmus.demon.co.uk
Contact Paul Rodriguez, Managing Director; Amy Coats, Copyright Manager

Recent work: BBC TV, Channel 4, Channel 5, Discovery. Facilities: music production, music publishing, music library, copyright clearance.

Nats Post Production

10 Soho Square, London W1D 3NT
t 020 7287 9900 f 020 7287 8636
e bookings@nats.ltd.uk
Contact Sara Hill, Bookings; Jo Manser; Louise Knight; Louise Thomas

One of Soho's leading facilities, Nats Post Production is fully equipped in all aspects of television post production, from offline to online, design and graphics, grade and audio dub. With over 40 suites, we strive to make sure your whole experience is as pleasant and productive as possible by offering you creative excellence, intelligent solutions and home comforts.

New Yorkshire Production Department (NYPD)

PO Box 67, Hessle, Hull HU13 0YG
t 01482 643677 f 01482 649480
e seanbell@nypd.co.uk w www.nypd.co.uk
Contact Sean Bell, Production Sound Mixer
Credits Radio Com Prod; Theme Park Sound; Station Imaging

One Stop Digital (OSD) Ltd

13 Perrymead, Prestwich, Manchester M25 2QJ
t 0161 773 2664 f 0161 773 8290 m 07973 480760
e mike@osd-uk.com w www.osd-uk.com
Contact Mike Thornton, Director, Director

Pampas Audio

7 Weybank, Bentley, Farnham GU10 5LB
t 01420 22739 f 01420 520583 m 07836 204091
e pmealing@talk21.com
Contact Peter Mealing, Audio consultant

Rainbow Post Production

16 Ingestre Place, London W1F 0JJ
t 020 7434 4566 f 020 7439 4565 w www.rainbowpost.com
Contact Nick Rogers, Dubbing Mixer; Louise , Bookings; Lyndsay , Bookings

Random Post Production

Artist's Court, Manette Street, London W1D 4AP
t 020 7434 3444 f 020 7434 3451
e edit@randompost.com w www.randompost.com
Contact Dan Weinberg; Sallyann Gray
Credits Computer Hackers (F); Harry At 18 (T); Young Musician of the Year (T)

Resolution

26 D'Arblay Street, London W1F 8EL
t 020 7437 1336 e bookings@resolution.tv w www.resolution.tv
Contact Christine Trouton, Facility Manager

Richmond Studios Ltd

83-84 George Street, Richmond TW9 1HE
t 020 8332 1690 f 020 8332 1691 m 07836 731918
e charlotte@richmondstudios.com w www.richmondstudios.com
Contact Charlotte Danaher, General Manager; Toby Alington, Director, Managing Director; Robert Grieves, Designer; Miles Tudor, DVD/IT Technician; Jonathan Potts, Video Editor; Andrea Hein, Project Manager
Credits DUP DVD (W); Ramones DVD (W); Cirque De Soleil - Alegria DVD (W); Brit Awards (T)

Sanctuary Town House Vision (THV)

150 Goldhawk Road, London W12 8HH
t 020 7932 3200 f 020 7932 3209
e thv@sanctuarystudios.co.uk w www.sanctuarystudios.co.uk
Contact Julian MacDonald, Head of Vision; D Ward, Group Sales Manager

Audio Postproduction Suite mixing stereo and 5.1, dialogue, effects tracklaying, ADR Voice Over and Foley for features, documentary, animation, broadcast and DVD.

Saunders & Gordon
30 Gresse Street, London W1T 1QR
t 020 7580 7316 **f** 020 7637 5085
e tlofts@sgss.co.uk **w** www.sgss.co.uk
Contact Tim Lofts, Facilities Director

Scramble Sound Ltd
8A Shelton Street, London WC2H 9JP
t 020 7240 6543 **f** 020 7240 6622
e post@scramble.co.uk **w** www.scramble.co.uk
Contact Amelia Jackson-Gray, Bookings; Sarah Sealey, Client Liaison Manager;
Karen Noden, Bookings
Credits Volkswagen GTI - Forever (Dir. Ringan Ledwidge) (C); Volkswagen Lupo
- Demon Baby (Dir. Frederick Bond) (C); Royal Marines - Strength Of Mind (Dir.
Ivan Zacharias) (I); Nike - Cage (Dir. Terry Gillian) (C)

Silk Sound Ltd
13 Berwick Street, London W1F 0PW
t 020 7434 3461 **f** 020 7494 1748 **i** 020 7434 7636
e bookings@silk.co.uk **w** www.silk.co.uk
Contact Paula Ryman, Studio Manager; Rebecca Parsons, Bookings Manager

Sound Heads Ltd
36/44 Brewer Street, London W1F 9LX
t 020 8432 2511 **m** 07775 572672 **e** nigel@soundheads.com
w www.soundheads.com
Contact Nigel Mills, Managing Director
Credits The Golden Bowl (F); Gosford Park (F)

Sound Monsters Ltd
4 Grafton Mews, London W1T 5JE
t 020 7387 3230 **f** 020 7387 0718 **e** info@soundmonsters.com
Contact Karl Mainzer, Dubbing Mixer; Cliff Jones, Dubbing Mixer; Rada
Danilovic, Assistant
Credits Our Sam (D); History Of DNA (D); Visions Of Space (D); Pyramid (D)

The Sound Store
8-9 Bayley Street, London WC1B 3HB
t 020 7637 7472 **f** 020 7436 4457 **e** store@editstore.org
Contact Eleanor Bradburne, Manager

Sounds in Motion Ltd
Media Centre, Culverhouse Cross, Cardiff CF5 6XJ
t 029 2059 0521 **f** 029 2059 0471
e enquiries@sounds-in-motion.co.uk
w www.sounds-in-motion.co.uk
Contact Ralph Evans, Director
Credits Roots Of Welsh (D); Magic Islands (D)

Soundworks
1-2 Mount Stuart Square, Cardiff Bay, Cardiff CF10 5EE
t 029 2033 1010 **f** 029 2033 1011
e info@soundworks.co.uk **w** www.soundworks.co.uk
Contact Greg Provan, Facility Manager; Simon H Jones, Creative Director;
Janet Jones, Financial Director; Stacha Kinor, Facility Co-ordinator; Dafydd
Jones, Senior Dubbing Mixer; Steve Castle, Dubbing Mixer
Credits Fireman Sam (A); The Seven Days That Shook Coronation St (T); The
Story Of Tracy Beaker (T); Wales Tourist Board (C); Hilltop Hospital (A)

Space Facilities Ltd
16 Dufours Place, London W1F 7SP
t 020 7494 1020 **f** 020 7494 2861
e bookings@space.co.uk **w** www.space.co.uk
Contact Tom McConville, Studio Manager; Marie McWilliam, Bookings Manager;
Rachel Grattage, Bookings Manager

Sprockets & Bytes
20 Richmond Hill, Clifton, Bristol BS8 1BA
t 0117 923 9210 **f** 0117 923 9310
e info@sprockets.co.uk **w** www.sprockets.co.uk
Contact Matt Coster, Facilities Manager
Credits Predators in Paradise (T); Different Ball Game (T); Teachers (T)

Stationhouse
Kensington, London W14
t 020 7602 9906
e jim@stationhouse.net **w** www.stationhouse.net
Contact Jim Betteridge, Proprietor
Credits J K Rowling (D); Film Focus (D); Alone (F); Paradise Grove (F)
Top quality Audio Post at a fraction of Soho prices.

Tamborine Productions
14 Livonia Street, London W1F 8AG
t 020 7434 1812 **f** 020 7434 1813
e tim@tamborine.co.uk **w** www.tamborine.co.uk
Contact Mark Blackledge, MD-Composer; Nick Harris, Sound Engineer; Tim
Dodd, Sales & Marketing Manager

Trident Sound Studios
17 St Anne's Court, London W1F 0BQ
t 020 7734 6198 **f** 020 7439 3813
e info@tridentsoundstudios.co.uk
w www.tridentsoundstudios.co.uk
Contact Peter Hughes, Managing Director
Credits Range Rover (C); Blakes 7 DVD Narrations (T); Stories In Art Videos (E)

TSI Post Production
TSI Video, 10 Grape Street, London WC2H 8DY
t 020 7379 3435 **f** 020 7379 4589
e bookings@tsi.co.uk
Contact Simon Peach, Managing Director; Andy Wright, Producer; Simon
Kanjee, Managing Director; Nathalie Roull; Shula Fitzgerald, Head of Sales;
Alan Cronin, Facility Manager; Julia Gonsalves, Head of Bookings
Credits Robbie Williams In Concert (T); This Morning (T); Sir Robert Winston -
The Human Instinct (T); They Think It's All Over (T)

Video London Sound Studios Ltd
16-18 Ramillies Street, London W1F 7LW
t 020 7734 4811 **f** 020 7734 0743
e info@videolondon.co.uk **w** www.videolondon.co.uk
Contact Beewan Athwall, Bookings Co-ordinator; Clifford Judge, Director
Credits The Lords Tale (D); Dalziel And Pascoe (T); Othello (T);
Hornblower (T)
Facilities include ADR, foleys, voiceovers, DVD and Dolby Digital.

Videosonics (Broadcast)
68A Delancey Street, London NW1 7RY
t 020 7209 0209 **f** 020 7419 4460
e info@videosonics.com **w** www.videosonics.com
Contact Dennis Weinreich, Managing Director; Richard Conway,
Project Development
Credits In This World (T); Foyle's War (T); Young Adam (T); Dr Zhivago (T)

Waterside Sound Studios Ltd
Waterside House, 46 Gas Street, Birmingham B1 2JT
t 0121 633 3545 **f** 0121 633 0480
e sound@waterside.co.uk
Contact Robin Ward, Director; Glyn Jones, Sound Engineer
Credits Panic Mechanics (T); Ten Things You Never Know (T); Waterworld (T);
Heart Of The Country (T)

Wild Tracks Audio Studios Ltd
Second Floor, 55 Greek Street, London W1D 3DT
t 020 7734 6331 **f** 020 7734 6195 **i** 020 7734 3645
e bookings@wildtracks.co.uk **w** www.wildtracks.co.uk
Contact Paul Headland, Managing Director; Liz Evans, Studio Manager
*Seven digital studios offering a complete post-production sound
solution. Networked DAR sound stations with tracklaying, sound-design,
surround-sound, OMFI import, autoconforming and DVD premastering.
Studio 7 with Dolby Commercials Licence for mixing in.*

World Wide Sound
21-25 Saint Anne's Court, London W1F 0BY
t 020 7434 1121 **f** 020 7734 0619
e sound@worldwidegroup.ltd.uk **w** www.worldwidegroup.ltd.uk
Contact Richard King, Managing Director

Wounded Buffalo Sound Studios
19A Hampton Lane, Bristol BS6 6LE
t 0117 946 7348 **f** 0117 970 6900 **e** info@woundedBuffalo.co.uk
Contact Helen Anderson, Manager
Credits Metrolands (F); Robbie the Reindeer (A); Mzima (D); Shanghai Vice (D)

Post Production Facilities
Sound Transfer & Duplication

Adluma Ltd
57 Sanderling Close, Letchworth SG6 4HZ
t 01462 648943 **f** 01462 648944
e sales@adluma.co.uk **w** www.adluma.co.uk
Contact Jane Fellowes, Managing Director; Andy Fellowes, Technical Director
Adluma Ltd - your specialist supplier for professional recording media.

Angell Sound Studios Plc
Top Floor, Film House, 142 Wardour Street, London W1F 8ZU
t 020 7478 7777 **f** 020 7478 7700
e info@angellsound.co.uk **w** www.angellsound.co.uk
Contact Penny Warnes, Studio Manager; Nick Angell, Manager; Jenny Sayers, Studio Bookings Manager; Claire Field, Studio Manager
Credits Big Issue (C); Drink Drive (C); Coca Cola (W); Hamlet (C)

Ascent Media
2 Golden Square, London W1R 3AD
t 020 7439 7138 **f** 020 7434 1907
e sally.hart-ives@ascent-media.co.uk **w** www.ascent-media.co.uk
Contact Sally Hart-Ives, Group Head of Sales; Sally Hart-Ives, Group Head of Sales

Ascent Media - Music & Agency
Video House, 48 Charlotte Street, London W1T 2NS
t 020 7208 2200 **f** 020 7208 2251
e claire.booth@ascent-media.co.uk **w** www.ascent-media.co.uk
Contact Claire Booth, Head of Music & Agency

Ascent Media Ltd
13 Hawley Crescent, London NW1 8NP
t 020 7284 7900 **f** 020 7284 1018
e michael.ashley@ascent-media.co.uk
Contact Michael Ashley, Head of Operations; Portia Napier, Head of Sales - ETV; Sally Hart-Ives, Group Head of Sales

BBC Post Production

BBC Post Production
(Sites across London, Bristol & Birmingham)
5550 Television Centre, Wood Lane, London W12 7RJ
t 020 8225 7702 (London) **t** 0117 9746 666 (Bristol)
t 0121 432 8621 (Birmingham)
w www.bbcresources.com/postproduction

dBm Ltd
The Loft, Mill Lane, Gaston Green, Little Hallingbury, Bishop's Stortford CM22 7QT
t 01279 721434 **f** 01279 721391
e info@dbmltd.com **w** www.dbmltd.com
Contact Richard Watts, Director; Janice Glen, Director

Digital Audio Technology Ltd
Phoenix Sound, Engineers Way, Wembley, London HA9 0ET
t 020 8450 5665 **f** 020 8208 1979
e jo@digitalaudiotech.com **w** www.digitalaudiotech.com
Contact Cathy Ferrett, Facilities Manager; Jo Harrison, Marketing Manager
Credits Braveheart (F); Ally McBeal (T); X-Files (T); The Full Monty (F)

Downsoft Ltd
Downsway House, Epsom Road, Ashtead KT21 1LD
t 01372 272422 **f** 01372 276122
e work@downsoft.co.uk **w** www.downsoft.co.uk

DTS (UK) Ltd
5 Tavistock Estate, Ruscombe Lane, Twyford RG10 9NJ
t 0118 934 9199 **f** 0118 934 9198
e dtsinfo@dtsonline.co.uk **w** www.dtsonline.com

Goldcrest Post Production Facilities
36-44 Brewer Street, London W1F 9LX
t 020 7437 7972 **f** 020 7437 5402 **m** 07836 204283
e mailbox@goldcrest-post.co.uk
Contact Poppy Quinn, Bookings and Customer Services Manager; Raju Raymond, General Manager

Graff Electronic Machines Ltd
Woodhill Road, Collingham, Newark NG23 7NR
t 01636 893036 **f** 01636 893317
e sales@graffelectronics.co.uk
w www.graffelectronics.co.uk
Contact Roger Platts, Sales and Marketing Manager

Grand Central Sound Studios
Craven House, 25-32 Marshall Street, London W1F 7ES
t 020 7306 5600 **f** 020 7306 5616
e info@grand-central-studios.com
w www.grand-central-studios.com
Contact Karen Crossley, Sales

John Claxton Associates Ltd
Monarch House, Victoria Industrial Estate, Victoria Road, London W3 6RZ
t 020 8357 5400 **f** 020 8357 5450

Keynote Audio Services
Smoke Tree House, Tilford Road, Farnham GU10 2EN
t 01252 794253 **f** 01252 792642
e sales@keynoteaudio.co.uk **w** www.keynoteaudio.co.uk
Contact Tim Wheatley, Sales Manager

•molinare
a television corporation company

Molinare
34 Fouberts Place, London W1F 7PX
t 020 7478 7000 **f** 020 7478 7199
e bookings@molinare.co.uk **w** www.molinare.co.uk
Contact Kate George, Facilities Manager
Credits Dorada Especial: Painting; AXN: Cornice; Walkers Dorito's: Idents; The Wind

For 30 years Molinare has been offering the best in Post Production, helping the best people make the best programmes, we have about the widest selection of facilities in one location in the industry. Based in the heart of Soho, we offer, 5 digital Online Suites, Editbox FX V8, Ursa Gold Telecine, High Definition Online, 10 Avid Offline suites and 2 Avid Online suites, 5 Audio Dubbing suites with voice over booths, Tracklay, Discreet Flint, Media Illusion, Drive in 1500 sq ft Video studio, 400 sq ft Virtual Studio, Duplication, Transmission Services, as well as the Molinare Design team for all your branding and design needs.

Selecta Sound
Sales Office, PO Box 4137, Hornchurch RM11 1GY
t 01708 453424 **f** 01708 455565 **m** 07779 140311
e select@classiques.demon.co.uk **w** www.selecta-sound.co.uk
Contact John Smailes, Proprietor

The Sound Company Ltd
23 Gosfield Street, London W1W 6HG
t 020 7580 5880 **f** 020 7580 6454
e info@sound.co.uk **w** www.sound.co.uk
Contact Dave Peacock, Studio Manager; Geoff Oliver, Managing Director; Eva Polnik, Bookings

TVS (London) Ltd
Unit 12 Nazeing Glassworks Estate, Nazeing New Road, Broxbourne EN10 6SU
t 0700 288 7887 **f** 0700 288 7000
e sales@tvslondon.com **w** www.tvslondon.com
Contact Nikki Birkinshaw, Sales Manager
Short run CD, DVD and VHS replication at sensible prices.

Unique Facilities
50 Lisson Street, London NW1 5DF
t 020 7723 0322 **f** 020 7453 1666
e info@uniquefacilities.com **w** www.uniquefacilities.com
Contact Shane Wall, Facilities Manager

Warwick Sound
111a Wardour Street, London W1F 0UJ
t 020 7437 5632 **f** 020 7439 0372 **m** 07909 923617
e info@warwicksound.com **w** www.warwicksound.com
Contact Ernie Marsh, Head of Sound

Post Production Facilities
Telecine Grading, Transfer & Duplication

Arion Facilities
Global House, Denham Media Park, North Orbital Road, Denham UB9 5HL
t 01895 834484 **f** 01895 833085
e sales@arion.co.uk **w** www.arion.co.uk

Arion Facilities offer a comprehensive range of post-production and duplication services to film, television and corporate clients. These include telecine, linear/non-linear editing, standards conversion and video/CD duplication.

The Ark Post Production Ltd
Suite 1B, 21-22 Poland Street, London W1F 8QQ
t 020 7437 0707 **f** 020 7287 4916
e bookings@theark.uk.com **w** www.theark.uk.com
Contact Matt Wyatt, Director; Tony Gorman, Head of Bookings

BBC Post Production

BBC Post Production
(Sites across London, Bristol & Birmingham)
5550 Television Centre, Wood Lane, London W12 7RJ
t 020 8225 7702 (London) **t** 0117 9746 666 (Bristol)
t 0121 432 8621 (Birmingham)
w www.bbcresources.com/postproduction

CD-RDirect.co.uk
Oakslade Studios, Station Road, Hatton CV35 7LH
t 01926 844005 **f** 01926 844045
e cd@oakslade.com **w** www.cd-rdirect.co.uk
Contact Caroline Kane, Sales Manager

ITFC
28 Concord Road, Acton, London W3 0TH
t 020 8752 0352 **f** 020 8993 6393 **w** www.itfc.com
Contact Cherry Cole, Director, Media Access Services; David Willis, Director; Chris Higgs, Director & General Manager

The London Studios Ltd

Upper Ground, London SE1 9LT
t 020 7261 3181 **f** 020 7737 8840
e post@londonstudios.co.uk
w www.londonstudios.co.uk
Contact Julie Sangan, Head of Post Production Sales

*Avid Offlines/Avid Symphony all on Avid Unity.
Avid Express. 7 digital Widescreen Linear suites.
6 Audio suites with Logic desks, audiofile
& voice over booths. 2 & 3D graphic areas.
2 Quantel Clipbox servers with access to
studios and Linear edit suites.*

Molinare
a television corporation company

Molinare

34 Fouberts Place, London W1F 7PX
t 020 7478 7000 **f** 020 7478 7199
e bookings@molinare.co.uk **w** www.molinare.co.uk
Contact Kate George, Facilities Manager
Credits Dorada Especial: Painting; AXN: Cornice; Walkers Dorito's: Idents;
The Wind

*For 30 years Molinare has been offering the best in Post Production,
helping the best people make the best programmes, we have about
the widest selection of facilities in one location in the industry.
Based in the heart of Soho, we offer, 5 digital Online Suites, Editbox
FX V8, Ursa Gold Telecine, High Definition Online, 10 Avid Offline
suites and 2 Avid Online suites, 5 Audio Dubbing suites with voice
over booths, Tracklay, Discreet Flint, Media Illusion, Drive in
1500 sq ft Video studio, 400 sq ft Virtual Studio, Duplication,
Transmission Services, as well as the Molinare Design team for
all your branding and design needs.*

![nats POST PRODUCTION logo]

Nats Post Production

10 Soho Square, London W1D 3NT
t 020 7287 9900 **f** 020 7287 8636 **e** bookings@nats.ltd.uk
Contact Sara Hill, Bookings; Jo Manser; Louise Knight; Louise Thomas

*One of Soho's leading facilities, Nats Post Production is fully equipped
in all aspects of television post production, from offline to online,
design and graphics, grade and audio dub. With over 40 suites,
we strive to make sure your whole experience is as pleasant and
productive as possible by offering you creative excellence, intelligent
solutions and home comforts.*

Pepper

3 Slingsby Place, Long Acre, Covent Garden,
London WC2E 9AB
t 020 7836 1188 **f** 020 7497 9305
e mailus@pepperpost.tv **w** www.pepperpost.tv
Contact Stephanie Goodwin; Helen Phelps; Jill Jones; Lisa Sweet
Credits Down To Earth (T); Spooks (T); Dr Zhivago (T); The Lost Prince (T)

Red Post Production

Hammersley House, 5-8 Warwick Street, London W1B 5LX
t 020 7439 1449 **f** 020 7439 1339
e production@red.co.uk **w** www.red.co.uk
Contact James Lamb, Producer; Fiona Byrne, Bookings; Stephen Luther,
Managing Director; Matt White, Senior Producer; Tara Geraughty, New
Business/Account Management; Tanya Johnson, Head Of Production; Annika
Ahl, Bookings; Aimee Posner, Bookings
Credits Blur - Crazy Beat (M); Tennants - Bollywood (C); S Club Movie -
Double Vision (F)

Soho Images

8-14 Meard Street, London W1F 0EQ
t 020 7437 0831 **f** 020 7734 9471
e emma.devonshire@sohoimages.com **w** www.sohoimages.com
Contact John Sears, Production Director; Len Thornton, Student and Short
Film Consultant; Paul Collard, Managing Director; Gordon Clampitt,
Commercials Director; Chris Bannister, Broadcast Sales; Nigel Horn, Features
Manager; Dave Kelly, Broadcast Manager
Credits The Magdalene Sisters (F); Bloody Sunday (F)

*Soho Images offers a complete camera to screen package for
Commercials, Features and Broadcast. We specialise in a range of film
and digital video post production services. Our Laboratory offers full
processing of 16mm and 35mm film, 24 hour rushes, PAL and NTSC
telecine transfers, 8/16/35mm gates, wet-gate option, sound-synching,
cinema bulk release prints, archive restoration and computerised
negative cutting. In conjunction with our sister companies we also
provide: film and video transfer and mastering (Standard Def or Hi-Def
formats), linear and non-linear editing (625/525/1080i), standards and
aspect ratio conversions, 2D and 3D graphics, titles and subtitling,
digital sound studios, dubbing facilities and complete DVD production.*

TV Set

22 Newman Street, London W1T 1PH
t 020 7637 3322 **f** 020 7637 1011
e info@thetelevisionset.co.uk **w** www.thetelevisionset.co.uk
Contact Terry Bettles, Managing Director; Alf Penn; David Yeo

VTR Ltd

64 Dean Street, London W1D 4QQ
t 020 7437 0026
Contact Mike Capon, Head of TV Production; Rod Shelton, Head of Digital
Cinema; Anthony Frend, Managing Director; Ellie Bourne, Contact; Lucy Clay,
Marketing Director

Windmill Lane Pictures

4 Windmill Lane, Dublin, Rep of Ireland
t +353 1 671 3444 **f** +353 1 671 8413
e tim.waller@windmilllane.com **w** www.windmilllane.com
Contact Tim Waller

Post Production Facilities
Video Editing

1410 Degrees Ltd

7 D'Arblay Street, London W1V 3FD
t 020 7287 1410 **f** 020 7287 1496 **m** 07976 289496
e davidchidgey@1410degrees.co.uk **w** www.1410degrees.co.uk

The 400 Company

Unit B3, The Workshops, 2A Askew Crescent, Shepherds Bush,
London W12 9DP
t 020 8746 1400 **e** info@the400.co.uk **w** www.the400.co.uk
Contact Mark Sloper, Director, Director; Paul Giordani, Business Development
Manager; Jo Haynes, Production Manager; Barry Woods, Facilities Manager

Avid Technology Europe

European Headquarters, Western Complex, Pinewood Studios,
Pinewood Road, Iver Heath SL0 ONH
t 01753 655999 **f** 01753 654999 **w** www.avid.com
Contact Sean Bradley, Sales and Marketing Director

AVIDly Creative Editing

m 07970 204214 **e** rdtv@btinternet.com
Contact Roger Dacier, Editor
Credits Tarrant On TV (T); Bloodline Of Dracula (D); Terror, Sex, And Other New
York Stories (D); Gooseberries Don't Dance (S)

BBC Post Production

BBC Post Production
(Sites across London, Bristol & Birmingham)
5550 Television Centre, Wood Lane, London W12 7RJ
t 020 8225 7702 (London) **t** 0117 9746 666 (Bristol)
t 0121 432 8621 (Birmingham)
w www.bbcresources.com/postproduction

bookingsbookings.com
e book@bookingsbookings.com **w** www.bookingsbookings.com
Contact A Bailey, Client Coordinator

Broadcast Television Facilities
Acuba House, Lymm Road, Little Bollington, Altrincham WA14 4SY
t 0161 9269808 **f** 0161 9299000 **m** 07974 151617
e info@broadcast-tv.co.uk **w** www.broadcast-tv.co.uk
Contact Robert Foster, Managing Director; Erin Mactague, Bookings Co-ordinator
Credits Brookside (T); Inside The Mind Of Roy Keane (T); Tonight With Trevor MacDonald (T); Cuba: The Other Side Of Armageddon (T)

Caseys Film & Video Ltd
316-318 Latimer Road, London W10 6QN
t 020 8960 0123 **f** 020 8969 3714
e tony@caseys.co.uk **w** www.caseys.co.uk
Contact Tony Weeks, General Manager; Sue McHugh, Bookings

Cine Wessex Ltd
Westway House, 19 St Thomas Street, Winchester SO23 9HJ
t 01962 865454 **f** 01962 842017
e info@cinewessex.co.uk **w** www.cinewessex.co.uk
Contact Ema Branton; Jenny Cave-Penney

Coach House Studios
Frithville Gardens, London W12 7JN
t 020 8740 8000 **f** 020 8743 8088 **m** 07850 755818
e coachhousestudio@hotmail.com
Contact John Walbeoffe, Managing Director
Credits Dr Zhivago (T); Murder In Mind (T); Jonathan Creek (T); Holby City (T)

Courtyard Productions
Little Postlings Farmhouse, Four Elms TN8 6NA
t 01732 700324 **e** yardley@littlepostlings.demon.co.uk
Contact Toni Yardley, Company Director/Producer; David Yardley, Editor
Credits The Borrowers (T); Kedleston Hall (D); If Wishes Were Horses (T); Two Men Went To War (F)

Creation Two
Unit 1, The Sandycombe Centre, Sandycombe Road, Richmond TW9 2EP
t 020 8332 0888 **f** 020 8332 1123
e production@creationcompany.tv **w** www.creationcompany.tv
Contact Steve Montgomery, Managing Director; Scott Drummond, Director; Louise Glen, Production Manager
Credits Surprise Wedding (T); The John Thaw Story (T); Cleo Around The World (T); Being Victoria Beckham (T)

Creative Staging
The Creative Studio, Church Path, Chiswick, London W4 5BJ
t 020 8994 3636 **f** 020 8994 3748
e hive@creativestaging.co.uk **w** www.creativestaging.co.uk
Contact Tony Campbell, Video Facilities Manager
Credits The Design Council; British Tourist Authority (I)

CTV Facilities
87 St John's Wood Terrace, London NW8 6PY
t 020 7483 6000 **f** 020 7483 4264 **w** www.ctv.co.uk
Contact Shelley Wallis, Post Production Manager; Janet Marbrook, Chief Executive

Dales Broadcast Ltd
Nettle Hill, Brinklow Road, Ansty, Coventry CV7 9JL
t 024 7662 1763 **f** 024 7660 2732 **m** 07803 584925
e sales@dales-ltd.com **w** www.dales-ltd.com
Contact Kate Boden, Marketing Director; Julian Boden, Managing Director
Credits Tickle, Patch And Friends (T); Young Choirs 2001 (T); Network Q Rally (T); Horseracing for Racetech, ATR And Channel 4 (T)

Dart Film & Video Services
196 Whitchurch Road, Cardiff CF14 3NB
t 029 2069 3100 **f** 029 2069 2555 **e** dart@ukgateway.net
Contact Bruce Rawlings, Senior Producer
Credits Unilever (I); Welsh Development Agency (C); United Nations (E)

Dateline Productions Ltd
84 Bennerley Road, London SW11 6DU
t 020 7978 7891

DGP
Portland House, 12-13 Greek Street, Soho, London W1D 4DL
t 020 7734 4501 **f** 020 7734 7034
e mail@dgpsoho.co.uk **w** www.dgpsoho.co.uk
Contact Mark Gardner, Managing Director; Rowan Bray, General Manager; Julian Day, Managing Director; Moira Brophy, Bookings Manager; Peter Hill, Sales
Credits World Chart Express (T); Gorillaz (W); Austin Powers In Goldmember (F); Murder In Mind (T)

DT Editing Services Ltd
Bridgeham Studios, Bridgeham Lodge, Broadbridge Lane, Smallfield RH6 9PS
t 01342 844448 **f** 01342 841582 **m** 07774 499883
e daren@dtediting.com
Contact Daren Tiley, Director, Director/Editor
Credits Creamfields Promo (C); Holiday With Craig Doyle (T); Fortune Finders (T); You Call the Shots (T)
Freelance off/online editor with 14 years broadcast experience working on non-linear AVID and linear editing suites. Offering editing with a difference in country surroundings near Gatwick Airport with great links to London. The studio has its own living area and is perfect for any broadcast work outputting to DigiBeta or DVCam. Phone Daren for excellent rates. Dry or wet hire.

Edit Heaven
Shacklewell Studios, 18 Shacklewell Lane, London E8 2EZ
t 020 7249 0438 **f** 020 7249 0494 **m** 07974 679199
e info@editheaven.com **w** www.editheaven.co.uk
Contact Bryan Comley, Facilities Manager; Michael Dixon, Facilities Manager

Edit Video Ltd
2A Conway Street, London W1T 6BA
t 020 7637 2288 **f** 020 7637 2299
e mail@editvideo.co.uk **w** www.editvideo.co.uk
Contact Jilly Byford, Director
Credits River Cottage III (T); The Who and Friends Live at the Albert Hall (W); Spared II (T)

Editorium
1 Chatsworth House, 7 Riverdale Road, Twickenham, London TW1 2BT
t 020 8892 4154 **e** allen@editorium.co.uk
Contact Nilgun Charlton, Manager

Editworks
77-79 Charlotte Street, London W1T 4PW
t 020 7079 2900 **f** 020 7079 2901 **e** alice@editworks.co.uk
Contact Alice Sagar-Musgrave, Facilities Manager
Credits Baddiel & Skinner Unplanned (T); So Graham Norton (T); Who Wants To Be A Millionaire? (T); Friends Like These (T)

Film Work Group
Top Floor , Chelsea Reach, 79-89 Lots Road, London SW10 0RN
t 020 7352 0538 **f** 020 7351 6479
Contact Nigel Perkins

Final Cut Ltd

Fenton House, 55-57 Great Marlborough Street,
London W1F 7JX
t 020 7556 6300 **f** 020 7287 2824
e finalcut@finalcut-edit.com **w** www.finalcut-edit.com
Contact Greg Caplan, Company Director; Zoe Henderson, Producer
Credits Mint Royale: Blue Song (M); BBC Radio 1: Kid (C); Ben: Symphonies (C);
Fray Bentos: He-Man (C)

Fine Cut Multimedia Ltd

The Exchange, Whitley Road, Benton, Newcastle upon Tyne
NE7 7XB
t 0191 270 1665 **f** 0191 266 4441
e mail@finecutmultimedia.com **w** www.finecutmultimedia.com
Contact Peter Groom, Sound Engineer

Frontierpost

66-67 Wells Street, London W1T 3PY
t 020 7291 9191 **f** 020 7291 9199
e info@frontierpost.co.uk **w** www.frontierpost.co.uk
Contact Beth Jeffreyes, Facility Manager; Fiona Cormack, Bookings
Co-ordinator
Credits So You Want To Adopt (E); The Christmas Truce (D); Wish You Were
Here? (T); Ground Force (T)

Frontline TV

35 Bedfordbury, Covent Garden, London WC2N 4DU
t 020 7836 0411 **f** 020 7379 5210
e info@frontline-tv.co.uk **w** www.frontline-tv.co.uk
Contact Gail Gilmartin, Facilities Manager; Charlie Sayle, Facilities Director;
Tracy Thomas, Director of Sales & Marketing
Credits Gareth Gates & Will Young (M); Shed Heads (T); Jennifer Lopez - This Is
me (C); Great Escapes (D)

GM Editing Ltd

Cumberland House, 80 Scrubs Lane, London NW10 6RF
t 020 8960 4482 **f** 020 8960 4089 **w** www.gmediting.com
Contact Mark Hands-Heart, Director; Gareth Maynard, Managing Director;
Linda O'Donoghue, Facilities Manager

Goldcrest Post Production Facilities

36-44 Brewer Street, London W1F 9LX
t 020 7437 7972 **f** 020 7437 5402 **m** 07836 204283
e mailbox@goldcrest-post.co.uk
Contact Poppy Quinn, Bookings and Customer Services Manager; Raju
Raymond, General Manager

Gray Audio Visual Video Facilities

34-36 Bickerton Road, London N19 5JS
t 020 7263 9561 **f** 020 7272 0146
e rob@gray-av.co.uk **w** www.gray-av.co.uk
Contact Rob Briancourt, Facilities Manager; Steve McHugh, Cameraman/Editor;
John Ayling, Director

Hammond AVS

64A Queens Road, Watford WD1 2LA
t 01923 239733 **f** 01923 221134 **m** 07836 235717
e info@hammonds-avs.co.uk **w** www.hammonds-avs.co.uk
Contact Mike Simpson, Business Development Manager

Inhouse Post Production Ltd

Shepperton Studios Building, 14 Studios Road, Shepperton
TW17 0QD
t 01932 592455 **f** 01932 592195
e contact@ihpp.co.uk **w** www.ihpp.co.uk
Contact Phil Hedgecock, Editor; Stewart Alves, Graphics; Kerry Osmond,
Bookings; Martyn Stretton, Managing Director

Input Video Group

The Production Centre, 191a Askew Road, London W12 9AX
t 020 8740 5222 **f** 020 8746 0811
e scheduling@input-video.co.uk **w** www.input-video.co.uk
Contact Christopher Payne, Facilities Manager; Diana De Magalhaes, Senior
Facilities Co-ordinator; Mark Hands-Heart, Group Client Director

Miles Johnson

TOVS Ltd, The Linen Hall, 162-168 Regent Street, London W1B 5TB
t 020 7287 6110 **f** 020 7287 5481
e info@tovs.co.uk **w** www.tovs.co.uk

Locomotion Digital Facilities

18 Greek Street, London W1D 4DT
t 020 7304 4403 **f** 020 7304 4400
e info@locomotion.co.uk **w** www.locomotion.co.uk
Contact Kevin Fawcett, Systems Co-ordinator; Andrew Newman, Marketing Director
Credits Hubba Bubba (C); Clean & Clear (C)

The London Studios Ltd

Upper Ground, London SE1 9LT
t 020 7261 3181 **f** 020 7737 8840
e post@londonstudios.co.uk **w** www.londonstudios.co.uk
Contact Julie Sangan, Head of Post Production Sales
*Avid Offlines/Avid Symphony all on Avid Unity. Avid Express. 7 digital
Widescreen Linear suites. 6 Audio suites with Logic desks, audiofile &
voice over booths. 2 & 3D graphic areas. 2 Quantel Clipbox servers with
access to studios and Linear edit suites.*

M2 Television

Ingestre Court, Ingestre Place, London W1F 0JL
t 020 7343 6543 **f** 020 7343 6555
e info@m2tv.com **w** www.m2tv.com
The Forum, 74-80 Camden Street, London, NW1 0EG
t 020 7343 6789 **t** 020 7343 6777
Contact Kabir Malik; Jennie Jones
*Based in Soho and Camden, we offer a full range of video and audio
post production as well as the award-winning co:de design. 5 digital
online suites, 5 Editbox FX online suites, 2 Symphony online suites, Avid
unity server, Clipbox video server, 14 Avid offline, 5 digital audio suites,
Hal, and Illusion.*

Marjon Facilities

Derriford Road, Plymouth PL6 8BH
t 01752 761115 **f** 01752 761132 **e** jbow@marjon.ac.uk
Contact Jenny Bow, Media Facilities Co-ordinator

Martin Sharpe Film & Television

18 Lanark Close, Ealing, London W5 1SN
t 020 8997 3714 **f** 020 8997 3714
e martin_roy_sharpe@compuserve.com
Contact Martin Sharpe, Editor
Credits A&E (T); The Vice (T)

Martyn Gould Productions

6 D'Arblay Street, London W1V 3FD
t 020 7437 3898 **f** 020 7287 2150 **e** mgp@darblaystreet.co.uk
Contact Martyn Gould, Managing Director

MGB Facilities Ltd

Sheepscar Court, Leeds LS7 2BB
t 0113 243 6868 **f** 0113 243 8886
e contact@mgbtv.co.uk **w** www.mgbtv.co.uk

Contact Mike Gaunt, Managing Director; Elaine Wigglesworth, Facility Manager
Credits Quick Grip (I); Sport On Five (T); Hasbro (W); BUPA (C)

Molinare

34 Fouberts Place, London W1F 7PX
t 020 7478 7000 **f** 020 7478 7199
e bookings@molinare.co.uk **w** www.molinare.co.uk

Contact Kate George, Facilities Manager
Credits Dorada Especial: Painting; AXN: Cornice;
Walkers Dorito's: Idents; The Wind

For 30 years Molinare has been offering the best in Post Production, helping the best people make the best programmes, we have about the widest selection of facilities in one location in the industry. Based in the heart of Soho, we offer, 5 digital Online Suites, Editbox FX V8, Ursa Gold Telecine, High Definition Online, 10 Avid Offline suites and 2 Avid Online suites, 5 Audio Dubbing suites with voice over booths, Tracklay, Discreet Flint, Media Illusion, Drive in 1500 sq ft Video studio, 400 sq ft Virtual Studio, Duplication, Transmission Services, as well as the Molinare Design team for all your branding and design needs.

Multicord

15 Glenavon, Chester Le Street DH2 2JL
t 0191 388 8979 **m** 07768 058900
e multicord@multicord.co.uk **w** www.multicord.co.uk

Contact Sara McKenzie, Director; Keith Marley

Nats Post Production

10 Soho Square, London W1D 3NT
t 020 7287 9900 **f** 020 7287 8636
e bookings@nats.ltd.uk

Contact Sara Hill, Bookings; Jo Manser; Louise Knight; Louise Thomas

One of Soho's leading facilities, Nats Post Production is fully equipped in all aspects of television post production, from offline to online, design and graphics, grade and audio dub. With over 40 suites, we strive to make sure your whole experience is as pleasant and productive as possible by offering you creative excellence, intelligent solutions and home comforts.

NLP

199 Upper Street, London N1 1RQ
t 020 7704 8333 **f** 020 7704 8444 **i** 020 7704 3607
e info@communicator.ltd.uk **w** www.communicator.ltd.uk

Contact Paul Drew, Managing Director

Oasis Television Ltd

6-7 Great Pulteney Street, London W1R 3DF
t 020 7434 4133 **f** 020 7494 2843 **e** sales@oasis.co.uk

Contact Pat Gale, Business Development Manager; Helen Leicester, Facilities Manager; Liz Hayward, Business Development Manager; Georgina Grant, Head of Bookings; Ray Nunney, Managing Director; Jennie Jones
Credits Reggae - The Story Of Jamaican Music (D); The Fall Of Milosevic (D); Messiah II (T); Red Cap (T)

Oculus Ltd

Millennium Studios, Elstree Way, Borehamwood WD6 1SF
t 020 8236 1336 **f** 020 8236 1144 **m** 07831 218391
e hire@oculus.ltd.uk **w** www.oculus.ltd.uk

Contact Helen Gatward, Post Production Manager
Credits Divorcing Jack (F); Importance of Being Ernest (F); Kiss Kiss Bang Bang (F)

The Old Kings Head Studios

m 07850 755818 **e** john@coachhousestudios.co.uk

Contact John Walbeoffe, Facility Manager

Omnivision

Pinewood Studios, Pinewood Road, Iver Heath SL0 0NH
t 01753 656329 **f** 01753 631146
e info@omnivision.co.uk **w** www.omnivision.co.uk

Contact Steve Rowsell, Facilities Director; Steve Rowsell, Director
Credits Die Another Day (T); Care Today, Hope Tomorrow (I); The Strawbs Live At Chiswick House (M); Only Food And Forces (T)

Peach Facilities Ltd

3 Slingsby Place, Long Acre, London WC2E 9AB
t 020 7632 4240 **f** 020 7632 4250
e info@peachfacilities.co.uk **w** www.peachfacilities.co.uk

Contact Russell Parrett; Tim Whitehead; Karen Davies

Pepper

3 Slingsby Place, Long Acre, Covent Garden, London WC2E 9AB
t 020 7836 1188 **f** 020 7497 9305
e mailus@pepperpost.tv **w** www.pepperpost.tv

Contact Stephanie Goodwin; Helen Phelps; Jill Jones; Lisa Sweet
Credits Down To Earth (T); Spooks (T); Dr Zhivago (T); The Lost Prince (T)

The Picture House Edit Suites Ltd

156 Holywood Road, Belfast BT4 1NY
t 028 9065 6769 **f** 028 9067 3771
e info@thepicturehouse.tv **w** www.thepicturehouse.tv

Poppy Films Ltd

24 Wells Street, London W1P 3PH
t 020 7637 0203 **f** 020 7580 9565
e pete@poppyfilms.com

Contact Farzana Ahmad, Managing Director

Post Production at Teddington Studios

Broom Road, Teddington TW11 9NT
t 020 8781 2735 **f** 020 8614 2078
e postprod@teddington.tv **w** www.teddington.co.uk

Red Post Production

Hammersley House, 5-8 Warwick Street, London W1B 5LX
t 020 7439 1449 **f** 020 7439 1339
e production@red.co.uk **w** www.red.co.uk

Contact James Lamb, Producer; Fiona Byrne, Bookings; Stephen Luther, Managing Director; Matt White, Senior Producer; Tara Geraughty, New Business/Account Management; Tanya Johnson, Head Of Production; Annika Ahl, Bookings; Aimee Posner, Bookings
Credits Blur - Crazy Beat (M); Tennants - Bollywood (C); S Club Movie - Double Vision (F)

The Reel Editing Company Ltd

65 Goldhawk Road, London W12 8EH
t 020 8743 5100 **f** 020 8743 2345 **e** penny@indepost.co.uk

Contact Penny Cassar, Facility Manager
Credits Royal Deaths & Diseases (T); Doctor Crippin (D); Coupling (T); Shooting Stars (T)

Salon Ltd

12 Swainson Road, London W3 7XB
t 020 8746 7611 **f** 020 8746 7613
e hire@salonrentals.com **w** www.salonrentals.com

Contact Justin Moyle, Manager

Second City Video

855 Bristol Road, Selly Oak, Birmingham B29 6ND
t 0121 472 6641 **f** 0121 471 1465
e terry@secondcity-studios.co.uk

Contact Terry Stanton, Proprietor

The Shed (A Farm Post Production Company)
2nd Floor, 22 Dean Street, London W1D 3RX
t 020 7479 7450 **f** 020 7479 7451
e susanne.wright@farmpost.co.uk
Contact Nicky Sargent, Director; Susanne Wright, Facility Manager

Silverwood Studios
London SW16
t 020 8764 6212 **e** info@silverw.co.uk **w** www.silverw.co.uk
Contact Tim Clarke, Director
Credits Understanding The Bible (E)

Studio Alba
54A Seaforth Road, Stornoway HS1 2SD
t 01851 701125 **f** 01851 701094 **m** 07740 785193
e info@studioalba.com **w** www.studioalba.com
Contact Willie Macleod, Facilities Manager

Tangram Post Production
1 Charlotte Street, London W1T 1RB
t 020 7437 8710 **f** 020 7439 0491
w www.tangrampostproduction.co.uk
Contact Lawrence Williamson, Partner; Simon Rose, Partner

Todd-AO Creative Services
13 Hawley Crescent, London NW1 8NP
t 020 7284 7900 **f** 020 7284 1018
e schedules@ascent-media.co.uk **w** www.ascent-media.co.uk
Contact Matt Bowman, Head of Production; Sam Webb, Head of Post
Production; Dick Knapman, Technical Manager; Sam Lucas, In House Producer

Triangle Television
81 Whitfield Street, London W1T 4HG
t 020 7255 5215 **f** 020 7255 5216 **e** bookings@facilities.co.uk
Contact Christian Downes, Post Production Manager
Credits If I Could - Wagon Wheels (C); Paul McCartney - Lover to a Friend (M);
So Solid Crew - 21 Seconds (M)

TSI Post Production
TSI Video, 10 Grape Street, London WC2H 8DY
t 020 7379 3435 **f** 020 7379 4589 **e** bookings@tsi.co.uk
Contact Simon Peach, Managing Director; Andy Wright, Producer; Simon
Kanjee, Managing Director; Nathalie Roull; Shula Fitzgerald, Head of Sales; Alan
Cronin, Facility Manager; Julia Gonsalves, Head of Bookings
Credits Robbie Williams In Concert (T); This Morning (T); Sir Robert Winston -
The Human Instinct (T); They Think It's All Over (T)

VET
The Lux Building, 2-4 Hoxton Square, London N1 6US
t 020 7505 4700 **f** 020 7505 4800
e facilities@vet.co.uk **w** www.vet.co.uk
Contact Scott Shand, Facilities Manager; Hinchee Hung, Facilities Director

The Whitehouse Post Productions Ltd
12-13 Kingly Street, London W1B 5PP
t 020 7287 3404 **f** 020 7287 9670
e lucie.georgeson@whitehousepost.co.uk
w www.whitehousepost.com
Contact Juliet Sturridge, managing Director; Jane Dilworth, Executive Producer
Credits McDonalds Being Six (C); Rebok Sofa (C)

Derek Wilson
TOVS Ltd, The Linen Hall, 162-168 Regent Street, London W1B 5TB
t 020 7287 6110 **f** 020 7287 5481
e info@tovs.co.uk **w** www.tovs.co.uk

XS Hire
Bramshill, Guildford Road, Ottershaw KT16 0QN
t 01932 454040 **f** 01932 454045
e enquiries@xshire.com **w** www.xshire.com
Contact Michelle Race, Facilities Manager
Credits The Last Detective (T); Daddy's Girl (T); William And Mary (T); Silent
Witness (T)

Post Production Facilities
Video Editing Non Linear

Ace Studio
27 Pilgrims Lane, Bugbrooke NN7 3PJ
t 01604 831800 **m** 07816 913980
e malcolm@acestudio.co.uk **w** www.acestudio.co.uk
Contact Malcolm Rivett-Carnac, Senior Editor

Andrew Shefford Video Productions
3 Springfield Road, Stoneygate, Leicester LE2 3BB
t 0116 270 3675 **m** 07740 853 109 **e** a_gaius@yahoo.com

Arion Facilities
Global House, Denham Media Park, North Orbital Road,
Denham UB9 5HL
t 01895 834484 **f** 01895 833085
e sales@arion.co.uk **w** www.arion.co.uk
*Arion Facilities offer a comprehensive range of post-production and
duplication services to film, television and corporate clients. These
include telecine, linear/non-linear editing, standards conversion and
video/CD duplication.*

Basement
60 Charles Street, Manchester M1 7DF
t 0161 273 8200 **f** 0161 273 6390 **w** www.the-basement.tv
Contact Wayne Pretl, New Media Manager; Jim Mooney, General Manager; Liza
Ryan-Carter, Senior Editor

Basement Multimedia Ltd
60 Charles Street, Manchester M1 7DF
t 0161 273 8200 **f** 0161 273 6390
e jim@the-basement.tv **w** www.the-basement.tv
Contact Liza Ryan-Carter, Senior Editor; Jim Mooney, General Manager

BBC Post Production

BBC Post Production
(Sites across London, Bristol & Birmingham)
5550 Television Centre, Wood Lane, London W12 7RJ
t 020 8225 7702 (London) **t** 0117 9746 666 (Bristol)
t 0121 432 8621 (Birmingham)
w www.bbcresources.com/postproduction

Broadcast Television Facilities
Acuba House, Lymm Road, Little Bollington, Altrincham WA14 4SY
t 0161 9269808 **f** 0161 9299000 **m** 07974 151617
e info@broadcast-tv.co.uk **w** www.broadcast-tv.co.uk
Contact Robert Foster, Managing Director; Erin Mactague, Bookings Co-ordinator
Credits Brookside (T); Inside The Mind Of Roy Keane (T); Tonight With Trevor
MacDonald (T); Cuba: The Other Side Of Armageddon (T)

Richard Calder
TOVS Ltd, The Linen Hall, 162-168 Regent Street, London W1B 5TB
t 020 7287 6110 **f** 020 7287 5481
e info@tovs.co.uk **w** www.tovs.co.uk

Classlane Ltd
Classlane Studios, Victoria Road, Beverley HU17 8PJ
t 01482 873390 **f** 01482 873389
e post@classlane.co.uk **w** www.classlane.co.uk
Contact D Beasley, Managing Director

Paul Clifton
TOVS Ltd, The Linen Hall, 162-168 Regent Street, London
W1B 5TB
t 020 7287 6110 **f** 020 7287 5481
e info@tovs.co.uk **w** www.tovs.co.uk

Ross Copeland
TOVS Ltd, The Linen Hall, 162-163 Regent Street, London
W1B 5TB
t 020 7287 6110 **f** 020 7287 5481
e info@tovs.co.uk **w** www.tovs.co.uk

Curious Yellow Ltd
33-37 Hatherley Mews, London E17 4QP
t 020 8521 9595 **f** 020 8521 4343
m 07718 155783 **i** 020 8521 5132
e paul@curiousyellow.co.uk **w** www.curiousyellow.co.uk
Contact Paul Penny, Production Manager; Tim Smith, Senior Editor; Flavio
Curras, Audio Port Engineer; Danny Bowes, Production Manager; Rikki Taraslas,
Producer; Paul Louis Henderson, Executive Producer
Credits Dance For Boys - National Theatre (E); Courier (S); Channel Fly -
Outside Broadcast (M); Chicane - Behind The Sun Tour (M)

Dales Broadcast Ltd
Nettle Hill, Brinklow Road, Ansty, Coventry CV7 9JL
t 024 7662 1763 **f** 024 7660 2732 **m** 07803 584925
e sales@dales-ltd.com **w** www.dales-ltd.com
Contact Kate Boden, Marketing Director; Julian Boden, Managing Director
Credits Tickle, Patch And Friends (T); Young Choirs 2001 (T); Network Q Rally
(T); Horseracing for Racetech, ATR And Channel 4 (T)

Darker Than Blue Media Services
PO Box 28314, London SE20 7WT
t 07092 366864 **f** 07092 366864 **m** 07788 441494
e info@dtbprod.com **w** www.dtbprod.com
Contact Dennis Morrison, Director
Credits Headworx Surf UK (T); Breakdance Special (M); Red (S)

Diva Pictures Limited
Ealing Studios, Ealing Green, Ealing, London W5 5EP
t 020 8758 8432 **f** 020 8758 8663 **m** 07956 251119
e steve@divapix.co.uk **w** www.divapix.co.uk
Contact Steve Teers, Managing Director; Cici Tang, Office Manager
Credits Monstrous Bosses (D); Jeremy Hardy Vs The Israeli Army (D); Fergus In
Ecuador (D); Bus Stop Art (D)

The Edit Centre
95 High Street, Kingswood, Bristol BS15 4AD
t 0117 967 6863 **f** 0117 967 6864 **m** 07733 451939
e editcentre@spectel.demon.co.uk
Contact Jill Laurence, Partner
Credits Stryker Howmedica (I); Harley Communications Agency (I); Lloyds TSB (I)

The Editworks
Austin House, 95-97 Ber Street, Norwich NR1 3EY
t 01603 624402 **f** 01603 624402 **e** info@theeditworks.co.uk

Andey Ford
TOVS Ltd, The Linen Hall, 162-168 Regent Street, London W1B 5TB
t 020 7287 6110 **f** 020 7287 5481
e info@tovs.co.uk **w** www.tovs.co.uk

Sue Giovanni
TOVS Ltd, The Linen Hall, 162-168 Regent Street, London W1B 5TB
t 020 7287 6110 **f** 020 7287 5481
e info@tovs.co.uk **w** www.tovs.co.uk

Kiera Gordon-Garrett
TOVS Ltd, The Linen Hall, 162-168 Regent Street, London W1B 5TB
t 020 7287 6110 **f** 020 7287 5481
e info@tovs.co.uk **w** www.tovs.co.uk

Nik Hayward
TOVS Ltd, The Linen Hall, 162-168 Regent Street, London W1B 5TB
t 020 7287 6110 **f** 020 7287 5481
e info@tovs.co.uk **w** www.tovs.co.uk

Headfirst Facilities Ltd
48 Lexington Street, London W1F 0LR
t 020 7287 2010 **f** 020 7287 2009
e info@headfirstpost.co.uk **w** www.headfirstpost.co.uk
Contact Andy Snowley, Facilities Manager

Mark Heasman
TOVS Ltd, The Linen Hall, 162-168 Regent Street, London W1B 5TB
t 020 7287 6110 **f** 020 7287 5481
e info@tovs.co.uk **w** www.tovs.co.uk

David Hill
TOVS Ltd, The Linen Hall, 162-168 Regent Street, London W1B 5TB
t 020 7287 6110 **f** 020 7287 5481
e info@tovs.co.uk **w** www.tovs.co.uk

Hillside
Merry Hill Road, Bushey WD23 1DR
t 020 8950 7919 **f** 020 8421 8085
e enquiries@hillside-studios.co.uk **w** www.hillside-studios.co.uk
Contact David Hillier, Head of Facilities
*Avid Symphony, Media Composer XL and Digibeta Suite. Dubbing to
picture with Soundtracs DS3 and Audiofile. Extensive effects/music
library.*

Hyper *active*

Hyperactive
5 The Royston Centre, Lynchford Lane, Ash Vale GU12 5PQ
t 01252 519191 **f** 01252 513939
e hire@hyperactivebroadcast.com
w www.hyperactivebroadcast.com
Contact Lawrie Read, Deputy Managing Director; David Reeves, Managing Director

Avids, Lightworks, and Steenbeck for dry hire. Avid On-line, Film Composers, Media Composers, G4 or NT and Unity MediaNet systems at highly competitive rates. Digital and Analogue VTR's and all film accessories available.

Imagine
4th Floor, 65 Westgate Road, Newcastle-upon-Tyne NE1 1SG
t 0191 230 0488 **f** 0191 230 0485 **m** 07802 422109
e garry@imagine-nonlinear.co.uk **w** www.imagine-nonlinear.co.uk
Contact Susan Cosgrove, Technical Director; Garry Cosgrove, Sales Director
Credits Danny And His Amazing Teeth (S); Secrets Of The Art Factory (T); Jools Holland's Piano (T)

Intrepid
19 Hartington Road, Millhouses, Sheffield S7 2LE
t 0114 236 3920 **f** 0114 236 3920 **m** 07759 120649
e info@intrepid.tv **w** www.intrepid.tv
Contact Mark Turnbull, Proprietor

Avid editing with award-winning editors, or dry hire

Kai Lawrence
TOVS Ltd, The Linen Hall, 162-168 Regent Street, London W1B 5TB
t 020 7287 6110 **f** 020 7287 5481
e info@tovs.co.uk **w** www.tovs.co.uk

Leitch
Holland Park House, Oldbury, Bracknell RG12 8TQ
t 01344 446000 **f** 01344 446100
e sales.europe@leitch.com **w** www.leitch.com
Contact Nigel Booth, Director Of Business Development; Dave Dougall, Director Of Sales & Marketing; Sara Tebb, Maroons Specialists

The Little Green Planet Editing Company
Burrows Lea Farm, Hook Lane, Shere GU5 9QQ
t 01483 209500 **f** 01483 209500 **m** 07941 821420
e littlegreenplanet@hotmail.com **w** littlegreenplanet.co.uk
Contact Byron Vaisey, Managing Director
Credits Pineapple Performing Arts School (I); The Politics Show (T)

Giles Llewellyn-Thomas
TOVS Ltd, The Linen Hall, 162-168 Regent Street, London W1B 5TB
t 020 7287 6110 **f** 020 7287 5481
e info@tovs.co.uk **w** www.tovs.co.uk

M2 Television
Ingestre Court, Ingestre Place, London W1F 0JL
t 020 7343 6543 **f** 020 7343 6555
e info@m2tv.com **w** www.m2tv.com
The Forum, 74-80 Camden Street, London, NW1 0EG
t 020 7343 6789 **t** 020 7343 6777
Contact Kabir Malik; Jennie Jones

Based in Soho and Camden, we offer a full range of video and audio post production as well as the award-winning co:de design. 5 digital online suites, 5 Editbox FX online suites, 2 Symphony online suites, Avid unity server, Clipbox video server, 14 Avid offline, 5 digital audio suites, Hal, and Illusion.

Matt Boney Associates
Woodside, Holdfast Lane, Haslemere GU27 2EU
t 01428 656178 **m** 07850 508082 **e** matt.boney@btclick.com
Contact Matt Boney, Proprietor
Credits Goodwood Revival Meeting (D); Goodwood Festival Of Speed (D)

Metropolis
30 Bloomsbury Street, London WC1B 3QJ
t 020 7927 9000 **f** 020 7255 2529
e mail@metropolispost.co.uk **w** www.metropolispost.co.uk
Contact Guy Morley, Director; Samantha Timms, Bookings Manager; Julian Sabath, Director

MGB Facilities Ltd
Sheepscar Court, Leeds LS7 2BB
t 0113 243 6868 **f** 0113 243 8886
e contact@mgbtv.co.uk **w** www.mgbtv.co.uk
Contact Mike Gaunt, Managing Director; Elaine Wigglesworth, Facility Manager
Credits Quick Grip (I); Sport On Five (T); Hasbro (W); BUPA (C)

molinare
a television corporation company

Molinare
34 Fouberts Place, London W1F 7PX
t 020 7478 7000 **f** 020 7478 7199
e bookings@molinare.co.uk **w** www.molinare.co.uk
Contact Kate George, Facilities Manager
Credits Dorada Especial: Painting; AXN: Cornice; Walkers Dorito's: Idents; The Wind

For 30 years Molinare has been offering the best in Post Production, helping the best people make the best programmes, we have about the widest selection of facilities in one location in the industry. Based in the heart of Soho, we offer, 5 digital Online Suites, Editbox FX V8, Ursa Gold Telecine, High Definition Online, 10 Avid Offline suites and 2 Avid Online suites, 5 Audio Dubbing suites with voice over booths, Tracklay, Discreet Flint, Media Illusion, Drive in 1500 sq ft Video studio, 400 sq ft Virtual Studio, Duplication, Transmission Services, as well as the Molinare Design team for all your branding and design needs.

Outpost Facilities Ltd
Pinewood Studios, Iver Heath SL0 0NH
t 01753 630770 **f** 01753 630771
e helen@out-post.co.uk **w** ww.outpostfacilities.co.uk
Contact Helen Pyrah, Facilities Manager; Nigel Gourley, Director; David Broscombe, Director; David Chisholm, Senior Editor
Credits BMW/Landrover (C); My Family (T); Meet My Folks (T); Teletubbies Everywhere (T)

OVC Media Ltd
88 Berkeley Court, Baker Street, London NW1 5ND
t 020 7402 9111 **f** 020 7723 3064
e eliot@ovcmedia.com **w** www.ovcmedia.com
Contact Eliot Cohen; Joanne Goldring-Cohen, Managing Director

Pace Productions
7 Barnsway, Kings Langley WD4 9PW
t 01923 269590
e info@paceproductions.com **w** www.paceproductions.com
Contact Chris Pettit, Director

PG Video Editing Ltd
Unit 52, Singer Way, Woburn Road Industrial Estate, Kempston, Bedford MK42 7AF
t 01234 844002 **f** 01234 844000 **m** 07970 029685
e paul@pgvideo.co.uk **w** www.pgvideo.co.uk

Portland Productions
1 Portland Road, Southall UB2 4BX
t 020 8574 5111 **f** 020 8843 9942 **m** 07710 549662
e riyaz@portlandproductions.co.uk
Contact Gillian Pyarali, Manager; Riyaz Pyarali, Proprietor

Positive Film & Television Ltd
73-75 Mortimer Street, London W1W 7SQ
t 020 7323 6956 **f** 020 7323 6957 **e** info@positive.co.uk
Contact Tim Jones, Post Production; Zelida Gordan, Camera Facilities

Tony Raffe
TOVS Ltd, The Linen Hall, 162-168 Regent Street, London W1B 5TB
t 020 7287 6110 **f** 020 7287 5481
e info@tovs.co.uk **w** www.tovs.co.uk

Glenn Rainton
TOVS Ltd, The Linen Hall, 162-168 Regent Street, London W1B 5TB
t 020 7287 6110 **f** 020 7287 5481
e info@tovs.co.uk **w** www.tovs.co.uk

Random Post Production
Artist's Court, Manette Street, London W1D 4AP
t 020 7434 3444 **f** 020 7434 3451
e edit@randompost.com **w** www.randompost.com
Contact Dan Weinberg; Sallyann Gray
Credits Computer Hackers (F); Harry At 18 (T); Young Musician of the Year (T)

Red Post Production
Hammersley House, 5-8 Warwick Street, London W1B 5LX
t 020 7439 1449 **f** 020 7439 1339
e production@red.co.uk **w** www.red.co.uk
Contact James Lamb, Producer; Fiona Byrne, Bookings; Stephen Luther, Managing Director; Matt White, Senior Producer; Tara Geraughty, New Business/Account Management; Tanya Johnson, Head Of Production; Annika Ahl, Bookings; Aimee Posner, Bookings
Credits Blur - Crazy Beat (M); Tennants - Bollywood (C); S Club Movie - Double Vision (F)

Red Square Editing
4th Floor, Circus House, 21 Great Titchfield Street, London W1W 8BA
t 020 7580 1880 **f** 020 7580 1890
e emily@redsquare.tv **w** www.redsquare.tv
Contact Tim Fulford, Director; Emily Sharp, Producer; Alex Hagou, Director; Rick Waller, Director; Tim Fulford, Director

Rod Howick Editing
3 Carlisle Street, London W1D 3BH
t 020 7437 0764 **f** 020 7437 3250

Chris Stott
TOVS Ltd, The Linen Hall, 162-168 Regent Street, London W1B 5TB
t 020 7287 6110 **f** 020 7287 5481
e info@tovs.co.uk **w** www.tovs.co.uk

Tangram Post Production
1 Charlotte Street, London W1T 1RB
t 020 7637 2727 **m** 07813 583735
w www.tangrampostproduction.co.uk
Contact Laurence Williamson, Partner; Simon Rose, Partner
Credits Trouble At The Top (D); The Decision (D); Fifteen (D)

Terry Jones Postproductions Ltd
Goldcrest International, 65-66 Dean Street, London W1D 4PL
t 020 7434 1173 **f** 020 7494 1893 **m** 07939 583512
e terryjonespost@btconnect.com **w** www.terryjonespostproductions.com
Contact Terry Jones, Managing Director
Credits Mattel - Living A Ballet Dream (D); Jungle Heat - Schweppes (C); Tenor - Smirnoff (C); New York City Ballet (D)

Susan Thomas
TOVS Ltd, The Linen Hall, 162-168 Regent Street, London W1B 5TB
t 020 7287 6110 **f** 020 7287 5481
e info@tovs.co.uk **w** www.tovs.co.uk

TVE Ltd
TVE House, Milton Business Centre, Wick Drive, New Milton BH25 6RH
t 01425 625020 **f** 01425 625021
e enquiries@tvehire.com **w** www.tvehire.com
Contact Sarah Ville, Business Development Manager

Two Plus One Ltd
1-2 Lower St James Street, London W1F 9EG
t 020 7287 2221 **f** 020 7437 4161
e sales@twoplusone.co.uk
w www.twoplusone.co.uk
Contact Martin Rogers, Sales and Business Development; Lyndsey McPherson, Office Manager; Joy Hancock, Managing Director; Natasha Linski, Sales & Business Development

Avid DS/HD editing suite, Avid Symphony Universal, Avid Media and Film Composers, Broadcast Dubbing, Dolby Digital Encoding and Decoding, DVD Authoring and Encoding incorporating: Sonic DVD Creator and Scenarist Systems, 2D Graphics. Based in relaxed and spacious surroundings with natural light.

Larry Walford
TOVS Ltd, The Linen Hall, 162-168 Regent Street, London W1B 5TB
t 020 7287 6110 **f** 020 7287 5481
e info@tovs.co.uk **w** www.tovs.co.uk

Jonathan Ward
TOVS Ltd, The Linen Hall, 162-168 Regent Street, London W1B 5TB
t 020 7287 6110 **f** 020 7287 5481
e info@tovs.co.uk **w** www.tovs.co.uk

Matt Wenner
90 Howard Road, Westbury Park, Bristol BS6 7UY
t 0117 942 7112 **f** 0117 942 7112 **m** 07623 783782
Credits Schooldays (E); Oldest Mummies In The World (D); Gerry Barnacle & Co - Sessions Musicians (M); Montlhery Vincent Records 50th Anniversay 2002 (D)

Post Production Facilities
Video Editing Offline

Adictive Editing Facilities
Studios Road, Shepperton TW17 0QD
t 01932 572124 **f** 01932 572134
e adictive.editing@sheppertonpostproduction.com
Contact Paul Stapley, Managing Director; Robin Harris, Production Supervisor
Credits Brit Awards (T); Elton John At The Royal opera House 2003 (T); Inspector Morse (T); Kevin And Perry Go Large (F)

BBC Post Production

BBC Post Production
(Sites across London, Bristol & Birmingham)
5550 Television Centre, Wood Lane, London W12 7RJ
t 020 8225 7702 (London) **t** 0117 9746 666 (Bristol)
t 0121 432 8621 (Birmingham)
w www.bbcresources.com/postproduction

Broadcast Television Facilities
Acuba House, Lymm Road, Little Bollington, Altrincham WA14 4SY
t 0161 9269808 **f** 0161 9299000 **m** 07974 151617
e info@broadcast-tv.co.uk **w** www.broadcast-tv.co.uk
Contact Robert Foster, Managing Director; Erin Mactague, Bookings Co-ordinator
Credits Brookside (T); Inside The Mind Of Roy Keane (T); Tonight With Trevor MacDonald (T); Cuba: The Other Side Of Armageddon (T)

Cornwall Media Resource
Royal Circus Buildings, Back Lane West, Redruth TR15 2BT
t 01209 218288 **e** info@mediaresource.freeserve.co.uk
Contact Antall Kovacs

The Edit Boutique Ltd
119E Cleveland Street, London W1P 5PN
t 020 7636 2625 **f** 020 7636 2424
e info@editboutique.co.uk **w** www.editboutique.co.uk
Contact Robert Nixon, Manager; Keith Gaisford, Managing Director

The Editpool
1 Wedgewood Mews, 12-13 Greek Street, London W1V 5LW
t 020 7734 4204 **f** 020 7851 6638 **m** 07778 635888
e grpool@theeditpool.com
Contact Geoff Pool, Managing Director

Elite Television
248 Meanwood Road, Leeds LS7 2HZ
t 0113 262 3342 **f** 0113 262 3798
e info@elitetv.co.uk **w** www.elitetv.co.uk
Contact Stuart Josephs, Managing Director

Evolutions Television Ltd
5 Berners Street, London W1T 3LF
t 020 7580 3333 **f** 020 7637 1942
e info@evolutionstelevision.com
w www.evolutionstelevision.com

Evolutions runs 15 Avid NT Offlines integrated into our technical infrastructure providing remote access to all VTR formats and our Avid Unity shared media network. Our team of experienced and creative editors, combined with comprehensive 24-hour technical support, provides an essential part of the service we offer. We also provide a full video duplication and new media service.

The Film Editors
6-10 Lexington Street, London W1F OLB
t 020 7439 8655 **f** 020 7437 0409
e postroom@thefilmeditors.com **w** www.thefilmeditors.com
Contact Pamela Power, Managing Director

Hamilton Ironside
12 Crown Terrace, Glasgow G12 9ES
t 0141 339 2279 **f** 0141 339 2279 **e** bawldnuss@btopenworld.com
Contact Phyllis Ironside, Managing Director; James Hamilton, Managing Director

Hyper*active*

Hyperactive
5 The Royston Centre, Lynchford Lane, Ash Vale GU12 5PQ
t 01252 519191 **f** 01252 513939
e hire@hyperactivebroadcast.com
w www.hyperactivebroadcast.com
Contact Lawrie Read, Deputy Managing Director; David Reeves, Managing Director

Avids, Lightworks, and Steenbeck for dry hire. Avid On-line, Film Composers, Media Composers, G4 or NT and Unity MediaNet systems at highly competitive rates. Digital and Analogue VTR's and all film accessories available.

Ian Weil Editing Services
39 Beak Street, London W1F 9SA
t 020 7287 2090 **f** 020 7287 4331 **e** ianweil@btinternet.com

Jim Bambrick Associates
2nd Floor, 118 Wardour Street, London W1F OTU
t 020 7434 2351 **f** 020 7734 6362 **e** bambricke@yahoo.com
Contact Victoria Allen, Post Production Manager; Aine Casey

The London Studios Ltd
Upper Ground, London SE1 9LT
t 020 7261 3181 **f** 020 7737 8840
e post@londonstudios.co.uk
w www.londonstudios.co.uk
Contact Julie Sangan, Head of Post Production Sales

Avid Offlines/Avid Symphony all on Avid Unity. Avid Express. 7 digital Widescreen Linear suites. 6 Audio suites with Logic desks, audiofile & voice over booths. 2 & 3D graphic areas. 2 Quantel Clipbox servers with access to studios and Linear edit suites.

Lynch Post Production
10 Dryburgh Gardens, Kelvinside, Glasgow G20 6BT
t 0141 945 1386 **f** 0141 334 0422
Contact Therese Lynch

M2 Television
Ingestre Court, Ingestre Place, London W1F OJL
t 020 7343 6543 **f** 020 7343 6555
e info@m2tv.com **w** www.m2tv.com
The Forum, 74-80 Camden Street, London, NW1 OEG
t 020 7343 6789 **t** 020 7343 6777
Contact Kabir Malik; Jennie Jones

Based in Soho and Camden, we offer a full range of video and audio post production as well as the award-winning co:de design. 5 digital online suites, 5 Editbox FX online suites, 2 Symphony online suites, Avid unity server, Clipbox video server, 14 Avid offline, 5 digital audio suites, Hal, and Illusion.

Monochrome Editing Ltd
Unit 61a, Pall Mall Deposit, 124-128, Barlby Road, London W10 6BL
t 020 8964 2111 **f** 020 8964 2358
e john@monochrome.fsbusiness.co.uk
Contact John McAvoy, Offline Editor/ MD; Ben Grove, Assistant Editor

Naisbitt & Co
117 Wardour Street, London W1F OUN
t 020 7287 6536 **f** 020 7287 5830 **e** postbox@naisbitt.co.uk
Contact Paul Naisbitt, Director

Nats Post Production
10 Soho Square, London W1D 3NT
t 020 7287 9900 **f** 020 7287 8636 **e** bookings@nats.ltd.uk
Contact Sara Hill, Bookings; Jo Manser; Louise Knight; Louise Thomas

One of Soho's leading facilities, Nats Post Production is fully equipped in all aspects of television post production, from offline to online, design and graphics, grade and audio dub. With over 40 suites, we strive to make sure your whole experience is as pleasant and productive as possible by offering you creative excellence, intelligent solutions and home comforts.

Nik Hindson Film Editing
8 Silver Place, London W1F OJU
t 020 7437 1052 **f** 020 7434 2400
Contact Sam Rice-Edwards, Contact; Nik Hindson, Contact

Rainbow Post Production
16 Ingestre Place, London W1F OJJ
t 020 7434 4566 **f** 020 7439 4565 **w** www.rainbowpost.com
Contact Nick Rogers, Dubbing Mixer; Louise , Bookings; Lyndsay , Bookings

Random Post Production
Artist's Court, Manette Street, London W1D 4AP
t 020 7434 3444 **f** 020 7434 3451
e edit@randompost.com **w** www.randompost.com
Contact Dan Weinberg; Sallyann Gray
Credits Computer Hackers (F); Harry At 18 (T); Young Musician of the Year (T)

Sanctuary Post
53 Frith Street, London W1D 4SN
t 020 7734 4480
e post@sanctuarystudios.co.uk **w** www.sanctuarystudios.co.uk
Contact Jason Elliott, Sales & Marketing Manager

Flame, DS editing, compositing and grading, on-line and off-line Avid editing, Audio, graphics, CD-Rom and DVD design / authoring and duplication services.

Steven Bell Editing Ltd

3 Meard Street, Soho, London W1F OEL
t 020 7734 7845 **f** 020 7734 7847
e steve@stevenbellediting.co.uk **w** www.stevenbellediting.co.uk
Contact Steven Bell, Editor

Victoria Real Ltd

International House, Queens Road, Brighton BN1 3XE
t 01273 702007 **f** 01273 706007
e enquiries@victoriareal.com **w** www.victoriareal.com
Contact Jamie Shaw, Head of IT & Facilities; Simon Hollobon, Facilities
Technician

Weil & Co

Beak Street, London WIF 95A
t 020 7287 2090 **f** 020 7287 4331 **e** ianweil@aesynet.co.uk
Contact Ian Weil

Post Production Facilities
Video Editing Online

Ace Editing

2-5 Rutland Studios, Cumberland Park, Scrubs Lane, London
NW10 6RE
t 020 8968 1090 **f** 020 8968 8844
e dominic@aceediting.co.uk **w** www.aceediting.co.uk
Contact Dominic Ruddy, Operations Manager

Arion Facilities

Global House, Denham Media Park, North Orbital Road,
Denham UB9 5HL
t 01895 834484 **f** 01895 833085
e sales@arion.co.uk **w** www.arion.co.uk

*Arion Facilities offer a comprehensive range of post-production and
duplication services to film, television and corporate clients. These
include telecine, linear/non-linear editing, standards conversion and
video/CD duplication.*

BBC Post Production

BBC Post Production
(Sites across London, Bristol & Birmingham)

5550 Television Centre, Wood Lane, London W12 7RJ
t 020 8225 7702 (London) **t** 0117 974 6666 (Bristol)
t 0121 432 8621 (Birmingham)
w www.bbcresources.com/postproduction

Blue Turtle Pictures

Percy House, 33 Gresse Street, London W1T 1QU
t 020 7637 2432 **f** 020 7323 1930
e blue@blueturtle.co.uk **w** www.blueturtle.co.uk
Contact Andi Osho, Director; Louise Hussey, Director; Graham Carr, Managing
Editor; Charlotte Briggs, Scheduling Manager

Broadcast Television Facilities

Acuba House, Lymm Road, Little Bollington,
Altrincham WA14 4SY
t 0161 9269808 **f** 0161 9299000 **m** 07974 151617
e info@broadcast-tv.co.uk **w** www.broadcast-tv.co.uk
Contact Robert Foster, Managing Director; Erin Mactague, Bookings Co-ordinator
Credits Brookside (T); Inside The Mind Of Roy Keane (T); Tonight With Trevor
MacDonald (T); Cuba: The Other Side Of Armageddon (T)

Broadley Editing

48 Broadley Terrace, London NW1 6LG
t 020 7258 0324 **f** 020 7724 2361
e admin@broadleystudios.com **w** www.broadleystudios.com
Contact Manny Elias, General Manager; Mark French; Alex McMillan

Capital Studios

Wandsworth Plain, London SW18 1ET
t 020 8877 1234 **f** 020 8877 0234
e info@capitalstudios.com **w** www.capitalstudios.com
Contact Bobbi Johnstone, Contact; Clare Phillips, Contact

*Fully equipped digital broadcast studios: 3000 sq ft (60x50x19.5)
and 2000 sq ft (50x50x19.5). Supported by galleries, dressing rooms,
wardrobe, green room and audience facilities. Tx lines, Cafe with
courtyard garden. New digital Post-Production facilities.*

Centreline Video

138 Westwood Road, Tilehurst, Reading RG31 6LL
t 0118 941 0033
e mike@video.demon.co.uk **w** www.centrelinevideo.com

Clark Facilities Ltd

37 Hugh St, London SW1V 1QJ
t 020 78288678 **f** 020 7233 9997 **e** mail@clarktv.com
Contact Selina Kay, Production Manager

Clear Ltd

Fenton House, 55-57 Great Marlborough Street,
London W1F 7JX
t 020 7734 5557 **f** 020 7734 4533
e clear@clear.ltd.uk **w** www.clear.ltd.uk
Contact Lucy Clay, Marketing Director
Credits Talking Heads (T); Virgin Records (C);
Robbie Williams – Rob By Nature (M)

Denham Productions

Quay West Studios, Old Newnham, Plymouth PL7 5BH
t 01752 345444 **f** 01752 345448
e peter-e@denhams.demon.co.uk
Contact Peter Edwards, Managing Director

Eclipse Presentations Ltd

Presentation House, 3 Croydon Road, Beckenham TN9 1QT
t 020 8650 5950 **f** 020 8650 4635
e info@eclipse-presentations.co.uk
w www.eclipse-presentations.co.uk
Contact Hugh Stewart-Thomas, General Manager

Edit 123 (Television Facilities) Ltd

123 Blythswood Street, Glasgow G2 4EN
t 0141 248 3123 **f** 0141 248 3423
e bookings@edit123.co.uk **w** www.edit123.co.uk
Contact Gill McFarlane, Facilities Manager
Credits Relocation Relocation (T); Thumb Bandits (T); Location, Location,
Location (T)

The Edit Store

8-9 Bayley Street, London WC1B 3HB
t 020 7637 7472 **f** 020 7436 4457 **e** store@editstore.org
Contact Ellenor Bradburn, Facilities Manager; Chantele Bigmore,
Facilities Manager

Eidos Interactive

Wimbledon Bridge House, 1 Hartfield Road,
London SW19 3RU
t 020 8636 3000 **f** 020 8636 3001
w www.eidosinteractive.com

Evolutions Television Ltd

5 Berners Street, London W1T 3LF
t 020 7580 3333 **f** 020 7637 1942
e info@evolutionstelevision.com **w** www.evolutionstelevision.com

Evolutions offer both linear and non-linear online editing facilities. We are one of London's largest Symphony facilities running five suites and also have two identical Sony Digital Online Suites. With our highly experienced, creative editing team we provide a high level of quality and service. We also offer a full duplication and new media service.

Eye Edit

62 Whiteley Road, London SE19 1JT
t 020 8761 1183 **f** 020 8761 1183 **m** 07836 799 030
e adriancharles@btinternet.com
Contact Adrian Charles

Golden Square Post Production

11 Golden Square, London W1F 9JB
t 020 7300 3555 **f** 020 7494 3288
e info@golden-square.co.uk **w** www.golden-square.co.uk
Contact Beth Vander, Producer; Ewan Macleod, Executive Producer; Lee Pavey, Producer; Sally Cooper, Producer

Hillside

Merry Hill Road, Bushey WD23 1DR
t 020 8950 7919 **f** 020 8421 8085
e enquiries@hillside-studios.co.uk **w** www.hillside-studios.co.uk
Contact David Hillier, Head of Facilities
Avid Symphony & Digibeta suite with in-house editors.

Image Creative

9 Newburgh Street, London W1V 1LH
t 020 7437 8217 **f** 020 7287 6950 **e** imageCR8@aol.com
Contact Tim Sparks, Manager

Key Video Communications

6 Prince Henry's Close, Evesham WR11 4NW
t 01386 765634 **f** 01386 765636 **m** 07976 365 841
e matthew@keyvideo.co.uk **w** www.keyvideo.co.uk
Contact Matthew Langmead, Proprietor

M2 Television

Ingestre Court, Ingestre Place, London W1F 0JL
t 020 7343 6543 **f** 020 7343 6555
e info@m2tv.com **w** www.m2tv.com
The Forum, 74-80 Camden Street, London, NW1 0EG
t 020 7343 6789 **t** 020 7343 6777
Contact Kabir Malik; Jennie Jones

Based in Soho and Camden, we offer a full range of video and audio post production as well as the award-winning co:de design. 5 digital online suites, 5 Editbox FX online suites, 2 Symphony online suites, Avid unity server, Clipbox video server, 14 Avid offline, 5 digital audio suites, Hal, and Illusion.

Mirage Television

53 Newington Road, Edinburgh EH9 1QW
t 0131 668 2010 **f** 0131 668 2243
e miragetv@compuserve.com **w** www.miragetv.com
Contact Yvonne Goodfellow, Producer

a television corporation company

Molinare

34 Fouberts Place, London W1F 7PX
t 020 7478 7000 **f** 020 7478 7199
e bookings@molinare.co.uk **w** www.molinare.co.uk
Contact Kate George, Facilities Manager
Credits Dorada Especial: Painting; AXN: Cornice; Walkers Dorito's: Idents; The Wind

For 30 years Molinare has been offering the best in Post Production, helping the best people make the best programmes, we have about the widest selection of facilities in one location in the industry. Based in the heart of Soho, we offer, 5 digital Online Suites, Editbox FX V8, Ursa Gold Telecine, High Definition Online, 10 Avid Offline suites and 2 Avid Online suites, 5 Audio Dubbing suites with voice over booths, Tracklay, Discreet Flint, Media Illusion, Drive in 1500 sq ft Video studio, 400 sq ft Virtual Studio, Duplication, Transmission Services, as well as the Molinare Design team for all your branding and design needs.

Nats Post Production

10 Soho Square, London W1D 3NT
t 020 7287 9900 **f** 020 7287 8636 **e** bookings@nats.ltd.uk
Contact Sara Hill, Bookings; Jo Manser; Louise Knight; Louise Thomas

One of Soho's leading facilities, Nats Post Production is fully equipped in all aspects of television post production, from offline to online, design and graphics, grade and audio dub. With over 40 suites, we strive to make sure your whole experience is as pleasant and productive as possible by offering you creative excellence, intelligent solutions and home comforts.

Paul Miller Post-Production

PO Box 201, Haslemere GU27 1XD
f 01428 648744 **m** 07778 853817 **e** pmpp@btinternet.com
Contact Nico Piazza, Bookings Manager; Paul Miller, Facilities Manager
Credits The Blue Beyond (D); Smirnoff World Tour (C); Cat Stevens Majicat Concert 1970 (M)

Peak White Facilities

1 Latimer Road, Teddington TW11 8QA
t 0870 740 5625 **f** 020 8977 8357 **w** www.peakwhite.tv
Contact Richard Bonfield, Manager; Andrea Anderson, Marketing Director

Peak White offer a range of post production services for broadcast and corporate clients. Linear and nonlinear online suites with in-house Editors. Digital Betacam tape suite with DVD, capgen, voiceover booth etc. Avid offline and online with DV Cam & Digital Betacam sources. Standards conversion, tape duplication & DVD authoring.

Pink Pigeon Post Production

74 Berwick Street, London W1F 8TQ
t 020 7439 3266 **f** 020 7439 3277
e info@pinkpigeon.net **w** www.pinkpigeon.net
Contact Simon Boyd, Director; William Timbers, Director
Credits Chrome Dreams (W); Mark Summers Management (W); The British Council (W)

Post Republic

Aradco House, 132 Cleveland Street, London W1T 6AB
t 020 7692 4110
e sally@postrepublic.tv **w** www.postrepublic.tv
Contact Sally Needham, Facilities Manager

Rainbow Post Production

16 Ingestre Place, London W1F 0JJ
t 020 7434 4566 **f** 020 7439 4565 **w** www.rainbowpost.com
Contact Nick Rogers, Dubbing Mixer; Louise , Bookings; Lyndsay , Bookings

Random Post Production

Artist's Court, Manette Street, London W1D 4AP
t 020 7434 3444 **f** 020 7434 3451
e edit@randompost.com **w** www.randompost.com

Contact Dan Weinberg; Sallyann Gray
Credits Computer Hackers (F); Harry At 18 (T); Young Musician of the Year (T)

Red Post Production

Hammersley House, 5-8 Warwick Street, London W1B 5LX
t 020 7439 1449 **f** 020 7439 1339
e production@red.co.uk **w** www.red.co.uk

Contact James Lamb, Producer; Fiona Byrne, Bookings; Stephen Luther, Managing Director; Matt White, Senior Producer; Tara Geraughty, New Business/Account Management; Tanya Johnson, Head Of Production; Annika Ahl, Bookings; Aimee Posner, Bookings
Credits Blur - Crazy Beat (M); Tennants - Bollywood (C); S Club Movie - Double Vision (F)

Remote Films

126 Bolingbroke Grove, London SW11 1DA
t 020 7738 2727 **m** 07901 716109
e berkeley@remote-films.com **w** www.remote-films.com

Contact Berkeley Cole, Director
Credits Tetleys (C); BT (C); Shock Movie Massacre (T); Outthere (T)

Richmond Studios Ltd

83-84 George Street, Richmond TW9 1HE
t 020 8332 1690 **f** 020 8332 1691 **m** 07836 731918
e charlotte@richmondstudios.com **w** www.richmondstudios.com

Contact Charlotte Danaher, General Manager; Toby Alington, Director, Managing Director; Robert Grieves, Designer; Miles Tudor, DVD/IT Technician; Jonathan Potts, Video Editor; Andrea Hein, Project Manager
Credits DUP DVD (W); Ramones DVD (W); Cirque De Soleil - Alegria DVD (W); Brit Awards (T)

Sanctuary Post

53 Frith Street, London W1D 4SN
t 020 7734 4480
e post@sanctuarystudios.co.uk **w** www.sanctuarystudios.co.uk

Contact Jason Elliott, Sales & Marketing Manager

Flame, DS editing, compositing and grading, on-line and off-line Avid editing, Audio, graphics, CD-Rom and DVD design / authoring and duplication services.

Studio M University of Westminster

Harrow Campus, Watford Road, Harrow HA1 3TP
t 020 8357 7303 **e** s.feldman@wmin.ac.uk

Contact Stephen Whaley; Sally Feldman

Two Plus One Ltd

1-2 Lower St James Street, London W1F 9EG
t 020 7287 2221 **f** 020 7437 4161
e sales@twoplusone.co.uk
w www.twoplusone.co.uk
Contact Martin Rogers, Sales & Business Development; Lyndsey McPherson, Office Manager; Joy Hancock, Managing Director; Natasha Linski, Sales & Business Development

Avid DS/HD editing suite, Avid Symphony Universal, Avid Media and Film Composers, Broadcast Dubbing, Dolby Digital Encoding and Decoding, DVD Authoring and Encoding incorporating: Sonic DVD Creator and Scenarist Systems, 2D Graphics. Based in relaxed and spacious surroundings with natural light.

Vivid Post Production

68 Wells Street, London W1T 3QA
t 020 7290 0700 **f** 020 7436 1819
e bookings@vividpost.com **w** www.vividpost.com

Contact Lucy Reid, Bookings Co-ordinator; Helen Connolly, Facilities Manager; Lesley Lund, Bookings Manager
Credits Girls Behaving Badly (D); Century Of The Self (D); The Pact (D); Averting Armageddon (D)

Xpression Post Production

Warwick House, Chapone Place, Dean Street, London W1D 3BF
t 020 7437 8182 **f** 020 7437 8183
e richard@xpression.tv **w** www.xpression.co.uk

Contact Steve Shears, Managing Director; Richard Meadowcroft, Managing Director

---

Post Production Facilities
Video Transfer & Duplication

Ascent Media Ltd

Film House, 14 Wardour Street, London W1F 8DD
t 020 7878 0000 **f** 020 7878 7800
e sally.hart-ives@ascent-media.co.uk

Contact Sally Hart-Ives, Group Head of Sales

Aztec Facilities Ltd

7 Charlotte Mews, London W1T 4ED
t 020 7580 1591 **f** 020 7580 1270
e info@azfac.com **w** www.aztecuk.net

Contact Sam Fraser, General Manager; Paul Johnson, Senior Librarian

BBC Post Production

BBC Post Production
(Sites across London, Bristol & Birmingham)

5550 Television Centre, Wood Lane, London W12 7RJ
t 020 8225 7702 (London) **t** 0117 974 6666 (Bristol)
t 0121 432 8621 (Birmingham)
w www.bbcresources.com/postproduction

Bob Ginger Partnership

19-21 High Street, Acton W3 6NG
t 020 8993 6772 **f** 020 8993 9982
e info@bobginger.co.uk **e** info@gingersnaps.co.uk
w www.bobginger.co.uk; www.gingersnaps.co.uk

Canon Video (UK) Ltd

15 Main Drive, East Lane Business Park, East Lane, Wembley HA9 7FF
t 020 8385 4455 **f** 020 8908 6785 **m** 07976 282819
e nathan@canonvideo.co.uk **w** www.canonvideo.co.uk

Contact Saylash Shah, Director; Mike Seaman, Sales Director

Cine Wessex Ltd

Westway House, 19 St Thomas Street, Winchester SO23 9HJ
t 01962 865454 **f** 01962 842017
e info@cinewessex.co.uk **w** www.cinewessex.co.uk

Contact Ema Branton; Jenny Cave-Penney

Cinram UK Ltd

6th Floor, 3 Shortlands, London W6 8RX
t 020 8735 9498 **f** 020 8735 9499
e uksales@cinram.com **w** www.cinram.com

Contact Chris Parry, Corporate Sales Executive; Jonathan Beddows, Commercial Director; Simon Staines, UK Key Accounts Manager

Classic Video Services

20 Tallon Road, Hutton Industrial Estate, Brentwood CM13 1TJ
t 0800 018 6564 **f** 01277 262625
e info@cvsinternational.co.uk **w** www.cvsinternational.co.uk

Copycats Video Ltd

The Metropolitan Centre, 26 Derby Road, Greenford UB6 8UJ
t 020 8813 2222 **f** 020 8813 2322
e sales@copycats.tv **w** www.copycats.tv

Contact Grahame Taylor, Technical Director; Beverley Harding, Sales Manager

Broadcast mastering including all DV, Beta SX/IMX Pal/NTSC with Alchemist conversions and ARC. VHS PAL/NTSC/SECAM duplication. CD/DVD replication. MPEG 1+2, AVI, Quicktime, RealVideo, Video CD, Floppy Disks.

Ascent Media - Music and Agency
(Formerly known as Tele–Cine)
Video House, 48 Charlotte Street, London, W1T 2NS
Claire Booth Managing Director
tel +44 (0) 20 7208 2200 fax +44 (0) 207208 2251
claire.booth@ascentmedia.co.uk

Aspect ratio conversions, Broadcast duplication
Broadcast standards conversion, Caption generation
Futuretel system– MPEG-1 & MPEG-2 encoder/decoder
CD burning, Omneon server
Quality assessment of broadcast masters
VHS duplication (PAL,NTSC & Secam), Video legalisers

 Stream Digital Media 61 Charlotte Street, London, W1T 4PF
Gareth Bourne Business Development
tel +44 (0) 20 7208 1567 fax+44 (0) 20 7208 1555
gareth.bourne@streamdm.co.uk
info@streamdm.co.uk www.streamdm.co.uk

Audio encoding for DVD, BEAM.TV encoding, upload and download
CD duplication and printing, DVD authoring – Encoding and
Duplication, DVD menu artwork design and creation, DVD-R and DLT
generation, Express DVD production, File transfer and conversion
Graphic design, Interactive CD-ROM production, Internet video
encoding, Quality assurance and testing, Storyboard creation,

Visiontext 48 Charlotte Street, London, W1T 2NS
Maggie Nuttall – Managing Director
tel +44 (0) 20 7016 2200 fax+44 (0) 20 7016 2222
maggie.nuttall@visiontext.co.uk www.visiontext.co.uk

Video-on-Demand
Teletext captioning (Europe)
Open captioning
Multilingual translations in 40 languages

CVB Duplication
179a Bilton Road, Perivale UB6 7HQ
t 020 8991 2610 **f** 020 8997 0180
e sales@cvbduplication.co.uk **w** www.cvbduplication.co.uk
Contact Phil Stringer, Managing Director; Adrian Tubman, Sales Manager
Credits Jaguar (C); The Post Office (C); Inland Revenue (C)

CVS International
1 Berkeley Street, London W1X 6BU
t 020 7224 3342 **f** 0845 100 2634
e info@cvsinternational.co.uk **w** www.cvs-international.co.uk

Deluxe Laboratories Ltd
North Orbital Road, Denham, Uxbridge UB9 5HQ
t 01895 832323 **f** 01895 832446 **w** www.bydeluxe.com
Contact David Dowler, Sales Director

Deluxe Video Services Ltd
Phoenix Park, Great West Road, Brentford TW8 9PL
t 0845 600 8900 **f** 020 8232 7601
e uksales@bydeluxe.com **w** www.bydeluxe.com
Contact William Coelho, Business Development Manager; Zoe Buckingham,
Head of Business Development

Dubbs
25-26 Poland Street, London W1F 8QN
t 020 7629 0055 **f** 020 7287 8796
e sales@dubbs.co.uk **w** www.dubbs.co.uk
Contact David Wilson, Sales Manager; Seb Tyack, Digital Media Producer;
Martin Rogers, Sales Manager; Lauren McCready, Business Development; Bill
Gamble, Customer Services Director

*Specialist duplication, replication and conversion facility, delivering
flexible, quality service and technical expertise that is geared to
respond to individual needs. Open 24 hours, 7 days a week.*

Duplication Express
Unit 9, City Business Park, Easton Road, Bristol BS5 0SP
t 0117 955 5599 **f** 0117 954 0567
e sales@dupexpress.co.uk **w** www.dupexpress.co.uk
Contact Adam Trewella, Sales/Account Manager; Grahame Conlon,
General Manager
Credits Aardman Animations (A); Allied Domecq (I)

evolutions

Evolutions Television Ltd
5 Berners Street, London W1T 3LF
t 020 7580 3333 **f** 020 7637 1942
e info@evolutionstelevision.com **w** www.evolutionstelevision.com

*Evolutions purpose-built duplication department provides a 24-hour
service and offers an impressive list of resources and services. Ranging
from multi format dubbing and cloning, aspect ratio conversion,
standards conversion, legalising, full technical assessments plus
worldwide delivery and distribution. We also offer a full range of post
production and new media services.*

Film & Photo Ltd
13 Colville Road, South Acton Industrial Estate, London W3 8BL
t 020 8992 0037 **f** 020 8993 2409
e info@film-photo.co.uk **w** www.film-photo.co.uk
Contact Tony Scott, Managing Director
Credits Ned Kelly (F); Johnny English (F); Die Another Day (F); Harry Potter (F)

Flix Facilities
5 Albany Road, Chorlton-cum-Hardy, Manchester M21 0AW
t 0161 882 2525 **f** 0161 882 2534
e mail@flixfacilities.com **w** www.flixfacilities.com
Contact Leo Casserly, Facilities Manager; Kath Jones, Office Manager; Leo
Casserly, Facilities Manager; Leo Casserly, Facilities Manager; Mark Wharton,
Senior Editor; Helen Kenny, Office Manager
Credits Welcome To Manchester (D); Engie Benjy (A); Close Up North (D); Bill
And Ben (A)

Frontline TV
35 Bedfordbury, Covent Garden, London WC2N 4DU
t 020 7836 0411 **f** 020 7379 5210
e info@frontline-tv.co.uk **w** www.frontline-tv.co.uk
Contact Gail Gilmartin, Facilities Manager; Charlie Sayle, Facilities Director;
Tracy Thomas, Director of Sales & Marketing
Credits Gareth Gates & Will Young (M); Shed Heads (T); Jennifer Lopez - This Is
Me (C); Great Escapes (D)

Future Video Services Ltd
Unit D, 2 Endeavour Way, Durnsford Road Industrial Estate,
London SW19 8UH
t 020 8938 7000 **f** 020 8947 8992
e sales@fvideo.com **w** www.fvideo.com
Contact James Brooker, Sales Executive

GAV Video Facilities

34-36 Bickerton Road, London N19 5JS
t 020 7263 9561 **f** 020 7272 0146
e rob@gray-av.co.uk **w** www.gray-av.co.uk
Contact Robert Briancourt, Technical Manager

Griffin Video Communications Ltd

53 Regent Place, Hockley, Birmingham B1 3NJ
t 0121 212 0044 **f** 0121 212 2114 **e** info@askgriffin.co.uk
Contact James Griffin, Managing Director; Pam Griffin, Studio/Facilities Manager

Hot Wachs Productions Ltd

26 Puller Road, Hemel Hempstead HP1 1QN
t 01442 385777 **m** 07973 360297 **e** hotwachs@aol.com
Contact David Wachs, Director
Credits The Life of Art (T); Picture Windows (T); Teletubbies (T)

Humphries Video Services Ltd

Unit 2, The Willow Business Centre, 17 Willow Lane, Mitcham CR4 4NX
t 020 8648 6111 **t** 020 7636 3636 **f** 020 8648 5261
e sales@hvs.bdx.co.uk **w** www.hvs.co.uk
Contact David Brown, Sales & Marketing Director; Jago Michell, Business Development; Emma Lincoln, Production Co-ordinator; Mike Hudson, Production Director

Video cassette duplication and standard conversion centre. From most formats to any cassette format in any world standard. Broadcast and corporate. CD and DVD authoring/replication.

International Broadcast Facilities

15 Monmouth Street, London WC2H 9DA
t 020 7497 1515 **f** 020 7379 8562
e ibf.admin@ibf.co.uk **w** www.ibf.co.uk
Contact James Puttock, Chief Executive of New Business Development; Dave Carstairs, Technical Director

Intervideo

87 Boundary Road, St Johns Wood, London NW8 ORG
t 020 7624 1711 **f** 020 7624 2683
e admin@intervideo.co.uk **w** www.intervideo.co.uk
Contact Gerry Wade, Technical Director; Clare Russell, Admin Manager; Trevor Nash, Managing Director

ITN Video Facilities

200 Gray's Inn Road, London WC1X 8XZ
t 020 7430 4303 **f** 020 7430 4381 **m** 07711 193 899
e pete.mills@itn.co.uk **w** www.itn.co.uk
Contact Peter Mills, Team Leader

j.c.a tv facilities

JCA TV Facilities

Monarch House, Victoria Road, London W3 6UR
t 020 8357 5400 **f** 020 8357 5450
e bookings@jcatv.co.uk **w** www.jcatv.co.uk
Contact Perry Foran, Sales Manager; Debbie Healy, General Manager

Jordan UK Ltd

67 Callcott Road, London NW6 7EE
t 020 7624 8080 **f** 020 7328 3273
e anne@jordanuk.co.uk **w** www.jordanuk.co.uk
Contact Anne Hardy, Project Manager; John Thwaites, Managing Director

The London Studios Ltd

Upper Ground, London SE1 9LT
t 020 7261 3181 **f** 020 7737 8840
e post@londonstudios.co.uk
w www.londonstudios.co.uk
Contact Julie Sangan, Head of Post Production Sales

*Avid Offlines/Avid Symphony all on Avid Unity.
Avid Express. 7 digital Widescreen Linear suites.
6 Audio suites with Logic desks, audiofile
& voice over booths. 2 & 3D graphic areas.
2 Quantel Clipbox servers with access to
studios and Linear edit suites.*

Macrovision UK

Charlwood House, The Runway, South Ruslip HA4 6SE
t 020 8839 0400 **f** 020 8839 0409
e info@macrovision.co.uk **w** www.macrovision.com
Contact Michael Welch, Sales & Marketing Manager

Masterpiece

Unit 14, The Talina Centre, Bagley's Lane, London SW6 2BW
t 020 7371 0700 **f** 020 7384 1750

Metro Broadcast

5-7 Great Chapel Street, London W1F 8FF
t 020 7434 7700 **f** 020 7434 7701
e info@metrobroadcast.com **w** www.metrobroadcast.com
Contact Elaine Jaxon, Duplications Manager; Paul Beale, Business Development; Mark Cox, Director

We offer a complete duplication service including multi-format VT, standards conversion, aspect ratio conversion, technical assessments and high definition. We also specialise in video and audio restoration and de-spot correction.

MGB Facilities Ltd

Sheepscar Court, Leeds LS7 2BB
t 0113 243 6868 **f** 0113 243 8886
e contact@mgbtv.co.uk **w** www.mgbtv.co.uk
Contact Mike Gaunt, Managing Director; Elaine Wigglesworth, Facility Manager
Credits Quick Grip (I); Sport On Five (T); Hasbro (W); BUPA (C)

molinare
a television corporation company

Molinare

34 Fouberts Place, London W1F 7PX
t 020 7478 7000 **f** 020 7478 7199
e bookings@molinare.co.uk **w** www.molinare.co.uk
Contact Kate George, Facilities Manager
Credits Dorada Especial: Painting; AXN: Cornice; Walkers Dorito's: Idents; The Wind

For 30 years Molinare has been offering the best in Post Production, helping the best people make the best programmes, we have about the widest selection of facilities in one location in the industry. Based in the heart of Soho, we offer, 5 digital Online Suites, Editbox FX V8, Ursa Gold Telecine, High Definition Online, 10 Avid Offline suites and 2 Avid Online suites, 5 Audio Dubbing suites with voice over booths, Tracklay, Discreet Flint, Media Illusion, Drive in 1500 sq ft Video studio, 400 sq ft Virtual Studio, Duplication, Transmission Services, as well as the Molinare Design team for all your branding and design needs.

MTS

PO Box 208, Old St Mellons, Cardiff CF3 9WG
t 029 2036 3311 **f** 029 2036 3315
e phil.mts@btinternet.com **w** www.multimediareplication.com
Contact Phil Silver, Director

Northern Video Facilities

9th Floor, Astley House, Quay Street, Manchester M3 4AE
t 0161 832 7643 **f** 0161 832 2818
e steve@northernvideo.co.uk **w** www.northernvideo.co.uk
Contact Steve Cooper-Bagnall, Managing Director

Oakslade Studios

Station Road, Hatton CV35 7LH
t 01926 844000 **f** 01926 844045
e suzanne@oakslade.com **w** www.oakslade.com
Contact Susan Bates, Facilities Manager
Credits Indian Karting Championships (C); Worcester County Council (W); BSSA (W); Cinderella To Princess - Virgin (I)

Outlook Audio Visual Ltd

The Courtyard, Orchard Hill, Little Billing, Northampton NN3 9AG
t 01604 788884 **f** 01604 788866
Contact Mark Shademan, Director

Peach Facilities Ltd

3 Slingsby PLace, Long Acre, London WC2E 9AB
t 020 7632 4240 **f** 020 7632 4250
e info@peachfacilities.co.uk **w** www.peachfacilities.co.uk
Contact Russell Parrett; Tim Whitehead; Karen Davies

Plato Video

3 Poole Road, Bournemouth BH2 5QJ
t 01202 554382

Professional Magnetics

Cassette House, 329 Hunslet Road, Leeds LS10 1NJ
t 0113 270 6066 **f** 0113 271 8106
e promags@aol.com **w** www.promags.com
Contact Hilary Rhodes, Sales Director

Profile Video Ltd

23 Gaisford Road, Cowley, Oxford OX4 3WA
t 01865 715429 **f** 01865 747559
e profilevideo@btconnect.com **w** www.profile-video.co.uk
Contact C Willson, Managing Director; P Skinner, Hire & Facilities Manager; D Woodbridge, Sales / Production Manager; G Bridges, Technical Manager

Quadrille Ltd

122 Ferry Road, Edinburgh EH6 4PG
t 0131 553 6789 **f** 0131 553 1771
e info@quadrille.tv **w** www.quadrille.tv
Contact Penny Dickson, Marketing Manager; Jeff Whitecross, Director

Rumble Productions

23 Macphail Street, Glasgow G41 DN
t 0141 554 6868 **f** 0141 554 6869
e mail@rumblepro.co.uk **w** www.rumblepro.co.uk
Contact Mark Butt, Director

Sain

Canolfan Sain, Llandwrog, Caernarfon LL54 5TG
t 01286 831111 **f** 01286 831496
e sain@sain.wales.com **w** www.sain.wales.com
Contact Dafydd Iwan, Director

Satellite Broadcast Facilities

18-20 Commercial Way, Park Royal, London NW10 7XF
t 0870 777 7888 **f** 0870 777 7800
e info@sat-facilities.co.uk **w** www.sat-facilities.co.uk
Contact Oliver Shawo, Sales & Marketing Manager; Aasha Patel, Accounts Manager

Stanley Productions

147 Wardour Street, London W1F 8WD
t 020 7494 4545 **f** 020 7437 2126
e sales@stanleyproductions.co.uk **w** www.stanleyproductions.co.uk
Contact Stanley Aarons, Managing Director

Thames Valley Video

660 Ajax Avenue, Slough SL1 4BG
t 01753 553131 **f** 01753 554505 **w** tvv@netcomuk.co.uk
Contact Nigel Morrice, Managing Director

TSI Post Production

TSI Video, 10 Grape Street, London WC2H 8DY
t 020 7379 3435 **f** 020 7379 4589 **e** bookings@tsi.co.uk
Contact Simon Peach, Managing Director; Andy Wright, Producer; Simon Kanjee, Managing Director; Nathalie Roull; Shula Fitzgerald, Head of Sales; Alan Cronin, Facility Manager; Julia Gonsalves, Head of Bookings
Credits Robbie Williams In Concert (T); This Morning (T); Sir Robert Winston - The Human Instinct (T); They Think It's All Over (T)

TV Set

22 Newman Street, London W1T 1PH
t 020 7637 3322 **f** 020 7637 1011
e info@thetelevisionset.co.uk **w** www.thetelevisionset.co.uk
Contact Terry Bettles, Managing Director; Alf Penn; David Yeo

Vanderquest

7 Latimer Road, Teddington TW11 8QA
t 020 8977 1743 **f** 020 8943 4812
Contact Nick Maingay, Managing Director

VCL Video

43-44 Hoxton Square, London N1 6PB
t 020 7729 6967 **e** info@vclvideo.com

Wheelers Post Production Film Services

4 Hansard Mews, London W14 8BJ
t 020 7603 0217 **f** 020 7603 5217
e wheelers@wheelers.co.uk **w** www.wheelers.co.uk
Contact Simon Wheeler, Managing Director

Post Production
Footsteps/Foley Artists

Peter Corley

41 Granville Road, Wood Green, London N22 5LP
t 020 8889 2420 **f** 020 8889 2420 **m** 07753 202385
e peter@corley46.freeserve.co.uk
Credits Raising The Dead (T); The King's Beard (A); Loop (F); Last Orders (F)

molinare
a television corporation company

Molinare
34 Fouberts Place, London W1F 7PX
t 020 7478 7000 **f** 020 7478 7199
e bookings@molinare.co.uk **w** www.molinare.co.uk
Contact Kate George, Facilities Manager
Credits Dorada Especial: Painting; AXN: Cornice;
Walkers Dorito's: Idents; The Wind

For 30 years Molinare has been offering the best in Post Production,
helping the best people make the best programmes, we have about the
widest selection of facilities in one location in the industry. Based in the
heart of Soho, we offer, 5 digital Online Suites, Editbox FX V8, Ursa Gold
Telecine, High Definition Online, 10 Avid Offline suites and 2 Avid Online
suites, 5 Audio Dubbing suites with voice over booths, Tracklay, Discreet
Flint, Media Illusion, Drive in 1500 sq ft Video studio, 400 sq ft Virtual
Studio, Duplication, Transmission Services, as well as the Molinare
Design team for all your branding and design needs.

Post Production **Supervisor**

Virginia Arendt
54 Chevening Road, London NW6 6DE
t 020 8964 4272 **m** 07973 433435 **e** varendt@cs.com

Roy Benson
10 Palace Court, Palace Road, London SW2 3ED
t 020 8671 2168 **m** 07905 625798 **e** roybenson7@aol.com
Agent Edit-Base, 70A Waldegrave Road, Teddington TW11 8NY
t 020 8614 6937 **e** alison@edit-base.co.uk
Credits John Harold's Circus (A); The Prince Of Pluto (A); The Herean Women
(F); To End All Wars (F)

Phil Brown
Edit-Base, 70A Waldegrave Road, Teddington TW11 8NY
t 020 8614 6937 **e** alison@edit-base.co.uk

Paul Bulmer
8 Marble Hill Close, Twickenham TW1 3AY
t 020 8892 3614 **f** 020 8892 3555 **m** 07710 328925
e paul@plt.co.uk
Agent Edit-Base, 70A Waldegrave Road, Teddington TW11 8NY
t 020 8614 6937 **e** alison@edit-base.co.uk
Credits White Oleander (F); Warriors (T); Club Le Monde (F); The Last Resort (F)

Jay Coquillon
Edit-Base, 70A Waldegrave Road, Teddington TW11 8NY
t 020 8614 6937 **e** alison@edit-base.co.uk

Eddie Daniels
3A Runnymeade Road, Canvey Island SS8 0EF

Deacy Bayford Associates
36 Carnarvon Road, Hayes UB3 1PU
t 020 8756 0797 **f** 020 8756 0797
e enquiries@dbapost.co.uk
Contact Linda Deacy, Director; Natalie Bayford, Director

Bruce Everett
Yeo Vale, Spreyton, Crediton EX17 5AX
t 020 7878 7803 **t** 020 7878 0000 **f** 0870 138 6233
m 07973 306515 **e** b.everett@btinternet.com
Credits Poirot (T); 10th Kingdom (T); Lost in Space (F); Band Of Brothers (T)

Tracey Gibbons
Edit-Base, 70A Waldegrave Road, Teddington TW11 8NY
t 020 8614 6937 **e** alison@edit-base.co.uk

Jonathan Haren
2 Hatfield Court, Avenue Crescent, London W3 8ER
t 020 8896 9354 **m** 07780 607090 **e** jonharen@msn.com
Credits Before You Go (F); Cheeky (F)

Howard Lanning
2 Fairview, Little Heath, Potters Bar EN6 1ND
t 01707 656244 **f** 01707 656244 **m** 07774 445749
Credits The Governor (T); Trial And Retribution IV (T); Harbour Lights (T); In
Deep I, II & III (T)

Richard Lloyd
Edit-Base, 70A Waldegrave Road, Teddington TW11 8NY
t 020 8614 6937 **e** alison@edit-base.co.uk

Cory McCrum-Abdo
18 Hampton Court Crescent, Graburn Way, East Molesley KT8 9BA
t 020 7863 0304 **m** 07904 957299
e cory.abdo@btopenworld.com
Credits Neverland (F); Dead Poet's Society (F); Conspiracy (F); The Lonely
Years / The Gathering Storm (T)

Shelley Powell
Room 7, 6 Brewer Street, London W1F 0SD
t 020 7494 3107 **f** 020 7437 1678 **m** 07989 499989
e shelley@waves.demon.co.uk
Credits Dr Zhivago (T); The Lost Prince (T); Spooks (T)

Michael Saxton
Edit-Base, 70A Waldegrave Road, Teddington TW11 8NY
t 020 8614 6937 **e** alison@edit-base.co.uk

Shadows on the Wall
The Grange, Barnack, Stamford PE9 3DU
t 01780 740232 **f** 01780 740237 **e** shadows@breathe.co.uk
Contact Nickie Stevens, Producer; Roy Beck, Producer

Jackie Vance
11 Gladsdale Drive, Pinner HA5 2PP
t 020 8866 1431 **f** 020 8866 1431 **m** 07768 794688
e jackie@vance0075.fsnet.co.uk
Agent Edit-Base, 70A Waldegrave Road, Teddington TW11 8NY
t 020 8614 6937 **e** alison@edit-base.co.uk
Credits Human Traffic (F); Asylum (F); The Intended (F); My Brother Tom (F)

Tania Windsor Blunden
75 Saint Margarets Grove, Twickenham TW1 1JF
t 020 8744 0459 **f** 020 8287 6649 **m** 07771 896606
e twindsor@globalnet.co.uk
Credits High Fidelity (F); Captain Corelli's Mandolin (F); Dirty Pretty Things (F);
Ned Kelly (F)

Post Production
Vision Effects, Digital

422 South
The Media Centre, 3-8 Carburton Street, London W1W 5AJ
t 020 7494 2422 **f** 020 7072 2429
e beccad@422.com **w** www.422.com
Contact Ellen Monaghan, Business Development; Becca Saraga, Head Of Production
Credits How Weird Are You? (T); Extreme Machine (D); Horizon - Dirty Bomb
(D); The Day The Earth Was Born (D)

BBC Post Production

BBC Post Production
(Sites across London, Bristol & Birmingham)
5550 Television Centre, Wood Lane, London W12 7RJ
t 020 8225 7702 (London) **t** 0117 974 6666 (Bristol)
t 0121 432 8621 (Birmingham)
w www.bbcresources.com/postproduction

Cine Image
7a Langley Street, Covent Garden, London WC2H 9JA
t 020 7240 6222 **f** 020 7240 6242
e mail@cineimage.co.uk **w** www.cineimage.co.uk
Contact Steve Boag, Partner

post production : footstep/foley artists, supervisor, vision effects digital

THE PRODUCTION GUIDE •465

Cinesite Europe Ltd

9 Carlisle Street, London W1D 3BP
t 020 7973 4000 **f** 020 7973 4040
e filmfx@cinesite.co.uk **w** www.cinesite.com
Contact Courtney Vanderslice, Head of Production
Credits Band Of Brothers (T); Harry Potter And The Philosopher's Stone (F)

Condor Post Production

54 Greek Street, London W1D 3DS
t 020 7494 2552 **f** 020 7494 1166
e anthea@condor-post.com **w** www.condor-post.com
Contact Minouche Kool, Managing Director
Credits The Jaffaman (S)

Digirama Ltd

Twickenham Film Studios, St Margarets,
Twickenham TW1 2AW
t 020 8607 8758 **t** 020 8891 2497 **f** 020 8607 8958
e digirama@goveyfilm.co.uk **w** www.digirama.co.uk
Contact Peter Govey, Creative Director

Digital Film @ the Moving Picture Company

127 Wardour Street, London W1F ONL
t 020 7434 3100 **f** 020 7287 5187
e mailbox@moving-pictures.com **w** www.moving-picture.com

Digital Film Lab

52 St John Street, London EC1M 4HF
t 020 7490 4050 **f** 020 7251 8430
e lon@digitalfilmlab.com **w** www.digitalfilmlab.com
Contact Helle Absalonsen, Facility Manager

Golden Square Post Production

11 Golden Square, London W1F 9JB
t 020 7300 3555 **f** 020 7494 3288
e info@golden-square.co.uk **w** www.golden-square.co.uk
Contact Beth Vander, Producer; Ewan Macleod, Executive Producer; Lee Pavey,
Producer; Sally Cooper, Producer

James Jordan

204 Northcote Road, London E17 7DH
t 020 8257 3926 **m** 07985 445745
e james.jordan66@ntlworld.com
Credits Majorie And Gladys (T); Daziel And Pascoe (T); Tipping The Velvet (T);
White Teeth (T)

Katherine Granger

4 Potland Street, St Albans AL3 4RB
t 01727 759189 **m** 07956 967984
e katherine.granger@ntlworld.com
Credits Tomb Raider (F); Something Stupid - Halifax (C); Pyramid (D);
Harry Potter (F)

Ken Lailey Effects

2 Cobbs Mill Cottage, Great Wishford, Salisbury SP2 ONX
t 01722 790225 **f** 01722 790225 **m** 07860 308469
e info@kenlaileyeffects.com **w** www.kenlaileyeffects.com
Contact Casper Lailey
Credits Warriors (T); Snatch (F); Lock Stock And Two Smoking Barrels (F)

The Mill

Shepperton Studios, Studios Road, Shepperton TW17 OQD
t 01932 592424 **t** 01932 592069
e info@mill.co.uk **w** www.mill.co.uk
Credits Mint Royale: Blue Song (M); Marmite: Guard

The Moving Picture Company (MPC)

127 Wardour Street, London W1F ONL
t 020 7434 3100 **f** 020 7287 5187
e mailbox@moving-picture.com **w** www.moving-picture.com
Contact Stephanie Bryan, Public Relations
Credits BBC Wild Weather (T); Madonna - Die Another Day (M); John West Tuna
(C); Harry Potter And The Chamber Of Secrets (F)

Nats Post Production

10 Soho Square, London W1D 3NT
t 020 7287 9900 **f** 020 7287 8636 **e** bookings@nats.ltd.uk
Contact Sara Hill, Bookings; Jo Manser; Louise Knight; Louise Thomas

*One of Soho's leading facilities, Nats Post Production is fully equipped in
all aspects of television post production, from offline to online, design
and graphics, grade and audio dub. With over 40 suites, we strive to
make sure your whole experience is as pleasant and productive as
possible by offering you creative excellence, intelligent solutions and
home comforts.*

Peerless Camera Company Ltd

32 Bedfordbury, Covent Garden, London WC2N 4DS
t 020 7836 3367 **f** 020 7240 2143
e andy@peerless.co.uk **w** www.peerless.co.uk
Contact Andy Fowler, General Manager; Caroline Waldron, Office Manager
Credits Twelve Monkeys (F); Lara Croft: Tomb Raider (F); Pinocchio (F);
Vertical Limit (F)

Lynn Perez

35 Tarner Road, Brighton BN2 9QT
t 01273 261961 **m** 07712 527693 **e** perezlynn@hotmail.com
Credits Wild New World (T); The Shopping News (F); Pitch Black (F)

Questech Ltd

Eastheath Avenue, Wokingham RG41 2PP
t 0118 978 4554 **f** 0118 979 4554 **e** info@charismatech.com
w www.questech.co.uk
Contact Elizabeth Allum, Sales Director

Reality Surgeons

193 Providence Square, London SE1 2DG
t 020 7232 2961 **m** 07803 391910
e e.king@realitysurgeons.co.uk **w** www.realitysurgeons.co.uk
Contact Edward King, Creative Director
Credits Nothing Personal (D); The Erased People (D); 21st Century War (D)

Smoke & Mirrors

57-59 Beak Street, London W1F 9SJ
t 020 7468 1000 **f** 020 7468 1001
e production@smoke-mirrors.co.uk **w** www.smoke-mirrors.co.uk
Contact Penny Verbe, Facility Director; Emma Ibbetson, Head Of Production;
Mark Wildig, Managing Director
Credits Stella Artois - Devil's Island (C); Tattoo Man (C); The Test -
The Chemical Brothers (M); Resident Evil - Title Sequence (F)

Sarah Soulsby MA (RCA)

29 Winterwell Road, London SW2 5JB
t 020 7737 4574 **m** 07989 798641 **e** sjlsoulsby@aol.com
Credits The I Inside (F); Randall And Hopkirk Deceased (T); Enemy At The Gates
(F); Below (F)

Triangle Post Production

81 Whitfield Street, London W1T 4HG
t 020 7255 5222 **f** 020 7255 5216
w www.triangletelevision.co.uk
Contact Tom Horton, Managing Director; Jonathan Chambers, Head of
Production; Christian Downes, Post Production Manager
Credits Sophie Ellis Bextor - Get Over You (M); Lexus - Store (C); Blue Featuring
Elton John - Sorry Seems To Be... (M); BBC News (C)

TSI Post Production

TSI Video, 10 Grape Street, London WC2H 8DY
t 020 7379 3435 **f** 020 7379 4589 **e** bookings@tsi.co.uk
Contact Simon Peach, Managing Director; Andy Wright, Producer; Simon
Kanjee, Managing Director; Nathalie Roull; Shula Fitzgerald, Head of Sales; Alan
Cronin, Facility Manager; Julia Gonsalves, Head of Bookings
Credits Robbie Williams In Concert (T); This Morning (T); Sir Robert Winston -
The Human Instinct (T); They Think It's All Over (T)

Visual Factory
21 Wigmore Street, London W1U 1PJ
t 020 7499 7544 **f** 020 7629 5020
e info@visualfactory.co.uk **w** www.visualfactory.co.uk
Contact Igor Sekulic, CEO; Ade Bello, Chief Financial Officer
Credits Young And Beautiful (F); My Wife Maurice (F); Just Visiting (F)

Vital Media Solutions
77 Oxford Street, London W1D 2ES
t 020 7399 1286 **f** 020 7659 2100 **m** 07714 695361
e odc@vitalmedia.co.uk **w** www.vitalmedia.co.uk
Contact Oli Da Costa, Proprietor/Digital Content Creator
Credits diabolikal.co.uk (W); Toni & Guy (I); The Banjo Account (A); Pop Will Shoot Itself (T)

Unique solutions in Motion-Graphics, Post, Online and Multimedia. Visit our website for news, projects and to view/request showreels.

Post Production
Vision Effects, Optical

BBC Post Production

BBC Post Production
(Sites across London, Bristol & Birmingham)
5550 Television Centre, Wood Lane, London W12 7RJ
t 020 8225 7702 (London) **t** 0117 974 6666 (Bristol)
t 0121 432 8621 (Birmingham)
w www.bbcresources.com/postproduction

DVD-UK
Downfiled Villa, 1 Downfield Road, Clifton, Bristol BS8 2TG
t 0117 973 7003 **f** 0117 973 7003 **m** 07050 048105
e info@dvd-uk.tv **w** www.dvd-uk.tv
Contact Laurie Jones, Managing Director

Peter Govey Film Opticals
Twickenham Film Studios, St Margarets, Twickenham TW1 2AW
t 020 8891 2497 **f** 020 8607 8958
e peter@goveyfilm.co.uk **w** www.goveryfilm.co.uk

Post Production
Vision Effects, Titles

52Post
4 Achilles Road, London NW6 1EA
t 020 7794 1236 **f** 020 7794 1236 **m** 07866 696059
e post52@mac.com **w** www.homepage.mac.com/post52
Contact Toby Brockhurst, VFX Supervisor; Lindsay Butler, Producer
Credits Marston's Pedigree (C); Ikea (C); American Cousins (F); Great Britons (C)

BBC Post Production

BBC Post Production
(Sites across London, Bristol & Birmingham)
5550 Television Centre, Wood Lane, London W12 7RJ
t 020 8225 7702 (London) **t** 0117 974 6666 (Bristol)
t 0121 432 8621 (Birmingham)
w www.bbcresources.com/postproduction

Big Squid
3 Berkeley Square, Bristol BS8 1HL
t 0117 914 0150 **f** 0117 914 0130
e richard@bigsquid.net **w** www.bigsquid.net
Contact Richard Higgs, Managing & Creative Director
Credits Raising Of The Monitor (T); DIY SOS (T); Cracking Contraptions (A); Killer Bees (T)

Capital FX
Denham Media Park, North Orbital Road, Denham UB9 5HG
t 01895 831931 **f** 01895 835338
e rick.corne@capital-fx.co.uk **w** www.capital-fx.co.uk
Contact Chester Eyre, Director of Operations; Fred Chandler, Consultant; Rick Corne
2nd Floor, 20 Dering Street, London W1F 1AJ
t 020 7493 9998 **f** 020 7493 9997
e ian@capital-fx.co.uk **w** www.capital-fx.co.uk
Contact David Smith, Producer; Ian Buckton, Director; Tim Baxter, Film Scanning & Recording; Simon Dowling, Head of Production; Jim Davey, Director of Digital Services

Graphic design for Film & TV, digital compositing, digital to film recording, video to film transfer, laser subtitling and video rostrum.

Diverse Post
6 Gorleston Street, London W14 8XS
t 020 7603 4567 **f** 020 7603 2148 **w** www.diverse.tv
Contact Fay Searl; Louise Townsend, Head of Post Production
Credits Slave Nation (T); Battle Center (D); Underworld (F)

Diverse Post offers a complete range of facilities that includes: Smoke, Digital online, Protools audio suite, subtitling, Avid offline and rushes transfer.

Evolutions Television Ltd
5 Berners Street, London W1T 3LF
t 020 7580 3333 **f** 020 7637 1942
e info@evolutionstelevision.com **w** www.evolutionstelevision.com

Evolutions visual effects artists use a diverse range of tools including Flame, Henry Infinity, Lightwave 3D, After Effects and Photoshop to consistently produce highly creative, innovative commercials, title sequences, promos, station idents, music videos and interactive media. We also offer a full range of post production services including duplication and new media.

Honey Brothers
293A Westbourne Grove, London W11 2QA
t 020 7221 5028 **f** 020 7221 5028 **m** 07973 266 864
e goddardski@dial.pipex.com **w** www.honeybrothers.com
Contact Mark Goddard, Partner; Daniel Goddard, Partner
Credits Bodysong (F)

Independent Media Support

21 Soho Square, London W1D 3QP
t 020 7440 5400 **f** 020 7440 5410
e ims@dial.pipex.com **e** london@ims-media.com
Contact Silvia Sheridan, Managing Director

Inter-Com Translations

Hurlingham Studios, Ranelagh Gardens, London SW6 3PA
t 020 7731 8000 **f** 020 7731 5511 **m** 07946 546531
e mail@intercom-translations.co.uk
w www.intercom-translations.co.uk
Contact Patrick Beacom, Partner; Carolina Lehrian, Partner

London Post

34-35 Dean Street, London W1D 4PR
t 020 7439 9080 **f** 020 7434 0714
e info@londonpost.co.uk **w** www.londonpost.co.uk
Contact Soraya Robertson, Bookings Manager; Verity Laing

television

M2 Television

Ingestre Court, Ingestre Place, London W1F 0JL
t 020 7343 6543 **f** 020 7343 6555
e info@m2tv.com **w** www.m2tv.com
The Forum, 74-80 Camden Street, London, NW1 0EG
t 020 7343 6789 **t** 020 7343 6777
Contact Kabir Malik; Jennie Jones

Based in Soho and Camden, we offer a full range of video and audio post production as well as the award-winning co:de design. 5 digital online suites, 5 Editbox FX online suites, 2 Symphony online suites, Avid unity server, Clipbox video server, 14 Avid offline, 5 digital audio suites, Hal, and Illusion.

molinare
a television corporation company

Molinare

34 Fouberts Place, London W1F 7PX
t 020 7478 7000 **f** 020 7478 7199
e bookings@molinare.co.uk **w** www.molinare.co.uk
Contact Kate George, Facilities Manager
Credits Dorada Especial: Painting; AXN: Cornice; Walkers Dorito's: Idents; The Wind

For 30 years Molinare has been offering the best in Post Production, helping the best people make the best programmes, we have about the widest selection of facilities in one location in the industry. Based in the heart of Soho, we offer, 5 digital Online Suites, Editbox FX V8, Ursa Gold Telecine, High Definition Online, 10 Avid Offline suites and 2 Avid Online suites, 5 Audio Dubbing suites with voice over booths, Tracklay, Discreet Flint, Media Illusion, Drive in 1500 sq ft Video studio, 400 sq ft Virtual Studio, Duplication, Transmission Services, as well as the Molinare Design team for all your branding and design needs.

Nats Post Production

10 Soho Square, London W1D 3NT
t 020 7287 9900 **f** 020 7287 8636
e bookings@nats.ltd.uk
Contact Sara Hill, Bookings; Jo Manser; Louise Knight; Louise Thomas

One of Soho's leading facilities, Nats Post Production is fully equipped in all aspects of television post production, from offline to online, design and graphics, grade and audio dub. With over 40 suites, we strive to make sure your whole experience is as pleasant and productive as possible by offering you creative excellence, intelligent solutions and home comforts.

Omnititles

28 Manor Way, London SE3 9EF
t 020 8297 7877 **f** 020 8297 7877 **m** 07889 627 001
e omnititles@ukgateway.net
Contact Isabelle Geesen-Leigh, Director

Screen Subtitling Systems

The Old Rectory, Church Lane, Claydon, Ipswich IP6 0EQ
t 01473 831700 **f** 01473 830078
e sales@screen.subtitling.com **w** www.screen.subtitling.com
Contact Victoria Orford, Marketing Manager; Gary Glover, Sales Group Manager; Brian East, Director; Simon Kane, Sales Manager; Keith Lucas, Sales Manager; Chris Woods, Managing Director

Screentext UK Ltd

PO Box 160, Faversham ME13 8TG
t 01787 478844
e subtitling@screentext.com **w** www.screentext.com
Contact David Packham

SDI Media UK Ltd

Cambridge House, 100 Cambridge Grove, London W6 0LE
t 020 8237 7900 **f** 020 8237 7950
e info@sdi-media.com **e** www.sdi-media.com
Contact Thomas Blomberg, Director

Slowly Making Smoke

8 Carnoustie Court, 17 Addiscombe Grove, Croydon CR0 5LR
m 07952 560858
e gareth@slowlymakingsmoke.com
w www.slowlymakingsmoke.com
Contact Gareth Qually, Director

Softel

7 Horseshoe Park, Horseshoe Road, Pangbourne, Reading RG8 7JW
t 0118 984 2151 **f** 0118 984 3939
e sales@softel.co.uk **w** www.softel.co.uk
Contact Gordon Hunter, Sales Manager

Trosol Ltd

Unit 1, Cwrt y Parc, Parc Ty Glas, Llanishen, Cardiff CF14 5GH
t 029 2075 0760 **f** 029 2068 1928
e subtitles@trosol.co.uk **e** data@trosol.co.uk **w** www.trosol.co.uk
Contact Deryk Williams, Managing Director; John Jones, Managing Director; Rhodri Evans, Head of Translation Services; Sion Morgan, Head of Subtitling
Credits Y Clwb Rygbi (T); Taro 9 (T); O Flaen Dy Lygaid (T); Ffermio (T)

VSI

Aradco House, 132 Cleveland Street, London W1T 6AB
t 020 7692 7700 **t** 020 7692 7702 **f** 020 7692 7711
e info@vsi.tv **w** www.vsi.tv
Contact Norman Dawood, Director; Carla Mercer, PA to Managing Director; Virginie Verdier, Head of Subtitling; Jenny Morris, Head of Voice-Overs; Lola Smith, Project Manager
Credits National Geographic - Africa (D); Heineken (C); What Lies Beneath (F)

Post Production
Voiceover Artists

Tahsin Akti
44A Russell Road, London W14 8HT
m 07812 457412
e tahsin.akti@bbc.co.uk **w** www.aktiv.freeserve.co.uk
Credits British Petroleum Training Video In Turkish (I); Turkish Phrasebook With Cassette (E); England 2006: World Cup 2006 Campaign (I); The World Is Not Enough (F)

Karen Archer
Castaway, 7 Garrick Street, London WC2E 9AR
t 020 7240 2345 **f** 020 7240 2772
e sheila@castaway.org.uk **w** www.castaway.org.uk

Jonathan Aris
Castaway, 7 Garrick Street, London WC2E 9AR
t 020 7240 2345 **f** 020 7240 2772
e sheila@castaway.org.uk **w** www.castaway.org.uk

Chris Armstrong
Castaway, 7 Garrick Street, London WC2E 9AR
t 020 7240 2345 **f** 020 7240 2772
e sheila@castaway.org.uk **w** www.castaway.org.uk

Greg Bance
126 White Hart Lane, London N17 8HS
t 020 8808 3951

Anna Barry
Castaway, 7 Garrick Street, London WC2E 9AR
t 020 7240 2345 **f** 020 7240 2772
e sheila@castaway.org.uk **w** www.castaway.org.uk

Tim Beckmann
Castaway, 7 Garrick Street, London WC2E 9AR
t 020 7240 2345 **f** 020 7240 2772
e sheila@castaway.org.uk **w** www.castaway.org.uk

Bill Bingham
Castaway, 7 Garrick Street, London WC2E 9AR
t 020 7240 2345 **f** 020 7240 2772
e sheila@castaway.org.uk **w** www.castaway.org.uk

Mark Bonnar
Castaway, 7 Garrick Street, London WC2E 9AR
t 020 7240 2345 **f** 020 7240 2772
e sheila@castaway.org.uk **w** www.castaway.org.uk

Robert Booth
Castaway, 7 Garrick Street, London WC2E 9AR
t 020 7240 2345 **f** 020 7240 2772
e sheila@castaway.org.uk **w** www.castaway.org.uk

Paul Broughton
Castaway, 7 Garrick Street, London WC2E 9AR
t 020 7240 2345 **f** 020 7240 2772
e sheila@castaway.org.uk **w** www.castaway.org.uk

David Browne
8 Greenfield Road, London N15 5EP
t 020 8802 4937 **m** 07754 176596
e david.browne@virgin.net **w** www.superbrowne.com
Credits Exit Festival, Serbia (C); Seven Seconds (S); Sunrise Double Glazing (C); The Sweet Smell Of Roses (A)

Michael Burrell
Castaway, 7 Garrick Street, London WC2E 9AR
t 020 7240 2345 **f** 020 7240 2772
e sheila@castaway.org.uk **w** www.castaway.org.uk

Liz Carling
Castaway, 7 Garrick Street, London WC2E 9AR
t 020 7240 2345 **f** 020 7240 2772
e sheila@castaway.org.uk **w** www.castaway.org.uk

The Chatterbox Studio
The Chattery, 19 Colwall Avenue, Hull HU5 5SN
t 01482 506983 **f** 01482 506983 **i** 01482 5722 48x2
e hazziesbox@aol.com
Contact Pete Haslam

Kieran Creggan
Castaway, 7 Garrick Street, London WC2E 9AR
t 020 7240 2345 **f** 020 7240 2772
e sheila@castaway.org.uk **w** www.castaway.org.uk

Niamh Daly
Castaway, 7 Garrick Street, London WC2E 9AR
t 020 7240 2345 **f** 020 7240 2772
e sheila@castaway.org.uk **w** www.castaway.org.uk

Sara Dee
m 07990 951703
e saradee@saradee.co.uk **w** www.saradee.co.uk

Emily Dormer
Castaway, 7 Garrick Street, London WC2E 9AR
t 020 7240 2345 **f** 020 7240 2772
e sheila@castaway.org.uk **w** www.castaway.org.uk

Michael Drew
Castaway, 7 Garrick Street, London WC2E 9AR
t 020 7240 2345 **f** 020 7240 2772
e sheila@castaway.org.uk **w** www.castaway.org.uk

Sharon Duce
Castaway, 7 Garrick Street, London WC2E 9AR
t 020 7240 2345 **f** 020 7240 2772
e sheila@castaway.org.uk **w** www.castaway.org.uk

Jonell Elliott
Castaway, 7 Garrick Street, London WC2E 9AR
t 020 7240 2345 **f** 020 7240 2772
e sheila@castaway.org.uk **w** www.castaway.org.uk

Tim Flavin
Castaway, 7 Garrick Street, London WC2E 9AR
t 020 7240 2345 **f** 020 7240 2772
e sheila@castaway.org.uk **w** www.castaway.org.uk

Maurice Gleeson
Castaway, 7 Garrick Street, London WC2E 9AR
t 020 7240 2345 **f** 020 7240 2772
e sheila@castaway.org.uk **w** www.castaway.org.uk

Iain Glen
Castaway, 7 Garrick Street, London WC2E 9AR
t 020 7240 2345 **f** 020 7240 2772 **e** sheila@castaway.org.uk
w www.castaway.org.uk

Garrick Hagon
Castaway, 7 Garrick Street, London WC2E 9AR
t 020 7240 2345 **f** 020 7240 2772
e sheila@castaway.org.uk **w** www.castaway.org.uk

Ian Hanmore
Castaway, 7 Garrick Street, London WC2E 9AR
t 020 7240 2345 **f** 020 7240 2772
e sheila@castaway.org.uk **w** www.castaway.org.uk

Tim Hardy
Castaway, 7 Garrick Street, London WC2E 9AR
t 020 7240 2345 **f** 020 7240 2772
e sheila@castaway.org.uk **w** www.castaway.org.uk

Jonathan Hart
Castaway, 7 Garrick Street, London WC2E 9AR
t 020 7240 2345 **f** 020 7240 2772
e sheila@castaway.org.uk **w** www.castaway.org.uk

Ruthie Henshall
Castaway, 7 Garrick Street, London WC2E 9AR
t 020 7240 2345 **f** 020 7240 2772
e sheila@castaway.org.uk **w** www.castaway.org.uk

Tamsin Hollo
Castaway, 7 Garrick Street, London WC2E 9AR
t 020 7240 2345 **f** 020 7240 2772 **e** sheila@castaway.org.uk
w www.castaway.org.uk

Tim Howar
Castaway, 7 Garrick Street, London WC2E 9AR
t 020 7240 2345 **f** 020 7240 2772
e sheila@castaway.org.uk **w** www.castaway.org.uk

Eiry Hughes
Castaway, 7 Garrick Street, London WC2E 9AR
t 020 7240 2345 **f** 020 7240 2772
e sheila@castaway.org.uk **w** www.castaway.org.uk

Lennie James
Castaway, 7 Garrick Street, London WC2E 9AR
t 020 7240 2345 **f** 020 7240 2772
e sheila@castaway.org.uk **w** www.castaway.org.uk

Ashley Jensen
Castaway, 7 Garrick Street, London WC2E 9AR
t 020 7240 2345 **f** 020 7240 2772
e sheila@castaway.org.uk **w** www.castaway.org.uk

Emily Joyce
Castaway, 7 Garrick Street, London WC2E 9AR
t 020 7240 2345 **f** 020 7240 2772
e sheila@castaway.org.uk **w** www.castaway.org.uk

Chris Langham
Castaway, 7 Garrick Street, London WC2E 9AR
t 020 7240 2345 **f** 020 7240 2772
e sheila@castaway.org.uk **w** www.castaway.org.uk

Jessica Martin
Castaway, 7 Garrick Street, London WC2E 9AR
t 020 7240 2345 **f** 020 7240 2772
e sheila@castaway.org.uk **w** www.castaway.org.uk

Ted May
Tudor Lodge, Castle Hill, East Leake LE12 6LX
t 01509 853698 **f** 01509 856143 **m** 07747 186 025
e ted@malevoiceover.com **w** www.malevoiceover.com

Philip McGough
Castaway, 7 Garrick Street, London WC2E 9AR
t 020 7240 2345 **f** 020 7240 2772
sheila@castaway.org.uk **w** www.castaway.org.uk

Gina McKee
Castaway, 7 Garrick Street, London WC2E 9AR
t 020 7240 2345 **f** 020 7240 2772
e sheila@castaway.org.uk **w** www.castaway.org.uk

•molinare
a television corporation company

Molinare
34 Fouberts Place, London W1F 7PX
t 020 7478 7000 **f** 020 7478 7199
e bookings@molinare.co.uk **w** www.molinare.co.uk
Contact Kate George, Facilities Manager
Credits Dorada Especial: Painting; AXN: Cornice;
Walkers Dorito's: Idents; The Wind

For 30 years Molinare has been offering the best in Post Production, helping the best people make the best programmes, we have about the widest selection of facilities in one location in the industry. Based in the heart of Soho, we offer, 5 digital Online Suites, Editbox FX V8, Ursa Gold Telecine, High Definition Online, 10 Avid Offline suites and 2 Avid Online suites, 5 Audio Dubbing suites with voice over booths, Tracklay, Discreet Flint, Media Illusion, Drive in 1500 sq ft Video studio, 400 sq ft Virtual Studio, Duplication, Transmission Services, as well as the Molinare Design team for all your branding and design needs.

Tracy-Ann Oberman
Castaway, 7 Garrick Street, London WC2E 9AR
t 020 7240 2345 **f** 020 7240 2772
e sheila@castaway.org.uk **w** www.castaway.org.uk

Barry Paine
Braeside Cottage, Rhodyate, Blagdon, Bristol BS40 7TP
t 01761 462256 **f** 01761 462256
e barry.paine@wildvoice.co.uk **w** www.wildvoice.co.uk
Credits The Natural World (T)

Paul Panting
Castaway, 7 Garrick Street, London WC2E 9AR
t 020 7240 2345 **f** 020 7240 2772
e sheila@castaway.org.uk **w** www.castaway.org.uk

Nigel Pilkington
Castaway, 7 Garrick Street, London WC2E 9AR
t 020 7240 2345 **f** 020 7240 2772
e sheila@castaway.org.uk **w** www.castaway.org.uk

Jeff Rawle
Castaway, 7 Garrick Street, London WC2E 9AR
t 020 7240 2345 **f** 020 7240 2772
e sheila@castaway.org.uk **w** www.castaway.org.uk

Struan Rodger
Castaway, 7 Garrick Street, London WC2E 9AR
t 020 7240 2345 **f** 020 7240 2772
e sheila@castaway.org.uk **w** www.castaway.org.uk

Michael Sheen
Castaway, 7 Garrick Street, London WC2E 9AR
t 020 7240 2345 **f** 020 7240 2772
e sheila@castaway.org.uk **w** www.castaway.org.uk

Shireen Shah
Castaway, 7 Garrick Street, London WC2E 9AR
t 020 7240 2345 **f** 020 7240 2772
e sheila@castaway.org.uk **w** www.castaway.org.uk

Nina Sosanya
Castaway, 7 Garrick Street, London WC2E 9AR
t 020 7240 2345 **f** 020 7240 2772
e sheila@castaway.org.uk **w** www.castaway.org.uk

Stephen Rhodes Promotions
81 High Street, Eaton Bray, Bedfordshire LU6 2DN
t 01525 222938 **f** 01525 222004
m 07734 113219 **i** 01525 229603
e stephen.rhodes@bramleybottomstudio.com
w www.bramleybottomstudio.com
Contact Alison Keenan, Partner; Stephen Rhodes, Partner
Credits Honda (I); British Steel (I); Edenvale (I); Marks And Spencer (I)

Judy Sweeney
Castaway, 7 Garrick Street, London WC2E 9AR
t 020 7240 2345 **f** 020 7240 2772
e sheila@castaway.org.uk **w** www.castaway.org.uk

Meera Syal
Castaway, 7 Garrick Street, London WC2E 9AR
t 020 7240 2345 **f** 020 7240 2772
e sheila@castaway.org.uk **w** www.castaways.org.uk

David Tennant
Castaway, 7 Garrick Street, London WC2E 9AR
t 020 7240 2345 **f** 020 7240 2772
e sheila@castaway.org.uk **w** www.castaway.org.uk

Steve Tompkinson
Castaway, 7 Garrick Street, London WC2E 9AR
t 020 7240 2345 **f** 020 7240 2772
e sheila@castaway.org.uk **w** www.castaway.org.uk

Sally Wallis
Castaway, 7 Garrick Street, London WC2E 9AR
t 020 7240 2345 **f** 020 7240 2772
e sheila@castaway.org.uk **w** www.castaway.org.uk

William Wilde
Castaway, 7 Garrick Street, London WC2E 9AR
t 020 7240 2345 **f** 020 7240 2772
e sheila@castaway.org.uk **w** www.castaway.org.uk

PRODUCTION

production : contents

Producers
Commercials & Promos

AI-Digital (Ad Infinitum Digital)
16A Grosvenor Avenue, London N5 2NR
e chris@ai-digital.com **w** www.ai-digital.com
Contact Chris Smith, Producer

Amy Appletonsmith
81 Bolingbroke Grove, London SW11 6HB
t 020 7738 1738 **f** 020 7564 3030 **m** 07831 772770
e amy@babefilms.com **w** www.babefilms.com

Baby
26A Parkway, Camden, London NW1 7AH
t 020 7482 6467 **f** 020 7482 6473
e mail@babyenterprises.com **w** www.babyenterprises.com
Contact Pam Asbury, Producer/MD; Lynnette Kyme, Producer/MD

Jacci Barrett
25 Kyrle Road, London SW11 6BD
t 020 7499 9199 **f** 020 7499 9699 **m** 07770 890608
e jacci@fatfish.co.uk

Blue Source
Saga Centre, 326 Kensal Road, London W10 5BZ
t 020 7598 9250 **f** 020 7598 9252
e info@bluesource.com **w** www.bluesource.com
Credits Fat Boy Slim: Bird of Prey (M); New Order: 60 mph (M); Dirty Vegas:
Days Go By (M); Bjork: Nature is Ancient

Ian Bouncer
13 Stevens Crescent, Bristol BS3 4UL
f 0117 330 1624 **m** 07974 834002
e ianbouncer@blueyonder.co.uk **w** www.ianbouncer.co.uk
Credits Lloyds TSB (I); Cable & Wireless (C); Microsoft (I); BT (C)

Lauren Campbell
The Production Switchboard, Northdown, Down Lane,
Compton GU3 1DN
t 01483 812011 **f** 01483 812027
aly@productionswitch.freeserve.co.uk
Credits Quest Telecommunications (C); Oil Of Olay (C); Ford (C); Ford

The Clinic
6A Poland Street, London W1F 8PT
t 020 7734 0599 **f** 020 7494 1184 **e** ml@the-clinic.co.uk
Contact Mark Lethem, Managing Director; Paul Donnellon, Director, Director

Patrick Duguid
30 Juer Street, Battersea, London SW11 4RF
t 020 7228 2722 **f** 020 7924 2729 **m** 07973 208916
e patrickduguid@yahoo.com
Agent The Production Switchboard, Northdown, Down Lane,
Compton GU3 1DN
t 01483 812011 **f** 01483 812027
e aly@productionswitch.freeserve.co.uk
Credits Tubby T (C); Addiction (C); Haagen Dazs (C)

John Fleming
1 Chatsworth Close, Borehamwood WD6 1UE
m 07836 703504
e john@thejohnfleming.com **w** www.thejohnfleming.com

The Good Film Company
The Studio, 5-6 Eton Garages, Lambolle Place, London NW3 4PE
t 020 7794 6222 **f** 020 7794 4651
e yanina@goodfilms.co.uk **w** www.goodfilms.co.uk
Contact Yanina Barry, Producer
Credits HBO - The Gathering Storm (C); Millennium Bridge (I); Wendy's
Hamburgers (C); Nestle - Acti-V (C)

Alan Graves
28 Bevin Court, Cruickshank Street, London WC1X 9HA
t 020 7419 4190 **m** 07816 979087 **e** alan@atomicarts.net
Credits Baby June (M); One Minute (C); Shoreditch (F); Seasons Alter (S)

Mike Griffin
58 Lawford Road, London N1 5BL
t 020 7254 5667 **f** 020 7254 5667 **m** 07775 657126
e michael_griffin@talk21.com

Brian Harding
12 Grove Avenue, London N10 2AR
t 020 8444 5317 **f** 020 8444 2113 **m** 07710 850373
e brianharding01@aol.com

Cleo Hodgkinson
37 Rylett Road, London W12 9ST
t 020 8743 7937 **m** 07956 435644
e aly@productionswitch.freeserve.co.uk
Agent Production Switchboard, Northdown, Down Lane,
Compton GU3 1DN
t 01483 812011 **f** 01483 812027
e aly@productionswitch.freeserve.co.uk
Credits Renault Cleo (C); Kingsmill (C); Sky TV (C)

Richard Holling
m 07831 498265 **e** richard@holling.co.uk

Megan Hollister
The Production Switchboard, Northdown, Down Lane,
Compton GU3 1DN
t 01483 812011 **f** 01483 812027
e aly@productionswitch.freeserve.co.uk
Credits Halifax (C); Whirlpool (C); Axa (C)

Jon Staton Productions Ltd
2 Percy Street, London W1T 1DD
t 020 7637 5825 **f** 020 7436 9740 **m** 07850 867624
e jstaton@dircon.co.uk **w** www.re-active.net
Contact Jon Staton, Executive Producer
Credits Safety

Matthew Jones
The Production Switchboard, Northdown, Down Lane,
Compton GU3 1DN
t 01483 812011 **f** 01483 812027
e aly@productionswitch.freeserve.co.uk
Credits Audi (C); Mastercard (C); Vodafone (C)

Sally Llewellyn
16 Oak Village, London NW5 4QP
t 020 7916 0238 **f** 020 7284 4442 **m** 07773 376277
e sally2@dircon.co.uk
Credits McCains - Vibes (C); Opodo (C); Coldplay - The Scientist (M)

London Joe Ltd
41 Rosenthal Road, Catford, London SE6 2BX
t 020 8698 1962 **f** 020 8473 3127 **m** 07798 527055
w www.london-joe.co.uk
Contact Joe Grossi, Producer/Managing Director; Carmen Vesztergom,
Company Secretary; Jillian Li-Sue, Director/Co-Producer
Credits Deutsche Telekom - M17 (C); Tutankamun - History (D); Teletubbies (T);
Puma - Woman Fragrance (C)
London Producer for German and US productions shooting in the UK.

Lyn MacDonald-Hill
The Production Switchboard, Northdown, Down Lane,
Compton GU3 1DN
t 01483 812011 **f** 01483 812027
e aly@productionswitch.freeserve.co.uk
Credits Max Factor (C); The Son (C); Natwest (C)

NS&H
93 New Kings Road, London SW6 4SJ
t 020 7371 5686 **f** 020 7371 5686 **m** 07957 254364
Contact Pat Firth

Tim Nunn
The Production Switchboard, Northdown, Down Lane,
Compton GU3 1DN
t 01483 812011 **f** 01483 812027
e aly@productionswitch.freeserve.co.uk

Stephen Plesniak
The Production Switchboard, Northdown, Down Lane,
Compton GU3 1DN
t 01483 812011 **f** 01483 812027
e aly@productionswitch.freeserve.co.uk
Credits UK Gold (C); Heinz (C); Brita Water (C)

Wendy Polowin
36B Spencer Rise, London NW5 1AP
t 020 7267 8179 **m** 07788 678498
Agent The Production Switchboard, Northdown, Down Lane,
Compton GU3 1DN
t 01483 812011 **f** 01483 812027
e aly@productionswitch.freeserve.co.uk
Credits Marbles (C); I Can't Believe It's Not Butter (C); Andrex Stress Relief (C)

QD Productions
93 Great Titchfield Street, London W1W 6RP
t 020 7462 1700 **e** andy.l@qotd.co.uk **w** www.qotd.co.uk
Contact Dave Wharin, Director- Design; Russell Hollinbery, Director- Design;
Julie Hawkins, Director- Commercials; Sophie Rodd, Director- Commercials;
Andy Leahy, Producer- Live Action; Andy Goff, Animator

Prudence Rex-Hassan
12 Upper Park Road, London NW3 2UP
t 020 7586 1905 **f** 020 7586 1905 **m** 07836 233492

Juliet Savigear
The Production Switchboard, Northdown, Down Lane,
Compton GU3 1DN
t 01483 812011 **f** 01483 812027
e aly@productionswitch.freeserve.co.uk
Credits Ondigital (C); Sugar Puffs (C); Burger King Drivethru (C)

Nicola Spence
Deerswood, Guilford Road, Loxwood RH14 0SE
t 01403 751744 **f** 01403 751745 **m** 07802 626498
Credits Pantene (C); Head And Shoulders (C)

Steve Jelly Promotions & Presentation
Brookmead Cottage, Chadhurst Farm, Cold Harbour Lane,
Dorking RH4 3JH
f 01306 640621 **m** 07768 400814 **e** steve@thebabyshop.net
Contact Steve Jelly, Managing Director

Melyssa Stokes
16 Lots Road, London SW10 0QF
t 020 7352 4132 **f** 020 7351 7971 **m** 07976 701790

Phil Tidy
The Production Switchboard, Northdown, Down Lane,
Compton GU3 1DN
t 01483 812011 **f** 01483 812027
e aly@productionswitch.freeserve.co.uk
Credits Alice (M); Oasis (M); Badly Drawn Boy (M)

TSI Post Production
TSI Video, 10 Grape Street, London WC2H 8DY
t 020 7379 3435 **f** 020 7379 4589 **e** bookings@tsi.co.uk
Contact Simon Peach, Managing Director; Andy Wright, Producer; Simon
Kanjee, Managing Director; Nathalie Roull; Shula Fitzgerald, Head of Sales; Alan
Cronin, Facility Manager; Julia Gonsalves, Head of Bookings
Credits Robbie Williams In Concert (T); This Morning (T); Sir Robert Winston -
The Human Instinct (T); They Think It's All Over (T)

new producers alliance

2003 marks the tenth anniversary of the New Producers Alliance, the national membership and training organisation which provides support for emerging film producers and filmmakers. The NPA undertakes a number of core activities including a Producer Training Programme, Networking Evenings, Business Breakfasts, Match Development Course, Master-classes and Screenings.

The UK film industry has expanded and evolved considerably during our organisation's lifetime through advances in technology and changes in the tastes of the film going public. The key issues of film training, financing, production, distribution and exhibition are now being tackled by a number of key industry organisations such as the UK Film Council, Skillset, PACT, The Nations and Regions and the New Producers Alliance among others.

Over the last few years, there has been some unfortunate downsizing by larger production companies, most notably Film Four and Granada Film. But we continue to see audience attendance figures rise, and though this is attributed to mainly mainstream American product drawing the masses to the multiplexes it is a healthy signal for film itself. Major tax incentives have been put in place to encourage film investment and these will run to 2005. Internationally there are seven co-production treaties at present and others planned, currently the UK Government is a signatory to bilateral co-production treaties with France, Italy, Germany, Canada, Norway, Australia and New Zealand.

The creation of the UK Film Council has made and will make a major difference to the industry. Most recently, it has led to the formation of nine regional film agencies in the UK. The UK Film Council not only invests in short films, development and feature films, it also has a major interest in funding training which plays an essential element in the stabilising and eventual growth of the UK industry. Major organisations, including the New Producers Alliance, BECTU, Directors Guild of Great Britain, Skillset, the CINEGUILDS, the new Regional Screen Agencies and the UK Media Desk, are working together and in conjunction with the UK Film Council to provide essential training for future filmmakers.

In 2002, the NPA presented over 50 educational events and training sessions reaching 2,750 filmmakers. Members' films received considerable acclaim, numerous awards and distribution. Features released in 2002 included WONDROUS OBLIVION Momentum; LAVA Winchester Films; SILENT CRY Optimum Releasing; NOISE CONTROL Sky TV; RIDERS Miramax. To find out more about how the NPA can help you, call us on 020 7580 2480 or visit our website for more information and forthcoming events www.npa.org.uk

---

Richard Weager
1 The Willows, 1025 High Road, London N20 0QE
t 020 8343 7911 **f** 020 8446 2508 **m** 07976 706240
e richard@weager.com
Credits New Order - 60mph (M); Amerada - Riggers (C); Avalanches - Frontier Psychiatrist (M); The Coral - Dreaming Of You (M)

Bruce Williamson
Production Switchboard, Northdown, Down Lane, Compton GU3 1DN
t 01483 812011 **f** 01483 812027
e aly@productionswitch.freeserve.co.uk
Credits Spec-Savers (C); Intercontinental Hotels (C); Smirnoff Ice (C)

Zap Production Services
1-2 Bromley Place, London W1T 6DA
t 020 7436 5577 **f** 020 7691 7282 **m** 07774 235141
e mail@zap-productions.co.uk **w** www.zap-productions.co.uk
Contact Mark Parsons

Producers **Film & TV**

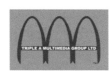

AAA Productions
GMC Studio, Hollingbourne ME17 1UQ
t 01622 880599 **f** 01622 880020
e productions@triple-a.uk.com **w** www.triple-a.uk.com
Contact Terry Armstrong, Managing Director; Jason Armstrong, Director

New Independent film and television company attached to Armstrong Multimedia Arts Academy and part of the Triple A Group of companies producing contemporary home-grown drama, music videos and documentaries.

Nick Abdo
t 020 7863 0304 **m** 07904 957299 **e** n.abdo@btopenworld.com

Jad Adams
2 Kings Garth, 29 London Road, London SE23 3TT
t 020 8699 6718 **m** 07939 635014 **e** julieandjad@btinternet.com

Alba Communications Ltd

Otterburn House, 8-12 Bromley Road, Beckenham BR3 5JE
t 020 8663 0990 **f** 020 8663 3800 **m** 07831 364075
e k-maliphant@ntlworld.com

Contact Ken Maliphant, Managing Director
Credits Tales Of The Bow (D); Visions Of War (D); Planes That Never Flew (D); The Executioners (D)

A unique network of 6 Production Companies with its own facilities and archive. Delivering over 20 hours of programming a year to US cable networks & worldwide distribution. A creative hothouse for innovative Writers, Researchers and Producers. Provides all executive production facilities, especially liaison with Broadcast and DVD clients.

All Set Productions

111 Sinclair Road, London W14 0NP
t 020 7602 5794 **f** 020 7602 5794 **m** 07759 211138
e info@allsetproductions.co.uk **w** www.allsetproductions.co.uk

Contact Jennifer Toynbee-Holmes
Credits National Health Breast Screening (I); The Family Health Nurse (I); The Living Body (T); Tomorrow's World (T)

An Acquired Taste TV

51 Croham Road, South Croydon CR2 7HD
t 020 8686 1188 **f** 020 8686 5928 **e** cbennetttv@aol.com

Contact Lesley Powell, Company Secretary; Colin Bennett, Managing Director
Credits The Motorsport Programme (D); Skateboarding Champs (T); London Light (D); Strictly Soho (D)

Dr Sadek Asha

24 Wakefield Road, Brighton BN2 3FP
t 01273 683858
e sadek.asha@ntlworld.com **w** www.findingmemet.com
Credits Finding Memet

Alex Azabal

1-14 Ovington Square, London SW3 1LN
t 020 7823 9085 **f** 0870 127 2253 **e** londonfilmlab@hotmail.com
Credits Nigel The Plonker (S); My Baby (S); Piece Of Cake (F); Oliver's Crimes (F)

Peter Barber Fleming

London Management & Representation, 2-4 Noel Street, London W1F 8GB
t 020 7287 9000 **f** 020 7287 3236

Bardot Films Ltd

28 Dover Park Drive, London SW15 5BG
t 020 8788 5152 **f** 020 8789 9239
e bardotfilms@aol.com **w** www.moviemgt.com
Contact Nigel Wooll, Producer

Harry Barnes

34 Aden Grove, London N16 9NJ
t 020 7241 2698 **e** harrybarnes@btinternet.com
Credits Discovery Today (T); Sea To Source (T)

Yoram Barzilai

Creative Media Management, Unit 3B, Walpole Court, Ealing Studios, Ealing Green, London W5 5ED
t 020 8584 5363 **f** 020 8566 5554
e enquiries@creativemediamanagement.com
Credits Hollywood Greats (T); Fear.com (F)

Adrian Bate

International Creative Management Ltd, Oxford House, 76 Oxford Street, London W1D 1BS
t 020 7636 6565 **f** 020 7323 0101 **w** www.icmlondon.co.uk

Mike Beale

London Management & Representation, 2-4 Noel Street, London W1F 8GB
t 020 7287 9000 **f** 020 7287 3236
Credits Without Prejudice (T)

Matthew Bird

45 Sunderland Road, London SE23 2PS
t 020 8291 0667 **m** 07778 738306 **e** matthew.bird2@virgin.net
Credits Anna Karenina (T); The Project (T); Boudica (T); Linda Green (T)

Blackowl Productions

Broadway Media Centre, 14 Broad Street, Nottingham NG1 3AL
t 01159 373889 **f** 01159 373889 **m** 07768 880685
e phil@blackowl.co.uk **w** www.blackowl.co.uk

Contact Phil Nodding, Managing Director; Chris Aldridge, Managing Director
Credits Golf Killer (S); Jim (S); Tales Of Sherwood (D)

Ello Bolz

International Creative Management Ltd, Oxford House, 76 Oxford Street, London W1D 1BS
t 020 7636 6565 **f** 020 7323 0101 **w** www.icmlondon.co.uk
Credits Undertaker's Paradise (F); Hot Gold (F); Best (F)

Simon Bosanquet

Peters Fraser & Dunlop, Drury House, 34-43 Russell Street, London WC2B 5HA
t 020 7344 1000 **f** 020 7836 9543
e postmaster@pfd.co.uk **w** www.pfd.co.uk

Ned Boulting

The Coachhouse, 112A Woodhill, London SE18 5JL
t 07956 137830 **e** ned.boulting@talk21.com
Credits Grandstand (T); Match Of The Day (T)

Ruth Boswel

129 Roseberry Road, London N10 2LD
t 020 8883 7330 **f** 020 8245 7054 **m** 07801 276973

Contact Ruth Boswell
Credits Gricers (F)

Pippa Brill

Peters Fraser & Dunlop, Drury House, 34-43 Russell Street, London WC2B 5HA
t 020 7344 1000 **f** 020 7836 9543
e postmaster@pfd.co.uk **w** www.pfd.co.uk

Dene Bristol

22 Canynge Square, Bristol BS8 3LA
t 0117 923 7925 **f** 0117 923 7925 **m** 07789 443118
e dene.bristol1@btinternet.com

British American Productions

t 020 7625 4514 **f** 020 7625 4514 **m** 07785 365294
Contact Paul Springer

Lucinda Broadbent

345 Renfrew Street, Glasgow G3 6UW
t 0141 332 2042 **f** 0141 332 2042 **m** 07790 036915
e lucinda@onetel.net.uk
Credits Two Day Coup (T); Macho (T); Lines In The Dust (T); Profile: Daniel Ortega (T)

Ewen Brown

Wizzo & Co, 35 Old Compton Street, London W1D 5JX
t 020 7437 2055 **f** 020 7437 2066
e wizzo@wizzoandco.co.uk **w** www.wizzoandco.co.uk

Andrew Buchanan

Free Hill House, Westbury-sub-Mendip, Wells BA5 1HR
t 01749 870404 **e** andrew.buchanan@lineone.net
Credits Toyota World Of Wildlife (T); The Great Elephant Rescue (T); Spinechillers (T); Built For The Kill (T)

Doug Bullock

128 The High, London SC016 1HA
t 0707 400 5000 **f** 020 8677 8486 **m** 07768 404380
e bullockdouglas@aol.com
Contact Doug Bullock, Producer

Chris Burt
Peters Fraser & Dunlop, Drury House, 34-43 Russell Street,
London WC2B 5HA
t 020 7344 1000 **f** 020 7836 9543
e postmaster@pfd.co.uk **w** www.pfd.co.uk

Josephine Calam
Peters Fraser & Dunlop, Drury House, 34-43 Russell Street,
London WC2B 5HA
t 020 7344 1000 **f** 020 7836 9543
e postmaster@pfd.co.uk **w** www.pfd.co.uk

Patricia Carr
Creative Media Management, Unit 3B, Walpole Court, Ealing
Studios, Ealing Green, London W5 5ED
t 020 8584 5363 **f** 020 8566 5554
e enquiries@creativemediamanagement.com
Credits Get Real (F); Hidalgo (F); The Mummy (F)

William P Cartlidge
Pinewood Studios, Iver Heath SL0 0NH
t 01753 651700 **f** 01753 630720 **m** 07836 518253
e billcartlidge@aol.com
Credits Incognito (F); The Scarlet Tunic (F); An Ideal Husband (F); Dinotopia (T)

Patrick Cassavetti
t 020 7289 8575 **f** 020 7289 8575 **m** 07785 326 167

Nicole Cauverien
Peters Fraser & Dunlop, Drury House, 34-43 Russell Street,
London WC2B 5HA
t 020 7344 1000 **f** 020 7836 9543
e postmaster@pfd.co.uk **w** www.pfd.co.uk

Simon Channing-Williams
9 Green Street, London W1D 4DQ
t 020 7734 7372 **f** 020 7287 5228
Credits Secrets And Lies (F); Topsy-Turvy (F); All Or Nothing (F)

Ted Childs
Peters Fraser & Dunlop, Drury House, 34-43 Russell Street,
London WC2B 5HA
t 020 7344 1000 **f** 020 7836 9543
e postmaster@pfd.co.uk **w** www.pfd.co.uk

Circle Multimedia Ltd
C/o 2nd Floor, The Quadrangle, 180 Wardour Street, London
W1F 8LB
t 01243 601482 **f** 01243 601482
m 07976 476692 **m** 0788 168857
e circlemultimedia@hotmail.com **w** www.circlemultimedia.com
Contact Anthony Straeger, Head of Production; Jenny Burgess, Executive
Producer; Janet Ives, Executive Producer
Credits Wire In The Blood (T)

Clarendon Film Productions Ltd
7 Trinity Crescent, London SW17 7AG
t 020 8488 9208 **f** 020 8488 3959
m 07802 252592 **e** 100532.362@compuserve.com
Contact Nigel Goldsack

Chris Clough
ICM, Oxford House, 76 Oxford Street, London W1D 1BS
t 020 7636 6565 **f** 020 7323 0101
Credits Born And Bred (T); Table Twelve (T); Without Motive (T); Black Cab (T)

Abigail Coult
2 Hillary House, Boyton Close, London N8 7BB

Christopher Courtney
Creative Media Management, Unit 3B, Walpole Court, Ealing
Studios, Ealing Green, London W5 5ED
t 020 8584 5363 **f** 020 8566 5554
e enquiries@creativemediamanagement.com
Credits Dies Irae (F); The War Bride (F)

David Courtney
London
m 07946 628355 **e** davidscube@hotmail.com
Credits National Geographic Channel Launch (T); Artsworld - Barker Loop (T);
Discovery People (D); The Clash - Westway To The World (D)

Paul Cowan
The Old Farmhouse, Weald, Bampton OX18 2HW
t 01993 850285 **f** 01993 851662 **m** 07836 788431
Credits The Krays (F); The Crying Game (F); Last Orders (F)

CTVC
Hillside, Merry Hill Road, Bushey WD23 1DR
t 020 8950 4426 **f** 020 8950 1437
e ctvc@ctvc.co.uk **w** www.ctvc.co.uk
Contact Nick Stuart, CEO; Ray Bruce, Head of Programmes
Credits Bethlehem Year Zero (T); Apostles; Dateline Jerusalem (T); Mystery Of
The Stroud (T)

D-L Productions
Quay House Cotehele, St Dominick, Saltash PL12 6TA
t 01579 351120 **m** 07885 813893 **e** rholmes@freenetname.co.uk
Contact Sue Dazziel, Managing Director; Rosemary Holmes, Director

Dashwood Productions (Assoc) Ltd
14 Victoria Grove, Bridport DT6 3AA
t 01308 459123 **f** 01308 459123
f 01308 420672 **m** 07970 981704
e angela@dashwoodprods.freeserve.co.uk **w** www.dashwood.tv
Contact Angela Howard-Bent, Director
Credits Rosamunde Pilcher (T); Family Affairs (T); The Scarlet Tunic (F)

Jane Dauncey
Peters Fraser & Dunlop, Drury House, 34-43 Russell Street,
London WC2B 5HA
t 020 7344 1000 **f** 020 7836 9543
e postmaster@pfd.co.uk **w** www.pfd.co.uk

Definition Films
194-196 Finchley Road, London NW3 6BX
t 020 7794 6500 **f** 020 7483 1300 **e** marshanlee@hotmail.com
Contact Marsha Nuriya Lee, Producer
Credits Secret Agent (F)

DMS Films Ltd
Argonaut House, 369 Burnt Oak Broadway, Edgware HA8 5X2
t 020 8951 6060 **f** 020 8951 6050 **e** danny@argonaut.com
Contact Daniel San, Producer
Credits Hard Edge; Understanding Jane

Carol Ann Docherty
Peters Fraser & Dunlop, Drury House, 34-43 Russell Street,
London WC2B 5HA
t 020 7344 1000 **f** 020 7836 9543
e postmaster@pfd.co.uk **w** www.pfd.co.uk

Eileen Docherty
Peters Fraser & Dunlop, Drury House, 34-43 Russell Street,
London WC2B 5HA
t 020 7344 1000 **f** 020 7836 9543
e postmaster@pfd.co.uk **w** www.pfd.co.uk

Mike Dormer
London Management & Representation, 2-4 Noel Street,
London W1F 8GB
t 020 7287 9000 **f** 020 7287 3236

ECM
9b Ladbroke Grove, Holland Park, London W11 3BD
t 020 7727 5752 **f** 020 7727 6803
e ecmproductions@ecm-group.co.uk
w www.ecminternational.com
Contact Chris Bonney, Chief Operating Officer; Paul Fraser, Head of
International Production; Barnaby Shingleton, Head of Interactive Television
Credits Double Cross (T); Popstars (T); Without Prejudice (T); Alternative Love (T)

Dave Edwards
48 Adelaide Road, Ealing, London W13 9EB
t 020 8567 3632 **f** 020 8933 5970 **m** 07785 394769
e daveedwards25@aol.com
Credits State Of Mind (T); Have Your Cake And Eat It (T); Love Or Money (T); Bait (T)

Eh! Communications Ltd
67 Northways, College Crescent, London NW3 5DP
t 020 7722 9731 **m** 07903 459955
e debradavis@eh-communications.co.uk
Contact Debra Davis, Managing Director; Alan Grindley, Director
Credits Canadian Crossing (T); Don't Leave the Seat Up (T); Mr Brian (T)

Charles Elton
Peters Fraser & Dunlop, Drury House, 34-43 Russell Street,
London WC2B 5HA
t 020 7344 1000 **f** 020 7836 9543
e postmaster@pfd.co.uk **w** www.pfd.co.uk

Aled Evans
London Management & Representation, 2-4 Noel Street,
London W1F 8GB
t 020 7287 9000 **f** 020 7287 3236

Ohna Falby
Wizzo & Co, 35 Old Compton Street, London W1D 5JX
t 020 7437 2055 **f** 020 7437 2066
e wizzo@wizzoandco.co.uk **w** www.wizzoandco.co.uk

Rosalind Farrimond
7 Meadow Lane, Southrepps, Norwich NR11 8NX
t 01263 833933 **f** 01263 833932 **m** 07774 712937
e rosalind.farrimond@btopenworld.com

Daniel Figuero
Pinewood Studios, Pinewood Road, Iver Heath SL0 0NH
t 01753 657104 **f** 01753 655025
e daniel@figuero.freeserve.co.uk
Credits The Scarlet Tunic (F); An Ideal Husband (F); The Bunker (F)

Helen Flint
Creative Media Management, Unit 3B, Walpole Court, Ealing
Studios, Ealing Green, London W5 5ED
t 020 8584 5363 **f** 020 8566 5554
e enquiries@creativemediamanagement.com
Credits Do Or Die (T); Bodily Harm (T); Second Generation (F)

Mary Fourt
75 Engadine Street, London SW18 5BZ
t 020 8870 6369 **f** 020 8488 8479
Credits Student Choice (E); Student Essentials (E)

Frigid Films Ltd
Host 21, Savile Mount, Leeds LS7 3HZ
t 01132 007022 **f** 01132 007021 **e** frigid@clara.net
Contact Bekki Rogers, Producer/Company Director
Credits Length (A); Red Wardrobe (S); Eulogy (S); Flood (S)

G Films
Pinewood Studios, Pinewood Road, Iver Heath SL0 0NH
t 01753 656799 **f** 01753 656799 **m** 07885 448067
e info@gfilms.co.uk **w** www.gfilms.co.uk
Contact Ian Garland, Producer

Sophie Gardiner
Peters Fraser & Dunlop, Drury House, 34-43 Russell Street,
London WC2B 5HA
t 020 7344 1000 **f** 020 7836 9543
e postmaster@pfd.co.uk **w** www.pfd.co.uk

Julie Gardner
International Creative Management Ltd, Oxford House,
76 Oxford Street, London W1D 1BS
t 020 7636 6565 **f** 020 7323 0101 **w** www.icmlondon.co.uk

Mervyn Gill-Dougherty
4 Leghorn Road, London NW10 4PH
t 020 7684 1661 **f** 020 7684 6111 **m** 07778 208 999
e mervyn@ideallondon.com
Credits Peak Practice (T); Holby City I (T); Cruel Train (F)

Nick Gillott
Creative Media Management, Unit 3B, Walpole Court, Ealing
Studios, Ealing Green, London W5 5ED
t 020 8584 5363 **f** 020 8566 5554
e enquiries@creativemediamanagement.com
Credits Event Horizon (F); Conspiracy: The Meeting At Wawsee (F);
The Swedish Job (F)

GJ Productions Ltd
7 Cornwall Crescent, Notting Hill Gate, London W11 1PH
t 020 7792 4321 **f** 020 7229 3623 **e** andy@filmx.f9.co.uk
Contact Charles Thompson, Producer; Renata Bovara, Script Advisor; Andy
Isaac, Producer

Nigel Goldsack
7 Trinity Crescent, London SW17 7AG
t 020 8488 9208 **f** 020 8488 3959 **m** 07802 252592
e nrgmmi@aol.com
Credits A Midsummer Night's Dream (F); The World Is Not Enough (F); The
Affair Of The Necklace (F); Ripley's Game (F)

Bridget Goodman
4 Edinburgh Road, London W7 3JY
t 07973 306357 **e** bridget.goodman@bgoodman.fsbusiness.co.uk
Agent Jessica Carney Associates, Suite 90-92 Kent House,
87 Regent Street, London W1B 4EH
t 020 7434 4143 **f** 020 7434 4173 **e** info@jcarneyassociates.co.uk
Credits The Basil Brush Show (T); EastEnders (T)

Helen Gordon-Smith
2 Varsity Row, Mortlake, London SW14 7SA
m 07887 607310 **e** contacthgs@aol.com
Credits Blind Date (T); This Is Your Life (T)

Yvon Grace
Pauline Asper Management, Jacobs Cottage, Reservoir Lane,
Sedlescombe TN33 0PJ
t 01424 870412 **f** 01424 870412 **e** pauline.asper@virgin.net

Conrad Green
Peters Fraser & Dunlop, Drury House, 34-43 Russell Street,
London WC2B 5HA
t 020 7344 1000 **f** 020 7836 9543
e postmaster@pfd.co.uk **w** www.pfd.co.uk

Virginia Green
10 Windamere Court, 47 St Johns Road, Woking GU21 1RA
t 01483 725983 **f** 01483 725983 **m** 07831 196822
e virginia_a0@ntlworld.com

Juliet Grimm
11 Russell Close, Chiswick, London W4 2NY
t 020 8995 1598 **f** 020 8747 8399 **m** 07798 604359
e julietgrimm@onetel.net.uk

Jasen Grindrod
London
t 020 7503 2571 **f** 020 7503 2571 **m** 07789 911002
e jasengrindrod@hotmail.com

Tim Hampton
International Creative Management Ltd, Oxford House,
76 Oxford Street, London W1D 1BS
t 020 7636 6565 **f** 020 7323 0101 **w** www.icmlondon.co.uk

Mary Hanover
Warren Farm, Wimbledon Common, London SW19 4UR
t 020 8947 8955 **m** 07957 358 883 **e** mhanover@aol.com
Credits The Real Sex And The City; Manhattan On The Beach

Sara Harkins
59 Holland Street, Glasgow G2 4NJ
t 0141 287 9514 **f** 0141 287 9515 **m** 07990 686930
e harkinsbarr@btopenworld.com

Pippa Harris
Peters Fraser & Dunlop, Drury House, 34-43 Russell Street, London WC2B 5HA
t 020 7344 1000 **f** 020 7836 9543
postmaster@pfd.co.uk **w** www.pfd.co.uk

Paul Harrison
Peters Fraser & Dunlop, Drury House, 34-43 Russell Street, London WC2B 5HA
t 020 7344 1000 **f** 020 7836 9543
e postmaster@pfd.co.uk **w** www.pfd.co.uk

Carrie Hart
67 The Chase, London SW4 0NP
t 020 7720 9091 **m** 07973 123482 **e** carriehart@easynet.co.uk
Agent The Production Switchboard, Northdown, Down Lane, Compton GU3 1DN
t 01483 812011 **f** 01483 812027
e aly@productionswitch.freeserve.co.uk
Credits Tele 2 (C); Ford (C); Cadbury's (C)

Patricia Harvey
2 Britannia Quay, River Road, Little Hampton BN17 5DB
t 01903 725471 **f** 01903 718249
e pat.harvey@talk21.com **w** www.patframes.co.uk

David Higginson
Creative Media Management, Unit 3B, Walpole Court, Ealing Studios, Ealing Green, London W5 5ED
t 020 8584 5363 **f** 020 8566 5554
e enquiries@creativemediamanagement.com
Credits Lava (F); Tom And Thomas (F); The Trench (F)

Claire Hobbs
33 Viceroy Close, Edgbaston, Birmingham B5 7US
t 0121 440 7311 **m** 07710 317097
e chobbs@dircon.co.uk **w** www.hobbs-schoon.co.uk
Credits The House That Mackintosh Built (D); Hi-Tech Vets (D); Going For A Song (T); Good Food Live (T)

Trevor Hopkins
Peters Fraser & Dunlop, Drury House, 34-43 Russell Street, London WC2B 5HA
t 020 7344 1000 **f** 020 7836 9543
e postmaster@pfd.co.uk **w** www.pfd.co.uk

Michael Houldey
14 Lowther Road, London SW13 9ND
e michaelh@uniprod.demon.co.uk
Credits Zoo (T); Hope For Helen (T); Airport (D)

Mike Hudson
108 Cowper Road, Hanwell, London W7 1EJ
t 020 8579 6749 **f** 020 8579 6749 **m** 07973 505960
e mike.hudson@msn.com
Credits Family Affairs (T); EastEnders (T)

Mark Huffam
International Creative Management Ltd, Oxford House, 76 Oxford Street, London W1D 1BS
t 020 7636 6565 **f** 020 7323 0101 **w** www.icmlondon.co.uk
Credits Captain Corelli's Mandolin (F); The Hours (F); Johnny English (F)

Imaginary Films
8 Cottons Garden, London E2 8DN
t 020 7613 5882 **w** www.filminvestment.co.uk/imagfilm/
Contact Ray Brady; Debra Brady; Chris Sutherland
Credits Team One (F); Day Of The Sirens (F); Kiss Kiss Bang Bang (F); Boy Meets Girl (F)

International Movie Management
Shepperton Studios, Shepperton TW17 0GD
t 01932 592061 **f** 01932 569527 **w** www.moviemgt.com
Contact Fred Muller, Producer; Nigel Wooll, Producer; Vicki Manning, Executive
Credits White Squall (F); GI Jane (F); Timeline (F)

Ira Trattner Productions
3rd Floor, 13 Campten Street, London W8 7EP
t 020 7727 0317 **f** 020 7727 0317 **m** 07813 800118
e itrattner@aol.com
Credits Sister, Sister (F); Off The Mark aka Crazy Legs (F); Two Men Went To War (F)

Jamie Wadhawan Associates
4 Lansdowne Court, 42 Lansdowne Crescent, London W11 2NW
t 020 7727 4194 **e** wadhawan@boltblue.com
Credits Man With A Hat (D); All I Know (D); Cain's Film (D); Sheep (F)

Peter Jaques
1 Buxton Road, London SW14 8SY
t 020 8392 9856 **f** 020 8392 9856 **m** 07860 511529
e Jaques@blueyonder.co.uk
Credits Anna And The King (F); Secret Society (F); Al's Lads (F)

Peter R Jones
34 Halesworth Road, London SE13 7TN
t 020 8692 8441 **e** picplan@talk21.com

Nell Jordan
Wizzo & Co, 35 Old Compton Street, London W1D 5JX
t 020 7437 2055 **f** 020 7437 2066
e wizzo@wizzoandco.co.uk **w** www.wizzoandco.co.uk

Mia Jupp
Linda Seifert Management, 91 Berwick Street, London W1F 0NE
t 020 7292 7390 **f** 020 7292 7391
e contact@lindaseifert.com **w** www.lindaseifert.com

Anna Kalnars
The Old Bakehouse, Buckland Court, Goveton, Kingsbridge TQ7 2DG
t 01548 856491 **f** 01548 856491 **m** 07967 662475
e anna-kalnars@beeb.net
Credits The Story Of Tracy Beaker: Series II (T); Silent Witness (T); Lenny Blue (T)

Laura Kanerick
Wizzo & Co, 35 Old Compton Street, London W1D 5JX
t 020 7437 2055 **f** 020 7437 2066
e wizzo@wizzoandco.co.uk **w** www.wizzoandco.co.uk

Deirdre Keir
t 020 8942 1002 **f** 020 8942 1002 **m** 07860 218487
e deirdrekeir@hotmail.com

Michael Kelk
3 Duxford Road, Whittlesford CB2 4NQ
t 01223 839248 **m** 07802 635 241 **e** michael.kelk@btinternet.com

Ruth Kenley-Letts
Peters Fraser & Dunlop, Drury House, 34-43 Russell Street, London WC2B 5HA
t 020 7344 1000 **f** 020 7836 9543
e postmaster@pfd.co.uk **w** www.pfd.co.uk

Keystone (Ealing) Productions Ltd
PO Box 10653, Ealing, London W5 4WR
t 020 8993 7441 **f** 020 8992 9993
e keystoneprod@dorm.co.uk **w** www.thedormgroup.com

Paul Knight
Peters Fraser & Dunlop, Drury House, 34-43 Russell Street, London WC2B 5HA
t 020 7344 1000 **f** 020 7836 9543
e postmaster@pfd.co.uk **w** www.pfd.co.uk

Matthew Kuipers
The Walled Garden, Hambleden RG9 6RJ
t 01491 571547 **m** 07768 825400
e matthew@kuipers.demon.co.uk
Credits Strictly Sinatra (F); Headless (T); Happy Together (T); The Great Ceili War (F)

Diana Kyle
London Management & Representation, 2-4 Noel Street, London W1F 8GB
t 020 7287 9000 **f** 020 7287 3236
Credits EastEnders (T); Grange Hill (T); Pig Heart Boy (T); Silent Witness (T)

L'Ocean Creative Projects
5 Darling Road, London SE4 1YQ
t 020 8692 0145 **f** 020 8692 0145 **m** 07958 317360
e roj@l-ocean.org **w** www.l-ocean.org
Contact Roger Elsgood, Creative Producer
Credits Shooting Stars (T); Fugitive Pieces; To the Wedding

Ingrid Lewis
70 Greyhound Road, London N17 6XW
t 020 8493 0405 **f** 020 8493 0405 **m** 07984 339444
Credits Siren Splits (T); The Scorman Trust (W)

The Light Club
2nd Floor, Enterprise House, 59-65 Upper Ground, London SE1 9PQ
t 020 7593 0440 **e** info@thelightclub.fsnet.co.uk
Contact Elinor Day, Producer; Shaun Dunn, Producer

John Lloyd
London Management & Representation, 2-4 Noel Street, London W1F 8GB
t 020 7287 9000 **f** 020 7287 3236
Credits Spitting Image (T); Not The Nine O'Clock News (T); Blackadder (T)

Philip Lloyd
103 Devonshire Road, Cambridge CB1 2AG
t 01223 132182 **m** 07813 132182 **e** philip.lloyd1@ntlworld.com
Credits The Tube (T); Collapsed (S); Ten Bulls (S)

Look-Hear
Westland Studios, PO Box 111, Watford WD17 1PQ
t 01923 225683 **f** 0870 705 3006
e jon@look-hear.com **w** www.look-hear.com
Contact Jon Danzig, Writer / Director

Paul Lowin
Creative Media Management, Unit 3B, Walpole Court, Ealing Studios, Ealing Green, London W5 5ED
t 020 8584 5363 **f** 020 8566 5554
e enquiries@creativemediamanagement.com
Credits Lion In Winter (F); In The Beginning (F); Hans Christian Anderson (F)

Lars Macfarlane
International Creative Management Ltd, Oxford House, 76 Oxford Street, London W1D 1BS
t 020 7636 6565 **f** 020 7323 0101 **w** www.icmlondon.co.uk
Credits Second Sight (T); Too Good To Be True (T); Second Nature (T)

Ian Madden
t 0141 946 0768 **f** 0141 945 5934 **m** 07831 851290
e ian.madden@btclick.com
Credits Storm Damage (T); Murder Rooms (T); Taggart (T)

John Mair
1 Oxfold Court, Northampton Road, Weston-on-the-Creek OX25 3QZ
t 01869 378156 **m** 07785 378156 **e** johnmair100@hotmail.com
Credits Harland And Wolff - A Day And A Night To Remember (T); Business Day (T); Crime Cracking Day (T)

Mallemaroking Productions
41 Caddington Road, London NW2 1RP
t 020 8830 5391 **f** 020 8450 1623 **e** mallema@dial.pipex.com
Contact Simon Kennedy, Producer; Sandra Rock, Production Manager
Credits Charging Into History (T); Cambridge Tradition (I); A Little Bit of Beatlemania (T)

Nick Martin
London Management & Representation, 2-4 Noel Street, London W1F 8GB
t 020 7287 9000 **f** 020 7287 3236
Credits Have I Got News For You? (T)

Susan Mather
19 Cheyne Walk, Chesham HP5 1AY
t 01494 785910 **f** 01494 785910 **m** 07976 733957
e sumather@waitrose.com

Dan Mazer
Peters Fraser & Dunlop, Drury House, 34-43 Russell Street, London WC2B 5HA
t 020 7344 1000 **f** 020 7836 9543
e postmaster@pfd.co.uk **w** www.pfd.co.uk

Janet McBride
5 Buchanan Gardens, London NW10 5AD
m 07973 255473 **e** jmcbride@freeuk.com
Credits TV's Naughtiest Blunders (T); Fantasy World Cup Live 1998 (T); Kirsty's Home Videos (T)

Nigel McCrery
Peters Fraser & Dunlop, Drury House, 34-43 Russell Street, London WC2B 5HA
t 020 7344 1000 **f** 020 7836 9543
e postmaster@pfd.co.uk **w** www.pfd.co.uk

Callum McDougall
International Creative Management Ltd, Oxford House, 76 Oxford Street, London W1D 1BS
t 020 7636 6565 **f** 020 7323 0101 **w** www.icmlondon.co.uk
Credits Harry Potter And The Prisoner Of Azkaban (F); The Beach (F); Die Another Day (F)

McKinnon Films
205 Royal College Street, London NW1 0SG
t 020 7267 5530 **f** 020 7267 4322
e mckinnonfilms@dial.pipex.com **w** www.mckinnonfilms.com
Contact Michael McKinnon, MD-Producer

John Mead
Gems, The Media House, 87 Glebe Street, Penarth CF64 1EF
t 029 2071 0770 **f** 029 2071 0771
e gems@gems-agency.co.uk **w** www.gems-agency.co.uk
Credits Caribbean Castaway (T); Highway (T); Get Fresh (T); The Last Long Haul (T)

Media Legal
West End House, 83 Clarendon Road, Sevenoaks TN13 1ET
t 01732 460592
Contact John Wheller, Director

Julian Meers
Linda Seifert Management, 91 Berwick Street, London W1F 0NE
t 020 7292 7390 **f** 020 7292 7391
e contact@lindaseifert.com **w** www.lindaseifert.com

Judith Millar
79 Harcourt Terrace, London SW10 9JP
t 020 7370 1830 **f** 020 7370 1830
Contact Judith Millar, Producer

Simon Moorhead
33 Porthall Place, Brighton BN1 5PN
t 01273 503074 **m** 07802 268953
Credits Haunted Halloween Live (T); London Boat Show (T); Neon (S); Ghostwatch Live (T)

Mosaic Films

8-12 Broadwick Street, London W1F 8HW
t 020 7437 6514 **f** 020 7494 0595
e info@mosaicfilms.com **w** www.mosaic.films.com
Contact Deborah Weavers, Production Manager; Colin Luke, Managing Director
Credits London - Pet Shop Boys (M); Tory Party Political Broadcast (I); Pakistan Daily (D); The Tube (D)

Frederick Muller

Flat2, 27 Lexham Gardens, London W8 5JJ
t 020 7244 7184 **t** +39 333 243 7297 **m** 07785 226252
e mullerfecon@compuserve.com
Credits Dirty Dozen II (T); James Clavell's Noble House (T); Fatherland (F); Tea With Mussolini (F)

Multi Media Arts (MMA) Ltd

Mauldeth House, Well Lawe, Manchester M21 7RL
t 0161 374 5566 **f** 0161 374 5535 **m** 07958 351662
e info@mmarts.com **w** www.mmarts.com
Contact Mike Spencer, MD; Mark Gorton, Creative Director
Credits Wild Shot (T); The Machine (T); Mad About Motors (T); Supporting X Series I & II (T)

Jimmy Mulville

London Management & Representation, 2-4 Noel Street, London W1F 8GB
t 020 7287 9000 **f** 020 7287 3236

Stuart Murphy

London Management & Representation, 2-4 Noel Street, London W1F 8GB
t 020 7287 9000 **f** 020 7287 3236

Christopher Neame

Elephant House, Chilham, Canterbury CT4 8DE
t 01227 732321 **t** 01227 7 **f** 01227 731641 **m** 07973 111360
e cn@goodboypix.go-plus.net
Contact Christopher Neame
Credits Bellman And True (F); Foreign Body (F); Monsignor Quixote (T); Feast of July (F)

Peter Norris

122 Worple Road, Isleworth TW7 7HU
t 020 8892 6882 **f** 020 8892 6882 **m** 07711 034707
e peternorris4@hotmail.com
Credits Between The Lines (T); Young Person's Guide To Becoming A Rock Star (T); My Uncle Silas (T)

Peter Norris

Peters Fraser & Dunlop, Drury House, 34-43 Russell Street, London WC2B 5HA
t 020 7344 1000 **f** 020 7836 9543
e postmaster@pfd.co.uk **w** www.pfd.co.uk

Nugus/Martin Productions Ltd

23 Golden Square, London W1F 9JP
t 020 7734 5428 **f** 020 7734 5420
e pn@nugusmartin-1.demon.co.uk **w** www.nugusmartin.com
Contact Philip Nugus, Managing Director

Pat O'Mahony

214 Stockwell Avenue, London SW9 9TB
t 020 7787 8804 **m** 07771 788680
e pat.omahony@ireland.com
Credits Hellraisers' Handbook (T); The Learning Zone (T); The Panel (T); Second Generation (D)

Pan-European Film & TV Productions

110 Trafalgar Road, Portslade BN41 1GS
t 01273 277333 **f** 01273 705451
e filmangels@freenetname.co.uk **w** www.filmangel.co.uk
Contact Penelope Joshi, Head of Legal & Copyright Sect; Karen King, Production Assistant Coordinator; Count De Straet Von Kollman KT, Producer; John Eagle, Assistant Producer; Countess Von Kollman, Producer Co-Ordinator; Petra Ginman, Production Head
Credits Lilith Rising (D); Iceni! (D); Boadicea - Queen of Death (F); Boudicca - A Celtic Tragedy (T)

Pratibha Parmar

Peters Fraser & Dunlop, Drury House, 34-43 Russell Street, London WC2B 5HA
t 020 7344 1000 **f** 020 7836 9543
e postmaster@pfd.co.uk **w** www.pfd.co.uk

Simon Passmore

The Coach House, 20A Park Road, Teddington TW11 0AP
t 020 8943 4697 **f** 020 8943 4901 **e** tylo@ukonline.co.uk
Credits An Evil Streak (T); Forgive And Forget (T); Pretending To Be Judith (T); Foyle's War (T)

Dan Paterson

Peters Fraser & Dunlop, Drury House, 34-43 Russell Street, London WC2B 5HA
t 020 7344 1000 **f** 020 7836 9543
e postmaster@pfd.co.uk **w** www.pfd.co.uk

Jacinta Peel

Peters Fraser & Dunlop, Drury House, 34-43 Russell Street, London WC2B 5HA
t 020 7344 1000 **f** 020 7836 9543
e postmaster@pfd.co.uk **w** www.pfd.co.uk

Nikki Penny

ADS, Shepperton Studios, Studios Road, Shepperton TW17 0QD
t 01932 592303 **f** 01932 592492 **e** ads@concept2100.co.uk
Credits Harry Potter And The Chamber Of Secrets (F); Gladiator (F); Dinotopia (F)

Geoffrey Perkins

London Management & Representation, 2-4 Noel Street, London W1F 8GB
t 020 7287 9000 **f** 020 7287 3236
Credits Ben Elton - The Man From Auntie (T); Game On (T); Spitting Image (T)

Therese Pickard

Debnershe, The Street, Shalford GU4 8BT
t 01483 539343 **f** 01483 539343 **e** therese.pickard@cs.com

Polarize Films

92 Wormholt Road, London W12 0LP
t 020 8749 3094 **f** 020 8749 3094 **m** 07952 249780
e tancredi@polarizefilms.co.uk
Contact Tancredi Medda, Director/Producer
Credits Sofa; Charlie (F); Disappearing World

Helena Pope

Peters Fraser & Dunlop, Drury House, 34-43 Russell Street, London WC2B 5HA
t 020 7344 1000 **f** 020 7836 9543
e postmaster@pfd.co.uk **w** www.pfd.co.uk

Jessica Pope

Peters Fraser & Dunlop, Drury House, 34-43 Russell Street, London WC2B 5HA
t 020 7344 1000 **f** 020 7836 9543
e postmaster@pfd.co.uk **w** www.pfd.co.uk

Line Postmyr

Wizzo & Co, 35 Old Compton Street, London W1D 5JX
t 020 7437 2055 **f** 020 7437 2066
e wizzo@wizzoandco.co.uk **w** www.wizzoandco.co.uk

Presentable Ltd

Ty Oldfield, Llandaff, Cardiff CF5 2PU
t 029 2057 5729 **f** 029 2057 5605
e all@presentable.co.uk **w** www.presentable.co.uk
Contact Chris Stuart, Creative Director; Rhiannon Murphy, Production Manager; Sian Williams, Multi-Camera Director; Chris Cadenne, Production Manager/PA; Megan Stuart, Managing Director
Credits Large (T); Mike Doyle (T); Late Night Poker (T)

Principal Media Group

Picture House, 65 Hopton Street, London SE1 9LR
t 020 7928 9287 **f** 020 7928 9886
e group@principalmedia.com **w** www.principalmedia.com
Contact Sarah Claxton, Head of Production
Credits Bugs! (F); Gentlemen's Relish (T); Hardcore (D)

Production Verité

22 Arlington Lodge, Baytree Lodge, London SW2 1RE
t 020 7274 1498 **f** 020 7274 1498 **m** 07957 149459
w www.momedia.fsnet.uk
Contact Mohamed Bouhda, Director
Credits Canal 5; North And South; Angola

Prussia Lane Productions Ltd

1A Upper Brockley Road, Brockley, London SE4 1SY
t 020 8692 6618 **m** 07976 165111
e mail@prussialane.freeserve.co.uk **w** www.prussialane.com
Credits Jamaica (S); Love is Not Enough (F); The Grimes (F);
Diary Of A Somebody (F)

Ron Purdie

Marsh Cottage, 135 The Marsh, Bath Road, Hungerford RG17 0SN
t 01488 682017 **f** 01488 682017 **m** 07836 287669
e ron.purdie@virgin.net
Agent Creative Media Management, Unit 3B, Walpole Court,
Ealing Studios, Ealing Green, London W5 5ED
t 020 8584 5363 **f** 020 8566 5554
e enquiries@creativemediamanagement.com
Credits Circus (S); The Stretch (F); The Bombmaker (F)

Paulette Randall

Pauline Asper Management, Jacobs Cottage, Reservoir Lane,
Sedlescombe TN33 0PJ
t 01424 870412 **f** 01424 870412 **e** pauline.asper@virgin.net

Rodney Read

45 Richmond Road, Twickenham TW1 3AW
t 020 8891 2875 **f** 020 8744 9603 **m** 07956 321 550
e rodney_read@hotmail.com

Mark Redhead

International Creative Management Ltd, Oxford House,
76 Oxford Street, London W1D 1BS
t 020 7636 6565 **f** 020 7323 0101 **w** www.icmlondon.co.uk

Storr Redman

Wizzo & Co, 35 Old Compton Street, London W1D 5JX
t 020 7437 2055 **f** 020 7437 2066
e wizzo@wizzoandco.co.uk **w** www.wizzoandco.co.uk

Redweather Productions

Easton Business Centre, Felix Road, Bristol BS5 0HE
t 0117 941 5854 **f** 0117 941 5851 **e**
production@redweather.co.uk
Contact Steve Spencer, Head of Production; Jonny Crew, Producer
Credits Smartronics (C)

Rewynd Productions

Ash Cottage, Church Street, Uplyme, Lyme Regis DT7 3TS
t 01297 445226 **f** 01297 444920 **m** 07771 617837
e rwyndham@aol.com
Credits ARD/SWR (T); Euronews (T); Carlton Westcountry (T)

Richmond Films & Television

PO Box 33154, London NW3 4LT
t 020 7722 6464 **f** 020 7722 6232 **e** mail@richmondfilms.com
Contact Sandra Hastie, Chief Executive/Producer
Credits The Office (T); Wavelength (T); The Lodge (T); Press Gang (T)

Jamie Riy

Linda Seifert Management, 91 Berwick Street, London W1F 0NE
t 020 7292 7390 **f** 020 7292 7391
e contact@lindaseifert.com **w** www.lindaseifert.com

Selwyn Roberts

Creative Media Management, Unit 3B, Walpole Court, Ealing
Studios, Ealing Green, London W5 5ED
t 020 8584 5363 **f** 020 8566 5554
e enquiries@creativemediamanagement.com
Credits Longitude (F); Pearl Harbour (F); Shackleton (F)

David & Kathy Rose

159 Earlsfield Road, London SW18 3DD
t 020 8874 0744 **f** 020 8874 9136 **m** 07885 227501
e info@theroses.co.uk **w** www.theroses.co.uk

Roxaboxen

19 Victoria Square, Dalcony, Clifton, Bristol BS8 4ES
t 0117 923 9111 **m** 07876 355430 **e** roxaboxen48@hotmail.com
Contact Diane Batson-Smith, President; Steve Abbot, Prominent Pictures -
President; David Nicolas, CineRoma - President / Producer; Susan Osman, Rich
Wins Director / Producer; Rowena Goldman, Producer / Development
Credits Panama (F); Andersonville (F); Good Burger (F); Rich Wins (F)

Charles Salmon

International Creative Management Ltd, Oxford House,
76 Oxford Street, London W1D 1BS
t 020 7636 6565 **f** 020 7323 0101 **w** www.icmlondon.co.uk
Credits Rhodes (T); Tom's Midnight Garden (T); Stranded (T)

Robbie Sandison

21 West End Park Street, Glasgow G3 6LH
t 0141 332 7721 **f** 0709 223 4201 **m** 07767 464 496
e robbie.sandison@virgin.net

Sarah Lawrence Productions

35 Heriot Row, Edinburgh EH3 6ES
t 0131 467 2397 **m** 07050 354090
e s.lawrence@blueyonder.co.uk
Credits New Year Texas Live Concert (T); Elaine C Smith (T); Perrier Awards Live (T)

Bill Shapter

11 Landford Road, Putney, London SW15 1AQ
t 020 8788 6244 **f** 020 8780 9323

Tom Sherry

Peters Fraser & Dunlop, Drury House, 34-43 Russell Street,
London WC2B 5HA
t 020 7344 1000 **f** 020 7836 9543
e postmaster@pfd.co.uk **w** www.pfd.co.uk

Debbie Shewell

Peters Fraser & Dunlop, Drury House, 34-43 Russell Street,
London WC2B 5HA
t 020 7344 1000 **f** 020 7836 9543
e postmaster@pfd.co.uk **w** www.pfd.co.uk

Mark Shivas

Peters Fraser & Dunlop, Drury House, 34-43 Russell Street,
London WC2B 5HA
t 020 7344 1000 **f** 020 7836 9543
e postmaster@pfd.co.uk **w** www.pfd.co.uk

Ruki Sidhwa

38a Cumberland Road, Hanwell, London W7 2EB
t 020 8579 5800 **m** 07778 873702 **e** rukisidhwa@lineone.net
Credits Animal Hospital (T); Crimewatch (T); Pet Rescue (T); Body Beautiful (T)

Amanda Silvester

Peters Fraser & Dunlop, Drury House, 34-43 Russell Street,
London WC2B 5HA
t 020 7344 1000 **f** 020 7836 9543
e postmaster@pfd.co.uk **w** www.pfd.co.uk

Skyline Films

PO Box 8210, London W4 1WH
t 020 8354 2219 **m** 07836 275584 **e** skylinefilms@aol.com
Contact Steve Clark-Hall, Producer; Mairi Bett, Producer
Credits Ali G In da House (F); Still Crazy (F); Saving Grace (F); The Gathering (F)

Smith & Watson Productions

The Gothic House, Fore Street, Totnes TQ9 5EH
t 01803 863033 **f** 01803 864219
e nick@smithandwatson.com **w** www.smithandwatson.com
Contact Nick Smith, Producer/Director; Chris Watson, Producer/Director; Cathy Waite, producer/Director

Joy Spink

International Creative Management Ltd, Oxford House, 76 Oxford Street, London W1D 1BS
t 020 7636 6565 **f** 020 7323 0101 **w** www.icmlondon.co.uk
Credits Final Demand (T); Waking The Dead (T); Auf Wiedersehen, Pet (T)

Standfast Films

The Studio, 14 College Road, Bromley BR1 3NS
t 020 8466 5580 **f** 020 8313 0443
Contact Anthony van der Elst, Producer

Steve Hoy Associates

49A Newport Road, Woburn Sands, Milton Keynes MK17 8UQ
t 01908 281135 **f** 01908 281135 **m** 07899 055702
e mail@stevehoy.com **w** www.stevehoy.com

William G Stewart

London Management & Representation, 2-4 Noel Street, London W1F 8GB
t 020 7287 9000 **f** 020 7287 3236
Credits Fifteen To One (T)

Stuff TV

132 Portland Road, Hove BN3 5QL
t 01273 775550 **m** 07702 025453
e mail@stufftv.com **w** www.stufftv.com
Contact Dave Thomas, Director; Rob Fletcher, Director

Saskia Sutton

12 Lansdowne Circus, Leamington Spa CV32 4SW
t 01926 335375
Credits Hotel Paradise (S); Movie Legends In Conversation (T)

Colin Swash

London Management & Representation, 2-4 Noel Street, London W1F 8GB
t 020 7287 9000 **f** 020 7287 3236
Credits Have I Got News For You? (T)

Elaine Taylor

Appartment 2, 5 Bewley Street, London SW19 1XF
t 020 8543 0284 **f** 020 8542 9798 **m** 07810 344644
e elainetaylor@onetel.net

Sue Taylor

36 Waddling Lane, Wheathampstead AL4 8RD
t 01582 831285 **m** 07836 223389
e taylorvision@compuserve.com
Credits Mopatop's Shop (T); Construction Site (T); The Hoobs (T)

Julian GA Thomas

Fordybrook House, Fordy Lane, East Hendred, Wantage OX12 8JU
f 01235 833439 **m** 07787 535678 **e** jgathomas@hotmail.com
Credits Howard Hall - Filming The Impossible (D); Barracuda - Deadly Shoals (D); Hidden Worlds (D); Moon Power (D)

Keith Thompson

International Creative Management Ltd, Oxford House, 76 Oxford Street, London W1D 1BS
t 020 7636 6565 **f** 020 7323 0101 **w** www.icmlondon.co.uk
Credits Bobbie's Girl (T); Oliver Twist (T); The Cry (T)

Tic & Tin Productions

PO Box 10653, Ealing, London W5 4WR
t 020 8993 7441 **f** 020 8992 9993
e ticandtin@dorm.co.uk **w** www.ticandtin.com

Annie Tricklebank

Peters Fraser & Dunlop, Drury House, 34-43 Russell Street, London WC2B 5HA
t 020 7344 1000 **f** 020 7836 9543
e postmaster@pfd.co.uk **w** www.pfd.co.uk

True TV & Film

2 Whitehill Street, Glasgow G31 2LJ
t 0141 554 1196 **f** 0141 554 1196 **m** 07714 986444
e b@truetvandfilm.co.uk
Credits Eastern Fling (T); Alexi Sayle's Dancing Tips (T)

Colin Tucker

Peters Fraser & Dunlop, Drury House, 34-43 Russell Street, London WC2B 5HA
t 020 7344 1000 **f** 020 7836 9543
e postmaster@pfd.co.uk **w** www.pfd.co.uk

Paul Tucker

The Mount, Mount Road, Chobham GU24 8AW
t 01276 858347 **m** 07802 849495 **e** marquisfilms@dial.pipex.com
Credits Veronica Gevrin (F); An Ideal Husband (F); Felicia's Journey (F); Nicholas Nickleby (T)

David Tyler

London Management & Representation, 2-4 Noel Street, London W1F 8GB
t 020 7287 9000 **f** 020 7287 3236
Credits Dinnerladies (T); TLC (T)

Zoe Uffindell

3 Plymouth Drive, Sevenoaks TN13 3RP
t 01732 456370 **f** 01732 456370 **m** 07831 545548
e zoe@panicproductions.co.uk
Credits Three Identites - One Life (I); The Sport Of Dance (T)

Ugly Duckling Films Ltd

1A Hollywood Road, London SW10 9HS
t 020 7376 7730 **f** 020 7376 7806 **m** 07802 774100
e lbausager@aol.com **w** www.uglyducklingfilms.com
Contact Winnie Li, Assistant Producer; Lene Bausager, Producer
Credits Pond Puppies (S); Stealing Rembrant (F); Boxed (F); Left Turn (S)

Umbrella Entertainment Productions

11 St Mark's Cresent, London NW1 7TS
t 020 7267 8834 **f** 020 7267 8846
e sandy@goodtime.demon.co.uk

Umbrella Productions Ltd

74 Victoria Crescent Road, Glasgow G12 9JN
t 0141 587 6146 **f** 0141 587 6147 **m** 07941 396642
e umbrella.productions@virgin.net
Contact Arlene Jeffrey, Line Producer; David Muir, Producer
Credits The Acid House (F); Skagerrak (F)

Nicola Usborne

Peters Fraser & Dunlop, Drury House, 34-43 Russell Street, London WC2B 5HA
t 020 7344 1000 **f** 020 7836 9543
e postmaster@pfd.co.uk **w** www.pfd.co.uk

Kevan van Thompson

Creative Media Management, Unit 3B, Walpole Court, Ealing Studios, Ealing Green, London W5 5ED
t 020 8584 5363 **f** 020 8566 5554
e enquiries@creativemediamanagement.com
Credits The Scarlet Pimpernel (T); Dust (F); Rockface (T)

Velvet Pictures Ltd

5 Lower Green Road, Esher KT10 8HE
t 020 8398 4529 **f** 020 8398 6043 **m** 07885 788527
e hq@velvetpictures.com **w** www.velvetpictures.com
Contact Keith English, Director; Claire Cottrell, Producer
Credits Top Dog (S)

Top dog has won awards in competitions and worldwide festivals.

Vixen Films
13 Aubert Park, Highbury, London N5 1TL
t 020 7359 7368 **f** 020 7359 7368 **e** kim@tgraham.demon.co.uk

Martha Wailes
m 07778 657088 **e** marthawailes@globalnet.co.uk
Credits Michael Palin's Hemigway Adveture (D); Maidens Of The Lost Ark (D)

Ann Walker
5 Belgrave Terrace, Hillhead, Glasgow GI2 8JD
t 0141 342 4340 **m** 07773 215606
e annworldwide@hotmail.com

Mike Wallington
1 Ravenslea Road, London SW12 8SA
t 020 8673 4550 **f** 020 8675 4760 **m** 07785 590 641
e mwallington@btinternet.com

Hugh Warren
Peters Fraser & Dunlop, Drury House, 34-43 Russell Street,
London WC2B 5HA
t 020 7344 1000 **f** 020 7836 9543
e postmaster@pfd.co.uk **w** www.pfd.co.uk

Richard Warren
9 Heather Wood, Forden, Welshpool SY21 8LQ
t 01938 580180 **f** 01938 580180 **m** 07949 652055
e 5warren@tiscali.co.uk

Jo Willett
Peters Fraser & Dunlop, Drury House, 34-43 Russell Street,
London WC2B 5HA
t 020 7344 1000 **f** 020 7836 9543
e postmaster@pfd.co.uk **w** www.pfd.co.uk

Kit Williams PGGB
Lodge Farm Cottage, Elvetham, Hook RG27 8AS
t 01252 842324 **f** 01252 842952 **m** 07860 587830
e kitjwilliams@aol.com
Credits Sex Chips And Rock 'N' Roll (T); Fortysomething (T); The Safe House
(T); Night And Day (T)

Lisa Williams
Peters Fraser & Dunlop, Drury House, 34-43 Russell Street,
London WC2B 5HA
t 020 7344 1000 **f** 020 7836 9543
e postmaster@pfd.co.uk **w** www.pfd.co.uk

Siân Williams
Felin lal, Bryneglwys, Corwen LL21 9LE
t 01490 450224 **f** 01745 583116 **m** 07977 757667
e dragonsian@hotmail.com **w** www.racingsnakefilms.com
Credits Infestation (F)

Lisa Williams-Callaway
8 Minister Court, Frogmore, St Albans AL2 2NF
t 01727 758660 **m** 07958 762131 **e** w.callaway@ntlworld.com
Credits Industrial Revelations (D); Dan Roamin (D); Dial A Date (T); Young,
Gifted And Broke (T)

Sarah Wilson
International Creative Management Ltd, Oxford House,
76 Oxford Street, London W1D 1BS
t 020 7636 6565 **f** 020 7323 0101 **w** www.icmlondon.co.uk

Ann Wingate
59 Ockendon Road, London N1 3NL
t 020 7354 2426 **f** 020 7354 3203
Credits My House In Umbria (F); Portrait Of A Lady (T);
Mid-Summer Nights Dream (F)

John Withington
t 020 7485 3690 **f** 020 7267 5430 **m** 07876 680 465
e john.withington@btinternet.com
Credits Strictly for the Birds (T); Clive Anderson's Euro Adventure (T); Secret City (T)

Wortman Productions UK
48 Chiswick Staithe, London W4 3TP
t 020 8994 8886 **m** 07976 805976 **e** nevillewortman@beeb.net

Yale College
Grove Park, Wrexham LL12 7AA
t 01978 3117 94x228 **f** 01978 291569
e spc@yale-wrexham.ac.uk **w** www.yale-wrexham.ac.uk
Contact Simon Collinge, Programme Area Leader

David Young
London Management & Representation, 2-4 Noel Street,
London W1F 8GB
t 020 7287 9000 **f** 020 7287 3236
Credits Jet Set (T); Friends Like These (T); Without Prejudice (T)

Neil Zeiger
Peters Fraser & Dunlop, Drury House, 34-43 Russell Street,
London WC2B 5HA
t 020 7344 1000 **f** 020 7836 9543
e postmaster@pfd.co.uk **w** www.pfd.co.uk

Zeno Film Productions Ltd
94 Lime Avenue, Lillington, Leamington Spa CV32 7DQ
t 01562 730270 **m** 07860 453321
e zeno@zenofilms.co.uk **w** www.zenofilms.co.uk
Contact Nick Hodgetts, Commercial Director; Adam Trotman, Creative Director
Credits There And Back Again (F); What It Is (T); Royal Televison Society Awards

Claire Zolkwer
London Management & Representation, 2-4 Noel Street,
London W1F 8GB
t 020 7287 9000 **f** 020 7287 3236
Credits Big Brother (T); I'm A Celebrity, Get Me Out Of Here (T); Pop Idol Extra (T)

ZR Production
1 Claremont Close, Stone ST15 8QE
t 01785 816210 **m** 07973 147507 **e** zcread@hotmail.com
Contact Zoe Read, Producer
Credits Steel Man (F); Fork (F)

Production Accountants

Ace Accounting Ltd
43 Kenwood Drive, Walton-on-Thames KT12 5AX
t 01932 247292 **f** 01932 267474 **m** 07879 428181
e mandy@calderhome.fsnet.co.uk
Contact Thomas Calder, Management Consultant; Amanda Calder,
Production Accountant
Credits Madonna - Who's That Girl? (D); Calendar Girls (F); Brit Awards 2003
(T); Lost Worlds (D)

AGN Shipleys
10 Orange Street, Haymarket, London WC2H 7DQ
t 020 7312 0000 **f** 020 7312 0022
e jobernss@agnshipleys.com **w** www.agnshipleys.com
Contact Ken Roberts, Partner; Steve Joberns, Partner

Craig Barwick
t 01628 524491

Charles Bates
Gems, The Media House, 87 Glebe Street, Penarth CF64 1EF
t 029 2071 0770 **f** 029 2071 0771
e gems@gems-agency.co.uk **w** www.gems-agency.co.uk
Credits The Gentleman Thief (T); Search (T); Paradise Heights (T); Shooters (F)

Bob Blues
2 Barley Mow Way, Shepperton TW17 0DU
t 01932 240502 **e** bobblues@msn.com
Credits Wind In The Willows (F); Amy Foster; Possession (F)

Neil Cairns
20 Dowanside Lane, Glasgow G12 9BZ
t 0141 357 5741 **m** 07941 311952 **e** nj.cairns@virgin.net
Credits Last Great Wilderness (F); 16 Years Of Alcohol (F); Solid Air (F); Bride Of Ice (F)

Martin Cook
5 Bainbrigge Road, Leeds LS6 3AD
t 0113 275 9576 **f** 0113 274 5686 **e** martin@leecook5.idps.co.uk
Credits Larkin - Love Again (T); Buried (T); There's Only One Jimmy Grimble (F)

Deborah Cooke
Gems, The Media House, 87 Glebe Street, Penarth CF64 1EF
t 029 2071 0770 **f** 029 2071 0771
e gems@gems-agency.co.uk **w** www.gems-agency.co.uk

Steve Cronick
Gems, The Media House, 87 Glebe Street, Penarth CF64 1EF
t 029 2071 0770 **f** 029 2071 0771
e gems@gems-agency.co.uk **w** www.gems-agency.co.uk
Credits Midsommer Murders (T); Ultimate Force (T); Sunset Heights (F); Snakes And Ladders (F)

Steven Edwicker
57 Sawley Road, Shepherds Bush, London W12 0LQ
t 020 8248 2586 **f** 020 8248 2586 **m** 07768 993997
e sedwicker@aol.com
Credits William And Mary (T); The Last Of The Blonde Bombshells (T); Trial And Retribution IV (T); The Commander (T)

Kevin Freemantle
21 Roe Green Close, Hatsfield AL10 9PD
t 01707 265460 **f** 01707 265460 **m** 07802 796421
e kevinfreemantle@hotmail.com
Credits Rough Treatment (T); Two Men Went to War (F); Mean Machine (W)

Charlotte Gerard
Alton Mill, Alton Pancras DT2 7RW
t 01300 348223 **f** 01300 348577 **m** 07775 526900
e charlotte.gerard@btinternet.com

Marilyn Goldsworthy
9 Eastern Drive, Bourne End SL8 5HQ
t 01628 529933

Handstand Productions
13 Hope Street, Liverpool L1 9BH
t 0151 708 7441 **f** 0151 709 3515 **m** 07778 660575
e info@handstand-uk.com **w** www.handstand-uk.com
Contact Nicholas Stanley; Lucy Dossor; Han Duijvendak
Credits Clocking Off (T); Merseybeat (T); The Virgin Of Liverpool (F); Revenger's Tragedy (F)

Sarah Hewitt
5 College Road, Colliers Wood, London SW19 2BP
t 020 8241 3507 **e** sarah.hewitt@virgin.net
Credits Room 101 (T); Spaced (T); Blind Date (T)

Simon Hill
Gems, The Media House, 87 Glebe Street, Penarth CF64 1EF
t 029 2071 0770 **f** 029 2071 0771
e gems@gems-agency.co.uk **w** www.gems-agency.co.uk
Credits Saving Private Ryan (F); The Birthday Girl (F); Miranda (F); Bend It Like Beckham (F)

Robert Hughes
41 Belle Vue Road, Wivenhoe CO7 9LD
t 01206 822723 **f** 01206 822723

Richard Hyland
t 020 7388 9618
Credits The Search for John Gissing (F); Intimacy (F); Darkness (F)

Janet Linton
Gems, The Media House, 87 Glebe Street, Penarth CF64 1EF
t 029 2071 0770 **f** 029 2071 0771
e gems@gems-agency.co.uk **w** www.gems-agency.co.uk
Credits Nicholas Nickleby (T); A Line In the Sand (T); Darwin (F); Best (F)

Sarah Lucraft
14 Jubilee Road, Downley HP13 5TW
t 01494 459603 **f** 01494 459635 **m** 07976 979449
e sarah.lucraft@ntlworld.com
Credits Trial And Retribution VII (T); The Lost Prince (T); Tabloid (F); Anita And Me (F)

Musicare
16/16A Thorpewood Avenue, London SE26 4BX
t 020 8699 1245 **f** 020 8291 5584
e sian.wynne@macunlimited.net
Contact Sian Wynne, Director
Credits The Fen Street Nativity (T); Media And Monarchy (T); The Major Years (T)

Nicholas Stanley - Handstand Productions
13 Hope Street, Liverpool I 1 9BH
t 0151 708 7441 **f** 0151 709 3515 **m** 07778 660 575
e info@handstand-uk.com **w** www.handstand-uk.com
Contact Nicholas Stanley, Director-Prod Accountant; Han Duijvendak, Director-Producer; Lucy Dossor, Director-Prod Accountant; Joanne McMahon, Office Manager
Credits Clocking Off (A); Mersey Beat (A); Revengers Tragedy (A)

Tracey Oakley
Gems, The Media House, 87 Glebe Street, Penarth CF64 1EF
t 029 2071 0770 **f** 029 2071 0771
e gems@gems-agency.co.uk **w** www.gems-agency.co.uk
Credits The Creatives (T); Metrosexuality (T); Station Jim (T); Sunday (T)

Osiris Organisational Services Ltd
27 Cromwell Avenue, New Malden KT3 6DN
t 020 8942 9800 **t** 020 8942 9811
f 020 8942 4142 **m** 07802 365793
e kd@osiris.gb.com **w** www.osiris.com
Contact Kerri Daly, Director; Albert Daly, Director

Maggie Phelan
t 01784 458940 **f** 07184 460488
e maggiephelan@compuserve.com
Credits The End Of The Affair (F); Nicholas Nickleby (T); Below (F)

Freya Pinsent
6 Rossiter Road, London SW12 9RU
t 020 8675 5950 **m** 07802 566639
e freyapinsent@lycos.co.uk
Credits Martha Meet Frank Daniel And Lawrence (F); Plunkett And Macleane (F); Margery And Gladys (T); Too Good To Be True (T)

Diane Pontefract
16 Claremont Road, Headingley, Leeds LS6 4EB
t 0113 275 7266 **f** 0113 275 7266 **m** 07786 465254
e diponte@aol.com
Credits Wings Of The Dove (F); The Cops (T); A&E (T); The Forsyte Saga (T)

Rennie Spiolek
Gems, The Media House, 87 Glebe Street, Penarth CF64 1EF
t 029 2071 0770 **f** 029 2071 0771
e gems@gems-agency.co.uk **w** www.gems-agency.co.uk
Credits Nicholas Nickleby (T); A Line In The Sand (T); Auf Wiedersehen Pet (T); The Queen's Nose (T)

Alec Thorne
Gems, The Media House, 87 Glebe Street, Penarth CF64 1EF
t 029 2071 0770 **f** 029 2071 0771
e gems@gems-agency.co.uk **w** www.gems-agency.co.uk
Credits Teachers Series II (T); Relic Hunter II (T); Trial And Retribution IV, V, VI (T); The I Inside (F)

Mrs Billie Watley
Barling Lodge, 11A Church Road, Barling Magna SS3 0LS
t 01702 217879 **f** 01702 217937 **m** 07702 477837
e billie.watmac@talk21.com
Credits Tourist Police (T); Dinner Ladies (T); Victoria Wood Xmas Special (T)

Peter Winstanley
5 Lascelles Road, Bournemouth BH7 6NF
t 01202 427944 **f** 01202 427944 **m** 07702 302404
e peterat94@aol.com
Credits Twelfth Night (T); Buried Treasure (T); Back Home (T); An Angel for May (F)

Sian Wynne
16 Thorpewood Avenue, Sydenham, London SE26 4BX
t 020 8699 1245 **f** 020 8291 5584
e sian.wynne@macunlimited.net

Production Assistants

Oliver Allgrove
The Production Switchboard, Northdown, Down Lane,
Compton GU3 1DN
t 01483 812011 **f** 01483 812027
e aly@productionswitch.freeserve.co.uk
Credits Bloody Nora (F); The Day Of Sirens (F); 16 Years Of Alcohol (F)

Amanda Bronkhorst
Production Switchboard, Northdown, Down Lane, Compton
GU3 1DN
t 01483 812011 **f** 01483 812027
e aly@productionswitch.freeserve.co.uk
Credits Benylin (C); OXO (C); Daewoo (C); Daewoo

Angela Beckles
88 Gellatly Road, New Cross, London SE14 5TT
m 07980 276536 **e** angiebeckles@aol.com
Credits The Oxfordshire Hour (T); Cheese (F); Animal/Vegetable/Machine (S); The Greek Man From Pakistan (S)

Isibeal Balance
Production Switchboard, Northdown, Down Lane, Compton
GU3 1DN
t 01483 812011 **f** 01483 812027
e aly@productionswitch.freeserve.co.uk
Credits HLA - Multi Historical Society (M); The Book Group (T); Simon (F)

Lara Baldwin
Production Switchboard, Northdown, Down Lane, Compton
GU3 1DN
t 01483 812011 **f** 01483 812027
e aly@productionswitch.freeserve.co.uk
Credits Clark's (C); Orange (C); Levi's (C)

Imogen Bell
The Production Switchboard, Northdown, Down Lane,
Compton GU3 1DN
t 01483 812011 **f** 01483 812027
e aly@productionswitch.freeserve.co.uk
Credits BBC Idents (C); MTV To Go (C); JT Roots (C)

Julia Biel
Experience Counts - Call Me Ltd, 5th Floor, 41-42 Berners
Street, London W1P 3AA
t 020 7637 8112 **f** 020 7580 2582

Ruth Bowles
10 Clandon Avenue, Egham TW20 8LP
t 01784 437921 **m** 07778 103315 **e** ruthadrian@supanet.com

Diana Bramwell
Experience Counts - Call Me Ltd, 5th Floor, 41-42 Berners
Street, London W1P 3AA
t 020 7637 8112 **f** 020 7580 2582

Marit K Brevik
19 Caring Lane, Bearsted, Maidstone ME14 4NJ
t 01622 736286 **e** brett.lockyer@tesco.net
Credits Richard Montgommery (D); Medical Accidents (D); Love Has No Fear (D)

Jeremy Burnage
The Production Switchboard, North Down, Down Lane,
Compton GU3 1DN
t 01483 812011 **f** 01483 812027
e aly@productionswitch.freeserve.co.uk
Credits Soft Cell (M); Sons And Lovers (T); Blackball (F)

Jeremy Burnage
95 Salterford Road, Tooting, London SW17 9TE
t 020 8682 2200 **m** 07808 177722
e jerry_burnage@hotmail.com
Credits Soft Cell (M); Sons And Lovers (T); Blackball (F)

Tricia Canavan
Experience Counts - Call Me Ltd, 5th Floor, 41-42 Berners
Street, London W1P 3AA
t 020 7637 8112 **f** 020 7580 2582

Clair Carney
384 Cable Street, Wapping, London E1 0AF
t 020 7790 8941 **m** 07956 543860 **e** claircarney@hotmail.com

Julie Church
Experience Counts - Call Me Ltd, 5th Floor, 41-42 Berners
Street, London W1P 3AA
t 020 7637 8112 **f** 020 7580 2582

Nikki Cockcroft
65 Avenue Road, Leamington Spa CV31 3PF
t 01926 882763 **m** 07973 295513 **e** nikki@bhdesign.ukf.net

Sarah Connors
The Production Switchboard, Northdown, Down Lane,
Compton GU3 1DN
t 01483 812011 **f** 01483 812027
e aly@productionswitch.freeserve.co.uk
Credits Al And Monkey (C); Out Of The Blue (M); KFC - Got Chicken, Got Soul (C)

Carolyn Davey
Experience Counts - Call Me Ltd, 5th Floor, 41-42 Berners
Street, London W1P 3AA
t 020 7637 8112 **f** 020 7580 2582

Jenny Drewett
m 07050 048969 **e** jenny.drewett@btopenworld.com
Credits The Club (T); The Weakest Link (T)

Sarah Ellis
The Production Switchboard, Northdown, Down Lane,
Compton GU3 1DN
t 01483 812011 **f** 01483 812027
e aly@productionswitch.freeserve.co.uk
Credits Axa (C); Whirlpool (C); Zipel (C)

Mary Gardner
t 07050 113039 **t** 020 8864 4805
Credits Tarrant On TV (T); Battle For The Planet (D); Gloria's Open House (T); Pavarotti Warchild Concert In Modena (M)
Wide experience of Broadcast Studios, OB's - especially entertainment, music and live.

Ellie Gleaves
Experience Counts - Call Me Ltd, 5th Floor, 41-42 Berners
Street, London W1P 3AA
t 020 7637 8112 **f** 020 7580 2582

Ellie Goodall
Experience Counts - Call Me Ltd, 5th Floor, 41-42 Berners
Street, London W1P 3AA
t 020 7637 8112 **f** 020 7580 2582

Jen Govey
One Tile Cottages, Robert Road, Hedgerley SL2 3YA
t 01753 646200 **f** 01753 646200 **m** 07721 451916
e jengovey@aol.com **w** www.jengo.8m.com
Credits What's A Carry On? (D); Mr Thunderbird (D); The Secret Agent (F); Something To Believe In (F)

Julia Guignabel
Production Switchboard, Northdown, Down Lane, Compton GU3 1DN
t 01483 812011 **f** 01483 812027
e aly@productionswitch.freeserve.co.uk
Credits McDonalds (C); Mattie (F); Blueberry (F)

Mickey Harding
Experience Counts - Call Me Ltd, 5th Floor, 41-42 Berners Street, London W1P 3AA
t 020 7637 8112 **f** 020 7580 2582

Jo Harrop
Production Switchboard, Northdown, Down Lane, Compton GU3 1DN
t 01483 812011 **f** 01483 812027
e aly@productionswitch.freeserve.co.uk
Credits Blink (C); Sky (C); Spirit Films (C)

Claire Hoath
Production Switchboard, Northdown, Down Lane, Compton GU3 1DN
t 01483 812011 **f** 01483 812027
w aly@productionswitch.freeserve.co.uk
Credits Burger King - Rose Hackney Barber (C); Rebranding - Two AM Films (T); BT Business - Hungry Man (C)

Chris Holbrook
Production Switchboard, Northdown, Down Lane, Compton GU3 1DN
t 01483 812011 **f** 01483 812027
e aly@productionswitch.freeserve.co.uk
Credits Sky TV (C); The Independent (C); Johnson And Johnson (C)

Jenny Hopwood
Experience Counts - Call Me Ltd, 5th Floor, 41-42 Berners Street, London W1P 3AA
t 020 7637 8112 **f** 020 7580 2582

Gill Horwood
Experience Counts - Call Me Ltd, 5th Floor, 41-42 Berners Street, London W1P 3AA
t 020 7637 8112 **f** 020 7580 2582

Sylvana Job
Experience Counts - Call Me Ltd, 5th Floor, 41-42 Berners Street, London W1P 3AA
t 020 7637 8112 **f** 020 7580 2582

Charlotte Johnson
55 Lonsdale Terrace, West Jesmond, Newcastle-upon-Tyne NE2 3HQ
t 0191 281 9597 **f** 0191 281 9597 **m** 07740 419665
e charlotte@charlottejohnson.co.uk
w www.charlottejohnson.co.uk
Credits Away Goals Rule (S); Learning To Drown (S); Bill & Bob (A); Frozen (F)

Demi Jones
The Production Switchboard, Northdown, Down Lane, Compton GU3 1DN
t 01483 812011 **f** 01483 812027
e aly@productionswitch.freeserve.co.uk
Credits Jacob's Crackers - Rules (C); Sony Playstation (C); Coi (C)

Dan Knight
The Production Switchboard, North Down, Down Lane, Compton GU3 1DN
t 01483 812011 **f** 01483 812027
e aly@productionswitch.freeserve.co.uk
Credits Zurich (C); Sunsilk (C); Harry Potter And The Philosopher's Stone (F)

Dan Knight
65A Regina Road, Finsbury Park, London N4 3PT
m 07977 589860 **e** danjknight@hotmail.com
Credits Zurich (C); Sunsilk (C); Harry Potter And The Philosopher's Stone (F)

Maria Kopanov
The Production Switchboard, Northdown, Down Lane, Compton GU3 1DN
t 01483 812011 **f** 01483 812027
e aly@productionswitch.freeserve.co.uk
Credits Pepsi (C); T-Mobile (C); Guinness (C)

Belinda Langford
34 The Warren, Worcester Park KT4 7DL
f 020 8330 2080 **m** 07956 417308
e belinda.langford@btinternet.com
Credits Children in Need Find a Fortune (T); Parkinson (T)

Helen Littlewood
The Production Switchboard, Northdown, Down Lane, Compton GU3 1DN
t 01483 812011 **f** 01483 812027
e aly@productionswitch.freeserve.co.uk
Credits Scene One (C); Swizzle (C); Clover (C)

Kin-Man Ly
The Production Switchboard, Northdown, Down Lane, Compton GU3 1DN
t 01483 812011 **f** 01483 812027
e aly@productionswitch.freeserve.co.uk
Credits Brave (C); Nytol (C); MTV On Air (T)

Carey Mann
Production Switchboard, Northdown, Down Lane, Compton GU3 1DN
t 01483 812011 **f** 01483 812027
e aly@productionswitch.freeserve.co.uk
Credits The Observer (C); West Life (M); Cold Play (M)

Cass Marks
The Production Switchboard, Northdown, Down Lane, Compton GU3 1DN
t 01483 812011 **f** 01483 812027
e aly@productionswitch.freeserve.co.uk
Credits Tyskie Beer (C); Ford (C); Mini Cab Safety (C)

Miranda Marks
Production Switchboard, Northdown, Down Lane, Compton GU3 1DN
t 01483 812011 **f** 01483 812027
e aly@productionswitch.freeserve.co.uk
Credits Planet Of The Apes (F); Dirty Pretty Things (F); Keen Eddie (T)

Victoria Mawden
The Production Switchboard, Northdown, Down Lane, Compton GU3 1DN
t 01483 812011 **f** 01483 812027
e aly@productionswitch.freeserve.co.uk
Credits Outbreak (D); Art Crimes (T); Orwell (D)

Hannah May
Production Switchboard, North Down, Down Lane, Compton GU3 1DN
t 01483 812011 **f** 01483 812027
Credits Rear Wing - Westlife (M); Rogue - Evening Standard (C)

Heather McDonald
78 Main Street, Kilmarnock KA3 4AG
t 01560 485828 **m** 07714 282181 **e** heathermay4@aol.com
Credits Celtic Connections (D); T In The Park (T)

Lucy McDowell
The Production Switchboard, Northdown, Down Lane,
Compton GU3 1DN
t 01483 812011 **f** 01483 812027
e aly@productionswitch.freeserve.co.uk
Credits AOL (C); Burger King (C); Coi (C)

Denise McShane
77A Kneller Road, Twickenham TW2 7DN
t 020 8898 5873 **e** denisemcshane@hotmail.com

Liz Minchin
Experience Counts - Call Me Ltd, 5th Floor, 41-42 Berners
Street, London W1P 3AA
t 020 7637 8112 **f** 020 7580 2582

Margaret Minchin
Experience Counts - Call Me Ltd, 5th Floor, 41-42 Berners
Street, London W1P 3AA
t 020 7637 8112 **f** 020 7580 2582

Gillian Moncrieff
Experience Counts - Call Me Ltd, 5th Floor, 41-42 Berners
Street, London W1P 3AA
t 020 7637 8112 **f** 020 7580 2582

Tracy Nicholles
Connections, The Meadlands, Oakleigh Road, Hatch End,
Pinner HA5 4HB
t 020 8420 1444 **f** 020 8428 5836 **m** 07831 305518
e mail@connectionsuk.com **w** www.connectionsuk.com

Julia Nyland
Experience Counts - Call Me Ltd, 5th Floor, 41-42 Berners
Street, London W1P 3AA
t 020 7637 8112 **f** 020 7580 2582

Gabrielle O'Connell
The Production Switchboard, Northdown, Down Lane,
Compton GU3 1DN
t 01483 812011 **f** 01483 812027
e aly@productionswitch.freeserve.co.uk
Credits The Clinic (C); John Clarke Productions (C); Cicada Films (D)

Pui
Production Switchboard, Northdown, Down Lane, Compton
GU3 1DN
t 01483 812011 **f** 01483 812027
e aly@productionswitch.freeserve.co.uk
Credits Stella Street (F); Mars Amicelli (C); VISA - Serious Pictures (C)

Patsy Richards
Experience Counts - Call Me Ltd, 5th Floor, 41-42 Berners
Street, London W1P 3AA
t 020 7637 8112 **f** 020 7580 2582

Rupi Randhawa
Production Switchboard, Northdown, Down Lane, Compton
GU3 1DN
t 01483 812011 **f** 01483 812027
e aly@productionswitch.freeserve.co.uk
Credits Xperiment (M); Medicine Eight (M); Gala Bingo (C)

Lynn Roberts
254 Sulivan Court, Parsons Green, London SW6 3DW
t 020 7736 0706 **m** 07773 714733
e lynndroberts@hotmail.com
Credits Wilfred (S); Ripe (S); Pigeon Eye (S); Cheese Makes You Dream (S)

Jonathan Scott
Production Switchboard, Northdown, Down Lane, Compton
GU3 1DN
t 01483 812011 **f** 01483 812027
e aly@productionswitch.freeserve.co.uk
Credits The Four Feathers (F); Comet (C); Keen Eddie (T)

Dominic Smith
Callbox Communications Limited, 66 Shepperton Studios,
Studios Road, Shepperton TW17 0QD
t 01932 592572 **f** 01932 569655 **m** 07710 572572
e callboxdiary@btinternet.com **w** www.callboxdiary.co.uk

Darko Stavrik
The Production Switchboard, North Down, Down Lane,
Compton GU3 1DN
t 01483 812011 **f** 01483 812027
e aly@productionswitch.freeserve.co.uk
Credits Gala Bingo (C); Marshalls (C)

Teletha Tapper
The Production Switchboard, Northdown, Down Lane,
Compton GU3 1DN
t 01483 812011 **f** 01483 812027
e aly@productionswitch.freeserve.co.uk
Credits Panasonic - Wedding (C); Guinness - Dwarf (C); Citroen - No Vat (C)

Meg Theakston
Redmayne, Bull Lane, Gerrards Cross SL9 8RF
t 01753 882541 **f** 01753 882541 **m** 07850 173790
e mtheakston@aol.com
Credits Prince Regent And Mrs Fitzherbert (T); Abbey National (I); Land Rover
(C); Don Quixote (T)

Margaret Thistle
Experience Counts - Call Me Ltd, 5th Floor, 41-42 Berners
Street, London W1P 3AA
t 020 7637 8112 **f** 020 7580 2582

Emma Thody
33 Park Drive, Morpeth NE61 2SX
t 01670 514 801 **m** 07879 645623 **e** emmathody@hotmail.com
Credits The Other Half (F); Die Another Day (F); Ticket To Ride (T); Danny And
His Amazing Teeth (S)

Barbara Thomas
Experience Counts - Call Me Ltd, 5th Floor, 41-42 Berners
Street, London W1P 3AA
t 020 7637 8112 **f** 020 7580 2582

Shari Tyrrell
12 Westfield Court, Catherine Road, Surbiton KT6 4HG
t 020 8549 6482 **m** 07889 073283 **e** sharityrrell@talk21.com

Mel Ward
Rydal Mount, Cold Hatton Heath, Telford TF6 6PZ
t 01952 541885 **f** 01952 541885 **m** 07774 114510
e mel.wardpa@virgin.net

Kathryn West
The Laurels, 6 Bredward Close, Burnham SL1 7DL
t 01628 665072 **f** 01628 665819 **m** 07714 126557
e kathrynawest@aol.com

Miles Wilkes
Production Switchboard, Northdown, Down Lane, Compton
GU3 1DN
t 01483 812011 **f** 01483 812027
e aly@productionswitch.freeserve.co.uk
Credits Heinz - Musical Plates (C); The Hideous Man (S); Flowers - Hints-Water (C)

Clare Wiltshire
m 07790 571083 **e** clarejane81@hotmail.com
Credits Cream Or Ice-Cream (S); Veggie Club (A); Ella (S); Stop 731 (F)

Lucy Witts
Production Switchboard, Northdown, Down Lane, Compton GU3 1DN
t 01483 812011 **f** 01483 812027
e aly@productionswitch.freeserve.co.uk
Credits Nike - Foot Locker (C); Kellog's Special K (C); Helen Of Peckham (F)

Claire Woods
The Production Switchboard, Northdown, Down Lane, Compton GU3 1DN
t 01483 812011 **f** 01483 812027
e aly@productionswitch.freeserve.co.uk
Credits Müller (C); Clinomyn (C); Kenwood Mixers (C)

Production **Buyers**

Anne Carlyle-Gall
The Buyers' Network, 12-16 Brunel Road, Acton, London W3 7XR
t 020 8749 5500 **f** 020 8749 4185 **m** 07973 683720
e anne@propbuyersnetwork.co.uk
w www.propbuyersnetwork.co
Credits Peter Ackroyd's London (D); Being Victoria (T); Reputations: Marie Antoinette (D)

Graham Curtis
4 Colville Drive, Bishops, Waltham SO32 1LT
t 01489 894553 **f** 01489 894553 **m** 07808 105087
e gthang@curtisg.fsnet.co.uk
Credits Ultimate Force II (T); Teachers (T); Midsomer Murders (T)

Judy Ducker
32 Kent Gardens, Ealing, London W13 8BU
t 020 8997 7957 **f** 020 8998 8763 **m** 07831 342785
e judy@kentgarden.demon.co.uk
Credits Around The World In 80 Days (F); Unconditional Love (T); Foyle's War (T); The Hours (F)

Suzie Finch
HERS
t 020 7608 3434 **f** 018 8425 1221
e hers@hersagency.co.uk **w** www.hersagency.co.uk

Marvin George
Gems, The Media House, 87 Glebe Street, Penarth CF64 1EF
t 029 2071 0770 **f** 029 2071 0771
e gems@gems-agency.co.uk **w** www.gems-agency.co.uk
Credits Hearts And Bones (T); Daylight Robbery (T); The Bill (T); The Asylum (F)

Julia Griffiths
t 020 7608 3434 **f** 018 8425 1221
e hers@hersagency.co.uk **w** www.hersagency.co.uk

Sara Grimshaw
85 Broom Park, Teddingdon TW11 9RR
t 020 8977 4386 **f** 020 8977 4386 **m** 07836 318157
e sarajgrimshaw@aol.com
Credits Spooks II (T); Buried Treasure (T); The Mayor of Casterbridge (T); NCS Manhunt (T)

Liz Hippisley
HERS
t 020 7608 3434 **f** 018 8425 1221
e hers@hersagency.co.uk **w** www.hersagency.co.uk

Clare Hunt
HERS
t 020 7608 3434 **f** 018 8425 1221
e hers@hersagency.co.uk **w** www.hersagency.co.uk

Rosalie Kenworthy-Neale
14 Launcelot Crescent, Thornhill, Cardiff CF14 9AQ
t 029 2062 8512 **m** 07050 106989
e rosie@kenworthy-neale.com **w** www.kenworthy-neale.com
Credits A Mind To Kill I (T); Tracy Beaker (T); Hedd Wyn (F); House (F)

Paula Lovell
t 020 7608 3434 **f** 020 8425 1221
e hers@hersagency.co.uk **w** www.hersagency.co.uk

Harriet Orman
ADS, Shepperton Studios, Studios Road, Shepperton TW17 0QD
t 01932 592303 **f** 01932 592492 **e** ads@carlincrew.co.uk
Credits The League Of Extraordinary Gentlemen (F); Mrs Caldicott's Cabbage War (F); About A Boy (F)

Sarah Raine
t 020 7608 3434 **f** 018 8425 1221
e hers@hersagency.co.uk **w** www.hersagency.co.uk

Mark Rimmell
12a St Johns Grove, London N19 5RW
t 020 7272 0645 **f** 020 7272 0645 **m** 07831 634 778
e m.rimmell@btopenworld.com
Credits The Exorcist The Beginning (F); In the Name of the Father (F); Longitude (T); Circle Of Friends (F)

Malcolm Rougvie
Gems, The Media House, 87 Glebe Street, Penarth CF64 1EF
t 029 2071 0770 **f** 029 2071 0771
e gems@gems-agency.co.uk **w** www.gems-agency.co.uk
Credits A Mind To Kill (T); The Bill (T); Jinnah (F); Sunset Heights (F)

Mike Smith
12 Newenden Close, Maidstone ME14 5RU
t 01622 678723 **f** 01622 678723 **m** 07860 389742
Credits Sparkling Cyanide (T); Margery & Gladys (T); Sons & Lovers (T)

Barbara Spiller
t 0113 250 0641 **f** 0113 236 0683 **m** 07860 919546
e barbaraspilleruk@aol.com

Charlotte Taylor
18 Eleanor Grove, Barnes, London SW13 0JN
t 020 8876 9085 **f** 020 8876 9085 **m** 07836 708 904
e charlotte-taylor@breathemail.net
Credits The Enemy (F); Three Blind Mice (F); Jason And The Argonauts (F); The Honey Trap (F)

Duncan Windram Wheeler
The Mechanics Institute, 7 Church Street, Heptonstall, Hebden Bridge HX7 7NS
t 01422 843407 **t** 020 8878 5450 **f** 01422 845070
m 07831 130841 **e** duncanwindramwheeler@hotmail.com
Credits Stig Of The Dump (T); Entering Blue Zone (F); One For The Road (F); The 51st State (F)

Production **Co-ordinators**

Alan Zafer & Associates Ltd
47-48 Chagford Street, London NW1 6EB
t 020 7723 0106 **f** 020 7724 6163 **e** productions@zafer.org.uk
Contact Alan Zafer, Managing Director; Alison Webb, Production Director

Phyl Allarie
Rose Cottage, Fulmer Road, Fulmer SL3 6HN
t 01753 662598 **f** 01753 664301 **m** 07836 319553
e allariep@aol.com

Richard Balshaw
26 Prince Leopold Street, Adamsdown, Cardiff CF24 0HT
m 07779 012007 **e** richard_balshaw@hotmail.com
Credits New To Q (T); Kerrang Awards (T); Base Beach MTV Aiya Napa (T)

Toni Barnett
Gems, The Media House, 87 Glebe Street, Penarth CF64 1EF
t 029 2071 0770 **f** 029 2071 0771
e gems@gems-agency.co.uk **w** www.gems-agency.co.uk
Credits Search For The Sons Of Abraham (D); Dad (T); My Hero (T); Judge John Deeds (T)

Scott Bassett
Gems, The Media House, 87 Glebe Street, Penarth CF64 1EF
t 029 2071 0770 **f** 029 2071 0771
e gems@gems-agency.co.uk **w** www.gems-agency.co.uk
Credits Askari (F); Beauty And The Beast (F); The Jealous God (F); The Mapleton Motor Marathon (F)

Alex Boyesen
7 Pointers Close, Isle Of Dogs, London E14 3AP
t 020 7538 8704 **f** 020 7538 8704 **m** 07770 270877
e alex@digitalmixes.co.uk **w** www.digitalmixes.co.uk

Claire-Louise Cooke
7 Halston Close, London SW11 6RH
t 07980 238134 **e** claire_cooke@yahoo.co.uk
Credits Extreme Machines Series V (D); Science Of Sleep/Science Of Dreams (D); Human Senses (D)

Mark Devlin
59 Clouston Street, Glasgow G20 8QW
t 0141 946 5972 **f** 0141 946 5972 **m** 07092 092923
e markdevlin@btinternet.com
Credits The Book Group Series II (T); Danny The Dog (F); Gas Attack (T); Nice Guy Eddie (T)

Suzanne Facenfield
Gems, The Media House, 87 Glebe Street, Penarth CF64 1EF
t 029 2071 0770 **f** 029 2071 0771
e gems@gems-agency.co.uk **w** www.gems-agency.co.uk
Credits Reputations (A); The Bill (T); Renford Rejects (T); The Swap (T)

Lorrain Fennell
160 Ashford Road, Iver Heath SL0 0QE
t 01753 798692 **m** 07850 350295 **e** lorfennell@hotmail.com
Credits The I Inside (F); Lara Croft And The Cradle Of Life: Tomb Raider 2 (F)

Bianca Gavin
Production Switchboard, Northdown, Down Lane, Compton GU3 1DN
t 01483 812011 **f** 01483 812027
w aly@productionswitch.freeserve.co.uk
Credits Three Man In A Restaurant (F); The Escapist (F); Suzie Gold (F)

Victoria Hawden
76a Tufnell Park Road, Holloway, London N7 0DT
t 020 7281 9758 **m** 07760 191519 **e** vichawden@aol.com
Credits Art Crimes (T); Orwell (T); Westlife 'Uptown Girl' (M); Gimme 6 (T)

Kelly Howard-Garde
31 Westwood Road, Barnes, London SW13 0LA
t 020 8878 2479 **m** 07941 308046
e kellyhoward-garde@another.com
Credits Posession (F); Spider (F)

Samantha Kaley
Gems, The Media House, 87 Glebe Street, Penarth CF64 1EF
t 029 2071 0770 **f** 029 2071 0771
e gems@gems-agency.co.uk **w** www.gems-agency.co.uk
Credits Talos The Mummy (F); Rock Face (T); New World Disorder (F); Britannic (F)

Victoria Leeson
82 Station Road, Epworth DN9 1JZ
t 01427 873770 **m** 07721 384855 **e** victorialeeson@hotmail.com
Credits Sex With Your Ex (D); Forbidden Fruit (D); Football Italia (T)

Fiona Lemon
43 Rosemont Road, London W3 9LU
t 020 8248 5653 **m** 07798 616929 **e** fiona_lemon@hotmail.com
Credits At The Live (T); Mike Neville Show (T); Home Shopping Europe (T)

Alison Liddle
Gems, The Media House, 87 Glebe Street, Penarth CF64 1EF
t 029 2071 0770 **f** 029 2071 0771
e gems@gems-agency.co.uk **w** www.gems-agency.co.uk
Credits Happy Birthday Shakespeare (T); Poirot (T); Casualty (T); Down To Earth (T)

Ingrid Litman
Flat 5, Capri Court, 2 Old Hospital Close, London SW12 8SS
t 020 8682 2581 **f** 0870 128 1898 **m** 07790 097364

Patsy de Lord
22 Felcott Road, Walton-on-Thames KT12 5NS
t 01932 229789 **m** 07970 200 203
Credits Sleeping Dictionary (F); The Mummy (F); 102 Dalmatians (F)

Kora McNulty
Gems, The Media House, 87 Glebe Street, Penarth CF64 1EF
t 029 2071 0770 **f** 029 2071 0771
e gems@gems-agency.co.uk **w** www.gems-agency.co.uk
Credits Being Mick (D); Milk (F); The Criminal (F); Honest (F)

Alexander Miller-Loeseke
21 Crescent Court, The Crescent, Surbiton KT6 4BW
t 020 8241 6478 **m** 07796 147324
e alexander@mundicnation.com

Mistral Film
31 Oval Road, London NW1 7EA
t 020 7284 2300 **f** 020 7284 0547
m 07712 675000 **m** 07768 876217 **e** sudo@mistralfilm.co.uk
Contact Keiko Sudo; Takashi Sudo

Rebecca Pope
Gems, The Media House, 87 Glebe Street, Penarth CF64 1EF
t 029 2071 0770 **f** 029 2071 0771
e gems@gems-agency.co.uk **w** www.gems-agency.co.uk
Credits Where The Heart Is (T); Married 2 Malcolm (F); Oklahoma (T); Joseph And His Technicolour Dreamcoat (F)

Primary Production (Services) Ltd
9 Cottages Grove, Surbiton KT6 4JH
t 020 8390 5870 **f** 020 8296 9280 **m** 07876 032 571
Credits Baby Father (T); The Bill (T)

The Production People
6 Cranley Road, Walton-on-Thames KT12 5BP
t 01932 221993 **f** 01932 223208 **e** storeytv@cix.co.uk

Karla Lesley Pugh
Eaton House, Elm Lane, Eaton, Grantham NG32 1SS
t 01476 870173 **f** 01476 870173 **m** 07816 643908
e fivestarcaterers@tinyworld.co.uk
Credits The Innocents (T); Close And True (T); Blue Dove (T); A Fish Out Of Water (T)

Charlene Sales
Gems, The Media House, 87 Glebe Street, Penarth CF64 1EF
t 029 2071 0770 **f** 029 2071 0771
e gems@gems-agency.co.uk **w** www.gems-agency.co.uk
Credits Harry And Cosh IV (T); Cavegirl (F); Adventure Inc (T)

Joan Schneider
Gems, The Media House, 87 Glebe Street, Penarth CF64 1EF
t 029 2071 0770 **f** 029 2071 0771
e gems@gems-agency.co.uk **w** www.gems-agency.co.uk
Credits Independence Day (F); From Hell (F); Blade II (F); Ancient Egyptians (F)

Kate Sinden
432 Muswell Hill Broadway, London N10 1BS
m 07957 922596 **e** kate@production-department.co.uk
Credits Fatboy Slim At Brighton Beach (M); Vodafone (C); Poison Arrow (F); Toto Live In Amsterdam (M)

Margaret Thompson
Gems, The Media House, 87 Glebe Street, Penarth CF64 1EF
t 029 2071 0770 **f** 029 2071 0771
e gems@gems-agency.co.uk **w** www.gems-agency.co.uk
Credits The Famous Jett Jackson (T); Domani (F); Ripley's Game (F); Les Liasions Dangereuses (F)

Sophie Treacher
Gems, The Media House, 87 Glebe Street, Penarth CF64 1EF
t 029 2071 0770 **f** 029 2071 0771
e gems@gems-agency.co.uk **w** www.gems-agency.co.uk
Credits Diggity (F); The Lost Battallion (F); George And The Dragon (F)

Unusual Rigging Ltd
The Wharf, Bugbrooke NN7 3QD
t 0870 868 7825 **f** 0870 744 4464
e info@unusual.co.uk **w** www.unusual.co.uk
Contact Denis Bramhall, Sales Manager; David Mayo, Marketing Manager

Clare Welsh
Gems, The Media House, 87 Glebe Street, Penarth CF64 1EF
t 029 2071 0770 **f** 029 2071 0771
e gems@gems-agency.co.uk **w** www.gems-agency.co.uk
Credits Relic Hunter III (T)

Production Companies
Animation

3 Bear Animations
Unit 45, Hartley Fold, Kirkby Stephen CA17 4JH
t 01768 371114 **t** 07970 945905 **f** 01768 371118
e doodi@3bears.co.uk **w** www.3bears.co.uk
Credits Car - Cumberland Building Society (C); Cowboy - Colorado National Lottery (C); Annecy International Animation Festival 2002 - Official Trailer (C); Plasticine - Dulux Paint (C)

Aardman Features
1410 Aztec West, Almondsbury, Bristol BS32 4RT
t 01454 859000 **f** 01454 614520
Contact Luke Smith, Camera Hire; John Bradley, Lighting Hire; Jan Sanger, Model Making; Marvin Denning, Studio Manager; Steve Pegram, Head of Features
Credits Chicken Run (F)

Am Bocsa Ltd
2 Parkside Street, Edinburgh EH8 9RL
t 0131 668 3749 **m** 07810 317126
e catriona.black@ambocsa.co.uk **w** www.ambocsa.co.uk
Contact Catriona Black, Managing Director
Credits Piobairean Bhornais (A)

Amedume Films
23 Tunley Road, Tooting, London SW17 7QH
t 020 8675 1203 **m** 07930 580012
e julius@amedumefilms.com **w** www.amedumefilms.com
Contact Adwoa Okyere, Producer/Company Secretary; Julius Amedume, Director
Credits The Meeting (S); The Phone Call (S)

Atomic Arts Ltd
3 Hanson Street, London W1W 6TB
t 020 7419 4190 **f** 020 7419 4194 **m** 07817 022336
e info@atomicarts.net **w** www.atomicarts.net
Contact Matt Clark, Producer; Alan Graves, Producer
Credits Body Hits (A)

Blue Sunflower
50 Eaglewharf Road, London N1 7ED
t 020 7490 2990 **f** 020 7336 7996
e niki@bluesunflower.com **w** www.silversunflower.com
Contact Niki Gibbs, Managing Director/Director

Bolexbrothers Ltd
Unit 3, Brunel Lock Development, Smeaton Road, Cumberland Basin, Bristol BS1 6SE
t 0117 985 8000 **f** 0117 985 8899
e mail@bolexbrothers.co.uk **w** www.bolexbrothers.com
Contact Cindy Jones, Production Assistant; Andy Leighton, Director
Credits Coca Cola (C); Nestea (C); Reebok (C); The Magic Roundabout (F)

Broadsword TV
Thorpe House, 79 Thorpe Road, Norwich NR1 3UA
t 01603 767493 **f** 01603 764946 **m** 07885 433507
e broadsword@televirtual.com **w** www.televirtual.com
Contact Tim Child, Managing Director

Clive Walley Films
Crymlyn Cottage Aber, Llanfairfechan LL33 0LU
t 01248 680500
Contact Clive Walley, Proprietor
Credits Aimfunds (C); Adagio (S); Light of Uncertainty (S); Procter & Gamble (C)

Collingwood O'Hare Entertainment Ltd
10-14 Crown Street, London W3 8SB
t 020 8993 3666 **f** 020 8993 9595
e info@crownstreet.co.uk **w** www.collingwoodohare.com
Contact Chris O'Hare, Managing Director; Tony Collingwood, Writer/Director; Helen Stroud, Head of Development
Credits Yoko! Jakamoko! Toto! (A); Eddy And The Bear (A); King's Beard (A)

Contraband Pictures Ltd
90 De Beauvoir Road, London N1 4EN
t 020 7254 9900
e info@contraband.co.uk **w** www.contraband.co.uk
Contact Kam Lau, Director; Kal Saber, Director; Wesley Dunton, Director
Credits Black Star Liner 'Rock Freak' (M); Jox McRox 'Go McMental' (M); Pussy 2000 'It's Gonna Be Alright' (M)

Cosgrove Hall Films
8 Albany Road, Chorlton-cum-Hardy, Manchester M21 0AW
t 0161 882 2500 **f** 0161 882 2555 **e** animation@chf.co.uk
Contact Mark Hall, General Manager; Iain Pelling, Managing Director; AJ Read, Head of PR & Marketing; Lee Marriott, Financial Director; Jane Wroe, Head of Personnel

Crazy Cartoon Company
C/o GL Publications, PO Box 168, Leeds LS15 9TJ
t 0113 260 0010 **f** 0113 232 6536
e crazycartoonco@aol.com **w** www.crazycartoonz.com
Contact Heather Pedley, Managing Director

Creative Film Productions Ltd
68 Conway Road, London N14 7BE
t 020 8447 8187
e pginfo@creativefilm.co.uk **w** www.creativefilm.co.uk
Contact Phil Davies, Producer
Credits Emma 18 (A); Home (A); Big Feet (A); Six Of One (A)

Ealing Animation
90 Brandon Street, London SE17 1AL
t 020 7358 4820 **f** 020 7358 4821
e admin@ealinganimation.co.uk **w** www.ealinganimation.co.uk
Contact Jilly Joseph, Assistant Producer; Richard Randolph, Producer
Credits Monty The Dog (A); Old Bear Stories (A); El Nombre (A); Dr Otter (A)

Elephant Productions
2 The Studio, 2 Rothamsted Avenue, Harpenden AL5 2DB
t 01582 621425 **f** 01582 767532
e elephant@elephant-productions.com
w www.elephant-productions.com
Contact Sarah Muller, Managing Director
Credits Johnny Casnova: Unstoppable Sex Machine (A); Animal School (A); Grizzly Tales for Grusome Kids (A)

Espresso Animation
5th Floor, 100 Oxford Steet, London W1D 1LN
t 020 7637 9090 **f** 020 7637 9339
e info@espressoanimation.com **w** www.espressoanimation.com
Contact Philip Vallentin, Director; Emma Maguire, Production Manager

Eyedentity Products
The Manor House, Church Hill, Saxmundham IP17 1EU
t 01728 603171 **m** 07770 616 445
Contact Nick Peters, Proprietor

Flicks Films Ltd
101 Wardour Street, London W1F OUG
t 020 7734 4892 f 020 7287 2307
e flicks@btconnect.com w www.flicksfilms.com
Contact Andy Dixon, Production Manager; Terry Ward, Managing Director; Mirella Barrow, Production Assistant
Credits Timbuctoo (A); Bananaman (A); Mr Men And Little Miss (A); Busy Buses (A)

Four Corners Vision
The Cedars, Andover Down SP11 6LJ
t 01264 335666 f 01264 335667 m 07899 653 923
e phamie@fourcornersvision.com
w www.fourcornersvision.com
Contact Phamie MacDonald, Head of Production

G28 Productions
10 Wheeler Gardens, Outram Place, Islington, London N1 OUW
t 020 7278 7696 m 07949 149142
e adwoa.okyere@group28.co.uk w www.group28.co.uk
Contact Aowoa Okyere, Producer/Director

Honeycomb Animation Enterprises Ltd
Berkeley House, 27 High Street, Cullompton EX15 1AB
t 01884 839202
e studio@honeycombanimation.co.uk
w www.binka.co.uk; www.honeycombanimation.com
Contact Sara Bar, Producer/Director; Simon Bar, Producer/Director; Susan Devey, Studio Manager
Credits Wolves, Witches And Giants (A); Grizzly Tales For Gruesome Kids (A); Lost In The Snow (A); Binka (A)

Ice Pics Animation
111A Wardour Street, London W1V 3TD
t 020 7437 3505 f 020 7287 0393 m 07973 508252
e mail@icepics.demon.co.uk w www.icepics.co.uk
Contact Mike Davies, Director

The Illuminated Film Company
115 Gunnersbury Lane, London W3 8HQ
t 020 8896 1666 f 020 8896 1669
e info@illuminatedfilms.com w www.illuminatedfilms.com
Contact Alison Gentleman, Assistant To Producer; Iain Harvey, Producer; Josie Law, Head Of Development
Credits The Very Hungry Caterpiller And Other Stories (A); T.R.A.N.S.I.T. (A); Christmas Carol-The Movie (A); War Game (A)

Krappo Films
213 Chester Road, Castle Bromwich, Birmingham B36 0ET
t 0121 749 4144 f 0121 747 3734
Contact Gavin Prime, Managing Director

Loose Moose Ltd
74 Berwick Street, London W1F 8TF
t 020 7287 3821 f 020 7734 4220
e info@loosemoose.net w www.loosemoose.net
Contact Ange Palethorpe, Director; Glenn Holberton, Producer; Penny Foster, Producer; Ken Lidster, Director
Credits Thunder Pig (S); Oscar Mayer Lunchables (C); Pepperami (C); Brisk Pepsi Lipton Iced Tea (C)

Lupus Films Ltd
Studio 7, 24-28 Hatton Wall, London EC1N 8JH
t 020 7419 0997 f 020 7404 9474 e liz@lupusfilms.net
Contact Camilla Deakin, Company Director; Ruth Kielding, Director of Comapny; Helen Kelsey, Production Manager; Elizabeth Hammond, Production Secretary; Sara Langton, Lawyer
Credits Little Wolf's Book Of Badness (A); Oscar Wilde Trilogy (A)

Martin Gates Productions
12 Mercer Street, London WC2H 9QD
t 020 7836 9674 f 020 7836 9712 e martin@martingates.co.uk
Contact Martin Gates, Chairman
Credits The Saveums (A); The Blobheads (A); Watership Down (A)

Nexus Productions
113-114 Shoreditch High Street, London E1 6JN
t 020 7749 7500 f 020 7749 7501
e info@nexuslondon.com w www.nexuslondon.com
Contact Charlotte Bavasso, Executive Producer, Executive Producer; Julia Parfitt, Producer; Producer; Chris O'Reilly, Executive Producer
Credits Miranda (F); Catch Me If You Can (F); Honda Campaign (C); Monkey Dust (T)
Nexus works with an international roster of directors producing high-quality animation for broadcast, commercials, music videos and title sequences.

Oscar Grillo & Ted Rockley Animations
11 Gordon Road, London W5 2AD
t 020 8991 6978 t 020 8728 2612 f 020 8991 6978
e klacto@klacto.com w www.klacto.com
Contact Ted Rockley, Director; Oscar Grillo, Director

Pepper's Ghost Productions
Clarendon House, 147 London Road, Kingston-Upon-Thames KT2 6NH
t 020 8546 4900 f 020 8546 4284 w www.tinyplanets.com
Contact Ben Lock, Head of Digital Production; Paul Michael, Managing Director; Ken Royall, Brand Manager; Carl Goodman, Head Of R&D
Credits Tiny Planets (A)

Presence Films Ltd
66A Great Titchfield Street, London W1W 7QT
t 020 7636 8477 f 020 7636 8722 m 07973 321 796
e alan@presencefilms.com
Contact Alan Dewhurst, Producer
Credits Lonely Boy (A); The Hound And The Fury (A)

Richard Purdum Productions
Unit 224, Aberdeen House, 22-24 Highbury Grove, London N5 2EA
t 020 7359 1777 e jill@purdums.com
Contact Katharine Tasker, Production Manager; Jill Thomas, Producer

Right Angle
2 Rock House, Saint Julian's Street, Tenby SA70 7BD
t 01834 845676 f 01834 845677 e right.angle@dial.pipex.com
Contact Penelope Middelboe, Producer

Sheila Graber Animation Ltd
50 Meldon Avenue, South Shields NE34 0EL
t 0191 455 4985 f 0191 455 3600 m 07931 792964
e sheila@graber-miller.com
Contact Jen Miller, Director; Sheila Graber, Director
Credits Mondrian (A); Sunderland College (C); Sign Post (W); www.signpostbsl.com (W)

Sherbet
112-114 Great Portland Street, London W1N 5PE
t 020 7636 6435 f 020 7436 3221
e info@sherbet.co.uk w www.sherbet.co.uk
Contact Rachel Matchett, Producer; Jonathan Bairstow, Producer; Jayne Bevitt, Producer
Credits Camouflage (S); Dove (A); Seat (A); Persil (A)

Silent Entertainment Ltd
Townhouse Studios, 150 Goldhawk Road, London W12 8HH
t 020 7917 2972 f 020 8743 5624
Contact Magnus Fiennes, Executive Producer; Chris Rice, Executive Producer; Bruno Davey, Development Assistant
Credits Freefonix (A)

Skryptonite
89 Giles Street, Edinburgh EH6 6BZ
t 0131 554 0194 f 0131 553 6007
e info@skryptonite.com w www.skryptonite.com
Contact Ken Anderson, Managing Director
Credits The Secret World OF Benjamin Bear (A); Wilf The Witch's Dog (A)

Studio AKA

30 Berwick Street, London W1F 8RH
t 020 7434 3581 **f** 020 7437 2309
e info@studioaka.co.uk **w** www.studioaka.co.uk
Contact Angela Edmonds, Producer; Sophie Goldstraw, Producer; Sue Goffe, Producer
Credits Natwest (C); Compaq (C); Vodafone (C); Orange (C)

Sundog Media

4 Carlton Terrace, Lipson, Plymouth PL4 8PR
t 01752 265562 **m** 07770 607 828
e info@sundog.co.uk **w** www.sundog.co.uk
Contact Kayla Parker; Stuart Moore

Tandem Films

26 Cross Street, London N1 2BG
t 020 7688 1717 **f** 020 7688 1718
e info@tandemfilms.com **w** www.tandemfilms.com
Contact Mike Bell, Producer; Alison Graham, Producer; Nigel Pay, Director; Daniel Grenves, Director
Credits Rockin' And Rollin' (S); How To Cope With Death (S); Flatworld (S); Manipulation (S)

Telemagination

Royalty House, 3rd Floor, 72-74 Dean Street, London W1V 6AE
t 020 7434 1551 **f** 020 7434 3344
e mail@tmation.co.uk **w** www.telemagination.co.uk
Contact Beth Parker, Head of Production; Denise Green, Producer; Marion Edwards, Managing Director/Executive Producer; Alan Simpson, Director of Animation; Lyndon Pickersgill, Head of Digital Facilities
Credits Metalheads (T); The Cramp Twins Series II (T); Little Ghosts (T); Pongwiffy (T)

Uli Meyer Animation Ltd

172A Arlington Road, Camden, London NW1 7HL
t 020 7284 2828 **f** 020 7284 2255
e info@ulimeyer.com **w** www.ulimeyer.com
Contact Christain Robertson, Producer; Matt Saxton, Producer
Credits The Lampies (T); Cookie Crisp (C); Lil Red (C); Space Jam (F)

West Highland Animation

Balquhidder, Lochearnhead, Falkirk FK19 8PQ
t 01877 384740 **f** 01877 384362 **e** leswesthi@aol.com
Contact Leslie MacKenzie, Director/Producer; Jim Stirk, Technical Director
Credits Am Baile (W); Peaten Shinnsrean - Pets Of Yore (A)

Production Companies
Commercials & Promos

@T.I.M.E Productions Istanbul

Meydan Sokak, 6/10 Akatlar, Istanbul 80630, Turkey
t +90 212 352 3991 **f** +90 212 352 3971
e mine@timeproductions.com **e** timeprod@superonline.com
w www.timeproductions.com
Contact Mine Kalpakcioglu, Executive Producer
Credits Swiss Telecom (C); Nokia (C); Badoit - Cinderella Mineral Water (C); Agents Secrets (F)

1759 Production Services

5 Canting Way, Pacific Quay, Glasgow G51 2QY
t 0141 427 3300 **f** 0141 427 3300
e info@1759.co.uk **w** www.1759.co.uk
Contact Ian Hopkins, Producer; Kirsten Bannerman, Location Manager; April Hopkins, Production Manager
Credits Mineral Water (C); Glenlivet (C); Ikea (C)

4 Minute Wonders

350 Saucatiehall Street, Glasgow G2 3JD
t 0141 332 0005 **m** 07880 634734
e ian@bigemedia.com **w** www.4minutewonders.com
Contact Bronagh Keegan, Creative Producer; Ian Crook, Director
Credits The Plan Man Story (T); 4 Minute Wonders Scheme (W)

Academy Commercials

16 West Central Street, London WC1A 1JJ
t 020 7395 4155 **f** 020 7240 0355
e post@academyfilms.com **w** www.academyfilms.com
Contact Elizabeth Gower, Executive Producer; Nick Morris, Executive Producer
Credits Stella Artois: Devil's Island (C); Groove Armada: Purple Haze (C); Levi's Engineered Jeans: Odyssey; 7UP: 'Little Red Riding Hood'

Addiction

Moray House, 23-31 Great Titchfield Street, London W1W 7PA
t 020 7637 8184 **f** 020 7637 8185
e info@addiction.tv **w** www.addiction.tv
Contact Max Garner, Head of Graphics Production; Abby Johnson, Head of Music Commercials; Slobhan Murphy, Head of Promotions; Fuzzy Sanders, Commercials Representative; Edwin John
Credits Terri Walker - Guess You Didn't Love Me (M); MJ Cole - Wonderin' Why (M); Northern Lite - Treat Me Better (M); Nike Run London - Chicken And Egg (C)

Angelic Films Ltd

The Mollies, Nash Lee Lane, Wendover HP22 6BG
t 01296 625414 **f** 01296 696323 **m** 07958 474 079
e mail@angelicfilms.com **w** www.angelicfilms.com
Contact Adam Coop, Producer; Zoe Farrell, Production Manager
Credits Novena - Stand (M); Anna (S); Roses Last Train (S); Spiked (C)

Arden Sutherland-Dodd

6 D'Arblay Street, London W1F 8DN
t 020 7437 3898 **f** 020 7287 2150
e nick@asdlondon.com **w** www.asdlondon.com
Contact Annie Irvine, Producer; Anthony Taylor, Producer; Will Cohen, Producer; Nick Sutherland-Dodd, Executive Producer
Credits Fray Bentos: He-Man (C); Camilla And The Queen (C); MTV Worldwide (C)

ASF Production Ltd

2 Teal Drive, Ducks Hill Road, Northwood HA6 2PT
t 01923 829410 **f** 01923 823310 **m** 07770 277637
e asfc@genmail.net
Contact Malcolm Bubb, Producer; Sarah Boitanna; Alan Spencer, Director/Managing Director
Credits Polish Up Your Nails (E); Animal Friends Insurance (C)

Babe Films

81 Bolingbroke Grove, London SW11 6HB
t 07831 772770 **f** 020 7564 3030
e mail@babefilms.com **w** www.babefilms.com

Bee's Pictures

Calle Cordoba 10B, Fuengirola, Malaga 29640, Spain
t +34 902 118531 **t** +34 95 2667073
f +34 902 118532 **f** +34 95 2664636
e beespics@beespics.com **w** www.beespics.com
Contact Belinda Lewin, Producer; Ivo Van Vollenhoven, Producer; Iohamil Navarro, Producer (Cuba); Simon Burge, Executive Producer

Believe Media

Dewhurst House, 3-6 Winnett Street, London W1D 6JY
t 020 7439 7100 **f** 020 7439 7200
e info@believemedia.co.uk **w** www.believemedia.co.uk

Bikini Films

60-62 Great Titchfield Street, London W1W 7QG
t 020 7323 0660 **f** 020 7323 0661 **e** info@bikinifilms.co.uk
Contact Matt Brown, Producer, Head of Production; Cindy Hanson, PA to Kate Elson; Austen Humphries, Executive Producer
Credits Kit Kat: Rap (Test) (C); Safe Turkey-Turkey Tussle - FSA (C); Incredible - Darius (M); Demons - FA Cup (C)

Black Dog Films Ltd

42-44 Beak Street, London W1R 3DA
t 020 7434 0787 **f** 020 7734 4978
e kai@rsafilms.co.uk **w** www.rsafilms.com
Contact Adrian Harrison, Managing Director; Kai Hsrung, Managing Director
Credits Radiohead - Like Spinning Plates (M); Röyksopp - Remind Me (M); Amon Tobin feat MC Decimal R - Verbal (M)

The Brave Film Company Ltd

5th Floor, Fenton House, 55-57 Great Marlborough Street, London W1F 7JX
t 020 7439 3093 **f** 020 7439 3192
e brave@bravefilms.com **w** www.bravefilms.com
Contact Emily Bliss, Head of TV, Managing Director; Roz Houchin, Directors' Representative; Vanessa Hetherington, Producer; Michelle Stapleton, Head of TV, Managing Director; Jessica Ensor, Producer
Credits BBCi: Fingers

Bullring

140 Battersea Park Road, London SW11 4NB
t 020 7720 5747 **f** 020 7720 5757
e info@bullring.fr **w** www.bullring.fr
Contact Christopher Granier-Deferre, Executive Producer; Serge Sabahi, Producer
Credits Paulina Rubio (M); Ronan Keating (M)

The Business Production Company Ltd

20 Fouberts Place, London W1F 7PL
t 020 7734 7752
Contact David Burgess, Head of Production

Chimera Films & Communications Ltd

Unit 203 Welsbach House, 3-9 Broomhill Road, London SW18 4JQ
t 020 8871 5127 **f** 020 8871 5128 **m** 07968 984727
e pro@chimerafilms.co.uk **w** www.chimerafilms.co.uk
Contact Yoshi Tezuka, Producer, Director/Producer
Credits Millennium - Kirin (C); Aerio - Suzuki (C); Sparky - Toyota (C); Miki House (C)

Chris Horton Films Ltd

19B Aldensley Road, Hammersmith, London W6 0DH
t 020 8741 3337 **f** 020 8741 9996 **m** 07802 717155
e chris@chris-horton.co.uk **w** www.chris-horton.co.uk
Contact Massimo Garlatti-Costa, Director; Chris Horton, Executive Producer; Paul Donnellon, Director; Voodoo Dog, Director; JC, Director; Yonni Usiskin, Production Assistant
Credits Drunken Fool - The Burn (M); Artist Logo - Eve (W); CBBC Xchange (C)

Commercials @ SMG

200 Renfield Street, Glasgow G2 3PR
t 0141 300 3000 **f** 0141 300 3152
e alan.jenkins@smg.plc.uk **w** www.smgtelevisionsales.co.uk
Contact Debbie Ross, Producer; Alison Gourlay, Producer; Gill McArdle, Producer; Alan Jenkins, Commercial Production Manager; Lorna Menzies, PA; Lesley Weir, Producer

Commercials Unlimited

Garden Studios, 11-15 Betterton St, Covent Garden, London WC2H 9BP
t 020 7470 8791 **f** 020 7470 8792
e mail@commercialsunlimited.net
w www.commercialsunlimited.net
Contact Neil Molyneux, Producer, Producer; Jo Marsden, Director, Producer, Producer; Simon Devine, Producer, Producer
Credits Credit Suisse (A); Peugeot (C); BT Openworld (C)

Constantine Sherlock Productions

85 Essex Road, London N1 2SF
t 020 7226 7277 **f** 020 7226 9563 **m** 07801 729491
e info@constantine-sherlock.com
w www.constantine-sherlock.com
Contact Hannah Sherlock, Executive Producer; Elaine Constantine, Creative Director; Gemma Cammidge, Production Assistant; Judy Parkinson, Research & Development
Credits Swapped (S); Baby You're My Light - Ricahrd Hawley (M); AXA Financial Services - Brand Moments (C); Familiar Feelings - Moloko (M)

Cowboy Films Ltd

11-29 Smiths Court, Great Windmill Street, London W1D 7DP
t 020 7287 3808 **f** 020 7287 3785
e info@cowboyfilms.co.uk **w** www.cowboyfilms.co.uk
Contact Robert Bray, Executive Producer; Charles Steele, Feature Film Producer; Natasha Marsh, Head of Development; Carly Stone, Production Assistant; Danielle Holton-Picard, Production Manager
Credits Batchelor's Saucy Noodles: 'Grandma', 'Licking Lezzi'; VW Polo: Whatever

DBI Communication

21 Congreve Close, Warwick CV34 5RQ
t 01926 497695 **e** davidimpey@dbicom.com **w** www.dbicom.com
Contact David Impey, Managing Director

Dene Films

Suite 6, Saville Exchange, Howard Street, North Shields NE30 1SE
t 01912 931860 **f** 01912 931861 **m** 07850 742770
e mail@denefilms.com **w** www.denefilms.com
Contact Steve Salam, Director, Producer, Producer/Director
Credits Worldchoice (C); First Sport (C); Northern Electric (C); Iveco Trucks (I)

Destiny AVP

1 Browning Close, Melton Mowbray LE13 1JW
t 01664 560813 **f** 08701 358132 **m** 07931 830067
e media@destinyavp.com **w** www.destinyavp.com

Directors Film Company of New York

1123 Broadway, Suite 1107, New York 10010, USA
t +1 212 627 4999 **f** +1 212 627 4499 **e** dfcnyc@aol.com
Contact Richard Coll

Dreamlight Pictures

12A Dominic Court, 43 The Gardens, London SE22 9QR
t 020 8299 3490 **e** info@dreamlight.co.uk
Contact John-Christian Jacques, Producer

The Duck Lane Film Company

2nd Level, 5 Carlisle Street, London W1D 3BL
t 020 7439 3912 **f** 020 7437 2260 **e** all@ducklanefilmco.com
Contact Rigby Andrews, Producer, Producer; Geraldine Lake, Production Manager

Eccentric Productions

Unit E, Sheen Stables, Hampton Works, London SW14 8AE
t 020 8876 5244 **f** 020 8876 8207 **e** info@eccentricprods.co.uk
Contact Mike Day, Producer; Trent Walton, Producer
Credits Photocopier Strikes Back (S); Marriage (S); Just Like My Dad (S); Flipped (S)

Echo Vision

The Old Piggery, Mapperton, Beaminster DT8 3NS
t 01308 862999 **f** 01308 862477
e studio@echo-vision.co.uk **w** www.echo-vision.co.uk
Contact Joe Lintell, Managing Director
Credits Baxter Healthcare (C); The Fish Run (D)

Exceeda Films

110-116 Elmore Street, London N1 3AH
t 020 7288 0433 **f** 020 7288 0735
e contact@exceeda.co.uk **w** www.exceeda.co.uk
Credits Glastonbury Festival 2002 (T); Nike - Freestyler (C); The Osbournes
Christmas Message (C); Star Wars: Episode 1 - The Phantom Menace Premiere
Visuals (F)

Eyeland Productions ltd

Unit 8, 9 Long Street, London E2 8HN
t 020 7749 5900 **f** 020 7739 3275
e mail@eyelandfilm.com **w** www.eyelandfilm.com
Contact Jonathan Bannister, Managing Director; Ben Bannister, Director;
Tim Pitman, Producer

Fat Fish Films

46 Maddox Street, London W1S 1QA
t 020 7499 9199 **f** 020 7499 9699 **m** 07770 890608
e jacci@fatfish.co.uk
Contact Jacci Barrett, Executive Producer

Ferocious Films Ltd

2-3 Bourlet Close, London W1P 7EJ
t 020 7251 3680 **f** 020 7637 5692 **m** 07718 822806
e ferocious@ferociousfilms.demon.co.uk
Contact Lucy Russell, Personal Assistant

Film It Sp Zoo

ul Wita Stwosza 17A, Warsaw
02 661, Poland
t +48 22 848 7811 **t** +48 22 848 3779
f +48 22 843 0607
e office@filmit.com.pl
w www.filmit.pl
Contact Dominika Grzegdala; Mira Klajnberg

Filma-Cass

Kocamansur Sokak 115/1, Sisli, Istanbul 80260, Turkey
t +90 212 233 6018 **f** +90 212 231 0227
e filmacass@filmacass.com.tr **w** www.filmacass.com.tr
Contact Ömer Vargi; Tamer Basaran; Bahadir Arliel; Elfin Yuksekteppe;
Oguz Peri

Flehner Films

Castillo 1366, Buenos Aires C 1414 AXD, Argentina
t +54 11 4771 0400 **f** +54 11 4771 6003
e rmazzeo@flehner.com.ar **w** www.flehnerfilms.com
Contact Rammero Mazzeo; Sergio Gullco
Credits Axe: 'Araña'; Renault Megane: 'Campo Traviesa'; Pajarito; Museum

The Flying Colours Film Company Ltd

11 Charlotte Mews, London W1T 4EQ
t 020 7436 2121 **f** 020 7436 3055
e fc@flyingc.co.uk **w** www.flyingc.co.uk
Contact Siobhan Buxton, Producer; Anne-Marie Perry, Producer; Michelle
Brooks, Production Assistant; Barry Aylett, Producer; Rachel Cotton
Credits Golden Grahams Cereal (C); Nationwide Building Society (C);
News of the World (C)

Fu-Cut-Wu

m 07941 802742
e charleswu@fu-cut-wu.co.uk **w** www.fu-cut-wu.co.uk
Contact Simon Gordon, Art Director; Charlie Wu, Director; Charles Fu, Producer
Credits New Drifters (M)

Music Video Production and Music Production. For any size pocket.

Garden Films

34 Lexington Street, London W1F OLH
t 020 7439 4080 **f** 020 7439 4083
e garden@gardenfilms.com
Contact Helen Conlan, Production Assistant; Jake Lloyd, Producer
Credits Carlsberg (C); Rover (C); McDonalds (C); British Gas (C)

Garretts

21 Little Portland Street, London W1W 8BT
t 020 7580 6452 **f** 020 7580 6453
e commercials@garretts.co.uk
Contact Sue Hildrey, Producer; Gerald Berman, Producer; Hans Elias, Producer;
Nat Taylor, Producer
Credits Welsh Tourist Board: Dog

Gerard De Thame Films

16-18 Hollen Street, London W1F 8BQ
t 020 7437 3339 **f** 020 7437 3338 **e** post@gdtfilms.co.uk

Glo & Co Ltd

5 Robertson Street, London SW8 3SH
t 020 7627 1982 **f** 020 7498 1370 **e** glo@gloandco.dircon.co.uk
Contact Glo Vanlinl, Managing Director

The Good Film Company

The Studio, 5-6 Eton Garages, Lambolle Place, London NW3 4PE
t 020 7794 6222 **f** 020 7794 4651
e yanina@goodfilms.co.uk **w** www.goodfilms.co.uk
Contact Yanina Barry, Producer
Credits HBO - The Gathering Storm (C); Millennium Bridge (I); Wendy's
Hamburgers (C); Nestle - Acti-V (C)

Gorgeous Enterprises

23/24 Greek Street, London W1D 4DZ
t 020 7287 4060 **f** 020 7287 4994
e gorgeous@gorgeous.co.uk **w** www.gorgeous.co.uk
Contact Paul Rothwell, Producer
Credits Audi - Drink Like a Fish (C); Boots 17 Make-up - Knock Out (C);
Aristoc - Wallet (C); NSPCC - Cartoon (C)

Grasshopper Films Ltd

3rd Floor, 14 Bacon Street, London E1 6LF
t 020 7739 7154 **f** 020 7739 6359 **m** 07956 435351
e info@grasshopperfilms.com **w** www.grasshopperfilms.com
Credits Britney Spears (D); Sharp Flatscreen TVs (C); Guerlain Perfume (C);
Macy Gray In Concert (D)

Great Guns

43-45 Camden Road, London NW1 9LR
t 020 7692 4444 **f** 020 7692 4422
e greatguns@greatguns.com **w** www.greatguns.com
Contact Laura Gregory, Managing Director/Producer; Geoff Stickler, Head Of
Production; Olivia Henley-Price, Producer; Polly Du Plessis, Producer; Sheridan
Thomas, Producer
Credits Rover - The Oddball Run (C); Milk - Bounce, Pants (C)

Harry Nash

Harry's House, 27-29 Beak Street, London W1F 9RU
t 020 7025 7500 **f** 020 7025 7501
e juliareed@harrynash.co.uk **w** www.harrynash.co.uk
Contact Julia Reed, Managing Director; Austen Humphries, Executive Producer
Credits Super Noodles (C): Salsa (C); Volkswagen Lupo (C); Wrangler (C)

Pier Hausemer

8 Stranraer Way, Islington, London N1 0DR
t 020 7700 2971 **m** 07971 589998
e piercamden@freeuk.com **w** www.offshorefilms.co.uk
Credits Chem5 (S); Livewire - It's not too late (M)

Horoscope Films Ltd

165 Farnview Court, Bawdsey Avenue, Newbury Park IG2 7TL
m 07949 238455 **e** nicolamillington@hotmail.com
Contact Nicola Millington, Producer; George Amponsah, Director
Credits One Plus One (D); Kit Kat (C); Daihatsu (C); Kodak (C)

Hotspur & Argyle

4th Floor, 25 Lexington Street, London W1F 9AG
t 020 7439 3130 **f** 020 7439 3075
e production@hotspurandargyle.co.uk
w www.hotspurandargyle.com
Contact Danny Fleet, Producer; Theo Delaney, Director; Juliet Smith, Production Assistant
Credits The Call (S); Sainsbury's (C); Imperial Leather (C); McDonalds (C)

Hungry Man UK

19 Grafton Mews, London W1T 5JB
t 020 7380 8280 **f** 020 7380 8299
e ukmail@hungryman.com **w** www.hungryman.com
Contact Mark Whelan, Production Assistant; Helen McLeish, Production Assistant; Adam Lyne, Head Of Production; Owen Harris, Director; David Levin, Director; Paul Norling, Director; John O'Hagan, Director; Bennett Miller, Director; Hank Perlman, Director; Russ Lamourcux, Director; David Shane, Director; Marcos Siega, Director; Bryan Buckley, Director; Allen Coulter, Director; Michael Cuesta, Director; Jim Jenkins, Director; Scott Vincent, Director; Matt Buels, Executive Producer; Helen MacCuish, Production Assistant
Credits MTV 9-11: Email

IDP Ltd

8A Delancey Passage, London NW1 7NN
t 020 7419 4655 **f** 020 7419 4660
e production@imagedynamic.co.uk
w www.idp.info; www.imgedynamic.co.uk
Contact Patrick Holtkamp, Producer
Credits Tom Jones (M); Hear'Say (M); Westlife (M); CNN (C)

Igloo

2nd Level, 5 Carlisle Street, London W1D 3BL
t 020 7734 0698 **f** 020 7437 2260 **e** info@iglooprod.com
Contact Rigby Andrews, Executive Producer; Giles Skillicorn, Producer; Geraldine Lake, Production Manager

Independent Films

7A Langley Street, London WC2H 9JA
t 020 7845 7474 **f** 020 7845 7475 **e** firstname@independ.net
Contact Tess Wight, Head of Music Videos; Vida Toombs, Assistant to Managing Director; Jani Guest, Managing Director; Dougal Meese, Production Assistant; Richard Packer, Managing Director; Elise Bennett, Head of Marketing & Promotion

Infinity Productions Ltd

13-14 Dean Street, London W1D 3RS
t 020 7434 4471 **f** 020 7434 4472
e info@infinityproductions.co.uk **w** www.infinityproductions.co.uk
Contact Mark Stothert, Executive Producer, Managing Director; Polly Fryer, Production Manager; Di Redvers, Director's Representative

Intro

35 Little Russell Street, London WC1A 2HH
t 020 7637 1231 **f** 020 7636 5015
e intro@intro-uk.com **w** www.intro-uk.com
Contact Julian House, Director, Senior Designer; Katy Richardson, Executive Producer, Executive Producer; Mat Cook, Director, Senior Art Director; Kate Dawkins, Director, Moving Image Designer; Nikki Hildesley, Producer, Producer; Julian Gibbs, Director, Director; Jo Marsh, New Business
Credits Mastercard Brits TVC (T); Doves - There Goes The Fear (M); BBC Athletics (T); Primal Scream - Kill All Hippies (M)

Jam Creative

22 Greek Street, London W1D 4DZ
t 020 7439 1600 **f** 020 7734 6276 **m** 07785 254 467
e mail@jamcreative.com **w** www.jamcreative.com
Contact Eddie Marshall, Producer

JK Advertising Ltd

730 Pershore Road, Selly Park, Birmingham B29 7NJ
t 0121 472 1000 **f** 0121 414 1290 **m** 07711 564121
e info@jkadvertising.co.uk **w** www.jkadvertising.co.uk
Contact Millan Joshi, IT Director

John S Clarke Productions

3 Alma Studios, 32-34 Stratford Road, London W8 6QF
t 020 7937 4373 **f** 020 7938 3253 **e** (name)@jscprods.com
Contact Gabrielle O'Connell, PA; John Clarke, Director; John Clarke

Joy Films

The Hat Factory, 16-18 Hollen Street, London W1F 8BQ
t 020 7287 0044 **f** 020 7287 0066 **e** info@joyfilms.co.uk
Contact Jeremy Barnes, MD; Desley Gregory, Exec Producer; Mehdi Norowzian, Director

Krygier Hirschkorn

6A Poland Street, London W1V 3DG
t 020 7434 1000 **f** 020 7434 1102
Contact Thomas Krygier; Pip McCall; Nick Hirschkorn; Franzi Hoch

Liberation Productions Ltd

7 Woodside Crescent, Glasgow G3 7UL
t 0141 332 4000 **f** 0141 332 4004 **m** 07732 108045
e warren@liberationproductions.com
w www.liberationproductions.com
Contact Warren Bader, Producer
Credits Tina Turner Silent Wings (M); First Direct (C); Royal Bank of Scotland (I); Coltas Reid Furniture (C)

Liquid Eyes Productions

t 07968 444530 **f** 01329 313351
e production@liquid-eyes.com **w** www.liquid-eyes.com
Contact David Cheng, Director; David Beavis, Director
Credits The South Bank Show - Soprano (T); The South Bank Show - JRR Tolkien (T); Monsters Inc - News Of The World (T); The Times 2003 (T)

Mad Cow Productions

75 Amberley Road, London W9 2JL
t 020 7289 0001 **f** 020 7289 0003
e info@madcowfilms.co.uk **w** www.madcowproductions.co.uk
Contact Anwen Rees-Myers, Executive Producer, Head of Production

Manifesto Film Productions

5A Irving Street, London WC2H 7AT
t 020 7930 5990 **f** 020 7930 5999
e info@manifes.com **w** www.manifes.com
Contact Daisy Hoque, Director; Edwin John; Aya Kobayashi, Producer; Ken Okubo, PA; Chris O'Reilly; Sam Takashima, Producer & MD
Credits Vodafone Japan (C)

Map Films

3 Bourlet Close, London W1W 7BM
t 020 7291 7840 **f** 020 7291 7841 **e** mail@mapfilms.com
Contact Stuart Macleod, Director; Giles Healy, Producer

Maverick Media

74 Newman Street, London W1T 3EL
t 020 7291 3450 **f** 020 7323 4143
e info@maverickmedia.co.uk **w** www.maverickmedia.co.uk
Contact Brian Hassan, Director; Daniel Outram, Director; William Jeffrey; Tristan Ramsey, Designer; Seamus Masterson, Director; Nigel Barton, Director; Levidi , Director; Jack O'Melli, Director; Denis McArdle, Director; Mahesh Mathai, Director; Justin Rogers, Director

MB Productions

33 Gay Street, Bath BA1 2HT
t 01225 314823 **f** 01225 444736 **m** 07831 145923
Contact Ian Simpson, Producer

Meantime Productions Ltd

165 Conway Road, London N14 7BH
t 01908 543265 **f** 01908 542850 **m** 07770 914 117
e meantimeproductions@supanet.com
w www.meantimeproductions.supanet.com
Contact Neil Lee, Location Manager; Luke Beauchamp, Managing Director

Mendoza Productions

75 Wigmore Street, London W1U 1QD
t 020 7935 4674 **f** 020 7935 4417 **m** 07973 258573
e info@mendozafilms.com **w** www.mendozafilms.com
Contact Louise Hooper, Production Assistant; Debby Mendoza, Producer; Wynn Wheldon, Producer

MG Films & Video Ltd

88 Albert Road, Caversham Heights, Reading RG4 7PL
t 0118 947 5600 **f** 0118 947 5600 **m** 07860 393945
e michel.gemmell@mg-films.co.uk **w** www.mg-films.co.uk
Contact Monika Wint, Producer; Michel Gemmell, Director
Credits Guinness - St. Patrick's Day (C); VW Castles (C)

Miracles Production

154 Upper Newtownards Road, Belfast BT4 3EQ
t 028 9047 3838 **f** 028 9047 3839 **m** 07831 661 603
e info@miraclesproduction.com
w www.miraclesproduction.com
Contact Gillian Devenney, Director/Producer; Dave Johnston, Director/Producer

Momentum Productions Ltd

90 York Road, Teddington TW11 8SN
t 020 8977 7333 **f** 020 8977 6999
e production@momentum.co.uk **w** www.momentum.co.uk
Contact Lucy Hampton, Production Manager

Mustard Films

The NCP Building, Level 3, 32 Brewer Street, London W1F 0ST
t 020 7434 2282 **f** 020 7434 2292 **e** shoot@mustardlondon.com

Mutiny Films Ltd

18 Soho Square, London W1V 3QL
t 020 7025 8710 **f** 020 7025 8100 **m** 07976 838487
e info@mutinyfilms.co.uk **w** www.mutinyfilms.co.uk
Contact Sam Eastall, Director; Adam Wimpenny, Director

Native Productions

6 Brewer Street, London W1F 0SD
t 020 7287 2433 **f** 020 7287 1357 **e** native.productions@virgin.net
Contact Charlie Hayter

Natural State

3 Eshton Road, Eastbourne BN22 7ES
t 01323 721603 **m** 07711 589610
e simonvieler@hotmail.com **w** www.obedientbone.com
Credits Suzi Quatro - No Choicec (C); Steve Winwood - Live Concert (C); Obedientbone - Tendril (C); MG Experience (C)

Nebraska Productions

12 Grove Avenue, London N10 2AR
t 020 8444 5317 **f** 020 8444 2113 **m** 07710 850373
e nebraskaprods@aol.com

Northlight Productions (London)

Northlight House, 7 Redbourne Avenue, London N3 2BP
t 020 8343 3161 **f** 020 8343 3203 **m** 07887 503 961
e kenw.little@virgin.net **w** www.northlight.co.uk
Contact Ken Little, Managing Director

Notorious Films (Europe) Ltd

117 Shaftesbury Avenue, London WC2H 8AD
t 020 7379 5511 **f** 020 7379 5544 **m** 07970 801386
e info@notoriousfilms.com **w** www.notoriousfilms.com
Contact Chia Tucker, Directors Representative And Public Relations; Laura Collins, Production Assistant/Office Manager; Sandra Yarwood, Producer; Severine Hamilton, Producer

Octavian Productions

3 South Down Crescent, Newbury Park IG2 7PT
t 020 8590 0160 **f** 020 8590 0160 **m** 07951 702946
e octavianprods@aol.com
Contact Socrates Pelendrides, Producer
Credits World Cup (D); Autism (D); Road To Ithaca (F)

Oil Factory Ltd

5th Floor, 26 Little Portland Street, London W1W 8BX
t 020 7255 6255 **f** 020 7255 6277
e production@oilfactory.net **w** www.oilfactory.com
Contact Toby Hyde, Head of Music Video; Paul Fennelly, Head of Production

On The Spot

c/ Alto de las Cabañas 5, Madrid 28230, Spain
t 636 0641 **f** 710 5038
e onthespot@onthespot.es **w** www.onthespot.es
Contact Mark Albela, Producer; Cayetano Chimeno, Production Manager; Ricardo Serrano, Production Assistant
Credits The Planets (M); Rover 25 (C); Play Skool (C); Hasbro (C)

The Online Video Production Company

8 Clooney Terrace, Londonderry BT47 6AR
t 02871 345945 **f** 02871 287116
Contact Paul McClintock, Managing Director
Credits RTE Ireland (T); TV 3 Ireland (T); UTV Live at 6 (T); BBC Newsline (T)

Outlaw Films

11 Southwick Mews, London W2 1JG
t 020 7262 2611 **f** 020 7262 2811
e production@outlawfilms.com **w** www.outlawfilms.com
Contact Bill James, Producer; Jeremy Goold, Producer

P4films

Cheltenham Film Studios, Arle Court, Hatherley, Cheltenham GL51 6PN
t 01242 542760 **f** 01242 542739 **m** 07831 342634
e info@p4films.com **w** www.p4films.com
Contact Phil Partridge, Producer; Peter Pullon, Director

Pagan Production Ltd

308 Westbourne Studios, 242 Acklam Road, London W10 5JJ
t 020 7575 3188 **f** 020 7575 3189 **e** info@paganproduction.co.uk
Contact Adam Saward, Managing Director

palmfiction.com

production and location services in spain

Palmfiction

Plaza de la Puerta Pintada 6, Palma de Mallorca 7002, Spain
t +34 971 711444 **f** +34 971 711445
e mail@palmfiction.com **w** www.palmfiction.com
Contact Alex Gegenfurtner; David Krause

Park Village Productions

1 Park Village East, Regents Park, London NW1 7PX
t 020 7387 8077 **f** 020 7388 3051 **e** reception@parkvillage.co.uk
Contact Freya Noble, Senior Producer

The Paul Weiland Film Company

14 Newburgh Street, London W1F 7RT
t 020 7287 6900 **f** 020 7434 0146
e action@paulweiland.com **w** www.paulweiland.com
Contact Mary Francis, Head of Production

Picasso Pictures Ltd

9-11 Broadwick Street, London W1F 0DB
t 020 7437 9888 **f** 020 7437 9040
e info@picassopictures.com **w** www.picassopictures.com
Contact Jane Bolton, Executive Producer; Jo Gallagher, Assistant Producer; Steve May, Director, Lighting & Generator Hire
Credits Silver Dead - Guinness (C)

Picture Coverage Ltd

23 The Crescent, Salford, Manchester M5 4PF
t 0161 745 8686 **f** 0161 745 8998
e mail@picturecoverage.co.uk **w** www.picturecoverage.co.uk
Contact Paul Francis, Director; David Gerrard, Director
Credits Videolinks (W); Hands (C); Plasplugs (C)

Playtime Pictures

26 Talbot Road, London W2 5LJ
t 020 7419 1501 **f** 020 7240 8883 **m** 07860 149459
Contact Tracey Adam, Producer

Power Media

Number 3, Bedfordbury, Covent Garden, London WC2N 4BP
t 020 7240 2828 **f** 020 7240 2282
e rachael@powerhousetv.co.uk **w** www.powerhousetv.co.uk
Contact Sam Wyner, Producer

The Producers

8 Berners Mews, London W1T 3AW
t 020 7636 4226 **f** 020 7636 4099
e info@theproducersfilms.co.uk **w** www.theproducersfilms.co.uk
Contact Jenny Edwards, Producer, Managing Director/Producer
Credits Lloyds TSB (C); Seeing Red (F); The Politician's Wife (T); Diet Coke (C)

PSA Ltd

52 The Downs, Altrincham WA14 2QJ
t 0161 9240011 **f** 0161 9240022 **m** 07713 214543
e tony@psa.u-net.com
Contact David Moss, Producer; Tony Smith, Producer
Credits ITV Weather Sponsorships (C); Coop Bank (C); Budget Insurance (C)

PTT Films - Production Team Of Turkey

Asmalimescit Minare Sok 23, Beyoglu, Istanbul 80050, Turkey
t +90 212 293 8473 **f** +90 212 293 8475
e sebnem@pttfilms.com **w** www.pttfilms.com
Contact R Sebnem Kitis

Raven Films Inc /Ravenous Pictures

16 West Central Street, London WC1A 1JJ
t 020 7395 4155 **f** 020 7240 0355
e post@academyfilms.com **w** www.academyfilms.com
Contact Lizie Gower, Managing Director; Nick Morris, Managing Director; Laura Kanerick, Music Videos; Tim Nash, Music Videos

Red Dragon

Unit 8, Sandhurst House, Wolsey Street, London E1 3BD
Contact Geoff Rogers, Director

Relative Normality

Unit F20, Argo House, Kilburn Park Road, London NW6 5LF
t 020 7644 0454
e mail@relativenormality.com **w** www.relativenormality.com
Contact Leon Mills, Director
Credits DJ Dee Kline - Don't Smoke (M); Lovestation - Teardrops (M); BVI/Disney - Toy Story II (M); BVI/Disney - Emperor's New Groove (C)

Republik Films

1 Marlborough Court, London W1F 7EE
t 020 7734 4048 **f** 020 7734 4047
e mail@republikfilms.co.uk **w** www.republikfilms.com
Contact J F, Executive Producer

RMC Ltd

4a Cadogan Sq, London Sw1X 0JU
t 020 7838 9119 **f** 020 7838 9229 **e** ramaco@global.com
Contact Ruck Strauss, Managing Director & Producer

Rom Media

52 Shaftsbury Avenue, London W1D 6LP
t 020 7287 0999 **f** 020 7287 8999
e mail@rom-media.com **w** www.rommedia.com
Contact Denise Connell, Producer; Daniel Figuero, Producer

Rose Hackney Barber

5-6 Kingly Street, London W1B 5PF
t 020 7439 6697 **f** 020 7434 4102
e info@rosehackneybarber.com
Contact Sandra Lawrence, Head of Music Video; Matthew Brown, Joint Managing Director; Tim Katz, Joint Managing Director
Credits Del Amitri - Just Before You Leave; Hamlet - Photo Booth (C); Impulse - Chain (C)

RSA Films Ltd

42-44 Beak Street, London W1R 3DA
t 020 7437 7426 **f** 020 7734 4978
e kai@rsafilms.co.uk **w** www.rsafilms.com
Contact Adrian Harrison, Managing Director; Kai Hsrung, Managing Director

Screenscope

Weald House, Pluckley, Ashford TN27 0SN
t 01233 840432 **f** 01233 840432 **e** astric1@btopenworld.com
Contact Michael Brandt, Managing Director

Shed Films Ltd

27 Britton Street, London EC1M 5UD
t 020 7490 2950 **f** 020 7336 7043 **e** noellep@globalnet.co.uk
Contact Noelle Pickford, Producer; Elaine Longster, Personal Assistant
Credits Firewalker

Silk Production

The Silk House, 13 Berwick Street, London W1F 0PW
t 020 7434 3461 **f** 020 7494 1748 **i** 020 7434 7636x2
e production@silkproduction.com **w** www.silkproduction.com
Contact Robbie Weston; Lee Climpson; Mike Blunt

Silver Productions (London) Ltd

Bridge Farm, Lower Road, Britford, Salisbury SP5 4DY
t 01722 336221 **f** 01722 336227 **m** 07899 927247
e info@silver.co.uk **w** www.silver.co.uk
Contact Simon Warne, Producer; Laura Rawlinson, Co-ordinator; Ethem Cetintas, Director; Ash Mills, Production; Riza Pacalioglu, Technical
Credits Beaulieu (C); Yes Car Credit (C); Hobbycraft (C); Hobbycraft (T)

Simpson Kennet Transparent

22 Poland Street, London W1V 8QQ
t 020 7287 9198 **f** 020 7287 9203 **m** 07774 235053
e sklfc@aol.com
Contact Eilon Kennet, Producer

Sneezing Tree Film Ltd

1-2 Bromley Place, London W1T 6DA
t 020 7927 9900 **f** 020 7927 9909
e sneezingtree@compuserve.com
Contact Christian Sandino-Taylor, Production Assistant; Brock Van Den Bogaerde, MD//Producer; Natalie Trieblasser, Production Assistant

Space City Productions

Suite 314, Bedford Chambers, London WC2E 8HA
t 020 7371 4000 **f** 020 7371 4001
Contact Jo Purefoy, Producer
Credits E-Shore (C)

Space City Productions

77 Blythe Road, London W14 0HP
t 020 7371 4000 **f** 020 7371 4001
e info@spacecity.co.uk **w** www.spacecity.co.uk
Contact Jo Purefoy, Producer; Zoe Lack, Producer; Roland Mizon, Marketing Manager; Claire Davies, Managing Director

Spoton (Film & TV Services) Ltd

Ormeau Business Park, 8 Cromac Avenue, Belfast BT7 2JA
t 028 9023 6111 **f** 028 9023 6068 **m** 07860 620743
e spoton.micky@virgin.net **w** www.spotontv.net
Contact Micky O'Neill, Producer/Director

Stark Films Ltd

3 Bromley Place, London W1T 6DB
t 020 7580 3870 **f** 020 7636 5412
e firstname@starkfilms.com **w** www.starkfilms.com

Contact Stephen Gash, MD
Credits McDonalds - Caravan (C); Adidas - Lee Evans (C); Art School Impulse (C); Virgin Atlantic (C)

Sterling Films Ltd

No 1 Stedham Place, London WC1A 1HU
t 020 7436 6279 **f** 020 8281 9059 **m** 07768 551532
e grahamfowler@sterlingfilms.fsworld.co.uk

Contact Graham Fowler, Managing Director

Studio

8 Conlan Street, London W10 5AR
t 020 8964 1109 **f** 020 8964 0126 **e** post@bigtvstudio.com

Contact Dawn Laren, Producer; Emmalou Johnson, Production Assistant; Jessica Dunn, Office Manager

Superkrush Productions

The Old Post Office, 5 Pink Lane, Newcastle NE1 5DW
t 0191 233 2001 **f** 0191 261 5746 **m** 07949 114857
e info@superkrush.com **w** www.superkrush.com

Contact Steve Brunton, Chief Editor; Chris Taylor, Director
Credits Childcare Information Service (C); The Secret World Of Me Unborn (S); Delicate (S); Madventures (D)

Tabletop Partnership

51-53 Mount Pleasant, London WC1X 0AE
t 020 7831 3033 **f** 020 7405 3721
e julian@julianseddonfilms.com
e alison@julianseddonfilms.com **w** www.tabletop.com

Contact Julian Seddon, Executive Producer; Alison Cooper, Producer

Tank Productions

6A Poland Street, London W1F 8PD
t 020 7434 0110 **f** 020 7434 9232
e editors@tankmagazine.com **w** www.tankmagazine.com
Contact Caroline Issa, Business Manager; Iram Quarishi, Tank TV

Thomas Thomas Films Ltd

14-19 Great Chapel Street, London W1F 8FN
t 020 7437 1112 **f** 020 7437 1113
e philippa@thomasthomasfilms.co.uk

Contact Philippa Thomas, Producer; Tracy Garfield, Producer; Alice Grant, Production Manager

Tick Tock Films

1 Littlewood Cottages, School Road, Drayton, Norwich NR8 6EP
t 01603 860984 **f** 01603 860984 **m** 07966 172909
e jf-edwards@hotmail.com

Contact Judith Carter Edwards

Toast TV Ltd

10 Frith Street, London W1D 3JF
t 020 7437 0506 **f** 020 7439 8852
e mail@toasttv.co.uk **w** www.toasttv.co.uk

Contact Fiona Watson, Director; Felicity Gradwell, Director
Credits British Telecom (I); Nike (I); Citroën (I); Camelot (C)

Tomboy Films Ltd

The Old Dairy, 13A Hewer Street, London W10 4DU
t 020 8962 3456 **f** 020 89623457
e info@tomboyfilms.co.uk **w** www.tomboy-films.co.uk

Treehouse North Productions Inc

345 Carlaw Avenue, Main Floor, Toronto M4M 2T1, Canada
t +1 416 861 1204 **f** +1 416 861 0220
e info@treenorth.com **w** www.treenorth.com

Contact Holly Nichols, Executive Assistant; Deb Feeney, Production Supervisor; Karen Silver, Executive Producer
Credits BMW (C); Honda (C); Chevrolet Trucks (C); Nike (C)

The Trouble With Harry Films

Also known as Trouble! Films, 98 Wardour Street, London W1F 0TL
t 020 7734 2214 **f** 020 7734 2214 **m** 07941 385770
e post@troublefilms.demon.co.uk

Contact Laine Lindsay Law, Executive Producer; Richard Gardner, Director
Credits Drum

TTO Films

Hardy House, 16-18 Beak Street, London W1F 9RD
t 020 7494 2414 **f** 020 7494 2417 **e** tto2ltd@easynet.co.uk

Contact Adrian Hughes, Producer; Lizzie Knowles, Production Manager; Kim Griffin, Producer

Unicorn Organisation Ltd

Pottery Lane House, Pottery Lane, London W11 4LZ
t 020 7229 5131 **f** 020 7229 4999 **m** 0410 356577
e nicholas.seligman@btclick.com

Contact Nicholas Seligman, Director

Unity Pictures

7A Newburgh Street, London W1F 7RH
t 020 7734 2888 **f** 020 7734 2999
e admin@unitypictures.co.uk **w** www.unitypictures.co.uk

Contact Chia Tucker, Production Manager; David Chiverton, Producer; Alon Ziv, Director; Hylton Tannenbaum, Director; Hilary Davis, Producer
Credits Art Crimes (T); Spitfire (C); Time Magazine (C); Spy TV (T)

Video Inn Production

Glebe Farm, Wootton Road, Quinton NN7 2EE
t 01604 864868 **e** andy@videoinn.co.uk

Contact Roger Bentley, Proprietor

Production Companies
Corporate & Non-Broadcast

1871 Productions

4th Floor, Windsor House, 40-41 Great Castle Street, London W1W 8LU
t 020 7631 4500
e info@1871productions.co.uk **w** www.1871productions.co.uk
Contact Giuliana Ostir, Executive Producer; Gaby Montanaro, Producer

20/20 Productions

4 Albany Lane, Edinburgh EH1 3QP
t 0131 556 2020 **f** 0131 556 2525
e info@2020productions.com **w** www.2020productions.com
Contact Fiona Bell

22 Ten

7 Primrose Street, Cambridge CB4 3EH
t 01223 561222 **f** 01223 569220
e studio22ten@ntlworld.com **w** www.22ten.co.uk
Contact C Hewitt
Credits London Underground (I); Dundee Science Centre (I); Pfizer UK (C); The Samaritans (C)

360 Degree.TV Ltd

t 01344 761315 **e** info@360degree.tv **w** www.360degree.tv
Contact John Chambers, Director

55degrees Ltd

73 Robertson Street, Glasgow G2 8QD
t 0141 222 2855 **f** 0141 222 2755
e mark@55degrees.co.uk **w** www.55degrees.co.uk
Contact Mark Magnante, Senior Account Executive
Credits The National Trust For Scotland (D); Glasgow City Council (E); Monsoon (I); Red Bull (C)

A+M Video Services

43 Dalry Road, Edinburgh EH11 2BU
t 0131 477 8686 **w** www.a-m-video.co.uk
Contact Alex Shaw, Public Relations

Abbey Video Productions
Woodlawn House, Woodlawn Grove, Woking GU21 4EF
t 01483 765605 **e** p.c.h@ntlworld.com
Contact Howell, Managing Director

Able Schott
Moon Cottage Studio, Higher Eype, Bridport DT6 6AS
t 01308 423095
e info@ableschott.co.uk **w** www.ableschott.co.uk
Contact G Cuddihy, Administrator; P Hulacki, Proprietor

Absolutely Visual
22 Cavendish Road, Sutton SM2 5ER
t 020 8661 7703 **f** 020 8661 0888 **m** 07715 749450
e info@absolutely-visual.co.uk **w** www.absolutely-visual.co.uk
Contact Noriko Brewster

Academy Productions
19 Fitzroy House, Wallwood Street, London E14 7AL
t 020 7536 0676 **m** 07803 923778
e info@academyproductions.co.uk
w www.academyproductions.co.uk
Contact David Waddell
Credits Fred The Fresher (I); Engineered Risks (D); Policing The Peace (D)

The Accidental Film Company Ltd
Unit 12, Acton Business Centre, School Road,
London NW10 6TD
t 020 8961 7945 **f** 020 8961 9037 **m** 07956 886138
e mail@accidentalfilm.co.uk **w** www.accidentalfilm.co.uk
Contact Chris How, Producer; Keir Husband, Producer
Credits Durex (I); British Gymnastics (I); Everest (I); Battersea Dogs Home (I)

Acrobat Televison
107 Wellington Road North, Stockport SK4 2LP
t 0161 477 9090 **f** 0161 477 9191 **m** 07850 919945
e info@acrobat-tv.co.uk **w** www.acrobat-tv.co.uk
Contact Jill Taylor, Media Director; Mike Clark, Editor; David Hill, Director/Producer
Credits Royal Yachting Association - Water Sports Training (I); Ski Club Great Britain - Snow Sports Training (I); Federation Of Tour Operators - Health And Safety (I)

Actionstream Direct Media Ltd
First Floor, 7-8 High Town, Hay-on-Wye HR3 5AE
t 01497 821458 **f** 01497 821460
e enquiries@actionstream.co.uk **w** www.actionstream.co.uk
Contact Lawrence Middleton Jones, Managing Director
Credits Loughborough University (W); Crathorne Hall Hotel (C); Hamleys (C); Harrods (C)

Active Image
Unit 5, Dunston Technology Park, Millennium Way, Dunston Road, Chesterfield S41 8ND
t 01246 450123 **f** 01246 450211
e mailbox@activeimage.demon.co.uk
Contact John Lister, Library Manager

Adelphi Medi Cine
32-38 Osnaburgh Street, London NW1 3ND
t 020 7387 3606 **f** 020 7387 9693
e sarahcb@medi-cine.com **w** www.medi-cine.com
Contact Sarah Barber, Managing Director

Airplay
The Manse, 39 Northenden Road, Sale M33 2DH
t 0161 962 2002 **f** 0161 962 2112
e mailbox@airplay.co.uk **w** www.airplay.co.uk
Contact Nick Porter, Sales Director; James Davidson, Company Director; Jonathan Boyne, Company Director; Peter Knott, Managing Director
Credits All Sports (C)

Alan Johnson & Partner
154 Pack Lane, Basingstoke RG22 5HR
t 01256 325419 **f** 01256 840930 **e** alanjohn@netcomuk.co.uk
Contact Alan Johnson, Partner

Alchemy Media
21A St Andrews Road, Hayling Island PO11 9JN
t 023 9246 1095 **f** 023 9246 1095
e info@alchemymedia.co.uk **w** www.alchemymedia.co.uk
Contact Richard Verney, Director
Credits Compass Group Facilities Management (I); CIWF - Farm Animals & Us (E); Ritazza Coffee Shop (C)

Allset Productions
111 Sinclair Road, London W14 0NP
t 020 7602 5794 **f** 020 7602 5794 **m** 07759 211138
e info@allsetproductions.co.uk **w** www.allsetproductions.co.uk
Contact Jennifer Toynbee-Holmes, Producer/Director
Credits World Health Organisation - The Community Health Nurse (I); NHS - Breast Screening Programme (I); The Living Body (T); Tomorrow's World (T)

Alpha Omega Productions
3 The Byre, Pump House Farm, Ongar Road, Kelvedon Hatch, Brentwood CM15 0LA
t 01277 365048 **f** 01277 365214 **m** 07973 763665
e tv@alphaomegaproductions.co.uk
Contact Martin McGahon

Amatis Films Ltd
PO Box 21, Tadworth KT20 5XZ
t 01737 215077 **e** info@amatis.eu.com **w** www.amatis.eu.com
Credits Academy Windows (C); Discovery Dock Property (C); Siemens Business Services Employee Communications (I); Toyota Concept Training Programme (I)

Anup Parmar Digital Video Productions
9 Hutchinson Terrace, London HA9 7TP
t 020 8908 2565 **m** 07879 400721 **e** anup.parmar@virgin.net
Contact Anup Parmar, Sole Proprieter/ Editor

ANV Productions
47A Kendal Street, London W2 2BU
t 020 7262 3074 **e** anvproductions@dsl.pipex.com
Contact Anthony Norris, Producer/Director

AR Communications
5 Kentish Gardens, Tunbridge Wells TN2 5XU
t 0870 321 7557 **f** 0870 321 7887
e info@ar-comms.com **w** www.ar-comms.com
Contact Alan Rustad, Managing Director

ARB Production Services
The Old Moat House, Aston, Stone ST15 0BJ
t 01785 811933 **f** 01785 8 **m** 07734 112517
e team@arbproductions.com
Contact Alan Reynolds, Creative Director

ArkAngel Productions
240 Kentish Town Road, London NW5 2AB
t 020 7267 9536 **m** 07932 378680
e care@arkangel.co.uk **w** www.arkangel.co.uk
Contact Susan Millard, Producer; Akeva Avery, Producer; Adam Gee, Executive Producer
Credits Merant - Waves Of Change (C); Open And Shut Case (D); Keep-Up-To-Date.TV (W); Mind Gym (W)

Atoll Productions
64 Gore Road, London SW20 8JL
t 020 8540 0700 **f** 020 8540 0700 **e** atollprod@aol.com
Contact Roy Perkins, Producer

AV Interactive Ltd
5 Wixford Lodge, Georges Elm Lane, Bidford-upon-Avon B50 4JS
t 01789 773535 **e** info@avi.co.uk **w** www.avi.co.uk
Contact Marc Edwards, Managing Director; Richard Bratton, Creative Director

AV Pro Media Ltd
Production House, 110 Alwoodley Lane, Leeds LS17 7PP
t 0113 261 1688 **f** 08701 386307
e video@avpromedia.tv **w** www.avpromedia.tv
Contact Simon Marcus, Director

AVC Media Enterprises Ltd
Wellington Circle, Altens, Aberdeen AB12 3JG
t 01224 248007 **f** 01224 248407
e avc@avcmedia.com **w** www.avcmedia.com

Contact Neil Gordon, Director of Media Productions; Frankie O'Kane, Production Co-ordinator; Simon Thorogood, Senior Producer; Mark Phillip, Senior Multimedia Designer
Credits Kirkwood Fyfe (C); Shell (I)

AVR Productions Ltd
38 Station Road, Lower Stondon, Henlow SG16 6JL
t 01462 850608 **f** 01462 850483
e info@avrproductions.co.uk **w** www.avrproductions.co.uk

Contact Gary Oaten, Director; Teresa Oaten, Secretary; David Howard, MultiMedia Developer; Richard Wood, Cameraman/Editor; Lee Blinco, Web Designer

AVT
AVT House, Stone Street, Brighton BN1 2HB
t 01273 299001 **f** 01273 299002
e mail@avtgroup.com **w** www.avtgroup.com

Contact Sharma Hadrill, Client Accounts Manager; Judi Tomlinson, Head of Production; Jon Fox, Head of Multimedia

AVTV
The Old Granary, Cotton End, Northampton NN4 8HP
t 01604 825500 **f** 01604 825501
e production@avtv.com **w** www.avtv.com

Contact Simon Parris, General Manager
Credits Whitebread Corporate Video & CD (I); Canada Life Multi-Media (W); Cool-I-Cam Commerical (C)

BA Video Communications
Government Buildings, Kingston Bypass Road, Surbiton KT6 5QN
t 020 8339 0203 **f** 0208 398 9854 **m** 07976 258598
e hughcapon@bavideo.demon.co.uk
w www.bavideocommunications.co.uk

Contact Andrew Brown, Writer/Editor; Hugh Capon, Director
Credits Shell International (I)

Backstage Films Ltd
39 Brunswick Gardens, London W8 4AW
m 07956 390603 **e** backstage.films@virgin.net

Contact Toby Daffarn, Director

The Barford Film Company
35 Bedfordbury, Covent Garden, London WC2N 4DU
t 020 7836 1365 **f** 020 7379 5210
e info@barford.co.uk **w** www.barford.co.uk

Contact Tim Mein, Managing Director; Angela Ridall; Colette Pearce, Producer
Credits Microsoft (I); M&C Saatchi (I); Ernst & Young (I)

Michael Barratt
Field House, Ascot Road, Maidenhead SL6 3LD
t 01628 770800 **f** 01628 627737 **m** 07768 613375
e mbarratt@compuserve.com

Barry Palin Associates
Unit 10, Princeton Court, 55 Felsham Road, London SW15 1AZ
t 020 8394 5660 **f** 020 8785 0440
e mail@barrypalinassociates.com

Contact Clare Sutton, Production Co-ordinator; Barry Palin, Executive Producer
Credits Energy, Waste And The Environment (I); The Courtesy Of Choice (I); Management Development Programme (I)

The Big Group
91 Princedale Road, London W11 4QT
t 020 7229 8827 **f** 020 7243 1462
e ed.riseman@biggroup.co.uk **w** www.biggroup.co.uk

Contact Ed Riseman, Director

Blackman Productions
47 Oxford Drive, London SE1 2FB
t 020 7827 0005 **f** 020 7827 0006
e johnb@blackman-productions.co.uk
w www.blackman-productions.co.uk

Contact John Blackman, Producer

Blow By Blow Productions
PO Box 565, Lincoln LN2 2YT
t 01522 754901 **m** 07850 521430
e andy@blowbyblow.co.uk **w** www.blowbyblow.co.uk

Contact Andrew Blow, Principal
Credits Making Choices (E); Young Entrepreneurs (E); Coastal Academy (E)

Bluefrog Studios
The Manor House, Oulston, York YO61 3RB
t 01347 868564 **f** 01347 868563 **m** 07968 822994
e studiobluefrog@yahoo.co.uk **w** www.bluefrogstudios.tv

Contact John Phillips, Managing Director; Jessica Savage, Studio Manager
Credits Illuminitis: VJ & Pop Promo (M); The York Millenium Bridge (D); Jonathan Cainer Astrological DVD (C); The Mirror's Astrology Ad Campaign 2001 & 2002 (T)

Complete facilities, green screen, private country location, accommodation available, ideal for corporate weekends/music recordings, whatever your production needs.

Blueline Productions Ltd
28B Victoria Road, Ruislip HA4 0AB
t 01895 635100 **f** 01895 635060
e david@blue-line.tv **w** www.blue-line.tv

Contact Sue Nash; David Tranter, Director

Bob Ede Film & Television Partners
18 Valiant Gardens, Portsmouth PO2 9NZ
t 023 9279 9811 **m** 07958 369557
e enquiries@bobedetv.com **w** www.bobedetv.com

Contact Lesley Ede, Producer; Bob Ede, Director
Credits Wightlink Ltd (I); Apollo Fire Detectors Ltd (I); Procter & Gamble Product Supply UK Ltd (I)

Brainwave Media Ltd
The New Granary, Station Road, Newport CB11 3PL
t 01799 542620 **f** 01799 541026 **m** 07970 205033
e production@brainwaveuk.com **w** www.brainwaveuk.com

Broadcast Media Services Ltd
The Media Centre, Faraday Road, Nottingham NG7 2DU
t 0115 955 3989 **f** 0115 955 3990 **m** 07831 692147
e andrew.ogoen@broadcastmedia.co.uk
w www.broadcastmedia.co.uk

Contact Lesley Wall, Business Manager; Andrew Ogoen, Director
Credits Manchester United - Red Rivals! (T); NTL: Video News Release (T); Lake District National Park (I); Lord Of The Rings - Games Workshop (I)

Buckmark Productions Ltd
Commer House, Station Road, Tadcaster LS24 9JF
t 01937 835900 **f** 01937 835901 **m** 07710 144495
e ed@buckmark.co.uk **w** www.buckmark.co.uk

Contact Ed Marks, Producer/Director

Camerson Productions
Deane, Basingstoke RG25 3AR
t 01256 780600 **f** 01256 782563
e contact@camerson.co.uk **w** www.camerson.co.uk
Contact Richard Cutler, Producer

Campbell Lloyd Video
3 Sunray Avenue, Hutton, Brentwood CM13 1PR
t 01277 225818 **e** mike@clvideo.freeserve.co.uk
Contact Mike Lloyd, Managing Director

Cathode Digital Video
5 Church Walk, High Street, Bletchingley RH1 4PD
t 01883 740024 **m** 07986 108811 **e** barrie@cathode.fsnet.co.uk
Contact Barrie Ward, Director
Credits Watson Wyatt - Financial News Channel (I); AON Kidnap (I); Pass You Riding Test With The Motor Cycle Industry (E); The Fond Guide To Passing Your Theory Test (E)

Centre Screen Productions
Eastgate Building, Castle Street, Castlefield, Manchester M3 4LZ
t 0161 832 7151 **f** 0161 832 8934
e info@centrescreen.co.uk **w** www.centrescreen.co.uk
Contact Sarah Jackson, Marketing Manager
Credits Local Primary Care Trust - HIV Awareness (E); North West Development Agency (I); Greater Manchester Passenger Transport Executive (E); Manchester Airport (I)

CI Vidcom
The Coachhouse Studio, The Coach Inn, Clynnog Fawr, Caernarfon LL54 5PB
t 01286 660212 **f** 01286 660785
e skypix@clara.co.uk **w** www.coachinn.com
Contact Stephen Williams, Technical Producer/Director

Classic Video Productions Ltd
19 Waterloo Street, Glasgow G2 6BT
t 0141 248 3882 **f** 0141 204 1535 **e** weestudio@aol.com
Contact Graham Bone

Clear Focus Productions
53 Lime Walk, Headington OX3 7AB
t 01865 744722 **m** 07050 103016 **e** clearfocusuk@yahoo.com
Contact Phil Gauron, Managing Director
Credits Remembering Anne Frank (D); Church Time (E); Looking Beyond The Brochure (E); Winning The Mind Game (D)

Cleveland Film Productions
5 Rainbow Court, Oxhey WD19 4RP
t 01923 254000 **m** 07740 902095 **e** michael@gosling.com
Contact Michael Gosling, Director

Comm:HQ
3 Lyne Court, Lyne Lane, Lyne KT16 0AW
t 01932 571006 **f** 01932 571008 **m** 07774 130871
e aok@commhq.co.uk **w** www.commhq.co.uk
Contact Michael Shackleton, Director

Communicator Ltd
199 Upper Street, London N1 1RQ
t 020 7704 8333 **f** 020 7704 8444
e info@communicator.ltd.co.uk **w** www.communicator.ltd.uk
Contact Paul Drew, Managing Director; Martin Collins, Creative Director

Compulsion Media
t 0870 011 8168 **f** 0870 011 8168
e info@compulsion-media.com **w** www.compulsion-media.com

Comtec
Unit 19, Tait Road, Croydon CRO 2DP
t 020 8684 6615 **f** 020 8684 6947 **m** 07958 967977
e info@comtecav.co.uk **w** www.comtecav.co.uk
Contact Danny Edwardson, Managing Director

Countrywise Communication
103 Main Road, Wilby NN8 2UB
t 01933 272400 **f** 01933 272800 **m** 07899 897690
e media@countrywise.com **w** www.countrywise.com
Contact Phillip Malone, Director; Josephine Rodgers, Director; Leora Pacheco, Production Co-ordinator

CreationVideo
38 Quick Road, London W4 2BU
t 020 8987 9363 **f** 0870 051 5610 **m** 07889 444963
e info@creationvideo.co.uk **w** www.creationvideo.co.uk

Creativ Video Ltd
15 Craven Close, Loughborough LE11 2SR
t 01509 211013 **e** philip@creativ.co.uk **w** www.creativ.co.uk
Contact Philip Francomb, Director; Kate Mendham, Project Manager
Credits Cascaid Careers CD-Rom & Video (E); Balfour Beatty Embedded Rail Track (I); John Harvard (Stratford-on-Avon) (D)

Creative Channel
Television Centre, La Pouquelaye, St Helier, Jersey JE1 3ZD
t 01534 816888 **f** 01534 816889
e creative@channeltv.co.uk **w** www.channeltv.co.uk
Contact David Evans, Producer; Kevin Banner, Managing Director; Sharon Reid, Production Coordinator; Sharon Campbell, Sales & Marketing; Stig Adeler, Producer; Gillian Smart, Sales & Marketing; Sharon Le Marinel, Production Co-ordinator

Creative Media - ITM Group
Latimer Square, White Lion Road, Amersham HP7 9JQ
t 01494 549525 **f** 01494 549465
e malcolm.bood@itm-group.co.uk **w** www.itm-group.co.uk
Contact Malcolm Bood, Managing Director

Creative Vision
The Old House, Fedw Hir, Llwydcoed, Aberdare CF44 0DX
t 01685 882011 **f** 01685 882048 **m** 07960 698417
e creativevision@tiscali.co.uk **w** www.fused.net/creativevision

Croft Video Productions
The Barn House, Whitbourne, Worcester WR6 5RT
t 01886 821599 **m** 07866 640 395
e cynthia@croftvideo.co.uk **w** www.croftvideo.co.uk
Credits The National Trust; Epson UK

Crown Business Communications
United House, 9 Pembridge Road, Notting Hill Gate, London W11 3JY
t 020 7727 7272 **f** 020 7727 9940
e info@crownbc.com **w** www.crownbc.com
Contact Steven Webb, Head of Production

CSN Digimedia
PO Box 2365, Iver SL0 9WD
t 01753 630701 **f** 01753 650686 **m** 07770 626631
e seen@csndigimedia.co.uk **w** www.csnvideo.com

CTN
200 Gray's Inn Road, London WC1X 8XZ
t 020 7430 4500 **f** 020 7430 4517
e info@ctn.co.uk **w** www.ctn.co.uk
Contact Bivyang Mistry, Finance Director; Benet Northcote, Head of Intercative Media; Gary Mitchell, Director of Programmes; Tristan Allsop, Executive Producer; Stephen Watson, Managing Director
Credits DTI (E); Vodafone (W); GlaxoSmithKline (W); Shell (I)

Cutting Edge Productions Ltd
27 Erpingham Road, London SW15 1BE
t 020 8780 1476 **f** 020 8780 0102 **m** 07710 409880
e norridge@globalnet.co.uk
Contact Julian Norridge, Director; Julian Norridge, Director
Credits Tourism Strategy - Department Of Culture, Media And Sport (I); Competition Policy - Office Of Fair Trading (I); Fighting Hate - Metropolitan Police (I); Preventing Deaths In Custody - Metropolitan Police (I)

Cwmni Da
Cae Llenor, Lon Parc, Caernarfon LL55 2HH
t 01286 685300 **f** 01286 685301 **e** post@cwmnida.co.uk
Contact Dylan Huws; Gwyn Williams
Credits Coast To Coast(+ITV) (T); Edgar Christian Lost On The Barrens (T); Susan Williams Ellis; Y Sioe Gelf

Cyclops
Guildford
t 01483 850190
e video@cyclops-tv.co.uk **w** www.cyclops-prods.co.uk
Credits Sentinels Of Britain - The Royal Observer Corps In World War II (D); Tocsin Bang-The Cold War Story Of The Royal Observer Corps (D)

Dave Knowles Films
34 Ashleigh Close, Hythe SO45 3QP
t 023 8084 2190 **f** 023 8084 1600 **m** 07740 284028
e mall@dkfilms.co.uk **w** www.dkfilms.co.uk
Contact Jenny Knowles, Producer/Scriptwriter; Dave Knowles, Director/Editor/Cameraman
Credits The Borouge Petrochemicals Project (I); Domino Consultancy (W); Saira's Life In Lakhabawal (E)

Davideo

69 Chichester Avenue, Netherton, Dudley DY2 9JL
t 01384 235009 **m** 07802 420 305
e david@davideo.co.uk **w** www.davideo.co.uk
Contact David Grayburn Hale, Proprietor

DC Entertainment

First Floor, 58 Charlotte Road, London EC2A 3QG
t 020 7739 7464 **f** 020 7739 8082
e info@dcentertainment.co.uk

Design Story

The White Cottage, Little Ickford, Ickford HP18 9HR
t 01844 338817
e alice@designstory.co.uk **w** www.designstory.co.uk
Contact Alice Story, Creative Director

DMI Productions

Unit 8, Littleton House, Littleton Road, Ashford TW15 1UU
t 01784 421212 **f** 01784 421213
e info@dmiproductions.co.uk **w** www.dmiproductions.co.uk
Contact Stuart Turner, Partner
Credits BVI-TV Web Launch (W); Film 48 (T); Disney Store Idents (C); Property
Apocalypse Now (I)

Eagle Vision

16 Hanson Street, London W1W 6UD
t 020 7436 2707 **f** 020 7580 5838
e eaglevision@supanet.com **w** www.eaglevision.free-online.co.uk
Contact John Court, Director, Managing Director

Edensun Films Ltd

58 Bargery Road, London SE6 2LN
t 020 8697 3968 **f** 020 8697 2206
Contact Marta Zaldivia, Director; Franklyn Jean-Jacques, Managing Director

The Edge Picture Company

7 Langley Street, London WC2H 9JA
t 020 7836 6262 **f** 020 7836 6949
e ask.us@edgepicture.com **w** www.edgepicture.com
Contact Philip Blundell, Managing Director

Edit Suite 7

C/o Autobond Ltd, Heanor Gate Road, Heanor DE75 7RJ
t 01773 530520 **f** 01773 769890 **m** 07712 295885
m 07967 672291 **e** editsuite7@hotmail.com
Contact Matt Saunders, Partner; Connor Gilmore, Partner
Credits Autobond Compact 52 (I); Autobond Compact 102 (I); Autobond MF 76
(I); Nyland Graphics Ltd (I)

Edric Audio Visual

34-36 Oak End Way, Gerrards Cross SL9 8BR
t 01753 481400 **f** 01753 887163
e info@edric-av.co.uk **w** www.edric-av.co.uk

Edward Widdowson Productions

47 Chenies Village, Chorleywood WD3 6EG
t 01923 283665 **e** epwol@worldonline.co.uk
Contact Edward Widdowson, Director

EFS Television Production & Motivation Sound Studios

35A Broadhurst Gardens, London NW6 3QT
t 020 7624 7785 **f** 020 7624 4879
e production@efstv.demon.co.uk **w** www.efstv.demon.co.uk
Contact Peter Walton, Managing Director

Elbow Productions Ltd

175 Victoria Park Road, London E9 7JN
t 020 8986 9021 **f** 08701 207823 **m** 07961 150139
e info@elbowproductions.com **w** www.elbowproductions.com
Contact Jan Lower, Director
Credits St Patrick Visitor Centre - Ego Patricius (E); Deadlines 20th Century War
Propaganda (D); Magna Science Centre - Water (W); V&A - Radical Fashion (I)

em:seven communications

Cambridge House, Cambridge Grove, London W6 0LE
t 020 8752 2200 **f** 020 8752 2201
e inspired@emseven.com **w** www.emseven.com
Contact Keith Pollard, Managing Director

EPM Production

Paulswell, West Linton EH46 7BH
t 01968 660984 **f** 01968 660984
e info@picturemachine.co.uk **w** www.picturemachine.co.uk
Contact Ken Andrew, Producer-Director

Eye Pro Ltd

Hollywood House, Hollywood Lane, Rochester ME3 8AR
t 01634 291301 **f** 01634 727200 **m** 07947 380170
e coop@ipro.tv
Contact Charles Cooper, Director; Jo Austen, Art Director
Credits Specialist Height Access (I); Task Force (I)
*Specialists in rigging and working at height. All staff IRATA trained and
qualified. Height Access trained cameramen also available.*

The Farrant Partnership

429 Liverpool Road, London N7 8PR
t 020 7700 4647 **f** 020 7697 0224 **m** 07768 285487
e mail@farrant-partnership.com
Contact Jean Stern, Partner; James Farrant, Partner

Fat Fudge Productions

150 Princess Drive, Seaford BN25 2TS
t 01273 470227 **f** 01273 470227
e info@fatfudge.co.uk **w** www.fatfudge.co.uk
Contact Jon Rhoades, Proprieter; Antony Elliott, Finance; Dave Gere, Producer;
Jude Dalton, Producer

The Film & Theatre CONNECTION Ltd

The Studio, 46 Marsh Road, Pinner HA5 5NQ
t 020 8866 1253 **f** 020 8866 5403 **m** 07785 333858
e info@cnxeurope.com **w** www.cnxeurope.com
Contact Adam Penny, Producer/Director; Peter Penny, Producer/Director
Credits Xerox Extreme (C); Christies - The Pause (I); Extreme Videos (I); Cities
For Cohesion (D)

Firehouse Productions

42 Glasshouse Street, London W1B 5DW
t 020 7439 2220 **f** 020 7439 2210
e postie@firehouse.biz **w** www.firehouse.biz

First Creative Ltd

Belgrave Court, Caxton Road, Fulwood, Preston PR2 9PL
t 01772 651555 **f** 01772 651777
e video@firstcreative.com **w** www.firstcreative.com
Contact Michael Mulvihill, Director

First Field

Unit B5, 3 Bradbury Street, London N16 8JN
t 020 7690 4990 **f** 020 7690 4494 **m** 07957 502150
e firstfield@clara.co.uk **w** www.firstfield.co.uk
Contact Greg Loftin, Producer

First Take

13 Hope Street, Liverpool L1 9BH
t 0151 708 5767 **f** 0151 709 2613
e all@first-take.demon.co.uk **w** www.first-take.demon.co.uk
Contact Mark Bareham, Director; Phil Morton, Finance; Lynne Harwood,
Director; Stephen Barr, Editor; Kath Peters, Development

Fleetwood Films

32 Minden Close, Chineham, Basingstoke RG24 8TH
t 01256 353444 **f** 044 1256 323636 **m** 07711 980032
e k.d.hicks@btinternet.com
Contact Keith D Hicks, Proprietor

Focal Point Television
Winters Farm Studios, Puttenham, Guildford GU3 1AR
t 01483 811999
e studio@focal-point.co.uk **w** www.focal-point.co.uk
Contact Peter Money, Producer; Seb Bone, Producer; Simon Bisset, Director
Credits Dave Matthew's Band - Plugging The Gap (M); History Of The British Police Force (D); Practical Guide To Divorce (D); DJ's Complete Guide (D)

Michael Fogarty
91 Sterndale Road, London W14 0HX
t 020 7602 0814 **f** 020 7603 6692
e video@avexcellence.prestel.co.uk

Forcefed Films
PO Box 37623 NW7 2XB
t 020 7748 3212 **f** 020 7748 3213 **m** 07970 602763
e info@forcefed.co.uk **w** www.forcefed.co.uk
Credits Compac (C); Hewlett Packard (C); Cystic Fibrosis Awards (I)

Frost Media
29 Chesterfield Road, Dronfield S18 2XA
t 01246 292751 **f** 01246 292296 **m** 07971 419730
e andrewwhiston@hotmail.com
Contact Andrew Whiston, Production Co-ordinator

Gateway Television Productions
Gemini House, 10 Bradgate, Potters Bar EN6 4RL
t 01707 872054 **f** 01707 888655
w www.gatewaytelevision.co.uk
Contact Graham Smart, Director

Gazebo Films
PO Box 9, Chipping Campdem GL55 6TX
t 01386 593770 **f** 01386 593770
e de@gazebofilms.co.uk **w** www.gazebofilms.co.uk
Contact David Eccles
Credits A Postcard From London (W); A Postcard From The Cotswolds (W); A Postcard From Shakespeare's Stratford (W)

Genesis
114 Whitchurch Road, Cardiff CF14 3LY
t 029 2066 6007 **f** 029 2066 6008 **m** 07796 262000
e alan@genesis-media.co.uk **w** www.genesis-media.co.uk
Credits ICT In Food And Textiles Manufacture (E); Art In Wales (E); C'Mon Make A Difference (C); No Need To Shout

Grant Corporate Media Ltd
DVP Studios, Linton House, 39-51 Highgate Road, London NW5 1RS
f 020 7485 9090 **m** 07970 610316
e sales@grantcorporatemedia.com
w www.grantcorporatemedia.com
Contact Alasdair Grant, Managing Director
Credits Weekend TV (T); 13 Episodes Trouble Series (T)

Green Field Television
Home Farm, Shere Road, Albury GU5 9BL
t 01483 202206 **e** info@greenfieldtv.com

Greg Younger Associates
Barons Croft, Hare Lane, Blindley Heath RH7 6JA
t 01342 832515 **f** 01342 833768
e gregassociates@aol.com **w** www.btinternet.com/~gya
Contact Chris Younger, Production Assistant; Tony Bastable, Director; Greg Younger, Producer

Grosvenor TV
The Café Royal, 68 Regent Street, London W1B 5EL
t 020 7439 4440 **f** 020 7439 0429
e grosvenortv@grosvenortv.com
Contact Des Good, Managing Director; Annabel Seaman, Production Assistant

Gym-TV
422 Studios, Battersea Road, Stockport SK4 3EA
t 0161 442 4205 **f** 0161 442 2677 **w** www.gym-tv.com

Hallmark Productions
30 Woodside Road, Lower Parkstone, Poole BH14 9JJ
t 0845 644 5406 **t** 01202 779000 **f** 01202 778059
e info@hallmarkproductions.co.uk
w www.hallmarkproductions.com
Contact Chris Hall, Head of Production; Rod Hewitt, Producer

Haylock Ltd
Oakhill, Barking Road, Barking, Ipswich IP6 8HG
t 01449 720228 **e** haylocks@talk21.com
Contact Peter Haylock, Director

HBL Media
14-18 Great Titchfield Street, London W1P 7AB
t 020 7612 1839 **f** 020 7636 7446 **m** 07855 044836
e duncan@hblmedia.com **w** www.hblmedia.com
Contact Duncan Pow, Assistant Producer; Steve Levinson, Director

Head To Head Communication
The Hook, Plane Tree Crescent, Feltham TW13 7AQ
t 020 8893 7766 **f** 020 8893 2777 **e** enquiries@hthc.co.uk
Contact Amanda Anderson, Business Development Director

Heavy Entertainment Ltd
222 Kensal Road, London W10 5BN
t 020 8960 9001 **t** 020 8960 9002 **f** 020 8960 9003
e info@heavy-entertainment.com
w www.heavy-entertainment.com
Contact David Roper, Managing Director; Nick St. George, Company Director
Credits Shine Communications (I); Royal Shakespeare Company (I); Lever Faberge (I); Queen Mary Unicersity Of London (W)

Henderson Grime & Associates Ltd
The Old Exchange, 514 Liverpool Road, Irlam, Manchester M44 6AJ
t 0161 775 7890 **f** 0161 775 7916
m 07770 340913 **i** 0161 777 8408
e ian@henderson-grime.com **w** www.henderson-grime.com
Contact Michael Henderson, Managing Director; Ian Grime, Live Events Director; Mark Hope, Creative Director; Mike Fallows, Studio Manager
Credits AG Barr (W); SAGE (I); Direct Line (C); Coca-Cola (C)

Hesketh Crean Consultants Ltd
PO Box 2903, London W1A 6BR
t 020 7495 7222 **f** 020 7399 9977
e info@heskethcrean.com **w** www.heskethcrean.com
Contact David Ryan, Head of Marketing; Rosie Dalling, Head of Marketing

HM Customs & Excise
4th Floor North, Portcullis House, 27 Victoria Avenue, Southend-on-Sea SS2 6AL
t 01702 367548 **f** 01702 367560 **e** paul.mercer@hmce.gsi.gov.uk
Contact Adrian Fox, Unit Manager; Vanessa Kingsley, Producer; Paul Mercer, Producer; Kelly Burfield, Producer; Frank Butler, Producer
Credits Managing Sickness Absence (I); Working With Diversity (I); Equal Rights And Wrongs (I); Human Rights Act (E)

HMX Corporate Communication
24 Green Lane, Radnage, High Wycombe HP14 4DN
t 01494 484820 **f** 01494 485068 **m** 07802 236500
e timhorrox@hmx.cc **w** www.hmx.cc
Contact Tim Horrox, Executive Producer

Hotshotz Shoot & Edit
m 07836 780053
e hotshotz@btopenworld.com **w** www.markewart.co.uk
Credits Vision Express (E); Orange Innovations (I); The Black And White Mortgage Company (I)

I-Vision
North Oxfordshire College, Banbury OX16 9QA
t 01295 252221 x259 **f** 01295 250381
e sstockle@northox.ac.uk
Contact Steven Stockley, Production Manager; Richard Hollingum, Audio Production Manager; Kevin Robbinson, Script Writer; Damien Homer, Production Manager
Credits Compassion Religious Video (I); The Experience Video Displays (I); Formula Schools 2001 (E); ACO Landrover Challenge 2002 (I)

Ian Gall Television
PO Box 403, Corsham SN13 9RZ
t 01225 811403 **f** 01225 811404
e rosie@iangalltv.com **w** www.iangalltv.com

Iceni Productions Ltd
19 Dawson Street, Birmingham B66 4JB
t 0121 601 0688 **f** 0121 601 0980
e info@iceniproductions.com **w** www.iceniproductions.com
Contact Cathy Bentley, Director; Andrew Jepson, Production Manager

IDS London
29 Worfield Street, London SW11 4RB
t 020 7228 1021 **f** 020 7228 8169 **e** tony@idslondon.co.uk
Contact Tony Jackson, Partner

Image Weaver
e luke@image-weaver.co.uk
Contact Luke Witcomb

Imperial College Video Productions
TV Studio, Exhibition Road, London SW7 2BT
t 020 7594 8135 **f** 020 7594 8138 **m** 07736 827000
e tvstudio@imperial.ac.uk **w** www.lib.ic.ac.uk/av
Contact Martin Sayers, Production Assistant; Colin Grimshaw, Studio Manager

The Indeprod People Company
891 Plymouth Road, Slough SL1 4LP
t 01753 567420 **f** 01753 567421
e info@indeprod.com **w** www.indeprod.com

Insight Production Services Ltd
t 01525 759047 **f** 01525 755317 **m** 07973 699464
e chris.walsh@insightproduction.co.uk
w www.insightproduction.co.uk

Interesting Television
Oakslade Studios, Station Road, Hatton CV35 7LH
t 01926 844044 **f** 01926 844045
e john@interestingtv.co.uk **w** www.interestingtv.com
Contact John Pluck, Director
Credits Reed Exhibitions (I); Ess Sharco (I); Pendolino Launch - Virgin Trains (I)

International Corporate Events Ltd
7 Gunnery Terrace, Leamington Spa CV32 5PE
t 01926 740550 **f** 01926 740559 **m** 07790 741818
e admin@ice-productions.com **w** www.ice-productions.com
Contact Cheryl Henson, Event Manager; Eric Zenwiner, Video Production; Sean Griffiths, Managing Director

Jack Morton Worldwide
16-18 Acton Park Estate, Stanley Gardens, The Vale, London W3 7QE
t 020 8735 2000 **f** 020 8735 2020 **w** www.jackmorton.com
Contact Heather Thompson, Team Manager

Jay Film & Video
Sandgate House, 102 Quayside, Newcastle-upon-Tyne NE1 3DX
t 0191 229 1717 **f** 0191 229 1818 **w** www.jayvideo.com
Contact Joanna Urwin, Producer

Jay TV Ltd
Newcastle Technopole, Kings Manor, Newcastle-upon-Tyne NE1 6PA
t 0191 229 1717 **f** 0191 229 1818
e production@jayvideo.com **w** www.jayvideo.com
Contact Joanna Urwin, Producer
Credits Sanyo (I); Nissan (I); Health And Safety Executive (I); Renault Training Video (I)

John McKenzie Productions
1 Horton Avenue, London NW2 2RY
t 020 8208 0363 **f** 020 8208 0363 **m** 07946 420 429
e movie@lineone.net
Contact John McKenzie, Director
Credits Haden Young Construction; Howarth Consulting International; Eversheds International Law Group

JTA
The Old Rectory, Ombersley, Worcester WR9 0EW
t 01905 823400 **f** 01905 823401
e info@jta.co.uk **w** www.jta.co.uk
Contact Brian Darnley, Director of Video & Events

Junction 7
36 Mortimer Street, London W1W 7RG
t 020 7307 9620 **f** 020 7307 9621
e info@junction7.com **w** www.junction7.com

JWP
Studio 1, Utopia Village, 7 Challot Road, London NW1 8LH
t 020 7758 3670 **m** 07973 962926
e info@utopiavillage.com **w** www.utopiavillage.com
Contact James Ward, Producer/Cameraman

Keep-Up-To-Date
156 Agar grove, London NW1 9TY
t 020 7267 9969 **m** 07932 378680
e susan@keep-up-to-date.co.uk
Contact Susan Millard, Producer; Akeva Avery, Editor
Credits www.keep-up-to date.tv (W)

Keyframe
Unity Court, 431 Meanwood Road, Leeds LS7 2LL
t 0113 246 5913 **f** 0113 234 0038
e info@keyframe.co.uk **w** www.keyframe.co.uk
Contact Helen Simpson, Production Manager

Klicks Photographic Ltd
3 Mallard Business Centre, Mallard Road, Bretton, Peterborough PE3 8YR
t 01733 333630 **f** 01733 331773
e klicksvideo@aol.com **w** www.klicksvideo.co.uk
Contact Ben Wright, Photographic Director

KTV
95 Beech Road, Harrogate HG2 8DZ
t 01423 873009 **f** 01423 873009 **m** 07885 541643
w www.ktvcvp.co.uk
Contact Tony Raffe, Editor

Landscape Film & Television Productions
PO Box 35, London SW11 3LB
t 020 7228 9734 **f** 020 7223 4872
Contact Andrew Davie, Producer/Director

Lane, Jefferies & Associates
2 Winchester Close, Hagley, Stourbridge DY9 0PW
t 01562 884585 **f** 01562 884585 **e** ljfireco1@aol.com
Contact D Lane, Producer; R Jefferies, Executive Producer
Credits A Special Risk (I); Tunnel Vision (E); Play Safe (E); Better Safe Than Sorry (I)
Specialist personal development and training resource producer for rescue services.

Leapfrog Productions
Number 7, 68 Broadwick Street, London W1V 1FA
t 020 7439 1019 **f** 020 7439 1021 **m** 0836 794739
e jacquihamilton@aol.com **w** www.leapfrog.co.uk

Lighthouse Productions
4 Court Street, Upton-upon-Severn WR8 0JT
t 01684 591594 **f** 01684 594586 **m** 07714 103821
e mal.luff@traplet.com
Contact Mal Luff, Video Production Manager

Lipfriend Rodd International Ltd
18 Spectrum House, 32-34 Gordon House Road, London NW5 1LP
t 020 7267 6066 **f** 020 7267 6455
e all@lipfriend-rodd.co.uk **w** www.lipfriend-rodd.co.uk
Contact Robert Lipfriend; Elliot Levi

London Scientific Films
Mill Studio, Crane Mead, Ware SG12 9PY
t 01920 444399 **e** lsf@londonscientificfilms.co.uk

The Loop Communication Agency
Hanover House, Queen Charlotte Street, Bristol BS1 4EX
t 0117 311 2040 **f** 0117 311 2041
e info@theloopagency.com **w** www.theloopagency.com
Contact Stephen Williams, Business Development Manager

Love Revolution Ltd
487A Smithdown Road, Liverpool L15 5AE
t 0151 734 5465 **f** 0151 734 5465
m 07974 951943 **i** 020 7494 8260
e b_viner@hotmail.com **w** www.tribemanagement.com
Contact Brian Viner, Producer - Music; Eugeuina Kelly-Viner, Director/Producer/Writer
Credits spon6elab.com (W); Box Of Ivails (S); Annies's Magic Pie Garden (S)

Maelgwn Productions
Llys Maelgwn, 112 Albert Drive, Deganwy, Conwy LL31 9YY
t 01492 584595 **f** 01492 584595 **m** 07759 544323
e dilwyn@maelgwn.freeserve.co.uk
Contact Dilwyn Roberts, Producer
Credits Llandudno Junction (D); Conwy - A Place In History (D); CCLT Promotional Video 2002 (I); RWF Freedom Of Conwy Parade 2002 (D)

Maritz
Alexander House, 3rd Avenue, Globe Park, Marlow SL7 1YW
t 01628 486 011 **f** 01628 496 264 **w** www.maritz.co.uk
Contact Julie Albury, Head of Production

MC Video Productions
23 Albion Hill, Exmouth EX8 1JS
t 01395 224647 **f** 01395 224647 **m** 07971 253028
e mcvideo@eclipse.co.uk **w** www.mcvideoptoductions.co.uk
Contact Chris Adams, Partner/Cameraman Editor; Joyce McCarthy, Production Manager

Meadow Productions Ltd
134 Knights Hill, West Norwood SE27 0SR
t 020 8761 6061 **m** 07930 254004
e victoria@meadowprod.freeserve.co.uk

Media Projects International Ltd
7 Cameron Lane, 12 Castlehaven Road, London NW1 8QW
t 020 7681 0552 **f** 020 7482 4995
e ml-mpa@blueyonder.co.uk **w** www.mediaprojects.co.uk
Contact Colin Payne, Director; Jayne Hobart, Production Manager

Media Tree
19-20 Romilly Street, London W1D 5AE
t 020 7437 3322 **f** 020 7437 3340
e main@media-tree.com **w** www.media-tree.com
Contact Carrie Stett, Production Director
Credits Scariest Places On Earth (T)

The Media Trust
3-7, Euston Centre, Regents Place, London NW1 3JG
t 020 7874 7600 **f** 020 7874 7644
e info@mediatrust.org **w** www.mediatrust.org
Contact Simon Gallimore, Production Director
Credits Scope Training Video, Fair Trade Foundation Promotional Video; Fair Trade Foundation (I); Scope Training (I)

MediaFour Ltd
Bailey Court, Green Street, Macclesfield SK10 1JQ
t 01625 423424 **f** 01625 423334
e suzanne.becerra@mediafour.co.uk **w** www.mediafour.co.uk
Contact Andrew Rushton, New Technology Manager; Liam Lockwood, DVD Engineer; Rick Lord, Facilities Contact; Vicky Fagan, Production Sales Contact

MedSci
Stoke Grange, Lidstone, Uxbridge Road, George Green SL2 6AG
t 01753 516644 **f** 01753 516965 **m** 07718 736 234
e info@medsci.co.uk **w** www.medsci.co.uk
Contact Peter Fogarty, Producer; Kerry Williams, Producer; Helen McDowell; Lucille Weinberger

Melusina Production Company Ltd
20 Cottesmore Road, Leicester LE5 3LN
t 0116 276 8111
e clive@melusina.freeserve.co.uk **w** www.melusinaproductions.com
Contact Tricia Rudkin, Company Secretary; Clive Ward, Creative Director/CEO
Credits No More Mr Nice Guy (T); BBC Clothes Show Live (T); Our Town Story Millennium Dome (T)

Mental-Health TV
Bishops Lodge, Oakley Green Road, Windsor SL4 5UL
t 01344 890099
e cardinalbroadcast@yahoo.co.uk **w** www.mentalhealth.tv
Contact Andrew Macaulay, Managing DIrector

Mezzo Studios Ltd
17 North Hill Road, Headingley, Leeds LS6 2EN
t 0113 203 6161 **f** 0113 203 6162
e tv@mezzostudios.com **w** www.mezzostudios.com
Contact Sue Underwood, Senior Producer; Lindsay Bentley, Producer; Howard Hesling, Business Development

MGA International
51 Monkhams Lane, Woodford Green IG8 0NN
t 020 8504 3877 **f** 020 8559 1674
e mail@mga-int.co.uk **w** www.mga-int.co.uk
Contact Laura Knap, Producer; Mario Grattarola
Credits Lake Vyrnwy (I); Harry's Bar (I); I Won't Be Back (I)

Michael Swerdlow Video Production
213 The Colonnades, Albert Dock, Liverpool L3 4AB
t 0151 707 1002 **f** 0151 707 1002 **m** 07770 800246
e michael@swerdlow.co.uk **w** www.swerdlow.co.uk
Contact Michael Swerdlow, Producer
Credits Liverpool Compact Marketing Video (I); Wigan Education Authority Training Video (I); Abbott Ireland Training Video (I)

Mighty Media
Long Boyds House, Hedsor Road, Bourne End SL8 5FJ
t 01628 522002 **f** 01628 526530
e info@mightymedia.co.uk **w** www.mightymedia.co.uk
Credits NAAFI (I); Johnson & Johnson (C); Boots (C); Alberto Culver (I)

The Mighty Pen Production Company
Riverside Studios, Crisp Road, London W6 9RL
t 020 8137 1085 **f** 020 8237 1001 **m** 07885 059586
e jsquire@mightypen.co.uk **w** www.mightypen.co.uk
Credits Growing Pains (I); Meaningful Day (I); A Journey into Light (I)

The Mills Video Company
11 Hope Street, Liverpool L1 9BJ
t 0151 709 9822 **f** 0151 709 6585 **i** 0151 707 2882
e sales@millsvideo.co.uk **w** www.millsvideo.co.uk
Contact Barrie Farrell, Head of Production; Rachel Ballard, Scriptwriter/Director; Andrew Mills, Managing Director
Credits Shotton Paper (E); Lever Faberge (W); Waltham (W); Lakeland Ltd (C)

Mirage Digital Video Productions
132 Holmfield Road, North Shore, Blackpool FY2 9PB
t 01253 596900 **f** 590368 **m** 07734 035838
e info@miragedigitalvideo.co.uk **w** www.miragedigitalvideo.co.uk
Contact Ashley Lewis, New Business Manager/Partner; Andy Houghton, Technical Manager/Partner

Mirage Events Ltd
Brewer Street Business Park, Brewer Street, Bletchingley RH1 4QP
t 01883 740400 **f** 01883 740111
e hannah@mirageevents.co.uk **w** www.mirageevents.co.uk
Contact Diane Green, New Business Manager; Julia Brewer, Director; Christian Marryat, Managing Director

Mission Pictures Ltd
23 Golden Square, London W1R 3PA
t 020 7734 6303 **f** 020 7734 6202 **e** info@missionpictures.net
Contact Sophie Meyer, Head of Development
Credits Millions (T); Gladiatress (T); Welcome To Sarajevo (F); Thunderpants (F)

MJ Productions Ltd
110 The Business Village, Broomhill Road, London SW18 4JQ
t 020 8877 9348 **f** 020 8874 9052
e mjpro@mjproductions.co.uk **w** www.mjproductions.co.uk
Contact Martin Johnson, Director

Mole Productions
2 Overton Cottages, East Kennett, Marlborough SN8 4EZ
t 01672 861188 **f** 07092 032073
e enquiries@moleproductions.com **w** www.moleproductions.com
Contact Tim Ashton, Partner
Credits Smith & Nephew: Endoscopy (I); NCSL New Heads Multi Camera
Conference (I); Business Link Gloucestershire: Setting Out In Business (E);
Johnson & Johnson: Silver Seminar (W)

Molton Rock
4H Peabody Buildings, Herbrand Street, London WC1N 1JS
t 020 7833 4302 **e** richie.wlnearls@virgin.net
Contact Keith Brookshaw, Production; Richie Winearls, Managing Director;
Sarah Harris, Marketing
Credits Kingsmill In The Community (I); Climate Change (I); Marry Me (S);
The Imitators (F)

Monroe Video Productions
8 Cornwall Court, Eaton Socon, St Neots PE19 8PR
t 01480 374036 **f** 01480 374036 **m** 07810 201111
e nigel.mvp@virgin.net **w** www.monroevideo.co.uk
Contact Nigel Cooper, Director, Director
Credits Glamour Photography Masterclass (E); You & Your Baby (E)

Moonstone Productions Ltd
Laurel House, Park Road, Paulton, Bristol BS39 7QQ
t 01761 416703 **f** 01761 411223
e info@moonstone-productions.com
w www.moonstone-productions.com
Contact Russel Michaeli, Project Development Manager; Emma Harrison,
Production Assistant; Kirsty Withyman, Production Director; Fiona Seton, Sales
Manager; Martin Roberts, Managing Director
Credits Atlantic City Promotional CDRom (W); Crystal Holidays Ski Video (I);
Sky Travel (T); Disneyland Paris (I)
Video and Multimedia specialists for the travel and leisure industry.

The Morrison Company
302 Clive Court, Maida Vale, London W9 1SF
t 020 7289 7976 **f** 0870 127 5065 **m** 07831 256 959
e don@morrisonco.com **w** www.morrisonco.com
Contact Don Morrison, Director

MST Television Ltd
1 Adpar Street, London W2 1DE
t 020 7724 8917 **f** 020 7262 8353
e info@msttelevision.co.uk **w** www.msttelevision.co.uk
Contact Clive Hayden, Managing Director

N8tivemedia Ltd
47-53 Fore Street, Ipswich IP4 1JL
t 01473 286400 **f** 01473 284299 **m** 07932 653785
e info@n8tivemedia.co.uk **w** www.n8tivemedia.co.uk
Contact Craig Clark, Managing Director; James Kindred, Studio Director

New Moon
5 Newburgh Street, London W1F 7RG
t 020 7479 7010 **f** 020 7479 7011
e production@new-moon.co.uk **w** www.new-moon.co.uk
Contact Sophie Broadbent, Production Manager; Caroline Rowland, Executive
Producer; Nicola Ash, Executive Assistant
Credits Accenture (I); J Sainsbury (I); The Metropolitan Police (I);
Dove Testimonials (C)

Noble Image Productions
80 High Street, Winchester SO23 9AT
t 01962 875475 **m** 07710 401639
e info@noble-image.co.uk **w** www.noble-image.co.uk
Contact Mike Dodd-Noble, Director
Credits Motorola; Coming Together; Connected Pl@net

Nomad Media
5 Copywell, Orcop HR2 8EP
t 01981 540509 **f** 01981 540509 **m** 07742 315089
e richard@nomadmedia.co.uk **w** www.nomadmedia.co.uk
Contact Richard Urbanski, Director, Director
Credits The Future At Risk (W); Down To The River (D); Taken Without Consent
(E); Roller Coaster (W)

Octopus Multimedia Ltd
Gauntley Court Studios, Gauntley Court, Nottingham NG7 5HD
t 0115 917 2222 **f** 0115 917 2211
e phil@octopusinfo.com **w** www.octopusinfo.com
Contact Philip Hucknall, Director

ON Communication
The Media Lab, 5 Fast St Helen Street, Abingdon OX14 5EG
t 01235 537400 **f** 01235 530581
e on@oncomms-tv.co.uk **w** www.oncomms-tv.co.uk
Contact Jane May, Business Assistant

One Box Productions Ltd
The Watermark, 9-15 Ribbleton Lane, Preston PR1 5EZ
t 01772 827766 **f** 01772 827733
e info@onebox.co.uk **w** www.onebox.co.uk
Contact David Langdon, Managing Director; Judith Langdon, Director; Chris
Horsfall, Producer/Director; Richard Garry, Post-Production Supervisor; Philip
Whiting, Programme Designer

Open Gate Picture Company
Spinney's End, Beeches Close, Kingswood KT20 6QA
t 01737 830119 **f** 07970 614733 **m** 07974 193556
e info@opengatepicturecompany.co.uk
w www.opengatepicturecompany.co.uk
Contact Jo Foot, Producer
*Christian company specialising in corporate/promotional films for
charitable organisations.*

Open Mind Productions
6 Newburgh Street, London W1F 7RQ
t 020 7437 0624 **f** 020 7434 9256
 clare@openmind.co.uk **w** www.openmind.co.uk
Contact Clare Hepper, Production Manager

Original Film & Video Productions
84 St Dionis Road, London SW6 4TU
t 020 7731 0012 **f** 020 7731 0027 **m** 07850 780370
e original.films@btinternet.com **w** www.originalproductions.co.uk
Contact Boyd Catling, Managing Director
Credits BT's Don't Stop (I); Top Of The Shoplifters (I); Night Or Day (D); My
Blind Ambition (T)

Ovation Productions
1, Prince of Wales Passage, 117 Hampstead Road, London NW1 3EF
t 020 7387 2342 **f** 020 7380 0404
e events@ovationproductions.com **w** www.ovationproductions.com

P&G Television
The Manor House Market Place, Mottram-in-Longdendale
SK14 6JD
t 01457 766000 **f** 01457 766660
e phil@videos-events.com **w** www.videos-events.com
Contact Phil Lingard
Credits Employment Service Gateway Project to the NHS Video (C); MMO_
Conference Opener Video (I); Connexions at Work (E)

Pantechnicon
90 Lots Road, London SW10 0QD
t 020 7351 7579 **f** 020 7351 0667
e info@pantechnicon.co.uk **w** www.pantechnicon.co.uk

Partners Walters Meacham
9 Jew Street, Brighton BN1 1UT
t 01273 297410 **f** 01273 297410
e info@partnerswm.com **w** www.partnerswm.com
Contact Alice Meacham, Director; Julie Munt, Project Manager
Credits Waitrose Management Development - Branding (W); BBC Training And Development - Safety At Work (W); BBC Worldwide - O2MO (W); Waitrose (W)

Paul Hughes Video Productions
10 Carbry Heights, Keady BT60 3AW
t 028 3753 1396
e info@phvideoproductions.com **w** www.phvideoproductions.com
Contact Paul Hughes, Proprieter

Performance Communications
2b The Broadway, Penn Road, Beaconsfield HP9 2PD
t 01494 670505 **f** 01494 672263
e paul@performancecommunications.co.uk
Contact Paul Kent, Proprieter

Periwinkle Productions Ltd
Old Bank House, Warsash, Southampton SO31 9FS
t 01489 572009 **f** 01489 571017 **m** 07850 674028
e gill.thomas@periwinkle-productions.com
Contact Gill Thomas, Managing Director

Persistence of Vision Productions Ltd
32 Waterside Court, Paper Mill Lane, Alton GU34 2PQ
t 01420 542108 **f** 0870 164 1842 **m** 07973 342005
e info@povprods.com **w** www.povprods.com
Contact Leigh Emmerson, Producer
Credits Short Circuit Racing (T); AA Frontline Training (I); Wildlife Photographer (D); Lifeboat Rescue (D)

Planet Multimedia
1 Canbury Park Road, Kingston-upon-Thames KT2 6JX
t 020 8974 6051
e planettv@online.ie **w** www.planetmultimedia.co.uk
Contact Eve Kirby, Bookings; Lindy Breekes, Manager; Ian Moriarty
Credits NBC TV UK View (D); Fighting For Fairness - The Police Federation (F); Plasma Promo - Samsung (W); Zyban Update - Smithkline Beecham (E)

The Presentation Group
Production House, 15 Brisco Avenue, Loughborough LE11 5HB
t 01509 215105 **f** 01509 231220
e enquiries@thepresentationgroup.net
w www.thepresentationgroup.net
Contact Anita Mullins, Senior Manager

Pretty Clever Pictures Ltd
Shepperton Studios, Studios Road, Shepperton TW17 0QD
t 01932 592047 **f** 01932 592454 **m** 07836 616981
e pcpics@globalnet.co.uk
Contact Gelly Morgan, Managing Director

The Promotional Video Company
First Floor, 38 Russell Road, Kensington, London W14 8HT
t 020 7460 1697 **m** 07977 269794
e info@promo-video.com **w** www.promo-video.com
Contact Martin Phillips, Proprieter

Prospectus
8 Flanchford Road, Stamford Brook, London W12 9ND
t 020 8743 9707 **f** 020 8743 9707
e richardduplock@compuserve.com

PT Productions Ltd
Cookley Farm House, Swyncombe, Henley-on-Thames RG9 6EJ
t 01491 641351 **f** 01491 642230
e info@pt-uk.demon.co.uk **w** www.ptproductions.co.uk
Contact Pam Taylor, Head of Production

Pukka Films Ltd
22/23 D'Arblay Street, London W1 8EQ
t 020 7866 0000 **f** 020 7866 0011
e info@pukkafilms.com **w** www.pukkafilms.com

Purple Flame Media
22 Wingfield Street, London SE15 4LN
t 020 7207 0091 **f** 020 7564 6346 **m** 07958 233550
e jay@purpleflame.com **w** www.purpleflame.com
Contact Jay Knox, Producer/Director; Phil Knox, Cameraman
Credits AIDS In Thailand (T); Slumlord's Losing Power (T); Team Building Works (I); Youth Crime In Peckham (T)

Purple Rage Productions
78 Water Street, Stoke-on-Trent ST4 2BH
t 01782 852835 **m** 07773 554194
e info@purplerage.co.uk **w** www.purplerage.co.uk
Contact Martin Roberts; Glyn Wade; Martin Griffiths
Credits Paint; The Mitchell High School Promo Video; Tullis Russell Health and Safety Video

Quadrant Television Ltd
17 West Hill, London SW18 1RB
t 020 8870 9933 **f** 020 8870 7172 **m** 07831 290085
e quadranttv@aol.com **w** www.quadrant-tv.com
Contact Nik Cookson, Managing Director

R Millichope Film & Video
1 Leacroft, London Road, East Grinstead RH19 1PL
t 01342 314128 **m** 07709 069348
e r.millichope@virgin.net **w** www.millichope.co.uk
Contact Ray Millichope, Director; Greg Millichope, Director//Producer
Credits Bank Of America - Data Upgrade (D); Canary Wharf - PLC (D); Citigroup (D)

Radical Departures
1 Gregories Court, Gregories Road, Beaconsfield HP9 1HQ
t 01494 689100 **f** 01494 689109
e media@radical-departures.com **w** www.radical-departures.com

Ragtime Video
50 Sterte Esplanade, Poole BH15 2BA
t 01202 672423 **f** 01202 672423
e brianjr@lds.co.uk **w** www.ragtimevideo.co.uk
Contact Mark Rigler, Editor; Brian Rigler, Managing Director; June Rigler, Finance

RailTraining.co.uk
Oakslade Studios, Station Road, Hatton CV35 7LH
t 01926 844001 **e** production@oaksdale.com
Contact Allison Bradley, Production Assistant
Credits Railtrack (I); Helping Hands (W); The LI Group (I)

Raw Business Communications Ltd
57-59 Woodside Terrace Lane, Glasgow G3 7YW
t 0141 333 0300 **f** 0141 333 0361
e raw@rawbc.co.uk **w** www.rawbc.co.uk
Contact Roy Wilson, Managing Director

Raw Business Communications Ltd
Northminster Business Park, Northfield Lane, York YO26 6QU
t 01904 783300 **f** 01904 783361
e raw@rawbc.co.uk **w** www.rawbc.co.uk
Contact Roy Wilson, Managing Director

Reach Out Productions
Rosebank House, Overton Park Road, Cheltenham GL50 3BP
t 0870 460 1920 **e** tv@reachout.co.uk **w** www.reachout.co.uk
Contact Kate Fann, Producer; Richard Tierney, Managing Director
Credits NFU Roadshow (I); Standard Life TCS (I); Stakeholder Pensions - Eagle Star (I); Inside Job - Channel 4 (D)

Real Spirit
Garden House, Woods Road, Ford End, Essex CM3 1LJ
m 07765 221627 **e** info@realspirit.co.uk **w** www.realspirit.co.uk
Contact Jonny Lang, Director

Red Balloon Enterprises

Royal London House, Christchurch Road, Bournemouth BH1 3LT
t 01202 504157 **f** 01202 504151
e stephanie@redballoon.co.uk
w www.s2b.bournemouth.ac.uk/html/red_balloon.html
Contact Stephanie Farmer, Media Producer
Credits Plymouth University (E); Bournemouth Education Diretorate (W); Just A Moment (T)

The Red Film Company

t 01748 886745 **e** john@red-film.co.uk **w** www.red-film.co.uk
Contact John Hall, Managing Director
Credits Samsung (I); Hitachi (I)

The Reel Thing

182 Brighton Road, Coulsdon CR5 2NF
t 020 8668 8188 **f** 020 8763 2558 **m** 07802 211587
e info@reelthing.tv **w** www.reelthing.tv
Contact Chris Day; Georgina Huxstep, Head of Production

Reeltime Productions Ltd

Unit 205, The Foundry, 47 Morris Road, London E14 6NJ
t 020 7515 8787 **f** 020 7515 8787 **m** 07957 202030
e info@reeltime.co.uk **w** www.reeltime.co.uk
Contact David Dunkley Gyimah, Co-proprietor/Creative Director; Charles Amponsah, Proprietor/Managing Director
Credits Richard Beer - The Artist (D); The Commission - Ghana High Commission (I); Avitas (M); Lennox Lewis - Before The Fight (D)

Renaissance Vision

256 Fakenham Road, Taverham, Norwich NR8 6QW
t 01603 260280 **f** 01603 864857 **e** bfg@renvision.co.uk
Contact Brian Gardner, Director

Resource Productions

8-67 Upton Park, Upton, Slough SL1 2GF
m 07715 975914
e dom.oliver@virgin.net **w** www.activearchive.org.uk
Contact Dominique Oliver, Producer
Credits What Are We Like? First Light (S); SYPC After Hours (A)

Retina Productions Ltd

United House, North Road, London N7 9DP
t 020 7697 0123 **f** 020 7697 0011
e look@retina-productions.com **w** www.retinaproductions.com
Contact Paul Jocelyn, Production Manager; Stephen Arkell, Managing Director/Executive Producer; Eugene Quinn, Producer; Mathew Avriel, Producer

Revival Productions

25 Messiter Mews, Willington, Derby DE65 6PG
t 01283 701594 **f** 01283 701594
e info@revivalproductions.co.uk **w** www.revivalproductions.co.uk
Contact Sandra Harrison, Producer/Director
Credits Turning Pages, Changing Lives (I); Refresh - Boots Opticians (I); Satelite 3 - British Airport Authorities (I); The Person Not The Problem (I)

Riverhouse Films

11 The Terrace, Barnes, London SW13 0NP
t 020 8392 9939 **f** 020 8878 9663
e colin@riverhousefilms.com **w** www.riverhousefilms.com
Contact Colin Webb, Managing Director; Emma Ogden, Director

Robert Fuller Associates

PO Box 257, West Winch, King's Lynn PE33 0XB
t 01553 773718 **f** 01553 773718 **m** 07767 843407
e robert@robertfullerassociates.co.uk
w www.robertfullerassociates.co.uk
Contact Robert Fuller, Producer

RTV Communications

10 Church Street, Hartlepool TS24 7DJ
t 01429 264673 **f** 01429 865416 **m** 07833 671030
e bmartin@ccad.ac.uk
Contact John Harris, Lighting cameraman; Bob Martin, Producer/Director

Sacha Video Productions

3 Pikes End, Pinner HA5 2EX
t 020 8866 2705 **f** 020 8429 8128 **m** 07980 862633
e info@sachavideo.co.uk
Contact Darren Silver, Director

Sand Pictures Ltd

22 Longmead Avenue, Bristol BS7 8QD
t 01179 249976 **m** 07711 807411
e daniel@sandpictures.co.uk **w** www.sandpictures.co.uk
Credits First Steps To Stress Management In The Workplace (E)

Satellite Productions

4A Marloes Road, London W8 5LJ
t 020 7373 3966 **f** 020 7373 3952 **m** 07973 781133
e sat-prod@virgin.net
Contact Nick Kelsey, Director

Schwops Productions

34 Ashton Road, Luton LU1 3QE
t 01582 412622 **f** 01582 412095
e enquiries@schwops.co.uk **w** www.schwops.co.uk
Contact Maureen Brown, Editor

Scope Productions Ltd

Keppie House, 147 Blythswood Street, Glasgow G2 4EN
t 0141 332 7720 **f** 0141 332 1049
e malcolmmccalister@scopeproductions.co.uk
w www.scopeproductions.co.uk
Contact Malcolm McCalister, Managing Director
Credits Motorola NSCG (I); Intelligent Finance (I); Morrison Bowmore Distillers (I); Xansa (I)

Secret River Productions

10 Forster Road, Beckenham BR3 4LJ
t 020 8325 1260 **f** 020 8325 1260 **m** 07976 692751
e b.oakley.secretriver@cwcom.net
Contact Richard Eccles, Personal Assistant; Ben Oakley, Director/Producer; Helen Brown, Producer
Credits Citroen (I); JVC (I); Unilever (I); Renault (I)

See Thru Watch Group Ltd

30A Powell Road, London E5 8DJ
t 020 8533 5338 **f** 020 8533 5339 **m** 07973 758764
e claude@seethruwatch.com **w** www.seethruwatch.com
Contact Claude Fisicaro, Director
We are an idea-rich company, providing solutions to corporate companies. We handle idents, animation, event and exhibition content, as well as CDRom/DVD production.

Sharkfin Productions

27 Clockhouse Place, Putney, London SW15 2EL
t 020 8788 2425 **m** 07790 908178
e jasper@sharkfinproductions.com **w** www.sfptv.com
Contact Japser Lloyd, Senior Producer
Credits OrangeArrow (I); ATP Tennis (T); TalkSport Marketing (C); FIFA World Cup 2002 (C)

Shelly Telly

63 Wymer Street, Norwich NR2 4BJ
t 01603 763358 **f** 01603 763358 **m** 07713 246613
e shell@shellytelly.co.uk **w** www.shellytelly.co.uk
Credits Remembering Our Friends (D); Give Us A Minute (E); The Living Memory Project (E); Circling The Line (S)

Shelton Fleming Associates

35 Chelsea Wharf, Lots Road, London SW10 0QJ
t 020 7351 2420 **f** 020 7351 9411 **i** 020 7349 4705
e experience@sheltonfleming.co.uk **w** www.sheltonfleming.co.uk
Contact Maurice Fleming, Managing Director; Siobhan Harnett, Senior Producer; Maria Apps, Onscreen Producer; Philip Burrows, Head of Business Marketing; Nicola Kirkby, Project Director

Solar Dreams Productions
1 Shelburne Court, 3 Carlton Drive, London SW15 2DQ
t 020 8789 9229 **m** 07985 200312 **e** juansolari@yahoo.com
Contact Giovanna Hennandez, Production Manager; Juan Solari, General Director

Spa Fax Inflight Entertainment
The Pump House, 13-16 Jacobs Well Mews, London W1U 3DY
t 020 7906 2001 **f** 020 7906 2006 **m** 07876 579695
Contact Ed Oppe, Head of Production

Speakeasy Productions Ltd
Wildwood House, Stanley, Perth PH1 4PX
t 01738 828524 **f** 01738 828419 **i** 01738 825006
e info@speak.co.uk **w** www.speak.co.uk
Contact Geoff Holder, Head of Production; Magnus Wake, Head of Post Production; Shona McGowan, Office Manager; Shona Johnstone, Office Manager
Credits ICT Works (I); Mysterious Scotland (T)

Spectel Communications
95 High Street, Kingswood, Bristol BS15 4AD
t 0117 967 6863 **f** 0117 967 6864 **m** 07866 468390
e info@spectel.demon.co.uk
Contact Jane Batt

Spiral Productions
Aberdeen Studios, London N5 2EA
t 020 7354 5492 **f** 020 7359 6123
e info@spiralproductions.co.uk **w** www.spiralproductions.co.uk
Contact Jonathan Gibbon, Managing Director
Credits Holocaust Exhibition - Imperial War Museum (W); Science Museum Welcome Wing (W); Glaxo Welcome (I)

Spoken Image Ltd
8 Hewitt Street, Knott Mill, Manchester M15 4GB
t 0161 236 7522 **f** 0161 236 0020
e multimedia@spoken-image.com **w** www.spoken-image.com
Contact Rachel Richardson-Jones, Producer/Director; David Harpham, Producer/Director; Steve Foster, Producer/Director; Geoff Allman, Managing Director
Credits Touchstones Museum (E); AGFA - Analogue Plates (W); www.the-shipman-inquiry.org.uk (W); English Partnerships - Expo Real (I)

Stable Recordings
Lochend, Beith KA15 2LN
t 01505 850488 **f** 01505 850658
e info@stablerecordings.com **w** www.stablerecordings.com
Contact Alistair Wilson, Partner; Alison Stevenson, Partner

Star Quality Video Productions
36 Mount Ephraim Lane, Streatham, London SW16 1JD
t 020 8769 6425 **e** starqualityvideo@aol.com
w www.starqualityvideoproductions.co.uk
Contact Don Reeve, Director

Startled Bunny Productions Ltd
109 Rothesay Avenue, Greenford UB6 OD3
t 07050 264755 **e** email@startledbunny.com
Contact Kevin King; Sheena King, Director
Credits North East Coastal Trail (D)

Suffolk Films Ltd
12 Bridge Street, Halesworth IP19 8AQ
t 01986 875875 **f** 01986 875111
e info@sfltv.co.uk
Contact Patrick Redsell, Managing Director; Jonathan Brinton, Chief Editor; Julia Frost, Production Administrator

Supernova
22 Hove Park Villas, Hove BN3 6HG
t 01273 323311 **f** 01273 326624
e service@supernovalearning.com **w** www.supernovalearning.com
Contact Gina Russell, Marketing; Vincent Thompson, Director; J Parry, Producer; J Parry, Producer
Credits Live And Learn (E); Easywriter (E); Recipe For Sucess (E)

Swingbridge Video
Norden House, 41 Stowell Street, Newcastle upon Tyne NE1 4YB
t 0191 232 3762 **f** 0191 232 3762 **e** swingvid@aol.com
Contact Hugh Kelly, Director

Tabard Productions
Adam House, 7-10 Adam Street, London WC2N 6AA
t 020 7497 0830 **f** 020 7497 0850 **e** info@tabard.co.uk
Contact John Herbert

Tads Europe Ltd
37 High Street, Shaftesbury SP7 8JE
t 01747 855888 **f** 01747 855889
e tads@tads.co.uk **w** www.tads.co.uk
Contact Simon Smith, Marketing Manager; Nic Dixon, Production Manager; Allison Williams, Fianance Director; Faye Harrison, Adminstration Co-Ordinator; Katy Smith, Production Adminstrator; Jack Wills, Managing Director

Take 1 Productions
PO Box 6010, Chelmsford CM1 2FT
t 01245 614161 **f** 01245 614160 **m** 07767 398133
e info@take1.co.uk **w** www.take1.co.uk
Contact Peter Curtis, Producer

Take 3 Productions
72-73 Margaret Street, London W1W 8ST
t 020 7637 2694 **f** 020 7637 4678
e mail@take3.co.uk **w** www.take3.co.uk
Contact Cecil Rowe, Director; Richard Smith, Director; Laura Hardman, Director; Christopher Bratt, Managing Director

Take One Business Communications Ltd
Phoenix House, Desborough Park Road, High Wycombe HP12 3BQ
t 01494 835444 **f** 01494 835440 **m** 07771 807817
e takeonetv@aol.com **w** www.takeonetv.com

TalkScience Ltd
Windsor
e contact@talkscience.co.uk **w** www.talkscience.co.uk
Credits EdiTrack: Training Rack (W); EdiTrack: Training Rack (I); Mammals Trust UK (W); Mammals Trust UK (I)

Tandem TV & Film Ltd
10 Bargrove Avenue, Hemel Hempstead HP1 1QP
t 01442 261576 **f** 01442 219250 **m** 07796 134007
e info@tandemtv.com **w** www.tandemtv.com
Contact Barbara Page, Director; Terry Page, Director
Credits History Today (I); Valuing Life - Living With Cancer (I); One For The Road (T); Emmy - The Little Spy (T)

Tantrwm Ltd
45F Oxford Street, Aberdare CF44 8BE
t 01685 886546 **f** 01685 886546
e info@tantrwm.co.uk **w** www.tantrwm.co.uk
Contact Andrew Chainey, Director; Al Wilson, Director; Mayda Wilk, PA
Credits Boys Of Black And Blue (S); Rhymny Partnership Community Story (I); Mobile Phone Sense (E); Cowboy Cabs - The Hidden Danger (E)

TAP Film & Video
39 Hillmarton Road, London N7 9JD
t 020 7700 2212 **f** 020 7700 2623 **m** 07831 167266
e tap@dial.pipex.com **w** www.tapfilm-video.co.uk
Contact Adrian Pearson, Proprieter/Creative Director; Wilfred Aquilina, Financial Director; Bridget Laing, Account Director; Ellen Kate, New Business Director

Tapestry Productions Ltd
The Coach House, Manor Cottage, Solihull B91 2BL
t 0121 711 3664 **f** 0121 711 3159
e tapestryprod@aol.com **w** www.tapestryproductions.co.uk
Contact Jonathan Trace, Managing Director
Credits British Council Horizons (I); Capital One Office Of The Year (I)

taylors.tv

17 Westbourne Avenue, London W3 6JL
t 020 8896 1247 **f** 020 8896 1247 **m** 07968 625634
e info@taylors.tv **w** www.taylors.tv
Contact Ian Puddick, Communications Director; David Taylor, Producer; Philip Taylor, Creative Director; Lalita Taylor, Producer
Credits Acton Community Forum - Community Forum (I); Shell Renewables - 2002 Into 2003 (I); The Company of Strangers (C); Stephen King's Black House (C)

CEO communications for Shell Renewables and Vodaphone, including '2002 into 2003' for Shell Renewables; CEO Phonecasts for Vodaphone; Direct to customer commercials for HarperCollins Publishers; 'Community Forum' launch video for Acton Community Forum. Ultra-current concept-to-creation producers to the highest standards.

tca: World Training

Lyndhurst Maypole Road, East Grinstead RH19 1HL
t 01342 301107 **f** 01342 301108 **m** 07949 886170
e cathybartrop@btconnect.com
Contact Cathy Bartrop, Producer
Credits Malaysia Truly Asia (I); Open your Mind to Norway (I); Cruising A World of Difference (I); Amazing Thailand (I)

That's A Wrap

Three Mills Studios, Three Mill Lane, London E3 3DU
t 020 8215 3373 **f** 020 8215 3421 **m** 07958 513495
e studio@thatsawrap.tv **w** www.thatsawrap.tv
Contact Daniel Backer, Producer; Robert Taylor, Scriptwriter; Samantha Tait, Producer/Director; Sigh Jones, Creative Director
Credits The Women's Freemasons (I); The Camden Jobtrain (E); Investors In People (I); The Dairy Council (E)

Theta Productions

6A Portley Wood Road, Whyteleafe CR3 0BP
t 01883 341485
e cd@thetaproductions.com **w** www.thetaproductions.com
Contact Chris Davies, Producer

Tigervision

27 Maiden Lane, Covent Garden, London WC2E 7JS
t 020 7438 9960 **f** 020 7438 9980
e production@tigervision.com **w** www.tigervision.com
Contact Stephen Hervieu, Managing Director
Credits SESGlobal (I); English National Ballet (I); EasyJet (I); Accenture (I)

Toast TV Ltd

10 Frith Street, London W1D 3JF
t 020 7437 0506 **f** 020 7439 8852
e mail@toasttv.co.uk **w** www.toasttv.co.uk
Contact Fiona Watson, Director; Felicity Gradwell, Director
Credits British Telecom (I); Nike (I); Citroën (I); Camelot (C)

Shoot and post postproduction under one roof.

Totem Event

Platt's Eyot, Lower Sunbury Road, Hampton-on-Thames TW12 2HF
t 020 8979 5225 **f** 020 8979 7885
e neil@totemevent.co.uk **w** www.totemevent.co.uk
Contact Neil Christie

Transfilm UK

Suite 62, Stockton Business Centre, 70 Brunswick Street, Stockton-on-Tees TS18 1DW
t 01642 608878 **f** 01642 634843
e sales@transfilm.fsnet.co.uk **w** www.transfilmuk.com
Contact Steve Wilson, Production Director
Credits Our Town (T); Roto-Glide - Implants International (C); Mission Antartica - Cleaning Up Antartica (T); JCM Company Video (I)

Turner Visual Communications

27 Business and Innovation Centre, Enterprise Park East, Wearfield, Sunderland SR5 2TA
t 0191 516 6344 **f** 0191 549 5808
e turner_visuals@compuserve.com
Contact Nicholas Downing, Managing Director; Hilton Davis, Production Manager

TV Choice

PO Box 597, Bromley BR2 0YB
t 020 8464 7402 **t** 01843 604633 **f** 020 8464 7845
e tv.choice@virgin.net **w** www.tvchoice.uk.com
Contact Norman Thomas, Director

Two Cats Can

6 Staplehall Road, Bletchley MK1 1BQ
t 01908 645646 **f** 01908 645646
m 07768 703625 **m** 07702 378439
e mags@twocatscan.fsnet.co.uk **w** www.twocatscan.co.uk
Contact Mags Noble, Company Secretary; Tony Coe, Director
Credits H2H Metropolitan Police/EBST (I); Disability Awareness CD ROM - The Open University (W); Gaining Ground - Spinal Injuries Association (E); Dreams And Nigtmares - Prince_Waterhouse Coopers (I)

Two Plus Two Multimedia Ltd

80B High Street, Burnham, Slough SL1 7JT
t 01628 600600
e sales@twoplustwo.co.uk **w** www.twoplustwo.co.uk
Contact Fiona Crosswell, Facilities Manager; Barry Tyler, Managing Director; Chris Tibbenham, Producer/Director

Uden Associates

Unit 37, Chelsea Wharf, Lots Road, London SW10 0QJ
t 020 7351 1255 **f** 020 7376 3937 **w** www.uden.com
Contact Michael Proudfoot, Creative Director

University of Leicester, AVS-Video

MSB, PO Box 138, University Road, Leicester LE1 9HN
t 0116 252 2914 **f** 0116 252 3993
e jems1@le.ac.uk **w** www.le.ac.uk/avs/
Contact Jon Shears, Video Production Manager

Vantage Point

1 First Avenue, Sherwood Rise, Nottingham NG7 6JL
t 0115 969 3636 **f** 0115 969 3434 **i** 0115 960 2226
e enquiries@vpoint.co.uk **w** www.vpoint.tv
Contact Theresa Guest, Administrator; Ian Sterling, Proprietor

Vera Media

30-38 Dock Street, Leeds LS10 1JF
t 0113 242 8646 **f** 0113 242 8739 **e** vera@vera-media.co.uk
Contact Al Grathwaite, Producer, Director; Catherine Mitchell, Producer, Director

Video Enterprises

12 Barbers Wood Road, High Wycombe HP12 4EP
t 01494 534144 **f** 01494 534145 **m** 07831 875216
e videoenterprises@btconnect.com
w www.videoenterprises-uk.co.uk
Contact Maurice Fleisher, Proprietor

Videotel Productions

84 Newman Street, London W1T 3EU
t 020 7299 1800 **f** 020 7299 1818
e mail@videotelmail.com **w** www.videotel.co.uk
Contact Stephen Bond, Managing Director

Vidox Video Productions

Vidox House, 139A Tankerton Road, Whitstable CT5 2AW
t 01227 770808 **f** 01227 772808 **m** 07802 500544
e info@vidox.co.uk **w** www.vidox.co.uk
Contact Mary Bekes, Managing Director; John Mcleod, Head of Post Production; George Bekes, Chairman

VisAbility Productions

Kingsland House, 23 Raeburn Avenue, Dartford DA1 3BQ
t 01322 400175 **f** 01322 294746
e visability@lineone.net **w** www.visabilityproductions.net
Credits Dfes (I); Greg Isaacs (C); Sussex Sharks (C)

Visible Productions Ltd

3 The Flag Store, Jubilee Yard, Queen Elizabeth Street,
London SE1 2LP
t 020 7403 9333 **f** 020 7403 5225
e visibleproductions@compuserve.com
e mike@visibleproductions.co.uk
Contact Mike Raggett, Director; Martine Coker, Production Assistant; Denise
Lesley, Producer
Credits AEA Technology Nuclear Engineering; National Express Coaches; IM:TV

Visual Communications

200 London Road, Southend-on-Sea SS1 1PJ
t 01702 339727 **f** 01702 431806
Contact Tony Hill, Managing Director

Visual Language Productions

217 Silver Road, Norwich NR3 4TL
t 01603 404440 **f** 01603 404433
e nda@btconnect.com **w** www.norfolkdeaf.org.uk
Contact Ian Smith, Producer
Credits National Department Of Health (I); Take It On (I); Not The Nightly News (I)

The Visual Link

Head Office, Kingstown Broadway, Carlisle CA3 0HA
t 01228 403900 **f** 01228 511267
e info@tvl.co.uk **w** www.tvl.co.uk
Contact Rob Johnston, Managing Director; Hilda Johnston, Systems Design
Director; Richard Bell, Chairman; Chris Packham, Company Secretary; Stuart
Jefferies, Production Director; Ewan Urquhart, Business Operations Director
Credits Parts Interpretation (I); www.firststate.co.uk (W); The Virtual Hotel (E);
Story Of Sellafield (I)

Vox Pops International Ltd

Bank House, 42 High Street, Ewell KT17 1RW
t 020 8786 8855 **f** 020 8393 9240
e john@voxpops.co.uk **w** www.voxpops.co.uk
Contact John Earnshaw, Director; Sara Sawbridge, Marketing Manager; Diane
Earnshaw, Managing Director

VSO

317 Putney Bridge Road, Putney, London SW15 2PN
t 020 8780 7586 **f** 020 8780 7576 **m** 07960 393785
e video@vso.org.uk **w** www.vso.org.uk
Contact Daniel Gifford, Video Worker; Andy Jones, Production Manager

Walnut Media Communications Ltd

Crown House, Armley Road, Leeds LS12 2EJ
t 08707 427070 **f** 08707 427080
e mail@walnutmedia.com **w** www.walnutmedia.com
Contact Geoff Penn, Director; Gary Nutland, Director

Wedding Videos Direct Limited

t 0800 917 8251 **f** 0152 942 1742
e info@videomakers.com **w** www.videomakers.com
Contact Jan Parry, Director; Helen Lem, Operations Manager; Gerry Roffey, Director

Whatever Pictures Ltd

13A Iliffe Yard, Kennington, London SE17 3QA
t 020 7708 3434 **f** 0870 135 3510 **m** 07767 687102
e alex@whateverpictures.com **w** www.whateverpictures.com
Contact Alex Lewis, Producer; Bruce Webb, Producer
Credits BBC Online Grand Tours (T); The Road To Success (T)

Wheel Track Television Productions

Field House, Forest Hill, Oxford OX33 1EF
t 01865 873078 **f** 01865 873593 **m** 07836 596596
e goffey@community.co.uk
Contact Linda Goffey, Company Secretary; Chris Goffey, Managing Director

White Hart Communicates

Upper Glyn Farm, Devauden, Chepstow NP16 6PN
t 01291 650761
e whitehart@btinternet.com **w** www.whitehart.co.uk
Contact Christine Brooks, Director
Credits Langley Holdings (C); Alfred McApine (F)

William Martin Productions

e info@wmproductions.co.uk

World Television

8 Fitzroy Square, London W1T 5HN
t 020 7388 8555 **f** 020 7387 8444
e info@world-television.com **w** www.world-television.com
Contact Jon King, Chief Operating Officer; Julie Gambling, Archive Manager;
Daniel Rivkin, Head of News & Web
Credits World Economic Forum (W)

World Wide Pictures

21-25 St Anne's Court, London W1F 0BJ
t 020 7434 1121 **f** 020 7734 0619
e info@worldwidegroup.ltd.uk **w** www.worldwidegroup.ltd.uk
Contact Sally Brincklow, Business Development; Jo Goodenough, Senior
Producer; Ray Townsend, Chairman; Chris Courtenay Taylor, Managing Director;
Hannah Mably, Producer; Reina Norris, Business Development
Credits The Learning Journey (E); ESA TV (T); Your Passport To Export Success
(I); Changing Neighbourhoods, Changing Lives (I)

Wren Media Productions

50 Rodney Crescent, Hoddesdon EN11 9EW
t 01992 471620 **f** 01992 447126 **e** wrenprod@aol.com
Contact John Perkins, Production Director

Wyatt & Wyatt

Old House Barn, Chidham Lane, Chidham PO18 8TF
t 01243 576986 **m** 07802 218751
e wyatt_wyatt@compuserve.com
Contact Sara Green, Production Manager; John Wyatt, Parnter; Helen Wyatt, Partner

Xube

Studio 14, 3rd Floor, 246 Stockwell Road, Brixton, London SW9 9SP
t 020 7737 6888 **f** 07031 152052
e info@xube.co.uk **w** www.xube.co.uk
Contact Richard Woolfenden, Director; Jeremy Henderson, Director
Credits Ferl Practitionners's Programme (W); Grosvenor Caledonian (C); BETT
Show Awards 2003 (E)

Zafer Associates

47-48 Chagford Street, London NW1 6EB
t 020 7723 0106 **f** 020 7724 6163 **e** productions@zafer.org.uk
Contact Alan Zafer, Creative Director

Production Companies
Film & TV

@T.I.M.E Productions Istanbul

Meydan Sokak, 6/10 Akatlar, Istanbul 80630, Turkey
t +90 212 352 3991 **f** +90 212 352 3971
e mine@timeproductions.com **e** timeprod@superonline.com
w www.timeproductions.com
Contact Mine Kalpakcioglu, Executive Producer
Credits Swiss Telecom (C); Nokia (C); Badoit - Cinderella Mineral Water (C);
Agents Secrets (F)

2am Films

1 Lawfords Wharf, Lyme Street, Camden, London NW1 0SF
t 020 7428 8800 **f** 020 7428 8801
e production@2amfilms.co.uk **w** www.2amfilms.co.uk
Contact Amanda Martin, Principal
Credits Volkswagen Passat: State Reception; Volkswagen Passat: Disturbance;
Volkswagen Passat: State Reception

The 39 Production Company Ltd

The Estate Offices, Knebworth House, Knebworth SG3 6PY
t 01438 814150
e henry.cobbold@btinternet.com **w** www.the39.com

3BM Television Ltd

63 Gee Street, London EC1V 3RS
t 020 7251 2512 **f** 020 7251 2514
e 3bmtv@3bmtv.co.uk **w** www.3bmtv.co.uk
Contact Simon Berthon, Managing Director; Maggie Still, Director; Daniel Korn, Director; Marlon Milne, Director; Jeremy Bennett, Director
Credits Kings And Queens (D); Adolf and Eva (T); Secrets of the Dead (T); Allies at War (T)

3sixtymedia

Quay Street, Manchester M60 9EA
t 0161 827 2020 **f** 0161 832 8809
e rachel.joseph@3sixtymedia.com
Contact Rachel Joseph, Sales Director

Absolutely Productions

Craven House, 121 Kingsway, London WC2B 6PA
t 020 7930 3113 **f** 020 7930 4114
e info@absolutely-uk.com **w** www.absolutely.com
Contact Miles Bullough, Managing Director
Credits Pub Quiz; Barry Welsh is Coming; Trigger Happy TV (T)

Abstract Images

117 Willoughby House, Barbican, London EC2Y 8BL
t 020 7638 5123 **f** 020 7638 5123
e productions@abstract-images.co.uk
Contact Howard Ross, Managing Director

Acacia Productions Ltd

80 Weston Park, London N8 9TB
t 020 8341 9392 **f** 020 8341 4879
e acacia@dial.pipex.com **w** www.acaciaproductions.co.uk
Contact Nikki Nagasiri, Senior Production Executive; Edward Milner, Managing Director
Credits Amazon - Special Report (T); No Easy Walk (D); Spirit Of The Trees (D); Vietnam After The Fire (D)

Acorn Films

56A Queenstown Road, London SW8 3RY
t 020 7978 2216 **e** acorn_films@beeb.net
Contact Rupert Davies-Cooke, Producer

ACP Television

Crosshands, Coreley, Ludlow SY8 3AR
t 01584 890893 **f** 01584 890810 **e** mail@acptv.com
Contact Richard Uridge, Creative Director; Sandra Keating, Managing Director
Credits Joined - The Secret World Of Siamese Twins (D); I Was Not Asleep - The Inside Story Of Selby (D)

Adam Media Limited

21 Dungarvan Avenue, Roehampton, London SW15 5QU
t 020 8876 3333 **f** 020 8876 3333 **m** 07785 357077
e adamprods@aol.com
Contact John McAdam BA (Hons), FRGS
Credits Golf - Etiquette, Decorum And The Game (D); Zulu Wars (T); Charities Unite (T)

Adrian Rowbotham Films

21 Eccleston Square, London SW1V 1NS
t 020 7976 6800 **f** 020 7976 6300 **m** 07860 459664
e avro@tagad.demon.co.uk
Contact Adrian Rowbotham, Director

Adventure Pictures

6 Blackbird Yard, Ravenscroft Street, London E2 7RP
t 020 7613 2233 **f** 020 7256 0842
e mail@adventurepictures.co.uk
Credits Orlando (F); The Tango Lesson (F); The Man Who Cried (F)

Agenda Productions

Woodstock Studios, 36 Woodstock Grove, London W12 8LE
t 020 8743 9255 **f** 020 8749 3376
e ap@tinopolis.com **w** www.tinopolis.com
Contact Rosie Riding, Production Co-ordinator; Clare Wilmshurst, Production Coordinator
Credits Orphans Of The Artist (D); Lahore Law (D); Shoot Out (D); Sleeping With The Enemy (D)

Aimimage Productions

Unit 5, St Pancras Commercial Centre, 63 Pratt Street, London NW1 0BY
t 020 7916 3734 **e** prods@aimimage.com

Airwaves Media Productions

58 Warsash Road, Warsash, Southampton SO31 9JA
t 01489 578850 **f** 01489 579007
e mail@airwavestv.com **w** www.airwavestv.com
Contact Steve Ancsell, Managing Director; Dick Johnson, Diector

AJT

Corner Cottage, Dike Hill, Low Harley, Rotherham S62 7UL
t 01226 745985 **f** 01226 243718 **m** 07831 709889
e timms@ajt.net.swinternet.co.uk
Contact Andrew Timms, Director

Al Fresco

44 Cathedral Road, Cardiff CF11 9WT
t 029 2072 6726 **f** 029 2072 6727
e alfresco@alfrescotv.com **w** www.alfresco.com
Contact Liz Lloyd-Griffiths, Managing Director; Rhian Williams, Producer; Sian Lloyd Jones, Admin; Melnir Mai Richards, Producer
Credits Jlynis Johns (D); John Belle (D); Welsh Down Under (T); Hot Houses (T)

Alan More Films

Pinewood Studios, Pinewood Road, Iver SL0 0NH
t 01753 656789 **f** 01753 650988 **m** 07768 840122
e almorefilm@aol.com
Contact Alan More, Producer; Judith More, Associate Producer

Alibi Productions

35 Long Acre, London WC2E 9JT
t 020 7845 0400 **f** 020 7379 7035
e apro@alibifilms.co.uk **w** www.alibifilms.co.uk
Contact Lucy Goodman, Producer/Childrens & Family Programming; Linda James, Managing Director; Lex Carey, Assistant; David Glennon, Financial Controller; Roger Holmes, Chief Executive Officer; Joanna Anderson, Producer; Vicky Licorish, Producer; Emma Drinkwater, Development Executive
Credits The Safe House (T); Sir Gadabout Series I & II (T); Goodbye Mr Steadman (T)

Alomo Productions

1 Stephen Street, London W1T 1AL
t 020 7691 6531 **f** 020 7691 6081 **w** www.freemantelmedia.com
Contact Claire Hinson, Managing Director
Credits The House Jack Built (T); Believe Nothing (T)

Alvin Rakoff Productions Ltd

1 The Orchard, Chiswick, London W4 1JZ
t 020 8994 1269 **f** 020 8742 0507 **m** 0780 8401999
e alvin@alvinrakoff.com **w** www.alvinrakoff.com
Credits A Dance To The Music Of Time; A Voyage Round My Father; Too Marvelous For Words

Amadeus Film Productions

104 Kingsley Way, London N2 0EN
t 020 8455 5267 **f** 020 8458 0988 **e** amadeus104@aol.com
Contact Rivka Gottlieb, Associate Director

Amazing Productions

31 Royal Crescent, London W11 4SN
t 020 7602 5355 **e** media@amazing.co.uk

Amber Films

5&9 Side, Newcastle-upon-Tyne NE1 3JE
t 0191 232 2000 **f** 0191 230 3217 **w** www.amber-online.com

Amnesty International

1 Easton Street, London WC1X 0DW
t 020 7413 5560 **f** 020 7413 5815
e avproduction@amnesty.org **w** www.news.amnesty.org
Contact Joanna Duchesne, Producer; Selina Nelte, Production Coordinator
Credits Afghan Voices: Untold Stories - The Hidden Face Of The War (T); Far From The Eyes Of Society (Bulgaria) (D); Justice Denied (Russia) (T); Colombia: The Hidden Tragedy (D)

Anatole Pictures Ltd

5 Elstree Gate, Elstree Way, Borehamwood WD6 1JD
t 020 8810 1286 **m** 07947 050499
e info@anatolepictures.com **w** www.anatolepictures.com
Contact Anna Mackenzie, Company Director/Producer
Credits Katyn Witness (F)

Andrews Marshall Communications

203-204 Great Guildford Business Square, 30 Great Guildford Street, London SE1 0HS
t 020 7928 7576 **f** 020 7928 7555 **m** 07867 847021
e swandyeandrews@hotmail.com
Contact Sandy Andrews, Managing Director
Credits Tower Hamlets- Mother Tounge Video (E); Cilt- Make It (E); QCA-Awarding Bodies Training Video (E)

Angel Eye Film & Television Ltd

1 New Burlington Street, London W1S 2JD
t 020 7437 0082 **f** 020 7437 0084
e office@angeleye.co.uk **w** www.angeleye.co.uk
Contact John O'Callaghan, Creative Director, Angel Eye Scotland; Richard Osborne, Company Director; James Harding, Company Director; Sally Martin, Senior Producer; Harriet Evans-Lombe, Head of Films; Rosalyn Ball, Technical Assistant
Credits The Last Chancers (T); Beginner's Luck (F); Will Durst Live At The Edinburgh Festival (T); The Estate Agents (T)

Anglia Television Ltd

Anglia House, Norwich NR1 3JG
t 01603 615151 **f** 01603 752282
e annedmonds@granadamedia.com **w** www.anglia.tv.co.uk
Contact Dave Wyatt, Postproduction; Ian Osborne, Studios
Credits Trisha (T)

Anglo-Fortunato Films Ltd

170 Popes Lane, London W5 4NJ
t 020 8932 7676 **f** 020 8932 7491 **w** www.digimotion.co.uk
Contact Luciano Celentino, Managing Director
Credits Was There A Way Out? (F); The Pinch (F); Gallan (F); Hobo (F)

Animaton Partnership

13-14 Golden Square, London W1F 9JF
t 020 7636 3300 **f** 020 7580 9153 **m** 07785 302298
e carl@animationpartnership.com
Contact Carl Gover, Managing Director

Antelope

Drounces, White Chimney Row, Emsworth PO10 8RS
t 01243 370806 **f** 01243 376985
e mick.csaky@antelope.co.uk **w** www.antelope.co.uk
Contact Mark Fletcher, Commercial Director; Leslie Woodhead, Producer/Director; Justin Johnson, Director of Production; Phillipa Le Grys, Office Coordinator; Mick Csaky, Chief Executive/ Creative Director
Credits A Cry from the Grave (T); Himalaya (C); Africa Now

Antena

Quebec House, Castlebridge, 5-19 Cowbridge Road East, Cardiff CF11 9AB
t 029 2031 2000 **f** 029 2031 2001
e swyddfa@antena.co.uk **w** www.antena.co.uk
Contact Peter Elias Jones, Director; Mike Griffiths
Credits The Great Divide (T); UNED PIMP 5 (T); The FlintStreet Nativity (T)

Apollo Television Ltd

The Studio, 21A Allensbank Road, Cardiff CF14 3PN
t 029 2025 1811 **f** 029 2025 1821
e info@teledu-apollo.demon.co.uk
Contact Paul Jones, Company Director; Launa Llewellyn-Davies, Director

APP Broadcast

Unit 7, 2 Exmoor Street, London W10 6BD
t 020 8964 4992 **f** 020 8960 0464
e info@appbroadcast.com **w** www.appbroadcast.com
Contact Andrew Preece, Director; Richard Simmonds, Director
Credits Sting - Live Webcast (W); 2003 America Cup (T); Ellen MacArthur (T)

APT Films

225A Brecknock Road, London N19 5AA
t 020 7284 1695 **f** 020 7482 1587
e admin@aptfilms.com **w** www.aptfilms.com
Contact Andy Porter, Company Director/Producer; Paul Morrison, Company Director; Tony Dowmunt, Company Director/Producer; Jonny Persey, Company Director/Producer; Jerry Rothwell, Company Director/Producer
Credits L8r (W); Solomon And Gaenor (F); Wondrous Oblivion (F); Skin Deep (S)

Aquila Films

19 Bishops Road, London N6 4HP
t 020 8340 9500 **f** 020 8348 4610
e andrea.florence@aquilafilms.com
Contact Andrea Florence, Senior Producer
Credits Return To The Wild (D)

Arcadian Productions Ltd

The Media Centre, 42 Bridgegate, Howdon DN14 7AB
t 01430 430100 **m** 07801 384670
e mail@arcadian-uk.com **w** www.arcadian-uk.com
Contact Sally Wells, Managing Director

Arena Films Ltd

2 Pelham Road, London SW19 1SX
t 020 8543 3990 **f** 020 8540 3992
Contact David Conroy, Managing Director

Argus Video Productions

52 Church Street, Briston, Melton Constable NR24 2LE
t 01263 861152 **f** 01263 861152 **w** www.norfolkvideos.co.uk
Contact Siri Taylor, Producer
Credits Kurt Schwitters In Western Norway (D); Chainsaw Safety (E); The Norfolk Coast (D); The Norfolk Broads (D)

Arista

70 Saint Michaels Road, Llandaf, Cardiff CF5 2AQ
t 029 2056 2245 **f** 029 2056 0991
Contact Owen Roberts, Producer/Director

Arlington Productions Ltd

Cippenham Court, Cippenham Lane, Cippenham, Nr Slough SL1 5AU
t 01753 516767 **f** 01753 691785

Armac Films

Appartment G/1, 69 Otago Street, Glasgow G12 8PQ
t 0141 337 2322 **f** 0141 357 3064 **m** 07850 090469
e armacfilms@ukbusiness.com **e** armacfilms@aol.com
w www.filmscot.co.uk
Contact Alex McCall, Director

Armadillo Productions Ltd

Invision House, Wilbury Way, Hitchin SG4 0XE
t 01462 427300 **f** 01462 427375 **e** patoma@rmonlin.com
Contact Manny Cohen, Managing Director

ARTTS Productions

Highfield Grange, Bubwith YO8 6DP
t 01757 288294 **f** 01757 288253
e info@arttsint.co.uk **w** www.arttsint.co.uk
Contact Duncan Lewis

ASA Communications

Ashleigh House, 42 Hammelton Road, Bromley BR1 3PY
t 020 8464 7929 **f** 020 8464 7930 **m** 07860 542352
e stephensaunders@asa-uk.tv
Contact Stephen Saunders, Film & Video Producer/Director

Ashford Entertainment

182 Brighton Road, Coulsdon CR5 2NF
t 020 8645 0667 **f** 020 8763 2558
e info@ashford-entertainment.co.uk
w www.ashford-entertainment.co.uk
Contact Georgina Huxstep, Head of Production
Credits Great Little Trains (T); Love Goddesses of... The World (T); 12,000 Mile Dream (T)

ASM Productions (a division of Marketmetro Ltd)

Media House, 17 Kedlestone Road, Peterborough PE2 8XL
t 01733 313773 **f** 01733 313773 **e** marketmetro@aol.com
Contact Julian Bray, Producer/Director
Credits Granada (C)

Assassin Films Ltd

74 Holland Park, London W11 3SL
t 020 7706 8352 **f** 0870 167 2981 **e** ludwin@dircon.co.uk
Contact Leslee Udwin, Producer/Company Director
Credits The One And Only (F); East is East (F)

Attaboy TV Ltd

Unit N107, 1-45 Westminster Business Square, Darham Street, London SE11 5JH
t 020 7642 3000 **f** 020 7642 3001
e info@attaboytv.com **w** www.attaboytv.com
Contact Loris Vigiani, Production Assistant; Michael Wood, Company Director; Daniel Allum, Company Director
Credits Celebrity SW (T); Shedheads (T); The Great Escape (D); Michael X (D)

Atticus Television Ltd

5 Clare Lawn, London SW14 8BH
t 020 8487 1173 **f** 020 8878 3821 **e** attw12@aol.com
Contact Bob Louis, Executive Producer

Audience Films

31 Samuel Manor, Chelmer Village, Chelmsford CM2 6PU
t 01245 493350 **m** 07774 292242 **e** td@audiencefilms.co.uk
Contact Terence Daw, Producer/Director/Writer

Avalon Television Ltd

4A Exmoor Street, London W10 6BD
t 020 7598 7280 **f** 020 7598 7281 **e** atv@avalonuk.com
Contact Jon Thoday, Executive Director; Richard Allen-Turner, Executive Director

Axiom Films

12 D'Arblay Street, London W1V 3FP
t 020 7287 7720 **f** 020 7287 7740
e mail@axiomfilms.co.uk **w** www.axiomfilms.co.uk
Contact Douglas Cummins, Managing Director; Melanie Robbins, Marketing & Publicity Executive; Rocio Freire-Bernat, Head Of Acquisitions

B-Line Productions Ltd

135 Sydney Road, London N10 2ND
t 020 8444 9574 **f** 020 8365 3664 **m** 07831 289283
e anniemoore@b-lineproductions.co.uk
w www.b-lineproductions.co.uk
Contact Paula Gau, Assistant Producer; Ruth Billings, Assistant Producer; Serena MacBeth, Director; Sarah Peat, Director; Annie Moore, Managing Director/Producer; Jon Walker, Editor
Credits Complementary Kids (D); For The Love Of Liddy (D); The Alternative (D)

Baker Street Media Finance Ltd

96 Baker Street, London W1U 6TJ
t 020 7487 3677 **f** 020 7487 5667
e enquiries@bakerstreetfinance.tv
Contact Keith Evans, Director; Bill Allan, Director
Credits I Capture The Castle (F); Anita And Me (F); Bloody Sunday (F); Saving Grace (F)

Balanced Productions

74 Moss Lane, Pinner HA5 3AU
t 020 8866 5271 **f** 020 8866 5271 **e** angela@spi.ftech.co.uk
Contact Angela Spindler-Brown, Managing Director

Bamboo Film & TV Productions

15 Rochester Square, London NW1 9SA
t 020 7916 9353 **f** 020 7485 4692
e 100411.2324@compuserve.com
Contact Rosemary Forgan, Managing Director

Bangaw

The Media Centre, Culverhouse Cross, Cardiff CF5 6XJ
t 029 2059 0225 **f** 029 2067 9160 **e** bangaw@msn.com
Contact Paul Apreda, Director
Credits Justice (T); Into the Valleys (T); Clublife (T)

Bard Entertainments Ltd

7 Denmark Street, London WC2H 8LZ
t 020 7240 7144 **f** 020 7240 7088
e office@bardentertainments.co.uk
w www.bard-entertainments.co.uk
Contact Margaret Mattheson, Producer/Managing Director
Credits AKA (F); Kin (F); Revenger's Tragedy (F); American Cousins (F)

Barry Hale Threshold Studios

69B Kettering Road, Northampton NN1 4AW
t 01604 250377 **f** 01604 233346
e info@thresholdstudios.com
Contact Barry Hale, Production Coordinator; Uzma Choudhry, Workshops & Training Coordinator
Credits Fresh From Dadesh (T); Underground High (T); Out Of Time (T); Songs Of Innocence (S)

BBC Wales

Broadcasting House, Llantrisant Road, Llandaff, Cardiff CF5 2YQ
t 029 2032 2000 **f** 029 2055 2973 **w** www.bbc.co.uk/wales
Contact Sian Owen, Head of Operations; Toby Grosvenor, Head of Operations

BEE'S PICTURES

Bee's Pictures

Calle Cordoba 10B, Fuengirola, Malaga 29640, Spain
t +34 902 118531 **t** +34 94 2667073
f +34 902 118532 **f** +34 94 2664636
e beespics@beespics.com **w** www.beespics.com
Contact Belinda Lewin, Producer; Ivo Van Vollenhoven, Producer; Iohamil Navarro, Producer (Cuba); Simon Burge, Executive Producer

Bentley Productions

Pinewood Studios, Pinewood Road, Iver SL0 0NH
t 01753 656594 **f** 01753 652638
e emma.kingsman_lloyd@crysalis.com
Contact Brian True-May, Producer/Managing Director
Credits Ultimate Force (T); Midsomer Murders (T)

Berwick Universal Pictures

45 Brookfield, London N6 6AT
t 020 7923 1998 **e** paul@paulyule.com
Credits Damned In The USA (D); Lone Star Hate (D); In The Footsteps Of Bruce Chatwin (D); The House Of War (D)

Bewick Films

The Captains Lodgings Bamburgh Castle, Bamburgh NE69 7DF
t 01668 214480 **f** 01668 214160
Contact John Mapplebeck, Producer
Credits Foot and Mouth (D); Twelve Men and a Boat (T); Soulway Harvest (T)

Beyond The Frame Ltd

49 Goodge Street, London W1T 1TE
t 020 7631 4441 **f** 020 7631 4449 **e** beyondtheframe@aol.com
Contact Jenifer Millstone, Producer; Victor Schonfeld, Producer
Credits The Animals Film (T); Shattered Dreams; Picking Up the Pieces (F); It's a Boy! (T); Loving Smacks (T)

production companies : film & tv

Big 30 Films

6 Cedar Way, Camley Street, London NW1 0PD
t 020 7387 2637
e production@big30films.com **w** www.big30films.com
Contact Paul Williams, Head of Production; Terez Mahr, Production Coordinator
Credits Gods Own County (D); Road To Hell (D)

Big Bear Films

36 Courtnell Street, London W2 5BX
t 020 7229 5982 **f** 020 7221 0676
e office@bigbearfilms.co.uk **e** www.bigbearfilms.co.uk
Contact Marcus Mortimer, Producer; John Stroud, Producer
Credits Strange Series I (T); My Hero Series IV (T)

Big H Productions

The Great Barn Studios, 9 Plaines Close, Cippenham SL1 5TY
t 01753 522984 **f** 01753 522984 **m** 07836 289877
e harryfr@another.com
Contact Harry Fayers-Rushton, Producer
Credits Green Fingers (F); Dr Surreal (F); The Late Twentieth (F); Free Spirits (F)

Big Wave Productions Ltd

156 St Pancras, Chichester PO19 7SH
t 01243 532531 **f** 01243 532153
e info@bigwavetv.com **w** www.bigwavetv.com
Contact Angela Palmerton, Producer, Production Manager
Credits Secret Weapons (T); The Bodysnatchers (T); Meerkat Madness (T); Poison (T)

Big;bam;boo;Films

Meadow's End, Turner's Mead, Chiddingfold GU8 4UD
t 01428 684481 **m** 07766 006805 **e** jeremy@bigbamboo.biz
Contact Jeremy Drysdale, Proprietor
Credits Grand Theft Parsons (F); Rotten (F)

Bino Honda

63 White Hart Lane, Barnes, London SW13 0PP
t 020 8878 7102 **f** 020 8392 8510 **m** 07802 353626
e bino@dircon.co.uk
Contact Bino Honda, Japanese Co-ordinator

Blackbird Productions

6 Molasses Row, Plantation Wharf, Battersea, London SW11 3TW
t 020 7924 6440 **f** 020 7924 4778
e enquiries@blackbirdproductions.co.uk
w www.blackbirdproductions.co.uk

Blackwatch Productions

752-756 Argyle Street, Glasgow G3 8UJ
t 01412 222640 **f** 01412 222646
e info@blackwatchtv.com **w** www.blackwatchtv.com
Contact Paul Gallagher, Writer/Director; Heidi Proven, Research & Development
Credits The Paranormal Peter Sellers (D); When Freddie Mercury Met Kenny Everett (D); Designer Vaginas (T); Bone Breakers (D)

Blakeway Production

32 Woodstock Grove, London W12 8LE
t 020 8743 2040 **f** 020 8743 2141 **e** admin@blakeway.co.uk
Contact Kate Macky, Head of Production
Credits Newton The Dark Heretic (D); Winstons War (D); Empire (D)

Blast! Films

2 Imperial Works, Perren Street, London NW5 3ED
t 020 7267 4260 **f** 020 7485 2340
e blast@blastfilms.co.uk **w** www.blastfilms.co.uk
Contact Madonna Baptiste, Head of Production; Mark Hayhurst, Producer; Penny Woolcock, Writer/Director; Edmond Coulthard, Managing Director

Blenheim TV Films Ltd

10 Blenheim Road, Shirburn, Watlington OX49 5DN
t 01491 614288 **f** 01491 612988
e enquiries@blenheimfilms.com **w** www.blenheimfilms.com
Contact Candida Brady, Producer; Titus Ogilvy, Director; Adam Clavering, Music Director
Credits Kids From Anna Scher (T); Waiting For Marco (T); Soul (T)

Blink Productions

181 Wardour Street, London W1F 8WZ
t 020 7494 0747 **f** 020 7494 3771
e info@blinkprods.com **w** www.blinkprods.com
Contact James Studholme, Executive Producer; Lauren Mott
Credits Clark's: Catwalk (C); Smirnoff: Trainer (C); Volkswagen: Toy Car; Microsoft XBox: Ear Tennis

Bliss Films

2 Kingsway Place, Sans Walk, London EC1R OLS
t 020 7336 7100 **f** 020 7336 7102
e reception@blissfilms.co.uk **w** www.blissfilms.co.uk
Contact Helen Hatfield, Managing Director
Credits Flora: Wedding; Fox's Biscuits (Test)

Blue Heaven Productions

45 Leather Lane, London EC1N 7TJ
t 020 7404 4222
e sarah@blueheavenproductions.freeserve.co.uk
Contact Christine Benson, Managing Director
Credits The Ruth Rendall Mysteries (T)

Blue Lemon Films

8 Dewhurst House, 3-6 Winnett Street, London W1B 6JY
t 020 7434 4134 **f** 365 9395 **m** 07866 515546
e bluelemonfilms@yahoo.com
Contact Francoise Higson, Director
Credits Rooftops (S); Man Alone (S)

Blue Orange Films Ltd

88 Park Avenue South, London N8 8LS
t 020 8341 9977 **f** 020 8340 9889
Contact Ruth Kenley-Letts, Producer

Bob Hope TV Productions

PO Box 134, Sittingbourne ME9 7TF
t 01795 844404 **f** 01795 843986 **e** bhtv@dial.pipex.com
Contact Bob Hope, Executive Producer; Beverley Nolker, Production Assistant//Executive Producer

Borzoi Broadcasting Company Ltd

3 Bearhurst Cottages, Henhurst Cross Lane, Cold Harbour, Dorking RH5 4LR
t 01306 712054 **f** 01306 713347 **m** 07890 867277
e bryanizz@aol.com
Contact Roger Hannah, Producer; Bryan Izzard, Head of Production
Credits Opera Babes In Jerusalem (T); Secrets Of The Shed (T); Russell Watson At Christmas (T)

Box Productions

28 St Margaret's Road, Oxford OX2 6RX
t 01865 311040 **f** 01865 311495 **e** seanmcphilemy@aol.com
Contact Sean McPhilemy, Managing Director

Boxwood Productions

18 Upper High Street, Shipton-under-Wychwood OX7 6DP
t 01993 832586 **f** 01993 832586 **m** 07860 461050
e boxwood@talk21.com
Contact Peter Champness, Producer

Boyana Film Company

Kino-center Boyana, Sofia 1616, Bulgaria
t +359 2 958 2766 **f** +359 2 958 6487 **m** +359 88 705556
e director@boyanafilm.bg **w** www.boyanafilm.bg
Contact Evgeny Mihailov

Bracan

Ty Cefn, Rectory Road, Canton, Cardiff CF5 1QL
t 029 2033 3200 **f** 029 2033 3833 **m** 07712 541702
e bracan@business.ntl.com **w** www.bracan.co.uk
Contact Catrin Lewis Defis, Producer; Branwen Cennard, Producer
Credits Iechyd Da - V & VI (T)

Breakfuture
38 Ringwood Ave, East Finchley, London N2 9NS
t 020 8444 3303 **f** 020 8374 2462
e pchipping@lineone.net **w** www.breakfuture.co.uk
Contact Peter Chipping, Director

Brechin Productions Ltd
7 High Park Road, Kew TW9 4BL
t 020 8876 2046 **f** 020 8392 2046
e clive@brechin.com **w** www.brechin.com
Contact Clive Doig, Managing Director / Producer
Credits Turnabout (T); See it, Saw It (T)

Brenda Rowe Productions
42 Wellington Park, Clifton, Bristol BS8 2UW
t 0117 973 0390 **f** 0117 973 8254
Contact Brenda Rowe, Producer
Credits Citzen's Arrest (T); Hotel (T)

James Brett
PO Box 2001, London W1A 1FY
t 020 7957 5323 **f** 020 7957 5324
e email@makefilm.net

Brian Waddell Productions Ltd
Strand Studios, 5-7 Shore Road, Holywood BT18 9HX
t 028 9042 7646 **f** 028 9042 7922 **e** strand@bwpltv.co.uk
Contact Jon-Barrie Waddell, Executive Producer; David Cumming, Head Of Development; J Brian Waddell, Chairman & Managing Director; Jane Coyle, Press & PR/Film & Drama Development; Richard Williams, Executive Producer; Irene Boyd, Company Secretary; Mark McMaster, Facilities Manager
Credits Chasing Time In (T); Ten Of The Best (T); Built To Measure (T); The Vibe (T)

The Bridge (Media, Film, & Studio Production) Ltd
11 Jew Street, Brighton BN1 1UT
t 01273 774888 **f** 01273 729915 **m** 07880 791035
e info@the-bridge.tv **w** www.the-bridge.tv
Contact Tony Steyger, Managing Director
Credits The Brighton Festival (D); A Sense Of Place (D); St Dunstans (D); Mercenaries (T)

Bridge Television Productions
Apt 5, 5 Cromwell Crescent, London SW5 9QN
t 020 7341 9694 **f** 020 7602 9325
Contact Laurence St John, Managing Director

Bright Filament Productions
Bath BA1 5TW
t 01225 474940
e info@brightfilament.com **w** www.brightfilament.com
Contact Diane Morgan; Phil Ashby, Producer
Credits Science Fair Behind The Scenes (E); Digital Radio Briefing (I)

Brighter Pictures
10th Floor, Blue Star House, 234-244 Stockwell Rd, Brixton, London SW9 9ST
t 020 7733 7333 **f** 020 7733 6333
e info@brighter.co.uk **w** www.brighter.co.uk
Contact Gavin Hay, Managing Director; Luke Wilkins, Assistant to the Managing Director
Credits Casino (T); Diet Another Day (T); Tabloid Tail (T); Get A New Life (T)

British Gothic Films
PO Box 61, Bideford EX39 1YJ
t 01237 477946 **f** 01237 477946 **m** 07939 224004
e mitch@britishgothic.com
Contact Mitchell Henderson, Director; Debi Nethersole, Executive Consultant
Credits Chaos (F)

Broadcast Media Ltd
59 Glebe Road, Norwich NR2 3JH
t 01603 471261 **f** 01603 471261 **m** 07710 433459
e andrew@broadcastmedialtd.co.uk
Contact Andrew Ridoutt, Lighting Cameraman
Credits Time Team (T); Gardeners World (T); Country File (T)

Bronco Films
The Producers Centre, 61 Holland Street, Glasgow G2 4NJ
t 0141 287 6817 **f** 0141 287 6817
e broncofilm@btinternet.com **w** www.broncofilms.co.uk
Contact Peter Broughan, Managing Director
Credits The Young Person's Guide To Becoming A Rockstar (T); Rob Roy (F)

Brook Lapping Productions Ltd
6 Anglers Lane, London NW5 3DG
t 020 7428 3100 **f** 020 7284 0626
e info@brooklapping.com **w** www.brooklapping.com
Contact Claire Healey, Head of Production
Credits Diana, Story of a Princess (T); The Death of Yugoslavia (T); End Game in Ireland (T)

Bubbaloosh Productions Ltd
44 Granville Street, Leamington Spa CV32 5XN
t 01926 422390
e gisele@bubbaloosh.com **w** www.bubbaloosh.com
Contact Gisele Ryan, Director
Credits Anything's Possible (F); A Full Life (F)

Buffalo Pictures Ltd
4th Floor, 48 Poland Street, London W1F 7ND
t 020 7439 0401 **f** 020 7439 0402 **e** buffalo@dial.pipex.com
Contact Natalie Hughes, Office Manager/PA/Development Associate; Philippa Braithewaite, Producer; Martin Clunes, Managing Director
Credits Hunting Venus (T); Staggered (F); Sliding Doors (F)

Burder Films
37 Braidley Road, Meyrick Park, Bournemouth BH2 6JY
t 01202 295395 **f** 01202 589089
e burderfilms@aol.com **w** www.johnburder.co.uk
Contact John Burder, Managing Director

The Bureau Film Company Ltd
3rd Floor, 28 Goodge Street, London W1T 2QQ
t 020 7580 8182 **f** 020 7580 8185
e mail@thebureau.co.uk **w** www.thebureau.co.uk
Contact Bertrand Faivre, Producer; Sol Gatti-Pascual, Producer; Matthew Debraconier, PA to Faivre
Credits Noi Albinoi (F); The Warrior (F)

Burnt Orange
21 Tamworth Street, Fulham, London SW6 1LG
m 07818 451232 **e** yoruba64@hotmail.com
Contact Tunji Akinsehinwa, Cameraperson; Debra Asante, Producer/Director/Writer; Oliver Noel, Producer/Director/Writer
Credits Virtuality (S)

Buxton Raven Productions
102 Clarence Road, London E5 8HB
t 020 8986 0063
Contact Jette Bonnevie, Producer

Cactus TV
Cactus Studios, 373 Kennington Road, London SE11 4PS
t 020 7091 4900 **f** 020 7901 4901
e touch.us@cactustv.co.uk **w** www.cactustv.co.uk
Contact Amanda Ross, Joint Managing Director; Simon Ross, Joint Managing Director
Credits Cliff Richard - The Hits I Missed (T); Songs Of Bond (T); The British Soap Awards (T); Richard And Judy (T)

Café Productions Ltd

Capital Court, Capital Interchange Way, Brentford TW8 0EX
t 020 8987 1063 **f** 020 8987 1070 **m** 07785 346958
e pat.footer@cafeproductions.com
Contact Pat Footer, Director of Production
Credits Spectacled Bears (D); Ten Plagues Of Egypt (D); $100 Taxi Ride (D); The Man Who Bought Mustique (D)

Caledonia Sterne & Wyld

147 Bath Street, Glasgow G2 4SQ
t 0141 564 9100 **f** 0141 564 9200
e info@caledonia-tv.com **w** www.caledonia-tv.com

Capricorn Productions

23-29 Albion Place, Maidstone ME14 5DY
t 01622 691431 **f** 01622 688249 **m** 07811 020421
e info@capricornproductions.co.uk
w www.capricornproductions.co.uk
Contact Ernie Brennan, Head of Production; Colin Furley, Chief Executive
Credits Kent County Council - SOLACE (I); Locate In Kent (I); Rural Partnership (D); Kent Messenger (I)

Cardinal Television

15A Clive Road, Cardiff CF5 1HF
t 029 2022 8807 **f** 029 2022 8925 **e** post@cardinal-tv.co.uk
Contact Dafydd Parry, Producer

Carey Films Ltd

5 Henshaw Lane, Yeadon, Leeds LS19 7RW
t 0113 250 6411 **f** 0113 210 9426
e owen@careyfilms.com **w** www.careyfilms.com
Credits Baby Blues (F)

Carnival (Films & Theatre) Ltd

12 Raddington Road, Ladbroke Grove, London W10 5TG
t 020 8968 1717 **f** 020 8968 0177
e info@carnival-films.co.uk **w** www.carnival-films.co.uk
Contact Brian Eastman, Producer; Maxine Tate, Head of Finance & Business Affairs
Credits Lucy Sullivan Is Getting Married (T); The Tenth Kingdom (T); As If I-III (T); Agatha Christie's Poirot (T)

Carpenter Communications

45 Holloway Lane, West Drayton UB7 0AE
t 020 8759 6292 **f** 020 8759 7165 **w** www.carpentercoms.co.uk
Contact John Carpenter, Managing Director
Credits Valencia Conference- Independant Travel Organisers Association (Marketeer Plc) (M); Eight Language Multi-Screen Conference- Armstrong (I); Ferrari Maserati North America (I)

CASE Film & Television

204 Mare Street Studios, 203-213 Mare Street, London E8 3QE
t 020 7296 0010 **f** 020 7296 0011
e case@casetv.com **w** www.casetv.com
Contact Sam Allen, Project Manager; Susan Francis, Joint Managing Director
Credits National Maritime Museum - Skin Deep Tattoo (W); V&A Museum - Family Online (W); Learn.co - Ancient Egypt (W); Learn.co - Celebrations (W)

Castle Haven Digital

Borgue, Kirkudbright DG6 4UD
t 01387 702013 **m** 07811 002046
e mail@castlehaven.com **w** www.castlhaven.com
Contact Rex Pyke, Producer

Catalyst Television

Brook Green Studios, 186 Shepherds Bush Road, London W6 7NL
t 020 7603 7030 **f** 020 7603 9519
e info@catalyst-films-tv.com
Contact Katherine Hedderly, Head of Drama Development; Gay Search, Company Director/Producer; Tony Laryea, Managing Director; Jo Sandilands, New Business Development
Credits Women Who Kill (D); Gardener's World (D)

Catherine Bailey Ltd

110 Gloucester Avenue, London NW1 8JA
t 020 7483 2681 **f** 020 7483 4541 **e** cbl@cbltd.net
Contact Catherine Bailey, Managing Director

Celador Film

39 Long Acre, London WC2E 9LG
t 020 7240 8101 **f** 020 7836 1117 **e** tvhits@celador.co.uk
Contact Clare Stewart, Senior Press Officer; Christian Colson, Head of Production & Development
Credits Dirty Pretty Things (F)

Celador Productions

39 Long Acre, London WC2E 9LG
t 020 7240 8101 **f** 020 7836 1117 **e** tvhits@celador.co.uk
Contact Steve Springford, Director of Production; Kate Perrior, Head of Press & Publicity; Clare Stewart, Senior Press Officer
Credits Commercial Breakdown (T); All About Me (T); The National Lottery-Winning Lines (T); Who Wants To Be A Millionaire? (T)

Celtic Films Ltd

21 Grafton, London W1 S4EU
t 020 7409 2080 **f** 020 7409 2383 **e** info@celticfilms.co.uk
Contact Rebecca Torman; Stuart Sutherland, Chief Executive Officer; Muir Sutherland
Credits Girl From Rio (F); A Life For Life (T); Sharpe (T)

Cerci Communications

26 Store Street, London WC1E 7BT
t 020 7692 6209 **f** 020 7436 7169
e events@buildingcentretrust.org
Contact Andrew Scoones, Manager

Chameleon Television

Television House, 104 Kirkstall Road, Leeds LS3 1JS
t 0113 244 4486 **f** 0113 243 1267 **e** allen@chameleontv.com
Contact Simon Wells, Producer; Patricia Doherty, Producer; Emma Ekelund, Assistant Producer; Richard Everiss, Producer; Justin Rowlatt, News Reporter; Anna Hall, Producer; Carl Dinnen, Producer/Reporter
Credits The Big Trip (T); College Girls (S); Dispatches (T); Crimefighters (T)

Channel 6 Productions Ltd

Standby Studios, Hempstead, Saffron Walden CB10 2PJ
t 01799 599350 **f** 01799 599906 **m** 07774 921528
e info@videoproduction.co.uk
Contact Andrew Sanders, Director

Chaplins Film & TV Ltd

Chaplins House, The Acorn Centre, Roebuck Rd, Hainault IG6 3TU
t 020 8501 2121 **f** 020 8501 3336 **m** 07974 673675
e enq@chaplinsfilm.tv.com **w** www.chaplinspantos.co.uk
Contact Laurence Barnett, Producer; Jim Holmes, Producer; Joe Wenburne, Producer

Charisma Films

Riverbank House, 1 Putney Bridge Approach, London SW6 3JD
t 020 7610 6830 **f** 020 7610 6836 **e** mail@charismafilms.net
Contact James Atherton; Alan Balladur

Charles Dunstan Communications

42 Wolseley Gardens, London W4 3LS
t 020 8994 2328 **f** 020 8994 2328

Chatsworth Television Ltd

97-99 Dean Street, London W1D 3TE
t 020 7734 4302 **f** 020 7437 3301
e info@chatsworth-tv.co.uk **w** www.chatsworth-tv.co.uk
Contact Nick Heyworth, Producer; Halina Stratton, Head of Licensing; Cynthia Kennedy, Head of Sales & Acquisitions; Rebecca Channon, Sales & Marketing Executive; Malcolm Heyworth, Managing Director
Credits The Crystal Maze (T); Treasure Hunt (T); Busy Buses (A)

Cheerful Scout Productions Ltd

25-27 Riding House Street, London W1W 7DU
t 020 7291 0444 **f** 020 7291 0445
e info@cheerfulscout.com **w** www.cheerfulscout.com
Contact Ben Ashmore, Manager; Rachel Pardoe, Facilities Manager

The Children's Film Unit
South Way, Leavesden WD25 7LZ
t 01923 354656 **f** 01923 354656 **m** 07729 869105
e cfilmunit@aol.com **w** www.btinternet.com/~cfu/
Contact Carol Rennie, Administrator

Christopher Swann Associates
89 Wendall Road, Stamford Brook, London W12 9SB
t 020 8749 9056 **f** 020 8740 9306 **m** 07747 775935
w www.swanntv.co.uk
Contact Francis Peters

Chromodynamic
77 Oxford Street, London W1D 2ES
t 020 7439 0400 **f** 020 7439 0300 **m** 07885 488300
e jb@chromodynamic.com
Contact Jon Blay, Producer

Chrysalis TV Midlands
1 The Square, 111 Broad Street, Birmingham B15 1AS
t 0121 697 1900 **f** 0121 697 1999 **w** www.chrysalis.com
Contact Paola Colpani, Deputy Managing Director; Zoe Norman, Head of
Production; Richard Pearson, Executive Producer; Elaine Bedell, Managing
Director; Debbie Vile, Production Manager
Credits Fifth Gear - James Bond Special; Greatest Cars In The World (T);
Fifth Gear (T)

CHX Productions Ltd
2nd Floor, Highgate Business Centre, 33 Greenwood Place,
London NW5 1LB
t 020 7428 3999 **f** 020 7428 3998
e mail@chxp.co.uk **w** www.chxp.co.uk
Contact Heather Hampson, Joint Managing Director

Cicada Films
1 Marylands Road, London W9 2DU
t 020 7266 4646 **f** 020 7289 2599
e cicada@cicadafilms.com **w** www.cicadafilms.com
Contact Natalie Burke, Assistant Producer; Chris Holland, Head of Production
Credits Oasis Of The Golden Mummies (D); Secrets Of The Sands (D); Emperors
Eternal Armies (D); The Real King Herod (D)

Clarion, Film & Television
The 1929 Building, Merton Abbey Mills, Watermill Way, London
SW19 2RD
t 020 8545 2000 **t** 070 9200 2806 **f** 070 9203 0160
e info@clariontv.com **w** www.clariontv.com
Contact Ahna Rosenska, Producer; Kieran Matthew, Director of Programmes;
Andrew Linton, Creative Director; Shaun Lee Bishop, Animation Designer;
Richard Hannah, Managing Director
Credits Picture Story - Colt (A); Direct Line Rescue (I); The Spoken World (T)

Clear Image
Lancashire Business School, Department of Journalism,
University of Central Lancashire, Preston PR1 2HE
t 01772 893733 **f** 01772 892907
Contact Paul Egglestone, Producer, Director

The Clear Picture Company
PO Box 12, Bakewell DE45 1ZP
t 01246 583005 **f** 01246 583645 **m** 07767 775253
e schaungilmartin@aol.com
Contact Shaun Gilmartin, Producer; Judy Laybourn, Producer

Cloud 9 Screen Entertainment Group
Sanctuary House, 45-53 Sinclair Road, London W14 ONS
t 020 7300 6623 **f** 020 7300 6529
e hannah.butler@sanctuarygroup.com **w** www.entercloud9.com
Contact Aky Najeeb, Managing Director; Raymond Thompson, Chief Executive
Credits Classic Collection (T); Atlantis High (T); Revelations: The Initial
Journey (T); The Tribe Series I-V (T)

COI Communications
Hercules House, Hercules Road, London SE1 7DU
t 020 7261 8767 **f** 020 7261 8776 **w** www.coi.gov.uk
Contact Jackie Huxley, Head of Television; Sally Whetton, Director of Broadcast

Coleridge Productions Ltd
Marjon, Derriford Road, Plymouth PL6 8BH
t 01752 761138 **f** 01752 636722
e mail@coleridgeproductions.com
w www.coleridgeproductions.com
Contact Adrian Emerson, Director; John Sheppard, Director

Colonial American Productions
The Waterfront, St Aubin, Jersey JE3 8AB
t 01534 743678 **f** 01534 746613
e colonial@itl.net **w** www.colonialtv.com
Contact Alastair Layzell, Executive Producer
Credits Heritage: Love It or Lose It! (T); Vintage & Veteran (T)

Comedy People Ltd
Elstree Film & TV Studios, Shenley Lane, Boreham Wood WD6 1JG
t 8324 2703
e enquiries@comedypeople.biz **w** www.comedypeople.biz
Contact Andrew Barclay, Director
Credits The Sitcom Trials (T); PETS (T)

Common Features
5 Charlotte Square, Newcastle-upon-Tyne NE1 4XF
t 0191 261 8808 **f** 0191 261 8809
e commonfeatures@compuserve.com
Contact Stewart Mackinnon, Producer; Bob Davis, Producer
Credits Julie Burchill - What Killed My Dad (D); The Little Life (F)

Continent Film Ltd
8 Cleveland Gardens, London W2 6HA
t 020 7262 4646 **f** 020 7262 3242 **m** 07771 581219
e joe@hollywoodclassics.com
Contact Michael Pakleppa, Director
Credits The Last Unicorn (F); 8 1/2 (F)

Convergence Productions
10-14 Crown Street, London W3 8SB
t 020 8993 3666 **f** 020 8993 9595 **e** info@crownstreet.co.uk
Contact Christopher O'Hare, Director
Credits David Starkey's Henry VIII (D); Plastic Fantastic (T); Private View (T)

Cork Films
51 Coleherne Court, The Little Boltons, London SW5 ODN
t 020 7244 8079 **f** 020 7244 8079
e emicorc@hotmail.com **w** www.corkfilms.co.uk
Contact Emily Corcoran, Managing Director
Credits Stranger Than Fiction (I); Life's A Drag (D); Snap (S); The Invitation (S)

Cracking Films
Halstead Croft, Shoreham Lane, Halstead, Sevenoaks TN14 7DD
t 01959 533718 **f** 01959 532028 **m** 07818 082066
e crackingfilms@yahoo.co.uk
Contact David Burrows Sutcliffe, Company Secretary
Credits Spy Trapper (F)

Crannog Films Ltd
46 Grafton Street, Dublin 2, Rep of Ireland
t +353 1 671 5677 **f** +353 1 671 5678 **e** crannogfilms@indigo.ie
Contact Conor Harrington, Managing Director

Crazy Films Ltd
42 Eastbourne Road, Hanworth TW13 5EY
t 020 8755 4348 **t** 020 8894 5885 **f** 020 8755 4388
m 07867 790482 **e** crazyfilms@lycos.co.uk
Contact Carlos Clarke, Director, Managing Director; Luke Harris, Creative
Director; Keith Wait, Company Secretary

Create TV & Film Ltd

Capital Point, 33 Bath Road, Slough SL1 3UF
t 08700 949400 **f** 01753 495225
e info@creativetvandfilm.com **w** www.creativetvandfilm.com
Contact Vanessa Chapman, Director, Film and TV; Bob Thompson, Head of Story and Character; Michael Carrington, Head of Programming
Credits Bionicle: Mask Of Light (F); Little Robots (A)

Creative Film Makers Ltd

Pottery Lane House, 34A Pottery Lane, London W11 4LZ
t 020 7229 5131 **f** 020 7229 4999
e nicholas.seligman@btclick.com
Contact Michael Seligman, Managing Director

The Creative Production Team Ltd

2 Dixwell Close, Gillingham ME8 9TB
t 01634 262606 **f** 01634 263606 **m** 07950 353802
e david@medbiz.co.uk
Contact David Neale, Producer; John Luton, Director
Credits Almarai Smoothy (C); Snailsbury Tales (C); Kenana Green Gold (C)

Croft Television

Croft House, Progress Business Centre, Whittle Parkway, Slough SL1 6DQ
t 01628 668735 **f** 01628 668791
e sales@croft-tv.com **w** www.croft-tv.com
Contact Terry Adlam, Managing Director

Cwmni'r Castell

10 Garth Road, Old Colwyn LL29 8AF
t 01492 512349 **f** 01492 574235 **e** cwmnicastell@aol.com
Contact Elwyn Williams, Producer/Director

Cynyrchiadau Huw Brian Williams Productions

6B & 8B Station Road, Radyr, Cardiff CF15 8AA
t 029 2084 4044 **f** 029 2084 2287
e cynhbwprod@ndirect.co.uk
Contact Rob Nicholls, Assitant Producer; Huw Williams, Managing Director/Director/Producer
Credits Sgiliaith (I); Tourism and the Environment (E); The Psychic Detective (T)

Daisybeck Productions

Elite TV House, 248 Meanwood Road, Leeds LS7 2HZ
e info@daisybeck.tv
Contact Paul Stead, Managing Director

Dakota Films Ltd

4A Junction Mews, London W2 1PN
t 020 7706 9407 **f** 020 7402 6111 **e** info@dakota-films.demon.co.uk

Dan Films Ltd

32 Maple Street, London W1P 5GD
t 020 7916 4771 **f** 020 7916 4773
e office@danfilms.com **w** www.danfilms.com
Contact Jonathan Taylor

Dandy Productions

Gainsborough House, 81 Oxford Street, London W1D 2EU
t 020 7903 5200 **f** 020 7903 5333 **e** info@dandytv.com
Contact Andy Williams, Creative Director; Dan Berlinka, Creative Director
Credits The Raoul Show ... With Raoul (T); Brush-Head Mini-Toons (A)

Dane Productions

Brook Cottage, Sutton Valence Hill, Maidstone ME17 3AS
t 01622 844300 **f** 01622 844300 **m** 07885 253617
e daneproductions@aol.com
Contact John Reynolds, Producer/Director
Credits Vauxhall (C); Pirelli Cables (C); Scottish Power (C)

Dareks Production House

58 Wickham Road, Beckenham BR3 6RQ
t 020 8658 2012 **f** 020 8325 0629 **m** 07973 664189
e david@dareks.fsnet.co.uk **w** www.dareks.fsnet.co.uk
Contact David Crossman, Director; Tom Dow-Smith, Lighting Cameraman

Darlow Smithson Productions Ltd

4th Floor, Highgate Business Centre, 33 Greenwood Place, London NW5 1LB
t 020 7482 7027 **f** 020 7482 7039
e mail@darlowsmithson.com
Contact Ulla Streib, Head of Production
Credits Driven (D); How The Twin Towers Collapsed (D); Lost Worlds (D); Touching The Void (F)

David Deyong & Associates

17 Cholmley Gardens, Aldred Road, London NW6 1AE
t 020 7794 8744 **f** 020 7813 0920 **m** 07958 911052
e susie_deyong@yahoo.co.uk
Contact Susie Deyong, Producer

David Furnham Productions

39 Hove Park Road, Hove BN3 6LH
t 01273 559731 **f** 01273 559731
Credits Cinema of Comic Illusions (D); Tatti - A Chance to Whistle (D)

David Paradine Productions

5 St Mary Abbots Place, London W8 6LF
t 020 7371 3111 **f** 020 7602 0411 **e** mail@paradine.demon.co.uk
Contact Shelly Safari, Personal Assisitant

David Taylor Associates Ltd

25 Wensley Drive, Hazel Grove, Stockport SK7 6EW
t 01625 850887 **m** 07816 149774 **e** dtaylor@clara.net
Contact David Taylor, Proprietor

David Wickes Productions Ltd

10 Abbey Orchard Street, Westminster, London SW1P 2LD
t 020 7222 0820 **f** 020 7222 0822 **m** 07786 070878
e wickesco@aol.com
Contact Heide Wilsher, Production Executive

DD Video

11 Churchill Court, 58 Station Road, North Harrow HA2 7SA
t 020 8863 8819 **f** 020 8863 0463
e office@ddvideo.co.uk **w** www.ddvideo.co.uk
Contact Steve Ayres, CEO; Richard Jones, Managing Director; Barney Ashton, Production Manager; Peter Fraser, Trade Sales; Tony Knight, Marketing; Colin Higgs, Marketing Manager
Credits Seaplanes And Flying Boats Of The Royal Airforce (D); Bristish Steam (D); Bristish Campaigns: Western Desert (D)

De Warrenne Pictures Ltd

St Anne's House, Diadem Court, London W1D 3EE
t 020 7734 7648 **f** 0709 236 7853
e mail@dewarrenne.com **w** www.dewarrenne.com

The Dead Good Film Company

35 Grange Road, Kings Heath, Birmingham B14 7RN
t 01214 497229 **e** info@deadgood.co.uk **w** www.deadgood.co.uk

Dean Brothers Productions

121 Horsham Avenue, Peacehaven BN10 8DT
t 01273 579612 **m** 07711 825662

Denis Tyler Ltd

59 High Street, Great Missenden HP16 0AL
t 01494 866262
e denistylerlimited@btinternet.com **w** www.denistyler.com
Contact Elizabeth Tyler, Managing Director

Dennis Woolf Productions

169 Didsbury Road, Stockport SK4 2AE
t 0161 442 8175 **f** 0161 442 8175

Dibb Directions

27 Lillian Road, Barnes, London SW13 9JG
t 020 8748 1579
Contact Mike Dibb, Director
Credits The Miles Davis Story (T)

Different Film Ideas Productions Ltd
38 Grange Road, St Anne's, Lytham St Anne's FY8 2BW
t 01253 640476 **m** 07860 577172 **e** PTW@parkinson@aol.com
Contact Paul Woods, Company Director/Producer
Credits Tobacco Seriously Damages Your Health (T); The Art of Dating Women (T)

Digital Imagemakers
PO Box 17, St Ives TR26 2YH
t 01736 797888 **f** 01736 796725
e info@digital-imagemakers.co.uk
w www.digital-imagemakers.co.uk
Contact Caitlin Ryan, Resources; William Heller, Senior Producer

Diplomat Films Ltd
Oakedene House, Parkfield Road, Altrincham WA14 2BT
t 0161 929 1603 **f** 0161 929 1604 **m** 07831 125090
e diplomatfilms@hotmail.com
Contact Keith Thompson, Producer/Managing Director; Alan Bleasdale,
Writer/Producer; Dawn Thompson, Company Secretary

Directors Film Company of New York
1123 Broadway, Suite 1107, New York 10010, USA
t +1 212 627 4999 **f** +1 212 627 4499 **e** dfcnyc@aol.com
Contact Richard Coll

DLT Entertainment UK Ltd
10 Bedford Square, London WC1B 3RA
t 020 7631 1184 **f** 020 7636 4571
Contact John Bartlett, Director Of Comedy & Drama; Gary Mitchell, Contact;
John Reynolds, Contact
Credits As Time Goes By (T); My Family (T)

DML Productions
4 Selwyn Road, Stamford PE9 1JW
t 01780 752294 **m** 07747 878646 **e** dmlproductions@lineone.net
Contact David Longstaff, Director

Domino Films
7 King Harry Lane, St Albans AL3 4AS
t 01727 750153 **e** jo@dominofilms.co.uk
Contact Joanna Mack, Director

Double E Productions Ltd
The Manse, New Street, Chulmleigh EX18 7DB
t 01769 580583 **f** 01769 580992 **e** sarah@doubleeprods.f9.co.uk
Contact Sarah Errington, Producer

Double Exposure
Unit 22-23, 63 Clerkenwell Road, London EC1M 5PS
t 020 7490 2499 **f** 020 7490 2556
e reception@doublex.com **w** www.doubledex.com
Contact Sarah Streatfield, Administration
Credits The Hairman (T); Film Focus Animation (T); Extra (T)

Double-Band Films
The Crescent Arts Centre, 2-4 University Road, Belfast BT7 1NH
t 028 9024 3331 **f** 028 9023 6980
e info@doublebandfilms.com **w** www.doublebandfilms.com
Contact Dermot Lavery, Director/Producer; Michael Hewitt, Director/Producer
Credits Beckham And The Battle With Argentina (D); Unfinished Business (D);
George Bests Body: Football Stories (D)

Dox Productions
84 Addison Gardens, London W14 0DR
t 020 7602 3094 **f** 020 7602 3771 **e** mail@tvdox.com
Contact Duncan Copp, Producer; David Sington, Executive Producer
Credits Horizon - The Secret Of El Dorado (D); Extreme Lives - The Great Dog
Race (D); Rocket Men Of Mission 105 (D); Equinox - Hunt For The Deathstar (D)

DPTV Productions
Overgare, Stuckenduff Road, Shandon G84 8NW
t 01436 820084 **f** 01436 820084
Contact Patricia Maclaurin, Director; David Peat, Director
Credits Development of Screenplay (T); BBC Gardening Series (T); BBC
Archives Series (T)

Dragonfire Entertainment Ltd
The Blue House, 6 Station Road, Hampton Village TW12 2BX
t 020 8255 3624 **f** 020 8255 3624 **m** 07747 043411
e russell@dragonfire.tv **w** www.dragonfire.tv
Contact Katharine Robson, Co-ordinator; Russell Jarman Price, Co-Managing
Director; Petter Wallace, Co-Managing Director
Credits Captain Sabertooth (F); Snow Children (T); Department Of Work And
Pensions (W)

The Drama House
Coach Road Cottages, Little Saxham, Bury St Edmunds IP29 5LE
t 01284 810521 **f** 01284 811425
e jack@dramahouse.co.uk **w** www.dramahouse.co.uk
Contact Jack Emery, Producer
Credits Witness Against Hitler (T); Suffer The Little Children (T); Breaking the
Code (T); Inquisition (T)

Dreamchaser Productions
Eblana House, Eblana Avenue, Dun Laoghaire, Ireland
t 230 3433 **f** 230 3349
e info@dreamchaser.ie **w** www.dreamchaser.ie
Contact Vasessa Moss, Production Co-ordinator
Credits Harley Davidson's 100th Anniversary Tour (T); U2 Elevation 2001: Live
From Boston (M); 3rd Brown Thomas International Fashion Show 2003 (T); U2
Beautiful Day (M)

Duke Marketing
Champion House, Tromode Business Park, Douglas IM99 1DD
t 01624 640020 **f** 01624 640001
e info@dukesales.com **w** www.dukesales.com
Contact Kelly Smith, International Sales Executive; Jon Quayle, Commercial
Director; Lauren Roberts, International Sales Executive

DVD Productions Ltd
16 Tournay Road, London SW6 7UF
t 020 7385 9207 **f** 020 7386 9836 **e** iain.j@uk.com
Contact Sophie Johnstone, Producer
Credits Policing The Future (D); The Man With No Name II (D); Steven And
Stanley (D); The Flying Con Man (D)

Eagle & Eagle
15 Marlborough Road, London W4 4EU
t 020 8995 1884 **f** 020 8995 5648 **e** producer@eagletv.co.uk

Eagle Eye Productions
Eagle House, 22 Armoury Way, London SW18 1EZ
t 020 7351 6429 **f** 020 7351 1018
e vic@production-department.co.uk
e lu@production-department.co.uk **w** www.eaglevision-int.com
Contact Perry Joseph
Credits Usher - Live (M); Fat Boy Slim - Big Beach Boutique II (M); Yes -
Symphonic Live (M); Diana Krall - Live In Paris (M)

Eagle Films Ltd
Lakewood, Heathfield, Cobham KT11 2QY
t 01372 844484 **f** 01372 501228 **m** 07939 501228
e eagle.films@virgin.net **w** www.eaglefilms.co.uk
Contact Ann Clifford, Writer; Martina Nagel, Director; Katrina Moss, Producer
Credits A Life Of Fire (D); A Story Of The Heart (D); Let's Do Lunch (S)

East Wind Films
Old Rectory Studios, Rosary Road, Norwich NR1 1TA
t 01603 628728 **f** 01603 664727 **m** 07836 263486
e averilbrennan@oldrectory44.freeserve.co.uk
Contact Averil Brennan, Producer; Jon Pusey, Development Executive; Gerry
Wigzell, Company Director; Peter North, Administrator
Credits Clear Conscience (T); Shadow Play (T); Deep Sleep (T); Trial by Fire (T)

eastNortheast Ltd
Glebe Farm, Wells Road, North Creake NR21 9LG
t 01328 730430 **t** 01328 730444 **m** 07818 041556
e info@eastnortheast.co.uk **w** www.eastnortheast.co.uk
Contact Jeremy Brettingham, Director
Credits Reeve Flooring (C); The Sailor's Tale (D); Barb Jungr Live (M);
Circle Line (S)

EBS Trust
12 Printing House Yard, Hackney Road, London E2 7PR
t 020 7613 5082 **t** 020 7613 5083 **f** 020 7613 5220
e mail@ebstrust.u-net.com **w** www.ebst.co.uk
Contact Janice Gardner, Project Executive; Jim Stevenson, Chief Executive Officer
Credits Truth Will Out (T)

Eco Productions
Newbolt Close, Paulerspury NN12 7NH
t 01327 811294 **f** 01327 811753 **m** 07711 239557
e eco1pro@aol.com
Contact Barbara Payne, Assistant Producer; Chris Payne,
Producer/Lighting Cameraman
Credits Golden River Traffic (W); Time Team - Behind the Scenes (D);
Island Gems (D)

Ecosse Films
Brigade House, 8 Parsons Green, London SW6 4TN
t 020 7371 0290 **f** 020 7736 3436
e info@ecossefilms.com **w** www.ecossefilms.com
Contact Douglas Rae, Executive Producer, Managing Director; Robert Bernstein,
Executive Producer, Head of Drama; Paula Howarth, Production Assistant
Credits Monarch Of The Glen (T); Mrs Brown (F); Charlotte Gray (F)

Eddy French Associates
90 Dean Street, London W1D 3SX
t 020 7434 1564 **f** 020 7494 1357
e eddy@eddyfrenchassociates.co.uk
Contact James Gooch, Editor

Eden Productions
24 Belsize Lane, London NW3 5AB
t 020 7794 1533 **f** 020 7794 1533 **e** nlander@cix.co.uk
Contact Nicholas Lander, Director

Edinburgh Film Productions
Traquair, Innerleithen EH44 6PP
t 01896 831188 **f** 01896 831199
Contact Robin Crichton, Director, Managing Director

Edinburgh Film Workshop Trust
56 Albion Road, Edinburgh EH7 5QZ
t 0131 656 9123 **f** 0131 656 9123 **e** post@eswt.demon.co.uk
Contact David Halliday, Producer

Einstein Entertainment
The Picture House, 4 Lower Park Row, Bristol BS1 5BJ
t 0117 927 7473 **f** 0117 923 0862 **e** jules.brown@einstein.tv
Contact Jules Brown, Head of Development; Jeff Dowson, Executive Producer
Credits Toffs Behind Bars (D); What Makes Jeffrey Tick? (T); Hard Bastards (T);
Real Dad's Army (T)

Electric Picture Machine Production
Paulswell, West Linton EH46 7BH
t 01968 660984 **f** 01968 660984
e kenandrew@picturemachine.co.uk
w www.picturemachine.co.uk
Contact Ken Andrew
Credits Middle of the Road Ltd (M); Near Project Edinburgh (I); Edinburgh
Military Tattoo (C)

Elgin Productions
68 Elgin Crescent, London W11 2JJ
t 020 7243 0660 **f** 020 7243 1317 **e** peterswain@elginmedia.com
Contact Peter Swain, Producer

ELK Productions
4 Church Road, East Molesey KT8 9DR
t 020 8224 8586 **f** 020 8224 8507 **m** 07711 757230
e elk@elkproductions.co.uk **w** www.elkproductions.co.uk
Contact Elisabet Wootton, Producer/Director
Credits Ideal Saturday (T); Cabin Fever (T)

Elmgate Productions
Shepperton Studios, Studios Road, Shepperton TW17 0QD
t 01932 562611 **e** elmgate@dial.pipex.com
Contact Chris Burt, Producer
Credits The Woman in Black (T); Goodnight Mister Tom (T); Rockface (T)

Endboard Productions Ltd
114A Poplar Road, Bearwood, Birmingham B66 4AP
t 0121 429 9779 **f** 0121 429 9008
e endboard@btconnect.com **w** www.endboard.com
Contact Sunandan Walia, Managing Director; Yugesh Walia, Chairman; Anna
Sommerville, Documentary Researcher
Credits Buddhas Of Suburbia (D); Days & Nights An Indian Jail (D); Bouncer (S)

Endemol UK
Shepherds Building Central, Charecroft Way, Shepherds Bush,
London W14 0EE
t 0870 333 1700 **e** info@endemoluk.com **w** www.endemoluk.com
Contact Symon Veglio; Chloe Power
Credits The Salon (T); Changing Rooms (T); Big Brother (T); Fame Academy (T)

Endgame Pictures
37b New Cavendish Street, London W1G 8JR
t 01274 589116 **m** 07736 709149
e endgamepictures1@hotmail.com **w** www.endgamepictures.com
Contact Graham Roberts, Managing Director/Producer; Heather Wallis, Writer;
Shirley Roberts, Company Secretary; Stephen Hay, Director

English & Pockett
e rob.machin@english-pocket.com **w** www.english-pocket.com
Contact Cynthia King, New Business Manager

Enteraction TV
8 Park Place, 12 Lawn Lane, Vauxhall, London SW8 1UD
t 020 7820 4470 **f** 020 7820 4471
e etv@enteractiontv.com **w** www.enteractiontv.com
Contact Mark Murphy, Managing Director

Entertainment Film Productions
Eagle House, 108-110 Jermyn Street, London SW1Y 6HB
t 020 7930 7744 **f** 020 7930 9399

Eon Productions
Eon House, 138 Piccadilly, London W1J 7NR
t 020 7493 7953 **f** 020 7408 1236 **w** www.007.com
Contact Michael Wilson, Executive Producer

Equilibrium Films
28 Sheen Common Drive, Richmond TW10 5BN
t 020 7602 1989
Contact John Miles, Producer/Director
Credits Burma's Final Solution (T); Conquering The Mountain Of Fire (T); The
Path To Manhood (T); Barefoot Amongst Tamil Tigers (T)

Escape Pictures (Worldwide) Ltd
13 Brackenwood Lodge, Prospect Road, Barnet EN5 5AQ
t 020 8275 0167 **f** 08701 675380
e mark@escapepictures.com **w** www.escapepictures.com
Contact Mark Johnson, Managing Director/Producer

Ettinger Brothers
Gladstone House, 2 Church Road, Liverpool L15 9EG
t 0151 734 2240 **f** 0151 733 2468
e philipettinger@blueyonder.co.uk
Contact Philip Ettinger, Managing Director

Event One

5 Carlisle Street, London W1D 3BL
t 020 7437 4040 **f** 020 7437 1111 **m** 07957 939072
e wilton@event-1.co.uk
Contact Nigel Wilton, Manager; Jeff Chegwin, Manager

Excelsior Group Productions

Dorking Road, Tadworth KT20 7TJ
t 01737 812673 **f** 01737 813163 **e** pip.burley@amserve.net
Contact Pip Burley, Chief Executive; Richard Bates, Executive Producer
Credits My Uncle Silas (T); A Touch of Frost (T); Darling Buds of May (T)

Eye 4 Films

2 Chitty Street, London W1T 4AP
t 020 7916 0157 **f** 020 8459 4875 **m** 07711 112850
e info@eye4films.com
Contact Tim Pearce, Managing Director; Mark Tiley, Head Of Development

Face Television

Unit 20, Intec 2, Wade Road, Basingstoke RG24 8NE
t 01256 350022 **f** 01256 350046 **m** 07767 887622
e paul@facetv.co.uk **w** www.facetv.co.uk
Contact Paul Friend, Producer/Director
Credits Wildlife Photographer (T); Lifeboat (T); Lifeboat Rescue (T); Wildlife SOS (T)

Fair Game Films Ltd

Garden House, 1 Hamilton Gardens, London NW8 9PS
t 020 7266 2686 **f** 020 7266 0211 **e** fgme@aol.com
Contact Stephen Bill, Director of Comapny; Alan Dossor, Director of Comapny; Irving Teitelbaum, Director of Comapny
Credits Maisie Raine (T); The Locksmith (T)

Fairline Productions

15 Royal Terrace, Kelvin Grove, Glasgow G3 7NY
t 0141 331 0077 **f** 0141 331 0066 **e** rockettv@aol.com
Contact Ricki Walker, Director

Fame - Film & Music Entertainment

34 Bloomsbury Street, London WC1B 3QJ
t 020 7636 9292 **f** 020 7636 9229
e info@fame.uk.com **w** www.fame.uk.com
Credits Under The Stars (F); Loving Glances (F); Falcons (F); Deathwatch (F)

The Farnham Film Company

34 Burnt Hill Rd, Lower Bourne, Farnham GU10 3LZ
t 01252 710313 **f** 01252 725855
e info@farnfilm.com **w** www.farnfilm.com
Contact Ian Lewis, Managing Director; Melloney Roffe, Head Of Production

Feature Films Ltd

Production House, 37 Blandford Hill, Milborne St Andrew DT11 0JB
t 01258 839000 **f** 01258 839111
e info@featurefilms.co.uk **w** www.featurefilms.co.uk
Contact Simon Curtis, Producer/Director

Festival Film & Television

Festival House, Tranquil Passage, London SE3 0BJ
t 020 8297 9999 **f** 020 8297 1155
e info@festivalfilm.com **w** www.festivalfilm.com
Contact Ray Marshall, Managing Director
Credits Mandancini (F); Catherine Cookson Dramas (T)

Ffilmiau Fflur Ltd

4 Garth Villas, Gwaelod-y-Garth, Cardiff CF15 9HL
t 029 2081 1582 **f** 029 2081 4096 **m** 07881 624991
e robin@ffilmiau-fflur.fsnet.co.uk **w** www.ffilmiau-fflur.co.uk
Contact Robin Davies-Rollinson, Producer/Director
Credits Y Delyn (F)

Ffilmiau Tawe

10 Clos y Maerdy, Garden Village, Gorseinon, Swansea SA4 4EA
t 01792 898221 **f** 01792 898221 **m** 07771 667046
e taweffilms@ntlworld.com
Contact Wyn Thomas
Credits David Thomas (T); Adardrycin Series II (T); Canrif O Brifyeyl (S); Eisteddfod Y Ddwyawdl (S)

Ffilmiau'r Bont

Y Ganolfan Deledu, Cibyn, Caernarfon LL55 2BD
t 01286 677225 **f** 01286 673077 **e** anharad@bont.tv
Contact Angharad Anwyl, Producer

Ffilmiau'r Nant Cyf

Moreia, Penrallt Isaf, Caernarfon LL55 1NS
t 01286 675722 **f** 01286 675159 **e** nant@nant.co.uk
Contact Robin Evans, Producer; Sue Water, Producer; Alun Ffred Jones, Producer; Emyr Davies, Producer
Credits Sgorio (T); Xtra (T); Rownd A Rownd (T); Oed Y Addewid (T)

Fflic Films

59 Mount Stuart Square, Cardiff Bay, Cardiff CF1 6DR
t 029 2040 9000 **f** 029 2040 9001 **e** fflic.zip@business.ntl.com
Contact Gwenda Griffith, Director

Fighting Films Ltd

1 Triangle House, 2 Broomhill Road, Wandsworth, London SW18 4HX
t 020 8874 3314 **f** 020 8874 8590 **e** info@fightingfilms.com
Contact Simon Hicks, Partner; Ian Sharples, Partner
Credits 1997 World Judo Championship (T); 2000 Sydney Olympics Judo (T); 2001 World Judo Championship (T); 2001 Moscow Grand Prix (T)

The Film & Theatre CONNECTION Ltd

The Studio, 46 Marsh Road, Pinner HA5 5NQ
t 020 8866 1253 **f** 020 8866 5403 **m** 07785 333858
e info@cnxeurope.com **w** www.cnxeurope.com
Contact Adam Penny, Producer/Director; Peter Penny, Producer/Director
Credits Xerox Extreme (C); Christies - The Pause (I); Extreme Videos (I); Cities For Cohesion (D)

Film & General Productions

4 Bradbrook House, Studio Place, London SW1X 8EL
t 020 7235 4495 **f** 020 7245 9853 **e** cparsons@filmgen.co.uk
Contact Davina Belling, Producer; Clive Parsons, Producer
Credits Hans Christian Andersen (T); The Queen's Nose (T); I Am David (F); Callas Forever (F)

The Film Exchange

7 Cornwall Crescent, Notting Hill Gate, London W11 1PH
t 020 7792 4321 **f** 020 7229 3623 **m** 07714 203374
e andy@filmx.f9.co.uk
Contact Renata Bovara, Script Editor; Harvey Robbins, Director

Film West

Windy Ridge, Goonbell Lane, St Agnes TR5 0PN
t 01872 552824 **f** 01872 553994 **m** 07866 498994
e freddie@palombo.co.uk
Contact Freddie Palombo, Cameraman
Credits Cricket Live NEC (T); Shadows Of Killimanjaro (F)

Filma-Cass

Kocamansur Sokak 115/1, Sisli, Istanbul 80260, Turkey
t 233 6018 **f** 231 0227
e filmcass@filmacass.com.tr **w** www.filmacass.com.tr
Contact Ömer Vargi; Tamer Basaran; Bahadir Arliel; Elfin Yuksekteppe; Oguz Peri

Filmhouse Ltd

2 Wedgwood Mews, 12-13 Greek Street, London W1V 5LE
t 020 7813 4800 **f** 020 7813 4808
e bookings@filmhouse.co.uk **w** www.filmhouse.co.uk
Contact Michael Günther; Darren Cathan

Filmnova Productions

Newcastle House, Albany Court, Monarch Road, Newcastle-upon-Tyne NE4 7YB
t 0191 272 7035 **f** 0191 272 7036
e info@filmnova.com **w** www.greatrun.org
Contact Peter Brown, Managing Director; Albert Mark, Marketing

Films of Record

2 Elgin Avenue, London W9 3QP
t 020 7286 0333 **f** 020 7286 0444 **m** 07958 577160
e films@filmsofrecord.com **w** www.filmsofrecord.com
Contact Sam Allen, Assistant To Roger Graef; Marja Kurikka, Office Manager; Roger Graef, Managing Director; Jane Bevan, Head of Production
Credits Police 2001 (D); Feltham Sings (D); September Mourning (D); Rail Cops (D)

Finola Dwyer Productions

53 Greek Street, London W1D 3DR
t 734 7065 **f** 734 4250 **e** kate@wildgaze.co.uk
Contact Amanda Posey, Producer/Company Director; Kate McCullagh, Assistant; Finola Dwyer, Producer/Company Director
Credits Backbeat (F); The Lost Son (F); Me Without You (F)

First Freedom Productions

15 Rochester Square, London NW1 9SA
t 020 7916 9355 **f** 020 7485 4692
 info@firstfreedom.co.uk **w** www.firstfreedomtv.com
Contact Natasha Sweeney, Producer; Graham Addicott, Managing Director

First Up Film Ltd

3 Sheldon Square, Paddington, London W2 6PS
t 020 7339 9000 **f** 020 7339 9017
e info@firstupfilm.biz **w** www.firstupfilm.biz
Contact Harry Hicks, Head of Film & TV; Steve McMellon, Head of Media Rights; Matthew Campling, Head of Script Development

Fisticuff Films

Fisticuff Films

15 Star Lane, Lymm WA13 9LE
t 01925 753893 **f** 01925 751455 **e** fisticufffilms@aol.com
Contact Karen Jones, Assistant MD; Martin Jones
Credits Red Hot Chili Peppers (M); United Utilities (I); Manchester Airport (I); BBC News (T)

Flame Television

6-9 Cynthia Street, London N1 9JF
t 020 7713 6868 **f** 020 7713 6999 **e** info@flametv.co.uk
Contact Claire Featherstone, Head of Production

Flashback Television

9-11 Bowling Green Lane, London EC1R OBG
t 020 7490 8996 **f** 020 7490 5610
e mailbox@flashbacktv.co.uk **w** www.flashbacktv.co.uk
Contact Tim Ball, Head of Production

Flick Features Ltd

3rd Floor, 179 Wardour Street, London W1F 8WY
t 020 7855 3636 **t** 020 7855 3634
e info@flickfeatures.co.uk **w** www.flickfeatures.co.uk
Contact Felicity Leabeater, Production Assistant; John Deery, Director; Esther Knight, Producer
Credits Conspiracy Of Silence (F)

Flint Films Ltd

8 Chesham Street, Brighton BN2 1NA
e info@flintfilms.co.uk
Contact Sarah Flint

Floella Benjamin Production Ltd

73 Palace Road, London SW2 3LB
t 020 8671 1628 **f** 020 8671 1626
Contact Keith Taylor, Director
Credits Taste Of Cuba (D); Jamboree (T); Statues And Monuments (D); Coming To England (F)

Flying Brick Films Ltd

41 Beck Road, London E8 4RE
t 020 7249 7440 **f** 020 7249 7440 **m** 07770 481977
e tpm44@aol.com

Flying Fox Films

37 Queen Street, Belfast BT2 8HD
t 028 9024 4811 **f** 028 9023 4699 **e** mail@flyingfoxfilms.com
Contact Catherine Gifford, Producer

Flying Machine Films Ltd

22 Keats Close, Wimbledon, London SW19 1TU
t 020 8543 3635 **f** 020 8543 3635 **m** 07770 846284
e flyingmachinefilms@hotmail.com
Contact Pearl Howie, Managing Director; Anthony Thompson, Executive Producer
Credits The Fat Project (E); Camden Young Women's Centre (E); Now Seal's Gone (M); Love Me Tender...ish (S)

Focus Films Ltd

The Rotunda Studios, Rear of 116-118 Finchley Road, London NW3 5HT
t 020 7435 9004 **f** 020 7431 3562 **e** focus@pupix.demon.co.uk
Contact Malcolm Kuhll, Head of Development; David Pupkewitz, Managing Director; Lucinda Van Rie, Co-Producer
Credits The Bone Snatcher (F); The Book Of Eve (F); Julia's Ghost (F); The 51st State (F)

Focus Productions Ltd

PO Box 173, Stratford-Upon-Avon CV37 7ZA
t 01789 298948 **t** 0117 904 6292 **f** 01789 294845
m 07901 978902 **e** maddern@focusproductions.co.uk
e martinweitz@focusproductions.co.uk
w www.focusproductions.co.uk
Contact Martin Weitz, Producer; Ralph Maddern, Producer
Credits Flying With Jemima (D); Fear Of The Falcon (D); The Copper Scroll (D); Cabot's Bristol (D)

The Food Channel Ltd

Hagley Road, Stourbridge DY8 1QR
t 01384 395654 **f** 01384 340582
Contact Jim Driscoll, Director of Broadcasting
Credits The Cornish Riviera Pasties (T); PC Pepper (T); The Shoe People (T)

Footstep Productions Ltd

2 Goldstone Close, Hove BN3 7PD
t 01273 552700 **t** 020 7836 9990 **f** 020 7836 9990
m 07710 298371 **e** footstepproductions@compuserve.com
e footstepproductions.com
Contact Colette Thomson, Director, Managing Director
Credits Work Talk (E); A Christmas Card From England (D); Voces Espanolas (E)

Forged Films Ltd

8 West Newington Place, Edinburgh EH9 1QT
t 0131 667 0230 **f** 0131 667 0230 **m** 07768 483969
e forgedfilm@aol.com

Formula Communications

2 Austins Place, The Old Town, Hemel Hempstead HP2 5HN
t 01442 250247 **f** 01442 261358 **w** www.formula-creative.com
Contact Steve Arnold, Director

The Foundation TV Productions Ltd

The Maidstone Studios, Vinters Park, Maidstone ME14 5NZ
t 01622 684632 **t** 01622 684575 **f** 01622 684421
e vanessa@foundationtv.co.uk **w** www.foundationtv.co.uk
Contact Gwen Hughes, Production Manager; Ged Allen, Joint Managing Director; Carol Stark, Business Administrator; Vanessa Hill, Joint Managing Director
Credits Eureka TV (T); Brilliant Creatures (T); Finger Tips (T)

Foyle Film Projects

7-8 Magazine Street, Derry BT48 6HJ
t 028 7126 0562 **f** 028 7137 1738
e info@nerve-centre.org.uk **w** www.nerve-centre.org.uk
Contact Jim Curran, Manager

Francesca Wilkinson Productions

19 Rothschild Road, London W4 5HS
t 020 8994 0348 **f** 020 8994 0348
e fw@fwproductions.f9.co.uk
Contact Francesca Wilkinson, Producer; David Burrows Sutcliffe, Company Secretary
Credits Party - Lenor (C); Snow - Wiskas (C); Wrong Shirt - Lenor (C); Harry - Slimfast (C)

Free At Last TV

2nd Floor, 5-7 Anglers Lane, Kentish Town, London NW5 3DG
t 020 7485 5000 **f** 020 7267 5441
e info@freeatlasttv.co.uk **w** www.freeatlasttv.co.uk
Contact Katie Kinnaird, Director; Barry Ryan, Managing Director; David Walton, Director; Veerinder Mann, Director
Credits Sex, Drugs, Ruck 'N' Roll (T); The Punk Years (T); The Spiderman Story (T); Rock 'N' Roll Myths (T)

Freedom Pictures Ltd

10 Rylett Crescent, London W12 9RL
f 020 8743 6981 **m** 07768 855746
e timwhite@freedompictures.co.uk
Contact Tim White, Managing Director/Producer; Jeanne White, Head of Development

Fremantle UK Productions

1 Stephen Street, London W1T 1AL
t 020 7691 6000 **f** 020 7691 6100
e feedback@fremantlemedia.com **w** www.pearsontv.com

FremantleMedia Thames

1 Stephen Street, London W1T 1AL
t 020 7691 6000 **f** 020 7691 6100 **w** www.fremantlemedia.com
Credits The Bill (T); Pop Idol (T)

Friday Productions

23a Saint Leonards Terrace, London SW3 4QG
t 020 7730 0608 **f** 020 7730 0608
Contact Georgina Abrahams, Producer

Front Page Films / Knatchbull Quinn Communications

23 West Smithfields, London EC1A 9HY
t 020 7329 6866 **f** 020 7329 6866
Contact Philip Knatchbull, Producer

Frontier Productions Ltd

51 Carlton Mansions, Randolph Avenue, London W9 1NR
t 020 7328 4823 **f** 020 7625 7459 **m** 07768 567545
e nickh@frontier-productions.com
w www.frontier-productions.com
Contact Nick Hadcock, Managing Director
Credits Timeseekers (A); Princely Returns (F); Chitral (F); Wisden Online (W)

FulcrumTV

254 Goswell Road, London EC1V 7RE
t 020 7253 0353 **f** 020 7490 0206
e info@fulcrumtv.com **w** www.fulcrumtv.com
Contact Martin Long, Head of Production; Richard Belfield, Joint Manager; Christopher Hird, Joint Manager; Tracey Gardiner, Head of Business Development
Credits Like It Is (F); The Luckiest Nut In The World (A); The Mystery Of The Black Mummy (T); Great Political Mistakes (T)

Fulmar Television & Film/Fulmar West

Pascoe House, 54 Bute Street, Cardiff CF10 5AF
t 029 2045 5000 **f** 029 2045 5111 **e** sam@fulmartv.film.com
Contact Sam Koger, Office Administrator; Judith Winnam, Head of Programmes; Ian Jones, Head of Development; Leana Cowley, Office Manager; Ruth Morgan, Head of Production; Jeremy Bugler, Managing Director
Credits Tin Gods II (D); Seven Days That Shook Coronation Street (D); When Steptoe Met Son (D); The Private Life of a Masterpiece: Michaelangelo's David (D)

Fulu International Films

88 The Green, Southall UB2 4BG
t 020 8843 1311
Contact Paresh Shah, Producer

Future Planet

5 Hillside Avenue, Mutley, Plymouth PL4 6PR
t 01752 664544 **f** 01752 664547
m 07831 658492 **i** 01752 664540
e danny@futureplanet.co.uk **w** www.futureplanet.co.uk
Contact Dak Burton, Director of Underwater Imagery; Martin Truman, Legal Director; Danny Bamping, Managing Director
Credits The Big Cat Flap (D); Stonehenge Solution (D); Wildboar In Britain (D); Diving The Bounty (D)

Gabriel Productions Ltd

Grey Courtledge, Richmond Road, Bath BA1 5PU
t 01225 311194 **f** 01225 484430 **e** janegabriel@compuserve.com
Contact Jane Gabriel, Producer/Director

Gabriela Productions

51 Goldsmith Avenue, London W3 6HR
t 020 8993 3158 **f** 020 8993 8216 **e** only4contact@yahoo.com
Contact Witold Starecki, Director
Credits Blooming Youth (D); Going Straight (D); Cybercops (D)

Gainsborough Productions

The Groom Cottage, Pinewood Studios, Studios Road, Iver Heath SL0 0NH
t 01753 651700 **f** 01753 656844
Contact John Hough, Director/Producer

Gala Productions Ltd

25 Stamford Brook Road, London W6 0XJ
t 020 8741 4200 **f** 020 8741 2323 **e** info@galaproductions.co.uk
Contact Beata Romanowski, Director, Director; David Lindsay, Executive Producer, Producer
Credits Entartete Musik (M); Mediterranean Cruise (I); Grenada - Luciano Pavarotti (M); Sentimento (C)

Gangster Pictures Ltd

Top Floor Suite, 67 Southbridge Road, Croydon CR0 1AG
t 020 8686 3879 **f** 020 8686 3879 **m** 07790 005416
e toby@gangsterpictures.com **w** www.gangsterpictures.com
Contact Leo Godsaw, Producer; Toby White, Producer
Credits The Quarry Men (F); Rachel Stamp (M); Snap (S)

GB Films

26 Ormonde Mansions, 110A Southampton Row, London WC1B 4BS
t 020 7404 2351 **f** 020 7404 2351 **m** 07770 737450
e jonathan.ruffle@gbfilms.com **w** www.gbfilms.com

Gearhouse Broadcast Production Solutions

Unit 14, Olympic Industrial Estate, Fulton Road, Wembley HA9 0TF
t 020 8795 1866 **f** 020 8795 1868
e skatz@gearhousebroadcast.com
w www.gearhousebroadcast.com
Contact Steve Katz

Generations

Meadow View, Newbridge, Cadnam, Southampton SO40 2NW
t 02380 813344 **f** 02380 813344 **m** 07850 566503
e jonbav@lycos.co.uk
Contact Jon Baverstock, Director
Credits FR 2002 - Edinburgh Festival

Genesis Media Group Ltd

114 Whitchurch Road, Cardiff CF14 3LY
t 029 2066 6007 **f** 029 2066 6008 **m** 07796 262000
e info@genesis-media.co.uk **w** www.genesis-media.co.uk
Contact Alan Torjussen, Producer/Director
Credits Ceiri And His Music (T); Dylan Thomas (T); Peter Warlock (T); Biology Collection (T)

Genre Vision

Legends house, 31 Oathall Avenue, Haywards Heath RH16 3ES
e infogenrevision@aol.com w www.genrevision.co.uk
Contact Vicky Fosh, Head of Development; Nicola Brooks, Writer/Producer;
Chaz Harris, Director/Writer/Producer
Credits Cursed And Blessed (T); You're In My Seat (S); Stealing A Career (S); In
Your Dreams (S)

Glasgow Television Productions Ltd

APT 0/1, 1010 Crow Road, Glasgow G13 1JN
t 0141 589 1669 m 07719 390487
e cmartin@glasgowtv.fsnet.co.uk
e mailto:cmartin@glasgowtv.fsnet.co.uk

Goldhawk Media Ltd

31A Hill Aveny, Amersham HP6 5BX
t 01494 729777 f 01494 729555
e info@goldhawk-media.co.uk
Contact Bernedette Bos, Managing Director

Granite Film & Television Productions Ltd

Vigilant House, 120 Wilton Road, Victoria, London SW1 1JZ
t 020 7808 7230 f 020 7808 7231 e research@granite.co.uk

Grant Naylor Productions Ltd

Suite 950-951, David Lean Building, Shepperton Studios,
Shepperton TW17 0QD
t 01932 592175 f 01932 592484 w www.reddwarf.co.uk
Contact Helen Norman, General Manager

Grasshopper Productions

28-31 High Street, Wimbledon Village, London SW19 5BY
t 020 8971 3706 w www.grasshopper.uk.com

Great British Films

3rd Floor, Hanover House, 118 Queens Road, Brighton BN1 3XG
t 01273 324122 f 01273 327105 e info@greatbritishfilms.com
w www.greatbritishfilms.com
Contact David Rogers, Executive Producer/Tax Consultant; Fiona Kihlstrom,
Investor Relations; Stella Litou, Film Executive; Adam Betteridge, Film
Consultant/Associate Producer; Christelle Conan, Tax Consultant
Credits Going Off Big Time (F); Mr In Between (F); Plots With A View (F);
Bollywood Queen (F)

Green Inc Film & TV Ltd

47A Botanic Avenue, Belfast BT7 1JL
t 028 9057 3000 f 028 9057 0057 e tv@greeninc.co.uk
Contact Stephen Stewart, Director
Credits Music Asides (T); It's Not the Answer (T); Patrick Kielty Almost Live (T);
Last Chance Lottery (T)

Green Umbrella Ltd

The Production House, 147A St Michael's Hill, Bristol BS2 8DB
t 0117 973 1729 f 0117 946 7432
e postmaster@umbrella.co.uk w www.umbrella.co.uk
Contact Gina Shepperd; Peter Jones, Chairman; Nigel Ashcroft, Managing
Director; Sara Compton, Head of Production
Credits Triumph Of Life (D); Journey To The Centre Of The Earth (D); Escape
From Berlin (D); Galileo's Daughter (T)

Greenlight Television

Tromode IM4 4QJ
t 01624 611601 f 01624 611602
e mail@greenlight-tv.com w www.greenlight-tv.com
Contact David Beynon, Director; Richard Nichols, Director; Rob Hurdman, Director
Credits American Le Mans Series (T); British Rally Championship (T); FIA
Sportscar Championship (T); Isle of Man TT (T)

Greenlit Productions Ltd

3rd Floor, 14-15 D'Arblay Street, London W1F 8DZ
t 020 7287 3545 f 020 7439 6767
e info@greenlit.co.uk w www.greenlit.co.uk
Contact Eve Gutierrez, Associate Producer; Jill Green, Managing Director;
Rachel Snell, Development Executive
Credits Trust (T); Menace (T); Foyle's War (T); The Swap (T)

Greenroom Digital Ltd

120-124 Curtain Road, London EC2A 3SQ
t 020 7426 5147 f 020 7729 6792
e jon@greenroom-digital.com w www.greenroom-digital.com
Contact Darren Hayles, Designer; Linda Revill, Producer; Jon Hamm, Creative
Director; Nick Hamm, Director
Credits Godsend (F); Martha Meet Frank Daniel And Lawrence (F); The Hole (F);
Talk Of Angels (F)

Greenwich Films

Studio 2B1, The Old Seager Distillery, Brookmill Road, London
SE8 4JT
t 020 8694 2211 f 020 8694 2971
e team@greenwichfilms.demon.co.uk
w www.greenwichfilms.demon.co.uk
Contact Liza Brown, Producer

Gwdihw Ltd

12 Twll yn y Wal, Caernarfon LL55 1RF
t 01286 675766 f 01286 671131
e post@gwdihw.demon.co.uk w www.gwdihw.demon.co.uk
Contact Sian Wheway, Producer; Dafydd Roberts, Managing Director
Credits Flight Over Snowdon (I); The Baby Business (D); Gradman (I)

Hadada Productions

31 Chitstade Gardens, London NW2 6EL
t 020 8208 2112 f 020 8208 2112
Contact Stella Osoba, Producer

Halcyon Productions

14 South Road, Grassendale Park, Liverpool L19 0LT
t 0151 427 7770 f 0151 427 7772
Contact Rob Rohrer, Director

Hallelujah Productions

34 Grosvenor Road, London W4 4EG
t 020 8995 9574 f 020 8995 9574
m 07712 175857 e hallelujah_productions@hotmail.com
Contact Michael Walker, Director; Paul Rattigan, Director
Credits Wild West (T)

Hand Pict Productions Ltd

20 Haymarket Terrace, Edinburgh EH12 5JZ
t 0131 346 1111 w www.handpict.com
Contact George Cathro, Producer/Director
Credits Do Organs Remember (T); From The Paisley To The Palace (T); Prison
Officer (T); Big Day (S)

Happy Pigs Productions

35 Walford Road, London N16 8EF
t 020 7690 1833 f 020 7690 1833 m 07808 403932
e happypigs.lilly@virgin.net w www.happypigs.com

Harbour Pictures

11 Langton Street, London SW10 0JL
t 020 7351 7070 f 020 7352 3528 e info@harbourpictures.com
Contact Nick Barton, Chief Executive
Credits Calendar Girls (F)

Harcourt Films

58 Camden Square, London NW1 9XE
t 020 7267 0882 f 020 7267 1064 e jmarre@blueyonder.co.uk
Contact J Marre, Producer
Credits Ladyboys (F); The Memphis Mafia (The Elvis Mob) (D); The Voice; The
James Brown Story (T)

Harlequin Communications Ltd

Enterprise House, Meadowcroft Business Park, Whitestake,
Preston PR4 4BA
t 01772 743100 f 01772 744453 m 07973 418852
e info@harlequincomms.com w www.harlequincomms.com
Contact Nigel Sharples, Managing Director

Hartswood Films
Twickenham Studios, The Barons, Twickenham TW1 2AW
t 020 8607 8736 **f** 020 8607 8744
Contact Beryl Vertue, Chairman; Debbie Vertue, General Manager

Hasan Shah Films Ltd
153 Burnham Towers, Adelaide Road, London NW3 3JN
t 020 7722 2419 **f** 020 7483 0662 **e** hsfilms@blueyonder.co.uk
Contact Hasan Shah, Producer/Director

Hat Trick Productions
10 Livonia Street, London W1F 8AF
t 020 7434 2451 **f** 020 7287 9791
e info@hattrick.com **w** www.hattrick.com
Contact Denise O'Donoghue, Managing Director

Hawdon Productions Ltd
3 Warleigh Manor, Bath BA1 8EE
t 01225 852900 **t** 01225 852235 **f** 01225 852235
e rhawdon@aol.com
Contact Robin Hawdon, Managing Director

Hay Fisher Productions
Unit 4, Roman Way, Business Centre, Droitwich Spa WR9 9AJ
t 01905 794411 **f** 01905 794800 **e** info@hayfisher.com
Contact Richard Hay, Managing Director

Healthcare Productions
Unit 104, Bridge House, Three Mills, Three Mill Lane, Bromley-by-Bow, London E3 3DU
t 020 8980 9444 **f** 020 8980 1901
e enquiries@helathcareproductions.co.uk
w www.healthcareproductions.co.uk
Contact Penny Webb, Managing Director; Ian Wood

Helifilms Ltd
Chalk Pit Farm Studios, Theale, Reading RG7 5EE
t 01189 305408 **f** 01189 303936 **m** 07831 631540
e sara@helifilms.com **w** www.helifilms.homestead.com
Contact Jerry Grayson, Director; Sara Hine, Producer; Mike Wright, Tech Director
Credits Black Hawk Down (F); Air Support & Island Escape (T); Space Academy (T); Space Cadet School (T)

Heritage Theatre Ltd
No 1, 8 Clanricarde Gardens, London W2 4NA
t 020 7243 2750 **f** 020 7792 8584 **m** 07768 570343
e rm@heritagetheatre.com **w** www.heritagetheatre.com
Contact Robin Lough, Director; Robert Marshall, Managing Director/Producer; Clare Rich, Director
Credits Betty Buckley - Live At The Donmar; Denial (T); Alone Together - Michael Ball (T); The Mysteries (T)

Hewland International
Spring House, 10 Spring Place, Kentish Town, London NW5 3BH
t 020 7916 2266 **f** 020 7916 2244 **w** www.hewland.co.uk
Contact Jane Hewland, Executive Producer/Director
Credits Dial-A-Date (T); Dream Team VII (T); Dream Team V (T)

Hideaway Productions
4 Nelson Road, London N8 9RU
t 020 8374 3367 **f** 020 8347 9761 **m** 07976 795570
e sl015c2150@blueyonder.co.uk
Contact Simon Lowe, Director
Credits Let's Make An Opera - Royal Opera House (E); Taj (W); The History Of Alton Towers (D); Sir Stanley Matthews - His Own Story (D)

High Ground Films
1 Aigburth Mansions, Mowll Street, London SW9 0EP
t 020 7564 3211 **f** 020 7564 3211 **m** 07890 100249
e jill@reportinternational.com
Contact Jill Daniels, Director
Credits Fool's Gold (D); I'm In Heaven (S); Killing Time (S); Next Year In Lerin (D)

High Tide Productions Ltd
7 Grasmere Road, Sheffield S8 0UL
t 0114 220 4014 **m** 07736 462536
e film@hightideproductions.co.uk
w www.hightideproductions.co.uk
Contact Carl Timms, Writer/Producer; Alan Tisch, Camera; Andrew Beatson, Editing/Camera
Credits In Toni's Footsteps (D)

Hilltop Pictures
57 Bridgman Road, London W4 5BB
t 020 8994 3575 **f** 020 8747 0416 **m** 07747 798863
e office@hilltoppictures.co.uk **w** www.hilltop-pictures.fsnet.co.uk
Contact Charlotte Hamp, Managing Director; Jeremy Hamp, Company Secretary

HLA
3rd Floor, 19-21 Great Portland St, London W1W 8QB
t 020 7299 1000 **f** 020 7299 1001 **e** post@hla.net
Contact Mike Wells, Managing Director; Helen Langridge, Managing Director
Credits Car Phone Warehouse (C); Yellow Pages (C); Independent Newspaper (C)

Holmes Associates Ltd
The Studio, 37 Redington Road, London NW3 7QY
t 020 7813 4333 **f** 020 7916 9172
e holmesassociates@blueyonder.co.uk
Contact Andrew Holmes, Managing Director

Hot Property Films
27 Newman Street, London W1T 1PP
t 020 7323 9466 **f** 020 7323 9467
e janine@hotpropertyfilms.com
Contact Janine Marmot, Producer
Credits Made In Heaven (F); Institute Benjamenta (F); I Could Read The Sky (F); Bodysong (F)

Hot Shot Films Ltd
37-39 Queen Street, Belfast BT1 6EA
t 028 9031 3332 **f** 028 9031 9287
e info@hotshotfilms.com **e** brendan@hotshotfilms.com
Contact Brendan Byrne, Managing Director

Hotbed Media Ltd
16 Regent Place, Hockley, Birmingham B1 3NJ
t 0121 248 3900 **f** 0121 248 4900 **m** 07949 240664
e mail@hotbedmedia.co.uk
Contact Simon Broadley, Head Of Development; Kelly Langley, Administration Manager; Dianne Moore, Finance Manager; Sara Jane Datta, Development Researcher; Johannah Dyer, Chief Executive
Credits Painting Stars (T); Everything Must Go (T); Songs Of Praise Christmas Special (T); 100 Worst Britons (T)

Hourglass Pictures Ltd
117 Merton Road, Wimbledon, London SW19 1ED
t 020 8540 8786 **f** 020 8542 6598
e pictures@hourglass.co.uk **w** www.hourglass.co.uk
Contact Martin Chilcott, Director; Jacqueline Chilcott, Head of Production
Credits Energy From Nature (T)

Hunky Dory Productions
Cambridge House, 135 High Street, Teddington TW11 8HH
t 020 8943 3006 **f** 020 8977 4464 **m** 07973 655510
e hunkydoryprods@aol.com **w** www.hunkydory.tv
Contact Adrian Hilliard, Managing Director

Hyphen Films
101 Wardour Street, London W1F 0UN
t 020 7734 0632 **f** 020 7439 3789 **e** nmk@hyphenfilms.com
Contact Nasreen Kabir, Director
Credits Spotlights And Saris: Making Bombay Dreams (D); Bollywood Gold (F); Bollywood Celebrities (F)

Iambic Productions Ltd

89 Whiteladies Road, Bristol BS8 2NT
t 0117 923 7222 **f** 0117 923 8343
e team@bristol.iambicproductions.com

Contact Angela Hall, Producer; Chris Hunt, Producer
Credits The London Masterclasses (T); The Voice Of Choice (T); Romeo & Juliet (T); An Enchanted Evening (T)

IBT Productions

3-7 Euston Centre, Regent's Place, London NW1 3JG
t 020 7874 7650 **f** 020 7874 7644 **m** 07931 543544
e mail@ibt.org.uk **w** www.ibt.org.uk

Contact Mark Gallaway, Director; Cathy Workman, Assistant to Director

ICE Ltd

PO Box 2904, Kenilworth CV8 2HL
t 01926 864800 **m** 07790 741818
e admin@ice-productions.com **w** www.ice-productions.com

Contact Cheryl Henson, Account Manager; Sean Griffiths, Managing Director; Liam Griffiths, Media Production
Credits Minolta (I); Merril Lynch (I); Orange (I); HSBC (I)

Icon Films

4 West End, Somerset Street, Bristol BS2 8NE
t 0117 924 8535 **f** 0117 942 0386
e info@iconfilms.co.uk **w** www.iconfilms.co.uk

Contact Harry Marshall, Creative Director; Patrice Hornibrook, Company Manager; Laura Marshall, Managing Director
Credits Great Cats Of India (D); A Different Ball Game (D); White Slaves, Pirate Gold (D)

Ideal World Productions

3rd Floor, 77 East Road, London N1 6AH
t 020 7684 1661 **f** 020 7684 1441 **e** mail@ideallondon.com

Contact Zad Rogers, Creative Director; Hamish Barbour, Creative Director; Sue Oriel, Managing Director
Credits The Plan Man (T); Location Location Location (T); Relocation Relocation (T); Mechanoids (T)

Ignition Films

1 Wickham Court, Bristol BS16 1DQ
t 0117 958 3087 **f** 0117 965 7674 **m** 07977 470457
e ignition@blueyonder.co.uk
w www.ignition.purp.blueyonder.co.uk

Contact Alison Sterling, Producer; Terry Flaxton, Director

Illumina Ltd

8 Canham Mews, Canham Road, London W3 7SR
t 020 8600 9300 **f** 020 8600 9333
e illumina@illumina.co.uk **w** www.illumina.co.uk

Contact Andrew Chitty, Managing Director

Illuminations Films Ltd

19-20 Rheidol Mews, Rheidol Terrace, London N1 8NU
t 020 7288 8400 **f** 020 7359 1151
e griff@illumin.co.uk **w** www.illumin.co.uk

Contact Keith Griffiths, Managing Director; Pinky Ghundale, Assistant
Credits Dance Of The Wind (F); Institute Benjamenta (F); Little Otik (F); London Orbital (F)

Illuminations Television

19-20 Rheidol Mews, Rheidol Terrace, London N1 8NU
t 020 7288 8400 **f** 020 7359 1151
e illuminations@illumin.co.uk **w** www.illumin.co.uk

Contact John Wyver, Chairman; Linda Zuck, Managing Director
Credits The Eyes Series (T); Private Lives Of Pompeii (T); Macbeth (T); All About Desire (T)

Images First Ltd

10 Hereford Road, South Ealing, London W5 4SE
t 020 8579 6848 **w** www.images-first.com

Contact Tony Freeth, Managing Director
Credits You Can't Eat Potential (D); Fulfilling The Promise - Quality Protein Maize (D); Ethiopia - My Hope, My Future (D); Setting The Grassroots On Fire (D)

Imagicians Television Ltd

34 Fouberts Place, London W1F 7PX
t 020 8374 4429 **f** 020 8374 4436 **m** 07973 736502
e imagicians@blueyonder.co.uk **w** www.imagicians.tv

Contact Alan Scales, Managing Director
Credits Magic And Mystery Of The Crown Jewels (D); HM The Queen A Remarkable Life (D); The Royal Jewels (D); Royals And Their Pets (D)

Imagination Ltd

25 Store Street, South Crescent, London WC1E 7BL
t 020 7323 3300 **f** 020 7323 5801 **w** www.imagination.co.uk

Contact Sally Mason; Danny Coyle

Imago Productions

5th Floor, Grosvenor House, Norwich NR1 1NS
t 01603 727600 **f** 01603 727626
e mail@imagoproductions.tv **w** www.imagoproductions.tv

Contact Lauren Heffernan, Assistant to Managing Director/Publicity Coordinator; Vivica Parsons, Managing Director; Nathalie Humphreys, Creative Director; Bob Ottaway, Director of Operations; Charlie Robinson, Post Production Manager
Credits Killer Queens (T); The Biz (T); Arty Facts (T); Swimming Lions (T)

Impact Pictures

3 Percy Street, London W1T 1DE
t 020 7636 7716 **f** 020 7636 7814 **e** production@impactpix.com

Contact Judy Goldberg, Production Assistant

Impossible Pictures

45 Mortimer Street, London W1W 8HX
t 020 7580 4666 **f** 020 7636 8860
e info@impossiblepictures.co.uk

Contact Jasper James, Director; Tim Haines, Director

Inca (London) Ltd

67 Castelnau, Barnes, London SW13 9RT
t 020 8748 9600 **f** 020 8748 9607 **e** incaltd@dial.pipex.com

Contact Sue Draper, Production Manager
Credits Memphis Belle - The True Story (D); The Wonders Of Science (D); Tek Sing - China's Titanic (D); BBC World (C)

Independent Image Ltd

The Old Coach House, Overhills, Northdown Road, Woldingham CR3 7BB
t 01883 652113 **f** 01883 653290 **m** 07771 784322
e info@indimage.com **w** www.indimage.com

Contact David Wickham, Managing Director
Credits Quest For The Lost Civilisation (T); Interpol's Most Wanted (T); Cannabis From The Chemist (T); Chefs In The City (T)

Infinite Pictures Ltd

The Engine House, Flete Estate, Ermington PL21 9NX
t 01752 830000 **f** 01752 830001
e info@infinitepictures.com **w** www.infinitepictures.com

Contact Alison Burner, Production Manager; David Nottage, Managing Director; Lucy Mattison, General Manager; Matt Richards, Broadcast Director; Nick Dixon, Corporate Producer; carole Mattison, Broadcast Producer; Sarah Bell
Credits Boys Toys (T); Seventy Years Under The Stars (D); Christmas At The Cathedral (D); Britannia - A Ship Ashore (D)

Infonation

272A Earls Court Road, London SW5 9AS
t 020 7370 1082 **f** 020 7370 1082
e mail@infonation.org.uk **w** www.infonation.org.uk

Contact Fiona Connelly, Senior Producer; Jo Kelly, Production Manager; Jane Clarke, Head of Broadcast; Simon Frost, Production Manager; Ron Blythe, Managing Director
Credits Savage Seas (D); Beyond Babel (T); The Edge - Series I And II (T)

Initial
Sheperds Building Centre, Sharecroft Way, Shepherds Bush, London W14 0EE
t 08703 331700 f 08703 331800
e info@endemol.com w www.endemol.com
Contact Lawrence Jones, Managing Director
Credits Salon (T); Big Brother (T); Fame Academy (T)

Inspired Media Group
Avionics House, Naas Lane, Quedgeley, Gloucester GL2 4SN
t 01452 722202
Contact Elizabeth Mathews, CEO/Producer; Martin Myers, Head of UK Theatrical; Mark Chesney, Post Production Manager
Credits Filligoggin (T); Merlin The Return (F); CreationStation.tv (W); Viewing4Leisure (W)

Intermedia Film & Video (Nottingham) Ltd
19 Heathcote Street, Nottingham NG1 3AF
t 0115 955 6909
e info@intermedianotts.co.uk w www.intermedianotts.co.uk
Contact Ceris Morris, Director; Helen Solomon, Producer; Deborah Ballin, Head of Production; Jane McKeever, Development Producer; Laura Rees, Production Assistant
Credits DV Shorts - 8 X DV Short Dramas For EMMI And The Film Council (S); Shifting Units (S); First Cut - Carlton Television 2000-Present (T); Slot Art - Channel Four 2001 (S)

IQ Creations
103 Kingsway House, Kingsway, London WC2B 6AW
t 020 7692 0580 m 07801 548754 e iqcreations@yahoo.com
Contact Emmanuel Anyiam-Osigwe, Head of Research & Development; Al Raymore, Resources Co-ordinator; Neil Oyenekan, Creative Director

ISIS Productions Ltd
106 Hammersmith Grove, London W6 7HB
t 020 8748 3042 f 020 8748 3046 e isis-productions.com w www.isisproductions.co.uk
Contact Nick de Grunwald, Director; Jamie Rugge-Price, Director; Catriona Lawless, Production Co-ordinator
Credits South Bank Show (D); Classic Albums Series I-III (D)

It's Alright Ma Productions
Michelin House, 81 Fulham Road, London SW3 6RD
t 020 7838 6952 f 020 7838 6955
e info@itsalrightma.com w www.itsalrightma.com
Contact Staffan Tollgard, Company Director
Credits Kickstart (E); Dead Bolt Dead (F)

Jacaranda Productions
6 Studland Street, Hammersmith, London W6 0JS
t 020 8741 9088 f 020 8748 5670
e creatives@jacaranda.co.uk w www.jacaranda.co.uk
Contact Katy Eyre, Managing Director

Jane Walmsley Productions/Jam Pictures
8 Hanover Street, London W1S 1YE
t 020 7290 2676 f 020 7290 2677 e producers@jampix.com
Contact Jane Walmsley, Producer; Michael Braham, Producer
Credits Rudy; The Rudy Guiliani Story (T); A Tale of Two Movies (D); One More Kiss (F)

The Jim Henson Company
30 Oval Road, London NW1 7DE
t 020 7428 4000 f 020 7428 4001
e jstephenson@hanson.com w www.henson.com
Contact Angus Fletcher, Senior Vice President, International TV

John Hemson Associates
37 Vicarage Street, Woburn Sands, Milton Keynes MK17 8RE
t 01908 583062 f 01908 281035 m 07762 922551
e jha@powernet.co.uk w www.johnhemsonassociates.co.uk

John Mills Film & Television
4 Effingham Road, Surbiton KT6 5JY
t 020 8398 8084 f 020 8339 0760 e mills.film@virgin.net
Contact John Mills, Managing Director

Jolyon Symonds Productions Ltd
3 Newburgh Street, London W1F 7RE
t 020 7434 0942 f 020 7287 6304 e jolyon@jspl.freeserve.co.uk
Contact Jolyon Symonds, Managing Director; Clio Lee, Production Executive
Credits The Escapist (F); Kevin And Perry Go Large (F); The Last Yellow (F)

Julian Seddon Films
51-53 Mount Pleasant, London WC1X 0AE
t 020 7831 3033 f 020 7405 3721 m 07770 277289
e sarin@julianseddonfilms.com w www.tabletp.com
Contact Julian Seddon, Head of Production

Just About Productions
4-6 Northington Street, London WC1N 2JG
t 020 7916 6200 f 020 7692 9080
e info@justtv.co.uk w www.justtv.co.uk
Contact Olwyn Silvester, Managing Director; Steve Phelps, Creative Director
Credits Paranormal Files (T); Mark Thomas Weapons Inspector (T); Real Doctor Crippen (T); Amazing Story Of Jeremy Bamber (T)

K-lyx Media
Flat 5, 12 Glenmore Rd, London NW3 4BB
t 020 7794 9803 f 07977 437379 m 07976 257913
e info@k-lyx.com w www.k-lyx.com
Contact Robin Kershaw, Producer

Karen Hamilton Productions Ltd
4th Floor, 18-24 Shacklewell Lane, London E8 2EZ
t 020 7503 1640 f 020 7503 1659 e khamiltonprods@aol.com
Contact Karen Hamilton, Director
Credits Singing For Dear Life (D); Gold Fever (D); Kids Alone (D); Inside My Head (D)

Kemistry Ltd
Brook Green Studios, 186 Shepherds Bush Road, London W6 7LL
t 020 7371 3300 f 020 7603 9519
e info@kemistry.co.uk w www.kemistry.co.uk
Contact Richard Churchill; Catherine Gosling, Producer
Credits Extreme (F); BBC Discovery Channel (C); Monarch Of The Glen (T); Resident Evil (F)

David Kennaway
59 Sisters Avenue, London SW11 5SW
t 020 7924 7340 f 020 7924 7340 m 07850 729089
e david@kennawayfilms.com
Credits The Rocket Post (F)

Kensington Film Company
128 Kensington Church Street, London W8 4BH
t 020 7221 7166 f 020 7792 9288
e stacey-inter@btconnect.com
Contact T Stacey, Chairman

KEO Films
Studio 2B, 151-157 City Road, London EC1V 1JH
t 020 7490 3580 f 020 7490 8419
e keo@keofilms.com w www.keofilms.com
Contact Zam Baring, Director/Executive Producer; Hugh Fearnley-Whittingstall, Director/Executive Producer; Jaimie O'Cruz, Producer; Katherine Perry, Head of Production; Andrew Palmer, Executive Producer; Will Anderson, Head of Development
Credits My Body My Business (D); To The Ends Of The Earth - Dangerous Obsession (D); River Cottage Forever (T); Going To Extremes (T)

Key Productions
First Floor, Globe House, Globe Park, Moss Bridge Road, Kingsway West, Rochdale OL16 5EB
t 01706 644338 f 01706 712542 e keytv1@aol.com
Contact John O'Hara, Partner/Director; Trisha O'Hara, Partner/Producer
Credits Job Swap (D); Supervets (D); Living For The Moment (D); Quentin Willson's Bangers & Cash (D)

Kings Oak Films

118 Piccadilly Mayfair, London W1J 7NW
t 020 8202 4947 **f** 020 8202 4947
e info@kingsoakfilms.co.uk **w** www.kingsoakfilms.co.uk
Contact Lewis Critchley, Director; Peter Critchley, Web Master
Credits RSPCA Dogs Home (D); Dreams (A); Fremont Mysteriously Disappears
(S); Broadlands (S)

Kinsman & Co

17A Chepstow Crescent, London W11 3EA
t 020 7439 9666 **t** 020 7727 2455 **f** 020 7734 9124
e kinsmanco@hotmail.com
Contact Serena Davies, Production Manager
Credits Hotel; Busy Line

Kismet Film Company

25A Old Compton Street, London W1D 5JW
t 020 7734 0099 **f** 020 7734 1222 **e** kismetfilms@dial.pipex.com
Contact Michele Camarda, Managing Director / Producer
Credits Born Romantic; This Year's love (F)

Kudos Productions Ltd

65 Great Portland Street, London W1W 7LW
t 020 7580 8686 **f** 020 7580 8787
e reception@kudosproductions.co.uk
Credits Spooks (T); Among Giants (F); The Magicians House (T); Psychos (T)

Kult Fiktion

m 07711 784437 **e** kontakt@kultfiktion.com **w** www.kultfiktion.com
Contact S Bamberg, Producer; Ivor Benjamin, Producer

Kulture Vulture Productions

42B Woodville Gardens, Ealing, London W5 2LQ
t 020 8810 4721 **f** 020 8810 4721 **e** steverehman@hotmail.com
Contact Steve Rehman, Managing Director
Credits Norman On Norman (T); British Cinema (T); On Location (T)

La Plante Productions

Paramount House, 162-170 Wardour Street, London W1F 8ZX
t 020 7734 6767 **f** 020 7734 7878
e admin@laplanteproductions.com
w www.laplanteproductions.com
Contact Liz Thorburn, Managing Director; Lynda La Plante, Producer

Lancaster University Television

The Language Centre, Lancaster University, Bailrigg LA1 4YW
t 01524 593984 **f** 01524 593984
e d.blacow@lancaster.ac.uk **w** www.lancs.ac.uk/users/lutv
Contact David Blacow, Producer

Large Door Productions

3 Shamrock Street, London SW4 6HF
t 020 7627 4014 **f** 020 7627 2469 **e** ldoor@demon.co.uk
Contact John Ellis, Managing Director

Last Ditch Television

Ditchingham House, Ditchingham NR35 2JP
t 01986 892549 **f** 01986 892549 **e** lastditchtv@aol.com
Contact Andy Murrow, Managing Director
Credits Blast Off (T); Get Stuffed (T); That Prezzie Show (T)

Lateral Productions

42 Woodland Hill, London SE19 1NY
t 020 8761 3937 **f** 020 8761 3937 **m** 07860 406906
Contact Lizzi Becker, Executive Producer; Jill MacFarlane, Associate Producer

LATV Productions Inc

3rd Floor, 445-453 Hackney Road, London E2 9DY
t 020 7613 2820 **f** 020 7729 9060 **m** 07956 484610
e info@latv.co.uk **w** www.latv.co.uk
Contact Lanre Adegun, Producer, Director
Credits Temptation (F); This London I-III (F); Blue Cross Estates (I); Secrets (F)

Lawless Films

12 Drewstead Road, London SW16 1AB
t 020 7272 1478 **e** andydeemmony@aol.com
Contact Joanna Beresford, Managing Director
Credits Father Ted (T); 2DTV (T); Cutting It (T); The Lost Prince (T)

Leafcase

52 Achilles Road, London NW6 1EA
t 020 7435 5631 **e** vfairbinda@hotmail.com
Contact Vivian Woodruff, Partner

Left Handed Pictures Ltd

97 Old South Lambeth Road, London SW8 1XU
t 020 7735 2933 **t** 020 7820 1081
Contact Harriet Cruickshank, Managing Director

Leopard Films

Lion House, 191 Askew Road, London W12 9AX
t 020 8735 4000 **f** 020 8735 4001
e mail@leopardfilms.com **w** www.leopardfilms.com
Contact Susie Field, Production Manager; Julie Davies, Development Producer;
Jeremy Mills, Director; James Burstall, Director; Will Sergeant, Development
Producer; Nick Catliffe, Director
Credits America A List Comedy (T); Being Unfaithful (D); Cash In The Attic 2
(T); The Story Of Computer Games (D)

Libra Films

1 Hall Farm Place, Bawburgh, Norwich NR9 3LW
t 01603 749 068 **f** 01603 749 069 **m** 07850 847116
e n.lonsdale@internet.com
Contact Clive Dunn, Director/Producer

Libra Television

4th Floor, 22 Lever Street, Manchester M1 1EA
t 0161 236 5599 **f** 0161 236 6877
e hq@libratelevision.com **w** www.libratelevision.com
Contact Louise Lynch, Managing Director; Madeline Wiltshire, Managing Director
Credits Citizen Power (E); How To Be A Bully (E); History Busters (T);
Copycat Kids (T)

Like Minds Ltd

98 Handsworth Wood Road, Handsworth Wood, Birmingham
B20 2PN
t 0121 515 2921 **f** 0121 515 3989 **m** 07785 995489
e paulmartin@like-minds.co.uk **w** www.like-minds.co.uk
Contact Paul Martin, Senior Producer

Lilyville Screen Entertainment Ltd

7 Lilyville Road, Fulham, London SW6 5DP
t 020 7371 5940 **f** 020 7736 9431 **m** 07710 064663
e tony.cash@btclick.com
Contact Tony Cash, Managing Director
Credits Sex And Religion (T); Johathan Millers's St Matthew Passion (T); Simon
Schama's Landscape And Memory (T); Alan Bennett's Poetry In Motion (T)

Lindley Stone Ltd

46 Oak Village, London NW5 4QL
t 020 7267 5870 **f** 020 7267 2668 **e** linstone@btinternet.com
Contact Richard Lindley, Director; Carole Stone, Director

Lion Television Scotland

14 Royal Crescent, Glasgow G3 7SL
t 0141 331 0450 **f** 0141 331 0451
e mail@liontv6.demon.co.uk **w** www.liontv.com
Contact Chris Kelly, Executive Producer; Nan Gourlay, Production Manager
Credits The Day That Shook The World (C); Wills World (D); Nightmare Families
(D); Readers & Writers Roadshow (T)

Little Dancer Films

Avon Way, Naseby Road, London SE19 3JJ
t 020 8653 9343 **f** 020 8286 1722 **m** 07885 627091
e littledancerfilm@aol.com
Contact Robert Smith, Producer
Credits Love Child (F); Wild Flowers (F); The Cappuccino Years (T)

Little King Communications
The Studio, 2 Newport Road, London SW13 9PE
t 020 8741 7658 **f** 020 8563 2742 **e** littleking@squaremail.com
Contact Simon Nicholas, Managing Director

London Films
71 South Audley Street, London W1K 1JA
t 020 7499 7800 **f** 020 7499 7994
e luff@londonfilms.com **w** www.londonfilms.com
Contact Andrew Luff, Head of Sales

Lone Star Productions Ltd
19 Hopefield Avenue, London NW6 6LJ
t 020 8968 1863 **f** 020 8960 3045 **m** 07831 647253
e martin@lonestarproductions.co.uk
Contact Martin Rosenbaum, Producer

Longbow Productions Ltd
Fearnhead, Chillaton, Lifton PL16 0HS
t 01822 610210 **f** 01822 610177 **m** 07702 089686
e tom@longbowprods.co.uk **w** www.longbowprods.co.uk
Contact Tom Keene, Managing Director; Karen Woodward, Director;
John Oven, Director

Luk-Luk Productions
67 Stone Close, Seahouses NE68 7YW
t 01665 721195 **f** 01665 721195 **m** 07980 164047
e jimmynews@talk21.com
Contact Jimmy France, Producer
Credits Alnmaritec CD-ROM (W); Alkane Energy (I); Grace's Crumbling Statue
(T); The Rais Project (E)

Luna Films
59 Oakfield Road, London N4 4LD
t 020 8341 9591 **f** 020 8340 4301 **e** luna@gn.apc.org
Contact Holly Aylett, Director
Credits Quicksands (F); Gynaecological Chronicles (D); Footnote In History (D);
Tales Beyond Solitude (D)

The Luxury Travel Show Ltd
Suite 18, 95 Wilton Road, London SW1V 1BZ
t 07939 577859 **f** 07092 111417
e info@theluxurytravelshow.com **w** www.theluxurytravelshow.com

LWT Productions
The London Television Centre, Upper Ground, London SE1 9LT
t 020 7620 1620 **f** 020 7261 3201 **w** www.lwt.co.uk
Contact Simon Shaps, Managing Director of Granada Content

M Productions
A division of Metropolis Group, The Powerhouse, 70 Chiswick
High Road, London W4 1SY
t 020 8742 1111 **f** 020 8742 2626
e m@metropolis-group.co.uk **w** www.metropolis-group.co.uk
Contact Anouk Fontaine, Executive Producer
Credits Kerrang Awards (T); Romeo (M); Led Zepplin Live (M); Oasis - Songbird (M)

MAC Films
37 The Chase, Sutton Coldfield B76 1JS
t 0121 384 2093 **e** macmcarthur@compuserve.com
Contact Ian McArthur, Managing Director

Mac TV
Rigs Road Industrial Estate, Stornoway, Isle of Lewis HS1 2RF
t 01851 705638 **f** 01851 706577
e info@mactv.co.uk **w** www.mactv.co.uk
Contact Ann Morrison, Managing Director

Macheath Productions
Suite D, Business Development Centre, Stafford Park TF3 3BA
t 01952 201212 **f** 01952 290752 **m** 07785 394214
e andrew@macheath.u-net.com
Contact Andrew Higgs

Macmillan Media
729 Lisburn Road, Belfast BT9 7GU
t 028 9050 2150 **f** 028 9050 2151
e info@macmillanmedia.co.uk **w** www.macmillanmedia.co.uk
Contact Michael MacMillan, Managing Director

Magnetic Pictures
First House, 1 Sutton Street, Birmingham B1 1PE
t 0121 622 1582 **f** 0121 622 3080
e mail@magpix.co.uk **w** www.magpix.co.uk
Contact Andrew Price, Marketing Manager; Peter Barry, Facilities Manager
*Award winning, specialising in production for charities and
caring professions.*

Maiden Films
Niton Cottage, Munday Dean Lane, Marlow SL7 3BU
t 01628 890999
Contact Brian Jonson, Director

Main Image Ltd
39 Southgate Street, Winchester SO23 9EH
t 01962 870680 **f** 01962 870699
e main@main.co.uk **w** www.main.co.uk
Contact Eben Wilson, Head of Production

Mair Golden Moments
1 Oxford Court, Weston on the Green, Bicester OX25 3QZ
t 01869 351 167 **f** 01869 351 167 **m** 07785 378156
e johnmair100@hotmail.com
Contact John Mair, Managing Director

Malachite Productions
East Kirkby House, Spilsby PE23 4BX
t 01790 763538 **e** info@malachite.co.uk **w** www.malachite.co.uk
Contact Charles Mapleston, Director; Tracy Dean, Asscoiate Producer
Credits Portrait of Carol Shields (D)

Malone Gill Productions Ltd
27 Campden Hill Road, London W8 7DX
t 020 7937 0557 **m** 07710 344118 **e** malonegill@aol.com
Contact Lita Yong, Financial Director; Michael Gill, Consultant; Georgina
Denison, Managing Director
Credits Storm Chasers (D); Highlanders (D); Vermeer: Light, Love, and Silence
(D); The Face Of Russia (D)

March Hare Productions Ltd
Crosslands House, Ash Thomas, Tiverton EX16 4NU
t 01884 820877 **f** 01884 821328 **e** marchhare@eclipse.co.uk
Contact Roger Elliott, Producer/Drama; Annie Elliott, Producer/Docs

Matchbox TV Ltd
21 Serpentine Road, Sevenoaks TN13 3XR
t 01732 458228 **e** rufus@matchboxtv.com
Contact Rufus Roubicek, Executive Producer
Credits The King And I On Tour (D); Gangs Of New York British Premiere (D);
Blind School (D); Catch Me If You Can In London (D)

Maverick Television
The Custard Factory, Gibb Street, Birmingham B9 4AA
t 0121 771 1812 **f** 0121 771 1550
e mail@mavericktv.co.uk **w** www.mavericktv.co.uk
Contact Clare Welch, Head of Production; Alexandra Fraser, Strategic Director;
Jonnie Turpie, Chairman; Richard McKerrow, Creative Director
Credits Tainted Love (D); Celebrity Wheelchair Challenge (D); Whatever
Happened To The Slimmers Of The Year (D)

MBPTV
Saucelands Barn, Coolham, Horsham RH13 8QG
t 01403 741620 **f** 01403 741647
e info@mbptv.com **w** www.mbptv.com
Contact Alastair Martin-Bird, Managing Director; Philip Jennings, Director of
Production; Carl Heaysman, Manager; Nick Stucke, Editor
Credits Samsung Nations Cup Jumping (T); World Cup Show Jumping (T)

Meanpeach

11 Coniston Court, Hanover Hill, Weybridge KT13 9YR
t 01932 855598 f 01932 858724
e info@meanpeach.com w www.meanpeach.com
Contact Mike Walker, Director
Credits We Three Warriors (S); On A Life's Edge (S); Does God Play Football (F);
The Fall (F)

Media Flawless Productions

32 Lexington Street, London W1F OLQ
t 020 7292 6200 f 020 7292 6201
e info@flawless.com w www.flawless.com
Contact Neill Etheridge, Managing Director; Jenico Preston, Head of Marketing
Credits Holocaust Exhibition

Media Merchants Television Company Ltd

TV Centre, Vinters Park, Maidstone ME14 5NZ
t 01622 684622 f 01622 684627
e clare.joyce@gullane.com w www.gullane.com
Contact Neil Buchanan, Executive Producer; Pete Dunkerley, Head of
Production Finance; Matt Porter, Head of Production; Kate Worrall, Production
Secretary; Peter Urie, Vice President, Group Head of Production; Tim Edmunds,
Executive Producer
Credits Art Attack (T)

Media Nan Eilean Television

Pentagon Business Centre, 36 Washington Street, Glasgow G3 8AZ
t 0141 249 9999 f 0141 221 4477 e mne@btconnect.com
Contact Allan MacDonald, Managing Director

Media14

39 The Drive, Hertford SG14 3DE
t 01992 410838 f 01992 410838 m 07966 465613
e info@media14.com w www.media14.com
Contact Steve Fisher, Producer; Richard Fisher, Producer
Credits Wakestock 2002 - The Extreme Sports Channel (T)

Mentorn

43 Whitfield Street, London W1T 4HA
t 020 7258 6800 f 020 7258 6888
e mentorn@mentorn.co.uk w www.mentorn.co.uk
Contact Jane Rogerson, Head of Mentorn Scotland; Charles Thompson,
Managing Director; Alan Hayling, Director of Development; Eamonn Matthews,
Head of Mentorn Midlands; Lisa McFarland, Office Manager
Credits World's Worst Driver (T); Queen And Country (D); Robot Wars (T);
Question Time (T)

*Mentorn is one of the UK's most respected independent production
companies. We produce critically acclaimed programming across a
range of factual and entertainment genres for UK and international
broadcasters. We have three subsidiary companies: Folio, specialising in
popular factual programming; Mentorn Scotland, and Mentorn
Midlands which specialises in current affairs.*

Merchant Ivory Productions Ltd

46 Lexington Street, London W1F OLP
t 020 7437 1200 f 020 7734 1579
e miplondon@merchantivory.demon.co.uk
Contact Paul Bradley, Executive Producer
Credits The Golden Bowl (F); The Mystic Masseur (F); Le Divorce (F)

Merlin Broadcast Ltd/NewsNet UK Ltd

Aquaplan House, Burt Street, Cardiff CF10 5FZ
t 029 2048 8500 f 029 2045 0077 m 07974 4952010
e dmj@newsnet.co.uk w www.merlinbroadcast.com
Contact David Morris Jones, Managing Director

Mersey Film & Video

13 Hope Street, Liverpool L1 9BQ
t 0151 708 5259 f 0151 707 8595 m 07951 379270
e info@mersey-film-video.co.uk w www.mersey-film-video.co.uk
Contact Joanne Toomey, Producer / Development; Patrick Hall, Resources Manager
Credits Chinese Whispers - Millenium Film (D); Vilayat (D)

Mersey Film Productions Ltd

C/o David Lean Buliding, Shepperton Studios, Studio Road,
Shepperton TW17 OQD
t 01932 593599 f 01932 593167 m 07711 223288
e andybbirmingham@aol.com
Contact Andy Birmingham, Director

The Mersey Television Group Ltd

Campus Manor, Childwall Abbey Road, Childwall, Liverpool L16 OJP
t 01517 229122 f 01517 221969 w www.merseytv.com
Contact Andrew Gossage, Finance Director & General Manager
Credits Drug Runners (T); Grange Hill (T); Hollyoaks (T); Brookside (T)

Metro Video

33 Derby Road, Wirksworth DE4 4AS
t 01629 822998 f 01629 824238
Contact H. D. Barke, General Manager

Michael Howes Productions Ltd

6 Theed Street, Southbank, London SE1 8ST
t 020 7928 7851 f 020 7261 0919
Contact Michael Howes, Producer/Consultant
Credits Senko Dance (E); Parliament Of The Doomed (I); Sinfonietta (T); The
Singing Voice (D)

Michael Hurll Television

3rd Floor, Beaumont House, Kensington Village, Avonmore
Road, London W14 8TS
t 020 7605 1200
e adillon@uniquegroup.co.uk w www.uniquecomms.com
Contact Alex Hardcostle, Head of Comedy and Entertaiment; Michael Hurll,
Managing Director
Credits Entertaining Elvis (T); The All Star Aniaml Awards (T); Countdown To
The Comedy Awards (T); British Comedy Awards 2002 (T)

Millennium Business Communications Ltd

12A Church Yard, Hitchen SG5 1HR
t 01462 636800 f 01462 636900
e info@mnewm.co.uk w www.mnewm.co.uk
Contact Geoff Ide; John Hunter, Managing Director; Val Ellard

Mind Time Productions

95 Forest Drive West, Leytonstone, London E11 1JZ
t 020 8556 6203 f 020 8556 6203 m 07774 128174
e info@mindtime.co.uk
Contact Steve West, Partner; Anne Mitchell, Partner

Molehill Productions

86 Stoke Park Road, Bishopstoke, Eastleigh SO50 6BX
t 023 8061 5688 f 023 8061 2196 m 07721 653830
e graham.mole@btinternet.com
Contact Graham Mole, Producer

Monkey

192 St John Street, London EC1V 4JY
t 020 7250 0000 f 020 7250 0567
e laura@monkeykingdom.com w www.monkeykingdom.com
Contact Dom Loehnis, Managing Director; David Granger, Director of TV; Will
Macdonald, Creative Director
Credits Swag (T); Born Sloppy (T); Make My Day (T)

Monocle Films International

Monocle House, 181a Kennington Lane, London SE11 4EZ
t 020 7587 0335 f 020 7793 7074
e arnottdav@btopenworld.com w www.frenchcinema.ision.co.uk
Contact Jon Davies, Director
Credits Aprés Godard Quoi (S); St Batan - Festival Du Film (E);
Les Volets Sont Bleu (E)

Moondust Productions

22 Clarence Road, Tottenham, London N15 5BB
t 020 8802 3811 e nassim@moondustfilms.com
Credits The Winter Sun Is A Lie (F)

Moonstone Films

5 Linkenholt Mansions, Stamford Brook Avenue, London W6 0YA
t 020 8846 8511 **f** 0870 401 7171 **m** 07710 090239
e info@moonstonefilms.co.uk
Contact Tony Stark, Executive Producer

Morgan - Fiorentini Film Productions

87 Glynn Road, London E5 0JA
t 020 7682 1403 **f** 020 7682 1403 **m** 07976 295270
e m.f.films@virgin.net
Contact Dennis Morgan, Director; Anna Fiorentini, Producer
Credits AFTFS (I); Sisters (S); Calling The Shots (T); Honey - Time To Dance (M)

Movie Craft Ltd

35 Montague Road, London N15 4BD
e ps@moviecraft.ltd.uk **w** www.moviecraft.ltd.uk
Contact John Martin, Director
Credits Forever Joy (F)

Muscle Television

136 Old Lane, Little Hulton, Manchester M38 9SB
t 0161 790 0728 **m** 07989 089613
e muscletv@aol.com **w** www.muscletv.co.uk
Contact Tony Jewell, Producer/Director/Editor; Richard Litchfield, Presenter/Producer
Credits Gloria (M); Phallic (S); Red Box Requiem (S); Manchester Treats (T)

Music Box Ltd

30 Sackville Street, London W1S 3DY
t 020 7478 7356 **f** 020 7478 7407
e nickv@sunsetvine.co.uk **w** www.music-bx.co.uk
Contact Nick Vance, Head of Library Sales
Credits Forever (T); The Kerrang! Awards 2002 (T); MWA (T)

Music Theatre London Films

Chertsey Chambers, 12 Mercer Street, London WC2H 9QD
t 020 7240 0919 **f** 020 7240 0805
e musictheatre.london@virgin.net
Contact Clive Donner, Director; Tony Britten, Director
Credits Boheme (T)

MWTV

63 Southampton Street, Brighton BN2 9UT
t 01273 622043 **f** 01273 622043 **e** mwtv@hotmail.com
Contact Kevin Law, Head of Production; Carl Simons, Managing Director
Credits Maxim Vengerov-Playing By Heart (D); A Passion for Verdi-Jose Cura In Concert (T)

mykindofshow.com

105 The Custard Factory, Gibb Street, Birmingham B9 4AA
t 0121 693 1894 **f** 0121 693 1895
e mail@mykindofshow.com **w** www.mykindofshow.com
Contact Kirsten de Keyser, Executive Producer; Mark Rossiter, Head of Development; Sarah Reddi, Production Manager; Kate Hollingsworth, Researcher; Sam Evans, Producer / Director; Glynis Powell, Assistant Producer; Marika Jones, Camera Operator
Credits Mrs Bridges Boozers (T); Borscht, Blackbreads And Champagne (T); Tuscany To Go (T); Follow That Tomato (T)

Narrateo Ltd

21 Culverlanz Close, Stanmore HA7 3AG
t 020 7223 3326 **f** 020 7223 3326
e info@narrateo.com **w** www.narrateo.com

Nelson Films

48 Woodsford Square, London W14 8DP
t 020 7603 8987 **f** 020 7603 7665 **e** nelsfilms@dircon.co.uk
Contact David Harrington, Executive Producer, Producer

Nelvana Enterprises (UK) Ltd

4th Floor, 14 -16 Great Putney Street, London W1F 9ND
t 020 7439 6400 **f** 020 7439 6396
e lynn@uk.nelvana.com **w** www.neluana.com
Contact Cathy Laughtan, Managing Director; Marg Evans, Executive Assistant; Lynn Chadwick, Director For Sales

Nemo Media

74 Newman Street, London W1T 3EL
t 020 7436 9084
 stephen.colwell@nemo-media.com **w** www.nemo-media.com
Contact Stephen Colwell, Director of Programmes; Will Poole, Head of Production
Credits Korea At War (D); The Goodbye Plane (S); Meteor Chasers (D)

NFH Ltd

6 Flitcroft Street, London WC2H 8DJ
t 020 7691 4500 **f** 020 7691 4445
Contact Laura McDonald, Personal Assistant to Director

Noel Gay Television

Shepperton Studios, Studios Road, Shepperton TW17 0QD
t 01932 592575
Contact Lesley McKirdy, Head of Production

North South Productions

18 Oxford Gardens, Twickenham TW1 4PL
t 020 8892 0022 **f** 020 8892 7836 **m** 07973 745506
e mail@northsouth.co.uk
Contact Polly Magraw, Director; Susan Crawley, Company Director; Steve Bottomore, Producer
Credits Forum: Once Upon A Planet (E); Africa's Child (E); Wild India (D)

Objective Production Ltd

29 Mount View Road, London N4 4SS
t 020 8348 5899 **f** 020 8348 3277 **e** mpvine@aol.com
Contact Matt Crook, Head of Entertainment; Andrew O'Connor, Managing Director; Michael Vine, Company Secretary; Barry Read, Head of Production; Anthony Owen, Head of Magic Entertainment
Credits Psychic Secrets Revealed (T); Monkey Magic (T); Movie Mistakes (T); Fifty Greatest Magic Tricks (T)

October Films

Spring House, 10 Spring Place, London NW5 3BH
t 020 7284 6868 **f** 020 7284 6869
e info@octoberfilms.co.uk **w** www.octoberfilms.co.uk
Contact Tom Roberts, Managing Director; Denman Rooke, Executive Producer; Adam Bullmore, Executive Producer; Jane Manning, Head of Production; Angus MacQueen, Executive Producer

The Offline Editing Company Ltd

12 Poland Street, London W1F 8QB
t 020 7439 3321 **f** 020 7439 3341
e toecdigital@hotmail.com **w** www.offline-editing.co.uk
Contact Vanessa Myrie, Facilities Manager
Credits Morvern Callar (F); Baltimore (F); Parallel Universes (T); Live Forever (F)

One Two Nine Productions

129 Rosebery Road, London N10 2LD
t 020 8883 7330 **f** 020 8883 7330 **m** 08701 276973
e ROnetwonine@aol.com
Contact Ruth Boswell, Producer

Onedotzero Ltd

212C Curtain House, 134-146 Curtain Road, London EC2A 3AR
t 020 7729 0072 **f** 020 7729 0057
e info@onedotzero.com **w** www.onedotzero.com
Contact Claire Cook, Project Manager; Anna Doyle, Project Manager; Shane Walter, Director
Credits Salaryman VI (S); Onedottv (T); Onedottv - Global (T)

Open Media

The Mews Studio, 8 Addison Bridge Place, London W14 8XP
t 020 7603 9029 **f** 020 7603 9171
e contact@openmedia.co.uk **w** www.openmedia.co.uk

Open Mike Productions

Floor 3, Hammer House, 113-117 Wardour Street, London W1F 0UN
t 020 7434 4004 **f** 020 7434 4045 **e** mail@openmike.co.uk
Contact Andrew Beint, Head of Production

Open Road Films
The Studio, 37 Redington Road, London NW3 7QY
t 020 7813 4333 **f** 020 7916 9172
e openroadfilms@blueyonder.co.uk

Optomen Television
1 Valentine Place, London SE1 8QH
t 020 7967 1234 **f** 020 7967 1233
e otv@optomen.com **w** www.optomen.com
Contact Rachael Whalley, Head of Business Affairs; Susan Healy, Financial
Controller; Sue Hickman, Head of Sales; Patricia Llewellyn, Creative Director;
Richard Thomson, Head of Production; Peter Gillbe, Managing Director; Simon
Andreae, Head of Documentaries
Credits Two Men In A Trench (T); Police Camera Action (T); The Naked Chef (T);
Two Fat Ladies (T)

Opus Television
60 Severn Grove, Canton, Cardiff CF11 9EP
t 02920 223456 **f** 02920 377746 **e** opus@opustv.com
Contact Dudley Newbery, Chairman; J.M. Williams, Director; Hefin Owen,
Director; Eryl Phillips, Director
Credits Liangollen International Music Eisteddford (M); Opera's - Recordings
With Welsh National Opera (M); The Celts (D); Saints And Sinners (D)

OR Media
Capital Court, Capital Interchange Way, Brentford TW8 0EX
t 020 8987 1000 **f** 020 8987 1020
e info@ormedia.co.uk **w** www.ormedia.co.uk
Contact Lynn Osbourne, Managing Director
Credits Gate Crashers (T); Faces of Islam (T); Naseem Hamed - The Prince Who
is King (T)

Original Film & Video Productions Ltd
84 Saint Dionis Road, London SW6 4TU
t 020 7731 0027 **f** 020 7731 0027 **m** 07850 780370
e original.films@btinternet.com
Contact Boyd Catling, Director
Credits Don't Stop (I); It's The Smile (I); Night Or Day (D); My Blind Ambition (D)

Orlando Television Productions Ltd
Up The Steps, Little Tew, Chipping Norton OX7 4JB
t 01608 683218 **f** 01608 683364
e info@orlandodigital.co.uk **w** www.orlandodigital.co.uk
Contact Mike Tomlinson, Producer

Orpheus Productions
6 Amyand Park Gardens, Twickenham TW1 3HS
t 020 8892 3172 **f** 020 8892 4821
e richard-taylor@blueyonder.co.uk
Contact Richard Taylor, Proprietor

OSF
45-49 Mortimer Street, London W1W 8HX
t 020 7470 1300 **f** 020 7436 9421
e jsibson@sstar.uk.com **w** www.southernstargroup.com
Contact Peter Guest, Production Manager; Mark Strickson, Head Of
Programming; Simon Willock, Head Of Factual Programming for The Southern
Star Group
Credits Bug World (D); Industrial Revelations (D); The Elephant And The
Emperor (D); The Ladies Of Viramba (D)

Otmoor Productions
9 Turret House, New High Street, Oxford OX3 7BA
t 01865 744844 **f** 01865 744227 **m** 07836 378639
e otmoorproductions@compuserve.com
Contact John Edginton, MD
Credits Witness - The Killing of Sister Gilford (T); Everyman - Our Father the
Serial Killer (T); Omnibus - Syd Barrett: Crazy Diamond (T)

Outlaw Values
50 Bonnington Square, London SW8 7TQ
t 020 7820 1301 **f** 020 7793 9064
Contact Evan English, Managing Director

Outlook Media Ltd
Grove House, Barley Close, Lang Farm, Daventry NN11 5FW
t 01327 878476 **m** 07703 357967
e television@outlook-media.com **w** www.outlook-media.com
Contact Malcolm Adcock, Senior Producer
Credits Top Gear (T); BBC Current Affairs (T)

OVC Ltd
88 Berkeley Court, Baker Street, London NW1 5ND
t 020 7402 9111 **f** 020 7723 3064
e eliot@ovcmedia.co.uk **w** www.ovcmedia.co.uk
Contact Joanne Goldring-Cohen, Director

Pacific
5-7 Anglers Lane, London NW5 3DG
t 020 7691 2225 **f** 020 7691 2226 **e** rachel@pacific.uk.com
Contact Rachel Purnell, Managing Director; Fi Cotter - Craig, Managing Director

Palace Gate Productions
44 Elvaston Place, London SW7 5NP
t 020 7584 3025 **f** 020 7584 3025
Contact Robert Clamp, Producer

Paladin Invision Ltd
8 Barb Mews, London W6 7PA
t 020 7371 2123 **w** www.pitv.com
Contact William Cran, Joint Managing Director; Clive Syddall, Joint Managing
Director; Fiona Smith, Production Assistant
Credits Commanding Heights (D); Nelson's Trafalgar (D); PG Wodehouse - The
Long Exile (D); Harem (D)

palmfiction.com
production and location services in spain

Palmfiction
Plaza de la Puerta Pintada 6, Palma de Mallorca 7002, Spain
t +34 971 711444 **f** +34 971 711445
e mail@palmfiction.com **w** www.palmfiction.com
Contact Alex Gegenfurtner; David Krause

Panama Productions
Sovereign House, 12 Trewartha Road, Praa Sands, Penzance
TR20 9ST
t 01736 762826 **f** 01736 763328 **m** 07721 449477
panamus@aol.com **w** www.panamamusic.co.uk
Contact Roderick Jones, Managing Director

PanMedia
57A Jamestown Road, London NW1 7BD
t 020 7916 9916 **f** 020 7226 5916 **w** www.bbpr.com
Contact Frank Wintle, Director

Paper Moon Productions
Wychwood House, Burchetts Green Lane, Maidenhead SL6 3QW
t 01628 829819 **f** 01628 825949 **m** 07836 240815
e info@paper-moon.co.uk
Contact David Haggas, Producer
Credits Living With Diabetes (E); Out Of Control (E); Shamans And Science (E);
Bilbo And Beyond (D)

Paradogs Ltd
First Floor, 17-25 Cremer Street, London E2 8HD
t 020 7613 3001 **f** 020 7613 3001
e paradogs@pinkpink.demon.co.uk **w** www.paradogs.org.uk
Contact Steven Eastwood, Director
Credits I Make Things Happen (S); Those Who Are Jesus (D); The End (S);
Of Camera (S)

Parallax Independent
7 Denmark Street, London E2 6HU
t 020 7836 1478
e info@parallaxindependent.co.uk
w www.parallaxindependent.co.uk

Parallel Pictures Ltd
Pinewood Studios, Pinewood Road, Iver Heath SL0 0NH
t 01753 655191 **f** 01753 630663
e films@parallelpics.u-net.com
Contact Graham Bradstreet, Director; Mike Richards, Chairman; Bill Chamberlain, Managing Director; Lee Chamberlain, Business Affairs Manager; John Roddison, Finance Director
Credits Naked August (F); P.O.V (F); Far From China (F); Carmen (F)

Pathway Productions
22 Colinton Road, Edinburgh EH10 5EQ
t 0131 447 3531 **f** 0131 452 8745 **m** 07831 618633
e pathway@dial.pipex.com
Contact Laurence Wareing, Director - Audio Visual Production

Patricia Murphy Films Ltd
25 Arlington Road, Camden, London NW1 7ER
e patriciamurphyfilms@cwcom.net
Contact Patricia Murphy, Director
Credits Ignorance

Patrick Wallis Productions
The Old Courthouse, 26a Church Street, Bishops Stortford CM23 2LY
t 01279 501622 **f** 01279 501644 **m** 07836 604877
e patrick.wallis@virgin.net
Contact Patrick Wallis, Producer; Stephanie Trickett, Production Manager

Paul Berriff Productions
Cedar House, Heads Lane, Hessle HU13 0JH
t 01482 641158 **f** 01482 649692 **m** 07831 636133
e pberriff@aol.com
Contact Paul Berriff, Managing Director

PBF Motion Pictures
The Little Pickenhanger, Tuckey Grove, Ripley GU23 6JG
t 01483 225179 **f** 01483 224118 **e** image@pbf.co.uk
Contact Peter Fairbrass, Proprietor
Credits Oz Aerobics (C); Tiffany Chapman Workout (C); Sony PlayStation 2 - Shut Your Mouth (C); BMW Mini Cooper S (C)

PCI:Live
G4 Harbour Yard, CHelsea Harbour, London SW10 0XD
t 020 7544 7501 **f** 020 7352 7906
e www.pci@pci-live.com **w** www.pci-live.com
Contact Richard McHardy, Head of Business Development

Pearl Catlin Associates
The Production Centre, Clock House, Summersbury Drive, Shalford, Guildford GU4 8JQ
t 01483 567932 **f** 01483 302646 **m** 07861 677655
e pearl@onetel.net
Contact Pearl Catlin, Producer

Pelicula Films Ltd
Producers Centre, 59 Holland Street, Glasgow G2 4NJ
t 0141 287 9522 **f** 0141 287 9504 **m** 07710 215887
e pelicula.films@btinternet.com
Contact Mike Alexander, Producer/Director; Mark Littlewood, Director/Director of Photography
Credits Nanci Griffiths-Other Voices Too (T); Transatlantic Sessions 2 (T); Interrogation (T)

Peloton Productions Ltd
3 Gilbert Street, London W1Y 1RB
t 020 7491 8615 **f** 020 7409 1808 **m** 07768 615331
e jeff@pelotonmedia.co.uk **w** www.pelotonmedia.co.uk
Contact Jeff Emerson, Managing Director; Paul Thompson, Creative Director; Annie Thomas, General Manager

Penderyn Films Ltd
80 Kimberley Road, Pen y Lan, Cardiff CF23 5DN
t 029 2049 0781 **f** 029 2048 7945 **e** pennant.roberts@virgin.net
Contact Pennant Roberts, Director

Penguins With Freckles Ltd
16 Raleigh House, Albion Avenue, London SW8 2AF
t 020 7642 0869 **f** 0870 121 8803 **m** 07769 971706
e wbmalone@hotmail.com
Contact Warren Malone, Director

Peninsula Films
Canalot Studios, 230 Kensal Road, London W10 5BN
e info@peninsula-films.co.uk **w** www.peninsula-films.co.uk
Contact Julian Nott, Director
Credits Straight (S); Gambler's Guide To Winning (D); The Mystery Of Anastasia (D); Weak At Denise (F)

Penumbra Productions Ltd
80 Brondesbury Road, London NW6 6RX
t 020 7328 4550 **f** 020 7328 3844 **e** nazpenumbra@aol.com
Contact H Nazareth

The Periscope Project Company
PO Box 39740, London W4 1XZ
t 020 8994 3598 **f** 020 8994 1755
e paula@periscopeproject.com **w** www.periscopeproject.com
Contact Paula Gjesdal, Director; Helen Knott, Director
Credits EMI IJO: Heart Of Dance (I); Bonsoir Burkina (D)

Perpetual Motion Pictures
3rd Floor, 14-15 D'Arblay Street, London W1F 8DZ
t 020 7287 4400 **f** 020 7287 3567 **e** markshivas@hotmail.com
Contact Mark Shivas, Producer
Credits The Cambridge Spies (T)

Perx Productions
4 Fanthorpe Street, Putney, London SW15 1DZ
t 020 8780 9602 **m** 07889 844443
Credits Retrace (T); Just Us (T)

Peter Batty Productions
Claremont House, Renfrew Road, Kingston KT2 7NT
t 020 8942 6304 **f** 020 8336 1661
e peter@wbatty.freeserve.co.uk
Contact Peter Batty, Managing Director

Peter Williams Television
The Maidstone Studios, Vinters Park, Maidstone ME14 5NZ
t 01622 684545 **f** 01622 684606 **e** pwtv@dial.pipex.com
Contact Peter Williams, Chief Executive; Peter Crook, Business and Production Manager
Credits My Way (D); Secret Army (D); Hillary On Everest (D)

PeterPix Productions
Beacon House, Woodley Park, Skelmersdale WN8 6UR
t 01695 733310 **f** 01695 733310 **m** 07813 036405
e mail@peterpixproductions.com **w** www.peterpixproductions.com
Contact Peter Tong, Director, Director
Credits The Building Of Blackpool Tower (T); The Crematorium (F); Mrs H Of Baker Street (T); Gobsmacked! (F)
Upbeat English cinema, television and internet movie and programme makers.

Phantom Pictures
187 Haverstock Hill, London NW3 4QG
t 020 7419 6268 **f** 020 7419 5178
e contact@phantom-pictures.com
Contact Bob Portac, Producer
Credits Mr In-Between (F)

Phil McIntyre Productions
2nd Floor, 35 Soho Square, London W1Q 3QX
t 020 7439 2270 **f** 020 7439 2280 **e** reception@pmcintyre.co.uk
Contact Phil McIntyre, Executive Producer; Em Moscin, Head of Development; Kathryn Lowrey, Production Co-ordinator; Lucy Ansbro, Producer
Credits Victoria At The Albert (T); Phoenix Nights (T); Guest House Paradiso (F); Maybe Baby (F)

Photoplay Productions

21 Princess Road, London NW1 8JR
t 020 7722 2500 **f** 020 7722 6662
e photoplay@compuserve.com
Contact Patrick Stanbury, Director
Credits Cecil B. De Mille (D); The Tramp And The Dictator (D)

Picardy Media & Communication

1 Park Circus, Glasgow G3 6AX
t 0141 333 1200 **f** 0141 332 6002
e jr@picardy.co.uk **w** www.picardy.co.uk
Contact Karen Forster, Facilities Coordinator; Bill Fairweather, Client Manager
Facilities; Charles Kelly, Operations Director; John Rocchiccioli, Head Of Production
Credits Tanqueray (I); Finning (W); Coca Cola (W)

Picture Palace Films

13 Egbert Street, London NW1 8LJ
t 020 7586 8763 **f** 020 7586 9048
e info@picturepalace.com **w** www.picturepalace.com
Contact Malcolm Craddock, Chief Executive; Katherine Hedderly,
Head of Development
Credits Sharpe (T); The True Story of Stefan Kiszko (T); Rebel Heart (T)

Pie Films

PO Box 42301, London N12 9LN
f 07989 387371 **m** 07977 554079
e film@pie.uk.net **w** www.pie.uk.net
Contact John Burns, Director
Credits You Are A Monkey (S); Killing Time (S)

Pierrot Productions

35 Charlton Lane, Charlton, London SE7 8LB
t 020 8858 0846 **f** 020 8858 0846 **m** 07768 705003
e pierrotdocs@aol.com
Contact Paul Pierrot, Producer/Director
Credits The Mafia Cookbook (D); Marty Wilde Stage Show (M); Jukebox Heroes
(D); Diving With The Force (D)

Pillarbox Productions

32 Lonsdale Square, London N1 1EW
t 020 7700 0505 **f** 020 7700 1155 **e** mail@pillarbox.tv
Contact Clare Richards, Managing Director

Pilot Film & TV Productions

The Old Studio, 18 Middle Row, London W10 5AT
t 020 8960 2771 **f** 020 8960 2721
e info@pilot.co.uk **w** www.pilot.co.uk
Contact John DeAngelis, General Manager; Maud Nahmias, Marketing
Executive; Ian Cross, Managing Director
Credits Planet Food (D); Bazaar (D); Treks In A Wild World (D); Pilot Guides (D)

Pinewood Television Studios

Pinewood Road, Iver Heath SL0 0NH
t 01753 656638 **f** 01753 656103
e diana_crystalhoney@pinewood-studios.co.uk
w www.pinewood-studios.co.uk
Contact Diana Crystal Honey, Sales and Marketing Manager, TV

Pinwood Productions

Northcroft, Oakhill Avenue, Pinner HA5 3DL
t 020 8866 4857 **t** 020 8866 6043 **f** 020 8866 9661
e pinwood@cmc.uk.com
Contact Geoff Crocker, Producer, Producer

Pioneer Productions

Voyager House, 32 Galena Road, London W6 0LT
t 020 8748 0888 **f** 020 8748 7888
e pioneer@pioneertv.com **w** www.pioneertv.com
Contact Liam Brannan, Executive Assistant; Kirstie McLure, Head of
Production; Julia Behar, Finance Director; Sharon Goulds, Managing Director;
Becky Lee, Head Of Development; Stuart Carter, Managing Director; James
McGhie, Executive Assistant
Credits Space Shuttle: Human Timebomb (T)

Pixelle Ltd

84 Mercers Road, Tufnell Park, London N19 4PR
t 020 7263 7277 **f** 0870 163 9647 **m** 07941 829359
e jwilson@orion-systems.co.uk
Contact Jennifer Wilson, Managing Director / Executive Producer; Matthew
Spencer Brown, Company Secretary
Credits Filghtline Series I, II & III (D); Animal X Series I & II (D); Mapping Murder (D)

Planet 24 Productions Ltd

The Planet Building, 35-38 Portman Square, London W1H 6NU
t 020 7486 6268 **f** 020 7345 9400
Contact Justine Heggs

Planet Rapido

14-16 Great Pulteney Street, London W1F 9ND
t 020 7440 5700 **f** 020 7439 2733
e info@rapido.co.uk **w** www.planetrapido.com
Contact Peter Stuart, Managing Director; Isobel Oram, Head of Operations;
Mark Ford, Managing Director; Rose Murphy, Head of Resources
Credits 10 Ways To Kill An Alien (T); Is Harry On The Boat? (T); Eurotrash 16 (T)

Planet Wild Productions

Suite 204, Barclay House, 35 Whitworth Street West,
Manchester M1 5NG
t 0161 233 3090 **f** 0161 233 3098
e office@planetwild.co.uk **w** www.planetwild.co.uk
Contact John Moulson, Head of Factual Entertainment; Paula Trafford,
Managing Director; Oliver Lang, Head of Production
Credits Fleur's Story, Real Life (T); The Lives Of Jesus (T); Althorp (T); Back To
The Beach (T)

Plantagenet Films Ltd

Ard-Daraich Studio B, Ardgour, Fort William PH33 7AB
t 01855 841384 **f** 01855 841248 **m** 07876 368028
e plantagenetfilms@aol.com
Contact Norrie Maclaren, Director/Producer

Playback HD

422 Lanark Road West, Edinburgh EH14 5SN
t 0131 449 3864 **f** 0131 449 3864 **m** 07802 401371
e info@playbackhd.tv **w** www.playbackhd.tv
Contact Nigel Shepherd, Managing Director

PMA TV

80A Victoria Street, St Albans AL1 3XH
t 01727 845845 **f** 01727 845999
e info@pmatv.co.uk **w** www.pmatv.co.uk
Contact Adrian Bourne, Co-Director; Paul Musselle, Managing Director; Sally
Peters, Co-Director
Credits Legends (T); Bare Necessities (T); Internations Cup (T);
Ascar Motor Racing (T)

Point of View Production Company

2 Valletort Cottages, Valletort Lane, Stoke, Plymouth PL1 5PU
t 01752 568602 **f** 01752 551595 **m** 07710 094974
e pov@povprod.co.uk **w** www.povprod.co.uk
Contact Mike Ford, Director; Emma Ford, Director
Credits Changing Climate (D); Island Life (D)

Poisson Rouge Pictures

140 Battersea Park Road, London SW11 4NB
t 020 7720 5666 **f** 020 7720 5757
e info@poissonrougepictures.com
w www.poissonrougepictures.com
Contact Christopher Granier-Deferre, Producer; Alexandre Deon, Producer;
Neil Endicott, Head Of Development

POLAR Tele-Film Ltd

28 Trotter Way, Manor Park, Epsom KT19 7EW
t 01372 728938 **f** 01372 728665 **m** 07720 396755
e sales@polar-telefilm.com **w** www.polar-telefilm.com
Credits Revyjaget (D); Rammer Video (I); Opening Night (S); News Reports - NRK (T)

Portobello Pictures

PO Box 31579, London W11 3YA
t 020 7379 5566 **f** 020 7379 5599
e ericabraham@portobellopictures.com

Contact Judi Ferreira, Personal Assistant; Will Cookson, Production Assistant; Eric Abraham, Managing Director
Credits Forsythe Saga (T); Kolya (F); Dark Blue World (F)

Poseidon Productions

Hammer House, 117 Wardour Street, London W1F 0UN
t 020 7734 4441 **f** 020 7437 0638
e poseidon@posfilm.demon.co.uk

Contact April Turner, Personal Assistant; Nadine Limb, Personal Assitant; Frixos Constantine, Managing Director
Credits Anna Pavlova (F); Global Bears Rescue (A); Byzantine Cat (F); The Odyssey (A)

Posh Pictures

420 Sauchiehall Street, Glasgow G2 3JD
t 014 1353 0456 **f** 079 7408 1934 **m** 07989 385929
e mail@poshpic.com **w** www.poshpic.com

Contact Garfield Kennedy, Producer; David Griffith, Producer; David Ward, Director
Credits The Last Great Aventure (D); Changing Tombs (D); Tartan Shorts: All Over Brazil (S); The Fall Of Shug McCracken (S)

Pozzitive Television Ltd

Floor 5, Paramount House, 162-170 Wardour Street, London W1V 4AB
t 020 7734 3258 **f** 020 7437 3130

Contact Geoff Posner, Producer; David Tyler, Producer

Praxis Films Ltd

PO Box 290, Market Rasen, Lincoln LN3 6BB
t 01472 399976 **f** 01472 399976
e info@praxisfilms.com **w** www.praxisfilms.com

Premiere Productions

3 Colville Place, London W1P 1HN
t 020 7255 1650

Pressure Cooker Productions

66 Townsend Road, London NW8 6BS
t 020 7722 9314 **f** 020 7722 9314

Contact Wendy Meller, Producer; Ashley Dartnell, Producer

Principal Films

Picture House, 65 Hopton Street, Bankside, London SE1 9LR
t 020 7928 9287 **f** 020 7928 9886
e richard.sattin@principalmedia.com

Contact Miranda Collinge, Development Assistant; Rod Caird, Executive Producer; Mike Slee, Director; Richard Sattin, Chief Executive
Credits True Stories From The Morgue (T); Hardcore - True Stories (D); Comet Cover Up - Secret History (D)

Priority Productions

559 Kings Road, London SW6 2EB
t 020 7384 1531 **f** 020 7384 1486 **m** 07836 718632
e priorityp@aol.com

Contact Jeff Inman, Managing Director

Prisma Communications

92-93 Great Russell Street, London WC1B 3PS
t 020 7691 3060 **f** 020 7691 3070
e info@prismacomms.com **w** www.prismacomms.com

Contact Amanda MacKen\ie Stuart, Producer/Writer; Ildiko Kemeny, Producer; Robert Buckler, Producer/Writer
Credits Leo Burnett, AAR Reel (I); Geltronics 'Plain Talk. Practical Solutions' (I); London Business School for NTL (T)

Production Friend

e rick@productionfriend.demon.co.uk

Contact Rick Friend, Managing Director
Credits Non Possumus; Hair Today; More Tea Vampire

Production One Ltd

Dorchester House, Station Road, Letchworth SG6 3AW
t 01462 680860 **f** 01462 482616
e production@productionone.co.uk

Contact Julian Bennett, Managing Director

Victory Productions

PO Box 18976, London W14 8YF
t 020 7731 7810 **f** 020 7731 0322 **m** 07974 353529
e mail@vpuk.co.uk **w** www.vpuk.co.uk
Credits The River To Greyrock (F); Dead Wrong (F); The Arrangement (F)

Projectile Productions

3 Walton House, Thane Villas, London N7 7PD
t 020 7609 3873 **f** 020 7609 3873 **m** 07778 363492

Contact Gerard Tierney, Producer
Credits Mosaic (F)

Projector Productions

12-13 Poland Street, London W1F 8QB
t 020 7434 1110 **f** 020 7434 1115 **e** film@projector.co.uk

Contact Polly Cork, Development Executive; Trevor Eve, Managing Director; Rachel Gesua, Producer
Credits Twelfth Night (T); Alice Through The Looking Glass (T); Cinderella (T)

Prolific Films

90 Salusbury Road, London NW6 6PA
t 020 7372 5495 **f** 020 7372 5495 **m** 07904 413521
e jr@prolificfilms.freeserve.co.uk
w www.prolificfilms.freeserve.co.uk

Contact Julian Richards, Producer
Credits Queen Sacrifice (S); Darklands (F); Silent Cry (F); The Last Horror Movie (F)

Prospect Pictures

Capital Studios, Wandsworth Plain, London SW18 1ET
t 020 7636 1234 **f** 020 7636 1236
e pp@prospect.uk.com **w** www.prospect-uk.com

Contact Barry Lynch, Joint MD; Tony McAvoy, Joint MD
Credits Saturday Kitchen (T); Good Food Live (T)

Prospero Productions Ltd

Baytons Farm, Gloucester Road, Upleadon, Gloucester GL18 1EH
t 01531 822843 **f** 01531 821931 **e** prospero@argonet.co.uk

Contact Tim Rickard, Creative Director; Tish Faith, Producer

PTT Films - Production Team of Turkey

Asmalimescit Minare Sok 23, Beyoglu, Istanbul 80050, Turkey
t +90 212 293 8473 **f** +90 212 293 8475
e sebnem@pttfilms.com **w** www.pttfilms.com

Contact R Sebnem Kitis

Pukka Productions

Birchwood, 12 Furze Field, Oxshott KT22 0UR
t 01372 843457 **m** 07774 458598
e info@pukka.tv **w** www.pukka.tv

Contact Scott Thomas, Producer; Harlan Cockburn, Producer

Purple Genie Productions Ltd

PO Box 496, Orpington, Kent BR6 9WT
t 07973 658408 **t** 07979 210469 **f** 07966 155914
e info@purplegenie.co.uk **w** www.purplegenie.co.uk

Contact Paul Freeman, Producer; Neil Doughty, Producer
Credits Guest House (S); Harry's Game (S)

Quadrant
63 Cowbridge Road, Cardiff CF11 9QP
t 020 7836 5320 **f** 029 2023 7444
e enquiries@quadrant.uk.com **w** www.quadrant.uk.com
Contact Colin Stevens, Deputy Chief Executive

Quanta Ltd
Old Forge House, Rodbourne Road, Corston, Malmesbury
SN16 0HA
t 01666 826366 **f** 01666 824871 **e** quanta_films@yahoo.co.uk
Contact Daphne Jones, Secretary; Nicholas Jones, Chairman; Gema Jareno, Director
Credits Equinox (T); Panorama (T); Bookmark (T); Horizon (T)

Quirky Film & TV
Pinewood Studios, Iver SL0 0NH
t 01753 650070 **e** info@quirky.co.uk
Contact Angela Ewen, Assistant; Guy Hemphill, Development Manager; Steve
Sheen, Director; Ron Barkeham, Director

Ragdoll Ltd
Heath Farm, Iver Heath, Bucks SL0 0NH
t 01753 631800 **f** 01753 631831
e pinewood@ragdoll.co.uk **w** www.ragdoll.co.uk
Contact Sue James, Director of Production; Liz Queenan,
Head of Production Operations
Credits Teletubbies Everywhere (T); Boohbah (T); Brum (T); Badjelly The Witch (A)

Raindance Rawtalent
81 Berwick Street, London W1F 8TW
t 020 7387 3899
e rawtalent@raindance.co.uk **w** www.raindance.co.uk/rawtalent
Contact Carl Schonfeld, Producer; Elliot Grove, Executive Producer; Oscar
Sharp, Head of Development
Credits Day Of Reckoning (S); Table 5 (F)

Raindog Ltd
5 Park Circus Place, Glasgow G3 6AH
t 0141 572 0777 **f** 0141 572 0885 **e** info@raindog.org.uk
Contact Stuart Davids, Creative Director; Robbie Allen, Business Manager; Lee
Davidson, Development Executive
Credits Tinsel Town Series I & II (T)

Raintree Productions Ltd
Rushall House, Rushall, Diss IP21 4RX
t 01379 741557 **f** 01379 740148 **m** 07774 257459
e martinhubneruk@aol.com
Contact Martin Hubner, Producer/Director
Credits NatWest (C); Nationwide (I); British Gas (C); Associated Newspapers (C)

Ralph's Films Ltd
5 Carpenter Court, 37-41 Pratt Street, London NW1 0BJ
t 020 7362 0484 **f** 020 7267 0589
e infor@ralphsltd.co.uk **w** www.ralphsltd.co.uk
Contact Mark Riley, Managing Director
Credits Peace And Quiet (S); Frozen (S); Embryo (M); Pangloss (M)

Random Factor Productions Ltd
West View, Monks Hill, Smarden TN27 8QH
t 01233 770433 **f** 01233 770433 **m** 07989 349284
e adam@randomfactor.co.uk **w** www.randomfactor.co.uk
Contact Marios Hajipanayi, Producer; Adam Jeal, Director

Raw Charm Ltd
Ty Cefn, Rectory Road, Cardiff CF5 1QL
t 029 2064 1511 **f** 029 2066 8220
e pam@rawcharm.co.uk **w** www.rawcharm.tv
Contact Pam Hunt, Producer; Kate Jones-Davies, Producer, Director
Credits Hanar and Her Sisters (T); War Stories (T)

Razzmatazz Productions
48C Primrose Gardens, London NW3 4TP
t 020 7722 2065 **f** 020 7722 2065
e info@razzmatazzproductions.co.uk
w www.razzmatazzproductions.co.uk
Contact Jeremy Hoare, Director; Tony Ferris; David Hatter

RDF Television
140 Kensington Church Street, Notting Hill, London W8 4BN
t 020 7313 6700 **f** 020 7313 6777
e tv@rdfmedia.com **w** www.rdf.co.uk
Contact David Frank, Managing Director

Real Life Media Productions
Anstey House, 40 Hanover Square, Leeds LS3 1BQ
t 0113 234 7271 **t** 0113 220 6944
f 0113 244 2061 **m** 07831 140648
e info@reallife.co.uk **w** www.reallife.co.uk
Contact Simon Schofield, Director of Programmes; Ali Rashid, Managing
Director; Jenny Scott, Director of Productions
Credits Tudor Times (E); Mum, I'm A Muslim (D); Britain's Most Dangerous
Prisoner (D); The Brits Who Fought For Hitler (D)

Real to Reel Productions Ltd
61-63 Churchfield Road, London W3 6AY
t 020 8993 6000 **f** 020 8993 6006 **m** 07050 115007
e office@realtoreel.co.uk **w** www.realtoreel.co.uk
Contact Ian Johnson, Producer

Red Rose Chain
1 Fore Hamlet, Ipswich IP3 8AA
t 01473 288886 **f** 01473 288882
e info@redrosechain.co.uk **w** www.redrosechain.co.uk
Contact David Newborn, Director of Production; Jimmy Grimes, Director of
Communications; Joanna Carrick, Director of Creativity
Credits Bad Behaviour (S); Sparkleshark (S); Four Carrier Bags And A Buggy
(D); Moving On Up (S)

Redweather Productions
Eastern Business Centre, Felix Road, Bristol BS5 0HE
t 0117 941 5854 **f** 0117 941 5851
e production@redweather.co.uk **w** www.redweather.co.uk
Contact Steve Spencer, Head of Production

Reef Television
4th Floor, 8 Carnaby Street, London W1F 9PD
t 020 7287 7877 **f** 020 7287 7852
e mail@reeftv.com **w** www.reef.tv
Contact Tom Milligan, Company Director; Richard Farmbrough, Managing Director
Credits Put Your Money Where Your House Is, UK Style (T); Model Gardens,
UK Style (T)

Renegade Films
92-93 Great Russell Street, London WC1B 3PS
t 020 7691 3060 **f** 020 7691 3070 **m** 07710 410 362
e renprism@dircon.co.uk
Contact Robert Buckler, Producer/Writer
Credits Room To Rent (F); Last Result (F); Hotel Splendide (F)

Renovators Productions Ltd
The Old Courthouse, 26A Church Street, Bishops Stortford
CM23 2LY
t 01279 501622 **f** 01279 501644 **m** 07836 604877
e patrick.wallis@virgin.net
Contact Patrick Wallis, Producer; Stephanie Trickett, Production Manager

Renting Eyeballs Films
13-14 Dean Street, London W1D 3RS
t 020 7437 4417 **f** 020 7437 4221 **e** realcreate@aol.com

Robber Baron Productions
15 Henrietta Street, Covent Garden, London WC2E 8QG
t 020 7928 9240 **f** 020 7379 5518 **m** 07958 984286
e info@robber-baron.co.uk **w** www.robber-baron.co.uk
Contact Joseph Alberti, Producer
Credits URBrain (S); Danger Zone (S); Red Lines (S); On Edge (S)

Roberts & Wykeham Films Ltd
74 Iffley Road, London W6 0PF
t 020 8748 5008 **f** 020 8932 0861
e rwfilms@mac.com **w** www.rwfilms.co.uk
Contact Sadie Wykeham, Producer; Gwynne Roberts, Director, Producer
Credits Saddam's Ultimate Solution (T)

Robot Productions Ltd

2-3 Duck Lane, London W1F 0HX
t 020 7734 7773 **f** 020 7437 0544 **m** 07974 370544
e carlie@robotfactory.co.uk **w** www.robotfactory.co.uk
Contact Matt Tsang, Director; Phil Man, Director; Luke Halls, Director; Carlie
Mead, Production Manager
Credits Q Music Channel Rebrand (T); The Box Channel Rebrand (T); Trouble TV
Channel Rebrand (T); Kodak (C)

Robson Brown Film & Video Productions

Clavering House, Clavering Place, Newcastle-upon-Tyne NE1 3NG
t 0191 232 2443 **f** 0191 232 8745 **m** 07931 502902
e info@robson-brown.co.uk **w** www.robson-brown.co.uk
Contact Steve Hunneyset, Director of Film and Video

Rock Solid Entertainment

Suite 173, 77 Beak Street, London W1F 9DB
t 020 7738 2720 **f** 020 7439 3330 **m** 07801 061598
e nforzy@rocksolidentertainment.co.uk **w**
www.rocksolidentertainment.co.uk
Contact Nicolas Forty, Director
Credits Flash (C); Stone Henge (A); Effrakata (M); The Cage (S)

Rocket Pictures

1 Blythe Road, London W14 0HE
t 020 7603 9530 **f** 020 7348 4830 **e** luke@rocketpictures.co.uk
Contact David Furnish, Chairman; Ed King, Development Executive; Luke Lloyd
Davies, Assistant To Mr. Furnish; Steve Hamilton-Shaw, Managing Director/Head
Of Production
Credits Tantrums And Tiaras (D); Women Talking Dirty (F)

Roger Bolton Productions

9 Cynthia Street, London N1 9JF
t 020 7713 6868 **f** 020 7713 6999 **e** (name)@rogerbolton.co.uk
Contact Roger Bolton, Managing Director; Gabrielle O'Connell, Head of
Production; Claire Featherstone, Head Of Production

Rooftop Productions

35-41 Lower Marsh, London SE1 7RT
t 020 7523 2299 **f** 020 7523 2441 **m** 07973 408243
e info@rooftop-productions.co.uk
w www.rooftop-productions.com
Contact Cheryl Campbell, Executive Producer; Sophie Chalk, Development Producer
Credits Rooted (T); Drop the Debt; Takeaway; Volcano Stories

Rose Bay

13 Austin Friars, London EC2N 2JX
t 020 7670 1609 **f** 020 8357 0845 **e** info@rosebay.co.uk
Contact Mathew Steiner, Chief Executive; Simon Usiskin, Managing Director

Rosetta Pictures

12 Haycroft Rd, London SW2 5HZ
t 020 7737 6713 **f** 020 7737 6523
e rosetta@globalnet.co.uk **w** www.rosetta.co.uk
Contact Emma Crichton-Miller, Director

Rosso Productions

13 Fonthill Road, London N4 3HY
t 020 7281 4709 **f** 020 7281 4709
Contact Joanna Smith, Producer

RSPB Film Unit

The Lodge, Sandy SG19 2DL
t 01767 680551 **f** 01767 683262
e mark.percival@rspb.org.uk **w** www.rspb.org.uk
Contact Tim Norman, Film Library Manager; Lynda Whytock, RSPB Film
Collection Manager; Mark Percival, Head Of Production
Credits Sea Eagle - A Bird In Our Hands (D); Keeping Seabirds Off The Hook (D);
Unnatural Neighbours (D); The Undiscovered Country (D)

Ruby Films

Apartment 9, Goldcrest Building, 1 Lexington Street, London
W1F 9TA
t 020 7439 4455 **f** 020 7439 1649 **e** rubyfilm@dircon.co.uk

S&M Films Ltd

Westar Studios, Priory Way, Southall UB2 5EB
t 020 8848 7475 **f** 020 8848 7478
e admin@sandmfilms.com
Contact Shakila Taranum Maan, Director; Abi Ward, Personal Assistant;
Manjeet Singh, Producer
Credits Talking About Suicide (I); A Quiet Desperation (F); The Line (T);
Restless Sky (T)

Saltire Film & Television Productions Ltd

5 Queens Crescent, Glasgow G4 9BW
t 0141 332 3326 **f** 0141 332 3327 **e** info@saltirefilms.co.uk
Contact Peter Barber-Fleming, Managing Director; Audrey English, Documentary
Development Producer; Paddi James, Production Manager; Sarah MacKinnon,
Producer; Elaine Campbell, Production Manager; Anna Hunter, Researcher
Credits Gigha - Buying Our Island (D); Mandancin' (F); The Tartan Pimpernel
(D); Stairway 13 - The Ibrox Disaster (D)

*Specialising in drama and documentary, seeking co-production
opportunities and international expansion.*

Sarah Radclyffe Productions

5th Floor, 83-84 Berwick Street, London W1F 8TS
t 020 7437 3128 **f** 020 7437 3129 **e** mail@srpltd.co.uk

SATV Television Productions

15-17 Annandale Street, Edinburgh EH7 4AW
t 0131 558 8148 **e** mail@satv.co.uk **w** www.satv.co.uk

Scala Productions

15 Frith Street, London W1D 4RE
t 020 7734 7060 **f** 020 7437 3248 **e** scalaprods@aol.com

Scarab Films Ltd

St Martins Chapel, Bayham Street, London NW1 0BD
t 020 7482 3433
Contact Jamil Dehlavi, Managing Director
Credits The Blood of Hussain (F); Immaculate Conception (F); Jinnah (F)

Scimitar Films

219 Kensington High Street, London W8 6BD
t 020 7734 8385 **f** 020 7602 9217
Contact Michael Winner, Producer

Scorer Associates

10 Redland Terrace, Redland, Bristol BS6 6TD
t 0117 946 6838 **f** 0117 946 6840
e info@scorer.co.uk **w** www.scorer.co.uk
Contact Martin Dohrn, Director; Christine Owen, Managing Director;
Mischa Scorer, Director
Credits The Cultured Ape (D); In Search Of Killer Ants (D); Congo (D)

Scraggy Dog Productions Ltd

The Dog House, 192 Lightwoods Hill, Bearwood, Warley B67 5EH
t 0121 434 5767 **f** 0121 429 5727 **m** 07778 555275
e scraggydog@hotmail.com
Contact Paul Leather, Director/Producer; Helen Griffith, Producer
Credits The People's Park (E); Cephas (E); Parenting (I); Tall Order (M)

Scream Films

3 Mills Studios, Three Mill Lane, London E3 3DU
t 020 870 **f** 020 8215 3468
e susiedark@screamfilms.com **w** www.screamfilms.com
Contact Susie Dark, Head Of Production; Paul Flexton, Head Of Entertainment;
Jane Glasson, Head Of Development; Southan Morris, Director Of Company;
Sheila Risk, Researcher
Credits Dancercise With Lucy Benjamin (C); Hear Say: Here Today, Gone
Tomorrow (D); 2001: A Sex Oddity (T); Born Stars (T)

Screen Channel Ltd

29 Newman Street, London W1T 1PS
t 020 7436 4808 **f** 020 7323 5625
e productions@screenchannel.co.uk
w www.screenchannel.co.uk
Contact Peter Lowe, Managing Director
Credits Off The Beatles Track With Nigel Farrell (T); Inside Crime (T); Bulls And
Bears (T); Movie Nights (T)

Screen First Ltd

The Studios, Funnells Farm, Down Street, Nutley TN22 3LG
t 01825 712034 **f** 01825 713511 **m** 07774 714028
e paul.madden@virgin.net
Contact Mairede Thomas, Producer/Director; Paul Madden, Producer/Director
Credits Here Comes The Bogeyman (D); Ivor The Invisible (T)

Screen Production Associates Ltd

1st Floor, 13 Manette Street, London W1D 4AW
t 020 7287 1170 **f** 020 7287 1123
e enquiries@screenpro.co.uk **w** www.screenpro.co.uk
Contact Doug Abbott, Managing Director; Julia Vickers, Commercial Manager;
Piers Jackson, Producer; John Jaquiss, Managing Director
Credits The Case (F); The Truth Game (F); Club Le Monde (F)

Screen Scene Productions

81 Saltram Crescent, Maida Vale, London W93LS
t 020 8964 1144 **f** 020 8964 8902
e screenscene@hotmail.com

Screen Ventures

49 Goodge Street, London W1T 1TE
t 020 7580 7448 **f** 020 7631 1265
e info@screenventures.com **w** www.screenventures.com
Contact Naima Mould, Producer; Peter Neal, Producer/Director; Daniel Hagget;
Christopher Mould, Managing Director
Credits Room Full of Mirrors (D); Pavement Aristocrats (D); Life and Limb (T)

Screenhouse Productions

Chapel Allerton House, 114 Harrogate Road, Leeds LS7 4NY
t 0113 266 8881 **f** 0113 266 8882
e info@screenhouse.co.uk **w** www.screenhouse.co.uk
Contact Marty Jopson, Head of Intercative; Paul Bader, Managing Director;
Catherine Mounsey, Production Manager; Barbara Govan, Head of Development
Credits Walking The Line (T); Snapshots (T); Science Shack (T)

Screenworks

13 Dale Street, Carlisle CA2 5JT
t 07092 374726 **f** 07092 209617 **m** 07970 673002
e production@screenworks.uk.com **w** www.screenworks.uk.com
Contact Damon Beed, Production Executive; Sian Williams, Producer; Ian
Fleming, Cheif Executive
Credits Stingers (F); The Gatherers (F); Hollyoaks (T); Sweet Dreams (T)

Seaforth Studios

Seaforth House, 54 Seaforth Road, Stornoway, Isle of Lewis
HS1 2SD
t 01851 704433 **f** 01851 706406
e info@tarlas.com **w** www.studioalba.com
Contact Michael Skelly, Operations Manager; Murdo MacLeod, Managing Director

Seahorse Productions

63 St Georges Road, Kemptown, Brighton BN2 1EF
t 01273 624679 **f** 01273 887759 **m** 07771 522733
e seahorse-productions@lineone.net
Contact Andrew Miles, Producer

Seance Productions Ltd

55 Station Road, West Byfleet KT14 6DT
t 07811 637703 **e** mjgunn@seanceproductions.com
Contact MJ Gunn, Creative Director

Sear Communications

Biddenden Green Farm, Smarden TN27 8NJ
t 01233 770326 **f** 01233 770688 **m** 07831 531627
Contact Howard Williams, Managing Director

SeeHear Productions

Low Cottages, St Margaret's Road, Bungay NR35 1PL
t 01986 894500 **f** 01986 894505 **m** 07860 938993
e mail@seehearproductions.com
Contact Eddy Pumer, Music Producer/Composer; Roberta Pumer

SEL Presentations

1 The Quadrangle, Enbourne Gate, Enbourne Road, Newbury
RG14 6AL
t 01635 34445 **f** 01635 49992
e sales@sel-pres.co.uk **w** www.sel-pres.co.uk
Contact Andy Regent; Chrissie Eccleston

September Films

Glen House, 22 Glenthorne Road, London W6 0NG
t 020 8563 9393 **f** 020 8741 7214
e september@septemberfilms.com **w** www.septemberfilms.com
Contact Elaine Day, Head of Production
Credits The Real Sex In The City (T); Our Sam (D); Secrets And Lies (F);
Bridezillas (T)

Serendipity Picture Company Ltd

Media Centre, Emma-Chris Way, Abbeywood Park, Bristol
BS34 7JU
t 0117 906 6541 **f** 0117 906 6542 **m** 07889 615453
e tony@serendipitypictures.com
Contact Tony Yeadon, Producer/Director; Nick Dance, Producer/Cameraman
Credits A Garden For All Seasons (D); Sacred Landscape (D); Land Of Plenty
(D); Tasting South Africa (D)

Serious Pictures Film Co Ltd

1A Rede Place, London W2 4TU
t 020 7792 4477 **m** 07768 950973
e info@seriouspictures.com **w** www.seriouspictures.com
Contact Simon Bank, Head of Music Video; Donnie Masters, Managing Director;
Ann-Marie Morris, Office Manager; Carine Harris, Executive Producer; Verity
Louden, Commercials Representative

Seventh Art Productions

63 Ship Street, Brighton BN1 1AE
t 01273 777678 **f** 01273 323777
e info@seventh-art.com **w** www.seventh-art.com
Contact Angela Vermond, Office Manager; Jack White, Production Co-ordinator
Credits Great Artists with Tim Marlow (T); Ali (F)

Shining Light Productions

PO Box 5520, Westcliff SS0 9WE
t 01702 393758
e info@shininglightfilms.com **w** www.shininglightfilms.com
Credits Grave Mistakes (S); Making a Killing (F)

Sianco Cyf

36 Y Maes, Caernarfon LL55 2NN
t 01286 676100 **f** 01286 677616 **m** 07831 726111
e post@sianco.tv **w** www.sianco.tv
Contact Sian Teifi, Managing Director
Credits Marc (S); Bois Y Bac (D); Mas Draw (T); Tafarn Y Gwr Drwg (T)

Silent Sound Films Ltd

Cambridge Court, Cambridge Road, Frinton-on-Sea CO13 9HN
t 01255 676381 **f** 01255 676383
e thj@silentsoundfilms.co.uk **w** www.silentsoundfilms.co.uk
Contact Timothy Foster, Managing Director
Credits Harwich Film Festival; London Food Film Festival; Lucky Star

Silicon<19 Media

The Basement, 3A Lansdown Terrace Lane, Cheltenham GL50 2JU
t 01242 580929 **f** 01242 580929
e production@silicon19.co.uk **w** www.silicon19.co.uk
Contact Greg Browning, Creative Director
Credits The Essential Guide To Extending Your Home (I); Celluloid@22H (M);
WLTM (S); Rising Stars (D)

Silver Light Media

72 Staunton Road, Oxford OX3 7TP
t 01865 744451 **f** 01865 741352 **m** 07785 373306
e mail@silverlightmedia.com **w** www.silverlightmedia.com
Contact David Marlow, Managing Director

Silverapples Media Ltd
3rd Floor, Whiteleys, Queensway, London W2 4YN
t 020 7727 8030 **f** 020 7727 9030
e silverapples@silverapplesmedia.co.uk
Contact Brendan Hughes, Managing Director; Avril MacRory, CEO
Credits NHK Classics (D); Worldwide Women (D); Frankenstein (T); Forever Ealing (D)

Simple Productions
22 Scott's Sufferance Wharf, 5 Mill Street, London SE1 2DE
t 020 7231 4587 **e** athertonpn@aol.com
Contact Paul Atherton, Producer
Credits Environments For All - A New Beginning (D)

Simply Television Ltd
150 Great Portland Street, London W1W 6QD
t 020 7307 6000 **f** 020 7307 6001
w www.simplytelevision.com
Contact Paddy Smart, Marketing Manager; Avie Littler, Head of Production; Arnold Reicher, Head of Broadcast Marketing Division; Henry Scott, Director, Managing Director

Sinibad Films Ltd
5 Prince's Gate, London SW7 1QJ
t 020 7823 7488 **f** 020 7823 9137
e info@sinibad.co.uk **w** www.sinibad.co.uk
Contact Omar Al-Qaltan, Producer/Director; Michel Khleifi, Producer/Director; Anna Mackenzie
Credits Forbidden Marriages In The Holy Land; The Tale Of The Three Jewels; Wedding in Galilee

Six Foot High Films Ltd
15-17 Middle Street, Brighton BN1 1AL
t 01273 201322 **f** 01273 201323
e general@sixfoothighfilms.com **w** www.sixfoothighfilms.com
Contact Emma Farrell, Director
Credits Lost (C); Harper (C); Cupboard Love (S); Chicken Karma (S)

SKA Films Ltd
2nd Floor, 6 Salem Road, London W2 4BU
t 020 7243 9777 **f** 020 7437 3245 **e** skafilms@skafilms.com
Contact David Reid, Joint Head of Production; Matthew Vaughn, Producer; Manuel Puro, Head of Development; Adam Bohling, Joint Head of Production; Guy Ritchie, Director
Credits Mean Machine (F); Snatch (F); Lock Stock And Two Smoking Barrels (F)

Skreba Films
7 Denmark Street, London WC2H 8LZ
t 020 7240 7066 **f** 020 7240 7088
Contact Simon Relph, Producer

Skyline Productions
10 Scotland Street, Edinburgh EH3 6PS
t 0131 557 4580 **f** 0131 556 4377 **e** admin@skyline.uk.com
Contact Leslie Hills, Director

The Sladdinc Company
PO Box 116, Pudsey, Leeds LS28 5WL
t 0870 130 2297 **f** 0870 130 2297 **m** 07802 429021
e mail@sladdinc.com **w** www.sladdinc.com
Contact Jeremy Sladdin, Company Director
Credits Whatever Next? (S); Park Life (S); Bodyshop (S); Echoes (F)

Small Back Room Productions
Cawnpore House, 6 West Common Road, Uxbridge UB8 1NZ
t 01895 239166 **f** 01895 239166 **m** 07774 415702
e smallback@aol.com
Contact Charles Balchin, Managing Director

SMG TV Production
116 New Oxford Street, London WC1H 1HH
t 020 7663 2300
Contact Judy Counihan, Executive Producer

Smoking Dogs Films
26 Shacklewell Lane, London E8 2EZ
t 020 7249 6644 **f** 020 7249 6655
e info@smokingdogfilms.com **w** www.smokingdogfilms.com
Contact David Lawson, Producer; J Akomfrah, Director; Lina Gopaul, Producer
Credits Stan Tracy The Godfather Of British Jazz (D); Riot (D); Goldie, When Saturn Returns (D); The Wonderful World of Louis Armstrong (D)

Softly Softly Productions Ltd
Bury Farm House, Pegsdon, Hitchin SG5 3LA
t 01582 883480 **f** 01582 883152
e j.softly@softlysoftlytv.com **w** www.softlysoftlytv.com
Contact Richard Faria, Director; Joanna Softly, Director

Soho Communications
2 Percy Street, London W1T 1DD
t 020 7637 5825 **f** 020 7436 9740 **m** 07850 867624
e sohocom@re-active.net **w** www.re-active.net
Contact Jon Staton, Managing Director

Solo Films Ltd
1 Abbotswood Road, London SW16 1AJ
t 020 8769 2192 **f** 020 8677 4274 **m** 07949 151295
e solofilms@hotmail.com **w** www.solofilms.co.uk
Credits Small Time Obsession (F)

Somethin Else Sound Directions Ltd
Unit 1-4, 1A Old Nichol Street, London E2 7HR
t 020 7613 3211 **f** 020 7739 9799 **w** www.somethin-else.com
Contact Jez Nelson, Director; Bruce Hepton, Head of Television; Delilah Seale
Credits Pioneers (T); The Bug Detectives (T); London Jazz Festival 2002 (T); Free Will And Testament: Robert Wyatt Story (T)

South Street Productions Ltd
11 South Street, Harborne, Birmingham B17 0DB
t 0121 603 0071 **f** 0121 603 0071 **e** southstreet1@aol.com
Contact Richard Patching, Executive Producer
Credits One Lump Or Two? (T); Science Of Beauty (T); Outback Odyssey (T); Tasting Australia (T)

The Special Treats Production Company
96-98 Camden High Street, London NW1 0LT, Turkey
t 020 7387 4838 **f** 020 7529 8969
e thosenicepeople@specialtreats.co.uk
w www.specialtreats.co.uk
Contact Colin Burrows, Managing Director
Credits Shaken & Stirred... On Ice (D); The Navajo Codetalkers (D); Script To Screen (D)

Specific Films
25 Rathbone Street, London W1T 1NQ
t 020 7580 7476 **f** 020 7494 2676 **e** info@specificfilms.com
Contact Michael Hamlyn, Managing Director

Spellbound Productions
90 Cowdenbeath Path, London N1 0LG
t 020 7713 8066 **f** 020 7713 8067 **e** phspellbound@hotmail.com
Contact Paul Harris, Producer

Spice Factory
81 The Promenade, Peacehaven, Brighton BN10 8LS
t 01273 585275 **t** 01273 585304 **e** info@spicefactoty.co.uk
Contact Emily Kyriakides, Films Co-ordinator; Alex Marshall, Head of Business Affairs
Credits Angel For May (F); $teal (F); Bollywood Queen (F); Plots With A View (F)

Spire Films Ltd
7 High Street, Kidlington OX5 2DH
t 01865 371979 **f** 01865 371962 **e** mail@spirefilms.co.uk
Contact David Willcock, Director; Linda Flanigan, Diretcor
Credits Extreme Terrain; Fact or Fiction; Delia's How to Cook

Spirit Dance UK
30 Percy Street, London W1T 2DB
t 020 7813 3700 **f** 020 7813 3701
e admin@spiritdanceuk.com **w** www.spiritdanceuk.com
Contact Jonathan Insanally, Head of Spirit Dance UK

Sportshows Television Ltd
60 Parsons Green Lane, Fulham, London SW6 4HU
t 020 7731 4242 **f** 020 7731 4204
e info@sportshowstv.com **w** www.sportshowstv.com
Contact Clifford Webb, Chairman; Stuart Page, Director; Andrew Thornley, Sales and Marketing Manager
Credits PWA Windsurf World Tour (T); Wild Spirits (T); World Yachting (T)
Leading edge sports specialists in yachting, watersports and extreme sports.

Sportsweb
19 Heol y Delyn, Lisvane, Cardiff CF14 0SR
t 02920 2759 854 **f** 029 2066 4800 **m** 07721 834165
e martynwms@aol.com
Contact Martyn Williams, Executive Producer

Squeeze Productions Ltd
8 Flitcroft Street, London WC2H 8DJ
t 020 7010 7803 **f** 020 7010 7801
e info@squeezeproductions.com
Contact Maggie Swinfen, Production Manager; Nicci Crowther, Producer
Credits Are You Being Served (D); Power Of Choice (D); Energy (E)

John St Clair
Southacott Farm, Bratton Fleming, Barnstaple EX31 4TL

Stagescreen Productions
12 Upper Saint Martin's Lane, London WC2H 9DL
t 020 7497 2510 **f** 020 7497 2208 **e** stagescreenprods@aol.com
Contact Jeffery Taylor, Chief Executive Officer; Carolyn Jordan, Development Executive; Shailish Gor, Business Affairs; John Segal, Development Executive
Credits What's Cooking? (F); Foreign Affairs (T); Where Angels Fear To Tread (T); A Handful Of Dust (F)

Stagestruck Productions
Stowe March, Barnet Lane, Elstree WD6 3RQ
t 020 8953 8300 **f** 020 8905 1511 **m** 07000 227526
e simon.caplan@virgin.net
Contact Simon Caplan, CEO

Starlet Ltd
10 Morningside Park, Edinburgh EH10 5HB
t 0131 446 0011 **e** starlet@tinyonline.co.uk

Starnite
55 Heathlands, Swaffham PE37 7TG
t 01760 720140 **f** 01760 720140 **m** 07768 660524
e jake@jacee.demon.co.uk
Contact John Clarke, Managing Director

Steel Spyda Ltd
98 Undley, Laken Heath IP27 9BY
t 01842 862 880 **f** 01842 862 875
e office@steelspyda.com **w** www.steelspyda.com

Stephen Gammond Associates
24 Telegraph Lane, Claygate KT10 0DU
t 01372 460674 **f** 01372 460674 **m** 07931 782424
e stephengammond@hotmail.com
Contact Stephen Gammond, Producer

Stephen Weeks Company
Penhow Film Studio, Penhow, Newport NP26 3AD
t 01633 400 800 **f** 01633 400 990 **m** 07970 400800
e castles@compuserve.com
Contact Stephanie Cave, Secretary

Sterling Pictures
28 Goodge Street, London W1P 1FG
t 020 7323 6810 **f** 020 7323 6811
e admin@sterlingpictures.com **w** www.sterlingpictures.com
Contact Tedi De Toledo, Producer; Michael Riley, Producer
Credits Out Of Depth (F); Loop (F); In A Land Of Plenty (T); Lava (F)

Steve Orme Productions
1 Seaton Close, Mickleover, Derby DE3 0QH
t 01332 514616 **f** 01332 514616 **e** steve@steveorme.freeserve.co.uk
Contact Steve Orme, Managing Director

Steve Walsh Productions Ltd
78 Fieldview, London SW18 3HF
t 020 7223 6070 **f** 020 7924 7461 **e** steve@steve-walsh.com
Contact Steve Walsh, Managing Director; Wendy Wolfcarius, Head of Development
Credits Howdi Gaudi (A); The Intruder (F); A Monkey's Tale (A)

Stewart Mackay Associates
7 Tutton Hill, Colerne, Chippenham SN14 8DN
t 01249 712302 **f** 01249 701987 **m** 07974 315806
e stewart_mackay@btinternet.com
Contact Stewart MacKay, Manager
Credits Microsoft UK (I); Trials Of Mice (D); Waiting For A Killer (T); Fowld's In The Landscape (D)

Stirling Film & Television Productions Ltd
137 University Street, Belfast BT7 1HP
t 028 9033 3848 **f** 028 9043 8644
e alison@stirlingtelevision.com
Contact Jackie Newell, Producer/Director; Anne Stirling, Managing Director; Declan McCann, Editor; Lorainne McCotter, Producer/Director; Alison Auld, Production Manager; Grainne McColter, Producer/Director
Credits South City Beat (D); The Casualty (D); Sales Of The Century (D); Probable Cause (D)

Stiwdio Capel Mawr
Capel Mawr, Llanrug, Caernarfon LL55 4AE
t 01286 678102 **f** 01286 678102
Contact Dyfan Roberts, Producer; Angela Roberts, Head Of Development/Director
Credits The Adventures Of Ginny May (T); The Heather Mountain (F)

Storm Film Productions Ltd
32-34 Great Marlborough Street, London W1V 1HA
t 020 7439 1616 **f** 020 7439 4477
e sophie.storm@btclick.com **w** www.stormfilm.tv
Contact Sophie Inman, Production Manager

Storyland Productions
217 Brook Street, Broughty Ferry, Dundee DD5 2AG
t 01382 731188 **f** 01382 737738 **m** 07866 04640176
e mail@storyland.co.uk **w** www.storyland.co.uk
Contact David Evans, CEO; Vic Qinn, Director of Corporate Development; Joe Austen, Director
Credits Music And Moonlight (A)

Straight Forward Film & Television Productions Ltd
Ground Floor, Crescent House, 14 High Street, Holywood BT18 9AZ, Ireland
t 028 9042 6298 **t** 9065 1010 **f** 028 9042 3384
m 07831 189892 **e** enquiries@sforward.prestel.co.uk
Contact Joy Hines, Production Manager; John Nicholson, Managing Director
Credits A La Carte (E); Gift Of The Gab (E); Awash With Colour (E)

Strawberry Blonde Productions
47A Barnsbury Street, Islington, London N1 1TP
t 020 7689 8348 **f** 020 7689 8348 **m** 07961 129001
e gary@strawblonde.co.uk
Contact Gary McDonagh, Director/Producer
Credits Living With The Klan (D); VH1 100 Greatest Albums (T)

Strawberry Productions
36 Priory Avenue, London W4 1TY
t 020 8994 4494 **f** 020 8742 7675 **e** strawprod1@aol.com
Contact John Black, Managing Director

Stream Films Ltd
58 Kensington Church Street, London W8 4DB
f 08701 242253
e streamfilms@hotmail.com **w** www.reelplay.com/streamfilms
Contact Elena Lario, Director; Alejandro Gutierrez de Lario
Credits My Baby (S); Piece Of Cake (F); Nigel The Plonker (S); The Three Ages Of Crime (F)

Studio 13 Ltd
Unit 7, Liberty Centre, Mount Pleasant, Wembley HA0 1TX
t 020 8795 5413 **f** 020 8795 4613 **m** 07711 329576
e studio13@easynet.co.uk **w** www.studio13ltd.com
Contact Rekha Singh, Director; Amrit Basran, Director

Studio Alba
54A Seaforth Road, Stornoway HS1 2SD
t 01851 701125 **f** 01851 701094 **m** 07740 785193
e info@studioalba.com **w** www.studioalba.com
Contact Willie Macleod, Facilities Manager

Studio Arts Television Ltd
35 Larkspur Terrace, Jesmond, Newcastle-upon-Tyne NE2 2DT
m 07779 204036 **e** studioartstv@blueyonder.co.uk
Contact Trevor Hearing, Managing Director
Credits Willy's World (D); The Duchess And The Garden (D)

Studio Capel Mawr Ltd
Stiwdio Capel Mawr, Llanrug LL55 4AE
t 01286 678102 **f** 01286 678102 **m** 07880 714051
e capelmawr@talk21.com
Contact Dyfan Roberts, Company Director
Credits Angela Roberts (Waiter), The Heather Mountain (W); The Adventures of Sinny May (T); Stories in the Stones (D); The Heather Mountain (T)

Sugar Productions Ltd
12-28 Wood Lane, London
t 020 8746 7771
e info@sugarproductions.co.uk **w** www.sugarproductions.co.uk

Sunset & Vine North
Rushmere Lodge, Arthington Lane, Pool-in-Wharfedale, Leeds LS21 1JZ
t 0113 284 2400 **m** 07788 581154
e nicklord@sunsetvine.co.uk **w** www.sunsetvine.co.uk
Contact Nick Lord, Senior Producer

Sunset & Vine Productions
30 Sackville Street, London SW14 8NY
t 020 7478 7300 **f** 020 7478 7403 **w** www.sunsetvine.co.uk
Contact John Leach, Managing Director; Nick Vance, Head of Library Sales; Simon Potter, Senior Producer; Olly Slot, Head of Production; Tania Alexander, Senior Producer; Ian Sollors, Senior Producer
Credits Kerrang! Awards (T); Sport On 5 (T); Gillette World Sport (T); Channel 4 Cricket (T)

Sunset+Vine
30 Sackville Street, London W1S 3DY
t 020 7478 7300 **f** 020 7478 7407
e sandv@sunsetvine.co.uk **w** www.sunsetvine.co.uk
Contact John Leach, Managing Director; Olivia Slot, Head of Production; Nick Vance, Library Sales; Tania Alexander, Executive Producer, Music Box
Credits Toyota World Of Wildlife (T); Gillette World Sport (T); Sport On Five (T); Channel 4 Cricket (T)

Sunset+Vine is a world leader in sports programme production and international advertiser-supplied programming, producing over 2000 hours of television every year for around 250 broadcasters. Our subsidiary Music Box produces music and children's programmes for UK and international broadcasters and has one of the UK's largest libraries of interviews and clips.

Sunstone Films
36 Maryon Mews, London NW3 2PU
t 020 7431 0353
e sunstonefilms@aol.com **w** www.eremite.demon.co.uk
Contact Alan Ereira, Director

Supervision Ltd
92 Addington Village Road, Croydon CR0 5AQ
t 020 8251 9500 **f** 020 8251 9501 **m** 07831 606352
e chas@supervision.co.uk
Contact Charles Marriott, Director/Producer

Sweet Child Films
10 Richmond Road, Brighton BN2 3RN
t 01273 673171 **f** 01273 673172 **m** 07808 928485
e sweet@dircon.co.uk
Contact Amanda Lloyd, Producer
Credits Whoosh (S); eMale (S); The King (F); Dad Savage (F)

Table Top Productions
1 The Orchard, London W4 1JZ
t 020 8994 1269 **f** 020 8994 1269 **m** 07808 401999
e berry@tabletopproductions.com **w** www.tabletopproductions.com

Taft Television Associates
49 Eland Road, London SW11 5JX
t 020 7223 0906 **f** 020 7223 8530
Contact Alma Taft, Producer/Director

Tailor-Made Films
Unit 17, Waterside, 44-48 Wharf Road, London N1 7UX
t 020 7566 0280 **f** 020 7253 1117
e info@tailormadefilms.net **w** www.tailormadefilms.net
Contact Althea Doyley, Office Manager

Talent Television Ltd
1st Floor, MWB Business Exchange, 77 Oxford Street, London W1D 2ES
t 020 7659 2017 **f** 020 7659 2188
e entertainment@talenttv.com **w** www.talenttv.com
Contact John Cooper, Creative Director; Tony Humphreys, Managing Director; Hana Canter, Head of Production; Pete Ward, Head of Development
Credits Test The Nation (T); TV Scrabble (T); The Villa (T)

Talisman Films Limited
5 Addison Place, London W11 4RJ
t 020 7603 7474 **f** 020 7602 7422
e email@talismanfilms.com **w** www.talismanfilms.com
Contact Richard Jackson, Director; Andrew Lawton, Associate Producer; Caroline Oulton, Head of Television; Harry Oulton, Head of Development
Credits Starhunter 2300 (T); Rob Roy (F); Where There's Smoke (T); Complicity (F)

Talisman Television
2 Garden Walk, Ashton-on-Ribble, Preston PR2 1DP
t 01772 720602 **f** 01772 720602 **m** 07944 855628
w www.talismantv.com
Contact Jason Karl, Creative Director; Diana Jarvis, Production Director; Norie Miles, Associate Producer; Simon Castle, Financial Director
Credits Terrortower! (T); Theatre Of The Strange (D); Haunted Homes (T); Spectre Inspectors (T)

Talkback Productions
20-21 Newman Street, London W1T 1PG
e reception@talkback.co.uk **w** www.talkback.co.uk
Contact Peter Finchman, Chief Executive Officer; Sally Debonnaire, Managing Director
Credits I'm Alan Partridge (T); House Doctor (T); Brass Eye (T); Da Ali G Show (T)

Talking Heads Production Ltd
88-90 Crawford Street, London W1H 2BS
t 020 7258 6161 **f** 020 7258 6162 **m** 07778 354555
e info@talkingheadsproductions.com
w www.talkingheadsvoices.com
Contact Jennifer Taylor, Agent

Talking Pictures
45 Boston Road, Hanwell, London W7 3SH
t 020 8579 8444 **m** 07798 552539
e prod@media-studio.co.uk **w** www.media-studio.co.uk
Contact Satin Sohal, Director

Tall Order Productions Ltd

2 Greenfield Crescent, Birmingham B15 3BE
t 0121 456 2844
e tall-ord@tall-ord.co.uk **w** www.tallorderproductions.co.uk
Contact Robyn Woolston, Producer; Charles Nicklin, Director; Trish Putnam, Producer; Graham Thompson, Accounts; Milly Haddon, Production Assistant; Iolanda Vettese, Production Assistant; John Dixon, Director; Nick Birch, Producer; Ellie Barber, Production Administrator
Credits The Pitch (S); Shadow Of The Spitfire (F); Top Dog Of The Big Cats (D)

Tango Marketing & Management

2 Bradbrook House, Studio Place, Kinnerton Street, London SW1X 8EL
t 020 7235 6654 **f** 020 7823 1069
Contact Gill O'Neil

Tara Television

Studio 54, Grove Park, London SE5 8LE
t 020 7733 1806 **f** 020 7737 3901
e laurens@laurens.as **w** www.artsresidencies.com
Contact Laurens Postma, Director/Producer; Jane Gordon-Green, Director; Phillip Bartlett, Director
Credits Buskers Odyssey (T); Gummed Labels (T); Midnite Breaks (T)

Tartan Television

3-5 Torrens Street, London EC1V 1NQ
t 020 7278 9327 **f** 020 7278 9327

Taylored Productions Ltd

74 Victoria Crescent Road, Glasgow G12 9JN
t 0141 579 0500 **t** 0141 579 0546 **f** 0141 579 0600
e elly-tayloredpl@bigfoot.com
Contact Elly Taylor, Producer/Director
Credits Through Hell And High Water (D)

Technobabble

110-116 Elmore Street, London N1 3AH
t 020 7288 1116 **f** 020 7288 1119 **m** 07973 823801
e info@technobabble.demon.co.uk
Contact Jes Benstock, Director
Credits SK8N16 (D); Heroes Of Coke (W); Phosphenes (A)

Teledu Elidir

Alexander House, Excelsior Road, Cardiff CF14 3TD
t 02920 610555 **f** 02920 611555 **e** elidir@celtic.co.uk
Contact G Pritchard, Managing Director; Emlyn Davies, Company Chairman
Credits Cameleon (F); The Magic Microscope (T); Dechrau Canu, Dechrau Canmol (T); Adrenalin (T)

Teledu Seiont

Moria, Penrallt Isaf, Caernarfon LL55 1NS
t 01286 677595 **f** 01286 660874
e seiont@gwynedd.net **w** www.gwynedd.net/seiont/
Contact Loan Roberts

Teledu Tri Television

Scimitar Court, Cardiff Road, Taffs Well, Cardiff CF4 7RF
t 029 2089 0581 **f** 029 2081 1012
Contact Arwel Owen, Chairman/Producer

Telescope Pictures Ltd

Twickenham Film Studios, St Margarets, Twickenham TW1 2AW
t 020 8607 8875 **f** 020 8607 8879
e justinredtern@saqnet.co.uk
Contact Simon Bosanquet, Producer

The Television Corporation

30 Sackville Street, London W1S 3DY
t 020 7478 7300 **f** 020 7478 7407
e tvcorp@tvcorp.co.uk **w** www.televisioncorporation.co.uk
Contact George Carey, Director of Programmes; Tom Gutteridge, Creative Director; Martin Anderson, Director of Facilities; Jeff Foulser, Chief Executive

The Television Corporation is the UK's leading independent supplier of programmes to broadcasters worldwide. The group combines two of the UK's top production companies, Mentorn and Sunset+Vine, with the UK's premier facilities companies Visions and Molinare. The Group is also a world leader in creating, producing and distributing television formats and advertiser funded programming.

Credits: see listings for Mentorn, Sunset+Vine, The Television Corporation International Division, Visions and Molinare"

Television In Europe

33 Chester Close South, London NW1 4JG
t 020 7935 0984 **f** 020 7935 0984
Contact David Goldstrom, Executive Producer
Credits Weightlifting Champions, World & Europe (T); World Canoe Slacom Championships (T); Alpine and Nordic World Cup Skiing Host Broadcaster (T); Burchley Horse Trials (T)

Tempest Films Ltd

33 Brookfield, Highgate West Hill, London N6 6AT
t 020 8340 0877 **f** 020 8340 9309 **m** 07808 294808
e mail@temp-films.demon.co.uk
Contact Jacky Stoller, Managing Director
Credits Beck (T); Bliss (T); At Home With The Braithwaites (T); Rockface - Series I (T)

Ten-Alps Events

10 Blue Lion Place, Long Lane, Bermondsey, London SE1 4PU
t 020 7089 3686 **f** 020 7089 3696 **w** www.tenalps.com
Contact Timothy Spencer, Managing Director

Tenth Planet Productions

75 Woodland Gardens, London N10 3UD
t 020 8442 2659 **f** 020 8883 1708 **m** 07989 556075
e admin@tenthplanetproductions.com
w www.tenthplanetproductions.com
Contact Alexander Holt, Executive and Artistic Director; Susie Harriet, Executive Producer; Alex Scrivenor, Associate Director; Rainer Wiseman, Associate Director; Lucie Barat, Associate Director; Rebecca Long, Production Developer; Mark Underwood, Literary Manager
Credits Rapunzel (F); The Warrior King (F)

Terebi.Biz Ltd

21 York Mansions, 84 Chiltern Street, London W1U 5AL
m 07799 194737 **e** mail@terebi.biz **w** www.terebi.biz
Contact Tara Duffy, Executive Producer; Asif Zubairy, Executive Producer
Credits Roxy Music At The Apollo (M); Everyman (D)

Tern Television Productions Ltd

73 Crown Street, Aberdeen AB11 6EX
t 01224 211123 **f** 01224 211199
e office@terntv.com **w** www.terntv.com
Contact Harry Bell, Director of Develoment for Glasgow; David Strachan, Joint Managing Director; Gwyneth Hardy, Joint Managing Director
Credits Chancers (D); Mike Reid's Under Par (T); Weed It And Reap (T); Songs Of Praise (T)

Testimony Films

12 Great George Street, Bristol BS1 5RS
t 0117 925 8589 **f** 0117 925 7668
e mail@testimonyfilms.force9.co.uk
Contact Steve Humphries, Producer/Director
Credits The Real Tom Jones (T); BBC2 - Pocketful of Posies (D); Channel 4 - Married Love (D); ITV - Some Like It Hot (D)

Tetra Films Ltd

24 Stormont Road, London N6 4NP
t 020 8374 4553 **f** 020 8374 4553 **e** tetrafilms@blueyonder.co.uk **w** www.tetrafilms.demon.co.uk
Contact Alan Horrox, Executive Producer
Credits The Gift (T); What Katy Did (T); Treasure Seekers (T); Canterville Ghost (T)

That's A Wrap

Three Mills Studios, Three Mill Lane, London E3 3DU
t 020 8215 3373 **f** 020 8215 3421 **m** 07958 513495
e studio@thatsawrap.tv **w** www.thatsawrap.tv
Contact Daniel Backer, Producer; Robert Taylor, Scriptwriter; Samantha Tait, Producer/Director; Sigh Jones, Creative Director
Credits The Women's Freemasons (I); The Camden Jobtrain (E); Investors In People (I); The Dairy Council (E)

Thin Man Films

9 Greek Street, London W1D 4DQ
t 020 7734 7372 **f** 020 7287 5228
Contact Deborah Read, Director
Credits Secrets and Lies (F); Topsy -Turvy (F); All for Nothing (F)

Third Eye Productions

33 Gloucester Road, Kew, Richmond, London W10 5BN
t 020 8940 9062 **f** 020 8940 9062
e kerry@thirdeye.demon.co.uk **w** www.thirdeye.demon.co.uk
Contact Kerry McKinnell, Production Co-ordinator

Third Rail Films

41 Granville Road, Wood Green, London N22 5LP
t 020 8889 2420 **f** 020 8889 2420
e peter@corley46.freeserve.co.uk
Contact Elizabeth Adams, Producer; Peter Corley, Producer
Credits Dead On The Money (F); Eddy And The Bear (A); Last Orders (F); King's Beard (A)

Those People

Sophia House, 28 Cathedral Road, Cardiff CF11 9LJ
t 029 2066 0123 **f** 029 2066 4891
e office@thosepeople.co.uk **w** www.thosepeople.co.uk
Contact Neil Wagstaff, Director, Producer; Jason King, Director, Producer
Credits Fingal's Rule (S); Ellen (S); D48 NNY (S); All My Mum's Friends Must Be Dead (S)

Thrilanfere

33 Diamond Street, Saltburn TS12 1EB
t 0128 762 6988 **f** 020 8542 9798 **m** 07810 344644
e et_thrilanfere@onetel.net
Contact Elaine Taylor, Producer; Mark Elliott, Director

Tiger Aspect Productions

7 Soho Street, London W1D 3DQ
t 020 7434 6751 **f** 020 7434 1903 **e** tigeraspect@tigeraspect.co.uk
Contact Peter Bernett Jones, Chairman; Charles Brand, Joint Managing Director; Andrew Zein, Managing Director; Grey Brenman, Head of Drama; Paul Sommers, Head of Factual; Claudia Lloyd, Head of Animation; Clive Tullon, Head of Comedy
Credits Mr Bean The Animated Series (A); Swiss Toni (T); Howard Goodall's Great Dates (T); Teachers (T)

Tilling Productions

12 Park Place, Newdigate Road, Harefield UB9 6EJ
t 01895 824022 **f** 01895 824026 **m** 07798 803240
e info@tillingproductions.com **w** www.tillingproductions.com
Contact Michael Gold, Business Development; Ed Swatman, Producer; Chris Tilling, Director, Director

Tinopolis

Park Street, Llanelli SA15 3YE
t 01554 880880 **f** 01554 880881
e info@tinopolis.com **w** www.tinopolis.com
Contact Rhodri Williams; Alan Morgans, Head of Interactive; Glymnog Davis, Group Director; Adam Salkeld, Head Of Programmes

Tonfedd Eryri

Hen Ysgol Aberpwll, Bangor Road, Y Felinheli LL56 4JS
t 01248 671167 **f** 01248 671172 **m** 07831 251253
e swyddfa@tonfedd-eryri.com **w** www.tonfedd-eryri.com
Contact Norman Williams, Director; Hefin Elis, Director

Tony Kaye Productions

33 Tottenham Street, London W1P 9PE
t 020 7025 7542 **f** 020 7323 1711 **e** info@tonyk.ltd.uk
Contact Ron Holbrooke, Executive Producer
Credits Reebok - Time Out (C); Volvo - Twister (C); Dunlop - Unexpected (C); British Rail - Relax (C)

Topical Television

Radcliffe Road, Southampton SO14 0PS
t 023 8071 2233 **f** 023 8033 9835 **e** topical@topical.co.uk
Contact Diana Saggers, Production Manager
Credits Ridgeriders (T); Tell it to Me Straight (T); City Hospital (T)

Torpedo Ltd

91A Beulah Road, Rhiwbina, Cardiff CF14 6LW
t 029 2076 6117 **f** 029 2076 6116
e info@torpedoltd.co.uk **w** www.torpedoltd.co.uk
Contact Ceri Wyn Richards, Director; Mark Jones, Director
Credits Sea Stories (T); Jigsaw (T); Speak For Yourself (T)

Torque Media
Tel: 0044 (0) 1536 771 768

Torque Media

The Old Post Office, Main Street, Rockingham LE16 8TG
t 01536 771768 **f** 01536 772220
e admin@torquemedia.com **w** www.torquemedia.com
Contact David Harmon

Touch Productions Ltd

The Malthouse Studios, Donhead St Mary, Shaftesbury SP7 9DN
t 01747 828030 **f** 01747 828004
e enquiries@touchproductions.co.uk
w www.touchproductions.co.uk
Contact Malcolm Brinkworth, Managing Director; Erica Wolfe-Murray, Producer; Hilary Daniels, Production Co-ordinator; Denise Guest, Production Manager
Credits The Life Of A Ten Pound Note (T); Afghan Warrior - The Life And Death Of Abdul Hag (T); Simon's Heroes (T)

Trademark Films

Phoenix Theatre, 110 Charing Cross Road, London WC2H 0JP
t 020 7240 5585 **f** 020 7240 5586
e mail@trademarkfilms.co.uk
Contact Cleone Clarke, Assistant Producer; Karen Katz, Head of Development; David Parfitt, Producer
Credits The Madness Of King George (F); The Wings Of The Dove (F); Shakespeare In Love (F); I Capture The Castle (F)

TransAtlantic Films

Cabalva Studios, Whitney-on-Wye HR3 6EX
t 01497 831800 f 01497 831808
Contact Revel Guest, President; Cath Jones, Contact; Corisande Albert, Managing Director
Credits Science Of Sleep And Dreams (D); Legends Of The Living Dead (D); Extreme Body Parts II (D)

Transatlantic Films Production & Distribution Ltd

Studio 1, 3 Brackenbury Road, London W6 0BE
t 020 8735 0505 f 020 8735 0605
e mail@transatlanticfilms.com w www.transatlanticfilms.com
Contact Revel Guest, President; Corisande Albert, Managing Director
Credits 2025 (D); The Science Of Life (D); Legends Of The Living Dead (D); Extreme Body Parts (D)

Transmedia Pictures

Stowe March, Barnet Lane, Elstree WD6 3RQ
t 020 8953 8300 f 020 8905 1511 m 07000 227526
e simon.caplan@virgin.net
Contact Simon Caplan, CEO

Tricorn Associates

11 Wellesley Road, Chiswick, London W4 4BS
t 020 8995 3898 f 020 8747 8488 m 07736 601727
e ebennett@dircon.co.uk

True Vision

49A Oxford Road South, Chiswick, London W4 3DD
t 020 8742 7852 f 020 8742 7853
Contact Brian Edwards, Director and Head of Programmes

Tu Meke Productions Ltd

Apartment 1/2, 19 Westminster Terrace, Glasgow G3 7RU
t 0141 248 1852 f 0141 248 1852 m 07769 670093
e mail@tu-meke.com w www.tu-meke.com
Contact Andrew Hunt, Director/Producer
Credits Mandancin' (F); The Tartan Pimpernel (D); The Jesus Story (T); JFP (S)

Tubedale Films

Barley Mow Centre, 10 Barley Mow Passage, Chiswick, London W4 4PH
t 020 8994 6477 f 020 8995 0896 m 07711 656659
e films@tubedale.co.uk
Contact Carl Clifton
Credits L'Homme Du Train (F)

Tumbleweed Productions

35D Onslow Road, Richmond TW10 6QH
t 020 8948 3804 f 020 8948 3804
e info@tumble-weed.tv w www.tumble-weed.tv
Contact Jo Keaney, Contact; Elise Keusch, Contact

Turn On Televison Ltd

Warehouse 4, 121 Princess Street, Manchester M1 7AG
t 0161 247 7700 f 0161 247 7711
e mail@turnontv.co.uk w www.turnontv.co.uk
Contact Alison Higgins, Head of Production; Phil Niland, Head of Development; Angela Smith, Managing Director
Credits The Gym (T); When I Grow Up (T); Special Delivery (T); Tourist Police (T)

TV 6 Ltd

Unit 24, The Quadrangle, 49 Atalanta Street, London SW6 6TU
t 020 7610 0266 f 020 7610 1466 w www.tv6.co.uk
Contact Richard Reisz, Managing Director; Lesley Cherry, Head of Production

TWI

McCormack House, Burlington Lane, Chiswick, London NW2 5LT
t 020 8233 5300 f 020 8233 5301
e plewin@imgworld.com w www.imgworld.com
Contact Paula Lewin, Personal Assistant
Credits British Empire In Colour (D); Christopher Reeves (D); Sportaid: Superstars (T); Ryder Cup 2002 (T)

Award winning sports, F&E television production company, offering worldwide distribution and rights representation. Specialists in made-for-TV events, documentaries, highlights packages, live coverage, home video, inflight, multimedia and sponsorship.

Two Rivers Partnership

1st Floor, 13-14 Golden Square, London W1F 9JF
t 020 7287 9888 f 020 7434 9148
e info@tworivers.co.uk w www.tworivers.co.uk
Contact David Parvin, Proprieter
Credits Horrible Histories (C); Strepsils Sharp (C)

Two Sides TV

53A Brewer Street, London W1F 9UH
t 020 7439 9882 f 020 7287 2289 e info@twosidestv.co.uk
Contact Catherine Robins, Managing Director; Tracy Cooke, Production Manager
Credits Insect Antics (T); Little Antics (T); Bug Alert! (T); The Fantastic Flying Journey (T)

Twofour Productions Ltd

Quay West Studios, Old Newnham, Plymouth PL7 5BH
t 01752 333900 f 01752 344224
e enq@twofour.co.uk w www.twofour.co.uk
Contact Charles Wace, Managing Director
Credits Reach For The Stars (T); Ginger Nation (T); Taming Toddlers (T); The City Gardener (T)

Tyro Films & Television Ltd

The Coach House, 20A Park Road, Teddington TW11 0AQ
t 020 8943 4697 f 020 8943 4901
Contact Simon Passmore, Producer
Credits Seventeen (S); Out of Hours (T); Imogen's Face (T); Pretending To Be Judith (T)

Uden Associates

Unit 37, Chelsea Wharf, Lots Road, London SW10 0QJ
t 020 7351 1255 f 020 7376 3937 w www.uden.com
Contact Michael Proudfoot, Creative Director

The UK Film & TV Production Company Plc

3 Colville Place, London W1T 2BH
t 020 7255 1650 e info@fudakowski.com
Contact Peter Fudakowski, Chief Executive Officer
Credits Bugs (F); Helen West Investigates (T); Trial By Fire (T); he Last September (F)

United Television Artists Ltd

15-17 St Cross Street, London EC1N 8UW
t 020 7831 4433 f 020 7831 6633
e uta@unitedtv.co.uk w www.unitedtv.co.uk/uta
Contact Bill Kerr Elliott, Director

Upfront Television Ltd

39-41 New Oxford Street, London WC1A 1BN
t 020 7836 7702 f 020 7836 7701 m 07973 839 126
e upfront@btinternet.com w www.celebritiesworldwide.com
Contact Richard Brecker, Joint Managing Director; Claire Nye, Joint Managing Director

Utopia Productions

33 Whitepit Lane, Wooburn Green HP10 9HR
t 01628 525500 f 01628 525673
e stuartchapman@btclick.com w www.utopiaproductions.co.uk
Contact Stuart Chapman, Creative Director

Vashca

Unit 13, Shepperton House, 93 Shepperton Road, London N1 3DF
t 020 7359 2688 e info@vashca.com
Credits The John Holmes Story (T); Harry Partch (T); Touch The Truck (T)

Velocity Optics Ltd

1/8 Waters' Close, Edinburgh EH6 6RB
f 0131 554 5240 m 07970 571928 m 07971 835190
e markb@velocityoptics.com w www.velocityoptics.com
Contact Mark Bender, Proprietor
Credits Spinning Disks (F); Frontier (F); Dark Continent (F); Here Comes Trouble (F)

TWI *Archive*

www.twiarchive.com

contact: TWI Archive, McCormack House, Burlington Lane, London W4 2TH
Togo Keynes, Commercial Director
Tel: +44 (0)20 8233 5500/5300   Fax: +44 (0)20 8233 5301/6476
E-mail: twiarchive@imgworld.com

Ventura Productions Ltd
PO Box 100, Knowle, Solihull B93 9WH
t 01564 776888 **f** 01564 772720
e paulcolbert@ventura-productions.co.uk
w www.ventura-productions.co.uk
Contact Karen Lamb, Creative Director; Paul Colbert, Managing Director
Credits The High Definition Story (l); The Golden Jubilee (T); Fab Pads (T); Diana's Rock, The Paul Burrel Story (D)

Vicarious Productions
92 York Mansions, Prince Of Wales Drive, London SW11 4BN
t 020 7622 9307 **f** 020 7640 9980 **e** vicariousprod@aol.com
Contact Yvonne Cayle, PA; Carol Harding, Managing Director

Video Arts
6-7 St Cross Street, London EC1N 8UA
t 020 7400 4800 **f** 020 7400 4900
e sales@videoarts.co.uk **w** www.videoarts.com
Contact Martin Addison, Learning Resource Director; Marissa Vercizza, Production Manager; Margaret Tree, Managing Director

The Video Crew Ltd
30 Sherbourne Avenue, Bristol BS32 8BB
t 0117 931 2712 **m** 07970 836177

Visage Productions
40 New Bond Street, London W15 2RX
t 020 7659 1140 **f** 020 7629 8785
e television@visagegroup.com **w** www.visagegroup.com
Contact Bob Clarke, Chairman

Visionaires
Flat 2, 9 Colville Terrace, London W11 2BE
t 020 7727 1030 **f** 020 7313 9595 **e** marysoan@aol.com
Contact Mary Soan, Director

Visions (Digital Outside Broadcasting) Ltd
t 020 7478 7289 **f** 020 7478 7107
e vickib@visions-ob.co.uk **w** www.visions-ob.com
Contact Vicki Betihavas, Director of Sales & Marketing

Visionworks TV Ltd
56 Donegall Pass, Belfast BT7 1BU
t 028 9024 1241 **f** 028 9024 1777
e production@visionworks.co.uk **w** www.visionworks.co.uk
Contact Alan Morton, Producer

Vista Films Ltd
55A Chesson Road, West Kensington, London W14 9QR
t 020 7368 0591 **f** 020 7368 0591 **m** 07941 685612
e vista.films@virgin.net
Contact Lisa Renee, Director; Dina Jacobsen, Director; Tracey Thomson, Director
Credits Contact (S); Suite For Three Oranges (S)

Viva Films Ltd
46 Cascade Avenue, London N10 3PU
t 020 8444 5064 **f** 020 8444 1074
e viva.films@dial.pipex.com
Contact John Goldschmidt, Director and Producer

production companies : film & tv

Vivum Intelligent Media

17 Scawfell Street, London E2 8NG
t 020 7729 2749 f 020 7684 8128 m 07971 543703
e info@vivum.net w www.vivum.net
Contact Nick Rosen, Director
Credits Radio 4 News & Current Affairs; Channel 4 News (T)

Volcanika Ltd

111 Midhurst Road, Ealing, London W5 4JD
t 020 8579 1872 e mail@volcanika.com
Contact Silvia Perett, Producer/Director
Credits My Daily Everest (E); Smooth (C); PG Tips Roadshow Video (C);
Planet Holiday (T)

Volcano Films

47 Woodsome Road, London NW5 1SA
t 020 7424 0146 f 020 7424 0143 e volcfilm@dircon.co.uk
Contact John Dollar

Vortex Media Ltd

107 Trundleys Road, Surrey Quays, London SE8 5BD
t 020 7237 8450 f 020 7394 9204
e mail@vortexmedia.demon.co.uk
w www.vortexmedia.demon.co.uk
Contact Nick McAlpine, Producer

VTV Ltd

30 Sackville Street, London W1S 3DY
t 020 7478 7300 t 020 7478 7391
f 020 7478 7415 m 07775 853944
e vtv@venner.tv w www.venner.tv
Contact Carolyn Viccari, Managing Director; Brian Venner, Chairman
Credits Winter Paralympics 2002 (T); Tour De Langkawi 2002 (T); All England
Open Badminton 2002 (T); Tour De France 2002 (T)

W3KTS

10 Portland Street, York YO31 7EH
t 01904 647822 f 08700 554863
m 07831 378107 e chris@w3kts.co.uk
Contact Chris Wood, Director

Wag TV

2D Leroy House, 436 Essex Road, London N1 3QP
t 020 7688 1711 f 020 7688 1702 e post@wagtv.com
Contact Martin Durkin, Managing Director; Angela Neenan, Development
Producer; Katherine Ainger, Finance Director; Steven Green, Head of Production;
Alex Bledzki, Head of Facilities
Credits Hidden Sex (D); The Road To Santiago; Devine Designs (D); Gods In The Sky (D)

Walkabout Film & Television

PO Box 6, Moreton Hampstead TQ13 8WA
t 01647 441075 m 07974 353932 e mark@walkabouttv.co.uk
Contact Mark Twittey, Director
Credits International Red Cross (D); Disney (E); Holiday On Ice (C); Transco (E)

Wall To Wall

8-9 Spring Place, London NW5 3ER
t 020 7485 7424 f 020 7267 5292 w www.walltowall.co.uk
Contact Gavin Rota, Head Of Development; Alex Wood, Development
Department Assistant
Credits New Tricks (T); Five Things I Hate About You (T); Salvage Squad (D);
The Edwardian Country House (D)

Walsh Bros Ltd

24 Redding House, Harlingen Street, King Henry's Wharf,
London SE18 5SR
t 020 8858 6870 t 020 8854 5557 f 020 8854 5557
m 07879 816426 e walshbros@lycosmail.com
Contact Maura Walsh, Head of Development; David Walsh, Head of Finance;
John Walsh, Director, Managing Director
Credits Liberace (F); Headhunting The Homeless (T); Trex II (D)

Wark Clements & Company Ltd

Studio 7, The Tollgate, 19 Marine Crescent, Glasgow G51 1HD
t 0141 429 1750 f 0141 429 1751
e info@warkclements.co.uk w www.warkclements.co.uk

Wash House Films

1 Thurlestone Court, Victoria Road, Dartmouth TQ6 9HF
t 01803 833826 f 01803 832570
e production@washouse.net w www.washouse.net
Contact Sam Usher, Director; Andrew Brown, Director
Credits The Real Cost Of Diamonds (T); Riders And Rich Kids - Series I & II (T);
Snowbombing 2003 (T)

Water on the Rock Ltd

WOTR Ltd, PO Box 20, Leeds LS8 2ZZ
t 0113 265 0881 f 0113 265 0881
e info@wotr.co.uk w www.wotr.co.uk
Contact Patricia Grant
Credits Rosetta - Prime Donna Assoluta (F); Kingdom (F)

Waterside Productions

Waterside House, 46 Gas Street, Birmingham B1 2JT
t 0121 633 3525 f 0121 633 0480 m 07973 321704
m 07941 450245 e naden@amserve.com
Contact David Naden, Director
Credits First Cuts (T); Nasty Neighbours (F)

Wellington Films Ltd

3B Wellington Square, Nottingham NG7 1NG
t 0115 847 9388 f 0115 845 0013 m 07971 425440
e info@wellingtonfilms.co.uk w www.wellingtonfilms.co.uk
Contact Al Clark, Producer; Rachel Robey, Producer
Credits Fat Girls (M); Hear No Evil (T); A Nice Little Earner (S); The High Life (T)

Wessex Films

57 Abbots Park, London Road, St Albans AL1 1TP
t 01727 852879 f 01727 845775 m 07808 914212
e darylbristow@waitrose.com
Contact Peter Dolman, Producer; Daryl Bristow, Producer

Whitehall Films

10 Lower Common South, London SW15 1BP
t 020 8785 3737 f 020 8788 2340
e mwhitehall@email.msn.com

The Wickes Company

10 Abbey Orchard Street, Westminster, London SW1P 2LD
t 020 7222 0820 f 020 7222 0822 e wickesco@aol.com
Contact Susan Davies, Production Assistant; Heide Wilsher, Production Executive

Wide Vision Productions

87 Elm Park Mansions, Park Walk, London SW10 0AP
t 020 7352 1770 e rgbshepherd@msn.com

Wild Gaze Films

53 Greek Street, London W1D 3DR
t 734 7065 f 734 4250 e kate@wildgaze.co.uk
Contact Finola Dwyer, Producer/Company Director; Amanda Posey,
Producer/Company Director; Kate McCullagh, Assistant
Credits Fever Pitch (F)

Wild Productions

Randalls Farm House, Randalls Road, Leatherhead KT22 0AL
t 01372 079069 f 01372 375183 m 07836 635 269
e mail@wildproductions.co.uk w www.wildproductions.co.uk
Contact Simon Cowell, Director

Wildcat Films

Windy Hall, Alston CA9 3NJ
t 01434 381067 m 07802 406334
e mail@wildcatfilms.biz w www.wildcatsfilms.biz
Contact David Baillie, Managing Director
Credits Desert Geordies (D); Wildlife Cop (D); Angel Passes By (S); Vivid (S)

Windfall Films

1 Underwood Row, London N1 7LZ
t 020 7251 7676 f 020 7253 8468
e enquiries@windfallfilms.com w www.windfallfilms.com
Contact Kristina Obradovic, Head of Production
Credits Marrying A Stranger (T); Dam Busters (T); Commandos (T)

Windrush Productions Ltd/OOM

7 Woodlands Road, Moseley, Birmingham B13 4EH
t 0121 449 6439 **f** 0121 449 6439 **m** 07977 059378
e beboyyaa@hotmail.com
Contact Pogus Caesar, Executive Producer/Director; Emma Jeffares, Production Assistant/Researcher
Credits An Eye On X (S); Drumbeat (T); Forward Ever Backward Never (S); Xpress (T)

Winklemania Productions

Cromwell House, Cromwell Park, Chipping Norton OX7 5SR
t 01608 644444 **f** 01608 641722
e info@winklemania.net **w** www.winklemania.net
Contact Mark Iddon, Creative Director; Ellis Iddon, Managing Director; Phil Meagher, Managing Director
Credits Back To Sherwood (T); The Adventures Of Shirley Holmes (T); I love Mummy (T)

Wobbly Picture Productions

75 Engadine Street, London SW18 5BZ
t 020 8870 6369 **f** 020 8488 8479 **e** mail@wobbly.co.uk
Contact Mary Fourt, Producer/Director; John A Parry, Director
Credits University Choice (T); Ramp (W); Student Choice (D); Student Essentials (T)

Wonder Stuff Productions Ltd

48 St Peter's Street, Syston, Leicester LE7 1HJ
t 0116 260 3794 **f** 0116 260 3794 **m** 07980 669607
e louise@wonderstuffproductions.com
w www.wonderstuffproductions.com
Contact Louise Christie, Company Director/Producer; Graeme Christie, Company Secretary
Credits Hertfordshire Fire And Rescue Service (W); Farley On Farley (D); Sundissential (M); Sainsbury's (I)

Woodline Films

West Normanhurst, The Common, Cranleigh GU6 8NS
t 01483 271644 **f** 01483 271866 **m** 07770 233364
e glinwood@globalnet.co.uk
Contact Terry Glinwood
Credits The Pillow Book (F); Eight And A Half Women (F); Superstition (F)

Working Title Films

Oxford House, 76 Oxford Street, London W1D 1BS
t 020 7307 3000 **f** 020 7307 3002
Contact Eric Fellner, Co-chairman; Tim Bevan, Co-chairman
Credits The Guru (F); To Kill A King (F); The Man Who Wasn't There (F)

World of Wonder

40 Chelsea Wharf, Lots Road, London SW10 0QJ
t 020 7349 9000 **f** 020 7349 9777
e wow@worldofwonder.net **w** www.worldofwonder.net
Contact Helen Booth, Head of Production
Credits Party Monster (S); The Double Life of Jonathan King (T); Andy Warhol - The Complete Picture (T)

The Write Good Corporation Ltd

PO Box 204, Romsey SO51 6WB
t 01794 885801 **f** 01794 884747
e media@writegood.tv **w** www.writegood.tv
Contact Mikaela Bell, Head Of Production; Richard Digance, Chairman

X'cel FilmFabrik United

Studio 10, Church Studios, Camden Park Road, London NW1 9AY
t 020 7482 7200
e xcelfilmfabrik@aol.com **w** www.xcelsoundfabrik.com
Contact Alastair Gordon Scott, Director - Regisseur; Jenny Niehoff, Director's Assistant; Claudia Jakob, Producer
Credits Style (T)

XYTV Ltd

Anstey House, 40 Hanover Square, Leeds LS3 1BQ
t 0113 275 9835 **f** 0113 234 1456 **m** 07831 412154
e mail@xytvltd.co.uk
Contact Diane Myers, Producer/Director; Rachael Surtees, Head of Production; Rob Pendlebury, Head of Development; Beverley Doyle, MD/Producer
Credits American Vampires (T); Partners in Crime (T); The Alternative Christmas Message 2001 (T)

Y2K Film Productions Ltd

25 Cole Park Road, Twikenham TW1 1HP
t 020 8892 4505 **f** 020 8287 6589
m 07956 384682 **e** y2k@tuohy.co.uk
Contact Ken Tuohy, Producer
Credits Puckoon (F)

York Films of England

1 Chapel Court, Borough High Street, London SE1 1HH
t 020 7403 2721 **f** 002 7403 3494
e office@yorkfilms.com **w** www.yorkfilms.com
Contact David Taylor, Managing Director
Credits Spacefiles - The A-Z Of The Universe (T); Nobel's Greatest Hits (T); Stargazing (T)

Yorkshire Television

The Television Centre, Kirkstall Road LS3 1JS
t 0113 243 8283 **f** 0113 244 5107 **w** www.granadamedia.com
Contact Sasha Savage

Yorkshire Television Resources

The Television Centre, Leeds LS3 1JS
t 0113 243 8283 **f** 0113 245 4319
e jim.richardson@granadamedia.com
w www.yorkshire-television.tv
Contact John Surtees, General Manager; Peter Rogers, General Manager; Jim Richardson, Head of Sales and Planning
Credits Heartbeat (T); The League Of Gentlemen (T); Where The Heart Is (T)

YoYo Films & Tara Television

Studio, 54 Grove Park, London SE5 8LE
t 020 7737 3901 **f** 020 7737 3901 **m** 07855 303199
e yoyofilms@aol.com **w** www.laurens2000.com
Contact Janet Green, producer; Philip Bartlett, Producer; Laurens Postma, Managing Director
Credits Maqbarl (F); The Journey (D); The Snow (T); The Girls (M)

Zanzibar Film Productions Ltd

52 North Poulner Road, Ringwood BH24 3LS
t 01425 472892 **f** 01425 472892
e zanzibarfilms@aol.com **w** www.zanzibarfilms.com
Contact Matt Dickinson, Director; Chris Bradley, Producer
Credits Cloud Cuckoo Land (F); High Trails to Istanbul (D); Shetland Oil Disaster (I); Sheba's Greatest Treasure (D)

Zebra Film Productions Ltd

4 Leigh Road, Clifton, Bristol BS8 2DA
t 0117 970 6026 **f** 0117 973 6866 **e** info@zebrafilms.co.uk
Contact Richard Matthews, Managing Director
Credits The Natural World: Wild Indonesia (D); The Natural World: Octopus Hunter (D); Golden Seals Of The Skeleton Coast (D); Snake Hunter (D)

Zenith Corporate Communications Ltd

41 Balham High Road, London SW12 9AN
t 020 8675 4455 **f** 020 8673 9585 **e** info@zenith.co.uk
Contact Deborah Roslund, Managing Director

Zenith Entertainment Ltd

43-45 Dorset Street, London W1U 7NA
t 020 7224 2440 **f** 020 7224 1027
e general@zenith-entertainment.co.uk
w www.zenith-entertainment.co.uk
Contact Sarah Howie, Production Co-ordinator; Ivan Rendall, Director, Managing Director; Adrian Bate, Head of Film & Drama; Julian Scott, Head of Children's Drama & Animation; Alan Ravenscroft, Head of Features & Adult Education; Ed Braman, Executive Producer, Factual Programmes
Credits Two Thousand Acres Of Sky (T); Garden Rivals (T); SMTV (T); Byker Grove (T)

Zephyr Films

48A Goodge Street, London W1T 4LX
t 020 7255 3555 **f** 020 7255 3777 **m** 07768 270513
e chris@zephyrfilms.co.uk
Contact Damon McMinn; Merryn Conaway; Pippa Best, Head of Development; Chris Curling, MD; Phil Robertson, Producer
Credits Mathilde (F); Dark City (F); My Son The Fanatic (F); Secret Passage (F)

Zigzag Films LLP
27 St Peters Street, Stamford PE9 2PS
t 01780 754778 **m** 07774 138245
e ziggy@zigzagfilms.com **w** www.zigzagfilms.com
Contact Ziggy Uszkurat; Richard Day

Zip TV
59 Mount Stuart Square, Cardiff Bay, Cardiff CF10 5LR
t 029 2040 9000 **f** 029 2040 9001 **e** fflic.zip@business.ntl.com
Contact Richard Pawerko, Proprietor

ZKK
152-156 Kentish Town Road, London NW1 9QB
t 020 7482 5885 **f** 020 7482 5884 **e** films@zkktv.co.uk
Contact Laura Matthews, Head of Production

Zorba Films
18 Frankland Close, Croxley Green, Rickmansworth WD3 3AR
t 01923 777059 **f** 01923 777059 **m** 07860 852957
e maxim@time-lapse.co.uk
Contact Peter Rowe, Director of Photography

Production Companies
International

(h) Films Srl
Via Varese 12, Milan 20121, Italy
t +39 02 620051 **f** +39 02 6200 5215
e info@hfilms.net **w** www.hfilms.net

Accelerator Production
58 Wessels Road, Rivonia, Johannesburg 2128, South Africa
t +27 11 803 5578 **f** +27 11 803 5959
e jenny@acceleratorfilms.co.za **w** www.velocityfilms.com
Contact Jenny Leslie, Executive Producer

Altana Films
Girardot 1378, Buenos Aires C 1427 AKD, Argentina
t +54 11 4554 3940 **f** +54 11 4552 2547
e info@altana.com.ar **w** www.altana.com.ar
Contact Enrique Bacher

Aronis TV & Film Productions
4-6 Provelenghiou Street, Palio Iraklio, Athens 14122, Greece
t +30 210 288 1400 **f** +30 210 883 0872
e aaronis@mail.com
Contact Annabelle Aronis
Credits Emma Paya (M); Krezip (M); Schauma Scwartzkopf (T); Lux - Close-up (T)

Artcore Productions
Nieuwendammerkade 28A12, Amsterdam 1022 AB, Netherlands
t +31 20 531 8282 **f** +31 20 531 8280
e stef@artcore.nl **w** www.artcore.nl
Contact Monique van Beckhoven, Production Manager; Marco Both, Executive Producer/Managing Director; Stefany Rietkerk, Executive Producer/Managing Director; Danielle Lucassen, Production Manager
Credits NH Hotels (C); KPN (C); VW (C); Ben: Symphonies (C)

Banana *split*

Banana Split Polska
UL JS Bacha Street 28, Warsaw 02-743, Poland
t +48 22 843 3556 **f** +48 22 843 9458
e banana@banana.pl **w** www.banana.pl
Contact Jerzy Hamkalo, Producer; Ewa Jacuta, Manager/Producer; Magda Przezdziak, Production Manager
Credits You Decide (T); Chopin (F); Lech Beer (C)

◖ BEE'S PICTURES ◗

Bee's Pictures
Calle Cordoba 10B, Fuengirola, Malaga 29640, Spain
t +34 902 118531 **t** +34 95 2667073
f +34 902 118532 **f** +34 95 2664636
e beespics@beespics.com **w** www.beespics.com
Contact Belinda Lewin, Producer; Ivo Van Vollenhoven, Producer; Iohamil Navarro, Producer (Cuba); Simon Burge, Executive Producer

Big Fish Filmproduktion
Linienstrasse 214, Berlin 10119, Germany
t +49 30 2853 7610 **f** +49 30 2853 7633
e info@bigfish.de **w** www.bigfish.de
Contact Andrea Roman, Executive Producer; Henry Rehorek, Producer; Robert Gold, Executive Producer
Credits Riccardo Cartillone: Hand-Foot (C)

want to film in Brazil? We've got the muscle.

Clients: Marken Films, Diners, Sixt Rent a Car, Unilever, Flehner Films, Mercedes Benz, Bates South, Sorin Cine, Peluca Films, Nestlé, J.W.Thompson, Impiric, Wasabi Films, TBWA - Brahma, Vegaolmosponce, El Bagre Films and Lowe Lintas & Partners.

Contact: Cristian Marini / João Roni
Phone: +55 48 334 8893 • Fax: + 55 48 334 8135
Mobile: +55 48 99606944 • Site: www.oceanfilms.com.br
Mail: oceanfilms@oceanfilms.com.br

OceanFilms
PRODUCTION SERVICES

Blue Sky Croatia

Kamenarski Brijeg, Borovina 14, Zagreb 10000, Croatia
t +385 1 457 5082 **f** +385 1 457 5072
e mario@blueskycroatia.com **e** blueskycroatia@hotmail.com
Contact Sabrina Allaria, Producer; Mario Zvan, Executive Producer
Credits Kenya - White Terror (D); Dario's Sunchyme (M); Reebok (C); Lara Croft And The Cradle Of Life: Tomb Raider 2 (F)

Blue Sky Films

PO Box 25711, 00603 Lavington, Nairobi, Kenya
t +254 2 561841 **t** +254 2 577387 **f** +254 2 574164
e bluesky@africaonline.co.ke **w** www.blueskyafrica.com
Contact Sabrina Allaria, Executive Producer, Producer; Mario Zvan, Executive Producer; Jim Shamoon, Managing Director
Credits Kenya - White Terror (D); Dario's Sunchyme (M); Reebok (C); Lara Croft And The Cradle Of Life: Tomb Raider 2 (F)

British American Studio Enterprises (BASE)

Rua Tavares Bastos 414/66, Rio de Janeiro RJ 22221-030, Brazil
t +55 21 2558 5547 **f** +55 21 3235 4073
e nadkarni@alternex.com.br **w** www.basebrazil.tripod.com

BRW & Partners

Via Savona 97, Milan 20144, Italy
t +39 06 424121 **f** +39 06 424 1270
e info@brwpartners.com **w** www.brwpartners.com
Contact Federico Levizzani, Executive Producer; Liza Fisher Fores, Producer; Pamela Telloli, Producer; Barbara Brown, Producer; Claudio Cicoli; Federico Turchetti, Executive Producer; Federico Fasolino, Executive Producer; Emanuela Cavazzini, Executive Producer
Credits BMW: Privacy Not Included

Bus

Calle Vicente Jimeno 11, Madrid 28035, Spain
t +34 91 376 8170 **f** +34 91 386 6193
e info@bus-pro.com **w** www.bus-pro.com
Contact Marta Delgado, Producer; Pablo Nolla, Managing Director; Pilu Pilosio, Executive Producer; Joel Marsden, International Producer
Credits Coca Cola (C); Pepsi (C); TriNa (C); Smart (C)

C47 Films

Stollar Bela utca 22, Budapest 1055, Hungary
t +36 1 473 3110 **f** +36 1 473 3111
e alex.nemetz@c47films.com **w** www.c47films.com
Contact Alex Nemetz
Credits Eplus (C); Africola (C); Bluewin (C); Nintendo (C)

Directors Film Company of Amsterdam BV

Duivendrechtsekade 83, Amsterdam 1096 AJ, Netherlands
t +31 20 665 8965 **f** +31 20 694 9996 **e** dfc@euronet.nl
Contact Richard Coll; Piet-Hein Luykx

Duex

Viale Toscana 13/15, Milan 20136, Italy
t +39 02 5843 1097 **f** +39 02 5843 4048
e info@duex.it **w** www.duex.it
Contact Georgio Fantini, Executive Producer; Rino Sorrentino, Executive Producer
Credits MTV: The Chat (Test) (C); Laura Pausini (M); Piaggio (C); Meltin' Pot (C)

Easy Hell Productions

Warsaw, Poland
t +48 501 595000
e easyhell@easyhell.com.pl **w** www.easyhell.com.pl
Contact Tomek Hryniszyn, Producer; Magda Wolosz, Managing Director
Credits Smile (E); Sprite - Passion (C); Steam Engine Depot (D); Migraine (C)

embassy of dreams filmproduktion gmbh

Heβstrasse 74-76, Munich 80798, Germany
t +49 89 236 6630 **f** +49 89 2366 6333
e dream@embassy.de **w** www.embassy.de
Contact Helmut Hartl, Executive Producer

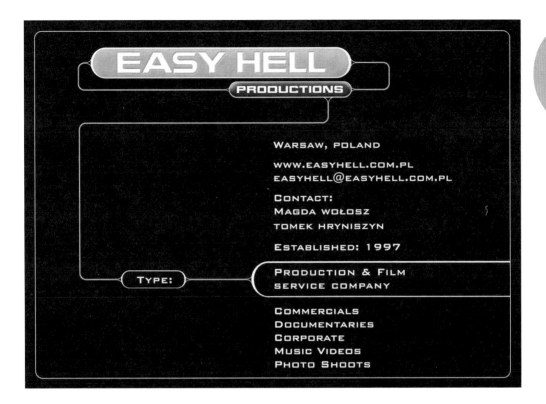

EASY HELL PRODUCTIONS

WARSAW, POLAND

WWW.EASYHELL.COM.PL
EASYHELL@EASYHELL.COM.PL

CONTACT:
MAGDA WOŁOSZ
TOMEK HRYNISZYN

ESTABLISHED: 1997

TYPE: PRODUCTION & FILM
SERVICE COMPANY

COMMERCIALS
DOCUMENTARIES
CORPORATE
MUSIC VIDEOS
PHOTO SHOOTS

FILM STUDIO
GRUPA ITI

PRODUCTION SERVICES
IN POLAND

WWW.ITIFS.COM
E-MAIL: OFFICE@ITIFS.COM
TEL.: +(48 22) 45 33 600

production house
wita stwosza 17a, 02-661 warsaw, poland
office@filmit.com.pl, www.filmit.com.pl
tel. /4822/ 848 78 11, 848 37 79
848 35 99, fax 843 06 07

The Family

The Family
Via Ariosto 6, Milan 20145, Italy
t +39 02 4851 9711 **f** +39 02 4810 0567
e info@thefamilyfilm.it **w** www.thefamilyfilm.it
Contact Stefano Quaglia, Executive Producer; Lorenzo Cefis, Executive
Producer; Lorenzo Ulivieri, Executive Producer
Credits Toyota: Racing (C); Laundry - Nintendo Game Boy Advanced (C);
Wildness - Chrysler Jeep (C); If - BMW (C)

Film It Sp Zoo
ul Wita Stwosza 17A, Warsaw
02 661, Poland
t +48 22 848 7811 **t** +48 22 848 3779
f +48 22 843 0607
e office@filmit.com.pl
w www.filmit.pl
Contact Dominika Grzegdala; Mira Klajnberg

www.filmmaster.com

Film Master Srl
Via Maroncelli 13, Milan 20154, Italy
t +39 06 290911 **f** +39 06 2900 7150
e nadia.migliori@filmmaster.com **w** www.filmmaster.com
Contact Karim Bartoletti, Executive Producer; Nadia Migliori, Office Coordinator
Credits Converse: Golf (C); RAI Institutional Campaign: Traffic Controllers (C);
Tonno Maruzzella; Sea

Filma-Cass
Kocamansur Sokak 115/1, Sisli, Istanbul 80260, Turkey
t +90 212 233 6018 **f** +90 212 231 0227
e filmacass@filmacass.com.tr **w** www.filmacass.com.tr
Contact Ömer Vargi; Tamer Basaran; Bahadir Arliel; Elfin Yuksekteppe; Oguz Peri

Filmitalli Oy
Pohjoisesplanadi 21B, Helsinki 100, Finland
t +358 9 622 6160 **f** +358 9 6226 1622
e hanna.salminen@filmitalli.fi **w** www.filmitalli.fi
Contact Minna Kemp; Mark Stubbs; Hanna Salminen
Credits BAM Blendamed (C); DNA Finland Ltd - The Bank (C); Milli Chokero (C);
OP Bank - The Wedding (C)

Filmworks
The Production Village, PO Box 37415, Dubai, United Arab Emirates
t +971 4 347 4909 **f** +971 4 347 4590
e info@filmwks.com **w** www.filmwks.com
Contact July Tracey

Final Touch Filmproduktion
Schulterblatt 58D, Hamburg 20357, Germany
t +49 40 432 1660 **f** +49 40 432 16666
e info@finaltouch.de **w** www.finaltouch.de
Contact Paula Bergner, Executive Producer; Rainer Spix, Producer
Credits Beck's (C); Nivea (C); Sleep ; Rots; Gun

FLEHNERFILMS
OTHER VISION. OTHER EXPERIENCE.

Flehner Films
Castillo 1366, Buenos Aires C 1414 AXD, Argentina
t +54 11 4771 0400 **f** +54 11 4771 6003
e rmazzeo@flehner.com.ar **w** www.flehnerfilms.com
Contact Rammero Mazzeo; Sergio Gullco
Credits Axe: 'Araña'; Renault Megane: 'Campo Traviesa'; Pajarito; Museum

Genius Loci
Strandvejen, Klampenborg, Copenhagen 2930, Denmark
t +45 2190 2980 **f** +45 3990 1898
e jacob@genius-loci-filmproduction.com
w www.genius-loci-filmproduction.com
Contact Jacob Jörgensen, Managing Director
Credits Ferrero Kinder (C); Copenhagen (T); Armani (C)

Graffiti Film
Ul Kolobrzeska 12, Warsaw 02-923, Poland
t +40 1 858 7488 **f** +40 1 858 7490
e szyperek@graffitifilm.com.pl **w** www.graffitifilm.com.pl
Contact Agnes Szyperek, Producer
Credits Wedding

Group Films
Margenat 73, Barcelona
8017, Spain
t +34 93 418 3302
f +34 93 212 6504
e barcelona@groupfilms.com
w www.groupfilms.com
Contact Nuria Gimpera, Executive Producer;
Barbara Muschietti, Head of Services; Anna
Bonet, Research & Development

Haibun Srl
Via Quadrio 20, Milan 20154, Italy
t +39 02 654863 **f** +39 02 655 4665
e haibun@haibun.com **w** www.haibun.com
Contact John Smith, Managing Director

Harold&Motion Pictures
Via Montemagno 15, Turin 10132, Italy
t +39 011 8195694 **f** +39 011 819566
e info@hmpictures.com **w** www.hmpictures.com
Contact Valter Buccino, Executive Producer; Enrico Grassi, Executive Producer,
Executive Producer; Emanuela Cavazzini, Executive Producer
Credits Swatch (C); Land Rover (C); Heineken (C)

Harold&Motion Pictures
Via Moscati 10B, Milan 20121, Italy
t +39 02 310 3411 **f** +39 02 310 341500
e info@hmpictures.com **w** www.hmpictures.com
Contact Valter Buccino, Executive Producer, Executive Producer; Enrico Grassi,
Executive Producer, Executive Producer; Richard Ronan, Executive Producer;
Michele Virgilio, Executive Producer; Luca Oddo, Executive Producer
Credits Swatch (C); Land Rover (C); Heineken (C)

Harold&Motion Pictures
Via G Nicotera 29, Rome 195, Italy
t +39 06 361 1497 **f** +39 06 361 0353
e info@hmpictures.com **w** www.hmpictures.com
Contact Valter Buccino, Executive Producer, Executive Producer; Enrico Grassi,
Executive Producer; Emanuela Cavazzini, Executive Producer
Credits Land Rover (C); Heineken (C); Swatch (C)

Filming in Turkey?

COMMERCIALS, FEATURE FILMS,
LINE PRODUCTIONS, POST PRODUCTION & RENTAL

Contact us.

Filma-Cass Film Yapim ve Pazarlama A.S

*Ayazağa Mah. G 40 Sk No : 303 / 4 Maslak 80670
Istanbul Turkey*

*Tel: (+90) 212 286 0940
Fax: (+90) 212 286 2082
e-mail: filmacass@filmacass.com.tr*

At Your Service...

...FOR ADVERTISING, MUSIC VIDEOS, DOCUMENTARIES

T: +39.02.5815331/ 89423036
F: +39.02.89423028
Via Novi, 4 - 20144 MILANO - ITALY
www.neuesentimentalfilm.com
E: milano@nsf.it

CONTACT
Francesca Chiappetta - Executive Producer
E: francesca.chiappetta@nsf.it

Annalisa Negri - Producer
E: annalisa.negri@nsf.it

Doing Time

Nescafé

Planet Funk

NEUE SENTIMENTAL FILM

Jodaf-João Daniel Films
Rua Gomes de Carvalho 1306, 4º Andar, Vila Olímpia,
São Paulo CEP 04547-005, Brazil
t +55 11 3044 2287 **f** +55 11 3044 2178
e jodaf@jodaf.com.br **w** www.jodaf.com.br
Contact Michel Tikhomiroff, Director; Sérgio Tikhomiroff, Executive Producer;
João Daniel Tikhomirof, Director
Credits Blockbuster - Editing (C); Sinaf - Jolly Good Fellow (T); Mizuno (T)

Kraftwerk Productions
Riddersvoldsgt 10, Oslo 258, Norway
t +47 2212 8720 **f** +47 2212 8721
e kraftwerk@kraftwerk.no **w** www.kraftwerk.no
Contact Knut Jensen; Guri Neby Hilland; Nils Kittilsen, Producer/Line Producer
Credits Stratos-Nidar: The Kid

La Fabrica Films
Montes de Oca #5, Colonia Condesa, Mexico City DF06140,
Mexico
t +52 55 5211 6213 **f** +52 55 5286 6345
e cesar@lafabrica.tv **w** www.lafabrica.tv
Contact Cesar Ahumada, Executive Producer; Alfredo Couturier, Executive Producer
Credits LG Electronics: Movie

Maximum Films Africa (Pty) Ltd
81 St Johns Street Gardens, Cape Town 8008, South Africa
t +27 21 461 3903 **f** +27 21 461 3925
e pendra@maximumfilms.com **w** www.maximumfilms.com
Contact Claire Dissel; Pendra Dissel, Managing Director
Credits Bubbaloo (C); Acuvue (C); Twingo (C)

Metro Films
Ul Dominikanska 9, Warsaw 02-738, Poland
t +48 22 843 2172 **f** +48 22 843 6626
e metro@metrofilms.com.pl **w** www.metrofilms.com.pl
Contact Marcin Wierzchoslawski, Producer

Monkey Films
Dr Roux 34, Barcelona 8017, Spain
t +34 93 252 5200 **f** +34 93 280 2555
e maria@monkeyfilms.com **w** www.monkeyfilms.com
Contact Tom Sabin, Director; Laura Rota, Assistant Producer; John Smith,
Managing Director; Maria Guerin, Executive Producer
Credits Toyota (C); Sony - Digital World (C); Audi - Kiss (C); Spiderman (F)

Movie Magic International
Via Bramante 29, Milan 20154, Italy
t +39 02 311971 **f** +39 02 317837 **e** commercials@hotmail.com

The Network Productions International
Old Castle Brewery, 6 Beach Road, Woodstock, Cape Town
7915, South Africa
t +27 21 448 0335 **f** +27 21 448 1766
e netprod@iafrica.com **w** www.thenetwork.co.za
Contact Liz O'Shaughnessy, Executive Producer; Duncan Robson, Director
Credits Isfahan (S); Canal Satellite (C); Volvo Ocean Race - UBS (C);
Le Sorcier - Saur (I)

NEUE SENTIMENTAL FILM

Neue Sentimental Milan
Via Novi 4, Milan 20144, Italy
t +39 02 581 5331 **f** +39 02 8942 3028 **e** milano@nsf.it
Contact Francesca Chiappetta, Executive Producer - Advertising & Music
Video Awards

Unique Film Opportunities

Prague, Czech Republic
www.ufopictures.tv

Partnership Pictures

Barrandov Film Studios, Krizeneckeho Namesti 322, Prague 5
152 53, Czech Republic
t +420 2 6707 2117 **f** +420 2 5181 4757
e office@partnershippictures.com
w www.partnershippictures.com
Contact Petr Keller, Managing Director; Lucien Tyssendier, Executive Producer;
Duncan Robson, Director, Director
Credits Hellboy (F)

Peluca Films

Congreso 3545, Capital Federal, Buenos Aires 1430, Argentina
t +54 11 4545 6200 **f** +54 11 4545 6200
e producciones@pelucafilms.com.ar
Contact Pompi Huarte, Producer; Jorge Di Benedetto, Producer; Ale Di Michele,
Producer; Fabio Cimmarusti, Producer; Andrea Dibaja
Credits Philips Batteries: Cemetery (C); mundocelular.com: 'Bill'

Piramide

Calle Diputación 37, Local 2A, Barcelona 8015, Spain
t +34 93 327 8500 **f** +34 93 327 8501
e service@piramideproductions.com
w www.piramideproductions.com
Contact Xavier Sorolla, Executive Producer; Olaf de Boer

PlanetB

Bosanska 28, Zagreb 10000, Croatia
t +385 1 377 6655 **f** +385 1 390 9121 **e** mario@planetb.hr
Contact Andrej Korovljev

Prizes:
5 Clios
5 Cannes Lions
1 London Advertising Awards
1 Grand Prix at Gramados
8 Fiap
Twice Best Iberoamerica Production House

www.pelucafilms.com

PTT Films - Production Team of Turkey
Asmalimescit Minare Sok 23, Beyoglu,
Istanbul 80050, Turkey
t +90 212 293 8473 **f** +90 212 293 8475
e sebnem@pttfilms.com **w** www.pttfilms.com
Contact R Sebnem Kitis

Skyfilm Studio
Hüvösvölgyi út 35, Budapest 1026, Hungary
t +36 1 275 3066 **f** +36 1 275 3069
e skyfilm@skyfilm.hu **w** www.skyfilm.hu
Contact Andrea Orban, Casting Director; Monika Nagy, Location Manager; Lidia Kecskemethy, Producer
Credits A Kind Of America (F); Nestlé (C); Panasonic (C); Amstel (C)

Stillking Films
Krizeneckeho nam 322, Prague 5 152 53, Czech Republic
t +420 2 073741 **f** +420 2 073742
e peanut@stillking.com **w** www.stillking.com
Contact Pavla Burgetova, Executive Producer
Credits Eurotel (C); Allianz (C); Pilsner Urquell (C); Pilsner Arquell (Clip)

STRAWBERRY FILMS

Strawberry Films
Bimbó út 141/B, Budapest 1026, Hungary
t +36 1 200 4040 **f** +36 1 200 6060 **m** +36 309 427589
e strawberry@strawberryfilms.hu **w** www.strawberryfilms.hu
Contact Melinda Szepesi, Producer, Producer; Katalin Krammer, Executive Producer, Executive Producer

Studio Arkadena
Brodisce 23, Trzin 1236, Slovenia
t +386 1 562 1627 **f** +386 1 562 1628
e arkadena@siol.net **w** www.arkadena.si
Contact Janez Kovic; Rok Ban, Producer; Leon Krpic, Producer

Sunflower Production
Vicolo Antoniniano 6, Via delle Terme di Caracalla 75, Rome 153, Italy
t +39 06 7725 0804 **f** +39 06 7045 4425
e rosaammaturo@sunflower.tv **w** www.sunflower.tv

SYNTHESIS ── FILM ──

Synthesis Film
Via Lazzaretto 15, Milan 20124, Italy
t +39 02 6698 0300 **f** +39 02 6698 3186
e info@synthesisfilm.com **w** www.synthesisfilm.com
Contact Marcello Noera, Executive Producer

Twin Film

Ortnitstrasse 20, Munich 81925, Germany
t +49 89 300 0860 **f** +49 89 3000 8640
e info@twinfilm.de **w** www.twinfilm.de
Contact Thomas Habermeyer, Producer; Andreas Habermeyer, Producer

UFO Pictures

Nad Spádem 17/202, Praha 4 140 00, Czech Republic
t +420 2 6121 3968 **f** +420 2 6121 4015
e into@utopictures.tv **w** www.utopictures.tv
Contact David Rauch, Executive Producer; Monika Splíchalová, Producer;
Jeffrey Brown, Producer/International Representative
Credits The Myth - Nick Cave And The Bad Seeds (D); Nissan (C); The Pied Piper
(F); Sprandi (C)

Velocity Afrika Production

38 Wessels Road, Johannesburg 2128, South Africa
t +27 11 807 0100 **f** +27 11 807 1208
e info@velocityfilms.com **w** www.velocityfilms.com
Contact Nicola Valentine, Executive Producer; Barry Munchik, Executive
Producer; Karen Kloppers, Head of Production; Peter Carr, Executive Producer;
Mark Gilbert, Executive Producer

Velocity Europe Production Services

Hermann-Behn-Weg 1, Hamburg 20146, Germany
t +49 40 4440 5823 **f** +49 40 410 2846
Contact Oliver Székessy, Executive Producer

Voodoo Productions

Calle Alegre de Dalt 55, 2C, Barcelona 8024, Spain
t +34 93 285 0229 **f** +34 93 210 5866
e contact@voodooproductions.net
w www.voodooproductions.net
Contact Txell Sabartés; Albert Brasó

Vulcan Films

Korkeavuorenkatu 2B, Helsinki 140, Finland
t +358 9 684 0620 **f** +358 9 6840 6240
e location@vulcanfilms.fi **w** www.vulcanfilms.fi
Contact Mika Sylvin

Production Companies
News

APP Sports News

Unit 7, 2 Exmoor Street, London W10 6BD
t 020 8964 4992 **f** 020 8960 0464
e info@appbroadcast.com **w** www.appbroadcast.com
Contact Andrew Preece, Director; Richard Simmonds, Director
Credits Sting - Live Webcast (W); Ellen MacArthur (T); 2003 America Cup (T)

APTN

The Interchange, Oval Road, Camden Lock, London NW1 7DZ
t 020 7482 7400 **f** 020 7413 8302
e aptnbookings@ap.org **w** www.aptn.com
Contact Bart Stobart, Non-Broadcast Clients/London; Roberto Soto, Broadcast
Clients/New York; Marisa Sgro, Non-Broadcast Clients/New York; Charlotte
DeJean, Broadcast and Non-Broadcast Clients/Washington DC; Neal Harrison,
Non-Broadcast Clients/London; Tim Rudell, Manager APTN Broadcast
Services/Washington DC

HUTC Ltd

35 Eagles Drive, Tatsfield TN16 2PB
t 01959 575779 **f** 01959 571350 **m** 07810 484044
e info@hutc.co.uk **w** www.hutc.co.uk
Contact David Painter, Managing Director; Pam Harris, Sales And Distribution

Independent Television News

200 Grays Inn Road, London WC1X 8XZ
t 020 7833 3000 **f** 020 7430 4016
e firstname.lastname@itn.co.uk **w** www.itn.co.uk
Contact Stewart Purvis, Chief Executive

International News Productions Ltd (INP)

2nd Floor, PA News Centre, 292 Vauxhall Bridge Road, London
SW1V 1AE
t 020 7963 7474 **f** 020 7963 7476
e broadcasting@pa.press.net **w** www.pa.press.net
Contact Sean Curtis-Ward, Head of TV & Radio; Jennifer McDermott, Office Manager;
Peter Wallace, News Operations Manager; Stephen Gardner, Managing Editor
Credits Battle For The Gulf - 10 Year Anniversary (D); Safe & Secure (SAS
Training Video) (S); Sat 1/N 24/Pro-7 News Daily Reports (T)

ITN News Services

200 Gray's Inn Road, London WC1X 8XZ
t 020 7430 4330 **f** 020 7430 4854 **w** www.itn.co.uk

Litmus Films

207 Pottle Street, Horningsham BA12 7LX
t 01985 845003 **f** 01985 845003 **m** 07740 619222
e info@litmusfilms.com
Contact Aileen Chen, Director; Robert Stern, Managing Director

Locum Productions Ltd

1 Hamilton Road, London TW8 0QE
t 020 8758 1178 **f** 020 8758 1178
e info@locum-productions.com
Contact Simon Cumbers, Director; Louise Bevan, Director
Credits CNN International; Wimbledon; BBC Foreign News

NewsRoomInk

Kensington Centre, 66 Hammersmith Road, London W14 8YT
t 020 7605 2164 **m** 07774 212125 **e** lgibbs@newsroomink.com
Contact Lorna Dean Gibbs

Reuters Television

85 Fleet Street, London EC4P 4AJ
t 020 7250 1122 **f** 020 7542 7574 **w** www.reuters.co.uk

Video Newsreels

Church Cottage Studios, Ruscombe, Twyford RG10 9UB
t 07710 611123
e gerry.clarke@btinternet.com **w** www.videonewsreels.co.uk
Contact Gerry Clarke, Managing Director

Production Consultants

Content is King (CiK)

15 Bowling Green Lane, London EC1R 0BD
t 020 7490 4600 **f** 020 7490 4492
e stephen.liddle@contentisking.co.uk **w** www.contentisking.co.uk
Contact Ewan King, Director; Rob Martindill, Production Manager

Cult TV

PO Box 1701, Peterborough PE7 1ER
t 01733 205009 **f** 01733 205009
e enquiries@cult.tv **w** www.cult.tv
Contact Paul Jones, Artist Acquisition; Idris Evans, Technical Director; Alex
Geairns, Executive Producer; Dave Mullin, Financial Director; John Godsland,
New Media Director

Andrew Edwards

Range 14, Communications plc, Newlands Annexe, 6 Veronica
House, London SE4 1NQ
t 020 8469 3764 **f** 0870 130 2375 **m** 07775 884477
e andrewedwards00_99@yahoo.com
e tidworth@yahoogroups.com
Credits Tidworth - The Future (D); Inside Housing Today (I)

Warwick Gee

Pyers Croft, Compton, Chichester PO18 9EX
t 02392 631339
Credits Omnibus (T); Arena (T); BBC Arts (T)

Gerry King Productions

29 Falstaff Close, Walmley, Sutton Coldfield B76 1YG
t 0121 351 3809 **f** 0121 351 3809 **m** 07850 469989
e gerry.king@limeone.net

Hornagold & Hills

3 Waterhouse Square, 138-142 Holborn, London EC1N 2HG
t 020 7822 7654 **f** 020 7822 7655
e bill.phelps@hornagold-hills.com **w** www.hornagold-hills.com
Contact Alex McDonald, Projects Manager; Bill Phelps, Partner
Credits Gardeners' World (T)

Iland Corporation

8 Malins Court, Nightingale Lane, London SW12 8NU
Contact Terence Iland, Director/Designer; Matthew Iland, Production Designer
Credits Excel-Lence 2001 (D); Digital Media World (D); International Display
Week (D); A View From The Wings (D)

Interactive Knowhow

9 Stonefield Mansions, Cloudesley Square, London N1 0HS
t 020 7837 5090 **f** 020 7837 5090 **m** 07958 357334
e info@interactiveknowhow.co.uk **w**
www.interactiveknowhow.co.uk

IPH Associates

t 020 7207 2966 **f** 020 8398 9928 **m** 07711 161856
e info@iphassoc.com
Contact Jed Leventhall, Contact; Barrie Leventhall, Contact
Credits My HFRC (T); Disney Channel Kids Awards (T); Lights, Camera,
Magic (T); tlc (T)

Peter R Jones

34 Halesworth Road, London SE13 7TN
t 020 8692 8441 **e** picplan@talk21.com

Le Park TV Ltd

Windmill Studios, 49-51 York Road, Brentford TW8 0QP
t 020 8568 5855 **f** 020 8568 4151 **m** 07836 689942
e info@leparktv.com **w** www.leparktv.com

Magic Lantern Productions Ltd

125 Bolingbroke Grove, London SW11 1DA
t 020 7738 9911 **f** 020 7223 9124
e anthony@magiclantern.co.uk **w** www.magiclantern.co.uk
Credits Cold Smoke (T); Teacher's TV (I); Broadband Britain (I); Broadband (I)

Medialink

7 Fitzroy Square, London W1T 5HL
t 020 7554 2700 **f** 020 7554 2710
e info@europe.medialink.com **w** www.europe.medialink.com
Contact Paul Harraghy, Head of Sales; Dominic Redfearn, Head of Production

Pauline Muirhead Productions (PMP)

41 Lanark Road West, Edinburgh EH14 5JX
t 0131 476 9598 **f** 0131 476 9598
e pmuirhead@tvcopro.com **w** www.csf.org.uk
Contact Pauline Muirhead, Producer

Phil Brown Production Resource Consultants

31 Southside, Congresbury, Bristol BS49 5BS
t 01934 833500 **f** 01934 877421
e philbrown@juliashortman.freeserve.co.uk
Contact Phil Brown, Managing Director

Plahyai Productions Ltd
156 Cuckmere Way, Hollingbury, Brighton BN1 8GH
t 01273 275185 **f** 01273 275185 **m** 07967 105254
e david.salmon2@ntlworld.com
Contact David Salmon, Managing Director

Production Partners
t 020 8977 6432 **m** 07831 802511
e ca.hawkins@ntlworld.com **w** www.productionpartners.tv
Contact Sally Lindsay, Company Director; Caroline Hawkins, Company Director

Psi Pi & Jujumi Productions
e jujumi@jujumi.com **w** www.jujumi.com
Contact Simon Hedley
Credits Nephalim (S); Dinner 'N' Drinks (W); Strawberries 'N' Cream (W); Eclipse (M)

Shooting Partners Ltd
9 Mount Mews, High Street, Hampton TW12 2SH
t 020 8941 1000 **f** 020 8941 0077
e mail@shooting-partners.co.uk
w www.shooting-partners.co.uk
Contact Jenny Bigrave, Production Coordinator; Mark Holdway, Displays & Projection; Phil White, Managing Director; Chris Dingley, Technical Director; Darrin Dart, Facilities Manager; Matthew Tomkinson, Head of Resources
Credits Brainteaser (T); Wish You Were Here...? (T); Laureus World Sports Awards (T); Spy TV (T)

Supotco Design Ltd
3-5 Valentine Place, London SE1 8QH
t 020 7928 5474 **f** 020 7928 6082 **m** 07774 116440
e info@supotco.co.uk
Contact Walter Dammers, Chief Executive

The Television Business
The Old Vicarage, Church Road, Emneth, Wisbech PE14 8AF
t 01945 467157 **m** 07970 088040 **w** www.thetvb.co.uk
Contact Mark Thatcher, Producer/Director; Lucy Mucillo, Production Co-ordination
Credits auction-world.tv (T); Ideal World (T); QVC UK & Germany (T)
Home Shopping specialists with a decade's experience in channel launches.

The Television Company (London) Ltd
8 Henley Prior, Collier Street, London N1 9JU
t 020 7713 6579 **f** 020 7713 6581
e tvco2000@aol.com **w** www.the-television-company.co.uk

Video & Film Production
Robin Hill, The Ridge, Lower Basildon RG8 9NX
t 0118 984 2488 **f** 0118 984 4316 **m** 07836 544955
e david.fisher@videoandfilm.co.uk **w** www.videoandfilm.co.uk
Contact David Fisher, Proprietor

Dorothy Viljoen
259 Kennington Road, London SE11 6BY
t 020 7735 2450 **f** 020 7735 3140 **e** viljoendot@aol.com

White Rabbit Productions Ltd
Upper Hattons Media centre, Upper Hattons, Peneford Hall Lane, Wolverhampton WV9 5BD
t 01902 682444 **f** 01902 840448
e audio@wrproductions.co.uk **w** www.wrproductions.co.uk
Contact Tim Sidwell

Production
Managers/Line Producers

Bruce Abrahams
16 Greville Road, Southville, Bristol BS3 1LL
t 0117 963 5515 **f** 0117 963 5515 **m** 07768 363783
e bruce_abrahams@hotmail.com
Credits Kerching! (T); Holby City (T); Casualty (T)

Catharin Alen-Buckley
15 Marlborough Road, London W4 4EU
t 020 8995 1884 **f** 020 8995 5648 **e** catharine@eagletv.co.uk

Jane Alexander
3 Georgina Court, Arlington Road, Twickenham TW1 2AT
t 020 8891 6980 **f** 020 8891 6980 **m** 07713 682578
e ja@janealexander.fsnet.co.uk

Mary Alleguen
10 St Catherine's Avenue, South Circular Road, Dublin 8, Ireland
t +353 1 454 3367 **f** +353 1 584481 **e** maryalleguen@eircom.net
Credits My Left Foot (F); Braveheart (F); Reign Of Fire (F)

Rosie Allsop
56 Chatsworth Avenue, London SW20 8JZ
t 020 8715 7545 **f** 020 8542 2071 **m** 07957 595375
e rosie_allsop@lineone.net
Credits Two Men In A Trench - Series II (D); The Ultimate Guide To Mummies (D); Secrets Of The Dead - Sounds From The Stone Age (T)

Philippa Atterton
71B Partickhill Road, Glasgow G11 5AD
t 0141 339 4434 **f** 0141 339 4434 **m** 07831 299937
e philippaatterton@aol.com

Zara Balfour
Callbox Communications Ltd, 66 Shepperton Studios, Studios Road, Shepperton TW17 0QD
t 01932 592572 **f** 01932 569655 **m** 07710 572572
e callboxdiary@btinternet.com **w** www.callboxdiary.co.uk

Erica Banks
6 Elmwood Gardens, Hanwell, London W7 3HA
m 07764 581585 **e** erica.banks@ntlworld.com
Credits Arts Features - BBC (D); Arena (D)

Annabelle Barr
Production Switchboard, Northdown, Down Lane, Compton GU3 1DN
t 01483 812011 **f** 01483 812027
e aly@productionswitch.freeserve.co.uk
Credits Andrex Stress Relief (C); Nescafe - Outlaw (C); Pizza Hut - Blink (C)

Maddy Barrington
49 Haverhill Road, London SW12 0HD
t 020 8675 1464 **m** 07850 070071
e weegee@madasafish.com
Credits Dreamspaces (T); Billy Connolly - A Bafta Tribute (T); The 74th Academy Awards With Jonathan Ross (T); The 75th Academy Awards With Jonathan Ross (T)

Jane Bartlett
t 020 7739 3379 **f** 020 7739 3379 **m** 07976 407418

Rauf Stuart Bayraktar
Promopromo, 1-6 Falconberg Court, Soho, London W1 3AB
t 020 7440 1090 **f** 020 7440 1099 **m** 07956 367396
e ensigne@ensigne.co.uk **w** www.promopromo.com
Credits Channel4 (C); E4 (C); Sci-Fi Channel (C)

Sue de Beauvoir
m 07778 034 129 **e** sue@suedebeauvoir.com
Credits Footballer's Wives (T); This Is Personal (T); The Gentleman Thief (T); Redcaps (T)

Liesbeth Beeckman
57 Lebanon Park, Twickenham TW1 3DH
m 07769 708751 **e** liesbeth_beeckman@hotmail.com

Kim Belcham
Production Switchboard, Northdown, Down Lane, Compton GU3 1DN
t 01483 812011 **f** 01483 812027
e aly@productionswitch.freeserve.co.uk
Credits Vodafone (C); Midland Bank (C)

Erica Bensly
The Production Switchboard, Northdown, Down Lane,
Compton GU3 1DN
t 01483 812011 **f** 01483 812027
e aly@productionswitch.freeserve.co.uk
Credits Lucky Break (F); Simon (F)

Hilary Benson
Gems, The Media House, 87 Glebe Street, Penarth CF64 1EF
t 029 2071 0770 **f** 029 2071 0771
e gems@gems-agency.co.uk **w** www.gems-agency.co.uk
Credits Down To Earth (T); Whistleblower (T); Mansfield Park (F);
Charlotte Gray (F)

Mairie Bett
International Creative Management Ltd, Oxford House,
76 Oxford Street, London W1D 1BS
t 020 7636 6565 **f** 020 7323 0101 **w** www.icmlondon.co.uk
Credits Long Time Dead (F); Ali G Indahouse (F); Dot The I (F)

Fiona Black
109 Finsbury Park Road, London N4 2JU
t 020 7359 1634 **m** 07970 117342 **e** fionablack@aol.com
Agent Gems, The Media House, 87 Glebe Street,
Penarth CF64 1EF
t 029 2071 0770 **f** 029 2071 0771
e gems@gems-agency.co.uk **w** www.gems-agency.co.uk
Credits Attachments (T); Holby City (T); Ants (A); Perfect (T); Sir Gadabout (T);
Jonathon Creek (T)

Laurie Borg
International Creative Management Ltd, Oxford House,
76 Oxford Street, London W1D 1BS
t 020 7636 6565 **f** 020 7323 0101 **w** www.icmlondon.co.uk
Credits Little Voice (F); The Four Feathers (F); If Only (F)

Anne Boyd
7 Gambetta Street, Battersea, London SW8 3TS
t 020 7720 1884 **m** 07946 638295
e anneboyd@tunamoon.demon.co.uk
Credits The Wedding Tackle (F); Chatterhappy Ponies (T); Beachcomber Bay
(T); Sir Gadabout (T)

Grant Branton
The Production Switchboard, Northdown, Down Lane,
Compton GU3 1DN
t 01483 812011 **f** 01483 812027
e aly@productionswitch.freeserve.co.uk
Credits Aqua Pura (C); Primal Scream (M); Backstage Kids (T)

Chris Brock
EXEC, 6 Travis Court, Farnham Royal SL2 3SB
t 01753 646677 **f** 01753 646770
e sue@execmanagement.co.uk **w** www.execmanagement.co.uk

David Brown
International Creative Management Ltd, Oxford House,
76 Oxford Street, London W1D 1BS
t 020 7636 6565 **f** 020 7323 0101 **w** www.icmlondon.co.uk
Credits Star Wars: Episode I - The Phantom Menace (F); Enigma (F); The
Importance Of Being Earnest (F)

Lin Brown
Carlton Television, 35-38 Portman Square, Marble Arch,
London W1H 6NU
t 020 7612 7458 **f** 020 7612 7528 **e** lin.brown@carltontv.co.uk
w www.carltontv.com

Helena Bullivant
9 Rosslyn Hill, London NW3 5VL
m 07973 509866
Credits Pornography- The Secret History of Civilisation (D); Hannibal (T);
Queen & Country (T)

Al Burgess
4 Blatch's Close, Theadle, Reading SL4 4EL
t 0118 930 2030 **m** 07785 993855
e al@burgess.demon.co.uk
Credits Shiner (F); Quicksand (F); Octane (F); LD50 (F)

Jo Burn
1 Cantelowes Road, London NW1 9XH
t 020 7267 7992 **m** 07778 998028 **e** joannaburn@aol.com
Credits The Mummy Returns (F); The Hours (F); Johnny English (F);
Thunderbirds (F)

Stuart Butterworth
34 Kimbell Gardens, London SW6 6QB
t 020 7610 9642 **m** 07889 505501 **e** stu@stu100.fsnet.co.uk
Agent The Production Switchboard, Northdown, Down Lane,
Compton GU3 1DN
t 01483 812011 **f** 01483 812027
e aly@productionswitch.freeserve.co.uk
Credits Lee Jeans (C); Honda (C); Daily Telegraph (C)

Anne Cafferky
28 Sandown Road KT10 9TU
t 01372 465044 **f** 01372 462591 **m** 07721 539688
e anne.morley@virgin.net
Credits The Truthabout Football (D); Geri's World Walkabout (D); The
Real.....Brian Clough (D); DNA (D)

Kitty Campbell
The Production Switchboard, Northdown, Down Lane,
Compton GU3 1DN
t 01483 812011 **f** 01483 812027
e aly@productionswitch.freeserve.co.uk
Credits Workline Balance (C); Smirnoff Absolute (C); The Fever (F)

Nicky Charles
Callbox Communications Limited, 66 Shepperton Studios,
Studios Road, Shepperton TW17 0QD
t 01932 592572 **f** 01932 569655 **m** 07710 572572
e callboxdiary@btinternet.com **w** www.callboxdiary.co.uk

David Cherrill
EXEC, 6 Travis Court, Farnham Royal SL2 3SB
t 01753 646677 **f** 01753 646770
e sue@execmanagement.co.uk **w** www.execmanagement.co.uk

Polly Chetwynd-Staplyton
The Production Switchboard, Northdown, Down Lane,
Compton GU3 1DN
t 01483 812011 **f** 01483 812027
e aly@productionswitch.freeserve.co.uk
Credits Ms. Dynamite (M); Gran (S); Der Grune Punkt - Rose Hackney Barber (C)

Julie Clark
35 Deodar Road, Putney, London SW15 2NP
t 020 8780 2650 **f** 020 8789 1474 **m** 07889 657647

Peter Clews
C/o 45 Neppoch Court, Hampton Park, Howick, Auckland, New
Zealand
e pclews@hotmail.com
Credits Junkyard Wars (T); Shipwrecked (D); Scrapheap Challenge (T); Faking It
USA (D)

Fiona Cockburn
Norton Paddox, Norton Lindsey, Warwick CV35 8JA
m 07885 453983
Credits Doctors (T)

Isobel Conroy
The Production Switchboard, Northdown, Down Lane,
Compton GU3 1DN
t 01483 812011 **f** 01483 812027
e aly@productionswitch.freeserve.co.uk
Credits BB6 Music (C); Mull Historical Society (M); Onwards (C)

pma: the production managers' association

The Production Managers' Association (PMA) is a professional body of Film, Television, Corporate and Multimedia production managers.

Within the industry, the Association provides a unique network for both freelance and permanently employed production managers, providing invaluable information and support, as well as regular social events, workshops and training courses. The Association is supported by sponsors from across the industry, who keep members up-to-date with matters relating to film and television production in the UK.

The PMA also provides an up-to-date availability list of experienced production managers, as a service for both its member and for those producers or production companies looking to employ a highly-skilled production manager. The list can be accessed on the PMA's own website, www.pma.org.uk or by calling the executive member responsible for employment. In addition to the availability list, the website can also be used to access members who speak a particular language, or to search for specific areas of experience or credit listings.

The PMA's membership currently stands at 180, and each member has at least six broadcast credits (or equivalent) as well as at least three years experience as a production manager. The experience of our members ranges across the board – from features to drama, to investigative films and documentaries, OBs and travel programmes, to magazine formats and quiz shows. The PMA offers each member a solid network of support and advice, which enables every production manager to bring to their work a unique and valued insight into the industry and how it operates.

The PMA offers:

Networking

Regular meetings for members to share work experiences and provide professional support for each other.

Employment availability list

Producers and production companies wishing to employ a production manager can see which members are currently available for work.

Annual directory of members

An established publication referred to throughout the industry, containing members' contact numbers and recent credits.

Business support helpline

Members can phone for free professional advice on tax, VAT, PAYE, payroll, employment and personnel, health and safety and commercial legal issues.

Social events

Hosted by our sponsors, members get a chance to keep abreast of industry developments and exchange ideas and information in an informal setting.

Training workshops

Bespoke courses provided for members covering areas such as health and safety, scheduling, new technology, and first aid.

The Forum

A members' private email newsgroup which taps into the vast wealth of experience of the membership. Over 180 members working in broadcast TV, commercials, feature films, corporate videos and multimedia with accumulated knowledge across every genre.

Bi-monthly newsletter

Members and sponsors hear news and views of the PMA and the industry at large.

The website

Contains members' credits, the availability list, contact details for the PMA, a diary of forthcoming events, 'The Forum', and details of our sponsors with links. A list of recommended production co-ordinators and their production credits now exists on our website for access by members only.

Pension scheme

PMA members can take advantage of preferential terms for Stakeholder and Personal Pension schemes, negotiated for us with two leading pension providers by our independent financial advisers.

PACT affiliation

Gives PMA members the benefit of PACT events and information.

Membership standards

To join, all members must have had at least 3 years experience in the industry and 6 broadcast credits as a production manager. Additional skills are also taken into consideration.

The Convent
25 Bury Street, Ruislip HA4 7SX
t 01895 472707 **f** 01895 635010 **m** 07905 923836
e the.convent@btopenworld.com
Contact Jonathan Musgrave, Producer/Production Manager
Credits Sunburn Hi-Definition Masterclass Workshop (E); Culture Jockey (I)

Brian Cook
EXEC, 6 Travis Court, Farnham Royal SL2 3SB
t 01753 646677 **f** 01753 646770
e sue@execmanagement.co.uk **w** www.execmanagement.co.uk

Hannah Cooper
The Production Switchboard, Northdown, Down Lane,
Compton GU3 1DN
t 01483 812011 **f** 01483 812027
e aly@productionswitch.freeserve.co.uk
Credits Cereal Bars (C); Campaign Screen (C); Cultura Trips (C)

Cormac Clarke
20A Ellerslie Road, London W12 7BW
t 020 8749 0806 **f** 020 8749 0806 **m** 07785 797822
e cormac.clarke@virgin.net
Credits Simply Shopping Channel (T); Xerox Business Television (I); SAGA
Crusie Holidays (C); Prepared For Capture (E)

Peter Cotton
Gems, The Media House, 87 Glebe Street, Penarth CF64 1EF
t 029 2071 0770 **f** 029 2071 0771
e gems@gems-agency.co.uk **w** www.gems-agency.co.uk
Credits Big Meg, Little Meg I, II (T); Valentine (T); Children's Ward (T); Heart (F)

Sophie Cowling
7 Gayville Road, London SW11 6JN
t 020 7228 1193 **m** 07798 600904
e aly@productionswitch.freeserve.co.uk
Agent The Production Switchboard, Northdown, Down Lane,
Compton GU3 1DN
t 01483 812011 **f** 01483 812027
e aly@productionswitch.freeserve.co.uk

Nick Crabb
The Production Switchboard, Northdown, Down Lane,
Compton GU3 1DN
t 01483 812011 **f** 01483 812027
e aly@productionswitch.freeserve.co.uk
Credits Lucozade Sport (C); Bertolli (C); Muller (C)

Andi d'Sa
97 South Hill Park, London NW3 2SP
t 020 7433 3391 **f** 020 7433 3391 **m** 07711 087471
e andi.dsa@virgin.net

Kate Dain
Gems, The Media House, 87 Glebe Street, Penarth CF64 1EF
t 029 2071 0770 **f** 029 2071 0771
e gems@gems-agency.co.uk **w** www.gems-agency.co.uk
Credits Dangerous Liasons (F); Blood In Their Eyes (F); The Visitor (F); An Ideal
Husband (F)

Hilton Davis
7 St Michaels Avenue, South Shields NE33 3AN
t 0191 455 6047 **m** 07990 785158 **e** hilton.davis@bbc.co.uk
Credits Excellence At Rof Birtley (I); Selling Skills At Pubmaster (I); Welcome to
Rhodia Chirex (I); The Supplier Of Choice (I)

Chloe Deverell
Flat B, 132 Upper Clapton Road, London E5 9JY
t 020 8806 3844 **e** fin_du_monde@hotmail.com
Credits Tour De Langkawi 2002 (T); Tour De France 2002 (T)

Sarah Dickens
Flat 10, 7 Bradstock Road, London E9 5BZ
t 020 8533 5601 **m** 07957 167441
e sarahdickens@hotmail.com
Agent The Production Switchboard, Northdown, Down Lane,
Compton GU3 1DN
t 01483 812011 **f** 01483 812027
e aly@productionswitch.freeserve.co.uk
Credits Audi (C); Absolut Vodka (C); BT (C)

Faye Dimdore
78 Christchurch Avenue, London NW6 7PE
t 020 8459 0400 **m** 07957 387648
Credits Vote 2001 BBC1 General Election Coverage (T)

Sassica Donohoo
Wizzo & Co, 35 Old Compton Street, London W1D 5JX
t 020 7437 2055 **f** 020 7437 2066
e wizzo@wizzoandco.co.uk **w** www.wizzoandco.co.uk

Brian Donovan
McKinney Macartney Management Ltd, The Barley Mow
Centre, 10 Barley Mow Passage, London W4 4PH
t 020 8995 4747 **f** 020 8995 2414
e fkb@mmtechsrep.demon.co.uk **w**
www.mckinneymacartney.com

Josephine Dunn
19 Mill Grove, 3 Water Lane, Whissendine LE15 7EY
t 01664 474517 **m** 07710 729613
Credits The Promise (F); Watercolour Challenge

Sarah Eatock
172 Purves Road, London NW10 5TG
t 020 8964 8054 **m** 07050 046847
e saraheatock@talk21.com
Agent The Production Switchboard, Northdown, Down Lane,
Compton GU3 1DN
t 01483 812011 **f** 01483 812027
e aly@productionswitch.freeserve.co.uk
Credits Godman (C); Burger King (C); Citroen (C)

Kirsten Eller
Gems, The Media House, 87 Glebe Street, Penarth CF64 1EF
t 029 2071 0770 **f** 029 2071 0771
e gems@gems-agency.co.uk **w** www.gems-agency.co.uk
Credits Life Force (T); The Queen's Nose (T); My Kingdom (F); Stig Of The Dump (T)

Jo Farr
Production Switchboard, Northdown, Down Lane, Compton
GU3 1DN
t 01483 812011 **f** 01483 812027
e aly@productionswitch.freeserve.co.uk
Credits My Wife Is An Actress (F); The Gathering (F); Calendar Girls (F)

Rebecca Ferrand
Gems, The Media House, 87 Glebe Street, Penarth CF64 1EF
t 029 2071 0770 **f** 029 2071 0771
e gems@gems-agency.co.uk **w** www.gems-agency.co.uk
Credits The Suicidal Dog (S); The Falklands Play (F); Search (T)

Danielle Fox
37 Rosemont Court, Rosemont Road, London W3 9LS
t 020 8992 7268 **f** 020 8993 7997 **m** 07957 432838
e danielle.fox@btconnect.com
Credits Kavanagh QC (T); The Jungle Book (F); The Haunting (F)

Rhun Francis
Flat 1, 471 Bethnal Green Road, London E2 9QH
t 020 7739 9242 **m** 07711 052375 **e** rhun72@hotmail.com
Agent The Production Switchboard, Northdown, Down Lane,
Compton GU3 1DN
t 01483 812011 **f** 01483 812027
e aly@productionswitch.freeserve.co.uk
Credits The Sun - Bizarre Album (M); Radio 2 - Friends (C); Great Britons (C)

Christopher Frederick
Home Farm, Batcombe, Shepton Mallet BA4 6HF
t 01749 850303 f 01749 850540 m 07976 177885
e christopherfrederick@lineone.net
Credits Calling the Wild (T); Kumbh Mela (D)

Alan Frost
Cherrywood, Crawley Down Road, Felbridge RH19 2PP
t 01342 300566 m 07710 498924 e alan@idealimage.co.uk
Credits Pipeline (S); The Tigers (I); My Family Tree (T)

Caz Fuller
68 Hemberton Road, London SW9 9LJ
t 020 7274 8183 m 07973 654637 e caz.fuller@virgin.net
Agent The Production Switchboard, Northdown, Down Lane,
Compton GU3 1DN
t 01483 812011 f 01483 812027
e aly@productionswitch.freeserve.co.uk
Credits Iceland (C); Pimms (C); Nectar (C)

Sarah Jane Gabb
Callbox Communications Limited, 66 Shepperton Studios,
Studios Road, Shepperton TW17 0QD
t 01932 592572 f 01932 569655 m 07710 572572
e callboxdiary@btinternet.com w www.callboxdiary.co.uk

Peter Gallagher
4 Winton Lane, Glasgow G12 0QD
t 0141 357 4374 e p.gallagher@netmatters.co.uk
Credits Ratcatcher (F); Sweet Sixteen (F); Bum's Rush (F); Danny The Dog (F)

Rachel Gasser
Flat 6, 130 Talbot Road, London W11 1JA
t 020 7229 8028

Trevor Gittings
Experience Counts - Call Me Ltd, 5th Floor, 41-42 Berners
Street, London W1P 3AA
t 020 7637 8112 f 020 7580 2582

Lucy Glyn
Wizzo & Co, 35 Old Compton Street, London W1D 5JX
t 020 7437 2055 f 020 7437 2066
e wizzo@wizzoandco.co.uk w www.wizzoandco.co.uk

Sharon Gold
Bookends, 83 Maynard Drive, St Albans AL1 2JX
t 01727 841177

Petrina Good
146 Landor Road, London SW9 9JA
t 020 7737 0974 m 07973 692652
e petrina.good@endemoluk.com
Credits Fear Factor (T); The Salon (T); Big Brother II & III (T)

Victoria Goodall
Gems, The Media House, 87 Glebe Street, Penarth CF64 1EF
t 029 2071 0770 f 029 2071 0771
e gems@gems-agency.co.uk w www.gems-agency.co.uk
Credits King Of LA (F); Ken Parker (F); Tulse Luper Suitcase (F); If Only (F)

Nigel Gostelow
International Creative Management Ltd, Oxford House,
76 Oxford Street, London W1D 1BS
t 020 7636 6565 f 020 7323 0101 w www.icmlondon.co.uk
Credits Captain Corelli's Mandolin (F); Below (F); RKO 281 (T)

John Gray
21 Binden Road, London W12 9RJ
t 020 8749 6667 f 020 8742 9690 m 07976 734564

Rupert Greaves
55 Baizdon Road, Blackheath, London SE3 0UN
t 020 7288 9440 m 07976 289580
Agent The Production Switchboard, Northdown, Down Lane,
Compton GU3 1DN
t 01483 812011 f 01483 812027
e aly@productionswitch.freeserve.co.uk
Credits DIY Hard (S); Pork Pie (C); Natwest (C)

Patricia Greenland
10 Theobalds Way, Frimley GU16 9RF
t 01276 685925 m 07802 717606 e greenland.p@virgin.net
Credits The Hidden City (T); Rehab (F); The Dwarfs (T)

James Gregory
t 020 8871 2727 t 020 7281 1644 m 07961 316864

Victoria Gregory
32 Longley Road, Flat A, Tooting, London SW17 9LL
m 07900 493666 e vickgregory@hotmail.com
Credits Macintyre Investigates (D); Modern Times (T); Changing Rooms (T);
Class Act (D)

Caroline Greig
Callbox Communications Limited, 66 Shepperton Studios,
Studios Road, Shepperton TW17 0QD
t 01932 592572 f 01932 569655 m 07710 572572
e callboxdiary@btinternet.com w www.callboxdiary.co.uk

Dewi Griffiths
138 Strathnairn Street, Roath, Cardiff CF24 3JQ
t 029 2025 7711 m 07831 554421 e dewigriff@aol.com

Groundwork Events
27 Willow Road, London NW3 1TL
t 020 7431 7171 f 0 7431 8773 m 07860 323249
e postmaster@groundwork-events.co.uk
w www.groundwork-events.co.uk
Contact David Wright, Technical Director
Credits Lancome Fashion Show (I); Oasis - Songbird (M)

Marisa Guagenti
Flat 6, 54 Battersea High Street, London SW11 3HX
t 020 7228 4920
Credits X-perimental (T); Modern Times (T); Celebrity Big Brother Live (T); The
Pepsi Chart (T)

Joanna Gueritz
9 Ivyday Grove, London SW16 2XE
t 020 8769 0506 f 020 8677 8854 m 07802 347397
e joanna@gueritz.co.uk
Credits Cold Comfort Farm (T); Baby Father (T); Ella & The Mothers (T)

Guy A Gilks
Kiln Cottage, Kiln Hill, Upper Basildon, Reading RG8 8TA
m 07850 717765 e guygilks@beeb.net

Sian Gwilliam
65 Tradescant Road, Stockwell, London SW8 1XJ
m 07958 385929 e sian.gwilliam@vmtv.tv
Credits BAFTA Awards (T); Big Brother (T); Celebrity Big Brother (T);
Boys And Girls (T)

Mike Hack
Experience Counts - Call Me Ltd, 5th Floor, 41-42 Berners
Street, London W1P 3AA
t 020 7637 8112 f 020 7580 2582

Matthew Hamilton
Jessica Carney Associates, Suite 90-92 Kent House,
87 Regent Street, London W1B 4EH
t 020 7434 4143 f 020 7434 4173
e info@jcarneyassociates.co.uk
Credits Inquisition (T); Plotlands (T); 2000 Acres Of Sky - Series 3 (T)

Steve Harding
EXEC, 6 Travis Court, Farnham Royal SL2 3SB
t 01753 646677 **f** 01753 646770
e sue@execmanagement.co.uk **w** www.execmanagement.co.uk

Ed Harper
Gems, The Media House, 87 Glebe Street, Penarth CF64 1EF
t 029 2071 0770 **f** 029 2071 0771
e gems@gems-agency.co.uk **w** www.gems-agency.co.uk
Credits Angel For May (F); Monsignor Renard (T); Cinderella (F); Redemption (F)

Victoria Hartley
12A St George Square, London SW1V 2HP
t 020 7630 1569 **m** 07956 158875 **e** bugsarella@easynet.co.uk
Agent The Production Switchboard, Northdown, Down Lane,
Compton GU3 1DN
t 01483 812011 **f** 01483 812027
e aly@productionswitch.freeserve.co.uk
Credits Renault Megane (C); Lighthouse Family - Dry (M); Chillout Album 2003 (M)

David Harvey
21 Water Lane, Twickenham TW1 3NP
t 020 8744 0123 **f** 07930 009360 **m** 07932 003827
e davidharvey00@hotmail.com

Alex Hedges
37 Shirland Mews, London W9 3DY
t 020 8964 9591 **m** 07909 517286 **e** alexhedges@yahoo.com
Agent The Production Switchboard, Northdown, Down Lane,
Compton GU3 1DN
t 01483 812011 **f** 01483 812027
e aly@productionswitch.freeserve.co.uk
Credits Kaliber (C); Army (C); McDonald's (C)

Geoffrey Helman
9D Logan Place, Kensington, London W8 6QN
t 020 7373 6288

Peter Hider
t 01344 466966 **f** 01344 466966 **m** 07850 555151
e hider@onetel.net.uk

Robert How
Gems, The Media House, 87 Glebe Street, Penarth CF64 1EF
t 029 2071 0770 **f** 029 2071 0771 **e** gems@gems-agency.co.uk
w www.gems-agency.co.uk
Credits The Parole Officer (F); The Cup (F); 24 Hour Party People (F);
28 Days Later (F)

Kate Howard-Smith
The Production Switchboard, Northdown, Down Lane,
Compton GU3 1DN
t 01483 812011 **f** 01483 812027
Credits Robinsons Fruit Shoot (C); Coca Cola (C); All Charged Up (C)

Sheila Humphreys
25 Springwell Road, Streatham, London SW16 2QU
t 020 8769 3436 **f** 020 8769 3436 **m** 07980 598899
e sheilaeobrien@aol.com

Louise Hunter
Flat 2, 10 Bernays Grove, Brixton, London SW9 8DF
t 020 7274 3110 **m** 07957 455391
e louisethehunted@hotmail.com
Credits MTV Total Request Live (T); Staying Alive 3 (T)

Maurice Hunter
10 River View Court, Llandarf, Cardiff CF5 2QJ
t 029 2055 5055 **f** 029 2055 5055 **m** 07885 317755
e maurice.hunter@virgin.net
Credits Oh Little Town Of Bethlehem (F); Civvies (F); Solomon And Gaenor; One
ot the Hollywood Ten

Georgina Huxstep
8 Chiswick Village, Chiswick, London W4 3BY
t 020 8994 3321 **f** 020 8996 0447 **m** 07973 396295
e george@georgie-girl.co.uk
Credits Homebase (I); Fetish Seen (T); Call Me (T); Catering For All Tastes (T)

Gemma Jackson
International Creative Management Ltd, Oxford House,
76 Oxford Street, London W1D 1BS
t 020 7636 6565 **f** 020 7323 0101 **w** www.icmlondon.co.uk
Credits Bridget Jones's Diary (F); Iris (F); Neverland (F)

Helen Jackson
46 Maple House, Idonia Street, London SE8 4LT
t 020 8691 1125 **f** 020 8691 1125 **m** 07973 835316
e hjhelga@aol.com
Credits Richard Taylor Interviews (T); BBC Blackwater (T); Streetmate (T)

Richard Johns
McKinney Macartney Management Ltd, The Barley Mow
Centre, 10 Barley Mow Passage, London W4 4PH
t 020 8995 4747 **f** 020 8995 2414
e fkb@mmtechsrep.demon.co.uk
w www.mckinneymacartney.com

Carolyn Parry Jones
Gems, The Media House, 87 Glebe Street, Penarth CF64 1EF
t 029 2071 0770 **f** 029 2071 0771
e gems@gems-agency.co.uk **w** www.gems-agency.co.uk
Credits Bad Girls (T); The Safe House (T); Goodbye Mr Steadman (T); Menace (T)

Sandra Jordan
71 Niton Street, London SW6 6NH
t 020 7835 1427 **f** 020 7610 1009 **e** sandy-s@btinternet.com
Agent The Production Switchboard, Northdown, Down Lane,
Compton GU3 1DN
t 01483 812011 **f** 01483 812027
e aly@productionswitch.freeserve.co.uk
Credits Baileys Minis - Bath And Massage (C); Tyskie Uncle Duncan (C);
Five Alive (C)

Selina Kay
5 Durham Road, East Finchley, London N2 9DP
t 020 8444 3611 **f** 020 8444 3633 **m** 07710 198200
e selina@clarktv.com

Emma Kellachan
15 Melling Street, Plumstead Common, London SE18 2EG
t 020 8854 5802 **m** 07941 135918
e emma@visualeyes.fsnet.co.uk
Credits Number 1 Longing - Number 2 Regret (F); Woosh (S); Ten Minutes (S);
Living it Up (T)

Paul Kelly
Orchard Cottage, Church Walk, Marston, Grantham NG32 2HL
t 01400 250252 **f** 01400 251007 **m** 07785 356 944
e 100415.1550@compuserve.com
Credits Skysports Boxing (T); Question Time (T); The Price Is Right (T)

Helen Kelsey
North Grange Farm, Halesworth Road, Saxmundham IP17 2JL
t 01728 660341 **f** 01728 660341 **m** 07711 782238
e helenmacdonogh@aol.com
Credits Hear' Say (M); Gender Trouble (D); Little Wolf's Book Of Badness (A); S
Club 7 Go Wild (T)

David Kenyon
13 Albert Road, Teddington TW11 0BD
t 020 8977 5195 **f** 020 8977 5195 **m** 07836 363222
e davidjkenyon@aol.com
Credits C5 Football (T); ITV Athletics (T); Commonwealth Games (T); Sydney
Olympics (T)

Mark Lavender
191 Trewhitt Road, Newcastle-upon-Tyne NE6 5DY
t 0191 224 4301 **f** 0191 224 4301 **m** 07710 064632
e mark@rsproductions.co.uk **w** www.rsproductions.co.uk
Credits How We Met (T); Learning To Drown (S); Away Goals Rule (S); Sunday Lunch (T)

Susan Lee
t 07971 676050
Credits Jamie's Kitchen (T); Whatever Happened To Food (D); Muhammad Ali: Through the Eyes of the World (D)

Denise Lesley
108 Woodyates Road, London SE12 9JL
f 020 8857 5193 **m** 07966 443034
e deniselesley@aol.com **w** www.pma.org.uk
Credits History File: The Cold War (T); History File: American Voices (E); Curriculum Bites: History (E); The Live Sessions: Georgie Fame And The New Blue Flames (I)

Cathy Lord
McKinney Macartney Management Ltd, The Barley Mow Centre, 10 Barley Mow Passage, London W4 4PH
t 020 8995 4747 **f** 020 8995 2414
e fkb@mmtechsrep.demon.co.uk
w www.mckinneymacartney.com

Veronica Lowes
4 The Embankment, London SW15 1LB
t 020 8788 7028 **f** 020 8789 2097 **m** 07860 286144
e vlowes@hotmail-com
Contact Veronica Lowes, Producer
Credits Services Company (C)

Graeme MacArthur
18 Shirley Avenue, Southampton SO15 5NG
t 023 8077 9287 **f** 023 8077 9289 **m** 07831 857837
e graeme@shirleyavenue.com
Credits McCready & Daughter (T); Monarch Of The Glen (T); Silent Witness (T); My Uncle Silas (T)

Jacob Madsen
Production Switchboard, Northdown, Down Lane, Compton GU3 1DN
t 01483 812011 **f** 01483 812027
e aly@productionswitch.freeserve.co.uk
Credits Patek Phillippe - The Time (C); Marianne Faithful - Sex Strangers (M); Chemical Brothers - The Test (M)

Carmel Maloney
International Creative Management Ltd, Oxford House, 76 Oxford Street, London W1D 1BS
t 020 7636 6565 **f** 020 7323 0101 **w** www.icmlondon.co.uk
Credits Forgive And Forget (T); Pretending To Be Judith (T); Messiah (T)

Sophie Marshall
t 020 8675 9738 **f** 020 8675 9608 **m** 07788 780885
Credits Benylin (C); Nat West (C); Smirnoff Ice (C); DFS (C)

M Martell
12 Grenville Place, Flat 7, London SW7 4RW
t 020 7835 1494 **f** 020 7835 0064 **m** 07831 465612
e martell333@aol.com

Alison B Matthews
5 Fish Street, Redbourn AL3 7LP
m 07976 246151
e dragon33@produxion.com
e alisonmatthews@btopenworld.com
Credits Judge John Deeds (T); Mersey Beat (T); The Bill (T)

Helen McAulay Stewart
Tumblewood, Radyr Court Road, Cardiff CF5 2QF
t 029 2055 2414 **f** 029 2055 2414 **m** 07778 175420
e helenmstewart@lycos.co.uk
Credits War Surgeons (D); Lucky Bag (T); A Light in The City (F); Bloody Towers (D)

Geraldine McCarthy
The Production Switchboard, Northdown, Down Lane, Compton GU3 1DN
t 01483 812011 **f** 01483 812027
e aly@productionswitch.freeserve.co.uk
Credits MTV To Go (C); Mastercard (C); Lynx Christmas Pack (C)

Shirley McIntyre
Orchard Cottage, Church Walk, Marston, Grantham NG32 2HL
t 01400 250252 **f** 01400 251007 **m** 07785 356945
e shirleyamcintryre@hotmail.com

Peter Miller
Gems, The Media House, 87 Glebe Street, Penarth CF64 1EF
t 029 2071 0770 **f** 029 2071 0771
e gems@gems-agency.co.uk **w** www.gems-agency.co.uk
Credits Last Flight Of Zulu Delta 576 (T); Wavelength (T); The Queen's Nose I,II,III,IV & V (T); Lifeforce (T)

Janine Modder
EXEC, 6 Travis Court, Farnham Royal SL2 3SB
t 01753 646677 **f** 01753 646770
e sue@execmanagement.co.uk **w** www.execmanagement.co.uk

Jacqui Moore
London
m 07973 800498 **e** moorejacqui@hotmail.com
Credits Oliver's Twist (T); Star For A Night (T); Banzai (T); Top Gear (T)

Simon Moorhead
Gems, The Media House, 87 Glebe Street, Penarth CF64 1EF
t 029 2071 0770 **f** 029 2071 0771
e gems@gems-agency.co.uk **w** www.gems-agency.co.uk
Credits Antelope South (C); National Geographic (C); Granada Sport (C)

MJ Morgan
Flat 2, 13 Pinfold Road, London SW16 2SL
t 020 8355 9773 **m** 07768 864556 **e** haha.films@virgin.net
Credits Mobo Awards (T); Dancestar Awards (T); Brian Wilson (M); Red Hot Chili Peppers (M)

Philip Morris
Gems, The Media House, 87 Glebe Street, Penarth CF64 1EF
t 029 2071 0770 **f** 029 2071 0771
e gems@gems-agency.co.uk **w** www.gems-agency.co.uk
Credits One Man's Heaven (F); Dragonworld (F); The Honey Trap (F); Relic Hunter (T)

Redmond Morris
International Creative Management Ltd, Oxford House, 76 Oxford Street, London W1D 1BS
t 020 7636 6565 **f** 020 7323 0101 **w** www.icmlondon.co.uk
Credits Interview With A Vampire (F); Michael Collins (F); The Actor (F)

Nick Mortimer
6 Lion Avenue, Twickenham TW1 4JG
t 020 8892 0999 **m** 07801 337165
Contact Nick Mortimer
Credits The Fitz (T); The Savages (T); The Estate Agents (T); Couplings - II (T)

Paul Munn
Gems, The Media House, 87 Glebe Street, Penarth CF64 1EF
t 029 2071 0770 **f** 029 2071 0771
e gems@gems-agency.co.uk **w** www.gems-agency.co.uk
Credits Rebel Heart (T); The Bomb Maker (T); Miracle At Midnight (F); St Patrick (F)

Paul K Munn
Experience Counts - Call Me Ltd, 5th Floor, 41-42 Berners Street, London W1P 3AA
t 020 7637 8112 **f** 020 7580 2582

Monica Murphy
Gems, The Media House, 87 Glebe Street, Penarth CF64 1EF
t 029 2071 0770 **f** 029 2071 0771
e gems@gems-agency.co.uk **w** www.gems-agency.co.uk
Credits Lunch (T); Mary Berry (T); Delia Smith's Winter Collection (T)

Angela Murray
2/1, 39 Byres Road, Glasgow G11 5RG
t 0141 334 0241 **f** 0141 579 4042 **m** 07768 388603
e angela.kh.murray@virgin.net
Credits Room For The Night (T); The Karen Dunbar Show (T); Still Game (T); Sixteen Years Of Alcohol (T)

Helen Murray
t 028 9127 1848 **m** 07711 010 916 **e** helenmurray@appleonline.net

Kate Murrell
Gems, The Media House, 87 Glebe Street, Penarth CF64 1EF
t 029 2071 0770 **f** 029 2071 0771
e gems@gems-agency.co.uk **w** www.gems-agency.co.uk
Credits West Eleven (T); The Stick Up (S); As If (T); Two Days (F)

Naseem Nathoo
68 Hartfield Crescent, London SW19 3SA
t 020 8542 1570 **f** 020 8542 1570 **m** 07931 336 028
e nasnat@breathemail.net

Rachel Neale
12 Melbourne Road, Teddington TW11 9QX
t 020 8943 0371 **f** 020 8977 7506 **m** 07860 766363
e rneale@dircon.co.uk
Credits To Kill A King (F); The Man Who Cried (F); Three Guesses (F); Wit (F)

Debbie Ninnis
The Production Switchboard, Northdown, Down Lane, Compton GU3 1DN
t 01483 812011 **f** 01483 812027
e aly@productionswitch.freeserve.co.uk
Credits Phoenix Blue (T); South Kensington (F); BT Business (C)

Zoe Norman
55 Warlock Road, London W9 3LW
t 020 8964 1242 **f** 020 8960 9374 **m** 07973 295 233
e zoepinicbrewer@yahoo.com

Kevin de la Noy
t 01753 646677 **f** 01753 646770
w www.exec6677.demon.co.uk/kdelanoy1.htm
Agent EXEC, 6 Travis Court, Farnham Royal SL2 3SB
t 01753 646677 **f** 01753 646770
e sue@execmanagement.co.uk **w** www.execmanagement.co.uk
Credits Saving Private Ryan (F); Mission:Impossible II (F); Ali (F)

Gabriella Panas
10 Belmont Court, Finchley Road, London NW11 6XS
t 020 8458 9661 **m** 07775 891047 **e** gabi@care4free.net
Credits What Women Want (T); Dispatches (T); Smash (T); South Bank Show (T)

Peter Pearson
1 Long Slip, Langton Green, Tunbridge Wells TN3 0BT
t 01892 862751 **f** 01892 861705 **m** 07778 474617
e pearsonpeter@clara.net

Tessa Pemberton
22 Nightingale Square, London SW12 8QN
t 020 8673 8011 **m** 07796 135726 **e** tessapemberton@clara.co.uk

Murray Peterson
m 07966 169728 **e** murray1000@hotmail.com
Credits Coupling (T); The Royle Family (T); Gimme Gimme Gimme (T); My Hero Series I-IV (T)

Cliff Pinnock
Jessica Carney Associates, Suite 90-92 Kent House, 87 Regent Street, London W1B 4EH
t 020 7434 4143 **f** 020 7434 4173 **e** info@jcarneyassociates.co.uk
Credits Our Friends In The North (T); Red Dwarf - The Movie (T); The Bill (T)

Juliet Poels
t 020 8875 1571 **m** 07973 823 064 **e** juliet_poels@hotmail.com
Credits Addicted to Death; Tales from the Black Museum

Carla Poole
24B Veronica Road, London SW17 8QL
t 020 8772 6580 **m** 07801 748684 **e** mail@carlapoole.com
Agent The Production Switchboard, Northdown, Down Lane, Compton GU3 1DN
t 01483 812011 **f** 01483 812027
e aly@productionswitch.freeserve.co.uk
Credits COI - Waste Awareness (C); Audi Of America (C); Orange (C)

Justine Randle
Gems, The Media House, 87 Glebe Street, Penarth CF64 1EF
t 029 2071 0770 **f** 029 2071 0771
e gems@gems-agency.co.uk **w** www.gems-agency.co.uk
Credits Oribble (T); Hearts And Bones (T); The Hosue That Jack Built (T); The Bill (T)

Annie Rees
117 Pembroke Road, Clifton, Bristol BS8 3EU
t 01173 309597 **m** 07831 223092 **e** annierees1@hotmail.com
Credits Gentlemen's Relish (T); Dirty Tricks (T); NCS (T); Servants (T)

Mary Richards
McKinney Macartney Management Ltd, The Barley Mow Centre, 10 Barley Mow Passage, London W4 4PH
t 020 8995 4747 **f** 020 8995 2414
e fkb@mmtechsrep.demon.co.uk
w www.mckinneymacartney.com
Credits Elizabeth (F); Notting Hill (F); Band Of Brothers (T)

Virginia Roberts
Wizzo & Co, 35 Old Compton Street, London W1D 5JX
t 020 7437 2055 **f** 020 7437 2066
e wizzo@wizzoandco.co.uk **w** www.wizzoandco.co.uk

Michael Robins
t 020 7354 0438 **f** 020 7354 0438 **m** 07771 743771
e michaelrobins@appleonline.net
Contact Michael Robins

Rupert Ryle-Hodges
4 Redesdale St, London SW3 4BH
t 020 7376 4673
Credits Keen Eddie (T); Messiah II (T); Armadillo (T); Dirty Pretty Things (F)

Beth Sanders
Top Floor, 63 Marchmont Street, London WC1N 1AP
e beth@pondlife.co.uk
Agent The Production Switchboard, Northdown, Down Lane, Compton GU3 1DN
t 01483 812011 **f** 01483 812027
e aly@productionswitch.freeserve.co.uk
Credits Mastercard (C); Coca-Cola (C); IBM (C)

Robbie Sandison
International Creative Management Ltd, Oxford House, 76 Oxford Street, London W1D 1BS
t 020 7636 6565 **f** 020 7323 0101 **w** www.icmlondon.co.uk
Credits The Choir (S); A&E (T); Where The Heart Is (T)

Paul Sarony
Gems, The Media House, 87 Glebe Street, Penarth CF64 1EF
t 029 2071 0770 **f** 029 2071 0771
e gems@gems-agency.co.uk **w** www.gems-agency.co.uk
Credits Criminals (F); Honest (F); A Rather English Marriage (T); Darwin (F)

Ian Scaife
The Banks, Common Road, Whiteparish SP5 2SU
t 01794 884898 **f** 01794 884898 **m** 07836 499504
e scaifey@tesco.net
Credits Trust (T); No Child Of Mine (T); Mosley (T); Second Sight (T)

Tracey Seaward
International Creative Management Ltd, Oxford House, 76 Oxford Street, London W1D 1BS
t 020 7636 6565 **f** 020 7323 0101 **w** www.icmlondon.co.uk
Credits The Serpent's Kiss (F); The Good Thief (F); Dirty Pretty Things (F)

Jane Shackleton
Wizzo & Co, 35 Old Compton Street, London W1D 5JX
t 020 7437 2055 **f** 020 7437 2066
e wizzo@wizzoandco.co.uk **w** www.wizzoandco.co.uk

Sandra Shuttleworth
179 Leighton Road, London
m 07771 602009 **e** sandrashuttleworth@virgin.net
Agent The Production Switchboard, Northdown, Down Lane, Compton GU3 1DN
t 01483 812011 **f** 01483 812027
Credits Entering Blue Zone (F); Suzie Gold (F); Nouvelle (C)

Farne Sinclair
7A Tomlins Grove, London E3 4NX
t 020 8983 0388 **m** 07946 854678
e farne.sinclair@principalmedia.com
Credits True Stories From The Morgue (T); Me and My Toyboy (T); Amnesia, Trapped in Time (T); Secret History (D)

SOL Productions Ltd
10A Twyford Avenue, London W3 9QA
t 0845 458 9740 **f** 0845 458 9741 **m** 07956 145049
e info@sol-productions.co.uk **w** www.sol-productions.co.uk
Contact Peter Stubbs; Johnny Blick
Credits Kit-kat - Nestle (C)

Andy Stebbing
Production Switchboard, Northdown, Down Lane, Compton GU3 1DN
t 01483 812011 **f** 01483 812027
e aly@productionswitch.freeserve.co.uk
Credits Tomorrow La Scala (F); Undercover Cops (D); Helen Of Peckham (F)

Peter Stenning
EXEC, 6 Travis Court, Farnham Royal SL2 3SB
t 01753 646677 **f** 01753 646770
e sue@execmanagement.co.uk **w** www.execmanagement.co.uk

Meinir Stout
Gems, The Media House, 87 Glebe Street, Penarth CF64 1EF
t 029 2071 0770 **f** 029 2071 0771
e gems@gems-agency.co.uk **w** www.gems-agency.co.uk
Credits D'Artangan (F); The Lost Batallions (F); Diggity (F); George And The Dragon (T)

Dusty Symonds
EXEC, 6 Travis Court, Farnham Royal SL2 3SB
t 01753 646677 **f** 01753 646770 **e** sue@execmanagement.co.uk **w** www.execmanagement.co.uk

Guy Tannahill
St Johns Mount, 45 Bodenham Road, Hereford HR1 2TP
t 01432 268793 **f** 01432 279999 **m** 07836 337199
e guy@dodo.co.uk
Credits Girl With A Pearl Earring (F); It Was An Accident (F); Possession (F); Spider (F)

Television Support Services
The Maidstone Studios, Maidstone ME14 5NZ
t 01622 684538 **f** 01622 684627 **e** peter.urie@gullane.com
Contact Peter Urie, Vice President, Group Head of Production
Credits Thomas the Tank Engine (T); Sooty (T); Art Attack (T)

Ruth Tester-Brown
26 Multon Road, Wandsworth Common, London SW18 3LH
t 020 8874 8336 **f** 020 8355 8804 **m** 07714 201881
e ruthtb@aol.com
Credits The Television Of The Year Party (T); 30 Years Of Billy Connolly (T); The National Television Awards 1998-2002 (T)

Artie Thomas
Gems, The Media House, 87 Glebe Street, Penarth CF64 1EF
t 029 2071 0770 **f** 029 2071 0771
e gems@gems-agency.co.uk **w** www.gems-agency.co.uk
Credits Noah's Ark (T); Labour Of Love (T); Daisies In December (F)

Karl Thurston-Brown
68A St James Street, Brighton BN2 1PJ
m 07866 941738 **e** ktbcurious@hotmail.com
Credits Save Our World Festival (E); Looking Glass - The Frame (E); Sussex Downs College Performance Arts (E); Fireraisers - This Rough Magic (E)

Ian Tootle
Gems, The Media House, 87 Glebe Street, Penarth CF64 1EF
t 029 2071 0770 **f** 029 2071 0771
e gems@gems-agency.co.uk **w** www.gems-agency.co.uk
Credits Mortimer's Law (T); The Creatives (T); A&E (T); Monarch Of The Glen (T)

Sue Tramontini
The Horses Pond, Nedging Tye IP7 7HJ
t 01449 744059 **f** 01449 744058 **m** 07770 870405
e suetram@aol.com
Credits Greetings From Grozny (D); Masterchef 1999 (T); Mission Wild (D); Warrior: From Civilian To Soldier (D)

Gary Tuck
35 Gladsmuir Road, London N19 3JY
t 020 7281 7688 **f** 020 7281 2622 **e** tuck@easynet.co.uk

Julia Valentine
Gems, The Media House, 87 Glebe Street, Penarth CF64 1EF
t 029 2071 0770 **f** 029 2071 0771
e gems@gems-agency.co.uk **w** www.gems-agency.co.uk
Credits Kin (F); Breve Traversee (T); Revenger's Tragedy (F)

Sarah Wadey
24 Earls Court Square, London SW5 9DN
t 020 7244 7043 **m** 07970 623062 **e** snappress@aol.com
Agent The Production Switchboard, Northdown, Down Lane, Compton GU3 1DN
t 01483 812011 **f** 01483 812027
e aly@productionswitch.freeserve.co.uk

Andrew Warren
10 Patten Road, London SW18 3RH
t 020 8874 9667 **f** 020 8333 2098 **m** 07831 719321
e andrew@awarren.demon.co.uk

Tony Waye
Gems, The Media House, 87 Glebe Street, Penarth CF64 1EF
t 029 2071 0770 **f** 029 2071 0771
e gems@gems-agency.co.uk **w** www.gems-agency.co.uk
Credits Tomorrow Never Dies (F); Goldeneye (F); Die Another Day (F); The World Is Not Enough (F)

Debbie Weinreich
Wizzo & Co, 35 Old Compton Street, London W1D 5JX
t 020 7437 2055 **f** 020 7437 2066
e wizzo@wizzoandco.co.uk **w** www.wizzoandco.co.uk

Sue Wesley
Tiverton House, Warwick road, Chadwick End, Solihull B93 0BU
t 01564 795569 **m** 07710 378867 **e** wesleysue@hotmail.com

Natalie Williams
Flat 1, 33 Ongar Road, London SW6 1SL
t 020 7381 2442 **f** 020 7385 0460 **m** 07771 976562
e nwilliams@winklefilms.com

Gary Williamson
International Creative Management Ltd, Oxford House, 76 Oxford Street, London W1D 1BS
t 020 7636 6565 **f** 020 7323 0101 **w** www.icmlondon.co.uk
Credits The Escort (F); My Uncle Silas (T); Stranded (T)

Brian Windus
19 Kilravock, London W10 4HX
t 020 8960 3214 **f** 020 8960 8324 **m** 07711 847774
e brianwindus@dial.pipex.com

Andrew Wood
12 Bridge Road, St Margarets, Twickenham TW1 1RE
t 020 8891 6790 **f** 020 8891 6790 **m** 07961 325029
e drew@fornalutx69.freeserve.co.uk
Credits London's Burning (T); Lighthouse Hill (F); Chaos And Cadavers (F); Ted And Alice (T)

Leopold Wurm
London
t 07626 921137 **m** 07720 639574 **i** +1 212 713 5528
e lwurm@mac.com
Credits Cut & Dry (F); Disney's World Of English (A)

Cyrus Yavneh
International Creative Management Ltd, Oxford House, 76 Oxford Street, London W1D 1BS
t 020 7636 6565 **f** 020 7323 0101 **w** www.icmlondon.co.uk
Credits Hard Rain (F); Town And Country (F); 24 (T)

Zap Production Services
1-2 Bromley Place, London W1T 6DA
t 020 7436 5577 **f** 020 7691 7282 **m** 07774 235141
e mail@zap-productions.co.uk **w** www.zap-productions.co.uk
Contact Mark Parsons, Line Producer

Elena Zokas
Gems, The Media House, 87 Glebe Street, Penarth CF64 1EF
t 029 2071 0770 **f** 029 2071 0771
e gems@gems-agency.co.uk **w** www.gems-agency.co.uk
Credits Ripley's Game (F); League Of Extraordinary Gentlemen (F); From Hell (F)

Production Secretaries

Clare Bennett
Gems, The Media House, 87 Glebe Street, Penarth CF64 1EF
t 029 2071 0770 **f** 029 2071 0771
e gems@gems-agency.co.uk **w** www.gems-agency.co.uk
Credits Relic Hunter III (T); The Tiger (T)

Sarah Bryant
Experience Counts - Call Me Ltd, 5th Floor, 41-42 Berners Street, London W1P 3AA
t 020 7637 8112 **f** 020 7580 2582

Eve Petcher
The Production Switchboard, North Down, Down Lane, Compton GU3 1DN
t 01483 812011 **f** 01483 812027
e aly@productionswitch.freeserve.co.uk
Credits Cold Mountain (F); Helen Of Troy (T); Keen Eddie (T)

Nina Sagemoen
Gems, The Media House, 87 Glebe Street, Penarth CF64 1EF
t 029 2071 0770 **f** 029 2071 0771
e gems@gems-agency.co.uk **w** www.gems-agency.co.uk
Credits English Goodbye (S); The Trouble With Men And Women (F); Les Liasions Dangereuses (F); Twelfth Night (T)

PRODUCTION FACILITIES

Production Facilities
Air Conditioning/Heating

Air Trembath
Felstead Road, Longmead Industrial Estate, Epsom KT19 9XS
t 01372 215000 **f** 01372 215008 **e** m.holiday@airtrembath.co.uk
Credits Red Cap (T); Harry Potter And The Philosopher's Stone (F); Band Of Brothers (T); Die Another Day (F)

Coglan Air Conditioning Services
Worting House, Basingstoke RG23 8PY
t 020 8202 4279

J Verhoeven (UK) Ltd
Brick Kiln Lane, Parkhouse Industrial Estate West, Chesterton, Newcastle ST5 7AS
t 01782 566054 **f** 01782 564754
e kellyeccleston@jverhoevenuk.fsbusiness.co.uk
w www.jverhoeven.com
Contact Kelly Eccleston, Promotion, Sales & Marketing

Production Facilities
General

ANGLIA
Television Limited

Anglia Studios
Anglia House, Norwich NR1 3JG
t 01603 615151 **f** 01603 752504
e angliastudios@granadamedia.com **w** www.angliastudios.com
Contact Dan Haddon, Location Services; Dave Wyatt, Head of Post Production; Jacky Lane, Head of Resources; Ian Osborne, Head of Studios; Beverly Bulcock, Head of Resources
Great kit, great people and the Norwich nightlife is brilliant.

Apex Television Production
Vision Centre, Eastern Way, Bury St Edmunds IP32 7AB
t 01284 724900 **f** 01284 700004
e sales@apextv.co.uk **w** www.apextv.co.uk
Contact Peter Creswell, Technical Director; Bernard Mulhern, Managing Director

Avonbridge Film Production
3 York Road, Edinburgh EH5 3EJ
t 0131 478 4439 **f** 0131 478 9344 **m** 07831 596510
e penny@avonfilm.com **w** www.avonfilm.com
Contact Penny Thomson, Director

Awfully Nice Video Company Ltd
30 Long Lane, Ickenham UB10 8TA
t 07000 345678 **f** 07000 345679 **m** 07860 343737
e nicevideo@aol.com **w** www.awfullynicevideo.com
Contact Keith Darbyshire, Director/Sound Recordist; Debbie Crook, Personal
Assistant/Bookings; Graham Maunder, Director/Lighting Cameraman
Credits Kirsty's Home Videos (T); World's Strongest Man (T); Olympic Preview
Show (T); Daz (C)

Barcud Derwen
74-78 Park Road, Whitchurch, Cardiff CF14 7BR
t 029 2061 1515 **f** 029 2052 1226 **m** 07970 112 903
e bryn@barcudderwen.com **w** www.barcudderwen.com
Contact Bryn Roberts, Managing Director; Tudor Roberts, Director; Stephen
Cowin, Director; John Gwynedd Jones, Director
Credits National Eisteddfod; Tom Jones Live at Cardiff Castle; Bryn Terfec Festival

BBC Resources

BBC Resources
Room 2119, Television Centre, Wood Lane, London W12 7RJ
t 020 8576 0907 **f** 020 8746 1024 **e** bbcresources@bbc.co.uk
w www.bbcresources.com

BKA Facilities
The Croft Studio, 24 Mill Lane, Wingrave, Aylesbury HP22 4PL
t 01296 681660 **f** 01296 681458 **m** 07836 280016
e bka.service@virgin.net
Contact Brian King

Bluefrog Studios
The Manor House, Oulston, York YO61 3RB
t 01347 868564 **f** 01347 868563 **m** 07968 822994
e studiobluefrog@yahoo.co.uk **w** www.bluefrogstudios.tv
Contact John Phillips, Managing Director; Jessica Savage, Studio Manager
Credits Illuminitis: VJ & Pop Promo (M); The York Millenium Bridge (D);
Jonathan Cainer Astrological DVD (C); The Mirror's Astrology Ad Campaign
2001 & 2002 (T)

*Complete facilities, green screen, private country location,
accommodation available, ideal for corporate weekends/music
recordings, whatever your production needs.*

Bow Tie Television
Unit 20, Bourne Industrial Park, Bourne Road, Crayford DA1 4BZ
t 01322 524500 **f** 01322 527777
e john@bowtietv.com **w** www.bowtietv.com
Contact John Knopp, Managing Director
Credits Endemol - King Of Sport (T); NHK Enterprises Europe Ltd - Red Demon (T)

BVC (Bath) Ltd
Kingston House, 2 Combe Park, Bath BA1 3NP
t 01225 428777 **f** 01225 429111
info@bvctelevision.co.uk **w** www.bvctelevision.co.uk
Contact Geoff Todd, Managing Director; Matthew Grant, Facilities Manager;
Marie-Louise Grant, Line Producer

Caravel Film Techniques Ltd
The Great Barn Studios, Cippenham Lane, Slough SL1 5AU
t 01753 534828 **f** 01753 571383
e ajjcaraveltv@aol.com **w** www.caravelstudios.com
Contact Anita See, Director

Castle Vale Community Radio Ltd
Lower Ground Floor, Topcliffe House, Hawkinge Drive,
Birmingham B35 6BT
t 01217 491343 **f** 01217 491829
e neil@cvcr.co.uk **w** www.cvcr.co.uk
Contact Neil Hollins, Manager

Cheltenham Film Studios
Arle Court, Hatherley Lane, Cheltenham GL51 6PN
t 01242 542700 **f** 01242 542701
e info@cheltstudio.com **w** www.cheltstudio.com
Contact Valerie Lane, Site Co-ordinator

Chris Potts Television Sound
131 Queen Elizabeth Way, Colchester CO2 8LT
t 077 6868 1062 **e** tvsound416@hotmail.com
Contact Chris Potts, Managing Director
Credits Newsnight (T); This Morning (T); World Cup (Korea) (T);
Comic Relief 2003 (T)

The Cutting Edge
44 Berwick Street, London W1F 8SE
t 020 7287 0080 **f** 020 7287 0090
e cuttingedge@claria.co.uk

DSA Production Services
1 Addley Court, 435 Chiswick High Road, London W4 4AU
t 020 8994 9445 **f** 020 8995 1347
e svend@dsaproductions.co.uk
Contact Svend Johannsen, Production Manager

Eardrum Productions
177 Wardour Street, London W1F 8WX
t 020 7287 2211 **f** 020 7287 2288
e info@eardrum.com **w** www.eardrum.com
Contact Martin Simms, Director; Janet Clarke, Production Manager
Credits Ford (C); Red Bull (C); Lenor (C); Nike (C)

Entec Sound & Light
517 Yeading Lane, Northolt UB5 6LN
t 020 8842 4004 **f** 020 8842 3310 **m** 07836 590057
e sales@entec-soundandlight.com
w www.entec-soundandlight.com
Contact Noreen Oriodan, Lighting Manager; Dick Hayes, Sound Manager
Credits Walkers Crisps (C); National TV Awards (T); Boys And Girls (T)

Films at 59 Ltd
59 Cotham Hill, Clifton, Bristol BS6 6JR
t 0117 906 4300 **f** 0117 923 7003
e info@filmsat59.com **w** www.filmsat59.com
Contact Mike Prudence; George Panayiotou, Facilities; Gina Fucci, Co-
ordinating Director

Free Range Television
2 Anvil Court, Venterdon, Stoke Climsland, Callington PL17 8PJ
t 01579 389389

Line-Up PMC
9A Tankerville Place, Jesmond, Newcastle-upon-Tyne NE2 3AT
t 0191 281 6449 **f** 0191 212 0913 **m** 07808 300906
e chrismurtagh@line-up.co.uk
Contact Chris Murtagh, Director
Credits APU (M); Black Voices (M); BSKYB Awards - Personality Of The Year (T)

LT Scotland
74 Victoria Crescent Road, Glasgow G12 1JN
t 0141 337 5000 **f** 0141 337 5050
e enquiries@ltscotland.com **w** www.ltscotland.com
Contact Tommy Cass, Media Producer

The Lucky Strike Company
82 Berwick Street, Soho, London W1F 8TP
t 020 7734 4424 **f** 020 7734 0544 **m** 07798 528276
e info@luckystrike.uk.com **w** www.luckystrike.uk.com
Contact Martin Bruce-Clayton, Producer; Phil Haselden, Managing Director;
Beth Sanders, Head of Production
Credits IBM (C); Kleenex (C); Fed Ex (C); New York Stock Exchange (C)

Meridian Broadcasting (Southampton)
Television Centre, Southampton SO14 0PZ
t 023 8022 2555 **f** 023 8033 5050
w www.meridian.tv.co.uk/facilities
Contact Ken Dawkins, Studio Manager; Paul Reece, Post Production Manager;
Ian Carley, Head of Graphics

Moviesmiths
Crofts House, Kirdford RH14 0JH
t 01403 820299 **m** 07802 874040
e info@moviesmiths.tv **w** www.moviesmiths.tv
Contact Roger Whitby, Partner

Moving Vision Ltd
Newbridge-on-Wye LD1 6LH
t 01597 860575 **f** 01597 860655 **m** 07721 429181
e mv@movingvision.co.uk **w** www.movingvision.co.uk
Contact Luke Wallich-Clifford, Director/Multi-Tasking; David Lawless,
Director/Multi-Tasking; John Lubran, Managing Director and Producer
Credits The General And The Scientist (T); Kingdom Of The Asante (D); Centre
For Alternative Energy (I); Deadline 2000 (T)

RTE TV Facilities
Donnybrook, Dublin 4, Rep of Ireland
t +353 1 208 3010 **f** +353 1 208 3034 **e** tvfacility@rte.ie
Contact Charles Byrne, Head of TV; Paul Tighe, Production, Planning
and Co-ordination

Sky Pictures Worldwide
The Coach House Studios, The Coach Inn Complex, Clynnog
Fawr, Caernarfon LL54 5PB
t 01286 660212 **f** 01286 660785 **m** 07767 607503
e skypix@clara.co.uk **w** www.skypix.co.uk
Contact Stephen Williams, Technical Director/Producer

SLV
70-74 Stewarts Road, London SW8 4DE
t 020 7720 6464 **f** 020 7622 3666
e facilities@slvision.co.uk **w** www.slvision.co.uk
Contact Dan Pope, Facilities Manager
Credits The South Bank Show (T); What Not To Wear (S); The Real Birth Show (S)

Sound Design
Dundas, Chavey Down Road, Winkfield Row, Bracknell RG42 7PB
t 01344 883620 **f** 01344 893620 **m** 07774 138136
e sounddesign@hotmail.com
Contact Courtenay Nicholas, Director/Acoustician

Sound Moves
The Oaks, Cross Lane, Smallfield RH6 9SA
t 01342 844190 **f** 01342 844290
e steve@sound-moves.com **w** www.sound-moves.com
Contact Steve Williams, Proprietor

TVMS
420 Sauchiehall Street, Glasgow G2 3JD
t 0141 331 1993 **f** 0141 332 9040 **e** peter@tvms.fsnet.co.uk
Contact Peter McNeill, Director/Camera
Credits The Vulcan Barge (I); 6000000 Is A Number (T)

Ucles Video Unit
1 Hills Road, Cambridge CB1 2EU
t 01223 553414 **f** 01225 552590 **e** thompson.su@ucles.org.uk
Contact Sue Thompson, Video Unit Manager

Video Production Workshop
16 Alfred Road, London W3 6LH
m 07956 529943
e philcamera@yahoo.com **w** www.videoworkshop.co.uk
Contact Phil Compton, Managing Director

Visions (Digital Outside Broadcasting) Ltd
t 020 7478 7289 **f** 020 7478 7107
e vickib@visions-ob.co.uk **w** www.visions-ob.com
Contact Vicki Betihavas, Director of Sales & Marketing

Westside Video Production
20 High Beeches, Gerrards Cross SL9 7HX
t 01753 890400 **f** 01753 890400
Contact Stuart Johnson, Managing Director

Production Facilities
International

@T.I.M.E Productions Istanbul
Meydan Sokak, 6/10 Akatlar, Istanbul 80630, Turkey
t +90 212 352 3991 **f** +90 212 352 3971
e mine@timeproductions.com **e** timeprod@superonline.com
w www.timeproductions.com
Contact Mine Kalpakcioglu, Executive Producer
Credits Swiss Telecom (C); Nokia (C); Badoit - Cinderella Mineral Water (C);
Agents Secrets (F)

Ardmore Studios
Herbert Road, Bray, Co Wicklow, Ireland
t +353 1 286 2971 **f** +353 1 286 1894
e film@ardmore.ie **w** www.ardmore.ie
Contact Kevin Moriarty
Credits Everlasting Piece (F); The Tailor Of Panama (F); The Count Of Monte
Cristo (F); Reign Of Fire (F)

Barrandov Studios
Krizeneckeho Namesti 322, Prague 5 152 00, Czech Republic
t +420 2 6707 1111 **f** +420 2 6707 2027
e info@barrandov.cz **w** www.barrandov.cz
Contact Jiri Matolin, Set Construction Department Manager; Robert Keil,
Production Services Manager; Petr Tolar, Post Production Manager; Ales
Bosticka, Film Labs Manager; Radomir Docekal, General Manager; Matous
Forbelsky, General Manager
Credits The League Of Extraordinary Gentlemen (F); Shanghai Knights (F); A
Sound Of Thunder (F)

British American Studio Enterprises (BASE)
Rua Tavares Bastos 414/66, Rio de Janeiro RJ 22221-030, Brazil
t +55 21 2558 5547 **f** +55 21 3235 4073
e nadkarni@alternex.com.br **w** www.basebrazil.tripod.com

Directors Film Company Of Amsterdam BV

Duivendrechtsekade 83, Amsterdam 1096 AJ, Netherlands
t +31 20 665 8965 **f** +31 20 694 9996 **e** dfc@euronet.nl
Contact Richard Coll; Piet-Hein Luykx

Egyptian Media Production City

Media Free Zone, Sixth of October City 12586, Egypt
t +20 2 840 0192 **f** +20 2 840 0261
e empc.chairman@menanet.net **w** www.egyptianmediacity.com
Contact Mona El-Sabbagh

Filma-Cass

Kocamansur Sokak 115/1, Sisli, Istanbul 80260, Turkey
t +90 212 233 6018 **f** +90 212 231 0227
e filmacass@filmacass.com.tr **w** www.filmacass.com.tr
Contact Ömer Vargi; Tamer Basaran; Bahadir Arliel; Elfin Yuksekleppe; Oguz Peri

MADE Srl

Via Carnevali 24, Milan 20158, Italy
t +39 02 3931 0390 **f** +39 02 3932 2505
e made@madefor.net
Contact Angela Latorraca, General Manager/Executive Producer; Federico Fasolino, Executive Producer; Enrico Mazzini, Producer

MADE Srl

C.so Sempione 9, Milan 20145, Italy
t 331 9976 **f** 3361 1655 **e** made@madefor.net
Contact Angela Latorraca, General Manager/Executive Producer; Federico Fasolino, Executive Producer; Enrico Mazzini, Producer

Maximum Films Africa (Pty) Ltd

81 St Johns Street Gardens, Cape Town 8008, South Africa
t +27 21 461 3903 **f** +27 21 461 3925
e pendra@maximumfilms.com **w** www.maximumfilms.com
Contact Claire Dissel; Pendra Dissel, Managing Director
Credits Bubbaloo (C); Acuvue (C); Twingo (C)

Mediterranean Film Studios

RL5, St Rocco Street, Kalkara CSP11, Malta
t +356 21 678151 **f** +356 21 674434
e info@mfsstudios.com **w** www.mfsstudios.com
Contact Cornelia Azzopardi-Schellmann

Opus Film

Ul Lakowa 29, Lódz 90-554, Poland
t +48 42 636 7059 **f** +48 42 636 7018
e opus@opusfilm.com **w** www.opusfilm.com
Contact Magda Przezdziak, Production Manager
Credits Roses (C); America (C); Coop (C); Ikea: Dog

Pioneer Productions

Hajógyári Sziget 130/1, Budapest 1033, Hungary
t +36 1 457 1050 **f** +36 1 388 8950
e main@pioneer.hu **w** www.pioneer.hu
Contact Jennifer Webster, Managing Director; Dorka Klim, Producer; Juci Darvas, Producer
Credits Dior Addict (C); Nike Puddles/Stream (C); Levi's Odyssey (C); Mini: Drunkard

PTT Films - Production Team Of Turkey

Asmalimescit Minare Sok 23, Beyoglu, Istanbul 80050, Turkey
t +90 212 293 8473 **f** +90 212 293 8475
e sebnem@pttfilms.com **w** www.pttfilms.com
Contact R Sebnem Kitis

Roma Studios Srl

Via Pontina Km 23, 270, Rome 128, Italy
t +39 06 501931 **f** +39 06 5019 3043
e info@romastudios.com **w** www.romastudios.com
Contact Uros Gorgone, Marketing Manager

Stillking Films

Krizeneckeho nam 322, Prague 5 152 53, Czech Republic
t +420 2 6707 3741 **f** +420 2 6707 3742
e michal@stillking.com **w** www.stillking.com
Contact James Ricketts, Marketing Director; Michal Skop, Head of Production; Pavla Burgetova, Executive Producer; Matthew Stillman, Managing Director; David Minkowski, Head of Film
Credits The Prodigy (M); Sony Playstation (C); Van Helsing (F); The Prodigy: Baby's Got a Temper

Studio Francesco Rapa

Via Dei Missionari 11, Naples 80125, Italy
t +39 081 593 5500 **f** +39 081 593 4440
e info@studiorapa.it **w** www.studiorapa.it
Contact Ivano Rappa

Studios Srl

Via Tiburtina 521, Rome 159, Italy
t +39 06 438 6792 **t** +39 06 438 6921 **f** 438 0392
e studios@diginet.it **w** www.studiosinternational.com
Contact Daniele Taddei, Chief Executive Officer

UFO Pictures

Nad Spádem 17/202, Praha 4 140 00, Czech Republic
t +420 2 6121 3968 **f** +420 2 6121 4015
e info@ufopictures.tv **w** www.ufopictures.tv
Contact David Rauch, Executive Producer; Monika Splíchalová, Producer; Jeffrey Brown, Producer/International Representative
Credits The Myth - Nick Cave And The Bad Seeds (D); Nissan (C); The Pied Piper (F); Sprandi (C)

Velocity Afrika Production

38 Wessels Road, Johannesburg 2128, South Africa
t +27 11 807 0100 **f** +27 11 807 1208
e info@velocityfilms.com **w** www.velocityfilms.com
Contact Nicola Valentine, Executive Producer; Barry Munchik, Executive Producer; Karen Kloppers, Head of Production; Peter Carr, Executive Producer; Mark Gilbert, Executive Producer

Velocity Afrika Production Services

30 Keerom Street, Cape Town 8001, South Africa
t +21 21 424 4971 **f** +21 21 424 6244
e karen@velocityfilms.com **e** barry@velocityfilms.com
w www.velocityfilms.com
Contact Jenny Leslie, Executive Producer; Barry Munchick, Managing Director; Nicola Valentine, Executive Producer; Karen Kloppers, Head of Production

Vidéorama

5 Boulevard de l'Océan Atlantique, Anfa, Casablanca 20050, Morocco
t +212 22 798585 **f** +212 22 798585 **e** vdr@iam.net.ma
Contact Ahmed Belghiti, Producer, General Manager

Production Facilities
Stages

3 Mills Studios
Three Mill Lane, Bromley-by-Bow, London E3 3DU
t 020 7363 3336 **f** 020 8215 3499
e info@3mills.com **w** www.3mills.com
Contact Candice McDonald, Studio Co-ordinator; Pat Perilli,
Studio Coordinator
Credits Code 46 (F); B&Q (C); Tim Burton's Corpse Bride (F); Bad Girls (T)

Alistage
Unit 2, Hotspur Industrial Estate, West Road, Tottenham,
London N17 0XJ
t 020 8808 5005 **f** 020 8801 9851
e sales@alistage.co.uk **w** www.alistage.co.uk
Contact Adrian Yates, Sales; John Dorman, Sales; Steve Ambler, Sales; Colin
Wright, Managing Director

Black Island Studios
Alliance Road, London W3 0RA
Contact Steve Giudici, Director

Bray Management Ltd
Bray Film Studios, Windsor Road, Windsor SL4 5UG
t 01628 622111 **f** 01628 770381 **m** 07836 629340
e b.earl@tiscali.co.uk
Contact Beryl Earl, Studio Manager
Credits Fimbles (T); Born And Bred Series II (T)

Duthy Hall Studios
Duthy Hall, Great Guildford Street, London SE1 0ES
t 020 7261 0360 **e** info@duthyhall.com
w www.duthyhall.com
Contact Lori Russell, Studio Manager; Malcom Russell, Manager

Ealing Studios
Ealing Green, London W5 5EP
t 020 8567 6655 **f** 020 8758 8658
e info@ealingstudios.com **w** www.ealingstudios.com
Contact Louisa Hadkinson, Bookings; Jeremy Pelzer, Studio Manager;
Gabrielle Kane, Commercial Manager; Kate Mansfield, Bookings Manager
Credits Roger Roger (T); Strange (T); Sir Gadabout, The Worst Knight In The
Land Series II (T); The Importance Of Being Earnest (F)

The Film Lab Ltd
Units 4&5, Pilot Close, Fulmar Way, Wickford SS11 8YW
t 01268 571408 **f** 01268 571221 **w** www.thefilmlab.com
Contact Brad Watson, Managing Director; Janice de la Mare, Finance Director
Credits The Church (F); Parking Space (S); Supermodels - The Plight Of (S);
Locks (S)

Hendon Film Studio Ltd
Goldsmith Avenue, London NW9 7EU
t 020 8205 2240 **e** hendonfilmstudio@aol.com
Credits Operation Good Guys Christmas Special (T); S19 (F)

Lee Studios Manchester
Manchester Road, Kearsley, Bolton BL4 8RL
t 01204 794000 **f** 01204 792111
e linda@lee.co.uk **w** www.lee.co.uk
Contact John Lawton, Operations Director; Linda Fisher, Studio Manager
Credits Clocking Off (T)

Millennium Studios
5 Elstree Way, Borehamwood WD6 1SF
t 02082 361400 **f** 02082 361444
e millennium@elstree-online.co.uk
w www.elstree-online.co.uk
Contact Ronan Willson, Studio Manager

Pinewood Shepperton
Pinewood Road, Iver Heath SL0 0NH
t 01932 592008 **f** 01932 592555
e gary_stone@shepperton-studios.co.uk
e natalie_may@pinewood-studios.co.uk
w www.pinewood-studios.co.uk
Contact Ray Pascoe, Preview Supervisor; Gary Stone, Sales and Marketing
Manager; Natalie May, Sales and Marketing Assistant

Twickenham Film Studios
The Barons, St Margaret''s, Twickenham TW1 2AW
t 020 8607 8888 **f** 020 8607 8889
e gerry@twickenhamstudios.com
w www.twickenhamstudios.com
Contact Gerry Humphreys, Post Production; Caroline Tipple, Production

Waagner Biro Stage Systems
4 Kempson Way, Suffolk Business Park, Bury St Edmunds IP32 7AR
t 01284 755512 **f** 01284 755516
e stagesystems-uk@waagner-biro.com
w www.waagnerbiro.com
Contact Iain Forbester, Managing Director

Production Facilities
Standards Conversion

Alken MRS
PO Box 33, Port Talbot SA13 1YZ
t 01639 895359 **f** 01639 898664
e sales@alkenmrs.com **w** www.alkenmrs.com/video
Contact Alan Kenyon, Proprietor

BBC Post Production
(Sites across London, Bristol & Birmingham)
5550 Television Centre, Wood Lane, London W12 7RJ
t 020 8225 7702 (London) **t** 0117 9746 666 (Bristol)
t 0121 432 8621 (Birmingham)
w www.bbcresources.com/postproduction

Copycats Video Ltd
The Metropolitan Centre, 26 Derby Road, Greenford UB6 8UJ
t 020 8813 2222 **f** 020 8813 2322
e sales@copycats.tv **w** www.copycats.tv
Contact Grahame Taylor, Technical Director; Beverley Harding, Sales Manager

Dubbs
25-26 Poland Street, London W1F 8QN
t 020 7629 0055 **f** 020 7287 8796
e sales@dubbs.co.uk **w** www.dubbs.co.uk
Contact David Wilson, Sales Manager; Seb Tyack, Digital Media Producer;
Martin Rogers, Sales Manager; Lauren McCready, Business Development; Bill
Gamble, Customer Services Director

*Specialist duplication, replication and conversion facility, delivering
flexible, quality service and technical expertise that is geared to
respond to individual needs. Open 24 hours, 7 days a week.*

Goldcrest Post Production Facilities

36-44 Brewer Street, London W1F 9LX
t 020 7437 7972 **f** 020 7437 5402 **m** 07836 204283
e mailbox@goldcrest-post.co.uk

Contact Poppy Quinn, Bookings and Customer Services Manager; Raju Raymond, General Manager

Humphries Video Services Ltd

Unit 2, The Willow Business Centre, 17 Willow Lane, Mitcham CR4 4NX
t 020 8648 6111 **t** 020 7636 3636 **f** 020 8648 5261
e sales@hvs.bdx.co.uk **w** www.hvs.co.uk
Contact David Brown, Sales and Marketing Director; Jago Michell, Business Development; Emma Lincoln, Production Co-ordinator; Mike Hudson, Production Director

Video cassette duplication and standard conversion centre. From most formats to any cassette format in any world standard. Broadcast and corporate. CD and DVD authoring/replication.

The London Studios Ltd

Upper Ground, London SE1 9LT
t 020 7737 8888 **f** 020 7928 8405
e sales@londonstudios.co.uk
w www.londonstudios.co.uk
Contact Penny Lent, Director of Sales, Marketing and Development

**Hat Trick Productions *Talkback Productions
*Blaze Television *Tiger Aspect Productions
*So Television *Avalon Television*

molinare
a television corporation company

Molinare

34 Fouberts Place, London W1F 7PX
t 020 7478 7000 **f** 020 7478 7199
e bookings@molinare.co.uk **w** www.molinare.co.uk

Contact Kate George, Facilities Manager
Credits Dorada Especial: Painting; AXN: Cornice; Walkers Dorito's: Idents; The Wind

For 30 years Molinare has been offering the best in Post Production, helping the best people make the best programmes, we have about the widest selection of facilities in one location in the industry. Based in the heart of Soho, we offer, 5 digital Online Suites, Editbox FX V8, Ursa Gold Telecine, High Definition Online, 10 Avid Offline suites and 2 Avid Online suites, 5 Audio Dubbing suites with voice over booths, Tracklay, Discreet Flint, Media Illusion, Drive in 1500 sq ft Video studio, 400 sq ft Virtual Studio, Duplication, Transmission Services, as well as the Molinare Design team for all your branding and design needs.

Peak White Facilities

1 Latimer Road, Teddington TW11 8QA
t 08707 405625 **f** 020 8977 8357 **w** www.peakwhite.tv
Contact Richard Bonfield, Manager; Andrea Anderson, Marketing Director

Peak White offer a range of post production services for broadcast and corporate clients. VHS duplication, standards conversion, and inter-format dubbing - Digital Betacam, Beta SP, DV, Hi-8, Umatic, DVD, all in PAL, NTSC and SECAM. Linear and nonlinear online edit suites with DV Cam & Digital Betacam.

Production Facilities
Studios

@T.I.M.E Productions Istanbul

Meydan Sokak, 6/10 Akatlar, Istanbul 80630, Turkey
t +90 212 352 3991 **f** +90 212 352 3971
e mine@timeproductions.com **e** timeprod@superonline.com
w www.timeproductions.com

Contact Mine Kalpakcioglu, Executive Producer
Credits Swiss Telecom (C); Nokia (C); Badoit - Cinderella Mineral Water (C); Agents Secrets (F)

124 Facilities

124 Horseferry Road, London SW1P 2TX
t 020 7306 8040 **f** 020 7306 8041
e 124facilities@channel4.co.uk **w** www.124.co.uk
Contact Diana Browne, Studio Co-ordinator

A+M Studios

The Royals, Victoria Road, London NW10 6ND
t 020 8233 1515 **f** 020 8233 1546
e studio@amhire.com **w** www.amhire.com
Contact Justin Brady, Studio Manager

Advanced Production Services

24 Park Royal Metro Centre, London NW10 7PA
t 020 8838 1133 **f** 020 8838 1173
e enquiries@advancedproduction.com
w www.advancedproduction.com
Contact Soussan Imani, Marketing Manager

After Image Ltd

32 Acre Lane, London SW2 5SG
t 020 7737 7300 **w** www.afterimage.co.uk
Contact Mark Lucas, Director; Jane Thorburn, Director

Air-Edel Recording Studios Ltd

18 Rodmarton Street, London W1U 8BJ
t 020 7486 6466 **f** 020 7224 0344
e air-edel@air-edel.co.uk **w** www.air-edel.co.uk
Contact Trevor Best, Studio Manager; Maggie Rodford, Managing Director

Anglia Studios

Anglia House, Norwich NR1 3JG
t 01603 615151 **f** 01603 752504
e angliastudios@granadamedia.com **w** www.angliastudios.com
Contact Dan Haddon, Location Services; Dave Wyatt, Head of Post Production;
Jacky Lane, Head of Resources; Ian Osborne, Head of Studios; Beverly Bulcock,
Head of Resources

Great kit, great people and the Norwich nightlife is brilliant.

Bagleys Studios

Kings Cross Freight Depot, Yorkway, London N1 0UZ
t 020 7278 2777 **f** 020 7837 7014 **m** 07788 723395
e classic@pwcsnet.co.uk **w** www.bagleys.net

Contact Alan Morris

BBC Scotland Resources Operations

Room G51, Broadcasting House, Queen Margaret Drive,
Glasgow G12 8DG
t 0141 338 2343 **f** 0141 338 2335
e resops.scotland@bbc.co.uk
w www.bbc.co.uk/scotland/resources
Contact Natalie Adams, Facilities Co-ordinator; Alex Gaffney, Sales & Marketing
Manager; Susie Miller, Marketing Assistant; Donagh Campbell, Facilities
Assistant
Credits Question Time (T); 50/50 (T); The Saturday Show (T); Live Floor Show (T)

B B C Studios

BBC Studios

The Hub, Television Centre, Wood Lane, London W12 7RJ
t 020 8576 7666 **f** 020 8576 8806
e tvstudios.sales@bbc.co.uk **w** www.bbcresources.com/studios

Big Shot Studios Ltd

Ascot Road, Keytec 7 Business Park, Pershore WR10 2JJ
t 01386 555667 **f** 01386 553678
e mail@bigshots.co.uk **w** www.bigshots.co.uk
Contact Keith Rowberry, Studio Manager

Blank Space Studios

10A Belmont Street, Chalk Farm, London NW1 8HH
t 020 7482 0957 **f** 020 7485 0957
e sue.blank-space-studios@vol.at **w** www.studiohire.co.uk
Contact Sue Parker, Director; Alexis Chabala, Studio Manager

Box Studios

15 Mandela Street, London NW1 0DU
t 020 7388 0020 **f** 020 7387 4259
e email@boxstudios.co.uk **w** www.boxstudios.co.uk
Contact Philip Bier, Director; Chris Gascoigne, Director

Broadley Studios

48 Broadley Terrace, London NW1 6LG
t 020 7258 0324 **f** 020 7724 2361
e admin@broadleystudios.com **w** www.broadleystudios.com
Contact Mark French; Alex McMillan; Manny Elias, General Manager
Credits Shell: The Edge (T); Moneygram TV (T); The Salon (T); Joan Armatrading (C)

*Central London location. Ideal for: White infinity, Chromakey,
Interviews, Links, Casting, Pack-shots. Lighting rig, Make-up room, Green
room, Production office.*

Capital Studios

Wandsworth Plain, London SW18 1ET
t 020 8877 1234 **f** 020 8877 0234
e info@capitalstudios.com **w**
www.capitalstudios.com
Contact Bobbi Johnstone, Contact; Clare Phillips, Contact

*Fully equipped digital broadcast studios: 3000 sq ft (60x50x19.5) and
2000 sq ft (50x50x19.5). Supported by galleries, dressing rooms,
wardrobe, green room and audience facilities. Tx lines, Cafe with
courtyard garden. New digital Post-Production facilities.*

Carlton Studios

Lenton Lane, Nottingham NG7 2NA
t 0115 964 5120 **f** 0115 964 5552
e paul.bennett@carltontv.co.uk **w** www.carlton.com
Contact Ian Squires, Managing Director; Suzanne Durance, Contact; Paul
Bennett, Controller of Operations
Credits Peak Practice (T); Family Fortunes (T); Get Your Own Back (T);
Crossroads (T)

Castle Studios (James Electrical)

Olmar Street, London SE1 5AY
t 020 7231 3387 **f** 020 7231 5030 **m** 07850 716814
Contact Steve James, Partner

Chalk Farm Studios

Units 2,3, & 7, 10A Belmont Street, London NW1 8HH
t 020 7482 1001 **f** 020 7267 3179
e manager.chalk-farm-studios@virgin.net
Contact Maria O'Hara, Manager

The Depot Studios

29-31 Brewery Road, London N7 9QH
t 020 7609 1366 **f** 020 7609 6844
w www.thedepotstudios.com
Contact Helen Hilton, Senior Partner

Dukes Island Studios

Dukes Road, Western Avenue, London W3 0SL
t 020 8956 5600 **f** 020 8956 5604
e info@islandstudios.net **w** www.islandstudios.net

Eastside Studios

40A River Road, Barking IG11 0DW
t 020 8507 7572 **f** 020 8507 8550
e elainenoy@btconnect.com **w** www.eastsidestudios.com
Contact Elaine Noy, Studio Manager

Elstree Film & Television Studios

Shenley Road, Borehamwood WD6 1JG
t 020 8953 1600 **f** 020 8905 1135
e info@elstreefilmtv.com **w** www.elstreefilmtv.com
Contact Neville Reid, Director of Studios; Paul Clark, Estates Manager; Mike
Scales, Communications & Site Services Co-Ordinator; Brian Coleman,
Hospitality; Julie Wicks, Director of Studios
Credits Enigma (F); Who Wants To Be A Millionaire (T); Star Wars - Attack Of
The Clones (F); Big Brother 3 (T)

Focal Point Studio

127 Camden Mews, London NW1 9AH
t 07071 888222 **e** rupert@focal-point-studio.com

Fountain Studios

128 Wembley Park Drive, Wembley HA9 8HP
t 020 8900 5800 **f** 020 8900 5802
e sales@ftv.co.uk **w** www.fountainstudios.tv
Contact Julian Cossick, Managing Director
Credits Bremner, Bird And Fortune (T); The Kumars At No 42 (T); Test The
Nation (T); Pop Idol (T)

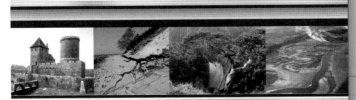
Glasgow TV & Film Studio

Glasgow Media Park, Craigmont Street, Glasgow G20 9BT
t 0141 305 6666 **f** 0141 305 6600

Contact Susan Haynes; Colin Gilbert, Director; Brian Clarke, Managing Director;
April Chamberlain, Director

Granada Media International

Granada Media International, London Television Centre, Upper
Ground, London SE1 9LT
t 020 7620 1620 **w** www.itv.com

The Greenford Studios

5-11 Taunton Road, Metropolitan Centre, Greenford UB6 8UQ
t 020 8575 7300 **f** 020 8839 1640
e studios@panavision.co.uk **w** www.panavision.co.uk

Contact Kate Tufano; Claire Peacock
Credits Sainsbury's (C); The Last Detective (T); Rockface II (T); Mean Machine (W)

Halliford Film Studios

Manygate Lane, Shepperton TW17 9EG
t 01932 226341 **f** 01932 246336 **m** 07967 593735
e sales@hallifordstudios.com **w** www.hallifordfilmstudios.co.uk

Contact Callum Andrews, Director/Studio Manager; Charlotte Goddard,
Director; Suzanne May, Director

Hanlon Studios

4-6 Minerva Road, Park Royal, London NW10 6HJ
t 020 8965 3335 **f** 020 8963 1250

Contact Jennifer Hanlon, Director

HDS Studios Ltd

Springfield Road, Hayes UB4 0LE
t 020 8573 4000 **f** 020 8561 7056
e info@hdsstudios.com **w** www.hdsstudios.com

Contact Dahl Bhabra, Studio Manager

Hillside

Merry Hill Road, Bushey WD23 1DR
t 020 8950 7919 **f** 020 8421 8085
e enquiries@hillside-studios.co.uk **w** www.hillside-studios.co.uk
Contact David Hillier, Head of Facilities

*1500 sq. ft. fully equipped multicamera studio with digital mixer and
production gallery. Interview studio, location unit, construction
facilities and landscaped grounds. Dressing rooms, office space,
restaurant and free parking.*

Holborn Studios

49-50 Eagle Wharf Road, Islington, London N1 7ED
t 020 7490 4099 **f** 020 7253 8120
e reception@holborn-studios.co.uk
w www.holbornstudios.com

The Hospital

19-21 Great Queen Street, London WC2B 5BE
t 020 7269 7990 **f** 020 7269 7998 **w** www.thehospital.co.uk
Contact Chris Collingham, Director Of Facilities

The Intrepid Aviation Company Ltd

Hangar 4, North Weald Airfield, North Weald CM16 6AA
t 01992 524233 **f** 01992 524225 **m** 07850 801491
e bpw@intrepidaviation.demon.co.uk
w www.deltaweb.co.uk/intrepid
Contact Brendan Walsh, Director

Island Studios Ltd

2 Dukes Road, Acton, London W3 0SL
t 020 8956 5600 **f** 020 8956 5604
Contact Steve Giudici, Director

H I L L S I D E

The complete package

- ● **Multi-Camera Studios**
- ● **Digital post-production**
- ● **Avid off-line & Symphony**
- ● **Linear on-line**
- ● **Soundtracs with Audiofile**
- ● **Green rooms & offices**
- ● **Restaurant & parking**

020 8950 7919

Email: mailbox@hillside-studios.co.uk
Merry Hill Road, Bushey, Hertfordshire, WD23 1DR
www.hillside-studios.co.uk

John Ash Photography
Church Farm, Ashchurch GL20 8JU
t 01684 291200 **f** 01684 291201
e ash-photography@ndirect.co.uk **w** www.ashphotography.com
Contact Sharon Ash, Managing Director

KD's Studio
78 Church Path, Chiswick, London W4 5BJ
t 020 8994 3142 **f** 020 8755 1124
e sue@kdees.co.uk **w** www.kdees.co.uk
Contact Kenny Denton, Managing Director

Kingston Inmedia
Chalfont Grove, Narcot Lane, Chalfont St Peter SL9 8TW
t 0845 123 7800 **f** 01494 876006
e vicki.redstone@kom.com **w** www.kingstoninmedia.com
Contact Vicki Redstone, Account Manager; Barrie Woolston, Head Of Studio K
Credits Blues Clues (T); World Cup Years (T); Fat Academy (T); Beachcomber Bay (T)

Location Lighting (London)
28 The Grangeway, Grange Park, London N21 2HJ
t 020 8364 3132 **f** 020 8373 1150 **m** 07836 639399
e mark.brennan@amserve.net
Contact Mark Brennan, Lighting Gaffer

London News Network
The London Television Centre, Upper Ground, London SE1 9LT
t 020 7827 7700
e denise.lister@lnn-tv.co.uk **w** www.lnn-tv.co.uk
Contact Denise Lister, Newsroom Manager

London Playout Centre (LPC)
1 Stephen Street, London W1T 1AL
t 020 7691 6900 **f** 020 7691 6919 **w** www.lpc.tv
Contact John Cooper, Director of Creative Services

The London Studios Ltd
Upper Ground, London SE1 9LT
t 020 7737 8888 **f** 020 7928 8405
sales@londonstudios.co.uk
w www.londonstudios.co.uk
Contact Penny Lent, Director of Sales,
Marketing and Development

*Hat Trick Productions *Talkback Productions
*Blaze Television *Tiger Aspect Productions
*So Television *Avalon Television

The Maidstone Studios
Vinters Park, Maidstone ME14 5NZ
t 01622 691111
e ianlindsay@maidstonestudios.com
w www.maidstonestudios.com

Malcolm Ryan Studios Ltd
48-52 Wimbledon Stadium Business Centre, Riverside Road,
London SW17 0BA
t 020 8947 4766 **f** 020 8947 9517
e info@malcolmryanstudios.com
w www.malcolmryanstudios.com
Contact Malcolm Ryan, Managing Director; Sylvia Meyborg, Studio Manager
Credits Citroen (C); Blazing Squad (M); Pulp (M)

mediahouse
3 Burlington Lane, Hogarth Business Park, Chiswick,
London W4 2TH
t 020 8233 6110 (Sales) **t** 020 8233 5400 (Switchboard)
f 020 8233 5401
e cportbury@imgworld.com **w** www.mediahouse.tv
Contact Cherry Portbury, Studio Sales Manager; Alistair Montgomery, Studio
Operations Manager
Credits GBTV (I); Partners Walters Meacham (I); British Comedy Awards 2002
(T); Faking It (T)

FILM STUDIOS

2 Sound Stages

60x60 and 60x40 (both with Cyc)

Large Backlot

Construction
Lighting
Catering
Off Street Parking

Production Offices, Dressing Rooms,
Make-up and Hairdressing

Contact: Callum Andrews or Suzanne May on
01932 226341 or Fax 01932 246336
or visit our website @ www.hallifordfilmstudios.co.uk

HALLIFORD STUDIOS LTD, MANYGATE LANE,
SHEPPERTON, MIDDX TW17 9EG

Mediapro Pictures

1 Studioului Street, Buftea 78910, Romania
t +4021 2051 840 **f** +4021 2051 871
e pictures@mediapro.ro **w** www.mediapropictures.com
Contact Adrian Sarbu, Chairman; Crenguta Alexandru, Chief Financial Officer;
Roxanda Gramada, Marketing Manager; Andrei Boncea, General Director;
Dragos Vilcu, Business Administration Officer; Gilda Velciu, Business
Administration Officer; Eugenia Balan, Chief Financial Officer
Credits Boudica (F); Callas Forever (F); Amen (F)

MILLBANK STUDIOS

Millbank Studios

4 Millbank, Westminster, London SW1P 3JA
t 020 7233 2020 **f** 020 7233 3158
e facilities@millbank-studios.co.uk **w** www.millbank-studios.co.uk
Contact Richard Rose, Managing Director; Pippa Walker, Head of Operations; Nick
Hattingh, Technical Operations Manager; Nicola Goulding, Head of Production

Miloco

36 Leroy Street, London SE1 4SP
t 020 7232 0008 **f** 020 7237 6109
e info@milomusic.co.uk **w** www.milomusic.co.uk
Contact Nick Young, Studio Manager; Mark Cox, Bookings Manager
Credits Persil (C); American Airlines (C)

molinare
a television corporation company

Molinare

34 Fouberts Place, London W1F 7PX
t 020 7478 7000 **f** 020 7478 7199
e bookings@molinare.co.uk **w** www.molinare.co.uk
Contact Kate George, Facilities Manager
Credits Dorada Especial: Painting; AXN: Cornice; Walkers Dorito's: Idents;
The Wind

*For 30 years Molinare has been offering the best in Post Production,
helping the best people make the best programmes, we have about
the widest selection of facilities in one location in the industry.
Based in the heart of Soho, we offer, 5 digital Online Suites, Editbox
FX V8, Ursa Gold Telecine, High Definition Online, 10 Avid Offline
suites and 2 Avid Online suites, 5 Audio Dubbing suites with voice
over booths, Tracklay, Discreet Flint, Media Illusion, Drive in
1500 sq ft Video studio, 400 sq ft Virtual Studio, Duplication,
Transmission Services, as well as the Molinare Design team for
all your branding and design needs.*

Nomad Studio Hire

George Leigh Street, School Buildings, Ancoats,
Manchester M4 5WD
t 0161 236 2008 **f** 0161 236 9621 **m** 07831 336140
e studionomad@aol.com **w** www.nomadstudios.co.uk

ntl:broadcast

ntl : Broadcast

Crawley Court, Winchester SO21 2QA
t 01962 822400 **f** 01962 822553
e satellite-info@ntl.com **w** www.ntlbroadcast.com

*From Virtual Studios and production through to digital server playout,
ntl:broadcast provides reliable end to end services for broadcast and media
clients from its Broadcast Media Centre at Feltham, SW London. Facilities
include virtual studios, online edit suites, graphic suites, audio suites, and
voiceover booths. Along with the ability to co-locate staff in the same
building, the Broadcast Media Centre also offers excellent satellite and fibre
connectivity to all the TV platforms.*

Optima Photographic Studios Ltd

The Chocolate Factory, 1st Floor Building D, Clarendon Road,
London N22 6XJ
t 020 8881 0064 **f** 020 8881 0064 **m** 07958 491481
e mail@optima-studios.co.uk **w** www.optima-studios.co.uk
Contact Edward Davies, Contact

Park Royal Studios

1 Barretts Green Road, London NW10 7AE
t 020 8965 9778 **f** 020 8963 1056
e mark@parkroyalstudios.com **e** francois@parkroyalstudios.com
w www.parkroyalstudios.com
Contact Rohan Paulo; Mark ; Francois van de Langaruis

Paul Cordwell

Unit 3, Century Park, Garrison Lane, Birmingham B9 4NZ
t 01217 668444 **f** 01217 668444 **m** 07831 416477
e paul@paulcordwell.co.uk **w** www.paulcordwell.co.uk
Contact Paul Cordwell, Contact

Picture It

50 Church Road, London NW10 9PY
t 020 8961 6644 **f** 020 8961 2969
e rosemary@picit.net **w** www.picit.net
Contact Trevor Hunt, Managing Director; Rosemary Element, Sales &
Marketing; Chris Sellers, Studio Manager

*1500 sq ft, 3-sided infinity cove, fixed lighting grid, production
gallery/vision mixing & talkback facilities, green room.*

Plough Studios

Unit Four, 9 Park HIll, London SW4 9NS
t 020 7622 1939 **f** 020 7627 5169
e cove@ploughstudios.com **w** www.ploughstudios.com
Contact Tim Edwards, Proprietor; Tim Wright, Proprietor; Quentin Wright, Proprietor

Riverside Studios

Crisp Road, London W6 9RL
t 020 8237 1000 **f** 020 8237 1001
e online@riversidestudios.co.uk **w** www.riversidestudios.co.uk
Contact Andy Scorgie, Head of Production; Nick Giles, Centre Manager; Jon
Fawcett, Hires Manager; Cheryl Ko, Reception; Jo Wallet, Studio Manager
Credits Recovered (T); Boys And Girls (T); Top Of The Pops (T)

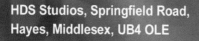

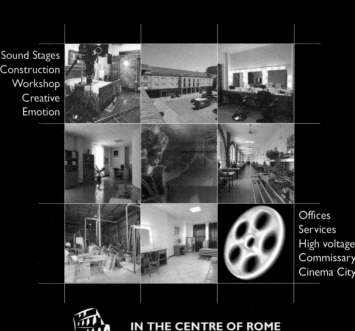

Sanctuary Westway Studios

8 Olaf Street, London W11 4BE
t 020 7221 9041 **f** 020 7221 9399
e westway@sanctuarystudios.co.uk
w www.sanctuarystudios.co.uk
Contact Steve Butt, Studio Manager; Kathy Hunter, Assistant Studio Manager

A centrally located studio complex incorporating four drive-on stages, all with solid cycloramas and lighting grids or chain tackle. In house Set Construction, Lighting, Scenery Hire, Production Offices, Make-up and Wardrobe Rooms, Art Department, Canteen & Catering, Car Park, Licensed Bar.

Sands Films

Grices Wharf, 119 Rotherhithe Street, London SE16 4NF
t 020 7231 2209
e ostockman@sandsfilms.co.uk **w** www.sandsfilms.co.uk
Contact Christine Goodwin, Director; Olivier Stockman, Director
Credits Little Dorrit (F); The Nutcracker (F); As You Like It (F); The Children's Midsummer Night's Dream (F)

SLV

70-74 Stewarts Road, London SW8 4DE
t 020 7720 6464 **f** 020 7622 3666 **m** 07799 690899
e shoot@slvision.co.uk **w** www.slvision.co.uk
Contact Dan Pope, Studio Manager; Tony Dow, Partner; Frank Don, Facilities Manager

Studio 1 Ltd

The Television Centre, Culverhouse Cross, Cardiff CF5 6XJ
t 029 2059 0104 **f** 029 2059 0502
e info@studio1tv.co.uk **w** www.studio1tv.co.uk

Studio Alba

54A Seaforth Road, Stornoway HS1 2SD
t 01851 701125 **f** 01851 701094 **m** 07740 785193
e info@studioalba.com **w** www.studioalba.com
Contact Willie Macleod, Facilities Manager

The Studio

21 Cabul Road, London SW11 2PR
t 020 7728 5228 **f** 020 7728 9975
e webmaster@the-studio.co.uk **w** www.the-studio.co.uk
Contact Emma Pascoe; Toby Tobias; Gemma Masters; Cressida Ranfield, Bookings Manager

Studios Srl

Via Tiburtina 521, Rome 159, Italy
t +39 06 438 6792 **t** +39 06 438 6921 **f** +39 06 438 0392
e studios@diginet.it **w** www.studiosinternational.com
Contact Daniele Taddei, Chief Executive Officer

Teddington Studios

Broom Road, Teddington TW11 9NT
t 020 8977 3252 **f** 020 8943 4050
e sales@teddington.co.uk **w** www.teddington.co.uk
Contact Cherry Portbury, Studio Sales Manager; Victoria Finlay, Client Liaison Manager; Lisa Lancaster; Zoe Thorn-Jones; Aidan Boulter
Credits Harry Hill (T); My Hero (T); Coupling (T); Men Behaving Badly (T)

FOCUS ON: ➤➤

Production Facilities
+ Studios

pages ...

Shooting in Amsterdam?

Take this test:

A.

B.

1. Before starting the day most Dutch citizens have a serving of whose Hash in the morning?

(Mom's)

(An old high school buddy)

A.

B.

2. Ever since the infamous "Windmill Incident of '94" local authorities encourage all visitors to shoot which well known Tulips?

(Keukenhof Park)

(Tony "Two-lips" Agnifilo)

A.

B.

3. Known for his fluid motion and vivid use of color, this Dutch artist was considered to be emotionally unstable and easily provoked.

(Vincent Van Gogh)

(Timmy Van Gogh)

not sure? call us.

directors film company

Executive Producer: richard coll

ph 3120.665.89.65 fax 3120.694.99.96
duivendrechtsekade 83
1096 aj amsterdam

ph 212.627.4999 fax 212.627.4999
1123 broadway, suite 1107
new york city 10010

providing worldwide film production services

ITALY
A.S.A.P. Production
Via Gran San Bernardo, 13
20154 Milano
tel: 0039 02 33608783 / 34938308
fax: 0039 02 33617967
email: info@asapps.it

MOROCCO
A.S.A.P. Marrakech
Rue Majoub El Rimiza, 1
40000 Marrakech
ph: 00212.44.446502
fax: 00212.44.446524
email: info@asapps.it

production service

Via Legnano, 26 · 20121 Milan · Italy
tel. +39 02 2900 6867 · fax 02 2900 6884

contact: Michele Virgilio,
Annalis Labat, Mariella Grandi

Via G. Nicotera, 29 · 00195 Rome · Italy
tel. +39 06 3611 497 · fax +39 06 3610 353

www.mrproduction.com
info@mrproduction.com

**for all your production needs
in Spain, Germany or the UK**

tel: +34 952 798129   fax: +34 952 795838
tel: +44 7949 949 534 fax: +44 1883 347086

tv, commercials, features, music videos,
documentaries, corporate videos
from Directors to runners
to make your shoot a pleasure
email: shoots@reelproduction.co.uk
web: www.reelproduction.co.uk

STUDIOS®
Stabilimenti Cinematografici e Multimediali

www.studiosinternational.com

BEE'S PICTURES
FOR ALL YOUR PRODUCTION NEEDS

SPAIN   ARGENTINA   CUBA   MOROCCO

www.beespics.com / www.loconation.com

STUDIO
FRANCESCO
RAPA SRL

Production Services and Casting
in Naples, Amalfi Coast

Via dei Missionari, 11 - 80125 Napoli (Italy)
+39.081.5935500 pbx +39.081.5934440 fax

www.studiorapa.it
info@studiorapa.it

Three Mills Studios
Three Mill Lane, London E3 3DU
t 020 7363 3336 **f** 020 8215 3499
e threemills@compuserve.com **e** info@threemills.com
w www.threemills.com
Contact Emma Pascoe
Credits Pure (F); Code 46 (F); Dream Team (T); Bad Girls (T)

Video Europe
The London Broadcast Centre, 11-13 Point Pleasant, London
SW18 1NN
t 020 8433 8000 **f** 020 8433 8001
e studios@videoeurope.co.uk **w** www.videoeurope.co.uk

Woburn Studios Ltd
Russell Farm, New Road, Maulden MK45 2BG
t 01525 408176 **f** 01525 840066
e info@woburnstudios.com **w** www.woburnstudios.com
Contact Neil Tkaczuk; Tim Liggins

The Worx
10 Heathmans Road, Fulham, London SW6 4TJ
t 020 7371 9777 **f** 020 7371 9888
e enquiries@theworx.co.uk **w** www.theworx.co.uk

Production Facilities
Video Editing

B B C Post Production

BBC Post Production
(Sites across London, Bristol & Birmingham)
5550 Television Centre, Wood Lane, London W12 7RJ
t 020 8225 7702 (London) **t** 0117 9746 666 (Bristol)
t 0121 432 8621 (Birmingham)
w www.bbcresources.com/postproduction

Bravo Post Production
22 Great Marlborough Street, London W1F 7HU
t 020 7287 7811 **f** 020 7287 7812
e mail@bravopost.co.uk **w** www.bravopost.co.uk

Clockhouse
34 Hanway Street, London W1T 1UW
t 020 7436 7702 **f** 020 7436 7679
e edit@clockhouse.co.uk **w** www.clockhouse.co.uk
Contact Graham Hobbs, Director; Tony Fox, Director; Drew Waugh, Producer
Credits Rebranding Royal Mail - SAP (I); Microsoft Business Solutions (I); Travel Solutions - TQ3 (I); The Best Run SAP - SAP (I)

Faction Films
26 Shacklewell Lane, London E8 2EZ
t 020 7690 4446 **f** 020 7690 4447
e faction@factionfilms.co.uk **w** www.factionfilms.co.uk
Contact Peter Day, Producer/Writer; Sylvia Stevens, Producer; David Fox, Director/Editor
Credits Tuna Heaven (D); 4Music: 4DJ (D); War Takes (D); Madame Kitty's Cathouse (D)

Graham Skelton Editing
Leafy Hollow, Lightwater Road, Lightwater GU18 5XB
t 01276 476540 **f** 01276 479008 **m** 07831 301500
e gs.edit@virgin.net
Credits Jack's Story - IUCA Gold Award Winner (T); Rally XS WRC 2002 (T); Football Italia (T)

Kindred Productions
Communications House, 12 Craufurd Rise, Maidenhead SL6 7LS
t 01628 625222
e kindredmedia@btinternet.co.uk **w** kindredproductions.co.uk
Credits Alan Titchmarsh Lighting (C); Picking Up The Pieces (I); Robin Of Sherwood (D)

●molinare
a television corporation company

Molinare
34 Fouberts Place, London W1F 7PX
t 020 7478 7000 **f** 020 7478 7199
e bookings@molinare.co.uk **w** www.molinare.co.uk
Contact Kate George, Facilities Manager
Credits Dorada Especial: Painting; AXN: Cornice; Walkers Dorito's: Idents; The Wind

For 30 years Molinare has been offering the best in Post Production, helping the best people make the best programmes, we have about the widest selection of facilities in one location in the industry. Based in the heart of Soho, we offer, 5 digital Online Suites, Editbox FX V8, Ursa Gold Telecine, High Definition Online, 10 Avid Offline suites and 2 Avid Online suites, 5 Audio Dubbing suites with voice over booths, Tracklay, Discreet Flint, Media Illusion, Drive in 1500 sq ft Video studio, 400 sq ft Virtual Studio, Duplication, Transmission Services, as well as the Molinare Design team for all your branding and design needs.

Stone Productions
Lakeside Studios, 62 Mill Street, St Osyth CO16 8EW
t 01255 822172 **f** 01255 822160 **m** 07768 470401
e info@stone-productions.co.uk
w www.stone-productions.co.uk
Contact J Stone, Partner; Kevin Stone, Partner
Credits NHS (C)

Production Facilities
Visual Display Systems

Barco
50 Suttons Park Avenue, Reading RG6 1AZ
t 0118 966 4611 **f** 0118 926 7716
e sales.uk.bps@barco.com **w** www.barco.com

Helen Flint
The Beehive, 36 Railwayside, Barnes, London SW13 0PN
t 020 8878 3766 **f** 020 8878 3766 **m** 07768 520334
e helenvflint@hotmail.com
Credits Perfect Strangers (T); Bodily Harm (T)

Moving Massage Centre, Vision Options Ltd
York House, 22 Old Shoreham Road, Brighton BN1 5DD
t 01273 385000 **f** 01273 549549 **m** 07970 861755
e voptions@aol.com **w** www.vision-options.co.uk
Contact Robert Douglas, Sales Director

SNP Group
Unit 8 Brentford Business Centre, Commerce Road, Brentford TW8 8LG
t 020 8580 0000 **f** 020 8580 9119
e visualsystems@snpgroup.com **w** www.snpgroup.com
Contact Caroline Travis, Marketing Executive; Scott Naylor, Managing Director; Steve Harper, Operations Manager

Windmill Studios
49-51 York Road, Brentford TW8 0QP
t 020 8568 0462 **f** 020 8568 4151
e info@windmillstudios.net **w** www.windmillstudios.net
Contact Simon Livingstone, General Manager
Credits Tommorrow Never Dies (F)

Promotional Merchandise

0800 Promote
14 Penhenden Lane, London N3 1TR
t 020 8371 8228 **f** 020 8371 8220
e sales@0800promote.com **w** www.0800promote.com
Contact Steve Harris, Director; Lesley Harris, Director

The Absolute Works Ltd
The Old Raven, Great Gap, Ivinghoe LU7 9DZ
t 08000 851724 **f** 01296 661918 **m** 07770 396809
e info@absoluteworks.com **w** www.absoluteworks.com
Contact Dian Parker, Director

Alexander Dunn & Company
Brook House, Downmill Road, Bracknell RG12 1QS
t 01344 411311 **f** 01344 860240
e sales@alexanderdunn.co.uk **w** www.alexanderdunn.co.uk
Contact Denise Hesselberger, Director

Amagination Merchandising & Promotions
280 Earlsfield Rd, London SW18 3EH
t 020 8874 2373 **f** 020 8874 2295 **e** siyeo@aol.com
Contact Simon Yeo, Director

Award International Ltd
Viking House, Cliftonville Avenue, Cliftonville CT9 2AQ
t 01843 295555 **f** 01843 295500
e sales@awardtp.com **w** www.awardtp.com
Contact Pete Gilbert, Marketing Director

Balloon Mad
Aston Road, Nuneaton CV11 5EL
t 024 7637 4425 **f** 024 7637 4424 **m** 07970 467354
e balloonmad@zoom.co.uk
Contact Y Bone, Partner; Ian Bone, Partner

Balloonland
12 Hale Lane, Mill Hill, London NW7 3NX
t 020 8906 3302 **f** 020 8906 1579
e info@balloonland.co.uk **w** www.balloonland.co.uk
Contact Pauline Zabaroff, Partner

Copycats
114 Hoe Street, London E17 4QR
t 020 8520 7711 **f** 020 8520 9776
e walthamstow@kindair.co.uk **w** www.copycats.co.uk
Contact Lydon Wall, Director; Peter Day, Director

Doppelgangers Ltd
30 North Street, Carshalton SM5 2HU
t 020 8669 1543
Contact David Mayo, Managing Director

Fat Dog Promotions Ltd
PO Box 20, Robertsbridge TN32 5ZE
t 01580 881000 **f** 01580 882000
e sales@fatdog.co.uk **w** www.fatdog.co.uk
Contact James Piddock, Sales Manager

Gold Star Printers & Embroiders
Units 5&6, Britannia Business Park, Quarry Wood Industrial
Estate, Aylesford ME20 7NT
t 01622 717332 **f** 01622 715508
e goldstaruk@ukonline.co.uk **w** www.goldstaruk.com
Contact Simon Dean, Managing Director

Marketing In Mind Ltd
64 High Street, Esher KT10 9QS
t 01372 463000 **f** 01372 463800
e sales@marketinginmind.co.uk **w** www.marketinginmind.co.uk
Contact Steve Wickes, Principal
Credits The Mummy Returns (F); Men Behaving Badly (T)

PS Graphics
Heath House, Ebberns Road, Hemel Hempstead HP3 9RD
t 01442 262100 **f** 01442 262500
e sale@psgraphics.co.uk **w** www.psgraphics.co.uk
Contact David Rickman, Sales Manager
Credits Foyles War (T); Dirty Pretty Things (F); The Calcium Kid (F); The Book Group II (T)

Sky Signs
Church Street, Deeping St James, Peterborough PE6 8HD
t 01778 345464 **f** 01778 341198 **e** icarus1@easynet.co.uk
Contact Bob Lavender, Managing Director

T-Shirt & Sons
Unit 3-5, Riverside Business Park, Lower Bristol Road, Bath
BA2 3DW
t 01225 442340 **f** 01225 445442
e sales@tshirtandsons.co.uk **w** www.tshirtandsons.co.uk
Contact Jonathan Lunt

Think Promotions
Unit 6H, Clapham North Business Centre, London SW4 6DH
t 020 7627 4930 **f** 020 7498 3615
e sales@thinkpromotions.net **w** www.thinkpromotions.net
Contact Hugh Alexander, Managing Director
Credits Channel 4 (C); ITV Digital (C); Virgin (C)

Walsh & Jenkins Plc
Power House, Powerscroft Road, Sidcup DA14 5EA
t 020 8308 6300 **f** 020 8308 6340 **i** 020 8300 0158
e edward@walsh-jenkins.co.uk **e** www.walsh-jenkins.co.uk
Contact Edward Howson, Specialist Executive

PROPS

Prop Crew

Sonny Anthony
Experience Counts - Call Me Ltd, 5th Floor, 41-42 Berners
Street, London W1P 3AA
t 020 7637 8112 **f** 020 7580 2582

DBW Atkinson
The Old Forge, 24 Bourne Avenue, Windsor SL4 3JR
t 01753 831432 **f** 01753 831432 **m** 07711 294009

Ken Augustin
EXEC, 6 Travis Court, Farnham Royal SL2 3SB
t 01753 646677 **f** 01753 646770
e sue@execmanagement.co.uk **w** www.execmanagement.co.uk

Lawrie Ayres
4 Scotney House, Petridge Road, Redhill RH1 5JG
t 01737 769963 **f** 01737 218378 **m** 07768 848961
Credits Lara Croft And The Cradle Of Life: Tomb Raider 2 (F); Kellog's Special K (C); Harry Potter And The Chamber Of Secrets (F); Cold Mountain (F)

Ken Bacon
31 Willow Road, West Bridgford NG2 7AY
t 0115 923 3798 **m** 07702 256 180
Credits Eyes Wide Shut (F); 102 Dalmatians (F)

David Cheesman
14 Beancroft Road, Marston Moretaine MK43 0PY
t 01234 766688 **m** 07767 324004
e david.cheesman1@btinternet.com
Credits Van Helsing (F)

Dan Coleman
Experience Counts - Call Me Ltd, 5th Floor, 41-42 Berners Street, London W1P 3AA
t 020 7637 8112 **f** 020 7580 2582

Kelvin Cook
11 Langton Way, Egham TW20 8DS
t 01784 455390 **m** 07976 442 652
e kelvincook@hotmail.com
Credits Pinnochio II (F); Sleepy Hollow (F); The Mummy (F)

Ron Dowling
334 Bromsgrove Road, Hunnington, Halesowen B62 0JW
t 0121 550 5945 **m** 07774 858014 **e** rondowling@ntlworld.com
Credits My Uncle Silus (T); There's Only One Jimmy Grimble (F); Last Orders (F); The 10th Kingdom (T)

David Hayden
5 Berkley Square, Newcastle-upon-Tyne NE3 2JB
t 0191 284 6598 **m** 07702 203818
Credits Wire In The Blood (T); Murder In Mind (T); Blue Dove (T); Al's Lads (F)

Mark Hedges
m 07050 241408
Credits Fields of Gold (T); Murder Rooms (T)

Valma Hiblen
15B Chadwell Street, London EC1R 1XD
m 07961 447741 **e** valhib@hotmail.com

Jack Lee
8 Princeton Close, College Gardens, Salford, Manchester M6 8QL
t 0161 737 0844 **f** 0161 737 0844 **m** 07850 551469
Credits Sparking Reactions - BNFL/The Science Museum (C); The Forsyte Saga II (T); Linda Green (T); Playing The Field (T)

Glyn Phillips
17 Dulais Drive, Aberdulais, Neath SA10 8HB
t 01639 773852 **m** 07977 757680 **e** terrie@ntlworld.com
Credits Anazapta (F); Testimony Of Taliesen Jones; Solomon And Gaenor

Ray Rose
39 Southwold Spur, Langley SL3 8XX
t 01753 593661 **m** 07701 243074 **e** rayruthrose@aol.com
Credits Die Another Day (F)

Bryn Siddall
Experience Counts - Call Me Ltd, 5th Floor, 41-42 Berners Street, London W1P 3AA
t 020 7637 8112 **f** 020 7580 2582

Mark S Sindall
41 Redheath Close, Leavesden, Watford WD25 7AH
t 01923 467031 **m** 07876 351081
Credits New Tricks (T); EastEnders (T)

George Smithson
Experience Counts - Call Me Ltd, 5th Floor, 41-42 Berners Street, London W1P 3AA
t 020 7637 8112 **f** 020 7580 2582

Graham Stickley
t 01784 450452 **m** 07711 265430
Credits Cold Mountain (F)

Prop Masters

Mark Allett
Bookends, 83 Maynard Drive, St Albans AL1 2JX
t 01727 841177 **e** bookgold@bookends.fsbusiness.co.uk

Aaron Batterham
Art Department, 51 Pratt Street, London NW1 0BJ
t 020 7428 0500 **f** 020 7916 2167 **m** 07973 639785
e info@art-department.co.uk

Pat Begley
Hillside, 35 Church Lane, Highfield, Southampton SO17 1SY
t 023 8055 0086 **f** 023 8055 0086 **m** 07979 095844
e pbegley@ntlworld.com **w**
www.freespace.virgin.net/patrick.begley
Credits Accellerator (F); In Deep III (T); Father Ted (T)

Nick Bowering
Bookends, 83 Maynard Drive, St Albans AL1 2JX
t 01727 841177 **e** bookgold@bookends.fsbusiness.co.uk

Clive Bowerman
Art Department, 51 Pratt Street, London NW1 0BJ
t 020 7428 0500 **f** 020 7916 2167 **m** 07973 639785
e info@art-department.co.uk

Simon Clift
Art Department, 51 Pratt Street, London NW1 0BJ
t 020 7428 0500 **f** 020 7916 2167 **m** 07973 639785
e info@art-department.co.uk

Roy Dawson
10 Armada Court, East Bracklesham Drive, Chichester PO20 8JA
t 020 7267 0516 **f** 020 7267 0516 **m** 07860 294757
Credits Trinity Mirror (C); Remember Me (F); Trial And Retribution IV (T)

Bob Edgecombe
Suz Cruz, Halliford Studios, Manygate Lane, Shepperton TW17 9EG
t 01932 252577 **f** 01932 253323 **m** 07956 485593
e zoe@suzcruz.co.uk **w** www.suzcruz.co.uk

Tony Fiori
Bookends, 83 Maynard Drive, St Albans AL1 2JX
t 01727 841177 **e** bookgold@bookends.fsbusiness.co.uk

Barry Gibbs
t 01953 789039 **m** 07970 171160 **e** bgibbsprops@hotmail.com
Credits Onegin (F); Captain Corelli's Mandolin (F); About A Boy (F); Time Line (F)

Russell Hanson
Agent Bookends, 83 Maynard Drive, St Albans AL1 2JX
t 01727 841177 **e** bookgold@bookends.fsbusiness.co.uk
Agent Art Department, 51 Pratt Street, London NW1 0BJ
t 020 7428 0500 **f** 020 7916 2167 **m** 07973 639785
e info@art-department.co.uk

Geoff Hartman
Bookends, 83 Maynard Drive, St Albans AL1 2JX
t 01727 841177 **e** bookgold@bookends.fsbusiness.co.uk

Paul Jeffries
Bookends, 83 Maynard Drive, St Albans AL1 2JX
t 01727 841177 **e** bookgold@bookends.fsbusiness.co.uk

Mike Killman
Flat B Sandy, 110 Bluehouse Lane RH8 0AR
t 01883 734779 **f** 01883 734779 **m** 07850 165409
Credits Poirot 2000 (T); Waking The Dead (T); Impact (T)

Brian Lofthouse
22 Alexandra Road, Borehamwood WD6 5PB
t 020 8953 6791 **t** 020 7607 3025 **f** 020 7607 5928
m 07710 660317 **e** brianlofthouse@hotmail.com
Credits The Project (T); Once Upon A Time In The Midlands (F); Helen West (T); Perfect (T)

Martin Carley Ltd
School Cottage, Roundhurst, Haslemere GU27 3BN
t 01428 643716 **f** 01428 658530 **m** 07770 317167
e martincarley@compuserve.com
Contact Martin Carley

Ray McNeill
25a Bedford Court, London N22 7AU
t 020 8888 5248 **m** 07973 616109 **e** rnmcneill@tinyworld.co.uk
Credits Daddy's Girl (F); Bend It Like Beckham (F)

Paul Miller
10 Clwyd Avenue, Dyserth LL18 6HN
t 01745 571466 **f** 01745 571466 **m** 07774 808756
e pmiller@onetel.net.uk
Credits Grolsch (C); Sainsbury's (C); Coca-Cola (C)

Terry Murrell
55 Grasmere Road, Lightwater GU18 5TL
t 01276 471824 **m** 07966 539 369 **e** murrelltj@aol.com
Credits Hero To Zero (T); The Bill (T); EastEnders (T)

Wesley Peppiatt
Bookends, 83 Maynard Drive, St Albans AL1 2JX
t 01727 841177 **e** bookgold@bookends.fsbusiness.co.uk

Prop Fiction
20 Aldworth Avenue, Wantage OX12 7EJ
t 01235 771566 **f** 01235 224762 **m** 07768 965107
e dickon.peschek@ntlworld.com
Contact Dickon Peschek, Prop Master; Darren Wisker, Prop Master/Standby; Rob Sellers, Prop Master/Standby
Credits Alibi (T); The Last Detective (T); The Cazalets (T); Johnathan Creek (T)

Ray Perry
28 Arundel Drive, Borehamwood WD6 2NE
t 020 8207 0134 **f** 020 8207 0134 **m** 07836 702624
Contact Ray Perry, Propmaster
Credits Kevin And Perry Go Large (F); Anita And Me (F); Buffalo Soldiers (F); Cold Mountain (F)

Nick Rose
124 Lyham Road, London SW2 5QA
t 020 8671 3067 **f** 020 8671 3067 **m** 07831 678668

Peter Saunders
Bookends, 83 Maynard Drive, St Albans AL1 2JX
t 01727 841177 **e** bookgold@bookends.fsbusiness.co.uk

Paul Smith
130 Benhurst Ave, Elm Park, Hornchurch RM12 4QP
t 01708 703367 **f** 01708 780350 **m** 07850 198186 **e** paulsmiffysmith@hotmail.com
Contact Paul Smith, Property Master
Credits Silent Witness (T); Night & Day (T); Waking The Dead II & III (T)

Ray Spencer
Bookends, 83 Maynard Drive, St Albans AL1 2JX
t 01727 841177 **e** bookgold@bookends.fsbusiness.co.uk

Ty Teiger
Bookends, 83 Maynard Drive, St Albans AL1 2JX
t 01727 841177 **e** bookgold@bookends.fsbusiness.co.uk

Terry Tague
Wooland House, Trefrew Road, Camelford PL32 9TP
t 01840 213030 **f** 01840 213030 **m** 07771 606 947
Credits Tom's Midnight Garden (F); Basil (F); Kavana QC (T)

Richard Tharp
Art Department, 51 Pratt Street, London NW1 0BJ
t 020 7428 0500 **f** 020 7916 2167 **m** 07973 639785
e info@art-department.co.uk

Colin Thurston
61 Dukes Wood Avenue, Gerrards Cross SL9 7JY
t 01753 887910 **m** 07957 929834 **e** crisidad@aol.com
Credits George And The Dragon (T); Sharp (T); The Monkey King (T); The Fourth Angel (F)

Nick Turnbull
Bookends, 83 Maynard Drive, St Albans AL1 2JX
t 01727 841177 **e** bookgold@bookends.fsbusiness.co.uk

Bruce Vincent
2 Meadow Mead, Radlett WD7 8ES
t 01923 857868 **f** 01923 857868 **m** 07939 286742

Lloyd Vincent
2 Meadow Mead, Radlett WD7 8ES
t 01923 857868 **m** 07957 293652
Agent Art Department, 51 Pratt Street, London NW1 0BJ
t 020 7428 0500 **f** 020 7916 2167 **m** 07973 639785
e info@art-department.co.uk
Credits Trial And Retribution VII (T); Cold Mountain (F); Jeep (C)

Chris Wade
Agent Bookends, 83 Maynard Drive, St Albans AL1 2JX
t 01727 841177 **e** bookgold@bookends.fsbusiness.co.uk
Agent EXEC, 6 Travis Court, Farnham Royal SL2 3SB
t 01753 646677 **f** 01753 646770
e sue@execmanagement.co.uk **w** www.execmanagement.co.uk

Steve West
Bookends, 83 Maynard Drive, St Albans AL1 2JX
t 01727 841177 **e** bookgold@bookends.fsbusiness.co.uk

Stephen Wheeler
29 Burbidge Road, Shepperton TW17 0ED
t 01932 229222 **f** 01932 229222 **m** 07768 362132
Credits Servants (T); The Dept (T); Two Men Went To War (F); Long Time Dead (F)

Matthew Wyles
Art Department, 51 Pratt Street, London NW1 0BJ
t 020 7428 0500 **f** 020 7916 2167 **m** 07973 639785
e info@art-department.co.uk

Props Action Vehicles

Action 1st Position Vehicles
27 Old Gloucester Street, London WC1
t 0870 830 0688 **f** 0870 830 0681 **m** 07860 373799
w www.1stpositionvehicles.co.uk
Contact John Noel, Proprietor
Credits Sony PlayStation - 'Medal of Honour' (C); Rescue Me (T); Two Men Went to War (F)

Action Ambulances
Matrix Business Park, Victoria Road, Dartford DA1 5AJ
t 07000 959697 **f** 07000 980980 **m** 07074 678999
action@ambulance.co.uk **w** www.ambulance.co.uk
Contact Clive Brady, Proprietor
Credits Silent Witness (T); TV Times (C); Barclays Bank (C); Baby Father (T)
We supply authentic ambulance and paramedic vehicles with uniformed crews.

Action Motor Cycles
139 Putney Bridge Road, London SW15 2PA
t 020 8877 3434 **f** 020 8877 3737 **m** 07836 637538
e panmanhd@dialstart.net **w** www.riverside-motorcycles.com
Contact Jeff Murphy, Proprietor
Credits Virgin Records Promo Parties (C); Westlife Christmas Pop Video (M);
Record of the Year Awards (T)

Action Ten Tenths Ltd
106 Gifford Street, London N1 ODF
t 020 7607 4887 **f** 020 7609 8124 **m** 07421 420489
e mike@tentenths.co.uk **w** www.tentenths.co.uk
Contact Michael Hallowes

Action Vehicles Ltd
Cracker Barrel Farm, Horsham Road, Beare Green, Dorking
RH5 4PQ
t 01306 710300 **f** 01306 710301 **m** 07836 734477
e darren@actionvehicles.com **w** www.actionvehicles.com
Contact Darren Litten, Director
Credits The World Is Not Enough (F); Tomorrow Never Dies (F); Harry Potter
And The Prisoner Of Azkaban (F); Die Another Day (F)

AgriPower Ltd
Broomfield Farm, Rignall Road, Great Missenden HP16 9PE
t 01494 866776 **f** 01494 866779
e sales@agripower.co.uk **w** www.agripower.co.uk
Contact Mick Greaves, Director

Ambulance Services Film Unit
t 01754 880960 **m** 07831 220299 **e** ambservice@aol.com
Contact Michael Newbold, Proprietor
Credits Family Affairs (T); EastEnders (T); The Bill (T)

American 50's Car Hire
Claygate, Enfield Road, Shotgate, Wickford SS11 8SD
t 01268 735914 **f** 01268 735914 **m** 07985 265474
e patron2@rayleighlo.freeserve.co.uk **w** www.american50s.co.uk
Contact Garry Darby, Proprietor

Autofilm
3 Field House, Rochdale OL12 0AA
t 01706 719911 **f** 01706 719922 **m** 07977 404931
e nvmackenzie@hotmail.com
Contact Wendy Noakley

Bells & Two-Tones
Sandpits Bungalow, High Street, Shirrell Heath SO32 2JN
t 01329 834234 **f** 01329 832862 **m** 07860 499421
e bellsntwos@aol.com **w** www.bellsandtwotones.co.uk
Contact Gillian Hebard, Partner

Ben Ford Horses & Carriages
Higher Parks, Morchard Bishop, Crediton EX17 6NW
t 01363 877766 **f** 01363 877754 **m** 07831 517097
Contact Maria Bisset, Proprietor
Credits Treflan (T); Servants (T); Berkeley Square (T); House Of Elliot (T)

Bicycles Unlimited
522 Holly lane, Erdington, Birmingham B24 9LY
t 0121 350 0685 **f** 0121 350 0685 **e** pinkertn@mwfree.net
Contact John Pinkerton, Managing Director

Bikes On Film
1 Walmer Court Yard, 225-227 Walmer Road, London W11 4EY
t 020 7229 8882 **f** 020 7229 8883 **m** 07771 595999
e mg@markgeorge.com
Contact Mark George, Proprietor

The British Commercial Vehicle Museum
King Street, Leyland, Preston PR5 1LE
t 01772 451011 **f** 01772 623404

The British Motor Industry Heritage Trust
Heritage Motor Centre, Banbury Road, Gaydon CV35 0BJ
t 01926 641188 **f** 01926 641555
e enquiries@heritage-motor-centre.co.uk
w www.heritage-motor-centre.co.uk

British Raceways Motorcycles
17 The Vale, Uxbridge Road, Shepherds Bush, London W3 7SH
t 020 8749 8181 **f** 020 8749 8181
e info@raceways.net **w** www.raceways.net
Contact R Emblen, Manager

Bromcount Ltd
Rosedean House, London Road, Windlesham GU20 6PJ
t 01276 474450 **f** 01276 451385
Contact Liz Piper; David Piper

Bygone Transport Services
42 Coniston Avenue, Queensbury, Bradford BD13 2JD
t 01274 881640 **f** 08700 940075
e keithajenkinson@autobusreview.freeserve.co.uk
Contact Keith Jenkinson, Director
Credits Taggart (T); Emmerdale (T)

Call-A-Car & Street Scenes
Capri House, Walton-on-Thames KT12 2LY
t 01932 223838 **f** 01932 269109
Contact Arthur Freakes, Managing Director

Carriages Vehicle Agency
147 Nork Way, Banstead SM7 1HR
t 01737 353926 **f** 01737 353926 **m** 07831 543210
w www.carriagesvehicleagency.co.uk
Contact Norman Hodkinson, Proprietor

Cars for Stars
Merle Common, Oxted RH8 0RP
t 01883 714184 **f** 01883 730420 **m** 07831 257890
e dave.garage@unipart.net **w** www.carzforstarz.com
Contact Ivor Stamp, Managing Director

Cars In Camera
Units 6, Cardiff Road Industrial Estate, Watford WD18 0DG
t 01923 817894 **f** 01923 238494
e info@carsincamera.com **w** www.carsincamera.com

Celebricar
47 Blantyre Crescent, Duntocher, Glasgow G81 6JN
t 01389 878235 **f** 01389 383988 **m** 07703 162164
e robryan47@hotmail.com
Contact Robbyie Ryan, Proprietor

Chelsea Scooters Ltd
334-336 Wandsworth Bridge Road, Fulham, London SW6 2TZ
t 020 7736 6670 **f** 020 7736 6670
e chelseascooters.ltd@virgin.net **w** www.chelseascootersltd.co.uk
Contact Ray Humphries, Director; Brian Humphries, Partner

Classic Car Hire
9 Chestnut Place, Johnston PA5 9SZ
t 01505 322879 **f** 01505 345547 **m** 07850 792519
Contact Alan Hardey, Vehicle Coordinator
Credits The Magdelane Sisters (F); The Key (T); Danny The Dog (F); Harry And
The Wrinklies (T)

Classic Vehicles Unlimited
Woodstock Lodge, Shipton Lane, Wiggington, York YO32 2RQ
t 01904 471248 **f** 01904 471249 **m** 07939 529451
w www.classicvehiclesunlimited.co.uk
Contact John Harrison
Credits Born And Bred (T); The Royal (T); Heartbeat (T); Fairytale - A True Story (F)

Steve Dent
Fieldways Farm, Harefield Road, Rickmansworth WD3 1PE
t 01923 779603 **f** 01923 776256 **m** 07989 566291

Dream Cars
11 Abbey Business Centre, 15-17 Ingate Place, Battersea,
London SW8 3NS
t 020 7627 5775 **f** 020 7498 7556 **m** 07973 400245
e info@dreamcars.co.uk **w** www.dreamcars.co.uk
Contact Stewart Homan, Partner

ES Services Ltd
1 Woodview Drive, Boghall Road, Bray, Rep of Ireland
t +353 1 286 0709
e vintagerollsroyce@eircom.net **w** www.angelfire.com/artcom/rolls
Contact Eamon Dunne, Proprietor

Gleneagles Chauffeur Drive Service
Gleneagles Garage, 155 Victoria Road, Wargrave, Reading
RG10 8AH
t 0118 940 3228 **f** 0118 940 4321
e glenlimos@aol.com **w** www.gleneaglescds.co.uk
Contact David Lowe, Director, Director

Ivan Dutton Ltd
Peacehaven Farm, Worminghall Road, Ickford, Aylesbury HP18 9JE
t 01844 339457 **f** 01844 338933
e info@duttonbugatti.co.uk **w** www.duttonbugatti.co.uk
Contact Timothy Dutton, Director
Credits Top Gear

JD Christian & Son
52 Station Road, Banks, Southport PR9 8BB
t 01704 227101
Contact Christian, Proprietor

Keighley & Worth Valley Railway
The Railway Station, Hawarth, Keighley BD22 8NJ
t 01535 645214 **f** 01535 647317
e admin@kwvr.co.uk **w** www.kwvr.co.uk
Contact Paul Brown, Chairman

Keith Abrehart Company
Brookfarm, Mill Lane, Frittenden, Cranbrook TN17 2DR
t 01580 852352 **f** 01580 852352
Contact Keith Abrehart, Proprietor

London Citybus TV & Promotions
PO Box 76, Croydon CR9 9LY
t 020 8651 1051 **f** 020 8651 1051 **m** 07860 332339
e tope@cbmservices.freeserve.co.uk **w** www.mediabus.tv

Motorhouse Hire
Weston Underwood, Olney MK46 5LD
t 020 7495 1618 **f** 01234 240393
e michael@motorhouseltd.co.uk
Contact Michael Geary, Managing Director

The National Classic Car Film Register
Raymonds, London Road, Rawreth, Wickford SS11 8UA
t 01268 781119 **f** 01268 786669 **m** 07702 538407
e info@executive-carhire.co.uk **w** www.executive-carhire.co.uk
Contact David Murrells, Director
Credits Paradise Heights (T); League Of Gentlemen (T); Hope & Glory (T)

PAS Special Projects
37 Carterknowle Road, Sheffield S7 2DW
t 0114 255 0098 **f** 0114 255 0681 **e** pas@btclick.com
Working military vehicles/tanks/equipment - WWII to present day.

Portobello Gold
95 Portobello Road, London W11 2QB
t 020 7460 4910 **f** 020 7229 2278 **m** 07774 264474
e mike@portobellogold.com **w** www.portobellogold.com
Contact Michael Bell, Proprieter

Production Cars (Ltd)
58 Lewin Road, Streatham Common, London SW16 6JT
t 020 8769 9867 **f** 020 8769 4076 **m** 07768 030560
e prodcars@aol.com
Contact Kevin Potter, Company Director

Production Profiles Ltd
164 Waldegrave Road, Twickenham TW1 4TD
t 020 8891 5194 **m** 07785 788494
e info@productionprofiles.co.uk **w** www.productionprofiles.co.uk
Contact Delena keenan; Joe Keenan, Director

Tall Ships Liverpool
11 Greenbank Drive, Sefton Park, Liverpool L17 1AN
t 0151 733 0699 **t** 0151 733 2860
f 0151 733 0699 **m** 07720 286669
e merseyheritage@btinternet.com **w** www.merseyheritage.com
Contact Susan Hanley-Place, Director, Chief Executive; Geoff Hanley, Ship Manager
Credits The Proposition (F); Sherlock Holmes (T); Coral Island (T);
Four Feathers (F)

Tall ships, form boats, away dressings, skilled extras, horse vehicles.

Ten Tenths
106 Gifford Street, London N1 0DF
t 020 7607 4887 **f** 020 7609 8124 **m** 07721 420489
e mike@tentenths.co.uk **w** www.tentenths.co.uk
Contact Michael Hallowes

TLO Film Services
Longclose House, Common Road, Eton Wick, Near Windsor
SL4 6QY
t 01753 862637 **f** 01753 841998
e info@tlofilmservices.com **w** www.tlofilms.com
Contact Tony Oliver; Mark Oliver

Vintage Carriages Trust
C/o Haworth Railway Station, Keighley BD22 8NJ
t 01535 680425 **f** 01535 610796 **m** 07979 837180
e admin@vintagecarriagetrust.org **w**
www.vintagecarriagetrust.org
Contact Paul Holroyd, Trustee; Michael Cope, Secretary
Credits Turner - The Man Who Painted Britain (T); The Hound Of The
Baskervilles (T); Sons And Lovers (T); The Forsyte Saga (T)

Props **Armourers**

Armoury In Action
PO Box 12, Pateley Bridge HG3 5XN
t 07050 079587 **f** 07050 079587 **m** 07702 205809
Contact Neil Mountain, Proprietor
Credits Grease Monkeys (T); Deathwatch (F); A Touch Of Frost (T); My Kingdom (F)

Artisan Armours
Hope Farm, Halegate Road, Halebank, Widnes WA8 8LZ
t 0151 425 2500

Corridors of Time (Historical Presentations Ltd)
Palace Street, Canterbury CT1 2DZ
t 01227 478990 **f** 01227 478991
e alanaxe@btopenworld.com **w** www.corridors-of-time.co.uk

Alan M Meek
180 Frog Grove Lane, Wood Street Village, Guildford GU3 3HD
t 01483 234084 **f** 01483 236684

Perdix Firearms
PO Box 1670, Salisbury SP4 6QL
t 01722 782402 **f** 01722 782790 **m** 07850 668678
e perdix@eclipse.co.uk **w** www.perdix.co.uk
Contact Gregg Pearson, Film Services Manager
Credits The Lost Prince (F); Eye Spy (F); Gosford Park (F)

Props **Hire General**

1st Place Product Props Ltd
30 Hight Street, Linton, Cambridge CB1 6HS
t 01223 894949 **e** steve@firstplace.demon.co.uk
Contact Read

303 Hire Company
Brunel House, 12-16 Brunel Road, East Acton, London W3 7XR
t 020 8743 7616 **f** 020 8749 9435
e martha_newman@excite.co.uk
Contact Martha Newman
Credits From Hell (T); Die Another Day (F); Harry Potter And
The Philosopher's Stone (F)

A+M Hire Ltd
The Royals, Victoria Road, London NW10 6ND
t 020 8233 1500 **f** 020 8233 1550 **w** www.amhire.com

Allprops Ltd
Unit 2, Acton Central Estate, 2A Rosemont Road, London W3 9LR
t 020 8993 1625 **f** 020 8993 7570 **e** allpropsltd@btconnect.com

Bettavision TV
1 Mount Parade, Cockfosters EN4 9DD
t 020 8449 4898
Contact Moss, Director

Breakaway Effects Ltd
Shepperton Studios, Studios Road, Shepperton TW17 0QD
t 01932 592446 **f** 01932 592442
w www.breakaway-effects.com
Contact Neil Upington, Director; Sean Ward, Director

British Turntable Company Ltd
Emblem St, Wood Meads, Bolton BL3 5BW
t 01204 525626 **f** 01204 382407
e info@turntable.co.uk **w** www.british.turntable.co.uk
Contact Mike Forrest, Partner

Camden Special Events
125 Brantwood Road, Tottenham, London N17 0DX
t 020 8801 4444 **t** 020 8961 6161 **f** 020 8801 4445
e sales@camdenfurniture.co.uk **w** www.camdenfurniture.co.uk
Contact Dawn Humphries, Sales Office; Rob Sheperd, Sales Director; Craig
Hammond, Project Manager

Display Electronics
Stanley Works, 29-35 Osborne Road, Thornton Heath CR7 8PD
t 020 8653 3333 **f** 020 8653 8888
e admin@electroprops.co.uk **w** www.electroprops.co.uk
Contact Dave Martin, Manager

Eccentric Trading Company Ltd
Unit 2, Frogmore Estate, Acton Lane, London NW10 7JQ
t 020 8453 1125 **f** 020 8961 4080
e info@eccentric-trading.co.uk **w** www.eccentric-trading.co.uk
Contact Spencer Jordan, Director

Electro Signs Ltd
97 Vallentin Road, London E17 3JJ
t 020 8521 8066 **f** 020 8520 8127
e info@electrosigns.co.uk **w** www.electrosigns.co.uk
Contact Chris Bracey, Managing Director

Entertainment Marketing
8th Floor, 1 Kingsway, London WC2B 6XD
t 020 7836 5550 **f** 020 7240 9990
e maggie@entmarketing.com **w** www.entmarketing.com
Contact Maggie Tetlow, Managing Director; Russell Human, Account Director

Envision Services Ltd
Unit 11 Walthamstow Business Centre, Clifford Road, London
E17 4SX
t 020 8503 3399 **f** 020 8503 2550 **m** 07768 002385
e envision@allplastics.co.uk **w** www.allplastics.co.uk
Contact A Donohue, Managing Director

Fab 'n' Funky
18-20 Brunel Road, London W3 7XR
t 020 8746 7746 **f** 020 8743 2662
e inquiries@fabbfunky.co.uk **w** www.fabnfunky.co.uk

Film Furniture
Moorside, Tockwith YO26 7QG
t 01423 359052 **f** 01423 358188
e claire@tomlinson.demon.co.uk **w** www.antique-furniture.co.uk
Contact Claire Wade, Customer Service Manager

Foxtrot Productions Ltd
Canalot Production Studios, 222 Kensal Road, London W10 5BN
t 020 8964 3555

Frontiers
37-39 Pembridge Road, London W11 3HG
t 020 7727 6132 **f** 020 7229 4835
Contact David Nall-Cain, Proprietor

Graham Barkley Backcloths
32-36 Telford Way, London W3 7XS
t 020 8743 1563 **f** 020 8743 8075
e backcloths@sanctuarystudios.co.uk
w www.sanctuarystudios.co.uk
Contact Paul Johnson, Manager
*Over 800 backcloths for hire to TV, photographers, theatres and event
organizers in a wide variety of sizes and subjects.*

Graham Harrison Framing
81 Southern Row, London W10 5AL
t 020 8969 4599 **f** 020 8964 0238 **e** graham@ghframing.com
Contact Graham Harrison, Proprietor

H&R Hire
14 Wendell Road, London W12 9RT
t 020 8743 1452 **f** 020 8746 0018
Contact Carol Hicks, Manageress

Roza Haghighat
12 Ludlow Close, Keynsham, Bristol BS31 2JS
m 07980 678759 **e** haghighat_roza@hotmail.com

Havenplan's Architectural Emporium
The Old Station, Station Road, Killamarsh, Sheffield S21 1EN
t 0114 248 9972 **t** 01246 433315 **f** 0114 248 9972

Jaques Samuel Pianos Ltd
Bechstein House, 142 Edgeware Road, London W2 2DZ
t 020 7723 8818 **f** 020 7224 8692
e props@jspianos.com **w** www.jspianos.com
Contact Daniel Thomas, Commercial Hires Manager

Keeley Hire (Film & TV) Ltd
Unit 4A, Charlton Mead Lane South, Hoddesdon EN11 0DJ
t 01992 464040 **f** 01992 462239
e sales@keeleyhire.co.uk **w** www.keeleyhire.co.uk
Credits Harry Potter I, II, III (F); Nicholas Nickleby (F); Gosford Park (F);
Timeline (F)

Langfords
Vault 10-8, London Silver Vaults, 53-64 Chancery Lane,
London WC2A 1QS
t 020 7242 6646 **f** 020 7242 6656
e mail@langfords.com **w** www.langfords.com
Contact Adam Langford, Partner

CHAMPAGNE BOLLINGER
Stage Champagne

Mentzendorff & Co. Ltd
Tel: 020 7840 3600 Fax: 0207840 3601
www.mentzendorff.co.uk

Lynn Westward Blinds
273 The Vale, Acton, London W3 7QA
t 020 8740 8756 **f** 020 8740 9836
e info@lynnwestward.com
Contact Lynn Smith, Director, Managing Director

Magical Mart
42 Christchurch Road, Sidcup DA15 7HQ
t 020 8300 3579 **f** 020 8300 3579
w www.johnstylesentertainer.co.uk
Contact B Styles, Proprietor
Credits The Harry Hill Show (T); Nicholas Nickleby (T); Tipping The Velvet (T); EastEnders (T)

Mayfair Gym Equipment Hire/Prop Hire & Deliver (PHD)
Popin Building, Unit 20, Southway, Wembley HA9 0HB
t 020 8903 7005 **f** 020 8900 2025 **m** 07973 501737
e mayfairgym@aol.com **w** www.prophireanddeliver.co.uk

Mentzendorff & Co Ltd
Prince Consort House, 27/29 Albert Embankment, London SE1 7TJ
t 020 7840 3600 **f** 020 7840 3601
e belinda@mentzendorff.co.uk **w** www.mentzendorff.co.uk
Contact Belinda Green

Morten Hire
6 Warburton Street, Didsbury, Manchester M20 6WA
t 0161 445 7629 **f** 0161 448 1323 **m** 07836 785154
e morten.booksellers@lineone.net
Contact John Morten

Newman Hire Co Ltd
16 The Vale, Acton, London W3 7SB
t 020 8743 0741 **f** 020 8749 3513 **e** info@newman-hire.co.uk
Contact D Newman, Managing Director; Terry Poole, Sales Manager; Raven King
Credits BT (C); Daniel Daronda (T); The Bond (F)

Palm Brokers
Cenacle Nursery, Taplow Common Road, Burnham SL1 8NW
t 01628 663734 **f** 01628 661047
e ask@palmbrokers.com **w** www.palmbrokers.com
Contact Beau Honey, Director

The Palm Centre
Ham Central Nursery, opposite Riverside Drive, Ham Street, Ham, Richmond TW10 7HA
t 020 8255 6191 **f** 020 8255 6192
e mail@palmcentre.co.uk **w** www.palmcentre.co.uk
Contact Martin Gibbons, Proprietor

Penfriend (London) Ltd
Bush House Arcade, Bush House, The Strand, London WC2B 4PH
t 020 7836 9809 **f** 020 7836 9809
e pen.london@btinternet.com **w** www.penfriend.co.uk
Contact Julie Gibbens, Shop Manager

Period Angling Props
Chalford Manor, Stoney Cross SO43 7GP
t 01590 675955 **f** 01590 679994
Contact John Cooper, Proprietor
Credits Foyle's War (T)

Period Props & Lighting Ltd
London
e pplprops@supanet.com
Contact R Jackson, Finance Director; Simon Stacey, Manager

The Piano Warehouse Ltd
30 Highgate Road, London NW5 1NS
t 020 7267 7671 **f** 020 7284 0083
e piano@piano-workshop.co.uk **w** www.piano-warehouse.co.uk
Contact Mike Neill, Bookings Manager

Picture Props Company Ltd
Brunel House, 12-16 Brunel Road, London W3 7XR
t 020 8749 2433 **f** 020 8740 5846 **w** www.propascene.com
Contact Janet Woodward, Manageress; Helen Aver, Manageress

Pilgrims Progress
1A & 3A Bridgewater Street, Liverpool L1 0AR
t 0151 708 7515 **f** 0151 708 7515 **m** 07808 899333
e pilgrimsprog@fsddial.co.uk **w** www.pilgrimsprogress.co.uk
Contact Selwyn Hyams, Proprietor
Credits Brookside (T); Liam (T); Hollyoaks (T); The Forsyte Saga (T)

Prop It Up
The Basement, Design Building, Television Centre, Wood Lane, London W12 7RJ
t 020 8576 7295 **f** 020 8576 7295 **e** eugene.slattery@bbc.co.uk
Contact Eugene Slattery

Prop.AG.anda Ltd
Unit 16 Faraday Court, Park Farm, Wellingborough NN8 6XY
t 0845 125 9591 **f** 0845 125 9591 **e** props@ukpropaganda.com
Contact Derek Peters, Production Co-ordinator; Lizzie Naylar, Production Co-ordinator; Ali Smith, Production Co-ordinator; John Mealing, Production Co-ordinator; John Perry, Managing Director

Props Galore (Part of Farley's)
15 Brunel Road, London W3 7XR
t 020 8746 1222 **f** 020 8354 1866 **e** propsgalore@farley.co.uk
Contact Pam Chester; Naomi Leigh, Manager

Real To Reel Ltd
Rolismead Horse, Wyke, Gillingham SP8 4NG
t 01747 822942 **f** 01747 861195
Contact Cullingford

Richard Bonner Pritchard
Porth-yr-Aur, High Street, Caernarfon LL55 1RN
t 01286 673835 **f** 01286 673835 **e** pg_amos@msn.com

Can't find an entry? turn to the alphabetical index starting on page 705

The Production GUIDE

Robert Johnson Coin Co Ltd
16 Little Russell Street, London WC1 A2HL
t 020 7831 0305 **e** rjcoinco@aol.com
Contact Robert Johnson, Director

Russell Beck Studios
Ground Floor, Richmond House, 1A Westgate Street, London E8 3RL
t 020 8985 1813 **f** 020 8525 1927
e russell@russellbeckstudio.co.uk
Contact Russell Beck, Proprietor; Patricia Beck, Administrator; Mike Garrett, Workshop Manager

Sanctuary Backcloths
32-36 Telford Way, London W3 7XS
t 002 8743 1563 **f** 002 8743 8075
e backcloths@sanctuarystudios.co.uk
w www.sanctuarystudios.co.uk
Contact Paul Johnson, Manager

Over 800 backcloths for hire to TV, photographers, theatres and event organizers in a wide variety of sizes and subjects.

Scenario (UK) Ltd
Westfield, Westland Green, Little Hadham SG11 2AL
t 08700 119567 **f** 01279 841459 **m** 07968 012726
e info@scenariouk.com **w** www.scenariouk.com
Contact Geraldine Coyle, Managing Director

Studio & TV Hire
3 Ariel Way, Wood Lane, White City, London W12 7SL
t 020 8749 3445 **f** 020 8740 9662
e info@stvhire.com **w** www.stvhire.com
Contact Matthew Fyson, General Manager

Tables Laid
Church Farm, Ashchurch GL20 8JU
t 01684 297999 **f** 01684 291201
e tableslaid@ision.co.uk
w www.ashphotography.co.uk/www.tableslaid.co.uk
Contact Sharon Ash

Vintage & Rare Guitars Ltd
6 Denmark Street, London WC2H 8LX
t 020 7240 7500 **f** 020 7240 8900 **m** 07958 622828
e enquiries@vintageandrareguitars.com
w www.vintageandrareguitars.com
Contact Adam Newman, Manager

Wall to Wall Communications
13 Manor Road, Wallington SM6 0BW
t 020 8647 4758 **f** 020 8669 1338
e info@walltowallcomms.co.uk **w** www.walltowallcomms.co.uk
Contact Barbara Calvert, Director; Helen MacDonald, Administration Manager
Credits Staying Up (T); Eastenders (T); Scene of the Crime (T); The Whistleblower (T)

Props Speciality

Adel Rootstein Display Mannequins
Shawfield House, Shawfield Street, London SW3 4BB
t 020 7351 1247 **f** 020 7376 5084
e sales@adelrootstein.co.uk **w** www.rootstein.com

Adrian Marchant Studios Ltd
Unit C, Roebuck Road, Chessington KT9 1EU
t 020 8397 5777 **f** 020 8397 6939
Contact Joan Cruse, Design Consultant

Angels
1 Garrick Road, London NW9 6AA
t 020 8202 2244 **f** 020 8202 1820
e info@angels.uk.com **w** www.angels.uk.com
Contact Paul Strutt
Credits Sleepy Hollow (F); Saving Private Ryan (F); Die Another Day (F); Gangs of New York (F)

Arthur Middleton
12 New Row, Covent Garden, London WC2 N4LF
t 020 7836 7042 **f** 020 7497 2486 **m** 07887 481102
e arthur@antique-globes.com **w** www.antique-globes.com
Credits Around The World In 80 Days (F); The Lost Prince (T); Harry Potter And The Prisoner Of Azkaban (F); Harry Potter And The Chamber Of Secrets (F)

Backgrounds
Unit 25, Waterside, 44-48 Wharf Road, London N1 7UX
t 020 7490 1181 **f** 020 7250 4104
Contact Rachael Chmielewski, Manager

BBC Special Effects

BBC Special Effects
Kendal Avenue, London W3 0RP
t 020 8993 9434 **f** 020 8993 8741
e special.effects@bbc.co.uk
w www.bbcresources.com/specialeffects

Beat About The Bush Ltd
Unit 23, Enterprise Way, The Triangle Business Centre, Salter Street, London NW1 6UG
t 020 8960 2087 **f** 020 8969 2281 **m** 07973 265793
e info@beataboutthebush.com
w www.beataboutthebush.com
Contact Bob Hall, Contact; Adrian Purbrick, Proprieter

British Cured Pilchards Ltd
Tolcarne, Newlyn, Penzance TR18 5QH
t 01736 332112 **f** 01736 332442
e nick@pilchardworks.co.uk **w** www.pilchardworks.co.uk

Buttons Saddlery
44 Guildford Road, Westend, Near Woking GU24 9PW
t 01276 857771 **f** 01276 857771 **m** 07881 933850
e adrian@buttonssaddlery.com **w** www.buttonssaddlery.com
Contact Adrian Benge, Partner
Credits Band Of Brothers (T); Lost In Space (F)

Candle Maker Supplies
28 Blythe Road, London W14 0HA
t 020 7602 4031 **f** 020 7602 2796
e candles@candlemakers.co.uk **w** www.candlemakers.co.uk
Credits Black Knight, The Mayor of Casterbridge, Possession

Compuhire (Eccentric Trading Co Ltd)
Unit 2, Frogmore Estate, Acton Lane, London NW10 7NQ
t 020 8963 7480
e info@compuhire.com **w** www.compuhire.com
Contact Mark Jordan, Director
Credits Love Actually (F); The Project (T); Three Blind Mice (F); EastEnders (T)

Cool Productions
4 Green Close, South Wonston, Winchester SO21 3EE
t 01962 884890 **f** 07970 094461 **m** 07976 249831
e crispin.coolpro@dial.pipex.com
Contact Crispin Lowrey, Director/Designer; Colin Lowrey, Director/Designer; Pauline Lowrey, Company Secretary

Deborah Hammond & Denise Hagon
37 Shakespeare Street, Stratford-upon-Avon CV37 6RN
t 01789 264114 **f** 01789 264114 **m** 07866 347021
Credits Monarch Of The Glen (T); Revelation (F); Poirot (T)

Dick George & Company
Signal House, Station Approach, Shepperton TW17 8AN
t 01932 240200 **f** 01932 242244 **e** info@dickgeorge.co.uk
Contact Dick George, Proprietor

Dorans Propmakers
53 Derby Road, Ashbourne DE6 1BH
t 01335 300064 **f** 01335 300064 **m** 07721 744774
e props@dorans.demon.co.uk
Contact Linda Doran, Director; Paul Doran, Director
Credits Hollyoaks (T); The Grimleys (T); CITV (T); The Hoobs (T)

Edmonton Machines Ltd
Unit 14-15, Great Cambridge Industrial Estate, London EN1 1SH
t 020 8344 4777 **f** 020 8344 4700
e edmmach@btinternet.com
Contact Melvyn Mattock, Managing Director

Essex Tube Windings Ltd
Macanie House, Dock Road, Tilbury RM18 7PT
t 01375 851613 **f** 01375 851717 **e** info@essextubes.com

Fairgrounds Old & New
Halstead, Fovant, Salisbury SP3 5NL
t 01722 714786 **f** 01722 714786 **m** 07710 287251
e s-vpostlethwaite@fovant.fsnet.co.uk **w** www.pozzy.co.uk
Contact Stephen Postlethwaite, Contact

Farley Spiller & Props Galore
1-17 Brunel Road, London W3 7XR
t 020 8749 9925 **f** 020 8749 8372
e props@farley.co.uk **w** www.farley.co.uk

FB Design Cabinet Makers
The Old Granary Workshops, Herriard Park, Basingstoke RG25 2PL
t 01256 381855 **f** 01256 381856 **m** 07802 564103
e sales@fbdesign.co.uk **w** www.fbdesign.co.uk
Contact David Forrest

Film Medical Services Ltd
5&7 Commercial Way, Park Royal, London NW10 7XF
t 020 8961 3222 **f** 020 8961 7427
e filmmed@aol.com **w** www.filmmedical.co.uk

Firebrand
Leacnaban Tayvallich, Lochgilphead PA31 8PF
t 01546 870310 **f** 01546 870310 **e** alex@firebrand.fsnet.co.uk
Contact Alex Hamilton

The Flower Shop
102 High Street, Bushey WD23 3DE
t 020 8950 3384
Contact Martin Roberts, Partner; Susie Roberts, Partner

Gardencraft
Tremadog, Porthmadog LL49 9RD
t 01766 513036 **f** 01766 514364
e sales@gcraft.co.uk **w** www.gcraft.co.uk
Contact Chris Shutes, Partner
Credits Big Breakfast (T); Down To Earth (T); Pie In the Sky (T); First Knight (F)

Golden Age Television Re-Creations
Beazleys, Chelmsford Road, Felsted CM6 3ET
t 01371 820155 **f** 0870 125 3762
e dicky.howett@btinternet.com **w** www.golden-agetv.co.uk
Contact Dicky Howett, Organiser
Credits Damage (M); Li-Lets (C); BBC Discovery Channel (C); Evelyn (F)

Gomm Metal Developments Ltd
10 Manor Way, Old Woking GU22 9JX
t 01483 764876 **f** 01483 767639 **w** www.racecar.co.uk/gomm
Contact Frank Gomm, Managing Director

Gresham Wood Industries
68 Bentfield Road, Stansted CM24 8HS
t 01279 816135 **t** 01279 813132 **f** 01279 814627
e sales@greshamwood.com **w** www.greshamwood.com
Contact Colin Marshall, Sales Director

Heads 'n' Tails
Bournes House, 41 Church Street, Wiveliscombe, Taunton TA4 2LT
t 01984 623 097 **f** 01984 624 445 **m** 07971 954508
e mac@taxidermyuk.com **w** www.taxidermyuk.com
Contact D. McKinley
Credits Gladiatriss (F); Gladiatriss (F); Harry Potter And The Chamber Of Secrets (F); 102 Dalmations (F)

Hector Finch Lighting
88-90 Wandsworth Bridge Road, London SW6 2TF
t 020 7731 8886 **f** 020 7731 7408
e hector@hectorfinch.com **w** www.hectorfinch.com
Contact Hector Finch; Caroline Wolf; Lolita Campbell

Hybrid Enterprises Ltd
Units 26-27 Armley Workshops, Pickering Street, Leeds LS12 2QG
t 0113 217 1300 **t** 01277 654862
f 0113 217 1300 **m** 07870 600273
e studio@hybridfx.com **w** www.hybridfx.com
Contact Mike Stringer, Technical Director; Mike Bates, Production Director; Ryk Fortuna, Lead Sculptor/Technician
Credits The National Geographic (D); The Royal (T); Ant 'N' Dec's Saturday Night Takeaway (T); The Two Towers (F)

Hyper Inflatables
5th Floor, Broadquay House, Prince Street, Bristol BS1 4DJ
t 0117 955 5544 **f** 0117 955 0786 **m** 07949 031772
e sales@hyper-online.com **w** www.hyper-online.com
Contact Mark Dando, Project Manager; Michael McCoy, Managing Director

The Ice Box
Units A35 & A36, New Covent Garden Market, London SW8 5EE
t 020 7498 0800 **f** 020 7498 0900 **m** 07850 801929
e info@theicebox.com **w** www.theicebox.com
Contact Phillip Hughes, Managing Director; Greg Pittard, Sales Manager; Iain Casey, Sales Manager
Credits Die Another Day Premiere (T); MTV European Music Awards Barcelona 2002 (T); BAFTA Awards 2002 (T); Scarlett Pimpernel (T)

Irvin Leisure Entertainment Ltd
Victoria House, Main Street, Hanworth TW13 6SU
t 020 8893 8993 **f** 020 8893 3037
e info@irvinleisure.co.uk **w** www.irvinleisure.co.uk
Contact George Irvin, Managing Director

Jim Laws Lighting
West End Lodge, Wrentham, Beccles NR34 7NH
t 01502 675264 **f** 01502 675565
e jimlawslighting@amserve.com
Contact Jim Laws, Proprietor
Credits Tipping The Velvet (T); Neverland (F); Topsy Turvy (F)

John Morgan Hire Company
Mustons Yard, Shaftesbury SP7 8AD
t 01747 850353 **f** 01747 850354 **m** 07836 616130

Living Props Ltd
Sevenhills Road, Iver Heath SL0 0PA
t 01895 835100 **f** 01895 835757
Contact Brian Maslin, Director

London Nursery Supplies Ltd
6 Hardy Passage, Berners Road, Wood Green, London N22 6NZ
t 020 8889 3003 **f** 020 8881 3003 **m** 07973 748438
e londonnursery@btconnect.com
Contact Mike Casbolt, Director

London Pupae Supplies
The Granary, Manor Farm, Horspath, Oxford OX33 1SD
t 01865 873255 **f** 01865 873055
e lpscontact@btconnect.com **w** www.oxfly.co.uk
Contact R Burgess, Director

Keir Lusby
Studio 22, Shepperton Studios, Studios Road, Shepperton TW17 0QD
t 01932 561717 **f** 01932 565898
e props@keirlusby.com **w** www.keirlusby.com

Manfred Schotten Sporting Antiques
109 High Street, Burford OX18 4RG
t 01993 822302 **t** 01993 822958 **f** 01993 822055
e sportandgames@schotten.com **w** www.schotten.com
Contact Louise Noorani; Philip Greenwood, Assistant; Manfred Schotten, Proprietor

McGill Signs
t 01494 483152 **f** 01494 483152
Contact Phill McGill, Proprietor

Neon Circus
25 Enterprise Way, London NW10 6UG
t 020 8964 3381 **f** 020 8964 0084 **m** 07831 614248
e info@neoncircus.com **w** www.neoncircus.com
Contact Sue Shepherd, Director; Anita Buxton
Credits Who Wants To Be A Millionaire? (T); Boys And Girls (T); Winning Lines (T); Ant And Dec's Saturday Night Takeaway (T)

Ochre
22 Howie Street, London SW11 4AS
t 020 7223 8888 **f** 020 7223 8877
e inquiries@ochre.net **w** www.ochre.net
Contact Solenne de la Fouchardiere

One Little Girl & A Can of Gasoline
299-300 Clare Street, Bethnal Green, London E2 9HD
t 07971 254617 **m** 07971 254617
e adam@canofgas.co.uk **w** www.canofgas.co.uk
Contact Adam Laurence, Director

Pollex Props
Leacnaban Tayvallich, Lochgilphead PA31 8PF
t 01546 870310 **f** 01546 870310
e alex@firebrand.fsnet.co.uk
Contact Alex Hamilton

Pollock's Toy Museum
1 Scala Street, London W1T 2HL
t 020 7636 3452
e toytheatres@pollocksweb.co.uk **w** www.pollocksweb.co.uk

The Printed Word
1-3 Telford Way, London W3 7XR
t 020 8740 8804 **f** 020 8740 1253
e printedword@dsl.pipex.com
Contact Barbara Horne, Partner; Judy Ducker, Partner

Professor Patten's Punch & Judy
14 The Crest, Goffs Oak EN7 5NP
t 01707 873262
e dennis.patten@btinternet.com **w** www.dennispatten.co.uk
Contact Dennis Patten, Proprietor

Proptics
32-33 Liddell Road, London NW6 2EW
t 020 7625 6391 **f** 020 7625 5386 **e** proptics@mistral.co.uk
Contact Carlo Manzi, Proprietor
Hire of spectacles, sunglasses, watches and jewellery - men's and women's. 1900 to the present day.

The Puppet Workshop Ltd
Unit 3, Commercial Mews South, Commercial Road, Eastbourne BN21 3XF
t 01323 417776 **f** 01323 644440
e puppet.workshop@virgin.net **w** www.puppets.co.uk
Contact Mel Myland, Director
Credits The Hunchback of Notredame (F); Rosie and Jim Stage Show (T); Ivanhoe (T); The New Aventures Of Pinocchio (F)

Replica Manufacturing Ltd
11A Uplands Business Park, Blackhorse Lane, London E17 5QJ
t 020 8523 3523 **f** 020 8523 3524
e sales@replica.co.uk **w** www.replica.co.uk
Contact Loraine Krell, Managing Director; Alan Crawford, Design Director

Soft Props
Unit 4, Camberwell Trading Estate, 117 Denmark Road, London SE5 9LB
t 020 7738 6324 **f** 020 7738 5198 **e** jackie@softprops.co.uk
Contact Jackie Anderson, Director

A Somerford
m 07803 207154 **e** alsomerford@ukonline.co.uk

Sugavision-Cannabis Props & Replica
8 Calais Gate, Cormont Road, London SE5 9RQ
t 020 7735 5468 **f** 020 7735 5468 **m** 07968 754813
e marko@sugavision.com **w** www.sugavision.com
Contact Marko Waschke, Designer
Credits Science Museum (E); Nikon - Digital (C); South West Nine (F); Saving Grace (F)

Totem Creative Associates
Arch 67, Putney Bridge, Station Approach, Fulham, London SW6 3UH
t 020 7736 1243 **f** 020 7736 1243 **e** totemcreative@hotmail.com
Contact Stefi Cottle, Partner; Tim Bailey, Partner

Turk Film Services Ltd
Turks of Sunbury, Thames Street, Lower Sunbury TW16 5QG
t 01932 782028 **f** 01932 780429
e jtweedle@turks.co.uk **w** www.turks.co.uk
Contact John Tweedle, Director

Two Dragons Oriental Antiques
8 High Street, Llanerchymedd LL71 8EA
t 01248 470204 **t** 01248 470100
f 01248 470040 **m** 07811 101290
Contact Tony Andrew, Proprietor

Vin Mag Archive Ltd
Vinmag House, 84-90 Digby Road, London E9 6HX
t 020 8533 7588 **f** 020 8533 7283
e piclib@vinmag.com **w** www.vinmag.com
Contact Tony Price; Kimberly Mills, Commercial Sales
Credits Edwardian Country House (T); Fame Academy (T); Icons (T); V Graham Norton (T)

The Vintage Home Store
105 Churchfield Road, London W3 6AH
t 020 8993 4162
Contact Sandy Stagg, Proprietor

Publications

The A to Z of Presenters & Voice Artists
123 Corporation Road, Gillingham ME17 1RG
t 01634 851077 **f** 01634 316771 **m** 07958 582270
e info@presenterpromotions.com **w** www.presenterpromotions.com
Contact Colin Cobb, Editor

Animation UK
The Tobacco Factory, Raleigh Road, Bristol BS3 1TF
t 0117 902 9953 **f** 0117 902 9967
e nick@animationuk.com **w** www.animationuk.com
Contact Nick Williams, Editor

Audio Media Europe
Atlantica House, 11 Station Road, St Ives PE17 4BH
t 01480 461555 **f** 01480 461550
e mail@audiomedia.com **w** www.audiomedia.com
Contact Paul Mac, Editor

Billboard
Endeavour House, 189 Shaftesbury Avenue, London WC2H 8TJ
t 020 7420 6003 **f** 020 7420 6014 **e** awhite@bpicom.com
Contact Adam White, Editor in Chief

Broadcast
33-39 Bowling Green Lane, London EC1R 0DA
t 020 7505 8000 **f** 020 7505 8050 **e** jonb@media.emap.co.uk
Contact Jon Baker, Publishing Director

Broadcast Hardware International
Editorial Office, 80 Hazel Drive, Woodley, Reading RG5 3SA
t 0118 926 2787 **f** 0118 926 9928
e david_j_sparks@compuserve.com
w www.broadcast-hardware.com

The Business of Film
1st Floor, 41-42 Berners Street, London W1T 3NB
t 020 7372 9992 **f** 020 7372 9993
e elspeth@thebusinessoffilm.com
w www.thebusinessoffilm.com
Contact Elspeth Tavares, Publisher and Executive Editor

Cable & Satellite Europe
Informa Media, Mortimer House, 37-41 Mortimer Street,
London W1T 3JH
t 020 7017 5314 **f** 020 7453 2351
e stewart.thomson@informa.com **w** www.informamedia.com
Contact Stewart Thomson, Editor

Commonwealth Broadcaster
CBA, 17 Fleet Street, London EC4Y 1AA
t 020 7583 5550 **f** 020 7583 5549
e cba@cba.org.uk **w** www.cba.org.uk
Contact Elizabeth Smith, Secretary General

Creation
Townhouse Media, 18 Charlotte Road, London EC2A 3PB
t 020 7749 1970 **f** 020 7729 6249
e helen.fowler@townhousemedia.com
w www.townhousemedia.com
Contact Helen Fowler, Advertising Manager

Creative Review
St Giles House, 50 Poland Street, London W1F 7AX
t 020 7970 4000 **f** 020 7970 6713
e moira@centaur.co.uk **w** www.creativereview.co.uk
Contact Patrick Bourgoyne, Editor; Moira Robertson, Advertising Manager

Crewfinder
Adleader Publications, 15 Chartwell Park, Belfast BT8 6NG
t 028 9079 7902 **t** 028 9070 1982 **f** 028 9079 1454
e mail@filmscan.ie **w** www.filmscan.ie
Contact Sharon McClenaghan, Sales Manager; Gavin Doherty, Production
Manager; Stan Mairs, Proprietor; Hilary Ingram, Administration Manager

Equity Magazine
Guild House, Upper St Martin''s Lane, London WC2H 9EG
t 020 7670 0259 **f** 020 7379 6074 **e** info@equity.org.uk
Contact Martin Brown, Editor

Filmlog
PO Box 100, Broadstairs CT10 1UJ
t 01843 860885 **f** 01843 860899
Contact Bobbi Dunn, Editor

Filmscan
Adleader Publications, 15 Chartwell Park, Belfast BT8 6NG
t 028 9079 7902 **t** 028 9070 1982 **f** 028 9079 1454
i 028 9079 8475 **e** mail@filmscan.ie **w** www.filmscan.ie
Contact Sharon McClenaghan, Sales Manager; Gavin Doherty, Production
Manager; Stan Mairs, Proprietor; Hilary Ingram, Administration Manager

Focal Press
Linacre House, Jordan Hill, Oxford OX2 8DP
t 01865 314945 **f** 01865 314572
e ge.kennedy@elsevier.com **w** www.focalpress.com
Contact Christina Donaldson, Associate Editor; Jenny Ridout, International
Publisher; Georgia Kennedy, Editorial Assistant; Emma Hales, Product Manager;
Duncan Enright, Senior Marketing Manager; Jennifer Welham, Publisher; Marie
Hooper, Senior Commissioning Editor; Beth Howard, Commissioning Editor

GTC Newsletter/ Zerb Magazine
Ewell House, Graveney Road, Faversham ME13 8UP
t 01795 591326 **f** 01795 534114
e ads@deeson.co.uk **w** www.gtc.org.uk
Contact James French, Editor - GTC Newsletter; Alison Chapman, Editor - Zerb;
Tom Alford, Advertising Manager

Hollywood Reporter
Endeavour House, 189 Shaftesbury Avenue, London WC2 8TJ
t 020 7420 6003 **f** 020 7420 6015
e rbennett@eu.hollywoodreporter.com
w www.hollywoodreporter.com
Contact Ray Bennet, European Bureau Chief

IBE (International Broadcast Engineer)
Queensway House, 2 Queensway, Redhill RH1 1QS
t 01737 768611 **f** 01737 855470 **m** 07860 208947
e sarahjifri@uk.dmgworldmedia.com **w** www.ibeweb.com
Contact Sarah Jifri, Editor

International Connection
Orchardton House, Auchencairn, Nr Castle Douglas DG7 1QL
t 0845 130 6249 **f** 0845 658 8329
e connect@bnw.demon.co.uk **w** www.britishfilm.tv
Contact Susan Foster, Managing Director; David Burbidge, Editorial Director
*Sponsored publication promoting film and television partnerships
throughout the world.*

Lighting & Sound International
38 St Leonards Road, Eastbourne BN21 3UT
t 01323 418400 **f** 01323 646905
e media@plasa.org **w** www.plasa.org
Contact Barry Howse, Advertising Manager; Lee Baldock, Deputy Editor; Tony
Gotteuer, Associate Editor; James Eade, Technical Editor; Jane Cockburn,
Advertising Coordinator; Ruth Rossington, Editor

Line Up
27 Old Gloucester Street, London WC1N 3XX
t 01905 381725 **f** 01905 381725
e editorlineup@cix.co.uk **w** www.ibs.org.uk
Contact Hugh Robjohns, Editor; Jo Pearson, Advertisement Manager; Adrian
Bishop-Laggett, Publishing Manager

Linsar Global Network
e sjthompson@beeb.net
Contact Sara Thompson, Writer/Press & Promotions
Credits Stiff Upper Lips (F); Best (F); Cinderella (T); Sons And Lovers (T)

M2 Communications
Corporate Offices, PO Box 505, Coventry CV1 1ZQ
t 024 7623 8200 **e** pw@m2.com **w** www.m2.com
Contact Darren Ingram, Managing Director

Middle East Communications
Icom Publications Ltd, Icom House, 1 Langhurstwood Road,
Horsham RH12 4QD
t 020 8642 1117 **f** 020 8642 1941
e admin@icompub.com **w** www.icompub.com
Contact Daniel Anderson-Ford, Editor; Lily Cliff, Production Director

Moving Pictures

2 Chitty Street, London W1T 4AP
t 020 7813 9500 f 020 7681 0501
e info@movingpicturesonline.com
w www.movingpicturesonline.com
Contact Leslie Felperin, Editor; Paul Chai, Editor

Passion Music Ltd

South Bank House, Skratch Music, A21 Crabtree Lane, London
SW6 6LW
t 020 7381 8315 f 020 7385 6785
e info@passion-music.com w www.passion-music.com
Contact Les McClutcheon, Director

PIA

Victoria Street, Cwmbran NP44 3YT
t 0870 321 6450 f 0870 321 6451
e info@pia.co.uk w www.pia.co.uk
Contact Alison Roberts, Deputy Project Manager; Gail Chester, Managing
Director

Presenters Contact File/A-Z of Presenters & Voice Artists

123 Corporation Road, Gillingham ME7 1RG
t 01634 851077 f 01634 316771 m 07958 582270
e info@presenterpromotions.com
w www.presenterpromotions.com
Contact Colin Cobb, Proprietor

Pro Sound News Europe

Ludgate House, 7th Floor, 245 Blackfriars Road, London
Bridge, London SE1 9UR
t 020 7921 8316 f 020 7921 8302
e djago@cmpinformation.com w www.prosoundeurope.com
Contact Dave Robinson, Editor; Richard Lawn, Advertisement Manager; Dan
Jago, Group Advertisment Manager

Production & Casting Report (PCR)

PO Box 11, London N1 7JZ
t 020 7566 8282 f 020 7566 8284 w www.pcrnewsletter.com
Contact Bobbi Dunn, Editor

The Production Guide

33-39 Bowling Green Lane, London EC1R 0DA
t 020 7505 8305 f 020 7505 8076
e theproductionguide@emap.com
w www.productionguideonline.com
Contact Mei Mei Rogers, Editor; Charles Said, Advertising Manager

Programme News

6/7 St Cross Street, London EC1N 8UA
t 020 7405 4455 f 020 7430 1089
e info@programmenews.co.uk w www.programmenews.co.uk
Contact Paul Weatherley, Editor; Connie Man, Marketing Manager; Caroline
Citrin, Editorial Director; Matt Skinner, Head of Editorial; Tamion Von Christian,
Researcher; Rachel Mackie, Commercial Director; Maggie Trott, Editor; Adam
Hamptom, Senior Researcher

Red Cinnamon

32 Regina Road, London W13 9EF
t 020 8621 5411 f 020 8931 3949 m 07968 819016
e david.highton@redcinnamon.co.uk w www.redcinnamon.co.uk
Contact David Highton, Director

Rockport RotoVision Apple Fairwinds

Sheridan House, 112-116A Western Road, Hove BN3 1DD
t 01273 716020 f 01273 716019
e keldiet@rotovision.com w www.rotovision.com
Contact Martha Killick, Marketing & Publicity; Susan Spratt,
Marketing/Publicity; Keldie Travis, Marketing Manager

Screen Digest Ltd

Lyme House Studios, 38 Georgiana Street, London NW1 0EB
t 020 7424 2820 f 020 7580 0060
e editorial@screendigest.com w www.screendigest.com
Contact Guy Bisson, News Editor

Screen International

33-39 Bowling Green Lane, London EC1R 0DA
t 020 7505 8080 t 020 7505 8099 w www.screendaily.com
Contact Ann-Marie Flynn, Publishing Director

shots

33-39 Bowling Green Lane, London EC1R 0DA
t 020 7505 8475 f 020 7505 8490
e info@shots.net w www.shots.net
Contact Lyndy Stout, Editor; Charles Said, Advertising Manager

The Spotlight

7 Leicester Place, London WC2H 7RJ
t 020 7437 7631 f 020 7437 5881
e info@spotlightcd.com w www.spotlightcd.com
Contact Kate Poynton, Editor; Ben Seale, Partner

The Stage Newspaper Ltd

47 Bermondsey Street, London SE1 3XT
t 020 7403 1818 f 020 7403 1418
e info@thestage.co.uk w www.thestage.co.uk
Contact Catherine Comerford, Managing Director/Publisher

Stage Screen & Radio

373-377 Clapham Road, London SW9 9BT
t 020 7346 0900 f 020 7346 0901
e janice@stagescreenandradio.org.uk w www.bectu.org.uk
Contact Janice Turner, Editor

Television - The Journal of the Royal Television Society

Holborn Hall, 100 Gray's Inn Road, London WC1X 8AL
t 020 7430 1000 f 020 7430 0924
e publications@rts.org.uk w www.rts.org.uk
Contact Steve Clark, Editor; Gordon Jamieson, Production/Advertising

Television Business International (TBI)

Mortimer House, 37-41 Mortimer Street, London W1T 3JH
t 020 7453 2300 f 020 7453 2351
e info.media@informa.com w www.informamedia.com
Contact Lydia Blackwood, Publisher; Sarah Walker, Editorial Director

Televisual

St Giles House, 50 Poland Street, London W1F 7AX
t 020 7970 6541 f 020 7970 6734
e james.bennett@centaur.co.uk w www.televisual.com
Contact Rebecca Allen, Advertisement Manager; James Bennett, Publisher;
Mundy Ellis, Editor

Variety

84 Theobalds Road, London WC1X 8RR
t 020 7611 4580 f 020 7611 4591
e comments@variety.cahners.com w www.variety.com
Contact Steve Gaydos, Managing Director, International

Variety's International Film Guide

84 Theobalds Road, London WC1X 8RR
t 020 7520 5222 t 020 7611 4580 f 020 7611 4581
w www.variety.com
Contact Steve Gaydos, Managing Director, International

Waterlow New Media Information

Paulton House, 8 Sheperdess Walk, London N1 7LB
t 020 7324 2345 f 020 7324 2312
e newmedia@waterlow.com w www.newmediainfo.com

The White Book

Inside Communications, Bank House, 23 Warwick Road, Coventry CV1 2EW
t 024 7657 1171 **f** 024 7657 1172 **m** 07733 308006
e michelle_tayton@mrn.co.uk **w** www.whitebook.co.uk
Contact Clair Whitecross, Business Manager; Michelle Tayton, Group Sales Manager

Who's Where

PO Box 100, Broadstairs CT10 1UJ
t 01843 860885 **f** 01843 860899 **w** www.pcrnewsletter.com

ZERB - Journal for the Guild of TV Cameramen

Sunnyside, Church Street, Charlbury OX7 3PR
t 01608 810954 **m** 01795 591326
e alichap@mac.com **w** www.gtc.org.com
Contact Tom Alford, Advertising Manager

Puppets

Hybrid Enterprises Ltd

Units 26-27 Armley Workshops, Pickering Street, Leeds LS12 2QG
t 0113 217 1300 **t** 01277 654862
f 0113 217 1300 **m** 07870 600273
e studio@hybridfx.com **w** www.hybridfx.com
Contact Mike Stringer, Technical Director; Mike Bates, Production Director; Ryk Fortuna, Lead Sculptor/Technician
Credits The National Geographic (D); The Royal (T); Ant 'N' Dec's Saturday Night Takeaway (T); The Two Towers (F)

Playboard Puppets

t 020 7226 5911 **e** thebuttonmoon@aol.com
Contact Ian Allen, Director

The Puppet Factory

Punch's Oak, Cleobury Road, Kidderminster DY14 9EB
t 01299 266634 **f** 01299 266561
e glyn@punch-and-judy.com **w** www.punch-and-judy.com
Contact Mary Edwards, Director

Recruitment

42nd Street Recruitment

2nd Floor, The Linen Hall, 162-168 Regent Street, London W1B 5TB
t 020 7734 4422 **f** 020 7287 5481
e steph@42ndstreetrecruitment.com
w www.42ndstreetrecruitment.com
Contact Christie Sinclair, Manager; Steph Rice, Recruitment Manager

Artism

1 Angel Court, London EC2R 7HJ
t 020 7886 9940 **f** 020 7886 9941
e info@artism.com **w** www.artism.com
Contact Barrie Poulter, Finance Director

BCP Search & Selection Ltd

9B Intec 2, Wade Road, Basingstoke RG24 8NE
t 01256 470704 **f** 01256 844054
e mail@bcprecruitment.co.uk **w** www.tvfutures.net
Contact Mike Jones, Director

Carreras Lathane Associates

4 Golden Square, London W1F 9HT
t 020 7439 9634 **f** 020 7434 9150
e info@carreraslathane.com **w** www.carreraslathane.com

The Davis Company

1st Floor, 45-49 Mortimer Street, London W1N 8JL
t 020 7580 4580 **f** 020 7580 4981
w www.daviscompany.co.uk
Contact Malcom Farquharson, Managing Director; Lucy Mortlock, Sales Promotion

DNP Media

4th Floor, 2 Wedgewood Mews, 12 Greek Street, London W1D 4BB
t 020 7439 3896 **f** 020 7734 7049 **e** john@dnpmedia.com
Contact John Dowson, Director; Adam Hollowood, Director
Specialists in Legal and Business affairs and Finance Recruitment for the TV/Film Industry.

Grapevinejobs.com

125 Parkway, Regents Park, London NW1 7PS
t 020 7387 5445
e admin@grapevinejobs.com **w** www.grapevinejobs.com

JFB

9 Wimpole Street, London W1M 8LB
t 07000 402532 **f** 07000 402531 **m** 07930 540870
e enquiries@jfb.co.uk **w** www.jfb.co.uk
Contact Chris Monckton, Managing Director

London Placements

43 Harrington Gardens, London SW7 4JU
t 020 7244 6258 **f** 020 7244 2900
e meagan@londonplacements.com
Contact Meagan Newman, Placement Programme Director

MRI Worldwide

Kensington House, 33 Imperial Square, Cheltenham GL50 1QZ
t 0870 777 0896 **f** 0870 777 0897
e info@mosaicss.com **w** www.mosaicss.com
Contact Lynne Witney, Director

NJD Group

Pinewood Studios, Pinewood Road, Iver Heath SL0 0NH
t 01753 630040 **f** 01753 630830
e jill@njdgroup.co.uk **w** www.njdgroup.co.uk
Contact Jill Britnell, Office Manager; Nicky Davis, Managing Consultant; Catherine Pianta-McGill, Senior Consultant

PRE Recruitment Ltd

Bank Chambers, 64 High Street, Epsom KT19 8AJ
t 01372 726111 **f** 01372 722345
e info@prerecruitment.com **w** www.prerecruitment.com
Contact Chris Smitheran, Recruitment Manager

The Presenters Contact File

123 Corporation Road, Gillingham ME7 1RG
t 01634 851077 **f** 01634 316771 **m** 07958 582270
e info@presenterpromotions.com
w www.presenterpromotions.com
Contact Colin Cobb, Proprietor

Pricejamieson

Pricejamieson House, 104-108 Oxford Street, London W1D 1LP
t 020 7580 7702 **f** 020 7436 4789
e broadcast@pricejam.com **w** www.pricejam.com
Contact Kate Williams, Manager of Media & Broadcast Division; Ann Jamieson, Managing Director

The Production Base Ltd

Leroy House, 436 Essex Road, London N1 3QP
t 020 7354 2299 **f** 020 7354 2294
e info@productionbase.co.uk **w** www.productionbase.co.uk
Contact Moray Coulter, Chief Executive Officer

Recruit Media Ltd

20 Colebrooke Row, London N1 8AP
t 020 7704 1227 **f** 020 7704 1370
e info@recruitmedia.co.uk **w** www.recruitmedia.co.uk
Contact Daniell Morrisey, Editorial Manager; Melanie Bennett, Managing Director; Victoria Lubbock, Chairperson

SDA Media Recruitment
6 Twyford Crescent, London W3 9PP
t 020 8993 8401 **m** 07801 938401
e jobs@sdarecruit.com **w** www.sdarecruit.com
Contact Simone Dawood, Director; Ayhan Dawood, Director

startintv.com
Pell Mell, Redmarley GL19 3HY
t 01531 650082 **f** 01531 650780 **m** 07787 888384
e mail@startintv.com **w** www.startintv.com
Contact David Wheeler, Co-Founder; Amanda Hammond, Director
CVs to Industry Professionals at their desks via email - free and confidential. From Runners to Presenters - a great route into TV for new talent.

Switched On Production Consultancy
PO Box 43820, London NW6 7WL
t 0870 011 1415 **f** 0870 011 0004
e justine@switchedonjobs.com **w** www.switchedonjobs.com
Contact Justine Young, Managing Director; Lisa Davies, Consultant

TheSource.tv Ltd
15 Sunnyside Road, London W5 5HT
t 020 8810 1474 **e** enquiries@thesource.tv **w** www.thesource.tv
Contact Sheila Diviney, Director; Christine Smith, Director

Tip Top Media
Suite 11, 2nd Floor, 5 Blackhorse Lane, London E17 6DS
t 020 8527 5353 **f** 020 8527 6060
e info@tiptopmedia.co.uk **w** www.tiptopmedia.co.uk
Contact Isha Kabba; Eddra Crook; Colin Edwards; Tom Robertson; Sharon Launers

Tiro Resource Solutions
6 Long Lane, London EC1A 9HF
t 020 7759 8000 **f** 020 7759 8001
e admin@tiro.co.uk **w** www.tiro.co.uk
Contact Tristan Ramus, MD

Rehearsal Rooms

Big City Studios
Montgomery House, 159-161 Balls Pond Road, London N1 4BG
t 020 7241 6655 **f** 020 7241 3006
w www.pineapple-agency.com
Credits Fame; Royal Shakespeare Company; Faking It (T); Whitney Houston (M)

Dance Works
16 Balderton Street, London W1Y 1TF
t 020 7629 6183 **f** 020 7499 9087
e info@danceworks.net **w** www.danceworks.net

English National Opera (ENO)
Lillian Baylis House, 165 Broadhurst Gardens, London NW6 3AX
t 020 7845 9500 **f** 020 7625 3398
e receptionlbh@eno.org **w** www.eno.org
Contact Christine Rogers

North Paddington Rehearsal Rooms
235 Lanark Rd, London W9 1RA
t 020 7624 4089
Contact Albert St Ange, Senior Youth Worker

Pineapple Dance Studio
7 Langley Street, London WC2H 9JA
t 020 7836 4004 **f** 020 7836 0803 **w** www.pineapple.co.uk
Contact Jennifer Wade, Studio Manager

Rambert Dance Company
94 Chiswick High Road, London W4 1SH
t 020 8630 0601 **f** 020 8747 8323
e cd@rambert.org.uk **w** www.rambert.org.uk
Contact Claire Drakeley, Company Administrator

The Red Rose Club
129 Seven Sisters Road, London N7 7QG
t 020 7263 7265 **f** 020 7274 0812 **w** www.redrosecomedy.co.uk

Soho Laundry
9 Dufours Place, London W1F 7SJ
t 020 7434 8570 **f** 020 7287 8763
e admin@setheatre.co.uk **w** www.setheatre.co.uk

RESEARCH

Research Services

BFI Information
21 Stephen Street, London W1T 1LN
t 020 7255 1444 **f** 020 7436 0165
e www.bfi.org.uk/nationallibrary/ask/ask.html
w www.bfi.org.uk/nationallibrary/services/index.html

British Universities Film & Video Council
77 Wells Street, London W1T 3QJ
t 020 7393 1500 **f** 020 7393 1555
e ask@bufvc.ac.uk **w** www.bufvc.ac.uk
Contact Murray Weston, Director; Luke McKernan, Head of Information

Broadcasters Audience Research Board (BARB)Ltd
18 Dering Street, London W1R 9AF
t 020 7529 5531 **f** 020 7529 5530
e enquiries@barb.co.uk **w** www.barb.co.uk
Contact Tony Wearn, Research Director

Building Research Establishment Ltd
Bucknalls Lane, Garston, Watford WD25 9XX
t 01923 664000 **f** 01923 664 010 **w** www.bre.co.uk

Campaign For Press & Broadcasting Freedom
2nd Floor, 23 Orford Road, Walthamstow, London E17 9JU
t 020 8521 5932 **e** freepress@cpbf.org.uk **w** www.cpbf.org.uk
Contact Tim Gopsill, Vice-Chair; Jonathan Hardy, National Secretary; Julian Petley, Chair; Barry White, National Organiser

Celtic Research, Genealogy
PO Box 5, Machynlleth SY20 9WA
t 01650 511719 **f** 01650 511826 **m** 07711 266202
e missingheirs@celticresearch.co.uk **w** www.celticresearch.co.uk
Contact Peter Birchwood, Proprietor
Credits Unsolved Mysteries (T); Find a Fortune (T)

Charta Research
75 Dunkeld Road, Sheffield S11 9HN
t 0114 236 4801 **f** 0114 236 4801 **m** 07754 014596
e charta@blueyonder.co.uk **w** www.charta-research.com
Contact Tim Cooper
Credits Peterloo (D); The Great Plague (D)

David Graham & Associates
33-39 Bridge Street, Taunton TA1 1TP
t 01823 322829 **f** 01823 323093
e enquiries@dganet.co.uk **w** www.dganet.co.uk
Contact Ali Vahdati, Contact

Film Research & Production Services Ltd
PO Box 28045, London SE27 9WZ
t 020 8670 2959 **f** 020 8670 1793
e frps@aol.com **w** www.filmresearch.co.uk
Contact Amanda Dunne, Researcher

FRPS Ltd
PO Box 28045, London SE27 9WZ
t 020 7736 9066 **t** 020 8670 2959
f 020 7348 7991 **f** 020 8670 1793 **m** 07710 930627
e frps@aol.com **w** www.filmresearch.co.uk
Contact James Webb, Researcher; Amanda Dunne, Researcher

Helen Harrison & Company Ltd
Manfield House, 1 Southampton Street, London WC2R OLR
t 020 7240 1606
e helen@helen-harrison.co.uk **w** www.helen-harrison.co.uk
Contact Patricia Jackson, Reservation Manager

John Frost Historical Newspapers
22B Rosemary Avenue, Enfield EN2 OSS
t 020 8366 1392 **f** 020 8366 1379
e andrew@johnfrostnewspapers.com
w www.johnfrostnewspapers.com
Contact Andrew Frost, Proprietor

LWT Information Research Unit
The London Television Centre, Upper Ground, London SE1 9LT
t 020 7261 3386 **f** 020 7737 8561
e fiona.sanson@granadamedia.com **w** www.granadamedia.com
Contact Fiona Sanson, Information Manager; Kirstie Jamieson,
Information Researcher

Mark Watts & Associates News Investigations
274 Hither Green Lane, London SE13 6TT
t 020 8461 0730 **f** 020 8461 0730 **m** 07973 720315
e Markwatts@talk21.com
Contact Mark Watts

News Team International Ltd
41-43 Commercial Street, Birmingham B1 1RS
t 0121 246 5511 **f** 0121 246 5101
e news.desk@newsteam.co.uk **w** www.newsteam.co.uk
Contact Cori Mitchell; Steve Chatterley, Commercial Manager

Quizmasters
11 Offley Road, Hitchin SG5 2AZ
t 01462 437009 **e** quizmastersuk@hotmail.com
Contact Jane Housham, Co-Founder
Credits Jeopardy (T); Take a Letter (T); Say the Word (T); All Shook Up (W)

RAJAR (Radio Joint Audience Research) Ltd
Gainsborough House, 81 Oxford Street, London W1D 2EU
t 020 7903 5350 **f** 020 7903 5351
e info@rajar.co.uk **w** www.rajar.co.uk
Contact Jane O'Hara, Managing Director

The Research Centre for Television & Interactivity
227 West George Street, Glasgow G2 2ND
t 0141 568 7113 **f** 0141 568 7114 **w** www.researchcentre.co.uk
Contact Carol Sinclair

Riley Research
1st Floor, 190 Ladbroke Grove, London W10 5LZ
t 020 8968 7236 **f** 020 8960 1678 **e** rileyresearch@virgin.net
Contact Ursula Riley, Proprietor
Credits The Sexual Century (D); Paying The Price: Killing The Children Of Iraq
(D); Orange (I); Orange

RSMB TV Research
114 St Martins Lane, London WC2N 4AZ
t 020 7240 6779 **f** 020 7836 6778 **e** cathie@rsmb.co.uk
Contact Catherine Robbins, Client Service Manager

Seafacs Information & Research
PO Box 317, Welwyn Garden City AL8 6DP
t 01707 334192 **f** 01707 324615
e seafacs@sir.co.uk **w** www.sir.co.uk
Contact Alex Powell

Teral Research Services
45 Forest View Road, Moordown, Bournemouth BH9 3BH
t 01202 516834 **e** terry@judgetread.fsnet.co.uk
Contact Terry Treadwell, Head of Research

Zooid Pictures Ltd
66 Alexander Road, London N19 3PQ
t 020 7281 2407 **f** 020 7281 2404 **i** 020 7263 1259
e pictures@zooid.co.uk **w** www.zooid.co.uk
Contact Richard Philpott, Managing Director; Dan Sinclair, Research Manager
Credits Red Consultancy (I); Dimplex (I); Frontline Documentary Strand (D);
Oxford University Press (E)

Researchers General

Sue Agyeman
28 Greenfield Gardens, Cricklewood, London NW2 1HX
m 07855 868704 **e** sagyeman@hotmail.com
Credits Fan-o-rama (T); Trisha (T); Kilroy (T); The Weakest Link (T)

Mark Arnold
m 07733 305875 **e** mark.a@lineone.net
Credits Hunt For The Malaria Vaccine (D); The Potters Bar Investigation (D);
September Mourning (D); Railcops (D)

Sheila Bailey
78 Avondale Road, Bromley BR1 4EZ
t 020 8460 4398 **e** sheila.bailey@bromley2.demon.co.uk
Credits Great Speeches (D); UK Confidential 2002 (D); Clive Anderson's
Conspiracies (D); Spend It Like ... The Beckhams (D)

Helen Bennitt
t 01872 554143 **f** 01872 554143 **m** 07775 994508
e helen.bennitt@hotmail.com

Emalone
109 Cavendish Road, Highams Park, London E4 9NG
m 07973 389 088
e graham@emalone.net **w** www.emalone.net/gb_cv.htm
Contact Graham Barnfield, Director; Paul Woodford, Head of Magnesium Films;
Graham Barnfield, Director
Credits Bad Lad Space Pirates (S); Yeast Extract (D)

Jenny Gordon
4A Park Road, Romley, Stockport SK6 4PG
m 07769 947093 **e** jenny.gordon@virgin.net
Credits Gym TV (I); Two's Country - Ship To Shore (T)

Head Start Research
119 Glenurquhart Road, Inverness IV3 5PD
t 01463 220539 **m** 07765 257547
e headstartresearch@myartism.com
Contact Malcolm Maccallum, Head of Research

Rachel Helyer Donaldson
7/3 Rothay Street, London SE1 4UD
t 020 7357 9372 **m** 07766 658017
e rhelyerdonaldson@london.com
Credits Sound Travels - Nathan Haines (D)

Christopher Howells
t 029 2059 3677 **f** 029 2067 9288 **m** 07710 851455
e christopher.howells@virgin.net
Credits Remember? (D); So What Do You Do All Day? (D); Magic Islands (D)

Angela Kidner
t 020 8892 6474 **f** 020 8892 6474 **m** 07768 097686
e angela@kidners.globalnet.co.uk
Credits Otherworld (F)

Joan Morris
10 Lena Gardens, London W6 7PZ
t 020 7603 2411 **m** 07931 734607 **e** joan@jmorris10.demon.co.uk
Credits BSE (D); Art Crime (D); Horticultural Therapy (D); Fisher Boxing Club (D)

Paul Morten
71 Victoria Road, Finsbury Park, London N4 3SN
t 020 8374 0622 **m** 07715 173715 **e** paulmorten01@hotmail.com
Credits Eurotrash (T); Fame Academy (T)

Mosaic Performance Projects
69 Hounslow Road, Twickenham TW2 7HA
e j.keefe@londonmet.ac.uk
Contact John Keefe, AD

New Solutions
Artists House, 14-15 Manette Street, London W1D 4AP
t 020 7434 3535 **t** 020 7413 2836
f 020 7434 3533 **m** 07768 392736
e gt@newsolutions.co.uk **w** www.newsolutions.co.uk
Contact Guy Tomlinson, Director
Credits Brand development - The Fimbles (T); Research - Sky Premium
Channels (T); Research/positioning for BBC/RHS Chelsea Flower Show (T);
Brand development - Agatha Christie (F)
For audience insight, ideas and building media properties as brands.

Angela Pollard
The Old School, Worthen, Shrewsbury SY5 9HT
t 01743 891912 **f** 01743 891142 **m** 07736 070906
e newsons@clara.co.uk

Nadaav Soudry
London
m 07966 290331 **e** nadaavsoudry@hotmail.com
Credits After Dark (T); Bombay Blush (T); Diners (T); Unthinkable (D)

David Wyatt
104 Alicia Gardens, Kenton, Harrow HA3 8JE
t 020 8907 9188 **f** 020 8907 9188 **m** 07720 741496
e dwyatt@tiscali.co.uk
Credits Story of Computer Games (T); Stars of Tomorrow (T);
South Bank Show - Cher (T); Legends (T)

RIGGING

Riggers

David Broadfoot
94 Hivings Hill, Chesham HP5 2PG
m 07818 807309 **e** dbfoot@hotmail.com
Credits Lenny Henry In Pieces (T); The Strangerers (F); Murphy's Law (T);
Spiceworld (F)

Neil Carr
30 Shirley Gardens, Barking IG11 9UZ
t 020 8594 1379 **f** 020 8507 1232 **m** 07860 963466
Credits ThunderBirds (F); Lara Croft And The Cradle Of Life: Tomb Raider 2 (F);
Star Wars - Episode Two (F)

Frederick Crawford
7 Kingsley Avenue, Boreham Wood WD6 4LY
t 020 8953 6300

James Dillimore
203 Morefield, Harlow CM18 7QL
m 07931 809607 **e** jim.rigger@ntlworld.com
Credits Lara Croft Tomb Raider II - The Cradle Of Life (F); Harry Potter And The
Prisoner Of Azkaban (F); Harry Potter And The Chamber Of Secrets (F); Harry
Potter & The Philosopher's Stone (F)

Eye Pro Ltd
Hollywood House, Hollywood Lane, Rochester ME3 8AR
t 01634 291301 **f** 01634 727200 **m** 07947 380170
e coop@ipro.tv
Contact Charles Cooper, Director; Jo Austen, Art Director
Credits Specialist Height Access (I); Task Force (I)
*Specialists in rigging and working at height. All staff IRATA trained and
qualified. Height Access trained cameramen also available.*

Jesse (James) Foster
78 Cranbrook Drive, Esher KT10 8DP
t 020 8398 3329 **m** 07816 530425
Credits End Game (F); The Gentleman Thief (T); Trust (T); Bertie And Elizabeth (T)

GP Scaffolding Ltd
10 Waverley Drive, Prescot, Liverpool L34 1PU
t 0151 449 1231 **f** 0151 449 1231 **m** 07889 440388
e g.coltman@tinyworld.co.uk
Contact Ged Coltman
Credits All BBC Golf (T); The Inspector Lynley Mysteries (T)

David Gray
218B Riverdale Road, Erith DA8 1QF
t 01322 433950 **f** 01322 433950 **m** 07788 498249
Credits Spider (F); Blackball (F); Our Mutual Friend; Ali G In da House (F)

Pat Hagarty
m 07885 353030
Credits Die Another Day (F); Roger Roger (T); Below (F)

Roy Lomas
34 Summerhill Park, Stormont, Belfast BT5 7HE
t 028 9087 8837 **m** 07968 155737 **e** r.lomas@tiscali.co.uk
Credits The Great Ceili War (F); Coronation Day (S); As the Beast Sleeps (S)

Charles Macher
t 020 8330 0879 **m** 07850 260099
Credits State of the Planet (D); Man And Boy (T); Emma Brody (T); Charlotte Gray (F)

Robert O'Neill
82 Leander Drive, Castleton, Manchester OL11 2XE
f 01706 351302 **m** 07740 471608
e castleton82@castleton82.fsnet.co.uk

Jamie Salvadori
Effects House, 62 Broadacres, Hatfield AL10 9LD
t 01707 894620 **f** 01707 262900 **m** 07939 222867
e jamiesalvadori@aol.com

Bob Schofield
15 Craig Drive, Hillingdon UB8 3HL
t 01895 444872 **f** 01895 444872 **m** 07774 979492
Credits Johnny English (F); Ella Enchanted (F); Below (F)

Dave Straiton
31 Crundale Crescent, Llanishen, Cardiff CF14 5PX
t 029 2040 8787 **f** 029 2040 8787 **m** 07889 644201
e david.straiton@ntlworld.com
w http://homepage.ntlworld.com/david.straiton

Frankie Webster
Elm Cottage, Chapel Croft, Chipperfield WD4 9EQ
t 01923 264389 **f** 01923 264389 **m** 07775 688771

Dave Weller
5 Sampage Close, Reading RG2 8VD
t 01189 867471 **f** 01189 867471 **m** 07889 951397
w www.daveweller.com

Rigging/Scaffolding Equipment

Anglian Access
Unit One, East Coast Storage, Clenchwarton Road, West Lynn, King's Lynn PE34 3LW
t 01553 770776 **f** 01553 770776
Contact Ken Rout, Partner; Wendy Rout, Partner

Castle Scaffolding Ltd
Heron House, Sandy Lane Industrial Estate, Wideopen, Newcastle-Upon-Tyne NE3 5HE
t 0191 217 0565 **f** 0191 217 0585
e castlescaffold@sagehost.co.uk **w** www.castlescaffold.co.uk
Contact Michael Mitchell, Director; Kevin Murray, Director

Flint Hire & Supply
Queens Row, London SE17 2PX
t 020 7703 9786 **f** 020 7708 4189
e sales@flints.co.uk **w** www.flints.co.uk
Contact John Mainey, Hire Manager; Alasdair Flint, Director; Ben Lyle, Administration

Hall Stage Ltd
The Gate Studios, Station Road, Borehamwood WD6 1DQ
t 020 8327 3818 **f** 020 8207 3657
e ch@hallstage.co.uk **w** www.hallstage.com
Contact Tony Bailey, Customer Services Manager; Richard Clarke, Sales; Doug Heather, Technical Manager; Charles Haines, Director
Track systems, Drapes, Counterweights and Rope, Powered Hoists and all associated stage/studio rigging equipment.

Jones Rigging Equipment
High View, Woburn Hill, Addlestone KT15 2QE
t 01932 847260 **m** 07810 812433
Contact Tony Jones, Director
Credits Harry Potter And The Philosopher's Stone (F); Enemy At The Gate (F); Gladiator (F); Cutthroat Island (F)

Morris Leslie Ltd
The Denes, Barnacres Rd, Hemel Hempstead HP3 8AP
t 01442 217217 **f** 01442 244646 **m** 07831 621840
Contact Allan Huggett, Depot Manager

Mushroom Event Services Ltd
3 Encon Court, Owl Close, Moulton Park, Northampton NN3 6HZ
t 01604 790900 **f** 01604 491118
e paulb@mushroomevents.co.uk **w** www.mushroomevents.co.uk
Contact Paul Butler, Sales Director; Ian Robson, Production Manager; Andy Slevin, Hire Manager

Outback Rigging Ltd
Unit 11, Kendal Court, Western Avenue Trading Estate, Kendal Avenue, London W3 0RP
t 020 8993 0066 **f** 020 8752 1753 **m** 07710 975678
e enquiries@outbackrigging.com **w** www.outbackrigging.com
Contact Bowie Ebrill, Technical Director; Stuart Cooper, Operations Director
Credits Smash Hits Awards (T); Brit Awards 2003 (T)

Steeldeck Sales Ltd
Kings Cross Freight Depot, York Way, London N1 0UZ
t 020 7833 2031 **f** 020 7278 3403
e steeldeck@aol.com **w** www.steeldeck.com
Contact Phil Parsons, Managing Director; Lynda Hall, Rentals Manager; Jo Fles, Sales/Office Manager

Swan Scaffolding Contractors Ltd
19 Skelcher Road, Shirley, Solihull B90 2EY
t 0121 744 4686 **f** 0121 744 4011 **e** swanscaff@talk21.com
Contact Liam Swan, Company Director

Tele Scaff Services
47-49 Brunel Road, London W3 7XR
t 020 8749 7305 **f** 020 8749 8750 **m** 07836 358459
e d.thomas@telescuff.freeserve.co.uk
Contact Dave Thomas, Director

TR Services (Bristol) Ltd
Units 11-12, Carrick Business Centre, Bonville Road, Brislington, Bristol BS4 5NZ
t 0117 300 9500 **f** 0117 300 9501 **m** 07973 156407
e trservicebristol@aol.com **w** www.trscaffolding-services.co.uk
Contact Alan Clark; John Hudson
Credits Teachers (T); Songs Of Praise (T); Casualty (T); Antiques Road Show (T)

Vertigo Rigging Ltd
Unit 1, Deptford Trading Estate, Blackhorse Road, London SE8 5HY
t 0208 694 6033 **f** 07071 200077
e info@vertigorigging.com **w** www.vertigorigging.com

Vincent Shaw
36 Kingswood Road, Leytonstone, London E11 1SF
t 020 8518 7077 **m** 07973 115216
Credits Sony Playstation (C); Bend It Like Beckham (F)

Runners

Alan Adair
Production Switchboard, Northdown, Down Lane, Compton GU3 1DN
t 01483 812011 **f** 01483 812027
e aly@productionswitch.freeserve.co.uk
Credits Anybody's Nightmare (T); The Vice IV (T); Ska Films (F)

Moncho Aldamiz
Callbox Communications Ltd, PO Box 66, Shepperton Studios, Shepperton Lane TW17 0DQ
t 01932 592572 **f** 01932 569655 **m** 07710 572572
e callboxdiary@btinternet.com **w** www.callboxdiary.co.uk

Harry Amies
Production Switchboard, Northdown, Down Lane, Compton GU3 1DN
t 01483 812011 **f** 01483 812027
e aly@productionswitch.freeserve.co.uk
Credits Wizard Books (C); Idlewild (M); Harry Potter Chamber of Secrets (F)

James Amos
Callbox Communications Ltd, PO Box 66, Shepperton Studios, Shepperton Lane TW17 0DQ
t 01932 592572 **f** 01932 569655 **m** 07710 572572
e callboxdiary@btinternet.com **w** www.callboxdiary.co.uk

Eva Arnold
The Production Switchboard, Northdown, Down Lane, Compton GU3 1DN
t 01483 812011 **f** 01483 812027
e aly@productionswitch.freeserve.co.uk
Credits Talisman Films (T); Ultimate Force II (T); Rockface (T)

Devina Artley
Callbox Communications Ltd, PO Box 66, Shepperton Studios, Shepperton Lane TW17 0DQ
t 01932 592572 **f** 01932 569655 **m** 07710 572572
e callboxdiary@btinternet.com **w** www.callboxdiary.co.uk

Cecile Baird
Callbox Communications Ltd, PO Box 66, Shepperton Studios, Shepperton Lane TW17 0DQ
t 01932 592572 **f** 01932 569655 **m** 07710 572572
e callboxdiary@btinternet.com **w** www.callboxdiary.co.uk

Mike Baldock
The Production Switchboard, Northdown, Down Lane, Compton GU3 1DN
t 01483 812011 **f** 01483 812027
e aly@productionswitch.freeserve.co.uk
Credits Godman (C); Rose Hacknoy - Barber (C); Suzie Gold (F)

Natalie Beer
The Production Switchboard, Northdown, Down Lane, Compton GU3 1DN
t 01483 812011 **f** 01483 812027
e aly@productionswitch.freeserve.co.uk
Credits Lego Starwars (C); BT Broadband (C); Just Jalle (M)

Sam Benjamins
18 Webster Road, London SE16 4DF
t 020 7450 3184 **m** 07958 373789
e samuelbenjamins@hotmail.com
Credits Mike Bassett: England Manager (F)

Dan Bevis
The Production Switchboard, Northdown, Down Lane, Compton GU3 1DN
t 01483 812011 **f** 01483 812027
e aly@productionswitch.freeserve.co.uk
Credits Brain Candy (T); Goodbye Mr Chips (T); Strange (T)

Ed Bishop
Callbox Communications Ltd, PO Box 66, Shepperton Studios, Shepperton Lane TW17 0DQ
t 01932 592572 **f** 01932 569655 **m** 07710 572572
e callboxdiary@btinternet.com **w** www.callboxdiary.co.uk

Tim Blair
48 College Road, London NW10 5ER
t 020 8968 5180 **m** 07971 808352
Agent Stella's Diary, 9 Hormead Road, London W9 3NG
t 020 8969 1855 **f** 020 8964 2157 **m** 07971 808352
e stella'sdiary@btinternet.com

Edward Boyd
Production Switchboard, Northdown, Down Lane, Compton GU3 1DN
t 01483 812011 **f** 01483 812027
e aly@productionswitch.freeserve.co.uk
Credits Bride Of Ice (F); Its In Our Hands - Bjork (M); The Day Britain Stopped (D)

Simon Brooks
7 Wern Road, Skewen, Neath SA10 6DN
t 01792 813930 **m** 07866 163871
e urwithbrooks@yahoo.co.uk

Emily Brown
Callbox Communications Ltd, PO Box 66, Shepperton Studios, Shepperton Lane TW17 0DQ
t 01932 592572 **f** 01932 569655 **m** 07710 572572
e callboxdiary@btinternet.com **w** www.callboxdiary.co.uk

Chris Burgess
Callbox Communications Ltd, PO Box 66, Shepperton Studios, Shepperton Lane TW17 0DQ
t 01932 592572 **f** 01932 569655 **m** 07710 572572
e callboxdiary@btinternet.com **w** www.callboxdiary.co.uk

Darren Capper
Callbox Communications Ltd, PO Box 66, Shepperton Studios, Shepperton Lane TW17 0DQ
t 01932 592572 **f** 01932 569655 **m** 07710 572572
e callboxdiary@btinternet.com **w** www.callboxdiary.co.uk

Despina Catselli
Callbox Communications Ltd, PO Box 66, Shepperton Studios, Shepperton Lane TW17 0DQ
t 01932 592572 **f** 01932 569655 **m** 07710 572572
e callboxdiary@btinternet.com **w** www.callboxdiary.co.uk

Charlotte Cave
Art Department, 51 Pratt Street, London NW1 0BJ
t 020 7428 0500 **f** 020 7916 2167 **m** 07715 093705
e info@art-department.co.uk

Nick Clarke
Callbox Communications Ltd, PO Box 66, Shepperton Studios, Shepperton Lane TW17 0DQ
t 01932 592572 **f** 01932 569655 **m** 07710 572572
e callboxdiary@btinternet.com **w** www.callboxdiary.co.uk

Dan Cleland
Callbox Communications Ltd, PO Box 66, Shepperton Studios, Shepperton Lane TW17 0DQ
t 01932 592572 **f** 01932 569655 **m** 07710 572572
e callboxdiary@btinternet.com **w** www.callboxdiary.co.uk

Matt Cole
3 Stannard Road, London E8 1DB
t 020 7249 3068 **m** 07960 665822
e mattcole75@yahoo.co.uk
Agent Callbox Communications Ltd, Box 66, Shepperton Studios, Shepperton TW17 0QD
t 01932 592572 **f** 01932 569655 **m** 07710 572572
e callboxdiary@btinternet.com **w** www.callboxdiary.co.uk
Credits Citroen (C); Citroen; Mastercard Mobo Awards (T); Touch Me, Tease Me - Godman (M)

Nick Collett
The Production Switchboard, Northdown, Down Lane, Compton GU3 1DN
t 01483 812011 **f** 01483 812027
e aly@productionswitch.freeserve.co.uk
Credits B.O.D.Y. (C); B&Q (C); British Telecom (C)

Tim Compton
Callbox Communications Ltd, Box 66, Shepperton Studios, Shepperton TW17 0QD
t 01932 592572 **f** 01932 569655 **m** 07710 572572
e callboxdiary@btinternet.com **w** www.callboxdiary.co.uk

Christopher Coote
Callbox Communications Ltd, Box 66, Shepperton Studios, Shepperton TW17 0QD
t 01932 592572 **f** 01932 569655 **m** 07710 572572
e callboxdiary@btinternet.com **w** www.callboxdiary.co.uk

Andrew Davis
Callbox Communications Ltd, Box 66, Shepperton Studios, Shepperton TW17 0QD
t 01932 592572 **f** 01932 569655 **m** 07710 572572
e callboxdiary@btinternet.com **w** www.callboxdiary.co.uk

Stephen Dipre
5 Orchard Close, Bexleyheath DA7 4RP
t 020 8303 8087 **m** 07974 314132
Credits Men Only (T); Phoenix Blue (F); Come Together (T); 40 (T)

Ben Domb
Callbox Communications Ltd, Box 66, Shepperton Studios, Shepperton TW17 0QD
t 01932 592572 **f** 01932 569655 **m** 07710 572572
e callboxdiary@btinternet.com **w** www.callboxdiary.co.uk

Lucy Egerton
Callbox Communications Ltd, Box 66, Shepperton Studios,
Shepperton TW17 0QD
t 01932 592572 **f** 01932 569655 **m** 07710 572572
e callboxdiary@btinternet.com **w** www.callboxdiary.co.uk

Jonnie Elf
The Production Switchboard, North Down, Down Lane,
Compton GU3 1DN
t 01483 812011 **f** 01483 812027
e aly@productionswitch.freeserve.co.uk
Credits Oil Factory - Supergrass (M); BT (C); Evening Standard (C)

Peter Foster
The Production Switchboard, North Down, Down Lane,
Compton GU3 1DN
t 01483 812011 **f** 01483 812027
e aly@productionswitch.freeserve.co.uk
Credits William And Mary (T); Hornblower (T); Gladiatress (F)

Phil Gilbert
The Production Switchboard, North Down, Down Lane,
Compton GU3 1DN
t 01483 812011 **f** 01483 812027
e aly@productionswitch.freeserve.co.uk
Credits Addiction (M); Addiction (C); Popworld (T)

Sam Gore
The Production Switchboard, Northdown, Down Lane,
Compton GU3 1DN
t 01483 812011 **f** 01483 812027
e aly@productionswitch.freeserve.co.uk
Credits Woodworks (C); Culturer (C); Carling (C)

Michael Goring
Flat D, 19 Pryland Road, London N5 2JB
m 07939 502851 **e** goringmichael@hotmail.com
Agent The Production Switchboard, North Down, Down Lane,
Compton GU3 1DN
t 01483 812011 **f** 01483 812027
Credits Matalan (C); Ready When You Are Mr McGill (F); Billy Elliot (F)

Tom Grady
Callbox Communications Ltd, Box 66, Shepperton Studios,
Shepperton TW17 0QD
t 01932 592572 **f** 01932 569655 **m** 07710 572572
e callboxdiary@btinternet.com **w** www.callboxdiary.co.uk

Amy Griffiths
Production Switchboard, North Down, Down Lane, Compton
GU3 1DN
t 01483 812011 **f** 01483 812027
e aly@productionswitch.freeserve.co.uk
Credits Krygier Hirschkorn (C); BT Business - Hungry Man (C); Godman (C)

Lee Groombridge
Callbox Communications Ltd, Box 66, Shepperton Studios,
Shepperton TW17 0QD
t 01932 592572 **f** 01932 569655 **m** 07710 572572
e callboxdiary@btinternet.com **w** www.callboxdiary.co.uk

Sam Haveland
Callbox Communications Ltd, Box 66, Shepperton Studios,
Shepperton TW17 0QD
t 01932 592572 **f** 01932 569655 **m** 07710 572572
e callboxdiary@btinternet.com **w** www.callboxdiary.co.uk

Tristan Hefele
Callbox Communications Ltd, Box 66, Shepperton Studios,
Shepperton TW17 0QD
t 01932 592572 **f** 01932 569655 **m** 07710 572572
e callboxdiary@btinternet.com **w** www.callboxdiary.co.uk

David Hewitt
Callbox Communications Ltd, Box 66, Shepperton Studios,
Shepperton TW17 0QD
t 01932 592572 **f** 01932 569655 **m** 07710 572572
e callboxdiary@btinternet.com **w** www.callboxdiary.co.uk

Hannah Holland
Callbox Communications Ltd, Box 66, Shepperton Studios,
Shepperton TW17 0QD
t 01932 592572 **f** 01932 569655 **m** 07710 572572
e callboxdiary@btinternet.com **w** www.callboxdiary.co.uk

Ben Holman
Callbox Communications Ltd, Box 66, Shepperton Studios,
Shepperton TW17 0QD
t 01932 592572 **f** 01932 569655 **m** 07710 572572
e callboxdiary@btinternet.com **w** www.callboxdiary.co.uk

Luke Howard
Callbox Communications Ltd, Box 66, Shepperton Studios,
Shepperton TW17 0QD
t 01932 592572 **f** 01932 569655 **m** 07710 572572
e callboxdiary@btinternet.com **w** www.callboxdiary.co.uk

Harriet Howe
Callbox Communications Ltd, Box 66, Shepperton Studios,
Shepperton TW17 0QD
t 01932 592572 **f** 01932 569655 **m** 07710 572572
e callboxdiary@btinternet.com **w** www.callboxdiary.co.uk

Paulette James
Callbox Communications Ltd, Box 66, Shepperton Studios,
Shepperton TW17 0QD
t 01932 592572 **f** 01932 569655 **m** 07710 572572
e callboxdiary@btinternet.com **w** www.callboxdiary.co.uk

Adam Jenkins
The Production Switchboard, North Down, Down Lane,
Compton GU3 1DN
t 01483 812011 **f** 01483 812027
e aly@productionswitch.freeserve.co.uk
Credits Daddy's Girl (T); Harry Potter And The Prisoner Of Azkaban (F);
Roger Roger (T)

Ben Jerrit
142 Fitzneal Street, London W12 0BB
t 020 8740 4615 **m** 07767 783984 **e** ben@jerrit.co.uk
Agent The Production Switchboard, North Down, Down Lane,
Compton GU3 1DN
t 01483 812011 **f** 01483 812027
e aly@productionswitch.freeserve.co.uk
Credits Braun (C); Silent Witness Series VI (T); Neverland (F)

Liam Johnson
The Production Switchboard, North Down, Down Lane,
Compton GU3 1DN
t 01483 812011 **f** 01483 812027
e aly@productionswitch.freeserve.co.uk
Credits Rogue Productions (C); Fifa (C); Pizbuin (C)

Joff Joyce
Callbox Communications Ltd, Box 66, Shepperton Studios,
Shepperton TW17 0QD
t 01932 592572 **f** 01932 569655 **m** 07710 572572
e callboxdiary@btinternet.com **w** www.callboxdiary.co.uk

Paul Kemble
Callbox Communications Ltd, Box 66, Shepperton Studios,
Shepperton TW17 0QD
t 01932 592572 **f** 01932 569655 **m** 07710 572572
e callboxdiary@btinternet.com **w** www.callboxdiary.co.uk

Maeve Kenny
Production Switchboard, North Down, Down Lane, Compton
GU3 1DN
t 01483 812011 **f** 01483 812027
e aly@productionswitch.freeserve.co.uk
Credits 4MC (C); The Times (C); MTV (C)

Anja Kirschner
Callbox Communications Ltd, Box 66, Shepperton Studios,
Shepperton TW17 0QD
t 01932 592572 **f** 01932 569655 **m** 07710 572572
e callboxdiary@btinternet.com **w** www.callboxdiary.co.uk

Anja Kristiansen
Callbox Communications Ltd, Box 66, Shepperton Studios,
Shepperton TW17 0QD
t 01932 592572 **f** 01932 569655 **m** 07710 572572
e callboxdiary@btinternet.com **w** www.callboxdiary.co.uk

Niki Levy
Callbox Communications Ltd, PO Box 66, Shepperton Studios,
Shepperton TW17 0QD
t 01932 572572 **f** 01932 569655 **m** 07710 572572
e callboxdiary@btinternet.com **w** www.callboxdiary.co.uk

Susanna Lindstrom
SBFC, Unit 8, Sandhurst House, Wolsey Street, London E1 3BD

Claire Luke
Callbox Communications Ltd, PO Box 66, Shepperton Studios,
Shepperton TW17 0QD
t 01932 572572 **f** 01932 569655 **m** 07710 572572
e callboxdiary@btinternet.com **w** www.callboxdiary.co.uk

Lucas Manley
Callbox Communications Ltd, PO Box 66, Shepperton Studios,
Shepperton TW17 0QD
t 01932 572572 **f** 01932 569655 **m** 07710 572572
e callboxdiary@btinternet.com **w** www.callboxdiary.co.uk

Scott Mason
The Production Switchboard, North Down, Down Lane,
Compton GU3 1DN
t 01483 812011 **f** 01483 812027
e aly@productionswitch.freeserve.co.uk
Credits Neil's Party (F); Dog (F); Outsider (C)

Cally Maycox
The Production Switchboard, North Down, Down Lane,
Compton GU3 1DN
t 01483 812011 **f** 01483 812027
e aly@productionswitch.freeserve.co.uk
Credits H30 (C); Independent (C); Brit Awards 2003 (T)

Paul McCann
Callbox Communications Ltd, Box 66, Shepperton Studios,
Shepperton TW17 0QD
t 01932 572572 **f** 01932 569655 **m** 07710 572572
e callboxdiary@btinternet.com **w** www.callboxdiary.co.uk

Jim Moran
Callbox Communications Ltd, 66 Shepperton Studios, Studios
Road, Shepperton TW17 0QD
t 01932 592572 **f** 01932 569655 **m** 07710 572572
e callboxdiary@btinternet.com **w** www.callboxdiary.co.uk

Jenny Mitchell
Callbox Communications Ltd, 66 Shepperton Studios, Studios
Road, Shepperton TW17 0QD
t 01932 592572 **f** 01932 569655 **m** 07710 572572
e callboxdiary@btinternet.com **w** www.callboxdiary.co.uk

Kate McDonough
Callbox Communications Ltd, Box 66, Shepperton Studios,
Shepperton TW17 0QD
t 01932 572572 **f** 01932 569655 **m** 07710 572572
e callboxdiary@btinternet.com **w** www.callboxdiary.co.uk

Malcolm McGilchrist
Callbox Communications Ltd, Box 66, Shepperton Studios,
Shepperton TW17 0QD
t 01932 572572 **f** 01932 569655 **m** 07710 572572
e callboxdiary@btinternet.com **w** www.callboxdiary.co.uk

Pete Mellor
Callbox Communications Ltd, Box 66, Shepperton Studios,
Shepperton TW17 0QD
t 01932 572572 **f** 01932 569655 **m** 07710 572572
e callboxdiary@btinternet.com **w** www.callboxdiary.co.uk

Jorge Menna
The Production Switchboard, North Down, Down Lane,
Compton GU3 1DN
t 01483 812011 **f** 01483 812027
e aly@productionswitch.freeserve.co.uk
Credits The Biography Channel (C); Four Day Fashion Shoot (C); Johnny English (F)

Francis Mildmay-White
Callbox Communications Ltd, PO Box 66, Shepperton Studios,
Shepperton TW17 0QD
t 01932 572572 **f** 01932 569655 **m** 07710 572572
e callboxdiary@btinternet.com **w** www.callboxdiary.co.uk

Humphrey Milles
Callbox Communications Ltd, Box 66, Shepperton Studios,
Shepperton TW17 0QD
t 01932 572572 **f** 01932 569655 **m** 07710 572572
e callboxdiary@btinternet.com **w** www.callboxdiary.co.uk

Robert Morgan
The Production Switchboard, North Down, Down Lane,
Compton GU3 1DN
t 01483 812011 **f** 01483 812027
e aly@productionswitch.freeserve.co.uk
Credits British Heart Foundation (C); T-Mobile (C); Suzie Gold (F)

Sam Morris
The Production Switchboard, North Down, Down Lane,
Compton GU3 1DN
t 01483 812011 **f** 01483 812027
e aly@productionswitch.freeserve.co.uk
Credits Coast (C); The Quarry (C); Sony Playstation (C)

Paul Mortimore
Callbox Communications Ltd, 66 Shepperton Studios, Studios
Road, Shepperton TW17 0QD
t 01932 592572 **f** 01932 569655 **m** 07710 572572
e callboxdiary@btinternet.com **w** www.callboxdiary.co.uk

Nick Moss
Callbox Communications Ltd, 66 Shepperton Studios, Studios
Road, Shepperton TW17 0QD
t 01932 572572 **f** 01932 569655 **m** 07710 572572
e callboxdiary@btinternet.com **w** www.callboxdiary.co.uk

Peter Murlis
Callbox Communications Ltd, 66 Shepperton Studios, Studios
Road, Shepperton TW17 0QD
t 01932 592572 **f** 01932 569655 **m** 07710 572572
e callboxdiary@btinternet.com **w** www.callboxdiary.co.uk

Stephan Norinder
The Production Switchboard, North Down, Down Lane,
Compton GU3 1DN
t 01483 812011 **f** 01483 812027
e aly@productionswitch.freeserve.co.uk
Credits Sports Relief (T); Sainsbury's (C); Johnny English (F)

Mel Nwanguma
The Production Switchboard, North Down, Down Lane,
Compton GU3 1DN
t 01483 812011 **f** 01483 812027
e aly@productionswitch.freeserve.co.uk
Credits Blink (C); Outsider (C); Keen Eddie (T)

Nnamdi Nwosu
Callbox Communications Ltd, 66 Shepperton Studios, Studios
Road, Shepperton TW17 0QD
t 01932 592572 **f** 01932 569655 **m** 07710 572572
e callboxdiary@btinternet.com **w** www.callboxdiary.co.uk

John Joe O'Driscoll
Callbox Communications Ltd, 66 Shepperton Studios, Studios Road, Shepperton TW17 0QD
t 01932 592572 **f** 01932 569655 **m** 07710 572572
e callboxdiary@btinternet.com **w** www.callboxdiary.co.uk

Sam le Page
Callbox Communications Ltd, PO Box 66, Shepperton Studios, Shepperton TW17 0QD
t 01932 572572 **f** 01932 569655 **m** 07710 572572
e callboxdiary@btinternet.com **w** www.callboxdiary.co.uk

Mark Palfreeman
Callbox Communications Ltd, 66 Shepperton Studios, Studios Road, Shepperton TW17 0QD
t 01932 592572 **f** 01932 569655 **m** 07710 572572
e callboxdiary@btinternet.com **w** www.callboxdiary.co.uk

Clara Paris
The Production Switchboard, North Down, Down Lane, Compton GU3 1DN
t 01483 812011 **f** 01483 812027
e aly@productionswitch.freeserve.co.uk
Credits Infinity (C); Outsider (C); American Girl (F)

Olivia PB
Callbox Communications Ltd, 66 Shepperton Studios, Studios Road, Shepperton TW17 0QD
t 01932 592572 **f** 01932 569655 **m** 07710 572572
e callboxdiary@btinternet.com **w** www.callboxdiary.co.uk

Augusta Peto
The Production Switchboard, North Down, Down Lane, Compton GU3 1DN
t 01483 812011 **f** 01483 812027
e aly@productionswitch.freeserve.co.uk
Credits Gorgeous (C); Infinity (C); BT Business - Hungry Man (C)

Amy Pettipher
Callbox Communications Ltd, 66 Shepperton Studios, Studios Road, Shepperton TW17 0QD
t 01932 592572 **f** 01932 569655 **m** 07710 572572
e callboxdiary@btinternet.com **w** www.callboxdiary.co.uk

Bobbie Pryor
Callbox Communications Ltd, 66 Shepperton Studios, Studios Road, Shepperton TW17 0QD
t 01932 592572 **f** 01932 569655 **m** 07710 572572
e callboxdiary@btinternet.com **w** www.callboxdiary.co.uk

Douglas Pye
The Production Switchboard, North Down, Down Lane, Compton GU3 1DN
t 01483 812011 **f** 01483 812027
e aly@productionswitch.freeserve.co.uk
Credits Future Shock (M); The Vessels (M); Comic Relief (C)

James Rice
Fairacre, Deadham Lane, Chalfont St Giles HP8 4HG
t 01494 874824 **m** 07711 886517
e jamesrice2000@hotmail.com
Agent The Production Switchboard, North Down, Down Lane, Compton GU3 1DN
t 01483 812011 **f** 01483 812027
e aly@productionswitch.freeserve.co.uk
Credits Playstation 2 (C); Orange (C); Virgin Megastore (C)

Max Rich
Callbox Communications Ltd, 66 Shepperton Studios, Studios Road, Shepperton TW17 0QD
t 01932 592572 **f** 01932 569655 **m** 07710 572572
e callboxdiary@btinternet.com **w** www.callboxdiary.co.uk

Fabien Riggall
The Production Switchboard, Northdown, Down Lane, Compton GU3 1DN
t 01483 812011 **f** 01483 812027
e aly@productionswitch.freeserve.co.uk
Credits The Hounds Of The Baskerville (T); Serious And Organised (T); The Great Ceili War (F)

Stevan Riley
The Production Switchboard, North Down, Down Lane, Compton GU3 1DN
t 01483 812011 **f** 01483 812027
e aly@productionswitch.freeserve.co.uk
Credits Moi Cesar (F); BT (C); Hornblower (F)

Kate Rudge
Callbox Communications Ltd, 66 Shepperton Studios, Studios Road, Shepperton TW17 0QD
t 01932 592572 **f** 01932 569655 **m** 07710 572572
e callboxdiary@btinternet.com **w** www.callboxdiary.co.uk

Lisa Ruff
Callbox Communications Ltd, 66 Shepperton Studios, Studios Road, Shepperton TW17 0QD
t 01932 592572 **f** 01932 569655 **m** 07710 572572
e callboxdiary@btinternet.com **w** www.callboxdiary.co.uk

Miss Shelley Rutter
48A Brendon Road, Watchet TA23 0HT
t 01984 634199 **m** 07790 576255 **e** shelleyrutter@yahoo.co.uk

Andy Seaton
Bookends, 83 Maynard Drive AL1 2JX
t 01727 841177 **e** bookgold@bookends.fsbusiness.co.uk

Sergei Serpuhov
Callbox Communications Ltd, 66 Shepperton Studios, Studios Road, Shepperton TW17 0QD
t 01932 592572 **f** 01932 569655 **m** 07710 572572
e callboxdiary@btinternet.com **w** www.callboxdiary.co.uk

Sophia Shek
Callbox Communications Ltd, 66 Shepperton Studios, Studios Road, Shepperton TW17 0QD
t 01932 592572 **f** 01932 569655 **m** 07710 572572
e callboxdiary@btinternet.com **w** www.callboxdiary.co.uk

Hannah Shields
Flat 1, 107 Middleton Hall Road, Kings Norton, Birmingham B30 1AG
t 0121 451 1396 **m** 07905 791735 **e** hannah_shields@hotmail.com
Credits Doctors (T); Dalziel And Pascoe (T); RHS Tatton Flower Show (T); Housecall (T)

Louis Smith
Callbox Communications Ltd, 66 Shepperton Studios, Studios Road, Shepperton TW17 0QD
t 01932 592572 **f** 01932 569655 **m** 07710 572572
e callboxdiary@btinternet.com **w** www.callboxdiary.co.uk

Danjel Starborg
Callbox Communications Ltd, 66 Shepperton Studios, Studios Road, Shepperton TW17 0QD
t 01932 592572 **f** 01932 569655 **m** 07710 572572
e callboxdiary@btinternet.com **w** www.callboxdiary.co.uk

Daniel Susman
Callbox Communications Ltd, 66 Shepperton Studios, Studios Road, Shepperton TW17 0QD
t 01932 592572 **f** 01932 569655 **m** 07710 572572
e callboxdiary@btinternet.com **w** www.callboxdiary.co.uk

Simon Tatum
Callbox Communications Ltd, 66 Shepperton Studios, Studios Road, Shepperton TW17 0QD
t 01932 592572 **f** 01932 569655 **m** 07710 572572
e callboxdiary@btinternet.com **w** www.callboxdiary.co.uk

Erica Taylor
The Production Switchboard, North Down, Down Lane,
Compton GU3 1DN
t 01483 812011 **f** 01483 812027
e aly@productionswitch.freeserve.co.uk
Credits Trial And Retribution VI (T); Dream Team (T); Bright Young Things (F)

Adam Teeuw
The Production Switchboard, North Down, Down Lane,
Compton GU3 1DN
t 01483 812011 **f** 01483 812027
e aly@productionswitch.freeserve.co.uk
Credits 4 Creatives (C); American Pop Idol (M); Evening Standard (C)

Gareth Thomas
Callbox Communications Ltd, 66 Shepperton Studios, Studios
Road, Shepperton TW17 0QD
t 01932 592572 **f** 01932 569655 **m** 07710 572572
e callboxdiary@btinternet.com **w** www.callboxdiary.co.uk

Jack Till
Callbox Communications Ltd, 66 Shepperton Studios, Studios
Road, Shepperton TW17 0QD
t 01932 592572 **f** 01932 569655 **m** 07710 572572
e callboxdiary@btinternet.com **w** www.callboxdiary.co.uk

Dan Turner
The Production Switchboard, North Down, Down Lane,
Compton GU3 1DN
t 01483 812011 **f** 01483 812027
e aly@productionswitch.freeserve.co.uk
Credits Kenco (C); Keen Eddie (T)

Russell Turner
Callbox Communications Ltd, 66 Shepperton Studios, Studios
Road, Shepperton TW17 0QD
t 01932 592572 **f** 01932 569655 **m** 07710 572572
e callboxdiary@btinternet.com **w** www.callboxdiary.co.uk

James Twyford
Callbox Communications Ltd, 66 Shepperton Studios, Studios
Road, Shepperton TW17 0QD
t 01932 592572 **f** 01932 569655 **m** 07710 572572
e callboxdiary@btinternet.com **w** www.callboxdiary.co.uk

Mari Tyson
Callbox Communications Ltd, 66 Shepperton Studios, Studios
Road, Shepperton TW17 0QD
t 01932 592572 **f** 01932 569655 **m** 07710 572572
e callboxdiary@btinternet.com **w** www.callboxdiary.co.uk

Gavin Watson
Callbox Communications Ltd, 66 Shepperton Studios, Studios
Road, Shepperton TW17 0QD
t 01932 592572 **f** 01932 569655 **m** 07710 572572
e callboxdiary@btinternet.com **w** www.callboxdiary.co.uk

Benjamin Whistle
The Production Switchboard, North Down, Down Lane,
Compton GU3 1DN
t 01483 812011 **f** 01483 812027
e aly@productionswitch.freeserve.co.uk
Credits KFC (C); Direct Line (C); Evening Standard (C)

Toby White
Callbox Communications Ltd, 66 Shepperton Studios, Studios
Road, Shepperton TW17 0QD
t 01932 592572 **f** 01932 569655 **m** 07710 572572
e callboxdiary@btinternet.com **w** www.callboxdiary.co.uk

Tony Whiteway
Callbox Communications Ltd, 66 Shepperton Studios, Studios
Road, Shepperton TW17 0QD
t 01932 592572 **f** 01932 569655 **m** 07710 572572
e callboxdiary@btinternet.com **w** www.callboxdiary.co.uk

Jamie Williams
Callbox Communications Ltd, 66 Shepperton Studios, Studios
Road, Shepperton TW17 0QD
t 01932 592572 **f** 01932 569655 **m** 07710 572572
e callboxdiary@btinternet.com **w** www.callboxdiary.co.uk

Magda Witko
Callbox Communications Ltd, 66 Shepperton Studios, Studios
Road, Shepperton TW17 0QD
t 01932 592572 **f** 01932 569655 **m** 07710 572572
e callboxdiary@btinternet.com **w** www.callboxdiary.co.uk

Adrian Woods
Callbox Communications Ltd, Box 66, Shepperton Studios,
Shepperton TW17 0QD
t 01932 572572 **f** 01932 569655 **m** 07710 572 572
e callboxdiary@btinternet.com **w** www.callboxdiary.co.uk

Duncan Wright
Callbox Communications Ltd, 66 Shepperton Studios, Studios
Road, Shepperton TW17 0QD
t 01932 592572 **f** 01932 569655 **m** 07710 572572
e callboxdiary@btinternet.com **w** www.callboxdiary.co.uk

SCRIPT SERVICES

script copyright

Copyright is the legal protection extended to the owner of the rights in an original work that he has created. First of all, always ask a lawyer's advice or seek out a more established professional film-maker. Or try the NPA or PACT and BECTU, which are trade bodies that give advice.

Some writers post themselves a copy and keep it, leaving the postmarked envelope unopened. You may also want to send a copy to your solicitor. If you are a member of BECTU you can post scripts or proposals to the union and they will register them at no cost, providing definitive proof that you own the copyright.

Writers must write their name and the date on the cover page of the script. In all correspondence you should state that the letter and script are "In Confidence". For more, check with the Writer's Guild. http://www.wggb.demon.co.uk.

Script Services

1st Transcriptions & Scripts Ltd
217 Northfield Avenue, West Ealing W13 9QU
t 020 8579 8388 **f** 020 8840 8833
m 07836 325586
e 1st@s4kmedia.tv
Contact Simon Bell; Tommy Wan

Various BBC + ITV programmes, children's TV, and adult channels. Continuing to serve the industry into the 21st century.

8 Ball Productions
'The Russetts', Bumpstead Road, Hempstead, Saffron Walden CB10 2PW
t 01799 599105 **f** 01799 599106 **m** 07710 644475
e 8ballproductions@amserve.net
Contact Ron Bennett, Proprietor

A4 Enterprises
61 Parry Road, Ashmore Park, Wolverhampton WV11 2PS
t 01902 722729 **f** 01902 722729 **m** 07740 244646
e kenneth.rock@btinternet.com

Ask Typewryte
11 Harford Walk, London N2 0JB
t 020 8444 7437 **f** 020 8444 7437 **e** typewryte@aol.com

Bill Bourne Associates
106 Rosendale Road, West Dulwich, London SE21 8LF
t 020 8670 3130 **f** 020 8244 8591 **e** bourneass@aol.com
Contact Dee Bourne, Production Manager

Century Quiz Promotions
100 Blantyre Road, Liverpool L15 3HT
t 0151 733 8676 **f** 0151 734 5740 **m** 07967 338676
e graeme@century-quiz.co.uk **w** www.century-quiz.co.uk
Credits Mastermind (T); The Weakest Link (T); University Challenge (T)

Christian Howgell
6 Leysfield Road, London W12 9JF
t 020 8932 3530 **f** 020 8932 3530
e christian@christianhowgill.freeserve.co.uk
Contact Christian Howgill, Producer/Writer
Credits Plato's Kiss (F); St Ambrose Of Orpington (F); Stealing a Kiss (F); Carrott Confidential (T)

Derek Cunningham Productions
6 Yarrell Mansions, Queen's Club Gardens, London W14 9TB
t 020 7385 0595 **e** cunningham@screaming.net
Contact Derek Cunningham, Writer / Director
Credits Reporting On Reuters (I); Law Of Armed Conflict (D); Pimopen (C); Bullshot (F)

Douglas Dougan
3 Lower Joppa, Edinburgh EH15 2ER
e mail@douglasdougan.co.uk **w** www.douglasdougan.co.uk
Credits Birds of Passage (F)

Lucy Edyvean
Flat 2, Cornwall Gardens, London SW7 4AL
t 020 7584 9758 **f** 0870 056 8557 **m** 07973 200197
e lucy@transcripts.demon.co.uk
Timecoded I/Vs - lucid, detailed, fast. Post production Scripts - the best.

Jane Fryers
Wizzo & Co, 35 Old Compton Street, London W1D 5JX
t 020 7437 2055 **f** 020 7437 2066
e wizzo@wizzoandco.co.uk **w** www.wizzoandco.co.uk

David Jay
16 Reade Road, Holbrook, Ipswich 1P9 2QL
t 01473 328283 **f** 01473 328283 **e** info@alphafilms.co.uk

Mo Johnstone
16 Tournay Road, London SW6 7UF
t 020 7385 7038 **f** 020 7386 9836 **m** 07785 226569
e mo.jo@ur.com
Credits Early Doors (T); Hewlett Packard (C); Abbey National (C)

London Pictures Ltd
Herne Farm, 41 Upper Heyshott, Petersfield GU31 4QA
t 01730 231141 **f** 01730 231141
e general@londonpicturesltd.com **w** www.londonpicturesltd.com
Contact Jo Crissey, CEO/Producer/Director; Jaki Crissey, Script Consultant; Nigel Winterbottom, Director; Rustin Holton, PR Manager
Credits Give And Give Again (S); Smarty Pants (S); Tape 7 (F); Merchant Of Venice (F)

Frances Mable
m 07768 760264
Credits My Hero Series I-IV (T); Bad Girls (T); Trial & Retribution III (T)

Hayley McKenzie
m 07813 031221 **e** hayleymckenzie@yahoo.co.uk
Credits Crossroads (T); Heartbeat (T)

Mike Mendoza Broadcasting
169 Old Fort Road, Shoreham Beach BN43 5HL
t 01273 462213 **f** 01273 462214 **m** 07808 342322
e mikemendozalbc@aol.com
Contact Mike Mendoza, Managing Director

The Phantom Captain
618B Finchley Road, London NW11 7RR
t 020 8455 4564 **f** 020 8455 4564
e ziph@macunlimited.net **w** hppt://phantomcaptain.netfirms.com
Contact Neil Hornick, Artistic Director

Reading & Righting
618B Finchley Road, London NW11 7RR
t 020 8455 4564 **f** 020 8455 4564
e ziph@macunlimited.net
w http://readingandrighting.netfirms.com
Contact Robert Lambolle, Chief Editor

S4K Media Group
t 020 8579 8388 **f** 020 8840 6810 **m** 07836 325586
e info@s4kmedia.tv

Sapex Scripts
Millennium Studios, 5 Elstree Way, Borehamwood WD6 1SF
t 020 8236 1600 **f** 020 8236 1591
e scripts@sapex.co.uk **w** www.sapex.co.uk
Contact Paul Sattin; Penny Sattin
Credits The Vice (T); The Lost Prince (T); The Hours (F); Harry Porter (F)

The Screenwriter's Store
Suite 121, Friars House, 157 Blackfriar's Road, London SE1 8EZ
t 020 7261 1908 **f** 020 7261 1909
e info@thesws.com **w** www.thesws.com
Contact Johanna Reder, Marketing Manager; Rinaldo Quacquarini, Company Director

The Screenwriters' Workshop
Suffolk House, 1-8 Whitfield Place, London W1T 5JU
t 020 7387 5511
e screenoffice@tiscali.co.uk **w** www.lsw.org.uk
Contact Katharine Way, Chairwoman; Rita Wheeler, Administration
Credits EastEnders (T); Doctors (T); The Bill (T)

Ann Simpson
t 01749 890689
Credits Eyes Wide Shut (F)

Susanna Lindstrom
SBFC, Unit 8, Sandhurst House, Wolsey Street, London E1 3BD

Take 1 Script Services Ltd
456-458 The Strand, London WC2R 0DZ
t 0800 085 4418 **f** 01580 715809 **m** 07711 531381
e info@take1scripts.com **w** www.take1scripts.com
Contact Dom Bourne, Managing Director
Credits Jackass The Movie (F); Eurotrash (T); Louis Theroux (T)

The Word Business
56 Leyborne Park, Kew, Richmond TW9 3HA
t 020 8948 8346 f 020 8920 9029
e j.mabbett@btinternet.com

The Word Store
PO Box 1536, Hanwell, London W7 1NF
t 020 8566 4188 f 020 8566 4189
e 106645.3316@compuserve.com
Contact Anne Silk, Proprietor

Wrap it Up
67 Brentham Way, Ealing, London W5 1BE
t 020 8998 6852 m 07973 198154
e victoria.gilbert@mcmail.com
Contact Victoria Gilbert, Proprietor

Security

Able Security
117 Waverley Road, Plumstead, London SE18 7TH
t 020 8317 6899 f 020 8317 6899 m 07771 848039
e tomgandl@tomsmail.com
Contact Tom Gandl, Proprietor
Credits City Hospital (T); Murder In Mind (T); Inspector Lynley Investigates (T);
Without Motive (T)

Advanced Vision Systems
Unit 2B, Raceview Business Centre, Hambridge Road, Newbury
RG14 5SA
t 01635 31466 f 01635 43996
Contact Roger Daymond, Partner

Communications & Surveillance Systems Ltd (Spymaster)
3 Portman Square, London W1H 9PS
t 020 7486 3885 f 020 7486 2655
e sales@spymaster.co.uk w www.spymasteruk.com

Crown Protection Services
The Pound, Cool Oak Lane, London NW9 7NB
t 020 8205 6000 f 020 8205 6005
e info@cgsplc.demon.co.uk w www.security-guards.com

Flir Systems International
2 Kings Hill Avenue, Kings Hill, West Malling ME19 4AQ
t 01732 221245 f 01732 843707
e sales@flir.uk.com w www.flir.com
Contact David Lancaster, Sales and Marketing Director

North Star Security Group
Parman House, Fife Road, Kingston-upon-Thames KT1 1SY
t 020 8546 8900 f 020 8546 6005
e enquiries@northstarsecurity.co.uk
Contact Martin Gauci, Proprietor

Paul Owens - Owens Security Group
118 Piccadilly, London W1J
m 07951 082944 e sven1885uk@yahoo.co.uk
Contact Paul Byrne, Associate; Paul Owens, Group Proprieter

Pulsar Developments Ltd
Spracklen House, Dukes Place, Marlow SL7 2QH
t 01628 474324 f 01628 474325
w www.pulsardevelopments.com
Contact Brian Murphy, Director; Terri Baker, Office Manager; Adam Hogg,
Consultant; Michael Goode, Company Secretary; Keith Roberts, Consultant

Reel Security Services
72 Gristhorpe Rd, Selly Oak, Birmingham B29 7SW
t 0121 472 4714 m 07976 983599
Contact Steve Hill, Proprietor & Director

Securiguard
Century House, Century Works, Pencil Green SA7 9BZ
t 01792 539999 f 01792 539997 e sgwells@aol.com
Contact Mark Davis, Managing Director

Show & Event Security
Consort House, 1 Aston Court, Stanningley Road, Leeds LS13 2AF
t 0870 366 5878 f 0870 366 5879
e simon.miller@showandevent.com w www.showandevent.com
Contact John Phillips, National Business Development Manager; Andrew
Stevens, Operations Manager; Simon Miller, Area Manager; Gary Pritchard,
TV/Film Locations Manager

Synectic Systems Ltd
Unit 3, Acorn Business Park, Woodseats Close, Sheffield S8 0TB
t 0114 255 2509 f 0114 258 2050
e sales@synectics.co.uk w www.synectics.co.uk
Contact Phillip Longley, Sales Director

Task International Ltd
22-26 Albert Embankment, London SE1 7TE
t 020 7582 9205 f 020 7793 1455 m 07956 239527
e security@task-int.com w www.task-int.com
Contact Bob Dyson, Marketing Manager

Unit Security
23B High Street, Chislehurst BR7 5AE
m 07831 571707
Contact Jason Moyce, Head of Security
Credits Nicholas Nickleby (T); The Calcium Kid (F); Suzie Gold (T); Ted And Sylvia (F)

Showreel Services

Debbie Flint Productions
PO Box 18, Banstead SM7 2WT
t 08702 259438 m 08702 259438
e debs@debbieflint.com w www.debbieflint.com
Contact Debbie Flint, Managing Director
Credits Best Direct (T); Simply Television (T); QVC - The Shopping Channel (T)

Frontline Television
35 Bedfordbury, Covent Garden, London WC2N 4DU
t 020 7836 0411 f 020 7379 5210
e gail@frontline-tv.co.uk w www.frontline-tv.co.uk
Contact Christine Cook, Business Development Manager; Gail Gilmartin,
Facilities Manager

Frontline TV
35 Bedfordbury, Covent Garden, London WC2N 4DU
t 020 7836 0411 f 020 7379 5210
e info@frontline-tv.co.uk w www.frontline-tv.co.uk
Contact Gail Gilmartin, Facilities Manager; Charlie Sayle, Facilities Director;
Tracy Thomas, Director of Sales & Marketing
Credits Gareth Gates & Will Young (M); Shed Heads (T); Jennifer Lopez - This Is
me (C); Great Escapes (D)

*We make showreel compilations, copies for TV transmission, repeater
reels, VHS copies etc of your TV commercials. We are unique in that we
hold secure and confidential reels of all your TV commercials – which
are always kept up-to-date. Storage and updating of your material (held
as a digital clone of your master tapes on Digi Beta) is free – all you pay
for are the compilations and copies made from your holding reel. All you
have to do is phone, fax or email orders to us - taking the hassle of
making agency showreels and Director's reels away from you.*

McLegend Productions
117B Crofton Road, Camberwell, London SE5 8LZ
t 07946 651593 m 07946 651593 e mcl_pro@yahoo.co.uk
Contact Michael McLegend, Graphic & Title Designer/Video Editor

Myshowreel.com
Rosebank House, Overton Park Road, Cheltenham GL50 3BP
t 0870 460 1920
e showoff@myshowreel.com **w** www.myshowreel.com
Contact Richard Terney, Managing Director

One Stop Presenters Shop
PO Box 18, Banstead SM7 2WT
t 0870 225 9438 **f** 0870 225 9438
e debs@debbieflint.com **w** www.debbieflint.com
Contact Debbie Flint, Managing Director

SOUND

Sound Assistants

Jaime Lunn
London
t 020 7388 9609 **m** 07950 260078
e info@twoears.co.uk **w** www.twoears.co.uk
Credits Orange Mobile Phones (C); Reign Of Fire (F); About A Boy (F)

Graham Spence
t 01289 302929 **e** the_masked_musician@yahoo.co.uk

Warren Spencer
Connections, The Meadlands, Oakleigh Road, Hatch End, Pinner HA5 4HB
t 020 8420 1444 **f** 020 8428 5836 **m** 07831 305518
e mail@connectionsuk.com **w** www.connectionsuk.com

Samantha Swinglehurst
Connections, The Meadlands, Oakleigh Road, Hatch End, Pinner HA5 4HB
t 020 8420 1444 **f** 020 8428 5836 **m** 07831 305518
e mail@connectionsuk.com **w** www.connectionsuk.com

Sound Boom Ops

Keith Batten
107 Tilsworth Road, Stanbridge LU7 9HY
t 01525 210819 **f** 01525 210819 **m** 07973 320178

Matthew Desorgher
Mansell Close, Towcester NN12 7AY
t 01327 350504 **f** 01327 350504 **m** 07802 540985
e matthew@desorgher.com **w** www.desorgher.com
Credits The Lost Prince (T); The Hole (F); 101 Dalmations (F); Kundun (F)

James Drummond
76 Glamorgan Street, Canton, Cardiff CF5 1QT
t 029 2033 1371 **f** 029 2066 6322 **m** 07966 231293
e james@boomop.co.uk **w** www.boomop.co.uk
Credits If You Help Me Read (C); Bay College (T); Belonging (T)

Sophie Jackson
83 Devon Road, Easton, Bristol BS5 6ED
t 0117 951 7767 **m** 07977 376027 **e** sophie@boomboom.co.uk
Credits Judge John Deed (T); EastEnders (T); Grange Hill (T)

Adam Margetts
Gems, The Media House, 87 Glebe Street, Penarth CF64 1EF
t 029 2071 0770 **f** 029 2071 0771
e gems@gems-agency.co.uk **w** www.gems-agency.co.uk
Credits Trial And Retribution IV (T); Sunburn II (T); Goal (T); City

Graham McCormick
Flat 1-2, 2 Trossachs Court, Woodside, Glasgow G20 7DH
t 0141 948 0098 **m** 07980 845162 **e** gmc_boomop@yahoo.co.uk
Credits Harry And The Wrinklies (T); Mining (T); Overnight Express (T); Your Diary (T)

Charles McFadden
5 Exmouth Road, Ruislip HA4 0UX
t 020 8845 0790 **f** 020 8845 0790 **m** 07944 862713
Credits The Inspector Lynley Mysteries (T); London's Burning (T); The Vice (T); Daniel Deronda (T)

Dick Philip
Gems, The Media House, 87 Glebe Street, Penarth CF64 1EF
t 029 2071 0770 **f** 029 2071 0771
e gems@gems-agency.co.uk **w** www.gems-agency.co.uk
Credits A Dangerous Man (T); Taggart (T); Pandaemonium (F); Intimacy (F)

Malcolm Rose
Bookends, 83 Maynard Drive, St Albans AL1 2JX
t 01727 841177 **e** bookgold@bookends.fsbusiness.co.uk

Spiros Spyrou
Gib Farm, Haworth Old Road, Hebden Bridge HX7 8RG
t 01422 845710 **m** 07785 231921

Rob Widger
68A Hencroft Street South, Slough SL1 1RE
t 01753 820158 **m** 07973 491087 **e** rob@wijhoops.freeserve.co.uk
Credits Human Remains (T); Big Train (T); The Bill (T)

Sound Equipment Hire

AFL Television Facilities Ltd
181A Verulam Road, St Albans AL3 4DR
t 01727 844117 **f** 01727 847649 **m** 07802 682424
e facilities@afltv.com **w** www.afltv.com
Contact Chris Blake, Director; Chris Blake, Director; Graham Howe, Lighting Cameraman; Dave Chapman, Director; Jenny Lane, Facilities Manager; Athos Gabriel; Athos Gabriel, Sound; Chris Blake, Director
Credits Cheer For Charlie (T); Time Team (T); Holiday (T)
Broadcast video shooting facilities with state-of-the-art equipment and top technicians plus the best service and backup. We supply Digital Single Camera Units and 2/3/4/5 Camera OB units.

Audiohire
133-137 Kilburn Lane, London W10 4AN
t 020 8960 4466 **f** 020 8964 0343
e admin@audiohire.co.uk **w** www.audiohire.co.uk
Contact Richard Zamet, Manager

Audiolink Radio Communications
Link House, Heather Park Drive, Wembley HA0 1SS
t 020 8900 2311 **f** 020 8900 1977
e info@audiolink.co.uk **w** www.audiolink.co.uk

Better Sound Ltd
31 Cathcart Street, London NW5 3BJ
t 020 7482 0177 **f** 020 7482 2677
e hire@bettersound.co.uk **w** www.bettersound.co.uk

Blitz Sound
100 Centennial Avenue, Elstree WD6 3SA
t 08701 621010 **f** 08701 621020
e enquiries@blitzsound.com **w** www.blitzvision.com
Contact Richard Rogers, Director

Briana Electronics
Grey Mullets, Seaview Promenade, St Lawrence, Southminster CM0 7NE
t 01621 779480 **f** 01621 778452
Contact B Pead, Proprietor

Canegreen Commercial Presentations Ltd
Unit 2, 12-48 Northumberland Park, London N17 0TX
t 020 8801 8133 **f** 020 8801 8139
e enquiries@canegreen.com **w** www.canegreen.com
Contact Yan Stile, Director
Credits Andrew Frengley, M.D

Charter Broadcast Ltd
Unit 4, Elstree Distribution Park, Elstree Way, Borehamwood WD6 1RU
t 020 8905 1213 **f** 020 8905 1424 **m** 07836 521987
e charter@charter.co.uk
Contact Helen Frost, Bookings Coordinator

Equipment hire company, offering a comprehensive range of broadcast video, audio, graphics and RF facilities for dry hire. In addition, Charter Broadcast offers Mobile Production Units and Flyaway Systems world-wide. Please contact us for further information or visit our website.

Concert Systems
Unit 4D, Stag Industrial Estate, Atlantic Street, Altrincham WA14 5DW
t 0161 927 7700 **f** 0161 927 7722
e hire@concertsystems.co.uk **w** www.concertsystems.co.uk
Contact Paul Tandy, Director

DPA Sound
11 Fairview Close, Tonbridge TN9 2UU
t 01322 863664 **f** 07974 421885 **m** 07973 147909
e andrew@dpasound.com **w** www.dpasound.com
Contact Andrew Latham, Sound Engineer

Edenfield Communications Ltd
2 Southview Place, Midsomer Norton, Radstock BA3 2AX
t 01761 414992 **f** 01761 411717 **m** 07958 578417
e mail@edenfield-communications.co.uk
w www.edenfield-communications.co.uk
Contact E Jakins, Director

Encore Group
Unit 8, 19 Wadsworth Road, Perivale UB6 7JD
t 020 8991 2612 **f** 020 8991 2616 **m** 07733 051546
Contact John Tinline, Managing Director

FX Rentals Ltd
38-40 Telford Way, London W3 7XS
t 020 8746 2121 **f** 020 8746 4100
info@fxgroup.net **w** www.fxgroup.net
Contact Nick Harris; Peter Brooks
Credits Lord Of The Rings - Two Towers (F)

Genesis Television Ltd
46 Broadwick Street, London W1V 1FF
t 020 7734 8100 **f** 020 7734 8200
e hire@genesishire.com **w** www.genesishire.com
Contact Tim Banks, Director; Leon Powell, Hire Manager

Hammerhead Television Facilities Ltd
9 Merchiston Mews, Edinburgh EH10 4PE
t 0131 229 5000 **f** 0131 429 4211
e scotland@hammerheadtv.com **w** www.hammerheadtv.com
Contact Chris Orvis, Production Sound Mixer; Gail Glenwright, Facilities Manager

Hammerhead Television Facilities Ltd
42 Webbs Road, London SW11 6SF
t 020 7924 3977 **f** 020 7924 2154
e london@hammerheadtv.com **w** www.hammerheadtv.com
Contact Will Wilkinson, Facilities Manager; Dan Jarmany, Facilities Manager

Hammerhead Television Facilities Ltd
Unit 22, Waters Edge Business Park, Modwen Road, Manchester M5 3EZ
t 0161 872 6200 **f** 0161 872 6300
e manchester@hammerheadtv.com **w** www.hammerheadtv.com
Contact Darren Carrig, Facilities Manager; Matt Turnbull

Hand Held Audio
Unit 2, 12-48 Northumberland Park, London N17 0TX
t 020 8880 3243 **f** 020 8365 1131
e info@handheldaudio.co.uk **w** www.handheldaudio.co.uk
Contact Mick Shepherd

Hocken Audio Visual Ltd
5 Waterhouse Lane, Kingswood KT20 6EB
t 01737 370371 **f** 01737 370372
e info@hockenav.co.uk **w** www.hockenav.co.uk
Contact Richard Haines, Managing Director

John Henry's Ltd
16-24 Brewery Road, London N7 9NH
t 020 7609 9181 **f** 020 7700 7040
e info@johnhenrys.com **w** www.johnhenrys.com
Contact John Henry, Managing Director
Credits CD:UK (T); Later With Jools Holland (T); Friday Night With Jonathan Ross (T); Parkinson (T)

Location Communications
99 Bolingbroke Grove, London SW11 1DB
t 020 7223 8166 **f** 020 7924 2879
Contact Jennifer King, Director

MAC Sound
1-2 Attenburys Park, Park Road, Altrincham WA14 5QE
t 01619 698311 **f** 01619 629423
e hire@macsound.co.uk **w** www.macsound.co.uk

Mediatech
Unit 16, Northfield Industrial Estate, Beresford Avenue, Wembley HA0 1YH
t 020 8903 4372 **f** 020 8900 2903 **m** 07785 516 804
e mediatech@mediatechav.com **w** www.mediatechav.com
Contact Bob Jackson, Director

National Sound Reproducers (NSR) Ltd
Lower Priory Farm, Clamp Hill, Stanmore HA7 3JJ
t 020 8954 7677 **f** 020 8954 9329 **m** 07768 815070
e ronwalker@natsound.fsnet.co.uk
Contact Ron Walker, Managing Director

NSR Communications
Stable End, Beesons Yard, Bury Lane, Rickmansworth WD3 1DS
t 01923 771693 **f** 01923 772128 **m** 07860 554327
e sales@nsrcommunications.co.uk
w www.nsrcommunications.co.uk
Contact Peter Walker, Chairman

sound : equipment hire

Pandora Productions
Unit 38, Hallmark Trading Centre, 4th Way, Wembley HA9 0LB
t 020 8795 2432 **f** 020 8795 2431 **m** 07811 226143
e pandoraprods@btconnect.com
Contact John Montier, Proprietor

Peter Webber Hire Ritz Studios
110-112 Disraeli Road, London SW15 2DX
t 020 8870 1335 **f** 020 8877 1036
Contact Lee Webber, Director

Picture Canning Company
55 Bendon Valley, London SW18 4LZ
t 020 8874 9277 **f** 020 8874 6623
e info@picturecanning.co.uk **w** www.picturecanning.co.uk
Contact Leslie Zunz, Managing Director; Paul Taylor, General Manager; Phil Wade, Managing Director
Credits Escape To The Country (D); Watchdog (T); Is Harry On The Boat (T); Holiday (D)

Re:Creation Sound Ltd
Unit B2, 83 Copers Cope Road, Beckenham BR3 1NR
t 020 8658 2260 **f** 020 8658 2261
e info@recreationsound.co.uk **w** www.recreationsound.co.uk
Contact Mark Trigg, Managing Director

RG Jones Sound Engineering
16 Endeavour Way, London SW19 8UH
t 020 8971 3100 **f** 020 8971 3101
e enquiries@rgjones.co.uk **w** www.rgjones.co.uk
Contact John Carroll, Hire Department Manager

Richmond Film Services
The Old School, Park Lane, Richmond TW9 2RA
t 020 8940 6077 **f** 020 8948 8326
Contact Nigel Woodford, Technical Director

Sigma Broadcast
m 07050 349521
e simon@sigmabroadcast.com **w** www.sigmabroadcast.com
Contact Simon Daniels, Proprietor

Skarda International Communication Ltd
7 Portland Mews, London W1V 3FL
t 020 7734 7776 **f** 020 7734 1360 **m** 07836 200700
e martin@skarda.net **w** www.skarda.net
Contact Martin Davidson, Managing Director
Credits Mikihouse (C); Winter Olympics (C)

Sound Hire
Unit 7, Kimpton Trade and Business Centre, Minden Road, Sutton SM3 9PF
t 020 8644 1248 **f** 020 8644 6642
e richard@sound-hire.com **w** www.sound-hire.com
Contact Richard Lienard, Proprietor

Soundkit Ltd
12 Earle Place, Canton, Cardiff CF5 1NZ
t 02920 342907 **f** 02920 231235 **m** 07973 346723
e martyn@soundkit.co.uk **w** www.soundkit.co.uk
Contact Martyn Richards, Director

Soundsense
5 Jasmin Close, The Rock, Telford TF3 5EJ
t 01952 403884 **f** 01952 401375
e info@soundsense.co.uk **w** www.soundsense.co.uk
Contact Derek Tallent, Managing Director

Tannoy
Rosehall Industrial Estate, Coatbridge ML5 4TF
t 01236 420199 **f** 01236 428230 **m** 07768 603249
Contact Andrzej Sosne, Sales & Marketing Director

Recent Credits:

BBC Television TUC live on BBC2 1999-2002

RTL Holland Wimbledon Tennis Championships
2001, 2002

TV2 Denmark
ARD Germany

Racetech ATR Horse Racing 1997-2003

- Digital Outside Broadcast Facilities
- Trucks
- De-rigs
- PPU
- Edit System

ABC (USA) Good Morning America live from Kuwait, Feb 2003

MTV Media Facilities for European Music Awards, Barcelona 2002, Tony Blair Iraq Debate March 2003

TTL are Alan Green, Nigel Cubbage and Mark Llewellyn. For the complete solution to your outside broadcast needs, call us now on 01737-767655.

Television Film Services
The Workstation, 15 Paternoster Row, Sheffield S1 2BX
t 0114 249 5902 **m** 07831 666899
e info@tfsuk.com **w** www.tfsuk.com
Contact Keith Silva, Hire
Credits Walking With Cavemen (T); Gentleman Thief (T); Cutting It (T); Black Water (T)

Tour Tech (UK) Ltd
3 Quarry Park, Moulton Park, Northampton NN3 6QB
t 01604 494846 **f** 01604 642454 **m** 07889 187736
e tourtecuk@aol.com **w** www.tourtech.co.uk
Contact Tom Gordon; Derek Fudge; Dick Rabel; Matt Rabel

W1 Productions
2nd Floor, Swiss Centre, 10 Wardour Street, London W1D 6QF
t 020 7494 4917 **f** 020 7494 4918 **m** 07770 623593
e info@w1productions.co.uk **w** www.w1productions.co.uk
Contact Stuart Turvill, Director; Curis Kyriacou, Director

The Warehouse Sound Services (Edinburgh)
23 Water Street, Leith, Edinburgh EH6 6SU
t 0131 555 6900 **f** 0131 555 6901 **e** info@warehousesound.co.uk
Contact Pete Harris, Hire Manager

Wavevend Radio Communications
17B Pindock Mews, Little Venice, London W9 2PY
t 020 7266 1280 **f** 020 7266 1290 **e** wavevend@freeuk.com
Contact Melvin Lind, Managing Director

Wood & Douglas Ltd
Lattice House, Baughurst, Tadley RG26 5LP
t 0118 981 1444 **f** 0118 981 1567
e info@woodanddouglas.co.uk **w** www.woodanddouglas.co.uk
Contact Peter Blakeborough, Sales Director

Sound Equipment Hire Communications

Audiosend Communications
39 Leinster Avenue, London SW14 7JW
t 020 8876 8553 **f** 020 8876 9381 **e** soundman@talk21.com
Contact Bridget Hayes, Managing Partner
Credits Mean Machine (W); White Teeth (T); Midsomer Murders IV & V (T); Swept Away (F)

Communication & Technical Services Ltd
17 Pages Walk, London SE1 4SB
t 020 7252 1849 **f** 020 7252 3241
e mail@ctslimited.co.uk **w** www.ctslimited.co.uk
Contact Mike McMinn; Keith Hardy

CTS
17 Pages Walk, London SE1 4SB
t 020 7252 1849 **f** 020 7252 3241
e hire@ctslimited.co.uk **w** www.ctslimited.co.uk
Contact Mike McMinn, Hire Manager

FAB Sound Services
Unit 8, Rufus Business Centre, Ravensbury Terrace, London SW18 4RL
t 020 8947 7738 **f** 020 8947 6608 **m** 07831 354550
e info@fabsound.co.uk **w** www.fabsound.co.uk
Contact Geoff Horne, Partner

Hand Held Audio
Unit 2, 12-48 Northumberland Park, London N17 0TX
t 020 8880 3243 **f** 020 8365 1131
e info@handheldaudio.co.uk **w** www.handheldaudio.co.uk
Contact Mick Shepherd

In Touch Communications
Units 1&2, Mitre House, 223-237 Borough High Street, London SE1 1JD
t 020 7666 6644 **f** 020 7666 6633 **w** www.intouchcomms.co.uk
Contact Jonathan Miller, Managing Director

Total Audio Solutions
Unit 3, Woden Court, Saxon Business Park, Bromsgrove B60 4AD
t 01527 880051 **f** 01527 880052
e hire@totalaudio.co.uk **w** www.totalaudio.co.uk

TTL Video Ltd
38 Holmethorpe Avenue, Redhill RH1 2NL
t 01737 767655 **f** 01737 767665
e ob@ttlvideo.com **w** www.ttlvideo.com
Contact Alan Green; Mark Llewellyn; Nigel Cubbage

Equipment and expertise in all areas of outside broadcast engineering.

Sound Equipment Hire Mixing/Recording

Class Audio
47 Ashwell Street, Ashwell SG7 5QT
t 01462 742914 **f** 01462 742522 **m** 07778 815344
e peter@classaudio.co.uk
Contact Peter Stoddart, Technical Director

Jules Dawton
95 Birchtree Avenue, West Wickham BR4 9EQ
t 020 8462 6371 **m** 07860 777687
e julesdawton@compuserve.com
Credits Danny, Champion Of The World (F); Mile High (T); Hollyoaks (T); Brookside (T)

FX Rentals Ltd
38-40 Telford Way, London W3 7XS
t 020 8746 2121 **f** 020 8746 4100
e info@fxgroup.net **w** www.fxgroup.net
Contact Nick Harris; Peter Brooks
Credits Lord Of The Rings - Two Towers (F)

Dave Morton
134 Monmmouth Road, Dorchester DT1 2DQ
t 01305 265066 **m** 07831 329688
Credits Big Brother (T); Survivor (T); TFI Friday (T)

Ovni Audio
33- 37 Hatherley Mews, Walthamstow, London E17 4QP
t 020 8509 0832 **f** 020 8521 6363 **m** 07949 269 516
e flavio.uk@ukonline.co.uk
Contact Flavio Curras, Proprietor

VME Ltd
Unit 4, Laburnam Park, 72 Knutsford Road, Alderley Edge SK9 7SF
t 01625 585525 **f** 01625 599155 **m** 07831 487366
e dion@vme.uk.com **w** www.vme.uk.com
Contact Andre Davie, Director; Paul Holland, Warehouse Manager; Dion Davie, Director
Credits Northern Utilities Water Board (C); The History Of British Serial Killers (D); Great British Disasters (D); Sky Sports Superleague (T)

The Warehouse Sound Services (Glasgow)
40 Carmichael Street, Govan, Glasgow G51 2QU
t 0141 445 4466 **f** 0141 445 3636
e glhires@warehousesound.co.uk **w** www.warehousesound.co.uk
Contact Ian Gibson, Branch Manager

Welsh Media Music
Gorwelion, Llanfynydd, Carmarthen SA32 7TG
t 01558 668525 **f** 01558 668750 **m** 07774 100430
e dpierce@welshmediamusic.f9.co.uk
Contact Dafydd Pierce, Sound Engineer/Recordist

Sound Equipment Sales & Spares

10 out of 10 Productions Ltd
14 Forest Hill Business Centre, London SE23 3JF
t 0845 123 5664 f 020 8699 8968
e sales@10outof10.co.uk w www.10outof10.co.uk

Abacus Electrics
10 Barley Mow Passage, Chiswick, London W4 4PH
t 020 8994 6477 f 020 8994 1766
e info@abacuselectrics.com w www.abacuselectrics.com
Contact Philip Plunkett, Proprietor

All Set Productions
Audio House, Progress Road, High Wycombe HP12 4JD
t 01494 511711 f 01494 539600
e info@audioltd.com w www.audioltd.com

Apple Sound Ltd
St Andrews Park, Queens Lane, Mold CH7 1XB
t 0870 741 0123 f 0870 741 0124
e office@applesound.co.uk w www.applesound.co.uk

ASAP Europe
Units C&D, Tower Bridge Business Complex, London SE16 4DE
t 020 7231 9661 f 020 7231 9111
m 07967 816961 m 07768 490922
e sales@asapeurope.com w www.asapeurope.com
Contact Robin Ashley, Director; Alan Stewart, Director

Aspen Media Ltd
222 Maylands Avenue, Hemel Hempstead HP2 7TD
t 01442 255405 f 01442 399944
e sales@aspen-media.com w www.aspen-media.com
Contact Chris Collings, Director; Graham Bryant, Service Manager; Stephen Scott, Sales Technical

Audio + Design (Recording) Ltd
Unit 3, Horseshoe Park, Pangbourne, Reading RG8 7JW
t 0118 984 4545 f 0118 984 2604 m 07785 238 091
e sales@proaudio.uk.com w www.proaudio.uk.com
Contact Richard Strang, IT Manager; Ian Harley, Managing Director

Audio Agency Europe
PO Box 4601, Kiln Farm, Milton Keynes MK19 7ZN
t 01908 510123
e info@audioagencyeurope.com w www.audioagencyeurope.com
Contact Paul Eastwood, Sales/Marketing

Audio Engineering Ltd
Micron House, 3 New Road, London N8 8TA
t 020 8341 3500 f 020 8341 5100
e sales@micronwireless.co.uk w www.micronwireless.co.uk
Contact Aldo Hakligil, Sales Manager

Audio Ltd
Audio House, Progress Road, High Wycombe HP12 4JD
t 01494 511711 f 01494 539600
e info@audioltd.com w www.audioltd.com
Contact Kishore Patel, Managing Director

Audio Reflections
3 Longwood Vale, Tingley, Wakefield WF3 1UL
t 01132 528850 f 01132 525943
e info@audioreflections.co.uk w www.audioreflections.co.uk
Contact John Bleakley, Managing Director

Audio-Technica
Unit 2, Royal London Industrial Estate, Old Lane, Leeds LS11 8AG
t 0113 277 1441 f 0113 270 4836
e sales@audio-technica.co.uk w www.audio-technica.co.uk
Contact Paul Maher, Managing Director

Autograph Sales Ltd
102 Grafton Road, London NW5 4BA
t 020 7485 3749 f 020 7485 0681
e sales@autograph.co.uk w www.autograph.co.uk
Contact Mike Mann, Technical Sales; Graham Paddon, Director; Andrew Latham, Sales; Rob Piddington, Director; Roger Harpum, Meyer Sales; Mike Charman, Clear-Com Sales

BBM Electronics Group Ltd
Kestrel House, Garth Road, Morden SM4 4LP
t 020 8330 3111 f 020 8330 3222
e sales@trantec.co.uk w www.trantec.co.uk
Contact Sho Kubo, Managing Director/Overseas Sales; Gary Waywell, Regional Sales Manager; Lisa Williams, Sales Enquiries

Bel Digital Audio
3 Horwood Court, Bletchley, Milton Keynes MK1 1RD
t 01908 641063 f 01908 6410 63x7
e mick@beldigital.co.uk w www.bel-digital.co.uk
Contact Mick Bernard, Director

Beyerdynamic (GB) Ltd
17 Albert Drive, Burgess Hill RH15 9TN
t 01444 258258 f 01444 258444
e sales@beyerdynamic.co.uk w www.beyerdynamic.co.uk
Contact Richard Clarke, Regional Sales Manager; Matt Nettlefolio, Product Manager; Jon Stanley, Product Manager; Paul Cooke, Product Manager; Barbara Mishon, Accounts Manager; John Midgley, Managing Director; Bob Harrison, National Sales Manager

BSS Audio
Cranborne House, Cranborne Road, Potters Bar EN6 3JN
t 01707 660667 f 01707 660755
e info@bss.co.uk w www.bss.co.uk
Contact David McKinney, UK Sales Manager

Canadian Instruments & Electronics
Widdowson Close, Blenheim Industrial Estate, Bulwell, Nottingham NG6 8WB
t 0115 977 0075 f 0115 977 0081
e info@cie-ltd.co.uk w www.cie-group.co.uk

Cunnings Recording Associates
Brodrick Hall, Brodrick Road, London SW17 7DY
t 020 8767 3533 f 020 8767 8525
e info@cunnings.co.uk w www.cunnings.co.uk
Contact Malcolm Cunnings, Manager

d&b audiotechnik
Locks Mill, Brewery Lane, Nailsworth GL6 0JQ
t 01453 835884 f 01453 834193 e info.gb@dbaudio.com

DACS Ltd
Unit A19, Stonehills, Shields Road, Pelaw, Gateshead NE10 0HW
t 0191 438 2500 f 0191 438 2511
e info@dacs-audio.com w www.dacs-audio.com
Contact Douglas Doherty, Managing Director; Lillian Davison, Office Manager; Max St John, Sales/Distribution; Steve Dawson, Technical Manager

Drawmer
Charlotte Street Business Centre, Charlotte Street, Wakefield WF1 1UH
t 01924 378669 f 01924 290460
e info@drawmer.com w www.drawmer.com

Focusrite Audio Engineering Ltd
Lincoln Road, Cressex Business Park, High Wycombe HP12 3FX
t 01494 462246 f 01494 459920
e sales@focusrite.com w www.focusrite.com
Contact Melissa Nightingale, Purchasing & Sales

Fritsch Sound
8 Mentmore Terrace, London E8 3PN
t 020 8985 3678 f 020 8985 3678
e bfritsch@freenetname.co.uk w www.fritschsound.co.uk
Contact Bertrand Fritsch, Acoustic Consultant
Credits The Copyist (S)

Hand Held Audio
Unit 2, 12-48 Northumberland Park, London N17 0TX
t 020 8880 3243 **f** 020 8365 1131
e info@handheldaudio.co.uk **w** www.handheldaudio.co.uk
Contact Mick Shepherd

Hayden Laboratories
Hayden House, Chiltern Hill, Chalfont St Peter SL9 9UG
t 01753 888447 **f** 01753 880109 **w** www.denon.co.uk
Contact Simon Curtis, Manager for Professional Equipment

Headset Services Ltd
Unit 5, 24 Cecil Pashley Way, Shoreham Airport, Shoreham-by-Sea BN43 5FF
t 01273 234181 **f** 01273 234190
e headsetservices@btinternet.com **w** www.headsetservices.com
Contact Mark Panton, Managing Director; John Kelly

HHB Communications Ltd
73-75 Scrubs Lane, London NW10 6QU
t 020 8962 5000 **f** 020 8962 5050
e sales@hhb.co.uk **w** www.hhb.co.uk
Contact Steve Angel, Sales Director

HW International
Brantwood Industrial Area, 167-171 Willoughby Lane, London N17 0SB
t 020 8808 2222 **f** 020 8808 5599
e hwinternational@dial.pipex.com **w** www.hwinternational.co.uk
Contact Dennis Harburn, Sales Director

HZ International
Combe House, Stoke St Michael, Radstock BA3 5HN
t 01749 840102 **f** 01749 840887 **m** 07769 893262
e sales@hz-international.com **w** www.hz-international.com
Contact Lynda Roch, Sales Director; Dave Roberts, Technical Director; Doug Siddons, Sales Manager

Impact Percussion
Unit 7, Goose Green Trading Estate, 47 East Dulwich Road, London SE22 9BN
t 020 8299 6700 **f** 020 8299 6704
e sales@impactpercussion.com **w** www.impactpercussion.com
Contact Paul Hagen, Proprietor

Industrial Acoustics Company
IAC House, Moorside Road, Winchester SO23 7US
t 01962 873000 **f** 01962 873111
e info@iacl.co.uk **w** www.iacl.co.uk
Contact Ian Rich, Manager, Studio Division

John Hornby Skewes & Co Ltd
Salem House, Parkinson Approach, Garforth, Leeds LS25 2HR
t 0113 286 5381 **f** 0113 286 8515
e info@jhs.co.uk **w** www.jhs.co.uk
Contact Neville Raine, Pro Audio Manager; Dennis Drumm, Sales Director

Klark Teknik Group
Walter Nash Road, Kidderminster DY11 7HJ
t 01562 741515 **f** 01562 745371
e pro_audio_group@compuserve.com **w** www.klarkteknik.com
Contact David Webster, Marketing Director; Tony Fryer, Financial Director; David Cooper, Sales Manager

Larking Audio
t 01462 492095 **e** info@tlcommerce.co.uk **w** www.larking.com
Contact Don Larking, Managing Director

Len Brook UK
Unit 2, Old Worverton Road, Old Wolverton, Milton Keynes MK12 5NP
t 01908 319360 **f** 01908 322752
e info@lenbrook.co.uk **w** www.lenbrook.co.uk
Contact Stephen Calder, Managing Director

Lindos Electronics
Saddlemakers Lane, Melton, Woodbridge IP12 1PP
t 01394 380307 **f** 01394 385156
e info@lindos.co.uk **w** www.lindos.co.uk
Contact Richard Lincoln, Development Manager

Location Technical Facilities
64 Oxford Road, New Denham, Uxbridge UB9 4DN
t 01895 813698 **f** 01895 813701
m 07770 876552 **e** willb@ltf-uk.com **w** www.ltf-uk.com
Contact William Blackham, Sales Manager

Mosses & Mitchell
Parkwood, Sutton Road, Maidstone ME15 9NG
t 01622 690 001 **f** 01622 690 002
e m&msales@arlen.co.uk **w** www.mosses-mitchell.com
Contact Peter Wilson, Sales and Marketing Manager

MTR Ltd
Ford House, 58 Cross Road, Bushey WD19 4DQ
t 01923 234050 **f** 01923 255746
e mtrltd@aol.com **w** www.mtraudio.com
Contact Tony Reeves, Managing Director

Neutrik (UK) Ltd
Columbia Business Park, Sherbourne Avenue, Ryde PO33 3QD
t 01983 811441 **f** 01983 811439
e sales@neutrik.co.uk **w** www.neutrik.co.uk
Contact Charles Cook, Sales Manager

OpTex UK
20-26 Victoria Road, New Barnet, London EN4 9PF
t 020 8441 2199 **f** 020 8449 3646
e info@optexint.com **w** www.optexint.com
Contact Edward Catton-Orr, Sales; Mike Robinson, Rentals

PRECO (Broadcast Systems)
3 Four Seasons Crescent, Kimpton Road, Sutton SM3 9QR
t 020 8644 4447 **f** 020 8644 0474
e sales@preco.co.uk **w** www.preco.co.uk
Contact W Costello, Managing Director

Prism Sound
William James House, Cowley Road, Cambridge CB4 0WX
t 01223 424988 **f** 01223 425023
e sales@prismsound.com **w** www.prismsound.com
Contact Jody Thorn, Sales

Raper & Wayman Ltd
3 Crusader Estate, 167 Hermitage Road, London N4 1LZ
t 020 8800 8288 **f** 020 8809 1515
e sales@raperandwayman.com **w** www.raperandwayman.com
Contact Keith King, Sales Office Manager; Rodney Wayman, Managing Director; Simon Stoll, Sales; James Bradley, Sales; Gary Ash, Distributed Products Manager

Recording Architecture Ltd
1 Greenwich Quay, Clarence Road, London SE8 3EY
t 020 8692 6992 **f** 020 8692 6957 **e** ra@aaa-design.com
Contact Nick Whitaker, Acoustic Consultant; Roger Darcy, Managing Director

RTS 1 Stop Ltd
Units M1 and M2, Prescot Trade Centre, Albany Road, Prescot L34 2UP
t 0151 430 9001 **f** 0151 430 7441
Contact John Fairclough, Managing Director

Rycote
Libbys Drive, Slad Road, Stroud GL5 1RN
t 01453 759338 **f** 01453 764249
e info@rycote.com **w** www.rycote.com
Contact Vivienne Dyer, Managing Director

Sadie UK

Studio Audio and Video Ltd, The Old School, High Street, Stretham, Ely CB6 3LD
t 01353 648 888 **f** 01353 648 867
e sales@sadie.com **w** www.sadie.com
Contact Jim Gross, Sales Manager

Sennheiser UK Ltd

3 Century Point, Halifax Road, High Wycombe HP12 3SL
t 01494 551551 **f** 01494 551550
e info@sennheiser.co.uk **w** www.sennheiser.co.uk
Contact Alan Johnson, Director of Sales; John Steven, Director of Marketing

Sevenoaks Sound & Vision

109-113 London Road, Sevenoaks TN13 1BH
t 01732 459555 **f** 01732 466226
e savenoaks@sevenoakssoundandvision.co.uk **w** www.sevenoakssoundandvision.co.uk

Shuttlesound Ltd

4 The Willows Centre, Willows Lane, Mitcham CR4 4NX
t 020 8640 9600 **t** 020 8254 5660
f 020 8640 7583 **f** 020 8640 0106
e info@shuttlesound.com **w** www.shuttlesound.com
Contact Paul Barretta, Managing Director

Sonifex Ltd

61 Station Road, Northants NN9 5QE
t 01933 650700 **f** 01933 650726
e sales@sonifex.co.uk **w** www.sonifex.co.uk
Contact Marcus Brooke, Managing Director; Jill Brown, Sales Assistant; Julian Speed, Sales Manager

SoundKit Ltd

12 Earle Place, Canton, Cardiff CF5 INZ
t 029 2034 2907 **f** 029 2023 1235 **m** 07973 346723
e martyn@soundkit.co.uk **w** www.soundkit.co.uk
Contact Martyn Richards, Proprietor

Stirling Syco

Unit 5, The Chase Centre, Chase Road, London NW10 6QD
t 020 8963 4790 **f** 020 8963 4799
e sales@stirlingsyco.com **w** www.sterlingsyco.com
Contact Andrew Stirling, Director

Studio Audio & Video Ltd

The Old School, High Street, Streatham CB6 3LD
t 01353 648888 **f** 01353 648867
e sales@sadie.com **w** www.sadie.com
Contact Jim Gross, Sales Manager

Studio Spares

61-63 Rochester Place, London NW1 9JU
t 08456 441020 **f** 020 7485 4168
e sales@studiospares.com **w** www.studiospares.com
Contact Barry Lambden, Director

Studiomaster

7 Eden Way, Page Industrial Estate, Leighton Buzzard LU7 4TZ
t 01525 217111 **f** 01525 378466
e enquiries@studiomaster.com **w** www.studiomaster.com
Contact Jim Khan

Tascam

5 Marlin House, Croxley Centre, Watford WD18 8TE
t 01923 438880 **f** 01923 236290 **m** 07779 795656
e sales@tascam.co.uk **w** www.tascam.co.uk
Contact Robin Ashley, Pro-Audio Sales Manager

Teac UK

5 Marlin House, The Croxley Centre, Watford WD1 8YA
t 01923 488880 **f** 01923 239260
e sales@tascam.co.uk **w** www.teac.co.uk
Contact Tony Gravel, Sales and Marketing manager

Turbosound Ltd

Star Road, Partridge Green RH13 8RY
t 0140 371 1447 **f** 0140 371 0155
e sales@turbosound.com **w** www.turbosound.com
Contact Alan Wick, Managing Director; Bill Woods, Sales Director

Tyrell

17-19 Foley Street, London W1W 6DW
t 020 7343 5500 **f** 020 7343 5501
e info@tyrell.co.uk **w** www.tyrell.co.uk

University Audio

3 Peas Hill, Cambridge CB3 2PP
t 01223 354237 **f** 01223 322079
Contact David Hyam, Director

V'Audio

36 Druid Hill, Stoke Bishop, Bristol BS9 1EJ
t 0117 968 6005 **f** 0117 968 6005
e ian@vaudio.co.uk **w** www.vaudio.co.uk
Contact Ian Vaudin, Proprieter

Sound Recordists

Ace - Sound

26 Elm Park Road, Finchley, London N3 1EB
m 07769 504882 **e** bisher@bisher.freeserve.co.uk
Contact Chris King, Sound Recordist
Credits CD:UK (T); Everyman (D); Johnny Vaughan (T); Have I Got News For You (T)

Aiden Communications

22 Manor Links, Bishops Stortford CM23 5RA
t 07050 802613 **f** 07050 802613 **m** 07850 015002
e denis@aiden-comms.co.uk **w** www.aiden-comms.co.uk
Contact Denis Stevenson, Proprietor

Ambience Digital Sound Design Services

Basement Flat, 25 Trinity Rise, London SW2 2QP
t 020 8671 4124 **f** 020 8671 4124 **m** 07939 369 310
e ambiencesoundservices@btopenworld.com
Contact Nicholas Stocker, Director

Joe Archer

TOVS Ltd, 162-168 Regent Street, London W1B 5TB
t 020 7287 6110 **f** 020 7287 5481
e info@tovs.co.uk **w** www.tovs.co.uk

Gary Bainbridge

TOVS Ltd, The Linen Hall, 162-168 Regent Street, London W1B 5TB
t 020 7287 6110 **f** 020 7287 5481
e info@tovs.co.uk **w** www.tovs.co.uk

Steph Baldini

Stella's Diary, 9 Hormead Road, London W9 3NG
t 020 8969 1855 **f** 020 8964 2157
m 07956 424881 **e** stella'sdiary@btinternet.com

Julian Baldwin

19 Lutyens Close, Stapleton, Bristol BS16 1WL
t 0117 965 6744 **m** 07973 730033 **e** julian.baldwin@bigfoot.com
Agent Connections, The Meadlands, Oakleigh Road, Hatch End, Pinner HA5 4HB
t 020 8420 1444 **f** 020 8428 5836 **m** 07831 305518
e mail@connectionsuk.com **w** www.connectionsuk.com
Credits French Experience (E); Italianissimo (E); Horizon (D); Panorama (T)

Dickie Batchelor

Callbox Communications Limited, 66 Shepperton Studios, Studios Road, Shepperton TW17 0QD
t 01932 592572 **f** 01932 569655 **m** 07710 572572
e callboxdiary@btinternet.com **w** www.callboxdiary.co.uk

Paul Bateman
18 Crofton Avenue, Orpington BR6 8DU
t 01689 811170 **m** 07768 528462 **e** paulbateman@supanet.com
Credits Esther Ranza (T); Roger Cook (D); Dealers Choice (T); Chicago -
The Works (D)

Dave Baumber
Cornerways Roberts Lane, South Littleton, Evesham WR11 5TN
t 01386 830084 **f** 01386 834737 **m** 07970 860880
e dave.baumber@btinternet.com
Credits Boys From the Black Stuff (T); Dangerfield (T); Casualty (T)

Phil Bax
28 Montague Road, Hanwell, London W7 3PQ
t 020 8567 7023 **f** 020 8567 7023 **m** 07956 150977
e phil.bax@mail.com
Credits John Meets Paul (D); Bethlehem Year Zero (T); It Ain't Necessary So
(D); 2000 Years (D)

Dominic Bekes
73 Old Bridge Road, Whitstable CT5 1RB
t 01227 273695 **m** 07770 583082
Agent Linkline, 6 Thirlmere Gardens, Wembley HA9 8RE
t 020 8908 6262 **f** 020 8904 5179
e mail@linklinecrew.com **w** www.linklinecrew.com

Adrian Bell
m 07836 322802 **e** mail@adrianbell.net **w** www.adrianbell.net
Credits The Nugget Run (S); A French Affair (D); Offside (T); The Bill (T)

Daniel Birch
Gems, The Media House, 87 Glebe Street, Penarth CF64 1EF
t 029 2071 0770 **f** 029 2071 0771
e gems@gems-agency.co.uk **w** www.gems-agency.co.uk
Credits Relative Strangers (T); H2 (F); East Of Harlem (F); The Roman Spring Of
Mrs Stone (F)

Steve Blincoe
TOVS Ltd, The Linen Hall, 162-168 Regent Street, London W1B 5TB
t 020 7287 6110 **f** 020 7287 5481
e info@tovs.co.uk **w** www.tovs.co.uk

Rene Borisewitz
41 St Gabriels Road, London NW2 4DT
t 020 8452 2666 **f** 020 8208 0828 **m** 07798 624725

John JB Bowman
Callbox Communications Limited, 66 Shepperton Studios,
Shepperton TW17 0QD
t 01932 592572 **f** 01932 569655 **m** 07710 572572
e callboxdiary@btinternet.com **w** www.callboxdiary.co.uk

Matthew Boyle
Grade One TV & Film Personnel, Elstree Studios, Shenley
Road, Borehamwood WD6 1JG
t 020 8324 2224 **f** 020 8324 2328
e gradeone.tvpersonnel@virgin.net

Benoit Bradley
Stella's Diary, 9 Hormead Road, London W9 3NG
t 020 8969 1855 **f** 020 8964 2157 **m** 07816 937532
e stella'sdiary@btinternet.com

John Brady
12 Blackmores Grove, Teddington TW11 9AF
t 020 8943 3897 **m** 07973 883320
Agent Linkline, 6 Thirlmere Gardens, Wembley HA9 8RE
t 020 8908 6262 **f** 020 8904 5179
e mail@linklinecrew.com **w** www.linklinecrew.com

Chas Braithwaite
Grade One TV & Film Personnel, Elstree Studios, Shenley
Road, Borehamwood WD6 1JG
t 020 8324 2224 **f** 020 8324 2328
e gradeone.tvpersonnel@virgin.net

Julian Brannigan
1 The Firs, Gosforth, Newcastle-upon-Tyne NE3 4PH
t 0191 284 3444 **m** 07850 325426
e julian@tvsound.demon.co.uk

Adam Brewer
TOVS Ltd, The Linen Hall, 162-168 Regent Street, London W1B 5TB
t 020 7287 6110 **f** 020 7287 5481
e info@tovs.co.uk **w** www.tovs.co.uk

Darrell Briggs
KT6 7TF
t 020 8288 1009 **m** 07803 937623
e darrellbriggs@breathe.com **w** www.darrellbriggs.com
Agent Callbox Communications Limited, 66 Shepperton
Studios, Studios Road, Shepperton TW17 0QD
t 01932 592572 **f** 01932 569655 **m** 07710 572572
e callboxdiary@btinternet.com **w** www.callboxdiary.co.uk
Credits Battlefield Detectives (D); Bad Blood (D); Black Boxers (D); Wilson (D)

Peter Brill
22 Northampton Drive, Kelvindale, Glasgow G12 OLE
t 0141 357 0617 **f** 0141 357 0617 **m** 07971 780572
e brillsound@classicfm.net
Credits Skagerrak (F); 2000 Acres Of Sky (T); Bait (T)

Briteaudio Ltd
401 Foundry House, 47 Morris Road, London E14 6NJ
t 07768 613159 **m** 07973 296456
e info@briteaudio.com **w** www.briteaudio.com
Contact Joff White, Company Director; Adam Brewer, Company Director

Broadcast Audio Ltd
93 Glengall Road, Woodford Green IG8 0DP
t 020 8504 3424 **m** 07973 837692
e mail@broadcaststudio.co.uk **w** www.broadcaststudio.co.uk
Contact Alex Charge, Managing Director

Steve Brodie
19 Vicarage Road, Thetford IP24 2LW
t 01842 763215 **f** 01842 763215 **m** 07889 993759
e steve@thesoundmonkey.co.uk **w** www.thesoundmonkey.co.uk
Credits An Audience With Diana Ross (T); Trisha (T); Top Gear (T);
Gardeners World (T)

Harry Brooks
Connections, The Meadlands, Oakleigh Road, Hatch End,
Pinner HA5 4HB
t 020 8420 1444 **f** 020 8428 5836 **m** 07831 305518
e mail@connectionsuk.com **w** www.connectionsuk.com

Rudi Buckle
14 Wood Bastwick Road, Sydenham, London SE26 5LQ
t 020 8778 7315 **m** 07973 238785
Agent International Creative Management Ltd, Oxford House,
76 Oxford Street, London W1D 1BS
t 020 7636 6565 **f** 020 7323 0101 **w** www.icmlondon.co.uk
Agent Linkline, 6 Thirlmere Gardens, Wembley HA9 8RE
t 020 8908 6262 **f** 020 8904 5179
e mail@linklinecrew.com **w** www.linklinecrew.com
Credits August (F); Hornblower (T); The Tenth Kingdom (T)

Callum Bulmer
87B Queens Crescent, Chalk Farm, London NW5 4EU
t 020 7692 1550 **t** 020 8969 1855 **m** 07956 424881
e lolita@davidbowie.co.uk
Credits Versace (D); BBC Holiday (T); BT Broadband (C)

Laura Burei
1 Alma Place, Upper Norwood, London SE19 2TB
t 020 8761 3589 **f** 07771 907630
Agent Linkline, 6 Thirlmere Gardens, Wembley HA9 8RE
t 020 8908 6262 **f** 020 8904 5179
e mail@linklinecrew.com **w** www.linklinecrew.com

Craig Burns
Callbox Communications Limited, 66 Shepperton Studios,
Studios Road, Shepperton TW17 0QD
t 01932 592572 **f** 01932 569655 **m** 07710 572572
e callboxdiary@btinternet.com **w** www.callboxdiary.co.uk

Stuart Burroughs
Callbox Communications Limited, 66 Shepperton Studios,
Studios Road, Shepperton TW17 0QD
t 01932 592572 **f** 01932 569655 **m** 07710 572572
e callboxdiary@btinternet.com **w** www.callboxdiary.co.uk

Cable Media Resources
8 Pleasant Grove, Shirley, Croydon CR0 8AS
t 020 8776 0687 **f** 020 8776 0687 **m** 07768 870242
cable-media@hotmail.com
Credits OB Sports (T); The Edit (T); Channel 4 News (T); Sunset And Vine (T)

Dave Calvert
97 Horse Shoe Lane East, Guildford GU1 2TW
t 01483 569357 **m** 07831 278725
Agent Linkline, 6 Thirlmere Gardens, Wembley HA9 8RE
t 020 8908 6262 **f** 020 8904 5179
e mail@linklinecrew.com **w** www.linklinecrew.com

Ken Campbell
14 Pegasus Place, St Albans AL3 5QT
m 07831 322642 **e** ken_com@bbcnet.com
Agent Jessica Carney Associates, Suite 90-92 Kent House,
87 Regent Street, London W1B 4EH
t 020 7434 4143 **f** 020 7434 4173 **e** info@jcarneyassociates.co.uk
Credits Silent Witness (T); Murphy's Law (T); Perfect (T)

Trevor Carless
3 Kiln Cottages, Wood Lane End, Hemel Hempstead HP2 4RE
t 01442 257325 **f** 01442 257325 **m** 07973 114032
e tcsound@talk21.com
Credits The Inspector Lynley Mysteries (T); The Vice (T); Truth (T)

Carreg Ateb
Y Ganolfan Deledu, Cibyn, Caernarfon LL55 2BD
t 01286 677134 **f** 01286 676101
e post@carregateb.com **w** www.carregateb.com
Contact Carys Lloyd Jones, Manager

David Crozier AMPS, CAS
The Old Cottage, Andrew Hill Lane, Hedgerley SL2 3UW
t 01753 642338 **f** 01753 644622 **m** 07850 206303
e crozier@globalnet.co.uk
Credits Ted And Sylvia (F); The Hours (F); Neverland (F); To Kill A King (F)

John Casali
21 St Julians Road, St Albans AL1 2AZ
t 01727 868025 **m** 07973 755529
Agent Linkline, 6 Thirlmere Gardens, Wembley HA9 8RE
t 020 8908 6262 **f** 020 8904 5179
e mail@linklinecrew.com **w** www.linklinecrew.com

Steve Chaplin
3 Huntingfield Road, London SW15 5HE
t 020 8878 4683 **m** 07876 708375 **e** scsoundrec@hotmail.com
Credits Harry's Bar (M); Elvis Pelvis (S); Ten Minutes; Little Scars (S)

Julian Chatterjee
224 Fernhead Road, London W9 3EJ
t 020 8962 9495 **f** 020 8962 9495 **m** 07785 540282
e julian.chat@virgin.com
Agent Stella's Diary, 9 Hormead Road, London W9 3NG
t 020 8969 1855 **f** 020 8964 2157 **m** 07785 540282
e stella'sdiary@btinternet.com

Arthur Chesterman
133 Palenell Park, East Sheen, London SW14 8JJ
t 020 8876 5421 **f** 020 8255 9099 **m** 07768 828954
e arthur@soundsgreat.org.uk **w** www.soundsgreat.org.uk
Credits Natural Wonders Of The World (M); A Little Bit Of Blanc (M); The Nash
Ensemble At Wigmire Hall (M); London Music Masterclasses (M)

Chris Corner
100 Monkseaton Drive, Whitley Bay NE26 3DJ
t 01912 790769 **f** 01912 790769 **m** 07798 687322
e corner@globalnet.co.uk
Credits Gloria (M); Spy Game (F)

Alex Christison
68 Seward Road, Badsey, Evesham WR11 7HQ
t 01386 830367 **f** 01386 830367 **m** 07767 200022
e christison@bigfoot.com

Murray Clarke
The Corner House, 28 St Michaels Close, Ashby-de-la-Zouch
LE65 1ES
t 01530 563521 **f** 01530 563524 **m** 07973 345115
e murray.clarke@virgin.net

Classic Sound Ltd
5 Falcon Park Industrial Estate, Neasden Lane, London NW10 1RZ
t 020 8208 8100 **f** 020 8208 8111
e classicsound@dial.pipex.com **w** www.classicsound.net

Clive Cowan Recording (CCR)
27 Stirling Avenue, Leigh-on-Sea SS9 3PP
t 01702 460451 **m** 07625 397858 **e** info@ccr.euromarques.com
Contact Clive Cowan MIBS
Credits TOF Watch - Organon Laboratories (E); Rise And Shine - Orange
Telecom (I); Hail The Chief (D); Service Training - Royal Bank of Scotland (I)

John Coates
254 Breedon Street, Long Eaton, Nottingham NG10 4FD
t 01159 722385 **f** 01158 497285 **m** 07850 255 365
e john.coates6@ntlworld.com
Credits Peak Practice (T); Twenty Four Seven (T); Soldier Soldier (T)

Keith Conlon
24 Tweedale Wharf, Madeley, Telford TF7 4EW
t 01952 581150 **f** 01952 581150 **m** 07831 511875
e keith.conlon@virgin.net
Credits UB40 (M); The Waiting (F); Chasing The Deer (F); Bargain Hunt (T)

Tom Cooke
Callbox Communications Limited, 66 Shepperton Studios,
Studios Road, Shepperton TW17 0QD
t 01932 592572 **f** 01932 569655 **m** 07710 572572
e callboxdiary@btinternet.com **w** www.callboxdiary.co.uk

Mike Cooper
Suz Cruz, Halliford Studios, Manygate Lane, Shepperton TW17 9EG
t 01932 252577 **f** 01932 253323 **m** 07956 485593
e zoe@suzcruz.co.uk **w** www.suzcruz.co.uk

Clive Copland
116 Mortlake Road, Kew, Richmond TW9 4AR
t 020 8876 3728 **f** 020 8876 3728 **m** 07956 374623
e clive@coplandsound.fsnet.co.uk
Agent EXEC, 6 Travis Court, Farnham Royal SL2 3SB
t 01753 646677 **f** 01753 646770
e sue@execmanagement.co.uk **w** www.execmanagement.co.uk
Credits Hound of the Baskervilles (F); Rockface II (T); In the Beginning (F);
Fidel! (F)

Alan Cridford
Carlin Crew Ltd, Shepperton Studios, Studios Road, Shepperton TW17 0QD
t 01932 568268 **f** 01932 571109
e carlin@netcomuk.co.uk **w** www.carlincrew.com

Phil Croal
Castleview, Hawthornden, Lasswade EH18 1EJ
t 0131 440 2335 **m** 07836 786335 **e** philcroal@ednit.co.uk
Credits Monarch Of The Glen (T)

Alistair Crocker
Creative Media Management, Unit 3B, Walpole Court, Ealing Studios, Ealing Green, London W5 5ED
t 020 8584 5363 **f** 020 8566 5554
e enquiries@creativemediamanagement.com
Credits Servants (T); Octane (F); The Full Monty (F)

John Crossland
17 Titchwell Road, Wandsworth, London SW18 3LW
t 020 8874 5401 **f** 020 8870 9470 **m** 07973 216253
e earsok@aol.com

Alun Curnock
TOVS Ltd, The Linen Hall, 162-168 Regent Street, London W1B 5TB
t 020 7287 6110 **f** 020 7287 5481
e info@tovs.co.uk **w** www.tovs.co.uk

Tom Curry
Flat 4, Ashton Court, 11 Elmwood Road, London SE24 9NU
t 020 7733 7654 **m** 07976 271287 **e** tomcurry@easynet.co.uk
Agent Stella's Diary, 9 Hormead Road, London W9 3NG
t 020 8969 1855 **f** 020 8964 2157 **m** 07976 271287
e stella'sdiary@btinternet.com

Peter Davey
TOVS Ltd, The Linen Hall, 162-168 Regent Street, London W1B 5TB
t 020 782 6110 **f** 020 7287 5481
e info@tovs.co.uk **w** www.tovs.co.uk

David Holmes Production Ltd
5 Sutton Avenue, Langley, Slough SL3 7AP
t 01753 537105 **f** 01753 537105 **m** 07836 234740
e info@dave-holmes.co.uk **w** www.dave-holmes.co.uk
Contact David Holmes, Director
Credits Malta Tourist Board (C); Connect For Better Business (I); Children In Need (T)

Malcolm Davies
69 Ivy Green Drive, Oldham OL4 4PR
t 0161 622 0155 **f** 0161 622 0166 **m** 07973 159320
e malcolm@manxmoviesound.com **w** www.manxmoviesound.com
Agent Gems, The Media House, 87 Glebe Street, Penarth CF64 1EF
t 029 2071 0770 **f** 029 2071 0771
e gems@gems-agency.co.uk **w** www.gems-agency.co.uk
Credits Dangerous Obsession (T); 16 Years Of Alcohol (F); Esther Kahn (F)

Julian Dawton
95 Birchtree Avenue, West Wickham BR4 9EQ
t 020 8462 6371 **m** 07860 777687
Agent Linkline, 6 Thirlmere Gardens, Wembley HA9 8RE
t 020 8908 6262 **f** 020 8904 5179
e mail@linklinecrew.com **w** www.linklinecrew.com

Giancarlo Dellapina
210 Gipsy Road, London SE27 9RB
t 020 8655 7303 **m** 07785 572229
Agent Linkline, 6 Thirlmere Gardens, Wembley HA9 8RE
t 020 8908 6262 **f** 020 8904 5179
e mail@linklinecrew.com **w** www.linklinecrew.com

Clive Derbyshire
International Creative Management Ltd, Oxford House, 76 Oxford Street, London W1D 1BS
t 020 7636 6565 **f** 020 7323 0101 **w** www.icmlondon.co.uk
Credits A Dance To The Music Of Time (T); RKO 281 (T); LD50 (F)

Bill Dodkin
42 Highwood Avenue, Bushey WD23 2AL
t 01923 241943 **f** 01923 241974 **m** 07774 923202
e billdodkin@ukonline.com.uk
Credits Mrs Caldicot's Cabbage War (F); Messiah II (T); Wire In The Blood (T); Dead Romantic (T)

Mike Donald
Suz Cruz, Halliford Studios, Manygate Lane, Shepperton TW17 9EG
t 01932 252577 **f** 01932 253323 **m** 07956 485593
e zoe@suzcruz.co.uk **w** www.suzcruz.co.uk

Doug Dreger
120 Maidstone Road, London N11 2JP
m 07778 917931
Agent Linkline, 6 Thirlmere Gardens, Wembley HA9 8RE
t 020 8908 6262 **f** 020 8904 5179
e mail@linklinecrew.com **w** www.linklinecrew.com

Roy Drysdale
Experience Counts - Call Me Ltd, 5th Floor, 41-42 Berners Street, London W1P 3AA
t 020 7637 8112 **f** 020 7580 2582

Richard Eades
22 Gransden Avenue, Hackney, London E8 3QA
t 020 8985 6305 **m** 07774 184570
Agent Linkline, 6 Thirlmere Gardens, Wembley HA9 8RE
t 020 8908 6262 **f** 020 8904 5179
e mail@linklinecrew.com **w** www.linklinecrew.com

Keith Edwards
8 Victoria Avenue, Porthcawl, Bridgend CF36 3HG
t 01656 782227 **m** 07774 459693
e kedwards@tvsound.freeserve.co.uk

Peter Edwards
t 0118 973 2268 **f** 0118 977 6400 **m** 07831 550850
e info@bcafilm.co.uk **w** www.bcafilm.co.uk

Russell Edwards
12A Hatchard Road, Archway, London N19 4NH
t 020 7272 6210 **m** 07768 124082
Agent Linkline, 6 Thirlmere Gardens, Wembley HA9 8RE
t 020 8908 6262 **f** 020 8904 5179
e mail@linklinecrew.com **w** www.linklinecrew.com

Eddie Elmhirst
49 Yarmouth Road, Thorpe St Andrew, Norwich NR7 0EW
t 01603 433189 **f** 01603 433189 **m** 07976 555563
e edmund.elmhirst@btopenworld.com
Credits Survival (D); BBC Natural History (D)

Terry Elms
Coombe Bury, 10 Drakes Close, Esher KT10 8PQ
t 01372 465903 **f** 01372 465903 **m** 07710 073513
Credits Ella And The Mothers (T); Goodbye Mr Steadman (T); The Cazalets (T); Jonathan Creek IV (T)

Bradley Elster
20 Regency Court, Park Close, London E9 7TP
t 020 8533 0387 **m** 07976 353442
Agent Linkline, 6 Thirlmere Gardens, Wembley HA9 8RE
t 020 8908 6262 **f** 020 8904 5179
e mail@linklinecrew.com **w** www.linklinecrew.com

Mikkel Eriksen
London
t 020 7388 9609 **m** 07950 260078
e info@twoears.co.uk **w** www.twoears.co.uk
Credits Dance Of The Vampire; Toni's War (D)

Russell Erskine
Callbox Communications Limited, 66 Shepperton Studios, Shepperton TW17 0QD
t 01932 592572 **f** 01932 569655 **m** 07710 572572
e callboxdiary@btinternet.com **w** www.callboxdiary.co.uk

David Ferguson
t 07932 023016 **e** locationsound@btopenworld.com
Credits Nation's Favourite Foods (D); Oasis - Songbird (M); The South Bank Show (T)

Renato Ferrari
28 College Road, Isleworth TW7 5DW
t 020 8560 7726 **m** 07973 550802
Agent Linkline, 6 Thirlmere Gardens, Wembley HA9 8RE
t 020 8908 6262 **f** 020 8904 5179
e mail@linklinecrew.com **w** www.linklinecrew.com

Tim Fraser
Agent Suz Cruz, Halliford Studios, Manygate Lane, Shepperton TW17 9EG
t 01932 252577 **f** 01932 253323 **m** 07956 485593
e zoe@suzcruz.co.uk **w** www.suzcruz.co.uk
Agent International Creative Management Ltd, Oxford House, 76 Oxford Street, London W1D 1BS
t 020 7636 6565 **f** 020 7323 0101 **w** www.icmlondon.co.uk
Credits Topsy Turvy (F); Cheeky (F); Calendar Girls (F)

Lee Gabriel
Grade One TV & Film Personnel, Elstree Studios, Shenley Road, Borehamwood WD6 1JG
t 020 8324 2224 **f** 020 8324 2328
e gradeone.tvpersonnel@virgin.net

Carl Gardiner
TOVS Ltd, The Linen Hall, 162-168 Regent Street, London W1B 5TB
t 020 7287 6110 **f** 020 7287 5481
e info@tovs.co.uk **w** www.tovs.co.uk

Ron Garson
12 Michael Close, Maidenhead SL6 4PD
t 01628 784789 **m** 07836 536044
Agent Linkline, 6 Thirlmere Gardens, Wembley HA9 8RE
t 020 8908 6262 **f** 020 8904 5179
e mail@linklinecrew.com **w** www.linklinecrew.com

Pete Gaudino
Suz Cruz, Halliford Studios, Manygate Lane, Shepperton TW17 9EG
t 01932 252577 **f** 01932 253323 **m** 07956 485593
e zoe@suzcruz.co.uk **w** www.suzcruz.co.uk

Andrew Gaze
43 Roseberry Gardens, Haringey, London N4 1JQ
t 020 8802 6784 **f** 020 8802 6784 **m** 07973 762013
Agent Stella's Diary, 9 Hormead Road, London W9 3NG
t 020 8969 1855 **f** 020 8964 2157 **m** 07973 762013
e stella'sdiary@btinternet.com

Mervyn Gerrard
Seaton Cottage, West Common, Gerrards Cross SL9 7RE
t 01753 889077 **m** 07860 742491 **e** hilaryt@compuserve.com
Agent Linkline, 6 Thirlmere Gardens, Wembley HA9 8RE
t 020 8908 6262 **f** 020 8904 5179
e mail@linklinecrew.com **w** www.linklinecrew.com
Credits Behind Closed Doors (T); Stig (T); Bad Girls (T)

Nick Giammetta
Connections, The Meadlands, Oakleigh Road, Hatch End, Pinner HA5 4HB
t 020 8420 1444 **f** 020 8428 5836 **m** 07831 305518
e mail@connectionsuk.com **w** www.connectionsuk.com

Tom Gibb
15A Spencer Park, Wandsworth, London SW18 2SY
t 020 8870 5983 **m** 07931 743313
Agent Linkline, 6 Thirlmere Gardens, Wembley HA9 8RE
t 020 8908 6262 **f** 020 8904 5179
e mail@linklinecrew.com **w** www.linklinecrew.com

Andrew Gleed
1 Pinels Way, Cressex, High Wycombe HP11 1TU
t 01494 451487 **f** 01494 451487 **m** 07956 287716
Credits Homefront: Inside Out (T); Countryfile (T); Backchat (T); Movie Nights (T)

Andy Glendinning
1B Wood End Gardens, Northolt UB5 4QH
t 020 8423 0575 **m** 07831 180893

Glowing Productions Inc
25 Nutleigh Grove, Hitchin SG5 2NH
t 07796 990962 **e** samswinglehurst@aol.com
Contact Samantha Swinglehurst
Credits BBC Education (T); The Score (T); Jail Break (T)

Goldcrest Post Production Facilities
36-44 Brewer Street, London W1F 9LX
t 020 7437 7972 **f** 020 7437 5402 **m** 07836 204283
e mailbox@goldcrest-post.co.uk
Contact Poppy Quinn, Bookings and Customer Services Manager; Raju Raymond, General Manager

Nic Grant
11 Holeyn Hall Road, Wylam NE41 8BB
t 01661 853513 **f** 01661 852152 **m** 07711 368604
e nic@nicsound.co.uk **w** www.nicsound.co.uk
Credits Emmerdale (T); Catherine Cookson (T); Aston Martin (C); Badger (T)

Brian Gray
42 Evelyn Road, Crookes, Sheffield S10 5FF
t 0114 266 6145 **f** 0114 266 6145 **m** 07956 654366
e brian@mosaicstudio.co.uk
w www.mosaicstudio.co.uk/location.shtml
Credits Pet Rescue (T); Baby Blues (F); Anatomy Of A Crime (T)

Al Green
Carlin Crew Ltd, Shepperton Studios, Studios Road, Shepperton TW17 0QD
t 01932 568268 **f** 01932 571109
e carlin@netcomuk.co.uk **w** www.carlincrew.com

Robin Green
Carlin Crew Ltd, Shepperton Studios, Studios Road, Shepperton TW17 0QD
t 01932 568268 **f** 01932 571109
e carlin@netcomuk.co.uk **w** www.carlincrew.com

Brian Greene
Experience Counts - Call Me Ltd, 5th Floor, 41-42 Berners Street, London W1P 3AA
t 020 7637 8112 **f** 020 7580 2582

Jim Greenhorn
International Creative Management Ltd, Oxford House, 76 Oxford Street, London W1D 1BS
t 020 7636 6565 **f** 020 7323 0101 **w** www.icmlondon.co.uk
Credits Iris (F); Last Orders (F); Bright Young Things (F)

Andrew Griffin
Carlin Crew Ltd, Shepperton Studios, Studios Road, Shepperton TW17 0QD
t 01932 568268 **f** 01932 571109
e carlin@netcomuk.co.uk **w** www.carlincrew.com

David Hall
Stockport
m 07973 385746 **e** david@dhsound.co.uk
Credits Linda Green (T); When Louis Met Jimmy (T); The League Of Gentlemen (T); Clocking Off (T)

Paul Hardy
Stella's Diary, 9 Hormead Road, London W9 3NG
t 020 8969 1855 **f** 020 8964 2157 **m** 07958 611099
e stella'sdiary@btinternet.com

Collins Harper
6 Bela Grove, Blackpool FY1 5JZ
t 01253 698921 **f** 01253 698921 **m** 07976 429844
e collins@chtv.freeserve.co.uk **w** www.chtv.freeserve.co.uk
Contact Collins Harper
Credits Richard And Judy (T); NTL (T); Tonight With Trevor McDonald (T); GMTV (T)

Ed Harris
TOVS Ltd, The Linen Hall, 162-168 Regent Street, London W1B 5TB
t 020 7287 6110 **f** 020 7287 5481
e info@tovs.co.uk **w** www.tovs.co.uk

Marc Hatch
28 Talbot Road, London W2 5LJ
t 020 8747 8741 **f** 07000 785821 **m** 07885 219402
e marc.hatch@mjhltd.freeserve.co.uk
Credits History Of Britain (T); Duty Beyond Call (S); The Tour (D)

Jeff Hawkins
7 Cherry Hill, St Albans AL2 3AT
t 01727 865932 **m** 07973 865309
Agent Linkline, 6 Thirlmere Gardens, Wembley HA9 8RE
t 020 8908 6262 **f** 020 8904 5179
e mail@linklinecrew.com **w** www.linklinecrew.com

Andy Hawley
10 Sherwill Close, Ivybridge PL21 9UW
t 01752 896696 **f** 01752 896696 **m** 07977 422543
e andy@thesoundbloke.freeserve.co.uk
Credits Countryfile (T); Big Cat Diary (T); Vets In Practice (T); Really Wild Show (T)

Allan Haynes
Dogwood House, Hall Moor Road, Hingham NR9 4LB
f 01953 851003 **m** 07774 806486 **e** dogwood@supanet.com
Credits Adnam's Beer (C); Ted's Tractors (D); PD James' Inspector Dalgliesh (T); Poldark (T)

Judi Headman
Grade One TV & Film Personnel, Elstree Studios, Shenley Road, Borehamwood WD6 1JG
t 020 8324 2224 **f** 020 8324 2328
e gradeone.tvpersonnel@virgin.net

Paul Hellard
Carlin Crew Ltd, Shepperton Studios, Studios Road, Shepperton TW17 0QD
t 01932 568268 **f** 01932 571109
e carlin@netcomuk.co.uk **w** www.carlincrew.com

Stephen Higgs
18 Balmoral Gardens, London W13 9UA
t 020 8567 4213 **f** 020 8567 2220
Credits Dangerfield (T); Casuality Series XIV & XV (T)

Bob Hill
Connections, The Meadlands, Oakleigh Road, Hatch End, Pinner HA5 4HB
t 020 8420 1444 **f** 020 8428 5836 **m** 07831 305518
e mail@connectionsuk.com **w** www.connectionsuk.com

Maurice Hillier
Creative Media Management, Unit 3B, Walpole Court, Ealing Studios, Ealing Green, London W5 5ED
t 020 8584 5363 **f** 020 8566 5554
e enquiries@creativemediamanagement.com
Credits New Tricks (T); The Stratosphere Girl (T); Love Again (T)

Andy Hoare
7B Ferme Park Road, Stroud Green, London N4 4DS
t 020 8374 8518 **f** 020 8374 8518 **m** 07970 070198
e andyhoare@locationrecording.co.uk
w www.locationrecording.co.uk
Contact Andrew Hoare, Sound Recordist
Credits Wasted (D); Perfect Match (T); Holiday Airport (D)

Mark Holding
McKinney Macartney Management Ltd, The Barley Mow Centre, 10 Barley Mow Passage, London W4 4PH
t 020 8995 4747 **f** 020 8995 2414
e fkb@mmtechsrep.demon.co.uk
w www.mckinneymacartney.com

John Hooper
Allington, Howards Lane, Addlestone KT15 1EX
t 01932 841116 **f** 01932 841116 **m** 07850 690049
e john.hooper@btinternet.com
Credits Oscar Charlie (T); Grange Hill (T); Miami 7 (T)

Jon Hose
Suz Cruz, Halliford Studios, Manygate Lane, Shepperton TW17 9EG
t 01932 252577 **f** 01932 253323 **m** 07956 485593
e zoe@suzcruz.co.uk **w** www.suzcruz.co.uk

Dick Hunt
Callbox Communications Limited, 66 Shepperton Studios, Shepperton TW17 0QD
t 01932 592572 **f** 01932 569655 **m** 07710 572572
e callboxdiary@btinternet.com **w** www.callboxdiary.co.uk

Tim Hunt
44 Hamilton Road, Southville, Bristol BS3 1PB
t 0117 966 8377 **m** 07774 232894
Agent Linkline, 6 Thirlmere Gardens, Wembley HA9 8RE
t 020 8908 6262 **f** 020 8904 5179
e mail@linklinecrew.com **w** www.linklinecrew.com

Dushko Indjic
Bookends, 83 Maynard Drive, St Albans AL1 2JX
t 01727 841177 **e** bookgold@bookends.fsbusiness.co.uk

Rupert Ivey
Creative Media Management, Unit 3B, Walpole Court, Ealing Studios, Ealing Green, London W5 5ED
t 020 8584 5363 **f** 020 8566 5554
e enquiries@creativemediamanagement.com
Credits Phoenix Blue (T); An Ideal Husband (T)

Martin Jackson
14 Willow Road, Thame OX9 3BE
t 01844 215415 **m** 07785 313455
Agent Linkline, 6 Thirlmere Gardens, Wembley HA9 8RE
t 020 8908 6262 **f** 020 8904 5179
e mail@linklinecrew.com **w** www.linklinecrew.com

Matthew Jackson
Callbox Communications Limited, 66 Shepperton Studios, Shepperton TW17 0QD
t 01932 592572 **f** 01932 569655 **m** 07710 572572
e callboxdiary@btinternet.com **w** www.callboxdiary.co.uk

Grayson James
Connections, The Meadlands, Oakleigh Road, Hatch End, Pinner HA5 4HB
t 020 8420 1444 **f** 020 8428 5836 **m** 07831 305518
e mail@connectionsuk.com **w** www.connectionsuk.com

Mark Jelbert
40B Hungerford Road, London N7 9LP
t 020 7607 7060 **m** 07050 117041
Agent Linkline, 6 Thirlmere Gardens, Wembley HA9 8RE
t 020 8908 6262 **f** 020 8904 5179
e mail@linklinecrew.com **w** www.linklinecrew.com

Mark Jenvey
11 Carleton Road, London N7 0QZ
t 020 7607 5977 **m** 07970 104272 **e** mark.jenvey@which.net

Robbie Johnson
217A Lordship Lane, London SE22 8JF
m 07740 422816 **e** robfewster@hotmail.com

Roger A Johnson
21 Church Garth Pemberton Gardens, London N19 5RN
t 020 7263 6466 **f** 020 7263 6466 **m** 07774 490480
e roger.a.johnson@btinternet.com

Peter Jones
17 Broadfields, East Molesey KT8 0BW
t 020 8398 5274 **m** 07973 909911
Agent Linkline, 6 Thirlmere Gardens, Wembley HA9 8RE
t 020 8908 6262 **f** 020 8904 5179
e mail@linklinecrew.com **w** www.linklinecrew.com

Simon Jones
30 Pimlico Road, Clitheroe BB7 2AH
t 01200 442245 **f** 01200 442245 **m** 07973 625665
e simon.jones@capelinmedia.co.uk **w** www.capelinmedia.co.uk

Steve Jones
Westfield Studios, Grubbs Lane, Essendon, Hatfield AL9 6EF
t 01707 644620 **f** 01707 664805 **m** 07778 963522
e tilbyjones@btopenworld.com
Credits BBC Digital Launch Idents (C); South Bank Show (T); Whickers World; Hollywood Women

Zoë Jordan
114D Fordwych Road, London NW2 3NL
t 020 8450 4440 **f** 020 8450 4440 **m** 07813 108176
e zoej@soundgirl.fsbusiness.co.uk
Credits Phat Phuc (T); Anything Is Happening (S); Have Sex Today (S); The Crucible (S)

Christian Joyce
EXEC, 6 Travis Court, Farnham Royal SL2 3SB
t 01753 646677 **f** 01753 646770
e sue@execmanagement.co.uk **w** www.execmanagement.co.uk

Dave Keene
Suz Cruz, Halliford Studios, Manygate Lane, Shepperton TW17 9EG
t 01932 252577 **f** 01932 253323 **m** 07956 485593
e zoe@suzcruz.co.uk **w** www.suzcruz.co.uk

Ron Keightley
Connections, The Meadlands, Oakleigh Road, Hatch End, Pinner HA5 4HB
t 020 8420 1444 **f** 020 8428 5836 **m** 07831 305518
e mail@connectionsuk.com **w** www.connectionsuk.com

Paul Kennedy
North Barn, Oasby, Grantham NG32 3NB
t 01529 455717 **f** 01529 455717 **m** 07976 438502
e paul@oasbybarn.co.uk **w** www.oasbybarn.com
Credits Massacre In Luxol (D); JK Rowling - Omnibus Special (D); Imagine (D); Empire (D)

James Kenning
16 Glebe Road, Warlingham CR6 9NJ
t 01883 625912 **m** 07710 146350
Agent Linkline, 6 Thirlmere Gardens, Wembley HA9 8RE
t 020 8908 6262 **f** 020 8904 5179
e mail@linklinecrew.com **w** www.linklinecrew.com

Paul Keyworth
56A Highbury Hill, London N5 1AD
t 020 7359 1388 **f** 020 7359 1388 **m** 07956 839425
e paul.keyworth@lineone.net **w** www.paulkeyworth.co.uk
Credits The Plantsman (T); Dream Spaces (T); Winter Flying Gardener (T); Tony And Georgio (T)

Chris King
Gems, The Media House, 87 Glebe Street, Penarth CF64 1EF
t 029 2071 0770 **f** 029 2071 0771
e gems@gems-agency.co.uk **w** www.gems-agency.co.uk
Credits Miss USSR (D); Comrades (F); Making Babies (D); Great Railway Journeys - Ben Okri (D)

Louis Kramer
48 Orchard Court, Orchard Park Avenue, Thornliebank, Glasgow G46 7BL
t 0141 638 2433 **f** 0141 638 2433 **m** 07980 920908
e louiskramer@onetel.net.uk
Agent Gems, The Media House, 87 Glebe Street, Penarth CF64 1EF
t 029 2071 0770 **f** 029 2071 0771
e gems@gems-agency.co.uk **w** www.gems-agency.co.uk
Credits The Book Group Series II (T); Regeneration (F); Gregory's Two Girls (F); Late Night Shopping (F)

Ashok-Kumar Kumar
2 Bouverie Road, Harrow HA1 4EZ
t 020 8537 2205 **f** 020 8537 2205 **m** 07973 728 131
Agent Gems, The Media House, 87 Glebe Street, Penarth CF64 1EF
t 029 2071 0770 **f** 029 2071 0771
e gems@gems-agency.co.uk **w** www.gems-agency.co.uk
Credits The One (T); Family Affairs (T); Green Fingers (F); The Honey Trap (F)

David Lascelles
9 Leigh Road, Cobham KT11 2LF
t 01932 868370 **m** 07850 674173
Agent Linkline, 6 Thirlmere Gardens, Wembley HA9 8RE
t 020 8908 6262 **f** 020 8904 5179
e mail@linklinecrew.com **w** www.linklinecrew.com

Grant Lawson
4C Southcombe Street, London W14 0RA
t 020 7602 2910 **m** 07768 778178
Agent Linkline, 6 Thirlmere Gardens, Wembley HA9 8RE
t 020 8908 6262 **f** 020 8904 5179
e mail@linklinecrew.com **w** www.linklinecrew.com

Chris Lebert
22 Grove Court, 37-39 The Drive, Hove BN3 3JG
t 01273 770770 **m** 07860 118163 **e** lebert@madasafish.com
Credits What Not To Wear (T); Beast Of The Amazon (D); Driven (T)

Pete Lee
Flat 4, 25 Uxbridge Road, Kingston-upon-Thames, London KT1 2LH
t 020 8408 2900 **m** 07974 416788 **e** pete.lee@bigfoot.com

Edward Leetham
44 Marsh Lane, Nantwich CW5 5LH
t 01270 625125 **f** 01270 629424 **m** 07976 215152
e edd@downstream.ltd.uk
Credits Horizon (T); Crimewatch (T); T Mobile (C); The 51st State (F)

Bill Lewis
5 Churchyard Cottages, Barden Road, Speldhurst, Tunbridge Wells TN3 0PS
t 01892 863776 **m** 07768 514324
Agent Linkline, 6 Thirlmere Gardens, Wembley HA9 8RE
t 020 8908 6262 **f** 020 8904 5179
e mail@linklinecrew.com **w** www.linklinecrew.com

Andy Lilley
Grade One TV & Film Personnel, Elstree Studios, Shenley Road, Borehamwood WD6 1JG
t 020 8324 2224 **f** 020 8324 2328
e gradeone.tvpersonnel@virgin.net

David Lindsay
23 Park Road, Twickenham TW1 2QD
t 020 8892 2956 **f** 020 8892 2956 **m** 07831 315 643
e davidlindsay@clara.co.uk
Credits Prometheus (F); Faking It - Drag Queen (T); Dove (C); Alfred Brendel At 70 (D)

Peter Lindsay
International Creative Management Ltd, Oxford House,
76 Oxford Street, London W1D 1BS
t 020 7636 6565 **f** 020 7323 0101 **w** www.icmlondon.co.uk
Credits The Beach (F); Captain Corelli's Mandolin (F); Johnny English (F)

Steve Linsey
62 Ryecroft Avenue, Whitton TW26 8NR
t 020 8898 1969 **m** 07973 666740
Agent Linkline, 6 Thirlmere Gardens, Wembley HA9 8RE
t 020 8908 6262 **f** 020 8904 5179
e mail@linklinecrew.com **w** www.linklinecrew.com

Roger Lucas
Thorny Lee Farm, Combs, High Peak SK23 9UT
t 01298 812467 **f** 01298 812467 **m** 07966 204605
e lucas@care4free.net
Credits Who Killed Simone Valentine (T); Battlefield Detectives (D); Secrets Of
The Dead (D)

Paul Lydon
Grade One TV & Film Personnel, Elstree Studios, Shenley
Road, Borehamwood WD6 1JG
t 020 8324 2224 **f** 020 8324 2328
e gradeone.tvpersonnel@virgin.net

Oliver Machin
Stella's Diary, 9 Hormead Road, London W9 3NG
t 020 8969 1855 **f** 020 8964 2157 **m** 07876 804924
e stella'sdiary@btinternet.com

Colin Macnab
14B Leven Terrace, Edinburgh EH3 9LW
t 0131 228 5646 **f** 0131 228 5646 **m** 07850 327614
e zerolevel@blueyonder.co.uk

Iain Macrae
Grade One TV & Film Personnel, Elstree Studios, Shenley
Road, Borehamwood WD6 1JG
t 020 8324 2224 **f** 020 8324 2328
e gradeone.tvpersonnel@virgin.net

Karl Madert
160 Kennington Park Road, London SE11 4DJ
t 020 7582 2370 **m** 07973 419167
Agent Linkline, 6 Thirlmere Gardens, Wembley HA9 8RE
t 020 8908 6262 **f** 020 8904 5179
e mail@linklinecrew.com **w** www.linklinecrew.com

Richard Manton
53 Trowley Hill Road, Flamstead AL3 8DL
t 01582 840552 **f** 01582 849030 **m** 07771 765942
e r_manton@yahoo.co.uk
Credits Our Mutual Friend (T); Shooting The Past; The Project (T); Great
Expectations (T)

Adam Margetts
Carlin Crew Ltd, Shepperton Studios, Studios Road,
Shepperton TW17 0QD
t 01932 568268 **f** 01932 571109
e carlin@netcomuk.co.uk **w** www.carlincrew.com

Scott Marshall
Bookends, 83 Maynard Drive, St Albans AL1 2JX
t 01727 841177 **e** bookgold@bookends.fsbusiness.co.uk

Mel Mason
165 Brookhill Road, London SE8 4JH
t 020 8265 2035 **m** 07930 361791
Agent Linkline, 6 Thirlmere Gardens, Wembley HA9 8RE
t 020 8908 6262 **f** 020 8904 5179
e mail@linklinecrew.com **w** www.linklinecrew.com

Richard Mason
Grade One TV & Film Personnel, Elstree Studios, Shenley
Road, Borehamwood WD6 1JG
t 020 8324 2224 **f** 020 8324 2328
e gradeone.tvpersonnel@virgin.net

Jeff Matthews
Gems, The Media House, 87 Glebe Street, Penarth CF64 1EF
t 029 2071 0770 **f** 029 2071 0771
e gems@gems-agency.co.uk **w** www.gems-agency.co.uk
Credits Belonging (T); Daisies In December (F); The Theory Of Flight (F);
Chameleon (F)

Chris McDermott
Suz Cruz, Halliford Studios, Manygate Lane, Shepperton TW17 9EG
t 01932 252577 **f** 01932 253323 **m** 07956 485593
e zoe@suzcruz.co.uk **w** www.suzcruz.co.uk

Kiff McManus
11 Dorchester Road, Weybridge KT13 8PG
t 01932 853538 **m** 07973 228584
Agent Linkline, 6 Thirlmere Gardens, Wembley HA9 8RE
t 020 8908 6262 **f** 020 8904 5179
e mail@linklinecrew.com **w** www.linklinecrew.com

George McMillan
218 Devonshire Road, London SE23 3TQ
t 020 8291 0894 **m** 07977 522294 **e** scotchegg25@hotmail.com
Credits Holiday: You Call The Shots (T); Without Predujice (T); Holiday (T)

Phil Middleham (MIBS)
Barton Farmhouse, Welford Road, Barton B50 4NP
t 01789 490356 **f** 01789 490353 **m** 07836 654066
e phil@pmiddleham.freeserve.co.uk
w www.pmiddleham.freeserve.co.uk
Credits Cardiff Singer Of the World (T); Top Gear (T); Antiques Roadshow (T)

Steve Middleton
3 Back Lane, Hardingstone, Northampton NN4 6BX
f 01604 661830 **m** 07770 275727 **e** steve@stevemiddleton.com
Credits Peugeot (I); Royal Trilogy (T); Pulling Power (T); Bargain Hunt (T)

John Midgley
Creative Media Management, Unit 3B, Walpole Court, Ealing
Studios, Ealing Green, London W5 5ED
t 020 8584 5363 **f** 020 8566 5554
e enquiries@creativemediamanagement.com
Credits The Importance Of Being Earnest (F); Enigma (F); Star Wars: Episode I -
The Phantom Menace (F); Harry Potter And The Philosopher's Stone (F)

Henry Milliner
t 01273 737086 **m** 07790 905475
e henrymilliner@soundrecording.freeserve.co.uk
Credits SAS Jungle, Are You Tough Enough? (T); Blue Peter (T); Is Harry On The
Boat (T); Changing Rooms (T)

Max Mills
Grade One TV & Film Personnel, Elstree Studios, Shenley
Road, Borehamwood WD6 1JG
t 020 8324 2224 **f** 020 8324 2328
e gradeone.tvpersonnel@virgin.net

Mary Milton
3 Pembery Road, Bedminster, Bristol BS3 3JR
t 0117 909 3306 **f** 0117 909 3366 **m** 07974 729064
e mary@marymilton.co.uk **w** www.marymilton.co.uk
Credits Mrs Rosenarne - The Queen Of Camborne (D); The Day I'll Never Forget
(D); Gaea Girls (D); Runaway (F)

George Mitchell
32 Craighirst Road, Milngavie, Glasgow G62 7RG
t 0141 956 6753 **f** 0141 956 1785 **m** 07813 859422
e geo.mitchell@btinternet.com
Credits Frontline Scotland (T); River City (T)

Jonathan Mitchell
Carlin Crew Ltd, Shepperton Studios, Studios Road,
Shepperton TW17 0QD
t 01932 568268 **f** 01932 571109
e carlin@netcomuk.co.uk **w** www.carlincrew.com

Mr J Moon
45 Scotland Road, Nottingham NG5 1JU
t 0115 978 7745
e john@realsound.fsnet.co.uk **w** www.realsound-uk.com

John Mooney
EXEC, 6 Travis Court, Farnham Royal SL2 3SB
t 01753 646677 **f** 01753 646770
e sue@execmanagement.co.uk **w** www.execmanagement.co.uk

Mario Mooney
EXEC, 6 Travis Court, Farnham Royal SL2 3SB
t 01753 646677 **f** 01753 646770
e sue@execmanagement.co.uk **w** www.execmanagement.co.uk

Gary Moore
Basement Flat, 9 Burlington Street, Bath BA1 2SA
t 01225 484212 **m** 07879 497 218 **e** gary.moore@pgen.net
Agent TOVS Ltd, The Linen Hall, 162-168 Regents Street,
London W1B 5TB
t 020 7287 6110 **f** 020 7287 5481
e info@tovs.co.uk **w** www.tovs.co.uk

Trevor Moore
179B Hammersmiths Grove, London W6 0NL
m 07958 762579 **e** therevtrev@hotmail.com

David WB Morgan
'Kielder', Y Pare, Groes-Faen, Pontyclun CF72 8NP
t 029 2089 0564 **f** 029 2089 0565
m 07770 890564 **e** dwbmorgan@aol.com

Robert Moro
Connections, The Meadlands, Oakleigh Road, Hatch End,
Pinner HA5 4HB
t 020 8420 1444 **f** 020 8428 5836 **m** 07831 305518
e mail@connectionsuk.com **w** www.connectionsuk.com

Peter Moscrop
21 Greenacres, Penclawdd, Swansea SA4 3GD
t 01792 850046 **m** 07889 487285

Stuart Moser
20 Copperkins Lane, Amersham HP6 5QF
t 01494 726785 **f** 01494 723925 **m** 07050 126981
e stuart.moser@talk21.com
Agent Gems, The Media House, 87 Glebe Street, Penarth
CF64 1EF
t 029 2071 0770 **f** 029 2071 0771
e gems@gems-agency.co.uk **w** www.gems-agency.co.uk
Credits Murder In Mind (T); Messiah (T); Rock Face (T); The Feast Of July (F)

Richard Munns
28 Charcroft Court, Westwick Gardens, West Kensington,
London W14 0BX
t 020 7603 5644 **m** 07771 758605
Agent Linkline, 6 Thirlmere Gardens, Wembley HA9 8RE
t 020 8908 6262 **f** 020 8904 5179
e mail@linklinecrew.com **w** www.linklinecrew.com

Chris Munro
EXEC, 6 Travis Court, Farnham Royal SL2 3SB
t 01753 646677 **f** 01753 646770
e sue@execmanagement.co.uk **w** www.execmanagement.co.uk

Ian Munro
EXEC, 6 Travis Court, Farnham Royal SL2 3SB
t 01753 646677 **f** 01753 646770
e sue@execmanagement.co.uk **w** www.execmanagement.co.uk

Paul Nathan
Suz Cruz, Halliford Studios, Manygate Lane, Shepperton TW17 9EG
t 01932 252577 **f** 01932 253323 **m** 07956 485593
e zoe@suzcruz.co.uk **w** www.suzcruz.co.uk

Annie Needham
Flat 5, 14 Boundaries Road, Balham, London SW12 8EX
t 020 8265 0778 **m** 07971 077616
Agent Linkline, 6 Thirlmere Gardens, Wembley HA9 8RE
t 020 8908 6262 **f** 020 8904 5179
e mail@linklinecrew.com **w** www.linklinecrew.com

Bob Newton
St Barnabas Old School, Ranmore Common, Dorking RH5 6SP
t 01306 886598 **f** 01306 886598 **m** 07850 331811
Agent Linkline, 6 Thirlmere Gardens, Wembley HA9 8RE
t 020 8908 6262 **f** 020 8904 5179
e mail@linklinecrew.com **w** www.linklinecrew.com

Howie Nicol
Suz Cruz, Halliford Studios, Manygate Lane, Shepperton TW17 9EG
t 01932 252577 **f** 01932 253323 **m** 07956 485593
e zoe@suzcruz.co.uk **w** www.suzcruz.co.uk

Colin Nicolson
International Creative Management Ltd, Oxford House,
76 Oxford Street, London W1D 1BS
t 020 7636 6565 **f** 020 7323 0101 **w** www.icmlondon.co.uk
Credits Still Crazy (F); The Magdalene Sisters (F); Once Upon A Time In
The Midlands (F)

Ninth Wave Audio
PO Box 5517, Birmingham B13 8QW
t 0121 442 2276 **f** 0121 689 1902 **m** 07770 364464
e ninthwave@blueyonder.co.uk

Keith Nixon
Grade One TV & Film Personnel, Elstree Studios, Shenley
Road, Borehamwood WD6 1JG
t 020 8324 2224 **f** 020 8324 2328
e gradeone.tvpersonnel@virgin.net

Derek Norman
Creative Media Management, Unit 3B, Walpole Court, Ealing
Studios, Ealing Green, London W5 5ED
t 020 8584 5363 **f** 020 8566 5554
e enquiries@creativemediamanagement.com
Credits Insiders (T); Strange (F); Ali G Indahouse (F)

Alan O'Duffy
39 Cambridge Drive, Potters Bar EN6 3ET
t 01707 653545 **f** 01707 663963 **m** 07973 728733
e soundman@oduffy.com **w** www.alanoduffy.com
Agent Callbox Communications Limited, 66 Shepperton
Studios, Shepperton TW17 0QD
t 01932 592572 **f** 01932 569655 **m** 07710 572572
e callboxdiary@btinternet.com **w** www.callboxdiary.co.uk
Agent Gems, The Media House, 87 Glebe Street,
Penarth CF64 1EF
t 029 2071 0770 **f** 029 2071 0771
e gems@gems-agency.co.uk **w** www.gems-agency.co.uk
Credits Merseybeat (T); Me Without You (F); Three Blind Mice (F); Devil's Gate (F)

Sean O'Malley
Grade One TV & Film Personnel, Elstree Studios, Shenley
Road, Borehamwood WD6 1JG
t 020 8324 2224 **f** 020 8324 2328
e gradeone.tvpersonnel@virgin.net

Simon Okin
McKinney Macartney Management Ltd, The Barley Mow
Centre, 10 Barley Mow Passage, London W4 4PH
t 020 8995 4747 **f** 020 8995 2414
e fkb@mmtechsrep.demon.co.uk **w** www.mckinneymacartney.com

Mark Owen
Grade One TV & Film Personnel, Elstree Studios, Shenley Road, Borehamwood WD6 1JG
t 020 8324 2224 **f** 020 8324 2328
e gradeone.tvpersonnel@virgin.net

Bob Owens
TOVS Ltd, The Linen Hall, 162-168 Regent Street, London W1B 5TB
t 020 7287 6110 **f** 020 7287 5481
e info@tovs.co.uk **w** www.tovs.co.uk

Paul Paragon
19 New Park Lane, Aston SG2 7ED
t 01438 880737 **m** 07973 222967
Agent Linkline, 6 Thirlmere Gardens, Wembley HA9 8RE
t 020 8908 6262 **f** 020 8904 5179
e mail@linklinecrew.com **w** www.linklinecrew.com

Simon Parmenter
14 Grove Gardens, Teddington TW11 8AP
t 020 8977 3454 **f** 020 8977 3225 **m** 07973 305189
e sparmenter@clara.net

Dick Philip
84 Courtland Grove, Thamesmead, London SE28 8PD
t 020 8311 5517 **m** 07711 553160
Agent Linkline, 6 Thirlmere Gardens, Wembley HA9 8RE
t 020 8908 6262 **f** 020 8904 5179
e mail@linklinecrew.com **w** www.linklinecrew.com

Matt Phillips
Flat3, 28 Park Hill, London W5 2JN
t 020 8810 5181 **m** 07968 971112 **e** matt@phillips01.fslife.co.uk
Agent Stella's Diary, 9 Hormead Road, London W9 3NG
t 020 8969 1855 **f** 020 8964 2157 **m** 07958 762579
e stella'sdiary@btinternet.com

Steven Phillips
9A Hillyfields Crescent, London SE4 1QA
m 07831 575214 **e** steve.phillips@ukf.net
Agent International Creative Management Ltd, Oxford House, 76 Oxford Street, London W1D 1BS
t 020 7636 6565 **f** 020 7323 0101 **w** www.icmlondon.co.uk
Credits The Commander (T); North Square (T); This Life (T); Anna Karenina (T)

Steve Picco
Grade One TV & Film Personnel, Elstree Studios, Shenley Road, Borehamwood WD6 1JG
t 020 8324 2224 **f** 020 8324 2328
e gradeone.tvpersonnel@virgin.net

Lucy Pickering
Flat 1, 12 Milton Road, London SE24 0NP
t 020 7501 9753 **m** 07976 287953
Agent Linkline, 6 Thirlmere Gardens, Wembley HA9 8RE
t 020 8908 6262 **f** 020 8904 5179
e mail@linklinecrew.com **w** www.linklinecrew.com

Simon Pinkerton
136B Anerly Road, London SE20 8DL
t 020 8776 6569 **m** 07831 252972
Agent Linkline, 6 Thirlmere Gardens, Wembley HA9 8RE
t 020 8908 6262 **f** 020 8904 5179
e mail@linklinecrew.com **w** www.linklinecrew.com

Charles Pitt
t 01249 462374 **f** 01249 462374 **m** 07836 343046
Credits Peter Kay (T); Hollyoaks (T); Brookside (T); Casualty (T)

Brian Powell
63 Chester Terrace, Brighton BN1 6GB
t 01273 565600 **m** 07850 100091
Agent Linkline, 6 Thirlmere Gardens, Wembley HA9 8RE
t 020 8908 6262 **f** 020 8904 5179
e mail@linklinecrew.com **w** www.linklinecrew.com

Nick Pratt
Grade One TV & Film Personnel, Elstree Studios, Shenley Road, Borehamwood WD6 1JG
t 020 8324 2224 **f** 020 8324 2328
e gradeone.tvpersonnel@virgin.net

Adam Prescod
16 Spezia Road, London NW10 4OJ
t 020 8965 1125 **m** 07836 623368
Agent Linkline, 6 Thirlmere Gardens, Wembley HA9 8RE
t 020 8908 6262 **f** 020 8904 5179
e mail@linklinecrew.com **w** www.linklinecrew.com

Graham Price
Ironclad, Benbow Waye, Moorings, Cowley UB8 2HD
t 01895 273653 **m** 07932 222551
Agent Suz Cruz, Halliford Studios, Manygate Lane, Shepperton TW17 9EG
t 01932 252577 **f** 01932 253323 **m** 07956 485593
e zoe@suzcruz.co.uk **w** www.suzcruz.co.uk

Jeff Price
Suz Cruz, Halliford Studios, Manygate Lane, Shepperton TW17 9EG
t 01932 252577 **f** 01932 253323 **m** 07956 485593
e zoe@suzcruz.co.uk **w** www.suzcruz.co.uk

Darren Pyke
Grade One TV & Film Personnel, Elstree Studios, Shenley Road, Borehamwood WD6 1JG
t 020 8324 2224 **f** 020 8324 2328
e gradeone.tvpersonnel@virgin.net

Billy Quinn
124 Richmond Park Road, Kingston KT2 6AJ
t 020 8546 7761 **f** 020 8546 7761 **m** 07812 604562
e billy.quinn@btinternet.com
Agent Stella's Diary, 9 Hormead Road, London W9 3NG
t 020 8969 1855 **f** 020 8964 2157 **m** 07812 604564
e stella'sdiary@btinternet.com
Credits Pick Up (F); Clap Le Monde (F); History Of The Novel (T)

Patrick Quirke
Gems, The Media House, 87 Glebe Street, Penarth CF64 1EF
t 029 2071 0770 **f** 029 2071 0771
e gems@gems-agency.co.uk **w** www.gems-agency.co.uk
Credits The Scold's Bridle (T); The Blonde Bombshell (F); Beech Is Back (T); Jeffrey Archer - The Truth (T)

Chris Renty
42 Langler Road, London NW10 5TL
t 020 8969 4484 **m** 07966 141366
Agent Linkline, 6 Thirlmere Gardens, Wembley HA9 8RE
t 020 8908 6262 **f** 020 8904 5179
e mail@linklinecrew.com **w** www.linklinecrew.com

George Richards
103 Elderfeild Road, London E5 0LE
t 01453 884775 **m** 07876 080504
e george@ukrecordist.co.uk **w** www.ukrecordist.co.uk
Credits I'll Sleep When I'm Dead (F); There's Only One Jimmy Grimble (F); Secrets and Lies (F)

Ian Richardson
Menai, Romilly Road, Cardiff CF5 1FH
t 029 2022 1938 **f** 029 2031 8346 **m** 07973 263784
e ian@filmsound.co.uk **w** www.filmsound.co.uk
Credits Tomorrow La Scala (F); The I Inside (F); Alone (F)

Adam Rickets
Grade One TV & Film Personnel, Elstree Studios, Shenley Road, Borehamwood WD6 1JG
t 020 8324 2224 **f** 020 8324 2328
e gradeone.tvpersonnel@virgin.net

Graig Rihoy
Flat 2, 240A Amhurst Road, London N1 7UL
t 020 7503 5068 m 07930 530325
e craigrihoy@yahoo.co.uk
Credits Hoxton Sings (D); Bury It (S); Second Generation (F); Inbetweeners (F)

Vaughan Roberts
The Old Bakehouse, 4 North Street, Marcham, Abingdon OX13 6NG
t 01865 392086 m 07887 504654
e robertsfamily@compuserve.com
Agent Callbox Communications Limited, 66 Shepperton Studios, Shepperton TW17 0QD
t 01932 592572 f 01932 569655 m 07710 572572
e callboxdiary@btinternet.com w www.callboxdiary.co.uk
Credits EastEnders (T); ITV - ITN (T); ITV Football (T); Panorama (T)

Nick Robertson
Suz Cruz, Halliford Studios, Manygate Lane, Shepperton TW17 9EG
t 01932 252577 f 01932 253323 m 07956 485593
e zoe@suzcruz.co.uk w www.suzcruz.co.uk

John Rodda
The Close, Great Somerford SN15 5JG
t 01249 720515 f 01249 720815 m 07785 504606
e jr@jrsound.com w www.jrsound.com
Credits The Lost Prince (T); Longitude (T); Dirty Pretty Things (F); 28 Days Later (F)

Keith Rodgerson
10 Leigh Road, Bristol BS8 2DA
t 0117 973 3848 f 0117 923 7791 m 07970 623262
e krbristol@ntlworld.com w www.keithrodgerson.com

Mike 'Golly' Russell
21 Bycullah Avenue, Enfield EN2 8DN
t 020 8367 8109 f 020 8367 8109 m 07990 503045
e mike@golly-russell.demon.co.uk
Agent Stella's Diary, 9 Hormead Road, London W9 3NG
t 020 8969 1855 f 020 8964 2157 m 07990 503045
e stella'sdiary@btinternet.com
Credits The Lives Of Animals (T); Endangered Species (F); Endangered Species (C); Den Of Lions (F)

Peter Sainsbury
Holly Tree House, Shoreheath Lane, Sulhamstead, Reading RG7 4EG
t 0118 983 2483 f 0118 983 5445 m 07973 271621
e peter.sainsbury@tesco.net
Credits Royal Navy Flight Safety Film (I); Leonardo (T); Shark! Beyond The Jaws (D)

Guy Satchwell
C/o Fyffe, 18 Kirk Street, Edinburgh EH6 5EZ
m 07050 353 913 e gsa@freeuk.com

Mike Savage AMPS, MIBS, MBKS
Manor Farmhouse, Stibbard Road, Fulmodestone, Fakenham NR21 0LX
t 01328 829353 f 01328 829741 m 07860 344311
e savagesound@aol.com w www.spotonsound.netfirms.com
Credits Summit 2002 (I); History Of Sex And Love With Terry Jones (T); I Love 70's/80's/90's (D); The Stringer (F)

Andy Shakallis
4 Hartfield Crescent, Wimbledon SW19 3SD
t 020 8544 0903 m 07802 584528
Agent Linkline, 6 Thirlmere Gardens, Wembley HA9 8RE
t 020 8908 6262 f 020 8904 5179
e mail@linklinecrew.com w www.linklinecrew.com

Stewart Shape
17 Northend, Bath Easton, Bath BA1 7EE
m 07970 792031
Agent Stella's Diary, 9 Hormead Road, London W9 3NG
t 020 8969 1855 f 020 8964 2157 m 07970 792031
e stella'sdiary@btinternet.com

Pasha Shilov
Bookends, 83 Maynard Drive, St Albans AL1 2JX
t 01727 841177 e bookgold@bookends.fsbusiness.co.uk

Mike Shoring
Cerring, Angel Mountain West, Newport SA42 0SR
t 01348 811382
Credits Dance Of The Dead (M); Jefferson In Paris (F); Howards End (F)

Mario Sierra
31 Stansfield Road, London SW9 9RY
f 020 7738 5151 m 07711 167637 e mario_sierra@yahoo.com
Agent Stella's Diary, 9 Hormead Road, London W9 3NG
t 020 8969 1855 f 020 8964 2157 m 07711 167637
e stella'sdiary@btinternet.com

Brian Simmons
EXEC, 6 Travis Court, Farnham Royal SL2 3SB
t 01753 646677 f 01753 646770
e sue@execmanagement.co.uk w www.execmanagement.co.uk

Rick Simon
Grade One TV & Film Personnel, Elstree Studios, Shenley Road, Borehamwood WD6 1JG
t 020 8324 2224 f 020 8324 2328
e gradeone.tvpersonnel@virgin.net

Andrew Sissons
Holywell, 58 Craigwell Avenue, Radlett WD7 7EY
t 01923 852146 m 07976 897883
Agent Linkline, 6 Thirlmere Gardens, Wembley HA9 8RE
t 020 8908 6262 f 020 8904 5179
e mail@linklinecrew.com w www.linklinecrew.com

Mark Skinner
TOVS Ltd, The Linen Hall, 162-168 Regent Street, London W1B 5TB
t 020 7287 6110 f 020 7287 5481
e info@tovs.co.uk w www.tovs.co.uk

Sounds Pro
4 Goss Barton, Kingsgrove, Nailsea BS48 2XD
t 01275 858156 m 07050 098093
e mikebird@soundspro.com w www.soundspro.com
Contact Mike Bird
Credits Casualty (T); Make My Day (T)

Soundscape Productions
108 Mearns Road, Clarkston, Glasgow G76 7UP
t 0141 638 3620 m 07860 216308
Contact Stuart Gillan, Sound Recordist/Mixer

Michael Spencer
Creative Media Management, Unit 3B, Walpole Court, Ealing Studios, Ealing Green, London W5 5ED
t 020 8584 5363 f 020 8566 5554
e enquiries@creativemediamanagement.com
Credits Roger Roger (T); Serious And Organised (T); Silent Witness (T)

Eva Springer
Callbox Communications Limited, 66 Shepperton Studios, Shepperton TW17 0QD
t 01932 592572 f 01932 569655 m 07710 572572
e callboxdiary@btinternet.com w www.callboxdiary.co.uk

Gary Staddard
Stella's Diary, 9 Hormead Road, London W9 3NG
t 020 8969 1855 f 020 8964 2157 m 07970 667937
e stella'sdiary@btinternet.com

Gary Stadden
28 Belmont Road, Kensington Park, Brislington, Bristol BS4 3PB
t 0117 904 4545 m 07970 667937
e info@garystadden.com w www.garystadden.com
Credits 30 Years Of Glastonbury (F); Living in Hope (F); Perfect Partner (T)

Roger Stamp
Experience Counts - Call Me Ltd, 5th Floor, 41-42 Berners Street, London W1P 3AA
t 020 7637 8112 **f** 020 7580 2582

Chris Stanway
61 The Rutts, Bushey Heath WD2 1LN
t 020 8950 1423 **m** 07973 119217
Agent Linkline, 6 Thirlmere Gardens, Wembley HA9 8RE
t 020 8908 6262 **f** 020 8904 5179
e mail@linklinecrew.com **w** www.linklinecrew.com

Sam Staples
6 Brendon Villas, Highfield Road, London N21 3HP
m 07976 903854
Agent Linkline, 6 Thirlmere Gardens, Wembley HA9 8RE
t 020 8908 6262 **f** 020 8904 5179
e mail@linklinecrew.com **w** www.linklinecrew.com

David Stephenson
11 The Avenue, Chobham GU24 8RU
t 01276 857036 **f** 01276 857757 **m** 07885 639332
e dasmix@aol.com
Credits Love Actually (F); The Good Thief (F); My House In Umbria (F); The Gathering Storm (T)

Mike Stephenson
Carlin Crew Ltd, Shepperton Studios, Studios Road, Shepperton TW17 0QD
t 01932 568268 **f** 01932 571109
e carlin@netcomuk.co.uk **w** www.carlincrew.com

Peter Stoddart
Experience Counts - Call Me Ltd, 5th Floor, 41-42 Berners Street, London W1P 3AA
t 020 7637 8112 **f** 020 7580 2582

Dave Stonestreet
Connections, The Meadlands, Oakleigh Road, Hatch End, Pinner HA5 4HB
t 020 8420 1444 **f** 020 8428 5836 **m** 07831 305518
e mail@connectionsuk.com **w** www.connectionsuk.com

Mark Swinglehurst
Grade One TV & Film Personnel, Elstree Studios, Shenley Road, Borehamwood WD6 1JG
t 020 8324 2224 **f** 020 8324 2328
e gradeone.tvpersonnel@virgin.net

Chris Syner
38 Drummond Road, Guildford GU1 4NT
t 01438 458120 **m** 07831 514410
Agent Linkline, 6 Thirlmere Gardens, Wembley HA9 8RE
t 020 8908 6262 **f** 020 8904 5179
e mail@linklinecrew.com **w** www.linklinecrew.com

Tango Romeo Ltd
209 Lascelles Hall Road, Huddersfield HD5 0BQ
t 01484 535006 **f** 01484 301966 **m** 07836 583422
e terry@tangoromeo.tv
Contact Terry Ricketts, Managing Director
Credits People of the Year Awards 2001 (T); British Superbikes 2001 (T); Premier League 2001/2002 (T)

Alan Taylor
TOVS Ltd, The Linen Hall, 162-168 Regent Street, London W1B 5TB
t 020 7287 6110 **f** 020 7287 5481
e info@tovs.co.uk **w** www.tovs.co.uk

John Taylor
30A Elers Road, Ealing, London W13 9QD
t 020 8840 1543 **e** johntaylorsound@aol.com
Agent International Creative Management Ltd, Oxford House, 76 Oxford Street, London W1D 1BS
t 020 7636 6565 **f** 020 7323 0101 **w** www.icmlondon.co.uk
Credits Bodily Harm (T); Daniel Deronda (T); Second Generation (T); Byron (T)

Yvonne Teacher
Connections, The Meadlands, Oakleigh Road, Hatch End, Pinner HA5 4HB
t 020 8420 1444 **f** 020 8428 5836 **m** 07831 305518
e mail@connectionsuk.com **w** www.connectionsuk.com

Nick J Thermes
3F2, 30 Polwarth Crescent, Edinburgh EH11 1HN
t 0131 228 1299 **f** 0131 228 1299 **m** 07836 233531
e nick@soundmixer.biz **w** www.soundmixer.biz
Credits Pasty Faces (F); Driving School; SAS Jungle, Are You Tough Enough? (T); Dog Soldiers (F)

Deke Thompson
34 Bellevue, Bangor BT20 5QW
t 028 9146 2204 **m** 07860 724135
e deke@dnet.co.uk **w** www.deke.info
Credits Ulster Orchestra

Helen Thompson
Suz Cruz, Halliford Studios, Manygate Lane, Shepperton TW17 9EG
t 01932 252577 **f** 01932 253323 **m** 07956 485593
e zoe@suzcruz.co.uk **w** www.suzcruz.co.uk

Graham Tobin
Grade One TV & Film Personnel, Elstree Studios, Shenley Road, Borehamwood WD6 1JG
t 020 8324 2224 **f** 020 8324 2328
e gradeone.tvpersonnel@virgin.net

Geoff Tookey
Connections, The Meadlands, Oakleigh Road, Hatch End, Pinner HA5 4HB
t 020 8420 1444 **f** 020 8428 5836 **m** 07831 305518
e mail@connectionsuk.com **w** www.connectionsuk.com

Will Towers
Carlin Crew Ltd, Shepperton Studios, Studios Road, Shepperton TW17 0QD
t 01932 568268 **f** 01932 571109
e carlin@netcomuk.co.uk **w** www.carlincrew.com

Martin Trevis
40 Wellington Road, Sandhurst GU47 9AY
t 01344 771511 **f** 01344 771511 **m** 07798 766171
e trevis@web-hq.com **w** www.trevis58.freeserve.co.uk
Credits Sons And Lovers (T); Mathilde (F); Anita And Me (F); The Heart Of Me (F)

Damian Turner
Grade One TV & Film Personnel, Elstree Studios, Shenley Road, Borehamwood WD6 1JG
t 020 8324 2224 **f** 020 8324 2328
e gradeone.tvpersonnel@virgin.net

Video Sound Services Ltd
11 Earls Road, Tunbridge Wells TN4 8EE
t 01892 530932 **t** 01622 630773
f 01892 526974 **m** 07973 831786
e sound@vssltd.demon.co.uk **w** www.vssltd.demon.co.uk
Contact Robert Edwards, Director; Ian Rosam, Director
Credits Premiership And World Cup Football (T); Des And Mel (T); Pop Idol (T); City Hospital (T)

Ian Voigt
McKinney Macartney Management Ltd, The Barley Mow Centre, 10 Barley Mow Passage, London W4 4PH
t 020 8995 4747 **f** 020 8995 2414
e fkb@mmtechsrep.demon.co.uk **w** www.mckinneymacartney.com

Richard Walcott
TOVS Ltd, The Linen Hall, 162-168 Regent Street, London W1B 5TB
t 020 7287 6110 **f** 020 7287 5481
e info@tovs.co.uk **w** www.tovs.co.uk

Chris Walker
106A Forest Road, Hackney, London E8 3BH
t 020 7683 0944 **m** 07768 288054
Agent Linkline, 6 Thirlmere Gardens, Wembley HA9 8RE
t 020 8908 6262 **f** 020 8904 5179
e mail@linklinecrew.com **w** www.linklinecrew.com

Michael Walker
133 Rhydpenau Road, Cyncoed, Cardiff CF23 6PZ
t 029 2076 4400 **m** 07831 623733 **e** mjwalk@ntlworld.com
Credits Tomorrow's World (T); Top Gear (T); Antiques Roadshow (T)

Christian Wangler
Creative Media Management, Unit 3B, Walpole Court, Ealing
Studios, Ealing Green, London W5 5ED
t 020 8584 5363 **f** 020 8566 5554
e enquiries@creativemediamanagement.com
Credits Two Brothers (F); East Is East (F)

Simon Ware
Northminster, Tuesley Lane, Godalming GU7 1SN
t 01483 421524 **m** 07768 734333
Agent Linkline, 6 Thirlmere Gardens, Wembley HA9 8RE
t 020 8908 6262 **f** 020 8904 5179
e mail@linklinecrew.com **w** www.linklinecrew.com

Mark Wellman
15 St Margarets, Creekmoor, Poole BH15 2DL
t 01202 658029 **m** 07971 011510 **e** markywellman@aol.com
Agent Stella's Diary, 9 Hormead Road, London W9 3NG
t 020 8969 1855 **f** 020 8964 2157 **m** 07971 011510
e stella'sdiary@btinternet.com

Gil Wells
2 Norfolk Rd, Brighton BN1 3AA
m 07810 698011 **e** chris@theagency.co.uk
Credits Amazing Race (T); Watchdog (T); Gillette World Sport Special (T);
Tomorrow's World (T)

Bruce White
137 Henry Doulton Drive, Tooting, London SW17 6DF
t 020 8682 2069 **f** 020 8682 2069 **m** 07768 403584
e brucewhite@clara.co.uk
Agent Gems, The Media House, 87 Glebe Street,
Penarth CF64 1EF
t 029 2071 0770 **f** 029 2071 0771
e gems@gems-agency.co.uk **w** www.gems-agency.co.uk
Credits Goodnight Mister Tom (T); Fortysomething (T); I Am David (F); The Swap (T)

Joff White
TOVS Ltd, The Linen Hall, 162-168 Regent Street, London W1B 5TB
t 020 7287 6110 **f** 020 7287 5481
e info@tovs.co.uk **w** www.tovs.co.uk

Steve Whitford
4 Bramble Hill, Chandlers Ford SO53 4TP
t 023 8026 6186 **m** 07973 168761
Agent Linkline, 6 Thirlmere Gardens, Wembley HA9 8RE
t 020 8908 6262 **f** 020 8904 5179
e mail@linklinecrew.com **w** www.linklinecrew.com

Katy Willett
Ganders Neck, Clun Road, Knighton LD7 1NE
t 01547 520328 **e** borderline@altword.com

Kevin Williams
Membury, Stry Isa, Hope LL12 9PT
t 01978 761959 **f** 01978 761959 **m** 07774 109622
e kbaal@care4free.net
Credits Sky Boxing (T); Grand Designs (T); Watercolours Challenge (T)

Mike Williams
88 Grove Road, London W7 3ES
t 020 8762 9799 **m** 07867 530149
Agent Linkline, 6 Thirlmere Gardens, Wembley HA9 8RE
t 020 8908 6262 **f** 020 8904 5179
e mail@linklinecrew.com **w** www.linklinecrew.com

Bruce Wills
International Creative Management Ltd, Oxford House,
76 Oxford Street, London W1D 1BS
t 020 7636 6565 **f** 020 7323 0101 **w** www.icmlondon.co.uk
Credits The Candelstine Marriage (F); Vanity Fair (T); Zhivago (T)

Martin Wilson
51 Bath Road, Atworth SN12 8JY
t 01225 708917 **m** 07813 609044
Agent Linkline, 6 Thirlmere Gardens, Wembley HA9 8RE
t 020 8908 6262 **f** 020 8904 5179
e mail@linklinecrew.com **w** www.linklinecrew.com

Jan Wisnieswski
9 Parkside Gardens, Winchester SO22 5NA
t 01962 849163 **m** 07860 336005 **e** jan@wisniewski.to
Agent Grade One TV & Film Personnel, Elstree Studios,
Shenley Road, Borehamwood WD6 1JG
t 020 8324 2224 **f** 020 8324 2328
e gradeone.tvpersonnel@virgin.net
Credits Chained (T); Playdays (T); Pet Rescue (T)

Wizard House Media Services
26 Blenheim Road, Bristol BS6 7JP
t 0117 974 3430 **f** 0117 974 3595 **m** 07785 575733
e mail@wizardhouse.org.uk **w** www.wizardhouse.org.uk
Contact John Wilson, Sound Recordist
Credits Commonwealth Games (T); Choir Of The Year (T); 200 Year House (D);
Murder Most Foul (D)

Ben 'Woody' Woodgate
TOVS Ltd, The Linen Hall, 162-168 Regent Street, London W1B 5TB
t 020 7287 6110 **f** 020 7287 5481
e info@tovs.co.uk **w** www.tovs.co.uk

Peter Woods
Blue Cedars, The Ballands North, Fetcham KT22 9HU
t 01372 378362 **m** 07774 607217
Agent Linkline, 6 Thirlmere Gardens, Wembley HA9 8RE
t 020 8908 6262 **f** 020 8904 5179
e mail@linklinecrew.com **w** www.linklinecrew.com

Anthony Wornum
t 020 8944 7221 **m** 07973 728125 **w** www.wornum.co.uk
Credits Omnibus (T); Seeing Salvation (T); Timewatch (T)

Tim Worth
12 The Garth, Hampton Hill TW12 1SR
t 020 8979 0773 **m** 07956 331320
Agent Linkline, 6 Thirlmere Gardens, Wembley HA9 8RE
t 020 8908 6262 **f** 020 8904 5179
e mail@linklinecrew.com **w** www.linklinecrew.com

Chris Wright
119B Tufnell Park Road, London N7 0PS
t 020 8373 1160 **m** 07930 557022
Agent Linkline, 6 Thirlmere Gardens, Wembley HA9 8RE
t 020 8908 6262 **f** 020 8904 5179
e mail@linklinecrew.com **w** www.linklinecrew.com

Jonathan Wyatt
EXEC, 6 Travis Court, Farnham Royal SL2 3SB
t 01753 646677 **f** 01753 646770
e sue@execmanagement.co.uk **w** www.execmanagement.co.uk

Paul Zanders

47 Carew Court, Basinghill Gardens, Sutton SM2 6AS
t 020 8643 1734 **m** 07768 501678
Agent Linkline, 6 Thirlmere Gardens, Wembley HA9 8RE
t 020 8908 6262 **f** 020 8904 5179
e mail@linklinecrew.com **w** www.linklinecrew.com

SPECIAL EFFECTS

Special Effects Designers

Peter Akass

The Keepers Cottage, Kerrow, Cannick
t 01456 415398 **f** 01456 415207 **m** 07747 616165
e www.earthwindfirefx@aol.com
Credits Balamory (T); Taggart (T); Strictly Sinatra (F); Monach of the Glen (T)

Jonathan Angell

2 Vicarage Cottages, Iford, Lewes BN7 3EJ
t 01273 479021 **f** 07970 039362 **m** 07973 220 023
e jonathanangell@lineone.net
w www.jonathanangell.com, www.jonathanangell.co.uk
Credits Sounds Of Thunder (F); Sleepy Hollow (F); First Knight: The Gauntlet Machine (F); Band Of Brothers (T)

Arcadia Models & Effects

9 Fairway Close, Park Street, St Albans AL2 2QX
t 07778 934954 **f** 01727 872352
Contact Alexander Gunn, Supervisor
Credits Lost In Space (F); Hidalgo (F); Dr Zhivago (T); Band Of Brothers (T)

Artem Special Effects

Perivale Park, Horsenden Lane South, Perivale UB6 7RH
t 020 8997 7771 **f** 020 8997 1503
e info@artem.com **w** www.artem.com
Contact Mike Kelt, Managing Director

BBC Special Effects

BBC Special Effects

Kendal Avenue, London W3 0RP
t 020 8993 9434 **f** 020 8993 8741
e special.effects@bbc.co.uk
w www.bbcresources.com/specialeffects

Bickers Action

Ivy Farm Works, High Street, Coddenham, Ipswich IP6 9QX
t 01449 761300 **f** 01449 760614
m 07831 132009 **m** 07836 606291
e action@bickers.co.uk **w** www.bickers.co.uk
Contact Paul Bickers, Managing Director; Dean Cox, Operations Manager
Credits Emmerdale (T); Cold Play - Scientist (M); Heartbeat (T); Die Another Day (F)

Stunt Engineering, Mechanical SFX, Camera Tracking Vehicles & Low Loaders.

Bob Smoke Special Effects

Epsilon Building, Walmgate Road, London WB6 7LR
t 020 8998 2000 **f** 020 8998 3393 **m** 07956 963742
e bobsmokefx@supanet.com
Contact Bob Smoke, Managing Director; Scott Peters, Technician
Credits Popstars (T); Carphone Warehouse (C); Shoreditch (F); Born Romantic (F)

Steve Bowman

41-44 Kendal Avenue W3 0RP
t 020 8993 9441 **f** 020 8993 8741 **m** 07973 719837
e steve.bowman@bbc.co.uk
w www.resources.gateway.bbc.co.uk/cvs/
Credits Lenny Henry In Pieces (T); They Think It's All Over (T); The Cruise Of The Gods (T)

Perry Brahan

t 01494 774321 **f** 01494 775432 **m** 07973 132 647
e perryb.asd@btinternet.com

Stuart Brisdon

t 020 8746 1056 **f** 020 8743 5715 **m** 07860 682 066
Credits Gosford Park (F); The Hours (F)

Chris Corbould

Firtree Farm, 101 Woodlands Road, Little Bookham KT23 4HN
t 01372 454088 **f** 01372 454088 **m** 07802 657318
e chriscorbould@aol.com
Credits Die Another Day (F); The Mummy (F); The World Is Not Enough (F)

David Harris Special Effects

Allwood, Perks Lane, Prestwood, Great Missenden HP16 0JG
t 01494 864713 **f** 01494 890344 **m** 07831 227005
e davidharrisspfx@compuserve.com
Contact Judith Harris, Special Effects Co-ordinator & Technician; David Harris, Special Effects Supervisor
Credits Rob Roy (F); Legionnaire (F); Gangster No 1 (F); Harry Potter And The Chamber Of Secrets (F)

Definitive Special Projects Ltd

PO Box 169, Ardeley, Stevenage SG2 7SG
t 01438 869005 **f** 01438 869006
e info@laserlightshows.co.uk **w** www.laserlightshows.co.uk
Contact Stephen Hitchins, Managing Director
Credits We Will Rock You; Raymond Gubbay Classical Spectaculars

The Especial Effects Company

86 Woodhurst Avenue, Pettswood BR5 1AT
t 07000 433332 **f** 01689 837251 **m** 07074 744 539
e espfx@specialeffects.uk.com **w** www.specialeffects.uk.com
Contact Phil Anderson, SFX Designer
Credits Scilent Witness, Inspector Morse, Murder Rooms; Murder Rooms II (T); Shooters (F); Robbie Williams 2001 Stadium Tour

Melvyn Friend

61 Manor Park Road, East Finchley, London N2 0SN
t 020 8993 9434 **f** 020 8993 8741 **m** 07973 719 986
e melvyn_friend@hotmail.com
Credits Egyptian Empire (T); Black Books (T); Casualty (T); Comic Relief-Nessie (T)

George Gibbs

7 Lammas Court, Windsor SL4 3ED
t 01753 853856 **f** 01753 853856 **m** 07885 430 100
e ggibbs2000@aol.com **w** www.filmtrickery.com
Credits The Man In The Iron Mask (F); Indiana Jones And The Last Crusade (F); 101 Dalmations (F); From Hell (F)

Indiwell Productions Ltd

Indiwell Farm, Swimbridge, Barnstable EX32 0PY
t 01271 830027 **f** 01271 831378
e info@indiwellproductions.co.uk **w** www.indiwell.co.uk
Credits Blue Planet Live (T); Proms In The Park (T)

Jamie Campbell Models & SPFX
77A St John's Wood High Street, London NW8 7NL
t 020 7722 0017 **f** 020 7722 1779 **m** 07932 153723
Contact Jamie Campbell, Art Director
Credits Animatronics And Industrial Design (C); Walking With Dinosaurs (T); Walking With Beasts (T)

Keith Edwards - Special Effects
14 Leaholme Gardens, Burnham SL1 6LD
t 01628 603024 **m** 07973 623118 **e** keith-edwards@beeb.net
Credits The World's Strongest Man (T); Children In Need (T); CBBC Roadshows (T); Blue Peter (T)

Kit West Productions
2 Albany Close, East Sheen, London SW14 7DX
t 020 8878 6745 **f** 020 8392 2948 **m** 07957 420247
e kitwestspfx@aol.com
Contact Kit West, Company Director
Credits Around The World In 80 Days (2003) (F); Ali (F); Blackdog (F); Enemy At The Gates (F)

Laser Creations International
55 Merthyr Terrace, London SW13 8DL
t 020 8741 5747 **f** 020 8748 9879
e contact@lci-uk.com **w** www.lci-uk.com
Contact Marlyn Weeks, Managing Director

Steve Lucas
t 020 8993 9434 **f** 020 8993 8741 **m** 07973 625782
e steve.lucas@bbc.co.uk
Credits French And Saunders (T); The League Of Gentlemen (T); Blackball (F)

The Matte Studios
43 Manor Way, London SE3 9XG
t 020 8852 7553 **f** 020 8852 7553 **m** 07947 420001
e replicapaintings@hotmail.com

Andy McVean
G14 Park Weston, 41-44 Kendal Avenue, Acton W3 0RP
t 020 8993 9442 **f** 020 8993 8741 **m** 07973 720305
Credits Jet Set (T); Comic Relief (C)

Peter Kersey Special Effects
Woodview, 5 Gurnells Road, Seer Green HP9 2XJ
t 01494 675087 **f** 01494 675087 **m** 07973 640688
e peter.kersey@ukgateway.net
Credits Ultimate Force II (T); Murder In Mind (T); Jonathan Creek (T); Midsomer Murders (T)

Special Effects **Facilities**

Airzone Events Ltd
The Stables, Lychgate Green, Titchfield, Fareham PO14 3LL
t 01329 665842 **f** 01329 511150 **m** 07973 891335
e email@airzoneevents.com **w** www.airzoneevents.com
Contact Berny Maginn

Any Effects
64 Weir Road, London SW19 8UG
t 020 8944 0099 **f** 020 8944 6989
e info@anyeffects.com **w** www.anyeffects.com
Contact Jules Pellici, Company Coordinator
Credits The Importance Of Being Earnest (F); Horatio Hornblower II (T); London's Burning (T)

Bristol UK Ltd (TM Products)
12 The Arches, Maygrove Road, London NW6 2DS
t 020 7624 4370 **f** 020 7372 5242 **m** 07802 874338
e tech.sales@bristolpaint.com **w** www.bristolpaint.com
Contact Mark Chapman, Director
Credits Ella Enchanted (F); Shanghai Knights (F); Harry Potter And The Chamber Of Secrets (F); Die Another Day (F)

Digitalia
6A Poland Street, London W1F 8PT
t 020 7287 9920 **f** 020 7287 9930
e info@digitalia.co.uk **w** www.digitalia.co.uk
Contact Heidi Wyithe, Producer
Credits Akasha Ganga (F); Hibbert Ralph (C); B-Boy Championship (T); What A Girl Wants (F)

Effects Associates
Pinewood Studios, Pinewood Road, Iver Heath SL0 0NH
t 01753 652007 **f** 01753 630127
e ea@effectsassociates.co.uk **w** www.cinesite.com
Contact Tim Field, General Manager; Carmila Gittens, Production Manager
Credits Underworld (F); Hellboy (F); Thunderbirds (F); Heartbeat (T)

Emergency House SFX
Manchester Road, Marsden, Huddersfield HD7 6EY
t 01484 846999 **f** 01484 845061 **m** 07836 674360
e sfx@emergencyhouse.com **w** www.emergencyhouse.com
Contact Evan Green-Hughes, Senior SFX Supervisor
Credits Wilbur Wants To Kill Himself (F); Wire In The Blood (T); A Touch Of Frost (T); My Kingdom (F)

Framestore CFC
9 Noel Street, London W1F 8GH
t 020 7208 2600 **f** 020 7208 2626
e info@framestore-cfc.com **w** www.framestore.com
Contact Andy Welsh; Stephanie Bruning
Credits Wrigley's: Dog Breath (C); Xbox Mosquito" (C); Walking With Beasts (T); Die Another Day (F)"

FX Projects
Studio House, 34 Rita Rd, London SW8 1JU
t 020 7582 8750 **f** 020 7793 0467 **e** cinebuild@btclick.com
Contact A Neale, Managing Director; Patrick Neale, Director

Glassworks
33-34 Great Pulteney Street, London W1R 3DE
t 020 7434 1182 **f** 020 7434 1183
e hector@glassworks.co.uk **w** www.glassworks.co.uk
Contact Hector Macleod, Managing Director
Credits Orange Arrows (A); Sprite (C); Kitekat (C); Bjork (M)

hotdog
2 Hillary House, Boyton Close, London N8 7BB
Contact Abigail Coult, Proprietor

Hothouse Models & Effects
10 St Leonard's Road, Park Royal, London NW10 6SY
t 020 8961 3666 **f** 020 8961 3777
e info@hothousefx.co.uk **w** www.hothousefx.co.uk

Hydro Gas & Chemicals Ltd
Unit 11, Central Park Estate, Staines Road, Hounslow TW4 5DJ
t 020 8384 5454 **f** 020 8384 5455 **m** 07000 245010
e mike.bell@hydro.com **w** www.dryice.gbr.fm
Contact Mike Bell, Depot Manager - Dry Ice

Just FX

Lincoln Parkhouse, Unit 4, Frontier Works, 33 Queen Street, Tottenham, London N17 8JA
t 020 8493 0527 **f** 020 8493 0528 **m** 07860 679616
e office@justfx.co.uk **w** www.justfx.co.uk
Contact Lincoln Parkhouse, Proprietor

Laser Hire

30 Water Street, Snow Hill, Birmingham B3 1HL
t 0121 2362 243 **f** 0121 236 0764 **m** 07836 526834
e Info@laserhire.co.uk **w** www.laserhire.co.uk/
Contact Keith Flunder, Managing Director
Credits The Good Thief (F); Coronation Street (T); Taggert (T); Kylie Minogue (M)

Pirate Models & Effects

St Leonard's Road, London NW10 6ST
t 020 8930 5000 **f** 020 8930 5001
e help@pirate.co.uk **w** www.pirate.co.uk
Contact Martin Godward, Technical Director

Theatrical Pyrotechnics Ltd

The Loop, Manston Airport, Ramsgate CT12 5DE
t 01843 823545 **f** 01843 822655
e pyrotech@manstona.fsnet.co.uk **w** www.tplpyro.co.uk
Contact Susan Sturges, Director; Malcolm Armstrong, Director; Ken Humphries, Technical Manager

Water Sculptures Ltd

St Georges Studios, St Georges Quay, Lancaster LA1 5QJ
t 01524 64430 **f** 01524 60454
e info@watersculptures.co.uk **w** www.watersculptures.co.uk
Contact William Elliot; Alasdair Elliot

Special Effects Operators

Add F/X

Meadow Cottage, Dean Way, Chalfont St Giles HP8 4LH
t 01494 870659 **f** 01494 876033 **m** 07973 638573
e tony@addfx.co.uk
Contact Tony Auger, Proprietor

Advantage FX

Keppel Gate, High Street, Lewknor, Watlington OX49 5TL
t 01844 352210 **f** 01844 352210 **m** 07774 720280
e ianwingove@advantagefx.co.uk
Contact Ian Wingrove
Credits Mission Impossible (F); Land Girls (F); Sleeping Dictionary (F)

Garry Cooper

6 Kingham Drive, Carterton OX18 3HU
t 07798 820074 **e** garry.cooper@talk21.com
Credits Harry Potter And The Chamber Of Secrets (F); Shanghai Knights (F); Under World (F); Band Of Brothers (T)

Elements Special Effects

Unit PO3 Acton Business Centre, School Road, London NW10 6TD
t 020 8961 4244 **f** 020 8961 4255
m 07968 613030 **m** 07968 613040
e johnny@elementsfx.co.uk **w** www.elementsfx.co.uk
Contact Johnny Rafique, Director; Nick Rideout, Director
Credits Charlie (F); Stella Artois (C); Suzie Gold (F); Goodbye Mr Chips (T)

John Hatt

41 Moor End, Holyport, Maidenhead SL6 2YJ
t 01628 638894 **f** 01628 638894 **m** 07802 247321
e john.hattsfx@btinternet.com **w** www.johnhatt.biz
Credits Dream Street (T); Lost In Space (F); Enigma (F); Die Another Day (F)

Live Action FX Ltd

152 Ayelands, New Ash Green, Longfield DA3 8JU
t 01474 874127 **f** 01474 874127 **m** 07947 835347
e info@LiveActionFX.com **w** www.LiveActionFX.com
Contact Stephen Miller M.I.Exp.E

Mario Grattarola, MGA Films

51 Monkhams Lane, Woodford Green IG8 0NN
t 020 8504 3877 **f** 020 8559 1674
e mail@mga-int.co.uk **w** www.mga-int.co..uk
Contact Mario Grattarola
Credits Harry's Bar; Millennium Dome Stero; Lake Vyrnwy

Mark Holt Special Effects

94 Pickford Lane, Bexley Heath DA7 4RT
t 020 8298 9438 **f** 020 8298 9450 **m** 07836 246237
e mark.holt@talk21.com
Contact Mark Holt, Contact
Credits Bright Young Things (F); Longitude (T); Dirty Pretty Things (F)

MTFX Ltd

Velt House, Velt House Lane, Elmore GL2 3NY
t 01452 729903 **f** 01452 729904
e info@mtfx.com **w** www.mtfx.com
Contact Mark Turner, Managing Director; Paula Davey, Administrative Assistant
Credits Hearts Of Gold (T); Servants (T); Blackwater (T); Casualty (T)

Snow Business

The Snow Mill, Bridge Road, Ebley, Stroud GL5 4TR
t 01453 840077 **f** 01453 840077
e snow@snowbusiness.com **w** www.snowfx.com
Credits Harry Potter And The Philosopher's Stone (F); Ted And Sylvia (F); Die Another Day (F); Band Of Brothers (T)

Tony Steers Prototypes

Calderpark House, 63 Calder Street, Lochwinnoch PA12 4DG
t 01505 843419 **f** 01505 842700 **m** 07887 780704
e tony.steers@prototypes.fsnet.co.uk
Contact Tony Steers, Proprietor
Credits Trainspotting (F); Shallow Grave (F)

Trevor Williams

Manor Field, Manor Close, East Horsley KT24 6SA
t 01483 282154 **m** 07956 382338
e trevor-williams@amserve.com
Credits Cold Mountain (F); Spy Game (F); The League Of Extraordinary Gentlemen (F); Gladiator (F)

Trilogy Special Effects

4 Stanley Hill Avenue, Amersham HP7 9BD
t 01494 721873 **f** 01494 721873 **m** 07778 750626
e tony-harding@btinternet.com
Contact Peter Kersey, Supervisor; Tony Harding; Chris Lawson, Supervisor
Credits Serious And Organised (T); Jonathan Creek (T); Ultimate Force (T); Tipping The Velvet (T)

Vision Effects

1 Arlington Drive, Ruislip HA4 7RJ
t 01895 679277 **f** 01895 679277 **m** 07775 627400
e avfx1@aol.com **w** www.visioneffects.co.uk

Anne Marie Walters

191 Tamar Way, Langely, Slough SL3 8SZ
t 01753 548159 **f** 01753 794281 **m** 07721 311426
e anniew@vossnet.co.uk
Credits Gladiator (F); Mummy Returns (F); Black Hawk Down (F)

Specialist Activity Advisors

Albany Kick Boxing
61A Camden Road, London NW1 9EU
t 020 7485 9993 **m** 07713 638233
e kwilson_57@yahoo.com **w** www.albanykickboxing.com
Contact Keith Wilson, Company Director
Credits Between The Lines (T); Kickboxing (T); Looking For Love (T)

Baby Wranglers
Chantry House, 4 Umbria Street, Roehampton, London SW15 5DP
t 020 8789 3232 **f** 020 8788 0758 **m** 07774 606814
e info@twizzle.co.uk
Contact Peter Robertson, Proprieter
Credits BT (C); Standard Life (C); Direct Line (C); Johnson & Johnson (C)

Greenwood Pursuits & Period Action
(Corporate Archery & Costumed Extras)
Newlands, Orpington Road, Badgers Mount, Sevenoaks TN14 7AQ
t 01959 534256 **f** 01689 850917 **m** 07774 458438
e john@greenwood-pursuits.fsnet.co.uk
Contact John Asmus, Proprietor

High Exposure (Climbing & Safety Services)
t 01855 811402 **f** 01855 811402 **m** 07881 784874
e dave@highexposure.co.uk **w** www.highexposure.co.uk

Hopkin Smith & Sons
Cwrt-Celyn Farm, Upper Boat, Pontypridd CS37 5BJ
t 029 2083 1658 **f** 029 2083 2734
e hopkinsmith@btconnect.com **w** www.adventurewales.co.uk
Contact Hopkin Smith, Proprietor

Outer Limits
Pwll y Garth, Dolwyddelan LL25 0HJ
t 01690 760248 **f** 01690 760248 **m** 07885 313455
e outerlimits@lineone.net
Contact Chris Butler, Director
Credits First Knight (F); Willow (F); Robin Hood (F); Merlin (F)

Simon Bornhoft Watersports
Middleton Cottage, Steels Lane, Chidham PO18 8TB
t 01243 572442 **e** simonbornhoft@compuserve.com
Contact Simon Bornhoft, Proprietor

Kevin West
The Old Forge, Catton, Walton-on-Trent DE12 8LN
t 01283 711122 **f** 01283 711166 **m** 07778 197462
e kevinwest@shelley38.freeserve.co.uk
w www.mycbsite.com/rocknrope

Windsport International
TR11 5UF
t 01326 376191 **f** 01326 376192 **m** 07974 194308
e brian.phipps@windsport.co.uk **w** www.windsport.co.uk
Contact Brain Phipps

Sponsorship

ABL Cultural Consulting
31 St Martins Lane, London WC2N 4ER
t 020 7420 9700 **w** www.ablconsulting.com

Arts Council England
14 Great Peter Street, London SW1P 3NQ
t 020 7333 0100 **f** 020 7973 6590
e enquiries@artscouncil.org.uk **w** www.artscouncil.org.uk

Arts Council England - East
48-49 Bateman Street, Cambridge CB2 1LR
t 01223 454400 **f** 08702 421271
e east@artscouncil.org.uk **w** www.artscouncil.org.uk
Contact Linda Brooklyn, Resources Officer

Arts Council England - East Midlands
St Nicholas Court, 25-27 Castle Gate, Nottingham NG1 7AR
t 0115 989 7520 **f** 0115 950 2467
e eastmidlands@artscouncil.org.uk **w** www.artscouncil.org.uk

Arts Council England - London
2 Pear Tree Court, London EC1R 0DS
t 020 7608 6100 **f** 020 7608 4100
e london@artscouncil.org.uk **w** www.artscouncil.org.uk

Arts Council England - North East
Central Square, Forth Street, Newcastle upon Tyne NE1 3PJ
t 0191 255 8500 **f** 0191 230 1020
e northeast@artscouncil.org.uk **w** www.artscouncil.org.uk

Arts Council England - North West (Liverpool)
107 Duke Street, Liverpool L1 4JR
t 0151 709 0671 **f** 0151 708 9034
e northwest@artscouncil.org.uk **w** www.artscouncil.org.uk

Arts Council England - North West (Manchester)
Manchester House, 22 Bridge Street, Manchester M3 3AB
t 0161 834 6644 **f** 0161 834 6969
e information.nw@artscouncil.org.uk **w** www.artscouncil.org.uk
Contact Howard Rifkin, Director, Visual and Media Arts

Arts Council England - South East
Sovereign House, Church Street, Brighton BN1 1RA
t 01273 763000 **f** 0870 242 1257
e southeast@artscouncil.org.uk **w** www.artscouncil.org.uk
Contact Sally Abbott, Director of Performing Arts

Arts Council England - South West
Bradninch Place, Gandy Street, Exeter EX4 3LS
t 01392 218188 **f** 01392 229229
e southwest@artscouncil.org.uk **w** www.artscouncil.org.uk

Arts Council England - Yorkshire
21 Bond Street, Dewsbury WF13 1AX
t 01924 455555 **f** 01924 466522
e tony.dixon@artscouncil.org.uk **w** www.artscouncil.org.uk
Contact Tony Dixon

The Arts Council of England
2 Pear Tree Court, London EC1R 0DS
t 020 7608 6100 **f** 020 7608 4100
e london@artscouncil.org.uk **w** www.artscouncil.org.uk
Contact Margery Allthorpe-Guyton, Director of Visual Arts

Arts Council of Northern Ireland
MacNeice House, 77 Malone Road, Belfast BT9 6AQ
t 028 9038 5200 **w** www.artscouncil-ni.org

Arts Council of Scotland
12 Manor Place, Edinburgh EH3 7DD
t 0131 226 6051
e help.desk@scottisharts.org.uk
e gillian.staniland@scottisharts.co.uk **w** www.sac.org.uk

Arts Council of Wales - Cyngor Celfyddydau Cymru
9 Museum Place, Cardiff CF10 3NX
t 029 2037 6500 **f** 029 2022 1447
e information@cc-acw.org.uk
Contact Peter Tyndall, Chief Executive

British Board of Film Classification
3 Soho Square, London W1D 3HD
t 020 7440 1570 **w** www.bbfc.co.uk

British Council Films & Television Department
11 Portland Place, London W1B IEJ
t 020 7389 3065 **w** www.britishcouncil.org/arts/film

JAGO DESIGN LTD, DESIGNED BY SOPHIE GRIFFITHS FOR FT.COM
ABOVE: FOUR 10" x 8" TRANSPARENCIES TAKEN BY RUTTERS' LOCATION PHOTOGRAPHER.
A SIMILAR SERIES OF SHOTS WERE TAKEN AT NIGHT IN ORDER TO CREATE A MATCHING NIGHTIME BACKDROP.
MIDDLE: FOUR TRANSPARENCIES MERGED AND MANIPULATED TO CREATE FINAL PANORMA IMAGE.
BELOW RIGHT: BACKDROP INSTALLED IN FT.COM STUDIO

location manipulation production

With over 25 years' experience in image origination and production for TV, stage, film and video, we offer the complete backdrop service. Rutters can handle the total project in-house, from 10" x 8" location photography to image manipulation, highest quality piezo digital printing and final installation.

The following are some of our recent projects:
Warner Bros Pictures: 'Harry Potter and the Philosopher's Stone', 'Harry Potter and the Chamber of Secrets'.
Carlton TV: 'Star Street'.
Paul Elliot Ltd: 'Stones in his Pockets'.
Jago Design Ltd: CNBC News Studio,
ITN General Election Studio, FT.com Studio.
LWT: 'Who's Afraid of the Ten Commandments',
'The Human Genome'.
The Jim Henson Company: 'Jack & The Beanstalk -
The Real Story'.
Pavilion Theatre Glasgow: 'Treasure Island', 'Aladdin'.
BBC: 'Love or Money', 'The Murder Rooms'.
Mermaid Design: BBC2 'Newsnight'.

Rutters

www.translights.com

Email: info-pg@translights.com
Telephone: +44 (0) 1799 531049 Fax: +44 (0) 1799 530651

FilmFour Lab
76-78 Charlotte Street, London W1P 1LX
t 020 7868 7700 **f** 020 7868 7766
Contact Robin Gutch, Head of FilmFour Lab

Media Antenna Wales
The Bank, 10 Mount Stuart Square, Cardiff Bay, Cardiff CF10 5EE
t 029 2033 3300 **f** 029 2033 3320
e sgrin@sgrin.co.uk **w** www.sgrin.co.uk
Contact John Berwyn Rowlands, Chief Executive

Sponsorship Film & TV

The British Film Commission
10 Little Portland Street, London W1W 7JG
t 020 7861 7860 **f** 020 7861 7864
e info@bfc.co.uk **w** www.britfilmcom.co.uk

STILLS

stills : contents	
Backings	636
Photographers	636
Processing	638

Stills Backings

Rutters
Eastgate House, 5 Eastgate, Great Chesterford, Saffron Walden CB10 1PA
t 01799 531049 **f** 01799 530651
e info@ruttersuk.com **w** www.ruttersuk.com
Contact Lynn Rose, PA; Paul Rutter, Managing Director

Stilled Movie Ltd
Shepperton Studios, Studios Road, Shepperton TW17 0QD
t 019 3259 2010 **f** 019 3256 8989 **m** 07860 399888
e alan@stilledmovie99.freeserve.co.uk
Contact Alan White, Proprietor
Credits Around The World In 80 Days (2003) (F); Die Another Day (F); The Hours (F)

Stills Photographers

Afshin Dehkordi Photography
19 Thursby Road, Woking GU21 3NZ
m 07968 726788 **e** afshin@ntlworld.com
Credits Raindance (S); Fallen Angels (F); Raindance

Alvey & Towers
Enterprise House, Ashby Road, Coalville LE67 3LA
t 01530 450011 **f** 01530 450011 **m** 07973 747957
e alveytower@aol.com **w** www.alveyandtowers.com
Contact Emma Rowen, Picture Library Manager

Simon Archer
45 Ash Grove Road, Ashleydown, Bristol BS7 9LF
t 01179 512996 **m** 07966 258014
e archerphotos@blueyonder.co.uk
w www.simonarcherphotography.co.uk

Graham Attwood
Flat 2, 22 Carlton Drive, London SW15 2BN
t 020 8789 5750 **f** 020 8789 5750 **m** 07973 182334
e grahamattwood1@aol.com

Matt Bright
5 Huddlestone Road, London NW2 5DL
t 020 8451 9727 **m** 07956 300113

Richard Campbell
30 Mansionhouse Road, Glasgow G41 3DN
t 0141 632 1020 **m** 07721 325326
e info@richardcampbell.sco.fm **w** www.richardcampbell.sco.fm
Credits Murder Rooms (T); Jo Brand's Hot Potatoes (T); Cowboys And Indians (S); Monarch Of The Glen (T)

Nigel Carter
52 Crabtree Lane, Ormskirk L40 0RN
t 01704 892683 **f** 01704 892683 **m** 07770 748926

Simon Cherry
19 Wendell Road, London W12 9RS
f 020 8740 1396 **m** 07956 598221 **e** simon.cherry@virgin.net

Stuart Chorley
19 St James's Lane, Muswell Hill, London N10 3DA
t 020 8883 0483 **m** 07956 283164
e stuart.chorley@btinternet.com
Credits LV Insurance (C)

Chris Frazer Smith Photography Ltd
1-7 Britannia Row, London N1 8QH
t 020 7359 4961 **f** 020 7359 5034 **m** 07831 376687
e chris@chrisfrazersmith.com
Contact Chris Frazer Smith
Credits Renault Laguna (C); Peugeot Boxer Vans (C); Atonement (C)

Christopher Hill Photographic
t 028 9024 5038 **f** 028 9023 1942
e chrishillphotographic@btclick.com **w** www.scenicireland.com
Contact Christopher Hill, Photographer

Alistair Cowin
London
t 020 7828 0626 **m** 07770 446229 **e** alcowin@aol.com

David Graham Photography
1 Hurst Road, Horsham RH12 2ES
t 01403 272760
e post@davidgraham.net **w** www.davidgraham.net

Dominic Photography
4B Moore Park Road, London SW6 2JT
t 020 7381 0007 **f** 020 7381 0008
Contact Catherine Ashmore, Partner

East Photographic
91 Rivington Street, London EC2A 3AY
t 020 7729 9002 **f** 020 7729 9004
e hq@eastphotographic.com **w** www.eastphotographic.com
Contact Nick Selby, Director

Carl Fox
C/o Penny Rich, 27 Hoxton Street, London N1 6NH
t 020 7613 3886

Katherine Griffiths
55 Carysfort Road, Stoke Newington, London N16 9AD
f 020 8760 5826 **m** 07905 266445 **e** kaffgvif@dircon.co.uk

Keith Hamshere
Ridge Cottage, The Hamlet, Potten End, Berkhamstead HP4 2RD
t 01442 863035 **f** 01442 863347 **m** 07836 733630
e khamshere@yahoo.com
Credits The World Is Not Enough (F); The Mummy Returns (F); Spy Games (F);
Die Another Day (F)

Mark Harwood
12 Waterside, 44-48 Wharf Road, London N1 7SF
t 020 7490 8787 **f** 020 7490 1009 **m** 07702 233721
e mark.harwood@macunlimited.net **w** www.markharwood.net

Robert Hind
12 Jenner Road, London N16 5SA
f 07790 480758 **m** 07976 442161
e robert@roberthind.co.uk **w** www.roberthind.co.uk
Credits Mercedes Benz (C); Mercedes Benz; The Criminal (F); Wildside (F)

The Image Studio
72A High Street, Chislehurst BR7 5AQ
t 020 8467 8151 **f** 020 8295 5909
e images@theimagestudio-uk.com **w** www.theimagestudio-uk.com
Contact Chris Johnson, Proprietor

John Cleare/Mountain Camera
Hill Cottage, Fonthill Gifford, Salisbury SP3 6QW
t 01747 820320 **f** 01747 820320
e cleare@btinternet.com **w** www.mountaincamera.com
Credits The Climbers (D); Surrender to Everest (D); Eiger Sanction (T)

Bill Kaye
146 Amyand Park Road, St Margarets, Twickenham TW1 3HY
t 020 8892 2304 **f** 020 8892 2521 **m** 07850 007492
e bill_kaye@bigfoot.com **w** blowupstills.co.uk
Credits Ted And Sylvia (F); Angela's Ashes (F); There's Only One Jimmy Gimble
(F); The Sleeping Dictionary (F)

Luke Kelly
222 St Leonard Road, London SW14 7BN
t 020 8878 2823 **f** 020 8878 2823

Living Light Ltd
54 Battery Road, Thamesmead, London SE28 0JT
t 020 8854 1412 **f** 0870 168 7054 **m** 07785 790613
e photo@livinglight.biz **w** www.livinglight.biz
Contact Jim Ashley-Down, Director
Credits My Divine (M); Royal Acedemy Of Arts (I); Witz End (I);
Hangman Studios (W)

Anthony MacDonald
Suite 128, 2 Old Brompton Road, London SW7 3DQ
t 020 7373 2602 **f** 020 7581 4445 **m** 07740 720470
e anthony@suite128.com **w** www.suite128.com

Jay Maidment
26 Clonmel Road, Teddington TW11 0SR
t 020 8943 4620 **m** 07771 711804 **e** jmaidphoto@aol.com
Credits Die Another Day (F); The World Is Not Enough (F); Band Of Brothers (T)

Marius Alexander Photography & Photo Library
2 West Park Place, Haymarket, Edinburgh EH11 2DP
t 0131 539 9100 **f** 0131 539 9100 **m** 07889 913485
e enquiries@mariusalexander.com
w www.mariusalexander.com
Contact Marius Alexander, Proprietor

Simon Mein
t 01798 344217 **f** 01798 344214 **m** 07949 706437

Micron Associates
34 Heath Croft Road, Four Oaks, Sutton Coldfield B75 6RL
t 0121 308 3106 **f** 0121 308 3106
Contact John Warren, Partner; John Warren, Partner

Nik Milner
Studio 202, Avro House, 7 Havelock Terrace, Battersea,
London SW8 4AS
t 020 7720 8123 **f** 020 7720 8123 **m** 07836 599233
e nik@nikmilner.com **w** www.nikmilner.com

Tom Mulvee
20 Haldon Road, Wandsworth, London SW18 1QB
t 020 8874 1141 **f** 020 8874 1141 **m** 07860 643873
e tom.mulvee@btconnect.com
Credits Beechams (C)

David Munns
Ethos Represents, 23 Albert Square, London SW8 1BS
t 020 7735 7006 **f** 020 7735 7009
e ethosrepresents@btinternet.com

Roberta Parkin
Creative Media Management, Unit 3B, Walpole Court, Ealing
Studios, Ealing Green, London W5 5ED
t 020 8584 5363 **f** 020 8566 5554
e enquiries@creativemediamanagement.com
Credits The Cup (F); Carmen (F)

Peter Sefton, Artistic Photography
34 Hillary Close, Ashby Fields, Daventry NN11 5SN
t 01327 878331 **m** 07702 626973
e art.photo.p.sefton@virgin.net
w www.artisticphotography.co.uk

Keith Pettinato
Unit 93, Cholmley Gardens, London NW6 1UN
f 020 8693 5551 **m** 07836 539671
e keithpettinato@hotmail.com

Redback Photography Ltd
26 Brent Terrace, London NW2 1BX
t 020 8458 7006 **f** 020 8458 7006 **m** 07768 807824
e neil@redbackuk.com **w** www.redbackuk.com
Contact Neil Hurley, Director; Richard Powers, Director
Credits Argos (I); Systemax (I); Universal Records (I); American Express (I)

Chris Ridley
6 Pindock Mews, London W9 2PY
t 020 7286 4843 **m** 07775 526586
e ridleyuk@aol.com **w** www.christopherridley.com

Robbie Jack Photography
45 Church Road, London W7 3BD
t 020 8567 9616 **f** 020 8567 9616 **m** 07774 235533
e robbie@robbiejack.com **w** www.robbiejack.com
Contact Robbie Jack, Proprietor
Credits Commercial Union (I); The Armando Ianucci Show (T); Weird Sister (T)

Georgina Slocombe
24 Hereford Square, South Kensington SW7 4TS
t 020 7373 1697 **f** 020 7373 1697 **m** 07831 290085

Stephen F Morley Photography
Harthanger, The Street, Lodsworth, Petworty GU28 9BZ
t 01798 861400 **f** 01798 861400 **m** 07860 733784
e morley400@aol.com
Credits Midsomer Murders (T); Ready When You Are Mr McGill (F); Foyles War
(T); Tipping The Velvet (T)

Peter Thiedeke
Ethos Represents, 23 Albert Square, London SW8 1BS
t 020 7735 7006 **f** 020 7735 7009
e ethosrepresents@btinternet.com

Underwater Images

First Floor, Gloucester House, 45 Gloucester Street, Brighton BN1 4EW
t 233773 **f** 01273 620673 **m** 07870 664673
e sean@underwaterimage@aol.com
w www.underwaterimage.co.uk
Contact Sean Clark, Proprietor
Credits BBC Southern Eye (T); South East Arts; Royal Photographic Society

Stills Processing

BlowUp

146 Amyand Park Road, St Margarets, Twickenham TW1 3HY
t 020 8892 2304 **f** 020 8892 2521 **m** 07850 007492
e angela_leahy@bigfoot.com **e** bill_kaye@bigfoot.com
w www.blowup.net
Contact Bill Kaye, Partner; Angela Leahy, Partner
Credits The Life Of David Gale (F); Johnny English (F); Harry Potter And The Chamber Of Secrets (F); Harry Potter And The Philosopher's Stone (F)

Pinewood Studios Ltd

Pinewood Road, Iver Heath SL0 0NH
t 01753 657198 **f** 01753 656252
e tim_forester@pinewood-studios.co.uk
w www.pinewood-studios.co.uk
Contact Graham Hartstone, Head of Post Production; Diana Crystal Honey, Sales and Marketing Manager, TV; Steve Gunn, Executive Director; Tim Forester, PDI Director

Sky Photographic Services Ltd

Ramillies House, 1-2 Ramillies Street, London W1F 7AZ
t 020 7434 2266 **f** 020 7434 0828
e info@skyphoto.demon.co.uk
w www.skyphoto.demon.co.uk/sky.html
Contact Mike Sherry, Managing Director

Storyboard Artists

Lee Andrews

34 Bonfield Road, London SE13 6BX
t 020 8297 9632 **m** 07764 192346
e mail@leeandrews.co.uk **w** www.leeandrews.co.uk
Credits Making Mistakes (S); Multiplex (F); Lynx (C); Baham (A)

Martin Asbury

Stonewold, Chapel Lane, Pitch Green, Bledlow HP27 9QG
t 01844 344688 **f** 01844 274680 **m** 07770 828679
e martin.ashbury@virgin.net **w** www.storyboardman.com
Credits Die Another Day (F); Harry Potter And The Chamber Of Secrets; The World Is Not Enough (F); Quills (F)

Adam Brockbank

49 Berrymede Road, London W4 5JE
t 020 8995 9501 **f** 020 8995 9501 **m** 07957 281020
e Badger.bank@virgin.net
Credits Harry Potter And The Prisoner Of Azkaban (F); Harry Potter And The Philosopher's Stone (F)

Robert Butler

20 Coniston Road, Bexleyheath DA7 6PY
t 01322 334756 **f** + 44 871 242 0386 **m** 07903 365688
e robert@constructivelines.com **w** www.constructivelines.com
Credits Johnson & Johnson (C); Sainsbury's (C); Eurostar (C); Oasis (M)

Francesca Cassavetti

t 020 8451 5803 **f** 020 8451 5803
e francesca.cassavetti@btopenworld.co.uk

John Challis

8 St John Mansions, Clapton Square, London E5 8HT
t 020 8533 9357 **f** 020 8533 9357 **m** 07714 956962
e jcmoody@nw3.net
Credits Petting - Andrex (C); Fruit Machine - Reef (C); Car Ride - Volkswagen (C); Ten Minutes Older/Addicted To The Stars (F)

John Greaves

44 Copthall Drive, London NW7 2NB
t 020 8959 1325 **f** 020 8906 4385 **m** 07867 803163
e greaves44@btinternet.com
Credits Blackball (F); The Thunderbirds (F); World Is Not Enough (F); Band Of Brothers (T)

Douglas Ingram

15 Uplands Park Road, Enfield, London EN2 7PU
t 020 8367 4646 **f** 020 8367 4646 **m** 07721 011331
e ingrampov@yahoo.co.uk
Credits Ford Puma (C); The Elegant Universe (D); Richard III (F); Foyle's War (T)

Barry Macey

Ivy Cottage, Aylesbury Road, Princes Risborough HP27 0JW
t 01844 343075 **e** barrymaceystudio@aol.com
Credits Pong Whiffy (T); Little Ghosts (T)

New Illustration Ltd

4 Almeida Street, London N1 1TA
t 020 7226 7349
Contact Clarissa New

Nicholas Pelham

t 01252 621588 **f** 01252 622110 **m** 07889 266269

Trevor Ricketts

C/o Ealing Animation, 90 Brandon Street, London SE17 1AL
t 020 7358 4823 **f** 0207358 4821 **m** 07770 954086
e trevorjricketts@aol.com
Credits Animal Stories (A); Sheeep (A); Angelina Ballerina (A); Mr Bean The Animated Series (A)

Stage One Storyboards

t 020 7494 3222 **f** 020 7494 3220
e stage.one@easynet.co.uk **e** olly@stageonestoryboards.co.uk,
w www.stageonestoryboards.co.uk
Contact Olly Dumas

Ada-Maria Wiggins

Gems, The Media House, 87 Glebe Street, Penarth CF64 1EF
t 029 2071 0770 **f** 029 2071 0771
e gems@gems-agency.co.uk **w** www.gems-agency.co.uk
Credits Pink Champagne (T); After Life (T); Private Life (S)

STUNT

Stunt Coordinators

Acrobat Productions

The Circus Space, Coronet Street, London N1 6HD
t 020 7613 5259 **f** 020 7613 5259
e info@acrobatproductions.co.uk
w www.acrobatproductions.co.uk

Role of the stunt coordinator

There are only around 300 recognised stunt performers in the UK, and much stunt work goes to a small proportion of these. But the profession is inundated with people longing to fling themselves through fake windows, dangle from aeroplanes or tumble down stairs.

To join this daredevil profession you have to be highly qualified in at least six sports or activities (this can often cost thousands of pounds). Skills such as trampolining or horse riding are helpful to have, but it's imperative to have a fighting qualification – fencing, boxing or a martial art.

Orchestrating or participating in fights makes up much of the stunt man's work. But there's another essential piece of paper: an Equity card. To acquire this you need to have at least 30 weeks' professional experience as an actor or performer. That's why many stunt people come from the circus or have toured with acrobatic groups. The majority are men; only around 15 per cent are women.

An organisation called The Joint Industry Stunt Committee sets the stringent requirements that stunt men must meet and the stipulations are approved by Pact, the BBC, ITV and Equity. Every two years the committee publishes the Stunt Register, which is a book listing all its members.

Many stunt men specialise in one particular field – such as driving like a madman – but it's also important that they remain versatile. Much of the work involves doubling for actors so it helps if the stunt man is of an average size and build.

Good stunt men get regular work by showing that they can perform safely. The trick is to create the illusion of danger rather than nearly killing yourself. Safety is ensured through a lot of hard work and expert know-how. It's the responsibility of the stunt co-ordinator to write a risk assessment report for each stunt. This has to satisfy the producers that no one is going to get hurt. While the stunt is filmed, the stunt co-ordinator also ensures that relevant medical professionals are on hand.

Accidents rarely happen but there's always a risk.

For instance, Sting performed his own stunt in Brimstone and Treacle by putting his hand through a breakable window made of sugar glass. He ended up with more than 30 stitches in his arm and couldn't play the bass on tour.

Another example is the potential hazards of a contraption called an air ram. This is a foot-plate that catapults the performer 30 feet into the air while setting off an explosion. Naturally, this gives the impression that the person has been blown up. But it takes an experienced performer to step on the plate and land correctly.

It takes a while for a new stunt worker to become established. Initially, stunt men join the Stunt Register as probationary members for three years, then become intermediary members for two years before gaining full membership.

After becoming well-known, many become stunt co-ordinators, which involves doing much more preparation at the pre-production stage. Occasionally, they train actors to perform their own stunts. But they also travel to assess the suitability of locations, employ the stunt performers and advise the director how to shoot the scene.

Some co-ordinators go on to become second-unit directors. Stunt co-ordinators are often ideally suited to this position because a second unit often concentrates solely on the action.

Pay depends on experience, and whether it is film or TV work. On average, a day-rate for a co-ordinator is around £500, and £300 for performers, who are also paid extra per take. In film, they often earn more because they do more takes. The amount per take can vary enormously depending on the nature of the action. One performer is rumoured to have earned as much as £35,000 for one stunt. Aerial and fire sequences generally pay best.

For further information contact
Equity Register of Stunt/Action Co-ordinators & Performers.
020 7379 6000 or www.equity.org/info@equity.org.uk

Writer: David Collins. Reprinted with kind permission from B+, the Broadcast monthly pull-out.

Roy Alon
14 Alwoodley Chase, Harrogate Road, Leeds LS17 8ER
t 0113 266 4050 **f** 0113 266 4050 **m** 07836 322 012
e roy@royalon.com
Credits Die Another Day (F); Peak Practice (T); A Touch of Frost (T)

Del Baker SACG
Hillside, Potters Lane, Well End, Borehamwood WD6 5NX
t 020 8386 4567 **f** 020 8207 4757 **m** 07770 870720
e delstunt@hotmail.com
Credits Entrapment (F); The Count of Monte Cristo (F); Kull the Conqueror (F); Smilla's Feelings for Snow (F)

Bickers Action
Ivy Farm Works, High Street, Coddenham, Ipswich IP6 9QX
t 01449 761300 **f** 01449 760614
m 07831 132009 **m** 07836 606291
e action@bickers.co.uk **w** www.bickers.co.uk
Contact Paul Bickers, Managing Director; Dean Cox, Operations Manager
Credits Emmerdale (T); Cold Play - Scientist (M); Heartbeat (T); Die Another Day (F)
Stunt Engineering, Mechanical SFX, Camera Tracking Vehicles & Low Loaders.

Andy Bradford
The Garden Flat, 35 Nassington Road, London NW3 2TY
t 020 7435 2856 **f** 020 7435 2856 **m** 07831 281320
e andyonemail@aol.com
Credits Clocking Off (T); Men Only (T); Spooks (T); Buried (T)

David Brandon
13a Lyttleton Road, London N2 0DR
t 020 8455 9291

Peter Brayham
64 The Gallop, Sutton SM2 5RY
t 020 8642 3936 **f** 020 8643 7213 **m** 07860 126395
w www.stuntnet.co.uk/action/peter_brayham
Credits Cutting It (T); Vacuuming Nude In Paradise (T); Paradise Heights (T); State Of Mind (T)

Helen Caldwell
t 01628 531678 **m** 07836 642815

Jordi Casares

International Creative Management Ltd, Oxford House,
76 Oxford Street, London W1D 1BS
t 020 7636 6565 **f** 020 7323 0101 **w** www.icmlondon.co.uk
Credits Jason And The Argonauts (T); The Four Feathers (F); Die Another Day (F)

Simon Crane

International Creative Management Ltd, Oxford House,
76 Oxford Street, London W1D 1BS
t 020 7636 6565 **f** 020 7323 0101 **w** www.icmlondon.co.uk
Credits Saving Private Ryan (F); Terminator 3: Rise Of The Machines (F); Lara Croft: Tomb Raider (F)

Clive Curtis

Dollygate, Great Ponton, Grantham NG33 5DP
t 01476 530572 **f** 01476 530573 **m** 07831 850295
e clive_curtis@ellysmanor.co.uk
Credits Waking The Dead Series 3 (T); Man And Boy (T); The Crying Game (F); Princess of Thieves (T)

Eddie Daniels

3A Runnymeade Road, Canvey Island SS8 0EF

Bill Davey

11 Cranborne Ave, Tolworth, Surbiton KT6 7JP
t 020 8391 2629 **f** 020 8241 1943 **m** 07831 788138
e bill@nobull.fsbusiness.co.uk
Credits Rockface II (T); Murphy's Law (T); The Bill (T); Casualty (T)

Nrinder Dhudwar

158 City Way, Rochester ME1 2AU
t 01634 842519 **f** 01634 842519 **m** 07860 889500

Dorothy Anne Ford

Merry Acres, Sheepcote Dell Road, Beamond End, Amersham HP7 0QS
t 01494 717071 **f** 01494 713131 **m** 07860 333767
Credits Buffalo Soldiers (F); The Bill (T); Cromwell (F)

Elaine Ford

t 07074 735246 **f** 01747 820024 **m** 07836 633877
w www.stuntnet.co.uk/action/Elaine_Ford
Credits Friends (D); The Bill (T); Holby City (T)

Sarah Franzl

Holly Bushes, Leverstock, Green Road, Hemel Hempstead HP3 8LR
t 01442 253018 **f** 01442 239715 **m** 07831 465650
e sarahfranzl@compuserve.com

Nick Gillard

10 Kensington Place, Brighton BN1 4EJ
t 01273 680575 **m** 07775 912366 **e** Gillard3@aol.com
Credits Star Wars: Episode II- Attack of the Clones (F); Shaft (F); Star Wars: Episode I-The Phantom Menace (F)

Steve Griffin

58 Addlestonemoor, Weybridge KT15 2QL
t 01932 565686 **f** 01932 568934 **m** 07860 711009
e monsteraction@compuserve.com **w** www.stevegriffin.co.uk
Credits Charlie's Angels (F); Bad Boys 2 (F); The Italian Job (F); Terminator 3: Rise Of The Machines (F)

Guild of Stunt & Action Coordinators

72 Pembroke Road, London W8 6NX
t 020 7602 8319 **f** 020 7602 8319 **m** 07974 966665
e stunts.uk@btinternet.com
Contact Sally Fisher, Secretary

Richard Hammatt

Hyde Meadow Farm, Hyde Lane, Hemel Hempstead HP3 8SA
t 01932 266373 **f** 01923 260852 **m** 07836 642074
e richard@nineninecars.com

Frank Henson

32 St Peters Square, London W6 9NW
t 020 8748 9293 **f** 020 8748 9293 **m** 07860 208583
Credits The Mummy II (F); Heartbeats (T)

Mark Henson

t 01273 857036 **m** 07768 580595
Credits Cold Mountain (F); Mummy I&II (F); Saving Private Ryan (F); Die Another Day (F)

Dave Judge

Zero G Northern, Marazion, Stansfield Hall Road, Todmorden OL14 5LR
t 01706 812317 **f** 01706 812317 **m** 07774 101448
e dave@zero-gfilms.com
w www.stuntjudge.co.uk; www.zero-gfilms.com

Sean McCabe

t 020 8876 5308 **f** 020 8878 7203 **m** 07860 646381
e seanmccabe@compuserve.com
Credits Vertical Limit (F); Star Wars: Episode II- Attack of the Clones (F); Buffalo Soldiers (F)

Gareth Milne

20 Hermiston Avenue, Crouch End, London N8 8NL
t 020 8340 4742 **m** 07836 278778 **e** garethmilne@aol.com
Agent International Creative Management Ltd, Oxford House,
76 Oxford Street, London W1D 1BS
t 020 7636 6565 **f** 020 7323 0101 **w** www.icmlondon.co.uk
Credits Young Adam (F); Parole Officer (F); Essex Boys (F); Bloody Sunday (F)

Moelfre City Screen Services

Tyn-y-Cwm, Llanbister, Llandrindod Wells LD1 6UN
t 01597 840616 **e** megalith@megalithicsites.co.uk
Contact Tony Crerar, Screen Services

Donal O'Farrell

30A Newbridge Avenue, Sandymount, Dublin 4, Rep of Ireland
t +353 1 668 7045 **f** +353 1 668 7045 **e** stunts@eircom.net
Credits Head Rush (F); Watermelon (F); Song For A Raggy Boy (F); The Actors (F)

Greg Powell

International Creative Management Ltd, Oxford House,
76 Oxford Street, London W1D 1BS
t 020 7636 6565 **f** 020 7323 0101 **w** www.icmlondon.co.uk
Credits Mission Impossible (F); Lord Of The Rings: The Fellowship Of The Ring (F); Harry Potter And The Philospher's Stone (F)

Lee Sheward

Hunters Lodge, 264 Brooklands Road, Weybridge KT13 0QX
t 01932 850643 **f** 01932 858320 **m** 07831 474829
e leesheward@compuserve.com **w** www.leesheward.co.uk

Stuart St Paul

13 Mountview, Northwood HA6 3NZ
t 01923 820330 **f** 0870 161 7339 **m** 07775 768531
e ssp@indyuk.co.uk **w**
http://us.imdb.com/Name?St.+Paul,+Stuart

The Stunt Register

Guild House, Upper St Martins Lane, London WC2H 9EG
t 020 7379 6000 **f** 020 7379 7001
e info@equity.org.uk **w** www.equity.org.uk
Contact Tim Gale, Secretary to Stunt Committee

Chris Webb

7 Tasman Close, Rustington BN16 2BD
t 01903 786500 **f** 01903 786500 **m** 07973 465154
e stunts.uk@btinternet.com
Credits Children's Ward (T); The Human Face (T); The Heart Of Me (F)

Paul Weston

t 01707 879888 **f** 01707 879888 **m** 07860 878800
e pw.action@btinternet.com
Credits The Count Of Monte Cristo (F); Indian (F); Auf Wiedersehen Pet (T); Messiah II (T)

5 inches

90 mph/250 feet

mins 12 secs
ll body burns

150 feet +

Stunts?
Take zero chances.

When it comes to stunt work and SFX, Zero-g provides the film and tv
ndustry with the best people and equipment for the toughest jobs.

ave Judge
B.Eng. AIIRSM
unt Supervisor
unt performer
alth&Safety Advisor

VEHICLE CHASES, CRASHES, ROLLS, KNOCK DOWNS - MOTORCYCLE
STUNTS - WEAPONS - FIGHT SEQUENCES - CLIMBING/ HEIGHT WORK, RIG-
GING, HIGH FALLS - BUNGEE - CLOSE PROXIMITY EXPLOSIONS AND BOMB
RUNS - FULL AND PARTIAL BODY BURNS - WATERWORK - FIGHT TRAINING

zero-g LTD

T 020 7561 0404 or 070 7170 7770   F 020 7272 8675
info@zero-gfilms.com www.zero-gfilms.com
118, Piccadilly London W1J 7NW UK

zero limits film and tv

Rod Woodruff
Heathley, 12 Highfield Road, Walton On Thames KT12 2RJ
t 01932 700755 **t** 01932 700756 **f** 01932 700757
m 07850 059005 **e** rwtmp@aol.com
Credits Volvo (C); Subaru (C); Nissan (C)
Precision Driver: Specialist in car action sequences: Commercials: TV: Film.

Zero-G
3 Newman Passage, London W1T 1EF
t 020 7636 6633 **t** 07071 707770
f 020 7436 8342 **m** 07900 696919
e info@zero-gfilms.com **w** www.zero-gfilms.com
Contact Franz Pagot; Dave Judge, Director; Keiko Nagai, Director
Credits Ronan Keating (M); Goodbye Charlie Bright (F); The Killing Zone (F);
Fallen Angels (F)

Stunt Equipment Hire

Screen Stunt Supplies Ltd
Hunters Lodge, 264 Brooklands, Weybridge KT13 0QX
f 01932 850643 **m** 07000 478868
e info@stuntsupplies.co.uk **w** www.stuntsupplies.co.uk
Contact Lee Sheward, Stunt Co-ordinator
Suppliers of stunt and safety equipment to the film industry.

Tom Delmar - The Stunt Company
119B Guildford St, Chertsey KT16 9AS
t 07831 571127 **f** 07785 833373 **m** 07831 571127
e tom@stuntsupplies.com **w** www.stuntsupplies.com
Contact Tom Delmar, Stunt Co-ordinator
Credits Star Wars Episode II - The Attack Of The Clones (F); Snatch (F); Long
Time Dead (F); Boudicca - A Celtic Tragedy (T)

Stunt Performers

Acrobats Productions
The Circus Space, Coronet Street, London N1 6HD
t 020 7613 5259 **f** 020 7613 5259 **m** 07771 907030
e roger@acrobatproductions.co.uk
w www.acrobatproductions.co.uk
Contact Roger Robinson, Director

David Anders
76 Long Readings Lane, Slough SL2 1PZ
t 07000 326 3377 **f** 07000 326 3377 **m** 07074 263377
e actiononscreen@aol.com
Credits Lara Croft: Tomb Raider (F); Messiah II (T); Silent Witness (T); Casualty (T)

Daniels Film
3A Runnymeade Road, Canvey Island SS8 0EF
Contact Eddie Daniels

Sean Murphy
18 Marine Parade, Barmouth LL42 1NA
t 01341 281023 **m** 07901 780686
Credits Mortal Kombat II (F)

Richard Dwyer - Stunts
PO Box 361, London TW5 0YQ
t 08700 130108 **m** 07956 341370
e richard@rdstunts.com **w** www.rdstunts.com
Contact Richard Dwyer, Director
Credits Suzie Gold (T); Ella Enchanted (F); Below (F); 28 Days Later (F)

Stunt Action Specialists
110 Trafalgar Road, Portslade BN41 1GS
t 01273 230214 **f** 01273 708699
e wayne@stuntactionspecialists.co.uk
w www.stuntactionspecialists.com
Contact Wayne de Strete, Managing Director

Sy Hollands
Coppice Farm, Akeley Wood, Akeley MK18 5BN
t 01280 823199 **f** 01280 823190 **m** 07831 392589
e ratts@compuserve.com
Credits Titanic (F); 101 Dalmations (F); Lara Croft: Tomb Raider (F); Saving
Private Ryan (F)

Stunt Wire Specialists

Steve Crawley
35 Wood Lane Close, Iver Heath SL0 0LH
t 01753 652570 **f** 01753 652570 **m** 07710 525587
Credits Die Another Day (F); Tomb Raider II (F); The World Is Not Enough (F)

Flying by Foy
Unit 4, Borehamwood Enterprise Centre, Theobald Street,
Borehamwood WD6 4RQ
t 020 8236 0234 **f** 020 8236 0235
e mail@flyingbyfoy.co.uk **w** www.flyingbyfoy.co.uk

Specialist Wire Rigs Ltd
32 Downside Rd, Risinghurst, Headington OX3 8HP
t 07000 947371 **f** 01628 530557 **m** 07767 775 760
e kevin@specialist-wire-rigs.co.uk
w www.specialistwirerigs.co.uk
Contact Kevin Mathews, Proprieter
Credits Sleepy Hollow (F); Star Wars: Episode I - The Phantom Menace (F);
Harry Potter & The Philosopher's Stone (F)

Stunt Rigging
Woodlands Cottage, Basingstoke Road, Greeham RG19 8HR
t 01635 269699 **f** 01635 269699 **m** 07860 267678
e kevinwelch@stuntrigging.co.uk
Contact K Welch, Proprietor; Caroline Botha, Manager
Credits Harry Potter And The Prisoner Of Azkaban (F);
The World Is Not Enough (F)

Kevin Welch
Woodlands Cottage, Basingstoke Road, Greenham RG19 8HR
t 01635 269699 **f** 01635 269699 **m** 07860 267678
e kevinwelch@stuntrigging.co.uk
Credits The World Is Not Enough (F); Harry Potter And The Chamber Of Secrets
(F); Harry Potter And The Prisoner Of Azkaban (F)

Bob Wiesinger
10 Blaydon Court, Northolt UB5 4DW
t 07000 947339 **f** 0796 8253071 **m** 07973 662393
e bobwirefx@aol.com
Credits The Empire Strikes Back (F); Star Wars (F); Superman (F); Harry Potter
And The Philosopher's Stone (F)

Systems Consultancy

ATG Broadcast
4 Shaftsbury Industrial Centre, Letchworth SG6 1HE
t 01462 485444 **f** 01462 485777
e sales@atgbroadcast.co.uk **w** www.atgbroadcast.co.uk
Contact Alan Pimm, Sales Director

Frank Bamgboye
100 Sandymount Avenue, Stanmore HA7 4TX
t 020 8954 8613

Cooper Consultancy
27 Masons Way, Corsham SN13 9XW
m 07887 947533 **e** cooper.com@virgin.net

CPS
158 Little Hardwick Road, Aldridge, Walsall WS9 0SF
t 0121 353 5705 **f** 0121 353 5705 **e** csiddell@compuserve.com
Contact Christopher Siddell, Managing Director

Keith Ealey

8 Horder Road, London SW6 5EE
t 020 7736 5593 **f** 020 7736 5593 **m** 07710 356448
e kesys008@aol.com
Contact Keith Ealey, Proprietor
Credits The Weather Programme (T)

Andrew Eio

Suite 3, Old Props Building, Pinewood Studios, Iver Heath SL0 0NH
t 01753 653456 **f** 01753 654507 **m** 07710 597774
e andrew@bionicdigital.co.uk **w** www.bionicdigital.co.uk

Electronic Media Systems Ltd (EMS)

256 Waterloo Road, London SE1 8RF
t 020 7202 2140 **f** 020 7202 2141
e phil@ems-group.co.uk **w** www.ems-group.co.uk
Contact Phil Holland, Business Development Director; Alistair McDonald,
Proposals Manager; Graham Wilson, Technical Director

Feltech Electronics Ltd

2 Sphere Industrial Estate, Campfield Ross, St Albans AL1 5HT
t 01727 834888 **f** 01727 848704
e sales@feltech.co.uk **w** www.feltech.co.uk
Contact Peter Fell, Managing Director; Ben Holman, Sales Co-ordinator

Gawton Associates Ltd

Gawton Farmhouse, Gawton, Bere Alston, Yelverton PL20 7HW
t 01822 840355 **f** 01822 841529 **m** 07977 049440
e raybgawton@aol.ocm
Contact Ray Bragg, Managing Director
Credits Media Centre System Consultancy - Falmouth College (T); Project
Management - Thomson (T); Playout And System Consultancy - NTL (T); Playout
System Consultancy - Network Seven (T)

KP Associates

Elley House, Elley Green, Corsham SN13 9TX
t 01225 812588 **e** kevin@kevinhunt.co.uk

Laser Communications

5 Kernthorpe Road, Kings Heath, Birmingham B14 6RA
t 01214 446080 **f** 01214 446080 **m** 07092 127919
e iain.welsh@laser-communications.co.uk **w** www.laser-
communications.co.uk

Megahertz Broadcast Systems Ltd

1 College Business Park, Coldhams Lane, Cambridge CB1 3HD
t 01223 414101 **f** 01223 414102
e frances@megahertz.co.uk **w** www.megahertz.co.uk
Contact Paul Ager, Procurement Manager; Stephen Burgess, Technical
Director; Ray Sillampalam, Head of Sales; Frances Jarvis, Commercial Director

Television Systems Ltd

Unit 4, Kings Grove, Maidenhead SL6 4DP
t 01628 687200 **f** 01628 687299 **m** 07787 531614
e russellg@televisionsystems.ltd.uk
w www.televisionsystems.com
Contact John Pinniger, Marketing Manager; Russell Grute, Sales Manager

Visuals

55 Selwood Road, Hook, Chessington KT9 1PT
t 020 8397 1567 **f** 020 8287 8618
e visuals@bigfoot.com **w** www.visuals.freeserve.co.uk
Contact Alan Moss, Consultant Engineer

Systems Integrators

Broadcast Service Centre Ltd (BSC)

2 Andromeda House, Calleva Park, Aldermaston, Reading RG7 8AN
t 0118 981 0804 **f** 0118 981 0698 **m** 07778 153937
e info@bscltd.co.uk **w** www.bscltd.co.uk
Contact David Reid, Director

Fischer Connectors

Unit 6, Stratfield Park, Elettra Avenue, Waterlooville PO7 7XN
t 023 9224 1122 **f** 023 9225 7596
e sales@fischerconnectors.co.uk **w** www.fischerconnectors.co.uk
Contact Ray Quinn, Managing Director

NH Evolution

36 Stratton Road, Sunbury TW16 6PQ
t 01932 883866 **f** 01932 883866 **m** 07751 404241
e nigel@holden1.ndo.co.uk

Pyser-SGI Ltd

Fircroft Way, Edenbridge TN8 6HA
t 01732 864111 **f** 01732 865544 **m** 07785 725826
e sales@pyser-sgi.com **w** www.pyser-sgi.com
Contact Paul Goodwin, Broadcast Division Sales Director

Michael Sellman

45 The Drive, Rickmansworth WD3 4EA
t 01923 720726 **e** sales@michael-sellman.com

Team 4

Latimer Square, White Lion Road, Amersham HP7 9JQ
t 01494 549400 **f** 01494 549454 **m** 07836 242795
e paul.valint@itm-group.co.uk **w** www.itm-group.co.uk
Contact Paul Vanlint, Director

TGA Electronics Ltd

181 Station Drive, Four Ashes, Wolverhampton WV10 7BU
t 01902 791325 **f** 01902 790344 **m** 07860 454359
e tga.tim@virgin.net **w** www.tgaelectronics.co.uk
Contact Tim Gray

Thear Technology Ltd

TTL House, Sheeptick End, Lidlington MK43 0SF
t 01525 841999 **f** 01525 841009 **e** service@theartechnology.co.uk
Contact Rod Thear, Managing Director
Credits Otari (C); Sony Broadcast (C)

Video Engineering

4 Woodgates Farm, Woodgates End, Broxted, Dunmow CM6 2BN
t 01787 461434 **f** 01787 461672 **m** 07957 230018
e videoengineering@compuserve.com
Contact Teresa Firlit

Vision Power (UK) Ltd

Unit 4, Montague Works, 90-92 Queensbury Road, Wembley
HA0 1QG
t 020 8998 8848 **f** 020 8998 6170
e vision.power@btinternet.com
Contact Bipin Patel, Managing Director

TELECOMMUNICATIONS

Telecommunications **General**

Adam Phones Ltd

5 Dolphin Square, Edensor Road, London W4 2RG
t 020 8742 0101 **f** 020 8742 3679
e moreinfo@adamphones.com **w** www.adamphones.com
Contact Sunita Sharma, Hire Department

*Mobile phone hire at the lowest prices ever. Over fourteen years
experience of supplying film and TV production clients ensures our
mobiles are a support, not another source of anxiety.*

Applied Satellite Technology
Airport House, Purley Way, Croydon CR0 0XZ
t 020 8781 1844 **f** 020 8781 1846 **m** 07860 245 623
e astlondon@aol.com **w** www.satcomms.com
Contact Chris Wood, Managing Director

Aquarius Communications
15 Warburton Street, Manchester M20 6WA
t 0161 434 5666 **f** 0161 434 5656
Contact Martyn Pardoe, Managing Director

Avoca
View Point, Basing View, Basingstoke RG21 4RG
t 01256 799845 **f** 01256 799844 **w** www.avocacom.net

British Monomarks Ltd
27 Old Gloucester Street, London WC1N 3XX
t 020 7419 5000 **f** 020 7831 9489
e sales@monomark.co.uk **w** www.britishmonomarks.co.uk

Cabletime Ltd
64 Greenham Road, Newbury RG14 7HX
t 01635 35111 **f** 01635 35913 **w** www.cabletime.com
Contact David Ridley, Service Manager; Terry Jones, Production Manager

Cellhire Plc
Park House, Clifton Park, York YO30 5PB
t 01904 610610 **f** 01904 611028
e rentals@cellhire.com **w** www.cellhire.com

Communication Spares (UK) Ltd
Empress House, 42 Empress Parade, Chingford Road, London
E4 8SL
t 020 8531 1909 **f** 020 8531 0008
e sales@csuk.co.uk **w** www.csuk.co.uk
Contact Steve Brown, Proprietor

CSA Ltd
Knight Road, Rochester ME2 2AX
t 01634 715544 **f** 01634 715742
e international.sales@cs-wireless.com **w** www.csa-wireless.com
Contact Helmut Helmberger, Marketing Sales Director

Echo Communications Ltd
Echo House, 27-33 Burr Road, London SW18 4SQ
t 020 8870 4000 **f** 020 8871 4007
e info@echocomms.co.uk **w** www.echocomms.co.uk
Contact Simon Turner, Sales Manager

Enterprise Control Systems
31 The High Street, Wappenham NN12 8SN
t 01327 860050 **f** 01327 860058
e sue@enterprisecontrol.co.uk **w** www.enterprisecontrol.co.uk
Contact Sue Haysey; C Bullock, Managing Director

Fibernet Bespoke Networks
Rosalind House, Jays Close, Viables, Basingstoke RG22 4BS
t 01256 858685 **f** 01256 858601 **w** www.fibernet.co.uk
Contact Patrick Daniels, Business Development Manager

Intercity Mobile Communications Ltd
101-114 Holloway Head, Birmingham B1 1QP
t 0121 643 7373 **f** 0121 643 6160
Contact Nikki Windridge, Contact; Jan Stolarska, Personnel Manager

Intext Media (UK) Ltd
3-5 Islington High Street, London N1 9LQ
t 020 7745 2510 **f** 020 7745 2511
e info@intextmedia.com **w** www.intextmedia.com
Contact Caroline Griffiths, Managing Director

iSky
Clevedon Hall, Victoria Road, Clevedon, Bristol BS21 7RQ
t 0800 252032 **f** 01275 344101
e response@isky.co.uk **w** www.isky.co.uk
Contact Maggie Evans, Head of Marketing

iTouch
Avalon House, 57-63 Scrutton Street, London EC2A 4PF
t 020 7613 6000 **f** 020 7613 6006
e info@itouch.co.uk **w** www.itouch.co.uk
Contact Graham Thorley, Media Sales Manager

Loral Skynet
MWB Business Exchange, Liberty House, 222 Regent Street,
London W1B 5TR
t 020 7297 2067 **f** 020 7297 2173 **w** www.cyberstar.com
Contact Chris Chaney, UK Director; Howard Farr, Vice President

Marconi Plc
Regent's Place, 338 Euston Road, London NW1 3BT
t 020 7543 6900 **f** 020 7493 1974 **w** www.marconi.com

Motek Portable Products
Sandtoft Industrial Estate, Belton, Doncaster DN9 1PN
t 01427 873391 **f** 01427 874037
e sales@motek.co.uk **w** www.motek.co.uk
Contact Allan Layfield, Sales Manager; Alison Barker, Marketing Manager; Phil
Bayliss, Sales Co-ordinator

Nortech
Blackdyke Road, Kingstown Industrial Estate, Carlisle CA3 0PJ
t 01228 544678 **f** 01228 515370
e claire@nortech-radiocomms.co.uk
w www.nortech-radiocomms.co.uk
Contact Claire Andrews, Sales Manager; Simon Osman, Director

North East Radio Communications
Bewick Street, Willington Quay, Wallsend NE28 6SR
t 01912 621221 **f** 01912 634004 **e** sales.nerc@dial.pipex.com
Contact Brian Maine, Service Manager; Stephen Smith, Sales

ntl
NTL House, 9000 Cambridge Research Park, Eley Road,
Waterbeach CB5 9TF
t 01223 567200 **f** 01223 567222 **w** www.ntl.com
Contact Richard Crane, Assistant Managing Director

Parris-Wolfe Communications Ltd
Trade Tower, Plantation Wharf, Battersea, London SW11 3UF
t 020 7738 1111 **f** 020 7738 0111
e enquiries@parris-wolfe.com **w** www.parris-wolfe.com
Credits Alicia Keyes Tour (W); Rolling Stones Tour (W)

Radiocoms Systems Ltd
170A Oval Road, Croydon CR0 6BN
t 020 8680 1585 **f** 020 8686 9433
Contact Lee St Pier, Area Manager

Syscom Systems Ltd
12 London Road, Liphook GU30 7AN
t 01428 722065 **e** talkbacksys@aol.com
Contact Keith Banham, Director

Telewest Communications Plc
Cable House, 1 Waterside Drive, Langley SL3 6EZ
t 01753 810810 **f** 01753 810818 **w** www.telewest.co.uk
Contact Chris Neary, Managing Director

TTI Ltd
Unit 1, The Ringway Centre, Edison Road, Basingstoke RG21 6YH
t 01256 330366 **f** 01256 330410
Contact Tracy Wilkinson, Administration Manager

TVL Ltd
The Media Centre, Culver House Cross, Cardiff CF5 6XJ
t 029 2059 0159 **f** 029 2059 0386
e phil@tv-links.demon.co.uk
Contact Richard Pimlott, Director; Phil Hallinan, Director

Vodafone Hire Solutions
2-3 The Argent Centre, Pump Lane, Hayes UB3 3NE
t 0870 900 9809 **f** 08709 009810
e hire@vodafone.co.uk **w** www.vodafone-hiresolutions.co.uk
Contact Debbra Moses, Operations Manager

Telecommunications
Interactive TV

Downtime Media Productions Ltd
38 Academy Apartments, Institute Place, London E8 1JZ
t 020 8510 9500 **m** 07932 074621 **e** dtmprods@hotmail.com
Contact John Denton, Senior Producer
Credits Interactive Games (T); Better Homes and Gardens Australia (T); Interactive Wine Guide - Mobile and IDTV (W)

Production of high quality, cross platform programmes for the converging technologies of interactive TV, web and mobile services. Consultancy services.

Original Thinking Group
5th Floor, 6 Ramilles Street, London W1F 7TY
t 020 7479 4050 **f** 020 7479 4051 **m** 07973 185795
e liam.westley@originaltg.com **w** www.originaltg.com
Contact Liam Westley, Chief Technology Officer
Credits Sky Gamestar (T); Sky One (T); Sky News (T)

Telecommunications
Mobile Interactive Services

BBC Audiocall
Woodlands, Wood Lane, London W12 0TT
t 020 8433 3670 **f** 020 8433 3993
e audiocall@bbc.co.uk **w** www.audiocall.co.uk
Contact Marc Humphrey, Sales Manager; Tamara Suaznabar, Sales Executive; Andrew Jackson, Sales Executive
Credits Children In Need (T); Bargain Hunt (T); Fame Academy (T); Big Brother (T)

Mediation Technology
2 Sidney Gardens, Haslingfield, Cambridge CB3 7NA
t 01223 872340 **f** 07092 308912 **m** 07710 170481
e info@mediation.co.uk **w** www.mediation.co.uk
Contact Geoff Vincent, Partner
Credits WH Smith People's Choice Book Awards (W); Granada Reports (T); The Late Debate (T)

Teletext Ltd
101 Farm Lane, Fulham, London SW6 1QJ
t 020 7386 5000 **f** 020 7386 5002 **w** www.teletext.co.uk
Contact Michael Stewart, Managing Director; Jonathan Crebes, Mobile Manager

Theatres **Preview**

Bloomsbury Theatre
15 Gordon Street, London WC1H 0AH
t 020 7679 2777 **f** 020 7383 4080
e blooms.theatre@ucl.ac.uk **w** www.ucl.ac.uk/bloomsburytheatre

Century Screening Rooms
Twentieth Century Fox, 31-32 Soho Square, London W1V 6AP
t 020 7753 7135 **f** 020 7753 7138 **m** 0=44 7976 248818
e projection@foxinc.com

City Screen Ltd
11 Rupert Street, London W1V 7FS
t 020 7851 7041 **f** 020 7851 7060
e othercinema@picturehouses.co.uk
Contact Paul Homer, Manager; Melanie Crawley, Business Development Manager

Commonwealth Conference & Events Centre
Kensington High Street, London W8 6NQ
t 020 7603 4535 **f** 020 7603 4525
e conference@commonwealth.org.uk
w www.commonwealth.org.uk
Contact David French, Chief Executive

De Lane Lea Ltd
75 Dean Street, London W1D 3PU
t 020 7432 3800 **f** 020 7432 3838
e info@delanelea.com **w** www.delanelea.com
Contact Katrina Rochowski, Office Manager; Anna Billington, Bookings; Yazz Rajeeball, Bookings; Peter Joly, Managing Director; Mica McGrath, Bookings
Credits Billy Elliot (F); Ned Kelly (F); Dirty Pretty Things (F); The Lost Prince (T)

The Most Competitive and Versatile Audio Post House in London.

Eden Court Theatre
Bishop's Road, Inverness IV3 5SA
t 01463 239841 **f** 01463 713810
e cmarr@eden-court.co.uk **w** www.eden-court.co.uk
Contact Colin Marr, Theatre Director

Hoxton Hall
130 Hoxton Street, London N1 6SH
t 020 7684 0060 **f** 020 7729 3815
e office@hoxtonhall.co.uk **w** www.hoxtonhall.co.uk
Contact Chris Bowler, Director

Institut Francais
17 Queensberry Place, London SW7 2DT
t 020 7073 1350 **f** 020 7073 1355
e box.office@ambafrance.org.uk **w** www.institut-francais.org.uk
Contact Vincent Melilli, Director; Alexandre Minski, Head of Marketing

Liverpool Everyman & Playhouse
13 Hope Street, Liverpool L1 9BH
t 0151 708 0338 **f** 0151 709 0398
e info@everymanplayhouse.com **w** www.everymanplayhouse.com
Contact Tim Brunsden, General Manager

Mr Young's Preview Theatre
14 D'Arblay Street, London W1F 8DY
t 020 7437 1771 **f** 020 7734 4520
e info@mryoungs.com **w** www.mryoungs.com
Contact Jim Archer, Manager; Reuben Barnes, Manager

Planet Hollywood Preview Theatre
13 Coventry Street, London W1D 7DH
t 020 7437 7827
Contact Annabella Wilkinson; Annabella Wilkinson, Events Organiser; Reg Lackman, Projectionist

The Royal Society Of Arts
8 John Adam Street, London WC2N 6EZ
t 020 7930 5115 **f** 020 7321 0271
e conference@rsa.org.uk **w** www.theplacetomeet.org.uk
Contact Nicki Kyle; Anna Clover, Conferencing

Scottish Mask & Puppet Theatre Centre
8-10 Balcarres Avenue, Kelvindale, Glasgow G12 0QF
t 0141 339 6185 **f** 0141 357 4484
e info@scottishmaskandpuppetcentre.co.uk
w www.scottishmaskandpuppetcentre.co.uk

Contact Malcolm Knight, Executive Director
Credits Cultural Diversity Programme (E); The Magic Of Masks And Puppets (E); HND Puppet Theatre Arts (E); Treasures: Malcolm Knight Mask Man (T)

Screen West
136-142 Bramley Rd, London W10 6SR
t 020 7565 3102 **f** 020 7565 3077
e sarah.alliston@jbcp.co.uk **w** www.screenwest.co.uk
Contact Sarah Alliston, Manager

Showroom Cinema
Paternoster Row, Sheffield S1 2BX
t 0114 276 3534 **f** 0114 249 3204
e info@showroom.org.uk **w** www.showroom.org.uk

Southport Theatre & Floral Hall Complex
Promenade, Southport PR9 0DZ
t 01704 540454 **f** 01704 536841
e southporttheatre@clearchannel.co.uk
w www.southport-floralhall.co.uk

Contact Lisa Chu, Area General Manager; Emma Baldwin, Marketing Manager; Sarah Burton, Venue Manager

Ster Century UK Ltd
3rd Floor St George's House, Knoll Road, Camberley GU15 3SY
t 01276 605605 **f** 01276 605600
e reception@stercentury.co.uk **w** www.stercentury.net
Contact Selwyn Grimsley, Chief Operating Officer

Watermans
40 High Street, Brentford TW8 0DS
t 020 8232 1010 **t** 020 8232 1020 **f** 020 8232 1030
e info@watermans.org.uk **w** www.watermans.org.uk

Contact Jon Brighton, Technical Director; Jan Lennox, Director; Matthew Pritchard, Programme Administrator; Jennie Gentles, Marketing Director

Tourist Boards
Embassies, Consulates

Afghanistan Embassy
31 Princess Gate, London SW7 1QQ
t 020 7589 8891 **f** 020 7581 3452

Antigua & Barbuda High Commission and Tourist Office
15 Thayer Street, London W1U 3JT
t 020 7486 7073 **f** 020 7486 1466
e antbar@msn.com **w** www.antigua-barbuda.com
Contact Sandra Scotland; Joyce Fyfe; Curliss Bart, Information Counsellor

Australian Tourist Commission
1st Floor, Gemini House, 10-18 Putney Hill, London SW15 6AA
t 020 8780 2229 **f** 020 8780 1496
w www.media.australia.com, www.australia.com
Contact Kate Kenward, PR Information Manager

Austrian National Tourist Office
PO Box 2363, London W1A 2QB
t 020 7629 0461 **f** 020 7499 6038
e info@anto.co.uk **w** www.austria-tourism.at/

Bahamas Tourist Office
3 The Billings, Walnut Tree Close, Guildford GU1 4UL
t 01483 448900 **f** 01483 571846
e btogfd@bahamas.com **w** www.bahamas.com
Contact Jeremy Bonnett, General Manager

Bahrain Embassy
30 Belgravia Square, London SW1 8QB
t 020 72019170 **f** 020 7201 9189

Belgian Tourist Office
217 Marsh Wall, London E14 9FJ
t 020 7531 0392 **f** 020 7531 0393
e consumer@belgiumtheplaceto.be
w www.belgiumtheplaceto.be
Contact Sue Heady, Press Manager

Brazilian Consulate
32 Green Street, London W1K 7AT
t 020 7399 9000 **f** 020 7399 9100
e info@brazil.org.uk **w** www.brazil.org.uk

Cayman Islands Department of Tourism
6 Arlington Street, London SW1A 1RE
t 020 7491 7771 **f** 020 7409 7773
e info-uk@caymanislands.co.uk **w** www.caymanislands.co.uk
Contact Vicki Sacker, Office Administration Manager

Chile Tourist Information
12 Devonshire Street, London W1G 7DS
t 020 7580 1023 **f** 020 7323 4294
e cglonduk@congechileuk.demon.co.uk **w** www.visitchile.org
Contact M Condesa

Costa Rica Embassy
Flat 1, 14 Lancaster Gate, London W2 3LH
t 020 7706 8844 **f** 020 7706 8655
e info@embcrlon.demon.co.uk **w** www.embcrlon.demon.co.uk
Contact Lorena Villalobos, Attache (tourism)

Cyprus Tourism Organisation
17 Hanover Street, London W1S 1YP
t 020 7569 8800 **f** 020 7499 4935
e ctolon@ctolon.demon.co.uk **w** www.cyprustourism.org

Danish Tourist Board
55 Sloane Street, London SW1X 9SY
t 020 7259 5959 **e** dtb.london@dt.dk **w** www.visitdenmark.com

El Salvador Embassy
Mayfair House, 39 Great Portland Street, London W1W 7JZ
t 020 7436 8282 **f** 020 7436 8181
e embasalondres@netscapeonline.co.uk

Embassy Of Czech Republic
26 Kensington Palace Gardens, London W8 4QY
t 020 7243 1115 **f** 020 7727 9654 **e** london@embassy.mzv.cz
Contact Katrina

Embassy of Iceland
2A Hans Street, London SW1X 0JE
t 020 7259 3999 **f** 020 7245 9649
e icemb.london@utn.stjr.is **w** www.iceland.org/uk

Embassy of the Democratic Republic of Congo
38 Holne Chase, London N2 0QQ
t 020 8458 0254 **f** 020 8458 0254

Embassy of the Islamic Republic of Iran
16 Princes Gate, London SW7 1PT
t 020 7225 3000 **f** 020 7589 4440
e info@iran-embassy.org.uk **w** www.iran-embassy.org.uk

Ethiopian Embassy
17 Princes Gate, London SW7 1PZ
t 020 7589 7212 **f** 020 7584 7054
e info@ethioembassy.org.uk **w** www.ethioembassy.org.uk
Contact Andy Charles; Ephrem Mehret-Ab

Finnish Tourist Board
PO Box 33213, London W6 8JX
t 020 8600 5680 **t** 020 7365 2512 **f** 020 8600 5681
e finlandinfo.lon@mek.fi **w** www.finland.tourism.com/uk
Contact Paivi Kemppainen, Marketing Manager

Gambian National Tourist Office
57 Kensington Court, London W8 5DG
t 020 7376 0093 **f** 020 7938 3644
e office@ukgta.fsnet.co.uk **w** www.gambiatourism.info

German National Tourist Office
PO Box 2695, London W1A 3TN
t 020 7317 0908 **f** 020 7495 6129
e michael.helmerich@d-z-t.com **w** www.germany-tourism.de
Contact Michael Helmerich, Press Officer

Ghana High Commission
13 Belgrave Square, London SW1X 8PN
t 020 7201 5900 **f** 020 7245 9552 **w** www.ghana-com.co.uk
Contact Mr Andoh, Information Office

Gibraltar Tourist Board
Arundel Great Court, 178-179 Strand, London WC2R 1EL
t 020 7836 0777 **f** 020 7240 6612
e info@gibraltar.gov.uk **w** www.gibraltar.gov.uk
Contact Albert Poggio

Grenada Board Of Tourism
1 Battersea Church Road, Battersea, London SW11 3LY
t 020 7771 7016 **f** 020 7771 7181
e grenada@cibgroup.co.uk **w** www.grenadagrenadines.com
Contact Sharon Bernstein, Representative

Guyana High Commission
3 Palace Court, Bayswater Road, London W2 4LP
t 020 7229 7684 **f** 020 7727 9809
Contact Merion Herbert, First Secretary

Honduras Embassy
115 Gloucester Place, London W1U 6JT
t 020 7486 4880 **f** 020 7486 4550
e hondurasuk@lineone.net

Hong Kong Tourism Board
6 Grafton Street, London W1S 4EQ
t 020 7533 7100 **f** 020 7533 7111
e lonwwo@hktourismboard.com
w www.discoverhongkong.com

ICEP Portuguese Trade & Tourism Office
22-25A Sackville Street, 2nd Floor, London W1S 3LY
t 020 6364 0610 **f** 020 7494 1868
e tourism@portugaloffice.org.uk **w** www.portugalinsite.com
Contact Jose Preto da Silva, Director

Indian Government Tourist Board
7 Cork Street, London W1X 2LN
t 020 7437 3677 **f** 020 7494 1048
e info@indiatouristoffice.org.uk
w www.indiatouristoffice.org.uk
Contact Mrs Alkohli, Director; Alkohli, Director

Indonesian Embassy
38 Grosvenor Square, London W1K 2HW
t 020 7499 7661 **f** 020 7491 4993
e kbri@indolondon.freeserve.co.uk
w www.indonesianembassy.org.uk

Israel Government Tourist Office
UK House, 180 Oxford Street, London W1D 1NN
t 020 7299 1113 **f** 020 7299 1112 **w** www.go-israel.co.uk
Contact Heather Freedland, PR Manager

Italian State Tourist Office
1 Princes Street, London W1B 2AY
t 020 7408 1254 **f** 020 7399 3567
e italy@italiantouristboard.co.uk **w** www.enit.it

Kenya High Commission
45 Portland Place, London W1B 1AS
t 020 7637 2371 **f** 020 7323 6717
e kcomm45@aol.com **w** www.kenyahighcommission.com
Contact Steve Crawley, Manager

Lebanon Embassy
Information Office, 15 Palace Gardens Mews, Kensington,
London W8 4RA
t 020 7229 7265 **f** 020 7243 1699

Maison De La France
178 Piccadilly, London W1J 9AL
t 020 7399 3535 **e** info@mdlf.co.uk **w** www.franceguide.com
Contact Ann Noon, Head of Press

Malaysia Tourism Office
Malaysia Tourism Promotion Board, 57 Traflalgar Square,
London WC2N 5DU
t 020 7930 7932 **f** 020 7930 9015
e info@tourism-malaysia.co.uk **w** www.tourismmalaysia.gov.my
Contact Yazid Mohamed, Director

The Mersey Partnership
5th Floor, Cunard Building, Pier Head, Liverpool L3 1ET
t 0151 237 3925 **f** 0151 237 3938
e rachel.woods@merseyside.org.uk **w** www.merseyside.org.uk
Contact Rachel Woods, Marketing Assistant; Thomas O'Brien, Cheif Executive

Mexico Tourism Board
Wakefield House, 41 Trinity Square, London EC3N 4DJ
t 020 7488 9392 **f** 020 7265 0704
e uk@visitmexico.com **w** www.visitmexico.com
Contact Manuel Diaz-Cebrian, Director

Moroccan National Tourist Office
205 Regent Street, London W1B 4HB
t 020 7437 0073 **f** 020 7734 8172
e mnto@morocco-tourism.org.uk **w** www.visitmorocco.com
Contact A Al Kasmi; Aziz Mnii, Trade and Media Officer

Netherlands Board of Tourism
PO Box 30783, London WC2 6DH
t 020 7539 7957 **f** 020 7539 7953
e smartens@holland.com **w** www.holland.com/uk
Contact Andrew van der Feltz; Anette Hendrickx

Nigerian High Commission
9 Northumberland Avenue, London WC2N 5BX
t 020 7839 1244 **f** 020 7839 8746
w www.nigeriahigncommissionuk.com

Northern Ireland Tourist Board
St Anne's Court, 59 North Street, Belfast BT1 1NB
t 028 9023 1221 **f** 028 9024 0960
e info@nitb.com **w** www.discovernorthernireland.com
Contact Mark Alexander, Deputy Chief Executive; Mo Durkan, Press Office Manager

Oman Embassy
167 Queens Gate, London SW7 5HE
t 020 7225 0001 **f** 020 7589 2505
e omanembassy@omanembassy.fsnet.com

Pakistan High Commission
34-36 Lowndes Square, London SW1X 9JN
t 020 7664 9200 **f** 020 7664 9224
e pareblondon@supanet.com **w** www.pakmission-uk.gov.pak

Peru Embassy
52 Sloane Street, London SW1X 9SP
t 020 7235 1917 **f** 020 7235 4463
e carlosrossi@peruembassy-uk.com **w** www.peruembassy-uk.com
Contact Carlos Rossi

Romanian National Tourist Office
22 New Cavendish Street, London W1G 8TT
t 020 7224 3692 **f** 020 7935 6435
e uktouroff@romania.freeserve.co.uk
Contact Dan Gaman, Director

Royal Embassy Of Saudi Arabia
30 Charles Street, London W1X 8LP
t 020 7917 3000 **f** 020 7917 3065
e info@intourist.co.uk **w** www.saudiembassy.org.uk

Salt Marsh Partnership
The Copperfield, 25 Copperfield Street, London SE1 0EN
t 020 7928 1600 **f** 020 7928 1700
e geoff@saltmarshpr.co.uk **w** www.saltmarshpr.co.uk
Contact Selena Parish, Contact

Seychelles Tourist Office
36 Southwark Bridge Road, London SE1 9EU
t 020 7202 0722 **f** 020 7928 0722
e seychelles@hilsbalfour.com **w** www.aspureasitgets.com
Contact Debbie Walker, Sales and Marketing Manager

Singapore Tourism Board
1st Floor, Carrington House, 126-130 Regent Street, London W1B 5JX
t 020 7437 0033 **f** 020 7734 2191 **w** www.visitsingapore.com
Contact Anna Rajah, Marketing Manager

Sudan Embassy
3 Cleveland Row, St James, London SW1A 1DD
t 020 7839 8080 **f** 020 7839 7560
e www.sudan-embassy.co.uk
Contact Sadi Bakheid, Press Officer

Switzerland Tourism
Swiss Centre, 10 Wardour Street, London W1D 6QF
t 0800 1002 0030 **f** 0800 1002 0031
e info.uk@switzerland.com **e** res.uk@switzerland.com
w www.myswitzerland.com

Tanzania High Commission
43 Hertford Street, London W1Y 7DB
t 020 7499 8951 **f** 020 7491 9321
e tanzarep@tanzania-online.gov.uk **w** www.tanzania-online.gov.uk
Contact Simon May

Tourism Ireland
Nations House, 103 Wigmore Street, London W1U 1QS
t 020 7518 0800 **f** 020 7493 9065

Tourism New Zealand
New Zealand House, Level 7, 80 Haymarket, London SW1Y 4TQ
t 020 7930 1662 **f** 020 7839 8929
e info@nztb.govt.nz **w** www.purenz.com

Tunisian National Tourist Office
77A Wigmore Street, London W1U 1QF
t 020 7224 5561 **f** 020 7224 4053 **e** tntolondon@aol.com
Contact Ahmed Essaies, Director

Uruguay Embassy
140 Brampton Road, London SW3 1HY
t 020 7589 8835 **f** 020 7581 9585
Contact The Ambassador, Cultural Attache

Venezuela Embassy
1 Cromwell Road, London SW7 2HW
t 020 7584 4206 **f** 020 7589 8887
e informationdepartmentvenezlon@venexlon.demon.co.uk
w www.venezlon.demon.co.uk
Contact The Ambassador, Attache Cultural

Visit Scotland
19 Cockspur Street, London SW1Y 5BL
t 0131 332 2433 **f** 020 7930 1817 **w** www.visitscotland.com

Wales Tourist Board
Visit Britain Centre, 1 Regent Street, London SW1Y 4XT
t 0870 121 1251 **f** 020 7808 3830
e info@visitwales.com **w** www.visitwales.com
Contact Haf Jones

Yemen Embassy
57 Cromwell Road, London SW7 2ED
t 020 7584 6607 **f** 020 7589 3350
Contact Abraham Alkater, Financial and Administrative Attaché

Zambia National Tourist Board
2 Palace Gate, London W8 5NG
t 0207 589 6655 **f** 0207 584 6346
e zntb@aol.com **w** www.zambiatourism.com

Tracking Vehicles

A1 Grip/Camera Tracking Cars
1 Hurstlands, Oxted RH8 0HF
t 01883 712426 **f** 01883 712426
e jose.decozar@btopenworld.com **w** www.a1grips.co.uk

BBC Outside Broadcasts

BBC Outside Broadcasts
Kendal Avenue, London W3 0RP
t 020 8993 9333 **f** 020 8993 4510
e ob@bbc.co.uk **w** www.bbcresources.com/ob

Bickers Action
Ivy Farm Works, High Street, Coddenham, Ipswich IP6 9QX
t 01449 761300 **f** 01449 760614
m 07831 132009 **m** 07836 606291
e action@bickers.co.uk **w** www.bickers.co.uk
Contact Paul Bickers, Managing Director; Dean Cox, Operations Manager
Credits Emmerdale (T); Cold Play - Scientist (M); Heartbeat (T); Die Another Day (F)
Stunt Engineering, Mechanical SFX, Camera Tracking Vehicles & Low Loaders.

Central Film Facilities
Unit 1, Marshbrook Business Park, Church Stretton SY6 6QE
t 01694 781418 **f** 01694 781468
m 07971 546647 **w** www.centralfilmfacilities.com
Contact Charles Mansell, Partner; Paul Mansell, Partner; Bridget Freeman, Office Manager
Credits Birthday Girl (T); Cold Feet (T); Coca Cola (W); At Home With The Braithwaites (T)

Close Encounters Film Action
t 07000 326 3377 **f** 07000 326 3377 **m** 07074 263377
e actiononscreen@aol.com
Contact David Anders, Stunt Engineer
Credits Navy in Action (F&I) (F); Indian (F); Deceit (F)

Mansfields

Bentalls, Pipps Hill Industrial Estate, Basildon SS14 3BX
t 01268 520646 **f** 01268 526865
m 07887 517533 **i** 01268 280235
e mike@mansfieldsdesign.co.uk **w** www.trackingcar.co.uk
Contact Andy Frankland, Operations Director; Mike Hayward, Sales and Marketing Manager
Credits Fiesta (I); Jaguar XS (I)

Nine Nine Cars

Hyde Meadow Farm, Hyde Lane, Hemel Hampstead HP3 8SA
t 01923 266373 **f** 01923 260852 **m** 07785 382448
e richard@nineninecars.com **w** www.nineninecars.com
Contact Richard Hammott; David Hammott

Off Trax

Wharf House, Brentwaters Business Park, The Ham, Brentford TW8 8HQ
t 020 8232 8822 **f** 020 8232 8877
e mail@offtrax.co.uk **w** www.offtrax.co.uk
Contact Crispin Kyle, Facilities Manager

Translation Services

Acroama

4A Duck Lane, Soho, London W1F OHY
t 020 7287 2075 **f** 020 7287 2045
e sales@acroama.co.uk **w** www.acroama.co.uk
Contact Brendan Weaney, Operations Director
Credits The Tiger In The Snow (T); Elvis In Hollywood (F)

Allmedia Translations

157A Nelson Road, London N8 9RR
t 020 7248 0263 **f** 020 7248 1291 **e** info@allmediatrans.co.uk

American Pie

179 Kings Cross Road, London WC1X 9BZ
t 020 7278 9490 **f** 020 7278 2447 **m** 07956 364724
e bacon@langservice.com **w** www.americanization.com
Contact Josephine Bacon, Managing Director; Zuzana Zabkowa, Translation Manager
Credits Experiments In Tunis (T); Trial Of Kurt Waldheim (T); Executions (T); Young Indiana Jones (T)

Expert translation, interpreting, foreign language typesetting and voice coaching. Owner Equity and NUS member, 20 years in the profession. Tape translation and transcriptions with timecodes.

APA Translations

91 Princes Avenue, London W3 8LY
t 020 8752 1944 **f** 020 8752 1918
e ana@apatrans.demon.co.uk **w** www.apatrans.com
Contact Ana Soto, Director

APT Transtelex Plc

585A Fulham Road, Fulham Broadway, London SW6 5UA
t 020 7381 0967 **f** 020 7381 0960
e marketing@aptplc.net **w** www.aptplc.com
Contact Charles Jamieson, Director; Andrew Clementson

Aradco VSI Ltd

Aradco House, 132 Cleveland Street, London W1T 6AB
t 020 7692 7700 **f** 020 7692 7711
e info@aradco.com **w** www.aradco.com
Contact Vicky Voyatzi; Richard Dawood

Barbara Back

63 Philbeach Gardens, London SW5 9EE
t 020 7373 5783

The BigWord Company

59 Charlotte Street, London W1T 4PE
t 020 8866 2135 **f** 0870 748 8001
e info@thebigword.com **w** www.thebigword.com
Contact Chloe Leach, Marketing Executive

Biznet Professional Translation & Voiceovers

63 Abingdon Villas, London W8 6XA
t 020 7565 0909 **t** 08000 565453
f 020 7565 0111 **f** 020 7937 1447
e translate@biznetserv.com **w** www.biznetserv.com
Contact Mary O'Byrne, Account Manager; David Levin, Managing Director; Basil Short, Transcription Services; Jerome Alexander, Voiceover Bookings; David Thomas, Interpreter Bookings; Allison Colenutt, Translation Bookings
Credits Discovery Channel (T); Fiat (C); Fiat; Fiat

Elena Crompton

2 Yester Drive, Chislehurst BR7 5LR
t 020 8467 3542 **f** 020 8467 3542 **m** 07703 313164
e ecrompton@yester2.demon.co.uk

Foreign Versions Ltd

Bakerloo Chambers, 304 Edgeware Road, London W2 1DY
t 020 7723 5744 **f** 020 7723 5018
e info@foreignversions.co.uk **w** www.foreignversions.co.uk

German Accurate Translations

81 Chambers Lane, London NW10 2RN
t 020 8459 5023 **f** 020 8459 5023
e michaelmertl@aol.com **w** www.mmertl.com

IMS

Manor House, Soho Square, London W1D 3DP
t 020 7440 5400 **f** 020 7440 5410 **m** 07710 348288
e mark.robinson@ims-media.com
Contact Mark Robinson, Head Of Operations

INTER-COM Translations

Inter-Com Translations

Hurlingham Studios, Ranelagh Gardens, London SW6 3PA
t 020 7731 8000 **f** 020 7731 5511 **m** 07946 546531
e mail@intercom-translations.co.uk
w www.intercom-translations.co.uk
Contact Patrick Beacom, Partner; Carolina Lehrian, Partner

Looking for a dependable professional team, with a major client list to handle your foreign versions? All languages, all subjects. Translations, transcriptions, time-coded scripts, subtitling, type-setting, interpreting, voiceovers.

Kenrick Translation Services
17 Howards Lane, Putney, London SW15 6NX
t 020 8789 0896 **f** 020 8789 0897 **e** kenrick1@onetel.net.uk
Contact Michael Wakefield, Chairman; John Trechman, General Manager

Lesley Howard Languages
27 Ryland Road, London NW5 3EH
t 020 7267 2677 **f** 020 7482 4822
e lingua@atlas.co.uk **w** www.lesleyhoward.net
Contact Lesley Howard, Managing Director

Password International
118 Chevening Road, Queens Park, London NW6 6TP
t 020 8723 8841
e translations@password-eu.net **w** www.password-eu.net
Localisation services for corporate materials, games, instructions, training and the internet.

Pratima Dave Translation Services
32 Winton Avenue, New Southgate, London N11 2AT
t 020 8888 9373 **f** 020 8889 6998 **e** pratimadave@aol.com
Contact Pratima Dave, Proprietor

Pudsey Translators & Interpreters
2 Church Lane, Pudsey LS28 7BD
t 0113 239 3301 **f** 0113 236 1651 **m** 07957 246666
e translators@bakerharding.co.uk
Contact Liz Navin-Jones, Partner

QTransco Ltd
8 St Marys Way, Guilford GU2 8JY
t 01483 870231 **f** 01483 870229 **m** 07718 207092
e info@qtransco.com **w** www.qtransco.com

Take 1 Script Services Ltd
456-458 The Strand, London WC2R 0DZ
t 0800 085 4418 **f** 01580 715809 **m** 07711 531381
e info@take1scripts.com **w** www.take1scripts.com
Contact Dom Bourne, Managing Director
Credits Jackass The Movie (F); Eurotrash (T); Louis Theroux (T)

foreignvoices.co.uk

Translations To Picture
24 Hawgood Street, London E3 3RU
t 020 7517 3550 **f** 020 7537 2839 **m** 07956 577668
e info@foreignvoices.co.uk **w** www.foreignvoices.co.uk
Contact Susan Cunningham, Production Assistant; James Bonallack, Director

A one-stop shop for timed translations, foreign voices in 25 languages — listen to them now at www.foreignvoices.co.uk, subtitling and our in-house Sadie suite from £60 per hour to picture.

UPS Translations
111 Baker Street, London W1U 6RR
t 020 7837 8300 **f** 020 7486 3272
e info@upstranslations.com **w** www.upstranslations.com
Contact Bernard Silver, Chairman & Managing Director; Justin Silver, Marketing Director; Sarah Parkhurst, Head of Translation
Credits A Short Film About Projectors (S); Auf Wiedersehen Pet (T); Hard To Believe (C); In Desert And Wilderness (F)

Foreign-language transcription, script translation, voiceover artistes, coaching, subtitling, lipsync and interpreters, in all the world's languages. The Language Division of United Publicity Services Plc.

VSI
Aradco House, 132 Cleveland Street, London W1T 6AB
t 020 7692 7700 **t** 020 7692 7702 **f** 020 7692 7711
e info@vsi.tv **w** www.vsi.tv
Contact Norman Dawood, Director; Carla Mercer, PA to Managing Director; Virginie Verdier, Head of Subtitling; Jenny Morris, Head of Voice-Overs; Lola Smith, Project Manager
Credits National Geographic - Africa (D); Heineken (C); What Lies Beneath (F)

TRANSPORT
Transport **Captains**

Gary Birmingham
349 Hanworth Road, Hampton TW12 3EJ
t 020 8941 6255 **f** 07980 687499 **m** 07973 848464
e gary.birmingham@virgin.net
Credits To Kill A King (F); Neverland (F); The Four Feathers (F)

Peter Graovac
25 Ember Gardens, Thames Ditton KT7 0LL
t 020 8398 4439 **f** 07092 003052 **m** 07970 074627
e pgraovac@aol.com
Credits Band Of Brothers (T)

Robbie Ryan
47 Blantyre Crescent, Duntocher, Glasgow G81 6JN
t 01389 878235 **f** 01389 383988 **m** 07703 162164
e robryan47@hotmail.com

Transport **Vehicle Hire**

1st Direct Vehicle Rentals
628 Streatham High Road, Streatham, London SW16 3QL
t 020 8679 5110 **f** 020 8679 6869 **m** 07887 516111
e 1st.direct@dial.pipex.com **w** www.1stdirectvehiclerentals.co.uk
Contact Simon Bates, Main Contact

Air-Rider
18 Gisburn Mansions, Tottenham Lane, London N8 7EB
t 020 8341 5871 **f** 020 8341 9827 **m** 07836 519902
Contact Greg Haynes, Proprietor

Alan Sycamore Motor Homes
1 Shenley Road, Whaddon MK17 0LW
t 01908 501896 **f** 01908 501896 **m** 07836 253343
e motorhomes@alan-sycamore.freeserve.co.uk
Contact Alan Sycamore, Proprietor
Credits The Corrs (M); BBC (C); HSBC (C)

Allander Coaches
Unit 19, Cloberfield Industrial Estate, Glasgow G62 7LN
t 0141 956 5678 **f** 0141 956 6669
e enquiries@allandertravel.co.uk **w** www.allandertravel.co.uk
Contact M Brown, Company Secretary; G Wilson, Transport Manager
Credits Harry Potter And The Prisoner Of Azkaban (F); Harry Potter And The Philosopher's Stone (F); First Knight: The Gauntlet Machine (F)

Apex Car & Van Rental
Vulcan Road South, Norwich NR6 6AG
t 01603 488688 **f** 01603 482382
e mikegotterson@apexcarrental.co.uk
w www.apexcarrental.co.uk
Contact Robbie Gleeson, Film/TV Rental Coordinator; Mike Gotterson, Sales Executive; Steve Ruddock, Rental Manager; Allison Ing, Rental Coordinator
Credits Serious & Organised (T); Iris (F); Band Of Brothers (T); The Hours (F)

Bernal Services Ltd
92 Perryn Road, Acton, London W3 7LU
t 020 8743 6889 **f** 020 8743 6889 **m** 07831 378883
Contact BW Peters

Bus Shot Location Vehicle Hire
27 Sandy Lane South, Wallington SM6 9RF
m 07768 104261 **w** www.busshot.co.uk
Contact George Dunkley

Cabervans
Gourock PA19 1BA
t 0845 644 4775 **f** 01475 638775 **m** 07860 413434
e cabervans@lineone.net **w** www.cabervans.com
Contact Patricia McKenzie, Partner; Colin McKenzie, Proprietor
Credits Harry Potter And The Chamber Of Secrets (F); Jonathan Creek (T); Harry Potter And The Philosopher's Stone (F); Monarch Of The Glen (T)

Call-A-Coach
Capri House, Walton-on-Thames KT12 2LY
t 01932 223838 **f** 01932 269109
Contact Arthur Freakes, Managing Director

Computer Cab Plc
Hygeria, 66-68 College Road, Harrow HA1 1BE
t 020 7286 2728 **f** 020 7286 7259
e ccinfo@comcab.co.uk **w** www.computercab.co.uk
Contact Mike Galvin, Managing Director

Dartford Motors
Heath Lane Upper, Dartford DA1 2TW
t 01322 223112 **f** 01322 289138
e dartfordmotors@virginnet.com **w** www.dartfordmotors.com
Contact John Turnbull, Manager

Dennis Diners
Unit 14, Honeybourne Airfield, Weston Road, Honeybourne WR11 7QF
t 01386 833733 **f** 01386 833798 **m** 07973 628219
e sales@ddslv.com **w** www.ddslv.com
Contact Kate Dennis, Contact; Doug Dennis, Contact
Credits Dinosaur Hunters (T); Starlight (T); DIY SOS (T); Casualty (T)

DJK Film Services
Unit 22B, Moss Lane Industrial Estate, Moss Lane, Royton, Oldham OL2 6HR
t 01616 335620 **f** 01616 335620 **m** 07831 550178
e djkfilms@hotmail.com
Contact Dave Kipling, Proprieter
Credits French And Saunders Christmas Special (T); Last Of The Summer Wine (T); Below (F); Murphy's Law (T)

Elite American Trailers
Lower Grange Park, Chacombe, Banbury OX17 2EL
t 01295 711157 **f** 01295 712119 **m** 07798 665001
w www.elite-american-trailers.co.uk
Contact Mark Bowes, Director
Credits Wire In The Blood (T)

Elite Helicopters
Hanger 3, Goodwood Aerodrome, Chichester PO18 OPH
t 01243 530165 **f** 01243 539921 **m** 07768 314273
e ops@elitehelicopters.co.uk **w** www.elitehelicopters.co.uk
Contact Glenn Curtis, Managing Director; Sharon Douglas, Operations Director

Elite Motor Homes
Lower Grange Park, Chacombe, Banbury OX17 2EL
t 01295 711157 **f** 01295 712119 **m** 07798 665001
e elitemotorhomes@lineone.net **w** www.elite-motorhomes.co.uk
Contact Mark Bowes, Director
Credits British American Racing F1 Team (C); Waking The Dead (T); Once Upon A Time In The Midlands (F)

Film Service Transport
Pinewood Studios, Pinewood Road, Iver SL0 0NH
t 01753 630364 **f** 01753 630241
e transcamera@btconnect.com **w** www.studioworkshop.co.uk
Contact Nick Gill, Operations Manager; Ben Gill, Managing Director
Credits Gosford Park (F); Shackleton (F); Spy Games (F)

Gee Whizz Transport Services Ltd
10 Oaklands, Argyle Road, Ealing, London W13 OHG
t 020 8997 1578 **f** 020 8997 1578 **m** 07860 385227
Contact Kathy Gee, Director; Simon Gee, Director; James Hall

Gemini Travel
Unit 20, Sterling Complex, Farthing Road, Ipswich IP1 5AP
t 01473 462721 **f** 01473 462731
e ed@geminiofipswich.co.uk **w** www.geminiofipswich.co.uk
Contact Ed Nicholls, Director

GH Lucking & Sons
Commerce Road, Brentford TW8 8LX
t 020 8569 9030 **f** 020 8569 9847 **e** markd@lucking.co.uk
Contact Mark Dooner, General Manager

Hi-Deck Cruisers
4 Reeves Piece, Bratton BA13 4TH
t 01380 831206 **f** 01380 831206 **m** 07787 534535
e hideckcruisers@btinternet.com
Contact Jeff Sears, Proprietor

HNA Facilities - Home N Away
Unit 16, Redbank Court, Manchester M4 4HF
t 0161 832 1199 **f** 0161 832 2299 **m** 07860 339449
e hire@homeaway.co.uk **w** www.homeaway.co.uk
Credits Forsythe Saga (T); Real Men (T); Spooks (T); The Inspector Lynley Mysteries (T)

Howard Ray Driver Services
65A Church Road, London SW13 9HH
t 01932 241401 **f** 01932 246939 **m** 07939 026208
e howardray@hotmail.com **w** www.howardray.co.uk
Contact Nataye Saunders-Griffiths, Director; Howard Ray, Director
Credits Keen Eddie (T); Ultimate Force (T); Murder In Mind (T); Midsomer Murders (T)

Lancaster Private Hire Ltd
9A Craven Terrace, London W2 3QD
t 020 7262 7282 **f** 020 7724 0331 **m** 07802 222951
e sales@lancaster-online.co.uk **w** www.lancaster-online.co.uk
Contact Ernie Hall, Customer Liasion Manager
Credits The Weakest Link (T)

Lift & Shoot
99 Bolingbroke Grove, London SW11 1DB
t 020 7223 8166 **f** 020 7924 2879
Contact Jennifer King, Director

Limolux Transportation
Unit 19, Shepperton Studios, Studios Road, Shepperton TW17 OQD
t 01932 592344 **f** 020 7286 7555 **m** 07860 315463
e www.limolux-transport@talk21.com
Contact Michael Marks, Proprietor

Davy Liver
72-76 Duke Street, Liverpool L1 5AA
t 0151 709 4646 **f** 0151 708 0906 **e** leepeacock@daveyliver.co.uk

Location Cars Ltd
68 Lucas Street, London SW1V 3EH
t 020 7834 7293 **f** 020 7834 3388
Contact Ivan Green, Managing Director

Location Transport Ltd
Sandsend, Monument Lane, Lymington SO41 5SE
t 01590 678999 **f** 01590 678999 **m** 07831 371808
e jon@locationtransport.com
Contact Jon Oldfield, Director
Credits Stretford Wives (T); Tipping The Velvet (T)

Locations Unlimited
Riverside Park, Bent Ley Road, Meltham, Holmfirth HD9 4AP
t 01484 851999 **f** 01484 850999 **m** 07976 533 775
e tony@locations-unlimited.co.uk **w** www.locations-unlimited.co.uk
Contact Tony Watson, Proprietor
Credits Cromwell (T); The Gunpowder Plot (T); The Lawless Heart (F)

London Travel Services Ltd
Featherstone Gardens, Borehamwood WD6 2LW
m 07885 300808 **e** ltravel@ntlworld.com **w** www.ltravel.co.uk
Contact Peter Hedges, Director

Marscom
Haulage Yard, Wyck Beacon, Bourton-on-the-Water GL54 2NE
t 01451 821289 **f** 01451 810423 **m** 07774 213 183
e horseboxes@marscom.fsnet.co.uk **w** www.marscom.co.uk
Contact Michael Gowers, Director

Memories For Tomorrow
4 London Road, Bishop Stortford CM23 5ND
t 01279 654789 **f** 01279 657434 **m** 01279 307020
w www.stortvalleycoaches.co.uk
Contact Andy Mahoney, Chairman

Miles & Miles Ltd
18 Petersham Mews, London SW7 5NR
t 020 7591 0555 **f** 020 7581 2259
e bookings@milesandmiles.com **w** www.milesandmiles.co.uk
Contact B Thompson, Operations Manager

Production Support Services Europe
196 St Albans Road West, Hatfield AL10 0ST
t 01255 672114 **f** 01255 672115 **m** 07976 151590
e production.europe@btopenworld.com
Contact Gary Fletcher, Proprietor

Radio Taxis London Ltd
Mountview House, Lennox Road, London N4 3TX
t 020 7272 5471 **f** 020 7281 5709
e moulders@radiotaxis.co.uk **w** www.radiotaxis.co.uk
Contact Peter Crawley, Business Development Manager

Redburn Transfer Ltd
Redburn House, Stockingswater Lane, Enfield EN3 7PH
t 020 8804 0027 **f** 020 8804 8021
e sales@redburn.co.uk **w** www.redburn.co.uk
Contact Chris Redburn, Sales Manager

Rentaplus Ltd
74 Glenthorne Road, Hammersmith, London W6 0LR
t 020 8748 8112 **f** 020 8748 5966
e den4ccl@yahoo.co.uk **w** www.rentaplus.co.uk
Contact Denise McDonald, Director; Linda St Jean, Manager; Christopher Ridgeon, Operations Manager

The Scene Store Ltd
PO Box 79, Radlett WD7 8ZR
t 01923 857274 **f** 07092 248719
e mail@scenestore.co.uk **w** www.scenestore.co.uk
Set storage, transport, art department crewing and set re-furbishment.

Screen Facilities Ltd
Saxon Park, Hanbury Road, Stoke Prior, Bromsgrove B60 4AD
t 01527 576777 **f** 01527 576280
e screenfac@screengroup.co.uk **w** www.screengroup.co.uk
Contact Graham Whitehouse, Contact; Dawn Hudson, Contact

Sharp's Reliable Wrecks
Inverness Railway Station, Academy Street, Inverness IV1 1LE
t 01463 710048 **f** 01463 713777
w www.sharpsreliablewrecks.co.uk
Contact Michael Sharp, Partner

Southern Film Services
Unit A4, Canal Bridge Yard, Byfleet Road, Newhaw, Weybridge KT15 3JE
t 01932 845526 **f** 01932 845527 **m** 07860 259751
e sfilms@netcomuk.co.uk **w** www.sfilms.co.uk
Contact David Catchpole, Proprietor; Sean Battrill
Credits Smack The Pony (T); The Muskeeter (F); Vicar of Dibley (T); Lost In Space (F)

Speedy Hire Centres (Southern) Ltd
Northern Way, Bury St Edmonds IP32 6NL
t 01284 760842 **f** 01284 764932
e info@speedysouth.co.uk **w** www.speedyhire.co.uk
Contact Valarie Lockhart, PA; Kate Nice, PA to Managing Director

Steve Lang Facilities
207A Heath Road, Hounslow TW3 2NU
t 020 8568 2173 **f** 020 8568 2178 **m** 07836 244483
e slfac@supanet.com
Contact Steve Lang, Proprietor; Susan Lang, Film Location Transport

Studio Workshops Ltd
Pinewood Studios, Pinewood Road, Iver SL0 0NH
t 01753 656375 **f** 01753 630241
e swell@easicom.com **w** www.swell-trans.co.uk
Contact Nick Gill, Manager; Ben Gill, Managing Director
Credits Shackleton (T); Die Another Day (F); Spy Game (F); Gosford Park (F)

Supreme Car Hire Ltd
Stour Wharf, Stour Road, London E3 2NT
t 020 8986 5000 **f** 020 8986 8444
Contact Clifford Humphries, Managing Director

Trans-Executives Ltd
134 Hendon Lane, London N3 3PS
t 020 8343 1322 **f** 020 8343 1314
Contact George Maile, Director

Translux International
245 Warwick Road, London W14 8PX
t 020 7348 0770 **f** 020 7603 8168
m 07966 556272 **m** 07966 556273
e info@translux.com **w** www.translux.com
Contact Aubrey Tredget, Marketing & Booking

Transtrucks Ltd
Supreme House, Stour Wharf, Stour Road, London E3 2NT
t 020 8986 5000 **f** 020 8986 8444
Contact Clifford Humphries, Managing Director

Warner's Film & Location Transport
204 Regents Park Road, London NW1 8BE
t 020 7586 6060 **f** 020 7483 1755
e vans@warners2000.freeserve.co.uk

Warner's Film & Location Transport
12-16 Brunel Road, London W3 7XR
t 020 7586 6060 **f** 020 7483 1755
Contact Rupert Talbot-Dunn, Proprietor; Daniel Dunphy

Watkins & Sole Transport Ltd
Unit 6/11, Galleymead Road, Colnbrook, Slough SL3 0EN
t 01753 683647 **f** 01753 682405
Contact Michael Higgins, Managing Director

Michael Webb
Holdings Farm, The Barracks, Hook RG27 9NW
t 01256 768395 **m** 07860 246966
e info@mwfacilities.com **w** www.mwfacilities.com

Wheels World Wide Ltd
3 Springbok Farm, Alfold, Cranleigh GU6 8HT
t 01403 753340 **f** 01403 753340 **m** 07799 116558
e wheelsworldwide@hotmail.com
Contact Jim Moran, Director

Travel Agents, Consultants

Arctic Experience
29 Nork Way, Banstead SM7 1PB
t 01737 218810 **f** 01737 214245
e marketing@discover-the-world.co.uk
w www.arctic-experience.co.uk
Contact Joanne Bower, Marketing Consultant

Capable Travel
31 Old Bailey, London EC4M 7QJ
t 020 7489 8787 **f** 020 7236 7901
e sales@capabletravel.com **w** www.capabletravel.com

Cee Bee Travel
Shepperton Marina Building, Felix Lane, Shepperton TW17 8NJ
t 01932 254873 **f** 01932 244402 **e** cbfly@aol.com
Contact Caroline Bequette, Proprieter

CI Travel Consultants
Studio 16, Shepperton Film Studios, Shepperton TW17 0QD
t 01932 592323 **f** 01932 592417 **m** 07973 688020
e ci.travel@virgin.net
Contact Steve Garner, Proprieter; Debbie Hunter, Sales and Marketing
Manager; Joanne Newman, Operations Manager
Credits Buffalo Soldiers (F); Swept Away (F); Ted And Sylvia (F);
British Comedy Awards (T)

CIS Travel
5 Hobart Place, London SW1W 0HU
t 020 7393 1234 **f** 020 7393 1275 **m** 07831 276195
e lon@chapman-freeborn.com **w** www.chapman-freeborn.com
Contact Carol Norman, Managing Director

Danube Travel Ltd
3rd Floor, 6 Conduit Street, London W1S 2XD
t 020 7493 0263 **e** holidays@doubletravel.freeserve.co.uk
Contact Georgina Berenyi, MD

Major Travel
28-34 Fortess Road, London NW5 2HB
t 020 7393 1060 **f** 020 7267 6780 **m** 07957 371845
e sales@majortravel.co.uk **w** www.majortravel.co.uk
Contact Simon Triggers, Manager

Network Travel Services Ltd
4 The Broadway, Hanwell, London W7 3SS
t 020 8579 5433 **f** 020 8840 1721 **e** nts@networktvl.com
Contact Graham Mablin, Director

Screen & Music Travel Ltd
Colne House, High Street, Colnbrook SL3 0LX
t 01753 764050 **f** 01753 764051 **m** 07836 205063
e travel@screenandmusictravel.co.uk
w www.screenandmusictravel.co.uk
Contact Michele Griffiths, Groups Manager; Maureen Grieve, Managing
Director; Susi Dillon, Branch Manager; Colin Doran, Manager - Group Projects;
Sue Drinkwater, Managing Director; Gina Wilson, Director; Stephen Bellingham,
Senior Travel Consultant; Sarah Downing, Senior Travel Consultant
Credits Ground Force (T); Olympic Games - Sidney 2000 (I); Walking With
Dinosaurs (T); Captain Corelli's Mandolin (F)
The programme makers travel agent.

Specialised Travel Ltd
12-15 Hanger Green, London W5 3EL
t 020 8799 8310 **f** 020 8998 7965
e admin@stlon.com **w** www.stlon.com
Contact Patrick Mylon, Business Travel Manager; John Gordon - Jones,
Director of Business Travel; Richard Savage, Chairman/CEO

The Travel Company
Garden Suite, Pinewood Studios, Pinewood Road, Bucks SL0 0NH
t 020 7170 4434 **f** 020 7170 4534 **m** 07970 060825
e sales@thetravel.co.uk **w** www.thetravel.co.uk
Contact Kevin King, Head of Sales; Michele Bibby, Operations Director; David
Whittaker, Joint Managing Director; Mike Walley, Joint Managing Director

Travel Incorporate
Sunlife, 85-103 Queens Road, Reading RG1 4BT
t 0118 955 3302 **w** www.travelinc.co.uk
Contact Jeremy King, Managing Director

VC Associates
Hop Cottage, Church Road, Kenardington, Ashford TN26 2NG
t 01233 733 733 **f** 01233 733 998 **m** 07785 267929
e victoriacocking@aol.com
Contact Victoria Cocking, Partner; Tim Cocking, Partner

Wollaton Travel Services
177A Bramcote Lane, Wollaton, Nottingham NG8 2QJ
t 0115 928 8739 **f** 0115 928 9186
Contact Derek Read, Proprietor

TV

TV Satellite & Cable

The Adult Channel (HVC)/Playboy Channel
Aquis House, Station Road, Hayes UB3 4DX
t 020 8581 7000 **f** 020 8581 7007
w www.theadultchannel.co.uk
Contact David Porter, General Manager

Apna TV
C/o Media Moguls, 42 Theobalds Road, London WC1X 8NW
t 020 7831 2525 **f** 020 7242 2860
e harish@apnatv.freeserve.co.uk **w** www.apnatv.com
Contact Harish Joshi, Director

BBC News 24

BBC Television Centre, Wood Lane, London W12 7RJ
t 08700 100883 **f** 08700 100884 **w** news.bbc.co.uk

BBC Parliament

4 Mill Bank, London SW1P 3JA
t 020 7973 6189 **f** 020 7233 2070
e parliament@bbc.co.uk **w** www.bbc.co.uk/bbcparliament
Contact Peter Knowles, Channel Editor

Bravo

160 Great Portland Street, London W1W 5QA
t 020 7299 5358 **f** 020 7299 5340 **w** www.bravo.co.uk
Credits World Famous For Driving Around (T); International King Of Sports (T); Combat Cars (T); World Of Pain (T)

BSkyB Ltd

Grant Way, Isleworth TW7 5QD
t 020 7705 3000 **f** 020 7705 3030 **w** www.sky.com
Contact Chris Haynes, Head of Press and Publicity

Cable & Satellite Mediacast

Reed Exhibition Companies, Oriel House, 26 The Quadrant, Richmond-Upon-Thames TW9 1DL
t 020 8910 7910 **f** 020 8940 2171
e RECinfo@reedexpo.co.uk **w** www.mediacast.co.uk

Cable & Satellite Transmissions (CAST) Ltd

66 Newman Street, London W1T 3EQ
t 020 7436 5692 **f** 020 7580 9676
e gtrickey@cast.tv **w** www.teddington.co.uk

The Cartoon Network

Turner House, 16 Great Marlborough Street, London W1F 7HS
t 020 7693 1000 **f** 020 7693 1020 **w** www.cartoonnetwork.co.uk
Contact Andy Bird, President

Challenge TV

160 Great Portland Street, London W1N 5TB
t 020 7299 5000 **f** 020 7299 6000 **w** www.flextech.co.uk
Contact Jonathan Ellis, Advertising Manager

The Chinese Channel (TVBS)

Teddington Studios, Brom Row, Teddington TW11 9NT
t 020 8614 8300 **f** 020 8943 0982
e tvbs@chinese-channel.co.uk **w** www.chinese-channel.co.uk
Contact Regina Chan, Project Coordinator

Christian Communications Network Europe Ltd

646 Shore Road, Whiteabbey, Belfast BT37 0PR
t 028 9085 3997 **f** 028 9036 5536
e ccn@ccneurope.org.uk **w** www.ccneurope.org.uk
Contact Sandra Mathers, Director of Administration; Karen George, Company Secretary

CNBC Europe

10 Fleet Place, London EC4M 7QS
t 020 7653 9300 **f** 020 7653 5956 **w** www.cnbceurope.com

CNN Cable News Network

16 Great Marlborough Street, London W1F 7HS
t 020 7693 1000 **f** 020 7693 1552
e cnnlondon@turner.com **w** www.cnn.com
Contact Tony Maddox, Senior Vice President

The Disney Channel

566 Chiswick High Road, London W4 5AN
t 020 8636 2000 **f** 020 8636 2202
e name.surname@disney.com **w** www.disneychannel.co.uk
Contact Paul Robinson, Managing Director; Howard Myers, Director of Production; Nick Richards, Director of Marketing; James Neal, Director of Programming and Acquisitions

EMAP Performance

Mappin House, 4 Winsley Street, London W1W 9HF
t 020 7436 1515 **f** 020 7376 1313
e gillian.short@emap.com **w** www.emap.com
Contact Gillian Short, PA; Dee Ford, Managing Director

ESPN Classic Sport

Hogarth Business Park, 3 Burlington Lane, Chiswick, London W4 2TH
t 020 8233 5300 **f** 020 8233 6619 **e** jbaker@espn-cs.com
Contact Jamie Baker, Director of Production, Europe

Eurosport

Lachan House, 84 Theobalds Rd, London WC1X 8RW
t 020 7468 7777 **f** 020 7468 0024
e enquiries@eurosport.co.uk **w** www.eurosport.com
Contact Michelle Gui, PR Manager; Martin Johnstone, Head of Press and PR
Credits Tour De France (T); World Superbikes (T); Moto GP (T); International Football (T)

Extreme Sports Channel

131-151 Great Titchfield Street, London W1W 5BB
t 020 7244 1000 **f** 020 7244 1001
e group@extreme.com **w** www.extremeinternational.com
Contact Alistair Gosling, MD/CEO

FilmFour Channel

124 Horseferry Road, London SW1P 2TX
t 020 7396 4444 **t** 020 7306 8509
t 020 7306 8155 **f** 020 7306 8368 **w** www.filmfour.com

Fox Kids

Fox Kids Centre, 338 Euston Road, London NW1 3AZ
t 020 7554 9000 **e** name@foxkids.co.uk **w** www.foxkids.co.uk

God Digital

Crown House, Borough Road, Sunderland SR1 1HW
t 0870 444 0660 **t** 0870 607 0446 **f** 0191 568 0879
e name@godnetwork.com **w** www.godnetwork.com
Contact Rory Alec, Managing Director

Granada Men & Motors

Franciscan Court, 16 Hatfields, London SE1 8DJ
t 020 7578 4040 **f** 020 7578 4058
e enquiries@gsb.co.uk **w** www.gsb.co.uk
Contact Maureen Fuller, Head of Marketing
Credits Havoc (T); Bike Spot Weekly (T); MCN (T); Used Car Heaven (T)

Granada Plus

Franciscan Court, 16 Hatfields, London SE1 8DJ
t 020 7578 4040 **f** 020 7578 4058
e plus@gsb.co.uk **w** www.gsb.co.uk
Contact Maureen Fuller, Head of Marketing
Credits Agatha Christie's Poirot (T)

Granada Sky Broadcasting Ltd

Franciscan Court, 16 Hatfields, London SE1 8DJ
t 020 7578 4040 **f** 020 7578 4058 **w** www.gsb.co.uk
Contact Tora Young, Marketing Executive; Gary Shoefield, Director Of Programming; Lesley Johnson, Channel Manager

The History Channel

Grant Way, Isleworth TW7 5QD
t 08702 403000 **f** 020 7941 5187
e elizabeth.curwen@bskyb.com **w** www.thehistorychannel.co.uk
Contact Martin Morgan, Executive Producer; Louise Dillon, Acquisitions Manager; Richard Melman, Head of Programming; Emily Lloyd, New Media Manager

Independent Television Commission (ITC)

33 Foley Street, London W1W 7TL
t 020 7255 3000 **f** 020 7306 7800
e publicaffairs@itc.org.uk **w** www.itc.org.uk
Contact Bradley Brady, Senior Media and PR Officer

Japan Satellite TV (JSTV)
3rd Floor, 65 Clifton Street, London EC2A 4JE
t 020 7426 7330 **f** 020 7426 7339
e info@jstv.co.uk **w** www.jstv.co.uk
Contact Mr Kitagawa, Managing Director

Living TV
160 Great Portland Street, London W1W 5QA
t 020 7299 5000 **f** 020 7299 6000 **w** www.flextech.co.uk
Credits 6ixth Sense (T); Tiny Living (T)

Motorola BCS Limited
Imperium, Imperial Way, Reading RG2 0TD
t 0118 975 5555 **f** 0118 975 3933 **w** www.motorola.com

The Movie Channel
Sky, Grant Way, Isleworth TW7 5QD
t 020 7705 3000 **f** 020 7705 3030
e skydigital@bskyb.com **w** www.sky.com
Contact James Baker, Head of Network Programming

MTV Europe
17-29 Hawley Crescent, London NW1 8TT
t 020 7284 7777 **f** 020 7284 7788 **w** www.mtv.co.uk
Contact Brent Hanson, President/ Chief Executive

Music Choice Europe
Fleet House, 57-61 Clerkenwell Road, London EC1M 5LA
t 020 7014 8700 **f** 020 7253 8460
e sales@musicchoice.co.uk **w** www.musicchoice.co.uk
Contact Simon Bazalgatte, Chief Executive Officer; Margot Daly, Chief
Executive Officer

National Geographic Channel
6 Centaurs Business Park, Grant Way, Isleworth TW7 5QD
t 020 7705 3000 **f** 020 7805 2297
w www.nationalgeographic.co.uk
Contact Marc Ollington, Senior UK Marketing Executive

Nickelodeon
15-18 Rathbone Place, London W1T 1HU
t 020 7462 1000 **f** 020 7462 1030 **w** www.nick.co.uk

ntl (Glasgow)
ntl House, 60 Maxwell Road, Glasgow G41 1PR
t 0141 564 0000 **f** 0141 564 0350

ntl (Luton)
Wigmore House, Wigmore Lane, Luton LU2 9EX
t 01582 610000 **f** 01582 610100 **e** david.thatcher@ntl.co.uk
Contact David Thatcher, Managing Director

ntl (Northants)
NTL Switch 2, Kingsfield Business Park, Gladstone Road,
Northampton NN5 7RX
t 01604 451111 **f** 01832 210455 **w** www.ntl.com
Contact Vicky Keen, Marketing and PR Co-ordinator

ntl (Swindon)
Hawkesworth Estate, Newcome Drive, Swindon SN2 1TU
t 0179 333 4370 **f** 0179 333 4301
Contact Keith Hamish, Regional Installation Manager

ntl (Wokingham)
300 Wharfdale Road, Winersh, Wokingham RG41 5TZ
t 0118 954 4000 **f** 0118 954 4001 **w** www.ntl.com
Contact Robert Halhead, Managing Director

ntl:broadcast

ntl : Broadcast
Crawley Court, Winchester SO21 2QA
t 01962 822400 **f** 01962 822553
e satellite-info@ntl.com **w** www.ntlbroadcast.com

ntl Communications
ntl House, Bartley Wood Business Park, Hook RG27 9UP
t 01256 752000 **w** www.ntl.com

The Paramount Comedy Channel
180 Oxford Street, London W1D 1DS
t 020 7478 5300 **f** 020 7478 5442
e tony.orston@paramountcomedy.com
w www.paramountcomedy.com
Contact Tony Orsten, Managing Director

Performance - The Arts Channel
New Pathe House, 57 Jamestown Road, London NW1 7XX
t 020 7424 3688 **f** 020 7424 3689
e info@performancetv.co.uk **w** www.performance-channel.com
Contact Bob Lynton, General Manager

QVC - The Shopping Channel
Marco Polo House, Chelsea Bridge, 346 Queenstown Road,
London SW8 4NQ
t 020 7705 5600 **f** 020 7705 5601
e richard_burrell@qvc.com **w** www.qvcuk.com
Contact Mark Suckle, Chief Executive

Racing Channel
Satellite Information Services Ltd, 17 Corsham Street, London
N1 6DR
t 020 7253 2232 **f** 020 7490 0017
e racingchannel@satelliteinfo.co.uk
Contact George Irvine, Director of Programming

Satellite Information Services
Satellite House, 17 Corsham Street, London N1 6DR
t 020 7696 8002 **f** 020 7251 3737
Contact Alan Sale, Senior Engineer; Ben Honey

The Sci-Fi Channel
5-7 Mandeville Place, London W1U 3AR
t 020 7535 3500
Contact Tor McLaren, Director of Broadcast; Jason Thorp, Director of
Programming; Janet Goldsmith, Managing Director
Credits Head F**k (T); S.F.G (D); Unthinkable (D)

Setanta Sport
52 Haymarket, London SW1Y 4RP
t 020 7930 8926 **f** 020 7930 2059
e setantauk@aol.com **w** www.setanta.com
Contact Leonard Ryan, Managing Director

Simply Television Ltd
150 Great Portland Street, London W1W 6QD
t 020 7307 6000 **f** 020 7307 6001
w www.simplytelevision.com
Contact Paddy Smart, Marketing Manager; Avie Littler, Head of Production;
Arnold Reicher, Head of Broadcast Marketing Division; Henry Scott, Director,
Managing Director

Sky Movie Max
6 Centaurs Business Park, Grant Way, Isleworth TW7 5QD
t 020 7705 3000 **f** 020 7705 3030 **w** www.sky.co.uk
Contact James Baker, Head of Content & Creative Affairs

Sky Movies Cinema
6 Centaurs Business Park, Grant Way, Isleworth TW7 5QD
t 020 7705 3000 **f** 020 7705 3030 **w** www.sky.co.uk
Contact James Baker, Head of Content & Creative Affairs

Sky News (Belfast Bureau)
Floor 2, Fanum House, 108-110 Great Victoria Street, Belfast
BT2 7BE
t 028 9023 4098 **t** 028 9023 4099
Contact Kieran Gaffey; Gary Honeyford

Sky One
6 Centaurs Business Park, Grantway, Isleworth TW7 5QD
t 020 7705 3000 **f** 020 7705 3030 **w** www.skyone.co.uk
Contact Joel Pilkington, Senior Commission Executive

Sky Sports
6 Centaurs Business Park, Grant Way, Isleworth TW7 5QD
t 020 7705 3000 **f** 020 7705 3030 **w** www.bskyb.com

Sky Sports 1
6 Centaurs Business Park, Grant Way, Isleworth TW7 5QD
t 020 7705 3000 **f** 020 7705 3030 **w** www.skysports.co.uk
Contact Andy Melvin, Director

Sky Sports 2
6 Centaurs Business Park, Grant Way, Isleworth TW7 5QD
t 020 7705 3000 **f** 020 7705 3030 **w** www.skysports.co.uk
Contact Andy Melvin, Director

Sky Sports 3
6 Centaurs Business Park, Grant Way, Isleworth TW7 5QD
t 020 7705 3000 **f** 020 7705 3030 **w** www.skysports.co.uk
Contact Andy Melvin, Director

Sky Travel
British Sky Broadcasting Ltd, Grantway, Isleworth TW7 5QD
t 020 8705 3200 **f** 020 8705 3030 **w** www.sky.co.uk
Contact Delia Bushell, General Manager

Television X - The Fantasy Channel
Northern & Shell Tower, 4 Selsdon Way, City Harbour, London
E14 9GL
t 020 7308 5090 **f** 020 7308 6001
e pauldunthorne@navnet.co.uk **w** www.fantasy121.co.uk
Contact Paul Dunthorne, Station Controller

Telewest Broadband
Communications House, Scimitar Park, Courtauld Road,
Basildon SS13 1ND
t 01268 471000 **f** 01268 470199 **w** www.telewest.co.uk
Contact Adam Singer, Chief Executive; Keith Martin, Head of Calls

Telewest Broadband
1-4 Fowler Court, Fowler Road, West Pitkerro Industrial Estate,
Dundee DD5 3RU
t 01382 525150 **f** 01382 520001 **w** www.telewest.co.uk

Telewest Broadband
Unit 4, Bankhead Avenue, Bankhead Industrial Estate,
Glenrothes KY7 6JG
t 01592 595857 **f** 01592 590001 **w** www.telewest.co.uk

Telewest Broadband
Communications House, 1 Dukesway West, Team Valley,
Gateshead NE11 0PN
t 0191 420 2000 **f** 0191 420 2001 **w** www.telewest.co.uk
Contact Bruce Langham, Regional Managing Director; Charles Burdict,
Regional Managing Director

Telewest Communications (Avon)
700 Waterside Drive, Aztec West, Almondsbury, Bristol BS32 4ST
t 0117 983 9000 **f** 0117 983 9966 **w** www.telewest.co.uk

Telewest Communications (Scotland)
1 South Gyle, Crescent Lane, Edinburgh EH12 9EG
t 0131 539 0002 **f** 0131 539 0003
e enquiries@telewest.co.uk **w** www.telewest.co.uk
Contact Bruce Langham, Regional Managing Director

Travel Channel
66 Newman Street, London W1P 3LA
t 020 7636 5401 **f** 020 7636 6424
e gareth@travelchannel.co.uk **w** www.travelchannel.co.uk
Contact Gareth Davis, Head of Production; Alison Rice, Director of Programmes

Triangle
Whitfield House, 81 Whitfield Street, London W1A 4XA
t 020 7255 5215 **f** 020 7255 5216 **e** bphillips@facillties.co.uk
Contact Tanya Fitzgerald

TV & Broadcast Services
University of Plymouth, Hoe Centre, Notte Street, Plymouth
PL1 2AR
t 01752 233640 **f** 01752 233638 **e** dhurrell@plymouth.ac.uk
Contact David Hurrell, Manager
Credits MRCSTU (E)

TV-Shop Broadcasting Ltd
19 Norfolk Road, London NW8 6HG
t 020 7722 0242 **f** 020 7722 6973 **m** 07768 402116
e polesuperpole@aol.com
Contact Tony Pole, Consultant

UCB Europe
PO Box 255, Stoke-on-Trent ST4 8YY
t 01782 642000 **f** 01782 641121
e ucb@ucb.co.uk **w** www.ucb.co.uk/

UK Gold
2nd Floor, 160 Great Portland Street, London W1W 5QA
t 020 7765 0103 **f** 020 7765 0876
e ukgold@bbc.co.uk **w** www.flextech.co.uk
Contact Katie Barnard, Channel Editor

UK Style
160 Portland Street, London W1W 5QA
t 020 7299 5000 **w** www.uktv.co.uk
Contact Roly Keating, Head of Programming; John Keeling, Controller

UK TV
UK Television, 2nd Floor, 160 Great Portland Street, London
W1W 5QA
t 020 7299 5000 **e** john.keeling@bbc.co.uk
Contact Dick Emery, Chief Executive; David Dorans, Director of New Media;
Nick Betts, Commercial Director - Programming; John Keeling, Controller; Julia
Weston, Marketing Director

VH1
17-29 Hawley Crescent, London NW1 8TT
t 020 7284 7777 **f** 020 7284 6466 **w** www.vh1.co.uk
Contact Sam Curlewis, Press Officer

Viasat Broadcasting Group
Viasat Broadcast Centre, Unit 7, Horton Industrial Park,
Horton Road, West Drayton UB7 8JD
t 01895 433433 **f** 01895 446606 **w** www.viasat.se
Contact Maurice Firman, Director of Broadcasting Operations

Video Communication Consultants
Manor Cottage, Winderton, Banbury OX15 5JF
t 01608 685647 **f** 01608 685911 **m** 07771 574402
e alan.joy@virgin.net

Vision Channel
Vision Studio, Heritage House, Eastcot Road, Swindon SN1 3LF
t 01793 511244 **f** 01793 511211
e info@visionchannel.co.uk **w** www.visionchannel.co.uk

Zone Vision
105 Salusbury Road, London NW6 6RG
t 020 7328 8808
Contact Chris Sharp, General Manager; Chris Sharp, Director of Sales
and Acquisitions

Terrestrial

Addictive Television

The Old House, 39A North Road, London N7 9DP
t 020 7700 0333 **f** 020 7700 0303
e mail@addictive.com **w** www.addictive.com
Contact Graham Daniels, Producer; Nick Clarke, Producer; Jim Waters, Production Manager
Credits Spaced Out (T); Transambient (T); Mixmasters (T); The Web Review (T)

Assembly Film & TV

Riverside Studios, Crisp Road, London W6 9RL
t 020 8237 1075 **f** 020 8237 1071
e judithmurrell@riversidestudios.co.uk **w** www.chrysalis.com
Contact William Burdett-Coutts, Chief Executive
Credits Jo Brand's Hot Potatoes (T); Black Books (T)

BBC Television

BBC Television Centre, Wood Lane, London W12 7RJ
t 020 8743 8000 **w** www.bbc.co.uk
Credits BBC One: Rush Hour

Capital TV Ltd

Aquaplan House, Burt Street, Cardiff CF10 5F2
t 029 2048 8500 **f** 029 2025 0703 **e** news@capital-tv.co.uk
Contact David Morris Jones, Chief executive; Alan Carter, Director of Engineering; Della Knite, Director Human Resources; Gideon Wilkins, Head of Sales

Carlton Television

101 Saint Martin's Lane, London WC2N 4RF
t 020 7240 4000 **w** www.carlton.com

Central Television

Central Court, Gas Street, Birmingham B1 2JT
t 0121 643 9898 **f** 0121 634 4606
e newsdeskwest@carltontv.co.uk **w** www.carlton.com
Contact John Toolan, News Editor

Channel 4 International

124 Horseferry Road, London SW1P 2TX
t 020 7396 4444 **w** www.c4i.tv

Channel 4 Television

124 Horseferry Road, London SW1P 2TX
t 020 7396 4444 **w** www.channel4.com

Channel 5 Broadcasting (C5B)

22 Long Acre, London WC2E 9LY
t 020 7550 5555 **f** 020 7550 5554 **w** www.five.tv
Contact Paul Leather, Head of Publicity

Dream Media Group

77 Kennylands Road, Sonning Common, Reading RG4 9JR
t 0118 972 1221 **m** 07790 869 621
e info@dreammediagroup.co.uk **w** www.dreammediagroup.co.uk

Fusion FM

270 Woodstock Road, Oxford OX2 7NW
t 01865 557000 **f** 01865 553355
e admin@oxfordchannel.com **w** www.oxfordchannel.com
Contact Nigel Taylor, Managing Director

GMTV

The London Television Centre, Upper Ground, London SE1 9TT
t 020 7827 7000 **f** 020 7827 7001 **e** talktous@gmtv.co.uk
Contact Nicky Johnceline, Head of Public Relations

Grampian Television (Dundee)

Dock Street, Harbour Chambers, Dundee DD1 3HW
t 01382 591000 **f** 01382 591010 **m** 07803 970492
e craig.millar@smg.plc.uk
Contact Craig Millar, Reporter

Grampian Television (Inverness)

23-25 Huntley Street, Inverness IV3 5PR
t 01463 242624 **f** 01463 715384 **e** nicola.mcalley@smg.plc.uk
Contact Nicola McAlley, Scottish Reporter

Grampian Television Ltd

Queen's Cross, Aberdeen AB15 4XJ
t 01224 846846 **f** 01224 846800
e gtv@grampiantv.co.uk **w** www.grampiantv.co.uk
Contact Derrick Thomson, Managing Director; Henry Eagles, Head of News and Current Affairs; Bert Ovenstone, Head of Public Relations; Donald MacDonald, Senior Producer; Craig Wilson, Senior Producer; Iain MacDonald, Resources Manager
Credits Desert Island Chefs (T); People Show (T); Crossfire (T); North Tonight News (T)

Hanrahan Media

PO Box 163, Stratford-upon-Avon CV37 8NG
t 01789 450182 **f** 01789 450143
e admin@hanrahanmedia.com **w** www.hanrahanmedia.com
Contact Gill Carter, Production Manager; Catherine O'Riordan, Editor; Will Hanrahan, Managing Director
Credits Your Stars (T); Most Haunted Live (T); Soap Star Lives (T); Star Lives (T)

HTV Group Ltd

HTV Wales Media Centre, Culverhouse Cross, Cardiff CF5 6XJ
t 029 2059 2500 **w** www.htvwales.com
Contact Elis Owen, Director of Programming (HTV Wales); Jane McCloskey, Director of Programming (HTV West and Carlton West Country); Jeremy Payne, Managing Director

HTV West The Television Centre, Bath Road, Bristol BS4 3HG
t 0117 972 2722 **w** www.htvwest.com
Contact Elis Owen, Director of Programming (HTV Wales); Steve Egginton, Head of News; Tom Archer, Controller of Network Programming; James Garrett, Head of Features & Current Affairs; Jane McCloskey, Director of Programming (HTV West and Carlton West Country); Jeremy Payne, Managing Director
Part of the Carlton Communications Group.

ITV 1 Wales

The Television Centre, Culverhouse Cross, Cardiff CF5 6XJ
t 029 2059 0590 **f** 029 2059 7183
e public.relations@htv-wales.co.uk
Contact Sion Clwyd Roberts, Business Affairs Manager; Elis Owen, Controller and Director of Programmes

LWT

The London Television Centre, Upper Ground, London SE1 9LT
t 020 7620 1620
e christy.swords@granadamedia.com **w** www.lwt.co.uk
Contact Christy Swords, Managing Director

Maya Vision International

43 New Oxford Street, London WC1A 1BH
t 020 7836 1113 **f** 020 7836 5169
e info@mayavisionint.com **w** www.mayavisionint.com
Contact John Cranmer, Designer/Technical; Rebecca Dobbs, Producer; Sally Thomas, Producer; Michael Wood, Writer/Presenter; Barbara Bouman, Researcher; David Wallace, Director
Credits The Real History Show (T); In the Footsteps of Alexander the Great (T); Hitler's Search for the Holy Grail (T); Conquistadors (T)

Philips Digital Networks

Unit 4, Elmwood, Chineham Business Park, Crockfort Lane, Basingstoke RG24 8WG
t 0870 906 9500 **f** 0870 906 9455
w www.digitalnetworks.phillips.com
Contact Siraj Marzban, Area Manager

SIX TV - The Oxford Channel
270 Woodstock Road, Oxford OX2 7NW
t 01865 557000 **f** 01865 553355
e admin@oxfordchannel.com **w** www.oxfordchannel.com
Contact Nigel Taylor, Managing Director

Tyne Tees Television
Television Centre, City Road, Newcastle-upon-Tyne NE1 2AL
t 0191 261 0181 **f** 0191 261 2302
e tyne.tees@granadamedia.com
Contact Norma Hope, Head Of Regional Affairs

UTV
Havelock House, Ormeau Road, Belfast BT7 1EB
t 02890 328122 **f** 03890 246695
e info@utvlive.co.uk **w** www.utv.com
Contact John McCann, Managing Director
Credits Lesser Spotted Ulster (T); UTV Live (T); The Kelly Show (T)

UNDERWATER

underwater : contents	
Equipment Hire	658
Services	658
Health & Safety	659
Cameramen	660
Specialists	662

Underwater & Marine
Equipment Hire

Action Underwater Studios Ltd
ESAB Industrial Site, Hertford Rd, Waltham Cross EN8 7RP
t 01992 718485 **f** 01992 719546
e aus01@tinyonline.co.uk **w** www.actionunderwaterstudios.co.uk
Contact Doug Green, Managing Director
Credits The Hours (F); Sexy Beast (F); Hood/Bismark (D); Dirty Pretty Things (F)

Allchorn Pleasure Boats
1 Offham Close, Eastbourne BN23 8LU
t 01323 410606 **f** 01323 460840 **m** 07855 791555
e allchorn_boats@hotmail.com
w www.allchornpleasureboats.co.uk

Beaumaris Marine Services
The Anchorage, Rosemary Lane, Beaumaris LL58 8ED
t 01248 810746 **f** 01248 810746 **m** 07860 811988
e cerismar@hotmail.com **w** www.puffinisland.co.uk
Contact Dave Jones, Proprietor
Credits HTV Wales (T); Helly Hanson (C); Braveheart (F)

Collins & Chambers
197-199 Mare Street, London E8 3QF
t 020 8985 0752 **f** 020 8985 3123 **e** nautilus@talk21.com
Contact A Marshall, Managing Director

Eyewitness Ltd
The Drove, Sherfield English Road, Plaitford, Romsey SO51 6EF
t 01794 322500 **f** 01794 323601 **m** 07711 845108
e eyewitnessrental@aol.com **w** www.eyewitnessuk.co.uk
Contact Slim MacDonnell, Managing Director; Sandra James, Facilities Manager
Credits Loch Ness (T); Roger Roger (F); Harry Potter And The Prisoner Of Azkaban (F); Monarch Of The Glen (T)

Searchwise Ltd
Unit 6, Broomiesburn Road, Ellon Industrial Estate, Ellon AB41 9RD
t 01358 722990 **f** 01358 722933 **m** 07831 568558
e sales@searchwise.co.uk **w** www.searchwise.co.uk
Contact Pat Kelsall, Director; Alaistair Blanch, Operations Manager

Tritech Rentals
Peregrine Road, West Hill Business Park, West Hill, Aberdeen AB32 6JL
t 01224 744111 **f** 01224 741771
e rental@tritech.co.uk **w** www.tritech.co.uk

Underwater Studios
ESAB Industrial Site, Hertford Rd, Waltham Cross EN8 7RP
t 01992 718485 **f** 01992 719546 **m** 07730 064451
e aus01@tinyonline.co.uk **w** www.actionunderwaterstudios.co.uk
Contact Doug Green, Manager
Credits The Hours (F); Harry Potter And The Prisoner Of Azkaban (F); Sexy Beast (F); Snatch (F)

Underwater & Marine
Services

Anchor Marine Film & Television Ltd
Spikemead Farm, Poles Lane, Lowfield Heath RH11 0PH
t 01293 538188 **f** 01293 551558 **m** 07831 568684
e amsfilms@aol.com
Contact Tony Tucker, Marine Co-ordinator
Credits The Russian Bride (T); Down To Earth (T); Importance Of Being Earnest (F); Anna And The King (F)

Anglesey Sea Zoo
Brynsiencyn, Anglesey LL61 6TQ
t 01248 430411
e fishandfun@seazoo.demon.co.uk **w** www.angleseyseazoo.co.uk
Contact Alison Lea-Wilson, Partner; Karen Tilson, Curator; Helen Evans, Business Administrator

Aquarius Marine Group Ltd
Mill Lane, The Beckery, Glastonbury BA6 9NT
t 01458 834734 **f** 01458 834734 **m** 07860 811303
e info@aquariusmarine.com **w** www.aquariusmarine.com
Contact Tony Wynes, Director
Credits The Lost Seals (T); Harvest Moon (T); The Bill (T); Manchild (T)

BBC Outside Broadcasts

BBC Outside Broadcasts
Kendal Avenue, London W3 0RP
t 020 8993 9333 **f** 020 8993 4510
e ob@bbc.co.uk **w** www.bbcresources.com/ob

Charlie Bennett Underwater Productions
13A Station Terrace, London NW10 5RT
t 020 8968 9348 **m** 07702 263952 **e** chazben@aol.com
Credits Green Eyed Monster (T); Drebbels Submarine (D); Nembrotha Diving (I); Frou Frou (M)

Cameras Underwater
East Island Farmhouse, Slade Road, Ottery St Mary EX11 1QH
t 08700 660384 **f** 08700 660385
e sales@cameras-uw.co.uk **w** www.camerasunderwater.co.uk

Chas Newens Marine Company Ltd
The Boathouse, Embankment, London SW15 1LB
t 020 8788 4587 **f** 020 8780 2339 **m** 07801 474975
e info@chastheboat.com

underwater : health and safety

The UK Diving at Work Regulations 1997. S.I. 2776. apply to all divers and impose duties on producers, production companies and those who manage divers. The previous regulations were often avoided and were exempted in parts for "journalists". To help production staff understand the basic requirements of these regulations the Association of Media Divers has put together the following guide.

To help understanding and compliance to the Regulations, the Health and Safety Executive (HSE) publish an Approved Code of Practice (ACoP) for each of six industries that require Diving at Work. The Media Diving Projects ACoP is specific and detailed. A large input into its composition came from a group of diving film technicians, identified by the HSE as the Author Group, and who have since formed the Association of Media Divers. It applies to all areas of the 'Media' except large scale construction projects and the use of explosives, for these the ACoP for Inshore Diving should be followed. The HSE has recently published Diving Information Sheet Number 8 (benign conditions). This is not an alternative to the AcoP; it is supplementary and does not remove the requirement to comply with it. The HSE is pursuing a much more vigorous campaign of inspections and site visits.

Client

Under Paragraph 4 of our Media ACoP the onus is put on the Client – generally the Producer – to put in place his or her way of complying with it. The Client should:

a   Appoint a competent Contractor (para. 5). The Contractor must have supplied the Health & Safety Executive with particulars as listed (para. 7) The contractor is responsible for the safe organisation of the diving event (para. 6)

b   Establish clearly the employer of the divers. A diver 'Works' underwater if he/she breathes a compressed gas and accepts any form of commission or request. Payment is not a criteria.

c   Provide sufficient detail of the project to enable it to be carried out safely (para. 4)

d   Make available to the appointed contractor all information and knowledge available to themselves about the prospective dive site, location or set, or to state that no information is available to enable the contractor to plan accordingly (para. 4)

e   Ensure that any other equipment and personnel under their control does not affect the safety of the diving project (para. 4)

Under Para.4, the code also identifies others who may be responsible: Event Promoters, Sponsors, Publishers, Agencies, Film and TV production companies, also owners of dive sites/locations and the operators of vessels used in the diving project.

f   Co-operate with the Contractor and his/her appointed Supervisor (they may be the same person) and others so as to enable them to fulfil their obligations.

The Supervisor cannot dive and may be thought of as the Diving Safety Officer. He/she is the only person who can give the divers instructions or authorise their requests. Supervisors co-ordinate, and communicate very closely with the director and cameraman to facilitate their creative ideas with safe diving practices. The Supervisors are required to make the divers safe, for example remove them from the water should any other activity compromise their safety.

Sufficient time should be allowed for the project to be thoroughly planned. It could also save money.

It can now be possible for a partly trained or even untrained Presenter or artist to take part in a dive, the safety of which must be assessed in the contractor's risk assessment. Specific safety arrangements and additional fully trained attendant diver(s) to be noted in the dive rules. All divers (including artists) must accede to a medical examination and hold a certificate of medical fitness to dive, issued by an HSE-approved medical examiner of divers.

Contact details of approved doctors are available from the HSE on 0141 275 3029.

Contractor

To identify 'competence' the Producer may wish to consider items required of the contractor such as:

a   The diving project plan and rules.

b   The risk assessment for previous dives.

c   His/her records of equipment maintenance/ testing.

d   The logs and records of previous dives, divers and personnel.

e   Is their day-to-day work in the media business? Will you both be able to communicate creative ideas and implement them safely?

f   Whether they are a member of the Association of Media Divers and dive to their rules.

Details of your insurance may need to be checked.

A trail of verifiable records will follow the progression of the 'Duty of Care' from the 'Client' to the Contractor and then on down through the Supervisor to the Diver and his/her equipment.

The paragraphs referred to are those in the ACoP. The HSE was consulted in the preparation of this guide, which however is not definitive.

They are at www.hse.gov.uk/spd/noframes/spddiv.htm

Copies of the 'The Diving at Work Regulations' 1997 S.I. 2776 ISBN 0 11 065170 7 and
'Media Diving Projects', Approved Code of Practice ISBN 0 7176 1497 2 are available from:
HSE Books Ltd, PO Box 1999, Sudbury, Suffolk CO10 6FS. Tel 01787 881165, Fax 01787 313995.
© Association of Media Divers Nov. 2002
With thanks to the Association of Media Divers for supplying this information.
For further information please contact 020 8567 4213.

John Close
29 Merchants House, 66 North Street, Leeds LS2 7PN
t 0113 244 1348 **f** 0113 244 1372 **m** 07850 589728
e JCloseencounters@aol.com

Commercial Diving & Marine Services
Ashley House, Malt Kiln Lane, Appleton Roebuck YO23 7DT
t 01904 744424 **f** 01904 744724 **m** 07860 847247
e cdms@diving-serv.co.uk
Contact Steven Fila, Contracting Operations Manager

Dive Force Marine
10 Cheapside Parade, North Circular Road, Palmers Green,
London N13 5ED
t 020 8803 0241 **f** 020 8803 6994
e enquiries@diveforce.co.uk **w** www.diveforce.co.uk
Contact Terry Wheal, Director

Diving Services UK
24 Copthall Lane, Chalfont St Peter, Gerrards Cross SL9 0DB
t 01753 891074 **f** 01753 891074
e info@divingservicesuk.com **w** www.divingservicesuk.com

Marine Film Services Ltd
15 Church Road, East Molesey KT8 9DR
t 020 8224 9246 **f** 020 8224 9265 **m** 07973 411120
e info@marinefilm.co.uk **w** www.marinefilm.co.uk
Contact Richard Carless, Proprietor
Credits LD50 (F); Bright Young Things (F); Die Another Day (F)

Moonsail
Pankina, Croit-e-Quill Road, Lonan IM4 7JG
t 01624 861127 **f** 01624 861127 **m** 07624 450146
e mclark@enterprise.net
Contact Mike Clarke, Proprietor

Ocean Leisure
11-14 Northumberland Avenue, London WC2N 5AQ
t 020 7930 5050 **f** 020 7930 3032
e info@oceanleisure.co.uk **w** www.oceanleisure.co.uk
Contact I Ballard, Financial Controller; Tom Rowlands; Tara Priestley

Oceanic Ltd
Pelagic House, Dunkeswell, Honiton EX14 4RB
t 01404 891819 **f** 01404 891909
e info@oceanicuk.com **w** www.oceanicuk.com
Contact Kelvin Richards, Managing Director

Runnymede Dive
Unit 11, Eversley Way, Thorpe Industrial Estate, Egham TW20 8RG
t 01784 436909 **f** 01784 436909
e runnymededive@compuserve.com **w** www.runnymededive.co.uk
Contact Bob Harris, Contact; Steve Panrucker, Contact

Scubacam Ltd
Unit 19, Oliver Business Park, Oliver Road, Park Royal, London
NW10 7JB
t 020 8961 5333 **f** 020 8838 0656
e scubacam@btconnect.com **w** www.scubacam.co.uk
Contact John Johnson, Managing Director

SDM Commercial & Yacht Marine Services
3 Gordon Close, Binstead, Ryde PO33 3RB
t 01983 615289 **f** 01983 615289 **m** 07770 453521
e simon.mayne3@virgin.net
Contact Simon Mayne, Director

Specialised Diving Services
24 Harrier Drive, Poole BH21 1XE
t 01202 841932 **f** 01202 841932 **m** 07885 941969
e info@specialised-diving.co.uk **w** www.specialised-diving.co.uk
Contact Phil Richards, Diving & Safety Supervisor
Credits Casualty (T); Journey To The Bottom Of The Sea (D); Body Hits (E)

Splashsports Services
Unit 26, West Gorgie Park Industrial Estate, Hutchison Road,
Edinburgh EH14 1UT
t 0131 455 8788 **f** 0131 455 8787
e info@splashsports.co.uk **w** www.splashsports.co.uk
Contact Kevin Brown, Edinburgh Sales Manager; Richard Niven,
Managing Director
Credits Monarch Of The Glen (T); Chewing the Fat (T); Taggart (T);
2000 Acres Of Sky (T)

Square Sail Shipyard Ltd
Charlestown Harbour, St Austell PL25 3NJ
t 0 1726 70241 **t** 0 1726 67526 **f** 0 1726 61839
e info@square-sail.com **w** www.square-sail.com
Contact David Redhead, Marine Manager; Robin Davies, Managing Director;
Ray Atkin, Harbour Manager
Credits Saving Private Ryan (F); Count Of Monte Cristo (F); Longitude (T);
Hornblower III (T)

Submex Ltd
21 Roland Way, London SW7 3RF
t 020 7373 3069 **f** 020 7373 7340 **m** 07802 785050
e submex@dircon.co.uk **w** www.under-water.co.uk/submex
Contact John Bevan, Managing Director
Credits Scrapheap (T)

Tenrag Yacht Charters Ltd
Tenrag House, Freepost CU986, Preston, Canterbury CT3 1EB
t 01227 721874 **f** 01227 721617
e info@tenrag.com **w** www.tenrag.com
Contact Roger Garnett, Managing Director

Thanetcraft Ltd
29 Pope's Grove, Twickenham TW1 4JZ
t 020 8894 5218 **f** 020 8894 5218
e sales@thanetcraft.com **w** www.thanetcraft.com
Contact John Armstrong, Managing Director

TWI's Underwater Facilities
Aurora Court, Barton Road, Riverside Park, Middlesborough
TS2 1RY
t 01642 210512 **f** 01642 252218
e twinorth@twi.co.uk **w** www.twi.co.uk
Contact Jim Sheppard, Underwater Manager

The Water Babies
Little Grange Farm, Woodham, Mortimer CM9 6TL
t 01245 222771 **f** 01245 227711 **m** 07710 021010
e guytrench@aol.com
Contact Guy Trench, Managing Director

Underwater Cameramen

Axtell Underwater Video
68 Rockley Road, Hamworthy, Poole BH15 4HA
t 01202 718522 **f** 01202 710037 **m** 07973 772349
e steve.scuba@virgin.net
w www.axtell-underwater-video.com
Contact Steve Axtell, Proprietor
Credits Underwater Specialist In The Red Sea (E); Underwater Cameraman In
The Red Sea (D)

Blue Fin Television Ltd
34 Fitzwilliam Road, London SW4 0DN
t 020 7622 0870 **f** 020 7720 7875 **m** 07973 502349
e antleake@bluefin-tv.demon.co.uk **w** www.bluefintv.com
Contact Anthony Leake, Head of Cameras; Diane Porter, Bookings
Credits The Fugitives (T); Vandals (D); Escape From Experiment Island (T); The
South Bank Show (T)

Companies worked for:
Oil Factory
BRW Milan
Outsider
Mustard
RSA
Bullet
Cineteam Rome
Howard Guard
Procine
The Directory
Darling films
Storm films
Atomic Worx
Space City
Saga films
Fugitive
XTV
Atit
Channel 4
BBC

Award
Winning DoP
(The
New York
Film Festival
twice)
GBCT, BAFTA,
DGGB, IAWF,
AoP member

Franz Pagot MBKS

Director of Photography
Underwater Cameraman

(+44) 07770 520 757

BBC approved

Features, TV, commercials and promos (Adidas, Toyota, Red Cross, Mumm, Pepsi, Speedo,
Utterly Butterly, WWF, COI, Black Lines, The Uninvited, Out of the Blue, The Corridor,
Bocelli, Joey Tempest, Jelisha, TBell, Afterhours, BBC 999, Child of our time, Blue Peter,
Scrapheap, and many more)

HSE Diving contractor-TDI Rebreather-IANTD AdvEANX
mail@franzpagot.com   www.franzpagot.com

Jason Bulley

104 Hassall Road, Sandbach CW11 4HL
t 07775 595 559 **f** 01270 766 960
e JasonBulley@aol.com **w** www.cinematography.net/underwater
Agent Suz Cruz, Halliford Studio, Manygate Lanes,
Shepperton TW17 9EG
t 01932 252577 **f** 01932 253323 **m** 07956 485593
e zoe@suzcruz.co.uk **w** www.suzcruz.co.uk

Celtic Diving & Media Services

Main Street, Goodwick SA64 0BN
t 01348 874752 **f** 01348 879694 **m** 07816 640684
e celticdiving@ukonline.co.uk **w** www.celticdiving.co.uk
Contact Mark Deane, Sole Proprieter
Credits It's Out There (W); Obs Spot (E); Agneta (S); It's No Fun Being No.2 In
The Food Chain (D)

John Cocking

Cuckoo Barn, 3 Church Court, Church Street, Denby Village
DE5 8PG
t 01332 781511 **f** 01332 780206 **m** 07831 200977
e j.cocking@netmatters.co.uk **w** www.contact-uk.com\johncocking
Credits Bjork (M); Rank/Warner Hotels (I)

Richard A Edwards

5 Windsor Close, St Ives, Ringwood BH24 2LJ
t 01425 472377 **f** 01425 473779
e richard@underwatercameraman.org
w www.underwatercameraman.org

Hugh Fairs

7 Claygate Road, Dorking RH4 2PR
t 01306 889250 **m** 07770 321940
e hugh.fairs@ntlworld.com **w** www.underwater-camera.com
Credits 999 (T); Coronation Street (T); Green Eyed Monster (T); Hornblower II (T)

Filmways

f 01306 889250 **m** 07770 321940
e hugh.fairs@ntlworld.com **w** www.underwater-camera.com
Contact Hugh Fairs, Proprietor
Credits Coronation Street (T); Scrapheap I, II & III (T); Hornblower II (T)

Rob Franklin

8 Winchendon, Alyesbury HP18 0EH
t 01296 658960 **m** 07973 196002 **e** rob.franklin@virgin.net
Credits Human Body - Imax (D); National Geographic - Africa (D)

Jeff Goodman

The High Barn, Sancreed, Penzance TR20 8QY
t 01736 788705 **f** 01736 788705 **m** 07050 173433
e jeffgoodman@supanet.com **w** www.jeffgoodman.supanet.com
Credits Commercial Diving (I); Indonesia (D); Giants (D); Kindred Spirits (D)

Henderson Underwater Images

14 Mellorbrow, Mellor, Blackburn BB2 7EX
t 01254 812993 **f** 01254 814244 **m** 07976 265847
e dave@scubamad.com
w www.henderson-underwater-images.co.uk
Contact Dave Henderson, Proprietor
Credits Underwater Specialist In The Red Sea (E); Underwater Cameraman In
The Red Sea (D)

Zena Holloway

2 Manor Court Road, London W7 3EL
t 020 8567 5249 **f** 020 8567 5249 **m** 07710 037715
e z3n4@lineone.net
w www.peterbailey.co.uk/holloway/holloway.html

Slim MacDonnell

The Drove, Sherfield English Road, Plaitford, Romsey SO51 6EF
t 01794 322500 **f** 01794 323601 **m** 07711 845108
e eyewitnessrental@aol.com **w** www.eyewitnessuk.co.uk
Credits Daddy's Girl (T); Building The Impossible (T); Fame Academy (T);
Leonardo Da Vinci (T)

Franz Pagot MBKS

f 020 7281 8520 **m** 07770 520757
e franz@acqua.demon.co.uk **w** www.franzpagot.com
Credits Love, Honour & Obey (2nd Unit) (F); Black Lines (F); World Wildlife Fund (I)

*Underwater Cameraman HSE qualified and BBC approved, TDI Full Closed
Circuit Rebreather, IANTD Adv EANX, HSE Diving Contractor. Many
features and commercials credits and several awards. GBCT BAFTA DGGB.*

Simon Rowles

11 Kenley Road, St Margarets, Twickenham TW1 1JT
t 020 8891 5765 **f** 020 8891 5765 **m** 07702 364023
e s.rowles@virgin.net
Credits Jesus In The Himalayas (D); The Dream Team (T); Comedy About Us (C);
Lloyds (C)

Mike Valentine

31A Hollywood Road, London SW10 9HT
t 020 7351 1504 **f** 020 7351 1504 **m** 07880 746292
e valentinefilms@clara.net **w** www.valentinefilms.com
Credits Shanghai Knights (F); Tomb Raider II (F); Die Another Day (F); The Hours (F)

Ian F T Young

57 Rowan Close, London W5 4AL
t 020 8567 1568 **f** 020 8567 1568 **m** 07802 883943
e ianftyoung@eircom.net

Underwater **Specialists**

The Antique Diving Company

28 Ashburnham Road, Eastbourne BN21 2HX
t 01323 737939 **f** 01323 737939 **m** 07050 040701
e leachy001@hotmail.com
Contact Paul Leech, Proprietor

Commercial & Leisure Video Productions

4 North Point, Emerald Quay, Shoreham Beach, Shoreham
Harbour, Shoreham-by-Sea BN43 5JX
t 01273 455100 **f** 01273 455100 **m** 07885 211269
e gary@yachttuition.co.uk **w** www.yachttuition.co.uk
Contact Gary Williams, Company Proprieter

Divers II Divers International

Cedar Lodge, 14 Hardingham Street, Hingham NR9 4JB
t 01953 850814 **f** 01953 851577 **e** divers2divers@orangenet.co.uk
Contact Jonathan Conte, Managing Director

Future Planet Ltd

One Chapel Platt, Exeter EX3 0HE
t 01392 875446 **m** 07767 446250
e dan@underwaterimages.co.uk
w www.underwaterimages.co.uk
Contact Dan Burton
Credits The Fishmonger (S); Deepest Diver (D); Death Of A Battlecruiser (D)

In Depth Solutions

129 Lavenham Road, London SW18 5ER
t 020 8874 6343
e mike@indepthsolutions.co.uk **w** www.indepthsolutions.co.uk
Contact Mike Seares, Director
Credits Blockbuster (C); Casualty (T); Leviathan (F); You Only Breathe Twice (D)

Little Dippers Ltd

PO Box 3223, Brighton BN1 3TY
t 01273 328275 **f** 01273 328275 **m** 07767 824733
e info@littledippers.co.uk **w** www.littledippers.co.uk
Contact Lauren Heston, Director

Kevin Matthews
t 07000 947371 **f** 01628 530557 **m** 07767 775760
e kevin@specialistwirerigs.co.uk **w** www.specialistwirerigs.co.uk
Credits Star Wars: Episode I - The Phantom Menace (F); Sleepy Hollow (F); Band Of Brothers (T)

John Miles
Flat 2, Auriol Mansions, Edith Road, London W14 OST
t 020 7602 1989 **m** 07930 622964 **e** equilibrium.films@virgin.net
Credits Green Hell; Underworld; Conquering Mountain of Fire

Christopher Morris
20 Ulva Road, Putney, London SW15 6AP
t 020 8488 0877 **f** 020 8488 0876 **m** 07785 541006
e chris@smilecheese.com **w** www.smilecheese.com
Credits Ministry Of Sound (M); Mind Hunters (F); London's Burning (T)

Ocean Optics Underwater
13 Northumberland Avenue, London WC2 N5AQ
t 020 7930 8408 **f** 020 7839 6148
e optics@oceanoptics.co.uk

Oceanic Film Studio
Pelagic House, Flightway, Dunkeswell Industrial Estate, Honiton EX14 4RB
t 01404 891819 **f** 01404 891909
e kelvinr@oceanicuk.com
Contact Kelvin Richards, Managing Director

Franz Pagot MBKS
f 020 7281 8520 **m** 07770 520757
e franz@acqua.demon.co.uk **w** www.franzpagot.com
Credits Love, Honour & Obey (2nd Unit) (F); Black Lines (F); World Wildlife Fund (I)

VIDEO

Video Co-ordinators

BKA Facilities
The Croft Studio, 24 Mill Lane, Wingrave, Aylesbury HP22 4PL
t 01296 681660 **f** 01296 681458 **m** 07836 280016
e bka.service@virgin.net
Contact Brian King

Ira Curtis Coleman
t 01923 237575 **f** 019 2323 7616 **m** 07710 247787
e bitsoft@talk21.com
Credits Lighthouse (S); Worst Witch (T)

Abigail Coult
2 Hillary House, Boyton Close, London N8 7BB

Inbox Solutions Ltd
Greenford UB6 7QN
m 07439 012249
e stevec.inbox@virgin.net **w** www.inboxsolutions.co.uk
Contact Steve Campbell, Director
Credits Lara Croft: Tomb Raider (F); Dinotopia (T)

Video Equipment Hire

AEL Video
13A Airport Road West, Belfast BT3 9ED
t 028 9088 3555 **f** 028 9088 3539 **e** aelvideo@adt.co.uk
Contact Roy Porter, Hire Manager; Mark Ross, Sales Manager

Altered Images
The Gate House, 2 Richmond Road, Old Isleworth TW7 7BL
t 020 8568 4466
e sales@alteredimagesltd.com **w** www.alteredimagesltd.com
Contact Libby Pickett, Business Development Manager

AT Communications Ltd
13-19 Gate Lane, Boldmere, Sutton Coldfield B73 5TR
t 0121 354 7582 **f** 0121 354 7669
e mick@atcomms.co.uk **w** www.atcomms.co.uk
Contact Andrew Thomas, Managing Director

AVCOM
Stanlake Mews, London W12 7HS
t 020 8735 3422 **t** 020 8735 3410
f 020 8735 3429 **m** 07973 425375
e info@avcomhire.com **w** www.avcomhire.com
Contact Linda Goodlip, Rental Co-ordinator; Eric Bastin, Managing Director

Blitz Communications Ltd
100 Centennial Avenue, Centennial Park, Elstree WD6 3SA
t 0870 162 1000 **f** 0870 162 1111
e enquiries@blitzvision.com **w** www.blitzvision.com
Contact Andy Watterston, Sales Director

Bow Tie Television
Unit 20, Bourne Industrial Park, Bourne Road, Crayford DA1 4BZ
t 01322 524500 **f** 01322 527777
e john@bowtietv.com **w** www.bowtietv.com
Contact John Knopp, Managing Director
Credits Endemol - King Of Sport (T); NHK Enterprises Europe Ltd - Red Demon (T)

Broadcast RF
Unit 16, Acorn Industrial Park, Crayford Road, Dartford DA1 4AL
t 01322 520202 **f** 01322 520204
e hire@broadcastrf.com **w** www.broadcastrf.com
Contact Mark Houghton, General Manager

Broadcast Services
The Coach House, Ruxbury Road, Chertsey KT16 9EP
t 01932 570001 **f** 01932 570443
e hire@broadcast-services.co.uk **w** www.broadcast-services.co.uk
Contact David Scrutton, Director; Peter Scrutton, Director; Darren Moss, Hire Manager

Capitol AV Ltd
143 Clocktower Road, Isleworth TW7 6DT
t 020 8569 9958 **f** 020 8569 9961
e info@capitolav.co.uk **w** www.capitolav.co.uk
Contact Kris Hill, Senior Account Manager; Ian Leslie, Managing Director; John Yardley-Turpin, Sales Director; Ralph Taylor, IT Project Manager

Chapter
Market Road, Canton, Cardiff CF5 1QE
t 029 2031 1050 **f** 029 2031 3431
e tony.whitehead@chapter-online.co.uk **w** www.chapter.org
Contact Tony Whitehead, Cinema Programmer; Jamie Rees, Cinema Assistant; Graham Jones, Projectionist; Glen Manby, Head Projectionist

Charter Broadcast Ltd

Unit 4, Elstree Distribution Park, Elstree Way, Borehamwood
WD6 1RU
t 020 8905 1213 **f** 020 8905 1424 **m** 07836 521987
e charter@charter.co.uk
Contact Helen Frost, Bookings Coordinator

Equipment hire company, offering a comprehensive range of broadcast video, audio, graphics and RF facilities for dry hire. In addition, Charter Broadcast offers Mobile Production Units and Flyaway Systems worldwide. Please contact us for further information or visit our website.

Computec AV Ltd

G7 G9-G12, Hastingwood Trading Estate, 35 Harbet Road,
London N18 3HT
t 020 8807 4457 **t** 020 8807 2002 **f** 020 8807 3818
e rentals@computecgroup.com **w** www.computecav.co.uk
Contact Nish Kahn, Manager

Connections Communication Centre Ltd

Palingswick House, 241 King Street, Hammersmith, London
W6 9LP
t 020 8741 1766 **f** 020 8563 9134
e info@cccmedia.co.uk **w** www.cccmedia.co.uk

Creative Technology ltd

307-309 Merton Road, London SW18 5JS
t 020 8877 5700 **f** 020 8877 1980
e info@ctlondon.com **w** www.ctlondon.com
Contact Guy Mapley, Director of Sales; Emma Holden, Sales

Euro Screens Ltd

Unit 4, Laburnam Park, 72 Knutsford Road, Alderley Edge SK9 7SF
t 01625 590033 **f** 01625 590033 **m** 07831 487366
e postmaster@vme.uk.com **w** www.euroscreens.co.uk

Fine Point Broadcast

Furze Hill, Kingswood KT20 6EZ
t 0800 970 2020 **f** 0800 970 2030
e hire@finepoint.co.uk **w** www.finepoint.co.uk
Contact Roger Wedlake, Chief Engineer; Colin Smith, Hire Co-ordinator; Linda Pressley, Hire Co-ordinator; Sam Barley, Hire Co-ordinator

Gearhouse Broadcast Ltd

Unit 14, Olympic Industrial Estate, Fulton Road, Wembley HA9 0TF
t 020 8795 1866 **f** 020 8795 1868
e uk@gearhousebroadcast.com **w** www.gearhousebroadcast.com
Contact Andy Hayford, Hire Manager; Jason Doherty, Account Manager - UK Rental; Stephen Ratcliff, Account Manager - UK Rental; Jon Sugden, Audio
Credits I'm A Celebrity, Get Me Out Of Here (T)

Genesis Television Ltd

46 Broadwick Street, London W1V 1FF
t 020 7734 8100 **f** 020 7734 8200
e hire@genesishire.com **w** www.genesishire.com
Contact Tim Banks, Director; Leon Powell, Hire Manager

Gordon Audio Visual Ltd

Symes Mews, 37 Camden High Street, London NW1 7JE
t 020 7387 3399 **f** 020 7383 7411
e sales@bigtelly.com **w** www.bigtelly.com
Contact John Talbot

Hammerhead Television Facilities Ltd

42 Webbs Road, London SW11 6SF
t 020 7924 3977 **f** 020 7924 2154
e london@hammerheadtv.com **w** www.hammerheadtv.com
Contact Will Wilkinson, Facilities Manager; Dan Jarmany, Facilities Manager

Hammerhead Television Facilities Ltd

Unit 22, Waters Edge Business Park, Modwen Road,
Manchester M5 3EZ
t 0161 872 6200 **f** 0161 872 6300
e manchester@hammerheadtv.com **w** www.hammerheadtv.com
Contact Darren Carrig, Facilities Manager; Matt Turnbull

Hammerhead Television Facilities Ltd

9 Merchiston Mews, Edinburgh EH10 4PE
t 0131 229 5000 **f** 0131 429 4211
e scotland@hammerheadtv.com **w** www.hammerheadtv.com
Contact Chris Orvis, Production Sound Mixer; Gail Glenwright, Facilities Manager

HCVF Television & Video Productions

67 Kenneth Street, Inverness IV3 5QF
t 01463 224788 **f** 01463 711460 **m** 07860 285872
e info@hcvf.co.uk **w** www.hcvf.co.uk
Contact Jim Eglinton

The Hire Company
4 Lower Park Row, Bristol BS1 5BJ
t 0117 927 7473 **f** 0117 923 0862 **m** 07860 341141
Contact Jeffrey Berning, Managing Director; Andy Bennett, Hire Manager

The Hire Company (UK) Ltd
Unit 18, Priory Industrial Park, Highcliffe, Christchurch BH23 4HD
t 01425 272002 **f** 01425 270094 **m** 07885 959128
e mail@thehireco.co.uk **w** www.thehireco.co.uk
Contact Pat Holdway, Hire Assistant; Scott Clarke, Hire Manager

HOTCAM
t 020 8742 1888 **e** info@hotcam.co.uk **w** www.hotcam.co.uk

Interbroadcast
22 Newman Street, London W1T 1PH
t 020 7580 5524 **f** 020 7637 1011
e interbroadcast@tvsetgroup.co.uk
Contact Mark Phillips; Terry Bettles

Leightons of Leeds
Webster Row, Wortley Moore Road, Leeds LS12 4JF
t 0113 279 5755 **f** 0113 279 5719
e leofleeds@aol.com **w** www.members.aol.com/leofleeds
Contact Owen McKee, Managing Director; Lee Williams, Managing Director

McMillan
22 Soho Square, London W1D 4NS
t 020 7070 7200 **f** 020 7070 7201
e mcmillan@mcmillan.co.uk **w** www.mcmillan.co.uk
Contact Fazal Shah, Hires Manager; Kay Gilmour, Director

As Premier Resellers, McMillan are a leading broadcast equipment supplier, with confidence in their high level of service and offer special hire rates to new clients.

The Mike Pia Video & Film Company
Saint Pancras Commercial Centre, 63 Pratt Street, London NW1 0BY
t 020 8203 8155 **f** 020 7485 3205 **m** 07956 142541
e marieni@ibm.net
Contact Marie Nicolas, Manager; Christian Malone

NCV Distribution Ltd
Unit 2, Loughlinstown Industrial Estate, Ballybrack, Rep of Ireland
t 282 6444 **f** 282 6532 **e** sales@ncv.ie
Contact Jeanette Long

Newland Electronics Ltd (Newcastle)
The Exchange, Whitley Road, Benton, Newcastle upon Tyne NE7 7XB
t 0191 215 0088 **f** 0191 266 4298 **e** newland@dial.pipex.com
Contact Alan Harrison, Managing Director

On Sight
14-15 Berners Street, London W1T 3LJ
t 020 7637 0888(24hr) **f** 020 7637 0444
e hire@onsight.co.uk **w** www.onsight.co.uk
Contact Sam Higham, Bookings Co-ordinator; Gemma Hoppenbrouwers, Hire Co-ordinator; Tony Maher, Hire Manager; Angi King, Bookings Manager; Terry Millard, General Manager; Eve Ray, Bookings Co-ordinator

Picture Canning Company
55 Bendon Valley, London SW18 4LZ
t 020 8874 9277 **f** 020 8874 6623
e info@picturecanning.co.uk **w** www.picturecanning.co.uk
Contact Leslie Zunz, Managing Director; Paul Taylor, General Manager; Phil Wade, Managing Director
Credits Escape To The Country (D); Watchdog (T); Is Harry On The Boat (T); Holiday (D)

Picture It
50 Church Road, London NW10 9PY
t 020 8961 6644 **f** 020 8961 2969
e rosemary@picit.net **w** www.picit.net
Contact Trevor Hunt, Managing Director; Rosemary Element, Sales & Marketing; Chris Sellers, Studio Manager

Comprehensive range including plasmas, projectors, cameras and vision mixers.

The Picture Works Ltd
33 Rosemont Road, Wembley, London NW3 6NE
t 0845 310 8321 **f** 0845 310 8320 **m** 07971 958780
e info@pictureworks.co.uk **w** www.pictureworks.co.uk
Contact Carolyn Price, Director; Robin Wealleans, Director

Presentation Services Ltd
The Heights, Cranborne Industrial Estate, Potters Bar EN6 3JN
t 01707 648120 **f** 01707 657072
e psl@presservgroup.com **w** www.presservgroup.com
Contact Gary Davis, Vice Chairman; Darren Glossop, Director; Chris Scadding, Director; Irene McLean, Director

Presteigne Broadcast Hire
The Studios, Cocks Crescent, New Malden KT3 4TA
t 020 8336 2345 **f** 020 8336 0333
e hire@presteigne.co.uk **w** www.presteigne.co.uk
Contact Emma Levin, Senior Sales Manager; Jane Harris, Finance Director; Peter Gates, Operations Manager; Mike Ransome, Managing Director
Credits Commonwealth Games 2002 (T); BBC Football (T)

PSL Proquip

The Heights, Cranborne Industrial Estate, Potters Bar EN6 3JN
t 01707 648120 **f** 01707 648127
e nick.pask@presservgroup.com **w** www.presservgroup.com
Contact Nick Pask, Division Manager; Tim Olwer, Manager
Credits Die Another Day (F); Pride Of Britain Awards (T); My Kind Of Music (T)

Screenco Ltd

4 Concorde Close, Sopwith Park, Segensworth, Fareham PO15 5RT
t 01489 560900 **f** 01489 560901
e mikew@screenco.com **e** shelleep@screenco.com
w www.screenco.com
Contact Mike Walker, Director of Sales & Marketing; Shellee Pegg, Sales
& Project Co-ordinator; Graham Filmer, Director & General Manager
Credits Royal Variety Performance (T); TOTP Awards (T); BBC Sports
Personality Of The Year (T); Smash Hits Poll Winners Party (T)

Shooting Partners Ltd

9 Mount Mews, High Street, Hampton TW12 2SH
t 020 8941 1000 **f** 020 8941 0077
e mail@shooting-partners.co.uk **w** www.shooting-partners.co.uk
Contact Jenny Bigrave, Production Coordinator; Mark Holdway, Displays
& Projection; Phil White, Managing Director; Chris Dingley, Technical Director;
Darrin Dart, Facilities Manager; Matthew Tomkinson, Head of Resources
Credits Brainteaser (T); Wish You Were Here...? (T); Laureus World Sports
Awards (T); Spy TV (T)

Transmission (TX) Ltd

Unit 2A, Shepperton Studios, Studios Road, Shepperton TW17 0QD
t 020 8547 0208 **f** 01932 572571 **m** 07769 688813
e info@ttx.co.uk **w** www.ttx.co.uk
Contact Steve Lloyd, General Manager; Melanie Parkin, Bookings Contact;
Peter Hughes, Bookings Contact; Malcom Bubb, Bookings Contact
Credits The Hoobs (T); Doctors (T); Teletubbies (T)

*TX supply a comprehensive range of Video & Sound equipment for hire.
Including Digi Beta, Hi Def & DVCAM Camera Packages. Portable
Triax/CCU Production Units, Time-lapse Facilities, Cable Free Systems,
Minicams, Microwave Links, Jimmy Jibs, Lightweight Track & Dollies, Edit
VTR's, Kino Flos, HMI's, Sunguns — see website.*

TTL Video Ltd

38 Holmethorpe Avenue, Redhill RH1 2NL
t 01737 767655 **f** 01737 767665
e ob@ttlvideo.com **w** www.ttlvideo.com
Contact Alan Green; Mark Llewellyn; Nigel Cubbage
Equipment and expertise in all areas of outside broadcast engineering.

VCS

22 Woods Way, Goring Business Park, Goring-by-Sea, Worthing
BN12 4QY
t 01903 700499 **f** 01903 242588 **m** 07885 205100
e pete@vcs-av.co.uk **w** www.vcs-av.co.uk
Contact Pete Ewens, Director

Video Europe

The London Broadcast Centre, 11-13 Point Pleasant, London
SW18 1NN
t 020 8433 8000 **f** 020 8433 8001
e hire@videoeurope.co.uk **w** www.videoeurope.co.uk

Video Playback Company

Pinewood Studos, Pinewood Road, Ivor Heath SL0 0NH
t 01753 652 452 **f** 01753 652 090
e kevin.selway@videoplayback.co.uk **w** www.videoplayback.co.uk
Contact Kevin Selway, Proprietor

Whitwam

Unit 3, Chaucer Business Centre, Euston Lane, Winchester
SO23 7RR
t 01962 870408 **f** 01962 850820 **m** 07768 306123
e service@whitwamltd.uk **w** www.whitwamltd.uk
Contact Dave Harding, Director; Steve Birnage, Client Accounts

Video Equipment
Sales & Spares

All Systems International

Unit 4, Fleetsbridge Business Centre, Upton Road, Poole BH17 7AF
t 01202 680998 **f** 01202 680455
e asicavicom@aol.com **w** www.asicavi.com
Contact Z Sabawi, Managing Director

Altered Images

The Gate House, 2 Richmond Road, Old Isleworth TW7 7BL
t 020 8568 4466
e sales@alteredimagesltd.com **w** www.alteredimagesltd.com
Contact Libby Pickett, Business Development Manager

*We supply Hi-Definition, acquisition, graphics, post, non-linear editing,
presentation & communication products. In addition, we provide
complete turnkey solutions, maintenance and now equipment hire.*

Aztek Video

Preswylfa, Garth Road, Bangor LL57 2RT
t 01248 362021 **f** 01248 371895
e sales@aztekvideo.com **w** www.aztekvideo.com

Boxer Scotland

Unit 1, Millenium Court, Burns Street, Glasgow G4 9SA
t 0141 564 2710 **f** 0141 564 2719
e info@bsaltd.co.uk **w** www.bsaltd.co.uk
Contact Stuart Currie, Managing Director; Richard Devlin, Tech Support; John
Dormer, Data Systems; Alan Aitken, Broadcast Systems; Brian Young, Sales

Boxer Systems Ltd

4 Allied Business Centre, Coldharbour Lane, Harpenden AL5 4UT
t 01582 466119 **f** 01582 768489
e info@boxer.co.uk **w** www.boxer.co.uk
Contact Jon Phillips, Sales Manager

Campower Remu

27 West Wratting Road, Balsham CB1 6DX
t 01223 890000 **f** 01223 892529
e info@campower.co.uk **w** www.campower.co.uk
Contact Brenda Williamson, Partner

Crane Communications

77 Abetta Parade, Belfast BT5 5LA
t 028 9045 6071 **f** 028 9045 4961
e crane@cranecommunications.co.uk
w www.cranecommunications.co.uk
Contact Roy Logan, Managing Director; David McConkey, Managing Director

DS Video Facilities

Britannia Way, Unit 27, Metro Centre, Coronation Road,
London NW10 7PR
t 020 8965 8060 **f** 020 8453 0885
e bob.poole@btclick.com **w** www.dsvideo.co.uk
Contact Bob Poole, Sales Manager

DT Electronics Ltd
Eastwood Business Village, Harry Weston Road, Coventry CV3 2UB
t 024 7643 7437 **f** 024 7643 7401
e sales@dtelectronics.com **w** www.dtelectronics.com
Contact Zoe

E-Mediavision.com
19 Park Avenue, Hounslow TW3 2NA
t 020 8755 2014 **f** 020 8230 7828 **m** 07949 085178
e info@e-mediavision.com **w** www.e-mediavision.com
Contact Joe Conto, Technical Director; Kash Acharya, Managing Director; Andy Biscoe, Sales Director

Edirol (Europe) Ltd
Studio 3,4, 114 Power Road W4 5PY
t 020 8747 5949 **f** 020 8747 5948
e info@edirol.co.uk **w** www.edirol.co.uk
Contact Massimo Barbini, Managing Director; Simon Lowther, Sales Manager; Phil Palmer, Product Specialist

Electrosonic
Hawley Mill, Hawley Road, Dartford DA2 7SY
t 01322 222211 **f** 01322 282282
e info@electrosonic-uk.com **w** www.electrosonic.com
Contact Yvonne Hegarty, Advertising and Promotion

ES Video
6 The Riverside, Farnham GU9 7SS
t 01252 823850 **f** 01252 711702
m 07748 148696 **m** 07887 698928
e r.everard@esvideo.com **w** www.esvideo.com
Contact David Boothman, Sales Consultant; Richard Everard; Ian Dudley, Sales Consultant

Evertz Europe Ltd
Unit 1, Alderhouse, High Road, Rayleigh SS6 7SA
t 01268 779234 **f** 01268 779234 **m** 07786 512144
e uksales@evertz.com **w** www.evertz.com
Contact Harold Griffiths, UK Sales Manager
HDTV Video & Audio Equipment Manufacturers.

First Choice Solutions
1L Merrow Business Centre, Merrow Lane, Guilford GU4 7WA
t 01483 302333 **f** 01483 306789 **e** team@fcs.demon.co.uk
Contact Jim Inskip, Director

FSL International Ltd
PO Box 7290, Maldon CM9 8WP
t 01621 869111 **f** 01621 869111
e sales@fslinternational.co.uk **w** www.fslinternational.co.uk
Contact J Andrews, Director, Managing Director; H Potter, Sales Support

Fumeo Video Systems
5 Wellin Close, Edwalton NG12 4BL
t 0115 846 0022 **f** 0115 846 0033
Contact Roy Tidmarsh, Sales Manager

Global Distribution/Glyph Technologies
The Old School House, Ashdon, Saffron Walden CB10 2FT
t 0870 464 0600 **f** 0870 464 0601
e uksales@globaldistribution.com **w** www.globaldistribution.com
Contact Richard Berry, Marketing Director

H Preston Professional Video
107 Worcester Road, Malvern, Worcester WR1 1EP
t 01684 575486 **f** 01684 5755 94 **m** 07778 284 976
e jpreston@hpreston.co.uk **w** www.hpreston.co.uk

Hague Camera Supports
Mile End Road, Colwick, Nottingham NG4 2DW
t 0115 987 0031 **f** 0115 987 2900
e info@b-hague.co.uk **w** www.b-hague.co.uk
Contact Robert Scotton, Director

Harpers AV Ltd
3 Woking Business Park, Albert Drive, Woking GU21 5JY
t 01483 757577 **f** 01483 729449
e sales@harpersav.com **w** www.harpersav.com
Contact Ken Foster, Sales Manager

Hi Tech Systems Ltd
Homecroft, Oakley Lane, Oakley, Basingstoke RG23 7JZ
t 01256 780880 **f** 01256 782600
e sales@hitechsys.co.uk **w** www.vtrcontrol.com
Contact Tom Favell, Managing Director

Holdan Ltd
Unit 2, Waterside Business park, Hadfield, Glossop SK13 1BE
t 0845 130 4445 **f** 01457 850964
e sales@holdan.co.uk **w** www.holdan.co.uk
Contact Paul Armitage, Sales & Marketing

Horsham Hi-Fi Home Cinema
28 Queensway, Horsham RH13 5AY
t 01403 272931 **f** 01403 251587 **m** 07890 390310
e jeff@homecinema.uk.net **w** www.projectorsareus.com
Contact Jeff Paynter, Partner; Jan Paynter, Partner

IDX Technology Europe
Unit 34, Metropolitan Centre, 3 Taunton Road, Greenford UB6 8UQ
t 020 8813 1666 **f** 020 8813 1777
e idx.europe@idx.tv **w** www.idx.tv
Contact Spencer Doran; Kevan Parker, Technical Sales

IMP Electronics
Rocol Building, 3 Glebe Road, Huntingdon PE29 7DL
t 01480 411822 **f** 01480 411833
e sales@imp-electronics.co.uk **w** www.imp-electronics.co.uk
Contact Gill Ashby, Managing Director

LRC Broadcast
3-5 Whitfield Street, London W1T 2SA
t 020 7323 2117 **f** 020 7323 2191
e sales@lrcbroadcast.com **w** http://lrcbroadcast.com

MCD Broadcast Auctions
The Coach House, Ruxbury Road, Chertsey KT16 9EP
t 01932 571911 **f** 01932 571831
e auction@mcdauctions.co.uk **w** www.mcdauctions.co.uk
Contact Mark Walton, Auctioneer

Mediaplus AV Ltd
3 Mills Studios, 3 Mills Lane E3 3DU
t 020 8709 8582 **f** 020 8709 8339
e bianca@mediaplus-av.com **w** www.mediaplus-av.com
Contact Gerard Kirwin, Technical Manager

Mitcorp UK Ltd
5A Greenock Road, Acton, London W3 8DU
t 020 8752 1414 **f** 020 8752 0707
e lauradodds@mitcorp.co.uk **w** www.mitcorp.co.uk
Contact Laura Dodds, Marketing Executive; Lisa Sheikh, Marketing Executive

MVS Video
Alkham Valley Road, Folkestone CT18 7EH
t 01303 891468 **f** 0 7092 094431 **m** 07831 183256
e sales@mvsvideo.co.uk **w** www.mvsvideo.co.uk
Contact P Maxted, Engineer; P Marshall, Partner; S Marshall, Partner
Sales: Service and Production in Kent.

New Media Research (NMR)
5 Charlotte Mews, London W1P 1LP
t 020 7255 2700 **f** 020 7255 2702
e info@nmr.com **w** www.nmr.com
Contact Neil Anderson, Sales & Marketing Director

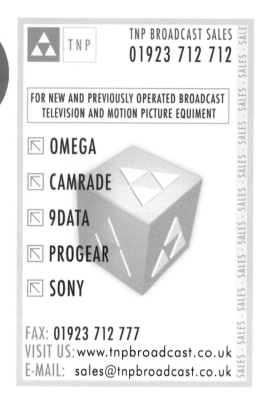
OpTex UK
20-26 Victoria Road, New Barnet, London EN4 9PF
t 020 8441 2199 **f** 020 8449 3646
e info@optexint.com **w** www.optexint.com
Contact Edward Catton-Orr, Sales; Mike Robinson, Rentals

PEC Video Ltd
65-66 Dean Street, London W1D 4PL
t 020 7437 4633 **e** sales@pec.co.uk **w** www.pec.co.uk
Contact Dan Wheeler, Sales Manager

Piks Video Engineering
55 Bendon Valley, London SW18 4LZ
t 020 8877 9669 **f** 020 8877 0394 **m** 07774 250794
e piks@picturecanning.co.uk **w** www.piks.co.uk
Contact Mark Calvert, Chief Engineer

Prokit
111 Power Road, London W4 5PY
t 020 8995 4664 **f** 020 8995 4656
e enquiries@prokit.co.uk **w** www.prokit.co.uk
Contact Mark Holmes, Managing Director; Sue Holmes, Director

Pure Digital
Home Park Estate, Kings Langley WD4 8LZ
t 01923 260511 **f** 01923 270188
e sales@videologic.com **w** www.videologic.com
Contact Paul Smith, Sales; Marsha Watson

Quadrant Visual Solutions (Birmingham)
4 Parkway Industrial Estate, Heneage Street, Ashton,
Birmingham B7 4LY
t 0121 359 6377 **f** 0121 359 2041
e sales@quadrantsolutions.com **w** www.quadrantsolutions.com

Reflex Ltd
Unit 1, Bennet Court, Bennet Road, Reading RG2 0QX
t 01189 313611 **f** 01189 314439
e info@reflex.co.uk **w** www.reflex.co.uk
Contact Chris Axford, Sales Manager; Roland Dreesden

Shannon Audio Visual Ltd
Unit 6G, Eastway Business Park, Ballysimon Road, Limerick,
Rep. of Ireland
t +353 6 141 2744 **f** +353 6 141 2123
e info@sav.ie **w** www.shannonsideav.ie
Contact Dirdre O'Donnelly, Marketing Manager

TNP Broadcast
Watford, Hertfordshire
t 01923 712712 **f** 01923 712777 **m** 07973 729423
e sales@tnpbroadcast.co.uk **w** www.tnpbroadcast.co.uk
Contact Tim Constable, Sales Executive; Garry Martin, Sales Executive; Howard
Rose, Managing Director; Matt Robins, Sales Executive

Top-Teks Ltd
Top-teks, 14 Park Place, Newdigate Road, Harefield UB9 6EJ
t 01895 825619 **f** 01895 822232 **m** 07831 866615
e gwen@top-teks.co.uk **w** www.top-teks.co.uk
Contact Mike Thomas, Sales Director; Gwen Thomas, Managing Director

TriMedia Broadcast
72-73 Margaret Street, 1st Floor, London W1N 7HA
t 020 7580 0043 **f** 020 7636 0112
e info@trimedia.co.uk **w** www.trimedia.co.uk
Contact Sheri Candler, Marketing; John Donovan, Managing Director; Ed
Silvester, Technical Support

True Colours Distribution Ltd
Suite 8, Great Bramshot Farm Barns, Bramshot Lane, Fleet
GU51 2SF
t 01252 788910 **f** 01252 786000
e sales@true-colours.net **w** www.true-colours.net
Contact Iain Campbell, Director; David Raymen, Director

Video Implementation Ltd
The Granary, Wood Hill Lane, Long Sutton RG29 1SU
t 01256 861005 **m** 07860 269708
e frank@video-implementation.co.uk
w www.video-implementation.co.uk
Contact Frank Page, Technical Manager

Video Rescue Ltd
Unit 19, The Markham Centre, Station Road, Theale, Reading
RG7 4PE
t 0118 9306900 **f** 0118 9306901
e info@videorescue.co.uk **w** www.videorescue.co.uk
Contact Ben Pearce; Chris Allen; Dominic Harland

*Services include: Consultation, Sales, Configuration, Manufacture,
Installation, Training and Support.*

Vistek Electronics
Wessex Road, Bourne End SL8 5DT
t 01628 531221 **f** 01628 530980
e sales@vistek.tv **w** www.vistek.tv
Contact Andrew Osmond, Managing Director; Mark Gardner, Sales Director;
Andrew Osmond, Managing Director

Visual Impact (Northern)
7-8 Dalby Court, Gadbrook Park, Northwich CW9 7TN
t 01606 42225 **f** 01606 49161 **e** sales@visnorth.visuals.co.uk
Contact David Phillips, Director

WTS
Unit 23, River Road Business Park, 33 River Road, Barking
IG11 0DA
t 020 8594 3336 **f** 020 8594 3338
e sales@wtsbroadcast.com **w** www.wtsbroadcast.com
Contact Ofir Mor, Sales Manager

Video Playback Operators

ASE Broadcast & Film Services
Geddes House, Parleyhill, Culcross KY12 8JD
t 01383 880602 **f** 01383 880737
m 07774 492085 **e** ase@asebroadcast.co.uk
Contact Andrew Steele, Partner
Credits Flash (C); Texaco (C); Ikea (C); Safeway (C)

David Atkinson
TOVS Ltd, The Linen Hall, 162-168 Regent Street, London W1B 5TB
t 020 7287 6110 **f** 020 7287 5481
e info@tovs.co.uk **w** www.tovs.co.uk

Azmat International
EXEC, 6 Travis Court, Farnham Royal SL2 3SB
t 01753 646677 **f** 01753 646770
e sue@execmanagement.co.uk **w** www.execmanagement.co.uk
Contact Sue Jones; Pam Riley

Stephen Barber
TOVS Ltd, The Linen Hall, 162-168 Regent Street, London W1B 5TB
t 020 7287 6110 **f** 020 7287 5481
e info@tovs.co.uk **w** www.tovs.co.uk

Richard Bardsley
TOVS Ltd, The Linen Hall, 162-168 Regent Street, London W1B 5TB
t 020 7287 6110 **f** 020 7287 5481
e info@tovs.co.uk **w** www.tovs.co.uk

Mark Bassenger
EXEC, 6 Travis Court, Farnham Royal SL2 3SB
t 01753 646677 **f** 01753 646770
e sue@execmanagement.co.uk **w** www.execmanagement.co.uk

Charles Bata
15 Quennel Mansions, Weir Road, London SW12 0NQ
t 020 8673 3855 **m** 07956 261312 **e** karelbata@yahoo.com
Credits British Airways (C); Paul McCartney (M); BBC Sport (T); Crimestrike (F)

Julian Bennet
Connections, The Meadlands, Oakleigh Road, Hatch End, Pinner HA5 4HB
t 020 8420 1444 **f** 020 8428 5836 **m** 07831 305518
e mail@connectionsuk.com **w** www.connectionsuk.com

BKA Facilities
The Croft Studio, 24 Mill Lane, Wingrave, Aylesbury HP22 4PL
t 01296 681660 **f** 01296 681458 **m** 07836 280016
e bka.service@virgin.net
Contact Brian King

Buddy Blackwell
EXEC, 6 Travis Court, Farnham Royal SL2 3SB
t 01753 646677 **f** 01753 646770
e sue@execmanagement.co.uk **w** www.execmanagement.co.uk

Perry Blakemore
TOVS Ltd, The Linen Hall, 162-168 Regent Street, London W1B 5TB
t 020 7287 6110 **f** 020 7287 5481
e info@tovs.co.uk **w** www.tovs.co.uk

Bob Bridges
EXEC, 6 Travis Court, Farnham Royal SL2 3SB
t 01753 646677 **f** 01753 646770
e sue@execmanagement.co.uk **w** www.execmanagement.co.uk

Kevin Brookner
EXEC, 6 Travis Court, Farnham Royal SL2 3SB
t 01753 646677 **f** 01753 646770
e sue@execmanagement.co.uk **w** www.execmanagement.co.uk

Trevor Cairns
EXEC, 6 Travis Court, Farnham Royal SL2 3SB
t 01753 646677 **f** 01753 646770
e sue@execmanagement.co.uk **w** www.execmanagement.co.uk

Alex Cambell
Connections, The Meadlands, Oakleigh Road, Hatch End, Pinner HA5 4HB
t 020 8420 1444 **f** 020 8428 5836 **m** 07831 305518
e mail@connectionsuk.com **w** www.connectionsuk.com

Guy Caplin
Connections, The Meadlands, Oakleigh Road, Hatch End, Pinner HA5 4HB
t 020 8420 1444 **f** 020 8428 5836 **m** 07831 305518
e mail@connectionsuk.com **w** www.connectionsuk.com

Alex Claydon
11 Oriel Drive, London SW13 8HF
t 020 8274 0573 **f** 020 8274 0573 **m** 07974 751855
Agent EXEC, 6 Travis Court, Farnham Royal SL2 3SB
t 01753 646677 **f** 01753 646770
e sue@execmanagement.co.uk **w** www.execmanagement.co.uk

Julian Elvins
Connections, The Meadlands, Oakleigh Road, Hatch End, Pinner HA5 4HB
t 020 8420 1444 **f** 020 8428 5836 **m** 07831 305518
e mail@connectionsuk.com **w** www.connectionsuk.com

Maureen Godfrey
TOVS Ltd, The Linen Hall, 162-168 Regent Street, London W1B 5TB
t 020 7287 6110 **f** 020 7287 5481
e info@tovs.co.uk **w** www.tovs.co.uk

Casper Gordon
EXEC, 6 Travis Court, Farnham Royal SL2 3SB
t 01753 646677 **f** 01753 646770
e sue@execmanagement.co.uk **w** www.execmanagement.co.uk

Davey Graham
EXEC, 6 Travis Court, Farnham Royal SL2 3SB
t 01753 646677 **f** 01753 646770
e sue@execmanagement.co.uk **w** www.execmanagement.co.uk

Rashid Haddou-Riffi
Connections, The Meadlands, Oakleigh Road, Hatch End, Pinner HA5 4HB
t 020 8420 1444 **f** 020 8428 5836 **m** 07831 305518
e mail@connectionsuk.com **w** www.connectionsuk.com

Marcus Hanbury
Connections, The Meadlands, Oakleigh Road, Hatch End, Pinner HA5 4HB
t 020 8420 1444 **f** 020 8428 5836 **m** 07831 305518
e mail@connectionsuk.com **w** www.connectionsuk.com

Dan Hartley
m 07887 548640 **e** mail@danhartley.co.uk

Bryan Hinds
Connections, The Meadlands, Oakleigh Road, Hatch End, Pinner HA5 4HB
t 020 8420 1444 **f** 020 8428 5836 **m** 07831 305518
e mail@connectionsuk.com **w** www.connectionsuk.com

Peter Hodgson
49 Cannonbury Avenue, Pinner HA5 1TP
t 020 8868 7546 **f** 020 8868 7546 **m** 07831 399506
e peter@monitorvideo.co.uk
Credits Hudson Hawk (F); Indian Jones and the Last Crusade (F); Batman (F)

Ichi Ichimura
Connections, The Meadlands, Oakleigh Road, Hatch End, Pinner HA5 4HB
t 020 8420 1444 **f** 020 8428 5836 **m** 07831 305518
e mail@connectionsuk.com **w** www.connectionsuk.com

Tina Jagger
TOVS Ltd, The Linen Hall, 162-168 Regent Street, London W1B 5TB
t 020 7287 6110 **f** 020 7287 5481
e info@tovs.co.uk **w** www.tovs.co.uk

David James
TOVS Ltd, The Linen Hall, 162-168 Regent Street, London W1B 5TB
t 020 7287 6110 **f** 020 7287 5481
e info@tovs.co.uk **w** www.tovs.co.uk

Nick Jordan
Connections, The Meadlands, Oakleigh Road, Hatch End,
Pinner HA5 4HB
t 020 8420 1444 **f** 020 8428 5836 **m** 07831 305518
e mail@connectionsuk.com **w** www.connectionsuk.com

Nick Kenealy
EXEC, 6 Travis Court, Farnham Royal SL2 3SB
t 01753 646677 **f** 01753 646770
e sue@execmanagement.co.uk **w** www.execmanagement.co.uk

Tom Laurie
EXEC, 6 Travis Court, Farnham Royal SL2 3SB
t 01753 646677 **f** 01753 646770
e sue@execmanagement.co.uk **w** www.execmanagement.co.uk

Stephen Lee
EXEC, 6 Travis Court, Farnham Royal SL2 3SB
t 01753 646677 **f** 01753 646770
e sue@execmanagement.co.uk **w** www.execmanagement.co.uk

Aslan Livingstone-Ra
Connections, The Meadlands, Oakleigh Road, Hatch End,
Pinner HA5 4HB
t 020 8420 1444 **f** 020 8428 5836 **m** 07831 305518
e mail@connectionsuk.com **w** www.connectionsuk.com

Andy Macdouall
Connections, The Meadlands, Oakleigh Road, Hatch End,
Pinner HA5 4HB
t 020 8420 1444 **f** 020 8428 5836 **m** 07831 305518
e mail@connectionsuk.com **w** www.connectionsuk.com

Sandip Mahal
Connections, The Meadlands, Oakleigh Road, Hatch End,
Pinner HA5 4HB
t 020 8420 1444 **f** 020 8428 5836 **m** 07831 305518
e mail@connectionsuk.com **w** www.connectionsuk.com

Derek McGurk
Connections, The Meadlands, Oakleigh Road, Hatch End,
Pinner HA5 4HB
t 020 8420 1444 **f** 020 8428 5836 **m** 07831 305518
e mail@connectionsuk.com **w** www.connectionsuk.com

Neil McLeod
TOVS Ltd, The Linen Hall, 162-168 Regent Street, London W1B 5TB
t 020 7287 6110 **f** 020 7287 5481
e info@tovs.co.uk **w** www.tovs.co.uk

James Millham
TOVS Ltd, The Linen Hall, 162-168 Regent Street, London W1B 5TB
t 020 7287 6110 **f** 020 7287 5481
e info@tovs.co.uk **w** www.tovs.co.uk

Jeremy Nathan
EXEC, 6 Travis Court, Farnham Royal SL2 3SB
t 01753 646677 **f** 01753 646770
e sue@execmanagement.co.uk **w** www.execmanagement.co.uk

Dave Newis
EXEC, 6 Travis Court, Farnham Royal SL2 3SB
t 01753 646677 **f** 01753 646770
e sue@execmanagement.co.uk **w** www.execmanagement.co.uk

Robin Nurse
TOVS Ltd, The Linen Hall, 162-168 Regent Street, London W1B 5TB
t 020 7287 6110 **f** 020 7287 5481
e info@tovs.co.uk **w** www.tovs.co.uk

ONE 8 SIX Ltd
12 Garrick Centre, Irving Way, London NW9 6AQ
t 020 8203 8155 **f** 020 8457 2445
e info@one8six.com **w** www.one8six.com
Contact Marie Nicolas, Manager; Craig Game, Client Contact

Martin Pearson
TOVS Ltd, The Linen Hall, 162-168 Regent Street, London W1B 5TB
t 020 7287 6110 **f** 020 7287 5481
e info@tovs.co.uk **w** www.tovs.co.uk

Michael Peat
TOVS Ltd, The Linen Hall, 162-168 Regent Street, London W1B 5TB
t 020 7287 6110 **f** 020 7287 5481
e info@tovs.co.uk **w** www.tovs.co.uk

Paul Puttick
TOVS Ltd, The Linen Hall, 162-168 Regent Street, London W1B 5TB
t 020 7287 6110 **f** 020 7287 5481
e info@tovs.co.uk **w** www.tovs.co.uk

Craig Robins
TOVS Ltd, The Linen Hall, 162-168 Regent Street, London W1B 5TB
t 020 7287 6110 **f** 020 7287 5481
e info@tovs.co.uk **w** www.tovs.co.uk

Antony Robinson
TOVS Ltd, The Linen Hall, 162-168 Regent Street, London W1B 5TB
t 020 7287 6110 **f** 020 7287 5481
e info@tovs.co.uk **w** www.tovs.co.uk

Darryl Rose
TOVS Ltd, The Linen Hall, 162-168 Regent Street, London W1B 5TB
t 020 7287 6110 **f** 020 7287 5481
e info@tovs.co.uk **w** www.tovs.co.uk

RT Video
7 Warren Road, Woodley, Reading RG5 3AP
t 0118 969 6632 **f** 0118 969 6632 **m** 07973 286933
e rtvideo@hotmail.com
Contact Ross Taggart
Credits Waitrose (C)

Stephen Rudder
EXEC, 6 Travis Court, Farnham Royal SL2 3SB
t 01753 646677 **f** 01753 646770
e sue@execmanagement.co.uk **w** www.execmanagement.co.uk

Andy Sandom
56 Hawthorne Avenue, Ruislip HA4 8ST
t 020 8582 3950 **f** 020 8582 3950 **m** 07976 270729
e sandom@lineone.net

Mark Schafer
Connections, The Meadlands, Oakleigh Road, Hatch End,
Pinner HA5 4HB
t 020 8420 1444 **f** 020 8428 5836 **m** 07831 305518
e mail@connectionsuk.com **w** www.connectionsuk.com

Andrew Shields
30 Kirkstall Road, London SW2 4HF
t 020 8671 1544 **t** 020 8203 8155 **f** 020 8671 1544
m 07973 769935 **e** ashi3333@aol.com
Agent EXEC, 6 Travis Court, Farnham Royal SL2 3SB
t 01753 646677 **f** 01753 646770
e sue@execmanagement.co.uk **w** www.execmanagement.co.uk

Sally Ann Shortman
TOVS Ltd, The Linen Hall, 162-168 Regent Street, London W1B 5TB
t 020 7287 6110 **f** 020 7287 5481
e info@tovs.co.uk **w** www.tovs.co.uk

Steve Smith
Grade One TV & Film Personnel, Elstree Studios, Shenley Road, Borehamwood WD6 1JG
t 020 8324 2224 **f** 020 8324 2328
e gradeone.tvpersonnel@virgin.net

Will Smith
Casarotto Ramsay & Associates Ltd, National House, 60-66 Wardour Street, London W1V 4ND
t 020 7287 4450 **f** 020 7287 9128
e agents@casarotto.uk.com **w** www.casarotto.uk.com

Simon Starr
TOVS Ltd, The Linen Hall, 162-168 Regent Street, London W1B 5TB
t 020 7287 6110 **f** 020 7287 5481
e info@tovs.co.uk **w** www.tovs.co.uk

Simon Thompson
TOVS Ltd, The Linen Hall, 162-168 Regent Street, London W1B 5TB
t 020 7287 6110 **f** 020 7287 5481
e info@tovs.co.uk **w** www.tovs.co.uk

Mark Tomlinson
TOVS Ltd, The Linen Hall, 162-168 Regent Street, London W1B 5TB
t 020 7287 6110 **f** 020 7287 5481
e info@tovs.co.uk **w** www.tovs.co.uk

Chris Warren
EXEC, 6 Travis Court, Farnham Royal SL2 3SB
t 01753 646677 **f** 01753 646770
e sue@execmanagement.co.uk **w** www.execmanagement.co.uk

Garie Wetherill
EXEC, 6 Travis Court, Farnham Royal SL2 3SB
t 01753 646677 **f** 01753 646770
e sue@execmanagement.co.uk **w** www.execmanagement.co.uk

Tracie Wetherill
EXEC, 6 Travis Court, Farnham Royal SL2 3SB
t 01753 646677 **f** 01753 646770
e sue@execmanagement.co.uk **w** www.execmanagement.co.uk

Vision Mixers

Chris Allen
Grade One TV & Film Personnel, Elstree Studios, Shenley Road, Borehamwood WD6 1JG
t 020 8324 2224 **f** 020 8324 2328
e gradeone.tvpersonnel@virgin.net

Moyra Bird
Experience Counts - Call Me Ltd, 5th Floor, 41-42 Berners Street, London W1P 3AA
t 020 7637 8112 **f** 020 7580 2582

Ian Blease
TOVS Ltd, The Linen Hall, 162-168 Regent Street, London W1B 5TB
t 020 7287 6110 **f** 020 7287 5481
e info@tovs.co.uk **w** www.tovs.co.uk

Kate Campbell
Connections, The Meadlands, Oakleigh Road, Hatch End, Pinner HA5 4HB
t 020 8420 1444 **f** 020 8428 5836 **m** 07831 305518
e mail@connectionsuk.com **w** www.connectionsuk.com

Brad Crockford
Agent TOVS Ltd, The Linen Hall, 162-168 Regent Street, London W1B 5TB
t 020 7287 6110 **f** 020 7287 5481
e info@tovs.co.uk **w** www.tovs.co.uk
Agent Connections, The Meadlands, Oakleigh Road, Hatch End, Pinner HA5 4HB
t 020 8420 1444 **f** 020 8428 5836 **m** 07831 305518
e mail@connectionsuk.com **w** www.connectionsuk.com

John Dodge
Experience Counts - Call Me Ltd, 5th Floor, 41-42 Berners Street, London W1P 3AA
t 020 7637 8112 **f** 020 7580 2582

Amanda Fairrington
TOVS Ltd, The Linen Hall, 162-168 Regent Street, London W1B 5TB
t 020 7287 6110 **f** 020 7287 5481
e info@tovs.co.uk **w** www.tovs.co.uk

Mark Foster
Flat 2, 44 Denton Road, Crouch End, London N8 9NS
t 020 8340 9091 **m** 07788 675530
e mark.vision-mixer@virgin.net
Agent Grade One TV & Film Personnel, Elstree Studios, Shenley Road, Borehamwood WD6 1JG
t 020 8324 2224 **f** 020 8324 2328
e gradeone.tvpersonnel@virgin.net
Credits Britain's Brainiest Kid Grand Final 2002 (T); Celebrity Big Brother (T); SMTV/CDUK (T); V Graham Norton (T)

Sarah Giles
Gems, The Media House, 87 Glebe Street, Penarth CF64 1EF
t 029 2071 0770 **f** 029 2071 0771
e gems@gems-agency.co.uk **w** www.gems-agency.co.uk

Kay Harrington
TOVS Ltd, The Linen Hall, 162-168 Regent Street, London W1B 5TB
t 020 7287 6110 **f** 020 7287 5481
e info@tovs.co.uk **w** www.tovs.co.uk

Alison Jones
Experience Counts - Call Me Ltd, 5th Floor, 41-42 Berners Street, London W1P 3AA
t 020 7637 8112 **f** 020 7580 2582

Mary Kellehar
t 020 8876 8103 **f** 020 8392 1347 **m** 07958 501489
Credits Family Affairs (T); EastEnders (T)

Greg Livermore
Grade One TV & Film Personnel, Elstree Studios, Shenley Road, Borehamwood WD6 1JG
t 020 8324 2224 **f** 020 8324 2328
e gradeone.tvpersonnel@virgin.net

Anne McCaw
11 Gortin Drive, Belfast BT5 7ES
t 02890 482571 **m** 07715 143971

Julie Michel
TOVS Ltd, The Linen Hall, 162-168 Regent Street, London W1B 5TB
t 020 7287 6110 **f** 020 7287 5481
e info@tovs.co.uk **w** www.tovs.co.uk

Julie Miller
Grade One TV & Film Personnel, Elstree Studios, Shenley Road, Borehamwood WD6 1JG
t 020 8324 2224 **f** 020 8324 2328
e gradeone.tvpersonnel@virgin.net

Laureen Chau Morrow
Grade One TV & Film Personnel, Elstree Studios, Shenley Road, Borehamwood WD6 1JG
t 020 8324 2224 **f** 020 8324 2328
e gradeone.tvpersonnel@virgin.net

Tracy Myers
Experience Counts - Call Me Ltd, 5th Floor, 41-42 Berners Street, London W1P 3AA
t 020 7637 8112 **f** 020 7580 2582

the guild of vision mixers

Back in the Seventies, several attempts were made to form some sort of association to bring vision mixers together. Initially, such stalwarts as Dave Hanks, Daphne Renny and Ken Angus met to discuss the issues of the day.

In the early Eighties, two Thames people, driven by the attractions of a mainly social association, wrote a letter to all known vision mixers and video and film editors in the U.K. inviting them to form an organisation. The Association of Vision Editors was established. In 1984 it was decided to rename the group as The Guild of Vision Mixers, which is now the UK-based organisation that seeks to represent the interests of vision mixers working in TV production throughout the UK and Ireland.

When the Guild was formed most vision mixers were employed on the staff of the BBC and the ITV companies. At one time, Thames Television employed seven vision mixers, with a similar number at LWT. During this period, only a handful of freelancers existed. However, in the early nineties, there were major changes in the ITV franchises and many vision mixers entered the freelance market. In addition, the BBC downsized their vision mixing department and yet more people left and became freelance.

With no work base to meet at and with very few jobs requiring more than one or two vision mixers, those employed in this field rarely saw each other. Also vision mixers who were still staff rarely met with those who were freelance. The Guild of Vision Mixers provided the platform necessary to facilitate contact.

As well as the developments in employment and staffing, there has been a technological revolution in vision mixing. Programme production demands have meant many more cameras and vision sources to cope with, along with the widespread use of digital video effects and electronic graphics.

The Guild of Vision Mixers works to ensure that the interests of members are protected adequately. Aims of the Guild include the maintenance and improvement of the status of vision mixers, the advancement of their skills, and the preservation of professional standards in television production.

Main meetings are organised from time to time at various venues, such as studio centres and the premises of equipment manufacturers. In addition to being the chance to catch up on the latest industry developments, meetings are also very much a social occasion.

An Executive Committee of four members runs the Guild on an entirely voluntary basis. Peter Turl is Chairman, Graham Giles is Treasurer and Membership Secretary, Sara-Jayne Phillips is Project Manager, and Stuart Owen has joined the team as Honorary Secretary.

A Website Manager has been appointed and the Guild plans to re-launch its website in April 2003. The website will include all the latest news and events, details of the latest equipment and a freelance directory with online CV service.

The Guild Of Vision Mixers

Maria Needle
Experience Counts - Call Me Ltd, 5th Floor, 41-42 Berners Street, London W1P 3AA
t 020 7637 8112 **f** 020 7580 2582

Manny Neto
TOVS Ltd, 162-168 Regent Street, London W1B 5TB
t 020 7287 6110 **f** 020 7287 5481
e info@tovs.co.uk **w** www.tovs.co.uk

Jez Nicholson
45 Romulus Court, 1 Justin Close, Brentford TW8 8QW
t 020 8847 5184 **m** 07966 399157
e jeremy67@btinternet.com
Credits Britain's Most Wanted (T); Art Attack (T); Catchphrase (T)

Martin Perrett
Experience Counts - Call Me Ltd, 5th Floor, 41-42 Berners Street, London W1P 3AA
t 020 7637 8112 **f** 020 7580 2582

Peter Phillips
Experience Counts - Call Me Ltd, 5th Floor, 41-42 Berners Street, London W1P 3AA
t 020 7637 8112 **f** 020 7580 2582

Dave Potter
Grade One TV & Film Personnel, Elstree Studios, Shenley Road, Borehamwood WD6 1JG
t 020 8324 2224 **f** 020 8324 2328
e gradeone.tvpersonnel@virgin.net

Janice Reed
Experience Counts - Call Me Ltd, 5th Floor, 41-42 Berners Street, London W1P 3AA
t 020 7637 8112 **f** 020 7580 2582

Ian Rowan
4 The Woodlands, Esher KT10 8DB
t 020 8398 9817 **m** 07976 442492 **e** ian.rowan@talk21.com
Credits I'm A Celebrity Get Me Out Of Here! (T); Channel Four Racing (T); National Lottery Winning Lines (T); Who Wants To Be A Millionaire? (T)

Simon Sanders
Experience Counts - Call Me Ltd, 5th Floor, 41-42 Berners Street, London W1P 3AA
t 020 7637 8112 **f** 020 7580 2582

Roz Storey
6 Cranley Road, Walton-on-Thames KT12 5BP
t 01932 221993 **f** 01932 223208 **m** 07976 756262
e storeytv@cix.co.uk
Credits Proms In The Park (T); Popstars - The Rivals (T); Who Wants To Be A Millionaire? (T)

Stuart Suckling
Experience Counts - Call Me Ltd, 5th Floor, 41-42 Berners Street, London W1P 3AA
t 020 7637 8112 **f** 020 7580 2582

Nick Swain
Agent TOVS Ltd, The Linen Hall, 162-168 Regent Street, London W1B 5TB
t 020 7287 6110 **f** 020 7287 5481
e info@tovs.co.uk **w** www.tovs.co.uk
Agent Experience Counts - Call Me Ltd, 5th Floor, 41-42 Berners Street, London W1P 3AA
t 020 7637 8112 **f** 020 7580 2582

Peter Turl
147 Ship Lane, Farnborough GU14 8BJ
t 01252 514953 **f** 01252 514953 **m** 07971 818183
e peter.turl@ntlworld.com
Agent Experience Counts - Call Me Ltd, 5th Floor, 41-42 Berners Street, London W1P 3AA
t 020 7637 8112 **f** 020 7580 2582
Credits Kilroy (T); The Weakest Link (T); Channel Four Racing (T)

Paul Robert Walker
5 Motcombe Road, Heald Green, Cheadle SK8 3TP
t 0161 437 5372 **f** 0161 437 5372 **m** 07831 237006
e paul.vision-mixer@amserve.com
Credits Robot Wars (T); James Last In Concert (M); Question Time (T); Coronation Street (T)

WARDROBE

Wardrobe General

BBC Costume + Wigs

BBC Costume & Wigs
Victoria Road, London W3 6UL
t 020 8576 1761 **f** 020 8993 7040
e costume@bbc.co.uk **e** wigs@bbc.co.uk
w www.bbcresources.com/costumewig

Charades
12 Vincent Street, St Helens WA10 1LF
t 01744 737909 **e** charades@talk21.com
Contact Betty Avery, Proprietor

Clencast
PO Box 1305, Glasgow G51 4WE
t 0141 445 1045 **f** 0141 445 1045
e clencast@hotmail.com **w** www.braveheartscotland.com
Contact Helen Craig, Production Manager; Pamela Wallace, Production Manager; Seoras Wallace, Site Director

Tabitha Doyle
t 020 7352 1598 **f** 020 7352 1598 **m** 07956 158113

Katrina Frith
t 020 8351 6028 **m** 07970 275871 **e** katrina_frith@hotmail.com
Credits Murder In Mind (T)

Jenny Hawkins
t 01372 469283 **m** 07774 759442 **e** earlywrap@yahoo.com

Mark Holmes
92B Rotherfield Street, London N1 3BX
t 020 7704 0980
Credits Possession (F); Evita (F); The Tailor Of Panama (F); Shadowlands (F)

Andy Huggins
Hengrove Cottage, Chivery, Tring HP23 6LE
t 01296 625508 **e** huggy@huggins.fsworld.co.uk

Ruth Kirton
21 Marsh Court, Pincott Road, South Wimbledon, London SW19 2LD
t 020 8241 5614 **f** 020 8241 5614 **m** 07785 756333
e ruthkirton@yahoo.com
Credits The Acid House Trilogy (T); Virtual Sexuality (F); The Vice III (T); Once Upon A Time In The Midlands (F)

Laurence Corner Theatricals
62-64 Hampstead Road, London NW1 2NU
t 020 7813 1010 **f** 020 7813 1413
w www.laurencecorner.com
Contact Kim Jamilly, Director, Director
Vast selection of military outfits. Huge stock of headwear. Catalogue on request.

Judith More
Bramblewood, Collum Green Road, Farnham Common SL2 3RH
t 01753 642628 **f** 01753 644904 **m** 07768 846646
e frocksjm@aol.com

Mycoal Warm Packs Ltd
Unit 1, Imperial Park, Empress Road, Southampton SO14 0JW
t 023 8021 1068 **f** 023 8023 1398
e sales@mycoal.co.uk **w** www.mycoal.co.uk

Adam Preston
Casarotto Ramsay & Associates Ltd, National House, 60-66 Wardour Street, London W1V 4ND
t 020 7287 4450 **f** 020 7287 9128
e agents@casarotto.uk.com **w** www.casarotto.uk.com

Lindsay Pugh
23 Second Avenue, London W10 4RN
t 020 8968 5413 **f** 020 8968 5413 **m** 07768 733 143
e linspins@dircon.co.uk
Credits Mists of Avalon (F); The Hours (F)

Diane Stevens
Flat B, 19 Ashmead Road, London SE8 4DY
t 020 8691 1414 **f** 020 8691 1414 **m** 07957 449 177
e diane.stevenS@tesco.net

Van Peterson Designs
194-196 Walton Street, London SW3 2JL
t 020 7584 1101 **f** 020 7581 9686
e vpshop@vanpeterson.com **w** www.vanpeterson.com
Contact Sandra Burrows, Manager

Vicky West
t 020 8341 6137 **m** 07973 744526 **e** vickywest@orange.net
Credits Silent Witness (T); Goodnight Sweetheart (T); In Defence (T); My Family (T)

Michael Weldon
t 020 8558 5895 **f** 020 8558 5895 **m** 07939 207833
e michael@costume-designers.com
Credits Murder Rooms (T); Bad Girls IV (T)

Wardrobe
Assistants/Dressers

Tanya Aanderaa
London
t 020 8288 3890 **f** 020 8241 6478 **m** 07968 979510
e tanya@skogenart.com **w** www.skogenart.com

Sheryl Brittian
13 Hawfinch Close, Southampton SO16 8HQ
t 023 8073 0361 **f** 023 8073 0361 **m** 07752 384082
Credits Ruth Rendell Mysteries (T); Teddybears (T); Mrs Bradley Mysteries (T); Hope And Glory (T)

Helen Godwin
Experience Counts - Call Me Ltd, 5th Floor, 41-42 Berners Street, London W1P 3AA
t 020 7637 8112 **f** 020 7580 2582

Diedre Hall
Orchard Cottage, High Street, Colne Huntingdon PE28 3ND
t 01487 842564

Kirsten Marshall
Flat 12, Casterbridge, 84 Doods Road, Reigate RH2 0NR
t 01737 247040 **m** 07767 777714 **e** d.marshall@euphony.net
Credits Punch (S); David Copperfield (T)

Frances Miles
Experience Counts - Call Me Ltd, 5th Floor, 41-42 Berners Street, London W1P 3AA
t 020 7637 8112 **f** 020 7580 2582

ON & OFF
101 Chalton Street, London NW1 1SP
m 07989 965883 **e** onandoff2002@hotmail.com
Contact Lene Langgaard, Partner; Sam Burdon, Partner

Anthony Vasey
Flat 2 145 Church Street, Whitby YO22 4DE
m 07850 624796
Credits Starlight Express (F)

Weather Information

Noble Denton Weather Services
131 Aldersgate Street, London EC1A 4EB
t 020 7606 4961 **f** 020 7606 5085
e ndws@nodent.co.uk **w** www.nobledenton.co.uk

Racemet Radar Systems
86 West Street, Marlow SL7 2BP
t 01628 481600 **f** 01628 478847 **m** 07767 450989
e racemet@aol.com **w** www.racemet.com
Contact Peter Morton, Logistics Manager; David Morton, Manager - Operations

Weather Services International Ltd
22-24 Vittoria Street, Hockley, Birmingham B1 3PE
t 0121 233 7600 **f** 0121 233 7666
e info@wsieurope.com **w** www.weather.co.uk
Contact Louis Bucciarelli, Sales Director - Media; Abby Wilkes, Partner

Wigs

A&A Hair Studios
8-10 Tanfield, Edinburgh EH3 5HF
t 0131 556 7057 **f** 0131 556 3223
e sales@aestudios.co.uk **w** www.aestudios.co.uk
Contact Susan Barton, Office Manager

Angels Wigs
1 Garrick Road, London NW9 6AA
t 020 8202 2244 **f** 020 8202 1820 **e** info@angels.uk.com
Contact Ben Stanton, Contact

Banbury Postiche Ltd
Little Bourton House, Southam Rd, Banbury OX16 1SR
t 01295 750606 **f** 01295 750751
e general@banburyhair.com **w** www.banburyhair.com
Contact Nick Allen, Sales Director
Credits Crossroads (T); Casualty (T); Harry Potter And The Philosopher's Stone (F)

BBC Costume + Wigs

BBC Costume & Wigs
Victoria Road, London W3 6UL
t 020 8576 1761 **f** 020 8993 7040
e costume@bbc.co.uk **e** wigs@bbc.co.uk
w www.bbcresources.com/costumewig

London Wigs (London & New York Wig Company)
Unit 107, Blackfriars Foundry, 156 Blackfriars Road, London SE1 8EN
t 020 7721 7095 **f** 020 7721 7026 **e** info@londonwigs.com
Contact Alex Rouse, Director; Astrid Schikorra, Manager; Jan Archibald, Director

Marian Wilson Wigs
59 Gloucester Street, Faringdon SN7 7JA
t 01367 241696 **f** 01367 242438 **m** 07973 698609
e willy@wilmawigs.freeserve.co.uk
Contact Marian Wilson

Natural Image
60 Low Friar Street, Newcastle-upon-Tyne NE1 5UE
t 0191 261 1622 **f** 0191 261 1622
Contact Jill Ward, Contact

Pam Foster Associates
Unit 009, The Chandlery, 50 Westminster Bridge Road, London SE1 7QY
t 020 7721 7641 **f** 020 7721 7409
Contact Janice Mackay, Director

Ray Marston Wig Studio Ltd
No 4 Charlotte Road, London EC2A 3DH
t 020 7739 3900 **f** 020 7739 3800
e wigstudio@raymarstonwigs.co.uk

Sarah Phillips & Company Ltd
Unit 11, Tottenham Green Co-operative Workshops, 2 Somerset Road, London N17 9EJ
t 020 8808 2171 **f** 020 8808 2157
e sarah_weatherburn@hotmail.com
Contact Sarah Weatherburn, Proprietor
Credits Harry Potter And The Philosopher's Stone (F); Harry Potter And The Chamber Of Secrets (F); Lord Of The Rings II (F); Lord Of The Rings I (F)

Thomas-Wigmakers

Acorn House, 1 Old Taunton Road, Bridgwater TA6 3NY
t 01278 431991 **f** 01278 431991 **m** 07801 668163
e thomaswigs@talk21.com
Contact Mike Drew, Partner; Belynda Drew, Partner

Wig Specialities Ltd

173 Seymour Place, London W1H 4PW
t 020 7262 6565 **f** 020 7723 1566
e wigspecialities@btconnect.com **w** www.wigspecialities.co.uk
Contact Richard Mawbey, Managing Director
Credits French And Saunders (T); Churchill-The Gathering Storm (F); Nicholas
Nickleby (T); Titanic (F)

Writers

Duncan Abbott

30 Carden Road, London SE15 3UD
t 020 7732 9777 **f** 020 7732 9777 **m** 07970 943844
e da@enricosmog.com
Credits Stress And Strain (E); Backcycler (I)

Paul Abbott

Casarotto Ramsay & Associates Ltd, National House,
60-66 Wardour Street, London W1V 4ND
t 020 7287 4450 **f** 020 7287 9128
e agents@casarotto.uk.com **w** www.casarotto.uk.com

Gill Adams

Curtis Brown, Haymarket House, 28-29 Haymarket, London
SW1Y 4SP
t 020 7396 6600 **f** 020 7396 0110 **e** cb@curtisbrown.co.uk
Credits Jack in the Box (T)

Judith Adams

Alan Brodie Representation, 211 Piccadilly, London W1J 9HF
t 020 7917 2871 **f** 020 7917 2872
e info@alanbrodie.com **w** www.alanbrodie.com

Kay Adshead

Peters Fraser & Dunlop, Drury House, 34-43 Russell Street,
London WC2B 5HA
t 020 7344 1000 **f** 020 7836 9543
e postmaster@pfd.co.uk **w** www.pfd.co.uk

Joe Ainsworth

The Dench Arnold Agency, 24 D'Arblay Street, London W1F 8EH
t 020 7437 4551 **f** 020 7439 1355
e contact@dencharnoldagency.co.uk **w** www.dencharnold.co.uk

Michael Aitkens

Peters Fraser & Dunlop, Drury House, 34-43 Russell Street,
London WC2B 5HA
t 020 7344 1000 **f** 020 7836 9543
e postmaster@pfd.co.uk **w** www.pfd.co.uk

Dare Aiyegbayo

20 Malmsey House, Vauxhall Street, London SE11 5LT
t 020 7735 0699 **m** 07958 406558 **e** aiyegbayo@talk21.com
Credits The Mechanic (S); Ruby's Slippers (S); Family Affairs (T)

Ed Allen

International Creative Management Ltd, Oxford House,
76 Oxford Street, London W1D 1BS
t 020 7636 6565 **f** 020 7323 0101 **w** www.icmlondon.co.uk

Tom Allen

Peters Fraser & Dunlop, Drury House, 34-43 Russell Street,
London WC2B 5HA
t 020 7344 1000 **f** 020 7836 9543
e postmaster@pfd.co.uk **w** www.pfd.co.uk

Amapola Productions

305 Hood House, Dolphin Square, London SW1V 3NH
e poppysmith@onetel.net.uk
Contact Poppy Smith, Writer/Producer

Hossein Amini

Curtis Brown, Haymarket House, 28-29 Haymarket, London
SW1Y 4SP
t 020 7396 6600 **f** 020 7396 0110
e cb@curtisbrown.co.uk
Credits The Dying of the Light (T); Four Feathers (F); Gangs of New York (F)

Giles Andreae

Peters Fraser & Dunlop, Drury House, 34-43 Russell Street,
London WC2B 5HA
t 020 7344 1000 **f** 020 7836 9543
e postmaster@pfd.co.uk **w** www.pfd.co.uk

April De Angelis

Casarotto Ramsay & Associates Ltd, National House,
60-66 Wardour Street, London W1V 4ND
t 020 7287 4450 **f** 020 7287 9128
e agents@casarotto.uk.com **w** www.casarotto.uk.com

Jean Anouilh

Alan Brodie Representation, 211 Piccadilly, London W1J 9HF
t 020 7917 2871 **f** 020 7917 2872
e info@alanbrodie.com **w** www.alanbrodie.com

John Arden

Casarotto Ramsay & Associates Ltd, National House,
60-66 Wardour Street, London W1V 4ND
t 020 7287 4450 **f** 020 7287 9128
e agents@casarotto.uk.com **w** www.casarotto.uk.com

Sophie Arnold

Peters Fraser & Dunlop, Drury House, 34-43 Russell Street,
London WC2B 5HA
t 020 7344 1000 **f** 020 7836 9543
e postmaster@pfd.co.uk **w** www.pfd.co.uk

Jean Ashe

Brie Burkeman, 14 Neville Court, Abbey Road,
London NW8 9DD
t 07092 239113 **f** 07092 239111 **e** brie.burkeman@mail.com

Richard Askwith

Brie Burkeman, 14 Neville Court, Abbey Road,
London NW8 9DD
t 07092 239113 **f** 07092 239111 **e** brie.burkeman@mail.com

Geoffrey Atherden

Peters Fraser & Dunlop, Drury House, 34-43 Russell Street,
London WC2B 5HA
t 020 7344 1000 **f** 020 7836 9543
e postmaster@pfd.co.uk **w** www.pfd.co.uk

Eileen Atkins

International Creative Management Ltd, Oxford House,
76 Oxford Street, London W1D 1BS
t 020 7636 6565 **f** 020 7323 0101 **w** www.icmlondon.co.uk

Kate Atkinson

Casarotto Ramsay & Associates Ltd, National House,
60-66 Wardour Street, London W1V 4ND
t 020 7287 4450 **f** 020 7287 9128
e agents@casarotto.uk.com **w** www.casarotto.uk.com

Sir Alan Ayckbourn

Casarotto Ramsay & Associates Ltd, National House,
60-66 Wardour Street, London W1V 4ND
t 020 7287 4450 **f** 020 7287 9128
e agents@casarotto.uk.com **w** www.casarotto.uk.com

Ivor Baddiel
London Management & Representation, 2-4 Noel Street, London W1F 8GB
t 020 7287 9000 **f** 020 7287 3236
Credits BAFTA Awards (T); MTV Europe Music Awards (T); Alistair McGowan's Big Impression (T); The Saturday Show (T)

Sarah Bagshaw
Peters Fraser & Dunlop, Drury House, 34-43 Russell Street, London WC2B 5HA
t 020 7344 1000 **f** 020 7836 9543
e postmaster@pfd.co.uk **w** www.pfd.co.uk

Louise Bagshawe
Peters Fraser & Dunlop, Drury House, 34-43 Russell Street, London WC2B 5HA
t 020 7344 1000 **f** 020 7836 9543
e postmaster@pfd.co.uk **w** www.pfd.co.uk

Darren Bailie
Peters Fraser & Dunlop, Drury House, 34-43 Russell Street, London WC2B 5HA
t 020 7344 1000 **f** 020 7836 9543
e postmaster@pfd.co.uk **w** www.pfd.co.uk

Bain & Armstrong
Linda Seifert Management, 91 Berwick Street, London W1F ONE
t 020 7292 7390 **f** 020 7292 7391
e contact@lindaseifert.com **w** www.lindaseifert.com

Nicola Baldwin
Curtis Brown, Haymarket House, 28-29 Haymarket, London SW1Y 4SP
t 020 7396 6600 **f** 020 7396 0110 **e** cb@curtisbrown.co.uk
Credits Where the Heart Is (D)

JG Ballard
Casarotto Ramsay & Associates Ltd, National House, 60-66 Wardour Street, London W1V 4ND
t 020 7287 4450 **f** 020 7287 9128
e agents@casarotto.uk.com **w** www.casarotto.uk.com

Matthew Bardsley
Peters Fraser & Dunlop, Drury House, 34-43 Russell Street, London WC2B 5HA
t 020 7344 1000 **f** 020 7836 9543
e postmaster@pfd.co.uk **w** www.pfd.co.uk

Mike Barfield
London Management & Representation, 2-4 Noel Street, London W1F 8GB
t 020 7287 9000 **f** 020 7287 3236

Debbie Barham
Casarotto Ramsay & Associates Ltd, National House, 60-66 Wardour Street, London W1V 4ND
t 020 7287 4450 **f** 020 7287 9128
e agents@casarotto.uk.com **w** www.casarotto.uk.com

Greg Barker
Casarotto Ramsay & Associates Ltd, National House, 60-66 Wardour Street, London W1V 4ND
t 020 7287 4450 **f** 020 7287 9128
e agents@casarotto.uk.com **w** www.casarotto.uk.com

Patrick Barlow
Casarotto Ramsay & Associates Ltd, National House, 60-66 Wardour Street, London W1V 4ND
t 020 7287 4450 **f** 020 7287 9128
e agents@casarotto.uk.com **w** www.casarotto.uk.com

Peter Barnes
Casarotto Ramsay & Associates Ltd, National House, 60-66 Wardour Street, London W1V 4ND
t 020 7287 4450 **f** 020 7287 9128
e agents@casarotto.uk.com **w** www.casarotto.uk.com

John Barton
Casarotto Ramsay & Associates Ltd, National House, 60-66 Wardour Street, London W1V 4ND
t 020 7287 4450 **f** 020 7287 9128
e agents@casarotto.uk.com **w** www.casarotto.uk.com

Ray Battersby
21 Samoa Way, Eastbourne BN23 5BA
t 01323 471011 **m** 07813 646532 **e** raybattersby@email.com
Credits Life On The Edge (I); BMW 7 Series (T); The Knowledge (T); Not To Worry (I)

Belinda Bauer
Peters Fraser & Dunlop, Drury House, 34-43 Russell Street, London WC2B 5HA
t 020 7344 1000 **f** 020 7836 9543
e postmaster@pfd.co.uk **w** www.pfd.co.uk

Katie Baxendale
Peters Fraser & Dunlop, Drury House, 34-43 Russell Street, London WC2B 5HA
t 020 7344 1000 **f** 020 7836 9543
e postmaster@pfd.co.uk **w** www.pfd.co.uk

Richard Bean
Peters Fraser & Dunlop, Drury House, 34-43 Russell Street, London WC2B 5HA
t 020 7344 1000 **f** 020 7836 9543
e postmaster@pfd.co.uk **w** www.pfd.co.uk

Alistair Beaton
London Management & Representation, 2-4 Noel Street, London W1F 8GB
t 020 7287 9000 **f** 020 7287 3236
Credits Not The Nine O'Clock News (T); It'll All Be Over In Half An Hour (D); Downwardly Mobile (T); Dunrolin' (T)

Philip G. Bell
30 Lords Meadow, Redbourn AL3 7BX
t 01582 792333 **e** philip@mindings.co.uk
w www.mindings.co.uk

Gerald Benedict
Brie Burkeman, 14 Neville Court, Abbey Road, London NW8 9DD
t 07092 239113 **f** 07092 239111 **e** brie.burkeman@mail.com

Alan Bennett
Peters Fraser & Dunlop, Drury House, 34-43 Russell Street, London WC2B 5HA
t 020 7344 1000 **f** 020 7836 9543
e postmaster@pfd.co.uk **w** www.pfd.co.uk

Caspar Berry
Curtis Brown, Haymarket House, 28-29 Haymarket, London SW1Y 4SP
t 020 7396 6600 **f** 020 7396 0110 **e** cb@curtisbrown.co.uk
Credits Byker Grove (T); Steroid Blues (F); Bedhead (T)

Maurice Bessman
The Dench Arnold Agency, 24 D'Arblay Street, London W1F 8EH
t 020 7437 4551 **f** 020 7439 1355
e contact@dencharnoldagency.co.uk **w** www.dencharnold.co.uk

Bevan & Stevens
North Lodge, Waverley, Farnham GU9 8ET
t 01252 725843 **f** 01252 725843 **e** witcheshouse@onetel.co.uk
Contact John Bevan, Writer/Director

Smita Bhide
Casarotto Ramsay & Associates Ltd, National House, 60-66 Wardour Street, London W1V 4ND
t 020 7287 4450 **f** 020 7287 9128
e agents@casarotto.uk.com **w** www.casarotto.uk.com

Tony Bicât
London Management & Representation, 2-4 Noel Street, London W1F 8GB
t 020 7287 9000 **f** 020 7287 3236
Credits Christmas Present (T); The Scold's Bridle (T); Lost Belongings (T); An Exchange Of Fire (T)

Michael J Bird
Peters Fraser & Dunlop, Drury House, 34-43 Russell Street, London WC2B 5HA
t 020 7344 1000 **f** 020 7836 9543
e postmaster@pfd.co.uk **w** www.pfd.co.uk

Penny Black
Alan Brodie Representation, 211 Piccadilly, London W1J 9HF
t 020 7917 2871 **f** 020 7917 2872
e info@alanbrodie.com **w** www.alanbrodie.com

Stuart Black
79 Charlbert Court, Eamont Street, St Johns Wood, London NW8 7DB
t 020 7722 7636 **f** 020 7722 7636 **e** stublack@onetel.com

Lucy Blincoe
International Creative Management Ltd, Oxford House, 76 Oxford Street, London W1D 1BS
t 020 7636 6565 **f** 020 7323 0101 **w** www.icmlondon.co.uk

Simon Block
International Creative Management Ltd, Oxford House, 76 Oxford Street, London W1D 1BS
t 020 7636 6565 **f** 020 7323 0101 **w** www.icmlondon.co.uk

Chris Boiling
Culverhouse & James Personal Management, Shepperton Studios, Studio Road, Shepperton TW17 0QD
t 01932 592151 **f** 01932 592233
e dculverhouse@onetel.net.uk **e** jilljames4@aol.com

Dermot Bolger
Curtis Brown, Haymarket House, 28-29 Haymarket, London SW1Y 4SP
t 020 7396 6600 **f** 020 7396 0110 **e** cb@curtisbrown.co.uk
Credits The Disappearance of Finbar (F); The Journey Home (F); A Second Life (F)

Edward Bond
Casarotto Ramsay & Associates Ltd, National House, 60-66 Wardour Street, London W1V 4ND
t 020 7287 4450 **f** 020 7287 9128
e agents@casarotto.uk.com **w** www.casarotto.uk.com

Simon van der Borgh
C/o John Rush, Sheil Land Associates, 43 Doughty Street, London WC1N 2LF
t 020 7405 9351 **f** 020 7831 2127
e simonvanderborgh@hotmail.com
Credits The Elephant In The Dark (F); The Allens (F); Boney And Betsy (F)

Adam Bostock-Smith
Casarotto Ramsay & Associates Ltd, National House, 60-66 Wardour Street, London W1V 4ND
t 020 7287 4450 **f** 020 7287 9128
e agents@casarotto.uk.com **w** www.casarotto.uk.com

Colin Bostock-Smith
Casarotto Ramsay & Associates Ltd, National House, 60-66 Wardour Street, London W1V 4ND
t 020 7287 4450 **f** 020 7287 9128
e agents@casarotto.uk.com **w** www.casarotto.uk.com

Alain de Botton
Peters Fraser & Dunlop, Drury House, 34-43 Russell Street, London WC2B 5HA
t 020 7344 1000 **f** 020 7836 9543
e postmaster@pfd.co.uk **w** www.pfd.co.uk

John Bowen
Casarotto Ramsay & Associates Ltd, National House, 60-66 Wardour Street, London W1V 4ND
t 020 7287 4450 **f** 020 7287 9128
e agents@casarotto.uk.com **w** www.casarotto.uk.com

TR Bowen
Peters Fraser & Dunlop, Drury House, 34-43 Russell Street, London WC2B 5HA
t 020 7344 1000 **f** 020 7836 9543
e postmaster@pfd.co.uk **w** www.pfd.co.uk

David Bowker
Peters Fraser & Dunlop, Drury House, 34-43 Russell Street, London WC2B 5HA
t 020 7344 1000 **f** 020 7836 9543
e postmaster@pfd.co.uk **w** www.pfd.co.uk

Susan Boyd
Peters Fraser & Dunlop, Drury House, 34-43 Russell Street, London WC2B 5HA
t 020 7344 1000 **f** 020 7836 9543
e postmaster@pfd.co.uk **w** www.pfd.co.uk

Derek Boyle
International Creative Management Ltd, Oxford House, 76 Oxford Street, London W1D 1BS
t 020 7636 6565 **f** 020 7323 0101 **w** www.icmlondon.co.uk

Braithwaite & Alexander
Linda Seifert Management, 91 Berwick Street, London W1F ONE
t 020 7292 7390 **f** 020 7292 7391
e contact@lindaseifert.com **w** www.lindaseifert.com

Colin Brake
Peters Fraser & Dunlop, Drury House, 34-43 Russell Street, London WC2B 5HA
t 020 7344 1000 **f** 020 7836 9543
e postmaster@pfd.co.uk **w** www.pfd.co.uk

Sally Brampton
Peters Fraser & Dunlop, Drury House, 34-43 Russell Street, London WC2B 5HA
t 020 7344 1000 **f** 020 7836 9543
e postmaster@pfd.co.uk **w** www.pfd.co.uk

Bertolt Brecht
Alan Brodie Representation, 211 Piccadilly, London W1J 9HF
t 020 7917 2871 **f** 020 7917 2872
e info@alanbrodie.com **w** www.alanbrodie.com

Howard Brenton
Casarotto Ramsay & Associates Ltd, National House, 60-66 Wardour Street, London W1V 4ND
t 020 7287 4450 **f** 020 7287 9128
e agents@casarotto.uk.com **w** www.casarotto.uk.com

Simon Brett
Casarotto Ramsay & Associates Ltd, National House, 60-66 Wardour Street, London W1V 4ND
t 020 7287 4450 **f** 020 7287 9128
e agents@casarotto.uk.com **w** www.casarotto.uk.com

Irena Brignull
Casarotto Ramsay & Associates Ltd, National House, 60-66 Wardour Street, London W1V 4ND
t 020 7287 4450 **f** 020 7287 9128
e agents@casarotto.uk.com **w** www.casarotto.uk.com

Francesca Brill
The Dench Arnold Agency, 24 D'Arblay Street, London W1F 8EH
t 020 7437 4551 **f** 020 7439 1355
e contact@dencharnoldagency.co.uk **w** www.dencharnold.co.uk

Daniel Brocklehurst
Peters Fraser & Dunlop, Drury House, 34-43 Russell Street,
London WC2B 5HA
t 020 7344 1000 **f** 020 7836 9543
e postmaster@pfd.co.uk **w** www.pfd.co.uk

Neil Bromley
Culverhouse & James Personal Management, Shepperton
Studios, Studio Road, Shepperton TW17 0QD
t 01932 592151 **f** 01932 592233
e dculverhouse@onetel.net.uk **e** jilljames4@aol.com

Christopher Brookmyre
Peters Fraser & Dunlop, Drury House, 34-43 Russell Street,
London WC2B 5HA
t 020 7344 1000 **f** 020 7836 9543
e postmaster@pfd.co.uk **w** www.pfd.co.uk

Edel Brosnan
Curtis Brown, Haymarket House, 28-29 Haymarket, London
SW1Y 4SP
t 020 7396 6600 **f** 020 7396 0110 **e** cb@curtisbrown.co.uk
Credits Always And Everyone (T); EastEnders (T); Casualty (F)

Ben Brown
Curtis Brown, Haymarket House, 28-29 Haymarket, London
SW1Y 4SP
t 020 7396 6600 **f** 020 7396 0110 **e** cb@curtisbrown.co.uk
Credits The Arrangement (F); Inspector Rebus (T)

Craig Brown
Peters Fraser & Dunlop, Drury House, 34-43 Russell Street,
London WC2B 5HA
t 020 7344 1000 **f** 020 7836 9543
e postmaster@pfd.co.uk **w** www.pfd.co.uk

Moira Buffini
Peters Fraser & Dunlop, Drury House, 34-43 Russell Street,
London WC2B 5HA
t 020 7344 1000 **f** 020 7836 9543
e postmaster@pfd.co.uk **w** www.pfd.co.uk

Mike Bullen
International Creative Management Ltd, Oxford House,
76 Oxford Street, London W1D 1BS
t 020 7636 6565 **f** 020 7323 0101 **w** www.icmlondon.co.uk

Amelia Bullmore
Peters Fraser & Dunlop, Drury House, 34-43 Russell Street,
London WC2B 5HA
t 020 7344 1000 **f** 020 7836 9543
e postmaster@pfd.co.uk **w** www.pfd.co.uk

Gregory Burke
Alan Brodie Representation, 211 Piccadilly, London W1J 9HF
t 020 7917 2871 **f** 020 7917 2872
e info@alanbrodie.com **w** www.alanbrodie.com

Richard Burke
Culverhouse & James Personal Management, Shepperton
Studios, Studio Road, Shepperton TW17 0QD
t 01932 592151 **f** 01932 592233
e dculverhouse@onetel.net.uk **e** jilljames4@aol.com

Stephen Burns
Michelle Kass Associates, 36-38 Glasshouse Street, London
W1B 5DL
t 020 7439 1624 **f** 020 7734 3394

Richard Burridge
Peters Fraser & Dunlop, Drury House, 34-43 Russell Street,
London WC2B 5HA
t 020 7344 1000 **f** 020 7836 9543
e postmaster@pfd.co.uk **w** www.pfd.co.uk

Mark Burt
International Creative Management Ltd, Oxford House,
76 Oxford Street, London W1D 1BS
t 020 7636 6565 **f** 020 7323 0101 **w** www.icmlondon.co.uk

Mark Burton
London Management & Representation, 2-4 Noel Street,
London W1F 8GB
t 020 7287 9000 **f** 020 7287 3236
Credits Smith And Jones (T); Chicken Run (F); Have I Got News For You? (T); 2DTV (T)

Bussell & Sbresni
Linda Seifert Management, 91 Berwick Street, London W1F 0NE
t 020 7292 7390 **f** 020 7292 7391
e contact@lindaseifert.com **w** www.lindaseifert.com

Justin Butcher
Peters Fraser & Dunlop, Drury House, 34-43 Russell Street,
London WC2B 5HA
t 020 7344 1000 **f** 020 7836 9543
e postmaster@pfd.co.uk **w** www.pfd.co.uk

David Butler
Peters Fraser & Dunlop, Drury House, 34-43 Russell Street,
London WC2B 5HA
t 020 7344 1000 **f** 020 7836 9543
e postmaster@pfd.co.uk **w** www.pfd.co.uk

John Byrne
Casarotto Ramsay & Associates Ltd, National House,
60-66 Wardour Street, London W1V 4ND
t 020 7287 4450 **f** 020 7287 9128
e agents@casarotto.uk.com **w** www.casarotto.uk.com

Tara Byrne
Culverhouse & James Personal Management, Shepperton
Studios, Studio Road, Shepperton TW17 0QD
t 01932 592151 **f** 01932 592233
e dculverhouse@onetel.net.uk **e** jilljames4@aol.com

David Cairns
Culverhouse & James Personal Management, Shepperton
Studios, Studio Road, Shepperton TW17 0QD
t 01932 592151 **f** 01932 592233
e dculverhouse@onetel.net.uk **e** jilljames4@aol.com

Patricia Calder
Culverhouse & James Personal Management, Shepperton
Studios, Studio Road, Shepperton TW17 0QD
t 01932 592151 **f** 01932 592233
e dculverhouse@onetel.net.uk **e** jilljames4@aol.com

Richard Cameron
Curtis Brown, Haymarket House, 28-29 Haymarket, London
SW1Y 4SP
t 020 7396 6600 **f** 020 7396 0110 **e** cb@curtisbrown.co.uk
Credits Lessons for the Loveless (T); The Horse Marine (T); Stone,
Scissors, Paper (T)

Shenagh Cameron
Curtis Brown, Haymarket House, 28-29 Haymarket, London
SW1Y 4SP
t 020 7396 6600 **f** 020 7396 0110 **e** cb@curtisbrown.co.uk
Credits EastEnders (T)

Alexandra Carew
Brie Burkeman, 14 Neville Court, Abbey Road, London NW8 9DD
t 07092 239113 **f** 07092 239111 **e** brie.burkeman@mail.com

Alexander Carey
International Creative Management Ltd, Oxford House,
76 Oxford Street, London W1D 1BS
t 020 7636 6565 **f** 020 7323 0101 **w** www.icmlondon.co.uk

Bob Carlton
Casarotto Ramsay & Associates Ltd, National House,
60-66 Wardour Street, London W1V 4ND
t 020 7287 4450 **f** 020 7287 9128
e agents@casarotto.uk.com **w** www.casarotto.uk.com

Justin Cartwright
Peters Fraser & Dunlop, Drury House, 34-43 Russell Street,
London WC2B 5HA
t 020 7344 1000 **f** 020 7836 9543
e postmaster@pfd.co.uk **w** www.pfd.co.uk

Daragh Carville
Casarotto Ramsay & Associates Ltd, National House,
60-66 Wardour Street, London W1V 4ND
t 020 7287 4450 **f** 020 7287 9128
e agents@casarotto.uk.com **w** www.casarotto.uk.com

Tony Casement
Culverhouse & James Personal Management, Shepperton
Studios, Studio Road, Shepperton TW17 0QD
t 01932 592151 **f** 01932 592233
e dculverhouse@onetel.net.uk **e** jilljames4@aol.com

Cat & Frog Productions
65 Woodlands, Esher KT10 8B2
t 020 8398 3161 **f** 020 8398 3161 **m** 07957 438497
e lesroy@freeserve.co.uk
Contact Lesley North, Director

Michele Celeste
e m.celeste@btinternet.com
w http://members.tripod.com/mivheleceleste/
Credits Obeah (F); Aetna (F)

Mark Chappell
Curtis Brown, Haymarket House, 28-29 Haymarket, London
SW1Y 4SP
t 020 7396 6600 **f** 020 7396 0110 **e** cb@curtisbrown.co.uk
Credits My Life in Film (T); Cold Feet (T); Brouhaha (T)

Monique Charlesworth
Peters Fraser & Dunlop, Drury House, 34-43 Russell Street,
London WC2B 5HA
t 020 7344 1000 **f** 020 7836 9543
e postmaster@pfd.co.uk **w** www.pfd.co.uk

Chris Baker & Andy Day
Peters Fraser & Dunlop, Drury House, 34-43 Russell Street,
London WC2B 5HA
t 020 7344 1000 **f** 020 7836 9543
e postmaster@pfd.co.uk **w** www.pfd.co.uk

Chris Thompson & Peter Reynolds
Linda Seifert Management, 91 Berwick Street, London W1F 0NE
t 020 7292 7390 **f** 020 7292 7391
e contact@lindaseifert.com **w** www.lindaseifert.com

Caryl Churchill
Casarotto Ramsay & Associates Ltd, National House,
60-66 Wardour Street, London W1V 4ND
t 020 7287 4450 **f** 020 7287 9128
e agents@casarotto.uk.com **w** www.casarotto.uk.com

Boyd Clack
Casarotto Ramsay & Associates Ltd, National House,
60-66 Wardour Street, London W1V 4ND
t 020 7287 4450 **f** 020 7287 9128
e agents@casarotto.uk.com **w** www.casarotto.uk.com

Catrin Clarke
Peters Fraser & Dunlop, Drury House, 34-43 Russell Street,
London WC2B 5HA
t 020 7344 1000 **f** 020 7836 9543
e postmaster@pfd.co.uk **w** www.pfd.co.uk

Wensley Clarkson
Linda Seifert Management, 91 Berwick Street, London W1F 0NE
t 020 7292 7390 **f** 020 7292 7391
e contact@lindaseifert.com **w** www.lindaseifert.com

Grae Cleugh
Curtis Brown, Haymarket House, 28-29 Haymarket, London
SW1Y 4SP
t 020 7396 6600 **f** 020 7396 0110 **e** cb@curtisbrown.co.uk

Vicky Clever
Curtis Brown, Haymarket House, 28-29 Haymarket, London
SW1Y 4SP
t 020 7396 6600 **f** 020 7396 0110 **e** cb@curtisbrown.co.uk
Credits A & E (T); Casualty (T); Peak Practice (T)

Alan Clews
Alan Brodie Representation, 211 Piccadilly, London W1J 9HF
t 020 7917 2871 **f** 020 7917 2872
e info@alanbrodie.com **w** www.alanbrodie.com

Andrew Clifford
London Management & Representation, 2-4 Noel Street,
London W1F 8GB
t 020 7287 9000 **f** 020 7287 3236
Credits Smack The Pony (T)

John Clifford
Alan Brodie Representation, 211 Piccadilly, London W1J 9HF
t 020 7917 2871 **f** 020 7917 2872
e info@alanbrodie.com **w** www.alanbrodie.com

Mark Clompus
International Creative Management Ltd, Oxford House,
76 Oxford Street, London W1D 1BS
t 020 7636 6565 **f** 020 7323 0101 **w** www.icmlondon.co.uk

Nathan Cockerill
Linda Seifert Management, 91 Berwick Street, London W1F 0NE
t 020 7292 7390 **f** 020 7292 7391
e contact@lindaseifert.com **w** www.lindaseifert.com

Lin Coghlan
Peters Fraser & Dunlop, Drury House, 34-43 Russell Street,
London WC2B 5HA
t 020 7344 1000 **f** 020 7836 9543
e postmaster@pfd.co.uk **w** www.pfd.co.uk

Bradley Cole
Peters Fraser & Dunlop, Drury House, 34-43 Russell Street,
London WC2B 5HA
t 020 7344 1000 **f** 020 7836 9543
e postmaster@pfd.co.uk **w** www.pfd.co.uk

Tony Coll
31 Clyde Road, Totterdown, Bristol BS4 3DH
t 0117 987 0442 **m** 07813 480986
e tony.coll@btinternet.com
Credits Bristol Royal Infirmary - Department Of Health Public Inquiry (I);
Ministry Of Defence - Construction Laws (I); The Singapore Show (I); Norwich
Union - Live Stage Show (I)

John Collee
Peters Fraser & Dunlop, Drury House, 34-43 Russell Street,
London WC2B 5HA
t 020 7344 1000 **f** 020 7836 9543
e postmaster@pfd.co.uk **w** www.pfd.co.uk

Rob Colley
Casarotto Ramsay & Associates Ltd, National House,
60-66 Wardour Street, London W1V 4ND
t 020 7287 4450 **f** 020 7287 9128
e agents@casarotto.uk.com **w** www.casarotto.uk.com

Tim Connery
International Creative Management Ltd, Oxford House,
76 Oxford Street, London W1D 1BS
t 020 7636 6565 **f** 020 7323 0101 **w** www.icmlondon.co.uk

Michael Cook
Casarotto Ramsay & Associates Ltd, National House,
60-66 Wardour Street, London W1V 4ND
t 020 7287 4450 **f** 020 7287 9128
e agents@casarotto.uk.com **w** www.casarotto.uk.com

Brian Cooke
Peters Fraser & Dunlop, Drury House, 34-43 Russell Street,
London WC2B 5HA
t 020 7344 1000 **f** 020 7836 9543
e postmaster@pfd.co.uk **w** www.pfd.co.uk

Steve Coombes
Linda Seifert Management, 91 Berwick Street, London W1F ONE
t 020 7292 7390 **f** 020 7292 7391
e contact@lindaseifert.com **w** www.lindaseifert.com

Ben Cooper
Casarotto Ramsay & Associates Ltd, National House,
60-66 Wardour Street, London W1V 4ND
t 020 7287 4450 **f** 020 7287 9128
e agents@casarotto.uk.com **w** www.casarotto.uk.com

Matthew Cooper
Peters Fraser & Dunlop, Drury House, 34-43 Russell Street,
London WC2B 5HA
t 020 7344 1000 **f** 020 7836 9543
e postmaster@pfd.co.uk **w** www.pfd.co.uk

Paul Copley
Casarotto Ramsay & Associates Ltd, National House,
60-66 Wardour Street, London W1V 4ND
t 020 7287 4450 **f** 020 7287 9128
e agents@casarotto.uk.com **w** www.casarotto.uk.com

Antony Cotton
Peters Fraser & Dunlop, Drury House, 34-43 Russell Street,
London WC2B 5HA
t 020 7344 1000 **f** 020 7836 9543
e postmaster@pfd.co.uk **w** www.pfd.co.uk

Frank Cottrell Boyce
International Creative Management Ltd, Oxford House,
76 Oxford Street, London W1D 1BS
t 020 7636 6565 **f** 020 7323 0101 **w** www.icmlondon.co.uk

Victoria Coules
Peters Fraser & Dunlop, Drury House, 34-43 Russell Street,
London WC2B 5HA
t 020 7344 1000 **f** 020 7836 9543
e postmaster@pfd.co.uk **w** www.pfd.co.uk

Ben Court
Curtis Brown, Haymarket House, 28-29 Haymarket, London
SW1Y 4SP
t 020 7396 6600 **f** 020 7396 0110 **e** cb@curtisbrown.co.uk
Credits Marion Again (T); The Hole (F); Cracks (F)

Noël Coward
Alan Brodie Representation, 211 Piccadilly, London W1J 9HF
t 020 7917 2871 **f** 020 7917 2872
e info@alanbrodie.com **w** www.alanbrodie.com

Nancy Crane
Casarotto Ramsay & Associates Ltd, National House,
60-66 Wardour Street, London W1V 4ND
t 020 7287 4450 **f** 020 7287 9128
e agents@casarotto.uk.com **w** www.casarotto.uk.com

David Cregan
Casarotto Ramsay & Associates Ltd, National House,
60-66 Wardour Street, London W1V 4ND
t 020 7287 4450 **f** 020 7287 9128
e agents@casarotto.uk.com **w** www.casarotto.uk.com

Philip Crispin
Alan Brodie Representation, 211 Piccadilly, London W1J 9HF
t 020 7917 2871 **f** 020 7917 2872
e info@alanbrodie.com **w** www.alanbrodie.com

Penny Croft
London Management & Representation, 2-4 Noel Street,
London W1F 8GB
t 020 7287 9000 **f** 020 7287 3236
Credits Follow Your Stars (T); Life Without George (T)

Greg Cruttwell
The Dench Arnold Agency, 24 D'Arblay Street, London W1F 8EH
t 020 7437 4551 **f** 020 7439 1355
e contact@dencharnoldagency.co.uk **w** www.dencharnold.co.uk

Mike Cullen
Curtis Brown, Haymarket House, 28-29 Haymarket, London
SW1Y 4SP
t 020 7396 6600 **f** 020 7396 0110 **e** cb@curtisbrown.co.uk
Credits The Cut (F); Silent Witness (T); Rebus 'Dead Souls' (T)

Carol Cullington
Culverhouse & James Personal Management, Shepperton
Studios, Studio Road, Shepperton TW17 0QD
t 01932 592151 **f** 01932 592233
e dculverhouse@onetel.net.uk **e** jilljames4@aol.com

Richard Curtis
Peters Fraser & Dunlop, Drury House, 34-43 Russell Street,
London WC2B 5HA
t 020 7344 1000 **f** 020 7836 9543
e postmaster@pfd.co.uk **w** www.pfd.co.uk

Neil D'Souza
Curtis Brown, Haymarket House, 28-29 Haymarket, London
SW1Y 4SP
t 020 7396 6600 **f** 020 7396 0110 **e** cb@curtisbrown.co.uk
Credits Tender Coconuts (T)

Sarah Daniels
Casarotto Ramsay & Associates Ltd, National House,
60-66 Wardour Street, London W1V 4ND
t 020 7287 4450 **f** 020 7287 9128
e agents@casarotto.uk.com **w** www.casarotto.uk.com

Danny Robins & Dan Tetsell
Peters Fraser & Dunlop, Drury House, 34-43 Russell Street,
London WC2B 5HA
t 020 7344 1000 **f** 020 7836 9543
e postmaster@pfd.co.uk **w** www.pfd.co.uk

Rosie Dastgir
Curtis Brown, Haymarket House, 28-29 Haymarket, London
SW1Y 4SP
t 020 7396 6600 **f** 020 7396 0110 **e** cb@curtisbrown.co.uk
Credits Night Nation (S); City (T); Neighbourhood (F)

Richard Davidson
Peters Fraser & Dunlop, Drury House, 34-43 Russell Street,
London WC2B 5HA
t 020 7344 1000 **f** 020 7836 9543
e postmaster@pfd.co.uk **w** www.pfd.co.uk

Jim Davies
The Dench Arnold Agency, 24 D'Arblay Street, London W1F 8EH
t 020 7437 4551 **f** 020 7439 1355
e contact@dencharnoldagency.co.uk **w** www.dencharnold.co.uk

Mark Davies
Alan Brodie Representation, 211 Piccadilly, London W1J 9HF
t 020 7917 2871 f 020 7917 2872
e info@alanbrodie.com w www.alanbrodie.com

Rib Davis
Peters Fraser & Dunlop, Drury House, 34-43 Russell Street,
London WC2B 5HA
t 020 7344 1000 f 020 7836 9543
e postmaster@pfd.co.uk w www.pfd.co.uk

Clive Dawson
51 Roundwood Way, Banstead SM7 1EH
t 01737 354179 f 01737 354179
e postmaster@screenwriting.demon.co.uk
w www.screenwriting.demon.co.uk
Agent Peters Fraser & Dunlop, Drury House, 34-43 Russell
Street, London WC2B 5HA
t 020 7344 1000 f 020 7836 9543
e postmaster@pfd.co.uk w www.pfd.co.uk
Credits Casualty (T); The Bill (T); The Bunker

Martin Day
Cranstock, 60 Preston Road, Yeovil BA20 2BY
t 01935 420973 f 07005 980651 m 07770 958917
e marty@v21.me.uk w www.martinday.co.uk
Agent Culverhouse & James Personal Management,
Shepperton Studios, Studio Road, Shepperton TW17 0QD
t 01932 592151 f 01932 592233
e dculverhouse@onetel.net.uk e jilljames4@aol.com
Credits The Dust Commision - Pilot (T); Family Affairs (T)

Eric Deacon
The Dench Arnold Agency, 24 D'Arblay Street, London W1F 8EH
t 020 7437 4551 f 020 7439 1355
e contact@dencharnoldagency.co.uk w www.dencharnold.co.uk

James Dean
Curtis Brown, Haymarket House, 28-29 Haymarket, London
SW1Y 4SP
t 020 7396 6600 f 020 7396 0110 e cb@curtisbrown.co.uk
Credits The Dentist Who Wanted To Talk Dirty In Italian (F)

Geoff Deane
Linda Seifert Management, 91 Berwick Street, London W1F 0NE
t 020 7292 7390 f 020 7292 7391
e contact@lindaseifert.com w www.lindaseifert.com

Frank Deasy
Peters Fraser & Dunlop, Drury House, 34-43 Russell Street,
London WC2B 5HA
t 020 7344 1000 f 020 7836 9543
e postmaster@pfd.co.uk w www.pfd.co.uk

Elizabeth Delaney
Culverhouse & James Personal Management, Shepperton
Studios, Studio Road, Shepperton TW17 0QD
t 01932 592151 f 01932 592233
e dculverhouse@onetel.net.uk e jilljames4@aol.com

Simon Delaney
International Creative Management Ltd, Oxford House,
76 Oxford Street, London W1D 1BS
t 020 7636 6565 f 020 7323 0101 w www.icmlondon.co.uk

Maria Delgado
Alan Brodie Representation, 211 Piccadilly, London W1J 9HF
t 020 7917 2871 f 020 7917 2872
e info@alanbrodie.com w www.alanbrodie.com

Nell Denton
Culverhouse & James Personal Management, Shepperton
Studios, Studio Road, Shepperton TW17 0QD
t 01932 592151 f 01932 592233
e dculverhouse@onetel.net.uk e jilljames4@aol.com

Anne Devlin
Alan Brodie Representation, 211 Piccadilly, London W1J 9HF
t 020 7917 2871 f 020 7917 2872
e info@alanbrodie.com w www.alanbrodie.com

Dolly Dhingra
Peters Fraser & Dunlop, Drury House, 34-43 Russell Street,
London WC2B 5HA
t 020 7344 1000 f 020 7836 9543
e postmaster@pfd.co.uk w www.pfd.co.uk

Des Dillon
London Management & Representation, 2-4 Noel Street,
London W1F 8GB
t 020 7287 9000 f 020 7287 3236

Stephen Dinsdale
Curtis Brown, Haymarket House, 28-29 Haymarket, London
SW1Y 4SP
t 020 7396 6600 f 020 7396 0110 e cb@curtisbrown.co.uk
Credits The Dentist Who Wanted To Talk Dirty In Italian (F)

Christophe Dirickx
Peters Fraser & Dunlop, Drury House, 34-43 Russell Street,
London WC2B 5HA
t 020 7344 1000 f 020 7836 9543
e postmaster@pfd.co.uk w www.pfd.co.uk

Jasmin Dizdar
Casarotto Ramsay & Associates Ltd, National House,
60-66 Wardour Street, London W1V 4ND
t 020 7287 4450 f 020 7287 9128
e agents@casarotto.uk.com w www.casarotto.uk.com

John Docherty
Curtis Brown, Haymarket House, 28-29 Haymarket, London
SW1Y 4SP
t 020 7396 6600 f 020 7396 0110 e cb@curtisbrown.co.uk
Credits Morwenna Banks Show (T); Jack Docherty Show (T); The Creatives (T)

Jeff Dodds
6 Eccles Road, Holt NR25 6HJ
f 01263 711982 e doddsjeff@hotmail.com
Credits Heartbeat (T); Truth (T); Peak Practice (T)

Liana Dognini
Casarotto Ramsay & Associates Ltd, National House,
60-66 Wardour Street, London W1V 4ND
t 020 7287 4450 f 020 7287 9128
e agents@casarotto.uk.com w www.casarotto.uk.com

Chris Dolan
Peters Fraser & Dunlop, Drury House, 34-43 Russell Street,
London WC2B 5HA
t 020 7344 1000 f 020 7836 9543
e postmaster@pfd.co.uk w www.pfd.co.uk

Samantha Doland-De Vaux
Culverhouse & James Personal Management, Shepperton
Studios, Studio Road, Shepperton TW17 0QD
t 01932 592151 f 01932 592233
e dculverhouse@onetel.net.uk e jilljames4@aol.com

Paul Dornan
Curtis Brown, Haymarket House, 28-29 Haymarket, London
SW1Y 4SP
t 020 7396 6600 f 020 7396 0110 e cb@curtisbrown.co.uk
Credits My Wonderful Life (T); Mad Dog Days (T); Expiration Date (F)

Roger Drew
Casarotto Ramsay & Associates Ltd, National House,
60-66 Wardour Street, London W1V 4ND
t 020 7287 4450 f 020 7287 9128
e agents@casarotto.uk.com w www.casarotto.uk.com

Eddie Dujon

Carmonlaw House, 179 Cambridge Heath Road, Betnhal Green, London E1 5QH
t 020 7375 2218 **f** 020 7375 2219 **m** 07973 208920
e edujon@carmonlaw.fsnet.co.uk

Sarah Dunant

London Management & Representation, 2-4 Noel Street, London W1F 8GB
t 020 7287 9000 **f** 020 7287 3236

Adrian Dunbar

The Dench Arnold Agency, 24 D'Arblay Street, London W1F 8EH
t 020 7437 4551 **f** 020 7439 1355
e contact@dencharnoldagency.co.uk **w** www.dencharnold.co.uk

Kevin Dunk

15 Guest Road, Hunters Bar, Sheffield S11 8UJ
m 07786 380273 **e** kevdunk22@yahoo.co.uk

Christopher Dunlop

Alan Brodie Representation, 211 Piccadilly, London W1J 9HF
t 020 7917 2871 **f** 020 7917 2872
e info@alanbrodie.com **w** www.alanbrodie.com

Frank Dunlop

Casarotto Ramsay & Associates Ltd, National House, 60-66 Wardour Street, London W1V 4ND
t 020 7287 4450 **f** 020 7287 9128
e agents@casarotto.uk.com **w** www.casarotto.uk.com

Nell Dunn

Alan Brodie Representation, 211 Piccadilly, London W1J 9HF
t 020 7917 2871 **f** 020 7917 2872
e info@alanbrodie.com **w** www.alanbrodie.com

Shaun Dunn

Peters Fraser & Dunlop, Drury House, 34-43 Russell Street, London WC2B 5HA
t 020 7344 1000 **f** 020 7836 9543
e postmaster@pfd.co.uk **w** www.pfd.co.uk

Roger Dunton

63 Cedar Court, Rye Street, Bishops Stortford CM23 2HB
t 01279 505560 **f** 01279 506601 **m** 07860 679603
e roger.dunton@virgin.net **w** www.rogerdunton.co.uk

Eamonn O'Neill, James O'Neill & Martin Shea

Peters Fraser & Dunlop, Drury House, 34-43 Russell Street, London WC2B 5HA
t 020 7344 1000 **f** 020 7836 9543
e postmaster@pfd.co.uk **w** www.pfd.co.uk

Richard Easter

Casarotto Ramsay & Associates Ltd, National House, 60-66 Wardour Street, London W1V 4ND
t 020 7287 4450 **f** 020 7287 9128
e agents@casarotto.uk.com **w** www.casarotto.uk.com

Bob Eaton

Alan Brodie Representation, 211 Piccadilly, London W1J 9HF
t 020 7917 2871 **f** 020 7917 2872
e info@alanbrodie.com **w** www.alanbrodie.com

David Edgar

Alan Brodie Representation, 211 Piccadilly, London W1J 9HF
t 020 7917 2871 **f** 020 7917 2872
e info@alanbrodie.com **w** www.alanbrodie.com

Neil Edwards

Culverhouse & James Personal Management, Shepperton Studios, Studio Road, Shepperton TW17 0QD
t 01932 592151 **f** 01932 592233
e dculverhouse@onetel.net.uk **e** jilljames4@aol.com

Charlotte Eilenberg

Alan Brodie Representation, 211 Piccadilly, London W1J 9HF
t 020 7917 2871 **f** 020 7917 2872
e info@alanbrodie.com **w** www.alanbrodie.com

David Eldridge

International Creative Management Ltd, Oxford House, 76 Oxford Street, London W1D 1BS
t 020 7636 6565 **f** 020 7323 0101 **w** www.icmlondon.co.uk

Tim Elgood

Culverhouse & James Personal Management, Shepperton Studios, Studio Road, Shepperton TW17 0QD
t 01932 592151 **f** 01932 592233
e dculverhouse@onetel.net.uk **e** jilljames4@aol.com

Ben Elton

Casarotto Ramsay & Associates Ltd, National House, 60-66 Wardour Street, London W1V 4ND
t 020 7287 4450 **f** 020 7287 9128
e agents@casarotto.uk.com **w** www.casarotto.uk.com

Ed Emery

Alan Brodie Representation, 211 Piccadilly, London W1J 9HF
t 020 7917 2871 **f** 020 7917 2872
e info@alanbrodie.com **w** www.alanbrodie.com

Michael Ennis

Curtis Brown, Haymarket House, 28-29 Haymarket, London SW1Y 4SP
t 020 7396 6600 **f** 020 7396 0110 **e** cb@curtisbrown.co.uk
Credits Taggart (T); Where The Heart Is (T); Faraway Home (F)

Tony Etchells

Peters Fraser & Dunlop, Drury House, 34-43 Russell Street, London WC2B 5HA
t 020 7344 1000 **f** 020 7836 9543
e postmaster@pfd.co.uk **w** www.pfd.co.uk

Peter Ettedgui

International Creative Management Ltd, Oxford House, 76 Oxford Street, London W1D 1BS
t 020 7636 6565 **f** 020 7323 0101 **w** www.icmlondon.co.uk

Mark Ezra

The Dench Arnold Agency, 24 D'Arblay Street, London W1F 8EH
t 020 7437 4551 **f** 020 7439 1355
e contact@dencharnoldagency.co.uk **w** www.dencharnold.co.uk

Hilary Fannin

Casarotto Ramsay & Associates Ltd, National House, 60-66 Wardour Street, London W1V 4ND
t 020 7287 4450 **f** 020 7287 9128
e agents@casarotto.uk.com **w** www.casarotto.uk.com

David Farr

Peters Fraser & Dunlop, Drury House, 34-43 Russell Street, London WC2B 5HA
t 020 7344 1000 **f** 020 7836 9543
e postmaster@pfd.co.uk **w** www.pfd.co.uk

Robert Farrar

Michelle Kass Associates, 36-38 Glasshouse Street, London W1B 5DL
t 020 7439 1624 **f** 020 7734 3394

Toby Farrow

Curtis Brown, Haymarket House, 28-29 Haymarket, London SW1Y 4SP
t 020 7396 6600 **f** 020 7396 0110 **e** cb@curtisbrown.co.uk

John Fay

Culverhouse & James Personal Management, Shepperton Studios, Studio Road, Shepperton TW17 0QD
t 01932 592151 **f** 01932 592233
e dculverhouse@onetel.net.uk **e** jilljames4@aol.com

Steven Fay
Culverhouse & James Personal Management, Shepperton Studios, Studio Road, Shepperton TW17 0QD
t 01932 592151 **f** 01932 592233
e dculverhouse@onetel.net.uk **e** jilljames4@aol.com

Simon Fellowes
Peters Fraser & Dunlop, Drury House, 34-43 Russell Street, London WC2B 5HA
t 020 7344 1000 **f** 020 7836 9543
e postmaster@pfd.co.uk **w** www.pfd.co.uk

James Fenton
Peters Fraser & Dunlop, Drury House, 34-43 Russell Street, London WC2B 5HA
t 020 7344 1000 **f** 020 7836 9543
e postmaster@pfd.co.uk **w** www.pfd.co.uk

Johnny Ferguson
Curtis Brown, Haymarket House, 28-29 Haymarket, London SW1Y 4SP
t 020 7396 6600 **f** 020 7396 0110 **e** cb@curtisbrown.co.uk
Credits Gangster No. 1 (F); My Boy (F); Magnificat (F)

Chris Fewtrell
Casarotto Ramsay & Associates Ltd, National House, 60-66 Wardour Street, London W1V 4ND
t 020 7287 4450 **f** 020 7287 9128
e agents@casarotto.uk.com **w** www.casarotto.uk.com

Eduardo de Filippo
Alan Brodie Representation, 211 Piccadilly, London W1J 9HF
t 020 7917 2871 **f** 020 7917 2872
e info@alanbrodie.com **w** www.alanbrodie.com

John Finch
Peters Fraser & Dunlop, Drury House, 34-43 Russell Street, London WC2B 5HA
t 020 7344 1000 **f** 020 7836 9543
e postmaster@pfd.co.uk **w** www.pfd.co.uk

Jon Stephen Fink
Michelle Kass Associates, 36-38 Glasshouse Street, London W1B 5DL
t 020 7439 1624 **f** 020 7734 3394

Alex Finlayson
Alan Brodie Representation, 211 Piccadilly, London W1J 9HF
t 020 7917 2871 **f** 020 7917 2872
e info@alanbrodie.com **w** www.alanbrodie.com

John Finnemore
Peters Fraser & Dunlop, Drury House, 34-43 Russell Street, London WC2B 5HA
t 020 7344 1000 **f** 020 7836 9543
e postmaster@pfd.co.uk **w** www.pfd.co.uk

Tim Firth
Alan Brodie Representation, 211 Piccadilly, London W1J 9HF
t 020 7917 2871 **f** 020 7917 2872
e info@alanbrodie.com **w** www.alanbrodie.com

Joe Fisher
Curtis Brown, Haymarket House, 28-29 Haymarket, London SW1Y 4SP
t 020 7396 6600 **f** 020 7396 0110 **e** cb@curtisbrown.co.uk
Credits The Titchbourne Claimant (F); Wanting It (T); The Writer (F)

Nick Fisher
Linda Seifert Management, 91 Berwick Street, London W1F ONE
t 020 7292 7390 **f** 020 7292 7391
e contact@lindaseifert.com **w** www.lindaseifert.com

Ian Fitzgibbon
Curtis Brown, Haymarket House, 28-29 Haymarket, London SW1Y 4SP
t 020 7396 6600 **f** 020 7396 0110 **e** cb@curtisbrown.co.uk
Credits Paths to Freedom (T); Fergus' Wedding (T)

Lucy Flannery
The Dench Arnold Agency, 24 D'Arblay Street, London W1F 8EH
t 020 7437 4551 **f** 020 7439 1355
e contact@dencharnoldagency.co.uk **w** www.dencharnold.co.uk

Charlie Fletcher
International Creative Management Ltd, Oxford House, 76 Oxford Street, London W1D 1BS
t 020 7636 6565 **f** 020 7323 0101 **w** www.icmlondon.co.uk

John Fletcher
Peters Fraser & Dunlop, Drury House, 34-43 Russell Street, London WC2B 5HA
t 020 7344 1000 **f** 020 7836 9543
e postmaster@pfd.co.uk **w** www.pfd.co.uk

Piers Fletcher
Peters Fraser & Dunlop, Drury House, 34-43 Russell Street, London WC2B 5HA
t 020 7344 1000 **f** 020 7836 9543
e postmaster@pfd.co.uk **w** www.pfd.co.uk

Emma Forrest
Casarotto Ramsay & Associates Ltd, National House, 60-66 Wardour Street, London W1V 4ND
t 020 7287 4450 **f** 020 7287 9128
e agents@casarotto.uk.com **w** www.casarotto.uk.com

Gez Foster
Curtis Brown, Haymarket House, 28-29 Haymarket, London SW1Y 4SP
t 020 7396 6600 **f** 020 7396 0110 **e** cb@curtisbrown.co.uk
Credits Live and Kicking. V, VI (T); SMTV (T)

Sharon Foster
Alan Brodie Representation, 211 Piccadilly, London W1J 9HF
t 020 7917 2871 **f** 020 7917 2872
e info@alanbrodie.com **w** www.alanbrodie.com

Tim Fountain
Curtis Brown, Haymarket House, 28-29 Haymarket, London SW1Y 4SP
t 020 7396 6600 **f** 020 7396 0110 **e** cb@curtisbrown.co.uk

Lee Fowler
1 Bluebell Close, Ashford TN23 3NG
t 01233 500928 **f** 01233 500928 **m** 07980 661118
e leefowler@compuserve.com
Credits Turning Passion Into Profit (E); Career Advice (E)

David Fox
Culverhouse & James Personal Management, Shepperton Studios, Studio Road, Shepperton TW17 0QD
t 01932 592151 **f** 01932 592233
e dculverhouse@onetel.net.uk **e** jilljames4@aol.com

Donna Franceschild
Alan Brodie Representation, 211 Piccadilly, London W1J 9HF
t 020 7917 2871 **f** 020 7917 2872
e info@alanbrodie.com **w** www.alanbrodie.com

Paul Fraser
Casarotto Ramsay & Associates Ltd, National House, 60-66 Wardour Street, London W1V 4ND
t 020 7287 4450 **f** 020 7287 9128
e agents@casarotto.uk.com **w** www.casarotto.uk.com

Michael Frayn
Peters Fraser & Dunlop, Drury House, 34-43 Russell Street,
London WC2B 5HA
t 020 7344 1000 **f** 020 7836 9543
e postmaster@pfd.co.uk **w** www.pfd.co.uk

Richard Free
Casarotto Ramsay & Associates Ltd, National House,
60-66 Wardour Street, London W1V 4ND
t 020 7287 4450 **f** 020 7287 9128
e agents@casarotto.uk.com **w** www.casarotto.uk.com

Esther Freud
International Creative Management Ltd, Oxford House,
76 Oxford Street, London W1D 1BS
t 020 7636 6565 **f** 020 7323 0101 **w** www.icmlondon.co.uk

Rosemary Friedman
Linda Seifert Management, 91 Berwick Street, London W1F ONE
t 020 7292 7390 **f** 020 7292 7391
e contact@lindaseifert.com **w** www.lindaseifert.com

Raymond Friel
International Creative Management Ltd, Oxford House,
76 Oxford Street, London W1D 1BS
t 020 7636 6565 **f** 020 7323 0101 **w** www.icmlondon.co.uk

Jeremy Front
Casarotto Ramsay & Associates Ltd, National House,
60-66 Wardour Street, London W1V 4ND
t 020 7287 4450 **f** 020 7287 9128
e agents@casarotto.uk.com **w** www.casarotto.uk.com

Lisa Fulthorpe
Linda Seifert Management, 91 Berwick Street, London W1F ONE
t 020 7292 7390 **f** 020 7292 7391
e contact@lindaseifert.com **w** www.lindaseifert.com

James Gaddas
Darley Anderson Literary TV & Film Agency, Estelle House,
11 Eustace Road, London SW6 1JB
t 020 7385 6652 **f** 020 7386 5571
e enquiries@darleyanderson.com

Ted Gannon
The Dench Arnold Agency, 24 D'Arblay Street, London W1F 8EH
t 020 7437 4551 **f** 020 7439 1355
e contact@dencharnoldagency.co.uk **w** www.dencharnold.co.uk

Adam Ganz
Peters Fraser & Dunlop, Drury House, 34-43 Russell Street,
London WC2B 5HA
t 020 7344 1000 **f** 020 7836 9543
e postmaster@pfd.co.uk **w** www.pfd.co.uk

Anthony Garrick
36 Hatfield Road, Chiswick W4 1AF
t 020 8995 1943 **f** 020 8995 1943 **e** anthony-garrick@b.net

Kate Gartside
Peters Fraser & Dunlop, Drury House, 34-43 Russell Street,
London WC2B 5HA
t 020 7344 1000 **f** 020 7836 9543
e postmaster@pfd.co.uk **w** www.pfd.co.uk

Dan Gaster
Casarotto Ramsay & Associates Ltd, National House,
60-66 Wardour Street, London W1V 4ND
t 020 7287 4450 **f** 020 7287 9128
e agents@casarotto.uk.com **w** www.casarotto.uk.com

Nigel Gearing
Peters Fraser & Dunlop, Drury House, 34-43 Russell Street,
London WC2B 5HA
t 020 7344 1000 **f** 020 7836 9543
e postmaster@pfd.co.uk **w** www.pfd.co.uk

Adam Gee
240 Kentish Town Road, London NW5 2AB
t 020 7267 9536 **m** 07787 501148
e adam@arkangel.co.uk **w** www.arkangel.co.uk
Credits To Boldly Go (D); Ideas Into Action (E); Keep-Up-To-Date.TV (W);
Mind Gym (W)

Pam Gems
Casarotto Ramsay & Associates Ltd, National House,
60-66 Wardour Street, London W1V 4ND
t 020 7287 4450 **f** 020 7287 9128
e agents@casarotto.uk.com **w** www.casarotto.uk.com

Andrea Gibb
Curtis Brown, Haymarket House, 28-29 Haymarket, London
SW1Y 4SP
t 020 7396 6600 **f** 020 7396 0110 **e** cb@curtisbrown.co.uk
Credits Golden Wedding (S)

Linda Gibson
Peters Fraser & Dunlop, Drury House, 34-43 Russell Street,
London WC2B 5HA
t 020 7344 1000 **f** 020 7836 9543
e postmaster@pfd.co.uk **w** www.pfd.co.uk

Peter Gill
Casarotto Ramsay & Associates Ltd, National House,
60-66 Wardour Street, London W1V 4ND
t 020 7287 4450 **f** 020 7287 9128
e agents@casarotto.uk.com **w** www.casarotto.uk.com

Phil Gladwin
Curtis Brown, Haymarket House, 28-29 Haymarket, London
SW1Y 4SP
t 020 7396 6600 **f** 020 7396 0110 **e** cb@curtisbrown.co.uk
Credits The Bill (T); Grange Hill (T)

John Godber
Alan Brodie Representation, 211 Piccadilly, London W1J 9HF
t 020 7917 2871 **f** 020 7917 2872
e info@alanbrodie.com **w** www.alanbrodie.com

Roger Goldby
Casarotto Ramsay & Associates Ltd, National House,
60-66 Wardour Street, London W1V 4ND
t 020 7287 4450 **f** 020 7287 9128
e agents@casarotto.uk.com **w** www.casarotto.uk.com

Richard Goleszowski
Curtis Brown, Haymarket House, 28-29 Haymarket, London
SW1Y 4SP
t 020 7396 6600 **f** 020 7396 0110 **e** cb@curtisbrown.co.uk
Credits Rex the Runt (A); Tortoise and the Hare (A); Creature Comforts (A)

Iain Gonoude
Culverhouse & James Personal Management, Shepperton
Studios, Studio Road, Shepperton TW17 0QD
t 01932 592151 **f** 01932 592233
e dculverhouse@onetel.net.uk **e** jilljames4@aol.com

Carl Gorham
Curtis Brown, Haymarket House, 28-29 Haymarket, London
SW1Y 4SP
t 020 7396 6600 **f** 020 7396 0110 **e** cb@curtisbrown.co.uk
Credits Hospital (T); Stressed Eric (A); Meg and Mog (A)

Steve Gough
The Dench Arnold Agency, 24 D'Arblay Street, London W1F 8EH
t 020 7437 4551 **f** 020 7439 1355
e contact@dencharnoldagency.co.uk **w** www.dencharnold.co.uk

Mark Grant
Casarotto Ramsay & Associates Ltd, National House,
60-66 Wardour Street, London W1V 4ND
t 020 7287 4450 **f** 020 7287 9128
e agents@casarotto.uk.com **w** www.casarotto.uk.com

Rob Grant
Curtis Brown, Haymarket House, 28-29 Haymarket, London SW1Y 4SP
t 020 7396 6600 **f** 020 7396 0110 **e** cb@curtisbrown.co.uk
Credits The 10 Per Centers (T); Dark Ages (T); The Strangerers (T)

Helen Greaves
Peters Fraser & Dunlop, Drury House, 34-43 Russell Street, London WC2B 5HA
t 020 7344 1000 **f** 020 7836 9543 **e** postmaster@pfd.co.uk
w www.pfd.co.uk

Graham Greene
Alan Brodie Representation, 211 Piccadilly, London W1J 9HF
t 020 7917 2871 **f** 020 7917 2872
e info@alanbrodie.com **w** www.alanbrodie.com

David Greig
Casarotto Ramsay & Associates Ltd, National House, 60-66 Wardour Street, London W1V 4ND
t 020 7287 4450 **f** 020 7287 9128
e agents@casarotto.uk.com **w** www.casarotto.uk.com

Noël Greig
Alan Brodie Representation, 211 Piccadilly, London W1J 9HF
t 020 7917 2871 **f** 020 7917 2872
e info@alanbrodie.com **w** www.alanbrodie.com

Rachel Gretton
Curtis Brown, Haymarket House, 28-29 Haymarket, London SW1Y 4SP
t 020 7396 6600 **f** 020 7396 0110 **e** cb@curtisbrown.co.uk
Credits A & E (T); Casualty (T); Peak Practice (T)

James Greville
Curtis Brown, Haymarket House, 28-29 Haymarket, London SW1Y 4SP
t 020 7396 6600 **f** 020 7396 0110 **e** cb@curtisbrown.co.uk
Credits Gricers (F); Crocodile Snap (S)

Annie Griffen
Curtis Brown, Haymarket House, 28-29 Haymarket, London SW1Y 4SP
t 020 7396 6600 **f** 020 7396 0110 **e** cb@curtisbrown.co.uk
Credits Coming Soon (T); The Book Group Series II (T); The Island (T)

Trevor Griffiths
Peters Fraser & Dunlop, Drury House, 34-43 Russell Street, London WC2B 5HA
t 020 7344 1000 **f** 020 7836 9543
e postmaster@pfd.co.uk **w** www.pfd.co.uk

Tony Grisoni
Casarotto Ramsay & Associates Ltd, National House, 60-66 Wardour Street, London W1V 4ND
t 020 7287 4450 **f** 020 7287 9128
e agents@casarotto.uk.com **w** www.casarotto.uk.com

Jeff Gross
The Dench Arnold Agency, 24 D'Arblay Street, London W1F 8EH
t 020 7437 4551 **f** 020 7439 1355
e contact@den120charnoldagency.co.uk **w** www.den120charnold.co.uk

Nick Grosso
Curtis Brown, Haymarket House, 28-29 Haymarket, London SW1Y 4SP
t 020 7396 6600 **f** 020 7396 0110 **e** cb@curtisbrown.co.uk

Tony Grounds
Peters Fraser & Dunlop, Drury House, 34-43 Russell Street, London WC2B 5HA
t 020 7344 1000 **f** 020 7836 9543
e postmaster@pfd.co.uk **w** www.pfd.co.uk

Simon Grover
3 Clifton Street, St Albans AL1 3RY
m 07951 290732 **e** sgrover@onetel.net.uk
Credits Bobinogs (A); Fimbles (T); Tweenies (T)

John Hales
Linda Seifert Management, 91 Berwick Street, London W1F ONE
t 020 7292 7390 **f** 020 7292 7391
e contact@lindaseifert.com **w** www.lindaseifert.com

Suzie Halewood
International Creative Management Ltd, Oxford House, 76 Oxford Street, London W1D 1BS
t 020 7636 6565 **f** 020 7323 0101 **w** www.icmlondon.co.uk

Jonathan Hall
Alan Brodie Representation, 211 Piccadilly, London W1J 9HF
t 020 7917 2871 **f** 020 7917 2872
e info@alanbrodie.com **w** www.alanbrodie.com

Matthew Hall
Casarotto Ramsay & Associates Ltd, National House, 60-66 Wardour Street, London W1V 4ND
t 020 7287 4450 **f** 020 7287 9128
e agents@casarotto.uk.com **w** www.casarotto.uk.com

Roger Hall
Casarotto Ramsay & Associates Ltd, National House, 60-66 Wardour Street, London W1V 4ND
t 020 7287 4450 **f** 020 7287 9128
e agents@casarotto.uk.com **w** www.casarotto.uk.com

William Hall
PO Box 1294, London N6 4TW
t 020 8340 0003 **f** 020 8340 0003
e william@wohall.fsnet.co.uk

Peter Hamilton
Curtis Brown, Haymarket House, 28-29 Haymarket, London SW1Y 4SP
t 020 7396 6600 **f** 020 7396 0110 **e** cb@curtisbrown.co.uk

Robert Hammond
The Dench Arnold Agency, 24 D'Arblay Street, London W1F 8EH
t 020 7437 4551 **f** 020 7439 1355
e contact@den120charnoldagency.co.uk **w** www.den120charnold.co.uk

Christopher Hampton
Casarotto Ramsay & Associates Ltd, National House, 60-66 Wardour Street, London W1V 4ND
t 020 7287 4450 **f** 020 7287 9128
e agents@casarotto.uk.com **w** www.casarotto.uk.com

James Handel
Peters Fraser & Dunlop, Drury House, 34-43 Russell Street, London WC2B 5HA
t 020 7344 1000 **f** 020 7836 9543
e postmaster@pfd.co.uk **w** www.pfd.co.uk

Steve Handley
Peters Fraser & Dunlop, Drury House, 34-43 Russell Street, London WC2B 5HA
t 020 7344 1000 **f** 020 7836 9543
e postmaster@pfd.co.uk **w** www.pfd.co.uk

Gordon Hann
Peters Fraser & Dunlop, Drury House, 34-43 Russell Street, London WC2B 5HA
t 020 7344 1000 **f** 020 7836 9543
e postmaster@pfd.co.uk **w** www.pfd.co.uk

Chris Hannan
Alan Brodie Representation, 211 Piccadilly, London W1J 9HF
t 020 7917 2871 **f** 020 7917 2872
e info@alanbrodie.com **w** www.alanbrodie.com

Stewart Harcourt
Peters Fraser & Dunlop, Drury House, 34-43 Russell Street, London WC2B 5HA
t 020 7344 1000 **f** 020 7836 9543
e postmaster@pfd.co.uk **w** www.pfd.co.uk

Mike Harding
Casarotto Ramsay & Associates Ltd, National House, 60-66 Wardour Street, London W1V 4ND
t 020 7287 4450 **f** 020 7287 9128
e agents@casarotto.uk.com **w** www.casarotto.uk.com

Chips Hardy
Linda Seifert Management, 91 Berwick Street, London W1F 0NE
t 020 7292 7390 **f** 020 7292 7391
e contact@lindaseifert.com **w** www.lindaseifert.com

Peter Harness
Curtis Brown, Haymarket House, 28-29 Haymarket, London SW1Y 4SP
t 020 7396 6600 **f** 020 7396 0110 **e** cb@curtisbrown.co.uk
Credits 57 Cairo Road (T); The Chocolate Billionaire (F)

Joanne Harris
Brie Burkeman, 14 Neville Court, Abbey Road, London NW8 9DD
t 07092 239113 **f** 07092 239111 **e** brie.burkeman@mail.com

Paul Harris
102 Eaton Place, London SW1X 8LP
f 020 7235 8441 **m** 07710 281306 **e** paul.harris@forayfilms.com
Credits Closing The Deal (S)

Zinnie Harris
Casarotto Ramsay & Associates Ltd, National House, 60-66 Wardour Street, London W1V 4ND
t 020 7287 4450 **f** 020 7287 9128
e agents@casarotto.uk.com **w** www.casarotto.uk.com

Carey Harrison
London Management & Representation, 2-4 Noel Street, London W1F 8GB
t 020 7287 9000 **f** 020 7287 3236

Carol Harrison
Alan Brodie Representation, 211 Piccadilly, London W1J 9HF
t 020 7917 2871 **f** 020 7917 2872
e info@alanbrodie.com **w** www.alanbrodie.com

David Harrower
Casarotto Ramsay & Associates Ltd, National House, 60-66 Wardour Street, London W1V 4ND
t 020 7287 4450 **f** 020 7287 9128
e agents@casarotto.uk.com **w** www.casarotto.uk.com

Harry Venning & Dave Ramsden
Peters Fraser & Dunlop, Drury House, 34-43 Russell Street, London WC2B 5HA
t 020 7344 1000 **f** 020 7836 9543
e postmaster@pfd.co.uk **w** www.pfd.co.uk

Dylan Harvey
International Creative Management Ltd, Oxford House, 76 Oxford Street, London W1D 1BS
t 020 7636 6565 **f** 020 7323 0101 **w** www.icmlondon.co.uk

Jonathan Harvey
International Creative Management Ltd, Oxford House, 76 Oxford Street, London W1D 1BS
t 020 7636 6565 **f** 020 7323 0101 **w** www.icmlondon.co.uk

Lynne Harwood
Culverhouse & James Personal Management, Shepperton Studios, Studio Road, Shepperton TW17 0QD
t 01932 592151 **f** 01932 592233
e dculverhouse@onetel.net.uk **e** jilljames4@aol.com

Vaclav Havel
Casarotto Ramsay & Associates Ltd, National House, 60-66 Wardour Street, London W1V 4ND
t 020 7287 4450 **f** 020 7287 9128
e agents@casarotto.uk.com **w** www.casarotto.uk.com

Giles Havergal
Alan Brodie Representation, 211 Piccadilly, London W1J 9HF
t 020 7917 2871 **f** 020 7917 2872
e info@alanbrodie.com **w** www.alanbrodie.com

John Hawkesworth
Casarotto Ramsay & Associates Ltd, National House, 60-66 Wardour Street, London W1V 4ND
t 020 7287 4450 **f** 020 7287 9128
e agents@casarotto.uk.com **w** www.casarotto.uk.com

Jane Hawksley
Casarotto Ramsay & Associates Ltd, National House, 60-66 Wardour Street, London W1V 4ND
t 020 7287 4450 **f** 020 7287 9128
e agents@casarotto.uk.com **w** www.casarotto.uk.com

Elizabeth Heery
Peters Fraser & Dunlop, Drury House, 34-43 Russell Street, London WC2B 5HA
t 020 7344 1000 **f** 020 7836 9543
e postmaster@pfd.co.uk **w** www.pfd.co.uk

John Hegley
Peters Fraser & Dunlop, Drury House, 34-43 Russell Street, London WC2B 5HA
t 020 7344 1000 **f** 020 7836 9543
e postmaster@pfd.co.uk **w** www.pfd.co.uk

Olivia Hetreed
Curtis Brown, Haymarket House, 28-29 Haymarket, London SW1Y 4SP
t 020 7396 6600 **f** 020 7396 0110 **e** cb@curtisbrown.co.uk
Credits Children of the News Forest (F); Ballet Shoes (T); Girl with a Pearl Earring (F)

Stan Hey
Linda Seifert Management, 91 Berwick Street, London W1F 0NE
t 020 7292 7390 **f** 020 7292 7391
e contact@lindaseifert.com **w** www.lindaseifert.com

Simon Hickson
Casarotto Ramsay & Associates Ltd, National House, 60-66 Wardour Street, London W1V 4ND
t 020 7287 4450 **f** 020 7287 9128
e agents@casarotto.uk.com **w** www.casarotto.uk.com

Christopher William Hill
Alan Brodie Representation, 211 Piccadilly, London W1J 9HF
t 020 7917 2871 **f** 020 7917 2872
e info@alanbrodie.com **w** www.alanbrodie.com

Lindsey Hill
Bucks Farm, Goose Green RH20 2LR
t 01798 815092 **f** 01798 815094 **m** 07713 250881
e hilllinds@aol.com
Credits Crossroads (T); EastEnders (T); Wing And A Prayer (T)

Ed Hime
International Creative Management Ltd, Oxford House, 76 Oxford Street, London W1D 1BS
t 020 7636 6565 **f** 020 7323 0101 **w** www.icmlondon.co.uk

Michael Hirst
Peters Fraser & Dunlop, Drury House, 34-43 Russell Street, London WC2B 5HA
t 020 7344 1000 **f** 020 7836 9543
e postmaster@pfd.co.uk **w** www.pfd.co.uk

Andrew Hislop
Michelle Kass Associates, 36-38 Glasshouse Street, London W1B 5DL
t 020 7439 1624 **f** 020 7734 3394

Ian Hislop
Casarotto Ramsay & Associates Ltd, National House, 60-66 Wardour Street, London W1V 4ND
t 020 7287 4450 **f** 020 7287 9128
e agents@casarotto.uk.com **w** www.casarotto.uk.com

Tony Hoare
International Creative Management Ltd, Oxford House, 76 Oxford Street, London W1D 1BS
t 020 7636 6565 **f** 020 7323 0101 **w** www.icmlondon.co.uk

Grace Hodge
Peters Fraser & Dunlop, Drury House, 34-43 Russell Street, London WC2B 5HA
t 020 7344 1000 **f** 020 7836 9543
e postmaster@pfd.co.uk **w** www.pfd.co.uk

John Hodge
Peters Fraser & Dunlop, Drury House, 34-43 Russell Street, London WC2B 5HA
t 020 7344 1000 **f** 020 7836 9543
e postmaster@pfd.co.uk **w** www.pfd.co.uk

Jo Hodges
Curtis Brown, Haymarket House, 28-29 Haymarket, London SW1Y 4SP
t 020 7396 6600 **f** 020 7396 0110 **e** cb@curtisbrown.co.uk
Credits Silent Film (S); Portobello Road (T)

James Hogg
Peters Fraser & Dunlop, Drury House, 34-43 Russell Street, London WC2B 5HA
t 020 7344 1000 **f** 020 7836 9543
e postmaster@pfd.co.uk **w** www.pfd.co.uk

Dominic Holland
Peters Fraser & Dunlop, Drury House, 34-43 Russell Street, London WC2B 5HA
t 020 7344 1000 **f** 020 7836 9543
e postmaster@pfd.co.uk **w** www.pfd.co.uk

Tony Holland
Peters Fraser & Dunlop, Drury House, 34-43 Russell Street, London WC2B 5HA
t 020 7344 1000 **f** 020 7836 9543
e postmaster@pfd.co.uk **w** www.pfd.co.uk

Richard Hollands
Brie Burkeman, 14 Neville Court, Abbey Road, London NW8 9DD
t 07092 239113 **f** 07092 239111 **e** brie.burkeman@mail.com

Wayne Holloway
Curtis Brown, Haymarket House, 28-29 Haymarket, London SW1Y 4SP
t 020 7396 6600 **f** 020 7396 0110 **e** cb@curtisbrown.co.uk
Credits Rock A Bye Baby (T)

Robert Holman
Casarotto Ramsay & Associates Ltd, National House, 60-66 Wardour Street, London W1V 4ND
t 020 7287 4450 **f** 020 7287 9128
e agents@casarotto.uk.com **w** www.casarotto.uk.com

Ben Hopkins
Curtis Brown, Haymarket House, 28-29 Haymarket, London SW1Y 4SP
t 020 7396 6600 **f** 020 7396 0110 **e** cb@curtisbrown.co.uk
Credits The Owl Service (F); Stones in his Pockets (F); Simon Magus (F)

Elizabeth Hopley
Alan Brodie Representation, 211 Piccadilly, London W1J 9HF
t 020 7917 2871 **f** 020 7917 2872
e info@alanbrodie.com **w** www.alanbrodie.com

Justin Hopper
Peters Fraser & Dunlop, Drury House, 34-43 Russell Street, London WC2B 5HA
t 020 7344 1000 **f** 020 7836 9543
e postmaster@pfd.co.uk **w** www.pfd.co.uk

David Horlock
Alan Brodie Representation, 211 Piccadilly, London W1J 9HF
t 020 7917 2871 **f** 020 7917 2872
e info@alanbrodie.com **w** www.alanbrodie.com

Nick Hornby
Casarotto Ramsay & Associates Ltd, National House, 60-66 Wardour Street, London W1V 4ND
t 020 7287 4450 **f** 020 7287 9128
e agents@casarotto.uk.com **w** www.casarotto.uk.com

Israel Horovitz
Alan Brodie Representation, 211 Piccadilly, London W1J 9HF
t 020 7917 2871 **f** 020 7917 2872
e info@alanbrodie.com **w** www.alanbrodie.com

Anthony Horowitz
Peters Fraser & Dunlop, Drury House, 34-43 Russell Street, London WC2B 5HA
t 020 7344 1000 **f** 020 7836 9543
e postmaster@pfd.co.uk **w** www.pfd.co.uk

David Howard
Peters Fraser & Dunlop, Drury House, 34-43 Russell Street, London WC2B 5HA
t 020 7344 1000 **f** 020 7836 9543
e postmaster@pfd.co.uk **w** www.pfd.co.uk

Howe & Preddy
Linda Seifert Management, 91 Berwick Street, London W1F ONE
t 020 7292 7390 **f** 020 7292 7391
e contact@lindaseifert.com **w** www.lindaseifert.com

Fiona Howe
London Management & Representation, 2-4 Noel Street, London W1F 8GB
t 020 7287 9000 **f** 020 7287 3236

John Howlett
Alan Brodie Representation, 211 Piccadilly, London W1J 9HF
t 020 7917 2871 **f** 020 7917 2872
e info@alanbrodie.com **w** www.alanbrodie.com

Kimberley Huggins
53 Longfield Lane, West Cheshunt EN7 6AE
t 020 7717 6455 **m** 07808 402597 **e** kimbly@dsl.pipex.com
Credits Illusion (T); Child's Play (T); Sins Of The Fathers (F); It's Only Love (F)

Declan Hughes
Curtis Brown, Haymarket House, 28-29 Haymarket, London SW1Y 4SP
t 020 7396 6600 **f** 020 7396 0110 **e** cb@curtisbrown.co.uk
Credits 20 Grand (F); Younger than Springtime (F)

Phil Hughes
Casarotto Ramsay & Associates Ltd, National House, 60-66 Wardour Street, London W1V 4ND
t 020 7287 4450 **f** 020 7287 9128
e agents@casarotto.uk.com **w** www.casarotto.uk.com

William Humble
Peters Fraser & Dunlop, Drury House, 34-43 Russell Street, London WC2B 5HA
t 020 7344 1000 **f** 020 7836 9543
e postmaster@pfd.co.uk **w** www.pfd.co.uk

Moray Hunter
Curtis Brown, Haymarket House, 28-29 Haymarket, London
SW1Y 4SP
t 020 7396 6600 **f** 020 7396 0110 **e** cb@curtisbrown.co.uk
Credits Morwenna Banks Show (T); Jack Docherty Show (T); The Creatives (T)

Angela Huth
Casarotto Ramsay & Associates Ltd, National House,
60-66 Wardour Street, London W1V 4ND
t 020 7287 4450 **f** 020 7287 9128
e agents@casarotto.uk.com **w** www.casarotto.uk.com

Colin Hutton
Curtis Brown, Haymarket House, 28-29 Haymarket, London
SW1Y 4SP
t 020 7396 6600 **f** 020 7396 0110 **e** cb@curtisbrown.co.uk
Credits The Last Post (F); Numb (F)

Jeremy Hylton Davies
Culverhouse & James Personal Management, Shepperton
Studios, Studio Road, Shepperton TW17 0QD
t 01932 592151 **f** 01932 592233
e dculverhouse@onetel.net.uk **e** jilljames4@aol.com

Chrissie Illey
International Creative Management Ltd, Oxford House,
76 Oxford Street, London W1D 1BS
t 020 7636 6565 **f** 020 7323 0101 **w** www.icmlondon.co.uk

Will Ing
Casarotto Ramsay & Associates Ltd, National House,
60-66 Wardour Street, London W1V 4ND
t 020 7287 4450 **f** 020 7287 9128
e agents@casarotto.uk.com **w** www.casarotto.uk.com

Caroline Ip
Curtis Brown, Haymarket House, 28-29 Haymarket, London
SW1Y 4SP
t 020 7396 6600 **f** 020 7396 0110 **e** cb@curtisbrown.co.uk
Credits Marion Again (T); The Hole (F); Cracks (F)

Jeremy Isaacs
Peters Fraser & Dunlop, Drury House, 34-43 Russell Street,
London WC2B 5HA
t 020 7344 1000 **f** 020 7836 9543
e postmaster@pfd.co.uk **w** www.pfd.co.uk

Debbie Isitt
Curtis Brown, Haymarket House, 28-29 Haymarket, London
SW1Y 4SP
t 020 7396 6600 **f** 020 7396 0110 **e** cb@curtisbrown.co.uk
Credits Nasty Neighbours (F); Faghags (F); The Illustrated Mum (T)

Helen Jacey
Casarotto Ramsay & Associates Ltd, National House,
60-66 Wardour Street, London W1V 4ND
t 020 7287 4450 **f** 020 7287 9128
e agents@casarotto.uk.com **w** www.casarotto.uk.com

Kit Jackson
Peters Fraser & Dunlop, Drury House, 34-43 Russell Street,
London WC2B 5HA
t 020 7344 1000 **f** 020 7836 9543
e postmaster@pfd.co.uk **w** www.pfd.co.uk

Leigh Jackson
Peters Fraser & Dunlop, Drury House, 34-43 Russell Street,
London WC2B 5HA
t 020 7344 1000 **f** 020 7836 9543
e postmaster@pfd.co.uk **w** www.pfd.co.uk

Clive James
Peters Fraser & Dunlop, Drury House, 34-43 Russell Street,
London WC2B 5HA
t 020 7344 1000 **f** 020 7836 9543
e postmaster@pfd.co.uk **w** www.pfd.co.uk

Corinne James
2 Manor Cottages, Somerford Keynes, Cirencester GL7 6DL
t 01285 862269

Donald James
Linda Seifert Management, 91 Berwick Street, London W1F 0NE
t 020 7292 7390 **f** 020 7292 7391
e contact@lindaseifert.com **w** www.lindaseifert.com

Stephen Jeffreys
Casarotto Ramsay & Associates Ltd, National House,
60-66 Wardour Street, London W1V 4ND
t 020 7287 4450 **f** 020 7287 9128
e agents@casarotto.uk.com **w** www.casarotto.uk.com

George Jeffrie
Curtis Brown, Haymarket House, 28-29 Haymarket, London
SW1Y 4SP
t 020 7396 6600 **f** 020 7396 0110 **e** cb@curtisbrown.co.uk
Credits Smack the Pony (T); The People's Harry Enfield (F)

Ann Jellicoe
Casarotto Ramsay & Associates Ltd, National House,
60-66 Wardour Street, London W1V 4ND
t 020 7287 4450 **f** 020 7287 9128
e agents@casarotto.uk.com **w** www.casarotto.uk.com

Guy Jenkin
London Management & Representation, 2-4 Noel Street,
London W1F 8GB
t 020 7287 9000 **f** 020 7287 3236
Credits Not The Nine O'Clock News (T); Crossing The Floor (T); Drop The Dead
Donkey (T); Jeffery Archer: The Truth (T)

Amy Jenkins
Casarotto Ramsay & Associates Ltd, National House,
60-66 Wardour Street, London W1V 4ND
t 020 7287 4450 **f** 020 7287 9128
e agents@casarotto.uk.com **w** www.casarotto.uk.com

Laura Jewell
Casarotto Ramsay & Associates Ltd, National House,
60-66 Wardour Street, London W1V 4ND
t 020 7287 4450 **f** 020 7287 9128
e agents@casarotto.uk.com **w** www.casarotto.uk.com

Alex Johnston
Curtis Brown, Haymarket House, 28-29 Haymarket, London
SW1Y 4SP
t 020 7396 6600 **f** 020 7396 0110 **e** cb@curtisbrown.co.uk

Charlotte Jones
Peters Fraser & Dunlop, Drury House, 34-43 Russell Street,
London WC2B 5HA
t 020 7344 1000 **f** 020 7836 9543
e postmaster@pfd.co.uk **w** www.pfd.co.uk

Debbie Jones
Casarotto Ramsay & Associates Ltd, National House,
60-66 Wardour Street, London W1V 4ND
t 020 7287 4450 **f** 020 7287 9128
e agents@casarotto.uk.com **w** www.casarotto.uk.com

Ed Jones
Peters Fraser & Dunlop, Drury House, 34-43 Russell Street,
London WC2B 5HA
t 020 7344 1000 **f** 020 7836 9543
e postmaster@pfd.co.uk **w** www.pfd.co.uk

Gareth Jones
London Management & Representation, 2-4 Noel Street,
London W1F 8GB
t 020 7287 9000 **f** 020 7287 3236

Ken Allen Jones
Pauline Asper Management, Jacobs Cottage, Reservoir Lane,
Sedlescombe TN33 0PJ
t 01424 870412 **f** 01424 870412 **e** pauline.asper@virgin.net

Laura Jones
Casarotto Ramsay & Associates Ltd, National House,
60-66 Wardour Street, London W1V 4ND
t 020 7287 4450 **f** 020 7287 9128
e agents@casarotto.uk.com **w** www.casarotto.uk.com

Marie Jones
Curtis Brown, Haymarket House, 28-29 Haymarket, London
SW1Y 4SP
t 020 7396 6600 **f** 020 7396 0110 **e** cb@curtisbrown.co.uk

Terry Jones
Casarotto Ramsay & Associates Ltd, National House,
60-66 Wardour Street, London W1V 4ND
t 020 7287 4450 **f** 020 7287 9128
e agents@casarotto.uk.com **w** www.casarotto.uk.com

Neil Jordan
Casarotto Ramsay & Associates Ltd, National House,
60-66 Wardour Street, London W1V 4ND
t 020 7287 4450 **f** 020 7287 9128
e agents@casarotto.uk.com **w** www.casarotto.uk.com

JT Electrons
42 Torridge Road, Thornton Heath CR7 7EY
t 020 8665 6595 **f** 020 8665 6595 **e** istc@istc.org.uk
Contact John Tooze, Proprietor

Saurabh Kakkar
Peters Fraser & Dunlop, Drury House, 34-43 Russell Street,
London WC2B 5HA
t 020 7344 1000 **f** 020 7836 9543
e postmaster@pfd.co.uk **w** www.pfd.co.uk

Jackie Kay
Peters Fraser & Dunlop, Drury House, 34-43 Russell Street,
London WC2B 5HA
t 020 7344 1000 **f** 020 7836 9543
e postmaster@pfd.co.uk **w** www.pfd.co.uk

David Keating
International Creative Management Ltd, Oxford House,
76 Oxford Street, London W1D 1BS
t 020 7636 6565 **f** 020 7323 0101 **w** www.icmlondon.co.uk

Paul Kellett
Linda Seifert Management, 91 Berwick Street, London W1F 0NE
t 020 7292 7390 **f** 020 7292 7391
e contact@lindaseifert.com **w** www.lindaseifert.com

Andrew Kemble & John Pape
Linda Seifert Management, 91 Berwick Street, London W1F 0NE
t 020 7292 7390 **f** 020 7292 7391
e contact@lindaseifert.com **w** www.lindaseifert.com

Edward Kemp
Alan Brodie Representation, 211 Piccadilly, London W1J 9HF
t 020 7917 2871 **f** 020 7917 2872
e info@alanbrodie.com **w** www.alanbrodie.com

Sarah Kennedy
Casarotto Ramsay & Associates Ltd, National House,
60-66 Wardour Street, London W1V 4ND
t 020 7287 4450 **f** 020 7287 9128
e agents@casarotto.uk.com **w** www.casarotto.uk.com

Stephen Keyworth
Peters Fraser & Dunlop, Drury House, 34-43 Russell Street,
London WC2B 5HA
t 020 7344 1000 **f** 020 7836 9543
e postmaster@pfd.co.uk **w** www.pfd.co.uk

Raymond Khoury
International Creative Management Ltd, Oxford House,
76 Oxford Street, London W1D 1BS
t 020 7636 6565 **f** 020 7323 0101 **w** www.icmlondon.co.uk

Thomas Kilroy
Alan Brodie Representation, 211 Piccadilly, London W1J 9HF
t 020 7917 2871 **f** 020 7917 2872
e info@alanbrodie.com **w** www.alanbrodie.com

Clive King
Linda Seifert Management, 91 Berwick Street, London W1F 0NE
t 020 7292 7390 **f** 020 7292 7391
e contact@lindaseifert.com **w** www.lindaseifert.com

Danny King
Darley Anderson Literary TV & Film Agency, Estelle House,
11 Eustace Road, London SW6 1JB
t 020 7385 6652 **f** 020 7386 5571
e enquiries@darleyanderson.com

Steven Knight
Peters Fraser & Dunlop, Drury House, 34-43 Russell Street,
London WC2B 5HA
t 020 7344 1000 **f** 020 7836 9543
e postmaster@pfd.co.uk **w** www.pfd.co.uk

Malcolm Kohll
The Dench Arnold Agency, 24 D'Arblay Street, London W1F 8EH
t 020 7437 4551 **f** 020 7439 1355
e contact@dencharnoldagency.co.uk **w** www.dencharnold.co.uk

Ash Kotak
Peters Fraser & Dunlop, Drury House, 34-43 Russell Street,
London WC2B 5HA
t 020 7344 1000 **f** 020 7836 9543
e postmaster@pfd.co.uk **w** www.pfd.co.uk

Larry Kramer
Casarotto Ramsay & Associates Ltd, National House,
60-66 Wardour Street, London W1V 4ND
t 020 7287 4450 **f** 020 7287 9128
e agents@casarotto.uk.com **w** www.casarotto.uk.com

Anna Kythreotis
The Dench Arnold Agency, 24 D'Arblay Street, London W1F 8EH
t 020 7437 4551 **f** 020 7439 1355
e contact@dencharnoldagency.co.uk **w** www.dencharnold.co.uk

Rosemary Lane
34 Smithies Road, Abbey Wood, London SE2 0TG
t 020 8311 2046 **m** 07730 349753
Credits Picture Of Dorian Gray (E); The Private Life Of Queen Anne (E); What
The Dickens (S); Burke And Hare, Thieves In The Night (F)

Daniel Lapaine
Peters Fraser & Dunlop, Drury House, 34-43 Russell Street,
London WC2B 5HA
t 020 7344 1000 **f** 020 7836 9543
e postmaster@pfd.co.uk **w** www.pfd.co.uk

Bryony Lavery
Peters Fraser & Dunlop, Drury House, 34-43 Russell Street,
London WC2B 5HA
t 020 7344 1000 **f** 020 7836 9543
e postmaster@pfd.co.uk **w** www.pfd.co.uk

Elizabeth Lawrence
Peters Fraser & Dunlop, Drury House, 34-43 Russell Street,
London WC2B 5HA
t 020 7344 1000 **f** 020 7836 9543
e postmaster@pfd.co.uk **w** www.pfd.co.uk

Karen Laws
Casarotto Ramsay & Associates Ltd, National House,
60-66 Wardour Street, London W1V 4ND
t 020 7287 4450 **f** 020 7287 9128
e agents@casarotto.uk.com **w** www.casarotto.uk.com

Lawson & Phelps
Linda Seifert Management, 91 Berwick Street, London W1F ONE
t 020 7292 7390 **f** 020 7292 7391
e contact@lindaseifert.com **w** www.lindaseifert.com

James Lawson
Pauline Asper Management, Jacobs Cottage, Reservoir Lane,
Sedlescombe TN33 0PJ
t 01424 870412 **f** 01424 870412 **e** pauline.asper@virgin.net

Pete Lawson
Casarotto Ramsay & Associates Ltd, National House,
60-66 Wardour Street, London W1V 4ND
t 020 7287 4450 **f** 020 7287 9128
e agents@casarotto.uk.com **w** www.casarotto.uk.com

Steve Lawson
Culverhouse & James Personal Management, Shepperton
Studios, Studio Road, Shepperton TW17 0QD
t 01932 592151 **f** 01932 592233
e dculverhouse@onetel.net.uk **e** jilljames4@aol.com

Jessica Lea
Peters Fraser & Dunlop, Drury House, 34-43 Russell Street,
London WC2B 5HA
t 020 7344 1000 **f** 020 7836 9543
e postmaster@pfd.co.uk **w** www.pfd.co.uk

Peter Learmouth
Peters Fraser & Dunlop, Drury House, 34-43 Russell Street,
London WC2B 5HA
t 020 7344 1000 **f** 020 7836 9543
e postmaster@pfd.co.uk **w** www.pfd.co.uk

Alison Leathart
Michelle Kass Associates, 36-38 Glasshouse Street, London
W1B 5DL
t 020 7439 1624 **f** 020 7734 3394

Carenza Lewis
Peters Fraser & Dunlop, Drury House, 34-43 Russell Street,
London WC2B 5HA
t 020 7344 1000 **f** 020 7836 9543
e postmaster@pfd.co.uk **w** www.pfd.co.uk

Jonathan Lewis
Curtis Brown, Haymarket House, 28-29 Haymarket, London
SW1Y 4SP
t 020 7396 6600 **f** 020 7396 0110 **e** cb@curtisbrown.co.uk
Credits Truth (T)

Matthew Leys
Casarotto Ramsay & Associates Ltd, National House,
60-66 Wardour Street, London W1V 4ND
t 020 7287 4450 **f** 020 7287 9128
e agents@casarotto.uk.com **w** www.casarotto.uk.com

Nell Leyshon
Peters Fraser & Dunlop, Drury House, 34-43 Russell Street,
London WC2B 5HA
t 020 7344 1000 **f** 020 7836 9543
e postmaster@pfd.co.uk **w** www.pfd.co.uk

Sue Limb
Peters Fraser & Dunlop, Drury House, 34-43 Russell Street,
London WC2B 5HA
t 020 7344 1000 **f** 020 7836 9543
e postmaster@pfd.co.uk **w** www.pfd.co.uk

Seth Linder
The Dench Arnold Agency, 24 D'Arblay Street, London W1F 8EH
t 020 7437 4551 **f** 020 7439 1355
e contact@denwhen charnoldagency.co.uk **w** www.dencharnold.co.uk

Douglas Lindsay
Darley Anderson Literary TV & Film Agency, Estelle House,
11 Eustace Road, London SW6 1JB
t 020 7385 6652 **f** 020 7386 5571
e enquiries@darleyanderson.com

Geoff Lindsey
Curtis Brown, Haymarket House, 28-29 Haymarket, London
SW1Y 4SP
t 020 7396 6600 **f** 020 7396 0110 **e** cb@curtisbrown.co.uk
Credits The Bill (T); Crossroads (T)

Robert Llewellyn
Peters Fraser & Dunlop, Drury House, 34-43 Russell Street,
London WC2B 5HA
t 020 7344 1000 **f** 020 7836 9543
e postmaster@pfd.co.uk **w** www.pfd.co.uk

Tim Loane
International Creative Management Ltd, Oxford House,
76 Oxford Street, London W1D 1BS
t 020 7636 6565 **f** 020 7323 0101 **w** www.icmlondon.co.uk

Amanda Lomas
Peters Fraser & Dunlop, Drury House, 34-43 Russell Street,
London WC2B 5HA
t 020 7344 1000 **f** 020 7836 9543
e postmaster@pfd.co.uk **w** www.pfd.co.uk

Deric Longden
Peters Fraser & Dunlop, Drury House, 34-43 Russell Street,
London WC2B 5HA
t 020 7344 1000 **f** 020 7836 9543
e postmaster@pfd.co.uk **w** www.pfd.co.uk

Khurram Longi
Peters Fraser & Dunlop, Drury House, 34-43 Russell Street,
London WC2B 5HA
t 020 7344 1000 **f** 020 7836 9543
e postmaster@pfd.co.uk **w** www.pfd.co.uk

Jack Lothian
Curtis Brown, Haymarket House, 28-29 Haymarket, London
SW1Y 4SP
t 020 7396 6600 **f** 020 7396 0110 **e** cb@curtisbrown.co.uk
Credits Late Night Shopping (T)

Doug Lucie
Alan Brodie Representation, 211 Piccadilly, London W1J 9HF
t 020 7917 2871 **f** 020 7917 2872
e info@alanbrodie.com **w** www.alanbrodie.com

Claire Luckham
Alan Brodie Representation, 211 Piccadilly, London W1J 9HF
t 020 7917 2871 **f** 020 7917 2872
e info@alanbrodie.com **w** www.alanbrodie.com

Christopher Luscombe
Alan Brodie Representation, 211 Piccadilly, London W1J 9HF
t 020 7917 2871 **f** 020 7917 2872
e info@alanbrodie.com **w** www.alanbrodie.com

Garry Lyons
Alan Brodie Representation, 211 Piccadilly, London W1J 9HF
t 020 7917 2871 **f** 020 7917 2872
e info@alanbrodie.com **w** www.alanbrodie.com

Holly Lyons
London Management & Representation, 2-4 Noel Street,
London W1F 8GB
t 020 7287 9000 **f** 020 7287 3236
Credits 24/Seven (T); Girls In Love (T)

Andy Macdonald
International Creative Management Ltd, Oxford House,
76 Oxford Street, London W1D 1BS
t 020 7636 6565 **f** 020 7323 0101 **w** www.icmlondon.co.uk

RD MacDonald
Alan Brodie Representation, 211 Piccadilly, London W1J 9HF
t 020 7917 2871 **f** 020 7917 2872
e info@alanbrodie.com **w** www.alanbrodie.com

Sharman Macdonald
Alan Brodie Representation, 211 Piccadilly, London W1J 9HF
t 020 7917 2871 **f** 020 7917 2872
e info@alanbrodie.com **w** www.alanbrodie.com

Stephen MacDonald
Alan Brodie Representation, 211 Piccadilly, London W1J 9HF
t 020 7917 2871 **f** 020 7917 2872
e info@alanbrodie.com **w** www.alanbrodie.com

Barbara Machin
Pauline Asper Management, Jacobs Cottage, Reservoir Lane,
Sedlescombe TN33 0PJ
t 01424 870412 **f** 01424 870412 **e** pauline.asper@virgin.net

Douglas Mackinnon
Curtis Brown, Haymarket House, 28-29 Haymarket, London
SW1Y 4SP
t 020 7396 6600 **f** 020 7396 0110 **e** cb@curtisbrown.co.uk
Credits Truth (T); The Vice (T); Nice Guy Eddie (F)

James MacManus
Linda Seifert Management, 91 Berwick Street, London W1F 0NE
t 020 7292 7390 **f** 020 7292 7391
e contact@lindaseifert.com **w** www.lindaseifert.com

Don MacPherson
Casarotto Ramsay & Associates Ltd, National House,
60-66 Wardour Street, London W1V 4ND
t 020 7287 4450 **f** 020 7287 9128
e agents@casarotto.uk.com **w** www.casarotto.uk.com

Richard Maher
Peters Fraser & Dunlop, Drury House, 34-43 Russell Street,
London WC2B 5HA
t 020 7344 1000 **f** 020 7836 9543
e postmaster@pfd.co.uk **w** www.pfd.co.uk

Mick Mahoney
Peters Fraser & Dunlop, Drury House, 34-43 Russell Street,
London WC2B 5HA
t 020 7344 1000 **f** 020 7836 9543
e postmaster@pfd.co.uk **w** www.pfd.co.uk

Paul Makin
The Dench Arnold Agency, 24 D'Arblay Street, London W1F 8EH
t 020 7437 4551 **f** 020 7439 1355
e contact@dencharnoldagency.co.uk **w** www.dencharnold.co.uk

Mark Mills
International Creative Management, Oxford House,
76 Oxford Street, London W1D !BS
t 020 7636 6565 **f** 020 7323 0101 **w** www.icmlondon.co.uk
Contact Sue Rogers, Agent

Marks & Gran
Linda Seifert Management, 91 Berwick Street, London
W1F 8EH
t 020 7292 7390 **f** 020 7292 7391
e contact@lindaseifert.com **w** www.lindaseifert.com

Andrew Marshall
Curtis Brown, Haymarket House, 28-29 Haymarket, London
SW1Y 4SP
t 020 7396 6600 **f** 020 7396 0110 **e** cb@curtisbrown.co.uk
Credits Scary Poppins (F); Strange (T)

Cheryl Martin
Peters Fraser & Dunlop, Drury House, 34-43 Russell Street,
London WC2B 5HA
t 020 7344 1000 **f** 020 7836 9543
e postmaster@pfd.co.uk **w** www.pfd.co.uk

Mick Martin
Alan Brodie Representation, 211 Piccadilly, London W1J 9HF
t 020 7917 2871 **f** 020 7917 2872
e info@alanbrodie.com **w** www.alanbrodie.com

Nicholas Martin
Peters Fraser & Dunlop, Drury House, 34-43 Russell Street,
London WC2B 5HA
t 020 7344 1000 **f** 020 7836 9543
e postmaster@pfd.co.uk **w** www.pfd.co.uk

Matthew Faulk & Mark Skeet
The Dench Arnold Agency, 24 D'Arblay Street, London W1F 8EH
t 020 7437 4551 **f** 020 7439 1355
e contact@dencharnoldagency.co.uk **w** www.dencharnold.co.uk

Carole Matthews
Darley Anderson Literary TV & Film Agency, Estelle House,
11 Eustace Road, London SW6 1JB
t 020 7385 6652 **f** 020 7386 5571
e enquiries@darleyanderson.com

Tim May
London Management & Representation, 2-4 Noel Street,
London W1F 8GB
t 020 7287 9000 **f** 020 7287 3236

Lise Mayer
International Creative Management Ltd, Oxford House,
76 Oxford Street, London W1D 1BS
t 020 7636 6565 **f** 020 7323 0101 **w** www.icmlondon.co.uk

Jenny Mayhew
Michelle Kass Associates, 36-38 Glasshouse Street, London
W1B 5DL
t 020 7439 1624 **f** 020 7734 3394

Paul Mayhew-Archer
Casarotto Ramsay & Associates Ltd, National House,
60-66 Wardour Street, London W1V 4ND
t 020 7287 4450 **f** 020 7287 9128
e agents@casarotto.uk.com **w** www.casarotto.uk.com

Stephen McAteer
The Dench Arnold Agency, 24 D'Arblay Street, London W1F 8EH
t 020 7437 4551 **f** 020 7439 1355
e contact@dencharnoldagency.co.uk **w** www.dencharnold.co.uk

Nichola McAuliffe
Peters Fraser & Dunlop, Drury House, 34-43 Russell Street,
London WC2B 5HA
t 020 7344 1000 **f** 020 7836 9543
e postmaster@pfd.co.uk **w** www.pfd.co.uk

Richard McBrien
Peters Fraser & Dunlop, Drury House, 34-43 Russell Street,
London WC2B 5HA
t 020 7344 1000 **f** 020 7836 9543
e postmaster@pfd.co.uk **w** www.pfd.co.uk

Ruth McCance
Peters Fraser & Dunlop, Drury House, 34-43 Russell Street,
London WC2B 5HA
t 020 7344 1000 **f** 020 7836 9543
e postmaster@pfd.co.uk **w** www.pfd.co.uk

Martin McCardie
Curtis Brown, Haymarket House, 28-29 Haymarket, London
SW1Y 4SP
t 020 7396 6600 **f** 020 7396 0110 **e** cb@curtisbrown.co.uk
Credits Innitiation (T); Tinsletown (T)

Anthony McCarten
Casarotto Ramsay & Associates Ltd, National House,
60-66 Wardour Street, London W1V 4ND
t 020 7287 4450 **f** 020 7287 9128
e agents@casarotto.uk.com **w** www.casarotto.uk.com

Nicola McCartney
Peters Fraser & Dunlop, Drury House, 34-43 Russell Street,
London WC2B 5HA
t 020 7344 1000 **f** 020 7836 9543
e postmaster@pfd.co.uk **w** www.pfd.co.uk

James McClure
Peters Fraser & Dunlop, Drury House, 34-43 Russell Street,
London WC2B 5HA
t 020 7344 1000 **f** 020 7836 9543
e postmaster@pfd.co.uk **w** www.pfd.co.uk

Stephen McDool
Linda Seifert Management, 91 Berwick Street, London W1F ONE
t 020 7292 7390 **f** 020 7292 7391
e contact@lindaseifert.com **w** www.lindaseifert.com

Peter McDougall
Peters Fraser & Dunlop, Drury House, 34-43 Russell Street,
London WC2B 5HA
t 020 7344 1000 **f** 020 7836 9543
e postmaster@pfd.co.uk **w** www.pfd.co.uk

Philip McGough
Peters Fraser & Dunlop, Drury House, 34-43 Russell Street,
London WC2B 5HA
t 020 7344 1000 **f** 020 7836 9543
e postmaster@pfd.co.uk **w** www.pfd.co.uk

Roger McGough
Peters Fraser & Dunlop, Drury House, 34-43 Russell Street,
London WC2B 5HA
t 020 7344 1000 **f** 020 7836 9543
e postmaster@pfd.co.uk **w** www.pfd.co.uk

McGrath & O'Driscoll
Linda Seifert Management, 91 Berwick Street, London W1F ONE
t 020 7292 7390 **f** 020 7292 7391
e contact@lindaseifert.com **w** www.lindaseifert.com

Frank McGuinness
Casarotto Ramsay & Associates Ltd, National House,
60-66 Wardour Street, London W1V 4ND
t 020 7287 4450 **f** 020 7287 9128
e agents@casarotto.uk.com **w** www.casarotto.uk.com

Diane Mcinernery
Curtis Brown, Haymarket House, 28-29 Haymarket, London
SW1Y 4SP
t 020 7396 6600 **f** 020 7396 0110 **e** cb@curtisbrown.co.uk
Credits Miracle Police (T); Widows Peak (T)

John McKay
Casarotto Ramsay & Associates Ltd, National House,
60-66 Wardour Street, London W1V 4ND
t 020 7287 4450 **f** 020 7287 9128
e agents@casarotto.uk.com **w** www.casarotto.uk.com

Malcolm McKee
Alan Brodie Representation, 211 Piccadilly, London W1J 9HF
t 020 7917 2871 **f** 020 7917 2872
e info@alanbrodie.com **w** www.alanbrodie.com

Peter McKenna
Peters Fraser & Dunlop, Drury House, 34-43 Russell Street,
London WC2B 5HA
t 020 7344 1000 **f** 020 7836 9543
e postmaster@pfd.co.uk **w** www.pfd.co.uk

Stephanie McKnight
Casarotto Ramsay & Associates Ltd, National House,
60-66 Wardour Street, London W1V 4ND
t 020 7287 4450 **f** 020 7287 9128
e agents@casarotto.uk.com **w** www.casarotto.uk.com

Colin McLaren
Curtis Brown, Haymarket House, 28-29 Haymarket, London
SW1Y 4SP
t 020 7396 6600 **f** 020 7396 0110 **e** cb@curtisbrown.co.uk
Credits Home (S)

Linda McLean
Casarotto Ramsay & Associates Ltd, National House,
60-66 Wardour Street, London W1V 4ND
t 020 7287 4450 **f** 020 7287 9128
e agents@casarotto.uk.com **w** www.casarotto.uk.com

Kenneth McLeish
Alan Brodie Representation, 211 Piccadilly, London W1J 9HF
t 020 7917 2871 **f** 020 7917 2872
e info@alanbrodie.com **w** www.alanbrodie.com

John McNally
Michelle Kass Associates, 36-38 Glasshouse Street, London
W1B 5DL
t 020 7439 1624 **f** 020 7734 3394

Conor McPherson
Curtis Brown, Haymarket House, 28-29 Haymarket, London
SW1Y 4SP
t 020 7396 6600 **f** 020 7396 0110 **e** cb@curtisbrown.co.uk
Credits The Actors (F)

Jim McRoberts
Michelle Kass Associates, 36-38 Glasshouse Street, London
W1B 5DL
t 020 7439 1624 **f** 020 7734 3394

Shane Meadows
Casarotto Ramsay & Associates Ltd, National House,
60-66 Wardour Street, London W1V 4ND
t 020 7287 4450 **f** 020 7287 9128
e agents@casarotto.uk.com **w** www.casarotto.uk.com

Anthony Meech
Alan Brodie Representation, 211 Piccadilly, London W1J 9HF
t 020 7917 2871 **f** 020 7917 2872
e info@alanbrodie.com **w** www.alanbrodie.com

Martin Meenan
Peters Fraser & Dunlop, Drury House, 34-43 Russell Street,
London WC2B 5HA
t 020 7344 1000 **f** 020 7836 9543
e postmaster@pfd.co.uk **w** www.pfd.co.uk

Paul Mendelson
Alan Brodie Representation, 211 Piccadilly, London W1J 9HF
t 020 7917 2871 **f** 020 7917 2872
e info@alanbrodie.com **w** www.alanbrodie.com

Jed Mercurio
International Creative Management Ltd, Oxford House,
76 Oxford Street, London W1D 1BS
t 020 7636 6565 **f** 020 7323 0101 **w** www.icmlondon.co.uk

Johnny Meres
Curtis Brown, Haymarket House, 28-29 Haymarket, London
SW1Y 4SP
t 020 7396 6600 **f** 020 7396 0110 **e** cb@curtisbrown.co.uk
Credits Out of Tune (T)

Peter Meyer
Alan Brodie Representation, 211 Piccadilly, London W1J 9HF
t 020 7917 2871 **f** 020 7917 2872
e info@alanbrodie.com **w** www.alanbrodie.com

Jake Michie
Peters Fraser & Dunlop, Drury House, 34-43 Russell Street,
London WC2B 5HA
t 020 7344 1000 **f** 020 7836 9543
e postmaster@pfd.co.uk **w** www.pfd.co.uk

Lizzie Mickery
Alan Brodie Representation, 211 Piccadilly, London W1J 9HF
t 020 7917 2871 **f** 020 7917 2872
e info@alanbrodie.com **w** www.alanbrodie.com

John Milarky
Michelle Kass Associates, 36-38 Glasshouse Street, London
W1B 5DL
t 020 7439 1624 **f** 020 7734 3394

Mark Millar
London Management & Representation, 2-4 Noel Street,
London W1F 8GB
t 020 7287 9000 **f** 020 7287 3236

Martin Millar
JT Management, 55 Fairbridge Road, London N19 3EW
t 020 7272 4000 **f** 020 7272 4000
e julia@jtmanagement.co.uk

Peter Milligan
Peters Fraser & Dunlop, Drury House, 34-43 Russell Street,
London WC2B 5HA
t 020 7344 1000 **f** 020 7836 9543
e postmaster@pfd.co.uk **w** www.pfd.co.uk

Bob Mills
Peters Fraser & Dunlop, Drury House, 34-43 Russell Street,
London WC2B 5HA
t 020 7344 1000 **f** 020 7836 9543
e postmaster@pfd.co.uk **w** www.pfd.co.uk

George Milton
International Creative Management Ltd, Oxford House,
76 Oxford Street, London W1D 1BS
t 020 7636 6565 **f** 020 7323 0101 **w** www.icmlondon.co.uk

Dominic Minghella
Casarotto Ramsay & Associates Ltd, National House,
60-66 Wardour Street, London W1V 4ND
t 020 7287 4450 **f** 020 7287 9128
e agents@casarotto.uk.com **w** www.casarotto.uk.com

Simon Mirren
Curtis Brown, Haymarket House, 28-29 Haymarket, London
SW1Y 4SP
t 020 7396 6600 **f** 020 7396 0110 **e** cb@curtisbrown.co.uk

Adrian Mitchell
Peters Fraser & Dunlop, Drury House, 34-43 Russell Street,
London WC2B 5HA
t 020 7344 1000 **f** 020 7836 9543
e postmaster@pfd.co.uk **w** www.pfd.co.uk

Gary Mitchell
Peters Fraser & Dunlop, Drury House, 34-43 Russell Street,
London WC2B 5HA
t 020 7344 1000 **f** 020 7836 9543
e postmaster@pfd.co.uk **w** www.pfd.co.uk

Julian Mitchell
Peters Fraser & Dunlop, Drury House, 34-43 Russell Street,
London WC2B 5HA
t 020 7344 1000 **f** 020 7836 9543
e postmaster@pfd.co.uk **w** www.pfd.co.uk

Peter Moffat
Peters Fraser & Dunlop, Drury House, 34-43 Russell Street,
London WC2B 5HA
t 020 7344 1000 **f** 020 7836 9543
e postmaster@pfd.co.uk **w** www.pfd.co.uk

Steven Moffat
London Management & Representation, 2-4 Noel Street,
London W1F 8GB
t 020 7287 9000 **f** 020 7287 3236
Credits Press Gang (T); Coupling (T)

Sarah Moffett
Peters Fraser & Dunlop, Drury House, 34-43 Russell Street,
London WC2B 5HA
t 020 7344 1000 **f** 020 7836 9543
e postmaster@pfd.co.uk **w** www.pfd.co.uk

Richard Monks
Curtis Brown, Haymarket House, 28-29 Haymarket, London
SW1Y 4SP
t 020 7396 6600 **f** 020 7396 0110 **e** cb@curtisbrown.co.uk
Credits ; Rolling Home (T)

Ben Moor
Curtis Brown, Haymarket House, 28-29 Haymarket, London
SW1Y 4SP
t 020 7396 6600 **f** 020 7396 0110 **e** cb@curtisbrown.co.uk
Credits ; My Last Week with Modolia (T)

Davey Moore
Culverhouse & James Personal Management, Shepperton
Studios, Studio Road, Shepperton TW17 0QD
t 01932 592151 **f** 01932 592233
e dculverhouse@onetel.net.uk **e** jilljames4@aol.com

Carmel Morgan
Peters Fraser & Dunlop, Drury House, 34-43 Russell Street,
London WC2B 5HA
t 020 7344 1000 **f** 020 7836 9543
e postmaster@pfd.co.uk **w** www.pfd.co.uk

Peter Morgan
International Creative Management Ltd, Oxford House,
76 Oxford Street, London W1D 1BS
t 020 7636 6565 **f** 020 7323 0101 **w** www.icmlondon.co.uk

Michael Morpurgo
London Management & Representation, 2-4 Noel Street,
London W1F 8GB
t 020 7287 9000 **f** 020 7287 3236
Credits Out Of The Ashes (T)

Grant Morris
The Dench Arnold Agency, 24 D'Arblay Street, London W1F 8EH
t 020 7437 4551 **f** 020 7439 1355
e contact@dencharnoldagency.co.uk **w** www.dencharnold.co.uk

Judy Morris
International Creative Management Ltd, Oxford House,
76 Oxford Street, London W1D 1BS
t 020 7636 6565 **f** 020 7323 0101 **w** www.icmlondon.co.uk

Stuart Morris
Culverhouse & James Personal Management, Shepperton
Studios, Studio Road, Shepperton TW17 0QD
t 01932 592151 **f** 01932 592233
e dculverhouse@onetel.net.uk **e** jilljames4@aol.com

Bill Morrison
Alan Brodie Representation, 211 Piccadilly, London W1J 9HF
t 020 7917 2871 **f** 020 7917 2872
e info@alanbrodie.com **w** www.alanbrodie.com

Blake Morrison
Peters Fraser & Dunlop, Drury House, 34-43 Russell Street,
London WC2B 5HA
t 020 7344 1000 **f** 020 7836 9543
e postmaster@pfd.co.uk **w** www.pfd.co.uk

John Morrison
Culverhouse & James Personal Management, Shepperton Studios, Studio Road, Shepperton TW17 0QD
t 01932 592151 **f** 01932 592233
e dculverhouse@onetel.net.uk **e** jilljames4@aol.com

Sir John Mortimer QC CBE
Peters Fraser & Dunlop, Drury House, 34-43 Russell Street, London WC2B 5HA
t 020 7344 1000 **f** 020 7836 9543
e postmaster@pfd.co.uk **w** www.pfd.co.uk

Chloe Moss
Casarotto Ramsay & Associates Ltd, National House, 60-66 Wardour Street, London W1V 4ND
t 020 7287 4450 **f** 020 7287 9128
e agents@casarotto.uk.com **w** www.casarotto.uk.com

Simon Moss
Peters Fraser & Dunlop, Drury House, 34-43 Russell Street, London WC2B 5HA
t 020 7344 1000 **f** 020 7836 9543
e postmaster@pfd.co.uk **w** www.pfd.co.uk

Stephen Mulrine
Alan Brodie Representation, 211 Piccadilly, London W1J 9HF
t 020 7917 2871 **f** 020 7917 2872
e info@alanbrodie.com **w** www.alanbrodie.com

Rona Munro
International Creative Management Ltd, Oxford House, 76 Oxford Street, London W1D 1BS
t 020 7636 6565 **f** 020 7323 0101 **w** www.icmlondon.co.uk

Jimmy Murphy
Casarotto Ramsay & Associates Ltd, National House, 60-66 Wardour Street, London W1V 4ND
t 020 7287 4450 **f** 020 7287 9128
e agents@casarotto.uk.com **w** www.casarotto.uk.com

Phyllis Nagy
Casarotto Ramsay & Associates Ltd, National House, 60-66 Wardour Street, London W1V 4ND
t 020 7287 4450 **f** 020 7287 9128
e agents@casarotto.uk.com **w** www.casarotto.uk.com

Trevor Neal
Casarotto Ramsay & Associates Ltd, National House, 60-66 Wardour Street, London W1V 4ND
t 020 7287 4450 **f** 020 7287 9128
e agents@casarotto.uk.com **w** www.casarotto.uk.com

Nick Newman
Casarotto Ramsay & Associates Ltd, National House, 60-66 Wardour Street, London W1V 4ND
t 020 7287 4450 **f** 020 7287 9128
e agents@casarotto.uk.com **w** www.casarotto.uk.com

Nicholas Hicks-Beach & Shelley Miller
Peters Fraser & Dunlop, Drury House, 34-43 Russell Street, London WC2B 5HA
t 020 7344 1000 **f** 020 7836 9543
e postmaster@pfd.co.uk **w** www.pfd.co.uk

David Nicholls
International Creative Management Ltd, Oxford House, 76 Oxford Street, London W1D 1BS
t 020 7636 6565 **f** 020 7323 0101 **w** www.icmlondon.co.uk

Peter Nichols
Alan Brodie Representation, 211 Piccadilly, London W1J 9HF
t 020 7917 2871 **f** 020 7917 2872
e info@alanbrodie.com **w** www.alanbrodie.com

William Nicholson
Peters Fraser & Dunlop, Drury House, 34-43 Russell Street, London WC2B 5HA
t 020 7344 1000 **f** 020 7836 9543
e postmaster@pfd.co.uk **w** www.pfd.co.uk

Susan Nickson
Casarotto Ramsay & Associates Ltd, National House, 60-66 Wardour Street, London W1V 4ND
t 020 7287 4450 **f** 020 7287 9128
e agents@casarotto.uk.com **w** www.casarotto.uk.com

Carol Noble
International Creative Management Ltd, Oxford House, 76 Oxford Street, London W1D 1BS
t 020 7636 6565 **f** 020 7323 0101 **w** www.icmlondon.co.uk

Jeff Noon
Michelle Kass Associates, 36-38 Glasshouse Street, London W1B 5DL
t 020 7439 1624 **f** 020 7734 3394

Sam North
Casarotto Ramsay & Associates Ltd, National House, 60-66 Wardour Street, London W1V 4ND
t 020 7287 4450 **f** 020 7287 9128
e agents@casarotto.uk.com **w** www.casarotto.uk.com

Sally Norton
Peters Fraser & Dunlop, Drury House, 34-43 Russell Street, London WC2B 5HA
t 020 7344 1000 **f** 020 7836 9543
e postmaster@pfd.co.uk **w** www.pfd.co.uk

Jonathan Nossiter
Curtis Brown, Haymarket House, 28-29 Haymarket, London SW1Y 4SP
t 020 7396 6600 **f** 020 7396 0110 **e** cb@curtisbrown.co.uk
Credits ; Sunday (T)

Lisa O'Donnell
London Management & Representation, 2-4 Noel Street, London W1F 8GB
t 020 7287 9000 **f** 020 7287 3236

Sean O'Hagan
Casarotto Ramsay & Associates Ltd, National House, 60-66 Wardour Street, London W1V 4ND
t 020 7287 4450 **f** 020 7287 9128
e agents@casarotto.uk.com **w** www.casarotto.uk.com

Eugene O'Brian
Curtis Brown, Haymarket House, 28-29 Haymarket, London SW1Y 4SP
t 020 7396 6600 **f** 020 7396 0110 **e** cb@curtisbrown.co.uk
Credits ; Pure Mule (T)

Harriet O'Carroll
Peters Fraser & Dunlop, Drury House, 34-43 Russell Street, London WC2B 5HA
t 020 7344 1000 **f** 020 7836 9543
e postmaster@pfd.co.uk **w** www.pfd.co.uk

Jo O'Keefe
Peters Fraser & Dunlop, Drury House, 34-43 Russell Street, London WC2B 5HA
t 020 7344 1000 **f** 020 7836 9543
e postmaster@pfd.co.uk **w** www.pfd.co.uk

Mary O'Malley
Alan Brodie Representation, 211 Piccadilly, London W1J 9HF
t 020 7917 2871 **f** 020 7917 2872
e info@alanbrodie.com **w** www.alanbrodie.com

Mark O'Rowe
Curtis Brown, Haymarket House, 28-29 Haymarket, London SW1Y 4SP
t 020 7396 6600 **f** 020 7396 0110 **e** cb@curtisbrown.co.uk

Phil O'Shea
The Dench Arnold Agency, 24 D'Arblay Street, London W1F 8EH
t 020 7437 4551 **f** 020 7439 1355
e contact@dencharnoldagency.co.uk **w** www.dencharnold.co.uk

Meredith Oakes
Casarotto Ramsay & Associates Ltd, National House, 60-66 Wardour Street, London W1V 4ND
t 020 7287 4450 **f** 020 7287 9128
e agents@casarotto.uk.com **w** www.casarotto.uk.com

Richard Ommanney
Curtis Brown, Haymarket House, 28-29 Haymarket, London SW1Y 4SP
t 020 7396 6600 **f** 020 7396 0110 **e** cb@curtisbrown.co.uk
Credits ; Three Up, Two Down (T)

Rosamund Orde-Powlett
Curtis Brown, Haymarket House, 28-29 Haymarket, London SW1Y 4SP
t 020 7396 6600 **f** 020 7396 0110 **e** cb@curtisbrown.co.uk
Credits ; The Surgeon (T)

Will Osborne
Peters Fraser & Dunlop, Drury House, 34-43 Russell Street, London WC2B 5HA
t 020 7344 1000 **f** 020 7836 9543
e postmaster@pfd.co.uk **w** www.pfd.co.uk

Philip Osment
Alan Brodie Representation, 211 Piccadilly, London W1J 9HF
t 020 7917 2871 **f** 020 7917 2872
e info@alanbrodie.com **w** www.alanbrodie.com

Howard Overman
Peters Fraser & Dunlop, Drury House, 34-43 Russell Street, London WC2B 5HA
t 020 7344 1000 **f** 020 7836 9543
e postmaster@pfd.co.uk **w** www.pfd.co.uk

Gary Owen
International Creative Management Ltd, Oxford House, 76 Oxford Street, London W1D 1BS
t 020 7636 6565 **f** 020 7323 0101 **w** www.icmlondon.co.uk

Allen Palmer
Casarotto Ramsay & Associates Ltd, National House, 60-66 Wardour Street, London W1V 4ND
t 020 7287 4450 **f** 020 7287 9128
e agents@casarotto.uk.com **w** www.casarotto.uk.com

Philip Palmer
Curtis Brown, Haymarket House, 28-29 Haymarket, London SW1Y 4SP
t 020 7396 6600 **f** 020 7396 0110 **e** cb@curtisbrown.co.uk
Credits ; Rebus - Dead Souls (T)

Gary Parker
Casarotto Ramsay & Associates Ltd, National House, 60-66 Wardour Street, London W1V 4ND
t 020 7287 4450 **f** 020 7287 9128
e agents@casarotto.uk.com **w** www.casarotto.uk.com

Ged Parsons
Casarotto Ramsay & Associates Ltd, National House, 60-66 Wardour Street, London W1V 4ND
t 020 7287 4450 **f** 020 7287 9128
e agents@casarotto.uk.com **w** www.casarotto.uk.com

Stuart Paterson
Alan Brodie Representation, 211 Piccadilly, London W1J 9HF
t 020 7917 2871 **f** 020 7917 2872
e info@alanbrodie.com **w** www.alanbrodie.com

Ian Pattison
Peters Fraser & Dunlop, Drury House, 34-43 Russell Street, London WC2B 5HA
t 020 7344 1000 **f** 020 7836 9543
e postmaster@pfd.co.uk **w** www.pfd.co.uk

Stel Pavlou
Linda Seifert Management, 91 Berwick Street, London W1F 0NE
t 020 7292 7390 **f** 020 7292 7391
e contact@lindaseifert.com **w** www.lindaseifert.com

Daniel Peacock
Linda Seifert Management, 91 Berwick Street, London W1F 0NE
t 020 7292 7390 **f** 020 7292 7391
e contact@lindaseifert.com **w** www.lindaseifert.com

Edwin Pearce
Peters Fraser & Dunlop, Drury House, 34-43 Russell Street, London WC2B 5HA
t 020 7344 1000 **f** 020 7836 9543
e postmaster@pfd.co.uk **w** www.pfd.co.uk

Colin Heber Pearcy
Peters Fraser & Dunlop, Drury House, 34-43 Russell Street, London WC2B 5HA
t 020 7344 1000 **f** 020 7836 9543
e postmaster@pfd.co.uk **w** www.pfd.co.uk

Allison Pearson
Peters Fraser & Dunlop, Drury House, 34-43 Russell Street, London WC2B 5HA
t 020 7344 1000 **f** 020 7836 9543
e postmaster@pfd.co.uk **w** www.pfd.co.uk

Joe Penhall
Curtis Brown, Haymarket House, 28-29 Haymarket, London SW1Y 4SP
t 020 7396 6600 **f** 020 7396 0110 **e** cb@curtisbrown.co.uk
Credits Last King of Scotland (F); Enduring Love (F)

Julian Perkins
Culverhouse & James Personal Management, Shepperton Studios, Studio Road, Shepperton TW17 0QD
t 01932 592151 **f** 01932 592233
e dculverhouse@onetel.net.uk **e** jilljames4@aol.com

Adam Pernak
Casarotto Ramsay & Associates Ltd, National House, 60-66 Wardour Street, London W1V 4ND
t 020 7287 4450 **f** 020 7287 9128
e agents@casarotto.uk.com **w** www.casarotto.uk.com

Arzhang Pezhman
Curtis Brown, Haymarket House, 28-29 Haymarket, London SW1Y 4SP
t 020 7396 6600 **f** 020 7396 0110 **e** cb@curtisbrown.co.uk

Sarah Phelps
Peters Fraser & Dunlop, Drury House, 34-43 Russell Street, London WC2B 5HA
t 020 7344 1000 **f** 020 7836 9543
e postmaster@pfd.co.uk **w** www.pfd.co.uk

Holly Phillips
International Creative Management Ltd, Oxford House, 76 Oxford Street, London W1D 1BS
t 020 7636 6565 **f** 020 7323 0101 **w** www.icmlondon.co.uk

Giles Pilbrow
London Management & Representation, 2-4 Noel Street,
London W1F 8GB
t 020 7287 9000 **f** 020 7287 3236
Credits 2DTV (T)

Darryl Pinckney
Peters Fraser & Dunlop, Drury House, 34-43 Russell Street,
London WC2B 5HA
t 020 7344 1000 **f** 020 7836 9543
e postmaster@pfd.co.uk **w** www.pfd.co.uk

Alan Pollock
Alan Brodie Representation, 211 Piccadilly, London W1J 9HF
t 020 7917 2871 **f** 020 7917 2872
e info@alanbrodie.com **w** www.alanbrodie.com

Bernard Pomerance
Alan Brodie Representation, 211 Piccadilly, London W1J 9HF
t 020 7917 2871 **f** 020 7917 2872
e info@alanbrodie.com **w** www.alanbrodie.com

Eve Pomerance
Alan Brodie Representation, 211 Piccadilly, London W1J 9HF
t 020 7917 2871 **f** 020 7917 2872
e info@alanbrodie.com **w** www.alanbrodie.com

Jeff Pope
Peters Fraser & Dunlop, Drury House, 34-43 Russell Street,
London WC2B 5HA
t 020 7344 1000 **f** 020 7836 9543
e postmaster@pfd.co.uk **w** www.pfd.co.uk

Mike Poulton
Alan Brodie Representation, 211 Piccadilly, London W1J 9HF
t 020 7917 2871 **f** 020 7917 2872
e info@alanbrodie.com **w** www.alanbrodie.com

Paul Powell
Casarotto Ramsay & Associates Ltd, National House,
60-66 Wardour Street, London W1V 4ND
t 020 7287 4450 **f** 020 7287 9128
e agents@casarotto.uk.com **w** www.casarotto.uk.com

John Preston
Peters Fraser & Dunlop, Drury House, 34-43 Russell Street,
London WC2B 5HA
t 020 7344 1000 **f** 020 7836 9543
e postmaster@pfd.co.uk **w** www.pfd.co.uk

Rebecca Prichard
Casarotto Ramsay & Associates Ltd, National House,
60-66 Wardour Street, London W1V 4ND
t 020 7287 4450 **f** 020 7287 9128
e agents@casarotto.uk.com **w** www.casarotto.uk.com

Georgia Prichett
Peters Fraser & Dunlop, Drury House, 34-43 Russell Street,
London WC2B 5HA
t 020 7344 1000 **f** 020 7836 9543
e postmaster@pfd.co.uk **w** www.pfd.co.uk

Jonathan Priest
40 Brodrick Road, London SW17 7DY
t 020 8767 0811 **f** 020 8767 9546 **m** 07973 406 417
e scripts@creative-writer.com **w** www.creative-writer.com

Peter Prince
Casarotto Ramsay & Associates Ltd, National House,
60-66 Wardour Street, London W1V 4ND
t 020 7287 4450 **f** 020 7287 9128
e agents@casarotto.uk.com **w** www.casarotto.uk.com

Deirdre Purcell
Curtis Brown, Haymarket House, 28-29 Haymarket, London
SW1Y 4SP
t 020 7396 6600 **f** 020 7396 0110 **e** cb@curtisbrown.co.uk
Credits Falling For A Dancer (T)

Neal Purvis
Casarotto Ramsay & Associates Ltd, National House,
60-66 Wardour Street, London W1V 4ND
t 020 7287 4450 **f** 020 7287 9128
e agents@casarotto.uk.com **w** www.casarotto.uk.com

Joanna Quesnel
Peters Fraser & Dunlop, Drury House, 34-43 Russell Street,
London WC2B 5HA
t 020 7344 1000 **f** 020 7836 9543
e postmaster@pfd.co.uk **w** www.pfd.co.uk

Roy Radford
Contemporary Quills, Buttercup Cottage Studio, South Zeal,
Okehampton EX20 2JU
t 01837 840547 **f** 01837 840547
e timestealers@onetel.net.uk
Credits Time Stealers (A); Heritage Of A Market Town (D); Sincerely
Yours Faihtfully (T)

Ursula Rani Sarma
Casarotto Ramsay & Associates Ltd, National House,
60-66 Wardour Street, London W1V 4ND
t 020 7287 4450 **f** 020 7287 9128
e agents@casarotto.uk.com **w** www.casarotto.uk.com

Peter Ransley
Peters Fraser & Dunlop, Drury House, 34-43 Russell Street,
London WC2B 5HA
t 020 7344 1000 **f** 020 7836 9543
e postmaster@pfd.co.uk **w** www.pfd.co.uk

Frederic Raphael
Alan Brodie Representation, 211 Piccadilly, London W1J 9HF
t 020 7917 2871 **f** 020 7917 2872
e info@alanbrodie.com **w** www.alanbrodie.com

Andy Rattenbury
International Creative Management Ltd, Oxford House,
76 Oxford Street, London W1D 1BS
t 020 7636 6565 **f** 020 7323 0101 **w** www.icmlondon.co.uk

Terence Rattigan
Alan Brodie Representation, 211 Piccadilly, London W1J 9HF
t 020 7917 2871 **f** 020 7917 2872
e info@alanbrodie.com **w** www.alanbrodie.com

Mark Ravenhill
Casarotto Ramsay & Associates Ltd, National House,
60-66 Wardour Street, London W1V 4ND
t 020 7287 4450 **f** 020 7287 9128
e agents@casarotto.uk.com **w** www.casarotto.uk.com

Jay Rayner
Peters Fraser & Dunlop, Drury House, 34-43 Russell Street,
London WC2B 5HA
t 020 7344 1000 **f** 020 7836 9543
e postmaster@pfd.co.uk **w** www.pfd.co.uk

Corin Redgrave
Alan Brodie Representation, 211 Piccadilly, London W1J 9HF
t 020 7917 2871 **f** 020 7917 2872
e info@alanbrodie.com **w** www.alanbrodie.com

Nick Reed
Peters Fraser & Dunlop, Drury House, 34-43 Russell Street,
London WC2B 5HA
t 020 7344 1000 **f** 020 7836 9543
e postmaster@pfd.co.uk **w** www.pfd.co.uk

Morna Regan
Alan Brodie Representation, 211 Piccadilly, London W1J 9HF
t 020 7917 2871 **f** 020 7917 2872
e info@alanbrodie.com **w** www.alanbrodie.com

Christina Reid
Alan Brodie Representation, 211 Piccadilly, London W1J 9HF
t 020 7917 2871 **f** 020 7917 2872
e info@alanbrodie.com **w** www.alanbrodie.com

David Reid
Peters Fraser & Dunlop, Drury House, 34-43 Russell Street,
London WC2B 5HA
t 020 7344 1000 **f** 020 7836 9543
e postmaster@pfd.co.uk **w** www.pfd.co.uk

John Retallack
Alan Brodie Representation, 211 Piccadilly, London W1J 9HF
t 020 7917 2871 **f** 020 7917 2872
e info@alanbrodie.com **w** www.alanbrodie.com

Anna Reynolds
International Creative Management Ltd, Oxford House,
76 Oxford Street, London W1D 1BS
t 020 7636 6565 **f** 020 7323 0101 **w** www.icmlondon.co.uk

Yasmina Reza
Casarotto Ramsay & Associates Ltd, National House,
60-66 Wardour Street, London W1V 4ND
t 020 7287 4450 **f** 020 7287 9128
e agents@casarotto.uk.com **w** www.casarotto.uk.com

Graham Rhodes
35A Esplanade Road, Scarborough YO11 2AT
t 01723 367251 **m** 07774 415674
e grhodes@globalnet.co.uk
w www.geocities.com/grahamrhodes
Credits Drug Rape (E); Yager (W); Launch - Volkswagen Golf (I); Life Of
Beatrix Potter (D)

Frank Ricarby
International Creative Management Ltd, Oxford House,
76 Oxford Street, London W1D 1BS
t 020 7636 6565 **f** 020 7323 0101 **w** www.icmlondon.co.uk

Stephen Rice
PO Box 5714, West Mersea CO5 8UH
t 01206 385586 **f** 01206 385586
e riceys@screamings.freeserve.co.uk
w www.screamings.freeserve.co.uk
Credits Between The Wars (S)

Jonathan Rich
Peters Fraser & Dunlop, Drury House, 34-43 Russell Street,
London WC2B 5HA
t 020 7344 1000 **f** 020 7836 9543
e postmaster@pfd.co.uk **w** www.pfd.co.uk

Jamie Richards
Casarotto Ramsay & Associates Ltd, National House,
60-66 Wardour Street, London W1V 4ND
t 020 7287 4450 **f** 020 7287 9128
e agents@casarotto.uk.com **w** www.casarotto.uk.com

Jonathan Richardson
Curtis Brown, Haymarket House, 28-29 Haymarket, London
SW1Y 4SP
t 020 7396 6600 **f** 020 7396 0110 **e** cb@curtisbrown.co.uk
Credits Two Minus One (S); Stone Tears (S)

Gillian Richmond
Casarotto Ramsay & Associates Ltd, National House,
60-66 Wardour Street, London W1V 4ND
t 020 7287 4450 **f** 020 7287 9128
e agents@casarotto.uk.com **w** www.casarotto.uk.com

Riley & Cecil
Curtis Brown, Haymarket House, 28-29 Haymarket, London
SW1Y 4SP
t 020 7396 6600 **f** 020 7396 0110 **e** cb@curtisbrown.co.uk
Credits Puny Humans (T); Black Books (T); Gnomes (A)

Aileen Ritchie
Casarotto Ramsay & Associates Ltd, National House,
60-66 Wardour Street, London W1V 4ND
t 020 7287 4450 **f** 020 7287 9128
e agents@casarotto.uk.com **w** www.casarotto.uk.com

Robert Lambolle Services (Reading & Righting)
618B Finchley Road, London NW11 7RR
t 020 8455 4564 **f** 020 8455 4564
e ziph@macunlimited.net
w http://readingandrighting.netfirms.com
Contact Robert Lambolle, Director

June Roberts
Peters Fraser & Dunlop, Drury House, 34-43 Russell Street,
London WC2B 5HA
t 020 7344 1000 **f** 020 7836 9543 **e** postmaster@pfd.co.uk
w www.pfd.co.uk

Rony Robinson
Peters Fraser & Dunlop, Drury House, 34-43 Russell Street,
London WC2B 5HA
t 020 7344 1000 **f** 020 7836 9543
e postmaster@pfd.co.uk **w** www.pfd.co.uk

Tony Roche
Casarotto Ramsay & Associates Ltd, National House,
60-66 Wardour Street, London W1V 4ND
t 020 7287 4450 **f** 020 7287 9128
e agents@casarotto.uk.com **w** www.casarotto.uk.com

Kenneth Rock
61 Parry Road, Ashmore Park, Wolverhampton WV11 2PS
t 01902 722729 **f** 01902 722729 **m** 07740 244646
e kenneth.rock@btinternet.com **w** www.bscw.co.uk

Christopher Rodriguez
Alan Brodie Representation, 211 Piccadilly, London W1J 9HF
t 020 7917 2871 **f** 020 7917 2872
e info@alanbrodie.com **w** www.alanbrodie.com

Jane Rogers
Peters Fraser & Dunlop, Drury House, 34-43 Russell Street,
London WC2B 5HA
t 020 7344 1000 **f** 020 7836 9543
e postmaster@pfd.co.uk **w** www.pfd.co.uk

Nicholas Rohl
Casarotto Ramsay & Associates Ltd, National House,
60-66 Wardour Street, London W1V 4ND
t 020 7287 4450 **f** 020 7287 9128
e agents@casarotto.uk.com **w** www.casarotto.uk.com

Tim Rose Price
London Management & Representation, 2-4 Noel Street,
London W1F 8GB
t 020 7287 9000 **f** 020 7287 3236
Credits The Serpent's Kiss (F); Rapa Nui (F); A Dangerous Man (T)

Michael Rosen
Peters Fraser & Dunlop, Drury House, 34-43 Russell Street,
London WC2B 5HA
t 020 7344 1000 **f** 020 7836 9543
e postmaster@pfd.co.uk **w** www.pfd.co.uk

Amy Rosenthal
Casarotto Ramsay & Associates Ltd, National House,
60-66 Wardour Street, London W1V 4ND
t 020 7287 4450 **f** 020 7287 9128
e agents@casarotto.uk.com **w** www.casarotto.uk.com

Jack Rosenthal
Casarotto Ramsay & Associates Ltd, National House,
60-66 Wardour Street, London W1V 4ND
t 020 7287 4450 **f** 020 7287 9128
e agents@casarotto.uk.com **w** www.casarotto.uk.com

Miles Ross
Peters Fraser & Dunlop, Drury House, 34-43 Russell Street,
London WC2B 5HA
t 020 7344 1000 **f** 020 7836 9543
e postmaster@pfd.co.uk **w** www.pfd.co.uk

James Rourke
Peters Fraser & Dunlop, Drury House, 34-43 Russell Street,
London WC2B 5HA
t 020 7344 1000 **f** 020 7836 9543
e postmaster@pfd.co.uk **w** www.pfd.co.uk

Ben Rowell
Peters Fraser & Dunlop, Drury House, 34-43 Russell Street,
London WC2B 5HA
t 020 7344 1000 **f** 020 7836 9543
e postmaster@pfd.co.uk **w** www.pfd.co.uk

David Rudkin
Casarotto Ramsay & Associates Ltd, National House,
60-66 Wardour Street, London W1V 4ND
t 020 7287 4450 **f** 020 7287 9128
e agents@casarotto.uk.com **w** www.casarotto.uk.com

Jack Russell
Peters Fraser & Dunlop, Drury House, 34-43 Russell Street,
London WC2B 5HA
t 020 7344 1000 **f** 020 7836 9543
e postmaster@pfd.co.uk **w** www.pfd.co.uk

Willy Russell
Casarotto Ramsay & Associates Ltd, National House,
60-66 Wardour Street, London W1V 4ND
t 020 7287 4450 **f** 020 7287 9128
e agents@casarotto.uk.com **w** www.casarotto.uk.com

Catherine Ryan
14 Course Road, Ascot SL5 7HL
t 01344 626399 **m** 07973 748244
e cath.ryan@cryan.demon.co.uk

Hugh Rycroft
London Management & Representation, 2-4 Noel Street,
London W1F 8GB
t 020 7287 9000 **f** 020 7287 3236

Tad Safran
Peters Fraser & Dunlop, Drury House, 34-43 Russell Street,
London WC2B 5HA
t 020 7344 1000 **f** 020 7836 9543
e postmaster@pfd.co.uk **w** www.pfd.co.uk

Clara Salaman
Peters Fraser & Dunlop, Drury House, 34-43 Russell Street,
London WC2B 5HA
t 020 7344 1000 **f** 020 7836 9543
e postmaster@pfd.co.uk **w** www.pfd.co.uk

Kevin Sampson
Peters Fraser & Dunlop, Drury House, 34-43 Russell Street,
London WC2B 5HA
t 020 7344 1000 **f** 020 7836 9543
e postmaster@pfd.co.uk **w** www.pfd.co.uk

Leslie Sands
Peters Fraser & Dunlop, Drury House, 34-43 Russell Street,
London WC2B 5HA
t 020 7344 1000 **f** 020 7836 9543
e postmaster@pfd.co.uk **w** www.pfd.co.uk

Lee Santana
Casarotto Ramsay & Associates Ltd, National House,
60-66 Wardour Street, London W1V 4ND
t 020 7287 4450 **f** 020 7287 9128
e agents@casarotto.uk.com **w** www.casarotto.uk.com

Tony Sarchet
London Management & Representation, 2-4 Noel Street,
London W1F 8GB
t 020 7287 9000 **f** 020 7287 3236
Credits High Stakes (T)

James Saunders
Casarotto Ramsay & Associates Ltd, National House,
60-66 Wardour Street, London W1V 4ND
t 020 7287 4450 **f** 020 7287 9128
e agents@casarotto.uk.com **w** www.casarotto.uk.com

David Savage
Brie Burkeman, 14 Neville Court, Abbey Road, London NW8 9DD
t 07092 239113 **f** 07092 239111 **e** brie.burkeman@mail.com

SCA Scripts
177 Bideford Green, Linslade, Leighton Buzzard LU7 2TS
t 01908 262560 **f** 01908 267078 **e** writers@northern-light.co.uk
Contact Stewart Hildred, Writer

Joanna Scanlan
International Creative Management Ltd, Oxford House,
76 Oxford Street, London W1D 1BS
t 020 7636 6565 **f** 020 7323 0101 **w** www.icmlondon.co.uk

Eric-Emmanuel Schmitt
Alan Brodie Representation, 211 Piccadilly, London W1J 9HF
t 020 7917 2871 **f** 020 7917 2872
e info@alanbrodie.com **w** www.alanbrodie.com

Claire Schrader
Michelle Kass Associates, 36-38 Glasshouse Street, London
W1B 5DL
t 020 7439 1624 **f** 020 7734 3394

Howard Schuman
Casarotto Ramsay & Associates Ltd, National House,
60-66 Wardour Street, London W1V 4ND
t 020 7287 4450 **f** 020 7287 9128
e agents@casarotto.uk.com **w** www.casarotto.uk.com

Debé Scott
6 Stoney Lane, Thaxted CM6 2PF
t 01371 831613
e fadein@onetel.net.uk **w** www.web.onetel.net.uk/~fadein
Credits Bird's Eye; Streaks-Ahead

Gavin Scott
Linda Seifert Management, 91 Berwick Street, London W1F 0NE
t 020 7292 7390 **f** 020 7292 7391
e contact@lindaseifert.com **w** www.lindaseifert.com

Scripts
St Johns Building, 43 Clerkenwell Road, London E1M 5RF
t 020 7608 2095 **t** 020 7253 6779 **f** 020 7608 1642
e scripts.typing@virgin.net
Contact Richard Linford, Chairman/Managing Director

Scriptwriting/Story Consultant
40 Cliftonville Road, Woolston, Warrington WA1 4BH
t 01925 813018 **f** 01925 813018 **m** 07944 857840
Contact Peter Tonkinson

*Coronation Street. Theatre. Comedy. Corporate Video. Script Editor.
Story Consultant.*

Gerald Seymour
Peters Fraser & Dunlop, Drury House, 34-43 Russell Street, London WC2B 5HA
t 020 7344 1000 **f** 020 7836 9543
e postmaster@pfd.co.uk **w** www.pfd.co.uk

Paulene Shannon
Culverhouse & James Personal Management, Shepperton Studios, Studio Road, Shepperton TW17 0QD
t 01932 592151 **f** 01932 592233
e dculverhouse@onetel.net.uk **e** jilljames4@aol.com

Alan Sharp
Peters Fraser & Dunlop, Drury House, 34-43 Russell Street, London WC2B 5HA
t 020 7344 1000 **f** 020 7836 9543
e postmaster@pfd.co.uk **w** www.pfd.co.uk

Wallace Shawn
Casarotto Ramsay & Associates Ltd, National House, 60-66 Wardour Street, London W1V 4ND
t 020 7287 4450 **f** 020 7287 9128
e agents@casarotto.uk.com **w** www.casarotto.uk.com

Ben Silburn
Casarotto Ramsay & Associates Ltd, National House, 60-66 Wardour Street, London W1V 4ND
t 020 7287 4450 **f** 020 7287 9128
e agents@casarotto.uk.com **w** www.casarotto.uk.com

Shawn Slovo
Casarotto Ramsay & Associates Ltd, National House, 60-66 Wardour Street, London W1V 4ND
t 020 7287 4450 **f** 020 7287 9128
e agents@casarotto.uk.com **w** www.casarotto.uk.com

Rob Shearman
Curtis Brown, Haymarket House, 28-29 Haymarket, London SW1Y 4SP
t 020 7396 6600 **f** 020 7396 0110 **e** cb@curtisbrown.co.uk

Kirsten Sheridan
Curtis Brown, Haymarket House, 28-29 Haymarket, London SW1Y 4SP
t 020 7396 6600 **f** 020 7396 0110 **e** cb@curtisbrown.co.uk
Credits The Bench (S); Patterns (S); Disco Pigs (F)

Ned Sherrin
Casarotto Ramsay & Associates Ltd, National House, 60-66 Wardour Street, London W1V 4ND
t 020 7287 4450 **f** 020 7287 9128
e agents@casarotto.uk.com **w** www.casarotto.uk.com

Colin Shindler
International Creative Management Ltd, Oxford House, 76 Oxford Street, London W1D 1BS
t 020 7636 6565 **f** 020 7323 0101 **w** www.icmlondon.co.uk

Frank Shouldice
Peters Fraser & Dunlop, Drury House, 34-43 Russell Street, London WC2B 5HA
t 020 7344 1000 **f** 020 7836 9543
e postmaster@pfd.co.uk **w** www.pfd.co.uk

Joe Shrapnel
Curtis Brown, Haymarket House, 28-29 Haymarket, London SW1Y 4SP
t 020 7396 6600 **f** 020 7396 0110 **e** cb@curtisbrown.co.uk
Credits Only Children (T)

Simon Sharkey
C/o Rochelle Stevens, 2 Terretts' Place, Upper Street, London N1 1QZ
t 020 7359 3900
Credits Down To Earth (T); The Bill (T); Murder In Mind (T)

Martin Sherman
Casarotto Ramsay & Associates Ltd, National House, 60-66 Wardour Street, London W1V 4ND
t 020 7287 4450 **f** 020 7287 9128
e agents@casarotto.uk.com **w** www.casarotto.uk.com

Peter Shrubshall
Casarotto Ramsay & Associates Ltd, National House, 60-66 Wardour Street, London W1V 4ND
t 020 7287 4450 **f** 020 7287 9128
e agents@casarotto.uk.com **w** www.casarotto.uk.com

Simon Stephens
Casarotto Ramsay & Associates Ltd, National House, 60-66 Wardour Street, London W1V 4ND
t 020 7287 4450 **f** 020 7287 9128
e agents@casarotto.uk.com **w** www.casarotto.uk.com

Dave Simpson
The Dench Arnold Agency, 24 D'Arblay Street, London W1F 8EH
t 020 7437 4551 **f** 020 7439 1355
e contact@dencharnoldagency.co.uk **w** www.dencharnold.co.uk

Julian Sims
Peters Fraser & Dunlop, Drury House, 34-43 Russell Street, London WC2B 5HA
t 020 7344 1000 **f** 020 7836 9543
e postmaster@pfd.co.uk **w** www.pfd.co.uk

Lemn Sissay
Peters Fraser & Dunlop, Drury House, 34-43 Russell Street, London WC2B 5HA
t 020 7344 1000 **f** 020 7836 9543
e postmaster@pfd.co.uk **w** www.pfd.co.uk

Steven Sivell
Brie Burkeman, 14 Neville Court, Abbey Road, London NW8 9DD
t 07092 239113 **f** 07092 239111 **e** brie.burkeman@mail.com

Madeleine Sizer
t 01366 382420 **m** 07785 540710 **e** riprods@msn.com

Michael Marshall Smith
Curtis Brown, Haymarket House, 28-29 Haymarket, London SW1Y 4SP
t 020 7396 6600 **f** 020 7396 0110 **e** cb@curtisbrown.co.uk

Murray Smith
Curtis Brown, Haymarket House, 28-29 Haymarket, London SW1Y 4SP
t 020 7396 6600 **f** 020 7396 0110 **e** cb@curtisbrown.co.uk
Credits Paradise Club (T); Legacy (T); The Fixer (T)

Neville Smith
Casarotto Ramsay & Associates Ltd, National House, 60-66 Wardour Street, London W1V 4ND
t 020 7287 4450 **f** 020 7287 9128
e agents@casarotto.uk.com **w** www.casarotto.uk.com

Olly Smith
C/o Ben Hall, Curtis Brown, Haymarket House, 28-29 Haymarket, London SW1Y 4SP
t 020 7396 6600 **f** 020 7396 0110 **f** 020 7396 0111
e info@ollysmith.co.uk **w** www.ollysmith.co.uk
Credits Metalheads (T); Bounty Hamster (T); Pingu (T); Hot Reels (T)

Steve Smith
Alan Brodie Representation, 211 Piccadilly, London W1J 9HF
t 020 7917 2871 **f** 020 7917 2872
e info@alanbrodie.com **w** www.alanbrodie.com

Sam Snape
83 Vanbrugh Court, Wincott Street, London SE11 4NR
t 020 7582 5148 **f** 020 7840 0352 **m** 07976 294896
e samsnape@aol.com
Credits Taming The East (F); Taps Workshop (E); Business Simulation (W); All Creatures Great And Small (T)

Ashmeed Sohoye
Curtis Brown, Haymarket House, 28-29 Haymarket, London SW1Y 4SP
t 020 7396 6600 f 020 7396 0110 e cb@curtisbrown.co.uk
Credits Tottenham I, II (T)

Andrea Solomons
London Management & Representation, 2-4 Noel Street, London W1F 8GB
t 020 7287 9000 f 020 7287 3236
Credits My Family (T)

Sam South
59 Frome House, Rye Hill Estate, Peckham Rye, London SE15 3JF
e sam.south@btinternet.com w www.belindablanchard.com
Credits Mr Bakewell (T); Letting Go @ Sophie's (T)

Dame Muriel Spark
Casarotto Ramsay & Associates Ltd, National House, 60-66 Wardour Street, London W1V 4ND
t 020 7287 4450 f 020 7287 9128
e agents@casarotto.uk.com w www.casarotto.uk.com

Si Spencer
Culverhouse & James Personal Management, Shepperton Studios, Studio Road, Shepperton TW17 0QD
t 01932 592151 f 01932 592233
e dculverhouse@onetel.net.uk e jilljames4@aol.com

Christian Spurrier
Peters Fraser & Dunlop, Drury House, 34-43 Russell Street, London WC2B 5HA
t 020 7344 1000 f 020 7836 9543
e postmaster@pfd.co.uk w www.pfd.co.uk

Marc Starbuck
Peters Fraser & Dunlop, Drury House, 34-43 Russell Street, London WC2B 5HA
t 020 7344 1000 f 020 7836 9543
e postmaster@pfd.co.uk w www.pfd.co.uk

Gordon Steel
Alan Brodie Representation, 211 Piccadilly, London W1J 9HF
t 020 7917 2871 f 020 7917 2872
e info@alanbrodie.com w www.alanbrodie.com

Jessica Stevenson
Casarotto Ramsay & Associates Ltd, National House, 60-66 Wardour Street, London W1V 4ND
t 020 7287 4450 f 020 7287 9128
e agents@casarotto.uk.com w www.casarotto.uk.com

Ena Lamont Stewart
Alan Brodie Representation, 211 Piccadilly, London W1J 9HF
t 020 7917 2871 f 020 7917 2872
e info@alanbrodie.com w www.alanbrodie.com

Brian Stirner
Michelle Kass Associates, 36-38 Glasshouse Street, London W1B 5DL
t 020 7439 1624 f 020 7734 3394

James Stock
Alan Brodie Representation, 211 Piccadilly, London W1J 9HF
t 020 7917 2871 f 020 7917 2872
e info@alanbrodie.com w www.alanbrodie.com

Richard Stoneman
Linda Seifert Management, 91 Berwick Street, London W1F ONE
t 020 7292 7390 f 020 7292 7391
e contact@lindaseifert.com w www.lindaseifert.com

Kay Stonham
Casarotto Ramsay & Associates Ltd, National House, 60-66 Wardour Street, London W1V 4ND
t 020 7287 4450 f 020 7287 9128
e agents@casarotto.uk.com w www.casarotto.uk.com

Tom Stoppard
Peters Fraser & Dunlop, Drury House, 34-43 Russell Street, London WC2B 5HA
t 020 7344 1000 f 020 7836 9543
e postmaster@pfd.co.uk w www.pfd.co.uk

David Storey
Peters Fraser & Dunlop, Drury House, 34-43 Russell Street, London WC2B 5HA
t 020 7344 1000 f 020 7836 9543
e postmaster@pfd.co.uk w www.pfd.co.uk

Mike Stott
Peters Fraser & Dunlop, Drury House, 34-43 Russell Street, London WC2B 5HA
t 020 7344 1000 f 020 7836 9543
e postmaster@pfd.co.uk w www.pfd.co.uk

Alexander Stuart
Peters Fraser & Dunlop, Drury House, 34-43 Russell Street, London WC2B 5HA
t 020 7344 1000 f 020 7836 9543
e postmaster@pfd.co.uk w www.pfd.co.uk

Allan Sutherland
London Management & Representation, 2-4 Noel Street, London W1F 8GB
t 020 7287 9000 f 020 7287 3236

Jason Sutton
International Creative Management Ltd, Oxford House, 76 Oxford Street, London W1D 1BS
t 020 7636 6565 f 020 7323 0101 w www.icmlondon.co.uk

Suzan St Maur
6 Mount Pleasant, Aspley Guise, Milton Keynes MK17 8LA
t 01908 587050 m 07767 354090
e suze@suzanstmaur.com w www.suzanstmaur.com
Contact Suzan Maur, Corporate Scriptwriter

Eamonn Sweeney
Peters Fraser & Dunlop, Drury House, 34-43 Russell Street, London WC2B 5HA
t 020 7344 1000 f 020 7836 9543
e postmaster@pfd.co.uk w www.pfd.co.uk

Michael Tait
Peters Fraser & Dunlop, Drury House, 34-43 Russell Street, London WC2B 5HA
t 020 7344 1000 f 020 7836 9543
e postmaster@pfd.co.uk w www.pfd.co.uk

CP Taylor
Alan Brodie Representation, 211 Piccadilly, London W1J 9HF
t 020 7917 2871 f 020 7917 2872
e info@alanbrodie.com w www.alanbrodie.com

Ken Taylor
Peters Fraser & Dunlop, Drury House, 34-43 Russell Street, London WC2B 5HA
t 020 7344 1000 f 020 7836 9543
e postmaster@pfd.co.uk w www.pfd.co.uk

Sue Teddern
Linda Seifert Management, 91 Berwick Street, London W1F ONE
t 020 7292 7390 f 020 7292 7391
e contact@lindaseifert.com w www.lindaseifert.com

Matthew Temple
1C Mabley Street, London E9 5RH
t 020 7682 1521 m 07941 000086
e matthewtemple@blueyonder.co.uk
Credits The 11 O'Clock Show (T)

Michael Thomas

Peters Fraser & Dunlop, Drury House, 34-43 Russell Street, London WC2B 5HA
t 020 7344 1000 **f** 020 7836 9543
e postmaster@pfd.co.uk **w** www.pfd.co.uk

Emma Thompson

Peters Fraser & Dunlop, Drury House, 34-43 Russell Street, London WC2B 5HA
t 020 7344 1000 **f** 020 7836 9543
e postmaster@pfd.co.uk **w** www.pfd.co.uk

Jane Thornton

Alan Brodie Representation, 211 Piccadilly, London W1J 9HF
t 020 7917 2871 **f** 020 7917 2872
e info@alanbrodie.com **w** www.alanbrodie.com

Jamie Thraves

Curtis Brown, Haymarket House, 28-29 Haymarket, London SW1Y 4SP
t 020 7396 6600 **f** 020 7396 0110 **e** cb@curtisbrown.co.uk
Credits The Low Down (F)

Derek Threadgall

10 Robjohns Road, Chelmsford CM1 3AF
t 01245 259806 **m** 07712 378320
Credits Welcome (I); British Gas (C)

Nick Tigg

Peters Fraser & Dunlop, Drury House, 34-43 Russell Street, London WC2B 5HA
t 020 7344 1000 **f** 020 7836 9543
e postmaster@pfd.co.uk **w** www.pfd.co.uk

Claire Tomalin

Peters Fraser & Dunlop, Drury House, 34-43 Russell Street, London WC2B 5HA
t 020 7344 1000 **f** 020 7836 9543
e postmaster@pfd.co.uk **w** www.pfd.co.uk

Peter Tong

Beacon House, Woodley Park, Skelmersdale WN8 6UR
t 01695 733310 **f** 01695 733310 **m** 07813 036405
e peter.tong@virgin.net
Credits Hitwoman (F); The Crematorium (F); Mrs H Of Baker Street (T); Gobsmacked (F)

Andy de la Tour

Peters Fraser & Dunlop, Drury House, 34-43 Russell Street, London WC2B 5HA
t 020 7344 1000 **f** 020 7836 9543
e postmaster@pfd.co.uk **w** www.pfd.co.uk

Catherine Tregenna

International Creative Management Ltd, Oxford House, 76 Oxford Street, London W1D 1BS
t 020 7636 6565 **f** 020 7323 0101 **w** www.icmlondon.co.uk

Michel Tremblay

Alan Brodie Representation, 211 Piccadilly, London W1J 9HF
t 020 7917 2871 **f** 020 7917 2872 **e** info@alanbrodie.com **w** www.alanbrodie.com

Martin Trenaman

Casarotto Ramsay & Associates Ltd, National House, 60-66 Wardour Street, London W1V 4ND
t 020 7287 4450 **f** 020 7287 9128
e agents@casarotto.uk.com **w** www.casarotto.uk.com

William Trevor

Peters Fraser & Dunlop, Drury House, 34-43 Russell Street, London WC2B 5HA
t 020 7344 1000 **f** 020 7836 9543
e postmaster@pfd.co.uk **w** www.pfd.co.uk

Paul Tucker

Casarotto Ramsay & Associates Ltd, National House, 60-66 Wardour Street, London W1V 4ND
t 020 7287 4450 **f** 020 7287 9128
e agents@casarotto.uk.com **w** www.casarotto.uk.com

Mark Tuohy

Alan Brodie Representation, 211 Piccadilly, London W1J 9HF
t 020 7917 2871 **f** 020 7917 2872
e info@alanbrodie.com **w** www.alanbrodie.com

Bert Tyler-Moore

Curtis Brown, Haymarket House, 28-29 Haymarket, London SW1Y 4SP
t 020 7396 6600 **f** 020 7396 0110 **e** cb@curtisbrown.co.uk
Credits Smack the Pony (T); The People's Harry Enfield (F)

Julian Unthank

Peters Fraser & Dunlop, Drury House, 34-43 Russell Street, London WC2B 5HA
t 020 7344 1000 **f** 020 7836 9543
e postmaster@pfd.co.uk **w** www.pfd.co.uk

Jjo Unwin

International Creative Management Ltd, Oxford House, 76 Oxford Street, London W1D 1BS
t 020 7636 6565 **f** 020 7323 0101 **w** www.icmlondon.co.uk

Andrew Upton

Peters Fraser & Dunlop, Drury House, 34-43 Russell Street, London WC2B 5HA
t 020 7344 1000 **f** 020 7836 9543
e postmaster@pfd.co.uk **w** www.pfd.co.uk

Stuart Urban

Linda Seifert Management, 91 Berwick Street, London W1F ONE
t 020 7292 7390 **f** 020 7292 7391
e contact@lindaseifert.com **w** www.lindaseifert.com

Ziggy Uszkurat

27 St Peters Street, Stamford PE9 2PS
t 01780 766934 **m** 07774 138245
e ziggy@zigzagfilms.com **w** www.zigzagfilms.com

David Varela

Alan Brodie Representation, 211 Piccadilly, London W1J 9HF
t 020 7917 2871 **f** 020 7917 2872
e info@alanbrodie.com **w** www.alanbrodie.com

Richard Vincent
Peters Fraser & Dunlop, Drury House, 34-43 Russell Street,
London WC2B 5HA
t 020 7344 1000 **f** 020 7836 9543
e postmaster@pfd.co.uk **w** www.pfd.co.uk

Nick Vivian
International Creative Management Ltd, Oxford House,
6 Oxford Street, London W1D 1BS
t 020 7636 6565 **f** 020 7323 0101 **w** www.icmlondon.co.uk

Stephen Volk
Linda Seifert Management, 91 Berwick Street, London W1F 0NE
t 020 7292 7390 **f** 020 7292 7391
e contact@lindaseifert.com **w** www.lindaseifert.com

Robert Wade
Casarotto Ramsay & Associates Ltd, National House,
60-66 Wardour Street, London W1V 4ND
t 020 7287 4450 **f** 020 7287 9128
e agents@casarotto.uk.com **w** www.casarotto.uk.com

Mark Wadlow
International Creative Management Ltd, Oxford House,
76 Oxford Street, London W1D 1BS
t 020 7636 6565 **f** 020 7323 0101 **w** www.icmlondon.co.uk

Mat Wakeham
Casarotto Ramsay & Associates Ltd, National House,
60-66 Wardour Street, London W1V 4ND
t 020 7287 4450 **f** 020 7287 9128
e agents@casarotto.uk.com **w** www.casarotto.uk.com

Stephen Wakelam
Alan Brodie Representation, 211 Piccadilly, London W1J 9HF
t 020 7917 2871 **f** 020 7917 2872
e info@alanbrodie.com **w** www.alanbrodie.com

Tina Walker
Culverhouse & James Personal Management, Shepperton
Studios, Studio Road, Shepperton TW17 0QD
t 01932 592151 **f** 01932 592233
e dculverhouse@onetel.net.uk **e** jilljames4@aol.com

Enda Walsh
Curtis Brown, Haymarket House, 28-29 Haymarket, London
SW1Y 4SP
t 020 7396 6600 **f** 020 7396 0110 **e** cb@curtisbrown.co.uk
Credits The Rose of Tralee (F)

Rupert Walters
Peters Fraser & Dunlop, Drury House, 34-43 Russell Street,
London WC2B 5HA
t 020 7344 1000 **f** 020 7836 9543
e postmaster@pfd.co.uk **w** www.pfd.co.uk

Ben Ward
Curtis Brown, Haymarket House, 28-29 Haymarket, London
SW1Y 4SP
t 020 7396 6600 **f** 020 7396 0110 **e** cb@curtisbrown.co.uk
Credits Tri-Zone (T); SMTV (T)

Julie Wassmer
Michelle Kass Associates, 36-38 Glasshouse Street, London
W1B 5DL
t 020 7439 1624 **f** 020 7734 3394

Fletcher Watkins
Peters Fraser & Dunlop, Drury House, 34-43 Russell Street,
London WC2B 5HA
t 020 7344 1000 **f** 020 7836 9543
e postmaster@pfd.co.uk **w** www.pfd.co.uk

James Watkins
Peters Fraser & Dunlop, Drury House, 34-43 Russell Street,
London WC2B 5HA
t 020 7344 1000 **f** 020 7836 9543
e postmaster@pfd.co.uk **w** www.pfd.co.uk

Lucy Watkins
Peters Fraser & Dunlop, Drury House, 34-43 Russell Street,
London WC2B 5HA
t 020 7344 1000 **f** 020 7836 9543
e postmaster@pfd.co.uk **w** www.pfd.co.uk

Andy Watts
London Management & Representation, 2-4 Noel Street,
London W1F 8GB
t 020 7287 9000 **f** 020 7287 3236
Credits My Parents Are Aliens (T)

Katharine Way
Peters Fraser & Dunlop, Drury House, 34-43 Russell Street,
London WC2B 5HA
t 020 7344 1000 **f** 020 7836 9543
e postmaster@pfd.co.uk **w** www.pfd.co.uk

Weatherone Ltd
178 Rectory Road, Sutton Coldfield B75 7RT
t 01212 404367 **f** 01216 816659 **m** 07767 277 952
e mart@weatherone.tv
Contact Mart Gottschalk, Executive Producer

Chris Webb
Peters Fraser & Dunlop, Drury House, 34-43 Russell Street,
London WC2B 5HA
t 020 7344 1000 **f** 020 7836 9543
e postmaster@pfd.co.uk **w** www.pfd.co.uk

Paul Webb
Peters Fraser & Dunlop, Drury House, 34-43 Russell Street,
London WC2B 5HA
t 020 7344 1000 **f** 020 7836 9543
e postmaster@pfd.co.uk **w** www.pfd.co.uk

Paula Webb
Jessica Carney Associates, Suite 90-92 Kent House,
87 Regent Street, London W1B 4EH
t 020 7434 4143 **f** 020 7434 4173
e info@jcarneyassociates.co.uk
Credits Baby Father (T)

Arabella Weir
Casarotto Ramsay & Associates Ltd, National House,
60-66 Wardour Street, London W1V 4ND
t 020 7287 4450 **f** 020 7287 9128
e agents@casarotto.uk.com **w** www.casarotto.uk.com

Fay Weldon
Casarotto Ramsay & Associates Ltd, National House,
60-66 Wardour Street, London W1V 4ND
t 020 7287 4450 **f** 020 7287 9128
e agents@casarotto.uk.com **w** www.casarotto.uk.com

Colin Welland
Peters Fraser & Dunlop, Drury House, 34-43 Russell Street,
London WC2B 5HA
t 020 7344 1000 **f** 020 7836 9543
e postmaster@pfd.co.uk **w** www.pfd.co.uk

Timberlake Wertenbaker
Casarotto Ramsay & Associates Ltd, National House,
60-66 Wardour Street, London W1V 4ND
t 020 7287 4450 **f** 020 7287 9128
e agents@casarotto.uk.com **w** www.casarotto.uk.com

Matthew Westwood
International Creative Management Ltd, Oxford House,
76 Oxford Street, London W1D 1BS
t 020 7636 6565 **f** 020 7323 0101 **w** www.icmlondon.co.uk

Iain Wetherby
Peters Fraser & Dunlop, Drury House, 34-43 Russell Street, London WC2B 5HA
t 020 7344 1000 **f** 020 7836 9543
e postmaster@pfd.co.uk **w** www.pfd.co.uk

Paul Wheeler
Peters Fraser & Dunlop, Drury House, 34-43 Russell Street, London WC2B 5HA
t 020 7344 1000 **f** 020 7836 9543
e postmaster@pfd.co.uk **w** www.pfd.co.uk

Philip Whitchurch
Casarotto Ramsay & Associates Ltd, National House, 60-66 Wardour Street, London W1V 4ND
t 020 7287 4450 **f** 020 7287 9128
e agents@casarotto.uk.com **w** www.casarotto.uk.com

Ted Whitehead
Casarotto Ramsay & Associates Ltd, National House, 60-66 Wardour Street, London W1V 4ND
t 020 7287 4450 **f** 020 7287 9128
e agents@casarotto.uk.com **w** www.casarotto.uk.com

Alan Whiting
The Dench Arnold Agency, 24 D'Arblay Street, London W1F 8EH
t 020 7437 4551 **f** 020 7439 1355
e contact@dencharnoldagency.co.uk **w** www.dencharnold.co.uk

Ed Whitmore
Peters Fraser & Dunlop, Drury House, 34-43 Russell Street, London WC2B 5HA
t 020 7344 1000 **f** 020 7836 9543
e postmaster@pfd.co.uk **w** www.pfd.co.uk

Marrisse Whittaker
Culverhouse & James Personal Management, Shepperton Studios, Studio Road, Shepperton TW17 0QD
t 01932 592151 **f** 01932 592233
e dculverhouse@onetel.net.uk **e** jilljames4@aol.com

Christopher Wicking
Michelle Kass Associates, 36-38 Glasshouse Street, London W1B 5DL
t 020 7439 1624 **f** 020 7734 3394

Dan Wicksman
88A High Street, Hornsey, London N8 7NU
t 020 8341 7139 **m** 07905 611762
e danwicksman@yahoo.co.uk
Agent Culverhouse & James Personal Management, Shepperton Studios, Studio Road, Shepperton TW17 0QD
t 01932 592151 **f** 01932 592233
e dculverhouse@onetel.net.uk **e** jilljames4@aol.com
Credits De Madra A Hija (F); The Tribe (T); Doctors (T); Gagging For It (T)

Michael Wilcox
Alan Brodie Representation, 211 Piccadilly, London W1J 9HF
t 020 7917 2871 **f** 020 7917 2872
e info@alanbrodie.com **w** www.alanbrodie.com

Emlyn Williams
Alan Brodie Representation, 211 Piccadilly, London W1J 9HF
t 020 7917 2871 **f** 020 7917 2872
e info@alanbrodie.com **w** www.alanbrodie.com

Roy Williams
Alan Brodie Representation, 211 Piccadilly, London W1J 9HF
t 020 7917 2871 **f** 020 7917 2872
e info@alanbrodie.com **w** www.alanbrodie.com

Phil Willmott
Curtis Brown, Haymarket House, 28-29 Haymarket, London SW1Y 4SP
t 020 7396 6600 **f** 020 7396 0110 **e** cb@curtisbrown.co.uk

Gerald Wilson
Brie Burkeman, 14 Neville Court, Abbey Road, London NW8 9DD
t 07092 239113 **f** 07092 239111 **e** brie.burkeman@mail.com

Tom Wnek
Peters Fraser & Dunlop, Drury House, 34-43 Russell Street, London WC2B 5HA
t 020 7344 1000 **f** 020 7836 9543
e postmaster@pfd.co.uk **w** www.pfd.co.uk

David Wolstencroft
Curtis Brown, Haymarket House, 28-29 Haymarket, London SW1Y 4SP
t 020 7396 6600 **f** 020 7396 0110 **e** cb@curtisbrown.co.uk
Credits Psychos (T); Jerusalem (T)

Annie Wood
Linda Seifert Management, 91 Berwick Street, London W1F 0NE
t 020 7292 7390 **f** 020 7292 7391
e contact@lindaseifert.com **w** www.lindaseifert.com

David Wood
Casarotto Ramsay & Associates Ltd, National House, 60-66 Wardour Street, London W1V 4ND
t 020 7287 4450 **f** 020 7287 9128
e agents@casarotto.uk.com **w** www.casarotto.uk.com

Kate Wood
The Dench Arnold Agency, 24 D'Arblay Street, London W1F 8EH
t 020 7437 4551 **f** 020 7439 1355
e contact@dencharnoldagency.co.uk **w** www.dencharnold.co.uk

Barry Woodward
Culverhouse & James Personal Management, Shepperton Studios, Studio Road, Shepperton TW17 0QD
t 01932 592151 **f** 01932 592233
e dculverhouse@onetel.net.uk **e** jilljames4@aol.com

Harry Wootliff
International Creative Management Ltd, Oxford House, 76 Oxford Street, London W1D 1BS
t 020 7636 6565 **f** 020 7323 0101 **w** www.icmlondon.co.uk

John Wrathall
Peters Fraser & Dunlop, Drury House, 34-43 Russell Street, London WC2B 5HA
t 020 7344 1000 **f** 020 7836 9543
e postmaster@pfd.co.uk **w** www.pfd.co.uk

Michael Wynne
International Creative Management Ltd, Oxford House, 76 Oxford Street, London W1D 1BS
t 020 7636 6565 **f** 020 7323 0101 **w** www.icmlondon.co.uk

Art Young
Culverhouse & James Personal Management, Shepperton Studios, Studio Road, Shepperton TW17 0QD
t 01932 592151 **f** 01932 592233
e dculverhouse@onetel.net.uk **e** jilljames4@aol.com

Richard Zajdlic
Peters Fraser & Dunlop, Drury House, 34-43 Russell Street, London WC2B 5HA
t 020 7344 1000 **f** 020 7836 9543
e postmaster@pfd.co.uk **w** www.pfd.co.uk

Michael Zucker
The Dench Arnold Agency, 24 D'Arblay Street, London W1F 8EH
t 020 7437 4551 **f** 020 7439 1355
e contact@dencharnoldagency.co.uk **w** www.dencharnold.co.uk

index : companies

AaCcDdEeFfGgHhIiJjKkLlMmNnOoPpQqRrSsTtUuVvWwXxYyZz

Wherever the action is

APTN Library

Contact Ed Everest, Rob Hollier or Jane Carroll:

Tel +44 (0)121 327 2021   Fax +44 (0)121 327 7021

email 021info@carltontv.co.uk   web www.carlton021.net

CARLTON
O21

Banana *split*

Carlton 021

AaBbCcDdEeFfGgHhIiJjKkLlMmNnOoPpQqRrSsTtUuVvWwXxYyZz

AaBbCcDdEeFfGgHhIiJjKkLlMmNnOoPpQqRrSsTtUuVvWwXxYyZz

Carlton 021

AaBbCcDdEeFfGgHhIiJjKkLlMmNnOoPpQqRrSsTtUuVvWwXxYyZz

Wherever the action is

AaBbCcDdEeFfGgHhIiJjKkLlMmNnOoPpQqRrSsTtUuVvWwXxYyZz

|---|---|
Debbie Shepherd Casting	155
Deborah Goodman Publicity	396
Deborah Hammond and Denise Hagon	594
Debrouillard Ltd	112
Decent Exposure TV Ltd	112
Deep Blue	398
Deepwater Blue	412
Definitely Red	437
Definition Design Ltd	300
Definition Films	475
Definitive Special Projects Ltd	631
Delamar Academy Of Make-Up, The	276
Delaney Lund Knox Warren	54
Delicious Digital Ltd	412
Deloitte & Touche	295
Deloitte & Touche Consulting Group	297
Deluxe Digital Studios	242
Deluxe Laboratories Ltd	462
Deluxe London	292
Deluxe Video Services Ltd	462
Dench Arnold Agency, The	65
Dene Films	492
Denham Productions	459
Denis Tyler Ltd	518
Denman Casting Agency	63
Denmead Marketing (Europe) Ltd	398
Dennis Dillon	305
Dennis Diners	651
Dennis Lyne Agency	58
Dennis Woolf Productions	518
Denton Wilde Sapte	321
Dentsu Holdings Europe Ltd	54
Department Of Culture, Media & Sport (Media Division)	299
Department Of Trade & Industry (DTI), The	299
Depot Studios, The	574
Derek Cunningham Productions	609
Derek Hill Consultancy	239
Derek Williams Film Editors Ltd	433
Derek's Hands	63
Design Story	501
Designlab Systems Ltd	242
DeSisti Lighting (UK) Ltd	340
Destiny AVP	492
Devlin, Mark	488
Devon Marquee Company Ltd	352
Dewsbury College	273
Dewynters	54
Dexia Banque Internationale a Luxembourg	297
DGP	242, 451
DHL International (UK) Ltd	182
Di Carling Casting	155
Diary	186
Dibb Directions	518
Dick George & Company	594
Dick Hunt	623
Different Film Ideas Productions Ltd	519
Digi Consoles	282
Digi-Box.co.uk Ltd	239
Digirama Ltd	466
Digital Arts World	398
Digital Audio Company, The	445
Digital Audio Research Ltd	282
Digital Audio Technology Ltd	437, 445, 448
Digital Film @ the Moving Picture Company	466
Digital Film Lab	466
Digital Garage Company Ltd, The	114, 120, 186
Digital Group Ltd, The	242

Digital Imagemakers	519
Digital Oasis	406
Digital Video Show, The	398
Digital Vision Motion	325
Digital Vision Music	330
Digitalia	632
Digiverse Ltd	242
Dimes & Sillitoe Ltd	396
Dinedor Management	65
Diplomat Films Ltd	519
Direct Image Productions Ltd	406
Direct Lighting	337
Direct2 Music Management	419
Directors & Producers Rights Society	97
Directors Film Company Of Amsterdam BV	352, 368, 550, 571

Directors Film Company Of New York	352, 492, 519
Directors Guild of Great Britain, The	97
Disney Channel, The	654
Display Electronics	592
Diva Pictures Limited	455
Dive Force Marine	660
Divers II Divers International	662
Diverse Post	437, 467
Diving Services UK	660
DJK Film Services	651
DK-Audio (UK) Ltd	282
D-L Productions	475
DLA	321
DLT Entertainment UK Ltd	519
DMC Business Machines Plc	425
DMI Productions	501
DML Productions	519
DMS Films Ltd	475
DNA Consulting	318
DNP Media	599
DO Productions	368
Docklands Light Railway	342
Doctor Doalot Unit Doctors	400
Doctors Direct PLC	399
Documentary Video Associates	437
Dolby Laboratories	282
Dolly Brook Casting Agency, The	63
Domaine	325
Dominic Photography	636
Domino Films	519
Domino Systems	319
Don Grant Design	86
Donald Smith Promotions Ltd	398
Doner Cardwell Hawkins	54
Doppelgangers Ltd	587
Dorans Propmakers	595
Dorchester, The	314
Doreen Jones Casting	155
Dorling Kindersley Ltd	239
Dorset Square Hotel	314
Double E Productions Ltd	519
Double Exposure	519
Double-Band Films	519
Downes Presenters' Agency	67
Downhall Broadcast Solutions	279
Downlink Communications Ltd	426

Downsoft Ltd	449
Downstream Ltd	242
Downtime Media Productions Ltd	645
Dox Productions	519
DPA Sound	612
DPTV Productions	519
Dragonfire Entertainment Ltd	519
Drake Electronics Ltd	282
Drama House, The	519
Drawmer	616
Dream Cars	591
Dream Media Group	657
Dreamchaser Productions	519
Dreamlight Pictures	492
Drew & Company	321
DRS Construction	165
Drunken Angel Entertainment	368
DS Video Facilities	666
DSA Production Services	569
DSM Video Ltd	244
DT Editing Services Ltd	451
DT Electronics Ltd	667
DT Productions	437
D-Tek	337
DTL Broadcast Ltd	282
DTS (UK) Ltd	449
Dubbs	244, 462, 572
Dubois Ltd	282
Duchy Parade Films Ltd	218
Duck Lane Film Company, The	492

Duex	550
Duke Marketing	519
Dukes Hotel	314
Dukes Island Studios	574
Dundee Airport	102
Dune Films	368
Duplication Express	462
Durham Wildlife Trust	72
Duthy Hall Studios	572
DVA Ltd	437
DVD Productions Ltd	519
DVD R Direct	244
DVDi	244
DVD-UK	467
Dwight Cavendish Systems Ltd	286
Dyer & Bradbury	412

Ee

E TO E Ltd	429
E2V Technologies	282
Eagle & Eagle	519
Eagle Eye Productions	519
Eagle Films Ltd	519
Eagle Helicopters	104
Eagle Vision	501
Eagle Vision Productions	244
Ealing Animation	489
Ealing Studios	572
Eamonn O'Neill, James O'Neill & Martin Shea	682
Eardrum Productions	569
East Anglian Film Archive	325
East England Arts	296

Carlton 021

AaBbCcDd**Ee**FfGgHhIiJjKkLlMmNnOoPpQqRrSsTtUuVvWwXxYyZz

AaBbCcDdEeFfGgHhIiJjKkLlMmNnOoPpQqRrSsTtUuVvWwXxYyZz

AaBbCcDdEeFfGgHhIiJjKkLlMmNnOoPpQqRrSsTtUuVvWwXxYyZz

FLEHNERFILMS

OTHER VISION. OTHER EXPERIENCE.

Gg

Carlton 021

AaBbCcDdEeFf**GgHh**IiJjKkLlMmNnOoPpQqRrSsTtUuVvWwXxYyZz

Hh

(h)

Wherever the action is

AaBbCcDdEeFfGgHhIiJjKkLlMmNnOoPpQqRrSsTtUuVvWwXxYyZz

AaBbCcDdEeFfGgHhIi JjKkLl MmNnOoPpQqRrSsTtUuVvWwXxYyZz

Wherever the action is

LICHTENBERG
production & mediaservice

Carlton 021

Wherever the action is

AaBbCcDdEeFfGgHhIiJjKkLlMmNnOoPpQqRrSsTtUuVvWwXxYyZz

NEUE SENTIMENTAL FILM

Carlton 021

Wherever the action is

Carlton 021

AaBbCcDdEeFfGgHhIiJjKkLlMmNnOoPpQqRrSsTtUuVvWwXxYyZz

Wherever the action is

AaBbCcDdEeFfGgHhIiJjKkLlMmNnOoPpQqRrSsTtUuVvWwXxYyZz

Carlton 021

Wherever the action is

AaBbCcDdEeFfGgHhIiJjKkLlMmNnOoPpQqRrSsTtUuVvWwXxYyZz

Wherever the action is

index : contacts

Aa

AaBbCcDdEeFfGgHhIiJjKkLlMmNnOoPpQqRrSsTtUuVvWwXxYyZz

AaBbCcDdEeFfGgHhIiJjKkLlMmNnOoPpQqRrSsTtUuVvWwXxYyZz

index : contacts

AaBbCcDdEeFfGgHhIiJjKkLlMmNnOoPpQqRrSsTtUuVvWwXxYyZz

AaBbCcDdEeFfGgHhIiJjKkLlMmNnOoPpQqRrSsTtUuVvWwXxYyZz

Cc

AaBbCcDdEeFfGgHhIiJjKkLlMmNnOoPpQqRrSsTtUuVvWwXxYyZz

AaBbCcDdEeFfGgHhIiJjKkLlMmNnOoPpQqRrSsTtUuVvWwXxYyZz

AaBbCcDdEeFfGgHhIiJjKkLlMmNnOoPpQqRrSsTtUuVvWwXxYyZz

AaBbCcDdEeFfGgHhIiJjKkLlMmNnOoPpQqRrSsTtUuVvWwXxYyZz

AaBbCcDdEeFfGgHhIiJjKkLlMmNnOoPpQqRrSsTtUuVvWwXxYyZz

AaBbCcDdEeFfGgHhIiJjKkLlMmNnOoPpQqRrSsTtUuVvWwXxYyZz

AaBbCcDd**Ee**FfGgHhIiJjKkLlMmNnOoPpQqRrSsTtUuVvWwXxYyZz

Ff

AaBbCcDdEeFfGgHhIiJjKkLlMmNnOoPpQqRrSsTtUuVvWwXxYyZz

AaBbCcDdEeFfGgHhIiJjKkLlMmNnOoPpQqRrSsTtUuVvWwXxYyZz

AaBbCcDdEeFfGgHhIiJjKkLlMmNnOoPpQqRrSsTtUuVvWwXxYyZz

AaBbCcDdEeFfGgHhIiJjKkLlMmNnOoPpQqRrSsTtUuVvWwXxYyZz

AaBbCcDdEeFf**GgHh**IiJjKkLlMmNnOoPpQqRrSsTtUuVvWwXxYyZz

index : contacts

AaBbCcDdEeFfGgHh**Ii**JjKkLlMmNnOoPpQqRrSsTtUuVvWwXxYyZz

AaBbCcDdEeFfGgHhIiJjKkLlMmNnOoPpQqRrSsTtUuVvWwXxYyZz

AaBbCcDdEeFfGgHh**Ii**JjKkLlMmNnOoPpQqRrSsTtUuVvWwXxYyZz

AaBbCcDdEeFfGg**Hh**IiJjKkLIMmNnOoPpQqRrSsTtUuVvWwXxYyZz

764 · THE PRODUCTION GUIDE

AaBbCcDdEeFfGgHhIiJjKkLlMmNnOoPpQqRrSsTtUuVvWwXxYyZz

AaBbCcDdEeFfGgHhIiJjKkLlMmNnOoPpQqRrSsTtUuVvWwXxYyZz

AaBbCcDdEeFfGgHhIiJjKkLlMmNnOoPpQqRrSsTtUuVvWwXxYyZz

AaBbCcDdEeFfGgHhIiJjKkLIMmNnOoPpQqRrSsTtUuVvWwXxYyZz

index : contacts

AaBbCcDdEeFfGgHhIiJjKkLlMmNnOoPpQqRrSsTtUuVvWwXxYyZz

AaBbCcDdEeFfGgHhIiJjKkLlMmNnOoPpQqRrSsTtUuVvWwXxYyZz

AaBbCcDdEeFfGgHhIiJjKkLlMmNnOoPpQqRrSsTtUuVvWwXxYyZz

AaBbCcDdEeFfGgHhIiJjKkLlMmNnOoPpQqRrSsTtUuVvWwXxYyZz

AaBbCcDdEeFfGgHhIiJjKkLlMmNnOoPpQqRrSsTtUuVvWwXxYyZz

AaBbCcDdEeFfGgHhIiJjKkLlMmNnOoPpQqRrSsTtUuVvWwXxYyZz

index : contacts

AaBbCcDdEeFfGgHhIiJjKkLlMmNnOoPpQqRrSsTtUuVvWwXxYyZz

AaBbCcDdEeFfGgHhIiJjKkLlMmNnOoPpQqRrSsTtUuVvWwXxYyZz

AaBbCcDdEeFfGgHhIiJjKkLlMmNnOoPpQqRrSsTtUuVvWwXxYyZz

AaBbCcDdEeFfGgHhIiJjKkLlMmNnOoPpQqRrSsTtUuVvWwXxYyZz

AaBbCcDdEeFfGgHhIiJjKkLlMmNnOoPpQqRrSsTtUuVvWwXxYyZz

AaBbCcDdEeFfGgHhIiJjKkLlMmNnOoPpQqRrSsTtUuVvWwXxYyZz

AaBbCcDdEeFfGgHhIiJjKkLlMmNnOoPpQqRrSsTtUuVvWwXxYyZz

Uu

AaBbCcDdEeFfGgHhIiJjKkLlMmNnOoPpQqRrSsTtUuVvWwXxYyZz

AaBbCcDdEeFfGgHhIiJjKkLlMmNnOoPpQqRrSsTtUuVvWwXxYyZz

AaBbCcDdEeFfGgHhIiJjKkLlMmNnOoPpQqRrSsTtUuVvWwXxYyZz

If you or your company would like a free listing in The Production Guide 2004, simply take a photocopy of the form below, complete and return it to:

The Production Guide, 33-39 Bowling Green Lane, London EC1R ODA

Fax it to: 020 7505 8076

If you need help filling in this form please email theproductionguide@emap.com or call 020 7505 8371

THE PRODUCTION GUIDE FREE ENTRY REGISTRATION

Individual/Company Name: _____

Address: _____

_____

Town/City: _____ Postcode: _____

Tel: _____ Fax: _____

Mobile: _____

Email: _____

Website: _____

Company Contact 1: Name: _____ Position: _____

Company Contact 2: Name: _____ Position: _____

Company Contact 3: Name: _____ Position: _____

Credits:
*(Please indicate what type of production your credits are: Animation; Commercial; Documentary; Educational; Feature Films; Industry/Corporate Video; Short Film; Television; Web/Multimedia)

Title 1 _____ Type* _____

Title 2 _____ Type* _____

Title 3 _____ Type* _____

Title 4 _____ Type* _____

Categories: I would like my free listing to be located under the category of (see categories on pages 6-11)

_____

For duplicate listings or more advertising and promotional opportunities email

samantha.turner@emap.com

or contact the sales team on +44 20 7505 8062.

Closing date for free listing in The Production Guide 2004 - 1st February 2004.

index : advertisers

post production terms

2K
Short for the image size of 2048 x 1556 pixels. Commonly used resolution for digitising full frame 35mm film for effects.

3:2 Pull-down
Telecine process used to create 60 fields [30fps] for 525/NTSC video from 24fps film material. The first film frame is repeated to create two fields and the subsequent frame is repeated three times. [12 frames x 2 = 24, 12 frames x 3 = 36, equals 60 fields]. This keeps the film duration the same for the Theatrical and Television versions.

525
Short for 525/59.94Hz component system used in USA and Japan. [See component]

625
Short for 625/50Hz component system used in UK, Europe, Australia and other parts of the world. [See component]

Aa

Analogue
Method of recording pictures or audio using a variable voltage level signal. The signal degrades on each generation.

Anamorphic
[see FHA]

ARC - Aspect Ratio Conversion
Equipment used to change the aspect ratio of TV images. Common examples are producing 4:3 or 14:9 from a 16:9 Master.

Aspect Ratio
The shape of the TV or Film image expressed as units of width against units of height. Old TV Pictures are 4:3 [also can call 12:9], widescreen TV is 16:9. Modern Feature films are usually 1.85:1 or 2.35:1.

Auto Conform
Process of recreating the offline edit in an online suite from the master rushes using the timecodes contained in the EDL file.

Bb

Best Light
The Telecine transfer of film to tape, usually carried out in one pass with grading adjustment made on the fly. Mostly used for rushes transfers. Often confused with Technical Grade.

BITC - Burnt In Timecode
Master timecode that is displayed in the image to which it refers. Often used on viewing VHSs to provide accurate frame references.

Blue Screen
[See Chroma Key]

Cc

Centre Cut Out
To make a 14:9 Letterbox or 4:3 Full Frame image from the middle of a 16:9 wide-screen master, with the loss of image from the sides.

Chroma Key
The process of shooting against a coloured background [normally green or blue] which is removed in post production to allow the foreground to be placed over any background.

Chrominance
The colour part of a television signal that relates to the hue and saturation but not the brightness of the image.

Closed Caption
Information that is recorded in a non-visible part of TV image that can be read by a Closed Caption Reader to generate Subtitles on the viewers Television set.

Colour Correction
[See Grade]

Compression
The processes of reducing the amount of digital information required to record or transmit images and/or audio. The final quality will depend on the amount of compression applied - The more data used the better the quality, higher compression will result in poorer quality.

Component signal
A component video signal has separate luminance and chrominance information. This results in a better quality picture than a composite signal. BetacamSP, Digital Betacam and D1 and examples of component formats.

Composite signal
A composite video signal has combined luminance and chrominance information using on of tree encoding standards - PAL, NTSC or SECAM. This results in a picture quality that is lower than component signals. 1-inch, D2 and VHS are examples of composite formats.

Compositing
Term referring to the combination of different picture elements and effects to produce a final "composite" image.

Conform
[see Auto Conform]

Cross Conversion
Changing video material from one High Definition format to another.

CSO - Colour Separation Overlay
Usually BBC term for Chroma Key.

Dd

DA-88/DA-98
8-track digital audio tape.

DAT - Digital Audio Tape
2-track digital audio tape.

De-spot
The removal of film dirt and sparkle on Telecine transfers.

DF Timecode - Drop Frame Timecode
The process used to match the timecode on 525/NTSC masters. 525/NTSC is usually refered to as being 30fps, but actually runs at 29.97fps, thus the timecode drifts out in relation to the picture. Drop Frame timecode overcomes this problem by skipping 2 frames every minute [except at every 10 minute interval], this brings the timecode back in line with the video.

Digital
Method of recording pictures or sound with a binary signal [ones and zeros].
The signal can be copied without any loss of quality.

Digital VTR
Video Tape Recorder that stores pictures and audio in digital form. Examples are D1, Digital Betacam, HDCAM, D5 and DVCAM.

Dissolve
Video transition where the outgoing picture is reduced in level to zero, whilst the incoming picture is increased in level from zero. Also known as a mix.

Dolby 5.1
Digital surround sound system with separate front left and right and centre, rear left and right and sub-bass channels.

Dolby Surround
Analogue surround system with four audio channels - front left, centre, right and rear surround [LCRS] that are encoded into two combined channels, Left Total and Right Total [Lt, Rt]. These two signals are separated on playback by a Pro Logic decoder to give LCRS.

Down Conversion
Changing video material from a High Definition format to a Standard Definition format.

Drop Out
Loss of picture and/or audio information resulting from damage or imperfections in the tape stock.

Dry-gate
Telecine transport for moving the film through the optical path.

DVD - Digital Versatile Disk
A high density storage format that is the same size as a CD. These are either single sided with single or dual layers or double sided with single or dual layers depending on the capacity.

DVD-R
One time recordable DVD

DVE - Digital Video Effects
Generic term for any piece of equipment that manipulates the shape, size, position and orientation of an image.

DVNR - Digital Video Noise Reducer
Device for reducing or removing film grain and scratches or electronic noise from pictures. Excessive use can create disagreeable artefacts.

Ee

EDL - Edit Decision List
Offline edit decisions saved as a computer file, usually on floppy disk for use in an online session to auto-conform the offline edit at online quality.

post production terms

Ff

FHA – Full Height Anamorphic
Commonly used to refer to the horizontal squeezing of a wide-screen 16:9 picture so that it can be recorded using a 4:3 tape format.

Field
One television frame is made up of two different interlaced fields, each of which is displayed for half the duration of the frame.

Filmic Effect
Television systems display approximately twice as many images per second than compared to film. Filmic effect combines the two different fields of a television frame to reduce the number of images displayed per second. This gives specifically shot material a visual quality similar to film.

Flex File
Data file that is created during the film rushes transfer that relates the keycode numbers from film to the timecode of the rushes tapes. Necessary if the film is going to be cut.

fps
the number of complete images displayed per second.

Frame

Gg

Garbage Matte
A rough matte uses to remove unwanted objects such as lamp stands, wires and rigs from chroma key sequences.

Grade
The process of changing the colour balance of an image, either to create a dramatic effect or to match the scene with the others in the sequence of the film. Usually carried out in Telecine, but limited grading can be achieved in online suites.

Grade 1 Monitor
Very high quality monitors made to very high specifications. These can be accurately aligned to industry standards, thus enabling pictures displayed on different monitors to match.

Green Screen
[see Chroma Key]

Hh

Handles
Additional material before the in-point and after the out-point that is loaded into an edit system to allow cut points to be extended if required.

HD – High Definition
Television format offering increased resolution compared to standard definition television. It also has an aspect ratio of 16:9. Currently being adopted in USA and Japan.

Hz – Hertz
Engineering term for number of cycles per second. Usually refers to number of images per second, 50Hz for 625/PAL and 60Hz for 525/NTSC.

Ii

Illegal Colours
Luminance or Chrominance levels that fall outside of the limits defined for each format. These can cause problems during transmission as well as playback. Colours that are legal in on video format can become illegal once converted to another video format.

Interlace
Video scanning where each frame is made up of two fields, each of which makes up half of the image. The first field comprises odd numbered lines, whilst the second field is made up of even lines.

Kk

Keycode
Numbers and barcodes along the edge of film that identify each film frame and can be automatically read by Telecine and neg cutting equipment. Used to relate each film from to each video frame during rushes transfer and subsequent editing.

Key Frame
Markers within an effects sequence that are used to adjust the profile of any transition.

Keying
Layering of different picture elements using either a separate matte or by creating a matte using the luminance or chrominance content of the foreground image.

Ll

Letterbox
Method of displaying or recording pictures with a wider aspect ratio than the screen. The image has black bars top and bottom.

Linear Editing
Tape-based system where scenes are laid down in order on tape. If a scene is changed in duration, then all the following material must be laid down again.

LTC - Longitudinal Timecode
Timecode that is recorded along the tape that can that is read when the tape is being shuttled at high speed.

Mm

Matte
A separate [usually] black and white signal that is used to separate parts of the image during compositing.

Motion Control
Computer controlled camera that can be programmed to follow a specific path for special effects shots. The move can be accurately repeated each time to allow each path to be overlayed.

MPEG - Moving Picture Experts Group
Compression standard for moving pictures. MPEG1 uses a high compression rate and is usually used for CD Rom, whilst MPEG2 has a lower compression rate [and hence better quality] and is used for DVD, video on demand and Digital Television transmission.

Nn

NDF - Non Drop Frame
Timecode that identifies every frame of 525/NTSC material. As these systems operate at 29.97fps, the 30fps Non Drop Frame timecode will slowly drift from actual running time – by 18 frames every 10 minutes.

Non-Linear Editing
Method of editing using disk storage, where scenes can be played back in any order or length. Shot durations and positions can be changed without having to replace the following material.

NTSC - National Television Standards Committee
Composite encoding system used for recording and transmission in USA, Canada and Japan. NTSC is often incorrectly used to refer to 525 component formats.

Oo

Offline
Editing process using lower cost, lower quality equipment, where the structure of the programme is created. The offline system then produces an EDL which is used in an online suite to recreate the programme from the master rushes.

OMFI - Open Media Framework Interchange
Standard for interchange of video and audio media between different applications and equipment, e.g. transferring audio media from an edit system to the dubbing theatre.

One Light
Transfer of film material where the grading is established on the first shot then all the material is transferred using these settings. Commonly used for rushes transfers.

Online
Higher cost editing systems using the EDL produced in the offline to reconstruct the programme using the full quality rushes material. Also when all dissolves, effects and titles are added.

Opengate
Method of exposing film to use the area reserved for the audio track and therefore increasing the available picture area. Used for widescreen formats such as Super 35mm or Super 16mm. The Telecine transfer also needs to be carried out opengate to capture the entire picture.

OSC/R
Software system that references the film's keycode numbers to the video's timecode. Using the offline EDL, OSC/R will produce a list of keycode references that are used to cut the negative.

Overlength
Cut negative [usually S16mm] that has been assembled into programme order with 20 frame handles at each cut.

Pp

PAL - Phase Alternate Line
Composite encoding system used for recording and transmission in UK, Europe and Australia. PAL is often incorrectly used to refer to 625 component formats.

post production terms

Perf
Short of film sprocket or perforation, used to transport the film through the camera or Telecine gate.

Pillar box
Method of displaying or recording pictures with a narrower aspect ratio than the screen. The image has black bars at the left and right of picture.

Plug Ins
Third party software that adds extra functions to computer applications. Used to add specific effects not offered by the original manufacturer.

Pre-read
Recording technique on suitably equipped VTR [e.g. Digital Betacam] where the source pictures are played back and recorded on the same machine.

Progressive
Video standard where each line of the frame are displayed continuously from top to bottom in one pass. There are no fields as used in interlaced systems.

Promist
A Camera or Telecine filter that adds a diffusing effect to the picture. A similar effect can be created electronically in some online suite.

Rr

Real Time
Any operation that can be achieved in the running time of the material to which it is being applied.

Rendering
Process that is required when effects cannot be created in real time. The duration required to produce the final rendered version [that can be played in real time] depends on how complex the effect is.

Resolution
The measure of the finest detail that can be reproduced by the television system being used.

Ss

Safe Action Area
The part of the picture that is considered to be the area that is visible on a correctly adjusted domestic television. There are different areas for 16:9 and 4:3.

Safe Title Area
The area inside of safe action where critical elements such as text and graphics are placed, thereby ensuring they are not lost on a poorly adjusted television. There are a number of different standards [4:3, 14:9 and 16:9] depending on the final broadcast medium.

SD – Standard Definition
Television formats such as 625/PAL or 525/NTSC.

SECAM – Sequential Colour and Memory
Composite encoding system used for transmission, mainly in France. It is only relevant as a transmission standard and not used in post production.

Shoot and Protect
Widescreen shooting technique where critical action is framed more centrally, therefore making the widescreen master suitable for transmission in other aspect ratios.

Stabilise
Electronic method where unwanted movement, such as film weave or camera shake is removed from an image. To achieve this, it is necessary to slightly zoom into the original picture.

Standards Conversion
Process of changing from one television format to another. This may require a number of format changes including either the removal or creation of lines and a change of frame rate., again by either removal or creation.

Stripped Stock
Tape stock that has been pre-recorded with black and timecode. This is needed for insert editing.

Tt

Tape Grade
Colour Correction that is performed from a master tape rather than film elements. To get the best results, the material to be graded will be created from technically graded rushes.

Technical Grade
The Telecine transfer of film to tape, where the material is adjusted to ensure as much of the original image is maintained without any crushing of the blacks or whites. This material will later be auto conformed and tape graded to produce the final master.

Telecine
Machine used to transfer film to tape in real time. Each frame of film is scanned and converted into the required video standard. Used in conjunction with a colour corrector to create the final look of the material.

TIFF [.TIF]
Short for Tagged Image File Format. A bit-mapped file format used widely used for image transfers.

Time Lapse
Shooting technique where a very slow film speed is used [e.g. 1-frame per hour]. When played back at normal speeds, gives the impression of time being speeded up.

Timecode
A unique number given to each video frame, comprising of hour, minutes, seconds and frames. Used to identify each frame as well as required for accurate editing.

Timeline
A graphical representation of an editing sequence, showing each edit and its duration along a line representing time.

Uu

Underscan
Mode of operation for broadcast monitors, where the entire picture area, including those normally crop by domestic television sets, can be displayed.

Up Conversion
Changing video material from a Standard Definition format to a High Definition format.

Up-res
Process where the number of pixels used to represent an image is increased by interpolating the existing pixels, to produce a larger format. This process does not increase the resolution above that of the original image.

Vv

Vari-speed
Effect where the speed of film or video material is either increased or decreased. This can be carried out in either a linear way across the whole scene, or gradually increased or decreased to give a smoother transition.

Vistavision
Film format where the 35mm negative is passed through the camera horizontally rather than vertically, thereby increasing the negative area available and with it the resolution of the image. Usually used for effects shots.

VITC - Vertical Interval Timecode
Timecode that is recorded within the non-visible part of the picture. Unlike Longitudinal Timecode, VITC can be read when the tape is stationary.

VTR
Abbreviation for Video Tape Recorder.

Ww

Warp
Process were all or part of the frame is distorted as if it were an elastic surface.

Wet-gate
Telecine gate where the film is submersed in a solution whilst it passes through the optical path. The solution has the same optical properties as the film and helps to disguise any scratches during the transfer. It also helps to remove any dirt that might be present on the film.

Wide-screen
Term used to refer to pictures wider than 4:3. usually used to describe 16:9 television but also applies to 1.85:1 or 2.35:1 film aspect ratios.

Xx

X Axis
Denotes horizontal axis of a picture; to move a picture in the X axis is to move it left or right.

Yy

Y Axis
Denoted the vertical axis of a picture; to move a picture in the Y axis is to move it up or down.

Zz

Z Axis
Denotes the central axis of a picture; to move a picture in the Z axis is to move towards or away from the viewer.

Thanks to Pepper for compiling the glossary

production terms

Aa

A & B roll
Alternative shots in a film production go on to two separate reels – the first to roll A, the second to B, the third to A etc. Makes the joins less obvious and makes effects like wipes and mixes easier. Also called "chequer-boarding".

Aerial shot
A shot taken from a high building, crane, plane or helicopter. Not necessarily a moving shot.

Ambience
The noise that is in the background of the sounds you want to record.

Bb

Barn doors
Metal flaps attached to the front of a lamp that give the user much more selectivity over the lighting.

Best boy
Term used by the lighting gaffer and the senior grip for their number two.

Blow up
An optical enlargement of a film from one gauge to another, such as 16mm up to 35mm. The opposite of a blow up is a reduction print.

Boom
Long pole used to mount microphones above people's heads and out of shot. The holder of the pole is called the boom operator

Bridging shot
A shot used to cover a jump in time or place or other discontinuity. Common examples are falling leaves, maps, changing calendar pages and newspaper headlines.

Buzz track
A recording of the ambient sounds present at any location – distant traffic, bird sound, air conditioners etc. Can be used to cover any gap, or to disguise a jump when dialogue has been recorded with two slightly different background levels.

Cc

Close-up
A shot in which a character's face and shoulders are the main image, or where a single object or parts of objects are the main image.

Crane
A camera platform that can be raised and lowered. Generally mounted on a rolling base.

Dd

Digital Betacam
Digital videotape format that records video on half-inch tape.

Dissolve
This type of transition can suggest the passage of time and refers to a soft transition between two sequences or scenes. The first image gradually dissolves or fades out and is replaced by another that fades in over it.

Dolly
A set of wheels and a platform upon which the camera can be mounted to give it mobility.

Dubbing
Replacing the dialogue of a film. Can be done to translate the film into another language or to replace dialogue not recorded (deliberately or accidentally) during the shoot.

Ee

Edge numbers
Numbers printed on the edge of film stock (every foot). This allows the editor, director, laboratory or computer to find a specific frame very easily.

Effects track
Separate soundtrack that contains all the non-dialogue sounds. Can be recorded synchronously with the picture or recorded wild.

Ff

Filter
Glass attachments usually put in front of the lens to modify the light entering the camera. They can change the colour of the light or give a soft feel to the picture.

Flare
Bright white or coloured blob or streak on the image caused by a light shining directly on to the lens.

Foley
System for adding sound effects to a film and generally making the soundtrack more interesting. The person responsible for this is called a foley artist.

Frame
One complete video image, or two video fields. There are 25 frames in one second of PAL video. Also a single film image.

Gg

Gaffer
Chief electrician. Works to the DoP/ cinematographer.

Grip
Person (or people) in charge of moving camera dollies, tripods etc. The main grip is often referred to as the key grip.

Hh

High key
Scene lit so that it contains few dark areas. Contrast is low and shadows are not very deep.

Humidity sensor
A device in a video camera that prevents it working when there is too much moisture present.

Ii

Inter-positive
A colour master positive print.

Jj

Jump cut
Cut where there is no match between the two shots. A jump cut ignores continuity of time, place and action. It can make the viewer jump and wonder where the narrative has got to.

Junior
A 2-kilowatt lamp with a fresnel lens.

Kk

Key light
The main light on a subject. In drama it simulates natural light. It reveals the shape of people and things.

Kinescope
A film recording of a video image displayed on a specially designed television monitor. Also called Kine. Only means of recording TV programmes before video recorders and tape were invented.

Ll

Lip sync
Relationship between the movements of a performer's mouth and the words you hear. If they occur simultaneously, the shot is said to be in sync.

Loop
Short piece of magnetic tape joined end-to-end so as to provide constant sound when played.

Low key
Scene lit so that areas of darkness predominate. Contrast is high.

Mm

Master shot
A shot that tries to contain the majority of the action. A long take of an entire scene, generally a relatively long shot that facilitates the assembly of component closer shots and details.

Montage
An edited sequence of two or more shots that have no logical connection, but which, when put together, suggest something not specifically shown.

Nn

Negative
Most film productions are shot on negative film – the actual stuff that goes through the camera is black where the scene was white and vice versa.

NTSC - National Television Standards Committee
Television standard used in USA, Canada, Japan and Mexico.

Oo

Overcranking
Shooting film faster than the usual 24 or 25 frames a second to produce a slow-motion effect.

Pp

Pan
Movement of the camera from left to right or right to left around the imaginary vertical axis that runs through the camera.

Point of view shot (PoV)
A shot that shows the scene from the specific point of view of one of the characters.

Prime lens
A non-zoom lens. Generally gives better picture quality and can enable the camera to shoot with less light than a zoom lens requires.

Qq

Quick release
A latching device for quickly mounting and removing the camera from the tripod.

Rr

Radio microphone
A microphone that works with a receiver to allow the user freedom of movement.

Raw stock
Unexposed film.

Reverse angle
A shot that complements a previous shot – in a drama, a shot of the second participant.

Rough cut
The first edit.

Rushes
The first quick print of a film.

production terms

Ss

Saturation
The purity of a colour.

Second unit
Additional crew used when more than one camera is needed on a scene (eg a car crash) or to pick up additional shots in which the main cast doesn't appear (an airliner landing, for instance).

Shooting ratio
Ratio of amount of film or tape shot to that used in the final production.

Shutter
The device that allows light on to a film for a short time, closes off the light while the film is moved to the next frame, then allows the light through again.

Steadicam
A system that permits hand-held shooting with an image steadiness comparable to that of a tracking shot done on a dolly.

Storyboard
A sequence of sketched frames showing the basic shots for a scene of a film or television programme. It is drawn during the planning/ development stage, and gives the director a chance to try out ideas without spending much money.

Sync (synchronisation)
Picture and sound exactly in time with each other.

Tt

Tilt
The camera looks up or down, rotating around the axis that runs from left to right through the camera head.

Timecode
A numerical code expressed as hours, minutes, seconds and frames to give each frame a unique address for location purposes as well as being vital for synchronising VTR for example.

Tracking shot
A shot where the camera is moved by means of wheels. The movement is normally quite steady and can be fast or slow.

Uu

Undercrank
Shooting film slower than the usual 24 or 25 frames a second in order to make action in the finished shot appear faster.

Vv

VCR
Video cassette recorder.

Voice-over (V/O)
The voice of an unseen narrator.

Vox pop
Technique of asking a number of people for their views on one subject. The result is a series of short shots showing the replies.

Ww

Walk-through
Rehearsal of a scene without trying for a performance.

Whip pan
A fast pan in which the shot deteriorates to a blur.

Wide angle
Lens with a short focal length, therefore a wide angle of view. Used close to a subject, it can distort the view.

Wild track
Sound recorded on location independently of the picture.

Wipe
An optical effect in which an image appears to wipe over or push aside the previous shot.

Xx

Xenon
A very bright, daylight-balanced projection lamp, or a projector with a xenon lamp. A xenon lamp is not interchangeable with a tungsten lamp or arch lamp, but requires a different lamp housing on the projector. Because xenon lamps are daylight-balanced it is sometimes advisable with colour film to have the lab make a print that is balanced for xenon. This is sometimes called a 5,400K print, the colour temperature of daylight.

Zz

Zoom
A shot using a lens whose focal length is adjusted during the shot.